ISBN 978-1-5280-3641-2
PIBN 10915188

1 MONTH OF
FREE
READING

at

www.ForgottenBooks.com

By purchasing this book you are eligible for one month membership to ForgottenBooks.com, giving you unlimited access to our entire collection of over 1,000,000 titles via our web site and mobile apps.

To claim your free month visit:

www.forgottenbooks.com/free915188

English
Français
Deutsche
Italiano
Español
Português

www.forgottenbooks.com

Mythology Photography **Fiction**
Fishing Christianity **Art** Cooking
Essays Buddhism Freemasonry
Medicine **Biology** Music **Ancient**
Egypt Evolution Carpentry Physics
Dance Geology **Mathematics** Fitness
Shakespeare **Folklore** Yoga Marketing
Confidence Immortality Biographies
Poetry **Psychology** Witchcraft
Electronics Chemistry History **Law**
Accounting **Philosophy** Anthropology
Alchemy Drama Quantum Mechanics
Atheism Sexual Health **Ancient History**
Entrepreneurship Languages Sport
Paleontology Needlework Islam
Metaphysics Investment Archaeology
Parenting Statistics Criminology
Motivational

REPORT

OF THE

INDUSTRIAL COMMISSION

ON

TRANSPORTATION,

INCLUDING

REVIEW OF EVIDENCE, TOPICAL DIGEST OF EVIDENCE,
AND TESTIMONY SO FAR AS TAKEN
MAY 1, 1900.

VOLUME IV
OF THE COMMISSION'S REPORTS.

WASHINGTON:
GOVERNMENT PRINTING OFFICE.
1900.

MEMBERS OF THE INDUSTRIAL COMMISSION.

A. 156924

Senator JAMES H. KYLE, Chairman.

Senator BOIES PENROSE.   Mr. ANDREW L. HARRIS.

Senator STEPHEN R. MALLORY.   Mr. ELLISON A. SMYTH.

Senator JOHN W. DANIEL.   Mr. JOHN M. FARQUHAR.

Representative JOHN J. GARDNER.   Mr. EUGENE D. CONGER.

Representative WILLIAM LORIMER.   Mr. THOMAS W. PHILLIPS.

Representative L. F. LIVINGSTON.   Mr. CHARLES J. HARRIS.

Representative JOHN C. BELL.   Mr. M. D. RATCHFORD.

Representative THEOBALD OTJEN.   Mr. JOHN L. KENNEDY.

Mr. LEE MANTLE.   Mr. ALBERT CLARKE.

WILLIAM E. SACKETT, Secretary.

[Extract from act of Congress of June 18, 1898, defining the duties of the Industrial Commission and showing the scope of its inquiries.]

SEC. 2. That it shall be the duty of this commission to investigate questions pertaining to immigration, to labor, to agriculture, to manufacturing, and to business, and to report to Congress and to suggest such legislation as it may deem best upon these subjects.

SEC. 3. That it shall furnish such information and suggest such laws as may be made a basis for uniform legislation by the various States of the Union, in order to harmonize conflicting interests and to be equitable to the laborer, the employer, the producer, and the consumer.

2

UNITED STATES INDUSTRIAL COMMISSION,
Washington, D. C., May 14, 1900.

SIR: I have the honor to transmit herewith, on behalf of the Industrial Commission, a preliminary report to Congress on the subject of Transportation, prepared in conformity with an act of Congress of June 18, 1898.

The Commission is not prepared at present to make recommendations to Congress or to the State legislatures, but contemplates the making of such recommendations hereafter.

Respectfully,   JAMES H. KYLE,
Chairman.

The SPEAKER OF THE HOUSE OF REPRESENTATIVES.

REVIEW OF EVIDENCE.

INTRODUCTION.

The Industrial Commission has taken the testimony of many witnesses on the subject of transportation, especially railway transportation. These witnesses include representatives of all the important organizations of railway employees, representatives of many organizations of shippers and commercial bodies, as well as other shippers, officers of railways and of railway associations, members of the Interstate Commerce Commission, and special students of transportation questions—college professors and others. Several witnesses have also testified as to lake, canal, and ocean transportation. While detailed and specific statements as to the conditions of labor and traffic have not usually been sought, many general statements as to these conditions have been obtained, and although there is, of course, not a little difference of opinion, certain conclusions as to facts emerge with fair clearness from the testimony. Naturally, there is even greater difference of judgment as to needed legislation; but here again it is possible to gather some fair conclusions concerning the preponderance of opinion among those most interested, as to some of the important problems now before the people. The Commission has not, however, completed its investigation of transportation. It is expected that additional testimony will be taken as to all phases of the subject, but more especially as to certain topics which have been investigated least fully, such as ticket brokerage, capitalization of railways, consolidation of railways, state railway commissions, taxation, conditions of water transportation, etc.

The wide-reaching social and economic influence of the means of transportation is indicated by the fact that questions relating to them have been discussed to a greater or less extent by the witnesses in connection with almost all the other investigations of the Commission—notably those on agriculture, trusts and industrial combinations, and capital and labor. The evidence in these investigations should be consulted in connection with the present volume.

FREIGHT DISCRIMINATIONS BETWEEN INDIVIDUALS.

There is a general consensus of opinion among practically all witnesses, including members of the Interstate Commerce Commission, representatives of shippers, and railway officers, that the railways still make discriminations between individuals, and perhaps to as great an extent as ever before. In fact, it is stated by numerous witnesses that discriminations were probably worse during the year 1898 than at any previous time. It is admitted that there is great difficulty in proving individual cases where shippers have been given special rates or other favors, but the witnesses declare that it is common knowledge among all familiar with the subject that such concessions are largely granted.[1] The arguments pre-

---

[1] Knapp, pp. 129, 132, 139, 142; Prouty, pp. 150–152; Clements, p. 159; Cowen, pp. 313–316; Blanchard, pp. 683, 684; Ingalls, pp. 286, 297; Spencer, pp. 273, 279; Ripley, pp. 594, 596; Stickney, pp. 460–462; Bird, pp. 470, 471; Morton, pp. 490, 493, 494; Kelley, pp. 185, 186; Vanlandingham, pp. 194, 207; Dousman, pp. 353, 359; Neall, pp. 173, 174.

sented by many railway officers in favor of pooling assert directly or indirectly the existence of discriminating rates. The representatives of the railways declare that so long as competition exists the attempt to get traffic by secret rates must continue.

It is thought generally that there has been a considerable improvement in the situation during the year 1899. This is attributed in part to the exceedingly heavy traffic which rendered it unnecessary for railroads to secure shipments by discriminating rates, and in part to a better spirit among the railways themselves. In the latter part of 1898, Messrs. Cowen and Murray, receivers of the Baltimore and Ohio Railroad, addressed a letter to the Interstate Commerce Commission declaring that the practice of granting rates below the published tariffs was so general as seriously to reduce the revenues of the railroads. More than 50 per cent of the traffic, at least on certain roads, was affected. The receivers expressed a determination to cooperate in the enforcement of the law. Later, conferences were held between the Interstate Commerce Commission and railway officers, which led to a general attempt to reduce the extent of the evil. Many witnesses, however, including representatives of the railroads, think that the improvement is only temporary and that when the present rush of traffic has ceased discriminating rates will be granted more and more.

A few witnesses are inclined to think that discriminations are not at present a very serious evil and are not likely to become such, especially since the published freight rates are now so low that no considerable concessions can be made from them with profit to the railroads; but the evidence is preponderatingly strong on the other side.[1]

Methods and forms.—The methods by which discriminations are granted are stated by the witnesses to be very numerous. It is claimed by some that direct rebates and secret rates are still frequently granted; commissions are paid for securing freight; goods are billed at less than the actual weight; traffic within a State not subject to the interstate-commerce act is carried at lower rates; allowances and advantages are made in handling and storing, etc. Several witnesses refer to the practice of shipping goods under a false classification. Sometimes this is done without the knowledge of the railways, but in other cases they apparently connive. Thus, fine hardware may be shipped as some low-class kind of iron. A few specific instances of discriminations of different sorts were mentioned before the Commission, but no detailed evidence was taken to prove the exact character and amount of these discriminations.[2]

Effect of discriminations.—It is very generally acknowledged that discriminating favors are granted chiefly to large shippers at the expense of small shippers. This is natural, since the railways compete more actively for the traffic which a large shipper can furnish. It is claimed, also, that the effect of the penalties of the interstate-commerce act has been still further to limit the preferences to a few shippers, since this makes it more possible to secure secrecy. There seems, accordingly, to be weight in the suggestion made by several witnesses that railway discriminations tend to foster trusts and combinations; a position which was especially upheld by numerous witnesses in the investigation of the Industrial Commission on trusts. Mr. Blanchard and one or two other witnesses declare that it is in no way the purpose of railways to favor combinations or men of great wealth; in fact, they would prefer not to do so, since it gives these large shippers power to force still greater concessions. But the railways are in no position to refuse the demands of such shippers.[3]

---

[1] Tucker, pp. 558, 559; Callaway, pp. 231, 234; Bird, p. 471; Woffinden, p. 565.

[2] Gallagher, pp. 541-543; Fuller, pp. 442, 443; Prouty, pp. 149, 150; Snydacker, pp. 398-400; Blanchard, pp. 625, 675; Knapp, p. 132; Kelley, p. 186; Vanlandingham, pp. 210, 211.

[3] Knapp, pp. 139, 142; Prouty, pp. 147, 148; Blanchard, pp. 683, 684; Reagan, p. 342; Bird, pp. 470, 471; Ripley, pp. 594, 596.

Carload and part carload shipments.—Witnesses on behalf of the railroads justify different rates on goods shipped in full carloads and in part carloads, and there appears no special objection to this practice on the part of other witnesses, so far as the differences are reasonable. It is claimed, however, that on shipments to the Pacific coast the rate on part carloads has been as much as 50 per cent higher than on carloads, the difference amounting to more than the possible profit of the dealer, and that this arrangement has practically prevented Eastern jobbers from selling directly to retailers in the Pacific States.[1]

Private cars.—It is the practice of the railways, as was brought out clearly in the evidence, to allow the owners of private cars a mileage rate of from 6 mills to 1 cent per mile for the use of their cars. A very large proportion of the shipments of fruit and of dressed beef is made in such cars. Although the same mileage rates and the same freight rates are perhaps open to all shippers, only those possessed of very large capital are in a position to furnish private cars in sufficient numbers to carry on an important business. It is claimed by nearly all witnesses testifying on the subject, including several railway officers, that the mileage is excessive and represents an exceedingly high profit on the cost of the cars, to that extent giving the owner of private cars an advantage over his competitors. Many of the railways apparently would be glad to supply the needed cars themselves and to refuse to haul private cars, but without an agreement on the part of all the competing lines it is impossible for them to do so.[2] One or two witnesses think that the peculiar character of these cars makes it unwise that the railways should own them, and that the mileage rate is probably not excessive.[3]

Penalties for discriminations.—Several witnesses, especially railway officers, incline to the opinion that the existing law prohibiting discriminations would be more effective if the penalty of imprisonment were abolished and a high fine, to be assessed primarily upon the corporation rather than upon individuals, made the sole penalty. It is also claimed that railway officers, who are most likely to have definite evidence concerning discriminations, will not testify against one another if the result may be imprisonment, but that they would have no such scruple if the punishment were pecuniary only.[4] It is suggested by some that each carload or shipment carried at a discriminating rate should be made the basis of a separate fine. Mr. Knapp, of the Interstate Commerce Commission, and one or two other witnesses, however, think that the threat of imprisonment is more effective than that of a fine, and especially urge that the mere granting of a right to sue for damages on account of discriminations is of very little effect in enforcing the law.[5] Other witnesses suggest the inspection of books and accounts as a means of obtaining evidence and as a remedy for discriminations. (See p. 23.)

THE ALLEGED ELEVATOR MONOPOLY.

A considerable amount of testimony has been taken concerning the practice of the large elevator owners, especially at Chicago, in buying grain, and concerning its effect upon commission merchants, country grain dealers, and farmers.

The evidence is clear that the great terminal elevators at Chicago, and to a less degree in other grain markets, are owned by a comparatively few men or firms; that the owners of public elevators, where grain may be stored at fixed charges by any holder, also control great private elevators; that they themselves buy a very large proportion of the grain which comes into the public elevators; and

---

[1] Vanlandingham, pp. 207, 210.

[2] Knapp, p. 141; Prouty, p. 151; Kelley, p. 187; Vanlandingham, pp. 209, 210; Greeley, pp. 373, 378; Dousman, p. 362; Callaway, p. 230; Ingalls, pp. 301, 302; Kennard, pp. 363–365.

[3] Bird, pp. 475, 476; Fish, p. 336.

[4] Ripley, p. 595; Morton, p. 495; Ingalls, pp. 296, 297; Hyland, pp. 351, 352; Carter, p. 585; Dousman, p. 361; Bird, p. 471.

[5] Knapp, p. 137; Spencer, p. 274; Reagan, p. 350.

that the business of handling grain on commission has been very greatly reduced by this practice. The elevator owners admit that they are very large buyers of grain. It is claimed by their opponents also, although the evidence is less definite, that these same owners of terminal elevators own or control most of the country elevators and warehouses; that in fact practically all the elevators along the lines and at the terminals of each railway system are in the hands of a single organization.[1]

The opponents of these large dealers admit that the elevator owners pay more for grain to the local dealers and farmers than the commission merchants and small dealers can pay, but they declare that this is due to various unfair advantages. Thus, the elevator owners themselves are exempt from the terminal storage and transfer charges which must be paid by other persons—three-fourths of a cent for transfer and the first 10 days storage—which is alleged to be much more than the actual cost. It is further declared that the elevator owners receive great advantages from the railways in the forms of allowances for handling grain and of direct freight discriminations. In fact, it is held by many witnesses that the railway companies or their officers are largely interested in the elevators and in grain buying. The evidence as to discriminations in favor of the elevators is chiefly indirect, based either on general belief or on the known fact that the elevator owners often pay more for grain at country stations than the price at Chicago, Kansas City, or Milwaukee, minus the full freight rate, would warrant. The excess in the price offered was shown to be sometimes as high as 2 or 2½ cents on both wheat and corn. It was also stated that in 1890 a rebate of 5 cents per hundred was proved before the Interstate Commerce Commission to have been granted to certain elevator owners.[2]

It is also alleged that the Eastern railways have largely leased their transfer elevators, for transferring grain from Western to Eastern cars, to private companies which also deal in grain, and that the charges made by these companies are excessive, so that they have an advantage over competitors.

The elevator owners deny that the charge of ¾ of a cent for handling grain is excessive; the law permits 1¼ cents to be charged, while the actual charge is the lowest known anywhere. They deny also that the railways operate elevators directly, or, in the cases where they own them, have given special favors in leasing them to the present operators; though no very detailed evidence is presented. Mr. Webster, of the Armour Elevator Company, claims that that company actually owns most of its numerous elevators and pays high rentals for the remainder, while Mr. Counselman declares that the elevators on the Rock Island were built and paid for by his own firm. Mr. Webster also denies that the elevator owners receive discriminating rates from the railways.[3]

In view of the quite general acknowledgment among railway men that discriminations in favor of large shippers are still conspicuous, there seems to be a considerable probability that the claim that these large elevators receive favors from the railways, in one way or another, has some basis.

The elevator men explain further the reasons for their buying grain and for their advantages over competitors. They claim that the establishment of through rates on grain from the Mississippi River and other Western points to the seaboard lower, than the sum of the local rates from those points to Chicago and from Chicago east, gave an advantage to Eastern commission merchants and buyers, and Chicago elevator owners found it necessary to buy grain on a large scale and handle it in the same way, on through rates, in order to keep their ware-

---

[1] Vanlandingham, p. 199; Carter, pp. 583, 584; Greeley, pp. 371, 373; Dousman, p. 354.

[2] Barry, p. 260; Bookwalter, pp. 573-576; Gallagher, p. 545; Vanlandingham, pp. 198-200; Greeley, p. 373; Dousman, p. 355; Carter, p. 584; Bacon, p. 427.

[3] Webster, pp. 413-416; Counselman' pp. 385-388.

houses from standing idle. Moreover, the competition of the newer markets of Minneapolis, Duluth, Kansas City, and elsewhere forced these men to buy grain to protect Chicago as a market. The advantages which have made it possible for them to compete successfully with other markets, and largely to take business away from commission merchants, arise from their large capital, which enables them to carry large quantities of grain in anticipation of favorable markets, from the elimination of commission and other intermediate charges, and from the ability to forego a part or all of the normal charge for actual elevator service. The elevator owners have the same advantage over commission merchants that any business man has who furnishes himself with all accessory materials and facilities, instead of obtaining them from others, especially from his competitors.[1] One or two witnesses, however, claim that, as regards local buying, the small dealer, who has perhaps other business during the season when there is little grain buying, can handle the grain business more cheaply than a great concern.

Effect on prices.—The opponents of the elevator owners declare that there is a growing monopoly of the local elevators, those on each line of railway being largely controlled by a single firm. While there is still sometimes competition and while in such cases the large buyers pay the higher prices, sooner or later all competitors will be driven out and the farmer will be at the mercy of the great elevator owners. It is maintained, moreover, that where different elevator owners operate along the same line of railway they do not actively compete. On the contrary they meet daily on the Chicago Board of Trade and agree as to the prices which they will pay, at least as to certain territory. No evidence is presented to show specific cases where prices have been depressed by elevator owners.[2]

To these charges the elevator owners[3] reply that, at least along many railroads, they do not control any large proportion of the local elevators. They buy largely from the local dealers, who compete among themselves; and there is nothing to check the competition of the different elevator concerns. There are few railroad stations which do not have two or more buyers. No agreement exists for limiting competition or fixing prices, except that certain leading Chicago elevator men do discuss daily the prices which they will pay in Kansas and other parts of the West, where the Chicago market comes into severe competition with other grain markets. The purpose is to agree upon a price high enough to bring the grain to Chicago. At practically all stations local dealers receive daily bids for their grain from a large number of buyers—often from 5 to 20. The existence of these competing bids is admitted by some of the opponents of the elevators.

Two country grain dealers from Iowa and Nebraska also testify that in their towns there are competing grain buyers, and that each of the local dealers receives bids directly from various elevator owners at Chicago and also from other markets, there being often a considerable range in the prices offered.[4]

The elevator owners maintain that the farmers are not only not injured by the existence of these large buyers, but that they are benefited by the elimination of various commissions and profits which were formerly paid by grain in its progress from the producer to the consumer, and by the many economies which elevator owners are able to effect. The elevator owner is satisfied with a little profit on a large business.[5]

The two local grain dealers referred to above also declare that the farmer benefits by the elimination of middlemen under the present practice. Moreover

---

[1] Webster, pp. 400–411; Counselman, pp. 382–389; Bartlett, p. 393.

[2] Dousman, p. 355; Greeley, pp. 371–376; Bookwalter, p. 576; Gallagher, p. 545; Vanlandingham p. 200; Sager, p. 451; Carter, p. 586.

[3] Counselman, pp. 384, 387; Bartlett, pp. 393–395; Webster, p. 416.

[4] Burke, pp. 465–467; Hulbert, pp. 486–489.

[5] Counselman, p. 384; Bartlett, pp. 393, 395; Snydacker, p. 396; Webster, pp. 405–415; Bookwalter, p. 574.

the reduction of the risk borne by the local dealer, from the fact that he receives bids for his grain on the track every day, enables him to work on a narrower margin.

Quality of grain.—It is claimed by certain witnesses that the owners of public warehouses have an unjust advantage over competing grain dealers from the fact that they are able to deliver to those who hold storage certificates the poorest quality of grain which will meet the official grade, while the owners themselves can take the best quality, for which they are able to obtain a higher price. The representative of a prominent milling company especially declares that millers are forced to disregard official inspections in order to prevent the warehousemen from giving them inferior qualities.[1] The elevator owners, on the other hand, declare that their practice of mixing and cleaning grain for the purpose of improving the grades is beneficial to all concerned; that there are no instances proved where unjust discriminations as to the quality of grain have been made, and that it is absurd to expect them to furnish to the public grain better than the official inspection requires.[2] There seems little doubt, however, that opportunities do exist for the warehousemen who store grain for the public and who are also grain owners to get an advantage in the way suggested. This seems the more probable from the fact, brought out in the testimony of one or two witnesses who are especially familiar with grain inspection, that the official grading of grain is necessarily imperfect.[3]

EXPORT GRAIN RATES AND FLOUR SHIPMENTS.

It appears clearly from the evidence that the railways have of late made specially low rates on grain hauled to the seaboard for export, while higher rates have been maintained on grain intended for domestic use and on flour, whether for domestic use or export. The chief complaint as to this practice comes from the American millers. Although the evidence is not entirely clear on this point, it is stated that these special export rates have been granted for the most part only since February 1, 1899. The discriminations were so great at times during 1899 that, while the Chicago miller would have to pay 21 cents per 100 pounds to get his flour to New York, the English miller could take wheat from Chicago to New York for 13 cents. The discrimination on shipments from points on the Mississippi and Missouri rivers to the Eastern seaboard and to the Gulf ports was even greater. The Interstate Commerce Commission investigated this subject, and issued an order on August 9, 1899, that the difference between export rates on wheat and on flour should not exceed 2 cents per hundred from Chicago, although the commission admits that it doubts its power in the matter.

It appears that some slight changes in rates were made soon after this order, and that on November 1, 1899, the export rates on grain were raised so that the difference from Chicago to the seaboard was 2 cents, as suggested by the Commission. The through grain rates from the Mississippi River, however, were changed to a less extent, so that it would still cost from 3 to 7 cents more for a miller at Chicago, Milwaukee, or Indianapolis to carry grain from the West to his mill and flour from the mill to the seaboard than it would cost the English miller to take grain from the Mississippi River to the coast, while there were differences of about the same amount between export wheat and domestic wheat, putting the miller on the seacoast at a like disadvantage as compared with the English miller.[4]

The evidence seems conclusive that the effect of this discrimination has already been disastrous to our milling interests, and that probably, even with the dif-

---

[1] Carter, pp. 582, 583; Sager, pp. 450–452; Dousman, p. 356; Greeley, p. 371.
[2] Webster, pp. 411, 413; Vanlandingham, pp. 200, 201.
[3] Clark, pp. 431–433; Evans, p. 440.
[4] Knapp, pp. 134, 142; Prouty, p. 146; Vanlandingham, p. 195; Barry, p. 249; Bacon, pp. 422–425; Sager, pp. 446, 447; Evans, pp. 435, 436; Gallagher, pp. 539, 540.

ference in rates reduced as already shown, it will continue to be injurious. Although very large flour shipments continued to be made early in 1899, in order to meet previous contracts or to dispose of stocks on hand, there was later in the year a great decrease in the demand for American flour. The exports from Minneapolis during September, 1899, were one-fourth less than during September, 1898, while exports from Duluth decreased more than one-half. At present American flour has a reputation which tends to keep up the demand, but when it is found that European millers are able to secure the same quality of grain and, owing to lower freight rates and cheaper labor, to turn it into flour at a reduced price, the American millers will probably find it very difficult to export, especially since the margin of profit in milling is very low.[1]

Justification of discriminations discussed.—The representatives of several railways, as well as one or two shipping merchants, declare that it is justifiable to make lower rates on grain for export than on grain for domestic use. The price of grain in foreign markets is determined by the competition of sources of supply all over the world, and American grain can be sold there only if it meets the market price. At times the conditions of competition are such that only by making a very low freight rate could American wheat be sold at all. The low export rate relieves the country of a surplus and is beneficial to the farmers; it is similar to the practice of manufacturers in selling their surplus abroad at lower prices than at home. If the railroads were compelled to make an equally low rate on grain for domestic use, they would be unable to make any profit whatever.[2]

One or two representatives of the railways also assert that the competition of Canadian carriers is more severe as to export grain than as to domestic grain, and that lower export rates are thus forced upon American railways.[3]

On the other hand, Mr. Prouty, of the Interstate Commerce Commission, declares that the investigation of that body showed that the market conditions in Europe during 1899 did not necessitate low export rates, but that the reduction in these rates was due primarily to the bitter competition of the American trunk lines. Several other witnesses hold the same opinion, and especially contend that these low export rates scarcely existed prior to 1899, and that no special change in conditions has arisen to necessitate them. America can produce grain as cheaply as any country, and lower export rates are less justifiable on grain than they would be on manufactured products.[4]

Railway officers also defend the making of lower rates on grain as compared with flour. The chief argument is that grain is easier and cheaper to handle, both as regards the weight which can be loaded into cars and as regards terminal services. Moreover, water competition is stronger in the case of wheat than of flour, especially because of the greater convenience with which grain can be loaded and unloaded from vessels. It is claimed also that railways can get full train loads of grain, and can get them at times when shipments are especially desired. Railways always charge higher rates for more valuable and more elaborated products than for cheaper crude products.[5]

Other witnesses,[6] however, declare emphatically that the railways can handle flour as cheaply as wheat. Flour for export, which is always in bags, can be piled up so as to make the load quite as heavy as that of wheat, and equal to the

[1] Barry, pp. 243, 246; Vanlandingham, p. 196; Sager, pp. 447, 448, 453; Gallagher, pp. 539, 545, 546, Evans, pp. 435–437.

[2] Neall, p. 166; Kelley, p. 188; Callaway, p. 234; Spencer, pp. 276, 281; Fish, pp. 336, 337; Tucker, p. 563; Snydacker, p. 397; Blanchard, pp. 628, 629; Gallagher, p. 543.

[3] Blanchard, p. 628.

[4] Prouty, pp. 146, 147; Vanlandingham, p. 195; Morton, p. 490; Barry, pp. 247, 248; Bacon, pp.424,425.

[5] Callaway, pp. 232, 233; Bird, pp. 473, 474; Tucker, pp. 563, 564; Blanchard, pp. 672, 673.

[6] Barry, pp. 244–250; Vanlandingham, pp. 197, 203–205; Bacon, p. 424; Evans, pp. 435–438; Sager, pp. 449, 450; Gallagher, pp. 540, 541, 543; Neall, pp. 164–166.

full capacity of the car. If the actual weight of carloads of flour averages less than that of wheat, it can be due only to the fault of railways, which often furnish small, old-fashioned cars for flour shipments. The expense of handling at terminals is not to be considered, since the cars are loaded by the miller and unloaded by the consignee. Grain shipments tend to concentrate themselves during a short period after harvest, when they interfere with other shipments and prevent the securing of return loads. The gradual shipment of flour throughout the year is an advantage to the railways. It should be to the interest of the railways also to favor milling interests because of the traffic in mill supplies and in the goods consumed by mill employees. One or two witnesses think that the reason for discrimination is that railways are interested in grain elevators and are themselves dealers in grain (see above, p. 8), while others believe that the officers of railways are interested in the terminal elevators and transfer facilities at the seaboard ports, especially at New York, and derive a profit from handling grain. This last argument is specifically denied by the representatives of the railways.[1]

Import rates.—It appears also from the testimony that railways sometimes make lower rates on goods imported from other countries than on the same goods produced in this country. Indeed, instances were mentioned in which the through rates, including ocean transportation, from European countries to inland points, or to the Pacific coast, have been considerably lower than the rates from points in this country, over the same routes, to the same destination.[2]

Remedy.—In view of the discriminations which are thus shown to have existed between the rates on goods exported or imported and goods of domestic origin and destination, it is urged by several witnesses that the power of the Interstate Commerce Commission be specifically extended to cover export and import traffic. It is claimed by some that the commission already has such power, but this is denied by many railway men, and the courts have held, as regards import traffic, that the commission has no power.[3]

DISCRIMINATIONS BETWEEN PLACES.

Many witnesses presented evidence concerning what they considered to be unjust discriminations in rates as between different places. Mr. Knapp points out that such discriminations are not secret, but result from unfairness of published tariffs.[4]

Long and short haul.—The form of place discriminations which is most conspicuously recognized in the interstate-commerce act is that of higher rates for a shorter distance over the same track than for a longer one. The so-called long and short haul clause of the act, however, declares such differences illegal only where conditions are similar, and it has been held by the courts that dissimilarity of conditions is caused by water competition, and even by competition among railways themselves. The witnesses point out that terminal points are naturally subject to such competition to a far greater degree than intermediate points. In the Southern States, largely on account of water competition along the Atlantic and Gulf coasts, and in the Western States also, on account of ocean transportation, the rates to terminal points are often conspicuously lower than those to intermediate points. The policy of the railways is stated by the members of the Interstate Commerce Commission to be to charge a gradually increasing rate to local points according to distance, until the rate becomes such that it would cost no more to ship the goods through to the terminal point and back to the local station.

[1] Blanchard, p. 673.
[2] Vanlandingham, p. 205; Prouty, p. 146; Reagan, pp. 340, 349; Morton, p. 493; Kindel, p. 290; Kelley, p. 188.
[3] Vanlandingham, p. 213; Gallagher, p. 589; Sager, pp. 447, 453; Barry, pp. 246; Reagan, p. 349.
[4] P. 133.

Since terminal charges are an important factor in rates, the intermediate rate may thus be materially higher than the through rate.[1]

Numerous specific instances were submitted by a witness residing in Colorado to show that the rates for the shorter haul from Chicago and other Eastern points to that State were much higher than those for the haul to Pacific coast points. Moreover, the rates on various commodities from Colorado to the Pacific coast and other Western points were shown to be often higher than those from Eastern points to the same destination. Thus the freight on books from Chicago to San Francisco was $1.75 per hundred pounds, and from Denver to San Francisco $3. The rate on boots and shoes from Chicago to Denver was $2.05, and from Chicago to San Francisco $1.50, etc. The witness claimed that the jobbing and manufacturing interests of Colorado have been very greatly injured by these discriminations.[2]

Other instances of higher rates for shorter hauls over the same road were mentioned by witnesses in connection with more general complaints as to differences in rates, often by separate roads, in favor of one market as against another.

A few witnesses think that the provision that dissimilar conditions may justify lower rates to competitive than to intermediate points should be repealed, or at least that the Interstate Commerce Commission should be given final authority to decide as to the justice of rates to different places on the same line.[3]

Several representatives of the railroads, owever, declare that discriminations between long and short hauls are made only under stress of necessity, and that if the rates for the shorter hauls are themselves reasonable, there should be no objection against lower rates to through points. At least one of these witnesses thinks that the entire long and short haul clause should be dropped from the interstate-commerce act.[4]

Other place discriminations.—Most of the discriminations between places of which complaint was made are between different terminal points or central markets, as distinguished from discriminations between terminal and intermediate points. Frequently the rates complained of are not made by the same railway system, but by different ones, with or without agreement among themselves. Thus the trunk lines from the West to the Eastern seaboard compete actively, especially for the export traffic in grain and grain products. It is a matter of indifference often to grain shippers whether their goods go by way of New York, Philadelphia, Baltimore, or other ports. Each railroad and each terminal point considers itself entitled to a certain proportion of traffic, and naturally the opinion of each differs from that of the other. In the particular case referred to an agreement was reached more than 20 years ago permitting railroads reaching Philadelphia to charge a rate 2 cents less per hundred pounds than those reaching New York, and granting those reaching Baltimore and more southern ports a similar "differential" of 3 cents. Each of the ports is inclined to complain that this adjustment of differentials is unfair.[5]

Similar adjustments of rates have been made with a view to putting the leading cities of the central West more or less on a par as distributing points for goods shipped from the East and as marketing points for grain and other products. Railway officers point out the immense difficulty of adjusting rates so as to do justice to different sections and cities, and the practical impossibility of satisfying all. They declare that the attempt of each railway, each section, and each city to get the largest possible proportion of traffic has been the chief cause of rate wars and disturbances, especially in the Northwestern States.[6] Since repre-

[1] Knapp, pp. 134, 137; Clements, pp. 154, 155; Vanlandingham, pp. 202, 206.

[2] Kindel, pp. 251-264.

[3] Dousman, p. 361; Bacon, p. 420; Clements, pp. 154, 155; Reagan, p. 342; Hyland, p. 352.

[4] Spencer, pp. 275, 281, 284; Blanchard, p. 628; Tucker, p. 560.

[5] Kelley, pp. 185, 186; Neall, p. 173; Callaway, pp. 224-226; Blanchard, p. 673.

[6] Blanchard, pp. 630, 631; Bird, p. 472; Ripley, pp. 597, 598.

sentatives of each of the leading cities are prepared to make complaints against each of the others, a large number of such conflicting complaints being actually made before the Industrial Commission,[1] it becomes very difficult for any public authority to decide as to the justice of the rates in any particular case.

Special reference was made by several witnesses to the effect of transportation by way of the Gulf of Mexico and the railways of the central West upon rail rates between that section and the Eastern seaboard. Some witnesses think that an undue proportion of traffic is diverted to Kansas City, St. Louis, New Orleans, and Galveston, and that the rail rates favor those points, while other witnesses think that the natural conditions—distances, grades, etc.—would justify the Southern ports in demanding a much larger proportion of the traffic than they actually receive.[2]

POOLING.

A large number of witnesses discussed the question of permitting railways to make pooling and other agreements. It was pointed out that pools were to be distinguished from other agreements as to rates or as to other matters. In the pool an agreement is made as to the proportion of business to be allotted to each of the roads entering the arrangement. Either tonnage is diverted from the roads receiving more than the agreed proportion or a money payment representing the profit on the surplus tonnage is made. Pooling agreements seldom fix rates, although, of course, rates are in practice greatly affected by them.[3]

The interstate-commerce act specifically prohibits pools, while the antitrust act of 1890 has been interpreted as prohibiting associations and agreements among railways with a view to fixing rates. It is now advocated by many witnesses that railways should be permitted to make agreements of any kind, and that pooling contracts should be not only legalized, but made enforceable by law. The chief difficulty, it is said, with the pools which formerly existed was that they were outside of the pale of the law, and that there was no way of punishing a railway belonging to a pool which should attempt to divert traffic to itself or should refuse to divide returns. The advocates of pooling include nearly all of the railway officers who appeared before the Commission. A number of shippers, representatives of commercial bodies, members of the Interstate Commerce Commission, and other expert students of transportation also favor pooling, but usually only with the proviso that much more effective governmental control than at present be exercised over rates and over pooling contracts. It was declared by two or three witnesses also that a very general consensus of opinion in favor of pooling exists on the part of other persons throughout the country.[4]

Arguments against pooling are vigorously presented by Mr. Stickney, of the Chicago Great Western Railway, by two officers representing the Chicago Board of Trade, by Mr. Vanlandingham, the commissioner of the St. Louis Traffic Bureau, and by one or two others; their general position being that the practice would tend to maintain high rates by checking the legitimate competition between railways. Mr. Vanlandingham, however, would permit railways to agree as to rates.[5]

---

[1] Complaints regarding discriminations against Chicago, Kennard, p. 365; Mallory, p. 588; discriminations against St. Louis, Vanlandingham, pp. 194-199, 206; against Kansas City, Bookwalter, pp. 570-578; Mallory, p. 588; against Milwaukee, Bacon, p. 418; against La Crosse, Dickinson, p. 549; against Norfolk, Nebr., Fuller, pp. 442-446; against Grand Rapids, Musselman, p. 556.

[2] Vanlandingham, pp. 197, 206; Knapp, p. 133; Callaway, p. 225; Fish, pp. 321-330.

[3] Newcomb, p. 97; Cowen, p. 314; Blanchard, pp. 677, 643, 665; Ingalls, pp. 286, 297.

[4] Public officers, etc.: Knapp, p. 138; Prouty, p. 150; Newcomb, pp. 96-98; Johnson, p. 62; Reagan, p. 345; Seligman, pp. 614-617. Railway men: Blanchard, pp. 640-649; Woffindin, pp. 565, 566; Callaway, pp. 235-238; Ingalls, pp. 286, 296-300; Spencer, p. 280; Cowen, pp. 314, 315; Bird, p. 474; Tucker, pp. 558-561; Morton, pp. 491, 495, 499; Ripley, p. 593. Shippers: Neall, p. 173; Evans, p. 441; Kelley, pp. 190, 191; Counselman, pp. 390, 391; Bacon, pp. 420, 426.

[5] Hyland, pp. 351, 353; Vanlandingham, pp. 214, 216; Stone, pp. 532-535; Stickney, p. 463; Carter, p. 585.

Pooling and competition.—The argument in favor of pooling rests on the position, as stated by several witnesses, that competition between railways is abnormal and destructive, tending to reduce rates to an unprofitable figure, to cause sudden fluctuations injurious to the stability of business, and to induce discriminations between individuals. Several witnesses maintain that the conditions of competition in the railway business are entirely different from those in the production and sale of ordinary commodities; that the poorest railway, such as one which is in the hands of receivers, and therefore not forced to pay dividends, can cut rates with a view to diverting traffic unduly, and can thereby force other railways to make unprofitable rates. The experience of the past with rate wars is referred to as evidence of the destructive character of railway competition. It is pointed out that the control which the Government can and does exercise over railway rates makes competition unnecessary, in a way which would not be true as to other business.[1]

At the same time the defenders of pooling claim that pools would not absolutely prevent competition and would not permit railways to charge excessive rates. The competition of water carriers, not only those immediately parallel to railways but often those far distant, would in many cases keep down rates. The chief influence affecting rates is the competition of different markets, frequently of markets all over the world. If the railways in one section should attempt to maintain excessive rates, products of that section could not compete with those of another section, perhaps far removed. Reasonable competition, moreover, still exists among pooled railroads themselves, especially in the way of offering greater facilities and conveniences, for the sake of justifying a claim to a larger proportion of the business. The experience of the country with pools in the past is cited as showing that rates have not been maintained at excessive figures, but have actually been reduced under pools. It is also asserted that pooling is recognized in all leading European countries as a necessary remedy for excessive rate cutting and discriminations, government roads even entering pools with private lines, and that it has not tended toward excessive rates.[2]

On the other hand, it was claimed by two or three witnesses that competition is as natural, necessary, and beneficial in the railway business as in any other; that pooling would mean nothing else than monopoly, and that pools in the past have had injurious effects, tending toward excessive rates, and not preventing other evils.[3]

Pooling and discriminations.—Pooling is especially advocated by railway officers and others on the ground that it would tend to check discriminations between persons and between places, which it is claimed are the natural result of excessive competition. It is urged that the only method by which discriminations can be prevented is by interesting the railways themselves to prevent them.[4]

A few witnesses, however, maintain that railways would still be inclined to grant discriminating rates for the sake of increasing their proportion of traffic, in order to secure a larger allotment when the proportions of the roads in the pool should be fixed for the next time.[5]

To this it is replied that as a matter of fact the proportion of business allotted to each road is determined by other considerations than temporary changes in tonnage.[6]

Control of pooling by the Interstate Commerce Commission.—All of the members of the Interstate Commerce Commission, general students, and representatives of

---

[1] Knapp, p. 138; Seligman, p. 615; Blanchard, pp. 635–640; Ripley, pp. 593, 594; Tucker, pp. 560, 561.

[2] Blanchard, pp. 643–647, 651–656, 664; Ripley, pp. 593, 595; Cowen, pp. 314, 315; Ingalls, p. 299; Callaway, pp. 235–238; Newcomb, p. 96.

[3] Stone, p. 532–537; Stickney, p. 460.

[4] See especially Blanchard, pp. 644, 675, 683; Ripley, pp. 594, 596; Tucker, p. 558; Musselman, p. 557, and other witnesses already referred to generally.

[5] Vanlandingham, pp. 214, 216; Hyland, p. 351; Greeley, p. 374; Stone, p. 535.

[6] Ripley, p. 596.

shippers who favor pooling think that the Interstate Commerce Commission should be given a very great degree of control over the terms of pools, and especially over the rates on pooled roads. Otherwise it is feared that extortionate rates may result from the removal of competition. Mr. Clements, of the Interstate Commerce Commission, is disposed to doubt the possibility of proper regulation, and hence the wisdom of permitting pooling at all. The majority of the railway officers who testify on this subject also express themselves as willing to concede such control to the commission, and there is no specific opposition to it. The degree of control suggested by the various witnesses of course differs. Many go so far as to favor giving the commission absolute power to approve or disapprove a pooling agreement or to discontinue it at any time, and also to fix rates finally so far as they apply to pooled traffic.[1] A few railway men think that the commission should be given little more power over the rates under pools than over rates in general.[2]

REASONABLENESS OF FREIGHT RATES.

There is comparatively little complaint on the part of witnesses before the Industrial Commission concerning excessive freight rates, aside from the complaints regarding discriminations between individuals and places.

On the other hand, many witnesses, including both representatives of railways and others, maintain that American freight rates are reasonable, and are, in fact, remarkably low. Some of these witnesses point out the great complexity of the influences affecting the carrying of freight, and the consequent difficulty of determining whether a particular freight rate is just. The justice of rates can be judged only by comparison between different commodities and different places, and by considering the profits of the railway. It is insisted that it is ordinarily impossible for freight rates to be excessive upon any railway or in any section of the country, on account of the competition of products and markets themselves. Rates must be made such that goods can be produced and marketed, and this fact not only is of prime importance in determining relative rates on different commodities, but also practically prevents unfairly high rates.[3] For this reason the proposition[4] that railway rates should be made strictly uniform on the basis of mileage is declared to be neither feasible nor necessary to secure justice. The differences of conditions, both as to the expenses of transportation and as to competition for markets, necessitate different charges in different parts of the country.[5]

It is shown further by the testimony that freight rates in the United States have decreased steadily and with considerable rapidity during the past 30 years. Numerous specific statistics concerning the decrease in rates are presented. For example, it is stated that the average rate per ton per mile in 1873 was 2.21 cents, and in 1895, 0.839 cent. At the same time it is claimed that the profits of the railway business have declined, the present returns on securities being, on the average, exceedingly low. Opinion as to the last matter will, of course, depend on the belief as to the extent to which railway securities represent actual investment of capital. (See p. 19.) It is also stated by many witnesses that the freight rates in this country are materially lower than in foreign countries, although it is admitted

---

[1] Knapp, pp. 138, 141; Prouty, p. 150; Clements, p. 157; Ingalls, pp. 287, 299; Cowen, p. 315; Counselman, p. 391; Kelley, pp. 190, 191; Bacon, p. 421. See also statements of witnesses above named.
[2] Morton, pp. 491, 495, 499; Blanchard, pp. 640, 643, 678, 682.
[3] Blanchard, pp. 626, 627, 630; Newcomb, pp. 96, 99–101; Callaway, pp. 223, 226, 235; Stickney, pp. 460–463; Tucker, p. 559.
[4] Dousman, pp. 359–361.
[5] Morton, pp. 498, 499.

that some of our local rates are as high as those abroad, the average being reduced by our low through rates on long hauls. No detailed comparisons of American and foreign freight rates have been thus far submitted.[1]

CLASSIFICATION OF FREIGHT.

There is a movement of considerable strength in favor of a uniform system of classifying freight over the entire country. This is advocated by many shippers, and some of them are inclined to believe that the Interstate Commerce Commission should be given power to establish such a uniform classification, or at least to require the railways to do so. There are at present three different systems of classification—the Official, applying north of the Potomac and east of the Mississippi (with certain exceptions as to traffic west of Chicago); the Southern, applying south of the Potomac and east of the Mississippi, and the Western. It is claimed by shippers that great inconvenience occurs on account of the differences under these systems. It is impossible for shippers to ascertain accurately the rates on any particular commodity where it passes from one region to another having a different classification. The differences also give rise to discriminations between shippers. Thus goods shipped from Eastern points through Chicago to points in Wisconsin and Illinois come under the Official classification, while similar goods shipped directly from Chicago, from Mississippi River points, or other points in that section, come under the Western classification, by which the rates are likely to be higher, putting the Western shipper at a disadvantage in competition.[2]

A number of railway officers also expressed themselves in favor of uniform classification, and some of these believe it to be feasible to make the classes absolutely alike in all sections.[3]

Others, while admitting the desirability of more uniform classification, think that absolute uniformity is out of the question, and that the railroads should be left to approach more and more toward uniformity as their experience and interests may dictate. It is pointed out that the number of classifications, and the number of classes in each, have been greatly reduced in recent years, and that the railways themselves some time ago actively sought to secure a single classification, although the attempt failed on account of the opposition of certain railways in different sections to the assignment of particular commodities. It is urged by some witnesses with considerable force that the conditions of different sections necessitate differences in classification. In each section the goods which are most largely produced there must be given favoring rates in order that they may compete in the world market; while it would be unjust to require similarly low rates on railways in a section where little of such commodities is carried. It is declared that these differences in conditions have necessitated the adoption of special "commodity rates" outside of the regular classifications, and that even if a uniform classification should be established as regards most articles, these special rates on the more bulky commodities would still be necessary.[4]

There is evident a desire, however, on the part of both railways and shippers, that a greater degree of uniformity should be secured, and many favor conservative action of Government to further the movement. Most railway officers think that the railways themselves should frame the classification, even if uniformity be required by law, and comparatively few witnesses favor giving a Government commission entire control of classification.[4]

---

[1] Newcomb, pp. 101, 108; Blanchard, pp. 630, 631; Callaway, p. 223; Cowen, pp. 315, 318; Clements, pp. 153, 161; Morton, p. 498; Ripley, p. 593; Vanlandingham, pp. 201, 204; Spencer, pp. 278, 279; Stone, pp. 536, 538; Seligman, p. 614; Lewis, p. 733.
[2] Newcomb, p. 100; Knapp, p. 142; Kelley, p. 191; Emerson, p. 483; Dickinson, pp. 548, 550.
[3] Ripley, pp. 568-570; Morton, pp. 491, 496, 497; Ingalls, p. 300.
[4] Blanchard, pp. 626, 627, 632-634, 676; Vanlandingham, pp. 202-204; Spencer, p. 277; Cowen, p. 217; Callaway, p. 237; Kelley, p. 191.

PASSENGER TRAFFIC.

Reasonableness of fares.—Little complaint has been made by witnesses on the ground that passenger fares are excessive or discriminating, although two or three declare that our fares are considerably higher than those in European countries.[1] Representatives of the railways, on the other hand, especially defend the reasonableness of American passenger charges. They think that satisfactory comparisons with other countries are impossible because of the European practice of establishing different classes with widely different fares. It is claimed, too, that the average service in America is very much superior in comfort, speed, and other regards to that in Europe. So far as differences in fares exist in different parts of the United States, these are justified chiefly on account of the differences in the density of traffic and in the consequent cost of transportation, while other special reasons account for particular variations in rates.[2]

Passes.[3]—There seems to be a general agreement among all classes of witnesses that the issue of free passes is carried to a degree which makes it a serious evil. It is generally claimed that fewer passes are issued now than ten or fifteen years ago, and that the railways themselves are more and more inclined to reduce the number. It appears, however, that passes are still frequently granted to the members of State and national legislatures and to public officers of many classes; that they are sometimes issued to shippers and thus may constitute a form of freight discrimination; while they are largely issued in exchange for newspaper advertising and for other services and to employees of railroads. Some witnesses think that the revenues of railways are reduced appreciably by granting free transportation, and that thus indirectly the fares of paying passengers are increased, but others think that the extent of the practice is not sufficient to have this effect. Stress is often laid on the opinion that the issue of passes to public officers and legislators involves an element of bribery; although some witnesses claim that this is not true, but that the practice is simply a conventional one due to respect for public authorities.

Most of the witnesses believe that practically no passes should be issued except to the employees of the issuing railway themselves, although some would favor issuing them to employees of other railways traveling on official business. Perhaps a majority of the witnesses consider legislation on the matter unnecessary, but not a few believe that laws would be helpful in aiding the railways to check the evil. Several States already have laws prohibiting the issue of passes to public officers, but one witness maintains that the effect of such laws is really to increase the number of passes, since officers, being unable to use them personally, demand them for their friends and supporters.

Ticket brokerage.[4]—Most witnesses so far heard on this subject are representatives of railways, and these almost uniformly favor legislation prohibiting the sale and purchase of unused parts of passenger tickets. This position is also taken by several other witnesses. The witnesses who discuss the subject most fully declare that ticket "scalping" usually consists in the purchase and sale of parts of tickets which have been issued by railways at less than the regular rates for some justifiable reason, with the understanding that the entire ticket shall be used by the original buyer. For example, round-trip tickets are sold at reduced rates. So, too, through tickets

---

[1] Weyl, p. 758; Lewis, p. 733; Seligman, p. 614; Johnson, p. 61.

[2] Blanchard, pp. 618–620; Callaway, p. 229; Ingalls, p. 292; Spencer, p. 275; Morton, pp. 490, 498; Cowen, p. 310; Johnson, p. 61.

[3] Knapp, pp. 135, 136; Prouty, p. 152; Reagan, pp. 341, 342; Ingalls, pp. 293–295; Fish, pp. 334, 335; Spencer, p. 270; Callaway, p. 229; Bird, pp. 468, 469; Morton, p. 490; Cowen, pp. 310–313; Blanchard, pp. 620, 621, 669; Stickney, pp. 456, 457; Dickinson, pp. 552–554.

[4] Blanchard, pp. 621–623, 666–671; Morton, pp. 489, 500; Spencer, pp. 269–272; Ingalls, pp. 293, 294; Cowen, pp. 309, 310; Stickney, p. 457; Callaway, p. 227; Bird, p. 469; Reagan, p. 350; Johnson, p. 61; Wilson, p. 768; Fish, p. 333; Vanlandingham, p. 214.

are often issued over connecting lines, making a trip considerably longer than the shortest possible railway route; these tickets must necessarily be sold at the same price as those over the direct line, so that there is opportunity for scalping the separate coupons. It is maintained that the railways already usually provide for the redemption of unused parts of tickets at a rate such as to make the fare for the distance actually traveled the same as that which would have been paid if the ticket for that distance had been bought in the first place. At any rate, the witnesses would be willing that a law prohibiting scalping should include a requirement that unused tickets be redeemed in this way. It is claimed that the fear of unauthorized use of reduced-fare tickets has a material effect in preventing the sale of such tickets by the railroads. The general public suffers more from this effect, perhaps, than from the increase of ordinary fares necessitated by loss of revenue to the railways through scalping.

These witnesses claim also that ticket brokerage leads to many fraudulent and illegitimate practices, such as the alteration of dates, the forging of signatures, the counterfeiting of tickets, and the stealing of tickets by railroad employees. Moreover, railways themselves have often connived with ticket brokers by selling them tickets at reduced rates with a view to secretly drawing a larger proportion of traffic than they could secure under open and equal rates. Opinions differ as to the extent of this latter practice at present, although most witnesses think it is not so common as formerly. Some believe that if the railways should cease to patronize the brokers they would be driven out of business, but the more common opinion seems to be that a large part, perhaps the most, of their business comes from other sources.

Although various methods have been proposed by which the railways themselves should check the sale of unused parts of tickets, it is claimed that none of them is thoroughly effective and that the only sufficient remedy is to be found by direct legislation, either by Congress or by the States.

CAPITALIZATION OF RAILWAYS.

It has been suggested that judgment as to the reasonableness of rates and fares from the standpoint of the earnings of railways will depend largely upon the question whether or how far their capital is inflated. Several witnesses declare, in general terms, that the amount of the stocks and bonds of most railways is far greater than their original cost or the cost of reproduction, and that even the bonds in many cases exceed the actual cost of construction. No detailed investigation of this subject was made. Some of the witnesses advocate that hereafter the issue of stocks should be controlled carefully by State authorities or, so far as constitutionally possible, by Federal authorities.[1]

Most of the arguments in opposition to this view are also of a general nature, pointing to the great increase in the value of terminals and of rights of way, to the large expenditure of earnings for improvement of properties, etc., as indicating that American railways, whether at first overcapitalized or not, are not now overcapitalized. It is also urged that overcapitalization in any case has practically no effect on rates, which are determined by competition (a statement which is questioned by one or two other witnesses), and that it does not deceive investors, since the market value of the stock is dependent on actual earning power.[2]

One witness presents detailed comparisons, showing that during the past decade the capitalization of American railways has increased only in proportion to the increase of mileage, while the capitalization of British railways has increased much more rapidly and is now fully four times as great per mile as that of American lines.[3]

[1] Reagan, pp. 341–345; Knapp, pp. 144, 145; Clements, p. 160; Johnson, pp. 60, 62; Seligman, pp. 609, 610.
[2] Callaway, pp. 227, 228; Ingalls, p. 298; Cowen, p. 318; Newcomb, pp. 100, 101; Morton, p. 501.
[3] Fish, pp. 326–332.

CONSOLIDATION OF RAILWAYS.

Several witnesses refer to the recent well-known tendency toward consolidation in the ownership of railways. These consolidations take the form either of the establishment of long connecting systems, or, in some cases, of the common ownership of parallel and previously competing lines. Little detailed evidence as to the extent of this process of consolidation was presented. Members of the Interstate Commerce Commission declare that, although consolidation may result in certain advantages, it also necessitates more effective supervision.[1]

Railroad officers assert that consolidation has been forced in certain cases by the prohibition of pooling. It is also justifiable, they say, on account of the great economies in management and the improved facilities which are thus made possible. It is claimed that rates have been reduced, service improved, and discriminations checked by the consolidations hitherto made.[2]

The only representative of railway labor who mentions this subject sees nothing in consolidation to which to object.[3]

PROPOSED INCREASE OF POWERS OF INTERSTATE COMMERCE COMMISSION.

There is a very general feeling shown by the witnesses representing shippers, by members of the Interstate Commerce Commission, and others, that the interstate-commerce act should be amended so as to increase the powers of the Interstate Commerce Commission in one way or another. It is asserted that the commission has found its powers constantly decreased, especially by the interpretations of the courts, and that its influence is at present chiefly an educational one.[4] The evils of railway management, these witnesses claim, are still many. The public character of railways, their great influence upon the general welfare, and their dependence on the State for their privileges, justify a greater degree of Government regulation of railways than of almost any other branch of industry, and a degree materially greater than is at present exercised.

Several railway officers recognize the public character of railroads, and some are willing that a greater measure of power should be given to the Interstate Commerce Commission. These same witnesses and others, however, argue that the rights of railways must also be considered, and that legislation must not prevent the furnishing of proper service, the payment of proper wages, or the earning of a fair return on the investment. It is thought by some of these witnesses that the public is disposed to be unduly hostile to railways.[5]

General power of commission over rates.—It is proposed by two or three witnesses that the Interstate Commerce Commission should have power to prepare general freight classifications and schedules of rates in the first instance, instead of being confined as at present to action on complaints concerning established rates and to the mere ability to declare existing rates unreasonable without prescribing other rates.[6] Other witnesses think it would be sufficient to give the commission power to revise tariffs framed by the railroads, either on its own initiative or after complaint, and to reduce or change unreasonable rates, fixing the rate which shall prevail. Some of these witnesses hold that the decision of the

---

[1] Knapp, p. 141; Prouty, p. 153.
[2] Morton, pp. 490, 496, 497, 499; Spencer, p. 278; Ingalls, pp. 296, 298.
[3] Sargent, p. 70.
[4] Knapp, pp. 135, 139, 140; Clements, p. 159; Kindel, p. 261; Musselman, p. 557; and the same position is implied in the demand of many others for specific additions to the commission's powers.
[5] Ingalls, pp. 285, 288, 297; Ripley, pp. 594, 595; Blanchard, pp. 624, 625; Callaway, pp. 296, 297, 239; Bird, p. 479.
[6] Reagan, pp. 339, 345, 346; Woffindin, pp. 566, 567; Clements, pp. 155, 158, 161.

commission in these cases should be final and not subject to appeal to the courts. They urge that the commission has technical knowledge of railway matters which is wanting in the judges. Others would be willing to have the courts review the decision, although they would have it enforced pending appeal. Detailed arguments are not presented in favor of this position, but it is claimed generally that many unjust rates still exist, both rates excessive in their amount, and open rates which discriminate between different places or classes of traffic. The power simply to declare a given rate unreasonable is very ineffective.[1]

A few representatives of the railways would be willing to give the Interstate Commerce Commission power to revise rates or to fix them after complaint, but none of them thinks that the commission would be competent to fix rates generally in the first instance, and most believe that it should be confined, as at present, to declaring existing rates unreasonable.[2] It is argued that the making of rates even for a single railway or section of the country is an exceedingly difficult task, and that no body of men, even though all were experts, could fix rates for the entire country. The influences affecting freight traffic are so numerous and complicated, and so constantly changing, that only the highest skill can fix rates even approximately fair to all interests. Some witnesses claim that even to fix a comparatively limited number of rates, under the power of revision, would in many cases be beyond the competency of a body of five men not especially trained by actual experience in railway management.

It is urged especially in this connection by Mr. Blanchard that the power to fix rates is essentially a legislative one, and that it would be contrary to our principles of government to give one body the power to fix rates in the first instance, to investigate as to compliance with them, by inspecting the accounts of railways and otherwise, and to judge concerning their reasonableness and application. In England, which is appealed to as an example, rates are not fixed by the railway and canal commission, but by act of Parliament; the railway and canal commission is restricted, for the most part, to purely judicial functions, and acts only in case of complaint. Moreover the English commission is composed partly of life members, and partly of judges who, as judges, have life tenure. This gives the body a judicial spirit not found in the Interstate Commerce Commission, which is subject to political influences, and which changes frequently in its membership. For these reasons this witness especially opposes the suggestion that the Interstate Commerce Commission be given final power.

Enforcement of commission's orders pending appeal.—Those who favor an increase of the powers of the Interstate Commerce Commission often lay even greater stress on the desirability of making its orders binding on the railways pending appeal to the courts than on that of giving it more extended power as to fixing rates in the first instance.[3] The two positions are not always clearly distinguished, nor is issue always clearly drawn as to them between those witnesses who favor an increase in the regulation of railways and those who on the whole oppose it. Some railway officers are willing that the decisions of the commission should remain binding until declared unjust by the courts, although part of them apparently would wish to make this only as a concession in exchange for the privilege of pooling.

---

[1] Vanlandingham, pp. 212–214; Kennard, p. 367; Bacon, p. 419; Kelley, p. 192; Dousman, pp. 358–361; Stone, pp. 537, 538; Wilson, p. 767; Ronemus, p. 771; Dickinson, p. 549.

[2] Blanchard, pp. 661–665; Ripley, pp. 596, 597; Morton, pp. 492, 495, 496; Stickney, p. 463; Spencer, pp. 276, 282; Cowen, pp. 314, 315; Callaway, pp. 236, 237, 239; Bird, p. 479.

[3] Clements, pp. 155, 158, 161; Moseley, pp. 41, 43; Newcomb, pp. 103, 104; Bacon, pp. 419–422; Vanlandingham, p. 212; Dousman, pp. 358–361; Mallory, pp. 587, 588; Baker, p. 592; Barry, pp. 246, 247, 250; Carter, p. 585; Musselman, p. 557; Stone, pp. 537, 538; Ingalls, pp. 299, 300; Cowen, pp. 314, 315; Evans, p. 439.

Those who favor the enforcement of the decisions of the Interstate Commerce Commission pending appeal declare that at present the railways very frequently, perhaps usually, disregard the orders of the commission, and that the commission is compelled to bring suit before a court to enforce them. The court takes up the matter de novo, considering not merely the law, but also the facts, and often taking entirely new evidence. The case may then be appealed from one court to another, and it may be years before a final decision is reached. Meantime the rates complained of have remained in force, and the injury may easily have become irreparable, or the occasion for the complaint, being of a temporary nature, may have disappeared. The right of the shipper to collect damages in view of a past injury is decidedly ineffective, especially since the burden of excessive or discriminating rates may have been shifted in part by him upon the general community. It is claimed that on this account, as well as because of the expense of pushing a case to final conclusion, persons injured by the action of railways have almost ceased to appeal to the Interstate Commerce Commission for relief. Much more is accomplished by the action of associations of shippers in influencing railways directly.

Some representatives of the railways oppose also this increase of the power of the Interstate Commerce Commission, presenting similar objections to those mentioned above. It is argued that the railways may be injured just as truly as the shippers by being compelled to make rates unjust to themselves pending appeal, and that they have no such recourse in damages as the shippers have. The courts may not have the technical knowledge possessed by the commission, but their proceedings are subject to fixed rules and the judges are trained to consider the principles of law and the rights of property, while their tenure of office makes them much freer from political and personal influences.[1]

The conclusion seems clear from the testimony that the powers of the Interstate Commerce Commission at present are decidedly limited, probably somewhat more limited than was the intention of the framers of the interstate-commerce act. The suggestion is made by certain witnesses that some changes in the character of the commission itself, tending to make it more a judicial body, would make more justifiable an increase of its powers.

OTHER PROPOSED LEGISLATION.

Aside from the proposed legislation specially mentioned elsewhere, such as that regarding pooling, powers of the Interstate Commerce Commission, the issue of passes, ticket brokerage, railway labor, etc., various other suggestions have been advocated by one or more witnesses. The most important are the following:

1. *Membership of the Interstate Commerce Commission.*—It is thought that the Interstate Commerce Commission should be increased in number on account of the increase of railway business. A representative of the railways also urges that a certain proportion of the members should be railway men, familiar with the actual conditions of the business.[2]

2. *Conferences with railways.*—It is also suggested that special provisions should be made in the interstate-commerce law for conferences between the commission and representatives of the railways, with a view to promoting mutual understanding and harmony.[3] Such conferences already held are said to have proved very useful. In this connection it is also recommended that the commission should issue a monthly bulletin stating all complaints, without the names of the railways or the complainants.

---

[1] Blanchard, pp. 659–665; Spencer, pp. 282, 283; Tucker, pp. 558, 560; Stickney, p. 463.
[2] Blanchard, pp. 664, 665, 678.
[3] Blanchard, p. 665.

3. *Publicity of accounts.*—Numerous witnesses urge that all of the affairs of railways should be made much more public than at present. Publicity will tend to prevent excessive and discriminating rates on the one hand, and, on the other hand, will often dissipate prejudice against the railways by giving knowledge of actual facts. Indeed, it will promote mutual understanding and good feeling. For the sake of securing this publicity it is suggested that the Interstate Commerce Commission should have power to appoint inspectors to examine the books of railways, and also that reports should be required from the railways in much greater detail than at present. The public character of railway service is held especially to justify such publicity.[1] The advocates of publicity include several railway officers. On the other hand, two or three prominent railway officers think that little would be accomplished by the inspection of books, etc., and that perhaps some injustice would be done to the railways.[2]

4. *Construction of railways.*—Two or three witnesses representing the railways think that the United States and the separate States should restrict the construction of competing railroads as a protection to the existing lines. Additional railroads often involve a needless duplication of facilities, waste of capital, and excessive competition.[3]

5. *Control over water transportation.*—It is suggested by one or two witnesses that the absence of control by the Interstate Commerce Commission over water transportation results in unwarranted cutting of rates and unjust discriminations between persons and places, and it is thought that the power of the Commission should be extended to water carriers so far as regards coastwise, lake, and river traffic.[4]

6. *Control of shipments within States.*—It is urged, from both the standpoint of shippers and that of railways, that, if this were possible under the Constitution, it would be desirable that the National Government should have control over traffic within States as well as over interstate traffic. Much traffic moving wholly within a State is essentially interstate in character. Discriminations are often granted, it is claimed, on traffic within a State with a view to influencing shipments of interstate traffic; while inequalities as between different places easily arise from the absence of control over intrastate railways.[5]

GOVERNMENT OWNERSHIP.

Railroads.—Very few witnesses on transportation who have thus far appeared before the Commission have advocated government ownership of railways. Several witnesses in the trust investigation advocated public ownership of railways as the only effective means of preventing discriminations, and at least one witness in the transportation investigation suggests this as a sufficient ground for favoring public ownership.[6] Another witness submits a somewhat detailed argument in favor of the system, declaring that it will tend to reduce fares and rates, to develop the country more rapidly and equally, to improve the condition of railway labor, to prevent losses and wastefulness arising from excessive competition and from speculation, and to produce still other advantages. It is believed by this witness that satisfactory financial results could be obtained from the railroads by the Government, as has been the case with the government railways of Prussia. He does not believe that there would be as serious political evils as those

[1] Knapp, p. 144; Stone, p. 538; Reagan, p. 349; Prouty, p. 151; Bacon, p. 430; Clements, pp. 159, 160; Newcomb, p. 100; Johnson, p. 62; Ingalls, pp. 287, 297, 301; Spencer, pp. 274, 278; Morton, p. 500.
[2] Callaway, pp. 237, 238; Cowen, pp. 317, 318; Stickney, p. 464.
[3] Blanchard, pp. 663, 680; Ingalls, p. 287; Morton, p. 492; Ripley, p. 594.
[4] Johnson, p. 63; Kelley, p. 189.
[5] Vanlandingham, p. 214; Morton, pp. 492, 501.
[6] Greeley, pp. 379–381.

which exist at present from the interference of private railways in politics, but he declares that thorough civil-service reform would be essential to the greatest success.[1]

Several railway officers, on the other hand, declare that under private owner-ship American railways are furnishing better service at lower rates than the government railways of Europe. This statement is denied by one or two other witnesses, but no detailed evidence is submitted on either side. These officers insist that all government enterprises in this country are extravagantly managed and that government management of railways would necessarily be less econom-ical than private ownership. They urge especially the political danger of making so many persons dependent on government employment, as well as that likely to arise from sectional conflicts as to construction of railways, rates, etc.[2] Two or three other witnesses aside from railway officers express essentially the same opinions.[3]

Professor Seligman, of Columbia University, presents the argument against government ownership more fully and broadly. He declares that the large capital invested in railways and the great complexity of their management make them unfit for public control, at the present stage of American political develop-ment, although he approves government ownership in Germany. Individual initiative turns ability most strongly toward reducing the cost of service by improved methods.[4]

Government ownership of telegraphs and telephones.—On the other hand, Profes-sor Seligman thinks that the comparatively small capital involved in the telegraph and telephone business and the relative simplicity of their management favor public ownership, while the widespread social interest in these facilities makes government ownership, as against monopolistic private ownership, especially desirable. The telegraph and telephone are becoming as necessary as the post, and the same arguments which justify government control in one case justify it in the other.[5] England and nearly all the continental countries of Europe have public telegraph and telephone systems. Several other witnesses complain of the high charges for telegraph and telephone service in this country, and express them-selves in favor of putting these facilities under the Post-Office Department,[6] while one or two express themselves as satisfied with existing conditions.[7]

RAILWAY TAXATION.

The most detailed testimony concerning the subject of railway taxation is that of Professor Seligman.[8] He discusses the different methods of taxation, points out the great difficulty of avoiding double taxation as well as of preventing evasion, and reaches the conclusion that a tax based on net receipts is most equitable. Such a tax, however, would in practice be apt to result in evasions, unless there were a very thorough inspection of railway accounts by the Govern-ment. This difficulty has led many of our States to tax the gross receipts of railroads; a system which has many practical advantages, especially in view of the legal difficulties, under our Constitution, of the just taxation of stocks and bonds. The tax on gross receipts is also favored by Professor Johnson, of the

[1] Lewis, pp. 72–751.

[2] Cowen, pp. 319, 320; Fish, p. 338; Morton, pp. 492, 497-499; Spencer, pp. 279, 283, 284; Ingalls, p. 299; Ripley, p. 598; Callaway, p. 239.

[3] Knapp, p. 145; Newcomb, pp. 102, 103; Reagan, p. 347.

[4] Seligman, pp. 607-613.

[5] Seligman, pp. 610-612.

[6] Kennard, p. 366: Fuller, p. 446; Greeley, p. 381.

[7] Snydacker, p. 400; Counselman, p. 392.

[8] Pp. 599-606.

University of Pennsylvania,[1] Mr. Callaway,[2] of the New York Central, and Mr. Fish,[3] of the Illinois Central. Mr. Newcomb, of the division of agriculture, United States Census, however, favors the net-receipts tax on the ground that a gross-receipts tax tends to produce high rates and fares.[4]

Two or three other witnesses prefer the system of assessment of the physical property of the railways for the general property tax. Mr. Reagan thinks that the assessment in that case should be made by the State railway commission rather than by any other authority.[5]

GENERAL RELATIONS OF RAILWAY EMPLOYERS AND EMPLOYEES.

The commission has taken the testimony of the chief officers of all the leading organizations of railway employees, as well as some testimony of representatives of the railways and of other witnesses, as to the conditions of railway labor.

Qualifications.—Some few complaints were made concerning the tests as to physical ability, eyesight, etc., and concerning the age limits fixed as conditions for employment on certain railways.[6] Railway officers state that somewhat strict conditions regarding the use of intoxicants are usually imposed.

Union membership.—It appears from the testimony that most railways make no discrimination against members of the various brotherhoods and other organizations in granting employment or in the conditions of work; but it is claimed that occasionally there is such discrimination, especially against prominent union leaders. Although the United States statute of 1898 prohibiting this practice is not perhaps openly violated, men can be refused employment, denied promotion, or discharged, on various pretexts, where the real ground is objection to union membership. Several witnesses think that for the sake of reaching these exceptional cases the law should be made even more stringent and the penalty more severe than at present. This subject connects itself closely with that of blacklisting.[7]

Discharge and suspension.—It is also claimed by several witnesses that injustice is sometimes done in the discharge of railway employees. Thus men are at times discharged on account of personal whims and prejudices on the part of their immediate superiors, and without proper hearing. Employees are also sometimes suspended for various periods of time on account of offenses or neglect of duty, and occasionally, it is held, the charges are unwarranted or the penalties unduly severe. A few witnesses think, accordingly, that some legal restriction should be placed upon the discharge and suspension of railway employees, such as a requirement that they be given a hearing, preferably before a high officer of the railway company, or even before a specially constituted court.[8] A prominent railway officer, however, urges that such a requirement would seriously interfere with effective discipline, and that it would be unjust in view of the responsibility of the employer for his servants,[9] while the chief officers of the leading railway orders, in a joint statement, express doubt as to the desirability of legislation, holding that these organizations themselves afford a considerable degree of protection against unjust dismissals.[10]

Blacklisting.—Testimony was submitted to show that the practice of blacklisting, in one form or another, has been quite extensive during the past decade, although it is admitted that since the prohibition of the practice by the United

[1] P. 63.
[2] P. 228.
[3] P. 332.
[4] Pp. 101, 105.
[5] Reagan, p. 348; Cowen, p. 319.
[6] Clark, pp. 110, 111; Arthur, p. 119. See comments of railway presidents: Callaway, pp. 217, 218, 221; Spencer, p. 265; Ingalls, p. 292.
[7] Sargent, pp. 90, 91; Arthur, pp. 123, 124; Moseley, p. 36; officers of railway orders, pp. 760, 763, 765, 768; Murphy, p. 777.
[8] Sargent, pp. 65, 88; Clark, p. 113; Arnold, p. 763; Murphy, p. 778; Wilson, p. 765; Ronemus, p. 768
[9] Walker, p. 772.
[10] P. 760.

States arbitration act of 1898 it exists for the most part only in a secret form which is very difficult to reach. Railway officers, in fact, claim that the practice is largely dying out.[1] It appears clearly that men who took part in the Chicago strike of 1894 found it exceedingly difficult to obtain employment thereafter. Witnesses believe that there was an understanding among the railways that those who had taken part in the strike should not be employed. The letters which were given them by their former employers sometimes contained a statement of the fact that they had engaged in the strike. In other cases the very date of the letters gave a clue to employers. It is stated, also, that blacklists containing the names of strikers, and especially of leaders, were circulated among the railways.[2] Several witnesses think the requirement made at present by most railways, that applicants for employment must submit letters of recommendation from their former employers, has somewhat the effect of the former blacklists, especially since, as some believe, secret marks are at times attached to the letters to indicate that the person is not to be employed.[3]

Several witnesses accordingly urge that the existing penalties for the practice of blacklisting should be made even more severe with a view to checking these alleged secret practices.[4] One witness thinks that the employer should be required to give a discharged employee a copy of every statement sent, even though by request, to any other employer. Two or three others doubt the necessity of further legislation, one railway switchman especially declaring that the requirement of recommendations from former employers has a good effect in raising the standard of service and shutting out those not worthy of employment.[5]

Railroad Y. M. C. A. and hospitals.—Two or three railway officers testify that, at least on their own roads, considerable effort is made to provide for the improvement and comfort of the men by the establishment of Young Men's Christian Associations, and of hospitals, the expense being borne in part by the company.[6]

WAGES AND HOURS OF LABOR.

A number of witnesses testify concerning the wages of different classes of railway employees. There is little complaint on the part of men employed on trains. They are for the most part paid for the distance traveled, a certain distance constituting a day's work and any travel beyond that being paid for as overtime.[7] On the other hand, track hands, especially those of the lowest grade, claim that they are underpaid.[8] No special legislation in regard to wages is suggested.

On account of the nature of train service the hours of labor are necessarily very irregular. A certain distance must be covered before a train crew can be relieved, and the time required may be short or, under exceptional circumstances, may be exceedingly long. Trainmen are not inclined to complain, especially in view of the fact that they are usually paid extra wages when they travel more than a certain distance or when they are at work continuously for more than 10 or 12 hours. Laws have been passed in some States to restrict the number of hours which trainmen can work without being given rest, the main object being to protect the public safety. Most representatives of the railway employees are not disposed to advocate any legislation, beyond perhaps some provisions of this sort.[9]

[1] Cowen, p. 308; Spencer, pp. 264, 265; Ingalls, p. 288; Walker, p. 772.
[2] Strong, pp. 503-524; Moseley, p. 8.
[3] Clark, p. 112; Sargent, p. 65; Wilson, p. 52; Arthur, pp. 123, 124; Strong, p. 524.
[4] Joint answer of chiefs of railway orders, p. 760; Arnold, p. 763; Strong, p. 523; Murphy, p. 777.
[5] Wilson, p. 765; Ronemus, p. 768; O'Rourke, pp. 528, 529.
[6] Callaway, pp. 218, 220; Ingalls, pp. 289, 290.
[7] Sargent, pp. 64, 65; Arthur, pp. 117, 127; Callaway, p. 217; Ingalls, p. 287; Blanchard, p. 642.
[8] Wilson, pp. 46, 50; Spencer, p. 288.
[9] Sargent, pp. 66, 86-88; Clark, p. 110; Callaway, p. 218; officers of the brotherhoods, p. 761. For opposing views see Ronemus, p. 769; Arnold, p. 763; Murphy, p. 779.

These witnesses, however, favor, on the whole. as regards most occupations, the legal 8-hour day.

On the other hand, it is claimed by several witnesses that the hours of track-men, stationmen, telegraphers, etc., are often unduly long, and that it is possible to shorten them by employing more men. The chief officers of the brotherhoods of locomotive engineers, locomotive firemen, railway trainmen, railway conductors, and railway telegraphers, in a joint statement, express themselves in favor of legally limiting the hours of employees not in train service to 10 hours, while some others urged 8 hours as the legal limit for these employees.[1]

It is claimed by representatives of the railways, and apparently conceded by representatives of employees, that there has been a material decrease in the running of trains on Sunday, and that it is the general purpose of the railways to relieve their men on that day as far as possible. It is pointed out, however, that a certain number of passenger trains are demanded on Sunday and that live stock and perishable freight must be carried through. An absolute prohibition of Sunday traffic, moreover, would often result in stopping trains at inconvenient places and in keeping men from getting to their homes. It is admitted that the laws which exist in several States, restricting the operation of Sunday trains, are often evaded in various ways.[2]

LABOR ORGANIZATIONS, STRIKES, ETC.

The railway brotherhoods.—Several witnesses testify concerning the organization, character, and working of the great railway brotherhoods and orders. It appears clear, both from the statements of the officers of these organizations and from those of the railway presidents and other persons, that these bodies are generally conservative and have been highly beneficial, not only to their members, but to the railway service generally. Much attention is paid by them to elevating the character and morale of the members. Mutual insurance is a prominent feature in nearly all the bodies, and it has apparently worked very successfully. The relations between the brotherhoods and the railways are usually friendly, although a few of the railways refuse to recognize them. In many cases contracts concerning wages and conditions of labor are made directly between railways and the brotherhoods, while in other cases the railways discuss these matters with the representatives of the brotherhoods although contracts are not made directly with them. It is claimed that the organizations do not seek to antagonize nonunion labor, although as a matter of fact on many railways very nearly all of the employees belong to the organizations. Two or three witnesses distinguish sharply between these standard brotherhoods and orders and such temporary organizations as the American Railway Union, which are claimed to be under the control of professional agitators.[3]

Strikes.—It is stated by certain railway employees that strikes are probably somewhat less common on railways than in many other employments. It is admitted that strikes upon railways are more serious in their effects upon the community than those in any other industry.[4] Several witnesses refer more or less incidentally to the great strike of 1894. It appears that it was formerly the rule of the organizations of railway employees, at least of the Brotherhood of Locomotive Engineers, to refuse to haul cars from any road upon which the mem-

---

[1] Wilson, pp. 50, 51, 766; Ronemus, p. 769; Arnold, p. 763; Murphy, p. 779; officers of brotherhoods, p. 761.

[2] Sargent, pp. 66, 86, 87; Cowen, pp. 303, 304; Ingalls, p. 288; Spencer, pp. 265, 266; Callaway, p. 218.

[3] Arthur, pp. 116–122; Clark, pp. 110, 113; Wilson, pp. 48, 50, 51–54; O'Rourke, pp. 525–527; Sargent, pp. 67, 68, 87, 91, 92; Moseley, pp. 36, 43, 44; Callaway, pp. 221, 222; Ingalls, p. 291; Fish, pp. 327, 328; Cowen, p. 307; Spencer, pp. 266, 268.

[4] Sargent, pp. 68, 71; Arthur, pp. 120, 126, 128; O'Rourke, p. 528; Strong, p. 506; Callaway, p. 221.

bers of the organization were engaged in a strike; but this practice having been enjoined by the courts it has been discontinued.

Injunctions in strikes.—Much testimony was presented concerning alleged abuses of the power of injunction by. the courts in connection with railway strikes. Instances were mentioned in which injunctions have prohibited the most ordinary of acts connected with the carrying on of a strike, such as consultation by officers of organizations with one another and with the strikers, and requests, quite without any element of intimidation, to employees or to applicants for employment to refrain from working.[1] In other cases injunctions have been issued to restrain employees from performing criminal acts, such as destroying the property of employers. It is claimed by witnesses that this practice is unwarranted, since sufficient remedy exists under the criminal laws, and that, in fact, a person who is accused of violating an injunction of this class is deprived of the right of trial by jury, as well as of the ordinary protection of the rules of criminal procedure. Judges, moreover, it is held, are apt to be prejudiced against those accused of contempt in violating their orders. Several witnesses accordingly favor legislation restricting the power of the courts in issuing injunctions. Most of these suggestions are somewhat indefinite in their nature, but the chief officers of the leading railway orders, in a joint reply to a schedule of inquiries, declare themselves in favor of a national law, similar to that already enacted in Kansas, dividing contempts of court into two classes. Indirect contempts—those committed outside of the court—would under such a law be tried by procedure similar to that in criminal cases, and the decision would be subject to appeal.[2]

Especial complaint is made against the attempt on the part of the courts in one or two instances to compel specific performance of service on the part of employees. Thus, during the Northern Pacific Railway strike of 1894 an injunction was issued by a Federal district judge prohibiting the employees of that road from quitting or conspiring to quit employment in such a way as to cripple the property or hinder the operation of the railroad. This decision, to be sure, was afterwards reversed by the Circuit Court of Appeals on the ground that it was an invasion of natural liberty, although the court held that under certain circumstances a combination to quit employment in this way might be held an illegal conspiracy. In another case, when a strike was in force on the Toledo, Ann Arbor and North Michigan Railway, an injunction was issued restraining the employees of the Lake Shore and various other railways from refusing to handle cars and freight coming from the Ann Arbor road. The court held that an injunction could legally be issued not only against the railways themselves, but against their employees, in a case of this kind. Apparently this decision has remained in force. It is pointed out by the witnesses that the courts are especially inclined to issue injunctions regarding employees of railways in the hands of receivers, and, indeed, that sometimes without the previous issue of an injunction certain acts of employees upon railroads in the hands of receivers have been held to be in contempt of court.[3]

Arbitration.—The United States arbitration act of 1898 provides that either party to a labor controversy on interstate railroads may apply to the Commissioner of Labor and the chairman of the Interstate Commerce Commission to act as mediators. If mediation fails the parties may each appoint an arbitrator and a third shall be appointed by the Commissioner of Labor and the chairman of the Interstate Commerce Commission. It appears from the testimony that in

[1] Moseley, pp. 9-11; Sargent, p. 89; Arthur, p. 119.
[2] Moseley, pp. 12, 13; Johnson, p. 63; Sargent, pp. 65, 66; Wilson, p. 766; Ronemus, p. 769; Murphy, pp. 779, 780; officers of the railway orders, pp. 761, 762.
[3] Moseley, pp. 8-13; Sargent, pp. 65, 66, 71-74, 89; Arthur, pp. 119, 120.

only one case has there so far been any application for mediation, and the employers in that case refused to accept mediation or arbitration. Some of the officers of the railway brotherhoods, however, think that the act has had a beneficial moral effect and needs no amendment.[1] Several officers of railways are satisfied with the act, but express the opinion that railways will not arbitrate any really important question, such as the rate of wages or the right of the railways to employ and discharge whom they will. The question of wages is so vital to the financial interest of the railroads that they would be unwilling to trust it to the decision of outside authorities.[2]

Compulsory arbitration is deprecated by most of the representatives of the railway employees, as well as by the officers of two or three railways who testified concerning the matter.[3] A few witnesses, however, think that it should be compulsory upon the parties to railway disputes to submit their differences to the Interstate Commerce Commission or some other body, which should have full power to investigate. The decision should not, most of these hold, be enforceable at law, but it is believed that public opinion would compel the parties to conform to the recommendations of the arbitrators.[4] The influence of public opinion is chiefly relied upon also by those who think the existing statute sufficient.

EMPLOYERS' LIABILITY.

A large number of witnesses representing railway employees, as well as two or three general witnesses not connected with railways, express themselves strongly in favor of some extension of the liability of railway employers for injuries to their employees. The railway officers who appeared before the Commission presented little specific opposition to this demand.

The common-law doctrine concerning employers' liability, and the modifications made by existing statutes, are summarized with considerable care by two or three of the witnesses, a large number of court decisions being referred to. The employee, it is said, is supposed to assume the ordinary risks of employment as to which he has or may be presumed to have knowledge. On the other hand, the employer is liable for defects in machinery or appliances of any sort, of which, by taking reasonable care, he might have had knowledge, as well as for failure to provide such facilities and appliances as reasonable care would demand. It is not, however, necessary, in the opinion of most courts, that the very best appliances should be furnished by the employer, although it appears that the recent tendency of the courts has been toward making greater requirements of the employer, especially as regards railroads. The employer is also liable for failure to make proper rules for the conduct of work. Comparatively little complaint is made by the witnesses as to the extent of the liability of employers in these regards. No witness, in fact, demands that the law of employers' liability shall be made as broad as in Great Britain, where the employer is liable for a limited amount of damages on account of injury from any cause whatever, in the absence of contributory negligence on the part of the employee injured.

The chief demand of the railway employees is that railways should be made responsible for injuries arising from the acts of fellow-servants. The common-law doctrine is that the employer is not liable if he has exercised reasonable care in selecting his servants; he is ordinarily liable only for the acts of those having positions of superintendence, designated as vice-principals. With regard to rail-

---

[1] Sargent, pp. 68, 69, 94, 95; Knapp, pp. 129-131; Moseley, p. 37; Wilson, pp. 766-767; officers of railway brotherhoods, pp. 68, 69, 762.

[2] Ingalls, p. 291; Cowen, p. 309; Callaway, pp. 221, 222; Fish, p. 324.

[3] Officers of railway brotherhoods, pp. 68, 69, 762, 764; Callaway, p. 221; Walker, pp. 773-776; Knapp, p. 131.

[4] Arthur, p. 125; Wilson, pp. 766, 767; Ronemus, p. 770; Murphy, p. 780.

ways, the decisions of the American courts appear to be exceedingly conflicting in defining those who are considered fellow-employees as distinguished from vice-principals. Perhaps in the majority of instances, however, it is held that all persons not possessing the power of direction, although they are in an entirely different branch of the service, are fellow-servants. Thus, the railway company is not liable for injuries to men on trains arising from the negligence of switchmen or trackmen, and vice versa.

This common-law doctrine has been modified by statute in a number of States, at least to the extent of declaring that the railway shall be liable for injuries by acts of employees in a different branch of the service. Several witnesses, however, desire that laws of this nature shall be made uniform as far as possible, preferably by Federal enactment; and most of these think that the employer should be made liable for injuries to employees arising from the act of any other employee. It is declared that the employees have no choice whatever with regard to the fellow-servants with whom they are forced to work; whereas the employer picks out his men and should be responsible for his choice. It is said that where the liability of employers for the acts of fellow-servants has been extended by statute, they have become more careful in selecting their men, while, on the other hand, there has been no increase of carelessness on the part of the employees.[1] Mr. Callaway, president of the New York Central, thinks that railways would not especially object to being made liable for injuries to employees through negligence of fellow-servants, provided a similar liability were imposed upon other employers and provided a reasonable limit to the damages collectible were fixed.[2]

Complaint is also made by various witnesses on the ground that the Federal courts, before which a large proportion of suits for damages on account of injury are brought, do not conform in their decisions to the statute law or the decisions of the courts of highest resort of the State in which the injury occurs. Frequently, it is claimed, the railways by some device carry damage cases before the Federal courts for the express purpose of evading the statute or the rule of the State courts. These witnesses favor an act of Congress requiring the Federal courts to conform their decisions to those of the courts of last resort of the several States.[3]

RELIEF FUNDS OF RAILWAYS.[4]

It appears from the evidence that some half dozen of the leading railways of the country have established relief departments, supported mainly by assessments upon the men, while the railways perform the necessary routine business without charge and sometimes make regular contributions to the fund or supply deficits. Employees contributing to the fund are entitled to certain payments in case of death by accident or to weekly allowances during incapacity.

Complaint is quite general that contribution to these funds is practically compulsory on the part of the employees of the railways maintaining them. Three of the railways openly compelled their employees to join the relief departments up to the time of the enactment of the United States arbitration act of June 1, 1898, which prohibited such compulsion. It is stated by several representatives of the railway employees that excuses are still often given for refusing employment to those who are unwilling to become members of the relief department, or that they are not kept in the line of promotion, or are discriminated against in various

---

[1] Sargent, pp. 66, 74, 75, 89; Moseley, pp. 21-28, 81, 82; Wilson, pp. 53, 54; Clark, p. 115; officers of railway orders, pp. 762, 764, 769; Murphy, p. 780.

[2] Pp. 222, 225.

[3] Moseley, pp. 29, 30, 40, 41; officers of railway brotherhoods, pp. 762, 764, 769; Sargent, p. 93; Clark, p. 115.

[4] Johnson, pp. 57-60; Sargent, pp. 67, 89-91; Arthur, pp. 121, 122, 125; Wilson, pp. 47, 48, 767; Moseley, pp. 31, 82; Cowen, pp. 304-308.

ways. Witnesses claim that employees who are members of such departments often lose in independence, since they do not wish to forfeit their interest in the fund by striking or leaving employment. Mr. Cowen admits that on the Baltimore and Ohio Railroad the applicant for employment must consent to contribute to the relief department, although he says that this does not constitute compulsion, since no one is forced to apply for employment.

It is also declared that the railways maintaining relief funds require those who accept payments from them to release the company from all further liability for damages. This practice is opposed strongly on the ground that the employees pay a full, and in some cases an exorbitant, rate for their insurance in the relief department, and that the receipt of money from the fund should not therefore be any bar to the collection of damages. It is admitted by Mr. Cowen that this requirement exists, at least on the Baltimore and Ohio, although he declares that the fact that the men have the right to sue for damages if they are willing to run the risk, relinquishing their claim upon the insurance fund, is a sufficient answer to complaints. The act of June 1, 1898, declares that the employer shall not be released from liability beyond the amount of his own contribution to the relief fund, but Mr. Cowen says that on the Baltimore and Ohio an absolute release is still required from those accepting relief from the fund.

Most witnesses on this subject urge that the law of 1898 in these two regards should be made more stringent.

SAFETY APPLIANCES AND ACCIDENTS.

The United States act of 1893, requiring railways, on or before January 1, 1898, to equip their engines and cars with air brakes, automatic couplers, and proper handholds, was only partly complied with by the railways at that date, and an extension of two years was granted by action of the Interstate Commerce Commission. It appears from the testimony before the Industrial Commission, mostly taken before January 1, 1900, that the railways for the most part had met the requirements of the act, and there appears to be no general complaint. It is believed by witnesses, including several railway officers, that the use of these appliances will have a very material effect in decreasing injuries to employees. A few witnesses recommend that acts similar to that of 1893 should be passed by all of the States with reference to railways lying wholly within their borders.[1]

Report of accidents.—The members of the Interstate Commerce Commission think that railways should be required to report somewhat more in detail than at present concerning accidents, and this suggestion is upheld by representatives of the railway brotherhoods.[2]

OCEAN AND LAKE TRANSPORTATION.

American merchant marine.—The Industrial Commission has not sought thus far to make a detailed investigation on the subject of measures for developing an American merchant marine. Several witnesses in connection with other investigations of the commission have commented incidentally on the desirability of such measures. In the present investigation one witness, Mr. Neall, presents statistics showing the exceedingly small proportion of American ocean vessels, as compared with the total shipping of the world and as compared with the freight exported and imported by this country. The witness estimates that American-owned vessels actually suitable for transoceanic traffic have not over 800,000 gross tons register out of more than 27,000,000 gross tons for the world's shipping. Our

---

[1] Moseley, pp. 32, 59; Clark, p. 115; Arthur, p. 126; brotherhood officers, pp. 763, 767; Callaway, pp. 219, 220; Spencer, p. 268; Cowen, p. 308; Knapp, p. 131; Sargent, p. 93.

[2] Moseley, pp. 37, 38; officers of brotherhoods, p. 763; Sargent, p. 93; Clark, p. 114; cf. Stickney, p. 456.

American shipyards, he says, scarcely build any ordinary freight steamers, being entirely occupied with naval vessels and high-grade passenger vessels; and the cost of freight steamers here is very materially higher than abroad. Since he believes it would be impossible, even with the help of subsidies, for American shipyards to turn out within a reasonable time any large number of the kind of vessels specially needed, Mr. Neall advocates the passage of a law permitting Americans to buy vessels abroad and to place them under the American flag, these vessels to be prohibited from coastwise traffic.[1]

Condition of American seamen.—Only one witness, Mr. Furuseth, the secretary of the Sailors' Union of the Pacific, has been examined on this subject. He states the amendments to the navigation laws which are advocated by the Seamen's Union, and presents a detailed account of the existing conditions among seamen in defense of these demands. The chief proposals are that the practice of permitting sailors to make "allotments" of their wages in advance be prohibited on the ground that it promotes the evil of crimping; that masters be required to pay sailors the wages due at any port, so that they may quit employment and not be forced, as at present, to continue service for the full period of time agreed upon, usually 12 months; that the required air space in the forecastle for each sailor be increased; that the majority of the crew be given the right to demand a survey of the condition of the vessel to assure themselves of its safety; that a certain standard of skill and experience be established for "able seamen," to prevent the shipping of incompetent men, which not only depresses wages but endangers the safety of the vessel and increases the work and responsibility of the experienced men; and that there be required a standard number of men for vessels according to their tonnage and rigging, to prevent the common evil of undermanning.[2]

Lake transportation.—A considerable amount of testimony was presented showing the magnitude of the traffic on the Great Lakes, the importance of its influence on rail rates, and the rapid increase of shipping and of traffic. No special legislation was advocated for furthering lake navigation, aside from general improvements of the waterways from time to time. Some witnesses, as we have seen, favor putting water carriers under the interstate-commerce act. Improvement of the Erie Canal and the construction of a ship canal from the lakes to the Mississippi are advocated by some witnesses.[3]

---

[1] Neall, pp. 166–184.   [2] Furuseth, pp. 686–709.   [3] Keep, pp. 710–724; Carter, pp. 578–582.

TOPICAL DIGEST OF EVIDENCE.

[Prepared by E. Dana Durand.]

I. CAPITALIZATION, CONSTRUCTION, AND CONSOLIDATION OF RAILWAYS.

A. Are American railways overcapitalized?—Very little evidence was submitted to prove that railways are at present overcapitalized, but that they are is implied in the testimony of those who favor Government restriction. See paragraph B, below. The subject was not investigated in detail by the Commission.

Mr. CLEMENTS, a member of the commission, testifies that it is impossible to estimate even roughly what proportion of the $11,000,000,000 capitalization of the railways of the United States represents actual money cost. He knows that many roads are capitalized at at least twice the original investment. (160.)

Mr. FISH, of the Illinois Central, presented a table comparing the changes in mileage, receipts, and capitalization of American railways from 1890 to 1898 with the corresponding changes in Great Britain. While the number of miles of railroad in the United States has increased 18.06 per cent during these eight years, the capitalization of our railways has increased only 14.64 per cent, the capitalization per mile of track remaining almost precisely the same. The gross receipts have increased 18.58 per cent, the gross receipts per mile having thus only very slightly increased, 0.45 per cent.

In the United Kingdom, on the other hand, while the number of miles operated has increased 7.9 per cent since 1890, the total capitalization of railways has increased 26.41 per cent, the capitalization per mile 17.15 per cent, the total gross receipts 20.39 per cent, and the gross receipts per mile 11.57 per cent.

The capitalization of American railways is $60,343 per mile; that of British railways (at $5 per pound) $261,895. The capitalization per mile in Great Britain has increased $38,345 since 1890. Although, on the whole, the English railways are better built than ours, there are many points in which ours excel.

In regard to railways in the South in particular, Mr. Fish says that much of their property was destroyed during the war and their capital was thus lost. There was a considerable amount of inflation and overcapitalization, going as far as rascality, during the reconstruction period, but the water in the stock has since been wiped out by reorganization.

Generally speaking, in fact, there has been a very great decrease in the fixed charges of American railways during the past ten years, even more from the reduction in the rate of interest than from reduction of capital. In most of the recent reorganizations bondholders have had to reduce their rate of interest from 7 to 3 or 4 per cent. (330–332.)

Mr. FISH says, further, that the capital of the Illinois Central Railroad has been increased from $38,881,000 at the close of the war to about $186,000,000. This increase is partly accounted for by the purchase of additional lines, but still more by the thorough reconstruction and reequipment of the system. Thus the weight of rails has been greatly increased during the past 10 years. Added capital is secured by the sale of bonds or stocks, as the condition of the market makes most desirable. Bonds have for a long period been sold at better prices than those of any other railway. In 1895 3 per cent bonds were floated. Bonds have always been sold at par or but a little below par. Stock has never been issued below par. It is first offered to stockholders at that rate, and what is not taken by them has always been sold at par, except once, when a premium was secured. Besides improvements made with new capital, probably $20,000,000 of current earnings have been spent in making improvements. Moreover, there has been a very large natural increase in the value of the right of way and real estate of the Illinois Central, which has not been represented by added capitalization. An expert estimate by the mayor of Chicago has recently placed the value of the terminals of the railway in that city at $34,500,000, but the land stands on the books at probably $200,000. Early in the history of the railway large cash payments were made by the stockholders, and, although some of the stock was issued during the war on the basis of an inflated currency, there is absolutely no water in the present capitalization.

The Illinois Central has always paid semiannual dividends, the rate during recent years being 5 per cent. (326, 332.)

Mr. CALLAWAY, of the New York Central, declares that the practice of watering stock is practically obsolete. It has usually been found that overcapitalized companies very soon go into the hands of receivers. There are still roads whose stocks were originally largely watered, but the value of their properties has usually greatly increased. Thus the value of the real estate owned by the New York Central in New York City has increased till it amounts to fully the entire capital of the road. The methods of different railways as to expenditure for improvements vary materially. Many of them have improvement funds, supplied by issues of bonds and stocks, for the more important outlays. The Lake Shore has made it a practice to charge nearly all improvements to operating expenses. (227, 228.)

Mr. Callaway thinks that the practice of letting contracts for the construction of new lines to railroad officers themselves has been almost altogether discontinued, and that, in fact, the railways generally are managed very honestly. (226, 227.)

Mr. INGALLS, of the Chesapeake and Ohio, declares that the present capitalization of the railways of the country since their reorganization is less than the cost of reproducing them. Immediately after the civil war the people were anxious to get railways. Companies received land and other inducements, which they turned over to contractors, who issued bonds and stocks almost without limit. Reorganizations have proved necessary, and in many cases have been very severe in their effects on investors. The present cost of getting terminals in the cities would be enormous. The cost of right of way in the rural districts has also increased greatly, while outlay for equipment is very large. (298.)

Mr. COWEN, of the Baltimore and Ohio, is also of the opinion that none of the large and well-established railroads, certainly none of those east of the Mississippi and north of the Ohio, could be reproduced for their existing capital. Nevertheless there have been many mislocations of railways, representing a waste of capital. (318.)

Mr. VANLANDINGHAM, commissioner of the St. Louis Traffic Bureau, says that on most of the railways, especially in the West, stocks have been issued largely as bonus in connection with bonds. This is necessary on account of the risk of building in a new territory. Sometimes the development of the territory brings large profits to persons securing stocks in this way. (210.)

Mr. SARGENT, grand master of the Brotherhood of Locomotive Firemen, says that the increase of securities adds to the burden of the railways, and often leads to reduction of wages, foreclosures, and other evils. (70.)

B. Effects of overcapitalization and government control.—Mr. REAGAN, of the Texas railroad commission, declares that Congress and the several States should prohibit the issue of stocks and bonds by railroads except for money paid, labor done, or property actually received. The constitution and laws of Texas contain such provisions, designed to protect the people from imposition by means of watered and fraudulent stocks and bonds. A further statute of Texas, passed in 1893, provides that no bonds or other indebtedness shall be created over and above a reasonable value of the railroad property, except that in case of emergency the railroad commission may permit additional bonds to an amount not over 50 per cent above the value of the property. In order to prevent overcapitalization the railroad commission has made a careful valuation of the various railroads. The average value per mile has been found to be $15,759 and the aggregate value $141,117,176, the capitalization of the companies being $362,953,383. The method adopted by the commission in making valuations is to ascertain the actual amount of cutting and filling and the character of the material, and to learn from construction companies and manufacturers the actual cost of cutting, grading, ties, rails, rolling stock, etc. The value of the right of way is also ascertained, and an allowance of about 6 per cent is made to cover the cost of charter fees and engineering and counsel expenses, and another allowance of about 6 per cent to cover interest during the period of construction. Although opportunity has been given for doing so, not one of the valuations thus made has been contested. (341, 342.)

Mr. Reagan criticises the dictum of the United States Supreme Court in the case of Smythe v. Ames as to the method of valuing the property of railways. He declares that there is no just relation between the original cost of construction and the present value. The railroads may have been built when material and labor were high or upon an excessive contract. Similarly, the amount spent in making permanent improvements may be greater than the present value. The amount and market value of bonds and stocks can be no just measure of the future value of a railroad, especially since market values fluctuate constantly and often violently, because of speculation and manipulation. The safer method is that employed by the Texas commission—ascertaining the present cost. At the same time the railways are entitled to demand revaluations of their property from time to time in view of the improvements made and of the increased value of terminal property, etc. (343–345.)

Mr. KNAPP, chairman of the Interstate Commerce Commission, does not think that overcapitalization of railways influences their rates materially where there is competition, although when the reasonableness of rates is questioned in the courts or otherwise the cost of the road must necessarily be considered, and the capitalization may affect the decision. He believes that Government supervision over the issue of stocks of railways is therefore justifiable. (144, 145.)

Professor JOHNSON believes that in the long run the watering of stock is likely to tend to increase railway charges and to decrease wages. The percentage of dividends materially affects the attitude of legislators and the public toward railways. There are nothing but rough estimates as to the real value of our railways. Very often new stock issued does represent increase in actual value and cost of plant. It is doubtful whether Congress has constitutional power to control the issue of railway stock, but the experience of Massachusetts and Texas seems to favor some Government regulation of its issue. (60, 62.)

Mr. NEWCOMB, chief of the division of statistics, United States Department of Agriculture, thinks it is doubtful whether watering of stock has ever had any material influence on rates or has deceived legislators or others as to their justice. At any rate, there is now no possibility of such deception, and watered stock is a matter of concern only to investors. The rates of freight are determined by world-wide competition in the disposal of products. To increase rates beyond a legitimate level would shut out many goods from transportation. Wages also are little affected. (100, 101.)

Moreover, Mr. Newcomb continues, the cost of a railroad is not to be estimated by the original cost of construction. Most of our roads were built cheaply at first and have been greatly improved either through expenditure out of earnings or through new capital. Terminals, tunnels, bridges, etc., are often overlooked in estimates of cost. (101.)

Mr. MORTON, vice-president of the Atchison, Topeka and Santa Fe Railway, thinks that little would be gained by Government supervision of issues of stock by railroads. He admits that there has been and is overcapitalization, but declares that the price of securities indicates it. He does not approve of the watering of stock. (501.)

C. Government regulation of construction of railways.—Mr. BLANCHARD, late commissioner of the Joint Traffic Association, believes that the construction of new railroads should be restricted by proper governmental safeguards. There are more miles of railroad in this country in proportion to the population and tonnage than in any other. Existing roads need protection. The multiplication of securities of new railroads is an evil similar to the watering of stock of existing roads. The restriction of railway construction in England is especially referred to. (663, 680.)

Mr. INGALLS, of the Chesapeake and Ohio, believes that the approval of the Interstate Commerce Commission should be required for the construction of every railway, in order to prevent the building of parallel lines which are of no advantage to the public. The commission should also require that sufficient capital be subscribed and fully paid up. If the Government is to regulate railways, it needs also to protect them. (287.)

Mr. MORTON, of the Atchison, Topeka and Santa Fe, also believes that the construction of railroads should be subject to Federal supervision. Unnecessary duplication of lines has been one of the chief causes of our last two financial panics. The witness thinks that there are provisions in the laws of many States intended to restrict improper construction of railroads. (492, 503.)

D. Consolidation of railways.—Mr. KNAPP, chairman of the Interstate Commerce Commission, testifies that the consolidation of railways has gone so far in certain sections of the country that pooling arrangements for the maintenance of rates are no longer desired by the railways. He believes that the effect of such consolidation, through the elimination of destructive competition, has been a general reduction of rates and impartial treatment of shippers. (141.)

Mr. PROUTY, of the commission, also believes that the tendency toward consolidation has been beneficial in the same ways as suggested by Mr. Knapp. This is especially seen in New England. At the same time he considers that this tendency makes public supervision all the more necessary. (153.)

Mr. MORTON believes that consolidation of railroads is very desirable. The country is bound to have either legalized pooling or consolidation or Government ownership, and the witness thinks that the second, in conjunction with the first, is the most advantageous. Consolidation tends to reduce charges, improve the service, advance wages, and check favoritism to individual employees. It means great economies in management generally, in advertising, in preventing the running of unnecessary trains, etc. Concentration will not necessarily tend to a complete union of roads throughout the country, but only of those competing among themselves in any one section. It can come only gradually, and meantime legalized pooling is desirable. (490, 496, 497, 499.)

Mr. SPENCER, president of the Southern Railway, likewise believes that consolidation is likely to greatly check discriminations. It may somewhat retard the diminution of railway rates, although the reduction of rates is primarily necessitated by commercial conditions, the necessity of getting products to market in competition with those of other localities. The interstate-commerce law has been more strictly observed by consolidated railways than by others; this is notably the case with the Southern Railway itself, which 5 or 6 years ago consisted of 35 or 36 separate corporations. The average rates have decreased on this system about 7 per cent, although they have not been reduced as much as they would have been, were it not for the fact that the lines had previously been often unable to earn interest. (278.)

Mr. INGALLS, of the Chesapeake and Ohio, thinks that consolidation will not entirely overcome competition, and that agreements between railways are consequently desirable. Consolidation has gone far in New England and the South, and with generally beneficial results; but the witness doubts whether it is practicable to consolidate the great trunk lines between the Mississippi River and the seaboard, on account of the many large local interests involved.

Mr. Ingalls does not think it likely that all the railways of the country will ultimately fall into the hands of two or three great corporations, and believes that such a result would greatly strengthen the movement for Government ownership, which he deprecates. (296, 298.)

In the investigation on trusts, Mr. STETSON, who has acted as counsel in various recent railway reorganizations, testified that they had been rendered necessary by the inability of the corporations to meet their fixed charges, an inability which has been due largely to ruinous reduction of railway rates, partly through legislation and partly through competition. The reorganizations have been made to avoid foreclosure, and also in order to bring in sufficient contributions of cash to improve the property and to wipe out floating indebtedness. Either the property of railways has deteriorated from an inability to make betterments while paying fixed charges, or they have been forced to incur floating debts. Although in some instances the amount of capitalization, including bonds and stocks, has been increased by reorganization, reduction of rates of interest on bonds has decreased the total fixed charges. (See Vol. I, on Trusts, pp. 977, 978.)

Mr. SARGENT, grand master of the Brotherhood of Locomotive Firemen, thinks the consolidation of railways under single management leads to economy in cost of service, and has not injured employees. In some cases, where small roads, paying low wages, have been taken into large systems, the employees have directly benefited. (70.)

Mr. STONE does not think that the forbidding of pooling has a tendency to bring about the consolidation of different lines of road. (538.)

E. Receivers.—Mr. VANLANDINGHAM believes that railroads in the hands of receivers, owing to the fact that they have no dividends to pay, are especially likely to cut rates and to make discriminations. The receiver is usually appointed by the influence of the majority bondholders, and since these bondholders frequently control the stock also, the receiver is apt to be the president of the railroad. The witness does not consider this fact injurious to the interests of the owners of the railroad, and probably not to the general public. It is not usually true that the insolvency has been due to bad management by the officers, but rather to the excessive capitalization. The reorganization after insolvency generally wipes out the original stocks, turning over the property to the holders of the first and second mortgages. (211, 212.)

F. Palace-car and other subsidiary companies (see also *Private cars*, p. 55).—Mr. CALLAWAY, of the New York Central, declares that although the railways have a contract with the palace-car companies to pay them a certain mileage in case the receipts from the cars do not exceed a certain figure, the business on all the important roads is such that the railways really make no payment at all for the use of the cars, and their profits accordingly are not decreased by this system. The attempt of railways themselves to operate sleeping cars has usually been a failure.

The bridge companies, which were formerly common, have mostly been merged into the railway companies, and toll for the use of bridges scarcely exists anywhere. (226, 227.)

Mr. INGALLS, of the Chesapeake and Ohio, says that, while it would be desirable for the railroads to own the sleeping and parlor cars if possible, the operation of through trains, together with the great demand for such cars on special occasions, makes it necessary that they be held by private companies. (302.)

Mr. VANLANDINGHAM, of the St. Louis Traffic Bureau: The so-called "car trusts" result usually from the poverty of the railroads, which makes them unable to buy cars directly. Some of the officers of the railroad form a separate company and build cars, which they lease to the railroad. The proportion which the payments to these "car trusts" bear to the total receipts of railways depends upon the credit and the standing of the railway companies. (209, 210.)

G. Land grants.—Mr. FISH, of the Illinois Central, refers to the fact that that road was granted by the Federal Government, through the agency of the State of Illinois, all the alternate sections of land on each side of the road originally built under the charter. The value of the sections reserved by the Government, which had been only $1.25 per acre, increased rapidly after the building of the road, and the lands were sold at from $2.50 up. The railway itself has sold 2,540,469 acres. (328.)

II. FREIGHT TRAFFIC GENERALLY.

A. Policy in fixing freight rates and influences affecting them.—Mr. BLANCHARD, late commissioner of the Joint Traffic Association, points out the very great complexity of the influences which must affect the determination of freight rates. There are often many different railroads reaching the same points, and these roads have unequal facilities, differ in length, etc. Rates are subject to competition between different markets all over the world, to water competition in many cases, and to countless other influences. Changes in the cost of operation and materials, such, for example, as the recent increase in prices of steel and other products, should influence rates. In view of these facts the success of the railways in securing uniform and fair rates, as between different commodities, sections, and places, is very remarkable. Such solutions can only be reached by conferences of railway officers, and it is now the tendency of the law to prohibit such conferences. The broad adjustments of rates which have been reached are quite generally satisfactory. Not one rate in a thousand is ever questioned by anyone. (626, 627.)

Mr. NEWCOMB, of the division of statistics, United States Department of Agriculture, says that there is no such thing as a rate which is excessive in itself. A rate must be compared with rates on other roads and for other products and must be judged by the earnings of the railway. For instance, where a lumber road is built which hauls lumber one way and nothing on the return trip, the rates would naturally be higher than where there are loads both ways. Rates must be classified for different products according to the amount of each shipped, and such classification must differ in different places. (99, 100.)

Mr. Newcomb declares, further, that it is impossible for railways to maintain rates such as to give them more than a normal profit, whether by means of pools, watering of stock, or otherwise. There is always a large amount of traffic which is on the margin of profitable shipment, and the rates must be kept low enough to secure it. Goods come into competition with others from all over the world, under varying conditions of transportation, so that the railways must haul them at such rates that they can be put on the market. (96, 101.)

Mr. CALLAWAY, of the New York Central, says that one of the chief influences affecting rates is the competition of producers in different localities, including, often, competition over the entire world. Even local rates are considerably affected in this way. Thus, if an industry has been established upon the New York Central, that railroad must make such rates that it can compete with some other establishment in the same business on the Pennsylvania Railroad or elsewhere. Unless a railroad looks after the producers along its lines those producers will be driven out of business and ultimately the railroad will be driven out of business. Similarly, the competition of producers in foreign countries makes it necessary to adjust rates to enable domestic producers to do business, and this influence is sufficient to prevent excessive charges in most cases. There would accordingly be little danger of extortionate charges if pooling were allowed among railways. Mr. Callaway illustrates this general argument by reference to his experience in being practically compelled to make special rates on copper from Butte, Mont., to enable mines there to compete with the Chile mines in the Liverpool market. (223, 226, 235.)

Mr. STICKNEY, president of the Chicago Great Western Railway, declares it is impossible by any theory to determine what shall be the just relation between charges for different classes of freight. Judge Cooley held that a reasonable rate must be based on the cost of carriage, but rates never have been so based and never can be. It does not cost more to haul a ton of first-class goods than one of fifth-class goods, but the rates can not be made the same. Rates must be made such in every case as to secure the traffic. It may be true that any particular commodity already produced must of necessity be moved over a particular railroad and must pay the rate fixed. But there is no necessity that the commodity shall be produced at that place. If rates on wheat from Dakota be made so high that the farmer can not afford to raise wheat he will stop raising it. If a stone quarry is discovered the owner must find out how much he can get for his product at the markets, and he will not quarry stone at all unless he can get railroad rates such as to enable him to do so at a profit. Practically, so-called local rates are always competitive.

Similarly it is impossible to keep rates fixed permanently after they have once been established. As conditions change, rates must change accordingly. Thus, in the case of flour shipments from Minneapolis, the rates must fluctuate frequently with the price of flour. The millers do not expect to make a profit of more than two or three cents per hundred pounds, and small differences in freight rates thus affect them. If the freight rates were uniform the mills could only be run at occasional seasons, especially since the mills seldom have facilities for storing large quantities of flour.

The attempt to maintain steady rates by traffic associations has always failed. Thus the Joint Traffic Association attempted to maintain rates on the trunk lines from 1894 to 1898, but they actually decreased, and even more rapidly than during the two years preceding 1894, which were years of hard times quite as much as those after 1894.

The witness especially deprecates increasing the powers of the Interstate Commerce Commission or of any other governmental body as regards rates. (460–463.)

Mr. EMERSON, a produce dealer of St. Paul, says that special rates are usually made on potatoes and similar bulky classes of produce. A uniform classification is, however, desirable in those cases where the goods are put under a general class. The witness cited instances where special low rates have been given on potatoes and similar products from the Northwestern States in view of heavy crops or other special market conditions, enabling products to be moved, which otherwise would not be. The volume of business in these products in the Northwestern States is much larger now than it was 10 years ago, and the railway rates are considerably lower. (484, 485.)

Mr. BACON, of the Milwaukee Board of Trade, says that the attempt to fix maximum rates for an entire State or section is likely to prove unsuccessful on account of the different conditions. Thus, in Illinois, where the law gives ample power, it has been found impossible to fix a maximum rate, in justice to some roads and to certain conditions, which shall not be considerably higher than the actual rates fixed by the railroads in most other cases. (421.)

Uniform mileage rates.—Mr. DOUSMAN, a grain shipper of Chicago, thinks that freight rates should be practically fixed, not changed from time to time. It is feasible to have uniform mileage rates between different places in the same general section of the country. The witness refers to the declaration of the president of a large Western railroad that that road would like to see its freight rates made permanent, but that each road fears that some other road will get the advantage, and hence tends to cut rates. (359, 361.)

Mr. MORTON, vice-president of the Atchison, Topeka and Santa Fe Railway, thinks that an attempt to fix railway freight rates on the basis of mileage would have the same effect upon business as a complete revolution in the customs tariff. Moreover, the mileage rate would necessarily have to be very high in order to be fair to railroads in the less populous sections. The time when the uniform rate can be established is very remote indeed. Crop conditions and other temporary circumstances must also be considered in making rates. (498, 499.)

B. **Are existing rates reasonable?**—1. *Generally.*—Mr. BLANCHARD, late commissioner of the Joint Traffic Association, declares it is not true that American railway rates are made arbitrarily or that they are excessive. The rates have been greatly reduced and the adjustments have been forced by natural laws of competition. There is no absolute standard by which to gauge the reasonableness of rates. The success of American railways in competing with water transportation would seem to indicate that their rates are exceedingly low. (630.)

Mr. COWEN believes that the railway rates in the United States are, if anything, abnormally low. In the central section of the country, he thinks, local rates are almost as low as through rates. On the Southern railways the local rates are higher, but this is justified by the sparse population and light traffic. The great mining and steel industries of Pennsylvania furnish exceedingly dense traffic to the railways; hence low local rates are possible. (818.)

Mr. RIPLEY, of the Atchison, Topeka and Santa Fe, says that the lines in the East are largely consolidated into a few hands; in New England there are practically only two railroad corporations, and yet there is less complaint there than in any other part of the United States. Things become more settled as a community becomes older; but Mr. Ripley thinks that the great reason for the tranquility in the Eastern States is that the people along the lines are interested in the railroad properties. (598.)

Compared with the rates in the past, and considering the improved methods of handling business, Mr. MALLORY thinks that existing rates are reasonable. (588.)

Mr. GALLAGHER states that at his mill, in Dallas, Tex., the freight paid on coal is nine times its value at the mine; and he knows of a mill in western Kansas where the freight paid on coal is ten times its value at the mine. (543.)

This question is also touched by many points in paragraph A, above.

2. *Mississippi Valley railroads.*—Mr. FISH, president of the Illinois Central, points out that the statistics show that the reduction in the number of employees during the hard times from 1893 to 1897 was twice as great relatively in the Mississippi Valley as in the other parts of the country. The average rate of transportation is less in the two chief groups of railways in that valley than in almost any other locality. There were more bankruptcies among these railways during the hard times than elsewhere. The witness implies that railway rates have been unduly reduced in that section. The physical condition of the railroads is now as satisfactory as that in the Eastern States, and earlier watered capital has been destroyed by reorganization. (321, 322, 330.)

3. *Decrease in rates.*—Mr. NEWCOMB, of the division of statistics, Department of Agriculture, says that a careful statistical comparison made by the Department of Agriculture shows that the average freight rate per ton per mile throughout the country has declined from 1.9 cents in 1867 to 0.8 cent in 1897. The former figure is probably too low, because statistics were available only from the largest roads, having the lowest rates. The average rate on the Hannibal and St. Joseph Railroad in 1870 was 3.194 cents; in 1897, 0.617; on the Union Pacific Railroad, 3.596 cents in 1869, 0.791 cent in 1897; Chicago, Milwaukee and St. Paul, 2.376 cents in 1865, 1.008 in 1897. On the Georgia Railroad the average rate in 1866 was 3.552 cents; in 1897, 1.112 cents. On the Louisville and Nashville, 3.007 cents in 1867, 0.791 in 1897. All the figures given are those in gold. (108.)

Mr. Newcomb refers especially to the reduction in freight rates on grain during the past forty years. The only case of increase was after the special reduction made in 1890 to relieve the farmers at a time of exceedingly low prices, but this increase did not bring rates back to their former level. The decrease in rates has been greater than the decrease in the price of grain. The average rate per ton per mile on grain in 1896 was only 44 per cent as great as in the years 1867-1872, while the average price of wheat was 67 per cent of the price at the former period, and the average price of other products from 44 to 65 per cent. The rate for all-rail transportation of wheat from Chicago to New York was 39 cents in 1858, 12.5 cents in 1897. The rate for part-rail and part-water transportation from Chicago to New York was 20.76 cents in 1868, 7.37 cents in 1897. In all-water transportation one bushel of wheat would pay for carrying 5.78 bushels in 1868, for 17.25 bushels in 1897. The rates on beef and live stock have decreased from one-third to one-half since 1879. (101, 108.)

Mr. BLANCHARD also compared the existing freight rates with those at earlier periods, to show the reasonableness of the present charges. In 1873 there were 70,268 miles of railway, and the average charge was 2.21 cents per ton per mile for 168,000,000 tons carried. In 1895 there were 179,162 miles of railway, and the average freight rate was 0.839 cent for 763,800,000 tons.

The reduction in dividends of railways also shows how low the rates are. The dividends per mile of railway in 1895 were equal to only 40 per cent of the dividends per mile of railway in 1872. The gross receipts upon each ton of freight moved in 1895 averaged 97 cents, regardless of distance, and 48 cents was the average receipt for each passenger carried. The dividend payments in that year were only equal to 7.2 cents per ton and 3.6 cents per passenger carried. The average rate of dividends on railway capital in 1895 was only 1.57 per cent, while 68 per cent of the entire amount of capital paid no dividends. (630, 631.)

Mr. CALLAWAY, president of the New York Central, thinks that railway rates have been reduced through competition of different kinds to such low figures that further extensive rate wars or serious discriminations between individuals or places will practically be impossible. Thus, on the New York Central the average rate received for hauling a ton of freight has been reduced from 1.88 cents in 1870 to 0.59 cent in 1898. These reductions have been rendered possible by cheaper cost of transportation, through use of larger cars and engines, superior rails, etc. (223.)

4. *Foreign freight rates and service* (see also under *Government ownership*, p. 125 ff).—Mr. VANLANDINGHAM, of the St. Louis Traffic Bureau, does not believe that the freight rates in this country are exorbitant. They average lower than in any European country, although this is not true of local traffic, the average being reduced by the low rates on general traffic. Comparisons are difficult on account of different methods. Thus in England transportation covers delivery to the place of business of the consignee. Wages are very much higher in this country than in Europe. (201, 204.)

Mr. SPENCER, of the Southern Railway, likewise declares that railway rates in this country are reasonable, being cheaper than anywhere else in the world. Although some of the short-haul rates are as high as in other countries, this is necessitated by the small amount of business. Undoubtedly the long hauls of American roads are one element in making the low rates possible. (278, 279.)

Mr. BLANCHARD says that American rates are certainly the lowest prevailing in any country and the service the quickest and best. In 1886 a British writer pointed out that the freight rate on grain and flour from Liverpool to Birmingham, 97 miles, was $3.01 per ton, while the rate from Chicago to New York, 1,000 miles, was $5.60 per ton. Another English writer, in 1886, said that the average ton-mile rate on English roads was probably not under 3 cents, which was three times the amount charged on the principal American lines. (630, 631.)

Mr. STONE believes that the facilities for the transportation of persons and of property are much better in this country than elsewhere and that the time of travel is shorter here and the regularity of service is greater. A commission from the Continent, which came here not many years ago to investigate the matter, reported that railroad travel here is much faster. Mr. Stone admits that the fairest comparison would be one between our railroads as a whole and the railroad service as a whole in western Europe, and that he has not seen a comparison made upon this line. He believes that there are more miles of road to the square mile in England and western Europe, and that discriminations are not a serious question there, as they are here. (536, 538.)

C. **Publication of tariffs.**—Professor JOHNSON and Mr. NEWCOMB both declare that publicity of railway rates is the first requisite of regulation. Books and accounts should be subject to inspection, on account of the essentially public nature of railway business. (62, 100.)

Mr. MORTON thinks that the requirement that railways shall post their rates conspicuously in every office is a good deal of a farce and causes unnecessary trouble and expense. Not one intelligent man out of a hundred can ascertain from the published tariffs any one rate within probably 24 hours. It might be possible to publish rates clearly if the attempt were not made to include so many stations. On the other hand, the requirement that rates shall be filed with the Interstate Commerce Commission is eminently desirable and has proved beneficial. The publication of passenger rates as distinguished from freight rates is desirable and not unduly complicated. (491, 493.)

Mr. STICKNEY says that while it is the clear intent of the interstate-commerce act that tariffs of local rates and also of joint rates should be posted in such a way that the ordinary shipper can himself ascertain the rates in any particular instance, the actual carrying out of this requirement is impossible. There are such innumerable railway stations and commodities that it would require several billions of rates to make a complete tariff. Several years ago the Western railways showed the Interstate Commerce Commission their printed tariffs, each having volumes as large as a small trunk, and although they admitted that the ordinary man could not ascertain the legal rate by inspecting these tariffs, the commission did not attempt to require anything further. The witness presumes that the tariffs filed by his own company with the Interstate Commerce Commission include 5,000 or 6,000 sheets. It is true, however, that the ordinary man usually learns the rates on standard products from his own local station to the leading markets. (458, 459.)

Mr. BIRD, general traffic manager of the Chicago, Milwaukee and St. Paul Railway, in reply to these statements of Mr. Stickney, says that the publication of rates with the Interstate Commerce Commission has been decidedly beneficial. The Western railroads as a rule maintain agencies in Washington especially to examine the tariffs of other roads. The courts hold that no tariff can be introduced as evidence in a suit unless it has been duly filed with the commission according to the law. (477.)

Mr. BLANCHARD, late commissioner of the Joint Traffic Association, does not believe that published tariffs are so complicated that experienced shippers and railway officers can not find the rates by means of them. There is not a large shipping firm in Chicago, for example, which does not keep tariff rates in its office. Most of the large shippers have special traffic managers to look after such matters. (674.)

D. Classification of freight.—1. *General principles.*—Mr. RIPLEY, chairman of the Western Classification Committee, explains that classification is the basis of freight rates. When an article is presented for shipment the classification is examined and the rate upon the article is determined by the class to which it is assigned. Bulk and value are the two controlling features in the classification of freight. Value determines what an article will stand; bulk represents the accommodation furnished by the carrier. Probably the greater quantity of freight consists of articles which are shipped at commodity rates outside of the classification, such as wheat, coal, pork, etc. (568, 569.)

Mr. TUCKER, chairman of the Central Freight Association, states that classification is based on value, bulk, and risk. The question what an article is able to stand, in view of its value, is also taken into consideration. (564.)

Mr. KELLEY, freight commissioner of the Trades League of Philadelphia, considers that the classification of the goods is the basis of the power of the railroads in influencing commodities. The railways at present can fix the final classification of any commodity, and there is no redress except by appeal to the committee of officials which makes the classification. (191.)

2. *Classification committees.*—Mr. RIPLEY, chairman of the Western Classification Committee, states that this committee establishes the freight classification for the roads between Chicago and the Pacific coast. The committee is composed of a delegate from each road, usually the assistant freight agent, sometimes the general freight agent or the traffic agent, sometimes the commercial and general agent. The by-laws of the committee provide for two meetings each year; but it is usually necessary to have an extra meeting. The chairman presides at meetings, decides questions on the construction of the classification in the intervals between meetings, and rules upon new articles presented for classification which are not already provided for. Changes are constantly made at the semiannual meetings, but they are not very numerous. All rulings are operative on the roads in the territory as soon as published. (567, 568.)

Mr. RIPLEY states that shippers have the privilege of appearing before the Western Classification Committee, in person or by attorney, and presenting their cases. He thinks that shippers are generally satisfied with their privileges in respect to the presentation of their desires before the Western Classification Committee. (570.)

Mr. BIRD says that business men and others wishing changes in classifications are permitted to appear before a subcommittee of the Western Classification Committee during some time before the meeting of the association itself. This subcommittee passes on the questions submitted in part and submits the others in due form to the association. Requests for changes are usually made by those who hope to get some special advantage for themselves at the expense of others. (478.)

Mr. TUCKER says that the Eastern Classification Committee is composed of 6 members of the Central Freight Association and 9 others; 15 in all. (558.)

3. *Uniformity of classification.*—Mr. NEWCOMB says that there are at present three more or less uniform systems of classification of freight in this country—one in the Northern and Central States (the Official), one in the Western States, and one in the South. These classifications differ in important respects, a thing which is justified by the differences in the character of the products chiefly hauled. A uniform classification for through freight would be desirable, but there would be too many exceptions as to local traffic. (100.)

Mr. REAGAN says that the State of Texas has adopted practically the Western classification, but has prohibited the railways from making certain reservations exempting themselves from liability. (350.)

Mr. RIPLEY, chairman of the Western Classification Committee, says there are three principal classifications in the United States—the Official, which covers the territory east of Chicago and the Mississippi River and north of the Ohio; the Southern, which governs south of the Ohio and east of the Mississippi, and the Western, which governs from Chicago to the Pacific coast. If freight is shipped from New York into the territory of the Western classification, through Chicago, it is rebilled under the Western classification. This is not uniformly true, however. For instance, freight from points east of Chicago consigned to St. Paul or Mississippi River points goes through on the Eastern classification. Mr. Ripley does not think that difference of classification is a source of much inconvenience to the shipper. It does, however, produce some unjust discrimination between places. For instance, a shipper in Chicago, sending to St. Paul or to Mississippi River points, is likely to be at some disadvantage as compared with an

Eastern shipper sending similar goods to the same points. This is because the Eastern classification is, upon the whole, somewhat lower than the Western. Many complaints on the part of shippers arise from these differences of classification, and often delay is caused in the delivery of freight. The witness has not known of any suit arising from such a cause.

In Illinois there is a classification framed by the Illinois board of railway and warehouse commissioners. Of course this applies only to business wholly in the State of Illinois. (568, 569.)

Mr. BIRD, of the Chicago, Milwaukee and St. Paul Railway, explains the reason why the Eastern or Official classification has been applied by the Western railroads as far as the Mississippi River. It was used by the railroads running directly from Eastern points to the Mississippi River, and roads from Chicago were forced to adopt the same classification on through traffic in order to compete in handling the goods. Thus, in one instance, the witness found that whisky was being shipped from Cincinnati to St. Paul at less than the rate from Milwaukee to St. Paul, whisky being fourth or fifth class at Cincinnati and first class under the Western classification.

The witness was a member of the committee which attempted to establish uniform classification throughout the country. Each section has made its classification with a view to promoting business and building up manufacturing in its own territory. Consequently each section must yield something to the other to secure uniformity; it is a matter of giving and taking. This committee prepared a classification which was agreed to by the roads west of Chicago and by several Eastern lines, but it was defeated by the vote of one or two of the trunk lines. Even if this uniform classification had been adopted, special commodity rates on grain, lumber, coal, etc., would still have been permitted, just as they are at present. (477, 478.)

Mr. KNAPP, of the Interstate Commerce Commission, believes that uniform classification of freight under public authority would lessen discriminations and be generally beneficial. The desirability of uniformity comes not so much from the difference in absolute expense of shipment of a given commodity under different classifications as from the fact that its relation to competing commodities is largely determined by classification. Thus the differences in rates between wheat and flour, referred to in another connection, are exceedingly important in their influence upon the milling business. (142.)

Mr. DICKINSON, of La Crosse, Wis., a manufacturer of agricultural implements, testifies that he has suffered serious injustice as a result of the differences between the existing classifications. For instance, under the Official classification, which rules in Michigan, certain sizes of packages of vehicles are shipped as first class. Under the Western classification, which governs in Wisconsin, practically all vehicles, except those of large and bulky structure, are shipped at 1¼ times first class. The classification at the initial point of shipment controls the rate to destination. From this it results that while a shipper of vehicles in Wisconsin has to pay 1¼ times first-class rates, a shipper in Michigan can reach the same points by payment of first-class rates only. Again, trouble arises from the different requirements as to packing. Under the Official classification cutters may be shipped in crates, set up, with the bows projecting, and without wrapping the projecting parts; under the Western classification the bows must be wrapped or a higher rate is charged. The railroad companies have also made a special ruling on buggies, which enables the Michigan manufacturers and the manufacturers in Chicago, Milwaukee, and Racine to ship vehicles to Iowa points at a rate that is sometimes even less than the first-class rate. Mr. Dickinson is obliged to pay 1¼ times first class on the same commodity to the same points. He considers this a gross injustice. He admits that there might be a particular instance in which a strictly uniform classification might work hardship, but, taking the country as a whole, he believes that the uniform classification would be the proper and right thing. He does not think that uniformity of classification can be hoped for except through governmental action. (548.)

Mr. Dickinson states further that the manufacturers in the West are dependent on commodity rates to put them in a position to compete with manufacturers farther east. He finds, however, that his own town is put at a disadvantage in respect to these rates as compared with St. Paul. The commodity rate on the witness's raw material, mostly iron and steel, is about one-half of the rate from Chicago to St. Paul on the finished product, but as it takes about two carloads of raw material in the rough to make one of finished product, this amounts to a discrimination against La Crosse. (550.)

Mr. RIPLEY is in favor of a uniform classification of freight for the whole United States. It should be framed by the railroads. The roads made an attempt some years ago to frame such a classification, and practically agreed upon it; but the agreement failed through the objection of a few roads. The objecting roads were principally in the East, although some of the Pacific coast lines also objected. The witness thinks that the trend of the changes which are made from time to time in the Western classification is toward uniformity. The framing of a classification is a very complicated matter, and it is doubtful whether one made by the Interstate Commerce Commission would give general satisfaction, at least at first. The classification which all the roads drew up some time ago, however, would be available as a basis. The witness would not anticipate any injury to the roads by a classification framed by the commission after a full hearing. It is perhaps hardly possible that a uniform classification will be attained, unless the framing of one is put into the hands of the Interstate Commerce Commission, or it is made mandatory upon the railroads to frame one. (568–570.)

Mr. MORTON believes that the universal classification is very desirable. He was a member of the committee appointed with a view to such classification. The attempt failed, because men in different sections desired different classifications on account of the commodities most largely carried in their sections. The witness thinks it would be to the interest of the railroads and of the public that some commission, p   under the supervision of the Interstate Commerce Commission, should frame a uniform classification. It would still be possible for different rates to be made upon the same classification, and for special commodity rates to be made as at present. (491, 496, 497.)

Mr. INGALLS, of the Chesapeake and Ohio. declares that differences in classification cause an immense amount of trouble. He thinks that uniform classification would not necessitate making the same rates in every section. (300.)

Mr. BLANCHARD, late commissioner of the Joint Traffic Association, declares that he is in favor of uniform classification so far as it is practicable. The railways themselves ought to formulate classifications. Assignment of articles to classes is a very important element in deciding what the rate on those classes shall be, and the railways should determine these classes for the same reason that they should determine the original rates. It might be wise to permit the Interstate Commerce Commission to order the railroads to adopt a uniform classification by a certain date, leaving it to the railways themselves to work out the classification. In case of failure to adopt a classification, the commission might perhaps put one in force.

At the same time the importance of uniform classification, Mr. Blanchard thinks, has been overestimated. Its adoption would not stop discriminations. The chief advantage would be in securing unbroken through rates. Moreover, there are many difficulties in the way of uniform classification. Despite these difficulties, however, the number of classes has been greatly reduced, as well as the number of classifications. The eastward tariffs of the Central Traffic Association formerly contained 13 classes; these have been merged into 6, exclusive of commodity rates. (633, 676, 677.)

Mr. Blanchard says further that there are many reasons which warrant differences in charges and in classifications in different sections of the country. In a section where there is a large and regular traffic in some one commodity, such as cotton, live stock, or manufactured products, it is proper that a lower rate should be made on that commodity than in a section where the traffic is very light. Thus, the large concentration of manufacturing industries in New England justifies lower rates on manufactured products from that section than in the regions where manufactures are little developed. Other items in the classification must be affected by canal, ocean, and river transportation. This is especially true as to transcontinental traffic. On account of the numerous influences which affect the transportation of commodities in different sections, it is necessary to have special commodity rates intermediate between the various classes. It is desirable that these should be reduced in number as far as possible, but they can not be entirely done away. Moreover, to establish uniform classification for interstate traffic would also necessitate changes in regard to State traffic. The present classifications have been adopted in view of the circumstances and conditions in their respective regions. The system of freight classification in England and on the continent of Europe is, roughly speaking, similar to that in this country. (632–634.)

Mr. VANLANDINGHAM, freight commissioner of the St. Louis Traffic Bureau, does not think that a uniform classification by statute is advisable or even possible without many exceptions of particular commodities. The territory in which an article is produced in large quantities must naturally have a lower rate on that article to the central market than prevails in territories where it is carried in small quantities. Water transportation also makes modifications in classifications necessary; in Pacific coast traffic there are nearly 1,500 exceptions to the general classifications. The railways themselves are seeking uniformity in classification as rapidly as possible. There were fully 20 different classifications fifteen years ago. The classification committees of the different sections meet yearly, and often have hundreds of applications for changes. One difficulty encountered by the railways in trying to get uniform classification, which would also arise in trying to fix a uniform classification by national authority, grows out of the classifications prescribed on particular commodities for traffic within various States by statutes of those States, as in Illinois

The Official classification has only six classes; the Western is much higher on general merchandise, and lower on the products of the country; the Southern is more largely based on quantities than on the value of goods, on account of water competition. (202–204.)

Mr. SPENCER, president of the Southern Railway, believes that greater uniformity of classification than now exists is desirable, but regard must always be given to the different conditions in different sections. Classification amounts to the fixing of rates. Many articles have been taken out of the regular classes and given special commodity rates. Thus in the State of Alabama as soon as the iron business was introduced and largely developed it became absolutely necessary to make a special commodity rate for iron, such as was not necessary before. The railway must thus always consider local conditions, must take into account the markets to which local products can go, and the prices which can be obtained. While the original theory in fixing classification was probably to impose all the traffic would bear, the method is now to constantly whittle away rates according to constantly changing conditions. (277.)

Mr. COWEN, of the Baltimore and Ohio, thinks that uniformity in classification is out of the question for a country so large and with so great a traffic as the United States. But the railways themselves are tending to secure uniformity as far as possible. (217.)

Mr. CALLAWAY, president of the New York Central, does not understand all of the reasons for differences in the classification of commodities in different sections of the country, but admits that there are differences in conditions. (237.)

Mr. KELLEY, of the Philadelphia Trades League, believes that on the whole a uniform system throughout the country would be very desirable, although it would take a considerable time and much labor to prepare one, and although there are often reasons why classifications should differ somewhat in different territory. At present, under the three classifications which prevail in different sections, the shipper, who can not be familiar with them all, or even with a single classification, on account of its complexity, does not know when he ships goods what the freight to some distant point will be. Shippers themselves, rather than buyers, usually determine the route of shipment. The witness believes that, individually, railroads do not depart materially from the general classification adopted for their respective sections of the country. (191.)

E. Miscellaneous questions.—1. *Through freight rates.*—Mr. BLANCHARD testifies that through freight rates and fares were formerly made by adding up the various local rates with the terminal charges, etc. The rules and responsibilities of the different carriers forming the links in the through lines were dissimilar and even clashing. Transfers were numerous and the time of through transit very long. At present through routes have been arranged either by actual consolidation of ownership or by joint agreements of different kinds, and now more and better through routes are offered to shippers in this country than in any other. The result has been economical to the railroads in car supply and return loads, and advantageous to the general public in quicker time and lower charges. It is not necessary to pass laws to induce railways to make proper through connections. The self-interest of the carriers themselves will regulate the matter. At present any road, which can offer reasonable facilities and which will divide charges as satisfactorily as existing connecting lines, can usually secure through rates from any important railroad connecting with it. It is true that railways sometimes have preferences for particular roads. Thus a group of roads under common ownership will naturally tend to prefer one another in their shipments. So, too, if one connecting line has a reputation for demoralizing rates and injuring both shippers and carriers it will naturally be less favored than more conservative lines. (627, 632.)

2. *Fast freight lines.*—Mr. NEWCOMB, of the Department of Agriculture, says that there are many lines of freight cars going by special names which traverse two or more lines of railways. Their purpose is to secure a reputation or trade name for through traffic. Through traffic arrangements of some sort are absolutely essen-

tial. There were formerly some fast-freight lines which were incorporated and separate from the railways, but the Empire Line and the Merchants' Despatch are the only ones of this kind now. Others are merely cooperative arrangements among connecting roads. Each puts in a number of cars and pays expenses and divides receipts in proportion to its mileage. The railway companies consider the separate, incorporated fast-freight lines disadvantageous. (98.)

3. *Competition of Canadian railroads* (see also under *Grain shipments*).— Mr. MORTON, vice-president of the Atchison, Topeka and Santa Fe Railway, complains of the fact that the Canadian Pacific Railroad is permitted to carry freight from one State in our Union to another through the Dominion of Canada, and especially of the fact that it demands that the American transcontinental lines shall charge 10 per cent higher rates than the Canadian road. He thinks that this practice should be prohibited by law. (492.)

Mr. PROUTY, of the Interstate Commerce Commission, referred to the practice of permitting goods to be carried by the Canadian railways from one part of the United States to another in bond. The practice is opposed by those railways which do not participate in the traffic brought by the Canadian roads.

4. *Export of butter and cheese.*—Mr. KENNARD, of the Chicago Butter and Egg Board, says that the export trade in butter and cheese is quite large, amounting to millions of dollars yearly, but that it is hindered by lack of shipping facilities and is not increasing in amount. There is only one steamship line from New York which will carry shipments of butter, and the freight rates on this line are almost prohibitive. Chicago dealers ship largely by way of Montreal, the freight rate being only about one-half that from New York. Owing to these lower Canadian rates the exportation of butter and cheese has developed enormously, although the witness does not know how far the statistics distinguish between the product made in Canada and that shipped through Canada from the United States. The shipments of cheese from Montreal from May 1, 1899, to November 1, 1899, were about seven times as great as those from New York, and the shipments of butter about four times as great. The Canadian steamers would only take American products when they can not get the products of their own country, and they keep their freight rooms open, excluding American products, up to within three days of sailing. Mr. Kennard thinks that American shipping should be encouraged in order to remedy this difficulty. (368.)

5. *Weight of shipments.*—Mr. EMERSON, a produce dealer of St. Paul, says that shippers of bulk vegetables, especially potatoes, frequently have difficulty on account of the apparent shrinkage in weights. Where these dealers ship to other persons the lack of proper supervision by the railroad over the discharge of the freight sometimes permits part of the goods to be taken away, either by accident or intentionally, without being weighed. The goods are paid for by the discharge weight. In other cases on shipments made to the dealer the car is found to contain less weight than the amount billed by the person loading it, but the consignee is compelled to pay freight at the higher rate. In the case of potatoes there is naturally a slight shrinkage, chiefly due to the evaporation of moisture, but it should not exceed two per cent, whereas some of the discrepancies which the witness has met with have been much larger. The difficulty of lack of supervision over the discharge of cars is found chiefly in medium-sized markets. The witness thinks it would be possible for the railroads to exercise proper supervision without employing many more men; at any rate, shippers would be willing to pay for necessary supervision. Where potatoes and similar articles are shipped in barrels instead of in bulk, little difficulty occurs.

In this connection the witness declares that the track scales used by the railways are often inaccurate. He has weighed the same car on the same day on the scales of two different railroads at St. Paul and found a difference of nearly 3,500 pounds. (480–485.)

Mr. KENNARD says that great inconvenience is caused to dealers by the different weights fixed for bushels of different products in the various States. Sales of all sorts of products should, if possible, be made by weight instead of measure. (369.)

6. *Perishable products.*—Mr. KENNARD, vice-president of the butter and egg board, successor of the Chicago Produce Exchange, says that that board meets daily to give opinions and to vote on the market price of butter and eggs and to consider the interests of business. Many of the members are interested in the handling of other perishable farm products. There are about 200 or 250 firms in Chicago in these general lines. These dealers use refrigerator cars largely, and are charged very high rates. In the case of fruit products, for example, in addition to an extra freight rate for the use of refrigerator cars, there is a charge for icing, which the dealers think should be omitted. (363.)

Mr. EMERSON complains that the increase of the minimum carload of fruit from 20,000 pounds to, he thinks, 26,000, compels the loading of cars almost or quite to the roof. The result is injurious to the product, because of the generation of heat and of its tendency to rise to the top of the car. Potatoes are often injured from the same cause. (482, 483.)

7. *Terminal charges, live stock, Chicago.*—Mr. MALLORY states that a charge of $2 per car on live stock sent to the Union stock yards at Chicago was added to the regular tariff on June 1, 1894, and is still collected by all roads. The excuse for the imposition was that on the same day the Union Stock Yards and Transit Company, which owns tracks in and about the stock yards, imposed a trackage charge of 80 cents per car upon most of the roads and $1.50 per car upon others, which used the company's tracks for a longer distance. This is aside from the charge made to stock owners by the stock-yard company for feed and yardage. By the decision of various courts and commissions, the terminal facilities must be furnished by the railroads and must be included in their rate. Consequently any charge for them must be entirely separate from the charges which shippers have to pay to the stock-yards company. The live-stock exchange took the matter up with the Illinois Board of Railroad Commissioners, and obtained a decision that the terminal charge was unjust, unreasonable, and illegal. The matter was afterwards taken to the United States court in Chicago and a similar decision was obtained; the railroads were ordered to desist from making the charge, and they did so until the court of appeals reversed the decision of the lower court on a technicality. Complaint was made to the Interstate Commerce Commission, and the commission, after a full investigation, ordered the railroads to cease collecting the charge. The railroads refused to obey the order. The commission appealed to the United States court to enforce the decision, and at the time of Mr. Mallory's testimony the court had the case under advisement.

The Cattle Growers' Association, which is the largest association of its kind in this country, and is composed largely of Texas, Montana, and other range people, has joined the Chicago live-stock men in their fight. (587, 588.)

8. *Chicago Belt Railroad.*—Mr. GREELEY says that the usual charge for transferring grain around the Chicago Belt Railroad is about $3 per car, which he considers excessive. He does not know concerning the power of the Interstate Commerce Commission in regard to this railroad. (881.)

Mr. VANLANDINGHAM refers to the abuse of the belt-line system around Chicago for the purpose of making discriminations in favor of that city and of particular shippers. The allowances made by the trunk lines to the belt lines for handling their cars have been so large that the belt lines have been able to make large rebates. The belt lines claimed not to be amenable to the interstate-commerce act. The Interstate Commerce Commission, however, has ruled against this practice. (208, 209.)

9. *Furnishing of cars.*—Mr. CALLAWAY states that his own and other railways sometimes find it difficult to furnish cars to shippers promptly. He admits that railways ought to be compelled to take care of their customers, but declares that the inequality of the business at different times makes complete supply of the demand occasionally impossible. (232.)

10. *Express companies.*—In the opinion of Mr. INGALLS, of the Chesapeake and Ohio, the earnings of the express companies are not increasing relatively to those of railways, especially those of the fast freight trains which the railways are running. He believes that on the Chesapeake and Ohio the earnings of the companics amount to only about 1 per cent of the freight receipts. (301.)

11. *Freight bureaus.*—Mr. KELLEY, president of the National Association of Freight Commissioners, and freight commissioner for the Trades League of Philadelphia, testifies that there are about 25 freight bureaus in the different States similar to the Trades League of Philadelphia. This consists of merchants organized for the purpose of furthering the mercantile interests of the city by securing fair rates of transportation to and from the city. The freight bureau acts as the mediator between the transportation companies and the members of the association in case of grievances, and also furnishes advice to shippers. The Philadelphia bureau, for example, has presented a number of grievances and has succeeded in having Philadelphia shippers and merchants placed on a parity with those of other cities. The railway companies usually give fair consideration to questions raised by these bureaus, knowing that they represent probably the major proportion of the shipping interests of their respective cities, and that they are familiar with the subjects discussed.

The National Association of Freight Commissioners has for its purpose the discussion of matters of transportation of a national character, the presentation of resolutions to Congress, etc. It has an executive committee, which takes up important matters during the intervals between the national conventions. (185, 187, 193.)

Mr. VANLANDINGHAM, of the St. Louis Traffic Bureau, similarly points out that such bureaus are able to influence railway officials materially. The usual method of action is to visit the traffic officer of the railway company and confer with him informally. He will often be much more frank than if the investigation were a public one, and the fact that the representative of the traffic bureau is familiar with railway matters, so that he is not forced to believe all the arguments of the traffic manager as he pleases to give them, and that he has behind him the moral influence of a large body. enables him often to secure important changes. (208.)

III. DISCRIMINATIONS BETWEEN INDIVIDUALS.

A. **Existence of discriminations.**—1. *General affirmation.*—Mr. KNAPP, Mr. PROUTY, and Mr. CLEMENTS, members of the Interstate Commerce Commission, all agree in the opinion that numerous and secret discriminations are still made by railways, notwithstanding the interstate commerce act, although there has, in their opinion, been a marked improvement during the past year. They attribute these discriminations to competition between carriers, and the attempt to secure business in whatever way is possible, rather than to a desire to injure or favor any shippers. It is poverty which leads to dishonest action.

Mr. PROUTY declares that he has no doubt that during 1898 the demoralization of rates by discriminations was about as bad as it could be. Competitive traffic did not pretend to move on the published rates. At Portland, Oreg., it was found that large shippers telephoned to the agents of the different railways, got the best rates possible, billed their goods at the published rates, and afterwards received the difference. This witness also points out that railways in the hands of receivers have been among the most serious offenders, although since about the beginning of 1899 the courts appointing receivers have been more strict in keeping them within the law.

Mr. KNAPP, especially, believes that since the action of the receivers of the Baltimore and Ohio Railroad in the latter part of 1898, in acknowledging the extensive practice of discriminations and agreeing to aid in the future in preventing them, there has been a very marked improvement of conditions. The managers of many railroads had become impressed with the danger to their finances from the reduction of rates to many special shippers. They believed that, since practically all railways made these special rates, no one really gained largely in traffic. Moreover, rates at first granted secretly tended afterwards to become published rates, at less than profitable figures. The Baltimore and Ohio Railroad simply took the initiative in a movement favored by many other railways, especially of the Northeast. This changed attitude of the railways, together with the increased amount of traffic, and with the narrow margins which now remain for making concessions, has, in the opinion of Mr. Knapp, largely done away with direct discriminations on the trunk lines, although grain for export, packing house products, and some other classes of traffic are perhaps still subject to dis criminating rates.

Mr. PROUTY, however, declares himself less optimistic as to present conditions regarding rates, and Mr. CLEMENTS implies that he considers discriminations between persons, as well as between places, to be still a serious evil. (Knapp, 132, 139, 142, 143; Prouty, 150–152; Clements, 159.)

Mr. COWEN, president of the Baltimore and Ohio Railroad. says that the letter written by him and Mr. Murray to the Interstate Commerce Commission in 1898 was occasioned by the great reduction in the revenues of that railway from the secret cutting of rates. The granting of rebates and lower rates affected a great deal more than 50 per cent of all the traffic at that time. All packing-house products and iron and steel products were getting cut rates. The system is contrary to the public welfare and injurious to the railways. Excessive competition and open rate cutting are the chief causes leading to discriminations. All sorts of methods were being employed. There is much less abuse in this way at present. but the witness fears that when the great demand for transportation again falls off new discriminations will be made. Pooling is the only remedy. (313–316.)

Mr. BLANCHARD, late commissioner of the Joint Traffic Association, says that the practice of granting discriminating rates differs in extent at different times and in different sections of the country. The actual amount is difficult to ascertain, since the offending companies never divulge their actions to anyone. The witness believes, however, that discriminating rates have increased steadily since about the first year after the passage of the interstate commerce act, and that

they will continue to increase in the absence of pooling. Throughout his argument in favor of pooling the serious character and results of discriminating rates
are repeatedly referred to. (625, 626.)

Mr. Blanchard declares further that it is usually the shippers who demand
rebates, and threaten to transfer their patronage to other lines, rather than the
railway companies which solicit traffic. The railways have no desire to build up
large shippers. (683, 684.)

Mr. INGALLS, president of the Chesapeake and Ohio, also says that the practice
of granting discriminations in favor of individuals has varied greatly at different
times. Thus in 1885 there were many discriminations. The interstate commerce
act checked them for a few years, but they increased until in 1894 and 1895 the
evil was about as bad as possible. During 1896 competing railways made joint
agreements which almost prevented discriminations, but the decision of the
Supreme Court in the trans-Missouri case under the antitrust act caused anarchy
in railway rates. The conferences between the Interstate Commerce Commission
and the railways have resulted in a great improvement, but Mr. Ingalls fears that
when the present rush of business has ceased the railways will gradually drift
back into their old ways until they are permitted to form agreements. (286, 297.)

Mr. FISH, of the Illinois Central, also speaks of the decrease in discriminations
due to the conferences with the Interstate Commerce Commission, to abundant
traffic, and to the consolidation of railways. (336.)

Mr. SPENCER, president of the Southern Railway Company, believes that discriminations in favor of individuals are still largely granted by the railways.
The object is to get business without enabling competitors to find out how it is
obtained. If the law were obeyed which requires rates to be made known, and
three days' notice of reduction to be given, the competitor would have the same
opportunity to make bids for traffic. The evil takes many forms, including
direct rebates, commissions, car mileage, underbilling, and billing to the wrong
destination.

Mr. Spencer declares, however, that the Southern Railway is not making any
discriminations between individuals, aside from the general difference between
carload rates and part-carload rates. This was not true of the separate lines
which were consolidated a few years ago into the Southern Railway, and the
witness thinks that consolidation generally tends greatly to reduce discriminations. Throughout the South rates are much more uniformly maintained now
than five years ago. Shippers have confidence that other shippers are not getting
advantages, and hence do not themselves apply for advantages. (273, 279.)

Mr. BIRD, of the Chicago, Milwaukee and St. Paul, also testifies that railway
rates are not maintained as the law requires, but believes that the number of
instances of violation is much less than is generally supposed. However, on account
of the severe penalties, the railways are apt to confine their discriminations to the
largest shippers, who will help them in concealment, and these shippers need
favors less than the others. Generally speaking, a large volume of business tends
to steady the rates. (470, 471.)

Mr. HYLAND says that there is no necessity for railroads to make private discriminations in order to compete. Only three days' notice of reduction in rates made
for the purpose of securing business is required by the law. Mr. Hyland declares
that the long and short haul clause of the interstate-commerce act is especially
important and should be strictly enforced. Railways should be willing to give
up any part of their traffic which can not be carried on legitimately. (352.)

Mr. STICKNEY, president of the Chicago Great Western Railway, declares that
published tariffs are not maintained by railroads and can not be maintained.
Moreover, he does not think that uniformity of rates between different shippers
is natural or necessary. The producer of transportation, like the producer of
other commodities, should be free to sell for all he can get and to make different
prices to different persons if necessary. "If I was a banker and found a merchant that had an idea that somebody had to buy his goods I would not allow
him to do business at my bank." It takes two to make a bargain. Mr. Stickney
discusses quite fully the conditions which must be considered in making freight
rates, his evidence on this subject being summarized in another place. (460–462.)

Mr. MORTON, of the Atchison, Topeka and Santa Fe Railroad, thinks that discriminations, whether between individuals or localities, should be prohibited.
There certainly do exist unjust discriminations of both classes, although it is
not always easy to decide what are fair rates as between different communities,
and what constitutes discrimination. A man who ships a single carload should
receive as low a rate as one who ships 100 carloads.

The witness thinks that preferential rates are probably given on as large a proportion of the business as before the interstate-commerce act, or even larger,
although the number of persons who receive these rates is smaller. Practically

all the methods which human ingenuity can devise are employed to evade the law. Frequently lower rates are granted on shipments within a State as compensation for furnishing interstate shipments. If a single railroad believes that the interstate-commerce act is a farce, and makes special rates, its practice goes far toward demoralizing the rates of other roads. The witness declares that there is one railroad from Chicago to the Missouri River which is doing double the business it ought to do if it maintained rates. A few years ago a number of railroads in that section tried to maintain absolutely the interstate-commerce law, and brought suit against this particular road. Its president admitted the charges, but nothing was done. (490, 493, 494.)

Mr. KELLEY, freight commissioner for the Trades League of Philadelphia, is of the opinion that rates have been better maintained during the year 1899 than before. He attributes this less to the fact of the abundance of traffic. which does not in the past seem to have prevented discriminations, than to the conferences between the Interstate Commerce Commission and the trunk line officials. Discriminations by false classifications, private cars, and similar methods still exist. (185, 186.)

Mr. VANLANDINGHAM, commissioner of the St. Louis Traffic Bureau, believes also that published rates have for the most part been maintained during 1899, but that the discriminations during 1898 were worse than at any time during the past quarter of a century. They were made by numerous methods, such as payment of commissions for securing business, allowance of direct rebates, transportation of grain on export rates when really intended for domestic use, allowances to elevator owners for loading and unloading, payments for the use of private cars, etc. (194.)

Mr. Vanlandingham further declares that in his position he learns of many illegal discriminations between individuals, perhaps as many in favor of individuals whom it is his interest to proteet as in favor of others. He believes that usually such discriminations in favor of individuals in one city are made by railways in the belief that they would otherwise lose business by reason of discriminations made in favor of some other place or individual. He thinks that the evil of discriminations is likely to get worse and worse, until it becomes so great that the railways will agree to put things back to the proper basis again. (207, 208.)

Mr. DOUSMAN, a grain shipper of Chicago, testifies that he frequently received rebates on grain shipments before the interstate-commerce act. Since that time, his opposition to freight discriminations being well known, he has scarcely been offered rebates and certainly would not accept them. On this account he has practically been driven out of business. The witness believes from his experience that discriminations are worst when there is the most traffic to move. Discriminations were temporarily checked when the interstate-commerce law went into effect, but gradually increased and have continued ever since. Place discriminations of all kinds are especially deprecated by this witness. The practical effect of the interstate-commerce law has been to lessen the number of persons to whom railroads grant favors, but probably not to lessen the amount of such favors. With every man on the same basis all danger from large combinations of capital will disappear. (353, 359.)

Mr. NEALL, a shipping merchant of Philadelphia, believes that discriminations still exist. He even thinks that they are justified in certain cases in order to off-set discriminations between places made legally under the tariffs. Thus, Philadelphia has repeatedly complained that the freight rates on the trunk lines to that port are relatively higher than to other ports, so that traffic is diverted from Philadelphia. The only way in which the railways, which are under agreement as to differential rates to different ports, can do justice to Philadelphia is by making discriminations in favor of individuals at that city, and Mr. Neall is inclined to think that the fact that Philadelphia has been receiving a fairer proportion of freight during the past year than hitherto is largely due to the existence of such individual departures from published tariffs. Mr. Neall admits that the harbor of Philadelphia is not equal in some regards to those of other ports.

In view of the discriminations which exist among railways Mr. Neall advocated pooling, under proper restrictions and under the supervision of the Interstate Commerce Commission. (173, 174.)

Mr. STONE, of the Chicago Board of Trade, thinks there is generally less complaint of discrimination when business is good than when it is bad. At the present time he believes that there is less unjust discrimination than there has been during the last four or five years, and perhaps during the decade just closing. In a place like Chicago or any large city he thinks the merchants are more alert than people in smaller places, and there is not apt to be so much discrimination between them. Railways would be more cautious about allowing discrimination where public opinion furnishes such a search light than they would be in a community dominated by one large business. He has no information about local discriminations between great cities like Chicago and smaller places. He does not believe pooling would prevent unjust discrimination. (584, 535.)

Mr. WOFFINDIN, chairman of the Chicago east-bound freight committee, thinks it quite probable that there is a good deal of freight discrimination, but he has no means of knowing it. He is of opinion, however, that the public rates are now so low that any lower discriminating rates would involve a loss. (565, 566.)

Mr. GALLAGHER is inclined to think that there is less discrimination in the trunk-line territory than in the West; at least, not so much is heard about it. (545.)

2. *Denial of discriminations.*—Mr. TUCKER, chairman of the Central Freight Association, says that there never was a time when there was less rate trouble than now. He thinks that as a rule more has been said about rate troubles than has been justified. He does not know of any discriminations, and he does not think any discrimination could long continue without being known to everybody. It is natural for a shipper to feel that he is not getting as low rates as others, but Mr. Tucker thinks he is mistaken as a rule. He does not think there is any case in which large shippers get advantages over smaller ones; though "of course, a man that is a large shipper and does a large wholesale business, like several packers or large grain men, naturally have more power than the smaller dealer. That is exemplified in almost every commercial transaction."

It is, of course, possible that there might be a system of drawbacks without its being publicly known. If, as stated, the Santa Fe paid $7,000,000 in drawbacks in the years preceding its bankruptcy, that was not known at the time to the other roads. Mr. Tucker thinks, however, that the other roads would have known if the Santa Fe had got a greater tonnage than it would otherwise have got. He does not think that any pirating of rates can result in increased tonnage, because it will soon be met by a competitor. (558–561.)

Mr. CALLAWAY, of the New York Central, thinks that the freight rates have been reduced to such a low figure that considerable discriminations between individuals are impossible. He implies that special rates to certain shippers, not necessarily more favorable than those to other shippers on the same line, are sometimes made to enable those shippers to compete with producers on other lines of railway and even in other countries. The private-car system constitutes a form of discrimination, although the rates are open to all such shippers. The witness admits, also, that pooling would be somewhat beneficial in its influence upon discriminations. (231.)

Mr. Callaway is positive that the New York Central adheres strictly to published rates at present. He had not understood that extensive rebates were distinctly proved against the Atchison, Topeka and Santa Fe Railroad. (234.)

Mr. EVANS, a miller of Indianapolis, thinks that there has been very little discrimination between individuals in regard to the shipment of grain products. Practically all shippers have paid published rates. (440.)

Mr. EMERSON, a produce dealer of St. Paul, thinks there are probably no discriminations between different shippers in handling vegetables and similar products in connection with that market. (484.)

Mr. MALLORY believes that the rates on live stock are exactly the same to all shippers. The great packers, who own cattle cars, have an advantage to the extent of the profits the cars bring them; but he believes that they have to pay the same tariff rates as others. (588, 589.)

3. *Specific instances of discriminations.*—Mr. GALLAGHER states that he has all the documents to prove a shipment of grain from Minnesota to Texas at a rate very much less than the published rate. (542.)

Mr. FULLER, of Norfolk, Nebr., says that he knows of instances where jobbers in that city have received rebates from the published freight rates. One leading dry-goods firm has assured the witness that it secures a rebate of 25 per cent. A wholesale grocery house did business at Norfolk on the basis of 25 per cent rebate. and abandoned its business when this rebate was withdrawn. The Chicago, St. Paul, Minneapolis and Omaha Railroad at that point does not publish its tariff in the office, but claims to comply with the law by posting a card stating that the tariff rates can be ascertained by applying to the agent. The witness also refers to other railway practices which he considers unjust. (442, 443.)

(See also *Discriminations against St. Louis*, p. 65.)

4. *Standard Oil Company.*—Mr. PROUTY, of the Interstate Commerce Commission, testifies that, while the Standard Oil Company perhaps receives no direct rebates or discriminations, it is favored in various ways by the railroads. These are cited as illustrations of the methods by which, under the law, inequalities may still exist, as between different shippers. Thus the freight rate from Cleve.

land to Boston was formerly 22 cents per hundred pounds alike on iron articles, grain, and petroleum. But since the interstate-commerce act the rates have been changed, so that the rate on grain is 15 cents per hundred pounds, on iron 20 cents, and on petroleum 24 cents. Again, on almost every commodity through rates are made from Cleveland and other Western points to points reached by the New York, New Haven and Hartford Railroad. On petroleum there are no through rates, but a local rate is added to the Boston rate. Moreover, the New York, New Haven and Hartford Railroad prescribes that petroleum and its products shall be in the second class of freight unless the person to whom it is shipped has a private siding or tank opposite the rails, in which case it is fifth class, the rate for fifth class being probably one-half that for second class. These arrangements, the witness believes, are explainable by the fact that the Standard Oil Company ships oil from its seaboard refineries to Boston largely by tank steamers, and distributes it from there for a comparatively short distance at the local rates. The railroad can, to be sure, make more money by transporting on the local than on the through rate, but there is no justification for denying the through rate to one particular commodity. There is no power now, however, to prevent such discriminations.

Mr. Prouty also refers to the differences in rates between shipments from Cleveland to New Orleans, and from Whiting, near Chicago, to New Orleans. Whereas the average rate on about 25 articles is about 2 cents higher from Cleveland than from Chicago, the rate on petroleum is 8 cents higher. The Standard Oil Company is the only shipper of oil from Whiting.

Mr. Prouty believes that the commission should have the power to establish through rates. (149, 150.)

Mr. KINDEL, manufacturer, of Denver, testifies that the Standard Oil Company, although it does not itself largely own wells in the Colorado fields, controls the refining business and buys practically all of the crude oil. The freight rates from the East are such that there can be practically no competition with the local product of the Standard. The Standard did cut prices for a time to 5 cents per gallon until competitors were driven out, but now, notwithstanding the nearness of the supply, oil costs 100 per cent more in Denver than in Chicago. Moreover, the freight rate on oil from Colorado to the Pacific coast is 96 cents per hundred, while that from Chicago through Colorado is 78¼ cents per hundred. (259.)

Mr. SPENCER declares that the Standard Oil Company receives no special favors from the Southern Railway. It is paid mileage on its tank cars, but this arrangement is open to any shipper who furnishes a car. The private-car system is injurious to the railways, but they are unable to do away with it. (280.)

5. *Railway discriminations on export shipments.*—Mr. SNYDACKER, a grain merchant and exporter of Chicago, testified concerning the rates of transportation from Chicago to the seaboard, especially on export grain. His first statement was to the effect that the rates for all-water or part-rail and part-water transportation from Chicago were entirely a matter of trade and barter between the individual shipper and the transportation company. Mr. Snydacker's firm has a man in charge of the export business who is supposed to get rates as cheap as any that are made. The witness implied that, so far as export rates are concerned, it is not illegal for the railroad company or the transportation company to carry grain at a lower rate for one person than for another. The method is the same as that regarding ocean tonnage. Mr. Snydacker afterwards stated, however, that he was satisfied that his firm shipped grain on the basis of published tariff export rates, and did not solicit or obtain rates below these or below the rates given competitors. Nor does his firm receive any commissions or other indirect favors. It does not hold grain for any length of time at the seaboard, and hence could not receive advantages in storage. There appears no reconciliation of these somewhat conflicting statements. (398–400.)

B. **Methods of discriminations.**—1. *Generally.*—Mr. BLANCHARD says that discriminations are chiefly granted by means of secret rebates or by combinations of rates on inward and outward traffic. To a less degree they arise from special advantages in terminal facilities, in charges for switching and similar services, in storage periods, from car mileage, quicker time, allowances in weights, etc. Railways also favor certain shippers by leasing them elevators or making special elevator contracts. All discriminations are vicious and indefensible. (625.)

Mr. KNAPP is especially specific in his statements. He believes that direct payment of rebates is comparatively rare, but other methods of discrimination are endless. Thus, in certain cases railways maintain their interstate rates rigidly, but secure business by making concessions on purely State traffic. Commissions are paid to agents of shippers; shippers are favored in the purchase of supplies;

or, in many instances, the weight of shipments is underbilled. Several parties are now under indictment for misdescription of goods, by which they are brought under a class bearing a lower freight rate than that to which they really belong. (132.)

Several other witnesses, in their general statements as to the existence of rebates, already summarized, mention these various devices incidentally.

Mr. GALLAGHER refers to the straw-man system of discrimination and to discriminations by advances of money upon shipments. The straw-man system he describes in the following terms: "Instead of billing that stuff to the man I have sold it to I bill it to a fictitious man, or straw man. On the bills he is the actual shipper. I do not see him at all, don't know anything about him, but he bills the stuff to the man that I want it to go to, my customer, and it will go through all right, and by and by the straw man sends me a check for a rebate. You can not find him; at least I have not been able to do it. That was also described to me by a man who practices it." (541, 542.)

2. *Misdescription of goods.*—Mr. BLANCHARD says that many frauds are practiced upon the railways by the misdescription of goods, and that this results in discriminations between shippers. In 1898 the Westbound Inspection Bureau of the trunk lines from Boston, New York, and Philadelphia discovered 270,000 cases of misrepresentation. Thus, a box containing silks may be represented as containing shirtings. The witness has recently heard a hardware manufacturer speak jocularly of putting a single piece of iron pipe in each box of brass goods shipped, and billing the whole as iron pipe at much lower rates. The railways are more and more striving to inspect such shipments, but they would be greatly strengthened in doing so by permission to pool. (675.)

Mr. KELLEY believes that the chief difficulty encountered by Philadelphia shippers in recent years has been on account of the wrong classification of hardware shipped from certain southwestern cities, Louisville and others, in competition with Philadelphia manufacturers. High-priced commodities which should bear the first-class rate were shipped as saddlery and other low-priced commodities at sixth-class rates. The witness believes that the railroad companies were not aware of this misrepresentation. (186.)

Mr. VANLANDINGHAM, commissioner of the St. Louis Traffic Bureau, believes that freight can scarcely be shipped under a false classification, or at less than its real weight, without the knowledge of railway officers. He believes, however, that there is a considerable amount of discrimination by this method. It has been felt especially in regard to hardware shipments from St. Louis. The railways, for example, have allowed large shippers to load cars with different classes of articles, which should pay separately the higher part carload rates, and have then charged at full carload rates. There is little difficulty from such abuses in territory west of the Mississippi River, since freight is inspected and weighed in practically every case by officers of an association representing the railways jointly and not any individual road. The chief difficulty which arises under this system is in deciding what constitutes the proper classification of particular commodities. (210, 211.)

3. *Underbilling of weight.*—Mr. GALLAGHER regards underbilling as one of the worst evils in the transportation business to-day. Millers have told him within a week that they have been solicited by the railroad companies to ship 200 barrels of flour and bill at 100. Where Mr. Gallagher lives peaches are shipped to Salt Lake City at four boxes to 100 pounds; he has a friend living 350 miles farther west who ships six boxes to 100 pounds, shipping to the agent of the railroad. (541, 543.)

Mr. Gallagher suggests that underbilling might in some cases be detected by authorizing a Government officer to break the seal of a car and examine its contents in cases of suspicion. (546.)

4. *Intrastate discriminations.*—Mr. GALLAGHER has heard of a practice of giving lower rates on special articles of freight within the borders of a State in consideration of the consignment of large amounts of interstate business, but he has no positive information upon this subject. (542, 543.)

Messrs. KNAPP and MORTON also refer to this practice. (132, 502.)

5. *Furnishing of cars.*—Mr. DOUSMAN says that at times railways apparently discriminate between shippers in the promptness with which they furnish cars, and he cites one recent instance in which an order for shipment was delayed an entire month. (355.)

6. *Carload and part-carload shipments.*—Mr. VANLANDINGHAM, commissioner of the St. Louis Traffic Bureau, testifies that the differences in rates on part carloads as compared with full carloads of goods are very much greater on the Western railways than on the Eastern. By an agreement made in 1898 between the

railways and the jobbers of the Pacific coast, a minimum difference of 50 cents per hundred pounds between the carload and the part-carload rate was established. This difference is greater in the case of many commodities than the possible profit upon the goods. The arrangement is intended to shut out the jobbers of Chicago, St. Paul, and other Eastern cities from selling directly to retailers on the coast. The retailers are practically put at the mercy of the local jobber. Similar extensive differences between the carload and part carload rates exist on railways leading to Texas. Discriminations between shippers are sometimes made by allowing one shipper to fill up a car with several different commodities, which should bear separate part-carload rates, and carrying them all at the lower carload rate. (207, 210.)

C. Mileage on private cars.—Members of the Interstate Commerce Commission point out that the use of cars belonging to shippers often constitutes a means of discrimination between individuals. Some shippers own thousands of these cars, and the railways pay them a rate of mileage for the use of them so high as to amount to a very large profit, even on the entire business of the shipper. Shippers take pains often to send these cars by unnecessarily long routes and not to load them to their full capacity, in order that the mileage may be as much as possible.

The so-called fast-freight lines and through-freight lines, like the Red Line, Merchants' Despatch, etc., are usually understood to have no special rates. Usually they are simply combinations among the railways themselves for through traffic. One line which operates over the New York Central as a separate company receives perhaps 10 per cent of the freight charge for its services in collecting freight. (KNAPP, 141; PROUTY, 151.)

Mr. KELLEY, of the Philadelphia Freight Bureau, also considers the private car system a means of discrimination. The mileage of three-fourths of a cent per mile allowed by the Eastern railroad companies to the owners is excessive. The railway companies get an advantage, perhaps, by making such an allowance in securing more of the business of particular large shippers. (187.)

Mr. VANLANDINGHAM, of the St. Louis Traffic Bureau, agrees in the opinion that the private-car system constitutes a method of discrimination. The allowance made by the railways west of the Mississippi River on refrigerator and similar cars is 1 cent per mile in both directions. The shorter railway lines are forced often to pay mileage on the basis of the length of the longer railways in order to secure the business of these cars. The practice of using private box cars, which prevailed up to two or three years ago, is largely ceasing, since the railways have reduced the mileage on such cars to 6 mills. The cars mostly used are stock cars, which are largely owned by companies controlled by the officers of the railways themselves, and refrigerator cars, which are owned by large meat packers and beer shippers, either directly or by means of subsidiary companies, organized partly for the purpose of evading the law. (209, 210.)

Mr. GREELEY, a commission merchant of Chicago, says that firms in which P. D. Armour is interested own between 10,000 and 20,000 private cars. The mileage on cars generally amounts, he thinks, to 25 or 50 per cent per year on the value of the car. Private cars are by no means confined to handling products which are perishable. The witness believes that even where railroads could use cars of their own, private-car shippers are so powerful as to compel them to use private cars and pay mileage. The owners of these cars make so much money from them that competition against them is impossible. (373, 378.)

Mr. DOUSMAN, a Chicago grain shipper, refers to an instance in which a certain grain shipper having asked for one 1,000-bushel car was furnished with two smaller cars belonging to a private-car company. The object of this was to enable the railroad to pay a large amount in mileage to this company, which seems to have practically forced the railroad to help it to maintain its large profits on that feature of its business. The railroads would like to abolish the private-car system, but can not do it so long as any one road permits these cars to be used. The system is simply an indirect method of cutting rates. (362.)

Mr. BACON, of the Milwaukee Board of Trade, thinks that private cars are a convenient means of making discriminations, but he is not aware that they are used in the grain business. (430.)

Mr. CALLAWAY, president of the New York Central, likewise thinks that great abuses arise from the private-car system, especially in the case of dressed beef refrigerator cars. The most of the railroads, he thinks, pay a mileage of 1 cent per mile, although the New York Central has refused to pay more than three-fourths of a cent, since its income from the freight would have been practically nothing at the other figure. The railways themselves are all anxious to break up the practice, but no railroad dares to build and operate the cars, since all of its traffic in dressed beef would immediately be turned away to other railroads. If the railways were allowed to pool and divide their traffic they could agree in refusing to haul such private cars, and would then be able to furnish cars themselves. The railways pay to one another six mills mileage for the use of cars, and they calculate that this is a fair payment for interest and repairs. In view of the enormous distances which are covered by the dressed-beef cars the profits from their mileage are very high. The cars are carried back practically empty, but this would still be the case if the railways owned refrigerator cars. It would be much cheaper, however, for the railways to operate their own cars. Most of the beef shipped for Eastern consumption is already dressed. The witness does not think that individual discriminations are made in the shipment of dressed beef. The rates are open to all shippers. But it requires large capital to establish a refrigerator-car system, and practically only three or four establishments control the business.

The railways do not especially object to the use of private cars for iron, steel, oil, and similar shipments, where the rate of mileage is usually only 6 mills. (230–232.)

Mr. INGALLS, of the Chesapeake and Ohio, also believes that the use of private cars benefits large shippers at the expense of small shippers. He thinks that the owners may get 15 or 20 per cent on the investment in these cars. Up to five years ago the trunk lines largely refused to run private cars, but the restrictions have gradually been dropped, and although the railways would like to refuse to haul them and to substitute their own cars, they are unable to do so, since they can not make pooling agreements. (301, 302.)

Mr. KENNARD, a commission merchant, of Chicago, declares that there is discrimination in favor of a few large fruit shippers in shipments from California to the East. These concerns apparently own the refrigerator cars for the most part. They can, accordingly, get cars in any number for their own use at the time wanted, while private growers or small shippers must pay to them a considerable premium to get cars—$60 to $90. This arrangement often practically shuts out the smaller shipper. (363, 364.)

Mr. Kennard declares that owners of private cars often load them in part with commodities bearing a high class of freight, but have them billed at rates applicable only to the lower class, of which part of the load consists. (365.)

Mr. MALLORY states that no cattle shippers engaged exclusively in the live-cattle business, so far as he knows, own cars. Very few concerns devoted exclusively to shipping live stock would handle business enough to warrant their keeping a line of cars. The great packing houses, such as Armour & Co. and Swift & Co., do have cattle cars of their own, though they also ship cattle in the railroad cars. These concerns have an advantage to the extent of whatever profit their cars bring them, and it would seem to be more proper that the railroad company should conduct its business with its own cars. (589.)

Mr. BIRD, of the Chicago, Milwaukee and St. Paul Railway, says that until recently the railroads had not enough cars to meet emergencies in busy seasons, and were glad to use cars belonging to private owners. Many classes of manufacturers wish cars having a special capacity or character. Finally the development of the packing business made the use of refrigerator cars necessary on a large scale. While the railways would be glad to furnish all the cars for ordinary business, and in fact do so for the most part, the witness doubts whether it would be to their advantage to attempt to furnish refrigerator cars. The number of cars actually used under private ownership is much less than would be necessary if every company solicited the business and had a sufficient number to carry all that it could possibly get at any time. The packers bear their own risks as regards the preservation of the meat shipped, in the absence of special delay on the part of the railroad. It requires technical knowledge to be sure that the car is in proper condition for shipping meat, and the railways would not like to be responsible. The payment of mileage to the owners of private cars is not an injustice to other shippers. The owner has his money invested and is entitled to something for the use of cars, just as any other manufacturer having superior facilities is entitled to the benefit of his investment. Railroads ordinarily pay one another six mills per mile for the use of common cars costing perhaps $400 or $425. Refrigerator cars cost $900 to $1,000, and the mileage of one cent is therefore not to be considered excessive. (475, 476.)

Mr. FISH, of the Illinois Central, while recognizing the abuses of the private-car system, thinks that they are less serious than formerly, and that, as the cost of constructing and repairing cars is tending to increase on account of the larger size and the greater complexity, the time will come when the undue profit of the owners from mileage will be reduced to a reasonable amount. The railways are becoming better able to buy their own equipment, and can resist demands for higher mileage rates. (336.)

D. Effects of discrimination on combinations, etc.—Mr. KNAPP, chairman of the Inter-state Commerce Commission, believes that railway discriminations of all kinds tend, generally speaking, to benefit great shippers and manufacturers, men of wealth, at the expense of the masses of the people. Farmers and small producers get no favors. He believes that trusts and monopolies would not be dangerous to the social welfare if they had no advantage from the railways. Almost the only unfair advantage which can come between the producer and the consumer of staple commodities comes through transportation. Under ordinary circumstances anyone can buy wheat or corn, can build a mill and grind it, or establish a store and sell it: but the opportunities for the transportation of wheat and corn are limited, and through them discriminations may be made. A few years ago anyone could buy grain west of Chicago, and there were many buyers; but at present, through the action of railways, one buyer takes all the grain on one line of railroad, and there is practically no competition. (147, 148.)

Mr. BLANCHARD, of the former Joint Traffic Association, admits that discriminations are chiefly in favor of large shippers and that they tend to destroy small producers and dealers. He does not say directly that discriminations have fostered trusts or that the railways are the parents of trusts, but he admits that if present tendencies continue trusts will undoubtedly be placed at an advantage. The witness denies that the railroads have any desire to favor large shippers or trusts. They know that to strengthen shippers will enable them to make yet greater demands from the railways. In every city the aggregate of freight from small shippers is greater than that from the principal large shippers. There is no railroad company which would not desire to see fewer favors granted to trusts and combinations. (683, 684.)

Mr. RIPLEY, president of the Atchison, Topeka and Santa Fe Railroad Company, says that the railroads want equal rates, but the large shippers do not. All the large shippers, however they may theorize about the desirability of equal rates, believe in their hearts, and act upon the belief, that their large business entitles them to concessions. Believing this, they are actively engaged in finding ways to evade the law. Comparatively few of the railroads are strong enough to resist the pressure which such men can bring to bear. There are so many ways in which concessions may be made without violating the letter of the law that it is impossible to prevent discriminations by statute. It is very difficult to obtain evidence of evasions of the law, made by indirect methods. Discriminations will continue until it becomes the interest of the carriers, as it is not now, to maintain equal rates. Discrimination between individuals has been much more rife since the attempt was made to prevent it by law than it ever was before. (594, 596.)

Mr. REAGAN, of the Texas railway commission, declares that railway discriminations not only injure shippers, increasing the cost to the smaller and poorer shippers for the benefit of the few, but that they generally injure the revenues of the railroads. They should be prohibited under penalties which would make them a felony. (342.)

Mr. COWEN does not think that the railway discriminations are more generally in favor of so-called trusts than of other large shippers. This is certainly true about the great combinations in the steel industry. The rates to all iron and steel producers have been unjustly low during 1899 in view of the high prices of those products. (317.)

E. Remedies for discriminations.—Most representatives of the railways think pooling the only effective remedy for discriminations. See pp. 97, 98.

Mr. DICKINSON says that it is not so much a question what the absolute rates are which he pays, provided they are equitable as compared with those which his competitors pay. He himself pays the full tariff rates. He has no personal knowledge of rebates, but no intelligent man can say that he does not hear a good deal in regard to them. He believes that rates ought to be alike to all, and that the railroad companies should not favor any industry or any individual as against another, or monopolize any industry through its control of transportation. The witness formerly felt that the best service ought to come from unrestricted competition; but he is convinced that the only remedy for the troubles that exist is Congressional control of the railroads, and he has reached the conclusion that the railroads themselves, as well as the public, would be benefited by a control outside of themselves. (551, 552.)

Mr. TUCKER, chairman of the Central Freight Association, does not consider it right that the men best able to pay the tariff rate should get rebates and special favors. He would approve of a system of regulation to stop all rebates and discriminations, and he believes that the reliable roads would approve of it. (561.)

1. *Publicity.*—Mr. Spencer believes that complete publicity of railway affairs and accounts is the most effective remedy for discriminations, although the prevention of illegal actions is, in any case, difficult. (273, 279.)
See also pp. 117, 118.

2. *Enforcement of existing laws.*—Mr. KNAPP, chairman of the Interstate Commerce Commission, sees no effective way to enforce the provisions of the laws against railway discriminations, except by making violations criminal misdemeanors. No suit for damages is sufficient. The corporations themselves, rather than some agent who is not the real offender, should be indictable. At the same time the law should be made somewhat specific as to what is required, and the penalties should be also more accurately prescribed. Thus the present requirement as to publishing rates is very vague and should be made more specific. (187.)

Mr. CLEMENTS, a member of the commission, sees no reason why courts should not be empowered to enjoin officers or agents of railways from continuing any practice in violation of law. He believes, also, that the seizure of goods in transit, where they are carried in violation of the law, would be desirable. (160.)

Mr. NEWCOMB, of the division of statistics, Department of Agriculture, says that the burden of excessive or discriminating rates is shifted in varying degrees upon consumers and others, so that it is impossible for the courts justly to determine the amount of damages to aggrieved parties. (99.)

Mr. FISH does not think that the inspection of railway books by Government officers would result in the discovery of many abuses or in securing evidence for prosecution. He believes that sufficient remedies exist under the present law if it is vigorously enforced and if the offenders are actually punished by fines and imprisonment. The difficulty at present is largely in the failure of the persons injured to make complaint. (338.)

Mr. CARTER knows no better method of preventing discriminations than to enlarge the powers of the Interstate Commerce Commission and to enforce the law. (584.)

3. *Shall punishment be by fine or imprisonment?*—Mr. RIPLEY, of the Atchison, Topeka and Santa Fe, thinks that fines upon the corporation offending would check discriminations much more effectively than the threat of imprisonment. Railroad managers meet their competitors from time to time, and very few men would be willing to inform the authorities of anything that would criminate their acquaintances. The existing law is an absolute failure. There has never been a conviction under it, or if there has been a conviction it has been nominal. (595.)

Mr. MORTON also disapproves of the imprisonment clause, thinking that it prevents effective enforcement. He favors a very heavy fine, both on the shipper receiving the cut rate and on the railroad. Shippers practically always know when they are receiving cut rates, and are as much at fault as the railroads. (495.)

Mr. INGALLS, of the Chesapeake and Ohio, agrees in thinking that the imprisonment feature of the interstate-commerce law prevents it from being effective. People do not consider the making of different prices to different individuals a crime in ordinary business, and public opinion is not prepared to enforce the penalty of imprisonment upon railway officers for making discriminations. The violation of the law should be made punishable by fines, and the witness thinks it possible by putting a fine upon every bill of lading to make this an effective punishment. (286, 297.)

Mr. HYLAND, of the Chicago Board of Trade, thinks that violation of the interstate-commerce law should be punished by fines against the railway companies rather than penalties upon individuals. Each carload or part carload shipped in violation of law should constitute a separate offense; the penalty should be double the gross earnings for the service performed, and should be divided equally between the informant and the Government. Some one official of each railroad should be held accountable for the strict maintenance of rates. (351, 352.)

Mr. VANLANDINGHAM, of the St. Louis Traffic Bureau, takes practically the same position as Mr. Hyland. (214.)

Mr. CARTER thinks it likely that evidence of discriminations could be got more easily if the penalty were a fine than it can be while the penalty is imprisonment. (585.)

Mr. DOUSMAN, a grain shipper of Chicago, believes that a fine is a more effective penalty than imprisonment, especially because railway officers will not testify against one another so long as the imprisonment penalty exists. (361.)

Mr. BIRD, general traffic manager of the Chicago, Milwaukee and St. Paul Railway, declares that the penalties against discriminations are so severe as practically to make it impossible to learn the truth. They encourage great ingenuity in covering up discriminations. The way to prevent discriminations is to remove the possibility of gain by placing heavy fines upon the railroad companies themselves, which would then see to it that their employees complied with the law. It would require great provocation or influence to induce a railroad officer to testify against another railroad officer if it might result in sending him to jail, while he would feel no such reluctance if the penalty were a fine. (471.)

Mr. SPENCER, president of the Southern Railway, on the other hand, believes that the penalty of imprisonment for violations of the interstate commerce act should be retained. Fines of the amount of $5,000 could be paid repeatedly by many railways out of the profits of illegal business. It is not a hardship to imprison subordinates for knowingly violating the law under direction of their superiors, and, furthermore, the persons really responsible can usually be ascertained if sufficient effort is made. (274.)

Mr. REAGAN believes that the penalty of imprisonment as for felony should be imposed in cases of violation of the interstate-commerce act, and believes that it would be possible to enforce such a penalty, although he knows of no instances where it has yet been done under the Texas railway commission statute. (342, 350.)

IV. DISCRIMINATIONS BETWEEN PLACES—LONG AND SHORT HAUL.

A. Existence and causes of place discriminations generally.—The members of the Interstate Commerce Commission who testified before the Industrial Commission agree in believing that inequalities in rates between different places, including especially discriminations in favor of terminal points having a longer haul, but also other differences, are exceedingly numerous, and constitute perhaps the most injurious feature of railway discriminations. Place discriminations are made, not by departure from published tariffs, but by unfair tariffs themselves.

Differences in rates over the same road, according to the direction of shipment, are also common, and are claimed to be justifiable often to prevent cars from being returned empty. (See also *Southern States*, p. 63)

All of the Interstate Commerce Commissioners called attention to the fact that these place discriminations, like long and short haul discriminations, are often defended by railroads as being necessary to meet water competition.

Mr. KNAPP and Mr. CLEMENTS pointed out what great effects upon the prosperity of individuals, towns, and sections of the country would result from apparently slight differences in railway rates. Thus a difference of $2 in the terminal charges on each car of live stock at Chicago, which a certain court considered insignificant, amounts to half a million dollars during the year. A difference of 2 or 3 cents in the freight rate on wheat from a certain section in Iowa was estimated to represent a difference of $5 per acre in the value of land. The margin on which many lines of business are done is so slight that small differences may completely change the location of a manufacture or the profits of a business. An increase in the average rate of freight per ton per mile of 1¼ mills would represent an added revenue of about $100,000,000 to the railroads and corresponding outlay by the public. Mr. Knapp calls attention to the inequality in the conditions of competition between different producers brought about by such differences in rates, whether these differences be over the same railroads or over different ones, and whether the favored shipper be a small producer or a combination. The margin of profit in most lines of business is so small that a slight adjustment of rates will exclude one shipper from a particular consuming territory, while benefiting another shipper. (KNAPP, 133–135, 142; PROUTY, 148, 149; CLEMENTS, 154, 157.)

Mr. BIRD, of the Chicago, Milwaukee and St. Paul Railway, declares that fully 75 per cent of the rate disturbances in the West and Northwest originate primarily in the question as to what is a fair relation of rates between competing markets. There is nothing in the interstate-commerce act by which such a fair relation can be determined. Thus, one road may make the rate on some heavy class of goods, such as iron, but little more from St. Louis to St. Paul than the rates on another road from Chicago to St. Paul or from Milwaukee to St. Paul, although the difference in distance is very considerable. It will be impossible to remedy these injustices unless the Interstate Commerce Commission is given power to prescribe minimum rates as well as maximum rates. If it orders that one railroad shall not make more than a certain difference between different places, there is nothing at present to keep another railroad from reducing its rates in the same proportion. There is no doubt that towns are created or destroyed by the mere matter of the relation of railway rates. (472.)

Mr. DICKINSON, manufacturer, La Crosse, Wis., states that a railroad general manager said to him that the rates are made on a basis which is not calculated to favor the Western manufacturers in shipping East. It has been the practice of certain railroads to try to build up certain trade centers. Some people are very much dissatisfied with this, but others, perhaps, feel as well satisfied to have a center built up where they can get their materials on short notice without a great difference in freight. On general principles it would seem that business should be built up where there are natural advantages for it. Any discrimination on the part of the railroad diverts the development from a place where it is natural to one where it is unnatural. The witness considers, however, that the question must now be considered in the light of existing conditions. The business of the West to-day, especially the manufacturing business, has been largely built up by what may be called favors in the way of commodity rates, particularly where the roads may have united upon some one town against another where the natural advantages are greater. Whatever the injustice of this course may have been in the first place, the proposition to change it must now be considered in the light of the fact that large and prosperous communities so built up are in actual existence. Towns which have continuously received such privileges may be considered to have acquired a certain vested right in them, and the witness does not consider that there has been any such continuous protest on the part of other communities as might have interfered with the valid establishment of such a vested right. He mentions particularly the iron and steel manufacture, which is not natural to the West, as an instance of businesses built up by such discriminations. (550, 551.)

Mr. TUCKER says that the rates from all points on the east bank of the Mississippi River to the Eastern seaboard are the same, and that the Western roads haul at the same rate to all points on the east bank of the Mississippi. By this means equal through rates through all gateways are obtained. (562.)

Mr. RIPLEY, president of the Atchison, Topeka and Santa Fe Railroad Company, says that the adjustment of rates between different localities can never be made satisfactory to everybody. Every road is interested in a particular locality, and the result must always be a compromise, which generally is not satisfactory to anybody, and is very unsatisfactory to a great many. The endeavor has been to do the fair thing. There have been so many opposing interests that it has been impossible to do anything very unfair, although it is not an exact science. There have been many cases in which Mr. Ripley would have been glad to place the entire responsibility on an outside body, such as the Interstate Commerce Commission, and have them say what should be done. (597, 598.)

Mr. BLANCHARD declares that the practice of granting discriminating rates to individuals often results in considerable discriminations between places. Shippers at one place who believe that their rivals are getting special discriminating rates are apt to combine and obtain special rates for their own market. Thus sometimes departures from tariffs become the rule as to certain shipping points. Individual discriminations are granted more in favor of shippers at central points than at local stations. Aside from discriminations of this class, there are differential rates and apparent discriminations between localities which are often justifiable. Each railway is inclined to build up its own important towns by specially favorable rates. Many influences combine to complicate the problem of a fair adjustment of rates between different places. (626, 627.)

Mr. DOUSMAN, a grain shipper of Chicago, believes that in the same general section of the country railroad freight rates should be made strictly uniform, so much per ton per mile, regardless of the character of the roads. The railroad that carries goods cheapest in this country is the Chesapeake and Ohio, which runs over mountains and through tunnels. "Differentials are inventions of the devil." Practically 75 per cent of the business of every railroad is its own natural business, which it can do better than any other. If the remaining 25 per cent of competitive business be allowed to distribute itself naturally, on the basis of open and stable rates, the railroads and the general community will be benefited. (361.)

Percentage rates.—Mr. TUCKER, chairman of the Central Freight Association, states that the system of fixing rates to the seaboard from large portions of the country upon the basis of certain percentages of the Chicago rates was established some 15 or 20 years ago, through what was called the joint rate committee. The east bank of the Mississippi pays 116 per cent of the Chicago rate, and the percentage system extends as far east as Buffalo. Buffalo pays, he thinks, two-thirds of the Chicago rate. The 100 per cent territory runs up into Michigan, and the percentage gradually decreases as one advances toward the East. The decrease is not exactly proportional to the distance. The rate per ton per mile is somewhat higher for the shorter distance. This is proper, because the terminal expense is the same for a haul of 50 miles as for a haul of 500. There have been some changes in the percentage basis for certain towns since the arrangement was first made, but the changes have been few, and there has been little complaint. If the shippers of any town thought their rate too high, they would make their complaint to the general freight agent of their road. If any road felt that its town was injured by an unjustly high rate, it would, no doubt, get such an injustice corrected. As a rule the Eastern connections take it for granted that the men where the traffic originates know most about the situation, and carry out what they suggest. So the question of maintaining or reducing rates rests chiefly with the road that first receives the freight. (561–563.)

Mr. MUSSELMAN, president of the Grand Rapids Board of Trade, states that the rate from Grand Rapids to the seaboard is 96 per cent of the Chicago rate, and that he believes that Grand Rapids is justly entitled, on the actual mileage basis, to a 90 per cent rate. Grand Rapids was on a 100 per cent basis up to 1891. At that time the Grand Rapids Board of Trade undertook to get the rate changed to the 90 per cent basis, and succeeded in getting a reduction to 96 per cent. Mr. Musselman believes that the present basis still amounts to a discrimination against his town. (556.)

B. Long and short haul discriminations generally.—Mr. BLANCHARD states the principle of the long and short haul clause in the interstate-commerce act as follows: An interstate rate or fare made between any two points shall not be exceeded by the rate on the same article moved over the same line in the same direction under similar circumstances and conditions. He regards the requirement as just in the majority of cases, but declares there are some justifiable exceptions, especially on account of water competition or the competition of Canadian railroads. He mentions a number of specifie instances justifying lower rates to through points.

Mr. NEWCOMB, of the division of statistics, Department of Agriculture, says that under this provision of the interstate-commerce act the courts have interpreted "dissimilar conditions" to include conditions of competition and other conditions which make the provision practically ineffective. The witness does not consider a change of the law sufficiently important to be pressed if it is likely to arouse opposition to other needed legislation. (104.)

Mr. BACON, of the Milwaukee Board of Trade, thinks that the provision in the long and short haul clause as to the dissimilarity of circumstances and conditions should be stricken out, leaving it, however, to the Interstate Commerce Commission to suspend the operation of the clause where judged expedient, as in the case of water transportation. The decision of the Supreme Court that railroad competition justifies lower rates for longer hauls seems to the witness unwarranted. (420.)

Messrs. KNAPP, PROUTY, and CLEMENTS, of the Interstate Commerce Commission, are unanimous in saying that the discriminations between long and short hauls made by railways are exceedingly numerous, and are probably the most serious abuse now existing. The evil is most conspicuous in the Southeastern States and in the far Western States. These States are peculiarly situated with reference to water transportation, and the railways defend the lower rates to terminal points on this account. Mr. Clements, however, points out that no such great inequalities in rates exist in the vicinity of the Great Lakes of the North. The Supreme Court holds that a dissimilarity in conditions sufficient to justify departure from the rule of the law is made by competition, whether by water or among railways themselves. Mr. Clements points out that the railways never did, before the interstate-commerce act, charge less for longer hauls than for shorter ones, except on account of competition, and he would favor inserting a clause in the law by which competition should not be allowed to count as constituting dissimilar circumstances. Ownership of property in particular towns by railway officers is pointed out as another influence leading to discriminations.

Mr. Knapp and Mr. Clements agree that the method of adjusting rates as between competitive and noncompetitive points on the same road is usually that the rates to the noncompetitive points increase with the distance until the rate equals the through rate to the terminal point plus the local rate back from the terminal point to the point of destination. It would thus be as cheap to send the goods through and back again as to stop them off; but of course, as a matter of fact, they do not go through. Mr. Clements especially declares that since rates include terminal charges, the dealer in the small town has to pay practically four terminal charges, besides the charge for transportation pure and simple for a distance greater than that to the terminal point, whereas the dealer at the terminal point has to pay only two terminal charges. It is as cheap to ship goods, for example, to a point 50 miles beyond Atlanta as to a point 50 miles this side. The effect of the prevalence of this practice in the South is seen in the marked difference between the prosperity of the few trade centers and that of the small intermediate towns, whereas the small towns of the North often show a high degree of prosperity. It is impossible to establish manufacturing enterprises in small towns in the face of such discriminations. (Knapp, 134, 137; Clements, 154, 155.)

Mr. VANLANDINGHAM, freight commissioner of the St. Louis Traffic Bureau, also comments on the disregard of the long and short haul rule in the Southeastern States on account of water competition. He is not sure that the effect is altogether injurious to local stations. The jobbing houses at the central points may be able to sell goods at lower rates to the local stations, through having a lower freight rate, than would probably be secured if all the rates were made uniform. Mr. Vanlandingham further points out that the interpretation of the courts regarding the long and short haul clause puts the water carriers at a disadvantage in competition. The railways can make their rates to the few points reached by the water carrier so low as to drive it out of business, while holding up their rates to intermediate territory. (202, 206.)

Mr. SPENCER, president of the Southern Railway, thinks that if the rates for shorter hauls are themselves reasonable in view of the amount of traffic and the cost of service, there should be no objection to the railways making whatever rates are necessary to meet competition or to develop traffic to through points. Otherwise it might not get the long-distance traffic at all. In sparsely settled regions the amount of business is less, and the cost of construction and operation is always relatively greater, and often absolutely greater. It would be impossible to satisfy all communities in any case, since no two persons or communities will consider in the same light the unlike conditions which exist in different cases. Large cities, by the very nature of things, have certain advantages in business over small places, and this advantage must extend to railway transportation. (275, 281, 284.)

Mr. TUCKER, chairman of the Central Freight Association, considers that there are strong arguments against the long and short haul clause. The competition of the Galveston route to Liverpool from Kansas City, for instance, forces the making of very low rates from Kansas City eastward. The long and short haul clause compels the making of the same rates from intermediate points, where there is not the same competition, the same necessity. (560.)

Mr. CALLAWAY, president of the New York Central, says that it is the policy of the Vanderbilt lines to make local rates substantially proportional to through rates, under the belief that local business and local prosperity can not be built up at rates so high that competitive business could be done much cheaper. (282.)

C. Specific cases of place discriminations, water competition, etc.—1. *Differentials as to Eastern ports.*—Mr. KELLEY, freight commissioner for the Trades League of Philadelphia, testifies that that city is peculiarly situated between New York and Baltimore, and has only 4 trunk lines from the West. Its coastwise trade is practically limited to a single line of steamers running to Norfolk. The city is allowed a differential of 2 cents as compared with New York on grain freight rates from Western points, while Baltimore has a differential of 3 cents; i. e., the rates are respectively so much lower than those to New York. (185, 186.)

Mr. NEALL, a shipping merchant of Philadelphia, also speaks of the existing differentials. He considers that Philadelphia is unfairly discriminated against still, especially because of the larger differentials allowed to the more southern ports. (173.)

Mr. CALLAWAY, of the New York Central, testifies that the existing practice of allowing differentials on shipments from the West to Philadelphia, Baltimore, and other more southern p s as compared with New York was established about 20 years ago, when the average freight rates were very much higher than at present, ranging from 52 to 60 cents. At present the rates on grain, for example, have been reduced to 15 or 18 cents, and the differential is thus proportionately greater, and, in the opinion of the witness, excessive. At present, by an arrangement with the Baltimore and Ohio and Chesapeake and Ohio, the experiment of making the differential only 1 or 1½ cents on export grain is being tried, but on other commodities the 3-cent differential is retained. Improvements in the ports of Baltimore and other Southern cities have also lessened the justifiability of such a differential. The terminal changes are, so Mr. Callaway thinks, adjusted in practically the same way at each of these ports. The New York Central has an extensive system of lighters, and its freight rate includes the charge for carrying the grain to the side of the ship in the lighter, but not for transferring it to the ship. As a matter of fact, most grain coming from Chicago goes by way of the Great Lakes, so long as they are open, and the New York Central. The Southern ports are less used for Chicago shipments, but St. Louis shipments go to them, as well as to the Gulf ports. Mr. Callaway is not prepared to say that a complete removal of the differential, so as to make the rates from the Western points to Eastern ports uniform, would be acceptable or even tolerable for the Chesapeake and Ohio and Baltimore and Ohio railroads; but he is convinced that the present differential is too high. Permission to the railways to pool their business would undoubtedly do away with this complication. (224–226, 235.)

Mr. BLANCHARD refers to the establishment of the present differential rates as between the leading Eastern seaboard points. The system was first adopted in 1877, after the railways had squandered millions of dollars in rate wars. Irregularities in steamship sailings and rates, with many other complicating elements, made the adjustment of rail rates on goods intended for export at the different ports exceedingly difficult. Often the railroads had made through rates from inland points to foreign ports, and had afterwards found the entire inland charge absorbed by the increased ocean rates. After a long discussion an agreement was reached fixing differences in charges over the lines reaching the various ports. (673.)

Mr. SNYDACKER, a grain merchant of Chicago, also refers to the differential in favor of Baltimore and other Southern ports and to the relative decrease of the export business through New York. He says that the terminal charges for grain at New York may also be higher than at other ports. (397.)

2. *Southern States.*—Mr. KNAPP, of the Interstate Commerce Commission, thinks injustice is done by the Southern railways in charging more for shipments going north than on those going south. (135.)

Mr. SPENCER, president of the Southern Railway, declares that the reason why higher rates are frequently charged for hauling products from the South to the North than vice versa is not because the dominating load goes north, and the cars would often be empty if lower rates were not made from the North. The direction of the dominating load varies at different seasons of the year. The classes of freight on which the rate from the South to the North is high are largely fruit and vegetables, which are exceedingly perishable, which require a special class of equipment and especially high speed of transportation, and with which a large amount of ice must usually be hauled free. (275.)

Mr. VANLANDINGHAM testifies that rates from the Northeastern States to the Southeast have been lower than from Chicago, St. Louis, and Cincinnati, thus injuring the general merchants and manufacturers of these more western cities. The Interstate Commerce Commission has four times ruled against this discrimination, but its order has never been obeyed. (202.)

3. *Shipments by way of Gulf of Mexico and their effect on other routes.*—Mr. VANLANDINGHAM, of the St. Louis Traffic Bureau, testifies that there has been a very large increase in ocean transportation from Galveston and other Gulf ports, and consequently in railway transportation from the middle West to the Gulf. Every freight rate from west of the Mississippi River as far north as the Platte River is affected by Gulf competition, which practically determines the freight rates to the Atlantic seaboard. The Illinois Central also carries a considerable traffic to the Gulf. The ocean freight rate is about 4¼ cents per hundred higher from Gulf ports than from Atlantic ports. The difference between export rates and domestic rates on the railways leading to the Gulf is even higher than on those leading to the eastern seaboard.

Mississippi River transportation also has a considerable influence. This influence varies according to the condition of the river, but often practically determines the rail rate on grain from St. Louis to Baltimore. The river traffic has, however, fallen off somewhat as compared with several years ago, and may be still further injured by the excessive competition of railways. (197, 206.)

Mr. KNAPP, of the Interstate Commerce Commission, says that the freight rates from New York to Chicago, St. Louis, and Kansas City have for years been adjusted with reference to one another. The first-class railway rate to Kansas City has been $1.47. Recently the Kansas City, Pittsburg and Gulf, being in the hands of receivers, in connection with the Mallory Steamship Line, made a rate of 80 cents from New York by way of Galveston. This has since been abandoned by order of the court in charge. (133; see also Mr. KENNARD, p. 364.)

Mr. VANLANDINGHAM also refers to the recent adjustment of rates from Eastern points, extending as far west as Buffalo, by way of ocean carriers to Galveston and thence to Missouri River and other Western points, by which shipments could be made as cheaply as from Chicago or St. Louis to the same place. This abuse has been remedied at present. (202.)

Mr. KENNARD, of the Chicago Butter and Egg Board, also refers to the fact that in April, 1898, the railroads entering Kansas City and other Kansas points charged the same rates from those points to the seaboard as was charged from Chicago to the seaboard. The cut was first made by a railroad not entering Chicago, but those which do reach that city were then compelled to meet the cut. The object of this arrangement is largely to develop the business of the through fast-freight lines on the Eastern roads. The witness thinks that Gulf competition has little to do with the practice, which is decidedly injurious to the interests of Chicago. (365.)

Mr. CALLAWAY, president of the New York Central, likewise refers to the increased competition of the Gulf ports with the Atlantic ports in export trade, and declares that practically all the rail rates have been reduced by this competition. It is no longer possible to increase the rates on grain over the railways when navigation on the Great Lakes closes. The competition of the St. Lawrence for grain shipments also keeps down rail rates. The freight rates are also affected by the ocean rates, since the railways must enable American products to be exported in competition with foreign products. (225.)

Mr. FISH, president of the Illinois Central Railroad Company, on the other hand, thinks that the Gulf ports do not get a natural proportion of traffic. He points out the immense importance of the territory tributary to the Mississippi River. It contains 41 per cent of the area of the United States and nearly half its population. Because of the constant reduction in freight rates the matter of railway grades is increasingly important in determining the direction of railway traffic. The level prairies of the Mississippi are specially favorable. New Orleans is the natural outlet of this great valley. The air-line distance from Chicago to New York is 709 miles, and to New Orleans 826 miles; but owing to the mountainous character of the Eastern States, the shortest railroad from Chicago to New York, 912 miles, is of the same length as the shortest to New Orleans. On this shortest line to New York, moreover, there is a dead lift in altitude of 1,571 feet, while the lift to New Orleans is only 214 feet.

The following table shows the short-line distance by rail from the leading interior grain markets to New York and New Orleans. respectively:

	To New York.	To New Orleans.	Saving to New Orleans.
	Miles.	*Miles.*	*Miles.*
Chicago, Ill	912	912	0
Duluth, Minn	1,390	1,337	53
Minneapolis, Minn	1,332	1,279	53
St. Paul, Minn	1,321	1,268	53
Sioux City, Iowa	1,422	1,258	164
Omaha, Nebr	1,402	1,070	332
Dubuque, Iowa	1,079	988	91
St. Louis, Mo	1,058	695	363
Peoria, Ill	1,006	860	146
Cairo, Ill	1,089	554	535
Evansville, Ind	989	708	281
Louisville, Ky	867	746	121
Nashville, Tenn	939	557	382
Denver, Colo	1,932	1,356	576
Kansas City, Mo	1,335	878	457

New Orleans has six great railroad systems, reaching a very wide extent of territory, with a total mileage of 19,086 miles. Although the railroads of the South immediately after the war were largely physical and financial wrecks, they have gradually improved, until now in safety, speed, and regularity of service they equal, if they do not excel, the Eastern railroads.

In view of these facts a much larger proportion of traffic, especially for export purposes, ought to be carried by way of New Orleans than is now carried. The railways do not discriminate in favor of that point, but, if anything, against it. Only 16.4 per cent of the freight carried by the Illinois Central Railroad in 1898 was through freight. The gross receipts of all the railroads entering New Orleans during 1898 were 30 per cent more than the value of all imports and exports at New Orleans. (321-324.)

It is not true, Mr. Fish continues, that the exportation rates on grain and other products from Chicago by way of New Orleans regulate the rates by way of New York, but vice versa. The witness does not think that the difference in the distance from New Orleans to Liverpool accounts for the small proportion of business at New Orleans. The distance is perhaps 50 per cent greater and the average time of the ocean voyage is relatively still longer by way of New Orleans as compared with New York. But the vessels from New Orleans avoid the most northern course, and the duration of the voyage is relatively less important in the case of products exported, where there is little haste for delivery. The imports by way of New Orleans are especially light. That city was formerly the market for nearly everything brought into the Mississippi Valley, and it is still the natural gate for the entrance of coffee and many other products. Although the import traffic is so small, the north-bound freight on the Illinois Central is usually about equal to that south bound, so there is no special expense from hauling empty cars.

The barge transportation on the Mississippi River is a much less important factor than formerly, since the rail rates have been made practically as low as the water rates.

There is constant competition between business by way of New Orleans and Cairo and by way of Kansas City and Galveston. (329, 330.)

4. *Discrimination against Chicago.*—Mr. KENNARD also points out that the freight rate on cheese and similar articles from Wisconsin to Chicago is higher than that from Michigan and New York to Chicago for similar distances. The railroads assign as the justification for the lower freight rates going west the fact that cars largely go back empty. (365.)

Mr. MALLORY considers that the terminal charge of $2 per car on cattle brought into Chicago (see p. 48) amounts to a discrimination against Chicago in favor of Kansas City and other markets. It has diverted a good deal of business from Chicago. The feeling of injustice which it gives rise to is more effective in driving away business than the money demand in itself. Competing markets use it as an argument against shipping to Chicago. (588.)

See also paragraph 3, above.

5. *Discriminations against St. Louis.*—Mr. VANLANDINGHAM, commissioner of the St. Louis Traffic Bureau, testifies that that organization consists of about 2,200 merchants and manufacturers, and that it was organized largely for the purpose of removing railway discriminations against St. Louis as compared with Chicago and other cities. It is believed that in various ways St. Louis is put at a disadvantage in securing trade, although some of these inequalities have been recently removed. Mr. Vanlandingham does not think that railways usually make place discriminations with a view to injuring or benefiting any city, but simply with a view to their own earnings. They frequently do not know or think of results.

One method by which Chicago has been favored is by export freight rates. Thus the rate from Kansas City to Chicago on grain intended for export has been 3.2 cents lower than on grain for local consumption, a distinction which was not made in regard to shipments through St. Louis. As a matter of fact, practically all the grain has been shipped to Chicago on these export rates, even when intended for domestic use, thus giving that city a general advantage. Moreover the practice of allowing to certain large firms owning elevators a sum ranging from one half to 1½ cents per bushel has been established on practically all of the railway lines leading into Chicago, but not on those leading to St. Louis. This and other advantages enable Chicago to control 85 per cent of the export freight business.

The witness admits that there will always be, under any circumstances, some advantage to Chicago in securing a large tonnage. on account of its location and its lake transportation, although export trade by way of the Mississippi River and the Gulf railroads is helping St. Louis to keep up its business. (194, 197-199, 206.)

6. *Discriminations against Kansas City.*—Mr. BOOKWALTER states that grain rates to Kansas City are disproportionately high as compared with the rates to points east and south. The town of Wahoo is 229 miles from Kansas City and 523 miles from St. Louis, and is reached by the Burlington and the Union Pacific. The rate from Wahoo to Kansas City is 14 cents, and to St. Louis it is also 14 cents. Grain can be shipped by the Union Pacific through Kansas City to St. Louis for 14 cents, but if it is billed to Kansas City and then rebilled to St. Louis the charge is 21 cents, the proportion accruing to the Union Pacific being 7 and 14 cents, respectively. From Doniphan, Kans., the rate on corn to Kansas City, 50 miles, is 7 cents. The rate to Chicago by way of St. Joseph, 522 miles, is 15 cents. The rate to Chicago by way of Kansas City, 43 miles farther, is 19 cents. The rate to St. Louis by way of Kansas City is 14 cents. The rate from Humboldt to Kansas City, 120 miles, is 8 cents. The rate to Chicago, 571 miles, is 17½ cents. Shepard, Iowa, on the Maple Leaf, is 167 miles from Kansas City, and grain billed from that point to St. Louis would be hauled through Kansas City in order that Maple Leaf might get the full amount of their mileage. The rate for the 167 miles to Kansas City is 10 cents; for the 528 miles to St. Louis it is 12 cents. (572-576.)

Mr. Bookwalter states also that Kansas City is discriminated against in favor of other towns on the same lines of road, in that grain can not be stopped in transit at Kansas City without an additional charge of from 1 cent to 7 cents a hundred. There is a switching charge besides, if the car is transferred from one road to another. At other points, like Topeka, there is no additional charge for stopping and milling in transit and there is no switching charge. This discrimination ruins both the grain business and the milling business of Kansas City. The local mills can pay more for grain than Kansas City millers, because they can manufacture it for export equally well, and they have an advantage in the total freight. A representative of Armour & Co. stated, in an investigation relative to the New York grain business, that one-sixteenth of a cent per bushel will determine where grain shall go. It is now impossible for Kansas City to handle grain, except for local consumption, and except poor grades that can not be sent to more distant markets.

The witness says further that a great deal of both oatmeal and corn meal used to be manufactured at Kansas City for the Southern market. Oats for oatmeal come chiefly from the central portion of Nebraska, where the white oats, which are desirable for oatmeal, are largely raised. The rate on oats from Wahoo to Kansas City, 229 miles, is 14 cents; the rate from Wahoo to Memphis, directly through Kansas City, is 19 cents, 5 cents for an additional 484 miles. If the oats are billed to Kansas City and then billed to Memphis the rate is 24 cents, a penalty of 5 cents for stopping and manufacturing at Kansas City. The oatmeal mill at Kansas City can not now get oats to run more than a small part of the time. Kansas City used to send a great deal of corn meal to Texas. The rate from Wahoo to San Antonio is 39 cents. If the corn is stopped at Kansas City and manufactured the rate is 44 cents. As a result, the corn is now shipped to Texas and manufactured there. Mr. Bookwalter does not think it is more expensive to carry the manufactured product than to carry the grain. The difference of charge between the grain and the manufactured product has been in force only about 2 years. (570–573.) (Compare *Export and domestic grain and flour rates*, p. 74.)

Mr. Bookwalter thinks that the grain tributary to Kansas City is diverted less to St. Louis than to Chicago and the South. When local market conditions make it better to send to Galveston, very little is handled in the Santa Fe elevator at Kansas City; if it is best to send to Chicago, very little is handled in the Rock Island elevator.

The witness believes the policy of discrimination against Kansas City has been dictated by the desire of the through roads to carry grain as far as possible on their own lines. However, the Union Pacific, which ends at Kansas City, makes the same discriminations in favor of other markets which are made by the roads which run to those markets. It is compelled to accept the terms made by the other roads, because, if it did not, they would revenge themselves upon it elsewhere. (572, 577.)

7. *Discriminations against Milwaukee.*—Mr. BACON, representing the Milwaukee Board of Trade, testifies that the Interstate Commerce Commission in 1898 issued an order requiring the reduction of differentials granted on grain shipments in favor of Minneapolis as compared with Milwaukee. The differential as fixed by the commission would just about equal the excess in the cost of transportation from Minneapolis to the seaboard. The railroad companies, after some delay, reduced their differentials, but only about one-half as much as the order of the commission required. The commission reaffirmed its order, but the railways failed to conform to it. This is due to the influence of the Chicago and Northwestern Railroad, which controls the Chicago, Minneapolis and Omaha Railway, and therefore finds it advantageous to favor Minneapolis. (418.)

8. *Discriminations against La Crosse.*—Mr. DICKINSON, of La Crosse, Wis., a manufacturer of agricultural implements, states that La Crosse and Chicago are at practically the same distance from Madison, Wis., but that his concern found itself unable to do business in Madison. On investigation he discovered that while the rate from La Crosse to Madison was 19 cents a hundred on agricultural implements and vehicles by the carload, the rate from Chicago was 12½ cents. After much trouble he succeeded in getting the rate from La Crosse reduced to 12½ cents. He then discovered that there had for some time been in existence a rate of 8 or 8½ cents on the same class of goods between Madison and Chicago; and that while the third-class rate from La Crosse to Madison was 28 cents a hundred, Chicago and Milwaukee had a rate on all kinds of agricultural machinery, in less than carloads, of 15 cents per 100. These discriminations made it impossible for manufacturers and dealers in La Crosse to do business in the territory referred to. La Crosse establishments succeeded in getting these special rates in favor of their competitors abolished; but one of the roads renewed the discriminating reduction, and it then continued until within 2 months of the time of Mr. Dickinson's testimony, although it was then abolished again. Mr. Dickinson believes that the only way in which such difficulties and injustices can be avoided is by increasing the power of the Interstate Commerce Commission. (549.)

9. *Discriminations in Nebraska.*—Mr. FULLER, of Norfolk, Nebr., declares that that city is discriminated against by the railroads. It has a population of about 5,000, while Fremont, the nearest large town, has a population of about 10,000. Norfolk stands practically alone in a territory having a radius of 75 miles. It has railroads diverging in 5 directions. Norfolk has grown very slowly, while Fremont has grown steadily, and this fact is to be attributed to the advantages given to Fremont manufacturers and jobbers in freight rates. Thus Fremont is given a through rate from Chicago and Eastern points the same as the rate to the Missouri River, while 45 cents per hundred, first class, is added to the Missouri River rate for shipments to Norfolk. So, too, the local rates, especially from Sioux City to Norfolk, are higher than those from Sioux City to many other points. The rate per mile on first-class freight from Sioux City to Norfolk, 75 miles, is 12 cents; from Sioux City to Alcester, S. Dak., 77 miles, 7.79 cents; from Lincoln to Dakota City, Nebr., 78 miles, 6.41 cents; from Sioux City to Beemer, Iowa, 168 miles, 5.24 cents. The witness thinks that these differences in rates are not justifiable on any ground. The railways claim that the lower rates accorded to Fremont are due to competition. The Nebraska railroad commissioners, when appealed to, have held that the discriminations complained of were on interstate business and not subject to their jurisdiction. The matter has not yet been acted upon by the Interstate Commerce Commission. (442–446.)

10. *Pacific coast traffic and Colorado points.*—Mr. VANLANDINGHAM says that the freight rates to the Pacific coast, from all parts of the East as far as the Mississippi River, are the same, an arrangement which takes away from the nearer points their advantage of location in selling goods to the Far West. This arrangement is explainable largely by the competition of water transportation from the Eastern seaboard to the Pacific coast. Goods are sometimes shipped from St. Louis to New York and thence to the Pacific States by vessel. There is no direct transportation by water from Gulf points to the Pacific coast. The Southern Pacific Railway Company owns the Morgan Line of steamships, running from New York to New Orleans and Galveston. By the economy of water transportation that railroad is able to handle 65 per cent of all the traffic from the East to Pacific coast points as far north as San Francisco, and to dictate rates upon the other railroads practically as far north as Portland. (207, 208.)

Mr. KINDEL, manufacturer, of Denver, declares that there are very many serious discriminations in rates against Colorado points, especially as compared with Pacific coast points. Up to 1895, for example, the railroads hauled rails from Chicago through Colorado to San Francisco for 60 cents per 100, while the Colorado Fuel and Iron Company was charged $1.60 for a haul 1,000 miles shorter. This discrimination has been checked by an order of the Interstate Commerce Commission, that the rates from Pueblo to California shall not exceed 75 per cent of the rates from Chicago. The witness has been driven out of the manufacture of upholstering goods and of spring beds in Denver because of similar differences. He wished to manufacture albums in Denver, but was forced to locate in Chicago because the freight rate on books from Chicago to San Francisco was $1.75 per 100 and from Denver to San Francisco $3, while the Denver manufacturer had to pay 37 cents freight on his raw material from Chicago to Denver. So, too, the freight rate on books from Chicago to New York is 75 cents, from Denver to New York $2.72. The difference in rates on coal oil has been so great that oil has sometimes been shipped from Chicago to San Francisco and back again to Denver. (See *Standard Oil Company,* p. 52.)

Other discriminating rates mentioned by the witness are as follows: Sugar is carried from San Francisco to Denver at 75 cents; to Omaha at 50 cents. Boots and shoes are carried from Chicago to Colorado common points at $2.05 per 100; California at $1.50 per 100. If a jobber in Colorado wishes to ship boots and shoes to California he must pay $3, making a total freight rate of $5.05 from Chicago to California in this way. Cotton piece goods under commodity rates are shipped from Boston to the Missouri River for 52 cents per 100, while the rate from the Missouri River to Denver is $1.25 for a haul of one-third the distance. The rate through Denver to California is only $1.

It appears that many of these discriminations referred to by the witness arise from special commodity rates outside of the regular classification rates; but even as to these latter rates there are marked differences. On first and second class goods the transcontinental rate is now the same as that from the seaboard to Denver. On the other classes the tariffs are, respectively, Denver, $2, California, $2.20; Denver, $1.75, California, $1.90; $1.60 and $1.50, $1.40 and $1.45, $1.20 and $1.25.

Mr. Kindel says, further, that whereas the railroads have admitted that freight can be hauled profitably at 2⅖ mills per ton per mile, Colorado rates are as high as 91 mills per ton per mile.

The explanation advanced by the railways regarding the lower freight rates to the Pacific coast—that they are necessary on account of water competition—is, Mr. Kindel thinks, only partly to be accepted. This would not justify the through rate from the Missouri River to the Pacific coast of only 50 cents on certain products, on which the rate is 75 cents from New York. Moreover, there are discriminations in favor of Salt Lake City on shipments from Eastern points as compared with Denver. These apparently arise largely from the granting of commodity rates on certain products to Salt Lake which are refused to Colorado. Thus the machinery manufactured at Chicago is shipped to Salt Lake at the same rate as to Denver, and owing to the difference in local rates it is cheaper for the buyer at Grand Junction, Colo., to secure his machinery from Salt Lake than from Denver, which is nearer. The third-class rate from the Missouri River to Colorado on ordinary commodities is 80 cents, to Utah common points, $1.55; but on oilcloth and linoleum, for example, Utah has a commodity tariff of only $1.09, the same articles being shipped to California at 75 cents.

As a matter of fact, the witness thinks the Southern Pacific Railway practically dictates California rates from the East, and it is largely for this reason that rates discriminate against Colorado.

The effects of this system, Mr. Kindel declares, have been largely to destroy the manufactures of Colorado, and to a considerable extent the jobbing business also. Only those persons are successful in business in Colorado who secure discriminating rates below the published tariffs. The witness admits that he himself obtains such rates and is thus able to continue business, but deprecates the necessity of thus violating the law. He believes that the reason why the Denver Board of Trade has not only raised no objection to the discrimination against that city, but itself petitioned the Interstate Commerce Commission to exempt Colorado from the provisions of the long and short haul clause of the interstate-commerce act, is that that body is composed of the wealthier manufacturers and dealers, practically all of whom receive large rebates from the railways. There are a number of jobbing houses in Denver which are raising no complaints, but the witness believes it is for this same reason. As a matter of fact, the discriminations have driven a great many jobbing houses out of business. Especially representatives of large Eastern firms have withdrawn their houses to Missouri River points, whence they ship directly to California retail stations. They are able to do this profitably, because the railways permit them to stop off their cars at one station after another, paying through freight rates to the last station.

The manufactures of Colorado, the witness believes, have been largely destroyed by these discriminations. Thus woolen mills, glass mills, and a large paper mill have been driven out. Colorado has cheap wool and coal, and should be able to manufacture many classes of goods. In the case of the paper mill referred to, the railways lowered the freight rate on paper immediately after it was started from more than $1 to 25 cents per hundredweight. The witness quotes Gen. Irving Hale to the effect that it is essentially the discriminating freight rates which have prevented the growth of Colorado manufacturing industry.

The witness admits that the smelting industry in Colorado is in a prosperous condition, and makes no complaints regarding freight rates. He attributes this fact largely to the interest which the officers of the railroads themselves have in mining and smelting works. It is true, also, that a cotton factory is successfully operated at Denver, cotton being hauled from Texas at fair rates.

On being questioned as to the motive of the railways in thus discriminating against the industries of Colorado, Mr. Kindel says that most of the directors and other officers, even of railways having their termini at Denver, live in New York and give little thought to the prosperity of Colorado.

The witness at first stated that unfavorable freight rates had largely prevented the exportation of agricultural products from Colorado. He afterwards admitted, however, that large quantities of flour, cattle, horses, potatoes, and melons are exported; that the agricultural production of that State was on the whole increasing, and that the State in any case has to import certain of its agricultural products from Nebraska and Kansas.

Mr. Kindel also refers to alleged discriminations in local rates, as between Denver and Pueblo. Shippers of the latter city complain that they are discriminated against. The witness does not attach much weight to this statement, though he admits that sometimes rates from Denver are adjusted so that goods can be shipped through Pueblo at the same cost as if shipped directly from Pueblo.

The railroad commission which formerly existed in Colorado was abolished in 1893, under the influence, Mr. Kindel claims, of the railways. The officers of railroads take active part in Colorado politics and have great influence. (251–264.)

D. Discriminating import rates.—Mr. REAGAN, of the Texas railroad commission, refers to the complaint brought before the Interstate Commerce Commission in 1889 as to the practice of the Pennsylvania Railroad and other railroads in charging lower rates, even 50 per cent lower, on goods carried under through bills of lading from foreign ports than on domestic traffic. The defendant substantially admitted the facts, and the commission ordered the discriminations to cease, holding that the interstate-commerce law applied to such shipments. This decision was upheld by the circuit court and the circuit court of appeals, but was reversed by the Supreme Court of the United States, although the Chief Justice and two other justices dissented. Justice Harlan, in his dissenting opinion, stated that the records showed that the rates on certain classes of goods from Liverpool to San Francisco by way of New Orleans were 102 cents per hundred pounds, while the rates from New Orleans to San Francisco over the same railroads were 288 and even 370 cents per hundred. Mr. Reagan thinks that Congress should legislate or remedy the lack of power in this direction.

Mr. Reagan quotes from the opinion of the Interstate Commerce Commission above referred to, to the effect that the authority of the United States to regulate is strictly limited to the territory of the United States. He suggests, without making the matter entirely clear, that the decision of the court permitting through freight rates on imported goods at rates lower than the domestic rates involves an extension of the power of the court outside of the limits of the United States. (340, 349.)

Mr. KELLEY, freight commissioner of the Trades League of Philadelphia, and Mr. VANLANDINGHAM, freight commissioner of the St. Louis Traffic Bureau, likewise believe that injustice is done by allowing lower freight rates on imported goods than on domestic shipments. Rates are so arranged in many cases that goods can be shipped from Liverpool to Western points for less than the freight from New York to Chicago, St. Louis, or Kansas City. These special rates are made by agreements between the foreign shipper, the ocean line, and the railway company, with a view to enabling goods to be shipped which would otherwise not be shipped at all. (187, 205.)

Mr. KINDEL, a manufacturer of Denver, also refers to the fact that goods can be brought to that city from Liverpool by way of Gulf ports very much cheaper than from New York and other Eastern points, which forces buyers to patronize the foreign product. (260.)

Mr. PROUTY also testifies that the freight rates on goods imported from other countries are often lower than those on domestic goods. Thus the rates from Liverpool to San Francisco through New Orleans on many articles are not more than one-half the rates from New Orleans to San Francisco. (146, 151.)

Mr. MORTON, of the Atchison, Topeka and Sante Fe, declares that he has known instances where goods have been carried from Hamburg to Denver for less than the rates from Chicago to Denver, an unnecessary discrimination against American producers. On the other hand, where the rate is from Hamburg to San Francisco, the goods going entirely by water, the question of fair rates becomes a different one. (490, 493.)

V. EXPORT AND DOMESTIC GRAIN AND FLOUR RATES.

A. Existence of differences in rates.—Mr. KNAPP, of the Interstate Commerce Commission, refers to the differences in freight rates between grain intended for exportation, on the one hand, and grain intended for domestic consumption and flour on the other, and Mr. PROUTY describes them more in detail. The Interstate Commerce Commission has held that railways are bound to publish schedule rates in the case of export traffic, although the railways have objected to this position. A recent investigation showed that the freight on wheat from Kansas City to Galveston, if the wheat was intended for domestic use, was 27 cents, while the rate on wheat intended for exportation was 10 cents. From the Mississippi River to New York the rate on domestic wheat was 20 or 21 cents, on export wheat 12 or 13 cents. By similar differences between the rate on export wheat and that on flour ground in this country, whether intended for domestic or export use, a Chicago miller, for example, would have to pay about 21 cents per 100 pounds to get either wheat or flour to New York, while the English miller could take his wheat to New York from Chicago for 13 cents. The freight rate on flour in some instances was as much as 11 cents more than that on wheat. Since a rate of profit of from 2 to 3 cents per 100 pounds of flour is regarded as a good one, our millers could not grind for the export trade against such a discrimination. (134, 142, 146.)

The Interstate Commerce Commission issued an order on August 7, 1899, that the difference between export rates on wheat and flour rates should not exceed 2 cents per 100 pounds and declaring that public policy demanded that they should be the same. The railways appear to have conformed in part to this order, but after some delay.

Mr. VANLANDINGHAM, of the St. Louis Traffic Bureau, submitted the following statement as to the differences in effect September 18, 1899: From East St. Louis the rate on domestic grain to Newport News, Norfolk, and Baltimore, except on corn and corn products, was 20 cents, and on corn and corn products 18 cents; for export the rate on corn, wheat, barley, and rye was 13½ cents. From Chicago the domestic rate on grain and products was 17 cents, and on corn and corn products 15 cents; for export corn, wheat, barley, and rye, 12½ cents; oats, 14½ cents. To Philadelphia the rate on domestic grain was 21 cents from East St. Louis; corn products, 19 cents; export corn, wheat, barley, and rye, 14 cents; oats, 16 cents; from Chicago, domestic, 18 and 16; export, 13 and 15. To New York, domestic, from East St. Louis, 23 and 21; export, 15 and 17; from Chicago, domestic, 20 and 18; export, 14 and 16. The differences on shipments to Gulf ports were even greater. (195.)

The witness also submitted the following table showing the differences in rates on flour and wheat existing under the tariff adopted September 18, 1899 (195):

	Flour.	Wheat.	Difference in favor of wheat.
From East St. Louis, when from beyond, to—	Cents.	Cents.	Cents.
Baltimore	20	13½	6½
Philadelphia	21	14	7
New York	23	15	8
Boston	23	15	8
Portland	23	15	8

These differences Mr. Vanlandingham considers excessive, but he doubts the power of the Interstate Commerce Commission to control export rates.

Mr. INGALLS, of the Chesapeake and Ohio Railroad, testifying on October 16, 1899, speaks of a recent reduction of the difference between rates on wheat and flour, but is doubtful whether this is so much the result of the decision of the Interstate Commerce Commission as of the increase of rates on wheat by agreements among railways, made possible by the exceedingly large demand for transportation. (300, 301.)

Mr. BACON, a grain merchant of Milwaukee, testifying in November, 1899, says that changes were made in the freight rates on grain and flour November 1. Both were advanced, but the rate on grain was advanced the more, so that the difference between export grain and flour rates from Chicago and Milwaukee to the seaboard is only 2 cents per 100 pounds, as prescribed by the Interstate Commerce Commission, and there is the same difference between rates on export grain and domestic grain. Nevertheless, millers at Chicago or Milwaukee are still at a considerable disadvantage, owing to the fact that through export rates from the Mississippi River and farther western points to New York are considerably less than the domestic rate on grain to Chicago or Milwaukee plus the rate on the manufactured product to the seaboard. The witness presented a table showing that it would cost from 4 to 7 cents per 100 less to send wheat from Columbus, Nebr., Sioux City, and other Iowa points to New York than to send the same wheat to Chicago and the flour made therefrom to New York. Another table shows that it would cost from 4 to 5½ cents less to send grain from these same points to New York for export than for domestic use. Milling-in-transit rates are not granted on grain for export purposes. (422–425.)

Mr. SAGER, secretary of the Northern Milling Company of Chicago, confirms the testimony of Mr. Bacon as to the existing differences in the freight rates on flour and grain. The differences are much less than those which formerly existed. Nevertheless, the Chicago miller has to pay the local rate of about 5 cents per 100 on grain from the Mississippi River to Chicago, and in addition must pay 2 cents per 100 more on flour from Chicago to the seaboard than the export rate on wheat from the Mississippi River to the seaboard, which is the same as that from Chicago. (446, 447.)

Mr. EVANS, a miller of Indianapolis, testifying in November, 1899, says that the rates from Chicago to the seaboard since November 1, 1899, have been 20 cents for grain and 22 cents for grain products, and from the Mississippi River 20 cents and 24 cents, respectively. Even with the discrimination between grain and grain products thus reduced the effect upon flour and corn mills in the interior cities is still serious. The witness submitted a table showing that the cost of delivering corn, at an original price of 30 cents per bushel, in New York for export purposes would be 76.07 cents per 100 pounds. If the corn be ground in Indianapolis, paying a milling privilege of 1½ cents per 100 pounds and the higher freight rate on milled products, it would cost 79.07 cents to deliver it in New York. (435, 436.)

Mr. GALLAGHER states that there had been for months up to November, 1899, a gradually increasing discrimination between wheat for export and flour for export. He believes that it was at one time 8 cents, before that 5 cents, and before that 3 cents. In the tariff dated November 1, 1899, the rate on flour for export from St. Louis to New York is 27 cents, to Philadelphia 25 cents, and to Baltimore 24 cents; on wheat for export the rate to New York is 20 cents, to Philadelphia 19 cents, and to Baltimore 18½ cents. Though the railroads claim that the commission has no authority to make such orders at will, they have issued a tariff which complies with its order, so far as rates from Chicago are concerned. The export rate from Chicago is now only 2 cents higher on flour than on wheat. The discrimination in other parts of the country, including St. Louis, is as great as before. The new Chicago rate was made on November 1, at a time when rates generally were advanced. The rate on flour was not reduced, but the discrimination was reduced by advancing the rate on wheat. (539, 540.)

B. Effect of differences on American millers.—Mr. BARRY, secretary of the Millers' National Association, is fullest in his description of the effects of these discriminating rates on American millers. His testimony was given before the change of rates in November.

The millers' association was organized in 1873, primarily for the purpose of checking litigation concerning patents and saving expense in that regard. Since 1890 it has acted in other directions for the benefit of the trade, urging pure-food laws, considering tariff measures, etc., and it is now active in opposing these discriminations. It has not sought to influence prices, and can never do so, since the interests associated are so diverse. The organization is affiliated with various State organizations of millers. It has a membership in 24 States, its members having 120,000 barrels daily capacity. In certain European countries the organizations of millers include even a larger proportion of those engaged in the industry and are more effective. (240–243.)

Mr. Barry calls attention to the great importance of the milling industry in this country and to the fact that it is widely scattered, including many small producers. The capacity of the mills of the country is excessive, which renders the export trade of even greater importance than it would be otherwise. Competition has driven millers to increase the size of their plants in order to reduce cost, so that it is estimated that the mills could in 90 days make into flour every bushel of wheat raised in a year.

Mr. Barry further says that up to within two years there have been practically the same freight rates on flour and wheat for both domestic and export use. The growing disparity has come about by the decrease in the export rates on wheat, the flour rate remaining practically the same. The witness cited as one instance the fact that the export rate on flour from Missouri River points by way of Chicago has been 24½ cents to the seaboard; the export rate on wheat only 12 cents. The effect of this discrimination must be serious upon the milling industry. Although the exportation of wheat has been larger during 1899 than during 1898, the amount of flour exported from Minneapolis during the month of September, 1899, was 362,810 barrels, as compared with 485,534 in September, 1898. Exportation from Duluth for the same months has been 79,295 barrels and 173,135 barrels, respectively, showing a net decrease of 93,830. The most serious effect is likely to be on the small millers. They can not manufacture as cheaply as the large Minneapolis and other mills, and these, if excluded from foreign markets, will sell their surplus product in competition with the small mills. The witness quoted a letter from a London dealer which declares that the discrimination against flour is undoubtedly injuring the American trade and is a fine thing for the English miller, having the same effect as if the English Government should place a duty of perhaps 6 cents per 100 pounds on flour. It is often difficult for American millers to dispose of their by-products satisfactorily, and though bran can now be packed in very condensed form for transportation, the low export rate on wheat prevents a good foreign market for American bran. (240–243, 246.)

Mr. VANLANDINGHAM thinks that if the present discriminations continue flour shipments will be very largely prevented. As a matter of fact, they have increased much less rapidly than grain shipments during the past four years, and were even lower in 1898 than in 1894, as shown by the following table: (204, 205.)

Year.	Wheat.	Flour.
	Bushels.	*Barrels.*
1894	88,415,230	16,859,533
1895	76,102,704	15,268,892
1896	60,650,080	14,620,864
1897	79,562,020	14,569,545
1898	148,231,261	15,349,943

The effect of this discrimination, if continued, Mr. SAGER declares, must be ultimately to destroy the American industry of milling for export. At present the reputation of American brands prevents them from being entirely shut out from the foreign market. But when foreign consumers find that millers on their own side can furnish them with flour made from the best American wheat at a lower price, the American trade will be lost. The foreign millers have cheaper labor and the cost of their plants is less. The American export trade in flour has grown steadily and has been very large, but the mill in which the witness is interested, at any rate, has never done so little export business as during 1899. The fact that official statistics show that the export of flour for the first 9 months of 1899 was somewhat greater than for the first 9 months of 1898 is explained by the existence of many contracts made in 1898 which had to be filled in the spring of 1899, as well as by the fact that a large amount of export flour went to the seaboard in the fall of 1898, but was not shipped until 1899. The millers of the country think that Congress should come to their aid in protecting the American industry, especially for the sake of American labor.   (447, 448, 453.)

Mr. GALLAGHER states that our flour export trade has rapidly diminished since February, 1899. The St. Louis miller has to pay what is practically an export duty of 7 cents per 100 pounds, or about 15 cents a barrel, on his flour. This the American miller can not afford to do; his profit is not so great. The American miller is under some natural disadvantages as compared with the foreign miller using American grain. The export grain goes directly from the field toward the sea. The miller often has to ship his grain 200 or 300 miles at local rates and perhaps away from the sea. The milling-in-transit privilege sometimes modifies this disadvantage, but does not overcome it, and this privilege does not exist generally, but only in certain territories.   (539, 545, 546.)

Mr. Gallagher says, further, that St. Louis has manufactured soft-wheat flour for export for 50 years or more. When the crop fails in the district from which the St. Louis mills are accustomed to buy, they have to go to Indiana, or even to Ohio or to Chicago, for wheat. The mills of St. Louis and its suburban towns have a capacity of over 27,000 barrels per day, and employ 1,100 men exclusively engaged in that business, besides truck drivers, men working in the mills, etc. The consumption of wheat is much larger in St. Louis than in Chicago.

Mr. EVANS says that the result of the discriminations which have existed during 1899 has been to divert trade very largely from American mills and to favor foreign mills, both as regards corn products and as regards flour. The witness quoted from various letters from dealers in English cities and in Amsterdam referring to the impossibility of selling American products in competition with the existing low prices of the foreign mills. There has never been a time in the past 20 years when the mills have been so largely shut down or running on half time. This means a loss to many classes of people, especially to the employees of the mills. On the other hand, the witness has been told that the English mills are running at a rate never before known.   (437.)

C. Are lower export rates justifiable?—*Affirmative.*—Mr. NEALL, a shipping merchant of Philadelphia, believes that it is justifiable to charge lower freight rates on goods intended for exportation than on those for domestic use. This practice benefits the producer, notably the farmer. If the farmer sought to force the large surplus production of corn and wheat down the mouths of the inhabitants of the United States, who are all sufficiently supplied, the price would be materially cut down. In the foreign market grain can be sold only if the price is made low enough to compete with the products of Argentina, Russia, and Hungary.   (166.)

Mr. KELLEY agrees with Mr. Neall in justifying the lower rates on goods intended for export than on other goods.   (188.

Mr. CALLAWAY, president of the New York Central, also thinks that low export rates are necessary to meet foreign competition, and that the ability to dispose of surplus products, especially of grain, in this way is a great advantage to American producers. If the railways were compelled to make domestic rates as low as those frequently necessary for export, they would have to go out of the export business. But the proportion of the export business is enormous. About 80 per cent of the provisions shipped from the West to the seaboard go abroad, and practically all of the grain. Mr. Callaway does not admit that the railways haul export goods at a loss. No intelligent man would take traffic which did not pay a reasonable profit. But the entire bulk of a railway's business must be averaged in calculating profit. Thus the New York Central carries about 15,000 freight cars per day. If the number were reduced to 10,000 at the same rates the railroad probably could not live. The margin, however, on export traffic is often exceedingly small. (232–234.)

Mr. SPENCER, president of the Southern Railway, states the argument in favor of permitting lower export rates in very much the same terms. If the domestic rate itself is reasonable, all things considered, no one is harmed by making a special export rate, necessary to meet competition in foreign markets. The only possible harm would come to the railway in case it made the rate too low. The recent competition of transportation by way of the Gulf has compelled the reduction of rates from Chicago and St. Louis to the Eastern seaboard, although the effect of this competition has probably been exaggerated. (276, 281.)

Mr. FISH, of the Illinois Central, says the practice of the railways in making lower export rates is similar to that of manufacturers who try to keep foreign markets in order to relieve themselves of surplus product, even at a loss. Railways must either lose the business entirely, and American producers lose foreign markets, or special rates must be made. In the case of the Illinois Central, although about 85 per cent of the total tonnage is local, most of the grain hauled to New Orleans is for export. The export business also is done more economically than the local business. Shipments are made by train loads, and the cars are unloaded very promptly, whereas in the case of local shipments they are often delayed several days. (336, 337.)

Mr. TUCKER, chairman of the Central Freight Association, considers that it is proper to make a lower rate on grain for export, just as manufacturing concerns or mines sell their surplus at lower rates than they charge to their regular customers. A low export rate on grain enables the surplus crop to be got rid of, meets foreign competition which does not have to be met in local traffic, and is on the whole the best policy for the country at large. Besides, the export traffic is very large in volume; both export grain and export flour can be moved in heavy carloads, and so can be moved with fully as much profit to the railroad as other freight in smaller volume. (563.)

Mr. SNYDACKER, a grain merchant of Chicago, thinks also that it is just and desirable to make freight rates for export grain such as to enable American grain to compete in foreign markets. He believes it to be a serious offense to divert grain to domestic consumption when it has been billed for exportation at a lower rate. (398.)

Mr. BLANCHARD, late commissioner of the Joint Traffic Association, presents a similar line of argument in favor of lower export rates. He thinks that such special rates are justifiable, not only as regards grain, but also as regards flour cattle, meat products, cotton, tobacco, and much other exported merchandise Lower rates are often necessary to meet foreign competition, and there is no good reason why the domestic rates, if reasonable in themselves, should be reduced on account of the reductions in export rates, especially since a reduction of domestic through rates carries with it many intermediate rates. The present practice helps all of the producing interests of the country.

Mr. Blanchard adds that the competition of Canadian carriers for American grain often makes it necessary to reduce rates on export shipments, a similar reduction not being necessary on domestic shipments.

This witness points out further that a considerable amount of grain and similar products goes abroad on through bills of lading from inland points to foreign ports. It may be greatly to the national advantage to make such through rates. On account of the frequent changes in ocean rates, a through rate which is disadvantageous to a port at one time may very soon become beneficial to it. (628, 629.)

Mr. GALLAGHER thinks that the roads are justified in making the rates on grain and flour for export lower than the rates on the same things for domestic use. (543.)

Negative.—Mr. PROUTY, of the Interstate Commerce Commission, says that although the railways have assigned as a justification for such discriminations the necessity of meeting competition in markets abroad, investigation by the commission showed that this claim was not justified, but that the discriminations had been due to competition among the railways at home. The American farmer therefore received no benefit, the foreign consumer reaping the entire advantage.

These discriminations are partly defended on the score of water competition; for example, by way of Montreal. How far the railways succeed in recouping themselves by such low rates can not be estimated. The fixed charges must be paid in any case, and the additional cost of handling an increased amount of business can not be estimated by itself. The low rate from Kansas City to Galveston was defended on the ground that the ocean rate from there to Liverpool was higher than from New York. The commission, at any rate, ordered that the rate on flour or on grain for domestic use should not exceed the export grain rate by over 2 cents. (146, 147.)

Mr. GALLAGHER thinks lower export rates in themselves advantageous to farmers, but declares that grain is bought up by railroads and elevators and run out of the country by the train load, taking advantage of a rate, often secret, which the farmer gets nothing out of. (540, 541.)

Mr. VANLANDINGHAM, freight commissioner of the St. Louis Traffic Bureau, considers that at some periods a lower export rate is doubtless necessary to secure foreign markets against competition of other countries. The railways are sometimes unable to make the domestic rates as low as the export rates which are necessary. But this has not been true during 1898 and 1899, since our grain would have gone abroad to as great an extent in any case. (195.)

Mr. MORTON, vice-president of the Atchison, Topeka and Santa Fe Railway, does not think that lower rates on imported or exported articles than on domestic traffic are usually justifiable. The recent low rates on export traffic have been caused by excessive competition among American carriers, and not by the necessity of meeting foreign competition. There must be some elasticity in the rates on manufactured goods, since we are only beginning to extend our foreign markets largely. America can produce cereals as cheaply as any country, and there is no need for low export rates on them. (490.)

Mr. BARRY does not think that the exceedingly low export rates on wheat are necessary in order to enable American products to compete in foreign markets. He thinks the cost of transportation in this country tends to determine the Liverpool price of wheat, rather than that price determines the transportation charges. He admits that the Liverpool price of grain largely determines the American price. He insists, however, that there is demand for American wheat regardless of the competition of other countries, on account of its superior quality, and especially that American flour has a preference among foreign consumers. It would be to the advantage of the American grain producer to sell his product as far as possible to American mills, since the foreign demand for American flour is steadier than that for wheat and would tend to keep up the price of wheat. (247–251.)

Mr. BACON does not consider lower rates on export shipments of grain justifiable. They have never been considered necessary until within the past two years. They are not essential to hold European markets. The price in Liverpool is only one of many elements in fixing prices to American producers. Even if rates on flour and grain be made the same, the existence of an export rate lower than the domestic rate would at least injure millers on our eastern seaboard. (424, 425.)

D. Are lower rates on grain than on flour justifiable?—*Affirmative.*—Mr. CALLAWAY, president of the New York Central, thinks that flour will bear a higher freight rate than grain. At any rate, there is no considerable profit in hauling flour at present rates (October, 1899). The competition is very keen, especially since the "Soo Line" was built from Minneapolis directly to tide water. Water competition also keeps rates on flour down. The witness believes that his own road has complied with any finding the Interstate Commerce Commission may have made on this subject. It is the purpose of the railways to foster traffic, and if it be found that American flour industries are being repressed by rail rates, the rates will be reduced. But the millers continue to ship at present rates and are making money. (232, 233.)

Mr. BIRD, of the Chicago, Milwaukee and St. Paul, thinks that the interstate commerce act does not apply to export business. The lower rates which are often made on wheat as compared with flour are partly explainable, in his opinion, by the fact that water competition is specially strong in the case of wheat, and water carriers are not subject to the interstate-commerce act. At the same time the recent specially low export rates on wheat were due essentially to the contest for supremacy between the various trunk lines. The witness does not believe that the ownership of terminal facilities by railway officers has had anything to do with it. A further justification for lower rates on grain may be found in the fact that a heavier load of grain can be shipped in a car than is usually shipped of flour. Nevertheless, Mr. Bird sees no reason why, other conditions being equal, wheat grown in the Northwestern States should be carried for export at so cheap a rate that the foreign miller can compete with our own millers in grinding American wheat. (473, 474.)

In explanation of the fact that the difference between the rates on export grain and on flour is greater from the Mississippi River points to the seaboard than from Chicago, and greater than the limit prescribed by the Interstate Commerce Commission, Mr. Bird stated that the Western roads could not reduce their through rates without the cooperation of the Eastern roads, especially, apparently, of those which run directly from the Mississippi River to the coast. (477.)

Mr. TUCKER, chairman of the Central Freight Association, says that transportation rates are really based on value, bulk, and risk. The terminal expense is another element to be considered in determining the rates. The manufactured article should always be charged more than the raw material, and, as a rule, it is of less weight in proportion to bulk. Export flour is sent from Minneapolis in carloads about two-thirds as large, he thinks, as carloads of wheat. He is not clear whether the railroads may not be in part responsible for this by furnishing smaller cars for flour than for wheat. It is a matter of evidence that the export flour is worth just about as much as wheat; but the witness queries whether this may not result from using a poor wheat for export flour. The witness does not believe that the railroads are themselves owners of wheat, and therefore discriminate against American flour. He does not think that such a thing could long continue without its being known to those not in it. (563, 564.)

Mr. BLANCHARD is not clear as to whether differences between rates on wheat and flour are entirely new developments or have long been in existence. He thinks that such differences are justifiable. He has, indeed, heretofore heard of complaints made by grain shippers on the ground that the railways carry a barrel of flour weighing 216 pounds at the same rate as 200 pounds of wheat (presumably on domestic shipments). He thinks that it is the intention of the carrying companies to put the two articles on the same footing wherever practicable. He suggests that the lake vessels are able to handle wheat much more economically than flour, and that the railroads are compelled to meet their rates. He thinks it is also cheaper for the railways themselves to handle bulk grain than flour. The loads are heavier.

Mr. Blanchard says further that the railways, at least at New York, by contract with the New York Produce Exchange, deliver bulk grain in canal boats or otherwise at the ocean vessels themselves, including storage, without extra charge, and apparently this is not the case with flour. It is not true, as is sometimes contended, that there is a charge of 3 cents per 100 pounds for this transfer of grain, and that the fact that railway officers are interested in the transfer business at New York accounts for their preference for grain. As a matter of fact, the differential by which the freight charge on grain by way of New York is 3 cents higher than by way of Baltimore or other Southern ports was made more than 20 years ago, and entirely independently of any consideration as to the exact cost of transfer facilities at New York. The witness implies that the cost of the transfer is often more than 3 cents per 100 pounds, and says that the Erie Railroad formerly found it necessary to restrict somewhat the options given to shippers as to the numerous points about New York Harbor to which grain could be delivered without special charge. (672, 673.)

Negative.—Mr. BARRY says that the various arguments presented by the railway companies in justification of the differences between the rates on flour and wheat are not warranted by the facts. The railroads can handle flour as cheaply as wheat. Cars can be loaded to the full weight capacity with export flour, since the bags in which the export shipments are always made can be piled up nearly to the roof, especially at the ends of the car. Cars are never more than half filled with wheat, since the greater weight of wheat would break down the running gear. The average weight of flour shipments may be less per car, but this is because the railways have seen fit to furnish largely small, old-fashioned cars for flour shipments.

The argument that wheat can be secured abundantly at the times when it is most needed for transportation is more than offset by the fact that the largest demand for wheat transportation is immediately after harvest, and that the railways are often unable to secure return shipments sufficient to fill the large number of cars then used. The shipments of flour are quite steady throughout the year and can be counted upon.

The real reason, Mr. Barry thinks, why favoring rates have been made on export wheat shipments rather than on flour shipments is that the railways have been largely interested in elevators and have found it to their interest to secure a foreign market for their product. Moreover, the small number of important wheat exporters and the large business which each controls enables these to a considerable degree to dictate to the railways. He admits that these large firms, of which there are practically only five in Chicago, are often able to furnish full train loads of wheat for shipment, which is more than the millers can do. Mr. Barry believes that some of these large export dealers have discriminating rates lower than those published, and it is possible there may be discriminations between the different large dealers themselves. See on this point p. 79. (241–244, 249.)

Mr. vANLANDINGHAM does not admit the claim of the railways that these differences in charges are justified by the greater cost of handling flour. As much of flour for export is shipped in a car as of wheat. The shipper in each case loads the car, while the railway company usually loads the flour on the steamer, and at some of the Gulf and south Atlantic ports also pays the elevator charges for loading the wheat on the steamer. Flour for domestic use is hauled at the same rate as grain, although cars are not loaded to their full capacity. Mr. Vanlandingham thinks that the real basis for the difference on export shipments is that the railroads can get large quantities of wheat at almost any time when they happen to have empty cars to go East, and that this is not true of flour. There are only about twenty firms engaged in the export grain business, and these often have large stocks on hand. The millers are distributed over a large territory, and there are, perhaps, 5,000 firms. The matter of by-products does not justify higher rates on flour, since the miller in Europe gets better prices for his by-products than the American miller. (204, 205.)

Mr. BACON does not think that the difference between the rates on flour and grain is justifiable. There never was any such difference until very recently, when export rates have been introduced for the first time as regards wheat, but have not been applied to flour. Before this change about equal quantities of American wheat and flour went abroad, but American millers have since been at a disadvantage. (424.)

Even a difference of 2 cents per 100 pounds in favor of grain as compared with milled products, according to Mr. EVANS, is a serious injury to domestic millers, and the witness thinks that it is not justified by any of the arguments presented by the railways. It has not been shown that it costs more to handle flour. There is a considerable loss in quantity in shipping unground wheat. Cars can be loaded as heavily with flour as with grain. The witness has found that 16 cars taken consecutively from the books of his mill have averaged a weight of 63,000 pounds to the car. Numerous railway officers have told the witness personally that they did not approve of the discrimination. Mr. Ingalls, president of the Chesapeake and Ohio and Cleveland, Cincinnati, Chicago and St. Louis railroads, in a letter to the witness, has expressed himself as opposed to the reduction in the wheat rate which caused this discrimination. The discrimination has been in existence only since February 1, 1899, and no new reasons have come into existence since that time for maintaining it. (435–438.)

Mr. SAGER also denies that there is any justification for the difference in rates between grain and flour. Millers can load 60,000 pounds of export flour on a 60,000-pound car, although the custom in the domestic trade has been to put 150 barrels—somewhat less than the total capacity—in a car. The millers load the flour themselves. The witness thinks that the probable explanation of the difference in charges is that certain officers of the railroads are interested in elevators and other terminal facilities for handling wheat. It is for the interest of the railroad stockholders to give the millers favorable rates. The mills become centers of population, and give the railroads business in hauling milling supplies as well as hauling the goods used by the operatives. (449, 450.)

Mr. GALLAGHER says the millers are ready to comply with any reasonable demand of the railroads in respect to the loading of cars, but they claim that the largest and best cars are furnished for shipping wheat and older and smaller cars for shipping flour. If proper equipment is furnished the millers will furnish carloads of flour of any size that the railroads desire. Mr. Gallagher states, however, that when railroads are specially desirous of business they can get train loads of grain more readily than they can get train loads of flour, and this leads to special cuts. (540, 541.)

Mr. GALLAGHER argues that the railroads themselves can not afford to destroy the export business of the American mills because of the large incidental traffic which mills give the railroads. He estimates the amount of freight, in the shape of coal, lumber, machinery, bags, cooperage, and other supplies for which the mills are responsible, at 88,000 tons more than the annual exports of grain. On a large part of this material the railroads receive high rates of freight. Further, both this traffic and the mill freights of grain and flour come regularly to the railroads throughout the year. (543.)

Mr. NEALL, a shipping merchant of Philadelphia, believes that some higher charge on flour shipments than on grain shipments is justified by the greater ease of handling the grain through elevators, etc. But he has estimated rather carefully that the difference should not exceed 2 or 3 cents per hundred, whereas the actual difference in freight rates has been at times as high as 7½ cents. A difference of 2 or 2½ cents, moreover, is all that the traffic will stand. The by-products of the miller should enable him to pay that much more on his flour. The witness believes that at present competition is keeping the margin between wheat and flour down to about the figure named. (164–166.)

Ocean freight rates on flour and wheat.—Mr. NEALL also points out that a lower ocean freight rate on grain than on flour is justified. It costs about 8 cents per ton to load grain upon a ship and 37½ cents to load flour. A ton of grain will stow in about 50 cubic feet, while 60 to 65 cubic feet is required for flour on account of the use of bags.

Some higher charge upon oats than upon wheat is justifiable in ocean transportation on account of the necessity of tramping down the oats. Flour bears the lowest rate among mill products on account of its condensed weight. (164–166.)

Mr. BARRY does not think that the difference between the ocean freight rates on flour and wheat is any element in the present difficulty regarding export flour shipments. Some difference in ocean transportation is justifiable by the greater cost of handling and carrying flour. The flour shipments are not usually made on through rates to foreign markets, but the rates of ocean transportation vary frequently, and the price of the American product in Europe is changed accordingly. The witness thinks that the ocean steamships seldom have any difficulty in securing full loads of flour promptly. (244, 245, 249, 251.)

Mr. GALLAGHER says that the difference between the ocean rates on grain and flour may sometimes run as high as 5 cents, though if there is no grain available, and flour can be got, the flour may be taken low. As a general thing he thinks the difference would range from 1 to 3 cents. (539.)

E. Milling-in-transit rates.—Mr. BARRY states that the railways usually make it a practice in sections of the country where milling is a prominent industry to haul grain on through rates from West to East, allowing it to be stopped off and milled at any point between by payment of an additional rate of about 2 cents, simply to cover the cost of stopping and unloading and loading the car. Small millers as well as large ones have the advantage of this practice where it exists at all. (243.)

Mr. GALLAGHER states that milling-in-transit rates do not exist generally, but only in certain territories. There are no such rates which are of great value to St. Louis. Wheat can be shipped from western Kansas and stopped for milling anywhere. This wheat, however, is hard wheat and is not suitable for the St. Louis mills, which are almost exclusively soft-wheat mills. The Minneapolis mills profit largely by the milling-in-transit privilege. Their wheat generally comes from the North and the West. One cent per 100 is the general charge for milling in transit. (546.)

Mr. BOOKWALTER states that grain from the West can be stopped at any station on the roads running into Kansas City, such as Topeka, ground, and forwarded, for instance, to New York without any charge above the through rate from the original point. But if the grain is billed to Kansas City, although it is never removed from the car, an additional charge of from 1 cent to 7 cents per 100 is imposed. This places Kansas City at a fatal disadvantage. (571.)

VI. GRAIN ELEVATORS AND GRAIN BUYING.

A. Alleged monopoly of elevator owners.—Mr. CARTER, a commission merchant, states that the railroad people have built large elevators in Chicago, and formerly had them managed by men who were simply managers of the elevators and custodians of other people's property. Now each of these elevators has been turned over to some one large concern, which undoubtedly has the use of it at a merely nominal rent, while any other grain shipper or receiver must pay three-fourths of a cent for having grain handled through the elevator and held 10 days. Mr. Carter does not think that any of the public elevators are now managed by men who are not engaged in the grain business. Efforts have been made to correct this evil by the action of the board of trade, and also to put greater safeguards by legislation about the handling of public property. Elections in the board of trade have turned upon this issue, and the board has never failed to elect officers who have stood for the handling of public property by disinterested parties. But the efforts to bring about a better condition have not yet succeeded. As a rule, a single operator, to whom the terminal facilities of a road in Chicago have been turned over, controls the grain business along that line of road and does no considerable business on any other line. (583, 584.)

Mr. GREELEY, a commission merchant of Chicago, declares that the original purpose of the public warehouses was that they should be simply custodians of grain for the public. After the interstate-commerce act was passed the railroads, in order to cover up the granting of rebates, saw fit to make arrangements with the owners of public elevators by which favors could be granted in an indirect manner to them and to others, and this led the warehousemen to become dealers in grain. At least 75 per cent of the grain in public elevators sooner or later becomes the property of the warehousemen. The charges to private persons for handling and storing grain are excessive. The transfer charge is three-fourths of a cent per bushel, and the storage charge three-fourths of a cent per bushel for the first 10 days and one-fourth of a cent for each succeeding 10 days. The witness understands that certain transfer elevators connected with Eastern railroad lines receive from railroad companies $1.50 per car for transferring grain and make a profit, while the charge to shippers is about $12 per car. The owners of a warehouse avoid this high storage and transfer charge, having to pay only the actual cost, which is much less. The witness thinks that the capital invested by them in the elevators is usually practically nothing, since they are "presented with the elevators by the railroad companies." Owing to these advantages the warehousemen can pay more for grain than others and consequently secure the largest proportion of it. One result of this practice is that the large elevator companies are driving the small country elevators and grain merchants out of business. Sooner or later this process will be completed, and the one buyer will fix the price to the producer. (370-377.)

Mr. DOUSMAN, a grain shipper, says that in earlier days most grain was consigned to Chicago from the West and reshipped there, without through rates. Soon after the interstate-commerce act was passed it became the custom for elevator proprietors at Chicago to become grain buyers in that city and also along the railroads. These elevators arrange to secure through rates on grain from the Mississippi River to New York. Apparently, they are sometimes allowed a certain amount by the railways for transferring the grain in the elevators. As a matter of fact, a large proportion of the elevators in Chicago are now owned or controlled by the railroads, and the witness is inclined to think that the railroads should consider elevator charges as a part of their through rates.

It was also formerly the custom that the elevator owners acted simply as agents, their elevators being public storehouses. But at present the owners of elevators buy most of the grain. The fact that they charge three-fourths of a cent per bushel to those using the elevator, which apparently is more than the actual cost warrants, gives them an advantage over other buyers. The country buyer of grain, who is frequently a merchant, sells to the elevator company; or the company itself often has elevators along the road and buys directly. The witness implies that in many cases there is practically only one such general buyer on a particular line of railroad, although he refers also to the fact that in some cases country grain merchants receive daily offers from 5 to 25 different dealers. He thinks that small concerns can handle grain business more economically than large ones. (354-356.)

Mr. CLARK, secretary of the Grainers' National Association, disapproves of the practice of the elevator owners in buying grain themselves. The Illinois Grainers' Association, which is chiefly made up of commission men and country grain shippers, opposed the enactment of the law permitting public warehousemen to buy grain, as against the best interests of the trade. Most of the public elevators in Chicago are owned by the railroads, although operated by individuals. (434.)

Mr. WEBSTER points out that the act passed by the legislature of Illinois in 1897 permitting public warehousemen to buy grain, was passed after very free discussion in that body and in the press. The vote showed a very large majority in its favor in each house, and an attempt to repeal the law in 1899 was defeated by an even more decisive vote. (409.)

In reply to a question as to the alleged control of the barley trade of the United States by Mr. P. D. Armour, Mr. GREELEY said that although Mr. Armour is a very important factor in the market, other elevators also hold large quantities of barley. (380.) Mr. Counselman declares that the claim that Mr. Armour controls the barley trade is ridiculous. The witness himself handles eight or nine million bushels of barley a year. (390.)

B. Interest of railways in elevators.—Mr. BARRY, secretary of the Millers' National Association, thinks that a large proportion of the elevators, not merely in the cities, but along the railway lines, are controlled by railways or their officers. These elevators doubtless have a considerable effect in controlling the prices of grain to the farmers. Millers are not especially injured by them, since the small millers buy grain largely at the mill from the farmers, and the large mills usually have elevators of their own. (250.)

Mr. BOOKWALTER says that eight railroad systems control the grain-producing territory, and every one of these systems is going into the grain business as fast as it can. When the business has been brought into the hands of eight roads, with storage capacity enough to take care of the crop, the local dealer will have to go out of business entirely, unless some remedy can be found. Mr. Bookwalter can not say that the grain is dealt in directly by the railroads, but certain persons can handle it on these roads when nobody else can. He thinks we are rapidly approaching the condition in which a trust will absolutely control the handling, and thereby the price, of grain. He would require the railroads to attend strictly to the railroad business and go out of the grain business and any other; that is the only remedy. (576.)

Mr. GALLAGHER does not consider that companies chartered to operate railroads should be allowed to engage in the grain business. He believes that ownership of elevators by railroads inevitably results in the control of the grain business by the railroads, in the destruction of all competition, and in the establishment of a monopoly. Wherever the road controls the business one finds little elevators abandoned and run down. This shows the destruction of competition. Where competition disappears the price of grain to the farmer is certain to go down. (545.)

Mr. BOOKWALTER states that the Union Pacific has an elevator in Kansas City. The Burlington has none at present, but it is understood that it is going to build one. Mr. Counselman, who operates on the Rock Island, and Mr. Richardson, who operates on the Santa Fe, have elevators in Kansas City. The Peavey Elevator Company of Minneapolis operates on the Union Pacific, west of Kansas City, and is building a line of elevators. It tries, first, to buy out the local man at a station, if he will sell; if not, it builds an elevator beside him. There are two public elevators in Kansas City, with a capacity of 400,000 to 1,000,000 bushels. The total elevator capacity in Kansas City is about 6,000,000. The understanding is that the elevators are owned by the railroads, though they are operated by private parties. Mr. Bookwalter does not think that the railroads ought to be permitted to go into the grain business or any other business. (573–575.)

Mr. SNYDACKER says that his firm leases elevators along the line of the railways, and has one leased in Chicago. (397.)

Mr. WEBSTER says that Armour & Co. own practically no elevators along the lines of the railways, although they own all of those which they operate in Chicago except three, which are leased at a high rental. Mr. Armour is interested in various railroads, but receives no advantages from them in transportation rates or otherwise. (413, 416.)

C. Freight discriminations and allowances in favor of elevators.—Mr. VANLANDINGHAM, commissioner of the St. Louis Traffic Bureau, says that on each of the leading railways from grain-producing sections to Chicago, allowances, ranging from one-half to 1½ cents per bushel, are made on grain to one or two favored firms having a large number of local grain elevators, nominally as compensation for gathering the grain, loading it, and shipping it at times when the railways can most conveniently care for it. The favored elevators are thus enabled to pay higher prices for grain. The average profit in handling grain is less than 1½ cents per bushel, and smaller buyers can thus easily be driven out of business. Mr. Counselman, who controls one such system of elevators, testified before the Interstate Commerce Commission that his warehouses were paying three-fourths of a cent per bushel more than the market prices for August corn at the Mississippi River, being able to make a profit by so doing. The small shipper being driven out of business the large dealer is in a position to depress the price of grain to the producer, although the witness thinks that the prices can not be lowered much below the amount of this allowance without calling in new buyers or enabling the farmer to ship directly.

Many of these systems of elevators, especially those at terminal points, are owned by railways themselves, or by their officers, but the allowances are just as likely to be granted to distinct companies. The practice described does not, Mr. Vanlandingham thinks, prevail at St. Louis or upon the railroads reaching that city, but he believes that it is general on the Chicago railroads. (198-200.)

Mr. GREELEY is inclined to think that every one of these public warehousemen in Chicago receives special freight rates and considerations, and that they are also notified in advance of changes to be made in rates, so getting an advantage over their competitors.

Mr. Greeley says further that the Eastern railroads have arranged with certain favored elevator men to transfer grain from Western cars to Eastern cars, putting the transfer houses owned by the railroad in the charge of these favored individuals. These persons are themselves grain dealers and competitors of the men who products they handle, which gives them an unjust advantage. (370, 377.)se

Mr. DOUSMAN declares that one of the chief reasons why the elevator business has been largely centralized in a few companies is the discriminations in their favor by the railroads. In one instance brought before the Interstate Commerce Commission by the Chicago Board of Trade in 1890, it was shown that regular buyers of grain along Western railroads had found themselves forced to sell to certain individuals, and this was due to the receipt of a rebate of 5 cents per 100 by these favored individuals. The matter was not pushed to a final decision, because Mr. Counselman, the head of the elevator system on the Rock Is a1 Railroad, declared that he could not testify without incriminating himself. (354–856.)

Mr. BOOKWALTER believes that the large elevators get favors from the railroads which enable them to pay more for grain than others can pay, and to drive others out of business. For instance, two days before his testimony there was bid for No. 3 corn, Chicago terms, on track at Humboldt, 120 miles from Kansas City, 25¼ cents. The rate to Chicago is 17½ cents, or 9.8 cents a bushel; that would make the corn cost 35.3 cents at Chicago, if the tariff rate were paid. The best corn was worth that day in Chicago 33½ cents. The Peavey Elevator Company, of Minneapolis, which is getting control of the grain business on the Union Pacific west of Kansas City, offered one-fourth of a cent more for corn along the Union Pacific road a few days before Mr. Bookwalter's testimony than the Kansas City price on the same day, less the freight to Kansas City. Again, in testimony before the Interstate Commerce Commission a year or two ago, it was stated by an elevator man that the railroad company paid him as much as 4 cents per 100 for running grain through the house, as an elevator charge. This was really a drawback on the freight and would give him the absolute control of the business on that road. (574–577.)

Mr. CARTER has no doubt that the large dealers in grain who control the business along several roads centering in Chicago have lower freight rates than the ordinary buyer. He believes that one reason why the roads would wish to concentrate business in the hands of one man is that rebates can be paid to one and kept secret; if they were paid to a dozen, the secret could not be kept. He instances a man who has done business with a line of road for not more than a year, and so has not had opportunity to become established and make friends there, and yet is getting perhaps nine-tenths of the grain that comes in over that road. He had done a grain business of a general character in years past, and had shown no great ability. He does not now do any considerable business except on the one line which he has a connection with. If his very large business there were due to his great skill this would have shown itself in former years and would now show itself in other districts. This particular man in not interested, Mr. Carter thinks, in the road which he is connected with; but he suggests that an arrangement could easily be made by which half a dozen silent partners could enjoy the profits. (583, 584.)

Mr. BACON, of the Milwaukee Board of Trade, thinks that the great elevator owners undoubtedly receive advantages from the railways. As evidence he submits an instance in connection with the Milwaukee Elevator Company, which is understood to be controlled largely by P. D. Armour. Postal cards sent out by this company to Kinbrae, Minn., and Flandreau, S. Dak., offered prices for wheat at Milwaukee ranging, if full freight rates were paid by the buyer, from 0.95 cent to 2¼ cents more than the price of wheat at Milwaukee on the particular day. Similarly, the price offered for oats, freight rates counted, would make the cost at Milwaukee from one-sixth to nearly one-half cent more than the price at Milwaukee, oats always being handled on a small margin. The inference is that the buyer must receive some advantage in freight rates. Mr. Armour is also a director in the Chicago, Milwaukee and St. Paul Railway, which extends from the points named to Milwaukee. The ownership of elevators by the buyer can not explain this difference in price. Elevators are lately used but little for storing grain, and, moreover, the proprietors would have as much advantage from buying grain at Milwaukee at market rates and storing it in their own elevators as in buying it at other points.

Such discriminating rates are usually made wherever there is competition, whether it be between different marketing points or simply between different railroads.

Generally speaking discriminations are still frequent, although they are confined to a smaller number of beneficiaries than formerly. The witness has heard of instances where rebates have been paid by railway officials in currency and without any receipts. Some grain shippers secure advantages by paying what are known as proportional rates on shipments to Chicago or Milwaukee with the understanding that the grain is to be forwarded for export purposes. There is nothing to compel the grain actually to be forwarded, and an advantage is obtained in this way. There is, in fact, a general impression that elevator owners at Chicago and Milwaukee receive advantages.

The St. Paul road owns all the elevators at its Milwaukee terminals, but leases most of them to the Milwaukee Elevator Company and one to F. Kraus & Co. (427-429.)

Mr. GALLAGHER does not think that low freight rates on grain, made in the manner in which the roads actually make them, are of any benefit to the farmer. The reason is, however, that the low export rates are obtained only by particular persons. If everybody had the low rate it would be better for the farmer. He gives an instance of a large mill which contracted with the railroads to ship 17,000 bags of flour, 400 to a car, at a rate of 5 cents. "They slapped in one of these midnight tariffs, published the tariff, and gave notice of withdrawal just as quick as he filled the contract." (543, 544.)

Mr. Gallagher admits that the price of grain to the farmer may occasionally be raised by means of cuts in freight rates, when there are competing lines of railroad and also competition in the buying of grain on that account. (541.)

D. General explanation of business by elevator owners.—The witnesses representing the great elevator companies reply generally to the complaints against them by explaining the reasons why the warehousemen have become grain buyers, the causes of their success, and the sources of complaints.

Mr. WEBSTER, president of the Armour Elevator Company, says that about the middle of the century Chicago, St. Louis, and Milwaukee became the primary markets for the rapidly developing grain production of the Western and Northwestern States. These Western States have increased their production until 10 of them produce from 55 to 67 per cent of the grain crops of the country. But meantime the development of railroads, of lake transportation, of local mills, and of other cities has diverted much of the grain trade from Chicago, as is shown by the statistics of the receipts at that point as compared with the total production. Minneapolis, through its flour mills, has become the greatest primary wheat market in the world, although it does not handle as much grain, aside from that turned into flour, as Chicago. Duluth is second to Minneapolis. Chicago comes next, while the wheat receipts of Kansas City are almost equal to those of Chicago. There are a great many other widely separated markets on the Great Lakes and elsewhere. Grain no longer seeks a market at Chicago; Chicago markets must seek the grain.

Immense elevators had been built to accommodate the great quantities of grain which formerly sought Chicago. Owing to the changes just mentioned much of this elevator space would have become idle if the proprietors had not determined to buy grain themselves and thus bring it to Chicago for handling and storage. They were able to do this to better advantage than commission merchants for various reasons. The value of the grain could be increased by cleaning. The proprietors could include the storage charges in the cost to them of the grain, especially since they were enabled to use space which otherwise would have remained idle. By doing business on a large scale, including storage, filling of orders, and shipping of cargoes, the elevator owners could afford to pay higher prices to farmers than commission men. Moreover, the elevator men sell largely for export trade and have facilities for choosing the best markets and securing the most favorable ocean rates. In fact, their advantage over the small dealer is simply that which comes legitimately to any person in any line of business who supplies himself directly with needed appliances, raw materials, etc., avoiding the payment of profits to other persons.

Mr. WEBSTER declares that he knows of no discriminations in freight rates in favor of elevator owners. The published rate obtains in all cases. There is a discrimination in favor of points on and west of the Mississippi River from the fact that grain can be shipped to the seaboard on through bills of lading at less than the sum of the local rates from the point to Chicago and from Chicago to the seaboard, an arrangement which is not made as regards points between the Mississippi River and Chicago. (415.)

It is true that many of the public elevators have found it to their advantage to become private elevators, especially because the use of machinery for cleaning grain is prohibited in public elevators; but the use of such machinery is advantageous to the producer, as was shown after an exhaustive judicial investigation as to a similar practice in Kansas City. Nothwithstanding the advantages of private elevators, there are, according to a detailed list of warehouses submitted by the witness, public elevators in Chicago having a capacity of 28,600,000 bushels, the i t elevators having almost exactly the same capacity. The legislature of Illinois, in accordance with the constitution of 1870, has passed laws regulating public warehouses, especially such as mix grain together so that that owned by different persons can not be distinguished. Licenses must be obtained and bonds given, while the grain is carefully inspected. The public elevators of Chicago handle about 25 per cent of the grain received at that city.

It is doubtless true that the commission merchants who formerly handled the grain passing through Chicago have found their business taken away largely by the purchase of grain by elevators, and they naturally feel bitter. But the system is much more economical and advantageous to the grain producer than that which formerly existed. Besides, the competition of other cities would have taken away the business of these merchants in any case. Moreover, they can move elsewhere to carry on business, and the elevators can not be moved. The purchase of grain by elevators has also, Mr. Webster thinks, become the common practice at other grain cities besides Chicago. (400–411.)

Mr. COUNSELMAN, a grain-shipping merchant of Chicago, declares that the practice of the elevators in buying grain is a matter of recent growth. Formerly the railroads had a local rate on grain from the West to Chicago and another local rate to Eastern points from Chicago. Commission merchants then handled grain on commission and stored it in the public elevators, and the elevator owners felt no necessity for buying grain. The railroads then introduced a through rate from Western points to the seaboard less than the sum of the two local rates. The Eastern grain buyer could therefore afford to go into the Western region and buy grain, paying more for it than could be paid if it were brought to Chicago on the local rate and afterwards shipped from there. So, too, the grain buyers in Minneapolis and the Northwestern points were able to pay more for grain in northern Iowa and adjacent regions, shipping it by water from Duluth. The elevator companies at Chicago were accordingly forced to buy grain to protect their own interests and to keep Chicago in the front as a grain market. The commission merchants who were unable to compete with the large elevator concerns have been those who complained concerning the elevators. The elevator companies mostly take advantage of this lower through rate, which is made through Chicago itself. This through rate is open to all persons, and the grain buyer has the privilege of shipping grain out from Chicago by lake or by rail or of stopping it there, paying the local rates. (382, 383.) Mr. BARTLETT confirms this testimony n ally. (393.)

Mr. Counselman suggests that this discrimination in favor of through rates is injurious and should be abolished. (392.)

Mr. WEBSTER, of the Armour Elevator Company, also refers to this through rate as injurious, especially to intermediate points between the Great Lakes and the Missouri River, which have to pay the local rate. It is probably a factor in causing the elevators to buy grain. (416.)

Mr. COUNSELMAN admits that the great elevator companies have an advantage over smaller commission merchants and grain dealers in handling grain. The charge of three-fourths of a cent per bushel for handling grain is not excessive. The State law of Illinois permits 1¼ cents to be charged, and this is the rate prevailing at Minneapolis, Duluth, New York, and Boston. The charge includes the transfer of grain from the cars and storage for 10 days. Nevertheless, the owner of the elevator naturally has an advantage because of his possession of these facilities, and it is impossible by any fair method to put the small dealer, who has less capital and less satisfactory facilities, on a par. The cleaning of grain by warehousemen, raising its grade, is also a source of profit. The elevator man on account of his advantages can pay the most for grain, and accordingly gets the grain. The small dealer must accumulate 5,000 bushels before he can sell his grain in the speculative market, and during the process would have to pay storage on the grain in the elevator and lose interest and insurance charges. Accordingly the small dealer mostly sells grain on the track and does not put it in elevators. Moreover, the large business and the opportunity for storage of the elevator proprietor enable him to sell in the best foreign market and at the most favorable times. There is nothing to prevent any person from building elevators who has the capital. The elevator companies have no exclusive arrangements with railroads, nor do the railroads themselves usually own any elevators. Mr. Counselman declares that he owns and has paid for with his own money the elevators along the Rock Island Railroad. The railroads do not care to go into the grain business and it is not permitted by their charters. They could not compete with the great elevator men, who sell grain in the markets over the entire world.

The complaints concerning the existence of private elevators as distinguished from public elevators are entirely unwarranted. In fact, speculators frequently urge that there should be fewer public elevators in order that less grain might be kept in stock, and that speculation might be freer accordingly. The witness owns public elevators, and they are open for use, but he does not care to do that kind of business especially. The total capacity of the public elevators of Chicago is at least 23.000,000 bushels, and that of the private elevators probably not much over 10,000,000 bushels. (385–389.) (As to these figures, compare Mr. Webster's statement, p. 82, above.)

E. Effect of grain buying by elevators on prices to farmers.—Mr. SAGER refers to the practice of a few large buyers and elevators in meeting daily on the Chicago Board of Trade to fix the price of grain for certain sections of the country. He does not altogether know the motive, but presumes that they intend to keep from competing with one another and paying too high prices. Although they are not the exclusive buyers in these sections, they are much more generally represented there than any other buyers, and they get most of the grain. (451.)

Other witnesses, as seen under Section A, also think that for the most part the business of grain buying on each railroad system is confined to one concern, and that this must ultimately have a depressing effect on prices to farmers.

Mr. CARTER thinks it certain that unrestricted competition gives the best results for the producer. In the end the farmer will not be benefited by the operation of the large institutions which are monopolizing the grain business. When there is only one concern to buy grain along a given road, a condition of affairs which is probable, the farmers will not get a better price for their grain. (586.)

Mr. COUNSELMAN declares emphatically that there is no combination between the elevators in Chicago or along the different railroad lines, and that the price to farmers is not fixed by any agreement. The railroads, in fact, will not permit the exclusive ownership of elevators at any one point along their lines. The small grain dealer receives offers from a score of sources every morning for his grain on the track. Moreover, the railroads will furnish cars and the farmer can ship his grain himself, and sell it on the track in Chicago without putting it in elevators or paying elevator charges at all. (384.)

Mr. BARTLETT also declares that there is no agreement whatever between his firm and any other firm or elevator company. His firm buys a considerable amount of grain on the Rock Island road, where the elevators are chiefly controlled by Mr. Counselman. Mr. Bartlett controls no elevators on that road, but buys directly from local grain dealers, who still handle the great bulk of the grain. It is true that the prices paid by different elevator men at the same points are usually the same, or nearly so, but this is necessary, because they all operate under similar conditions and sell their grain in the same markets. They would have no object in overbidding one another in buying grain. (393, 394.)

It is true, Mr. COUNSELMAN admits, that four or five men who deal on the board of trade meet daily and discuss the price which shall be paid for grain along certain lines of railroad. This is done, Mr. Counselman declares, because of the competition of other markets with the Chicago market. These dealers are determined to pay the farmer as much for his grain as those in any other city, and are simply fighting for the Chicago market. (387.)

Mr. BARTLETT also refers to the daily agreement between certain large elevator men as to the price of grain in the territory west of the Missouri River. This, he declares, is made in order to meet the competition of buyers who ship grain from that region by way of the southern Atlantic ports or of the Gulf ports. It is necessary in order to protect Chicago as a grain market. Chicago dealers are practically unable to buy grain in Kansas at all on account of the competition of the Gulf and the lower freight rates in that direction. At certain seasons of the year, however, corn can not be sent by way of the Gulf for fear of its germination. (394, 395.)

Mr. Webster makes a similar explanation as to the agreements concerning prices. (416.)

Mr. COUNSELMAN further says that it is true that he and other grain deal-ers sometimes pay more for grain from Nebraska, at a greater distance, than from Iowa. This is largely due to the superior quality of grain from Kansas and Nebraska, caused by the dryer climate. But the fact that the railroads make their rates for the longer distance little greater than for the shorter distance also accounts for this practice. In part, this adjustment of rates, the witness implies, is unjust. (392.)

Mr. Counselman says that the practice of the great elevator companies in buying and holding grain is advantageous to the producers, not only from the fact that commissions are saved, but from the fact that temporary surpluses are carried by the buyers until needed. The large elevator companies especially deal in grain for European consumption. There are many times when there is no demand for American grain in Europe, and the buyers must carry it until consumption overtakes supply. Thus, Argentina during the fall of the year sup-plies the European demand largely. There being no elevators or speculative system, grain from that country is all dumped on the market in a short time, and afterwards the American grain can be sold at a fair price. (384.)

Mr. BARTLETT also refers to the fact that elevator men hold grain until needed for European markets, and that at certain seasons Argentina practically controls those markets. (393, 395.)

Mr. BARTLETT says, further, that 25 years ago practically all grain paid a profit to the local grain dealer and a commission at Chicago to the commission mer-chant there, and another commission at the eastern seaboard to the merchant who sold it to the exporter. Certain Eastern firms then began to buy grain directly from the local Western elevator man or dealer, leaving out the Chicago commis-sion merchants. The grain dealers in Chicago were finally forced to adopt a similar system, and now Mr. Counselman, the firm in which the witness is inter-ested, and others, have in many instances become the only middlemen between the farmer and the foreign consumer. They operate country elevators and buy the grain directly, selling it abroad or wherever the market is most favorable. The elimination of these numerous commissions is a benefit to the producers. (393.)

Mr. SNYDACKER agrees with the testimony of Mr. Bartlett. He declares that the present method of handling grain is a survival of the fittest. The old system of handling on commission gradually dwindled. The smaller the number of men who must be supported by the handling of grain between the producer and the consumer the greater the advantage to both producer and consumer. Fifteen years ago the commission merchant at Chicago got a commission of 1 or $1\frac{1}{4}$ cents per bushel on wheat, and there were several other commissions or profits at different points on the same grain. Now an elevator company is content with a profit of 1 cent per bushel between the producer and the consumer in Europe. (396.)

Mr. WEBSTER, president of the Armour Elevator Company, states the effect of the purchase of grain by elevators upon the prices received by the producer in very much the same terms as Mr. Bartlett. He adds that in earlier years farmers were practically forced to sell their grain to one local dealer. There were few towns and few elevators and the local dealers expected a profit of from 3 to 8 cents per bushel. Many new towns have grown up, competing with one another, while at nearly every town there are from two to six grain buyers. The witness thinks that the average profit of country grain buyers now is from $2\frac{1}{4}$ to 3 cents per bushel. Formerly these grain buyers consigned grain to Chicago commission mer-chants. These sold it to other commission merchants in the East, representing Eastern buyers. The Eastern buyer, whether he exported the grain or sold it to Eastern mills, expected a liberal profit. All of these profits and commissions have been greatly reduced by the practice of the elevators of buying grain. Since the ultimate market price is fixed abroad by the competition of the entire world, any reduction in intermediate charges necessarily comes to the benefit of the pro-ducer. In fact, the wholesale grain buyer, who is also an elevator proprietor, now often pays the farmer more than the current Chicago prices would seem to warrant. He is forced to do this to meet the competition of other marketing points, and he counts on making up the difference by doing business on a very large scale. In fact, he must be a buyer over a very large extent of territory in order to get enough grain to keep his elevators busy. He is able to offer higher prices especially because he exports much of what he buys and has special advan-tages in selecting his foreign markets and securing the cheapest market rates. Moreover, the elevator man often buys grain with a speculative purpose, expect-ing to store it for some length of time in anticipation of a higher price. Being the owner of the elevator, he may at times cut into the allowance for elevator charges, since the actual cost of handling may be somewhat less than the charge to outside dealers storing grain. The witness refers by way of illustration to similar economies which have been made by carrying on the packing and provision business on a large scale. (405–410.)

Mr. BOOKWALTER states that though he has not been in the grain business 10 years, he has seen the customary margin decrease from a cent a bushel on wheat and half a cent on corn and oats to half a cent on wheat and a one-fourth of a cent on corn. (574.)

Mr. BURKE, a grain dealer of Friend, Nebr., thinks that the present method by which the great elevator owners in Chicago and elsewhere buy grain directly from the country dealers is very beneficial to the farmers and satisfactory to such dealers. Several years ago the dealers found it necessary to calculate on about a 5-cent margin on every bushel of grain, in order to protect themselves against variations in the market before the time when they should succeed in actually delivering or selling it. Now the dealers receive bids every morning for the grain on hand and can sell it immediately without taking any risk whatever. The result is that they are satisfied with a profit of from 2 to 3 cents per bushel on wheat and from one-half to 1 cent per bushel on corn, and the farmer gets the advantage accordingly. Moreover, the farmers themselves can get the same shipping facilities as the local grain dealers, and can ship directly to the large grain centers, as, in fact, they quite often do.

The witness sometimes still ships grain to the central markets. He is not sure whether he could get the same freight rates as the great elevator owners, but presumes he could. When grain is shipped in this way, a commission must be paid to a merchant at the central market, which is avoided by selling directly.

The witness does not think that any group of elevator men control the market in Nebraska. He gets bids for grain from Armour & Co. and other large Chicago dealers, though it is possible that they do not compete strongly against one another. But bids are received daily from St. Louis, Kansas City, and often from Galveston, St. Joseph, and other points. These differ frequently by one-fourth or one-half of a cent, and there seems to be no collusion between buyers at the different markets. During the year 1899 little grain has gone from Friend to Chicago, most being sent to Kansas City, where the prices are somewhat better. (465–467.)

Mr. HULBERT, a grain dealer of Fontanelle, Iowa, says that the margin of local grain dealers in handling corn is now about 1 cent or 1½ cents, as compared with 3 cents or 4 cents 7 or 8 years ago. The difference is partly explained by the fact that corn was formerly bought with snow and other impurities and had to be cleaned, and was also usually shelled by the buyer. At present corn is shelled and cleaned to a considerable extent by the farmers. At the same time the witness thinks that the recent practice of the local dealers in selling their purchases directly to large elevator owners and dealers at Chicago, instead of sending it for sale on commission, has been beneficial to the farmers in securing higher prices. The witness has often shipped grain to Chicago and sold it there, but thinks that he can now always get a price a cent or more higher by selling it on the track in Iowa. The witness thinks that probably these large dealers have some advantages in freight rates, which explains the fact that they are able to pay more for grain than, if the full freight rate were paid, could be received at the market price in Chicago. At the same time they have many advantages in handling grain. They have the necessary machinery for cleaning wheat and improving its grade, as well as for handling it generally.

The witness knows nothing about any agreement for fixing the prices between these different purchasers. Bids are usually received from several different purchasers at Chicago, and also from other markets, and the witness does not believe that any agreement among the Chicago buyers would affect the business from the other cities. Corn is largely sold at St. Louis, Peoria, and even Louisville. The witness supposes that buyers at Louisville have in view seaboard inspection and weights, and that they haul corn over lines which give them better rates than Iowa shippers can get themselves.

Mr. Hulbert thinks that the farmers of Iowa have no special grievances against transportation companies, although it is often difficult for those who wish to ship grain directly to get cars promptly. Moreover, the shipper is required to load his car within 48 hours, which is often a difficult thing for a farmer to do. (486–489.)

Mr. FULLER, of Norfolk, Nebr., says that at that town there are two competing grain dealers, although, perhaps, they do not compete very strongly against one another. The feeding of stock furnishes a strong competitive market for grain, especially for corn. The witness does not know of any special complaints on this subject. (445.)

F. Effect on speculative prices.—Mr. GREELEY declares that the hoarding of large stocks of grain in the public elevators of Chicago gives an advantage to the bear speculators, favoring the short sellers at the expense of the buyers and tending to depress the price of grain generally. The warehousemen desire to hold the grain as long as possible in order to earn the carrying charge paid by speculative owners. Consequently, if a condition of the market can be produced which will force a man who has bought grain for future delivery to sell it out ahead for another deferred delivery the warehouseman will gain. The bear speculators or short sellers, with this immense quantity of grain in sight, can count on getting grain to fill their contracts at the last moment, while the buyer is frightened by the immense stock on hand. The bear speculator in the meantime uses all his efforts to depress the markets. The fact that the warehousemen deal and speculate in grain, and that they do not have to pay storage rates, gives them an advantage in forcing men who buy for future delivery to sell out at a lower price.

The existence of this large supply of grain also promotes the bucket-shop business. The bucket-shop proprietors are mostly short sellers, who are enabled to count on fulfilling their contracts if necessary. It has been estimated that there are about 10,000 bucket shops in the United States, and they trade in 30,000,000 bushels of grain per day. The result of this bucket-shop speculation, and of the similar though less extensive abuses under the Board of Trade, is a tendency greatly to depress the price of grain. The witness attributes the lower prices which have prevailed for the last 10 years largely to this influence, and thinks that the panic of 1893 and the political discontent of the Western States during recent years are explainable by the same cause. Often speculation depreciates the value of a new crop long before it exists. The witness thinks that the ultimate remedy for this evil, which has its origin in railroad discriminations in favor of public warehouses, must be Government ownership of railroads. (371–378.)

Mr. Greeley says, further, that so far as public warehousemen are buyers of grain it is to their advantage to depress the price to the farmer, since the insurance and interest on the investment are thus made less. (380.)

The claim that it is to the interest of the elevator owners to keep down the price of wheat is characterized by Mr. COUNSELMAN as ridiculous. The witness says that he does not speculate in grain. He buys it and sells it as soon as possible, either in Chicago or in Eastern markets or in Europe. Very little grain is held in his elevators for any length of time. It is true that a considerable amount of grain is constantly at Chicago, but this is necessary to prevent frequent corners on the market. (386.)

Mr. WEBSTER declares that it is entirely impossible for elevator owners or large grain dealers to manipulate the market, just as it has always proved impossible for any speculator or group of speculators to control prices. If the elevators tried to force up prices the immense amount of grain coming from all parts of the country would make this impossible, while to attempt to force down prices makes the market the target of buyers from all over the world. With the world market for grain supplied from Argentina, Russia, and many other different sources, the natural laws of supply and demand are more inexorable in the grain business than in almost any other. The elevators, therefore, are not responsible for bucket shops or bear raids. Armour & Co. have never been short on the grain market. It has been their policy to prevent depression of prices if possible. (410–413.)

G. Alleged discriminations by elevators as to quality of grain.—Mr. CARTER states that the fact that while the elevators are still used as public storehouses, the larger part of the grain in them belongs to the managers of them, gives a great opportunity for illegitimate profit. Out of 100 cars of grain inspected as of one grade, 8 or 10 cars may vary 1 cent or 5 or 6 cents in value from others. If all were simply put together into one bin the purchaser would get a fair average of the grade. Under the old system many grain dealers bought elevator receipts. To-day a careful man would not accept simply the inspection and receipt, but would want to see a sample of the grain itself. Otherwise he is likely to become compelled to take the very lowest quality that can be brought into the given grade. (582, 583.)

Mr. Greeley also says the public warehousemen mix different qualities of grain or sort them out in different ways. A shipper who buys grain from public warehouses will be furnished with a relatively inferior quality, while the warehouseman can offer for sale the slightly better grades, thus securing practically a monopoly of the selling business in Eastern markets. The owner of grain is supposed to be able to keep it in elevators in a special bin by itself, but as a matter of fact he can not get this privilege, and it seems almost impossible to get even general storage. The courts held some time ago that public warehousemen were not entitled to deal in grain, but the warehousemen secured an act of the State legislature, by corrupt means, as the witness believes, giving them specifically this power. (870–877.)

Mr. SAGER, secretary of the Northern Milling Company, of Chicago, declares that the practice of public warehousemen in buying and owning grain is injurious to the millers. There is a constant temptation for the warehouseman to give the lowest quality of grain which will meet the standard grade to the miller who buys grain on the exchange, while retaining for his own private sales or for the benefit of dealers associated with him the better qualities. The millers have found by experience that the warehousemen make these discriminations, and they now never accept wheat simply on State inspection, but hire private inspectors to see that they do not get the bottom of the grade. Because of these possibilities he thinks that it is improper to permit owners of public elevators to be dealers in wheat and to mix their own grain with that held for storage. The Chicago millers are compelled to buy large quantities of grain from the elevators. The witness has found that it is often impossible to buy grain from Western points and ship it to Chicago in competition with the great elevator owners and grain dealers, and he thinks that this is due largely to railroad discriminations made in favor of such persons. More that three-quarters of the grain used by the Northern Milling Company is bought in Chicago, and the proportion which must be so bought has been rapidly increasing. Even when grain is bought from a commission firm, that firm is often allied closely with some elevator owner. The capacity of the Chicago mills, when running constantly, is about 7,000,000 bushels. (450–452.)

Mr. WEBSTER says that it would be absurd to expect elevator proprietors, who may clean grain or store it simply, to furnish to the public better grain than the inspection department requires to meet the official grades. On the other hand, the witness declares that the most exhaustive investigation has failed to show a single instance in which a Chicago elevator proprietor has mixed or handled grain in his public elevator so as to give an advantage to himself. (411, 413.)

Mr. VANLANDINGHAM says that there are various public grain warehouses at Chicago and other terminal points which are for the most part controlled by the same persons who control the private warehouses. He does not think that the farmers, or even the shippers, are injured by the possible mixing of grain of different grades at these elevators, although it is true that grain once shipped there loses its identity. As a matter of fact, the grain is paid for in the first instance, not simply according to its general grade, but according to its special quality. There are in very large markets professional grain mixers who buy grain of different qualities, being willing to pay more than the average grade price for superior grain. These mixers then combine different grades, possibly sometimes to the injury of the buyer, but scarcely to the injury of anyone else. (200, 201.)

H. Grain inspection.—Mr. CLARK, secretary of the Grainers' National Association, says that the grading of grain has not been reduced to an exact science. Flaxseed inspection has been made very systematic, but the attempt to devise similar methods as to other grains has failed. Inspectors are not always in the same mood, and their judgment differs greatly. The millers frequently grade grain very differently from the official inspection departments, taking into account many characteristics of which the inspectors know nothing, such as the strength of the grain in gluten or in starch. The grading of barley by official inspectors at Chicago has been for years disregarded by the trade, the outward characteristics of barley being especially deceptive as to its value. The witness mentions one instance where a dealer paid 4½ cents more per bushel for a certain grade of oats than the ruling market price for that official grade.

The inspection methods of different cities differ materially. The rules of each market are made chiefly with a view to the general character of the grain coming from the region tributary to that market. Thus St. Louis gets certain qualities of grain which seldom come to Chicago, and vice versa. There is a growing approach toward uniformity in the rules of the different markets, but they are carried out with different degrees of accuracy. Peoria is the only market of importance west of Chicago that has a private inspection system. In most Eastern markets the inspection is not governed by State laws. The witness implies that public inspection is usually more satisfactory than private; but he disapproves the proposed national system of inspection as being impracticable. It has been suggested that national inspectors at Washington and their deputies in different sections of the country should make chemical analysis of any grain submitted to them. The different markets if left to themselves will work out a classification essentially uniform and to the best interests of the grain producers. In order to bring grain to the market each city will wish to make its rules as favorable as that of any other. (431–434.)

Mr. EVANS, a miller of Indianapolis, declares that persons handling grain throughout the entire country are interested in the inspection system at Chicago. He has found from experience that the inspection is often dishonestly rigid as regards grain coming into the city and dishonestly lax as regards that going out. He refers to specific instances in which grain shipped to Chicago has been reduced in grade and grain from Chicago found inferior to the grade fixed. He thinks that State inspection is apt to be irregular in quality, owing to political influences in appointments. The witness thinks, however, that national inspection is impracticable, on the whole. (440.)

Mr. DOUSMAN thinks that the temptations to grade grain unfairly under the existing system of inspection are undoubtedly great. The inspectors in Chicago are fairly well experienced and doubtless have the ability to grade grain rightly if they perform their duties faithfully. (356.)

1. Grain markets and prices (see also pp. 74, 81).—Mr. BOOKWALTER states that since 1895, when there was a shortage in the corn crop and 100,000,000 bushels of wheat was fed to stock, wiping out the immense visible supply, Chicago rather than Liverpool has controlled the price of wheat. It is true that it is often said that low cables from Liverpool put down the price in Chicago and high cables put it up; but Mr. Bookwalter thinks such statements are made chiefly to influence the speculative markets. The foreign cable of to-day is based on our market of yesterday. This is because the Liverpool market of a given date comes earlier; it closes very soon after the Chicago market begins. The influence of the markets of Chicago and Liverpool is mutual, but that of Chicago is the greater. (576, 577.)

Mr. GALLAGHER also thinks that the Chicago market exercises the principal influence upon the price of grain. The foreign markets control, of course, just so far as they are buyers. If there is a good demand in Liverpool, the foreign market is likely to influence our markets for the time being. St. Louis buys much more wheat than Chicago, on account of its large milling interests. (541.)

Mr. BOOKWALTER states that Kansas City is a higher market for grain than any other in the country, simply because it gets so little. The receipts of oats are only 4, 5, or 6 cars a day—merely what is consumed there. The wheat the city received last year was about 30,000,000 bushels from a territory that raised 240,000,000 bushels. Mr. Bookwalter recently made some investigation on the amount of grain shipped from various stations to Kansas City and to other markets. From Inman, a small station on the Rock Island, a shipper sent about 400 cars; 54 came to Kansas City; 227 stopped at a mill on the way to Kansas City. From Table Rock, 272 cars of corn were shipped; only 3 to Kansas City. "These were not shipped by dealers; they were shipped by farmers, who did not know any better." In 90 days preceding Mr. Bookwalter's testimony, 3 cars of corn a day, on the average, had been received at Kansas City from the Burlington system. He thinks the receipts ought to have been 150 cars. (572, 574.) Compare Mr. Webster's statement that Kansas City stands close to Chicago as a grain market (p. 81).

Mr. Bookwalter states that out of 500 cars, three days' receipts at Kansas City, less than 2 per cent was what is known as graded wheat; it ran from "rejected" to "4" and "3." This inferior wheat is sent to Kansas City, because that is the nearest market, and the wheat is not, as a rule, in a condition for long shipment; it is desirable to get it out of the car as soon as possible. Kansas City is the nearest place where it can be put into an elevator, scoured, dried, and stored. (572.)

Mr. GALLAGHER says that whenever the world has an overproduction it affects the price of wheat disastrously for the time being, but that overproduction can not have a depressing influence for any great length of time. (543, 544.)

VII. RAILWAY POOLS, ASSOCIATIONS, AND AGREEMENTS.

A. Forms and methods of pools.—(See also *Effect on discriminations*, p. 97.) 1. *Enforcement*.—Mr. BLANCHARD, late commissioner of the Joint Traffic Association, suggests the following as a form which, without legal technicalities, indicates the significance of pooling agreements: "The following railroads (naming them) operating from and through ——, to and through ——, hereby agree that to observe and give due effect to the tariffs from time to time legally issued, they will, from —— for a period of —— years from said date, divide their tonnage therefrom and thereto and the earnings produced thereby at the published rates substantially in the proportions in which the shippers have delivered it to them heretofore. The proportions in which the said business shall be carried by the several parties hereto shall be as follows: (Specifying the percentage due to each.) If any company carries more than its said proportion, it shall in the next month transfer such excess of tonnage, computed at the gross rates shown by said established tariffs, to the company or companies in deficit, or, failing to so transfer the tonnage, it shall pay money in an equal or agreed amount within 30 days thereafter." (677.)

Mr. Blanchard also says that pooling agreements do not themselves fix rates, but that rates may change frequently on all or a part of the roads during the agreement. (643, 665.)

Mr. Blanchard points out further that the pools which formerly existed affected only a comparatively limited traffic. Thus the Eastern pools related only to freight from Chicago, Peoria, Louisville, Cincinnati, Indianapolis, St. Louis, to Eastern points. The traffic from Buffalo and Albany, Washington, and other points—Rochester and Boston, for example—was outside the pool, and the same was true of traffic from Cleveland, Detroit, Toledo, Columbus, and other cities. (681, 682.)

Mr. RIPLEY, president of the Atchison, Topeka and Santa Fe Railroad, thinks that if pools are formed they should be formed for terms as long as 5 years. The longer they are the more stable they are likely to be. An agreement for 1 year has an element of temporariness which is unsettling. Mr. BLANCHARD and Mr. WOFFINDIN express the same opinion. (565, 566, 695.)

2. *Outside lines.*—Mr. BLANCHARD says that in the case of the two leading pools which existed before the interstate-commerce act, that between the Eastern lines and that between those west of Chicago, there were a considerable number of lines outside. No threats were made against outside companies who refused to do joint business with them. Nevertheless, the actions of these outside roads finally demoralized business. It appears that the outside roads were largely those connecting points not actually reached by the pooled roads, but nevertheless competing with them as to certain through traffic. In case pools should be permitted in the future, Mr. Blanchard thinks that the only means of influencing outside roads to enter the pool or maintain rates would be by refusing to receive their traffic on the same conditions existing between the concurring companies, or by collectively cutting rates against the outside lines. (681, 682.)

Mr. RIPLEY, president of the Atchison, Topeka and Santa Fe Railroad, would not object to the forcing of all the roads in a competitive district into a pool, but he thinks there are some reasons against it, and he does not think it necessary. If the law permitted the roads which desire united action to combine against the one which would not unite, they could fight it jointly and by legal means, and could effectually regulate it. The trouble now is that when one party "thinks that he can flock by himself," the law forbids the rest to combine against him. A pool among 4 or 5 competing lines would have a very steadying effect even if 1 line remained out, especially if deviations from public rates were punished by fines, and the law were well enforced. (595, 597.)

B. *Advocates of pooling.*—1. *General authorities.*—Messrs. KNAPP, PROUTY, and CLEMENTS, of the Interstate Commerce Commission, agree in favoring pooling on the part of the railways, but only in case much more effective control than at present over rates generally, and especially over pooling contracts, be given to the commission or some other authority. Mr. CLEMENTS especially fears the effect of pooling in raising rates generally. (138, 150, 157.)

Mr. NEWCOMB, of the division of statistics, Department of Agriculture, says that competition in railway rates tends to cause discriminations, and in many instances results in rates below the cost of service. The only remedies are Government ownership or pooling arrangements between railways under Government supervision. Pools are of two kinds, those which simply divide tonnage, and those which divide receipts, letting tonnage take care of itself, such division of profits being guaranteed by a deposit. When such pools were formerly made, before they were prohibited by the interstate-commerce act, they usually broke up soon, because they could not be enforced in the courts. It is now advocated that pools be legalized by an amendment of the interstate-commerce act so that they can be enforced by the ordinary procedure of securing damages for violation of contract. The majority of the railways favor this amendment, as well as a majority of the Interstate Commerce Commission, and many others. The opposition comes from a small part of the people who are ignorant concerning the effect of competition, from certain railway officers who object to the increased power which it is proposed to give to the Interstate Commerce Commission in connection with the change, and from trusts and combinations of shippers which are now able to dictate rates to their own advantage. The witness does not believe that pools would result in higher charges, except where rates are now unjustly low. The rates can never be much increased without shutting out a large amount of traffic which is on the margin of profitable shipment. Such pools should be, however, subject to the approval of the Interstate Commerce Commission, a thing which the railways themselves desire, and should be entirely public. In England pools have been found necessary; in France traffic is divided territorially, and in Belgium even the State-owned roads have been compelled to pool with private roads. (96–98, 103.)

Professor JOHNSON favors trying the practice of allowing the railways to make pools. The chief objection now raised comes from strong railways which are already getting satisfactory rates. Exorbitant rates are not likely to result, especially if proper Government supervision be maintained. (62.)

Mr. REAGAN thinks that in the absence of complete control over railway rates by the Interstate Commerce Commission, the next best method is to permit railways to make pooling contracts, subject to the approval of the commission, with an enforceable penalty for violation. This would go far toward preventing rate-cutting and discriminations. (345.)

2. *Representatives of railways.*—Mr. BLANCHARD believes that the only way to secure uniformity and stability of transportation charges is by association among the railways, by which it shall be made to their interest to secure that result. Every association of railways in the past has had for its primary object the same ends as those sought by the interstate-commerce act. Association and organization among railways is necessary in the same way that association and organization are necessary in any great business or interest having common purposes. Thus, the nation must have its Congress representing the separate States; the President must have his Cabinet bringing together the different Departments. The rates of transportation must be predetermined in order to be announced in accordance with the law. (640, 641, 683.)

According to Mr. Blanchard, the interests of railway investors and employees especially demand protection by permission to secure reasonable profits through a pooling system. The Eastern trunk lines reported in 1894 that their shareholders numbered 99,826; in proportion to mileage the total number of shareholders of all railways would be over 950,000, besides bondholders. There are nearly 1,000,000 railway employees. Since each adult may be supposed to represent five persons, the total number thus directly affected by railway earnings would be fully 10,000,000, aside from those interested in manufacturing railroad supplies. American railway wages are higher than those abroad, and no measure should be taken to force them down. (642.)

Mr. WOFFINDIN, chairman of the Chicago East-bound Freight Committee, favors legalized pooling, and supposes that if pools were legalized they would be under some governmental supervision. He would have pools formed for at least 5 years. The difficulties of creating pools are such that he does not think it would be practicable to readjust the basis of them annually. He thinks that a pool could be so formed that it would do away with discriminations and rebates. To make it operative, penalties for violation of the agreement would have to be provided. He does not wish to express an opinion upon the question whether these penalties should be fines or imprisonment. Fines would be more effective if they were severe enough and were enforced. The enforcement of any penalty seems to be, in the witness's opinion, a matter of some difficulty. (565, 566.)

Mr. CALLAWAY, president of the New York Central, advocates legalizing pooling, so that contracts shall be enforceable at law. Pooling has in the past been especially advantageous in enabling railways to resist the unjust demands of large shippers, especially of private car owners. Discriminations would be lessened and freight rates would not be increased, because of water competition and world-wide competition in regard to commodities. The difficulty with pooling hitherto has been that the various lines were not satisfied with their percentages of business, and there was no way of enforcing agreements and preventing cutting. Mr. Callaway would be willing to give the Interstate Commerce Commission supervisory veto power over pooling contracts. A further advantage of pooling would be the reduction of expenses of various kinds; for example, saving in the maintenance of city offices. Railways which are opposed to pooling are mostly such as connect with the various competing roads, so that they are practically in the position of large shippers. (235–238.)

Mr. INGALLS, president of the Chesapeake and Ohio, believes that the only remedy for excessive competition is to be found in pooling. Unrestrained competition injures railway, shipper, and general public. It is almost sure to result in bankruptcies and to increase speculation in railway securities. Discriminations, also, are due to excessive competition. Agreements between railways, including more than mere pools of traffic or of earnings, should be made legal and enforceable at law. The witness does not think there would be any danger of undue increase of rates if such agreements were permitted, particularly on account of competition of products. (286, 296–300.)

In the opinion of Mr. SPENCER, of the Southern Railway, the legalization of pooling contracts would diminish discriminations, though it would not necessarily do away with them. If pooling were allowed, some authority would have to be provided to prevent unreasonable rates under the pool. The witness does not think rates would for the most part be materially affected, although in the trunk-line territory some exceedingly low rates might be raised. (280.)

Mr. COWEN, president of the Baltimore and Ohio, thinks that if laws and court decisions had not interfered the railways, under the stress of necessity, would by this time have evolved a system of traffic associations and of pooling which would substantially have prevented discriminations. It was not the thought of the framers of the Sherman antitrust act that it should apply to railways as the courts have interpreted it. The witness favors granting permission to the railways to agree as to rates, including division of traffic, if necessary. He would be willing to have the Interstate Commerce Commission given the power to set aside such agreements without appeal if contrary to the public welfare.

Even if such agreements were permitted, true competition would not be destroyed. Properly there can be no such thing as different rates on different railroads for the same traffic; but with uniform rates competition occurs in furnishing facilities, handling traffic, and presenting inducements to the public. (314, 315.)

Mr. BIRD, general traffic manager of the Chicago, Milwaukee and St. Paul Railway, is very much in favor of pooling. The only persons who could object, provided the Interstate Commerce Commission had proper power to regulate pools, would be those who hope to get discriminating rates. The requirement of the interstate-commerce act that rates shall be reasonable is defeated by the prohibition of agreements concerning rates. Fluctuating rates can not be of advantage to anyone. (474.)

Mr. MORTON, vice-president of the Atchison, Topeka and Santa Fe Railway, declares that rate wars are always injurious to the general public, to the employees, and to the carrier. Stability in freight rates is as essential as in import duties. Uniformity of freights as between individuals is especially important to all classes. The witness accordingly advocates the legalization of pooling. This would tend greatly to prevent unjust discriminations between shippers and between places, to create stable rates, check disastrous competition, prevent the reduction of wages, and afford protection to the railroad investors. It is not in restraint of trade in the sense that ordinary combinations would be, since the Government undertakes to regulate railway charges. Unless pooling is permitted concentration of ownership will increase. Even with greater concentration pooling would still be advantageous. If a certain group of railways should be combined there is yet always a tendency toward competition between different markets. (491, 495, 499.)

Mr. FISH, of the Illinois Central, says that his own railway, since fully 85 per cent of its traffic is local, is not especially interested in pooling. It has not sought for competitive business, since there is not much profit in it. Nevertheless, the witness thinks pooling would be advantageous to many railways, although it will not be a panacea or prevent rate cutting and discriminations. (337.)

3. *Representatives of shippers.*—Most representatives of shippers favor pooling only on condition that effective public control be exercised. See Paragraph F.

Mr. KELLEY, freight commissioner of the Trades League of Philadelphia, thinks that unless pooling among railways is allowed they will be driven more and more into consolidated systems. The weaker railroads will be unable to compete and will be controlled by the stronger. All the railroads east of the Mississippi are likely in a few years to come into the hands of a very few men, who can fix rates to suit themselves. (190, 191.)

Mr. BACON, of the Milwaukee Board of Trade, favors permitting the railways to pool their earnings or traffic. This would be the most effective remedy for rate cutting and discriminations between persons and places.

The witness read from a letter of the secretary of the Chamber of Commerce of Milwaukee, declaring that that body has repeatedly advocated pooling. He also submitted a letter from Mr. Robert Eliot, a member of the Milwaukee Board of Trade, upholding the views just presented. (420, 426.)

Mr. COUNSELMAN, a grain dealer of Chicago, thinks that the only remedy for railroad discriminations and rate cutting is pooling. Even where some railroads are willing and able to do a satisfactory business at fair rates another road with inferior equipment and facilities will come in and try to get business by lower rates. It is true that railroads might try to increase their percentage under a pool by rate cutting, but in general this attempt would be made by the weaker roads, and the strong roads, which felt satisfied, would be likely quietly to buy control of them. The witness would favor giving the Interstate Commerce Commission absolute authority to limit the maximum rates to be charged under pools. Shippers should be allowed the privilege of sending freight over any line they preferred; the railroads would not care if this were permitted. (390, 391.)

4. *Public opinion concerning pooling.*—Mr. BLANCHARD quotes from a number of important authorities indorsing pooling. He says that practically all of the witnesses who appeared before the Cullom committee in 1886 favored pooling, although some desired certain restrictions. That committee reported in its bill a provision that the Interstate Commerce Commission should inquire further as to the wisdom of pooling and report to Congress. Judge Reagan, who was then chairman of House Committee on Commerce, was the most influential in amending the bill so as to prohibit pooling, and he has since changed his opinion and advocates permitting railroads to enter into traffic arrangements. The Interstate Commerce Commission has several times advocated pooling. Judge Cooley, its first chairman, has repeatedly defended the system. Very large numbers of commercial organizations and trade bodies have at different times declared in its favor, including the National Board of Trade. The national convention of State railway commissioners in 1894 and 1896 took a similar position. The minority of the Supreme Court of the United States in the case of the Trans-Missouri Freight Association declared that agreements as to reasonable rates conformed exactly to the purpose of the antitrust act. (641, 642, 648, 649.)

Mr. RIPLEY, president of the Atchison, Topeka and Santa Fe Railroad Company, thinks that the sentiment of nearly all the members of the mercantile community that have had the largest dealings with railroad companies is in favor of pooling. The chairman and the majority of the Interstate Commerce Commission, and, Mr. Ripley thinks, a majority of the State commissioners and a majority of the shippers of the country, are in favor of it. For every opinion against it, ten can be produced in favor of it, from merchants and shippers, State and interstate commissioners, students of political economy, and almost all who have dispassionately studied the transportation problem. (593.)

Mr. BOOKWALTER does not think the views of business men in his section of the country are well defined upon legalized pooling. (576.)

C. *Opponents of pooling.*—Mr. STONE, secretary of the Chicago Board of Trade, objects to railway pools, because "they are in restraint of trade, they prevent competition, they are monopolistic in purpose and effect, they are odious in law, they are subversive of the very interest which railways were created to conserve, viz, the general welfare, in so far as that welfare relates to the functions and obligations of a common carrier." The pools which formerly existed, "although ostensibly for the equalization of traffic compensation, for the encouragement of feeble lines, and opposed to any unfair and unjust proportion of remuneration received by great and controlling trunk lines, degenerated into a reckless and unscrupulous abandonment of the terms of such agreement, creating confusion, distrust, an unsettling of freight rates, antagonism, and a general warfare, resulting in disaster to many of the parties to the pools, as well as to the business interests generally." Mr. Stone does not believe, in view of the enormous extent of the business and the vast number of rates to be fixed, that it is practicable to place pooling under the control of the Interstate Commerce Commission in any sense that would protect the vast business interests of the country. (533–535.)

Mr. HYLAND, traffic manager of the freight bureau of the Chicago Board of Trade, believes that a large majority of the members of that board and of the general public oppose legalization of railroad pooling as contrary to public policy and not calculated to secure the results claimed for it. In would, in fact, result in minimum service at maximum cost. Railroads would still continue to make special concessions in rates in order to establish their claim to an increased allotment in the pool, as has been especially demonstrated by the work of the Southwestern Railway Association. The witness thinks that the so-called strong lines, more than the weak ones, lead in violating traffic agreements.

On the other hand, Mr. Hyland would favor granting permission to railways to make agreements concerning rates, giving the Interstate Commerce Commission full power to regulate and control the rates. (351–353.)

Mr. VANLANDINGHAM, commissioner of the St. Louis Traffic Bureau, does not think that pooling is desirable either from the standpoint of the carriers or of the general public. It would not remove the incentive to reduce rates or to make discriminations. Mr. Vanlandingham, however, favors agreements as to rates.

The witness thinks that consolidation of railways is more advantageous than legalized pooling. He does not so much oppose pools themselves as the proposition to make the pooling contracts enforceable at law. (214, 216.)

Mr. STICKNEY, president of the Chicago Great Western Railway, does not think that pooling would realize the expectations of its advocates. If a pool should be formed on the lines between Chicago and St. Paul for the purpose of maintaining rates, St. Paul would be injured, unless pools were also formed on the roads from Chicago to Kansas City and other points. When it was possible to repudiate a pooling contract if it proved unfair, railroads were willing to pool; but if the contract is made binding, affecting, as it does, millions of dollars monthly, no railroad would ever make such a contract. (463.)

Mr. CARTER, a commission merchant, is unalterably opposed to pooling. He thinks railroads should be no more exempt from competition than other lines of business. Pooling would be less objectionable coupled with adequate authority in the Interstate Commerce Commission to regulate rates and to sanction, or refuse to sanction, any pooling contract; but we have not reached such a point in the supervision of railroad affairs that we can consider it from that standpoint. (585.)

See also under paragraph F.

D. Railway competition—should it exist?—1. *Negative.*—Mr. KNAPP, chairman of the Interstate Commerce Commission, believes that it is unwise to attempt to foster competition among railways or to treat them as purely private businesses are treated. In ordinary business, where property and things, as distinguished from public services, are dealt in, there should be the greatest freedom of contract, and no attempt to impose uniform prices. In fact, competition means discrimination; that is, difference in prices at different times and places and between different individuals. Thus, with regard to trusts and combinations, it will probably not be possible to control them by means of fixing prices. If prices were fixed it would be impossible to compel producers to sell any more than to compel consumers to buy. On the other hand, in railroad service competition is possible as regards only a small portion of the entire territory and population of the country. To most people railroad service must be monopolistic. It is, moreover, essentially public service. There can, accordingly, be no gain from freedom of contract or from lack of uniformity in charges, but, on the other hand, industrial freedom can not be secured without equality in charges. On account of the public nature of railways, the people can interfere directly, as they are not justified in doing in regard to ordinary business. Even such regulation as is now applied to railways would be out of the question as regards truly competitive business.

It may be true, Mr. Knapp admits, that competition among railways, in its broadest sense, has reduced rates over the entire country, but at the same time it has caused many discriminations, and the same advantages can be better secured by public regulation. The antitrust laws and the prohibition of pooling have not been of any benefit whatever to producer or consumer; but have been a chief cause of discriminations. (138.)

Mr. NEWCOMB declares that discriminations in railway rates spring almost always out of excessive competition, and can be prevented only by allowing pooling or some other form of combination between railways. Competition in other lines of business results in uniform prices, but in the case of railways the patronage of large shippers is so important that special rates will be made to secure it, often at less than the cost of service. The interstate-commerce act has failed to check such discriminations, and although there is at present a cessation of them for the most part, it can not be permanent so long as competition is compelled by law. The antipooling clause has tended to increase discriminations, and no government supervision can prevent them. (95–97.)

Professor SELIGMAN, of Columbia University, says that both competition and monopoly have their good sides and their bad sides. Through the force of competition new efforts are continuously made and new machines are introduced, by which cost of production is lowered. All progress, which depends directly upon the lower cost of production, depends indirectly upon the competition between producers. This competition works through the effort of every buyer to get a little lower price than his neighbor gets. Competitive enterprise means preferring one customer to another, giving advantages to the large buyer over the small. When competition is applied to a public or quasi-public institution, like the railway, this feature of competition is inconsistent with the highest social utility. Everybody ought to be put on the same level. Competition should continue in respect to the constant effort to obtain the best appliances and to give the best service; but there ought not to be any competition as to rates. It is out of competition in rates that discriminations, both personal and local, come.

The good side of monopoly is that it may prevent the difference in the treatment of individuals which is due to competition. Of course, there may be personal discriminations due to the whim of the monopolies, and the experience of California, where there is practically no competition in the railroad business, shows that there may be just as serious evils under the monopoly system as under the competitive system. In France also, where each railway has a monopoly of its own field, the evils of noneffective management, lack of facilities, etc., are prominent. The question is whether it is not possible to devise some scheme which shall reduce the evils of both systems to a minimum and increase the advantages of both systems, competition and monopoly.

The witness believes that pools and traffic associations are the best system thus far devised for getting these advantages. Pooling need not bring any cessation of competition as regards facilities. Each railway in past pools has tried to increase its efficiency and its traffic in order to pave the way for an increase of its percentage when the pool should be renewed. But a well-devised pool avoids the evils of competition, cut rates, personal discrimination, and, to a certain extent, illegitimate and indefensible local discrimination. It would not do to allow the railways to do what they choose with their pools. It is necessary to regulate and restrict them. The railways must be regarded, not as a private business, but as a trust for the public.

Wherever any vestige of competition among railroads is left, in all countries of the world, there are pools and traffic associations. Even where the government runs the railways it forms pools and traffic associations with privately owned railways. Such facts show that there is some underlying cause which makes these things inevitable. (615-617.)

Mr. BLANCHARD points out that competition as applied to railways is essentially different from that in ordinary commercial transactions. The contests between buyers and sellers in ordinary cases are carried on under fair conditions. Differences in the conditions and facilities of the sellers, in the outlook of the market, in the credit of buyers, etc., justify different charges for the same goods. But when railways compete they are not governed by uniform rules applying openly and impartially to all. One company can reduce its rates from various motives, and thereby force all other companies connecting the same points to meet the rate. There can not be different rates for the same haul. Moreover, the cutting of rates between two points will affect the rates between altogether different points which compete for certain classes of traffic. Thus, to reduce the through rates from St. Louis to Boston would affect the rates from Chicago to every seaboard city. Moreover, under the law concerning long and short hauls a cut in competitive rates to terminal points affects also the rates to numberless intermediate points which can not legally exceed the through rate. When competitors in ordinary lines of ·business lose money by unduly low prices they fail and go out of business. Insolvent railways are required to continue in business and are often the most dangerous competitors. (635-637, 653.)

Mr. Blanchard declares further that competition between railways induces secret rates and discriminations, so that it can not be considered fair. By such discriminations the one railway is injured by losing its profit and its competitor by losing its business, while the merchant or producer competing with the favored shipper may be ruined. If all of the railways should give one grain shipper an advantage of a cent per 100 pounds, he might ultimately control the grain markets of the nation, and the same tendency exists to a less degree wherever a discrimination is granted. Some shippers become dealers in rebated railway earnings and make their profit chiefly from this source. In fact, those who chiefly oppose pooling are shippers and railways which profit by disobeying the law requiring uniform rates. (635, 636, 655.)

Many prominent authorities, Mr. Blanchard declares, have expressed themselves clearly as to the impossibility or undesirability of railway competition. Thus Interstate Commerce Commissioner Schoonmaker has stated that it is a "now fully demonstrated fallacy that unrestricted competition among railways is a public benfit." Judge Cooley and Mr. Knapp of the commission have expressed similar opinions. In 1882 a joint report by Messrs. Thurman, Washburn, and Cooley declared that "this is not what in other business is known and designated as com. petition." The Cullom committee in 1886 attributed personal discriminations largely to competition. The convention of State railway commissioners in 1899 declared that the policy of unrestricted competition has been steadily working out its own destruction. The great English commission on railways in 1882 declared that reliance on competition to regulate railway rates was a failure. (637, 638.)

Mr. Blanchard says further that competition in railway rates is as impracticable and undesirable as competition between different officers in the Government service. Uniform rates to all persons and stable rates are as important in railway service as in taxation and postal charges. The Government assures to all persons the impartial and unabated collection of its charges. The witness presented statistics of the amount of Government bonds and interest charges as compared with those of railways to indicate the relatively greater importance of just railway charges than of just Government charges.

Mr. Blanchard declares that if the Government itself owned the railways it would have to apply the same rules as to uniform charges which apply in the custom-houses and the post-offices, and no one would think of declaring that this system was in restraint of trade or of legitimate competition. So, too, if the Government should operate a single railway, such as the Union Pacific, it would find that it could fix its rates only after consultation with other companies performing similar service, as has already been shown by the experience of government railways in Europe. (638–640.)

Mr. RIPLEY says that when competition in freight rates has had full sway it has unsettled values, disarranged the plans of merchants, and wrought general destruction, and the tendency of it is to concentrate business in a few hands and to drive out the small trader. (593, 594.)

Mr. GALLAGHER is informed that rate wars have frequently been started for the purpose of lowering the price of stocks after inside speculators have made heavy sales. (542.)

Mr. TUCKER says that railroading is simply a commercial transaction; it is selling transportation. Railroads, however, unlike other commercial enterprises, are obliged to sell at a common price, and he does not consider that transportation is a thing to be sold or bartered at varying prices as commodities are. It is the nation's business to see that discriminations in the price of transportation cease. (560, 561.)

Mr. SARGENT, grand master of the Brotherhood of Locomotive Firemen, says that rate wars are injurious to all parties concerned. The moment a company begins carrying goods and passengers at less than cost it must discriminate against other persons or places, or must make unwarranted economies at the expense of the condition of the road or of the employees. Rates have often been put in force which anyone could tell at a glance to be far below the cost. If railway officers can not prevent such disastrous competition, the Government should step in and fix the rates. (69.)

Mr. O'ROURKE, switchman, of Chicago, believes that the interest of railroad workers demands profitable rates for the railroad companies. Whatever strengthens the earning powers of the company will be beneficial to the man who works for it. The most prosperous corporation is the most agreeable one and the most profitable one to work for. Excessive competition and rate wars, resulting in the performance of service by the companies at a loss, must result in diminution of the earnings of the workmen. (526.)

2. *Affirmative.*—Mr. STICKNEY, president of the Chicago Great Western Railway Company, criticises the position of Mr. Knapp as to the desirability of uniformity in railway rates. The sale of transportation is like the sale of other commodities. A manufacturer may put out a catalogue of goods with certain prices, but the real prices will be different unless customers are found at the published prices. We may want uniform charges on railways, but we can not get them, any more than it can be made possible for the poor man to buy ordinary commodities as cheaply as the rich. If a railroad can not sell its transportation at one price it should be allowed to lower the price immediately without any publication of notice. (460. See also p. 92, above.)

Mr. STONE believes that in railroad business, as well as in other kinds of business, competition is the best regulator of prices and the best incentive to progress. It is competition, not the will of railroads, which has reduced our transportation rates and given us the facilities for transportation of persons and property which Mr. Stone believes to be better than those of any other country. Competition has been of benefit to those railroads which have been most subject to it. He instances the great trunk lines which have had to compete with the cheap transportation of the Great Lakes and the Erie Canal. The railroads had to reduce their rates, but the volume of business increased so largely as to make them the most prosperous lines of railway in the country. Mr. Stone would not, however, have the Government reduce the rates, in the expectation that such a reduction would have the same favorable effect. He thinks that competition will fix rates better than the Government can. He apparently prefers the introduction of competition by the building of parallel lines of roads to Government regulation, which might be intended to have a similar effect upon rates. (533, 536, 537.)

E. **Effects of pooling.**—The opinions of various witnesses as to the effects of pooling have already been stated in connection with their general arguments for or against the practice, paragraphs B and C. See also *Consolidation of railways,* p. 37; *Discriminations between individuals,* p. 43.

1. *Rates and competition.*—Mr. BLANCHARD holds that railway pooling would not merely be beneficial to the railways, but also to shippers and the general public. The benefit to railroads may be measured by the evils of unrestricted competition already mentioned. If pools were permitted for reasonably long terms bad methods would be forgotten, and the railways would abolish needless officers and save many expenses growing out of excessive competition. (683.)

The effect upon rates could not be to make them unreasonable. For one thing, pooling agreements do not specify rates, as is frequently supposed. They provide a division of tonnage or earnings for a fixed period of time, whereas conditions of various sorts may cause fluctuations in the rates during the agreement. More over *some* standard of rates must be reasonable. If the rates charged by railways in pools are thus reasonable, it is entirely impossible to show how the public interest is affected by any division of the proceeds among the railways. It is only when pools are used to sustain excessive rates that they are objectionable, and then the remedy lies in the correction of the rates and not the prohibition of pooling.

In Mr. Blanchard's opinion, however, competition would still be a sufficient preventive of excessive rates under pools. There would still be a fair competition between the pooled railways themselves, in the way of furnishing improved facilities or otherwise attracting traffic. The most important competition, however, would be that between railways in different sections, created by the laws of trade and the endeavor to reach common markets. The competition of water carriers has been an effective element in the past, and would continue to be. The competing water routes or railways need not be close at hand. A route from Chicago through Canada, or from Cincinnati to Newport News, fixes rates from Pittsburg to New York. (688.)

Mr. Blanchard criticises especially the arguments of Mr. Prouty on this subject in an article in the Forum. Mr. Prouty speaks of the monopolies which would arise if the six railroads connecting Chicago and Kansas City should combine. Mr. Blanchard replies that river traffic between Kansas City and St. Louis, traffic by way of rail and water to the Gulf, traffic between Omaha, Sioux City, and St. Paul, and Chicago, and still other traffic, would compete with that over the pooled railways and would prevent unjust charges. Pooling would not give the carrier absolute power over rates. Mr. Prouty himself has spoken of water competition as a potential factor, and of reduction in rates between Chicago and New York forcing down rates at other points. Mr. Prouty's statement that it is reasonably certain that railway lines terminating at Galveston would pool with lines terminating at Boston is unwarranted; such a pool is highly improbable and without precedent. Anything like a universal pool is out of the question. (666.)

The pools which existed before 1887 had none of the disastrous effects which are now held up as likely to result from pooling. They did not stop the construction of new lines nor destroy competition. Although there were no water routes from Pittsburg and other interior points to the coast, those points were given the advantage of the same rates to New York as Buffalo, which had canal competition. The railways sought to build up a large local and through traffic at low rates. The trunk line association reduced tariff rates from 71 cents in 1877, when first organized, to 50 cents in 1886, and there is no instance of rates having been advanced unless to restore unjustifiable rate-war reductions. (643–647, 653–656.)

The witness points out further that a combination among railways is not similar in character to an industrial trust. Railway rates and fares must be publicly announced, must be actually or tacitly approved by the Government, and are subject to a much greater degree of competition, in the way of water routes, foreign markets, etc., than trusts are subject to. Railways must make public reports. Railways never tend to restrict trade, but always to enlarge it. No railway is ever closed by a pool, or driven out of business by competition, whereas trusts may close part of their own plants or force competitors to close theirs. In every way the situation and conditions are different.

Our experience with telegraphs, Mr. Blanchard declares, shows the advantage of combination. Formerly there were disastrous contests in rates, private discriminations, and other evils. The Western Union Company after its consolidation introduced economies, increased facilities, reduced charges, and especially made its rates uniform to all persons. (645–647.)

Mr. RIPLEY says that no pool can change the general laws of competition. There is no possible danger of an extortionate rate; there is no such thing in this country, and it is impossible. (593, 595.)

Referring to the statement of Mr. Stone (p. 532), that the Southwestern Traffic Association was a "vampire, which for a decade sucked the lifeblood of the commerce of the Missouri Valley," Mr. Ripley points out that during the decade referred to, say from 1877 to 1887, the population of Kansas City increased from 58,000 to 156,000, and that of Omaha from 25,000 to 110,000, and that the whole Missouri Valley was in a state of great prosperity. It is untrue that rates were advanced under this pool. Advances may have been made at times on certain commodities, but far more rates were reduced, and the general average for the 10 years would show a steady reduction. It is not claimed that the agreement worked perfectly or that no discriminations existed, but discriminations were far less common and less disastrous than those which have existed since the passage of the interstate-commerce law. When at intervals the pool was temporarily broken and competition had full sway, the result was unsettling of values, disarranging of the plans of merchants, and general destruction. (593.)

2. *Effect on discriminations.*—Mr. BLANCHARD insists that pooling is the only effective remedy against discriminations. It must be made to their interest not to discriminate or to allow discriminations. Those directly in contact with railway affairs must remedy the evil. Only the possibility of agreeing for a considerable length of time will make possible the abandonment of existing methods and the establishment of effective instrumentalities for checking discriminations. The witness denies that there would be a considerable temptation for one railway to increase its share of business by discriminations. Each railway would have to account for all traffic at the tariff rates, and if it secured an excess of traffic by rebates, it would lose not only by having to pay the rebates, but by having to account for its excess tonnage. Under pools there would be more uniform and rigid inspection of shipments, tending to check the increasing practice of misdescription of goods on the part of the shippers which results in discriminating advantages. Intermediate towns would be benefited by pooling, since the discriminations which are now made chiefly in favor of terminal points and shippers at those points would be done away with. (644, 675, 676, 683.)

Mr. RIPLEY, president of the Atchison, Topeka and Santa Fe Railroad Company, says that pooling is not a cure-all, but is the best known remedy for discriminations between individuals and localities. Mr. Ripley quotes an Interstate Commerce Commissioner as saying that the prohibition of pooling in the interstate-commerce act defeats the whole purpose of the law; that the law prescribes uniform rates and forbids the only known plan by which rates can be kept uniform. Mr. Ripley asserts that discrimination can never be prevented by law; it can be prevented only by making it the interest of the railroads to maintain equal rates. This can be done only by allowing the formation of pools.

Mr. Ripley thinks that the prohibition of pooling by the interstate-commerce law has done more to concentrate business in a few hands and drive out the small trader than could have been accomplished in a century of the old methods. (594, 596.)

Mr. TUCKER, of the Central Freight Association, is inclined to think that the legalized pool, under proper conditions, is the greatest incentive to stability and maintenance of reasonable rates. He thinks that pooling would do away with discrimination, and that it would also remove the feeling which shippers sometimes have that they are discriminated against, when they really are not. (558.)

Mr. MUSSELMAN thinks that pooling should be legalized under the supervision and direction of the Interstate Commerce Commission. There would not then be any inducement to cut rates. The railroads could carry freight at a lower rate, because they would not be carrying a large amount of freight at less than cost, suffering a loss which must be made up on the rest of the freight. The roads say that they do not cut rates east of Chicago, but they do cut the rates from Chicago and from the Mississippi River points to the seaboard, and the trunk lines carry this cut-rate freight across the Middle States and accept their proportion of the rate. The shippers in Michigan, Ohio, and Indiana must necessarily pay higher rates to make up for the unjustly low rates which the more distant shippers get. (557.)

Mr. VANLANDINGHAM, however, thinks pooling would not check discriminations or rate wars. A company which by chance has been allotted more than its proportion of traffic will cut rates to keep its proportion up. Since changes in allotments are made from time to time, each road will be tempted to cut rates in order to increase its volume of business so that it will receive a greater proportion the next time—a practice which has been the means of breaking up all previous pools. The large shipper would still be able to dictate to the railroads and to secure discriminations by offering to the railroads as an organization large shipments at times when they were especially desired. Since the pools would not affect local business, people living at small stations would clearly not be benefited. Mr. Vanlandingham believes that it would be possible to check rate cutting and discriminations legally without pooling agreements. Even weak as the interstate-commerce law is, he thinks that 85 per cent of the rate cutting which existed during 1898 was wiped out during 1899, largely through the influence of the law, and if the law be properly amended it can be made much more effective. (214, 216.)

Mr. HYLAND presents practically the same argument. (351.)

Mr. STONE thinks that pools are based on the amount of traffic which each road has previously carried. It is not necessary, however, that this be made the basis, and it is probably modified by other considerations. If this basis were followed strictly the force of competition and the consequent tendency to discrimination would hardly be lessened. Each road would still desire to increase its business, with a view to the next traffic division. (535, 539.)

Mr. RIPLEY, president of the Atchison, Topeka and Santa Fe Railroad Company, on the other hand, states that no pool was ever formed on the basis of the proportion of the business done by each railroad the previous year. Such an arrangement would give the same incentive to make concessions that now exists. When there were pools, some of the railroad people sometimes thought that by increasing their tonnage one year through illegitimate methods, they could secure a larger percentage in the pool the next; but they very seldom succeeded. Nobody would be willing to recognize the business done by illegitimate methods as the basis of division. The proportion was sometimes settled by mutual agreement, but usually there was a provision for leaving it to an arbitrator in case of failure to agree. (596.)

3. *Selection of routes.*—Mr. VANLANDINGHAM thinks that the shippers would, if the pool involved division of traffic and not merely of earnings, be deprived of their right to ship freight over any line they saw fit. Shippers often have good reason for selecting particular lines. (214.)

Mr. BLANCHARD holds that under pools shippers could still continue to choose their own routes. Only the traffic of consenting shippers would be transferred. If smaller shippers consented to such a transfer for the sake of preventing discriminating rates, this would serve as an argument in favor of pooling. As a matter of fact, pools provide for dividing competitive traffic substantially in the proportion of the previous tonnage of the roads, so that little diversion of tonnage or revenue is necessary. In the last year of the eastward pools from Chicago and other cities the tonnage actually changed from one route to another was only 2.2 per cent of the total, and the transfer of earnings on pooled freight only about 2½ per cent. (644, 645.)

Mr. CALLAWAY also thinks shippers could choose their own routes, the railways dividing earnings instead of tonnage when necessary. (236.)

F. Control of pooling by Interstate Commerce Commission.—Many witnesses, including representatives of the railways, think that considerable control over the formation of pools, and over rates among them, should be given to the Interstate Commerce Commission. The following witnesses mention this point incidentally in connection with their arguments favoring pooling: NEWCOMB (108), JOHNSON (62), REAGAN (345), WOFFINDIN (565), CALLAWAY (236).

The members of the Interstate Commerce Commission believe that a large measure of control over the contracts between railways and over their rates ought to be given to the commission. Otherwise, freedom of contract might become a means of increasing rates generally and injuring the public. Mr. Clements especially insists that railways have usually sought to make pools in order to get more money out of the business, and that consequently unregulated pooling might tend toward excessive rates. There might be some difficulty in imposing effective checks upon rates under the pooling system. (KNAPP, 138; PROUTY, 150; CLEMENTS, 157.)

As to the attitude which the railways would be likely to take toward a proposition for the repeal of the antipooling clause, coupled with supervisory control over pooling and rates, Mr. Knapp stated that a change would doubtless be favored by some roads which at present suffered from sharp competition to such a degree that they would be willing to submit to rather drastic requirements. On the other hand, some railroads have, by consolidations and otherwise, got into a position where they do not suffer from excessive competition and do not care for pooling. At the same time the great combinations, whose shipments are so large as to be of first consequence to carriers, will be likely to oppose such legislation and to influence the railways to oppose it. (141.)

Mr. BIRD thinks the Interstate Commerce Commission should have the right to approve the rates under pools in the first instance and to discontinue the pool at any time if the rates were unjust. (474.)

Mr. RIPLEY, president of the Atchison, Topeka and Santa Fe Railroad Company, says that he would not object to a revision by the Interstate Commerce Commission of the rates charged by a pool, although some railroads might. (595.)

Mr. INGALLS would even be willing to have the decisions of the commission concerning the reasonableness of rates under agreements final without appeal, (800), and a similar position is taken by Mr. COWEN (315) and Mr. COUNSELMAN. (391.)

Mr. KELLEY thinks pooling should be subject to the supervision of the Interstate Commerce Commission, at least to the extent of allowing the commission to declare pooling contracts unreasonable and inoperative until upheld by a judicial body. (190, 191.)

Mr. BACON holds that rates fixed under pooling contracts should require the approval of the Interstate Commerce Commission and be subject to change by it at any time. The actual rates should be fixed by the commission where necessary, rather than maximum and minimum rates. (421.)

Mr. MORTON advocates giving the Interstate Commerce Commission power to revise the rates fixed by the pool whenever complaint should be made. It would be as important for it to prevent rates unreasonably low as unreasonably high. In case of appeal to the courts, the witness would be willing that the decision of the commission should remain in force temporarily, at least as regards rates under pooling contracts. The witness thinks further that the commission should have some control over the rates of railroads which should refuse to enter pools. Especially ought the roads which should enter the pool to be protected against secret and preferential rates made by any outside line. The witness has known of cases hitherto where pools have been made without bringing in all the roads in a section, the pooled roads acting as a unit in meeting competition of the outside lines. (491, 495, 496, 499.)

Mr. EVANS, a miller of Indianapolis, says that the general feeling among the millers seems to be in favor of pooling, but only under the supervision of the Interstate Commerce Commission. (441.)

Mr. BARRY, of the Millers' National Association, would not favor pooling unless the power of the Interstate Commerce Commission was very greatly enlarged. Under the present law pooling would simply strengthen the position of the railways in their unjust action toward shippers. (247.)

Mr. BLANCHARD suggests, incidentally, that the "interposition of the courts under an amended and swifter procedure, or due enlargement of the powers of the Interstate Commerce Commission, would fully protect the shippers and others involved." He would be willing that the agreements themselves should be submitted to the commission. But apparently he would give the commission no other power as regards rates under pools than as regards rates in general. For his opinion as to this power see p. 113. (640, 643, 678, 682.)

Mr. FULLER, of Norfolk, Nebr., is opposed to permitting railways to pool, since it would practically prohibit competition, unless the Interstate Commerce Commission be given thorough control over the pool. (445.)

G. Pooling in foreign countries.—Mr. BLANCHARD cites a number of authorities to show the existence of pooling in foreign countries, even in the case of government-owned railroads. He says that a series of conferences were held from 1874 to 1890, between representatives of Switzerland, Austria-Hungary, Belgium, Germany, Italy, and the Netherlands, with a view to adjusting tariffs on international competitive traffic. Such an agreement was ratified by all the participating nations, and went into effect in 1893. (640.)

In England, where railways are all privately owned, several writers declare that pools are common. Mr. Acworth says that there seems to be no popular objection to them, and that the railways continue to compete for traffic, notwithstanding their division of earnings. He mentions two specific pools as illustrations. The royal commission of 1887, appointed to inquire into the railway system, advocated permitting railways to pool without any control further than that the particulars of the agreement should be made public in the locality. In a prominent case before the courts the vice-chancellor declared that such agreements were legal in principle, and were not prejudicial either to the shareholders or to the public, and this appears to be the uniform attitude of the courts. (649, 650.)

The pools in England, Mr. Blanchard continues, are usually called joint purses. Aside from the regular pools there are associations of committees of railway managers, which agree as to rates. There are various district committees which hold stated meetings. If a company desires to change its rate, it consults its competitors and connections in conjunction with these committees. The result is that there is a great stability and uniformity in the rates, and practically no discrimination. The witness has been told by railroad officers that more than 99 per cent of the entire business of the British Islands is probably carried on established rates. Mr. Blanchard also refers to the railway clearing house in Great Britain; but its purpose is simply the adjustment of accounts, and it does not constitute a pool or an association for fixing rates. (664, 680.)

Mr. Blanchard refers especially to the testimony of President Hadley, of Yale University, before the Senate select committee on interstate commerce in 1885.

President Hadley then declared that no nation has succeeded in prohibiting discriminations and pooling at the same time. In Europe general' pools are organized much more completely than we have any conception of in this country, and are not merely recognized, but enforced by law. This is true in France, Belgium, and Austria, and to a less extent in Italy. And in most of these countries the pools include government railways and private railways alike. Thus, about 1860, the competition between the government railroads and the private companies in Belgium led to discriminations, in which the Government itself was the worst sinner, as well as to disastrous rate wars, and the difficulty was only terminated by an inflexible pooling agreement. The railroads of Prussia were also largely pooled before the government owned practically all of the lines. (651, 652.)

H. Traffic associations and other agreements.—1. *Argument favoring.*—The distinction is drawn by several witnesses between pools and other forms of agreement, such as those regarding rates. These latter are also advocated, even by two witnesses who oppose pooling. See Paragraphs B and C; INGALLS, COWEN, HYLAND, VANLANDINGHAM. (214.)

Mr. BIRD, of the Chicago, Milwaukee and St. Paul Railway, complains of the injustice of prohibiting agreements between railways as to rates. Since the decision of the supreme court in the trans-Missouri Freight Association case the gatherings of railway officers for the discussion of rates can not be called associations. There is simply a conference and a statement by different officers of what their own roads think ought to be done or will themselves do. But there is no way to prevent discriminations and fluctuations of rates without such conferences, and more formal agreements are desirable. For instance, if one of the roads from the Missouri to Chicago makes a different through rate from the other, since the through rate is also the maximum rate for a large number of smaller intermediate points, and since the two roads are only a few miles apart, the towns on the one road are discriminated against by the lower rates on the other. (478.)

2. *Kansas City Lines.*—Mr. BOOKWALTER has little doubt that some sort of agreement, probably not amounting to a pool, exists on the roads running into Kansas City. This is indicated by the fact that the Union Pacific, which ends at Kansas City and has elevators there, makes the same discriminations against Kansas City and in favor of other markets which are made by roads which run to those other markets. The Union Pacific is compelled to accept the terms made by the other roads, because if it did not they would revenge themselves upon it elsewhere. (573, 576, 577.)

3. *Joint Traffic Association.*—Mr. BLANCHARD says that the Joint Traffic Association was in existence for about 3 years, until held illegal by the United States Supreme Court. It included substantially all the railways south of the Great Lakes and the St. Lawrence River and east of a line from St. Louis to Chicago. There were 32 signers to the agreement. The roads affected carried about 78 per cent of the tonnage of the United States, but the agreement related to through traffic only. It was also provided that any company not a member of the association might appear and argue its case. The association appointed 9 managers. These 9 discussed 22,000 subjects during their administration. (678, 681.)

4. *Central Freight Association.*—Mr. TUCKER, chairman of the Central Freight Association, states that this organization is the successor of the Central Traffic Association. It is composed of about 60 railroads. The boundary of its territory runs from Chicago west to the Mississippi River at Burlington, down the Mississippi and up the Ohio to Pittsburg; thence to Buffalo, then, crossing the Canadian frontier, up to Mackinaw, down the east bank of Lake Michigan, and back to Chicago. The association holds meetings twice a month, attended usually by the general freight agents or the freight traffic officials of the different lines. The purpose of these meetings is to consult about matters of common interest and to see what are the necessities for reduction or advance of rates. There is no binding agreement between the roads; each road is at liberty to do as it pleases. If any road desires to make any given rate it is customary to communicate the desire or intention to the other roads interested. The question will then be discussed and each road will state what it wishes to do. Mr. Tucker does not think that any pressure is brought to bear on the individual members to charge a rate agreeable to all. In the end all the roads must necessarily adopt the lowest rate which any road insists upon making. There could not be an understanding that different roads should charge different rates on the same traffic; those that charged the higher rates would get no business. In case any member of the association makes a cut rate the only action taken is the action of the individual roads in meeting it. The association as such takes no action. Mr. Tucker does

not remember any case in which correspondence on such a subject has passed through the association.

Besides the information supplied to the association by each of its members, the association gets information of all new tariffs from the files of the Interstate Commerce Commission at Washington. (557-559.)

5. *Chicago East-bound Freight Committee.*—Mr. WOFFINDIN, chairman of the Chicago East-bound Freight Committee, states that this organization is a statistical bureau, of which 10 eastern trunk lines, and also the C. & E. I. and C., I. & L., are members. The several roads are represented upon the committee by their principal freight officials in Chicago. The committee keeps a record of all the industries around Chicago and the connection they have had with various roads, the various rates they get, and what rates should be fixed to reach them. It keeps a record of minimum rates, so that it can know at any time what the minimum rate is from Chicago to any Eastern point. If a road reduces the rate, the committee makes a record of the change and advises the other roads. It receives from the several roads the same tariffs which they file with the Interstate Commerce Commission. It has nothing to do with the rate-making power, and the witness is not in a position which enables him to judge as to the existence of rebates or other forms of freight discrimination. (565.)

VIII. PASSENGER TRAFFIC.

A. Passenger fares.—1. *General influences affecting.*—Mr. BLANCHARD, late commissioner of the Joint Traffic Association, enumerates various causes for the differences in passenger rates which exist in different parts of the country. Among these are provisions of charters and laws, the dissimilar volume of passenger traffic on different lines, inequality in the cost of railway construction and operation (as, for example, the differences between mountain roads and those in level country), differences in the cost of terminal facilities, competition of electric roads, of water routes, and of Canadian railways, etc. Special rates are sometimes made for certain classes as an aid to freight development. The special equipment of limited trains, involving greater expense and permitting only a smaller number of passengers per car than is customary on ordinary trains, as well as the higher speed of these trains, justifies a higher charge. On the other hand, railways which reach the same points as other lines, but which offer inferior or slower service, are justified in demanding differential rates in order to tempt passengers to take their routes. The large and regular volume of certain local travel justifies lower charges to commuters. In fact, the conditions of railway travel in the leading geographical sections of the country, of which the witness enumerates 7, justify differences in railway charges by sections. Similar causes lead to the different conditions imposed upon and prices charged for commutation, excursion, mileage, and similar tickets. Differences in rates are as justifiable in this country as they are in foreign countries, where different classes of traffic are recognized. Nevertheless, there is a steady tendency to reduce the disparity in rates according to natural laws. Growth of population, further consolidation of railways, and other influences will tend to make fares steadily lower and more uniform, and legislation is not necessary nor helpful. (618-620.)

2. *Existing rates.*—The average passenger rate on the New York Central Railroad, according to Mr. CALLAWAY, is only 1.82 cents per mile. The company is allowed to charge only 2 cents on its main line, and the highest rate on the branch lines is 3 cents. Mileage books are issued at 2 cents, which are good on the branch lines. (229.)

On the Chesapeake and Ohio, Mr. INGALLS testifies, the local passenger rates are all based on 3 cents per mile, while the through rates average about 2 cents. On account of the sparse population, higher local rates are necessary, and even then local trains lose money. The average receipt from passengers on the Chesapeake and Ohio is a trifle over 2 cents per mile, and on the Cleveland, Cincinnati, Chicago and St. Louis a trifle under 2 cents. (292.)

According to Mr. SPENCER, of the Southern Railway, the somewhat higher passenger rates in the Southern States are necessary on account of the sparse population and the consequent small amount of passenger business. The average rate on the Southern Railway system, however, was only 2¼ cents in 1898. (275.)

Mr. MORTON, vice-president of the Atchison, Topeka and Santa Fe Railway, declares that passenger rates in this country will average lower than those in any other country, and that the character of the service is better. The charges for sleeping cars especially are lower, and the cars superior. (490, 498.)

3. *Devices for stimulating traffic.*—Upon its being pointed out to Mr. COWEN, of the Baltimore and Ohio, that there is relatively less passenger travel in this

country than in Europe, he said that he thought the railways did everything possible to stimulate traffic. The practice of granting special rates to parties, which has finally been upheld by the courts, has built up a considerable traffic, especially by way of allowing theater companies to visit small towns. The use of mileage books accomplishes many of the results obtained by the "round-about" ticket and other passenger devices of European countries. (310.)

Mr. DICKINSON desires a general mileage book, good either over the whole United States or over large portions of the country. He admits that the difficulty in adjusting such a book without injustice either to the roads in mountainous and thinly settled regions or to the travelers in level and thickly settled regions would be considerable, but says that the railroads always seem to be able to surmount difficulties when they want to do so. It would not be necessary, however, that the mileage book be absolutely universal. The witness thinks that passengers can be carried in Wisconsin or Minnesota as cheaply as in New York or Ohio; and there would seem to be no difficulty in issuing mileage books which should be good at least over very large portions of the country. (555, 556.)

Professor JOHNSON believes that the American people, contrary to common opinion, do not travel as much relatively as those of Europe. We need cheaper service, cheaper sleeping-car accommodations, excursion rates, etc. The reduction of rates in Austria-Hungary in 1890 immediately caused great increase in travel. (61.)

4. *American and European passenger rates.*—(See also pp. 125 ff.—Mr. WEYL submitted the following table, comparing the passenger traffic of European countries with that in the United States. He points out on the basis of this table that in proportion to population the American people take a considerably smaller number of trips than the English or Germans, and even less than the French, Belgians, and Swiss. The average distance traveled per passenger is considerably greater in the United States, and the total number of miles traveled by all passengers is greater; although in proportion to the population the total number of miles traveled is only about as great as in Germany or France, and probably considerably less than in Great Britain. Our receipts per passenger are considerably higher than those of other countries, our fares averaging from three-fourths to 1¼ cents. High fares in America are associated with comparatively empty trains. The comparison frequently made between fares on American railways and first-class fares on the Continent is unjust, since, as is seen by another table presented by the witness, the great mass of travel in Europe is in the third-class cars, while in Germany a considerable proportion is also in the fourth class. The proportion of third-class traffic is 90 per cent in Great Britain, and in the other countries ranges from 71 per cent in Italy to 92 per cent in Norway. (758, 759.)

Country.	Year.	Number of passengers (in millions).	Number of passenger miles (in millions).	Number of passengers per head of population.	Number of passenger miles per head of population.	Average length of trip in miles.	Receipts per passenger.	Receipts per passenger per mile.	Number of passengers per train.	Revenue per passenger train mile.	Passenger density (passenger miles divided by miles of railroad).	Freight density (ton miles divided by miles of railroad) not tons.
						M.	Cts.	Cts.		Cts.		
Germany	1897-8	692.5	10,058	13.2	192	14.5	15.7	1.08	71	77	342,000	661,000
United Kingdom	1897	1,030.4	----	27.0	----	17.4	----	----	----	----	283,000	373,000
France	1897	396.7	7,227	10.3	188	18.3	27.8	1.17	----	----	289,000	234,000
India	1897	151.2	5,931	0.5	20	39.2	11.4	0.27	189	62	289,000	234,000
United States	1898	501.2	13,380	8.0 (6.6)	214 (189)	26.7	52.6	1.97	215 / 39	60 / 77	72,000	618,000

B. Passes.—Mr. KNAPP, chairman of the Interstate Commerce Commission, believes that the granting of free passes and special privileges to individuals in passenger traffic is a serious evil. In most cases the granting of such passes has some motive of self-interest, although the half rates granted to clergymen are apparently due to unselfish motives. Members of State and National Legislatures, judges, and public officers are quite regularly offered free transportation, although they do not always accept it. The law, where it prohibits the giving of passes to such persons, is evaded in various ways. Thus they may ostensibly be granted for newspaper service, or be limited to transportation within a State where there is no law against it, although in practice accepted in other States.

The witness thinks that it is possible, as he has heard it claimed, that the actual revenues received by the railroads on their passenger business do not exceed 75 or 80 per cent of what they would be if the full published rates were paid by all passengers. Thus by the elimination of free transportation, as well as of the abuse of round-trip tickets by scalpers, the passenger rates throughout the country could be materially reduced. The granting of passes to employees of other railroads is also carried too far. (135, 136.)

Mr. PROUTY, another member of the Interstate Commerce Commission, does not consider the abuse of passes as serious as Mr. Knapp does, but suggests that an effective remedy would be secured by requiring the railroads to file with the Interstate Commerce Commission lists of all passes issued, to be open to public inspection. (152.)

Mr. REAGAN, chairman of the railroad commission of Texas, declares that free passes are not given for charitable purposes, but usually to public officers and other influential persons, or to large shippers as an inducement for freight traffic. The system involves the taxing of a part of the people for the benefit of a few. The Texas constitution contains a large number of exceptions to the provisions prohibiting discrimination between individuals, so that practically the railroad commission is unable to prevent the abuse of the pass system. (341, 342.)

Mr. WILSON, grand chief of the Brotherhood of Railroad Trackmen, and Mr. RONEMUS, grand chief of the Brotherhood of Railway Carmen, think that the issue of free transportation should be restricted to railway employees and Government employees in the Railway Mail Service, declaring that passes are issued largely for corrupt political purposes, and that favors are extended to men who can well afford to buy tickets. Mr. Ronemus thinks that a uniform rate of 1 cent per mile should be made to all railway employees and their families. (768, 771.)

Mr. INGALLS, of the Chesapeake and Ohio, thinks that the granting of passes is discrimination in favor of individuals, which should be considered a violation of law. There has been a great decrease in the practice during the past 10 or 15 years, but the witness presumes that it is still large. Passes on the Chesapeake and Ohio, and the Cleveland, Cincinnati, Chicago and St. Louis, are not, he thinks, more than one-tenth as numerous as they formerly were. A great majority of the railway managers are tired and sick of issuing passes.

It is still the practice on the railways represented by the witness to grant passes to members of State legislatures and of Congress, so far as they live on the line of the railroad, good for the session. Since it is an immemorial custom, this practice could not be discontinued without a law prohibiting it. Passes are not issued to judges or to officers of municipalities, although State officers are granted passes. Mr. Ingalls does not admit that any political influence is sought through the issue of passes.

The witness is in favor of absolutely prohibiting the granting of passes except, perhaps, to employees of the road itself. It creates a better feeling among employees to be somewhat liberal in granting passes to them and their families. The registration of passes with the Interstate Commerce Commission might have some beneficial effects, but the list would be so large that few people would ever look through it. (293-295.)

Mr. FISH, of the Illinois Central, believes that the evils of passes would have been largely prevented under the interstate-commerce act but for the long list of exceptions allowed. The witness does not believe in giving something for nothing under any circumstances. If value is received from employees or others it should be paid in money and not by transportation. Mr. Fish has been told that sometimes there is value received from members of legislatures to whom passes are granted. He favors abolishing passes altogether, including special rates to clergymen. He does not think, however, that the loss of earnings through the issue of passes is significant. People who receive passes would not travel without them for the most part. (334, 335.)

Mr. SPENCER, president of the Southern Railway, thinks that the granting of passes constitutes an abuse throughout the entire country, although he hopes that it is less on the Southern Railway than on some others. He would like to see all passes prohibited by statute. Railroad men themselves should pay fare on other railroads at the expense of the railway employing them, if the journey be upon official business. (270.)

Mr. CALLAWAY, president of the New York Central, testifies that no passes are issued by that road except by Mr. Depew or by Mr. Callaway. He grants them practically only to railroad employees, and he does not think that the revenues of the railroad are affected by these passes. They largely go to persons who would not travel otherwise. A New York law prohibits the granting of passes to public officers. (229.)

Mr. BIRD, general traffic manager of the Chicago, Milwaukee and St. Paul Railway, declares that the practice of issuing passes benefits the few at the expense of the many. Railroad companies themselves are trying to limit passes to their own employees or to the employees of other companies necessarily traveling on official business. In the latter case the issue is merely an exchange which evens itself up. The witness would consider it just to limit the use of passes by employees to travel on the company's business exclusively, but thinks that to try to do so would lead to corruption and excuses for traveling on the company's business. It is not practicable for the railways to abolish passes to public officers unless all do it; and legislation to assist them in the movement is very desirable. There is probably less of free transportation in the Northwestern States now than 5 or 6 years ago. On the Chicago, Milwaukee and St. Paul passes are issued, practically, only by the president. The witness does not think that the entire amount of free traffic would be more than about 1 per cent of the passenger earnings of the railroads. (468, 469.)

Mr. MORTON, vice-president of the Atchison, Topeka and Santa Fe Railway, declares that passes are given for personal, official, and commercial reasons, and in exchange for advertising, services, etc. In almost all cases the reasons for issuing them are bad ones. Even railroad officials or employees traveling on other lines should be required to pay fare. At a meeting of the executive officers of the Western, Northwestern, and Southwestern railroads in October, 1899, it was recommended that free transportation should be done away with except to railroad employees and greatly reduced in their case. These recommendations being submitted to the officers of 265 railroads representing 184,000 miles, practically all of the mileage of the country, favorable replies were received from 129 railroads representing 150,590 miles. (490.)

Mr. COWEN, of the Baltimore and Ohio, also thinks the pass system is abused, although he would not favor trying to prohibit it, unless it is used as a means of discrimination between shippers—a practice which has greatly decreased in recent years. The issue of passes to public officers is not in the nature of bribery, but has grown out of long custom from which it is impossible to break away. It is true that passes granted to prosecuting officers of counties are probably issued in consideration of the many offenses against railroads which these officers are called on to prosecute. The witness has heard it stated by a prominent railway officer in New York that the prohibition of passes to State officers has resulted in even more passes being granted, since officers now demand them for their friends and supporters, and the railways are not in a position to refuse.

Mr. Cowen does not think it possible to remedy this abuse by legislation, since the opinion of the people generally, and especially that of railway officers, is not ready to support such laws. The railways must work out relief from the practice themselves. In New England, where the railway business is largely monopolized, passes are probably not issued to such an extent as in other places. (310-313.)

Mr. BLANCHARD, late commissioner of the Joint Traffic Association, says that passes are sometimes issued to shippers in such a way as to constitute unjustifiable discrimination. Nevertheless, when a shipper is also a railway officer there is no reason why he should be refused a pass even if it helps him as against his competitor. Passes issued to persons accompanying live stock are necessary to secure proper care for the animals. Some passes issued to manufacturers may be wholly or partly compensated for in freight rates; the two things should be dissociated. Passes issued for charitable reasons are sometimes abused. Passes given in exchange for newspaper advertising are convenient to both sides and save the keeping of accounts. The witness would favor limiting passes of railway employees to those connected with the company itself and the members of their families. The unwarranted issue of passes to legislators and public officers can be most effectively checked by legislative action; but such passes are usually complimentary to public position and seldom have corrupt motives or influence. (620, 621, 669.)

Mr. STICKNEY, president of the Chicago Great Western Railway Company, says that if there had never been passes granted it would be a good thing not to permit them, but to prohibit or stop issuing them now immediately might cause too much disturbance. He believes that Congressmen are not given passes by his road, nor the members of the judiciary of the States. Nevertheless, railroads often find that there are men to whom it is not to their interest to refuse passes if asked for. Legislation on the matter is probably not desirable. At any rate, whatever penalty is imposed must be small if there is any hope of enforcing it. (456, 457.)

Mr. DICKINSON testifies that his State, Wisconsin, has enacted an antipass law, applying only to public and State officials. From the fact that people who hold quasi-public positions have had passes he infers that the law has not been enforced. He does not know of anything to justify the giving of passes, except to railroad employees. He considers that railroads may properly favor their employees in this way, just as other business institutions are accustomed to grant favors to their employees which they do not grant to outsiders. Although mercantile houses do not often, perhaps, make presents to their employees, they do regularly sell goods to their employees at less than the regular price. This seems to be a courtesy of similar character to the grant of a pass by a railroad. The witness supposes that railroads grant passes to their employees of all grades, though doubtless more freely to the higher ranks. He understands that such passes are now limited for the most part to transportation over the line on which the man is employed. Although the railroad is in theory a public institution, it is also in part a private institution, and the granting of favors to its men is not so objectionable as the granting of favors by a purely governmental establishment would be. (552–554.)

Mr. Dickinson states that people often seem able to get free transportation who can not apparently be of any value to the railroad; at least people who are not in a position to furnish the railroads with any business. He thinks that newspaper men do not generally have passes in his region, but that their transportation is rather in the way of mileage. He notices that public men of various grades are likely to get them, and he mentions that a councilman in St. Joseph was able some time ago to accommodate him with transportation from St. Joseph into Nebraska and back. (554, 555.)

C. **Ticket brokerage.**—1. *Existence and character of evil.*—Mr. BLANCHARD, late commissioner of the Joint Traffic Association, declares that the practice of ticket brokerage reduces railway revenues. It forms the basis of many secret and fraudulent devices which result in unjustifiable discriminations in fares. Unauthorized persons secure the advantage of special rates granted to trade bodies, conventions, etc. Scalpers incite railroad wars in order to procure tickets.

The opportunities for ticket scalping are made very numerous by the practice of issuing, for the convenience of passengers, through tickets for long distances over various routes. Each railway offers tickets over a multiplicity of connections. For example, a ticket may be sold from Philadelphia by way of Buffalo, Cleveland, and Toledo, to Cincinnati, at a rate based upon a direct route to Cincinnati. The opportunity for using the various coupons for scalping is manifest. (621, 622.)

Mr. Blanchard also declares that railways often connive with ticket brokers. By furnishing them tickets at reduced rates a company is able to violate the law by cutting rates without due notice. This practice is less extensive than formerly. The witness refers to one instance when a new line was opened from Buffalo to New York, which disposed of perhaps 10,000 tickets directly to speculators. Afterwards a better understanding was reached between the competing roads and an offer was made to redeem these tickets at a profit to the scalpers, but they refused to return them. Even where railroads have not furnished tickets directly to scalpers they have sometimes referred passengers to brokers' offices as places where tickets, as the result of the ordinary practice of selling unused parts of tickets, could be secured more cheaply. These practices have been in part curtailed by the appointment of agents to visit scalping offices and "test the market."

Scalpers also secure tickets at times from conductors and from clerks and ticket distributers in the general offices. The witness cited one particular case where a chief ticket clerk was found to be getting three times his salary by selling tickets to brokers.

Scalpers often mislead buyers of tickets by false information as to routes, checking of baggage, sleeping cars. etc. Railway companies are ready to offer all necessary information correctly. (621–623. 666, 667.)

Mr. MORTON, vice-president of the Atchison, Topeka and Santa Fe Railway, declares that ticket scalping is tolerated in no other country and should be abolished here. There should be national legislation on the subject for the sake both of the public and of the railroads. There is always more or less transportation furnished by dishonest employees of railroads to ticket brokers. Moreover, railroad companies often secretly assist the scalpers, although the business obtained in this way is less than that which the public gives to the brokers. Probably united action by the railroads would drive the brokers out of business. (489, 500.)

Mr. SPENCER, of the Southern Railway, declares that this practice is exceedingly injurious to the railways, and therefore prevents them from affording as great facilities to the public as they could otherwise. In fact, if the practice were abolished, the general tendency toward lowering passenger rates would probably be somewhat accelerated. The sale of unused parts of tickets to scalpers is morally wrong. In the case of cheaper through tickets and return tickets there are legitimate reasons for granting lower rates. The ticket is bought with the supposed intention on the part of the buyer to use the entire ticket, and he is acting fraudulently if he stops off at an intermediate station or does not return, and sells his ticket. Railways themselves are usually entirely willing to prevent loss to a man who finds it impossible to complete his journey by refunding to him such a part of the money paid that the cost of his transportation to the point reached is the same that he would have paid if he had bought a ticket to that point originally. This is clearly all that the buyer can ask for.

The witness thinks, however, that one of the chief evils of ticket scalping is that certain railways themselves employ the ticket brokers to sell tickets at cut rates. They thus escape the necessity of publishing their true rates and giving the due notice of changes required by law, and their competitors are unable to act intelligently in meeting them. The railway which obeys the law is thus at a serious disadvantage.

In case scalpers' tickets are presented to a railway with its knowledge, it is the usual policy not to recognize them unless there is some danger that a court decision may be made against the railway for refusing. Railways would not especially object to transferring tickets if the same prices were received for the transportation. In case of injury to a person carried on a scalper's ticket, the railway would be apt to claim that it was bound by no liability. (269, 272.)

Mr. INGALLS, of the Chesapeake and Ohio, also considers this practice injurious. It constitutes a great temptation to conductors to dispose of tickets to brokers. On account of the abuse of round-trip tickets, the granting of special low rates for excursions is considerably checked. It would be in this special regard that the general public would be benefited by abolishing ticket brokerage, rather than in any general lowering of the rates. Ticket scalping cuts into the revenues of railways very largely.

Although a few years ago a number of railways made it a practice themselves to sell tickets to brokers, most of these have gone into bankruptcy, and the practice is apparently not common. There is complaint that the West Shore Railroad still sells tickets to brokers. The railways themselves, nevertheless, if they would all agree to limit their tickets to single trains, could immediately check the practice of ticket scalping. (293, 294.)

In the opinion of Mr. COWEN, of the Baltimore and Ohio, the practice of ticket brokerage has often been the cover for many illegitimate practices, although this is not necessarily true of the business of the brokers. The railways formerly employed brokers during rate wars, but to remove the connivance of the railways would not destroy the brokerage system. Although the prohibition of ticket scalping would probably not lower general rates, the witness believes that there are cases where special low rates can not be given for fear of this practice. (309, 310.)

Mr. FISH, of the Illinois Central, thinks that since the railways are prohibited from selling tickets for more than the advertised rates, they should be protected against sale below those rates by others. Although brokers do some honest business, they could not maintain themselves except by dishonest practices, such as altering the dates on tickets. To some extent railways doubtless connive with brokers by furnishing them tickets at cut rates. (333, 334.)

Mr. WILSON, grand chief of the Brotherhood of Railroad Trackmen, declares that ticket brokerage should be abolished on account of the unnecessary losses to railway earnings arising from the practice, which tend to reduce wages and to cause other evils. (768.)

2. *Justification of ticket brokerage.*—Mr. STICKNEY, president of the Chicago Great Western Railway, declares that, although his view is unpopular with railroad men, he sees no reason why a person who buys a through ticket and only uses part of it should not sell the unused part. When it is suggested that the ticket be redeemed by the company, the reply is that it is not easy to find the company's office or to make the arrangement. To punish a man for buying and selling the unused part of the ticket would be outrageous. The witness presumes, however, that the bulk of the business of the scalpers is given them directly by the railroads. At any rate, legislation in the matter is not desirable. (457.)

3. *Remedies.*—Practically all the witnesses, expressly or by implication, favor legislation prohibiting ticket brokerage. They mostly are willing to require railways to redeem unused parts of tickets.

Mr. BLANCHARD declares that the railway companies are unable entirely to check the scalping of tickets. All the different means of identifying holders of tickets are evaded in various ways, some of which are specifically mentioned. The railways are always willing to return to the holders of unused parts of tickets any amount not exceeding the fare which duly accrues for the distance actually traversed. In fact, passengers often sell unused tickets for less than the railways would pay, although Mr. Blanchard admits that they sometimes save money by selling their tickets. The railways have been seeking to reduce the opportunities for scalping by the sale of limited tickets at reduced fares. These tickets are good only on a single day, and can not well be sold.

The suggestion that ticket scalping be checked by requiring the name of every man who buys a ticket to be placed upon it is impracticable on account of the great rush of traffic at many ticket offices. The same difficulty confronts the proposition to have the selling price printed on the face of every ticket, with the proportion of the whole fare accruing on each coupon, and with the assurance that any coupon will be redeemed.

The witness is not certain as to the effect of the purchase of a scalped ticket upon the liability of the railroad for injury to a passenger. If there were distinct fraud, as by the signing of a false name, the railway should probably be exempt from liability.

Commenting on the decision of the court of appeals of New York, holding the antiscalping law unconstitutional on the ground that a ticket once bought becomes the property of the purchaser, to dispose of as he sees fit, Mr. Blanchard declares that the ticket is not the property of the purchaser, but of the carrier. It is simply an evidence of a contract of transportation, and the railroad has the right to demand its surrender when the contract has been fulfilled. The railroad, in fact, could take up the ticket when the train first started. Freight bills of lading must be surrendered to the railway when the goods are delivered. No one would think of authorizing the scalping of freight bills as the scalping of tickets is authorized. The whole system of ticket brokerage is, in the opinion of the witness, immoral and illegal. (622, 623, 666–671.)

Mr. Blanchard states that during the recent hearings before the committees of Congress on the antiscalping bill, practically all of the newspapers, mercantile associations, railway officers, and railway commissioners of the country were strongly in favor of the bill. Ticket brokerage was defended by not over 3 railroads, and was chiefly upheld by 560 brokers. There can be no doubt that the only proper officers to sell tickets are the duly chosen agents of railroads. (621.)

Mr. CALLAWAY, of the New York Central, thinks that this practice is one of the most demoralizing features of railway business. He declares that it has been abolished by law in nearly every country in the world except the United States, and that it is prohibited in Pennsylvania, Illinois, New Jersey, Montana, North Dakota, Minnesota, Texas, North Carolina, New York, Florida, and Indiana. One of the chief difficulties is that brokers deal largely in forged and stolen tickets. (227.)

Mr. BIRD, of the Chicago, Milwaukee and St. Paul, says that the constant effort of the railroads to limit the use of through tickets at reduced rates has largely lowered the profits of ticket brokers, although there are special cases of such low through rates. Improved methods of regulating mileage books have also made it more difficult to transfer them through ticket brokers. Thus, in the Northwestern States, a "traveler's permit" is issued, by which the passenger pays always his local fare, but has the amount entered in a little book, and after traveling 2,000 miles, can get from the railway the difference between what he has paid and the special 2,000-mile rate. The only business of consequence left to the broker is that which is furnished by the railways themselves. The original practice of allowing brokers reasonable commissions for selling tickets in times of rate wars was not especially injurious, but in many cases the commissions offered are so great that the brokers can profitably sell tickets at less than the open rates. The railroads are generally in a position to stop this practice. The strongest lines in a group are forced to follow the practices adopted by the worst and weakest lines. The witness believes that legislation by Congress and the States on the subject is desirable. (469.)

Mr. REAGAN, of the Texas Railroad Commission, believes that it should be made a penal offense to engage in the business of ticket scalping, and perhaps even for the purchaser of a single ticket to sell it to another person. In that case the law, like that in Texas, should provide that the purchaser who does not use a ticket can have it redeemed by the railway. Ticket scalping enables railroads themselves to underbid each other and make discriminations, and leads to many frauds. (350.)

Mr. FISH thinks that if statutes should require that every ticket should be stamped with the price at which it is sold, and that an unused coupon should be redeemable within 30 days by railways, the practice of ticket scalping would be destroyed. He does not think that it would be desirable to compel railways to redeem small parts of tickets or coupons. (333, 334.)

Professor JOHNSON believes that the practice of ticket brokerage should be done away by law. The railways are unable to do this alone, especially because some roads are always sure to refuse to cooperate. In fact, the system is often employed as a device for cutting rates in order to get business, the cuts being concealed in this way. The losses which railways suffer by ticket brokerage undoubtedly tend to reduce wages. (60, 61.)

Mr. SARGENT, grand master of the Brotherhood of Locomotive Firemen, says that this practice offers a convenient way for evading the law and making discriminations. Losses caused by it must be made up at the expense of someone. Those who live in large places secure an advantage over others. Many brokers resort to fraudulent and criminal methods—forgery, counterfeiting, and misrepresentation. Employees are enticed to defraud the company and altercations with passengers are caused. Counterfeit cards of membership in railway brotherhoods have been sold by brokers. (70.)

Mr. WILSON, grand chief of the Brotherhood of Railway Trackmen, has found from his own experience that tickets for any considerable distance can always be bought from scalpers for less than the regular fare. Such tickets have no signature, and he has known them to be bought by scalpers directly from agents who have quoted higher rates just before. He believes this practice, by reducing railway profits, tends to keep down wages. (46, 58.)

Mr. VANLANDINGHAM favors a law prohibiting ticket scalping. (214.)

IX. GENERAL LEGISLATION CONCERNING RAILWAYS.

A. Principles of legislation generally.—1. *Public character of railways.*—The members of the Interstate Commerce Commission who testified before the Industrial Commission were unanimous in their opinion that control over railway rates and over pooling agreements, as well as the requirement of publicity of railway affairs, is thoroughly justified by the public character of railway services. Mr. KNAPP declares that various practices, discriminations, etc., among railways might perhaps be justified if only the private financial interests of the railways were to be considered. But where the public interest is concerned such practices must cease. The impossibility of effective competition among railways, together with the absolute necessity of their services, renders them public agencies. The passenger makes use of the railway rather by virtue of his political rights than by contract. The passenger ticket is more in the nature of a tax receipt than evidence of a bargain. Mr. CLEMENTS also insists that if the public has any rights at all with regard to railways it has absolute right to inspect and control them, subject only to the limitation that property shall not be confiscated or taken without due process of law. (Knapp, 135, 139, 140; Clements, 159.)

Other witnesses often refer incidentally to the public character of railways as justifying various regulations.

2. *Claim of railways to fair treatment.*—Mr. BLANCHARD, late commissioner of the Joint Traffic Association, says that cities, States, and the General Government at first granted all sorts of privileges and advantages to railways, but that afterwards the attitude of the public changed to one of opposition. Most of the railways first constructed sought to connect important objective points. Their local traffic was inadequate, and they had to wait for a long time before the slow development of the territory traversed made them profitable. Many of the roads defaulted in their interest payments and were reorganized. There has been a steady decrease in charges and a steady improvement in service; but in spite of that fact public appreciation of the railway service has lessened, and legislators have been inclined to increase restrictions of all sorts. The railways have sought to obtain legitimate protection in exchange for their services and in view of the restrictions placed upon them, but they are met with constant opposition. (624, 625.)

Mr. INGALLS, president of the Chesapeake and Ohio, declares that three interests must be considered in attempting regulation: (1) The property must be kept up in satisfactory condition so that passengers can be carried with safety and dispatch and the freight handled regularly and promptly. (2) The employees must be paid promptly and fairly and their interests protected. If the revenues are insufficient to pay fair wages, the character of the service is injured and safety and proper transportation lessened. (3) Patrons must be served at a cost as reasonable as is consistent with the previous requirements and with a fair return to the investors on their property.

When railways were first established the investment was a hazardous one;

securities were issued with little regard to values, and in many cases were afterwards wiped out by foreclosure. The new owners of the reorganized companies endeavored to earn an income in any possible way. This caused public dissatisfaction, and the courts finally held that the railways were public servants, subject to control over their rates, provided a fair revenue be left for the capital invested. Many States appointed commissions, and some endeavored to fix charges absolutely by law. The latter practice has been largely abandoned as unsatisfactory.

Mr. Ingalls believes that the public character of railways thoroughly justifies any necessary regulation. They are quasi-public corporations and should be managed to the satisfaction of the people, and especially with their thorough knowledge. But the chief legislation which the witness considers necessary is the legalization of pooling in order to prevent the existing rate cutting and discriminations. (285, 286, 297.)

Mr. RIPLEY, president of the Atchison, Topeka, and Santa Fe Railroad Company, says that the railroads are entitled, in all fairness and justice, to ask that one of the following courses be pursued:

1. Remove the restrictions and turn the roads loose.
2. Accord them that protection to which they are justly entitled.
3. Buy them.

If a railroad is a private corporation solely, the Government has no right to interfere with its business; if it is a public or a quasi-public institution, the Government ought to protect its interests. The attitude of the American people toward the railroads is grossly unfair and even dishonest. The railroads have restrictions without protection. (594, 595.)

Mr. Ripley says that the state has not assumed in this country to regulate the price of any commodity except railroad transportation. If the revenues of a private corporation are limited by law the state owes that corporation protection. That is, the Government has no right, while it limits the charges of the railroads, at the same time to forbid them to adopt reasonable methods for maintaining fair rates. Nothing more than the opportunity to maintain fair and reasonable rates has ever been asked by the roads. The roads might well ask for more than the mere permission to pool—for instance, laws prohibiting the building of unnecessary roads and confirming each existing line in the sole occupancy of its territory. (594.)

B. Working of interstate-commerce act.—Mr. BLANCHARD declares that the interstate-commerce act has been effective in protecting the public and has been unjust to railways. He attributes its chief failure to the prohibition of pooling. The exclusion of the water carriers from the application of the law has been unfair to the railways. The law did not foster harmony between the Government officers and the carriers. It has failed to prevent discriminations, in spite of its severe penalties, because, preventing pooling, it has not enlisted the interests of the carriers. Nevertheless, the act has been beneficial in securing greater publicity of rates, in checking open rate wars, in more fairly adjusting long and short haul rates, and in its educational effect upon the railways and public opinion. (657, 658.)

Mr. SPENCER thinks that the commission has already accomplished much good in requiring publicity of rates, in systematizing accounts and records, and, to a less extent, in prosecuting violations of the law. Its powers in this last regard should be increased. (282, 283.)

Mr. CALLAWAY, president of the New York Central, says that almost invariably his own road complies with the orders of the Interstate Commerce Commission, and he believes that most railways do the same. The commission, in fact, usually agrees with the position taken, at least by his own railway. If not, publicity and the influence of public opinion are enough to enforce the commission's orders. (236, 237.)

Mr. COWEN, of the Baltimore and Ohio, declares that as a matter of fact there are very few complaints as to the reasonableness of rates. Most shippers are powerful enough to look after their own interests. The chief value, moreover, of a commission like the Interstate Commerce Commission is that it brings public opinion to bear upon the railways. Most of the important work of the commission is done without technical litigation. In 95 cases out of 100 the railways comply with suggestions of the commission. (314, 315.)

Mr. SARGENT, grand master of the Brotherhood of Locomotive Firemen, says that as yet the Interstate Commerce Commission has scarcely possessed power to accomplish anything except to collect statistics. It has had a beneficial moral effect, but should be given much greater power. In this way its services might become of great value to the country, the railroads, and the employees. The witness would not favor, however, giving the commission power to settle disputes between employees and railways. (94.)

Mr. KINDEL, a manufacturer, of Denver, thinks that the interstate-commerce act at present is a mere farce. The long and short haul feature seems to him the most important part of the law, and this is practically not carried out at all. The witness thinks that the amendments proposed in the Cullom bill, in the Fifty-fifth Congress, would meet the needs of the case for the most part. (261.)

Other opinions as to the working of the present act appear in connection with arguments as to proposed changes.

C. General amendments proposed to interstate-commerce act.—Mr. VANLANDINGHAM, commissioner of the St. Louis traffic bureau, recommends the following changes in the act to regulate commerce:

1. The findings of the Interstate Commerce Commission should be binding within 30 days and enforceable at law unless upon appeal to the courts they are found to be unjust. The commission should not have the authority to fix rates generally, but should be authorized to order reduction of rates found to be exorbitant, and to determine the relation of rates as between localities and commodities.

2. Absolute publicity should be required regarding all rates or regulations affecting transportation, whether in domestic or export and import traffic. The railways at present hold that they are not required to publish their export rates. Railways should also be required to furnish to shippers, boards of trade, etc., on request, copies of all tariffs that affect such shippers or members of such organizations, whether such tariffs apply directly to the locality or to rival localities. At present men who are not posted do not know how to get information as to tariffs.

3. All traffic moving by rail, or partly by rail and partly by water, including export and import traffic, should be subject to the interstate-commerce act, the proportion of rates accruing to the inland carrier being subject to the same control as purely domestic traffic.

4. Railways should be prohibited from making lower rates on grain to the seaboard for export than on flour or grain products for export.

5. The penalty of imprisonment against persons who pay or accept less than the published tariff rates, except shippers who obtain lower rates by fraudulent misrepresentation, should be repealed. The purpose of this is to secure testimony. Moreover, the imprisonment clause, as regards officers and agents of railroads, should be abolished, since railway, men will not furnish testimony against others so long as it remains. There should be substituted fines against the companies themselves primarily, and also against their officers, those against the companies being not less than $5,000, or double the revenue receied by the company at unlawful rates, where this is greater than $5,000.

6. Railways should be permitted to agree upon reasonable rates and to maintain voluntary associations for the maintenance and promulgation of such rates, the compilation of statistics, and the transaction of other joint work. On the other hand, pooling is not necessary or desirable. Agreements of this nature should be filed with the Interstate Commerce Commission and subject to its control.

7. There should be no change requiring longer notice as to reduction or advance in tariffs than is required at present.

8. Ticket scalping should be prohibited.

9. The Interstate Commerce Commission should be required to render its decisions not later than 90 days after the close of testimony, unless longer time is given by mutual consent.

10. If it were possible to require the various States to repeal all laws in conflict with the act to regulate commerce, and to adopt it as law for intrastate business, or if it were possible to transfer the entire control of commerce to the Federal Government, such changes would be desirable. (212–214.)

Mr. BLANCHARD, while opposing most of the suggested extensions of the power of the Interstate Commerce Commission, is willing somewhat to increase its prerogatives. He thinks that proposed amendments to the act should be made only after conference between the various interests involved. Railways should be consulted as well as shippers and the general public. The public certainly has an interest in railway affairs which justifies regulation, but the rights of railways should also be protected. The work of the commission has hitherto been very beneficial, especially by correcting misunderstandings on the part of both the railways and the public, increasing knowledge on both sides. The railways have usually been inclined to follow the suggestions made. The requirement of a uniform system of accounts has doubtless been beneficial. An amendment to the law should provide for more frequent conferences between the Interstate Commerce Commission and the railways, in which perhaps interested shippers might also participate.

The commission should be enlarged to seven members, especially in view of the increased railway business of the country. Some, at least, of these members should be railway men. It is as absurd to constitute a railway commission with a provision that no member shall own a share of railway stock as it would be to exclude army officers from membership in a committee concerning coast defenses. The interests and the opinions of the railways would thus be brought into touch with the commission. It would be possible to find railway officers who would be impartial. The people trust their Senators and Representatives to legislate concerning industrial interests and do not prohibit them from holding stocks or acting as officers of corporations.

, The Interstate Commerce Commission should provide for greater publicity by issuing at least every month a bulletin stating all the complaints coming before it. These statements should be in impersonal form, naming only the points and rates complained of, and not naming the railways or the complainants. This would have a very desirable effect upon public opinion and would tend to make the railways more conservative and careful in conforming to law. (664, 665, 678, 679.)

Messrs. PROUTY and CLEMENTS, of the Interstate Commerce Commission, agree in believing that its power should be increased if effective regulation of railway rates is to be secured. Especially if the railways are to be given the right to pool, the commission or some similar authority must be given thorough control over pooling contracts. Inspection of books by representatives of the commission is especially advocated, as well as the power to fix through rates, which is now entirely denied. (150, 155, 158, 161.)

Mr. GALLAGHER would provide uniform classification, with Government supervision, in the belief that it would do away with rate cutting in many cases where classification is now changed to produce a cut rate. He would have the Interstate Commerce Commission empowered to enforce its rulings, the rulings to stand until reversed by the courts. He would introduce Government inspection of railroad accounts, bringing the records of the roads under the supervision of the Treasury Department, if necessary, by means of an internal-revenue tax, which the shipper, if necessary, might pay. He would punish infractions of the law with fines, and not with imprisonment; he thinks we should get conviction quicker by releasing the shipper, unless he can be shown to be a party to the fraud. He is not clear whether the words "under substantially similar circumstances and conditions" should be eliminated from the long and short haul clause. (547.)

Mr. DICKINSON would permit the railroad companies to make rates in the first instance, but would give the Interstate Commerce Commission authority to revise rates, and to enforce their decisions. He would also have the books of railroad companies examined by Government examiners. Mr. Dickinson was formerly of opinion that unrestricted competition would give the best railroad service, but has been forced to the conclusion that the railroads should be placed under governmental control. He believes that there is a strong and growing sentiment in his State, Wisconsin, in favor of Government control and of the increase of the powers of the Interstate Commerce Commission. He has been compelled to conclude that there is no other remedy for the existing troubles in transportation, and that the railroads themselves, as well as the public, would be benefited by a control outside of themselves. (549, 552.)

Business within States.—Mr. MORTON declares that Federal regulation of railways can never be entirely satisfactory until Congress has power to regulate business within the States, as well as interstate traffic. Rates within the State are intimately related to the interstate rates. For instance, rates from St. Louis to Kansas City, entirely within Missouri, are and must be on the basis of rates from Chicago to Kansas City. Discriminations in favor of individuals are often made on shipments within a State, there being no law against them, and this affects interstate traffic also. Many shipments entirely within a State are really only the beginning of shipments of an interstate nature. State railroad commissions often take action which practically nullifies orders issued by the Interstate Commerce Commission. Thus, in Texas particularly, the State commission is inclined to regulate rates so as to confine business as far as possible to the State and its citizens; "they are States' rights people." In Iowa and Nebraska somewhat the same tendency exists. The witness would be inclined to favor a constitutional amendment giving Congress power over all railroad business. (492, 501, 502.)

Telegraph and express companies.—Mr. PROUTY, of the Interstate Commerce Commission, sees no reason why express companies could not be subject to the control of the Interstate Commerce Commission, although he believes there are few complaints against them. The control of telegraph companies, he thinks, would more appropriately be given to the Post-Office Department. (152.)

D. Proposal to give final power over rates to Interstate Commerce Commission.—This proposition takes the form of giving the commission power either to fix all rates finally in the first instance, or to fix them on complaint, without appeal. The two forms can not always be distinguished in the discussions.

1. *Advocated.*—Mr. REAGAN, chairman of the railroad commission of Texas, believes that the Interstate Commerce Commission should be empowered to make and maintain freight and passenger rates as regards interstate and foreign commerce, and that the States should similarly regulate State traffic. He considers this entirely practicable, even with the present number of employees of the Interstate Commerce Commission, in view of the experience of the Texas railroad commission. The decisions of the commission should be subject to appeal to the courts on questions of law only, not on questions of fact.

Mr. Reagan also believes that to give the Interstate Commerce Commission power to reduce rates, even if it could not fix them generally, would go far toward remedying existing evils. He believes also that the commission has the necessary technical knowledge. The Texas railroad commission exercises absolute control as regards shipments within the State, shipments from without the State to points within the State being out of its jurisdiction. In deciding as to the justice of rates the Texas commission is forced for the most part to consider only the earning capacity and expenses of the railroads as regards their State traffic. Many considerations affecting the profits and character of the business must necessarily be disregarded on account of the excessive complexity and detail. There is, in fact, no science in rate making. Rates must be on the basis of experience from day to day. Uniform rates on all classes of goods, for example, are out of the question. In fact, it is not necessary to consider all theoretical conditions affecting railway traffic, but the actual working of rates can be studied by experience. Nevertheless, the reports of the Texas railroad commission do show statistically many of the controlling influences entering into the cost of transportation, and questions growing out of competition are also considered in fixing rates. (339, 345, 346.)

Mr. WOFFINDIN, chairman of the Chicago East-Bound Freight Committee, thinks that a reasonable rate fixed by the Government might benefit the strong roads and protect them against weaker roads who might be undertaking to reduce their proportionate expense of operation by cutting rates and so increasing their tonnage. He sees no objection to governmental fixing of rates, provided the rate is made with due regard to the rights of the roads as well as to the interest of the public. He has no reason to suppose that the action of Congress would not be reasonable on both sides, and he has every reason to believe that if the facts were properly placed before a board like the Interstate Commerce Commission their action would be reasonable. His experience is that the commission has always been patient in hearing both sides. He thinks the reputable roads would be glad of anything that would insure them stable, and at the same time reasonable, rates. There would have to be some power to arbitrate between the roads and the public, and he does not see why the Interstate Commerce Commission should not be as able to make a proper decision as any other body. (566, 567.)

Mr. CLEMENTS, of the Interstate Commerce Commission, is doubtful whether it would be practicable for the commission to have absolute responsibility for establishing freight rates throughout the entire country, but a body of experts could be appointed temporarily to revise existing tariffs and classifications with very beneficial results. The rates then established could be revised and corrected from time to time on the basis of experience.

The Interstate Commerce Commission ought to have power not simply to decide that a particular rate is unjust, but to prescribe a rate which shall be in force until conditions change. The commission formerly held that it had such authority to fix rates for the future, and frequently did so; but the courts afterwards decided that it had no such authority. Virtually the commission has been deprived of 1   all the power which it was originally intended to possess. (155, 158, 161a)most

Mr. KENNARD, of the Chicago Butter and Egg Board, thinks that many existing difficulties concerning freight rates and classification would be remedied by giving the Interstate Commerce Commission power to revise tariffs. The witness thinks that the action of the railways in making classifications, especially, is exceedingly arbitrary. (367.)

Mr. WILSON, grand chief of the Brotherhood of Railroad Trackmen, and Mr. RONEMUS, grand chief of the Brotherhood of Railway Carmen, think that the Interstate Commerce Commission should be given power to determine freight and passenger rates on all interstate roads. It should consider the actual investment in the roads and should fix the rates high enough to let reasonable wages and other expenses be paid and a reasonable dividend be earned. (767, 771.)

2. *Deprecated or criticised.*—Mr. BLANCHARD, late commissioner of the Joint Traffic Association, opposes strongly the proposed extensions of the powers of the Interstate Commerce Commission. He declares that the proposal that it shall fix rates, either directly, in the first instance, or by revising and changing them with conclusive authority, is a proposal to place legislative powers in the hands of the commission, and that it should not possess at the same time legislative, judicial, and administrative powers. The enormous complexity of rate problems makes it out of the question for a small body of unskilled men to determine them. Review by the courts would be insufficient protection to the railways. In fact, the only case where the courts would be inclined to overturn the findings of the commission would be where the railway was shown to be operating at a loss, and thus deprived of its property without due process of law.

The system in England, which is often appealed to as justifying added powers for the Interstate Commerce Commission, really gives the railway and canal commission only judicial powers to act in case of complaint. So far as rates are fixed by Government they are fixed by act of Parliament, and the procedure is very careful. The carriers are required to transmit to the board of trade—an entirely different body from the railway and canal commission—their classifications and schedules of rates. The board must hear all parties, and then, if it agrees with the railways as to the proposed schedules, or if it frames others for itself, embraces them in a "provisional order" to be transmitted to Parliament as a bill. In Parliament, if there be any objections to the bill, it is carefully considered by a select committee, and the rates only become binding after adoption by Parliament. The power to fix rates is certainly a legislative one, and it is entirely out of harmony with our principle of the division of powers to give that authority to an administrative body like the Interstate Commerce Commission, especially if it be also given judicial power to enforce the law.

The claim that if the commission were given power to fix rates it would merely act in case of complaint in changing and revising the rates, is scarcely upheld by the previous attempted acts of the commission. At present it has, under the law, no power to make rates at all, and yet it at one time attempted to fix the rates on all classes of commodities from Chicago and Cincinnati to points in four Southern States, virtually affecting all the rates to the South. The power to change a rate is virtually the power to fix rates. (661–665, 675.)

Mr. RIPLEY, president of the Atchison, Topeka and Santa Fe Railroad Company, says that it would be better for the railroads if all rates were enforced as published, but it would not be practicable to intrust the fixing of rates to any governmental body. Conditions vary so rapidly that there must be a certain amount of elasticity in the rates. The business is a sensitive one, and the same reasons exist for quick action in the changing of rates that exist in the selling of merchandise. Changes should be made honestly and publicly. It would not be possible, however. to intrust the matter to anybody many miles away. The Interstate Commerce Commission might have power to pass on the rate after it is fixed. At any rate, that would be better than the conditions we have now. It is a power that might be subject to very great abuse, and it is a larger power than is wielded by the President, or anybody in the United States. (596, 597.)

Mr. MORTON, vice-president of the Atchison, Topeka and Santa Fe Railway, declares that he is not in favor of letting the Government fix the maximum and minimum rates for railways unless it at the same time fixes the prices of railway supplies, wages, and other elements of cost. He is willing that the Interstate Commerce Commission should revise rates on complaint, and apparently that its decision should stand until reversed by the courts. He thinks that the recommendations of the Interstate Commerce Commission generally have been wise and beneficial, both to the public and to the railroads, and that the railroads have usually followed its suggestions. The commission should have power to declare rates unreasonably low as well as unreasonably high. A low rate is often made for the purpose of diverting business illegitimately, to the injury of some particular industry or locality. One of greatest difficulties met by railroads is to fix justly the relative rates from competing markets. There should be some tribunal, such as the Interstate Commerce Commission, with final power to settle disputes as to differentials and similar questions. (492, 495, 496.)

Mr. SPENCER does not think that the Interstate Commerce Commission would be able to adjust railway rates throughout the United States. The problem is too large. Rates can not be fixed arbitrarily, but must be determined by experience on the basis of the constant friction of commerce and competition, which only the railway officers can understand. (282.)

Mr. COWEN, of the Baltimore and Ohio, says it would be impracticable on account of the magnitude and complexity of the task for five men to fix rates generally for all traffic. (314, 315.)

Mr. NEWCOMB, of the Department of Agriculture, would favor increasing the power of the Interstate Commerce Commission to regulate rates, but he believes that in each case careful investigation should be made, since many causes affect the justice of rates. Blanket orders covering a large number of rates and topics should be avoided. (99.)

Mr. CALLAWAY, of the New York Central, would be willing to give the commission supervisory power over pooling contracts, and with the commission as now constituted would be willing to submit to it questions as to the relativity of rates between commodities and localities. But it would be impossible for the commission to fix rates generally, the matter is so complex and the country so large. Nor would it be entirely safe to give the commission absolute power to reduce rates fixed by railways. Railways must sell their transportation to the best advantage, and the difficulties of securing entirely just rates are very great. The witness admits, however, the possession of public franchises by the railways and their quasi-public character. and declares that the railways are willing to accept reasonable regulations. He does not think railways would object if the decisions of the Interstate Commerce Commission should go into immediate effect until overruled by the courts on appeal. (236, 237, 239.)

Mr. BIRD, of the Chicago, Milwaukee and St. Paul, thinks that the Interstate Commerce Commission should have greater power. At any rate, when its decisions are appealed to the courts, the trial should be on the basis of the testimony before the commission, unless some new issue has been raised. But to give the commission general power to make rates would defeat itself. It would be entirely incompetent to handle such an enormous task. (479.)

Mr. KELLEY, freight commissioner of the Trades League of Philadelphia, is of the opinion that the powers of the Interstate Commerce Commission should be enlarged by giving it control of the classification of freight, of pooling, and of rates. He would not allow it absolutely to fix rates, but would limit its power to that of revision; but if the commission declares rates or pooling contracts unreasonable, they should not go into force until upheld by a judicial body. The membership and opinions of the commission are constantly changing, and although they have greater technical knowledge than the courts, it would be unsafe to make their decision final. (190-192.)

Mr. CARTER thinks that the railroad company should be permitted to arrange its rates, subject to reasonable restrictions. They should be fairly remunerative. They should be such that all shippers over the line might have the advantages that the largest businesses have to-day. The great trouble to-day is the preferences that are given. The Interstate Commerce Commission should have the power of revising rates. (585.)

E. Proposal to make orders of Commission binding pending appeal.—*Advocated.*—It is the opinion of many witnesses that the Interstate Commerce Commission should be given power to enforce its own orders, and that they should be operative pending appeal to the courts. This is especially urged by members of the commission itself.

Mr. CLEMENTS, in particular, urges that the decisions of the Interstate Commerce Commission should be operative and binding until reversed by some court of higher authority. At present the railways can simply disregard any action of the commission, and the burden is upon the commission to bring suit and have its order enforced by the courts. The matter is taken up practically de novo in the Federal circuit court, and may then be appealed to the circuit court of appeals, and thence to the Supreme Court. In the meantime three or five or seven years may have passed, while the rates complained of have been in daily continuous operation, and the evil effects, for which immediate remedy was desired, have been continuing. Often, in fact, by the time a decision is rendered it is no longer of any use. Nor is the possibility of obtaining damages for the injury which has occurred by any means a sufficient remedy. (155, 156, 158, 161.)

Mr. MOSELEY, secretary of the Interstate Commerce Commission, declares that experience has shown the need of further powers to secure effective administration of the interstate-commerce act. The act requires that all rates shall be reasonable and just, but the Supreme Court in 1897 decided that the commission was not authorized to prescribe rates for future observance, but only to condemn rates already existing and complained of. As a matter of fact, no one has recovered a cent from the carriers on account of unreasonable rates, because of the large expense of litigation and because a person who pays excessive rates often shifts the burden on the consumer, and has little motive to bring suit. If carriers fail to comply with orders of the commission suit must be brought, and the average time necessary to secure a final decision by the Supreme Court has been 4 years. In the case of discrimination it is held that the railway can not be prosecuted unless someone has paid the higher rate. The published rates may be so high that no one ever uses them, as was the case with the rates on cattle on the Atchison, Topeka and Santa Fe, where the shipping was entirely controlled by a monopoly. The commission should be authorized to make its orders as to rates effective until the carrier shows them to be unlawful before a court. (41, 43.)

Mr. NEWCOMB, of the division of statistics, Department of Agriculture, thinks the law should be amended so as to give practical finality to the orders of the Interstate Commerce Commission. At present. where railways refuse to obey orders, the commission is forced to carry the matter to the courts, which maintain that they have a right to hear the case practically as a new one, so that it is almost impossible to get the commission's decrees enforced. The courts are not experts, as the commissioners are, in matters of transportation. The power of the commission over freight rates should be final, although it should be exercised with great care. The courts might perhaps be allowed to refer matters back to the commission for further consideration. (103, 104.)

Mr. BACON, a member of the Milwaukee Board of Trade, says that he took an active part in the enactment of the interstate-commerce law and has watched its working. He thinks that the powers of the Interstate Commerce Commission should be strengthened. It should be permitted to revise rates in particular cases and its orders should go into effect pending appeal to the courts, since otherwise the railways, as at present, could delay cases almost indefinitely. The courts should pass only upon the law and not on the facts, since the commission, being an expert body, is better able to judge these. There would be no danger of ultimate injustice of the orders, since rates which are practically confiscatory are held unconstitutional by the Supreme Court. The injury to the railroads pending a decision would be much less than that to the public when unjust rates are continued pending a decision. The practice of fixing maximum and minimum rates to be applied in general sections all over the entire country is not desirable, on account of the differences in conditions in different cases. (419–423.)

Mr. SAGER, of the Northern Milling Company, Chicago, says that the millers generally favor giving the Interstate Commerce Commission power to effectively carry out its orders, especially with a view to protecting the milling industry against existing discriminations. (450, 454.)

Mr. VANLANDINGHAM, of the St. Louis Traffic Bureau, declares that if officers of freight bureaus and large shippers find it impossible to get redress of grievances from railway companies themselves they seldom appeal to the Interstate Commerce Commission, since it is practically powerless to remedy existing evils. He recommends the granting of power to the commission to enforce its decisions unless on appeal to the courts they be proved unjust, although he would not give the commission power to fix rates generally, but only to act on complaints. (212.)

Mr. DOUSMAN, a grain shipper of Chicago, believes there should be a uniform classification established by the Interstate Commerce Commission, and rates should be allowed to vary in different sections upon the same classification, subject to revision by the Interstate Commerce Commission. The commission's decision should be subject to review by the courts, but should be operative until proved unjust. The power of injunction should, if possible, be taken from the courts as regards rates fixed by the commission. Delay would not necessarily result from this, since the courts can decide emergency and constitutional cases quickly. The Interstate Commerce Commission might also be allowed to fix maximum and minimum rates generally. The witness is not an advocate of low rates simply. The business community can not get proper service unless the railroads make money. Moreover, good railroads need to be protected against undue rate cutting by poor ones. and to this end the witness favors allowing the railroads to pool with proper supervision by the Interstate Commerce Commission. (358–361.)

Mr. MALLORY, chairman of the railroad committee of the Chicago Live Stock Exchange, considers that the interstate-commerce law is defective, particularly in that the commission lacks the power to enforce its findings. He cites the experience of the Chicago live stock men in their efforts to secure the removal of the terminal charge of $2 per car on live stock at Chicago. This charge was imposed 5½ years before Mr. Mallory's testimony. It had been declared to be unreasonable and illegal by the Illinois board of railroad commissioners. by the United States court at Chicago (though this decision was reversed by the court of pleas on a technical point), and then by the Interstate Commerce Commission. When Mr. Mallory testified the matter was still in the United States courts.

Some method of prompt redress and of preventing arbitrary action by the roads is urgently needed. (587, 588.)

Mr. BAKER states that he is entirely in accord with Mr. Mallory's views as to the need of strengthening the interstate-commerce act so as to give a prompt and effective remedy for unjust and arbitrary action of the railroads. He believes that the same views are practically universal among men in the live-stock business. As representative of the National Live Stock Association, he participated in the recent meeting looking to action for securing legislation in this direction. He believes that the bill which his association supports provides for public inspection of railway accounts. (592.)

Mr. BARRY, secretary of the Millers' National Association, is also of opinion that the Interstate Commerce Commission should be given authority to make its orders mandatory until reversed by some court. Although some of the investigations of the commission have had a beneficial effect, it is at present able to accomplish little. The millers generally favor the Cullom bill as introduced in the Fifty-fifth Congress, and commercial organizations and farmers are generally in favor of some such measure. The witness does not think that many of the railways would strongly oppose such a change in the law, although some few of them would do so.

This witness likewise refers to the disadvantage of the present arrangement by which the person injured or the Interstate Commerce Commission must appeal to the courts to enforce the order of the commission, the case being taken up de novo by the courts. (246, 247, 250.)

Mr. CARTER, a commission merchant, considers that every finding of the Interstate Commerce Commission should go into effect at once and that any rate fixed by it should stand pending appeal. (585.)

Mr. MUSSELMAN, president of the Grand Rapids Board of Trade, feels that to make complaint of any abuse to the Interstate Commerce Commission, with its lack of power to enforce compliance with its orders, would be a waste of energy. He desires that the powers of the commission be enlarged and that it be enabled to make its orders mandatory and operative. He believes that if the commission had such power many unjust discriminations would be speedily remedied and the people's interest would be better guarded. (557.)

Mr. STONE would give the Interstate Commerce Commission the power to fix a reasonable rate, after a hearing, and make its order effective pending an appeal. He would also give the commission power to examine the accounts of railroads as the accounts of national banks are now examined. (537, 538.)

Mr. INGALLS, president of the Chesapeake and Ohio, declares that he does not think that 5 independent men like the members of the Interstate Commerce Commission would be likely to make rates especially unfair to railways. They could not make rates so bad as some of the railway managers themselves if they tried. But to fix general tariffs would be beyond their power. The work is very extensive and very difficult, and tariffs must be changed continually. The witness would be willing that the commission should determine as to the existence of discriminations between localities and shippers, or should decide special cases as to the reasonableness of rates. Its decision could remain in force until overruled by the courts. The decision of the commission as to rates underpooling agreements might be final. (299, 300.)

Mr. COWEN, of the Baltimore and Ohio, would also be willing to give the Interstate Commerce Commission power to decide in any litigated case whether a given rate was reasonable or unreasonable, the decision to remain in force pending appeal to the courts. He thinks that most railway men, however, do not agree in this opinion. It is generally opposed by the Southern and Northwestern lines and by the New England roads, while the roads in the interior sections are divided in opinion. (314, 315.)

3. *Deprecated.*—Mr. BLANCHARD thinks that the demand of the commission that its orders should go into effect until declared unlawful by the courts, unless on the very face of the record the courts should declare the findings erroneous, is unjust. The court could seldom say that an error or injustice was shown on the very face of the record; so the commission's orders would usually remain in force throughout the proceedings, and injustice would often be done for a long time to the railways.

The commission in its past actions has often shown itself wise, and the railways have usually accepted its rulings. Nevertheless, it has often shown that it has prejudged the case and has been biased. The decision of the commission is not similar to that of a board of arbitration, since both parties agree to submit the question in the case of arbitration and since both have a voice in the selection of the arbitrators. The witness does not desire that the railways should be entirely free from control, but he is not willing that 5 governmental officers should replace them as managers of their vast property. The railways certainly possess some vested rights.

Mr. Blanchard declares further that the English railway and canal commission, which is cited as justifying increased powers in the Interstate Commerce Commission, is different in its constitution and powers and offers no precedent. The English body consists of two commissioners who hold office during good behavior, and three ex-officio members, who are at the time and continue to be judges of the superior courts, and who act for 5 years. One of the appointed commissioners must have had experience in railway affairs. The commission, as thus constituted, is evidently more a judicial body than the Interstate Commerce Commission. Moreover, the English commission has no administrative powers, but only judicial powers. For the most part it can act only in case of complaint, although it has certain powers as to approving agreements between railways, ordering through rates, and ordering changes in canal rates in case a railway owns a canal and tries to divert traffic from it to the railway. It is not charged with detecting violations of the law itself and has no authority to investigate accounts or institute complaints in its own name. The Interstate Commerce Commission, on the other hand, has large administrative and inquisitorial powers, which have a strong tendency to deprive it of the judicial temperament. In fact, to permit the Interstate Commerce Commission to render final judgment against a railroad would be like allowing a party to be judge in his own cause or like permitting a man to be convicted of murder by the grand jury which indicted him. There is an appeal from the decision of the British railway and canal commission as to questions of law, notwithstanding the fact that it is itself constituted as a a judicial body.

Mr. Blanchard points out further that the conditions of railway traffic in England are different, so that greater restrictions upon railway rates would be justifiable there than in this country. The freight rates are about double those in this country. The railways are more fully protected in many regards by the law. Thus their stations are more carefully policed, the liability for damages is more fairly interpreted, etc. Moreover, the construction of new competing roads is carefully regulated. Before a line can be built it must be demonstrated that it is a reasonable public requirement, while with us the building of parallel lines is often unwisely encouraged. Mr. Blanchard also speaks in some detail of the permission of pooling in England. (659–665.)

Mr. SPENCER, of the Southern Railway, does not believe that the commission should be permitted to amend and rectify rates, except under the right of appeal to the courts, while its decisions, if appealed from, should not remain in force until upheld by the court. Otherwise the railway may have suffered for two or three years by being forced to maintain an unreasonably low rate pending the trial. If a shipper, on the other hand, is injured during the duration of the suit he can collect damages. If on account of the smallness of the debt he will not take the trouble to collect them, that is no reason why the railways should pay him what is not due. The members of courts are supposed to be trained jurists, and they have a greater responsibility than the members of the Interstate Commerce Commission. If, however, the commission itself were constituted as a court, with life membership, and with a court's powers and responsibilities, the witness would be willing to submit the question of reasonable rates to its final decision. (282, 283.)

Mr. TUCKER, chairman of the Central Freight Association, thinks that the reasonableness of rates should be left to the courts. He would not have the railroads compelled to conform to rates fixed by the Commission until the court should rule otherwise. He does not think it possible for the Interstate Commerce Commission to have properly in view the tonnage, the expenses, the risks, and all the circumstances which make a given rate necessary. (558, 560.)

Mr. STICKNEY, president of the Chicago Great Western Railway, declares that the Interstate Commerce Commission has all the powers it ought to have. Nevertheless, it is, as a whole, little more than a farce, although it has had some educational influence. Its powers ought not to be final, since in taking evidence it does not follow the rules of courts. In fact, the less government interference in the case of railways the better. (463.)

F. Publicity of accounts and books.—*Advocated.*—All of the members of the Interstate Commerce Commission who appeared before the Industrial Commission believe that the essentially public character of railway service justifies the requirement of much greater publicity of railway affairs than is now secured. No effective regulation is possible without thorough knowledge. This publicity can be best promoted by permitting public examiners to inspect the books and accounts of railroads at any time. Such inspection is fully as justifiable in the case of railways, with their immense influence upon the public welfare, as in the case of banks and insurance companies. Government inspection of these latter concerns has been distinctly beneficial. Many criminal violations of law by railways, such as granting of rebates, are covered up by deceptive entries in the books, and can not be ascertained readily when, as sometimes happens, the books are brought into court in case of suits. It requires expert skill and often long investigation to make the publicity of books effectively beneficial. In connection with such a system of inspection the requirement of uniform methods of bookkeeping might be advantageous. Mr. Clements, however, does not think that publicity alone, without power to punish or regulate, would be a sufficient remedy for existing abuses. (KNAPP, 144; CLEMENTS, 159, 160.)

Mr. NEWCOMB thinks the powers of the Commission to secure statistics and to inspect accounts, etc., should be extended. For instance, it is desirable to know the freight rates on different classes of traffic for through and local business, which we are not now able to ascertain. (104.)

Professor JOHNSON declares that publicity is essential as the very foundation of supervision by public authority. Rates published must be strictly observed, and accounts of railways must be open to inspection to show such observance. (62.)

Professor SELIGMAN thinks that the prescription of uniformity of accounts, and Government inspection of accounts, of transportation companies, are not only advisable but imperatively necessary. Such regulations would not only be useful for purposes of taxation, but they are needed on account of many other questions of the relations between railways and the Government. (605.)

Mr. INGALLS, president of the Chesapeake and Ohio, believes that the public character of railways justifies the most thorough possible publicity, and that publicity is the most effective remedy for all existing evils. He advocates the examination of the books of railways by public inspectors in the same manner as the books of banks are examined. The various scandals and false accountings, with their injustice to the public, and especially to stockholders and investors, would thus be prevented, and discriminations also would be checked. (287, 297, 298, 301.)

Mr. SPENCER, of the Southern Railway, thinks that publicity is the chief remedy for discriminations as well as for unjust rates and other abuses. As a matter of fact, if discriminations were abolished, nine-tenths of the problem of Government supervision of railroads would disappear. The witness recognizes the fact that railways are quasi-public corporations, and that if rates actually became burdensome direct legislation would be justifiable, but he thinks that rates are not often unreasonable, and that publicity is a sufficient remedy. He would have no objection to the establishment of inspectors who should examine the books of railways, provided they would use ordinary respect for the private part of the business, especially not revealing information to competitors. To some extent the railways might evade the inspection by various methods, and for this reason the witness thinks that the criminal phase of the interstate-commerce act should not be abandoned. (274, 278.)

Mr. MORTON, of the Atchison, Topeka and Santa Fe, believes that the more publicity is required of railroads the better. The immense importance of railway rates and of fair treatment of all shippers justifies the requirement of such publicity. (500.)

Deprecated.—Mr. CALLAWAY, president of the New York Central, does not approve of requiring the books of railways to be open to the inspection of examiners, although as far as his own road is concerned there is nothing in the books which the world can not see. Competitors might be given information to the detriment of the railway under this system. The sworn statements made to the various State railway commissioners and to the National Government already give all necessary information. (237, 238.)

In the opinion of Mr. COWEN, of the Baltimore and Ohio, the inspection of railway books by public officers would not accomplish any particular good, although it might prevent suspicion and discontent on the part of the people, and is not especially objectionable. At present people wishing information concerning railways consult Poor's Manual rather than the publications of the Interstate Commerce Commission or other official bureaus. (317, 318.)

Mr. STICKNEY, of the Chicago and Great Western, opposes the inspection of railway accounts by Government officers or any interference by Government with private business affairs. He even thinks that the national-bank examiners have burst more banks than they have ever saved. (464.)

G. National charters.—Mr. BLANCHARD, late commissioner of the Joint Traffic Association, thinks that national charters for interstate railways would be undesirable. There would result a constant conflict with the rights of the State.

Moreover, there are important railroads which lie wholly within one State, and yet do a large interstate traffic. Furthermore, incorporation under national laws would give an erroneous feeling that the National Government had a right to control the traffic within the States upon such railroads.

H. State railway commissions.—Mr. REAGAN, of the Texas railroad commission, believes that Congress should prohibit the Federal courts from issuing injunctions during the pendency of suits to prevent the enforcement of rates fixed by the Interstate Commerce Commission or State railroad commissions, until the rates have been found unjust or illegal. Some deference is due to the actions of railway commissions, and the power of injunction is too great and too dangerous to be intrusted to the arbitrary will of any one judge. (344.)

The Texas railroad commission has absolute power in fixing rates, subject only to appeal to the courts. The constitutionality of the statute was upheld in the case of Reagan v. The Farmers' Loan and Trust Company by the Supreme Court of the United States. The railways at first opposed the law, but most of them now claim that it is beneficial to them as well as the public, stopping the cutting of rates and the wasting of revenue. The commission has power to examine the books of railways, and has used it to advantage; and Mr. Reagan favors giving similar power to the Interstate Commerce Commission. (339, 44, 349.)

X. TAXATION, ESPECIALLY AS APPLIED TO RAILWAYS.

A. General discussion of railway taxation.—Professor SELIGMAN, of Columbia University, presented a general discussion of corporate and especially railway taxation.

1. *General principles of taxation.*—Professor Seligman considers that taxation is not only to be utilized for fiscal purposes, but also for such social purposes as are approved by the majority. There are two classes of thought on this subject throughout the world. One is that of the extreme individualists, such as Hon. David A. Wells, who believe that as soon as taxation is used for other purposes than revenue it is not taxation but confiscation. On the other side are the socialists, who maintain that the great problem to-day is the social and economic problem; and that a tax is not a tax unless it has a social object. Professor Seligman thinks the great mass of scientists and statesmen will confess that both the theory of the subject and the history of the world show that taxation must be utilized for both purposes; that the primary end is to secure revenue, but that we must not shrink from utilizing taxation for any desirable end for which taxation is a workable means. (605.)

The difficulties of taxation problems arise largely from the fact that our legal and constitutional conditions are not in harmony with our economic conditions. In the long run, law is nothing but the outcome of economic conditions. As economic conditions change, the law necessarily follows. But the change takes time, and in the interval of maladjustment we are subject to evils such as we see. (602.) The tax situation may be much improved if the legislators will realize that they can take only one step forward at a time. (608.)

The wealth of the nineteenth century consists, far more largely than in past times, of what is known as personalty. The largest part of this personalty under modern conditions consists of corporate securities. The problem of just taxation, therefore, is very largely the problem of corporation taxation. (599.)

The problem of corporation taxation may be approached from several points of view. In the first place, there is the general question of revenue—what revenue we can get or ought to get from transportation and other corporations; second, there is the question of justice to the various individuals interested in the corporations. There are also questions of a different class arising out of the relations of the State governments and the Federal Government. (599.)

2. *Federal and State taxation.*—Professor SELIGMAN considers it a primary principal that the Federal Government and the State governments should draw their revenues from different sources so far as possible. He points out that this has always been our general policy. The Federal Government has largely depended upon the so-called indirect taxes, and has seldom touched those sources of taxation which are depended on by the States. He considers it an unfortunate exception that the Federal Government has recently levied a tax on inheritances. In our leading States, like New York, Pennsylvania, and Massachusetts, there is a well-marked tendency to derive State revenues in increasing proportions from inheritances and corporations, relegating the general property tax to the local divisions. This is a wise policy, and Federal taxation of interstate commerce would bring in a further disturbance of it by interfering with the power of the States to collect a large portion of their revenues from corporations. This seems

a sufficient reason why the Federal Government should not make taxation of corporations a source of revenue, though it is entirely possible that Federal taxation might well be laid on corporations for other purposes. (599, 600.)

On the other hand Professor SELIGMAN does not consider that any difficulty is likely to arise from constitutional impediments to taxation of railroads by the United States. The Government has a right to tax any corporation, whether created by itself or not. The gross receipts tax during the civil war, though economically a direct tax, was considered by the courts an indirect tax and constitutional. The stamp tax has recently been upheld as a tax on business, and the Government is now taxing inheritances; though the constitutionality of this tax is still unsettled. (608.)

8. *Interstate complications—Double taxation.*—The problem of corporate taxation is much complicated by the fact that a corporation may have its legal situs in one State and its actual property in another, and may be owned in a third. So far as domestic corporations are concerned the State is at perfect liberty to levy a franchise or excise tax, measured by the total receipts of the corporation. A tax can not be levied by a State upon gross receipts, so far as those receipts are derived from interstate commerce. But through a fiction of the law, a tax under the name of a franchise tax or an excise tax is held to be valid, though the value of the franchise or excise is measured by the gross receipts. Such a tax, however, can be levied by any State only upon corporations which it has chartered. Under modern conditions a large part of the corporations doing business in any State are, as a rule, chartered by other States. A franchise tax upon such foreign corporations is held by the Supreme Court of the United States to be a tax upon business; and it can not be levied upon receipts derived wholly or in part from interstate commerce. It results that a great mass of corporate business can not be reached by any tax on receipts. Some States attempt to solve the problem by taxing the corporations upon valuation or upon capital stock, and in some cases also upon bonded indebtedness. (600,601.)

Again, the taxation of corporations which do business in several States, upon their capital stock, is subject to great difficulties in the determination of the amount upon which the tax should be levied. The Western Union Telegraph Company does business, perhaps, in every State. If its entire stock were taxed in every State, the company would be taxed 50 times. There has been a tendency in the last few years, as in the taxation of express and telegraph companies in Ohio and Illinois, and in a few other cases, to tax that proportion of the valuation which is employed within the State. In the case of transportation companies this proportion is measured by mileage. While a division on the basis of mileage is not altogether fair, and would be entirely unfair if it were extended to small subdivisions, some of which include great terminals, it serves tolerably as a basis of State taxation. It seems the only practical way to levy a tax based upon the value of a corporation's capitalization. (601, 603, 604.)

The same difficulties in avoiding or adjusting double taxation which we have in the United States are found in all modern federal governments. They are found in Germany and in Switzerland, and will appear in Australia under the new form of government. They are perhaps most prominent here, because the legal idea of State sovereignty is strongest here. In Canada, where the provinces are not legally sovereign, the problem does not exist. (600.)

Professor SELIGMAN suggests two general lines in which advance toward the correction of the evils of double taxation may be made. One is to try to secure uniformity of State action, perhaps through Federal pressure. Many of our existing evils arise from the diversity, complexity, and opposition between our State laws. If the Federal Government would enact a law for the calling together of annual conventions of State commissioners to meet with Federal commissioners who should be appointed, and to consider the questions involved from the point of view of general utility, the views of the State executive authorities and ultimately the action of the State legislatures might gradually be brought into harmony and unity. A Federal officer or commission appointed for the purpose would be desirable, because Federal officers would naturally take the national rather than the State point of view.

The second way would be by the direct intervention of Federal authority. While it would be unwise for the National Government to make corporations a source of direct revenue to itself, it might make itself an agency for collecting revenues from them, to be afterwards distributed to the States. Such a plan is followed in England as to the inheritance taxes, and Germany and Switzerland follow a similar plan to some extent. In our own country we have the precedent of a distribution of money by the Government to the States. While the witness would not advise the adoption of this plan until the futility of the first plan has been shown, he would consider it perfectly legal and constitutional and an available way out of our difficulties if no better way is found. If it were adopted, the rights of the stock and bond holders, as well as the location of the railways, ought to be considered in arranging the division. (602, 603, 607–609.)

4. *Taxation of capital stock and bonds.*—Professor Seligman would consider it best to tax the market value of capital stock rather than its par value. He considers that every real economic increase of capital ought to be taxed. Water is not an economic increase of capital, because it does not increase the earning capacity of the company. A tax upon watered stock might perhaps be desirable to check watering; at least that end is desirable. The difficulty is that a tax would strike the honest in trying to reach the dishonest. There may be an increase of capital which seems to be water and yet is not. We may not be able to tell until some years have elapsed. It is true there is sometimes an increase of capital stock for mere jobbing purposes, and this may for the time being increase the credit of the stock, and cause it to sell at higher rates. But it is frequently difficult to draw the line between what is fictitious and what is actual capital. The Massachusetts method of dealing with stock watering is better. (609, 610.)

Professor Seligman says that it is manifestly unfair to tax corporations upon capital stock, excluding bonds. Two corporations may have each a capital stock of $100,000, but one may have a further working capital, represented by bonds, of $200,000. The second corporation has an actual capital three times as great as the first. The particular form of document issued to investors does not affect the economic conditions of the problem. The second corporation ought to pay three times as much tax as the first. But the United States courts have held that a tax upon the bonds of a foreign corporation is a tax upon the bondholders; and, consequently, since the State has sovereignty only within its own borders, no State can reach corporation bonds which are held outside. However defensible this decision may be legally, it is economically incorrect. The possibility of a just system of taxation based on capitalization is destroyed by it. If you try to tax corporation bonds, and can tax them only so far as they are owned within the State, you will soon have no bonds within the State to tax. (601, 608.)

5. *Taxation of net receipts.*—Professor SELIGMAN considers the taxation of net receipts more equitable than any other system. Everywhere else in the world where transportation companies are taxed, with the exception of the cantons of Switzerland, the tax is based somewhat on the net receipts. He does not consider, however, that under our present conditions such a tax is practically desirable. The great corporations could easily succeed in so scaling down the nominal net receipts that they would not have any receipts to tax. The difficulty would appear especially in the case of manufacturing corporations. In order to make the tax successful as to any class of corporations, net receipts would have to be defined as they never have been defined before, even by the Interstate Commerce Commission. Yet it would be possible by careful statutory definition of net receipts, by prescription of uniformity of accounts, and by Government inspection of accounts, to reach such a public knowledge of the net receipts of quasi-public corporations as should make the tax on their net receipts practicable and just. (604, 605.)

6. *Taxation of gross receipts of railroads.*—Professor SELIGMAN says that the practical difficulties of the taxation of net receipts have led the most of our States, so far as they tax receipts at all, to base the tax on gross receipts. This system is theoretically far less good, but has many practical advantages. The difficulties which our constitution puts in the way of any State tax on receipts are referred to above. (See *Interstate complications, Double taxation*, p. 120.) Professor Seligman believes that the taxation of gross receipts in Wisconsin is comparatively light, and that the interstate railways have acquiesced in it without raising much objection. In other States, as Maine, where it was sought to get a large part of the revenue from this object, the corporations have fought the law and have succeeded in fighting it. (603, 604.)

7. *New Jersey tax system and corporation law.*—Professor SELIGMAN considers that the tax system of New Jersey is on the whole very wise, and that the entire system of corporation law of New Jersey is in some respects in advance of the systems of many other States. New Jersey is peculiarly situated, in that a great deal of property belongs legally to her which belongs economically to New York. Rules which might apply to her might not altogether apply under other circumstances. (606.)

B. **Special cases and opinions.**—1. *General property tax on railways.*—Mr. REAGAN, of the Texas railroad commission, favors the general property tax on the basis of the actual value of the property of railroads. He thinks that the State railroad commission rather than anybody else should fix the valuation, since it alone has the means of knowing the facts concerning railroad property. Thus the Texas railroad commission has valued one road, capitalized at $60,000 per mile, at $18,000 per mile, while the assessment for taxation is only $8,000 per mile. The witness does not favor a tax on the value of railway franchises in addition to the tax on property or on earnings, nor does he favor taxing both property and earnings. (348.)

Mr. COWEN does not think that the methods of taxation in the States reached by the Baltimore and Ohio system are especially unjust. In many of these States the physical property of the railways is assessed to the general property tax, by State officers, the valuation being distributed among the localities. This system is preferable to the gross receipts tax which prevails in Maryland and Ohio, since it avoids difficulty as to the question of taxing receipts from interstate traffic. (319.)

Mr. SPENCER, of the Southern Railway, declares that under the general property tax in the Southern States the assessed value of railway properties is often much too high. The assessment is usually based upon the mileage, with special assessments of depots and such property and of rolling stock. (282.)

2. *Gross receipts tax on railways.*—Mr. CALLAWAY, president of the New York Central, thinks that the taxation of gross earnings is the fairest method, and approves the graduation of the tax according to the amount of earnings. He says that under the general property tax the New York Central, especially on account of the high assessments of its terminal properties, pays no less than 12 per cent of its net earnings in taxation. A gross earnings tax at such a rate as that applied in Michigan would not amount to more than 3 or 4 per cent of the net earnings. Taxation of net earnings is not desirable, because the Government is entitled to some payment from the railways whether they are earning any profit or not, and because interest on the bonds, which often constitute the chief cost of the railway, is deducted in calculating net earnings. (228.)

Professor JOHNSON would be inclined to tax railways on their gross earnings. A license tax is most satisfactory of all. The general property tax results in a score of different tax rates. Since the rates and fares of railways largely depend on influences which they can not control, it is probable that a tax on gross earnings can not be shifted. The Supreme Court has decided that the States can tax railway property only so far as it lies within their own boundaries, but has upheld the Ohio law, which has put a liberal interpretation on what property lies within such boundaries. (63.)

The Illinois Central, by the contract in its charter with the State of Illinois, declared fixed by the constitution, pays 7 per cent on its gross receipts to the State. While Mr. FISH considers the gross receipts tax the fairest, he declares that this percentage is excessive. It was based on the supposition that operating expenses would be not over 50 per cent of the gross receipts. As a matter of fact, exclusive of taxes, the operating expenses of the railroad are now about 62¼ per cent. Such rates as prevail in the West, 2¼ to 4 per cent, would be fairer. (232, 233.)

3. *Net receipts tax.*—Mr. NEWCOMB, of the division of statistics, Department of Agriculture, says that scarcely any two of the States have the same system of taxation. Where a State attempts to secure a higher tax from railways than its neighbors, the effect is often to increase rates or decrease facilities for its own citizens, since taxes are largely shifted. A tax on net earnings is the only just and scientific one. Taxation of the property of a railroad is impracticable on account of its character and location, and because of the peculiar relation between its visible property and its franchises, stocks, bonds, etc. A tax on gross earnings is likely to lead to high rates, giving a smaller total of gross earnings but added profits through a lower percentage of operating expenses. The proposition to tax interstate commerce for the benefit of the Federal Government might tend to check the territorial division of labor, but is worthy of consideration. It is just to differentiate the methods of taxing railways from those of taxing other forms of property, for different incomes are different in their nature and in the degree to which they are earned. It is difficult to establish a uniform system of taxation among different States on account of the limitations of their constitutions. (101, 102, 105, 106.)

C. The general property tax.—Professor SELIGMAN remarks that questions of taxation do not present the same difficulty in the agricultural States of the South and West as in the highly developed industrial States of the North and East. In the agricultural States the general property tax still serves fairly successfully. The more highly developed States are getting rid of it, at least for the general revenue of the State. Besides New Jersey there are other States, Connecticut among them, which do not levy any State tax on general property. At the time of the testimony New York had a plan under consideration by which the same result was to be reached. The general property tax is suitable to a certain stage of economic development, and everywhere in the world at a certain stage of economic development it is found. It was found in Europe in the Middle Ages, and it has prevailed in our own country; but when the fit stage is passed the property tax is bound to go. The general property tax, maintained under unfit conditions, resolves itself into a tax on real estate, plus a more or less wild guess at the personal property. (602, 603, 607.)

In a great many of the States the complaint of the farmers that they bear more than their share of taxation is just. The reason is that while the chickens and cows are assessed to the farmers the personal property in the cities largely escapes taxation. Professor Seligman has no faith in the possibility of enforcing the personal property tax by means of any system of listing or by any severity of penalty. The law recently enacted in Illinois is simply another example of the new broom sweeping clean. It works as long as everybody believes that the law is going to be enforced, but it takes only a very short time for everybody to conclude that the law will not be enforced. (607.)

Mr. Newcomb says that he would favor abolishing the personal property tax and laying a general tax on real estate, including the improvements. He would not abandon franchise and internal-revenue taxes and others having special advantages. It is not necessary or just that all classes of property and income should be taxed in the same way. Different incomes differ in their nature and in the degree to which they are earned. (105, 106.)

D. Franchise taxation.—Professor Seligman remarks that three different rights are given to corporations by government. First, the right to become a corporation. That is paid for in New York, as in most other States, by incorporation fees or bonuses on charters. The second right is the franchise, not to become, but to be, a corporation. That is paid for by so-called franchise or license taxes levied at intervals upon capital stock or upon gross receipts or otherwise. The third right is a privilege of certain corporations to make use of the streets and highways, by going either below or above them. It is this third privilege which the Ford franchise tax law of New York seeks to reach. It applies only to those quasi-public corporations which are sometimes called municipal monopolies— street railways, gas companies, electric-light, steam-heat, and power companies, etc. Such companies own little or no real estate. The streets, where the principal business is done, do not belong to them. The value of their property as a whole is very much more than the value of their tangible assets. This difference between the value of their tangible assets and the total value of their whole property is what the Ford bill tries to reach. Professor Seligman considers such a tax entirely proper, and thinks that all franchises of a quasi-public nature ought to be paid for over and above the general rate of taxation. (606, 610.)

E. Taxation of inheritances.—Professor Seligman regards taxation of inheritances as proper and highly desirable for the States. It is one of the means by which the States will be enabled to separate their sources of general revenue from the sources of revenue of their subdivisions; and this is the first step to be accomplished in the reform of State taxation. For this very reason it is undesirable that the Federal Government tax inheritances. Such a tax will make it more difficult for the States to obtain a large revenue from this source, and so will constitute an interference in the progress of reform of State taxation. (599, 603.)

XI. GOVERNMENT OWNERSHIP OF RAILWAYS AND TELE-GRAPHS.

A. Advocates of government ownership of railways.—Mr. Greeley, a commission merchant of Chicago, thinks that no legal regulation will prevent railroad discriminations and abuses. Pooling would not prevent special rates; it has been tried many times and found wanting. The only remedy, therefore, is Government ownership of railroads, and in order to make this feasible the standard of the civil service must be greatly raised. Even as it is, however, aside from excessive payments which it has been forced to make to the railroads, Mr. Greeley believes that the United States post-office is run on as cheap a basis as any private institution in the world. Government ownership would reduce freight rates about one-half. It would not do to take away the right of employees to vote under Government ownership. Mr. Greeley thinks, also, that the United States Government should operate public grain warehouses. (379–381.)

Mr. Lewis, of Cumberland, Md., submitted a written argument in favor of Government ownership of railroads.

Mr. Lewis believes that under Government the following objects may be attained:

First. The just security of the capital invested upon the basis of its commercial worth. Precarious securities will become things of the past.

Second. Uniformity and equality of freight rates among shippers; the elimination of quasi-natural discriminations as well as willful.

Third. A half-cent passenger rate per mile over the entire country.

Fourth. An 8-hour day for all railway workers, and the consequent employment of 165,000 of the unemployed to fill this one-fifth reduction in time.

Fifth. The greater development of the natural resources of the country by a sensible application of the capital now invested in " parallels," etc.

Sixth. A juster distribution of railway mileage to the population and area of the several States. The grossest inequality is the necessary effect of the present system.

Seventh. The establishment of a system of postal express, which it seems might be conducted, in conjunction with the post-office, at half the present cost to the public.

Eighth. The institution of accident insurance for passengers, employees, and freight under certain limitations.

Ninth. The emancipation of public men from the evil influences of railway "politics," and the attainment of free elections.

Tenth. The adoption by the Government of punitive freight rates, when considered necessary to destroy existing trusts and discourage the formation of others. (724.)

1. *Estimated financial results.*—Mr. LEWIS gives a detailed estimate of the receipts and expenditures of the railroads under Government ownership, from which he deduces a net revenue to the Government of over $70,000,000 per annum. Forty million dollars is due to the elimination of State taxation of the railroads. A saving of $165,000,000 in the annual interest charge is expected, because of the ability of the Government to borrow at one-half the rate of interest which the railroads, on the average, have to pay. Seventeen million dollars is to be saved by the elimination of some 1,500 railway presidents, who "in most instances represent the financing rather than the actual management of the railroads." The superintendents, the actual trained railroad men, would be retained. Other large savings are $12,500,000 for legal expenses, advertising, and commissions; exclusive use of shortest routes, $15,000,000; savings by uniformity of rolling stock, machinery, accounts, etc,, under single control, $15,000,000; abolition of fund for legislation, corruption, lobbies, etc., $10,000,000; elimination of pass evil, $5,000,000; elimination of " outside agencies," $11,000,000. On the other hand Mr. Lewis allows an additional cost of $90,000,000 for reducing the hours of labor of all railroad men to 8 per day, and adding one-fifth to the number of men, paying all the same wages per day which are now paid. He adds a further sum of $6,000,000 to raise the average daily wages of the trackmen from $1.17 to $1.30. (735–741.)

When Switzerland purchased her railroads in 1898 she fixed their value by capitalizing the average net profits of the roads for the previous 10 years. Mr. Lewis would have the United States follow a similar plan, capitalizing the interest paid on bonds at 5 per cent, the dividends paid on stock at 6 per cent, and the rent paid for equipment, terminals, etc., at 12 per cent. He would have the existing owners paid the full value of their property, as so arrived at. He estimates that the entire funded debt, stock, and rented property would be covered by a cash payment of about 6¼ billions of dollars. (727–729.)

If the railroads were bought for 6¼ billions of dollars the debt of the United States would then be less than $100 per head of population. The debt of France is about $162 per head, and the 3 per cent bonds of France are above bar. Moreover, the purchase of the railways would not involve a real increase of debt, since the railroads would be an asset fully equal in value to the face of the bonds issued. Mr. Lewis would have the bonds exchangeable at will for Treasury notes and the notes exchangeable at will for bonds. He believes that such bonds to the necessary amount could be floated at 2¼ per cent. (731.)

Mr. Lewis notes that from 1890 to 1897, the last year covered by his statistics, the amount of passenger travel in the United States did not vary more than 7 per cent. The amount of freight business showed a fairly steady increase. From these facts Mr. Lewis draws the conclusion that while on any one road the results of operation may greatly vary from year to year, the results of the operation of the whole system of the country are calculable. It is possible to foretell the results of railway management as a whole, just as it is possible to foretell the experience of life insurance companies. The elimination of the element of risk, by uniting all the railroads in a single system, furnishes an additional argument for the ownership of all by the Government. (738.)

2. *Security of property.*—Mr. LEWIS gives quotations of stocks and bonds of 30 principal railways for 1897 and 1898, showing that the value of stocks fluctuated from 30 to 300 per cent, and the value of bonds from 5 to 100 per cent, in each of these years. This reduces the ownership of such securities, he says, to a matter of gambling. Government purchase would substitute Government bonds, stable in value, for these so fluctuating issues of the railways, and would offer a secure investment for savings instead of a temptation to speculative gambling. (726, 727.)

3. *Extension of the system.*—Mr. LEWIS believes that the railway system would be more wisely extended by governmental action than under the stress of competitive private interests as at present. To prevent the improper building of new roads through political influence, he suggests that, while all roads should be built and operated by the Federal Government, States and counties thinking themselves entitled to new roads should bond themselves to cover the cost of construction. If the traffic of the new roads should justify their construction, the Federal Government should pay the cost. If not, the local bodies which had them built should bear the burden. (742.)

Mr. Lewis estimates that perhaps one-fourth of the capital now invested in railways is wasted in duplication. He considers that such waste would be entirely saved for the future by Government ownership. (741.)

4. *Freight rates under Government ownership.*—According to the Interstate Commerce Commission's Report, the average receipts from freight service in 1896 were 8.6 mills per ton per mile. Mr. LEWIS suggests that under Government ownership there should be adopted, generally speaking, a uniform rate of about 8 mills per ton per mile. He does not desire, however, that freight should be carried like letters, without reference to actual cost of service. (732.)

Mr. Lewis suggests that if the Government owned the railroads there should be a commission to determine when an industrial organization had become a trust, and the Government should then impose double freight rates upon the products of such trusts, or prohibit the transportation of them altogether. (748, 749.)

5. *Reduction of passenger fares.*—Mr. Lewis states that a reduction of passenger fares of about 40 per cent in Austria-Hungary increased passenger traffic 50 per cent. He believes that a reduction of passenger fares in the United States to one-half cent per mile would increase the number of passenger miles traveled from 13 billions, in 1896, to at least 26 billions. The number of passengers could be doubled without any appreciable increase of cost, for the number of passengers per train averages only about 41 or 42, and the capacity of the trains is several times as great. It costs no more to haul a full train than an empty one. Mr. Lewis bases the argument for so radical a reduction of fares not so much upon the probability that it would pay in a pecuniary sense, as upon the educational and refining influences of travel, and upon such considerations as the ready movement of laborers from place to place as their services might be demanded; in other words, upon general social utility. In the management of the railroads, as in the management of the post-office, considerations of profit should be eliminated and only social utility should be considered. (733, 734.)

6. *Postal express.*—Mr. Lewis states that something above 40 per cent of the gross receipts of the express companies goes for payment for railroad transportation, and the remainder goes largely for supporting independent offices and warehouses, for handsome salaries, dividends, etc.; the only service performed by them which is of social utility being delivery by wagons in cities. He believes that with governmental ownership of railroads and management of the express business in connection with the post-office the business could be conducted at about one-half of the rate now charged by private companies. (745, 746.)

7. *Accidents.*—The witness gives figures to show that the proportion of passengers killed in the year 1890 was, for the United States, 1 to 1,721,786; for Germany, 1 to 9,262,092; for Austria-Hungary, 1 to 17,109,734; the number of passengers injured, for the United States, 1 to 203,064; for Germany, 1 to 1,805,323; for Austria-Hungary, 1 to 1,291,300. Of the men employed on the railroads the number killed in 1890 was, for the United States, 1 in 306; Germany, 1 in 750; Austria-Hungary, 1 in 1,067; of men employed there were injured, in the United States, 1 in 33; Germany, 1 in 169; Austria-Hungary, 1 in 292. Mr. Lewis believes that the great contrast between the United States on the one hand and Germany and Austria-Hungary on the other is to be attributed to the difference between private and governmental management. Many of the accidents in the United States Mr. Lewis believes to be due to the excessive amount of work demanded of railway employees. (743.)

Moreover, Mr. Lewis would unite with Government ownership of railroads a system of governmental accident insurance, designed particularly for the benefit of railroad employees, but available also to passengers. As indicating the social inefficiency of existing accident insurance companies, he points out that they return to the insured in payment of losses only about $6,000,000 for $16,000,000 collected in premiums. (744, 745.)

8. *Political effects, civil service.*—Mr. LEWIS considers that the railroads, instead of getting into politics through public ownership, would be less in politics than now. The postal service, with its nearly 200,000 employees, is relatively free from politics, as compared with the railroads. The railroads constantly interfere with Congress, legislatures, county and city officials, and the courts. (746, 747, 750, 751.)

Mr. Lewis says that no one, he believes, has ever advocated public railways without demanding at the same time a thorough enforcement of genuine civil-service reform. (746, 747.)

He adds that the presidencies of railroads are largely occupied by men who have no practical knowledge of railroad affairs, and many of the lower offices are filled by favoritism. Nepotism is more rampant in railway management to-day than in any of the departments of the public service. Under public ownership the railway service would be confined to trained railway men. No one should be eligible for advancement but some railway man who had passed a suitable examination, and promotion should also be determined in part by the record of each man's errors in his previous work, as in the postal service. The post-office is on the whole the best-managed industrial enterprise in the United States. The record of business failures, showing an average bankruptcy among private business enterprises of some $200,000,000 per annum for the last 20 years, seems to Mr. Lewis to indicate the inefficiency of private management. (746, 747.)

Referring to the aphorism that the least government is the best government, Mr. Lewis remarks that the systematic exercise of power by any set of persons is in itself government, whether the power is exercised under the name of government or not. The railroad managers at the present time exercise enormous power over their employees, not only as to their economic condition, but even as to their social and political action. Moreover, the railroads are able to wield political power, not only by their influence over their employees, but also by their direct interference with Congressmen, legislators, governors, judges, and tax assessors. The post-office exercises little influence, if any, upon our Government. The privately owned railroads exercise enormous influence upon it. Public ownership of them would result in a diminution, instead of an increase, of their governmental influence. (749–751.)

B. Opponents of government ownership.—Professor SELIGMAN, of Columbia University, says that we have in this country 3 different stages of economic life existing at the same time—the frontier life in some of the Western States, purely agricultural communities in some of the Southern States, and most fully developed industrial communities in a few Eastern and Northern States. This is one of the reasons why the solution of all economic problems is so much more delicate in the United States than in any of the compact and complete communities of the Old World. It has taken those communities 1,000 or 2,000 years to get a development which we are getting through in a few decades. Some of our States are, practically, as regards certain economic conditions, where Europe was in the Middle Ages. (607, 608.)

The great end of individual initiative in general is to turn ability toward the reduction of cost of production by inventions, etc. All progress consists of lowering the cost of production by driving out old processes and introducing new. This method of improvement results not only in lower prices for the community, but in higher wages for the operative, as well as prosperity for the employers. (611.)

Professor Seligman says that three considerations determine the desirability of Government ownership of any industry : First, the existence or nonexistence of widespread social interests. Second, the amount of capital invested; the need of large capital is an objection to Government ownership. Third, the complexity of the management; public authorities can best handle businesses which are comparatively simple, and whose methods are likely to change but little. (610.)

The witness, while favoring Government ownership of telegraphs, is distinctly opposed to public ownership of railroads in the United States. Two of the criteria named seem to him to be conclusive against it. (1) In the railway service we have the greatest possible amount of capital invested. If the Government owned the railroads their revenues and expenditures would be two or three times as great as all the rest of our revenues together. The whole budget of the country would be thrown out of gear, and everything would depend upon the success and prosperity of the railway system. (2) The requirements for skill in management are of the highest. The greatest salaries in this country, salaries from $25,000 to $100,000, are given to the railway presidents, and deservedly so. The Government could not hope to compete successfully in such a line of business with private individuals. A democracy will not pay very high salaries to public officers, and with low salaries the temptation to the highest order of ability would not be great enough. It is true that governmental service has an attractiveness which compensates in part for loss of salary, but under the present necessarily materialistic drift of our people, with a whole continent to conquer, this incentive to public service can not be sufficient to attract the highest order of talent. There are numerous instances of men quitting the Government service because of small salaries, and many of the men of the first class who do serve the Government for comparatively small pay are men of independent means. In Prussia the conditions are different, and to a certain extent in France. This is one of the reasons which make public ownership of railroads in Prussia feasible and desirable.

A third objection to Government ownership of railroads in this country is the fact that the States would be deprived of the income which they derive from taxation of the railroads. (606, 610–613.)

Mr. KNAPP, chairman of the Interstate Commerce Commission, is inclined to believe that, while Government ownership would prevent discriminations between individuals and while the published rates would be observed, political influences would be so brought to bear that discriminations between different places and sections of the country might be even more serious than at present. At the same time the immense number of railway employees would make them a dangerous political influence under Government ownership. (145.)

Mr. NEWCOMB, of the divison of statistics, Department of Agriculture, thinks that Government ownership would be one of the two possible methods of preventing unjust competition and discrimination. There would be, theoretically, great saving in the "cost of production," by a consolidation of the entire railway system; but such a consolidation could not be allowed in the hands of a private individual, while to put it under the Government would at present be unwise. Government business usually costs twice as much as private business, and it would require fully a generation for us to secure an administrative system competent to handle the railway business properly. We must try to regulate first and later may look for Government ownership. (102, 103.)

Mr. REAGAN, chairman of the railroad commission of Texas, thinks that Government ownership of railroads would necessarily increase the cost of transportation greatly. Everything which the Government does requires more time, men, and money than like things done by private enterprise. Public ownership would tend to eliminate discrimination because of the absence of the motive to get the most freight possible for an individual road. But it would give to the President the power, directly or indirectly, of appointing 900,000 employees in the service of the railroads and would enable him to practically perpetuate himself in office, would subvert the system of government, and destroy public liberty. (347.)

Mr. COWEN, of the Baltimore and Ohio, believes that Government ownership would be "sublime folly." He refers with approval to the opinion of Mr. W. H. Mallock, that labor is very greatly benefited by the ability employed in the management of capital. Labor, in the sense of manual work, is not the chief producer of wealth. Private ownership of capital, and of the rewards for its management, is necessary in order to stimulate men of ability to their highest effort. Government ownership would destroy the motive of private gain, which is essential to successful business. (319, 320.)

Mr. MORTON, vice-president of the Atchison, Topeka and Santa Fe Railway, thinks that Government ownership would necessarily greatly increase the expense of railway management. Rates in this country under private ownership are lower and the service better than where the Government owns the roads. The post-office is perhaps the most extravagantly managed business in the country, and most people are not aware of the large annual deficit. Moreover, political difficulties would result from Government ownership. There would still be a tendency toward discrimination, especially between different sections of the country and under party influences. There would be difficulty in adjusting rates in accordance with changing conditions. (492, 497–499.)

Mr. SPENCER, of the Southern Railway, believes that there would be no necessity for discrimination between individuals or places under Government ownership, although it would require strong action of the Government to prevent undue modifications of rates at the demand of different sections of the country. Government ownership would probably result, on the other hand, in undue rigidity of rates as regards commodities, in view of conditions of business and competition.

It would also prevent rapid improvement in facilities. German railways, for example, have nothing like the promptness, efficiency, or luxury of American lines. The introduction of politics also would be a great evil.

The experience of the States of this country in building and operating railways has been very unsuccessful. Georgia long ago leased its railroad, preferring that to direct management. North Carolina still operates one railroad, but unsuccessfully. The Cincinnati Southern Railway, built by the city of Cincinnati, has finally been leased at a rate $400,000 less than the annual interest. The cost of construction was enormous, and for twenty-three years it has not earned interest. (279, 283, 284.)

Mr. INGALLS, of the Chesapeake and Ohio, is of the opinion that railways owned by governments have never been managed as well as those under private ownership. The United States has astonished the world with its transportation facilities. (290.)

Mr. RIPLEY, president of the Atchison, Topeka and Santa Fe, would not object, as a railroad man, to Government ownership of the roads, but would be sorry to see it as a citizen. There would be a considerable saving in the stoppage of the waste which is incident to all competition. "But governmental methods, as we know them, and as applied to governmental affairs now, would result in a very large deficit in the operation of railroads, unquestionably. The influence of politics and politicians on the railroad business would be, I think, exceedingly disastrous, and any elective officers who were in a position to influence the policy of the railroads, and who would also be desirous of pleasing their constituents, would find the two things irreconcilable. Everybody would want a branch railroad and everybody would want as many trains as possible on it, whether they paid or not, and the price of the election of a Congressman or Senator would be his ability to get things out of the Government in the way of transportation."

Mr. CALLAWAY, president of the New York Central, thinks that Government railways would have to be managed by experts in the railway business, and that methods of fixing rates, etc., would not be materially different from those at present. The railways would become a dangerous political factor. Government ownership has never been a great success—it was abandoned in Canada—nor does the witness understand where the money would be obtained to pay for the railroads. (239.)

Mr. STICKNEY, of the Chicago Great Western, thinks that even under Government ownership railway rates would have to be fixed strictly along the line of what the traffic would bear, just as Government taxes are fixed in practically the same way. The maximum revenue rate would have to be ascertained and then enforced. (464.)

C. Experience of other countries.—Mr. LEWIS states that in Germany the government-owned railroads paid a net profit of $119,000,000 in 1890, and that the net profit of the German system has increased 41 per cent during 10 years. One may ride 4 miles third class in Germany for a cent, and 10 miles for a cent on the Berlin road. In Belgium, under government ownership, fares and freight rates have been reduced one-half and the wages of employees have been doubled. In Australia one may ride 1,000 miles first class for $6.50, and workingmen may ride 3 miles for a cent. In Siberia workingmen ride at the rate of $6 for 2,000 miles. Mr. Lewis quotes Professor Ely as stating that every man he met in Germany considered the test of experience as demonstrating the superiority of public ownership, and that "even those who were once bitterly opposed to the undertaking are now convinced of their error, and no one wishes to return to private ownership." (747, 748.)

On the other hand, several witnesses declare that American passenger rates average as low as those abroad, and that the service is superior, while freight rates are lower here than in any other country. See under "Reasonableness of rates," pp. 41, 101.

Professor SELIGMAN states that only one country in Europe, Prussia, has made a change from private ownership to public ownership of railroads. In Belgium and also in Australia the Government railroad systems are being greatly extended. Even in Australia conditions are somewhat different from those in this country. The drift toward governmental aid and interference in Australia has always been greater than here, because of the economic conditions. Australia is a vast arid table-land, where nature is not bountiful and where an individual can scarcely cope with the difficulties of nature; the people have always had to have the aid of the government to develop the country. In this country, the most fruitful on the globe, the people have always thought that they could develop the country most by depending on themselves. (613, 614.)

Professor Seligman believes the government ownership of railroads in Germany to be desirable, although it would be undesirable in the United States. This is partly due to the difference between the governmental service of the two countries. It is partly due also to the fact that the private railways of Germany had always been accustomed to far greater governmental interference than we have had. The German government officials were always accustomed to consider questions of rates and tariffs. The capital invested in railroads per mile is 2 or 3 times as much in Germany as in the United States. (614.)

Professor Seligman states that passenger fares in Germany are somewhat less than in this country, though it is difficult to make a comparison, because of the system of first, second, and third class rates. Freight rates here are very much lower, because of our long-distance traffic. The public patronage of the railroads on the continent of Europe is much less than in America. The reason is that the social conditions in many regions are still almost medieval and the peasants travel very little. It is mostly for this reason that Australia and Hungary have so greatly reduced their passenger fares under the zone system, in order to stimulate intermunicipal travel. (614.)

Professor Seligman says also that Prussia is a very peculiar and exceptional country in respect of the standard of its civil service. In Prussia there is a successful income tax; no one who realizes the differences between political conditions in Prussia and the United States would dare to state that an income tax would be as successful here. In Prussia, and to a certain extent in France, the very best men go into public business and administration. The witness hopes the same will be true in this country some day; possibly the assumption by the Government of more work may lead individuals to be willing to sacrifice themselves for public good. At present, however, men of the highest order of business ability can in general be secured only by higher pay than our democracy is willing to give to public officers. It is probably true that the Government can get the same talent cheaper than a private corporation. There are well-known instances of men who have left more remunerative private work for comparatively small-salaried Government positions. These are, however, often men of independent means; and there are numerous instances of men quitting Government service because of small salaries. (613.)

D. Public opinion as to Government ownership.—Mr. GALLAGHER thinks there is a very dangerous tendency toward Government ownership throughout the Western country, and that the feeling or theory has grown very greatly within recent months. The people feel that they are not justly dealt with; are not getting what is due them. They see that they can buy a postage stamp as cheap as anybody can; can go through the custom-house as cheap as anybody can; " and are getting around to the idea that they could go to the station agent's office and buy a railroad ticket as cheap as anybody if Uncle Sam had control of it." The dissatisfaction comes not from high rates, but from unequal rates. He thinks that the greater desire for Government ownership in the West than in the East is perhaps caused by the greater discriminations in the West. (545.)

Mr. DICKINSON says that there is some sentiment in his State—Wisconsin—in favor of Government ownership of railroads. He would not say that it is a general sentiment, but it is greater than it was two decades ago, and possibly greater than it was one decade ago. It does not arise, he thinks, from a desire of ownership, but from the belief that the public is not fairly treated by the railroads. If shippers were to understand that the Interstate Commerce Commission would absolutely put down all discriminations, it might be that the sentiment in favor of Government ownership would be considerably weakened. Government officials themselves might discriminate, though the witness would not expect such action generally. (553.)

E. Municipalization of street-railway service.—Professor SELIGMAN, applying his three criteria of the desirability of government ownership to the question of municipal ownership of street railways, says that the complexity of management of the street railways is far less than in the steam railways, but is greater than in the telegraph or waterworks. The capital invested is tremendous. For that reason, chiefly, but also because the methods of street railway management have been revolutionized within a few years, and in another 5 or 10 years may be revolutionized again, he thinks that the safer plan for the present is governmental regulation rather than governmental management. Everybody is agreed, however, that the relations between government and the street railways—honorable, straightforward relations—have not been as close as they should be. (617.)

F. Government ownership of the telegraph.—Professor SELIGMAN considers that upon the basis of his three criteria of the desirability of government ownership, namely, widespread social interests, amount of capital invested, and complexity of management, the argument for Government control of the telegraph is substantially as strong as for Government ownership of the postal service. (1) Unfortunately in this country the telegraph is not used by every one; but this is because the charges are so much higher and the facilities so much less than in other countries, where the telegraph service is managed by the Government. (2) As regards the capital invested, the requirements, though greater than in the case of the post, are yet very small as compared with other interests. The cost of putting up poles and stringing wires is relatively slight. If the existing companies were bought out there would be a capital outlay, but even then it would be insignificant when compared with the capital invested in ordinary enterprises or the means of transportation. (3) As to complexity of management, while the telegraph makes possibly a somewhat higher demand than the postal service upon the skill of its managers, and while somewhat more effort is required to keep the service up to the level of the advances of science, the business is yet very simple as compared with others; for instance, with the railroads. The great end of individual initiative in industry in general is to turn all ability toward the reduction of cost by inventions, etc. Experience shows that " even such sleepy administrations as those of France and of England " keep the telegraph service on a level with new inventions. That the post is a public service with us and the telegraph is not is an historical accident, due to the fact that the telegraph was not invented until 1844, and that the postal service grew up in the seventeenth and eighteenth centuries. If the postal service had not been in the hands of the Government in the colonies and in the time of Hamilton we should have had the same discussion of Government posts v. private posts as of Government telegraph v. private telegraph. (610–612.)

Professor Seligman says that in every other country in the world, including the most advanced democratic communities like Switzerland and Australia, the telegraph is in the hands of the government. It was practically in Government hands in our own country when it was first established in 1844. The Government decided not to go on with it, for they thought that it would not amount to anything, and did not wish to commit the Government to a hazardous experiment.

It is probably true that the Government would not make as much money out of the telegraph as the Western Union Telegraph Company makes. Its object would be to make no profit at all, but to run the service just as the postal service is run. Any possible profits would reduce the rates. (611.)

Professor Seligman says that in arguing for government ownership of the telegraph and the telephone he assumes that along with it there would go a very progressive development of our civil service. He does not think there have been any great political dangers in our postal service. If there have been, they have been more than counterbalanced by the political dangers that would have existed if the postal service had been private. The political dangers of government ownership of the telephone and the telegraph are minimized by the fact that the capital invested in them is small. (612.)

Professor Seligman would be in favor of the purchase by the Government of the existing telegraph and telephone systems. He is always opposed to governmental competition with private enterprises. "Although the assumption is that the private enterprise will be brought up to the level of the governmental efficiency, the practical result is always that the governmental agent is pulled down to the level of the private." (612.)

Mr KENWARD, of the Chicago Butter and Egg Board, states that the expense of telegraph and telephone service in the business of handling perishable goods is very great and that the service is far from satisfactory. He refers to the much lower charges in European countries under government ownership, and advocates putting the telegraphs and telephones under the Post-Office Department. In many lines of business the telephone and telegraph service is as important as the mail. At present there is practically no competition between the two great telegraph companies. The charge for messages is made excessive by the payment of dividends on an enormous capitalization. The witness thinks that the opinion of the business men in Chicago generally is in favor of the position stated. (366.)

Mr. FULLER, of Norfolk, Nebr., says that there are constant complaints among the business men of that place concerning the high tolls charged by the Western Union Telegraph Company. He sees no reason why the United States should not control the telegraphs as the leading European countries do. (446.)

Mr. GREELEY, a commission merchant of Chicago, is decidedly in favor of a postal telegraph system. He declares that it is a crime for a man to have the right to a private wire, as well as for the telegraph company to give the quotations to bucket shops. (881.)

Mr. SNYDACKER, a grain merchant of Chicago, says that he sometimes finds the telegraph service in connection with his business a little slow and the prices somewhat high. His firm operates private telegraph wires, a privilege which is open to anyone who can pay for it. (400.)

Mr. COUNSELMAN says that elevator men have occasion to use the telegraph very largely in their business, but he considers the rates fair and the service satisfactory. (392.)

G. Public ownership of the telephone.—Professor SELIGMAN says that the arguments for a Government telephone are not quite as strong as for a Government telegraph, because the complexity of management of the telephone is a little greater; yet he thinks that the telephone ought certainly to be publicly owned. On the whole, especially in view of the increased possible use of the long-distance telephone, a national system rather than a municipal system seems to be desirable. England has recently passed a law in accordance with this idea, which will result in the absorption of the entire system by the government at the expiration of the existing company's charter in 1911. The telephone will be a part of the post-office. Almost all European governments, Germany, France, Norway, Switzerland, and also Australia, run the telephone as a part of the postal system. The telephone exchanges should be placed in charge of the local postmasters. (612.)

XII. RAILWAY LABOR.

A. Employment and discharge.—1. *Conditions of entering employment.*—Mr. CALLAWAY, president of the New York Central Railroad, testifies that no tests are made as a condition of employment on that road except willingness to obey reasonable rules and tests of the eyesight and hearing for persons required to take signals. Men are discharged or suspended for various offenses, according to their previous records and to the seriousness of the offenses. No restriction is put upon membership in organizations.

The use of intoxicating liquors on the road or about the premises of the company is strictly prohibited, and no one will be employed or retained who is known to be in the habit of drinking intoxicating liquors. Men are not discharged for occasionally taking a drink, but are not allowed to operate trains if intoxicated or known to be habitually intoxicated. (217, 218, 221.)

Mr. CLARK, grand chief of the Railway Conductors, says that railroad companies are becoming more rigid in making physical examinations of applicants for employment. In many cases they refuse employment simply because a man has lost a finger or has been otherwise slightly crippled, without being in any way incapacitated. The reason for this is said to be that men have sometimes secured employment and then claimed damages for imaginary injuries on the strength of previous disablement. This, however, can not be a sufficient reason, since at the time of entering the service a record is made of all such existing disabilities. (111.)

Mr. ARTHUR, g   chief of the Locomotive Engineers, believes that some of the examinations of applicants for engineers' positions recently conducted have been u   in excluding experienced men because of alleged defects in sight or hearing. (119.)

Mr. CLARK says that some railway companies have recently established the custom of refusing to employ new men as brakemen or firemen who are beyond a certain age, ranging from 28 to 40. Their purpose seems to be to relieve themselves of the obligation of caring for a large number of men who have grown old in the service without having rendered them an extended period of service. The practice also is likely to influence employees to be less independent, making them very careful before leaving a position. It must have the effect of checking the best young men from going into railway work. (110, 111.)

Mr. ARTHUR has heard complaints, only indirectly, that some railway companies refuse to employ men who are over 45 years of age. He has never known of a case of a man being retired at that age. (119.)

On the Chesapeake and Ohio, according to Mr. INGALLS, no man who drinks while on duty is retained, and young men who drink while off duty are not promoted and are continually watched. The railway brotherhoods are the most effective influences in enforcing temperance. (292.)

Mr. SPENCER says that on the Southern Railway no man who habitually uses liquor is employed in train service. (264.)

2. *Discrimination against union members.* (See also p. 142.)—The chief officers of the respective orders of Railway Conductors, Locomotive Engineers, Locomotive Firemen, Railway Trainmen, and Railway Telegraphers, in reply to the inquiries of the Industrial Commission, declare that the right of a railway employee to hold membership in any reputable organization should be inalienable, and that there should be swift and severe punishment for discrimination against members of organizations. However, it is only the action of a few railway managers which makes such legislation necessary or desirable. (760.)

Mr. ARNOLD, of the Locomotive Firemen; Mr. WILSON, of the Railroad Trackmen, and Mr. RONEMUS, of the Railway Carmen, express similar opinions in their answers, favoring strict legislation. (763, 765, 768.)

Mr. MURPHY, an attorney at law of Denver, declares that the provision of the act of June 1, 1898, which prohibits discrimination against members of labor unions in seeking employment upon railways, as well as the similar statutes of many States, are in practice violated with impunity. The witness declares that there is one trunk line running west from Chicago which maintains a large detective corps for the purpose of ascertaining whether employees become members of labor organizations, and that a convenient time and excuse are soon found for discharging those who are members. On the other hand, the greater number of railways have no opposition to the brotherhoods. Mr. Murphy suggests that it be made criminal to procure or furnish evidence concerning employees' membership in labor organizations. (777.)

Mr. ARTHUR, of the Locomotive Engineers, says that soon after the centennial of 1876 the employees of the Reading Railroad asked for higher wages, but were met with the demand that they all resign their membership in the railway brotherhoods. By unanimous vote they refused to do so and struck, and their places were filled by other men. This opposition of the Reading system to brotherhood men has continued ever since. Under the receivership of Mr. McLeod, however, one man who had been discharged on account of membership in a brotherhood was reinstated when it was shown that he had not signed the agreement that he would not join any labor organization. (123, 124.)

As to this case, Mr. MOSELEY, secretary of the Interstate Commerce Commission, says that some time ago the receivers of the Reading Railroad revived a former regulation, which had become a dead letter, requiring all employees to drop their membership in labor organizations. A representative of the brotherhoods, Wilkinson, brought suit against the receivers, but the court maintained that the employees themselves must appear, in spite of the danger of being discharged and blacklisted. Three of them finally did bring suit, and were discharged, but the court decided that the receivers could use their employees as they saw fit. As a result of this injustice the railway men secured the enactment of a Pennsylvania statute, and the incorporation in the arbitration act of 1898 of a provision, prohibiting such coercion of employees. (36.)

3. *Discharge and suspension.*—Mr. SARGENT, grand master of the Locomotive Firemen, says that railway employees are discharged for violation of rules, responsibility for accidents, insubordination, intoxication, and occasionally for incompetence. Suspension from duty without pay and systems of merit and demerit markings are employed as penalties in many cases. The practice of suspension has often resulted in injustice. Men have been laid off without any cause assigned and with no opportunity for hearing. The railway brotherhoods have secured the adoption of a rule requiring their members to be given a hearing within 5 days after suspension or discharge, and if the employee is shown to be innocent of the charge made, he is to be returned to service and paid for lost time. The length of suspension for different offenses is fixed. (65, 88.)

Mr. CLARK, grand chief of the Railway Conductors, says that the former practice of suspending men for from 10 to 60 days for violation of rules or other offenses has been practically everywhere replaced by what is known as the Brown system of discipline. A record is kept of each man's service. Any offense is entered and may be offset by a certain number of months of good service or by special meritorious acts. When a certain number of demerit marks have been received, dismissal follows. (113.)

Mr. MURPHY, an attorney at law of Denver, thinks that some restriction should be placed upon the discharge of railroad employees. Railroad work requires a high degree of skill, and a person specially trained in one department is not able to fill positions in other departments of the railway or in other occupations. It is to the interest of the railroads and the general public that men should remain in the same line of work. Often persons in positions of superintendence discharge employees out of caprice or for the sake of securing positions for their own friends. It would be well to have a labor court to give hearings to aggrieved employees, although of course railways should not be prevented from reducing expenses. On some roads the brotherhoods have been strong enough to secure contracts that none of their members shall be discharged without a hearing, and this practice has been beneficial both to the employees and to the companies. (778.)

The chief officers of the leading railway orders, in a joint reply to inquiries by the Commission, are disposed to doubt the advantage of legislation regulating the discharge of railway employees. They hold that the organizations themselves afford a considerable degree of protection against unjust dismissals. (760.)

Mr. ARNOLD, of the Locomotive Firemen, expresses the same opinion. (763.)

Mr. WILSON, of the Railway Trackmen, and Mr. RONEMUS, of the Railway Carmen, on the other hand, think that laws should be passed requiring that good reasons for discharge should be given and that the discharged employee should have an opportunity to state his side of the case before a competent officer of the employer, such as the general manager. (765, 768.)

Mr. WALKER, chairman of the directors of the Atchison, Topeka and Santa Fe Railway, thinks it would not be advisable to regulate the discharge of railway employees by law. Their service is one involving the safety of life and property for which the employer is pecuniarily responsible, so that he must be absolutely let alone in his choice and retention of servants. (772.)

B. Blacklisting.—1. *Existence of the practice generally.*—Mr. MOSELEY, secretary of the Interstate Commerce Commission, says that after the Chicago railway strike of 1894 a large number of employees found it impossible to obtain employment again. To many of them certificates of good character were given by the railways, but by a form of reading or by some secret mark these papers proved to be notices to other employers that the person was blacklisted. As a result of this abuse Congress included in the arbitration act of 1898 a prohibition against attempting to conspire to prevent any employee from obtaining employment. The evil is one which it is difficult to prevent, evasion being easy, and the witness has no suggestion to make for strengthening the law. (8.)

Mr. CLARK, of the Railway Conductors, says the practice of blacklisting was formerly common. The witness knows of one case in Florida where a conductor was offered a better position on another road. His own road kept him as long as possible, not desiring him to make the change, and, when he had taken the new employment, sent a letter to the other road advising that he be not employed, so that he was afterwards discharged. The abuse has been greatly reduced by legislation. The practice now is for railway companies to give men who leave the service a letter stating what their service has been and the reason for leaving it. Very often the reason is stated to be "unsatisfactory service." The witness has known of one instance where an employee received a letter of high commendation, but was at the same time on the blacklist. He has heard rumors that letters themselves are sometimes marked so as to indicate that the man should not be employed. (112.)

Mr. SARGENT, of the Locomotive Firemen, says that this practice was formerly very common, but has largely been done away with by laws. It is now the custom to require men entering employment to submit a statement of their former employment, and their former employers can then be asked for information. This practice has the same effect as the old blacklist. Many companies furnish their employees statements of their service when they leave. The trade unions have had a strong influence in preventing unreasonable dismissals. (65.)

Mr. WILSON, secretary of the Locomotive Firemen, thinks a majority of railways have some understanding among themselves, by which all employees who have been discharged are required to present to any other road a letter as to their competence from their immediate superior in the previous employment. The witness has been told that there are certain private marks by which it is known whether such letters mean what they say or the opposite. (52.)

Mr. ARTHUR, of the Locomotive Engineers, does not know from personal knowledge that engineers have been blacklisted. He has been told by men that they have been discharged after a few days of work under a new employer, and they have attributed this to some notice received from their previous employer. During the strike of 1894 those who left employment were given letters as to their service, but the date of these letters being the same as that when the strike was begun they served to prevent their holders from securing employment. The Philadelphia and Reading Railroad has at various times refused to employ union men, and has been accused of blacklisting them. (123, 124.)

Mr. STRONG, an attorney at law of Chicago, says that he has evidence of the continuance of the practice of blacklisting up to within 3 or 4 months of the time of his testimony, November 22, 1899, and that the system extends to all the principal railroads in the United States and even down into Mexico. (524.)

Mr. COWEN, president of the Baltimore and Ohio Railroad, says that it is the practice to suspend men for various offenses for periods varying according to the nature of the offense. The railway does not exchange blacklists with other roads, although possibly this may have been the practice earlier. Mr. Cowen does not know whether the divisions are always notified of the discharge of men from other divisions. (303.)

Mr. SPENCER, president of the Southern Railway, testifies that on that system lists of men discharged are kept, but these lists are not exchanged with other companies, since there is no reason for pursuing a man, or undertaking to decide for others whom they shall employ. The practice, Mr. Spencer thinks, is dying out. (264, 265.)

Mr. INGALLS declares that on the Chesapeake and Ohio blacklists are not exchanged with other railroads. If one division of the railway discharges a man no other division can employ him without the consent of the general manager. (288.)

Mr. WALKER, chairman of the directors of the Atchison, Topeka and Santa Fe Railway, declares that blacklisting is largely an imaginary grievance, and that if a servant is unfaithful it is not only the right but the duty of the master to tell the truth upon inquiry. (772.)

2. *Chicago strike.*—Mr. STRONG believes that the idea of blacklisting first took form among the railroads centering in Chicago in 1893. The General Managers' Association of Chicago, which embraces 24 roads, appointed a committee which made a report on May 18, 1893, containing the following clauses:

"The matter of the establishment of an employment bureau: The subject has been discussed at great length, and it is the opinion of the committee that such a bureau would be of advantage to the association—

"First. In assisting them in the procurement of men, both under ordinary conditions and in times of emergency.

"Second. In assisting the roads to guard against the employment of a man who has been proved unworthy on some other road.

"Third. In abolishing the state of affairs with which we are all familiar, that is expressed, when a man is disciplined, by the statement that ' your road is not the only road in Chicago,' and that ' employment can readily be obtained on some other road,' although an offense has been committed."

Thirteen out of 20 railroads present voted to adopt it, but the rules of the association provided that whenever any scheme was proposed which required any expenditure of money, as this did, it should not take effect unless the vote was unanimous; so it was defeated. During the strike of 1894, however, a plan which had the same effect was adopted. Mr. John Eagan was selected to take charge of the whole strike, and to get employees for all of the different railroads.

Mr. Strong says that the association's committee disclaimed the idea of blacklisting, but this very disclaimer seems to him to show that they were conscious that their proposition meant nothing else. There had been growing friction between the railroads and their employees, resulting largely from the workings of what the association's committee calls "discipline." By discipline Mr. Strong understands the system of suspensions and fines for sundry offenses, often, he says, of a trivial character. Frequently, in Mr. Strong's opinion, discipline fell upon the wrong man, and frequently it was unjustly severe. (503–505, 510.)

Mr. STRONG states that his attention was called to blacklisting in the fall of 1895. He was then called suddenly into the case of Fred R. Ketcham against The Chicago and Northwestern Railroad Company. Becoming deeply interested in the matter, he put an advertisement in the Chicago Evening News, asking any men who thought they had been blacklisted to come to his office and make their statements to him, and bring such letters as they had that they thought were evidence of the blacklisting agreement. Mr. Strong received 500 statements with letters corroborating them. In June, 1896, he filed some 50 cases, including some against nearly every railroad in Chicago. Mr. Strong gives in some detail the experience of a considerable number of the strikers of 1894, or of men who were denied work on the ground that they had sympathized with the strikers. The case of Mr. Ketcham, who brought the first suit, is typical. Mr. Strong's statement of his case is as follows: He testified that he quit the employment of the Chicago and Northwestern Railroad Company during the railway union strike, and remained at home, not going near any railroad during the trouble; that about July 3 of that year Superintendent J. C. Stuart came to his house and asked him to take out a train; that he refused, as he considered it dangerous; that he was not at this time a member of the American Railway Union, but afterwards joined it about July 20; that he had been in the employ of the defendant company about 10 years; that upon his refusal Stuart "threatened him with arrest, adding that he had sympathy for his family, and that if he did not take out the train he would find hard work getting a job from any other road." Having heard of the black list, he went to the Chicago Great Western Railway and secured a situation as conductor of one of its freight trains July 28, and made one trip to Dubuque, Iowa, and back, arriving home July 31, at 5; that at 7 he was arrested by a United States marshal and kept in custody several days until he could give a bond for $3,000, but was never prosecuted, no evidence being offered against him; that August 6 he went to Superintendent Stuart and asked him for a clearance, and was given a letter showing how long he had been in the employ of the Chicago and Northwestern, but at the bottom was the following: "Left his post during American Railway Union strike and was active in persuading others to do likewise. When he returned for duty his place was filled."

On the same day he returned to the Chicago Great Western for duty and was told by Train Master J. B. Strong and Superintendent J. A. Kelly that he was discharged, Superintendent Kelly telling him that he was a good man and he would like to keep him, but could not unless he first obtained a "clearance" from the Northwestern. When asked why he was discharged Kelly said, "Because he had heard he was a Northwestern striker." Ketcham then asked where he got his information, and Kelly replied, "From the one we all get it from." Ketcham then asked if he was blacklisted, and Kelly replied, "You can call it that or anything you're a mind to. I can't put you back to work unless you bring a 'clearance' from the Northwestern. I am sorry, but it comes from above me."

The following facts also appeared from Ketcham's testimony: After being discharged from the Chicago Great Western he applied to several other roads for employment, but was everywhere refused, and never secured railroad employment after the strike. In the autumn of 1897 he worked as stationary engineer at the Michigan Central Railroad elevator at Kensington, but was discharged about 2 weeks before the trial, for the alleged cause that business was slack, though the elevator was running full time, and continued to do so after his discharge just as it had been doing previously.

About 35 other men who had quit various roads during the strike testified that they had applied to all the roads in Chicago, were told the roads needed men, but were denied employment because they did not have "clearances." The clearance was a letter from the road which the man had last worked for, giving a full statement of his record. The essential thing seemed to be an assurance that the man had not taken part in the great strike. The railroad managers admitted that they were in the habit of writing to each other for the record of men who applied to them for work. This appeared in repeated instances in which men had at first been employed and were afterwards discharged, admittedly without any fault in their services. Sometimes they were made to sign a formal application for employment and, although temporarily given work, were afterwards discharged with a statement that their applications had been rejected. The rejection was stated, in some instances, to be due to information that the men had participated in the strike. The railroads denied that there was any actual blacklist, or list of men to whom employment was to be refused. A messenger boy in the office of the superintendent of terminals of the Illinois Central Railroad, however, testified that he was instructed to make 50 mimeograph copies of a list of 524 names; that he addressed and mailed 49 copies of this list, 1 to each official of the Illinois Central Railroad who hired men, and 1 marked "private" to every railroad in Chicago. A copy of this list came into Mr. Strong's hands. The messenger boy's testimony seems to have been in some degree corroborated by the statement of the superintendent of the Chicago and Grand Trunk Railway that he saw a copy of the list in the office of the attorney of the defendant railroad. (503-519.)

Mr. STRONG says that out of 30,000 men who went out in the Chicago strike of 1894 only about 31 were proved to have been reemployed, and fully one-half even of these were men who returned to work before July 10, when notified by the railroads to do so, and hence were really not strikers. This statement seems to refer, however, to individual instances proved in court. Mr. Strong says in another connection that a great many were taken back to work after the suits were begun against the railroads, and when the roads saw what damages they were liable to for refusing employment. He knows of probably 50 or 60 men who, finding it impossible to get work under their own names, changed their names and by this means got employment. He elsewhere estimates the number of men who were blacklisted at "fully half of the men who went out here." He also mentions that Mr. W. G. Brimson, of the Calumet and Blue Island road, testified that he had secured work on other roads for a good many of the strikers by leaving out the fact that the men had been in the strike when he answered inquiries about their record, implying that if he had mentioned this fact the men could not have gotten employment. (513, 517, 522-524.)

3. *Is blacklisting justifiable?*—Mr. STRONG says that no one questions the right and duty of the railroad to report to another the name of a drunken or careless employee, as the public is interested in having sober and careful men operate the trains. But if railways combine to keep men from work simply because they have struck to better their condition, though they have violated no

law, such an act is unlawful and dangerous to the public welfare. The men do not complain that they lost their old positions. They complain that their old employers vindictively pursued them and prevented them from getting employment elsewhere. If a man who quits the employ of another can not get work in his chosen occupation without obtaining his former employer's consent, he becomes a slave. He will not dare resist any oppression his employer may see fit to impose upon him, because he knows he can not leave and get employment elsewhere. Mr. Strong believes that it is the purpose of the railroads to reduce their men to this condition, and that the employees of the railroad companies are to-day absolutely terrorized. He says that men who were in the strike of 1894, and who are now employed, have told him that the punishment and suffering of the men who went out during the strike have been so severe that they do not dare to form another union or present a grievance, for fear of being discharged and blacklisted; that they are burdened with extra duties and dare not complain. The objection of the railroads seems to be especially against the heads of the union. To strike at the heads of the union is to destroy the union. If they are to be singled out and punished, men will hesitate before accepting these positions. A railway vice-president recently said to Mr. Strong, "The people who own this country propose to run it," and he explained that by the owners he meant " those who own the property." Mr. Strong believes that the course of the railroads has been dictated by the feeling and intention which this man expressed.

Mr. Strong considers that political bondage as well as industrial bondage must result if employers are permitted to exclude men from work for taking part in strikes or other efforts to better their condition. No man can be a proper elector who is afraid to assert his rights, and it will come to pass, if it has not already, that the workmen will not dare to exercise the elector's franchise according to their own will. Moreover, to exclude a man from means of honest livelihood is to make him a criminal or a pauper. It is in the highest degree required by the public interest that every man be given an opportunity to work in that calling in which he is skilled. (513, 514, 516, 518, 521, 523.)

Mr. O'ROURKE, switchman, of Chicago, thinks that a system of blacklisting is now in use by the railroads, but does not think that it works against the laboring man. It tends to place a premium on good character, good conduct, and good service, and to shut out those who are not worthy of employment. In an individual case it might be an evil system, in enabling railroad officials to shut out a man against whom they had a grievance from employment on any other road, and it is true that the situation has been more disagreeable in Chicago than elsewhere; but considering the whole body of employees in the United States he believes the system works well. Mr. O'Rourke apparently considers agitators to be among those who may properly be excluded from employment. He says that the switchmen's union is demanding that men making application for membership "must show as good a character as any railroad company has ever asked of any man." "In the growth of the organized railway labor to-day no shelter is being given to the agitator." To have been actively engaged in the strike of 1894 is a reason for exclusion from Mr. O'Rourke's union. (528, 529.)

4. *Remedies for blacklisting.*—Mr. STRONG considers that there is only one way to settle the contest between labor and capital regarding public transportation. He thinks it will be necessary for the Government to take control of the railroads and put the men on the civil-service list. In the absence of Government ownership he would make blacklisting a felony, punishable by imprisonment of the officers who may be concerned in it. To permit the blacklisting of those who may have done unlawful acts in furtherance of a strike would be to make any law against blacklisting entirely ineffective. It is very easy to trump up some charge of an unlawful act. Besides, such permission of blacklisting is wrong in principle. A man ought to be punished according to law for any unlawful act he may do. He ought not to be starved to death as a punishment. (523.)

The grand chiefs of the leading railway orders in their reply to the schedule of inquiries concerning railway labor favor the enactment of laws with a penalty sufficiently severe to outweigh the desire to violate the law by the secret practice of blacklisting. Existing laws are sufficient to check open blacklisting. (760.) Mr. ARNOLD, of the Locomotive Firemen, expresses a similar opinion (763), while Mr. WILSON, of the Railway Trackmen, and Mr. RONEMUS, of the Railway Carmen, think that the practice is decreasing, and that further legislation will be either ineffective or unnecessary (765, 768).

Mr. MURPHY, an attorney at law of Denver, says that there is great difficulty in getting evidence concerning blacklisting. He thinks that even the practice of giving a statement concerning a discharged employee to an inquiring employer, which has always been permissible at law, is pernicious. The bare statement of certain happenings or acts of a servant may make him appear an undesirable employee, in the absence of an explanation of the circumstances. It should be made unlawful for any person to furnish a statement to any other employer concerning an employee without first furnishing the employee a true copy. (777.)

C. **Wages of railway labor.**—1. *Rates.*—Mr. SARGENT, chief of the Locomotive Firemen, states that the standard rate of wages for passenger engineers is 3½ cents per mile; for freight engineers 4 cents; and for firemen 58 per cent of engineers' pay. Freight conductors receive 3 cents per mile, and brakemen two-thirds as much. Passenger conductors receive from $100 to $125 per month, and brakemen from $50 to $70. Station agents receive from $40 to $85 per month, according to the importance of the station; train dispatchers $125 per month. In the Southern States colored men are employed largely as brakemen and firemen at much cheaper rates. (64, 65.)

Mr. BLANCHARD, late commissioner of the Joint Traffic Association, submitted the following as a comparison of railway wages in the United States and Europe:

Country.	Per day.		Per month.
	Engineers.	Firemen.	Conductors.
United States	$3.65	$2.05	$82.40
England	$1.25 to 1.87	$0.75 to 1.12	30.40
France	1.00 to 1.16	.75 to .83	
Germany	.81 to 1.25	.62 to .81	28.30
Belgium	.81 to .89	.50 to .60	
Holland	.83 to 1.04	.54 to .72	
Hungary			32.40

Mr. ARTHUR, chief of the Locomotive Engineers, says that the wages of engineers have been materially increased by the efforts of the Brotherhood of Locomotive Engineers. At the time of its organization engineers were paid $60 per month. Now they receive 3½ cents per mile in passenger service and 4 cents per mile in freight service, 100 miles or less in a run constituting a day's work. The wages of engineers were kept up on almost all roads despite the depression of 1893. This fact is, of course, partly due to the practice of paying by the run, since the men actually earned less when there was less business for the railroads. The engineers have little to complain of concerning wages. The wages are the same as have prevailed for the past 15 years, and their purchasing power is greater than before. (117, 127.)

Mr. WILSON, of the Brotherhood of Railway Trackmen, states that roadmasters receive from $60 to $150 per month; section foremen from $1.05 to $2 per day, and track hands from 47½ cents to $1.25 per day. The lowest wages are paid in the Southern States. The employment of the track hands is chiefly in the summer, so that many of them are forced to become tramps in the winter. The witness believes that the Interstate Commerce Commission should be given power to aid these men to get better pay. Sometimes railways furnish little houses near the track free of rent to trackmen. The excessive competition of railways, rate wars, etc., are responsible for these low wages. (46, 50.)

According to Mr. CALLAWAY, president of the road, the employees of the New York Central are partly paid by distance traveled, especially in the case of trainmen, and partly by the number of hours of service per day. The average wages are as follows:

Telegraph operators, $52.50; block-signal men, $46.50; other signalmen, $49, which includes baggagemen, station clerks, etc.; enginemen, $114, although their wages vary from $90 to $175; firemen and wipers, $59, firemen getting from $50 to $84; conductors, $86; baggagemen and trainmen, from $40 to $70; mechanics and helpers in shops, $49; other shopmen, $40; roadmasters, from $100 to $125; track foremen, from $40 to $50; track laborers, $35.50; switchmen, flagmen, watchmen, etc., $40; mechanics and helpers on road, $56; employees of floating equipment, $58. There are no deductions from wages unless the men give orders for payment of rent, board, etc., out of their earnings. (217.)

Mr. SPENCER says that the wages on the Southern Railway are about the same as on the other railways in the South. They are somewhat lower than in the North, but not, as Mr. Spencer thinks, largely on account of the competition of colored labor. Colored labor is not employed for the more responsible positions. Although there is a relatively larger supply of labor as compared with the demand in the Southern States, this is less true of skilled labor, such as that necessary for many railway positions. The business of the Southern railways is for the most part less complex than in the North, since the traffic is not so dense, and less skilled and less difficult labor is required. The cost of living is also materially lower. (264, 267.)

Mr. INGALLS testifies that about 20,000 men are employed on the Cleveland, Cincinnati, Chicago and St. Louis, and the Chesapeake and Ohio Railroads. The men are paid monthly, clerks and agents by monthly rates, track and shop men on the basis of the hours worked, and trainmen by mileage. The trackmen are paid about $1 a day. On some roads during 1895 and 1896 the witness thinks that the wages of this class fell to 90 cents, and occasionally to 75 cents. Their hours are long and they may be considered, perhaps, the hardest worked and poorest paid of American laborers. At the same time, they often own their own houses, and their work requires little skill, although Mr. Ingalls admits that considerable responsibility rests upon them. (287, 288)

Mr. FISH testifies that during the period of great depression, from 1893 to 1897, the Illinois Central Railroad was obliged largely to reduce the number of men employed. It was also necessary to reduce the number of hours of work per day in the shops. The wages, however, were not cut at all. The witness is inclined to think it would have been more for the advantage of the employees if wages had been reduced, since the number of employees and number of hours would not then have had to be cut so much. Thus, the railroad could have employed shop hands in building new cars and engines, but, instead, was compelled to buy a considerable number from manufacturers having lower wage scales. The reason why wages were not reduced was that there was apprehension of strong opposition from the employees, and possibly of a strike. The railway had for years been paying a standard scale. (324–327.)

See also Paragraph L, below.

2. *Methods of fixing wages.*—Mr. ARTHUR says that early in the history of the Brotherhood of Locomotive Engineers the organization began to send committees to the railway companies to discuss wages and conditions of employment. These committees would present a statement of their demands, and when an agreement had been reached it would be put in form and signed by both parties. In this way grew up the system of fixing wages by joint agreement or contract, which now prevails in the case of about 90 per cent of the railways. Such agreements are indefinite in their duration and may be terminated on from 30 to 60 days' notice. The railways have practically never violated them, but the employees did so at the time of the Chicago strike of 1894. (117, 127.)

Mr. SARGENT states that the wages of railway trainmen and telegraphers are mostly fixed by joint agreement between their organizations and the railways. Approximately uniform rates exist in the North Central States. Payment is by the mile in freight service, and usually by the month in passenger and station service. (64, 65.)

Mr. Sargent says also that trainmen are usually paid for overtime on a fair basis, but in many cases telegraphers and yardmen are not, although working more than 12 hours. Sunday work is paid at the same rate as other work. (66, 86.)

On the Baltimore and Ohio, according to Mr. COWEN, the train hands are paid by the miles run. Overtime is allowed for excess mileage or for work after 12 hours in case the trainmen are unable to get their trains over the required distance within that time. There is no extra compensation for Sunday work. Trackmen and similar employees work 10 hours daily. (303.)

3. *Influences affecting wages.*—Professor JOHNSON says that the rate of wages on railways has been found in Europe to vary according to the rates for other occupations in the same locality, and presumably the same is true in this country. Anything which affects the earning power of the railway is likely to influence wages. The losses due to ticket brokerage, and the necessity of paying dividends on watered stock, are both likely to reduce wages. (60.)

Several witnesses suggest that whatever affects railway rates unfavorably is likely to injure the employees. See pp. 39, 95.

D. Hours of Labor.—1. *Duration generally.*—Mr. SARGENT, of the Locomotive Firemen, says that trainmen have little occasion for complaint as to hours. Telegraphers and yardmen, however, often have to work 12 hours per day, and are not always paid overtime for longer hours. Ten hours is the day for trainmen. If a locomotive fireman makes a 100-mile run he is counted as having worked a full day, no matter how many hours are required. Often in this way he may earn pay for 2 days' work in 1, or for 9 or 10 days' work in a week. Frequently, when there is a rush of business, men are required to work overtime. There are certain rules of the railways and the brotherhoods as to giving a number of hours' rest after a certain amount of work has been performed, but circumstances prevent even this, sometimes, from being carried out. Special conditions of weather, etc., may make necessary continuous labor for 36 hours or more. The railway managers are disposed to be fair; they pay for overtime. The crowding might be prevented by employing more men to work during the busy season, but this would leave men idle later on, and is opposed by the employees themselves. They prefer to work hard and make extra pay at times, getting more rest with moderate wages at other seasons. The hours of firemen used to be much longer than at present; even after the organization of the brotherhood they were formerly 12, but now the limit is 10 hours, wherever the length of time determines the day, except that hostlers usually work 12 hours per day. (66, 86–88.)

Mr. CLARK, chief of the Order of Railway Conductors, says that it is difficult to state the average number of hours worked by conductors. They are considerably shorter than a few years ago, because of the more rapid transportation of freight, although in some cases there is a disposition to require conductors to run longer distances than before. During a rush of business, hours are sometimes excessive, since railway companies do not wish to put on new men, especially on account of the possibility of accident. The companies, however, do not desire to work the men beyond their physical capacity, and it is the general rule that men who have been on duty for 16 hours may demand at least 8 hours rest. (110.)

Mr. WILSON, chief of the Railway Trackmen, states that on some railways the required hours for trackmen are 10 or 11, while on others they are from daylight to dark. Laborers are paid for overtime, nights, and Sundays, but foremen are not. The hours should be shortened by adding more men. (50, 51.)

Mr. CALLAWAY says that, on the New York Central, station employees are sometimes necessarily employed for very long hours, although during much of the time they have little or nothing to do. Telegraph operators are not required to work more than 12 hours, and in some signal towers where many levers are used 8 hours constitutes a day's work. On passenger trains the hours average less than 10 per day. In freight service they are sometimes 12 hours during the 24, but the men receive sufficient rest before another run. (218.)

Mr. INGALLS testifies that on the Chesapeake and Ohio and the Cleveland, Cincinnati, Chicago and St. Louis the outside limit of labor is 10 hours. This is the usual requirement for track labor. Shopmen more often work 9 and even 8 hours. On passenger trains the hours are not usually over 5 or 6 and sometimes less. Freight runs are scheduled at 8, or more often 10 hours. The purpose is to arrange the divisions of the railway so that good wages can be made by going over the division on a mileage rate. (287, 288.)

Mr. SPENCER says that on the Southern Railway the hours vary according to the service. Laborers ordinarily work longer than trainmen. The outside limit for engineers is 12 hours, and they often work much less. (265.)

2. *Proposed legal regulation of hours.*—The chief officers of the leading railway brotherhoods, in their joint reply to a schedule of questions, declare that it is impracticable to fix arbitrarily the hours of labor of train and engine men on account of the necessity of changing crews only at established points. The hours of labor of yard and office men should be shortened; for train dispatchers and yard employees 8 hours should constitute a day. For all other classes 10 hours should be recognized as a day's work, and there should be extra pay for extra hours. (761.)

Mr. WILSON, of the Railway Trackmen, thinks that those not engaged in operating trains should not be required to work more than 8 hours except in cases of emergency, believing that they become more fatigued in that length of time than men on trains would during 10 or 12 hours. (766.)

Mr. RONEMUS, of the Brotherhood of Railway Carmen, thinks that in every department 8 hours should be the maximum day's work. In most cases of shop work men would perform as much work in 8 as in 10 hours. The only reason why there is not more agitation for shorter hours is the fear of reduced wages. (769.)

Mr. ARNOLD, secretary of the Locomotive Firemen, thinks that Federal legislation regulating the hours of continuous labor is desirable, especially for the sake of promoting safety. (763.)

Mr. MURPHY, an attorney at law, of Denver, declares that on account of the exacting and exhausting character of railway work it is for the interest of the public that no man should be permitted to be on duty more than 12 hours out of 24 in train service, while in yards and machine shops, where the service will not be impaired by one set of employees relieving another, 8 hours should constitute a day's work. Reduction of the hours of labor will raise the standard of health and of character. (779.)

Mr. WALKER, chairman of the directors of the Atchison, Topeka and Santa Fe Railway, on the other hand, declares that legislation concerning hours of labor is unnecessary. At present, overtime is paid for under duly established schedules. When trains are delayed it would be impossible to tie them up at a stated hour. Cases where employees are overworked are very exceptional. (772.)

3. *Sunday labor.*—According to Mr. SARGENT very little Sunday work on railways is done in the New England States, although perishable freight and some passenger cars are carried. In other parts of the country also there has been a marked decrease in Sunday work during recent years. The railway managers are disposed to do as little of it as possible, but the public insists on a certain amount of passenger traffic, and perishable freight, live stock, etc., must be transported. The railway brotherhoods have all taken a stand against Sunday labor, but recognize the necessity of a certain amount of it. Whether the employee who works on Sunday will get a day's rest during the week depends upon the amount of business. At present he is not likely to do so. Sunday work on railways should be abolished as far as practicable. At present it is paid for at the same rates as work on other days. (66, 86, 87.)

Mr. COWEN, president of the Baltimore and Ohio, says that it is the object of the railways to reduce the running of Sunday trains as much as possible. At the same time it is more economical to use the plant 7 days a week than 6, and in any case it is impossible to stop Sunday work altogether or even any large part of it. Through freight moves on Sunday much as on other days, but the fact that the stations are practically shut on Sunday curtails local business especially.

In the States where the operation of trains on Sunday is limited by law, practically no attention is paid by the Baltimore and Ohio to the statute. There have been some complaints, especially as to the running of excursion trains, but no prosecutions. (303, 304.)

On the Chesapeake and Ohio, according to Mr. INGALLS, only train men work on Sunday. They receive the same pay as for other days. It is unwise for any employer to work his men more than 6 days in a week, but nevertheless laws prohibiting the running of trains on Sunday are injurious. They often injure shippers, and prevent men from reaching their homes for Sunday. The Virginia law permits perishable freight to be carried on Sunday, and Mr. Ingalls admits that frequently on his road long trains of coal cars are run through with single carloads of hogs to legalize the traffic. (288.)

Sunday labor on the Southern Railway, according to Mr. SPENCER, its president, is not paid for at higher rates. Many local passenger trains are not run on Sunday, but through trains must be. In Georgia and one or two other States the running of freight trains except for perishable freight is prohibited on Sunday. Such laws are, Mr. Spencer thinks, exceedingly injurious. It is the desire of railways to move as little freight as possible on Sunday, but if the freight must absolutely be stopped at a fixed hour it may render necessary additional facilities, yards, etc., and it tends to keep the men away from home over Sunday oftener than if no such law existed. Trains having only a small quantity of perishable freight along with other cars are sometimes run. This is in a certain sense an evasion, but if the railways were not permitted to haul other cars along with perishable freight they would often have to refuse to haul perishable freight altogether. (265, 266.)

Mr. CALLAWAY, president of the New York Central, says Sunday labor is necessary for part of the freight crews, especially on account of perishable freight. The pay for Sunday work is the same as for other days, by the mile. In the case of some passenger employees who have to work more than two Sundays during the month the pay is double for such extra Sunday work. Dead freight is usually allowed to lie over from morning to night on Sunday. (218.)

E. The railway brotherhoods and orders.—1. *Relations to one another.*—Mr. ARTHUR, Chief of the Locomotive Engineers, says that the various railway brotherhoods, except the Locomotive Engineers, have formed a federation. The question of joining this federation was thoroughly discussed by the Engineers and defeated. The witness maintains that it is undesirable for engineers to delegate authority over their actions to conductors, firemen, and others. Moreover, the public will cease to consider the separate brotherhoods as individual organizations, and will look only to the federation. The avowed aim of the federation, to coerce railways into submission by the threat of general strikes, is not approved by the witness. The policy of his organization has been to cultivate friendly relations with employers, not to coerce them. (122.)

2. *General organization of brotherhoods—Locomotive Engineers.*—Mr. ARTHUR says that this body was organized in 1863, with the object of promoting the interests of locomotive engineers generally. It now includes about 90 per cent of all

the engineers in the country. The organization sought almost from the beginning to protect its members and secure better conditions from employers, a thing which was not attempted by other railway brotherhoods until much later. Its chief purpose, however, was to improve the character of its members, check intoxication, etc., and its influence in this direction has been very important. (116–118.)

For the central organization of the brotherhood the dues are $2.50 per year, in return for which the members receive the monthly journal. From this source and from profits on other printing the organization has a sufficient fund for current purposes, out of which an annual appropriation for charity, amounting last year to $42,000, is made. There is also an assessment for the contingent fund, to be used in case of strikes. This fund has not been called upon for a number of years, and amounts to about $100,000. Local lodges have additional dues of from $4 to $6 per year. (120, 121.)

Order of Railway Conductors.—Mr. CLARK, grand chief, says that this organization includes at present 22.700 members, of which about 1,500 are in Canada and Mexico. The total number of conductors employed in the United States is about 24,000. The organization has only been active in pushing the interests of employees in labor disputes, etc., since about 1890, and in that time has succeeded in raising wages and reducing hours in many parts of the country, in promoting the independence of its members, and in checking discharges for unjust causes. (110, 113.)

Brotherhood of Railway Trackmen.—According to Mr. WILSON, grand chief. this organization was established about 7 years ago. Till recently only section foremen and roadmasters were eligible, but it is now open to laborers also. The organization as yet, however, includes only about 6,000 of the 180,000 track employees. Its membership is mostly confined to the South and West. It is not associated with the Federation of Railway Employees. which in fact restricts its membership to those employed on trains. Nevertheless the members of the other railway brotherhoods have encouraged this organization. The monthly dues of the brotherhood are 25 cents, while an insurance fee of $1 is also collected. When a member dies or is totally disabled a payment of $1,000 is made; for partial disablement, $500. The slow growth of the organization may be partly due to the practical compulsion of contributions to the insurance funds of some railway companies. (48, 50.)

Switchmen's Union of America.—Mr. O'ROURKE, of Chicago, a member of Switchmen's Union No. 36, states that the membership of that lodge is about 65 or 70. There are 3 or 4 other local unions of switchmen in Chicago. Mr. O'Rourke does not think that a quarter of the switchmen of Chicago belong to the switchmen's union. The total number of switchmen's local unions is 158. The union was reorganized after the strike of 1894, and has had a wonderful growth during the past 5 years. The sick benefits are arranged by the local unions according to their several desires. The union has effected insurance for all its members with a separate organization—the Imperial Mystic Legion—an insurance company doing business under the laws of Nebraska. This arrangement was made in the autumn of 1899. (525–527, 530.)

American Railway Union.—Mr. O'ROURKE considers that a large number of the officers and members of the American Railway Union, especially in Chicago, were professional agitators. He apparently regards the influence of such men as opposed to the interests of organized labor, and considers that the great strike of 1894 was due to evil counsel. Perhaps one-fourth of the present members of Mr. O'Rourke's switchmen's union were among the strikers in 1894. (527, 529.)

Mr. O'Rourke believes that more men who are in active service are members of the various railway unions to-day than at any previous time, even at the time of the greatest strength of the American Railway Union. It was not necessary to be in active service to be a member of that union, and Mr. O'Rourke thinks that one-third of its members were not in active service. This large proportion of unemployed men was due to the slack business of that time, the years 1893 and 1894. (527.)

3. *Purposes, advantages, and effects.*—Mr. MOSELEY, secretary of the Interstate Commerce Commission, declares that the only way by which the workingmen can maintain themselves against great combinations of capital is by thorough organization. Thereby they will be able to preserve their individuality and to improve their situation socially and in the public eye. (43.)

Mr. Moseley has always found the officers of the various railway brotherhoods to be of high character, conservative, and law abiding. They have asked for no legislation which is not justified by humanity and civilization. One of the main purposes of the organizations is mutual insurance. (44.)

Mr. SARGENT, grand master of the Locomotive Firemen, says that the railway brotherhoods are each confined to men in a particular department. Their purposes are to obtain better conditions as to wages, hours, and surroundings, to elevate the profession; to influence legislation, to obtain financial aid for afflicted members and their families, and to furnish out-of-work benefits to members on strike. They have had very beneficial effects. Probably 80 per cent of the employees belong to them. They do not interfere with nonmembers. (68.)

Mr. WILSON, of the Railway Trackmen, says that the railways are easily able to replace men who are dissatisfied unless they are very thoroughly organized. Without organization and public opinion little improvement in the conditions of railway trackmen can be anticipated. Already increases in wages have been secured by organization on 8 or 9 different systems, and reduction of hours on 2 or 3. The railways do not like to oppose the organization directly, but through the road masters they have to a certain degree done so. The organization, however, is doing much to bring closer relations between the road masters, section foremen, and ordinary track laborers. (51, 52, 54.)

Mr. ARTHUR says that one of the chief purposes in the organization of the Brotherhood of Locomotive Engineers was to check the intoxication and vice which were then prevalent among railway employees. In this the organization has been very successful. Application for membership is carefully investigated, and a man must be of good character to secure admission. In 1 year 172 members were expelled for intoxication. The result of this strict system has been that indulgence in intoxicating liquors is now rare among engineers. (116, 117.)

Mr. SARGENT also says that the use of intoxicating liquors is discountenanced by the railway brotherhoods in every way, as well as by the rules of many railway companies. It has greatly decreased in recent years. (69.)

4. *Insurance features of brotherhoods.*—Mr. SARGENT testifies that railway brotherhoods make insurance of their members against death or disability an important feature. The amount of insurance ranges from $400 to $5,000, and it is furnished on a mutual assessment plan at actual cost. The various brotherhoods have already paid out in round numbers $20,000,000 for benefits. The Brotherhood of Locomotive Firemen is furnishing insurance at a cheaper rate than any other organization whatever. It has a rigid medical examination. The cost of an insurance of $1,500 in 1898 was only $16 per member. The reason for this low cost is that most of the members are young and able-bodied, since, when they become older, they are usually promoted to be engineers. The organization also pays benefits for various disabilities not covered by the other railway brotherhoods. Thus, it pays for the loss of a hand or a foot, for blindness, and during the continuance of consumption, paralysis, or Bright's disease. In the local lodges this organization also provides for sick benefits. Railway employees would all prefer insurance in the brotherhoods to relief funds maintained by the companies. (67, 91, 92.)

There is also established near Chicago a home for aged railway employees which is supported by voluntary contributions from the lodges of the various railway brotherhoods. It now contains 22 inmates. (92.)

The insurance system of the Brotherhood of Locomotive Engineers was established in 1867. It is operated on the assessment plan, and policies are for either $750, $1,500, $3,000 or $4,500. About $8,000,000 has been paid to widows and orphans. The local lodges often have assessments and benefits for sickness or injury. The cost of insurance in the general organization has never exceeded 1½ per cent. Men are paid for the loss of a hand, foot, or eye the same amount as for death. The insurance department is incorporated and legally separate from the brotherhood itself. This was found necessary to comply with State laws. (ARTHUR, 117, 121, 126.)

Mr. ARNOLD, grand secretary of the Locomotive Firemen, favors the enactment by Congress of a law giving to all labor organizations the right to carry on insurance business strictly among their members without requiring incorporation or license from any State except the State where the headquarters may be located. (764.)

5. *Attitude toward nonmembers.*—According to Mr. MOSELEY, the railway brotherhoods show no antagonism toward railway men who do not belong to the organizations. (36.)

The Brotherhood of Locomotive Engineers, says Mr. ARTHUR, does not attempt to dictate to employers whom they shall employ, nor does it put any obstacles in the way of nonunion men. It relies on its record to influence men to join the union. (118.)

6. *Relations to employers* (see also as to *Discrimination in employment*, p. 131; as to *Wage contracts*, p. 138).—Mr. ARTHUR declares that engineers and other railway

employees stand in special need of organization for mutual protection, because each employee is subject to so many superior officers serving in different capacities. The Brotherhood of Locomotive Engineers has established committees to present grievances to employers and discuss matters with them. It does not attempt to dictate whom the railroads shall employ, but seeks only justice for its members. The principle followed has usually been that of the golden rule, and if the railway managers had met the employees in the same spirit there would have been no strikes or difficulties. As a matter of fact, the relations between the railways and the men have usually been very friendly. (117, 118, 123.)

Mr. SARGENT says that for the most part the relation between the various brotherhoods and their employers is a pleasant one. The witness has seldom found officers with whom he could not negotiate and usually reach results acceptable to his organization. Some railway managers, however, consider these organizations injurious to their interest, and use the system of benefit funds and other means to hinder men from joining them. In some cases, too, members, especially leaders in the organization, are discriminated against as to conditions of employment or promotion, or an intimation is made that this is likely to be the case in such a way that violation of law can not be proved. (87, 91.)

Mr. MOSELEY says that a large number of railways are now conforming to rules, regulations, and rates of pay agreed upon between the representatives of the various brotherhoods of employees and the railway managers. There is a feeling of entire accord. The passage of the arbitration act of 1898 has still further promoted this harmony. (36, 37.)

Mr. CALLAWAY, of the New York Central, testifies that a large proportion of the men on that system are members of the various brotherhoods, and that the railway makes no opposition to such membership. The witness personally in his long experience has had little difficulty with the brotherhoods. At first they were inclined to abuse their new power and to make arbitrary demands, but they have become more reasonable and are now largely benevolent associations. They have improved both the morale and the intelligence of the men.

The New York Central has had few difficulties with strikes. The last one was several years ago, and was due to the demand of the employees in the yards to be allowed practically to select their own immediate superiors. In this case the employees were unsuccessful. Mr. Callaway also refers to earlier strikes on the Union Pacific and the Missouri Pacific. (221, 222.)

Mr. INGALLS, president of the Chesapeake and Ohio and the Cleveland, Cincinnati, Chicago and St. Louis, says that he himself and these railways generally are in favor of the organization of their employees, and that contracts are made with the organizations. It is thought, however, that telegraph operators and confidential employees ought not to belong to organizations, and that it is desirable, on account of their smaller number and the variety of their work, to deal with them individually. These railways have never had serious difficulty with strikes. (291.)

While Mr. FISH, of the Illinois Central, is in favor of ordinary railway brotherhoods and organized labor generally, he thinks that the temporary organizations, especially of railway employees, which have sometimes been made through the influence of professional agitators, are essentially "labor trusts." They are irresponsible and injurious. The American Railway Union was a type of these organizations. The Illinois Central does not, Mr. Fish thinks, make contracts directly with the brotherhoods, although their grievance committees are dealt with by officers of the railway. (327, 328.)

On the Baltimore and Ohio, according to Mr. COWEN, agreements as to wages, etc., are made with committees of the men rather than of the brotherhoods. But the officers of the railway also discuss questions regularly with the brotherhoods. The witness thinks that the brotherhoods believe that they have been fairly treated by the railway. (307.)

Mr. SPENCER, of the Southern Railway, believes that a large proportion of the railway employees in the Southern States belong to the brotherhoods. His own company has no objection to the unions, but, on the contrary, frequently discusses questions with them in a friendly manner, although no contracts are made with them. This company has had no strikes or general complaints. Wages have been increased during the past year or two, making up for the reductions which were made during 1892 and 1893. The question of this increase was discussed in perfectly good temper. (266, 268.)

7. *Incorporation of trade unions.*—Mr. CLARK, of the railway conductors, sees no serious objection to incorporation of trade unions, but believes that it will be some time before it will meet with general approval. (116.)

Mr. ARTHUR says that objections to incorporation have been raised by delegates of the Brotherhood of Locomotive Engineers, on the ground that each individual member of the organization could then be sued for acts of the organization. The insurance departments of the railway brotherhoods are incorporated, being legally independent of the brotherhoods themselves. The custody of funds of the brotherhoods is protected by requiring bonds from financial and other officers. (126.)

F. Strikes.—1. *Strikes generally.*—Mr. SARGENT, of the Locomotive Firemen, says that railway strikes are chiefly due to difficulties as to wages or to resistance to unfair conditions of employment. They are resorted to only when all other means of adjustment have failed. They have been highly beneficial in their results to railway employees. The railway brotherhoods are strong advocates of arbitration. (68.)

Mr. ARTHUR says an authorized strike of Locomotive Engineers requires the approval of the Grand Chief Engineer of the brotherhood. It is Mr. Arthur's policy to refuse that approval unless the cause is just. The effect of the organization has been to decrease the number of strikes. (128.)

Mr. O'ROURKE, switchman, of Chicago, hopes that the time has come when there will be no more strikes. He considers that they are to be prevented by closer association and better understanding between employer and employee. In particular he believes that strikes will be prevented, and the interests of organized labor will be furthered, by the exclusion of agitators from labor organizations (528.)

Mr. SARGENT says that the general modern doctrine as to the right of labor to combine or strike is that any body of men may associate themselves for the purpose of bettering their condition in any way, may demand wages at their own rates, and choose their own employers, provided a like liberty is accorded to everyone else. (71.)

Mr. STRONG says that the employees of the railroads are under no obligation to stay at their work a moment. The railroads exercise the right to discharge men without any notice whatever. If the men leave without notice they are only exercising the same right. The railroads can not properly construe such leaving of employment as an offense, comparable with drunkenness, or carelessness in the performance of duty. (522.)

Mr. WALKER, chairman of the directors of the Atchison, Topeka and Santa Fe Railway, declares that there can be no question of the right of workmen to strike, but that the moment they have struck they cease entirely to be employees and have absolutely no claim upon the property of their former employers. They may negotiate for reinstatement, but they can not justly interfere with the operation of the business by other persons. In fact, public opinion has now generally come to recognize that strikers are not justified in employing violent measures of any sort. The witness, however, thinks that employees are justified in forming a combination for their mutual benefit. (774.)

2. *Boycotts.*—According to Mr. ARTHUR, it was formerly the rule of the Brotherhood of Locomotive Engineers that where a duly authorized strike was made on any road the members of the organization on other roads should refuse to haul its cars. Such refusal was enjoined in the case of the Toledo, Ann Arbor and North Michigan Railroad strike, and the order was upheld by the United States Supreme   Court. This rule of the organization has accordingly been abandoned. (120, 126.)

3. *Railroad strike of 1894.*—Mr. STRONG, an attorney at law of Chicago, says that the strike of the railroad men in 1894 was brought about altogether by generous sympathy with the Pullman men, and was meant to induce the railroads to persuade the Pullman Company to arbitrate its differences with its employees. The strikers had no idea of tieing up the traffic of Chicago, at least for more than a few days. The destruction of property which actually took place has been greatly exaggerated, according to Mr. Strong. He says that the Labor Commission reported, after careful investigation, that the railroads lost in property, including the hire of 3,000 deputy marshals and other incidental expenses, a total of $685,783. (506.)

Mr. Strong says that within 10 or 12 days after the commencement of the Pullman strike there were 1,600 families in Pullman, who had been employees of the Pullman Company from 5 to 20 years, and who were absolutely destitute of the necessaries of life, depending on public charity for support; showing, as he thinks, that they had not been able to accumulate enough out of the pittance they had received to support them for 2 weeks. (505.)

Mr. O'ROURKE, switchman, states that fully 90 per cent of the switchmen of Chicago went out in the strike of 1894. Two-thirds of them, he believes, are now at work in Chicago as switchmen. A great number of the officers and members of the A. R. U. Mr. O'Rourke considers to have been professional agitators, especially in Chicago. (529.)

G. Injunctions in strikes.—1. *Intimidation of employees, etc.*—Mr. MOSELEY, secretary of the Interstate Commerce Commission, submitted a large number of abstracts of decisions of courts in which injunctions had been issued forbidding the intimidation of persons seeking employment or of those already employed to prevent them from working. In the various cases the methods of supposed intimidation are defined and enjoined specifically; such as displaying banners before the premises of the employer, publishing placards and other statements addressed to employees, uttering menaces and threats, including even mere requests not to enter upon or continue work. Thus in one case a notice to a foreman of the shops of a railroad requesting him to stay away from work until the strike was settled, but adding, "In no case are you to consider this an intimidation," was still held to be a threat. Under the interstate-commerce act and the antitrust act various injunctions to prevent interference with the conduct of railways by intimidation or threats have also been issued. In one case, however, an injunction to prevent persecution of plaintiff's company by strikes, boycotts, violence, or intimidation was refused, since no threat to do any unlawful act was shown. (9–11.)

According to Mr. SARGENT, of the Brotherhood of Locomotive Firemen, on trial of the habeas corpus proceedings to secure the release of Debs et al., the court held that the United States had a right to remove any obstructions on highways over which mails must be carried, to supervise interstate commerce so as to prevent great public inconvenience, and to enjoin all persons from interfering with those engaged in the operation of roads in the hands of receivers, or engaged in interstate commerce, or carrying United States mails. A violation of such an injunction may be punished as contempt. 158 U. S., 564. (73.)

2. *Compulsory performance of service.*—Mr. MOSELEY shows also that in various cases injunctions have been issued by the courts to compel railway employees to perform particular services. This is especially common in the case of railways under receivership. In 1893 Judge Jenkins, of the United States circuit court, enjoined the employees of the Northern Pacific Railroad, about 12,000, from quitting the service of the receivers with the object of crippling the property or embarrassing its operation. The United States circuit court of appeals, however, reversed the order as an invasion of natural liberty. In another case one Lennon was punished for contempt of court in refusing to handle cars from the Ann Arbor Railway, he being an engineer of the Lake Shore and Michigan Southern. In this case it appears that the injunction was issued without any hearing of the railway employees and in the office of the railroad itself. (See fuller account of these cases below.) The witness advocates a bill prohibiting courts of the United States from enforcing specific performance of contracts for personal service by injunctions. (8, 12, 13.)

3. *The Northern Pacific case, 1894.*—Mr. SARGENT, of the Locomotive Firemen, says that in 1894 Judge Jenkins issued an order enjoining the employees of the Northern Pacific Railway, then in the hands of a receiver, "from combining and conspiring to quit, with or without notice, the service of said receivers with the object and intent of crippling the property in their custody or embarrassing the operation of said railroad, and from so quitting the service of said receivers, with or without notice, as to cripple the property or to prevent or hinder the operation of said railroad." (60 Fed. Rep., 803.) This matter was afterwards brought before the circuit court of appeals, and it was held that it would be an invasion of one's natural liberty to compel him to work for or remain in the personal service of another. The fact that employees of railroads might quit under circumstances that would show bad faith or disregard of contract does not, the court holds, justify a departure from the general rule that equity alone will not compel the affirmative performance of simply personal services. Since these employees had entered service under a general contract which did not limit their right to quit the service, it would not be illegal or criminal for them, by peaceable cooperation, persuasion, and conference, to assert their right to refuse further service, even though they expected that their quitting simultaneously without notice would temporarily inconvenience the receivers and the public. Any loss due to such quitting would be merely incidental to the situation and not legally chargeable upon the employees. On the other hand, there might be circumstances where the employees could be held guilty of a conspiracy in combining to wrong others or the public, and such a conspiracy is illegal, even though no act be performed toward carrying it out. Any combination which had for its object to cripple the property in the hands of the receivers and embarrass the operation of the railroad either by disabling the engines, cars, or other property, interfering

with their possession or use, or employing force, threats, or other wrongful methods against the receivers and their employees, would be illegal conspiracy. (See 63 Fed. Rep., 310.)   (65, 66, 73, 74.)

Mr. Sargent declares that there had been no intention on the part of the employees of the Northern Pacific Railroad to strike previous to the issuance of the injunction by Judge Jenkins. The receivers had issued a new and lower schedule of wages, in violation of an existing contract with the organization of the employees. While the representatives of the men were consulting with the company the injunction restraining them from quitting service was issued. Its ultimate result was to bring about a general strike, and, had it not been for the restraining influence of the organization leaders, there might have been a rebellion among the men. The injunction also restrained the leaders of the various brotherhoods from even advising or counseling with the employees of the road. Thus the witness was served with such an injunction at his office in Indiana. (89.)

Mr. ARTHUR, chief of the Locomotive Engineers, confirms the testimony of Mr. Sargent regarding the causes of the difficulty and the nature of the injunction in this case. He and others in the office of the Brotherhood of Locomotive Engineers at Cleveland were enjoined from talking, counseling, conferring or advising with the members of the brotherhood employed on the Northern Pacific. It was, of course, impossible for a body of men to quit employment without to some extent crippling the business, as the injunction undertook to restrain the employees from doing.   (119.)

In 1894 the receivers of the Union Pacific Railway followed the example of those of the Northern Pacific Railway in petitioning for an injunction to prevent employees from striking when a reduced schedule of wages should be put in force. This injunction was granted by the lower court, but reversed by the higher Federal court.   (62 Fed. Rep., 7.)   (SARGENT, 74.)

4. *Toledo, Ann Arbor and North Michigan case.*—Mr. SARGENT says that in 1893, in the case of the Toledo, Ann Arbor and North Michigan Railroad Company *v.* The Pennsylvania Company et al., it was held that a combination to induce the officers and engineers of a common carrier to refuse to receive and handle interstate freight from another carrier is a criminal offense, and that the carrier injured has a cause of action against all those engaged in it. An injunction may be issued to restrain the chief member of such a conspiracy from giving such an order, or to compel him to rescind it. An injunction may also be issued to compel such a carrier and its employees to haul the cars of the other company, and this is binding on all officers and employees whether they be made parties or not. Employees can evade this obligation only by quitting the service of the company. (54 Fed. Rep., 730, 746.)   (72; see also 65, 66.)

Mr. ARTHUR says that the strike on the Ann Arbor road was caused by its president breaking a contract with the railway brotherhoods in reducing wages. Although evidence as to this contract was produced in court, the judge granted an injunction restraining the employees of other railroads from refusing to haul cars of the Ann Arbor road in through traffic. This order was sustained by the United States Supreme Court under the antitrust law. Owing to this decision the Brotherhood of Locomotive Engineers has abandoned its former rule for boycotting traffic from roads on which authorized strikes are in force. In addition to this injunction the officers of the brotherhoods were enjoined from advising or consulting with their men.   (119, 120.)

5. *Receivers protected by injunction.*—Mr. MOSELEY says that the courts have issued numerous injunctions to restrain employees from interfering with the operation of railways by receivers. Apparently injunctions are issued under these circumstances against acts which would not be restrained if the railway were not under receivership. It has also been held that, in the absence of injunction, an attempt to interfere with the management, or cripple the property, or intimidate employees or those seeking employment, is a contempt of the court appointing the receiver. In another case a person attempting to induce men to quit work for a receiver was arrested. The action of the lower court in the Northern Pacific case, however, where it was sought to enjoin all the employees from quitting work, was overruled by the United States circuit court of appeals. (11, 12.)

Mr. SARGENT, as illustrating this practice, says that in 1885 the Wabash Railroad was in the hands of a receiver. The chairman of a committee of striking employees sent notice to the foremen of the various shops of the road requesting them to stay away from the shop until the strike should be settled, but adding, "In no case are you to consider this an intimidation." The courts held that this was an unlawful interference with the receiver's management and a contempt of court.   (24 Fed. Rep., 217.)   In another case in 1885 it was held that the employees of a receiver are guilty of contempt of court if they resort to threats or violence, or seek to overawe others by preconcerted demonstrations of force, in order to induce them to leave employment and thus hinder the operation of the road. Where a party of men combine to do an unlawful thing, and one of them does an act which the others do not, all are responsible for his act. (U. S. *v.* Kane et al., 23 Fed. Rep., 748.) (71, 72.)

6. *Restriction of use of injunctions.*—Mr. MOSELEY declares that the frequent use of injunctions is exasperating to the wage-worker and is tending to bring the Federal judiciary into disrepute. The employees are not given a fair hearing, but employers seem to secure injunctions for the asking, as in the Lennon case. The witness admits the duties of railway employees toward the public as a third party; but he believes that railway employees recognize those duties and should have accordingly a special protection. (12, 13.)

Professor JOHNSON says that railways have found the injunction an important means of securing their ends in disputes with their employees. They have at times taken occasion to attach mail cars to as many trains as possible for the sake of the protection of the courts. The witness believes that some statutory limitation will have to be placed on the use of the injunction. (63.)

The chief officers of the leading railway orders, in a joint reply to a schedule of inquiries, declare themselves in favor of a bill, which has already been introduced at a previous session of Congress, dividing contempts of court into two classes, those committed in the presence of the court and those not committed in its presence. The latter, which are called indirect contempts, should be treated by different procedure from direct contempts. A written accusation should be made and the accused required to answer. The trial should proceed upon testimony as in criminal cases; the accused should be entitled to be confronted with the witnesses, and the court should have the option of summoning a jury. Especially should the judgment be subject to appeal to higher courts. The text of the proposed law is submitted in full. The witnesses declare that the criminal laws are brought into contempt by the too liberal use of injunctions. In fact, where men simply exercise their inalienable right to cease work, and where they pay due regard to the public safety, there is no occasion for an injunction of the Federal courts at all. (761, 762.)

These officers maintain also that the enjoining of men from taking concerted action in leaving the employ of railways or from using proper and peaceable means to induce others to do so is unjust and should be prohibited. The criminal code provides proper penalties for criminal actions. (65, 66.)

Mr. ARNOLD, of the Brotherhood of Locomotive Firemen, also favors the bill providing for two classes of contempt, and thinks that the court should not be given the right to imprison for contempt committed without the direct knowledge of the courts. (764.)

Mr. WILSON, of the Brotherhood of Railway Trackmen, thinks that either party in an injunction case should have the right to have disputed questions of fact tried by jury; but otherwise that the procedure of injunction should not be done away. (766.)

Mr. RONEMUS, of the Railway Carmen, declares that no injunction should be used against employees until they have had an opportunity to answer. Injunctions against men who have committed no actual offense and do not contemplate doing so are un-American. (769.)

Mr. MURPHY, an attorney at law of Denver, declares that where injunctions are issued in connection with strikes they usually forbid acts which are already illegal and criminal under statutes, and that they are accordingly unnecessary. Moreover, the issue of such injunctions deprives citizens of the right of trial by jury, which has always been considered absolutely essential to securing justice. The judge who acts in an injunction case must decide that certain acts have been committed, a question which properly belongs to the jury. The strict laws of evidence which would be applied in criminal cases do not necessarily govern the judge in a case for contempt. The judge is biased on the ground that his authority has been disregarded. The witness would apparently favor the prohibition of injunctions in connection with strikes. (779, 780.)

Mr. WALKER, chairman of the directors of the Atchison, Topeka and Santa Fe Railway, sees no reason for interfering with the well-established rules of equity concerning injunctions. There may be errors in the decisions of the lower courts concerning such matters, but the body of the law is composed of the decisions of the courts of last resort. (772.)

H. **Arbitration.**—1. *Generally.*—The officers of the leading railway brotherhoods, in a joint statement, declare that the brotherhoods are strong advocates of conciliation and arbitration. Their experience with these methods has been satisfactory.

Compulsory arbitration would involve permanent boards and would take away the very spirit of arbitration. Two cases of arbitration under the Canadian law on the Grand Trunk Railway have recently been settled by award in favor of the employees. (68, 69, 94, 95.)

Mr. ARTHUR, grand chief engineer, says the policy of the Brotherhood of Locomotive Engineers has been to conciliate employers, sending committees to discuss difficulties with them, and referring unsettled matters to the chief officers of the organization. (125.)

Mr. INGALLS, president of the Chesapeake and Ohio, thinks that moral suasion and mediation between parties in labor disputes is advantageous. There must be consideration on both sides. The railways which he represents would not, however, be willing to arbitrate the question of an increase in wages, without some limitation, such as that the wages should not exceed those of rival lines; they could not afford to leave the final decision to anyone but their own directors. (291.)

Mr. CALLAWAY, president of the New York Central, does not think that arbitration of labor disputes on railways is likely to be of great importance. Compulsory arbitration is out of the question. There is no way of compelling men to continue work if they do not wish to. On the other hand, the railways will not voluntarily submit disputes involving really vital matters to the decision of outside authorities. They must have employees who will carry out orders and obey instructions. The influence of a change of even 10 per cent in the rate of wages upon the earnings of a railway company is so great that Mr. Callaway, at any rate, would hardly be willing to submit a question involving such an increase to arbitration. (221, 222.)

Mr. FISH, of the Illinois Central, thinks that the chief objection to the arbitration of railway matters is the impossibility of maintaining effective discipline over the men if authority is divided. The railways are held responsible to the people, and must have discipline. (324.)

2. *United States arbitration act of 1898.*—Mr. KNAPP, chairman of the Interstate Commerce Commission, testifies that the United States arbitration act of June, 1898, has as yet had no direct effect upon the settlement of labor disputes concerning railways. The act provides that either party to a controversy may apply to the Commissioner of Labor and the chairman of the Interstate Commerce Commission to act as mediators. If the mediation fail, the parties, if they agree to arbitrate, each appoint one arbitrator, and a third is appointed by the Commissioner of Labor and the chairman of the Interstate Commerce Commission. In only one instance so far has there been any application for mediation. This came from the side of the employees, and there appeared to be clearly a situation within the contemplation of the law. The officers of the common carriers, however, declined all offers of conciliation and refused to arbitrate, declaring that the controversy related only to wages, and that the influence of the rate of wages upon profits was so great that they could not afford to submit the determination to any other authority.

Mr. Knapp is of the opinion that resort to arbitration must necessarily be voluntary, and, accordingly, that if other railroads take the same position as was taken in this case, law can accomplish nothing. He thinks, further, that if the attempts at conciliation by the Commissioner of Labor and chairman of the Interstate Commerce Commission in any case shall prove unsuccessful, the parties will not be willing to arbitrate, since the decision of the third arbitrator would be likely to be practically the same as that of the officers just named who appointed him.

The witness, however, is able to suggest no amendment to the measure. (129–131.)

Mr. MOSELEY, secretary of the Interstate Commerce Commission, says that the arbitration act enables employees and employers to come together without any surrender of ground. The Government itself steps in and urges arbitration, and the side which refuses to arbitrate is likely to receive public condemnation. The relations between railways and their employees have never been so harmonious as since the passage of this law, and it meets the approval of all railway men. (37.)

The chief officers of the leading railway brotherhoods think that the act of June 1, 1898, has not yet been given a fair test; indeed, there has been no occasion to take advantage of it. If proper earnestness be shown by Government officials, it may have good results. They have no changes to suggest. (68, 69, 762.)

Mr. WILSON, of the Brotherhood of Railway Trackmen, however, points out that the act does not apply to employees except those engaged in the operation of trains. Out of 823,476 employees, 596,859 have no protection under the law. The measure should be extended to them. Moreover, the witness thinks that the Interstate Commerce Commission should be made a tribunal before which all c asses of railroad employees could present their grievances. It should be the duty of the commission to take testimony and make a public record of their opinion as to the justice of the case. Public opinion would then have great influence in compelling railways to accept the decision. (766, 767.)

Mr. RONEMUS, of the Railway Carmen, favors a somewhat similar system to that proposed by Mr. Wilson. (770.)

Mr. ARTHUR thinks it is just to compel the parties to arbitration, especially in the case of railways, to abide by the awards of the arbitrators. The existing United States arbitration act, however, is of great advantage without the compulsory clause, since public opinion will be a powerful influence in compelling both sides to accept arbitration when either asks for it, and to abide by the decision. However, there has been no experience on the part of the Locomotive Engineers under this law. (125.)

Mr. COWEN, of the Baltimore and Ohio, does not think that the arbitration act will have any effect. Railway companies will not permit outside authorities to fix wages, especially since no power can bind the employee unless practical slavery be introduced. (309.)

3. *Compulsory arbitration.*—The chief officers of the five leading brotherhoods of railway employees are opposed to compulsory arbitration, as involving involuntary servitude. (762.)

Mr. ARNOLD, secretary of the Brotherhood of Locomotive Firemen, is of the same opinion. (764.)

Mr. MURPHY, an attorney at law of Denver, thinks that compulsory arbitration is both practicable and advantageous. Corporations, being creatures of the law, can be made to submit to any condition imposed upon them. The great interest which the public has in the conduct of railways, and in preserving the general stability of business, would justify any interference with labor disputes in this way. (780.)

Mr. WALKER, chairman of the directors of the Atchison, Topeka and Santa Fe Railway, in reply to a schedule of inquiries concerning railway labor, submitted a detailed argument against compulsory arbitration. The witness recognizes the right of laborers to strike and to form unions, but he declares that during strikes they have no rights whatever as regards the property of their employers. As a matter of fact, the strike is ultimately the only effective way of settling labor disputes. Force, not in the sense of physical force, but of economic ability to resist, must be ultimately decisive.

Arbitration which is compulsory is a contradiction of terms. Arbitration can only mean a contract to submit questions to a decision, and it is enforceable as a contract and not otherwise. Compulsory arbitration would involve the right of one party to compel another to appear before a tribunal, and this would be essentially a judicial proceeding. Moreover, there are some things which, from their very nature, can not be arbitrated. Thus, if the workmen assert a claim that no one shall be employed who does not belong to a given labor union, the employer having the inherent and essential right to employ whom he will, there is no question for arbitration. A merchant would be justified in refusing to arbitrate the price of his goods.

It is very difficult to find men to whom questions concerning labor disputes may be prudently submitted. The universal tendency of arbitrators is to split the difference, and this inevitably gives advantage to the workmen, especially since the pecuniary risk of the employer is much greater than that of the laborer. Moreover, arbitrators are bound by no rules of law, and they are apt to be prejudiced in favor of the supposedly weaker party.

Finally, the laborers can not be effectively bound by the decision of arbitrators. The decision may be binding upon the labor union, but the union can not control the actions of its members, who are always at liberty to withdraw. The employer, on the other hand, is bound.

As a matter of fact, Mr. Walker thinks, workingmen are not anxious to submit questions to arbitration until they have found that they are unable to obtain their demands in any other way. They seldom think of arbitrating until a strike has proceeded so far as to become apparently a failure. This feeling is fostered by the leaders of many labor unions, who find their chief advantage during the period of the strike. (773–776.)

I. **Accidents and injuries.**—1. *Safety appliances—United States act of 1893.*—Mr. MOSELEY, secretary of the Interstate Commerce Commission, says that by this act railways were required within 5 years to equip freight trains with air brakes and train brakes sufficient to enable the engineer to control the train directly, and to equip all cars with automatic couplers and with hand holds. At the end of this time some roads had almost entirely failed to comply with the act, and as those which had done so were by the law practically punished by being prohibited from hauling the cars of other roads not so equipped, the Interstate Commerce Commission extended the time for 2 years, to January 1, 1900. The witness does not think further extension will be asked for or necessary. (32.)

Mr. CLARK, chief of the railway conductors, says that the extension of time for 5 years asked by the railroads was opposed by the various railway brother-hoods, and they succeeded in having the time reduced to 2 years. The same testimony is given by Mr. ARTHUR, who adds that some of the roads had been prevented from complying with the law by the depression in railway business, but that others had simply neglected to do so, although their earnings were ample. (115, 126.)

The officers of all the leading railway brotherhoods declare that they think the railways are doing all they can to comply with the law concerning safety appli-ances, and that no further legislation is necessary. (763, 767.)

Mr. KNAPP, chairman of the Interstate Commerce Commission, testified in October, 1899, that very rapid advance was being made by railroads in equipping their cars with the safety appliances required by law, and he did not think that there would be an application for extension of the time for equipment beyond January 1, 1900. (131.)

Several railway officers testified on this subject before the expiration of the time limit for the equipment of cars, January 1, 1900.

Mr. CALLAWAY said that the New York Central had entirely and promptly com-plied with the requirements of the act of Congress as to safety appliances. All its cars have automatic couplers and handholds and about 68 per cent of the freight cars have air brakes. There was some difficulty at first in securing suffi-ciently strong couplers, but this has now been remedied. During the period of transition there has been no marked decrease in the number of accidents, but when all cars are properly equipped the witness believes that there will be decidedly fewer casualties.

The New York Central is equipped throughout with the block-signal system, which gives information to coming trains of any difficulty. Stoves have been replaced altogether by steam heat, but the witness is doubtful whether this decreases risk materially. The cars of this road are largely lighted by Pintsch gas, and some experiments are being made with electric lighting, which has hith-erto scarcely proved satisfactory. The system is almost altogether double tracked. (219, 220.)

Mr. INGALLS said that the Chesapeake and Ohio and the Cleveland, Cincinnati, Chicago and St. Louis railroads expected to have their equipment of safety appliances complete by January 1, 1900. (291.)

Mr. SPENCER, of the Southern Railway, said that that system expected to com-ply with the requirements concerning safety appliances by January 1, 1900, a large proportion of the cars being already equipped. The master car builders' vertical car coupler is used. (268.)

Mr. COWEN, of the Baltimore and Ohio, stated in October, 1899, that a large proportion of the cars of that company had been equipped with air brakes and automatic couplers. A certain proportion of the cars are not worth the expense of putting on these appliances. They will be used in local traffic and will grad-ually go out of service altogether. The reason why the process of equipping cars has been necessarily slow is that no large proportion of cars could be taken out of service without interfering with the business of the country. The new equip-ments have been put on chiefly at times when the cars were taken into the shops for repairs and reconstruction. (308.)

Mr. MOSELEY states that there was a great dispute among railway men as to the relative merits of the vertical-plane coupler, which had been approved by the master car builders, and the link-and-pin coupler, similar in form to the old hand couplers. The former was finally generally approved. Its special advantage is that it holds the cars closely together, preventing slack. This coupler was free from patents. The act likewise required that the drawbars of cars should be of a standard type. This was fixed by the American Railway Association at not less than 31¼ nor more than 34½ inches, and railways have generally complied. (33.)

Mr. SARGENT, of the Locomotive Firemen, says that the cost of air brakes is $29.75 per set. If they are applied to cars having substantial foundation brake gear, the cost of putting on the brakes should not exceed $5; if new foundations and brake gear are necessary, about $20.

The cost of putting automatic couplers on new cars should not exceed from $13 to $20. On old cars there may be added expense for strengthening the draft timbers, etc., but this expense would be necessary in any case, since old cars of light capacity are unfit for use along with modern heavy cars and engines. At any rate most cars now used are new, since there has been a marked tendency to increase the size of cars in recent years. (67, 68.)

2. *Effect of safety appliances.*—Mr. MOSELEY says that the result of the requirement concerning couplers and air brakes has been greatly to reduce accidents. Considering the amount of freight handled, only about half as many men were killed and half as many injured in 1897 as in 1893. The number killed was 1,067 less. The change has also resulted in saving loss of links and the breakages in the old style of coupler, involving considerable expense. The requirement as to air brakes was necessary especially to prevent the rear-end collisions which were formerly frequent. It is proving an economy to railways. Trains can make much faster time, because they need not take so long to slow down, and the capacity of cars can be increased. Where an employee formerly handled 200 tons of train load he can now handle 600 or 800. (32–34.)

Mr. KNAPP says that the effect of the change already seems to be a decided decrease in the casualties to the employees. At the same time, on account of differences in the equipment on different cars, imperfect appliances, and lack of experience, there might be expected to be numerous accidents during the period of transition, so that the full effect can not be judged. (131.)

Mr. SPENCER expects that casualties will be considerably diminished by these appliances, although the results of individual carelessness can not be eliminated. He does not think that the amount of labor required on trains will be reduced by them. The use of air brakes on passenger trains has not lessened the number of employees. The work of operating trains is actually becoming more complicated. Nevertheless, these devices help in securing efficiency and apparently reduce the relative demand for labor, although not causing absolute reduction in numbers. (268, 269.)

Mr. INGALLS thinks the law of 1893 was a wise one. The real test of its efficiency in preventing casualties will be made after January 1. The railways which are fully equipped will then refuse to exchange cars with those which are not. (291.)

Mr. COWEN says that although the use of these appliances probably adds considerably to the safety of the employees there are some new dangers connected with them, such as from the necessity of getting under the cars to fix the pipes on the air brakes. (309.)

Mr. STICKNEY, president of the Chicago Great Western Railway, thinks that the use of safety appliances will probably reduce the number of accidents and result in a considerable saving to the railroads. He does not believe that there has been much reduction in the number of accidents up to the present time, but that was perhaps not to be expected. (455.)

3. *Proposed State law as to safety appliances.*—Mr. MOSELEY favors the enactment of uniform laws by the separate States requiring railways lying wholly within a State to equip their engines with power driving-wheel brakes and their cars with train brakes, automatic couplers and drawbars of standard height, and hand holds, as well as to block all frogs, switches, guard rails, etc., to prevent the catching of feet. This bill, which is submitted in full, is similar to the existing United States act requiring safety appliances on interstate railways. (39.)

Mr. SARGENT advocates the law proposed by the Interstate Commerce Commission, for enactment by separate States, requiring the use of automatic couplers and continuous brakes. There are many roads lying wholly within single States which yet haul cars in interstate traffic, and employees on these should be protected. (93.)

4. *Blocking of frogs.*—Mr. MOSELEY declares that men have been killed in the District of Columbia recently for lack of proper blocking of switch frogs. He accordingly recommends a bill for requiring them to be properly blocked in the Territories of the United States and in the District of Columbia. (38.)

Mr. CLARK says that the proposed law requiring the blocking of frogs in the District of Columbia, the Territories, etc., is of less importance than it would have been before the introduction of automatic couplers. These obviate the necessity for going between cars, and it was principally while doing so under the old system that accidents from catching the feet in frogs occurred. (115.)

5. *Report of accidents.*—Mr. MOSELEY favors a requirement that in case of accident resulting in killing or injuring employees or others railways should notify the Interstate Commerce Commission at once, giving it an opportunity to investigate as to the cause. Railways should also report accidents, with their causes and results, each month instead of annually, as at present. None of these reports should be made the basis for damage suits. The witness submitted the form of a bill for this purpose. (37, 38.)

This measure is also commended by the officers of the 5 great railway brotherhoods in their joint reply to the schedule of inquiries as to railway labor.   (763.)

Mr. SARGENT also advocates this proposal.   (93.)

Mr. CLARK, of the Railway Conductors, declares that the condition of the railways and the welfare of railway employees are matters of general public interest. The presentation of statistics concerning accidents is of great importance.   Such statistics had much influence in securing the passage of the act requiring the use of automatic couplers and brakes, and more detailed information than is now received would be of material value.   (114.)

Mr. STICKNEY, president of the Chicago Great Western Railway, does not believe that a requirement that the railroads should report the details of accidents to the Interstate Commerce Commission would secure very much definite information.   Railway companies themselves try to discover the causes of accidents, but in some cases reach only indefinite results.   Still such a requirement would not work any particular hardship to the railroads.   (456.)

6. *Contribution by railways to injured persons.*—Professor JOHNSON says that, aside from benefit funds maintained by certain railway companies, it is quite a common practice for these and other roads to contribute to injured employees or to the families of those who are killed.   Moreover, those who are injured so as to be unable to perform hard labor are often given some subordinate position, such as that of watchman.   (59.)

According to Mr. CALLAWAY, it is the practice of the New York Central to allow persons injured half pay during the time of disability, or, in case of permanent incapacity, to provide them, if possible, with some light employment at a gate or signal tower, or in some such place.   Similar arrangements are made for the benefit of older men.   The company has no regular pension system, but frequently does grant pensions to individuals at various rates.   The railroad has no hospitals of its own, but these are scarcely necessary, as it has arrangements with private hospitals at various points.   The men largely belong to associations for mutual relief, and many also insure with accident insurance companies.   (218, 219.)

7. *Hospital associations.*—Mr. SARGENT says that these are maintained by various railways, and where honestly conducted are of great benefit.   Thus the Southern Pacific Railroad collects 50 cents per month from firemen and a proportionate sum from all other employees, including the president and managers, and the hospital facilities furnished are very acceptable to the employees.   The funds thus accumulated may become very large.   Recently the Union Pacific hospital department was investigated in the courts, and it was found that the funds had been mismanaged and diverted from their purpose.   (92.)

The Chesapeake and Ohio Railroad has recently established a hospital which cost the railway $75,000, and which, Mr. INGALLS declares, is very complete.   It is supported by assessment upon all employees who care to have the privilege of its use.   Even the officers are nominally assessed, although Mr. Ingalls has commuted his own payment.   The railway is also hoping to establish a pension system for disabled or superannuated employees.   (289, 290.)

J. **Liability of railways for injuries to employees.**—1. *Assumption of risk by employees.*—Mr. SARGENT, of the Locomotive Firemen, submitted a paper summarizing the common-law doctrines as to employers' liability.

Where an employment is accompanied with risk, of which those who enter it have or are presumed to have notice, they can not, if they are injured by exposure to such risks, recover from the employer.   By contract to perform hazardous duties the employee assumes such risks as are incident to their discharge, including such as arise during the course of employment, if he had or was bound to have knowledge thereof.   He does not, however, assume the risk of danger arising from unsafe or defective methods, machinery, or other instrumentalities, unless he has or may be presumed to have knowledge or notice thereof; and the burden of proof that an injured employee had such knowledge or notice of the defect or obstruction causing the injury is upon the employer.   (75.)

2. *Who can sue for injury.*—All of the States and Territories within the United States have a statute giving the right to the person injured to bring suit for damages, and in case the injury is fatal, then the statute provides either that the widow or heirs of the decedent, or the representatives of the decedent (his executors or administrators), shall have the right to sue, and to derive benefit from any recovery that may be had.   (SARGENT, 75.)

3. *Defective appliances and rules.*—An employer is liable in damages to his employee where the employee, free from negligence, sustains an injury through the employer's negligence.   Such negligence may consist in the doing of something by the employer which, in the exercise of ordinary care and prudence, he ought not to have done, or in the omission of any duty or precaution which a prudent, careful man would or ought to have taken.

It is the duty of the master to furnish his servant with such appliances, tools, and machinery as are suited to his employment and may be used with safety; and he is responsible for all defects which he should or could have known, but failed through negligence to learn of, or which, having learned of, he failed to remedy.

A railroad company is liable for injuries occasioned by its negligence in failing to keep its track or roadbed or other surroundings under its control in proper condition; however, its duty is only to use reasonable care.

Employers are not required to furnish the best and latest improved machinery, but only such as is reasonably safe and suitable.

A master who sets a servant to work in a place of danger without giving him such warnings and instructions as the youthfulness, inexperience, or lack of capacity of the servant reasonably requires, is guilty of negligence and liable to the servant for any injury arising therefrom.

It is the duty of employers to make such regulations for their employees as will give them reasonable protection; and employees are bound to obey all lawful and reasonable commands of their employers, and an injury resulting to the employee while disobeying rules would not entitle him to recover damages. (SARGENT, 74.)

Mr. MOSELEY, secretary of the Interstate Commerce Commission, says that the common law, as affirmed by numerous decisions in this country, holds a master liable for injury to his servants resulting from defects in machinery or appliances of which he might have known by the exercise of ordinary care. But it is ordinarily held not necessary that he furnish the very best appliances known, and the continued use of an appliance which has long been used safely does not imply negligence. The tendency is in the State courts toward greater liberality toward the employee. In the Greenlee case in North Carolina, May, 1898, it was held that the railroad was liable because it did not use safety appliances which experience had shown to be best. In another case in the same State this doctrine was reaffirmed as being as old as the law itself: "When safer appliances have been invented and have come into general use, it is negligence per se for the master to expose his servant to the hazard of life or limb from antiquated appliances which have been generally discarded by the intelligence and humanity of other employers." Economy of expenditures on the part of the railroad is not to be deemed superior to the conservation of life and limb. (25–28.)

4. *Liability for acts of fellow-servants.*—Mr. SARGENT states the common-law doctrine as to the liability of employer for injuries to employees through the acts of fellow-servants as follows: Where a master uses due diligence in selecting competent, trusty servants, and furnishes them with suitable means to perform the services in which they are employed, the master is not answerable to one of them for an injury received through carelessness and negligence of another while both are engaged in the service.

All who serve the same master, work under the same control, derive authority and receive compensation from the same common source, and are engaged in the same general business, though it may be in different grades or departments of it, are fellow-servants who take the risk of each other's negligence. (75.)

Mr. MOSELEY, secretary of the Interstate Commerce Commission, says that most cases where persons are injured through the acts of coemployees or fellow-servants in the United States are decided under the common-law doctrine, not being regulated by special statute. That doctrine relieves the employer from liability in case he has used reasonable care in selecting his servants. The only question, therefore, is the correct definition of fellow-servants. As to this point, the numerous cases cited by the witness show marked divergences, but the greater number appear to consider all employees of the same master or company, whether they have power of direction or not, as fellow-servants. Thus it is held that the servant causing and the servant sustaining the injury need not be engaged in the same kind of work, and one may be the superior of the other. Thus on buildings and in cases of laborers working by gangs generally, one having direction as a boss is still regarded as a fellow-servant. But in Illinois, where their employment does not require cooperation and result in mutual contact such that each might influence the other toward safety or caution, servants of the same employer are not fellow-servants; habitual association is necessary. In regard to railways specifically, many decisions hold that trainmen are all fellow-servants of one another and also of trackmen, employees in shops, telegraph operators, switchmen, etc. There are, however, numerous conflicting decisions; for example, conductors and engineers are held the superiors of brakemen, as vice-principals. In Gulf, C. & S. F. Ry. Co. *v.* Warner, the court defines fellow-servants to be those engaged in a common service, in the same grade of employment, working together at the same time and place, and working to a common purpose.

The doctrine of fellow-servants has been abrogated as regards railway employees by the statutes of several States, notably Texas, where the act has been held constitutional.

Uniformity in the law is very desirable and should be secured by a Federal statute. Mr. Thomas G. Shearman especially urges that under modern conditions the liability of common carriers should be extended rather than, as court decisions often tend to do, restricted. (21-25, 28).

Mr. WILSON, of the Railway Trackmen, declares that the fellow-servant doctrine in many States is so interpreted as to work great injustice to railway employees, especially trackmen. The laws and court decisions vary greatly in different States. (53, 54.)

Mr. COWEN, president of the Baltimore and Ohio, says that the attitude of the courts and of the statutes regarding the liability of railroads for the acts of fellow-servants differs considerably in different States. There would be some advantage in a uniform rule. In Ohio, without statute, the courts have been inclined to consider many railway employees as being superior officers for whose acts the company is liable. (304.)

According to Mr. INGALLS, president of the Chesapeake and Ohio, the attitude of courts and juries toward the railways in suits for damages for personal injury, both to employees and others, is different in almost every State. In Kentucky his railway has never, except during the past year or two, had fair treatment. In most States the attitude toward railways is much better now than 10 or 20 years ago. As a railway manager Mr. Ingalls would like to have the liability for injury limited, but he thinks it would be a mistake from the standpoint of the public. (289.)

5. *Proposed extension of liability.*—Mr. SARGENT says that laws modifying the doctrine as to fellow-servants, so as to extend the liability of railway companies, have been passed in Texas, Missouri, Wisconsin, Florida, Georgia, Iowa, Kansas, Massachusetts, Minnesota, Ohio, and other States. The effect of the law has been or will be, the witness hopes, to induce employers to be more careful in selecting men, and to make the men more careful of their fellow-employees. Railway employees would prefer to prevent accident rather than to secure indemnity.

Since men have no choice as to who shall be their fellow-employees, and often know nothing about their character, the company should be responsible for their acts. The courts and laws regularly free railways from liability where injury is due simply to natural risks or to contributory negligence by the person injured. Where the railways fail to furnish proper appliances liability should attach to them for accidents. (66, 89.)

Mr. CLARK, of the railway conductors, thinks full liability should attach to railway companies for injuries in any way due to improper equipment of roadbed or to acts of fellow-employees. Railway men have no choice as to those with whom they work, and should not suffer for their incompetence or negligence. (115.)

Mr. MOSELEY is scarcely in favor of the proposal to make the employer liable for all injuries or deaths, however caused, and even though due to the fault of the employee himself. Men should understand that they owe care and caution not only to themselves, but to their employers. But employers should be held responsible for using unsafe appliances, or employing incompetent men to manage or direct. In the case of railways, trackmen and laborers, at any rate, should not be held fellow-servants of trainmen. (32.)

While Mr. Moseley would not favor action by Congress without the fullest investigation, he believes that a national law defining the liability of railways for injury to their employees would be desirable. Railway men are engaged in a semipublic employment. The courts hold nearly all railways to be engaged in interstate commerce, so that the Federal courts are those in which damage suits are usually tried. Experience shows that the decisions of these courts are very conflicting and even unjust, and unless Congress deals with the subject this judge-made law will continue largely to govern these cases. The following bill has been drafted for this purpose (31, 40.)

"*Be it enacted by the Senate and House of Representatives of the United States of America in Congress assembled,* That the provisions of this act shall be held to apply only to common carriers engaged in interstate and foreign commerce and to their employees engaged in the service of such common carriers as such.

"SEC. 2. That where, after the enactment of this act, personal injury is caused to an employee by reason of the negligence of any person in the service of the employee's employer, the employee, or, in case of his death, his representatives, shall have the same rights to compensation and remedies against the employer as if the employee had not been an employee of, nor in the service of, the employer, nor engaged in his work: *Provided,* That an employee or his representatives shall not be entitled under this act to any right of compensation or remedy against the employee's employer in any case where the employee knew of the negligence which caused his injury and failed, without reasonable excuse, to give or cause to be given within a reasonable time information thereof to his employer, or to some person superior to himself in the service of his employer; but nothing contained in this proviso shall apply to any case where such employee is injured contrary to the provisions of the act to promote the safety of employees, and so forth, approved March second, eighteen hundred and ninety-three.

"SEC. 3. That a contract whereby an employee relinquishes any right under this act shall not, if made before the accrual of the right, constitute a defense to any action brought for the recovery of compensation under this act."

The chief officers of the leading railway orders also favor the passage of the above bill. (762.) Mr. ARNOLD, secretary and treasurer of the Brotherhood of Locomotive Firemen, takes the same position. (764.) So do also Mr. WILSON, of the Brotherhood of Railroad Trackmen, and Mr. RONEMUS, of the Brotherhood of Railway Carmen. The latter declares that the effect of such a measure would be to force employers to exercise the greatest care in selecting fit men. (766,769.)

Mr. MURPHY, an attorney at law of Denver, thinks that a uniform law making all common carriers liable for the negligence of a fellow-servant would not be unjust to the employer, since he selects and directs each employee, while the employee has no choice as to his fellow-servants. (780.)

Mr. CALLAWAY, president of the New York Central, thinks that railways would not object especially to being made liable for injuries to employees through negligence of their fellow-servants, provided a similar liability were imposed upon other classes of employers, and provided a reasonable limit of liability were fixed. As the law now stands, persons injured often recover damages through the sympathy of juries, and frequently to excessive amounts. (222, 223.)

6. *Uniformity of decisions.*—Mr. MOSELEY states that in the case of the Baltimore and Ohio Railway Company *v.* Baugh the railway company claimed citizenship in Maryland by virtue of its incorporation in that State, and hence obtained a removal to the circuit court of the United States from the State courts of Ohio, where the accident occurred. By section 721 of the Revised Statutes, the laws of the several States must be regarded as rules of decision at common law in the United States courts, unless a Federal law provides otherwise. The lower courts in this case followed the rule of law in Ohio as settled by the State courts, in the absence of statute, and granted damages for the injury. This was overruled by the Supreme Court, which held that there is no common law for the Federal courts, but that there is a " general law " to be settled by the United States courts, with no obligation to follow the decision of State courts. Justice Field dissented vigorously from this decision. He declares that the court had previously, in Wheaton *v.* Peters, held that there was no such thing as the " general law " of the country. The justice of the claim by which a corporation, by a mere fiction as to its citizenship, removes a case to the Federal court is also denied. The witness calls attention to the fact that had the employee been injured on a railroad p - leling the Baltimore and Ohio, but owned by an Ohio corporation, he would have obtained damages. A foreign corporation, simply by being such, escapes the obligation of the Ohio common law. Several Federal judges have officially referred to the decision as being against the trend of former cases. The decisions of Federal courts themselves have been very conflicting, and this last decision makes more conspicuous the need for a uniform definition of liability by Federal statute. (29, 30, 40, 41.)

In the absence of such a uniform Federal statute Mr. Moseley thinks that advantage would come from the passage of such a bill as the following:

"*Be it enacted by the Senate and House of Representatives of the United States of America in Congress assembled,* That the decisions of the courts of last resort in the several States shall, except where the Constitution, treaties, or statutes of the United States otherwise require or provide, be regarded as rules of decision in trials at common law in the courts of the United States in cases where such decisions apply, and no distinction in this regard shall be made between cases involving questions of general and those involving questions of special or local law."

The chief officers of the leading railway brotherhoods also express themselves in favor of the bill proposed by Mr. Moseley. They doubt the possibility of taking jurisdiction entirely away from the Federal courts, but think that the decision of some one court should be made the rule and followed in all cases to which it can be justly applied. (762.) Mr. ARNOLD, of the Brotherhood of Locomotive Fire-

men, is also in favor of this bill (764); while Mr. RONEMUS, of the Brotherhood of
Railway Carmen, believes that the Federal courts should as far as possible follow
the decisions of the State courts. (769.)   Mr. SARGENT also advocates this law
and thinks it would be of great benefit to railway employees.   (93.)

Mr. CLARK says that he and the organization which he represents—the Order of
Railway Conductors—favor the act for requiring Federal courts to conform their
decisions to the State laws and decisions.   (115.)

7. *Employers' liability in Great Britain.*—Mr. MOSELEY says that prior to 1880
the common-law doctrine of liability obtained in Great Britain.   By the act of
that year the employer was made liable for injuries to workmen caused by defects
of machinery, by negligence of a person in the employer's service intrusted with
superintendence or authority over the injured person, by any act or omission in
obedience to the orders or by-laws of the employer, or by the negligence of any
person in charge of a railway signal.   This act is still in force.   In 1893 a bill
sought to extend liability to include all acts of fellow-servants, but it failed of
passage.   The workmen's compensation act of 1897 makes the employer liable for
all injuries, even if purely fortuitous, unless caused by serious and willful misconduct of the employee injured.   The amount of compensation for different
cases is fixed.   Contracting out is prohibited.   Most employers have insured
themselves against accident, the rates of insurance being considerably raised.
(28, 29.)

K. Relief funds and departments maintained by employers. 1. *Description.*—Professor
JOHNSON, of the University of Pennsylvania, testifies that six leading railways—
the Baltimore and Ohio, Pennsylvania lines, east and west of Pittsburg, Burlington, Reading, and Plant systems—have relief departments for the insurance of
employees against accident and sickness.   Previous to the United States arbitration act of 1898, contribution to these by employees was compulsory on three of
the lines.   It is still practically compulsory, since those who do not join are discriminated against in the conditions of employment.   The contributions of members range from 75 cents to $3.75 per month, the former sum securing a death
benefit of $250.   Benefits for accident and sickness range from $1 to $1.50 per
week.   The railways themselves pay the expense of administration and supply
any deficit.   Their proportion of the total cost ranges from 16 to 20 per cent.

Under these arrangements the employees contract that the benefits paid shall
offset any damages for injury or death, and this contract is usually held legal by
the courts.   The system is thus an economical one for the railways, and the more
so because it gives them more control over their employees, especially in time of
strike.   Nevertheless, the railways often make additional contributions in particular cases of accident, and they often give injured employees some position not
requiring hard labor.   The examination of employees as a condition of membership in the association has also been beneficial.   The cost of insurance under this
system and in the railway brotherhoods is practically the same, but the latter
method is to be preferred for other reasons.   The railway relief departments tend
to prevent their members from joining the brotherhoods on account of the expense
of double insurance.   There are also certain relief associations of a more voluntary nature formed among the employees of certain other railways; thus there
are six in New England.

Perhaps the dominant motive of the railway companies which have established
benefit funds is to hold their employees more closely under control.   In time of
strike the employee is in doubt whether to remain with the company or to act
with the union, often sacrificing his rights in the benefit fund.   However, it is
usually provided that the employee can continue his payments and retain his right
for 9 months while he is out of the employ of the company.   (57-60.)

2. *Compulsory contributions.*—Mr. SARGENT, of the Locomotive Firemen, says
that it is impossible to secure evidence that the present law prohibiting compulsion of employees to contribute to relief funds is violated.   Contribution to
the fund is not now made an open condition of employment, but if an applicant
refuses to join the relief association, when it is called to his attention at the time
of his application, he has no way of knowing but this is the reason for refusing to
give him work.   The Pennsylvania Railroad has always had a nominally voluntary association.   The more subservient employees are inclined to join it, and, as
in the case of other roads, they may be given the impression, rightly or otherwise,
that they will be promoted more rapidly by doing so; but an independent man is
not compelled to join the association—hundreds of them do not—and they may
prefer to risk fewer chances of promotion for the sake of being free.   Some railways consider the brotherhoods injurious to their interests and use this method
of influencing employees to stay out of them.   (67, 89-91.)

Mr. ARTHUR, of the locomotive engineers, says that railway employees prefer
insurance in their own organizations rather than in those controlled by railway

companies, but the complaints concerning the companies' funds are not very definite or general. When the relief system was first established by the Pennsylvania Railroad there was strong opposition to the compulsory feature, and this was afterwards abandoned. The witness has heard no complaints concerning the system on that road. There have been some complaints as to the Baltimore and Ohio, but the witness knows of men who have secured employment on that road without being required to join the benefit association, and has heard no complaints from these men. The railway funds have, however, kept many from taking insurance in the brotherhoods. (121,122,125.)

Mr. WILSON, of the Railway Trackmen, says that some trackmen have declined to join their brotherhood because they were compelled to pay for insurance maintained by railway companies, and could not afford to insure twice. On the Plant System there is little opportunity of securing employment unless one also applies for membership in the insurance association. (47, 48.)

Mr. MOSELEY, secretary of the Interstate Commerce Commission, says that prior to the United States arbitration act of 1898 employees were virtually required to contribute to relief funds as a condition of employment. Coercion in this regard was prohibited by that act, and the witness does not believe that any force, as contemplated by that act, has since been exerted. (31, 32.)

Mr. COWEN, president of the Baltimore and Ohio Railroad, discusses somewhat fully the nature and effect of the relief system of that road. The employees and the railway jointly contribute to a fund for providing relief. When the system was first established it was not compulsory for men to enter the relief department, but employees who now enter the service must agree to join. No change has been made since the act of 1898. There is no compulsion, since an applicant need not take employment unless he chooses.

As a matter of fact, the system is approved, the witness declares, by 99 per cent of the men. The relief department was formerly a separate corporation. The charter of this corporation being repealed, it was reorganized as a voluntary association. There was no compulsion upon the men to enter the reorganized department, but fully nineteen-twentieths of the members did enter it of their own free will, after ten years' previous experience. No complaint is heard that those who are outside the department are not placed in the line of promotion. The effect of the entire system upon the relations of employer and employee is ery good. Litigation has been practically wiped out by this arrangement. (304–308.)

3. *Exemption from liability through relief departments.*—Mr. WILSON thinks that railway companies having relief departments should not be permitted to manage them in such a way as to prevent injured employees or their heirs from collecting the amount of damages to which they are justly entitled. By way of illustration, the witness declares that the Atlantic Coast Line has recently organized a relief department charging $36 per year on $1,000 insurance, with provision for a small weekly benefit. The employee is thus required to pay exorbitantly for insurance, and in order to collect the insurance must sign a release relieving the company of liability. The injured person is not altogether deprived of the right to sue for damages, but can not do so if he accepts benefits from the fund. (767.)

Mr. RONEMUS, of the Brotherhood of Railway Carmen, also declares that participation in any relief fund should not bar an employee from collecting damages for injuries. Most relief associations are more expensive than the same amount of insurance outside, especially in the brotherhoods. This witness also objects to the relief departments on the ground that applicants for employment may be rejected because they can not pass the rigid examination required for entering relief departments. (770.)

Mr. SARGENT declares that although the employers contribute somewhat to these funds, the employees pay practically the full cost of insurance. This system is bitterly opposed by the employees, because of its paternalism, because of the forfeiture of sums paid in by change of employment, and because of the compulsion to contract to exempt the employers from liability, notwithstanding that the employees have paid the full value of the insurance. (67.)

Mr. COWEN admits that on the Baltimore and Ohio the employee is required to sign a contract when he accepts relief from the relief department that he will not sue the railway company, although there is no agreement made in advance not to sue.

The attention of the witness being called to the section of the United States arbitration act of June 1, 1898, which prohibits employers from making it a condition of entering employment that the applicant shall agree to contribute to any such fund, or that he shall release the employer from legal liability for injury to an amount exceeding the proportion of the relief fund contributed by the employer, Mr. Cowen declared that no change of practice had been made by his company since that act. If the act aimed to prevent railroad companies from making agreements with their intended employees as to contributing to a relief fund, the act is invalid, and the only way to test its constitutionality is by not complying with it. As a matter of fact the railway is in no sense released from liability. The requirement is simply that when the employee accepts payment from the relief fund he must give an absolute release of further liability. This contract is not made in advance, and if he prefers to take his chance, he can sue for damages. Although the railway company itself contributes directly only from one-sixth to one-fifth of the payments to the relief fund, the service which its clerks and officers perform in managing the business of the fund is an important contribution. (304–308.)

4. *Savings fund, Baltimore and Ohio.*—Mr. COWEN also describes the savings-fund system which has been established by the Baltimore and Ohio Railroad. There are few savings banks in the region through which this railway passes. Employees are allowed to make deposits with the company. On this they are guaranteed 4 per cent. The moneys deposited are loaned to employees, chiefly for the purpose of building homes. The fund has been so prosperous that during 1899 the depositors received interest at $5\frac{1}{4}$ per cent, and hundreds of employees have obtained homes through this system. The deposits at the end of the fiscal year 1899 were $1,168,000, the deposits made during that year being $393,000. The fund is managed by the officers of the railroad without expense to the depositors. (306.)

I. General conditions of labor—Miscellaneous.—1. *Labor on Illinois Central.*—Mr. FISH says that the Illinois Central and the Yazoo and Mississippi Valley Railroad have 28,750 employees. Men are employed regardless of membership in labor organizations. Pains are taken to keep them from working too many hours without proper sleep. Rules regarding intoxication are strictly enforced. On one division of the road a hospital has been established by the company, and is maintained by assessments on the men, which are, however, voluntary. The companies expected to conform to the law regarding safety appliances by January 1, 1900. (333.)

2. *Labor on Chicago Great Western.*—Mr. STICKNEY, president of the Chicago Great Western Railway Company, says that his road has had no special difficulties in the way of strikes. It never hesitates to treat with organized labor. The usual hours of work, except for trainmen, are 10 per day. Trainmen work by the hour. It is not the intention of the company to have the men work on Sundays more than is absolutely necessary. There is no provision for a fund for sickness or disablement. (455.)

3. *Railway trackmen.*—According to Mr. WILSON. grand chief of the Railway Trackmen, the road masters on the railways are the heads of employment, except where the trackmen are very thoroughly organized. They can employ and discharge men at will. Partly from necessity, in order to secure the approval of their superiors, they are inclined to be severe with their men. The road masters and foremen are harmonious in their relations, but often have little care for the track laborers. The chances for promotion to positions as foremen are fair, but road masters are often civil engineers without previous practical railway experience. It requires several years to become a thoroughly efficient track hand. The Brotherhood of Railway Trackmen is doing much to promote harmony between these different classes. (52, 54.)

There are about 180,000 men employed in maintaining the tracks and roadbeds of American railroads. Of these about 2,000 are road masters, covering from 100 to 150 miles of track each. · About 30,000 are section foremen, each covering a few miles of track, for which he is personally responsible. These men are almost always faithful to duty, and few accidents occur through their fault. The trackmen are employed by these foremen. Scarcely half as many are employed in winter as in summer. The trackmen are paid exceedingly low wages. The witness believes that 90 per cent of them are American citizens. On the Pacific coast some Chinamen are employed, and in New England there are many foreigners, but elsewhere nearly all are Americans. (45, 46, 50.)

4. *Switchmen.*—Mr. O'ROURKE states that the wages of switchmen in Chicago are 25 cents an hour for what is called p   switching during the day and for helping, and 27 cents at night. Some of the railroads work their men as little as 10 hours a day; some 11, many 12, some 15 and 16. There is no complaint about the long hours; if there were, the men might change to shorter runs. Some prefer to work the long hours and make more, and others would rather have less and work only 10 or 11 hours. There has been no change in switchmen's wages in 4 or 5 years. More men are now employed on account of the increased business,

and the men are working more hours. The switchmen's wages are entirely satisfactory, and the switchmen have had no grievances of any kind against the railroads. (530.)

Mr. O'Rourke supposes that there are 900 to 1,000 switchmen in Chicago. He does not believe that a quarter of them are members of the switchmen's union. Many of them are members of other organizations—the conductors' organization and the trainmen's organization. These are men who were out of work in their own line and who came to Chicago and got employment as switchmen. (530.)

5. *Car repairers.*—Mr. RONEMUS, grand chief of the Brotherhood of Railway Carmen, states that repairers of cars are subjected to many inconveniences and hardships. Loaded cars are often in need of repair and are repaired on the track, usually without any shed or other covering. The men are required to keep at work constantly, regardless of rain, sleet, and all other conditions of the weather. Railways should be required to erect suitable sheds over at least part of the repair track. (770.)

6. *Relations of employer and employees.*—Mr. O'ROURKE, switchman, of Chicago, believes that the interests of railroad labor will be best furthered by closer association between employer and employee; that all forces which tend to cause hostile feelings between them are wrong, and those who encourage such feelings are the foes of labor. He hopes that the time has come when there will be no such thing as a strike. He and his associates look for industrial peace. Organized railway labor to-day offers no shelter to the agitator. The policy of the switchmen's unions in Chicago is to exclude agitators from membership. (526, 527, 529.)

Mr. MOSELEY, secretary of the Interstate Commerce Commission, says that most railway managers are progressive men and have done much in the interest of their employees. They have established hospitals, relief funds, Young Men's Christian Associations, etc. The American Railway Association and the Master Car Builders' Association have recommended the best safety appliances and regulations; but in the absence of law some few employers refuse to perform their duties properly. The managers feel a certain opposition to restraint, but the public has a clear right to regulate enterprises to which they have given such great privileges as to railways. (43, 44.)

Mr. CLARK, of the Railway Conductors, says some of the most serious disputes as to labor matters have occurred on roads operated by receivers. The railway men believe that reductions in wages have been undertaken which would not have been tried if the support of the Federal courts had not been expected. (116.)

7. *Profit sharing, etc.*—Mr. INGALLS, president of the Chesapeake and Ohio, declares himself strongly in favor of profit sharing as applied to railways. The plan of the Illinois Central in getting the men to buy stock is perhaps somewhat dangerous, because stocks go up and down in value. It is preferable to let the wages paid be considered as representing a certain capital, and make a payment upon that capital out of profits. This practice creates better feeling among the men, secures better work, and checks trouble with strikes. The difficulty so far has been that railways have been too poor to be sure of paying regular dividends. (290.)

Mr. FISH, president of the Illinois Central Railroad, says that it is the practice of that company, on the first of each month, to authorize the sale of one share of stock to each employee at the current market price. Payment may be made by installments in sums of $5 or multiples thereof. Interest at 4 per cent is allowed on partial payments. The number of employees thus holding stock is 705, and their holdings amount to 2,554 shares.

The general ownership of stock in the Illinois Central is widely distributed. The average holdings of each investor are from 85 to 90 shares. Much more than a majority of the stock is held by the 5,194 persons who own less than 100 shares each, the total number of stockholders being 6,526. A block of 40,000 shares is held by a group of Dutch investors, who issue certificates in the Dutch language based upon them. (325–327.)

Mr. SARGENT, of the Locomotive Firemen, says that the system by which the employees of the Illinois Central Railroad are permitted to purchase stock at special rates has been taken advantage of by many employees. It is generally considered acceptable and is promoting harmonious relations. The man who has an interest in a business will naturally be more devoted to its success. (92.)

8. *Railroad Y. M. C. A.*—Mr. CALLAWAY states that branches of the railroad Y. M. C. A. are located at nearly all the large terminal stations and yards of the New York Central Railway. The buildings have often been furnished by the railroad company, and Mr. Vanderbilt has frequently furnished libraries and other facilities. The secretaries are usually paid by the company. Many employees

have homes of their own, but a large proportion of the others avail themselves of the privileges of the Y. M. C. A. Lodgings and meals are provided at low rates; there are bath rooms, reading rooms, and other conveniences. (220.)

9. *Colored labor.*—Mr. SPENCER, of the Southern Railway, testifies that colored men are employed as trainmen and firemen, but not as conductors and engineers, and scarcely at all as switchmen. Their wages are usually about 10 per cent less than those of whites doing the same work. (266, 267.)

Mr. ARTHUR, chief of the Brotherhood of Locomotive Engineers, says that by action of the convention of this organization in 1873 colored men were made ineligible for membership. They are opposed by the white members in the South, where the organization has a large constituency, and they are also less competent than white men. (118, 119.)

XIII. LAKE TRANSPORTATION.

A. Volume and character of traffic.—Mr. KEEP, secretary of the Lake Carriers' Association, states that the great item of freight on the lakes is ore. This business has increased immensely in the last few years. The total shipments of iron ore by lake during 1899 were 17,901,000 gross tons, of which 4,101,675 tons came from Lake Michigan ports, and the rest from Lake Superior. The total traffic through the Soo Canal in 1899 was 25,255,810 tons, of which about 60 per cent was ore. Of the grain traffic, probably about 80 per cent goes to Buffalo, the remainder going to the Georgian Bay, to Erie, to Ogdensburg, and down the St. Lawrence. In 1899 the grain receipts at Buffalo were 153,000,000 bushels, besides 10,000,000 barrels of flour. In 1898 they were 204,000,000 bushels of grain and 12,500,000 barrels of flour. The falling off was due principally to the labor controversy at Buffalo in May, which shortened the season, and the very high rates which prevailed for carrying iron ore, so high that the railroads were able to compete actively in the carriage of grain.

The east-bound movement of freight on the lakes is two or three times as large as the west bound. The most of the boats return west light. Coal is the only large item of west-bound shipment. There was shipped last year from Buffalo 2,648,425 tons of anthracite coal by lake, and 126,140 tons of bituminous. These figures include shipments to all ports, but the greater part goes to various American ports. The most of the bituminous coal that is shipped by lake goes from Cleveland, Toledo, and Ashtabula. No coal is received from Canada into the United States by lake; the movement is the other way. Coal is shipped on Lake Ontario, from Charlotte and Oswego and other points, to Toronto and other points in Canada. It is also shipped from Buffalo and from Ohio ports. (715-717.)

The ore boats are likely to carry a load or two of grain in the spring before the ore movement begins and another load or two in the fall after the ore movement ends. The Strait of Mackinac sometimes opens before the St. Marys River, and boats can go from Chicago with a load of grain earlier than from Lake Superior with ore. In the fall the ore freezes in the pockets, and it becomes difficult to load vessels, whereas grain can still be loaded from the elevators. (717.)

Loading and unloading.—Since lake vessels are in commission only about two-thirds of the year, the question of dispatch in port is of very great importance. The machinery for loading and unloading has been greatly improved within a few years. A vessel now reaches Buffalo with 260,000 or 270,000 bushels of wheat in the morning, and is unloaded, gets a load of coal, and leaves the same night. (721.)

Opening of navigation—Insurance.—Mr. KEEP states that the lake season begins with the opening of the Strait of Mackinac—about the 20th of April. Insurance begins when the strait is reported open. Insurance policies expire at noon on some specified day—some on December 1, some on December 5, some as late as the 12th. If the vessel is on a voyage at that time the insurance covers her until she completes the voyage. (721.)

Navigation laws.—Mr. KEEP states that the navigation laws forbidding the participation of foreign vessels in the coastwise trade of the United States apply to lake commerce. He does not consider that these laws are of much value to the lake-vessel owners, since even the commerce between American and Canadian ports is almost entirely in the hands of American vessels. During 1899 American vessels carried about 97 per cent of the freight through the St. Mary's Falls Canal. (722, 723.)

B. Character of vessels—Amount of tonnage.—Mr. KEEP says that the ordinary lake vessel is built to carry bulk freights—coal, ore, lumber, or grain. The transportation companies affiliated with the railroads own what are called package-freight boats, built with an extra deck, giving a place between the decks, in which package freight or miscellaneous merchandise is carried for the lake-and-rail route. These boats also have a hold in which they carry grain or coal. A few other owners have built their boats with decks, so that they may charter them for the season to some of these companies that are short of boats. But this custom is rather disappearing, since the great object of the lake-vessel owner in building a boat is the speedy handling of cargo, which is hindered by decks. (714.)

Alexander McDougall invented the whaleback, and interested some New York capitalists in a shipyard. A fleet of about 30 boats was built, under the name of the American Barge Company. No other company has built whalebacks. This company is now building one boat which is not a whaleback. No whaleback is at present under construction. These boats are not by any means the largest on the lakes. The witness thinks Mr. Rockefeller had some interest in the whaleback enterprise, and it is understood that he has bought the whole fleet since the close of navigation in 1899. (714, 718.)

Tonnage.—Mr. KEEP states that the total number of vessels on the lakes was 3,162 on June 30, 1899, out of a total of 22,728 vessels of all kinds in the United States. The tonnage on the lakes was 1,446,348 tons, against 2,614,869 tons on the Atlantic and Gulf coasts, 539,937 tons on the Pacific coast, and 263,084 tons on the Western rivers; a total of 4,864,238 tons. A little less than one-third of the whole tonnage of the country is on the lakes. In 1886 there were 6 steel vessels on the Great Lakes; in 1891 there were 89; in 1899 there were 296. (713, 718.)

Mr. KEEP states that at the time of his testimony, February 19, 1900, there were building in the lake shipyards vessels of a capacity of 185,500 tons and a cost of $8,902,000. This is the greatest tonnage and the greatest value of ships ever built on the lakes in one year. In 1898, at the same time, vessels were building of 71,400,000 tons capacity and of a value of $2,974,000. Among those now under construction are two boats larger than were ever launched on the lakes, namely, 498 feet long, with an estimated capacity in gross tons on 18-foot draft of 7,900 tons. The boats building are practically all of steel. Nearly all the shipbuilding is in American yards; only some $400,000 out of the total of $8,900,000 is Canadian. The largest cargo brought from the upper lakes to Lake Erie down to 1891 was 3,527 tons, and the largest cargo that passed through the St. Marys Falls canal in 1899 was 8,215 tons. The advantage of the large boat is that with a comparatively small increase in the crew and in the expense of running the carrying capacity is greatly increased. (713, 718, 719.)

Mr. CARTER also states that the tonnage of lake shipping will be much increased during the coming year. Several carriers of the largest size are building. It could not be otherwise, since the lake carrying business has been very remunerative during the past year, and boats have made contracts during the last few months to carry ore at one-third of what it can be carried for by rail. (581.)

C. Ownership of vessels.—Mr. KEEP, secretary of the Lake Carriers' Association, states that out of about 600 vessels in the association 72 are owned or controlled by companies having affiliations of some kind with the railroads. These boats have a net registered tonnage of 122,000 out of a net registered tonnage in the association of 760,000. Mr. Keep gives in detail the names of the lake transportation companies which are affiliated with the several roads. The Standard Oil Company has one tank boat on the lakes, carrying oil in bulk from Chicago to Duluth. Mr. Rockefeller owns the Bessemer Steamship Company, which has quite largely handled the Carnegie ore. It is understood that Mr. Rockefeller has recently bought the whole whale-back fleet of about 30 boats. The Carnegie people are now building about half a dozen boats. Many mining companies have affiliated companies which own ore-carrying vessels. Very few vessels are now owned by individuals. Vessels are becoming too large and expensive. No boats are sailed by their owners except some of the smaller lumber schooners. Boats are owned by groups of men who frequently form a separate corporation for each boat, though the ownership of several boats may be identical. (713, 714, 716.)

Mr. CALLAWAY testifies that the New York Central owns a line of lake boats running to Milwaukee, Chicago, and Duluth. An attempt is made to agree with leading competitors as to rates, but the chief competition is from tramp steamers, and the company is practically compelled to meet their rates. Although Chicago is about as far from Buffalo as Duluth, the Duluth rate must be higher in order not to ruin intermediate rail business. (239.)

D. Passenger boats.—Mr. KEEP, secretary of the Lake Carriers' Association, states that the Great Northern Railroad has two passenger boats nearly 400 feet long, and costing about $800,000 each, running between Buffalo and Duluth, and making a round trip of 2,000 miles in 6½ days. They do not carry any freight. Their season is very short, only from June to September; but during the season they are crowded. There are other boats which do a large passenger business in connection with the package-freight business, as between Buffalo and Cleveland, between Cleveland and Detroit, and night service between Detroit and Mackinaw, Chicago and Mackinaw, and Chicago and Milwaukee. The only international service, except that on the St. Lawrence River and the ferry service at Detroit, is that of one or two boats daily in the summer between Toronto and the mouth of the Niagara. (720.)

E. Freight rates and methods of business.—Mr. CARTER, a grain shipper of Chicago, states that a large number of different persons own vessels on the lakes, and that there are usually several people with whom a shipper may contract. A boat is generally chartered and loaded with grain by one shipper. The shipper may contract with the owner, but usually contracts with the vessel agent, who arranges before the boat comes in to have a load ready as soon as the boat can take it. A great deal of package freight is transported on the lakes, such as flour and pork. It is carried largely on the regular lines, and the business is done very much as similar business is done on the railroads. (581, 582.)

Mr. KEEP states that on ore the freight rate is now largely a season rate made on contracts. On grain the rate fluctuates from time to time, according to the supply of boats and the demand. The rate fluctuates so rapidly and the amount of business done at different times and under different rates varies so much that it is very difficult to make a fair average of the rates for the season. (719.)

Combination on freight rates.—Mr. KEEP says that there was some talk two or three years ago, during a very dull season, of an effort to get the vessel owners to agree on a minimum freight rate; but it was given up as impossible. The witness never heard of any other attempt to control lake freight rates. Mr. CARTER also says that there has never been a successful combination to maintain rates upon the lakes, and he does not think that anything of the kind would be possible at present. (581.)

Statistics of rates.—(See also under *Railway Freight Rates*, p. 39).—Mr. KEEP states that it is difficult to give the rate on wheat to Buffalo, as most of it is contracted through at a rate which includes both lake and rail, and it is impossible to say what the rail rate east of Buffalo is. He, however, states the highest rate from Chicago to Buffalo for 1898 as $3\frac{1}{4}$ cents per bushel, and the lowest as $1\frac{1}{4}$ cents, with an average of $1\frac{1}{2}$ cents for the season; and for 1899 the highest $3\frac{1}{4}$ cents, the lowest $1\frac{7}{8}$ cents, and $2\frac{1}{4}$ cents the average. In 1891 the rates on ore from Lake Superior ports to Lake Erie ports varied from 90 cents to $1.50 a ton, the average being about $1.15 or $1.20. In 1898 most of the ore was brought down at 65 cents. The vessel has to pay for loading and unloading out of these freights.

1897 and 1898 were dull years, but in 1899 the smaller boats had perhaps as prosperous a year as they ever had. The larger vessels had made contracts which compelled them to carry throughout most of the season at a low rate. Many of the smaller vessels which took their chances on getting cargoes from trip to trip got exceedingly high rates. The variation was as great as between 60 cents a ton, the season contract rate, made in the winter of 1898 and 1899, and $2, the rate which prevailed for some time during the season of navigation. The owner of a vessel that carries 1,000 tons or 2,000 tons may very well take his chances on getting cargoes from trip to trip, but a boat of 7,000 tons or 8,000 tons can not so easily pick up loads, and safety requires that such boats should make contracts in advance. (714–717, 719, 722.)

Mr. CARTER states that within the last two years coal has been carried from Buffalo to Chicago as low as 20 cents per ton; a great deal has been carried at 25, 30, and 35 cents. Ore has been carried from Lake Superior ports to Buffalo for 40 cents, and large contracts have been made at 45 cents. During this year the maximum rate for ore was $2. (581.)

Lake transportation and rail transportation.—Mr. KELLEY, freight commissioner of the Trades League of Philadelphia, considers that the practice of the railways in greatly reducing their freight rates during the season of navigation on the Great Lakes in order to compete, especially in the transportation of grain, is likely to result ultimately in driving the lake vessels out of business, after which rates will be put up and kept up. The same practice in regard to river and coastwise transportation has had the effect which he fears in this case. It is true that the railways themselves own lines of lake boats which they operate in conjunction with their land lines. This practice itself has some dangers, since water transportation is not under the Interstate Commerce Act and railways owning boats may thus make discriminations on through traffic. But most of the steamers owned by the railways are regular lines carrying general merchandise of high class, paying higher rates of freight. Wheat, ore, and similar bulky products, having low freight rates, are largely transported in full cargoes by tramp steamers built especially for such traffic, and it is against these that the cuts in railway rates are injurious. Railways sometimes carry freight at a loss for the purpose of competing with water traffic, depending on higher-class commodities for their profit. This is probably true in railway competition with the Erie Canal. (188, 189.)

Mr. DOUSMAN, a grain shipper of Chicago, does not believe that freight rates on the trunk lines have been made low through the competition of lake carriers so much as through competition between the railroads themselves. Each of the great railway lines east of Buffalo has its own line of lake steamers, and the witness knows of no regular independent lake lines, although there is usually little trouble in chartering tramp steamers. The lake freight rates have been very low for several years. The rate in 1899 was only 2 cents per bushel on grain, and it has been as low as 1 cent. There is considerable danger that independent lake boats would be driven out of business by the lines controlled by railways if it were not for the competition of the Erie Canal with the railways from Buffalo to New York. (357.)

Mr. KEEP, secretary of the Lake Carriers' Association, states that the railroads do not make as much difference in their rates as formerly between the season of navigation and the winter season. (718.)

F. Grain shipments—methods, routes, etc. (see also as to *Export rates*, p.69 ff.).—Mr. WEBSTER, president of the Armour Elevator Company, says that the cheapest route for grain shipment from Chicago is usually by way of the Great Lakes, although frequently the railroads are forced to cut their rail rates to meet the water rates. The favorite routes are from Chicago to Buffalo and thence by the Erie Canal or by rail to New York, Boston, and Philadelphia; from Chicago to Erie and thence to Philadelphia or Baltimore; from Chicago to Fairport, Ohio, and thence to Baltimore; from Chicago to Port Huron, Sarnia, Owen Sound, and other Lake Huron ports, and thence by rail through Canada to Montreal, St. Johns, Portland, or Boston; from Chicago by the Great Lakes and the Welland Canal to points on Lake Ontario and thence by barge down the St. Lawrence to Montreal or by rail to Portland or Boston. A new and very advantageous route has recently been established, by water to some port on Lake Huron, thence by rail to Coteau Point, from which the grain is carried by barges to the ocean vessels at Montreal. The Erie Canal at present to some extent regulates rail rates east of · Buffalo, but the limited capacity of the boats, equal to more than 15 per cent of the grain passing through Buffalo, makes this influence less important than is often supposed. If the canal is enlarged more and larger boats will be built and the canal will mainly control transportation rates. The Canadian routes are at present the cheapest, and only lack of ocean tonnage has prevented Montreal from doing still larger business. The witness thinks that the United States Government should use its best efforts to improve the water routes from the West to the seaboard. (412.)

Mr. CARTER, of Chicago, commission merchant, states that the slowness of the increase of the through shipments of grain to New York by lake and canal is due to the fact that the Erie Canal is not in condition to handle the trade. Much grain that is shipped to Buffalo by water is forwarded from there by rail. In 1898 the greater part of the grain left Chicago by water. This was not true in 1899, because of the low rates for export by rail. (578, 579.)

Mr. Carter states that water transportation offers great advantages over the best facilities that the railroads can furnish. For the year 1897 the average all-rail rate from Chicago to New York on corn was 11.43 cents per bushel. During the season of navigation of that year the average rate by lake and canal, including the charge at Buffalo, was 4.53 cents per bushel. For 1898 the average all-rail charge on corn was 9.8 cents, and on wheat 12 cents. The average charge by lake and canal, exclusive of charges at Buffalo, was 3.81 cents on corn, and 4.45 cents on wheat. The charges at Buffalo for this year are excluded because they were very irregular, and a fair average can not be obtained. They ran from three-fourths of a cent to nothing. On the amount of grain exported during the year 1898, the difference between the all-rail charges and the lake-and-canal charges would be about $25,000,000. A great deal of grain is shipped to Buffalo by lake and thence by rail. This is cheaper than shipping all rail, but not so cheap as shipping all water. During some years the rail rate is cut very close to the water rate during the season of navigation; and in other years it is not. During the 20 years past the average rail rate has been at least 25 per cent higher during the winter than during the season of navigation. (578, 579.)

Mr. Carter says that he buys the most of his grain in Chicago and sells much of it there. His trade has always been largely confined to Illinois. Since his shipments are rather small they go mostly by rail. For a single carload, which is regarded as a retail shipment, railroad transportation is the most desirable because, among other reasons, by this means the identity of the shipment is pre-served. (582.)

Mr. TUCKER states that the rate from Chicago to Buffalo has been as high as 3 and 4 cents a bushel during 1899; in 1898 it was three-fourths of a cent. (558.)

Buffalo transfer charges and elevator combination.—Mr. KEEP, secretary of the Lake Carriers' Association and of the Buffalo Merchants' Exchange, states that the elevator charges on grain at Buffalo had never been less than seven-eighths of a cent per bushel before 1898. In 1898 there was no combination of elevators and no fixed rate. In 1899 an elevator combination was again formed and the rate was made one-half cent per bushel. The present elevator association includes only working elevators which have rail connections. Houses that are not work-ing or that are on islands and can only unload into canal boats have not been taken in. The association is a pooling arrangement. Some of the elevators in it are owned by individuals, some by companies, and some by railroads. The associa-tion elevators did almost all the business in 1899, though a few canal houses which were not taken in did a little business in loading grain into canal boats. (721.)

G. Lake Carriers' Association.—Mr. KEEP states that the Lake Carriers' Association began some 14 or 15 years ago in the joining of a few vessel owners, chiefly of Buffalo, to forward their common interests in such matters as the building of needed lighthouses and legislation with reference to channels. About the same time the Cleveland Vessel Owners' Association was formed at Cleveland. Its purpose was slightly different; it was largely to look after business matters con-nected with the running of boats, and particularly the supplying of labor. The Cleveland association opened shipping offices and put shipping masters or employ-ment agents in charge. In 1890 a question arose in which the Cleveland and the Buffalo associations took diametrically opposite sides. Out of this arose the con-solidation of the two organizations into the Lake Carriers' Association in 1891. Since that time the Lake Carriers' Association has been the only association of vessel owners on the lakes. It embraces about 600 vessels out of 3,162 lake ves-sels of all kinds; but its tonnage is a little over 1,000,000 tons out of 1,400,000 tons all told, and the association vessels have probably from four-fifths to nine-tenths of the freight-carrying tonnage.

The work of the association is to interest itself in legislative matters relating to the lakes, trying to get needed channel improvements and improvements in the aids to navigation, so far as they are of general concern, the supplying of many private lights, and the maintenance of shipping offices. Since Canada has a rela-tively small interest in lake navigation, the Canadian government does not estab-lish sufficient lights on its side; and there are certain places on the American side where lights have been deficient. The Lake Carriers' Association has built and sustained many lights at its own expense, particularly at vital points in the St. Mary's, Detroit, and St. Clair rivers, where vessels pass through crowded, nar-row channels. Some which the association used to maintain have been taken over by the United States Government; but there are at least six lights in the lower Detroit River which the association has maintained for 10 years.

The Association maintains shipping offices at Chicago, South Chicago, Milwau-kee, Cleveland, Toledo, Ashtabula, and Buffalo, for the furnishing of men to vessels.

The association, as such, owns no vessels and is not engaged in the transpor-tation business. It has never made any attempt to control or regulate freight rates. (709, 710, 713, 723).

The fleets of the iron and steel manufacturers and also the boats owned by companies affiliated with the railroads are in the association. (713.)

Mr. CARTER, a commission merchant of Chicago, states that the Lake Carriers' Association tries to regulate wages, and looks after the interests of the lake carriers generally. It would try to fix freight rates if it could, but it has never succeeded in fixing a rate that has stood for any length of time. It does not control the tonnage of the lakes, and it has members who have no tonnage on the lakes. One of the leading men of Chicago, who has been one of its officers, has owned nothing but tugs for towing ships into Chicago. (582.)

H. Improvement of lake navigation.—*Improvement of " Soo" Canal.*—Mr. KEEP states that there were two blockades in the Soo River during 1899, which cost the vessels $1,000,000 in delay. The channels are only 300 feet wide in several places. If an accident happens to a 400 or 500 foot boat which wrecks it across the chan-nel, no boat can pass until the wreck is removed. Two plans of improvement are proposed—one to widen the channel to a minimum of 600 feet, the other to make a second 300-foot channel. The second plan is the better, because two 300-foot channels could not be blocked by a single accident, while one 600-foot channel could.

The last figures for the Suez Canal traffic are those for 1897. They amount, in ship tonnage, to 7,899,373 tons. During the same year the traffic through the St. Mary's Falls Canal was 18,982,755 tons, and in 1899 it was 21,958,347 tons, though this canal is open less than 8 months in the year. (720.)

Mr. Keep states that there was originally only about 9 feet of water in the shallow parts of the St. Mary's and Detroit rivers. The available draft is now 18 feet on an average. With this draft the largest vessels now building will carry about 9,000 tons of freight. The Government is engaged in dredging a channel to be 20 feet deep in still water and 21 feet where subject to wave action. (722.)

A power canal is building to draw water from Lake Superior or from St. Mary's River above the rapids and return it to the river below the rapids. It is proposed that this canal shall carry a volume of water equal to 50 per cent of the flow of St. Mary's River at low water. The engineer of the power company has estimated that if no compensatory works to obstruct the fall in the rapids were built, the canal would lower the level of Lake Superior 2 feet. The company proposes to build compensatory works. The Lake Carriers' Association showed, in a hearing before the River and Harbor Committee, that a diminution of 1 inch in the available draft of water in the Soo Canal and the harbors of Lake Superior would cause a loss of $150,000 a year to the vessels. (717.)

Canal tolls.—Mr. KEEP says that the Canadian government formerly charged a toll of 20 cents per ton on all freight carried through the Welland Canal, but gave a rebate of 18 cents if the freight went to Montreal, and no rebate if the freight stopped at an American port. The United States retaliated by levying discriminating tolls on Canadian vessels at the St. Mary's Falls Canal. As a result, the rate for the Welland Canal was made uniform at 10 cents, whatever the destination of the freight. The Canadians have since completed a canal of their own at St. Mary's Falls, but the policy of discriminating tolls has not been renewed. There are no tolls at either of the St. Mary's Falls canals, to either Americans or Canadians. (723.)

. Labor on lake vessels.—*Lake Carriers' Association—wages card.*—Mr. KEEP says the Lake Carriers' Association issues a card, called its wages card, from time to time, stating the maximum wages which the members will pay different classes of employees. Only members of the association are bound by it, and the members are at liberty to get their men cheaper if they can. The policy of the association is to pay liberal wages in good times and to reduce the wages in hard times, when the vessels can not make any money. The men seem generally to have been satisfied with the card of late years; there has been almost no controversy with labor. Wages were much higher in 1899—a prosperous year—than in 1898; and the wages card for the spring of 1900 will doubtless be higher than that of the spring of 1899. The card is changed from time to time during the season in accordance with the supply of men and the demand for them, as well as in accordance with the rates of freight. (710, 711, 719.)

Labor unions.—The Lake Carriers' Association recognizes committees from organized seamen. The men sometimes send in communications when they know that the association's wages card is about to be altered, and these communications are taken into consideration.

The labor organizations on the lakes have not been very active of late years. There are a seamen's union, a firemen's union, and an engineers' organization. (710, 711.)

Labor troubles and strikes.—Mr. KEEP states that there has been very little trouble between employers and employees since his connection with transportation on the lakes. On one occasion a few years ago the schooner *Mabel Wilson* lay at the breakwater at Buffalo with a crew of nonunion men, and a boat load of union men went out from the city and pulled off the crew and assaulted the captain. Two of the ringleaders were sent to State prison by the United States court. The witness does not know the cause of the controversy. (710.)

The grain shovelers who struck at Buffalo in the spring of 1899 were not employees of the Lake Carriers' Association. They were employees of a contractor, with whom the association had made a contract to do the necessary shoveling for the grain elevators at Buffalo for the entire season. There were two unions of the men at Buffalo, whose demands seem to have been identical. Mr. Keep does not make clear the origin of the difficulty. He states that in the end the question became one of personal animosity, and that the men declined to work for the contractor on any terms.

The grain fleet which had been loading all winter at Western ports came to Buffalo as soon as the Strait of Mackinac opened, arriving mostly on the 3d or 4th of May. The shovelers had determined that they would not work under the contract system, but would return to the system of shoveling under boss

scoopers at the different elevators, which had prevailed before the contract system was adopted. The Lake Carriers' Association adopted a resolution on May
3, declaring that the contract system had corrected many abuses, furnished good
wages, saved vessels from delays and extortions, and been a marked advantage
to the grain trade of Buffalo, and that the association would stand by its contractor and insist on the performance of the work under his contract. Finally
Bishop Quigley, of Buffalo, undertook, primarily at the suggestion of the representative of the Lake Carriers' Association, to reconcile the contending parties.
After his efforts had continued nearly a week, the following basis of settlement
was signed by the representatives of the association and the attorney for the
shovelers. From its terms some of the grievances and demands of the men may
be inferred.

"First. That the price of $1.85 per thousand bushels should be paid to the
men actually doing the work of shoveling, with not exceeding one foreman at
each elevator leg; no other person to participate therein.

"Second. Each gang to select a timekeeper from its own number.

"Third. The timekeeper and the inspector provided for at the conference to
have free access to bills of lading and other documents showing the quantity of
grain elevated.

"Fourth. Wages to be paid at elevator offices.

"Fifth. No bar bill or other accounts to be deducted from wages.

"Sixth. No boss or paymaster to be directly or indirectly connected with any
saloon.

"Seventh. An inspector to be appointed by the bishop to see that the provisions of the agreement were carried out, and to report any violation to the
bishop and to the Lake Carriers' Association; the inspector to be removable by
the bishop with power to appoint another, if necessary, to be paid by the Lake
Carriers' Association.

"Eighth. Bishop Quigley to have power to appoint a disinterested arbitrator
to hear and finally determine complaints."

The scoopers did not, however, return to work. They alleged acts on the part
of the contractor inconsistent with the agreement. The Lake Carriers' Association withdrew from further negotiations. On May 23, through the continued
efforts of Bishop Quigley, a settlement was finally reached on which the men
returned to work. (711–713.)

J. Canals (see also *Grain transportation*, p. 163).—*Erie Canal.*—Mr. KEEP states
that the business of the Erie Canal is decreasing. and, so far as the grain business
is concerned, must disappear if present conditions continue. The business is not
profitable enough to justify building new boats. The number of boats in condition
to carry grain decreases year by year. Even if rates advance there are not boats
enough to do any large business. The canal ought to be abandoned or practically
built over. A small improvement would be of no value. A State commission in
New York has just reported to the governor, urging that the canal be made
capable of handling boats 25 feet wide and 150 feet long, with a draft of 10 feet, and
that single locks be arranged to take in two of these boats at once. The idea is
that boats would travel in tows of 4,000 tons made up of 1 canal steamboat and
3 barges. The estimated cost is about $58,500,000 for the Erie Canal proper, and
$3,500,000 additional for the Oswego Canal. (722.)

Mr. CARTER, a commission merchant of Chicago, thinks that the Erie Canal
should be improved and given a depth of at least 10 feet. He does not think
that navigation of canals by the ships of the Great Lakes is likely to be brought
about. These vessels are built very expensively and provided with powerful
engines. Much cheaper boats would answer just as well for the slow movement
along the canal, and would involve less expense. Grain should be carried on
barges fitted for competing with the railroads, on which the unit is the train load,
amounting now to from 1,200 to 2,000 tons of actual burden. The barge need not
necessarily be of similar capacity to a train of cars, as many questions besides
that of the wages necessary to handle the barge must be considered. (579.)

Chicago drainage canal.—Mr. KEEP states that the lowering of Lakes Huron
and Michigan, to be expected from the Chicago drainage canal, varies from 3
inches to 7 or 8 inches in the estimates of different engineers. The most serious
effect, so far as yet appears, is the effect on the harbor of Chicago itself. It is
making a dangerous current in the Chicago River, and it has lowered the water in
the upper part of the Chicago River 2 feet. Over the Washington street tunnel,
where the draft of vessels is limited, the water is lowered about 6 inches.
Improvement of the Chicago River without increasing the draft of water through
the canal would be simply a harbor improvement and would not affect lake navi-

gation. The proposal to make the drainage canal navigable for vessels of light draft is of interest to the lake carriers only as it might affect the amount of water abstracted from Lake Michigan. If that amount were largely increased it would have a very serious effect on lake navigation. (717, 718.)

Mr. CARTER, a commission merchant of Chicago, says that the Chicago drainage canal is constructed with a depth of 22 feet, and is 28 miles long. He thinks the United States Government ought to take up this work and complete it, making a navigable channel from the Great Lakes to the Mississippi. A careful estimate has been made of the cost of completing a 16-foot channel from the termination of the drainage canal, through the Desplaines River and the Illinois River, to the Mississippi. The estimate is less than $125,000,000. There is not 16 feet of water in the Mississippi up to the mouth of the Illinois, but that would be a matter for the Mississippi River Commission to attend to. The United States Government has taken charge of the Chicago River and is deepening the water there. The volume of water which the canal will carry to the Mississippi will be of great aid in giving the required depth to the Illinois River and to the Mississippi itself. Several merchants of St. Louis, whom Mr. Carter has talked with, believe that the additional water will be of great advantage to them when the Mississippi is low. Mr. Carter does not clearly advocate the 16-foot channel, but many men think it desirable that deep-water navigation be provided throughout the whole distance from the Great Lakes to the mouth of the Mississippi. Mr. Carter does not think that such a waterway would be a dangerous rival of the Erie Canal. "In some respects it would add to the volume of business which is now going by the eastern route." Since the Illinois River is a navigable river the deepening of it would necessarily be under the control of the National Government. The United States Government has done nothing more with the Desplaines River than to make surveys. (580, 581.)

Mr. Carter states that the Illinois and Michigan Canal is still operated by the State of Illinois. (581.)

XIV. OCEAN TRANSPORTATION.

A. Different methods of shipment in different ports.—Mr. NEALL, a shipping merchant of Philadelphia, testifies that at different Atlantic ports the methods of shipment of ocean freights differ materially. New York, being the most important port, is reached by a large number of regular steamship lines runn ng to many different ports, and it is not necessary to arrange for means of transportation in advance to any such degree as in the other cities. At Boston, also, there are few tramp steamers, but many regular sailings of freight vessels to Liverpool and some to other ports. The freight room on these vessels is largely engaged in advance through the agents of railways. The bulk of the grain transported from Philadelphia, Baltimore, Norfolk, and Newport News is taken by tramp steamers, and these are largely chartered in advance for full cargoes. These tramp steamers will carry freight to ports practically never reached by regular lines, although their rates to ports reached by regular lines would be higher. (161–163.)

B. Rates. (See also as to *Flour shipments*, p. 77).—Mr. NEALL testifies that in the case of flour shipments, through rates from the inland points to Liverpool or other foreign ports are usually made. The steamship lines offer ship room to the railways from time to time, for a particular vessel or period, at a certain rate, and the railways make through rates accordingly, apparently sometimes varying their own rates slightly to fill the room offered. It was formerly the practice to ship flour in large quantities to Eastern ports without such arrangements for through shipment, and the same is still true, mainly, regarding grain.

There is no agreement among the freight carriers of the North Atlantic as to rates, and the rates vary greatly, according to the supply and demand. There is, in fact, competition for vessels from the traffic of the entire world. Tramp steamers, owned in England, may be sought for transportation from American ports, and at the same time they may have offers to carry cargoes to or from ports throughout the world. The regular lines also vary their rates frequently, according to the supply of tramp steamers, the amount of freight seeking transportation, etc. Rates may be changed sometimes twice in one day.

Ocean freight rates, unlike rail rates, depend more upon the space occupied than upon the weight. Railway cars are seldom filled to their full bulk capacity, since the weight of most products is too great. The ocean carrier can scarcely be overloaded as to weight. Indeed, concentrated weight is desirable. The differences in ocean freight rates between different products depend to a considerable degree upon the cost of handling the product in loading and unloading, and upon the amount of waste space caused by the shipment. Thus grain can be more cheaply handled than flour, and occupies about one-sixth less space per ton. (163-165.)

C. American merchant marine and its encouragement. 1. *Time charters.*—Mr. NEALL testifies that during the last year or two it has become increasingly common for Americans to secure charters of foreign vessels for considerable periods, running from 6 months to 2 years. The owner furnishes the officers, crew, and engine stores, but has no further control of the vessel. The lessee furnishes coal, and is able to use the vessel between whatever ports he sees fit. The great advantage of this practice is that it prevents delay in shipments and enables vessels to visit ports which are not commonly reached. (168, 189.)

2. *Small tonnage of American merchant marine.*—Mr. NEALL, a shipping merchant of Philadelphia, believes that the entire tonnage of American vessels fitted for transoceanic traffic does not exceed 300,000 tons gross register. He estimates that the total gross tonnage of the steam and sailing vessels of the world is about 28,000,000 tons.

	Tons.
Total steam tonnage (gross), in vessels of 100 tons or over, of the world	20,800,000
Total sail tonnage (net), in vessels of 100 tons or over, of the world	6,800,000
	27,600,000
Of above Great Britain owns, say, one-half	13,900,000
Of above United States owns, say, one-eleventh	2,400,000
Of above Germany owns	2,400,000
And Norway is next with	1,700,000

The exports of the United States amount to about 30,000,000 tons of freight and the imports to about 7,500,000 tons. Although the United States is credited with the ownership of vessels having a register of 2,400,000 tons, Mr. Neall, by taking the character of each individual vessel into consideration, estimates that only 296,185 tons are represented by vessels suitable for transoceanic traffic, as shown in the following table:

	Tons.
140 steamships, with aggregate gross register of	399,425
52 ships, with aggregate gross register of	111,433
14 barks, with aggregate gross register of	18,870
88 schooners, with aggregate gross register of	115,101
294 Total gross register	644,829

From this total should be deducted, as not intended, and in reality unsuitable, for the transoceanic trade, having been constructed especially for the requirements of coastwise or near-by commerce—

169 vessels of gross register	348,644

Leaving as suitable and available for transoceanic traffic 125 vessels of gross register	296,185
Of which are steam, 47 vessels, gross register	149,040
And of these latter 23 steamers with gross register	73,420

were built abroad, and subsequently, under various conditions, granted United States register.

In making this estimate Mr. Neall has excluded all vessels of less than 1,000 tons burden, because they can not possibly compete in the transoceanic trade. Sailing vessels more than 20 years old have been excluded as unsafe. Although we have a considerable tonnage in coastwise steamships, these have not coal capacity sufficient for crossing the ocean, and their construction, especially the high superstructure, makes them also unfit for North Atlantic navigation. Mr. Neall submitted a list of all the American vessels of more than 1,000 tons gross register sailing from ocean ports, together with an enumeration of the reasons in each case for excluding such as are deemed unfit for ocean traffic.

Mr. Neall says further that there is no trans-Atlantic steamship line composed wholly of American-built vessels, part of those of the American Line being of foreign construction. Not over three trans-Pacific lines are composed of American vessels. (166-168, 175-184.)

3. *Reasons for small tonnage.*—Mr. Neall does not enter into detail as to the reasons for the comparatively small proportion of American shipping, further than to point out that the cost of constructing steam vessels, especially the lower grades, tramp steamers, etc., is much higher in this country than in England. Previous to 1860, when ocean transportation was confined practically to wooden vessels, the United States excelled all other countries in its proportion of shipping and in its success in the business. This superiority is attributed by Mr. Neall less to the discriminating duties than to the ability of Americans to construct better and faster ships and to man and navigate them more ably. While our shipyards have built some fast ocean-going liners and numerous war vessels,

they have practically never built an ordinary ocean tramp, which is the kind of vessel that handles the great bulk of commodities.

Although the difference in the cost of construction of such vessels between this country and Europe is less than formerly, Mr. Neall believes that a substantial tramp steamer of 7,000 tons dead-weight capacity can be built in Great Britain at a cost of $42.50 or $45 per ton, while it would be impossible, even aside from the present high price of iron, to buy them here at less than $65 or $70 per ton. On higher-class vessels, where there is more joiner work and other fine work, the difference between Europe and America is less. Mr. Neall does not explain fully the reasons for this higher cost in the United States. It can not be due to the higher cost of steel and iron or of wood, nor does he believe that American labor is, in view of its higher efficiency, necessarily dearer. But our shipyards are comparatively few, and those which we have are taxed to their fullest capacity to build high-grade vessels, and could not, if they would, build any considerable number of ordinary steam vessels within a reasonable length of time. For these reasons Mr. Neall thinks it would not be unjust to American shipbuilders to permit Americans to buy vessels abroad for navigation under the home flag, in view of the immediate and pressing need for an American merchant marine. (168–172.)

4. *Purchase of vessels abroad.*—Mr. NEALL accordingly recommends that, aside from any other measures in the shape of subsidies or postal payments designed to build up an American merchant marine, laws should be passed permitting American citizens to buy foreign vessels and put them under the United States flag. He would prohibit craft thus purchased from being used in American coastwise trade or in trade with any foreign port within 500 miles of the shores of the United States proper; and would provide that these vessels should have a dead weight capacity of not less than 5,000 tons for steamers or 2,500 tons for sailing vessels, and that they should not be over 5 years old at the time of purchase. If further restrictions seemed necessary it might be enacted that the number of ships thus bought should not exceed 500,000 tons net register, and that a duty of $1 per ton for 5 years should be levied upon them.

Mr. Neall states that the Norwegians have made an extensive practice of buying foreign-built vessels and putting them under the home flag, and that they have made large profits by doing so. At present a large proportion of the vessels thus bought by the Norwegians have been leased by them to Americans on time charters, running for 6 months to 2 years, at high rates.

Were an American merchant marine thus established, Mr. Neall believes that the vessels could be run with sufficient economy to compete in the world traffic. It is true that the wages of American sailors are higher than those of foreign sailors, although the difference is less than formerly, the average pay of an English seaman having been raised to about £4 10s. The food furnished on American vessels is also of better quality, and in other ways the cost of navigation is somewhat higher. But the witness is confident that this difference is not sufficient to necessitate higher rates of freight on American vessels than on those owned abroad, nor to preclude the earning of a fair profit, especially as our vessel owners learn the economies which are employed in other countries. (169–171, 177.)

5. *Discriminating duties.*—Mr. NEALL does not believe that the system of discriminating duties would be an effective one in building up an American merchant marine; nor does he attribute the earlier development of American shipping to the duties which then existed. Unless the discriminating duty be excessively high the foreign vessel owner would bid for traffic with a view to the duty and would still underbid the American owner. (172, 173.)

6. *Coastwise trade.*—Mr. NEALL testifies that under the existing laws only American-built vessels can be employed in American coastwise trade. The men employed in that business, however, have been very enterprising, and have kept the demand for transportation fairly supplied. (172, 174.)

7. *Shipping bounties and labor.*—Mr. FURUSETH, secretary of the Sailors' Union of the Pacific, does not think that the payment of bounties to American vessels would have any effect upon the condition of the men. As a general thing he has never seen any master of a vessel paying more than he had to pay or giving better food than he had to give. He has some question whether the proposal to subsidize the fishermen, in the form in which it is made, does not make the seamen subject to impressment. That is the chief reason why the convention of seamen in Chicago condemned that bill. The following paragraphs make clear Mr. Furuseth's opinion on the subject of bounties. (699–700.)

"None of the schemes that I have seen so far, or heard discussed so far, has anything in it that would in any way increase the number of real American sailors, or cause any American boy to go to sea, or stay at sea, or in any way make it any easier for the merchant marine or Navy to obtain real American sailors.

" Q. You would think, however, that some of these measures might be taken to increase the business of the American merchant marine?—A. Yes; probably.

" Q. Well, then, if these measures were accompanied by such measures as you suggest for the improvement of the condition of the sailors, you think it would be of general benefit to the country?—A. Then the improvement, so far as the sailor is concerned, would come from the measures accompanying the measure, and not from the original measure."

" Q. Do you think the bounties proposed in these subsidies, in these bills, to the fishing fleet are going to be of any advantage in bringing more into that, and then ultimately augmenting the marine?—A. No; not a bit of it.

" Q. You think it will be simply absorbed where it is?—A. The seamen, instead of getting $20 a month, will get $19 a month from the man who hires him and $1 from the Government. It is simply another way of subsidizing the vessel, that is all—adding so much to the subsidy paid to the owner of the vessel—and will not do the sailor one iota of good."

D. Condition of American ocean seamen.—1. *United States law relating to seamen.*— Mr. FURUSETH, secretary of the Sailors' Union of the Pacific, states that the law relating to seamen passed by the Fifty-fifth Congress has been of great benefit on the whole, though there were certain mistakes in it, particularly the repeal of some of the old law which had worked well. On the whole, foreign laws regarding seamen are not better than those of the United States, though they are better in some particulars.

The Seamen's Union, however, has drafted a bill to amend the laws relating to American seamen. Its proposals are to abolish crimping, so far as it can be abolished by law; to increase the space in the forecastle; to give the seamen a right to one-half of what is actually due him in every port; to give the majority of the crew, exclusive of officers, the right to call for a survey of the vessel; to establish a standard of skill and experience for those who sign as able seamen, and to provide a standard number of men to be carried by vessels according to their tonnage and rigging. (691–693.)

Mr. Furuseth supposes that the reforms which the Seamen's Union desires will probably make the running of vessels a little more expensive. The cost of running a vessel includes so many things that the wages of the men are only a small part of it. The cost of running does not by itself determine the possibility of competition. It is said that when the American merchant marine was practically supreme, 50 years ago, American vessels could get a higher rate than those of other nations, because of the better stowing and better care of cargoes, and the faster time they made. No doubt increased wages and improved condition and treatment of the men would result in getting a better class of men and better service, which would tend to make up for the higher wages. (699.)

The witness takes up the conditions of seamen and the proposed reforms in detail.

2. *Hiring of sailors—Crimps.*—Mr. FURUSETH says that when a master needs a crew he commonly goes to a shipping master or "crimp" and makes a contract with him to furnish a crew. The crimp and the master agree upon the wages to be paid. The crimp secures a crew from men who come to his office or by dealing with the keepers of sailors' boarding houses, and is usually paid for his services by the sailor with an "allotment" or order on the ship.

The law formerly allowed a sailor to make an "allotment" for not more than $10 a month, but the last Congress changed it to not more than one month's wages. The allotment usually goes, not to a bona fide creditor, but to a crimp, to be divided between him and the ship captain and perhaps the keeper of a sailor's boarding house. The Seamen's Union does not desire that the possibility of making an allotment to a man's family or relatives be removed—to remove it would be a great hardship; but the allotment to creditors is a means of robbing the sailor. Indeed, the law forbidding more than one month's allotment to creditors is constantly violated, and it is very hard to get evidence of violation because the sailor is immediately carried away out of the jurisdiction. (690–692, 696.)

If this allotment to original creditors were abolished, and a law were made entitling the seaman to one-half what he has actually earned in every port where the vessel loads or delivers cargo, and if the seaman were given the full right to quit wherever he is, the crimp would have to go out of business. Plymouth, Portsmouth, and Sheerness, the three man-of-war ports of England, used to have the worst crimp dens in the United Kingdom; but when the Admirality decided to pay their men monthly wherever they happened to be, these dens were wiped out. (691.)

3. *Payment of sailors' wages and compulsory service.*—Mr. FURUSETH states that sailors' articles now usually provide for service for 12 months, and no money dur-

ing the interval except at the master's option. Often the master will absolutely refuse to make any payments. That generally means that he intends to misuse the sailor so that he will run away and forfeit his pay. The sailor, poor and under the necessity of getting employment, has no option but to sign the contract. The Seamen's Union is trying to induce Congress to provide that a sailor may quit his employment in any port and receive all the money that he has earned. (695, 696.)

Up to 1898 a seaman was subject to imprisonment for refusing to continue to labor, in the United States as well as out of the United States. If he left his employment he might be imprisoned, kept in jail for an indefinite period at his own expense, then taken on board the vessel against his will, and compelled to proceed to sea and do the work for which he had engaged. If he refused to work he was subject to penal or to corporal punishment and to being placed in irons on short rations. If he deserted, the master might offer a reward for his detection and return to the vessel. Eighty men were thus reclaimed in Callao last year, one in Singapore, and one in Yokohama; one, in Singapore, was punished besides. The present law of the United States in respect to forcing seamen to specific performance of their contracts of service, however, is better than that of most other nations, except England. Since 1898 there has been no penalty for desertion in a home port. The sailor can take his clothes and go, but he forfeits all the money he has earned. The Seamen's Union desires Congress to so change the law that the sailor will be free to quit in any port, and to get his money, too. (686, 691, 695.) The sailor still commonly says after shipping, "I have sold myself." An effort was made to establish the freedom of sailors from compulsory service under the thirteenth amendment to the Constitution, but the Supreme Court held that that did not apply to seamen. Efforts have been made to get Congress to abolish the law under which a sailor can be seized and returned by force to his vessel, but so far without success. The witness states that if sailors were free to quit at will vessels would be under no difficulty in getting new crews. The usual thing is to pay the sailors or drive them out when a vessel comes into port for some time, and let the vessel lie without sailors until she is ready for sea again, and then hire new ones. (707.)

4. *Dependent seamen.*—Mr. Furuseth says that Congress appropriates annually a certain amount of money for the return of sick and disabled seamen to the United States. It would be much better if the return to the United States were abolished and the sailor were left free to quit. As to the statement that many sailors who have left their vessels become dependent, and have to be sustained and sent home at the expense of the Government, the witness says that the most of such men were probably driven out of the vessels they were in, without receiving any pay for the work they had done. A vessel lying in a port waiting for cargo does not wish to keep the men on board. By the law of 1884 the master may discharge the men, if they consent to be discharged, by paying them what is due them. If a man is offered his discharge and his pay and refuses to take it, he will invariably be treated so that he will leave in a week or two without his pay. Sometimes masters will refuse to give a discharge when it is asked for, and then will so abuse the man that he will run away and leave his pay behind him.

5. *Wages and economic condition of seamen.*—Mr. FURUSETH states further that the absence of any standard of qualification for seamen results in the fixing of wages at such a point as the idle men in a seaport, without regard to knowledge of the sea, can be induced to accept. Wages of seamen are determined entirely by the port, and not by the flag. Seamen's wages in New York City are the same to the American, Dutch, German, English, or Norwegian ship. There is no such thing as American wages; it is international wages. Seamen's wages vary much. They will run from $15 in the port of New York up to $30 in different American ports. In Sunderland, England, they are fully as high as in New York. In Liverpool they are usually lower. They are lower still in Antwerp and in Mediterranean ports. In San Francisco and on Puget Sound deep-water wages are about $20; in New York, at the present time, about $18. English sailors get between £4 and £6 a month.

These are all white men's wages. Asiatics ship in Hongkong and Yokohama, and their wages are $16 Mexican. About one-quarter of our merchant marine is manned by Asiatic seamen. All these statements refer to the foreign trade or deep-water wages. The wages in our coastwise trade are higher than in the foreign trade, and higher than in any other coastwise trade except that of Australia. Coastwise wages at New York are at present from $18 to $25. In San Francisco they run from $30 to $40, and in a few cases to $45. In fact, the general condition of sailors in the coastwise trade is better than in the deep-sea trade. The witness ascribes this partly to the fact that from 1874 up to 1890 the men in the coastwise trade were free to quit. Being free to quit, they were free to organize. Besides, the work is harder, and a better class of men is needed. (687-689, 697, 698.)

While the wages of men working ashore have increased, the wages of seamen have been stationary. The cost of living has increased in about the same ratio as shore wages; and the result is that the seaman's wages are not sufficient to keep himself, far less a family. The condition is the same in other countries as in the United States. Norway used to furnish a great number of seamen. The Norwegian sailors were better off than the ordinary mechanics on shore. But now the condition of shore employment has so improved that the standard of living of the shore mechanic has risen vastly above that of the seaman. Norwegian vessels are now very largely filled with Swedes and Finns. The case is the same in England. A man can earn more on shore than at sea, and can be at home with his family. Though a boy may go to sea from notions of romance, he will leave it when he has made one or two trips, and finds out what the life is, what the work is, and what wages he is likely to get. The first thing a sailor does when he comes into New York is not, as the shore people think, to go and get drunk; he looks around and tries to find other employment. He becomes a bridge builder, or an architectural ironworker, or a gripman on the street cars, positions where his training in climbing and in quick thinking and quick work are of value. Seventy-five per cent of the men who work at architectural ironwork in Philadelphia, Boston, and Chicago are sailors. Aside from the actual economic debasement of the sailor's condition, there is a loss of social caste which results from this economic debasement. The ordinary man ashore speaks of the sailor as a poor fellow, who would not go to sea if he could do anything else. The remedy for this state of things is to improve the general condition of the men so that it shall be equal with that of other ordinary mechanics. (697, 698.)

6. *Permanency of employment.*—Mr. FURUSETH states that in the Continental and English marine men usually ship for a year, and stay in the same vessel about a year or two. He does not speak of the regular liners, as he never sailed in them. It appears from a British consular report, quoted by the witness, that on the well-known and wealthy English lines the same picked men continue to be employed from voyage to voyage and year to year. (694, 695, 703.)

7. *Nationality of seamen.*—Mr. FURUSETH states that about one-fourth of the American merchant marine is manned by Asiatic seamen, Japanese, Chinese, Lascars or East India sailors, and Tagals or "Manila men," together with Turks and Arabs. Even in the coastwise trade, although the vessels must be American, there is no such requirement as to seamen, and on the Pacific coast not more than 10 per cent are American born. On that coast, the Scandinavians, including with them the Finns, probably predominate; next would be the Germans, and Americans last of all. The conditions are not very different in the Atlantic coastwise trade.

It is a very rare thing to have an Asiatic on a German, Scandinavian, or French vessel. On English vessels they are to-day as common as on American. No other nation uses them to any extent.

Some of the foreigners referred to above are naturalized citizens, and some others have declared their intention to become citizens. Prior to 1893 about one-half of the coasting seamen on the Pacific coast belonged to these classes. The witness does not know what the proportion is now. (689, 690.)

The vessels that trade between Hongkong and San Francisco and Puget Sound, whether under the American or English or Japanese flag, sign all their men in China or Japan. They carry white quartermasters and white officers, but no white men as sailors, as firemen, or in the steward's department. Although the wages of the Asiatics are only about $16 Mexican, they can not be much cheaper than white men, because about twice as many Chinamen as white men are needed to do the same work. They are said to be more docile, and not so apt to get drunk or leave the vessel. Where real seamen are needed in a storm or disaster they are practically useless, for they have not the coolness, courage, or strength of the average white man. (708.)

Seamen are exempt both in the immigration laws and in the Chinese exclusion laws; so that neither of these laws gives any protection to the American sailor. (709.)

Mr. NEALL says that the law provides that only Americans may hold official positions upon vessels engaged in the coastwise trade. There is no such limitation as regards common sailors, however, and the witness estimates that 50 per cent of the sailors on these ships are of foreign birth, especially Germans, Danes, and Scandinavians. It is not true that on the Pacific Ocean the vessels engaged in the coasting trade are largely manned by Chinese and Japanese, the existing laws relating to the Chinese practically preventing their employment in this way. (172, 174, 175.)

8. *Undermanning of vessels.*—Mr. FURUSETH quotes with approval a British Parliamentary report dealing with the impossibility of a contract on equal terms between employer and employee in respect to sea service. Many considerations, such as rigging, sail area, steering gear, winches, number of fires, coal consumption, position of bunkers, etc., must be taken into account in determining the proper crew for a ship. The seaman can have no adequate knowledge of such considerations nor of the extent of the work to which he binds himself. If the crew of an undermanned ship refuse to serve, they are liable to imprisonment. If they do serve and by working for their lives succeed in reaching their destination, they will have established their number as a proper crew for the vessel until a further reduction is made. (702.) The only country that has a definite law about the manning of vessels, says Mr. Furuseth, is New Zealand. Labor-saving machinery has somewhat reduced the number of men needed to work a vessel, but the number of men carried has been decreased disproportionately to the need. There are vessels on the Pacific coast which while sailing in the foreign trade carried 18 and 20 men, but now carry 10. The witness mentions 1 ship which used to carry 36 men and now carries 14. He estimates that she should have 24. In 9 vessels out of 10, if the ship is taken aback, the only thing to do is to depend on the strength of the gear. The yards can not be swung quickly enough to prevent damage, for lack of men. American vessels carry less men than those of Europe. Holland carries most, Denmark next, Sweden next, then Norway and Germany, then England. and last the United States. The number of men carried varies somewhat with the wages. If wages go up a vessel usually takes 1 or 2 men less. (687, 688.)

Mr. Furuseth states that most sailing vessels now have a steam donkey winch, which is used in going in and out of port for lifting anchor and hoisting sails; but at sea steam is not kept up in it. The principal labor-saving devices aside from this are double topsail yards, double gallant yards, patent blocks with small inside rollers, and the use of softer, better rope—manila rope. (687–688.)

9. *Food and drink of seamen.*—The food of seamen, Mr. FURUSETH states, is regulated by law. Up to 1898 the requirement was fully 50 per cent poorer than the food provided for the prisoners in Sing Sing. It was exactly equal to the English contract scale, about 50 per cent below the German scale, and about 100 per cent below the Danish scale. The existing American scale is better. Mr. Furuseth gives in detail these comparative scales. He says that the only complaint which he would make of the American scale is that the water should be increased from 4 quarts a day to 6 quarts, and the butter from 1 ounce to 2. In fact, however, the scale is not in general operation. It is not given in the deep-water vessels, and even not in some of the coastwise vessels. (686, 693, 694.)

Mr. Furuseth quotes at length, although without special reference to this point, an English consular report in which the enforcement of total abstinence from liquor on British sailing vessels is declared to result in increased excesses on arrival in port. It is stated that a daily ration of spirits works well in the English navy, and that, since the proportion of total abstainers in the navy is incomparably higher than in the merchant service, it can not be considered fatal to the cause of temperance. (704.)

10. *Air space for seamen.*—The air space in the forecastle, where the seamen live, is regulated by law. The requirement for steamers is that each man have 72 cubic feet of air space, and not less than 12 feet of floor space; that is, a space 6 feet long, 6 feet high, and 2 feet wide. By a change made 8 years ago, the requirement for sailing vessels thereafter built or rebuilt was changed to 100 cubic feet. Seventy-two cubic feet is the requirement in England and Germany; but inasmuch as German and English ships do not carry loads on the decks, where the houses usually are, they have no special temptation to narrow the space for the men. In England the space actually given is usually about 100 to 120 feet. (686.)

11. *Watches on shipboard.*—Mr. FURUSETH explains in detail the division of the 24 hours into 7 watches. He states that in some vessels it is the custom to keep all the men on deck during the daytime; that is, to have both watches on deck during the period from 12 to 4 in the afternoon. This gives too little sleep and rest, and makes the men too much subject to sleepiness to be effective at the wheel or on the outlook during the night.

Another custom has recently grown up which is called the Kalashi watch; that is, all hands on deck all day and called out whenever they are wanted during the night; but on deck steadily through the night only a watchman, a lookout man, the wheelman, and the officers on the bridge. If a disaster happens at night to vessels so managed, the men come from the forecastle half asleep, the light half blinds them, and for the first 15 minutes they are practically useless. Besides, it is, of course, much harder for the men to work all day and be called out at night also. This practice enables vessels to run with 2 or 3 men less than they would otherwise have to have. It is used on practically all of the passenger steamers on the eastern coast of the United States. It is not so much used on the Pacific coast and has not been applied in Europe.

No man is capable of proper lookout or proper work at the wheel for more than 2 hours at a time. In a storm or on very serious occasions 1 hour is long enough, and sometimes too long. In the Great Lakes, on freight steamers, at least, men stand at the wheel for 4 hours, sometimes as much as 6 hours. (700–701.)

12. *Examination of ships by sailors.*—Mr. Furuseth says that it is impossible for sailors to control their own actions with regard to the kind of ship, seaworthy or not, which they shall sail in. They do not always ship in the port in which they join the vessel. Men may ship in Boston and Philadelphia for a vessel in New York, with no opportunity to inspect her. (701.)

13. *Loss of life on passenger vessels.*—The witness attributes the great loss of life in certain disasters to passenger vessels to the insufficiency of life-saving apparatus and the insufficient number of the crew. He implies that the fact that the Cunard Line has never lost any passengers is due to the carrying of a larger number of skilled men than other lines carry. According to the witness, accidents between 3 and 6 in the morning, particularly about 4, are most likely to result disastrously. Sailors call this period "the graveyard watch." About 4 in the morning one watch leaves the deck, and another, which has had but 4 hours' sleep that night, comes up. (700.)

14. *Denial of shore leave.*—Mr. Furuseth quotes, as expressing the condition and feeling of seamen generally, an English consular report on the condition of seamen in the British merchant marine, in which very serious complaint is made of the denial of shore leave while in port. In the British navy shore leave is granted freely when opportunity offers, and the same custom prevails in the steam merchant marine. In sailing vessels, however, men are kept for weeks together in harbor without being permitted to step off the ship. The report regards this grievance as by far the chief incentive to desertion and to the minor offense of absence without leave. (704, 705.)

15. *Corporal punishment of seamen.*—Mr. Furuseth states that the United States law forbidding corporal punishment of seamen is constantly violated. The most common form of punishment is a blow over the head with a belaying pin—a stick like a policeman's club. Such blows are given by officers in sudden passion and without any control from superior officers. In continental and English vessels such occurrences are very rare. (692.)

16. *Qualifications of seamen.*—Mr Furuseth says that an "able seaman" is a healthy man in his active years, accustomed to the sea, who has received the peculiar training that makes it possible for him to apply his wits to conditions as they come. The Seamen's Union desires a law providing that an able seaman must be more than 18 years of age, and must have had 3 years experience at sea. (708, 709.) The law at present does not set any standard of qualification. Anybody whom the captain considers a seaman is a seaman, whether he has ever been at sea or not. Custom used to determine the qualification. Four years' apprenticeship is still customary in England. In most countries apprenticeship has been abolished. In German and Scandinavian countries the standards are stricter; a boy goes to sea as a boy; about the second year he will be called a young man; the third year and the fourth year an ordinary seaman; after about 4 years he will rank as an able seaman. The American Navy has a very exacting standard of skill—the old standard of years ago. Not more than 15 per cent of the men engaged as seamen on the Great Lakes would pass the naval standard as able seamen. The vast majority would not pass as ordinary seamen. About one-half of the men on the Atlantic and the Pacific coasts might pass as able seamen, one-quarter as ordinary seamen, and one-quarter would be called landsmen. Even as to officers, including the master, our law has not until recently prescribed any qualification, except that they should be citizens. (687.)

17. *Labor unions of seamen.*—Mr. Furuseth, secretary of the Sailors' Union of the Pacific, says that there have been organizations of the seamen on the Lakes, with short intermissions, since 1868, on the Pacific coast since 1885, and on the Atlantic coast since 1890. In 1892 the local unions were organized into an international union, and were affiliated with the American Federation of Labor. The membership is nearly 5,000. The general objects are to improve the condition of the seamen,

industrially and socially, and to improve the maritime law. There is a funeral benefit for the burial of dead members, and in case of shipwreck and loss of clothing the organization pays a sum not exceeding $50 to buy a new outfit. The three local organizations, on the Lakes, on the Atlantic, and on the Pacific, deal with matters of wages each for itself. There is a national card transferable from one local union to another, and men engaged in the lake trade can pass to either of the ocean organizations, and vice versa. There is no traveling benefit. There are no rules as to apprenticeship. The national body has had four conventions. The convention formulates a legislative programme, and gives instructions to the legislative committees; but there is full cooperation between the legislative committees and the executive committees. (685–686.)

Mr. Furuseth says that the wage question would settle itself with sailors if they were given the opportunity to help themselves—the opportunity to organize. The sailor can not effectively organize because he can not quit his employment; he can not strike. (698.)

18. *Homes for aged and disabled sailors.*—Mr. Furuseth says that the Sailors' Union looks on homes for sailors as eleemosynary institutions, which are in one way a good thing, but tend in the wrong direction, in that they perpetuate the treatment of sailors as children. He doubts whether it would be a proper thing for the United States to establish such homes. In case of disability, there are marine hospitals, supported by the United States Government, and including a farm in Arizona or New Mexico, where consumptives are sent. The witness entirely approves of these hospitals. Sailors used to contribute 40 cents a month to them before the passage of the law of 1884, but now they are supported out of the tonnage dues on vessels. The Sailors' Snug Harbor in New York is the outcome of private benevolence. The institution has become very rich. (696, 697.)

XV. MISCELLANEOUS EVIDENCE NOT RELATING TO TRANSPORTATION.

A. Trusts and combinations.—Mr. Moseley, secretary of the Interstate Commerce Commission, thinks that discrimination in railway rates has been one of the main advantages accruing to large combinations. Trusts tend to lessen the number of employers and of employees. The workman is in danger of losing his individuality and becoming a mere dependent part of the machinery of the establishment. He will be unable to find other employers if he refuses to work for the combination which controls the entire business. (43.)

Mr. Sager, secretary of the Northern Milling Company of Chicago, thinks that industrial combinations are not necessarily bad; that they can effect great economies, and are the natural economic result of existing conditions; but he does not believe in monopolies and regrets to see the small individual proprietors driven out of business. (454.)

Mr. Counselman, an elevator owner of Chicago, declares himself in favor of large aggregations of capital, but not of combinations possessing power to control prices absolutely. He had some experience in dealing with the American Tin Plate Company, and thinks its prices are probably reasonable in view of the high cost of raw materials. (390, 391.)

Mr. Carter, a grain dealer of Chicago, does not think that the trust, in and of itself, if founded on actual values, need frighten anybody. He believes that the two greatest questions before the people are, first, the prevention of preferences in freight rates; second, the prevention of overcapitalization. He considers that absolute equality of opportunity is all that any man is entitled to. He does not believe that large concerns, dependent altogether on hired assistants, can overcome, in legitimate competition, the smaller man who maintains a direct supervision of his business. (583–585.)

Mr. Dickinson has heard it charged very strongly that the railroads have obtained a monopoly of coal mining in the East, but he does not think that such a monopoly exists generally throughout the country. There is a large mining district in Illinois, and he has not heard it charged that the industry is there monopolized by the railroads. (553.)

United States Flour Mill Company.—Mr. Barry testifies that this company has been recently organized with a capital, he believes, of $15,000,000. It includes 24 large mills in several Northwestern cities. The capacity of these mills is not over 50,000 barrels per day, no attempt being made to control the output or prices. The object of the combination was, by having a large capacity in different advantageous localities, to make the business more independent of local conditions and to reduce the cost of management and of selling. The good will of the plants entering the combination was a very considerable element in the price paid for them. (242.)

B. Agriculture.—Mr. NEWCOMB, of the Department of Agriculture, says that the difficulties under which farmers labor are due partly to the fact that our public-land systems and railroad grants induce producers to settle beyond the range of profitable production, and partly to the lack of organization and of knowledge as to methods and conditions of the industry. This lack of knowledge the Department of Agriculture is seeking to remedy by its reports and statistical information. Its monthly estimates of crop conditions and probable production are secured through about 60,000 correspondents, who exercise great care and intelligence. The witness considers them far more accurate than any estimates of dealers. These reports are useful to dealers and speculators, but do not therefore injure farmers. By greater knowledge of conditions, speculators tend to fix prices more evenly and accurately, so that there is less difference between prices at harvest and through the year. (106, 107.)

Mr. Newcomb declares that speculators perform a useful function in distributing agricultural products. By their familiarity with conditions of production and consumption they are able to estimate the probable future prices, and thus to make prices throughout the year more uniform than they would otherwise be. The price at harvest is thus kept up more nearly to the level of the price later on. Speculation in farm products may, in abnormal cases, be detrimental, but not usually. The price of farm products is ultimately fixed by the cost of production to the man whose production is the most expensive, but whose product is necessary to supply the demand. This ultimate price is largely fixed in the Liverpool market. The practice of selling options can not long mislead dealers as to the true grain supply. (107, 109.)

Duties on grain and grain products.—Mr. EVANS, a miller, of Indianapolis, points out that most European countries and some other countries, such as Brazil, have established discriminating duties against American flour as compared with wheat, thus seeking to develop their own milling industry. The witness thinks that by treaties or otherwise the United States should seek to prevent such discriminations. A department of commerce might be beneficial in accomplishing such results. (439.)

Adulteration of flour.—Mr. BARRY, secretary of the Millers' National Association, says that flour has in recent years been very largely adulterated with a by-product of glucose or starch, or even with white earth, to the great detriment of the flour product. The mixed-flour law, passed by the Fifty-fifth Congress, has entirely stopped this practice. (240.)

C. The cattle business.—Mr. BAKER, secretary of the Chicago Live Stock Exchange, says that there seem to have been about 52,000,000 cattle in the country 6 years ago, and there seem to be about 10,000,000 less to-day. It would take perhaps 3 or 4 years, with a continuance of high prices, to make up this deficiency. An animal can be bred and put on the market in 18 months or 2 years, but since it is necessary to supply the current demand as well as to make up the shortage, it will take a longer time than that to catch up. At the same time the consumption is heavier than it has been. (592.)

Mr. MALLORY states that men in the live stock trade do not figure, as the Agricultural Department does, on the whole number of cattle supposed to be in the United States. So far as trade and values are concerned, it is the supply and demand in the market that governs, and not what exists in the country. Mr. Mallory does not consider the live stock statistics of the Agricultural Department to be of any value whatever. There are no statistics of live stock in this country which he considers reliable. (589–591.)

Mr. Mallory says that the price of cattle has been considerably higher since 1899, perhaps $1 to $1.50 per hundred, than during the preceding 3 or 4 years. Hogs have not risen so much; perhaps 25 cents to 50 cents per hundred. Fat cattle had gone down just before Mr. Mallory's testimony, November 24, 1899. Stock cattle had declined a little. The decline in hogs came in October, as it generally does in the fall. Mr. Mallory attributes the rise of live stock in 1899 not so much to the shortage of supply as to the increase of demand. The laboring man uses a larger percentage of his earnings for meat in prosperous times, and during this year he has been well employed at fair wages. Mr. Mallory thinks the consumption of meat is from 35 to 40 per cent greater than it was 8 years ago. He admits that there has been a relative shortage, and that this has of course helped to raise the price.

The witness thinks that the so-called shortage of live stock in 1899 was the result of the depression of 2 or 3 years before. At that time the prices were very low and a great many people became discouraged and threw their cattle on the market. This process was also increased by the eating out and fencing up of the Western ranges; but if the owners had not been discouraged by low prices, they would have found places to feed and mature many of the cattle which they did throw prematurely on the market. (589–592.)

Mr. Mallory says that when beef reaches a certain price consumption will decrease, and if pork is relatively lower many consumers will take up with pork; if mutton is lower the demand for mutton will increase; the people are not dependent upon any one class of meat. (591.)

Mr. Mallory states that one part of the Spanish war advanced the prices of meat and another part decreased them. The amount of meat spoiled and thrown away was not large enough to affect the market at all. The feeling which arose from the condemnation of the meat, and the newspaper discussion of it, had an unfavorable effect upon the market, which lasted several months. (590.)

Mr. Mallory states that changes of the price of live stock affect all the markets at about the same time. "The telegraph works very promptly. If Chicago declines other markets decline, and if they decline it has a sympathetic effect upon Chicago." (589, 590.)

D. Immigration.—Mr. CLARK, chief of the Railway Conductors, declares that there is practical unanimity among the railroad brotherhoods in favor of very close restriction of immigration. They do not feel its effects directly, but since the lower classes of American labor are displaced by foreigners, who are willing to live in a manner which Americans will not endure, these classes seek employment in the higher grades of labor, which are thus indirectly affected. The witness would favor increasing the period of residence before naturalization, perhaps to as much as 21 years. (113, 114.)

Mr. ARTHUR says that the Brotherhood of Locomotive Engineers is in favor of restricting immigration, which indirectly affects their prosperity by creating a large surplus of labor. The witness would advocate an educational test and also the requirement of property of at least $500 for admission into this country. He would also limit the ballot in all cases to those who are able to read and write English. (124, 125.)

E. Department of commerce.—Mr. KENNARD, of the Chicago Butter and Egg Board, thinks that the interests of agriculture and of business have been greatly promoted by the work of the United States Department of Agriculture, and believes that a similar department of commerce would prove of great advantage. (366.)

F. The Mississippi River lumber industry.—Mr. DICKINSON states that the logs avail able for mills along the Mississippi River are disappearing, and a good many of the mills are gone, and others will have to go. This is true all the way up and down the Mississippi River. The witness thinks the lumbermen have felt pretty well satisfied with the way they have been treated by the railroads. (550.)

655A—TR——12

INDEX OF REVIEW AND DIGEST.

TESTIMONY.

INDUSTRIAL COMMISSION.

TRANSPORTATION.

TOPICAL PLAN OF INQUIRY OF SUBCOMMISSION ON TRANSPORTATION.

PART I.—TRANSPORTATION BY LAND IN ITS RELATION TO LABOR EMPLOYED THEREIN.

CHARACTER OF DUTIES AND CLASSIFICATION OF EMPLOYEES OF RAILROADS AND OTHER CARRIERS BY LAND; THEIR QUALIFICATIONS.

WAGES OF EMPLOYEES.
  1. Terms and conditions of employment; rates of wages of different classes of employees; basis and stability thereof; reductions and deductions, and their causes; discharge and suspension and the reasons therefor; blacklisting discharged employees; compulsory performance of service under mandatory injunction; proceedings for contempt, to that end, when railroad is in the hands of a receiver; power of courts in such cases under recent decisions.
HOURS OF LABOR OF EMPLOYEES OF RAILROADS AND OTHER CARRIERS BY LAND.
  2. Usual hours of labor exacted of different classes of employees.
  3. Sunday labor and overtime; conditions under which required and compensation therefor; limitation thereon by State laws, and effect thereof on employees, carriers, and the public.
LIABILITY OF RAILROADS TO EMPLOYEES FOR INJURIES SUSTAINED BY THE LATTER IN PERFORMANCE OF DUTY.
  4. Extent of modification by statute of common-law rule as to negligence of fellow servants; legislation of the States thereon, and effect thereof; statutes authorizing persons dependent on employee to sue for damages when employee has been killed through negligence of railroad.
  5. To what extent has doctrine of risks contemplated by voluntarily engaging in a dangerous occupation been modified by statute and judicial decisions? In what States has this been done?
  6. Limited liability legislation as applicable to railway employees, its nature and effect.
  7. Inadequate or defective appliances.
PROVISION FOR SICK AND DISABLED EMPLOYEES.
  8. Aid and benefit features of employees' associations; conditions and extent of relief.
  9. Relief and aid to sick and disabled employees, by railroads and other carriers by land; conditions and extent thereof; its effect on relations of employer and employee.
SAFETY APPLIANCES ON RAILROADS.
  10. Automatic couplers, air-brakes, and hand-holds, on passenger and freight cars; percentage of freight cars so equipped; cost of such safety appliances on old and new cars; cause of delay by railroads in complying with requirement of act of Congress relating to safety appliances on freight cars.
  11. Effect of increased use of automatic couplers, air-brakes, and hand-holds on freight cars on number of casualties to railway employees.
  12. Other methods and devices for insuring safety of employees and passengers on railroads.
ASSOCIATIONS AND ORGANIZATIONS OF EMPLOYEES OF RAILWAYS AND OTHER CARRIERS BY LAND.
  13. Their nature, purposes, and effect; proportion of employees belonging to them; extent of their control of their members; their effect on employees who are not members of such organizations.

3

DISPUTES AND DIFFERENCES BETWEEN EMPLOYERS AND EMPLOYEES.

14. Usual subjects thereof.
15. Strikes, their causes; methods used in conducting them; their effects; their efficacy as a means of settling differences between railway employers and employees.
16. "Boycotts;" in what do they differ from strikes.
17. Conciliation, mediation, and arbitration, and other methods of composing differences between railway employers and employees; consideration of State and Federal laws providing for conciliation, mediation, and arbitration.
18. State and Federal laws designed to repress strikes; judicial construction thereof and decisions thereon; anti-trust law as affecting railway strikes; transportation United States mail; its effects on strikes.
19. Compulsory arbitration; arguments for and against.
20. Use of intoxicants by railway employees; to what extent prohibited by employers; effect of such prohibition; observance thereof.

RAILWAY METHODS IN RESPECT OF RATES, NEW BOND ISSUES, INCREASES OF CAPITAL STOCK AND CONSOLIDATION OF LINES, AS AFFECTING RAILWAY EMPLOYMENT AND RAILWAY WAGES.

21. Effects of rate wars and unrestrained rate competition upon railway employment and railway wages.
22. Effect of ticket brokerage upon railway employment and railway wages.
23. Effect of watering stock and unnecessary additions to bonded indebtedness upon railway employment and railway wages.
24. Effect of railway consolidations upon railway employment and railway wages.

PART II.—DIVISION A.—TRANSPORTATION BY LAND IN ITS RELATION TO THE PUBLIC.

IN RELATION TO PASSENGER TRAVEL.

25. Passenger rates; differences in different parts of the United States; causes and effects; local and through rates.
26. The practice of giving passes and reduced rates of fare to individuals; to whom, under what circumstances, and for what consideration are passes and reduced rates so granted by railway companies; effect of the practice on railway receipts; its effect on the traveling public; other effects thereof.
27. State laws prohibiting State officials from accepting or using passes; reasons for such laws; what States have enacted such laws; to what extent are they observed.
28. Advisability of effectually prohibiting the giving of such passes and reduced passenger rates to anyone; of limiting the giving of such special privileges to railway officials and employees.

TICKET BROKERAGE.

29. In what the practice consists; mileage books and excursion tickets; number of people engaged in the business; by whom carried on; effect on passenger travel, interstate and intrastate; to what extent is it supported or encouraged by railroads, and for what purpose.
30. State laws prohibiting it; what States have enacted such laws.
31. Arguments for and against the abolition of ticket brokerage as now conducted.

DIVISION B.—TRANSPORTATION BY LAND IN ITS RELATION TO THE CARRIAGE OF GOODS AND COMMODITIES.

UNJUST DISCRIMINATIONS AND UNDUE PREFERENCES BY RAILROADS.

32. Against persons; against places; against other railways; manner of making the same; rebates, concessions, commissions; lower relative rates as between places; lower relative rates as between connecting railways; long and short haul; its meaning; when higher rates for short haul justified; when not justified; "Chicago Belt Lines;" their operation, and effect on rates of transportation through Chicago to the Atlantic seaboard and to the West; the "Free Cartage" case; effect of decision of the Supreme Court of the United States in that case.
33. Effect of unjust discriminations and undue preferences on persons, places, and the public; how they affect the producer, the middleman, and the consumer.

INTERSTATE COMMERCE COMMISSION—Continued.

55. Its procedure in determining questions submitted to it; delay incident thereto; procedure in courts to review its decisions; defects therein and proposed remedies therefor.

56. English Railroad Commission; English laws against unreasonable rates, unjust discrimination and undue preferences; leading English court decisions on these questions.

GOVERNMENT OWNERSHIP OF LAND TRANSPORTATION.

57. Ownership and operation of street-car and suburban railways by munici- palities; its advantages and objections thereto.

58. Ownership and operation by the United States of railroads engaged in interstate commerce; arguments for and against it.

59. Consideration of other methods of ownership and operation of railroads proposed as beneficial to the public.

TELEGRAPH AND TELEPHONE LINES.

60. Cost per mile of constructing and operating such lines in this country; number of interstate lines in the United States, exclusive of those owned and operated for their own use by railways; their mileage; amount of stock per mile issued; amount of bonded debt per mile thereof; consideration for such stock and bonds; total capital; gross earnings; net earnings; interest on bonds; dividends on stock; annual amount devoted to construction, equipment, repair, and betterments; surplus, how disposed of; charters of various States; State taxation and supervision.

61. Schedule of rates; basis thereof; rates for similar service in Great Britain and on the Continent; cause of excessive rates in this country as com- pared with those in Great Britain and on the Continent.

62. Consideration of advisability of the United States controlling telegraph and telephone lines for the use of the public as part of the postal system of the country.

PART III.—DIVISION A.—TRANSPORTATION BY WATER,

IN ITS RELATION TO EMPLOYEES ON VESSELS ENGAGED IN COMMERCE.

63. Our navigation laws as affecting employees on vessels engaged in com- merce on the high seas; classes, manner, and terms of employment; treatment and provision for comfort and health on shipboard; disci- pline and penalties for its breach; redress of grievances at home and abroad; hospitals; sailor boarding houses; "crimps" and boarding mas- ters; wages, reductions, deductions, and forfeitures; when performing duty of stevedores; desertion, penalties therefor; discharge, at home and abroad; when vessel sold or wrecked in foreign country; inspection of American vessels at home and abroad; what restraint on the over- loading of vessels; consideration of general condition of our merchant sailors engaged in commerce on the high seas; abuses of and defects in system g   them; consideration of measures to correct them; proposed amendments to our navigation laws; foreign navigation laws; comparison with ours.

64. In its relation to employees in lake, river, and canal transportation.

DIVISION B.—TRANSPORTATION BY WATER IN RELATION TO THE PUBLIC.

VESSELS ENGAGED IN COMMERCE.

65. Proportion of American vessels engaged in our foreign commerce as com- pared with vessels under foreign flags so engaged; "lines" under our flag engaged in foreign commerce; "lines" under foreign flags so engaged; annual earnings of American vessels engaged in our foreign commerce; of foreign vessels engaged therein; "tramp" steamships; respects in which they differ from "liners;" relative cost of building, equipping, and running them; comparison of number of tramp steam- ships under American flag engaged in our foreign commerce with those of Great Britain, France, Germany, Russia, Italy, Holland, Sweden and Norway, and Spain.

66. Comparison of cost of building and equipping vessels for ocean commerce in this country with that of similar vessels in foreign countries; cost of operating them as compared with foreign vessels of similar character, comparison of wages of officers and crew of American vessels with those of foreign vessels; respects in which American shipowners are at a dis- advantage as compared with foreign shipowners.

VESSELS ENGAGED IN COMMERCE—Continued.

67. Forms and characters of aid and subsidy to foreign vessels; to American vessels; résumé of laws of foreign countries intended to develop their merchant marine; registry laws of the United States; their effect on shipbuilding and on shipowning in this country.

68. Laws and regulations of the United States relating to transportation of passengers and freight on the high seas; accommodations for and treatment of passengers, cabin and steerage; immigrants, and laws relating to them; defects in such laws and proposed amendments; inspection; observance of our laws by foreign vessels engaged in transportation of passengers and freight; effect of quarantine and health laws on our ocean commerce; vessels engaged in transportation of live stock on high seas; laws and regulations relating thereto.

69. Our coastwise commerce; rates per mile for passengers and freight as compared with rates for similar service under like conditions in coast trade of other countries; competition between railway and water transportation on the Atlantic, Pacific, and Gulf seaboards; comparison of rates coastwise, where there is railway competition, and rates foreign from our seaboard.

70. Through bills of lading and through passenger tickets to and from the interior of the United States, from and to foreign countries and domestic ports; immigrant tickets.

71. Our commerce on the Great Lakes; its tonnage and number of vessels as compared with tonnage and number of American vessels engaged in our ocean commerce; as compared with number and tonnage of such foreign vessels; closed season on the Great Lakes; effect of the closing of lake navigation on rates of transportation between the Mississippi Valley and the seaboard; importance as a factor in maintaining reasonable rates; efforts to control freight rates on the Great Lakes; methods employed to that end.

72. Our river commerce; its tonnage; causes of decline thereof; railway competition by steamboat and barge lines controlled by competing railways; methods employed in such competition; cutting rates and "freezing out" competing steamboat lines; ultimate effect thereof on river commerce and transportation rates; consideration of the question of public policy involved in such methods and of restraining legislation.

73. Our canal commerce; its tonnage; its decline and causes thereof; where competing with railway transportation its influence on rates.

WASHINGTON, D. C., *December 6, 1898.*

TESTIMONY OF MR. EDWARD A. MOSELEY,

Secretary of the Interstate Commerce Commission.

The commission met at 11 a. m., December 6, 1898, Vice-Chairman Phillips presiding. Mr. Edward A. Moseley, secretary of the Interstate Commerce Commission, testified. Mr. Phillips suggested that the witness be guided by the syllabus on transportation in giving his testimony.

Mr. MOSELEY. I desire to say that I am here in the capacity of an American citizen, who for many years has paid a good deal of attention to the relations between employer and employee, particularly in connection with railroad labor. I was at one time an officer in one of the largest labor organizations in this country, and have always taken a great interest in this subject. Then, as the secretary of the Interstate Commerce Commission, I have been brought into more or less intimate connection with the railroads and the relations which they bear to the public and to their employees, as well as to each other. It must be understood, however, that I do not in any manner represent the Interstate Commerce Commission, but I am here solely as a citizen whose whole heart is wrapped up in the subject of the relations between capital and labor and the proper position which they should occupy to each other. I therefore gladly make such suggestions as appear to me and which, I trust, will prove of interest to this commission. In doing so I am happy to follow the suggestion of Mr. Phillips, your chairman, whom I have long known as the friend of those interests which I desire to conserve so far as I can.

The first part of your "Topical plan of inquiry" relates to the "Character of duties and classification of employees of railroads and other carriers by land; their qualifications." First, regarding the wages of employees, I desire to pass that and come to the question of blacklisting discharged employees and compulsory performance of service under mandatory injunction.

Q. (By Mr. FARQUHAR.) Which section?—A. That is Part I, Section I, "Wages of employees." I do not now know of any demand by the employed that further legislation be had in regard to blacklisting in amendment of the law as it now stands. It forbids blacklisting. I allude to section 10 of the arbitration act of June 1, 1898.

After the "Chicago strike" there was a large number of employees thrown out of employment who have never been able to obtain employment again. It is alleged that these men would go to the railway managers and ask for certificates of good character to enable them to get employment elsewhere, but that the certificate obtained worked them harm rather than good, for by a method of writing the certificate or by use of certain watermarks, or other means, the paper of apparent recommendation proved to be notice to the person receiving it that the applicant was blacklisted; that there was a very large amount of this blacklisting done even where to all outward appearances strong letters of recommendation had been given. So much of a wrong had this become that when the arbitration act was enacted by the last Congress, approved June 1, 1898, in the tenth section, which is next to the last section, it is positively forbidden in any way to blacklist a man, and is made a misdemeanor to do so. I call the attention of the commission to this law. It is the act concerning carriers engaged in interstate commerce and their employees. I will read section 10:

"That any employer subject to the provisions of this act and any officer, agent, or receiver of such employer who shall require any employee, or any person seeking employment, as a condition of such employment, to enter into an agreement, either written or verbal, not to become or remain a member of any labor organization, corporation, association, or shall threaten any employee with loss of employment, or shall unjustly discriminate against any employee because of his membership in such labor corporation, association, or organization; or who shall require any employee, or any person seeking employment, as a condition of such employment, to enter into a contract whereby such employee or applicant for employment, shall agree to contribute to any fund for charitable, social, or beneficial purposes to release such employer from legal liabilities for any personal injury, by reason of any benefit received from such fund beyond the proportion of the benefit arising from the employer's contribution to such fund; or who shall, after having discharged an employee, attempt or conspire to prevent such employee from obtaining employment, or who shall, after the quitting of an employee, attempt or conspire to prevent such employee from obtaining employment, is hereby declared to be guilty of a misdemeanor, and, upon conviction thereof in any court of the United States of competent jurisdiction in the district in which such offense was committed, shall be punished for each offense by a fine of not less than one hundred and not more than one thousand dollars."

Blacklisting, of course, is one of those evils which is extremely difficult to meet—to make any law which is effective against the practice. If a person does not wish to employ a man, or wants to see that someone else does not employ him, the methods of doing so and preventing the applicant from gaining employment on other railroads are easily found, and it is very hard indeed to reach it by effective legislation. Congress has, however, put its stamp of disapproval on it and made it a misdemeanor, and I do not now know how to strengthen the law in this particular; still, I believe there is a necessity for at least making the attempt to stamp out blacklisting effectively, and I urge this commission to fully consider this subject with that end in view.

"COMPULSORY PERFORMANCE OF SERVICE UNDER MANDATORY INJUNCTION."

Some time ago an engineer in the service of the Lake Shore and Michigan Southern Railway was charged with contempt and punished. Lennon was a locomotive engineer in the service of the Lake Shore, and a member of the Brotherhood of Locomotive Engineers. The engineers of the Toledo and Ann Arbor line had gone out on a strike and the Brotherhood had requested its members on the Lake Shore not to haul the Ann Arbor cars. The Ann Arbor got an injunction against the Lake Shore and its employees, prohibiting them from refusing to haul its cars. Lennon refused to take a car from the Ann Arbor road, though ordered to do so. Judge Ricks ordered his arrest and found Lennon guilty of violating the injunction in refusing to haul such car, adjudged him to be in contempt, and fined him $50 and costs, or else remain in jail until the fine should be paid. Lennon took out a writ of habeas corpus, which was denied. He then appealed to the Supreme Court of the United States, which dismissed the appeal, holding that it had no appellate jurisdiction in the case. Then he went to the circuit court of appeals, which affirmed the decree of the circuit court, wherefrom he obtained a writ of certiorari from the Supreme Court, which affirmed the decision of the circuit court of appeals. Lennon staid in jail for some time, but finally paid his fine. Such "proceedings for contempt" ought to be fairly looked into, whether the road is in the hands of a receiver or not, as the question is one in which the railroad brotherhoods of the country are to-day very much interested. Such employees should not be punished for contempt for acts done outside of the purview of the court. This matter has proceeded to such an extreme that in a case on the Northern Pacific Railroad the judge of the court enjoined Mr. Arthur, chief executive officer of the locomotive engineers; Mr. Sargent, chief executive officer of the firemen; Mr. Clark, chief executive officer of the conductors; Mr. Wilkinson, chief executive officer of the trainmen; Mr. Ramsey, chief executive officer of the telegraphers, and Mr. Wilson, chief executive officer of the Switchmen's Mutual Aid Association—all heads of their various brotherhoods and hundreds of miles away—from in any way consulting with the members of their brotherhoods in regard to the question of wages, or the hours of labor, or in regard to any question which was then in dispute.

In this connection I will read a memorandum which I have upon injunctions to restrain strikes, boycotts, and conspiracies against interstate commerce.

"INJUNCTIONS TO RESTRAIN STRIKES, BOYCOTTS, AND CONSPIRACIES AGAINST INTERSTATE COMMERCE.

"Strikers refusing to work, and intimidating employees by threats or menaces to prevent them from continuing in the performance of their duties or employment, will be enjoined. (Lake Erie and W. R. Co. v. Bailey, 61 F. R., 494; Wick China Co. v. Brown, 164 Pa., 449; McCandless v. O'Brien, 21 Pitts. L. J. N. S., 435; Perkins v. Rogg, 28 Ohio L. J., 32; Murdock v. Walker, 152 Pa., 595; Cœur d'Alene Consol. Min. Co. v. Miners' Union, etc., 51 F. R., 260.)

"Where the request to quit was accompanied by the intimation that there will be bloodshed and riot, an injunction was allowed. (N. Y., L. S. and W. R. Co. v. Wenger, 17 Week. L. Bull., 306.)

"Interference with business by preventing the employment of sailors for a steamship owned by subjects of Great Britain will be enjoined on the ground of preventing multiplicity of suits and inadequacy of remedy at law; but it can not be granted under the antitrust law in a suit brought by any party except the United States Government. (Blindell v. Hagan, 54 F. R., 40; 56 F. R., 696.)

"An injunction was granted against displaying banners in front of plaintiff's premises calculated to injure his business and to deter workmen from entering his employ. (Sherry v. Perkins, 147 Mass., 212.)

"An injunction was granted against members of a labor union who boycotted plaintiffs because they refused to reinstate discharged employees. (Brace Bros. v. Evans, 5 Pa. Co. Ct. Rep., 163.)

"A boycott against a newspaper for publishing 'patent insides,' which reduced wages, was enjoined. (Barr v. Essex Trades Council (N. J.), 30 Atl. Rep., 881.)

"A boycott against a printing office for refusal to unionize the same and pay laborers union prices, was enjoined. (Casey v. Cinn. Typ. Union, 45 F. R., 135.)

"A court of chancery can enjoin false publications tending to injure trade. (Collard v. Marshall (1892), 1 Ch., 571.)

"Printing and publishing placards for the purpose of intimidating workmen, as a part of a scheme to prevent work and destroy the value of plaintiff's property, was enjoined. (Springhead Spinning Co. v. Riley, L. R. 6 Eq., 551.)

"An association devoting funds to support striking workmen was enjoined from misappropriating such funds. (Warburton v. Huddersfield Ind. Soc. (1892), 1 Q. B., 213.)

"An injunction against libelous circulars denouncing plaintiff's workmen as "scabs" will not be granted where it is not shown by the evidence whether employees were compelled to leave through moral suasion or by intimidation, or whether alienated customers derived their information from the circulars or from other sources. (Richter v. Journeyman Tailors' Union, 24 Ohio L. J., 189.)

"A court of equity will prevent a combination to interfere with or injure plaintiff's business by force, threats, intimidation, or menace of harm or violence. (Sweeny v. Torrence, 11 Pa. Co. Ct. Rep., 497.)

"Peaceable persuasion of employees to quit, and paying their expenses, and posting in the union labor halls the names of contributors to the funds, was not enjoined. (Rogers v. Evarts, 17 N. Y. Supp., 264.)

"If there is no irreparable injury and the strike is over, the dissension of the trial court in refusing to grant perpetual injunction will not be reviewed. (Reynolds v. Everett, 67 Hun., 294; 144 N. Y., 189.)

"Where plaintiff's hands were enticed away, but no coercion is shown to be committed or intended, an injunction was refused. (Johnston Harvester Co. v. Meinhardt, 9 Abb. N. C., 393; 24 Hun., 489.)

"Equity will not enjoin a blacklisting of employees. (Worthington v. Waring, 157 Mass., 421.)

"Indictment under United States Revised Statutes, sections 5399, 5440, making it criminal to obstruct justice in the Federal courts or to conspire to do so, not alleging that the defendants conspired to violate the injunction of the court which had been issued or to interfere with its proceedings and not alleging notice to the defendants of the pendency of proceedings or issue of injunction, was invalid, although it alleged a conspiracy to intimidate employers to discharge the employees. (Pettibone v. U. S., 148 U. S., 197.)

"An injunction was refused to prevent persecution of plaintiff's company by strikes, boycotts, or violence, or intimidation, as no threat to do any unlawful act was shown. (Mayer v. Journeyman S. C. Ass'n., 47 N. J. Eq., 519.)

"A conspiracy to destroy or injure the business of another, or doing violence to his property or property rights, where the injury is threatened and imminent and will become irreparable to the suitor, or intimidation of workmen, will be enjoined; but in this case an injunction was refused because the petition did not show that the damages would be irreparable, and failed to connect the defendants directly with the damages shown. (Longshore Pr. and Pub. Co. v. Howell, 26 Oreg., 527; 28 L. R. A., 464, the notes to which make up most of this brief.)

"Under the interstate commerce act, a combination or conspiracy of persons to hinder, obstruct, or interfere with the business or management of any interstate railroad company by threats, intimidation, force, or violence against such railroad companies or their employees in the discharge of their duties, will be enjoined. (Sou. Cal. R. Co. v. Rutherford, 62 F. R., 796; U. S. v. Workingmen's Amal. Council, 54 F. R., 994; 57 F. R., 85; U. S. v. Elliott, 62 F. R., 801; U. S. v. Agler, 62 F. R., 824; C. C. and Q. R. Co. v. C. C. R. and N. R. Co., 34 F. R., 481; Toledo A. A. and N. M. R. Co. v. Penn. Co., 54 F. R., 730, 746; Farmers' Loan and T. Co. v. N. P. R. Co., 60 F. R., 803; U. S. v. Debs, 64 F. R., 724; 158 U. S., 564.)

"Under the antitrust act, a conspiracy and combination to hinder the operation of railroads engaged in interstate commerce will be enjoined. (U. S. v. Elliott, supra; U. S. v. Agler, supra.)

"Prior to the United States antitrust act, the circuit courts of the United States had not equitable jurisdiction to prevent such acts. (U. S. v. Agler, supra, but see U. S. v. Debs, supra.)

"Arthur's disclaimer of knowledge of a prior injunction against the railroads and their employees was held immaterial to the question of the injunction against him. (Toledo, A. A. and N. M. R. Co. v. Penn. Co., 54 F. R., 730.)

"Employees will be restrained from enforcing rules of their labor union which injure the company or the public, and they need not be made parties defendant. (Toledo, A. A. and N. M. R. Co. v. Penn. Co., 54 F. R., 746; ex parte Lennon, 64 F. R., 320; 150 U. S., 393.)

"In the Debs Case, supra, an injunction was granted against the officers of the A. R. U., and all persons combining with them, to desist and refrain from hindering, obstructing, or stopping any of the business of certain railroads as common carriers of passengers, freight, or mails, and from entering the premises of said roads for any of said purposes, and from compelling or inducing, or attempting to compel or induce by threats, intimidation, persuasive force, or violence, any of the employees to refuse or fail to perform any of their duties as employees on any of the roads engaged in interstate commerce or carrying mails; and from compelling or inducing, or attempting to compel or induce by threats, intimidation, force, or violence any of said employees to leave the service, and from preventing any person by such means from entering the service, and from doing any act in furtherance of any conspiracy or combination to restrain the railroad companies or receivers in the control of the same, and from ordering, directing, aiding, assisting, or abetting any person to commit any of said acts. Interference by intimidation or force with receivers in the management of a railroad preventing employees from working is a contempt of court, and the order appointing a receiver in effect prohibits any disturbance of possession. (Secor v. Toledo, P. and W. R. Co., 7 Biss., 513; King v. Ohio and M. R. Co., 7 Biss., 529; Thomas v. C., N. O. and T. P. R. Co., 62 F. R., 803.)

"The order of the Brotherhood of Locomotive Engineers preventing the handling of freight of certain roads was contrary to the interstate commerce act. (Waterhouse v. Comer, 55 F. R., 149.)

"The United States anti-trust law does not apply to all attempts to restrain commerce between the States by strikes and boycotts, but applies to monopolies. (U. S. *v.* Patterson, 55 F. R., 605.)

"Any interference with the possession of receivers by attempts to control the management, or cripple the property, or hinder or obstruct its operation, or intimidate the employees or persons desirous of obtaining such employment; or any acts of violence directed against such receiver or the property or employees, in pursuance of a conspiracy to cripple the operation of the business intrusted to the receiver, is a contempt of the court appointing him and will render the parties liable. (Re Higgins, 27 F. R., 443; Frank *v.* Denver and R. G. R. Co., 23 F. R., 757; U. S. *v.* Kane, 23 F. R., 748; Arthur *v.* Oakes, 63 F. R., 310; Secor *v.* Tol., P. and W. R. Co., 7 Biss., 513; King *v.* O. and M. R. Co., 7 Biss., 529; Waterhouse *v.* Conner, 55 F. R., 149.)

"A request to engineers of a railroad not to act without the consent of the strikers was a threat and intimidation. (Re Doolittle, 23 F. R., 544.)

"A receiver of a railroad is not bound by an agreement, made before his appointment, between the railroad company and its employees, whereby the latter are not to be discharged except for cause, to be determined by arbitrators. (In re Seattle, L. S. and E. Ry. Co., 61 F. R., 541.)

"An injunction to prevent discharge because member of labor organization was denied. (Platt *v.* Phila. and R. R. R. Co., 65 F. R., 660.)

"A boycott by the members of trades unions or assemblies (which term, in law, implies a combination to inaugurate and maintain a general proscription of articles manufactured by the party against whom it is directed) is unlawful, and may be enjoined by a court of equity. (Oxley Stove Co. *v.* Coopers' Int. Union of N. A., 72 F. R., 695: Hopkins *v.* Oxley Stove Co. (same case on appeal), 83 F. R., 912.)

"A conspiracy to prevent the loading or unloading of a vessel, except by such labor as may be acceptable to defendants, may be enjoined, though no particular overt act against that particular vessel is alleged or proved. (Elder *v.* Whitesides, 72 F. R., 724.)

"An injunction will be granted where members of labor organizations conspire unlawfully to interfere with the management of the business of a corporation, and to compel the adoption of a particular scale of wages, by congregating riotously and in large numbers at and near the works of the corporations for the purpose of preventing persons, not members of said organizations, from entering the employ of the corporation or remaining therein, by intimidation, consisting in physical force or injury, actual or threatened, to person or property. The jurisdiction of equity is not ousted because the acts complained of may also be the subject of indictment. (Consolidated Steel and W. Co. *v.* Murray, 80 F. R., 811; Mackall *v.* Ratchford, 82 F. R., 41.

"A notice to the foreman of the shops of a railroad, requesting him to stay away from work until the strike was settled, 'But in no case are you to consider this an intimidation,' signed by the chairman of the committee of striking employees, is a threat and renders him guilty of contempt of court. (Re Wabash R. Co., 24 F. R., 217; U. S. *v.* Berry, 24 F. R., 780.)

"An injunction can not make men continue in the service, and an injunction against interference with the employees of a receiver can not make it any more of a contempt, as the law itself imposes an injunction, and injurious effects are caused by injunctions, creating the belief that it is not an offense to interfere if no injunction was issued. (Ames *v.* Union Pac. R. Co., 62 F. R., 7.)

"The marshal, without warrant, properly arrested a person interfering with the management of a railroad in the hands of a receiver by attempting to induce men to quit work, but as the prisoner was held in custody for a month without examination, he was released on habeas corpus. In this case there was an order of court directing the marshal to attack all persons interfering with the possession of the receiver. (Re Acker, 66 F. R., 290.)

"Telegraphers were enjoined from interference with property, operations, or employees of the receiver, and rules were issued against persons interfering. (Telegraphers *v.* Comer, unreported, but referred to in Waterhouse *v.* Comer, 55 F. R., 149.)

"Where the receiver refused an interchange of freight on account of a boycott by Brotherhood of Engineers, but rescinded his order or disclaimed all connection with the chief of the brotherhood, the petition for injunction was allowed to remain on file for future action, if necessary. (Beers *v.* Wabash, St. L. and P. R. Co., 84 F. R., 244.)

"On December 13, 1893, Judge Jenkins, of the United States circuit court, issued an injunction in the case of F. L. and T. Co. *v.* N. P. R. Co., supra,

restraining the employees of the Northern Pacific Railroad, about 12,000 in number, from 'combining and conspiring to quit, with or without notice, the service
of the receivers, with the object and intent of crippling the property in their custody or embarrassing the operation of the railroad, and from so quitting the service of said receivers, with or without notice, as to cripple the property or prevent
or hinder the operation of said railroad.' A second writ of injunction was issued
December 22, 1893, containing in addition a clause enjoining all persons from
'ordering, recommending, approving, or advising others to quit the service of the
receivers of the Northern Pacific Railroad Company on January 1, 1894, or at any
other time.' On mature consideration, however, this extraordinary clause was
withdrawn on petition of the principal labor organizations among the employees.
The court, however, refused to modify the original injunction forbidding the
employees from quitting the service of the receivers. An appeal was consequently carried to the United States circuit court of appeals, which, October 1,
1894, overruled the court below on the ground that an equity court should not
intervene to compel the effective performance of a contract. (See Arthur v.
Oakes, 63 F. R., 310.) Said Mr. Justice Harlan in that decision: 'It would be an
invasion of one's natural liberty to compel him to work for or to remain in the
personal service of another. One who is placed under such constraint is in a
condition of involuntary servitude, a condition which the supreme law of the
land declares shall not exist within the United States or in any place subject to
their jurisdiction. * * * In the absence of legislation to the contrary, the
right of one in the service of a quasi public corporation to withdraw therefrom at
such time as he sees fit, and the right of the managers of such a corporation to
discharge an employee from service whenever they see fit, must be deemed so far
absolute that no court of equity will compel him, against his will, to remain in
such service or actually perform the personal acts required in such employments,
or compel such managers, against their will, to keep a particular employee in
their service.' 'Whether organized labor has just grounds to declare a strike or
boycott is not a judicial question,' said Judge Caldwell in his able dissenting
opinion in the Oxley Stove Company Case, supra. 'These are labor's only
weapons, and they are lawful and legitimate weapons; and so long as in their
use there is no force or threats or violence, or trespass upon persons or property,
their use can not be restrained. Laborers are not wards of chancery. A court
of chancery has no more authority to interfere with labor organizations in the
conduct of their business than it has to interfere with the business of corporations
and trusts and other combinations of capital in the conduct of their business; and
in the case of a strike or a boycott, as long as each side is orderly and peaceful,
they must be permitted to terminate their struggle in their own way, without
extending to one party the adventitious aid of an injunction.'"
    I know of nothing more exasperating to the wage worker than the apparent
arbitrary action of the courts in the issuance of mandatory injunctions in this
class of cases and subsequent proceedings for contempt.
    This use of the injunction fills many of those who are deeply interested in the
welfare of their country with great alarm. It is a matter of the greatest surprise
to Englishmen to observe the way in which the power of the court is strained in
this respect. An injunction is never issued there without the greatest deliberation. In this country it seems to be had for the asking, particularly whenever an
employer desires to get the influence of the court thrown into the scale in his
favor when a dispute between himself and his workmen arises. Whatever warrant there may be for the Federal courts to interfere in disputes between the
carriers engaged in interstate commerce and their employees, it is straining power
for the Federal judges to interfere in those disputes which are simply between
those engaged in ordinary industrial pursuits and their employees. It is bringing the Federal judiciary into disrepute, and if something is not done to curb this
unjustifiable act on the part of some of the Federal judges it will surely bring
disaster to our institutions.
    In the first place, a railroad employer or manager, anticipating a difficulty
which is apparently about to take place, rushes to a friendly court. I want to
state just for a moment in regard to this Lennon case. It is stated that the judge
in this case was at his home in Cleveland and was summoned by telegraph; was
rushed through in the special car of the corporation to Toledo; went to the
offices of the railroad company, where the railroad officials presented their side of
the case to him behind the closed doors of the railroad corporation, and where
also he issued the injunction, and the first knowledge that the men had of the action
was when the injunction was served on them. They had no opportunity—there
was no chance for them to say a word, and there was no chance for them to
explain to the court. The court took the one side at once and threw its whole
influence to the railroad.

This commission will give the railroad employees, through their representatives, an opportunity to be heard, and they will convince you that this is a question which needs the most careful consideration on your part. This is a matter which concerns every wage worker in the country. Their representatives will fairly present this question to you. There ought to be a law prohibiting courts of the United States from enforcing the specific performance of contracts for personal service by writs of injunction. The following bill to to this effect has been suggested:

' A BILL to prohibit courts of the United States from enforcing the specific performance of contracts for personal service by writs of injunction or other legal proceedings.

" SECTION 1. *Be it enacted by the Senate and House of Representatives of the United States of America in Congress assembled,* That no judge of any court of the United States shall enforce or attempt to enforce the specific performance of any labor contract, or contract expressed or implied, for continuous personal service by the writ of injunction or any other legal process whatever: *Provided,* That the right of action at common law for damages for breach of such contracts is not hereby abridged."

Though since the passage of the arbitration bill of June, 1898, I seriously doubt if any Federal judge will ever undertake again to force men against their will by injunction.

I do not come here—neither will the railroad employees through their representatives come here—and say that there are not circumstances under which a railroad employee is just as much bound to continue his employment as is a pilot on board ship in a dangerous sea way. A railway engineer dissatisfied with the terms of his employment has no business to leave a train load of passengers out on a prairie. A freight engineer has no right to leave his train in a position where it endangers the lives of others. There is right and reason in all things. The railway employee recognizes that to a certain extent he is performing a public service, and to that extent he is a public servant; that the railroad is performing a public service and he, as a servant of the railroad, owes a duty to the public which those engaged in the ordinary industrial pursuits do not. The man engaged in the cotton factory, the man engaged in any ordinary vocation, can leave his employment at any time, at any hour, and in any way, and the public can not properly question his right to do that; but in the case of the railroad and the railroad employee the great overpowering third party, the public, has certain rights, and the railway employees recognize those rights. In that respect I think they differ from other organizations or employments. They stand on a different plane, occupy a different relation to the public; and as the general public has a right to demand from them certain service, they must have equal right to demand and expect from Congress such measures of protection as are warranted. If not provided for by the National Government they are practically without such protection. Questions concerning those engaged in the ordinary industrial pursuits are largely matters for the several States to deal with.

Before leaving this subject, I desire to call attention to the Royal Commission on Labor, whose investigations began May 1, 1891, and whose final report was submitted June, 1894, in two volumes, the majority report signed by nineteen and the minority by four commissioners. Their work is comprised in 65 blue books, 25 being taken up with the testimony of witnesses. In addition to these reports, the blue book contains separate statements of the individual views of certain members of the commission of much interest and value.

I will read the propositions stated by Sir Frederick Pollock in the minority report of the Royal Commission on Labor:

"Let us apply these principles (previously considered by Sir Frederick in his minority report) to some of the ordinary facts of trade disputes. I submit the following propositions as being fairly deducible:

"(1) Neither an arrangement for a strike, immediate or contingent, among workmen in any trade, nor an agreement for a lockout among masters, is an enforceable contract; but neither is in itself punishable or wrongful.

"(2) A strike (or lockout) begun without breach of any existing contract does not necessarily involve any wrongful act.

"(3) But if a strike is begun by stopping work in breach of an existing contract, the employer probably has a right of action against the promoters of a strike for procuring that breach of contract. A workman would have the same right against anyone who procured his employer to dismiss him in breach of existing terms, either individually or by way of general lockout. And generally whatever can be said of a workman's freedom to choose his employer may be said of an employer's freedom to choose his workmen.

"(4) Individual workmen are free to renew or not to renew their contracts, or to enter or not to enter into contracts with other employers, as they think fit. And all persons are free, if they think fit, to lay before workmen, individually or collectively, facts and reasons in favor of their doing or not doing any of these things. The like as to customers resorting or not resorting to any particular place of business or dealing with any individual trader.

"(5) But no one is free to deprive an employer of his workman's services, or of the custom of those who may deal with him, by violence or unlawful interference of any kind with person or property, nor by threats thereof. Any such act is a trespass against the employer as well as against the workman or customer intimidated. And the rule seems to extend to threats of doing harm by means of a breach of contract or other definite civil wrong.

"(6) An agreement not to work with or not to employ any particular class of persons (as a rule of a trades union not to work with nonunion men, or of an association of masters not to employ members of a particular union) is probably 'in restraint of trade' and not enforceable, but not wrongful.

"(7) Any of the acts above mentioned which is not wrongful in itself does not become wrongful.

"(a) Merely because done by a number of persons acting in concert; or

"(b) Merely because those persons give notice to an employer or other person concerned of their intention to do such acts.

"It seems, therefore, that an employer has not any civil right of action against, e. g., the officers of a trade union who threaten him with a strike of union hands (not involving violence or breach of contract), if he continues to employ nonunion men in general, or particular men objected to by the union.

"(8) It is not that interference with a man's business by persons having no definite interest of their own to serve thereby (for example, an agreement not to deal with a certain trader at all, or to prevent others from doing so) might not be held to be without just cause or excuse, and therefore an actionable wrong, even if it did not involve the committing, procuring, or threatening of any breach of the peace, or breach of contract, or other specific wrongful act.

"If any one thinks that the law laid down by the House of Lords does not sufficiently protect individual freedom of action, he may partly console himself reflecting on the obvious fact that, whatever the law may be, there will still be a thousand ways beyond the reach of legal process in which a majority in any trade or society can make it unpleasant for the minority to differ with them. Ultimately the rights of minorities can be secured only by securing general respect for every citizen's lawful freedom of action and discussion; and this must be the work of enlightened public opinion, and not of legal definitions; judgments and statutes, which embody, or ought to embody, the best wisdom and experience of the nation may do something to guide and form public opinion; they can not take its place.

"I am not aware of any existing legislation which, with regard to civil liability, could be held to affect the results of common-law principles.

"This statement concludes nothing as to the criminal law. Many civil wrongs (including some of those above mentioned) are certainly not criminal offenses. On the other hand, acts which are not a civil wrong to any definite person may be deemed so contrary to the public welfare that they are made a punishable offense. 'There are some forms of injury,' both civil and criminal, 'which can only be effected by the combination of many persons.'

"Things which are harmless or trifling when done by one or by a few may be a nuisance, or a danger to the public peace, and therefore criminal, when done and repeated by the multitude."

Sir Frederick, after making the foregoing summary of principles as related to the civil law, then proceeds to consider the bearing of the criminal law upon cases of strikes, lockouts, etc. (See Id., pp. 160,161.)

These reports, majority and minority, 1894, of above commission are most valuable, and should be in the library of this commission.

A very condensed epitome of some 240 pages, called the Labor Question, was printed shortly after the report in 1894 by T. G. Spyers, precis or special writer to the commission, covering their three years of investigation and summarizing the results. I also submit for your consideration some extracts from this epitome, with minutes of observation made in reading his very interesting summary of that important investigation.

TRADE UNIONISM AS RELATED TO AND CONNECTED WITH SOCIALISM.

Socialism may be defined as the blending of political and industrial functions. It contemplates the state becoming the sole landlord, the sole capitalist, and the sole employer of labor. It derives its strength from the political enfranchisement of the industrial class, which has had the effect of directing the action of the state to the solution of industrial problems.

Another force and influence connected with trade unionism is cooperation, or the association of workmen to become their own employers. Its success may be said to have originated with the establishment of the Rochdale Pioneer Society, in 1844. It now embraces no fewer than 1,624 societies, which have an aggregate capital of over £16,000,000, and do a trade of about £50,000,000 a year, at a net profit of nearly £5,000,000.

"The labor movement," says the author in summing up the foregoing considerations, "is a complex, genuine, human force, at once too vigorous to perish and too strong to be crushed. The problem, therefore, is to bring it into harmony with existing industrial conditions and to turn it from the abuses of industrial warfare to the uses of industrial peace." (Pages 1–10.)

"Collective bargaining" is a phrase invented to express the attitude of trade unionism and is said to be its very essence. Viewed internally its policy is "collectivism;" viewed externally its policy is "bargaining." Trade unionism does not allow its members to fight their battles individually and separately, but aims to focus the efforts of all upon a common object, and then as a "collective" body, as a unit, demand and "bargain" for a higher rate of wages or other concession from employers.

At the beginning of the century the "combination acts" expressly forbade a number of men from agreeing together to send in on the same day their notices to quit work. But these acts have been repealed. Even in England they could not stand against the force of public sentiment. Compare the spirit of such acts with the late decision of Mr. Justice Harlan, of the United States circuit court of appeals. The repeal of the oppressive acts and the interpretation of the law as laid down by Justice Harlan mark decided progress and give encouragement to trade unionism.

The evidence before the royal commission relating to the development, organization, and conduct of strikes was very full and interesting. The methods pursued by the trade unions were what are termed "picketing," that is, stationing men in the neighborhood of a place where a strike is going on to inform the workmen of the fact, collection of subscriptions for maintaining the strike, efforts to extend the strike over a larger and larger area, and consolidation of the federation.

The employers resorted in their methods to blacklisting, employing and organizing nonunionists, extension of the lockout over larger areas, and eviction.

All these means and methods are of course exactly parallel with the means and methods used in the late strikes and lockouts in the United States.

The conspiracy and protection of property act, now in force in England, while expressly declaring the legality of "picketing" for the purpose of giving information, forbids any person from intimidating or persistently following another to induce him to quit work, under penalty of imprisonment or fine. No doubt our own courts would sustain the principle involved in this law.

"One of the most interesting features of industrial politics," says the author, "is the way in which trade unions generally contrive to make their hold over their members effective. The most common device is to create a fund for the purpose of providing friendly society benefits, and to give to each member a direct personal interest in keeping up his connection with the organization. The success of this policy is evidenced by the fact that the unions that give the most benefits of this kind are at once the strongest and the *best able to command the confidence of the employers.*"

The last clause I have underscored to call attention to a fact that obtains in this country as well as in England. Our brotherhoods of locomotive engineers, of locomotive firemen, of trainmen, of conductors, it is not too much to say, command the respect and confidence of their employers largely by reason that the brotherhoods are drawn together by their benefit funds into a consolidated and well-organized body of moral, industrious, and self-respecting men. For, be it observed, temperance, sobriety, and moral character are, by brotherhood rules, made a condition precedent to membership and to enjoyment of benefit funds. (See these provisions set out in Sixth Annual Report of Interstate Commerce Commission, for 1892, p. 333.)

The author sums up as follows: "The essence of trade unionism is 'collective bargaining,' and 'collective bargaining' is made possible when the rival organizations of employers and employed, being imbued with a desire for industrial peace, survive the hostilities they originally came into existence to conduct and provide their representatives with definite and homogeneous constituencies." (Pages 11–31.)

Conciliation and arbitration.—The difficulty of obtaining suitable and competent arbitrators was shown by the evidence before the commission. Trade-unionists said that the clergy, judges, barristers, mayors, members of Parliament were objectionable. They either would not be possessed of the technical skill requisite, or they would not be disinterested. Disinterestedness and sympathy, as well as acquaintance with the technicalities involved in the dispute, are indispensable qualities for a successful arbitrator.

The main obstacle to compulsory State arbitration is the absence of a body of law on which decisions could be based.

Arbitration in trade disputes must be suffered to develop. It can not be manufactured and its growth can not be forced; and the author comes to the conclusion that compulsory State arbitration, in the absence of a body of law on which to base decisions, is impossible. Voluntary State arbitration which did not base its awards upon a knowledge of the traditions and customs of the trade and the district, would not be accepted. There must be found competent and disinterested arbitrators, well acquainted with the traditions and customs of the particular industry involved in the dispute, acquainted, too, with the practical work and technicalities of true industry. (Pages 32-47.)

The question of industrial remuneration is next considered.

Mr. Giffin put in evidence some interesting figures, showing the average annual income of the adult male laborer to be £60, and of laborers of every age and sex £48; and stated that of a total national income of £1,500,000,000 about £633,000,000 was appropriated to the manual laborers in the form of wages, as against £867,000,000 appropriated otherwise.

But a very large portion of the £867,000,000 represents wages other than the wages of manual labor; yet, notwithstanding this and other exceptions mentioned, the main statement may be taken as a rough and approximate showing of the relative income derived by the labor of England.

Thereupon follows a discussion of the question whether the rate of wages should be fixed by law—either specifically or by fixing a minimum price—and the author says that "the large majority of the representatives of all classes in the industrial world concurred in expressing emphatic disapproval of State action in fixing the rates of wages."

But although the workers desire the Government to do nothing toward fixing the rates of wages as a Government, they want it to do a great deal as an employer of labor. All the socialist and trade-union representatives agreed in thinking that the Government ought to lead rather than follow the market in determining the wages of its own employees; it should pay the full trade-union rates, and should take care that its contractors did the same. This point was brought very prominently forward by the socialists, who must have felt that the grievances of Government employees in regard to their low scale of wages constituted a standing argument against their favorite doctrine that industrial functions are better discharged by political than by purely industrial bodies.

Profit sharing is discussed in the light of the evidence adduced before the commission. This is a device for minimizing the fluctuations in the profits and wages themselves by throwing them upon a third fund created for that purpose, in which both parties, employer and employee, have an equal interest. Thus wages are paid at a fixed rate, and profits are also paid at a fixed rate, and what is left is divided between the wage and profit earners respectively.

It is plain that if the scheme is to work at all neither profits nor wages must be fixed so high as to leave nothing in the third fund to be divided. So much as to sharing the profits. But how about sharing the losses? Will the workmen share losses as well as profits? The fact is that the authors of such schemes have never provided any machinery by which losses are to be shared. Every system yet propounded presupposes an established and successful—profitable—business.

For these and other reasons, Mr. Giffen pointed out that profit sharing was unlikely to solve the whole problem of industrial remuneration.

There are at present a total number of 77 profit-sharing firms, the largest being the South Metropolitan Gas Company, which employs only nonunionist workers. The plan of this company in its details is merely a means of insuring against strikes and trade unionism. The workmen, however, support it, because the company pays the full rate of trade-union wages, and there is nothing to gain by refusing to accept the bonuses, if any.

It is clear that the natural attitude of trade unionism is hostile to profit sharing.

There is to be noted a certain kinship between profit sharing proper and the following methods of remuneration: Cooperative production, where the workers monopolize both profits and management: industrial partnership, where they share, but do not monopolize them; gain sharing, or associated piecework, where groups of men share in such portion only of the profits as is derived from economy of labor, and piecework proper, where individuals are paid according to the value of their work. All these are methods of payment by result, and therefore out of a different fund from the wages which are advanced before the result is achieved. For this reason it is the natural instinct of the trade unions to oppose them; the evidence given by their representatives before the commission proves that, in the absence of any special reason to the contrary, they generally do so. (Pages 48–66.)

The subject of "Hours of labor" comes next. It is asked, Whence comes the demand for a regulation of the hours of labor? The demand does not represent the unanimous voice of the workers. It does not proceed from any of the 6,000,000 nonunion workers, who, whether from principle or force of circumstances, do not demand any system of industrial regulation whatever. It does not proceed from all even of the 1,000,000 trade unionists. Thus, the representatives of the organizations of hand nail makers, of nut and bolt makers, of coopers, and of the Boot and Shoe Operatives' Union, informed the commission that neither employers nor employed could exist under any system of regulations that prevented them from making up in good times for their losses incurred in periods of depression. In some cases, moreover, where the union officials are in favor of regulating and reducing the hours, the members themselves are opposed to it. Thus, Mr. Trow, representing the Associated Iron and Steel Workers' Union of Great Britain, said that an attempt on the part of an employer, acting in conjunction with the union executive, to introduce an eight-hour day in his works, had recently failed, owing to the determined opposition of the men, who positively refused to work under the new arrangements. In most unions, finally, where there is a majority of members in favor of regulation, there is a strong minority against it. But in spite of this, however, it seems that the principle of depriving the individual of his full freedom of contract in settling his hours of labor is accepted by the bulk of the trade-unionists of the country.

Second, as Mr. Mann pointed out, such freedom is irrevocably lost already inasmuch as modern business establishments can be conducted only on the basis of uniformity in the men's hours of labor. The individual has practically no voice in determining how long he is to work; he must work either the same hours as his fellows or not work at all.

That is true, but the author omits to remark that a proper law prescribing the hours of labor would take into account the whole "modern business establishment," and would fix, say, an eight or ten hour day, applying to every workman therein.

One can not fail to notice that this want of unanimity among British workmen of which the author speaks shows conclusively how clearly, among English workmen, subsistence presses upon wages; for if large masses of men demand freedom to contract, say, for a fifteen or eighteen hour day of labor, they do so, in fact, under compulsion of hunger or the fear of it. Does such a sentiment obtain in the United States? Certainly not.

The commission seem to approve of the general plan of empowering the local authorities of each district within their respective jurisdictions to make provision for regulating the hours of and portion of a trade within such jurisdiction on petition of a majority of the workers concerned. (Pages 67–84.)

"The employers' liability act" of 1893 anticipated, in some degree, the report of the commission upon this branch of its inquiry.

According to the common law, the liability of masters with respect to the personal safety of their servants was considered to arise solely from the terms of the contract of service. And, in the absence of express provisions to the contrary, every such contract was held to imply an undertaking on the part of the master to exercise due care to associate his servants with competent persons as mates and superiors. But here the master's responsibility was held to cease. Provided that he had exercised due care in the selection of the members of his staff, he was not held liable for the results of their subsequent actions toward one another. The absence of such liability was expressed in positive language in the well-settled doctrine of "Common employment" and of "Fellow-servants."

The extension of employers' liability to cases of pure accident is supported on the ground that, inasmuch as somebody must suffer, and the work that occasioned the accident was for the benefit of the employer, it is more just for the employer to suffer than the worker. The pleas of acquiescence and contributory negligence are of a quibbling nature and are provable on such flimsy grounds as to be a source of great injustice.

Various modifications of the law, objections to and arguments in favor of the law, are considered; also the practice of "contracting out;" that is to say, entering into an agreement whereby the workman renounces the rights conferred on him by the act, and often his common-law rights also, to be indemnified for injury. (Pages 85–100.)

" Factory acts" were investigated and considered. These acts relate to sanitation, safety and accidents, methods of paying employees, "sweating," employment of women, "young persons," and children, etc., and upward of sixty amendments were proposed by witnesses. (Pages 101–125.)

In Chapter V the socialistic questions are passed in review: Government employment as a substitute for private employment; nationalization of mines, railways, and canals; municipalization of land, water, and gas supplies, tramways, dwelling houses, hospitals, docks, factories and workshops, etc.—in fact, the whole brood and spawn of notions and isms fathered by all the dreamers abroad, from Fourier to Karl Marx, and from Henry George and Bellamy to Peffer, at home.

The extension of the direct functions of the State to the various industrial functions is advocated on two distinct grounds: (1) That employment by purely industrial firms is inferior; and (2) that it is insufficient.

To make the State the sole employer of labor, the sole landlord, and the sole capitalist is the ultimate good of the socialist; and as a step toward the attainment of that good witnesses representing these ideas informed the commission that they desired to organize all local industries under municipal and county authorities. They even considered that the time had come when the State should enter into possession of all mines, with a view to intrusting their management to the county councils and confiscating the mining royalties; should buy out the railroad and canal companies, with a view to managing them directly through a public department. Further than that, they believed that the more wealthy municipalities, at least, should at once proceed to purchase the land in the towns and suburbs for the letting of small holdings to laborers; to buy out the water, gas, and street railroad or tramway companies; to build artisans' dwellings; to entirely support and control the hospitals; to purchase and administer all docks, and to start factories and workshops for doing the work which they would otherwise give to contractors.

In relation to Government ownership and control of railroads, Mr. Mann testified that the State, "instead of consulting the interests of a body of shareholders, should aid both at making traveling expenses as cheap as possible, and also at releasing railway employees from the long hours and other hardships which they are at present called upon to endure."

Mr. Webb's evidence was to the same effect.

Mr. Hyndman expressed himself as follows: "The first industry that the State should take over is the railways. They are the great highways of the country, but they have been converted by capitalist Houses of Commons in the past from being worked in the interest of the community to being worked in those of shareholders and directors. The cost of the acquisition by the State of this vast property would probably amount to about £1,100,000,000, but the money would be well spent. On becoming possessed of the means of transport the State should at once proceed to reduce its cost. The New York Central Railway, for example, compares very favorably in this respect with the London and Northwestern. During 1891 the average train loads on the former line were 250 tons, and the working expenses 285 pence per ton per mile; whereas on the latter the average train loads were only 65 tons, while the working expenses amounted to 658 pence per ton per mile. Yet the New York Central pays higher wages than the London and Northwestern, and at the same time charges less than one-third as much for its fares."

Yes, true; but the witness forgot to observe that the New York Central is not a Government-owned railway, and that the low rates are the natural result of competition.

" The worker's sole object," says the author, " is to get more wages for less work. The socialist may prove that State employment ought, logically, to enable him to get what he wants. But will it? Or, rather, since the State is already a very large employer of labor, does it? A review of the large portion of the evidence that related to the employees of the Government will enable the reader to supply the answer."

The evidence referred to, given by the socialists themselves, is a curious jumble and medley of facts unrelated to the conclusions drawn and openly contradicting their own theories, as the author, in his running criticism, abundantly shows.

The author proceeds to review the evidence touching the various kinds of "municipal ownership" as proposed by the socialists.

As to General Government ownership and control of industries the discussion is endless, both in England and in this country. In regard to Government ownership of railroads in the United States the discussion ought to be concluded, at least for the present, if facts are to govern the decision.

Note, for example, a statement recently prepared by the Interstate Commerce Commission, in compliance with a resolution of the Senate and submitted August 27, 1894.

"The freight rates," says this statement (page 7), "in the United States are, in general terms, only five-eighths of those charged on the Continent of Europe and a little less than one-half of those which prevail in Great Britain." As shown elsewhere in this statement, the railways on the Continent of Europe are largely owned and operated by Government. In Belgium, 71.81 per cent of the railway mileage is both owned and operated by the Government; in Denmark, 76.96 per cent so owned and operated; in France, 16.89 per cent; in Norway, 95.67 per cent; in Portugal, 37.86 per cent; in Prussia, including Finland, 50.75 per cent; in Sweden, 33.69 per cent; while in Austria-Hungary, 39.98 per cent of the mileage is owned and 73.35 per cent operated by the Government; and in Germany, 88.42 per cent is owned and 89.52 per cent is operated by the Government. (Page 6.)

See in this statement a mass of information compiled under "Views of various writers." (Page 9 et seq.)

The unemployed.—How can employment be provided was another question investigated by the commission. A wide diversity of views was expressed by the witnesses, some advocating the establishment of a national control labor bureau, others the encouragement of agriculture, others the formation of labor colonies, etc. (Pages 150–174.)

Mr. John Burns, the prominent labor leader, urged the Government to utilize the 18,000 offices as employment bureaus—a sample of the general socialistic tendency so prone to look to the Government in every stress and emengency. (See his article in Nineteenth Century for December, 1892.)

There is little in this part of the testimony that is relevant to conditions existing in the United States.

Some special subjects—mines and quarries, transport trades, agriculture, labor departments, and labor councils—are reviewed, and we come finally to the—

Recommendations of the commission.—As the result of its inquiries the commission have issued a blue book, containing two principal reports, one signed by 19 and the other by 4 of its members, and the recommendations contained in these reports may be briefly summarized as follows:

With reference to strikes and lockouts, the majority of the commission recommend an amendment to section 7 of the "Conspiracy and protection of property act" of 1875, relating to "picketing," so as to read, "uses or threatens to use violence to such other person," instead of "uses violence to or intimidates such other person."

As to arbitration, the majority desire to empower municipal and county councils to establish industrial courts to decide questions arising out of existing contracts or trade customs; to give one of the central government departments an adequate staff, with adequate means to procure, record, and circulate information relating to the work of voluntary conciliation boards, and, by advice and assistance, to promote their more rapid and universal establishment; and to give a public department, on receipt of a sufficient application from the parties interested or from local conciliation boards, power to appoint a suitable person to act as arbitrator, either alone or in conjunction with local boards or with assessors appointed by the employers and workmen concerned.

With reference to hours of labor, the majority propose to give a secretary of state power to regulate the hours of labor in any industry which he may certify to be, in his opinion, dangerous or injurious to health. Such orders they consider would be final if protected persons—i. e., women, young persons, and children are concerned—but as regards adult males, the orders should lie for a certain time upon the tables of both Houses of Parliament before becoming law.

A minority of the commission refer to employers' liability, and declare that the bill passed by the House of Commons, but rejected by the House of Lords, in 1893 embodied the reforms which they were disposed to recommend. They say that they are utterly opposed to any wage-earner being allowed to "contract out" in return for some individual advantage—"a privilege contrary, as they assert, to the whole principle of our industrial legislation."

It would seem that the majority of the commission were silent upon the above subject.

Upon the factory act, etc., the majority express the opinion that an act should be passed compelling every owner of workshops to obtain a certificate of the fitness of his premises and of the workshops of outworkers to be used for industrial purposes, especially in the case of manufacturers of clothing, books, and cheap furniture, and in case of bakehouses and laundries. They also recommended that young persons be prohibited from working overtime in certain trades.

With reference to state and municipal employment the minority recommended that all public bodies giving employment should, in explicit and widely advertised notice, adopt the eight-hour day; trade-union conditions and a minimum wage of 21s. per week; the express binding of public contractors, where such are employed, to adopt the same conditions; the establishment of a dock and harbor board composed of representatives of the London county council, the town council of West-ham, and other public bodies concerned, of the shipowners and of the dock laborers, with   to take over and administer the dock and wharves below London Bridge, etc. power

The majority would seem to have made no recommendation upon this subject.

With reference to the unemployed, the majority consider that public authorities should hold overwork, needed but not urgent, with a view to furnishing employment in times of depression. The minority, on the other hand, recommend the undertaking of public works of a useful character, full wages being paid to the employed; the experimental establishment of labor colonies, and the grant of old-age pensions.

In the matter of mines the minority recommend the passage of an eight-hour law and the increase of the inspection force by the addition of practical working miners or miners' agents.

Upon this subject no recommendation of the majority appears.

As to transport trades, the majority recommend the amendment of the law, so that the wives of seamen may receive their husbands' pay fortnightly to the extent of one-half the pay due; the minority recommending, among other things, a weekly payment of two-thirds the pay due.

With reference to agriculture, the minority recommended Parliament to confer upon parish councils in Great Britain the same power of providing cottages as is possessed by boards of guardians in Ireland and by town councils throughout the Kingdom, and to make compulsory the laborers' (Ireland) act of 1881.

The majority are silent upon this topic.

Finally, touching the functions of the labor department, the majority recommended the engagement, under the department's direction, of a staff of skilled investigators to inquire into the conditions of labor and the formation of a census of occupations; the minority, on the other hand, favoring the foundation of a new department with many additional and enlarged functions.

"*The liability of railroads to employees for injuries sustained by the latter in the performance of duty*" and the "extent of the modification by statute of common-law rule as to the negligence of fellow-servants; legislation of States thereon and the effect thereof, etc." Upon this point I will preface my remarks by this statement: that so far as railroad employees are concerned there is hardly a case in which they are interested, suit for damages or any other matter, which does not ultimately reach the Federal courts, and if the Congress of the United States does not in some way undertake to legislate in regard to the matter or to control it, the existing state of affairs will continue, which is that in almost every court of the United States—Federal courts of the United States—there seems to be a different rule; there is no uniformity whatever upon the subject.

Hours of labor of employees of railroads and other carriers is not a subject upon which I care to dwell. That will be done by those representatives of labor who are thoroughly informed upon the subject. I desire, however, in this connection, to call your attention to section 9 of the arbitration act, as follows:

"Sec. 9. That whenever receivers appointed by Federal courts are in the possession and control of railroads, the employees upon such railroads shall have the right to be heard in such courts upon all questions affecting the terms and conditions of their employment, through the officers and representatives of their associations, whether incorporated or unincorporated, and no reduction of wages shall be made by such receivers without the authority of the court therefor upon notice to such employees, said notice to be not less than twenty days before the hearing upon the receivers' petition or application, and to be posted upon all customary bulletin boards along or upon the railway operated by such receiver or receivers."

I have undertaken to compile a statement as to the present condition of the law, or the interpretation which has been made of the law in regard to the liability of the employer, particularly for acts done by a fellow-servant, also by defective appliances. I spent a good deal of time in investigating this subject, and I am very glad to furnish the Commission with the following statement:

AUTHORITIES UPON THE LAW OF DAMAGES CAUSED FROM INJURIES RECEIVED (1) BY NEGLIGENCE OF A FELLOW-SERVANT AND (2) BY DEFECTIVE APPLIANCES.

1. *The negligence of a fellow-servant.*—To constitute fellow-laborers within the meaning of the doctrine which protects the master from responsibility for injuries sustained by one servant through the wrongful act or carelessness of another, it

is not necessary that the servant causing and the servant sustaining the injury shall both be engaged in precisely the same, or even similar acts, nor need their work be the same. The negligent servant may be superior to the injured servant, in his grade of employment. (Bartonshill Coal Co. *v.* Reid, 3 Macq., 295; Blake *v.* Me. Cent. R. Co., 67 Me., 60; Lawley *v.* A. R. R. Co., 62 Me., 463; Albro *v.* Agawam Can. Co., 6 Cush., 75; Thayer *v.* St. L. A., etc., R. Co., 22 Ind., 26; Hoinagle *v.* N. Y. C. and H. R. Co., 55 N. Y., 608; Malone *v.* Hathaway, 64 N. Y., 5; Peterson *v.* Whitebreast C. and M. Co., 5 Iowa, 673; McLean *v.* Blue Point Gravel M. Co., 51 Cal., 255; Collier *v.* Steinhart, 51 Cal., 116; O'Conner *v.* Roberts, 120 Mass., 227; Zeigler *v.* Day, 123 Mass., 152; Shanck *v.* N. C. R. Co., 25 Md., 462; Brown *v.* Maxwell, 6 Hill, 592.)

A common laborer conveyed to and from his labor by the railroad company employing him is a coemployee of those who have charge of the train conveying him. (Kan. Pac. R. Co. *v.* Salmon, 11 Kan., 83; Gillshannon *v.* Stony Brook R. Co., 10 Cush., 298; Seaver *v.* B. and M. R. Co., 14 Gray, 466; Tunney *v.* Midland R. Co., 1 L. R. C. P., 291; Russell *v.* Hudson R. Co., 17 N. Y., 134.)

A fellow-servant is anyone who serves and is controlled by the same master. Common employment is service of such kind that, in the exercise of ordinary sagacity, all who engage in it may be able to foresee when accepting it that, through the carelessness of fellow-servants, it may probably expose them to injury. (McAndrews *v.* Burns, 30 N. J. L., 117.)

A proper test is, whether the negligence of one servant was likely to inflict injury on another. (Valtez *v.* O. and M. R. Co., 85 Ill., 500; C. and A. R. Co. *v.* Murphy, 53 Ill., 336.)

In Illinois it is held that when servants are not associated together in the discharge of their duties, where their employment does not require cooperation, and does not result in mutual contact or bring them together in such relation that they may exercise upon each other an influence promotive of safety or caution, the reason of the rule making those in different departments coemployees does not apply. (C. and N. W. R. Co. *v.* Sevett, 45 Ill., 197; Ryan *v.* C. and N. W. R. Co., 60 Ill., 171; T. W. and W. R. Co. *v.* O'Conner, 77 Ill., 391; C. and N. W. R. Co. *v.* Moranda, 93 Ill., 302.)

A carpenter working as such for a railway company, while being conveyed to or from his work, is not a fellow-servant of the employees running the train or repairing the track. (O'Donnell *v.* Allegheny V. R. Co., 59 Pa. St., 239.)

A conductor being conveyed on his employers' railroad, under instructions to proceed to a certain point and there take charge of a train, is a fellow-servant of those who have the management of the cars in which he is riding. (Manville *v.* C. and T. R. Co., 11 Ohio St., 417.)

If the parties are subject to the same general control and the employment is a common one, they are coservants, although engaged in separate and distinct departments of the service. (Ohio and M. R. Co. *v.* Hammersley, 28 Ind., 371; Col. and Ind. Cent. R. Co. *v.* Arnold, 31 Ind., 174; Slattery *v.* T. and W. R. Co., 23 Ind., 81; Whaalan *v.* M. R. and L. E. R. Co. 8 Ohio St., 249; Ry. Co. *v.* Lewis, 33 Oh. St., 196; Hodgkins *v.* Eastern R. Co. 119 Mass., 419; Foster *v.* Minn. Cent. R. Co., 14 Minn., 360; Coon *v.* Syracuse and U. R. Co., 5 N. Y., 492; Banlec *v.* N. Y. and H. R. Co., 59 N. Y., 356; Sammon *v.* N. Y. and H. R. Co. 62 N. Y., 251; Kielley *v.* Belcher S. M. Co., 3 Sany., 500; Cooper *v.* M. and P. D. C. R. Co., 23 Wis., 668; C. and A. R. Co. *v.* Murphy, 53 Ill., 336; St. L. and S. E. R. Co. *v.* Britz, 72 Ill., 256.)

Where one railway company runs trains on the track of another the servants of either company are not coservants of the servants of the other. (Smith *v.* N. Y. and H. R. Co., 19 N. Y., 127; Carroll *v.* M. V. R. Co., 13 Minn., 30; N. and C. R. Co. *v.* Carroll, 6 Heisk, 347; Sawyer *v.* R. and B. R. Co., 27 Vt., 370; C. R. R. Co. *v.* Armstrong, 49 Pa. St., 186.)

Servants of subcontractor building bridges on line of railway are not coservants of those operating the road and managing trains. (Donaldson *v.* Miss. and Mo. R. Co., 18 Iowa, 280.)

Servants of a contractor and those of a subcontractor are not coservants. (Goodfellow *v.* B. H. and E. R. Co., 106 Mass., 461; Corley *v.* Harris, 11 Allen, 113; Abrahams *v.* Reynolds, 5 H. and N., 142; Murphy *v.* Corolli, 3 H. and C., 462; Riley *v.* State L. S. S. Co., 29 La. Am., 791; Svenson *v.* S. S. Co., 57 N. Y., 108; Young *v.* N. Y. C. R. Co., 30 Barb., 229; Murray *v.* Currie, 6 L. R. C. P., 24; Hunt *v.* Pa. R. Co., 51 Pa. St., 475; Hass *v.* Phila. and S. M. S. Co., 88 Pa. St., 269.)

Engineers and brakemen are in the same class or line of employment and fellow-servants. (L. and N. R. Co. *v.* Robinson, 4 Bush, 507; Sherman *v.* Roch. and S. R. Co., 17 N. Y., 153.)

So are a brakeman and a switch tender. (Slattery *v.* T. and W. R. Co., 23 Ind., 81.)

So are a car repairer and an engine driver having charge of a switch engine. (C. and A. R. Co. v. Murphy, 53 Ill., 336.)

So are laborers on a construction train and the conductor of the same having charge of them. (C. and A. R. Co. v. Keefe, 47 Ill., 108.)

So is a person employed to couple cars and the engineer and conductor having charge of them. (Wilson v. Madison, etc., R. Co., 18 Ind., 226.)

So are the engineer of a general train and the hands employed in loading and unloading. (Ohio and Miss. R. Co. v. Tindall, 13 Ind., 366; contra, Dobbin v. R. and D. R. Co., 81 N. C., 446.)

So are the master machinist having charge of the machinery and control of the engineers and firemen on the railroad. (Fort v. M. Pac. R. Co., 2 Dill., 259.)

So are a trackman to follow passenger trains in a hand car and see that the track is in order and the managers of the train. (Coon v. S. and V. R. Co., 5 N. Y., 492.)

So are those running a passenger train and a laborer employed to gravel new and unfinished track. (Boldt v. N. Y. C. and H. R. R. Co., 18 N. Y., 432.)

Unless they are subject to the same general control, the fact that they are engaged in the same common pursuit does not make them coservants. (Svenson v. S. S. Co., 57 N. Y., 108; Abrahams v. Reynolds, 5 H. and N., 142.)

An express agent in the employ of an express company is not a coemployee of the train hands on the train on which he travels. (Yeomans v. C. C. S. Nav. Co., 44 Cal., 71.)

At common law, the employer is not liable for damages for injuries caused to an employee by his fellow-servant. Statutes of States seek to define what is a fellow-servant and to limit the class. Thus, at common law, the engineer and fireman of a locomotive engine are fellow-servants, and their common employer, the railroad company, is not liable to either for the negligence of the other.

So, at common law, a car inspector is a fellow-servant with a freight brakeman and therefore the common employer is not liable to the brakeman for the negligent act of the the inspector. (See Reno on "Employer's liability acts," p. 113.)

Recovery from injuries from negligence of coservants is only precluded as against the common employer; the rule does not apply as to strangers. (Busch v. Buffalo C. R. Co., 29 Hun., 112.)

Where the owners of two steamboats agree to divide profits at the end of the season they are partners, but the crew of either boat are not fellow-servants of the crew of the other. (Connolly v. Davidson, 15 Minn., 519.)

Roadmaster having charge of repairs to a culvert is a coservant with the workmen repairing same. (Lawley v. Androscoggin R. Co., 62 Me., 463.)

A train hand is not a fellow-servant of a person who was engineer, conductor, superintendent, and master of a gravel and material train, and had entire charge of that branch of the business on a section, with power to employ and discharge men. (Dobbin v. R. and D. R. Co., 81 N. C., 446.)

When the servant, by whose negligence other servants of the common employer have received injury, is the alter ego of the master and to whom everything has been left, his negligence is the negligence of the employer, for which the latter is liable. (Malone v. Hathaway, 64 N. Y., 5; Corcoran v. Holbrook, 59 N. Y., 517; Murphy v. Smith, 19 C. B. N. S., 361; Laving v. N. Y. C. and H. R. R. Co., 49 N. Y., 521; Siegel v. Schantz, 2 T. and C. (U. Y.), 353; Wright v. N. Y. C. R. Co., 28 Barb., 80; Flike v. B. and A. R. Co., 53 N. Y., 551; Brothers v. Carter, 52 Mo., 373; Allen v. New Gas Co., 1 L. R. Ex. D., 251; Grizzle v. Frost, 3 F. and F., 622; Munson v. Oriental Pr. Wks., 11 R. I., 187; Brickner v. R. R. Co., 46 N. Y., 672; Brabbitts v. R. R. Co., 38 Wis., 289; Tarlant v. Webb, 18 C. B., 797; Ford v. Fitchburg R. Co., 110 Mass., 240; Kelly v. Norcross, 121 Mass., 508; also see Hough v. Tex. and Pac. R. Co., 100 U. S., 213; especially note in Law Ed., 612.)

An engineer on one train is a fellow-servant of a conductor of another train on the same road. (Oakes v. Mase, 165 U. S., 363.)

A conductor and hands on a work train and a section foreman in charge of a hand car are fellow-servants of a laborer on the hand car under the orders of such foreman when, through their negligence, he is injured by a collision of the train with the hand car. (Martin v. A., T. and S. F. R. Co., 166 U. S., 339.)

A railroad company is not required to adopt extraordinary tests for discovering defects in a locomotive boiler or any of its machinery, and the burden of proof is on an employee to show that the injury received was caused by the master's negligence. (Tex. and Pac. Ry. Co. v. Barrett, 166 U. S., 617.)

A master is responsible to servant for carefulness and competency of coservants. (Neb. Ry. Co. v. McDaniels, 107 U. S., 454; 27 Law Ed., 605; note to Baugh case, 37 Law Ed., 773.)

A brakeman on a regular train of a railroad and the conductor of a wild train on the same road are fellow-servants, and the railroad company is not responsible for injuries happening to the former by reason of a collision of the two trains. (Mo. Pac. R. R. Co. *v.* Poirier, 167 U. S., 48.)

The law of Kansas making a railroad company liable to an employee for the negligence or mismanagement of other employees of the same company is not in conflict with the fourteenth amendment to the Constitution. (Mo. Pac. Ry. Co. *v.* Mackey, 127 U. S., 205.)

The courts have declared the following fellow-servants:

A freight-train engineer and a yard clerk. (N. Y. and N. E. R. Co. *v.* Hyde, 56 Fed. Rep., 188.)

One who takes the number of each car and locomotive engineer. (Beuhring *v.* C. and O. R. Co., 37 W. Va., 502.)

A railroad fireman of one train and the engineer and fireman of another train. (Cole *v.* No. Cent. R. Co., 12 Pa. Co. Ct., 573; Enright *v.* T., A. A. and N. M. R. Co., 93 Mich., 409.)

A common day laborer and brakeman and engineer. (Mo. Pac. R. Co. *v.* Hawbly, 154 U. S., 349; 38 Law Ed., 1009, and many cases cited in footnote.)

A railroad engineer is not a fellow-servant of one who is in the exclusive employ of a coal company. (Cent. R. of N. J. *v.* Stoermer, 51 Fed. Rep., 518.)

A gripman on a cable car and the crew of a wrecking train are not fellow-servants. (West Chicago S. R. Co. *v.* Dwyer, 57 Ill. App., 440.)

Some more cases as to who are fellow-servants are collected in a footnote to Cent. R. R. Co. *v.* Keegan, 160 U. S., 259; 40 Law Ed., 418. Also footnote to B. and O. R. Co. *v.* Baugh, 37 Law Ed., p. 773.)

The engineer and fireman of a locomotive running alone and without any train attached are fellow-servants of the railroad company. (B. and O. R. R. Co. *v.* Baugh, 149 U. S., 368. See extensive notes on Iowa and Miss. employee's liability act in 9 Am. and Eng. R. Cas. (U. S.), 9 and 97.)

Damages received by a laborer in a roundhouse through the negligence of an engineer in blowing down the engine can not be recovered under the Massachusetts statute. (Perry *v.* Old Colony R. R. Co., 41 N. E. Rep., 289.)

A car cleaner engaged inside a passenger coach on a side track; another coach was kicked against it at an unusual rate of speed by a switching crew; damages awarded for injury done to such car cleaner. (Mitchell *v.* N. P. R. R. Co., 70 Fed. Rep., 15.)

The constitutional provision of Mississippi abrogating assumption of risk theory does not license recklessness or carelessness by the employees and give them a claim to compensation for injuries thus suffered. (Buckner *v.* R. and D. R. R. Co., 18 So. Rep., 449.

A car repairer working in a separate yard from a "hostler" is not a fellow-servant of such hostler, nor of the switchman in such other yard, particularly while on a car under orders to proceed to another place and assist in repairing damages caused by a wreck. (San Antonio and A. P. Ry. Co. *v.* Keller, 32 S. W. Rep., 847.)

A wiper in a roundhouse who was injured while assisting in coaling an engine by its being negligently removed by a co-employee can recover damages, and the receiver of the railway company is within the provisions of the Minnesota "fellow-servant act." (Mikkelson *v.* Truesdale, 65 N. W. Rep., 260.)

Both the conductor and engineer of a train are the superiors of a brakeman on the same train, and the railroad company is liable for injuries sustained by such brakeman in a collision caused by the negligence of the conductor in running his train in a depot yard at night without a sufficient headlight. (Crisswell *v.* Montana Central Ry. Co., 42 Pac. Rep., 767.)

A hostler, whose duty it is to bring the engines into the roundhouse and take them out when necessary, and a boiler washer, whose duty it is to clean the boilers ot the engine so as to fit them for further service, are, as a matter of law, fellow-servants. (M. K. and T. Ry. Co. *v.* Whittaker, 33 S. W. Rep., 716.)

The employer's act of Alabama makes a carrier liable for negligence of co-employees, without reference to the care and diligence used by the carrier in the selection of its employees. (Culver *v.* Ala. Md. Ry. Co., 18 Sou. Rep., 827.)

A carrier is liable in damages for death of an engineer who was killed in a collision caused by his engine running into an unlighted switching engine moving around in the yards. (San Ant. and A. P. R. R. Co., *v.* Harding, 33 S. W. Rep., 373.)

A brakeman of a railway company was injured by the negligence of his foreman; held that the carrier was not responsible, as the brakeman and the foreman of the drill crew, of which the brakeman was a member, are fellow-servants. (Cent. R. R. Co. *v.* Keegan, 16 Sup. Ct. Rep., 269.)

An engineer directed a brakeman to put on the brake, and it was the duty of the deceased to obey such direction, upon which the train was wrecked and brakeman killed. The engineer and brakeman are not fellow-servants and the carrier is liable. (Tex. Cent. Ry. Co. v. Frazier, 34 S. W. Rep., 664; 36 ib. 432.)

A switch engineer who had no authority or control over a switchman, but who belonged to the same crew, by negligence causes an injury to the switchman. The carrier is not liable as these employees were fellow-servants. (Gulf, C. and S. F. Ry. Co., v. Warner, 35 S. W. Rep., 364.) In this decision the court defined fellow servants to be: Employees who are engaged in a common service, in the same grade of employment, working together at the same time and place, and working to a common purpose.

The master's liability does not depend upon gradations in the employment. The test is, the servant must be employed in different departments, which in themselves are so distinct and separate as to preclude the probability of contact and of danger of injury by the negligent performance of the duties of the servant in the other department. (Sou. Pac. Co. v. McGill, 44 Pac. Rep., 302.)

The master owes a servant entering his employment the duty to provide a reasonably safe place to work in, to provide reasonably safe tools, appliances, and machinery, to employ safe and competent coservants, and to adopt and promulgate safe and proper rules for the conduct of the business. (North. Pac. R. R. Co. v. Peterson, 16 Sup. Court Rep., 843.) In this case the Supreme Court of the United States held that a day laborer on an extra gang on a hand car and a foreman of the gang are fellow-servants.

For using in a negligent manner a defective appliance furnished by the master the latter might be liable if a coemployee were thereby and in consequence thereof injured. As the master furnished the defective appliance it would be no answer to say that it was negligently used. But, on the other hand, the master would not be responsible for the negligent use of a proper appliance. (North. Pac. R. R. Co., v. Charles, 16 Sup. Ct. Rep., 849.)

The fellow-servant act of Texas does not apply to street railroads, as they are not "railroad corporations." (Riley v. Galv. City Ry. Co., 35 S. W. Rep., 826.)

A superintendent of a convict camp and a convict are not fellow-servants, as the convict's servitude was involuntary. (Buckalew v. Tenn. C. and I. Co., 20 Sn. Rep., 606.)

If the superintendent of a log company and vice-principal negligently and improperly directed the plaintiff to work on the log deck with him without giving him necessary or proper warning or instruction as to the danger and hazard of working there, for the lack of which he got injured, this must be regarded as the negligent act of the defendant, for which it would be liable. (Klochinski v. Sholes Lumber Co., 67 N. W. Rep., 934.)

A conductor directing and controlling the movements of a train is a vice-principal of the master, and not a fellow-servant of his brakeman. (Spencer v. Brooks, 25 S. E. Rep., 480.)

A carrier is liable for a defective ladder on a freight train because of which a freight conductor was injured, where by the use of ordinary care it could have been known that the ladder was in such condition. (Ill. Cent. R. R. Co. v. Hilliard, 37 S. W. Rep., 75.)

A train dispatcher is not a fellow-servant of trainmen in charge of a train; but a local telegraph operator at the station, who receives and delivers the orders of the train dispatcher is a fellow-servant of such trainmen. (Oreg. S. L. and U. N. Ry. Co. v. Frost, 74 Fed. Rep., 965.)

A motorman on an electric car and the track repairer in employ of the same corporation are fellow-servants. (Landquist v. Duluth St. Ry. Co., 67 N. W. Rep., 1006,)

A conductor of a train used in connection with a bridge gang is not a fellow servant of members of the bridge gang under the " fellow-servant act of Texas." (M. K. and T. Ry. Co. v. Hines, 40 S. W. Rep., 152.)

A boss directing an act in the execution of his duty merely as foreman of a gang and coemployee of the injured employee, is not liable for damages. (Maher v. Thropp, 35 Atl. Rep., 1057.)

The head of a gang of workmen who has charge of a particular department in the erection of a building is a fellow-servant with the workmen in his gang— following the Baugh Case. (Coulson v. Leonard, 77 Fed. Rep., 538.)

A shift boss in a mine is not a fellow-servant with a man under his employ. (McMahon v. Ida Mining Co., 70 N. W. Rep., 478.)

A master violates his duty and is guilty of culpable negligence whenever, without warning, he exposes his servant knowingly to a risk of injury which is not obvious and was not known to the servant. (Gorven v. Bosh, 76 Fed. Rep., 549.)

A conductor is a fellow-servant with a brakeman and other servants on a train, not a vice-principal. (Jackson v. N. and W. R. R. Co., 27 S. E. Rep., 278.)

An overseer of Government fortifications in personal charge of the work is not a fellow-servant with a laborer in his hire. (Atkins v. Field, 36 Atl. Rep., 375.)

A conductor and an engineer on a train are not fellow-servants under the fellow-servant act of Texas. (Culpepper v. Int. and G. N. R. R. Co., 40 S. W. Rep., 386.)

"Common service" means the particular thing or work being performed for the employer, at the time of the accident, and out of which it grew, jointly, by the employees sought to be held fellow-servants. So, members of two different train gangs, attached to two different trains, are not in a "common service," and therefore are not fellow-servants. (Patterson v. Houst. and Tex. C. R. R. Co., 40 S. W. Rep., 442.)

The fellow-servant act of Texas is constitutional. (Mo., K. and Tex. Ry. Co. v. Hannig, 41 S. W. Rep., 196.)

An employee of an American railway company on a train running from Vermont to a point in Canada is killed within the territory of Canada. The circuit court of appeals of the United States declared that his legal representatives could sue in the United States, but that the law of Canada making the carrier liable whether the injury was caused by negligence of a fellow-servant or not should be the law of the case. (Boston and Me. R. R. Co. v. McDuffey, 79 Fed. Rep., 934.)

A member of a gang doing the same work and receiving the same pay as other members of the gang, but who exercises authority over the gang, is still a fellow-servant. (Moore Lirve Co. v. Richardson Adnex, 28 S. E. Rep., 334; Railway Co. v. Becker, 39 S. W. Rep., 358; Hunter v. K. C. and M. Ry. Co., 85 Fed. Rep., 379.)

Statutes of a State as to fellow-servants do not encroach upon Federal authority, and constitute the laws of the State which Federal courts are bound to administer in suits arising within the State. (Hunter v. K. C. and M. Ry. and Br. Co., 85 Fed. Rep., 379; C., M. and St. Paul Ry. Co. v. Solan, 169 U. S., 133.)

A foreman of a section gang is not a fellow-servant of the men belonging to the gang under him, for the reason that they are under his control and direction in the performance of their duties. (St. L., I. M. and S. Ry. Co. v. Rickman, 45 S. W. Rep., 56.)

When an injury is caused partly by the negligence of a fellow-servant, and partly by the failure of the master to provide the servant a reasonably safe place at which to work, the negligence of the fellow-servant will not exonerate the master. (Stucke v. Orleans R. R. Co., 23 Sm. Rep., 342.)

In this State (Illinois), in order that one servant should be the fellow-servant of another, their duties must be such as to bring them into habitual association, so that they may exercise a mutual influence upon each other promotive of proper caution. (Edward Hines Lumber Co. v. Ligas, 50 N. E. Rep., 225.)

It must be conceded that the courts have indulged in much refinement of reasoning on the question of who are fellow-servants, and that the grounds on which many decisions have been based on either side of the question are not altogether satisfactory. (Walker v. Gillett, 52 Pac. Rep., 442.)

A vice-principal for whose negligence an employee will be liable to other employees must be either—First, one in whom the employer has placed the entire charge of the business, or of a distinct branch of it, giving him not mere authority to superintend certain work or certain workmen, but control of the business, and exercising no discretion or oversight of his own; or, secondly, one to whom he delegates a duty of his own which is a direct, personal, and absolute obligation, from which nothing but performance can relieve him. (Prevost v. Citizens' Ice and Refrigerating Co., 40 Atl. Rep., 88.)

In all the cases decided in Pennsylvania under the statute requiring operators of mines to employ mine bosses, it is held that these mine bosses are fellow-servants with the miners and employees in the mines. (Williams v. Thacker C. and C. Co., 30 S. E. Rep. (W. Va.), 107.)

A winchman operating the engine and a member of a stevedore gang are not fellow-servants. (The Lisnacrieve, 87 Fed. Rep., 570.) But where the regular winchman is absent and a common laborer, like the libelant, was at the winch, then the temporary winchman is a fellow-servant with the stevedores. (The Anaces, 87 Fed. Rep., 565.)

2. Defective appliances.—A master is liable to his servant for injuries resulting from defects in machinery or appliances of which he might have known by the exercise of ordinary care. (Bier v. Standard Mfg. Co., 130 Pa., 446; East St. Louis Pach and P. Co. v. McElroy, 29 Ill. App., 504; Union Pac. R. Co. v. Fray, 43 Kans., 750; Dutzi v. Geisel, 23 Mo. App., 676; Donaline v. Enterprise R. Co., 32 S. C., 299; Washington and G. R. Co. v. McDade, 135 U. S., 554 (34, 235), 18 Wash. L. Rep., 526; Southwest Virginia Imp. Co. v. Andrew, 13 Va. L. J., 634, 17 Wash. L. Rep., 599; Humphrews v. Newport News and M. V. Co., 33 W. Va., 135, 39 Am. and Eng. R. Cas., 363; Hoffman v. Dickinson, 31 W. Va., 142; Kaspari v. Marsh, 74 Wis., 562.)

An employer does his duty when he provides in such manner as is fairly and reasonably prudent and safe, and when he furnishes appliances which, although not the best that can be obtained, may be used without danger. (McCombs v. Pittsburg and W. R. Co., 130 Pa., 182; Ballard v. Hitchcock Mfg. Co., 51 Hun, 188; Kaye v. Rob Roy Hosiery Co., 51 Hun, 519; Lehigh and W. Coal Co. v. Hages, 5 L. R. A., 441, 128 Pa., 294; Carlson v. Phenix Bridge Co., 55 Hun, 485; Galveston, H. and S. A. R. Co. v. Garrett, 73 Tex., 262.)

An employee is warranted in acting upon the assumption that machinery which he is required to use is safe and adapted to the service in which he and it are employed. (Galveston, H. and S. A. R. Co. v. Garrett, 73 Tex., 262; Covey v. Hannibal and St. J. R. Co., 27 Mo. App., 170; Bowers v. Union Pac. R. Co., 4 Utah, 215.)

It is the duty of the master to use reasonable diligence to guard against the risk of accident to his employees, and to make such reasonable repairs or changes as may be necessary to remove such risk. (McDonald v. Chicago, St. P., M. and O. R. Co., 41 Minn., 439.)

A servant can not recover for an injury resulting from defective machinery or appliances unless the master knew, or ought to have known, of the defect and the servant was ignorant thereof and had not equal means of knowledge. (Humphrews v. Newport News and M. V. Co., 33 W. Va., 135; Bailey v. Rome, W. and O. R. Co., 49 Hun, 377; Chicago and A. R. Co. v. Stites, 20 Ill. App., 648; Washington and G. R. Co. v. McDade, 135 U. S., 534 (34–235), 18 Wash. L. Rep., 526; Goltz v. Milwaukee, L. S. and W. R. Co., 76 Wis., 136, 41 Am. and Eng. R. Cas., 282.)

It is the duty of a railroad company to inspect the cars of another company used upon its road and see that they are in proper condition so as to be safe for the use of employees. (Goodrich v. New York Cent. and H. R. R., 5 L. R. A., 750; 116 N. Y., 398; 41 Am. and Eng. R. Cas., 259.)

It is the duty of a railroad company in employing a brakeman to provide its cars with safe and suitable brakes and adapted to be used by him. (Carpenter v. Mexican Nat. R. Co., 17 Wash. L. Rep., 630; 39 Fed. Rep., 315.)

A railroad company owes an employee the duty of keeping in a reasonable safe and secure condition a stage or platform constructed for the use of men engaged in unloading coal cars standing on a trestle. (Sellbrok v. Langdon, 55 Hun, 19.)

Injury to a brakeman from collision of the train with an animal which has come upon the railroad track through a defective fence makes the company liable for the damages under the New York general railroad act of 1850, section 44, which imposes upon railroad companies the absolute duty to fence their tracks. (Donnegan v. Erhardt, 7 L. R. A., 527; 119 N. Y., 468; 42 Am. and Eng. R. Cas., 580.)

It is the duty of the master to provide his servants with a safe working place and with safe machinery and appliances and to keep them in repair. (Indianapolis and St. L. R. Co. v. Watson, 114 Ind., 20; Cullen v. National Metal Roof Co., 46 Hun, 562; Rice v. King Phillip Mills, 144 Mass., 229; Atchison, T. and S. F. R. Co. v. McKee, 37 Kan., 592; Thorn v. New York City Ice Co., 46 Hun, 497; Nelson v. Allen Paper Car Wheel Co., 29 Fed. Rep., 840.)

A railroad company is under a legal duty not to expose its employees to dangers arising from such defects in foreign cars as may be discovered by reasonable inspection before such cars are admitted into its trains. (Balt. and P. R. Co. v. Mackey, 157 U. S., 72.)

A railroad company which fails to have modern coupling devices on its freight cars is guilty of continuing negligence and is liable for injuries incurred in coupling such cars by hand. (Greenlee v. Southern Ry. Co. (N. C.), 30 S. E., 115.)

Railroads, though not bound to their servants to supply them with the best of everything in the way of machinery and appliances, are bound to furnish such as are being used by well-regulated and conducted railroads, well constructed, and kept in repair. (Toledo, W. and W. R. Co. W. Fredericks, 71 Ill., 294; Mansfield Coal and C. R. Co. v. McEnery, 91 Pa., 185; 36 Am. Rep., 662; Cooper v. Central R. Co., of Iowa, 44 Iowa, 134; Brown v. Accrington Cotton Spinning and Mfg. Co., 3 Hurlst and C., 511; McGinnis v. Canada Southern Bridge Co., 49 Mich., 466; Little Rock and Ft. S. R. Co. v. Duffey, 35 Ark., 602; Toledo, W. and W. R. Co. v. Asbury, 84 Ill., 429; King v. Boston and W. R. Corp., 9 Cush., 112; Cagney v. Hannibal and St. J. R. Co., 69 Mo., 416; Disher v. New York Cent. and H. R. R. Co., 94 N. Y., 622.)

A railroad company is liable for an injury to an employee from a defective side stake on a lumber car. (Bushby v. New York, L. E. and W. R. Co., 107 N. Y., 374.)

A railroad company is liable for negligence in not providing and keeping a ladder on a freight car next to a caboose in good repair, so as to make it safe for the conductor to pass up and down it in the discharge of his duties, where he is not chargeable with negligence in using it. (Goodman v. Richmond and D. R. Co., 81 Va., 576.)

An employer is not liable for injuries caused by defects in machinery, if they could not be known or be supposed to exist, after the exercise of ordinary care, skill, and diligence. (Gulf C. and S. F. R. Co. v. Wells, 81 Tex., 685.)

An employer is not required to furnish his employee with such appliances as combine the greatest safety with practical use, but only to exercise such care in their selection as a prudent man would exercise for his own protection. (Sappenfield v. Main Street and A. P. R. Co., 91 Cal., 48; Brymer v. Southern Pac. Co., 90 Cal., 496.)

A railway company is bound to use a high degree of care in furnishing and keeping in repair machinery which its servants are required to use; but is not bound to furnish machinery that is absolutely safe. (International and G. N. R. Co. v. Williams, 82 Tex., 342.)

The use of an appliance or machine which has been in daily use for a long time, and has uniformly proved safe and efficient may be continued without imputation of negligence. (Sappenfield v. Main Street and A. P. R. Co., 91 Cal., 48; Brymer v. So. Pac. Co., 90 Cal., 496.)

For the above and many other similar authorities on this point, see note to Richmond and Danville Railroad Company v. Elliott (149 U. S., 266) in 37 Law Edition (U. S. Rep.), page 728.

As to liability of railroad companies to switchmen or brakemen for injuries while coupling cars, see note to Kohn v. McNulta (37 Law Ed., p. 150).

While it is true that a servant who enters the employment of another assumes the ordinary risks of business, this would not include the risks of working with unsafe appliances; for the master is bound to supply his servants with sound and safe appliances, and to keep the same in sound and safe condition. (Bussey v. Char. and W. C. Ry. Co., 30 S. E., 477.)

The duty of a railway company toward an employee, to inspect cars coming from other roads, is not limited to cars which are to be hauled over its own road, but extends to cars which it switches from another road, to which they are to be returned after loading.

An employee of a railway company has the right to rest on the assumption that appliances furnished are free from defects discoverable by proper inspection, and is not submitted to the danger of using appliances containing such defects because of his knowledge of the general methods adopted by the employer in carrying on his business, or because, by ordinary care, he might have known of the methods, and inferred therefrom that danger of insufficient appliances might arise. (Tex. and Pac. R. Co. v. Archibald, 170 U. S., 665.)

The failure to provide the necessary appliances is the causa caucaus. The defendant, however, frankly asks us to reconsider and overrule the Greenlee case. That case was the expression of no new doctrine, but the affirmation of one as old as the law, and founded on the soundest principles of justice and reason, to wit: That when safer appliances have been invented, tested, and have come into general use, it is negligence per se for the master to expose his servant to the hazard of life or limb from antiquated appliances which have been generally discarded by the intelligence and humanity of other employers. (Witsell v. R. R. Co., 120 N. C., 557.) This must be so if masters owe any duties to their employees and unless economy of expenditures on the part of the railroad management is to be deemed superior to the conservation of the lives and limbs of those employed in their operation. The court refused to overrule the Greenlee decision.

The defendant was bound to exercise reasonable care in providing suitable machinery, instruments, means, and appliances for its work. The providing of suitable links for coupling the cars of the train fell within this duty. This was a duty which belonged to the defendant as master, and could not be delegated. It should use proper care to furnish secure and proper masters over any duties to their employees; and unless economy of expenditures on the part of the railroad management is to be deemed superior to the conservation of the lives and limbs of those employed in their operation. The court refused to overrule the Greenlee decision. (Troxler v. Southern R. R. Co. N. C., March, 1899, not yet reported.)

The defendant was bound to exercise reasonable care in providing suitable machinery, instruments, means, and appliances for its work. The providing of suitable links for coupling the cars of that train fell within this duty. This was a duty which belonged to the defendant as master, and could not be delegated. It should use proper care to furnish secure and proper links and to keep them in such a condition that they should be proper and sufficient for work to be done by them. The defendant should use reasonable care to prevent the use of unsuitable and dangerous links. (Judge Blodgett's charge to the jury in Miller v. N. Y., N. H. and H. R. R., superior court of Mass., October, 1898.)

NEGLIGENCE OF FELLOW-SERVANTS.

The great conflict of authority respecting the rule as to when two employees are fellow-servants has caused various States of the Union to pass acts upon the subject. The proposed object of such acts is, generally, to correct either a previous bad statement or a previous bad judicial decision. Alabama, Massachusetts, Colorado, Indiana, and other States have passed employer's liability acts based upon the English act of 1880. In the case of railroad employees, these acts give the employee a right of action against their employers for injuries caused by reason of the negligence of any person having charge or control of certain railroad instrumentalities.

In some States the defense of fellow-servant's negligence has even been abolished in certain cases by statute; other States have no legislation upon the subject; and the United States Supreme Court has decided in the Baugh case, "against the trend of some former cases," as Judge Acheson says, that in the absence of State legislation the question is not one of local law upon which the Federal courts are bound to follow the State decisions, but is one of general law upon which the Federal courts may exercise their independent judgment, uncontrolled by local decisions. Thus appears the anomalous condition of suits for damages in a State, based upon the same facts, which are governed by different principles of law, dependent upon whether the suits are brought in the courts of the State or in the courts of the United States. There is great need of legislation by Congress upon this point. A uniformity is very much to be desired in the legal principles governing such cases.

Again: A Federal court which sits in one State may enforce the statute of another State, where the injury occurred, although the local State courts of the State wherein the Federal court sits have refused to enforce such statute. Even a decision by a State court that no action can be maintained under a statute of another State is not binding upon a Federal court sitting in the first State in another like case: Cox Case (145 U. S., 593). There the "general law" doctrine also intervened and overrode the local statute. New legislation is necessary along this line, too, in order to clear up such conflict and confusion and to establish a uniform mode of procedure in all the Federal courts.

"The stubborn resistance of business corporations," said Mr. Thomas G. Shearman, an attorney of the New York bar who has repeatedly represented railway companies and other corporations, "common carriers and mill owners to the enforcement of the most moderate laws for the protection of human beings from injury, and their utter failure to provide such protection of their own accord, ought to satisfy any impartial judge that true justice demands a constant expansion of the law in the direction of increased responsibility for negligence, instead of attempts, unfortunately too common, to restrict such responsibility by introducing new exceptions."

DEFECTIVE APPLIANCES.

The weight of authorities establishes that a carrier is bound to the exercise of reasonable care with reference to all the appliances of its business, and is bound to protect its employees from injury therefrom by reason of latent or unseen defects so far as such care can do so; but the carrier is not an insurer to its employees against injury, and is only chargeable for damages happening to its employees from defective appliances when negligence can properly be imputed to the carrier.

I believe that an investigation by this commission will show that the time has come when the Congress of the United States should declare itself in regard to these unsettled questions which are being so differently determined by different courts, and for which there exists no fixed rule of decision.

In England considerable progress has been made in that direction. The state of the law there, as I understand it, is as follows:

Under the old common law the employer was only liable in damages for injuries caused to anyone by the negligence of his servants, and then an exception was made when the person knowingly incurred the risk. The courts held, on the ground that a workman when he engaged himself in any service he was aware that in all employments the risk of injuries by the negligence of fellow-employees will be incurred, that an employer was not, therefore, liable to the workman for the injuries thus incurred. The first step to relieve the employee of this hardship was the employers' liability act of 1880. At the time of its passage business men all over the country predicted ruin to the employers, but during nearly two decades of operation the predictions have not been fulfilled, and on the contrary it has been seen that the principle enunciated could be further invoked. A bill entitled the employers' liability act of 1893 was introduced in Parliament by Mr. Asquith, but it did not become a law. It was constructed along the lines of the act above mentioned, but in addition prohibited "contracting out." The workmen's compensation act of 1897, operative July 1, 1898, and introduced by Mr. Chamberlain, is a further evolution of the principle. It, too, practically prohibits "contracting out" and at the same time makes the employer virtually the insurer of the employee. Instead of the negative exposition, this new act declares the employer liable for all injuries and excepts those occasioned by the serious and willful misconduct of the employee. A schedule of compensations or damages for which the employer is variously liable is included in the act. These liabilities are so large that employers are compelled to resort to insurance companies, or for cheaper indemnity, to mutual combinations. Contrary to expectations the insurance companies have raised their charges very much, but it is conservatively hoped that the experience of a short period of time will prove the lack of necessity for such advances in rates.

This act, by fastening the liability upon the employers, makes a great stride toward the principle that the trades and industries in which an employee is engaged at the time of the injury should bear the burden of the relief and maintenance of the injured man and those dependent upon him.

Q. (By Mr. C. J. HARRIS.) Is there something about limit of liability in the English law?—A. The bill provides "That where personal injury is caused to a workman by reason of the negligence of any person in the service of the workman's employer, the workman, or, in case of the injury resulting in death, his representatives, shall have the same right to compensation and remedies against the employer as if the workman had not been in the employer's service. An exception to this is made where the workman, knowing of the negligence, failed, without reasonable excuse, to notify employer, etc. A contract made before the accrual of the right is not a defense. The employer, however, in case he has contributed to a fund providing any benefit for the workman, when sued shall be entitled, in the place of the workman, to any money payable out of the fund. And if the employer is sued and payment of a fine, under any act of Parliament in respect to the same cause of action, has not been paid, the workman shall not be entitled thereafter to receive any such fine."

Q. Do you know, as a matter of fact, whether they have limited liability by legislation there?—A. To the extent I have stated.

The act of 1880 makes the employer liable for injuries to the workman caused by defect of machinery, negligence of a person in the employer's service intrusted with superintendence or with authority over the injured man, or any act or omission done or made in obedience to the orders or by-laws of the employer, or by the negligence of any person in charge of railway signals, etc., while the bill of 1893 would make the employer liable to the injured workman where the injury was caused by the negligence of any person in the service of the employer. Both place the workman in the same position as if he were not in the service of the employer. By the act of 1880 the employer was protected by exceptions in which he was morally innocent, while bill 118 excepts him only when the employee, knowing of the negligence, failed without reasonable excuse to notify the employer, etc. The bill adds, further, that a contract made before the accrual of the right is not a defense. On the other hand, by it the employer, when he has contributed to a fund providing any benefit to the workman and the employer is sued, he is entitled, in the place of the workman, to any money payable out of the fund. And if sued and payment of a fine under any act of Parliament in respect to the same cause of action has not been paid by the employer, the workman shall not be entitled thereafter to any such fine. Unlike the act, the bill does not limit the amount of damages recoverable, nor does it limit the time within which the action must be brought. Both provide that the action must lie in the county court, but can be carried into a higher court.

In some of our own States we have limited liability; that is, that a death claim can not exceed $5,000. It is so in Massachusetts. Damages recoverable for death through negligence: $5,000 in Colorado, Connecticut, Illinois, Massachusetts, Maine, Minnesota, Missouri, New Hampshire, New York, Oregon, Pennsylvania, Wisconsin, West Virginia—13; $10,000: in District of Columbia, Ohio, and Virginia—3. Now, at least, the Congress should either do that or it should endeavor to secure harmony of decisions of State and Federal courts.

The case of Baltimore and Ohio Railroad against Baugh (United States Supreme Court Reports, vol. 149, p. 368) is a very peculiar case. I want to state something about it in an offhand way. Baugh was an employee on the Baltimore and Ohio Railroad; he was injured, and brought a suit in the State court. The Baltimore and Ohio Railroad, on the ground that it was a foreign corporation, had this case removed to the United States circuit court. It was tried in the United States circuit court. The court followed the decisions of the State court and damages were awarded Baugh. The case then went to the Supreme Court of the United States on appeal from this decision—made by court of the carrier's own choosing—and the Supreme Court held that the railroad was not liable. Now, you see this curious state of affairs: Here are two parallel roads. If the Baltimore and Ohio had been a corporation of the State of Ohio his case would have been maintained in a State court, where undoubtedly he would have obtained redress; but here was a foreign corporation paralleling a State road, and Baugh was injured with impunity. The fact of being a foreign corporation deprived him of the protection of the laws of his State and he could not recover for his injury. The court said that "there is no common law in the United States, but there is a general law;" and that seems to mean that any particular case is judged by such construction as any particular judge may see fit to find, without precedent to guide him. Here you will find what some of the United States court judges have said in regard to the Baugh decision:

"Against the trend of some former cases." (Judge Acheson, in Pull. P. Co. v. Harkins, 55 Fed. Rep., 932.)

"As a United States circuit judge, it becomes my duty to conform to the view so strongly announced as is the utterance of the Supreme Court in the Baugh Case." (Judge Lurton, in Harley v. L. and N. R. Co., 57 Fed. Rep., 144.)

"The Baugh and various other decisions may be characterized, at least, as conflicting." (Judge Ross, in Bank of N. A. v. Rindge, 57 Fed. Rep., 279.)

"The rule declared by the Supreme Court in the Baugh Case is claimed to be broader, more comprehensive, and far-reaching than any heretofore announced by that court." (Judge Woods, in N. and N. R. Co. v. Ward, 61 Fed. Rep., 927.)

"It is insisted that these and other cases," including the Baugh Case, "show the existence of some general law separate from and independent of the law of the land prescribed by the States. This does not, in my opinion, follow." (Judge Grosscup, in Swift v. Phil. and R. R. R. Co., 64 Fed. Rep., 59.)

"The Ross Case, while left to stand upon ground apparently inconsistent with the general principles announced in the Baugh Case, is nevertheless, in terms, expressly approved in the opinion of the court in the latter case, and the principles upon which it rested are there carefully distinguished." (Judge Gilbert, in No. Pac. R. Co. v. Beaton, 64 Fed. Rep., 563.)

"Our decisions above referred to were each predicated on the rulings made in the Baugh Case, which set at rest some of the doubts that had been raised, and corrected certain deductions that seemed to be warranted by some expressions found in the earlier case of Railway Co. v. Ross." (Judge Thayer, in Balch v. Haus, 73 Fed. Rep., 974.)

"In Finley v. Railroad Company I attempted to distinguish the facts and principles involved in the case on trial from those presented in Railroad Co. v. Baugh, and follow the decision of the supreme court of this State in Mason v. Railroad Company. The circuit court of appeals overruled my views of the law of the case. I now feel constrained to strictly observe the positive decisions of the United States appellate courts, clearly expressed in learned and elaborate opinions." (Judge Dick, in Wright v. So. Ry. Co., 80 Fed. Rep., 260.)

Here are a number of conflicting opinions—one judge says it is right and one judge says it is wrong; and if this commission can not come to the point where it feels that after a fair examination of this whole subject there ought to be a national law defining the liability of employers, at least it should recommend action such as is contemplated by the following proposed act:

"AN ACT to secure harmony in decisions of State and Federal courts.

"*Be it enacted by the Senate and House of Representatives of the United States of America in Congress assembled*, That the decisions of the courts of last resort in the several States shall, except where the Constitution, treaties, or statutes of the United States otherwise require or provide, be regarded as rules of decision in trials at common law in the courts of the United States, in cases where such decisions apply, and no distinction in this regard shall be made between cases involving questions of general and those involving questions of special or local law."

It seems to me that, as the time has come when almost every case involving railway employees reaches the courts of the United States, Congress can well enact legislation in regard to that class which the courts must follow.

Q. (By Mr. PHILLIPS.) Who suggested that law?—A. I wrote it.

Q. (By Mr. KENNEDY.) Do the State courts accept the decisions of Federal courts as higher than their own?—A. No, I think not; but the Federal court is presumed, where the statute of any particular State is in question, to follow the statute of that State and the decisions of the courts, as far as applicable to the case at issue. I have also here a bill which was introduced at my request by Mr. McEttrick, of Boston, in the Fifty-third Congress. I hardly expected that any legislation could there be accomplished, but I believed that time would bring the question to the front. The bill was prepared with the greatest care, and is in line with the English bill of 1893 regarding the same subject. The bill is as follows:

"A BILL relating to the liability of employers engaged in interstate and foreign commerce for injuries to their employees.

" *Be it enacted by the Senate and House of Representatives of the United States of America in Congress assembled,* That the provisions of this act shall be held to apply only to common carriers engaged in interstate and foreign commerce and to their employees engaged in the service of such common carriers as such.

"SEC. 2. That where, after the enactment of this act, personal injury is caused to an employee by reason of the negligence of any person in the service of the employee's employer, the employee, or, in case of his death, his representatives, shall have the same rights to compensation and remedies against the employer as if the employee had not been an employee of, nor in the service of, the employer, nor engaged in his work: *Provided,* That an employee or his representatives shall not be entitled under this act to any right of compensation or remedy against the employee's employer in any case where the employee knew of the negligence which caused his injury and failed, without reasonable excuse, to give or cause to be given within a reasonable time information thereof to his employer, or to some person superior to himself in the service of his employer; but nothing contained in this proviso shall apply to any case where such employee is injured contrary to the provisions of the act to promote the safety of employees, and so forth, approved March second, eighteen hundred and ninety-three.

"SEC. 3. That a contract whereby an employee relinquishes any right under this act shall not, if made before the accrual of the right, constitute a defense to any action brought for the recovery of compensation under this act.

"SEC. 4. That where an employer has contributed to a fund providing any benefit for an employee, or his representatives in case of injury or death, then, in the event of the employee or his representatives neglecting to sue the employer for compensation, instead of claiming against the fund, the employer may be released from legal liability to the amount of the proportion of the benefit arising from the employer's contribution to such fund."

The act referred to in section 2 of the bill just read is properly known as the "Coupler bill" or "Safety appliance act," which in section 8 provides that it can not be urged in defense by the railroad company that an injured employee knew of the failure to provide the appliances which this law requires and continued in service, and did not call the attention of his employer to the matter.

Q. Have some States adopted laws similar to that proposed by you?—A. Yes, indeed. The States to a greater or less extent are doing so. Every session, I might say, increases the number, and this is well, for it supplements what Congress has done.

(Mr. Moseley here read section 3 of the bill mentioned.)

This is to prevent an employer from forcing an employee to sign an agreement releasing him from claim for damages by reason of the negligence of the employer.

(Mr. Moseley here read section 4 of the bill mentioned.)

And I would state in explanation of it that the Baltimore and Ohio Railroad and other railroads—the Chicago, Burlington and Quincy Railroad, etc.—have what is called a relief fund, and every employee was required to contribute a certain amount of his earnings to the fund.

Q. Required by whom?—A. By the employer, who also contributes to the fund.

Q. (By Mr. FARQUHAR.) Is that contribution on the part of the employees perfectly voluntary?—A. Hardly, sir; it was virtually a condition of employment. It is voluntary in name; but if a man does not see fit to contribute, the road will probably find somebody better fitted to hold his position than himself.

Q. Has there not been a decision of the Illinois courts in regard to that within a year?—A. Yes, sir; so I understand. I have forgotten for the moment. This requirement is a condition of employment by some roads, and it had reached a point which it was believed called for action. Congress recognized this, as you will see by referring to section 10 of the "Act concerning carriers engaged in interstate commerce and their employees."

The employers' liability bill was introduced prior to the passage of the bill I have just mentioned, and very properly provided that only to the extent to which a man has contributed to a fund shall it be used as an offset against any claim which he rightly has for damages.

Q. (By Mr. KENNEDY.) Are railroad relief societies considered by employees as in some instances used to take away their allegiance from their unions and to put it where their money is?—A. That is a matter I will try to explain. Before the statute was enacted it became so onerous to the men that a desire was expressed to provide for it in what is called their bill—arbitration bill. Congress responded to this and made it law that it should not be made a condition of employment or a condition of remaining in employment to contribute to any fund, etc., and since the passage of that law, June 1, 1898, I do not think that any railroad has endeavored to force their men in the slightest way in this respect.

Q. (By Mr. C. J. HARRIS.) In view of the decisions of the courts, will it be advisable to attempt liability legislation in this country to cover this whole ground?—A. Limited as to the amount recoverable? You do not mean that if a man is killed, whether it is his own fault or not, then he gets so much? That is the case now, I believe, in Germany.

Q. Is that class of legislation being passed by foreign countries?—A. Yes, sir; particularly in Germany.

Q. What would be the effect here of such legislation?—A. This is a question of such importance that I can not properly answer it offhand. As a matter of present impression, I believe it would not be fair to go to that extent. Let men understand they owe some care and caution when engaged in their work not only to themselves, but to their employers. If a man is killed by his own negligence, purely as a matter of risk of his employment, he has been receiving increased compensation, or is presumed to be, for the hazardous employment he is engaged in. But where an employer has failed to put on an appliance which the law requires, or uses an unsafe one, or where the employer employs a man to manage or direct who is not a proper person and shows by his conduct he is not, I believe the employer should pay.

Again, to carry the fellow-servant idea to the extent of claiming that an Italian laborer, digging along the railroad track with a boss who says, standing over him, "Go ahead, what are you looking at," when he lifts his head—to maintain that he is a fellow-servant of an engineer who comes down a track at a tremendous rate of speed and cuts him in two, is not just from my point of view. He is kept at work by the representative of the corporation, who does not allow him to look up for safety, who says, "I am your eyes." To say the engineer is a fellow-servant and the railroad is not responsible is not right.

Q. Are not the State courts, as a rule, becoming more liberal toward the employee?—A. Yes; there is a recent case in North Carolina where the judge took very advanced grounds. A person was injured. It was held, by reason of the fact that the railroad did not use the appliance which experience had shown to be the best—safety appliances—that the railroad was liable. This was the Greenlee Case, decided by Judge Clark in May, 1898. In 1893 the safety-appliance law went into effect. The first provision was that the engineer, on and after five years from the date of passage of the law, should be enabled to control his train from the cab; and just as the passenger train was at that time being controlled, so it was required that railroads should not run freight trains which were not capable of being controlled by the locomotive engineer—that is, by the use of the air brake and train brake; and that a necessary proportion of the cars should be equipped to enable them to do it. Of course that would vary. On roads running across the prairie it would not be necessary to have so many cars equipped as it would be in a mountainous country to enable an engineer to control his train. This was the first provision. The second provision was that, after five years, no railroad engaged in interstate commerce should use cars which required men to go between them to couple them, and it stopped there; otherwise it would have been as gigantic a job as was ever forced upon anybody, as you can well imagine. If the law had said that any particular device was to have been used it would have cost the railroads additional millions in paying royalties, etc. over the proper cost for the adoption of an automatic coupler to have applied them; and you can imagine what it would have meant to have turned the railroads over to the tender mercies of the patentee; but it was left to the economies of railroad transportation and those who made a study of them to work out the method of coupling which would relieve the men from the danger of going in between the cars to couple and uncouple. What should be used to accomplish this end resulted in a great struggle. A great many roads were in favor of what is known as the Janney type of coupler, which is a vertical plane coupler, and which had been adopted by the Master Car Builders, while others advocated the continuance of the old type, the link and pin, which was claimed (and I believe it is true) could be made, and was made, automatic, so that this also could be used without men going in between the cars. Now the contest came between the two types of couplers, and it resulted in the general adoption of the M. C. B. coupler. The exigencies of railway operation require that the slack, which all of us have heard about, must be done away with, for to properly work the air brake you must have a solid train. Otherwise, when you undertake to use an air brake each car becomes a battering-ram, so to speak. It is therefore necessary to make the train as solid as possible.

It is now claimed that a solid train can be moved with less power than can one with slack between the couplers. So the contest went on, and finally out of it the Master Car Builders' type of coupler won. Now, this type of coupler at the time the law went into effect was free from patents, anybody could use it—anybody could build upon that type of coupler. Of course there were certain claimed improvements on it upon which there were patents, but the general type of the coupler was free from patent rights and a road could go into the market and get couplers as good as anyone else had without paying a royalty.

Q. (By Mr. FARQUHAR.) Was this coupler the property of the Master Car Builders' Association and given to all the roads as a benefit?—A. Hardly that. The first type was what was known as the Janney type, but Janney, prior to the passage of this law, released all claims he had to the patent to what was known as the contour line, so that anybody could make the M. C. B. coupler prior to the passage of the law. If they saw fit to use that style of coupler, they could do it without paying royalty to anyone.

Q. Was this coupler adopted by the Master Car Builders' Association?—A. Yes; and it has worked out so that about 75 per cent of the cars are now equipped with the M. C. B. type of coupler.

The next thing in the bill were the hand-holds. Many roads used no hand-holds or grab irons on their freight cars, though recommended to do so by the American Railway Association and the Master Car Builders' Association; some had them in one place on the car and some had them in another. The law required that all railroads should have hand-holds at the ends and sides of the cars. That was particularly important during the transition period, where the coupling had to be made between the old-fashioned coupler and the Master Car Builders' coupler, and therefore the switchmen had to get between the cars more than ever to couple up. Then another provision of the law was that the drawbars of the cars should be of a maximum or standard height. Now Congress, instead of undertaking to determine itself or leaving it to public officials to do, left the railways themselves, through the American Railway Association, to establish and determine the height, which they did. And 31½ inches was fixed to be the minimum height and 34½ the maximum height for drawbars—3 inches variation being allowed. This resulted in the saving of many lives. Penalties were fixed for failure to comply with the law, and then, as I have stated before, though an employee knew there was failure to comply with the law, that could not be raised as reason why the railroads should not be compelled to pay for injuries. A duty was also imposed upon the Interstate Commerce Commission to grant additional time to the railroads, if they, after full hearing, believed that it should be done. When the act was about to apply to drawbars and hand-holds the railroads asked a short additional time in which to comply, and after notice to all the railroad organizations in the country, and as far as could be the railroad employees interested, and after full hearing, a short extension was granted, both as regards the hand-holds and drawbars. So effectively had the law been observed that when it went into effect it is said the Pennsylvania Railroad held in its yards over 2,500 cars one night until hand-holds were put on them, and the Reading held some 3,000, and this was the fact all over the country. The commission has an employee who is a practical railroad man who goes all over the country, examines the freight cars, and it is surprising to find how few cars there are that are not equipped with hand-holds or cars which vary in height, and then it is some fractional part of an inch, and generally they are too high rather than too low—the car repairers being fearful that the cars may settle down too far. Then when it came to the question of an extension of time in which to equip with couplers and of having the cars equipped with a sufficient number of air brakes and train brakes, the railroads also asked for further time and demanded that they be given five years. They had already had five years, and it was found that certain railroads had not equipped 2 per cent of their cars in that whole period. Other roads—many of them—were fully equipped. Now the inhibition of the law was that you should not haul or permit to be hauled on your line; anybody could have a car equipped in any manner desired; it was only when they undertook to haul it that the law applied; for that reason, if the Louisville and Nashville Railroad's cars were not equipped, the Pennsylvania Railroad could not haul them, and to that extent was punished for the failure to comply with the law of the other road.

655A——3

Q. Was there any penalty attached to that law?—A. Yes; $100 for every violation. Therefore, after a full hearing, the commission failed to grant five years, but taking into account the great financial depression through which the roads went and the railway employees having agreed, as far as their view could be ascertained through their representatives, an extension of two years from January 1, 1898, was granted. The result has been, I believe, that one-half of the cars at least, which were not equipped at that time, have been equipped, and I have little idea that any railroad will ask for a further extension.

Q. (By Mr. C. J. HARRIS.) Have you statistics showing the results of this change of appliances?—A. I believe it can be fairly claimed the adoption of this humane law by Congress has resulted in the saving of very many lives. In 1893 there were over 280 more men killed in coupling and uncoupling cars alone than there were in 1897, and over 4,000 more men were injured than in 1897, so that there are only one-half the number of men killed in coupling cars alone, and nearly one-half of those injured as formerly—a saving to the Republic of American citizens, because these are all men in the full vigor of life—than were the casualties resulting from the Spanish-American war, that changed the whole map of the world. In 1897 there was a regiment of men, 1,067, less employees killed on the railroads of the United States than there were in 1893. Of course you must take into account the amount of freight handled, the number of men employed; but in looking at it in that view, there is about one-half as many killed and half as many injured as there were when this law was enacted. How much of this is due to the enactment of the law I leave others to determine. A short time ago Mr. Francis P. Hopwood, who is the railway secretary of the British Board of Trade, came to this country to look into the workings of this law; and while there has sprung up in Great Britain the same opposition encountered here (the expense of the change in Great Britain it is claimed would be about £7,000,000, or $35,000,000), I believe Great Britain will ultimately follow our example and enact a safety-appliance law.

I hope no one will understand that, from any remarks of mine, I believe the individual railroad manager is a hard-hearted man—that he has not a due regard for the welfare of men employed by him. The railway managers have as big hearts and, in the main, are as kind as anybody else. The Pennsylvania Railroad raised no opposition to the passage of this law, in fact was friendly to it. The Chicago and Northwestern and other railroads took the same position, while still others I could name fought the bill with all the power they could.

Q. Has there been a decrease of expense to the railroads from the time of making this change?—A. The loss in coupling pins and the links and the breakages which occur in drawbars—connected with the old style of coupler—is great; I have figures which show that it costs over $2 a year to maintain each car; whereas it is found that the new type of coupler does not cost 50 cents to maintain, and if that ratio is carried out the result of this law is ultimately going to be a saving to the railroads of over a couple of millions a year in that respect. Now, another thing It should be borne in mind the absolute necessity that the freight locomotive engineer should control his train, particularly when running on a single track with passenger cars ahead of his freight train. The rear-end collisions at times in the history of railroads have been appalling, largely occasioned by freight trains running into the rear of passenger trains that have become stalled; but with the use of the air brake the control of the freight train is almost as complete as the passenger train. Freight trains can make a much faster time because the engineer does not have to shut off steam miles away and whistle for brakes. Now they can run right up to a station before shutting off steam. It is increasing the facilities with which freight trains can be handled, and has enabled the railroad management to meet another great exigency of economy in present railway management. You will recall the time when the carload was 20,000 or 24,000 pounds. Trains are now being run where the capacity of cars is from 80,000 to 100,000 pounds. Of course the railroad employee is performing a very much larger service than he ever did. His wages are not being reduced, but you have got to bear in mind that where an employee hauled or handled 200 tons in a train he can now handle 600 or 800.

Now, coming to the "associations and organizations of employees of railways and other carriers by land." Here is an act to legalize incorporation of national trades unions with the right to appear by their representatives, and that is a thing which the workmen of the United States, the people of the United States, scarcely realize. It is hardly known that there is such a law on the statute books. They have all the rights of an incorporation. If there is any advantage to be gained in the incorporation of capital, they have the same right to have a corporation where labor is the fundamental object.

The act referred to is as follows:

"[PUBLIC—No. 90.]

"AN ACT to legalize the incorporation of national trades unions.

" *Be it enacted by the Senate and House of Representatives of the United States of America in Congress assembled,* That the term "national trade union," in the meaning of this act, shall signify any association of working people having two or more branches in the States or Territories of the United States for the purpose of aiding its members to become more skillful and efficient workers, the promotion of their general intelligence, the elevation of their character, the regulation of their wages and their hours and conditions of labor, the protection of their individual rights in the prosecution of their trade or trades, the raising of funds for the benefit of sick, disabled, or unemployed members, or the families of deceased members, or for such other object or objects for which working people may lawfully combine, having in view their mutual protection or benefit.

"SEC. 2. That national trade unions shall, upon filing their articles of incorporation in the office of the recorder of the District of Columbia, become a corporation under the technical name by which said national trade union desires to be known to the trade; and shall have the right to sue and be sued, to implead and be impleaded, to grant and receive, in its corporate or technical name, property, real, personal, and mixed, and to use said property, and the proceeds and income thereof, for the objects of said corporation as in its charter defined: *Provided,* That each union may hold only so much real estate as may be required for the immediate purposes of its incorporation.

"SEC. 3. That an incorporated national trade union shall have power to make and establish such constitution, rules, and by-laws as it may deem proper to carry out its lawful objects, and the same to alter, amend, add to, or repeal at pleasure.

"SEC. 4. That an incorporated national trade union shall have power to define the duties and powers of all its officers, and prescribe their mode of election and term of office, to establish branches and subunions in any Territory of the United States.

"SEC. 5. That the headquarters of an incorporated national trade union shall be located in the District of Columbia.

"Approved, June 29, 1886."

It was amended by the act of June 1, 1898, as follows:

"SEC. 8. That in every incorporation under the provisions of chapter five hundred and sixty-seven of the United States Statutes of eighteen hundred and eighty-five and eighteen hundred and eighty-six it must be provided in the articles of incorporation and in the constitution, rules, and by-laws that a member shall cease to be such by participating in or by instigating force or violence against persons or property during strikes, lockouts, or boycotts, or by seeking to prevent others from working through violence, threats, or intimidations. Members of such incorporations shall not be personally liable for the acts, debts, or obligations of the corporations, nor shall such corporations be liable for the acts of members or others in violation of law; and such corporations may appear by designated representatives before the board created by this act, or in any suits or proceedings for or against such corporations or their members in any of the Federal courts."

Now, sections 9 and 10 of the act of June 1, 1898, are as follows:

"SEC. 9. That whenever receivers appointed by Federal courts are in the possession and control of railroads, the employees upon such railroads shall have the right to be heard in such courts upon all questions affecting the terms and conditions of their employment, through the officers and representatives of their associations, whether incorporated or unincorporated, and no reduction of wages shall be made by such receivers without the authority of the court therefor upon notice to such employees, said notice to be not less than twenty days before the hearing upon the receivers' petition or application, and to be posted upon all customary bulletin boards along or upon the railway operated by such receiver or receivers.

"SEC. 10. That any employer subject to the provisions of this act and any officer, agent, or receiver of such employer who shall require any employee or any person seeking employment as a condition of such employment to enter into an agreement, either written or verbal, not to become or remain a member of any labor corporation, association, or organization; or shall threaten any employee with loss of employment, or shall unjustly discriminate against any employee because of his membership in such a labor corporation, association, or organization; or who shall require any employee or any person seeking employment as a condition of such employment to enter into a contract whereby such employee or applicant for employment shall agree to contribute to any fund for charitable, social, or beneficial purposes; to release such employer from legal liability for any personal injury by reason of any benefit received from such fund beyond the proportion of the benefit arising from the employer's contribution to such fund; or who shall, after having discharged an employee, attempt or conspire to prevent such employee from obtaining employment, or who shall, after the quitting of an employee, attempt or conspire to prevent such employee from obtaining employment, is hereby declared to be guilty of a misdemeanor, and, upon conviction thereof in any court of the United States of competent jurisdiction in the district in which such offense was committed, shall be punished for each offense by a fine of not less than one hundred dollars and not more than one thousand dollars."

These enactments were largely brought about by an act of injustice by the receivers of the Reading Railroad, which was approved by a Federal court. Some time ago the Reading Railroad revived a regulation which had become an absolute dead letter to the effect that no employee should become a member of a labor organization, and if he did he should be discharged. The general manager of the railroad company called upon some of the railroad employees to come to his office and told them to cease their membership, and demanded that they hand to him the charters and documents belonging to the lodge in the place, and said he must carry out the directions of the receivers. "If you do not do it, I shall turn you off," said he. These men appealed to their brotherhoods, and particularly to the Brotherhood of Railroad Trainmen. They were all interested in it. At my suggestion they came to Washington to see Mr. Olney, who was at that time Attorney-General of the United States, and consulted with him about their rights. The Attorney-General believed that they were wrongfully treated, and said he would see what could be done. He sent for the counsel of the Reading Railroad and urged him to rescind the order. The counsel said he would take it before the receivers and would endeavor to get them to do it. In a few days Mr. Olney got word from them that they proposed to carry out their rule, that any man belonging to a labor organization should be discharged.

Q. (By Mr. FARQUHAR.) Was that the order of the receivers that was to be carried out?—A. The order of the receivers. Mr. Olney then suggested that before anything should be done in the courts they return and remonstrate individually with every receiver. They did so, but to no purpose, as they were virtually shown the door. Then Mr. Olney said, "Bring your bill in the court, asking the courts to enjoin the receivers," and the bill was brought. It was decided to have counsel, and the best that could be had in Philadelphia and Washington was obtained and went into the United States court there. The first thing the counsel for the railroad said was that this man Wilkinson, a representative of the brotherhood which brought the suit, was not an employee of this railroad, and was not a proper party complainant. Mr. Wilkinson's counsel replied that if he divulged the names of the men in whose behalf he was appearing they would be put on the blacklist and discharged, and he did not want to offer them up for that purpose. Mr. Olney believed it was fair; that the bill should be brought by Mr. Wilkinson. The court held that if they wanted relief they must appear themselves, and dismissed the bill. The case was then brought in the name of three employees, who were offered up as a vicarious sacrifice. As was known, the men were discharged, and, to the credit of the Pennsylvania Railroad, they took care of them. Mr. Olney filed a statement as "amicus curiæ." I commend it to your attention as a fair presentation of the right of men to organize. And I want to say to the credit of the railroad employees, they went down to Harrisburg and got a law passed that would now put a receiver in jail who followed this precedent. The judge, however, rendered an opinion, though there were eight States in this Union that made it a criminal offense to deny a man employment or refuse to continue his employment because he belongs to a labor organization, that these receivers could use their employees as they saw fit.

I have no particular statistics, but a large number of the railroads in the United States to-day are being run upon rules and regulations, and rates of pay, which have been agreed to between the representatives of the various organizations and the railroad managers. At this time there is a feeling of perfect accord between the employer and employees, as far as I can learn, and, while there are a great many men engaged in railway employment who do not belong to an organization, still there is no antagonism on the part of the members of these organizations and those who do not belong to them, and who do not receive all the benefits of the combination which these organizations confer. Of course, these organizations not only have the question of wages, hours of service, and everything of that sort to deal with, but they all also have the beneficial insurance features. The railway employment is so hazardous that they can not obtain insurance elsewhere, except in rare instances; they therefore insure themselves through their organizations. A man joins the organization largely by reason of the fact that he desires to protect his family against the contingency of death or injury.

Q. Have the five brotherhoods insurance companies of their own?—A. All of them have, and the amounts of benefits they have paid runs into the millions.

DISPUTES AND DIFFERENCES BETWEEN EMPLOYERS AND EMPLOYEES.

One object of the arbitration bill passed June 1, 1898, which applies only to railroads and their employees, was that without any surrender apparently of any ground which either side held—without any appearance of giving in—arbitration could be brought about. The Government, through its officers, after endeavoring to settle the matter by conciliation, steps in and says to the disputants, "This difficulty has gone far enough and you had better agree to arbitration." Now, under these circumstances the side that will not arbitrate will receive the public condemnation, for the public knows who is in the wrong; so now the wronged have a means of reaching public sentiment, of enlisting the public with them, avoiding strikes which interrupt the public in the enjoyment of transportation facilities, and which turn the people against the strikers, no matter if their cause is just. What has been the result? I have asked every one of the representatives of the organization, and they say that the relations have never been so pleasant as since the passage of the law. It has been said to me, "We do not want to invoke the operation of that law, and our employers do not, and therefore they meet us on common ground with good feeling, and while we have to give in at times they also give in; but we meet and we know if we do not settle it between ourselves, the Government will step in." Since the passage of that law there has not been the slightest murmur, and it meets the approval of every railroad man I have met. There are some who predict that there will not be any more strikes. We really believe it is the era of good feeling.

Now, another matter. If not a sparrow falls to the ground without Divine knowledge, why should American citizens, our people, be maimed and killed and no record of the circumstance attending the casualty kept? I believe there should be a requirement in case of a collision or where persons or employees are killed or injured upon the railroads that the Interstate Commerce Commission should be notified of it at the time it occurs. It would do very much to decrease the number of accidents upon our railroads. When you open the light of day upon such things, and give the public an opportunity of ascertaining the cause of injury to a man, either a passenger or an employee, you will find that eventually the number of killed and injured will be decreased.

Q. Have the railway commissioners of some of the States the right to do that?—A. Quite a number of them have. Under their State laws they have the opportunity to investigate these facts. Many of our states have railway commissions, while others of them pay no attention to the matter. The National Government statistics furnished by the roads also require revised classification. For instance, a man is hurt; he is reported as injured in coupling cars when the real fact is he is running down a track and tumbles over a tie and falls down and gets hurt. He is reported as injured in coupling cars simply because he is engaged in that occupation. The means are not at hand to ascertain the actual facts. The commission has no means of learning the real cause of the injury.

Q. Could the interstate commerce law be amended to reach such a case as that?—A. I do not think there is the slightest doubt of it. I have a bill amending the act to promote the safety of employees, etc., which covers this point, I think. It is as follows:

"*Be it enacted by the Senate and House of Representatives of the United States in Congress assembled,* That there be added to the act entitled 'An act to promote the safety of employees and travelers upon railroads by compelling common carriers engaged in interstate commerce to equip their cars with automatic couplers and continuous brakes and their locomotives with driving-wheel brakes, and for other purposes,' approved March 2, 1893, the following:

"SEC. 9. That where any collision of trains where one of the trains is a passenger train shall occur on a railroad of any common carrier engaged in interstate commerce by railroad, or where any passenger train, or any part of a passenger train accidentally leaves the rails, it shall be the duty of the general superintendent or general manager, or other officer in general charge of the movement of trains on said road, immediately thereafter to transmit a full and detailed report under oath of such accident, and the causes thereof so far as known, to the Interstate Commerce Commission at their office at Washington, D. C. It shall also be the duty of any such common carrier to make to the Interstate Commerce Commission a monthly report under oath of all accidents which may occur to its passengers or employees, whether attended with loss of life or personal injury, and such report shall state the causes and circumstances connected therewith. That any common carrier failing to make such report within ten days after the end of any month, or failing to make report of any collision or cars leaving the rails accidentally, as herein required, within ten days after the occurrence of such accident, shall be deemed guilty of a misdemeanor, and, upon conviction thereof by a court of competent jurisdiction, shall be punished by a fine of not less than one hundred dollars, and not more than five hundred dollars for each and every offense, and for every day during which it shall fail to make such report after the time herein specified for making the same. The failure of the superintendent, general manager, or other officer in charge of the movement of trains, to make report to the Interstate Commerce Commission as herein required, shall be deemed the offense of the carrier as well as of such officer himself.

"Sec. 10. The Interstate Commerce Commission is authorized to prescribe for such common carriers a method and form for making the reports in the foregoing section provided."

This bill was introduced by Senator Pettigrew in the Fifty-fifth Congress, and is Senate bill No. 3244.

Q. Would such reports to the commission open the doors a good deal to suits for damages?—A. I should not want to have the facts used in that way; none of these reports should be used in any damage suits, and it might be provided in the act that they should not be.

The intent is to call the attention of the public to accidents upon the roads. Of course to-day every accident is supposed to be annually reported to the Interstate Commerce Commission, and they have authority to ask for it. They may not have authority to ask for a monthly report. They can ask for annual reports, but that hardly gets at it. Reports at the time of the accident are what are desired.

Another thing, right here, almost under the shadow of the dome of the Capitol, men have been killed within the last few years by having their feet caught in frogs, and there they have been held as in a vise, and the train backs down on them and kills them. I now recall a case. It was a particularly distressing case. This poor fellow had a wife and a number of children. When he was killed, for a few hours everybody would tell you all about it. I followed the thing up. A dozen hours had not gone by before nobody knew anything about it at all; even his wife did not. She said: "I do not dare say anything about it, because my brother-in-law is employed on the railroad, and if I say anything about it he will get his discharge."

I will read a bill which will cover this matter. I think it fully avoids any requirement which would force the railroads to adopt any particular device.

"*Be it enacted by the Senate and House of Representatives of the United States of America in Congress assembled,* That all persons, companies, or corporations owning and operating a railroad or railroads or operating a railroad owned by another person, persons, company, or corporation within the military reservations of the United States, the Territories, or the District of Columbia, shall be, and are hereby, required, within six months after the passage of this act, to so adjust, fill, or block, or securely guard the frogs, switches, and guard rails on their roads (with the exception of guard rails on bridges), so as to thoroughly protect and prevent the feet of employees or other persons from being caught therein.

"Sec. 2. That within ten days after compliance with this act by persons, corporations, or companies to whom it applies, such persons, corporations, or companies shall make report of the fact to the United States Interstate Commerce Commission.

"Sec. 3. That any person or persons, railroad company, or corporation owning and operating a railroad or railroads in any of the States or Territories, military reservations, or the District of Columbia, who shall fail to comply with the provisions of this act, shall be fined in a sum not less than five hundred dollars, nor more than two thousand dollars, in the discretion of the court, for each offense, and the neglect of any such person, company, or corporation to comply with the provisions of this act shall be deemed a violation of the same.

"Sec. 4. That the penalties herein prescribed shall be recovered by action brought in the United States district courts; and it shall be the duty of the United States district attorneys for said courts having jurisdiction in the premises to institute and prosecute such action for violations occurring therein, upon duly verified information coming to him of the occurrence of such violations.

"Sec. 5. That all persons, companies, or corporations owning or operating railroads in said States or Territories, reservations, or District of Columbia, shall, in addition to the penalties prescribed in this act, be liable for any damage resulting from the failure to comply with the provisions thereof, such damage to be recovered by the persons injured, or his or her legal representatives."

I also have another bill to which I would call the attention of this commission:

"AN ACT to promote the safety of employees upon railroads by compelling persons, firms, companies, and corporations operating railroads to equip their cars and locomotives with automatic couplers, continuous brakes, and grab irons; their locomotives with driving-wheel brakes; to provide a standard height for drawbars for freight cars and engines; and to adjust, fill, or block all frogs, switches, guard rails, and all other obstructions which are a part of, or are near, their tracks as to prevent the feet of employees from being caught therein.

"SEC. 1. *Be it enacted by the Senate and House of Representatives in general assembly met, and it is hereby enacted by the authority of the same:* That from and after the first day of January, nineteen hundred, it shall be unlawful for any person, firm, company, or corporation engaged in operating any railroad within this State to use on his or its line any locomotive engine in transportation between points or places in this State which is not equipped with a power driving-wheel brake and appliances for operating the train-brake system; or to run any train used in such transportation after said date that has not a sufficient number of cars in it so equipped with power or train brakes that the engineer on the locomotive drawing such train can control its speed without requiring brakemen to use the common hand brake for that purpose.

"SEC. 2. That on and after the first day of January, nineteen hundred, it shall be unlawful for any such person, firm, company, or corporation to haul, or permit to be hauled, or used on his or its line any cars or locomotives used in transportation between points or places within this State not equipped with couplers coupling automatically by impact, and which can be uncoupled without the necessity of men going between the ends of the cars.

"SEC. 3. And from and after the first day of January, nineteen hundred, it shall be unlawful for any such person, firm, company, or corporation to use any car in such transportation that is not provided with secure grab irons or hand holds in the end and sides of each car for greater security to men in uncoupling cars.

"SEC. 4. That the standard height of drawbars for freight cars and locomotives measured perpendicular from the level of the tops of the rails to the centers of the drawbar shanks, for standard-gauge railroads in this State shall be a maximum height of thirty-four and one-half inches for empty cars, and a minimum height of thirty-one and one-half inches for loaded cars; and for narrow-gauge railroads in this State the standard height of drawbars shall be a maximum height of twenty-six inches for empty cars, and a minimum height of twenty-three inches for loaded cars. And after the first day of January, nineteen hundred, no cars, either loaded or unloaded, shall be used in transportation within this State which do not comply with the standard above provided for.

"SEC. 5. That from and after the first day of January, nineteen hundred, every person, firm, company, or corporation engaged in operating any railroad within this State shall have all frogs, switches, guard rails, and other constructions which are a part of, or are near, his or its tracks so adjusted, filled, or blocked as to prevent the feet of any railroad employees being caught therein.

"SEC. 6. That any such person, firm, company, or corporation using any locomotive engine running any train, or hauling, or permitting to be hauled, or used on his or its line any car or engine, or having on his or its line any frog, switch, guard rail, or other construction in violation of any of the provisions of this act shall be liable to a penalty of one hundred dollars for each and every such violation, to be recovered in a suit or suits to be brought by the attorney-general in any court of competent jurisdiction; and it shall be the duty of the attorney-general to bring such suits upon duly verified information being lodged with him of such violation having occurred. And it shall also be the duty of the ——— of this State to lodge with the attorney-general information of any such violations as may come to his knoweldge: *Provided,* That nothing in this act contained shall apply to trains composed of four-wheeled cars, or to locomotives used in hauling such trains.

"SEC. 7. That any employee of any such person, firm, company, or corporation who may be injured by any locomotive, car, train, frog, switch, guard rail, or other construction in use contrary to the provisions of this act shall not be deemed to have assumed the risk thereby occasioned, although continuing in the employment of such persons, firm, company, or corporation after the unlawful use of such locomotive, car, train, frog, switch, guard rail, or other construction had been brought to his knowledge."

(Mr. Moseley's testimony was continued on December 7.)

Mr. MOSELEY. With some care I prepared the statement which I handed you yesterday, "Authorities upon the law of damages caused from injuries received (1) by negligence of a fellow-servant, and (2) by defective appliances," which I again desire to call your attention to, as it affects railroad employees, because almost all their cases sooner or later get into the Federal courts—the State courts have little to do with the suits of railroad employees for damages for negligence on the part of the employers.

Q. (By Mr. PHILLIPS.) Have you any law to suggest to meet this question of a fellow-servant?—A. Yes; to the extent of the bill I suggested yesterday, but I would not ask this commission to report to Congress a bill, or assume there was necessity for a national law regarding the liability of employers for injuries to employees, without the fullest investigation and without the opportunity being given to be heard. I mean by that, as it is a matter which would entail a large number of damage suits upon railroad corporations from time to time, therefore they ought to have full opportunity to be heard, but I do believe it is a question which sooner or later Congress must deal with.

Q. Do you think that a fellow-servant could be defined in a general law?—A. I do not think there is any trouble in defining what a fellow-servant is. Many of the States are undertaking to define it. As I said yesterday, the railroad employees of the country are engaged in a semipublic employment—in a national work; if they obtain any redress at all, they must obtain it through the Congress of the United States. I have not gone into the field of the ordinary industrial pursuits or the relation between an employer and employee in such industrial pursuits, because I believe these matters are very largely under State control and one which the people of each State should settle for themselves, as far as the relations between one citizen and another of that particular locality is concerned. But when we come to the railroad employee the case is different, for there is hardly a railroad in the United States that the courts have not held by their rulings are engaged in interstate commerce and therefore under national control, and where any difficulty occurs between employer and employee the Federal courts are the ones that are resorted to, that they may put the strong arm of the Federal power into the scales. Also wherever a case occurs of damage by accidents or any cause it is almost sure to reach the Federal courts. Therefore I believe these are matters which, if Congress itself does not deal with and does not bring about uniformity in by legislation—why decisions are as varying as are the ideas of the several judges—judge-made law will continue to largely govern the determination of all these cases. For that reason particularly I believe it is a matter which Congress may well devote its attention to, particularly in view of the fact that it has for a long time become more and more emphasized by the courts that the railroad employee is a servant of the public, not particularly a servant of the citizen of any particular locality, but he is a servant of the public at large, and his responsibilities and his duties to that public are constantly being put before him. He is constantly being reminded by the courts of them, and therefore if you are going to put the railway employee in this position he certainly has a right to expect that public which he serves or the representatives of it will see that he is protected in those things in which he is justly entitled to protection. As I said in the Fifty-third Congress, after a good deal of study on the subject, I drew a bill and handed it to a friend of mine then in Congress, and he introduced it, and that was the bill relating to the liability of employers engaged in interstate commerce to their employees which I read yesterday. If the commission does not go as far as that, I think they at least should recommend to Congress, after an examination of the subject, to define a fellow-servant and how far the employer is liable for the acts of a fellow-servant.

I will read a "memorandum of the case of Baltimore and Ohio v. Baugh," in the Supreme Court of the United States, which I have prepared, and to which I referred yesterday:

"Section 721 of the Revised Statutes declares that 'the laws of the several States, except where the Constitution, treaties, or statutes of the United States otherwise require or provide, shall be regarded as rules of decision in trials at common law in the courts of the United States in cases where they apply.' It would seem that the term 'laws' here used would include not only the statute laws of the States, but also those which are expressed in the decisions of their judicial tribunals. In the recent case, however, of the Baltimore and Ohio Railroad Company v. Baugh, a majority of the Supreme Court of the United States (Justice Brewer delivering the opinion) held that in a case involving a question of 'general laws,' the United States courts were not bound to follow the decisions on that question of the supreme court of the State in which the cause of action arose. This case illustrates in a most striking manner the necessity for some more explicit legislation on this subject. The plaintiff, Baugh, was a citizen of Ohio, and the defendant, the Baltimore and Ohio Railroad Company, a corporation created by the laws of Maryland. The suit was brought originally in one of the courts of the State of Ohio, but the defendant claimed citizenship in Maryland by virtue of its incorporation in that State, and on this ground obtained a removal of the action to the circuit court of the United States for the southern district of Ohio. The ground of action was damages alleged to have been sustained by the plaintiff while discharging his duty as fireman on a locomotive of the defendant, and he obtained a judgment in the circuit court for $6,750.

"Under the decisions of the supreme court of Ohio on the question of law involved the plaintiff was entitled to this judgment, and the Federal circuit court in rendering it followed the rule of law as settled by the State court. The United States Supreme Court, however, on appeal, reversed this judgment, adopting a different rule of law and ignoring the decision of the supreme court of the State in which the cause of action arose. The important question is, not whether the view of the law taken by the United States Supreme Court or that held by the State court was correct, but whether such an inharmonious administration of the law should be allowed to continue—whether the right of recovery by a citizen who claims to have been injured in his reputation or person or property shall depend upon the forum in which his case may be tried—whether on a mere fiction a suit commenced in one court where a recovery could be had may be removed to another in which it may be defeated. In his dissenting opinion in this case, Justice Field vigorously presents the facts and the glaring injustice of such a system of jurisprudence. He says, 'The present case presents some singular facts. The verdict and judgment of the court below were in conformity with the law of Ohio, in which State the cause of action arose and the case was tried, and this court reverses the judgment because rendered in accordance with that law and holds it to have been error that it was not rendered according to some other law than that of Ohio, which it terms the general law of the country. This court thus assumes the right to disregard what the judicial authorities of that State declare to be its law, and to enforce upon the State some other conclusion as law which it has never accepted as such, but always repudiated. The fireman, who was so dreadfully injured by the collision caused by the negligence of the conductor of the engine that his right arm had to be amputated from his shoulder and his right leg was rendered useless, could obtain some remedy from the company by the law of Ohio as declared by its courts; but this court decided, in effect, that that law thus declared shall not be treated as its law, and that the case shall be governed by some other law which denies all remedy to him. Had the case remained in the State court, where the action was commenced, the plaintiff would have had the benefit of the law of Ohio. The defendant asked to have the action removed, and obtained the removal to a Federal court because it is a corporation of Maryland, and thereby a citizen of that State, by a fiction adopted by this court that members of a corporation are presumed to be citizens of the State where the corporation was created; a presumption which, in many cases, is contrary to the fact, but against which no averment or evidence is held admissible for the purpose of defeating the jurisdiction of a Federal court. (Railroad Co. v. Letson, 2 How., 497; Cowless v. Mercer Co., 7 Wall., 121; Paul v. Virginia, 8 Wall., 168-178; Steamship Co. v. Tugman, 106 U. S., 120.) Thus in this case a foreign corporation, not a citizen of the State of Ohio, where the cause of action arose, is considered a citizen of another State by a fiction, and then, by what the court terms the general law of the country, but which this court held in Wheaton v. Peters has no existence in fact, is given an immunity from liability in cases not accorded to a citizen of that State under like circumstances. Many will doubt the wisdom of a system which permits such a vast difference in the administration of justice for injuries like those in this case between the courts of the State and the courts of the United States."

I would add, if this man was injured on a railroad paralleling the Baltimore and Ohio, which was an Ohio corporation, and unless by some means they were able to get it into a Federal court, he would probably obtain damages; yet here in the case of a foreign corporation paralleling a State road and the employee, a citizen of Ohio, can not get relief. Therefore I say to this commission, and beg your attention to the subject, either to suggest to Congress the passage of a national employers' liability act, or else the passage of some act which will tend to bring about uniformity in this question of employers' liability.

In regard to the relations of railroads to the public, it is almost sufficient to say that the Interstate Commerce Commission has been for nearly twelve years asking Congress for legislation which its experience in administering the act to regulate commerce has shown to be indispensable to effective regulation in the public interest. As secretary of the commission, I have no other views on this subject than those which have been expressed by the commission itself in its reports to Congress. Each of those reports constitutes the record of a year devoted to the work of regulation. The chairman and other members of the commission wish me say that they will be glad to give you the benefit of their views as to any of these matters at any time. One or two of the conditions now prevailing will, however, doubtless interest you at this time, and I will mention them briefly.

The act to regulate commerce requires that all rates shall be reasonable and just. It also provides that the commission shall execute and enforce its provisions. For fully ten years the commission proceeded upon the idea that its duty to execute and enforce the law involved the issuance of orders to carriers not to exceed the rate shown to be reasonable or just after complaint, hearing, and investigation. In 1897 the Supreme Court said that this view was wrong; that the commission was not authorized to prescribe rates for future observance by the carriers, and that the commission could only condemn the rate complained of, and incidentally award reparation. (The Freight Bureau Cases, 167 U. S., 479.) Condemning the present rate and awarding reparation is theoretically the remedy at common law, but as a matter of practice no one ever recovered a cent from a carrier for charging an unreasonable rate. In other words, the common law did not and does not afford a remedy. But beyond that, merely proceeding to recover excessive charges is no remedy. First, because the expense always involved in litigation must generally, of itself, deter the institution of such a proceeding. Second, because the person entitled to reparation is generally not the person who is injured. The rate, however excessive, is supposed to be published, and the goods have been bought and sold on the basis of that rate. Obviously the persons most likely to suffer injury are the producer and consumer, and sometimes the retailer, not the middleman or jobber, who is most frequently the shipper, and therefore the one who might be held entitled to recover the excess charge.

Q. (By Mr. C. J. HARRIS.) If parties do not obey decisions of the commission are they obliged to do so or not?—A. Yes, sir; the carriers do very often comply with the orders of the commission. But they will not if they consider that anything vital is involved. Of course the commission may bring suit in court to compel obedience to its order. The average time consumed in reaching final adjudication in such cases by the Supreme Court has been about four years. This practically denies the relief that obedience to the order might afford, and, in fact, enables the carrier to snap its fingers at the rulings of the commission. Now, if the commission were empowered, after hearing and investigation in particular cases, to fix the maximum reasonable and just rate, and if the law also provided that the order of the commission should become effective unless the carrier shows it to be unlawful upon application to the court for review, the result would be that relief would be granted as to all future shipments to the producer, to the consumer, to the retailer, and to all parties interested; and such relief would be summarily enforced unless the carrier could promptly show material error in the decision of the commission. A decision finding that the rate on flour from Minneapolis to Boston is 10 cents too high and an order not to charge, say, more than 20 cents for that service would benefit the Western miller and the New England consumer, as well as all intermediate handlers of that commodity. If you can say what the rate is to be, you benefit all who are commercially interested. If you can merely say the present rate in a particular case is wrong, you benefit only the man who has paid that rate in the case in question. As the law now stands, the commission can not order carriers to observe the rates which it finds, on investigation, to be actually reasonable—sufficient for the service rendered—and those orders which it does issue are practically nonenforceable because of inevitable long delay in the courts under the present procedure. When the act was passed it was supposed that the commission had full power to correct the tariff rates, and that its orders, except on plain showing of material error by the commission, would be summarily enforced by the courts. The commission can not determine and order the proper rate, and when it asks the court to enforce any order that it makes the case must be tried de novo, and, as before stated, the average time consumed in the courts has been about four years. Another present condition is shown in cases under the tenth, or penal, section of the law. If the published rate from Washington to New York is $6.50 and the road carries a man for $3, the company's agent can not be convicted of unjust discrimination unless it be shown that somebody paid the $6.50 rate. And so it is with freight. The published rate may be so high that a shipper can not use it, but at the same time the railway agent may give a favored large shipper a much lower rate, and he will, in consequence, gradually secure a monopoly of the business.

Q. (By Mr. PHILLIPS.) Would that result in small shippers not being able to ship at all?—A. Precisely so. We have had plenty of such cases, but the courts will not hold it to be unjust discrimination unless someone, by actually paying a higher rate, is shown to have been wronged. In one case nearly $12,000 were expended in proof in a case against the former receiver and president of the Santa Fe road. It appeared that some millions of dollars had been paid out by that road in rebates, and that large amounts were paid to shippers of cattle. But it was not practicable to prove who was injured. Those who actually shipped had a monopoly of the trade.

No one thing has operated to the advantage of the large shipper—the trust—or to the detriment of the small shipper—the individual manufacturer or dealer—so much as this vicious railway practice of allowing rebates from tariff rates to large customers. Indeed, it has been said that without railway favors the industrial combination could not exist. Whether that statement is accurate or not, it is acknowledged by all who have given thought to the matter that cutting off this railway rebate advantage would most seriously cripple these great foes to individual enterprise.

The tendency of trusts is to lessen the number of employers, of establishments, and employees, and this to my mind is the alarming feature about them.

When establishments are many and a man who has spent his best energies, the efforts of the best years of his life, in acquiring a trade, finds himself differing with his employer as to hours of labor, conditions of service, or wages, he loses no whit of his manhood, no particle of his independence, for the reason that, if the differences are irreconcilable, the workman can lay down his tools and seek another situation.

But when the trust absorbs the scattered establishments into one organization, closes the more expensive and less profitable, and concentrates the production into a few favored localities, the workman is in danger of losing his identity as a man, sinking into the dependent condition of a part of the machinery of the institution. He becomes in a measure helpless, for an individual difference now with his employer means a loss of his means of livelihood—a shutting of the only door of opportunity to work at his chosen vocation. The responsibilities of family cares, which should add dignity and nerve to the man, are only weakness and a burden to the machine and make cowards of brave men for very love's sake. He dare not risk their lives and happiness by so much as a feeble protest at the wrong against which his manhood revolts, in fear that, losing his one chance of employment, he must start life anew or enter the ranks of the day laborer, already overcrowded and underpaid.

There is but one way which suggests itself to me by which labor may combat the evil of the trust, and that is far from being entirely effective. It is by thorough organization. This will not control—indeed, should not interfere with—the management or financial success of the institution. It will not always save the reduction of establishments and employees. But it will have the effect of preserving his identity and manhood; will give him the courage that is always born of numbers; secure an audience, the whole public, if necessary, for the relation of his wrongs; insure him, as an integral part of the machinery, the wholesome respect of the administration of the establishment.

With all his fellow-craftsmen behind him, his situation becomes infinitely improved, not only socially but in the public eye. His pleas and demands receive consideration, when delivered through the megaphone of his order, whether in the shop, in legislative halls, or in the courts, to say nothing of the beneficiary effects of such organization in substantial relief as well as social sentiment. Every encouragement should be given to organization; every trade should be organized; and when the wage-earners stand shoulder to shoulder the trust must still be feared, but its evils will have been mitigated so far as labor can accomplish such a result.

There are no more progressive men in any walk in life than the managers of railways, and to say that they are other than fair and considerate would not be just; indeed it is difficult to find among them individuals who are not all that anyone has a right to expect so far as the treatment of their employees is concerned. Many of them have sprung from the ranks. One speaks of the railway corporation, but he speaks of it collectively. It must be understood that the railways have done a great deal in the interest of their men, as their railway hospitals, their relief associations, their work under the auspices of the railway branch of the Young Men's Christian Association, and many other agencies for good will testify. No remarks that I have here made are made with any view of disparaging in the least degree the managers of railways, for whom I have the greatest respect, but it is to state conditions as they exist as fairly as I can. Great credit is due and should be accorded the American Railway Association and the Master Car Builders' Association, both of which had established such rules as to safety appliances and regulations as would, if they had been carried out by every railroad, made legislation unnecessary. It was from the very fact that their recommendations were being lived up to by some roads and not by others that the chaotic condition existed which required the law to unravel and correct. Both of these associations have done a great deal for the railway employees as well as having been of great advantage in devising means looking to economy in railway operation. There is no class of men in the country more ready to respond to the calls of humanity and of justice than are those who operate railroads.

But in the matter of railway regulation, it is difficult for some railway managers to believe that business methods which are in use in every line of business should, if adopted and pursued in the operation of railways, be made criminal violations of law. The railway manager in the past has believed that his first duty was to the stockholders and investors in his property, and he neither relishes nor admits the right of interference in what was so long a private institution that he has forgotten in a measure his own official character and the rights of the public in an enterprise which the people have chartered by their votes, have given their lands for the right of way, have granted the supreme weapon of eminent domain to coerce unwilling individuals, have given millions of acres and billions of dollars to establish, and which in the opinion of many people, intelligent and otherwise, the people should themselves own. If open to criticism on any point, it is not a lack of humanity to their men, not in the intelligent management of the stupendous business under their control, not in the liberal and progressive spirit in which they have carried that management to the front rank in the world's system for safety, speed, comfort, and luxuries of transportation—but in an impatience of restraint, a resentment against suggestions from without, a failure to see good in the law, or good will in those called on to enforce it, though of both there are abundant evidences that only the willfully blind can fail to see.

When I first came to Washington, I early recognized the advantage of location, and opportunity, in the matter of furthering legislation, in the interest of the wage-worker, particularly of the employees of railways, now some 874,000 in number, the public character of whose employment, secures them greater attention and consideration, at the hands of Congress, than the average bread-winners in other vocations.

To assist so far as was in my power in this regard I deemed my duty, found in that effort the keenest pleasure, and it is with no little pride that looking backward over that twelve years the boast is mine that nothing was left undone on my part to help the cause as I saw the situation then or recall it now.

You will therefore understand with what satisfaction I have hailed the creation of this commission, which, though it secures not a line of legislation directly, will have performed a great work of education and reform by its exhaustive investigation. It is the forum for the presentation of those questions which vitally affect the life of the nation, questions of vastly more importance than those connected with our foreign relations, and upon the proper settlement of which the stability of our Government depends.

In these years of effort for the amelioration of the condition of labor and of intimate intercourse with the officers of their associations who so ably represent them, I have been more and more impressed with the high character of both.

The representatives of the railway employees who have been sent here to ask for legislation in their behalf command respect and win regard, and with those who do the no less important local work are imbued with a sense of responsibility not only to the men they serve but the country at large. They are conservative, law-abiding men, and they have neither asked nor advocated any legislation which can not be justified upon the ground of right, or defended from the vantage ground of humanity and a higher civilization.

I have memoranda of the bills I have suggested as follows:

"An act for the protection of railroad employees by requiring railroads to block their frogs, switches, guard rails, etc.

"An act to secure harmony in decisions of State and Federal courts to overcome the injustice to employees occasioned by decisions of the character of the Baltimore & Ohio against Baugh.

"An act relating to the liability of employers engaged in interstate and foreign commerce for injuries to their employees, to bring the United States in this respect as near as may be to the laws of Great Britain in regard to employers' liability.

"An act to promote the safety of employees and travelers by requiring carriers to report all collisions and accidents which may occur upon railroads engaged in interstate commerce, with the causes and circumstances connected therewith limited to certain classes of accidents. This is in line with the laws of Great Britain.

"The suggestion that the States that have not done so as far as may be enact laws in line with the car-coupler or national safety-appliance law. Otherwise controversies are likely to arise as to whether the liabilities have occurred under the law; that is, whether the cars are engaged in interstate commerce."

WASHINGTON, D. C., *March 1, 1899,*

TESTIMONY OF JOHN T. WILSON,

Grand Chief, Brotherhood of Railway Trackmen of America.

The Commission met at 11 a. m., March 1, 1899. Chairman Kyle presided and introduced the witness, Mr. John T. Wilson, Grand Chief of the Brotherhood of Railway Trackmen of America.

Mr. WILSON. I have prepared a paper pertaining to matters upon which I suppose the Commission desires to hear from me (reading):

The United States Industrial Commission, Washington, D. C.

GENTLEMEN: In obedience to your request for me to assist your honorable body in its efforts to obtain information which will enable it to recommend the enactment of laws to meet the problems presented by labor, agriculture, and capital, as I represent an organization composed of a class of men employed in transportation, known as the maintenance-of-way department employees, employed by railway companies engaged in interstate commerce, it is for that class of men I speak authoritatively. As I understand, your desire is to discover the actual conditions of the industrial workers of the country, and to discover causes for suffering, for injustice and inequality, so that you may be able to suggest remedies, I will explain the present condition of maintenance-of-way employees, and relate some of the causes which I believe aided in producing present industrial conditions.

There are in the United States 180,000 miles of railway, and according to the last report of the Interstate Commerce Commission about 180,000 men are employed in the maintenance-of-way department. This vast army of industrial workers is divided into three classes.

First. The class known as road masters numbers about 2,000, each having from 100 to 250 miles of track under his jurisdiction. Their divisions are cut into subdivisions called sections. The sections are from 5 to 10 miles each in length. On each section is employed a foreman who has a few assistants or laborers known as section hands. Road masters receive instructions from and make reports to division superintendents. They (the road masters) are fairly well paid, the minimum wage being about $60 a month and the maximum about $150 per month. The majority of the road masters seem to be in sympathy with the men under them, but they are not permitted to have anything to say about the terms of employment, the rate of wages they shall receive, the number of hours foremen and laborers will be required to work each day, etc., these matters being determined by higher authority, but on almost every large system of railway, some one is put in charge of a division in the capacity of road master who is ambitious to excel all other road masters on the system, and in order to have it said that he is the best road master on the system, he becomes a very hard master, drives the men under him from daylight till dark, and maintains his division at a minimum cost. As the higher officials are on the lookout for men who can produce the greatest results at the least cost, he becomes a favorite and is held up as an example for all other road masters on the system to follow. The most of them are poor men and are anxious to hold their positions; therefore, they feel compelled to be exacting and work the men under them to their full capacity from morning till night.

Second. The men in charge of subdivisions, known as section foremen, receive their instructions from and report to the road master. They number about 30,000. They are personally responsible for the condition of the track under their jurisdiction at all times, and are, in my judgment, the most important class of men engaged in operating railroads.

These men are required to work several years as laborers on track in order to learn enough about controlling men, repairing and maintaining tracks, to be qualified to assume the responsibilities of a track foreman.

The lives of the traveling public and the safety of commercial traffic are in their hands. They have more to do and more to look after to keep the track in a safe-running condition than any other class of railway employees. The track out of line, surface or gauge not properly tied or spiked, a guard rail out of place, or a mismatched joint, and many other little things that must receive their attention each day, would, if neglected, result in wrecking trains and destroying life and property. But few accidents on railroads can be traced to the negligence or carelessness of these men. They are always at their posts of duty without regard to hot or cold weather. At night, during storms and heavy rains, track foremen promptly leave their beds and patrol their track to see that all is safe for the passage of trains, and if the track has been obstructed by washouts or other causes it is usually discovered and red lights or other danger signals are displayed at proper distances from the place of danger, signaling engineers in charge of engines pulling approaching trains to stop and avoid danger.

They are paid by the month and are supposed to be on duty at all times. If they work every Sunday during a month and a dozen nights they receive no extra pay for extra service; their wages amount to from $1.05 to $2 a day, according to locality, cost of living, etc.

Third. The laborers who assist track foremen, known as track hands, are subject to the foreman's orders; the foremen usually hire and dismiss them to suit their own convenience. According to the report of the Interstate Commerce Commission, they number about 150,000, but I do not think more than half that number are employed during the winter months. It is customary for the companies to employ several men on each section during the summer months to assist in putting the track in good condition while the weather is good, the days are long, and at the proper time to repair the road bed, and to discharge them in the fall. Many of the foremen are only allowed one or two assistants during the winter months, and in some instances they are required to lose several days each month, and the foremen are required to walk over their track alone.

The track laborers are usually paid by the day; they receive from 47½ cents to $1.25 a day, according to locality, cost of living, etc. Think of it! More than 50,000 men work for the railway companies for from 47½ cents to $1.25 a day during six months in the year, receiving barely enough to subsist upon during the time of employment, and in the fall of the year, when the cost of living is high and employment is hard to obtain, they are turned out to tramp, beg, starve, or steal and become criminals.

I do not doubt that your honorable body will have men before it who enjoy all of the necessaries of life and many of the luxuries, and they will tell you things are all right as they are, and that the men in whose behalf I am speaking are Dagos, Hungarians, Polanders, Negroes, Mexicans, and Chinese, but in my opinion 90 per cent of these men are American citizens. They go to our polling places and vote, though I do not contend that they vote intelligently, but under improved conditions and more favorable circumstances many of them would become more useful and intelligent citizens, and add to our national strength.

Having related prevailing conditions among the men I am speaking for, as viewed from my standpoint, I will endeavor to explain what I believe to be some of the causes for the undesirable state of affairs.

Under our unrestricted competitive system almost every oppressor imagines he is being oppressed, and to some extent it is true, but the stronger members of society prosper under it, become rich and powerful, while the weaker ones are crushed, reduced to industrial slavery and abject poverty. The men who shape and determine the policies to be maintained by the different railway companies do not, it seems, understand the public, and the public does not understand them. Those who have invested their money in railway enterprises have done a great deal toward developing our country and advancing civilization, but without the aid and cooperation of the public our vast railway systems would be worthless to their owners; therefore railway companies, their employees, and the public should be on the best of terms. Transportation companies should not be allowed to discriminate against small shippers in favor of large ones; they should not be permitted to give millions of dollars' worth of transportation each year to men of political influence who are able to pay their fares, and then expect in return for it legislation favorable to their interests at the expense of the public. Such things arouse suspicion in the minds of the public, create prejudice, and are injurions to both. Rate wars between transportation companies should be abolished. A large per cent of their gross earnings, amounting to millions of dollars each year, is wasted in useless competition for business. I have heard men engaged in the ticket-brokerage business say that general passenger and ticket agents can not be relied upon to carry out agreements after entering into them. It is not an uncommon thing for them to meet and agree to maintain certain rates over certain competing lines to given points, and in less than three days for some or all of them to send agents to offer to supply them with tickets for less than the rate agreed upon. I can nearly always buy a railroad ticket cheaper from a ticket broker than I can obtain it from a company's regular ticket agent.

If the earnings of the road expended in this way were equally distributed among employees, it would enable them to supply themselves and families with the necessary comforts of life and abolish the causes for complaints on account of overwork and underpay.

In my judgment, the system under which the railways are operated at the present is having a demoralizing influence on the public. Were it possible to maintain present rates under judicious management, the earnings would furnish sufficient revenue with which to pay all employees living wages without requiring any of them to work an unreasonable number of hours in any one day, and leave plenty of surplus with which to pay investors a reasonable per cent on money invested. As railway companies hold valuable franchises by consent of the public, and as they are semipublic enterprises, I have no hesitancy in saying it would be a blessing to all concerned if Congress would enact laws to create and authorize commissions to harmonize conflicting interests. Under the present system, employees having just grievances in many instances are afraid to make complaints or to unite with their fellow-workmen for the purpose of presenting their grievances in a proper manner. If there existed a commission before which all classes of employees, from the president, who presides over the meetings of the boards of directors, to the humble trackman, who drives the sprikes and tamps the ties, could appear and present their grievances without fear of being discharged, a better understanding would be arrived at and a more just and equitable system could be adopted and put into practical operation.

As I understand your commission has been created by Congress to act as a mediator between the industrial workers and Congress, and as I desire to aid you in your laudable undertaking to the extent of my ability in my humble way, I will refer briefly to general causes, as I see them, which produce idleness and suffering among the toilers and wealth producers of the nation.

It should be understood that wage earners are not business men; they are capable of producing wealth, but depend upon others to provide ways and means. A demand for their labor must be created by the men who own the means of production and have possession of the things created by labor. Notwithstanding the majority of recruits to the United States Army were drawn from the army of unemployed, many of our citizens are in destitute circumstances and can not find employment; they can not sell their labor at any price. Such a condition is deplorable; it causes the citizen to degenerate and become a beggar, if not a criminal; degrades our Government, and weakens our national strength. Industrial panics such as we have recently passed through not only cause wage earners to suffer, but affect those who have possession of the wealth created by labor; they found no market for their products because the wealth producers, who should be the greatest consumers, were deprived of an opportunity to work and to earn sufficient wages to keep their consuming capacities anything like equal to their producing capacities. The natural result was commercial stagnation and industrial panic, which can not be traced to any natural cause. The causes were superficial—overproduction by some, under-consumption by others, and blind, selfish greed in others, who imagined that instead of creating wealth to be used by all, it should be created for gain for a small per cent of our citizens.

The change of conditions demands a change in methods. The young man in the East who has been crushed to the wall by competition, can not do as did the young man of a half century ago—" Go West and grow up with the country." Competition is as keen in the West as it is in the East; the land that was public a few years ago is occupied by settlements and cities to-day; our railways have been constructed, our cities have been built; machines that enable one workman to produce as much as was produced by ten a few years ago have been invented and are now in practical operation. The burden of public taxes upon the shoulders of labor (labor creates all wealth and pays all taxes) is increasing; the weakest members of society are found among the wealth-producing classes.

I ask the questions: Will our national representatives protect us against blind, heartless, and soulless capitalism? Will they be statesmen, protectors of equal rights, and saviors of our country by seeing to it that we are allowed to enjoy the things we need and are willing to work for in a country we have helped to develop? Or will they serve the class that wants more than they have any use for?

In my judgment, the questions your honorable commission is called upon to help solve are complex. It is hoped your time and energy will not be expended in theorizing, but that your investigations will enable you to see things as they are, for you have conditions to deal with that should and must be changed in order to preserve the rights of the people and to prevent the greatest nation on earth from retrograding.

Again referring to the men I represent and am authorized to speak for, I will state that there are about 200,000 carmen and shopmen employed by the railway transportation companies, whose conditions are but very little, if any, better than the conditions surrounding the men employed in the maintenance of way department. The trackmen, carmen, and shopmen, and their families are far greater in number than the entire population of the Island of Cuba. Our Government has expended many millions of dollars and sacrificed the lives of many of our citizens to aid the Cubans in their struggle to improve their condition, and I say unhesitatingly that before hostilities began on the Island of Cuba, the citizens of that Island upon the whole, were in no worse condition than are the men for whom I speak and who are citizens of the United States.

Q. (By Mr. KENNEDY.) Do the other brotherhoods recognize your organization, and are you federated with them?—A. We have no alliance with any other organization composed of railway employees or any other labor organization in the country.

Q. Do the men in your organization feel that they are neglected by the other organizations and that the other organizations do not do all they should in the way of bettering the poorer paid labor engaged in transportation?—A. I have heard members of our organization say the classes of railway employees that are well organized and are able to command living wages have become selfish and are unsympathetic; but, speaking as the chief representative of the organization, I will say that the members of other organizations have done considerable to encourage our people to organize by advising them and explaining to them how they could benefit themselves by entering into an organization, finding out what their grievances are, what they are entitled to, and how to contend for it.

Q. (By Chairman KYLE.) Is it the wish of your organization to be allied with these railway organizations? Do you desire to be connected with them?—A. I wrote Mr. Clark, the President of the Federation of Railway Employees, to know if an application from our organization for membership in the federation would be acceptable. He replied, saying that at that time they did not desire to extend the scope of the federation except to men employed in operating trains.

Q. On what ground did he take that position? Does he consider your class of workmen unskilled?—A. I will give my opinion. I believe that the only reason our organization is excluded from the federation is because it is young and has not done very much to show that our people are capable of self-government.

Q. (By Mr. KENNEDY.) What percentage of employees in the maintenance of way department of railroads are in your organization?—A. We have about 6,000 men enrolled. According to the report of the Interstate Commerce Commission there are about 180,000 men employed in the maintenance of way department. Our organization has only been in existence seven years, and we have not had time to give anything like the majority of our class an opportunity to become members of the organization.

Q. Is the ability of your members to support the organization very limited?—A. They are not able to pay very much.

Q. Are you personally in favor of governmental control of railroads?—A. Under our present partisan political system, no.

Q. You spoke about commissions adjusting matters and bringing about better conditions. Do you mean State and national commissions?—A. I think the Interstate Commerce Commission should be given more authority. It should be authorized to determine what the railway companies shall charge. I think their authority should be extended so they can require the railroad companies to charge 3 cents a mile if it is necessary to accumulate revenue enough to pay its employees living wages and the stockholders reasonable dividends.

Q. Are you familiar with the railroad pooling bill now pending in Congress?—A. I understand its objects.

Q. Are the railroad people generally in favor of that bill?—A. I think they are.

Q. Would such a law be a step in the direction of governmental control of railroads?—A. I suggested in my paper that a commission, with the authority to settle disputes between companies and employees and determine rates, should be provided by the Government, as the railroad companies are semipublic institutions.

Q. Have you beneficial societies that are promoted by the railroad companies?—A. When a member dies we pay his beneficiary $1,000; if he is partially disabled, we pay him $500; if he is totally disabled, we pay him $1,000. We collect $1 a month from each member to meet these demands.

Q. Do the railroad companies contribute to those benefits?—A. No; the railroad companies have never extended any favors to our organization, except in a few instances when we managed to get committees before the proper officers of the roads, and pictured our condition in such a way as to arouse their sympathy. In that way we secured an increase of a few dollars a month for each man.

Q. I see from a recent number of the Trainmen's Journal that they think the part of the arbitration law which forbids the companies compelling employees to go into these beneficial associations is a failure. They think those societies promoted by the railroads are injurious to their unions. Have you any such difficulty as that in your organization?—A. Some of our class of men have said that they would like to become members of the association, but they were compelled to carry insurance and pay for it in insurance associations gotten up by the companies, and with their small wages they could not afford to carry insurance in both societies. To some extent they are injurious, and especially to the beneficiary department of our organization.

Q. What I gathered from that journal is this: If a man seeks employment on a railroad the company will have no need for him unless an application for membership in its beneficial society accompanies his application, and that a man who is already an employee of the company knows that if he does not become a member of the beneficial society he is not in the line of promotion. I should like to know whether such a state of affairs affects your organization?—A. You mean to ask me whether the insurance societies that are maintained by the employees and managed by the company's officials affect our organization or not. Is that it?

Q. Yes.—A. To some extent, they do.

Q. (By Mr. RATCHFORD.) Are the men you represent covered by life insurance, or sick, or accident insurance that is compulsory, and of which the railroad companies are the chief promoters?—A. Some of them are.

Q. You know of such cases in existence at the present time?—A. All of the employees on the Plant System are. The Plant System officials require their employees to contribute to the company's beneficial department.

Q. Is it compulsory?—A. Yes; compulsory.

Q. Is the employment contingent upon their agreeing to it?—A. When a man makes application for employment, if he does not also make application for benefits at the same time his application for employment will more than likely not be noticed. In order to get employment, of course they apply for insurance in the company's beneficial society.

Mr. KENNEDY. The Trainmen's Journal says that is the way the new arbitration law is evaded; that they do not tell a man they do not want him, that he can not be in their employ because he is not a member of that beneficial society, but they ascertain whether he desires to become a member of it, and if he does not they have no employment for him.

Q. (By Mr. FARQUHAR.) You say you have 6,000 men enrolled in your organization?—A. Yes.

Q. And that it has been in existence seven years?—A. Seven years.

Q. And you made the statement that 180,000 men are employed in the maintenance-of-way department in the country?—A. Yes.

Q. What are your monthly union dues?—A. Three dollars a year—25 cents a month; and each member gets with his membership the monthly official organ without paying anything extra.

Q. Has that $1 a month that you have for your benefit association covered the death losses at the rate of $1,000, the partial injury at $500, the total injury at $1,000?—A. We have paid all legitimate claims and have a little surplus on hand out of the money collected at the rate of $1 a month on the thousand.

Q. So that on the three classes of benefits your assessment of $1 a month has been sufficient, with your organization of 6,000 men, to promptly pay policies, as they are called?—A. At a cost of $12 a year to the insured members.

Q. Have you any knowledge of the differences of cost between your voluntary organization of $12 a year to attain these benefits and the regular railroad insurance? What is the difference of cost?—A. I could not answer that question correctly, but in some instances they charge a little more.

Q. How much more, do you suppose?—A. From $3 to $8 dollars a year on the thousand.

Q. Have any of the railroad officials made any objections to your insuring yourselves instead of taking the insurance provided by the railroad companies?—A. The tendency has been to discourage men who might have become members of our association, and encourage them to accept employment and also insurance against disability, death, etc., in the associations managed by company officials.

Q. Do you think that possibly the railroad managers favor what you might call railroad insurance rather than the brotherhood insurance?—A. Yes.

Q. Are the men in your organization employed, as you might call it, locally; that is, are they people who live in villages or in hamlets by the line of road and have homes, or are they sometimes merely transient boarders?—A. A large per cent of the laboring class in the maintenance-of-way department are what you might term transient.

Q. Is there any change in the class of men employed as trackmen during late years?—A. During the last few years there has been a better class of men seeking employment in the track department. Mechanics and artisans employed in other lines of industry have been turned out and many of them have made application for employment on the track.

Q. Has the stress of circumstances forced skilled artisans to take the work if they can get it?—A. Yes.

Q. You say the lowest price is 47 cents a day?—A. Forty-seven and one-half cents.

Q. And extends to $1.25?—A. Yes.

Q. At that scale of wages what is the character of their maintenance and living? Do they have places of their own where they hire rooms so as to get along as cheap as they can?—A. Some of them are men of families and the companies furnish little houses for them to live in.   They are usually built near the track.

Q. (By Chairman KYLE.) Rent free?—A. Yes; rent free.

Q. (By Mr. FARQUHAR.) That is, they take an old box car or anything else that gives shelter, so as to have a home of some kind?—A. House them in different ways.

Q. (By Chairman KYLE.) On the Union Pacific road I noticed they employed Chinamen to a great extent; the company furnished a section house, in which the Chinamen lived and boarded themselves—furnished their own bedding and bought rice, and so on.   I want to know whether that is customary to-day?—A. A few sections to-day on the Pacific coast are kept up by Chinamen and the companies furnish houses or box cars for them to live in.   The foremen are Americans, speak the English language, and they have interpreters.   They tell the interpreters what to have done and they instruct the Chinamen in their own tongue.

Q. (By Mr. FARQUHAR.) Do you know what the wages of those men are?—A. On the Union Pacific, I believe, they pay the Chinamen from 75 cents to $1 a day, and the Americans are paid a little more—$1.25.

Q. What is the length of service of the oldest trackman you have worked with and have known; that is, in connection with one road?—A. I have known men who have stayed on one section of track for forty years.

Q. You used the word "transient" before.—A. I was then referring to laborers. I never knew a laborer to remain on one section more than fifteen or twenty years.

Q. Are not those transients generally aliens?—A. Through the Middle States they are very nearly all Americans; on the Pacific coast and in the New England States they have a great many aliens—Chinamen and Italians—and through the South, including all of the Southern States and the Middle States from Colorado back this way, very nearly all are Americans.

Q. How strong is your organization in the South?—A. The bulk of our membership is in the Southern and Western States.

Q. Are colored men admitted?—A. Colored men are not admitted.

Q. Among the trackmen of the South and West is there quite a percentage of colored men in the service?—A. In the Southern States the majority of the laborers are colored.

Q. Have you any idea what wages they are paid?—A. The wages are smaller in the Southern States than anywhere else.   Some roads pay as little as 47¼ cents a day.

Q. Where in the United States are the most foreigners employed on track work?—A. On the Pacific coast and in the New England States.

Q. You still believe that 90 per cent are American citizens?—A. Yes; I think 90 per cent are Americans.

Q. Of your organization?—A. So far as our organization is concerned, they are all Americans.   I believe 90 per cent, including all classes employed in the maintenance-of-way department, are American citizens.

Q. (By Mr. A. L. HARRIS.) Do you mean they are American born or naturalized Americans?—A. Some of them come from other countries, of course, and then become naturalized.

Q. Have you ever come across, in your investigations, anything bearing on the alien contract-labor question or the padrone system?—A. No, I have never come in contact with contract labor.

Q. Have you had many strikes?—A. We have never had a strike.

Q. Is it because your men are contented with wages and hours? Is that the reason you avoid strikes, or do you not feel strong enough to be aggressive?—A. I believe if we can get our people organized and teach them what their rights are and how to contend for them in the proper way, we can accomplish more for them than can be accomplished by engaging in strikes and causing the officials to become antagonistic to the purposes and aims of our organization.

Q. How about your hours; are there any set number of hours that your maintenance-of-way department men are required to work?—A. On some lines they work them ten and eleven hours a day and on others from daylight until dark.   In fact during the time I was running a section I received instructions to the effect that I should be at the place where I was to work during the day by the time I could see how to work, and remain there as long as I could see how to perform work.

Q. Was there any payment for overtime?—A. The laborers are paid for overtime if they work nights or Sundays; but the class known as foremen do not receive any extra pay on any road that I know anything about, even if they work every Sunday during the month and a dozen nights.

Q. (By Mr. RATCHFORD.) Are the foremen eligible to membership in your organization?—A. Our organization is composed principally of foremen; in fact, until two years ago no one who did not fill the position of foreman was admitted to membership.

Q. (By Mr. FARQUHAR.) Do you know any way to shorten the hours of the trackmen?—A. Put on more men and work them fewer hours. To illustrate: Ten men will do as much work in eight hours as eight men will do in ten hours. During summer when the days are long and the men work fourteen hours, if the time they are required to work is cut down to eight hours, you see it would furnish employment for more than half as many more men.

Q. Do you think that your labor on the maintenance of the track, the general labor, is any more exhaustive than farm work?—A. Much more; much harder; yes. The handling of materials, cross-ties and heavy steel rails, with a few men; lifting heavy cars, all make it much harder than work performed by the agricultural worker.

Q. (By Chairman KYLE.) Have you ever worked on a farm?—A. I have worked both on a farm and on the track; yes, I was raised on a farm.

Q. (By Mr. FARQUHAR.) What proposition do you make in the matter of either shortening the time or advancing the pay of this laboring class that is working for 47½ cents up to $1.25?—A. I should say if you reduce the hours you require those men to work and give them a little more time for intellectual development, and pay them a little more wages so they can supply themselves with the necessaries of life, books, and other things necessary to intellectual development, they will become better citizens.

Q. Are there many who are anxious to take the places on the roads at 47½ cents a day?—A. I know of locomotive engineers, who have been receiving from $5 to $8 a day, who have accepted positions on the track for $1.25 a day. I do not know of men who received very good wages going into the localities where the wages are so small and seeking those positions. In fact, I do not know of but one road that pays as low as 47½ cents a day; that is the C. F. and Y. V. Division of the Atlantic Coast Line. It is a road that runs through North Carolina, and the other roads that run through that section pay from 60 to 90 cents.

Q. Are there not enough of the unemployed near your roads who would fill the places, if you came into any struggle with the railroads, in order to shorten your hours or advance your wages? Are there enough of the unemployed to defeat your purpose?—A. Without the aid of public sentiment their places would be filled.

Q. Do you not also think a strong organization of other elements—the five brotherhoods—have in a measure helped you?—A. I believe that were it not for the influence of organized labor in the United States, the workingman would not receive more than 50 cents a day in any place in the United States. My opinion is based on the wages paid to men in countries where they have no labor organizations, such as Russia, China, Italy, Spain, Japan, and others.

Q. If you made an appeal to the managers of the railroads for an increase of wages or the shortening of your hours, would you be met with the general answer that has been given for twenty or thirty years, that the managers can find plenty of men to fill these places at the rates they are giving?—A. I have met managers who said to me, "We can get plenty of men to take the places if you people are dissatisfied." In turn I asked them if they did not think there was a principle of right involved in the wage question, and have always been successful in securing some concession for the men I represented.

Q. As a leader in your organization, knowing the men you have to deal with, knowing the roads that give the employment, what importance do you attach to public opinion and your organization in securing a remedy?—A. Without them we could not expect to be successful in our efforts to improve our conditions.

Q. Have you had, of late years, any raise of wages on any of the roads—on your brotherhood lines?—A. We have secured an increase of wages on eight or nine different systems and reduced hours on two or three.

Q. Were those roads in the hands of receiverships or were they in the hands of the owners?—A. Some of them were in the hands of receivers and some were not.

Q. Do railroad hands fare better in many ways under a receiver than under the corporations proper?—A. The receiver seems to be more liberal in the expenditure of moneys, allows a greater number of men to do a certain amount of work, and furnishes more material to work with than companies that are run independently by their own agents.

Q. And would that lead you into the argument that governmental control would be better still than the receivership?—A. I do not think I would advocate that the Government own the railroads as Government property at the present time under our present system. I do think the Government should say how these enterprises should be managed; that the men who manage these roads should not be allowed to discriminate against shippers or passengers; that they should not be allowed to give away free transportation to buy the good will of men of political influence, and they should not be allowed to be governed exclusively by the organized bodies in distributing wages. Take a class of men that is fairly well organized; they are like a trust; they come very near dictating their own terms.   Then take the other classes that are more illiterate, composed of the weaker members of society, and they do not know how to organize; they are simply at the mercy of the stronger members of society, and the company will raise the wages of the man who is already well paid, and take it away from the poor fellow who can not help himself and who is working for starvation wages to begin with.

Q. That may lead to the idea that the strongest organized union or brotherhoods of the country would always get the best wages.—A. There is no question in my mind that they will.

Q. Is the desire of your organization to make it thirty times as strong as it is now?—A. The object of our organization is to make better men, better citizens, and better conditions for the class of men the organization was established for.

Q. What is the success of your organization in seven years; are you advancing and increasing in membership and financial strength?—A. Personally I am proud of the record we have made during the past seven years. We have done a great deal to alleviate suffering and toward encouraging our people to make an effort to help themselves

Q. (By Mr. KYLE.) Do the railroads encourage your organization, or do they look upon it with disfavor?—A. The railroads are very diplomatic, or the men that manipulate the affairs of the companies are. They fear force. They don't antagonize a strong organization, and they do not like to be placed on record as antagonizing a weak organization. At the same time, they will permit the little fellows to do it for them. For instance, the first class of men referred to in my paper are known as road masters. A few of them are members of our association, but they have an independent association of their own and meet annually. A letter was presented and read at one of their conventions, outlining the purposes for which our organization had been established, and requesting them to cooperate with us in our efforts to improve our conditions in a legitimate way; and one of them maintained that if they encouraged our class of men to organize, after a while, if one of them should want to discharge one of us, the organization would question their right to do so, and bring about an investigation; in other words, the organization could dictate to them whether they could discharge a man or not.

Q. When you have wrongs to redress, do you go to the road masters themselves or to the superintendents of the road, or where?—A. Well, in an unorganized state, the road master is considered the head of the department. General managers have said on the witness stand, Until the majority of a class become members of an organization they will not recognize the organization; that they would leave such things as adjusting grievances to the heads of departments. As we are in an unorganized state, you might say the road master discharges the men under his jurisdiction at will.

Q. Do the railroads blacklist members of your organization, as is sometimes done in the case of men called trainmen?—A. All classes of railroad employees are subject to the black list. A majority of railways have an understanding, and they have rules. To illustrate: If you have charge of a division of road, and they dismiss you for cause or without a cause, if you go to another road in search of employment, they will ask you where you worked last; did you get a clearance from that company? Unless you can produce a letter from your immediate superior on the line you have been working for, showing where you have been, what you have been doing, and that you have made a good record, the man that you make application to for employment would simply say, "I do not need any more men."

Q. Does that refer to the Chinaman, the Hungarian, the Pole, or whoever comes along that wants a job?—A. That does not go below the foremen in the roadway department.

Q. (By Mr. KENNEDY.) Is that letter written in such form that it is sometimes taken to be a notice of blacklist?—A. I have heard it said that they have certain private marks by which they understand whether the letter means what it says or whether it means the opposite.

Q. (By Mr. KYLE.) What are the chances for promotion in your line of work?—A. The chances to be promoted to a foreman, if a man is reasonably intelligent and energetic, are fairly good; but the chances to go higher than the position of foreman are not very good.

Q. Are the higher positions chosen from your ranks?—A. On some lines they are and on some they are not. A great many of our road masters are civil engineers, men who never worked on a track a day in their lives, and do not even know how to handle the tools used to keep the track in proper condition.

Q. Your observation is that railway companies desire to put that system in operation?—A. The tendency is to have all the positions that pay well filled by the engineer class and not the working class.

Q. (By Mr. FARQUHAR.) Do you mean what might be called the educated class?—A. The educated class.

Q. (By Chairman KYLE.) Is it the policy of the companies to promote brakemen to the positions of conductors?—A. I am speaking only of maintenance-of-way department employees.

Q. (By Mr. KENNEDY.) Has your organization petitioned Congress and State legislatures for the passage of anti-scalping bills?—A. I believe I have written a few personal letters in regard to that matter.

Q. Asking for the passage of such bills?—A. Yes.

Q. (By Chairman KYLE.) Against ticket scalping?—A. Asking them to pass legislation in opposition to the scalping system.

Q. Is not that in favor of the present anti-scalping bill that is before Congress?—A. I have not read the present bill before Congress.

Q. (By Mr. KENNEDY.) Have you said in your statement that you could always get cheaper transportation by going to the scalpers than you could by purchasing from the railroads' regular agents?—A. If I am going a considerable distance such is always the case.

Q. (By Chairman KYLE.) Can you do this and maintain your honesty and integrity in every instance?—A. I have even gone to the company's regular agent and asked him, "What is your rate to a certain point?" and he would state the rate. Then, upon stepping across the street and asking a scalper, "Can you save me anything on a ticket?" stating the point that I wanted to go to, I do not remember that at any time I failed to get a ticket for from $1 to $5 cheaper than I could have bought it from the company's regular agent.

Q. A legitimate ticket?—A. No name on it. In some instances the broker stepped over to the office and bought the tickets from the company's regular agent.

Q. (By Mr. KENNEDY.) The same office?—A. The same office I had asked for rates.

Q. You say you have petitioned Congress to pass such a bill as that?—A. I have written to members of Congress personally in regard to the matter, and have also spoken to them about it when I have met them at different places.

Q. (By Mr. RATCHFORD.) In the paper you have read you state, I believe, that there were 180,000 trackmen employed in the United States. By the word "trackmen" do you mean section men or section foremen?—A. I mean all classes employed in the maintenance of way department.

Q. Including foremen?—A. Including roadmasters, foremen, and laborers that work on track, bridges, etc.

Q. In addition to that now, you stated, I believe, that there were 200,000 men employed in the car and shop works?—A. Yes.

Q. That is 380,000. In one of your statements you say that 90 per cent of those men are Americans; that means 90 per cent of the whole, shop and track men?—A. In my judgment 90 per cent of the whole are American citizens.

Q. In speaking of transient employees in your paper do you refer to all of them —shop men, track men, etc., as transient employees.—A. Largely so, in all three of these departments; but all of those transient men are not foreigners or aliens; many of them are Americans. They work during the summer months in one locality and then roam looking for work during the winter months, and wherever they happen to be located in the spring of the year, they drift back on the track.

Q. Is the fact that they have become transients due, not to any fault of their own or to their own restlessness, but to the fact that their employment gives out at certain seasons of the year?—A. That is right.

Q. I understand that the employers' liability laws vary very much in the different States as regards the protection afforded railroad employees. We would like to have your views in that connection.—A. The fellow-servants laws in some States are very unjust to the railway employees. For instance, in the State of Missouri some three or four years ago a track walker was going over the track carrying his tools, looking to see that everything was all right and in proper condition so that life and commerce could pass over those rails safely. The company wanted to deliver a message to this track walker. They gave it to a locomotive fireman, who wrapped the message around a lump of coal, and in passing this track walker on an engine, threw it off, striking him in the face and knocking one eye out, and he was not able to recover a cent for damages.

Q. Do the liability laws vary very much in the different States in the cases of men losing their lives in the employ of the company and in the discharge of their duty?—A. Very much, indeed.

Q. (By Mr. A. L. HARRIS.) What State has the best and most liberal laws toward the employee or the fellow-servant?—A. I can not answer that question.

Q. (By Mr. RATCHFORD.) Could you tell us what State has such laws as might be called the worst laws, from the standpoint of the workingman?—A. I would not care to answer that question without referring to records concerning those matters.

Q. Ninety per cent of the people you represent being American citizens, you are not hampered very much in your business by reason of foreign immigrants?—A. Except on the Pacific coast and in the New England States.

Q. (By Mr. FARQUHAR.) What class of laborers are the graders and construction laborers? Do they affiliate with you?—A. Under our laws they would not be eligible to membership in our organization. The men who do the grading and constructing are made up of all classes, from all countries.

Q. (By Mr. RATCHFORD.) What are the relations between the roadmasters and section foremen to the men who perform the labor?—A. The relations existing between the roadmasters and the foremen are very harmonious. The foremen are very much oppressed on account of having but a few men to perform a great amount of work, and by being stinted with material, etc., but ordinarily they feel that the roadmaster is doing all he can for them, and the reason why he is not supplied with more men and material to carry on his work is beyond the roadmaster. The feelings of sympathy toward the poor fellow that works with his tamping bar and pick and shovel has not been such as I would like it to be.

Q. Has not been as strong on the part of the foremen?—A. Neither upon the part of the roadmaster or foreman as I would like to see it.

Q. Are the men who are working on the section obliged to work during bad weather, during heavy rain storms, etc.?—A. When they receive orders from the foreman to do work that should be done on the section, it is like receiving orders from a military officer, with this exception: they can either do what they are instructed to do or leave. Our objects are to create better conditions in our department and to induce a better element to come into our ranks so that we can have this class of work done with a more intelligent class of men; in fact, a first-class trackman must be a skilled workman.

Q. (By Chairman KYLE.) The ordinary trackman?—A. An ordinary trackman, to be considered first-class, must be a skilled workman. It will take him four or five years to be a first-class trackman.

Q. I understood you to say, a minute ago, that many of these men were unskilled workmen.—A. They are not first-class. They are what you might term make-shifts. The foreman often has a gang of men and not one of them knows how to drive a spike. He has to take his hammer and gauge and drive the spike himself. He has to get down and show them how to do it.

Q. (By Mr. FARQUHAR.) Are not your section bosses coming nearer the workingman than they have been before, through your organization?—A. A better feeling between the men is being cultivated all round where the influence of the organization has been extended.

Q. Do you know a better way to maintain that sympathy than through your organization?—A. It is the only effort that has ever been made that has produced good results.

Q. Is it a fact that in the economical management of railroad beds, and the whole equipment, the necessary needs of the beds come from the men who are working below—the laborer—then to the section boss, then to the roadmaster, and then into the civil engineers' department, and that there is a unifying of all these interests on the road, and is it not becoming more so through organization?—A. It seems to be having a good effect.

Q. Is that the measure you would desire to carry out through the organization itself?—A. Yes; we desire to cultivate harmonious relations between all classes in our department.

Q. Does it come from a realization that the interests of the men are the interests of the road and the interests of the road are the interests of the men?—A. Yes.

Q. Why is it you do not find greater strength on the northern roads?—A. There has not been any effort on our part to extend the work of organization through that country. Our organization has not been in existence long. The organization not being in existence but a few years, we had all we could do at home.

Q. Have you any "organizers"

Q. What districts of the country do they cover? A. One of them is in Arkansas, two of them are in north Carolina, and one of them is in Florida at the present time.

Q. Was there ever any organization of what you might call the laboring part of the road—the track part of the road—in the North before you came up?—A. They have had local organizations, but they never accomplished anything.

Q. (By Chairman KYLE.) Do you think that railroad companies generally could afford to pay greater wages than they are paying for this class of work? Is that the opinion of your organization as a body?—A. I maintain that if the money that railroad companies seem to think they have to expend in competing with other lines was saved, and the free transportation they give away was sold for money, their incomes would be increased so that they would be able to pay living wages to all classes of their employees.

Q. You think it is bad management, then, on the part of the companies, of their own business affairs?—A. I think it is bad management on the part of the companies if their receipts do not enable them to treat all their employees as well as they treat some of them. They can increase their income by doing away with this unnecessary expenditure of money.

Q. You think the giving away of transportation, giving rebates in freight rates, etc., is one cause?—A. In other words, I think something should be done to protect railroad companies against themselves.

Q. What do you think about the salaries paid to the high officials of railroads? Do you think they pay too much for the salaries of presidents, managers, attorneys, etc., and too little to others?—A. I maintain that the money paid out for services by the railroad companies is not equitably distributed; some of them are paid more than they need and more than they are entitled to, and others are compelled to work for a great deal less than a man can work for and maintain himself in a manner becoming an American citizen.

Q. Do you think that the railways in issuing watered stock, etc., compel themselves to cut the rates of these workingmen?—A. I think every drop of water that has been poured into railroad stocks should be squeezed out.

Q. You think there is revenue enough, then, derived from freight and passenger traffic throughout the United States, to pay good living wages to every workingman on the railroads?—A. If the railroad business was properly managed.

Q. If they were paying interest on legitimate bonds and stocks?—A. There would be plenty of money to pay living wages to all men engaged in operating roads, and to pay the stockholders reasonable dividends on their investments, in my opinion.

Q. (By Mr. A. L. HARRIS) Under the benefit insurance, which you say companies require employees to take in an indirect way, is the fact of insurance having been paid or due ever plead at law by the company in defense when an injury is sustained?—A. In some instances, they make the employee accepting a position agree that money paid in that way shall indemnify the companies or shall protect the companies from loss on account of personal injury, etc.

Q. (By Mr. A. L. HARRIS.) Is it a contract not to bring suit against the company in case of injury?—A. Yes; and when an employee is injured or killed and leaves a widow, if the company has two or three thousand dollars that belongs to her according to right of contract and for which her husband has paid, she feels that she should deal more leniently with the company, and it assists them in making compromises and settling claims for death or disability for less than they would under other circumstances. There is no doubt in my mind that these schemes are of great advantage to the railroad companies; they assist them in keeping their employees unorganized. The Plant System, for instance, has a man for general superintendent by the name of Denham, who organized an insurance scheme for the company. The locomotive engineers were induced by him to withdraw from their own organization and to take policies with the company, and I have been informed that no organization can do anything with any class of employees on the road. One of our organizers reports that he can not obtain members on the system on account of the men being compelled to insure with the company.

Q. Is it a selfish motive the railroads have in view when they compel the employee to insure? Is it for their own protection?—A. Men who are well paid in the different departments can simply request a man working for them to do a thing and he does it, You know, if you have had any experience with men working under you, that a request from an employer to an employee is almost equal to a demand. In that way they succeed in weakening the organizations, and at the same time reduce the companies' liabilities.

WASHINGTON, D. C., *March 3, 1899.*

TESTIMONY OF PROF. E. R. JOHNSON,

Of the University of Pennsylvania.

The commission met at 11.30 a. m., March 3, 1899; Vice-Chairman Phillips presided, and introducing Mr. E. R. Johnson, said he was a professor of transportation and commerce in the University of Pennsylvania

Mr. JOHNSON. Mr. Phillips very kindly sent me a request to come over to meet the members of the commission this morning, and I came over with the supposition that I would be interrogated rather than give any formal discussion. I am not a technical man nor a practical transportation man, and probably my evidence will not be so useful to the commission as that of men of more practical training. My work during the last seven years has compelled me to acquaint myself with transportation literature. I have made two investigations for the department of labor, one on railway relief departments and one on the relief and insurance features of the brotherhoods, the latter being concerned with the brotherhoods as a whole, although emphasis was laid upon their relief features.

These studies have given me some insight into the railway organizations and their beneficial features. I have also followed during the last few years the work of the Interstate Commerce Commission. I notice that a good part of your outline deals with the work of State regulation. I may say that I have taken some interest in the studies which others are conducting on the subject of railway taxation, and perhaps the taxation of railways is a subject concerning which I have at least general information. Some years ago I prepared a monograph on inland waterways, which was published by the American Academy of Political and Social Science, and at that time I got some knowledge of water transportation. I say these things to you simply to indicate where the lines of my study have run, in order that you may interrogate me to better advantage.

Now as regards your outline, my first observation is that it is very comprehensive. I see the commission has in reality proposed to prepare a treatise covering the whole subject of transportation in all its various phases. I trust the commission will be able to carry out its plan. If it does I think it will result in the publication of one or more volumes that will be of use, not only to the legislatures of the States and to Congress, but also to every other student of the subject. The first part of your report deals with railway labor. I will say I think that the subject of railway labor in this country needs to be investigated, and it occurs to me that the United States department of labor ought to authorize some such a study of American railway labor as it has authorized and published on railway labor in Europe. I dare say all the members of the commission know that the Bulletin of the department of labor for January, 1899, contains a monograph of some 60,000 words in length on railway labor in Europe. It was prepared by Dr. Walter E. Weyl, a young man who has been studying with us at the University of Pennsylvania for the past three years. He has made a very valuable report, and what I think we now need is some such study for our own country as Dr. Weyl got out for Europe.

On page 4 of the outline it might be well to insert under "4" "And also a discussion of the recent laws of England and France." Part 4, as you will note, deals with "Extent of modification by statutes of common-law rule as to negligence of fellow servants; legislation of the States thereon, and effect thereof; statutes authorizing persons dependent on employee to sue for damages when the employee has been killed through negligence of railroad." That, it seems to me, is a very important part of the commission's outline, and I dare say the commission knows that in 1837 there was a decision of the English courts which modified the common law. In 1880 and 1897 there were statutes enacted by which the English law was very much modified in the interest of the employee. The Massachusetts and Alabama statutes, I believe, are copied after the English law of 1880.

Q. (By Mr. PHILLIPS.) What are the titles of your publications in the Bulletin of the department of labor?—A. One report was made in January, 1897, on Railway Relief Department, and another report on Brotherhood Relief and Insurance was published last July.

On the subject of automatic couplers, of course you won't expect me to make any observations; that question is well covered in the last annual report of the Interstate Commerce Commission; they have gone into the question thoroughly. We are all aware Great Britain seems about to adopt measures very similar to those we have adopted in this country.

Q. (By Mr. KENNEDY.) Did you investigate the question of relief associations from the standpoint of the employees themselves; did you go to them for data?— A. I got all my material from the secretaries of the brotherhoods.

Q. Did you find they were entirely satisfied with these relief societies which are promoted and in part sustained by the railroad companies?—A. No; they are not. There is some friction, indeed, between the relief features of the brotherhoods and the railway relief associations. Some of the railway companies having relief associations, three of them, until the passage of the arbitration law in 1898, made membership in their relief department compulsory; and in view of the fact that a majority of railroad men could not afford to carry insurance in the relief departments and in the brotherhoods, both the relief departments rather worked against the beneficial departments of the brotherhoods.

Q. Did it lessen their allegiance to the brotherhood organization?—A. Yes; and made it rather difficult for a man who was to be a member of the relief department to join the brotherhoods. For instance, a prominent official of an important railway corporation told me in a confidential conversation that he did not care whether the membership in the relief association was compulsory or not. At that time his railway made membership in his association compulsory; but he stated that he did not care whether it was compulsory to join the association or not, for the reason that the indirect pressure that the corporation could bring to bear would accomplish the same result.

Q. Did they force the employees?—A. Yes. From the testimony that has come to me I have come to believe that the employees of the corporations having voluntary relief departments feel rather insecure if they are not members of relief associations, because if it is necessary to lay off men, the men who are picked out to be laid off are the men who are not members of the association.

Q. (By Mr. FARQUHAR.) Will you explain the difference between relief and benefits proper of the brotherhoods and the railway departments, and name the prominent railways that have the beneficial associations.—A. There are six large corporations that have these relief departments: The Baltimore and Ohio, the Pennsylvania lines east and west of Pittsburg, the Burlington system, the Reading and Plant systems. The contributions to the relief associations are compulsory; that is, the contributions of members of associations are deducted from their monthly pay, and they range from 75 cents, in multiples of 75 cents up to, I think the highest is, $3.75 a month, and the benefits which they derive from them are a death benefit, $250 for a 75 cent per month payment, and then an accident and sickness relief, which ranges from $1 to $1.50 a day, beginning usually after the first week of illness. Three of these six corporations made membership compulsory until 1898. The brotherhoods provide in general for a considerably larger death benefit than the relief associations do, but the brotherhoods in their central organizations do not make any provisions for sickness and accident relief. That relief, however, is to a large extent accomplished through the lodges and divisions of the brotherhoods. Many lodges have a relief organization; that is, they have a distinct association for sickness and accident. I have made a report on a few of these lodges in my report to the department of labor, and I find that their members are getting as much relief in accident and sickness as members of the relief associations secure. I said that the central organizations of the railroad brotherhoods do not give relief in case of accident or sickness; they do in case of permanent disability, and sometimes in cases of sickness which results from any permanent disability, but the kinds of sickness are very carefully marked out. I tried to make a conscientious and perfectly fair comparison of the actual results of relief in the two organizations; that is, the associations which the corporations supported, and the associations which were entirely supported by the brotherhoods, and the results to which I came were practically negative; that is, the amount of effective relief accomplished is practically the same. I have given a comparative table in the Bulletin and my conclusions are based on the table.

Q. (By Mr. PHILLIPS.) Is that in the July, 1898, Bulletin?—A. Yes. The results of my study were that the amount of relief which the railway employee got was practically the same whether he got it from the brotherhood or from the relief association. I think, however, the employees get a great many advantages from the brotherhoods which they do not get if they are not members of the brotherhood, and the relief associations tend to prevent the development of the brotherhoods.

Q. (By Mr. FARQUHAR.) Do the railroads contribute to these relief funds at all, or is the draft made entirely on the wages of the employees?—A. They contribute what amounts to from 16 to 20 per cent of the actual expenses of the relief association. They contribute all the office expenses and the expense of managing the association; that is, the officers and staff of the relief departments are members of the regular railway staff, and the railway relief association have full use of the facilities for telegraphing and railway mail. Furthermore, the railway companies also obligate themselves to make up any deficiency that may arise in settling the obligations which the associations assume, and some corporations have contributed substantially for this purpose. The actual contributions on the part of the rail-roads range from 16 to 20 per cent of the total contributions. In England the corporations contribute one-half.

Q. (By Mr. NORTH.) Is that a voluntary contribution?—A. Yes. I do not think, however, that the railroad corporations are necessarily more just there. A comparative scale of wages in England and America was gathered by Dr. Weyl.

Q. Are you able to give the commission information as to the uniformity in the wages which exists between the different parts of this country?—A. That subject is taken up in the annual reports of the statistician to the Interstate Commerce Commission.

Q. Have you an impression on that subject; that is, as to the causes of differences?—A. My impression on what data I have seen on the subject is that the differences are due to exactly the same cause in this country as in Europe, namely, that the wages in the railway service were determined by the conditions governing labor in the different parts of the country where railway men work. In other words, wages are fixed by the general standards that govern all classes of labor.

Q. Is that the operation of the law of supply and demand?—A. Dr. Weyl has compiled statistics from France and other countries showing that the general labor supply controls wages in the transportation as well as in other industries, and when we study the causes of differences in this country, I think we will find the same thing true.

Q. (By Mr. FARQUHAR.) Do you find, in your investigations of the benefit arrangements in lodges and brotherhoods, that within the last eight or ten years the rate has become very high because there is no new blood coming into the organization itself to sustain the association?—A. If you have the report here, I can show you just what the members have contributed per thousand dollars, insurance. You will find on pages 571–586, inclusive, Volume III, Bulletin, Department of Labor, a statistical presentation of the amounts contributed and distributed by the associations for a series of years. There is no evidence of a rising cost per thousand dollars of insurance carried. New blood is being taken into the brotherhoods rapidly.

Q. In some of those brotherhoods do the members have to carry two classes of insurance, one in the railway relief department and one in the brotherhood?—A. Some of them do, but the tendency is to forego the membership in the brotherhood if they are obliged to join the relief association.

Q. Are the assessments taken out of the wages anyway, one being voluntary and the other involuntary on the part of the men?—A. Yes; that is true.

Q. (By Mr. RATCHFORD.) Is the insurance which they secure through membership in the relief associations partly supported by the corporations usually termed compulsory by the railroad employees?—A. As I said a few minutes ago, in the case of three corporations it actually was compulsory until 1898, and from what I can find out, railway employees feel that they are not so secure without being members of the relief associations, even if it is not compulsory.

Q. Do you regard such insurance as being just to the employees?—A. I must say that if we have to choose between the two, as we apparently must to some extent, I should choose the brotherhood as being more just—the brotherhood plan rather than the relief department plan.

Q. What has this form of insurance, supported by the companies, to do with the employers' liability law? Are the employees, in connecting themselves with such insurance companies, not under obligation to exempt their employers from damages in case of accident or death while in the discharge of their duties?—A. You of course know that the rules of all the relief associations which are organized by the corporations have a contract clause in the rules by which a man signs away his right to sue for damages in case of accident if he accepts remuneration through the relief associations, and the general practice of the courts has been to hold those contracts as legal.

Q. Does not the use of the funds of the relief departments, together with other considerations, such as exemption from the liability laws, indemnify the company for the interest they have in the funds of that association?—A. I should answer unhesitatingly, yes. I think the corporations have organized the relief departments not from philanthropy but because it is good business. The railway companies, however, pay interest on the funds of the relief departments.

Q. (By Mr. KENNEDY.) Is it a fact that the railroad companies promote these insurance associations to be inimical to the railroad organizations; that it is intended in time of trouble, in the case of strikes, for instance, to place the railroad employee in a quandary as to whether he shall follow his union or remain with the company?—A. I agree with you that that has perhaps been the dominant motive. I think it would be unfair to the railroads, however, if we did not accede to them the desire to raise the morale of the service, and they certainly do raise the general standard of efficiency through the examination the employees are obliged to pass because of the relief departments. I think men like Dr. Barnard, who organized the first railroad relief association in this country, were men who were prompted by philanthropic motives, but I think the economic motive is the motive of the corporations. It does bind the employees to the corporations.

Q. I have just read Dr. Weyl's article and I notice that there are railroads in England that pension their employees. Do you know whether these pension funds are affairs of the company or whether they are built up by associations on the wages of employees?—A. In England they are a part of the relief associations and they are fathered by the corporation.

Q. (By Mr. PHILLIPS.) In the case of injury of an employee, are they as liable to bring action for damages against the railroad if they belong to this association?—A. They very seldom do it.

Q. (By Mr. FARQUHAR.) Can they do it if they have a contract?—A. If it is believed there is a good case against the corporation and more can be secured through the courts than from the death benefit, his heirs may decide to take the legal action instead of the benefit.

Q. (By Mr. SMYTH.) Are the brotherhoods incorporated? Is there any way in which an injured person could bring any action against the officials of the brotherhoods?—A. The brotherhoods are not incorporated, but the insurance association of the engineers is incorporated; that is the only incorporated body, I believe.

Q. Is the man who may be injured entirely at the mercy of the brotherhood? Do they pass upon it?—A. They pass upon it. I never observed any complaint on that score.

Q. What would be the condition of a man who has been sick a couple of months? Does the railroad still keep him insured?—A. Provision is made for that; a man may be absent from service for nine months without sacrificing his membership.

Q. If a railway engineer or fireman is sick and does not work for two months and receives no pay from the railway company, is he kept insured?—A. He has to keep up his assessments. Perhaps I do not understand your question. While he is sick and receiving benefits he makes no contributions. If, however, he is laid off by the railroad corporation temporarily, because they have restricted their labor force, he can continue his regular assessments and retain his membership.

Q. (By Mr. FARQUHAR). Does he have to continue, then, whether employed or unemployed?—A. Yes.

Q. Is it true that there is some little advantage in the corporation insurance, as they call it, in this fact, that most of the railroads, after an employee is injured, say by the loss of an arm, so that he is incapacitated for hard labor, usually take care of that man by giving him a watchman's position, or some place which, under his disablement, he can fill?—A. It is customary to do that, and corporations make contributions which they are not obliged to make to aid their needy employees, men who have been in their service. This form of relief to injured employees is not confined to the companies having relief departments; it is the general practice. You will, however, find in the reports of the relief associations that contributions on the part of corporations to aid the aged are quite considerable. On the whole, corporations, as far as they can, manifest a desire to treat their employees so that the employees will feel that the corporation is fair to them.

Q. (By Mr. PHILLIPS). I presume you have a very considerable amount of authentic information on this question that would be valuable to this commission.—A. I think if you will take my report as a basis of your investigation of railway employees' relief, together with the various secretaries' reports for the past year or two, you can bring my work down to date, and will have pretty much what you wish with one exception. I have not worked up in detail the smaller insurance and relief associations of employees that are connected with one system. For instance, there are in New England six associations, among them the Old Colony Association. The Lehigh Valley and the Great Northern Association are typical of those outside of New England. They represent a phase of the subject—of the support by the corporations of insurance and relief. These small associations of employees are connected with only one road, and they usually are assisted more or less by the corporations, as in the case of the Lehigh Valley, Old Colony, Great Northern, and others that might be mentioned.

Q. At some future time will you give this commission an outline of what you think ought to be done to bring the investigation up to date?—A. I shall be pleased to do so.

Q. (By Mr. FARQUHAR.) Have you made any investigation as to the extent of the interest of the railroad employees in the corporations as held out by the Illinois Central?—A. I have followed in a general way the scheme of the Illinois Central, and am perhaps a little more familiar with the Pennsylvania savings fund and the Baltimore and Ohio building and loan arrangement. There are other corporations which have similar arrangements, but I have not the information in detail.

Q. (By Mr. SMYTH.) If an employee is insured both in the brotherhood and in the railroad beneficial fund, would he derive benefits from both in case of accident?—A. Yes. In the case of volunteer relief associations of the Pennsylvania Railroad type, you will find a large number of men who are members of both.

I should like to say just a word on the subject of rates in your outline, if I may pass to page 7. I would suggest that you put here before "21" a division devoted to the study of the general causes affecting railway rates in different parts of the United States. There has been a study of the causes affecting rates and fares made by Dr. Weyl. The study was published in the annals of the American Academy, and that article of some thirty pages in length, it seems to me, is a good and a clear analysis of the causes affecting rates and to some extent wages; but the question of wages has not been studied in detail, and I think it would be well to include in the investigation of the commission an investigation of those causes which obtain in different parts of the country, to see whether the railroad service in this country, as apparently it is in Europe, is subject to the same influences that affect the labor market generally.

Q. (By Mr. KENNEDY.) Have you anything to say under that head as to the effect of ticket brokerage upon railway employment and the railway wages?—A. I know nothing about that; I don't know whether it would be possible to trace any connection between ticket brokerage and railroad employment and railroad wages other than the general relation that ticket brokerage does undoubtedly decrease the receipts of the railway corporations somewhat, and to that extent it may have the effect of preventing them from paying as high wages as they otherwise would pay. Ticket brokerage does have some effect on the financial standing of corporations.

Q. The question I want to ask does not seem to be outlined: Do railroad companies share their prosperity with their employees? For instance, the C. B. and Q. R. R. has not within the past year, I understand, increased the wages of its employees. The stock of that railroad company the day war was declared with Spain was down to 88 cents. That was a low market. It is now in the neighborhood of 146. Is it a fact that the railway organizations or companies do not share their prosperity with their employees as a rule, and will not do it unless they are forced to do so by strong labor organizations?—A. I do not think the railroad corporation will increase wages beyond the ordinary scale unless it is compelled to do so under the influence of organized labor.

Q. (By Mr. PHILLIPS.) Do railroads in the hands of receivers pay the same wages as railroads that have very large net earnings?—A. Yes.

Q. Do those that are losing money or are not making money pay about the same rate as those that are making large profits?—A. The wages of the railway employees are fixed by the wages paid by other corporations, are they not?

Q. Calling attention now to 23, "Effect of watering stock and unnecessary additions to bonded indebtedness upon railway employment and railway wages." Have you any remarks to make?—A. It is usually said that the watering of stock or the unnecessary additions to bonded indebtedness do not affect the scale of wages paid or the rates charged by railroads. I question whether the statement in that form is true. In the long run, say in the course of twenty-five years, a corporation that has a very large capitalization will be able to secure for the owners of the capital a larger amount from the earnings than they would secure if the capitalization represented the actual value of the property. I think it can hardly be questioned that the public is influenced by the fact that railroads have very small earnings in proportion to capitalization. Dividends of a small per cent constitute an argument against State interference of any kind that imposes burdens upon a corporation.

Q. Have you information as to the amount of capital stock of the various railroads in the United States, and also about the actual cost of the same?—A. Nobody knows.

Q. Is there about one-third actual cash and two-thirds water?—A. You may find various estimates; we have nothing but estimates.

Q. (By Mr. A. L. HARRIS.) What becomes of the substance when water is put in?—A. Water means the capitalization of future hopes, and after these hopes are realized then the water becomes actual value.

Q. Are there not times when we consider that stock is water when really the companies are raising money to better their road, rebuild it almost?—A. Yes; and the additions in capital account may make the road actually increase in value: I do not think it is fair to call all new stock water, when the property does actually increase in value largely.

Part II takes up "Transportation by land in its relation to the public." Passenger travel in this country is relatively undeveloped. We are not large travelers. It is a common supposition that the Americans are extensive travelers, but the Europeans travel much more in proportion to the population. I published a short article in the Chicago Record last year, in which I brought out some of the figures regarding passenger travel. The figures disprove the common supposition that we are great travelers by rail in this country. What we need is not a better service, but a cheaper service in this country. I see that a move has been made by the Baltimore and Ohio Railway for cheaper sleepers, a move which is in the direction of cheaper service. When we get rid of ticket brokerage, as I think we shall, the railroads will be able to devote more attention to the excursion business and to offering special attractions for travelers, in some such manner as they do in Great Britain. In 1890 the reduction in rates in Hungary and Austria was followed by an immense amount of traffic, but there was very little travel before this change was introduced.

Q. (By Mr. KENNEDY.) Have you anything to say about the practice of giving passes, State laws prohibiting them, etc.?—A. I think it is something that ought to be prohibited by law. I think passes ought without exception to be restricted to actual employees of the railway corporations, and there is no doubt in my mind that the influences of the pass system upon our legislatures and judiciary are altogether bad.

Q. (By Mr. PHILLIPS.) Have you anything further to state in regard to ticket brokerage?—A. Nothing, except that, from the standpoint of the development of passenger traffic, it is to my mind essential that ticket brokerage should be done away with.

Q. (By Mr. KENNEDY.) Who should do away with ticket brokerage—the railroads themselves, or should it be done by national legislation?—A. I don't think the railroads themselves will be able to do away with it, unless they succeed in cooperating. There is nothing in the way of their cooperating excepting their own inability to do so, but that is quite sufficient.

Q. Is it their fault that the ticket brokerage system exists?—A. I think the railroads, as a whole, would be very glad to do away with ticket brokerage, but there will always be roads that will refuse to act with the others.

Q. Why do they refuse?—A. Ticket brokerage is one device used by competing roads to get business. The ticket brokerage is kept up, of course, as a part of a plan of discrimination. That is, the roads which have a desire to cut rates are really responsible for the maintenance of the ticket-brokerage business.

Q. Do not you believe there are greater evils that should be remedied by Congress?—A. I agree with you. I think the strengthening of the authority of the commission is of much more importance, but, personally, I shall be glad to see the ticket-brokerage law passed.

Q. (By Mr. PHILLIPS.) Has any member of the commission any question to ask under Division B, page 9?—A. There is a great mass of evidence on that division of your outline that has been collected during the last thirty years by the various reports, such as the Windom, Hepburn, and Cullom, and by the investigation of the Interstate Commerce Commission.

Q. We will pass to page 11. As regards question No. 36, "Reparation to individuals for damage from unjust discriminations, undue preferences, and unreasonable rates." There is no remedy, would be the answer, would it not?—A. Of course, if a man has been charged an excessive rate in the past he can secure damages equal to the difference between the sum he was charged and the amount he ought to have been charged; that is no real remedy for the damage he has suffered. He may have suffered a thousand times that damage. I am heartily in accord with the position taken by the chairman of the Interstate Commerce Commission. I should very much like to see the plan of regulation that is advocated by the Interstate Commerce Commission put into law. It would probably lessen to a large extent the amount of damages the public would suffer from discriminations. The individuals who are discriminated against will always be unable to collect damages equal to the amount of their losses.

Q. (By Mr. SMYTH.) Is there no legal remedy?—A. No.

Q. (By Mr. PHILLIPS.) Do you think there should be a publication of freight rates?—A. Undoubtedly; I think this is the first thing to be done in railway regulation, and I should insist on full publicity of rates as the first requisite in railway legislation.

Q. Have you anything to say on "Joint traffic associations and pooling contracts?"—A. The University of Pennsylvania is going to publish a study on "Railway cooperations" that will contain some historic material that may be of service.

Q. How soon will that be out?—A. In a few weeks.

Q. (By Mr. SMYTH.) If the pooling system could be established under the authority of the Interstate Commerce Commission, would it result to the benefit of all classes?—A. I am in favor of trying it.

Q. (By Mr. PHILLIPS.) Under Governmental supervision?—A. Yes. I think the chief opponents of railroad pooling at the present time are the big corporations that are getting a satisfactory rate. I believe there are a great many factors affecting railroad rates, and if the railroads of the country are allowed to cooperate they will not be able to charge exorbitant rates. I don't anticipate exorbitant rates as a result of railway combination.

Q. What are your views in regard to the "Consideration or advisability of requiring all books and accounts of interstate railroads to be open at all times to inspection by United States examiners?"—A. I think that is a very important question, and I am decidedly in accord with Prof. Henry C. Adams. I regard the railroad service as essentially a public service, and see just as good reason for publicity of the workings of railway corporations as I do for banking corporations. I think publicity would be in nowise unjust to the railways, and would be of immense public advantage.

Q. On page 12: "Consideration of advisability of prohibiting by law the increase of stock by interstate railways without a governmental permit therefor, after application and hearing?"—A. I have given that question some thought, but it is a question with me whether Congress could accomplish anything; indeed, I do not know whether Congress could control the issue of stock. I am not lawyer enough to know whether Congress could actually control the stock of corporations chartered by the States. I dare say that members of this commission can answer that question. My experience of Massachusetts and Texas, as far as I can gather from official sources, seems to be in favor of such laws. The report of the Massachusetts commission, and the reports I have received from Texas, seem to indicate that the laws regulating stock issues are working well.

The study of "Railroad charters in various States" is one, I think, that ought to be made, and I hope the commission will lay some emphasis on that phase of its investigation. The subject has been taken up in a general way by Dr. Meyer, of the University of Wisconsin. He is making a special study of railways of the State of Wisconsin, and as a basis of his investigation he has made some study of the charters granted to railroad corporations in other States, in order to compare Wisconsin with the other States. We have suffered, of course, in this country very greatly from the variation of charter regulations and the vacillating policy followed by the States from time to time, and it seems to me a good deal of light will be thrown upon the railroad question by a careful study of railroad charters. We do not know very much about them. In 1850 or 1851 the charters granted by the six New England States were published in two volumes. They are in the office of the Interstate Commerce Commission.

As regards railway taxation, Prof. Henry C. Adams has a scheme for Federal taxation of railways instead of State taxation, which he has published in a recent number of the Review of Reviews.

Q. (By Mr. RATCHFORD.) Do you believe railroads should be taxed according to their net earnings?—A. I should be inclined to tax them on their gross earnings. A license tax, it seems to me, is the best of all. I think the States will come to that presently. Of course there are some States that have adopted that method. Wisconsin has, and Illinois has for a part of her railways. This is a sure way to collect the tax. If you resort to the general property tax for railroads, it results, as it does in my own State of Pennsylvania, in the railroads being taxed a score of different rates.

Q. (By Mr. SMYTH.) Would not taxation on gross earnings tend to decrease the betterments on the road?—A. If you made it so excessive as to be a burden. The amount of the burden imposed by the tax depends upon whether it is a tax that the roads are able to shift on the travelers and shippers. Probably it is not a tax that they can shift, because the rates and fares are largely controlled by factors over which the railways themselves have only a small control; consequently when you put a tax burden on a corporation such as a railway, the burden rests there.

Q. (By Mr. A. L. HARRIS.) Would you use the entire funds arising from the tax for State business, or would you distribute it pro rata among the counties through which the road passes?—A. That is a question to be determined by local conditions.

Q. (By Mr. FARQUHAR.) Has a State granting a charter to an original company which ultimately went beyond the bounds of the State, a right to assess the whole property? Take, for instance, the Pittsburg and Fort Wayne road, having an Ohio, Indiana, and Illinois charter. Have any of these States the right to assess on the whole property of the system?—A. I have not carefully studied the decisions of the Supreme Court in the Ohio tax case, but as I understand these decisions the States have a right to tax property within the State only. The Ohio law, however, places a very liberal interpretation on what is in the State, and the Supreme Court has upheld that interpretation, I believe. Dr. Howe, of Cleveland, has recently sent the American Academy of Political and Social Science at Philadelphia a paper on the taxation of railways in Ohio. The paper will soon be published.

Taxation upon business done opens a large field for taxation, of course. In Kentucky and Indiana the laws are similar to the Ohio law. I regard transportation as a legitimate object of taxation.

Q. (By Mr. PHILLIPS.) Would you tax express companies, sleeping-car companies, etc.?—A. All forms of transportation I regard as legitimate objects for taxation. I am of the opinion that we will get the same kind of transportation if we impose upon the transportation companies the ordinary tax that we impose upon property generally.

Q. Have you any information to give in regard to the history of injunctions?—A. That question opens a large field for discussion—the question whether or not it is desirable to limit the common law by statute regarding the use of the injunction. I am inclined to think we shall decide to place some limitations by statute upon the common law in regard to injunctions. I do not pretend to be lawyer enough to form a definite programme.

Q. (By Mr. RATCHFORD.) Do you believe the issuing of injunctions in case of strikes of railway employees is adopted by corporations to aid them in reaching their ends?—A. Yes.

Q. Do you find they are intended for that purpose?—A. Yes. The corporations that pray for injunctions have found the injunction a very efficient means of accomplishing their ends.

Q. Is it not a fact that the transportation of the United States mails very largely assists corporations in obtaining those injunctions?—A. Of course it does.

Q. I should like to have you explain wherein the United States mails are interfered with and to what extent, and a comparison between the transportation of mails in the United States and in foreign countries, where the injunction is not so freely resorted to—in England, for instance?—A. I am afraid I do not possess the information necessary to answer your question. This much I do know, that the railroads attach mail cars in the case of a strike to as many trains as possible in order to avail themselves of the protection of the national laws in regard to carrying mails, and probably they have abused their privilege in that regard.

Q. (By Mr. PHILLIPS.) We would like to hear from you concerning transportation by water.—A. I think the commission will have great difficulty in getting hold of any really accurate and reliable information in regard to transportation by water. The statistics are collected only in part, and those that are collected are notoriously inaccurate, so that I do not anticipate, if I may be frank, that the commission will be able to secure very much reliable data in regard to inland transportation. The statistics of the transportation on the Great Lakes, prepared by Mr. Tunnell and published by the United States Treasury Department, is a very comprehensive study, but I understand that the author had to draw his statistics from sources which he found to be extremely inaccurate. We have very incomplete statistics of our traffic by rivers and canals, and they are by no means accurate. In regard to the relation of rivers and canals to railway commerce, it seems to me that the Interstate Commerce Commission is right in its recommendation that carriers by water as well as carriers by rail should be obliged to report to the commission, and that all carriers should be subject to a like degree of regulation. Probably there should be some action by law to prevent the freezing out of competing steamship lines that is resorted to on the part of railways. Of course it will have to be more than simply a prohibition, such as the State of Pennsylvania has put in her constitution, and which has been a dead letter. I do not think the day of water transportation is altogether past. I think that carriers by water will play an important part in our transportation business in the future, even in competition with the railroads, but the traffic will have to be carried on more highly developed and more efficient waterways than those that were constructed thirty or forty years ago.

Q. (By Mr. A. L. HARRIS.) Do you refer to the canals?—A. Yes, and to the improvement of rivers. The time of the strictly barge canal is very nearly past. Large barges of several hundred tons are being built, and will continue to carry an important part in our traffic on the larger natural and artificial waterways.

Q. (By Mr. PHILLIPS.) Have you anything else to say to the commission?—A. My monograph on inland transportation contains considerable information that may be of interest to the commission.

WASHINGTON, D. C., *March 16, 1899.*

TESTIMONY OF MR. FRANK P. SARGENT,

Grand Master of the Brotherhood of Locomotive Firemen.

The commission met at 11 a. m., Vice-Chairman Phillips presiding. Mr. Frank P. Sargent, Grand Master of the Brotherhood of Locomotive Firemen, testified.

Mr. Sargent presented a paper signed by the chiefs of the five railway organizations, the same being in answer to Part I of the syllabus on transportation, which was read by the secretary, as follows:

MARCH 10, 1899.

WM. E. SACKETT, Esq.,
    Secretary Industrial Commission, Washington, D. C.

DEAR SIR: We hand you herewith answers on our part, as representatives of our organizations, to the questions propounded in the syllabus of inquiry relative to transportation, sent out by the Industrial Commission. We have hastened preparation of this, and hand it to you in a less complete form than it would otherwise have been made because of the seeming anxiety on the part of the commission to get some evidence or information from us. As indicated in the answers, we shall expect to supplement them with definite information which has been sought and which at the present writing is not at hand.

Yours, very truly,

P. M. ARTHUR,
    Grand Chief Brotherhood of Locomotive Engineers.
F. P. SARGENT,
    Grand Master Brotherhood of Locomotive Firemen.
E. E. CLARK,
    Grand Chief Order of Railway Conductors.
R. H. MORRISSEY,
    Grand Master Brotherhood of Railroad Trainmen.
W. V. POWELL,
    Grand Chief Order of Railroad Telegraphers.

Answers on part of the Brotherhood of Locomotive Engineers, Brotherhood of Locomotive Firemen, Order of Railway Conductors, Brotherhood of Railway Trainmen, and Order of Railroad Telegraphers to questions propounded in Topical Plan of Inquiry of Subcommission on Transportation of the Industrial Commission.

First. The employees in branches of service represented by the above-named organizations are quite generally employed at rates of compensation and under terms of employment mutually agreed upon between the officers of the railway company and committees representing the men. In addition to these rules, the men are subject to the rules of the company relative to movement of trains, conduct of men, and care of property intrusted to their care.

The basis of pay for engine men and for train men in freight service is the number of miles run, with a minimum allowance as agreed upon. Train men in passenger service are generally paid by the month, although on many important roads they are paid by the mile or the trip. There are certain rates which are recognized as standard and which are in force, or are very closely approached, on all important lines west of the Hudson River and north of the Ohio River, and west of the Mississippi River. The standard for engineers in passenger service is 3½ cents per mile; in freight service, 4 cents per mile; for firemen, is 58 per cent of the engineers' pay. The standard rate for conductors in freight service is 3 cents per mile; for brakemen, 66⅔ per cent of the conductors' pay. Passenger conductors get from $100 to $125 per month, and passenger brakemen from $50 to $70 per month. The standard pay for yard foremen is 27 cents per hour for day work and 29 cents per hour for night work, and for yard switchmen is 25 cents per hour for day work and 27 cents per hour for night work.

In the Southern States colored men are used a great deal as firemen and brakemen. This practice has a strong tendency to unfavorably affect the rates of pay of men on neighboring roads, for the colored men work much more cheaply than white men could be induced to or than they could find it possible to do.

Telegraphers, train dispatchers, and station agents are generally paid by the month, and it is but of comparative recent date that the unfavorable and unsatisfactory conditions which have surrounded them in their work have been ameliorated to an appreciable degree. The rates of pay in this service varies with the importance of the station at which the men are employed.

The standard rate for train dispatchers is $125 per month, working in 8-hour tricks. The standard for station agents and telegraphers is fixed by establishing a minimum salary, and adding thereto as is proper in consideration of the responsibility assumed and the work performed. The pay of station agents and telegraph operators runs from $40 to $85 per month.

As a rule, the rates of wages are quite stable, the wages of the men who work by the mile or the trip being affected by the volume of business. Some few reductions in rates were made during the business depression of 1893-94. The earning power of the whole was seriously curtailed by the great falling off in the volume of business.

A few railway companies conduct relief associations for their employees and deductions from the wages of the employees are made therefor. In some few instances hospital associations are conducted on similar plan and deductions for their support are made. The practice of fining men for breakages or minor offenses has been practically abolished in deference to the wishes of the employees.

Men are discharged for violation of rules, responsibility for accidents, insubordination, intoxication, dishonesty, and occasionally for incompetency. Suspension from duty without pay is frequently made as a punishment for the less flagrant offenses. The plan of keeping record of men's conduct by a system of merit and demerit entries has of late quite generally taken the place of suspension as punishment.

The practice of blacklisting exemployes was for some time indulged in to a great extent. Vigorous laws, both State and national, have put a stop to the practice of voluntary blacklisting. The practice generally followed now is to require from the men entering the employ a statement of his former experience and employment, and to inquire from his former employers as to his leaving their employ. This practice has, in reality, the effect of the old blacklist, while at the same time it does not render those who follow it amenable to the law. A great many companies give the employee a service letter upon his leaving, which letter shows his term of service, character of services rendered, and cause for leaving. Through the influence of the organizations unjust or unreasonable dismissals and suspensions are becoming fewer in number and fewer in proportion to the whole.

We do not know of any specific instance in which it has been openly sought to compel men to work for a railway company against their will, by the exercise of the power of the courts through the channel of injunction, except when Judge Jenkins of the Federal court in Wisconsin enjoined the employees of the receivers of the Northern Pacific Railway from quitting the service of the receivers, with or without notice, in such manner as to hinder the operation of the road. Motion was made to modify the injunction in this particular, and was denied. Appeal was taken to the United States court of appeals and Judge Jenkins' decision on the motion to modify was reversed.

In connection with some troubles between the engineers and firemen and the Toledo, Ann Arbor and North Michigan Railroad, some orders were issued by Judges Ricks and Taft of the Federal courts which were believed to be intended to force men on that or other railroads to continue in the performance of their work even against their will. If additional information in this connection, which we are seeking, is secured, it will accompany this or be handed the commission later. The issuance of writs enjoining men from taking concerted action in leaving the employ of an employing railway company or to use proper and peaceable means to induce others to leave or to refrain from entering the service of such employer, and the punishment of men for contempt under strained interpretations of the actions and intentions of the men is wrong and should be made impossible by United States statute. The criminal code provides prohibition of, and punishment for, criminal acts. The code should be depended upon rather than to permit one judge to decide one way and another to decide in direct contradiction therewith. We are hardly competent to discuss this subject from the standpoint of one well versed in law, but we are well satisfied that a thorough study of it will convince the commission that the powers of the courts have been misused and abused in these connections and that it will be well to limit by statute their power, to the end that the dignity of the courts as well as the rights of the people may be preserved.

Second. Road, train, and engine men have little or no complaint as to hours of service. They are generally paid for all excess hours and the necessity for their being wide awake acts as a protection against unreasonable demands upon them. Ten hours for 100 miles is the standard rule in freight service for road men. Yard men are frequently required to work 12 hours for a day, which we consider as excessive when compared with the requirements in other occupations. The number of hours for these men should be but 8, and certainly not over 10. The telegraphers have much to complain of in this direction, as they are frequently required to remain on duty long hours.

Train and engine men, as a rule, are paid overtime on a very fair basis. Telegraphers are allowed overtime on many roads, but on many more they are not. Twelve consecutive hours is considered a sufficiently long day for them, and in our opinion telegraphers who, having worked 12 consecutive hours, are called for duty during the next succeeding 12 hours, should be allowed extra pay for time so used.

Third. Sunday work is compensated for at the same rates as if performed on any other day. The running of trains on Sunday should be abolished as far as is practicable.

Fourth. Fellow-servant laws, under which the employing railway company is liable for damages for personal injuries sustained through the neglect or incompetence of fellow-servants, have been enacted in several States, among which are Texas, Missouri, Wisconsin, Florida, Georgia, Iowa, Kansas, Massachusetts, Minnesota, Montana, and Ohio.

The effect of this has been the collection of damages in many cases where otherwise it would have been impossible, and we hope the effect has been or will be to induce the companies to be more careful in the selection of men, and the men more careful of their fellow-employees. We would prefer to prevent the injuries rather than to secure indemnity therefor. The men have no choice as to who their fellow-employees shall be. All are selected by the officials of the company, and hence the company should assume responsibility for their acts. Railroad companies have recently adopted, with practical unanimity, the requirement of a searching physical examination of all applicants for employment, under which the man who has suffered amputation of a portion of a hand or foot, or who has suffered from some other injury while in the service of some railway company is refused employment by other companies. If a man who has sustained such injury, which in reality does not prevent or hinder him from performing in an able manner the duties of his position, or who has attained a certain age which leaves him the prime of life yet to be lived, is to be refused employment under the operation of a rule adopted in concert or contemporaneously by the railroads, it seems but fair that the employee should look to the railroads for compensation for his injury, or pension for his age.

We believe it to be the generally accepted rule that persons dependent upon an employee may sue for damages on account of the death of such employee through the negligence of the railroad company, and if such negligence be shown may recover.

Fifth. The generally accepted doctrine of risks contemplated by voluntarily engaging in dangerous occupations has, we believe, been upheld and the companies held to be free from liability if the injury or death was clearly shown to be the result alone of such natural risks, or of contributory negligence on part of the injured.

Sixth. We do not know of any limited liability legislation which applies to railway employees in any manner different from that in which it applies to all others. We have as yet felt no serious effects from this source.

Seventh. Beyond a reasonable desire to get as much service as practicable from material or appliances on hand, the railroads generally provide adequate and proper appliances. In instances where this is not done, liability should very properly attach to the negligent company.

Eighth. The employees in the departments represented by the names of the organizations on whose part these answers are submitted have very thoroughly organized associations, one feature of which is insurance of members against death or total disability. The insurance is furnished the members on the mutual assessment plan and at actual cost. Members are insured in sums ranging, at their option, from $400 to $5,000. The only conditions imposed upon the member are that he shall remain a member and pay all assessments in accordance with the rules. The sums already paid out for these purposes by these organizations aggregate, in round numbers, $20,000,000. Temporary sick or disability benefits are provided by many local branches, and in that way many millions more have been distributed among the needy members.

Ninth. Relief associations, ordinarily termed " voluntary," are maintained by a few railway companies. Employees contribute, through deductions from their earnings, to such association and receive certain sick and other benefits, as provided in the rules. The companies contribute something to such relief feature, but a careful comparison shows that the sums paid by the individual employee fully covers the cost of carrying his risk. The term." voluntary " as used in the name of these associations is a misnomer, as, in fact, if an applicant for employment does not signify a willingness to participate in such association he is not given employment.

The number of railway companies conducting such associations is not large and their number does not now seem to be increasing. This is undoubtedly due very largely, if not entirely, to the bitter opposition on part of the employees to the establishment of such associations. They object to such paternalism being exercised over them by their employer; they object to paying for such protection only to have all sums paid in forfeited at any time when they may find it necessary or desirable to accept employment elsewhere, or when the company sees fit to dispense with their services; they object to paying full value for the insurance granted and then having the acceptance of the benefit for which they have paid operate as an effectual bar to their recovery for personal injury under the common law.

The maintenance of such associations by railway companies is generally obnoxious to the employees and is generally looked upon by them as an effort on part of the employer to secure a species of domination over the employee and his acts.

Tenth. We can best answer by referring to the proceedings of hearing had before the Interstate Commerce Commission in January, 1898, on petition from various railway companies for an extension of time within which to comply with the provisions of the law requiring the use of hand holds, power brakes, and automatic couplers. The Interstate Commerce Commission issued at that time a table of statistics, showing the percentage of cars and engines then equipped. Further authentic information on this subject is found on pages 86 and 87 of the Twelfth Annual Report of the Interstate Commerce Commission.

As to the cost of these appliances on old cars, evidence varies. It is more expensive to apply them to some cars than to others, dependent upon the construction of the car. We do not think, however, that the cost of attaching them to old cars is an important question any longer to a road which has made any reasonable effort to comply with the provisions of the law. The capacity of cars has been multiplied of late years, and if the new cars put in service since the enactment of this law have been properly equipped, the number of old ones which will be fit for use in interstate traffic after January 1, 1900, the date to which the Interstate Commerce Commission extended the time within which railway companies might comply with the law, will be very small.

As to the cost of putting these appliances on new cars, we find that the evidence varies. The manufacturers are unwilling to make estimates of the cost of putting the appliances on the cars, explaining that the several ways of putting them on make it difficult for them to determine. The cost of first-class vertical-plane couplers, f. o. b. at the factory, is from $12 to $18 per pair. To this cost must be added about $1.50 per pair for uncoupling rods, their brackets, lag screws, and labor to apply them to a new car. To this again must be added the freight on the couplers.

The first cost of material to be applied to an old car is the same, but whatever is realized from the sale of the old coupler and its links and pins for scrap iron should be deducted from the estimate of the cost of equipping an old car. It has been stated that the cost of changing from the old link-and-pin coupler to the vertical plane is from $25 to $40 per car. In this estimate is included the renewal of draft timbers and center sills or adding heavier and more expensive draft rigging. This does not seem to properly belong in this account, for the old and light capacity cars are unfit for use among the modern heavy and large capacity cars or for hauling with the modern giant locomotives with the old draft rigging. This rigging would probably have to be changed in order to use the car, whether automatic couplers were used or not.   Exact and reliable detailed information on this subject can best be secured from master car builders or superintendents of motive power and machinery.

The Westinghouse quick-action air-brake apparatus for freight cars is sold at $35 per set, f. o. b. at their works, and a rebate of 15 per cent is allowed all holders of a certain agreement with this company under which 95 per cent of the purchasers buy these supplies.   This makes the net cost of this apparatus for a freight car $29.75.   If an old car requires new foundation brake gear, the cost of putting that in and applying the air-brake apparatus is in the neighborhood of $20.   If the existing foundation brake gear is substantial enough for use with air brake, the cost of applying the apparatus should not be more than $5.

The main reason given by railroad managers for failure to complete the equipment of their cars and engines within the time fixed by law was the financial embarrassment caused by the panic of 1893 and desire to get what wear they could out of rolling stock not worth equipping.

Eleventh. Is best answered by figures given on page 88 of the Twelfth Annual Report of the Interstate Commerce Commission, to which we respectfully and proudly refer.

Twelfth. We have, at this time, nothing to recommend.

Thirteenth. There are many organizations of employees other than those for whom we speak.   We will confine our statements to our own and the others will undoubtedly speak for themselves.

Our organizations are of the trade-union nature; that is, each composed of the men in a particular department.   Their purposes are to obtain and retain fair and reasonable compensation for services performed; reasonable hours of labor and pay for excess hours; reasonable and fair conditions of employment; to protect against injustice to members; to elevate the profession; to exert a healthy influence upon legislative matters affecting the interests of those who make up the organizations, and to afford financial aid to the afflicted members, the widows and the orphans; and to furnish out of work benefits to members legally engaged in a conflict with their employers.   The effect of their efforts has been widely and generally successful.   They have accomplished to a great degree the purposes sought.

Of the number of employees in the departments represented, probably 80 per cent are members.

These organizations do not undertake to control their members except by requiring them to conform to the lawfully expressed will of a constitutional majority, which will of the constitutional majority governs in all things.

They do not interfere with the employee who is not a member, nor with his right to work.   They depend upon their standing, reputation, and works to attract to them all worthy and well-qualified employees.

Copies of the laws of our organizations are handed you herewith.

Fourteenth. Disputes of a serious nature are generally over the rates of compensation or an effort to impose some condition of employment which is considered unjust or unfair.

Fifteenth. So far as we are concerned, strikes are caused only when all other means of reaching an adjustment have failed and a principle is involved which can not be surrendered.

If a strike is decided upon, it is put into effect by withdrawing the members from the service of that employer, leaving him free to replace them with such as he can get or to make terms under which his old employees are willing to return to his service.

The effect of a strike is generally measured, so far as the principals therein are concerned, by the degree of success which either attains.   Strikes are not desired either by the railway companies or the railway employees.   On the whole, and taking into consideration the moral effect, the railway employees believe that much good has come to them as a result of their protective policy and the actions which they have found it necessary to resort to thereunder.

Sixteenth. A strike consists of the concerted and peaceable retirement from the employ of a certain employer on part of certain of his employees, leaving said employer to get along as best he can without them.   A boycott is an effort to injure the employer or his business in other ways, such as seeking to induce as many as possible to refrain from patronizing the employer or his business, pending the settlement of the dispute.

Seventeenth. We are strong advocates of the practice of applying the principles of conciliation, mediation, and arbitration to the settlement of any differences between railroads and their employees.   We earnestly sought the enactment of the bill approved June 1, 1898, entitled "An act concerning carriers engaged in interstate commerce and their employees," a copy herewith submitted.

Our experience with arbitration has been such as to commend it to our favor. We are at all times ready to accept it in its full spirit as a means of settlement of disputed points. Its effect, where tried, has been to establish more firmly feelings of confidence between the men and the officers in charge.

Eighteenth. If the laws are construed and applied in the spirit intended by the lawmakers, we have no criticism or suggestions to offer. Strained constructions and abuse of power under mandamus or injunction proceedings should be made impossible by legislative enactment.

Nineteenth. Under our acceptance of the term "arbitration," its whole virtue and vitality would be destroyed by making it compulsory. If made compulsory, permanent boards would probably be a necessity, and the objections to that practice are too obvious to invite discussion.

Twentieth. The use of intoxicants by railway employees is a practice which has very rapidly grown less of late years. Our organizations use every possible influence against it, and with great success. Strict rules have been adopted by many railway companies on this subject, and they are generally observed carefully by the employees.

It follows, without argument or room therefor, that the less the railway employees use intoxicants the better off they are from every standpoint of view.

Twenty-first. Railroads have but one commodity to sell, viz, transportation. The merchant who offers two or more lines of goods can, in competing with other dealers, sell one line at, or below cost, and possibly recoup himself on the other line or lines. The moment a railroad company begins carrying goods or passengers at less than the cost of the transportation furnished a condition is created under which the company must make up the loss by discriminating against other patrons or localities, by recovering the loss through economies practiced at the expense of the physical condition of the property, the character of the service rendered, or the employees, or by quietly charging the loss to the profit and loss account. If the first alternative is followed, the text and the spirit of the laws of the nation are violated; if the second be chosen, either the public or the employees are made to pay for losses unnecessarily and inexcusably sustained; if the last be adopted and followed to its logical conclusion, bankruptcy must come with all its attendant ills. Competition in railroad rates is simply ruinous. Most absurd lengths are gone to in a reckless underbidding of one another with an utter disregard as to how far the rates quoted may be below the cost of the service.

While we can not now point to specific cases of the wages of railway employees having been unfavorably affected as a direct result of rate wars or unrestrained competition, we can clearly and easily see how such evil effects to the employees may reasonably be expected to follow such unrestrained competition. If the practice of accepting business at a loss is continued, after all other economies have been inaugurated the wages of the employees will naturally become the object of consideration or attack. It is, and shall be, the purpose of our organizations to resist any reductions in the wages of the men, but we do not think it necessary or even pardonable to bring about a contest or a conflict on that point through such seemingly senseless rate wars as have been indulged in by the railway companies. While opposing the introduction of rates by commissions on the ground that they were so low as to be ruinous to the companies, some of the companies in connection with their competitive rate wars have put in force rates so low as to put to shame anything proposed by anti-railroad legislators or commissioners, rates which the veriest tyro would recognize at a glance as far below the actual cost of the service rendered.

It appears that Congress found it necessary, in order to prevent unfair discrimination, to exercise its right to control interstate traffic and to put a stop to arrangements or agreements between the common carriers under which certain rates should be maintained. It appears to us that there is just as much unfair discrimination possible and practiced under unrestrained competition as was, or could be, under pooling arrangements or traffic agreements. We have been of the opinion that the Government should be very careful in exercising or extending its right of control of the railways; but if the railway officers themselves can not, or will not, prevent such ruinous and disastrous wars under the guise of competition, the Government should assume the role of guardian for them, and in the interests of the shippers, the dealers, the traveling public, and the railway employees, take such steps as may be necessary to establish and enforce a minimum scale of rates, or to in some other way effectually stop these insane departures from business principles which seem to be becoming somewhat periodical in their recurrence. The whole business and laboring world are more interested in stability of rates than they are in the question of whether or not those rates are a fraction too high.

Twenty-second. The business of ticket brokerage as carried on in the United States affords a convenient and easy way through which the laws may be violated and discriminations indulged in. It gives to middlemen, for whose existence there is no excuse, a very large amount of money which properly belongs in the coffers of the railways or in the pockets of the people. If the earnings of the railways are reduced through the dealings of the brokers the railways will seek to make it up elsewhere, and the people who know the ropes and who reside in or travel from large cities or centers have a decided advantage over those who are not so fortunately located. If ticket brokerage consisted only of dealing in legitimate tickets, we would not feel that it was so much a matter of proper concern to us. The facts are, however, that in addition to whatever of such dealing they can secure, many ticket brokers resort to schemes and acts which are simply fraudulent and criminal. Forgery, counterfeiting, and misrepresentation as to identity are freely practiced. Ticket brokers' offices are made fences for the reception and sale of transportation which is known to be altered, forged, or counterfeited. Counterfeit receipts for dues paid, and counterfeit cards of membership in our organizations have been sold over the counter of ticket brokers' offices. Conductors in the discharge of their duties are frequently forced into altercations with passengers who, knowingly or unwittingly, have purchased worthless tickets from such offices, and in some instances have been shot down in cold blood by such passenger. Trusted employees have been enticed into wrongdoing which was made possible by the existence of the ticket broker's office and the methods followed therein. Grave suspicion has been cast upon many upright men, and many innocent men have lost their positions on account of transactions which were carried on through, or by, some ticket scalper, and which the employee could not explain because he knew nothing about it.

The natural and legitimate revenues of the railways are seriously invaded or affected by this agency. The interests of the employees are wrapped up in the earning power or capacity of the road, and hence the employees pronounce against the business of ticket brokerage largely for the same reasons given in favor of putting a stop to rate wars.

Twenty-third. Increasing the interest-bearing debt of a railway company or adding to the securities upon which it is sought or intended to pay dividends or returns is simply adding to the burden, already heavy in most instances. The stock of the road may not receive any dividends, but the interest on the bonds must be paid or receiverships, foreclosure sales, and reorgnizations follow. Not infrequently, under the protecting wing of the Federal courts, reductions in the wages of the employees are undertaken which would not be undertaken were it not for the protection which the company expects from the court. Unnecessary additions to the fixed charges of a railway should not be permitted.

Twenty-fourth. There is no doubt but that consolidation of railway lines under one management has effected economies in the management and in the traffic and accounting departments. It is not our experience that the large masses of the employees are unfavorably affected by such consolidations. On the contrary, we can cite instances where the employees of a small railway which paid poor wages and afforded very unsatisfactory conditions of employment have been greatly benefited by that line being absorbed by some large system, and the employees thereby brought under the operations of the higher rates of pay and much more advantageous conditions of employment which obtained on the absorbing system.

Q. (By Mr. KENNEDY.) Mr. Sargent has another very important paper. I should like to have it introduced at this point so that it may be printed in the testimony immediately following the paper just read.

Q. (By Mr. PHILLIPS.) Mr. Sargent will state the character of the paper.

Mr. SARGENT. In connection with the paper which has just been submitted by the secretary I wish to say that it is the reply of the five railway organizations. We had a conference in the city of Chicago shortly after receiving your topical plan of inquiry, and we thought best to appoint a committee to prepare answers, and Mr. E. E. Clark, of the Order of Railway Conductors, and myself were selected to prepare the answers and submit them to the commission after they had been referred to Mr. Arthur, Mr. Powell, and Mr. Morrissey, chief officers of the other organizations. We complied with instructions, held another conference, to which this was referred, and it has been approved by all, and the signatures of approval accompany the answers. In addition to that there was referred to me, as a special matter, the first proposition wherein you ask in relation to the inquiry as to the compulsory performance of service and the mandatory injunction and proceedings for contempt when the railroad is in the hands of a receiver, and the question respecting the liability of railroad companies to their employees for injuries sustained while in the performance of duty. We have had this looked up very carefully, and here you will find some of the many important cases which have come up in the years past, wherein injunction and mandatory proceedings have been brought while railroads were in the hands of a receiver, and also as to the application of the liability of railroad companies to their employees for injuries sustained in the performance of duty, covering every State in the Union. We submit it to you, as we believe it will aid in arriving at such conclusions as you may wish in regard to the matters referred to in your inquiry. This is in addition to the document read by the secretary. It contains the cases, special references thereto, quotes the authorities, and goes into details, and I think you will find it embraces nearly every State in the Union. It is quite a lengthy document, and it will not be necessary to read it. It also has several of the decisions of the United States Supreme Court. (The paper here referred to follows:)

BEFORE THE INDUSTRIAL COMMISSION OF THE UNITED STATES.

TOPICAL PLAN OF INQUIRY.

First. In relation to the inquiry as to compulsory performance of service under mandatory injunction and proceedings for contempt when a railroad is in the hands of a receiver; also as to powers of courts in such cases. (See p. 3 of Topical Plan of Inquiry.)

Second. Respecting the law of liability of railroad companies to their employees for injuries sustained while engaged in the performance of duty. (See p. 4, sections 4 and 5, Topical Plan of Inquiry.)

MODERN GENERAL DOCTRINE.

In England and in the United States it is lawful, and, it may be added, commendable, for any body of men to associate themselves together for the purpose of bettering their condition in any respect, financial or social. The very genius of free institutions invites them to higher levels and better fortunes. They may dictate their own wages, fraternize with other associates, choose their own employers, and serve man and mammon according to the dictates of their own conscience. But while the law accords this liberty to one, it accords a like liberty to every other one, and all are bound to so use and enjoy their own liberties and privileges as not to interfere with those of their neighbors. (Beach on Monopolies and Industrial Trust, pp. 288–289 (1898).)

RECEIVERS AND THEIR EMPLOYEES.

In 1885 the Wabash road was in the hands of a receiver and there was a lockout in some of the company's shops, and two employees who acted as a committee on behalf of the locked-out and striking employees were punished for contempt by being sent to jail for a term. The syllabi of the case is as follows:

"A writer, signing himself chairman, sent the following notice to the various foremen of the shops of the Wabash company during the strike organized to resist a reduction of wages, the railroad being at that time in the hands of a receiver appointed by the United States circuit court:

" 'OFFICE OF LOCAL COMMITTEE, *January 17, 1885.*

" '——, *Foreman:*

" ' You are requested to stay away from the shop until the present difficulty is settled. Your compliance with this will command the protection of the Wabash employees. But in no case are you to consider this an intimidation.'

"*Held*, that this was an unlawful interference with the management of the road by the receiver, and a contempt of court, for which the writer should be punished." (24 Fed. Rep., 217.)

Where employees of a railroad company that is in the hands of a receiver appointed by the court are dissatisfied with their wages paid by the receiver they may abandon the employment and by persuasion or argument induce other employees to do the same; but if .hey resort to threats or violence to induce the others to leave, or accomplish their purpose, without actual violence, by overawing the others by preconcerted demonstration of force, and thus prevent the receiver from operating the road, they are guilty of contempt of court and may be punished for their unlawful acts.

Where a party of men combine with intent to do an unlawful thing, and in the prosecution of that unlawful intent one of the party goes a step beyond the balance of the party and does an act which the balance do not themselves perform, all are responsible for what one does. It is essential, however, that there should be a concert of action—an agreement to do some unlawful thing. (Opinion by Justice Brewer. United States v. Kane et al. (1885), 23 Fed. Rep., 748.)

In the following case, after an injunction had been issued against one railroad company and its employees, commanding it to afford the same facilities to a certain other road that it afforded to all other roads, it was held that employees who refused to handle cars of such other road and quit the service of the company rather than handle such cars would not be guilty of contempt of court; but any employee refusing to handle such cars, though not being served personally with an injunction nor a party of the suit, although learning that such an injunction had issued, and his remaining in the service of the company and refusing to handle the cars of the road in question would be guilty of contempt.

Where a labor organization has declared a boycott against a railroad, and connecting roads are therefore refusing or seem about to refuse to afford equal facilities to the boycotted road, in violation of section 3 of the interstate-commerce act, they may be compelled to do so by mandatory injunction, since the case is urgent, the rights of the parties free from reasonable doubt, and the duties sought to be enforced is imposed by law.

A mandatory injunction restraining a railroad company from refusing equal facilities to a connecting line, in violation of section 3 of the interstate-commerce act, is binding upon all officers and employees of the respondent having proper notice thereof whether they are made parties or not.

A court of equity has power to contrive new remedies and issue unprecedented orders to enforce rights secured by Federal legislation provided no illegal burdens are imposed thereby. (Toledo, A. A. & N. M. Ry. Co. v. Pennsylvania Co. et al. (March 25, 1893), 54th Fed. Rep., 746.)

Circuit courts of the United States have jurisdiction of a bill in equity to restrain violation of the interstate-commerce law to the irreparable injury of complainant, because of the subject-matter, and without regard to the citizenship of the party.

A combination to induce and procure the officers of a common carrier corporation subject to the provisions of the interstate-commerce act, and its locomotive engineers, to refuse to receive, handle and haul interstate freight from another like common carrier in order to injure the latter, is a combination or conspiracy to commit the misdemeanor described by section 10 of the interstate-commerce act, and, if any person engaged in it does an act in furtherance thereof, all combining for the purpose are guilty of criminal conspiracy, as denounced by section 5440, Revised Statutes.

If the common carrier company against whom such a conspiracy is directed is injured by acts done in furtherance of it, it has a cause of action for its loss against all those engaged in the conspiracy.

The employees, while in the employ of the defendant company, may obey this mandatory injunction, but may, without contempt of court, avoid or evade obedience thereto by ceasing to be such employees; otherwise the injunction would, in effect, be an order compelling the employer to continue the relation of servant to the complainant—a kind of order never yet issued by a court of equity.

A preliminary injunction may issue against the chief member of such a conspiracy as that above described to restrain him from giving the order and signal which will result and is intended to result in the unlawful and irreparable injuries to the complainant. Where such chief member has already issued such an unlawful, wilful, and criminal order, the injurious effect of which will be continuing, the court may by mandatory injunction compel him to rescind the same, especially when the necessary effect of the order or signal is to induce and procure flagrant violations of an injunction previously issued by this court. (Toledo, A. A. and N. M. Railway Co. v. Pennsylvania Co. et al. (April 3, 1893), 54th Fed. Rep., 730.)

It would be an invasion of one's natural liberty to compel him to work for, or to remain in the personal service of, another. One who is placed under such restraint is in a condition of involuntary servitude, a condition which the supreme law of the land declares shall not exist within the United States, or in any place subject to their jurisdiction.

The fact that employees of railroads may quit under circumstances that would show bad faith on their part, or a reckless disregard of their contract, or of the convenience and interests of both employer and the public, does not justify a departure from the general rule that equity will not compel the actual, affirmative performance of merely personal services, or (which is the same thing) require employees, against their will, to remain in the personal service of their employer.

These employees having taken service first with the company, and afterwards with the receivers, under a general contract of employment which did not limit the exercise of the right to quit the service, their peaceable cooperation, as the result of friendly argument, persuasion, or conference among themselves, in asserting the right of each and all to refuse further service under a schedule of reduced wages, would not have been illegal or criminal, although they may have so acted in the firm belief and expectation that a simultaneous quitting without notice would temporarily inconvenience the receivers and the public. If in good faith, and peaceably, they exercise their right of quitting the service, intending thereby only to better their condition by securing such wages as they deem just, but not to injure or interfere with the free action of others, they can not be legally charged with any loss to the trust property resulting from their cessation of work in consequence of the refusal of the receivers to accede to the terms upon which they were willing to remain in the service. Such a loss, under the circumstances stated, would be incidental to the situation, and could not be attributed to employees exercising their lawful rights in orderly ways, or to the receivers when, in good faith and in fidelity to their trust, they declare a reduction of wages, and thereby cause dissatisfaction among employees, and their withdrawal from service.

According to the principles of the common law, a conspiracy upon the part of two or more persons, with the intent, by their own combined power, to wrong others or to prejudice the rights of the public, is in itself illegal, although nothing be actually done in execution of such conspiracy. This is fundamental in our jurisprudence. So, a combination or conspiracy to procure an employee or body of employees to quit service in violation of the contract of service would be unlawful, and in a proper case might be enjoined if the injury threatened would be irremediable at law.

It seems entirely clear, upon authority, that any combination or conspiracy upon the part of these employees would be illegal which has for its object to cripple the property in the hands of the receiver, and to embarrass the operation of the railroads under their management, either by disabling or rendering unfit for use engines, cars, or other property in their hands, or by interfering with their possession, or by actually obstructing their control and management of the property, or by using force, intimidation, threats, or other wrongful methods against the receivers or their agents, or against employees remaining in their service, or by using like methods to cause employees to quit, or prevent or deter others from entering the service in place of those leaving it.

(In the opinion circumstances are described under which courts of equity will interfere by injunction to prevent strikes, or what is termed illegal interference with property.) (Arthur et al. v. Oakes et al. (Oct. 1, 1894), 63d Fed. Rep., 310.)

In re Debs et al. was a habeas corpus proceedings to procure the discharge of the defendant who had been committed to jail for contempt of court.

The defendants were charged with ordering members of their organization and others to refuse handling Pullman cars, as there was a strike and lockout at the Pullman works. They were enjoined from in any way interfering with the employees working on roads engaged in interstate commerce, some of which roads were in the hands of receivers, and particularly on account of these roads having contracts with the United States to carry its mail.

In the opinion it was held that the United States had the right to remove obstructions on both natural and artificial highways over which it was necessary for it to carry its mails, and also that owing to great public inconvenience and injury it had a right to supervise interstate commerce, and that after an injunction was issued to prevent the defendants from interfering with the operation of roads in the hands of the receiver, or other roads engaged in interstate commerce and the carrying of United States mail, if violated, the defendants might be punished for contempt. In all such cases the Federal courts had power to enjoin all persons from any interference with the discharge of the duties before mentioned; and whether or not any person was actually served with such injunction if he had notice of it in any manner, it was binding upon him. (The above fairly states the substance of the opinion.) (In re Debs et al. (May 27, 1895), 158 U. S., 564.)

In an order issued by Judge Jenkins in 1894 the court went so far as to enjoin employees from quitting or leaving the service of the receivers, either collectively or individually. A part of the order is as follows:

And from combining and conspiring to quit, with or without notice, the service of said receivers, with the object and intent of crippling the property in their custody or embarrassing the operation of the said railroad, and from so quitting the service of the said receivers, with or without notice, as to cripple the property, or to prevent or hinder the operation of said railroad. (Farmers' Loan and Trust Co. *v.* Northern Pac. Ry. Co. et al., 60th Fed. Rep., p. 803.)

The receivers of the Union Pacific Railway in 1894 filed a petition in Judge Dundy's court at Omaha to annul the existing schedule of wages between employees and the company, and in lieu thereof prayed to put into force others which the receivers filed in court. The new schedules made many changes in the existing rules and reduced the wages of certain classes of employees. Also the receivers prayed for an injunction enjoining the employees from striking or interfering with the receivers in the management of the road, when their schedule should go into force. The court granted the injunction, which forbid the employees from striking or quitting the service of the company, the order of the court being more sweeping, if anything, than that of Judge Jenkins, which has been hereinbefore given. However, it might be stated that before Judge Dundy's order became effectual, steps were taken to bring the matter before a court that had more extended jurisdiction, and the whole matter was brought before Judge Caldwell, circuit judge, and Ryner, district judge, who ordered a full and complete investigation of the matters in dispute between the employees and receivers; and after such hearing Judge Caldwell rendered an opinion, in which Judge Ryner concurred, sustaining the position taken by the employees. (See Ames et al. *v.* Union Pac. Ry. Co. et al. (April 5, 1894), 62d Fed. Rep., 7.)

NOTE.—The injunction referred to issued by Judge Dundy seemingly has not been reported.

Where employees of a railroad company, though in remaining in its employment, refused to perform their duties of operating its trains so long as Pullman cars are hauled, though the company is bound by contract to carry them, thus interrupting interstate commerce and the transmission of the mails, and subjecting the company to suits and great irreparable damages, injunction will issue requiring them to perform their duties during the continuance in the company's employment. (Southern Cala. Railway Co. *v.* Rutherford et al. (June 3, 1894), 62d Fed. Rep., 796.)

PART SECOND.

Respecting the law of liability of railroad companies to their employees for injuries sustained while engaged in the performance of duty, and also persons who may recover damages.

General rule.—An employer is liable in damages to his employee where the employee, free from negligence, sustains an injury through the employer's negligence. Such negligence may consist in the doing of something by the employer which, in the exercise of ordinary care and prudence, he ought not to have done, or in the omission of any duty or precaution which a prudent, careful man would or ought to have taken.

It is the duty of the master to furnish his servant with such appliances, tools, and machinery as are suited to his employment and may be used with safety; and if the master fails to use ordinary care in the selection or inspection and care after such selection of the appliances his neglect, ignorance, or defects therein will not excuse him from liability for an injury caused thereby. He is responsible for all defects in machinery or appliances for which he should or could have known, but failed through negligence to learn of, or which, having learned of, he failed to remedy.

A railroad company is liable for injuries to its employees occasioned by the company's negligence in failing to keep its track or roadbed or other surroundings under its control in proper condition; however, its duty in this respect is only that it is required to use reasonable care in keeping them in safe condition.

Employers are not required to furnish the best and latest improved machinery, but only such as is reasonably safe and suitable.

A master who sets a servant to work in a place of danger without giving him such warning and instructions as the youthfulness, inexperience, or lack of capacity on the part of the servant reasonably requires, is guilty of negligence and liable to the servant for an injury arising therefrom.

It is the duty of the employers to make and promulgate such rules and regulations for the government of their employees as will, if observed, give them reasonable protection; and employees are bound to obey all lawful and reasonable commands of their employers, and an injury resulting to the employee while disobeying rules would not entitle him to recover damages.

ASSUMPTION OF RISK BY EMPLOYEES.

General doctrine.—Where an employment is accompanied with risk, of which those who enter it have, or are presumed to have, notice, they can not, if they are injured by exposure to such risks, recover compensation for injuries from their employer. By contract to perform hazardous duties the employee assumes such risks as are incident to their discharge, and he assumes not only the risk existing at the beginning of his employment, but also such as arises during its course, if he had, or was bound to have, knowledge thereof. He does not, however, assume the risk of danger arising from the unsafe or defective methods, machinery, or other instrumentalities unless he has, or may be presumed to have, knowledge or notice thereof; and the burden of proof that an injured employee had such knowledge or notice of the defect or obstruction causing the injury is upon the employer.

The employee also assumes all risk of latent defects in appliances or machinery, unless the master was negligent in not discovering such defects.

Fellow-servants.—The general rule at common law is that he who engages in the employment of another for the performance of specified duties and services for compensation, takes upon himself the natural and ordinary risks and perils incident to the performance of such services. The perils arising from the carelessness and negligence of those who are in the same employment are no exception to this rule, and where a master uses due diligence in the selection of competent, trusty servants, and furnishes them with suitable means to perform the services in which they are employed, the master is not answerable to one of them for an injury received in consequence of the carelessness and negligence of another while both are engaged in the same service.

All persons are fellow-servants where they are engaged in the same common pursuit under the same general control.

All who serve the same master work under the same control, derive authority and receive compensation from the same common source, and are engaged in the same general business, though it may be in different grades or departments of it, are fellow-servants, who take the risk of each other's negligence.

(The above is the general doctrine as to liability of employers to their employees and of the assumption of risk by the employee. However, there are many distinctions and modifications of the doctrine stated, so that each particular case is largely governed by the facts. As for instance, where an employee knew of a danger and his master promised to remedy it on condition that the employee continue work, if, in the meantime, such employee was injured, he could recover, not having assumed the risk. It would take too much space to point out these distinctions here, and perhaps would in no way be profitable, under the circumstances, to pursue their investigation.)

Who can sue for injury.—All of the States and Territories within the United States have a statute giving the right to the person injured to bring an action for damages, and in the event the injury is fatal, then the statute provides either that the widow or heirs of the decedent may bring an action for the recovery of pecuniary damages, or if the widow or heirs be not given such right, the personal representatives of the decedent, which would be his executors or administrators, are given the right to sue, and as the personal representatives sue for the benefit of the estate, and as the widow and heirs participate in the proceeds of the estate, then they are permitted to derive benefit from any recovery that might be had, much the same as if they themselves were entitled to sue.

State rules respecting liability of the employers for injuries and assumption of risk of employees, and doctrine of fellow-servant.

ALABAMA.

Where two persons are employed in the same general business by a common employer, if one is injured by the negligence of the other the employer is not responsible. (Mobile and Ohio R. Co. *v.* Thomas, 42 Ala., 672.)

All employees are fellow-servants when they come within general rules, stated hereinbefore. They assume the ordinary known risks incident to the employment, and also injuries by carelessness or negligence of fellow-servants.

ARIZONA.

In this State apparently there is no legislation on the subject of employers' liability.

It was held that a section foreman, injured through the misconduct of a conductor of a train upon which the former was riding, in hurriedly directing him and his men to get on the train, so as to get the train out of the reach of an approaching one, was the fellow-servant of such conductor. The reason given was that the section foreman had no duties to perform on the train, and was not, as to his duties, subject to the control or directions of the conductor, and therefore was entitled to recover. (McGill v. Southern Pac. R. Co., 83 Pac., 821.)

However, in another case, where a conductor and foreman of a section crew were engaged in clearing the track of a wreck on a section of the road under the latter's charge, they being under control of a superior, and the foreman was injured while riding on a train in charge of such conductor from the place of work, it wa held that they were fellow-servants. (Southern Pac. Co. v. McGill, 44 Pac., 802s)

ARKANSAS.

It was held where work was such as required a skillful or careful supervision, and where such supervision is necessary to the safety of the laborers engaged upon the work, it is the master's duty to bestow and, if he appoints an agent to perform that duty, he is responsible for his negligence. (Bloyd v. St. Louis and S. F. R. Co., 22 S. W., 1089.)

A train dispatcher who controls the movement of trains represents the company and is not a fellow-servant of an engineer injured in a collision resulting from his negligence. (Little Rock and M. R. Co. v. Barry, 23 S. W., 1097.)

Also, one who has the power to employ and discharge laborers is the vice-principal, as regards the duties to warn such laborers of special risks in their employment. (Fort Smith Oil Co. v. Slover, 24 S. W., 106.)

(In this State it has been held that a brakeman and car repairer, a yard master and car inspector, a foreman of a gang of bridge carpenters, and one of the workmen, were fellow-servants. General doctrine as to assumption of risks prevails.)

CALIFORNIA.

Whether the negligent act of a section foreman of a railroad company, by which an accident is caused to a section hand, is a personal duty which the company owes to the section hand as its employee, or whether the accident is in consequence of the negligence of another person employed by the same employer, within the meaning of section 1970 of the civil code, must be determined, not from the grade or rank of section foremen, but from the character of the act causing the injury.

If the act is one which it is the duty of the company to perform toward the section hand, the section foreman, in performance of such duty, acts as the agent of such company, for which the employer is responsible; but if it is not one of the duties of the company (like in common work that any workman would be expected to do), the foreman and section hand are fellow-servants, and the foreman is alone responsible for an accident to a section hand resulting therefrom.

The law recognizes no distinction growing out of the grades of employment of the respective employees. * * * The duties which a railroad corporation owes its servants, and which it is required to perform, are to furnish suitable machinery and appliances by which the service is to be performed, and to keep them in repair and order; to exercise ordinary care in the selection and retention of sufficient, competent servants to properly conduct the business in which the servants are employed, and to make such provisions for the safety of employees as will reasonably protect them against the dangers incident to their employment.

The performance of this duty can not be shifted by it to a servant so as to avoid responsibility for injuries caused to another servant by its omission; but where a section foreman left a switch open and a section hand was injured, it was held that a foreman and section hand were fellow-servants. (Davis v. Southern Pac. R. Co., 98 Cal., 19.)

In this State an employee was allowed to recover damages on account of proper machinery not having been selected; also on account of the improper construction of a roadbed; also where a boy was injured on account of a defective platform while he was endeavoring to adjust a belt.

It has been held that a train dispatcher and a material man on a road, were not fellow-servants; also where a foreman of a gang of men to whom the stevedore delegated the entire management of the work of unloading a vessel with full discretion to control and supervise it was not a fellow-servant with his subordinates; and also it was held that a hod carrier injured by the unsafe manner in which a scaffold was constructed was not a fellow-servant with the carpenter. However, a brakeman and conductor on a railroad train are held to be fellow-servants, and the foreman of a mine and the miner employed to work under his directions are fellow-servants. An engineer and conductor upon a railroad train are likewise held to be fellow-servants. Likewise a foreman and engineer of a ferryboat are held to be fellow-servants. Nor is the employer liable for any injury to one fellow-servant by another while engaged in the master's work.

COLORADO.

After referring to the rules established in several of the States, it is said: The better rule, as we extract from the best-reasoned cases, is that for the acts of the vice-principal done in the scope of his employment, and such as properly devolve upon the master in his general duty to his servant, the master is liable; while for all such acts as relate to the common employment and are on a level with the acts of fellow-laborers, except such acts done by the vice-principal against the reasonable objection of the injured servant, the master is responsible. In other words, the test of liability is the character of the act rather than the relative rank of the servant (Deep Mining Drainage Co. v. Fitzgerald, 43 Pac., 210.)

In this State where a superior employee gave direction to stop a car, and the appliance used to accomplish such stoppage was defective, it was held that the superintending employee was a vice-principal and the injured one could recover. Likewise, a foreman having authority to hire and discharge is not a fellow-servant of other employees.

A person employed by a mine owner to timber a drift, so as to provide a safe place for the miners running their shaft in which to work, is not a fellow-servant of the miners.

A teamster engaged in hauling coal for a tramway company is a fellow-servant with an employee in charge of one of its boilers.

CONNECTICUT.

The rule which exempts the master from liability for negligence of the fellow-servant applies not only in cases in which the servant injured is engaged in the same grade of employment as the servant whose negligence occasioned the injury, but also in cases in which the two servants are engaged in different grades of employment, if the services of each are directed to the same general end. It also applies to cases where the injured servant is of a grade of the services inferior to that of the servant whose negligence occasioned the injury, though the inferior in grade is subject to the orders of the superior; and it is not essential, in order to exempt the master from liability, that the injured servant at the time of receiving the injury should be engaged in the same particular work as the servant by whose negligence the injury was occasioned. If both servants are in the employment of the same master, work under the same control and in the same general business, and derive authority and compensation from the same common source, the master is not liable, but this rule has no application where the servant sustains an injury through a master's negligence alone, or through the negligence of the master combined with the negligence of a fellow-servant. In respect to appliances furnished for the use of his employees, the master's duty is that of reasonable care to provide such as are suitable. (Wilson v. Willimantic Linen Co., 50 Conn., 433.)

Also held that a train dispatcher was not a fellow-servant with the engineer, the engineer being bound to obey the orders of the dispatcher.

DELAWARE.

Those who perform duties personal to the master are, in respect to such duties, vice-principals. A general manager or overseer or superintendent of machinery represents the master. (Foster v. Pussey, 8 Houston, 168; 14 Atl., 545.)

(In this State the general common-law doctrine seems to prevail.)

FLORIDA.

A fellow-servant is one engaged with another under a common master and in the same common employment, so that they are brought into contact with each other, notwithstanding they are subject to the orders and under the exclusive control of separate bosses and foremen and at different work in the same service.

For illustration: If one was engaged as a common laborer to work on the roadbed of a gravel train, he would not be a fellow-servant with the engineer or conductor on a passenger train, but would be a fellow-servant with all employed on the roadbed or gravel train, if his employment was in a common work and brought him in immediate contact with them and risk through them, although working under orders of a different boss or foreman in said common work.   It was held that one of the shovelers upon a gravel train and the engineer were fellow-servants in respect to the act of the engineer in putting the handling of his engine into the hands of his fireman, who was either careless or unskilled in the management of such machines,   (Parrish v. Pensacola and A. R. Co., 28 Fla., 551; 9 So. Rep., 696.)

This State at present has the following enactment: If the person injured is himself an employee of the company, and the damage was caused by another employee of the company and without fault on the part of the person injured, his employment by the company shall be no bar to recover, and no contract which restricts such liability shall be legal or binding.   It was held that this act having been borrowed from Georgia and having received a construction there in effect that the right of the employee to recover depends upon his being entirely free from fault or negligence, such construction became a part of the law of Florida. (Duval v. Hunt et al., 34 Fla., 85; 15 So. Rep., 876.)

(The doctrine is laid down also in this State that where the master delegates to the servant any duty which is personal to himself, as, for instance, the providing of suitable machinery or inspecting a roadbed, or the like, the act of the servant is held to be that of the master, and it is immaterial whether the servant occupies a high or low position.)

GEORGIA.

This State abolished the common-law rule by statute as far as it extends to master and servants on railroads.   Section 2083 of the code of 1882 provides that railroad companies are common carriers, and liable as such.   As such companies have many employees who can not possibly control those who should exercise care and diligence in the running of trains, such company should be liable to such employees as to passengers for injuries received from the want of such care and diligence.   Section 3036 of the code provides substantially as hereinbefore given as the Florida law.

However, in this State it was held that the statute did not apply where a receiver was in charge of the road, and that the common-law doctrine prevailed. (Henderson v. Walker et al., 55 Ga., 481.)

Under the statute any supposed fault of the employee, however slight, which contributed to the injury for which he sues, would defeat his action.   (Kennedy v. Central R. Co., 61 Ga., 590.)

IDAHO.

The general common-law doctrine seems to prevail.   In this State where a miner while ascending a ladder in the mine was injured by being struck with a drill which was being lowered down the shaft by a blacksmith, it was held that he could not recover; that each employee was the fellow-servant of the other. (Snyder v. Viola Mining and S. Co., 26 Pac., 127.)

ILLINOIS.

Where an employee is hurt in an employment wholly separate and disconnected from that of the servant who caused the injury, a recovery may be had, where there is negligence, the same as in other cases.   A clerk in a depot, a carpenter employed constructing and repairing cars in a shop, or other persons disconnected with the management of trains and its officers, may recover where, by the carelessness of those running trains, he is injured.   The rule only applies that a fellow-servant can not recover for the injury occasioned by the fellow-servant where they are engaged in the same department of business.   The object of this rule is to make each servant vigilant in seeing that the others are careful, prudent, and faithful in the discharge of their duties; and if not, that it shall be to their interest to report all derelictions that occur. (Pittsburg, F. W. and C. R. Co. v. Powers, 74 Ill., 341.)

Persons may be fellow-servants, although not strictly in the same line of employment.   One person may be employed to transact one department of business, and another may be employed by the same master to transact a different and distinct branch of business, but if their usual duties bring them into habitual association, so that they may exercise a mutual influence upon each other promotive of proper caution, such persons might be regarded as fellow-servants. (Rolling Mill Co. v. Johnson, 113 Ill., 64; Joliet Steel Co. v. Shields, 146 Ill., 603.)

In this State it has been held that any duty personal to the master, though delegated to a servant, the master would be held liable for the acts of the servant; as where a laborer in a lumber yard was injured by following the direction of the superintending employee in the yard, he was permitted to recover. Also it has been held that an assistant superintendent is the representative of the company and not a fellow-servant of a conductor. Also where an employee was injured by an iron girder, the defective condition of which was known to the foreman, he was held not to be a fellow-servant of the injured employee. Also a pit boss in a mine and a superintendent of a mine were held not to be fellow-servants with injured employees. But according to the rule stated brakemen on train are fellow-servants, and where a head blacksmith who, while proceeding with a number of other employees upon a train to remove a wreck, was injured by the negligence of the engineer, who also acted as conductor, it was held that all such employees were fellow-servants. (Abend v. T. H. and I. R. Co., 111 Ill., 202.)

An engineer upon a switch engine and a switchman working with him are held fellow-servants. Where a conductor was killed by a collision of two trains, and the collision was brought about by the negligence of employees on the other train, all were held to be fellow-servants, and no recovery could be had. Also an engineer operating an engine letting down a cage to the bottom of the shaft and a track layer at the bottom were held fellow-servants. (Niantic Coal and Mining Co. v. Leonard, 126 Ill., 216.)

Also, locomotive engineers of the same road are fellow-servants. Switchmen belonging to different switching crews are fellow-servants. Likewise a hostler and his helper were held to be fellow-servants, though a track employee and locomotive engineer were held not fellow-servants. And where an engineer was killed by the explosion of a boiler he was held not a fellow-servant with those whose duty it was to furnish a safe boiler. Also a railroad laborer, whose duty it was to unload rails from cars, was held not a fellow-servant with the engineer.

(The rule seems settled that the employees, although working for the same master, if they are engaged in different departments of work, where their association is such that they can not influence the acts of employees engaged in different grades of service, then they are to be considered as not being fellow-servants. But, on the other hand, if servants in two different grades mingle together in the performance of their respective duties, so that the action of each may have some bearing toward influencing the acts of others, then in such case they are fellow-servants.)

INDIANA.

SEC. 1. *Be it enacted by the General Assembly of the State of Indiana,* That every railroad or other corporation, except municipal, operating in this State, shall be liable for damages for personal injuries suffered by any employee while in its service, the employee so injured being in the exercise of due care and diligence, in the following cases:

First. Where such injury is suffered by reason of any defect in the condition of ways, works, plant, tools, and machinery connected with or in use in the business of such corporation, when such defect was the result of negligence on the part of the corporation, or some person intrusted by it with the duty of keeping such way, works, place, or machinery in proper condition.

Second. Where such injury resulted from the negligence of any person in the service of such corporation to whose order or direction the injured employee at the time of his injury was bound to conform and did conform.

Third. Where such injury resulted from the act or omission of any person done or made in obedience to any rule, regulation, or by-law of such corporation, or in obedience to the particular instructions given by any person delegated with the authority of the corporation in that behalf.

Fourth. Where such injury was caused by the negligence of any person in the service of such corporation who has charge of any signal, telegraph office, switch yard, shops, roundhouse, locomotive engine, or train upon a railway, or where such injury was caused by the negligence of any person, coemployee, or fellow-servant engaged in the same common service in any of the several departments of the service of any such corporation, the said person, coemployee, or fellow-servant at the time acting in the place and performing the duty of the corporation in that behalf, and the person so injured obeying or conforming to the order of some superior at the time of such injury having authority to direct; but nothing herein contained shall be construed to abridge the liability of the corporation under existing laws.

SEC. 2. Neither an employee, nor his legal representative, shall be entitled under this act to any right of compensation or remedy against the corporation in any case where the injury results from obedience to an order which subjects the employee to palpable danger, nor where the injury was caused by the incompetency of the coemployee, and such incompetency was known to the employee injured, or such injured employee, in the exercise of reasonable care, might have discovered such incompetency, unless the employee so injured gave, or caused to be given, information thereof to the corporation or some superior intrusted with the general superintendence of such coemployee, and such corporation failed or refused to discharge such incompetent employee within a reasonable time, to investigate the alleged incompetency of the coemployee or superior, and discharge him if found incompetent.

SEC. 3. The damages recoverable under this act shall be commensurate with the injury sustained unless death results from such injury, when in such case the action shall survive, and be governed in all respects by the law now in force in respect to such actions: *Provided*, That where any such person recovers a judgment against a railroad or other corporation, and such corporation takes an appeal, and pending such appeal the injured person dies, and the judgment in the court below is thereafter reversed, the right of action of such person shall survive to his legal representatives.

SEC. 4. In case any railroad corporation which owns or operates a line extending into or through the State of Indiana and into or through another or other States, and a person in the employ of such corporation, a citizen of this State, shall be injured as provided in this act, in any other State where such railroad is owned or operated, and a suit for such injury shall be brought in any of the courts of this State, it shall not be competent for such corporation to plead or prove the decisions or statutes of the State where such person shall have been injured as a defense to the action brought in this State.

SEC. 5. All contracts made by a railroad or other corporation with their employees, or rules or regulations adopted by any corporation, releasing it or relieving it from liability to any employee having a right of action under the provisions of this act, are hereby declared null and void. The provisions of this act, however, shall not apply to any injuries sustained before it takes effect, nor shall it affect in any manner any suit or legal proceedings pending at the time it takes effect.

IOWA.

The code, section 1307 provides:

"Every corporation operating a railway shall be liable for all damages sustained by any person, including employees of such corporation, in consequence of the neglect of agents or by the mismanagement by engineers or other employees of the corporation, and in consequence of the willful wrongs, whether of commission or omission, of such agents, engineers, or other employees, when such wrongs are in any manner connected with the use and operation of any railroad on or about which they shall be employed, and no contract which restricts such liability shall be legal or binding."

Under the law a receiver was held liable the same as if the corporation were managing the road. However, one must be doing something tending toward the operation and management of the road to be within the benefit of the provision of the act, for it was held that a laborer in a machine shop of a railway company who was injured by a locomotive driving wheel which the plaintiff and other employees were moving was not within the benefits of the act, and that he was in no manner connected with the management of the railroad. (Potter *v.* C. R. I. and P. R. Co., 46, Iowa, 400.)

Also a sweeper in the roundhouse was not within the act, nor was an injured wiper within the act. Likewise a coal shoveler, a member of a construction gang, one engaged in elevating coal to the tender of engines, were all held not to come within the meaning of the act.

KANSAS.

The Iowa statute just given was adopted by the State of Kansas. The courts of Kansas have more liberally construed the law in favor of the employees than has the Iowa courts, and the statute was held to apply where one employee was injured by the negligence of another while both were engaged in the roundhouse in putting an engine in condition for immediate use. (C. R. I. and P. R. Co. *v.* Stahley, 62 Fed., 363).

KENTUCKY.

The rule that where one or two fellow servants is injured by the negligence of the other, the common laborer is not liable therefor, does not apply in a case of willful neglect if the two servants are not coequals. An engineer and a brakeman on the same train are not coequals, and the company is liable for the death of the latter caused by the willful neglect of the former. (Louisville and N. R. Co. *v.* Brooks, 83 Ky., 129.)

Though when one coequal injures another the injured employee can not recover. (Louisville, C. and L. R. Co. *v.* Cavens, 9 Bush., 559.)

Employees of one train with reference to those controlling another are regarded as agents of the company, and are not fellow servants. (Louisville, C. and L. R. Co. *v.* Cavens, 9 Bush., 559.)

Where a car repairer went under a car to repair it at the direction of the conductor the company was held liable, and where an engineer of a train was injured in a collision with a freight train, on account of the neglect of the train dispatcher, it was held that the company was liable. Also that a railroad yard switchman and a locomotive engineer were not fellow-servants. (Louisville and N. R. Co. *v.* Sheets, 13 S. W., 248.)

LOUISIANA.

In this State, while the Roman law instead of the common law was adopted and prevails, yet from all of the decisions it would appear that the common-law doctrine and the decisions of other States under it are followed in this State with respect to the liability of railroad companies to their employees. And the doctrine of fellow-servants which exists in the common-law States seems to be adopted by this State.

MAINE.

The common-law doctrine seems to be in full force and closely adhered to respecting the liability of masters to their servants, and also the doctrine of fellow-servants as explained under the decisions of the various common-law States is given full effect in this State.

MARYLAND.

The common-law doctrine seems to be in full force in this State respecting the relation of employer and employee, and it was held that a train dispatcher, employed by the division superintendent, though he has power to employ and discharge brakemen and firemen and has general charge of the movements of trains, is a fellow-servant of an engineer, who is also subject to the directions of the division superintendent. (Norfolk and W. R. Co. *v.* Hoover, 79 Md., 253; 29 Atl., 994.)

MASSACHUSETTS.

The common-law doctrine governs the relation of employer and employee in this State.

MICHIGAN.

In this State the general common-law doctrine prevails, but courts have construed the doctrine of fellow-servant very liberally in favor of the employee, more so than some of the other States, and it has been held where the train dispatcher of the railroad company who has absolute control over the moving of its train, and is charged with the duty of directing its movements, is not a fellow-servant of the employees in charge of the trains, who are bound to obey his directions. (Hunn *v.* Michigan Cent. R. Co., 78 Mich., 513; 44 N. W., 502.)

Likewise, section men and operatives of trains are not fellow-servants. An assistant roadmaster was held not a fellow-servant with an employee on a train. A fireman and engineer, however, were held to be fellow-servants. (Henry *v.* Lake Shore M. S. R. Co., 49 Mich., 495.)

An engineer of one train and a conductor of another were held fellow-servants. Also a conductor directing the unloading of a freight car is a fellow-servant of the brakeman doing the work.

655A——6

MINNESOTA.

Chapter 13, laws of 1887, provides that every railroad company owning or operating a railroad in this State shall be liable for all damages sustained by any agent or servant thereof by reason of the negligence of any other agent or servant thereof, without contributory negligence on his part, when sustained in this State, and no contract, rule, or regulation between such corporation and any agent or servant shall impair or diminish such liability, provided, that nothing in this act shall be so construed to render any railroad company liable for damage sustained by any employee, agent, or servant while engaged in the construction of any road or any part thereof not open to public travel or use. This statute, like the Iowa statute, applies only to those actually engaged in the moving of trains. With reference to other employees and their employer the common law doctrine prevails.

MISSISSIPPI.

Every employee of a railroad corporation shall have the same right and remedies for an injury suffered by him from the act or omission of the corporation or its employees as are allowed by law to other persons not employees, where the injury results from the negligence of a superior, agent, or officer, or of a person having the right to control or direct the service of the party injured, and also when the injury results from the negligence of a fellow-servant engaged in another department of labor from that of the party injured, or of a fellow-servant on another train of cars, or one engaged about a different piece of work.

The constitution of 1890, section 193, provides that every employee of a railroad corporation shall have the same rights and remedies for any injury suffered by him from the acts or omission of said corporation, or its employees, as are allowed by law to other persons not employees where the injury results from the negligence of a superior, agent, officer, or of a person having the right to control or direct the service of the party injured. Under these laws it was held that a fireman of an engine and a telegraph operator were engaged in different departments or by different pieces of work, within the meaning of the law. (Ill. Cent. R. Co. v. Hunter et al., 12 So., 482.)

MISSOURI.

In this State the common law doctrine governing the relation of employer and employee prevails. With respect to employees in different grades of employment the courts have construed the law somewhat favorably toward the employee; as, where a switchman was under the orders of a yard master, it was held that he was not a fellow servant of the latter. (Taylor v. Mo. Pac. Ry. Co., 16 S. W., 206.)

A railroad track layer and locomotive engineer were held not fellow-servants; nor a train dispatcher with the employees moving the train.

MONTANA.

Section 697, statute of 1888, provides that in every case the liability of the corporation to the servant or employee acting under the orders of his superior shall be the same in case of injury sustained by the default or wrongful acts of his superior, or to an employee not appointed or controlled by him, as if such servant or employee were a passenger.

Under such section it was held that a conductor was a vice-principal as to a fireman, and that a conductor and engineer of a train are the superior of brakemen on the same train within the meaning of the statute. (Crysswell v. Mont. Cent. R. Co., 42 Pac., 767.)

NEBRASKA.

The general common-law doctrine seems to prevail in this State, but the courts seemingly have construed the law most favorably to the employee, and wherever any person was acting in an authoritative position over the employee the courts have held him to be a vice-principal, as a conductor of a gravel train on a railroad with a gang of men under his control was held to be, as to such men, a vice-principal, and also a vice-principal as to the subboss under his control. (Burlingtou and M. R. R. Co. v. Crockett, 26 N. W., 921.)

NEW HAMPSHIRE.

In New Hampshire the common-law doctrine appears to prevail respecting the relation of master and servant, and also with respect to the doctrine of fellow-servant, although apparently the decisions of the court in deciding a question as to who are fellow-servants do not draw the lines very strictly against the injured employee.

NEW JERSEY.

The common-law doctrine prevails in this State. However, it has been said: "It is a matter of judicial disagreement whether the master can discharge the duty of examining and ascertaining whether appliances have become unfit or unsafe from wear and tear or otherwise, and the similar duty of keeping tools and appliances in repair, by selecting and employing competent persons to make inspections and repairs. In our courts it is held that the master's duty may be thus discharged." (Essex Electric Co. v. Kelley, 29 Atl., 427.)

In this State the law is construed very strongly against the injured servant.

NEW MEXICO.

Section 2308–2310 (1885), Compiled Laws, provides in substance that where any person comes to his or her death by reason of the negligence or carelessness or criminal action of an agent, officer, or employee of a railroad company his or her representative may recover of the company $5,000. But the courts have construed this section as giving only a right of action to the personal representatives or heirs of the decedent, and have held that it does not in any way do away with the common doctrine as between the master and servant.

NEW YORK.

In this State the common-law doctrine prevails. And it was held that an engineer of a gravel train and a laborer were fellow-servants. (Russel v. Hudson R. R. Co., 17 N. Y., 134.)

Though it was held that the failure of a conductor of a freight train to employ or secure a brakeman in a case where one employee failed to appear, and in starting the train with insufficient force, as a result of which negligence a brakeman was killed, was held not the neglect of the fellow-servant, the court holding that the conductor represented the company in the duty which he was performing or failed to perform. (Flike v. Boston and Albany Ry., 53 N. Y., 549.)

In general the scope of decisions are most unfavorable to the injured employee.

NORTH CAROLINA.

The general common-law doctrine prevails in this State.

NORTH DAKOTA.

The general common-law doctrine prevails in this State.

OHIO.

Ohio, in 1890, enacted a law which, without setting it out verbatim, the title will give a correct idea of its scope: "For the protection and relief of railroad employees; forbidding certain rules, regulations, contracts and agreements, and declaring them unlawful; declaring it unlawful to use cars or locomotives which are defective, or defective machinery or attachments thereto belonging, and declaring such corporation liable in certain cases for injury received by its servants and employees on account of carelessness or negligence of fellow-servants or employees."

Under the law, it was held that an engineer in charge of a locomotive, who has authority to direct and control a fireman on such locomotive, is a superior within the meaning of the statute. (Railroad Co. v. Margrat, 51 Ohio St., 130.)

The law makes the company responsible for any injury to a servant that results from any other employee who has the control, direction, or superintendence of or over the injured employee.

OREGON.

The general common-law doctrine prevails in this State.

PENNSYLVANIA.

The general common-law doctrine prevails in this State. But it has been held that a boiler maker in the machine shop of a railroad company is not such a coemployee of an engineer on a locomotive as will relieve the company from his negligence in repairing a boiler. (Penn. and N. Y. C. and R. Co. v. Mason, 100 Pa. St., 239.)

Also a train dispatcher who has power to move trains and make new schedules is not a coemployee with the train men. (Lewis et al. v. Seifert, 116 Pa. St., 628.)

RHODE ISLAND.

The general common-law doctrine seems to prevail in this State.

SOUTH CAROLINA.

The general common-law doctrine appears to prevail in this State. The decisions are not altogether in harmony, some construing the law most in favor of the master and others seemingly in favor of the employee; as, for instance, where it was the duty of a certain employee to keep machines in repair, and a shuttle was thrown from a machine which was defectively repaired and injured another employee, it was held that the injured employee could not recover. (Gunter v. Graniteville Mfg. Co., 15 S. C., 443.)

However, a locomotive engineer and track laborer were held not fellow-servants. (Calvo v. Charlotte C. and A. R. Co., 23 S. C., 526.)

Also a conductor of a train was held to be the representative of the company and not a fellow-servant with other employees operating the same train under his orders. (Boatwright v. North Eastern R. Co, 25 S. C., 128.)

Though it was held where a fireman was injured on account of the negligence of a conductor leaving cars on a track over which the fireman must pass in the discharge of his duties, was a fellow-servant of such fireman. (Coleman v. Wilmington C. and A. R. Co, 25 S. C,. 446.)

SOUTH DAKOTA.

The common-law doctrine seems to prevail in this State.

TENNESSEE.

In this State the common-law doctrine seems to prevail, but the decisions are somewhat conflicting.

An engineer in charge of a train was held to be not a fellow-servant of a brakeman on the same train acting under his orders. (East Tenn., etc., v. Collins, 1 Pickle, 227.)

Also a conductor was held to be a vice-principal as to other trainmen. (Ill. Central Ry. Co. v. Spence, 93 Tenn., 173.)

It was held that the engineer and hands employed on a locomotive are fellow-servants. (Nashville and Chattanooga R. Co. v. Elliott, 1 Cold, 611.)

TEXAS.

Chapter 91, laws of 1893, is intended to modify the common law, the title of which is "An act to define who are fellow-servants and who are not fellow-servants, and to prohibit contracts between employer and employees based upon the contingency of the injury or death of the employee, limiting the liability of the employer for damages."

But, notwithstanding this statute, the courts apparently draw largely on the common-law decisions to enable them to apply the principles of law relating to master and servant and coemployees.

UTAH.

This State has a statute defining who are fellow-servants, which declares that any person having superintendence or direction over another is not a fellow-servant with such employee. In other respects the common-law doctrine prevails.

VERMONT.

The common-law doctrine seems to prevail in this State; but the decisions are somewhat favorable to the injured employee.

The common-law doctrine prevails in this State.

The common-law doctrine prevails in this State. And it was held that a conductor on one train and a brakeman on another were not fellow-servants. (Daniel *v.* Chesapeake & O. R. Co., 36 W. Va., 397.)

In 1893 the following law was enacted:

"Every railroad or railway company operating any railroad or railway, the line of which shall be, in whole or in part, within this State, shall be liable for all damages sustained in this State by an employee of such company without contributory negligence on his part.

"First. When such injury is caused by any defect in any locomotive engine, car, rail, track, machinery, or appliance required by said company to be used by its employees in and about the business of such employment, when such defect could have been discovered by such company by reasonable and proper care, tests, or inspections; a proof of such defect shall be presumptive evidence of knowledge thereof on the part of such company.

"Second. Or while such employee is engaged in operating, running, riding upon, or switching passenger or freight or other trains, engines, or cars, and while engaged in the performance of his duty as such employee, and which such injury shall have been caused by the carelessness or negligence of any other employee, officer, or agent of such company in the discharge of, or for failure to discharge, his duty as such. No contract, receipt, rule, or regulation between any employee and a railroad company shall exempt such corporation from the full liability imposed by this act."

To the general rule as stated there are well-defined exceptions, one of which arises from the obligation of the master not to expose his servants, when conducting his business, to perils or hazards against which they may be guarded with proper diligence on his part, therefore it has no application to the character and condition or the appliances which are furnished for the use of the employees. Such duty is personal to the master and those who are performing duty are charged with the master's duty though they are employed in a distinct and independent department of the service. (Hough *v.* Railway Co., 100 U. S., 213.)

As to fellow-servants, this court has held that a gang of men and their foreman were fellow-servants. Likewise that an engineer and fireman were fellow-servants. (Baltimore and O. R. Co. *v.* Baugh, 149 U. S., 368.)

It might be said that where cases have come into the Federal courts the common-law doctrine respecting the duties of master and servant and the doctrine of fellow-servant as known to the common law has generally been applied. Of course, where an injury occurs in a particular State that has a statute the Federal courts, if called upon to administer the law, as a general thing will follow the construction placed upon such statute by the State courts.

Mr SARGENT. I wish to say further that I appear here this morning on behalf of the organization which I represent, only. The other gentlemen, representing the organizations named in this answer, are ready at any time to come before the commission to answer any questions which the commission may see fit to put to them relative to their respective organizations, or the work done by the men whom they represent. I am here this morning to answer any questions which the commission desires to put to me, but I wish it understood that I am not here in the capacity of a representative of the five railway organizations.

Q. (By Mr. FARQUHAR.) Have you a regular scale of wages?—A. Yes; we have a published book of schedules which shows the rates paid to firemen on nearly all the railways of the country. The report of the Interstate Commerce Commission shows the wages of every railway employee by a table of statistics, which the commission will find a very valuable book. It gives each railroad and exactly what it cost to operate it, what it earns, what its engineers earn, what its firemen earn, what its brakemen and section men earn, and covers the whole list of employees.

Q. (By Mr. KENNEDY.) How much labor is there on railroads without giving rest on Sunday?—A. That depends entirely upon the section of the country. Throughout the New England States very little Sunday work is done.   The trains there are usually run on Saturday night, and the men are relieved very early Sunday morning and during the day.   Except some of the local trains in and out of the cities, the train service is nearly abandoned.   That you will all understand if you will travel through New England and want to get anywhere on Sunday. In the West, however, we find the freight service, especially on Sundays, very active.   This is due largely to the desire on the part of shippers to get their stock into the markets early on Monday morning.   The stock trains on Saturday night start out and take advantage of Sunday and get into Chicago in order that they may deliver the stock early on Monday morning.   So that the railroad men throughout the West are pretty busily engaged on Sunday.   There are some trains, you will find, that are a necessity on Sunday.   We have discovered that it is not the desire of the railway operators to run Sunday trains, but there is a demand for a certain amount of Sunday business, and the railroads have to meet that demand.   The shippers of stock want their stock in the market early in the morning on Monday.   To get it there it has to leave Omaha and St. Paul and those northern points Saturday night to be delivered, and therefore those trains have to be run.   There has been a disposition manifested on the part of the railroad companies to abolish Sunday work just as far as they can do it, and there is a great deal less Sunday work done to-day than there was five or six years ago.   The organizations have gone on record as against Sunday labor.   The men want Sunday to be with their families; they think they should have it; they believe when they have worked six days there should be a day for rest, and that should be on Sunday.   At the same time, they realize that there is a certain demand of the public which the railroad companies must respond to.   Talk of taking off Sunday trains out of Chicago, for instance; those limited trains that run every day in the year for the accomodation of passengers!   The public would rebel against it; they must be run.   There must be a certain amount of transportation on Sunday that never can be overcome.   We believe there should be and there is generally a disposition on the part of the railroad companies to abolish Sunday traffic just as far as it is practicable to do it.

Q. Are the employees who work Sunday given a day of rest out of the seven days?—A. That depends entirely upon the rush of business during the week.   If business is light they may get a day lay-over during the week; but the way business is now on the railroads, men are doing 9 and 10 days a week.   The men get a day's pay for a certain trip.   Every time they make that trip it is a day.   They get in two or three extra days a week by coming back on those trips.   Each of those trips might consume from 9 to 12 hours.

Q. (By Mr. PHILLIPS.) Do they get two or three hours' sleep?—A. Sometimes they do not sleep at all.

Q. (By Mr. KENNEDY.) Is there a maximum number of hours fixed beyond which railroad firemen and engineers, for instance, shall not work in the 24?—A. We have a rule which is in force on many roads, where a man shall not be required to go out without 6 or 8 hours' rest, unless he feels pleasant to go.

Q. (By Mr. FARQUHAR.) Is that not a matter for State legislation?—A. Yes; I believe the State could regulate that by law.   At the same time take, for instance, the State of New York, where they have a law providing so many hours shall constitute a day.   I think you will find upon investigation that the men work to exceed that time.   Of course the company pays them overtime.

You can not put railroad men in the transportation department upon the same basis upon which men work at trades, in factories, and shops.   The handling of transportation is an entirely different matter.   For instance, I am called to-day to go out upon a run.   I am on duty 36 hours before I am relieved.   Certain conditions may arise, as have this year to my knowledge—storms and conditions of weather—whereby the men are on duty for 36 hours before they are relieved from their engines.   Those are conditions that can not be controlled by any specified law or regulation.   We believe that there is manifest on the part of the railways a disposition to be as fair and equitable in the establishment of hours of labor for train-service employees as is practicable with the business to handle.   At the present time the railroads are flooded with business and the men are working constantly, you might say, many of them under very severe strain.   If a man is not able to go out, does not feel that he can go, as a general rule he has no trouble in getting excused, if they have a man to place in his position.   Oftentimes trains are held while the men get a sufficient amount of rest to go out and perform their duty.

Q. (By Mr. Phillips.) Could that be obviated by employing a larger number of men, or is it difficult to get trained men?—A. No; you can get plenty of men. It might be obviated to a certain extent by increasing the number of employees and increasing the machinery, but when the dull time comes there would be that army of idle men. The men in the railway train service do not want an overproduction; they do not want the railroads loaded down with a great army of men in order that they may have it easy the whole year round. They are willing to take it rougher and work a little harder in the busy season, and then when the dull season comes there is plenty of time to rest up and earn fair wages. The railroad employees have an understanding with the employers that there shall be no more men employed than is necessary to move the traffic with dispatch, and during the busy times they take advantage of it and earn big wages, and when the dull season comes, of course, they earn an average wage.

Q. (By Mr. Conger.) Then, employees are generally satisfied and are not seeking additional legislation against long hours?—A. The train service with which I am associated, the firemen, are not seeking any legislation to reduce the hours in which they work. They have gone on record as against Sunday labor. They do not want to do Sunday labor when it is not an absolute necessity. They do not want these railroad corporations to work Sunday simply to accommodate themselves. They are willing to perform those duties which the public desire and compel them to perform. The agitation of the Sunday question on the railroads has reduced the amount of labor on Sunday to a marked degree all over the country. There are some sections of the country where the trains do not run on Sunday; neither come in nor go out. There are some small roads which do not pretend to work on Sunday where a few years ago everything ran. There is a disposition to hold trains on roads and not send them out, except where they carry perishable freight, dispatch freight, and live stock. Of course, you understand that now live stock takes precedence over humanity. Passenger trains are side-tracked for live stock trains. Live stock has precedence over first-class passenger trains, and I have gone out of Chicago on first-class passenger trains and seen stock trains on their way to New York pass us and we had to give way to them; they had the preference over everything.

Q. (By Mr. Farquhar.) Do the through freights run on the New England roads on Sunday?—A. Yes; what they call perishable freights; nearly all the local trains are tied up on Sunday. I have had some experience trying to get out of Boston on Sunday, and I have found it was a difficult thing to do.

Q. What are the relations between the operators and your brotherhood?—A. I have been associated with the Brotherhood of Locomotive Firemen as its chief executive for 14 years, and I have yet to find the first railroad officer with whom I could not do business and reach results that were acceptable to the organization which I represent. I can only speak for the firemen. To-day, throughout this entire country, we believe—and we form that belief from the treatment of our men and the readiness with which committees are received who wait upon the officers—there are pleasant relations existing between the firemen and their employers.

Q. Is there at times a little friction, over insurance matters for instance?—A. Friction breaks out between the railway employees and their operators just as it breaks out in church societies. Everything can not be expected to be peace and harmony at all times. I speak in general terms. We might single out certain instances in which we have had contention with railroad officers, and there are on record a few instances where the employees have withdrawn from the service; but to-day the relations which exist between the locomotive firemen and the railway companies of this country is of a most agreeable character, and we feel very well satisfied. We are reaping some of the rewards which patience brings, getting a little better wages in some localities since prosperity returned, and we hope to have better conditions. At the present time our men are earning good money, have plenty of work, and there is a demand for our men. One of the best evidences of the relations between the Brotherhood of Locomotive Firemen and the railway managers or operators is the fact that we are supplying a great many of our members to-day to the railway companies who are in need of experienced men; they telegraph to our office and ask us to supply the demand. That is an evidence of the feeling that exists between the companies and the organization. If they did not have respect for us and the work in which we are engaged they would not ask for our men to take service on their lines.

Q. (By Mr. Kennedy.) What are the usual hours of labor of locomotive firemen?—A. The usual hours of labor of locomotive firemen are 10; 10 hours constitute a day's work. If we work to exceed 10 hours we get a pro rata wage for the extra work. There are some places where they work 11 and some where they work 12, but the average hours of labor for the locomotive firemen are 10 hours or a run of 100 miles. If we run 100 miles that makes a day; if we make that run in 2 hours or 2½ we get a full day's pay. When they make the run back the same day, they make 2 days in 1. We have firemen that make 2 days in 1 by having made 200 miles in 10 hours.

Q. Does your organization favor shorter hours?—A. Yes, and so far as possible we have established 10 hours. It used to be 12, and before the organization came into existence there was no limit to the hours. Men used to work 24 hours and only get 1 day, and 15 hours and get 1 day; but when the organization came into existence it began to establish a maximum day and we have been very successful in establishing the 10-hour rule.

Q. Do your sympathy and support go out to all organizations that are struggling for a shorter work day?—A. Yes, and our organization is on record in favor of the establishment of the 8-hour rule for all employees. At the same time we question whether we would be able to introduce that successfully on railroads in the transportation department; but in the shops and on the sections, and wherever the men could work on an 8-hour basis, we want it done and we have advocated it. I tried to introduce the 8-hour rule a few days ago, and I felt very much encouraged from the conversation I had with the officers of a company in regard to working the switching crews on the 8-hour basis. Possibly, after a while that may come about.

Q. (By Mr. RATCHFORD.) Do monthly payments to railway employees operate as an incentive to exacting longer hours and greater number of days in the month from the employee than would be exacted if the same employee were paid by the day?—A. Yes; unless there is a rule specifying what their hours should be.

Q. Does such a rule exist?—A. We have men employed as hostlers at $90 per month. Their work is specified so that 12 hours constitute a day. And there are night men and day men; that fills in the 24 hours. There is a rule that they shall not work to exceed 12 hours a day, and if they work over that they get pro rata overtime. In the recent conference or settlement with the Grand Trunk, of Canada, the operators there were paid on the monthly basis and they have been compelled to work from 12 to 14 and 16 and 18 hours, just as the conditions of service required at the different stations. The schedule which has gone into effect and under which they work now provides a monthly salary and that 12 hours shall constitute a day, and if they work to exceed that 12 hours, they get overtime, which is added to their monthly compensation.

Q. In your paper you also made reference to the suspension of employees without pay. What are we to understand from the word "suspension" in the sense in which you used it?—A. It refers to an employee who was taken out of service for some alleged violation of the rules by an officer of the company and is held off for an indefinite length of time, and during that time, of course, no compensation is allowed him. He may be off 30 days; he may be off 60 days, and sometimes they have been off for 6 months. Investigation is finally held and he is returned to service. During that time he has had no earning capacity and we have believed that it was a gross injustice to railway employees, and the organizations have introduced a rule, which you will find in most of our schedules, that if a fireman is taken out of service, suspended, or discharged, he shall have a hearing within 5 days. If he is innocent, he shall be returned to service and paid for all time lost. By the establishment of that rule we have to a considerable extent lessened that evil of suspension. It still exists, however, among a great many of the different classes of employees, and that is what I think is referred to in that.

Q. In such cases is the employee paid the wages earned up to the date of his suspension?—A. He is paid up to the date he is taken out of the service. In days gone by if a superintendent or a train master did not feel just right, and an employee happened to do something that did not meet his views, he would send him home, and the employee might go around and try to get some knowledge of what their intentions were. He could get no information. He was kept out of service for an indefinite length of time—told that he was suspended. Afterwards he would be permitted to come back into the service. All that time has been lost. We believe that if a railroad employee is taken out of the service, he should know what he is taken out of the service for. He should be given an opportunity to be heard before his employer. If he can prove his innocence, he should be returned to service and paid for the time lost. If he is found guilty and 30 days' or so suspension is to be inflicted, we have a rule of punishment for offenses. A man may be suspended 30 days or he may be suspended 60 days for a specific violation of a rule, which violation has been determined after investigation.

Q. You referred also in your paper to the injunction order of Judge Jenkins being reversed by a higher court. What, in your opinion, was the effect of that proceeding among the railway employees and upon injunction proceedings generally?—A. I can speak of the effect upon the railway employees. It created a spirit of rebellion among them. It was a dangerous act on the part of the judge, and came very near at that time bringing about the most serious complications in the Northwest that this country ever saw; and had it not been for the influence of those who were at that time directly connected with the organizations there would have been an uprising on the Northern Pacific Railroad which would have been more disastrous, in my judgment, than the one in 1894. You will understand that prior to the issuing of this injunction there was no agitation, no disposition on the part of railroad employees to involve the Northern Pacific Railroad in a strike. The company had issued a schedule to take effect on a certain day, without any consideration or regard for the employees with whom they had a schedule at the time. The contract, as it was termed by the employees, was then in effect. Without any consideration of this the schedule was issued. The men came forward, through their representative committees, to have a hearing with the management and with the receivers. While this hearing was in progress, while the committee was in session deliberating with the officers of the road, Judge Jenkins issued his order, in which he restrained the men from leaving the service of the company, with or without notice—one of the most far-reaching injunctions ever issued in the annals of the courts. I was served with that injunction in my own office in Terre Haute, Ind., and I had not been near the Northern Pacific property, had not even been called into consultation with the men, yet I was restrained from even advising or counseling with the men or performing the duties which my office required. The men resented any such injunction and were very much worked up over it. Immediately the officers of the organization went forward, counseled with the men, and got the injunction modified, and it pacified the men to a certain extent, but it was the beginning of what finally terminated in the revolution which occurred in 1894 in the Northwest. Had that injunction never been issued by Judge Jenkins there never would have been a strike along the line of the Northern Pacific on the part of the railway employees in the company's service, but the issuing of that injunction so incensed the men that even after its modification they still felt the sting, and in 1894 the strike took place, and I believe that it was largely caused by the injunction of Judge Jenkins.

Q. Did the injunction restrain you from counseling with your men?—A. Yes.

Q. Verbally, by correspondence, or otherwise?—A. Yes, sir.

Q. (By Mr. KENNEDY.) In discussing the liability of railroads for injury, etc., you said the employees have no choice in the selection of the men employed by the railway. Do you have a certain choice through having 80 per cent of the employees in your organizations?—A. In answering that question as we do, we speak of the employee as he is received into the railroad service. We have no choice as to the character or qualifications of the man who to-day applies to the Southern Railway for employment. We are not consulted in the matter, neither are the employees on the road consulted. Any man who makes application for employment to the motive power department or the transportation department is heard without any regard to the employees then in service. Of course there are men who are hired by virtue of their membership in the organization upon recommendations which come from the organization to which they belong or of former employers; but the employees directly employed on the Southern Railway have no voice in the selection of their immediate associates. For instance, you are a conductor; you go out to-day upon the road in charge of your train. The train master has hired two men. He does not consult you in regard to hiring those men. You report to go out on your train, and there are two men you have never seen. You do not know them. You know nothing of their qualifications. They are sent there with instructions to go out with you as your brakemen. That is what we desire to convey in that answer, that the employee has no choice in his associate employees. You go on the road and an accident occurs through the carelessness or the negligence or lack of ability on the part of one of those men assigned to you. You have had no choice in the selection of your crew. You had to take out whoever the company designated.

Q. Are these so-called voluntary relief associations looked upon by employees generally as a menace to their labor organizations?—A. Yes, sir; they are.

Q. Do they believe that the railroad companies in promoting them seek to divide the employees' allegiance in time of trouble between their unions and their insurance?—A. They do.

Q. There is a part of section 10 of the act of June 1, 1898, which says that no railroad company or corporation, etc., shall require any employee or person seeking employment as a condition of such employment to enter into a contract whereby such employee or applicant for such employment shall agree to contribute to any fund for charitable or social or beneficia. purposes. Is that part of the act effective or is it evaded by the railroad companies?—A. So far as I know, there has been no evidence brought to us of any violation of it by the railroad companies. No complaint has been filed by any of our men, and I have understood from the representatives of the other organizations that they have received no knowledge of it. I think the railroad companies, if they had anything of that kind in their application blank, have had it stricken out since that law was passed, and I do not understand to-day that it is one of the conditions of employment that a man shall join the association for mutual insurance which they may have; that is, it has not been brought to our notice.

Q. One of the organs of one of the organizations you are associated with says it is practically nullified in this way: If a man applies for employment and his application for employment is not accompanied by an application for membership in the benefit society, they do not want men; and if he accompanies it with the other application his chances are better for securing employment. Is that a fact?—A. I will answer that by saying, in my judgment, it would be very hard to prove that the company compelled a man to file an application for membership in the relief department as one of the conditions of employment. I can understand how I could go into the office of the superintendent of the Baltimore and Ohio Railroad and make application for employment. He would hand me an applica-- tion blank. He might say: "Mr. Sargent, we have here, as you know, a voluntary relief association. If you care to join it, you will fill out that blank." He would give me an application for employment, accompanied by the application for membership in the voluntary relief association. If I took that as a condition of employment, I would have to fill it out; in all probability I would fill it out if I wanted employ- ment under those conditions. If, on the other hand, I said: "I do not care to join any relief association. I am a member of the Brotherhood of Locomotive Firemen, and we have our own insurance features in the organization." If I filled out an application for employment and in a few days was notified that my application for employment was rejected, it might be true that the reason my application for employment was rejected was because I had not applied for mem- bership in the relief association; yet that fact could not be established. I have no doubt that there are times when that has its influence as it does on some of the roads in the way of preferment for promotion, Men receive preferment in the line of promotion because of their connection with the mutual insurance asso- ciation, while another man, who has only his affiliation with the organization, is kept back. He is told sometimes by subordinates: "You are standing in your own light. Why do you not join the relief? That will fix you all right." Yet at the same time if you would attempt to show that the Pennsylvania Railroad, if you please, was forcing its men to join the relief, you could not do it. You could not make a case. When that was first introduced it was the organizations which caused it to be changed from compulsory to voluntary, and it has been voluntary ever since. Nevertheless the influence is used and the impression is conveyed to the man that if he will join the relief he will be better off for it; and of course there are lots of fellows who lean that way; but if a man is independent he would not have to join the relief, because there are hundreds of men in the employment of the Pennsylvania Railroad Company who have not contributed anything to the relief association.

Q. Are they, too, promoted?—A. They gradually work up, but some of them believe that they would get along more rapidly if they belonged to the relief; but they have that force of character in respect to their organization that they will not yield, and they shovel a few more shovelfuls of coal rather than take promo- tion at the expense of the benefits of their organization. When you come to ask me the question if that act has been violated, I can not say that it has, because I have never known of it.

Q. The Journal of the Brotherhood of Railroad Trainmen said, editorially, that those things had been done, and said also that a man in the employ of the com- pany who was not a member of the relief association generally understood that he did not stand in the line of promotion the same as the man who did become a member of the association. How about that?—A. That is made to show you the effect. For instance, the railroad company does not want its men to belong to the organization. It circulates the idea that if you leave the organization you will get promotion. There are men who will accept that as a bite and a number of men leave their organization. At the same time if you bring that railroad official before this commission, or put him on the stand, he will make oath that the company did not attempt to prevent its men from belonging to an organiza- tion; yet we know that those things are done in that way. A part of the act you referred to applies to that proposition.

Q. (By Mr. FARQUHAR.) Is it a fact that the desire very often of operators of railroads where these benefit organizations are would naturally be to try to bring the employees nearer to them in interest by making propositions of insurance or uniting with the employees and securing better insurance? Is it not a matter of self-interest on the part of railroad operators to do that?—A. The fair railroad operator who is most solicitous of his employees is always willing that they should obtain the benefits of insurance from such sources as they prefer. The record these organizations have made, the Brotherhood of Locomotive Firemen having paid $6,000,000 to its crippled and maimed, and widows and orphans of those who have been killed, satisfies the railroad operator that the insurance which the firemen get through their organization is a far better benefit to them than any insurance that the railroad company could possibly introduce. Hence they do not encourage, and they do not desire to introduce, the relief scheme. But you find a railroad operator who looks upon these organizations as institutions that ought to be crushed because they presume to have too much to say about the hours of labor, the wages, and the rates under which men shall work, the man who does not appreciate the value of these organizations, scheming to introduce some plan whereby he can have a hold upon his employees. While he comes out in that philanthropic way, with his paternal care for his family, his ambition is to keep those men out of these organizations, because he prefers that the men in his employ shall not have the advantage of the insurance of the organizations, and that he be not required to meet and treat with them in such affairs as wages and the hours of labor and the rights of the men. That is my observation.

Q. Are your beneficial and relief associations operated as cheaply, and do they give equal or better benefits, as do the usual paternal organizations?—A. The Brotherhood of Locomotive Firemen stands to-day, acknowledged by all the insurance and fraternal societies of the world, as furnishing insurance at a cheaper rate than any other institution known to man. That is a statement that has been made by the insurance experts and by the representatives of fraternal societies. The men joining the Brotherhood of Locomotive Firemen, in the first place, have to pass a rigid medical examination, as rigid as any old-line insurance company that you can name. Upon his admission into the order he takes out his policy of $1,500 or $1,000. The cost last year for carrying that insurance policy, meeting all the deaths and disabilities which have occurred in our organization, for the $1,500 policy, has been $16 to the individual member.

Q. (By Mr. KENNEDY.) What would it cost him in the locomotive engineers' organization?—A. In the locomotive engineers' organization it would be considerably larger, on account of their large death rate. We have this advantage, which no other organization has: The fireman enters the Brotherhood of Locomotive Firemen and takes out his insurance; he remains with us, say, 5 or 6 or 8 years; he is promoted to be a locomotive engineer; he steps from our organization into theirs; they have an insurance; he drops the insurance of the Locomotive Firemen and takes it up in the Brotherhood of Locomotive Engineers; a young man fills this man's place; so that we have all young, able-bodied men, in the full vigor of life. After they have been with us a few years they step into the other organization; so that we are virtually made up of young blood.

I want to go a little further on the insurance question. We pay not only for deaths, but for the loss of a hand above the wrist, a foot above the ankle, blindness, consumption, paralysis, Bright's disease of the kidneys. Name me an association or an insurance society in the world that has as liberal a policy for its insured members. There is not one. The risks which we take are most hazardous, and next to the risk of the brakeman. With the automatic couplers and safety appliances the risk on the brakemen has been considerably reduced, while that on the firemen has not been reduced at all. None of these organizations pay for any such disabilities as we pay for. The engineers only pay for the loss of life and the loss of eyesight, and you will find on investigation that the firemen's insurance is a remarkable one, and a great many have asked how we could carry our insurance as we do. You understand, it is because of the young blood.

Q. (By Mr. FARQUHAR.) In the general paper read there was a statement made as to out-of-work benefits. What are they?—A. We have in our local lodges what is known as weekly benefits. A man is out of work and has not the means for his support; there is a weekly contribution made out of those funds for his maintenance and the maintenance of his family. A great deal of money is paid out in that way. That is not taken into consideration in our insurance at all. That is an outside feature. We have sick benefits. If a man is sick, he is paid so much a week during his sickness.

Q. (By Mr. KENNEDY.) Are there benefits in any of the orders for members who have become too old to work?—A. I believe the Brotherhood of Locomotive

Engineers has something of that kind. We have never had that, because we have no old men with us.

Q. If the members of your order could exercise their free will, would they go en masse into your benefit societies and let the companies' associations severely alone?—A. The locomotive firemen in this country are practically all members of the Brotherhood of Locomotive Firemen, regardless of reliefs or any insurance schemes which the companies introduce; we have practically over 29,000. If you will take the statistics of the Interstate Commerce Commission showing the number of locomotive firemen employed, you will find we have nearly the entire number in our organization. You will find, if you have the sentiment of the men employed on these railroads where they have voluntary relief associations, they would tell you that they have done a great deal of good in many instances. There are some features about the voluntary relief which the men would probably speak well of; but if they were given their own option in the matter, the railroad companies would have no insurance features whatever; they would much prefer not to have anything of that kind in connection with the employment on the railroad. I would ask the commission, if it has not already looked into this matter, to make some inquiries in regard to hospitals which are provided by the railroads. That is a feature that is very commendable where it is honestly conducted. The road on which I was employed, the Southern Pacific, has its hospital, and every month a certain amount is taken out of the employees' wages—firemen, for instance, 50 cents—and that is placed in what is known as the hospital fund. If a fireman is taken sick or injured, he is cared for at the hospital, and all his medical attendance and nursing and treatment is given him. In a country like Arizona or those Western countries along the line of those overland roads, the hospital feature has been very acceptable to the men and they take an interest in it. The roads there have shown a very fair disposition by electing from the ranks of the men members of the hospital board, and the men feel that they have a representation in the management and direction of the affairs of the hospital feature; but in the insurance features the men are not represented in that way, as a general rule.

Q. (By Mr. PHILLIPS.) Do the railroads contribute to the hospital fund?—A. I think all railroad employees contribute according to their wages, and I presume that would affect the president.

Q. Would it affect the president and the managers as well?—A. The president and the managers and all the officers are assessed so much a month, according to their salaries. The fund becomes enormous, and, of course, in some instances it has created a good deal of trouble. A little over a year ago the Union Pacific hospital department was severely overhauled by the telegraphers, and it was before the courts. It will be very interesting to look up that case, and you will get some valuable information as to how that particular feature is arranged. There the trouble was due to mismanagement. The funds of the men, which were supposed to be devoted to hospital advantages, were diverted, scandal arose, and the court overthrew the hospital department and ordered the money paid back to the men in proportionate shares.

Q. In what State was that?—A. That was along the line of the Union Pacific Railroad. I think the case was heard before Judge Sanborn in St. Paul. The hospital feature and the insurance feature should be kept distinct and apart, because they are two different propositions.

Q. (By Mr. FARQUHAR.) Have you in or near Chicago a home for aged railway employees?—A. Yes; the organizations have a home at Highland Park, which is maintained by the voluntary contributions of members of the organizations. They have 22 inmates there at the present time—aged engineers, firemen, conductors, and trainmen.

Q. (By Mr. PHILLIPS.) Do all the organizations contribute?—A. Yes; every organization contributes freely and voluntarily toward the maintenance of that home. It is not compulsory. It is supported by the lodges. The ladies have their lodges, and they contribute largely to the support and maintenance of the home.

Q. (By Mr. FARQUHAR.) Do you know of a proposition made by the president and directors of the Illinois Central Railroad to employees to invest in the stock of the road, and on better terms possibly, than those on which the common stock is offered?—A. We have a large number of our members who are employed on the Illinois Central Railroad who have shares of stock, and it is regarded as very acceptable. There is no railroad company in the United States to-day where there are more pleasant and harmonious relations existing between employer and employee than on the Illinois Central, and we believe it is working to a good advantage. A man who is interested in a concern will naturally take a little more interest than though he had no investment there. That is natural. If we enter into a little business and all put in our mite we all feel that we have a personal interest in the success and prosperity of the property, and I believe the employees on the Illinois Central to-day, who know that their affairs are properly handled, that they are fairly treated, paid good wages, and that their organizations are encouraged take more interest in the success of the carrying on of the business of the Illinois Central Railroad than they otherwise would. That has been my observation.

Q. (By Mr. KENNEDY.) Some time ago Mr. Moseley, secretary of the Interstate Commerce Commission, was before this commission. He submitted five proposed laws in the interest largely of the railroad workers of the country. The first one is "An act to secure harmony in decisions of State and Federal courts." It is a brief one, and it is the only one I shall read in full [reading]:

"An act to secure harmony in decisions of State and Federal courts.

"*Be it enacted by the Senate and House of Representatives of the United States of America in Congress assembled,* That the decisions of the courts of last resort in the several States shall, except where the Constitution, treaties, or statutes of the United States otherwise require or provide, be regarded as rules of decision in trials at common law in the courts of the United States in cases where such decisions apply, and no distinction in this regard shall be made between cases involving questions of general and those involving questions of special or local law."

Would such a law meet your approval?—A. We believe the enactment of this into a statute would be of great assistance to the railroad employees and avoid carrying a case from a State court to a Federal court where they can get a contrary decision. We believe the decisions should be uniform, in line with what this act provides, and I will say for the organizations that if this bill is introduced we shall give it our support, believing it will be helpful to us.

Q. The other one is to be entitled "An act to promote the safety of employees and travelers upon railroads, by compelling common carriers engaged in interstate commerce to equip their cars with automatic couplers and continuous brakes, and their locomotives with driving-wheel brakes, and for other purposes."—A. That we approve of, and we have already taken steps to have it introduced in the Minnesota and other State legislatures. The purpose of that is this: There are some roads that can not be classed as interstate roads. They do not run out of the State. They, however, connect with interstate roads and will be required to handle interstate cars. We think that that corporation should be required to equip its cars with safety appliances, so that the men employed on that road shall have the same security in the discharge of their duties on the rail as any other railroad employees, and that they should not have the privilege of dodging behind the technical point that they are not an interstate road; that whenever their cars are turned over to another road they should be equipped. We believe the enactment of that law in every State will avoid any of these differences arising.

Q. Would you approve a Federal law of the same character?—A. Yes. We have lots of roads out West that run but a few miles, but they connect with large trunk lines.

Q. Another proposed act is in line with what you said you were in favor of this morning, compelling railroads to give full and detailed information in regard to accidents and to send that information to the Interstate Commerce Commission.— A. We believe that that should be done; we believe that every possible authority should be given to the Interstate Commerce Commission, so that they can obtain complete statistics as to accidents and deaths and all the information that is necessary to be had. We pay them a big salary, and they ought to be able to do something that will benefit us.

Q. You are in favor of this proposed personal-liability law?—A. We have had that up for some time. We have been working on that line for several years. I can speak for all the associations on those measures, because we have discussed them among ourselves in conferences and they meet our views and approval. If they are introduced, we shall set our representatives to work to endeavor to bring influence to bear to have them passed. Their success will depend largely upon whether or not the commission here. gives them favorable indorsement. What I want to impress upon the minds of the commission is this: We anticipate that these bills will be very carefully considered by the commission, and the approval by the commission of these bills would. carry with it a great deal more weight than it would be possible for us to expect to carry; therefore we shall look to this commission for their opinion of these measures, and if the commission approves these bills we shall feel more satisfied, perhaps, than we would at present of the justice of them, and that would cause us to renew our energies to have them enacted.

We expect great things from this commission. Whether we will be disappointed or not remains to be seen. We anticipate that this commission, after it gets through its investigations, is going to present to Congress some recommendations which will be of great value to the working people of all classes—railroad men and all others who work for a living—and therefore we present these matters to you, as a basis of thought coming from us, with the hope that you will find much in them that is of value, and when you come to make your recommendations to Congress that we will find our suggestions formulated into measures that we can look forward to as being very helpful.

I think the Interstate Commerce Commission can be of great value to the country, to the railroads, and to the railroad employees, providing it is clothed with power to do something; but I have yet failed to discover wherein the Interstate Commerce Commission has got any power to do anything, except to go about the country and ask questions and get opinions when they can, and, if they can not, go without. I believe the Interstate Commerce Commission should have all the authority possible delegated to it by statute, so that when anything arises in which the transportation and railroad companies and the public is equally interested they should have the authority to go and investigate; to do those things that would remedy the evils which exist. That is the way I feel about the Interstate Commerce Commission. We have a great deal of regard for the commission. The railroad organizations were kindly treated by the commission 2 years ago, when the question of extending time on the application of safety appliances was considered. The railroads came forward and asked 5 years' extension of time. We protested against it. We appreciated the fact that it was necessary to extend the time, but not for 5 years. We were treated kindly by the commission, and we learned more of its workings at that time than we ever knew before. The commission is very valuable if it is clothed with authority. When you can only sit around a table and issue orders, and then, if the railroads want to carry them out do so, and if not ignore them, the commission is of very little value.

Q. (By Mr. PHILLIPS.) Do you think it has been of great influence so far?—A. They have done very good service.

Q. Even if they have no authority, has their moral effect been very beneficial to the railroad service of the country?—A. Yes, sir.

Q. (By Mr. KENNEDY.) Would you have the powers of the Interstate Commerce Commission enlarged in such a way that grievances of railroad employees against companies might be brought before it?—A. No; we do not propose to turn our affairs over to any such commission. We have gone just as far as we care to in regard to help from the Interstate Commerce Commission in the arbitration act. We want both the Interstate Commerce Commission and the Commissioner of Labor to use their influence so that a strike can be avoided. We do believe, however, that the Interstate Commerce Commission should compile annually statistics of wages, hours of labor, the number of employees on each railroad, and all conditions of employment, as a matter of reference, accessible to everybody. In case of grievances on any railroad, and if we should wish to make comparisons, we could turn to the Interstate Commerce Commission's record and find what every railroad in New England is paying firemen, number of hours work, wages, etc. We believe that authority should be delegated to the Interstate Commerce Commission. We believe this belongs to the commission. I presume these statistics are partially compiled by the Commissioner of Labor, but I believe that the railroad part of it should be in the hands of the Interstate Commerce Commission, because they have access, or should have access, to all affairs of a railroad. I believe railroads should submit these rates, and from such reports the Interstate Commerce Commission should compile tables, showing the wages of men employed on all railroads in the United States; that should be compiled yearly. If we had a yearly report, you could very easily turn to that and see what the wages are on all roads.

I believe the interests of railroad employees are best taken care of by the organizations to which they belong. Railroad men have faith in their organizations. The methods which these organizations have adopted are honorable and fair, and the course which we take in the adjustment of our disputes are commendable. Under the act to which you referred, which provides arbitration where the parties in dispute agree to it, the influence of the chairman of the Interstate Commerce Commission could be used to good advantage, and we believe that that is as far as we should go in that direction. We don't believe railroad employees' differences with their employers should ever be in the hands of the Interstate Commerce Commission to be disposed of; we don't have much faith in that way of settling disputes.

Q. (By Mr. PHILLIPS.) Have you had any case under the arbitration law which took effect in June, 1898?—A. Not under that law, but under the application intended by it, during the last six months, there have been two cases on the Grand Trunk Railroad that have been settled by arbitration in line with what that law intends shall be done when the parties can not agree.

Q. Were they settled satisfactorily?—A. Yes; with satisfaction to both sides. Our organization was the first to be brought into the conflict with the Grand Trunk Railroad Company by the discharge of several of our members. The case was taken up; we pursued the matter until we could not agree. We then submitted to arbitration, and a decision was rendered in our favor. Shortly after that the question of wages came up with telegraphers on the Grand Trunk, and several telegraphers were discharged because of their prominence on the committee. The matter looked very serious for a time, but it resulted in an agreement to arbitrate. That question was settled satisfactorily; the telegraphers who were discharged were returned to the service, their wages increased and hours reduced, and a schedule made which was very acceptable to the men; and the board of arbitration were very unanimous in their award, regarding it as a successful affair. I was very sorry that did not happen in our country. It happened across the line, but, at the same time, it is carrying out the idea which that law is intended to carry out on the railroads of the United States, and I believe that it has demonstrated to the railroad managers in this country that arbitration is the proper way of settling these matters when they and the parties controlling the men can agree.

Q. Did the railroads make practically no opposition to the passage of the law?— A. How could they? It would be against public sentiment. The public believe in settling matters by arbitration. How could they oppose a law of that kind? Is not that a just way to settle disputes? It was the railway organizations' policy as far back as during the strike on the C., B. and Q. The railroad organizations have always wanted arbitration.

Q. (By Mr. KENNEDY.) Is there any organization of the employees of the great express companies of the country?—A. They have an organization of express messengers, I think. I do not know how large a membership they have.

Q. Are they affiliated with your organization?—A. No, sir.

WASHINGTON, D. C., *March 2, 1899.*

TESTIMONY OF MR. H. T. NEWCOMB,

Chief of the Section of Freight Rates, Division of Statistics, United States Department of Agriculture.

The commission met at 11 a. m., Vice-Chairman Phillips presiding. Mr. H. T. Newcomb, chief of the section of freight rates in the Division of Statistics, United States Department of Agriculture, appeared as a witness. The vice-chairman stated that the witness would testify in regard to transportation, especially in connection with the agricultural industry. The topical plan of inquiry on transportation was taken up.

Mr. NEWCOMB. I would like to commence with the topical plan of inquiry on transportation at Division B of Part II, because it seems to me that the primary purpose for which we have our railway transportation system is the carriage of commodities; that the transportation of passengers is an adjunct to that, and that the relations of employees to the railways, however important they may be, should be treated in a way that can be assimilated to whatever treatment we find necessarily growing out of the relations between the transportation agencies, as carriers of commodities, and their patrons. Discriminations among persons, whether as producers or consumers located at single points, or as residents of different localities, or as manufacturers, producers, or consumers of different commodities, appear to me to spring almost wholly out of competition between the separate agencies which make up our transportation system, the competition that causes these discriminations usually being that between rival carriers which seek to perform identical services, each making bids to shippers for the privilege of carrying their commodities. Competition in its ordinary and usual form, as we all understand it, between sellers of a commodity, results in a series of offers which, if competition is free and open, finally result in a common price that is open to all. Competition among railways does not have that effect. The interests of large shippers are so prominent that it is decidedly profitable for the carrier to make a special effort to get their traffic as against the traffic of smaller shippers. There is no minimum limit to the rates that can be made for specific services, and competition of this kind actually brings the rates, in many instances, very far below the cost of the service.

Q. (By Mr. NORTH.) Do you state that as a fact generally?—A. Not as a fact as regards the whole transportation system, but as regards the points at which there is competition among carriers offering to perform the same services. A great portion of the total railway traffic is not taken subject to that kind of competition, and thus arises a very prolific cause of discrimination. The rates are low at the points where actual competition exists and high at the points where it does not exist, because of the necessity of the carrier recouping itself for losses at competitive points. In a progressive country like this, where we are requiring additional capital all the time for new transportation agencies, the rate can not permanently go much below the rate in other industries.

It would be very difficult indeed to overstate the detrimental effects of this kind of discrimination. Ability in business affairs becomes, in consequence of these practices, absolutely no safeguard against disaster in the conduct of industry. The man who can obtain these illegitimate favors from railroads has an advantage that can not be offset in any way.

Q. Is that done to the same extent now that is was formerly?—A. I think there has been very little improvement in that regard. There have been, since the interstate-commerce law was passed, occasional periods when discriminations due to rate-cutting were uncommon, and I might say, at the present time the published rates are quite well observed; there is said to be very little discrimination of this kind, and there has not been since the 1st of January. The railroads and the Interstate Commerce Commission have evidently gotten together and through some means an agreement has been reached through which it is hoped rates will be maintained. I do not look for any permanence of that condition. I do not believe, under the conditions of the law that imposes competition and prohibits agreement between carriers in regard to rates, that there can be any permanence in it. Traffic conditions are, however, unusually favorable just now and while they last any arrangement may suffice.

Q. Do you believe it is an evil beyond remedy?—A. Beyond remedy, unless the carriers are allowed to get together, and the interests of particular carriers in taking traffic away from their rivals is done away with entirely and the route traversed by shipments made as nearly absolutely indifferent as possible.

Q. (By Mr. A. L. HARRIS.) Would that be done by the pooling system?—A. Yes, in so far as the pooling system is effective it would. That is the only object of the pooling system.

Q. Has not that been forbidden and wiped out?—A. It has.

Q. (By Mr. PHILLIPS.) Provided there was a pooling system among the various railroads, would they not advance the price and eliminate competition through selfish motives rather than diminish it?—A. I am inclined to think that it would not, except in particular cases where the rates are already too low. The prices which the railroad can exact for a given volume of business is strictly limited by the necessity of moving the business. The railroad is always carrying for a great many people who are absolutely on the margin of profitable production, and any increase of its rates would tend to prevent the moving of that traffic. Then, we must always bear in mind that the low rate on competitive business is made to the few and at very few points, and often to very few shippers at those points; that a great majority of the patrons of the railroad have to give their business to a particular line, and that there is no competition as to them. The Iowa railroad commission, in 1878, after considering the question of the pool between Omaha and Chicago, reported that they considered it the only means by which the through business could be made to bear its just proportion of the fixed charges of the railroads.

Q. (By Mr. A. L. HARRIS.) If pooling is such a good thing, why should it be wiped out?—A. The testimony taken before the Committee on Interstate Commerce of the United States Senate previous to the passage of the insterstate-commerce law does not show any particular desire for the prohibition of pooling, and I have not been able to find that any very definite or general sentiment of that kind has existed at any time. The men most acquainted with the nature of pooling agreements and their effect on transportation at that time, testified with practical unanimity in favor of an effective system of pooling under proper governmental supervision. The railroads at that time were asking that the Government supervise the pools. Mr. Albert Fink, at that time chairman of the Trunk Line Association, very strongly urged that the Government provide some effective supervision of those pools. Of course, one great defect was that the contracts were understood to be such as could not be enforced in the courts. No carrier that I know of ever went to the courts seeking the enforcement of a contract of that kind. The pools were usually temporary affairs, and only one case of continuous operation during a long period is on record—that of the Chicago-Omaha pool.

Q. What is the real difference between pooling and what is known as joint traffic association?—A. The pools are of two classes, either agreements to divide business—that is, tonnage in which the tonnage is actually diverted is put into a pool, and if one receives more than its allotted proportion, the surplus tonnage is actually diverted to other roads; or of another class in which a deposit of money is made, generally subject to the order of a commissioner, and balances are settled by the transfer of a portion of the earnings from business in excess of that allotted. In the Trunk Line pool it was provided, I think, that 40 per cent of gross returns should be considered the expense of conducting the business, and that the remaining 60 per cent should be put into the pool and distributed according to the agreed percentages. The joint traffic association is popularly supposed to have been intended to accomplish the division of traffic in some manner that was never developed. It did not appear in the contract, and if they had any such intention it was never executed so far as public records show. You must remember that it was under fire from the start and if the managers ever intended to do anything of the kind they did not have any opportunity. The joint traffic association was never very effective in any way.

Q. (By Mr. RATCHFORD.) What has governmental management of railroads, under receiverships, to do with the matter under discussion; does such management encourage or discourage discrimination?—A. So far it has very clearly tended to encourage it. Roads under receivers have frequently been the worst rate cutters and most demoralizing to rate situations.

Q. Is it a fact that when railroads are not operated upon a profitable basis, and when the management of such railroads see that they are destined to fall into the hands of receivers, that discrimination, or cutting of prices, begins there in order to divert traffic to their road prior to a receiver being appointed?—A. I do not know of any specific instance of that kind. It may have happened. It does not sound unreasonable at all. I think it is altogether possible that something of that kind may have occurred in the last four or five years, during which the railroads have been expecting and hoping that Congress would make some modification in the antipooling clause of the interstate-commerce law. It may be that some of the roads have tried to increase their earnings with the specific purpose of obtaining large percentages in whatever pools may be created.

Q. (By Mr. FARQUHAR.) Is it a fact that in all the preliminaries before making a pool, it has been the uniform practice with roads that were competent at that time, through rolling stock, etc., to cut rates in order to get a large pro rata of the pool itself?—A. I think it has been done.

Q. Has it not been the trouble in the last 25 years?—A. The latter half of the last 25 years we have not had pools. Recently, I think (from the hope that they might soon be legalized), it has been a part of the trouble.

Q. Do you think that the roads themselves, after their pools are formed, have sufficient honor in their directories to sustain an honorable pool?—A. I would rather not put it that way. It is an historical fact, however we explain it, that pooling agreements have not been observed; that every pool has sooner or later broken down and been followed by a rate war, but so has every other situation among the railroads.

Q. (By Mr. A. L. HARRIS.) Why should it not be made a legal, binding contract?—A. That is precisely what I would desire to have done.

Q. (By Mr. FARQUHAR.) Were it possible under the interstate-commerce law, or any law we could make in this country, to legalize a pool, from your past experience and knowledge of the management of pools in this country, do you think there is sufficient honor among the railroads to sustain a pool?—A. I do not think that there is sufficient honor among any set of public men or business men anywhere to sustain any arrangement that is seriously contrary to their business interests, but I do believe that it can be made desirable for the railways, or a great majority of them, to maintain those pools most of the time.

Q. Can you propose any safeguard to make them observe the pool unless it has governmental supervision?—A. Simply the ordinary legal safeguard we have when we make contracts, that we can go into court and enforce them through damages or otherwise. I do not hope for any solution of the railway problem that will be satisfactory to everybody. I believe we can minimize the number of discriminations and that the legislation of the last few years—the antipooling clause of the interstate-commerce law and all legislation of a similar character—has tended to multiply discriminations.

Q. So you think if pooling were established it would lessen the faults?—A. Yes. I think the contract must take the form of a pool in some way. I do not think there is any use in being afraid of the word "pool" at all. We have what in common parlance we call a "railroad system." We find that it is not coordinated to such an extent as to be a system at all in many respects. One of the respects is this question of rates. We all realize that these rates should be equal and open, and we find one thing—the Interstate Commerce Commission has made it as clear as it can be made in the English language—competition, at the root of it. I believe the way to get rid of that condition is to get rid of competition as much as you can. You can not get rid of it entirely by any means short of absolute consolidation of the railroads.

Q. (By Mr. NORTH.) Would governmental supervision of the railroads accomplish that purpose?—A. I do not believe governmental supervision will do it. No governmental supervision has done it.

Q. Has it been done in England, Germany, or France?—A. In Germany the Government owns the railways and makes its own rates. In England they pool. In France they have divided the country territorially, so that there is no such thing as competition. In Belgium they had rate wars between the State railroads and the privately owned railroads, and they had discriminations, and finally the State railroads were compelled to go into pools with the other roads.

Q. (By Mr. FARQUHAR.) What is the relationship of those fast freight lines; for instance, the Blue Line and a dispatch company?—A. There are two kinds of fast freight lines. There is the fast freight line which is actually incorporated, or a joint stock company, doing business with special privileges over particular lines. There are other fast freight lines, like the Blue Line and most of those in existence, which are, in substance, merely names and trade-marks for particular routes. The latter are cooperative lines. Each road puts in a number of cars, generally proportional to its mileage in the route. For instance, there is a line from Boston to Chicago, formed by the Boston and Albany, the New York Central, and the Lake Shore and Michigan Southern; they put in cars in proportion to their mileage in that route, and they pay the expenses and divide the receipts in the same proportions. They have a common manager; they have joint soliciting agents; and it is simply a trade-mark or a means of securing business. Each important road has a great many fast freight lines, although there has been some effort lately to consolidate them; and we actually find the Michigan Central, the Lake Shore, the Pennsylvania, and such roads competing against themselves in the Chicago markets for business through their separate agencies of this sort. It is just another agency of competition.

Q. Do you refer to fast freight lines that are really owned by the roads themselves?—A. Yes; and I only recall two others—the Empire Line and the Merchants' Despatch; they are the only incorporated fast freight lines I recall now.

Q. That are not owned by the railroad?—A. Yes. There was a time when there were more, but they have gradually disappeared, and they are generally regarded by the railroad people themselves as bad things, although I presume that does not refer to the Pennsylvania line. Their line—the Empire Line—seems to be doing a good business in a good way.

Q. (By Mr. A. L. HARRIS.) Are the stockholders and managers of fast freight lines officers of the railroads?—A. I think that is one of the things that is past now; that was true at one time. I think attempts to make money by inside corporations of that kind have ceased entirely.

Q. (By Mr. FARQUHAR.) Is it a fact that old lines—the Blue Line and others— were at one time independent of the railroads in rates, and made their own arrangements for equipment and everything else for the road?—A. I do not know of any lines existing now that were not always cooperative lines.

Q. Were the arrangements with those fast freight lines always satisfactory to the public and to the lines themselves? Was there ever any fault on the prorating of that class of freight?—A. I do not believe that has ever been a matter of importance to the general public.

Q. Did you ever hear of any public outbreak against the prorate that was formed by these lines at that time?—A. No.

Q. Was there such a thing as managing a prorating, and fairness in the transit of merchandise at one time?—A. Will you please tell me what you mean by prorating?

Q. Take the freight the Blue Line itself carried to Chicago from the East—every single line got its prorate from the Blue Line itself in the carriage of freight by its mileage. The Blue Line itself had to settle with the company.—A. That is prorating between connecting lines. I do not know that that is a subject in which the public has any particular interest. I do not know that there is any dissatisfaction in regard to it now or that there ever has been. Through lines are an almost universal incident of railroad business.

Q. (By Mr. RATCHFORD.) We learn that corn raised in the State of Illinois can be and is shipped into the plains of Lombardy, Italy, at a lower price than the Italians can raise corn there. Is that correct?—A. I do not know. We are shipping corn there all the time. We do not export anything unless we can put it in a foreign market at a lower price than it can be put there by somebody else. We do not export it unless they have something we want that we take in exhange—that we can get that way easier than we can make it at home. I believe that exchange is a desirable one to make.

Q. (By Mr. FARQUHAR.) Will you take up topics 36, 37, 38?—A. I would like to say a little in regard to 35 before I do that. In regard to 35, I wish to suggest that rates of transportation are unjust or just in comparison with other charges; that there is no such thing as a rate that is excessive in itself; that the only study of railway charges must be a comparative study; the relations among charges on similar products and of particular charges to the total earnings of the railway itself. I think that is perfectly clear if we consider the business of a single railroad. Take one such as they sometimes build them in my State—Michigan—for lumbering purposes. The road may be built and for some time carry nothing but timber or lumber. Take it at a time when it is only carrying one commodity. The reasonable and just rate on that single commodity would be one that would pay the wages and the other costs of operation, taxes, and a reasonable return on the capital. Now, let that railroad find it possible to get another commodity, say flour, for a return load. Of course lumber would only move in one direction. Say it could get a return load for its cars. I think it is a matter that must be absolutely clear to all of us that some reduction on the rate on lumber would be absolutely necessary at once. I think those two rates must be decided together. Of course in ordinary cases each of our railroads has a great complex of articles that make up its traffic. You must study the rates comparatively. You can not study them alone. There is no such thing as a rate that alone is excessive.

In regard to 36, I do not believe that there is any possible remedy after the discrimination has been made. The burden of an excessive and unjust rate is always more or less shifted. It is always excessive to some one by the amount of the advantage accorded to the man who gets the more favorable rate, and this excess is distributed among consumers in various degrees. It passes along much as taxation is shifted and transferred, and you can not ascertain and hand damages over to the aggrieved parties by any possible judicial process.

Referring to 37, through freight rates and routes are very important incidents of the transportation service—absolutely necessary in order to have a satisfactory service. The railways have established them, and the railway system has been tending toward unification. Many of you remember that you traveled over railroads of 6-feet gauge. You remember when narrow-gauge railroads were plentiful. You remember how the railways of the South were changed from the 5-feet gauge in order that cars might be interchanged with the roads of the North. The Atlantic and Western, now the New York, Pennsylvania and Ohio, was built with the 6-feet gauge in order specifically to prevent the transfer of cars, and in order that money might be spent at the terminus to unload and reload freight. You are now almost as liable to see a Union Pacific car on the Baltimore and Ohio track as one belonging to the road itself. Through rates and routes have been generally established. Those have been tendencies, I believe, that have not been very much affected by legislation, and, without saying that the Government should not interfere with that tendency, either to expedite or retard it, I believe that legislation in that direction ought to be undertaken with the greatest care. It is a very delicate subject, and I should be very much inclined to demand most satisfactory reasons before trusting it to anything but the natural operation of the forces we have already observed. And the same thing applies with perhaps not quite so much force to the question under 38. It is absolutely necessary that rates should be just as between the different patrons of the railways, in order that business may go ahead and true individualism may have play; and I think some strengthening of the authority of the Interstate Commerce Commission is advisable, but I would want to make it very clear in any legislation that rates are only to be changed by their order after the most careful investigation in specific cases, and that blanket orders, such as that in the Cincinnati Chamber of Commerce case, should not be considered proper from that body. You remember that was the case where rates for a very large section of the South were modified in a single order. It seems to me that is a dangerous power to trust anywhere. The movement in rates should be a gradual tendency to more symmetrical arrangement; and business conditions and business arrangements, even though they are not perfect in their own adjustment, should not be violently disturbed at any time. It will be very well to permit the commission to establish maximum and minimum rates under suitable limitations after careful consideration, and at the same time to prevent very general orders. There was one in the food products case in 1891, I think, of much the same character.

Q. (By Mr. PHILLIPS.) If these people are permitted to pool their interests and make through freight rates, will they not be governed by selfish considerations rather than for the whole people?—A. I think it is exceedingly desirable that there should be a commission with supervisory authority in case we are to permit pooling, or in case we are to go on as we are; even more necessary if we are to go on as we are.

Q. (By Mr. FARQUHAR.) Would it be well to have modified pooling at first as an experiment, giving the Interstate Commerce Commission sufficient authority under the law to carry it out?—A. I would not propose any pool—rather, should not advocate any pooling system—that did not provide public supervision. The contract ought to be a public one, filed with the commission, and the commission ought to have power to object to it and to require changes in the rates and conditions of operation under the contract; and no one objects to that at present.

I would suggest, in regard to 39 (publication of freight rates), that the publication of charges for railroad services is the foundation of any supervision by public authority which can be had at all. If we are going to have Federal supervision it is absolutely essential that the rates should be public, and those which are public should be observed; and some means of doing that must be had before we can have effective Federal supervision. At the present time in the United States we have three general freight classifications—one that applies, roughly, west of a line drawn from Chicago to St. Louis and the Mississippi River; one that applies east of that line and north of the Potomac and Ohio rivers, and one that applies south of that line and east of the Mississippi. Those classifications differ in very important respects, which grow out of the character of the traffic and the different territories. A uniform classification on through business would be a desirable thing. The railroads have confessed their inability to make such a classification and have indicated their desire to have one by having a joint committee try to make one. That committee existed for 3 or 4 years, but they gave it up as an impracticable thing; at least, impracticable to harmonize the relations between different railroads. If such a classification were had it would be necessary to make careful provision for exceptions in the interest of local traffic. Of course, the relations between the rates on cotton and rates on lumber can not be the same, properly, in Mississippi and Georgia that they are in Michigan and Wisconsin, and any classification must be elastic enough to permit of just discrimination among commodities in favor of those which are moved in especially large quantities in particular districts. Lumber, meat, and grains must have different rates in certain regions from those that are applied with propriety in localities where they do not move largely. I do not believe that the classifications are material causes of unjust discrimination. Classification may occasionally result in unjust discrimination, but it is not the root of the evil, or even the immediate source of evil.

Public regulation also requires, in addition to the publication of rates, some supervision of the accounting departments of railways. You can not tell whether a railroad is observing its rates or not, or whether its earnings are reasonable upon its capital or not, unless you can step in and find out how its earnings are distributed among the different accounts and generally supervise the accounting system; and I believe an important forward step is to extend the work of the Bureau of Statistics of the Interstate Commerce Commission.

I do not believe that the issuing of fictitious stock is an important factor in the railroad situation. I do not see in what way it can affect the rates to be obtained by the railway, or injuriously affect the public as distinct from the purchasers of railway securities, unless it is a means of deceiving legislators who have to legislate upon railway matters.

Q. In other words, do you think it lies more in the Stock Exchange of New York than elsewhere?—A. Yes. Its power to deceive legislators, if it ever had any such power, which is rather doubtful, has certainly been exploded by this time. The railway stocks and bonds decide upon what terms the surplus earnings shall be distributed between holders, and nothing more.

Q. (By Mr. PHILLIPS.) Do the railroad people endeavor to pay less wages and charge higher rates in order to pay interest on this capital and give it a market value?—A. Oh, they would like to, but they can not.

Q. (By Mr. FARQUHAR.) What are you going to do with watered stock where they pay no dividends at all and yet pay wages?—A. They have to hire labor in the market and pay market prices for the kind of labor they require.

Q. Do you think the water is paid for through wages?—A. I am certain that it is not paid for through wages, and I am also certain that it is not paid for through high rates. I do not believe it is in the power of most railroads to impose, I am certain it is not in the power of railroads to collect, a higher interest on money in the railroad business than the average amount collected in the other lines of industry. In explanation of that, the railroad carrying wheat from Minnesota to its market has to compete with railroads carrying wheat from other points. If it has wheat for export, it has to compete with transportation lines and producers in the Argentine Republic and Australasia and Russia and anywhere else where wheat can be produced, and the price the railroad obtains must be well within the price at which wheat is delivered in Liverpool. The railroad is always carrying for a large number of purchasers who are on the margin of profitable production. If the rate was raised a penny on the hundred pounds or a half cent on the bushel, sooner or later they would be forced out of production. The road is constantly meeting demands from other shippers who want lower rates in order to get into the market, and the tendency is downward rather than upward. It is said sometimes that the railroads raise their rates on agricultural products when prices are high. I can not speak for cotton rates; I have not studied them. For seven years with the Interstate Commerce Commission and four years with the Agricultural Department, I have watched the grain market with a great deal of care, and I only know of but one general advance in grain rates. In 1890 rates were reduced after a long investigation by the commission. Rates were generally reduced. What they called an emergency rate was put in, in order to save the producers, who were in a desperate condition on account of the low prices, and a part only of that reduction was put back in the following year, when prices were higher, and rates never got back to the point where they were before. Otherwise the rates have steadily declined. In a pamphlet published by the Agricultural Department on that subject I have gone into comparisons of that character, and have, I think, shown conclusively that the average rate obtained by the railroads in this country has declined very much more than the prices of agricultural products, comparing with the average for the years 1867 to 1872, using the average of these years as a basis.

Q. (By Mr. A. L. HARRIS.) On the gold basis?—A. On the gold basis; yes. The average rate per ton per mile charged by the railroads now is only 44 per cent of that average. That was for 1896, the latest year that could be given at the time the pamphlet was made up. The average rate of the railroads was 44 per cent of the average of the former years, and the average per cent of the price of wheat was 67. The average price of oats was 49, and rye 51; corn, 44; hay, 56; potatoes, 50; buckwheat, 53, and tobacco, 65. Of course, cotton could not be brought into that comparison, on account of the higher prices during the civil war.

In regard to 46, I do not wish to say anything except a word of remonstrance in regard to the common practice of supposing that the cost of a railroad as it exists now is to be measured by the actual cost of constructing the railroad at first. Most of our railroads have been built as cheaply as possible in order to enable them to handle traffic, and they have been improved afterwards, often by actually raising additional capital by selling more securities. The progress of our railway system from cheap roadbed, light rails, and poor equipment to heavy rails, good equipment, block-signaling system, and all that, has been accomplished after the roads have been put into operation. Terminals, tunnels, bridges, and other items of extraordinary cost that raise the average are usually omitted when people say that these railroads can be duplicated for $10,000, $15,000, or $20,000 a mile. Our roads are all being rebuilt. Those that have not taken it up must do it.

The subject of taxation of railroads is a subject of great complexity. Scarcely any two States have the same system. Some try to tax them on their property just as other property is taxed. To tax them on net earnings is probably the only scientific tax. I am inclined to think that the State which taxes railways higher than they are taxed by other States discriminates against its own citizens by limiting the agencies by which they market their products—practically imposes an export tax on its own products. The tax is shifted to the shipper, and it is in the nature of the business that it must be shifted. The express company, the sleeping-car company, and the fast freight line all ought to be regulated as far as possible, just as railroads are. It was a mistake to leave them out of the original law.

Q. Are the tax laws in the different States upon railroad property uniform?—A. No; there are scarcely two States that have the same tax.

Q. For instance, the State of New Jersey raises for State purposes about $1,000,000, and other States assess upon the value of the property. Do other States help to pay the taxes of New Jersey because the shipper has to help pay the tax?—A. Of course, you have splendid illustrations in that case, where those expensive terminals exist in the State of New Jersey, and they can practically tax the people in New York and the West for State purposes in that way very effectively.

Q. Have you given any thought to the question of the unification of tax laws?— A. I have given a great deal of thought to it, but I have never seen a thoroughly practical method. I would like to call the commission's attention to the work of Prof. Henry C. Adams, The Science of Finance, and to his proposals in that direction. I am not myself in full agreement with him, but as far as State taxation goes I think I can most heartily approve his plan. I am doubtful as to the effect of the method by which he proposes to tax interstate railway companies for the benefit of the General Government, but if the tax was tolerably certain to be moderate I would favor it; but whether it might not be a dangerous tax, one that would retard the territorial division of labor, I am not yet prepared to express myself on that. It might be dangerous in that way. He gives a very comprehensive suggestion in that line and in the line of taxation generally. He proposes a system for all governments—includes everything, from municipal taxation to national taxation.

Q. (By Mr. PHILLIPS.) Is he connected with the Interstate Commerce Commission?—A. He is the statistician there, and professor of political economy in the University of Michigan.

Q. (By Mr. A. L. HARRIS.) Is that not a Government publication?—A. No.

Q. (By Mr. KENNEDY.) I would like to hear from you upon Government ownership of land transportation?—A. To my mind there are two practicable methods of dealing with the railway situation: One of these is the plan which has been adopted in England, and which has been so far tried in this country, but not thoroughly—the regulation of railroads by commissions having supervisory power, and perhaps mandatory power to a limited extent; the other way is absolutely to take hold of transportation agencies and operate them by the Government. We have undertaken the commission system, and it might be argued that we ought to give it a thorough test before adopting another; no such thorough test has been given it; the law has been in effect, now, since 1887, 12 years nearly, and the law has never been in satisfactory shape; it has always contained this clause which the present chairman of the commission has declared is directly antagonistic to the whole purpose of the law—the antipooling clause. It has always tended to perpetuate competition, while prohibiting the means by which competition is generally made effective. The result of that has been that the usual means have been resorted to, in violation of the law. In other words, the railroad business of this country has been conducted for some time on an indictable basis.

Q. (By Mr. RATCHFORD.) In either case are recommendations practically governmental regulations, whether it be managed by commission or by Government?—A. Yes. I think that is all there is to the question of governmental ownership; whether that is the most satisfactory expedient of regulation is the question. There are objections to the plan of taking over the railroads, and there are arguments in favor of it. It seems to me that the economic argument, as distinct from the political argument—that is, considering the way we may produce with the least expenditure of energy or the least "cost of production," as the economists say— is wholly in favor of the actual consolidation of the whole railway system. That is as far as the economist can take you. The question as to who shall own the consolidated system or who shall operate it is a political question wholly; and, to my mind, the question whether the Government shall own it is one to be decided by the way in which we regard our present administrative agencies. As a matter of course, we could not permit a consolidated railway to be owned by a private corporation. If we believe our present Federal agencies are developed to the extent that they could properly manage an agency employing nearly a million of men and collecting a revenue of more than a billion dollars annually, I should think the argument was decidedly in favor of Government ownership, provided regulation by commission should fail; but no adequate test of that has been made.

Q. (By Mr. C. J. HARRIS.) Have you, in your statistics, ever gone into the economy of private and public management of business? In other words, is not every line of business that is run by the Government nearly twice as expensive as it would be if conducted by an individual?—A. So far as that administrative question goes, I wish to say that it seems to me that it is absolutely fatal to the governmental ownership of railways at present.

Q. (By Mr. PHILLIPS.) How would it apply to the mail service?—A. The mail service generally is conducted on a better basis than anything else the Government does. I should say it would require the development of a generation at least to give us an administrative system in this country that could handle railroads even decently. We are spending in everything we undertake, unless it be in the postal service and possibly the Bureau of Engraving and Printing—in almost everything we undertake we are expending $1 where 50 cents would be ample. It amounts to that in every agency of the Federal Government that I know of. I believe the proposition can not be overcome on other grounds, but we should unquestionably try the political expedient, which is simpler, at first, and that is through the exercise of the power to regulate interstate commerce by Congress.

I say the interstate commerce law is inadequate, and I would like to indicate in what way it could be improved: First, and as almost the only essential thing in that, I believe in the substitution for the present antipooling clause of a clause which will permit the railways to distribute their traffic among themselves according to agreed percentages, tnose contracts to be under the supervision of the Interstate Commerce Commission, to be public, and the commission to have power to require them to be suspended, or the rates to be changed, or the other practices corrected if found obnoxious to the public welfare. I do not care very much what shape that amendment takes so long as it embodies those principles. The railroads, ever since the law has been passed, have been urging that that be done. The House of Representatives has passed a bill once providing for it. A majority of the members of the Interstate Commerce Commission are understood to have approved it. The present chairman has approved it very heartily. In the last report he has put it very forcibly. It has been approved by the convention of State railroad commissioners; it has been approved by conferences of representatives of boards of trade and other representatives of municipal concerns. Mr. Reed has spoken in favor of it on the floor of the House. Senator Cullom has approved it, and every man who has made a thorough study of transportation, as far as I know. Judge Reagan, who drew and insisted upon the antipooling clause, has recommended it.

The opposition is of three classes: First, that coming from a small portion of the public that is still ignorant concerning the effect of competition in producing unjust discrimination and believes it to have substantial efficacy in regulating rates, and that it may even secure reductions in the general averages; second, from a class of railway officials who, while desiring pooling, object to measures providing for it, because they have also included amendments intended to strengthen the powers of the Interstate Commerce Commission, which they believe contrary to public policy; and, third, the really dangerous opposition comes from the trusts and powerful combinations of shippers who, through the control of enormous traffic, are able to dictate to the railways the terms upon which they will purchase transportation. These people are able to dictate rates to the railroads and get unfair profits and unfair advantages over their competitors from the necessity the railroad is under of taking traffic at whatever rates they are willing to pay. I will venture to say here, and if you will call railroad men and traffic men before you you will get more definite information from them—I will venture to assert that there has not been a rate on sugar from New York, Philadelphia, or any of the great refining cities, promulgated by the railways within the last 10 years, that has not first been submitted to the sugar trust. And you can go right through the list of organizations of that kind in this country and you will find they are the ones that make the rates on their own products. The reason, as I believe, that the Patterson bill, providing pooling and increasing the authority of the Interstate Commerce Commission, was not passed in 1894 was the underhanded and secret opposition of the trusts. That being the situation, it seems to me that we ought to get whatever legislation legalizing pooling we can get, with so much other amendment to the interstate-commerce law as is possible. That law ought to be amended so as to give substantial finality to the findings of the commission. The commission investigates a case by methods similar to those adopted by the courts. It cites witnesses, and the parties are represented by counsel, having due notice, and all the regular forms of procedure adopted by the courts. It issues an order and the railroad refuses to obey it, and the commission, or some party interested, has permission to go to the court and seek a decree enforcing that order, and the court is instructed to proceed by rather less formal procedure than usual, but that does not amount to much, and the court goes into it and it declares it has the right to hear that case as a new case, and the commission's findings are simply prima facie evidence of the facts it found, and they are subject, like all prima facie evidence, to rebuttal. Very often railroads make a very different showing before the courts from the one they made before the commission—set up a new defense—and it has been very difficult, practically impossible, to get the commission's decrees enforced. The courts are not experts in the matter of transportation, and the members of the commission are. They might be much better experts than some of them are if they were selected with more care, but by keeping them there a long time they necessarily become better acquainted with transportation matters than the courts, and when they find anything it should be final, unless the courts should decide to send it back to them and ask them to hear further evidence on particular points, but I do not believe that ought to be insisted upon. If it can not be obtained in its fullness, we ought to take what we can get rather than go on as we are. The same thing applies to the commission's power to name rates. That seems to be a proper thing, but if it can not be obtained I would prefer to get as near that as we can. Try it and trust to the future for remedial legislation. There are other minor matters in which improvements might be made. I do not see much in the commission's desire to have the long and short haul clause in the law remodeled. If the rate is obnoxious to the long and short haul principle and can not be reached by that section it can be under the third, and I would not cumber a new law with anything that is useless.

Q. (By Mr. A. L. HARRIS.) What is the long and short haul?—A. No carriers shall be permitted to charge more for a short intermediate haul than for a longer haul over the same line in the same direction, except under dissimilar circumstances and conditions. Interpretations by court · have made the section practically inoperative by holding that all differences and competition of any character can be introduced to show dissimilarity in the circumstances and conditions. For myself, I think that is a proper interpretation of the law as it stood; the commission does not think so. It thinks it should be modified so as to give the commission power to prohibit a higher charge for an intermediate haul. That could not do any harm if it could be enacted, but if it arouses opposition to the legislation, it seems to me it might well be abandoned. I would insist very strongly that the statistical agencies and all the purely visitorial functions of the commission be extended as much as possible. But amendments of that character we know meet with much opposition. Through the statistician the commission ought to be able to get full returns. He ought to have classified returns. For instance, he gives a rate which represents an average rate per ton per mile for the United States. He also gives that for ten geographical groups, which is a good figure, but it does not mean very much. We ought to have a rate applicable to different classes of traffic. We ought to know the rate per ton per mile on through business and local business, and agricultural products, perhaps on particular kinds of agricultural products, and on the products of the mines, and forest products, and classify our statistics in order to put more definite information into the hands of those who are to legislate and to regulate rates.

In connection with 57 (Government ownership of land transportation), it seems to me that this requires a modification of what I said in regard to the Government ownership of interstate railways. The question of Government ownership of municipal transportation lines is very much of the same kind, but the possibilities of administration in municipal affairs are so much better at present that we may well proceed to train administrators in our better governed cities by taking over their transportation agencies. I would put the street railways in large cities on the same plane as the waterworks and the sewerage system. I would include the telephone service and such things. I think they are proper subjects for municipal development, and it is very important also that we should have such training schools for men who are to administer the affairs of this country. Our administration is weak because we have given it very little to do.

Q. (By Mr. PHILLIPS.) Will your recommendations for remedial legislation be largely to increase the power or the authority of the Interstate Commerce Commission?—A. I believe, certainly and definitely, that we should take the present legislation as a basis, and the recommendations of the commission should be followed in most particulars—in all particulars, with the exception that the essential thing is the subordination of competition, and if we can get that we should make such concessions as are necessary in order to get it, and every necessary concession that can properly be made. We should unite all men who want pooling in favor of the amendment of the interstate-commerce law. We should get them all together, and that is the only way to secure this legislation against the opposition of the ignorant and the dishonest.

Q. Would you at some time suggest to this commission more definitely your views in the line of law that you would recommend?—A. I would oblige the commission in any way possible, but it seems to me the Interstate Commerce Commission has made very definite recommendations on that subject. I agree with the Interstate Commerce Commission in every particular on theoretical grounds. On practical grounds I am willing to make concessions, and I believe the character of these concessions are best decided in the committees of the two Houses. I do not believe you would gain anything by what I might submit.

Q. Have they recommended anything in relation to uniform taxation?—A. That is outside of their province. There was introduced at the opening of the first session of the present Congress in the Senate, by Senator Cullom, a bill which is understood to contain the wishes of the commission. At the time that was introduced pooling was left out. Mr. Morrison was at that time one of the commissioners. I think at the present time if they drew one that pooling would be put in, but even then it was understood they were quite willing that the provision in the Patterson bill might be added. I think I am stating, in this particular, the views of the commission, although I do not represent them in any way.

Q. (By Mr. KENNEDY.) Have you noticed that the Senate has abandoned all the remedial legislation proposed by the Interstate Commerce Commission with the single exception of the antiscalpers' bill?—A. I knew that it had been done.

Q. Does there seem to be much hope of getting anything?—A. There has been disagreement among the railroads as to what concessions they were willing to make in regard to legislation, and I think that has stood in the way. Those differences have almost disappeared. It is understood that one prominent railroad sent its agents here and opposed the passage of the Patterson bill when it was thought it might come to a vote in the Senate, and I believe that is true. There have been very unfortunate differences of that kind among the railroads on account of the demand for substantial changes in the other portions of the law. I think it would be well to do whatever is necessary in order to get the railroad people themselves to unite in favor of legislation. Of course, if you get the legislation you have not got the pools, and have no great certainty that you will be able to get them, but we hope that the various financial interests will concentrate their influence in such shape as to prevent further competition where pools are practical. This (pooling) is not a panacea; it is not a remedy that is going to cure everything, and it is not a remedy that is going to prevent discrimination altogether, but I believe it is going to prevent much of it.

In regard to the taxation of the railroads, it is believed that the only altogether just method of taxing the railroads is to tax the net earnings. Of course, if that means is adopted, some method by which net earnings on interstate business can be separated from net earnings of State business must be adopted. That involves statistical agencies, probably those of the Interstate Commerce Commission.

Q. (By Mr. A. L. HARRIS.) May that in many States require amendments to the constitutions?—A. I suppose that is possible.

Q. (By Mr. FARQUHAR.) Is it generally the custom in the Western States to attempt to tax railroads on gross receipts?—A. Several States tax them on gross receipts.

Q. Would there be any difficulty between taxation by the National Government and by the States?—A. Yes; of course. Grave difficulties are in the way of a uniform system, on account of limitations in our State constitutions. A great many of our States have distrusted their legislators, so that they have tried to tie them up in every possible way. It is one of the most unfortunate results of that practice.

Q. (By Mr. RATCHFORD.) Why do you think that railroad property should be taxed on net earnings?—A. The tax on the property of a railroad seems to be an impracticable tax on account of its character and on account of the relation of the franchise to its visible property, and the fact that it is a double tax, if you attempt to reach personalty also and tax stocks and bonds in the hands of their owners. It may promote such things as are suggested, where New Jersey was aole to tax terminals and thus tax the people in other States. A tax on gross earnings is objectionable because it may make it of advantage to the railroad to maintain high rates and a smaller total of gross earnings than if they were not taxed. That is purely a mathematical question. It may enable a railroad to obtain a larger net income by maintaining high rates and doing a small business with a lower percentage of operating expenses to gross earnings than by doing a larger business at lower rates with a greater total of earnings and a higher percentage of expenses to the gross returns.

Q. (By Mr. FARQUHAR.) Do you believe the same rule of taxation should apply to the farm, the mill, and the factory?—A. I do not; I do not believe they are to be regarded as constituting homogeneous property; they are employed for such different purposes. I would favor a general real estate tax. I believe it would be entirely to the advantage of the farmer to get rid of all taxes on personal property as such. They bear most heavily on the localities where there is the least personal property. I think the labor commission of the State of Illinois has shown that conclusively in a very elaborate study. I think it is true also in Ohio. The tax has been very disadvantageous to the farmers.

Q. (By Mr. A. L. HARRIS.) Would you exclude improvements from taxation?—A. No; I am not an advocate of that.

Q. (By Mr. SMYTH.) Then you do not believe in the single-tax theory?—A. Not as that word is used. I do not propose that as the only tax, either, so far as the general property tax goes. I would not have that. I would substitute for that a general real estate tax and other tax. If street railroads continue to be operated independently in our cities, I would have a franchise tax; and I certainly should not do away with internal-revenue taxation. It is a very satisfactory means of taxation, and easily collected.

Q. (By Mr. RATCHFORD.) Is the difference, in your opinion, between the two methods due to the relation of the property to the public?—A. The distinction in the method of treatment, you mean? If you mean that, I would say it is in the relation which the property bears to the man who owns it.

Q. Do you believe the same methods of taxation should apply to the farm, the mill, and the factory that apply to railroad property?—A. No.

Q. Is your belief on that point founded on the relationship which the public bears to the property to be taxed?—A. Both on that and the relation which the property has to other capital; that is, products employed for the creation of other products. The criterion for a tax, it seems to me, is the ability of the man called upon to pay it; that may be one thing to a farmer with a small farm, finding it difficult to earn wages for himself, let alone any interest on his capital, and a very different thing to the owner of a very productive factory, who is perhaps the owner of a patent, or in some other way able to obtain a monopoly price for his goods. He should be taxed very differently. I should say that a tax which would adjust itself to an income is a proper tax; but that is not an income tax, because incomes are different. If you have an income derived from investments, stocks and bonds, and I have an income obtained from delivering public lectures, they are very different. Yours is permanent; mine depends upon my health, conduct, and various other things, and I should not be taxed as high on mine as you on yours; and I think that excludes a nondifferentiated income tax—if that character of analysis were carried out in the direction I have indicated.

In regard to the general subject of agriculture, I would like to say that a great difficulty, and one fruitful cause of complaint against the railroads, has arisen from the fact that our public-land system induced producers to go beyond the region of profitable production. They were lured by a system which appealed to the land hunger of the Anglo-Saxon race, and called them out there, and they have had a loss to divide and not a profit. The railroads themselves were taken out there by land grants which were uneconomic, and many of the evils were produced by bringing producers where producers should not have gone for generations.

I have a very strong belief that the great difficulty with the farmer, aside from that I have indicated, is that the farmer constitutes an industrial class by himself. The Western farmer particularly has been lured out there, and society is rather responsible for his being there and must pay the penalty in hearing his complaints and in finding some way to make things easier for him. The other difficulty of the farmer is the lack of organization—the lack of knowledge of his own industry— and what can be done is in the line of the work that the Department of Agriculture is doing now. It is a general bureau of information for the farmers, and it should study market conditions statistically, as it does scientific methods of agriculture, and bring all those facts and methods home to the farmer in the plainest possible way, and help him in every practical way. It should be to the farmer what the associations of bankers and the railroad associations and all those other things are to industries in which individuals have the power and means of combination. I do not mean combination to monopolize their product, but combination to study their business. Development lies along that line. Strengthen our Federal agencies and our State agencies. That line of thought has suggested to me a study of the effect of speculation in food products. Of course I am engaged on the statistical work of the Department of Agriculture, and a large portion of our work is to promulgate from time to time estimates of crop conditions, and we continually hear from farmers who tell us that our work has only been helpful to the speculator, and I think it has been believed at times in the Department that that work could not help anybody but the speculator unless we were able to put our estimates in the hands of the farmer himself before or as soon as they can be had by the speculator. I hold that that is utterly impracticable. We can not reach the farmers by telegraph, and speculators, as a matter of fact, get the information by telegraph. We can post estimates in the post-offices and public places, as the Weather Bureau does its prognostications, but even that will be after the speculators have read them in the daily press.

Q. (By Mr. A. L. HARRIS.) Are you able to get prospective views on the crops?— A. Yes.

Q. (By Mr. FARQUHAR.) Are they made monthly?—A. Yes; except during the winter months. On the 10th of March (1899) we give a report covering the distribution—that is purely a statistical inquiry that does not relate to prospects— but next month we give our first report on prospects of winter grains, and from then to the time when the grains are harvested we give out estimates of the probable production. They are not expressed in estimates of bushels, but in estimates of percentages of a normal crop; but, as I said, it has often been suggested that these reports are only beneficial to the speculators, and the Department, under the administration of Mr. Morton, I believe, thought that the only way to make them beneficial was to put them in the farmers' hands. The statistical study of grain prices for a very extended period will show, however, a smaller difference now between harvest prices and the price in early spring, before the new crop becomes available, than there was 35, 40, or 50 years ago; and the reason of that is the creation of exchanges where there is a continual market. The speculator also has a definite function in the way of being an expert estimator of the probable value per unit of quantity of the succeeding crop.

Q. (By Mr. PHILLIPS.) How do you get accurate information in regard to crop prospects in the various States?—A. We have a very elaborate system of correspondence; we have about 60,000 correspondents who furnish voluntary reports.

Q. (By Mr. SMYTH.) Is it all very much a matter of guess?—A. They are mostly farmers.

Q. (By Mr. KENNEDY.) Township correspondents?—A. Yes. I think the estimates we give are generally good. It surprised me 4 years ago, when I first commenced to handle the thing, how much care and intelligence they put in it for nothing.

The man who buys grain performs a function in distributing. He is a capitalist. Several of them get together in an exchange; they consider all the conditions they can find—the more the better—and they estimate the prospective value of the crop, and the investor who distributes his purchases over different systems of road profits by their knowledge. No matter how depraved speculators may be— practical gamblers—they want to get all the facts they can obtain, and if we get out the report and it does not reach anybody but these men, if it removes indefiniteness it removes some of the difference between the harvest price and the price when the product is marketed, and that benefits the farmer.

Q. (By Mr. A. L. HARRIS.) Do the grain dealers in the grain centers have a system of collecting statistics that is almost equal to that of the Department?—A. I think not. I think their system is not worth much at all except as they are able to correct it every month from what we give them.

Q. Do they correspond with grain dealers in almost every town in the United States where grain is sold?—A. I doubt it. I do not believe we know very much about these independent sources of information. To correspond with all the grain dealers would be very expensive, and to tabulate the reports after they were received would be expensive. I think those men are mostly men who have been in our Department at one time or another. I think most of them are well acquainted with the grain trade and can make shrewd guesses without much foundation.

Q. Are your reports put in the papers?—A. Yes; given to the Associated Press on the afternoon of the 10th, and telegraphed all over the country.

Q. And in that way reach the producer?—A. Yes.

Q. (By Mr. FARQUHAR.) Is it a fact that in all the great grain markets like Chicago the price lists carry the entire sales of the day—carry the entire visible supply of grain, and that even these reports, which are to regulate prices, are supplemented by private circulars by the whole of these great grain commission men of the country?—A. Yes.

Q. Do you think the information that comes through these price lists, the daily newspapers, and the private circulars, comprehend all that needs to be known as to the regulation of prices?—A. I should not say that. I should say, Get all the facts you can. The more you get the better. The more thoroughly you eliminate the speculative element the more accurate information is obtainable, and the higher prices the farmer gets.

Q. Do you think the stability of railroad rates is one of the best things the farmer and producer can have?—A. It is absolutely necessary. Fluctuating rates would be like a fluctuating tariff.

Q. Does it give an opportunity to the speculator and gambler?—A. Yes.

Q. (By Mr. A. L. HARRIS.) What have you to say on topic 43, Part II (Increase or decrease in transportation rates during the past fifty years)?—A. I made a calculation, and the force under my direction worked for nearly a year on this little pamphlet, and as a result of a most careful inquiry, and most conscientiously performed, I think I might say we find that, measured in gold, the average rate per ton per mile throughout the United States has declined from 1.9 cents in 1867 to 8 mills in 1896. That is the general average. Now, I want to establish one limitation: I consulted every possible source of information. This inquiry was conducted with the utmost care. We were only able to get these figures for about one-fourth of the railroads in the early years. For the late years the figures represent all the railroads. The reason for that is that accounting methods had not developed in 1867 to the extent that permits us to get these figures. The legitimate inference from that is—the necessary inference—that the accounting methods were best developed on the roads that did the most business. The roads that did the most business were the ones that charged the lowest rates. Therefore my table does not show the full decline in rates; only shows part of it.

Q. Have you any tables showing the decrease in freight rates, say from Chicago to New York, per hundred pounds on agricultural products?—A. The rate for rail transportation for wheat from Chicago to New York in 1858 was 39 cents nearly—38.61 cents per bushel. That is in gold. In 1897 it was 12.5 cents a bushel. The decline is distributed pretty evenly after 1862. The rate was actually raised from 1858 to 1862. The maximum was $0.4237, and the decline since then is pretty even.

Q. Have you a table showing the rate from Chicago to New York, part rail and part water?—A. That goes back to 1868. At that time the rate was 20.76 cents per bushel, and in 1897 it was 7.37 cents. In 1867 the export price of a bushel of wheat was 92 cents in gold. The rate by lake and canal—I gave you the rate by lake and rail, but the rate by lake and canal was 15.95 cents, and 1 bushel of wheat would pay for carrying 5.78 bushels from Chicago to New York. In 1897 the export price of a bushel of wheat was 75 cents. The rate by the Great Lakes and the E   Canal was 4.35 cents, and 17.25 bushels could be carried for the price of 1 bushele

Q. What are the rates for general farm products, such as beef, pork, and corn?—A. I can give you meats. The classification varies very greatly. Most of the farm products are in the lower classes. The rate on packed meats from Cincinnati to New York by rail was 4.88 cents in 1868 per 100 pounds; in 1897 it was 26 cents. The rate on dressed beef from Chicago to New York by rail has declined from 81 cents per hundred in 1872 to 45 cents in 1897. The rate on sheep—live cattle from 61 cents in 1879 to 30 cents in 1897; that on hogs from 45 cents in 1879 to 30 cents in 1897; that on cattle from 47 cents in 1879 to 28 cents in 1897. I have never known a substantial advance in rates on agricultural products except in the single case where they put back in 1890 a portion of the reduction which was made in view of the desperate condition of the Western corn producers in the former year.

Q. Taking the roads west of the Missouri, has there been a decline also since those roads were constructed?—A. I will give you some illustrations. The average rate of the Hannibal & St. Joseph Railroad in 1870 was 8.194 cents per ton per mile; in 1897 it was 0.617. The average rate of the Union Pacific Railway per ton per mile has declined from 3.596 cents in 1869 to 0.962 cents in 1897.

I will give you an instance in the South: The Louisville and Nashville Railroad, 3.007 cents in 1867, and 0.791 cents in 1897. The Chicago, Milwaukee and St. Paul Railway obtained 2.376 cents in 1865, and 1.008 cents in 1897.

Q. (By Mr. C. J. HARRIS.) Have you investigated how our freight rates here compare with foreign countries?—A. It is very difficult to make comparisons of that kind on account of the difference in the character of the traffic.

Q. My impression is that our rates are very much cheaper; is that correct?—A. The average length of haul in this country for a ton of freight is 125 miles, and in England, France, and Germany it must be very much less. They would have higher rates, of course. The rate per ton per mile should decrease with the length of haul, and those comparisons are unsatisfactory. Our rates are lower per ton per mile.

Q. Have you the Southern down there as a system?—A. As a system? In all these comparisons we were compelled to use the road now operating under that name and the smaller road operating then; for instance, this comparison of the Chicago, Milwaukee and St. Paul should be much more favorable, for in the early days they operated only a small line in Wisconsin, I believe, and ran through a smaller part of country than is occupied by their line now.

I have here the Georgia Railroad, which obtained 8.552 cents in 1866, and 1.112 cents in 1897, per ton per mile. Here is the Norfolk and Western, which obtained 2.695 cents in 1870, and only 0.446 cents in 1897.

Q. (By Mr. PHILLIPS.) Was that figured in gold?—A. All the figures in this pamphlet are in gold.

Q. (By Mr. SMYTH.) Have you information relating to the South Carolina railways?—A. Yes; I have the South Carolina Railway as far back as 1872. It secured 3.254 cents in 1872, and 1.160 cents in 1897. I have some comparisons of passenger rates, if you care to have me put them in.

Q. Do they show about the same decline?—A. Not so much decline. The development there has been in the character of the service. You go faster and safer, and you have to pay for it.

Q. (By Mr. RATCHFORD.) Do the figures you have given on rates in 1897 show that the transportation of agricultural products on some of the Western roads was still cheaper than between New York and Chicago? The Milwaukee and St. Paul, I believe, was $.006.—A. I was giving you general averages on all their business. Even then I think that would hardly hold true. I think that grain rate from Chicago to New York, and the other rates dependent upon it on the percentage system, which makes nearly all the rates throughout the country on grain dependent upon it, is one of the lowest rates, outside of some of the rates on bituminous coal. It is one of the lowest rates for railway transportation. This year it has been extremely low.

Q. Can you give us any information on the effect of so-called corn and cotton gambling?—A. I tried to take that up a little while ago. It seems to me that the whole effect of speculation is to even prices, to approximate the harvest price to the price at the time the crop is nearly exhausted, and in that way it is beneficial to the farmer. Of course when it takes such abnormal forms as it did last year for a period it will be detrimental, but that is an evil which must be borne occasionally for the sake of the general benefit.

Q. What is your opinion in regard to its effect upon prices for the world?—A. None at all, unless it is to average them.

Q. Where are the prices of farm products fixed?—A. Fixed at the point where the marginal increment of the necessary supply is produced. The man to whom it costs the most to produce—he who contributes the last amount that is required to make up the entire supply demanded by the world—fixes the price. If he did not get his cost of production he would go out of business, and the price would have to be raised until he was brought back into business. Of course, that is the general tendency. Occasionally some fellow is producing below the margin of profitable production.

Q. (By Mr. A. L. HARRIS.) As produce centers do Liverpool, New York, or Chicago fix the prices?—A. It is fixed in Liverpool, as far as that is concerned. It is the Liverpool price which makes up the cost of production, but in the long run that price must pay for the producing of the last increment of the supply.

Q. It is claimed that selling options misleads the merchant in Liverpool, and in that way makes rates or raises the price without relation to the amount of produce; is there any foundation for that?—A. It may be true temporarily, but the merchant in Liverpool who is liable to be misled does not survive. He goes out of business, and a more sophisticated merchant takes his place.

Q. Do supply and demand, after all, regulate it?—A. I believe that is so.

WASHINGTON, D. C., *April 18, 1899.*

TESTIMONY OF MR. E. E. CLARK,

Grand chief conductor, Order of Railway Conductors; and chairman of the executive committee of the Federation of American Railway Employees.

The commission met at 10.30 a. m., Mr. C. J. Harris presiding. Mr. E. E. Clark, of Cedar Rapids, Iowa, testified.

Q. (By Mr. KENNEDY.) Please state your name, place of residence, and your official relation with railroad organizations.—A. E. E. Clark, Cedar Rapids, Iowa, grand chief conductor, Order of Railway Conductors, and chairman of the executive committee of Federation of American Railway Employees.

Q. How large a per cent of railroad conductors of the United States and Canada are in your organization?—A. Our membership is at the present time about 22,700; I say about; it does not vary over 50 from that. We have probably 1,200 members in Canada and 300 or 350 in Mexico. The Interstate Commerce Commission report, in good times, on our railways about 24,000 conductors employed in the United States.

Q. Your association having answered the topical plan of inquiry on transportation pretty fully, I would suggest that you take it up and see if there is any special topic in it that you would care to speak about now.—A. I will simply say that when this topical plan of inquiry was sent to us we arranged to answer it concisely, and, as we thought, comprehensively, in a written communication, which we filed with the commission, and naturally we incorporated in that what we thought was important, and what we specially cared to state, and I am here today in answer to the urgent invitation of the secretary of the commission. I do not think that I could with any advantage, either to ourselves or to the commission, take this plan up, because it would be a repetition of what we have already said. I am here at the invitation of the commission to answer any questions the commission cares to ask.

Q. (By Mr. C. J. HARRIS.) What are the usual hours of conductors?—A.. It is a very difficult thing to state what the usual hours are. The average number of hours on duty for conductors at the present time are considerably shorter than they were a few years ago, brought about by the demand for more and more rapid transit of freight.. Freight trains run cars daily faster than they did, consequently the number of hours on duty is shortened. Again, as influencing the situation, the general disposition of railroad companies is to lengthen the distance of the run, and where this has been done the number of hours are approximately the same.

Q. Are you paid by the length of the run?—A. The general basis of pay is by the mile.

Q. Is there any serious complaint in regard to the hours of work of railway conductors at the present time?—A. No; there is no serious complaint at the present time, and I might say no complaint at any time unless in the time of great rush of business, where business is so heavy that it necessitates keeping motive power and cars moving all the time, and naturally railroad companies in times of that kind desire to put on as few new men as possible, because the more new men put on they feel the more possibility of accident; they rather depend on the old men, and sometimes there is a disposition to keep them going too long.

Q. If you make extra runs you make extra pay in those busy seasons?—A. Yes; and I may say it is conceded by the managements of the roads that they do not want men to work beyond their physical ability, and it is the general rule that our agreements with companies provide that after a man has been on duty 16 hours he may demand 8 hours rest; that does not mean if he is delayed by accident; nor can a man demand rest in the middle of a division.

Q. (By Mr. KENNEDY.) I understand that some of the railroads of the United States are adopting a policy of refusing employment to men who have passed the age of 30 years, no matter how much experience they have had in the railroad business. Can you give the commission any information on that subject?—A. There seems to be growing up at the present time a general disposition among railroads to establish certain rules limiting the employment of men. Some companies provide that they will not hire a man as brakeman or fireman who is past a certain age. Some of them put it as low as 28, and some roads have a limit as high as 40 years of age. They direct their subordinate officials who have the employment of men to refuse employment to men who are past this age, and of course the subordinates have no choice but to carry it out.

Q. (By Mr. C. J. HARRIS.) What is the reason of that?—A. The only reason I ever heard assigned by railway officials was that they had a large number of men growing old in their service, and that there was a moral obligation, I think, to take care of those men by furnishing some sort of employment for those who had grown too old to follow in the capacity they were employed. If they hired a man of 20 years of age and had no bad luck they might expect to get 30 years of service out of him by the time he was 50, where, if 40, only 10 years of service would be gotten out of him. There may be room for suspicions as to other influences that are at work in that direction. I do not know that we would be justified in expressing any suspicions. We simply know that is a fact, and we think it is an unfair decision.

Q. (By Representative GARDNER.) If you had to express a suspicion, what would you say?—A. I would say one reason is that it has the effect of overstocking the market with experienced men. There is no use trying to dodge the fact that labor is governed more or less by the law of supply and demand. It may be it is looked upon as an influence calculated to make men extremely careful about losing a position.

Q. (By Mr. RATCHFORD.) Do the brotherhoods agree to the dismissal of their members because of old age?—A. Certainly not. If they undertook to dismiss our members because they got to be 40 years of age we would take care of that. It is where they are dismissed for something else, or out of a position, perhaps resigned a position 2 or 3 years ago; when they try to go back to work on the railroads they will not hire them.

Q. Where railroad companies dismiss any of their employees on the supposed ground that they are becoming aged, is that cause ever assigned by the companies for such dismissal?—A. No; I do not know of any instance where this cause has been assigned for dismissal. It is occasionally assigned as a cause for placing a man in some other employment. I want to carry that a little bit further. While appreciating fully the difficulties that would stand in the way of the enactment of any law, or the effort to enforce any law, requiring a corporation or any individual to give employment to any person they do not want, it does seem to me that if the railroad companies collectively, by understanding, if no direct understanding can be shown, adopt this policy, in the first place it is going to force the organizations to a more rigorous, and, if I may use the term, arbitrary, position in regard to dismissal of members for other causes, and, if there be any such thing as collective moral obligation, and I think there is, I believe if railroad companies are going to say railroad employees who have passed the age of 40 shall not be given employment again in that capacity, that some responsibility for the subsistence and maintenance of the men who have worn themselves out in the service should attach to the railroads or public, or the railroads and public jointly, because men have worn themselves out in the service.

Q. (By Representative GARDNER.) Suppose it was settled that a railroad man applying for a position after a given age, 30 years, would not be given employment, would not that operate to prevent young men from going into the railroad service?—A. It must operate as a preventive of the best quality of young men going into the service. They probably will have a sufficiency to fill vacancies, but they will not get the same class of ability that they get now; can not, because young men would have nothing to look to in the future.

Q. (By Mr. KENNEDY.) I understand that some railroads discharge men from their employment or refuse employment to men who have received some slight injuries; for instance, the loss of a finger, which does not incapacitate them from work, but the company alleges that it does, and treat them as if they had received a total disability. Can you say anything about that?—A. Railroad companies are generally adopting much more rigid physical examination of applicants for employment, and it is a fact that some of them refuse employment to a man simply because of the loss of a finger or thumb or something of that kind.

Q. (By Mr. FARQUHAR.) Do you mean by that, employment in the same class in which he received his injury, or employment as watchman or in some other position on the railroad?—A. I refer simply to a man who is out of employment altogether. The loss of a finger does not prevent a man satisfactorily and efficiently peforming the duties he performed before that finger was taken off. Some of the most efficient trainmen and conductors are men who have lost one or more fingers from one or both hands. It does not operate to prevent him performing his duties; but if he has been unfortunate enough to lose a position on one road, and goes to another road for employment, they refuse him employment because of that physical disability—the amputation of a finger. Now, naturally, with the adoption of automatic couplers, the percentage of the men who will be minus one or two fingers will be smaller than in years gone by.

Q. (By Representative GARDNER.) What could be the reason for refusing employment because a man lost a finger?—A. I think it is carrying to an absurd extremity the ideas that have been advanced by some of the railroad companies' surgeons. They claim to know of instances where men have secured employment, and later, as a result of some slight or possibly imaginary accident, have established a claim against the company for damages on account of physical injuries received, and that after the collection of those damages the same man has gone to some remote part of the country and secured employment from some other railroad company, and done the same thing there.

Q. (By Mr. C. J. HARRIS.) For the same accident there?—A. For the same disability.

Q. (By Representative GARDNER.) Can that be true in the case of lost finger?—A. No; they adopt a plan of physical examination. The lost finger is something on its face and can be recorded and shown when men enter their employ. These minor injuries, such as the loss of a finger, have never been considered serious things by train men. If a man had that misfortune and the company paid his wages while laid up he has been perfectly willing to sign a release; but if the loss of a finger is going to operate against his securing employment elsewhere the same as if he lost a hand I do not know any reason why the same liability should not attach to the company in whose service he received the injury.

Q. (By Mr. CONGER.) In your opinion, is a conductor 50 years of age as efficient as one 25 years of age?—A. Yes; that is, assuming a man of 50 years is physically all right—in good health—I think he is a better conductor.

Q. (By Mr. KENNEDY.) Experience makes him a better conductor?—A. Ought to; he has had experience, and he has a fount of knowledge he has gathered in that way which is of inestimable value in time of emergency. He is a more conservative man and takes less chances than a young man would.

Q. So that a conductor that has had experience and has passed 30 years of age is as valuable or more valuable to the railroad service than a man under 30?—A. I think so; yes.

Q. (By Mr. C. J. HARRIS.) Do they apply 30 years as a limit to conductors?—A. Some roads do. What I mean by that is, they decline to hire a man past 30 years of age.

Q. (By Mr. KENNEDY.) I have here a magazine article on the question of blacklisting, which seems to show pretty conclusively that it has been practiced extensively by railroads in that part of the country. Can you give the commission any light on that subject?—A. I can not give any reliable information as to the particular points in the case in mind. I am not acquainted with it. I had nothing whatever to do with the case. There is no doubt but that has been indulged in a good deal in years gone by. I have in mind one case that happened to one of our members in the State of Florida. He was in the employ of what is known as the Florida East Coast Line Railroad as a conductor. He was offered a position on another railroad, which he thought was more advantageous to him than the one he had, and he asked to be relieved for the purpose of going to take this new position. The company did not show any disposition to release him; in fact, required him to go out and continue several days after he wanted to be released, and he finally was required to take his run down to a place called Palm Beach, down at the south end of the peninsula, and he did so, and there he quit, insisting on being released. He went to the other railroad and was employed as a conductor, was sent out to learn the road, as we term it (they send a man out to learn the road when they have an opportunity to do so), and the general superintendent of the East Coast Line a day or two or three thereafter wrote a letter to the general superintendent of the road that had employed him, advising him not to employ the man, and on·the strength of that letter he let him go, would not give him employment. He brought suit against the Florida East Coast Line in the State courts of Florida and secured and collected damages.

Q. (By Mr. C. J. HARRIS.) Did he give sufficient notice of his intention to leave?—A. Yes.

Q. What is the rule in that case?—A. There is no written rule; a week or 10 days is always considered reasonable. Wherever I have known of a rule of that kind being established, it has been 10 days. I might add here that I think the practice of blacklisting has been very materially reduced by the enactment of laws, state and national, against it. I do not think blacklisting is indulged in to any great extent. The practice generally adopted now by railroad companies is to give a man a service letter when he leaves their service, stating when he entered, in what capacity employed, what date he left, and reasons for leaving. Of course their reasons are very often stated in the words "unsatisfactory service," which may mean one of a hundred things.

Q. (By Representative GARDNER.) The statement has been made to me by an ex-railroad employee here in Washington that he was discharged from the service of a company and received a very good letter, one strongly recommending him—everything he could ask for—and that he went from company to company, and his letter never availed; that the explanation was that it was written on paper containing a watermark or other sign agreed upon by the companies as a blacklist. Do you know of anything of that kind?—A. Nothing but rumors. I know of one instance that happened a few years ago, since my official connection with this organization. I investigated the case personally and found out where a division superintendant gave an employee leaving his service a letter of recommendation as you say, commending him highly, and recommending him to his employers, and at the same time I know that same man was on the blacklist of that company. It is a very large system.

Q. He was prevented by the blacklist and not by the letter of recommendation. This gentleman claimed that this letter of recommendation was in itself a blacklist.—A. I have heard that statement made, but I never found any evidence of it.

Q. (By Mr. RATCHFORD.) Is there, or is there not, a pretty well-established custom among railroad officials providing for temporary suspension of employees for some wrong or supposed wrong they may have committed in their work?—A. That used to be practically universal, but I think we may safely say now that on the majority of the roads—that is, a majority of the mileage of the country—what is called the Brown system of discipline, or modification of it, is in force, which is punishment without suspension. They keep records of men—all sorts, the merit and demerit entries—in a book. Instead of suspending men from service with loss of pay, they enter up 10 days' suspension against him, and for some meritorious act they give him a credit mark, and 6 months good record will erase 10 days' suspension, the idea being to keep the record of the men in that way and prevent the loss of employment; and it also prevents the necessity of keeping so many men on the extra list to take the place of men temporarily suspended; and the employee who is guilty of a minor offense is reprimanded and is informed that an entry is made against his record, and he goes on with his work, and when they receive a certain number of demerit marks—reach a certain maximum—or when the record is such as to justify dismissal, dismissal follows.

Q. Will you briefly outline the old plan of suspension?—A. The old plan of suspension was, when a man was guilty of a minor offense or oversight, they simply suspended him from duty; he lost his pay for 10, 20, 30, 40, 50, or 60 days.

Q. Have you ever known of a case in which a man was punished who was not guilty?—A. Oh, yes; a great many of them.

Q. Do you regard the change from that system to the present system as being an advantage to members of your brotherhood?—A. I regard it so; yes. It is so generally accepted by our brotherhood.

Q. (By Mr. KENNEDY.) What can you say as to betterment that has resulted from your organization; something of the condition of conductors before you had an organization and since?—A. Since our organization really assumed the position of a labor organization, and took up questions of relations of members with their employers, which commenced in 1890, the wages of conductors on practically all of the railroad mileage west of the State of Pennsylvania, south of the Ohio River, and north of the St. Lawrence River, have been increased from 5 to 25 per cent; their hours of labor have been lessened, conditions of employment have been improved, they are paid for excess hours or overtime, as we term it, which they were not paid for before, and the positions are more stable; and in the State of Pennsylvania, and east of there, there has been a great deal done in that same direction, but not so much—not quite so general. The New England States have more stable conditions than the western roads, and arrangements have been such as to make it very pleasant for the employees. They make an effort to get a man home as much as possible, instead of giving him a long run away from home, keeping him away two, three, or four days. They make the runs short, so that they are home for everything except their dinner, and the rates of wages there are better in comparison with the amount of work required than in the territory west and south and in Canada.

Q. Has your organization promoted independence on the part of the men, and done away with obsequiousness of the employees toward the employer?—A. We think so. In saying that, I do not want to say the organization has had influence in making them insubordinate; at the same time they have never lost sight of duties.

Q. Have discharges for alleged causes been less frequent on railroads than prior to the time your organization became influential?—A. Yes; a marked difference.

Q. (By Mr. RATCHFORD.) Do you attribute that, or any part of that, to the higher qualifications and standard of organized men?—A. I think that has some effect. I think the men have reached a higher limit of excellence in the performance of their duties all around, and I think that the knowledge on the part of the railroad officials of the organization's purposes to afford the men every protection that can be afforded them, is calculated to make them much more careful in making decisions.

Q. (By Mr. KENNEDY.) What do you know to be the sentiment of organized labor engaged in transportation on the subject of immigration?—A. Ordinarily, I might say, with practical unanimity the members of the railroad brotherhoods are in favor of very close restriction of immigration. We believe that this is necessary to the best interests of the workingmen of this country. We do not feel directly the effects of immigration—that is, the class of men commonly called immigrants do not come over here to get employment in train and engine service on the railroads—but we recognize the different branches or classes of working people in the United States, as arranged in a sort of a circuit, through which any evil effects are bound to be felt all the way down; as, for instance (of course I do not speak authoritatively, from the standpoint of a coal miner, but I simply make this general statement), a few years ago the coal miners of the State of Pennsylvania were a great deal higher caliber of manhood than at the present day. Now you may take the coal miners or any other class of employees who are able to earn reasonable wages and maintain their families, and who try to live something like Americans ought to live, if you bring in foreigners who live and work cheaper, at wages that these men can not work at and live, you crowd them out. The only thing this man can do is to seek employment in the next (what, you may say) higher paid place. We can not see how the best paid classes of labor in the United States can help but feel an interest in and be affected by conditions that surround and control the very poorest paid classes.

Q. Has your organization ever taken official action on that question?—A. No; excepting to pronounce in a general way in favor of restriction of immigration.

Q. Have you any suggestions to make as to the nature of an immigration law that would be effective, in the interest of our people?—A. I have my own idea. The organization has never pronounced in favor of any particular line.

Q. What are your ideas about it?—A. I had to stay in this country 21 years before I could vote. I do not know why anyone else coming here should not do the same. I believe it is all right to admit, to a reasonable extent, immigrants who make good citizens, who cast their lot with this country, who attempt to stay here and raise their children here. I do not believe in admitting any who come here simply because conditions are better than in the old country, who live like so many swine and send all their money out of the country, as a great many do.

Q. Do you believe if this commission were to recommend to Congress legislation that would restrict immigration, that organized labor throughout the country would support such recommendations?—A. In my judgment it would.

Q. (By Mr. RATCHFORD.) What qualifications should be fixed; what standard is necessary?—A. I do not know that I could define in exact terms my idea of the standard that is necessary; but I can not lose sight of the fact that we have a Chinese exclusion act, and while we have a Chinese exclusion act we are admitting a whole lot more just as bad as Chinese. I would put them in a bunch and put them under the same act.

Q. (By Mr. KENNEDY.) The commission will at some time in the future, I think, consider some proposed bills in the interest of the railroad organizations, and I will read to you the title of them; they were submitted to the commission by Mr. Moseley, the secretary of the Interstate Commerce Commission. The first is a proposed bill to require railroads to make detailed reports to the Interstate Commission of every accident. Does your order favor such a bill as that; and what have you to say as to what should be embraced in such a bill?—A. I believe that the public should take a great deal of interest in the welfare of the railroad employee. We have no Government railroads in this country, and I can not say that I am in favor of Government ownership or control of our railroads to the extent of controlling the operation of them, but I believe employees are in a sense public servants. They serve the public and the public should have the widest possible information as to the conditions under which they work. I believe that the question of the injuries received by the railroad employees is a matter of general public interest. If we had not been able to show by absolutely reliable statistics the number of men who were killed and injured annually in the railroad service in the United States, we never would have secured the passage of the law providing for the use of automatic couplers and brakes. Now in view of the conditions that we have before referred to, and the effect that the minor injury received a few years ago sometimes has on a man to-day, I see no reason why it would not be consistent and of very great value to have all these injuries reported to the Interstate Commerce Commission for the purpose of preparing reliable statistics on that subject.

Q. How much of a report do they make in regard to accidents?—A. They simply report the number injured.

Q. Do they give the cause?—A. They give no details, except that in some cases the number injured coupling cars are kept by themselves; that is, they are gathered in an independent group. They say, "Injured by falling from moving train," but there is nothing said as to what caused the man to fall from the train or what other thing there was that caused him to be "injured while making a coupling."

Q. (By Mr. C. J. HARRIS.) What is the condition of safety appliances now?—A. As near as we can observe (I get it from reports recently promulgated by the Interstate Commerce Commission) they are shaping themselves very satisfactorily.

Q. Are there any suggestions you would make from your experience?—A. Nothing from a national standpoint. I think that the act we now have, under the extension that was granted by the Interstate Commerce Commission, and our understanding that they will require strict compliance with those provisions, would do all that is necessary.

Q. Anything to complain of just now?—A. No. It will be necessary for some States to require the equipment of cars used only in State traffic.

Q. (By Mr. KENNEDY.) The next is a proposed bill to cover such a case as that known as the Baugh case, on the Baltimore and Ohio Railroad, to bring about harmony in State and Federal decisions.—A. The case referred to is one in which an injured employee brought suit against a railroad company in the State of Ohio. The case was removed to the Federal courts and the decision rendered by the Federal courts was almost diametrically opposed to the decision that would be expected under the State law or decision that would have been handed down by the State court, and the idea is that the decisions of the Federal courts in the State should conform to State laws.

Q. Your organization is in favor of such a bill as that?—A. Yes; we think that is only reasonable and fair.

Q. Another is a proposed employers' liability bill.—A. I think I have outlined our position on that in regard to minor disabilities and the age limit fixed by the railroad companies. I believe full liability should attach to the railroad company for injuries received while in their employ which are in any sense attributable to or the result of improper equipment, improper condition of roadbed or track, negligence, incompetency, or act of fellow employee; and I want to supplement in that regard what is said in our written answer, that a man has no choice as to whom he works with. If we take any given railroad, the Baltimore and Ohio, for instance, right out of Baltimore the trainmaster employs the trainmen. I, as a conductor, am going on that train; the trainmaster says who is to go with me as a brakeman; I have no choice whatever until I have tried that man and find him incompetent and inefficient; then I can object to keeping him any longer. A conductor has nothing to say about what engineer or fireman shall go out with him. The company has absolute control of these things, and inasmuch as the employee has no choice whom he will work with, that company should be responsible for the acts of its agents in assigning the men and the employment of the men.

Q. Another: Proposed bill to provide for blocking frogs in the District of Columbia, Territories, and on Government reservations. Are you familiar with that bill?—A. Yes; and I will be frank enough to admit that the matter of blocking frogs is not of as much importance as some think it to be, and especially at this time when the general increase in the number of cars that are equipped with automatic couplers obviates the necessity of men going between cars so much to couple and uncouple. Where men get caught in the guard rail or frog, in 9 cases out of 10 it is where they get in between cars to uncouple or to couple. The pin occasionally gets stuck in the link, and in trying to loosen it while the cars are moving a man walks along with the cars and unfortunately walks into the frog, falls down, and the cars go over him; and there have been a great many accidents of that kind. Now instead of going in there to pull that pin, with the cars equipped with modern couplings he stays at the outer edge and pulls it from the corner of the car. With the automatic coupler there is very little occasion to step in between the cars. If he does not have to step in between the rails he can not get stuck in the frog. The only danger after these things are completed will be that the men in running across the yard might possibly get stuck in them, but I think the chances are very remote.

Q. (By Mr. C. J. HARRIS.) Have there been any strikes of your organization in late years?—A. Not since 1893, I think it was.

Q. Are you able to settle by conciliation with the managers, as a general thing, your difficulties?—A. Yes.

Q. (By Mr. KENNEDY.) Have you anything further that you think important to talk about?—A. Only one thought that occurs to my mind; that extension of time, granted by the Interstate Commerce Commission, within which the railroads should comply with the safety-appliance act. It has been charged that the officers of these organizations agreed to that at the behest of the railroad companies, and that charge came from those who have no influence or any interest in railroad matters, and I do not think it would be made by any person who was present at the meeting or who would read the proceedings of the committee. These organizations seek in all things to be fair. We realized that some of the railroad companies had been absolutely unable to comply with the law within that time and keep out of the hands of receivers. A good many got in the hands of receivers without complying with it. We opposed any extension that would have the effect of nullifying the spirit of the law, and the fact that the request of the railroad companies for an extension of time for 5 years was cut down, through our opposition, to 2 years, I think, speaks for itself.

Q. (By Mr. C. J. HARRIS.) That is satisfactory, is it?—A. Yes; it was accepted y us as a reasonable decision in the face of conditions then existing.

Q. (By Mr. RATCHFORD.) Speaking of railroads going into the hands of receivers, have you covered that subject as fully as you care to in this paper?—A. You mean as to conditions that put them in the hands of receivers?

Q. Any phase of it.—A. Some of the most troublesome questions and cases we have ever met have been in connection with receiverships, and we confidently believe that in some instances reduction in pay of the men have been undertaken immediately after a road went into the hands of a receiver which would not have been undertaken under any circumstances if they had not expected the support of the Federal court. That was more notably true of the Union Pacific Company than any other, excepting the Northern Pacific. In the Northern Pacific they expected and got the support of the Federal court. In the Union Pacific they expected and got it so far as the district court was concerned, but the circuit court set it aside.

Q. Have you anything to say as to incorporation of trade unions?—A. I think, perhaps, it will be some time before the idea will be generally accepted. At the same time, it looks to me as if the logical conclusion is the incorporation of the trade unions and labor organizations under conditions which place them on a fair basis, as compared with incorporations that are for pecuniary profit, or the incorporations by which the men are employed. I see no serious objection to it.

Q. Can you give us an estimate of the total number of railway employees of all classes that are out of employment at present time?—A. No; I should not care to make a guess at that, because it would be a guess pure and simple.

Q. Can that information be had by consulting the reports of the railroad commissioners of the different States?—A. I do not think so.

Q. Can that information be had from any source?—A. They report the number of men employed at various times both in the State and interstate commerce reports, but I have never seen anything in the reports of the number of unemployed.

STATE OF IOWA, *County of Linn.*

I swear that the statements made by me of my own knowledge in the foregoing report of my testimony before the Industrial Commission are true, and that all other statements I believe to be true.

E. E. CLARK.

Sworn and subscribed before me this 4th day of October, 1899.

ORANGE SACKETT,
Notary Public, in and for Linn County, Iowa.

WASHINGTON, D. C., *April 20, 1899.*

TESTIMONY OF MR. P. M. ARTHUR,

Grand chief engineer of the Brotherhood of Locomotive Engineers.

The commission met at 10.30 a. m., Vice-Chairman Phillips presiding. Mr. P. M. Arthur, of Cleveland, Ohio, grand chief engineer of the Brotherhood of Locomotive Engineers, testified.

Q. (By Mr. PHILLIPS.) How long have you occupied the position of grand chief of your organization?—A. Twenty-five years last February. Prior to that I was their auditor. I have been identified with the organization from its inception. It was organized in the city of Detroit in April, 1863. The object of the organization was to promote the welfare and interests of locomotive engineers, elevate their standing and character in society as men, provide for the widows and orphans of their members, and protect their labor. None but those who are familiar with the conditions of railroad men prior to that time can form any just estimate of the work of the organization. It may not be generally known to the public at large that railroad men in the early days, speaking of them as a whole, were given to habits of dissipation and vice. Intoxication was quite general; habits were bad, which finally led up to the formation of this brotherhood for the purpose of bettering the condition of the men. That was the primary object. It is the great mission of the brotherhood. At that time the question of wages was not raised at all. After awhile that question came up. An effort had been made some 10 years before the brotherhood was established, on a road where I was employed, to obtain a slight increase of pay. At that time the wages of locomotive engineers throughout the country was $60 a month, firemen $30, freight brakemen $25, freight conductors $40, passenger conductors $60. Those were the almost uniform rates of pay for that class of service up to the formation of the brotherhood. After that we appointed committees on the roads where our brotherhood was established. They were known as general boards of adjustment, whose duties were, if any difference came up between the company and the men, to investigate and ascertain the facts. If they found upon investigation that the grievances were just, they waited upon the officers of the road. If they went to effect a settlement with the general manager of the road, and they were not satisfied and wanted the protection of the organization, they were required to send for the chief executive. It was his duty on receipt of the communication from the committee to proceed at once to the road and seek a conference with the general manager, and president if necessary, and use all honorable means to effect a peaceable and amicable adjustment of the differences that he found existing between the men and the company. In nearly every case, with few exceptions during my administration of 25 years, we succeeded in effecting an amicable adjustment, establishing what we call written agreements between the company and the men; so that to-day we have written agreements embodying the rate of pay, the rules for the government and protection of the men, with 90 per cent of the roads in the country. We have succeeded, through the efforts of our organization, in increasing the wages of locomotive engineers from $60 per month to 3½ cents in passenger service, and 4 cents in freight, per mile run. The firemen, through their organization, increased their wages in proportion.

Q. Please state what constitutes a run, so that we may have a basis for comparison.—A. A hundred miles or less constitutes a day's work, 3½ cents in passenger service and 4 cents in freight, through, I might say, the Middle and Western States. In the Southern States the rate is 3 and 4 for the same class of service. There has always been a difference between the South and the North in that respect. One hundred miles or less constitutes a day's work; 10 hours or less constitutes a day's work. In 1867 we established an insurance department. It is conducted on the assessment plan; it was patterned after the metropolitan police force of the city of New York at that time. Through that department we have paid to the widows and orphans nearly $8,000,000. We issue four policies; we may take one of the four, $750, $1,500, $3,000, and $4,500 is the limit. A large number of our subdivisions also have what they call weekly beneficial assessments which pay $10 and $12 a week in case of sickness or injury. It is a rare thing now to find a locomotive engineer, a member of our brotherhood, who indulges in anything intoxicating. The laws of the organization prohibiting it are very strict. In order to become a member of our brotherhood a man must be a man of good moral character, temperate habits, able to read and write, and have had 1 year's experience as a locomotive engineer. He fills out an application, which is referred to an investigating committee which investigates into the character and standing of the applicant, and upon their recommendation he is admitted. I have no doubt it will surprise the commission, but, as I have often said it from the public platform, I do so to convince the people that we are endeavoring to carry out the objects for which the brotherhood was formed—in 1 year we expelled from our organization for intoxication 172 members. That was about the fifth year of the existence of our organization. Our laws are very rigid in that respect. It becomes the duty of the division, when they expel a member for intoxication, to notify the company, so if they retain him in their service they do it on their own responsibility; but I have known the company to do it after they were notified. Some have in many instances cooperated with us in ridding the service of that class of men. Others have not paid any attention to it. We did not receive for many years the assistance and cooperation of the railroad companies that we were entitled to in that direction, but of late years we have. I think that we have convinced them by our work that we are sincere and honest in our efforts to give to the railway companies a more reliable, trustworthy class of men. We have done that. We have always claimed that we were in a position to judge better than any officer of the company, and to detect the men in wrongdoing, because we are mingling together day and night, while the officers are at home or asleep. In that way we have been very successful in ridding the service of that class of men. We have always aimed, as an organization, to do what was right and just between the companies and the men. Our policy in dealing with these questions has been to bring the parties together, and sit down and talk the matter over and reason together, and wherever the circumstances would warrant concessions being made upon either side we have always been willing to make them. We believe in that line of policy being pursued in the adjustment of grievances and differences, as they will spring up between the employer and employee. Men employed in railway service differ very much from men engaged in other pursuits, from the fact that they are subject to so many different masters. You may commence with the roundhouse foreman, if you please; then comes your yard master, your train dispatcher, your master mechanic, the division superintendent, general manager, etc.; he is subject to them all. It has occurred very frequently where men occupying positions like roundhouse foremen in a little heat have dismissed or suspended men from the service without just cause. That is what really caused the brotherhood to establish these general committees. We believe in protecting the men in everything that is right and just. We have never dictated to a railroad whom they shall or shall not employ. We have asked the railroad companies to give the oldest men in the service, if competent and worthy, a preference of engines and runs. We have succeeded in many places in having that embodied in our written agreements, but we have never resorted to coercive measures to bring it about. We have never attempted to interfere in any way with the railroad company employing men, whether they belonged to our organization or not.

Q. Do they employ many who do not belong to your organization?—A. Oh, yes; quite a number. The majority of engineers of this country, as well as of Canada—of course we include the entire continent—90 per cent of them are promoted from firemen, and it is optional with a man whether he becomes a member of our organization or not. We offer no incentive; we place no obstacles in his way. If our record as an organization is not sufficient to convince him that it is to his interest to be a member thereof he remains out.

Q. (By Mr. KENNEDY.) What is the total number, approximately, of engineers in the country, and how many are in your organization?—A. I think I would be safe in saying that we have 90 per cent of the locomotive engineers of the country in our organization. I should say perhaps there are between 35,000 and 36,000 in the United States and Canada.

Q. (By Mr. FARQUHAR.) Was there an organization of locomotive engineers under the so-called Knights of Labor?—A. No.

Q. Yours, then, is the only organization of the locomotive engineers in America?—A. Yes.

Q. (By Mr. KENNEDY.) Are the Mexican engineers in your organization?—A. There is only one native locomotive engineer who is not a member of our brotherhood. In our constitution we have the color line. A man can not belong to the brotherhood unless he is a white man.

Q. (By Mr. FARQUHAR.) In case of a man being dropped from your organization for intemperance and for satisfactory reasons to your organization, is he, by that one dereliction of duty, shut out from your organization and from employment on another road?—A. He is expelled from the organization, but we do not as an organization interfere with his getting employment elsewhere, if anyone wants to employ him.

Q. (By Mr. PHILLIPS.) What is your reason for excluding colored men from the brotherhood, and are colored engineers employed on the railroads in the South?—A. None that I know of. The only reason that I can assign is this, that in 1873 a delegate from San Francisco brought the question before the convention, as they had a colored man running between Truckee and Wadsworth, on some division of the Southern Pacific road. The question up to that time had not been raised, and he brought it up before the convention, which resulted in a resolution being passed at that convention prohibiting colored men from joining the organization.

Q. (By Representative LIVINGSTON.) Why?—A. I can not assign any reason for it, simply the judgment of the delegates.

Q. What was the reason given by the delegates at the time of passing that resolution?—A. None, whatever, that I know of. A delegate is not required in a convention to give his reason; he exercises his prerogative and uses the ballot. A great many things were said, but no particular reason assigned. We did not want them.

Q. Can you not assign the reason why you do not want them now?—A. Yes; the reason that I would give is, we do not want them. They will not have them in the Southern States. Our organization is well represented in the Southern States, and certainly it would not be right for me, as executive officer, to go contrary to the wishes of the membership in the South.

Q. Would they receive them in Pennsylvania and New York?—A. No.

Q. Then will you not say it covers the whole territory?—A. We do not recognize any particular territory.

Q. (By Mr. KENNEDY.) Would a railroad receive them anywhere in the country?—A. The railroad engineers would not.

Q. Have the companies colored engineers in Pennsylvania?—A. They have not any.

Q. Do corporations and people whose employees have places where life and property are at stake every moment exclude ignorant, careless, and indifferent people, whether they are black or white, and seek to get intelligent, trustworthy, and competent agents?—A. Yes; and we seek, as an organization, to furnish them with that class.

Q. You say you have those written agreements with about 90 per cent of the railroads of the country. Have the men in your organization ever violated those agreements?—A. Yes, some of them have.

Q. Have the railroads ever violated them?—A. Not before the men did. I am sorry to say that a good many of our men became involved in that trouble of 1894, and by doing so they violated the agreement they had with the company and violated the laws of the organization, for which they were punished.

Q. Is there any age limit fixed by the railroad companies beyond which they will not employ men as engineers?—A. I could not give you anything officially. I could only give you that from hearsay, from complaints made to me by some of my men, in which they say that some of the companies refuse to employ a man if he is over 45 years of age. There has been, in the last few years, introduced on a number of roads what they call a personal examination with regard to vision and hearing, and quite a number of old experienced men have been taken off the road for defective vision and defective hearing. And, according to the statements made to me, I have said, and I wish to repeat it here, that the examinations that our men have been required to undergo, if the statements made to me are true, were unfair and unjust; and we have succeeded in having them somewhat modified. We admit that a man requires good vision and good hearing; but when you take a man into a dark room and require him to name the different colored worsteds and detect the tick of a watch so many feet away and so on, I consider that unnecessary, uncalled for, and unfair. If a man has good eyesight and can distinguish the different-colored signals used by a railroad day and night, and has run a locomotive 35 or 40 years, I never could understand why he should undergo such an examination to make him qualified to run.

Q. (By Mr. FARQUHAR.) Would a man who has been in continuous service with a road for 25 or 30 years be allowed to pass the 45-year limit as long as he remained an efficient engineer, or would he be retired at 45 years?—A. I have never known of any such cases yet. We had 1 man running on the Baltimore and Ohio road here who ran up until he was 80 years of age; and he ran the fast line between Washington and Baltimore, and was then retired on a pension. We have men still running locomotives, who are all the way from 45 and 50 to 60 years of age. I ran a locomotive myself for 20 years, and I have been off for 25. A good deal depends upon the man and the care he has taken of himself.

Q. (By Mr. KENNEDY.) Will you tell the commission your experience with injunctions and the manner of their service upon you?—A. Yes; my experience has not been very pleasant with some of the injunctions that have been issued and the decisions rendered by some of our judges. Take, for instance, the case on the Northern Pacific road. There never was a more unjust act perpetrated on men than there was on that occasion. Each one of us in the office was served in Cleveland. Men who never go out of the office, whose duties never take them out of the office to do any business with the companies, were served with injunctions granted by Judge Jenkins, of Milwaukee, which prohibited me and every other man from talking, conferring, counseling, or advising with our men. I think that was very unfair and unjust. In the first place, the road was in the hands of receivers. The receivers, without consulting with the men, got up a new schedule of wages, which was a reduction from what the men were receiving. There may have been some talk among the men; there was a good deal of dissatisfaction; but they could have no strike on that road or any other road without first calling upon the executive officers of the organization and having a meeting with the management. So that this talk and the reason assigned for getting out these injunctions was all uncalled for; there was nothing to it. Finally we met the receivers and talked the matter over with them and arrived at an amicable adjustment for the time being, but the injunction was there all the same; and I remember Judge Jenkins, in his ruling, made use of this expression, "The men have a right to quit work individually or collectively if they want to, but they have no right to quit work if it cripples the business of the road. Whoever heard of a body of men quitting that it did not affect or cripple the business, whatever they were engaged in? Then Judge Taft, or, rather, Judge Ricks, issued an injunction in the case of the Toledo, Ann Arbor and North Michigan road, which amounted to the same thing, prohibiting advising and counseling with the men, which I think was very unjust. I think there ought to be something done to strip some of these judges of a little of their authority when it is exercised in the wrong direction.

Q. Has such use of the injunction had a tendency to lower respect for the courts among your membership?—A. Most decidedly.

Q. (By Mr. FARQUHAR.) Was it on the application of the railroad managers that these injunctions were issued?—A. It was on the application of the receivers in the case of the Northern Pacific; there were no managers; but in the case of the others it was on the request of the officials of the road.

Q. Were those injunctions called out by public opinion at any time, in your recollection?—A. Not that I am aware of.

Q. Or by any newspaper discussion?—A. No; they were issued at the request of the company. Take the case of the Toledo and Ann Arbor road. We exercised every honorable effort with Mr. Ashley; we even offered to work for him for a less rate of pay than any other road was paying. He positively refused. Consequently the men decided to quit, and we sustained them in quitting and gave them the protection of our brotherhood. We did what we thought we had a right to do, but since the decision of the Supreme Court we learn that we did not have the right. We had in our organization a rule that prohibited our men from handling cars of a company where there was a strike—a legal strike—in force. Consequently, when we decided to quit on that road we notified the chairmen of the committees of the adjoining roads that there was a legal strike in force upon the Toledo, Ann Arbor and North Michigan road, and to notify the general managers of that fact, which they did. Of course, our men, understanding the laws of the brotherhood, refused to handle Ann Arbor cars. Then the injunction was issued to put a stop to it, and our men were arrested. We appealed it to the circuit court and the circuit court sustained the lower court, and we brought it to the Supreme Court at Washington and they sustained it. Consequently we have eliminated the rule.

Q. Was the basis of the decision there on the interstate-commerce clause?—A. Yes; and the antitrust law, I think.

Q. Was the reason assigned by Mr. Ashley, when he asked for a reduction of wages on the Toledo and Ann Arbor road there, that the finances of the road compelled him to do that?—A. No; I am sorry to say young Mr. Ashley did not assign any reason. One year before we had a dispute with his father, the ex-governor, which was submitted to arbitration, and the arbitrators made an award and young Mr. Ashley never carried it out, and that feeling of discontent and dissatisfaction continued to exist which culminated in the strike. Mr. Ashley did not advance any argument except "I won't; I won't."

Q. Previous to this injunction did you have a written contract with Mr. Ashley and the road?—A. Yes.

Q. And the infraction of that contract was through Ashley and the company?—A. Yes.

Q. In a case of that kind is it common, when you make application for the dissolution of an injunction, to bring forward this written instrument of agreement and to show that you are holding to the terms of your agreement?—A. When the papers were served upon me I was sitting in the depot at Toledo. I read them over and I said to the United States marshal, "I will obey the order of the court." I immediately returned home and consulted my attorney, and he told me what to do and I did it. At the hearing before Judges Taft and Ricks all that was brought out, and it had no weight upon the decision rendered by the court.

Q. Did the court take into consideration the written instrument of agreement between the men and the road?—A. No; Judge Taft went so far as to say in his ruling that I was a conspirator.

Q. Independent of the writing or agreement?—A. Yes; independent of anything that was produced in court.

Q. (By Mr. PHILLIPS.) Was the written agreement produced in court?—A. I was under oath. It was not called for. The statement under oath called for it and was given by me.

Q. (By Mr. KENNEDY.) Would you have any objection to telling the commission something about the nature of the different funds which your organization has been building up?—A. Not the least. We have, you might say, three separate funds. One is the current fund, drawn from to pay the general expenses, salaries, printing, and so on; another is known as the charity fund, the widow and orphans' fund, if you please; the other is known as the contingent fund, to be drawn from in case of emergency, or, in other words, in case of a strike. You know we have had strikes; we are not ashamed of them, and we make provision for all those things. Our current fund is drawn from at each convention. We have, in the first place, what we call a charity blank, which is filled out by persons who need assistance and signed by the officers of the division. They are brought to the convention; they are submitted to our executive committee, who investigate and recommend an allowance. The convention in the first place sets apart so much to be given away to charity. Last year they gave away $42,000. That is about the average which they give in that direction. Of course, that reduces the current fund somewhat. We have had no occasion to draw from the contingent fund for a number of years, so it is growing.

Q. Would you care to state the size of it?—A. It is in the neighborhood of, perhaps, $100,000. I could not state the exact figures without looking it up, because I am not the financial officer and do not pay as much attention to the details in that direction as he does.

Q. What is the assessment upon your members for these different funds?— A. What is known as the grand dues is $2.50 a year, for which they receive a copy of our monthly journal. Then the local dues paid to the local divisions average from $4 to $6 a year. So that you may say that the total dues for membership would be from $8 to $9 a year.

Q. Are these different funds of your grand organization built up from this $2.50 or are they partly built up from the $4 to $6 paid into the locals?—A. No; they are built from the $2.50 and the profits on printing. We furnish all the printing of different documents of the subdivisions, on which there is a profit, and that goes into the general fund. For instance, from the publishing of our monthly journal there is quite a revenue derived, and quite a revenue from our constitutions and by-laws and all other documents required by the subdivisions, and all that goes into the current fund, out of which they contribute $42,000 at each convention.

Q. Is this fund of $100,000 practically the same as the defense fund among the conductors?—A. Yes; simply that we call it the contingent fund instead of the defense fund.

Q. (By Mr. FARQUHAR.) Is your insurance regarded among your brotherhood as less onerous than the usual rates of fraternal insurance?—A. I can say this: The rate has never yet exceeded 1½ per cent. Some years the rate of mortality is higher than others—and the number of accidents; but the rate has never yet exceeded, to my knowledge, since its formation in 1867, 1½ per cent. We think it is one of the best. It is better than we can get in any old-line company from the fact that we pay for the loss of a hand, arm, limb, or eyesight of one or both eyes, the same amount as we do for death.

Q. Is it the desire of your brotherhood to maintain among yourselves this insurance solely, or to agree to the cooperation of the companies in furnishing a part of the insurance?—A. Our men, speaking of them as a whole, prefer their own. It is only of recent date that the railroad companies have taken any steps to make provision for their men. I remember when it was first introduced in the Pennsylvania system. It created a great deal of dissatisfaction, so much so that I was called to the city of Philadelphia. They were all worked up, excited; did not want it; would not have it. We took the matter up with the committee and we looked it over, and I said. " If you can get the company to eliminate this obligatory clause there are no objections to it." I advised them to go and wait upon Mr. Pugh, or the president if necessary, and ask him to eliminate that obligatory clause. They did so, which was satisfactory. I said, " As long as this matter is left optional for you to take or leave it alone, you have no right to find any fault." The company did eliminate the obligatory clause and left it optional with the men, and it was not but a little while before they all went into it.

Q. Then the striking out of this clause has made it voluntary on the part of the men?—A. Yes.

Q. And is it still satisfactorily in existence?—A. As far as the Pennsylvania system is concerned, I have heard no complaints, and I have heard of many who have gone into it.

Q. Would the firemen acquire a larger sum of insurance by taking the cooperation of the railroads?—A. No; I think not.

Q. Would they pass your limit of 4,500?—A. Oh, no; that is the limit with us.

Q. (By Mr. KENNEDY.) Is there no feeling among the engineers that the railroad companies promote these beneficiary societies for the purpose of dividing the allegiance of the engineers between their organization and their interest in the fund controlled by the company, so that in time of trouble they would hesitate what to do?—A. There have been such expressions made by individuals, but I can not say that it is a general feeling. There have been quite a number of complaints made about the way it is managed on the Baltimore and Ohio system, but as I have said, I have heard no complaints from the Pennsylvania system. You talk with some of our men and you will find that quite a number have a feeling of distrust concerning it; they think it is done, you may say, to wean the men away from their own or win them over. I have said this, that we, as an organization, long before the railroad companies took any interest in that direction, made provision for the men, and we think we are entitled to the preference.

Q. (By Mr. FARQUHAR.) And you think that provision is ample?—A. Oh, of course, that has kept out of our insurance a great number who would have gone into it had it not been for that.

Q. Will you tell the commission something about the relations your organization bears toward the other organizations in railroad transportation?—A. Our relations are friendly, although we are not a part of the federation. We believe in cooperation, and we have, in every instance where a wish has been expressed by our men and the others, cheerfully cooperated with them in the adjustment of grievances, and we will continue to do so. The question of the Brotherhood of Locomotive Engineers joining the federation was submitted to our last convention. It was thoroughly discussed and defeated. Prior to that they had system federations, which left it to the men on the system to determine whether they would have it or not. It was adopted on quite a number of systems, and the other organizations at their conventions delegated authority to their executive officers to formulate a plan and submit it to the membership of their organizations, which they did, and it was adopted. It is known as the national federation, which abolished system federation. Consequently we are outside of the federation, yet our relations are friendly—I can speak personally for myself—with the other executive officers; they are of the most friendly character, and, so far as I am concerned and the organization I represent is concerned, nothing will be done to disturb those relations if we can possibly avoid it. We believe in being on friendly terms with everybody; but when the delegates, who are the lawmaking body of our brotherhood, pass upon the question and decide it, that settles it for the time being.

Q. In other words, you mean that you hold to the autonomy of your own organization and cooperate in a friendly way with like organizations in transportation?—A. Yes; that is our position exactly.

Q. (By Mr. KENNEDY.) What is the principal reason why you do not go into the federation with the other trades?—A. I will answer your question just the same as I told Brothers Clark, Morrisey, Sargeant, and Powell in the city of Washington some time ago. They asked me my reasons for opposing federation. I said, " I am not willing to delegate the power and authority to a conductor, a telegraph operator, a fireman, or a brakeman to say whether the engineers shall quit work or not. I want that question to be decided by engineers, not by anybody else." That is one of my principal reasons. Another reason is, the moment you federate you lose your identity as an organization. No matter how you may do it, the public will look upon it that you have become a part of the federation, and you will be known then as the American Federation of Railway Employees only; there will be no Brotherhood of Locomotive Engineers, or Brotherhood of Locomotive Firemen, or Order of Railway Conductors, or Order of Railway Telegraphers. I may be mistaken. We are the pioneers in the work of reformation among railway men. For years we were the only organization that claimed to be a protective organization. For 22 years the Order of Railway Conductors was known as a nonprotective organization; the same way with the Brotherhood of Locomotive Firemen up to 1885; and for 30 years we went right along adjusting our grievances, making agreements with the companies without the aid or assistance of anybody. We have treated everybody well so far as we knew how, and I never could understand, and I do not know to-day, why it is necessary for the locomotive engineers to federate with others. For what purpose? Might never made right. Some, however, advance this argument: If a delegation representing every branch of the service walks into the office of the general manager he would not dare say no. Well, that remains to be seen. I do not believe that we ought to win by resorting to coercive measures, nor do I believe you would be received in the same spirit if you would approach him in that coercive way. Again, it may be selfish, but federation would mean that each organization would have to spend its time and money in adjusting other people's differences. Personally I have always been opposed to it, and there has never been any argument advanced by anyone to convince me that it was necessary for the Brotherhood of Locomotive Engineers to federate with the organizations for its future good.

Q. You have taken lessons then from the causes which have brought about the downfall of the Knights of Labor?—A. Of course I have had my own notion and my own view about these things. I differ with a great many men as to how a labor organization ought to be conducted. I have gone on the principle that we should all be willing to do by other people as we would like to have them do by us; that is my way of doing business, and I wish to say here, for the information of the commission, that if the railway managers of this country had received us as we have always been willing to meet them, so far the Brotherhood of Locomotive Engineers is concerned, we never would have had any trouble; there never would have been any strikes.

Q. (By Representative LIVINGSTON). I believe they say the same thing of you—if you would have done what was right they would have. How do you harmonize those two statements?—A. Let us take the facts. You are the general manager, if you please, of a road whose stock is quoted at 145 or 150, recognized as one of the leading and richest corporations in the West. Your men approach you and want you to pay as much as your competitors. You say, "I won't do it." We try to convince you of the fairness of our proposition. You still refuse; you are stubborn; you will not do it; the men decide to quit. Who is to blame?

Q. Has your organization lessened the number of wrecks, loss of property, loss of lives, and things like that, and by that means improved the situation all along the line?—A. We have assisted the companies in ridding the service of a great many incompetent men.

Q. Does not that help the service?—A. Yes.

Q. Have you lessened the loss of life and property by your organization to a very large per cent?—A. We have, I think.

Q. (By Mr. KENNEDY.) I have here a magazine article, which seems to show pretty conclusively that the practice of blacklisting has been carried on quite extensively in some parts of the country, especially in that great railroad center Chicago? Do you know anything about that question?—A. No.

Q. It is published in the Arena, and the author of it is Mr. William J. Strong, the attorney who won that suit for Fred R. Ketcham, one of the strikers who was blacklisted in the strike of 1894, and the jury gave him a verdict of twenty-one thousand and odd dollars.—A. I could not say from personal knowledge, you understand, that any company had blacklisted the engineers. I have heard that such things have been done. Statements have been made by some of my men in which they say like this: "I have been discharged for belonging to the brotherhood; have applied for employment on another road; I was given employment, went to work, and in a few days I was notified that my services were no longer required." They attributed it to some notice the road had received from the last road where they were employed, but I could not state positively that a man was blacklisted. You of course remember the trouble of 1894. Quite a number of our men became involved in that trouble. It occurred on a certain day in June. Those men who voluntarily quit, asked for letters from their former employers. They were given letters in which it stated the date they quit.

Q. (By Mr. FARQUHAR.) And the date corresponded——A. With the date of the strike, and consequently when they sought employment and produced this letter; that seemed to shut them out. Of course I have read of cases. I think I read of the case you speak of, where men have recovered, and I think they ought to. I do not think you have any right to place any obstacles in the way of any man obtaining employment to earn a livelihood for himself and his family, because if he does not suit you he may suit someone else. It is all wrong and ought not to be allowed.

Q. (By Mr. KENNEDY.) Was it ever alleged that there was a blacklisting feature connected with the trouble on the Reading road some years ago when it was in the hands of receivers?—A. No. I will give you the history of the Reading road. Of course Mr. Gowan is dead and gone. During the Centennial of 1876 the Reading road carried a great many passengers, did an immense business very successfully. After the Centennial the men made application for a slight increase of pay. Instead of granting it, along in the following month of March, I think it was, Franklin B. Gowan, as president of the road, issued his printed circular, requesting his engineers to leave the brotherhood or leave his service. It was a peremptory demand. Men were handed those circulars, some of them, while oiling their engines at the station. We were sent for. We met with the men at Philadelphia. The question came up, whether they would remain with the Reading Company or with the brotherhood. They decided by unanimous vote to remain with the brotherhood. Consequently, they all quit in a body, with the exception of 12, expecting by so doing that the company would not be able to fill their places, but they did. They filled their places. Those men scattered over the country, and the brotherhood paid them under the laws of the organization so much a month for 3 months. The men who took the places of our men joined the Knights of Labor later on, and afterwards had a strike, and some of the old men, who lost their jobs in 1877 and were still in that section of the country, took the places vacated by the Knights of Labor, and for so doing they were charged with being scabs. During the strike on the Chicago, Burlington and Quincy road a gentleman came to Chicago and represented himself as being master of the Knights of Labor lodge at Reading. He stated that many of our men had taken the places of their men, and if I would call them off he would take his men back home. He had brought a carload to Chicago. I told him I had no authority to do that, but I would request the chairman of our executive committee to go to Philadelphia and investigate, and if he found our men had taken the places vacated by those men to ask them to withdraw and promise them pay from the brotherhood. He went to Philadelphia and investigated and found it was not so. Somehow or other this telegram that I gave to the chairman of our committee got into the newspapers, which angered Mr. Corbin, who turned against our brotherhood. Up to that time he had been our friend, but would not employ after that time a brotherhood man on the Reading road, and that gave rise to what you speak of, blacklisting the men.

Q. The road was in the hands of receivers part of that time?—A. No; that was later on. Later on, when Mr. McLeod was receiver—that was the last time I had anything to do with the Philadelphia and Reading road; he afterwards went to the New England road—2 of our men were discharged. It was represented to me that ·they were discharged for joining the brotherhood. I took it up with Mr. McLeod at that time. He produced a paper that one of our men had signed on entering the service of the company, wherein he agreed not to join any labor organization. He turned to me and asked me if I sustained men in violating an agreement of that kind. I said, "No, sir. If that man signed that paper which you produce, I have nothing further to say. In this case," I said, "here is another young man who has never signed any paper and was called into the office by Mr. Swigert (who was the general superintendent) and asked if he was a member of the brotherhood, and when he answered in the affirmative, he was discharged. I want you to reinstate that young man." He said, "Where is he?" I said "Down stairs." "Bring him up." I brought him up. He asked the young man the question and he answered it just as he told me, and he reinstated that young man and paid him for what time he was off, which was all we could ask. That satisfied me that they were not proscribing men for belonging to the brotherhood. They preferred, when they entered the service, that they should not be members of any organization, but if they employed them and it came to the knowledge of the officials that they were members they were not disturbed for that.

Q. What were Judge Paxon's relations to your organization?—A. That occurred with the trainmen, I believe. He was charged with discharging 2 members of the Brotherhood of Trainmen. He was charged with being an avowed enemy to organized labor. For that reason organized labor protested against his appointment. I did not know the gentleman. All I know is what I have been told.

Q. Your organization among others?—A. Yes.

Q. What is the attitude of your organization on the subject of immigration?—A. That question has not been brought before our convention, yet I feel safe in assuming the responsibility of speaking for the organization on it: We are in favor of restricting immigration, believing it would be for the best interests of the country at large.

Q. (By Mr. PHILLIPS). Your organization is not directly affected by it?—A. No.

Q. (By Mr. KENNEDY.) How about indirectly?—A. It is indirectly affected in this way, just the same as any other branch of industry, that after awhile it creates a large surplus of workmen.

Q. (By Mr. FARQUHAR.) How do you propose to restrict, educationally?—A. I would have it educational.

Q. (By Representative LIVINGSTON.) Is that the only restriction you would put on it?—A. No; I would add property; that is, a financial test.

Q. How much would you require each immigrant to own and possess in his own right in money or anything else?—A. I do not think I would be justified in prescribing a limit. If he had anything at all, he ought to have sufficient so he would not become dependent on the community.

Q. What do you think that ought to be?—A. I think it ought to be at least $50°.

Q. (By Mr. KENNEDY.) Do you think your organization would support a bill in Congress restricting immigration?—A. I think it would; yes.

Q. (By Representative LIVINGSTON.) Any other way in which you would restrict it?—A. I do not know of any other way.

Q. Would you restrict them in their rights of becoming citizens?—A. Perhaps I have peculiar views upon that question. If I had my way I would qualify the ballot. I would not allow any man to vote who could not read or write.

Q. English or German or Italian?—A. Could not read the ballot that was printed for him in this country.

Q. That means English?—A. That is my answer. I regard the ballot, the way it is used now, as a farce and a mockery. Men go up to the polls and deposit a ballot at the behest of somebody else and do not know what they are doing.

Q. You think, then, the commission should recommend to Congress a bill with all those disqualifying schemes in order to have these elements eliminated wholly?—A. Yes, I think it should.

Q. (By Mr. FARQUHAR.) What are your views on compulsory arbitration?—A. I have always been in favor of arbitration, but there has been so much said, and a great deal of opposition manifested, on compulsory arbitration, that I have dropped that part of it. Still I never could understand why there should be reasonable objections raised to compulsory arbitration, so far as it applies to railroads. They have the Interstate Commerce Commission that regulates and controls the railroad companies in regard to rates, which makes it compulsory on the part of the companies to submit to the rulings decided upon.

Q. Do not the Interstate Commerce Commission claim they have not enough power to carry out what they find?—A. They want more, and I guess they will get it.

Q. (By Representative LIVINGSTON.) Arbitration, to be arbitration, must be compulsory, must it not?—A. I think so; unless there is some way to compel parties to abide by the award, some penalty attached—it is left simply to their honor.

Q. (By Mr. PHILLIPS.) Did you not embrace your views, as well as the views of the brotherhood generally, in an arbitration bill which has recently become a law?—A. Yes.

Q. (By Representative LIVINGSTON.) What is your opinion of the last act; does it cover the ground?—A. It covers the ground as far as it goes; it is simply this: public sentiment is worth a great deal to any party engaged in a dispute; and if it is known to the public that one party to a dispute offers to arbitrate and the other refuses, we would have public sentiment in our favor. That is one advantage to be derived from the arbitration bill.

Q. How much effect on corporations, moneyed syndicates, does public opinion have when they take a near cut to get a thing?—A. When public sentiment is thoroughly aroused it generally has its effects sooner or later, and will continue to. We can not afford to ignore it.

Q. Have you had any cases of arbitration under the law passed by the last Congress?—A. No; fortunately for us there has been no occasion. We have been able so far to adjust every case we have had. We have had some 7 or 8 cases. I just returned from St. Paul, where we had a case. President Stickney and I had a very pleasant conference and succeeded in effecting a very amicable settlement; consequently, so long as that can be done there will be no occasion to avail ourselves of that law.

Q. (By Mr. PHILLIPS.) If you did not agree in the case to which you refer, would you have to offer to arbitrate under this law?—A. Yes, we would have made the effort.

Q. Do you have an idea that the existing law had anything to do with your settling that, knowing that it would be appealed to?—A. I think not. I think that the man we had to deal with, being a fair man, known as such, had more to do with it than anything else—the disposition to listen and do what was right.

Q. (By Mr. KENNEDY.) Have any of your organizations made any criticism as to the operation of section 10 of that law?—A. Not that I am aware of.

Q. It has been stated that it is evaded by the railroad companies, in some cases, by not having employment for a man who applies for work and does not express a desire to become a member of the beneficial association. Do you know anything about that?—A. In a general way, we have heard complaints, but nothing official. I know this, that men have entered the service of the Baltimore and Ohio Company without being required to take it out; that is, it was not one of the conditions upon which they were employed. It is pretty generally understood that in accepting service they also become a member of that relief association.

Q. It is believed to operate in this way, that if they come and ask for employment, and also signify a desire to become members of that association, they get employment, and if not they do not get employment?—A. There may be something in that. Still, I have sent quite a number of engineers there and have not heard any complaint from them on that question, and I very seldom allow myself to form any opinion on rumor. If I get anything official, authentic, then I am prepared to pass on it; but you know men talking say a great many things sometimes, and when you come to investigate them there is really nothing in them.

Q. (By Mr. FARQUHAR.) Has the question of incorporating your organization been before your annual meeting at any time?—A. Yes; our insurance departments were incorporated. We were obliged to have them incorporated, and they have their own officers now, and a board of trustees. That was brought about through the action of 2 men who joined our brotherhood in the city of New York. When a man joins the brotherhood he is required to take out and carry at least one insurance policy. After they became members they refused to comply with that law, consequently they were expelled. They laid their case before an attorney in the city. This was some 5 years ago; and we learned for the first time that we were doing business in the State of New York contrary to law as an insurance association. As soon as we learned that we consulted an attorney and he told us to become incorporated and take out a license. They had to have their own trustees, and in that way the insurance department became incorporated; but the brotherhood proper is not, and some objections have been raised by the delegates to becoming incorporated because they say each individual member could be sued and recovered against in case of trouble, and consequently there has never been any effort made to become incorporated.

Q. Was it your opinion that it was rather unsafe for the labor organizations to become incorporated?—A. According to that ruling. Now, for instance, Mr. Ashley sued me for $300,000 damages. He sued me as an individual, as an officer of the association, on account of telegrams I sent out. We learned from our attorneys that they could recover; it would depend upon the jury how much judgment they got; but through the attorneys it was settled out of court on the payment by us of $2,500. That grew out of cars of this company being detained with perishable freight.

Q. (By Mr. PHILLIPS.) Would not the incorporation of labor organizations free the individual members from legal responsibilities?—A. They tell me not—if he had anything they could get.

(Q. By Mr. FARQUHAR.) Then you do not think that there is any advantage to the labor organization in its becoming incorporated, unless it is to cover funds of the organization or the insurance?—A. They require bonds. We are under bonds for $25,000. Mr. Ingraham and the officers of the insurance department and the secretaries of the local divisions handling money are all under bonds, so that the members are protected in that way.

Q. (By Mr. KENNEDY.) Have you had any experience with boycotts, or do you resort to it in your organization?—A. We did until the Supreme Court decided against it. They called it the boycott. If we had a strike, if you please, on the Pennsylvania road, under our rule the members of the brotherhood on any other road would not be permitted to handle the Pennsylvania cars, but the Supreme Court decided it unlawful, consequently we eliminated the rule.

Q. Have you anything to say about proposed legislation to strengthen the Interstate Commerce Commission outside of what you have said in your statement to the commission?—A. Nothing, unless it is that they ought to have power to punish for violation of any State law; upon investigation, they ought to have the power to punish the guilty.

Q. Do you believe railroad companies should be compelled to file with the Interstate Commerce Commission a full detailed account of all accidents, giving the causes of the accidents, names of the persons maimed or killed, etc.?—A. Railroad companies, just as individuals, ought to be compelled to comply with any law enacted by the Government. I do not know why a railroad company should be relieved or released from compliance with the law any more than an individual. In regard to the equipment of cars, you remember the time expired the 1st of last January. The railroad companies appeared before the Interstate Commerce Commission and appealed for an extension of 5 years. The representatives of the organizations thought that too long, and they protested against it.

Q. (By Representative LIVINGSTON.) On what ground?—A. Some of them had made no effort to comply with the law. We can not understand why they should be permitted to ignore the law any more than anybody else. Whenever they assign a good reason—poverty was the principal one—then it should be considered. Then the companies passed through a very serious time, just the same as the country at large. Under those circumstances they were entitled to consideration; but where a company took the position that they did not do it and at the same time acknowledged that they had been paying 8 per cent dividends right along, we did not think that a very good reason for noncompliance with the law.

Q. Are the railroads agreed upon uniform couplings?—A. I do not know whether they are or not.

Q. Does not that law require it?—A. It does not bind them to any particular coupling.

Q. The law requires that cars should be of the same height and have uniform couplings?—A. Yes.

Q. Have they attempted to comply with that?—A. I believe they have, so far as I know.

Q. (By Mr. FARQUHAR.) What is the usual duration of these written agreements between the companies and the men?—A. They are unlimited. Some of them embody a clause for 30, 60, 90 days' notice if either party desires a change.

Q. (By Mr. KENNEDY.) It is you who propose agreements to railroad companies, is it?—A. Of course in the early days it was something new for a committee to wait upon a railroad management. I believe I was the first to help make a written agreement with a railroad company in regard to wages and rules for the protection and government of the men. In some of the agreements 30 days' notice is required; others, 60; some, 90. If you desire any change you have to give that length of notice; and what led up to the agreement was simply this: The committee got together and presented a paper to the company; it was taken up and discussed; it was then reduced to writing by the company and printed, and went out as an agreement between the engineers and the company, signed by the general management and the chairman and secretary of the committee. That was the origin of them.

Q. (By Mr. PHILLIPS.) Do most of the railroads sign such contracts?—A. Yes.

Q. (By Representative LIVINGSTON.) Have you ever made a test in the courts of those cases, where contracts have been violated, for damages?—A. No.

Q. (By Mr. PHILLIPS.) What effect, if any, has the watered stock of railroads upon the employees?—A. That would only come up in a discussion between the committees and the company if they pleaded poverty. They generally go prepared to come back at that argument.

Q. Is it not a fact that there is a very large per cent of watered stock in a large number of railroad companies?—A. I would not like to say that; personally, I never knew it. We never trouble ourselves about them if they give us what we want.

Q. Is it your opinion that the employees could not receive better wages than they do if they were not compelled to work, or did not work, for companies which have a large amount of watered stock?—A. The railroad men in this country, as a rule, for the last year or two, have had no occasion to complain so far as relates to their wages, and with few exceptions they have been maintained all through the panic. We did in 1893 submit to a slight reduction on two or three roads, where we were called upon. For instance, the Louisville and Nashville requested a reduction; on the Southern they made a slight reduction, and on the Wabash. But outside of them the wages have been maintained, among the trainmen especially, so that they have been given no occasion to complain so far as that goes. We are getting the same rate of pay to-day—I am speaking now of the engineers, and the same may be said of the firemen—that we have been receiving for the last 15 years, with a few exceptions, and we are pretty well satisfied with the rate of pay we are now receiving, with one or two exceptions. Our men on the Southern Railway here have been striving to get their reduction restored, but Mr. Spencer has given very good reasons. He simply said to the committee he could not do it at that time; but he has agreed to take the matter up next August, and we expect then, when they are in a position to do it, that they will restore the 10 per cent, and I think they will.

Q. (By Representative LIVINGSTON.) Can you buy as much now with a dollar as you could 10 or 15 years ago, or more?—A. I think in some cases more.

Q. You are really getting more wages now than ever?—A. Yes.

Q. (By Mr. KENNEDY.) Were your scales pretty well maintained during the financial depression of 1893, until recently?—A. Yes; with few exceptions—the roads that I have mentioned.

Q. Was there a falling off in the number employed?—A. Oh, yes. You see, men employed in the train service as a rule are paid by the trip or mile. Their wages depend upon the amount of business done. That is one reason why we have not been called upon to submit to a reduction in prices, because there have been cases where men would not earn over $35 or $40 a month. If there were no trains to run there was no pay.

Q. The members of your organization are steadfast in their loyalty to the organization, are they?—A. As a rule; yes. Of course in 1894 a few of them broke away.

Q. (By Representative LIVINGSTON.) That 1894 scrape settled the fact whether they were loyal, did it not?—A. A large majority.

Q. (By Mr. KENNEDY.) The railroad engineers are in a position, practically, to enforce their reasonable demands and their rights?—A. We feel that we are, if driven to it.

Q. (By Mr. FARQUHAR.) Do you think your strength gives your men an incentive to strike when they have a difficulty that is not very great?—A. No.

Q. Do you think, on the other hand, that your strength restricts striking?—A. Yes; in the first place they can not have a legal strike without the consent of the grand chief engineer, and they never will get it unless they have a just cause. They know that.

Q. (By Mr. KENNEDY.) Has there been more or less striking since the organization of railway engineers?—A. Of course we know of no strikes among railroad men prior to the formation of our brotherhood.

Q. (By Representative LIVINGSTON.) You are speaking of one class of railroad men; not for the conductors, are you?—A. Yes; I speak for the train service so far as it relates to strikes, because I am familiar with it.

Q. Does not a strike depend upon an organization?—A. Not always.

Q. How can you strike unless there is an organization?—A. I will cite a case on the New York Central road. I never was employed on any other road. At the close of the war, the shopmen, the section hands—everyone but trainmen—went out on a strike. They had no organization. It was simply this: It started down in the city with the laborers on the street. They formed together and drove every man out of the shop who was not receiving over $1.50 a day.

Q. You would not call that a strike?—A. It was a mob; they drove every man away. I have no doubt that the organization would like to have a law whereby an employee could recover for injuries received through the negligence of another employee, provided they could prove that this employee was incompetent and that was known to the employer.

Q. Suppose that employee to whom negligence is chargeable was not a member of your organization and the man hurt was?—A. We would not discriminate.

Q. (By Mr. FARQUHAR.) Then you think that the railroad companies ought to assume a little more liability in respect to accidents and damages than they do at present?—A. I do.

Q. Have you taken any action toward laying this requirement before legislatures or Congress?—A. Only in this way: The 5 organizations have decided to send a representative to Washington to look after legislation, and in that way protect the interests of the organization better than it would to have quite a number. We have a representative at Washington during the sitting of Congress. Then in each State we have a legislative board, which is supposed to look after legislation.

STATE OF OHIO, *County of Cuyahoga:*

I swear that the statements made by me of my own knowledge in the foregoing report of my testimony before the Industrial Commission are true, and that all other statements I believe to be true.

P. M. ARTHUR.

Sworn and subscribed before me this 2d day of October, 1899.

WM. H. MARLATT,
Notary Public, Cuyahoga County, Ohio.

WASHINGTON, D. C., *October 5, 1899.*

TESTIMONY OF HON. MARTIN A. KNAPP,

Chairman Interstate Commerce Commission.

The commission met at 10.40 a. m., Vice Chairman Phillips presiding. Hon. Martin A. Knapp, of New York, chairman of the Interstate Commerce Commission, being first duly sworn, testified as follows:

Q. (By Senator MALLORY.) Judge Knapp, we recognize the fact that you are better acquainted with these subjects than the commission itself is, and we would prefer that you pursue such a course of statement as may seem best to you.—A. Well, you will permit me to say that I should prefer to be interrogated. I have made no special preparation for appearing before this commission for two reasons: I understood, in a general way, that you desire to make inquiry in respect to discriminations in freight charges, and that is a very broad subject. It covers nearly the whole railroad question. It is in a way the railroad problem, and I could not foresee whether you desired information respecting the causes of discrimination, the facts of discrimination, the effects of discrimination, or the methods by which discriminations might be prevented; but as either one of these phases of the subject would require volumes, I may say, to exhaust, I could not, by any special preparation, anticipate the direction which your inquiries might take. And then, for a minor reason, I felt indisposed to appear to desire to utilize this commission as a medium for exploiting any views which I may entertain. If I can give you any information or make any suggestions respecting the subject of your investigation which will be valuable, I shall be very glad to serve you in that way.

Q. Is there no other branch of the subject that you have contemplated testifying on besides the subject of discrimination?—A. Well, I observe in the topical statement which your commission has issued that your investigation begins with the subject of the relations between railway corporations and their employees, and it occurred to me that perhaps you might desire to know something about the arbitration act which has now been in effect for something over a year. That measure was approved, I think, in June, 1898, and its substantial provision is to the effect that whenever a controversy arises respecting wages, hours of employment, or other conditions of service which actually interrupts or threatens to interrupt the movement of interstate commerce, either party to the controversy may apply to the Commissioner of Labor and the chairman of the Interstate Commerce Commission, whose duty it is, on such application, to put themselves in communication with the parties and endeavor, by mediation and conciliation, to bring about a friendly settlement. Failing in that effort, they are required to use their offices with a view of inducing the parties to enter into an arbitration; and if that method of settlement is accepted on their recommendation, then each of the parties appoints one arbitrator, and if the two thus chosen are unable to agree upon a third, the third arbitrator is to be appointed by the Commissioner of Labor and the chairman of the Interstate Commerce Commission. In only one instance has there been any attempt made to settle a controversy under the provisions of that act since it became a law. The controversy in that case related solely to the wages of a certain class of employees. It did not appear whether the controversy had assumed such a serious aspect as to actually threaten a strike or other interruption of the movement of commerce by the carriers complained of. Consequently the Commissioner of Labor and myself both agreed that the applying parties should make a written application, setting forth a state of facts which would confer jurisdiction upon us under the terms of the law, as otherwise it might be claimed that there was no controversy, and therefore we were not authorized to interfere. That view was acquiesced in by the applying parties, and presently a written application and statement of facts was presented, which upon its face showed a state of things plainly within the contemplation of the law; and thereupon copies of that complaint were sent to each of the carriers against which it was directed, with a request that they promptly answer in writing. They complied with that request, and within a few days those answers were received. Upon examination it appeared that, while the Commissioner of Labor and myself were treated with the utmost courtesy and the language of the answers was framed in the most respectful form, nevertheless they were substantially refusals to accept our offers of conciliation. In a word, they met the application at the threshold with a substantial declination to accept our friendly offices even to the extent of bringing about a settlement by conciliation, and of course accompanied that with a point-blank refusal to consent to arbitration. Briefly stated, their position was that where the controversy related only to wages, in view of the fact that the amount paid for wages is so large a percentage of the gross earnings of railroad carriers, they could not in justice to themselves or their stockholders submit that question to the determination of any other tribunal than themselves. In other words, that it was their right and their duty to decide for themselves without interference or advice as to the justice of the compensation paid by them.

Q. I infer, then, that the application for arbitration or conciliation was made on the part of the employees, and the refusal on the part of the employers?—A. That is the fact. Under these circumstances, the tender of mediation having been declined, we were clearly of the opinion that our duty was discharged and that there was nothing further that we could do, and the applying parties were so informed and furnished with copies of all correspondence; and there the matter, so far as we have any official knowledge, came to an end.

Q. (By Mr. FARQUHAR.) Who were the parties to this case?—A. I would prefer not to disclose the names of the parties, for the reason, and solely for the reason, that the representatives of the employees in this case were desirous that no publicity should be given to this controversy and no newspaper comment result from it; and it is entirely in obedience to their wish that I ask to be excused from disclosing the names of the carriers or the names of the employees who made the application. I have no personal objection whatever.

655A——9

Q. (By Senator MALLORY.) Is that the only case that has arisen, to your knowledge, under that act of 1898?—A. That is the only instance in which any effort has been made to apply or utilize the arbitration law. I might add, what is the obvious conclusion, that the carriers in declining to accept the mediation of the officials named in the act, whose duty it is to tender their friendly offices for that purpose, virtually put themselves in the position, I think, of refusing obedience to the law. That is to say, after conceding that a controversy existed, as they did, and declining the official mediation which the law provides for, they in effect took the position that they would not accept the method of settlement which Congress has provided.

Q. Well, the law is purely voluntary?—A. Entirely so.

Q. (By Professor JOHNSON.) Do you think there are subjects of controversy that could arise that might be settled by this law, judging from your experience in this case?—A. Well, I can understand that if a controversy related to hours of employment or other conditions of service and that controversy was recognized as actually serious, and threatening to interrupt commerce, the mediatory offices of the Commissioner of Labor and the chairman of the Interstate Commerce Commission might be accepted, but, of course, I can not determine what would be done in any case until it arises.

Q. (By Senator MALLORY.) Had you, before making your proffer of mediation, examined into the facts alleged by the parties seeking your intervention?—A. Only to the extent of hearing the statement of their representative. He was invited to disclose to us, as fully as he desired, the circumstances out of which the controversy arose and the reasons which, in his judgment, warranted the class of employees he represented in demanding higher wages.

Q. In your judgment, then, and in the judgment of the Commissioner of Labor it was a proper subject for such action as Congress authorized to be taken under those circumstances?—A. I think it was clearly a situation within the contemplation of the law.

Q. After that experience, have you been able to form any opinion as to the utility of that law in cases of serious differences between the employers and employees of railroads?—A. No; the single instance in which attempt has been made to apply that law hardly warrants any general deduction, and I am no more competent, I think, to express an opinion on that subject than any other gentleman.

Q. Has it occurred to you that any amendment to that law, looking to the meeting of such a case as that, would be advisable?—A. I am not able to suggest any specific amendment which seems to me calculated to overcome the inherent and fundamental difficulty in all such cases. The very idea of arbitration, it seems to me, implies a voluntary submission; and having reference to the voluntary acceptance by both parties to the controversy of that method of settlement, I do not quite see how the law in that regard could be materially improved. If that method of settlement is accepted, it seems to be ample enough to permit an adjustment of almost any sort of controversy between railway management and railway employees; but if it is not voluntarily accepted of course there must be a deadlock in all cases.

Q. Do you know whether there are any laws of similar character in the States?—A. I know that there are State laws on the subject.

Q. Do you know anything about the working of those laws?—A. Only in the most general way.

Q. I believe this is the only piece of legislation that Congress has ever enacted on the subject of conciliation and arbitration?—A. I so understand it.

Q. And the status of that is now, after this one experiment, that if either side to a controversy between railroad employers and employees is not willing to submit the differences to mediation, that effectually bars any conciliation?—A. Yes. To put it in another way, if the railways generally, when application is made under the terms of this law, take the position which the carriers in this instance took, that they will not even accept the tender of mediation, of course nothing can be accomplished under the law.

Q. If I remember, you said that the reason assigned for that was that this was so vital a matter that they could not afford to submit. Is that a brief statement of it?—A. That was the position of the carriers—that in view of the very large percentage of their earnings which goes to employees, they regarded the question of wages as so vital to their financial solvency that they could not relinquish exclusive jurisdiction over that subject.

Q. Have you given any consideration to the question of compulsory arbitration?—A. Only in the most general way.

In further answer to the question you asked me a moment ago, as to whether this law can be improved in any way, and without proposing to suggest any respect in which it can be profitably amended, I venture to make this comment upon the theory and plan of that enactment. It seems to me that the practical result will be in every case, even where the tender of mediation is accepted, either to bring about a settlement by methods of conciliation or a refusal to arbitrate. In other words, if the Commissioner of Labor and the chairman of the Interstate Commerce Commission, acting upon an application of this sort, enter into communication with the railroad management interested and do not succeed in bringing about an adjustment of the difficulty by that friendly mediation which, of course, would involve conferences now with one side, now with the other, and a most informal and at the same time most exhaustive examination of all the facts and circumstances in the case—if that does not result in a settlement, naturally the carrier would refuse to arbitrate for the reason that, as each side to the controversy would select one arbitrator, and as the third, who would ordinarily be the determining factor, is to be chosen by the Commissioner of Labor and the chairman of the Interstate Commerce Commission, if the first two chosen did not agree, it would hardly be expected that the third arbitrator would entertain a different view of the situation from the view taken by the chairman of the Interstate Commerce Commission and the Commissioner of Labor in the first instance, and therefore that the carrier or the employee would not accept any other result than to act on the recommendation of the officials in the first instance. As to whether the law can be improved in that respect I do not now undertake to say.

Q. Does not that view, if it is correct, bring that legislation down to a very unimportant position as a factor in the settlement of such troubles?—A. It certainly does; as I said, if the railroads generally take the position which was taken in this instance, that they will not accept the mediation provided by the statute.

Q. I am referring to your last remark in regard to the statement that you do not think it will ever reach beyond the period of conciliation; it will never reach arbitration.—A. I make that suggestion. It seems to me, in the nature of the case, if the method of settlement which this law contemplates is accepted by both parties, either there will be an adjustment as a result of the mediation of the officials charged with that duty, or a refusal to arbitrate, which would leave the matter just where it was at the outset; in other words, you come then to the question whether there can be any compulsory arbitration.

Q. I understand that you have not given that question sufficient consideration to justify you in expressing an opinion. Is there anything else on this branch of the subject that you care to state?—A. I observe that one of the subdivisions of this Part I relates to safety appliances. I can add nothing of value to what appears in the more recent reports of the commission to Congress, and to the statistical information, which will be placed at your disposal by our secretary, showing the present state of railway equipment.

Q. Under those statements it appears, I believe, that there has been considerable advance in the application of these safety appliances to railroads in the past, since the passage of that act?—A. Oh, a very rapid advance.

Q. And I also understand that, of course, we will have the fact in a statistical form, but I would like to have you state it. It is also a fact that there has been a very decided decrease in the fatalities and casualties to employees?—A. I think that is a justifiable inference from the data we collect. Of course, this should be borne in mind: During the period of transition from the old link-and-pin coupler to the automatic device, the danger in making couplings between a car that is automatic and one that is not is probably somewhat increased. Then there is further the want of familiar acquaintance, on the part of employees, with the new devices; and very recently our attention has been informally brought to a somewhat interesting feature of that subject, which is this, that a part of the automatic-coupling device which consists of what is known as the releasing rig, the lever to be used by the employees to avoid the necessity of going between the cars, either by reason of improper construction or imperfect adjustment, frequently gets out of order, and therefore the trainman is unable to unlock cars which are coupled by the automatic coupler without going between the cars, and sometimes the lever will not remain in position without being held there, which would compel the trainman, of course, to walk along if the train was moving, both of which things, of course, are quite as dangerous, and perhaps the former is more dangerous than the conditions which existed under the old link-and-pin coupler. So that until we get an automatic coupler in very general use, with all its appliances in perfect condition, so that they will operate according to their design, we can not certainly tell to what extent it will prove a life and limb saving device. My belief is that when those conditions are realized the loss of life and injury to employees will be very greatly reduced.

Q. Well, the air brake has advanced *pari passu* with the coupling, has it not, in being applied to freight cars?—A. Broadly speaking, I think that is the fact. The present indications are that by the 1st of January the safety appliances will be so nearly completed or applied to so large a percentage of the cars that there will be no application for an extension of the time for completing that equipment, and that pretty much all of the equipment engaged in interstate transportation will be equipped in accordance with the provisions of this law.

Q. Now, those two branches I believe you have disposed of. Will you take up now the question of discriminations, and in the first place will you state whether or not, in your judgment, discriminations are practiced by railroads in this country?— A. Undoubtedly, at the present time.

Q. In what form or method is the discrimination against individuals most usually practiced?—A. Well, generally speaking, of course, by some secret arrangement which results in one person getting a more favorable rate of transportation than another person under the same conditions. The methods by which that result can be accomplished are limitless. I think it can be fairly stated at the present time that the instance of the actual repayment, to the shipper, of rebates is comparatively rare. Where concessions of the sort I am now referring to are made, they are brought about in some other way.

Q. Why should there be a cessation of the rebate system and the continuance of other systems? Is it because the rebate system is more open and more liable to detection than the other methods?—A. That is doubtless the controlling reason. Of course the law specifically prohibits transactions of that kind, as, indeed, it aims to prohibit all methods which practically accomplish the same result. And just now, as you are probably all aware, nearly every railroad in the country has all the business it can do. The necessity, therefore, to secure business by making concessions is not as great as it is when the volume of traffic is below the present standard. And then rates generally have been very much reduced, so that the margin of concessions which can be made and leave any profit at all to the carrier or any justification to the carrier for taking the traffic is in many cases and in a large part of the country exceedingly small. Then, I think I am warranted in saying that, through voluntary action and perhaps a better recognition of duty to the law and to the public, unusual efforts have been made during the last year by railroad officers to observe tariff rates.

Q. You speak of concessions. Could you mention specifically some of the different forms or any form in which concessions are made other than the rebate? We would like to get hold of some practical illustration of how such things are done.— A. As I said, the possibilities in that direction are almost unlimited. I hardly know where to begin to illustrate the range of methods which would have the result of giving one person better rates than others. Sometimes it is said that where a given road is largely engaged both in State and interstate business, as most of them are, they observe rigidly their interstate rates and secure business by making concessions to shippers on purely State traffic. That, you can see, is a wide opportunity.

Q. (By Professor JOHNSON.) I do not mean to ask you to state them, but I would like to ask you if you know that such instances actually exist?—A. In the nature of the case, I can have no such official knowledge. I can only say that such information comes to me as leads me to believe that what amounts to such concessions are made in that way. Then, of course, through the payment of commissions, through the purchase of supplies, the variety of ways is almost unlimited.

Q. (By Senator MALLORY.) Have you ever heard it said that there is any considerable discrimination effected by means of false weighing or improper weighing?— A. Oh, yes.

Q. Of bulk goods?—A. Oh, yes. The infirmity of human nature finds expression in that way very frequently.

Q. Well, have you had your attention called to any one of these various methods of concessions that seem to be more common, more usually practiced than any other?—A. Well, passing for the moment, then, to discriminations which are effected by such devices as false billing, false weighing, misdescription of goods, our information shows many instances in which practices of that kind have been indulged in. In fact, it is a matter of more or less public knowledge that several parties are now under indictment for misdescription of goods. As, for example, a large hardware house, having very extensive dealings over a large section of the country, ships a carload of goods described as nails, if you please, which are taken at a comparatively low rate. That car, upon examination, would be found to contain shelf hardware, fine cutlery, tools, and various other commodities which, if carried according to the classification, would bear a much higher rate.

Q. And that is done in single instances to the detriment of others, is it?—A. Undoubtedly. To illustrate, and without mentioning names or places, which I assume you do not care to know about, complaint came from one great trade center in the country, where there are numerous houses dealing in that general class of merchandise, that their trade in a certain section of the country was materially affected and injured by practices of their rivals at another trade center sending goods into the same consuming territory under false billing and false weighing; and without going into details, I think there were circumstances in that case which justified the accusation.

Q. As a general rule, why is it that one party is discriminated against and another is discriminated in favor of; what consideration is there for that distinction?—A. The general answer to the question is the competition between the carriers. Where two or more rival roads are actively competing for the carriage of goods from one producing section to another consuming section, or between any two great centers of trade, and there is not business enough for them all, it is a natural, if not an inevitable, result that efforts will be made by each of them to a greater or less extent to secure business by some sort of concessions. In other words, the competition between the carriers is the excuse always advanced, and probably the actual reason in nearly every instance for the discriminations which occur. I have no knowledge of any instances in which discriminations of that sort were made by arbitrary action of the carrier—that is, through any desire to help one man or injure another. That may have influenced concessions in incidental cases, but ordinarily, I think, it is the competition between the carriers and the necessity which they avow of getting business which leads to these secret practices. Of course, coupled with that all the while is also the sharp competition between different producing and consuming territories.

Q. Well, then, according to your view of it, in prosperous times, when the railroads have about all they can do, naturally there is less of this than there is when times are dull and they have to hustle for trade?—A. That we should all expect to happen, and that does happen.

Q. Can you give us some idea of how discriminations between places are carried on or practiced?—A. Let me approach an answer to that general question by a preliminary statement. I think it is well to keep in mind, and perhaps to emphasize, a point which seems to me often lost sight of, and that is the difference between those discriminations which are effected as between individuals through concessions from the published rates and those discriminations between communities or commodities which result although the published rate is rigidly enforced. What we ordinarily mean by individual discriminations—that is to say, the circumstances under which a shipper at a given place gets more favorable rates than his rival at that place—are always brought about by some departure from the published tariff. Of course there is the open rate appearing upon the tariffs of all the roads; everybody knows what it is, and therefore if one person is favored against the others that means, of course, that that person gets something off or something below the published tariff, and, as you all understand, there may be the most rigid and absolute observance of the published tariffs and yet the most serious discrimination result because the tariffs themselves are improperly or unfairly adjusted as between different communities or different articles of traffic.

Q. In the case of discriminations against individuals, as I understand it, it is by reason of the nonobservance of the tariff rates which may be adjusted?—A. Yes.

Q. And in the other, it is by the observance of an unfair tariff?—A. Precisely. You may have a perfectly just tariff, just as between communities, as between individuals, as between commodities; and then injustice may result from departures from that tariff. You may have perfect observance of tariffs and yet great injustice because the tariffs themselves do not fairly and equitably adjust the burdens of transportation as between different communities or different articles of traffic.

Q. Can you give us an illustration, from your experience, the past experience of the commission, of a case of that kind, of discrimination between places? I am speaking now of flagrant discrimination, something that is palpably a discrimination in favor of one place as against another on the line of a railroad.—A. Well, I venture to take a situation that is pretty well known as an illustration. For many years there has been a basis of rates from the Atlantic seaboard, the great manufacturing territory of the country, to the western cities of distribution or consumption, so that the rates from, say, New York, for example, to Chicago and St. Louis and Kansas City, are adjusted with reference to each other with, I may say, a fair recognition of distance and other conditions of locality; and it so happens that the rate on first-class goods from New York City, all rail, to Kansas City is, I think, $1.47, and proportionately less to St. Louis and Chicago; and on that general basis all the rates over the most important section of the country are adjusted; and you can readily see that the maintenance of rates in particular localities depends upon maintaining the general basis of rates, otherwise the whole transportation system would be thrown into disorder. Now, not long ago there was constructed what is known as the Kansas City, Pittsburg and Gulf road, running almost directly from Kansas City to the Gulf of Mexico. That road became insolvent and receivers were appointed.

That railroad, in connection with the Mallory Steamship Line, which takes goods from New York to Galveston, after various intermediate reductions, finally put in a rate from New York City to Kansas City at 80 cents as against $1.47 by the all-rail lines, with the result that a very considerable amount of traffic moved by a circuitous route approximately $2\frac{1}{2}$ times as long as the direct route, making, of course, higher rates from New York to St. Louis and from New York to Chicago than from New York to Kansas City, a condition which, in a way, is illogical, and so, of course, can not permanently continue. I am not saying now whether the interested carriers were justified or not; that is not the point; but the effect, of course, was to bring about discriminating rates between the greatest trade centers of the country, because any-one can see that the rate from New York to Kansas City should not be lower than the rate from New York to St. Louis or from New York to Chicago. And yet during the last three or four months that has been the actual condition, that a very con-siderable amount of traffic has gone from New York to Kansas City, by way of Gal-veston, at a rate only a little more than half the standard rail rate from New York to that city.

Q. Can you say what conditions brought that about?—A. Well, I only know the excuse which, I understand, is put forward by the receivers of that road. They insist that they were entitled to what is known as a differential; that is, by reason of their circuitous route, the greater length of time which it would require to take traffic from New York to Kansas City by that route, the cost of marine insurance, and all that sort of thing, they could not get any of the business at the same rates as the all-rail lines; and therefore they ought to be allowed to charge somewhat less, with a view of getting what they claimed was their share of the business. And it was the refusal of the other lines, the all-rail lines, to concede the differential claimed which led them to get the differential by force. I may add, for your information, that by recent action of Judge Thayer, who appointed these receivers, they have been ordered to restore the rates which existed at the time this controversy arose. Of course, all that was complicated, and I mention it to illustrate the intricacies of the whole situation; that is, the water lines down to Savannah and Charleston and then the rail lines from there across the country to the same destination.

Take another illustration drawn from a very recent investigation and which, very likely, Commissioner Prouty will speak on more fully in some of its other aspects. We have been investigating the exports of grain and grain products, and the fact appeared that in some instances and through some of the gateways, through some of the ports, the rate on flour exported was often as high as 11 cents per 100 pounds above the rate on wheat. Now, obviously, if there is any such difference as that or anything approximating such a difference between the rates on exported wheat and exported flour, there can be no exportation of flour, and of course the mills and millers of the country who have large investments and large capacity for supplying the foreign demand for flour would be, if that state of things continued, entirely shut out of the business and the exportation would go abroad in the form of wheat and the flour would be made by the foreign miller rather than the domestic miller, and yet all those discriminations, as you see, can be accomplished with absolute adher-ence to published rates. They were not, as a matter of fact, in this case; but that is quite possible. Of course I assume that you are all perfectly familiar with that class of discriminations which has been the subject of repeated and grievous complaint which results from the disregard of what is known as the long and short haul clause. The act to regulate commerce contemplated that carriers subject to its provision should not in any case charge more for a short distance than for a long distance in the same direction, where the short distance was included in the long distance, except under conditions which would warrant the commission in allowing that exemption from the general rule. Well, without going into that subject, because I could spend a whole session talking about it, the Supreme Court has construed that section or provision of the act in such a way as to make it substantially nugatory, and as a matter of fact, especially in the territory south of the Potomac and east of the Missis-sippi River, the injury to small towns which results from higher rates to them from the great centers of production than to the larger cities of the South more distant, has been serious and is still serious. To a great extent similar conditions exist with refer-ence to the transcontinental traffic, rates all rail to the Pacific-coast terminals being ordinarily much higher than to many places in the interior. Of course the justifica-tion put forward in all those cases is the competition of water carriers and the neces-sity, often actually a justification fairly satisfactory in many instances, that they must approximate the rates of the water carrier or else they can not get any of the busi-ness. But whatever may be their necessity or justification, the fact remains that the interior town is put at a serious and often at a fatal disadvantage.

Q. There is a species of discrimination to which my attention has been called which you have not mentioned exactly; at least, I do not think it falls under any of these heads; and that is the charging of different rates over the same road in different directions, on the same line of road. For instance, from my State, Florida, up to New York, and the same cars coming back, there is a different rate per hundred charged?—A. Oh, yes.

Q. Now, the excuse that is offered for that, the reason, as I understand it, is that they have to bring the cars back anyhow; they have to get down South from here, and it is better to get something than nothing for it. Have you had occasion to consider the validity of that excuse or reason?—A. Oh, yes, in numerous cases; that is, to consider the general question which that situation raises. I recollect, without being able to give exact figures, an investigation in which it appeared that a certain railroad system charged a good deal more for carrying petroleum products south bound in tank cars to certain interior destinations than it charged for carrying cottonseed oil, a much more valuable product, in the contrary direction in the same cars.

Q. Now the reason, I suppose, is the same in that case as it was in the one to which I referred. Is that, in your judgment, a sufficiently strong reason to justify the discriminations which are practiced?—A. I do not hesitate to say that I do not think it is sufficient. Of course, gentlemen, you all understand, I assume that it depends on the point of view. If you accept railroad transportation as a purely private enterprise, to be conducted like a farm or factory, then the financial interest of the carrier may justly lead it to many and obvious discriminations; but if you say, as I think we are all now disposed to say and presently everybody will say, that railroad transportation is not a commodity, not a private enterprise, but purely a public service, and that public rights are to be considered at least equally with the rights of the carriers, then, of course, the asserted justification often entirely fails, and discriminations, which might be excused on the theory of private enterprise, become palpably insufficient and inadequate when you contemplate the railroad system as an agency of the State.

Q. Of course, I do not undertake to cover all these various kinds; but there is another species of discrimination which I would like to hear something from you on, as to its character and its extent, and that is the granting of free passes. You say that you know of no instance, or if there are instances they are very few, in which individuals are discriminated against because of their personality or discriminated in favor of because of their personality. The matter of granting passes to individuals over their roads by the railroads of this country, as I understand it, is a very general practice?—A. Your question very properly implies a criticism upon my general statement, which was designed to apply to rates of transportation of freight.

Q. I did not intend any criticism.—A. I know you did not; but I ought to have modified it in the direction of freight. Undoubtedly, when it comes to granting free passenger transportation the action of the carriers is in a sense arbitrary; of course, doubtless always influenced by considerations of self-interest. They presumably expect that they will receive corresponding advantages, or at least they find themselves placed in a situation where they can not well afford to refuse, as they think, the demands for free transportation. Of course, that is not an evil of the first magnitude as compared with the other subjects to which I have alluded, and yet it is one of very considerable importance, and one which in my judgment is without any excuse.

Q. It is the abuse of the principle more than anything else, of the principle that railway rates should be equal and fair in their application to the individual?—A. To give an illustration to the extent to which that sometimes occurs, although the general conditions are nothing like what this instance would indicate, a gentleman told me that on one occasion he came from Chicago to Washington just along in the latter days of November, and every other passenger in the Pullman car, besides himself, was a member of Congress or other Government official, with their families, and that he was the only passenger who paid a cent for transportation from Chicago to Washington, either for his passage or for his Pullman car.

Q. (By Mr. FARQUHAR.) Is there any remedy for such a condition of things that you could suggest?—A. Well, I should despair, Mr. Chairman, if there was not a remedy for what I regard as so grievous an injustice.

Q. Is it not a fact that this class of discrimination against the paying passenger is usually extended by free passes to all the legislatures of the State and to Congress itself?—A. Well, it is a general fact, as I understand, that representatives both in the State and National legislatures are very generally, if not always, offered free transportation. I am aware that it is not accepted in all cases.

Q. After the passage of the interstate commerce bill, was it not a fact that all the passes that had been issued to members of Congress and legislatures were taken in by the roads?—A. I do not know what the fact was in that regard. I was not a member of the commission until several years after; but I have some sympathy with the view which is expressed in some such fashion as this, that the law is used by the railroads when they do not want to give free transportation, and when they do want to do it they find a way to do it.

Q. Is the usual plan adopted by the railroads of issuing passes for newspapers or newspaper men?—A. Oh, that is one of the forms which the transaction takes.

Q. Also for advertising?—A. Yes, a pass that permits of free transportation in some way is furnished ostensibly for newspapers as consideration for advertising their time tables, etc., and then the recipients of these favors distribute them to their friends. And then I happen to know in many cases that passes are given which on their face are limited to transportation within the State, there being, except in some States, I think, no law against it; so that if a person is fortunate enough to have passes of that character covering the territory of one, two, or a dozen States through which he desires to go, why, he finds a method of getting himself carried without paying much, although he may have no pass for the whole journey.

Q. Has your commission ever investigated how far the pass system enters into the passenger system of the country; that is, the proportion of passes to the paid fares?—A. No.

Q. Not even one small case?—A. Not with a result which would enable me to answer your present question, or showing the percentage. It is very difficult to estimate. There are free passes of all the sorts that have been alluded to and perhaps some others. There is the free transportation given sometimes to the shippers as a consideration for getting their business; there are reduced rates for round-trip tickets, which are manipulated through the scalping offices. It would be impossible to say to what extent that results in diminished revenue to the carrier. I have heard it claimed—I know nothing about it, and make the statement only on that information—that probably the actual revenues received by all the railroads of the country from their passenger business did not exceed 75 or 80 per cent of what they would be at the published rates multiplied by the journeys actually taken.

Q. If it would be possible to abolish this pass system, which is just as bad a discrimination as the freight, in fact worse, what effect do you think it would have on the cash fare—would it lower the rates of a paying passenger or would not the railroads charge the same, taking the usufruct of the whole for themselves?—A. What would result I can not say.

Q. What would be your opinion, in your Interstate Commerce Commission, about a question of that kind?—A. I should feel warranted in answering your question this way: If we could eliminate the free transportation and bring this public service down to the impartial conditions where every person who uses it pays his proper share, I believe the passenger rates throughout the country could be materially reduced and still the railroads have better returns from that branch of their service than they have at the present time.

Q. Is it possible to amend the interstate commerce bill to abolish passes?—A. I think so, surely, and a good many other things that now occur.

Q. (By Mr. RATCHFORD.) Is it not a fact that professional men and ministers of the gospel usually are provided with passes?—A. I am not aware that professional men as a class ordinarily receive any concessions, but clergymen as a rule get half rates.

Q. (By Mr. KENNEDY.) Does the practice extend to Federal and State judiciary and district attorneys?—A. I do not know. I think the practice is diverse. My opinion is that in many sections of the country the judiciary, both Federal and State, have free transportation. In some cases it is not accepted. In some States it is prohibited, in others it is in a way recognized as one of the perquisites and emoluments of the office.

Q. (By Professor JOHNSON.) It was testified before your commission by an officer of the Louisville and Nashville that his railroad gave passes to judicial officers.—A. Yes; but there is no such general practice, I mean to say, as corresponds with the arrangement in which clergymen get half rates. That is quite universal.

Q. (By Mr. RATCHFORD.) What can be the motive of that?—A. In the case of clergymen?

Q. Yes. What is the motive of the railroad?—A. Broadly stated, charity; consideration for their profession; benevolence, and, presumably, unselfish. It is in harmony with the general sentiment and action which prevails that gives concessions to the clergy in other directions.

Q. It would seem, then, the transportation companies, in giving passes and discriminating rates, have motives other than unselfish motives in some cases?—A. Oh, yes. So far as a corporation can be unselfish, I think railroads are as corporations unselfish.

Q. (By Mr. FARQUHAR.) Is it not a fact also that the parties who apply for passes may have some claim on the railroad—for instance, boards of assessors in cities, aldermen, councilmen, and sealers of weights and measures, clear down to the rodmen who belong to the engineering department—and while they have a pull, as it is popularly called, that pass is usually handed to anybody and everybody having no rights whatever to free transportation?—A. That may be the case, but I do not know of any such instances.

Q. Have you ever had before your commission any question of that kind regarding the class of people who really do receive passes—the list that was published by order of the Senate through request of Senator Chandler with respect to a road in New England?—A. Oh, yes; there was an investigation in the case of the Boston and Maine Railroad, and they were required to disclose to the commission the classes of persons to whom they gave free transportation. That investigation was published at the time and was afterwards, as you mention, published by some resolution introduced by Senator Chandler. I should take pleasure in furnishing a report of the commission in that case, and I might say that is a fairly typical case.

Q. Could you succinctly state it to the commission now—the facts?—A. The statute contemplates a state of things in that regard which if realized would express the view of the commission, unless I should say the statute does not go far enough. It seems to me the permission of law giving to one railroad the right to carry employees of another railroad free is a privilege which results in abuse.

Q. (By Mr. PHILLIPS.) Are there not a number of leading central points that are made equal, and shippers ship business through intermediate points to that point, beyond, and then reship perhaps 100 or more miles back in order to get a reduced rate, when the railroad would not stop the freight at the point?—A. Oh, yes—the situation which results from what is called the long and short haul clause. In such cases the general plan on which rates are made is this: The rate to the interior and noncompetitive point increases gradually with distance until it comes to a point where it equalizes the lower through rate plus the local back from that destination to the point in question. Of course they can not make it any higher, because otherwise they would ship through and ship back. The rates to these interior points, as a matter of fact, are equivalent to the through rate plus the local back. Of course the shipment does not go through. It is stopped off at its actual destination.

Q. (By Senator MALLORY.) Has your attention been called to the fact, in connection with the subject of discrimination, that certain railroads are going into other business than railroading and transportation per se; engaging in mercantile business, by the formation of companies in which their directors are the directors, separate and distinct, working in with the railroads?—A. I have no special information on this line. In a general way I think more or less of that thing occurs, but of course that is a natural outcome of existing conditions. It is asserted that there are instances in which the officers and managers of railroads have been interested in the development of towns through the personal ownership of land and in some particular line of business in which they were stockholders or otherwise interested, and that rates have been adjusted with a view of favoring those localities or those industries. That is a perfectly natural outcome, and undoubtedly things of that kind have occurred frequently.

Q. Has your attention been called to the concrete case of railroads combining or associating with or owning elevators—grain elevators—in Chicago and controlling the business of the elevator?—A. Yes; we have some information on that subject; but, if it is agreeable to you, may I suggest that you interrogate Commissioner Prouty, who is to follow me as a witness, and who is more familiar with the particular facts in that direction than I am.

Q. (By Mr. KENNEDY.) You stated it was possible to abolish this system of giving passes and stopped there. Would you state to the commission what you would suggest as an amendment to the interstate-commerce law to carry out that suggestion?—A. The best answer I can give to that question is to refer you to what the commission has stated in its last two annual reports to Congress and the recommendations which are put in the form of proposed amendments which appear in these reports. I am perfectly willing to express my own views, but they have been stated in these reports and in these recommendations with deliberation and with the attempt to be accurate, and reference to them would, I think perhaps, be more satisfactory to you than anything I could now say on the spur of the moment.

Q. Can you say briefly what these recommendations are?—A. That would lead us into a pretty long chapter; we should have to start at the beginning. It is apparent that any system of railway regulation begins with the requirement that the carrier publish its rates. I can not conceive of any legislation which amounts to anything or which purports to accomplish anything in the way of railway regulation that would not require as the foundation a publication of tariffs; the announcement to the public of the charges which the railroad proposes to apply. Now, starting with that proposition, which I think commends itself to the intelligent reflection of everybody, you have two general classes of questions immediately arising. One question is, How are you going to secure the observance by the carriers of the published rate? How are you going to prevent departures from it? How are you going to put a stop to these individual discriminations which result in one individual obtaining the same service on more reasonable terms than another individual in like situation? Now, I do not know any way to handle that question except the way the present law proposes—that such transgressions are criminal misdemeanors and to be punished as such, because any civil remedy would be entirely unavailing. No suit for damages would be brought because the amount involved in any particular case is so inconsequential as to afford no remedy whatever; therefore we can only do what this law seeks to do—that is to say, treat transgressions of that kind as criminal violations of the penal law, to be punished as such; and I think that is a proposition which we must all accept in any view or any theory of public regulation. Now, that being so, the moment you say a transgression of that kind is a misdemeanor, you are obliged to treat it just as you would any other sort of criminal offense. You can not have any special way of dealing with it, and, therefore, a misdemeanor that comes from giving rebates would be prosecuted in the same way, by the same tribunals, as a misdemeanor under the postal, revenue, or any other laws of the United States—indictment, trial by jury, and all that sort of thing. Now, I conceive that more exact and unambiguous statements of the duty of the carrier to publish its rates (for the present law is very crude and imperfect in that respect), coupled with exact and determinable penalties for disregarding that duty, would help very materially to put a stop to the discriminations of that nature. Of course I do not hesitate to express here an opinion which I have long entertained. We shall not, in point of fact, under any system of laws secure exemption from injustice of that character as long as we attempt to keep up the compulsory competition of railroad carriers, which laws—mistaken, in my judgment—we now attempt to enforce. In other words, they create conditions which the necessities of human nature will compel to result in discriminations of the sort which we have now under consideration.

Q. (By Senator MALLORY.) That compulsory competition—do you mean by that the law which prohibits pooling?—A. Yes, and the antitrust law.

Q. You think the repeal of that clause would be conducive to fairer treatment of the public by the railroads?—A. I do, indeed.

Q. Has the commission made such recommendation?—A. Not as a commission; not exactly that recommendation. The commission's views, deliberately expressed, as I have stated, on that subject appear in these reports to Congress. I do not wish to be misunderstood on this point. While I believe these laws in their application to railroad transportation are unwise and against public interest, against the general good of the average citizen, I am not in favor of repealing them without at the same time having legislation which will enable the public to prevent a greater evil which exists or might exist under changed conditions.

Q. Your idea is that the repeal of the antitrust law and antipooling clause of the interstate-commerce law would be a long step in the direction of securing more equitable treatment of the public and individuals by the transportation companies. In addition to that you also would be in favor of specifically making misdemeanors of the violations of the law?—A. That is it. I put the two things together. I believe that rights of contract with each other which are now denied and prohibited ought to be granted to the railroad carriers, because they are engaged in a public service; but as a part of any such scheme of legislation I want a much more accurate and comprehensive definition of their legal duties, and a grant of power to the public authority, whether represented by a commission or some other tribunal, to prevent any abuse of the privilege.

Q. A supervisory power over the right to contract?—Yes, or over the results of the contract, which is the rates. That is a matter the public is interested in.

Q. As a matter of detail in regard to this provision for punishing infractions, on whom would you impose the penalty? Railroad employees are generally simply agents for their superior. Would there not be some question there as to justice, if you impose the penalty upon the man who actually committed the act and did it at the instance of a superior?—A. Plainly enough, the corporations ought to be indictable and punishable, and that is one of the glaring imperfections of the present law, that the corporation, which is the principal, which is the real offender, is not amenable to criminal process, but only the agent or representative of that corporation.

Q. (By Professor JOHNSON.) In addition to what you have already stated on discrimination, I think the commission would like to hear you state concisely the class of shippers that under existing conditions are most favored as a result of these discriminations.—A. It is doubtful whether I can add anything to what is commonly known on that subject. In the nature of the case it must happen where railroads are in actual and sharp competition with each other that the shipper whose business is of the most consequence or largest in volume is the one whose favor is likely to be secured.

Q. Let me put my question a little more concretely: Is it the meat packer and miller, or the wholesale grain dealer—are those classes now receiving special favors?—A. Undoubtedly.

Q. The favors, then, do not go to the benefit of the consuming public or to the general producing public?—A. No; and if I might be allowed to digress a moment or enlarge a little on what I have tried to say, it all depends on the point of view and on the ends that we seek to secure. Now, there seems to be a vague popular notion that the public generally gets the same benefit from the competition of railroads that it gets from the competition of farmers or manufacturers, but I think that is a very mistaken idea. The industries and occupations of the world are so distributed that what we call competition results to pretty nearly equal advantage everywhere and to every person. If the resident of a remote hamlet thinks the crossroads merchant charges him more than he ought to, there is another little store only a mile or two away where he can get the same article. Generally speaking, competitive conditions are so general, so diversified, so complete all over that when it comes to the articles of use, wear, and consumption one man is not charged much more than another in purchasing the same thing at the same place; but when it comes to this railroad service, a moment's reflection shows you that only a small portion of territory and only a small portion of the population are so situated that they can have the benefit of railroad competition. Competition, it seems to me, objectively considered, is simply the power to choose between two or more persons who can furnish the same article; that is the objective value of competition to him. As I said, there are only a few people comparatively who have any actual choice between railroad carriers. To much the largest number of people in this country, by far the largest number, and throughout the greatest part of its territory, railroad service is and always has been an actual monopoly, and the result of the competition which grows out of rival railroads gives this opportunity for choice only to a few persons in some of the great centers. Now, if I may be permitted to suggest a further word, which will give you some information of the way I look at this matter from an economic point of view—as I said before, I want not only to consider the point of view, but the result to be accomplished. Now, I want to say this: First, on what I call actual property—I mean the things we eat, use, and wear, the products of human labor and skill—possibly some of us do, but I do not want uniform prices under present conditions. We want every producer to be perfectly free to get just as much as he can for anything he has to sell, and we want every consumer to be perfectly free to buy everything he wants as cheap as he can. We want the utmost freedom of contract between buyer and seller in everything that relates to property. Therefore, it seems to me, all those conditions which tend to abridge that freedom of contract, whether by controlling and limiting production, controlling markets, or in whatever ways which operate against the general good of the public, ought to be prevented, if they can be, because it seems to me this freedom of contract between buyer and seller of property is the very foundation of industrial freedom. I can not conceive of commercial liberty that does not involve that absolute freedom of contract; but when you come to railroad transportation, that is not property, but public service, which the State might lawfully do by its own direct agency, but which from motives of expediency only it commits to private corporations to perform, you do not want uniform prices; you do not want any freedom of contract at all; you want every person to get exactly the same advantage under like circumstances as every other person, therefore you want quite a different thing from what you want with respect to property; you want uniform charges; you want the burden of transportation to be just as nearly equal as possible on one person as on another. Therefore, all that tends under proper limitations to bring about absolute uniformity of charge and impartial treatment by those who perform a public service is a thing to be commended and encouraged by legislation. Why, gentlemen, it seems to me you can not have industrial freedom, commercial liberty in its full sense, without rates and charges for public transportation which are in the nature of monopoly. That is the thing that ought to be equal to everybody. That is the element which in no instance ought to cut any figure. So I say we mistake as to the results we desire to accomplish; we mistake the thing which would be to the general public benefit when we say those who are engaged in a purely public service shall not enter into contract relations with each other for the purpose of performing that service on terms of impartiality. I will put it in another way: Competition is simply discrimination. When you analyze that thing you call competition, what is it? Simply the right of every man who has a piece of property to sell to one man at one price, and to another man for another price, or to vary that price to the same person when he thinks best. Of course railroad service can not be conducted on any such principle. Look at the conditions to-day. Suppose you have 2 great department stores in a town which supply its trade. Now, suppose the law required of those 2 stores what it now requires of the railroads—first, that they should publish all their charges on every article that they sell and that they should not vary the price to increase it without 10 days' notice, or reduce it without 3 days' notice; and suppose, in addition to that, it was made a criminal offense for them to vary on any article under any circumstances; and suppose they were required to report every year their capital, earnings, number of employees, wages, dividends, and all that sort of thing. Under that would there be any competition? If there was, it would be a competition in violation of that law which required them never to charge, in violation of their published rates; and that is the sort of competition we get now in railroad service. When tariff rates are actually and rigidly observed in all cases, there is no competition in rates; and when there is competition in rates it is when private concessions are made which result in giving one man an advantage over another. I do not mean to say that competition between carriers has not been a most powerful influence in bringing down the charges for railroad transportation to their present low level. Undeniably it has, and I am not at all suggesting that they should be allowed indefinitely and at pleasure to combine with each other without restrictions and conditions which give public authority adequate control over their rates and charges; but I do mean to say that you will not get that impartial treatment which every person is entitled to have and at the same time actual competition between the carriers.

I want to add another thought, which lies at the bottom of the whole thing; I do not ride on the railroad by virtue of any contract, but I use the agencies of the public carrier in the exercise of my political rights. I have just as much right to ride on the cars as I have to be protected in my person and property by the police administration; just as much right as I have to submit any controversy to the adjudication of our legal tribunals. I can not be excluded. The relations between railroads and patrons are not contract relations; the ticket is not evidence of a bargain; it is more in the nature of a tax receipt; it shows I have paid money which any person might pay and get the same service, and from which no person can be excluded. The merchant who sells goods has a right to stand on his threshold and say I can not enter his store. He has a right to refuse to sell me goods. He has a right to make one price to me and another to my neighbor at the same moment, but no railroad man can stand in his station and say I can not enter or say I shall not have all the privileges of service which his company can offer on exactly the same terms as any other man. I say you can not practically have that and at the same time have that actual constant competition which goes on in the industrial world.

Q. (By Senator MALLORY.) I think it is generally conceded that the popular position in the United States against permitting railroads to pool is based on the apprehension that they will utilize it to increase rates exorbitantly. Is not your understanding that that is the objection?—A. Yes; and I may be permitted to say again: We bear a good deal about trusts and combinations these days, and I do not care to go into that subject, but there is another thought which may be perhaps worth considering. We find no way, under our free government and consistent with constitutional liberty, to control the prices of property by direct legislation. Now, I suppose the objection to that tendency, which is now so marked, is possibly, so far as it is intelligent and thoughtful, based on the belief that these combinations do, or the apprehension that they will, use their power in such a way as to compel the consuming communities to pay more than they ought to and more than they otherwise would. We can not control the price at which they shall sell anything, because even if we could fix the prices we could not compel them to sell any more than we could compel the consumer to buy. As long as we can not fix the price we try by indirect methods to accomplish the same result. We try to prevent the combination. I am not saying whether that is right or wrong. It is not my province to enlarge on that phase of the economic question. The point I wish to make is that when it comes to public service, like railroad transportation, we can go right to the end we aim at and fix the prices. It is entirely competent for the State legislature and for Congress by direct legislation to say how much any carrier shall charge on any commodity or between any places. Of course that power is subject to the same limitations which is put by the Constitution on all legislation, that no man's property shall be taken without due process of law and that every man shall have the equal protection of the laws. But under these limitations the power of Congress over interstate, and State legislatures over State traffic is plenary and exclusive. Therefore the objections to the railway combinations which apply to the industrial combinations have no foundation, because we can prevent any excesses or abuses of railway combination by direct legislation, because we have the authority to do it, unquestioned and ample.

Q. That is what I wanted to get at. The apprehension of the people of the United States, when this subject of pooling is brought up in Congress, is that by allowing them to combine and form pools they would put up rates exorbitantly, and thereby become oppressive. If they could be permitted to pool, and at the same time a lawmaking power be authorized to impose such wholesome restrictions upon extravagant rates as would insure reasonable rates, is it not your opinion that if the people could be brought to understand that they would acquiesce in it in view of the very manifest necessity for our giving some opening at least for them to make their own rates?—A. I do not at all doubt that is so. I think unless this question is clearly comprehended, unless it is comprehended by the ordinary man, what my distinguished predecessor, Judge Morrison, used to describe as the "low-down man"—if his interests are to be consulted, if his welfare is to be promoted, so far as it depends on public transportation we will undertake the elimination of all discrimination and bring transportation charges to one uniform basis. Now, it is easy to enlarge on that and suggest that the objections to this combination are not well founded, but I have no disposition to go into that. I desire to put my opinion solely on my observation and judgment of what is for the benefit of the average man. I do not believe the antitrust law or the prohibition of pooling in the effort to regulate commerce has ever been of one penny's benefit to the farmer from Maine to Texas, the wage-earner or the crossroads dealer, or the man in the ordinary walks of life, but it has practically, almost necessarily, resulted in giving the capitalists at great centers advantages to which they are not entitled and which in a large measure accounts for their enormous accumulations.

Q. Do you think if Congress were to show a disposition to repeal the antipooling clause, and at the same time put some supervisory control in the hands of somebody, whether a commission or some other body, so as to see that they should not become oppressive, that it would be acceptable to the railroads of this country?—A. It is not easy to answer that question. I could easily excuse myself by saying I do not know. So far as I can perceive, there is a considerable difference of opinion among railroad men, and certain great railroad corporations are now in a position where they do not want any legislation for themselves, and they are therefore unwilling to have any legislation which will be presumably or actually in the public interest. You know very well in some sections of the country, by methods of consolidation, and one thing and another, what we observe elsewhere as to competition between railroad carriers has been practically eliminated. Where that has been the result, so far as my knowledge goes, not only have rates not been advanced, but they have been somewhat reduced; the service has been improved and impartial treatment has resulted to everybody. From these sections of the country the commission rarely gets a complaint now, where the railroads by consolidation (and this is a process very rapidly going on, and liable to continue)—where the railroads by consolidation get more or less exemption from these competitive conditions. They are no longer, in the nature of things, in favor of the repeal of the present laws, and of course those roads or influences which they command will not be likely to favor legislation which would give the commission or any other tribunal any greater control than they now have (which is not very great) over their practices or their charges. So, when you consider the practical aspect of legislation, and the attitude of railroad management toward the general plans of legislation, which perhaps I have in a way suggested, you find the roads which do not need the privileges on their side will be against it presumably, and only the roads which do need it will favor it. That is so with roads and systems of roads in such sharply competitive relations to each other as to threaten their financial integrity and their future prosperity, and they will submit to very drastic conditions under which they will be allowed to relieve themselves, but roads which do not need that relief, of course, are not likely to favor the establishment of any commission or tribunal to have actual control over their practices and their charges. Then, again, it must be considered in a general way that the greater combinations whose shipments are so enormous as to be of first consequence to carriers are not likely to favor any scheme of legislation which would enable the roads to combine with each other to stand up against their inducements. My own belief is that influences emanating from these sources have been more potent than any other to prevent the passage of what I believe to be legislation in the interests of the great body of the people. As an illustration of that, and it is a phase of that competition which you ought to take into serious account, take the discrimination effected by the use of private cars—shippers' cars. Here is a great concern, no matter of what sort or in what business. Its shipments amount to train loads a day. Instead of using the agencies which the carrier ordinarily provides, it builds its own cars—in some cases up to thousands or tens of thousands. Now, these cars are carried by the railroad ordinarily under what is known as a mileage contract, on the theory that the shipper has furnished the vehicle as well as the traffic. The railroad allows the shipper so much a mile for every mile that car is hauled. The result is, these cars being kept in active service, the mileage amounts to an enormous profit, not only on the cost of building the cars, but a very large profit on the business in which they are engaged.

Q. (By Professor JOHNSON.) In regard to the discriminations which result from traffic classifications, I think it will be a safe deduction from your testimony to say the establishment of a uniform classification by public authority would lessen discrimination to some extent?—A. I think so. We have now three general classifications: what is known as the official classification, covering trunk lines in the territory from the Atlantic seaboard north of the Potomac, west to the Mississippi or Chicago; the western classification, which takes in the territory west of the river; and the southern, which takes the territory south of the Potomac and east of the Mississippi River. These are diverse, and where commerce passes over one territory to another, with the result of change in the classification on the same article, the variation in charges frequently causes a discrimination. There should be but one classification.

Q. The placing of articles in classes in each of these classifications, I infer from what you state, often produces discrimination; articles are wrongly classed.—A. That brings up the whole question of relation of rates as between different commodities. If you divide the traffic into classes you must have a classification, which should be uniform; still the question is which class a given commodity shall take, because that will affect not only its rate but the relation of its rates to some other competing commodity. In the case of wheat and flour, the relation of rates between them will decide where the milling is to be done in this country, to say nothing about exports. If that disparity is inconsiderable, the milling will all be done pretty near the point of production; as it increases, the place of milling will be removed; and you could have such a relation as between wheat and flour, and it would not require a very great change. On so narrow a margin is that great business in flour and wheat transacted, it would not require such a great change to put a stop to the entire milling industry of Minneapolis. On account of the relation in rates the transformation of wheat into flour could be more advantageously and profitably effected along the eastern seaboard.

Q. Does not that condition of affairs exist at the present time? Is there not complaint, at the present time, on the part of the millers, as to the rates that have been fixed by the transportation lines, carrying wheat at a less rate than flour?—A. That is quite true, sir, though the complaint which has been the most pressed upon us of late relates mainly to export of both wheat and flour. Of course, there again you suggest a phase of the case which might be discussed indefinitely—what ought to be the relation of rates between export and domestic shipments. Is it the just thing that wheat and flour shall be carried across the Atlantic at a lower rate than it is carried to New York?

Q. (By Mr. RATCHFORD.) What is the general effect of a very low export rate on farm products?—A. If you will pardon me, I feel as though I had taken very much more time than I was warranted in taking, and Commissioner Prouty will follow me. It was he who wrote the report of the commission on this export investigation, and you are sure to get more valuable information from him than from myself.

Q. (By Mr. FARQUHAR.) Would you please answer in the case of discriminations? There are three parties interested—the producer, the shipper, and the consumer. Is it not a fact that the shipper gets the benefit of the discrimination entirely?—A. Well, that depends upon what you mean by the producer. If you take wheat, for example, I do not hesitate to say in my opinion the farmer, the man who actually raises the wheat, seldom gets any benefit from what you may call discrimination, and practically none at all from the competition between the railroad carriers, because he sells his wheat on a basis of the published tariffs, which presumably everybody pays, and generally the change or concession is made after he has parted with his wheat on that basis, and the commodity is concentrated in the hands of a few large dealers. Now, how far that results to the benefit of the consumer I am not able to say; but on the other hand, if you mean by the producer the great manufacturer, then it may be that the producer in that sense, who is also the shipper, gets the benefit of the discrimination. So these discriminations grow out of, as I have already stated, the relations of rates as between different localities, and that is a subject on which there could be indefinite inquiry and reflection. For example, if you have at Baltimore here some very large concerns making canned goods, and they are selling their product in the southern territory, and if at Pittsburg or Cincinnati there are some other very large concerns making canned goods and trying to sell them in the same territory, then if your adjustment of rates into that consuming territory, from Baltimore on the one hand and from Cincinnati on the other, is such as to give Baltimore an advantage, the Cincinnati dealer is practically shut out of that territory; and it does not matter, if the rate is actually observed, if it is an open rate to everybody, both from Cincinnati and from Baltimore, whether they become combined, or what you call a trust, having its plant at Baltimore, and being therefore the only producer at Baltimore—if the rates from Baltimore into the consuming territory are lower than they are from any other place where the same article is produced, the Baltimore producer, be he big or little, has practical control of that market.

Q. (By Mr. PHILLIPS.) Now, the newspaper press published a letter, probably the latter part of last year, which seemed to have been addressed to your commission from the receivers of the Baltimore and Ohio Railroad, from which it seems there had been discriminations up to that time, but they were to terminate on January 1, 1899. Did you or did you not receive such a letter?—A. We did; yes.

Q. Will you give us your views in regard to that?—A. Well, to fully explain all the circumstances connected with that communication, and the conditions out of which it arose, would require a recital of a considerable of recent railroad history. I said something in the early part of my examination about the absence of these secret discriminations, comparative absence of them at the present time, and perhaps it would not have been unfair to have mentioned this communication of the Baltimore and Ohio Railroad, and the attitude of that road at that time, as one of the influences which contributed to the improved state of things, aided by the enormous volume of traffic, and the other circumstances to which I alluded; but it is undeniably the fact, and so conceded by that railroad to be the fact, that it had allowed concessions which amounted to serious discriminations. I think the managers of that property, in connection with the managers of other great railroad systems in the east, about that time became very much impressed with the danger which threatened the financial solvency of all great railroads of the country. Now, an examination of the reports made by us for the year ending June 30, 1898, showed that about half of that railroad year had been a pretty prosperous one. As we understood, the first half of 1898 showed that the 8 trunk lines, on their business east of Buffalo and Pittsburg, took in about $250,-000,000. These roads traversed the most prosperous section of the United States, and these railroads, understood to be among the most prosperous institutions in the world, took in that year approximately two hundred and fifty millions, yet after paying operating expenses, taxes, and interest on bonds they virtually had nothing left. Only 3 of them paid dividends on their capital stock, and 2 of those, the 2 largest of all, paid the dividends, not out of the earnings during that year but out of accumulations during previous years. Now, that was the state of facts for railroad managers of trunk lines to confront, and I think they perceived, what seemed very plain to me, that there is nothing which makes against the integrity of railroad revenues in the long run like secret concessions. It is made to one; it gets to be known, or believed, or understood, and that intensifies the pressure of others, and so on, and ultimately that rate, first granted secretly, early finds expression in an open tariff to everybody; so the tendency goes on toward reduced rates, a tendency so marked at that time, in view of the volume of traffic moving then, as to lead even the managers of the New York Central and Pennsylvania to look on the future with serious apprehension. And so I think in a way, the letter of the Baltimore and Ohio may be regarded as an indication that railroad managers in that part of the country had, so to speak, suddenly become aroused to the necessity of taking some action that would protect their revenues and arrest this tendency, which would leave them solvent, and so the Baltimore and Ohio says, We will take a public position, and whatever rate we publish we will actually observe.

Q. And has that been done since, to your knowledge, largely with them and other roads?—A. Yes.

Q. But did discriminations continue since 1898 to January, 1899?—A. Well, generally speaking, as far as I have known, the rates since that time, in what is known as trunk-line territory, have been pretty rigidly maintained.

Q. But prior to that time there were large discriminations?—A. Undoubtedly, very grave demoralization of rates. Of course, as concerns the ordinary movement of merchandise in that territory, I think the published rates are very seldom departed from. When it comes to the movements, both for export and otherwise, of grain and packing-house products, and some things of that kind where transportation is partly in other territory than trunk-line country, and by other roads, partly for export, and rates are participated in by ocean carriers, I think it is not improbable that the published rate has been disregarded in some instances.

Q. Can there or can there not be a discrimination which is a just one? Are there not circumstances in which that could occur?—A. Well, the law uses the term "unjust discrimination," meaning by that that there may be discriminations which, nevertheless, are so excusable or so practically necessary in the conduct of business that a carrier practicing them ought not to be condemned.

Q. Can you instance a case of that kind?—A. Well, the most typical case is where water competition at the long-distance point compels the rail carriers to make approximately the same rate as the water carrier to that long-distance point, or else they do not get any business; and yet that is a rate which, if applied to all intermediate business, would not leave a reasonable revenue, reasonable from anyone's point of view. Now, there may be situations of that kind where the carrier is justified, in its own interest and in the public interest, in charging a higher rate to an intermediate point than to the long-distance point. That is discrimination, plain discrimination against the shorter-distance point, and yet may not be an unjust discrimination, all things considered. Of course as to the extent the short-distance should exceed the long-distance rate or whether that disparity should apply to all traffic are questions, and of course there is no end to incidental questions, but, broadly speaking, you see there may be occasions where there are discriminations which are not unjust either to the carrier or public.

Q. (By Senator MALLORY.) There is another branch of inquiry that is not strictly germane to this topic to which my attention has been called; that is, the inquiry as to the consideration and advisability of requiring books and accounts of the interstate railroads to be open at all times to inspection of United States examiners. It is a question that is only very remotely connected with the question of discrimination. I have been requested to ask you if you have any views to express on that subject?—A. My brief answer is this: I greatly believe in the virtue of publicity, and whatever may be said of other remedies against corporate abuses, there is one which seems to be valuable, almost uniformly admitted to be valuable, and that is publicity, and what I have in my mind might be illustrated by comparison. The General Government and the States as well take a most active supervision and control over our banks, both national and State, and yet, as between the banking business and the railroad business I regard the latter as most distinctively a public service in every way and entitled to have its transactions publicly known more than those of the banks, and I see no reason why a similar supervision may not be extended over the accounting and bookkeeping of the railroad carriers. I believe in it. I think, while the conditions are different, and the thing could not be so simply done, yet I think it ought to be open for some representative of public authority to walk into a railroad office at an unexpected moment and say, Gentlemen, I want to see your books, and I want to see them right now; and who should have the right to see them.

Q. (By Mr. PHILLIPS.) Would you believe the railroads should be compelled to take out a national charter when they had an international business and interstate-commerce business? Would there be any remedy in that?—A. That is a question which I have not considered. I suppose if anything of that kind should be done, it would be in reference to taxation or some other revenue purpose. I do not know. I have not considered that.

Q. (By Senator MALLORY.) There is another point to which I have been requested to ask your attention, and that is as to an expression of the advisability of prohibiting by law the increase of stock of interstate railways, without Government permit therefor, after application and hearing. Have you given that any consideration?—A. Well, I doubt if I could make any useful comment on that point. That is incidental to the more important principles involved in any adequate scheme of public regulation. I might observe this: I have not seen any instances in which the rates have seemed to much depend upon or be influenced by the capitalization of a road.

Q. You have never seen such a case?—A. I have not. The capitalization of the railroad, I think, cuts no figure in this rate question.

Q. I think I could call your attention to the case in which that very point seems to have been made, that the basis on which the rate should be fixed was the amount of capital invested in the railroad.—A. Oh, if you mean with reference to what the road ought to charge, of course it almost goes without saying that you will not get an ideal basis of rate making until you put some fair valuation on the railroad properties as a basis for determining the amount which they shall be permitted to earn; I simply mean that, broadly speaking, as to interstate traffic, especially this competitive traffic, and that is the traffic which creates the discriminations, it has not occurred to me that the rates of competitive roads are much influenced by the capitalization of the different roads.

Q. No, not competitive roads, but other than competitive roads.—A. When it has come to judicial investigation as to what is the proper rate to charge, then comes the question of capitalization, and very properly so.

Q. That involves the question whether or not it is a proper thing for the governments to exercise supervision over this matter of increasing capital stock unnecessarily or watering stock.—A. It would seem to me the very reason that applies to supervision over banks would apply to railroad corporations.

Q. (By Mr. FARQUHAR.) You have frequently said in your testimony that competition is the cause of discriminations.—A. Yes.

Q. And evidently to eliminate this competition there ought to have been an arrangement between the railroads so as to get uniform rates? That is, you would leave it to the railroads themselves whether by pooling or otherwise, to have uniform rates prepared for all? In other words, you would give contract power to the railroads themselves so that there could not possibly be any of this free competition or antagonism of roads in getting customers?—A. Substantially that. I would give to the carriers certain rights of contract with each other which are now denied and prohibited, but on condition that the public be protected against abuse of that privilege by such contemporaneous legislation as would give public authority ample power to control any abuses which might result from that combination.

Q. Now, were it possible to make practicable the proposition which is quite general in this country, of the Government ownership of all railroads, do you not think that that would solve the whole question of discrimination and regulation, by having the whole of those roads in the hands of public servants?—A. I will answer a part of your question first. I do not think it would at all stop discriminations, and to my mind that is one of the most serious objections to Government ownership of railroads; I mean as a present solution of the railroad question. Undeniably, under Government ownership this individual discrimination would disappear; the published rate would be observed; but the discriminations which might most grievously result from an unfair adjustment of public tariffs, as between communities and between commodities, might increase, intensified by the political control or influences which would be brought to bear upon that situation. I am so little disposed to say anything that should look like favoring Government ownership that if I thought it necessary I would say everything against it, and I feel very strongly on that precise point. Under Government ownership you would, of course, get rid of this private concession, but how would you see to it that rates were fairly adjusted so that the produce of this great country would circulate freely and in natural volume in different directions? How would you prevent political control, if I may so express myself, of rates which themselves would produce the most intolerable discrimination in favor of communities or sections of the country?

Q. Do you think there is any danger, when you speak of political control in the ownership of railroads, when you take into consideration the fact that the 800,000 employees of this country might possibly take one side of the political question?—A. That is so obvious an objection that it does not seem to me to need any comment.

WASHINGTON, D. C., *October 5, 1899.*

TESTIMONY OF HON. CHARLES A. PROUTY,

Member Interstate Commerce Commission.

The commission met at 2.15 p. m., Vice-Chairman Phillips presiding. At 3.30 Mr. Phillips introduced Hon. Charles A. Prouty, of Vermont, one of the members of the Interstate Commerce Commission, who, being first duly sworn, testified as follows:

Q. (By Senator MALLORY.) I will say to you, Judge Prouty, as I did to Mr. Knapp, that I would much prefer that you proceed on your own motion as to those points that you prefer to discuss.—A. Well, I have not any particular thing that I care to say to the commission. The chairman this morning covered the ground substantially, I think. If there is any point about which any member of the commission would like to interrogate me I shall be happy to answer that question.

Q. There is a point that I intended to refer to this morning in Mr. Knapp's testimony, which I omitted, and which I would like very much that you would devote some attention to, and that is embodied in topic 34 of the topical plan of inquiry on transportation—"Rates on imports and exports from and to the seaboard; in what do they differ from the rates on domestic products and commodities from and to the seaboard; if they are less, for what reason, and what is the effect on such difference?"—A. I have no particular knowledge and can make no particular statement as to the rates on imports. I know that in many cases rates from the seaboard to the point of consumption are very much less than in cases of corresponding domestic articles. The rates from Liverpool to San Francisco through New Orleans are not more than one-half on a great many articles what the rates from New Orleans to San Francisco are; but since I have been a member of the commission that subject has not been especially under consideration and I have no special knowledge about it. We have very recently investigated the question of export rates on grain and grain products, and, as the chairman stated, I prepared the opinion of the commission in that case. That does not give me any greater acquaintance with the subject than the other members of the commission have, although perhaps it ought to be, but I do not think it is, somewhat fresher in my mind for that reason. There were three points involved in that investigation: First, the comparative rate on grain from interior points to the seaboard, to New York, for instance, when intended for domestic consumption and when intended for export; second, the comparative rate on wheat and flour; and third, the publication of tariffs. The railroads have always claimed that they were under no obligation to publish their tariffs when the traffic was for export. That was entirely without the purview of the law. And we investigated that, among other things, and held that they were under the same obligation to publish schedule rates in case of export traffic that they were in the case of domestic traffic. Now, in reference to the relative rate on grain when for export and when for domestic consumption, we found this condition. I may get these rates wrong, because it has been some time since I looked into it particularly, but, generally speaking, the rate on wheat from Kansas City to Galveston, if that wheat was to be ground at Galveston and eaten up in Texas, was 27 cents a hundred pounds. The rate on wheat, if that wheat was to be exported from Galveston, taken over to Liverpool, and ground in England, was 10 cents a hundred pounds. The rate on wheat from the Mississippi River to New York, if that wheat was to be ground and eaten in New York, was about 20 or 21 cents a hundred pounds. If it was to be taken over to the other side and ground, it was 12½ or 13 cents a hundred pounds. That is to say, we found that the railroads were sometimes charging twice as much when the wheat was to be used at home as they did if the wheat or corn—for corn came into the investigation—was to be used abroad. Now, the railways said that that was necessary to meet market conditions abroad; that is to say, we could not sell our corn and wheat abroad unless they put in a lower rate which carried it abroad. Upon investigation it turned out to the satisfaction of everybody, and was admitted by the railroad companies themselves, that this was not true; that, looking merely at those rates which we had under investigation, there were no market conditions abroad which required charging a less rate on export than on domestic traffic. The rate had been charged entirely for the reason that our carriers were competing among themselves at home. Now, that being so, the low rate which was made on export traffic could not have benefited the American farmer. It benefited entirely the foreigner who ate the grain and who used the corn or the wheat. If the price is fixed in our country the farmer gets so much here anyhow; and of course, if the freight rate is low, the foreigner pays the price here plus the freight rate. On the other hand, if the price is fixed in a foreign country, then the farmer here gets the price abroad minus the freight rate, because he gets the benefit of the freight rates. We were satisfied, and the railroads admitted, that there were no market conditions which required this low rate; and it came to just this, that our railroads in the last year, under those low rates, because of their carrying the enormous amount of traffic along these lines, had been making a gratuitous present to foreigners of probably millions and millions of dollars which ought to have gone either into their own treasuries, or, if they did not need it, the American ought to have had the benefit of it in the way of a lower rate. While that was true, and while the railroads admitted it was, we had no power to stop it, and we were obliged to say that we could not undertake, with the power that the commission has, to prevent that discrimination. The question is complicated by water competition. This corn or wheat comes to Chicago, and it can go by water all the way from Chicago to Montreal, and can go by water all the way to New York, and that, of course, fixes the rate to Montreal and New York, and fixes the rate to every port through which it is exported; and that was one reason why, perhaps, we thought we ought not to interfere in that matter.

In reference to the flour rate, we found that the Chicago miller had paid about 21 cents a hundred pounds to get his wheat and flour, either in the shape of wheat or flour, to New York; that the English miller could take his wheat to New York for 13 cents. There was a clear discrimination, depending somewhat on the point of origin, but a clear discrimination of about 8 cents a hundred pounds in favor of the English miller. The testimony showed that on export flour a profit of from 2 to 3 cents a hundred pounds was regarded as a pretty good one by our millers, and of course our millers could not grind for the export market in the face of a discrimination of 8 cents, when all the profit they normally made was 5 cents. In that case we thought we should attempt to grant some relief, although our ability to do so was doubtful. We directed that the rate on flour should not exceed the rate on wheat by more than 2 cents a hundred pounds.

Q. Did you investigate at all as to the character of the rates, whether it was a paying rate for Galveston, that you were speaking of?—A. Twenty-seven cents and 10 cents.

Q. Did you inquire whether it was a paying rate really to the railroads, or whether it was a losing rate?—A. Yes, we inquired about that, but nobody can tell. Here is a railroad, here is the motive power, here are the cars; you must pay your fixed charges anyway. No man can tell whether it is good business or not good business to haul that stuff from Kansas City down to Galveston for 10 cents a hundred pounds; but it is only 900 miles from Kansas City to Galveston; it is 1,200 miles from the Mississippi River to New York. If it is good business to haul grain from the Mississippi River to New York for 12½ cents a hundred pounds, we certainly can not say that there may not be some money in hauling grain from Kansas City to Galveston at 10 cents.

Q. If that was a reasonable rate, the other rate must have been very extravagant?—A. That is the question. On all these Texas lines the percentage of operating expenses is very large, usually 90 per cent. The local traffic is light, and the through traffic is light. They must keep up their roads whether they carry the through traffic or not. We all felt that there was a grave inconsistency in these two rates and that the difference was altogether too wide, but we could not see how we had the power to remedy the difficulty.

Q. As I understood, you did not interfere with the Galveston rate?—A. No, we did not interfere with it; did not think we could. If the road carried any export business, the rate must be the same through Galveston as it is through New York. But the ocean rate from Galveston is high. The rate to New York was 12 cents, and the Galveston rate had to be as low as 10 cents or they could not do any business.

Q. Then the real reason, as you state, for that discrimination between rates for export and domestic consumption is competition to the seaboard by water?—A. No; the real reason is competition between carriers to the seaboard; that is what makes the low rate. Of course, the competition is between the point of origin and the point of destination; between, we will say, Chicago on the west and Liverpool on the east. The rate to Liverpool is made up of the freight rate to New York or somewhere else and the ocean rate to Liverpool. Now, the ocean rate to Liverpool is lower from New York than it is from Galveston. Therefore the freight rate to Galveston must be lower than the freight rate to New York.

Q. (By Mr. A. L. HARRIS.) I would like to ask whether or not the price of wheat in the foreign market had anything to do with the freight rate?—A. So far as we could learn, the price in the foreign market had not produced the slightest effect on freight rates; and, so far as we could learn, the freight rate did not produce any effect on the amount of grain sold in the foreign market. There might be conditions where it would, but the period which we investigated did not develop any of those conditions.

Q. (By Senator MALLORY.) This morning we had a very interesting statement from Mr. Knapp on the subject of discriminations. Is there anything that you would care to suggest in connection with that subject in addition to what he said?—A. No; I do not think that there is. The more you gentlemen look into it the more you will decide that the most important subject which you have to consider, or which can be considered in connection with the industrial operations of the country, is the freight rate. I do not think there is anything to-day which so contributes to build up the trusts and monopolies of this country, which you gentlemen are investigating, as the freight rate. I am not talking about this epidemic of combinations that is sweeping over this country now, which embraces a great many subjects into which the freight rate does not enter; but I do not believe that there is a great trust to-day anywhere—that is to say, in any one of the staple commodities handled in this country—which could have established or maintained itself in the face of absolute equality of the freight rate. I do not mean by that that every monopoly has a rebate. I do not mean by that that every monopoly enjoys some concessions in the rate; but I mean if you would strip these great combinations of all dominion over, and of all participation in, the making of the freight rate, not one of them would be a very dangerous element in our social polity.

Most people do not have the slightest appreciation how important a thing a slight change in the freight rate is. Some time ago the railroads centering in Chicago imposed a terminal charge on all cars of live stock shipped into Chicago. The Chi-

cago live-stock men objecting, and the ive-stock shippers down in Texas objecting, the commission took up the question and decided that the charge was unlawful
and ought not to be imposed. Subsequently a suit was brought before the circuit
court for the purpose of having the railroads prohibited from making that charge.
The court in deciding the question held that the commission in the preliminary proceedings was right in having made the order that the charge should not be made;
but said, in substance, this is such a small matter that it does not really seem worth
while to bother the court with it and bother the commission with it. Now, that
charge of $2 a car, applied to all the carloads of live stock that come into Chicago in
a year, amounts to half a million dollars, and that thing goes right along year after
year. That judge never had a case before him, and I doubt if he ever will have
such a case, which involved as much money as that question.

We heard a case the other day from Iowa, and as a result we decided that the
grain rate from a certain section of Iowa should be reduced about 2 or 3 cents a hundred pounds. Now you say, That does not amount to anything; that does not do the
farmer up there in Iowa any good. What does that mean to the farmer? It means that
the grain he raises and sends to market is worth about a cent a bushel more to him than
it otherwise would be. The testimony in that case showed us that land in that vicinity produces 30 bushels of corn to the acre on an average. Every man who owns an
acre of ground can get 30 cents a year more off it net than he could otherwise. That
means that his land is actually worth to him on a 6 per cent basis $5 an acre more.
I do not mean that it would sell for $5 an acre more now as a consequence of that
decision that the rate as charged was too high; but I mean that finally things will
find their market value, and the difference in that rate means an actual difference of
$5 an acre in the value of land in that section of the country.

I do not know just how broad your investigation has been here; I do not know
whether you have had occasion to inquire into the very narrow margin on which
business is done to-day. We have had some investigations which have brought it to
my attention, and it is a surprise to me. I may refer to some instances. Flour is
ground in this country at a profit of 2 or 3 cents a hundred pounds, 5 or 6 cents a
barrel. We had one investigation which developed the fact that coal was handled
on a margin, in cases of some large contracts, of 5 or 10 cents a ton. Our investigations have shown that half a cent a bushel is a good profit on grain. Now, just think
what that means. It means that if a grain dealer can get an advantage in the freight
rate of one-half a cent a bushel over his competitor it gives him the market. It
means that if a flour dealer can get an advantage of 2 cents a hundred over his competitor it gives him the market; and so with everything else in the same way. When
you think of that, you will see the importance of the freight rate; you will see what
an easy thing it is for these great combinations to so manipulate the freight rate that
they do obtain the market by obtaining this slight advantage. Now, I may say to
you furthermore—I do not want to weary you, I do not want to make a speech at your
expense—but I may say furthermore that if you will think about this thing, if you
will look into it, you will see that in the case of the staple commodities, the things
which we eat and wear and use, the things without which we can not sustain life, about
the only point between the producer and the consumer where anybody can obtain an
unfair advantage is the agency of transportation. Take wheat or corn; everybody can
buy it; everybody can buy the money with which he buys his wheat; everybody can
build a mill and grind it; everybody can have a store and sell it; but when it comes to
the question of transporting it from the grain fields or the station at the grain field to
the consumer it must go by one of some half dozen routes, and it can not go in any
other way; and, as I have said, about the only advantage which one man can get over
another is by manipulation in some way or other of the agencies of transportation.
Now, when you put these things together you see that inevitably the tendency of
this whole discrimination is to build up the great man and pull down the little one.
I do not care whether it is a city or whether it is an individual or what it is. The
discrimination builds up the big at the expense of the little everywhere. Go out
West to-day. A few years ago everybody bought grain west of Chicago; to-day one
man will buy the grain on one line of railroad, and nobody else can buy it on that
railroad. Another man buys grain on some other line of railroad, and nobody else
can buy it on that railroad. When those men have their elevators established, when
they have driven everybody else out of business, then they are in position to squeeze
the farmer and make him take less for his grain than he otherwise would. I have
on my desk at home a letter which was received by the commission a few days ago in
which the writer says that he has just traveled through the West in an attempt to buy
corn; that he finds that the corn is all bought by some half dozen men in just the
way I have indicated. He finds the prices fixed by these men; they agree what they
will pay; there is no competition out there really.

I have already said that it is not only the rebate, it is not only that sort of a discrimination which operates to the advantage of these monopolies. It has been said that the Standard Oil Company does not to-day pay or take any rebates. We all know what the history of that company was to begin with, but everybody else took rebates then and I suppose the Standard Oil was fortunate in being able to get twice what anybody else did. But they say that since 1887, since this law went into effect, they have not received any rebates. Assume for a minute that they have not, that is not all there is to it. It is not only by the payment of a rebate that you manipulate a freight rate. For the purpose of illustrating what I mean, I will take New Haven territory. That is up in my country and I know about it. Take the territory which is controlled by the New York, New Haven and Hartford Railroad to-day; that is, the whole State of Connecticut practically, part of Massachusetts, and part of Rhode Island. What is the condition of things there? We find this significant fact: In 1887, when this interstate-commerce law went into effect and the freight rate was first published, the rate from Cleveland, where a good deal of oil is refined, to Boston, on grain and grain products—if I get the figures right, it is a year or such a matter since I have looked at them—was 22 cents a hundred pounds; the rate on petroleum was 22 cents a hundred pounds; the rate on iron articles was 22 cents a hundred pounds; to-day the rate on grain is probably 15 cents a hundred pounds; the rate on iron articles is 20 cents a hundred pounds; the rate of petroleum from Cleveland to Boston is 24 cents a hundred. While the freight rate generally has declined, while the rate on every other article has declined, we find that the rate on petroleum has gone up. That is a very significant fact when you remember that the cost of transportation is less to-day than it was in 1887.

You come to another peculiar fact: On almost every commodity which you can ship from the West into New Haven territory there is a through rate from Chicago, Cleveland, and everywhere else to these different points. In the case of petroleum and its products there is no through rate. When you reach New Haven territory you strike a Chinese wall, and you can not get beyond that wall with a carload of petroleum unless you pay the local rate over the New Haven road to the destination. That is another significant fact, that while every other commodity takes a through rate into that territory, petroleum pays the local rate. Now, how is the petroleum business done in New Haven territory? The Standard Oil Company owns large receiving facilities at East Boston, and I am told it refines its commodity at seaboard points and transports it largely by tank boats to Boston. From Boston it distributes it through interior territory. Independent refiners at Cleveland and at other points in the West say the freight rate is such that they are unable to enter that territory in competition with the Standard Oil Company. If they had the through rate of 24 cents from Cleveland into that territory they might; but when you add to that rate the local rate of 10 to 20 cents, they can not do it. But suppose they could, here is another significant fact: The New Haven road says petroleum and its products shall be second class unless the party to whom it is shipped has a private siding or tank opposite the rails into which he can pump that petroleum, and in that case it is fifth class. Now, the Standard Oil Company has these tanks and private sidings all over this interior territory. The person without these facilities pays second class, and the person with these facilities pays fifth class. The fifth-class rate between Boston and New Haven is probably 10 cents a hundred pounds; it was about a year ago; and the second-class rate is probably 20 cents, a difference of 10 cents a hundred pounds. While, therefore, the Standard Oil Company does pay the published rate—it has gotten above the point of taking a rebate—it can make a rate, and the manipulation of these rates is just as effective to keep the independent people out of that territory as the payment of a rebate, and more so.

I will give you another instance, and that is the rate from Cleveland to New Orleans. The Standard people have some refineries at Cleveland, and there are a great many independent refineries at Cleveland; the Standard Company has also large refineries at Whiting, just out of Chicago, and theirs is the only company that has refineries at that point. There is a general relation of rates from Cleveland and Chicago to New Orleans. I had brought together the rates on about 25 articles, which pay substantially the same rate as petroleum ordinarily, and I find the Cleveland rate is about 2 cents higher than the Chicago rate on iron articles, acids, and everything of that grade. It costs about 2 cents more to send from Cleveland to New Orleans than from Chicago. Linseed oil took a rate of 16 cents from Chicago and 28 cents from Cleveland; but when you strike petroleum you find that whereas the rate from Cleveland to New Orleans is 31 cents, the rate from Chicago is 23 cents. Now, the independent refiner at Cleveland pays the 31 cents, and the only person who gets the benefit of the 23-cent rate is the Standard Oil people at Whiting.

That is the way in which the independent refiners claim the Standard Oil people manipulate rates to-day. Now, I do not think the property of the Standard Oil Company is not entitled to as much respect as the property of individuals; I do not believe any legislation against that company which is in any sense unjust would be wise or redound to the benefit of the country; but I do think the avenues of commerce, the arteries through which the lifeblood of this country circulates, should be unimpeded. I think the humblest shipper should have the same rates as the mightiest monopoly, and there ought to be some power to see that that is so.

Q. (By Senator MALLORY.) Have you any idea what influence it is that enables the Standard Oil Company to get such concessions as evidently it has in these rates?—A. Exactly the same influence which produces every discrimination—the interest of the party offering the discrimination somewhere, I suppose. In the case of the New Haven road, it is apparent. The New Haven road can make more money by transporting on a local than on a through rate. You ask me why the New Haven road does not adopt the same policy with reference to all commodities. Because the people of Connecticut, if they were compelled to pay a local rate on everything they use, eat, and wear, would send to the Capitol some Senators and Representatives who would endeavor to enact a law which would stop it; whereas they will get along with one or two commodities.

Q. Have you any suggestion as to a practical, expeditious remedy for such an evil as that, conceding it exists?—A. Of course I do not say it is an evil; I do not say it is an unjust discrimination. I state the facts as they appear. But assuming that this is an unjust discrimination against other commodities; that all commodities in New Haven territory ought to be treated alike; assuming all commodities ought to be carried on the through rate into New Haven territory, the only remedy is to endow somebody with the power to compel the New Haven road to make such a rate. There is no such power anywhere now.

Q. It is within the power of Congress to vest that power in somebody?—A. Undoubtedly.

Q. (By Mr. PHILLIPS.) Have you any knowledge that discriminating rates obtained up to the beginning of, say, 1899?—A. My knowledge on that subject would be twofold. In the first place, I should judge from complaints made to the commission and from investigations which the commission undertook. I was at Portland, for instance. We undertook an investigation there as to freight rates, and it turned out that every road running from Chicago west had an agent in Portland; and when any man wanted to ship anything from Chicago to Portland, he telephoned around to these agents and got the best rate he could, and the stuff was billed at the published rate, and he was afterwards paid the difference between the published rate and that rate. I make the same inference, from what railroad men tell me. They say a good many things to us in confidence that they do not say when they get onto the stand, and many things which we would not care to repeat to anybody else. While I am not at liberty to call any names, I have no doubt that during 1898 the demoralization of rates was about as bad as it could be. Competitive traffic did not pretend to move on the published rate. There was a paper in Chicago which quoted the actual rate just as the price of wheat is quoted. I am not so optimistic as my brother Knapp about the present condition. I would not like to say they are in all cases maintained, being under oath. I do not believe they are. They had a meeting in New York the other day to restore rates. I do not know just what that was for if rates are being maintained.

Q. (By Mr. A. L. HARRIS.) I hold in my hand the report of the commission of 1897. Amendments are recommended and written out in full. Have you any recommendations since 1897 as to amendments?—A. I think not.

Q. Are these amendments at the present time all you would suggest as a relief?—A. No; these amendments omitted provision for what I think is one of the most essential things. The commission has no power at all to establish a through rate. The transportation business of this country is done almost entirely on rates which are combinations of rates between different railroads. You can not control these rates; you can not handle these rates unless you have power to establish a through rate. But with that addition I think they do contain substantially all the amendments that might be desirable.

Q. That bill was introduced?—A. It was known as the Cullom bill.

Q. (By Mr. CLARKE.) You heard the testimony of Judge Knapp in favor of the freedom of contract between railroad companies; in other words, freedom to pool?—A. I did.

Q. Do you agree with that?—A. As the law stands now, I do not; as the law might stand, I do.

Q. How would you have it stand?—A. When it is possible for some tribunal to effectively control the rate, then I think railroad companies might safely be allowed to pool. So long as you treat transportation as a private concern, so long as the railways are given the right to make their own rates independent of all effective control, I do not think they ought to have the right to combine. At the same.time I believe, we must change our ideas on that subject. We must treat railroads as monopolies, and we must regulate them as monopolies.

Q. You are familiar with the subject of transit in bond across Canada, I suppose?—A. To a certain extent.

Q. Is it your understanding that the trunk lines are opposed to that privilege of allowing Canadian roads to make a differential?—A. What do you mean by trunk lines?

Q. I mean American trunk lines, wholly in this country.—A. I take it that those that do not participate in this traffic are opposed to it, and perhaps most of those that do would be in favor of it. The Grand Trunk road brings large quantities of that traffic down to the border at Niagara and passes it over to its various connections; and these connections, some of them, could not live for a month without it. I take it they would favor the practice, and the line that is independent of it would probably be opposed to it.

Q. If they had this freedom of contract how do you think it would affect the transit in bond?—A. Not at all.

Q. It would be continued the same as it is now, you think, substantially?—A. I think so. You understand the freedom of contract does not mean the railroad company is obliged to contract. It simply means they can contract. There is no way of making a man contract unless he wants to.

Q. (By Mr. A. L. HARRIS.) What action, if any, has Congress taken on the recommendation made by the Interstate Commerce Commission with reference to the law?—A. Senator Cullom has introduced a bill. There were one or two hearings before the Senate committee which nobody on the part of the Senate attended, if I remember; and I think that is the extent of the action. I do not know it, and I do not say it, but it is said that no action can be taken on an interstate-commerce law until the railroads consent to it.

Q. (By Senator MALLORY.) By the Interstate Commerce Commission or by Congress?—A. By Congress.

Q. Have you given any consideration to the point that Mr. Knapp referred to this morning in answer to the question of the commission concerning the advisability of the Government exercising the right of inspecting the books?—A. I think they ought to. I do not think there is any one thing which would so tend to stop the payment of rebates of various forms as that would.

Q. Just the mere thought that they are subject to inspection?—A. If some of the Government officials had the power to step into the office of a railroad company and examine their books, and they were required to keep books in a specified form, it would be very difficult to pay rebates. In January, 1899, the railroad companies began to maintain rates. I said to a railroad president, about the middle of January, "How does your road show in comparison with what it was before?" He said, "For January and February we do not expect any improvement, because we have to pay our former rebates out of January and February, but after that it begins to show." These rebates which the railroad companies paid were very serious things; they amounted to very large sums of money.

Q. Some enactment separate and distinct from the interstate-commerce act, establishing a corps of officials under the supervision of some department, and giving them the same powers that are possessed now by bank examiners, say, if carried out would have a great effect, in your judgment, in preventing and stopping discriminations in the shape of rebates, etc.?—A. I think it must, inevitably.

Q. (By Mr. FARQUHAR.) What have you to say about these private cars owned by shippers? What advantages do these shippers gain over the men that use the ordinary equipments of the road?—A. That, as Lord Dundreary said, is one of the things that no fellow can find out. That is one of the unfortunate things about it, and you can see to some extent how they are used. A packer owns a car; he gets on that car a certain mileage; if he can send it from Chicago to New York by a road that is 1,200 miles long, he gets so much more mileage than by sending over another road 918 miles long. There is an inducement to send it by the long haul. He never loads that car to the maximum weight, because he wants to get as much car mileage as he can. It is expensive to the railroads, unfair, and perhaps the most fruitful source of discrimination.

Q. What class of products are these cars chiefly used for?—A. I suppose more of them are used for transporting fresh beef and packing-house products than for any other purpose; but they are used, of course, for transporting live stock and fresh fruit from California east. I think in case of these cars they are generally used by some fruit association rather than by the shipper.

Q. We have in existence what are called the Red Line and Blue Line, the

Despatch, etc. What privileges have they over the general equipment of the road?—A. It is generally understood that these lines have no privileges. They are simply an association of railroads for the purpose of transporting freight; but there is one line which operates over the New York Central, an incorporated company, which receives, say, 10 per cent of the freight money for collecting and delivering to the railroad company the freight.

Q. Is it or is it not a fact generally understood, at least, that these lines are really a part of the railroads themselves?—A. They are simply an organization.

Q. And they just simply are an advertising feature of fast freight or something to gain business. Now, in the case of roads under receivers, do such roads participate in the deliberations of these traffic associations?—A. I think so. I understand they do. I do not want to say that, but my understanding is they do.

Q. Have the shippers any more privileges under a receivership than under an orderly managed road?—A. Until recently it has been understood that the roads in the hands of receivers were the worst violators of the law to be found anywhere, but recently, about the beginning of this year, some of the courts turned over a new leaf, and I do not think that has been so since. I think the courts came to the conclusion that this law must be obeyed, and notified the receivers to that effect.

Q. Was it not usually the instruction from the court that the receiver had the authority to make the rates to suit himself and get all the traffic on the road he could for the benefit of the stockholders and creditors of the road?—A. I do not know what the instructions were. I know what they were supposed to do.

Q. Was not that practically the result in the case of receivers?—A. I think that was the result, as a rule.

Q. And were these not placed in the hands of a receiver more for the purpose of reorganization?—A. The result is usually a reorganization. They usually go into the hands of a receiver because they can not pay their fixed charges.

Q. Now, is it not a fact in railroad management in this country, that a good deal of this cutting, rebating, and rate wars, and everything else has resulted from mismanagement; that the roads are not able to run as long as they cut rates to get traffic?—A. I do not know exactly what you mean. There are some roads undoubtedly that can not get what they think is their part of the traffic, unless they cut the rate, and they cut it for the   p   of getting that traffic. Whether that is mismanagement or not would depend ur ose

Q. Suppose they were under the agreement of the traffic association or anything of that kind, and they did not get sufficient traffic, on a road that would not draw traffic itself. Is it not a fact that a good deal of the cut rates come from these roads? Is it not the poverty of the road that will make it cut?—A. That is my understanding; but I do not know it.

Q. It is not dishonesty, but poverty?—A. It is not dishonesty which induces a road to cut; but it is dishonesty to cut. I do not think the railroads want to cut the rate because they like to be dishonest, but they have to.

Q. In prorating in a pooling organization, has it not been the custom on American roads to cut rates privately and quietly so as to get all the traffic that they can get for the pro rata when it comes to a pool division?—A. That is said to be so; that they all do it, whether weak or strong. They all want to establish the fact that the traffic belongs to them, so that when they make up the pool they can say they ought to have it.

Q. (By Professor JOHNSON.) In regard to the insolvency of roads it has been stated by some persons that it would be a good thing to establish a special tribunal consisting of specialists, which tribunal should look after the management of insolvent roads; what are your views on that?—A. I have never given the subject any consideration and have no views about it.

Q. Do you favor the supervision by your commission of the business of express and telegraph companies?—A. I do not see any reason why a telegraph company should be subjected to the supervision of our commission. I can see why an express company should be, perhaps, but I do not think any substantial complaint exists in this country about treatment by express companies.

Q. I understand it is claimed that telegraph rates are unnecessarily high. Do you see any reason why your commission is not the best authority that the supervision of the telegraph companies ought to be placed under?—A. I think that if we had the power to do what we are supposed to do now, we would have all that we could attend to.

Q. If the business of the telegraph companies is to be supervised, into whose charge should the business be put?—A. That comes more nearly the Post-Office Department than the railroad department. Perhaps you could supervise it under the Post-Office Department.

Q. (By Mr. FARQUHAR.) Do you care to state your opinion on the abuses of the pass system?—A. I do not think the abuses of the pass system as it exists to-day are as great as Chairman Knapp stated. That is, I do not believe that the revenues of the roads are depleted to that amount; but I do think that every man ought to pay his fare, and if you want me to suggest a remedy, all you have to do is to require the railroads to publish, and file with the Interstate Commerce Commission, or put somewhere, a list of every pass they issue, and let every man who wants to, look at it.

Q. You think an amendment of the interstate-commerce law covering that feature would remedy the whole matter?—A. If the roads obey it.

Q. Do you think the abolition of the pass system would result much in the lowering of the cash fare?—A. Perhaps not, because cash fares and freight all come together, and it might not. Fares are perhaps too high in some parts of the country now and in other parts they are low enough. I think myself we ought to have in this country some system like they have in Hungary, where a poor man who is willing to travel slowly and without the accommodations and conveniences we have now can travel cheaper. I think we ought to have some rate of that kind. Now, to-day every man pays substantially the same rate. In Canada they have a second class but they all go in first-class cars. It costs money to run a train fast. If we had some system of trains that ran slowly and carried people at a lower rate of fare it would be a good thing for the railroads and the public.

Q. You think we should have such a thing in the United States as first, second, and third class rates?—A. I do not think we could use different classes on the same train. I would advocate a difference of rates of fare on different trains.

Q. (By Mr. CLARKE.) You think railroad consolidation is on the whole beneficial?—A. I think that railroad consolidation tends to do away with discrimination. It does away with competition and to that extent prevents discrimination. Railroad consolidation in New England has proved to be a good thing, in my opinion. You know our territory is divided up there. We have the Boston and Maine and the New Haven Road. They control their own territory. I live in the Boston and Maine territory. Since the consolidation of that system our rates have been reduced; our service has been improved. New England is in my territory. I receive complaints from New England if there are any. I do not receive 1 complaint from New England where I receive 50 from the State of Ohio. At the same time the freight rate is higher in New England than almost anywhere else. The average over the country is about 8 mills a ton per mile, and in New England it is almost twice that.

Q. Suppose these great systems should be further consolidated, so that practically there would be only one system in the Eastern States, would you expect benefit or injury?—A. That would depend on the system. If the consolidation was carried out, that system would have it in its power to benefit or injure absolutely as it saw fit, as policy might dictate. Consolidation is bound to come in the United States unless something else comes first.

Q. Do you not think this tendency to consolidation makes it almost imperative that there should be supervision of these great roads?—A. Certainly I do. I do not think you can have a satisfactory railroad service until you have proper supervision. It is as much in the interest of the railroad as in the interest of the public.

WASHINGTON, D. C., *October 5, 1899.*

TESTIMONY OF HON. JUDSON C. CLEMENTS,

Member Interstate Commerce Commission.

The commission met at 10.40 a. m., Vice-Chairman Phillips presiding. At 2.10 p. m. Hon. Judson C. Clements, being duly sworn, testified on the subject of transportation as follows:

Q. (By Senator MALLORY.) I would like to call your attention to question No. 35 of the topical plan of inquiry on transportation, and ask if you have anything to say relating to the subject there referred to, "unreasonable and excessive rates."—A. It has frequently been asserted in recent years that there are practically no unreasonably high rates, and for proof of this it has been cited that the tendency of railroad rates for years past has been downward all the time; and while this statement is generally true, it is also a fact that rates covering large movements of property have within this same period been raised again and again. They have not always stayed down. They go down in rate wars and fierce competition and then go up again. This is not only true as shown on the tariff sheets with respect to miscellaneous freights, etc., but it is so with respect to the vast movement of grain from the West. Nevertheless, it is true as a general rule that the general result has been that rates are lower than they have been in years past, and decidedly so; but in almost every instance of gross discrimination in rates as between the localities I think there will be found two extremes—in the one case the rates to the competitive points are perhaps lower than they might be, particularly so as compared with the local rates, or the rates to intermediate or local points, so that where you find a rate that is pressed down below what is a reasonable rate this is counteracted in unreasonable rates to the numerous intermediate local stations. To illustrate: The rates from the East and from the North to Atlanta—I take that because that is a central city in that section of the country, where a trade-center system, as we call it, prevails, of lower rates to the trade centers, regardless of distances, and higher rates to the local stations, whether they are nearer or farther, because they are noncompetitive. Take the rates, for instance, to Atlanta from the East or from any point North, and the dealer at a local station 50 miles north of Atlanta will pay the through rate to Atlanta and the local rate back to the point through which the freight to Atlanta passes; but that destined to the local station 50 miles north stops there. There is no haul beyond usually, but the charge is made for it. Not only is that charge made for the haul to Atlanta, which is not actually made, but the local rate back again is charged; and so the through rate to the given station 50 miles this side of Atlanta, for illustration, is the sum of the rate to Atlanta and the local rate back. The Atlanta rate was made, presumably, to take care of 2 terminal services, 1 where the shipment begins and 1 in Atlanta, and the local rate from Atlanta to the local station back 50 miles also is in it. In the making of that rate there was taken into consideration, presumably, the expense of the 2 terminal services for that, so that the through rate, made up by this combination, to the nearer-distance point, is much higher in the aggregate than to the farther-distance point, and yet only have the 2 terminal services actually been performed, though the rate is made up as if there were 4. All practical railroad men agree and insist upon and testify that the terminal service is one of great importance, and that it is an expensive business to them to procure and maintain their terminal stations and do the switching and all those things incident to the movement of traffic and its delivery, and particularly it is a large proportion of the expense and service with regard to a short haul of 50 miles. With 2 terminal services in it a large proportion of that charge reasonably is creditable to the terminal service, so that I think in all cases of that kind of discrimination, or in most of them, there is an unreasonably high rate to the local stations, and the effect of this system is that the rate to a point 50 miles beyond Atlanta is just the same as to that point 50 miles this side. In each case it is assumed the traffic goes to Atlanta and is then shipped to that place on a through rate, and then out again, whether back or forward at the established local. Well, I do not want to enlarge upon this question, but I think gentlemen who travel through the Southern territory, particularly where this system prevails to its greatest extent, and then travel in the middle North, Ohio, Pennsylvania, and in the trunk-line territory, official classification territory, will readily see at a glance by the most ordinary observation the effect it has upon the country generally. In one section you will see in the North the prosperous cities and prosperous towns, small stations, suburban stations, and the smaller stations between the trade centers, between Pittsburg and Philadelphia and between Pittsburg and Columbus and Cincinnati, etc. When you go to the trade-center country of the Southeast, where this system prevails, you will see a prosperous Atlanta, Nashville, Knoxville, Birmingham, and so on, the recognized trade centers of importance, but between these you pass through towns that simply exist. They are in a struggle for existence. In some cases where they are nearer these larger places the stores that were filled with goods and with people dealing with merchants, and dealing with some degree of prosperity some years ago—many of them are unoccupied; and there is a vast difference between the rate to the trade center and to the intermediate stations, small noncompetitive stations, whether nearer or farther, which must tend to establish all of the manufacturing that goes to that country in these favored cities, because the freight rate is a serious matter for consideration with respect to people who are going to invest hundreds of thousands of dollars approximately in a plant that is going to continue and that can not be moved. It is a continuing tax upon their business to pay this difference for the smaller services, and it does not seem to me that it is well for the country at large that such a condition of things as that should be induced and encouraged. Neither do I think it is a good policy on the part of railroad management, but of course they assume they know more about their business than we do. But I have said more about that than I intended to, and my object in referring to it is to insist that there are many unreasonable rates in existence on the face of the tariffs.

Q. Do you mean they are unreasonable per se, or unreasonable by reason of the rates charged the cities at terminal points?—A. I think it is undue relation that works great prejudice and disadvantage to the intermediate station, and at the same time I think if the rates were properly adjusted it would result in the cutting down of these local rates; that they might be reduced in many instances.

Q. Well, there must be some potent cause of this regulation with respect to that Southeastern territory. Do you know what it is that has brought this state of things about?—A. Well, I have generally heard it assigned, when that system has been criticised by the commission—as it has been in numerous cases—I have generally heard it said that that territory was peculiarly situated with reference to water; that the Mississippi River and the other rivers to the Gulf and the Atlantic Ocean so surround that territory that there were so many points that could be reached by water, or partly by water, largely by water, that it necessitated a reduction, the making of low rates to these points. But that I do not think is borne out to any great degree, because the territory North, that of which I have spoken, is surrounded by a system of great lakes on the north and by the Mississippi River and Ohio River and Atlantic Ocean, the canals, and is subject to quite as many water influences, I think, as the South, except, perhaps, in winter time, when the lakes are closed.

Q. Have you had occasion to compare the local rates which prevail in that Southeastern section with the local rates which prevail in the other sections which you referred to, east of the Mississippi, north of the Ohio?—A. Well, the rates are usually lower in the North than they are in the South, both local and through. That is usually true.

Q. Then it would seem that the reason assigned does not apply to those local rates. May it apply to the terminal rates?—A. Yes. Another reason assigned for it is the sparseness of business and population. Of course, that is an influence; that is a reason in part for higher rates generally in the South, and I suppose a good reason for it is that the volume of business is not such as to support the roads on an even rate with the same kind of traffic in the North, where the volume is much greater.

Q. From your observation do you think it would be possible to arrange a different system of rates, local or intermediate, and terminal rates, for that section of the country that would give lower local rates, and at the same time not oppress the railroad?—A. Well, if the rule of the so-called fourth section, that they shall not be charged greater for a short haul than for a longer haul in the same direction, had been found to mean what it says, it would have corrected this condition of things. I do not mean an absolutely hard-and-fast rule without discrimination or relief from it under any circumstances; but as it is now, the carriers judge for themselves whether the circumstances and conditions are similar or not, and then they put in rates as they always did before. They never charged any more before the interstate-commerce law was passed for the short haul than the long one, except in the face of competition. Now they say that competition creates dissimilarity of circumstances, whether it is water competition or rail competition. Where two or more roads converge, that is rail competition, and that makes the situation dissimilar, and so changes it, and so it has been held that that may be a reason for finding these dissimilar circumstances and conditions. It has also been held that they may judge of it themselves and act upon it in the first instance, so we are right where we were before the law was passed in regard to that rule.

Q. (By Professor JOHNSON.) All that is needed to remedy the situation you depict would be an insertion in the law of a clause saying that competition between railways shall not constitute dissimilar circumstances within the meaning of the act?—A. Yes; and to enforce it and carry it out. Of course it might work some hardship somewhere if there were no exception to it, if the so-called rule of the fourth section was made operative in all cases, unless upon showing that relief ought to be had, and then the measure of relief might be granted upon hearing. Any case could be relieved that ought to be, where there is a good showing made to prevent particular cases of hardship.

Q. (By Senator MALLORY.) Does this difference between intermediate and terminal rates exist to the same extent in any other section of the country, to your knowledge?—A. It exists to a great extent in the far West.

Q. (By Professor JOHNSON.) In the Rocky Mountain territory?—A. Yes.

Q. (By Senator MALLORY.) Does there seem to be a general complaint in that section of the country against it?—A. There is more or less complaint from that section of the country, probably more from the Southeast than from the West. We hear of it oftener.

Q. Has any remedy suggested itself to you that you would be willing to outline?—A. None further than I have intimated, and such as the commission has heretofore recommended—that is, that the so-called rule should operate and be binding on the roads except where application is made for relief, and upon hearing by the commission or some tribunal authorized to hear the facts they might allow the higher charge for the shorter haul and fix the difference.

Q. The rate would have to be fixed at the starting out. Now, somebody would have to fix those rates. Suppose the railroads fixed the rates and the local or intermediate rates were complained against, brought to the attention of the commission. The commission would then have to consider whether those rates were reasonable, in view of all conditions existing. If they held they were unreasonable or excessive, or ordered them to be reduced—I understand that your idea is that they should be reduced; now, would the railroad companies' rate board have the right to appeal from that decision of the commission?—A. As the law is now they have the right. They are not required to take any notice of it now if they dispute it, and then the burden is on the commission to enter suit and establish the lawfulness of this order and have it enforced in court.

Q. Well, as I understand, your idea is that the onus should rest upon the corporation?—A. Yes; I think it would be better. The law now states that the finding of the commission shall be prima facie evidence of the correctness of the conclusions reached; and I think that it would be no hardship on the roads if the public tribunal, impartially devoting itself to these questions, after complaint made and notice to the carrier, full hearing, and taking of all testimony and argument, reaches the conclusion that a given rate is unreasonable and unlawful, either because too high or unjustly discriminatory, that the order of the commission or other impartial tribunal ought to go into operation and effect within a reasonably short time, unless the carriers can go into court and show that order to be unlawful. In all these cases it is the rate that is complained of—that is, it is the daily, continuing, operating rate, that is charged to-day, and to-morrow, and the next day, that is affecting a man's business, that he complains of, and if it is unlawful and hurtful and ruinous to his business he should have relief from it. As it is now he may bring his complaint and have a hearing, and all parties are heard fully, and it is decided by a public tribunal not interested in the question, and that tribunal makes an order which the law says shall stand prima facie, and yet they can ignore it. The commission must then institute a suit. It is tried in the circuit court de novo; new testimony may be taken and the whole matter gone over again after a great delay; volumes of briefs are written, and it passes up, and after awhile a decision is rendered and appealed. An appeal is taken to the circuit court of appeals, and the same thing is done again, except there is no new testimony taken, of course, and then to the Supreme Court, and in the meantime 3 or 4, 5 or 6 or 7 years have gone by before the controversy is ended. Now, what individuals or communities, understanding that they have to go through all of that, subject to all of that delay, have any sort of inducement to undertake to correct an oppressive rate? And then again the circumstances may be so changed in a man's business in all these matters that it may not be a matter of any interest to him when the judgment is rendered. His business may have been destroyed at that time by oppressive discriminating rates that injured his business, building up one man, his competitor, on one side of the street, by a discriminating rate; and this thing may go on until his business is injured or destroyed. What remedy is that for a man who has rights? If he has rights as to what the rate should be, he ought to have a remedy—that is, a practical and substantial one—that will right and correct a wrong; and I do not know a better way to do it than to let the orders of the commission go into effect 30 or 40 days after their rendition, provided the railroads do not go into court and obtain an injunction against them. If on the face of it, by investigation, the court can see that the commission made an error, then it can issue a restraining order or injunction and stop it until the matter can be heard on its merits, and if nothing of that sort appears there is certainly no hardship in its going into effect. Is not that better? It may be said that would be wrong to the roads, because the order might afterwards be reversed, and the commission found to be wrong on a full hearing, and in the meantime the carrier would be wronged in the matter of what he is unable to collect. In all these matters somebody has to take chances, and as it is now what becomes of the shipper, and what does he lose during this time between the decision of the commission and the final decision of the court? He is losing all the time by these effects of an unjust rate, and is suffering that which he can not recover.

But it may be said by some that after the final decision of the court he may recover reparation or damage and get it back; but every man of the least bit of experience in these matters will know that nobody is going to get substantial relief in that way. Usually the transactions are so numerous and it takes so many suits that it would be folly to enter upon an effort of that sort.

Q. (By Mr. PHILLIPS.) Have you not frequently found against the railroads a large amount of money?—A. Not very frequently.

Q. Are there not cases now pending before the courts under which you have found a large amount of money due the shippers?—A. Yes; we have in some cases. Under the law as it now is the commission is authorized to find and report what reparation shall be made. Now, we have ordered that in some cases, and in some cases the roads have paid it. In other cases they have resisted, and in those cases the suits are now pending in court to enforce such orders. But it is extremely injurious to a man's business which depends upon reasonable and just rates, which are affecting him from day to day, that he must wait for an accumulation of the wrongs and then bring a suit for recovery; and then the difficulty of finding what carrier shall be responsible, just how much, who shall be responsible for it, and all of the uncertainties pertaining to litigation of that sort make it an insufficient remedy for a man who has suffered an actual wrong.

Q. (By Senator MALLORY.) Is it your opinion that competition that exists now between railroads, and between railroads and water transportation, is to any extent responsible for this condition?—A. Well, undoubtedly the competition between carriers has reduced the rates to the trade centers and competitive points lower than other places, and so has water reduced them.

Q. Would the doing away of that competition, in your judgment, have a beneficial effect?—A. Well, if all the competition was done away with it would seem that there would be no particular inducement for discriminations, and it would go far to do away with discriminations; but I have always been apprehensive that it would have a different effect in respect to the reasonableness of rates. All of these combinations, such as pooling and contract relations between competing carriers, their leading purpose, as I have always understood it, is to get rid of competition in order to get more money out of the business.

Q. Which would equalize rates and prevent discriminations?—A. Well, it would result in equalizing; it would do away with the temptation to discriminate.

Q. Would it reduce or would it do away with the complaint of excessive rates?—A. Well, I am afraid it would aggravate the cause of complaint as to excessive rates.

Q. Well, do you not think it would be feasible to permit the transportation companies to make pooling contracts and at the same time to put some wholesome restraints upon them that would prevent them from charging excessive rates?—A. Well, that might do; that would depend a good deal upon what the restraint was and how it was to be applied.

Q. If you could open the door for them to harmonize their rates, as you might say, automatically, among the railroads themselves, establish an equal rate and at the same time put a check upon them, so that they would not be able to charge excessive or extortionate rates, would not that do away to a great extent with much of the cause of complaint against the railroad system of this country?—A. I have no doubt it would, if that can be accomplished effectively. The difficulty has always been, to my mind, about whether that would be effected or not. If the competition was gone and there was practically one management, so that undoubtedly there would be no temptation to discriminate, as there is now by rebates and otherwise, at the same time it would be much more in their power to get more out of it than they do now—tax the public more; and every slight raise in rates makes a vast difference in the charge to the public. We give a great deal of our attention to the silver question, and the tariff question, and the internal revenue, about how the tariff shall bear and how it shall be distributed, and a good deal of money is appropriated and expended to prevent cheating in respect to imports, not only to protect the Government in getting its revenue, but also to protect the honest importers against the smugglers; lots of money is expended for that purpose, justly so and necessarily so; so in regard to the internal revenue we expend a great deal of money to suppress the moonshiner, not simply to protect the Government in getting all its revenue, but also to protect the honest distiller who is paying his tax. In other words, to prevent unjust discrimination. But here is a business which collects from the people of the United States nearly $1,200,000,000 a year, which is more than twice as much as the Government collects out of the internal revenue and tariff put together; more than twice as much as both, and yet it is full of opportunities for discrimination between localities and individuals, tenfold more hurtful than anything that can be done under the tariff laws and the internal-revenue laws to individuals and communities. The rate of freight now, I believe, is about 8½ mills per ton per mile. An increase of about a mill and a half, which would seem to be a very small amount on a ton a mile, would make a revenue of over $100,000,000 increase to the railroads, and all of it would come out of the public. A very slight increase, made possible by any means, however insignificant it may look when expressed in mills, means a great sum. That increase would amount in a year to more than twice as much as the dividends paid to the roads on their stock in the last year.

Q. Are not the freight rates in the United States really less than they are in any other country, on an average?—A. I do not know how that is. I have heard very many statements about that, but I have never seen an authentic statement that was entirely satisfactory. They are less than in some countries. The investment in ld   roads is a great deal less than in some other countries where the freights are highing

Q. Do you think it is feasible for a body such as the Interstate Commerce Commission, with the information and experience which that commission possesses, to establish freight rates for the country at large, for the railroads all over the United States?—A. Well, it would be a great undertaking to do it originally, in the first instance, and I should hardly say that any commission ought to be charged with such responsibility and such duty as that. I am afraid it would not be within their power to do it at one time, and yet these things are a matter of growth. I think that a commission of experts could take the present tariffs, present classification, and construct from it, by revision and hearings and consideration of these matters, within a year or two, a much better system than we have now. It would be a matter of growth, a matter of revision and correction, based upon experience and information and observation, and it would have to be brought about by a system that would not permit this constant fluctuation.

Q. Is not that very fluctuation something that, under existing conditions of railroads in this country, is almost absolutely necessary?—A. Well, you mean it is due to competition, I suppose.

Q. Yes; competition.—A. Yes; largely so.

Q. They are obliged to change those rates to meet exigencies arising out of business?—A. Yes; the suggestion I made a little while ago in regard to the long and short haul, if it was made enforceable, would go very far to correct many of these rate wars and fluctuations, in my judgment. If a road running from New York to Atlanta—taking that for an illustration now—when it reduced its rate 100 per cent in order to get freight, knew that it had to reduce all its intermediate rates down there, it would hesitate a very long time. It would be a restraint, a wholesome one, against this reckless plunging into rate wars in particular localities. But I do not wish to be understood as advising the power to be conferred on the Interstate Commerce Commission, or any other tribunal, of making all the rates for all the roads of this country. The commission has never suggested that or asked it.

Q. Yet the equalization of freight rates has, I think, presented itself to the attention of the thinking people. I do not mean to say making them exactly alike, but to equalize them as far as practicable.—A. Yes.

Q. There is no authority now in anybody to do that?—A. No.

Q. Would not that be a proper subject for careful consideration in connection with our railroad problem?—A. Yes.

Q. Of vesting that power in somebody?—A. Undoubtedly it presses itself all the time. I think there ought to be a corrective power; there ought to be revisionary power in the Interstate Commerce Commission, or some other tribunal, upon cases in controversy, where the facts are found and the conclusion reached, to correct the rate; not simply to declare the rate in existence to be bad or unlawful, but to prescribe what it shall be, not perpetually, not forever, not unchangeably, but until other conditions grow up, a showing of which, by a full hearing and fair trial, will indicate the proper change to be made. The anomaly, it seems to me, in this class of controversies is that when two people of the country have a controversy about any matter it must go to a court or public tribunal to be tried by an impartial body; but as to the rate, although the law says that it shall be reasonable and just—and every rate that is not reasonable and just is unlawful—yet a man that uses the railroad must pay it, and he can not go into any tribunal, as the law is now, that has power to make any other rate. It is true, we heard this morning of one rate that had been changed (see testimony of Hon. Martin A. Knapp, pp. 133, 134); but that was raised, it was not reduced; and I suppose that is based upon the fact that the railroad was in the hands of the court. That probably could not be done by a court any more than by the commission in respect to a road that was not run by the court. But here you are bound to submit to the unlawful rate, no matter how unlawful it may be; you are bound to submit to it if you use the railroad, or else you must submit to the determination of the railroad manager, who is a party interested in the controversy, and his determination must control.

Q. You spoke of letting the rate stand as fixed by the commission or whatever body had that power, unless the railroad or transportation company could show good ground for an injunction. I do not suppose you mean to mark that out as the only procedure?—A. No; I simply mean that I think that after the commission has deliberated on the case and both sides have been fully heard, it being an impartial body established for that purpose, its finding ought to stand until a court finds to the contrary. In other words, every litigant is entitled to his day in court, and the commission is not a court, and therefore he must have a court pass upon the rightfulness of it; he must have an opportunity and time within which to present it to the court.

Q. (By Professor JOHNSON.) Do you think that the competition among producers is a force that will prevent exorbitant rates? You have not mentioned that in your remarks thus far that I could discover.—A. Do you mean the producers of goods?

Q. Yes, the producers of commodities of any kind that seek markets and reach those markets by transportation agencies. The competition of producers in given markets, of course, is a well-known phenomenon, and some writers lay much stress on that force as being one which will prevent excessive charges, even if you give the railroad corporations the power to cooperate in rate making. I think the commission would like your views on the operation of that force.—A. Well, I do not think that that is sufficient to prevent the exaction of exorbitant rates. If there is actual competition between railroads and it is carried on, that will tend to do it very much as charges for everything else are affected where there is free and full competition.

Q. Do you think the competition among carriers with each other at the present time has a stronger effect upon rates than the competition of producers with each other?—A. Well, they are so interwoven together that it is hard to tell which has the greater force. The competition of producers would not amount to much but for the railroads, because what is produced does not get very far but for the railroads. The circle of competition between producers before there were any railroads was very limited, and these questions did not trouble the country like they do now. It is the means of communication and transportation from the places of production to the places of consumption that affect the charges in all these things, and the one is dependent upon the other.

There is just one other matter I had in mind to refer to, and that is in regard to the power of inspection. It was referred to this morning in the testimony of Chairman Knapp (p. 144). The Government has the closest scrutiny over the banks. What they do in volume is a small matter compared to what the railroads do, and the number of people they touch and affect in their business is very small in comparison to the touch that the railroads have upon the public and its business generally; and the Government does not hesitate to send one of its agents into the bank at any time, with or without notice, to look into it from beginning to end to see what transactions it is dealing in, whether or not it is injuring business, whether it is violating any law or not; and that is done in large part for the protection of the people. So, with the insurance companies the States do the same thing, and it does not seem to me that any of these things compare in magnitude or in their effect upon the people with the business of the railroad companies. Many of these secret criminal violations of law, such as rebates and the like of that, were covered up in various ways in the books and offices, when they were called claims for loss and damages, presented as such, but which were rebates pure and simple. If the officer of the Government could walk in and call for Book A and the vouchers pertaining to the entries upon it, etc., and look through it like he does in a bank, these things can be found out. As it is now, how are you going to prove it? You go and call for the books and papers from the railroad officers and they bring them down and present them to you; but who can tell about what is in them? Who can do anything with them in the sessions of a court? It requires more time; it requires detailed examination by an expert who knows about books and has days and weeks to go through them and cull out and find out these things and explain them before a court can do anything with them or act upon them. But this is usually said to be an unnecessary interference with private affairs. I do not see that there are any private affairs in respect to the management of the railroad business in regard to transportation, if the public has any rights in it at all. If it is a private business, then there ought not to be any interstate-commerce law. If it is a public service and the public is entitled to equality of treatment and has rights in the matter, then it is but reasonable that they should have the means of finding out whether they are being wronged or not.

Q. (By Senator MALLORY.) You have no doubt as to the power of Congress to enact such legislation?—A. I see no reason for any doubt about it at all. The expressions of the courts seem to ascribe to Congress the fullest power in respect to interstate commerce, so that it does not confiscate property, a limitation that applies to all acts. These secret devices are so numerous and there are so many ways of concealing them that, unless you have access to their books and papers, you can not find out much about them; and even then it would be a matter of very great difficulty; but it would be more dangerous for them to do it than it is now.

Q. (By Professor JOHNSON.) Would you not have to accompany your inspection with a prescription as to accounts—uniformity of accounts?—A. Well, I think it would become necessary to have a uniformity of bookkeeping, and the present act hints at that and contemplates coming to that end at some time; uniformity of bookkeeping and keeping of accounts so that in all offices you would find about the same class of accounts on the same books.

It seems to me another wholesome thing would be to empower and require the courts, in cases of habitual and constant practices of paying rebates and of known violations of law, such as have been going on a few years back, where there was scarcely any attempt to conceal it except the detailed evidence of it that would be necessary in a criminal court—otherwise it was generally confessed that there was a general violation of law by rebates and by reducing the rates in one way and another—in a case of that kind, where a railroad is in that practice, and it is shown to the court on an application made, I do not see any reason why the court should not be required and empowered to enjoin any officer or agent of the road, from the president down, to cease and desist from that practice. Other people are enjoined in large numbers against violations of law, and I do not see why the whole company could not be enjoined in that way. If that were done, then a given instance being presented would require somebody to go to jail for contempt.

Q. It seems to me that would be taking the enforcement of criminal law out of the hands of the ordinary judicial machinery and substituting common law for statute law?—A. Well, it would be analogous to some things that are done now to preserve order and prevent general violations of law, whether it is good policy or not. Then, again, I think there is some language in the present antitrust law about the seizure of property in movement where it is being dealt with by practices in violation of law. I do not know that any case has ever been made, but if such remedies for unjust discriminations under the interstate-commerce law were applied in respect to that as are applied in regard to the internal-revenue law and the customs law, and property that was moving in fulfillment of contracts in violation of law was subject to seizure and condemnation, then it would make the road rough and hard, and that would tend to stop it. These things might be called harsh laws, but we have them in respect to all these other matters. They are effective; nothing else seems to answer the purpose, and no mild temporizing with this matter is going to make the condition any better than it is. It is true that publicity has a good effect and tends to improve the condition even when there is no power to enforce anything, because it exposes and holds up the wrongdoing and tends to cause correction of some of the worst things brought to light from time to time. But that is never going to be sufficient of itself in my judgment.

Q. (By Mr. PHILLIPS.) Has your commission ever made inquiry to ascertain the total amount of capitalization of all the railroads in the United States?—A. Well, their annual reports to us show that.

Q. Can you summarize it so as to give approximately the whole amount of capitalization?—A. I had those figures in my mind recently, but I am not sure what they are now.

Q. I mean the capitalization, and then the amount invested.—A. I am not sure what it is, but we have it in our reports and statistics accurately and definitely; something like $11,000,000,000, I think, is the capitalization.

Q. Have you any idea about how much actual money has been invested of this capital; can you approximate that?—A. No; I have no idea. I only know in respect to a great many of these roads that they are capitalized at least at twice as much as the original investment was. I only know that because of testimony brought into cases where they have had controversies, and the question of rates was up and the showing has been made. I do not know how many, but that has been shown at least in some cases. The commission has never had the means to ascertain what the original investments were. Many of these roads were built so long ago that I do not know of any way to ascertain that. Certainly we have not done so.

Q. Have you figures in regard to the entire bonded indebtedness of the railroads of the United States?—A. Yes.

Q. You have not that with you?—A. I do not quite remember what that is. Separate from the stock?

Q. Yes.—A. Oh, all those figures can be readily furnished you by the secretary, classified in any way you want them. They appear in our annual report.

Q. (By Senator MALLORY.) At present the chief and most conspicuous, and really probably the only material, source of complaint against our railroad transportation companies arises out of this question of discriminations?—A. That is far the greater cause of complaint.

Q. Of course, there are cases, as you said, of excessive rates?—A. Well, there are cases of that sort, and a good many complain of excessive rates; that is, in a good many of the complaints that come to the commission. But you can readily see that the shipper who makes complaint hardly has any means of measuring or estimating what would be a reasonable rate except by comparison; consequently in nearly all of these complaints references are made to other rates which they think are more favorable to some other community than theirs, or on some other commodity, and so they, nearly all of them, have in them the feature of alleged discrimination; also, a good many of them, that the rates are unreasonably high. It would be difficult for shippers generally to know whether a rate was unreasonably high or not except by comparison. There is hardly anything to judge by. They do not know what a road costs; they do not know what it costs to operate it; they do not know what proportion of the business of that road is made up of the particular kind of freight that they are complaining about; and it is hardly to be expected that the people generally, the individual shippers generally, would know whether the rates they were paying were unreasonably high or not by any means they can judge them by except comparison.

Q. (By Mr. A. L. HARRIS.) I would like to ask whether or not in the first years of the Interstate Commerce Commission it was not able to make a finding and fix a rate on that finding for the future?—A. Well, it so understood it and did it for about ten years. The commission understood that was within its authority.

Q. By what power was that taken away?—A. Well, the courts decided afterwards that it never had such authority.

Q. (By Senator MALLORY.) Virtually now, the commission is bereft of almost all of the power that was originally intended?—A. Yes, that is the way we understand it.

WASHINGTON, D. C., *October 6, 1899.*

TESTIMONY OF MR. FRANK L. NEALL,

Shipping merchant, Philadelphia, Pa.

The commission met on Friday, October 6, 1899, Vice-Chairman Phillips presiding. Mr. Frank L. Neall appeared at 10.55 a. m., and, after having duly affirmed, testified as follows:

Q. (By Senator MALLORY.) I believe your name is Frank L. Neall?—A. Frank L. Neall.

Q. Where do you reside?—A. Philadelphia.

Q. What is your occupation?—A. Shipping merchant, steamship agent; generally interested in transportation; also some banking business.

Q. Your business then gives you more or less extended acquaintance with the inland and ocean transportation of goods in this country?—A. It does.

Q. Is there anything now connected with that business on which you would like particularly to express criticisms, as to the abuses or suggestions of amendment?—A. I can not say that there are any subjects of abuse that I would care to be heard on; but I think I have knowledge on the general subject of ocean and inland transportation, and in correspondence with your committee, or those associated with it, certain suggestions were made that I might testify to, and if it is your pleasure, I will be glad to do so.

Q. We would be very grateful to hear you on any matter that your attention has been called to.—A. I am not in the habit of addressing audiences and, therefore, after making some short statements, if the committee sees fit to direct questions, I would be glad to answer them to the best of my ability.

In correspondence with Professor Johnson, I asked him if he would indicate a few subjects or a few lines on which it would probably be agreeable for the committee to hear me, and one of the suggestions was the relations of the railways to the business of ocean transportation. They are so intimately related and interdependent that it is difficult to separate them, at least as regards the immense volume of the export and import trade of the country. Of course, that does not have any relation to the inland carriage or the portion of property conveyed for domestic consumption. The relations of the ocean and inland carrier differ very materially at some of the ports. I will instance some differences between Boston, New York, Philadelphia, Baltimore, Norfolk, and Newport News. I do not purposely exclude the Southern ports, such as Charleston, Savannah, Mobile, Pensacola, New Orleans, and Galveston, but I am not so familiar with the details of their business as I am with the more Northern ports. Our relations with the export business via Boston are almost all what you might call definite. The property goes to Boston because specified there for the purpose of being exported, very often by previously designated or definite lines of transportation. In many articles of export, for instance, they have no local market. Grain and provisions and oil cake are in certain quantities specified, and only for export.

655A——11

Now, New York has immense receipts for export, and innumerable steamers visit that port seeking cargo in some respects, but most largely the regular line steamers carry the freight.   I suppose New York has 4 times, even 5 times, probably, more direct regular lines of steamers plying to all parts of the world than any of the other ports mentioned.   So that you bring to New York a great volume of the products of the United States and there meet the collected steamships, and they are able, to a very great extent, to arrange between themselves without any previous conference, you might say; whereas if an indefinite number of steamers were to go to Philadelphia or Baltimore, Norfolk or Newport News without the cargoes having been previously provided for them, they would be unsuccessful in securing them.

Q. They would lose a great deal of time?—A. They would lose a great deal of time, and, in the second place, they would not get it.

Q. In regard to this Boston business, as I understand, most of this product goes to Boston for the purpose of immediate shipment by water?—A. yes.

Q. Now, unless there was some provision and arrangement to meet the possibility, it would sometimes happen, probably, that there would be a large accumulation of cargo without any vessels to carry it, unless there was some arrangement made to meet it. Now, are we to infer that every cargo is arranged for when it is shipped to Boston, that there shall be a ship to take it to Europe or wherever it may go?—A. There are substantially no tramp steamers visiting Boston.   They have regular sailings averaging 30 or more per month.   The dates of these steamers do not change; they sail on fixed dates.   The agents of these steamers know in advance what steamers will sail in November and December and they make their previous provision for them just as you intimate.

Q. As a rule, do these vessels mostly combine passengers and freight, or are they freight vessels?—A. Substantially freight vessels.   A few of them take some passengers, but they are usually what is known as freighters—Warren, Leyland, and there are other lines, with the Cunard the only one taking a few passengers.   They do take largely cattle at times.

Q. (By Mr. CLARKE.) And the Dominion Line also, I suppose?—A. In the winter time I believe the Dominion Line goes from there, but in the summer time the Dominion Line goes from Montreal.

Q. I think this summer they have been running from Boston also.—A. That is quite possible.

Q. They go to Liverpool?—A. Yes.   There are 21 sailing per month from the port of Boston to Liverpool, and in this particular she far outranks New York.

Q. (By Senator MALLORY.) So the shipping merchants can always count on having a ship for their cargo on a certain day?—A. Yes; that freight room is placed through the agents of the railroad.   Generally they engage so many loads of wheat, corn, or oats, so many tons of oil cake, so many packages of provisions, which are to be there by a certain time.

Q. In Philadelphia are not the conditions much the same?—A. Much the same as in Boston.

Q. Not many tramp steamers go there?—A. Not for general cargo; but the bulk of our business is by tramp steamers for grain as from Baltimore, Norfolk, and Newport News.   New York and Boston are the reverse; they have the regular lines which do the bulk of their trade.

Q. Now, is there any difficulty in the matter of getting ocean transportation at times like this, when, I believe, there is great demand for it?—A. It is rather excited at the present moment, owing to the British Government having taken 75 or more vessels ordinarily engaged in the trans-Atlantic trade, for carrying mules, men, etc., to Africa.

Q. Situated as Philadelphia is, with a certain large quantity of grain to ship within a given time, and her chief reliance the tramp steamer—in a case of this kind, what would they do?—A. As a rule, Philadelphia, Baltimore, Norfolk, and Newport News all look ahead for their requirements to a considerable extent.   At the present time vessels are probably engaged for 7,000,000 bushels that can either load largely at Philadelphia, Baltimore, Norfolk, or Newport News, according as the parties who have chartered them eventually determine.   The out-port must always have a large credit balance of tonnage chartered ahead.   The immediate effect of the British Government going into the freight market has been to advance the rates of freight enormously in the last 2 weeks, in some directions 75 per cent.   London freight room from New York within 3 weeks has been 3d.; yesterday 4d. was offered; and by reason of some of the London carriers having combined, they are asking even more.   This has seriously affected all the tramp steamers.   We have this morning the refusal of a vessel at 3s. 3d.; that same vessel would have been glad 3 weeks ago to take 2s. 6d.; that is a difference of nearly 33 per cent.   As a rule, you can get your tonnage, but you must pay a higher rate by reason of these demands.

Q. Take business such as that conducted at the ports other than Boston and New York, as you have mentioned. Is there not considerable inconvenience and risk arising from the necessity of having to charter these vessels so far ahead, as to freight rates?—A. When you charter ahead to any considerable extent the chances are you are selling ahead. You are buying your corn or your wheat or your oats, and at the same time you are engaging your steamers, chartering them; and, as a rule, they are calculating to carry pretty good stocks of grain at these ports. When they can not cover themselves by the purchase of the identical delivery they want, they go into the New York market and buy an option, or the Chicago market and buy options temporarily against that g .

Q. I was speaking with reference to the inconvenience of this method of doing business. Instead of having reliable lines so that you can count on for your shipments, you have to go out in the market sometimes, I suppose, as much as two months ahead and charter your vessels?—A. Certainly. It is an entirely separate and distinct kind of business. That is what might be called a full-cargo business versus the line-steamer business; and it is on the full-cargo business that Philadelphia, Baltimore, Norfolk, and Newport News recoup themselves and counterbalance to a considerable extent the advantages which New York has from her innumerable regular steamship lines; and the regular direct steamship lines very often go to ports that the full cargoes do not go to. The direct steamships as a rule take cargo to those specific, direct ports at a proportionately lower rate than the tramp steamer will take it there, because the direct line takes a certain amount of grain and has to sail on the regular sailing day. Then she takes oil cake, and can take the grain she requires as ballast at a lower rate than the tramp steamer will take a full cargo.

Q. (By Professor JOHNSON.) I think it will be well for you to describe the manner in which the Minneapolis miller actually ships a consignment of flour from Minneapolis to Liverpool via Boston—what the arrangements really are that are made in connection with the movement of that consignment of flour to Liverpool via Boston.— A. The Minneapolis miller has, say, 50 cars of flour that he wishes to ship to Liverpool. He canvasses among the different railroad agents there—and most of them are supplied with rates of freight either via Boston, New York, Philadelphia, Baltimore, or Newport News—and he says he will have 50 cars of flour to ship in November, and he gets them to bidding on it. He says, I have the property; now, what will you take it at? One man says, I will take it at so many cents a hundred through, maybe Boston or maybe New York, or it maybe Newport News; and we will say the rate would be—I won't undertake to mention an actual rate—say, 35 cents a hundred from Minneapolis to Liverpool. One man will bid for that transaction, 35 cents; another man will come up and say, here, we want some for that steamer that sails in November and we will take it for 34 cents. So that is the cheapest rate by the differ- ential line; that is the rate that will get that property as a rule. Then the goods are shipped in cars which are transported by the railroad to the docks at Boston or any of the other cities. It is unloaded on to the docks, where it remains until the seagoing vessel is ready to receive it, or if the vessel comes alongside that dock it is loaded directly into it. If it is necessary to lighter to her, it is transferred by lighter to the seagoing craft. It is then carried to Liverpool and delivered to the consignee specified in the original through bill of lading.

Q. What contract or relationship exists between the inland carrier and the owner of the vessel?—A. That depends on circumstances.

Q. The man in Minneapolis is able to give a rate from Minneapolis to Liverpool over 2 carriers?—A. Yes.

Q. Does that mean there has been a previous contract or agreement between the 2 carriers?—A. Generally. Very often the ocean carrier will say to the railroad, We have so much room which we can give you for November at such and such a rate. The inland carrier adds to that ocean rate the inland rate, which makes the sum at which he undertakes to handle the goods.

Q. Is there an agreement among the freight carriers of the North Atlantic to which they adhere in the matter of freight, of grain traffic, or other lines of traffic?—A. I do not think there is. You mean as to rates of the steamship lines?

Q. Yes.—A. No. There could not be. It is too varying a quantity. I have just given you that instance of the raise from 3d. to 4d. in London. They are regulated almost entirely by supply and demand, and the urgency for freight.

Q. It is a matter of open competition then?—A. Forced competition.

Q. (By Senator MALLORY.) The freight rates, as I understand, from the interior of this country to Europe, vary considerably from time to time?—A. Yes; largely by the exigency of the demand of the ocean carriers.

Q. The variation is more due to the ocean carrier than the inland carrier?—A. The ocean carriers vary frequently every day in the week, but the inland carriers comparatively seldom.

Q. The transportation charge from the interior of the country to the seaboard for export is generally staple; I mean it holds pretty much the same figure without any startling or rapid changes?—A. It has been been holding at a pretty minimum figure for some years, and with the number of lines of transportation it seems unlikely that it should hereafter assume any very high figure, I should think.

Q. Is the competition between Boston, Philadelphia, New York, Baltimore, and Newport News a factor in keeping these rates at a reasonable and staple figure?—A. Yes. That is what we have to work for.

Q. (By Professor JOHNSON.) It would be a safe inference from what you said a few minutes ago that the major part of the Minneapolis flour is shipped by special contract rather than by any previously published rates of the inland carriers?—A. I do not think any considerable amount of flour is shipped away from Minneapolis unless the freight is previously arranged for. You know that used to be done to an enormous extent. Freight would be shipped through from Minneapolis and all western points and collected at New York, where they often offered very great inducements to have the freight shipped in that way, such as storage from 1 to 3 or 6 months, but as a rule now, the property, before it leaves the point of manufacture, has been contracted for very largely through to the destination.

I see another notation by Professor Johnson—"the extent to which the ocean business is subject to competition and the extent to which competition has been eliminated." The extent to which the ocean business is subject to competition is, probably the broadest and widest that could be conceived of. It is nothing unusual for us to have 2 or 3 steamers offered to us from London, which is the headquarters of tonnage. These vessels would be offered for 2s. 9d. per quarter, or 3s. a quarter, from what are called picked ports, such as the northern range, which, is New York, Philadelphia, Baltimore, Newport News, to certain specified ports in Europe. In the morning we get a cable, "Can not renew refusals; Argentina offering better prices; Danubian demand increasing; large eastern inquiry." So the vessel we get in America, you may say, for ocean transportation has to be taken in competition with the other foreign markets of the world. The owner sits there in his office, and does not care much whether she goes to America, Argentina, the Danube, or the East Indies. Ocean rates are subject to that kind of competition, and if we are not giving but 3s. a quarter, we must advance the rate, so that we will attract them as against the inquiries from other portions of the world. Does that measurably answer your inquiry?

Q. You might perhaps state to us what portion of the ocean transportation is taken by steamers that are contracted for in this way, and whether all regular liners are subject to this arrangement?—A. On the contrary, they are always on the alert. If they find that there are not steamers enough, as they did yesterday, or that rates are higher, the rates are advanced. They will advance their rates twice in a day if necessary. We took grain to Rotterdam early this week at 2s. 6d. a quarter; later on we took it at 2s. 9d.; yesterday, just before I came here, we took some at 3s., and refused to take more at 3s. because we feel the tendency is upward.

Q. (By Mr. CLARKE.) Right on that point I would like to inquire whether you take grain at a lower rate than flour?—A. As a rule, yes.

Q. Why is that?—A. For the reason that grain stows in about 50 cubic feet as against 60 to 65 cubic feet that flour stows in. The grain costs about 8 cents a ton to handle and to put into a ship, and flour costs 37½ cents to load and put into the ship. Grain is more economically handled; and we can take a room like this and get in it from one-fifth to one-sixth less tons of flour than corn or wheat. The flour comes in sacks and the grain in bulk.

Q. (By Senator MALLORY.) You just pour the wheat into the compartment of the ship?—A. A man goes into the bin and pushes it up into the corner and all round, and the compartment is filled; but when you put flour in there is more or less broken stowage; you can not get the ends together. When you come to the corner of a room you have room for half a bag of flour but you have not room for a whole bag, and you lose that space.

Q. (By Mr. CLARKE.) Does most of the export flour go in bags or barrels?—A. Nine-tenths of it goes in bags; only to South America, substantially, and West Indies, and to a few special points, is any flour exported in barrels.

Q. What are the bags, paper or cloth?—A. I never saw any paper; they are very largely burlap, which is imported, and then exported on a drawback; or muslin.

Q. Are you aware of the recent advance in the inland rate on export grain and flour?—A. I was present in New York at the hearing before the Interstate Commerce Commission on that subject, and I took occasion to testify—give my opinion—as to what I thought was a just and equitable difference between the two, which was that flour on ocean transportation, at least, should be not exceeding 2 to 3 cents per hundred more than grain.

Q. Well, is there any such reason appertaining to the inland transportation?—A. There is more or less difference in the cost of handling it.

Q. Is export grain as easily handled for transportation overland as export flour?—A. Well, there are special provisions made for the more economical handling of grain, by reason of the export elevators into which it is delivered upon arrival at the seaboard; and the car containing 1,000 bushels of grain is very expeditiously handled, and with very little manual labor. Every sack of flour has to be man-handled, as it were; but there were arguments used, which I think were very unjust and very unfair, in reference to flour, calculating on a much greater difference than the 2 or 3 cents which I referred to.

Q. Did your estimate of that difference cover both ocean and land transportation, or only ocean transportation?—A. Well, I am afraid I expressed myself very awkwardly a moment ago. The question I thought of, ocean transportation, was not particularly before the commission. It was on the question of inland transportation. We settle that ourselves by charging a higher rate for flour than for grain, and we have no difficulty in getting that; but my testimony was directed particularly to the inland question, and I thought the 2 or 3 cents, as an extreme, would be a full and fair difference, considering the amount of grain versus flour that you could put in a car, considering the labor involved in the loading and unloading a car, and the time that would naturally be involved in the emptying a car of grain versus one of flour.

Q. You make reference to the difference as a through shipment, say from Minneapolis to Liverpool?—A. Which would be a through shipment of flour, but there would be no through shipment of grain. There is very little grain shipped on through bills of lading. I am afraid I am not making that very clear to you.

Q. (By Mr. RATCHFORD.) Is there any variation in the cost of exporting different classes of grain?—A. You mean aboard the steamer?

Q. Yes.—A. Yes.

Q. Handling a ship?—A. Yes.

Q. What are the differences, and why?—A. When we come to stow the corn and the wheat, we pay the stevedores $2 a thousand for it; when we come to store the oats, we pay $3.50 a thousand, for the reason that the oats, because of their spongy character, are required to be tramped, and there is more labor involved in the stowage of them.

Q. The variation, then, is due to the loading of it?—A. The cost of handling, yes.

Q. Is there any variation in the cost of exporting the different flours and mill materials—breadstuffs?—A. Yes; a large difference. Flour is exported the cheapest of all flour-mill products, and then you have the bran and middlings, and all the various by-products. Corn meal and cornuda and all these various products are more bulky. A sack filled with flour weighs so many pounds. If you fill it with any other by-products, it does not weigh two-thirds or one-half as much, but it takes the same space, and therefore we have to raise the rate on it.

Q. (By Professor JOHNSON.) Then the rates are really determined ultimately by the space the product occupies?—A. On ocean carriage more than on inland carriage. If you fill a modern car with the legal weight of wheat, you bring it up about level with the car door; if you fill it with corn you bring it probably a foot higher, because the corn is lighter. Now, if you fill it with oats, you must put in a temporary door, and fill it nearly up to the roof. But the railroad will very often get the full maximum weight of any one of the three in there. In the steamship, however, you can not do that. Our problem is, to fill a vessel and to load her at the same time, and we must have concentrated weight largely to do that. In other words, we have a great big square bin, which is comparable to this room. Now, if we fill that with wheat weighing so many pounds, we get so many bushels; if we fill it with corn weighing 56 pounds, we get a smaller number of bushels; but if we fill it with oats weighing 36 pounds, you see what a small weight we get. It is all paid by weight. We do not care what a man puts in there, so it loads the vessel properly, and balances her and stiffens her. If the shipper will say, "I will give you so many pounds sterling freight," so long as we got the same amount of freight we would not object to that small difference in stevedoring.

Q. (By Senator MALLORY.) You said in your judgment, I believe, that 2 to 3 cents was a reasonable and fair margin between flour and wheat?—A. Between flour and heavy grains; for inland transportation I think that is fair.

Q. For inland transportation? Has that difference been considerably higher at different times?—A. Yes; I understand that the millers complain that it has been as high as 7½.

Q. I think it has been testified to here that it has been even higher than that?—A. Yes. I heard one of the officials of the Grand Trunk at this same meeting; he said the rate ought to be 50 per cent higher. I did not agree with him at all. I think 2½ cents is all that could be reasonably charged, and all that could be exacted or collected.

Q. Have you any idea of the reason why these exorbitant rates were charged?—A. I probably could not do better than to recite the information furnished by one of these traffic officials. An official of the Grand Trunk said it ought to be 50 per cent more. He may have had some sad experience. He may have been compelled to carry flour in cars or warehouse for 2 or 3 months at a time, and he may have had that in his mind. But for a reasonably prompt movement of both grain and flour, 2 to 2½ cents difference is all that ought to be exacted from the millers, and all that traffic can stand or actually will be paid.

Q. Can you say about what the difference is now?—A. I do not think it is more. I think competition is keeping it down to about that. For you see now, to be more exact, we are having a car famine in some lines of business. It is more a question of getting a car and asking for the rate afterwards. Generally they ask a rate and then have the car sent; now they send a car and ask for the rate afterwards.

Q. (By Mr. A. L. Harris.) How long has this difference in the rates existed between wheat and flour?—A. Always. The gradual tendency has been to decrease the difference.

Q. So the condition now is better for the American miller than it was in former years?—A. Yes; better. It never was less than it is, except under special circumstances, when great competition may have cut the rates.

Q. Then this difference in rates between wheat and flour in your judgment is made up in profit to the American miller, is it? He is still able to manufacture flour and ship it at a profit, as the grain dealer can ship wheat, or he can ship wheat before it is ground?—A. And if the differences are very fairly divided I think the advantage which the miller has with his by-product would enable him to pay that much more rail freight on the flour that he exports.

Q. The difference in the rate you suggest you think would not injure the American miller?—A. No; I think not. If not out of order I would like to state that I am a thorough believer in export rates on the products of the West being accorded at lower figures than are accorded domestic shipments.

Q. (By Senator Mallory.) That is done now generally, is it not?—A. That is done. It is generally a question of locality.

Q. (By Mr. Phillips.) Will you please give us your reasons therefor?—A. One of the principal reasons is that the condition of lower rates on the surplus export products of the United States operates in favor of the producer and farmer in the West as a protection, just as the United States tariff assists the eastern manufacturer in keeping out foreign goods unless they pay a heavy duty. In other words, the average export of corn, I presume, might be put down, in recent years, to 200,000,000 bushels. Wheat varies from 100,000,000 to 160,000,000 bushels, and the surplus, the export of oil cake and other articles, proportionately. Now, this surplus that the farmer has on hand must be gotten rid of. If it is not gotten rid of, or if he undertook to force that 200,000,000 bushels of corn or the 150,000,000 bushels of wheat down the mouths of the inhabitants of the United States, who are all sufficiently supplied, he would cut the price down, and very soon reduce, from necessity, the tonnage production. When that man ships out his maize or his wheat, or oil cake, or his petroleum, or whatever it may be, he meets the competition of the Argentine and the Danube and the Russias and Hungary or France, and he can only sell it, provided he is able to present a substantially good article, at about the same price as his competitors. Now, personally, I can not see what objection, for instance, the eastern producers of wheat and corn, articles of that kind, would have to conceding to the western producer the lower export rate, for the reason that if that western producer does not get rid of his surplus abroad he will come into the East and reduce the market price here by this small surplus, compared to the total production, and reduce prices to an unremunerative point.

Q. Now, you can go on with the next.—A. "The place of the American vessel owners in the business of ocean transportation. Can they compete; and if not, what is necessary to enable them to compete?" I was saying to Professor Johnson and Senator Mallory this morning that within the last few days, while having a general knowledge of the tonnage of American vessels versus that of foreign vessels, I had had occasion to examine into the subject more thoroughly, and I was simply astounded at the result. The steam tonnage of the world at the present time represents a gross tonnage of 21,000,000; sailing tonnage is represented by 7,000,000; that makes a total steam and sailing tonnage of the world, according to the last report of Lloyd's Register, of 28,000,000 tons. That refers to all the tonnage of all the vessels; that is, of sail and steam, of all the nations of the world—vessels of 100 tons and over, either steam or sail.

Q. That is gross tonnage?—A. The 21,000,000 is gross of the steamers, and the 7,000,000 is net of the sailing vessels; but taking the total as 28,000,000 tons, if you add 50 per cent to it, that would make 42,000,000 tons, and that would make, as near, I believe, as you can get to it, the carrying capacity of all vessels of all nations of the world in dead weight tons.

Q. That is ocean tonnage, is it?—A. I meant to say registered steam and sailing vessels of the world over 100 tons register or upward.

Q. Does that include lakes and rivers?—A. Lakes and rivers, oceans and everything; of every vessel that is registered or known in the world, either steam or sail, of 100 tons or over. Now, that being 28,000,000 tons, if you will add to that 50 per cent, it would make 42,000,000, and you have the capacity of all steam and sailing vessels in the world to transport in.

Q. (By Professor JOHNSON.) That represents the freight that they can actually carry?—A. Yes.

Q. If all loaded at one time?—A. Yes. Now, bearing on that subject, it would appear that the exports of the United States last year amounted to something over 30,000,000 tons of freight. That makes corn, 5,000,000 tons; wheat, 4,000,000 tons; oil, 3,500,000 tons; coal, 4,500,000 cotton, 2,000,000; flour, 1,600,000, something over 30,000,000 tons that we export per annum. Now, to go back to the subject: "The place of the American vessel owners in the business of ocean transportation. Can they compete; and if not, what is necessary to enable them to compete?" I am going to make a statement now which probably will be challenged, but I believe it to be absolutely correct. There are not now available for trans-Atlantic or trans-Pacific ocean carriage vessels under the American flag, sail or steam, of less than 20 years of age, of the capacity of over 300,000 tons register. I think that the records show us accredited altogether with 2,000,000 tons register. In other words, on the Atlantic coast and Pacific coast to-day under the American flag all steam vessels and sailing vessels available and ⌄uitable to cross the Atlantic to the Continent and the United Kingdom, to cross the Pacific to Honolulu or Manila, there is only a tonnage of vessels represented of 300,000 tons gross register.

Q. How did you get your knowledge?—A. By carefully going over the American Register and Lloyd's Register and other data. I had a man at work for a part of 2 days. It was so startling that I wanted it proved, and I believe it is correct. If you can bring out that fact I think it is one of the most important features, if you will permit me to say so, that your commission could draw to the attention of the public.

Q. (By Senator MALLORY.) In making that estimate, where did you draw the line as between the vessels capable of going across the Atlantic and Pacific and those not capable of doing that? What size did you strike out on the tonnage?—A. I took the position that people are not in business generally for fun, but to make money. Now, no steamer of 1,000 tons can pretend to live in a trans-Atlantic trade. I took out sailing vessels that were 20 years old, because you would not wish to ship goods in them. They will do for long voyages, for coal and like that. Then we would say that the coastwise steamships of the United States, like the *El Sud*, etc., that are built to go around this coast, and have 5 or 6 days coal in them and probably carry 2,000 tons or 2,500 tons of cargo. I say that vessel is neither suitable, from her construction, overhang, and superstructure, to go across the Atlantic, and if she was, she could not possibly make both ends meet to go across and come back. In making that statement I have not undertaken to make a forced showing at all, but carefully eliminated all vessels of which you, as a practical man, would say, "I would not take that vessel." You would not take the Winsor steamers; you would not take the Ward liners, that go to Habana in 3½ days; you would not take the Mallory steamers that go to New Orleans and Galveston, simply because they can not stand mid-Atlantic weather with their overhang. There is not enough carrying capacity to pay the man if he gets across, he can not take enough freight to pay him for the expense. So I only took vessels of 1,000 tons or over. I know that no vessel of 1,000 tons can engage in any trans-Atlantic trade and make both ends meet. I know that as a practical steamship man, running steamers, and being conversant with them.

Q. (By Mr. PHILLIPS.) Now, we understand you that this 300,000 tons is ocean tonnage; it does not include lakes and inland rivers?—A. I would like to make that thoroughly understood. At the present date there are not American vessels available for the trans-Atlantic or trans-Pacific trade, having a united registered tonnage of 300,000 tons, that are less than 20 years of age.

Q. We understood you to state that this forty-odd millions of tons capacity embraced both ocean and inland traffic. That includes lakes and rivers of the world as well as oceans?—A. Yes.

Q. Now, can you tell how much American tonnage we have in addition to this, on the lakes and the rivers of the United States?—A. According to records, 2,100,000 tons; but you can not get a lake steamer from the Great Lakes or any of those modern steamers through the canals; you can not get them through the canals down here. If they did come they would be knocked into smithereens by a great storm. It is so improbable that it need not to be compared.

Q. (By Senator MALLORY.) Right on that point you have spoken of the impossibility of using for trans-Atlantic trade such vessels as are now engaged in the coastwise trade down to New Orleans and Galveston from New York, and the Ward line to Habana and Mexico. Some of them are large enough. Some of those vessels are 3,000 tons, and yet you seem to think they are not strong enough or capable of standing Atlantic gales, because of their peculiar build?—A. Their superstructure, their housing and so on, are such that no one would put that kind of structure on vessels that are going to make those trips.

Q. Are they all constructed with that high superstructure?—A. More or less so. They have the passenger accommodations; and even those vessels at the present time are mostly owned by the Government.

Q. Now, one of the lines, the El Sud and the El Nord, have built some vessels ——A. (Interrupting.) Yes; the Mexico and Havana have been built within the last six months.

Q. Those vessels all have superstructure and have passenger room on deck?—A. Yes.

Q. But is not that merely an incident? Can not that be removed without affecting the shipping capacity at all, making a smooth-deck ship?

The WITNESS. How much do these vessels carry?

Senator MALLORY. Some register 3,000 tons.

The WITNESS. What is the dead-weight capacity?

Senator MALLORY. Greater than that; I do not know. If they register 2,500, they probably carry 4,500 tons freight.

The WITNESS. I guess their registry is largely made up of these housings, are they not?

Senator MALLORY. Now that, of course, is excluded by the registered tonnage. The registered tonnage is much less than the actual displacement. The proportion is not quite 2 to 1, but something like that.

The WITNESS. I recognize the difference of the net register and gross register and the tonnage capacity. If you take the net register and add half to it you have the gross register, as a rule, in the trans-Atlantic trade. If you add 50 per cent to the latter you have the dead-weight capacity. That dead-weight capacity always includes coal and anything of that nature, for which you would charge 600 or 800 tons. But after you charged all of these things it would not make any difference in my statement. I allowed more leeway than that in that estimate of 300,000 tons.

Q. (By Mr. PHILLIPS). You can take up the next question in order: "What laws, if any, do you think ought to be enacted on the part of Congress and the States in the interest of ocean transportation?" That is the question. "Can they compete; and if not, what is necessary to enable them to compete?"—A. While the ocean transportation was confined to wooden walls, we never had to ask any odds of anybody, that is, before 1860. When the tonnage of the world was contained in wooden vessels, the United States wooden walls commanded a premium over any other vessels that were on the seas, and the owners were as prosperous as you could ask them to be. After that the transition came to iron, and subsequently to steel steamers, and as strange as it may appear, for some reason or other, America has never built what might be called an ocean tramp. I think there has never been an American ocean craft or tramp of that kind built. Americans are not permitted to import or hold, substantially, foreign vessels, although probably at this time it is one of the most legitimately profitable industries in the world. The records of the British shipping show innumerable instances where within the last 10 years individuals or firms owning 1 or 2 steamers have developed their plants until to-day they own 20. All the increase in the British tonnage has very largely been made out of accretions from the returns of vessels they have managed. We have amongst our list of correspondents many people who comparatively a few years ago had 3 or 4 steamers. Now they have or represent 10 or 12, very largely made out of their profits. The United States has built up an export trade for her manufactured products which in the last 2 years has been considerably increased. It has been made possible by a character of subownership by Americans of foreign vessels. During that time there has been an innovation in transportation, practically—that is, what are designated as time charter parties. There are hundreds of vessels of that kind now chartered by British, Norwegian, German, and other owners, to Americans, and it gives the Americans for the time being—the time generally being fixed as 6 months to 2 years—it gives them the sole.

virtually the absolute control of that vessel. To give you an illustration of it: A company that we represent has a half dozen vessels at the present time owned on time charter for practically a year. We are able to control the movements of each of those vessels, virtually, as though we owned her, every dollar's worth. We have the right to send her to any port of the civilized world. If it had not been for that character of vessels, the American manufacturers would have found the greatest difficulty in getting their products out of the country, to their destinations in Europe, Asia, Africa, Japan, and Java, wherever the vessels go. Up to within a short time, if you wanted to ship, say, a cargo of locomotives to Vladivostock, or some of these out-of-the-way places, you would have to take a list of probably 50 steamers. When you would go to 1 owner, he would say, I do not want your locomotive freight; and when you would go to the next owner, he would say, That will make my vessels too late to go to China, and I do not want to take that freight; and the next man that comes along will say, I have not got large enough hatches for locomotives. Now, all you have is to go to the London or New York market, and you will find somebody who will take the freight either to South Africa, Australia, New Zealand, and any part of China or Manila. Simply say you want to ship so many thousand pounds of stuff, and you will find somebody who has such a time charter. A score of them will name you a rate.

Q. (By Senator MALLORY.) Does the charter of these vessels name the captain and subordinate officers?—A. A clause of the charter party is substantially this: The owner is to supply officers and crew, and engine stores, and pay ordinary consul's fees. Further than that he does absolutely nothing. He supplies the officers and crew and grubs them, as they call it, and the engine stores; then he is done. The next clause in the charter party says that if for any reason the captain or officers are unsatisfactory, or do not perform their duties to the satisfaction of the time charterers, the owners, on reasonable complaint, shall change them.

Q. Well, the owner pays the officers and crews, then?—A. The owner pays the officers and crews, and the time charterer furnishes the coal.

Q. Then the crew and master are paid European wages?—A. The crew and master are paid European wages.

Q. Which are less than American wages?—A. Somewhat less, but nothing like as great a difference as there was a few years ago. They have got wages of the men on the other side up to about £4 10s. now.

Q. (By Mr. CLARKE.) Is not the cost of keeping them a good deal less?—A. The foreign vessels are kept on a much lower range of diet than the American. You could keep them practically on the same rate; but they set a better table on the American vessels, as a rule.

Q. They eat oftener than the Americans; I understand the Norwegians eat 4 meals a day.—A. It is fish for breakfast, fish for dinner, and fish for supper, and fish soup. We have 4 vessels on time charters. The officers of those vessels are types in themselves. You do not want anything more intelligent, more interesting and more efficient in their way. And the owners are just sitting back and making 20 or 25 per cent per annum on their vessels, and it is for you gentlemen to devise some way so that America can get a chance at that kind of business.

Q. (By Professor JOHNSON.) You charter these vessels because you can not buy them?—A. We charter them. We can not get them under the American flag. Of course we would get American vessels if we could do so, but they do not exist.

Q. (By Senator MALLORY.) Have you any suggestions to make as to such legislation as will bring this about—this consumation so devoutly to be wished?—A. Well, I would like to make one suggestion in that connection, which would be to make it possible for Americans, under the most rigid restrictions from participation in coastwise trade of the United States or any trade within a few miles of it, that they should be able to own vessels that would be foreign vessels, improved vessels. I would not favor any law which would get a lot of superannuated tramps or old vessels. I would bring vessels from 2, 3, or 4 years of age. I think it would be a grand step forward for this country if she would enact such wise laws as would prevent the interference with the coastwise carrying trade, which we consider belongs especially to us, and which ought to, and which would enable American capital to seek what I consider one of the most profitable sources of investment at the present time—that is, owning what are called transient or tramp steamers, and running them in the general commerce of the world. We are excluded from that now, and the only way we can transport in one of those vessels now is by first paying the real owner 20 to 25 per cent profit, and we must make our profit on top of that.

Q. Do you know anything about the ability of shipbuilders in this country—say Philadelphia, Newport News, or elsewhere—to build iron or steel ships as cheaply as they can on the Clyde or other shipbuilding portions of the United Kingdom?—A. I know some little about it.

Q. I have seen it stated that the Cramps could build ships now as cheaply as they can on the Clyde.—A. You do not literally mean now, but within the next few years. Of course everything is going up. I do not believe you could contract in the United States for half a dozen tramps, say, of 6,000 or 7,000 tons, for delivery within the next 2 years. If you look that right in the face you have 2 years to look forward to.

Q. Is it a fact that the improvements of shipbuilding in this country have made such advances and the cheapening of the work has gone on so that we can now build them ton for ton as cheaply as the English can?—A. I do not believe anything of the kind; but I do not believe that there is the same difference that existed some time ago. I have knowledge in our business in connection with sale and purchase of vessels and correspondence with shipbuilders, and so on, of what tramp steamers, and so on, cost abroad. I cabled within the last 72 hours to have that verified. The present price for a substantial tramp steamer of 7,000 tons dead-weight capacity is £8 10s. per ton; that is, $42.50, roughly—call it $45—the cost in American money. If that was built by the Americans they would put $2.50 extras on; they would put better winches and a little heavier bottom and probably a little more water ballast. You can contract abroad now at $45 a ton. Before this difference in iron I believe that you could have contracted, possibly, for—during the depression, say—you could have contracted for 2 or 3 tramps, possibly, here at $65 or $70 a ton. I do not believe at any time you could have contracted at a lower price than that; but I do not think that is a comparison, for this reason, that we have very few shipyards; and it is as if we had very few shoemakers. For instance, if you pay $7.50 for your boots and shoes, and that shoemaker is kept very busy at $7.50, he is not very likely to solicit some hod carrier that comes along and wants a pair of $1.75 or $2 shoes. He can make them, but he can not make as much as if he sells $7.50 shoes, and he is not going to cater to that class of trade so long as he can get the other trade.

Q. Then your belief and experience are, in regard to large construction, that there is a decided difference in the cost price of vessels that can be built in the United States, as compared with those built in England or Scotland?—A. I make a distinction between transient vessels; on these I believe the difference will be at least $15 to $20 a ton more cost to buyer here, but on the higher-class vessels (ocean greyhounds), that require so much joiner work, etc., the percentage of difference between European and American prices is not as great.

Q. But it is on the common carrying vessel?—A. The common American tramp will cost the buyer from $15 to $20 more, because we charge more here.

Q. (By Mr. KENNEDY.) If the Baldwins and other manufacturers of American locomotives can make locomotives and sell them in England in competition with English manufacturers and in other parts of the world, why is it that American shipbuilders can not build ships as cheaply as the English can?—A. The reason that the Baldwins made some of these English contracts recently was entirely because they could deliver the goods almost offhand, and buyers could not find anybody abroad that could deliver them within 12 months. That is the reason they got those contracts, particularly the English contracts.

Q. Well, the American locomotives have been going to all parts of the world in competition with the others?—A. Yes; there has been a tremendous business done, and very often on account of time; and there is no doubt but what we have got up to that point. The same thing is true of steel rails. Steel rails during this depression were sold very largely to the British Government, and the British officials were taken to task on it and asked why they did it, and after beating around the bush for a while, they said: We did it because we needed 70,000 tons (I believe it was), and we bought them in America because we could buy them $31,000 cheaper than in England. We have got to that point on steel rails and locomotives where we can compete with the world, but we have not got there on steamers. Now, are you going to keep us a few more decades where we are, or are you going to give us a chance?

Q. (By Senator MALLORY.) We have fixed the fact of the cost of building in this country as against others.—A. The tramp steamers, I meant.

Q. I mean tramp steamers, or, say, freight-carrying steamships; and that may be accepted as settled, for the present at least, as a factor against America building steel or iron steamships of that class. Now, in addition to that we must consider the cost of running these vessels. I asked you, with regard to these chartered vessels, whether the crew and officers were paid by the owners of the ship or by the charter party, and you stated, by the owners of the ship. In other words, they received European wages. Can you state what is the per cent of difference between wages paid the average American sailor, or fireman, or stoker, mate, and captain, and the wages paid the sailors and officers of the vessels of France, Italy, England, Norway, and Sweden, or any of these continental countries that are commercial countries?—A. We have all that data as a matter of record in our office. I have a general idea, but I would prefer to give it to you exactly rather than by percentage now. If you will formulate your questions so as to ask what all nations pay their men at the present time, including, of course, the United States, I will be glad to give you the information.

Q. We would like to have it, as it is a matter of importance.—A. I can say, in a few words, the difference is not as great as sometime ago, but there is a difference.

Q. (By Mr. A. L. HARRIS.) I would like to ask to what extent the difference in cost of labor in this country in shipyards, and the cost of labor in foreign countries in shipyards, goes to make up this difference of 20 per cent?—A. The labor, I believe, is largely the element. Of course, it can not be steel and it can not be iron, and it can not be wood, because we know we are producing that as cheaply as any people in the world; but when you come to the question of labor, I am reminded of what an old Dutch captain of ours said sometime ago to me. He said: "It is cheaper for me to metal my vessel in Philadelphia, and pay $2.50 wages, than it is for me to go to Rotterdam and employ labor there at $1 a day. I get so much more out of the labor, and it takes so much less time for the work to be completed." So, while the labor over there is cheaper on the face of it, the labor here is—when you come to take the work it produces—not unnecessarily dear.

Q. (By Mr. CLARKE.) Is that true of every department of the work?—A. No; I think it would be more true of the commoner parts of the labor.

Q. (By Mr. PHILLIPS.) Then what goes to make up this difference in the cost, if the steel is as cheap and the wood is as cheap and the labor, while paid more, is more efficient?—A. I do not wish to undertake to dodge the question; but, as I stated, there have been no tramps built, and we have nothing to guide us very well. If anybody should offer tramps, transient steamers, or freight steamers, more properly called, because there is a feeling against that word tramp, but it is so customary now; we hardly ever speak of them except as that—if anyone was to offer American tramp steamers now of 7,000 tons capacity at $50 to $55 a ton, I believe they could find buyers for all that could be put on the market, and they would go out, notwithstanding they would be handicapped by the enhanced cost. At 7,000 tons—I am speaking of cost per ton, dead-weight capacity—and if you take it at 7,000 tons, and multiply that by 55, you get $385,000. You must immediately pay a large interest and insurance account, because you must insure that enhanced value; but even at that, you an go into that very remunerative trade legitimately, and get your dividends regularly.

Q. (By Professor JOHNSON.) It seems to be the opinion of the Commissioner of Navigation that it costs considerably more to navigate vessels under the American flag than under a foreign flag; that the cost of operating a vessel after it is constructed is a serious item that ought to be considered. What is your experience in regard to that?—A. That was measurably answered when the question of wages and what is termed grubbing came up. There is no doubt but what all foreign vessels are operated, both in manning and provisioning them, at a cheaper rate than American vessels are. But this difference I am confident at the present time is not as great as it was formerly.

Q. (By Senator MALLORY.) If your ideas were to be carried out, that is, for Congress to amend our navigation laws to such an extent as to enable parties to go into the markets of the world and lease such vessels as they want to put in the foreign trade of the United States, excluding them rigidly from our coastwise trade?—A. Or do any trading within a thousand miles of the United States.

Q. Now, if that could be carried through, would not the fact that there is an additional cost in maintaining and operating the ships abroad, by the higher wages which the American seamen have always obtained, the higher wages which the American ship officers, masters, and mates have always received, and also the better quality of living aboard ship which has been enjoyed, I think, by our sailors as distinguished from sailors from almost all nations of the world, would that not make the cost of running the ships so much greater as to necessitate our vessels charging a higher rate of freight than tramps of England or other commercial nations?—A. I should say most emphatically, no. It might result in reducing our percentage of profit until we got to understand and practice some of the economies that foreign nations use, but it would not prevent our having a very remunerative business. In addition to this ownership of foreign vessels, or right to buy foreign vessels, I do not say but what it might be well to encourage by subsidies; but in addition to subsidies, I would give the right, under rigid restrictions, of the purchase of modern tonnage to every man, if you choose, until you get something to be afraid of, and then limit the amount. I would give American citizens the right to purchase them and put them under the flag and subject to the rights of the Government under certain conditions. I quote that condition because it would take too long to build up our marine in any other way. You can not construct a shipyard plant as you can put up a lot of tents. You know it takes years to get the proper force and machinery together, and then after that it takes the first year and a half or 2 years to build a vessel and launch it.

Q. Has your business enabled you to form any idea of the supply of tonnage for our coastwise trade as to its being abundant or otherwise?—A. The coastwise trade is in the hands of certain interests who are alive to the demands of that trade, and I think they have been very clever, as a rule, in keeping the demand supplied.

Q. Well, there is no such disparity between American tonnage for our coastwise trade and the trade itself as there is between ocean-going steamers?—A. You can not compare them really, because the first is sufficiently—you might say amply—supplied, and literally there is not anything of the other.

Q. And according to your judgment it would be years now before we could even make any appreciable start in the way of supplying ocean carrying ships?—A. Of our own construction. That is indisputable, I consider it. I hope you will not think I am too positive.

Now, I am not going to stop on that 300,000 tonnage question until I furnish you a list. I will furnish you a list of all the vessels that I have included in that. That is the simplest way to do it, and then allow anyone else to put in any others that they may find suitable to go across the Atlantic and Pacific.

Q. In your experience with foreign shipowners, have you encountered the fact that many individual ships, old ships, from the greater shipowning nations could be put in trade to make money?—A. We have had a rather unique experience of that character. I have one man in mind there that we bought probably 10 vessels for within the last 15 years. He generally bought old American or old English ships, and has put them under the Dutch or German flag, and in every case he has, by his careful management and economies and so on, paid for them within a reasonable length of time. I do not think at the present that he is in debt over a few thousand pounds.

Speaking again about the people of other nations buying foreign vessels and running them, the Norwegians did that about 5 to 8 years ago to a very considerable extent. I am very glad you asked that question. We have a knowledge of the names and the details of them. They bought British tramps of 2,500 to 3,500 tons capacity. That was about as large as the old vessels were. They took them and made money out of them; and those same men have taken that money (we do not sell them any second-class vessels now) and they have gone right into England and bought new steamers. And this same set of men from whom we have to-day four Norwegian steamers chartered are the same men that formerly bought those second-hand vessels. Now they go and build new vessels and launch them themselves and run them. They are the people that are making this 20 to 25 per cent profit on their vessels.

Q. These new vessels are built out of the old vessels?—A. Out of the profits of the old vessels largely.

Q. Are the Norwegians doing that now—continually buying ships?—A. Their great specialty was sailing vessels a few years ago. They have gone out of that, and are selling them off as rapidly as possible and going into steam.

Q. (By Mr. CLARKE.) I would like to inquire, Mr. Chairman, if Mr. Neall has considered the subject of a revival of the discriminating-duties laws which prevailed in the early history of our Government?—A. I have at times given some little thought to that subject, but when I got hold of a piece of lead pencil and figured what it amounted to, it seemed to me that it would, in the first place, be very inefficient and ineffective, and it would be a direct bid for all other nations to in some way discriminate against us; and I can not see how it would be any different from a case of lifting yourself up by your suspenders.

Q. How could they discriminate against us any better than they did before?—A. Will you state your proposition definitely, what you propose in the discrimination? I am familiar in a measure with those laws, but if I could get something specific and definite so that I could get it down to dollars and cents per vessel, it would suit me a great deal better.

Q. Without going into figures, the substance of the policy is that goods imported in vessels not owned in this country will pay a higher duty than goods imported in vessels of American ownership. That is the discriminating duty that prevailed successfully in the early history of our Government, and under which American shipping took precedence of all the shipping in the world. Now, what would you say to a revival, a gradual revival perhaps, of that policy?—A. I do not think that necessary. I would not like to admit that I thought that a discriminating duty had necessarily very much to do with the supremacy of our former tonnage position. I think it was much more because we built a better and a tighter ship, a faster ship, one that was more ably manned and commanded, and that we could make the passage between giv shorter time than the vessels of any other nations, and when we got to our port of delivery we delivered the cargo in better shape. I think that was the reason.

Now, when I made my answer a few moments ago in reply to the discriminating-duty question I recalled a few things, taking up that question and reducing it to so many cents per ton, with respect to a number of principal articles of our imports, which might be said to be the rough articles—sugar, ore, and all the principal articles. I will speak of that for a moment. Now, the duty on ore is about 45 cents a ton, and on sugar was a cent a pound, roughly. May I ask you to take the question of ore, which next to sugar is probably the largest single article of import, and say what discriminating duty you would put on ore imported by American vessels?

Q. I am not testifying.—A. I did not mean to put that question to you in any impolite or improper way; I only wanted to get the information. I will then in one sense answer it. I thought that if, for instance, you take the duty on ore as 45 cents, or 40 cents, and put a 25 per cent discriminating duty in favor of ore imported in American vessels, that would be 10 cents a ton. Ten cents a ton is 5 pence a ton. When you come to get to your market at Elba, or Huelva, or Poti, or Rio, you find, for instance, 3 vessels in port; an American vessel carrying 5,000 tons is alongside a British vessel carrying 5,000 tons and alongside a Norwegian vessel carrying 5,000 tons. A man wants to ship 5,000 tons of ore to Philadelphia. He goes to the American vessel and says, "What do you charge?" The captain says, "I will bring that for 12s. 6d. a ton"; and the American captain says to him, "Look here; you remember now if you ship by my vessel you get a discriminating duty of 25 per cent." He says, "I know. That is 5d. per ton off this 12s. 6d." He goes to the Norwegian or the British vessel and says, "What are you going to charge me to take this ore to Philadelphia"? The captain says, "I will take that at 12s." Now, that man is going to follow you down according to any discriminating duty that you get on that ore, just as long as you go down, and he will still have something left at the end.

Q. You think he will reduce again?—A. Yes; and I think that the law would act mainly in so many ways to irritate foreign nations to make discriminations against us in other ways, of port charges, or light dues, or harbor dues, or something of that kind; that it would do more harm to the enterprise than good.

Q. Is it not a fact within your knowledge that shortly after the discriminating duties were repealed in the forties, that prevailed from 1817 to 1846, inclusive, American shipping began to decline, and has declined almost ever since?—A. I will answer you frankly, and say that I have very little knowledge of any of these subjects prior to 1861, when I entered business, and I have not been such a student as would put me in a position to answer that question. I am not evading it; I would answer you frankly if I had the information, but really I am without it.

Q. (By Mr. PHILLIPS.) We would be pleased to have anything from you of your own that you have to submit to the commission.—A. I do not know whether it would be amiss to refer to a subject intimately connected with transportation, and that is the question of pooling. I had the pleasure, without his knowledge probably, of meeting Senator Mallory here in 1894, at the time the Patterson pooling bill was up, and there were some committees down here which were very strongly opposed to pooling, unless it was under the supervision of the Interstate Commerce Commission. Now, I do not wish to appear as an advocate of pooling, certainly not unless under proper restrictions and the supervision of the Interstate Commerce Commission; but it is a very difficult question, and I suppose some of the brightest minds have given a good many years of their lives to find a way out of the transportation complications without approaching the subject of pooling, which I believe is the means which the transportation companies present as the only remedy from their standpoint. Now, I spoke a little while ago about my being connected with some committees that were protesting against discriminations in Philadelphia. Those discriminations, to be absolutely frank, were probably discriminations to remedy which required the perpetration of discriminations of another character. In other words, our port was suffering grievously in the early nineties from a diversion of traffic to New York, to Baltimore, to Newport News, and so on; and we took very decided grounds in advocating that transportation companies should not be permitted to do that. Now, probably they could not and did not bring about a different state of affairs, unless they themselves were in some way parties to another character of discriminations which involved the meeting of the differential rates to other ports. In other words, if a lot of export property is located at Chicago, and some line with a right to charge a low rate offers to take that property at that low rate, no other line is likely to get it unless they take it at about the same rate. Now, that can not probably be under the present condition of affairs; that can not be done unless one line does what the other does. That was the feature in regard to discrimination that I wanted to refer to, and whether pooling is the way out or not I do not know; but I think that not only the merchant but the railroad officials themselves would be glad if any better means than that were found to accomplish substantially the same result and enable them to retain what would seem to be their fair, reasonable share of the traffic of each port.

Q. (By Senator MALLORY.) Does not Philadelphia get her due share now of that Western traffic?—A. At the present time and for the last year or more I think she does get her fair reasonable share. The exports last year showed that.

Q. Do you know what that is due to?—A. No. I can only imagine that it is by meeting rates that are made by other ports. I am confident of that, because I know Philadelphia has had her share.

Q. Have you lowered your port charges at all?—A. No; the port charges are as favorable, as economical, in Philadelphia as at any other port, and that was the basis we made in our discrimination arguments; that we could take a ton of import traffic or export traffic and handle it between vessels and between the ocean carrier and the inland carrier, either way, east bound or west bound, as economically as it could be done elsewhere, almost more economically than it could be done at a good many other ports; and therefore, if we did not get our share of the traffic, there was some other reason. We furnished the resistance, so that the traffic followed that line which offered the least resistance.

Q. Have there been any new connections made whereby Philadelphia has had another route west, or the west has had another route to Philadelphia, since 1894, the time to which you refer?—A. No. We have had practically four trunk lines both then and now.

Q. Now this condition whereby Philadelphia has her due proportion of that traffic has been brought about by some cause——A. (Interrupting.) Not incident to the establishment of additional lines.

Q. Some cause independent of Philadelphia, of the city itself; some other influence or advantage of commerce?—A. Well, our harbor has been improved and our channel has been somewhat deepened, although it is very far short of what we ought to have yet.

Q. What have you in your channel?—A. Well, we can not and we do not claim over 25 feet. We have to anchor going up or down. If we draw over 22 feet we have to anchor at some time. You start a vessel away from Philadelphia and she can not go out without anchoring if she draws over 23 feet 6 inches, in an ordinary tide. We have several shoals, you know, down the river.

Q. Well, from your remarks we infer, or I would infer at least, that you are in favor of permitting the railroad transportation lines of this country to make pooling contracts under certain conditions?—A. Well, I have never had any different views from that. That was the position we took of the Patterson bill. The elimination of four words changed the whole bill.

Q. (By Mr. RATCHFORD.) What proportion of the Atlantic coast trade is carried on by American steamers and American sailors?—A. Absolutely every ton of it. It is impossible for a foreign vessel to load a barrel of flour and deliver it at New Orleans or Boston or any other American port. She can not even take it to San Francisco.

Q. Is the same true of the Pacific coast?—A. Yes. You can not load a ton at an American port on a foreign vessel and deliver it at another American port, even if you round the horn between taking it aboard and delivering it.

Q. (By Mr. CLARKE.) In other words, protection is applied to the coastwise traffic and not to the trans-Oceanic traffic?—A. Well, protection is applied to the coastwise traffic certainly, and always has been; but assistance is not applied to the trans-Oceanic.

Q. (By Senator MALLORY.) Protection is applied to the ocean trade so far as the purchasing and owning of ships is concerned now, and none but an American citizen can own an American ship, and none but an American-built ship can be owned by an American citizen.

Q. (By Mr. PHILILPS.) Do other nations have these same regulations and laws in regard to their coastwise trade; England, for instance?—A. I think not. We have never had enough to make it worth while, and I do not think there is anything to prevent our American ships from going to Liverpool and loading a cargo of coal and taking it around to London.

Q. (By Professor JOHNSON.) I think some 40 years ago they had that restriction as to the coastwise trade.—A. I never heard of any such restrictions.

Q. (By Mr. KENNEDY.) While foreign-built ships are excluded from the coastwise trade of the United States, foreigners are not excluded from manning those ships?—A. Yes; from any official position on them, captain, mate, and so on.

Q. And sailors?—A. There are not many questions asked about the sailors any more when an American ship comes to port. You do not suppose when an American ship comes in she gets American sailors. Probably the American sailors will all leave the American ship after she is in Liverpool or Antwerp or Hamburg 24 hours. Then she gets a new crew.

Q. Is it true that there are more foreigners on our coastwise ships than there are Americans?—A. I should not like to say that there were more foreigners, but I should think probably 50 per cent were foreigners at least.

Q. Fifty per cent?—A. Yes. You could pick out isolated cases where you would find a schooner sailing from some port that would have a great many New Englanders on board, and then you would have another that would have only three American citizens in the crew. The officers and engineers must all be Americans.

Q. One of the officers of the Atlantic Coast Seamen's Union has sent a statement to the commission stating that there are more foreign seamen in that trade than there are Americans.—A. There are a great many Germans and Norwegians and Danes and Swedes that come over here on their vessels; and, as you were saying some time ago, the wages being so much higher, they leave the trans-Atlantic ship and ship coastwise on some American vessel.

Q. Is it because there are better conditions on those vessels?—A. Somewhat better wages and better grub.

Q. (By Mr. RATCHFORD.) Have you anything to say as to the nationality of those men who man the ships on the Pacific Ocean?—A. I do not suppose they are materially different in nationality from what they are here.

Q. Are there not large numbers of Chinese and Japanese crews there in American vessels?—A. American vessels, no. You very rarely see Chinese sailors in an American vessel; they would not be allowed. The vessel that brings a single member of its crew, or even a steward, into port, is under certain restrictions. One of our Norwegian steamers trading here regularly for some 6 or 8 months, has had Chinese cooks, and they have to make certain provisions every time that vessel comes into port to see that the custom-house officials are sure that they are aboard when the vessel goes out. It is a great detriment that it has to be done. The vessel is subject here to all sorts of unnecessary inconveniences. I will say, as a matter possibly of information that a number of British steamers within the last 2 or 3 years have come here with complete crews of Lascars. They are secured out in the East Indies at a good deal cheaper rate of wages than the British seamen get, and the British get somewhat cheaper than the American, so that it has been very much more profitable for those owners; but not as profitable as it might appear on the face of it, because they have to take more of them to get the same result.

There is just one more point I would mention, and that is to give you an idea of the volume of remunerative business or money which we are kept out of by not having a marine. Within the last 8 weeks we have collected for British and foreign shipowners over $600,000 of freight money on cargoes which they had delivered.

Q. (By Senator MALLORY.) Philadelphia and New York?—A. Philadelphia and New York, yes; we have collected over $600,000 in the last 8 weeks.

Q. (By Professor JOHNSON.) I would like to ask Mr. Neall how much he thinks we pay foreign vessels for the carriage of freight?—A. I thought probably you would ask that question, and I thought I would try and see if I could check some figures I have recently issued.

Q. Would it be a great trouble to you to complete such a notation and send it to us?—A. No; I will do so. (See supplemental statement, p. 176.)

Q. (By Senator MALLORY.) Can you state exactly how many regular lines of American steamships, ocean going, sail out of the ports of the United States at the present day?—A. Do you mean for trans-Atlantic and trans-Pacific ports and to the West Indies?

Q. Trans-Atlantic or trans-Pacific; nothing in the West Indies or domestic ports; across the Atlantic and across the Pacific. What regular lines are solely American lines?—A. Not a single one on the Atlantic seaboard, and I should very much doubt if there were three on the Pacific.

Q. Can you mention those on the Pacific?—A. I had in my mind the Honolulu, or the Seattle connections of the Northern Line. I can not tell you exactly what they are. That is another question I would rather answer specifically. (See supplemental statement, p. 176.) There is no line out of the United States that is composed solely of American boats which cross the Atlantic. The American Line is pretty near it, with the *St. Paul*, the *St. Louis*, the *New York*, and *Paris;* but they are supplemented with the British boats and the Belgian boats.

Q. They have American vessels with American registry on that line; those four? A. Those 4; and up to the time the Government took them, they had the *Ohio, Indiana, Pennsylvania,* and *Illinois.* The Government bought the *Illinois* and has chartered the 3 other boats.

Q. That really is the only pretense to an American line on the Atlantic or on the Pacific?—A. That is absolutely the only American-built and American-owned transatlantic line on the Atlantic coast.

Q. So far as built is concerned, they are not even all American built?—A. No; the *New York* and *Paris* are not.

(At a later date the following supplemental statement was submitted by Mr. Neall as a part of his testimony:)

PHILADELPHIA, *October 12, 1899.*

UNITED STATES INDUSTRIAL COMMISSION,
Washington, D. C.

GENTLEMEN: *Statement to the effect that the merchant marine of the United States (steam and sail) of 1,000 tons gross register and upward, and under 20 years old, flying the American flag, and suitable and available for trans-Atlantic or trans-Pacific trade, does not exceed a total of 300,000 tons gross register.*

Complying with the promise which I made at the hearing before your commission on 6th instant, to substantiate with details the assertion then made by me as above recited, I inclose herewith an itemized record, which I believe to include the rig, name, gross register, place, and date of building, and port of registry of every American steamer and sailing vessel comprised in the foregoing category.

Surprising as the figures given in my testimony may have appeared, they are indeed an understatement of vital facts intimately associated with the continued prosperity of the commercial interests of the United States. The value of the merchandise exported by the United States to foreign countries during the last calendar year (that is, ending December 31, 1898), was in round numbers $1,200,000,000; the value of our imports of foreign merchandise during the same period was roundly stated at $600,000,000, making the sum total of exports and imports for 12 months upward of $1,800,000,000, an aggregate movement of merchandise of the value of $150,000,000 per month.

The aggregate weight of the exports as above was about 30,000,000 tons (of 2,240 pounds), of which—

	Tons.
Corn contributed, say	5,000,000
Wheat	4,000,000
Lumber, timber, staves, etc	3,000,000
Oils	3,000,000
Coal	2,300,000
Cotton	2,000,000
Flour and meal	1,700,000
Provisions, beef, pork, lard, etc	1,200,000
Oil and cotton-seed cake and meal	700,000
Iron and steel (pig and manufactured), etc	700,000
Fertilizers	500,000

The imports for same period may be approximated in weight as 7,500,000 tons (of 2,240 pounds), of which may be noted, in part—

	Tons.
Sugar, amounting to	1,600,000
Coal	700,000
Chemicals, drugs, dyes, etc	600,000
Hemp, jute, sisal, and other vegetable fibers and manufactures thereof	500,000
Iron ore, iron, steel, etc	400,000
Coffee, cocoa, etc	400,000
Cement	350,000
Salt	150,000
Rice	100,000
Wool, and manufactures of wool, etc	100,000
Wines, spirits, etc	50,000

In other words, the actual export and import ocean traffic out of and into the United States during the last calendar year aggregated a total of over 37,000,000 gross tons, dead weight, say over 3,000,000 tons per month.

In this connection it may be noted that, according to Lloyd's Register of British and Foreign Shipping—

	Tons.
Total steam tonnage (gross), in vessels of 100 tons or over, of the world is	20,800,000
Total sail tonnage (net), in vessels of 100 tons or over, of the world is	6,800,000
	27,600,000
Of above Great Britain owns, say, one-half	13,900,000
Of above United States owns, say, one-eleventh	a2,400,000
Of above Germany owns	2,400,000
And Norway is next with	1,700,000

a Less than 300,000 tons of the United States total suitable and available for transoceanic traffic.

The statements A, B, C, and D, which I append hereto, embrace all the United States vessels at present suitable and available that could possibly participate in the movement of this enormous transoceanic traffic, which traffic actually, not theoretically, now exists, and must be carried by the vessels of some nation or nations, and h volume of which should naturally increase as the years go by. The statements shew—

	Tons.
140 steamships, with aggregate gross register of	399,425
52 ships, with aggregate gross register of	111,433
14 barks, with aggregate gross register of	18,870
88 schooners, with aggregate gross register of	115,101
294 Total gross register	644,829

From this total should be deducted, as not intended, and in reality unsuitable for the transoceanic trade, having been constructed especially for the requirements of coastwise or near by commerce—

169 vessels of gross register	348,644
Leaving as suitable and available for transoceanic traffic 125 vessels of gross register	296,185
Of which are steam, 47 vessels, gross register	149,040
And of these latter 23 steamers with gross register	73,420

were built abroad, and subsequently, under various conditions, granted United States register.

NOTE.—All vessels have been numbered on each of the Schedules A, B, C, and D, and the deductions on each schedule are itemized and reasons assigned for the exclusions.

In view of the foregoing facts, the question which was put to me by your committee, "What laws, if any, do you think ought to be enacted on the part of Congress or the States in the interest of ocean transportation?" may, it seems to me, be answered as follows:

In addition to such assistance as the United States Government may see fit to extend to merchants, shipowners, or shipbuilders in the shape of subsidies, bounties, or postal considerations, in order to encourage the building of the higher class of merchant steamers, suitable, if required, to be used by the United States Government as auxiliary cruisers, transports, etc., and to assist in maintaining the mail service with other countries, and without questioning the great value of the existence of such a fleet to the General Government, as well as to our maritime and commercial interests at large, let us with the greatest possible promptness have enabling acts passed by the next Congress granting to citizens of the United States—

(a) The right to purchase foreign bottoms, steam and sail, and put them under the protection of the United States flag, with such restrictive conditions as will amply protect the existing coastwise merchant marine. These conditions should include the prohibition of the foreign-built craft from ever engaging in our coastwise trade or in trade with any foreign port within, say, 500 miles of the shores of the United States proper, as existing on January 1, 1898; and these foreign vessels so acquired should each have a dead-weight capacity of not less than, say, 5,000 tons, if steamers, or, say, 2,500 tons, if sailing vessels; further, they should not be over 5 years old at time of purchase.

(b) Should this project for any reason seem not to be practicable, then I would suggest the consideration by Congress of legislation permitting our citizens to purchase and place under the United States flag the same kind of tonnage as mentioned above, and under the same character of rigid restrictions as to employment, but with the additional provisos that such purchases of foreign-built tonnage must, as an experiment, not exceed a total of, say, 500,000 tons net register, and that on them must be paid, as duty to the United States Government, the sum of $5 per net registered ton, say $1 per ton on date of admission to American registry and $1 per ton annually thereafter until the entire $5 per ton shall have been paid.

What seems to be especially needed, if American-owned vessels are to participate to any appreciable degree in transporting between our shores and those of foreign countries the great commerce that is continually passing across both the oceans that wash our coasts, is that our merchants should have the facility of flying our flag, not alone on high-class passenger and mail steamers, but also on the plain, economically constructed, unpretentious freighters which are called "tramps;" for it is this latter class of vessel, that travels with an average speed of 8 to 10 knots per hour, that transports by far the greater bulk of the world's ocean commerce. Some such legislation as has been indicated in general terms above would, it seems to me, be a practical step toward the attainment of that end, at absolutely no cost to our Government and to the material profit of American citizens.

Neither would there be injustice wrought thereby to American shipyards, from which there is not to-day afloat a single ocean "tramp," and which shipyards, in all probability, could not within 2 years from this date build and place in commission a couple of dozen such steamers of 7,000 tons dead-weight capacity each; and in this connection, promptness, as well as practical action, is an essential factor.

In conclusion, I would mention as a pertinent illustration of the desirability—I might almost add necessity—for some such legislation as is suggested above, that for many years it has been customary for Norwegian merchants and shipowners, purely as a commercial transaction and without governmental aid, and without a home commerce in which to engage these vessels, to buy foreign-built freight steamers (and more recently to have them especially constructed for them in foreign shipyards) place them under the Norwegian flag, and engage them in the transportation of merchandise in every part of the world. At the present time, for instance, there are no fewer than 55 such steamers, averaging over 3,000 tons gross register each, flying the Norwegian flag (see Statement E herewith). These are mostly under time charter, and in the majority of cases to merchants of the United States, making a fleet whose aggregate dead-weight carrying capacity is materially greater than that of the entire list of steamships now under the United States flag, suitable and available for transoceanic commerce. These Norwegian steamers are less than 5 years old, with the exception of 21, which latter were built, 10 in 1891, 3 in 1892, 4 in 1893, and 4 in 1894. These steamers pay their Norwegian owners, as a rule, from 15 to 25 per cent per annum profit on the investment, besides the profit which they may yield to the American or other subcontractors, or time charterers. The equivalent of this fleet, which aggregates 169,900 tons gross register, could be built to-day in foreign shipyards for, say, $11,500,000, but the cost to the present owners was materially less than this.

If American ownership of modern foreign-built ocean freight steamers were promptly authorized by Congress, I believe it would prove a safe, popular, and remunerative additional source of investment for funds of American citizens, and would be widely availed of throughout the United States.

Yours, very truly,

FRANK L. NEALL.

NOTE.—In considering the relations of the terms net register tonnage, gross register tonnage, and dead-weight capacity, as applied to the ordinary modern tramp steamer, a reasonably accurate practical rule is that 50 per cent added to the tons net register will give the approximate tons gross register, and 50 per cent added to the tons gross register will give the approximate tons of dead-weight capacity.

F. L. N.

———

A.—*List of all merchant steamships of 1,000 tons gross register or over, under 20 years of age, hailing from Atlantic, Pacific, and Gulf ports of the United States.*

STEAMERS.

No.	Name.	Owners.	Gross tonnage.	Built.	Year.	Home port.
1	Admiral Dewey ..	American Mail S. S. Co .	2,104	Philadelphia, Pa..	1898	Perth Amboy, N. J.
2	Admiral Farragut	....do	2,104	....do	1898	Do.
3	Admiral Sampson	....do	2,104	....do	1898	Do.
4	Admiral Schley ..	....do	2,104	....do	1898	Do.
5	Advance	Panama R. R. Co	2,604	Chester, Pa	1883	New York.
6	Alabama	Baltimore S. P. Co	1,938	Sparrows Point, Md.	1893	Baltimore, Md.
7	Alameda	Oceanic S. S. Co	3,158	Philadelphia, Pa..	1883	San Francisco.
8	Alamo	C. H. Mallory & Co	2,942	Chester, Pa	1883	New York.
9	Algonquin	W. P. Clyde & Co	2,832	Philadelphia, Pa..	1890	Do.
10	Alleghany	Merchants & Miners' T. Co.	2,014	....do	1881	Baltimore, Md.
11	Allianca	Panama R. R. Co	2,985	Chester, Pa	1886	New York.
12	Arkadia	Miller, Bull & Knowlton	2,238	Stockton, England	1895	Do.
13	Atlanta	Sound and bay boat	2,094	Philadelphia, Pa..	1896	Alexandria, Va.
14	Atlas	Standard Oil Co	1,942	Chester, Pa	1898	New York.
15	Berkshire	Merchants & Miners' T. Co.	2,014	Philadelphia, Pa .	1891	Baltimore, Md.
16	Caracas	Red D Line	2,584	....do	1889	Wilmington, Del.
17	Carib	W. P. Clyde & Co	2,087	Port Glasgow, Scotland.	1882	New York.
18	Catania	H. S. Tweedie	2,635	Glasgow, Scotland	1881	Do.
19	Charles F. Mayer.	Consolidated C. Co	1,218	Wilmington, Del .	1884	Baltimore, Md.
20	Charlotte	Sound and bay boat	1,746	Philadelphia, Pa...	1889	Do.
21	Chatham	Merchants & Miners' T. Co.	2,728	....do	1885	Do.
22	Chattahoochee ...	Ocean S. S. Co	2,676	Chester, Pa	1882	Savannah, Ga.
23	Cherokee	W. P. Clyde & Co	2,556	Philadelphia, Pa .	1886	New York.

A.—*List of all merchant steamships of 1,000 tons gross register or over, under 20 years of age, hailing from Atlantic, Pacific, and Gulf ports of the United States—Continued.*

STEAMERS—Continued.

No.	Name.	Owners.	Gross tonnage.	Built.	Year.	Home port.
24	China	Pacific M. S. S. Co	5,060	Govan, Scotland..	1889	New York.
25	City of Augusta ..	Ocean S. S. Co...........	2,869	Chester, Pa	1880	Savannah, Ga.
26	City of Birmingham.	.....do	3,066	.....do	1888	Do.
27	City of Columbia.	.....do	1,869	Greenpoint, N. Y .	1880	New York.
28	City of Kingston..	Puget Sound & Alaska S. S. Co.	1,117	Wilmington, Del .	1884	Port Townsend, Wash.
29	City of Lowell....	Sound and bay boat	2,975	Bath, Me	1894	New London, Conn.
30	City of Puebla....	Pacific Coast S. S. Co ..	2,623	Philadelphia, Pa .	1881	New York.
31	City of Seattle....	Sound and bay boat	1,411	.....do	1890	Tacoma, Wash.
32	City of Topeka ...	.....do	1,057	Chester, Pa	1884	New York.
33	City of Worcester.	.....do	2,489	Wilmington, Del .	1881	New London, Conn.
34	Columbia.........	Oregon R. & N. Co......	2,721	Chester, Pa	1880	Portland, Oreg.
35	Columbia.........	N. American M. S. S. Co .	2,976	Glasgow, Scotland	1883	Tacoma, Wash.
36	Comal	C. H. Mallory & Co	2,934	Chester, Pa	1885	New York.
37	Comanche.........	W. P. Clyde & Co	3,202	Philadelphia, Pa .	1895	Do.
38	Concho...........	C. H. Mallory & Co	3,724	Chester, Pa	1891	Do.
39	Conemaugh	Empire Transportation Co.	2,328	Sunderland, England.	1882	Do.
40	Corona	Pacific Coast S. S. Co ..	1,492	Philadelphia, Pa .	1888	Portland, Oreg.
41	Costa Rica.......	Pacific M. S. S. Co......	1,783	Chester, Pa	1891	New York.
42	Cottage City......	Sound and bay boat.....	1,885	Bath, Me	1890	Do.
43	Curacao	Pacific Coaster	1,503	Philadelphia, Pa .	1895	Do.
44	Dorchester	Merchants & Miners' T. Co.	2,537	Wilmington, Del .	1889	Baltimore, Md.
45	El Dorado	Southern Pacific Co	3,531	Philadelphia, Pa .	1884	New York.
46	El Mar...........	.....do...............	3,531	.....do	1889	Do.
47	El Monte..........	.....do...............	3,531	.....do	1886	Do.
48	El Norte..........	.....do...............	4,604	Newport News,Va.	1899	Do.
49	El Paso	.....do...............	3,531	Philadelphia, Pa .	1884	Do.
50	El Sud...........	.....do...............	4,572	Newport News,Va.	1899	Do.
51	Essex............	Merchants & Miners' T. Co.	2,530	.....do	1890	Baltimore, Md.
52	Evelyn	Miller,Bull & Knowlton.	1,963	Southampton, England.	1883	Philadelphia.
53	Excelsior	Southern Pacific R. R ...	3,263	Wilmington, Del..	1882	New Orleans, La.
54	Finance	Panama R. R. Co	2,603	Chester, Pa	1882	New York.
55	Florida	Plant Line	1,786	Port Glasgow, Scotland.	1887	New Haven,Conn.
56	Georgia..........	Baltimore S. P. Co......	1,749	Wilmington, Del..	1887	Baltimore, Md.
57	Gloucester........	Merchants & Miners' T. Co.	2,541	Sparrows Point, Md.	1893	Do.
58	Guyandotte.......	Old Dominion Line	2,350	Chester, Pa	1882	New York.
59	Havana...........	N. Y. & Cuba Mail S. S.Co.	5,667	Philadelphia, Pa .	1899	Do.
60	H. F. Dimock	Metropolitan S. S. Co ...	2,625	.....do	1884	Boston, Mass.
61	H. M. Whitney....	.....do...............	2,706	.....do	1890	Do.
62	Hartford	Sound propeller	1,337	.....do	1892	Hartford, Conn.
63	Herman Winter ..	Metropolitan S. S. Co ...	2,625	.....do	1887	Boston, Mass.
64	Horatio Hall	Sound and bay boat	3,167	Chester, Pa......	1898	Portland, Me.
65	Howard	Merchants' & Miners' T. Co.	2,551	Wilmington, Del .	1895	Baltimore, Md.
66	Hamilton	Old Dominion S. S. Co..	3,127	Chester, Pa......	1899	New York.
67	Indian	Boston Line............	1,576	Wilmington, Del .	1890	Boston, Mass.
68	Iroquois	W. P. Clyde & Co	2,948	Philadelphia, Pa .	1888	New York.
69	Jamestown	Old Dominion S. S. Co..	2,898	Chester, Pa......	1894	Do.
70	Jefferson	.....do...............	3,127	.....do	1899	Do.
71	John Englis	Sound steamer.........	3,094	.....do	1896	Portland, Me.
72	Juniata...........	Merchants' & Miners' T. Co.	2,551	Wilmington, Del .	1897	Baltimore, Md.
73	Kansas City	New Eng.& Sav'h S.S.Co.	3,679	Chester, Pa......	1889	Savannah, Ga.
74	Kershaw	Merchants' & Miners' T. Co.	2,600	Wilmington, Del .	1898	Baltimore, Md.
75	La Grande Duchesse.	Plant Line..............	5,017	Newport News, Va	1896	New Haven,Conn.
76	Lampasas	C. H. Mallory & Co.....	2,942	Chester, Pa......	1883	New York.
77	Leelanaw	Saginaw S. S. Co........	1,923	Newcastle, England.	1886	Do.
78	Leona	C. H. Mallory & Co.....	3,328	Chester, Pa......	1889	Do.
79	Mae	Miller,Bull & Knowlton.	2,201	Toledo, Ohio	1899	Do.
80	Maine	Sound steamer..........	2,395	Wilmington, Del .	1891	Providence, R. I.
81	Mariposa	Oceanic S. S. Co	3,158	Philadelphia, Pa .	1883	San Francisco.
82	Matanzas.........	James E. Ward & Co	3,094	Belfast, Ireland ..	1888	New York.
83	Matteawan........	Pacific tramp	3,301	S. Shields, England.	1893	Do.
84	Mexico...........	James E. Ward & Co	5,667	Philadelphia, Pa'.	1899	Do.

A.—*List of all merchant steamships of 1,000 tons gross register or over, under 20 years of age, hailing from Atlantic, Pacific, and Gulf ports of the United States*—Continued.

STEAMERS—Continued.

No.	Name.	Owners.	Gross tonnage.	Built.	Year.	Home port.
85	Miami	Pacific coast	3,019	Sunderland, England.	1891	New York.
86	....do	Coaster	1,741	Philadelphia, Pa.	1897	Do.
87	Middletown	Sound and bay boat	1,554	....do	1896	Philadelphia.
88	Mineola	Pacific Improvement Co.	2,438	Sunderland, England.	1887	San Francisco.
89	Mohawk	Sound steamer	2,783	Chester, Pa	1896	New London, Conn.
90	Mohegan	Sound and bay steamer.	2,783	....do	1896	Do.
91	Monmouth	....do	1,440	Philadelphia, Pa	1888	New York.
92	Nacoochee	Ocean S. S. Co.	2,680	Chester, Pa	1882	Savannah, Ga.
93	Nantucket	Merchant and Miners' T. Co.	2,599	Wilmington, Del.	1899	Baltimore, Md.
94	Navahoe	W. P. Clyde & Co	1,637	Hamburg, Germany.	1880	New York.
95	New Hampshire	Sound and bay steamer.	2,395	Wilmington, Del.	1892	Providence, R. I.
96	New York	American Line	10,674	Clydebank, Scotland.	1888	New York.
97	Newport	Pacific M. S. S. Co.	2,735	Chester, Pa	1880	Do.
98	Newport News	Sound and bay steamer.	1,535	Newport News, Va.	1895	Washington, D. C.
99	Nueces	C. H. Mallory & Co	3,367	Chester, Pa	1887	New York.
100	Olivette	Plant Line	1,611	Philadelphia, Pa	1887	New Haven, Conn.
101	Olympia	N. American M. S. S. Co.	2,837	Glasgow, Scotland	1883	Tacoma, Wash.
102	Oneida	W. P. Clyde & Co	1,322	Leith, Scotland	1885	New York.
103	Orizaba	Ward Line	3,496	Chester, Pa	1889	Do.
104	Paris	American Line	10,668	Clydebank, Scotland.	1889	Do.
105	Parthian	Boston Line	1,683	Wilmington, Del	1887	Boston, Mass.
106	Pensacola	L. & N. R. R. Co	1,696	West Hartlepool, England.	1888	Pensacola, Fla.
107	Peru	Pacific Mail S. S. Co.	3,528	San Francisco, Cal.	1892	New York.
108	Philadelphia	Red D Line	2,520	Philadelphia, Pa.	1885	Wilmington, Del.
109	Pomona	Pacific coaster	1,264	San Francisco, Cal.	1888	New York.
110	Ponce	N. Y. & P'to Rico S. S. Co.	3,503	Wilmington, Del	1899	Do.
111	Princess Anne	Old Dominion S. S. Co.	3,078	Chester, Pa	1897	Do.
112	Queen	Pacific Coast Co	2,728	Philadelphia, Pa.	1882	San Francisco.
113	Richard Peck	Sound or bay boat	2,906	Wilmington, Del	1892	New Haven, Conn.
114	Roanoke	Old Dominion S. S. Co.	2,354	Chester, Pa.	1882	New York.
115	St. Croix	....do	1,993	Bath, Me	1895	Eastport, Me.
116	St. Louis	American Line	11,629	Philadelphia, Pa	1895	New York.
117	St. Paul	....do	11,629	....do	1895	Do.
118	....do	Alaska Commercial Co.	2,144	San Francisco, Cal.	1898	San Francisco.
119	San Blas	Pacific M. S. S. Co.	2,075	Chester, Pa	1882	New York.
120	San Jose	....do	2,080	....do	1882	Do.
121	San Juan	....do	2,076	....do	1882	Do.
122	San Marcos	C. H. Mallory & Co	2,839	....do	1881	Do.
123	Santa Rosa	Pacific Coast S. S. Co	2,416	....do	1884	San Francisco.
124	Saginaw	W. P. Clyde & Co	1,884	Barrow, England.	1883	New York.
125	Seguranca	Ward Line	4,033	Chester, Pa	1890	Do.
126	Seminole	W. P. Clyde & Co	2,556	Philadelphia, Pa.	1886	Do.
127	Seneca	Ward Line	2,729	Chester, Pa	1884	Do.
128	Spartan	Boston & Phila. S. S. Co.	1,595	Wilmington, Del.	1883	Boston, Mass.
129	Specialist	Mobile	2,801	Sunderland, England.	1890	Mobile, Ala.
130	S. T. Morgan	Va. & Carol. Chemical Co	1,836	Wilmington, Del.	1898	Richmond, Va.
131	Tallahassee	Ocean S. S. Co	2,677	Chester, Pa	1882	Savannah, Ga.
132	Umatilla	Oregon R. & Nav. Co	3,069	....do	1881	New York.
133	Unionist	Mobile	2,157	Sunderland, England.	1888	obile, Ala.
134	Valencia	Pacific Whaling Co	1,598	Philadelphia, Pa.	1882	San Francisco.
135	Vigilancia	Ward Line	4,115	Chester, Pa	1890	New York.
136	Walla Walla	Oregon R. & Nav. Co	3,069	....do	1881	Do.
137	Washtenaw	Saginaw S. S. Co	2,896	West Hartlepool, England.	1887	Do.
138	Willamette	Pacific Coast Co	2,562	Chester, Pa	1881	Do.
139	Winifred	Miller, Bull & Knowlton.	2,456	Bath, Me	1898	Do.
140	Yucatan	Ward Line	3,525	Chester, Pa	1890	Do.

Total gross register tonnage, 399,425.

Detailed analysis of deductions of steamers unsuitable or unavailable for trans-Atlantic or trans-Pacific trade.

Tons.

1, 2, 3, 4, under 10 years' mail subsidy with United States Government between United States and West Indies... 8,416
14, bulk-oil coastwise steamer... 1,942
13, 20, 29, 31, 32, 33, 42, 62, 64, 71, 80, 87, 89, 90, 91, 95, 98, 113, sound and bay steamers.............. 39,046
5, 11, 54, Coastwise steamers of Panama Railroad Co... 8,192
6, 56, bay boats belonging to Baltimore Steamship Co.. 8,687
8, 36, 76, 78, 99, 122, Coastwise steamers Mallory Line, New York, Galveston 22,076
9, 23, 37, 68, 128, Coastwise steamers W. P. Clyde & Co... 14,089
10, 15, 21, 44, 51, 57, 65, 72, 74, 93, Coastwise steamers of Merchants and Miners' Transportation Co. 24,665
22, 25, 26, 27, 92, 131, Ocean Steamship Co., New York, Boston, and Savannah 15,837
45, 46, 47, 48, 49, 50, 53, Southern Pacific Co. Coastwise steamers, New York, New Orleans........ 26,563
58, 66, 69, 70, 111, 114, 115, Old Dominion Steamship Co. coastwise, New York, Chesapeake, etc.... 18,927
67, 105, 128, Boston and Philadelphia coastwise steamers.. 4,854
59, 84, 103, 125, 127, 135, 140, Ward Line, New York and Cuba Mail Steamship Co................. 29,232
60, 61, 63, Metropolitan Steamship Co., coastwise steamers, New York to Boston.................... 7,956
19, Consolidated Coal Co., coastwise coal steamer 1,218
75, 100, Plant Line Coast steamers, Florida to Cuba, Boston, Halifax.................................... 6,628
73, coastwise steamer, Boston to Savannah.. 3,679
41, 107, 119, 120, 121, Pacific Mail Steamship Co. of coastwise fleet 11,542
130, Virginia and Carolina Chemical Co., coastwise steamer 1,836

Total deductions.. 250,385

Leaving as suitable and available steam tonnage for trans-Oceanic trade..................... 149,040

B.—*List of all merchant sailing vessels of 1,000 tons gross register or over, and under 20 years of age, hailing from Atlantic, Pacific, or Gulf ports of the United States.*

SHIPS.

No.	Name.	Gross tonnage.	Built.	Year.	Home port.
1	A. G. Ropes	2,460	Bath, Me	1884	New York, N. Y.
2	A. J. Fuller	1,848	.....do	1881	Do.
3	Abner Coburn	1,972	.....do	1882	Bath, Me.
4	Aryan	2,123	Phippsburg, Me...........	1893	Do.
5	Arthur Sewall	3,209	Bath, Me	1899	Do.
6	Bangalore	1,743	Stockton, England	1886	New York, N. Y.
7	Benjamin F. Packard	2,156	Bath, Me	1883	Bath, Me.
8	Berlin	1,634	Phippsburg, Me	1882	Do.
9	Charles E. Moody...........	2,003	Bath, Me	1882	Do.
10	Charmer	1,885	.....do	1881	New York, N. Y.
11	Clarence S. Bement........	1,998	Philadelphia, Pa	1884	Philadelphia, Pa.
12	Commodore T. H. Allen	2,390	Richmond, Me.............	1884	Bath, Me.
13	Cyrus Wakefield	2,118	Thomaston, Me...........	1882	New York, N. Y.
14	Dirigo	3,004	Bath, Me	1894	Bath, Me.
15	E. B. Sutton	1,826	.....do	1881	New York, N. Y.
16	Edward Sewell	3,539	.....do	1899	Bath, Me.
17	Emily Reed	1,564	Waldoboro, Me	'880	New York, N. Y.
18	Emily F. Whitney	1,317	Boston, Mass.............	1880	Boston, Mass.
19	Erskine M. Phelps	2,998	Bath, Me	1898	Bath, Me.
20	George Curtis...............	1,837	Waldoboro, Me	1884	Boston, Mass.
21	Governor Robie	1,712	Bath, Me	1883	Bath, Me.
22	Henry Failing...............	1,976	.....do	1882	Portland, Oreg.
23	Henry Villard...............	1,552	.....do	1882	New York, N. Y.
24	Henry B. Hyde..............	2,583	.....do	1884	Do.
25	I. F. Chapman...............	2,145	.....do	1882	Do.
26	Iroquois.....................	2,120	.....do	1881	Bath, Me.
27	James Drummond...........	1,556	Phippsburg, Me	1881	Do.
28	John Currier	1,945	Newburyport, Mass	1882	Boston, Mass.
29	John McDonald	2,281	Bath, Me	1883	New York, N. Y.
30	Joseph B. Thomas...........	1,988	Thomaston, Me...........	1881	Thomaston, Me.
31	Kenilworth	2,298	Port Glasgow, Scotland.....	1887	New York, N. Y.
32	Kennebec	2,126	Bath, Me	1883	San Francisco, Cal.
33	Luzon	1,390	Boston, Mass	1881	New York, N. Y.
34	Marion Chilcott	1,737	Glasgow, Scotland.........	1882	Port Townsend, Wash.
35	Mary L. Cushing	1,658	Newburyport, Mass	1883	New York, N. Y.
36	May Flint	3,577	Dumbarton, Scotland	1880	Do.
37	R. D. Rice..................	2,263	Thomaston, Me...........	1883	Do.
38	Reuce	1,924	Kennebunk, Me...........	1881	Bath, Me.
39	Roanoke	3,539	Bath, Me	1892	Do.
40	S. D. Carleton	1,882	Rockport, Me.............	1890	Rockport, Me.
41	S. P. Hitchcock	2,305	Bath, Me	1883	New York, N. Y.
42	St. Frances	1,898	.....do	1882	Do.
43	Sam Skolfield, 2d...........	1,603	Brunswick, Me............	1884	Portland, Me.
44	Servia	1,866	Bath, Me	1883	Bath, Me.
45	Shenandoah.................	3,406	.....do	1890	Do.

B.—*List of all merchant sailing vessels of 1,000 tons gross register or over, and under 20 years of age, hailing from Atlantic, Pacific, or Gulf ports of the United States*—Continued.

SHIPS—Continued.

No.	Name.	Gross tonnage.	Built.	Year.	Home port.
46	Susquehanna	2,744	Bath, Me	1891	Bath, Me.
47	Tacoma	1,738	....do	1881	San Francisco, Cal.
48	Tillie E. Starbuck	2,025	Chester, Pa.	1883	New York, N. Y.
49	W. F. Babcock	2,130	Bath, Me	1882	Bath, Me.
50	William H Macy	2,202	Rockport, Me.	1883	Rockport, Me.
51	William H. Smith	1,978	Bath, Me	1883	New York, N. Y.
52	William J. Rotch	1,717	....do	1881	New Bedford, Mass.
	Total	111,433			

NOTE.—The foregoing 52 ships, aggregating 111,433 tons gross register, are assumed to be all suitable for trans-Oceanic trade.

C.—BARKS.

1	Abby Palmer	1,943	Dumbarton, Scotland	1893	San Francisco, Cal.
2	Adam W. Spies	1,235	Newburyport, Mass.	1884	New York, N. Y.
3	Adolph Obrig	1,448	Camden, Me.	1881	Do.
4	Benjamin F. Hunt, jr.	1,258	Newburyport, Mass.	1881	Boston, Mass.
5	Francis S. Hampshire	1,079	Richmond, Me	1881	New York, N. Y.
6	Holliswood	1,141	Boston, Mass	1893	Do.
7	James W. Elwell a	1,192	Bath, Me	1892	Bath, Me.
8	Matanzas	1,028	....do	1889	New York, N. Y.
9	Olympic	1,469	....do	1892	New Bedford, Mass.
10	Pactolus	1,673	....do	1892	Do.
11	St. James	1,578	....do	1888	New York, N. Y.
12	St. Katherine	1,263	....do	1890	Do.
13	Saranac	1,080	Kennebunk, Me.	1880	Do.
14	Wilna	1,483	Freeport, Me	1888	San Francisco, Cal.
	Total	18,870			

a Barkentine.

NOTE.—The foregoing 14 barks, aggregating 18,870 tons gross register, are assumed to be all suitable for trans-Oceanic trade.

D.—SCHOONERS.

No.	Name.	Gross tonnage.	Built.	Year.	Home port.
1	Alice E. Clark	1,621	Bath, Me	1898	Portland, Me.
2	Alice M. Colburn	1,603	....do	1896	Bath, Me.
3	Alicia B. Crosby	1,113	....do	1889	Portland, Me.
4	Alma E. A. Holmes	1,208	Camden, Me	1896	Philadelphia, Pa.
5	Anna Murray	1,534	....do	1899	New York, N. Y.
6	Augustus Hunt	1,200	Bath, Me	1882	Bath, Me.
7	Augustus Welt	1,221	Waldoboro, Me.	1889	Boston, Mass.
8	Bayard Barnes	1,005	New London, Conn.	1891	New Haven, Conn.
9	Benjamin A. Van Brunt	1,191	Bath, Me	1891	Perth Amboy, N. J.
10	Benjamin F. Poole	1,155	....do	1886	Providence, R. I.
11	Blanche H. King	1,156	....do	1888	New York, N. Y.
12	C. S. Glidden	1,245	Thomaston, Me.	1898	Thomaston, Me.
13	Cassie F. Bronson	1,124	Bath, Me	1886	New York, N. Y.
14	Charles Davenport	1,297	....do	1890	Bath, Me.
15	Charles A. Campbell	1,576	....do	1890	New York, N. Y.
16	Charles L. Davenport	1,032	Thomaston, Me.	1890	Thomaston, Me.
17	Charles P. Notman	1,518	Bath, Me	1894	Bath, Me.
18	Clara A. Donnell	1,177	....do	1889	Do.
19	D. H. Rivers	1,072	Thomaston, Me.	1890	Thomaston, Me.
20	David P. Davis	1,231	Bath, Me	1893	Bath, Me.
21	Eagle Wing	1,232	Kennebunkport, Me.	1891	Fall River, Mass.
22	Edith Olcott	1,194	Bath, Me	1890	New York, N. Y.
23	Edward E. Briry	1,613	....do	1896	Bath, Me.
24	Edward J. Berwind	1,141	Camden, N. J	1894	Philadelphia, Pa.
25	Edwin R. Hunt	1,132	Bath, Me	1892	Bath, Me.
26	Eva B. Douglass	1,098	....do	1886	New York, N. Y.
27	Fanny C. Bowen	1,007	....do	1891	Fall River, Mass.

List of all merchant sailing vessels of 1,000 tons gross register or over, and under 20 years of age, hailing from Atlantic, Pacific, or Gulf ports of the United States—Continued.

D.—SCHOONERS—Continued.

No.	Name.	Gross tonnage.	Built.	Year.	Home port.
28	Frances M	1,228	Phippsburg, Me	1896	Bath, Me.
29	Frank A. Palmer	2,014	Bath, Me	1897	Do.
30	George Bailey	1,245	....do	1890	Perth Amboy, N. J.
31	George A. McFadden	1,070	....do	1888	Bath, Me.
32	General E. S. Greeley	1,306	Westhaven, Conn	1894	New Haven, Conn.
33	George E. Walcott	1,553	Bath, Me	1890	Portland, Me.
34	George M. Grant	1,254	Westhaven, Conn	1889	New Haven, Conn.
35	George P. Davenport	1,461	Bath, Me	1891	Bath, Me.
36	Gov. Ames	1,778	Waldoboro, Me	1888	Providence, R. I.
37	Gracie D. Buchanan	1,140	Bath, Me	1888	New York, N. Y.
38	Hattie P. Simpson	1,295	Waldoboro, Me	1891	Boston, Mass.
39	Henry J. Smith	1,108	Thomaston, Me	1890	Thomaston, Me.
40	Henry O. Barrett	1,807	Bath, Me	1899	Bath, Me.
41	Henry S. Little	1,096	....do	1889	Perth Amboy, N. J.
42	Henry W. Cramp	1,629	Camden, Me	1896	Fall River, Mass.
43	Horace W. Macomber	1,050	Newburyport, Mass	1890	Boston, Mass.
44	Inca	1,014	Port Blakeley, Wash	1896	San Francisco, Cal.
45	Independent	1,157	Bath, Me	1891	Bath, Me.
46	J. Holmes Birdsall	1,520	Camden, Me	1894	Philadelphia, Pa.
47	James W. Fitch	1,120	Waldoboro, Me	1890	Boston, Mass.
48	John Twohy	1,019	Newburyport, Mass	1891	Do.
49	John B. Manning	1,190	Wilmington, Del	1899	New York, N. Y.
50	John B. Prescott	1,454	Camden, Me	1899	Taunton, Mass.
51	John F. Randall	1,643	Bath, Me	1891	New York, N. Y.
52	Katherine D. Perry	1,125	Camden, Me	1891	Do.
53	Lewis H. Goward	1,191	Bath, Me	1895	Bath, Me.
54	Lizzie H. Brayton	1,126	....do	1891	Fall River, Mass.
55	Lucinda Sutton	1,486	Westhaven, Conn	1891	New Haven, Conn.
56	Lucy H. Russell	1,166	Bath, Me	1887	Port Jefferson, N. Y.
57	Lydia M. Deering	1,224	....do	1889	Bath, Me.
58	Lyman M. Law	1,300	Westhaven, Conn	1890	New Haven, Conn.
59	M. D. Cressy	2,114	Bath, Me	1899	Bath, Me.
60	Marguerite	1,553	....do	1889	Fall River, Mass.
61	Maria O. Teel	1,125	Newburyport, Mass	1890	Boston, Mass.
62	Marjory Brown	1,210	Wilmington, Del	1889	Perth Amboy, N. J.
63	Mary Manning	1,233	Camden, Me	1894	Do.
64	Mary E. Palmer	1,526	Bath, Me	1895	Bath, Me.
65	Mary E. H. G. Dow	1,264	....do	1894	Do.
66	Mary Adelaide Randall	1,166	....do	1891	Port Jefferson, N. Y
67	Mary T. Quinby	1,172	Thomaston, Me	1899	Thomaston, Me.
68	Massasoit	1,377	Bath, Me	1889	Fall River, Mass.
69	Monhegan	1,080	Rockland, Me	1890	New York, N. Y.
70	Mount Hope	1,105	Camden, Me	1887	Fall River, Mass.
71	Nathaniel T. Palmer	2,441	Bath, Me	1899	Bath, Me.
72	O. H. Brown	1,051	....do	1889	Perth Amboy, N. J.
73	Percy Birdsall	1,127	Wilmington, Del	1890	Do.
74	Rachel W. Stevens	1,211	Bath, Me	1898	Norwalk, Conn.
75	S. P. Blackburn	1,756	....do	1896	Bath, Me.
76	Sagamore	1,415	Kennebunk, Me	1891	Fall River, Mass.
77	Sarah C. Ropes	1,135	Bath, Me	1891	Portland, Me.
78	Sarah W. Lawrence	1,369	Wolf River, Miss	1886	Fall River, Mass.
79	Stella B. Kaplan	1,078	Bath, Me	1891	Greenpoint, N. Y.
80	Three Marys	1,151	....do	1891	New York, N. Y.
81	Viking	1,017	....do	1888	Do.
82	W. Wallace Ward	1,245	Westhaven, Conn	1888	New Haven, Conn.
83	Wesley M. Oler	1,061	Bath, Me	1891	Dennis, Mass.
84	William B. Palmer	1,805	....do	1896	Bath, Me.
85	William C. Tanner	1,083	....do	1890	Do.
86	Willi m H. Clifford	1,593	....do	1895	Do.
87	William J. Lipset	1,026	Camden, N. J	1893	Somers Point, N. J
88	William K. Park	1,252	....do	1889	Do.
	Total	115,101			

NOTE.—Of the foregoing 88 schooners, aggregating 115,101 tons gross register, only 12 (Nos. 7, 14 16, 21, 29, 33, 36, 44, 52, 64, 82, 84), aggregating 16,842 tons gross register, have ever made a trans-Atlantic or trans-Pacific voyage. At the present time (October, 1899) but one schooner (No. 44) of the entire list is engaged in transoceanic business, the remainder being employed in the coastwise or other near-by trade, for which they were especially designed.

It is assumed that only those schooners of the above list which have made transoceanic voyages are suitable and available for transoceanic trade.

E.—*List of steamers under the Norwegian flag, averaging over 3,000 tons, gross register, owned by Norwegians, and engaged in transoceanic commerce.*

No.	Steamer's name.	Gross tonnage.	Year built.	Home port.	Where built.
1	Aggi	3,277	1891	Bergen	Newcastle, England.
2	Avona	2,965	1891	....do	Stockton, England.
3	Bjorgvin	2,792	1891	....do	South Shields, England.
4	Drot *a*	2,931	1891	....do	Bergen, Norway.
5	Langfond	2,552	1891	Stavanger	Newcastle, England.
6	Norge	2,979	1891	Bergen	Stockton, England.
7	St. Andrews	3,066	1891	Tonsberg	West Hartlepool, England.
8	Taurus	2,123	1891	....do	Do.
9	Tyr	2,268	1891	Bergen	Sunderland, England.
10	Ulriken	2,377	1891	....do	Do.
11	Aladdin	3,082	1892	....do	Stockton, England.
12	Caprivi	2,932	1892	....do	Do.
13	Songa	3,024	1892	....do	Sunderland, England.
14	Eva	2,987	1893	....do	Stockton, England.
15	Frey	3,015	1893	....do	Do.
16	Horda	2,927	1893	....do	Do.
17	Oscar II	3,060	1893	....do	West Hartlepool, England.
18	Fortuna	2,994	1894	....do	Stockton, England.
19	Bogstad *a*	3,058	1894	Christiania	Christiania, Norway.
20	Lovstakken	3,105	1894	Bergen	Stockton, England.
21	Lyderhorn	3,075	1894	....do	Do.
22	Blaamanden	3,144	1895	....do	Do.
23	Eidsvold	3,535	1895	....do	Do.
24	Florida	3,537	1895	....do	Do.
25	Hanseat	3,358	1895	....do	Newcastle, England.
26	Mathilda	3,480	1895	....do	West Hartlepool, England.
27	Nordkyn	3,244	1895	....do	Stockton, England.
28	Olaf Kyrre	3,063	1895	....do	South Shields, England.
29	Rauma	3,048	1895	....do	Middlesboro, England
30	Tiger	3,273	1895	Tonsberg	Stockton, England.
31	Tyr	2,225	1895	....do	Sunderland, England.
32	Urd	3,049	1895	Bergen	Stockton, England.
33	Liv	3,068	1896	....do	Do.
34	Norman Isles	3,455	1896	Tonsberg	Sunderland, England.
35	Unique	2,036	1896	....do	Do.
36	Admiral Ihlen	2,045	1897	Christiania	Stockton, England.
37	Fridtjof Nansen	3,275	1897	Bergen	South Shields, England.
38	Titania	3,613	1897	Tonsberg	Sunderland, England.
39	Alf	3,078	1898	Bergen	Stockton, England.
40	Guernsey	4,445	1898	Tonsberg	Sunderland, England.
41	Peter Jebsen	3,578	1898	Bergen	South Shields, England.
42	Sanna	3,392	1898	....do	West Hartlepool, England.
43	Storfond	3,516	1898	Stavanger	Port Glasgow, Scotland.
44	Symra	3,006	1898	Bergen	Stockton, England.
45	Trold	3,292	1898	Tonsberg	Sunderland, England.
46	Universe	2,585	1898	....do	Do.
47	Aker	2,964	1899	Christiania	Stockton, England.
48	Bergenhus	3,606	1899	Bergen	West Hartlepool, England.
49	Hero	3,800	1899	Drammen	Sunderland, England.
50	Nordpol	3,830	1899	Bergen	Newcastle, England.
51	Otta	3,240	1899	....do	Sunderland, England.
52	Ulabrand *a*	2,011	1899	Tonsberg	Copenhagen, Denmark.
53	Ran	3,022	1899	Bergen	West Hartlepool, England.
54	Thordis	3,736	1899	Tonsberg	Sunderland, England.
55	Thyra	3,812	1899	....do	Do.
	Total	169,900			

a Nos. 4, 19, and 52 built in Norway and Denmark.

WASHINGTON, D. C., *October 6, 1899.*

TESTIMONY OF MR. N. B. KELLEY,

President National Association of Freight Commissioners, member of the Committee on Transportation of the National Board of Trade, and Freight Commissioner for the Trades League of Philadelphia.

The commission met at 2.20, Vice-Chairman Phillips presiding. Mr. Phillips introduced the witness, Mr. N. B. Kelley, of Philadelphia, who, having first duly affirmed, testified as follows:

Q. (By Senator MALLORY.) What is your name?—A. N. B. Kelley.

Q. Your residence?—A. Philadelphia.

Q. What is your occupation?—A. I am freight commissioner for the Trades League of Philadelphia, which is a corporation of merchants organized for the furthering of the interests of the mercantile community of the city of Philadelphia. Under the direction of that organization it has what is known as the freight transportation bureau, which looks after the interests of the shippers to and from the port of Philadelphia

Q. Are you connected in any capacity with any other commercial body of Philadelphia?—A. No.

Q. Will you state the purpose and object of this organization you have just mentioned?—A. The organization is formed for the purposes of protecting the interests of business men of Philadelphia as regards legislation, discrimination, or anything that might be a detriment to the city of Philadelphia.

Q. Well, now, of the transportation bureau, particularly.—A. The transportation bureau is formed for the purpose of acting as a mediator between the transportation companies and the merchants, members of the association. They have the benefit of the advice of the freight commissioner without any expense other than membership in the organization. We take up questions of rates and claims and all grievances that we may have against transportation companies or water lines operating to and from the city of Philadelphia.

Q. That character of organization is not peculiar to Philadelphia alone, is it?—A. No; there are about 25 freight bureaus in the United States.

Q. They are in the principal cities, I suppose?—A. Principal cities—Chicago, St. Louis, New Orleans, Savannah, Charleston, Cincinnati, Philadelphia, Pittsburg. Kansas City, and a few other of the Western cities.

Q. Will you state, if you can, to the commission your method of action when there is a grievance of which you merchants have just cause to complain; the course of procedure that you follow in order to rectify it?—A. We take up the grievance with the railroad company at fault, and if it is a case of discrimination and is not corrected, we then present the matter to the Interstate Commerce Commission and take it up through them. We are peculiarly situated in Philadelphia. We have New York on one side of us and Baltimore on the other, and we practically have only 4 trunk lines. If a line that is running into New York is enabled to make lower·rates to the merchants there than we can secure for Philadelphia, it acts as a discriminating influence against the merchants of Philadelphia doing business; and when we find that such is the case we take it up with the lines having their termini in our city, with a view to securing a rate which will put us on a parity with New York. We do not ask for anything lower than a rate that will put us on a parity with other cities on the Atlantic seaboard. Take for instance, on grain. We have a differential of 2 cents under New York, and Baltimore has a differential of 3 cents under New York, 1 cent under Philadelphia. If we know that the tariff is being maintained on grain to New York and Baltimore we have no complaint. And I would like to say that during the past year, at least since the letter sent to the Interstate Commerce Commission by the President of the Baltimore and Ohio Railroad Company, rates have been better maintained, so far as my knowledge goes, than they have at any time during my connection with this organization, which has been during past five years.

Q. Do you mean that the rates are kept more equitable and without being unjustly discriminatory to any particular place?—A. Yes; I believe, in other words, that the railroad companies have adhered more closely to the published tariff rates. A large volume of traffic has passed through the various ports. They have all received their fair share of it, and there has been no necessity for making any reductions in the rates.

Q. You are of opinion, I judge, from that remark, that when there is an abundance of traffic there is less unjust discrimination in regard to individuals?—A. Strange to say, I do not think that that has been so in the past. It seems to me, from my own experience, that the railroad companies have made greater efforts to secure business when there has been an abundance of traffic, in the past, than when there was a scarcity of business; but, as I say, since the 1st of January I think they have adhered to the tariff rates, so far as I know.

Q. What do you ascribe that to? A. Competition. You mean as to adhering to the rates? The Interstate Commerce Commission, through its chairman, I believe, invited the presidents and managers of the various trunk lines to a conference with the idea of devising some plan by which rates could be better maintained, and I think, as a result of these various conferences that they have had with the trunk line officials, great good has been accomplished. Prior to the decision of the United States Supreme Court, of course, they had their own joint traffic associations and they were supposed to maintain the rates through those associations. The commission, I think, felt possibly that by getting together and talking the matter over they could come to some agreement by which the rates could be maintained.

Q. You say that in matters of discrimination you present them to the railroads in question, transportation companies, and if they fail to comply with what you believe to be a reasonable request you make complaint to the Interstate Commerce Commission?—A. Yes.

Q. Have you done that often?—A. Not frequently; no.

Q. Have you done it recently?—A. We have not had occasion to go before the commission or to apply to the railroads operating from our own city this year. We are frequently discriminated against, not only by the railroads but by shippers, and we have one case now before the commission in which we think the discrimination is caused on the part of the shipper rather than the carrier.

Q. Will you explain what you mean by that exactly?—A. Yes; the greatest difficulty we have to contend with in the way of discrimination is falsely billing and falsely misrepresenting the character of the freight shipped, either by the shipper or the railroad companies; in this case it was the shipper. I will cite the case, if you like. We are shippers of large quantities of hardware from Philadelphia to the South. We have several of the largest hardware houses in the United States located in Philadelphia. During the latter part of last year we found it was very difficult to sell the Southern merchants. The matter was presented to me by 1 or 2 of our hardware houses; and upon investigation I found that certain houses in the Southwest were underbidding the Philadelphia merchants very materially. The rates from the Southwest to these particular points in North and South Carolina ought to be about the same as from Philadelphia. So far as we could learn the rates were the same. But upon presenting the matter to the Interstate Commerce Commission, they delegated a representative to investigate this matter, and they found that certain houses in Louisville were shipping hardware to points in the South as well as the Southwest and misrepresenting to the railroad companies the contents of the cars. They were shipping what we call shelf or high-class hardware as saddlery or other low-priced commodities of hardware; in other words, they were securing the benefit of a sixth-class rate on traffic that should bear a first-class rate. Therefore, naturally our people could not begin to compete with them without they resorted to the same practice. That case, I think, is now in the courts both in Texas and in Louisville, Ky.

Q. You say they were misrepresenting the character of this freight to the railroad companies?—A. Yes.

Q. This was done on a considerable scale in order to make itself felt as far as Philadelphia?—A. Yes.

Q. Do you mean to say that the railroad companies were not cognizant of this misrepresentation?—A. To my knowledge they were not.

Q. Philadelphia and the points that you have reference to in this illustration have also water communication, have they not?—A. Yes.

Q. Well, did that discrimination, occasioned by representing the freight at a false classification, amount to so much of a discrimination as to enable the Western hardware men to overcome the advantage which you had by way of water transportation as well as land transportation?—A. Yes; I regret to say that the water transportation of Philadelphia coastwise is very limited. In fact, Philadelphia occupies the position of only having one line between it and the South, and that point is Norfolk, Va.

Q. You do not get below there?—A. We do not get below there, and therefore all business for southern territory must either go by way of Baltimore, by rail from Philadelphia to Baltimore and thence by steamer, or go by steamer from Philadelphia to Norfolk and thence by rail the remainder of the trip. And the difference in the water rate is so small that it would cut no figure in a discrimination of this kind. The differential would only be about 5 or 6 cents a hundred pounds.

Q. Is that abuse continued now?—A. Well, we think that that abuse has temporarily been stopped, because there has been no decision rendered by the courts as yet. We tried to get an indictment before the grand jury in Louisville, but were unsuccessful, and we are still investigating the matter and hope to be able to punish those people there either by fine or imprisonment, whatever the courts may determine, under the interstate-commerce law.

Q. How long have you been connected with this league?—A. About 5 years.

Q. During that time, will you state whether you have had occasion to intervene in behalf of the merchants of Philadelphia on many occasions with the different railroads in Philadelphia?—A. We have had a number of grievances against the railroads during that time which, upon presentation to the railroad companies, have been settled satisfactorily to the merchants. In other words, the railroad companies have protected us when there was rate cutting. We were put on a parity with the other cities.

Q. What influence did you bring to bear to bring that about?—A. Simply by pointing out to them that we would lose this business if we could not compete with the rates named to other cities.

Q. Is it not a fact that in a great majority of instances the intervention of these leagues in behalf of the merchants of the cities that the leagues represent are successful with the transportation companies in cases where there are abuses of that character?—A. I think that the railroad companies, as a rule, consider seriously all questions that are brought to them by these various freight commissioners, knowing that they represent probably the better, the major portion of the shipping interests of the particular locality in which they exist, and also knowing that they are familiar with the subjects that they bring before them. It was thought some time ago that these organizations were antagonistic to the railroad companies. I do not think the railroad companies think so now. I believe they think that they are a benefit to them, because they very often prevent a great deal of their time and the time of their officials being taken up by merchants when they had any grievance. This is now settled directly through these bureaus.

Q. You have mentioned this system of false classification as one method of discrimination against particular localities. Can you give an account of any other practice by which the interests of Philadelphia are discriminated against?—A. Not as applying to Philadelphia locally.

Q. Well, speaking more broadly, then.—A. I think there are a number of discriminations on the part of carriers that affect certain interests, speaking generally.

Q. Will you mention them?—A. Well, I think this system of private cars is a discrimination. These large packing houses have private cars, and they are at an advantage over a competitor who is compelled to ship his commodity in the railroad companies' cars by reason of the fact that the railroad companies pay them ¾ of a cent a mile for the use of the cars.

Q. Well, now, let us come to that for a moment. A private car is the result of energy and enterprise on the part of the owner of the private car. He built that car and put his capital into it.—A. Yes.

Q. And of course he is entitled to any legitimate benefit that he can get therefrom. Now, where does the illegitimate benefit come to him from the use of the private car? What is there in the system which prevails now that gives him an undue advantage?—A. I think the discrimination or the undue advantage that he gains is by reason of the high rates that he gets for the use of that car. I think the railroads could very well afford to handle their cars and make money on the price they pay them for the use of them.

Q. What advantage is there to the railroad company from the use of this private car to justify paying exorbitantly for the use of it?—A. That I can not say; I can not answer that question.

Q. You know only that the evil exists?—A. I only know that the evil exists, but why it exists I can not say. As I say, we do not feel the effect of that in Philadelphia as much probably as they would in some of the other seaboard cities.

Q. Well, is there not something in the fact that by giving this payment the railroad gets more of the business of a particular individual than it would otherwise get?—A. Possibly that is so; it may get an advantage in that way.

Q. You do not know that, however; it is only a surmise?—A. Yes.

Q. Is there any other method of discrimination that you know of that your attention has been called to, not particularly confined to Philadelphia?—A. I personally can not see any reason why the railroad companies, in conjunction with the steamship companies, should make a lower rate, for illustration, from Liverpool to Chicago than is made in many instances from New York to Chicago on what is known as import traffic. I think that is a discrimination which operates against the merchants.

Q. Now, before you go any further, have you anything to say as to the discriminations made in export rates? There are discriminations made on both export and import rates.—A. The witness (Mr. F. S. Neal) whom you had before you this morning testified very particularly on that subject, and I can only reiterate what he said.

Q. I did not know but what you might differ with him.—A. No, I agree with him.

Q. Now, then, to come back to the import rates, can you give the commission some idea of the average difference between freights—say of imports from Liverpool to Chicago via Philadelphia or by way of New York, and from New York to Chicago and Philadelphia to Chicago?—A. I could not give you the difference now, but I could obtain the figures and send them to you.

Q. Well, we would be very much obliged if you would do that. It is a considerable difference, is it?—A. There is on some commodities considerable difference; yes.

Q. Do you know what reason is assigned for that?—A. No; I do not.

There is another practice which prevails among railroads during certain seasons of the year. The question of the American merchant marine was brought to your attention this morning by the witness, and it reminded me of the fact that while our merchant marine on the ocean is very small—in fact comparatively nothing—if the practice which is pursued by the railroad companies during the lake season continues, after a time we will lose considerable of that traffic also. Strange to say, the railroad companies at the beginning of the opening of lake traffic usually reduce their rates on commodities that are carried in large quantities, like sugar and coal, which is the life of the lake trade; and they reduce those rates to such an extent that they are commencing to take that traffic away from the lake trade, and immediately after the lake season they restore their rates.

Q. Has not that been characteristic of the railroad transportation lines wherever they come in competition with water lines? Is not that, you might say, essential?—A. Well, I think it is.

Q. Have they not done it on rivers?—A. Wherever they have water competition they usually do it on these low-priced commodities that they are carrying in competition.

Q. (By Mr. FARQUHAR.) You speak of the competition in the lake trade as between the railroads and the water. Do not the railroads own their own lines of ships on the lakes?—A. They own their own lines for carrying general merchandise; that is, I can not say that they own them, but they operate them in conjunction with the railroads. But I am speaking now of low, coarse freights that are carried by what are known as tramp steamers on the lakes, not as to the regular lines. The regular-line boats do not carry those low, coarse freights as a rule. They generally try to get a commodity that pays a higher rate of freight—general merchandise.

Q. You mentioned the case of carrying coal. Does not the Lackawanna carry its own coal?—A. The Lackawanna carries its own coal, probably. I do not think it carries anything like the quantity that is shipped to the West.

Q. In the freight boats that ship ores, do they not get exactly the same as the liners themselves?—A. I doubt it.

Q. How is it possible, then, to support the other lines?—A. Well, the other lines are operated, as I said a few minutes ago, by the railroad companies. They are worked in conjunction with the railroad companies, and they get the light or high-class freight that pays, where the tramp boat would not get anything of that kind, because she does not carry a general cargo. She carries a cargo of grain, for instance, or a cargo of coal, or a cargo of ore, or a cargo of oil.

Q. Can the regular railroad freighter carry at a greater price than the free freighter can?—A. Do you mean to say can she get a higher rate?

Q. Yes.—A. There would be no way of carrying it by lake except by the regular lines. These very low priced commodities, I have just said—they would not like to load and put a full cargo of coal with general merchandise.

Q. Regular rates are established on coal, for instance, at Buffalo, which is the greatest coal port of the world. The 7 or 8 trunk lines in that city, the lines of railroads, largely have their regular lines of boats which they use for their own traffic during navigation?—A. Yes.

Q. And when there is a surplus to be carried they bring in these freight boats, putting them on the same freight rate as other long-haul freight, do they not?—A. You mean to say that they charter these outside boats that do not belong to their lines?

Q. Always.—A. I do not think they charter outside boats for the purpose of carrying any low commodities now. If there was sufficient traffic west bound or east bound of general merchandise, and the railroad companies or water lines saw it was to their advantage to charter an extra boat, if they could go and get a boat at a price that they thought would enable them to make some profit at the time, they would undoubtedly charter it.

Q. Well, when they all have their own boats in use, of course?—A. Yes.

Q. These outside boats get the current rate, do they not, from Buffalo to Duluth, Chicago and Milwaukee?—A. They get the current rate; yes.

Q. So that practically speaking, when you mentioned the competition of the railroads you did not seem to take into account the fact that the railroads own their own transportation boats on the water?—A. But they do not own them all.

Q. I speak of trunk lines. They own the water transportation, do they not?—A. I think the statistics will show you that the percentage of boats owned by the railroads is very small in comparison with the total amount of tonnage.

Q. (By Mr. RATCHFORD.) Is it not a fact that the railroad companies are largely interested in those boats in cases where they do not own the whole line themselves?—A. Well, that I can not say. I expect that they must have some interest in the boats. I can only speak for one line which is operated on the lakes, which I am familiar with, and that is what is known as the Erie and Western Transportation Company. Those boats are operated in conjunction with the Pennsylvania Railroad Company and those boats are not owned by the Pennsylvania Railroad Company.

Q. (By Mr. FARQUHAR.) They are time-chartered boats?—A. No; they are boats owned by the Erie and Western Transportation Company, which is a separate and distinct corporation. I am very familiar with that because I worked for that company and I know just what it is. Now, they have probably in their fleet 16 or 18 steamers, but they could not afford to use one of those boats to carry a cargo of coal to Duluth or Chicago and exclude other freight, because there would not be sufficient money in it for them. But there are boats on the lakes that are built for the express purpose of carrying full cargoes, not general cargoes, and those are the boats that are suffering as a result of this competition, or will suffer, in my opinion.

Q. (By Senator MALLORY.) I understood you to say that if that kept up it would diminish the number of boats very greatly; those independent general cargo boats?—A. Yes, I think it will divert the traffic from the lakes to the rail.

Q. Do you know any other case in which there is a line of freight boats owned by any line of railroad that is tributary to the lakes?—A. I do not know positively, although I think the New York Central own their boats. They have a line. I think they own them. And the Great Northern Railroad own theirs.

Q. Do you think it good policy for a railroad corporation to own steamboats engaged in the transportation of freight on a line parallel with their railroads? Do you think there is anything against public policy in the principle?—A. Only this, that the rates by water are not controlled by the interstate law; the rates by rail are supposed to be, and, therefore, a railroad owning its own boats might be in a position to discriminate, whereas by carrying the freight all rail it would be more apt to be shown.

Q. The point I wanted to get at particularly was as to the injury that may result to the general public from the monopoly occasioned by such a proceeding as that. In the first place, railroad corporations are created, as a general rule, for land transportation?—A. Yes.

Q. Not for water transportation; they are not authorized, as a general rule, except in special instances, to engage in water transportation, except where that water transportation is supplementary or complementary to their land transportation; but in some sections of this country railroad corporations have deliberately gone to work and put in on rivers—this, of course, is not testimony; I am merely giving it as an illustration—competing lines of steamboats with other river lines for the purpose of breaking down those lines of transportation, and as soon as they have succeeded in breaking down the river competition, why, up go the rates again?—A. Yes.

Q. Now, what I want to get at is whether there is any such process as that going on on the lakes?—A. Well, the information that I am giving you now in that connection is my own thought. I have not any facts or figures to give you, but that is the theory that I advance, that in time it will force these boats off the lakes, and then these rates will go up, as you state. The same practice has been in force for a long time in the river and coastwise water transportation.

Q. Until a short time ago they carried a bushel of wheat all the way from Duluth to Buffalo, 1,000 miles, for a cent and a half. Is there any possibility of any railroad doing that within the next thousand years?—A. Railroad companies have been known to carry freight at a loss for the purpose of competing with water traffic and depending, as I stated before, on the higher class commodities to make their money. The railroads of the United States to-day, statistics show, only pay 1½ per cent interest on the amount of capital invested. Take as an illustration the Erie Canal. The railroads running from Buffalo to New York can compete with canal business on the Erie Canal during the season of canal navigation, and they do do it.

Q. (By Mr. PHILLIPS.) Carry freight cheaper?—A. They compete; I do not know whether they make any lower rates.

Q. (By Senator MALLORY.) Is there anything else you want to say on this particular point of discrimination?—A. I would like to say I have been an advocate of pooling for several years, because I believe that if such laws are enacted by Congress as would permit the railroad companies to pool it would do away to a very great extent with these failures. Competition means discrimination. I think it is a great deal better for the commercial community at large to permit the railroad companies to pool, and know that the rates are uniform and stable, than it will be for them to go on as they are now, gradually acquiring the weaker railroads and practically controlling them. If they keep on at the rate they are going, in. a few years the railroads of this country east of the Mississippi River will be in the hands of a very few men, and then they will be in a position to make rates to suit themselves.

Q. (By Mr. FARQUHAR.) You say competition is the parent of discrimination?—A. I think so; yes.

Q. (By Senator MALLORY.) How would this pooling business prevent this tendency to consolidation which seems to be in operation now, not only in railroads, but in almost everything else? It has been operating probably for a very great number of years in the case of railroads, and we see it every day. How would giving them the right to pool prevent that tendency to combination; and if it does prevent that tendency, would that necessarily be a benefit?—A. I believe the fact that the railroad companies are not able to control the situation has been the cause of these so-called combinations in railroads. I think that is undoubtedly what led up to that condition.

Q. In other words, you think the weaker railroads, being unable to maintain themselves in that violent, fierce competition that arose out of these conditions, became exhausted, were driven to the wall, or gobbled up by and consolidated with the stronger ones?—A. I believe in competition, but in legitimate competition; I do not think it is legitimate competition where a road is in the hands of a receiver and has to pay no dividends on its capital stock and cuts the rate to such a point that it compels a standard trunk line, like the New York Central or the Pennsylvania, to make a rate to meet the competition. I do not think that is healthy competition. I think competition where it is the markets, the deliveries, and so on is all right.

Q. Does your idea of permitting transportation companies to make pooling contracts stop at that, or would you go further and put some supervisory control over the making of such contracts?—A. Undoubtedly I would want to see the contracts made under the control of a disinterested body; in other words, I am only in favor of pooling under control and supervision of the Interstate Commerce Commission.

Q. There seems to be a general acquiescence in the idea, except on the part of the railroads themselves, but they do not seem, as far as my observation has gone, to approve of that. They do not want to be hampered by having to submit their contracts to the approval of anybody.—A. I do not think they object so seriously to the contracts as to giving the commission the power to fix rates; some of the rates at least.

Q. (By Mr. KENNEDY.) Are you in favor of pooling under the supervision of the Interstate Commerce Commission with its present powers, or would you have the powers of the commission enlarged before permitting pooling under their direction?—A. I would like to see the commission's powers enlarged. You, in all probability, will find that the Western people are opposed to pooling. I understand you have a witness coming from St. Louis to-morrow who is a member of the St. Louis Traffic Bureau, and he undoubtedly will be opposed to it.

Q. (By Senator MALLORY.) Under any conditions?—A. I think under any conditions. I probably may be selfish in advocating pooling. I advocate pooling because I think it would be to the best interests of the Atlantic seaboard. He would probably oppose it because there are a number of lines running into St. Louis, and he can make better terms on account of the competition on the number of lines he has to work with. But I think, for the benefit of the community at large, if uniform rates and staple rates could be brought about, it would be better for the public.

Q. In connection with this subject, have you considered the question of classification as connected with discrimination?—A. I think classification is the basis of the rate-making power of railroads.

Q. What is your judgment of the advisability of having a uniform system of classification in this country?—A. I am much in favor of the uniform system of classification, and I think it ought also to be under the control of the Interstate Commerce Commission.

Q. That would be the only way to effect it, under some Government agency?—A. You can readily see the classification is really the rate-making power. A commodity is classed under a certain head, first, second, third, or fourth class, as it may be. The railroad companies make the classification; the merchants do not make it. If they make a commodity second class that we think should be fourth class, they get the second-class rate, and we have no means of securing redress except by application to the association classification committee, and if they do not grant it we have to pay second-class rate on that commodity.

Q. The making of a classification is not an arbitrary power, but there is some reason for that classification?—A. The railroad companies always have good reasons for them. Then there are 3 classifications, Official, Western, and Southwestern, and they vary. A commodity in one classification may be of another when it reaches the territory of the Western association, and that, to the shippers, very often is inconvenient. That is one of the reasons for favoring uniform classification, which will cover the railroads of the country, rather than have 3 classifications. There are good reasons why the classification is higher in one territory than another; the district may be sparsely settled.

Q. Do you think it would be practical for any central authority, in view of all the various and diverse interests and reasons why classification should be different, to bring them to a uniform system, or anything approximating a uniform system?—A. I think it might be done. It would take considerable time and labor to do it.

Q. (By Professor JOHNSON.) You have had a great deal of experience, of course, in the shipment of goods. You have the experience of the merchants of your association in the shipment of goods, and you, of course, are in the Official classification territory?—A. Yes.

Q. I would like to ask you whether there is one uniform classification in this so-called Official territory, or whether there are numerous differences practiced on the part of the various railroad companies that amount to a diversification in classification; whether we really have one classification in that territory or whether we have several?—A. Well, I can not say that the railroads would deliberately permit the shipper to classify an article under something other than the proper head it belongs to in the classification. The shippers have resorted to that practice. They use the classification of another article.

Q. So far as you know, do any railroad lines maintain for any portion of their business anything else than the Official?—A. So far as I know, they adhere to the Official classification.

Q. Could you tell us what actual disadvantage it is to a hardware merchant who wants to sell goods in Denver, a Philadelphia hardware merchant, what disadvantage it is that there are two classifications that he has to use?—A. In making the rate, say he gets a third-class rate to Chicago; when the goods reach Chicago he gets a second-class rate from Chicago to Denver; you can not figure on that rate from Chicago to Denver unless you are familiar with the classification.

Q. Both rates are published, are they not?—A. Yes. The publication of rates is a farce, in my opinion, so far as being a benefit to the shipper is concerned. Under the interstate-commerce act the tariffs are posted in the freight station. The shipper never goes to the station; he sends his truckman. The only way the merchant can secure the rate is to go to the railroad company. He goes to the railroad office, or to my office, and I secure the rate for him.

Q. That is because the rate is changed so frequently?—A. No; it is not because it is changed so frequently; it is because he is not familiar with the classification question. He has the Official classification back in his office, and if he wanted to find out what some particular article would be classified under he probably could find it, and maybe not. The easiest way is to go to the railroad and ask the rate to Chicago on hardware or whatever it might be.

Q. (By Senator MALLORY.) With reference to this matter of publication of freight rates, is it not a fact that it is rare for the shipper, say, buying in Philadelphia from Denver or from one of the cities in the South, say Atlanta, to himself investigate the different rates or different classifications on different kinds of goods?—A. He generally depends on the shipper; he depends on the shipper giving him the lowest possible rate to the point to which the goods are to be shipped. If it happens to be a point where there is water competition, of course the rate is lower by water than the rail rate, and the usual procedure would be for the merchant to ask him whether he wanted his goods to go by water or by rail. The rate he generally arranges at this end of the line, unless he gets special instructions. Sometimes the consignee will give directions to route the freight by certain lines either on account of friendship for the agent who happens to be in that city or on account of his getting a concession from one of the competing lines.

Q. (By Mr. CLARKE.) Considering that the sum paid for freight in this country is greater than all the taxes, do not you think it would be putting a tremendous responsibility, a very great power, in the hands of the Interstate Commerce Commission to fix the rates?—A. Yes; I do.

Q. Do you think it would be safe for the people to intrust such a vast power to, say, 5 men?—A. No; I do not think so, for this reason: the complexion of the commission is constantly changing, and I think it is absolutely impossible for any 5 men to make rates for the railroads of the United States. When I said that I wanted to have pooling under the control of the Interstate Commerce Commission, I did not intend to say that I wanted them to have the power of fixing the rates also.

Q. Do you know of any State in the Union which makes it the part of the railroad commissioner to fix rates?—A. I am not sure, but I think Texas does. Texas and Missouri, I think.

Q. (By Mr. RATCHFORD.) Would the power of fixing the rate, in your judgment, be safe in the hands of a commission, say, composed of one representative from each State in the Union?—A. I do not think I would like to answer that question. I am in doubt about it.

Q. (By Professor JOHNSON.) How do you make any distinction between the fixing of rates as an initiatory process and the fixing of rates in a revisionary way, when you condemn the power? For instance, when you spoke against the advisability of giving the Interstate Commerce Commission power to fix rates, did you have in mind the prescribing of a general schedule of rates or power to revise rates that have been promulgated by private authority?—A. I had in my mind when I spoke the idea that the pooling contracts be submitted to a commission, and if, in their opinion, they seemed unreasonable, they could be carried to the courts.

Q. Irrespective of the question of pooling, on rate making, do you make any difference between the first process of creating and the power of revision?—A. No.

Q. Does it not seem to you that the two functions are very different?—A. I do not think I quite understand your question.

Q. One way of fixing the rates would be for the Interstate Commerce Commission to go to work and get out a schedule of rates, and promulgate it, and compel the railroads to observe that schedule; another way would be to allow each railroad to make its schedule, and each combination of companies, and put them in force, subject to the revisionary power of the National Government. Now, would you oppose the one the same as the other?—A. I would prefer the latter.

Q. Would you oppose the latter?—A. That would depend entirely on what the scope of the power of the commission might be.

Q. Of course you are familiar with the fact that it is the latter power the Interstate Commerce Commission desires subject to the superior power of the courts?—A. Yes.

Q. (By Senator MALLORY.) As I understand, your idea is that this power should be given to the Interstate Commerce Commission for the purpose of approving or disapproving contracts entered into regarding the transportation of freight by corporations; that power should be given the Interstate Commerce Commission to approve or disapprove them. If they disapprove them, then it should be taken to a judicial body or court, and ultimately determined by the action of that appellate body?—A. Yes.

Q. Do you think an ordinary judge of a United States district court or circuit court is better qualified to determine what should be a reasonable or just rate than a commission like the Interstate Commerce Commission, whose members have been devoting years to the study of this question?—A. I was referring more particularly to some specific rate that might be named that might be unreasonable. There is or there was a bill pending in Congress to the effect that any 2 or 3 railroads that choose to go into a combination for the purpose of pooling traffic and earnings may do so, but they must submit that contract to the Interstate Commerce Commission; and if there are any rates that are too high, according to the Interstate Commerce Commission, they have the right to order a reduction; and if the railroads do not agree to that, they can take it to the courts.

Q. To come to the practical point, the method by which this can be done: Is it reasonable to suppose a single judge who has never had any business of that kind before him, no familiarity with railroad matters, is better qualified to determine as to the reasonableness or unreasonableness of a rate than the members of the Interstate Commerce Commission, or men specially selected with reference to their adaptability for the purpose?—A. That is a pretty broad question. I would not like to say what, in my opinion, would be the proper thing to do.

Q. (By Mr. KENNEDY.) You stated you were in favor of the enlarging of the powers of the Interstate Commerce Commission, and now you say you are opposed to them fixing the rates or revising the rates. In what way would you have their powers enlarged?—A. I think it would enlarge the powers of the Interstate Commerce Commission if they were permitted to veto rates, such rates not to be permitted to remain in force until decided by the judicial body. I do not think the merchant would suffer by reason of the rates not being enforced. That would certainly enlarge the powers. And there are a number of other ways in which they might be enlarged. From the national board of trade petition after petition has gone to Congress for the enlargement of the powers of the Interstate Commerce Commission. I am not prepared just at this time to state how the commission's powers should be enlarged, but that is all on record.

Q. Would not the vital matter of enlarging the powers come down to the question of rates?—A. That is one way, but there are a number of other ways in which they could be given authority that would be of importance to the commercial community. I have some resolutions here, presented by the national board of trade to Congress, on that subject, which I will be very glad to leave with the commission, covering the last 3 or 4 years.

Q. (By Professor JOHNSON.) Could you give us in a few words an account of the purpose and activity of the National Association of Freight Shippers?—A. It is for the purpose of taking up matters regarding methods of transportation, and in the event of any matters of a national character that can be presented to Congress, we frame resolutions and send them to Congress. For instance, we have already presented resolutions on uniform classification and on the antiscalping laws and a number of other subjects. It is about on the same order, so far as transportation is concerned, as the National Board of Trade. We only take up national questions.

Q. (By Mr. PHILLIPS.) Are you in favor of or against scalping—these resolutions presented to Congress?—A. We are opposed to it.

Q. Could you give some reasons to the commission why your association takes this position as regards scalping?—A. We think it is for the best interests of the traveling public that this practice should not be permitted. We think if we do not have scalping, in all probability we can get lower passenger rates.

Q. (By Mr. KENNEDY.) Do you believe, also, you will get lower passenger rates if the system of free passes is abolished?—A. That is a question I do not know much about. It is a passenger question.

Q. Do you not suppose they affect the rates more than the scalping question?—A. I understand it is a very serious evil, but I understand the roads are trying to abolish passes.

Q. (By Mr. FARQUHAR.) You think it would be better for the railroads to go to Congress for a law abolishing all passes than to abolish the broker?—A. I am not familiar with the passenger end of it at all; I do not know how far that evil exists.

Q. (By Professor JOHNSON.) You are president of the National Association of Freight Shippers?—A. Yes.

Q. You have an office as president where you conduct business?—A. We meet once a year in Washington.

Q. Your activity is practically confined to the period of your convention?—A. Yes. We have an executive committee. When any important matter takes place during the year, we call the executive committee together and act on it.

Q. This national organization, in fact, enters complaint as a national association, in case of a complaint?—A. Yes, as a national association.

Q. As in the case of the transportation committee of the National Board of Trade?—A. They do not do so.

Q. They are a committee for recommending?—A. Yes; that is all.

WASHINGTON, D. C., *October 7, 1899.*

TESTIMONY OF MR. A. J. VANLANDINGHAM,[1]

Commissioner St. Louis Traffic Bureau.

The commission met at 11.10 a. m., Chairman Kyle presiding. Mr. A. J. Vanlandingham, being duly sworn, testified as follows:

Q. (By Senator MALLORY.) What is your name?—A. A. J. Vanlandingham.

Q. Where do you reside?—A. St. Louis, Mo.

Q. What is your business?—A. Commissioner of the St. Louis Traffic Bureau.

Q. Will you state briefly what your duties are in connection with that office?—A. The St. Louis Traffic Bureau is an organization of the St. Louis merchants and manufacturers, having about 2,200 members. The object of the bureau is to secure to

---

[1] Since deceased.

St. Louis fair and reasonable rates for transportation into and out of St. Louis, as compared with other cities, in order that our merchants and manufacturers may be able to meet the competition in what we consider St. Louis territory, of merchants and manufacturers of other cities.

Q. How long has that traffic association been in existence?—A. The present organization has been in existence two years and a half. The St. Louis Traffic Association, which was its predecessor, was organized in 1890.

Q. Will you state what was the cause that led to its organization?—A. It was indirectly organized by reason of a similar organization at Kansas City, of which I was commissioner. It was directly organized for the purpose of removing discrimination that was supposed to exist and did exist as against the city of St. Louis as compared with Chicago and other cities.

Q. Has it been efficacious in removing any discrimination?—A. I think so. They think well enough of it to pay about $15,000 a year for its maintenance.

Q. Illustrate as briefly as you can, but covering as much of the matter as you can, the character of the principal discriminations which led to this action on the part of the merchants of St. Louis.—A. I do not understand.

Q. What was the method or character or form of discrimination practiced against St. Louis?—A. Of course the general practice was one of tariff rates. Wherever the St. Louis merchant had an inside rate, if there was any, he kept it to himself, a rebate or lower rate than the published tariff. My office never takes any cognizance of a proposition where a St. Louis man is supposed to have a rate different from the published tariff. If it is a Chicago or a Kansas City man, we investigate. Consequently as to rates of that kind we will not make any investigation as to any complaints that may be made as against St. Louis. Rates generally have been maintained at the published tariff during the year 1899. There were fewer rates maintained in 1898 than at any time within my knowledge of the railroad business, and I have been in the railroad business for 28 years.

Q. In what form were these discriminations?—A. In every method that it is possible to cut a rate.

Q. Can you give us an illustration?—A. One method is the payment of commissions to secure business.

Q. Payment of commissions to merchants?—A. Payment of commissions to merchants. Of course you understand in this testimony my testimony on this proposition is not testimony that could be taken into court, because I do not know of these things directly, only indirectly. Another method is by direct rebates—that is, simply so much off the tariff. Another method is by allowing a larger proportion to one line as its division of the rate than the regular division, that proportion being paid to the shipper to secure his business. Another method is by what you might say is a manipulation of rates, changing the destination in transit to a basis that will make a lower proportion. As an illustration, the rate on grain for export from Kansas City or from the Missouri River to Chicago has been 3.2 cents lower per hundred pounds than when for local consumption. The consequence has been, and proved before the Interstate Commerce Commission, that all the grain moved from west of the Mississippi River to Chicago has been going into Chicago on the basis of the through rate—that is, billed to Chicago for export. It goes into the Chicago elevator and it may go out to New England. This is a general proposition. It goes into an elevator in Chicago and it may go out by rail. If it does it goes out at 80 per cent of the published Chicago export rate; if it goes for export, 80 per cent of the Chicago–New York rate, less 3 cents. We will say the rate was 13 cents; 3 cents was deducted for New York terminals, and 80 per cent of the rate plus this 3 cents; 8 plus 3, or 11 cents, was the rate and not 13, as published. It might go by water. It was shown in the testimony that if it went by water no record was taken other than at Buffalo. The water carriers of Chicago will not keep a record of destination except to Buffalo. There it goes to the railroads. The statement "It went to Chicago for export" was a subterfuge, and the rate was cut by 3 cents a hundred pounds.

Q. Do you mean to say that to take advantage of this difference between export rates and rates for domestic consumption, all that went through Chicago went at export rates?—A. All corn and wheat; it did not apply to so great an extent on oats; it did to the same degree, but it was not noticeable to so great an extent.

Q. In that case, then, there seems to have been no discrimination between those shipping from west of Chicago to Chicago?—A. There was this discrimination: when I say all the grain, I mean all the grain that was handled by the freight shippers on these roads. There was also another termination through the St. Louis gateway. St. Louis is a competitor for Western grain. We were discriminated against to the extent of the 3.2 cents a hundred pounds, because the rate to Chicago and through was 3.2 cents less than when shipped through St. Louis. The consequence was the grain that would ordinarily move in both directions through both cities had an undue preference to Chicago on the north and through Kansas City, a preference that was natural to a certain extent, to the Gulf.

Q. Was not that legitimately due to the lake transportation competition?—A. The lake competition has been felt always, and they have had an advantage on this ground in Chicago. In the published tariff the lake competition would have been met through the St. Louis gateway. The rates are so adjusted as to meet these situations on an agreed basis.

Q. What is the reason, in your judgment, for the difference between export rates and rates for domestic consumption, to the East on grain?—A. At some periods an export rate lower than an inland rate is probably necessary. It has not been necessary during 1898 and 1899. Our grain would have gone abroad to as great an extent, so far as the rate is concerned, if it had paid the same as the inland rates. The reason it applies on Western grain is the competition of the Gulf as against Atlantic ports. All New England rates are based upon the New York rate; that is, the rate once given from Chicago to New York fixes every rate from Dubuque on the north and Cairo on the south to every point east of Buffalo and Pittsburg.

Q. On the Atlantic?—A. On the Atlantic, yes. Now, to reduce the domestic rate to the export rate, necessary to meet the export rate through the Gulf ports, would have made so low a rate that the railroads did not feel they could afford to do so, and consequently they made this through arrangement of a lower proportionate rate for export than for domestic consumption.

Q. There was no necessity for it during 1898 and 1899?—A. None; as far as the value of the grain was concerned. It is necessary sometimes to meet the competition of other countries on wheat but not on corn.

Q. Can it be laid down as a general proposition that when there is a demand for our product there is no necessity for the difference?—A. Yes; when there is a large crop of wheat in the Argentine Republic or Russia, sufficiently great—or even Indian wheat sometimes—to control the price, then to move for export it is frequently necessary to make a lower rate than the domestic rate, for the same reason I stated a while ago, that the export business is not sufficient in volume to pay to reduce the entire domestic product of the territory covered.

Q. These differences between export and inland rates are unnecessary to-day, are they not?—A. Yes; I have the rates to-day if you want them.

Q. We would like to have them.—A. Using East St. Louis and Chicago as the points for eastbound traffic, the rate on domestic to Newport News, Norfolk, and Baltimore, except on corn and corn products, is 20 cents, and on corn and corn products 18 cents; for export, the rate on corn, wheat, barley, and rye is 13½ cents from East St. Louis. From Chicago the domestic rate on grain and products is 17 cents, and on corn and corn products 15 cents; for export, corn, wheat, barley, and rye 12½ cents, and on oats 14½ cents. To Philadelphia, the rate on domestic, the same proposition, is 21 cents from East St. Louis, corn products 19 cents; export, corn, wheat, barley, and rye 14 cents, and oats 16 cents. From Chicago, domestic 18 and 16; export, 13 and 15. To New York, domestic, from East St. Louis 23 and 21; export, 15 and 17. From Chicago, for domestic, 20 and 18; export, 14 and 16. That was the situation in effect September 18, 1899.

Q. Do you think at the present time there is any occasion for this difference as between export and domestic?—A. Not so far as the shipper is concerned.

Q. Is flour included in that?—A. I have a statement as to flour, which I would like to put in as a whole, with your permission.

Q. You may read it.—A. (Reading:) "The development of Gulf ports has caused a reduction in grain rates from the West to Atlantic ports and to Gulf ports far below the rate on grain to the same ports for domestic consumption, and, strange to say, the rate on flour and grain products for exports has not been reduced in the same degree, so that for the past year or more there has been a grave discrimination against American flour in favor of wheat. The difference between export flour and wheat rates to the seaboard for export, effective September 18, 1899, is as follows:

From East St. Louis, when from beyond, to—	Flour.	Wheat.	Difference in favor of wheat.
	Cents.	Cents.	Cents.
Baltimore	20	13½	6½
Philadelphia	21	14	7
New York	23	15	8
Boston	23	15	8
Portland	23	15	8

"The miller loads the flour, the grain shipper loads the wheat; elevator charges on export wheat are included in the inland rate; seaboard charges are always included in the export flour rate. Export flour can be loaded to the marked carrying capacity of the car. The millers will gladly accept an export flour rate based upon cars being loaded to marked capacity of car. It was demonstrated in testimony before the Interstate Commerce Commission taken June and July, 1899, that if present relative rates between flour and wheat are continued our exports of flour, in proportion to exports of wheat, would be largely decreased.

"Exports of wheat as compared with flour, 5 years, ending December 31, 1898, were:

Year.	Wheat.	Flour.
	Bushels.	*Barrels.*
1894	88,415,230	16,859,533
1895	76,102,704	15,268,892
1896	60,650,080	14,620,864
1897	79,562,020	14,569,545
1898	148,231,261	15,349,943

"Wheat exports, 1898, were 67 per cent greater than in any year for the past 5 years, and show an increase over 1897 of 85 per cent. Flour exports for 1898 were 9 per cent less than 1894, and show an increase over 1897 of but 5 per cent. American millers claim that flour exports would have increased in the same degree as wheat but for the discrimination against flour made by American railroads, in transporting wheat far below the rate charged for transporting flour."

In connection with my testimony I desire to submit as part of the same a decision of the Interstate Commerce Commission on export and domestic rates, decided August 7, 1899, calling special attention to the following clauses of that decision. (Reading:)

"The profit to American millers in manufacturing flour for export is from 1 to 3 cents per 100 pounds; but the freight rates on wheat and flour show a difference in favor of the English miller of from 4 to 11 cents per 100 pounds, and, other things being equal, such discrimination is clearly prohibitive on the American manufacturer. The published railroad rates on both wheat and flour for export have been the same up to a recent period, and the carriers have exacted such rates except where lower rates on wheat were induced by competition. Water competition on the Great Lakes limits rail rates to the various ports on both wheat and flour during the navigation season, and to a degree before the opening and after the close of navigation, and the published and actual water rates on wheat have been from 2 to 4 cents lower than those on flour. To a limited extent the cost of service may be greater in the transportation of export flour than of export wheat. The export rate on flour includes delivery on board ship, while the rate on wheat ordinarily does not, and at New York an additional charge of about 1¼ cents per bushel for loading wheat is made. Exportation of flour has steadily increased, but for the last 6 years the increase has not been marked, and a decrease is shown by comparing exports of 1894 with 1898."

Rates through Gulf ports and generally South Atlantic ports on wheat include elevation at seaboard and 15 days free storage, which seems to have not been clearly proven to the commission.

Based on the foregoing, the commission held:

"1. That public policy and good railway policy alike seem to require the same rate on export wheat and export flour, but the duties of the commission are confined to administering the act to regulate commerce, and in view of all the conditions shown in the investigation the somewhat higher rate on export flour than on export wheat is not in violation of the statute.

"2. That the published difference in rates is too wide, and that the rate on flour for export should not exceed that upon export wheat by more than 2 cents per 100 pounds.

"3. That the relations of rates on domestic shipments of flour and wheat are not involved in this decision, as the export and domestic freights are handled under different conditions."

The decision was rendered on August 7, sixty days ago. An advance has been made on both grain and flour rates, east bound, since that date, but no attempt has been made by the railroads to comply with the order of the commission, and so far no railroad has signified its intention to obey the order, and under the present law I doubt if there is any legal process by which the millers or the Interstate Commission can enforce the railroads to obey it.

The United States has from the beginning fostered American industries in assessing its import duties, and if there is any law that can be enacted that will prevent the discrimination of American railroads against American millers, in relative rates on wheat and flour for export, it will in my opinion prove valuable to American industries, to the wheat producers, and of general value to all American interests.

Q. What, in your judgment, is the reason for the continuance of this very wide discrimination against flour?—A. The answers given by the railroads are with reference to the difference in cost. If that be true all their domestic rates are wrong, for all their domestic rates in the territory north of the Ohio and east of the Mississippi are the same on wheat and flour for domestic consumption.

Q. The same from Chicago to New York?—A. The same from Chicago to New York and from any inland point in New England. Not only is that true, but the flour for domestic consumption is not loaded to the full marked capacity of the car. A carload of flour is 24,000 pounds. The carload effective the 1st of July is 30,000. For export, flour can be loaded as heavily as wheat, to the marked capacity of the car. In addition to this difference in inland rates you must remember the flour has also to pay a higher ocean rate, which the miller expects to a certain extent, because the flour can not be loaded as readily as wheat in the steamers. So it does not show the total discrimination in favor of wheat as against flour.

Q. As an actual fact, the shipment of flour from our inland points, like St. Louis and Chicago, to Europe is relatively much more expensive than the shipment of the grain out of which the flour is made?—A. You mean more expensive to the carrier?

Q. No; more expensive to the shipper.—A. Much more so; yes. It will average as much as 13 cents a hundred.

Q. Have you any idea as to what the effect of that will be if it is persisted in?—A. In a conversation with Governor Stannard, the largest manufacturer of flour at St. Louis, he stated he had been practically out of flour export for 60 days, and if present conditions continued he would be out much longer; that the millers could not stand this situation. That is felt to such an extent that the Millers' Association is now arranging for a meeting in Chicago to prepare an amendment, a proposed law on this subject. That meeting will be held some time next month.

Q. You speak of the rates north of the Ohio. Does that include Newport News, Baltimore, and Norfolk?—A. Yes; it includes the South Atlantic ports, the territory commonly called the "official classification territory," the lower port of Norfolk up to and including Montreal.

Q. Does that territory include the Southeast; New Orleans, say?—A. Yes.

Q. You say the rates to New Orleans and the Gulf ports affect the Atlantic seaboard rates. To what extent do they affect them?—A. The largest grain-producing States are Nebraska and Kansas, I believe, Iowa, Nebraska, and Kansas, particularly of corn. The rates on grain from Illinois south to Kankakee and New Orleans at the present time is 12 cents per hundred for export. That would naturally make the rate from the same territory to the South Atlantic ports. The average difference in the ocean rate is about 4½ cents per hundred; that is, the ocean rates are 4½ cents lower at Atlantic ports than at New Orleans and Galveston under natural conditions. Of course, this varies with the demand for tonnage. Every rate from west of the Mississippi River up to the Platte River, to a certain extent the north line of Nebraska, is affected by the Gulf competition; that is, more or less of all grain that originates west of the Missouri River and south of the north Nebraska line, and in Iowa west of Des Moines and south. The Chicago, Burlington and Quincy, leading from Des Moines to Omaha, is affected by Gulf competition, and all of Illinois on the line of the Illinois Central only; that is, I mean it is the only business which does actually move south from Illinois that affects other territory to a very great degree. Prior to the opening of the Gulf ports, prior to 1889, immediately at the close of navigation at Chicago, the rate on corn to the eastern seaboard was advanced to 25 cents per hundred pounds. The rate I have just given you for export is considerably less, and the rate has not advanced to the eastern seaboard within the last five years after the close of navigation.

Q. By reason of Gulf competition?—A. By reason of Gulf competition.

Q. Has that business through the Gulf ports increased to your knowledge during the last five years?—A. Very greatly. Galveston has increased in grain more than 1,000 per cent in the last five years.

Q. Is the same relation observed between the export rates and the inland rates from these Gulf ports?—A. A much greater difference. The rate from Kansas City to Galveston for export on wheat and oats is 15 cents; on corn, 13 cents, and on rye and barley, 16 cents. The local rate to Galveston is 37 cents, and to New Orleans it is 19 cents; not so great to New Orleans.

Q. Do you know of any reason why there should be so much greater discrimination between those two Gulf ports and the Atlantic ports?—A. Nothing, only the traffic reason that the railroads do not consider the export great enough to pull down their business. These export rates are all published.

Q. How are the export rates to the Gulf ports as between flour and wheat?—A. The differences are not so great at the Gulf ports. At St. Louis they do not reach the Gulf ports except occasionally at New Orleans. New Orleans, Pensacola, and Mobile are principally export points to Cuban ports.

Q. (By Mr. CLARKE.) The route for export is Newport News?—A. Newport News and Norfolk very largely. We do more from these ports than others. We do export quite a little from New Orleans by way of barge lines.

Q. (By Senator MALLORY.) The rates observed by railroads are all published regularly, are the not?—A. A great many are not published.

Q. What I want to get at is this, whether the rates that are published as rates of railroads are always observed in their dealings with shippers?—A. No.

Q. Are they ever observed, in your judgment?—A. Yes; they have been reasonably well observed this year. I do not think, with the exception, possibly, of grain and grain products, the packing-house products, and possibly a few other commodities of large volume, of that nature that rates have been different from the published rates this year. And even in these cases the discriminations have been by manipulations such as I have referred to, in Chicago, by divisions of rates, or manipulations of that nature, and by allowances to elevators. That is one of our worst forms of discrimination.

Q. Will you explain that?—A. One of the methods of allowances to elevators is where a certain large grain-producing road has 1 or 2 favored firms who have a large number of local elevators along the lines of these roads. Those elevators are allowed an elevator allowance of, say, from one-half to 1½ cents a bushel for gathering this grain and shipping it at such times as the railroads can take care of it. That is supposed to be the reason it is given. I recall one line that has an elevator at Kansas City and a number of elevators at local points. The Kansas City elevator is allowed three-fourths of a cent a bushel to unload grain from that line promptly when it comes in over that line. When it comes in the country elevator is allowed three-fourths of a cent a bushel for collecting that grain and holding it until the cars can be gotten to these elevators. The owner of that elevator is one of the largest exporters in this country. He also has this opportunity at Chicago, by billing for export and then distributing it wherever it is most satisfactory. The rival buyer at that station is soon out of business, for he must sell his grain to this man.

Q. Why can he not build his own elevators?—A. He could build the elevators, but he can not get the railroad company to make allowances. These elevators would not make a reduction to this firm, for this firm did not have a contract for the exclusive business over the line.

Q. Then, it is through preference on the part of the railroad that this particular elevator man is enabled to carry on his business?—A. It is through that that he is enabled to force his competitors out of business in that particular line.

Q. (By Mr. CONGER.) Is it your idea, then, that St. Louis is discriminated against in favor of Chicago by this system of elevators that you have been describing?—A. Yes; St. Louis is discriminated against. It happens to be; but I do not mean to say that Chicago is the only point that has this method.

Q. St. Louis has it as well?—A. St. Louis has not; but a method of this nature applies to a number of Chicago points. All points taking a hundred per cent rate are Chicago points; that is, a hundred per cent of the Chicago and New York rate. Those discriminations exist down as far as the St. Louis district, as Beardstown.

Q. Does this system enable the Chicago elevator man to reach out into the territory for grain and ship it to Chicago that would naturally go to other grain-distributing points like Omaha, St. Louis, and Kansas City?—A. It enables the Chicago firms to control 85 per cent, very nearly, of the export business of the points.

Q. I have heard it said that in certain portions of Nebraska where the grain would naturally go to Omaha, Chicago operators come into Nebraska and pay a cent or 2 cents more a bushel than they did in Iowa, a point nearer Chicago. Do you know anything of that nature?—A. Mr. Counselman testified before the Interstate Commission that he was paying for western grain at the Mississippi River three-fourths of a cent more per bushel than the market price in Chicago—for August corn; that he was doing this for the reason that he exported it at a profit in doing so.

Q. Your idea is that he was able to do it because of this export rate?—A. Not only the export rate but by the manipulation of 1.8 cents per hundred in the rate between the Mississippi River and the Chicago point—1.8 was elimitated from the profit by manipulation.

Q. (By Mr. CLARKE.) Mr. Counselman and his company are the owners of the terminal elevators at Chicago in connection with Rock Island?—A. I was going to say that I do not care to specify names.————————————

Q. This came out somewhat in connection with the work of the subcommission west?—A. There are 4 other firms of the same nature in Chicago.

Q. There were about 9 brought out in the decision of the court there; and does not what you say with reference to this matter apply to all terminal elevators in Chicago?—A. Yes; each one of these elevators is favored by the same particular line.

Q. Is it not true that these terminal elevators are owned very largely by this railroad company?—A. Yes; that is true of the Counselman elevators, and I suppose of all others.

Q. They have the favors that are granted?—A. Yes; he rents them.

Q. (By Mr. Conger.) Just a question or two further on another subject, and that is in regard to these differences in freight rates on wheat and flour. I think you have testified that the difference the railroads have been charging has ranged from 4 to 11 cents, have you not?—A. That is correct.

Q. Could you state from what point of those elevators this difference is made?—A. Well, that 4 to 11 cents was brought out in testimony before the Interstate Commerce Commission. Those tariffs were then in effect. The tariffs were all changed on September 16. They have been changed twice since that hearing; and while there are doubtless some differences made, the miller in St. Louis who would buy at the local station in Missouri would pay the local rate into St. Louis; he would pay 1½ cents bridge toll on his flour, and then he would pay the East St. Louis rate, so it would make 11 cents. There are a number of cases where that still applies on the large volume that the miller actually buys. My quotation was from the actual tariff paid from East St. Louis. All our rates in East St. Louis start from the east bank of the river, and we must pay the bridge toll to get over.

Q. Do you know if the Minneapolis millers have to contend against this discrimination?—A. The Minneapolis millers at the time of the hearing had 1½ cents on export for domestic flour. That has been withdrawn, so unless they have the same basis through the Canadian Pacific or through the "Soo" they are still doing that. The Minneapolis millers have an advantage over the millers further south; over districts that are not amenable to the commission.

Q. (By Professor Johnson.) I would like to ask if it is possible for St. Louis to compete with Chicago, owing to the railroad facilities that Chicago has in this connection?—A. St. Louis has as good railroad facilities as Chicago. She has not as good water facilities.

Q. These great terminal elevators are located in Chicago?—A. We have some elevators there, but they do not belong to the railroad. I want to say our condition in St. Louis has been improved in relation to Chicago since this hearing, as it should be. We are not in as bad a condition as we were some time ago. The condition against us now is about only half as bad as when this hearing was had.

Q. (By Senator Mallory.) Do you not think there always will be some difference in favor of Chicago, in view of its location?—A. There will be, always, in view of the volume of tonnage.

Q. It has a very decided water transportation during many months of the year, which St. Louis has not?—A. Yes.

Q. Do you complain of the fact that the elevators are owned by the railroads, or do you complain of the abuses that result from it?—A. I was not testifying by way of complaint; I was simply giving the situation as it exists. The elevators that are not owned by the railroads—frequently discriminations are just as great as where they are so owned. Now, in this Kansas City proposition that I gave the elevators are owned by a private company. The abuse is in allowing large shippers such an advantage that it throws the business naturally to one or two firms, who by agreement among themselves can pay their own prices just sufficiently above the other rate to prevent the man who has no rate from competing with them. That is where the injury, as I see it, is to the producer, as well as to the man who tries to buy against the large dealer.

Q. Well, along the lines of road, for instance, where the private companies have been building elevators, do you not think it is a good business proposition on the part of the railroads to build them in order to concentrate their shipments of grain?—A. I think so. I think that was particularly necessary on some of the northern lines at t e time they were built, for the reason that they could get no private companies to do so.

Q. Is it a fact that the farmer who grows the grain is practically compelled to sell to the elevators where they are owned by private individuals as well as where they are owned by the railroads, and sell at their prices?—A. 1½ cents a bushel is more than the average profit, and so long as the elevator company pays a little inside of that freight rate it can pay a higher price to the farmer than he can ship it himself for; consequently he is practically compelled to sell to the man who has the rate.

Q. Has the farmer any redress in that case?—A. I do not see that he has.

Q. He is obliged to sell his grain to the elevator, and the very existence of the elevator makes it necessary not only for him to do so, but also, if I understand the proposition correctly, affords him a better price than he could possibly dispose of it for in any other manner?—A. You understand that there are very few points where there are not 2 elevators, or 2 shippers, one being a large shipper and the other being a smaller shipper; or, in another case, there are 2 shippers, both buying from the farmer, but one shipper sells to the large dealer, for the reason that his prices are higher than anyone's else.

Q. (By Mr. CLARKE.) Does it make any difference whether one or a dozen buy?—A. It does not make any difference, if all could sell to this one firm.

Q. (By Mr. RATCHFORD.) What remedy have you to suggest, if any?—A. I think I have got that under the proposed changes in the interstate-commerce act. I think I cover that.

Q. (By Mr. A. L. HARRIS.) What is the effect, after the independent buyer has been driven out along the line of the railroad, on the price of grain to the farmer? In other words, does the same condition of affairs exist now as existed when Mr. Counselman bid for wheat, where there is no competition now?—A. My answer would be general on that proposition, that a buyer will never pay anything more for what he buys than he is compelled to, and he will pay just such a price as will enable him to get the business and to keep his competitor, who has no rate, from getting it.

Q. Well, after the competition is driven out, does that condition of affairs then exist, that he pays what he pleases?—A. Well, I would say it would be injurious to the man who had grain to sell, by reason of his selling for lower prices.

Q. Then the farmer can not expect a continued higher price for grain after the business goes into the hands of a single buyer?—A. No; but the buyer will be continually held down by the difference between his rate. There is always some buyer left who would be in that territory for the cut prices based on public traffic.

Q. Well, is not the independent dealer handicapped?—A. He is handicapped to the extent that the elevator owner or preferred buyer would know his rate.

Q. If the independent buyer along the line of a road consigns his grain to Chicago, is there a public warehouse that he can consign it to and get this same wheat?—A. There are a large number of commission men and a number of public warehouses. There is a question as to the public warehouses in Chicago being in reality private warehouses that I am familiar with; but there are public warehouses there to which grain can go.

Q. Are they controlled by the same person that controls the private warehouses?—A. Yes; that is my understanding.

Q. Then is there any danger of mixing grain, mixing a lower grade with a higher grade to bring the two up to a higher grade, that will give an advantage to a private buyer?—A. The grain that goes into a public elevator goes in there and never comes out a higher grade than the inspector will permit to go through as the class of grain that is being inspected out; in other words, I think all grains become one grade; that is, become two or three grades. Of course, the danger you speak of exists in any elevator. That is understood. That is not a proposition where I think the shipper is injured, because he sells his grain on the market basis, upon what it actually is. If it is a higher grade, we will say No. 2 wheat, the grain mixer will pay a higher price for it than if it was a barely No. 2, for the reason that he wants it to grade up his low-grade wheat; consequently I do not think that particular proposition is injurious to the farmer.

Q. Will not No. 2 wheat sell for the same whether it weighs 58 pounds or whether it weighs 62 pounds?—A. No; it will not on the St. Louis market, and I do not think it will on the Chicago market.

Q. I am speaking with regard to the farmer. Then, they may sell 58-pound wheat the same as 62?—A. I imagine he does. The high-grade wheat is bought to bring up the low grade.

Q. (By Mr. CONGER.) This evil of mixing grains, though, would militate against the independent buyer, would it not, if not against the seller?—A. I do not think the mixing of grain injures anybody but the man who buys the wheat for use, and probably the farmer who gets no better price for his high-grade wheat than for poorly graded No. 2.

Q. You said a moment ago that you thought the purchaser of the grain at a local station would pay a higher rate for it if it was an extra quality. Tell me what the object would be for the independent buyer to pay more for that grain that is a little better, if it is to go into the public warehouse and come out just equal to that grade?—A. Oh, I either misunderstand your proposition or you misunderstand my answer. I had referred to the independent shipper into a market. There are grain mixers at every market; also professional mixers. They are there to buy this grain as it goes on the market. They will buy it from Armour or any large shipper the same as anybody else. They pay for sound wheat a certain price under the No. 2; say it is 55-pound wheat—some is as low as 50; occasionally then they will pay for wheat that will grade higher than No. 2, which is 60-pound—they will pay higher than the No. 2 price, as sample wheat. That grain goes to the mixing elevator and is mixed and then sold.

Q. Do I understand that this mixing is done in the small elevators at the country stations?—A. It is done at both places, but usually in the city. There is some mixing at the country stations, but they do not get enough variety of wheat, enough classes of wheat to mix at the country, and it has to go to the large center to get the different varieties to grade it up or down. If the mixing is to be done in the city by the public elevator man or the private elevator man I can not see what the purpose or object would be for the independent or small buyer to pay more for this grain if it is going into this public elevator and the benefit goes to the man who does the mixing. The proposition is that the buyer who buys on the market pays more than he would for simply an average grade.

Q. (By Senator MALLORY.) To go back to this matter of private elevators. I understood you to say that there were no railroad elevators in St. Louis. You mean by that to say there are no elevators that have these preferences shown them or given them?—A. No. Unfortunately, that is brought about by local conditions; by the bankruptcy of our elevator system there.

Q. They have none in St. Louis of that kind?—A. Two of the railroads are part owners of the Consolidated Elevator Company, which is now in the hands of a receiver. A few years ago the elevators at St. Louis were all consolidated into one company. Prior to that time the Missouri Pacific owned one, the Burlington one, and, I think, the Wabash one. Those elevators were sold to this central company, and each seller took stock in the central company, and that company has been in the hands of a receiver, and the receivership has just been foreclosed to the new company organized to take care of it.

Q. Is that practice of giving certain elevators the preference in rate on the published rates indulged in generally?—A. I have no idea that it has been indulged in at St. Louis. I do not want to be understood as saying that.

Q. What I want to get at is whether that is the general practice now.—A. That is the general practice of moving the grain through.

Q. So much so now that it may be laid down as general in the grain-shipping business?—A. Yes.

Q. That certain elevators are gradually getting the benefit?—A. Certain elevators and certain large shippers.

Q. Certain large shippers?—A. Most of these large shippers, instead of owning elevators, buy from the people that are located along the lines, and in that case the rate is made through a manipulation.

Q. Now, with regard to the question of freight rates in general, have you any criticisms to make on the published freight rates of the United States generally? I mean those which are held up to the public. Are they exorbitant?—A. Not generally so; no. I do not think the rates generally charged in this country are, taking the rate within itself, exorbitant.

Q. Do you know how they compare with the freight rates on the Continent?—A. The general rates in this country are far lower than they are in European countries. That is the only thing that brings down the general rate proposition—the length of the haul in this country. Our local rates for short distances are higher than they are in Europe.

Q. The average rate is lower?—A. The average rate is lower.

Q. But the local rates are higher?—A. The local rates are higher.

Q. Have you any idea what is the percentage of excess on the part of the American local rates?—A. No, I have not. I made a comparison some years ago, but it would be out of date now. I did not figure up the per cents even then.

Q. What is your observation as to the observance of the long and short haul rule by the railroads that you have intercourse with?—A. It has never been obeyed in the territory south of the Ohio River and east of the Mississippi River. It has not been obeyed since the Troy decision. Rates through the Southeast have never been on the basis of the long and short haul clause; but I can tell you how they are made. The rates through the Southeast are made on a combination of locals through to a junction point. For instance, the rate to a given point between Atlanta and Macon, Ga., will be the rate to Atlanta plus the local rate out of Atlanta to that point; and the rate to Macon plus the rate back to that point is less. Whichever is lower will be the local rate to that point. You will find the rates from all territories north of the Ohio River and east of the Mississippi are lower to Savannah, Charleston, Jacksonville, and Port Royal than they are to any intermediate point. They will be lower to Augusta than to the first point north of Augusta.

Q. (By Professor JOHNSON.) Why is it that the Southeastern section has always adhered to this basing point system?—A. The local conditions in the South are so different from those in other parts of the country, particularly on account of the water competition. The Southeast has a coast line all the way round from New Orleans up to the Virginias. It requires a different classification and a different method of making rates. What its effect on the man at a local station is I am unable to say. There are two sides to that proposition. He pays the higher rate on his through business, but the question is whether the commission or jobbing house does not pay a lower one than it would if all were brought down to a level. Which is correct I am unable to say. The railroads maintain that the present condition is better for the shipper as well as themselves.

There is another discrimination, more particularly in reference to the Ohio River and the territory of the Southeast. The merchandise rates through to the Eastern seaboard and all the Southeast are lower than they are from our territory. A few years ago, after the rate war, in trying to arrive at a division of the business, it was found that the most of their business into that territory in the way of merchandise went there from the East, and that most of the provisions went there from Chicago and across the Ohio River and through Memphis. They so adjusted those rates as to force in a measure the provisions from this territory where they naturally originated and force merchandise other than iron articles from the Eastern seaboard. The consequence is that the boot and shoe dealers and general merchants of Chicago, St. Louis, and Cincinnati are at a disadvantage as compared with the merchants in the East to all territory east of the Mississippi line and east of Kentucky. That matter has been before the Interstate Commerce Commission four different times and has been decided in favor of the Cincinnati Freight Bureau and the Chicago Freight Bureau, and two of the cases were appealed to the courts and one of the cases decided in favor of the complainants; but still it has never been obeyed from that particular point. That was the Social Circle case.

Q. (By Senator MALLORY.) What is your judgment as to the local rates that prevail in your territory and in the Southeast generally, as to their being reasonable or otherwise; the rates that are not between terminal points?—A. The local rates in Illinois reached by us—that is, immediate local rates—are governed by the statute of Illinois and are not unreasonably high.

Q. Are they observed?—A. Generally speaking, yes; although there is nothing in the statute that would prevent them from being cut if competition required it. There is a pool in the State of Illinois on these rates paid there.

Q. Railroad pool?—A. Yes. I say it is a pool; it is a tonnage division business that holds up competitive traffic.

Q. How about the rates in this other section; that is, in your jurisdiction?—A. I do not know of any rates that are injurious. That is, I do not know of any rates so high as to be injurious to the people. There are a great many that are so adjusted as to be injurious, for the reason that some other cities have a lower rate or a lower basis, but whether the rate within itself is too high I am unable to say.

Q. Well, relatively?—A. Relatively there are a great many rates that are out of line.

Q. What is the motive for that discrimination?—A. Well, it is from various causes. One of the causes which has given the most trouble in my office for the past 6 months has been the desire of the railroads to secure business that did not legitimately belong to them. I had a condition on the Missouri River, that will expire on the 15th of October, whereby rates from all points in the East, beginning with Portland, Me., on the north and Norfolk on the south, extending as far west as Pittsburg and Buffalo to the Missouri River, by way of Galveston, and worked from Galveston on to Missouri River points, as low as rates from Chicago to the same points, as low as the rates from the same territory to St. Louis, when you count the bridge toll, added to our East St. Louis rate. That is in a way to be remedied now, by order of the judge of the United States circuit court. The line that was making the rate being in the hands of a receiver, he decided the rate in effect from the Eastern seaboard would be too low and ordered it advanced. If there had been no receiver, or if the receivers had not applied to the court for relief, I do not think we would have had any.

Q. You have had some experience with the classification of freight?—A. Yes.

Q. Will you state to the commission the salient or distinguishing features of the different classifications that you are acquainted with?—A. There are 3 different classifications in the United States at the present time. Within the last 15 years there were 20. At the present time all the territory east of the Mississippi or north of the Ohio, including the Virginias, takes the official classification, and the territory west of the Mississippi River, including as far as the Pacific coast, takes the Western classification. The territory south of the Ohio and east of the Mississippi takes the Southern classification. The State of Illinois has a classification within the State established by the railroad commission. The State of Iowa has one established by the commission. Those classifications are as near the same as the standard classification in the territory as in the opinion of the commission is best; that is, they make a number of commodity exceptions. The lowest classification, taking into consideration the principal classes, is the official. They only have 6 classes. The Western is much higher on general merchandise and lower on the products of the country. The Southern is very largely an any-quantity classification, for the reason that I just gave—on account of water competition. It has been a theory among shippers that a uniform classification was an absolute necessity. I do not believe a uniform classification without a great many commodity exceptions is a possibility.

Q. Why?—A. The territory in which an article is produced in quantities must naturally have a lower rate on those commodities to the central markets than where those commodities are consumed in much smaller quantities, of course. For instance, in your territory, the southeast, cotton piece goods are fifth-class in the classification, in the third-class of the official classification, and the first-class in the western classification. In may be that the western should be as low as third, but I do not think it should be as low as fifth. Otherwise it would bear its full share of the traffic burden on all traffic of that class shipped in the territory. The western classification is very largely to the consumer and to the retail dealer or jobber for consumption, while in the manufacturing districts it goes to the central markets for redistribution. The same proposition applies on iron articles. Take the Birmingham district—the freight rate on iron should vary with the price of pig iron, between the minimum and maximum rates. In other words, as the price of pig iron goes down the rate on pig iron is reduced to the Ohio River and the Mississippi River. As it advances, for every dollar's advance there is an advance of 25 cents in freight rate until it reaches the maximum.

Q. Well, is not that feature observable in all kinds of classifications; that is, the product in a particular section is classified, whether it be manufactured or natural product, lower than in any other classification?—A. Yes. That is the reason I say a uniform classification established by any arbitrary order would be very injurious to many people. In the Pacific-coast traffic there are nearly fifteen hundred exceptions to the classification, brought about by water classification around by the Pacific mail and Cape Horn and other competition.

Q. Do you think it would be possible for any central body to form a just and fair classification to both shipper and producer for the whole United States?—A. I do not believe it could be done by anybody, unless it was the railroad people themselves, and they are doing it as fast as circumstances will permit.

Q. You spoke of a classification established by the State of Iowa and also by the State of Illinois. Do you know anything about how that works?—A. The official classification of Illinois is based upon the western classification, with the proviso that no rate shall be higher than that classified by the official. In other words, it has a low rate, and applies it except on a number of articles, such as canned goods, sugar, coffee, and articles of that kind, which are classified in one class lower than either classification markets. That is to enable the jobber in the State to distribute through the State. The Iowa classification is the western classification brought up from time to time with a few exceptions of the same nature. Now, another trouble in the way of a uniform classification is the recent statute rates that are in effect, mostly as a maximum tariff, on about 25 or 30 commodities, that are lower in some cases than either one of the classifications made.

Q. Is there any observation, in the making of classifications, of the local State business—any consideration of that brought into the classification?—A. Yes. Now, the next meeting of the western classification committee will be held in Milwaukee next Monday. I issued a circular to the members of our different committees, calling attention to that meeting, and asking if anyone had any article that was wrongly classified or that injured them by the classification now in effect. At each of these meetings there are from 100 to 500 applications for changes. The argument is presented as to the way they are needed, one of the arguments being the classification in other territory. There is a blank that is furnished. If lower than the official, you state what the classification is. There is a continuous effort to bring the classifications nearer together by the railroads themselves wherever it is possible. The differences are not nearly so great now as they were 2 years ago, or even a year ago.

Q. Can you tell whether any considerable road, in its classification, draws a distinction between its local business, the business inside of certain State lines, and business that is interstate in its classification?—A. No; except where, in Texas, they are required by the Texas commission. As I stated a while ago, there are orders of the commission, but no road of its own volition makes a difference.

Q. If intrastate commerce is to have any weight in existing classifications, would it not be a very disturbing element in the case of the establishment of a classification by a central bureau, in Washington, which could only deal with interstate commerce and not with intrastate commerce?—A. It would be a very serious objection, and it is a serious drawback even in the making of rates as it is now. These conflicts between State and interstate laws are met with every day on all questions of traffic.

Q. (By Mr. CLARKE.) Concerning the difference in charges between local and other rates, yo say they are higher for the local?—A. Yes.

Q. Is it not true that the relative labor cost of handling local freight is greater than that of handling through freight?—A. Yes; it costs no more to load a shipment to cross the continent than it would to load it to go 10 miles. It costs no more to unload it at destination in either case. Consequently, the greater the load the lower the proportionate expense of transportation. I did not intend to be understood as claiming any serious discrimination on this proposition. The differences are great; whether they are too great I have not made sufficient investigation to say.

Q. You say also that the local rates in this country are higher than they are in Europe; still the through rates are lower?—A. Yes.

Q. Is not that difference accounted for largely by the labor cost?—A. I think that enters into it quite extensively. It is very difficult to compare our methods with the European methods anyway, for their methods are so different in handling traffic from ours. In England transportation covers store-door delivery in every case; that is, on ordinary merchandise. They furnish wagon transportation within the city, while with us, there are only a few points where that is true, and even then only in a few territories.

Q. Is it your understanding that the wages of the railroad employees are higher in this country than in Europe?—A. Very much so.

Q. Now, I would like to bring your attention to the difference between the export rates of flour and wheat. If I understood you, you testified that the local rates by rail in this country for consumption in this country are the same on flour and wheat?—A. In a great part of this country they are, yes.

Q. But the export rates are widely different, and you think that difference is too great?—A. Entirely so; yes.

Q. Now, what, in your opinion, is the cause of that excess? Is the difference made by the railroad companies or by the steamship companies?—A. My testimony covered only the railroad rate to the seaboard. There is a difference still to be added growing out of the steamship company's rate. The steamship company usually charges more for flour than wheat. The difference in the inland rate to the seaboard is where the discrimination exists, as I see it, against the American miller. The American miller will ship as much flour in a car for export as the American wheat shipper will ship wheat, in hundreds of pounds. The elevator company loads the wheat. At Gulf ports and at some of the South Atlantic ports the railroad company pays the elevator charges to get it aboard steamer. They also put it aboard steamer in the case of flour. Now, I can not see, other than the insurance risk, where there should be any difference between flour and wheat under those conditions. And I think the commission's decision that 2 cents would be a reasonable difference is certainly all that the wheat shippers should ask, or all that the railroad companies should ask, for the difference in transportation.

Q. Does it seem to you therefore that the difference, as made by the railroad companies, is practically dictated by the steamship companies?—A. No; the difference is made because you can get a large quantity of wheat to move out almost any moment. You can not get a large quantity of flour to move at the same time. Flour moves, a steady movement, say, of from 1 to 10 and 20 cars a day. You can go into St. Louis or Chicago to-day, and if you make a low enough rate you can get a contract for almost any quantity of wheat, but you can not do that for almost any quantity of flour. It is a question of competition between carriers that has brought about this situation.

Q. And you say you think the difference is excessive?—A. Yes.

Q. Who dictates that excess? A. The carrier.

Q. Which carrier?—A. The inland carrier.

Q. Why?—A. Wheat and flour, going east go very largely at times when empty cars are on the Mississippi River and in Chicago to go east. In other words, it is to get a return load. The elevator company, as I say, has the grain and can get those cars to come back quickly. The flour shipper does not carry a very large stock of flour on hand and has to grind his flour very frequently after he makes his sales.

Q. That explanation would seem to account for a resonable difference, but I can not see that it accounts for an unreasonable difference?—A. Well, the unreasonable difference is brought about by the anxiety of the outside railrod man to get business.

Q. (By Mr. FARQUHAR.) Is not there a reason in the fact that the foreign miller gets the advantage of the by-product in the grinding of the flour?—A. On the contrary, the miller on the other side gets better prices for his by-products than the miller or this side does.

Q. Yes; but he gets the by-product by getting the grain. If he got the flour, there is no by-product on the other side. Do you not take that into account?—A. Well, I can not see where that is of any consideration, to be considered by the American railroad men.

Q. Well, would it not be a consideration in this fact, that nearly all the tonnage is foreign tonnage that takes the American grain?—A. Yes.

Q. Is it not an advantage to the ship broker there to get the grain for the foreign miller?—A. That is true as to the ocean rate.

Q. That is the very rate that is complained of, is it not?—A. No. The rate we complain of is the rate that the railroad company makes to the seaboard on flour hauled in the same train; that he charges on flour from 6½ to 8 cents per 100 pounds from St. Louis, for example, higher than on wheat loaded about the same minimum weight. That is aside from the ocean rate. The ocean rate, of course, is largely on foreign tonnage, and the Englishman would naturally rather have the wheat ground in his country than on this side. That is so much so in foreign countries that France has a duty on flour and does not take the duty off on flour when it does on wheat. But the American miller complains that the railroad company is putting a duty on his business even where there is no duty on the other side.

Q. You stated here that the inland rates on flour and grain were the same?—A. For domestic consumption.

Q. It would seem that the American railroad makes a discrimination as well as the foreign shipper?—A. Yes.

Q. Both of them are getting toll?—A. Both of them are getting toll.

Q. Owing to the fact that they are carrying the grain instead of the ground products, the flour?—A. Yes.

Q. Now, as I understood the question, really you do not know whether it was the foreign shipper or the two in conjunction that forced the grain shipment instead of the flour shipment. Evidently there is a choice somewhere. You claim that it is in the lesser amount of flour that fs in the market for the carriers. But should that lesser quantity make such a difference as to allow the American transportation line and the foreign steamship line both to get toll?—A. The foreign steamship line has a reason in the fact that package freight pays naturally a higher rate than bulk freight. The American railroad company has no excuse for this that I can see, other than the permanence with which he can get the shipment.

The millers are distributed over a very large territory. There are hundreds of mills through Kansas and Nebraska of 125 and 150 barrel capacity. They export their surplus; they sell all they can locally and export all they have left. If they can export all their surplus they can manufacture their local flour much cheaper, for the reason that they are running full capacity. I can give you an illustration that also illustrates the long and short haul proposition. A few days ago a steamer was in port at Norfolk that had 6,000 tons room. A railroad, which terminates at St. Louis, contracted at Kansas City for 3,000 tons of flour at 2 cents lower rate—this is flour, in this case—at 2 cents lower rate than it makes in St. Louis. The reason it gave was that this 3,000 tons was there ready to go. We did not have that much within ten days at all of our mills. Now, that steamer would go on demurrage at a certain time. The tonnage in sight made the rate. Now, that proposition applies on grain to a much greater extent, for the entire grain business of this country is done by about not to exceed 20 firms. The entire flour business is done by 5,000 firms. Now, you can go to one of these 20 firms and get more tonnage than you can go to probably 20 flour shippers and get.

Q. (By Senator MALLORY.) Do you know anything about the difference in the import rates and the domestic rates?—A. Yes.

Q. Is not there a similar difference between the import rates and the domestic or inland rates?—A. I have known tin-plate rates to be lower from Liverpool to Kansas City than the rate from St. Louis to Kansas City. These are illustrations that have come to my mind. The rate on queensware to the Missouri River from Liverpool is frequently lower than it is from East Liverpool, Ohio.

Q. Well, do you ascribe the same reason for this difference that you ascribe for the difference in the export rate?—A. No; I think that the influence of the man on the other side makes the rate. By agreement between the railroad company and the ocean line, they deduct a certain per cent of the rate necessary to get the business.

Q. (By Professor JOHNSON.) I would like to ask whether the Mississippi River traffic has any appreciable influence on St. Louis rates?—A. A very great one.

Q. Will you illustrate the way in which the Mississippi traffic affects the rates at St. Louis?—A. We have a barge line between St. Louis and Kansas City—St. Louis and New Orleans. We have several steamer lines running more or less regularly, and those lines naturally make a lower rate than the rail lines. It is hard to estimate the exact effect of water competition, for the reason that it is not only the traffic that the water carrier hauls but all the traffic that the railroad company hauls in competition with it. We know that the rate by barge from St. Louis to New Orleans very frequently makes our rate on grain from St. Louis to Baltimore; that the rate on flour from St. Louis to New Orleans by barge frequently makes our rate to the eastern seaboard by rail. It would be impossible to state exactly what effect it has, but we know it has a very satisfactory effect. In fact, if we had the lakes at St. Louis that Chicago has, I do not think I would have any excuse for testifying for St. Louis on grain rates.

Q. Is this Mississippi River traffic increasing or decreasing?—A. As compared with several years ago, it is not so great. The barge line last year hauled very little traffic for the reason that lower rates were made on export grain than ever known before. The rate from St. Louis to Baltimore was lower than the barge line figured they could haul to New Orleans at a profit, to say nothing of the fact that the ocean rate was higher from New Orleans than from Baltimore. But taking 1899 as compared with several years ago it shows an increase.

Q. You do not expect the river traffic to be driven out of existence?—A. No; although there is one thing in the interstate-commerce act that is liable to drive it out of the inland rivers to some extent. It did drive it out on the Missouri River while I was there. The long and short haul clause itself, the exception to it, makes it more favorable to the railroad company than to the water carrier. The water carrier is usually one steamboat, sometimes two, three, or four, while the railroad company has only involved the points that are reached by this water carrier, for the reason that it can evade the long and short haul clause when meeting water competition. The consequence is that they can bankrupt the water carrier frequently and still hold up their rates to intermediate territory.

Q. (By Senator MALLORY.) Has not that to some extent been done?—A. It has been done very greatly. It did drive the Missouri River Transportation Company out of existence.

Q. Has it affected the Mississippi also?—A. Yes; it bankrupted the Anchor Line of steamers.

Q. (By Mr. FARQUHAR.) Did the establishment of your barge system make much difference in the freight rates to the East?—A. Yes, I could furnish the commission a comparative statement showing the rates when the river is up so the barge line can go down, and when it is not; when normal conditions were in effect, say up to 2 years ago, before this class of competition became such a factor. If you would like to have it, I would be very glad to furnish a statement of that kind showing the comparative rates, as an illustration.

Q. That is, it changes the eastern rate—by the establishment of the barge system?—A. Yes. Part of the year the river is closed by ice, and other times the river is so low that the barges can not run. When they can run the rates show lower than when they can not.

Q. (By Professor JOHNSON.) I would like to have your opinion as to whether the rates from the central West to the Pacific West are higher than they need be. I had, for instance, a letter this morning from Richmond, Ind., from the Hoosier Drill Manufacturing Company, in which they say that they are shipping large quantities of goods to the seaboard and from the seaboard to Pacific coast points and thereby saving nearly a third on freight rates over what it would cost them to send the same goods direct by rail to the Pacific coast. I cite that as an illustration of an actual fact, with a view of asking whether your experience in St. Louis has given you any information as to whether these rates to the Pacific coast by rail might be made less. —A. We at St. Louis have on file with the Interstate Commerce Commission a complaint on that proposition which will be heard on October 30. The rates from all the territory on the east of the Mississippi River on commodities to the Pacific coast are the same. That is, the rate from St. Louis to San Francisco on nails is the same as it is from Pittsburg by rail. This particular proposition that you speak of—where is it—Richmond, Ind.?

Q. Richmond, Ind.—A. Well, they pay a combination up to the nearest point, and that point happens to be the eastern seaboard. The Pacific coast rates are very grossly discriminatory against the less than carload shipper. They also take away from the near-by shipper the advantage of location and distance. The grounds of our complaint before the commission are these: First, that on June 29, 1898, the railroads advanced their less than carload rates to a minimum difference of 50 cents a hundred pounds above the carload rate; and on a great many commodities the difference is greater than the profit on the goods. They also maintain the same rate from Pittsburg to the Pacific coast that they maintain from St. Louis to the Pacific coast. That complaint we have not gone into so much. That is more particularly a St. Paul and Chicago proposition, although we are equally interested. This was brought about by an agreement between the jobbers of the Pacific coast and the railroads reaching there; the agreement being that if the less than carload rates were advanced sufficiently to shut out the merchants of Chicago, St. Paul, and St. Louis, they would discontinue shipments by water on the business they controlled. A committee from those cities went to Monterey, before the hearing, and. also at Milwaukee and St. Paul, protesting against this change. The change was made, however, and has now been in effect, as I say, since June 28, 1898. In May of this year the two northern lines, the Great Northern and the Northern Pacific, finding that they were not getting as much business as they thought they ought to have from the Pacific coast jobbers, reduced their difference to 25 cents a hundred; so we have the anomaly of a lower rate from St. Louis to Portland than from St. Louis to Los Angeles, and this entire situation will be brought before the Interstate Commerce Commission at hearings that we are now arranging for.

Q. Does any of your traffic destined to Pacific seaboard points go to the Gulf and thence by water?—A. No; we have at times shipped from St. Louis to New York and thence by water. There is no direct transportation from the Gulf to the Pacific coast.

Q. How recent, as far as you know, have there been shipments from St. Louis to the Atlantic seaboard and thence around· by water?—A. Within the last 2 years, up to the time of the rate war between what is known as the Clipper Line of steamers and the Pacific Mail, and the direct rail lines, went out of existence—that is about a year and a half ago—we shipped lard and oleo oil and a number of commodities of that nature from Kansas City to the seaboard and thence by water to San Francisco.

Q. (By Mr. CLARKE.) Is it not true that the Southern Pacific Railroad has a line of steamers plying between Atlantic and Gulf ports and their eastern railroad termini at New Orleans and Galveston?—A. Yes; they own the Morgan line. The Southern Pacific, on eastern seaboard business—I think it was shown in testimony some time ago—handled 65 per cent of all the eastern business by way of New Orleans to the Pacific coast points; that is, as far north as San Francisco.

Q. By reason of having that line of steamers?—A. Yes.

Q. They are able to make lower rates than the all-rail lines to the Pacific, aren't they?—A. The Southern Pacific so far have been able to dictate all the rates to the Pacific coast south of Portland, and up to May 1 last making, you might say, all the rates to the Pacific coast.

Q. In that way they can get a great deal of the freight of the central West, can they not?—A. They get it, but they prefer getting it from the East, where they get the haul for their water line and their rail line also. The freight that originates in territory west of Pittsburg seeks very largely the Santa Fe, the Great Northern, and the Northern Pacific roads. By the way, I might add that in consequence of this reduction by the Great Northern and Northern Pacific roads the Pacific coast jobbers have a boycott on those lines at the present time. They are dependent upon us in the middle West to get their business from the Pacific coast.

Q. (By Senator MALLORY.) In your experience can you say that you have encountered many instances of unjust discriminations against individuals, in your official experience, by transportation companies?—A. I have encountered a great many illegal discriminations.

Q. I qualified by the word "unjust," not illegal but unjust, whether they are legal or illegal.—A. Yes; there are a great many that occur from time to time. I think we have had as many in favor of individuals in whom I am interested as against them.

Q. Those which are in favor of some must necessarily be against others? In other words, it would not be a discrimination in favor of somebody unless it was against somebody else?—A. Yes.

Q. Have you succeeded in many cases in correcting those discriminations?—A. Our office has succeeded in correcting a great many discriminations against the city of St. Louis; and in a similar office at Kansas City that I filled for 8 years, we corrected a great many discriminations that were in effect there.

Q. That is, as against Kansas City?—A. They were published tariff discriminations that I refer particularly to. We found a condition of rates there that would, if continued, have prevented the progress of such cities as Kansas City and St. Joseph.

Q. Well, these were simply discriminations that were committed openly and aboveboard, as it were?—A. Yes; those were discriminations on published tariff.

Q. You stated in your testimony originally that you encountered discriminations in favor of individuals in St. Louis, but that with those things you have nothing to do?—A. I shut my eyes to a discrimination that is reported to me as a St. Louis proposition, for the reason that it is not policy for me, as a representative of St. Louis, to make too close an investigation. When there is such a discrimination in favor of an individual in St. Louis, it is because a similar discrimination exists in favor of an individual somewhere else. I make an investigation as to the other city, and if I can get that corrected the one in our own city is corrected at the same time. So indirectly I do, but directly I do not, take up a proposition where a St. Louis man is supposed to have a discrimination.

Q. Well, if you find that a similar discrimination exists in favor of an individual outside of St. Louis, and also in St. Louis, and you can not correct it in the other city, you allow it to go on in St. Louis?—A. I have never found one of that nature. My experience on both sides of this proposition is that when a lower rate than tariff is made it is because the line that makes it thinks it is losing business by reason of a lower rate to some other place or some other individual. If that is not the case at that particular moment it will be very soon; and matters will continue to grow worse and the discriminations will be greater as between individuals until they get so bad that the railroads will get together and put things back to a proper basis again.

Q. In other words, the evil works out its own remedy in the course of time?—A. The evil works out its own remedy in time; in the meantime some one is suffering.

Q. May I ask you what method you employ to induce railroads that are thus discriminating to correct their ways or their tariff?—A. It is owing to circumstances. Usually by calling personally upon the traffic official of the company and discussing it with him informally. In that way it is understood by railroad men that I am not a detective, nor am I going to make any report against them. Consequently they will discuss a proposition with me and give me their reasons individually that they would not either in correspondence or would not admit openly that they were doing; and they frequently make suggestions to me as to what action I can take as against what they are supposed to meet that will probably help them to correct the situation. In other words, I try to apply, in my position, the same proposition as I would if I was doing the business of an individual firm; that is, I try to apply for the city of St. Louis the same methods that I would if I owned its business and was handling it.

Q. Well, behind you, behind your personal influence, is not there also a moral influence?—A. The moral influence of more than 2,200.

Q. That of itself has more weight with the transportation companies?—A. Yes; so much so that if necessity arises I could divert a large proportion of the business that those 2,200 people control. That is the power behind my work.

Q. And these organizations, such as this in St. Louis and those in others of the principal commercial centers of this country, railroad centers, have been brought about by reason of the existence of a system of discrimination that has been going on for years?—A. They have been brought about by that; also by the fact that when the shipper calls upon the traffic men he is always at a disadvantage, for the reason that he does not know the traffic man's side of the case. The traffic man gives the situation as he pleases, and unless you are familiar with his side of the proposition you must take what he says as true. A man in my position is supposed to have been familiar with the railroad side of the case before he took the position; consequently his knowledge of the railroad side is what the shipper pays for; and a great many cases of discrimination in rates continue because they have never been brought before the roads in such shape as to convince them that there were discriminations existing. I do not think that any railroad company for any length of time upholds discriminations against a community. What they do is to look out for the greatest amount of revenue they can get for the company.

Q. You speak of Chicago and other western cities, of discrimination there by reason of the elevator system. Is there any other method, any other thing, peculiar to the Chicago transportation business, particularly of grain, whereby there is an advantage gained in Chicago over St. Louis or other cities?—A. There is a situation there that I do not know that St. Louis is particularly interested in, but by which a reduced rate is secured. It is no particular benefit to Chicago, but it is a benefit to the western shipper. That is, by the manipulation through the belt lines around Chicago.

Q. Will you please explain that?—A. For instance, there are 3 belt lines touching the western lines and the eastern lines. The belt line is allowed a certain per cent of the rate by the eastern line. It is also allowed a certain per cent of the rate by the western line. Those two percents are great enough so that the belt line can afford to give back part of it to the man who routes his business through this belt line, and still have a profitable business. That has not been pursued as much this year as in former years. It used to be one of the greatest methods of cutting rates through that territory.

Q. In other words, there was a rebate to the shipper?—A. It was a rebate to the shipper paid by a line which claimed that it was not amenable to the interstate commerce act, because it paid it out of a proportion that accrued in the State of Illinois.

Q. (By Professor JOHNSON.) Was that position of the belt line upheld by the Interstate Commerce Commission?—A. No; they ruled against it.

Q. (By Senator MALLORY.) Have you had any occasion to consider the question of private cars and their influence upon transportation rates?—A. The private car influence is one of the methods of cutting rates. So long as they exist that can be done and still be within the law. For illustration, take any packing company. The car line is a separate corporation. The traffic manager of the packing house is usually the manager of the car line. He routes his cars so as to get the longest mileage. That is one method of cutting rates. They are paid so much a mile for the use of the cars; usually in the west it is 1 cent per mile in both directions, loaded or empty. East of the Mississippi River it is three-fourths of a cent. Now a great deal of the packing house product, in fact, the larger proportion of it, is controlled absolutely by the packer. He takes the long line; that gives him the most mileage. The short line man goes to him and agrees to allow the long line mileage if it is shipped over his line, and at 1 cent per mile or even three-fourths of a cent per mile the packer has a very nice revenue from his car department. It is also done sometimes by leasing the cars; getting so much rent for a car.

Q. Is there any other line of business in which private cars, privately owned cars, are employed to any considerable extent, besides the packing business?—A. Yes; the stock car business is the largest. The stock cars and refrigerator cars are the two largest lines of private cars at the present time. Up to 2 or 3 years ago there were a great many box cars of that nature, but they are very largely going out of existence, for the reason that about 2 years ago the car mileage was reduced by the railroad companies from three-fourths of a cent to 6 mills. That took off 1½ miles, or about 25 per cent off the earnings, and it has reduced the number of car lines. In fact, at the present time, the railroad companies will not haul private box cars if they can haul their own. I think that eventually the private box cars will be a thing of the past.

Q. You distinguish the box car from the refrigerator car?—A. Yes; there is more reason for the existence of the refrigerator than there is for the existence of any other line, for the reason that the refrigerator has to be built peculiarly for the class of business that it hauls, and the railroad avoids some risk if it hauls the traffic in the car of the owner. That is the railroad excuse for it, and I think there is considerable to be said on that side of the propositon.

Q. (By Mr. FARQUHAR.) Generally, who are the owners of these refrigerator and stock cars?—A. The stock car lines are very largely owned, or to a certain extent owned, by officers of railroads, and refrigerators are owned, with only two exceptions that I now recall, by packers or by beer shippers—by the shippers of those products.

Q. There is not such a thing as a car trust of that character, is there?—A. The car trust, as applied to car lines, I think is a misnomer. The car trust is usually where the car belongs to the railroad company—that is, has the name of the railroad company on the car. The car trust is one of the methods of the officers of a railroad to use their money or lend their money to the railroad company at a per cent. In other words, the railroad company needs a given number of cars and has not the money to buy those cars. The officers or their friends will form a car trust and lease those cars to the railroad company. I do not think that affects the shipper at all, nor does it have anything to do with the rate of transportation. That is simply a question as between the owners of the trust and the stockholders of the company. That also applies to locomotives quite frequently.

Q. These refrigerator cars, you say, are usually owned by the packers themselves?—A. By the corporation which the packers own.

Q. That is a question which I desire to know about. It is not the immediate packer at all, but a corporation operating rolling stock, independent of the packer, but he having the money control of it?—A. He has the money control and any profits. If they are organized for the purpose of evading the law, the rate paid to the car trust and the refrigerator company is not paid to the packer, for the reason that the refrigerator company is disobeying the law, if anyone. The refrigerator company is a transportation company, consequently it is a question between two transportation companies, and, so far as I recall, there is no law against it.

Q. (By Professor JOHNSON.) Now I would like to ask on this point as to what extent you think the earning of railroad companies are at the present time absorbed by these subsidiary or ancillary companies, bridge companies, car trusts, freight lines, palace car companies, etc.? Some years ago, I think, a large part of the earnings of transportation were absorbed by the corporations that were subsidiary. To what extent do you think that now exists?—A. I do not believe that I can answer that question satisfactorily to you. It is so largely a question to each particular railroad. It is entirely owing to the credit and standing of the railroad company itself. If the railroad company has not the money, or if the stockholders of the company are not willing to advance the money necessary to do this, someone must; and the officers of the company, who usually have the money, are willing to loan this money and take as security these trust bonds or trust certificates.

Q. Do you think the apparent earnings of railroad companies from the business of transportation, as manifested in the dividends on stock, would be very largely increased if the real earnings of transportation all found their way to the stockholders?—A. Well, the first stockholder of a railroad company did not put up any money for his stock to begin with. He simply got his stock for subscribing to the bonds, as a usual proposition.

Q. I suppose you are aware that a great deal is heard of small earnings of the railroad companies for the business of transportation. Are the earnings small, in your opinion?—A. In some territories; yes. The building of roads in a new territory must be on a basis that will give the man who ventures his money more than the ordinary interest, and the general method of doing that is to form your line, get all the donations you can toward building it, issue your bonds, and give probably for every $1,000 bond that is subscribed, say, $250, $500, sometimes $1,000 in stock, as a bonus, on the basis that this stock represents the donations that you give; and if your lines prove profitable the stock increases as the country is built up. That is what has increased the value of Western stocks and what has prevented some Western stocks from being any greater than they are. Now, what effect can trusts have on this proposition is something I can not answer.

Q. (By Senator MALLORY.) Any other question?—A. There was one question referred to this morning that I meant to have covered in regard to discriminations; that is the question of fraudulent representations by shippers.

Q. As to classes?—A. As to classification. Usually speaking, where this is very great it is by the knowledge of some railroad men. The railroad company could prevent it if particularly anxious to do so. I suppose Mr. Kelley probably covered that yesterday pretty fully, inasmuch as he and I have been working on the same cases in Texas and the Southeast.

Q. He referred to it. Is that, in your judgment then, an evil, to a considerable extent?—A. It is a very great evil in some particular lines of business. We have felt it more at St. Louis on this particular line of hardware than anything else, because the difference is so great between carload and less than carload rates to the territory in question, particularly in Texas. The difference on iron articles is 40 cents per 100 pounds, and on nails 35 cents, and on another class of iron, galvanized iron, 36 cents. The shippers who load a mixed car of 30,000—up to the 1st of July 24,000 was a carload—putting in nails, sheet iron, ordinary iron articles—that is, merchant iron—gets 40 cents less than the man who ships to the same city in less than car loads, and it puts the man who ships in less than car loads at a very great disadvantage; and we have spent a great deal of time—the cities of St. Louis, Chicago, Cincinnati, Philadelphia, and other cities—in trying to have this stopped. We do not have much trouble of that nature west of the Mississippi River, for the reason that the Western Weighing Association inspect at all points west of us. The trouble that we particularly refer to comes in Texas and the Southeast, where no such associations exist. There was an association for a while in Texas, but it is not there now.

Q. You think that a system of inspection would make that thing impossible?—A. The railroad companies themselves could correct that proposition if they would pursue the same methods in all territories as they do in the South. The temptation is quite great in a good many commodities.

Q. (By Mr. FARQUHAR.) What have you to say on the question of underbilling?— A. That is part of the same proposition that I made there. Underbilling can not be pursued if the railroad companies do not want it. It is not pursued in the territory west of Chicago and west of St. Louis, and this inspection bureau that I speak of is also a weighing association. They weigh all traffic not as individual railroads, so there is no temptation for their employees to give other than the correct weights. One of the troubles of having the inspector of the railroad inspect for himself or the weighmaster for himself is the temptation to secure the business by under-billing or misrepresentation of the contents. When that is done by an association of railroads the inspector is the employee of no one individual road, and he hold his position by being correct instead of the reverse.

Q. So that it needs the collusion of the officials of one or two roads, on any long haul, to make a technical underbilling?—A. Yes.

Q. And you say this inspection at the origin of the bill itself would obviate any collusion even on the part of the other roads?—A. Yes; this inspection, as applied in the territory I speak of, is not only at the point of origin, but it may be at any point between origin and destination. It may be when you bill out your freight that the railroad has no time to put either inspection or weight. It notes on the bill, "Shipper's weight" or "Not inspected." That is notice to the inspector or weigh-master at destination to reweigh the freight or inspect the contents. Wherever that system is in existence we have very little trouble in wrong classification, and most of the complaints that reach me in that case are brought about by the simple differ-ence of opinion as to what the classification should be and the misinterpretation by the inspectors themselves.

Q. That is, a difference in judgment between the inspectors themselves as to sec-ond or third or fourth class rates?—A. Yes. We had a very peculiar one this year, where a feather costing a cent doubled the rate on millinery.

Q. (By Professor JOHNSON.) You have explained several times about the differ-ence between rates for carload lots and for less than carloads. Are you in favor of having essentially the same rate on less than carload lots as on carload lots?—A. Not necessarily the same rate. The difference between carloads and less than carloads should not be so great on any merchandise commodities as to prevent a movement in both cases.

Q. Do existing practices discriminate very strongly against the small shipper?— A. The existing practices to a very large territory to-day do; to all the territory west of the Rocky Mountains and to all of Texas. We have no trouble of that kind in the Southeast, particularly between the Mississippi River and the East. In the first place, the difference between carloads and less east of the Mississippi River is fre-quently not over 3 cents a hundred, while on the Pacific coast it is 50, and in Texas it ranges from a minimum of 20 cents to a maximum of 45.

Q. (By Professor JOHNSON.) That operates against the buyers of the territory as between your city and San Francisco?—A. It places the retail buyer on a great many commodities entirely in the hands of the jobber that is near by him. The profit on nails, for instance, is less than 40 cents a hundred. That is the jobber's profit. The jobber's profit on almost everything, any heavy commodity, is less than that; and when the difference is so great that it confines the retail dealer to the jobber in his immediate locality, vicinity, he pays more for his goods than if he could have the competition of jobbers in other farther away cities as well as the ones close by.

Q. (By Senator MALLORY.) You have some experience, I suppose, with railroads in the hands of receivers?—A. Yes.

Q. Do you find any difference between dealing with them and railroads that are not in the hands of receivers?—A. Well, the railroad that is in the hands of a receiver has no interest to pay, and consequently it can and does carry freight frequently for lower rates than it would if it had its interest to pay. Another proposition that comes in there is that of a line that needs money. You see an interest debt is due at a certain time and the money must be had, and a rate can frequently be secured over such a line at that time on a large volume of tonnage to get the ready money, on the same principle that a merchant will sell his goods at cost to get the money to pay a note. That is another case where a man with a large volume of tonnage has the best of the man with a small volume.

Q. The roads in the hands of receivers, as a general thing, having no interest to pay, can do this. Do they cut rates?—A. Yes; the record of rate cutting will show that the greatest aggressors and some of the worst forms of abuse of the interstate com-merce act have been by lines in the hands of receivers.

Q. Discrimination—do they practice that also?—A. On the principle that any rebate is a discrimination against the man that does not have one, yes.

Q. (By Mr. KENNEDY.) United States officers violating the laws of the United States?—A. Yes.

Q. (By Professor JOHNSON.) Would you have the laws in regard to receiverships amended in any way?—A. I think the law is sufficient to cover it as it is if com-plaint was made. So far the only case we have had where complaint was made is the one I mentioned this morning, in the Missouri River case, where the receivers ap-plied, and, instead of getting a judgment, were required to restore their rates. That was not a rebate, but a rate published according to law, but a worse discrimi-nation than if it had been a rebate.

Q. The system of receiverships is very bad frequently; that is, the appointment of the former managers of the road as receivers?—A. The receiver usually is appointed by the influence of the majority bondholders; the majority bondholders usually control the stock, and for that reason they usually make the president the receiver—the president and receiver being the same man; that is more frequently the case.

Q. Is it not against public policy to have the management that brought the road into the condition of insolvency to continue in the management of the road while in insolvency?—A. I do not know that it is; that is, from the standpoint of the owner of the property. It may be against public policy from the standpoint of the public. I do not think there is any grievous wrong in that situation. It seems to me the man who owns the bonds has the right to say who shall be in control, and if his choice happens to be the officers of the company, and if they have served him satisfactorily as president and traffic manager, they should serve him satisfactorily as receiver.

Q. (By Senator KYLE.) More a matter for their lookout than the public?—A. Yes; as a general proposition receiverships of railroads are not brought about by the fault of the manager of the property.

Q. (By Mr. FARQUHAR.) Are they brought about for the purpose of reorganization?—A. Frequently, because the capitalization is greater than they can pay the interest on.

Q. That gives the opportunity of reorganization?—A. Yes; and sometimes the only method that can be pursued.

Q. That is done to force out the small lien holder?—A. It forces out the stockholder and sometimes the second mortgagee. Usually, however, the stock is wiped out and both mortgagees take the property.

Q. (By Senator MALLORY). What would you say was the crying abuse arising out of the railway system now prevailing in this country?—A. The inability to get legal relief of any nature.

Q. You think that is the great crying evil?—A. Men in my position do not apply to the Interstate Commerce Commission for the reason that after we have a decision we have still to go to the courts, where the whole case can be reopened and entirely new evidence presented, and the evidence you take before the commission has practically no value except what it may have developed that you did not know yourselves.

Q. Your answer relates to that kind of relief. I do not infer you mean the inability to get judgment against the railroad company for cutting off your leg or anything of that kind?—A. I referred to the traffic.

Q. Even when you have a decision of the Interstate Commerce Commission, you have taken a very small step toward correcting the abuse?—A. It is entirely with the railroad company, after you have your decision, to say whether they will obey it or not.

Q. Have you anything to suggest for the correction of that evil?—A. I have some rather pronounced views on the changes of the law.

Q. We would like to have them.—A. As it now stands, if we can not get relief from the railroad companies themselves, we accept the best we can get and try it again later on. When we apply to the commission, it is because we think we will develop something that will enable us to go before the railroad companies again, not with the expectation that the commission's order will be obeyed.

I have some memoranda here with regard to my views on the amendments to the act to regulate commerce.

(Reading:) "The Interstate Commerce Commission, under the law as it now exists and is interpreted by the courts, is powerless to remedy existing evils. Its lack of power is so well known, and its orders so seldom obeyed, that the shipping public have almost ceased to appeal to it for relief. First, because its orders are not obeyed, except when railroads interested decide it to their interest to do so; second, because delay in rendering a decision after cases are heard is generally so great that shippers eit er abandon their fight or compromise with the railroads before decision is secured. h

"The act to regulate commerce should be amended by Congress at the earliest moment possible—

"First. By making the findings of the commission enforcible at law, unless upon appeal to the courts they are found to be unlawful or unjust, and pending the decision of the courts on such appeal the findings of the commission should be made effective by all the railroads interested within 30 days after they are promulgated by the commission, and continue in effect until overruled by the courts or changed by authority of the commission.

"That while the commission shall not have the authority to fix the rates or say what rates shall be charged, they shall have authority to order reduction in rates where found to be exorbitant and to determine the relation of rates as between localities and commodities."

What I mean to explain there is the proposition we now have on grain and flour. They nave ruled that the difference on flour and wheat should not exceed 2 cents, the idea being that the railroads ought to be compelled to put that order in effect unless the courts should decide after a hearing that it was too small a difference. I do not ask that they should have authority to say the rate should be 10, or any given amount, but that the difference should be that.

Q. (By Professor JOHNSON.) The same would apply as between communities?—A. The same would apply as between communities. If the difference between St. Louis and Cincinnati and the south on a given commodity was 4 cents if St. Louis or Cincinnati was to apply to the commission for reduction or increase, whatever their order should be on that proposition, should go into effect until countermanded by the courts. (Continuing to read:)

"Second. By enforcing absolute publicity of all rates, rules, or regulations affecting transportation of persons or property, whether such rates, rules, etc., are between points in the United States, or export and import traffic. If lower rates are made from or to the seaboard for export, or on import, than on domestic traffic, such rates, rules, and conditions to be published in the same manner and under the same conditions as domestic traffic. The railroads interpret the proposition now that they do not have to publish their export rates. If you put the export grain rates out of the knowledge of the public, you might as well have all of them out of the knowledge of the public, because you have the ruling factor in the price of grain, so you do not know what it is. The same proposition would apply on imports. Where through rates and divisions are made on foreign traffic, said rates and divisions to be published in such manner as required by the Interstate Commerce Commission.

"By requiring railroads and other common carriers subject to the act to regulate commerce, not only to file copies of tariffs, rules, and regulations with the Interstate Commerce Commission, but also to furnish, on request, from boards of trade, exchanges, shippers, freight bureaus, and other commercial organizations, whose duties are to look after transportation problems for their respective cities and communities, copies of all tariffs that affect members of such organizations, directly or indirectly, whether such tariffs read to or from such cities, etc., or to rival cities, and in case of refusal of railroad companies to furnish such tariffs, the Interstate Commerce Commission shall have authority to order them furnished within a reasonable time, not longer than 30 days; and in the event any current tariff is found to be out of print, though still in use, the railroad company shall be required to furnish certified copies of same, including all amendments or corrections."

I make that point for the reason that frequently in making up a comparative situation as between one city and another you apply to a railroad company for the tariff from a given territory to a rival city. It is not refused, but they say it is out of print. The consequence is that a man who is not posted as to how to get that tariff does not get it. If I get an answer of that kind, and I only get it from one road, I write the auditor of the Interstate Commerce Commission for a copy of the tariff, and I get it. A great many applications of that kind are not furnished, however, for the reason that knowledge of how to get it is lacking. I only suggest that this be done where asked for. I do not think it is necessary to have these tariffs filed continuously with the merchants' exchanges or organizations of that kind, but they should be required to furnish them when asked for. That is one part of the publicity of the tariff, and I think if the Interstate Commerce Commission had nothing to do but secure absolute publicity of rates it would be worth all it has cost. A railroad company can not continuously discriminate in public tariffs without in the end getting into trouble. [Continuing to read:]

"Third. By making all traffic moving by rail or partially by rail and partially by water, whether domestic, export, or import traffic, amenable to the act to regulate commerce; on export and import traffic, the rates or proportion of rates accruing to the inland carrier to be amenable to the act to regulate commerce, and subject to the control of the Interstate Commerce Commission, and under same rules as apply to domestic traffic.

"Fourth. By prohibiting railroads from making or accepting lower rates or lower proportion of rates on grain to the seaboard for export than they at the same time accept on flour or grain products to the seaboard for export, provided grain products may be required to be loaded to the marked capacity of the car."

That is to counteract the decision in what is known as the Texas-Pacific case, under which the railroads claim that no export or import is amenable to the interstate commerce law, and they do not have to account to the commission for their rates.

It seems to me one of the worst forms of discrimination against American manufactures that I know of.   [Continuing to read:]

"Fifth. By repeal of the imprisonment penalty against the shipper or receiver who procures or accepts lower than lawful published tariff rates, whether such preferences be made by rebates, commissions, or otherwise, except that where a shipper, by fraudulent practices, procures lower than authorized published tariffs, the imprisonment clause shall be continued in effect against this class of shipper."

The object of that is to get testimony. You can not get testimony with reference to a violation of the act under the present law, because every receiver is just as much a criminal under the act as the man who made the rate.   [Continuing to read.]

"By repeal of the imprisonment clause against officers and agents of railroads, and substituting therefor money penalties upon any corporation, officer, agent, or any other person through whose instrumentality other than the lawfully published rates, rules, or regulations affecting the transportation of persons or property shall become operative or available; it being understood that such penalties against the railroad companies should be sufficiently great, not less than $5,000, or double the revenue received by the company at unlawful rates where greater than $5,000, and the railroad company itself shall be the party against whom the fine shall be assessed."

Q. How about a railroad in the hands of a receiver?—A. Make that a debt of the company, the same as any other debt of a company.

Q. You can not enforce it without the consent of the court which appoints the receiver.—A. I was not looking for all of the law points. I see your point clearly. So long as the law exists as it is now you will never get a railroad man to furnish any testimony against another railroad if the imprisonment clause remains in. If it is taken out as against the shipper, you might get some testimony from the shipper, but you will never get a complaint from the source where the proof can be gotten. If the law was so amended that it was to the interest of the railroad to complain against its rival, and imposed no penalty except a fine against the corporation, there would be no trouble about getting evidence, and the railroads themselves would furnish it; but a railroad man will come as close to perjury as possible to not convict his fellow-employee or the employee of another line, for the reason that the imprisonment penalty clause exists.   [Continuing to read:]

"Sixth. By restoring to railroads the authority they were supposed to have before the decision of the Supreme Court of the United States was rendered in the Trans-Missouri case, viz, by permitting them to agree upon reasonable rates and to maintain voluntary associations for the maintenance and promulgation of such rates, compilation of statistics, and transacting such other joint work of railroads, members of the association, as may not be in conflict with the fifth or antipooling section of the act to regulate commerce, it being understood that no change in the law that will legalize pooling of traffic or of earnings is indorsed by me. On the contrary, I am firmly of the opinion that such amendment is against the interests of the public and not needed by the railroads themselves.

"All agreements between railroads and other common carriers to be filed with the Interstate Commerce Commission not less than 10 days before going into effect; and if, on investigation, any clause in such agreement is contrary to any clause of the act to regulate commerce, said agreement shall be decided by the commission not in effect, and shall be corrected by the railroads to correspond with the opinion of the commission before becoming effective.

"Seventh. Proposed change in act to regulate commerce, requiring longer notice than 3 days for reduction in published tariffs and 10 days for an advance, would be injurious to the public, and of no benefit to the railroads. A reduction is sometimes absolutely essential to enable some classes of traffic to move at all, and if even 10 days' time is required to make the rate effective, the opportunity to move the traffic at all will have passed. The law of Kansas requires 60 days for an advance in rates; it frequently prevents reductions of great value to the people being made, because once reduced they must stay in effect for 60 days.

"Eighth. By adding a clause prohibiting ticket scalping, with provisions similar to the Sherman bill before the last Congress.

"Ninth. By requiring the Interstate Commerce Commission to render its decisions not later than 90 days after close of testimony in case, unless longer time is given by mutual consent of complainants and defendants.

"Tenth. If it were possible to require the various States to repeal all laws in conflict with the act to regulate commerce, and to adopt it as the law, between points within their respective States, we would then have an improved condition of value to all interests. The conflict upon the borders of adjoining States is frequently such as to create unjust discrimination between commodities."

If it were possible to withdraw from the States the authority governing rates, rules, and regulations of transportation between points within the respective States and make same, whether State or interstate, amenable to national laws, it would simplify and in the end would benefit all concerned.

Q. You said you did not think the legalization of any agreements, freight pooling agreements, between the railroads of the country is desirable or would be beneficial in any way; why do you think so?—A. It would not remove the incentive to reduce rates, but, on the contrary, it would increase the incentive to reduce rates under certain circumstances.

Q. I asked that because we have some very high authority for that view.—A. Theoretically the pooling proposition is a beautiful one, but not in actual practice. To put my answer in the form of a question, How are you going to get an agreement as to the proportion accruing to each line? After you have gotten that agreement the line that gets more to-day than it can haul is going to do something to keep its proportion from being below what it was allotted. If it is continually being paid earnings of money that it did not earn by hauling the traffic and continually having transferred to it tonnage that it did not get by solicitation, it is evident that it has been allotted too much or too great a proportion. To prevent that the line is going to pursue the same methods as it does now, even at the expense of having to pay over sometimes more than its proportion. Now, on the other side, these pooling agreements will be for given periods. The line that thinks its allotment too small can afford on a great volume of business to allow a rate continuously, even if it has to pay into the pool part of its earnings or has to divert its business and pay for it, in order that when the next allotment comes around it shall get a greater proportion. There is no law that I can see that will make me say how little of a given proportion of business I will accept. That has been the means of breaking every pool that has existed so far.

Q. Now, under the conditions that would exist if pooling was legalized railroads could go into these agreements, and these agreements if violated could be enforced in the courts. It can not be done now, but if it were legalized it could be done, and this disposition on the part of the railroads to violate the agreement, it seems to me, could be checked just exactly as the disposition on the part of individuals to violate their contracts is checked by penalties arising from the operation of the law.—A. Individuals violate their contracts and prices continuously.

Q. A man makes a contract to-day as to a certain thing and he fails to live up to it; the man who was to receive the benefit can recover as damages the amount of damage he sustained.—A. Admitting, which I do not admit, that the railroads would profit by a pool, by a legally authorized pool, where does the public come in? A pretty good evidence that that is not needed is that, even weak as the law is to-day, I will venture to say that at least 85 per cent of the rate cutting that was in existence in 1898 has been wiped out in 1899. Now, if we had a law that was enforcable, as to its violation, I do not believe any pooling clause necessary. I think it is unfortunate that the Supreme Court found that the trans-Missouri agreement was in violation of the trust law. It was not in violation of the pooling law. Now, I would like to see, for the benefit of the general public, the railroads have the authority to avoid discrimination in violating, cutting the rate. They can make the penalty as great as they please, but whenever you take away from the shipper the right to put his freight over any line he pleases you are taking something away from him. He may have very good reasons why he wants it to go over a certain line. That line may have its quota of tonnage and may not be able to take it. You take a shipper of poultry who has icing facilities along a certain line; his arrangements are such that he wants his freight to go over that line, and it goes to the railroad company and the railroad company finds it is ahead in its tonnage and gives it to its rival. The poultry may go through without being iced at all, or he may have to pay a higher price where it was iced than he would at his own ice house. There are various reasons he might have, and the reconsignment proposition—through one gateway and not through another. I think it would be very unfair indeed to take away from the shipper, where the tariff is the same by two different routes, the privilege of selecting by which line it shall go over.

Personally, as to what the railroad company does with its earnings, I do not think it is the shipper's business, but I do not think the law should be so as to give the railroads absolute power to divide the business or tonnage; it takes away the only power the shipper has.

Q. (By Senator KYLE.) Is not the universal argument of the railroad companies that they are held by the throat by the large shippers in the States?—A. The large shipper would hold them by the throat still. You take cotton ties in Texas as an illustration; a man finds he can give the railroads at a certain time a large tonnage when business is slight. He goes to the railroad companies as an organization, "if you make our rate so and so, we will give you that within certain months." That was done this past year on cotton ties and the rate was not known to the public until the sales had been pretty generally made. Now, there was not anybody but this large shipper in a position to go to the railroad and make this proposition and get this price. The small competitor would not be in it.

Q. There was no small competitor in that case, was there?—A. There were a lot of shippers that had a lot of cotton ties on hand, and it decreased the value of their stocks to the extent of the difference in rate.

Q. (By Senator MALLORY.) That is your conclusion, then, regarding pooling, that it will not work well because it deprives the shipper of the freedom of action which he now enjoys of shipping by what route he pleases?—A. That is one conclusion, and the other is that it is not a remedy for the evil, and the third is that it is not needed by the railroads themselves.

Q. (By Senator KYLE.) You do not think it would help out the small shipper?—A. It would not help the small shipper at all.

Q. That is the contention of the companies.—A. It seems to me at a small station the people will not be affected; the local business will not be pooled, because that belongs to that railroad anyway.

Q. (By Professor JOHNSON.) Is the prohibition of the right to assign freight over a common line a necessary feature of pooling?—A. It is one of the easiest methods.

Q. I know; but is it the necessary way?—A. You can pool your earnings or your traffic.

Q. I want to get your view on another question, which is germane, I think, to that. It is the evident tendency of the railroad corporations in this country to consolidate, is it not, in your judgment?—A. Yes.

Q. Will not that of itself serve as a corrective of this evil of discrimination?—A. Yes.

Q. The effect being that when you have 1 railroad where there are now 5—1 rail road corporation controlling 5 railroads, whereas to-day there are 5 distinct corporations competing with each other—the tendency will be to do away with the necessity for discrimination?—A. We have an illustration of that in the St. Louis, Peoria and Northern, built out of St. Louis and intended to go to Chicago, and 1 line to Clinton, Iowa, this year. As soon as it got to Peoria it became one of the greatest rate cutters between St. Louis and Chicago that we had. It belonged to no association and took what it could get. It had its right of way bought and the rails on the ground to build to Clinton, Iowa. The Chicago and Alton and the Illinois Central and the Missouri, Kansas and Texas formed a pool and bought the Chicago, Peoria and Northern Railroad. They sold the rails that were to be built to Clinton, Iowa, and the road becomes a part of the Alton and the Illinois Central; and that competitor is out of existence. I think that will be the end to the Pittsburg and Gulf; that it will be bought by a combination of roads that will control its rate making. Even then, as between combination and legalized pooling, I think the combination is the preferable one of the two, so far as the public is concerned.

Q. That is, looking at it particularly from the point of view—— A. (Interrupting.) Point of view of the city of St. Louis, which I represent, or the point of view of the shipper as a whole. There are a great many railroad men that do not consider pooling necessary.

Q. Their number has increased of recent years?—A. Yes.

Q. (By Senator KYLE.) The president of the Great Northern is opposed to it, I believe.—A. I think Milton H. Smith, of the Louisville and Nashville, is also opposed to it. If that pooling clause was repealed without any other change, I do not know that the public would be affected. They would still have the trust act back of it. I oppose the legalizing of pooling—not the pool itself.

Q. Would it not be legal if not prohibited by law?—A. What the railroads ask is to make their contracts between each other absolute; collectible by law.

Q. That would be done simply by repealing that?—A. They were not collectible by law prior to the interstate-commerce act; there are thousands of dollars to-day owing by railroad companies under the old pooling clause that were never paid.

Q. (By Professor JOHNSON.) They were illegal at common law?—A. As I understand it.

Q. (By Senator MALLORY.) On the ground of public policy?—A. Yes.

WASHINGTON, D. C., *October 8, 1899.*

TESTIMONY OF MR. SAMUEL R. CALLAWAY,

President New York Central and Hudson River Railroad Company.

The commission met at 2.40 p. m., Vice-Chairman Phillips presiding. Mr. Samuel R. Callaway, being duly sworn, testified as follows concerning the topics in the plan of inquiry on transportation:

Q. (By Senator MALLORY.) What is your name?—A. Samuel R. Callaway.

Q. Where do you reside?—A. New York City.

Q. What is your occupation?—A. President of the New York Central and Hudson River Railroad.

Q. How long have you been connected with the railroad business?—A. Since 1863.

Q. How long have you been connected with the New York Central system?—A. I have been president of the New York Central and Hudson River Railroad since a year ago last April. Prior to that I was president of the Lake Shore and Michigan Southern; president of the New York, Chicago and St. Louis; president of the Toledo, St. Louis and Kansas City. Do you want my history right back?

Q. No; just to show your acquaintance with railroad matters. You have been connected with railroads since 1861?—A. Since 1863. I have been connected with railroads from the Atlantic to the Pacific during that time.

Q. You have seen the syllabus of this subcommission on transportation of the commission?—A. Yes.

Q. And I believe you have prepared answers with reference to the inquiries propounded in that syllabus?—A. Yes.

Q. Now, in order to expedite matters as much as possible, will you just take that up as you have prepared them?—A. Shall I read them?

Q. Yes, if you please.—A. The first question seems to be divided into sections. In answer to section 1—"Terms and conditions of employment"—from any person entering the employ of the company we receive the assurance of his willingness to obey any reasonable rules that may be made.

Q. This is under the head of employees?—A. Yes; after being employed it depends upon the employee himself as to his remaining. So long as he faithfully discharges his duty, there is no reason why an employee should not remain in the service and be in line for promotion when the opportunity offers, which promotion is dependent upon such performance and further capacity for increased responsibility. There are no physical conditions required, except in case of employees who are required to take signals, such as enginemen, firemen, conductors, and trainmen, such employees having to pass an examination as to their eyesight and hearing.

Rates of wages of different classes of employees: Most of our men are paid for the number of hours' work and for the number of miles made, the average pay of employees being as follows: Telegraph operators, $52.50; block-signal men, $46.50; other signalmen, $49, which includes baggagemen, station clerks, etc.; enginemen, $114, although their wages vary from $90 to $175; firemen and wipers, $59, firemen getting from $50 to $84; conductors, $86, their baggagemen and trainmen's wages varying from $40 to $70; mechanics and helpers in shops, $49; other shopmen, $40; roadmasters and track foremen, $49.50, roadmasters being paid on an average from $100 to $125 per month, and track foremen from $40 to $50; track laborers, $35.50; switchmen, flagmen, watchmen, etc., $40; mechanics and helpers on road, $56; employees of floating equipment, $58.

Q. Do I understand you to say that all men on your road are paid by the hour?—A. By the trip—the trainmen largely.

Q. The trainmen are paid by the hour?—A. The men in the shops are paid by the hour. That is true of nearly all the men in the service, in the shops or on the trains.

Q. The men in the shops are paid by the hour and the trainmen by the number of miles they run?—A. Yes; and we have an average. Their wages are for a certain time and we have an average.

Wages, basis and stability thereof: This is arrived at by the amount of work, character and ability of the employee. Our rates themselves have not changed; the men being paid for the work done, being greater in some months than others. This, of course, does not apply to monthly men.

Reductions and deductions, and their causes: We have no reductions and no deductions, except for value received, such as rent, board, uniforms, etc. For instance, if a man puts an order in that his rent is to be deducted from his wages and gives it to the person from whom he rents or boards, we take that out; otherwise there are no deductions, excepting by arrangements with the employees themselves.

Q. Have you any specific number of hours per day for men to be employed in the train service?—A. We generally limit their time to 8 or 10 hours on a train; but of course that is subject to accidents or derailments, when they are paid for overtime, and they are not allowed to go out after they come in until they get a certain amount of rest. I think the limit is 8 hours.

Q. Then the trainmen, when they work over the ordinary time of necessity are paid regular rates?—A. They have a general scale of wages. I do not know what they are. I can furnish them to you if you desire to have them. We have a regular agreement in regard to these things.

Discharge and suspension and the reasons therefor: Discharge or suspension is determined by the man's individual record and the seriousness of the offense, each case being determined by itself. There are various reasons—neglect ot duty, insubordination, incivility, dishonesty, and similar conditions met with in all other business.

Usual hours of labor exacted of different classes of employees: Station employees have necessarily long hours, but there are stretches, sometimes for hours at a time, where at some stations they have little or nothing to do. For instance, at some of the country stations a train may come along in the morning, a train may come along at noon, or it may come along at night, and it makes a very long time; there is very little to do in the interim.

Telegraph operators are not required to work more than 12 hours; same with signalmen, and, in some towers where a large number of levers are employed, 8 hours constitute a day's work.

In the passenger-train service our men do not average as high as 10 hours steady work during the 24. In freight service it might be in some cases 12 hours, but they receive sufficient rest before again taking their run.

In answer to question 3—"Sunday labor and overtime; conditions under which required and compensation therefor; limitation thereon by State laws, and effect thereof on employees, carriers, and the public:" On account of the accumulation of fre'ght at the various terminals, it is necessary for our freight crews to work on Sunday in order to clean up and be ready for the next week's business, and, as train employees are paid by the mile, they receive same compensation as they would for similar service on week days. On some of our local passenger runs, where the runs are unusually hard and where they are required to work more than half of the Sundays in a month, conductors and trainmen are paid double for such Sunday work over and above two Sundays. Just as little as possible Sunday work is done, and only those are kept at work that are actually necessary for proper and· safe running.

Q. Would it be possible, do you think, to give up the Sunday freight business entirely?—A. I think not.

Q. Georgia, you know, has adopted that rule. The Georgia railroad commission prescribe a rule, if I am not mistaken, that prohibits the running of trains through the State of Georgia?—A. Yes; and they have the same law in Connecticut, too.

Q. In your judgment, could that be practically done, or could it be generally done without great detriment to the public interests?—A. No. We carry such a large amount of perishable freight that the stoppage of that freight would be almost an impossibility. I will say, personally, that I am very much opposed to Sunday work, and we limit it as much as possible. Dead freight we allow to lay generally from morning to night, but perishable freight must be run through, as have also passenger trains and the transportation of mails.

Aid and benefit features of employees' associations; conditions and extent of relief: Among the employees we find benefit associations, and accident insurance is maintained by the following brotherhoods: Brotherhood of Locomotive Engineers, Brotherhood of Locomotive Firemen, Brotherhood of Railway Conductors, etc. They all have assessment insurance.

Question 9. "Relief and aid to sick and disabled employees, by railroads and other carriers by land; conditions and extent thereof; its effect on relations of employer and employees." This company makes it a practice, where their employees are injured, to allow the injured person half time.

Q. Half pay during the time of his indisposition?—A. Yes; we have no pension fund, or anything of that kind on the road, but we have a very large pension roll, men that have been a long time in the service, and are incapacitated, and we put them on what we call the pension roll, subject to the board of directors and president, sometimes for half pay, sometimes for less, and sometimes for whole pay.

Q. Have you such institutions as railroad hospitals, that are maintained by contributions from the employees?—A. No. We run through a thickly settled country, and we have arrangements with hospitals at nearly every point where men are likely to be injured to take care of them.

Q. If I understand it, if a man is injured, without reference to whether through his own negligence or not, he is paid half pay?—A. Yes; he is paid half pay while he is in the hospital, or while he is laid up. Then, if they are incapacitated by reason of the loss of a leg or arm, we generally provide them with some place at a gate or signal tower or place of that kind, and give them light work.

Q. (By Professor JOHNSON.) Do you have any provision with regard to retiring men at a certain age?—A. No; we have nothing of that kind on the New York Central.

Q. Well, supposing a man reaches 60 years of age in your service and becomes incapable of future service, what have you planned to do with him?—A. Well, a man does not generally become incapacitated at 60. We have lots of men in the service 70 and 75.

Q. It is not your plan to turn men off at a certain age?—A. No. Of course these things are all regulated by officers, and they generally endeavor to be considerate and kind to the men and try and find them some light employment. We have a very large number of old men on the New York Central. It is an old road and the proportion of old men is very large.

Q. (By Senator MALLORY.) Are you acquainted at all with the rules and regulations governing these brotherhoods of locomotive engineers, and firemen and train hands, as to the benefits derived by the men pending their sickness or pending their disability? I understand, of course, that the railroad company pays half wages if the man is injured on the road and goes into a hospital. Now can you say whether they receive any assistance from their brotherhoods?—A. Well, I do not know as to that. I think a large number of our men insure themselves. We have 2 or 3 insurance companies working on the road, and they give these insurance companies orders on their pay for so much per month. The paymaster honors these orders, and I think the large bulk of men are insured in these accident-companies. I presume they are insured in their brotherhoods, but I know nothing about their rules.

In answer to question 10: "Automatic couplers, air-brakes, and hand holds, on passenger and freight cars; percentage of freight cars so equipped; cost of such safety appliances on old and new cars; cause of delay by railroads in complying with requirement of act of Congress relating to safety appliances on freight cars." Our passenger and freight cars are all equipped with M. C. B. couplers and hand holds and about 68 per cent of the freight equipment is equipped with air brakes. There was no delay on the part of this company in complying with the requirements of the act of Congress. That is, we were finished by the time of the first date. The first date, I think, was last December or last January.

Q. And you adhere to the type of the Master Car Builders' couplers. Is that the type that is prescribed by the Interstate Commerce Commission?—A. The Interstate Commerce Commission have prescribed the height, and there are certain rules; I do not know what they are; but we have, of course, complied with those. And they also prescribed in regard to the hand holds on a car. Whatever the law is, we have complied with it.

Q. Complied with it to the extent of 68 per cent of the freight cars?—A. All of our freight cars. Sixty-eight per cent are equipped with air brakes. We are not required to have them on all.

Q. Have you complied with the coupler requirements in full?—A. Yes.

Q. And you are able to say that all your freight cars have that coupler attachment now?—A. Yes.

Q. Have you investigated or inquired into the likelihood of there being a better system of appliances than those that are now in vogue; for instance, a better system of couplers? I remember when that was suggested in Congress, one of the great objections by certain representatives of the railroads was that the matter of couplers was in embryo; that they had not reached such a definite point that they could say that the best coupler had yet been developed; and that they might have to go to the expense of putting on a different style of Master Car Builders' couplers, which included 4 or 5 different styles, and in 3 or 4 years have to put on a coupler which was supposed to be better. Now, the question is whether they have reached a point where the coupler is satisfactory, so far as you know?—A. We had a great deal of difficulty with the couplers at first, but of late years I have heard of no trouble. They were not sufficiently strong in their parts, but that is remedied to-day, and I think the coupler we have to-day is satisfactory

In answer to question 11: "Effect of increased use of automatic couplers, air-brakes, and hand holds on freight cars on number of casualties to railway employees." There is no doubt that, after all freight cars are properly equipped, the number of casualties to railway employees will be materially reduced. In the transitory state at the present time, where some cars are equipped and some not, there does not appear to be any marked decrease in the number. It is really an element of danger now, because to couple the cars with a patent coupler to one with the old couplers is a dangerous operation.

Q. A man has to go in between the cars now to couple the patent coupler with the old link and pin coupler, just as he would with the old link and pin couplers?—A. Just the same.

Q. But that will be done away with when they are all equipped?—A. That will be done away with when they are all equipped; yes.

In answer to 12: "Other methods and devices for insuring safety of employees and passengers on railroads." This road is entirely equipped with block signals between New York and Buffalo, the object of which is to keep trains a safe distance apart, the result of which makes it impossible for two trains to come together without the cooperation of two or more employees failing to properly perform their duty at the same time. These block signals require block towers at various intervals on the road, and are to all intents and purposes watchmen, as, if anything is discovered out of the way on trains such as hot box or train parted, the information is immediately communicated to the next tower, the train being notified. This has proved itself to be of considerable value in times past. Not very many years ago coal stoves were used in coaches. Steam heat is now used, lessening the danger by fire in case of accident. I have my doubts about the value of steam. I think in cases of escaping steam there is about as much risk as by setting fire to the coach, but under the New York law we were obliged to do it and we did it.

Q. How about lights in the cars?—A. Our trains are lighted very largely by Pintsch gas and electricity. We are experimenting with electricity. Up to this time it has not been very satisfactory. I think most of our cars are equipped with Pintsch light.

Q. To what extent, if I may ask, are your roads double tracked or more than single tracked?—A. We have between Buffalo and Albany 4 tracks on the main line and 2 tracks on the West Shore; 1 track on the Niagara Falls line; and 1 track on the Auburn line; which gives us largely the use of 7 tracks between Albany and the contiguous points on the West Shore, through Medina to Buffalo. From Albany to New York we have 2 tracks on the West Shore, and 2 tracks on the New York Central as far as Sing Sing, and 3 tracks from Sing Sing to New York, and are practically operating 5, 6, or 7 tracks continuously.

Q. (By Professor JOHNSON.) How many tracks are there on the Rome, Watertown and Ogdensburg?—A. It is almost entirely a single-track road.

Q. Is that true of the system of the northern part of the State of New York?—A. What we call the village line, Niagara Falls line, has a double track. I have forgotten just how far it extends; but the rest of them are all single-track roads.

In answer to question 13—"Their nature, purposes, and effect; proportion of employees belonging to them; extent of their control of their members; their effect on employees who are not members of such organizations," Railroad branches of the Y. M. C. A. are located at nearly all of our large terminals and yards. They are presided over by a secretary, and a very large number of our employees in the train service make use of their accommodations, lunch rooms, etc., paying nominal dues, $3, or more if their purse may warrant. Sleeping rooms are provided for members, and they can be secured for the sum of 10 cents per night. They likewise have bath rooms, shower, plunge, etc., and each branch has a lunch room which is very largely patronized. We find, with these associations, the men in their spare time, when away from home, may be found there most of the time, keeping them out of places where they should not be. We have a large number of employees, however, who do not avail themselves of these privileges. The greater portion of them being home every night, they do not feel the need of the association as those who are away.

Our line, I may say, is largely equipped with men who have been in the service for a long time, and a great many of them own their homes, and of course they have no necessity for those places, and wherever there is a necessity, the railroad companies have generally built a building, and in many cases Mr. Vanderbilt has equipped it himself with a library and all other furnishings, and the men take hold of it, and we pay the secretaries generally.

Q. These advantages are open to all employees of the road who pay the dues?— A. Yes; these dues are for the maintenance of the reading or writing room and the maintenance of the lunch room, and the many things in connection with these rooms.

Q. (By Senator KYLE.) You serve meals there, do you?—A. Yes; we serve lunches. We have 4 rooms altogether in the vicinity of New York. We have quite a large room, and a hall and dining room opposite the depot in Albany, and most of our men go there to get lunches and meals.

Q. What did I understand you to say the charges for meals were to employees?— A. They run from 10 cents up. A man can go in there and get a nice lunch for 10 cents and he can get a good dinner for 25 cents.

Q. From freight trains operating back and forth the employees can go in there and get meals or lunches?—A. Yes; we have 2 in Albany, one opposite the passenger depot and one opposite the shops.

Q. They take the place of what are called eating houses?—A. The eating houses, I think, are for passengers. I think as a general thing these are exclusively for our own men. Eating houses are places where trains stop for passengers to get their meals.

In answer to question 14, which is in reference to strikes—We have had none in years. The last one was occasioned by the employees insisting upon naming their immediate superiors. I was not connected with the road at that time and I do not know anything about the merits of it. My understanding is that the switchmen insisted upon having the yardmaster one of their own men and one agreeable to them, and the company objected to this, and they had a strike, which was more or less serious.

Q. (By Senator MALLORY.) Do you know what the result of the strike was?—A. I do not.

Q. Whether the men accomplished their purpose or not?—A. I should take it that they did not, because we do not allow men to name their superiors now.

Q. Do you remember what year that was?—A. No. My recollection is that it was quite a serious strike. I recollect that they had a good deal of difficulty. I can get you the details if you care for them. This is a memoranda that the superintendent gave me. I asked him if they ever had any strikes, and he said this was the only one that they ever had—in connection with switchmen.

"State and Federal laws designed to repress strikes; judicial construction thereof and decisions thereon."—We do not know that the transportation of United States mail has any effect on strikes.

In regard to the use of intoxicants by employees, it is prohibited. We have men who look the employees over before we allow them to take trains out, and see that they are in proper condition. Men that are in the habit of using intoxicating liquors and let them get the worst of them are required to leave the service.

Q. (By Senator MALLORY.) Have you any rule prohibiting engineers or firemen from drinking at all—requiring them to be total abstainers?—A. I think not. Here is a copy of the rules, our book of rules; section 9 of the operating department states "that the use of intoxicating drink on the road or about the premises of the corporation is strictly prohibited. No one will be employed, or continued in employment, who is known to be in the habit of drinking intoxicating liquors." I do not think we have ever gone to the length of saying that a man can not take a drink if he wants to, but we endeavor to see when he goes on the train that he has not been drinking.

Q. (By Senator KYLE.) Certain roads make it absolutely prohibitory, do they not?—A. They try to. My judgment is that it is almost always more or less of a dead letter.

Q. (By Professor JOHNSON.) Have you any objection to the men joining the brotherhood?—A. Not at all.

Q. Do you make any inquiry, then, in regard to that matter?—A. No. So far as I am personally concerned I have never had any trouble with the brotherhoods. I have had a good many strikes, a great many troubles, particularly in the West. I was connected with the Union Pacific at the time of the Irons strike, and it was intended that the men on the Union Pacific should go out. That was the intention of the Knights of Labor. At this time they had 25,000 of our men in the Knights of Labor and they had elected all the judiciary in that part of the country in their control, and I had more or less trouble with them. It finally eventuated in a serious riot at Rock Springs. There were some men burned alive and the Government took hold of it, and it finally straightened itself out. And we had one out on the Missouri Pacific, with the result you all know about, when we had a very serious strike. But as a general thing I have gotten along very comfortably with the labor unions, and have not any particular objections to them so long as the men do the work for which they are paid.

Q. (By Senator KYLE.) Have you examined the bill passed by Congress the last year relating to arbitration between the men and their employers?—A. Yes.

Q. What do you think of the bill as it is passed?—A. I have never been able to see how such a commission can be successful, in that it has no power to compel both sides to adhere to the decision.

Q. At the same time you are in favor of compulsory arbitration as a rule?—A. I do not think there is such a thing as compulsory arbitration. There is no body of men in the world who would adhere to it. If all of the employees on the New York Central road desire to have their wages increased, or desire things that we do not want, and we say no, and we go to the board of arbitration, and the board of arbitration says no, how are they going to be compelled to continue to work? I had a very similar case on the Union Pacific. I made an agreement with the Knights of Labor there, and we had it in writing, and the men in Kansas City violated the agreement and went out, and I sent for the grand master and he said he was powerless to control it.

Q. The testimony of the employees was that if the bill was passed it would bring strikes down to a minimum?—A. I have no objection to arbitration. In fact I have no objection to almost anything that is reasonable, excepting this vital question in railroading, that it is an impossibility to surrender the management, as the people in control of the road are here looked to by the public to protect the lives of the passengers, and they must have employees on the road that will carry out orders and obey their instructions.

Now, as to arbitrating with the switchmen as to who should be the yardmaster at Albany—I do not think I should want to submit that to arbitration.

Q. I do not think the bill means anything of that kind. It provides for agreement to submit to arbitration.—A. I do not see any objection to that. I only point out the difficulties. We very rarely have any difficulties about questions that are not vital. For instance, the question of the amount the New York Central can afford to pay the employees; its wages are questions that vitally affect the property itself and that question must be determined by the directors.

Q. (By Senator MALLORY.) That is a question that under no circumstances you would want to submit to arbitration?—A. I should be very much disinclined to. Our pay roll is $17,000,000 a year, I think. Now, an increase, say, of 10 per cent of that would prevent our earning any dividends at all, excepting in certain years.

Q. (By Senator KYLE.) What are ordinarily the questions of dispute between employers and employees?—A. We very rarely have any. You know this is all in process of evolution. When these labor unions were originally started they were intoxicated with their own strength and power. They were just as unreasonable and arbitrary as they could be. You could not do anything with them. They would even object to the rules that regulated the running of trains. We have had them come in and say, "We will not have these rules; we must have some others." Then, as time went on, they found that such things would not work, and they have become more or less reasonable, and of late years we have had no trouble with them. So long as they are controlled by intelligence, and are reasonable in their demands, we do not have any trouble.

Q. In other words, the question is becoming simplified and each party works within his own sphere?—A. Yes; they have become largely organizations looking after their injured, sick, and aged. In many cases I think they have raised both the morale and intelligence of the men. That is particularly the case of the locomotive engineers. I think they are as high-toned and intelligent a class of men as you will find in any employment.

Q. (By Professor JOHNSON.) Do you have any contracts with the locomotive engineers in the brotherhood?—A. I can not answer that question. Personally I have made lots of contracts with them. I have not the slightest hesitation in making them.

Q. Their statements are that they have contracts, that they have considerably over 100 railways?—A. I have no doubt that they have; may be not contracts, but understandings with our superintendents; but whether they have anything in writing or not, I do not know.

Q. (By Mr. KENNEDY.) I believe you omitted in your statement any reference to topic No. 4, relative to negligence of fellow-servants. You had nothing to say about that, did you?—A. No; there is no answer to that question here.

Q. I should like to ask if you believe a laborer on a railroad who is injured through the negligence of an engineer and who has no voice in the selection of that engineer, should be prevented from getting damages from the railroad on account of that injury?—A. Well, that is a pretty broad and general question. I do not think railroads would have any objection to anything of that sort, if you apply it to everyone else. I do not know why you should pick out railroads. Why should not the farmer be liable if he injures an employee by the swinging of a scythe, or a manufacturer be responsible for damages that might arise to his employee by reason of negligence of fellow-employees? Why do you apply it alone to railroads? I think in England they have a limited liability act.

Q. (By Senator MALLORY.) Have some States in this country qualified that to a certain extent?—A. Yes. The laws are different in different States. As a general thing I think they succeed in collecting something. They make out a machine is out of order or something of that kind, and whenever they go before the jury, the sympathy of the jury is with the men nearly always.

Q. (By Senator KYLE.) That is possible upon the farm also, is it not?—A. I do not know as they have ever tried it on the farm; they seem to pick out railroads especially.

Q. (By Professor JOHNSON.) We have the written testimony of the chiefs of the brotherhoods on this point, and they are unanimous in a very strong demand for a modification of the common law on that subject. They seem to feel very strongly on that question.—A. I think if the liability was limited to a reasonable amount the railroads as a general thing would not object. The difficulty about all these things now is that damages are out of all reason.

Q. (By Senator MALLORY.) What have you to say on Topic 21—"Effects of rate wars and unrestrained rate competition upon railway employment and railway wages?"—A. I do not think there is much I can say about that. Of course if there is anything that injures railroads and depletes their revenues, it makes it more difficult for them to pay good wages.

Q. Rate wars and unrestrained competition—the effect of them upon the wages of employees of the railroad would, if injurious to the railroads, of course be injurious to the employees?—A. Yes; I think the employees are gradually coming around to that view of the case and are rather inclined to help the railroad in averting unfavorable legislation.

Q. From your knowledge would you say whether or not there is now as much likelihood of great rate wars as in the past—say 20 years ago?—A. I think not.

Q. What do you ascribe the change to?—A. Well, we handle on the New York Central road from 10,000 to 15,000 loaded cars a day. These cars come from every place in the United States mostly, excepting, perhaps, the far South. The rates are made subject to three competitive forces. The first is the competition of the railroads among themselves; the second is the competition of the waterways; and the third is the commercial conditions which exist and which are world-wide; that competition extends around the world. In 1870 we received 1.88 cents for every ton of freight we carried. Last year we received 59 mills.

Q. (By Representative LIVINGSTON.) From which did you derive the largest profit?—A. I am getting around to that question The fact is that the rates to-day are so low that there is nothing left to discriminate upon. The introduction of Bessemer steel rails in the place of iron, and the building of heavier cars and locomotives, has enabled us to carry, instead of as in 1870, 103 tons, we now average 322 tons to a train, and as far as the New York Central road is concerned, being a road of very low grades and hauling, perhaps, the largest trains of any road in the country, we can live and make a profit on these rates. Whether other roads can haul about 25 where we haul 80, and flourish on that, I do not know.

Q. (By Senator MALLORY.) These improvements—heavy rails, steel rails, heavier locomotives, etc.—of course, entail a large additional expense, I suppose. In fact, I would like to inquire as to the relative price of steel rails just before the recent raise in everything, the relative price of steel rails a year ago, and the iron rail of 20 years ago?—A. The iron rail of 20 years ago cost 3 or 4 times as much as the steel rail to-day, but the steel rail lasts so much longer and is so much less expensive to maintain that it enables us to work the roads very much cheaper than a few years ago. It is difficult to tell the exact cost. I have some statements here. Taking what is known as the New York Central System, which includes the lines west of Buffalo, that are controlled through the ownership of the stock, it earned last year about $100,000,000. Now, in 1870, we only had 1,800 miles of road as against 6,675 now, and the earnings of course were necessarily very much smaller then.

Q. Well, you can tell what the earnings per mile are; what the average was?—A. The average per ton is very much less. The average per ton then was 1.88 cents, as I say, and now, the last year, we earned but 59 mills.

Q. You think, then, that rates, reaching bed rock, you might say, as they are with you, and I suppose the same with other roads of the country, are a check upon anything like ruinous rate wars?—A. Yes. I will say in passing that the making of rates is also in process of evolution. I will give you the history of what is known as the dressed-beef case, as an illustration. In 1879 the dressed-beef industry was practically in its infancy. Certain new roads were built into Chicago and they could not secure any of the cattle traffic, for the reason that the cattlemen owned their own stock yards, or the railroads built them for them. Certain of the roads were anxious to have cattle carried on the hoof to tide water, for the reason that they used their cattle cars for west-bound traffic—coarse traffic, such as coke—and it became then a question as between dressed-beef roads, that were anxious to foster this dressed-beef traffic, and the roads that were anxious to carry cattle on the hoof to New York—a question for the supremacy. The rates were then between 80 and 90 cents on dressed beef, and the cattlemen claimed that they must have a relatively low rate in order to enable them to bring cattle on the hoof to tide water to ship abroad, and that brought on two or three rate wars, and the rates fluctuated from that day until quite recently. They submitted the case two or three times to arbitration—to Judge Cooley at one time: and a number of different men sat upon it for several weeks, and they decided that the relative rates should be 70 per cent higher for dressed beef than for cattle, in order to make the cattle rate an equivalent, and in order to enable these cattlemen or men who wanted to ship the cattle to New York, to do so. Now, that ran along for a little time, but every little while there would break out a war over this thing. Now we have got the rates down; the cattle rate is down to 25 and the dressed beef to 40 cents, and there is nothing to cut on.

Q. Further reduction would be absolutely ruinous?—A. Yes; we could not carry the business at all. I would say the same thing applies to the question of Southern ports. At one time the rates to the Atlantic ports were all about the same, and the Baltimore and Ohio built into Chicago, and they said they had a line a good deal shorter than ours, than the rest of us, to Baltimore, and that they were going to make a 3-cent less rate than we did to New York. I think they started in with a 5-cent less rate. At that time the rates were certainly 45 or 50 cents, and that brought on a rate war, which lasted for years and years, and finally that was submitted to arbitration, to Judges Cooley, Washburn, and Thurman, and they found the disadvantages were such at Baltimore that they should have a differential of 3 cents; and the disadvantages at Philadelphia were such that they should have a differential of 2 cents. These differentials were on 52 and 60 cent rates. Now, these rates have come down until the grain rate, I think, to-day, is only 15 or 18 cents, and these Southern ports continue this excessive differential.

Q. The differential has not been reduced with the reduction of the rate?—A. No, not proportionately. Now, the roads running from New York to Boston, and the roads running from Boston to Montreal, simply do the best they can, and that accounts for a great many of what are known as discriminations, the difficulties of meeting any competition that exists, and that we have no way of remedying.

Q. You say that was an arbitration?—A. Yes.

Q. Was the finding of that arbitration board binding on both parties, on all parties connected with it?—A. No; excepting the moral binding. I believe they agreed to submit it to arbitration.

Q. They were only morally bound to observe it?—A. Yes.

Q. And your road and the other roads are now discriminated against, and still adhere to that?—A. We still adhere to it, yes, excepting it is overcome by ocean rates and one thing and another.

Q. What year was that?—A. This was 20 years ago. It was about 1878 or 1879.

Q. Have these differentials been in existence in favor of Baltimore and Philadelphia within that time?—A. Yes. Quite recently, when we had a meeting with the Interstate Commerce Commission, I think perhaps a year ago, I induced Mr. Cowen and Mr. Ingalls, who represented the Baltimore and Ohio, and Chesapeake and Ohio, to try 1½ on export grain, and we are trying that now; but the other differential, on provisions and all other classes of freight, remains at 3 cents; so that the situation is full of difficulties. It is not a very easy thing to sit down and make rates for 15,000 cars of freight per day which are exactly just and equitable, but we simply do the best we can. The interstate-commerce law prohibits us making any division of the tonnage, which of course would stop the competition as between the railroads themselves; but it would not stop competition as between waterways and the competition of commercial conditions. For instance, if grain is only worth so much in Liverpool, so much in Nebraska, and so much in Chicago, and we have transportation to sell, all we can get is the difference in the values of the grain at these places.

Q. (By Mr. FARQUHAR.) I would like to inquire if there is at the present time an arrangement seeking to rectify the injustice of the differential between those 2 ports as discriminating against New York?—A. We have been at it regularly for 20 years, but have never succeeded.

Q. Do you see any way to remedy this matter?—A. My impression is that eventually the differential will have to be wiped out. The conditions are entirely different. Baltimore is just as good a port to-day as New York. At that time Newport News was not known. I do not know any reason why a man to-day from Chicago should not send a cargo of grain from Newport News or Baltimore and reach Liverpool just with the same advantage as he does from New York.

Q. In making that differential were the transfer terminal charges taken into account?—A. I think there is a misapprehension in regard to terminal charges at New York. They are absorbed entirely by the railroads, excepting putting the grain upon the vessel. For instance, we will make a rate from Buffalo to New York; I think the current rate of corn is 3 cents; we pass that through our elevator at Buffalo, and we bring it to New York. We pass it through the elevator there and put it on a lighter, and we take that lighter with one of our own boats alongside of the ship. Now, there is a charge for transferring that grain from that lighter to the ship.

Q. But your road carries all the charges up to the lighter reaching the side of the ship?—A. Yes; and we take that corn from Buffalo for 3 cents; and there is no transportation rate in the world to-day as cheap.

Q. Does the charge for transferring from the lighter to the ship enter into the brokerage or commission on the ocean freight?—A. That is taken care of by the shipper. There was an agreement at one time that the same charge should be made at Newport News and Baltimore, and we have some doubt as to whether it is actually made there now. The same rule applies to all our export grain coming to New York, wherever it comes from.

Q. In respect to all other trunk lines through the State of New York, do you think that same transfer charge is maintained? Do the other roads include every charge up to the barge alongside of the ship?—A. Yes, all the roads do; those that carry grain. Some of the roads do not care to carry grain; they have no lighters of their own. We have a very extensive lighterage system, built by the road, and I think 1 or 2 other roads have a lighterage system; but some of the roads have gotten so lately that they do not care very much to carry grain.

Q. (By Mr. C. J. HARRIS.) Do you find that the transportation by railroads is turned very much to these Southern ports as against New York?—A. It was when rates were very high; but the Southern ports are very largely abandoned by Chicago; they go south with their grain now, to St. Louis and the South. The large bulk of the grain, I take it, during the summer months comes to us from vessels from all ports. Now, that transportation is usually very small. It has been rather higher this year on account of the activity in the steel trade. The vessels, finding they could get better rates for ore, have gone into the ore-carrying business; but usually the competition between these boats makes transportation from Chicago to Buffalo almost nothing. Last year the rates got down, I think, as low as three-fourths of a cent a bushel, and that, added to our 3 cents, or whatever the rate we made from Buffalo to New York was, fixes largely the rates you can get for the railroad.

Q. (By Senator MALLORY.) In the winter, when navigation is closed on the lakes, your rates are increased, I suppose, from Chicago?—A. We can not increase them very much because of the other condition—of prices in Liverpool. The price in Liverpool really fixes the prices that you can get for transportation. When I say Liverpool I mean the great centers of the world.

Q. Has the competition in St. Louis, by way of Newport News, and in St. Louis and Kansas City, by way of the Gulf, had any effect on that?—A. Yes; a very serious effect. We now have to make the price practically from the Missouri River; before, Chicago and St. Louis were the common centers. St. Louis maintained a higher rate of, we will say, 5 cents. I do not know whether it is 5 cents or not. On lower classes the rates from St. Louis were 5 cents higher going out than from Chicago. Of course competition of the Gulf ports knocked that thing, because you can get a rate now from Kansas City to the Gulf about as cheap as you can get it from Chicago.

Q. Can you say whether that competition arising from the development of the grain business at Galveston, the grain business in New Orleans has affected the grain business in New York to any appreciable extent?—A. It has affected the earnings of the railroads. I think that they all make lower rates now than then.

Q. But the quantity of business—has that been affected materially, do you think?—A. I can not answer that question. It is very difficult, because the crops vary so and the conditions vary so. Say one year the crops are very large, and that affects very largely the tonnage to New York. It may not be a question of rates at all; it may be a question of conditions abroad.

Q. It has been testified to before this commission that the anticipation of the trouble between England and the Boers has increased the demand for the steamships so much that freights have gone up very high. Are contingencies like that also potential in determining the quantity of business done?—A. Very much so. It is a very potent factor in the competition in our export business, which is enormous. We are quoted export rates from New York every day, and we have to add that to the inland rates in order to make a through rate to Liverpool. The through rate to Liverpool practically has to be made the same now by all routes. Now, the rule on which this differential was built largely at the time was that these Southern ports could not get the boats to come there at the same price that they could get grain transportation. The conditions have very largely changed, and the competition on the St. Lawrence River has a very potent effect. You can ship grain from Chicago to Montreal and put it on board vessels there and land it in Liverpool. That is the competition we have to take into account in connection with the ocean transportation. In other words, the railroads are obliged to take into account the value of this grain in Liverpool, and their charges between Chicago and the West and Liverpool have to meet the conditions, otherwise they can not take the grain.

Q. (By Professor JOHNSON.) The complaint that comes to the notice of the public and this commission is almost entirely in regard to local rates, as far as the question of reasonableness is concerned. The influence of competition in other business is recognized by everybody. I would like to ask you, first, whether you think that there are competitive forces at the present time that are at all effective in the question of local rates?—A. I will answer very frankly by saying, in the year and a half of my connection with the New York Central I have never had any complaint of local rates excepting one, and that was in connection with a paper mill located on our line. They said they could not compete with some other paper mill that was located on the water, and we made rates in order to enable them to compete, as all intelligent railroad men have to do; otherwise we would close up that concern on our road.

Q. Are men coming to you who have capital to invest along the line of your road and questioning you about local rates prospectively?—A. They are putting up factories every day. There are half a dozen going up now on the New York Central line, right alongside of our road.

Q. Do you think that the competition of capital seeking investment is a source of importance at the present time in the matter of rates?—A. Yes. For instance, the paper business of the country is now handled very largely by one concern. Now, if we want to get a share of that paper business we have to enable the paper concerns along our road to compete with concerns in Maine, or along the waterway, otherwise the paper trust will close them up.

Q. Can you give any illustrations of other business?—A. I think in a general way that applies to everything. If the Pennsylvania have a concern over at Altoona and we have a concern in Albany in the same business and the Pennsylvania rates are lower than ours, they will tie up our business in Albany, and it is our business, as managers of railroads, to see that they do not, and we endeavor to meet these conditions.

Q. Then you would say the local rates, speaking in a general way, are subject to competitive forces?—A. Yes.

Q. I would like to ask to what extent you think the earnings of the general business of transportation are now absorbed by subsidiary corporations such as car trusts, bridge companies, palace car companies, etc.?—A. We have nothing of the kind, practically.

Q. Well, take the case of the Wagner Palace Car Company. I suppose that the Wagner Palace Car Company is very largely owned by men who own the New York Central System, is it not?—A. I do not know. We have no stock in the company, so I can not give any information.

Q. Do the earnings of the New York Central go, to an appreciable extent at least, to remunerate the Wagner Palace Car Company?—A. We do not pay the Wagner Palace Car Company anything. They provide cars and keep them up and collect the fares, and we have nothing whatever to do with them.

Q. Are not the profits of that company known to be large?—A. I do not know whether they are or not. I have usually understood they are not very large. That is a question of fact. I do not know what they are, so I can not tell you. They pay 6 per cent, I understand, on the stock. Now, if you ask me as to the desirability of railroad companies running their own sleeping cars, I will say that the thing has been a lamentable failure wherever it has been tried.

Q. (By Mr. CONGER.) Could you tell the commission whether it is customary for the palace car companies, the Pullman and Wagner, to receive compensation from the railroads for the use of the car on it, or whether those companies depend for their revenues on the fees that they receive from passengers?—A. They depend entirely on the revenue they receive from the passengers, as far as we are concerned.

Q. The New York Central does not pay the Wagner or Pullman companies for the use of the cars?—A. No. We would pay the Pullman Company if we wanted to borrow a car from the Pullman Company; but we have a contract with the Wagner Company under which they agree to supply the cars and trains at a changeable rate of mileage. For instance, if they earn $1,000 a year we pay so much, and if they earn $2,000 a year we pay so much. But they always earn an excess, so we pay nothing.

Q. Is it your idea that on most of the roads of the country the roads do not pay for the use of those cars?—A. Except on the small roads, where the earnings of the cars are very small.

Q. And then they have to pay something?—A. The contract is generally the same contract we have. Where the earnings of the car are notoriously too small to pay the expenses of the porter, etc., they pay 1 cent a mile and 1½ cents a mile, and so on; but on most of the larger roads I think the earnings of the car exceed the amount which they contract to pay.

Q. We would be justified in the conclusion, then, that practically none of the earnings of the railroad companies are diverted to the palace car companies?—A. So far as my knowledge goes.

Q. (By Professor JOHNSON.) Does your company have contracts with bridge companies?—A. We have no such contracts that I know of. We are operated, so far as I know, about as clear as anything that exists in the world. I have no stock in the company. I am simply the operating officer. I take care that nothing exists, so far as my influence goes, of the kind that has been suggested.

Q. So the earnings of your company, you think, in the case of transportation actually inure to the benefit of the stockholders?—A. Yes.

Q. Those relations did not exist a score of years ago, did they?—A. When you go back to 25 years ago—the whole thing is a process of evolution. These bridges were enormously expensive. I think that perhaps the first large one to be built was the bridge over the river at Albany. It cost a very great amount of money. It was built jointly by the capital of the New York Central and the Boston and Albany roads, in the proportion of one-fourth to three-fourths. Now, for a portion of the time afterwards they exacted a bridge toll on freight. It did not come out of the shipper; it came out of the connecting road. For instance, if the Lake Shore sent a car to New York, they would have to pay a certain toll for this bridge. But that has been out of existence for 20 years. Competition has driven that out. I do not know of any case where a bridge toll is exacted now. Then in the case of the Union Pacific, at Omaha, they exacted their toll for 20 years. I think that was all done away with by the competition of the roads coming in there from Kansas City and going up the west bank of the Missouri River. Of course that knocked out all bridge toll there.

Q. Can you tell the commission, with propriety, the manner in which you arrange for the construction of new lines, when you do construct them?—A. We have not constructed any lines since I have been connected with the road, so that I can not answer that question.

Q. Speaking generally, independently of your own line, so far as your knowledge goes, is it the practice of roads to let contracts to their officers and directors?—A. I do not know of any such thing. You hear of those things in the newspapers. My judgment is that the railroads of this country are honestly managed, as a whole. I do not know of any business that is managed any more intelligently or more honestly. I have never been asked to do anything that did not commend itself to my judgment by anybody connected with any road I have been connected with, and I have been connected with many of them. But I can only testify as to what I know myself, and I know myself that there is nothing of that kind in our company.

Q. (By Senator MALLORY.) Have you anything to say on the subject of ticket brokerage in general?—A. I would like to put a book in evidence here, the hearings before the Committee on Interstate and Foreign Commerce, if any of you gentlemen want interesting reading upon this. It is the most demoralizing thing there is in the country in connection with this business.

Q. What hearing is that?—A. The hearings before the Interstate and Foreign Commerce Committee. The Interstate Commerce Commission joined in asking Congress to abolish this. It is abolished in nearly every country in the world now except the United States. The difficulty is that these brokers deal largely in forged tickets and stolen tickets of all kinds.

Q. (By Professor JOHNSON.) Do you think the Pennsylvania law is efficient, as far as you know?—A. They prohibit it in Pennsylvania and, I think, in a number of States. It is prohibited entirely in Canada.

Q. In those States where it is prohibited, is there any illegitimate traffic?—A. I do not know. It is prohibited in Pennsylvania, Illinois, New Jersey, Montana, North Dakota, Minnesota, Texas, North Carolina, New York, Florida, and Indiana. I think it is generally conceded that the business is demoralizing. I do not know that there is anything more to say about it than has already been testified to on that.

Q. (By Senator MALLORY.) What have you to say on topic 23—"Effect of watering stock and unnecessary additions to bonded indebtedness upon railway employment and railway wages"?—A. Well, watering stock is practically obsolete. The difficulty most of the roads have had is keeping out of the hands of a receiver.

Q. Your opinion to-day is that the watering of stock is an obsolete practice?—A. Pretty much so.

Q. But there is none the less a good deal of watered stock in existence?—A. Oh, I imagine so, but I do not fancy there is more watered stock than the increase in the value of the property. But that is a question I am not competent to deal with; I have had nothing to do with it myself.

Q. You are a railroad man, and it just occurred to us that you might have some views on the subject.—A. I know of a great many roads that have been watered, and in a short time they went into the hands of a receiver; most all.

Q. (By Mr. C. J. HARRIS.) What is your experience in railroads in regard to the increase of their valuation? Have they not increased the same as the property on Broadway in New York City has increased?—A. It has advanced enormously.

Q. Has not the value of the terminals of those Western roads increased more enormously than the increase of real estate, probably, on Broadway?—A. I suppose our property in New York is worth more than the entire capital of the road. In fact, you can not duplicate it for anything. We find that out when we have to pay the taxes. They put up the taxes $211,000 last year on us. In New York we are paying 12 per cent on our net earnings; in New York alone we pay over $2,000,000 a year.

Q. (By Senator MALLORY.) What is the total amount of your taxes in New York?— A. They put it up $211,000 last year; that is the figure, I think, and we are waiting to hear from the franchise tax yet.

Q. (By Mr. C. J. HARRIS.) Twelve per cent on your net earnings?—A. Yes. Oh, we do not have such a nice, easy time as you think we do.

Q. (By Professor JOHNSON.) Your tax in New York is a general property tax, is it not?—A. Yes.

Q. Is there any form of tax that you would prefer to that?—A. Yes; I think the Michigan system is the fairest—tax on their earnings. We are perfectly willing to have the taxes go up when the earnings go up, but the trouble is that the taxes go up when the earnings go up, and they go on up when the earnings come down.

Q. Would you be in favor of the abolition of the general property tax and the substitution of a tax on the net earnings?—A. The Michigan tax is on gross earnings; and where a road is serving the country and getting a very small proportionate income for its service, I think it is fair to tax it at a lower rate than they would tax a road having a larger earning capacity, and that is practically what they do in Michigan. I managed three or four roads in Michigan, so I am familiar with it.

Q. I would like to ask you if there is any choice between a tax on net earnings and on gross earnings?—A. I do not think so.

Q. The tax on gross earnings might be more of a discouragement to business, might it not?—A. Oh, I would not like to give an opinion on that subject without knowing what the figures were. Our earnings are $100,000,000 a year. A tax of 1 per cent on gross earnings would produce just the same as a tax of 3 per cent on the net earnings, or 4—whatever the ratio is to the total. Our total taxes last year were something over $2,000,000, which was 12 per cent on our net earnings.

Q. (By Mr. C. J. HARRIS.) If a road had no net earnings, it would be rather a hardship to make it pay a tax on its gross earnings, would it not?—A. I should say yes; but still it should pay some tax, I suppose.

Q. (By Mr. CONGER.) Are net earnings usually considered the earnings after the interest on the bonds is paid, or before?—A. The interest is considered generally part of the expenses.

Q. Well, in such a case, if a road had been bonded for 2 or 3 times its actual cost or worth, it would be an injustice to the State, would it not, to levy the tax on net earnings rather than upon gross earning, because possibly all the net earnings would be used up in paying the interest on those bonds?—A. Yes; that was what I was going to say in answer to that. Of course, if the tax were made on the net earnings of the road, the probability is that the interest charges would be left out of the net earnings.

Q. (By Senator MALLORY.) How do you determine the net earnings; do you eliminate from that all improvements on the road and everything of that kind?—A. Well, it varies on different roads. The bulk of the roads were imperfectly built to start with, and they issued bonds and stock, and have an improvement fund to take care of their large improvements. For instance, we are building a new depot at Albany, and raising our tracks there and putting in new bridges. A large proportion of that will be charged to our capital account; it will not go into our expenses. In the elimination of grade crossings at Buffalo, Albany, and New York, and at these different places on our road, the cost is so much that we have to have a fund for that sort of thing. We would not have any net earnings if we should charge that to operating expenses. It varies on different roads. The Lake Shore is in better shape than any other of the Vanderbilt roads; they charge nearly everything to expenses there.

Q. (By Mr. CONGER.) In the Michigan system which you commended, the tax is upon gross earnings, is it not, and the per cent is graduated according to the earnings of the road?—A. Yes, I think that is a very fair tax. I think there has grown up a good deal of opposition to it in Michigan, through Mr. Pingree and his friends; but it has always seemed to me the fairest way to tax railways.

Q. (By Senator MALLORY.) What is the rate, if there is an established rate, and I suppose there is, over your whole system—passenger rate per mile?—A. It varies. In New York State, on our main line, we are not allowed to charge more than 2 cents.

Q. You charge the 2 cents, do you?—A. Two cents; yes. The thing is so diluted by excursions and cheap rates that we do not really earn 2 cents. We have to figure pretty carefully on that.

Q. (By Mr. C. J. HARRIS.) Are mileage books issued at the cheaper rate?—A. Under the New York law we issue mileage books at 2 cents, and they are good on our branch lines. Outside of the main line we get between 2 cents and 3 cents.

Q. (By Senator MALLORY.) Outside of the State of New York?—A. No, inside of the State of New York. This law, I think, was part of the original franchise of the road; I do not know how it came about; but we only charge 2 cents on the main line. We earn 1.82 cents a year on all our passenger business, average. It has been gradually coming down.

Q. You mean in the territory in the State of New York?—A. We are all in New York, you know. That is the New York Central report.

Q. I did not know but what you included the whole system.—A. The Lake Shore and Michigan Central are managed separately. We have the control of the stock, but we do not own the roads outright, and they are managed separately and issue separate rates; and these figures refer to ⌐ie New York Central rate.

Q. 1.82 cents per mile?—A. Yes.

Q. Can you state what is the highest rate per mile you charge in New York on your branch lines?—A. I think 3 cents is the highest. I have a memorandum here from the passenger agent that gives the figures. On the various branches of the New York Central Railroad, some of which run through sparsely settled portions of the country, and others through mountainous regions, the rates are from 2½ to 3 cents per mile. So I take it that there is no rate in excess of 3.

Q. From your statement, the cause of that is the sparseness of the population through which the road runs and also the cost of building the roads?—A. Take a line like our Montreal road; trains earn there in the winter very little, and we charge 3 cents there. Trains earn from 40 to 50 cents a mile; probably do not more than pay expenses.

Q. Have you anything to say on the subject of the pass system that seems to be universal in the United States; the giving of passes to individuals?—A. Personally I am opposed to passes. I would cut the whole thing off to-morrow if I had my way. When I went to the New York Central I took the passes entirely into my own hands, with the exception of those issued by Mr. Depew. He is chairman of the board and he issues some passes. We issue no passes now, practically, except to railroad people; that is, from my office. I do not think the effect on the revenue would amount to anything because the people that get the passes would not travel if they did not get them. They are largely the clerks in the offices and mechanics. For instance, we give passes to the men in the shops at Cleveland, on the Lake Shore. If a man wants to bring his family down to New York, we give him a pass. In 99 cases out of 100 he would not go without a pass; so that I do not think that the effect on the revenue is very great. But the system is bad, and I think eventually it will be discontinued.

Q. As I understand, then, your remarks relate to your railroad, and there is a very small number of passes given now except to employees?—A. I do not know what Mr. Depew does, but I do not think he issues very many. You know there is a law in New York that prohibits the issuance of passes to State officers. They used to give passes very largely. I can not testify as to what passes Mr. Depew issues, because I do not know; but I know as to passes issued from my own office; I issue them entirely under my own supervision; I do not allow anybody else to issue them on the road except myself.

Q. It does not do any particular good?—A. It does not do any particular good, but as far as I know it does not do any particular harm. I do not see any reason why a road should pass a man any more than a dry goods merchant should give him a hat or a coat.

Q. You do not think it interferes to any extent with the receipts of your railroad?—A. I do not think it does. If we stopped it to-morrow, I do not think it would earn enough to pay an extra dividend, because the bulk of the people who get passes would not travel otherwise.

Q. What have you to say on the question of unjust discriminations and undue preferences by railroads?—A. Well, I think, perhaps, I have answered that question very largely. We have no unjust discrimination that I know about.

Q. As against persons and against places. Now, without reference to your own road, have you anything to say on that subject? There is a general impression that discrimination is practiced to a very great extent by railroads throughout the United States, discriminations whereby individuals have advantages which the general public have not. Do you know anything about that, or have you anything that you care to say on that subject?—A. No; I have already said that the rates have got so low that I do not think that there is anything to discriminate on, and I think the thing is a bugaboo. We do not get any complaints about discriminations. They may exist on other roads. I am only talking about our own road. Of course I can not tell what is going on in other places.

Q. Do you know anything about the system of private cars which is now an institution in this country?—A. Yes; that is very bad; there is no question about it at all. It is just as bad as it can be.

Q. Will you explain what that system is?—A. In connection with this dressed-beef case that I illustrated we found when we came to adjust matters that there were some contracts by which a cent a mile was paid for cars—dressed-beef cars—and the cars are nearly all owned by the dressed-beef shippers, and the dressed-beef business is all controlled by three or four people, and they very largely control the rate at which they will give their cars, and you can take them or leave them, just as you please. If you do not take their cars, somebody else will.

Q. (By Mr. CONGER.) Is that rate of 1 cent a mile in force to-day?—A. Yes. It is not paid by us, I will say. We only pay three-fourths of a cent. When the rate got down to one-fourth of a cent I said we would go out of it and not pay the extra mileage; but it is in force in some other parts of the country on some roads, under contract.

Q. Is it not possible that the payment of this mileage by the roads to the owners of the cars gives them an advantage that keeps competition from the dressed-beef business?—A. Well, I do not know about that. The dressed-beef business is a very large business and it has drifted into the hands of very strong concerns, and whether any other concerns could come in and get a cent a mile, I do not know. I know they could not get it from us. We have been trying to break the practice up for years.

Q. (By Mr. FARQUHAR.) How would it do for the railroads themselves to run that class of cars? Then they could break it up.—A. They would not get any business. Every dressed beef shipper in the country owns his own cars.

Q. Then it is not a matter of choice with the railroads at all?—A. Not at all. We do not do foolish things from choice; I will say that. The thing is just as bad and stupid and foolish as can be, but what are you going to do about it? Now, we have built up these dressed-beef men, and they have all got their own cars, and they can dictate what they are going to pay. I am not speaking particularly of the dressed-beef men; but that applies not only to the dressed beef, but to the cattle business. The cattlemen nearly all own their own cars now.

Q. In case there was an authorization of pooling, could the railroads eliminate these privileges?—A. Certainly.

Q. From the dressed beef men?—A. Certainly; that is the only thing we can do with pooling. Now, a pool or a division of the business has very little effect on competition, because the competition between railroads is not very great to-day. The interstate law has forced a system of consolidation. It has had just the opposite effect from what was intended by its framers. It has forced these railroads to consolidate and come together to do that practically which was the only sensible thing for them to do. But if we could go to-day and say to the Pennsylvania road in Chicago, "Now, we will take 20 per cent of this dressed beef, and you can take 20 per cent, and the Erie 20 per cent, and somebody else take 20 per cent, and if you do not get 20 per cent we will pay you the same proportion of the earnings per car," we could then turn around to these dressed beef people and say, "We will not run these cars at all."

Q. (By Mr. CONGER.) You would be very apt to do that?—A. We would be very apt to do that. But we are perfectly helpless to-day. Suppose I should turn around and say to our dressed beef shippers, "I will not haul your cars." They would say, "All right; good-bye; we will get somebody else to haul them." The same thing practically applies to the cattle traffic of the country.

Q. (By Senator MALLORY.) That is a kind of an "Old Man of the Sea" that you have?—A. We have lots of them. If you will come up in New York and sit with me a week, I will show you a few.

Q. Will you be kind enough to explain how it is that this is such a burden? To what extent is that 1 cent a mile a real bonus to the dressed-beef men on these cars?—A. Well, railroads pay each other 6 mills, and we figure that that 6 mills will about take care of the interest on the cars and their repairs. The additional 4 mills, some portion of it, of course, would be deducted for the extra value of the dressed-beef car, the dressed-beef car being more valuable than the ordinary car. Just what that is, I do not know, but they make an enormous mileage as against our ordinary cars. They just keep these cars humping.

Q. What are those cars used for on the trip back from the Eastern seaboard, west?—A. Practically nothing. We unload them and get them back to Chicago just as quickly as we can. That was the original fight, as I told you. The Pennsylvania had a very large west-bound coke traffic, and they were very much disinclined to allow or foster this dressed-beef business, but they were forced into it.

Q. (By Mr. FARQUHAR.) You pay mileage on them both ways?—A. Yes. We only pay three-fourths of a cent, but there are certain roads that pay a cent.

Q. (By Mr. CLARKE.) If the roads owned the cars would you load them back?—A. No.

Q. They have to be of a peculiar construction?—A. Yes; they are practically refrigerator cars, and it would be dangerous to put any freight in that would be damaged by dampness. There is always more or less ice left in the boxes, so that it is a practical question. Then they are always in a hurry to get them back; they have a lot of beef waiting there. We could not have them around the line, so the result is that we would not probably load them.

Q. (By Mr. A. L. HARRIS.) Was the necessity of that in the beginning the cause of the dressed-beef men building their own cars?—A. I do not think the railroads ever built any dressed-beef cars to speak of. The fight was originally between the cattlemen and the dressed-beef men, and the railroads joined, as of course was their interest. The Northern lines could not get any cattle. The Grand Trunk, for instance, was interested in building up the dressed-beef traffic because it could not get any cattle; and then in time they forced the other roads to come in, because the cattle traffic was diminished to next to nothing, and the dressed-beef traffic became so large that all had to participate in it, or at least desired to participate in it, and the result is that we have to do just about as they tell us.

Q. (By Mr. FARQUHAR.) Is not your cattle traffic now confined just simply to exports?—A. Very largely to exports.

Q. Dressed beef takes the place now of the old markets of the East, where butchering was done?—A. Almost entirely; yes. The cattle traffic is practically out of the way except for export traffic, and in the West for range cattle, I presume—bringing range cattle in to the dressed-beef men. Chicago was originally the headquarters, but they have been working west all the time to Omaha and Kansas City, working west all the time, and that makes the transportation of cattle less and less every year.

Q. (By Senator MALLORY.) Have you ever considered the question of the legal right of railroads to transport cars owned by private individuals and not by the roads? Even if you did refuse they would pass over some other line.—A. We have generally wanted the business.

Q. Now, in the event that you should form a combine, could you refuse to take the dressed-beef men's cars?—A. I suppose we would have the right to do that if we were supplying cars of our own to these men. Of course we could not say to a man, "We will not take your freight;" but if we had our own cars there would be no law that would compel us to haul another man's car.

Q. (By Mr. PHILLIPS.) Does the running of these cars injure the railroads more, or the people, the public? You speak of it as being bad; now who is injured most by running the private cars over these roads?—A. The railroad, I take it. We pay a very large amount of money for the use of cars that we could supply ourselves at much less cost.

Q. Well, does it not also give them an advantage over other shippers that are engaged in the same line of trade, a very material advantage?—A. I think that question has practically been eliminated, because the arrangements are the same practically for all of them. I think that is pretty general now. I think that the arrangements that are made are generally made to cover all the shippers, large and small; but practically there are no small shippers of dressed beef; it requires such a large capital.

Q. But there are a great many cars for iron, steel, oil, ore, and coal; private cars owned by companies and individuals?—A. I think in most cases those cars come under our general rule. We only pay them 6 mills. We do not object to paying 6 mills, because we figure that is what it costs to keep our cars and pay the interest, and so long as they do not sidetrack our cars we do not object to running them. It is the excessive mileage we object to.

Q. (By Professor JOHNSON.) Speaking generally of running the private cars there, the owners of private cars have a force which, of course, compels the railroad to give a concession, does it not?—A. I do not think that the ownership of private cars, so far as I know, except the cattle cars and the dressed-beef cars, came about by reason of the fact that the railroads were not able to supply the facilities themselves. We will get 500 or 1,000 cars down into our coal regions and distribute them to our shippers; and some shipper says, "I can not carry on my business on these cars that I get, and if you will run my cars I will build them." But those cars are unprofitable, and they lie along the roads, and we had just about as soon the shipper did build his coal car.

Q. Then, private cars are not the cause of concessions in rates at the present time?—A. I do not think so, with the exception of this contract that I named. That is known to all the railroads, and I think it has been eliminated to a certain amount. But these dressed-beef people and these large shippers have become very conservative themselves. They do not want very low rates; they want stable rates. They do not want somebody to get a better rate than they get. If some one got a 40-cent rate, somebody else would not be better off; I think the dressed-beef men would prefer to have the rates stable. To-day the rate is 40 cents, with extra mileage allowance, and that is made under contract and can not be changed, and is known by all the railroads.

Q. (By Mr. C. J. HARRIS.) Do you furnish the shippers all the cars they require?—A. We endeavor to.

Q. Suppose you do not furnish them and some one suffers on the line of your road; what do you do for them? Ought not the Government or some power compel a railroad to furnish enough cars to do the business?—A. Well, I would answer that by saying that if you are only going to give us business for a week in the year, it would not be fair to ask the railroads to supply all the cars that are needed for that one week. But railroads ought to be compelled to take care of their customers. It becomes pretty serious in times like these. For instance, last year we had cars lying on the side tracks everywhere. We have built 6,000 cars in the year that I have been with the New York Central road, and we are going to buy more, trying to care for the large amount of business. We can not do it in 1 day; we can not get cars now, and can not get them built before next year.

Q. (By Senator MALLORY.) I understood you to say that there are no complaints, so far as you know, on your road as to excessive rates?—A. If there are I never hear of them.

Q. There is a distinction, of course, between your rates between your terminals and intermediate points?—A. Well, of course, we generally try to make the same rates throughout. I think that has been the system that has been practically adopted on all the Vanderbilt lines. We take care of our intermediate customers on the theory that we can not build up local business and do our competitive business very much cheaper.

Q. The theory then, as I understand, of your road is to foster anything in the way of enterprise along the line of your road?—A. That is what we try to do. We may fail in some cases.

Q. Have you anything to say regarding the fact that rates from Chicago and New York for exportation are less than rates from Chicago to New York for domestic use, or inland rates as distinguished from export rates?—A. I have already stated that it is necessary to meet the competition abroad, and so enable the people of this country to get rid of a large amount of business that perhaps they otherwise would not be able to do. Now, how it hurts anybody I do not know. We undoubtedly do charge lower rates on export business than we do on business going to New York. The business that goes to New York is domestic and used there, and the lower rates enable us to take a lot of this stuff from the far west and transport it so cheaply that it comes into competition with Russia and India, and every other country in the world, when it gets abroad, and I do not see that anybody is injured by it very much. If we were compelled to make all other rates to meet the export rates, it is a question if we would not have to go out of the export business. The proportion of the export business is enormous. Take provisions: I suppose that about 80 per cent of the tide-water provisions go abroad. Practically all the grain goes abroad; there is no grain that stops at New York any more.

Q. How about flour?—A. Of flour the proportion that goes abroad is very large.

Q. Still there is a large consumption on the Atlantic coast?—A. I suppose there is. I have not the figures in regard to flour.

Q. Well, there is a discrimination between flour as against grain, to which attention has been called here. Do you know anything about that?—A. Well, we have had a great deal of discussion about that, as to whether flour will not bear a higher rate than grain. My judgment is that it will. That is the way we have generally done with all these questions. We have said, Now, we will refer this to the Interstate Commerce Commission. They are an intelligent body of men and they are fair. And we have submitted the question to the Interstate Commerce Commission and they have generally found in our favor.

Q. But the discrimination, they think, is much too high. They put the limit, I think, at 2½ cents.—A. I think we complied with their finding, whatever it was. We nearly always do when the Interstate Commerce Commission makes a ruling or recommends anything.

Q. I know you do generally, so far as your road is concerned, but there are a great many other roads?—A. Well, the tariffs are generally the same on all roads. When I say our road, I mean these established tariffs. The competition on flour is very keen. It is probably the worst stuff we have to transport. It commences at Minneapolis, and originally the rate was maintained between Minneapolis and Chicago, at a certain figure, and then from Chicago eastbound. Then the "Soo Line" was built across there, making practically a line not any longer from Minneapolis to tidewater than from Chicago to tidewater, and they naturally took the position, "We are going to make the same rates from here as you fellows do from Chicago;" and the result was that the lines between Chicago and St. Paul commenced to scramble for this business and they adjusted the rates some way, I do not know just how, so that some of it goes to Montreal; but the water competition comes in there, and the competition from Duluth and Superior City and these Lake Superior ports to Buffalo, added to the canal rate from Buffalo to New York, makes the transportation almost nothing. We simply have to do the business the best we can. It has got down simply now as to how cheap we can do the business and make a profit. We can not extort anything out of anybody.

Q. (By Mr. Farquhar.) Have you a line of steamers from Buffalo to Duluth?—A. Yes. We have a line that we own entirely; the New York Central owns the entire capital stock of it. We have built 2 boats that carry 6,000 tons, and we are building engines to haul 3,000 tons from Buffalo to New York, and we take that stuff from Duluth to New York with 1 boat and 2 engines, 2 trains. Now, as to how the intermediate people are hurt, I do not see. They would not be any worse off if we said that we would not take this business at all.

Q. (By Senator Mallory.) Well, with reference to this flour and wheat business, the millers complain that after you reach a certain discriminating point—a certain amount of discrimination against flour—they can not ship flour to Europe at all.—A. My answer to that would be that that will not continue. You know they have all sorts of theories about these things, but they continue to ship right along, and they all continue to make money. Now, if that is a fact, and we find that our local flour industries are being depleted, then we will reduce the rate—have to.

Q. Well, that would be done on wheat?—A. But we have had no complaints from anybody on our line, so I do not know. I have never looked into it any further than this investigation before the Interstate Commerce Commission. I said there myself that if they would investigate and make a recommendation we would carry out the recommendation. I think they became convinced that flour could stand a higher rate than grain. The fact is we ought to get a higher rate for grain, but we can not.

Q. (By Mr. Clarke.) You make an inland minimum transit rate?—A. I can not answer that. Minimum transit rates are made very largely through the country, but I can not answer that. The matter has never come under my notice, and I can not say what has been done.

Q. (By Mr. Ratchford.) Referring to the subject of exports from Chicago, I understood you to state that those exports have to be shipped very cheaply in order to meet competition abroad. Are such exports shipped by the railroad companies, at present prices, at a profit for the companies, a reasonable profit?—A. I will say, in answer to that, that as an intelligent man I would not haul any traffic that I did not think paid us a reasonable profit. As to whether we could do all our business at that price I should say not. It would be impossible for us to haul all our business at the rate at which we are obliged to haul the export.

Q. Then it is not a reasonable proposition to say that you will haul all your business at that rate and make a reasonable profit?—A. That would depend on what you call a reasonable profit. We have to take the entire bulk of our business at an entire average per mile to produce a profit. For instance, the last statement I saw, we had 15,000 cars 24 hours east of Buffalo. Now, if you reduce that to 10,000 at the same price we could not probably live. If you reduce that to 5,000, we could not pay our wages to our employees. If you increase it to 20,000 we could probably do it at a little less cost than we do now; and that is what we are struggling to do all the time.

Q. The incentive in shipping these exports from Chicago at reduced rates over all the articles that are shipped for domestic purposes is what—in order to meet competition abroad?—A. Yes.

Q. That is the sole purpose, is it?—A. Yes, we have agents; export agents in Chicago, and export agents in New York, and they get the prices of these commodities in Liverpool every day, and they get the ocean freight. The whole thing has to be done as one; you must land that stuff in Liverpool. The rate on the ship and from the interior is added together to produce this result.

Q. Have you considered the general effect of that policy?—A. In what way?

Q. On the people of the United States generally?—A. I think it is very beneficial.

Q. Do you not think it is possible to export those goods so cheaply that they can be landed, for instance, in a European country cheaper than the European can raise them, and as a result, encourage immigration?—A. That is a force we can not control. We have a corn crop here of about 2,500,000,000 bushels a year. Now there is a very small portion of that consumed in the United States. What are you going to do with the surplus? How are you going to enable the farmer to sell it? The railroads come in and say, "We will help you to do this; we will enable you to compete with foreign countries; we will enable you to get this to Liverpool at a cheaper rate than we can take this stuff to New York City." Now that is the general theory on which we do this business. Whether it is right or wrong I do not know. I think if we were to stop it there would be a howl from the West that we would not get over very soon.

Q. (By Mr. PHILLIPS.) Is there any competition abroad with our corn?—A. Oh, yes.

Q. Any considerable amount?—A. I can not tell you, but it is quite considerable. It is growing all the time. We are interested all the time in getting our own corn over there and helping our own people; but what effect it will have, I can not say.

Q. (By Mr. RATCHFORD.) The point I wish to make is simply this: if we ship American corn, for instance, into the plains of Lombardy and Italy, is it not going to have the effect of starving the Italian who raises corn at home, or sending him to this country?—A. Well, I would not venture any opinion on that subject. We simply take the prices at Liverpool as the fixed value of that corn. We have no voice in making the value. We have to take facts as they exist.

Q. (By Mr. KENNEDY.) You said that of our corn crop of 2,500,000,000 bushels, only a small proportion was consumed at home. Do you not mean a small proportion of it is exported?—A. Oh, no; the export of corn is very large.

Q. It does not exceed half of the corn crop, does it?—A. Half would be quite large, of that enormous quantity. I am not speaking of corn particularly. Wheat, of course, is largely exported. You asked me why we were doing these things, and I am telling. That is our best judgment about it. We may all be wrong.

Q. (By Senator KYLE.) How do you estimate your rate in freight matters; do you consider your whole system together as one?—A. We know about what it costs to run a train.

Q. Sometimes you operate some lines of business even as low as cost, and you expect to make that up on something else?—A. I do not think I said that.

Q. Almost down to cost?—A. On a very small margin.

Q. Do you ever do that, run down to cost on some and make it up on others?—A. Well, it depends a good deal on circumstances. We would not naturally take business at a loss if we could avoid it.

Q. The cut is not on all articles, but on one of them?—A. The large bulk of business is the transportation of grain and provisions and dressed beef and coal. Of course, coal is a commodity that the rates are pretty well fixed on. They are very low and have been made low by competition, and they are pretty well fixed and determined. But the grain rates and the provision rates are fixed largely by the necessities abroad; and, as I say, they have gone down so low that there is nothing left; they can not get very much lower. We know at the end of the year, of course, what our profit per ton per mile is, and we know what our expenses per ton per mile are.

Q. (By Senator. MALLORY.) Can you state whether or not, as a rule, the published freight rates are adhered to in all cases?—A. So far as our line is concerned, I think they are.

Q. Do you know anything about other lines?—A. I do not know anything about anybody else's road.

Q. (By Senator KYLE.) You would have an opportunity to know in regard to them, would you?—A. Oh, no; except as I give orders about those things.

Q. On your own line you are positive they are adhered to?—A. I am.

Q. (By Senator MALLORY.) Do you think it would be practicable for a uniform freight rate on through freight to be established from Chicago to the different seaboard cities—New York, Boston, Philadelphia, Baltimore, and Newport News?—A. Well, that depends. I would like to have it. I do not know whether the other fellows would or not.

Q. Is it practicable to have it done?—A. But whether the Chesapeake and Ohio and Baltimore and Ohio could flourish under such a system I do not know. My own opinion is that the present differential rates are too high—that is, the facilities of those ports have so increased, they so approximate New York now, that the differences, which were established 20 years ago, when the rates were twice or three times as high as they are now, are too high.

Q. Is it practicable to make a uniform rate, under existing conditions, with competing roads running to all these different ports that I have mentioned?—A. I would not like to say that it was. If you ask me if it can be done, I would say that we have been working at it a long time and have failed to do it on account of the opposition of our competitors. Whether a system of that kind would not result in giving the Northern ports an excessive share of traffic I do not know. We would have to try it to find out.

Q. Well, if pooling were permitted and sanctioned by law—pooling of traffic, for instance, by railroads—could it be done, in your judgment, under that system?—A. Then it could be done undoubtedly, because the traffic could be assigned to the different roads.

Q. If roads were allowed, by the repeal of the pooling clause of the interstate-commerce law and by sanctioning contracts made for pooling, to do that, do you think that the discriminations, concerning which there are a great many complaints now, would be lessened?—A. I think they would.

Q. (By Mr. Farquhar.) Do you think that freight rates would be raised by a pool?—A. I think not. I do not think that they can raise freight rates.

Q. Will you give a reason for that?—A. When I say raise them I mean to any extortionate extent, because the waterways control that, and the present competition, as I have said, and the price of the commodity and labor. I will give you an illustration. When I was on the Union Pacific we had a large copper concern start up at Butte. Now, you would naturally think that a railroad out there could extort a very high rate from a corporation at Butte. But when you had to deal with it practically you would find that in order to make that copper concern flourish at Butte, Mont., you had to meet the competition and traffic in Chile bars at Liverpool that fixed the price that they could get for copper. The Chile bars in Liverpool were gotten out by cheap labor and very cheap water transportation, and the Butte copper was produced by the very highest paid labor in the world. They were paying $5 or $6 or $8 a day out there at that time. What was the result? Mr. Haggins would come down to my office in Omaha and say, "Here is the price that I can sell my copper in Liverpool. We can pay you so much for coal, coke, salt, and for fluxing material, and we pay you so much for ore over to the smelters, over to water, and we will pay you so much to take this stuff to New York." And then we had to figure out how nearly true that was, and we had either to close out Mr. Haggins entirely or we had to take his own rate. And the same thing to a greater or less extent exists all over this country. You can not take a man by the throat and say, "You have got to do so and so." If he can not pay that, you close him up; if you do that, you close your road up.

Q. So you do not think pooling would make any difference in the rates?—A. Not the slightest difference. Now, the trouble with pooling before was distribution of the business, so that it never amounted to anything. When we would meet at Chicago we would say, "We will take so much, and so and so will take so much," and we would have a jangle over that for two or three months perhaps, and then the fellow that had 10 per cent—he perhaps had a new road and increasing facilities—would say, "I am not going to stay here on 10 per cent any more," and he would go out and go to cutting rates and cut every other fellow that had a big percentage. And then one road would run ahead 100,000 tons and it would not pay up, and we would have a row and the whole thing would break up. Now, if the distribution of the business could be made legal, so that these traffic rates could be enforced, that class of competition that I have spoken of in reference to the dressed-beef business as between the railroads would be done away with. But we still have the commercial conditions and the competition of the waterways, which control very largely the transportation of this country.

Q. (By Mr. Clarke.) If pooling were legalized, you would not consider the desire of the shippers to have their freight go over some particular line?—A. I think that would have to be done by money distribution.

Q. Need it be done that way?—A. Oh, yes; for instance, if the New York Central was assigned 25 per cent of the traffic out of Chicago and could not limit its carriage to 25 per cent, it could pay over a certain percentage of the excess to the railroads of the division, deducting the cost of operation and collecting and all that sort of thing.

Q. In that case would the wish of the shippers be respected?—A. Oh, yes; we always respect them and never divert anything except with the consent of the shipper. Sometimes diversions are made, but it is so little it has never amounted to anything.

Q. (By Senator MALLORY.) Would you favor legislation granting the right to the railroads to pool their traffic and their profits, but giving to somebody, the Interstate Commerce Commission, or some other body, supervisory veto power over the contracts?—A. Yes.

Q. You would favor such legislation as that?—A. Yes. In other words, so far as the system I represent is concerned, we do not want to do anything that is not fair, right, and just, and if we can not agree with our shippers upon what is fair, we will be willing to have somebody else of intelligence say what is fair. We find the more these questions are discussed and the better understood the more the difficulties are appreciated. So far as I am concerned, I favor publicity. I never had a case before the Interstate Commerce Commission where they did not find with us when they came to get at the facts and the difficulties and understood the entire situation.

Q. Now, there has been some discussion as to giving the Interstate Commerce Commission the power to fix these rates, and this has been opposed by some of the roads.—A. I do not think it would be physically possible for them to fix the rates. We have traffic men all over the United States engaged in this thing for 24 hours a day, meeting all these conditions, and I do not think any body sitting here in Washington could do it.

Q. (By Mr. CLARKE.) Would you object to their having the power to reduce the rate after the companies themselves fix it?—A. I should think that might be dangerous; I should want to know who is going to do so first; for instance, I might be perfectly willing to have the present body of the Interstate Commerce Commission do it, but I do not know as I would want to agree to that for all time.

Q. Unless they had such power as that would they have any power practically to supervise railroads?—A. I do not think the majority of the people fly in the face of the sentiment of the community for any length of time. If the Interstate Commerce Commission will say to us that the rates are not reasonable I think we will reduce them, but they have never said so to us; in fact, they have said the other way, that they were too low.

Q. In the State of Massachusetts the legislature once authorized the railroad commissioners to fix the rates on the Housatonic Railroad because the road had practically defied the legislature and public sentiment. The power of the commission was exercised with great prudence and the effect was good upon the railroads of the State from that time henceforth. Now, there never has been any attempt on the part of the railroad commission or anybody else, any part of the public, to have that power made general, but it could be applied in the State much easier than it could be applied to interstate traffic. Therefore, if such power could be conferred on the Interstate Commerce Commission do you think it would have a wholesome effect in the general regulation of railroad traffic?—A. In other words, you mean the Interstate Commerce Commission should be empowered to take the place of the board of directors in the management of the New York Central and fix the rates. I do not think it would work. The country is so large as to make it physically impossible for these gentlemen to fix the rates.

Q. Could you tell what power they could have other than at present on that question?—A. I really do not know what their powers are, to say the truth. I am not a lawyer; I do not attempt to answer that question.

Q. (By Senator KYLE.) Have they any particular power?—A. I think they have a value in giving publicity to these matters. I have said we complied with their findings.

Q. You said you generally did.—A. In a general way, yes. In every case I have had before the Interstate Commerce Commission I think they have discovered the thing was not so far out of the way as they thought.

Q. (By Professor JOHNSON.) You said you had no objection to submitting to the Interstate Commerce Commission the relativity of rates on wheat and flour?—A. No.

Q. Would you have any objection to submitting the question of relativity of rates between New York and North Carolina?—A. We have already done it.

Q. Making that question general, the question of the relativity of rates between commodities or these localities, would you be willing to submit the question to a commission?—A. I certainly would to-day with the commission as constituted.

Q. The chairman of the Interstate Commerce Commission stated not 3 hours ago that that was practically the only question of rates that could come before that body.—A. Now, as to whether the roads that have lines running to the South would do that or not I can not say; I would be willing to do it.

Q. (By Mr. FARQUHAR.) You stated it would be a physical impossibility. now, out of all the railroads of the United States, suppose 300 contentions occurred in 24 hours, how can any body sitting in Washington settle it; and is not there in every freight office of the railroads a continuous contention of that kind?—A. That is what the traffic managers are there for. The railroads have transportation to sell, and sell it to the very best advantage. That is the English of it. But when you come to deal with the subject every day in the year and 24 hours in the day you will find there are a great many more difficulties in the way than you think for.

Q. (By Senator KYLE.) You go on the theory that the railroad is subject to the same limitations as the private individual in conducting a factory, steel works, ship-building works, etc. Is it not a consideration that the railroads have a valuable franchise? Has not that something to do with the rights of the Interstate Commerce Commission and the Government?—A. We are carrying a lot of roads like the West Shore and Nickel Plate that do not produce anything at all. If the Government will come in and protect the railroads and say that other railroads shall not be built within a certain distance——

Q. (Interrupting.) Railroads do not consider the franchise worth anything?—A. They consider the franchise as their life. It would be an absurd statement for me to make that the franchise was not worth anything, but this constant contention that the railroads are subject to different laws from what other business men are is a thing that I confess—you can not run a railroad any differently from what a steel plant is run.

Q. (By Mr. FARQUHAR.) Do you not think, under the law, the railroads do perform a quasi public function in the United States?—A. I am perfectly willing to admit that; yes.

Q. And they are subject to public regulations?—A. Yes; and we are quite willing to be regulated.

Q. So you would modify your expression and say that it is not simply a steel-plant matter altogether—the New York Central Railroad; that she has duties toward the State and has duties toward the nation?—A. Yes; and we have duties toward our patrons and endeavor to fulfill our duties intelligently and satisfactorily, so far as I know.

Q. The legislature of the State of New York has gone so far as to regulate your passenger affairs?—A. I was speaking of the management more particularly; the necessity that occurs from time to time to manage these things intelligently—things that come to our knowledge—as any other large business is conducted. I do not claim that we have any power to do as we please.

Q. (By Senator KYLE.) Did you suggest any amendment to the interstate-commerce law?—A. I have not been asked.

Q. (By Senator MALLORY.) I would like to learn from you whether you think it practical to establish a uniform system of classification in this country?—A. We have the uniform system of classification east of Chicago and St. Louis. Now, the conditions at the West and South are such that the roads do not think they are justified in joining our classification. I can not testify as to that, as I have no personal knowledge of the difficulties in the way.

Q. Have you given the subject any thought as to the conditions that cause or require differences in classification?—A. No; we have our own classification, and it is satisfactory to us. We wanted the others to join with us and they want us to join with them; and we make the best arrangement we can; but as to the local conditions I can not tell you.

Q. (By Professor JOHNSON.) You do not think both sections could operate under the same classification?—A. I have no judgment about it, as I do not know anything about it. I do not know anything of the reasons given for having a different classification. The managers of the roads out there say they can not do it, and I assume they have some good reason.

Q. (By Senator MALLORY.) Can you say whether or not differences in classification make differences in rates?—A. There is no question about it.

Q. Necessarily?—A. Yes. We may want to make a classification to foster some business on our line and some other road may not want to carry a small amount of that stuff under that classification. Classifications in the East are made under certain conditions that do not apply west of the Missouri River and the South.

Q. Have you given any thought to the advisability of requiring all books to be open to the inspection of examiners, as national banks are, for instance?—A. I do not see any particular necessity. We make sworn statements to the railroad commissioners of New York and all the States we run through and to the Government here. They have never been controverted, and I suppose if they were, and the authorities came to my office and asked permission to examine the books, I would allow them to do so. They are all sworn to.

Q. You see no necessity for legislation to that effect?—A. No; nor do I see what benefit legislation of that character would be.

Q. In your judgment, would there be any serious objection to it?—A. I could not answer that question. That would be a question for the board of directors on our road to answer. As far as I am concerned, we have nothing on the books that all the world might not see; but I would not like to give an opinion on the subject without consulting my fellow-directors.

Q. (By Senator KYLE.) You fear your competitors might get hold of some information?—A. Yes. We used to have on the Union Pacific a six-monthly examination, and our competitors got away with everything we had most effectually.

Q. (By Mr. C. J. HARRIS.) The great objection on the part of the railroads would be the great publicity it gave to their rivals; but if all had to do that, would not that objection be more or less removed?—A. I think the affairs of the railroads are practically public now. The New York Central annual report has in it everything we do and earn. I do not know any more information that a man could want than he could get in that book.

Q. These issues of stock are matters of public record?—A. They have to be. They brought in statements for me just before I left; books piled up to that high [indicating] for me to swear to for different commissions and for gentlemen over here at Washington, and I think they practically contain everything we have ever done. I do not think anybody ever looks at them.

Q. (By Senator MALLORY.) There has been considerable argument urged that it was desirable for the Government, the Interstate Commerce Commission, at least, to have officials, as we have bank examiners, to look into these matters to see that certain railroads—not the New York Central; not these good railroads that do not violate the law——A. (Interrupting.) They are all the same. When one railroad violates the law the other has to. I am not claiming anything exceptional.

Q. (By Professor JOHNSON.) Some years ago the Atchison road was discovered in discriminations amounting to several millions of dollars, and it is claimed by those who advocate this public accounting of railroads that the discriminations practiced by the Atchison never could have been made if the publicity of accounts had been in effect.—A. I do not know anything about the Atchison road. I saw the statements in the papers; I never heard anybody claim they were true.

Q. The examination of an accountant would clearly show just what had taken place?—A. As I understood the thing at the time, I did not understand it was a matter of discrimination, but of making false entries, and making a better showing of the earnings than actually existed.

Q. (By Mr. A. L. HARRIS.) Might it not, to protect the public against these false statements of earnings, be a good idea to have a public auditor to go through their accounts as they do through banks, to prevent fraud, you might say, on the public?—A. My only answer to that is, we make this statement under oath, and if any stockholder or anybody has any desire to examine the books, I do not think there will be any objection.

Q. Suppose in some of the railroads there might be mismanagement, as there might be in a bank that fails, would it not be advisable in a case of that kind to have some public auditing of accounts subject to the Government?—A. I have no views on that subject at all.

Q. (By Senator MALLORY.) Is there anything you would suggest as amendments to the interstate commerce law?—A. I think an amendment to divide the business in some way between the roads would be an advantage to both the railroads and the public.

Q. (By Senator KYLE.) A pooling clause?—A. You can call it a pooling clause or a division of the business. I think a majority of the commission think that way themselves, if not all of them. It would limit these abuses that I have shown here, and enable the railroads to make long-time contracts in which they could more materially reduce their expenses. In New York to-day the expenses of the Broadway offices must be enormous; they are of no particular use to the public or the railroads except as they are fighting each other for business.

Q. Some prominent railroad persons of the United States are opposed to the legalizing of pooling. What are their objects?—A. I do not know as I would like to say anything about our associates; but many people are interested in keeping the railroads fighting so as to help their own business. That must be very patent to everybody. No, there are certainly very strong railroad men that are opposed to the pool. If they keep the trunk lines east of Chicago and St. Louis fighting, they can get their own business transported lower. Practically they are large shippers.

Q. That is probably the whole of the opposition?—A. You asked me what I thought of it, and I have told you what I thought of it.

Q. (By Senator MALLORY.) There is, also, in connection with this Interstate Commerce Commission question, much complaint arising from the fact that the Interstate Commerce Commission is entirely emasculated as far as any power to enforce its decisions is concerned. It can not enforce anything. Practically the individual can only get a recommendation, and the railroad may observe it or not, just as it pleases. This Industrial Commission has had considerable testimony on that subject. Have you any suggestions on that point as to an amendment of the interstate-commerce law?—A. I presume you can not take away from the railroad companies their rights under the Constitution. In fact, I suppose there is no power that can compel railroads to carry freight for nothing; and if the findings in court were unjust or unreasonable, I suppose the railroad would do anything it could to protect itself; but we have never had any trouble with this commission, and I think we have carried out every recommendation they have made.

Q. The commission itself in its report calls attention to the fact that it can not enforce its decisions, and it is desirable that it be empowered by some method different from what now exists to see that its decisions are observed. That was a question I thought you might have some views upon.—A. What would you suggest?

Q. I have my own opinion, of course, and I tried to advocate it some years ago in the House of Representatives, and that was to make their decision go into effect and let the railroads who did not think they were just give them an appeal before somebody, either a court or other tribunal.—A. I do not think we would object to that.

Q. Have you ever given any thought to the subject of Government ownership of railroads; the feasibility of it aside from the desirability of it?—A. I suppose the railroads would have to be managed by experts—men who have been brought up with the railroad business and understood it—and I do not see that they would act any different from what they do now. It would become a large political factor. I do not think we would want it. We have practically a million of men in our employ to-day, nearly all voters. It has never been a great success where they tried it. They tried it in Canada and gave it up. They had a road and it went to seed. Nor do I understand where you are going to get the money to pay for them. It is a thing I have never given any consideration, because I did not think it was a very live question. We have live questions to consider most of the time.

Q. (By Mr. FARQUHAR.) You said your road owned a line of steamers from Buffalo to the upper lake ports?—A. Yes.

Q. In framing rates of part rail and part water, do your rates usually conform or are they agreeable to other trunk lines that own steamers on the lakes, too?—A. The lake line is managed entirely separate and the manager of that line endeavors to get his competitors to agree with him as to what the rate shall be; but the tramp steamers have a large influence. For instance, last year and the year before the rates on the tramp steamers became so low that we practically tied up our boats for a time. This year the fact is just the opposite; the tramp steamers have gone after ore and are making the rates so high we are practically getting the same rates over the lake as rail lines.

Q. What class of freight do they carry?—A. Copper, flour; all those coarse freights that come here.

Q. Carry any package freight?—A. Yes.

Q. Between Chicago and Milwaukee?—A. We run to Milwaukee, Chicago, and Duluth.

Q. Your own line of steamers would then come in competition with the open rates declared at Chicago, Milwaukee, Duluth, Detroit, Cleveland, and elsewhere, would it not?—A. Yes.

Q. You would not have an exclusive rate of your own but you would have to compete with the open rate at these harbors?—A. Yes; we have to meet, practically, a tramp rate. A vessel will come in there and make a rate to Buffalo, and it makes our through rate the same as the tramp rate. That is the practical effect of meeting that competition.

Q. And you think among the lines on the lakes there is somewhat of an agreement of a common rate for all?—A. Yes; they endeavor to adjust these rates. Of course, we could not make Chicago rates apply from Minneapolis or Duluth because it would ruin these intermediate rates, and so they make an agreement among themselves, on lake lines, to maintain a higher rate from Duluth than Chicago, though the distance is practically the same.

WASHINGTON, D. C., *October 9, 1899.*

TESTIMONY OF MR. FRANK BARRY,

Secretary of the Millers' National Association of the United States.

The commission met at 2.30 p. m., Chairman Kyle presiding. Mr. Frank Barry being duly sworn, testified concerning transportation as follows:

Q. (By Mr. C. J. HARRIS.) Will you give the commission your name, occupation and place of business?—A. Frank Barry, secretary of the Millers' National Association of the United States; residence, Milwaukee, Wis.

Q. How long have you been employed in this capacity?—A. Eleven years.

Q. Were you connected with the milling business previous to that?—A. I was.

Q. (By Mr. FARQUHAR). When was this millers' association organized and what are the objects of the association?—A. The Millers' National Association was formed June 17, 1873. The object of it at that time was to provide protection from patent litigation which was very general, owing to a change in the system of milling from the old form of grinding by stones to the Hungarian roller process. The fact that the Patent Office of this country was not up in the state of the art had caused a large number of patents to be issued which resulted in an immense amount of litigation. I do not suppose any industry was ever so oppressed with litigation over patents as the mills of those days. There were several sectional and State associations, and finally they all came into one national association, which handled test suits on all these conflicting patents bringing general results for the miller as a matter of economy in handling these troubles. The association continued in that field strictly until 1890, and at that time, having produced a condition of peace and quiet in patent matters, it was decided to continue the organization for the general benefit of the trade. The association has since that time interested itself not only in patent matters which have arisen, but has acted for the trade in other directions, such as the enactment of the pure-flour section of the war-revenue act. We endeavored to get this law through as special legislation, and failing in that, we tacked it onto the war-revenue act. We are now working on a pure-food law in general, and legislation of that nature. As tariff bills come before Congress, there are matters which interest millers vitally, which we promote their interests in. The national organization has never and never can have anything to do with prices, either of raw material or of the products, for the reason that interests are so diversified throughout the country that it is and would be impossible, if desired, to have anything to do with questions of prices. We never have had anything of that kind. That is the nature, as nearly as I can state it, of the work of the association.

Q. (By Mr. C. J. HARRIS.) Will you state what adulterations have been made in your line of goods, and what has been the effect on the trade?—A. The adulteration of flour was produced by the same general causes as the adulteration of all other food products, unscrupulous people endeavoring to reduce the cost; and as we showed the last Congress, the adulteration of flour with a by-product of glucose or starch had been going on until it had reached a percentage as high as 40 and 50 per cent. Then adulterators had gone still further and used even white earth. The condition was such that the integrity of our flour had been seriously injured abroad and was being injured, especially in the Southern States, here. We showed that this must result in time disastrously to the milling interests of the country. I will say the mixed-flour law, as it is called, has entirely put a stop to that.

Q. We would like to-day to bring out, so far as possible, the transportation questions connected with your association, the questions of freight discriminations, and ask you to say anything in regard to that which you have in mind?—A. I will say, in answer to that, it is a question which is of vital interest to us at present, and with your permission I would like to call your attention to one or two points in regard to the milling interests of the country. It is to-day the largest and most important manufacturing industry of our country. There are something over 16,000 flour mills in operation, and not above 400 of them, I believe, have a daily capacity of 500 barrels, showing that the larger number of the mills are broadly scattered and of small capacity. My reason for referring to that will appear. The amount of capital invested exceeds $250,000,000, and the annual product is about $600,000,000; the wages paid are above $28,000,000 a year. There have been estimated to be about 40,000 employees, and a large number of them are skilled workmen. The raw material which we use is the farmer's product, wheat; and the product of our mills is of probably more direct interest to every man, woman, and child in the country than any other manufactured article of this country.

When we consider the transportation feature, as looked upon by millers, there are several points I would like to speak of. We have attained in flour milling in this country a condition of overproduction which, I think, very few people realize. It is estimated at the present time that the flour mills of this country, by grinding to their full capacity, can within 90 days make into flour every bushel of wheat raised in the United States in a year. This condition of overproduction has not been occasioned by capital seeking investment in a very profitable line of manufacture, but has been occasioned principally by the fact that competition has driven millers to attain as l irge a capacity, as large a production, as possible, in order to reduce the cost per barrel; and they have forced their capacity far beyond what they should have. The condition of overproduction has been warranted to some extent by the fact that there has been a strong and growing demand for our product abroad. Almost all of the European countries furnish a steady demand—require flour made from our wheat. They do not require our wheat, it is the flour made from it. If they could get the wheat and have their millers grind it into flour, they would prefer to do so; but if they can not do that, experience and statistics will show you they will buy the flour and must have it to mix with their flour. The published rates of railroads, their tariffs, for the past 25 years, until within a period of less than 2 years, have shown a parity of rates on wheat and on flour not only for domestic use, but for export. These rate sheets will show universally that they have been at the same rate. During the past 1½ years or 2 years there has been a gradually growing discrimination in the rate charged for export wheat as against flour. I can show you by some figures the result that this is having on flour manufacturing.

Q. (By Mr. Conger.) Have these discriminations been in the way of an increased rate on flour or a decreased rate on wheat?—A. A decreased rate on wheat.

Q. The flour rate remaining the same as before?—A. The flour rate has remained practically the same.

Q. (By Professor Johnson.) What has brought down the wheat rate?—A. That is something difficult to state positively, but my belief is, the principal factor has been that the railway lines of this country have found it expedient in the conduct of their business to establish elevators, which, although they may be conducted in the name of elevator companies, are owned and conducted by the railroads or their directors. They have gathered the wheat into these elevators and they have had to move it. Since the interstate-commerce act has been in force they have had to publish the rates on which they move all merchandise, and that merchandise has been moved on these published rates. These published rates have been cut down to meet the desires of the railroad people for wheat, without a like reduction for flour. I believe that is the principal factor in this reduction of the wheat rate. We have had a case before the Interstate Commerce Commission this summer and have had repeated hearings, in New York, Chicago, St. Louis, and in Washington, where we went into this subject very exhaustively, and where we showed to the satisfaction of the Interstate Commerce Commission, according to their decision, that the railways of the country could carry export wheat to the seaboard practically as cheaply as flour. The Interstate Commerce Commission has held that public policy would dictate that wheat and flour for export should be carried at the same rate. We satisfied them of that. As to these points in detail, I would like an opportunity to touch upon them in a written argument; I can refer better to the points.

Q. (By Mr. C. J. Harris.) I would like to ask you if in this millers' association the members are scattered throughout the whole United States, or does it apply more especially to the Northwest?—A. No; we have a membership extending through 24 States of the Union, and the capacity of our membership is about 120,000 barrels a day. All of the larger, more progressive mills are members.

Q. (By Senator Kyle.) Do you have organizations in the several States?—A. Nearly every milling State has an association, and they are practically, although not formally, allied with the work of the national association.

Q. (By Professor Johnson.) Can you tell what percentage of the milling is done by Minneapolis, or mills in that vicinity?—A. Of the entire milling of the country, I could not state. I could get you the figures.

Q. Have the Minneapolis mills been crushing out the smaller mills to any extent recently?—A. I do not think so, any more than that any large center of manufacture in any line has advantages, especially in transportation rates, etc. Naturally, smaller mills, when they go up against a large mill, which can manufacture so that the cost per barrel is less than the smaller mill—can sell cheaper—they feel it is an oppression; but I have not noticed any disposition on the part of the Minneapolis mills to oppress. They may lose export trade which they have acquired and have had heretofore; if they lose that trade they must find a market for their product so as to maintain their standard of daily capacity. They then will ship two or three carloads down into Tennessee or Arkansas; they will send it to some point where it is thickly settled. The little miller who has had that trade can not supply it at the same price per barrel as such mills as the Pillsbury's and others. He thus indirectly feels the loss of export trade materially; though he does not export himself, he will feel the result of the loss of export trade on the part of the large mill in that way.

Q. (By Mr. C. J. HARRIS.) Unless the surplus is taken by export trade it must crowd down the home market?—A. Yes.

Q. (By Mr. FARQUHAR.) You have in your trade the so-called millers' trust. What are the views of that organization? What is its relation to the trade generally?—A. I assume you refer to the United States Flour Mill Company, recently organized by McIntyre. I think that has had no effect as yet on the milling trade. It was an organization formed to buy up these different milling plants, and is operating them. I have been inquiring and watching very carefully to see if there were any indications of cutting prices by that company. The assurances I have received are that they have maintained prices, and show no inclination to reduce them.

Q. How many mills are in that organization?—A. I think 24 at present.

Q. What capacity do these 24 bear to the whole milling capacity of the country?—A. I could not say.

Q. Ten per cent?—A. Oh, no. They can not make over 50,000 barrels a day, and in our association we make about 120,000.

Q. Does this organization seek to control merely the domestic trade, or does it have anything to do with the foreign trade?—A. They are very large exporters. I should say at a guess nearly 60 per cent of their product is exported now. I think they have been looking very largely to the export market.

Q. Could you give the commission an idea as to what brought about the formation of this organization among the millers; what particular thought is there in their association? What do they desire to conserve in the formation of an organization of that kind?—A. I think the sole reason for combining the mills was the idea of obtaining a very large capacity located in scattered, advantageous localities, where they would not be dependent on local conditions, so that if the mills could run advantageously in the Northwest, when they could not in the East, they would run strong there, and vice versa; so as to obtain the benefit of a diversified wheat market, and reduce the cost of management and cost of selling their products. That was stated to me.

Q. (By Mr. PHILLIPS.) What is the capital stock of the organization?—A. I believe $15,000,000 at the present time.

Q. Do you know on what basis they went into it? In estimating the value of each property, was it estimated on the capacity of the mill, number of barrels?—A. No The mills were bought on a basis of the appraisement of the value of machinery and plant by a special committee, and also a price agreed upon for the good will of the concern, and that was the expensive part of it.

Q. Was the capitalization much larger than the real value of these plants?—A. So far as I know, they paid a fair price for every property they bought.

Q. Did they pay an exorbitant price?—A. I could not say; it depends on a man's valuation of the property. They paid more for some plants than I would consider them worth.

Q. (By Mr. FARQUHAR.) Is that organization in its growth absorbing other mills?—A. I think not. Since they organized they have bought only one company, the Northwestern Consolidated Company of Minneapolis, comprising five mills there.

Q. (By Mr. KENNEDY.) Have any mills in the combination been shut down?—A. Yes.

Q. How many?—A. I could not say. In the Northwest several of these mills were not in operation, and I heard recently they were going to start them up.

Q. (By Mr. PHILLIPS.) Did they, as a rule, take stock or money in payment?—A. I think that was purely optional with the men that went in; I think they were permitted to do as they pleased. One friend of mine that went into the combination, I know took cash. He took some bonds, but did not take stock.

Q. Did they have both common and preferred stock?—A. Yes.

Q. Do you know the amount of each?—A. I could not say, just now.

Q. (By Senator KYLE.) Will this institution work in opposition to the national association?—A. They are most of them members. There could be no question of antagonism against the national association, because the national association is working for the good of the trade, and there is nothing to fight about there. It is simply a question of whether a miller is willing to spend his money to help along the work we are doing.

Q. Are all the mills usually identified with your association or the State associations?—A. No. Some States have no millers' association.

Q. The millers are not alive?—A. There is no such organization of millers in this country as there is in most every other country where milling is a prominent industry. In France a very large proportion of their mills are organized, and their association has become such a power in national legislation that they have been able to so legislate that they receive our wheat, which they must have, from this country free of duty, and impose a prohibitive duty on our flour; and then the French Government pays a bounty on every barrel of flour exported by its millers.

Q. There are certain advantages to be gained in every State by belonging to this association?—A. Yes, in the way of assisting in the work we are doing for the good of the trade.

Q. You have legislative advantages to be gained also, State as well as national?—A. State as well as national, yes. In Germany they have over 4,000 members in their national millers' association. Other countries are better organized for protective and advantageous work for millers than the United States.

Q. (By Mr. C. J. HARRIS.) You have milling-in-transit rates I suppose. Have you any remarks to make about that?—A. I think that railroads generally, throughout the country, where there are any considerable milling centers, or in States where milling is a prominent industry—I think they make, pretty generally, milling-in-transit rates. Take a load of wheat from a point West to a point East, as through wheat, and they will allow it to be milled at any point between these two points for an additional rate of two cents, the cost of simply stopping, unloading, and loading the car.

Q. What effect does that have on the smaller millers, is it advantageous or otherwise?—A. It is an advantage to any mill.

Q. Is it not an advantage to the large millers especially?—A. It is equally advantageous to the small miller in the territory where they get milling-in-transit; and the small miller can get it as well as the large one. Otherwise he would have to pay the local rate on wheat and the local rate on flour out. That is an illustration of the necessity for the same rate on flour as on wheat, which we simply asked to have maintained in our case before the Interstate Commerce Commission, and which is not allowed on export business. We are suffering from the discrimination of foreign governments in assisting foreign millers; but we can overcome that by the quality of our flour if we are not discriminated against by our freight carriers in this country; but not when they will carry our wheat and get it to the foreign country cheaper than we can get the flour into the market. The condition is shown very readily by a letter which I have here from a leading London flour dealer.

(Reading:)

LONDON, 41 SEETHING LANE,
September 2, 1899.

Messrs. THE C. MANEGOLD MILLING CO.,
Milwaukee, Wis.

DEAR SIRS: The flour trade continues to drag heavily and a week's fair business is followed by a long interval of abstention from buying. There is no confidence in present prices among consumers and they are simply purchasing from hand to mouth as circumstances necessitate.

The freight discrimination against flour is no doubt working very prejudicially against the trade and is a fine thing for the English miller. It amounts to the same as if our Government placed a duty of, say, 6 cents per 100 pounds on flour and allowed wheat to come in free. This is what every miller here has been agitating for for years, in order to keep American flour out of the market. It hardly seems possible that such an anomaly will be permitted by your Government to last for any length of time. Other countries are paying their manufacturers bounties in order to encourage trade.

Yours, truly,

For JOHN J. CARTER,
HENRY EASTWOOD.

Q. (By Mr. CONGER.) How long ago was that letter written?—A. The 2d day of September, 1899.

Q. The Interstate Commerce Commission made an order that the difference should not exceed a certain amount?—A. They have. Their order reads so that anybody may know what it means exactly. It reads that public policy demands that a rate on export wheat and flour should be the same, but that no greater differential than 2 cents should be allowed under any circumstances. With our business we maintain that there should be a parity. I do not know why any difference is allowed.

Q. Well, the difference in years past has been greater than 2 cents?—A. It stands to-day on Mississippi points and inland points—say in Wisconsin, where there is a difference, as high as 7¾ cents per hundred.

Q. (By Mr. CLARKE.) Should not there be a greater difference on account of the greater ease in loading wheat, and because it can be gotten into a smaller space?—A. We went into that subject quite extensively. I will show that in a written argument. We showed conclusively that railroads do handle flour as cheaply as they can handle wheat. Now, it is a fact that the railroads do supply larger cars for wheat. Their large modern cars which they build for the wheat business are of 70,000 pounds capacity. When you order a car for export flour they will send you a car of 20,000 pounds capacity; and when they come to talk about this the railroads claim that wheat is loaded heavier than flour, and they will show a lot of cars loaded with wheat at 70,000 pounds, and a number of cars loaded with flour at 20,000 pounds. But why? We showed conclusively that we did load flour to the limit when we got the cars. That is the reason why on export business they can show that we have shipped a lower average carload weight of flour than is customary to ship of wheat.

Q. Does that statement apply to vessels as well as cars?—A. No; there is no trouble about tonnage of vessels, I think, in anyway.

Q. Do they not prefer to carry wheat?—A. I think they do, but then the discrimination, so far as we are concerned, does not occur after it leaves the seaport. This discrimination which we are suffering from is on the part of railroads between points from which they are moving the flour to the seaboard.

Q. Most of these rates are joint rates between the carriers?—A. No; they make a rate to the seaboard, and then from the seaboard the rates are made from day to day by conditions governing.

Q. Practically it is a through rate, is it not?—A. No; the rates on which we ship export are usually not based upon the through rate to destination. The basis on which we figure is the domestic rate entirely, and then, added to that, the ocean rate.

Q. (By Mr. CONGER.) But is it not true that owing to the fact of the railroads having these large elevators and in the elevators storing the wheat, and carrying on their roads at their own convenience, they can handle wheat more economically than the flour, because the millers want the flour transported at their convenience rather than at the convenience of the carrier?—A. I claim and I believe we showed, that this very point lies on the side of flour. The flour goes steadily for export the year through. Wheat as a rule moves most abundantly just after harvest, and it is a fact that all railroads carrying large amounts of wheat do have to devote nearly all of their cars to the wheat service, and there frequently results a gorging of traffic, shutting out the use of these cars to any further purpose, and requiring a large number of cars to return westward empty; that costs money. Now, so far as concerns the storing of wheat, the railroad, or whoever owns the elevators, must buy that grain and make an investment in the elevator property, and the interest on such investment ought to be counted in this calculation, it seems to me, but it is not.

Q. If the differential had been 4½, as you stated, and the order of the Interstate Commerce Commission is obeyed, so in the future it will be but 2 cents, that order will give you a great deal of leeway, will it not?—A. Yes. Now, you are coming to the point I want to speak about particularly. Whenever we encounter difficulties in regard to discrimination against us, we go to the traffic manager of the railroad that we are dealing with and state our case to him. He says, "Yes, there is a seeming injustice in that. Now I would be glad to do something for you, but this is a rate which is agreed to by our traffic association and I am powerless, personally, to assist you, but I would refer you to Mr. So-and-so, who is chairman of the traffic association. Take that matter up with him." We go to Mr. So-and-so and take the matter up with him and he says, "Yes, that is a discrimination; that is wrong and bad, but I am powerless to do anything in this matter. That is an agreed rate, and unanimously agreed to by all of these railroads, and without a unanimous agreement to change it nothing can be done." We find that there is no recourse there. We have gone before the Interstate Commerce Commission with our grievance at a considerable expense and effort. We have submitted our case to it and have got a favorable decision from the Interstate Commerce Commission. We are now confronted with the problem of whether the railroads will or will not comply with that decision. We have been afraid that they will not.

Q. Have any of them as yet put the new rate in force as a result of the order? In other words, have any of them reduced the differential?—A. Not to my knowledge.

Q. We have had testimony to the effect that the New York Central was obeying all of the orders of the Interstate Commerce Commission—that is, was following out all recommendations or orders. Do you know if that road has reduced the rate?—A. I think not. I have received no notification of it. If it had I probably would have known it.

Q. If the New York Central shall obey that order, is it likely, in your opinion, that other competing railroads will have to follow, and reduce differentials?—A. If the New York Central, independent of the traffic association, will do this, every road of that traffic association will do the same thing. There is no question about that.

Q. Do you know, or have you any knowledge, what the reason is on the part of the railroads for charging more for flour than for wheat?—A. They have not done so at any period until comparatively recently—a year or two—and in that time the influences brought to bear on railroads have caused them to charge less for wheat than for flour.

Q. (By Senator KYLE.) I think it has been stated before the commission here that they could get a consignment of wheat more easily than flour, in large quantities at certain times; that they have flour for export purposes all the time, and therefore could afford to make better prices on wheat. Is that not true?—A. Unquestionably. Immediately after harvest, at that time of the year when I suppose the consignments are very acceptable to railroads, and later, when merchandise has not commenced to move—after harvest, of course, the wheat is there, and they can on that account obtain larger consignments of wheat than they can of flour, but I believe that to be really a disadvantage to the railroad.

Q. (By Mr. FARQUHAR.) Did you state that your product of flour is about even the 12 months of the year, which gives a very uniform tonnage for the road?—A. Yes.

Q. Can you, as secretary of this National Association, give a miller's reason, or a farmer's reason, or any producer's reason, why this differential should not be as it is?—A. We are firmly convinced it should not exist.

Q. Do you think there is a catering to drive the grain to Europe instead of the flour, so that the by-products may be had there instead of here?—A. We believe so, and we believe it is to the interests of railway owners and companies to move the wheat rather than to move the flour. That is what we have maintained and endeavored to show. My belief is that the discrimination against flour in favor of wheat has not been occasioned by ocean carriers to any extent. They would not have been affected in any way, so far. I believe they could affect us if they had a mind to exercise their power in rates for the benefit of their foreign miller; they could, but I have never yet seen any evidence of their having done so. The discrimination under which we suffer is from the rate of the American railways between the West and the seaboard.

Q. Is it not pretty generally the fact that the parties to a bill of lading, or the consignor and consignee, are the same parties?—A. On flour?

Q. On the grain shipped.—A. Well, I think that is a matter of business form.

Q. Well, independent of the form; I mean in the matter of ownership?—A. I do not know. In other words, as I understand it, you want to know whether the American shipper is his own consignee abroad and that wheat is sold to his interest there?

Q. Yes; and whether the consignor here is not the foreigner on the other side?—A. No; I am positive of that. The exporters of wheat in this country are comparatively few. There are a mere handful of them in number. The bulk of the wheat shipped, or practically all of the wheat exported from Chicago, is exported by 5 firms, and these 5 firms have, of course, great influence with the railroad companies on account of the bulk of the stuff they ship, and they obtain advantageous rates so as to be able to sell to the foreign demand as cheaply as possible. When it goes over there they get practically a commission on what passes through their hands.

Q. You think that the ownership really changes at tide water?—A. I believe so.

Q. (By Mr. A. L. HARRIS.) Will you please name these 5 firms?—A. I can not do it at present.

Q. (By Professor JOHNSON.) Those 5 firms get a special rate from the railroad by being able to consign their freight in train loads to the line of their choice, do they not?—A. Yes.

Q. It is an advantage that the millers do not have?—A. Yes.

Q. Then it is a very obvious reason, it would seem to me. for the concession on the part of the railroad.—A. Yes.

Q. The millers would like to have that made illegal, would they not? In other words, they would like to have the ratio between wheat and flour right, would they not?—A. Yes. We believe a parity should be maintained, as it was in former years.

Q. (By Mr. FARQUHAR.) Is it not a fact that in the milling business as well as others, the great centers of manufacturing or milling have advantages over all small places, and the great men, firms, and corporations, who control great bodies of products have an advantage over small owners all over the United States?—A. Undoubtedly.

Q. It is a rule of trade and has been a custom, and was the same before the great railroad corporations with their through systems came in, that large institutions do get better rates than small ones?—A. They do; yes.

Q. (By Mr. PHILLIPS.) Is there any discrimination in favor of any one of these 5 firms, or has there been, in freight rates?—A. That, of course, I am not prepared to say upon oath; I can not prove it. We are satisfied, however, that advantages have been obtained and are obtained. One of the largest dealers in Chicago export wheat is Counselman, and I believe he obtains advantages over some others.

Q. (By Senator KYLE.) Export wheat by the car?—A. Yes.

Q. (By Mr. PHILLIPS.) Has there been any complaint as between these firms in regard to one claiming discriminations against the other?—A. None that I know of.

Q. (By Mr. CONGER.) Is it your opinion that any exporter of flour has the same tonnage to offer the transportation companies that Mr. Counselman has in wheat? Do you suppose any exporter of flour has that tonnage to offer?—A. I do not think so; no. Now, one point I would like to call attention to, is in regard to the effect that discrimination is having on our export business, which is shown very plainly, as before stated, and which has been comparatively recent. A fair comparison would be to take the shipment of a number of barrels of flour exported, say, from Minneapolis or Duluth, which are two of the largest exporting centers of the country. Take the month of September, 1898. In the first week of September, 1898, from Minneapolis there were exported 112,358 barrels. For the first week of September, 1899, there were exported 87,600 barrels; showing what effect this discrimination is having upon us—a steady and marked change. The second week in September, 1898, there were 128,595 barrels, and the second week in September, 1899, there were 93,760 barrels. The third week in September, 1898, it was 127,841 barrels; the third week of September, 1899, it was 84,600 barrels. You see it is going down. In the fourth week of September, 1898, ending October 1, 1898, it was 116,640 barrels, and in 1899, the same week, it was 96,850 barrels. There was a total in 1898, in the month of September, of export shipments from Minneapolis of 485,534 barrels, against 362,810 barrels for the month of September, 1899, a net decrease of 122,624 barrels.

Q. (By Professor JOHNSON.) What was the decrease of wheat?—A. The wheat has shown a greater proportion of increase.

Q. Is it not due to better crops?—A. No.

Q. A better demand?—A. No. It is, I believe, because you can do better with your wheat than with flour, on account of the transportation rates.

Q. (By Mr. CONGER.) Do you know whether the Minneapolis millers manufacture as many barrels of flour this year as last?—A. Yes. They have been running very heavily this year.

Q. On account of the local markets?—A. And the little miller is the fellow that must squeal. Now, I will not carry the thing out by giving week by week the shipments from Duluth. The total shipments from Duluth in September, 1898, were 173,135 barrels against, in 1899, 79,295, a net decrease of 93,830 barrels.

Q. (By Professor JOHNSON.) In your written statement could you include a table showing the exportation of wheat and flour since 1896?—A. Yes; I will do that. I refer you to the Government Bureau of Statistics for these figures. Now, this will give you an idea how this great industry is suffering. After thinking the whole matter over, we have concluded to endeavor to obtain an amendment, if possible, in the next session of Congress, to the interstate-commerce act which will give to the findings of the Interstate Commerce Commission a mandatory effect, as of a court of record, which shall stand until reversed by the United States courts. We are acting to that end. The interests which we will gather together, the millers and farmers, and like interests, will support that measure. I have recently taken the subject up with some fifty national commercial organizations, and I have heard from probably two-thirds of them so far; they heartily enter into the spirit of this movement; and there will be an effort made in the next session of Congress to do one or two things— to make that interstate-commerce law what it was originally intended to be and to give the findings of that commission some effect, or else wipe it out so that it may not fool us any longer. We want it amended so that when decisions are made they will have some effect.

Q. (By Mr. FARQUHAR.) Have you derived, from the millers' association, any benefit from the Interstate Commerce Commission's investigation, so far?—A. No; I believe not.

Q. (By Mr. CONGER.) Have you had any cases before the commission previous to this one?—A. Oh, we have had several cases which have not been entered in the name of our association, but which we have assisted in, and they have been to some extent beneficial in their results. The first case we have acted in, as an actual association case, has been this one of discrimination.

Q. Then you mean to say that not in any one of these cases has the commission been of any service to you?—A. Never in any case that the association has handled. It remains to be seen what will come in regard to this case, whether their decision in this case we have just had before them will result in anything.

Q. (By Professor JOHNSON.) I want to ask if you intend to urge that the Interstate Commerce Commission be given authority to prosecute railroads to compel them to obey this order?—A. Yes; it is that form of amendment we desire, with some few changes, to the Cullom bill of the last Congress.

Q. Are you going to urge the Interstate Commerce Commission to prose te for the enforcement of this order of August 7?—A. That has not been decided yet. We will cross that bridge when we get to it.

Q. You say that order has been disregarded as far as you know?—A. I understand it will be. I have been told so by the traffic manager of one road. The bill which was introduced in the last Congress by Senator Cullom for the amendment of the interstate-commerce act is about what we want, with some few changes, which will not be material. The spirit of that bill is in accordance with our ideas.

Q. Please make a little fuller statement with regard to the cooperation which the millers' association expects to give the Interstate Commerce Commission.—A. The cooperation we expect to give them, you mean, in our effort to secure the enactment of the amendment?

Q. Yes.—A. I have been in consultation with some of the commissioners, and I think that their ideas for an amendment of the act are going to meet with ours very closely, and, unless something should come up which has not yet appeared, we shall indorse the bill which is approved by the commission.

Q. Do you know whether the lumbermen are going to cooperate, too?—A. The National Lumber Association has indicated its intention to do so.

Q. For this coming session, as I understand it?—A. Yes.

Q. That would give a pretty powerful force, would it not, these two associations?—A. There are so far 23, I believe, of the leading national commercial associations that we have been in correspondence with, that have indicated their desire and intention to work with us to secure this amendment by Congress. If the desire of the manufacturing public may have any effect on Congress, I think we will succeed.

Q. So far as you observe, the manufacturing and producing public are in support of the position taken by the association?—A. I think so.

Q. It is too early for you to say to what extent the railroads are agreed in their opposition, I suppose?—A. I do not anticipate very strong general objection on the part of the railroads to the amendment of this act. There will be some pretty strong opposition on the part of a few.

Q. In the southwest territory would that be?—A. Yes; there will be some opposition there, and my impression is there may be some from the East.

In regard to the matter of pooling, our view of it is that, under existing conditions, with the act as it is now, we certainly do not approve of so amending the law that railroads may be permitted to pool. When they show an inclination to obey the spirit of the law and to comply with it, and the law is in such shape that they will have to do so, then we have no objection whatever to pooling, provided the pooled rates be made subject to the approval of the commission, when they have mandatory power; but with the law as it is now, we will fight against that.

Q. (By Mr. C. J. HARRIS.) Well, without the existence of a pool do you not find that discriminations may be made to certain parties that are detrimental to the general body of your association?—A. But it would not be so difficult to overcome as discrimination made by a pool existing under approval of the commission. We figure that a pool would simply strengthen the railways under the present law in whatever position they might take, and until they have some distinctly controlling power over them in such matters, we do not believe in giving them any greater power than they have now. As I said a while ago, we go to the general traffic manager of a road and he refers us to the chairman of the traffic association, and we go to him and he throws us back again; so there is no recourse. We have no satisfaction from them, and yet they claim that they should be strengthened in their position by the power to pool. They are strong enough for us now.

Q. It has been stated here that the railroads had to regulate their price of transportation by the price of wheat in Liverpool; that they were governed almost entirely by that. Now, would that same rule apply to export flour?—A. I can not understand that the price of flour in Liverpool can regulate the cost of transportation in this country on either flour or wheat. I can see where the cost of transportation has and does affect the price of flour and wheat there, but I can not reverse the order of things.

Q. (By Professor JOHNSON.) If I remember, it was testified that the price of grain was not fixed in the Liverpool market for this country.—A. The assertion was made. I do not think there was any proof of it.

Q. What is your opinion; do you think the price at which grain is sold, for instance, on the Chicago market for export, is determined by the Liverpool quotations?—A. I think it very largely is.

Q. Well, do you think that the Liverpool quotation is, to any great extent, affected by the American transportation rates?—A. Yes, I think so. Of course where there is a published rate it becomes a part of the basis on which they figure to make the price. I am satisfied of that.

Q. Well, suppose the agitation which you are interested in, in connection with wheat and flour rates, should result in the raising of wheat rates, let us say, 10 per cent or 8 per cent, would that lessen the sales particularly?—A. I think it would lessen the sales of American wheat, and largely increase the sale of that wheat ground into flour. I think that it is not the wheat they want, but what is made out of the wheat that they must have; and I believe that if wheat is not shipped the flour will be, from this country, when conditions are such that it can be.

Q. You think if they could not get wheat they would have to buy our flour?—A. They would buy our flour; that has been shown. The wheat which they obtain from Argentine and India, to grind that alone, does not satisfy the demand there. They want flour made from our American hard wheat. There is a demand for it, and if they can not get it in the form of wheat, they will take it in flour, and I believe the loss in tonnage of wheat will be compensated for by the increase in tonnage of flour.

Q. If that is true, then the way to keep up the price of American wheat is to keep up the rates on wheat, transportation rates, is it not?—A. I do not know. We are not complaining on the rate on flour. In fact—and it is the peculiar condition of affairs—when we get before the railroads we do not ask for any lower rates on our product, but do ask for a higher rate on the raw material. It is a reasonable proposition.

Q. It would be much better for the American grain grower if the rates on export grain could be higher?—A. An advantage, certainly.

Q. It forces that grain into flour, and American flour abroad has such a strong position that it is able to fix the price?—A. Yes. Now, you will find, and I think I could prove to you, that if you leave it to the grower of the wheat he would rather find a regular market; and he would get a higher average price for wheat if he found that market in this country at the mill. You do not have to depend on the prices abroad for the exportation of it. It is collected to go into the elevators of the buyers, and these elevator companies offer a man so much money. Now, if he has no home market, in many cases if a milling business is cut down, and they can not buy his wheat, he must sell that wheat to the buyer for an elevator company, and when it is pushed forward he does not get the money out of the wheat that he would from his steady customer right there, from some miller who is grinding it and exporting what flour he does not sell in this country. The farmers understand it throughout the West and they would very much rather sell their wheat to the mills. I can point to cases where wheat has been sold for less money to the mill than the grower would have sold it to an exporting buyer.

Q. (By Professor Johnson.) Does the grain that is now shipped from our Pacific seaboard for the European markets reach there at approximately the same time that the grain reaches those markets from our central West, this side of the Rocky Mountains?—A. Well, I do not think there is any, except in Montana; not beyond Montana.

Q. Can the grain from California reach the European market as quickly as it can from Montana?—A. No.

Q. I saw in an article recently that with our present means of transporting from the Pacific to the European markets the Western cereals reached the European markets at approximately the same time that the cereals of the Eastern and central part of the United States were reaching the same markets, and the result was that a considerably lower range of prices for American cereals was realized than would be if the Western cereals would reach those markets considerably earlier. I would like to ask if this is a fact or not?—A. Well, I am not familiar with conditions except in wheat and flour. I do not think—in fact, I am positive that no wheat or flour from the Pacific coast States can reach Europe as quickly as flour that is shipped from east of the Rocky Mountains.

Q. (By Mr. Farquhar.) Is not a great deal of the grain of the coast now ground into flour and sold in the Orient?—A. Yes.

Q. (By Professor Johnson.) Is there not just as much variation in the freights from the Danubian principalities to Liverpool markets and from India to the Liverpool markets as from New York to Liverpool?—A. I am unable to answer that question; I do not know about it.

Q. (By Mr. Kennedy.) I believe you stated that the cost of transporting the wheat across the water did not affect the price of wheat and flour and did not affect the price of transporting to the seaboard in this country?—A. No; I meant to say that the export rate through from a Western point, say to a European port, is almost invariably figured on the basis of the export rate from that point to the seaboard, and then the rates from the seaboard are very frequently quoted from day to day by export agents there, as they can be obtained. The ship, for instance, will be ready to sail; if she can get so much more cargo within a certain time she will make a lower rate of export, and the agent will quote West his ocean rate. Now, that added to the regularly established rate to the seaboard, will be the export rate on that shipment, and if a request comes for a price on flour—a European request for the price of flour—it is quoted on the basis of the rate made by this steamship, sometimes a tramp and sometimes a regular steamer, plus the regularly established American railway rate.

Q. The gentleman who was here on Saturday as a representative of the city of St. Louis gave us an illustration which seemed to show why wheat was transported cheaper than flour. He said that a steamship might be at Newport News waiting for a cargo, and that it could easily get a cargo of grain when it could not get such a cargo of flour.—A. Yes; I have heard Mr. Vanlandingham say that. But I had agents for some years at every one of the Atlantic ports, watching and hastening forward our export business, and I have never yet seen a time when the docks of the transportation lines were not pretty well lined with flour, so that a flour cargo could be had if they wanted it; but they frequently let it lie there and made a bid for more flour, and if they happened to get it, they would take on the flour from the West; if not, they will load the flour on the dock. But I have never seen the time when they could not get flour for export to fill up a cargo. I have never experienced that. I do not mean to say that it has not occurred, because I do not know that.

Q. (By Mr. C. J. HARRIS.) I would like to ask you if this rate on wheat to New York would not work very materially in the interest of the seaboard towns as against the Western millers—this low rate on wheat to the East?—A. I have been talking entirely about the export wheat. Now, then, when wheat is shipped at the export rate it can not be unloaded at the seaboard; it must go abroad.

Q. That is the theory?—A. That is the theory.

Q. And the practice, probably?—A. And the practice, probably.

Q. So that does not enter into it at all?—A. No.

In regard to this matter of rates, I have another communication, that I picked up yesterday, that shows something of it. Now, the rate has been, from the Mississippi River to Chicago and Milwaukee, 7½; then from Chicago and Milwaukee to New York, 17 cents, making 24½ cents, the sum of the 2 local rates. I do not mean to say local flour rates; I mean the sum of the 2 export flour rates; that is, flour for export, 7½ cents from the Mississippi River to Chicago and Milwaukee, and 17 cents from Chicago to the seaboard, making 24½ cents. The railroads make an export rate from the Mississippi River to the seaboard of 12 cents, putting those millers east of the Mississippi River—for instance, we will say, of Milwaukee—at a disadvantage of 12½ cents. I have a letter from the Stern Milling Company, which says [reading]:

"SEPTEMBER 30, 1899.

"GEO. A. SCHROEDER, Esq.,
    "Mgr. Ch. of Com. Frt. Bureau, Milwaukee, Wis.

"DEAR SIR: On 'change yesterday morning we had a very vivid illustration of how the proportions of the cheap through rate from the Mississippi River on export wheat works to our detriment.

"There were several cars of wheat for sale at 71½ cents. The millers did not see their way to pay this pri e for the same, when they were sold to an exporter at 70 cents; and the seller of the wheat expressed the opinion that it paid him better to sell the wheat at 70 cents to the exporter than to sell at 71½ cents to the miller.

"The above illustration will show you how hard it is for us to buy wheat in competition with the exporter. We should like to have bought those 3 cars of wheat, but of course we could not buy them with so much advantage in favor of the exporter.

"Please submit the above to the proper officials for their enlightenment, and oblige,
    "Yours, very truly," etc.

That is simply an illustration of where discrimination works against us on local business. I think that is all in regard to rates that I have to offer.

Q. (By Mr. A. L. HARRIS.) When this case was heard before the Interstate Commerce Commission, were the railroads named in your petition present?—A. Yes.

Q. Now, as I understand from the law, as it now stands, no order is issued, but a mere notice to the railroads that such a finding was made?—A. The order has been issued—a formal order, as I understand it.

Q. The railroads may or may not pay any attention to that?—A. Yes.

Q. Then, you or the Interstate Commerce Commission have to take it to the circuit court?—A. Yes.

Q. When that gets there is it tried on the case you made in the Interstate Commerce Commission, or is it tried de novo, letting the railroad bring in all the evidence?—A. I have not taken a case that way to the court yet from the commission, but my impression is that it is tried de novo. I may be wrong about that.

Q. Up to that time you have no relief?—A. No.

Q. And the case being tried anew it may be a different case than the case you tried before the Interstate Commerce Commission?—A. Practically makes useless the effort that we originally made.

Q. Now, what you desire is to have an amendment to the law so that the Interstate Commerce Commission can enforce the orders they make, and if the railroads desire to take it to the circuit court they are to have that privilege?—A. That is the idea, yes.

Q. And then it is proper to open the case, maybe, in the circuit court?—A. Yes.

Q. And not a new case?—A. Yes; not a new one.

Q. One excuse that has been made for railroads charging more for wheat than for flour is that they are able to put a greater tonnage in the same car than they can of flour. Is that practical?—A. That is not true. They can load a car of flour to the same capacity that they can a car of wheat, but as I explained a while ago, when a car is ordered for loading wheat, they send one of the new large capacity cars of 70,000 pounds gross. They will send one of these and it will be loaded to its full capacity. A miller goes to a road and orders a car for flour for export and they will send him a 20,000-pound car to load with flour, and it will go. Now, the railroads show by facts and figures that the average car of wheat exceeds in weight, very far, the average car of flour; but we claim that is so, simply because they do not give us those big cars; and we showed it to the commission by facts and figures. We can load a car to its capacity to just as good an advantage with flour as with wheat. There is really nothing in that claim.

Q. You were speaking about the elevators being owned largely by the railroad companies, or officials of the railroad companies; does that elevator ownership extend along the lines of railroad?—A. Yes.

Q. As well as in the cities?—A. Yes.

Q. Are you acquainted with the condition of affairs in Chicago?—A. Somewhat.

Q. How many of the elevators, if you know, in Chicago are public elevators or warehouses?—A. Well, I can not say how many, but, you know, the Armour system of elevators there is a very prominent and strong system, and you know Mr. Armour's connection as a director of railroads would indicate that certain of the railroads may indirectly, if not directly, be interested in his system of elevators.

Q. How many railroads is Mr. Armour interested in?—A. It would be difficult for me to say that. I know he is a director of the Chicago, Milwaukee and St. Paul.

Q. How many railroads is Mr. Counselman interested in, or rather elevators on the particular lines of railroads?—A. I can not say.

Q. The railroads, or those in sympathy with the railroads, controlling the elevators out along the line of railroad—does not that work against the miller who wants to buy grain?—A. Well, I think it does. It would against the small miller, but some of the large millers have their own elevators, and they are interested in elevators to the extent that it makes them independent of control that would be injurious to them by the roads.

Q. Do the railroads give the millers an equal advantage—the miller's elevator—equal to the elevator owned by the firm in sympathy with the railroad?—A. I have not known anything to the contrary.

Q. Is there danger that such might be the case if the condition continued to spread, as now appears to be indicated?—A. Well, I think so, although, as I say, many of the small millers do get their wheat from farmers that bring it right into the hopper. The larger mills have their own elevators or have their interest in elevator systems that supply them, where they are sure of getting enough grain to run. I do not think there are many large mills that are dependent for their grain upon elevator systems owned and controlled by independent companies or railroads.

Q. Then, so far, the combination between the elevator firms and the railroads is not hurting the larger millers?—A. Only so far as the favoritism shown in the export rates on wheat has militated against the interests of the millers.

Q. Do you think that the elevator system as it now exists is beneficial to the farmer; is it conducive to his getting the highest price for his wheat?—A. Well, the general elevator system of the country, which is not connected directly with flour mills, I do not think is conducive, as conducted, to the profit of the farmer.

Q. (By Mr. RATCHFORD.) Do you include in that the elevators owned by independent companies?—A. No; I do not include them in that.

Q. (By Mr. C. J. Harris.) What I wished to bring out was this: Does he have any open market or is he in a pocket and forced to sell to these railroad elevators?—A. You will find that in the farming districts where they raise the wheat the prices are controlled largely by some elevator system.

Q. (By Senator Kyle.) If the farmers of the country possess their own elevators that will give them the means of carrying on their own business independently of them?—A. Yes.

Q. Do you know whether they ever entered into a combination with the elevator men of the West regulating the price of the grain?—A. No; I have never known of anything of that kind.

Q. (By Mr. Kennedy.) In reply to a question by Governor Harris you stated that you could load a car of given capacity as full of flour as you could with grain. Last week one witness explained to the commission how the car was filled to its utmost capacity with grain. I would like to have you explain how you place the same amount of flour in a car that you do of wheat?—A. The export flour is sacked exclusively; no barrel flour is ever exported; it is all sacked flour. Those sacks of flour will fill the car up to greater than the gross capacity at any time. It can be packed in.

Q. (By Mr. C. J. Harris.) Wheat never fills more than half the car?—A. No; it is filled up to the top of the grain doors. If you have more than that the running gear will break down; it will not stand the test. If you attempt to fill that car higher you will overload the car. Now when you put sacked flour into the car you can stack the sacks regularly within two feet of the roof, if necessary, putting it high in the ends and then coming toward the center doors and piling it up very easily.

Q. (By Mr. Kennedy.) I think this gentleman explained that men will go into the car and shovel the wheat into the corners and fill it up completely?—A. They do not fill the car anything like full to the top. They shovel the grain back, but they can not get above these grain doors or grain sides; otherwise the car would leak.

Q. (By Mr. C. J. Harris.) The grain doors are furnished by the railroads?—A. They are put to the expense of buying these grain doors in order to handle the wheat. There is another expense to them.

Q. (By Mr. Ratchford.) Can flour be loaded and shipped as cheaply by water as grain can?—A. I have no figures on that subject, but my belief is that it can not be handled as cheaply as grain.

Q. Do you believe there should be a slight difference by water?—A. I believe that, all things considered, it may cost a little more to handle flour by water than wheat.

Q. (By Mr. Farquhar.) Does this country ship much of the by-products of milling to Europe?—A. That has fallen off very largely.

Q. Is the reason that the American miller can not compete with the European miller in the by-products?—A. Yes; to some extent, there is a surplus of it.

Q. Can you find a market for all your by-product in this country?—A. It is sometimes difficult to.

Q. For instance, in the case of bran—have you not improvements now in your bran packers by which you can send, relatively, a great deal more than you used to to the European markets?—A. Yes.

Q. And yet you are not able to compete with the foreign miller?—A. The association which I have the honor to represent some years ago offered a prize for a bran packer which would produce certain results, and there was quite an effort made for a time to get such a packer, and it has been obtained and we can pack bran now, so far as weight and bulk are concerned that it can be shipped very advantageously; but the trouble is that we have no good export market for it now, owing to the fact that the wheat is carried over cheaper than our flour, and in that is carried our bran, etc., for the foreign miller to put on the market against us.

WASHINGTON, *October 10, 1899.*

TESTIMONY OF MR. GEORGE J. KINDEL.

Manufacturer, Denver, Colo.

The commission met at 2.30, Chairman Kyle presiding. Senator Kyle introduced the witness, Mr. George J. Kindel, of Denver, Colo., manufacturer of bedding, who, being first duly sworn, testified as follows concerning transportation:

Q. (By Senator Kyle.) Will you state your full name and address?—A. George J. Kindel; address, Denver, Colo.

Q. And your business?—A. The manufacturing of bedding.

I would say that my complaint is that my city, Denver, and State, Colorado, and all the territory embraced in the one hundred and fifth meridian section is violently discriminated against by the railroads and express company; that we are denied commercial equality, which forbids the development of our resources and the sacred right and duty of making ourselves sustaining. Our freight rates are anywhere from 100 to 300 per cent higher per ton per mile than those of our Eastern and Western com petitors.

My first complaint of railroad discrimination to the Interstate Commerce Commission was filed in February, 1892. In the spring of 1895 I learned that the Colorado Fuel and Iron Company had also filed a complaint, which was set for hearing in 30 days. I came on to Washington to learn why my complaint was not given a hearing. Judge Morrison, then chairman, called up the secretary and learned from him that for some reason or other it was pigeonholed. Judge Morrison suggested that I make an amended complaint and that both the Colorado Fuel and Iron Company and my complaint be heard at the same time.

The trial was held in May, 1895, in Denver. The result of the Colorado Fuel and Iron Company hearing was a ruling by the Interstate Commerce Commission that the railroads be made to carry their products from Pueblo to San Francisco for 75 per cent of the Chicago rate. Previous to the hearing, rails were carried from Chicago through Pueblo, or even via New Orleans, to San Francisco for 60 cents per hundredweight, while they were charging the Colorado Fuel and Iron Company $1.60 per hundredweight, notwithstanding the 1,000 miles shorter haul.

In my case, in behalf of Denver City, I was never given a ruling by the commission. On my product—comforters—I was obliged to pay $3 per hundredweight, Denver to San Francisco, while my competitors at Missouri River points—Chicago, St. Louis, and New York—were paying only $1 per hundredweight. At the hearing in Denver the traffic managers of the transcontinental lines wished to appease me, and gave me the $1 on comforters to San Francisco and southern California points without any order or ruling from the Interstate Commerce Commission.

My blanket complaint to the Interstate Commerce Commission covered the rates and classification to and from Denver, east, west, and south. In my opinion, the interstate law is an expensive farce, and unless the commission is given powers, as was suggested in the proposed Cullom bill, it will continue to simply be a subterfuge to railroads, who now fear it about as much as a bad boy would a cast-iron bulldog. The interstate law should be either strengthened and enforced or abolished. As it stands to-day it is simply an expensive statistical bureau. Of the personnel of the commission I take pleasure in saying (of those whom I have met, notably Judge Clements, of Georgia) that they are brainy and honorable men. The best address on transportation I ever heard was delivered by Judge Clements in Denver about 2 months ago. It would profit every American citizen to read it. By the way, he had a thing in point there, an extract from a speech of ex-President Harrison on the enforcing of the act or giving the commission power to act, in which he said: "In the Senate, when the bill was under consideration, ex-President Harrison, then a Senator, with great force and clearness stated the public grievance and the necessity for a remedy. He said:

"'What is it that the people complain of? What is the just grievance at the bottom of this great popular clamor against the railroad companies? I think, as both these bills admit, just two things: First, extortion, the charging, especially for local freight, of unreasonable rates, thus unduly burdening the local traffic for the maintenance of the railway; and, secondly, and chiefly, discriminations between shippers of the same class.

"'Mr. President, I do not stop to prove the existence of these evils. They are confessed of all fair men. I do not stop to prove—for proof is not needed—that the railroad companies, by these discriminations between individuals and between localities and by the unrestrained exercise of the power to establish rates, have assumed and do now exercise a most dangerous and unwarranted control over the commerce of this country.

"'I would regard it as an utterly futile piece of legislation if we should pass here a bill simply declaring the common law upon this subject.

"'What is the trouble? It is that the shipper needs to be reenforced in his contest with the railroad company. If some should ask me why it is, if the exaction of an unreasonable rate is now unlawful and the excess may be recovered back, that shippers do not recover it back; or if one should ask me why it is, if discriminations are illegal, that shippers do not expose them and recover their damages, my answer would be that it is an unequal contest to which the shipper is invited.

" ' I think, then, I may declare, with the approval of those who listen to me, that egislation upon this subject to be efficient must reenforce the shipper in his contest with these great railroad corporations.' "

In this same address Judge Clements stated that statistics prove that the entire volume of money in the United States was only $24.70 per capita, while the railroad earnings amounted to $16 per capita per annum; also, the earnings of the railroads amounted to over $1,200,000,000, while the entire income of Government dues amounted to but $500,000,000; in other words, the income of railroads exceeded that of our Government by 140 per cent.

As to my individual railroad experiences, I would say that I was driven out of the manufacturing of upholstering goods in Denver, and later that of spring beds, and more recently had to start the manufacturing of a silk album in Chicago because of discrimination in freight rates. The reason of that was, the rates were, books, Chicago to San Francisco, $1.75 per hundred; Denver to San Francisco, $3 per hundred. Paper and raw material, Chicago to Denver, 97 cents; making, to be added together, deducting the Chicago rate, a handicap of $2.22 per 100 pounds; and therefore I started the plant in Chicago. I intended to annex it to my mattress factory—the steam plant I have there—but I did not see how I could do it. Reversing the proposition, from Chicago to New York books are 75 cents per hundred, while from Denver to New York they are $2.72 a hundred. This explains that freight rates, and not demonetization of silver, have lost us our manufactories, a few of which I enumerate. Denver once had prosperous woolen mills, powder mills, nail factory, shoe factory, saddle factory, glass works, cement works, cooper shops, implement factory, hardware manufactory, car shops, rolling mills, envelope factory, match factory, mattress factory, white lead works, paper mills, etc.

Q. (By Mr. Phillips.) Are they in existence now?—A. No; they are all idle buildings. Denver is perhaps the only town where so much could be lost and never missed. I want to emphasize here that our Senator Teller recently made a statement—I picked it up in New York; a copy of the Republican of September 23—in which he goes on to say that the silver question is not a local matter. We can see its application in Colorado in that our industries are lessening daily, and it is naturally a question vital to us. But I will say here that if silver was 16 to 1 or even 6 to 1, if you please, that with the discriminatory freight rates of 100 to 300 per cent higher than anybody else pays, you can not establish any manufactories. That stands to reason. Now, in this case of the Colorado Fuel and Iron Company, rails at that time were 60 cents, iron bars 60 cents, iron billets and blooms 50 cents, while from Colorado and Pueblo, at which we have our great Colorado Fuel and Iron Plant, they were $1.60; and the railroads in that case, I remember, under oath stated that they had to carry the freight from Chicago to New Orleans, thence via the southern line to California, for 60 cents. They were making a profit. When you remember and reflect that after the rails got to New Orleans from Chicago they were 130 miles farther from their destination than at the initial point, it seems preposterous. But the commission in this case did make a ruling, and it was upheld by Judge Hallett of the United States court. In my case I have not had a ruling.

Q. (By Mr. Kennedy.) What was the ruling?—A. The Interstate Commerce Commission made a ruling and the judge upheld it. It was 75 per cent of the Chicago rate. That is the ruling. It is 45 cents now, instead of $1.60. They have reduced it that difference.

Q. (By Mr. C. J. Harris.) I do not think you understand the gentleman. This ruling was not in regard to your product, but in regard to the Colorado Fuel and Iron Company's product.—A. Oh, yes; it was that.

Q. They made no ruling in your case?—A. Not in my case, and I am here to find out why I am not getting a ruling.

Q. (By Mr. Kennedy.) That is what you came to Washington for?—A. Well, that and to come before you here.

Q. (By Representative Livingston.) Have we general prosperity now in this country?—A. I think we have in every place except Colorado.

Q. Have discriminating freight rates brought about that general prosperity?—A. I do not know whether any place is discriminated against like us.

Q. You are representing your local city?—A. Yes; Denver.

Q. Have you general prosperity at Denver?—A. No.

Q. Nobody prospering out there?—A. Yes; I am prospering to-day.

Q. Who is it that does not get a fair show in Denver?—A. All these different mills.

Q. What are they manufacturing?—A. The woolen mills that we had there have gone, and we have lost them, and to-day one of the great complaints we have to make is that the railroads charge a higher rate for the raw material than they do for the manufactured product.

Q. (By Mr. C. J. HARRIS.) Some of these concerns have been gone a long time, have they not?—A. In the past 10 years or more; gradually going.

Q. (By Mr. KENNEDY.) Do you get rebates or have you any discriminations made in your favor by the railroad companies?—A. Yes; and everybody that is prosperous.

Q. Will you explain to the commission how you secure such favoritism from the railroads?—A. By comparison of rates. For instance, one of the products I use is palm fibre from Africa.

Q. (By Representative LIVINGSTON.) You mix that with the wool?—A. No; mix it with cotton.

Q. Is not that a fraud on the consumer?—A. No: we brand it to you. We tell you on the face of it.

Q. That is adulterated stuff?—A. No; it is not adulterated at all. It is pure palm fibre (a plant).

Q. Why do you put that in with the cotton?—A. We advertise a palm fibre cotton-top mattress, and we sell it to you as such.

Q. You put it in because you get it cheaper than cotton?—A. The people want it. You come to me and want an all-fibre mattress, and I will sell it to you cheaper than I would a palm fibre cotton top.

Q. (By Mr. KENNEDY.) Please explain why it is that you get these favorable rates, and why these industries that were knocked out of Denver could not have gotten the same favoritism from the railroad companies?—A. I can not answer any more than that we had large jobbing houses, and they are gone.

Q. Tell us how you get the favoritism?—A. I told you, by comparison of rates. I will take New York as a basing point. I ship by Galveston to Denver, Omaha being relatively the same distance. From New York to Galveston they get a 59-cent rate, and we have a tariff that gives a $1.17 rate. I can not compete because the Omaha man comes back into my territory with these same goods and undersells me.

Q. You can bring these goods around by water and up from Galveston cheaper than the rate across the country from New York?—A. Oh, not necessarily that. There are these dispatch lines which run over all the roads, or nearly so, all over the country. There are the Lake route, the Newport News route, and the Kanawha dispatch, and the Cumberland. There are 6 of them; I can not recollect the names of all of them.

Q. (By Mr. RATCHFORD.) Do other shippers to and from the same points receive the same rates?—A. In Denver?

Q. Yes.—A. I do not know.

Q. You do not know whether they are paying a higher rate to the same points?—A. No; I do not know what others are paying. I know that the tariff is $1.17. I know I am not paying the tariff, and I feel that I am a rebater, subject to the law, and I dislike that sort of thing; I deprecate it.

Q. (By Mr. PHILLIPS.) Do you or do you not get rebates as against other people in Denver engaged in the same industry that you are?—A. Perhaps; I do not know. I presume I must, because the tariff is $1.17, and I am not paying the tariff.

Q. You have reason to believe that others engaged in the same line of business with you are paying the tariff?—A. I do not know of anything different. There is the tariff. They may be all alike. They may get a better rebate than I do for all I know.

Q. (By Representative LIVINGSTON.) Well, if they give you rebates, how can you complain of their rates?—A. I complain of the tariff they have in effect.

Q. If you get all the rebates you want, why do you complain?—A. I do not get all I want.

Q. You want more?—A. I want simply fair freight rates, so that I can compete with other people in my section. As I told you a while ago, I manufacture a book in Chicago. The rate from Chicago to San Francisco is $1.75, while from Denver·to San Francisco it is $3 a hundred. Now I would like to see those rates just. I can not see why Denver, being 1,000 nearer the Pacific coast, should pay $1.25 more than does Chicago, 1,000 miles further off.

Q. (By Mr. RATCHFORD.) What is the rate from Denver to Chicago?—A. $2.05.

Q. It would be cheaper almost for you to ship your material from Chicago by way of San Francisco?—A. Yes. We have done that on oil. Coal oil has been shipped from Chicago to San Francisco and back again.

Q. (By Mr. C. J. HARRIS.) Have you made a proper representation of these differences to the railroad authorities?—A. Yes, indeed; I have for the past 10 years.

Q. How many different lines have you in Denver?—A. I believe there are 12.

Q. How many to the coast?—A. To the coast—the Sante Fe makes a pretense to that business, the Rio Grande, the Midland and the Union Pacific. I guess that is all.

Q. You have 3 at least?—A. Yes.

Q. Do you mean to say that, after consultation with these 3 lines to the coast, they refused to take your business at a rate less than this same classification is carried from Chicago to the Pacific coast?—A. Until I made complaint to the Interstate Commerce Commission and had them there at the hearing. Then they offered to make me a dollar rate on comforters. I was paying $3.

Q. (By Senator KYLE.) On that one article alone?—A. Yes.

Q. How did they explain their extortionate charges before?—A. They do not try to make any explanations.

Q. (By Representative LIVINGSTON.) Do they not offer this explanation, that their train is made up at Chicago for the Pacific coast, and that they can haul through loads from Chicago on a much less tariff than they could stop at your place and take on additional cars and an additional amount?—A. Their chief explanation has always been water competition, but I have exploded that theory. They allege that water competition is the controlling factor. I recognize water competition as a controlling factor, but I deny that if the rate is 75 cents from New York, all rail overland to the Pacific coast, that Missouri River points should be given a 50-cent rate. The only argument I can see that they might advance is because of its proximity to the Pacific coast. But they also alleged that the ships did actually absorb the inland freights to the Atlantic coast and carried them around by the Horn. I then assumed that the railroads should raise their rates, add the 30 cents, if you please, that the ships absorbed, to the Missouri River rate of 75 cents, and the New York rate, and that would make it $1.05 instead of 50 cents. And we proved at the hearing that they actually had 75 cents from New York and 50 cents at Omaha, but when you struck Denver, it was $1.60 to Pacific coast points on the same articles. So your train making would apply to Missouri River points. It ought to affect them more seriously there than at Denver. There, you understand, they make it less.

Q. You can not ship by water at Denver?—A. No; not unless down the Platte River, and that is not very big.

Q. (By Mr. CONGER.) You are on water competition on the Missouri River practically?—A. They have had 3 steamboats. One burned up, and another sold out, and I do not know what became of the other.

Q. (By Mr. C. J. HARRIS.) If you can show these railroad companies that there is a profit in handling your business—these railroads are not overrun with other business, are they, at the present time?—A. No; not too much.

Q. Why is it that they are not anxious to build up industries and increase the freight on their lines?—A. I presume it is because the directors of the roads do not live in Denver; they live east. And the traffic managers in Denver, I will say, are my best friends. We have often argued the question why it should be. It is incomprehensible.

Q. (By Senator KYLE.) What is the eastern terminus of the Denver and Rio Grande?—A. Denver.

Q. So that the trains to the Pacific coast are not in competition with Chicago in that case?—A. I believe most of their freight goes by Pueblo; the B. & M. brings it to the D. & R. G. at Denver, and they take it on and pull it through.

Q. That one road is interested in building up Denver; it should be, in the nature of the case?—A. Yes.

Q. Where do the stockholders of that road live?—A. New York.

Q. (By Mr. C. J. HARRIS.) Have you been discriminated against, in comparison with people in the same line of manufacture?—A. Yes; I believe so, though I do not know exactly what the other people got. They brag on it, that they were keeping their heads shut and were getting the better of Kindel.

Q. (By Representative LIVINGSTON.) How about the Pacific Traffic Bureau; do you belong in Denver to it? Do you know anything about it?—A. No; any more than the St. Louis people invited me to intervene in behalf of Denver. That suit is substantially the same as I brought before the commission.

Q. Are you in that suit, of the St. Louis Traffic Bureau?—A. No; I am not in the Traffic Bureau, but they have invited me to participate or intervene on behalf of our section, in this suit.

Q. (By Mr. C. J. HARRIS.) Are there any other manufacturers of the same line of goods as yours in Denver?—A. Yes.

Q. How many others?—A. There are two of nearly equal size, and there are several smaller ones; that is, small shops.

Q. Do they complain of rates?—A. Yes; they necessarily see that they are damaged.

Q. Do they unite with you in this general demand?—A. No.

Q. Is your statement that they have better rates simply hearsay?—A. It is repeated to me from them; that is, through a third party. I will say this, that our chamber of commerce, that ought to look after this thing, even went so far as to petition the Interstate Commerce Commission to grant the petition of the railroads to abrogate section 4, Colorado westward, and that I was the only mortal man out of all the community west of the line from Duluth, Minn., to Sabine Pass, Tex., on which the transcontinental lines draw their arbitrary and imaginary line, who protested, and I am glad to say I won.

Q. (By Mr. KENNEDY.) Is there any business similar to yours at Pueblo, Colo.?—A. Yes.

Q. Do they complain that they are discriminated against in the interest of building up Denver?—A. I guess they do, to an extent.

Q. Do not the people of Pueblo complain that your railroads discriminate in favor of Denver generally, for the purpose of retarding the growth of Pueblo?—A. Yes; as we do at Denver. For instance, Pueblo gets a minimum rate of $1 on some products, while we are paying $2.60 from Denver to the Pacific coast. Now, that looks remarkable.

Q. Do you believe Pueblo is discriminated against in the interest of Denver?—A. Yes; in the same ratio that Denver is.

Q. Well, in the interest of Denver?—A. In some sections, yes; on some products.

Q. This is the idea: Do they not complain that the railroads desire to build up the city of Denver, and therefore discriminate against the city of Pueblo?—A. I have heard that statement made by shippers and manufacturers of Pueblo.

Q. Do you believe that is true?—A. Not to any great extent.

Q. (By Mr. PHILLIPS.) In some articles Pueblo gets an advantage over Denver, as I understand you?—A. No; it is not on the articles, but it is in some of the total rates. For instance, the first-class rate, Denver, off 125 miles, is only 15 cents, while the regular rate is 52 cents, I think. In that way they get the better at the nearby points of Pueblo westward.

Q. (By Mr. FARQUHAR.) Mr. Kennedy asked you a question there that you did not hardly answer as fully, I think, as the commission would like. Is there any discrimination in respect to State commerce; discriminating on local rates, as between Pueblo and Denver?—A. No.

Q. You know of nothing of that kind?—A. No.

Q. And the question of discrimination lies in interstate commerce?—A. Interstate.

Q. (By Mr. RATCHFORD.) You know that the citizens of Pueblo make complaint to that effect, do you not?—A. Yes; they make complaint. They reduced the regular first-class rates from 52 cents to 15 cents to meet Pueblo on the line westward.

Q. Is that regarded by the shippers of Pueblo as being a discrimination against their city?—A. Yes.

Q. Do the shippers from Denver get that 15 cent rate?—A. Yes.

Q. Is it uniform between them?—A. Yes.

Q. No discrimination between shippers from that point?—A. Not that I know of; never heard of any.

Q. (By Mr. KENNEDY.) Are you a member of the chamber of commerce of Denver or any other commercial body out there?—A. I used to be.

Q. Not now?—A. No.

Q. Is it composed of representative business men of the city of Denver?—A. Yes.

Q. Are they making any complaint similar to yours?—A. No; because they are all rebated. General Irving Hale, who gained fame in the Philippines, said of the railroads——

Q. (By Mr. C. J. HARRIS, interrupting.) What would be his ground for knowing much about the railroad situation?—A. He lived there. He was the manager of the General Electric Company. I quote him as a very exceptional man. He is the man that took the highest graduate per cent at West Point college. He is an authority on many things. He said: "With our wonderful variety of raw materials, manufacturing should be the foundation of Colorado's prosperity. Freight discriminations, the great barrier against manufacturing development and the worst obstacle to our general progress, not excepting silver demonetization, should be removed." He is a man of broad views.

Q. (By Representative LIVINGSTON.) He disagrees with you then?—A. No.

Q. He does not say that the demonitization of silver had nothing to do with it?—A. No; I did not say it had nothing to do with it. I say in the same manner, in the same sense, I mean, that it is freight discrimination and not free silver that has knocked out these factories. And I repeat that if silver were 16 to 1, or even 6 to 1, if there could be such a thing, that with the freight rates as they are, you can not build up manufactures in Colorado.

Q. (By Mr. C. J. HARRIS.) I should like to ask you if, as a manufacturer, you would say that Denver is well adapted as a manufacturing and distributing center for the rest of the United States?—A. At least westward.

Q. Are you not too far removed from the markets to bring your raw material out there and manufacture it and send it back to the centers of population? Can you hope for anything of that kind?—A. No; I do not hope for that.

Q. Is it the railroads or is it your geographical position that prevents it?—A. It is the railroads. Understand me, I do not mean that we should bring our hardwood from the East or iron from the East, or such materials as that, to manufacture implements in Colorado. That would be out of the question. But I do contend that where we have wool and coal that we ought to be able to manufacture woolen goods. We ought to be allowed to ship those goods out in competition with others and not at a higher rate per ton per mile.

Q. Are not your wages higher there in proportion to other parts of the country?—A. Necessarily they have to be higher, because railroad rates make everything else higher. I will give you another illustration. Sugar is carried from San Francisco to Denver at 75 cents; to Loveland it is 93 cents; but on farther, to Omaha, it is only 50 cents. There is another thing we complain of. Rates between St. Louis and Galveston. I will just mention the first class are, either way, $1.30 a hundred. Denver to Galveston is $1.30, but from Galveston to Denver is $1.80. And when you come down to the lower classes, say to the third class, Denver pays $1.10 from Galveston and 97 cents to Galveston. St. Louis, in either direction, has 97 cents.

Q. (By Mr. KENNEDY.) Is not Denver an exceptionally favored city as far as railroad rates are concerned?—A. No.

Q. Do you not say that they are all rebaters out there?—A. Well, I do not call that favorable if a man has to violate the law to live in the land. I stand self-confessed, but I deplore that condition.

Q. Are all the rest of them criminals, too?—A. Yes.

Q. (By Mr. FARQUHAR.) What is your transcontinental line from Denver?—A. They are part of all these running from New York through. Twenty-one roads (or lines) make up the transcontinental tariff.

Q. Now, is there any difference between your classification and your rate on the Santa Fe and what it would be if you took the Union Pacific up to Greeley?—A. No; the same thing. They are pooled.

Q. What effect has the Southern Pacific on your rates?—A. None East and North, but to Pacific slope and Gulf of Mexico the Southern Pacific practically controls rates.

Q. You can not get a better Pacific slope rate by reaching Texas and then coming up from Galveston on the Southern, can you, than you have by the through line?—A. No; because our railroads have seen fit, even when the war was on between the Mallory and the Lone Star lines, to fix an arbitrary rate onto the prevailing rate, say, of 25 cents a hundred; so we got no benefit. And in answer to your last question I would say that the Southern Pacific is a factor, and it has destroyed many of our rates. For instance, gloves from San Francisco to Denver, $2 a hundred. You ship the same packages back from Denver, which has 5,000 feet of elevation, to San Francisco, at the sea level, downhill, like a toboggan slide, and it is $3 a hundred downhil. to $2 up. So we can not begin to compete.

Q. (By Mr. C. J. HARRIS.) Well, there are two large mountain ranges more to cross, are there not, in going from the coast to Denver?—A. Yes, you must cross four; but the proposition remains the same. The initial point, Denver, is at 5,000 feet elevation, while San Francisco is at the sea level.

Q. You can not figure the rate on a mountain railroad that you can on the New York Central, that is down grade from the lake right down to New York City?—A. Oh, no. But under those circumstances I deny the right of the railroad to make a higher charge to Denver than they do to other points beyond.

Q. (By Mr. PHILLIPS.) Will you go on in your own way and state the discriminations against yourself and against others specifically? Have you any information that you could give the commission along that line?—A. I could give you a number of articles here to show you a comparison of rates. For instance, Chicago to California terminals, a 2,500-mile haul, boots and shoes, $1.50 a hundred. Chicago to Colorado common points, which include Denver, Pueblo, and 200 other stations, from Trinidad to Cheyenne, it is $2.05. If we want to ship those boots and shoes from Denver again to California points, we pay another $3, making $5.05. That is the proposition. I see you have a map here and the best way is to illustrate it on that [indicating on wall map of the United States]. Here is Chicago, Denver, and St. Joe; that would be a Missouri River point. Chicago to St. Joseph, Mo., the freight rate is 80 cents a hundred. From St. Joseph to the Pacific coast it is $1.50, the same as it is from Chicago. And this will illustrate why Marshall Field and Farwell and some of the larger jobbing houses we had in Denver had to withdraw from Denver and fall back to the Missouri River and east of that. The shipper on the Missouri River from Chicago can get his goods there for 80 cents and reship them to San Francisco for $1.50, while from Chicago to Denver it is $2.05, and from Denver to

San Francisco it is $3. We have had it to Galveston, Tex., and El Paso, Tex. Our first-class rates were, when I got Kindel's A. B. C. on freight rates out, from here to there, a 781-mile haul, $2 a hundred, while from Chicago to El Paso it was $1.62 a hundred.

Q. (By Mr. KENNEDY.) With your rebate, what did you actually pay?—A. I did not happen to ship to El Paso, and I was not subject to rebates, because I was fighting too hard. I was not in position to get rebates. Now I will just illustrate this, if you will allow me, in the old kindergarten fashion [pinning paper over Colorado on map]. We will assume that represents the State of Colorado; just follow it now. This is a large ranch, we will call it, inside of the State. We will assume that Denver is here. I come along to you gentlemen, and I say, "Gentlemen, I would like to build a toll road through your ranch." You agree on condition that I pay the expense, which means taxes, for keeping up the barbed-wire fences, and that I give you reasonable and fair rates. After having opened the toll road, I carry goods from your neighbor, Chicago, to Denver and charge you $2.05. I carry the same goods right on through to San Francisco for $1; the whole haul for $1.

Q. (By Mr. PHILLIPS.) Clear through to San Francisco?—A. Yes. Now, you complain to me and say, "Kindel, this is not according to agreement. I have given you this right of way through my ranch. Why do you do it?" Well, I will tell you it is water competition, some changing of the haul, or something or other. And I say, "I do not want any of your Populist ideas." You are for a time pacified. After a little you get overloaded on the goods you have been shipping in from Chicago and you wish to dispose of them. You find a market at San Francisco, and you come to me and say, "Kindel, what are you going to ask me for getting these goods on through to 'Frisco?" I tell you $3 a hundred. That makes $5.05. You begin to howl about this time and ask me what I mean by such an outrage. You say, "I have paid you $2.05. Now you charge me $3, while you carry the same goods from Chicago to San Francisco through my ranch for $1." And you get mad and say, "You take up your old road and get out of here, and I will put up a barbed-wire fence myself." That is the whole situation. I have given you one of the most violent cases. There are things just like it out there. It is just like that book freight case I was showing you. The rate from Chicago to San Francisco is $1.75. I pay 97 cents for the paper. When I want to ship from Denver to San Francisco I pay $3, making $3.97 against $1.75. Now, how can I manufacture books in Denver when I have to pay this double rate, as against Chicago paying $1.75? Going from Denver to New York I pay $2.72, and I pay from Chicago to New York only 75 cents. I just threw up my hands and started up my plant in Chicago. That is the reason why our factories are leaving us.

There is another remarkable thing here. There is one thing we are denied in Colorado, and that is commodity rates. There is a distinction between class rates and commodity rates. They give it any sort of a name to suit their convenience—terminal points, common points, and all other points, and God knows what not. The commodity rates on cotton piece goods from Boston to the Missouri River is 52 cents a hundred. From the Missouri River to Denver it is $1.25; 250 per cent higher freight rate for one-third of the haul. These same goods going through Denver to California are $1. If you stop them in Denver it is $1.75.

Q. (By Representative LIVINGSTON.) Have you a railroad commission in Colorado?—A. No; I am sorry to say that we are the only State out of 37 or more States that have had commissions that has allowed the railroads to repeal the act; and I was very much amused this summer to see that the railroad commissioners of the several States had their convention in the city that is paying one-third higher freight rates than any other city of its size on earth.

Q. Is not your remedy to go back and get your State commission organized there?—A. Yes; but you can not do it. I have lost hope. I simply mean to plod on the best I can and sell out and go to Australia. I am getting tired. I can not stand it much longer.

Q. Do the railroads handling the through traffic of Colorado and the West take any part in politics, as corporations?—A. Not as corporations.

Q. Do the officers take part in politics?—A. Yes.

Q. Has that had anything to do with the discriminations against your people?—A. I think so. They have elected officers that will do their bidding.

Q. (By Mr. PHILLIPS.) Have they been known to lobby against or in favor of them?—A. Against.

Q. (By Mr. RATCHFORD.) Are they ever known to defeat candidates opposed to their interests?—A. Decidedly.

Q. Can you give the commission any specific cases?—A. No; I only know 1 was in politics; got into it by this very presentation of discriminative freight rates.

Q. (By Representative LIVINGSTON.) If you should harmonize yourself with the politics of the railroads would they not stop these discriminations against you?—A. Well, I guess I have harmonized myself. That is why I am living on rebates.

Q. (By Mr. KENNEDY.) You say they are all harmonized; they are all rebaters?—A. All the prominent people and prosperous people. The thing is, it stands as a disgrace to the Government of the United States to allow the poor people to bear the brunt and the burden of taxation, whether railroad or otherwise. There is no sense, no logic, no consistency in the rates they make. You take coal oil. We have coal-oil fields in Colorado, and yet our coal oil costs 100 per cent more to-day in Denver than it does in Chicago. Take gasoline. I got fooled on it this spring. I bought a gasoline engine, figuring out the cost per hour, what it would be at a price of 7 or 9 cents per gallon. I bought the engine and attached it to my waterworks. To my surprise, the first gasoline I bought—I expected to pay 5 or 10 per cent more, but I did not expect to pay a hundred per cent higher. Our freight rates to the Standard Oil Company on oil from Colorado common points to the Pacific coast are 96 cents, while from Chicago right through our oil field there, it is 78½ cents; and the oil wells are controlled by the Standard people.

Q. (By Mr. C. J. HARRIS.) They control the Colorado output?—A. Yes. They buy the oil, for instance, from the several owners, and pay them so much, and they refine it.

Q. (By Representative LIVINGSTON.) Is it not true that between San Francisco and New York there is a wonderful competition in trade?—A. Yes; I guess there is.

Q. Is not that one reason why, going through to San Francisco, these cheap rates are given from Chicago; trying to divert the trade to the Pacific slope instead of going to the Atlantic coast?—A. Yes; it is competition all the time.

Q. It is competition between California and New York which oppresses you, and water transportation rates?—A. I will not say that at all. I will show you a sample where water competition had nothing to do with it at all. Machinery manufactured at Chicago is shipped to Denver at 80 cents a hundred—carload. The same thing goes through Denver to Salt Lake for 80 cents a hundred.

Q. What is it the other way?—A. I do not know; it is less usually. Let me point out. The point I want to make is that the paralleling of railroads is not the remedy to get fair rates.

Q. Not if one company owns all of them?—A. No; they are separate, decidedly separate. Their earnings, I know, are always pooled, but they are hostile to each other in every other way. We will assume one of you is a jobber of Chicago machinery at Denver; we will assume that another gentleman is a jobber at Salt Lake; we will assume I live at Grand Junction, Colo., here [indicating]. I want to buy 5,000 pounds of machinery. Where shall I get it? Certainly, with the patriotic spirit we all should have, I would like to buy the goods at Denver, but I am barred. Why? Because I should pay $1.75 from Denver to Grand Junction [indicating], while from Salt Lake back I pay only $1.10; 65 cents higher than for the farther distance. They have to carry through Grand Junction and back again, and yet I save 65 cents. In this case they have only the Western Rio Grande, but here we have the Midland and the Denver Rio Grande. Yet many people in our State believe the whole remedy lies in paralleling railroads. We have another here [indicating]. We have the foolishness of three railroads between Denver and Pueblo; three lines and three railroads operating over the lines. Rates have been reduced time and again, but they have not been reduced in the last 15 years or more between Denver and Trinidad; and yet we have three lines doing a starvation business.

Q. (By Mr. PHILLIPS.) Are there any companies or individuals refining oil near Denver, where you have a considerable oil field?—A. No; they have been knocked out by the Standard Oil Company.

Q. How?—A. By reducing the price of such and such a product. They did sell oil for 5 cents, and it lasted until they had them all out, and now it is 100 per cent higher than any other section of the country. It was so the last time I investigated it.

Q. Is there any competition there in the petroleum business?—A Not that I know of; it is all controlled by the Standard Oil Company.

Q. Not among yourselves or from abroad?—A. No. The prohibitive freight rates bar anybody from coming in. You can not play in.

Q. Do the Standard Oil Company or not ship oil from a distance; or do they refine the oil produced in your own field?—A. They produce most of it there.

Q. And refine it there?—A. Yes.

Q. Do they own the wells?—A. No; some of our wealthy men own the wells and sell the supply to them. I do not know but they do own some of the wells. I know Senator Hill is represented as being a large owner of oil wells. He does not refine anything, but produces it, and they refine it, and they control the market price. I complained of the excessive price of the oil to the Standard Oil managers, and they gave me this statement I have just made, that they had to buy the oil from Senator Hill and refine it: "Why don't you kick about them as well as us?"

Q. Have you any local directors on these lines of road living in Colorado?—A. We did have one; he is dead.

Q. You have none?—A. I do not know of any.

Q. Has there not been a great deal of complaint in the handling of petroleum in your section by the Standard Oil Trust?—A. Yes. The Pueblo people tried to interest me in a fight on the rate on oil, in which they proved they were denied the rate from Pueblo to the Pacific coast points that the Missouri River points had. They quietly made a price to compete with the Missouri River, and when the Standard Oil Company found that the oil emanated from the Florence wells they refused to receive it. I have a bunch of correspondence on that matter; but I could not take it up because I was too busy with other things. I have the correspondence yet.

Q. (By Mr. C. J. HARRIS.) How long has your State railroad commission been abolished?—A. Since 1893.

Q. Has there been any effort to reestablish it?—A. I tried it, but the railroads outdid me.

Q. Is there anything further you would like to testify to?—A. I have some rates here if you would like to go into the matter more extensively. Here are some of the things that catch Denver hard. I was an importer of metallic beds. I could ship metallic beds from Liverpool via Gulf to Denver $75 per car cheaper than I could ship from New York or Birmingham, Conn., via Gulf to Denver. I pleaded with the traffic managers to let me buy those goods in this country. It was the $75 per car more that stood in my way, but I could get no hearing until I finally failed in business and suffered the humiliation of an assignment through excess of freight. To-day I think that this is true. Crockery from Trenton, New Jersey, to San Francisco is 95 cents; Trenton to Denver, $1.53; from England via Gulf to Denver, $1.22. The crockery we are getting is chiefly from England. On oilcloth and linoleum—here is where they catch us on most of the commodity rates—Missouri River to Colorado common points, third class, 80 cents; Missouri River to Utah common points, third class, $1.55; but a Utah man ships his goods in under "commodity" tariff, and instead of paying $1.55 he pays $1.09. They have no "commodity" tariff to Denver. In the western classification oilcloth and linoleum are third class, but here they make it a "commodity," and instead of charging the class rate from Missouri River to California common points, third class, $2, they are shipped Missouri River to California common points, "commodity," 75 cents. So, you see, in that case the Missouri River rate to California common points is 75 cents, while from the Missouri River to Colorado common points it is 80 cents; 5 cents higher than if it went on 1,500 miles farther.

Since my agitation of this question they have advanced the rates on the transcontinental class from $2.40 to $3 a hundred, so they are the same in the first and second class as the Denver rate. We have no reduction; but they have advanced them in a way, while on the other class our rate is $2 as against $2.20; $1.75 as against $1.90; then $1.60 as against $1.50; $1.40 as against $1.45; $1.20 as against $1.25, and so on diminishing.

Q. (By Mr. KENNEDY.) I will ask you if you can state whether the people of Colorado suffer any discrimination against them in shipping out the products of the State, the metalliferous products and fruit and cattle?—A. There has been quite a little complaint, but they are adjusting that of late. I think it is more satisfactory to-day than it has ever been.

Q. Is it comparatively satisfactory to the people of Colorado?—A. I have heard no complaint, but I have been very busy.

Q. (By Mr. C. J. HARRIS.) I would like to ask if the tendency of rates has been down in the last five or six years?—A. Oh, yes; but not in proportion to other lowerings.

Q. Have they been reduced as much as one-half in the last five years?—A. No, they have not been reduced one-half. For instance, furniture rate was $1.85; I got it down to $1.45. I found they were shipping furniture from Chicago to Salt Lake City at a tariff of $1.05, and made the kick on it, and we were granted it. It was only after making an exposition of the discrimination. They generally give me what I need in my line. Since then it has been raised in maximum car lots from 12,000 pounds to 16,000 pounds, and $1.10 instead of $1.05.

Q. (By Representative LIVINGSTON.) Is your chamber of commerce making any effort to correct this evil?—A. Not that I know of. On the contrary, they have petitioned the Interstate Commerce Commission to abrogate the long and short haul clause, justifying and legalizing these terrible rates that are now in effect.

Q. Now, if your chamber of commerce have taken that position, what hope have you to correct the evil?—A. Through the law—interstate-commerce law—or through this Industrial Commission.

Q. You would like us to override the chamber of commerce of your own town?—A. Oh, no; I did not say that, because I would not consider it worth riding over or under.

Q. (By Mr. PHILLIPS.) Have you any remedy or any law to suggest to the commission that would be effective in remedying this evil?—A. Yes; I think the Interstate Commerce Commission ought to be given greater powers and that they should enforce the law.

Q. (By Senator KYLE.) Along what lines; have you thought of any particular amendment?—A. I studied carefully at that time the Cullom bill, and could not conceive of any reason why that was not all right.

Q. (By Representative LIVINGSTON.) What was your remedy?—A. The Cullom bill was the nearest approach to anything I could suggest.

Q. (By Mr. A. L. HARRIS.) The original or the amended one introduced a couple of years ago?—A. The one the Interstate Commerce Commission sent out. I think it must be the amended one.

Q. (By Mr. PHILLIPS.) You think that would be effective in preventing this discrimination?—A. Oh, yes; the whole interstate law, to my mind—the foundation of it—is section 4, that the shorter haul within the longer shall not be charged more than the long haul under similar circumstances and conditions.

Q. (By Senator KYLE.) It would be all right to strike out the one clause, "Under similar circumstances and conditions?"—A. Leave the whole thing.

Q. Make it mandatory?—A. Yes; you have got it.

Another point: The railroads assumed a few years ago, before the Interstate Commerce Commission, that they were carrying goods at 2⅖ mills per mile and making a profit. They put Mr. Smur on the stand as an expert witness, and I made him my witness and asked him: "What, in your opinion, would be a fair and reasonable rate to Colorado on my product?" He refused to answer. I asked him: "Would 100 per cent or 200 per cent be satisfactory; would 300, 400, 500, 600, 700, 800, 900, 1,000 per cent?" And Mr. Smur still refused to answer. Then I turned to the commission and said: "Your honors, I will relieve Mr. Smur of his embarrassment. We are not paying 1,000, but we are paying 2,000 per cent—91 mills per ton mile; and all the intelligence and energy in the world can not overcome that." That is why we are a one-lunged hospital and globe-trotter station.

Q. (By Mr. C. J. HARRIS.) To be just, have not some industries you mention failed from other causes than transportation rates? Did not the powder factory, for instance, burn up or blow up?—A. It did, I believe, after it was abandoned, so far as I remember. I know that the powder station quit. I am not satisfied with the rates.

Q. I simply wish to ask if some of these industries had not been financial failures from other causes than freight rates?—A. Primarily it was freight rates. We did have four glass works there run by different men. Each in turn thought he would make it go; and yet the railroads would bring in the minute the plant was started at such a price that he had to throw up his hands. We have a million-dollar paper mill there now and it has gone through bankruptcy twice. It is now in the hands of a receiver. Prior to the building of the paper mill they asked for a reduction of rate, which was excessive, and they refused to make it until after it had started, and then put in force a 25-cent rate, and of course it went up.

Q. (By Mr. A. L. HARRIS.) Where did the paper mill get its raw material?—A. There in Colorado; the wood—a very fine plant.

Q. What distance did that have to be shipped to Denver?—A. It is right handy, on the border of the mountains.

Q. How near do they get their coal for motive power?—A. About 20 miles. They could get it farther, the southern coal, but they have got good steam coal.

Q. The disadvantage of raw material was not the cause?—A. Oh, no; freight rates, positively.

Q. (By Mr. C. J. HARRIS.) Is the wood suitable for pulp?—A. Yes. They have made paper and they make it now, only for local use there. They can not get out; that is their complaint.

Q. (By Senator KYLE.) How about your smelting works for the reduction of ores? How about discriminations in that line as against Salt Lake City and Missouri?—A. I do not know. They seem to be satisfactory. I do not hear any complaint. They are smelting right along. It is the only industry we have. If you should take away mining we would not be in it at all. Our farming industry is the same way. They raise cereals but can not ship. Community after community comes there to locate and moves out again.

Q. I know that is true about your agricultural products, but I understand most of your mines are over west, about Grand Junction, Gunnison, etc., where you are nearer to Denver than to Salt Lake City, and yet I believe ore comes this way to Denver. They evidently do not make a distinction in favor of Salt Lake City in that line.—A. No, I guess not. Denver makes a great bid for the smelting works.

Q. Does Denver make the bid, or the railroads?—A. The railroads. They do not discuss rates in the Denver Chamber of Commerce, I suppose, the whole year through as much as we have here to-day.

Q. Are the directors of the road interested in the mining stocks?—A. They are all interested to a greater or less extent. It is contagious to be interested in mining, more or less.

Q. Personal interest may be a consideration in that industry?—A. Possibly.

Q. (By Mr. PHILLIPS.) Could agricultural products be raised profitably in Colorado provided you had fair freight rates?—A. Yes; if we had fair rates.

Q. And you are not so far from the markets of the world as to prevent it, if you had fair rates, and that is one reason why the agricultural interest is blighted in your State?—A. Yes.

Q. Is that the chief reason?—A. It is the only reason I know of.

Q. (By Mr. KENNEDY.) Did you not state just a moment ago there was no complaint made on account of freight rates out of the State on agricultural products, cattle, etc.?—A. No, I did not state that; I said mining, metalliferous ores.

Q. I asked if there was any discrimination against the people of Colorado in getting its production out, and you said no.—A. I take that back and most emphatically answer yes; on cattle, I know, and agricultural products, yet the Denver market is becoming better, satisfied because they are making some differential rates there. One of the things that suprised me was that the Colorado Fuel and Iron Company asked for a differential as against Chicago, and I only contended for the relative rate. [Reading]: "If Chicago ships through to the Pacific coast for $1, give me the $1 from Denver." I never got a ruling and the Colorado Fuel and Iron Company got 75 per cent of the Chicago rate.

Q. (By Mr. RATCHFORD.) Regarding the smelting subject in Denver—you have a smelting trust there?—A. Yes.

Q. The bullion is shipped at a favored rate?—A. I could not say; I do not hear anything about it.

Q. Have you any opinion in the matter?—A. I have no opinion in the matter. I know this: some men have always contended for it, but I claim some credit from my agitation of the railroad question.

Q. You have smelters operated by independent concerns or individuals, have you?—A. We have 1 that I know of.

Q. Is there lots of complaint on the part of its managers against the transportation charges?—A. I have heard of none from them.

Q. (By Mr. CLARKE.) Is the population of Colorado increasing or declining?—A. They claim it has increased, but they are mostly one-lungers and consumptives. We have now too many of that kind of people.

Q. What is the fact as to Denver?—A. They claim it has grown about 10,000.

Q. Is there a larger output of the mines from year to year?—A. Yes; it is increasing very rapidly.

Q. Is there a larger output from the farms from year to year?—A. They claim that for it in the annual reports of the Denver newspapers. How correct the statistics are I do not know.

Q. Is there a larger output of the manufactures of the State from year to year?—A. In certain directions, certain lines. Mining machinery is doing wonderfully. They are building up large plants of mining machinery; and our steel works, which has been favored with 75 per cent of the Chicago rate, is an immense institution; about twenty-odd million dollars incorporation.

Q. (By Mr. PHILLIPS.) Can they ship that mining machinery to other places, or is it used principally in Colorado?—A. The majority, I presume, is used in Colorado. Having lower rates to El Paso and Mexico points, they are now shipping that way largely.

Q. (By Mr. FARQUHAR.) Do you raise enough agricultural products to keep up the home consumption in Colorado?—A. I do not know. I presume so, because they ship out lots of flour.

Q. How long have you lived in Denver?—A. Since 1877.

Q. Before the people of Colorado went into farming, where did they get their produce from?—A. I presume—I never observed closely—from Utah and Missouri River points—Kansas and Nebraska.

Q. Were you not for a great many years entirely dependent on these two States for your eggs, butter, flour, and everything that enters into household consumption?—A. I would not be able to say yes or no, because I was interested only to the extent of finding them on the table.

Q. Would you say, now, that in the course of 10 or 12 years you have raised sufficient agricultural products to take care of your population?—A. I believe that is right. I know there is lots of produce brought in from Nebraska and Kansas now.

Q. Is there not a possible reason in that fact that quite a number of your manufacturers have had to go out of business, independent of railroad discrimination?—A. I think, as I said before, that is primarily the cause.

Q. (By Representative LIVINGSTON.) Have you a cotton factory there?—A. Yes, we have a cotton factory there.

Q. (By Mr. FARQUHAR.) Could you not get cotton goods cheaper from other places than you could manufacture them, and pay the wages?—A. I scarcely believe that. We are near Oklahoma and Texas and get now an 80 cent rate on cotton up. Our cotton fabrics would cost us from the Missouri River $1.25.

Q. They would cost you less from New England, the manufactured fabrics. At any time in your cotton manufactures, did you ever approach competition with eastern and southern manufacturers?—A. They do approach it by shipping to Missouri River points on some special rate. They are not paying the tariff.

Q. So you have to have an accommodating tariff to make the competition?—A. Yes. I had been shipping my goods into Utah for $1.15, when, if I stopped at Grand Junction, half way, it was $1.75. I simply met the competition.

Q. (By Mr. A. L. HARRIS.) Cattle and sheep are about the only commercial export you ship out of Colorado?—A. Yes, and some horses, too.

Q. (By Representative LIVINGSTON.) We eat your muskmelons and cantaloupes here now in Washington.—A. We have some fine ones. Our cantaloupes, coal and other mines are all right.

Q. Do you not ship potatoes?—A. Yes.

Q. Is it not true that ever since 1876 you have raised all your people want to consume?—A. No.

Q. Is it not true that Colorado has produced her own cereals and things of that kind since 1876?—A. No; I do not think so. It is competition of other points; Nebraska, Kansas, and perhaps some comes in from Wyoming.

Q. (By Mr. CONGER.) I want to ask you why your chamber of commerce does not take up this question of rates or differentials against Denver, if they are of the vital importance you consider them?—A. The only explanation I can make is that they are the greatest shippers; men like Charles Trich, the Moray Merchantile Company, and the Colorado Milling Company, each and every one of whom is satisfied with the rates they have. They do not care to discuss the question; they are satisfied to have it as it is without any newcomers in the field. The newcomers can not prevail under the published tariff rates. They have told me so.

Q. It must be then a majority of these big shippers are getting a rate that is satisfactory?—A. Colorado is controlled by a few men, who are favored by the railroads.

Q. In that case it would seem to me your complaint is one of discrimination between individuals rather than against Denver?—A. It is against Denver and individuals.

Q. (By Senator KYLE.) Do we understand from your testimony a large class of small dealers are discriminated against?—A. Yes; they are paying tariff rates while a few are paying rebated rates.

Q. (By Mr. CONGER.) Have you many wholesalers in Denver?—A. We have about 2 dry goods, 3 grocery, about 2 hardware, and 4 lumber concerns.

Q. They are satisfied with the rates they get?—A. Yes. We do not hear any complaint.

Q. Are they able to supply the retailers in surrounding towns in Colorado and the neighboring States, or are they supplied from Chicago?—A. They supply them from Denver.

Q. (By Mr. FARQUHAR.) Do the Chicago houses have branches in Denver?—A. Yes. One concern is called the Chicago Lumber Company. But the Chicago houses have withdrawn house after house that used to be there, and now the Missouri River shipper and the Chicago shipper will come to Colorado, travel over the interior of the State and make up a carload, for instance, of furniture and mattresses at 20 different points, and he will get enough orders to make a carload, and he brings out a carload, and a "one-hoss shay" performs the functions of the jobbing house. If it had to deliver to the several depots—that would be impossible. The freight is not collected until it reaches its destination, so that the Colorado shipper can not compete against Chicago and Missouri River shippers. That is why Marshall Field and Farwell and the larger houses have pulled out from Denver. There was no use doing business there and paying expense of storage, insurance, and the outlay of money for freight. They would have to pay the freight when shipped to Denver, but in the other case it is not collected until at the destination.

Q. (By Mr. CONGER.) Are these wholesalers members of your chamber of commerce that have to pay these excessive rates to which you refer?—A. They are members of the chamber of commerce.

Q. They are satisfied with the rates, you say?—A. Yes. They went so far as to be the only body west of a line from Duluth to West Sabine, Tex., when the railroads asked to abolish section 4, to beg the commission to grant the petition of the railroads

Q. This chamber of commerce must have in its membership a large majority of the representative business men of Denver?—A. Yes.

Q. If the majority is satisfied, what shall we do?—A. The majority of wealth holders; that ought to cut no figure; what we want is individual justice.

Q. You stated a little while ago that after the establishment of the paper mill the railroads made a rate on incoming paper of 25 cents a hundred?—A. Yes.

Q. From what point, Chicago or New York?—A. I forget the location, but I remember the amount.

Q. You do not know from which point?—A. I do not know. It was on the B. & M. Railroad.

Q. What was the rate on incoming paper before the establishment of that mill?—A. About $1.55. I am not sure about that rate. I remember they did complain very much of the excessive rate, and when they would not reduce it they built the paper mill; and after the mill was built it was reduced to 25 cents.

Q. What is the rate now?—A. I have not looked it up, but they will periodically bring in such loads of paper that this paper mill can not make a living.

WASHINGTON, D. C., *October 11, 1899.*

TESTIMONY OF MR. SAMUEL SPENCER,

President of the Southern Railway.

The commission met on Wednesday, October 11, 1899, Vice-Chairman Phillips presiding. Mr. Samuel Spencer, president of the Southern Railway Company, appeared at 10.40 a. m., and being duly sworn, testified as follows:

Q. (By Senator MALLORY.) What is you name?—A. Samuel Spencer.

Q. Where do you reside?—A. New York City.

Q. What is your occupation?—A. President of the Southern Railway Company and other collateral companies in that system.

Q. What territory is embraced by the Southern company, genera speaking?—A. Generally speaking, the territory south of the Potomac and Ohio and east of the Mississippi River. There are only three States within that territory not reached by the system, namely, Louisiana, Florida, and West Virginia.

Q. The Southern owns and operates its own lines and also operates leased lines, does it not?—A. Yes.

Q. How long have you been engaged in the railroad business?—A. About 30 years.

Q. Are you in any way connected with any other systems than the Southern?—A. Yes.

Q. Will you mention what they are?—A. I am director in the Erie, the Cheasapeake and Ohio, the Chicago, Milwaukee and St. Paul, and the Northern Pacific.

Q. Can you state about how many employees the Southern Railway has in its employ?—A. A little under 20,000, I think.

Q. Can you state about the average remuneration which these employees receive? I am speaking now with respect more to the subordinate employees—railroad train employees and clerks.—A. It would be difficult to give an average, they are of so many classes. I have not the average figures in my mind. They are paid substantially, in the various grades, what other railroads in that and other sections of the country are paying for the same service.

Q. Are they paid by the month, by the week, or how?—A. By the month or by the day or by the amount of service performed. The higher ranks of officers are paid by the year.

Q. Your locomotive engineers and firemen are paid by the run, are they not?—A. They are paid by the trip or run; yes, almost entirely. A few on small branches and unimportant runs are paid by the month, where the service is exactly alike for each day.

Q. Have you any rule on your road regarding indulgence in intoxicating liquor?—A. The rule is absolute that no man indulging in the use of intoxicating liquor is allowed in the train service to our knowledge.

Q. At any time, or when on duty?—A. At any time. I do not mean to say that the rule can or does extend to the point that no man ever, under any circumstances, takes a drink, because that is, of course, beyond our power to know; but if he is known to drink habitually, whether on duty or not, he is not allowed to remain in his position.

Q. In your system is there any system of keeping a list of men who are discharged and exchanging that list with other roads, commonly known as blacklisting?—A. No. We make no such exchanges. We keep a list of men that we discharge for cause, of course, but we do not exchange that list with other companies.

Q. Do you know whether this is done by any other systems?—A. I have not been for a number of years in close contact with these questions. My impression is that that system is dying out. It is not pursued because there is no reason for it. I do not think it is general. We feel that we have done our duty and treated our employees as they should be when we decide the question whether or not they shall remain in in our service. We have no reason for pursuing the man or undertaking to decide for some one else whether that person shall employ any particular man. That is a question that should be left to them.

Q. What, in general, are the usual hours exacted of your different classes of employees?—A. It is according to the work. The ordinary laborer, of course, performs duty for more hours and can perform duty for more hours than a man who is engaged in such responsible duties as locomotive engineer, for instance. There is a nervous, mental strain on the man running an engine that is not on a man swinging a pick on the track.

Q. Locomotive engineers, how long are they employed each day?—A. The outside limit, except in cases of accident or something of that kind, is 12 hours, and the hours run on down to 3, 4, 5, or 6 per day.

Q. Runs are arranged with reference to giving them not exceeding 12 hours constant work?—A. Yes; for instance, if a run is prolonged more than 12 hours in the ordinary course we pay extra time on it. Of course that puts a practical prohibition on it.

Q. I suppose you also exact Sunday work from them?—A. When necessary.

Q. Are they paid extra for Sunday work?—A. On the regular runs they are not paid extra. Where they perform Sunday work they have to perform it at the regular rates, is my impression.

Q. (By Mr. FARQUHAR.) What is your rule with respect to Sunday runs, passenger and freight?—A. The passenger trains when scheduled for Sunday run regularly, and that applies to the long, through runs. A great many of the local passenger trains do not run on Sunday, as they perform a local service and there is no question involved of accommodating persons who are traveling long distances and laying them over at unexpected places. The long-distance trains run 7 days in the week.

Q. How with respect to freight?—A. In some States we are not allowed to run freight between certain hours on Sunday.

Q. What States?—A. Georgia is one of them; North Carolina, I think, is another. I can not undertake to exhaust the list from memory. When not restricted by law in respect to freights the policy is to do as little freight work as possible on Sunday consistent with keeping the perishable freight that must be moved promptly. We avoid Sunday work of the freight men where it can be done without serious detriment to the transportation.

Q. (By Senator MALLORY.) Certain seasons of the year you have more perishable freight than others, I assume?—A. Yes.

Q. What is your opinion, if you have any, as to the desirability or advisability of such laws as that of Georgia which prohibits the running of freight trains on Sunday?—A. I think that is very objectionable.

Q. (By Mr. FARQUHAR.) Would you care to give your reasons for saying that it is objectionable?—A. No; not at all. In the first place, it is more expensive a good deal to the railroads to do the business that way. If they have a large volume of business—for instance, if freight is to be stopped at a fixed hour—it may be necessary to provide additional facilities, yards, roundhouses, and things of that kind, at some point where otherwise it would not be necessary if the runs could be regularly completed. In the next place, in the interest of the men themselves, our experience is that men are thrown away from their homes on Sunday to a very large extent by such a law by reason of their inability to complete a run and get back, and when they started away from home it was so far from Sunday that the trip could not be omitted so as to leave them at home. That is a pretty serious question with some men, because they are at greater expense when away from home than when at home, and if the railroad will watch the question and avoid running freight when it is practical to do so on Sunday, I think that the effect both on the men and upon the service to the public is beneficial by not having arbitrary restrictions as to certain days and certain hours.

Q. (By Mr. KENNEDY.) Are there at certain seasons of the year large volumes of perishable freight running through the State of Georgia that is affected by this law?—A. Yes; at certain seasons there is a great deal of perishable business going through Georgia. We are allowed to run certain classes of perishable freight, because the freight would otherwise spoil and become valueless.

Q. (By Mr. FARQUHAR.) Does the law detrimentally affect Georgia itself—the business of the State?—A. The effect would be remote. There might be some effect, but I think that would be secondary.

Q. (By Mr. KENNEDY.) Is there any possibility of evading the Georgia Sunday law?—A. I do not know. I have never studied that subject. I could not say.

Q. So many laws are evaded, I thought perhaps there might be some system of evading that law.—A. That is a question that I can not answer. I suppose it is possible. I do not recall the Georgia statute exactly. I have had knowledge of some cases where one car of perishable freight would be used, for instance, to take an entire train of nonperishable freight through along with it. I suppose it is something like that you had in mind. Let me follow that up a moment. Suppose the law was stringent enough that if perishable freight had to be hauled nothing that was nonperishable could go along with it, and suppose there was one car of perishable freight, a railroad would at once say, we do not want that freight, because we cannot afford to run a freight train a long distance for one car. A peach grower, for instance, of the State of Georgia must send his peaches long distances in order to get good prices, because they must go to a section of the country where peaches do not ripen at that period. If he had to lose the shipment of a car of peaches that ripened and were gathered on Saturday, because they could not move on Sunday, the loss of a carload of high-priced peaches to the farmer might be a very serious question.

Q. (By Mr. CONGER.) Do you know whether there have been any prosecutions against any road for violation of the Georgia statute?—A. I do not.

Q. (By Senator MALLORY.) Has your system any objections to your employees belonging to labor unions?—A. No; we make no objections.

Q. Does your system make provision at all for relief and aid to the sick and disabled employees?—A. No; not directly in the way that some companies do; not systematically. We frequently provide for relief in individual cases.

Q. Some companies have a system of deducting so much a month from each man's pay to accumulate a fund?—A. I am familiar with some such systems. The Southern does not do that.

Q. (By Mr. KENNEDY.) Are the employees of your road—conductors, firemen, engineers, and trainmen—organized?—A. I think so. Most of them are members of unions, I think.

Q. Are there colored firemen on your system?—A. Yes, a great many.

Q. Is there any trouble between the white labor and colored labor on that account? Do the white firemen object to the employment of colored firemen?—A. They may have some objections. These objections do not take any serious form; but the question is sometimes discussed, though there has never been any organized or real opposition to it.

Q. No objection of the firemen against the employment of colored labor in that capacity?—A. I do not recollect such. That thing may have taken place in the general manager's and general superintendent's offices without my having personal knowledge of it; not reached a point where action was required. My impression is that it has not, however.

Q. (By Mr. PHILLIPS.) In what other capacity, if any, are colored men employed on the system?—A. We employ them on the train as trainmen, what corresponded before the days of air brakes to brakemen.

Q. Are they employed as switchmen?—A. As a rule, not. There may be some exceptions, but, as a rule, not.

Q. (By Mr. KENNEDY.) The colored fireman can never hope to be an engineer in your system, can he?—A. Our policy is now not to make an engineer of him. What the future may develop I do not know, but we certainly do not now.

Q. (By Mr. RATCHFORD.) Are they promoted as conductors on your line?—A. No.

Q. Can not rise above the condition of firemen or trainmen?—A. Not in train service.

Q. Is there any discrimination in wages for the same class of labor, regardless of color?—A. Regardless of color? I am not sure that I know what you mean by that.

Q. The colored firemen, for instance, and white firemen—do they receive the same wages?—A. No; but when you said "regardless of color," I did not know that was what you meant. The colored fireman is paid less than the white fireman. That would naturally follow from this circumstance, if no other: There are white firemen always on the road who are candidates for promotion to engineers. These white firemen outrank, so to speak, the colored firemen, and we keep that line of white firemen moving up all the time, and they get the higher wages as firemen.

Q. They receive higher wages for their labor and also have the chance of promotion as against the colored men?—A. Yes.

Q. Is the same true with your trainmen?—A. Yes.

Q. How much difference is there in the wages of firemen and trainmen?—A. As compared with white, about 10 per cent.

Q. Are the different classes of labor on the Southern Railway paid about the same schedule of wages as paid on the other lines with which you are connected?—A. Substantially the same. There are differences in some particulars. The wages in a great many classes North rate higher than they are in any of the Southern States, on any railroads in the South.

Q. How do you account for that?—A. There are several reasons for it; market conditions may be one; the trainmen are running a much more complicated system in the North on the great railroads than in the sparsely settled country of the South. The running of a train on the railroad, to give an extreme illustration, which has one train a day is quite a different thing and quite a different responsibility on the part of the engineer and conductor from running a train on a railroad where there are 150 trains a day, and they are paid accordingly.

Q. So far as the actual labor and hours are concerned, they are about the same as on the other road?—A. Substantially so; not always same labor, either; approximately the same on hours. Of course, there are differences of detail on every railroad. The amount of labor in running an engine on a little branch road where probably there is not over a half train load to haul is a different thing from running a modern consolidation engine with 75 loaded cars behind it. The labor of the engineer is necessarily greater; the fireman's, too, because the fireman has to handle enough coal to haul 1,000 or 1,500 tons of freight, while the other man handles coal enough to haul 300 tons of freight.

Q. There is a contention among the railroad men of the South that the colored man is used to keep wages down; is that contention correct?—A. I do not think it is.

Q. Is it your opinion or experience that his working for less money than the white man has the tendency to keep wages down?—A. No; I do not think so.

Q. (By Professor JOHNSON.) In regard to the question of wages. I want to ask you a question in regard to the wages in the South. Is the cost of living for a considerable percentage of your employees appreciably less there than they are north of the Potomac and Ohio?—A. Undoubtedly.

Q. And I presume you would agree that that would probably affect the rate of wages?—A. I intended to embrace that in the general statement first made, that the market conditions, supply and demand, govern it; the climate, amount of clothing, and amount of fuel used, make a difference in the expense of living, not only for railroad men, but for everybody.

Q. (By Mr. FARQUHAR.) Does the labor supply enter into it?—A. The labor supply enters into it to a certain extent; but the labor supply, when you come to the skilled work of the engineer and the conductor, I do not think enters very much, because those men are built up to their positions, and if there are not enough there they soon come in from somewhere else. The ordinary laborer would be affected of course; but the ordinary laborer does not move about so much from place to place in response to calls of what you might call market conditions for labor.

Q. Have you or not at the South a greater demand for the places than you naturally would have in the North?—A. A greater demand?

Q. Is there not a larger supply for the market of labor in comparison with the positions?—A. In comparison to the amount of labor to be performed, yes.

Q. And the possible willingness on the part of the men in the South, where they have opportunities for only one kind of work, like those on a railroad—they are pretty apt to underbid among themselves, are they not?—A. Yes. That is what I attempted to describe previously, as the market condition of labor. Labor throughout the South is lower than in the North, taking the general average.

Q. (By Senator MALLORY.) Farm labor is lower, is it not?—A. Yes.

Q. Is that what you mean by labor being lower in the South?—A. Yes.

Q. Has it been your experience that there has been considerable complaint from the employees of your system because they do not receive enough wages? Have there been any strikes?—A. No; there is no general complaint among our employees. We have had occasion in the last 15 months to increase their pay, and that was following reductions which were made in 1892 and 1893, during the very depressed conditions. On the revival of business we have substantially restored those wages, and prior to that restoration this question was discussed, and always discussed with us in perfectly good temper, and there was never any real disagreement between us.

Q. Have there been any strikes on any of the roads of your system since you have been superintendent on account of a demand for an increase of wages?—A. No.

Q. (By Professor JOHNSON.) Do you have, as some lines have, contracts with the Brotherhood of Locomotive Engineers regarding hours of labor or other conditions of employment?—A. No; we have no contracts with them.

Q. (By Senator MALLORY). You deal directly with them?—A. We deal directly with the men. When I say that I do not mean to say that we will not recognize the Brotherhood officers. I have had consultation time and again with the Brotherhood officers, and we treat them as the representatives of our men, and as long as the discussion is reasonable and fair we discuss the question of relations with our men with anybody that they choose to have represent them. As a rule they represent themselves, and it is only occasionally that we have come in contact with the Brotherhood chiefs; but when they request it, we say, Yes, we are glad to see them.

Q. (By Mr. KENNEDY.) Would it be a matter of economy to recognize representatives of the men in a given line, for instance, instead of consulting individually with every employee?—A. Where there are a large number of employees it is impracticable to discuss with everyone, and they have to be grouped as to rates of payment, and then, no matter who comes to the front, if it was one individual we would not discuss with him his wages alone; we would discuss the wages of the group to which he belonged.

Q. (By Senator MALLORY.) To what extent has the Southern system complied with the requirement that it shall put automatic couplers and airbrakes on its freight cars?—A. The hand holds are all attached. That was out of the way sometime ago. Our situation to-day is, as to airbrakes, about 77½ per cent.

Q. On freight cars 77½ per cent?—A. Yes; 77½ per cent. As to automatic couplers, 91 per cent is about where we stand.

Our equipment will be completed on the 1st day of January, substantially, except some old cars that are probably not worth putting the improvements on; and they will be used on local short runs.

Q. (By Mr. KENNEDY.) That is the date of extension granted?—A. That is the date of the extension granted by the Interstate Commerce Commission—the 1st of January, 1900. Our work has been going on ever since that extension was granted at such a rate per month as would complete it. That is where we expect to stand on the 1st of January.

Q. (By Senator MALLORY.) What style of coupler do you use?—A. We use the Janney chiefl .

Q. The master car builders'?—A. The master car builders' vertical plane. We used a variation of some others, but we had to give them up, and we took the master car builders' vertical plane standard.

Q. In the course of the operation you have to use cars that are equipped with the automatic coupler in conjunction with cars that are still equipped with the old link and pin, do you, constantly?—A. Yes.

Q. The effect of that, I suppose, is to really nullify any advantage from the improved type, the men having to go in between the cars as they did before?—A. In making that particular coupling, an automatic coupler on one side is of no advantage at all.

Q. Do you know whether there has been any decrease in casualties on your system since your cars have been so largely equipped?—A. I can not give you figures as to that. Yes; there has been some improvement, undoubtedly.

Q. Do you think when the cars of the country, the freight cars, are generally equipped, that there will be a very considerable decrease in casualties?—A. That is a matter of opinion. I assume it is safe to say that casualties will be diminished; that they will be done away with I have not the slightest idea. You can not eliminate from that question the carelessness of the individual, and a very large percentage of the accidents come from the carelessness of the men, growing out of the habitual use of a dangerous implement.

Q. What was the cause of the delay in complying with that requirement, particularly on the part of the Southern railroads; I mean roads of the South?—A. The want of money, chiefly, I think.

Q. They simply did not have the means?—A. Did not have the means.

Q. (By Mr. FARQUHAR.) When you are entirely equipped with this new appliance do you think there will be any economic advantage in the appliances themselves as far as the labor is concerned?—A. You mean in the amount of labor employed?

Q. Yes.—A. Practically none.

Q. Then it just simply amounts to a matter of safety, if there is safety in it?—A. Safety and economy in other directions; the economy of efficiency. There is a very marked economy in that.

Q. What I wish to get at is whether the amount you expend in these appliances would be reimbursed in the running expenses of the road?—A. Well, the interest on them would probably be reimbursed. That is a very rough statement. I do not know, but I thought your question was directed to the point as to whether there would be less labor employed on those trains.

Q. Both questions, both as to numbers and then to the other?—A. The amount of labor employed will substantially not be diminished. When we began some years ago in applying the air brakes to passenger trains, long in advance of any thought of putting them on freight cars, 15 or 20 years ago, it was thought that the passenger trains would be run with less brakemen. The practical effect was that the same number of men were employed on the train except for a short period. There was a theory of economy, and they were dropped off; but they were soon put back, for the reason that the exigencies of modern travel require so many men on a train to look after the travelers and to protect them at the stations and keep the ice-water coolers supplied, and all that sort of thing. Practically the same number of men were employed on a train. The same experience has followed on the freight trains. The engines are getting more powerful, the tracks are getting in better condition, the cars are getting very much heavier, and therefore the handling of one of these trains requires a good deal more than the mere putting down of brakes, and these other things required will compel the employment of substantially the same number of men on trains as before.

Q. (By Mr. PHILLIPS.) Does this automatic coupler save you any men?—A. Oh, no. There must be a man present when a coupling is made to see that it is done. It is merely a question of whether that man goes in between the cars or whether he does not.

Q. (By Senator MALLORY.) Have you had occasion in your experience to consider the law recently passed by Congress, the last session or the session before last, I think it was, regarding the arbitration of disputes between railroads and their employees?—A. I read it after it was passed. I have never read it since.

Q. Do you know of any instance of its being appealed to to be applied in the settlement of difficulties?—A. Not one; not in my experience; I do not know of a case.

Q. Have you considered the question of the abolition of ticket brokerage by an act of Congress?—A. Yes.

Q. On interstate roads?—A. Yes; frequently and continuously.

Q. What is your opinion as to the desirability of that?—A. I think it is very desirable.

Q. With reference to the public as well as the railroads' interest?—A. I think it is desirable from both standpoints.

Q. In what way is it injurious to the railroad interests?—A. It results in a diminution of their revenue; it results in the misuse of their tickets, and therefore in their facilities afforded to the public for travel. It is the basis practically for frauds upon their treasuries.

Q. Do not some railroads—I will not say all—utilize ticket brokers for the purpose of selling their tickets and their books, mileage books?—A. I am sorry to say they do.

Q. Well, there must be some motive inspiring them to do that?—A. Yes.

Q. What is it?—A. It is the motive of securing an illegitimate agency for getting business.

Q. Competition, in other words, is at the bottom of it?—A. Well, yes. Competition is a very dignified name to apply to it.

Q. The struggle between railroads for passenger traffic is so intense that some of them have to adopt that device in order to get a ticket sold?—A. No; I do not think they have.

Q. You think not?—A. I admit they do resort to it, but I do not think they have to.

Q. (By Mr. KENNEDY.) Are not the railroads themselves responsible for the ticket brokerage system?—A. I do not know what you mean by "responsible for it." Some railroads, as I have just stated, do countenance it, and do sell their tickets through these agencies, and therefore they are responsible to that extent.

Q. I mean is not such a volume of business given to brokers by the railroads themselves as to enable them to continue in business, and without that recognition from railroads they would not be able to do enough to remain in business?—A. I am not sufficiently acquainted with the ticket-scalping business to answer that question. I do know that it does have an influence on that business, undoubtedly, but whether they would stay in business or go out of it in case railroad patronage should be withheld, I am unable to state.

I would like to add to the last question, asked by Senator Mallory: The fundamental objection to that system of doing business I think is its illegality. Some of us are obeying the law under a statute which requires that a rate shall not be reduced without 3 days' notice and shall not be raised without 10 days' notice. Now, if a railroad under the stress of competition, or anything else, sells a batch of its tickets at a figure sufficiently below the published tariff, which it is bound by law to observe, to enable a ticket broker to sell those tickets afterwards at a reduction, and that railroad uses that means of securing business, it is using a means which is forbidden by law, and therefore the railroad which obeys the law is at a serious disadvantage in comparison with the competitor who is willing to resort to that illegal means of doing business. I think fundamentally this whole question of transportation, like everything else, should be based upon a recognition of law as it exists.

Q. (By Mr. PHILLIPS.) Is that a State or national law to which you refer?—A. That is the interstate commerce law, and in most States where they have commission laws it is State law also that there must be public notice of reduction of rates.

Q. (By Senator MALLORY.) Then, the principal reason, in your jugdment, is, as I understand it, that it is immoral; that it is a flagrant violation of law, and that a flagrant violation of law has a necessarily deleterious effect on the public and everything else?—A. Yes; and, moreover, it puts the law-abiding citizens at a disadvantage. It has a business aspect as well as a moral one. An injury is being inflicted upon him because of the fact that he obeys the law.

Q. Do you not think that the generally recognized violation of any law has a bad moral effect on the community in which that violation is practiced?—A. I think so, undoubtedly. It weakens the moral force of the community at large.

Q. That being so, can you state to the commission to what extent the free-pass system, or free-transportation system, is practiced? I will not ask in reference to your railroad, but railroads in general in this country.—A. I will be very glad to have you specify.

Q. Well, your railroad.—A. The policy of the Southern is that its whole business shall be public to one and all. I have no objection to answering generally or specifically if you want it. The pass system has grown to be an abuse throughout the entire country, and it is an abuse on the Southern just as well as it is on other roads, but I hope not to the same extent; but it is an abuse, and one which at the moment we can not throw off.

Q. It is just as much prohibited or more prohibited than the ticket-brokerage system?—A. No; not so specifically provided for as the public notice of reduced ticket rate that I have spoken of. The language of the interstate commerce law upon that subject is such that the prohibition of passes is covered by a general clause. There is no specific law in regard to the free-transportation system only in the question of discrimination.

Q. It is included in that?—A. It is included in that, undoubtedly. But you can not put your finger on it with quite the same specificness as you can the other provision.

Q. You say it is generally abused. You mean by that that passes are given without consideration?—A. Without really a proper consideration, yes.

Q. Legitimate consideration?—A. Yes.

Q. And you think it is a general abuse?—A. I do. I think it is widespread all over this country.

Q. Do you not think it would be well, if it is feasible, to have legislation enacted that will prevent it?—A. I would like to see a statute passed that there should not be one issued to anyone. I should like, with others, to be made to pay my railroad fare over railroads everywhere the same as I pay my hotel bills. I have on several occasions voted in meetings on that question, and I have gone so far as to endeavor to bring about the abolition even of the exchange system of passage between railroads of their officers. If an employee of the Southern Railroad Company is traveling on the business of the company over another railroad he can pay his fare just as he pays his hotel bill when he gets at the end of the journey, and if it is a legitimate expense of the Southern he can get the amount back from the treasury of the company. That is the basis to which that thing ought to be reduced. That is very radical, but sometimes to make reforms you must take very radical steps, and I am thoroughly of the opinion that is one that ought to be taken.

Q. (By Mr. FARQUHAR.) Whether on the ticket or on the pass, there are certain conditions that the railroads have printed on there which exempt the company from liability for damage in case of accident or otherwise. Do you regard the printed matter on the tickets or passes there as a contract?—A. I do.

Q. Suppose, in case of an accident, you find the passenger has a scalper's ticket; do you think that your road is liable to the second party to that contract as much as to the first party of the contract?—A. That might involve a law question and I am a layman in respect to law. Our claim would probably be, if we could sustain it, that if the man bought the ticket illegitimately from a scalper, or if the company had never received proper consideration, there was no liability.

Q. Is not that one of the greatest contentions as to the desirability of a railroad ticket, bought out of a regular railroad office, and not bought illegitimately, that that railroad ticket shall carry the safeguard in it that the common carrier shall carry the passenger with safety as to life and limb; is not that contention made by railroads?—A. Yes, that would be one feature of it.

Q. That you would give the full insurance in fact on your ticket, and that you claim the broker or the scalper can not do that?—A. Yes. I do not know how much that would amount to. Possibly I may answer your question in stating it this way: I do not know that we would raise an objection to transferring that contract legitimately to any other individual at the same price. That is, if we sell John Smith a ticket, we have no particular objection to John Smith's transferring that contract to Bill Jones, if he does not do it in a way that is detrimental to us in that or other particulars. Now, the mere transfer of that one ticket, if we know of the transaction, would not affect us very much; but if transferred at a lower rate, and that results in demoralization of future business, there is another danger and another damage, and it is that damage which is the chief one to us. The mere transfer of a ticket from one passenger to another is of no great consequence to us.

Q. (By Senator MALLORY.) Well, is not the point made at the beginning, that is, that it is so unjust to these roads that will observe the law, a very strong argument? The road that observes the law does not raise rates or decrease rates, whereas another road, naturally indifferent about the law, undersells it.—A. That is where the damage is.

Q. Before leaving this point I would like to ask what rule you have in your system in regard to this ticket brokerage, these scalpers' tickets, as they are commonly called, when they are discovered in the hands of a passenger?—A. We do not recognize them; we try not to recognize them. I can not say that is absolutely so in all cases. We might get ourselves in a position where a decision in court would go against us on that, and, sometimes, it is not worth while for us in every case to put ourselves in a position to suffer damages in order to protect against one ticket.

Q. Well, there have been cases in court, to which attention has been attracted, in which roads have claimed the right to take away that ticket, take it up and put the traveler off the train, if he does not pay his fare; in other words, treat it as an absolute nullity. Does that rule prevail generally among railroads, do you think?—A. In practice I do not think it does on the regular unlimited ticket. If it was a limited ticket and the date had been altered, or something like that, that would be a clear case of fraud, and we would resist it. Or if a pass, for instance, had been issued to one person and sent into a ticket office or sold, and turned up in the hands of another individual, we would resist accepting it, of course, where we had good legal ground.

Q. (By Mr. KENNEDY.) Do the railroad men contend that if the ticket brokerage system were abolished they could give cheaper rates to the traveling public?—A. That may be an argument. I do not think there is any certainty or any concerted action or any obligation that that would follow. I do not know that it has ever gotten to that particular point. The practical effect might be as you suggest, if our revenue should be thus protected for a long series of years. The natural tendency of rates is always down.

Q. Is ticket scalping an evil of such magnitude as to compel you to keep rates up to assure revenue?—A. I do not think that is the reason that rates are kept to present level. I think the reasons are commercial. I do not think any one of these reasons would govern them. If the abuses were done away with I think the tendency might be, under the natural order of things, toward reduction. There are a number of things that happen all the time to reduce rates. Every railroad in this country almost will show year after year that the average amount received per passenger per mile is slightly diminished. The abolition of abuses is only one of the things that might have its effect in that direction; but there is not that intimate relation between the two things that your question would indicate. That is, if the abuses of scalping and passes were suddenly shut off, I do not think that the next day the rates would go down in consequence.

Q. In replying to Senator Mallory you spoke about the railroads not observing the law. Suppose two lines from New York to Chicago, one line 150 miles longer than the other, and the longer line seeks to get some travel by giving some business to scalpers, what law is thereby violated?—A. They have sold those tickets to a scalper

at less than the p   is e rate, otherwise the scalper would not buy them, and their
rate is published under dhe interstate-commerce law, which requires that the rate
shall not be reduced without 3 days' notice to the public.

Q. (By Mr. C. J. HARRIS.) If you have transportation to sell, and a person buys
so much of it and does not use that part of it, what is the objection to that man selling the remaining portion? That is done through ticket brokers oftentimes; but is
that any hardship to your railroad?—A. Yes; it is a distinct hardship to the railroad
and the railroad is perfectly willing to meet the position of the man you speak of by
giving him a return of his money if he does not want to use the balance of his ticket.

Q. Yes; but that is a rather difficult thing to do, and a rather roundabout process,
and it may take two or three weeks to get his money back, whereas he can step into
a broker's office and sell his ticket at once?—A. At a discount, and not at what the
railroad would give him—that is, so far as remuneration is concerned; and it is not
probable that he would be in need of money to the extent that he could not take
the legal way to have it properly done, and the difference would not weigh against
the matter being illegally done.

Q. Is there anything illegal or bad morally in a man selling transportation he has
already paid you for?—A. Yes; it is wrong, as it injures unnecessarily an existing
business. Now, if the ticket business were confined to that and it had no other effect
than that which you describe, I do not think you would find railroads objecting to
it very much. But the man who bought that ticket, bought it and made a contract
for transportation from point A to point B, and he either intended to go that whole
distance or he did not.

Q. Well, I spoke of mileage—1,000 or 500 mile ticket?—A. That is certainly wrong,
because we make a contract with that man for the use of that mileage ticket on the
theory that that man is to use it.

Q. Your road pursues that policy, but the northern roads do not.—A. I am not
discussing the difference between our policy and that of someone else; I am discussing what is a good fundamental principle for the conduct of this particular kind of
business.

Q. You stated you considered it illegal and immoral, whereas the New York-
New Haven permits it.—A. I did not intend to say that that particular transaction
was illegal and immoral, as you limit it in your statement, but I stated the use of
tickets by the brokers as they do use them is illegal and immoral. When I referred to
the illegal and immoral point I was talking about the railroad companies selling their
tickets to the brokers, and that was the point that was objected to at the time I made
that answer. I was not referring to the scalping of a partially used ticket. But I
did not finish my illustration with you. Now, this man buys a ticket to go from
"A" to "B" and he stops at "X" and sells the rest. The railroad will sell him a
ticket to "X" at a certain price, and it will sell him a ticket to "B" at an entirely
different price, and there may be perfectly legitimate reasons for the difference in
rate per mile between these 2 points. Now, if the man is only going to "X" he
may be perpetrating a fraud upon the railroad company by not buying a ticket to "X."

Q. (By Mr. CLARKE.) I would like to inquire, for the further elucidation of this
point in regard to selling the unused part of a through ticket: Suppose I should buy
a ticket from Chicago to Boston and use it to Albany, then for perfectly good reasons
and in good faith should not wish to use the remaining portion, is there any rule
among railroads by which I could get back money in proportion to the whole distance?—A. Not probably in proportion to the whole distance, and there is no such
rule that can be said to exist universally. What a great many railroads do do, and
what I am sure all roads under proper regulation of this kind would do, would be to
give you back the difference between the rate from Chicago to Boston, and the rate
from Chicago to Albany. That is, they would put you in the same position as if you
had known before leaving Chicago that you were going to stop at Albany and bought
an Albany ticket only.

Q. That often happens, I suppose, to passengers?—A. It does happen; we do it constantly. We sell constantly round-trip tickets, and the man goes to the end of his
destination and says he is not going back within the limit we gave him; say 10 days
or 2 weeks. We say, Then the consideration for giving you a round-trip ticket is at
at an end, because the consideration was you would make a round trip within a given
time, but if you wish to consider it a one-way trip we will refund to you what you paid
in excess of what the cost would have been for a one-way trip.

Q. Do you consider that difference perfectly equitable to the passenger?—A. Perfectly so. That is what we would have done if he had gone to the ticket office at first
and said, I want a ticket to go one way. We would have sold him a ticket, and we
put him right back and gave him the benefit of that, assuming that his change of
mind was for proper reasons.

Q. What method is provided for giving money back? Must he correspond with the general traffic agent?—A. As a rule he must put his ticket in at the office where he is, and ask them to correspond with the general ticket agent. Of course we must do it in some regular way. We would be perfectly willing to let any ordinary agent do it if the machinery for such a transaction could conveniently be placed in every agent's hands, but it can not.

Q. (By Mr. KENNEDY.) Is it not true that a large element of the public have discovered that they can cheapen their railroad rates in just the way that Mr. Clarke has illustrated, by buying a ticket farther than they intend to go and selling it to the scalper?—A. Yes; that is one of the fundamental abuses of the scalper's system.

Q. Particularly traveling men?—A. Men who travel a good deal have that advantage, because in this, like everything else, experience teaches them how. They find what they can do by traveling. A man who sits in his office and does not travel does not see these things.

Q. (By Senator MALLORY.) We will pass on now to the head of unjust discrimination and undue preferences by railroads. Can you say whether or not to your knowledge unjust discrimination in favor of individuals is practiced now by railroads?—A. I certainly think they are.

Q. Do you know in what shapes they are practiced, such things as rebates, for instance, and concessions and commissions?—A. There are various forms.

Q. What is the cause, in your judgment, of this discrimination?—A. To get business without the other fellow finding out how they get it.

Q. (By Mr. PHILLIPS.) What forms do they generally take in discrimination?—A. I claim not to be an expert in that business. Senator Mallory has named the chief ones. They are rebates and commissions on business, allowances for car mileage on cars owned by shippers, underbilling in weights, billing the goods at less weight than the actual weight, which has same effect as reducing the rate, and also billing to wrong destination—that is, beyond the destination really required and stopping the goods short, or billing to one destination and then diverting to another destination to which the rate is higher.

Q. (By Mr. FARQUHAR.) In other words, the variety is limitless—the methods of giving preferences to individuals over the general public?—A. I suppose there is no end to the catalogue of ingenuities that can be devised to evade the law, but the power to evade applies not only to transportation law, but to criminal law and every other.

Q. You think that is due to the desire to get traffic?—A. Yes.

Q. And not let the other fellow know anything about it?—A. Yes; because if the law was obeyed and the rate made known by 3 days' notice, the competitive carrier would have the same opportunity to reduce, probably only a few hours behindhand, but before the shipment could be made, which would be quite sufficient.

Q. The other fellow does not find it out at all?—A. He finds out after a while. He finds out that something is going on, but frequently does not find out specifically what it is.

Q. He finds out that somebody is shipping at less rates than the published rates?—A. Yes.

Q. And the effect of that is to cause the other fellow to reduce to special rates?—A. Yes.

Q. And that thing is going on generally?—A. Yes; in many cases.

Q. Is it not a very serious abuse?—A. The most serious of all that are known in the transportation business.

Q. We have had testimony here as to various kinds of discrimination, and I will not trouble you to go over the details of them—such as the discrimination by reason of the use of the elevators under the control of the railroads; discrimination by the mileage paid to special car owners, the dressed beef people—refrigerator cars generally. This has been testified to here as being a source of a very considerable abuse; that is, abuse in that they enable certain individuals to get their freight carried at less than published rates, and as such are reprehensible. Now, is there any suggestion you have to make which you think would meet this difficulty and do away with it in the way of legislation?—A. Suggestions as to preventing illegal action by additional statute are very difficult of accomplishment. I think that the great desideratum in this whole question, the thing that underlies the whole of it, is an enforcement of the law which requires absolute publicity in everything that is done in respect to rates, and I think that everybody's hand ought to be turned to accomplish that special purpose, because that will do away with more abuse, more evils than any other one thing that can be done, and I think a good rule, where you have quite a large problem ahead of you, is to see what one stroke will accomplish the most good, to begin with, where there must be a series of strokes at the best, and address yourself to that one. In this case the great point is, that the published rates shall be the rates on which all the business moves.

CEE. 18

Q. Well, that is the law now?—A. I know it is the law now. I am speaking of the enforcement of that law, and any steps that can be taken to aid in the enforcement of that, should be taken.

Q. Well, it has been suggested here that it would be beneficial for the Government to provide for railroad inspectors—as it provides for bank inspectors for national banks—whose duty it would be to go at any time and examine the records of railroads for the purpose of ascertaining whether they comply with the law or whether they violate the law in their rates. Do you think that would be feasible?—A. It would do some good in reaching results, and I have no objection to that plan. I have said to the Interstate Commerce Commission, on one occasion, that I should be perfectly willing to have all of the traffic business of the Southern inspected by licensed inspectors. These inspectors should be men who would not reveal what they saw in the books of any company to a competitor. These inspectors must be subject to the law and must be men of character, and the books must be examined just as banks are examined, and the railroad companies must feel that there would be ordinary business respect shown as to what is the private part of their business. Now, the difficulty about it would be to devise by statute a means of avoiding violations of law. This is a very difficult thing to accomplish, not only in transportation law, but in criminal law or any other. Now, suppose you have an inspector and he goes into a railroad office to inspect; he sees whatever is there. Of course he does not see what is not there. Suppose that particular railroad, if it is determined to violate the law, has an understanding, not recorded on the books, with some large shipper that in 12, 18, or 24 months hence, it will take this question up with him and make settlement. The inspector does not detect that. Of course, in time he may get around to the point of it after there is a payment made to that shipper. The inspector will then see that something of the kind has been done, but the transaction will then perhaps be 2 years old. I am merely pointing out one of the difficulties of meeting the evil by inspection. I do not know any way to finally compel the obedience to law except to punish the criminal. For that reason I have taken the ground—and my colleagues differ with me—that the criminal section of the interstate-commerce law should not be taken out ot it. I think it ought to be enforced and not repealed.

Q. You mean punish the individual?—A. Punish the individual as well as the corporation.

Q. It is very difficult to locate who is responsible.—A. It may be that it is very difficult sometimes, as in the Whitechapel murders in London, to find out who stuck that knife, but nevertheless you do not repeal criminal law on that account.

Q. The objection that has been raised, in my experience, as to the infliction of personal punishment on individuals, is that there is only one head and all the rest of the railroad employees are subordinate agents, from the general manager down, and it is pretty hard to punish a man for obeying a superior officer, the man himself possibly not knowing it is a violation of law, the same being the orders of a superior, when if he does not obey the order of the superior he will lose his place; and for that reason it has been contended that it is a great deal better to let the penalty apply to the road itself, and hold the road as indictable, and let it be tried and fined.—A. With a $5,000 penalty; that is the present law. Now, there are plenty of shippers in the United States who have enough business for the railroads to warrant some railroad in paying 25 such penalties in 1 year, and if that fine were the whole question they would pay it willingly to get the business and care nothing about it. Now, I do not agree at all in the view that it is a hardship upon a subordinate or upon a superior that he shall be required to obey the law even when he is face to face with the crucial point, "Must I obey the law or lose my situation?" The law does not recognize the right of a man to make a living illegally or criminally, and I do not see how he should be allowed to do it in the railroad business when he is not in any other. I am willing the penalty should be applied wherever it fits. There may be difficulties in reaching the right man, but the man who is responsible can be reached if sufficient effort is made. If you are the right man, or I am, no distinction should be made, whether it is the president or a subordinate.

Q. (By Senator MALLORY.) I do not think they would ever miss it if they hit the president.—A. Well, then, I am willing that it should be the president. If I can not choose properly whether I shall become a criminal or shall go out of business, I do not know as I deserve much sympathy.

Q. In the matter of long and short haul, I believe your road and all the other roads have different rates for terminal points and for intermediate points?—A. Yes.

Q. What is a just basis of the distinction between long haul and short haul rates, these short-haul rates being largely in excess pro rata of long hauls?—A. The basis or the fundamental principle is that the short-haul rate shall be a just and reasonable rate. With that fact established, if it is established, it is proper that the railroad should take the similar business from a longer distance at a less rate, because otherwise it might not get it at all, and there is no good reason why it should not be allowed to do that additional business.

Q. The intermediate rates being fair and just to the other rates?—A. The other rates are a question of commercial conditions of whether the railroad can secure the haul or not.

Q. In your judgment is that absolutely necessary in very many cases?—A. Yes; it is in sparsely populated countries and where railroads have cost a good deal in comparison with the amount of business that that country affords. The principle has been very aptly illustrated by this sort of a statement: You build your house on the shore of the Potomac River in a level flat country. To get to and from your house you drive, and you haul your provisions at less cost than a man who builds his house on a neighboring height, probably 1,000 feet up, but not very far away, because he prefers the view and the elevation and surroundings. Now, he has necessarily to pay more in the matter of cost of transportation up to his house than you have to yours in the valley, but it is his choice, and if he wants his house upon a hill he pays the penalty of having to walk up to it or be hauled up at an increased cost of exertion or of money, as the case may be, whenever he goes to it, as compared with the man who prefers to locate on the level. A set of men come to a place where there is no water competition at all and they build a town. Another set of men build a railroad through that town to some interior and elevated point beyond that has probably cost twice as much as if built on the level of a water course. In addition, it costs a large percentage more to operate to the higher level, and those who require the moving of the freight up that height should pay the increased cost. The people in the valley suffer the disadvantage of being down in a low flat country as compared with the man who built up on the height, but they save in cost of their transportation. The man on the height finally complains to the railroad that it will haul cheaper for the man in the valley, and why not for him on the hill? The railroad says, simply because it can not afford it and it is not reasonable. If the railroad had been asked to do these things at exactly the same rate at the beginning and before the railroad was built it would have said, "No, we do not care to build under those conditions. We will stay where we are on the low level and let these people on the hill do without a railroad." This is the fundamental principle of the whole thing. There are exceptions and modifications and variations of that idea in a thousand ways, but the fundamental idea of it is the same.

Q. In your judgment, then, this difference between long and short haul rates is essential to railroad management?—A. In certain localities.

Q. It is governed to a great extent by the conditions of the country through which the road runs?—A. Through which the road runs, and the water conditions as recognized by the interstate-commerce law.

Q. Germane to that then comes the other question as to passenger rates in different sections of the country. I believe it is a fact that in the South passenger rates are higher than in the North?—A. Yes.

Q. What would you ascribe that to?—A. Sparse population; the small amount of business for the passenger trains.

Q. I believe in my State they charge 4 cents a mile.—A. That is above the average for the South. Florida is one of the highest. We have none that are as high as 4 cents, but all are gradually diminishing. Our average rate for the whole Southern system, 6,000 miles of railroad, was 2¼ cents for the last year.

Q. There is a matter to which I would like to call your attention and hear your views on, and that is the complaint that is made as to the difference in the South of the rates for produce going north and for merchandise coming south. On vegetables and fruits from Florida, and, I suppose, from South Carolina and Georgia, going north the rates are considerably higher per 100 pounds than for merchandise coming south from New York or Philadelphia or Baltimore. So much difference is there that it is regarded as a very great discrimination against our products going north. Why is that?—A. For certain classes that is true.

Q. Well, take fruits and vegetables.—A. Fruits and vegetables in the first place must be run at very high speed, they are so perishable; and in the next place they must have a special class of equipment, and with a good deal of it there must also be hauled a large amount of ice free. The rates include that. Trains must be shorter on account of high speed. We get fewer tons behind 1 engine and in 1 car than we do with other classes of freight. Then there is a very large item of insurance in it. Running those articles at high speed the bill of damages in case of accident is very different from what it is with other classes of freight. All these things go to make up the necessity for the difference in rate per 100 pounds.

Q. Is there anything in the consideration that the trains coming south would come empty if they did not bring those freights?—A. No. On the contrary, I think you would find that that argument applied in the opposite direction.

Q. The reasons you have assigned us, then, you think are the principal reasons?—A. I think those are the governing reasons. Whether the dominating load goes one way or the other depends very much upon seasons of the year and upon a particular locality, as to what their products are. You go into a busy district and, whether it is North or whether it is South, the tonnage coming out of that district to the four points of the compass probably dominates over every other. Those cars have to go back empty, so your question could not be answered in any general way. Each case would have to be taken up specifically.

Q. Can you briefly state the reason why rates from the West to the seaboard, for export goods or export products, are less than on products in that direction for domestic consumption?—A. We need to meet a foreign market. It is a wider application of the principle of the long and short haul clause, as I announced it. If the rate from Chicago to New York is a reasonable one for the New York consumer, considering all the circumstances, and if the railroad or the grain merchant or the flour merchant in the West can put an additional amount of business through New York for Liverpool or Hamburg or Antwerp, there is no reason from the railroad standpoint and from the shippers' standpoint, or from the standpoint of New York consumers, why the rates should not be so adjusted, if possible, as to send that product abroad. If, in making the general adjustment as to price, it is found that the railroad must take less than its New York rate, then the railroad is simply doing its part in that general combination to forward the American product to a foreign market, and the New York consumer is not injured.

Q. I believe rates to-day are lower than they ever have been, are they not?—A. Well, I can not speak specifically of the trunk-line rates at the moment. Taking the year as a whole, I have no doubt they are lower.

Q. Have you had occasion to consider the effect of the development of the grain trade through Galveston and New Orleans upon the rates from Chicago to the Atlantic seaboard?—A. Only in a general way. I have not had any personal part in that question. I have to watch it more or less.

Q. It has been testified here that it has had a very modifying effect on the rates from Chicago and St. Louis to the seaboard.—A. Well, I have no doubt that it has had some. My own impression is that the effect of it has been much exaggerated.

Q. Your experience in the railroad business has been through pretty nearly all the various spheres of it?—A. Yes; substantially the whole.

Q. Do you believe that it is practicable for one central authority to establish rates for the whole United States? Suppose Congress should vest tthe Interstate Commerce Commission with power to fix rates for the United States at large, do you think it would be practicable for a body of men here in Washington to do that?—A. I do not. I am very sure it would not; that is, to do it with any wisdom. They can issue a military order on any line, but rates can not be adjusted arbitrarily.

Q. I mean with justice to the railroads and with justice to the public?—A. With justice to the railroads and the commerce of the country, it is certainly impracticable.

Q. Why is that?—A. In the first place, it is too large a problem for any five men or fifty men to handle the business of making those tariff rates. It would be impossible. Tariffs are the result of the constant friction of commerce. Now, nobody but the people who are engaged in the business can do it thoroughly. You can not do it by any central power. If every railroad in the United States was owned by one man and he attempted to make one rate bureau that would look after all of his rates, he would fail. He would be compelled to subdivide it for each section of the country, or for different commodities, and for different conditions, and place the responsibility for each group on those to whom the authority was delegated. There are railroads in this country to-day that are so large that no one man undertakes to make the tariffs. He does, in a measure, decide as to whether alterations of the tariff shall or shall not take place, but as to making it, he can not do it.

Q. Now, conceding it to be a fact that it is a physical and moral impossibility for any central authority here in Washington to make tariff rates for the United States, do you think it would be practicable for such an authority, such a body, to consider the question of correcting, amending, or rectifying rates that are already established, but which may be sources of complaint, upon hearing the complaints?—A. Oh, yes; that is practicable, but I do not think it would be wise; I do not think it would be productive of good.

Q. You think, then, that the best authority, the one which can be relied on to do justice to the public and the individual, is the railroad itself?—A. The railroad itself, with absolute publicity in everything it does. That is, the people who have spent their lives at that business and have grown up in it know what the real problem before them is.

Q. There seems to be much complaint, at least, as to the diversity of classification. I understand that there are three different classifications in the United States. Do you think it would be practicable for a central body like the Interstate Commerce Commission to classify freight for the whole United States?—A. No; scarcely. But I think there ought to be more uniformity of classification than there is.

Q. You think it practicable?—A. Yes; I think it would have to be done for different sections of the country probably, and with reference to the different conditions in those sections. I do not think a uniform classification for the United States would be just either to the public or to the railroads, because classification at last is a means of making rates, you know. That is all.

Q. What may be said to be the general rule underlying the making of classifications?—A. It is simply a means of classifying several articles into one group, so that in naming a rate you are not naming a separate rate on every commodity, but you are naming a rate upon a group of commodities for purposes of convenience; that is all.

Q. Some railroads will have a great deal of one particular group to deal with in transportation; others will have very little of that particular group. Does the fact of having more or less of that particular group exert an influence in its classification, as to its being class 1, 2, 3, 4, or 5?—A. Not so much in its classification, because that would be governed more by the question of the rate; but classification would enter into it, of course.

Q. It has been testified here that where you have a very large amount of a particular product which is handled by a particular road, that that necessitates that road making a different classification for that particular product than is made by another road which has very little of that particular product to handle?—A. Well, it might be necessary or it might not. The practical effect of that would be this: If a road has a very small amount of it, they do not care very much about it and do not want to be bothered with it as an exceptional thing, and they simply place it in some general classification, because there is not enough of it to cut any figure. These questions arise frequently when new developments take place in a particular section of the country. In a State very near you, Alabama, before there was a ton of pig iron made there, the probability is that if you had looked at the tariffs, you would have seen pig iron in some class. Of course, there was very little of it to move. If somebody had shipped 10 tons of it for some particular need in manufacturing, it did not cut any figure; but the moment the blast furnaces were established, it became a special product for that country. It could not go under a general class, and the question became what should be the necessity in the way of rates to put that pig iron into the markets of the world. That probably required several adjustments, and finally it did not take the form of classification at all. They simply made what they call a commodity rate and said, pig iron so and so, and there is nothing else in that class. That is a system of evolution. I am not speaking with knowledge, of course, as to Alabama iron. I had nothing to do with the Alabama tariff and had never seen one at that time, but that is probably what occurred. There was an evolution there working out by reason of a new industry and a very large one, which compelled the giving of a new rate on pig iron. For such reason, you can not make your classifications absolutely uniform. You may open a mine of a particular mineral that has never been known in that section of the country before; it is a new development and if you turn to the tariff sheet of the road, that mineral may not be mentioned at all, or it may be just arbitrarily placed in some classification, fixing a rate for it that would be absolutely prohibitory in moving it. Then the railroad man must take up the question as to where it can go and at what price, and to what extent he can lower the rate by changing the classification or by making a commodity rate, in order to start shipments.

Q. In making the classification in tariff rates, do the railroads, as a rule, follow the practice of imposing all the traffic will bear?—A. They probably did in the beginning.

Q. Do they continue to do it?—A. It is now done by a general whittling away of rates under constantly changing conditions. The thing has settled itself down to commercial conditions covering everything. The real problem of the railroad manager in rates is to meet new conditions and prevent making violent disturbances; I mean, if he is pursuing a legitimate business.

Q. You recognize the fact that there is a steady trend toward consolidation of railroad interests in this country?—A. Undoubtedly.

Q. That it is rapid?—A. Very rapid of late.

Q. What will be the effect of that on rates, do you think?—A. I do not think it will have any material effect on rates, unless it retards the ratio of diminution in rates. It may do that to some extent.

Q. The tendency undoubtedly is to do away with competition?—A. Yes.

Q. Well, if competition is done away with, then the incentive to reduce rates will not longer exist?—A. Well, I say it may retard that process of reductions, but part of the reduction of rates which is going on constantly in this country is the result of commercial conditions, of getting more products to market all the time, and that of itself is putting down the average rates, and will continue to do so.

Q. Without reference to competition?—A. Without reference to competition. Now, added to that is, of course, this irregular illegal action of which I have already spoken, where one man comes in and makes a private agreement with the shipper. The other road finds it out and thinks it is incumbent upon it to do the same thing, and the first thing you know you have a lower published rate than you had before. I do not think that the consolidations that have taken place already have increased rates. The steadiest rates in America to-day, where the interstate-commerce law is more rigorously observed in respect to fighting secret rates, is in the place where the consolidations have taken place.

Q. (By Mr. C. J. HARRIS.) If this consolidation continues will it not be necessary, for the protection of the public, that the Interstate Commerce Commission have more power, and will not the regulation of rates by legislatures be more necessary than it has been hitherto?—A. I do not think so.

Q. You think the railroads will take care of the public without that interference?— A. Yes; I go further than that. I think, if by any means, by consolidation or by statute or otherwise, you can do away with secret rates, the complaints upon the part of the public will almost entirely disappear simultaneously. I think there are numerous illustrations of that tendency in support of that statement.

Q. Well, suppose, with competition entirely done away with and the tendency on the part of all the railroads or any other corporations to make everything they can for their stockholders, the rates become burdensome to the public—they have been so in some instances—is there any way out of that but by this governmental interference that I have suggested?—A. Well, I should go back of what you say. It all depends upon what you mean by "burdensome to the public." Now, admitting your premises for the present, I should have to answer but one way: If these rates did become burdensome in the true sense, or if these railroads were disposed to take advantage of that condition of affairs and squeeze a lot of people out of business and all that, I think there should be some regulation, because no one recognizes more than I do that a railroad is a quasi-public corporation. It ought to have some regulation, but I think the best regulation of any business that is intended to serve the public is that it should be absolutely free from concealment. You will not have such abuses if everything that any railroad officer does is known. The corporation could not sustain itself. But as to burdensomeness of freight rates, those rates in this country now are cheaper than in any part of the world. Therefore you can not consider that the general level of rates in this country is unreasonable or burdensome. Now, we know that where consolidations have taken place rates have not been raised. The Southern Railway Company is probably as good an illustration of consolidation as exists in this or any other country. What is now the Southern Railway Company was, five or six years ago, something like 35 or 36 corporations. The rates have not been raised. The facilities I think every man who knows that country knows have been very largely increased. The properties are in better condition. Therefore I do not think the condition that you suggest will arise at all, and I think the logic of past events goes to show it. It is not so much what the shipper pays, provided it is not exorbitant, of course, and does not keep him out of the markets, as it is that the rates are so adjusted that no one has a better rate than another, and that no other community or locality that furnishes the same product has a relative advantage. If you will get the discriminations out of the way, I therefore say that nine-tenths of the whole problem of governmental supervision of railroads will disappear. You have two prominent illustrations of that to-day in this country, and I had occasion to say this to the Interstate Commerce Commission, and they assented to my two illustrations at that time. I said to them, and I venture the statement to you, that there are two sections of the country now from which there are fewer complaints than any others, namely, New England and those States south of the Potomac and Ohio and east of the Mississippi rivers. They all assented and said, "Yes, that is true." The reason for that is that in those two sections secret rates have largely disappeared.

Q. As a matter of fact have you not, since your consolidation there, materially lowered rates?—A. No, it has not materially lowered them, because we found those several properties in the hands of receivers, unable to earn anything to pay interest, and not a single one of them keeping up the properties over which these people had to ride or do business. Now, that was not a condition from which to lower rates at that time. The Southern has been in operation 5 years. During that time the average rates obtained have decreased about 7 per cent, notwithstanding that.

Q. (By Mr. RATCHFORD.) Referring to the subject of governmental ownership and operation, what, in your opinion, would be the result of that? Would it prevent discrimination?—A. Well, I do not see, if the roads were honestly managed by the Government, why should they discriminate. It would not do away with charges of discrimination; it would not do away with this community and this State petitioning the Government that another community and another State had an advantage. That relative adjustment between the different sections of the country would be a very serious problem unless the strong voice of the Government said, "Those are the rates and they will not be changed." If you get, so to speak, an imperial sort of government of the railroads, under governmental ownership, it might say arbitrarily what should be charged. That is what they do in Germany.

Q. Is it your opinion that under such management and operation the railroads of the country might be managed to the satisfaction of the whole people, or more so than they are to-day?—A. You mean by governmental ownership?

Q. Yes?—A. No.

Q. You do not believe it?—A. No; my opinion is—of course it is simply an opinion—that you would find a rigidity that would prevent the rapid improvement in transportation facilities that has been going on in this country for a quarter of a century or more.

Q. Are you referring to the present prevailing rates in this country when you say that they are the cheapest in the world? Is it not a fact that the short-haul rates in this country are among the highest in the world?—A. No.

Q. It is not?—A. No, it is not. We may have some short-haul rates that are as high as anywhere, where the roads are doing a very small amount of business. If you will analyze it you will probably find a very small amount of business hauled on such roads at a very high rate, in comparison with larger amounts moved by the long haul. But the average freight rates in America are the cheapest of any important civilized country in the world.

Q. Is it not by reason of the fact that the long hauls give an opportunity for cheaper rates, and are more prevalent here than elsewhere?—A. That is one reason they are more prevalent. Undoubtedly the long hauls of the American roads are one element that has enabled them to make these cheaper rates; our long distances have been a large element in that result.

Q. (By Mr. PHILLIPS.) Have you looked into the governmental ownership in Germany, for instance?—A. In a measure, yes. I can not say that I have been a close student, but I have watched it.

Q. Do you think it has been quite satisfactory in the German Empire?—A. I do not. Certainly when you travel over the German railroads you do not get anything like the promptness, or the efficiency, or the courtesy, or the luxury that you do in America; and as for the prompt movement of freight, why they do not know anything about it. It frequently takes longer to get a ton of freight across the German Empire than it would from here to San Francisco.

Q. (By Mr. CLARKE.) Do you not think that the introduction of politics into the management of railroads would be an evil greater than most of the evils from which the public suffers now?—A. It would be a tremendous evil.

Q. You have testified in regard to discriminations being practiced up to the present day. That is true on your system, as I understand, as well as on others?—A. No, I do not think we are discriminating. The rule has been laid down by our Southern officers strictly that we make no secret concessions to anybody. If anyone wants to ship over the Southern Railway he must ship at the published tariff, and we have lost some business by that, but we find by experience that in the end we get that business back.

Q. Is there no discrimination through the mediumship of commodity tariffs?—A. No; because the commodity tariff is open to anybody. If we make a commodity tariff it is for anybody who ships that commodity, not for any single individual.

Q. Do I understand that you carry pig iron or a highly finished product at the same rate?—A. Oh, no; it is not a discrimination to charge more for a piece of finished steel than it is for a ton of pig iron.

Q. You misunderstood me. Do you charge the same rate to any individual for the same article?—A. Yes; under like circumstances and conditions, from the same point of origin to the same point of destination.

Q. It applies to the petroleum industry as well as any other?—A. It applies to everything.

Q. Do you know how that is on other roads in the South?—A. Well, the rates as a rule in the South are very uniformly maintained now, and that is ascribable to the fact that a condition of confidence has grown up there which has done away almost entirely with the discriminations between individuals. The shippers do not expect that other shippers are getting an advantage, and therefore they do not complain and do not apply for such advantages. This was a very difficult thing to bring about. It did not exist 5 years ago.

Q. Are there not preferences given to a large shipper through the mediumship of his making some preparations for handling his goods or for receiving or storing them?—A. None out of the road; no. If a man builds his own warehouse alongside of the track we do not give him any less rate by reason of that. If it facilitates his business he is at liberty to do it, but we do not give him anything off the rate for it.

Q. And you give every other shipper and any other shipper the same rate?—A. The same rate precisely. The only distinction as to the amount of his business is, that there is a carload rate on some things and a less than carload rate, and if he ships 100 carloads he pays the same per car as if he ships 1; and the tariff shows the difference between the carload and less than carload; it is all on the bulletin board and posted, and he can inform himself as to what it is.

Q. As a matter of fact, has any large company, like the Standard Oil Company, for instance, any advantage in getting the business of the people along the line of your road over any other company?—A. No, unless they have superior advantages within their own business; none so far as the railroad company furnishes them.

Q. (By Senator MALLORY.) Are the rates charged for hauling those tank cars the same as are charged for hauling like cars for anybody else?—A. Yes. If a man owns his car, under the present car mileage system, we pay him the established rate of mileage on his car; but we do that for any man who furnishes his car. I should like to see that done away with, but we can not do it. The cars are there and everybody takes them and takes them at the established rate. We have to do the same thing or go without the business.

Q. (By Mr. PHILLIPS.) Then the different discriminations to which you alluded before do not exist in the South, so far as you know?—A. I will not say that. I say positively they do not exist on the Southern Railroad, and they do not exist to any considerable extent in the South.

Q. But you do believe that they do exist?—A. Oh, I think there are some, but I think they are very small in the South now.

Q. (By Senator MALLORY.) On the subject of pooling contracts—legalizing them—ti has been proposed and urged in Congress that the provision of the interstate-commerce law inhibiting the pooling of traffic and profits by railroads be done away with, and that such contracts be legalized. What do you think would be the effect of that on the question of discrimination that we have just heard so much of?—A. I think it would tend to diminish it; that it would necessarily do away with it I do not believe.

Q. There are several propositions in different forms. Among them is one which seems to have met with more favor than others, and that is that power should be given to the railroads to make such contracts as they please concerning their traffic and profits, but that it should be subject to supervision by some constituted authority, and the Interstate Commerce Commission has been suggested, to approve of such contracts or disapprove of them. Have you thought anything on that subject?—A. Yes; a great deal.

Q. What do you think of that?—A. I think that if the legalizing of pools is to be done, it will be necessary to provide for some power or authority to decide whether such pool would result in excessive or unreasonable rates. I should be entirely willing to have that done so far as the pool contract and the pooled traffic was concerned.

Q. You think, then, if that were permitted, that there would immediately be a perceptible cessation of this abuse of discrimination?—A. I think so. In certain localities it ought to have a good deal of effect in that direction.

Q. (By Mr. A. L. HARRIS.) What effect would that have upon through rates compared with the present?—A. I do not think it would affect them materially. It might affect them in trunk-line territory to some extent, in respect to the very low rates that have obtained there of late; but as to the average of those rates I do not think it would affect them materially. At all events, that would place it where, if it did affect them, the Interstate Commerce Commission could annul the contract at once, and that would be a protection against any undue increase of those rates.

Q. (By Senator MALLORY.) What is your experience with regard to the taxation of your railroads by the States? Have you any suggestions to make regarding that? Do you find that it is oppressve?—A. No; I have no suggestions. The taxation is very high.

Q. Generally is oppressive?—A. In some cases it is oppressive.
Q. (By Representative LIVINGSTON.) There is no way of avoiding it, is there, where you run through the States?—A. I do not know of any way that has been devised.
Q. In some of the Southern States they have a railroad commission?—A. Yes.
Q. You have no trouble with them?—A. I can not say that.
Q. No serious trouble over the question of discrimination?—A. No; I do not think we do. We do not have any trouble on the score of discrimination anyhow. We have almost ceased to have discriminations in the South.
Q. If you were discriminating——A. (Interrupting.) We would hear from it; we ought to.
Q. These State commissions would interfere?—A. If we were discriminating between individuals under like conditions we ought to correct it or pay the penalty. As common carriers we have no right to do it and we endeavor not to.
Q. (By Mr. RATCHFORD.) Does the same apply to localities?—A. Yes. But I said individuals in that case for this reason, that I have never seen two communities yet that had a question up between them that did not feel that they were discriminated against. Not that they intend to be unjust about it, but charges of discrimination between localities involve so thoroughly the question of like or unlike conditions that no two men look at it alike. If two men are shipping goods from A to B those conditions are exactly alike and there is no room for disagreement on conditions. But it is very much more difficult—the most difficult problem in the United States to-day—to adjust the rates between communities.
Q. It has been stated here that a ton of freight shipped from Chicago to Salt Lake City or to the Pacific slope will be shipped at a great deal less than the same ton of freight shipped from Denver to the Pacific coast. Now, the illustration that you make with reference to elevation, etc., hardly applies in that case. The distance from Chicago is in the neighborhood of 1,000 miles longer than it is from Denver. I should like to have you explain.—A. Well, I should hesitate to take up in detail a case of that kind in a country where I am not familiar with the rate conditions. Personally I have no knowledge of Salt Lake City and Denver or that section of the country and the rates that apply to it, and I have had no occasion to look into it, and therefore I should hesitate to give an opinion with regard to a specific case of that kind.
Q. I only referred to that for illustration.—A. Well, where the conditions are not essentially different I think the long and short haul clause of the interstate-commerce law ought to apply. That is, I do not think a railroad ought to arbitrarily charge more for a short distance.
Q. Do you know of any good reason why a ton of freight from a given point in the West, Chicago for instance, that is being shipped for export purposes, should be hauled to the Atlantic seaboard for a less price than a ton of the same freight that is used for domestic purposes?—A. In New York?
Q. Yes.—A. Yes; I can conceive that it can be very reasonable and very just to the community to do it.
Q. Why?—A. It might resolve itself into a question as to whether that ton of freight went abroad at all. Suppose the rate from Chicago to New York on that ton of freight for New York consumption is a perfectly reasonable rate; that is, not more than a reasonable compensation to the carrier for transporting it there. That is a sufficient reason for that rate being in existence. Now, suppose the price of that particular commodity at Antwerp is such that the man who has that ton of freight at Chicago can not sell it at Antwerp unless he can get something off the ocean freight and get a little off from the railroad freight, and then he gets his own profit down to a mere bagatelle for the purpose of starting the business in Antwerp. The combination of railroad rate to New York and ocean rate to Antwerp thus made is such that he can sell that ton of freight in Antwerp. Now, suppose on that ton of freight it has been necessary from Chicago to New York to name a less rate than was named the same day on a similar ton of freight from Chicago to New York for New York consumption. The New York man is not injured, because he has been paying a reasonable rate. It does not affect anyone else in America except that New York consumer. The article is going to Antwerp. This condition is a market condition entirely. Nobody has been injured. The man who shipped it has been benefited, because he has been able to market a ton of freight that he could not otherwise market, there being no market for it in this country at the moment, assuming that this market is supplied. The railroad is benefited to a very limited extent probably. It may make a very little, and it could not have hauled that freight except at the reduced rate, but it is willing to do that in order to get the additional ton of freight, and besides it aids in putting the American merchant or farmer into a market that they would not otherwise reach. Now, under all these circumstances I do not think there is anything unreasonable in taking that ton of freight at a less rate than they would take it from Chicago to New York.

Q. I take it that the cost of transportation is measured by the value of the article after it reaches its destination?—A. That is one element.

Q. That is the main element, is it not?—A. No.

Q. In both cases, both for foreign and domestic consumption, is not that the main element?—A. The main element deciding whether it would go or not?

Q. No; in determining the cost of transportation.—A. It has nothing to do with determining the cost of transportation, because the cost of transportation is fixed regardless of it; the cost of transportation would be the same if you doubled that rate.

Q. (By Representative LIVINGSTON.) Suppose you hauled that ton of freight from Chicago to New York and charged nothing for it; is anybody hurt?—A. Yes; the railroad is hurt.

Q. Anybody outside of the railroad?—A. No; I think not. I should think the railroad would have the entire burden in that case unless the shipper agreed to give up his ton of freight as well. He might do that.

Q. (By Senator MALLORY.) To go back to this question of the taxation of railways by the States, can you state what is the basis of the State taxation of railways, as far as the Southern road is concerned, or whether there is any particular system that is practiced by all the States, or whether they differ among themselves?—A. They differ more or less. In general terms, it is based upon the assessed valuation of the properties. The properties are valued by some constituted board, usually at the rate of so much per mile, and then the taxation rate is applied. Now, that system of assessment of valuation differs in almost every State.

Q. In some you think it is too high?—A. Oh, in some it is entirely too high.

Q. (By Representative LIVINGSTON.) Is the property divided into real estate and rolling stock?—A. It is divided into the roadbed and the personal moving property. Those are the two classes; that is, the roadbed, depots, etc., are in one class and the rolling stock and moving property in another. That is the general rule.

Q. (By Mr. C. J. HARRIS.) The tax is by the mile?—A. By the mile usually. The valuation of the road in different sections is valued per mile. They take up one section of the road and usually that follows the line of demarcation of the old chartered corporations, even if they have been consolidated into combinations. This plan is usually adhered to because it has become a habit or custom coming down from the old times.

Q. (By Senator MALLORY.) Do you think that the Interstate Commerce Commission is of any service at all?—A. Yes. .

Q. In what respect?—A. Well, they have accomplished a good deal in respect of publicity of rates and action; they have accomplished a good deal in the way of systematization of accounting and records, so that the work of all the railroads can be very much more intelligently examined; and then they have accomplished some good by their prosecution of people who are violating the law. They have not done a great deal of that.

Q. Do you think it would be advisable for them to be empowered to enforce their decrees on questions of discriminations and unjust tariffs?—A. On discriminations between individuals, yes; as to tariffs, no.

Q. The original intention of the interstate-commerce law, I believe, so far as the public understood it, was that the Interstate Commerce Commission would have the power to determine that a thing was contrary to law and that that would be observed until set aside by some superior judicial authority?—A. I do not know what your opinion was. I was very actively engaged in railroad traffic at that time, but I must say I never thought so, in respect to rates or tariffs.

Q. You do not think it would be advisable to give them power to see that their decrees are observed and their findings followed until an appellate court sets aside their decision?—A. No; I think if there is a controversy on that question it ought to go to court for decision.

Q. Would it not be better for Congress to say: "You are simply an advisory body," or to give them the power to see that their findings are put into effect until some appellate power sets them aside?—A. What is to protect the railroads? Suppose the court should finally decide that the rate was not unjust or unreasonable? The question of discrimination is different from the question of an unjust rate. A discrimination is a distinct offense under the law, and should be followed by punishment. I have no objection to the commission being given any power you please for such punishment, but when it comes to deciding a question as to whether a certain rate is reasonable or unreasonable, unless that tribunal is constituted as a court, with all the responsibilities of a court, instead of a commission, with its decisions subject to appeal to higher courts—in fact, put on the same footing of permanency as a United States court—I do not think that they ought to have such authority. Suppose that question is finally carried to court, and it is decided by the courts of highest jurisdiction that the rate which was reduced was a reasonable rate, what becomes of the railroad and its revenue in the meantime? It has suffered during the trials an unreasonable reduction of its rates, and these trials may occupy 2 or 3 years.

Q. That argument may be answered by just shifting positions. I do not know as it is an answer, but it is one of the cases where somebody has to suffer, and suppose the court itself sustained the Interstate Commerce Commission's finding?—A. Then the shipper can collect from the railroad company.

Q. Four or 5 years after the thing has transpired.—A. Damages are usually collected only at the end of lawsuits, are they not?

Q. In each case the matter is generally so small individual people are not disposed to go into lawsuits?—A. That is one of the necessities of business you can not undertake to provide for by statute. If a man on account of the smallness of the debt is not going to take the trouble to collect it, it is no reason why I should pay to him what is not due as a means of keeping him safe while he sues. I do not think that will follow.

Q. Going back to the matter of discrimination, which you say is a violation of law—not a question of judgment, but simply a question of fact—do these corporations discriminate or not between individuals? Would you give them the power in that case to enforce their decision?—A. Yes; I should have no objection to that, because I do not think any railroad company should be in a position to discriminate between individuals at any time or for any length of time, but I think they are entitled to the protection of common law as to whether their charges are reasonable or unreasonable, and if you constitute the Interstate Commerce Commission as a court, with all a court's powers and limitations and with life members, or constitute it as the English commission is, I have no objection to submitting that question of reasonable rates to such a United States court especially constituted for that purpose.

Q. What is there about a court that gives it any more ability to determine rates—an ordinary United States district judge sitting as a circuit judge in determining whether it is reasonable or not?—A. He is supposed to be a trained jurist.

Q. It is simply a question of fact, and that fact must be determined by information that covers a multitude of subjects, whether a rate is unreasonable or reasonable, and in my mind a railroad man is the only man who can settle it, an experienced railroad man. Our judges are not appointed because of a knowledge of railroad matters. I am surprised that you will let a judge decide it when you will not let a railroad commission decide it, a commission supposed to be constituted of men familiar with the subject. But I do not wish to argue the subject.—A. I will not prolong the discussion. I think there is a very marked distinction between the two cases.

Q. (By Mr. C. J. Harris.) You have been railroading in the South a long time. We have in North Carolina and other States samples of railroads owned and run by the State—government ownership. As a railroad manager, will you tell us what has been the result of such ownership of railroads?—A. I do not know. I have personal knowledge of but one case of railroad run by the State of North Carolina. I think there was another in former years, but I do not think it was successful, and certainly the one run by the State of North Carolina now is not successful.

Q. (By Representative Livingston.) Do you know anything about the running of the Georgia State Railroad for a long time—30 or 40 years?—A. It has not been run by the State within my recollection. Twenty or 25 years ago the State leased it. It was leased to Joe Brown and his associates first. I did not know much about railroading in the days when the State ran that road. After running it they leased it; they preferred to get out of it.

Q. I was going to suggest that if you knew the history of that it would answer the question.—A. I do not know the specific history. I know the fact that it has not been run by the State for a number of years. The State of North Carolina owns another railroad to-day that is leased to us.

Q. (By Mr. C. J. Harris.) Have you any knowledge as to the Cincinnati Southern, owned by the city of Cincinnati?—A. Yes, a very intimate knowledge of it.

Q. What success did Cincinnati have?—A. Very bad success running it themselves. It built it through a board of trustees, and then attempted to run it for a little while; then some organization of some sort other than the trustees was formed, and then it was leased. Those people who leased it have been paying the bill ever since. I happen, unfortunately, to be one of them.

Q. (By Senator Mallory.) You think that was due to the fact that it was owned and constructed by the city of Cincinnati, or a rather poor investment anyhow?—A. The fact is it cost a great deal of money; they built an enormously expensive road, and it is now getting up to the point for the first time where, at a reasonable rate of interest on the cost, it will pay its way; but for nearly 23 years it has not been making the interest. The city of Cincinnati has been losing at the rate of $400,000 a year. They leased it for $400,000 a year less than the interest on the cost.

Q. You would not consider that as being a parallel case with the railroad run by the State itself?—A. No; that was a business venture, and it never had any political effect. The city never managed the property in the sense of having its own employees for any length of time. It never got into politics. There was and is a nonpolitical board of trustees in charge of the property.

Q. (By Mr. KENNEDY.) Has there been a remarkable revival of business along the Southern system during the last year?—A. Yes; there has been within a year, but it began about a year and a half ago.

Q. Does it compare with the revival of business along the roads running east and west into the great, growing States of the West?—A. Not quite so large relatively, probably.

Q. Have you a car famine on that road?—A. Yes; we are taxed to the uttermost for every car we can command, and we are not promptly supplying all the demands.

Q. (By Mr. FARQUHAR.) While you are on the Government ownership of railroads, what is your opinion as to whether the interests of the general public would be better conserved under the control of the railroads by the Government, or by the competition that we are having now, as far as rates are concerned?—A. Well, that I could not answer so far as rates are concerned. That would depend entirely on what the Government desired to do in the management of the road. If it desired to increase the revenues of the Government very largely, it might do it temporarily by putting the rates up.

Q. Supposing that in the Government ownership there would be a maintenance of reasonable rates, do you think that would be of advantage to the whole commercial community—a maintenance of reasonable rates rather than the competition we are having now between traffic lines?—A. No; I think, under Government control, while you might and probably would get absolute maintenance, you might get a rigidity of rates that would not meet the commercial conditions of the country anything like as well as they are met now. I do not think America would grow in internal or foreign commerce with the roads under Government control as it is growing now.

Q. You think, under natural conditions the natural growth of commerce would be better conserved than it would be under Government ownership?—A. I do.

Q. Your idea as a railroad man, as widely as you know the whole system here, is that many of these discriminations have been in the advancement of new products, and also of the growth of communities, in certain classes of commerce?—A. Yes.

Q. That has been the custom of all railroad men, to meet these conditions and, as much as possible, to promote the enlargement of traffic by rates and otherwise?—A. Yes.

Q. In other words, you take the more general proposition that the larger the shipper and the larger that corporation—the more beneficial rate will go to the party that sends the most traffic?—A. Yes, that is the natural tendency.

Q. There is an advantage to the great shipper and the great city?—A. Undoubtedly there is; but that advantage should not take the form of discrimination. Undoubtedly the large city always has an advantage in dealing with any large problem over the small one, the same as accumulated capital has an advantage over individuals. The railroads that have a business going out of large cities can get their properties in shape to do that business better than if serving small communities producing small revenues.

Q. More economically?—A. More economically and with more facility and dispatch, and therefore they can meet the conditions of the market better.

WASHINGTON, D. C., *October 16, 1899.*

TESTIMONY OF MR. MELVILLE E. INGALLS,

President of the Cleveland, Cincinnati, Chicago, and St. Louis, and the Chesapeake and Ohio Railroad Companies.

The commission met at 10:40 a. m., Vice-Chairman Phillips presiding. Mr. Melville E. Ingalls, being first duly sworn, testified as follows:

Q. (By Senator MALLORY.) What is your name?—A. Melville E. Ingalls.

Q. Where do you reside?—A. Cincinnati.

Q. What is your occupation?—A. I am president of the Cleveland, Cincinnati, Chicago, and St. Louis Railway, and of the Chesapeake and Ohio Railway; those two systems, one north of the river and one south.

Q. How long have you been connected with the railroad business?—A. With the management of railways since 1871.

Q. Were you connected in any other way before that?—A. I was attorney for them; I was practicing law in New England previous to that.

The witness submitted the following written statement:

In legislating in reference to railways three things must be considered: First, the accommodation to the public (and the prime condition in this is safety) and after that facility. Last year over 500,000,000 people traveled over the railways of this country, and nearly 1,000,000,000 tons of freight were shipped. These figures are so immense that their presentation at first staggers the mind. The first thing, as I have said, is to see that this immense travel is handled with safety and dispatch, and that this immense tonnage is carried with regularity. To do this requires good tracks, good equipment, terminal stations, all costing large sums of money, and to-day much more than ever before, on account of the development of the country and the growth of cities and the increase in the price of terminal property. The revenues of the railways must be sufficient to provide for this, and any legislation which limits that revenue below this safety point is unwise and against the interests of the people.

The second consideration must be the prompt payment and welfare of the employees of the railways. Leaving out of consideration the vast number of people who incidentally are supported by the railways as manufacturers of supplies and producers of raw material, the men actually on the pay rolls of the railways of this country to-day are about 1,000,000, and they support a population of 4,000,000 or 5,000,000. The railways, in addition to the revenues for maintaining their property, as previously stated, must earn sufficient to pay this army of employees. More than $500,000,000 were paid out last year by the railways for wages. Any legislation which affects the welfare of 5,000,000 of your people should not be hasty nor in anger, but conceived with the greatest care. If you reduce wages you reduce the character of your service. The lives of thousands of your citizens are in the hands of even the humblest trackmen. No one, unless he reflects and has studied the situation, understands how the duties of the employees of a railway are all interwoven, and how the lives and safety of passengers and the protection of freight depends upon the intelligence and character of the employees, from the highest to the lowest. It is vital, therefore, to the interests of the service, to the interests of this country, that the railways should earn sufficient to pay their employees and pay them well.

The third interest to be considered, after having provided for the maintenance of the property and the payment of the employees, is to see that all its patrons are served fairly and well, and at as reasonable a cost as is consistent with the previous statements, and a fair sum to be returned to the proprietors for their investment. Too little consideration has been given in this country to the latter fact. There has been a feeling among many people that the railways were built by stock jobbers, managed for these purposes, and that the capital invested had not much claim to consideration. In many cases the courts have interfered, and I think the sober, honest, sensible people are at last coming to a point where they wish to do justice to the proprietary interests.

To sum up, therefore, legislation in reference to railways should be such as to allow revenues sufficent (first) to maintain the property and the service, (second) to pay the employees, and (third) to provide a sufficient return on the investment. When these three conditions are attained you will have placed this large interest, representing through its employees and its purchases at least one-tenth of the population of this country, in a sound and safe condition, where as citizens they can perform their duties to the Republic and become useful members of society.

For half a century the railways have been going through a species of development. At first every community was anxious to secure a railway, and all manner and sorts of inducements were given. It was a hazardous enterprise to undertake, and nearly all the early promoters failed in their undertakings and capital could not be induced to enter the field without large inducements; therefore, speculators and promoters seized upon the field, charters were obtained, aid solicited from State, city, and town, bonds and stock issued without much regard to values, and all sold or turned over to contractors to build the railway. These contractors and promoters sold the securities to the public. In most cases they were lost—wiped out by foreclosure. The new owners and proprietors of the reorganized companies endeavored to earn an income upon their investment in all ways possible, and this produced dissatisfaction with the public. The contest first began as to whether railway companies were like other business enterprises—independent and free to pursue their business, charging what they could get from the traffic and making what they could. After many years of litigation the courts finally settled the question, which to-day is practically agreed, that railway corporations were public servants, receiving certain rights from the people, in consideration of which the public had control over their rates and charges, always reserving the right, which the courts protected, that there should be revenue enough to pay a fair return upon the capital invested. Sta'e after State appointed commissions, who endeavored to control or influence railways in the interest of the public. The Massachusetts idea of the commission was that one should be appointed which should have authority to inquire and report, and their control of rates and the enforcement of their commands depended more upon moral suasion than anything else. Other States endeavored by legislation to absolutely fix tariffs and charges. As the country has progressed and improved the latter idea has been given up to a great extent, except in more ignorant communities and in cases where it is used for political capital. The wise and thinking people stood aghast at the thought that a few commissioners, selected usually for political qualifications, could make, manage, and control the tariffs upon which this enormous business depended for its safe and prosperous conduct. Finally, in 1886, the demand for legislation developed into an act of Congress creating what is known as the Interstate Commerce Commission, which, with some amendments, is substantially to-day as it was passed. The courts have decided that its powers do not extend to the making of tariffs, but in many other ways it has the broadest and most complete authority. This act prohibited the pooling or division of earnings, which had been the favorite method of maintaining tariffs previous to that act. After the passage of that law, however, by agreement and association rates were still fairly maintained. Later, however, the Sherman antitrust law was passed, which at the time was supposed by many people not to apply to railways, but since, by the decisions of the courts, it has been practically decided that it applies to nothing else but railways; and under the decision of the courts in the Trans-Missouri case it seems as if no agreement or arrangement or understanding of any kind can be maintained and that there is nothing left for the railways but anarchy. It left the railways in a most deplorable condition, and during the years 1897 and 1898 the practice of cutting rates and secret rebates seemed to run riot. Late in 1898 and early in 1899 the Interstate Commerce Commission took up the question with the leading railway managers of the country, for the purpose of securing a better maintenance of rates, to stop secret cutting, and especially to prevent the payment of rebates which it was supposed were being paid, although no legal proof could be obtained. This move upon their part was most commendable and has worked out with extraordinary results and has been beneficial to the railways and the public. So far during 1899 there has been greater freedom from secret rate cutting and rebating than probably has ever been known before in the history of railways. This has been done by the resolve of the controlling officials that there must be a change, and it has been made easier by the fact that there was a large amount of business offering, more, in fact, than the capacity of the railways to take care of. A pride has also grown up among managers in obeying the law and discontinuing such practices, and to-day where here and there a railway manager is supposed to be paying secret rebates he is not looked upon as in good standing in the fraternity. How long this condition of affairs can last without legislative aid is a grave question. It has also resulted in tariffs far below cost, in many cases, and unprofitable to the railways and not demanded by the public.

I think it is the belief of railway commissions, railway officials, and large shippers that there should be some legislation by which the agreements between railways could be legalized. It is usually called a "pool," but the term should be broader than that. It should be legislation authorizing railways to enter into agreements to maintain the published tariffs, with penalties and fines for breaking the same. In other words, this immense traffic should be made legal, rather than leaving it, as it is now, outside the law.

I am quite well aware that at present there are penal provisions for the punishment of violations against the present law. It is, however, this very provision that, in my judgment, renders the law ineffective. When you provide a punishment for an act committed by an official of a corporation in the way of business which is done every day by 90 per cent of the business men engaged in private affairs without punishment, you are making that a crime which the public conscience does not consider one, and therefore such a law has not the support of the public. The public will not support anyone, either a railway official or a business man, who gives information leading to conviction under such a law. The law should be changed making it an offense punishable by fine. You may make the fine $500, or $1,000, or $5,000, if you please. It will then be supported, and you will have no difficulty in getting evidence, and the law can be enforced.

It is hardly worth while to treat agreements of railway corporations as more sacred than any other of the business affairs of men or to throw around them greater punishments and penalties. My judgment is that what is necessary in the way of legislation is, first, that we should amend the interstate-commerce law as it exists by allowing railways to make agreements for the maintenance of tariffs and the division of business, all rates and tariffs under such agreements to be subject to the supervision of the Interstate Commerce Commission as to whether they are reasonable or not; that all violations of these agreements as between the railways themselves should be subject to damages by suits in the courts, like other ordinary affairs; that any shipper wronged could bring suit, or on any complaint of the public violations should be punished by fines. Then I should provide, further, for the greatest publicity of accounts and the affairs of these great corporations; that their accounts should be kept according to the rules prescribed by the Interstate Commerce Commission; that that commission should employ experts similar to those appointed by the bank examiner, who should at stated times, and at other times as the commission concluded wise, examine the accounts of all the railways and should make report of their affairs.

I would provide then, further, that no railway should be built except upon the approval of the commission, and no charter should be issued except a proper and sufficient capital was fully paid up. The time has gone by when it is necessary to allow what you might call "skylarking corporations" to be organized. Henceforth the railway business is to be a conservative, steady business, and if a new line is desired it should not be authorized unless capital is willing to take the risk. This will prevent the building of parallel and competing lines in the future which are of no use to the public.

The tendency with many writers and thinkers to-day is for the Government to own and manage these great highways. As the Government is at present constituted and managed, I should consider this a national calamity. To avoid it we should endeavor as far as possible to see that these corporations are treated fairly; that the public is also given proper consideration, and, above all, that the great army of employees is well taken care of. I am a believer myself in profit sharing as applied to railways, and that in the future it will work out the solution of the question between employer and employee and avoid strikes and friction. Many of the great corporations are working to this end by means of their pension lists, hospitals, etc.; but they can not make much progress in this line if they are to be hampered by legislation such as is applied to no other of the industries of this country.

It must be remembered that the great factor in the development and improvement of this country is the railways, and that anything that unjustly and unduly oppresses them hinders and retards the development of the country. It is time that we disregarded the cry of the demagogues against the railways and treated them like business corporations, necessary and essential to our progress and development. And, to repeat and sum up, it seems to me that for this purpose it is necessary that the present law should be amended by legalizing contracts between railways, subject to the inspection and approval of the Interstate Commerce Commission; that infractions of that law should be punished, like other business transactions, by a fine, and no attempt should be made to make it a criminal offense; that a more thorough inspection of the accounts of railways should be made and greater publicity given, so that the public may know what is being done, what they are buying and what they are getting, and that they should be protected from raids by speculators and blackmailers, and no rival line allowed except upon a hearing and a decision by the commissioners that such a line is needed.

Q. Can you state, Mr. Ingalls, about how many employees you have in service on your two systems?—A. We have a little over 20,000 names on the pay roll now.

Q. How often are they paid?—A. They are paid every month by a pay car that runs over the different divisions.

Q. What is the basis of payment? I expect it differs with the different character of employees.—A. It differs generally because, in the first place, there are different classes. There are the clerks and agents, who are paid by the month; the train men are all paid by miles; the machine men are paid by the month, but based on hours— so many hours a day; and the track men are paid by the month, but it is based on so many hours a day.

Q. Have you any limit as to the number of hours the men work?—A. Oh, yes. For the shop men the outside limit is 10 hours; it is more often 9, very frequently 8. The arrangement of the hours in the shops depends a good deal upon business. If business is pushing, we try to work 10 hours; moderately fair times, 9 hours; and very hard times we have got down to 8; and often in the winter, in the short days, we get down to 8. The track labor is supposed to be 10 hours the year round, but in the winter if they get in 8 hours they are very lucky; we are very lucky, rather.

Q. How about the train men, the engineers, and firemen?—A. Their pay is based on mileage, and we endeavor to keep our divisions so that the train men will make good wages by going over the division. They are more apt in good times to double up; that is, to do more work and get much more wages than is calculated on; very rarely less.

Q. Have you any limit in the number of hours that a locomotive engineer must work or is permitted to work?—A. Well, the limit is hardly in hours, because sometimes a man may get laid out and it may take him a long time to finish on his division and get back. We expect him to finish his division; and then the rule, which we carry out strictly, is that he shall not go out until he has had an equal number of hours rest. Ordinarily we would like to get our passenger engines in not less than 6 or 5 hours, often in 2½. Our freight runs are all scheduled to run from 8 to 10 hours. Usually 10 hours is what we try to do.

Q. (By Mr. KENNEDY.) You say that the track men are supposed to work 10 hours a day. The track men of nearly all the systems in the United States have sent in complaints to the commission that they are the hardest-worked and poorest-paid laborers in the United States. That is the burden of their complaint; and that their hours are excessive. They have to work night and day, and they get no pay for overtime. Can you say anything as to that condition of affairs?—A. Well, if they had left their case with the first statement——

Q. (Interrupting.) Poorest paid and hardest worked?—A. I should be rather inclined to agree with them. They are the poorest paid and hardest worked when you take the two together. There are not many occupations harder; but in connection with the pay, I think the hardest-worked men all over the world are what I call the dollar-a-day men; that is, the ordinary laborer, who does not get above that. The track man, we will say, gets in 10 hours and he gets a dollar a day. I guess, in the hard times of 1895 and 1896, he got in a good many places down to 90 cents, and perhaps 75; but I think we always paid the $1. But when you come to talk with them you will find they are the men who are at home every night; they have their own little houses; they can live cheaper, and their labor does not require so much skill as other men's; and it is as fair wages as are paid to ordinary rough labor in other walks of life. I do not think it is true of the long hours. I was telling, before I came in here, when I took the Chesapeake and Ohio Railway they had a rule there that the darkies who worked on the track should work from sun to sun. Well, of course, in the long summer days that made a very long day, but we changed to the ordinary 10 hours. Occasionally, if you have a wreck, the section men are turned out at all times of the night, and have to go out very often in stormy weather. I do not think he averages more than his hours; certainly not on our system.

Q. They claim that a great deal of responsibility rests upon them; that the safety of the traveling public is in a measure in their keeping, as it is in that of other railroad employees; and they claim that they ought to be better paid.—A. Well, of the 20,000 names on our pay roll you could pick out very few who did not carry the lives of the passengers in their hands.

Q. (By Senator MALLORY.) I was proceeding to ask you if you knew with regard to the existence of such a system as what is commonly known as the blacklisting of discharged employees; I mean the system that has given rise to considerable complaint in this country, whereby the name of the employee who is discharged is transmitted to some other railroad system and is there used to keep him from getting employment on that system.—A. I understand. We have nothing of that kind. That comes under the head of the general manager. I understand the only thing we have is that if 1 division discharges a man and his name is sent in to the superintendent no other division can employ him without the consent of the general manager. But I do not understand we have ever had anything like what is known as the blacklist system with other roads; not to my knowledge.

Q. Is there any difference between the Sunday labor and labor during the week days in your system; that is, do you have the same quantity done on Sunday that you have on week days, or is there a difference, only such work as is absolutely necessary being done on Sunday?—A. Well, we rarely open our shops on Sunday unless some extraordinary calamity has overtaken us. Our track men do no work on Sunday except, possibly, to inspect, or in case of a washout or accident. The only people who do Sunday work are the train men.

Q. Are they paid extra for that or do they receive the same pay?—A. No, the same thing.

Q. The Chesapeake and Ohio runs through what States; Virginia, West Virginia, Kentucky, and Ohio, does it?—A. Yes.

Q. Do either of those States prohibit transportation by rail on Sunday?—A. Virginia does.

Q. How about the other States?—A. There is no prohibition.

Q. What is your view about the interference with railroad traffic on Sunday by State laws; do you think there is any real benefit from it?—A. I think it is unwise.

I would like to explain that at a little length. In the first place, leaving out the religious side of the question, as a matter of getting the best results, a man who works men is very foolish to work them over 6 days in the week. In my judgment there should be 1 day of rest. Now, the question of absolutely prohibiting work on Sundays is very often more against the merchants than against the men. Over on the Chesapeake and Ohio, where we do an enormous business, we may get blocked up in the mountains by an accident. We come along on Sunday and our yards are full. Men want to get home; they can not leave. They can not put through the trains. And there is more complaint from the men over that than anything I have heard of on the road. The merchants and people fail to get their goods and they will complain. The only thing that I can see in its favor is where we run through communities or by churches. I believe in everybody conducting his business so as not to interfere with his neighbor; and if I want to go to church my neighbor should not be allowed to blow a locomotive whistle beside the church or a brass band be allowed to play there. That ought to be controlled; but it seems to me that it should be left to the local communities to make their local regulations. But if you have a State law as it is in Virginia, which, I think, has been declared constitutional, it leaves a chance for every little blackmailer to make a complaint and get your fine.

Q. But that law does not prohibit passenger traffic?—A. No, nor perishable freight; and the result is that you will see 49 cars of coal running down over the road and a car of hogs used to run them through; and we run our passenger trains and business through. There is a demand for passenger trains now.

Q. According to that, practically, there is not a great deal of observance of that law?—A. You might not have cars enough of hogs to go around.

Q. If you do have hogs enough to go around, you are very sure to run the trains?—A. As long as we can switch in perishable freight, I understand from our attorneys that we are safe. The Virginia people are the cleverest people in the United States. I do not know any State where property rights are so carefully observed as they are in Virginia; and we do not have any trouble, unless we strike somebody who wants to make a fine out of us. The people themselves are all with us; we do not have any trouble with them.

Q. What is your observation with regard to suits against your road for damages for injuring people, or any other kind of damage? Do you find that you have a fair show before the juries, as a general rule, or otherwise?—A. Well, we run through 11 States, and you can see the difference in almost every State. However, I have rarely heard of a complaint in Virginia or West Virginia. In Kentucky we never, except in the last year or two, have had any fair treatment. We settle everything we can, and what we can not settle we let go. The State is full of lawyers who take the cases on shares; and before the poor man's eyes get closed from an injury a lawyer has got hold of his widow and brings suit, and the juries do not have much regard for us. Sometimes we are able to take exceptions and save. In Ohio and the West we do not find very much trouble. We get treated much better to-day than we did 10 or 20 years ago.

Q. Is there any such thing as a limited liability law in any of the States through which your road passes?—A. Do you mean for death?

Q. Yes.—A. I think there is; I know there is in Ohio. I think there are in the other States. I would not want to state that. That is a matter of law which I do not carry in my mind. I feel quite sure there is, though.

Q. Is it better to have such laws with a limited liability as they have in New York, where, I think, $5,000 is the maximum amount which can be recovered for the death of an individual?—A. Well, speaking as a railway manager, I should rather have a limited liability. Speaking generally, in the interests of the public, I should say it was a mistake.

Q. On your system now have you any such thing as a provision for sick and disabled employees provided by the railway?—A. On the Chesapeake and Ohio we have established a hospital system. We have had rather an interesting and successful result there. Our general manager got very much interested in it and he took it up with the heads of these different brotherhoods and their representatives, and they appointed committees who examined into the different systems, and they finally agreed to it and fixed a form of assessment on those that belonged. We gave them a hospital which cost us $75,000, which, I think—at Clifton Forge—is as complete a hospital as there is in America, and everybody that can be is sent there, and medicines are distributed from there. They have a good surgeon and they have trained nurses. It has been running now for 2 years, and we are establishing branches at other places. It has really been a wonderful success.

Q. How is it maintained?—A. By assessment on the men; we take it out; it runs down. It runs from my assessment, say $6, down, I think, to 10 cents on some of the men.

Q. All the employees are assessed?—A. All the employees who will come in and pay. We let the men themselves settle that.

Q. That gives them the privilege of taking advantage of the facilities of the hospital?—A. They have the privilege of going to the hospital and being taken care of until discharged by the surgeon without any charge. They have the privilege of having medicines sent to them on the request of the local surgeons. If they are injured at a distance from this hospital, we have arrangements by which private hospitals take care of them and all is paid out of this fund. This fund is taken care of, and it has accumulated quite a little surplus.

Q. Do you know whether that feature of railroad management has become common at all in this country?—A. Well, I think in the last few years the managers are looking into it more and more. We hope now to add to this a pension system; our people are at work at it. I am a great believer in profit sharing as applied to railways. That is one of the dreams that I hope to see carried out; but it can not be until the railroads get a little steadier business and have some profits to share.

Q. (By Mr. FARQUHAR.) Does the assessment take in the officers of the railway as well as the employees?—A. Yes.

Q. And they are all assessed, from the president down?—A. The assessment is a nominal thing. They assessed me and I commuted mine by sending check for the whole amount at once. The higher officials do not use the hospital.

Q. (By Senator MALLORY.) Do you notice any effect that this has in harmonizing the employers and employees at all? Has it any effect in the direction of pleasant relations?—A. We have never had any trouble over there in 10 years. We keep on pretty good terms with our men. We have worked out more satisfactory results on that railroad through the Young Men's Christian Association than anything else. We have established branches on our railway and the men have taken it up and have gotten interested, and it has been 10 years since they have been on the road, and it has been a revolution.

Q. (By Mr. FARQUHAR.) In the matter of profit sharing, or rather the investment of the earnings of your employees in the stock of the railroad, you say you favor that. Is that very much the same plan as the Illinois Central has, or is there any difference?—A. No; their arrangement was to get the men to buy the stock, and that is a little dangerous, because stocks go up and down. I have been on a railway where the stocks went up and they made money, and then afterwards everybody would get disgusted because the stocks would go down and they would lose. My theory of profit sharing—if you will have your secretary to get you the history of the Orleans Railway in France, before it was taken by the Government, it was the best exemplification of profit sharing that there has ever been in the world and the most successful. When the Government took it it stopped. But if railroads can be put upon such a basis that they can pay steady dividends like other business, so that the men will know about what they are getting, then you can let their wages represent certain capital by the side of yours and make a certain division every year. So long as you can keep that up you will have better feeling among the men, better work, and less trouble with strikes. The danger has been that so many of our roads are so poor that they may pay a dividend one year and the next nothing, and then we might have friction. That is what has kept so many railway owners and managers from the plan.

Q. Then your idea is more on the real profits than on stock investment?—A. Yes; I do not want any men in mine holding stock because then, if it goes up or down, they are satisfied or dissatisfied. But if a man says, on his engine, "I am earning $2,000 a year; that represents so much capital invested; if the road get 5 per cent on its stock, I get 5 per cent on my wages in the year," he has something to work for and he is not going to have an accident if he can help it; neither is he going to strike and make trouble if he can help it.

Q. Do you not think really that that theory, if you may call it a theory, of labor capitalization, employees and capitalists being united as one in the interests of any corporation, whether a railroad or manufacturing concern, is the proper way?—A. I am a great believer in it; I think so.

Q. You think that goes a great way in solving a good deal of the strikes and difficulties and disputes between capital and labor?—A. I am quite sure of it. We have an institution in Cincinnati that has carried it on for several years, and it has been a perfect success.

Q. (By Senator MALLORY.) To what extent have your two systems complied with the requirements for automatic couplers and air brakes?—A. We are fully up to the requirements. On the 31st of December we will be all completed.

Q. Do you think there will be any appreciable beneficial effects from these automatic couplers and air brakes in the future, when all the roads get well supplied with them?—A. Oh, I am quite sure so; I think it was a wise law. I was in favor of it when it was passed. The only thing I did, I came on here and saw Senator Voorhees. That was to get the time extended; it was a question of finding capital to provide for it; but I think the principle of the law was right.

Q. Until the freight cars get generally equipped, however, it is very difficult to determine what is the real benefit arising from that, I suppose, because you have to work the link and pin coupler in with the automatic coupler, and a man has to go in between the cars anyhow?—A. That has been the difficulty, and you will not get to the real test until after the 1st of January. But, of course, after the 1st of January we who are equipped will refuse to exchange with those who are not, and that will immediately enforce a compliance with the law. We can not work an exchange and do business.

Q. Has your road any objection to your employees belonging to organizations—employees' organizations—and associations?—A. We have been rather in favor of that within certain limits. There are some classes of employees which we think ought not to belong; but we are rather disposed to favor generally the organizations.

Q. (By Mr. KENNEDY.) What class should be excepted, in your opinion?—A. Well, there are some people who come into confidential relations with the corporation, and we think their duty should be to the corporation, and they should not, perhaps, belong to the orders.

Q. You mean clerks, I suppose?—A. Well, I see in the newspapers—it has not come to me just yet—that out on the Big Four there is a row with the telegraph operators. Our management there think that the telegraph operators should not belong to the organization. That is a matter like our agents and our clerks; they should be dealt with separately. I mention that because that is in the newspapers. Our trainmen—we have contracts with all of them. We recognize their orders and make contracts with them.

Q. (By Senator MALLORY.) You do not do that with the telegraphers?—A. No; we do not think there is any necessity for it; they are in such confidential relation, doing business through our contracts for commercial business. We are very ready to treat with them individually. There is not enough of them either. We are always open to conference with them individually, but with our trainmen we could not do it.

Q. (By Mr. KENNEDY.) How could they harm the railroad company on account of these confidential relations, if they were organized?—A. Instead of each man's settling what he should do, his order would settle it for him, you know. I have not been into the case thoroughly, and I only mention it because I have seen the newspaper talk about it. But I asked our general manager what he thought about it, and he said he thought there ought to be a limit or a different arrangement there.

Q. Do you not find your organized employees, as a rule, very fair and liberal in their dealing with you?—A. We have got along better since we had organizations than we did before. The engineers, the conductors, the brakemen, and the firemen—we never object to deal with them as an organization.

Q. (By Senator MALLORY.) Have you had any serious strikes among your employees, on either of your systems, in recent years?—A. Never.

Q. Have you had any occasion to think over this recent law passed by Congress providing for mediation, conciliation, and arbitration of disputes between railroads and employees?—A. I looked at it when it was passed. It never has arisen in the way of business and I have never had occasion to consider it. Anything that tends to moral suasion and mediation between two parties is always good.

Q. If it is at all practicable?—A. You will get some people—some employees—that are so mad sometimes that nothing will prevent them from striking; and you will get some managers that will be so bad that the men will have to strike. If you have not common sense and consideration on both sides, you will have strikes.

Q. Do you think that any railroad in this country would be willing to submit the question of the wages that it pays or will pay to its employees to arbitration? Do you think it could afford to do it?—A. There would have to be some limitations on that, I expect. For instance, I should not want to submit the limit of wages paid by our corporation, except that they should not be raised above the limit of our competitors. In 1894, on our railway, we came very near having a strike, but it was voted down by the men. We had to reduce our wages; they got so high we had to. We were willing to arbitrate with the limitation that the wages should be paid the same as our rival lines. You will find that the men do not want to arbitrate on those lines. They are good traders; better than the managers. They will work and they will gain a point here and a point there, and they will gain. They will always get a little ahead.

Q. Is it not a fact that there are so many considerations which go to establish and determine the amount of wages that a road can pay to those different classes of employees, that the railroad can not afford to yield the question to the determination of anybody but its own directors?—A. I do not think they can afford to do that. I do not think as a good business proposition that we can afford to do that. They must keep within certain limits, if they are going to do business, and their directors ought to know that.

Q. Have you anything to say on the subject of arbitration at all, as between the men and employers of railroads?—A. I do not know that I have. Every man must take care of his employees.

Q. You are not impressed, then, with any immediate urgency for legislation on the subject?—A. The less outside influence there is, I think, the better I should consider it. Our men, I do not think, as a class, have any complaints, and we have none to make of them. We spend a great deal of time negotiating with them. I suppose probably an average of a month a year is taken up by our heads of departments negotiating with the men.

Q. What is your rule, if you have a rule, regarding men who are in the habit of drinking intoxicating liquors or drinking to excess?—A. Well, if a man drinks while on duty, we have no use for him. If he is a young man and drinks off duty, we do not promote him; we can not afford to.

Q. That rule is observed, is it, closely?—A. Absolutely.

Q. The fact that a man is a frequenter of bar rooms when off duty is equivalent to a black mark?—A. Yes; we are always watching for him to make a mistake.

Q. (By Mr. KENNEDY.) If he has reached middle life and drinks while on duty, does that interfere with his chances of promotion?—A. No; we keep him along. That is what we are trying to work out, a system of pensioning to take care of men who have been working for us a long time on our railroads. Now, we have a lot of old men that ought to be taken care of, and just how to do it we do not know.

Q. (By Senator MALLORY.) Is it generally understood among the men that the habitual indulgence in intoxicating liquor is against them and will ultimately result in their discharge?—A. Oh, yes; and then you will find that these unions all enforce that. They are about the best temperance lecturers there are. You take the Brotherhood of Locomotive Engineers, and if they find a man is drinking they will bring him up with a round turn.

Q. That is, practically, essential with the locomotive engineers and the firemen and the train hands generally; but how is it with the other employees?—A. You take the shop men, and we do not pay any attention to them when they are not in the shop. There is no need to watch them; they do not permit any accident. But a trackman that drinks we can not afford to keep, nor a switchman nor a trainman.

Q. (By Mr. CLARKE.) Do the laws of the several States through which you run prohibit the employing of drinking men on your railroads?—A. I think not. If they do, they have not been called to my attention.

Q. There are such laws in some States?—A. I think likely.

Q. (By Senator MALLORY.) What are the prevailing rates, first-class passenger rates, that you have?—A. Well, the local rates are all based on 3 cents, and through rates between the large cities will average about 2 cents.

Q. Is that local rate that you speak of common to the Chesapeake and Ohio and the other system also?—A. Yes.

Q. Three cents is higher than is usual in the Middle and New England States, I believe, is it not?—A. I think their local is based on that, but the system of commutation, round trip and half rates reduces it. Now, I think our average rate on the Big Four last year—I used the technical term for the Three C's—was a trifle under 2 cents; on the Chesapeake and Ohio it was a trifle over. But if a man comes along and asks for a ticket from one station to another on the road, 10 miles apart, for instance, it is always 3 cents.

Q. Why is it that the local rate is higher than it is in some other sections of the country?—A. I was not aware that it was.

Q. Take the New York Central, for instance?—A. New York State has a limit of 2 cents; that was the original law, I think. But you go down to New England and get on any of their local trains and then come down on to our road, and you will see why they ought to have a less rate. They are a bustling, thronging hive, and they fill up a train at one station and empty it at the next, and it is always full. You come down to the Chesapeake and Ohio railway and you will run 50 miles and never see anybody. It is the reverse of what it is in New England and New York. We have to give people a certain service. It is a remarkable thing on these roads. Our through trains make us the money and our local trains lose us the money; but we have to run a certain number of local trains.

Q. And what difference there is is due to the fact that it is a sparsely settled country and there is little travel and you have to run your trains anyhow?—A. That is it;

we have to run trains anyhow; and we have to charge all we can get; and it has been settled in the minds of passenger people that 3 cents is fair and as much as they can get.

Q. What is your idea on the subject of ticket brokerage and mileage books—A. Oh, I think it is very bad; bad for the railways; bad for the public, and bad for the men. It is the greatest temptation in the world to ruin your men, because a conductor handles a large amount of tickets, if he is right in with the ticket brokers. There are some bad men in all classes. There are probably good ticket brokers and bad ones, but the bad ones have the greatest chance in the world to seduce your men. We have had a great deal of trouble, and good men are ruined by tickets purchased of them which they do not turn in. Then it prevents giving reduced rates to the public because these tickets which are not used are taken up by scalpers and sold to our regular customers. And I can not see that there is any benefit to the public providing you have a law that the railway companies shall redeem their tickets at any authorized agency.

Q. You then would favor the abolition by act of Congress of the ticket brokerage system in this country under interstate-commerce rules, and the establishment of a system whereby tickets not used can be redeemed?—A. I think it would be in the line of good morals and good business.

Q. Have you any idea to what extent that interferes with the profits of the railroads, this ticket brokerage system? Does it cut a large hole in the profits of the railroads of this country or otherwise? You base your objection on the ground of the immorality of it. Is there any other objection?—A. Yes: it cuts into your revenue very largely. You give a low rate, for instance, for a passenger from Cincinnati to Chicago for a special trip up and back. Now, if that ticket can be sold coming back and be used by the brokers for 5 or 10 days and the general public you have cut off so much of your general business, and therefore you have to be very careful when you give those low rates.

Q. What have you to say on the subject of passes, free transportation?—A. Well, I have voted for the last five years—every time it has been up in our associations—in fact, I think I was the originator of the proposal that all passes should be abolished. You will find that most of the managers will go so far as to say that they will abolish all except to railway officials and employees, but that leaves the door open and they will pass many officials. I think every railroad should pass their employees over their own road, but if they want to travel on the other roads let them pay their way, and if it is on railway business, they will be repaid upon vouchers for their expenses; and if it is not then let them pay their way.

Q. The giving of passes without consideration, as is generally done—that is, without any money consideration—is a violation of the law as much as any other discrimination in favor of the individual?—A. I have always thought so.

Q. Have you any idea to what extent it exists as an abuse; is it large or small?—A. Well, very much less than it was. There has been a tremendous revolution in the last 10 or 15 years, so far as my observation goes; but yet I presume it is still very large:

Q. Do you know yourself or can you say whether to any extent passes are given to members of the legislature or members of Congress or Senators?—A. Well, our pass business is all run by one man. Our rule has been to give them to the people who live on our lines, during the session. We give that not as a compliment, but as a matter perhaps of right; it has grown up from immemorial custom.

Q. I did not exactly catch that. You give it to people living along the line?—A. For instance, if there is a member of the legislature—take Ohio; a member of the legislature lives on the line; we issue to him a pass good during the session of the legislature. It has been done, I think, for the last 30 years, and our people have concluded, I think, that it was a matter of custom; it had to be carried out until there was some general reform.

Q. Do you know whether that is done in Virginia or West Virginia?—A. There our local officials handle all those things and I can not tell you positively. I think the same principle generally prevails with all the railways all over the country. I think it is so general that the pass absolutely does no good; it is only the name of it. It would be just as well to wipe the whole thing out.

Q. (By Mr. KENNEDY.) You say that the ticket brokerage system cuts into your profits. Is it not a fact that the ticket brokerage system makes profits for some lines of railroads?—A. Well, I have never managed one that has.

Q. Have you not knowledge of railroad systems competing with others, resorting to the ticket brokers for the purpose of getting trade?—A. A few years ago we had several lines which sold tickets to the brokers for the sake of getting some money, ready money. That was done very largely by one or two lines. They broke up soon afterwards, however, and have been foreclosed.

Q. Do not some of the lines in New York which can not compete on an equality with the Pennsylvania and the New York Central do a good deal of their business through ticket brokers?—A. Well, the only complaint I have heard is—the West Shore, which really is the New York Central—there is a great deal of talk about what they do with ticket brokers by opposition lines; but I do not know anything about it.

Q. Do you believe that the railroads themselves are largely responsible for the existence of this ticket brokerage system?—A. They could stop it in a moment if they would. For instance, if they would make all their tickets train limits on the short line and without limit on the 3-cent local there would not be any difficulty; but it is like all other evils in this world; you have to get unanimous consent to do that; and as it is impossible to get that therefore they have to appeal to legislation. But if the entire railroad management could get together and make an agreement, a ticket broker could not live a week; he would die.·

Q. They make the necessity for good sound legislation on the subject, the railroads themselves?—A. Certainly, just as in every other case of legislation in this world for police or in the way of morals or anything else. There is always some one that will not conform, and you have to have legislation to protect the great majority.

Q. Would not this legislation that is spoken about protect the stronger lines against the weaker lines running in the same direction in the country?—A. I do not think so. If a weak line is not getting its share of the business, they can reduce their ticket rate. It is better to do it openly than through the brokers.

Q. (By Mr. FARQUHAR.) Could the abolition of the ticket brokerage there result in the lowering of the price of tickets to the cash-paying passengers?—A. It would lower excursion tickets to the cash-paying passengers; it would not lower, I do not think, the general tariff, but it would make more frequent excursions and lower rates.

Q. Well, would the abolition of the pass system make any difference to the cash-paying passenger? - A. I do not think so.

Q. So that the two reforms, the abolition of ticket brokerage and the abolition of the pass system, are not inviting to the general public who are paying their way on all the railroads?—A. Well, I think the ticket brokerage would help the general passenger, as I say, because there are reduced rates made between all important points which it would help. When it comes to the question of passes, I can not see how the general public get any interest in it except as it would make it fair for everybody, but I do not think it would affect the rate.

Q. Now as to the general views of the managers of the railroads of the country on this question of passes—is it or is it not a fact that they would as soon continue the pass system as not?—A. Well, the best answer to that is that I have no doubt that some railway managers would not think they made a success in life unless they could issue passes; but I think the great majority are tired and sick of it.

Q. Provided that it does not make any difference in the regular rate, do you not think that on the part of railroads discriminating as between the pass passenger and the paying passenger, that it is just as bad a discrimination as between the freight rates?—A. Where it exists, it is.

Q. Do you not think that it is an unjust discrimination against honest people who will pay, and in favor of the favored ones who will get passes?—A. Well, the language of the question being yours, I should answer yes. [Laughter.]

Q. Does your system of giving passes on your line extend down to members of the common council and officers of municipalities?—A. We never have issued those of late years.

Q. How long since you ceased to issue that class of passes?—A. I do not think we have issued any in 5 or 10 years, unless it would be on some special occasion, a matter where a local official wants to be interested. I know of one case where we took the common council of a certain city to another city to see an elevated road, to show what ought to be done; some special cases like that. Our passes are not over, I should think, one-tenth of what they were 10 or 15 years ago.

Q. Has it come under your observation that passes issued to aldermen of cities are not used by the aldermen themselves but used by any party that may need them or that can get them?—A. As we do not give them, I have not much observation on that. Our general rule is not to issue any of that class.

Q. Do you know of any cases on your road where your conductors take up a pass when they find that it is not being used by the party to whom the pass was issued by the passenger agent?—A. Generally there are passes bulletined all the time that are not in the hands of people entitled to them.

Q. What do you think of the plan of having all passes registered with the Interstate Commerce Commission?—A. It is much easier not to issue them; but I would not object to that.

Q. You think it would be a check on the pass system if they should make that law?—A. The register would be so large, taking 180,000 miles of railroad in this country, that nobody would ever look through it.

Q. Even if they did not, if there should be such a system of registry, would not that be sufficient to cause the legislators and members of Congress to take some action on it?—A. It might prevent some Congressmen or members of the legislatures accepting passes, if they knew that some reporter would be looking over the record and publishing it on them.

Q. (By Representative LIVINGSTON.) Could they not get that now if they wanted it?—A. Yes.

Q. Do you suppose any Congressman would hold a pass in his pocket a minute, if he knew any reporter would ask him?—A. I do not know about that. [Laughter.]

Q. (By Mr. CLARKE.) As far as your observation extends, do the roads which issue passes to members of the legislature living along their lines also issue passes to State officers and the judges of the courts?—A. We do not issue passes to the judges; we have discontinued that. The officers of the State, I think, always have their passes issued the first of the year when they are elected, without any question, and have had from time immemorial.

Q. You say you think it proper to issue passes to the employees of the road. Are attorneys considered employees?—A. If they are doing your work; working for you.

Q. Is it not a frequent practice with railroads to give a small retainer to a very large number of local attorneys all over the State?—A. I do not know what the general principle is. On our road we have one general attorney who manages all those matters; and his plan is to keep one man in every county who manages his business. He usually pays them a small salary and gives them transportation.

Q. Sometimes a large railroad system is very much interested in State legislation and State politics, I suppose?—A. Certainly.

Q. Through a large number of local attorneys a railroad can exert political influence, can it not?—A. Well, we have never tried it that way. I do not think there is enough that could be done in that line to affect legislation very much.

Q. You do not know of that having been done anywhere in this country?—A. No.

Q. You do not think it would be a common practice, then?—A. Oh, I think that would be too large a job for any railway to undertake. They may have one or two men who give them information and present their side of the case, but to control general legislation, I do not think that possible.

Q. In granting passes to the employees of the railroad, is it customary also to extend the privilege to their families?—A. That varies on different roads and different divisions. It is a sort of a feeling we have that it creates a better feeling with the employees to be rather liberal in passing them over your own line, and that it does not do any harm to have the employees on one division see the other divisions, and we are inclined to be very liberal with our own people.

Q. Would it be agreeable to you to see the entire pass system abolished, and whenever a railroad employee of any class rides on railroad business let him be reimbursed for the cost of his ticket?—A. Yes; I would be very glad to see that done; it would save us a good deal of trouble and a good deal of annoyance and criticism, which in many cases is unjust.

Q. On the whole, would not that be the most businesslike and useful system?—A. No question about it; instead of fussing with some judge or some members of Congress or some member of the common council that has a pass. The right thing to do is to pass a law prohibiting any passes, and then you will get at it.

Q. (By Senator MALLORY.) What is your opinion of the effect of discrimination by railroad companies, whether it is against individuals or in favor of individuals, in the matter of transportation of freight? Is it an abuse to-day of any considerable magnitude?—A. It is much less to-day than it has been, but I suppose it exists in some cases.

Q. Have you any reason to assign for its decrease as an abuse?—A. Well, these things go in waves. For instance, in the year 1885 there was a great discrimination; in 1886, the interstate commerce law was passed and for 2 or 3 years there was very little discrimination. It made a turning point around which the managers gathered. Then discrimination grew until, in 1894 and 1895, it was about as bad as it well could be. In 1896, there was scarcely any. The railways met in the trunk-line territory and made what was known as the joint traffic agreement, for which I had the honor to be responsible, which was imitated all over the country, and that steadied rates during 1896 and until in the spring of 1897, when in the trans-Missouri case the Supreme Court decided that the Sherman law, which the railways had supposed did not apply to them, applied to them and to no one else practically; then there was anarchy. That lasted until December, 1898, when the Interstate Commerce Commission took up the matter by consultation with the various railroad managers, and there were a great many hearings held like these here in Washington, and the result was that the managers and officials decided the thing must stop, that it should not go on, and since the 1st of January, 1899, as far as my observation goes, I have never known less discrimination or published rates better maintained.

Q. Do you not think the fact that railroads have now about all they can do in the matter of transportation and traffic has something to do with the cessation of discrimination?—A. That is one of the reasons I was glad to come before you, and hoped we would get some aid from your report. My judgment is when this rush of business is over the railroads will gradually drift back to their old ways, and we must have some legislation to help us. I want to impress on your minds the gravity of the situation. It is such an enormous interest. Here are one-tenth of all your people supported by the railroads, one-tenth of your people dependent on the railways, and all of your people dependent on the railways for their comfort. Here are a million of employés whose happiness and welfare depends on the railways. All these can not be taken care of unless the railways get proper rates, and it seems almost impossible in dull times for the railways to get fair rates under the present law, as there is no way in which they can make an agreement, and it is such an enormous business that you can not expect as a matter of honor to have it all carried out, and I believe it is the duty of Congress to take the matter up. Originally the railroads claimed they were not amenable to law like other corporations. That took twenty years to settle, but it was settled in 1885 and 1886. Now, the people having won the fight that they have the right to regulate the railroads, it is their duty to do it, and to aid the railroads and furnish them something for that regulation. I believe it is their duty to pass a law so that if John Jones makes a contract with Peter Jones that he will maintain rates between two points it should be a legal contract. If either breaks it, the other should have the right to bring suit for damages. If the public is injured they should have the right to complain and get their damages. In other words, I see more danger to this country by leaving these large interests outside of the law than there can be in any proper legislation. If they are not controlled it is going to bring trouble to business and financial interests, and it is breaking down the largest interests in this country.

Q. Does unrestrained competition produce seriously injurious effects on railroads?—A. It produces injury to railway, shipper, and the public.

Q. If you have unrestrained competition, is there any danger of the railroads having to go into the hands of receivers, many of them, in this country?—A. Most assuredly. Look at the history of the last 10 or 15 years. The only roads which have made money have been reorganized roads. Look at the securities wiped out.

Q. Have you thought anything of the fact of the distinction between railroad enterprise and ordinary business enterprise being very marked, and what may be a theory applicable to the ordinary private enterprise is not applicable necessarily to the railroad; that while competition may be the life of business in a certain line of business, competition between railroads is necessarily disastrous; have you thought of that?—A. I have, and that is true. If this country had decided in the beginning that they would not attempt to control railroads at all but had left them like other enterprises, you could afford to stand still and see them fight and destroy each other, but you have said that they are subject to certain restrictions, and now when you take this enormous business, and say you shall not make any arrangements or agreements, you are outside of the law; you have produced a condition of affairs where reorganizations and bankruptcies will go on. Securities will go out of the hands of the people into the hands of Wall street speculators, and will be used exactly like counters in a game of cards to count the gains and losses in Wall street. You have destroyed one of the greatest industries of the United States, which employs more men than any other interest in this country, and you say all this shall be managed without any laws. That is the situation to-day. No one feels it more than the Interstate Commerce Commission. They have done all they could, but they have no authority. Take the export business of this country. Your grain and meats are sold abroad and sold in competition with all the world. Why should you limit the carriage of that in this country? It does not help your own people, your own farmers. It makes a market for your producers, and the question of selling your surplus product is one that concerns every farmer, especially of the great West, and that business ought to be left just as free as any business to be competed for.

Q. That subject was investigated by the Interstate Commerce Commission—the difference between export and inland rates—I believe?—A. I think they are going to make some report as to the modification of the law.

Q. (By Representative LIVINGSTON.) Are you not overcoming competition largely by consolidations and combinations?—A. In some ways, but not entirely. I should like to answer that question at length. I have been somewhat a student of the problem for a number of years. I am not and never was one of the railroad managers who believe that they should be left to do their own sweet will without any legislation whatever. I think that some regulation is demanded because the railway enters so closely into the interests of all the people. At the same time, if the present situation should go on, it will result in the railways being owned and operated by the Government, which I believe will be disastrous to the progress of the country, to say nothing about the Government. Now, there must be something done to create more stability in the earnings of the railway. The interstate-commerce law, as first passed, I was in favor of. I believe it should be amended, insuring the greatest publicity in the world to the rates; that is your protection. The long and short haul clause has never interfered with our roads north of the river; south of the river they claim it has been disastrous, and there should be some consideration given to their complaints, I think. What I plead for is a law that will enable railways to make agreements for the maintenance of their published tariffs, agreements that can be enforced by the courts. It goes further and broader than the pool. The pool is a division of the business. I would go further than that, saying that the railways should be permitted to make agreements, for instance, between Baltimore and New York, that they would maintain this tariff. Now, these tariffs should be reasonable, and I would leave the question whether reasonable or not to some tribunal like the Interstate Commerce Commission, and if the railways made their agreement and a man should complain, the commission should hear and decide whether these rates were reasonable or not. Then I would abolish the criminal feature of the law, because I think you are trying to make a business transaction a crime, and the public will not support it. You can not get your evidence and it has not the sympathy of the community. It should be a question of fine. When the public is injured, a question of fines; and when the individual is injured, a question of damages.

Q. You say, "Making a business transaction a crime." Is that it, do you think?—A. A man selling goods is on the same basis as the railway man selling transportation. The public does not consider it a crime to sell the goods at a lower price to one than another. You have not educated your communities outside of the railways to the view that discrimination in selling transportation is a crime; therefore, when you hope to pass beyond what public opinion thinks is justified, you do not succeed. We have always thought, the greater majority of the railway managers have thought, if we could have a system of fines we could help ourselves to enforce them. These fines would be so burdensome as to aid in carrying out agreements.

Q. What you call a business transaction is the violation of law; it is doing something prohibited by law.—A. You have created the law yourselves.

Q. We have a right to create the law.—A. Certainly. It is only a question of policy, not of right.

Q. (By Mr. PHILLIPS.) How would you regulate these fines in case of large shippers? A fine of a few thousand dollars would not amount to anything.—A. I would put a fine on every bill of lading right along, and in that way you will break up any institution in the world in 6 months, if not stopped. As I was going on to say, you need some protection of law. I believe your present condition of affairs is building up your large shippers and large institutions and crushing out your small ones; it is so much easier dealing with one man than a hundred. You are crushing out all your small shippers. Your legislation is all for the powerful few. Keep the power in the Interstate Commerce Commission. I would go further. I would not have a railway built except when its location and plans are approved by the Interstate Commerce Commission, and the money put up to build it. I would not have any more stock jobbing and bonding.

Q. (By Mr. CLARKE.) You would not allow a local railroad to be built without applying to the Interstate Commerce Commission?—A. You can inside the State. They should go to the State commissions. I would stop these enterprises that are built for the sake of issuing securities. As I think one gentleman, a Senator in this country, said, the only use, to his knowledge, of a railway was to bond it and sell the bonds. I would stop that practice.

Q. (By Mr. C. J. HARRIS.) What is the mileage of the system that you represent?—A. We have about 1,500 miles south of the river and 2,500 north.

Q. What is your general bonded indebtedness?—A. We have about $60,000,000 on each division—$60,000,000 south and $60,000,000 north.

Q. What is your idea, in a general way, of the capitalization of railroads in this country—is it excessive or not?—A. I think it is away below what they have cost, especially since these reorganizations have been made.

Q. As a matter of fact, is not the bonded indebtedness of most of these new organizations as much as the roads cost in the beginning, taking their increase?—A. Oh, no; some of these reorganizations have been the most cruel things in the world on small investors—that have been reorganized on the basis of one-half or two-thirds of what they were worth.

Q. Could some of these roads be built to-day at less than their present bonded indebtedness?—A. I do not know of one. Take the lines that I represent; you could not begin to produce them for their bonded indebtedness.

Q. You spoke of their being crushed out by competition when business was slack. It is alleged by some that they have created so much capitalization that they are demanding more of the public than they ought to have. That is one of the great troubles with rates. I brought out this capitalization for that purpose.—A. If you will let me, I will answer that at length, reviewing the history. After our war ended everybody went to building railroads and it created a class of people called promoters and contractors. The people were anxious to get railways and they would grant charters, land, and other inducements. They would turn over all of these and as many of the bonds and stocks as the people cared to issue to these contractors, who would build the railroad. They would go to work and build the railroad maybe 100 miles or 1,000 and unload the stocks and bonds and securities for what they could get, usually at a profit, and the people who got these found themselves loaded up with a large amount of worthless securities. The people found themselves paying higher rates. That was the origin of the granger laws, which culminated back in 1870. From that time on there has been so much of that that there has been a reorganization of railroads. I suppose there never in the history of the world has been such wiping out of securities as there has been in this country in the last 5 years, and to-day I think your capitalization is below what your railroads would cost. The cost of lands in the cities is enormous. Take the Big Four railway, which runs through the cities of Cincinnati, Dayton, Springfield, Columbus, Cleveland, Indianapolis, and into St. Louis and Chicago—why there are millions and millions in their terminal facilities. I suppose you could not get the new location they have in the city of Cincinnati under a great many millions of dollars. Then you attempt to build a new railroad, and you cut up the farmers' land, and it all costs so much money; and their equipment is enormous; we have to have an enormous equipment. A proof that the public are not paying too much is the fact that the rates of fare and the transportation of freight were never so low or lower in any other country on earth. Since the 1st of January we have had tariffs, but the tariffs have been so low that we can not go on with the increased price of labor and material with these tariffs. If we can not get an agreement to maintain better tariffs there is going to be bankruptcies and reorganizations; and securities will be wiped out, employees' wages reduced, or employees dismissed, which is the more modern way to do it—with less men. I think that is to the interest of the country, and I hope your commission will find some way to get proper legislation. Then I believe further the Interstate Commerce Commission or some proper body should have authority to examine the books of all these roads every month, three months, or any time they pleased, and stop all these scandals and false accountings. There is your protection. Do not let any stocks or bonds be issued except on their certificate. I am not pleading here for the railroads to be let alone. I want them to be regulated even more than they are now, but I want you in consideration of that to give us some legal rights and make us legal bodies.

Q. The shippers—we have discussed their grievances, and the grievances of railroads; now it seems to me the interests of the investors and owners of these stocks and bonds ought to be promoted in some way by some Government supervision of some kind.—A. I think so. There are 3 duties on the railroad; first, that the physical condition of the railways should be kept in such shape that they can do the business properly; they should be allowed income enough for that; second, they should have enough to take proper care of their employees; third, the investor should have a fair return for his money. No legislation will be supported by the great thinking community, when they get around to it, that does not take care of these three things.

Q. (By Senator MALLORY.) You recognize the fact that the drift and tendency of railroads in this country to-day is to consolidate, I believe?—A. Yes.

Q. That in the last 4 or 5 years there has been a tremendous impetus in that direction?—A. Yes.

Q. What effect will it have on railroad transportation in this country, if that is kept up?—A. The problem about that is this: Out in New England they have practically eliminated competition by consolidation and the people there seem to be very well satisfied with the present situation. In the South they have done substantially the same thing. There are two or three companies and, being so few, they can get along comfortably. I doubt whether it is practicable to consolidate the great trunk lines because they have so many local interests and they are so large and enormous. For instance, there are about 7 or 8 lines that control all this immense business between the Mississippi River and the ocean, north of the Potomac. I do not think it would be possible to consolidate them, and so long as they are not consolidated they are going to fight when business is dull unless there is some way they can agree lawfully among themselves.

Q. Are there not competing lines in New England that have been consolidated— lines that run practically from the same point to the same point, just as your lines running from the west to the Atlantic seaboard?—A. I do not know of any consolidation between them.

Q. (By Mr. FARQUHAR.) The Boston and Albany?—A. The Vanderbilt interests and the New York Central; the Erie, the Lackawanna, the Lehigh Valley, the Pennsylvania, and the Baltimore and Ohio. These are all independent interests, and I can not conceive of anything that would produce a consolidation of these interests. I think that would be too much to attempt. They would have too many local interests.

Q. (By Mr. C. J. HARRIS.) What is the eastern terminal of the Chesapeake and Ohio?—A. Newport News, Hampton Roads.

Q. (By Senator MALLORY.) I am glad to hear you express that opinion. I have been very apprehensive it was going to result in 2 or 3 corporations owning all the railroads in the United States. You think, then, that is not going to be the result?—A. I think not, and I hope not, because when that comes you strengthen largely the party that wants the Government to own the railroads, and then you will be on evil times.

Q. Your opinion is it is impractical for this Government to own and conduct railroad trunk lines?—A. The genius of our Government could do anything, but I do not think it would be wise with our present system. And, above all, the governments in other countries never have managed the railroads as well as individuals, and I do not think they would do it with the same skill and energy here. This is a very large country, which depends almost entirely for its future on its transportation, and the competition between these lines, in a legitimate way, the fast trains and facilities for doing business will always be kept up. The railroads are what have built our country up. It is as easy to go from the Mississippi to New York to-day as it used to be to go 100 miles. We have astonished the world with our facilities for transportation. If the Government had the railroads that would all be stopped. You would have slow trains and bad service, just as they do in France and Germany.

Q. In the event that there was no power to restrain the rates which the railroads should be allowed to charge for freight and passenger traffic, do you think if they were allowed also to make these contracts you speak of, they would drift into exorbitant, extortionate, excessive rates?—A. No; their interests are too large; there is too much competition.

Q. You think that would regulate itself?—A. I do.

Q. You, however, are not unwilling, in the event the power to make traffic contracts is given to them, so they can enforce them in the courts, that the Interstate Commerce Commission be given a supervisory control over the rates?—A. I think that ought to be done to satisfy the people. I doubt if they would exercise it in one case in a hundred; but if the law did not put that in, the people would think they had been cheated. It ought to be in. As to rates, I am perfectly willing to try my case before the Interstate Commerce Commission. If, after I put in my proof, they decide against me, there must be something wrong with my rates.

Q. You would be willing the decision should stand until set aside by the courts?— A. Yes, so long as I maintained that agreement; and if I am not I can drop out and go it alone.

Q. You would be willing for the Interstate Commerce Commission to determine prima facie as to the existence of discrimination as between localities or individuals?— A. I have never objected to that, but I think there ought to be a right of appeal to the courts.

Q. Prima facie I mean?—A. I have no objection to that.

Q. The contention has been made here by an eminent railroad gentleman that if the power were given to the Interstate Commerce Commission to determine anything about rates, those rates should not go into effect; its decisions should not go into effect until sustained by the court; but when it came to the matter of discrimination he said he was perfectly willing to let the decision of the Interstate Commerce Commission as to the existence of discrimination stand until set aside by the courts. One, he held, was a matter so vital to the railroad company that he did not think it was just or reasonable to leave the matter of the rate to the decision of an outside party like the Interstate Commerce Commission so that it would take effect. Have you given the subject any thought?—A. A great deal. That has been discussed in our meetings, and we have had to think of it. We have hundreds of millions of property to look after. I do not sympathize very much with those people who are so afraid of a bad decision by the Interstate Commerce Commission as to rates. I would keep my right to go to the courts, because there might be a matter of principle involved; but here you have five independent men; they never could make a rate so bad as some of us have made ourselves if they tried. I would be perfectly willing that they should settle any special cases, after a hearing, whether the rate was reasonable or not, and let it go into effect, subject to revision by the courts. In case of discrimination, I would go one step further and provide that in case of an agreement between railroads for maintenance of tariffs and division of business, if the rates under that agreement established by them should be complained of, and the Interstate Commerce Commission, after a hearing, found they were unreasonable, their decision should stand so long as the railroads maintained that agreement. It seems to me that is an absolute protection to the people.

Q. (By Mr. PHILLIPS.) Do you think the Interstate Commerce Commission or any other body would be competent to deal with such a vast subject, in regard to the fixing of freight rates all over this country? Could they possibly hear and determine on such large interests?—A. There is the difficulty. If you say you give them power over the general fixing of rates, you make a mistake and overwhelm them. I would confine it to special complaints in regard to special rates or discriminations. These they have a right to hear; but when it comes to the general tariff of the Chesapeake and Ohio Road, with that they have nothing to do. . But if the people of Cincinnati complained that the rates from Cincinnati to Richmond are too high, let the Interstate Commerce Commission hear that question. If they decide it against me, I have the right to appeal to the court.

Q. Not to fix the general schedule?—A. No; you can not do that; it is too large. The moment you mention that the people say you are giving them power to fix the rates. You do not do anything of the kind. It is only to hear special cases.

Q. You think it is impracticable for anybody outside of railroad experts to make any rates generally for a system of railway, like the Chesapeake and Ohio, for instance?—A. I do not see how you can get men to do it. I have been in the business for 30 years and have a large staff of competent men who have served with me for years and it is a very difficult matter to fix the tariffs. We have to change them every day.

Q. You say the same thing with reference to making classifications?—A. It seems to me we ought to have the same classification all over this country. I have never justified the difference that has prevailed.

Q. There are now three, I believe?—A. Yes; and it creates an infernal amount of trouble, which it seems to me is unnecessary. But some of my railroad brethren are strong against it.

Q. Do you think it practical to have one classification for the Pacific and the same for the south Atlantic seaboard?—A. I do not see but you should let the gentlemen make their rates on the same classification. They do not have the same rate all over now. I do not see why the same classification should not go from the Atlantic to the Pacific, so that a man should know what class he is going in when he picks up the tariff.

Q. Do you notice any particular inconvenience arising from three systems of classifications?—A. It would not come to me, except occasionally I meet a merchant and he speaks of it. I suppose the freight agents, who get with the people more, would know. It has been discussed more as a general matter, as it comes to me.

Q. (By Mr. KENNEDY.) Do you carry much grain from the Northwest to Newport News?—A. Very large quantities.

Q. Yours is what is called a trunk line?—A. We think we are considerable of a trunk. Some of our opponents think we are more so.

Q. I see by the New York Herald of a recent date that the managers of the trunk lines, or committee, have agreed on a rate for wheat and wheat products from Chicago, I believe, to the seaboard, which is a practical compliance with the recent opinion of the Interstate Commerce Commission. Is that a result of that opinion—that rate—or did business reasons determine it outside of that?—A. I really do not know what influenced them. We have no interest in that. You see we have no local business at Newport News like they have in New York and New England; it is all export. We have always been in favor of making the same rate, if they wanted it, or a different rate; it did not concern us.

Q. You mean a difference of 2 cents between grain and grain products?—A. Yes; I think that was it.

Q. You do not know whether that was the result of the opinion of the Interstate Commerce Commission or not?—A. I think the railroads were so snowed under with business they could not manage it and were making the rates so low they were ridiculous, and that is a compromise, patched up to get better rates. That is usually the way they are made. We are an export line, you know; we do very little interior business.

Q. (By Senator MALLORY.) Your rates are fixed by the rates to New York?—A. Yes; New York and New England. We have to take our chances on whatever they make.

Q. I understood you to say you would be willing to have the Interstate Commerce Commission or some other central body have the power to send an official to investigate and inspect the books and accounts of interstate railroads from time to time?—A. Yes; very glad to have it.

Q. Have you any particular object in that?—A. Publicity helps.

Q. You would think the fact that it is open to public inspection would have a beneficial effect?—A. I think the difficulty with railroads is they have tried to keep to themselves, and have had a little hesitation in dealing with the Interstate Commerce Commission, and I think it has injured them. I think the greater publicity you get the better it will be.

Q. (By Mr. PHILLIPS.) You would be willing to have accounts examined into similarly to the inspections we have by the Government in case of national banks?—A. I think that is what we ought to have; yes.

Q. (By Mr. C. J. HARRIS.) Do you not think the general public have a rather distorted idea of the amount of abuse and the amount of discrimination that is made by railroads?—A. There is no doubt of that, and it is ministered to by every cheap political orator who wants somebody to abuse. I think the railway managers have been perhaps arbitrary and added to that feeling. I think it would be much better if we could get the railroads on a business basis and everything public.

Q. (By Mr. CLARKE.) You are not afraid of the people? You recognize that railroads are quasi public corporations?—A. That is right. We are there to manage them for the people, and there should be no reason why they should not be managed with the people.

Q. (By Senator MALLORY.) Have you any suggestions to make with regard to putting express companies under the Interstate Commerce Commission?—A. I do not know anything about that. They manage their own business by making agreements. I should be sorry to have them put on the same basis as railroads so they could not agree.

Q. The extent of the traffic that they take from the railroad companies, is that really an appreciable quantity as compared with railroad business generally?—A. I do not think so. The railroads with their fast trains of late years have been decreasing that. I think their earnings on the Chesapeake and Ohio are only about 1 per cent of the freight business.

Q. Do you know anything about this question of discrimination in favor of certain individuals by the mileage which is paid for the use of cars?—A. I hear it at almost every railroad meeting I attend. There is a great evil in the mileage of private cars. It is discrimination in business, and it certainly builds up the large shipper as against the small shipper. The large shipper will buy 500 freight cars; he gets a large mileage for these; he gets them handled promptly, otherwise he would not give you his business. I suppose he gets 15 to 20 per cent income on the investment from these cars, and the small shipper who is trying to compete with him in the next store, who does not own cars, will go into bankruptcy. The man who owns the cars gets passes for his agent to look after the cars, and undoubtedly the one who owns the cars does a great deal of buying himself.

Q. Of itself, do you think that is an evil?—A. I do, yes.

Q. Why, if you will be good enough to say?—A. It is an evil because it enables one man to get the advantage of another.

Q. Through the railroad?—A. Through the railroad. Yet it would ruin any railroad in this country that did not do as they are doing now, because it would take off a very large amount of traffic which is valuable.

Q. Have you any suggestions as to the method of stopping it, if it is an evil?—A. Amend your interstate-commerce law as I told you and there would not be any trouble. If I make an agreement with my opponent that we will divide the business from a certain point, and the man who owns the private cars wants to give his business to the other man, he may have it; he cannot hurt me any. As long as you leave me outside the law and I get my business as best I can I will treat with him. That is considered the legal way of beating your opponent.

Q. (By Mr. C. J. HARRIS.) Why should not railroads furnish exclusively the cars that are used in business, and why should not the law compel them to furnish cars?—A. Well, you had better generally amend the law instead of trying to reach the sore spots.

Q. If a railroad undertakes to perform public transportation and does not furnish sufficient cars to do the business, is it not rather derelict to the people?—A. That is not the question. They all try to furnish the cars, but they can not get the business if they do. For instance, I have seen the stock cars of the Chesapeake and Ohio stand idle in Chicago while we had contracts for transporting stock from Chicago to Liverpool via Newport News, and could not get it unless we took these special cars and let our own cars stand idle; and it costs us thousands of dollars for mileage.

Q. Has the supply of private cars arisen from inability of railroads to take care of shippers by furnishing cars?—A. In one way the refrigerator people originated this, but this evil has grown up from the decisions under the interstate-commerce law. It is the large shipper taking care of himself. It would never have been heard of if it had not been for it.

Q. (By Mr. CLARKE). You think it will eliminate the speculative features, so far as the owners of private cars are concerned, if the railroads are left free to contract between themselves?—A. That is it precisely. These large interests then would have to put in their cars on a fair mileage and we would get legitimate business.

Q. (By Mr. FARQUHAR). In such an arrangement as that, would you also take in the Pullman service?—A. I leave that to be regulated like the railway, the sleeping-car service. The proper thing to do would be for the railway to own its own sleeping cars, if they only ran over their own line, but with the different lines spread out, you would have to have too many cars on extra occasions, and you would have too much invested. For instance, to-day as I came through the office I was told we had some troops that called for 25 or 30 sleepers. If we undertook to carry that number of sleepers ourselves we would be killed by dead capital. I think your transportation companies should have some limitation on rates as other people, but I do not see how the railroads themselves could afford to furnish this equipment.

Q. Was there not an attempt on the part of some railroads to furnish these refrigerator and stock cars, and did they not have some, say, 15 to 20 years ago?—A. Later than that. When Mr. Roberts was alive, he did not run a private car over the Pennsylvania Railroad, and the other trunk lines agreed to that, but about 5 years ago, I guess, one of the trunk lines decided it could not carry that out. That let down the bars, and to-day private cars are running.

Q. Is it not a fact to-day, on the question of the private cars, that there is no railroad which can afford to have a quarrel with the owners of these cars on rates or anything?—A. We do not think so.

WASHINGTON, D. C., *October 21, 1899.*

TESTIMONY OF HON. JOHN K. COWEN,

President of the Baltimore and Ohio Railroad Company.

The commission met at 10.35 a. m., Senator Mallory presiding. Hon. John K. Cowen, of Baltimore, president of the Baltimore and Ohio Railroad Company, being first duly sworn, testified as follows:

Q. (By Senator MALLORY.) What is your name?—A. John K. Cowen.

Q. Where do you reside?—A. In Baltimore.

Q. What is your occupation?—A. I am president of the Baltimore and Ohio Railroad Company.

Q. How long have you been connected with railroad affairs?—A. Twenty-seven years.

Q. How long have you been in your present capacity with the Baltimore and Ohio Railroad?—A. Three years and nine months.

Q. Can you state about how many employees there are in the employ of the Baltimore and Ohio?—A. I think we have about 30,500 employees in the service of the Baltimore and Ohio direct. That does not include the employees of lines that we are interested in, such as the Baltimore and Ohio Southwestern and the Pittsburg and Western.

Q. How are those employees paid, by the month or by the week?—A. By the month or by the day.

Q. Depending on the character of their employment?—A. Yes.

Q. How do you pay the train hands, locomotive engineers, firemen, and other train employees?—A. We have an agreed scale with them, based generally upon miles run.

Q. An agreed schedule with them individually?—A. Yes.

Q. Or is it with any associations?—A. No. All the associations, I believe, are on our road, all the trainmen's associations, but our understanding is with the committees directly of our own men.

Q. You do not then know the associations at all in the transaction?—A. No.

Q. It is just simply the committees of the men?—A. Yes.

Q. Have you any system of suspension of men for dereliction of duty?—A. Oh, yes.

Q. That is, anything less than discharge?—A. Yes, they are suspended for minor offenses varying greatly according to the offense.

Q. What do you mean by suspension?—A. Oh, they may be put off for 30 days and then taken on again, or indeed for a longer period of time.

Q. Have you any such thing as the system of blacklisting discharged employees?—A. No.

Q. The system to which I refer is one which has gained some notoriety by reason of suits brought by the parties claimed to have been injured. The railroad discharging the employee passes his name as one discharged over to some other railroad interested.—A. No, we do not engage in that.

Q. (By Mr. FARQUHAR.) Are you aware that such a system did exist between railroads; of blacklisting in case of strikes and troubles of that kind on the road?—A. I think possibly at one time it did; but the extent to which it went, I do not know.

Q. Are other sections notified of discharges of the man on your own system?—A. I can not answer without asking the general manager whether we systematically notify each of our divisions of the reasons for the discharge. I do not know how that is, and without examination of the general manager I could not testify whether we have a system under which we notify the superintendents of the respective divisions of the discharge or not.

Q. (By Professor JOHNSON.) If a man sought employment, the first question asked him would be where he was formerly employed?—A. Undoubtedly that is the case.

Q. And if he were employed recently on a division, inquiry would be made?—A. That is right.

Q. (By Senator MALLORY.) How many hours out of the 24 are the employees of the Baltimore and Ohio expected to work?—A. My recollection is, in the train service, the day is figured on a mileage basis, and overtime is allowed for excess mileage, or after 12 hours.

Q. Do they receive additional pay for overtime?—A. Yes, they receive additional pay for overtime—in other words, 12 hours is the limit of a day's work.

Q. By train hands?—A. That is my recollection. Of course there are a great many of the train hands who make their mile days very much within that time, but we have an understanding that work over that period is to be paid for. If without fault they do not get their trains in or they are delayed and do not get their trains, they are entitled to pay for overtime.

Q. Well, is that also the length of work per day of the other employees, such as clerks and men engaged in other business than that of train hands?—A. No; our clerks come either at 8 or 9 o'clock and are discharged at 5, and in summer there is a half holiday on Saturday.

Q. Well, then, there are men employed on the tracks and sections, bosses and so on?—A. Yes.

Q. And section hands?—A. Yes.

Q. How are their hours of employment?—A. I would have to inquire exactly what their time is; but my belief is, trackmen, laborers, and employees generally work 10 hours per day.

Q. Do your men work on Sundays as a rule?—A. The train hands and those that are necessary for the running of them on Sunday do work.

Q. Do they receive any extra compensation for Sunday work?—A. No.

Q. (By Representative LIVINGSTON.) You said the train hands worked on both passengers and freights?—A. Yes, both the freights and passengers, but of course there are fewer trains running on Sundays than on week days. An effort is made to curtail the Sunday trains as much as possible.

Q. You try to curtail the freight trains on Sunday?—A. We do run freight trains on Sunday, but there is a less movement on Sunday always than on week days, and of course there are less men employed on Sunday than on week days.

Q. (By Senator MALLORY.) You only run those freight trains on Sunday that you can not avoid, I suppose?—A. Well, that is practically so.

Q. In some of the States through which the Baltimore and Ohio Railroad passes there are laws prohibiting the running of freight on Sunday, are there not?—A. Yes.

Q. How do you manage in those States?—A. Just run along; we have not been prosecuted. I believe we were prosecuted once in West Virginia, but the matter dropped. It has been sort of recognized as a necessity to continue the running of certain trains. There has been from time to time complaint, of course, local complaints, of running excursion trains, which are not absolutely necessary, but we do run excursion trains, and of those there have been complaints from time to time, but no prosecution. There has not been any actual prosecution.

Q. Do you remember whether West Virginia permits the running of freight trains under some exceptional circumstances?—A. No, my recollection is that it is absolute, but I have not the statute before me and I do not now speak with certainty.

Q. What is your opinion of such laws anyhow; do you think they amount to anything or are of any benefit to anybody?—A. I do not think they amount to anything or are any benefit to anybody. I have had the distinction of having my name mentioned in some of the church congresses for not stopping these trains on Sunday. I do not think it is possible to do it. I think there is a desire, as far as possible, to curtail the transportation, but it is not possible, I think, to stop it altogether or any very large part.

Q. (By Professor JOHNSON.) Is your particular objection to stopping freight business on Sunday that of reducing the working hours of your plant?—A. That is the economic side of it, undoubtedly.

Q. It must be more economical for you to work 7 days a week than it is 6 days a week?—A. Yes.

Q. That being the economical motive, I should think that your through-freight business would move on Sunday the same as any other day.—A. It does; but you will see at once that all of your stations are practically shut up on Sunday, and there is a necessity for very considerable curtailment for receipts and delivery and a good deal of curtailment of movement.

Q. You do not believe in restricting the movement of through traffic on Sunday?—A. I do not; I do not think it is possible.

Q. (By Senator MALLORY.) I believe you are an attorney at law and have had considerable experience with the matter of suits for damages against railroads by employees who have been injured on the railroad. You have had your attention, of course, called to the modification by statute in some of the States of the common law rule as to the negligence of fellow servants, whereby under certain circumstances even the negligence of a fellow servant is not a defense. Do you know whether that modification has gone into effect generally in the States of the United States?—A. I do not know how many States have adopted statutes modifying the fellow-servant rule.

Q. You know, however, that it has been done?—A. It has been done.

Q. Well, can you, from your observation of it, say whether it has had any injurious effect on the service of railroads by their employees?—A. I have had no experience with the law at all. Of course, there is Ohio, for example, through which we run, which has modified the old rule of non-liability for the act of a fellow servant a great deal by judicial decision.

Q. As to who was a fellow servant and who was not?—A. As to who was a fellow servant and who was not, and introduced the rule of liability for the act of a superior, defining a superior, and in such a case, for example, as where a conductor's negligence resulted in injuring a brakeman, recovery was allowed. That is the rule by judicial decision in the State of Ohio. That is not the rule in West Virginia, and is not the rule in Maryland, and is not the rule in Delaware, through which we run, and it is not the rule in Pennsylvania. I do not see that it has had any effect practically one way or the other.

Q. Your observation is that the courts have differed very much in their decisions regarding who are fellow servants?—A. Yes, quite so.

Q. Do you not think it would be well to have some uniformity of decision on that subject?—A. Well, I presume in some respects it might be well to have a uniform rule. But if I may be permitted to speak from my experience on the Baltimore and Ohio Railroad, I should say this: We have established a relief department which is supported in part by the company and in part, chiefly, however, by contributions made monthly by the men. Under the rules of the relief department, each employee is entitled in case of accidents to a certain sum; in case of death his family are entitled to a certain sum; in case of sickness he is entitled to the services of a physician and to a certain sum. And practically the effect of the relief department has been to almost entirely wipe out litigation with employees on account of injuries; not entirely, but almost entirely. I think really it is quite a rare case now for us to have much trouble with our employees. Under the rules they are, of course, entitled to sue and recover, but they are not entitled to both remedies; they are not entitled to their relief benefits and at the same time to damage. The effect is that they take what is certain and fixed instead of what may be uncertain.

Q. (By Professor JOHNSON.) I would like to inquire whether you have modified that rule any since the passage of the act of June 1st, 1898?—A. What act do you refer to?

Q. Arbitration and conciliation, in which that clause of your road was made illegal.—A. No, we have not modified our practice in relation to that. I do not understand that act to make illegal our clause. It is a mere matter of contract, and we do not endeavor to prevent an employee from suing for negligence which would entitle him to sue at all. We do not endeavor to curtail his privilege in that behalf; but we do say that if he sues, we will not contribute from any other fund to pay him for the same damages. I do not understand that the act of 1898 sought to prevent that. If it did, I should say unhesitatingly that it was invalid.

Q. (By Senator MALLORY.) It was never compulsory, was it, on the road?—A. No.

Q. A man need not have his wages docked for the purpose of providing for this fund if he did not wish it done?—A. No; it was not compulsory as to any person who was in the service when it was put into effect. If a person comes into the service now he agrees to go into the relief department.

Q. (By Mr. FARQUHAR.) He must voluntarily agree to it?—A. He can not get into the service without going into the relief department, unless he is over age and for some special reason is relieved.

Q: [Reading.] "Section 10. That any employer subject to the provisions of this act, and any officer, agent, or receiver of such employer who shall require any employee, or any person seeking employment, as a condition of such employment, to enter into an agreement, either written or verbal, not to become or remain a member of any labor corporation, association, or organization, or shall threaten any employee with loss of employment, or shall unjustly discriminate against any employee because of his membership in such a labor corporation, association, or organization, or who shall require any such employee or any person seeking employment, as a condition of such employment, to enter into a contract whereby such employee or applicant for employment shall agree to contribute to any fund for charitable, social, or beneficial purposes, to release such employer from legal liability for any personal injury by reason of any benefit received from such fund beyond the proportion of the benefit arising from the employer's contribution to such fund, or who shall, after having discharged an employee, attempt or conspire to prevent such employee from obtaining employment, or who shall, after the quitting of an employee, attempt or conspire to prevent such employee from obtaining employment, is hereby declared to be guilty of a misdemeanor, and, upon conviction thereof in any court of the United States of competent jurisdiction in the district in which such offense was committed, shall be punished for each offense by a fine of not less than $100 and not more than $1,000."

That is the act of June 1, 1898, and the question is whether you exact as a matter of compulsion that contribution of your employees in the contract of labor; that they must contribute to this benefit fund?—A. An employee entering our service now makes that agreement. He can stay out or he can come in, just as he chooses; but if he comes in he makes an agreement by which he enters the relief department.

Q. (By Mr. KENNEDY.) The Baltimore and Ohio insists that he shall enter into an agreement?—A. We do not insist anything about it. We say that if he comes in he shall make that agreement.

Q. Is not that in violation of that act?—A. I do not know. If it is sought by that act to change the agreement that is made between the railroad company and its employees, I should say that the act is invalid; that a party has a perfect right to make that agreement on his part and the railroad company has the right to make that agreement. I should take that position unhesitatingly, even if I thought that the act covered our department. It is an enormous advantage to the employees.

Q. As a lawyer, would you not take the position that the law should be complied with until declared unconstitutional?—A. No; I would not. On the contrary, the only way you are going to get a decision as to its constitutionality is not to comply with it.

Q. (By Professor JOHNSON.) I would like to read the clause of the act which I referred to. (Reading.) "To release such employer from legal liability for any personal injury by reason of any benefit received from such fund beyond the proportion of the benefit arising from the employee's contribution to such fund; or who shall, after having discharged an employee, attempt or conspire to prevent such employee from obtaining employment, or who shall, after the quitting of an employee, attempt or conspire to prevent such employee from obtaining employment, is hereby declared to be guilty of a misdemeanor, and, upon conviction thereof in any court of the United States of competent jurisdiction in the district in which such offense was committed, shall be punished for each offense by a fine of not less than one hundred dollars and not more than one thousand dollars."—A. Yes, we do not have any such; we have no contract that releases us from any liability whatever.

Q. Well, as I understand it, you do.—A. No; on the contrary, our liability for suits remains precisely the same as it was before. The only thing about it is that if he brings suit, he can not, in addition to getting his damages, at the same time get his relief benefits. So that is the distinction.

Q. (By Mr. FARQUHAR.) You base that on the fact that the railroad and the employees are cocontributors to this fund?—A. Precisely so. We do not ask him to release the company from any claim for damages because of its neglect. His rights there are absolute and complete.

Q. (By Professor JOHNSON.) But if he does sue, he loses his relief under your benefits?—A. Oh, undoubtedly; that is, by the terms of the common agreement.

Q. (By Representative LIVINGSTON.) That is mutual between the railroad and the employee, for this relief association?—A. Yes.

Q. And it is voluntary on the laborer's part, whether he goes into it or not?—A. Yes.

Q. (By Mr. KENNEDY.) In accepting that relief, is he not accepting his own relief, the main part of which he has built up himself?—A. It is his own contribution and the company's contribution together.

Q. (By Representative LIVINGSTON.) He can take the relief fund or take his chances of damages, as he chooses?—A. That is it. In this relief department, a great savings fund has been established in connection with it. The employees are entitled to make deposits at the company's agency for their moneys. They are guaranteed 4 per cent. The purpose of this fund, or the purpose of these deposits, I should say, is the creation of a fund to be loaned out to the employees for the purpose of purchasing homes, building homes, releasing liens, or paying off liens on their homes. Now, that has grown to very considerable proportions; and this year, for example, those deposits pay to the employee 5½ per cent. They can not get less than 4 and they are entitled to the increment of their fund, and they are now getting 5½ per cent; and the effect of it has been to furnish homes for hundreds and hundreds of our employees. I have here the statistics of that. It does not give the number of parties who have borrowed money, but the deposits at the end of the fiscal year 1899 were $1,168,000; the deposits during the fiscal year were $393,000 and the withdrawals were $180,000.

Q. (By Mr. KENNEDY.) Would you say how much the Baltimore and Ohio Railroad contributes to this fund and how much the men contribute to it—the proportion of each?—A. I can not give you that proportionately.

Q. Have you the figures on that?—A. I have not the figures here.

Q. (By Professor JOHNSON.) A year ago it ranged from ⅕ to ⅓.—A. In addition to that contribution you have to take into consideration a great many things. You take this savings bank. Now, here is a savings bank that pays 5½ per cent to those employees. One of the reasons it can do it is that the whole staff of the company are employed, and of course they are all paid by the company, and there is no charge on this fund. Its lawyers search titles; its agents receive the funds; its agents distribute the money, and all that. The same way in relation to the work of the relief department; everybody does something more or less in connection with the relief department. The committees invest the money, examine the security, and see that everything is right in relation to the mortgages, and all that; and that appears nowhere in the expense in connection with it. And that is one reason that this insurance, of course of a hazardous employment, is comparatively low. I have the whole literature of the subject, which I will be very glad to present to the committee.

Q. (By Mr. KENNEDY.) Do you believe that if the Baltimore and Ohio contribute only one-fifth, that it is just to deny the men the right to sue for damages when the great bulk of the benefit that they receive is something that they have contributed themselves?—A. I believe that the arrangement is not only a perfectly fair one, but I think it is one which is approved by 99 per cent of our men. The reason I think that is this: the association was originally organized as a separate corporation, called the Baltimore and Ohio Employees' Relief Association, organized under a special statute of Maryland. The reformers—if you will permit me to use that term, not improperly—were constantly insisting on modifying that statute to require this and to require that, until finally the statute was repealed. It was repealed apparently as a hostile act by the parties who had been seeking to amend the act itself. The fact about it is that the repealing act was drawn by myself, but as it came in as hostile legislation it went through. The act gave a year within which to settle up all the accounts of the old association. We then organized the relief department. Nobody was required to join the relief department; it was a perfectly voluntary act. That was what I meant when I said when the association was established nobody in the service was required to join. Second, when the law was repealed and the department organized nobody was required to join. But out of 20 odd thousand members 19 odd thousand became members of the relief department of their own free will, and they had nad at that time at least 10 years' experience; so therefore it is found to be a mutually beneficial thing and approved by the employees.

Q. Are the men on your line organized into the brotherhoods?—A. Yes; they are. All the brotherhoods are on our lines, all of them, and while I said to the Senator here that our agreements were with our men, were made with committees of our own men, we do meet regularly with the brotherhood committees, such men as Mr. Arthur and Mr. Clark, and others of that character.

Q. We have had men before the commission who testified that the men believe that the prime object of these relief associations which are promoted by the railroads is to divide the allegiance of the men, so that in time of trouble they will side with the railroads and desert their brotherhoods—stay where their money is. Have you heard any complaints of that kind?—A. No; I think that is just one of those vague suspicions that get into men's minds.

Q. It seems to be pretty universal with the brotherhoods?—A. As far as the road is concerned, I think the brotherhood people themselves would say that they have dealt with us with perfect fairness throughout; and that subject was never mentioned. Its effect is a little the other way in this. Some of our officers complain that the effect of the relief department is to create enormous pressure on them in case of discipline in favor of a person who has something in the relief department, and more especially a person who has borrowed money from the savings fund. Now, if he has to be disciplined, there is always brought up the question, "Well, I have borrowed $200 from the relief fund; how am I going to pay it back?" Our officers have very frequently spoken of that side of it. But my answer to that always is, "You have to take the bitter with the sweet. There is probably a little here and there where that pressure will be brought to bear, and you better yield to them in view of the larger good that comes from the establishment of a relief department." Take this savings fund. I remember when the savings fund was first established some watchman up in the mountains put in $1,200 that he had had in the chinks of his cabin. We run through a country not remarkable for savings banks. When we established the savings fund, my recollection is that between Baltimore and Chicago on our line there was not a savings bank, with the possible exception of Columbus, Ohio. To-day there are very few in these smaller towns—Columbus and Pittsburg, I should say. To-day in the smaller towns there are none, and this furnishes a means of enabling them to invest their funds—on the one hand to the thrifty, and on the other it furnishes a means of building up their homes. I do not believe that the effect of it at all—certainly I know the purpose of it is not such as the question indicates.

Q. (By Mr. FARQUHAR.) Do you hear any complaint among the men in your employ that those who are not in the association are not in the line of promotion?—A. No.

Q. (By Senator MALLORY.) According to your testimony it is not practicable for anybody to be out of it?—A. No. I have not heard any complaints of that kind.

Q. (By Representative LIVINGSTON.) Is there any complaint from the chiefs of these labor organizations against that?—A. No; not to us.

Q. (By Senator MALLORY.) What is your opinion as to the effect on relations of employer to employee of such relief associations as you have described?—A. I think they are very good.

Q. (By Professor JOHNSON.) I want to make sure that we understand each other in regard to this question of contract. As I understand, your statement was that you did not employ a man unless he was willing to become a member of the relief department, and in becoming a member of the relief department I understand that that man signs a contract saying that if he receives the benefits as a member of that relief department he will not sue the company for damages?—A. He signs a contract under which he is at perfect liberty to sue the company; but if he does sue the company for damages he will not get his benefits.

Q. Well, is it correct to put it this way: that if he signs a contract that he will either accept the benefits or refuse the benefits and sue the company, and reserve his right to sue the company?—A. He signs a contract saying that "If I accept the benefits I do not sue the company, or if I do not accept the benefits I am at entire liberty to sue the company and get all the damages which I am entitled to under the law."

Q. Then, if a man accepts the benefits and sues the company he violates the contract, does he not?—A. Yes. In other words, when he takes the benefits he gives an absolute release; he does not get them if he does not.

Q. The act says that if any officer shall require any person seeking employment to release such employer from legal liability for any personal injury beyond the proportion of the benefit arising from the employer's contribution to such fund, shall be so and so.—A. We do not require him to do that. He does not release us at all; he is entitled to get his entire damages. We do not ask him to release any portion of his claim for damages. That is not it; he does not release us at all for any claim for damages. What he does do, he gets his entire claim for damages; he gets it; he does not release us; he gets his judgment and collects it; but under those circumstances he does not get second pay by way of a contribution from the relief fund. So I think as far as that is concerned, we are entirely outside of that provision of the statute in our form of contract. Now, there may be some of the departments organized which exact in their contract a release of liability for injury; we do not.

Q. (By Senator MALLORY.) But suppose he gets his relief from the relief fund and gives his receipt, and then subsequently sues the railroad company?—A. Then the release, the receipt, is pleaded in bar of his action.

Q. Do you think that that plea would be sustained in view of that law?—A. Oh, yes; I have no doubt about it; it has been sustained over and over by the courts.

Q. (By Professor JOHNSON.) Since June 1, 1898?—A. There has been no decision, so far as I know, since that act; but I have no doubt about the validity of the plea.

Q. Speaking as a layman, it would seem to me that law prohibited such a contract.—A. The difficulty about it, I think, is that you are misunderstanding the term liability. We do not ask a man to release us from our liability; not at all. You see at once there it uses the term "proportion." We do not ask him to release us at all. Our liability to him is absolute; he can sue us. But the point about it is that if he wants to get the fund, he can not get it any more than if he had come and settled with us, without being in the relief department and had taken $500, and then sued us again and claimed that it was not enough.

I think the statement I gave of the large transfer at once to the relief department, voluntarily transferring to the relief department all of their interests in the old association and becoming members of the relief department shows their opinion of the arrangement. You see, each member of the old association was entitled to a certain share of its assets, and they assigned those assets to the relief department. The case went through the courts, and, as I say, over nineteen-twentieths of them came in.

Q. (By Senator MALLORY.) Will you state to what extent your road has complied with the requirement of the law as to automatic couplers and air brakes on freight trains?—A. I did not bring the data over, but permit me to speak from recollection. I will give you the exact data from the record. I should think that on automatic brakes we must have about 75 per cent, possibly 80 per cent; I think 75 per cent of our freight cars are equipped; and with the couplers not quite so large a percentage, possibly 70 per cent. That, I suppose, would be a compliance with the law as to brakes and not a compliance as to couplers yet. We have put them on as fast as we could practically; but then there is a certain portion of the cars which do not pay to put on the coupler and the brake and which will go out of service in the next 2 or 3 years. I suppose we will put out this coming year, say, 2,000 cars. Now, those 2,000 cars will do some service in commerce, and you can not well withdraw them from commerce, but at the same time they are not of enough value to put the brake or the coupler on. They are not fitted for it. That is all.

Q. Was not the Baltimore and Ohio equipping its freight cars with automatic couplers and brakes before the passage of the act requiring it?—A. Yes.

Q. It had made some considerable progress, had it not?—A. Yes.

Q. Well, what is the cause of the delay?—A. Well, the situation in relation to the putting on of these couplers is this, and the brakes. When a car is taken into the shop for the purpose of making what they call thorough repairs, which might be said to be a partial reconstruction of the car, then they apply the brakes and couplers if a car is fitted for it; but they do not bring them out of commerce for the purpose of making that application; and if they did, the commerce of this country would stop. In other words, if you withdraw all the cars that have not got brakes and couplers, or if during the past year you had withdrawn all the cars that did not have brakes and couplers, and put them in your shop, and thus delayed commerce, the commerce of the country, or a very large portion of it, would have stopped; and the fastest you can do it is to apply it to the brake and the coupler when the car in its natural operations is brought in for reconstruction. You know to-day the enormous car shortage that there is. Now, if we would stop 20 per cent of our cars or any large proportion of them for the purpose of applying the brake and the coupler, you would see that if we all did it the commerce of the country would suffer very severely. I think the railroads have done about as well as could be expected in complying with the law. As I say, we have our automatic brakes, and we are getting couplers on nearly all the cars that are fit to put them on.

Q. Do you think that the application of these improved devices to freight cars will result in the saving of life and preventing of casualties?—A. My general impression is that it does add to the safety of the employee; but I do not think we have enough experience yet to say whether or not it introduces a new set of dangers which will partly counterbalance the loss of life and limb with the old.

Q. Can you specify any further what they are?—A. Well, if an employee did not have to go under the car to fix pipes. He now gets under the car to fix them. That is quite an important item.

Q. In air brakes?—A. In air brakes he must get down under them, and he must adjust them. There is always a certain amount of danger attaching to that. There is some danger in the automatic coupling producing a certain amount of accidents by its falling on the track; and there are others belonging to it which require mechanical means to define; but my own judgment is that upon the whole it is a saving of life and limb. That is my deliberate judgment, but I do not think it is wise for us to jump to generalizations too quick until we get a little more light than we have to-day.

Q. Until the railroads become so generally equipped with automatic couplers, it will be very difficult, of course, to form any opinion as to the matter, from a life-saving point of view, by reason of the fact that where they use the other coupler—the link and pin coupler—in connection with the automatic coupler, it is just exactly as it was before?—A. Yes.

Q. The employee has to go in between the cars?—A. That is right.

Q. And the principle of the automatic coupler is not brought into operation at all?—A. Our technical men will say that it has saved accidents. To what extent they do not commit themselves, but they think that it has saved a certain amount of coupling accidents.

Q. Have the employees of the Baltimore and Ohio Railroad had any strikes since you have been connected with it, since you have been president of the railroad?—A. No; there has been no strike on the Baltimore and Ohio Railroad since 1877.

Q Have you given any consideration to the act of Congress providing for mediation, conciliation, and arbitration; the last Congress, I believe?—A. Very little.

Q. You have read it, I believe?—A. Yes.

Q. Have you any opinion to express concerning it as to its being a law that will have any beneficial effect, or any effect at all?—A. Well, of course, if you want me to give my frank opinion, I do not think it will have any.

Q. That is what we want.—A. I do not think it will have any.

Q. Have you any objection to stating why you do not think this law will have any effect?—A. Well, I do not think that you will get the railroad companies to permit an outside party to fix wages for their employees, with no power to bind the employee. There is no way to bind the employee that I know of unless you introduce slavery.

Q. What have you to say on the subject of ticket brokerage; as to its effect on railroads and railroad rates?—A. Well, I think that ticket brokerage gives rise to a good many evils. I do not know the extent to which it affects railroad rates. My chief experience with ticket brokers was before I became president of the company, and in those cases it consisted in prosecuting them for selling tickets that had expired and been doctored and all that sort of thing; and I really am not very well versed as to the effect of ticket brokerage on railroad rates. I knew, as an attorney, that they furnished a depot for all forms of illegitimate practices. The particular case I have in mind was where I prosecuted a fellow that must have sold $6,000 or $7,000 worth of passes. But I do not mean to say that that is true of the mass of the business. I do not know that it is, and I think possibly it would not be fair to make any inference from it. I say that is my connection with it; it has been on that side.

Q. You think they ought to be prevented by legislation from carrying on the business of ticket brokerage; I judge so from that?—A. I think it would be wise to provide for it by the sale of tickets by the railroads only or their agents, and with the right of redemption for unused portions by passengers.

Q. (By Mr. KENNEDY.) Can not the railroads themselves stop this practice of ticket brokerage?—A. Not entirely, but I think they have done a good deal toward saving it. I believe the railroads formerly employed these ticket brokers. It was a method of railroad rate wars.

Q. They founded it; they are responsible for the system?—A. I do not know whether they are responsible for the system, but they found it and they utilized it in rate wars just as we utilize anything in war, the first weapon that comes to hand.

Q. Do you believe that if a certain class of railroads would stop seeking trade through the ticket brokers' offices they would practically break up the system?—A. No; I think the ticket broker would remain; I think there are enough ways by which he gets tickets for sale.

Q. (By Professor JOHNSON.) In England and certain continental countries there are various special tickets of different classes issued by the railroad companies for the purpose of stimulating passenger traffic of different kinds. And it has often been said that the existence of the ticket broker in this country has prevented the railroad companies from stimulating certain kinds of passenger traffic, because if tickets got out they could not control them. I would like to ask you if the existence of ticket brokerage prevents the railroads from these efforts to stimulate passenger traffic, and thus takes away the benefits which come to the community from passenger travel?—A. Well, I am not enough of a passenger expert to answer that. I believe there have been instances when tickets were not given at lower rates because they did furnish a basis for ticket scalping; but whether that difficulty is very widespread or not I do not know.

Q. It is a curious fact that the passenger travel in this country is considerably less than it is in some other countries.—A. Is not that owing to our sparse population, probably?

Q. Is it owing to the fact that the railroad companies have not been able, as the British companies have been, to stimulate the traffic? Whenever a British company sees a possible traffic that can be developed, it puts in a special rate to develop that traffic; but, as I understand, the ticket-brokerage system practically prevents that in this country; so it has been testified.—A. Well, a passenger expert would know more about that. But my own experience is that our boys have been right lively in stimulating traffic.

Q. (By Mr. C. J. HARRIS.) Do you know, in that connection, any method of developing or increasing passenger traffic that has not been adopted?—A. (Laughing) No; I do not; I must say that I do not.

Q. You have suburban rates, you have mileage books, large party rates, and excursion rates?—A. I tried the question of the party rates in the Supreme Court when the Interstate Commerce Commission decided that you could not give a rate to 10 persons lower than you gave it to a single person traveling between the same points, and the Supreme Court reversed that view. That was a case where the theatrical and amusement traffic, the kind that Professor Johnson speaks of, was built up absolutely upon the low rate, 2 cents a mile. I suppose abolition would have done just what Professor Johnson indicates; it would have destroyed a great business, not only for the railroad company, but it would have destroyed the furnishing of amusements by good artists, the traveling troop of to-day that goes to the little town and furnishes the little town with a character of amusement which it would not get—and the larger cities, too—except for the lower rate, I think.

Q. (By Senator MALLORY.) Do you remember the title of that case?—A. It is The Interstate Commerce Commission v. The Baltimore and Ohio Railroad Company, and it is within the last 5 or 6 years of the United States Supreme Court reports.

Q. The court in that case held that there was no discrimination prohibited by the interstate-commerce law in allowing a cheaper rate for individuals, for 10, than there would be for one traveling between the same points?—A. Between the same points; going between the same stations on the same system.

Q. (By Professor JOHNSON.) On the continent of Europe they have a system called Randresser Billets, or roundabout tickets. A man may buy a ticket in almost any part of Europe and travel in a large circuit and get back to his point of departure and at a very greatly reduced rate. The French systems of railways have such a system over their lines within France. In Great Britain they have an enormous week-end traffic, as they call it, Saturday to Tuesday traffic. I would like to ask whether it would be possible to inaugurate for a group of systems, or any one of the large systems, schemes of tickets or classes of tickets of that character for the purpose of stimulating a kind of passenger movement that does not now take place, provided you could control the tickets that you issued?—A. Well, it may be possible; I do not know.

Q. (By Mr. C. J. HARRIS.) Would not your mileage book cover this run about business?—A. Mileage books cover a great deal of it.

Q. Covers the same field, I mean?—A. The mileage book undoubtedly covers a large portion of the field. I do not know whether it would cover it entirely.

Q. (By Senator MALLORY.) Has your attention been called to the practice of giving passes, by different railroads in the United States, to individuals?—A. Yes.

Q. If it is not asking a question too personal, does your railroad give passes to individuals?—A. Yes.

Q. Do you regard that as an abuse, ordinarily?—A. Yes; I think the system is abused.

Q. Is it not prohibited by the interstate-commerce law?—A. I will have to answer that by saying that the Interstate Commerce Commission called the railroads up to show their lists of passes and they gave their lists. As you know, we issue those passes to public men and various people. I said to a judge, "I am going to put your name at the head." He says: "You do so, and then tell the commission that this court has decided that hauling a fellow for nothing is not interstate commerce." (Laughter.) The commission has taken that view. I do not myself believe that there is anything in the act that prohibits it unless it is used as a means of discrimination. In other words, giving it to shippers for the purpose of influencing traffic or something of that kind. But outside of that I do not think there is anything in the act that prohibits it. But it is a source of a great deal of annoyance to railroads to know how to deal with it. I have heard, for example—I do not know whether this is so; you might have got it from Mr. Calloway; I was told so by a leading railroad man in New York—that the prohibition, in the New York constitution, of passes to New York State officers, State officials, had led rather to an increase than to a decrease of free transportation, because the officer had his coterie of constituents, or his ring, if you choose to call it that, and instead of contenting him with his own transportation they were bound to furnish a lot to his henchmen. In other words, I think that if it was examined very closely, it would be found to have just shifted the difficulty over into another direction. I can readily understand why that should be the case.

Q. Is there any particular class of citizens in the United States who are the special beneficiaries of passes, that you know of?—A. Well, there are a great many public officers who hold transportation. It is perhaps quite common. Of course, they interchange passes with each other, and there is, I presume, a certain number of passes given to influence shipments, though I think that latter is being curtailed all the time.

Q. To influence shipments over the road?—A. Yes, I think that is getting less and less all the time.

Q. Well, what are they given to public officers for now?—A. I do not hold the view that they are given to public officers as a bribe. I do not believe it affects a public official in any such way; but it has grown up, possibly wrongfully; still, it has grown up as act of courtesy to certain classes of officials to extend to them free transportation.

Q. Can you specify more particularly what classes of officials those are?—A. As an illustration, the prosecuting officers of a great many of our counties have transportation; and I suppose, if you got behind that, the real reason is that there are a good many offenses against railroads that are prosecuted by these gentlemen. They have occasion to employ the railroad in these prosecutions, and they are furnished with transportation. There are others as to whom the custom or habit has grown up to extend to them the courtesy of transportation; members of Congress, Senators, etc., who are living along your line or near to it; it is quite customary to give them transportation as a matter of courtesy. We do it, and I believe most of them do it.

Q. You have been a member of Congress, have you not?—A. Yes.

Q. Have you had any opportunity of observing to what extent the use of passes by members of Congress exists? Is it general?—A. I think it is quite general. The railroads, from their standpoint, would like to get rid of it.

Q. (By Mr. FARQUHAR.) Except in the case of employees of your own system, were the pass system entirely abolished, would it result in lower rates to the cash-paying public?—A. No, I do not think so.

Q. So that the abolition of the pass system would be more a matter of sentiment than it would be of economic benefit to the people who complain of it?—A. It might be an economic benefit to the railroad, but I do not see how the public would be interested. I do not think it would affect the passenger tariffs.

Q. (By Mr. C. J. HARRIS.) Has there not been a great decrease on all lines you are acquainted with in the giving of passes of late years?—A. I think so.

Q. Is it as low as one-tenth of what it used to be 5 years ago?—A. I think it has gone out of vogue very largely as a means of influencing shipments. I think those that are now given are largely acts of courtesy. A railroad is a great concern and it has various interests in various places, and the extending of free transportation may be all wrong and they would certainly like to get rid of it, but the custom has grown up which they can not very well break without offending a great many people.

Q. (By Mr. CLARKE.) Why are passes given to public officials rather than to private individuals, as a rule?—A. Because you are coming into contact with the public officials; that is the reason.

Q. Is it not the custom to grant passes to delegates to conventions in many places, especially if there is a close contest?—A. Not if we can help it. (Laughter.) We try to arrange for the delegates with the various committees and give them strictly a party rate.

Q. Has it come within your knowledge anywhere in the country that conventions have sometimes been packed by the free issue of passes by the railroad company?—A. I have never known it.

Q. You say passes are given to prosecuting attorneys?—A. I gave that as one illustration.

Q. I suppose that is to enable them to get evidence in offenses against railroad companies, is it not, conveniently and comfortably?—A. Against offenders against the company, yes; the prosecution of offenses in which the company is concerned.

Q. (By Mr. KENNEDY.) Has not a private citizen as much right to cheap transportation as any other—as a public official?—A. Absolutely.

Q. Well, are not the citizen's rights infringed somewhat when this class distinction is made and the public official is given free transportation while the citizen must pay full published rates?—A. He is not treated just as the other fellow, undoubtedly; and in one sense it may be said his rights are violated, but I think it is rather a far-fetched statement.

Q. (By Representative LIVINGSTON.) According to the head of the nation—the chief executive of the nation or the State—a special train is not done for the purpose of bribing him, is it?—A. No. All these things are acts of courtesy that are extended in the various relations of life.

Q. Then when the citizens of great cities go for some special purpose in behalf of the city they get passes; that is a courtesy accorded to the city, not done for the purpose of bribing the city?—A. No.

Q. (By Mr. CLARKE.) On the whole, do you not think it would be better to put the whole on a business basis?—A. I think it would.

Q. The officials of the railroad company or employees going on railroad business pay their fares and let the railroad reimburse them?—A. Yes. I would be very glad to see it done if it could be done.

Q. Do you not think it entirely practicable?—A. Not in the present state of public and railroad opinion.

Q. (By Senator MALLORY.) Legislative?—A. Yes; legislative. I have just given an illustration, I believe. Take the operation of the New York statute. You will find it has increased free transportation instead of decreasing it. We are confronted with certain conditions, old customs; how we are going to get rid of it I do not know.

Q. (By Representative LIVINGSTON.) If the pass system is abolished by law, still your special friends, as a matter of courtesy, could travel on your road without a pass? Could it not be done just as well?—A. There are ways in which it is done; furnish them tickets, you know.

Q. (By Mr. KENNEDY.) You would like to see a system of national laws that would absolutely prohibit all carrying of free passengers over the roads in the country?—A. If I thought the system of national laws would prohibit it, yes. As I do not think they would prohibit it I do not think it wise to encumber the statute books at the present time with that class of laws. I am perfectly aware you will find no other railroad president saying that. I am perfectly well aware that it is one of our troubles—the pass system. I would like to see it abolished. I know it is very easy to say "Just have a law abolishing it." I know most railroad executive officers will take this view and say "Give us that kind of act." I say, do not give us that kind of act at the present time, because I do not think it would be complied with. You want my frank opinion and I give it frankly.

Q. (By Representative LIVINGSTON.) If you did that you would have to stop doing other things on the same line. You give paupers free transportation, you give ministers reduced rates. Now, if you go back to the idea of all men, women, and children traveling on a railroad at one fixed price, these benefits to the pauper and minister, and excursion rates, everything of the kind, would have to go down with it, would it not? To give justice to the mass of the people you would have to put them all on a level?—A. Of course many of these things would pass away. I do not want to be misunderstood. I would like to see the whole system of free transportation, even as between railroads themselves, abolished, and let everybody pay fare. I do not believe that an act of that sort will be effective in the present state of public opinion. The time will come at last when we will all be educated up to where we can enforce it, but you all know no law is worth anything except as it is an embodiment of the customs of the hour. I said before a Congressional committee hearing many years ago, when the question of restriction of interstate-commerce law should apply, etc., that it was a great mistake to legislate against the customs of business or to legislate with the idea of simply enforcing it from the outside without having any cooperation from the inside, and I used this expression; it illustrates my idea, that "the fugitive slave law will not catch negroes in Massachusets; force bills will not force in South Carolina; prohibition will not prohibit in New York or Chicago."

Q. If the railroad managers themselves would be glad to dispense with the practice of granting free passes would not legislation be helpful to them?—A. Well, I really frankly doubt it. That is just my view of it. I think we have got to follow the scriptural rule "The kingdom of heaven is within you." There must be something come from within, because we must curtail it ourselves.

Q. My question is, to use the same rule, when the kingdom of heaven is within the railroad managers would not a little help from the outside make it more general?—A. It might.

Q. (By Mr. CLARKE.) Are you acquainted with the effect of the prohibitions in New York and Massachusetts on the granting of passes to the members of the legislatures of those States?—A. The only knowledge I have is, as I said a little while ago, I was informed by a leading railroad officer in New York that the effect of the amendment to the State constitution prohibiting the issuance of free transportation to State officers had rather increased the free transportation than decreased it, because instead of the issue to the State officer you issue to the State officer's friends. He could no longer get it for himself, so he got it for his friends and his friends are more numerous than himself.

Q. How is it in Massachusetts?—A. I do not know anything about that. I presume the New England roads can do a good deal more than some of the other roads. They are more of a monopoly there and can do pretty much as they please.

Q. (By Senator MALLORY.) Is it your opinion that at present the weight of public opinion is adverse to the granting of free transportation by railroads to individuals?—A. Well, I do not believe there is much public opinion on the subject; but what I fear is that there are not enough, if you choose to put it that way, in favor of it in the railroads themselves to comply absolutely with a statute of that kind as against the pressure that will be brought to bear on them.

Q. (By Representative LIVINGSTON.) Is it true that in some States recently they have passed an act requiring the railroads in those States to furnish the State officials with free passes?—A. I understand that is the law in New Jersey.

Q. Would not that remedy the trouble somewhat, if there is a trouble?—A. That is the view they entertained in that State. I would like to see it got rid of, but I do not want to advise legislation that I do not feel would be carried out, and I must say it does not look to me in the present state of railroad opinion that it will be carried out.

Q. (By Senator MALLORY.) The subject of discriminations is next—the discriminations against persons and against places. Have you any opinion as to the comparative number of discriminations now against persons as compared with the discriminations of 2 or 3 years ago of a similar class?—A. Of course I can not give you figures, but I should say that the discriminations were less, because the rates are very much better maintained than 2 years ago or a year ago.

Q. On general principles you would argue that where there is less cutting of rates there is less discrimination?—A. Oh, yes; it is the cutting of rates that leads to discrimination. Where the rates are maintained you can get along without discriminations.

Q. Then it may be stated, as a general rule or principle, that sharp competition between railroads begets discriminations?—A. When competition assumes the shape of contests about rates, yes.

Q. Is it not pretty apt to assume that shape?—A. It is in this country, because of our system of legislation, I think, in particular.

Q. Do you know the methods by which discriminations are practiced in favor of certain persons and against others—the different shapes which they take?—A. It is different; like giving these passes that we spoke of. It is just giving lower rates, and that is all.

Q. Have you ever heard anything of such things as rebates, concessions, or commissions?—A. That is what I mean by giving lower rates. You can give it by one form or the other, through a system of rebates or a system of giving commissions or through various methods; it is all one thing—giving one a lower rate than another

Q. In your judgment, is that discrimination against individuals, or, through individuals, against the public weal?—A. Undoubtedly.

Q. Is it not also, in your judgment, injurious to the railroads?—A. Undoubtedly.

Q. In your judgment, then, there is no equity about it?—A. I do not think it has any.

Q. And it ought to be corrected if it is possible to correct it?—A. I think so.

Q. Have you any suggestions to make as to how it can be corrected?—A. There is a question which brings up the self-government of the railroad system of the country. I think the railroads ought to be permitted to agree to maintain rates; form traffic associations for the fixing of reasonable rates, and, if necessary, to divide their traffic or earnings. That is the one suggestion that I have in relation to a better method of avoiding discriminations. I believe this, that if the interstate-commerce act had not contained the prohibition of pooling and there had been nothing in the antitrust act, such as the Supreme Court has found in it, to prohibit railroads from agreeing to maintain rates, that by this time there would have been evolved in the natural course of railroad development a system of traffic associations, of rate agreements, and of pooling which would have substantially prevented all discriminations. I think that clause of the interstate-commerce act and the subsequent action on the antitrust act has prevented a gradual evolution of a system under which the same rates would have been given to all and discriminations would have been abolished. Now, I think the first step would be to go right to the inhibition which the courts have found in the antitrust act, prohibiting all kinds of railroad agreements about rates, and to get rid of the fifth section of the interstate-commerce act that prohibits pooling of competitive traffic among carriers.

Q. Do you think it would be advisable to have any provision preventing railroads from charging unreasonable rates, or do you think they would necessarily charge reasonable rates?—A. That is the existing law. I do not think anything additional would be required. Suppose I state in general what my views are. I believe that an amendment of the act so as to authorize pooling and to authorize agreements for the maintenance of rates is all that is required. I believe the other provisions of the act, which prohibit unreasonable rates, unjust discriminations, and the undue preferences, are all that are required. That is my personal belief. Now, I recognize the fact that in order to get any amendment to the act the railroads and the Interstate Commerce Commission must get somewhere near together, and the Interstate Commerce Commission will not approve of an act that does not give them some more power than they have to-day. Upon the other hand, the difficulty with the railroads is to get them to assent to giving any additional power to the Interstate Commerce Commission over the question of rates. I have worked, as you know, for some years trying to harmonize the views, and I give my own suggestions now, which ought not be taken as that of the railroad men, because I do not think they are concurred in generally. I would be willing to meet the Interstate Commerce Commission's views halfway, to this extent at least, to vest that body with power in a litigated case to say whether the rate was or was not reasonable, carefully guarding the act so that the decision of that body, in one form or another, can be made the subject of judicial examination by a United States court, with right of appeal to the Supreme Court. This would require the act to be very carefully drawn in order to insure that the question that the Interstate Commerce Commission should decide should be a judicial one. Now, in a general way, the railroads south of the Potomac, the continental lines, and the Northwest roads, and the New England roads would be opposed to giving the Interstate Commerce Commission this right. The roads in the interior section of the country are divided on it, and a portion of them would assent to an increase of power of the commission over the rates covered by traffic agreements or pooling agreements, but not over other roads not covered by such agreements. There are others that would object to increasing the Interstate Commerce Commission's power in any respect. We have, therefore, got into a sort of cul-de-sac in regard to this legislation. I say I think nothing is required except to give the railroad companies the right to agree; restore to them freedom of contract, giving the commission the right to set aside that contract whenever it pleases if it finds it interferes with the public welfare. But the commission does not take that view. They want certain power over the rates and a large proportion of the railroads are afraid to give any additional power over rates. That is the condition of affairs to-day as I understand it. Personally, I should go to the extent that I have indicated, but my own personal views do not meet with the approval of railroad men generally.

Q. (By Mr. CLARKE.) In case of the exercise of additional power by the Interstate Commerce Commission which should go so far as to fix rates pending litigation, you would favor the enforcement of their rates while the litigation is pending?—A. No; I would not. I do not know of any instance where judgment is executed while the appeal is pending, and especially it should not be executed where, as in a case against railroads, the railroads would have no remedy, while the public has a complete remedy.

Q. In view of the law's delay, would the public have a remedy that would amount to anything in such case?—A. A complete remedy, in my judgment. The public means the shipper. Now, the shipper is the great big fellow. As a matter of fact, the shippers who control the shipments of this country are large people, and they can enforce their rights, and enforce them very effectively. When you come to think about it, I think it is an amazing thing (with the freight traffic of this country, which must be equal, measured by ton miles, to the freight traffic of the entire world outside of the United States) that there are an infinitesimal number of complaints as to the reasonableness of the rates. It shows there is really very little ground for complaint. I think that Senator Mallory has touched the real point, and that is whatever vices there are in the system of railroad transportation exist in the discriminations. I believe the discriminations have to be removed by the ability of the railroads to agree among themselves as to the maintenance of rates, and as to the means of doing that, if it should be necessary, to divide the traffic or the proceeds, the revenue therefrom. That is the rule in every other country on the globe, and there is no reason why it should not be the rule here. I have worked for some years to bring it about, and am only sorry that I have had no better success than I have. I am willing to go, as you see, a good way, but there is among the railroad men of the country a deeply inbred thought that any additional power given to the commission over rates would be a bad thing. They call it fixing the rates, and that feeling is so strong that at present I do not believe that the suggestion which I make, namely, that you should confine that power to saying what is a reasonable rate, with the right of review in such a form that there could be no question that there could be a review—I say I do not believe my suggestion of that will meet with very much approval.

Q. (By Mr. FARQUHAR.) Do you think there is a physical possibility of five men ever fixing the rates of traffic in this country?—A. No.

Q. Do you think there is any means of collecting a clerical force of experts that could do the work of the experts in the employ of the railroads to-day?—A. I think it is more difficult to fix the rate of transportation than it is the price of wheat. I think that is a much more difficult task, and, therefore, if the commission could be got to view the point in that light and to leave the act as it is, which prohibits unreasonable rates, which prohibits unjust discrimination and undue preference, and vest them with certain powers, and then add to it the simple right to agree, with a power in the commission to set the agreements aside without any appeal from their opinion—that would be the simplest thing to do that could be gotten through. I wish the commission could see it in that light, because I think their work can be more effective than if you invest them even with greater power. My experience with commissions and on commissions is this: A commission does not get its value merely by being able to render a judgment behind which is the sheriff or constable, but it gets its value from the fact that it brings you up against what might be said to be public opinion, and that has been true of the Interstate Commerce Commission. When they deliver their opinions and when they call us up, which is very frequently done in a case of complaint, it may be by letter or in any other form, and they indicate what their views are, after a discussion, in 95 cases out of 100 we will comply with their views without further inquiry, only making a fight where we feel a matter of principle is involved. Now, if you will take a list of the decisions of the Interstate Commerce Commission in a year you will see that they are very few, and you may not see what is the use of keeping up a commission that only does that little work; but the real work that the commission does is on the complaints that come in from towns and individuals or from communities and individuals and are adjusted without going through the technical form of litigation. In that way the commission does a very great service. Now, they have very large powers notwithstanding all that has been said on the subject, and if the railroads now will be permitted simply to agree to maintain the rates under forms of contract that would be deposited with them and subject to the r right of revocation and leave the act stand as it is, I believe that the railroad discriminations of the country would in the progress of time pass away, and that we would under their direction and guidance and under our own self-government evolve a system of traffic agreements and pooling arrangements which would do away with the tremendous strife of to-day. Now, the doing away with strife is not the destruction of competition. If you want to get down to the last analysis, let me illustrate what I mean in this way: Two fellows run a horse race; one cuts the hamstrings of the other's horse; that is not competition; he poisons his oats, that is not competition. Competition, of course, is striving to obtain the same thing at the same time, and each would be striving to win the race, but there is the necessary implication as to the striving to win the race that it shall be done according to the rules of the game. So with railroad competition you must agree to maintain rates. There can be no such thing as two railroads out of the same place charging different rates, or if they are different, the differentials will be only enough to make up the inequalities of one against the other. They must, therefore, be the same rates. But given the same rates, and the same rates to all, the competition occurs in furnishing the facilities, in the way in which you handle your traffic, in the way in which you present your case to the public, and that competition goes on just as vigorously under your rate agreement as it did before. The thing that is destroyed is the rate cutting, but the competition itself, which is striving for the same thing under the rules of the game established by long experience, goes ahead. That is what we should do here and that is what is done in England; it is done in Germany, and is done in other countries, and I think it was a great mistake when the interstate-commerce act prohibited pooling. And then as to the antitrust act prohibiting agreements for the maintenance of rates, there was not a man who voted for that act who ever dreamed that was the case. The report of the committee shows that railroad transportation was intended to be excluded from the act, but like many other acts, as we all know, the language of the act was so put that the court was obliged to say that an agreement to maintain reasonable rates was within the terms of the act and therefore void. That act has caught two classes of persons, first, the railroads and, next, Mr. Debs, and it was not intended to cover either. I do not know of an instance of legislation where the purpose of the legislation has been so changed, and set aside, and which has run out in an entirely different line, as in the case of the antitrust act. I think, therefore, allowing these agreements for the maintenance of rates and for the division of traffic is all that is really required. The practical difficulty is there, namely, that the Interstate Commerce Commission asks for more power and the railroads, or a large proportion of them, are afraid to give them any power about rates. I do think the power of the commission for good will be just as great without giving them any additional power, but they do not think so; therefore I have been willing from my standpoint to compromise. I do not say I am right. I must be wrong or there would be more general agreement with me.

Q. (By Mr. Kennedy.) I believe you and Mr. Murray sent a letter to the Interstate Commerce Commission in which you practically admitted that the practice of giving rates and making discriminations had been in vogue on the Baltimore and Ohio Railroad, and that the same system was in general vogue on the different systems of the country. Would you be willing to give the commission a few illustrations of the giving of rebates and the making of discriminations that would apply to the Baltimore and Ohio and the other systems of the country at that time?—A. The letter had reference to the fact that we were not charging our published rates. At the time that letter was issued I should say that the custom of giving rebates had become much more general and much more widely extended than it had been before, and that it covered a very great deal of the traffic; I do not know what percentage, but certainly a very great deal more than 50 per cent. If you want individual instances, not mentioning names, take such things as the packing-house product from the packers; none of them were carried at tariff rates at that time. Take certain classes of large manufactures—iron, steel—they were all getting cut rates. The whole system was bad; but the discrimination of last year was greater than ever before. Fellows would get a cut rate on a 50-cent shipment, a thing which got to be almost ridiculous, and it was a tremendous reduction of our revenues.

Q. (By Mr. Farquhar.) Had you to meet cut rates elsewhere in making your rates?—A. Oh, yes; they were all doing the same thing. There are certain difficulties about complying always with a published rate. Export traffic is a difficult thing to deal with. The rate on export stuff varies from day to day; indeed, it varies between certain hours of the day. The same steamer, as you know, carries traffic of the same kind at very varying rates. They must make up their cargo, and they make it up. The result is that the carrying out of the law as to export rates is a very difficult subject. We took it up before the commission and talked the matter over frankly with the commission. There is no doubt about it that the frank disclosures made before the commission last January resulted in a great deal of good, but it resulted from the fact that mind got close to mind and the railroad to the commission and the commission to the railroad. We told them the whole story and said, What can we do? They recognize there are certain difficulties, and among them the export traffic. It is not a question of discrimination, but a question of complying strictly, technically with the law about publishing your rates. The formality has been gone through of putting in a tariff every day, sometimes two a day, which seems rather absurd; but that did not give rise to the question of discrimination. That is always changing, the published rate, because there are certain things to which it can not always apply, and more particularly as to the export traffic; and the export traffic of the country is growing so fast that nothing should be done to cripple it. The Interstate Commerce Commission recognizes that; but these are things we will fight out and we are fighting them out and getting along, but the fundamental trouble mainly is, that we are prohibited from making any agreements, and we can not very well get along; we ought to have the power to agree.

Q. (By Mr. Kennedy.) Have the character of rebates or discriminations referred to in your letter been done away with?—A. Very largely. Not entirely, but largely.

Q. (By Mr. Clarke.) What is that due to, general prosperity?—A. Some railroad men would say it is, but I think it is due to our getting a little more sense, and to the fact that the absurdity of the rebate system forced itself home to us more than ever before; but, of course, we are aided now by the fact that there is a tremendous demand for transportation.

Q. (By Senator MALLORY.) Should there be a change in that respect do you not think there would be a return to the old method?—A. There is a tendency to do that. I think, however, when we run along for six months and maintain rates pretty well it helps to maintain rates in the future; but when traffic falls off there is a danger of the strife beginning again on the cut-rate principle, and for that reason we ought to have this power of agreeing and of enforcing our agreements, too.

Q. (By Mr. FARQUHAR.) What do you say as to the generally accepted public opinion that the so-called combinations or trusts, if rates or rebates were taken away from them, could not exist?—A. I do not think that is so. Of course that term "trust" is a little indefinite, but I suppose you would call the Federal Steel Company a trust?

Q. Certainly.—A. I suppose you would call the National Steel Company a trust and also the American Steel and Wire companies?

Q. Having trust characteristics, I would say.—A. But strange to say, you would not call the Carnegie Company a trust, and yet the Carnegie Company is larger than any of them. They are getting no favors that are not extended in the iron and steel trade generally now to others, and, moreover, I have heard two of these concerns say that the railroads were making great fools of themselves by not advancing their rates on iron and steel. They recognize as their product has advanced our supplies are costing us a great deal more than they did before, and that we should advance a certain amount. We would not have to advance a great deal; but 25 to 50 cents a ton on steel, whereas steel is now $33 as against $18; 25 to 50 cents a ton advance on transportation is not very much, and the fact about it is, these gentlemen, strange as it may appear, are in favor of us advancing. They recognize the fact that we have been too low; and we have been too low; we have been brought down, I do not say below the cost of transportation, but below the point where fair profit could be made for our stockholders and security given to our bondholders.

Q. (By Senator MALLORY.) Why don't you raise?—A. That is it; why don't we? That is one of the most curious problems in economics. We are trying to do it now, and by the 1st of November we will be able to do it somewhat possibly.

Q. How many classifications of freight are there in this country, of the railroads; do you know?—A. I do not know the number of classifications.

Q. How many different systems of classifications? Is there what is called the official classification?—A. Yes. I do not know the number. There is the southern classification and all that; I do not know the number.

Q It is testified to here, I believe, that there are three and they all differ?—A. Yes.

Q. And the differences existing between the different classifications frequently give rise to much that is incongruous and much that is disagreeable where the two classifications come together?—A. Yes.

Q. And when the rate based on one classification comes to the boundary line of the other classification it has to be changed because of the difference in classification. Have you any suggestion at all as to that, as to whether there should be but one classification in the United States?—A. I have not. I do not regard myself as sufficiently expert to give an opinion about that except in a general way. That must be left again to the traffic managers to be worked out.

Q. You think it impracticable for anybody except the traffic managers to arrange these classifications?—A. I think so. If this was not a single country, nobody would ever suggest that five men should arrange the schedules for half the world, and yet we have a traffic equal to that. The tendency, too, is to uniformity as much as possible. The various associations are all organized, the American association is organized with a view of getting standards, like standards of cars, standards of engines and all that, and standards of signals.

Q. It has been urged that unjust discrimination on the part of the railroads as against the public and individuals could be checked to a certain extent by some legislation that would authorize all interstate railroads to hold their books or accounts open at all times to the inspection of United States officials or examiners. Has that subject been called to your attention at all?—A. Yes; I have heard that subject discussed somewhat. I have no objection whatever to such a provision of law, but I do not believe, frankly, that it would be any good. I will give you a single illustration: Right up here in the Interstate Commerce Commission office you will find all the records, sworn to, containing everything about the railroads. It has a very fine statistical bureau, exceedingly capable men in it, and they get out the statistics, and get them out fully and completely; all about it. Now, if you want to know the statistics of railroads (just think of this for a moment), where do you go? You have never gone yet—you do not go to the Interstate Commerce Commission report, although they have a splendid statistical bureau, but you take the private compilation of Poor. You go to any banker or broker, any large lawyer's office in this country, and in it you find Poor's Manual; and yet here are the official statistics of everything. That private compilation, with which the Government has nothing to do, furnishes the so-called publicity, of which we hear so much, of railroad accounts.

Q. (By Mr. CLARKE.) Is not this preference for it largely due to the fact that it was published before the Interstate Commerce Commission was established, and therefore the people got accustomed to using it; and is it not also due to the fact that it gives a history of contracts between railroads, leases, etc, so that it is valuable for reference in that respect?—A. Yes; it does all these things, undoubtedly. Of course I know it is a common notion that what is called publicity to-day—that is, to have your accounts examined by somebody—is the remedy for a great deal, whereas I, myself, do not think it is a remedy for anything, although I have not the slightest objection to having my accounts gone over by any public accountant; but as to expecting results from it, I do not believe there will be any; I believe you will still go to Poor's Manual.

Q. You believe in publicity in some form, of course?—A. Yes.

Q. Do you think that a remedy for suspicion and discontent?—A. I do; that is right. But I suppose that some examination would be made of these aggregations of capital. If that was thought necessary for railroads it would probably be necessary for the others.

Q. (By Senator MALLORY.) If it could be done; that is, by Federal authority?—A. Yes.

Q. Can you say whether or not to-day the unreasonable increase of stock by interstate railways is an abuse of any magnitude?—A. I have not looked into the matter very carefully, but I do not believe any of the large and well-established railroads could be reproduced for their existing capital.

Q. You think, then, as a general rule among large roads of the United States, their capital really is less than what the value of the road is?—A. There may be a great deal of misplaced capital, and it may not be earning, you know, but I do not believe that, take the railroads as a whole, you could reproduce them, certainly east of the Mississippi and north of the Ohio—I do not believe you could reproduce the existing roads, take them all in all, for their present bond and stock; but it does not follow that their value is equal to their stock, because we know definitely—in other words, there are a great many mislocations, a great many things that do not pan out as the promoters expect them to pan out; but you take all of this enormous cost of getting into cities, and I do not see how it would be possible to incur all that expense without increasing the capital.

Q. There is an impression in the minds of a good many people that much of the difficulty of the railroad problem is due to the fact that the railroads have been over-capitalized, and that the effort to pay interest on excessive capital necessitates exorbitant rates that otherwise would not be required. What is your opinion about that?—A. I do not think there is a single thing in that; I do not think there is anything in it at all; and as to excessive rates, I declare, from my standpoint, the rates seem to be most abnormally low.

Q. The through rates, I believe, are undoubtedly very low?—A. Well, our local rates are low.

Q. But local rates generally are pretty high?—A. Well, I can not speak, of course, of "generally;" I can not speak of it; but my impression is that they are low. You get a railroad like the Baltimore and Ohio, whose traffic last year only averaged three mills and nine-tenths, and if you can get any nearer the vanishing point than that for carrying a ton a mile, I do not know what is the vanishing point. One mill a ton a mile on our traffic would have been $5,137,000. Sixty per cent of our tonnage must consist of articles like coal, coke, brick, sand, and stone—articles that are right along the tracks; they take this at very low rates, but our section, north of the Ohio and east of the Mississippi, I should say the local rates were down along with the through rates. Practically everything is on a through basis. Now, I do not know enough about New England to speak. I know nothing about that; that is a separate and distinct system up there; they have very great advantages over the rest of us.

Q. Do you know anything about the Southern, Southeastern Division?—A. I do not. The Southern rates I know are higher, but that is a very sparsely populated country, and they are bound to be higher, if a railroad can live at all. To show the difference in the density of traffic south of the Potomac and north, take Mr. Carnegie's concern at Pittsburg; they produce a tonnage in and out that is about 4½ times the tonnage of the entire cotton crop of the United States; under the control of one man. This of course is not in value, but it is the tons moved, from the railroads' standpoint. I can show you little towns in western Pennsylvania of 10,000 inhabitants that will produce a tonnage equal to the wheat tonnage of such roads as the Great Northern or the Northern Pacific. You would hear them say they haul sixty or seventy million bushels of wheat, and "millions" strikes you as enormous, and yet the towns in Pennsylvania with 10,000 inhabitants will produce a tonnage equal to the tonnage of one of these great big roads.

Q. Have you anything to say on the subject of taxation of railroads, based on your experience with your road; taxation by States?—A. By States; yes. I have found they differed in the different States. I have never found very much ground for complaint of the system that is in vogue in the States through which we go. Generally there is a system of taxing the physical property under a system of State assessment, and distributed through the counties and townships and school districts, that is working very well.

Q. When you say "physical property," you mean both real estate and movable?—A. Yes, that is right; rolling stock assessed according to the amount used in the State, and distributed among the counties. It has worked very well, that system with us. In addition to that, there is in the States of Ohio and Maryland a gross receipt tax. In Ohio there is a tax on the gross receipts by a sort of common understanding between the State officials and the railroad companies. They pay the tax, though I think a good deal of it is now a tax of both classes of receipts, State traffic as well as interstate traffic. In Maryland, by some arrangement, there is a tax of that kind. It is thought not to be excessive and is just submitted to. In the main I should say the taxation of the physical property is about as fair a way of taxing railroads as any other. The taxation of receipts does give rise, if taken by the State, to this question, which is a somewhat unsettled one, of whether the States have the power to tax receipts from interstate points. The taxation of the physical property, including the rolling stock, etc., gets rid of all questions of that kind. I should say there are counties in northern Indiana where railroads pay two-thirds of the tax.

Q. The subject of Government ownership of land transportation is one that has attracted some attention. Have you anything to say on the subject? What do you think of the scheme of Government ownership of interstate railroads?—A. I think it a most sublime folly. Of course, I am rather radical on that general subject of State ownership and State interference. I think the further we keep away from all of those nostrums the better we will be off. The most informing book I know of on the general topic of socialistic adventures is by Mr. W. H. Mallock, on Labor and Popular Welfare, and if there is any single point that ever was demonstrated, it was demonstrated by him that the great welfare of the world, especially of what we call laborers, defining a laborer as a man who burdens his hands and is of average intelligence—that the great welfare of that class arises from the fact of private ownership of private capital and giving to industrial power whether in the shape of the inventor or the organizer of industry, the rewards of the use of private capital. The astonishing thing that is demonstrated by the figures is that the fundamental concept of socialism is false, to wit, that labor, defining labor as I have defined it, is the great producer of wealth. Divorce it from the intellect that invents, and the intellect that organizes, and the labor of to-day would not be receiving a third of what it did at the beginning of the century; so that, taking an industry like railroads, which is next to the farming industry, out of the category, where there are thousands and thousands of the brightest minds who are at work in solving all of these problems, and making it a mere routine machine of the Government, is one of the greatest mistakes that this country could make—especially this country.

Now, I do not refer to political difficulties and all that sort of thing, but the economical result arising from the fact, you may say, of leaving the railroads to be developed as they have been developed, if you choose, by permitting them to operate under the stimulus of private cupidity; in other words, giving the rewards to the people who handle the tools—I say, the results which have come from that system are admirably presented by Mallock in his book, and it shows that it is the laborer who receives far more than he would receive if you took all the instruments of production and divided them out amongst all.

Q. (By Mr. KENNEDY.) Are not all those instruments of production produced by labor?—A. No; not labor in the sense which you are using the term.

Q. I understand it is generally used that way?—A. It is generally used that way, when it becomes the subject of socialistic argument.

Q. The man who invents is doing labor?—A. Of course, in that sense, yes. In that sense Commodore Vanderbilt was a laborer, and the organizing genius who puts together all these railroads is a laborer, but you hardly would address a fellow of that kind as "My fellow-laborer." You do not refer to them as laborers. The term does not have that meaning when you are using the term labor. Take these great properties, and the farms of the country, and turn them over to the State to operate, and you take away private motive; take away private cupidity and you have a very poor concern compared with what you have now.

We have in Maryland a capital illustration of State ownership. The bed of the Chesapeake Bay is capable of producing a wealth greater than all the corn of Illinois, the gold of California, and all the wheat of the Dakotas, and it is wasted; it is wasted, because we have made it a species of common ownership, regulating the fishing of oysters between two classes, called tongers and dredgers. Turn the bottom of that bed into private ownership, as private property, and Maryland will produce wealth greater than the cornfields of Illinois to-day; but it is going to waste now because of State ownership.

Q. (By Mr. CLARKE.) I want to ask you a question about the system of combination and interchangeable mileage tickets on different roads; are you familiar with the working of that in this country?—A. Not very familiar. That belongs to the passenger department. I know in a general way, but I am not very familiar with it.

Q. I hold in my hand the cover of a Northern mileage ticket bureau, 1,000 mile rebate ticket, covering a number of roads in Michigan and some in Wisconsin and Illinois, and perhaps some other States in the Northern-Central West?—A. Yes; we issue them.

Q. You issue them?—A. Yes; we issue interchangeable mileage tickets west of the Ohio.

Q. Does that system work well?—A. I so understand from the passenger department that it works very well.

Q. You do not understand that you lose money by allowing your receipts to be taken by other roads and accounted for to you?—A. No.

Q. Suppose these roads happen to be in bankruptcy or anything of that sort?—A. Well, we have had one case where we lost, but only one; and in relation to that, I think as a rule the traffic balances, whether they are passenger balances, or whether they are freight balances, in cases of bankruptcy of roads, are settled by the receivers of the bankrupt road. Whether that is strictly legal or not, I am not exactly prepared to say; but the fact that you must do business as a rule with that connecting road, compels you to pay the traffic balances. We did it with our receivership. I know they are looked upon as trust funds, which should be accounted for as trust funds, and go over to the party to whom they belong.

Q. You recognize that a ticket of this kind would be a public convenience?—A. Yes; it is a public convenience.

TESTIMONY OF MR. STUYVESANT FISH,

President of the Illinois Central Railroad Company, and President of the Yazoo and Mississippi Valley Railroad Company.

The commission being in afternoon session, Senator Mallory presiding, Mr. Stuyvesant Fish, being duly sworn at 2.45 p. m., testified on the subject of transportation as follows:

Q. (By Mr. C. J. HARRIS.) What is your full name and address?—A. Stuyvesant Fish; New York.

Q. What position do you hold with the Illinois Central Railroad Company?—A. I am President; also President of the Yazoo and Mississippi Valley Railroad Company.

Q. Any others?—A. Those are two independent and operating companies; the others are leased, and are subsidiary companies.

Q. If you have prepared a paper, and so wish, you may read it, and if any members of the commission desire to ask questions on any point they can do so.

The WITNESS:

Mr. Chairman and Gentlemen of the Commission, railroads are "of the people and for the people." They are permanently attached to the soil. Capital invested in them is irrevocably dedicated to a public service. It is presumably for these reasons that the commission, in investigating "questions pertaining to immigration, to labor, to agriculture, to manufacturing, and to business," have called so many railroad presidents.

However this may be, I take p eas re in answering your summons, well knowing that nothing can affect, for good or evil, any important interest in the United States without in like manner affecting the railroads.

You have heard and will hear from other railroad men representing different parts of the country. What I have to say will relate to the great central basin drained by the Mississippi River—the heart of the country, its granary, and its workshop—and New Orleans, the seaport of that basin.

The Mississippi River drains the whole of 9 States and Territories,[1] and parts of 23 other States,[2] not to speak of a considerable slice of the Dominion of Canada. Rejecting 8 States,[3] of which but a small portion lies within the valley, 24 States and Territories may be fairly considered as tributary to that river.

Its valley contains 1,240,039 square miles, or 41 per cent of the area of the United States, exclusive of Alaska and other outlying possessions. There dwell 35,000,000 of our people, or nearly one-half of our citizenship.

Its soil, beside feeding all of our own people, except those on the Pacific coast, yields the whole of our exportable surplus of live stock of every kind, and most of the breadstuffs. Its mines yield our petroleum oil and most of our coal, its forests supply our lumber, and its workshops turn out annually an increasing share of our manufactures.

In these days of large and increasing tonnage and of low and constantly falling rates for transportation by rail, the question of grades is becoming more and more controlling. It is, therefore, in the level prairies of the great valley that we must look for the solution of the problem of how to conduct transportation ever at or near, and often below cost, without so absolutely bankrupting the carriers as to close the highways of traffic. The accumulated surplus earned in previous good years, and the borrowing power based thereon, coupled with a rigid and distressing economy, barely kept the Western and Southern railroads from universal bankruptcy during the bad times from 1893 to 1897. On June 30, 1894, there were in the hands of receivers 40,818 miles of railroad, or nearly one-fourth of all in the United States (176,602). These bankrupts represented an investment of over $2,500,000,000.

The enforced economies of that year reduced the number of railroad employees by 93,994. The effect on those employed by manufacturers of railroad supplies in particular, and on immigration, labor, manufacturing, and business in general, while not specifically reported, is too well remembered to need repetition. While we all hope that those evil days have passed, never to return, may we not gather wisdom from that sad experience?

The statistical reports of the Interstate Commerce Commission divide the United States into 10 territorial groups.[4] The following table has been compiled from these reports:

---

[1] Kentucky, Tennessee, Arkansas, Indian Territory, Oklahoma, Missouri, Kansas, Iowa, and Nebraska.

[2] New York, Pennsylvania, Maryland, West Virginia, Virginia, North Carolina, Georgia, Alabama, Mississippi, Louisiana, Texas, New Mexico, Colorado, Wyoming, Montana, North Dakota, South Dakota, Minnesota, Wisconsin, Michigan, Illinois, Indiana, and Ohio.

[3] New York, Maryland, Virginia, North Carolina, Georgia, Texas, New Mexico, and Michigan.

[4] The Interstate Commerce Commission define these groups as follows:

Group I. This group embraces the States of Maine, New Hampshire, Vermont, Massachusetts, Rhode Island, and Connecticut.

Group II. This group embraces the States of New York, Pennsylvania, New Jersey, Delaware, and Maryland, exclusive of that portion of New York and Pennsylvania lying west of a line drawn from Buffalo to Pittsburg, via Salamanca, and inclusive of that portion of West Virginia lying north of a line drawn from Parkersburg east to the boundary of Maryland.

Group III. This group embraces the States of Ohio, Indiana, the southern peninsula of Michigan, and that portion of the States of New York and Pennsylvania lying west of a line drawn from Buffalo to Pittsburg, via Salamanca.

Group IV. This group embraces the States of Virginia, North Carolina, South Carolina, and that portion of the State of West Virginia lying south of a line drawn east from Parkersburg to the boundary of Maryland.

Group V. This group embraces the States of Kentucky, Tennessee, Mississippi, Alabama, Georgia, Florida, and that portion of Louisiana east of the Mississippi River.

Group VI. This group embraces the States of Illinois, Wisconsin, Iowa, Minnesota, the northern peninsula of the State of Michigan, and that portion of the States of North Dakota, South Dakota, and Missouri lying east of the Missouri River.

Group VII. This group embraces the States of Montana, Wyoming, Nebraska, that portion of North Dakota and South Dakota lying west of the Missouri River, and that portion of the State of Colorado lying north of a line drawn east and west through Denver.

Group VIII. This group embraces the States of Kansas, Arkansas, that portion of the State of Missouri lying south of the Missouri River, that portion of the State of Colorado lying south of a line drawn east and west through Denver, that portion of the State of Texas lying west of Oklahoma, and the Territories of Oklahoma, Indian Territory, and the portion of New Mexico lying northeast of Santa Fe.

Group IX. This group embraces the State of Louisiana, exclusive of the portion lying east of the Mississippi River; the State of Texas, exclusive of that portion lying west of Oklahoma, and the portion of New Mexico lying southeast of Santa Fe.

Group X. This group embraces the States of California, Nevada, Oregon, Idaho, Utah, Washington, the Territory of Arizona, and that portion of the Territory of New Mexico lying southwest of Santa Fe

Comparative distribution of railroad employees, by groups, for the years ended June 30, 1893 and 1894, respectively.

Group.	1893.	1894.	Decrease.	Per cent.
III	137,913	117,233	20,680	14.99
V..	66,419	58,182	8,237	12.40
VI...	170,336	144,168	26,168	15.36
VII..	26,567	23,878	2,689	10.12
VIII...	71,287	63,525	7,762	10.88
Total of the 5 groups in the Mississippi Valley......	472,522	406,986	65,536	13.87
I..	65,521	58,272	7,249	11.06
II...	224,360	208,910	15,450	6.89
IV...	42,805	39,107	3,698	8.64
IX...	35,727	31,258	4,469	12.51
X..	32,667	35,075	[1] 2,408	7.37
Total of the 5 groups in other parts of the country..	401,080	372,622	28,458	7.10
Total of all the United States........................	873,602	779,608	93,994	10.76

[1] Increase.

This shows that seven-tenths of all the railroad employees discharged during the year ended June 30, 1894, had been employed in the Mississippi Valley, and that while throughout the rest of the country 1 man in 14 lost his employment during that year, in the valley nearly 1 in every 7 met with like misfortune. The distress was most severe in Groups III and VI, comprising substantially the area bounded east by the Allegheny Mountains, south by the Ohio, and west by the Missouri and the Mississippi rivers. Virtually half (46,848) of all the men discharged lived in those two groups.

In Group III the rate per ton per mile is the lowest of any, and in Group VI it is lower that in any of the other six groups lying west of the Alleghenies. The rate in Group I, the New England States, is more than 40 per cent higher than that of Group VI, and more than double that of Group III.

Justice apart, is it wise for us, as a nation, to continue to thus rob the carrier Peter and his "hired man" in order to pay the shipper Paul?

New Orleans is the natural port of the Mississippi Valley. You are familiar with the struggle made by the people of the valley toward the close of the last century against the embargo laid by Spain and France on commerce through New Orleans, which led to and justified the so-called Louisiana purchase in 1803. Down to the breaking out of the civil war in 1861 the river carried the products of the valley to the Gulf, and brought back imported goods. During the four years of that war and the following period of misrule at the South, the very mouth of the river was allowed to fill up until only vessels of small draft could enter it, and transportation between the valley and the sea was forced into the unnatural channels provided by steep or circuitous railroads over or around the Allegheny Mountains.

That even the most direct of them is crooked is shown by the fact that while the short-line distances by rail from Chicago to New York and to New Orleans are identical, 912 [2] miles, the air line distances are—to New York, 709; to New Orleans, 826. That is to say, in running over the mountains 203 miles, or 28$\frac{6}{10}$ per cent, are added to the air-line distance, while in running down the valley only 86 miles, or 10$\frac{4}{10}$ per cent, are added thereto. The summit on the short line between Chicago and New York is nearly midway between those cities, at an altitude of about 2,161 feet above tide; the summit on the short line between Chicago and New Orleans is within 34 miles of Chicago, at an altitude of 804 feet above tide. As Chicago is 590 feet above the sea, the dead lift to New York is 1,571 feet and to New Orleans 214 feet. While it is true that other railroads running to New York by longer routes cross lower summits, the most level of them reaches an altitude approximating, if not exceeding, 1,100 feet above the sea, and is compelled to lift every ton it carries in either direction 500 feet vertically above the level of Chicago.

When order was finally restored at the South, its railroads were, without exception, physical and financial wrecks. It is within my knowledge that they were then, and long continued, incapable of competing with the lines to the Atlantic seaboard.

[2] The distances given in the Official Railway Guide for the passenger trains of the Illinois Central Railroad cover a detour made in order to serve the city of Memphis, and are some 10$\frac{6}{10}$ miles longer than as above stated. Freight trains take the shorter route.

That condition has with us passed, through the increase, in the past 18 years, of the capitalization of the Illinois Central Railroad Company from $38,831,000 to $185,996,925. We can now use the advantages of our geographical position and give the advantage of theirs to a large part of the people of the valley.

Other Southern and Western roads being in like case, natural conditions are being restored, and the products of the valley are once more seeking an outlet on short lines, over easy and generally descending grades, to the Gulf of Mexico.

In physical condition, in the safety, speed, comfort and regularity of service, the level and straight roads of the West and South equal, if they do not excel, those of the Eastern States. Why, then, should they not carry their fair share of the produce of the West to tide water from their own local stations and, in turn, supply the interior with foreign goods?

Of the 2,715,981 tons of grain, flour, and other mill products carried by the Illinois Central and the Yazoo and Mississippi Valley railroads during the year ended June 30, 1899, less than one-fifth (536,841 tons) were exported through New Orleans to European and other ports.

Although the corn crop of 1898 was of such notoriously poor quality, no complaint has been received of any damage from heating having occurred in the 12,544,857 bushels which were delivered by the Illinois Central and the Yazoo and Mississippi Valley railroads for export through New Orleans.

Of the 13,517,161 tons of freight carried last year by the Illinois Central Railroad, 83.6 per cent were local and 16.4 per cent through.

Of the 1,840,719 tons of freight carried last year by the Yazoo and Mississippi Valley Railroad, 83.9 per cent were local and 16.1 per cent through.

When I entered the service of the Illinois Central Railroad Company in 1871, the ratio of its local to through freights was almost exactly the same as at present, and it has since varied between very narrow limits, although the tonnage has increased more than tenfold.

The two companies which I have the honor to represent are and have been developing the latent resources of the States which they were incorporated to serve, without seeking new territory.

The line of equal railroad distances to New York and to New Orleans, respectively, may be said to begin on Lake Superior, at the boundary between Wisconsin and the upper peninsula of Michigan, and following the northern and eastern boundaries of Wisconsin to pass through Chicago, Ill., run thence southeasterly through Indianapolis, Ind., and Bristol Tenn., and to reach the Atlantic coast near Charleston, S. C. Every point to the south and west of that line is nearer by rail to New Orleans than to New York. It is in that part of the basin of the Mississippi River which lies west of that line that our exportable surplus of breadstuffs and packing-house products is made, and so long as water runs down hill and it costs more to move freight up hill, the natural tendency of that exportable surplus will be to reach the sea at New Orleans and the other Gulf ports.

The short-rail distances from some of the interior grain markets and packing-house centers to New York and to New Orleans, are:

	To New York.	To New Orleans.	Saving to New Orleans.
	Miles.	*Miles.*	*Miles.*
Chicago, Ill.	912	912	0
Duluth, Minn.	1,390	1,337	53
Minneapolis, Minn	1,332	1,279	53
St. Paul, Minn	1,321	1,268	53
Sioux City, Iowa	1,422	1,258	164
Omaha, Nebr	1,402	1,070	332
Dubuque, Iowa	1,079	988	91
St. Louis, Mo.	1,058	695	363
Peoria, Ill.	1,006	860	146
Cairo, Ill.	1,089	554	535
Evansville, Ind.	989	708	281
Louisville, Ky	867	746	121
Nashville, Tenn	939	557	382
Denver, Colo	1,932	1,356	576
Kansas City, Mo.	1,335	878	457

Terminating in New Orleans and radiating therefrom into the interior in all directions are 6 great railroads:

1. The Southern Pacific, operating 7,614 miles, and extending through Louisiana, Texas, New Mexico, Arizona, and California to Portland, Oreg., as well as through

Nevada and Utah to Ogden, with branches reaching into the Indian Territory and the Republic of Mexico.

2. The so-called Queen and Crescent Route, operating 1,155 miles in Louisiana, Mississippi, Alabama, Tennessee, and Kentucky, and reaching Cincinnati, Ohio.

3. The Louisville and Nashville Railroad, operating in its own name 2,988 miles, and controlling, through an ownership of stock, the Nashville, Chattanooga and St. Louis Railroad, which operates 1,189 miles, making together 4,177 miles.

The lines of these two companies lie in Louisiana, Mississippi, Alabama, Florida, Tennessee, Georgia, Kentucky, Illinois, and reach St Louis on the west, Cincinnati on the northeast, as well as all the lower crossings of the Ohio River, except Cairo.

4. The Texas and Pacific Railway, operating in Louisiana and Texas 1,492 miles. While this railway is affiliated with the so-called Gould system of railroads, which comprise in all 9,000 miles, reaching through Arkansas, Indian Territory, Missouri, Kansas, Colorado, and Nebraska to Denver, Omaha, Kansas City, and St. Louis, only the mileage actually controlled by the corporation operating in New Orleans, the Texas and Pacific Railway Company, is considered in this connection.

5. The Yazoo and Mississippi Valley Railroad, operating in Louisiana, Mississippi, Arkansas, and Tennessee, 969 miles.

6. The Illinois Central Railroad, operating in Louisiana, Mississippi, Alabama, Tennessee, Kentucky, Illinois, Indiana, Wisconsin, Iowa, Minnesota, and South Dakota, 3,679 miles.   Railroad mileage tributary to New Orleans, 19,086 miles.

No other port in the United States is served by railroads reaching, under single managements, so far and in such varied directions into the interior of the continent. That those railroads ought to bring to and carry from New Orleans vastly more than they do of goods for foreign commerce is shown by their gross receipts during the past year from the carriage of passengers and freight, being $130,637,703, or 30 per cent more than the *value* of all the imports and exports of New Orleans, which, in turn, amounted to $100,090,537.

Far from discriminating in favor of New Orleans, it is to be feared that its railroads, taken as a whole, have not done their full measure of duty by the port in which each of those above named terminates.

The testimony given before you by the residents of other railroad companies, as reported in the newspapers, has suggested the following remarks:

It does not seem to me that disputes over wages form so vital a question as to exclude arbitration so absolutely and universally as does the maintenance of proper discipline.   The duty of safely carrying passengers and freight has been by the State committed to corporations.   They can not share that responsibility with others, much less arbitrate with irresponsible strangers the method of its discharge.   Discipline, if peculiarly severe, will carry with it increased pay.   Wages, on the other hand, have been generally controlled by supply and demand, to the great gain in recent years of the employed.   That natural law will always control, except as its operation may be influenced by labor trusts seeking to prevent free men from selling their only capital, labor, in the best market.   By labor trusts I do not mean organized labor as exemplified by the Brotherhood of Locomotive Engineers, the Order of Railroad Conductors, and like useful and honorable organizations of intelligent railroad men, but the lawless and disorganized bodies of outsiders who know nothing of, and care nothing for, either the railroads or the high class of men whom they employ.

No reductions in pay were made on the Illinois Central Railroad during the long period of depression (1893 to 1897) from which we are emerging, excepting that in some parts of the country the fall in the wages of farm laborers necessarily affected, for a short season, those of our track hands.   But many of our men suffered severely through our diminished need of their services.   Making less use of our cars and engines, we had less of them to repair, and both the number employed and the hours of work in the shops were reduced.   It seemed to me then, and it seems to me now, that it would have been better for the men, if it had been possible for us, by reducing the scale of wages a little to have employed more men or to give them work on full time. Men in railroad shops are paid by the hour.   The question is whether the men and the communities in which they live would not have been benefited by adopting course B below, rather than adhering to A, as we were forced to do.

CASE A.

Reductions in force and in time.

Men in shop, say 100.

Full time, 6 days of 10 hours—6,000 units of pay per week.

Reduction in force from 100 to 75—men discharged 25.

Reduction in time to 5 days of 8 hours, or 40 hours per week.

Result:-75 men at 40 hours, or 3,000 units of pay per week, and pay roll diminished by one-half.

Reductions in wages.

Men in shop, say, as above, 100.
Full time, as above, 6,000 units of pay per week.
10 per cent reduction in wages, 5,400 units of pay per week.
15 per cent reduction in wages, 5,100 units of pay per week.
20 per cent reduction in wages, 4,800 units of pay per week.
25 per cent. reduction in wages, 4,500 units of pay per week.
Pay roll diminished as follows:
By 10 per cent reduction, 600 units of pay per week.
By 15 per cent reduction, 900 units of pay per week.
By 20 per cent reduction, 1,200 units of pay per week.
By 25 per cent reduction, 1,500 units of pay per week.

That the Illinois Central Railroad Company could have employed more shop hands in building new cars and engines if it could have secured their services on a lower scale and one commensurate with the reduced cost of living, is shown by its having bought *new* engines and cars, as follows:

New equipment bought by Illinois Central Railroad Company.

Year ended June 30—	Locomotives.	Passenger cars.	Freight cars.
1893	42	62	301
1894	49	....	2,581
1895	19	....	1,044
1896	45	1	2,596
1897	25	....	1,800
Total in 5 years	180	63	8,272

During the whole of this period we built but few cars (241) and no engines, because we could buy them from others more cheaply. Now that the car makers have restored their wages and advanced their prices we have begun to build cars freely. In the past 3 months we have built nearly 500 new cars and bought the material for 1,250 more, which should be completed before the end of next March.

As to average rates of transportation, the attention of the commission is called to a pamphlet herewith submitted on "Changes in the Rates of Charge for Railway and Other Transportion Services. Prepared under the direction of John Hyde, statistician, by H. T. Newcomb, chief of the section of freight rates in the Division of Statistics, Miscellaneous Series, Bulletin No. 15, United States Department of Agriculture, Division of Statistics."

That pamphlet contained the first, and, I might say, the only, statistical publication by authority of the Federal Government which has come to my notice, dealing with these important questions with sufficient candor and accuracy to be of real value in determining questions affecting the regulation of commerce. The attention of the commission is particularly called to Table 1, on page 12, under the heading of Freight traffic, and to Table 54, on page 63, under the heading of Passenger traffic, each of which gives the volume of traffic, efficiency of service, and earnings. These tables give an immense amount of accurate information for the long period of 30 years from 1867 to 1896.

Conformably to a suggestion made by one of your officers that the commission would be interested in the plan adopted by the Illinois Central Railroad Company for aiding its employees to buy stock of the corporation, permit me to say that, in brief, it amounts to this: On the 1st of each month the price of shares at the New York Stock Exchange is telegraphed to Chicago, and the paymaster is authorized to sell 1 share to each employee at that price. Payment is accepted in sums of $5, or any multiple thereof. Interest at 4 per cent per annum is allowed on the partial payments, and when an employee leaves the service he must either pay in full for his share and receive a certificate therefor or take his money, with the interest added.

The number of officers and employees, other than directors of the corporation, registered on the books of the company as stockholders is 705, and their holdings amount to 2,554 shares.

The stock is being gradually purchased by those resident on and near the line. In each of the 11 States in which the company is operating railways there are a number of stockholders, varying from 7 in Indiana to 767 in Illinois. The total number of stockholders in these 11 States is 1,126, and the number of shares held by them 33,995.

There are resident in the United States 3,868 stockholders, owning 346,207 shares, or over 57 per cent of the whole; in Great Britain, 2,543, owning 198,616 shares; elsewhere, 115, owning 55,125 shares.

Exclusive of one large block of shares, held for more than 30 years past in trust by a Dutch syndicate or administration office, against its own certificates, good to bearer, which are widely scattered among hundreds of owners, the average holding of the remaining proprietors registered on the company's books is 85⅔ shares. In the United States the average is 89½ shares.

All told, the books show 5 holdings of 5,000 shares or over; 85 of 1,000 shares or over; 93 of 500 shares or over; 694 of less than 500, but more than 100 shares; 455 of exactly 100 shares each, and 5,194 of less than 100 shares. The number of stockholders registered on the books is 6,526. Barely one-seventh of them own over 100 shares apiece.

Q. (By Professor JOHNSON.) I want to ask if you will tell us more about the increase in the capitalization of your company? You spoke of having grown from $38,831,000 to $185,996,925. How do you account, in the main, for that immense increase of capital; what has been done?—A. Additional lines have been bought, and the whole property has been rebuilt and reequipped; grades have been cut down; new and heavier engines have been bought; heavier rails have been bought; the whole property has been rehabilitated. Many things were added in these years; as, for instance, a bridge across the Ohio River at Cairo at a cost of $3,000,000 and over. I can not give you the figures, but it is not merely in the acquisition of new properties, but rather in thoroughly rebuilding the railroads and reequipping them. I can give you one figure which happens to come to me, which is typical. Ten years ago we did not have a rail in a track that weighed 67 pounds to the yard. To-day the average rail over the whole system weighs over 67½ pounds. In other words, all the little lateral lines have been brought up, and our lowest standard rail to-day on our main lines is 75, and it runs up to 85. Indeed, we have some 4 miles of 100-pound rails. That is simply typical of the whole matter.

Q. Has that increase of capital taken the form of stocks or of bonds?—A. Both; it takes the shape of stocks and bonds. We will sell stocks or bonds as the markets suit. At times it is advantageous to sell stocks; there is a demand for them. Of course we supply the public with stock at that time; and if there is a demand for bonds, we sell them; and our bonds have been sold at better prices than those of any other company in the United States. We have always been in advance on the rate of interest. We issued 6 per cent bonds during the civil war. We issued 5 per cent bonds as early as 1874.

Q. You might tell us whether these various issues were floated at par.—A. They were floated at pretty near par. There were some commissions off, but they were the ordinary reasonable bankers' commissions. They were not floated at any great discount. It was a discount that we took up in the current year's earnings. In 1886 we issued 3½ per cent bonds. We issued 4's about same time, in 1886. In 1895 we issued 3 per cent bonds.

Q. Now, what has been your practice in regard to stock issues?—A. We have never issued any stock below par. We have offered it to our stockholders at par, and that which they have not taken we have sold at the same price. There is one exception to that statement, where we sold our stock, a million dollars, at a premium; I forget how much; it is a good many years ago; but at a very considerable premium. We have never sold any stock below par.

Q. Have your stock issues been purchasable by the public generally?—A. They have been purchased as stock. We have offered it to our stockholders for 60 days or a limited time according to public notice, and then what they did not take the board of directors sold at the same price. Sometimes it takes a good long while to sell it, but we generally succeed.

Q. And you say there have been no sales below par?—A. No, not by the company; and one sale I remember very well, of a million dollars, at a considerable premium above par. My recollection is that it was about 30. It was a good many years ago.

Q. And that is equivalent to saying that every dollar of stock issued there represented so much value?—A. Yes; and more, too, primarily. Besides that, in the rehabilitation of the property, we have taken the current earnings in succeeding years by the millions—taken $3,000,000 in the last 2 years—and put it into the property and our capitalization does not represent by, it is safe to say, $20,000,000 what the property cost.

Q. Absolutely no water in it?—A. No; no water.

Q. The last paragraph of your printed statement reads: "All told, the books show 5 holdings of 5,000 shares, or over." Can you tell what percentage of your total shares or capitalization is represented by those 5 holdings?—A. Off-hand, I can not. The only large holding, the Dutch holding, I should think amounts to about 40,000 shares, $4,000,000. What the others are I really don't know at the moment.

Q. The question is whether a majority of the stock is in the hands of the five men?—A. Oh, no, nothing like it. The majority of stock is in the 5,194 small stockholders. I know that. I could not tell you how much it is. There is no other interest, I am very confident, that amounts to half that. There is 4,000,000 in 1, but bear in mind that is not one man, that Dutch administration office. I am very familiar with those people. I have known them for nearly 30 years. They have their own due bills out, their own certificates, and being the owner of one of their certificates, I can go in their office any business day and demand the Illinois Central stock. They are mere stakeholders, but the stock, as far as the company is concerned, is registered in their names. They do not, however, own a share of it, that administration office. I think that is quite a common thing in Amsterdam. It arose in this way, years ago. They wished to have the certificates in the Dutch language, which they could understand, and have somebody in Holland responsible for them. They take our certificates, lock them up in a safe, subject to the joint order of two banking firms that constitute the administration office, and of the notary public who enrolls their certificates. It is done under their notarial system. Then, if I buy one of their certificates in the market and go and tender it to them and say: "Here, I want to redeem this and take my Illinois Central stock," they must give it to me. They are very nice people. I do not want to say anything against those Dutchmen. They have been my friends all my life, but they no more own that stock than you gentlemen do. They are simply trustees.

Q. (By Mr. KENNEDY.) I would like to ask you to more clearly define what you mean by a "labor trust," as used in your paper?—A. Well, I do not want particularly to go into that. My idea is that there is somewhere or other a lot of people who make a profession of dealing in labor and dealing with labor, and those are the people I am afraid of, from the manifestations I have seen of them as professional agitators. Organized labor I understand perfectly. I understand the Brotherhood of Locomotive Engineers and other organizations. These other things have come up from time to time. They are ephemeral. They are not anything known to the law; corporations or anything tangible. They are irresponsible. They are the men who come in between us and our men, and get in control of these organizations that we were treating fairly; and our men now believe we are treating them fairly.

Q. You have nothing to fear from your own men being organized?—A. We do not fear it; but they do create a great deal of trouble; they have in the past—these disorganized people. I am an advocate of organized labor and organized everything. I do not think that anything strong and good has been done and come down in this world yet except by organized effort.

Q. Is this a fair characterization of them to call them a "labor trust," these labor organizations that you have in mind?—A. I would not call them organized labor; I have too much respect for organized labor.

Q. Then it is not a trust at all if it is not an organization?—A. I would not class them by the same name as the Brotherhood of Locomotive Engineers. These things are only organized for the moment.

Q. (By Professor JOHNSON). The American Railway Union?—A. Yes; that was a ty e of them. It was a thing that lasted for a while; a thing that grows up and then disappears.

Q. (By Mr. KENNEDY.) They were not all railroad workers?—A. The American Railway Union?

Q. Yes.—A. I do not know who they were. I would not like to say who they were. I know at one time they tried to make us believe that there were not any railroad men in those riotous gangs that were around our tracks in 1894 until somebody shot one of them, and we buried him, and found out who he was.

Q. Your suggestion was that it would have been better to reduce the wages of your men instead of reducing the number of employees. You say that you were not permitted to do that. I would like to ask you what there was in the way of your carrying that out?—A. It was the apprehension of disorganizing all our labor and having a strike in the shop. Not that the men threatened to strike. We were paying the regular standard railroad scale. We were earning some money. We were doing fairly well even in those times. Our company was paying dividends; but we were not in position to force that on our men. It was the apprehension of trouble with our men. We talked it over with the men. But it was not practical.

Q. You feared a strike?—A. We were not threatened. I want to say that in justice to our men; they did not threaten anything of the kind, nor did we get far enough for it, but we felt that they might. We were not in any position to do it. Their wages were not reduced at any time.

Q. Probably if the men were organized you would have pursued a different course?—A. I think not; we would have talked that in the same way.

Q. You would have reduced their wages instead of the number of men?—A. I do not think it would have turned on their organization; it would have turned on their expression of willingness to accept a lower wage; but you see there is a regular standard scale running through all the wages, and we pay and have paid for years the standard scale.

Q. (By Professor JOHNSON.) I would like to ask you if you have definite arrangements with the locomotive engineers or conductors or any other organization in regard to the scale of wages; whether that is an agreement between your company and the organizations?—A. I do not think it is; I think it is a matter between ourselves and the organization of our men—our own men; but I would not like to say positively.

Q. The organizations say they have a contract with you.—A. I am inclined to think they confuse the agreement which is made between what they call their general grievance committee and the corporation with the contract between the Brotherhood of Locomotive Engineers, if it is a corporation, and the company as a corporation, as we would know it as lawyers.

Q. Then you think this agreement is between your local grievance committee and your superintendent?—A. Yes; our master mechanic, or general manager, or whatever it is.

Q. (By Mr. FARQUHAR.) Might the Illinois Central Railroad be characterized as a land-grant railroad?—A. It did receive a land grant from the State of Illinois, the State having received it from the Federal Government.

Q. Do you recollect what the amount of the land grant was at that time?—A. It was every alternate section for 6 miles on each side of the railroad.

Q. The main line?—A. Main line and branches, as then defined. Seven hundred and six miles, built under the charter.

Q. Have you any figures to show how much that land grant would yield to the road?—A. No; I have not got it here, because it was sold many years ago; but I can tell you very closely what it was worth when it was granted. I can not tell you what it yielded.

Q. What was it regarded as worth at that time?—A. The circumstances were these: The lands had been in the market for a number of years—many years. There were no navigable rivers through them, and therefore there was very little settlement there. The Federal Government had marked those lands down to $1.25 an acre, and they granted to the railroad company the even numbered sections. In the act of 1850, granting the lands to the State of Illinois, they marked up the price of the alternate odd numbered sections reserved to the United States Government to $2.50. That practice was not followed in the other land grants generally afterwards, I learned later, but it was in ours. The effect was that the lands near our line reserved to the Government were sold rapidly at from $2.50 up. At that time, in 1850, there was a great deal of Mexican war scrip floating that could be bought for from 40 to 50 cents on the dollar, and with that Government lands could be bought, and were bought. Mr. John M. Douglas—not Stephen A.—told me that just before the Illinois Central charter was granted he bought 3 sections of land up in the northern part of the State—and it is very fine land, I know it—at Wadhams Station—just in that way. It cost him 50 cents an acre in cash. He was a lawyer in Galena at that time, and is dead now. He was a very accurate and truthful man.

Q. Have you disposed of all that land grant?—A. We have sold all we can sell. There are some remnants. The total sales to June 30, 1898, of donated lands aggregated 2,540,468.89 acres, leaving unsold at that time 53,645.99 acres. The whole area of donated lands amounted to 2,594,114.88 acres.

Q. (By Senator MALLORY.) Reverting to your argument, you say that in the year 1894 the men who lost employment on the Mississippi Valley railroads were nearly 1 in every 7, while in the rest of the country it was 1 in 14. Why was that?—A. I can not say exactly why, but the burden seemed to rest there, and particularly in those two groups, III and VI. The figures referred to in the text seem to show it. I suppose that constant reduction in rates had something to do with it, but I would not like to swear that it was the only thing. Business was bad all through that country. We had been going ahead very rapidly, but we had a check in the Upper Mississippi Valley, and we also had at the South a very serious check with the general stoppage of business; and the fall in the price of cotton came along about that time, a very serious fall. It is hard to say precisely what brought that about. The fact is there, and the coincidence of the lowness of the rate per ton per mile in Groups III and VI struck me with force enough to bring it to the attention of the commissioners; but I would not like to swear that that produced the discharge of those men; that would be going a little too far.

Q. Well, in your judgment is there not some connection between that condition and the discharge of the men?—A. I think there is, undoubtedly. We had been doing business at a loss, and when the railroads came to a realizing sense of it they simply discharged their men.

Q. From your statement and showing, the roads running down the Mississippi Valley, say from Chicago and St. Louis to New Orleans, ought to be able to haul freight at a less cost per ton per mile than the roads crossing the Allegheny and Blue Ridge mountains?—A. Give us the volume and we will do it.

Q. And I infer from your argument that you think that New Orleans ought to be a point of much greater exportation than it is. In your judgment does not the fact that New Orleans is 20 days distant from Liverpool, and even a longer distance from continental ports, while New York is only about an average of 8 or 9 for freight steamers, would not that have some qualifying effect on that matter?—A. I do not think it would on the freights made. As I understand, the time for freight, New York to Liverpool, is 10 days; New Orleans to Liverpool, 16 to 17; I think that is about the difference. That is more than the ratio of distances, but the New York ships would average better time; faster ships, perhaps. But that all goes into the question of rates. I do not think the time would control on exports when you consider what the exports are. They are cotton and products of cotton; they are grain and the products of grain; beef and the products of beef, including meats of all kinds; those are the great things—and lumber. Now, those things are not needed with great expedition, but dry goods are, and especially silk goods, and things that have to meet the fashion. Answering your question, I would say, on imports, yes; exports, no. The ocean rates from New Orleans are higher than from New York. That is the advantage New York has. New Orleans rates are higher. It is a longer journey; a journey, I should say, 50 per cent greater. On the other hand you keep in the Gulf Stream and away from Newfoundland. In the case of New Orleans the great circle from the point of Florida does not carry you so far north as the great circle from New York would.

Q. The same could be said of Galveston also?—A. It would apply generally. I tried to make my remarks apply to Gulf ports generally, although, of course, the specified points I had to name and the statistics I had to give relate to New Orleans. I do not know about the others.

Q. Is it not a fact that your export rates from Chicago via New Orleans to Europe regulate the export rates via New York to Europe?—A. No; just the contrary. They make the rates. New York has the good will of the business.

Q. (By Mr. Farquhar.) Has the question of return cargoes entered into that matter with you; return cargoes to New Orleans, character of cargo, etc.?—A. It is very light; yes. The imports via New Orleans are very light. Our north-bound freight, however, is not light by any means. We have bananas to carry North; we have sugar to carry North; and after we get a little way from New Orleans into the longleaf pine country we have lumber to carry North; and we also have cypress lumber, and the deciduous lumber, oak and ash, from all that territory; so that our northbound business and our south-bound business at times come very even. In the year 1898 it did not vary 1 per cent.

Q. (By Mr. Clarke.) Do you not carry a great deal of cotton also?—A. Well, not much North; but cotton preponderates South. New Orleans is the great market. We carried into New Orleans last year upward of a million bales of cotton. That is about one-tenth of all the cotton grown in the United States.

Q. (By Mr. Farquhar.) Until manufacturing occurs in the South and Southwest do you expect much of a return cargo to be shipped there, so as to make New Orleans a great depot?—A. Well, I have been expecting it so long. "Hope deferred maketh the heart sick." New Orleans used to market everything imported into the Mississippi Valley. In 1852 the Illinois Central Railroad was begun to be built, and its building was completed with English rails brought to New Orleans and carried up the Mississippi River. The other roads in Illinois at that time were built in that way.

Q. Was not that the time when the rivers there—the Ohio and Mississippi—controlled nearly all the carrying trade of that whole section?—A. Now, why should not the railroads of that section control the carrying trade of that section?

Q. Is it not because the manufacturing line is North?—A. Yes; but I am talking on import goods now. On the goods we are importing, why should they not come in that way?

Q. Is it not because you have a great open market right up in Chicago there that sets you right out in immediate contact with New York, and because you need to be in contact with the money market, too—the Wall street exchange?—A. I will agree with you; but in the coffee business—that is the natural way to bring it in here. Why should coffee, for instance, come from Rio Janeiro to Baltimore and come into Chicago and then drift down into the Mississippi Valley? Why should it not come to New Orleans? Why should it not come from La Guayra and Mexico?

Q. While the barge system was in existence on the Mississippi River what effect did it have on the rates?—A. It is still in existence; but it is not the factor it was. They used to take a great deal of grain and heavy freights, but our rates have got so low that, including the two elements of marine insurance and our better delivery at the point of destination, being able to switch all around towns, our rates are as low as theirs for practical purposes. The barge line has not been the factor it used to be in our business. I can give you a very good illustration of that in regard to another business—cotton. It used to be carried from Memphis to New Orleans in steamboats in large quantities—upward of a hundred thousand bales a year. I watched for 3 years the shipments from Memphis by boat to New Orleans, and they did not carry 1 bale in 3 successive years. The railroad rates had got so low, including marine insurance and the delivery, that we could take cotton from Memphis and contract to put it alongside a ship on a day certain, whereas a steamboat could not.

Q. What is the relative difference between the rates from Kansas City to Galveston and from Cairo to New Orleans?—A. I am sorry to state that I can not tell you; I do not follow the rates. I have very little to do with that business. I know there is that competition every day in the year. We are interested in the Kansas City situation in another way. The Memphis, Kansas City and Birmingham road brings us considerable freight at Memphis.

A question by Professor Johnson led up to a matter on which I wrote something. It was on that question of capitalization, and the thought came to me after I had prepared the paper already read to you. The facts are interesting, I think. (Reading.)

"As to capitalization: The statement that the railways of the United States are overcapitalized has been so often reiterated as to be quite generally believed.

"While I know not only that there is no water in the securities of the Illinois Central Railroad Company, but that their sum total does not represent by millions of dollars the cash actually spent on the property, permit me to call your attention to the following statements, taken, with respect to the railroads of the United States, from the statistical reports of the Interstate Commerce Commission, and with respect to those of the United Kingdom of Great Britain and Ireland, from the returns of the British board of trade.

"The statements contrast the situation in 1890—the first year for which the Interstate Commerce Commission published statistical reports—with the year 1898.

"It will be seen therefrom that, while the number of miles of railroad in the United States has increased 18.06 per cent, their capitalization, including both bonds and stock, has increased only 14.64 per cent; and that the increase in the capitalization per mile of railroad is $3, a sum too small to be expressed in percentages, less than one-half of one-hundredth of 1 per cent.

"Also that the gross receipts of the railroads in the United States have increased in almost exactly the same ratio as the miles operated, viz, 18.58 per cent, while their gross receipts per mile have increasd $30, or less than one-half ($\frac{45}{100}$) of 1 per cent. This in a country which has developed enormously in the meanwhile, and whose population is estimated by the Interstate Commerce Commission to be increasing at the rate of 1,250,000 per annum.

"On the other hand, in the same time in the United Kingdom the number of miles operated increased 7.9 per cent, the capital increased 26.41 per cent, the capital per mile operated increased 17.15 per cent, gross receipts increased in amount 20.39 per cent, and per mile operated, 11.57 per cent.

"While it is true that, as a whole, the English railways are better built than ours, there are many points in which ours excel them, and there are also thousands of miles of railroad in the United States which are well and permanently constructed.

"The capitalization, including bonds and stocks, of the railroads in the United States, is $60,343 per mile; that of the railways in Great Britain, £52,379 per mile, which, at $5 to the pound, equals $261,895.

"The increase in the capitalization of the railroads of the United States per mile in 9 years has been, as above stated, $3.

"The increase in the capitalization of the British railways per mile during the same 9 years has been £7,669, or, at $5 to the pound, $38,345.

"The figures are given as reported, without accepting responsibility for their accuracy."

Railways in the United Kingdom.

[Stated in dollars, £1 being taken as worth $5.]

	Year ended December 31—		Increase in 9 years.	
	1890.	1898.	Amount.	Per cent.
Miles operated	20,073	21,659	1,586	7.90
Capital paid up	$4,487,360,130	$5,672,342,310	$1,184,982,180	26.41
Capital paid up per mile operated	223,550	261,895	38,345	17.15
Gross receipts	399,743,510	481,262,505	81,518,995	20.39
Gross receipts per mile....................	19,915	22,220	2,305	11.57

Railways in the United States.

	Year ended June 30—		Increase in 9 years.	
	1890.	1898.	Amount.	Per cent.
Miles operated	156,404	184,648	28,244	18.06
Capitalization	$9,437,343,420	$10,818,554,031	$1,381,210,611	14.64
Capitalization per mile	60,340	60,343	3	1.00
Gross receipts.............................	1,051,877,632	1,247,325,621	195,447,989	18.58
Gross receipts per mile....................	6,725	6,755	30	.45

¹ Less than one-half of one-hundredth of 1 per cent.

I think there are some inaccuracies in the Interstate Commerce Commission's figures, and I have had a good deal of correspondence with them about that. I have been very much impressed with that difference within the last 10 years. What may have happened 40 or 50 years ago I do not know, but in the last 10 years the railroads of the United States have gone through a process of undercapitalization, not only as to the amount, but as to the rate of interest. In all the recent reorganizations the 7 per cent bonds which the bondholder had a right to exact under his contract have been put in at 3½ and at 4 or 3, or whatever the rate may be. There has been a tremendous undercapitalization in the last 10 years out of that. I can point out 6 miles of the Illinois Central Railroad on which we have spent $6,000,000 in the last 10 years and not $1 of capital has been issued for it. We may have borrowed a few dollars of money, but I mean no stock has been issued for it; and that is going on all over the country.

Q. Do the Interstate Commerce Commission or do you railway men ever take into account the amount of local stock and of common stock that by reorganization is entirely wiped out and does not appear on a single figure to-day? For instance, township stock, county, State, or city stock and private individual stock, taken up in these reorganizations, has been entirely wiped out of existence and never shows in any figures whatever on the record. Are there not millions involved in that way that never show up?—A. I had a personal experience on that line. In 1877 I came back into the Illinois Central service. I had been out for a while, and then came back, as secretary of a reorganization committee for the New Orleans, Jackson and Great Northern and the Mississippi Central Railroad, leading from Cairo to New Orleans, 567 miles. Those 2 concerns had a capitalization, as shown by their reports, of about $50,000,000. They were bankrupt; they were physical wrecks; and we went to work and in 5 years thoroughly rebuilt them. We relaid every bar of iron with new steel rails; we rebuilt all their engines and all their cars and added to them, and at the end of the time we turned them over with a capitalization of $28,000,000, and it went on the books of the Illinois Central at that figure, having in the meanwhile spent the earnings of 5 years, and that was all the money we could scrape together. The difference between the $50,000,000 and $28,000,000 was not what I spoke about earlier as being at least $20,000,000 in the Illinois Central ro ert which is not shown by capitalization there. I mean real property—real money applied to the purposes of the corporation. I should say there must be something like $20,000,000 of it. I would not like to swear to the figures, but it is many millions—I would certainly swear to that.

Q. (By Mr. KENNEDY.) Have you fixed any limit to your capitalization?—A. No; there is no limit; that is to say, it is authorized from time to time to be issued by our board of directors.

Q. (By Mr. C. J. HARRIS.) Have you been able to pay dividends in these depressing years?—A. Yes; we have always paid dividends. The Illinois Central Railroad has always paid a 6-monthly, semiannual dividend. We have paid in recent years at the rate of 5 per cent.

Q. (By Mr. CLARKE.) Was any of this shrinkage to which you referred traceable to the increased value in money?—A. No; the loss in those Southern railroads was due to two facts—the war and the reconstruction period. During the war the railroads were destroyed. I had in my possession—I suppose I have still—2 receipts given, 1 by a Federal officer and 1 by a Confederate officer, for the destruction of a bridge across Yalabusha River, near Grenada, Miss. It was in Forrest's country, where General Forrest was cavorting around there back of Memphis in north Mississippi. I merely mention that as showing what went on. Bridges were destroyed over and over again during the war. And then came the period of national political reconstruction and the period also of the reconstruction of these railroads; and there were carpetbaggers in both; there was rascality in the railroads.

Q. I suppose some of the earlier capitalizations of your various roads were on the greenback basis, and when we got to the gold standard of course there was a shrinkage?—A. Well, of course, there was a shrinkage; and as a result of that panic of 1873 the Illinois Central, which had been paying 8 to 10 per cent, had shrunk; they got down in 1877 to paying 4 per cent. But I do not know that there was any shrinkage in the capitalization; it was in the earning power.

Q. More millions of stock on a greenback basis would have to be issued than on the gold basis, of course, at a gold premium?—A. Some of our stock was issued during the war.

Q. I would like to inquire if there has been a large natural increase in the value of your locations, especially in cities?—A. I think there has been in Chicago, very large; and elsewhere, but chiefly in Chicago.

Q. Is that fully covered by your present capitalization?—A. No; our land in Chicago, as far as capitalized at all, stands on our books at just what it cost 40 or 50 years ago. That has never been marked up. Those things have stood.

Q. Your position, then, and your opportunity to do business, the value of which is constantly increasing, would bear in your judgment a much larger capital than is shown in the amount issued?—A. The mayor of the city of Chicago had an estimate made by experts within 2 or 3 years—I think it was Mr. Mayor Swift, the predecessor of the present mayor—of the value of the property of the Illinois Central Railroad on our first mile, and he brought in figures of about $34,500,000. I should say that that property probably stands on the company's books at $200,000. I do not know the figures. Now, that is the same unearned increment that any other owner of real property would have had if he bought it. When this company was organized with $17,000,000 of paid-in capital, the directors themselves paid in $2.50 per share, and made themselves personally liable for $97.50, and they were the first men in New York at that time. They were men like William H. Aspinwall and Jonathan Sturges, George Griswold and Ludlow—I can give you the names of all of them—merchants in good standing. They believed that the sale of the land would build the railroad, and therefore were willing to make themselves personally liable. Then came the panic of 1857 and these gentlemen, after indorsing the company's paper very largely, had great trouble to pull through, and they assessed themselves on that stock first $20 and then $10 more and then $10 more until every last dollar was paid in on that $17,000,000 of stock. Now, suppose those gentlemen, intelligent men, men of affairs, had gone into the city of Chicago and taken their $17,000,000 and bought corner lots and let somebody else build this fool railroad. It nearly broke them; it did break some of them. They had the money to do it, and they had the credit, and they could get money just as well for Chicago real estate as they could for the railroad.

Q. (By Professor JOHNSON.) There is a question connected with taxation on which I think I would like to hear from you. The Illinois Central pays to the State of Illinois a tax upon its receipts?—A. Yes.

Q. And the amount is fixed by the State constitution, I believe?—A. Yes; it is fixed in the charter, and then the constitution provides that it shall not be altered.

Q. Will you please give us your views on the question of taxation, as to the best system, and as to the working of the various systems?—A. It seems to me that a tax on gross receipts, if properly regulated as to per cent, would be the fairest tax. Seven per cent is undoubtedly excessive.

Q. That is, on gross receipts in the State of Illinois?—A. Yes; we pay 7 per cent, and that is undoubtedly excessive. It is very much more than other railroads pay, and it is more than the business will bear. That was accepted by my predecessors, and I do not complain. We have made our bargain with the State of Illinois and we have lived up to it and we shall; but that was predicated on the railroads in the New

England States showing, in the years previous to 1850, that they could be operated for less than 50 per cent of their gross receipts, payment of taxes and everything else.

Our people thought, and it is in writing that they said so, that the railroads in Illinois, on those flat prairies, with coal abundant under the soil, could be operated for less. Now, if we got 55 per cent of our gross receipts, after paying operating expenses, you know, if we had that left, we could afford to pay the State 7 per cent; but as a matter of fact, we have only less than 30; our operating expenses run up to about 70 per cent. Last year, including taxes, it came to 69.580 per cent—operating expenses, very nearly 70 per cent, leaving 30.420 per cent as net. Now I have deducted there all taxes, taking the whole railroad as a system. To take from a business which it costs 62½ per cent to operate 7 per cent out of the 37½ left is too large a proportion for a tax. We should get to some figures such as they have up in Wisconsin, 2½ to 4, varying with the different classes of railroads. My reason for believing that a tax on gross receipts is a fair thing is that it is a tax on the money which the railroads take from the people for transportation in a quasi public service. Now, it is not unfair to the railroads, it seems to me, that they should be taxed in proportion as they take, just as I might be taxed on my income. There is nothing unfair in that. Nobody pretended that there was anything unfair in an income tax properly adjusted.

Q. (By Senator MALLORY.) How many employees have you in connection with your system?—A. The 2 railroads, the Illinois Central and the Yazoo and Mississippi Valley, have 28,750.

Q. Has your system any objection to employing men who belong to labor organizations?—A. No; we employ them regardless of what they do in that respect.

Q. Have you any arrangement with the men providing for them in case of sickness or injury?—A. We have on one division; on the Louisville division. We have a hospital fund there. There is a small contribution by the men from their wages and the company contributes a house and the land. The details of that I am not very conversant with—whether we make a monthly addition to it or not.

Q. The money for running it comes out of the earnings of the men?—A. A part of it does, I know. The company furnishes them with a very nice house and a piece of land and all the transportation for the hospital, etc., of course; but whether we make a payment of money I do not know.

Q. Is it compulsory on the men to subscribe to it?—A. No.

Q. Or is it just a matter of their own?—A. They all do it, though. They see the advantage of that. It is in a country where hospitals are not as close together as they would be here—western Kentucky and along the Ohio River.

Q. What are your hours of labor for train hands—men who are connected with the running of trains? Do most locomotive engineers and train hands work by the mile?—A. Yes; and we watch those men very carefully. The master mechanic watches that; looks his men over to see that a man can not go out unless he has had his sleep, and all that sort of thing.

Q. Have you any rule regarding intoxication of employees?—A. Yes; especially the men on the trains.

Q. I assume that that is rigidly enforced?—A. Yes; that is enforced.

Q. To what extent has the Illinois Central complied with the law requiring automatic couplers and air brakes to be put upon freight cars?—A. I can give you that information down to the 30th of June. It is in Mr. Harahan's report. On the 30th of June we had 95.39 per cent of our freight equipment equipped with automatic couplers and we had 38.83 per cent of our freight equipment equipped with air brakes. Of course all the passenger equipment is equipped with both. We will conform with the law at the end of the year.

Q. Have you any complaint to make about the system of ticket brokerage as it is practiced in this country to-day?—A. I did not come here to make any complaint, if you ask me the question.

Q. Have you any criticism to make?—A. Yes; the thing is wrong, because the companies are not free merchants. They can not sell above their advertised rates, and under those circumstances it seems to me that we ought to be protected against such sale by others below our rates. While I know that other railroad men will not agree with me—I do not suppose anybody will agree with me—I have always thought that that thing could be cured by a very simple statute, which would require every ticket to be stamped with the price at which it is sold and to be redeemable by the company issuing it within 30 days, if presented, in proportion to the part used on any coupon; not on any piece of a ticket or on a piece of a coupon. A piece of a ticket would be cutting it up a little too small. But if there is a ticket sold from Boston by the Boston and Albany Railroad to Albany, by the New York Central Railroad and over the New York Central Railroad to Buffalo, and over the Lake Shore Railroad to Chicago, and so on across the continent, and a man does not use one of those coupons, I think he is entitled to have his money back; and if the price of the whole ticket is stamped on there, printed on there in plain figures, there will be no quarrel as to what the proportion is, and there will be no reason for the life of the ticket broker except forgery. He would be out of any honest business that he has. I admit that they have some honest business; but there would be no reason for their existence except some of the things that they are accused of doing—altering the dates and places. But I do not believe the other railroad men would agree with me in that. I proposed it years ago. I think that such legislation would kill the ticket broker so that you would never hear of him again.

Q. (By Mr. KENNEDY.) Is not the proportion of business which the ticket broker does on unused portions of tickets very small in comparison to the business that is turned over to him by the railroads themselves?—A. I do not know about that, frankly. I imagine that there are some of the weak roads that do that business. I know that it is in evidence in the Interstate Commerce Commission, reported in their first big investigation in Chicago 8 or 10 years ago, that they found the tickets of every railroad except the Illinois Central in the scalpers' offices. I have had no dealings with them, and I do not think our people have. I think you are right about that—that there is some of that business going on at times. I doubt whether there is just at this moment.

Q. The statement you just made in regard to the finding of the Interstate Commerce Commission would seem to bear that out.—A. This is 10 years ago—1888, I think it was—one of their first investigations.

Q. Can not the railroads correct this evil themselves without going to Congress for it?—A. I do not see how we can prevent any other railroad company which has a line to points which we reach selling that ticket at any price they please through a broker as long as a broker exists.

Q. Then part of your object in going to Congress will be to control the action of those other railroads as much as that of these scalpers?—A. Undoubtedly.

Q. (By Senator MALLORY.) There is a feature of discrimination in the practical working of the ticket brokerage business, is there not, as where a man gets a ticket to travel over a certain distance at a less rate than the advertised rate which the public is generally called on to pay?—A. You mean that the railroad company sells a ticket to the broker and pays him a commission for the sale out of which he scalps the rate?

Q. I do not care to go into any details of that kind. What I meant to say was this: The principle on which this business is done is such that a man who buys a ticket from a ticket broker gets a ticket, say, from here to New York, at a less rate than he will be able to get a ticket from the railroad company; he pays less for it, less than the published rates, and it is therefore an infringement of the law, a violation of the law, very plain and flagrant.—A. You and I are not prohibited from selling tickets at any price, as I understand it, under the statute nor from buying. The law does not prohibit me from buying a ticket for $20 and turning around and selling it to you for $15. It does as a railroad officer, but not as an individual.

Q. As an officer of the company, yes.—A. Undoubtedly; it would be a violation of the statute.

Q. What have you to say about the giving of passes by railroads to individuals, discriminating against other individuals?—A. I think the evil in that is largely due to the twenty-second section of the act to regulate commerce. After carefully drafting a bill prohibiting discrimination they provide in this way (reading):

"SEC. 22. That nothing in this act shall prevent the carriage, storage, or handling of property free or at reduced rates for the United States, or municipal governments, or for charitable purposes, or to or from fairs and expositions for exhibition thereat, or the free carriage of destitute and homeless persons transported by charitable societies, and the necessary agents employed in such transportation, or the issuance of mileage, excursion, or commutation passenger tickets; nothing in this act shall be construed to prohibit any common carrier from giving reduced rates to ministers of religion, or to municipal governments for the transportation of indigent persons, or to inmates of the (2) National Homes or State Homes for disabled volunteer soldiers and of soldiers' and sailors' orphan homes, including those about to enter and those returning home after discharge, under arrangements with the boards of managers of said Homes. Nothing in this act shall be construed to prevent railroads from giving free carriage to their own officers and employees, or to prevent the principal officers of any railroad company or companies from exchanging passes or tickets with other railroad companies for their officers and employees."

Now, there are 20 lines, half a page, of exceptions, and the law has so expressed them that you can not see the limits of the exceptions. There should be a provision there for commutation tickets and mileage tickets, and then strike out all exceptions looking for reduced rates for charity, for the United States Government, and for municipal governments, and, above all, for other railroad men—strike that all out; and about the employees of the company itself. Cut out all these exceptions and forbid discrimination absolutely. Each railroad company will take care of its own employees very easily by increasing their pay or giving them an allowance for traveling. The root of the evil is in the exchange of passes. If you can cut that out you have done a great deal toward the whole. Why should I, who happen to belong to the Protestant Episcopal Church, be called upon to carry a Roman Catholic or a Hebrew minister free?

Q. (By Professor JOHNSON.) Is not the granting of passes an illegal discrimination when you carry a man across the boundary of a State?—A. I would rather you would prove it by some other witness, gentlemen, to put it in all candor. (Laughter.)

Q. (By Senator MALLORY.) Do you regard it as an evil?—A. Yes. I am so constituted I do not believe in giving something for nothing under any circumstances. I think the evil of the pass situation is, seriously, this: It is the only way of getting value out of the treasury of the railroad company without leaving a voucher. There is no other way known to me.

Q. (By Professor JOHNSON.) Do not the railroad companies give these passes for value to be received?—A. Some of them, but the particular value received is not of record.

Q. It is not of record, but is it not in the form of favors of various kinds?—A. I am giving passes now to persons that are serving the company well, and they are entitled to it. I can defend hundreds of passes. There are reasons; but the same thing would enable me to go right to the treasury of the company and put in a voucher and give these men, say, $100, just exactly the same. If it is defensible for value received, it can be paid by money.

Q. (By Senator MALLORY.) What do you say about these passes given to members of the legislature and members of Congress and Senators?—A. I think the whole thing should be stopped.

Q. Do you think there is value received in this case?—A. I have been told there is at times.

Q. (By Mr. KENNEDY.) Do you think there is any chance of getting value received from the ministers by issuing them passes?—A. Hereafter?

Q. No, now.—A. I do not know. Yes; there is something in that if you consider the corporation as a moral being, which it is not. If you consider it simply as what it is—a corporation for gain—I do not see why the clergyman should be helped in his business any more than a shoemaker should be in his. They are both doing good and perhaps the shoemaker is doing the most good.

Q. The ministers come up almost unanimously and denounce to Congress the immoral practices of discrimination.—A. I am glad to see they are after it. It is their business to denounce immoral practices.

Q. (By Mr. FARQUHAR.) If the corporation is on the line of a moral being, what do you say of a community that leaves church property untaxed?—A. I would tax it.

Q. Has that the character of a moral being?—A. I would advocate taxing it. I do not see why Congress, in legislating on this subject, should put it in the hands of a manager of a railroad who belongs to some particular church to make this discrimination. I try to be honest in what I do, but belonging to one denomination I can see the demands of that denomination more clearly than I can any other. I am naturally so constituted. So far as the issuance of free transportation passes through my hands personally, a clergyman of the Protestant Episcopal Church would probably have someone whom I know who could come to me, while a clergyman of the Methodist Church, for instance, might not have a way of approaching me. If the other men who grant passes are in like case, why not strike it out absolutely and stop it? Why should not the law say there shall be no discrimination? Then I see no loopholes, rat holes, and no leaks. It is pretty high ground to take and I know most railroad men will not agree with me. I doubt if any of them will.

Q. Do you think if the pass system were abolished there would be any decrease of rate to the paying passengers?—A. No; I do not think it amounts to enough to affect the passenger earnings. All my railroad friends say, "Fish, what are you fighting for?" The thing does not amount to enough to make it worth while to stop it." I do not think it affects the revenue to any considerable extent. The people simply would not travel.

Q. (By Mr. KENNEDY.) Congressmen and legislators would travel, would they not? A. Members of Congress would travel, yes; but they are not many; 400 perhaps.

Q. State legislatures in every State?—A. Yes; but they would not go home on Friday; they would go up and sit 6 days in the week and stay a fortnight and get their mileage and adjourn.

Q. (By Senator MALLORY.) What is your judgment in regard to discriminations as practiced to-day compared with those practiced a year ago or two years ago?—A. I think the situation is good to-day. Rates are fairly well maintained generally over the United States to-day; better than they have been.

Q. What do you ascribe that to?—A. The conferences between the Interstate Commerce Commission and the railroad people have had a very good effect. Then the abundant crops and the immense amount of tonnage freight has had another, and the getting of certain railroads into fewer hands has had an effect—consolidation.

Q. You think consolidation has a tendency to affect competition?—A. It checks the destructive kind of competition.

Q. Competition is really the cause of discrimination?—A. Yes; I do not see anything else that could cause it.

Q. If there was no competition there would be no reason for discrimination, would there?—A. No more than in the sale of any other commodity.

Q. What is the principal method of discrimination now in existence that you know, if you know of any, whereby certain individuals get a benefit out of railroad transportation which others do not?—A. As I said before, I am not in that part of the business to any extent, but it is the little things that the Interstate Commerce Commission have talked about so much, the underbilling and underweighing, any kind of rebates, contracts, and everything else; I do not think there is any one worse than the others.

Q. They are not practiced as much now as they were?—A. No.

Q. One system to which our attention has been called by several witnesses is where mileage is paid for the use of private cars owned by firms or individuals, which is a considerable amount on each car. Have you given any consideration to that question?—A. Necessarily. I think that it is less of an evil than it was. The cost of repairing cars as they become larger and heavier and more complicated in their construction increases. . . By holding the rate of mileage down we will come to a point where there is no particular profit to the owners of the car; where the mileage will just pay for the wear and tear on the car; I think the two things will gradually come together on that.

Q. Are not this class of shippers who own these cars sufficiently powerful to compel the railroads to give them the rates of mileage they want?—A. I think they would have great difficulty in getting the rate raised again. You see, the railroads are getting much more powerful in the sense of being better able to buy equipment of their own. The day when the railroad went to the shipper to borrow equipment is past. As a rule, the railroads do not invest in that kind of car; the refrigerator car, for instance, for beef. Of course, these great packers do own refrigerator cars and they refuse to ship in anything else, and that is where they have it.

Q. Are they not sufficiently powerful to say to the railroad shipping it, for instance, if you do not give us this mileage, which we are accustomed to get from you, we will ship by another road?—A. They can get the mileage but as the car becomes more expensive I do not think they will find it easy to get more mileage. Suppose a refrigerator car costs $800; suppose the price goes up to $1,000—25 per cent increase; it will not get an increased mileage; the thing will tend to close itself up there.

Q. In your State do you recognize the distinction between export rates and what are known as inland rates?—A. We have to.

Q. Shipping down through the Mississippi Valley to New Orleans, for instance?—A. We have to.

Q. What do you mean by having to do it?—A. Here is grain, for instance, coming into our local stations in Illinois. That has to go to Liverpool and the ocean rate is so much. Now, we must either let that business go entirely or make a lower rate than the local rate on grain. We have done it over and over again. The question is up before the Interstate Commerce Commission now, and it has been for months, on that sort of discrimination.

Q. You think it is absolutely necessary for the business; if you do not make a discrimination there will be no export business?—A. Either that or to reduce our local rate to New Orleans to a point at which it would not pay us to haul it. Our condition is very different from that of the Eastern trunk lines because we have a grain producing country all along our road more or less until you get close to New Orleans and we have no large consumption of grain in New Orleans, only to feed that quarter of a million people; no flouring industry, especially; no manufacturing into crackers or anything of that sort; no glucose factory or things of that kind to consume corn, and our local shipment is small. Our rates are reasonable in there and our export business is large and in order to get to the port of New Orleans we have, at times, to make a lower rate than the local.

Q. I understand you to say, then, if you were prohibited from making discrimnaitions between your export and local rates you would not have that export business?—

A. We would have to give it up or carry our local way down below the cost on so small a volume as the local. You see we do this export business by the train load and deliver it into our elevators in New Orleans, and it goes on the ship, and we have these cars back on the track inside of a few hours. On the other hand, if we have to handle that grain through a house in sacks or something of that kind, we hold these cars around there waiting on the convenience of the consignee for days or weeks.

This difference between export rates and local rates arises from a commercial necessity which is universally recognized. The same is true in all business. Every merchant does it. Every manufacturer does it. He keeps the foreign markets as a place on which to throw his surplus and relieve himself, even if he has to do it at a loss. In Europe and especially in England it works clearly against the local consumer, because there the freight is carried from one border of the country clear through it to the other and out of the other side; either the consignee or the consignor, both of whom are foreign to that country, gains the whole advantage. With us the case is different. If there is a glut due to overabundant crops, overproduction in some point, we will say, in central Illinois, in so far as we relieve that glut by making a low rate on export, we raise the price on the farm of that grain, and help the producer to that extent. Moreover, this thing is an absolute necessity, if the United States are going to stay in competition with the other points of production like Argentina, India, Japan, Australia, and Asia. If we are to be cut off from the power to do the same thing that they do, we are at a disadvantage. It is not a thing the railroads seek or want to do, it is a thing they must do. The question of the legality of that discrimination is before the Interstate Commerce Commission and has been for a long time.

Q. The question of discrimination between flour and wheat has also, I believe, been before the commission; the rates from Chicago and the West generally to the Atlantic seaboard?—A. I do not think that applies on our business, so far as I know.

Q. The great point of objection to-day against railroads, one which is urged more than any other, is that of discrimination; and the railroad people, so far as we can judge, are inclined to think that is correct, and that that accusation would not necessarily be made against them if they had a right to deal more freely with each other and make contracts concerning the rates. What is your view about that?—A. I have never been an ardent advocate of the pooling bill, but I believe if I were differently situated, if the property I represent was differently situated, I should advocate that as ardently as the others. We had a very large per cent—84 per cent of local traffic— which is ours; and while the pool would affect more or less all of that, we have got that, which we live on, and we can stand it.

Q. It is yours?—A. It is ours. You see our position in regard to the grain business is that there is brought to our local stations somewhere from 70,000,000 to 90,000,000 bushels of grain in a year, one time and another, and we have never exported more than 23,000,000. Now, that local business we will haul somewhere. We may haul it to New Orleans for export, or we may haul it to other lines and give to Eastern trunk lines, but we will get something out of it always.

Q. Eliminating your position in connection with a road that is not harassed much by local competition?—A. (Interrupting.) We have lots of competition.

Q. Well, you have 84 per cent of your business pretty secure, you say?—A. No; I say that is our business. We are contented with it. If we went around and made 80 per cent of our business competitive, we might have four or five times as much competitive business but we might not make any more money. That is what I mean. We are attending to our own legitimate business in our own country, and getting 84 per cent local now. I saw the statement of one road that got 82 per cent competitive through and 18 local. If we could come to that position and retain the 84 which we have now, we would have that much in addition of the competitive business. We have not reached out for that business and do not want to. I do not think there is much profit in it.

Q. You do not agree, you say, with the sentiment which seems to be quite strong among railroad people that it would be a good thing for them to be allowed to make pooling contracts which would be valid?—A. I do; but I do not think it is going to be a panacea. I think it is but fair to give them the right to contract. I do not think it was fair of Congress to deprive them of that right. I am not at all opposed to the pooling bill, but I believe we will have wars and rumors of wars if the pooling bill is passed.

Q. (By Professor JOHNSON.) On this question of local and through rates, your statement is very strong. I should like for our information to know what you consider local and what through; what you consider the basis of your classification?— A. I telegraphed for that. I have it here. I guessed that question would come up. (Reading:) "Business moving between terminal stations of northern, western, and southern lines"—I will explain those terms later—"or over entire line is considered as through. Cincinnati also a terminal point. Example: Between Chicago and New Orleans, Cairo, Dubuque, Sioux City, East St. Louis; between New Orleans and Memphis, Louisville, Cairo, East St. Louis; between Sioux City and Dubuque, East St. Louis, Cairo, Memphis, New Orleans. All other freight considered local." That is the same classification which prevailed right along. I said I would define those terms. The terminal stations of the northern lines are Dubuque, Chicago, Cairo—a triangle; of southern lines, Cairo and New Orleans, with Memphis, Louisville, or Cincinnati on the flank.

Q. (By Senator MALLORY.) What do you think of the idea of Congress requiring a Government inspector to visit all interstate railroads and look into their business, and if he finds anything that is prohibited by the interstate commerce law make it public, make complaint?—A. I do not believe he will find much.

Q. I infer from that you do not approve of that plan of railroad restriction?—A. I do not think it is necessary to have that minute examination, which might also be called espionage, on a lawful business, in order to keep men who are addicted to unlawful practices from pursuing them. I think the thing to do is to fine the companies and enforce that law and put somebody in the penitentiary. We are told the interstate commerce law is violated continuously, and yet in ten years no one has been punished for it.

Q. (By Mr. KENNEDY.) Could we not find out a great deal more if we had such expert examiners?—A. If so, why does not somebody do it? It is not my business to go around and do it; nor do I think it is the business of the courts to do it. It strikes me it is the failure of the person who is hurt to make the complaint.

Q. (By Senator MALLORY.) These people complain that they are individuals and that they can not make any headway against a railroad, and I think the facts indicate the truth of that. Where a case of unjust discrimination or a case of excessive freight rate is charged against a railroad, the Interstate Commerce Commission may decide in favor of the complainant, but it would be years before the matter would be finally disposed of, by going up to the different courts on appeal, and really the case and everything else is forgotten. The man who brought the original suit is dead. Now, for that reason, by reason of the delay and the alleged injustice which arises out of that delay, it has been thought that by having an official whose duty it would be to call attention to these cases and make complaint—not necessarily to have a lawsuit, but to call the attention of the public to the fact—that it would be an amendment that would perhaps be very beneficial in checking such things?—A. The idea is a new one to me. I had not thought much about it; but I think it would be futile.

Q. You do not think they would be able to discover anything wrong?—A. Well, I do not mean thereby to say there is nothing wrong, but I do not see how an officer of that kind is going to find out very much, not enough to earn his salary.

Q. (By Professor JOHNSON.) Do you think the bank examiners are able to find out anything?—A. The worst fraud I ever knew of in a bank (I was a victim of it) was where the bank was robbed of $90,000, and it was only found out by accident the next morning, after the examining officer had given us a clean bill. We were robbed of $90,000 and no one knew it. It had been going on for months, and the books showed it, too.

Q. (By Mr. C. J. HARRIS.) What is your opinion as to Government ownership of roads?—A. I think it would be a bad day for the Government and a good day for the railroads. We would get out of a not over-profitable business, and I do not believe the Government could operate them within many per cent as cheaply as we do.

CHICAGO, ILL., *November 15, 1899.*

TESTIMONY OF HON. JOHN H. REAGAN,

Chairman of the Railroad Commission of Texas.

The subcommission on transportation met at 10 a. m., November 15, 1899, in Chicago, Representative Lorimer presiding. Hon. John H. Reagan was introduced as a witness and, being duly sworn, testified concerning transportation as follows:

Q. (By Mr. C. J. HARRIS.) Please state your name and address.—A. John H. Reagan; my post-office address is Palestine, Tex.; place of business, Austin, Tex.

Q. Please state your relations, officially and otherwise, in regard to the railroads of the country.—A. I am chairman of the railroad commission of the State of Texas.

Q. (By Representative LORIMER.) Have you a paper to submit?—A. If the commission will permit me I would like to read a statement and then subject myself to such examination as you wish to make.

I do not propose to discuss the question as to the details of railroad transportation, except as they may be necessarily involved in the consideration of the greater question of the solution of the railroad problem.

I propose first to make some suggestions as to necessary legislation by Congress as to interstate and foreign transportation, and by the State legislatures as to transportation beginning and ending in a State, which seems to me to be necessary for the proper settlement of this greatest of our economic questions.

1. Congress should empower the Interstate Commerce Commission to make, regulate, and maintain freight rates and passenger fares as these relate to interstate and foreign commerce. And the several legislatures should make like provision for State traffic.

This I believe to be entirely practicable. The railroad commission of Texas is clothed with these powers and duties. On the 30th of June, 1899, the aggregate mileage of railroads in the State of Texas was about 9,675 miles. With the large powers above referred to this system of railroads is successfully managed by 3 railroad commissioners, 2 rate men, 1 auditor, 1 engineer, a secretary, and 1 clerk, who does the shorthand and typewriting—9 in all. There are about 70 railroads in this system. On the 30th of June, 1898, there were in the United States 184,428 miles of railroad. The total number of railways in the United States on the 30th of June, 1897, was 1,987. For the same year there were about 130 persons, including the commissioners, employed in the service of the Interstate Commerce Commission. Now, if 9 persons were found sufficient for the management of 70 railroads in Texas, of 9,675 miles in length, with these powers and duties, is it not practicable for 130 persons to manage in like manner the 1,987 railroads of the United States with a mileage of 184,428 miles?

The right of the commission to make, regulate, and maintain rates should be subject to appeal to the courts on questions of law only, the facts found by the commission to be conclusive of their accuracy.

The establishment of independent and impartial tribunals of this kind, to stand between the railroads, generally demanding higher rates, and patrons, generally demanding lower rates, it seems to me it is the only way in which this problem can be properly and justly solved, and is probably the only alternative to Government ownership of railroads.

I am of opinion that the ownership of the railroads by the Federal Government would so increase the power and patronage of the Government as to cause a change of the character of the Government and endanger the liberties of the people.

2. On the 3d of December, 1889, the Board of Trade and Transportation of New York filed with the Interstate Commerce Commission a complaint against the Pennsylvania Railroad Company and others, charging, in substance, that the defendants, being common carriers, engaged in the transportation of property between New York, Philadelphia, and Chicago and other Western points, had, since April 4, 1887, in violation of the act to regulate commerce, been and were guilty of unjust discriminations, in that they had been and were in the habit of charging the regular tariff rates upon property when delivered to them in New York and Philadelphia for transportation to Chicago and other Western points, while charging other persons rates which were lower, and even 50 per cent thereof, for a like and contemporaneous service under substantially similar circumstances and conditions, when the property was delivered to them in New York or Philadel-

phia by vessels and steamship lines under through bills of lading from foreign ports and foreign interior points, issued under an arrangement between the defendants and such steamship lines and foreign railroads for continuous carriage at joint rates from the point or port of shipment to Chicago and other Western points, the defendants' share of such rates, as aforesaid, being lower than their regular tariff rates.

The defendants substantially admitted the facts as charged. The Interstate Commerce Commission, in a clear and very elaborate opinion, said to have been written by the late Judge Cooley, held that the interstate-commerce law applied to shipments of freight wholly within the United States, or shipped from a foreign country to any place within the United States, and carried to such place from a port of entry either in the United States or an adjacent country. And it held that such rates were unjustly discriminating, and ordered the railroads to forthwith cease and desist from carrying any article of imported traffic, shipped from a foreign port to any port of the United States or any port of entry in a foreign country adjacent to the United States, upon through bills of lading destined to any place within the United States, at any other than upon the inland tariff covering other freight from such port of entry to such place of destination, or at any other than the rates established in said inland tariff for the carriage of other and like kind of traffic, in the elements of bulk, weight, value, and expense of carriage.

The Southern Pacific Railway Company refused to obey this order, and the commission applied to the circuit court of the United States to compel obedience to its order. The circuit court of the southern circuit of New York adjudged the case in favor of the decision made by the commission, and on an appeal to the second circuit court of appeals, that court affirmed the decision of the circuit court of the southern circuit. And, on appeal of this case to the Supreme Court of the United States, the decision of the commission and the judgments of the circuit court and the circuit court of appeals were reversed, by a divided court; the chief justice and two of the justices dissenting.

The jurisdiction of the United States is limited to the territory of the United States, to the marine league from the shores of the United States, and to the decks of the vessels of the United States. The court, in reaching this decision, assumed jurisdiction over commerce on the high seas and in foreign countries, and the circumstances connected with it, to the extent of declaring that the rates of freight on railroads in foreign countries and on the ocean might be blended with the inland rates of the United States so as to make such inland rates lower than the rate for the same kind of shipments made wholly within the United States.

Mr. Justice Harlan, in his dissenting opinion, states that the records show that on certain kinds of goods, which he names, the rates from Liverpool and London by New Orleans and over the Southern Pacific system of roads to San Francisco is 107 cents per hundred pounds, while the rate from New Orleans to San Francisco for like merchandise over the same roads, and probably on the same trains, is 288 cents per hundred pounds. And he shows that on other classes of goods the rate from Liverpool and London, via New Orleans and the Southern Pacific Railroad, to San Francisco, is 107 cents, and the rate from New Orleans to San Francisco on the same kind of a shipment, is 370 cents per hundred pounds. In this way the decision of the Supreme Court of the United States provides for most burdensome and mischievous discriminations in freight rates against the merchants and manufacturers of the United States. And while doing this it puts it out of the power of the Interstate Commerce Commission to know what rates are being charged on such shipments, and opens wide the door to unjust discriminations and fraudulent practices.

This is the most serious blow which has been struck at the efforts of Congress to prevent cut rates, rebates and unjust discriminations in freight rates, and to protect the people against fraudulent devices in this respect.

My object in calling attention to this subject is to direct the attention of this Industrial Commission to it, in the hope that it will look into this question and urge upon Congress the great necessity of remedying the mischief caused by this decision of the Supreme Court, by proper legislation. If the members of this commission should think it proper to look into this question they will find an able review of it in the Tenth Annual Report of the Interstate Commerce Commission, pages 7-16.

3. The allowance of free passes by the railroad companies is not done as a matter of charity, for they are not, as a rule, given to the poor and needy, but for the most part to public officials and to influential persons. It is one method of unjustly discriminating in freight rates in a way that it is difficult, if not

impossible, to prevent, by furnishing free passes to shippers, their families, their agents, etc. And as the revenues of the roads must be kept up, it is the taxing of one part of the people for the benefit of another part of them which violates the commonest rules of right, and it is undoubtedly employed as one of the means of influencing public officials and members of legislative bodies in the performance of their official duties. It is unfair, unjust, and demoralizing, and should be prohibited by Congress and the several legislatures in their respective spheres of authority.

4. Congress and the several States should protect the public, and give permanence to the value of the stock and bonds of railroads, by prohibiting their issue except for money paid, labor done, or property actually received and applied to the purpose for which the corporation was organized.

Article 12, section 6, of the constitution of the State of Texas, provides as follows:

"No coropration shall issue stock or bonds except for money paid, labor done, or property actually received, and all fictitious increase of stock or indebtedness shall be void."

Article 4410 of tho Revised Statutes of Texas provides that:

"No railroad corporation shall issue any stock or bonds except for money, labor, or property actually received and applied to the purposes for which the corporation was organized; nor shall it issue any shares of stock in said company except at par a e, and actual subscribers who pay or become liable to pay the par value thereofx"lu

Such provisions enacted by Congress and the several States and enforced would protect the people from being imposed on and swindled by the sale and purchase of watered and fraudulent stock and bonds. It would give permanence to their value and make such securities safe in which to invest trust estate and the surplus funds of citizens, and it would give that character to such securities which spring from honest dealing and good faith.

5. If I may be oxcused, I will refer to another measure adopted by the legislature of Texas to prevent the evils of watered and fraudulent stock and bonds, to give permanent value to such securities issued by the railroad companies of Texas, and to fix, to some extent, a measure to govern the freight rates necessary to furnish just and reasonable revenue to the railroads, where the business on them is sufficient for that purpose. This is by the enactment of what is known as the stock and bond law of April 8, 1893. The second section of that law, article 4584b of the Revised Statutes, provides as follows:

"That hereafter no bonds or other indebtedness shall be increased or issued or executed by any authority whatsoever, and secured by a lien or mortgage on any railroad or part of a railroad, or the franchises of property appurtenant or belonging thereto, over and above the reasonable value of said railroad property; provided, that in the case of emergency, on conclusive proof shown by the company to the railroad commission that the public interest or the preservation of the property demands it, said commission may permit said bonds, together with the stock in the aggregate, to be executed in an amount not more than 50 per cent over the value of said property."

And this act of the legislature, and the eleventh section of the railroad commission law of this State, article 4584c of the Revised Statutes, makes it the duty of the railroad commission of the State "to ascertain, and in writing report to the Secretary of the State, the value of each railroad in this State, including all its franchises, appurtenances, and property.

This has been done by the commission; and the average value per mile of all the railroads in the State has been determined to be $15,759.02. And the aggregate value of all the railroads of Texas, so valued, on the 30th of June, 1899, was $141,117,176.53. Their value as capitalized by the railroad companies, including stocks and bonds, was $362,953,383. But these valuations do not include the new railroads built since the passage of the stock and bond law, act of the legislature of April 8, 1893, article 4584b of the Revised Statutes, which have only been preliminarily valued.

I had better state the plan adopted by the commission for making these valuations: The law requires the railroad companies to file with the commission profiles of their several roads. When this has not been done the commission directs its engineer, in connection with the engineer of the railroad company, to prepare a proper profile. These being of completed roads, the profiles disclose the character of the material through which the cuts and fills are made. We then collect evidence of construction companies, contractors and others, as to the cost of grading, and put that on our files. We, in like manner, obtain evidence of the cost of crossties and put that on files. In like manner we obtain evidence as to the value of iron and steel rails and fixtures, from manufacturers and others, the cost of engines and of all kinds of cars, from those who make them and from others, and place this evidence on file. So of every article which enters into the construction and equipment of the railroad. We also ascertain the value of the right of way. Having thus ascertained the value of the physical property of a railroad, we generally fix an arbitrary allowance to the company of about 6 per cent of our valuation of its property, to cover the cost of charter fees and for engineering service and counsel fees. And we make to the company another arbitrary allowance of about 6 per cent on our value of the property, to cover the interest on the cost of construction during the period of construction.

When this is done the law requires the commission to furnish a copy of its valuation to the railroad company, and give it a notice of forty days in which it may contest the accuracy of the valuation. We have done this in every case of valuation, and not one of our valuations, of all the railroads of Texas, has been contested. By our plan of valuation, if contested, we could ask what item in it was complained of and could from our files show the proof on which it was made.

The purpose of the legislature in requiring these valuations was twofold: first, to protect the patrons of the roads against rates of freight which would pay interest on watered and fraudulent stock and bonds, and, second, to enable the commission to know, with greater certainty, what freight rates and passenger fares would be required to pay the interest on the actual value of the roads.

I supposed that a statement like this, showing some of the means adopted in the State of Texas to secure fairness and justice between the people and the railroads, might be more acceptable to the members of the Industrial Commission than an attempt to make categorical answers to questions propounded by it.

In the following I shall refer to the numbers on the margin of your "Topical plan of inquiry."

No. 32. The practice, so prevalent among railroads, of making unjust discriminations as between persons, places, and railways, and of allowing rebates, cut rates, etc., should be prohibited under penalties, which would make the doing of these things a felony, and such is the law of Texas. These practices are conceived in fraud and operate to the injury of innocent people. They demoralize the public and as a general rule deplete the revenues of the railroads and benefit only the managers who perpetrate the frauds. The enforcement of the long and short haul policy is of paramount necessity. Without it a few great commercial and manufacturing centers would be built up, and the people of the smaller intermediate places would be rendered unable to do a mercantile or manufacturing business successfully. And the people between such great commercial centers would be taxed, by increased freight rates, with the cost of transportation to the great centers of trade.

So long as you make pecuniary penalties the temptation is so great that every man will take the risk of doing wrong. Of course the company can not answer in pecuniary damages, and if it is a penitentiary offense they can not substitute the company's liability, and they will be more careful; at least our legislature took that view of it.

No. 33. Unjust discriminations, the allowance of rebates, etc., as practiced, tend to reduce the cost of carriage of merchandise to the wealthy and large shippers, to increase the cost to the poor and small shippers, cause every merchant and shipper to fear that others are getting lower rates than himself, and to induce men, otherwise honest, to ask the railroads to violate the law for their benefit simply, as they suppose, as a matter of self-defense.

No. 39. It is due to the public, and necessary to secure fair dealing, that freight rates should be published. The method for this provided by the Texas law is "That each of said railroad companies shall cause said schedules (meaning the freight rates) and rules to be printed in type of a size not much less than pica, and shall have the same posted up in a conspicuous place at each of its depots so as to be inspected by the public."

No. 40. Answering the question as to the cases in which lower than the published rates are allowed in Texas, I quote from subdivision (h) of section 15 of the railroad commission law:

"Nothing herein shall prevent the carriage, storage, or handling of freight free or at reduced rates for the State, or for any city, county, or town government, or for charitable purposes, or to or from fairs and expositions for exhibition thereof, or the free carriage of destitute or indigent persons, or the issuance of mileage or excursion passenger tickets; nor prevent the railroad from giving free transportation to ministers of religion, or free transportation to the inmates of hospitals, eleemosynary or charitable institutions, and to the employees of the agricultural and mechanical departments of the State, or to the peace officers of the State; and nothing herein shall be construed to prevent the railroad from giving free transportation to any railroad officers, agents, employees, attorneys, stockholders or directors, or to the railroad commissioners, their secretary, clerks, and employees hereinbefore provided for."

And then, as if a sufficient number of persons had not been provided for, the section adds:

"Or to any person not prohibited by law, provided they, or either of them, shall not receive from the State mileage when such pass is issued."

That law was in force for 8 years, and the commission has diligently attempted to get it remedied so as to make it more reasonable. I have conferred with members of the legislature time and time again about it, but as long as they have free tickets, annual passes, they do not afford us any relief.

Q. (By Mr. C. J. Harris.) That provision is still in?—A. Yes. We have very fine legislation on the subject, according to the view I take of it, and I always look upon that as a disgrace to the State.

No. 50. I suppose reference is here made to the case of Smyth vs. Ames, 169 U. S. Reports. While the Supreme Court in this case announced some very important and valuable principles of law, there is a feature of the case which I take it could not have been fairly represented to the court, or understood by it.

In discussing the basis of the valuation of the property of a railroad it said:

"What the company is entitled to ask is a fair return upon the value of that which it employs for the public convenience."

And that statement is followed by the court with the further statement that—

"In order to ascertain that value, the original cost of construction, the amount expended in permanent improvements, the amount and market value of its bonds and stock, the present as compared with the original cost of construction, the probable earning capacity of the property under particular rates prescribed by State, and the sum required to meet operating expenses, are all matters for consideration, and are to be given such weight as may be just and right in each case."

Now, I submit, with all respect for that great court, that parts of the foregoing statement will not successfully bear criticism. For instance, what just relation is there between the "original cost of construction" and the present value of a railroad? It may have been built when material and labor bore a very high price, when stock and bonds were at a great discount, or upon an improvident and excessive contract, and, owing to the fall in prices or other causes, may not now be worth the half of what it cost "originally." The original cost of a railroad is not and can not be, in any sense, a just measure of its present value.

So the amount expended in permanent improvements can not be a just test of the present value of the property. The material for such improvements may have cost too high, the contracts for making them may have been improvident and excessive; such material and labor may have been greatly reduced in price.

And the "amount and market value of its bonds and stock" can not be a just measure of the future value of a railroad. There may have been an excessive issue of bonds and stock, as has often been the case, and our common experience teaches us that by speculation and manipulation the market value of stock and bonds of railroads are constantly and often violently fluctuating, so that they are not a reliable or fit measure for values of any kind.

Surely it will not be seriously assumed that these matters will be considered a standard by which the subsequent value of a railroad should be measured. I submit as a substitute for all this that a safer means of ascertaining the present value of a railroad would be for experts to ascertain, as actual facts, what it would cost now to obtain the right of way and build and equip a railroad, making reasonable additions to its value to meet engineering expenses, the fees of counsel, the interest on the money necessary for these purposes, and whatever additional amount might be found proper of actual ascertainable value. We could thus determine the value of a railroad upon the ascertained value of its elements, and we would not be driven to loose speculations, like those stated in the opinion of the court, in order to assume what the value of a railroad might be.

I am inclined to make this statement here: I believe, just as in this case, that in determining what the rates shall be the State should furnish sufficient revenues to offset the railroad company for their industry. It was assumed it was necessary to limit the rates on interstate shipments and to put into the amount loaned from the State the revenues derived from local State shipments. Now, then, to meet that case fairly, the State grants the charter and the franchises; it authorizes the construction of the railroad; it authorizes its operation; it authorizes the collection of fares and revenues, and yet it is assumed that, notwithstanding a part of the freight may be interstate freight, it is not entitled to pay for the carriage of freight across the State. It has always seemed to me, at any rate, when

I know that the State furnishes the means of transportation, that it ought to be credited with the amount it receives, though some other corporation in connection with the State have no right to it.

No. 51. This, I suppose, has reference to the case of Reagan vs. The Farmers' Loan and Trust Company, 154 U. S. In that case the Supreme Court sustained the constitutionality of the railroad commission law of Texas. The only suggestion I have to make about that case is, that the justice who delivered the opinion of the court discussed the freight rate case as extensively as if that had been a material issue in the case. The truth is, the railroad commission believed that they could win the case as to rates, as well as in reference to the constitutionality of the commission law, but their rates would have stood enjoined until the final disposition of the case by the Supreme Court of the United States, which might have been from 3 to 5 years, and which they felt would be a serious misfortune to the people of Texas, and therefore in the circuit court they withdrew their answer as to the facts of the case, in order to secure an early decision on the constitutionality of the law. This was the question before the court, and its early decision enabled the commission, with much less delay, to assume the control of the question of freight rates.

I never understood why the question of rates was discussed, because we abandoned it in the court below.

No. 52. Congress should prohibit the Federal courts from issuing injunctions pendente lite in cases in which suits may be brought to enjoin the enforcement of freight rates, until the rates are found to be unjust or illegal. Otherwise a judge at chambers, on an ex parte statement, may arrest the employment of rates which have been regularly made by proper authority, and in this way arrest the business of a great railroad, or a system of roads, or of a whole State, which has been the effect of some of the injunctions heretofore issued. The issuance of such injunctions is too great and too dangerous a power to be intrusted to the arbitrary will of any one judge or more without a previous lawful ascertainment whether they are just and legal or unjust and illegal. It is not safe to allow the judges to assume that rates made by lawful authority will cause irreparable injury before their justice or injustice can be determined by a court. When a State railroad commission, duly appointed and sworn, has agreed to freight rates, some deference is due to its official action and to the authority of the State it represents. At all events, courts should be prohibited from issuing temporary injunctions until both sides of the case have been represented and heard.

When an injunction is sought to prohibit the enforcement of freight rates which have been established in conformity with law, the right of way should be given such suits over other business in all the courts by Congress for interstate shipments and by the legislature for State shipments.

Now, gentlemen, I am at your service.

Q. (By Representative LORIMER.) You are the author of the Reagan bill?—A. I should make some explanation about that. The first bill introduced on that subject of pooling was introduced when I was in the Forty-fourth Congress, and was introduced by Mr. Hopkins, of Pennsylvania. I was on the Commerce Committee and took a very active interest in trying to get it considered by the committee, but failed to get it considered during that Congress. Hopkins didn't return to the next Congress; I was returned. I received a letter from him asking me to reintroduce the bill. I had already prepared a bill with a view to introducing it. I introduced a bill which contains the great remedial features of the interstate-commerce law, except as to the commission, and it passed the House several times— I think, as many as three times—before it went to the Senate. In the Senate it was amended, adding the commission features of it. The question of the commission now arose. I might say that the fear of whoever the President might be who would make the appointment of the commissioners influenced us somewhat, because we did not know but what the influence the railroads would bring to bear would lead to the appointment of commissioners who would not execute the law; so the law was made to point out what they could do and what they could not do, and fixed the penalty, to be thereafter determined by the courts. That was, of course, changed. I put in the House bill a provision that State courts should have concurrent jurisdiction with the Federal courts in civil cases. That passed the House, but the conference committee struck it out. I also provided in the bill for a penalty to be inflicted on the railroad companies afterwards proved to be the beneficiaries of rebates and cut rates. In the conference committee that was struck out, because it was decided that they would all be guilty alike and that the penalty should be put upon them alike. I think the main remedial features of that bill were embodied in the bill I got passed through the House several times.

Q. (By Representative OTJEN.) What Congress was that?—A. Forty-fourth Congress.

Q. (By Professor JOHNSON.) That was in 1879?—A. 1878. That was the time it was finally passed. Hopkins introduced the bill in 1876, and I introduced my bill first in 1878.

Q. (By Mr. C. J. HARRIS.) And are you satisfied with the results of that bill as it was afterwards passed by the House and finally adopted in Texas; are your people in Texas satisfied with it?—A. I think the law is a very good one. I think the law is all right if it is fairly and justly interpreted.

Q. (By Representative LORIMER.) That is, by the courts?—A. Yes.

Q. (By Mr. C. J. HARRIS.) You claim in your paper, which, of course, is testimony, that the Interstate Commerce Commission should have certain powers in regard to rate making?—A. Yes. I know the objection is made to that that the system would be so exclusively with the commission that it would be impracticable; but I have studied this question practically for the last 8 or 10 years, and. under a fair law, I don't see why it can not be done. Of course, a system of rates can be fixed to cover a great deal of country which would have the same rates. If it can not be done in that way I don't see that there is any other way that you can ever get that question fairly solved.

Q. Do you care to say anything in regard to pooling?—A. I have spoken on that subject at the meeting of the State railroad commissioners. I think if you can not have the rates fixed in that way the next best thing to do is to regulate by law. My idea has been that if we can not get a law regulating the rates, we ought to provide for agreements binding in force and subject to the approval of the railroad commission, and to be amended or revoked by the commission, and with provisions for the imposing of a penalty sufficiently severe on railroad directors for the violation of any of their contracts. A great many efforts have been made from time to time in the past to get out of rate wars and keep peace among the railroads.

Q. (By Professor JOHNSON.) It is useless to talk of pooling, is it not, unless you have a penalty for the violation of a contract and one that can be enforced by any company or by the United States against any company?—A. Yes; that under the control of the commission would go a great way toward preventing rate cutting and to secure a regular rule regulating rates. If we could not get good legislation which would enable the commission to make, regulate, and maintain rates, I think that would be the next best thing.

Q. Have you any suggestions to make as to the power of reducing rates and the power of controlling and regulating rates on the part of the United States commission? You are aware that the Interstate Commission has for several years been asking for power of reducing rates and regulating rates that had not been put into operation by the railroad companies themselves?—A. You will have seen from what I have said that my view is that the Interstate Commission should have the power of making, regulating, and maintaining rates. I think that the commission should have some power of reducing rates at all events.

Q. (By Representative LORIMER.) If they had the power of reducing rates, that would practically mean that they could establish rates?—A. It would help a great deal.

Q. (By Professor JOHNSON.) Do you think the commission possesses the technical knowledge to work out a schedule of rates for this country as a whole?—A. Yes: I don't doubt it. They have some very able experts there. It is the same practice that enables a commission to do that work in the State; it is only applying it on a larger scale. The principles are the same; there is no difference in them at all. We have a territory in the state of Texas that is larger than France and with nearly 10,000 miles of railroad and nearly 60 active operating roads. The commission under the law governing these great powers is composed of three commissioners, two expert rate makers, an auditor, secretary, engineer, and one clerk, and we maintain it although of course it is very hard work. However, it is necessary, so we maintain it although we can not have any specified hours; we work all day.

Q. (By Mr. KENNEDY.) Does your commission fix the rates of Texas?—A. Yes. We make the rates, regulate them, and have absolute control.

Q. State railroads only?—A. I mean State shipments.

Q. How would you arrange about the shipment of freight from St. Louis to Austin?—A. That would be under the control of the Interstate Commerce Commission.

Q. You would not control the rate in Texas where shipments are made from one State to another?—A. No; the Interstate Commerce Commission controls any rate if it is from one State to another; freight from another State or from a foreign country is out of our jurisdiction.

Q. (By Representative OTJEN.) You simply regulate the State traffic?—A. Yes; by law and by our action.

Q. (By Professor JOHNSON.) You spoke of the case of Smythe v. Ames in your testimony. I think you implied that a very important part of that decision seemed to be overlooked?—A. Yes; about the methods to be adopted as to certain values.

Q. In the fixing of rates now you can be guided, since that decision, only by the earning capacity of the railroads as regards their control of State traffic?—A. Yes; that is what I tried to deal with really. I have said that investigation will show that if that decision in that respect is carried out and enforced, it will bankrupt every railroad in the United States; I don't think there will be a single exception to it. When you take away the right from a State to embrace in its receipts pay for all the carriage done in it, you take from it the right to embrace in its receipts the cost of interstate shipments, and it makes the amount so low that it will not be commensurate with the value of the property and the operating expenses. The enforcement of that particular law will bankrupt every road in the United States.

Q. I was looking at that question from another standpoint altogether. It seems to me that a large part of the State traffic is but the initial or original proportion of other traffic; that most of the traffic which becomes interstate is in its initial stages State traffic, and from that point of view a considerable portion of the traffic within the State is really interstate, or in character it becomes interstate, and the railroads so regard it. If there is an all-through freight business and by allowing a charge on the all-through business of rates high enough to cover the cost of that business, would it not impose such a high local maximum of rates that it would be practically impossible for the State commission to regulate rates?—A. I think it would.

Q. You know this very question has arisen with regard to tickets. The rates fixed by ticket men have been set aside because of this ruling in Smythe v. Ames. Why do you offer your schedule in Texas?—A. In our State we are threatened with legislation on that very subject. This freight shipped on a published rate, which constitutes a contract between the railroad and shipper from one point to another in the State, causes some railroads to undertake to assume they must necessarily be interstate shipments; it must necessarily go somewhere else. Our law provides that our jurisdiction covers shipments from one point to another in the State of Texas. The action of the commission there is when the bill of lading calls for a shipment from one point to another in the State. That is the contract for the local State shipment.

Q. (By Representative LORIMER.) If the commission you suggest fixes the rate would it not be necessary for them to take into consideration every item of the expense?—A. It would seem theoretically that that would be necessary; practically it is never done, because the items that enter into it are so numerous that the degree in which they affect the rate is uncertain. They would have to be guided by experience from day to day, as there is no science in rate making. You can not make a science out of rate making; you have to be governed by experience from day to day, and how much a particular piece of freight costs, and what proportion it bears to the expense of carriage. There are a great many things you must necessarily put very low rates on. Then there are other things, very costly things, you put a very high rate on. There is no uniformity, because if you make a uniform rate it would make rates almost nothing on costly goods and almost if not quite prohibitive on these cheaper things. In theory it is necessary to consider everything, but so far as the practice is concerned it is not necessary to consider all these things, and it can not be done for the reason I stated—because the road has to be guided by every day's experience and the observation of what has been done before and the effect of it.

Q. What I wish to learn from you is, whether or not, ultimately, this commission that fixes the rate would not have to settle the rate of wages of the employees of the roads?—A. I don't think that would be necessary; I don't think one follows the other necessarily; that is a matter of contract between the corporation and its emyloyees.

Q. If every item of expense must be considered is not that one of the items.—A. Of course a part of the cost of transportation is the expense of the employees of the road.

Q. Would it not finally have control of the road and everything that goes to make up the road?—A. They would not undertake to determine a question which no commission has jurisdiction of, and which the courts alone have jurisdiction of, and would not undertake to determine the rate of wages. They might consider that in making up the rate on freight, but they would not determine that question independently.

Q. You think if they were to fix the rates they would have to take the wages into consideration?—A. They would necessarily consider everything that affected the cost of transportation so far as they practically could. The difficulty is that there is such an endless number of things that enter into th cost of transportation that you have to be guided by what has been done in the past, the experience of day to day and time to time, to ascertain what can be done in the way of carriage of any particular commodity and to make the carriage valuable to the public and at the same time secure the necessary revenue for the railroad; so that a railroad commission would not be embarrassed by such a question as that, with the opportunity of an examination to see what the carriage had been heretofore. Of course, to get down to the details would be a matter of infinite labor, and I suppose very unsatisfactory.

Q. It strikes me it will be necessary for the railroad company to go into all those details. All our railroads to-day, in considering the rate they make, take into consideration all those causes.—A. Our annual report shows the extent to which our commission goes into that subject. Of course we did not embrace every item, but we show a great many of the controlling influences that enter into the cost of transportation. These things are considered in connection with others. It is not only a question as to what is reasonable upon each commodity, but we have also to consider the questions growing out of competition.

Q. (By Professor JOHNSON.) In connection with this question of rates I would like to ask whether you think Government ownership, in case we should come to that, would mean the elimination of discrimination.—A. It is a very big question you are asking, and I have discussed it very fully on other occasions. Government ownership would, I think, necessarily make the cost of transportation much greater than its cost under the influence of private interests, corporate interests. They exercise all the economies they can in cheapening transportation and they have done a great deal of it from time to time. As they have made improvements of various kinds that facilitate and cheapen transportation, rates have gone down. If the Government owned the roads and appointed the employees the influence of private interests and corporate interests would go out of it, and all experience shows that everything the Government does requires more time, more men, and more money than the like thing done by the private individual or corporation. So I take it for granted, as the railroads are managed under corporate and private interests, the rates can be and as a rule will be cheaper than would be possible to make them if they were under the control of the Government. But there are other elementary troubles about that. There are now nearly 900,000 employees in the service of the railroads. They are men in the active years of life, energetic, intelligent men. Give the Government the appointment of these men in addition to the appointments it now makes and any man who is President can continue himself in office just as long as he wants to. I remember a speech made by Mr. Webster and one made by Mr. Calhoun over 50 years ago in their respective States, and each discussed the question and reached about the same conclusion. Each said that when the number of Government employees reached 100,000 it would endanger the character of the Government and the liberties of the people. There is now not less than 160,000 employees. Add the railroad employees to it and you have over 1,000,000 men under the control of the Government, with their families and their influences. To my mind Government ownership means the subversion of our system of government and the destruction of popular liberty.

Q. (By Mr. KENNEDY.) Has not experience shown that they were false prophets?—A. I do not know. It has not turned out that when we reached 100,000 we endangered the Government, but it is not safe to say they were false prophets, because I take it there is no man who has studied carefully the operations of this Government that does not see the increased danger of multiplication of offices under the Federal Government.

Q. (By Representative LORIMER.) They probably had in mind the population at that time.—A. Yes.

Q. (By Professor JOHNSON.) In my question I had another point in mind. The recognized evil of the transportation business is that of discrimination?—A. Yes.

Q. And it is claimed by those who do not believe regulation will be effective that we ought to deal with this question of discriminations by Government ownership. Would Government ownership necessarily eliminate discrimination?—A. It would have an influence in this way: Under corporate and private management the managers are interested in getting the most freight they can get. Under Government control that element would be absent from the managers of the road, they being under the employment of the Government and not interested in the aggregate amount earned by the railroads. It might have some influence in preventing discriminations in that respect.

Q. Would not the influence of localities result in discriminations between localities?—A. That might be.

Q. The valuation per mile you put on roads in Texas—is that on the basis of the taxation?—A. No; it does not control taxation.

Q. Are the stocks and bonds of the companies limited to the valuation of their roads?—A. All of the roads that have been built since the passage of the law. That, of course, is not retroactive. It is applied only on the new roads. It could not affect the stocks and bonds issued before the passage of the law.

Q. Suppose the railroad has increased its terminals in cities a good deal over what they originally cost, what effect would that have—simply to raise the price of stocks?—A. Our view—we have never practically acted on it—is that on account of increased value of the property a revaluation might be called for. If the conditions change I think they would have a right to a revaluation.

Q. Do you allow anything for improvements of railroads and betterments of conditions in making the rates for these railroads?—A. What we do is to take evidence of the value of the right of way, take evidence of the value of all that enters into construction and equipment of the road, then get its physical value, and then add to that arbitrarily an allowance in the aggregate of about 12 per cent. So we do not quite reach the subject of that question.

Q. Every railroad is trying to better itself; adds heavier rails; makes better bridges; has better ties, perhaps, and rock-ballasted roadbeds. Now, do you allow anything for that in your making of rates?—A. No; we take the value of the road; what it would take to rebuild the road. As I suggested, we have contemplated that as improvements are made and the value of the property increases corporations may demand a revaluation and would be entitled to it if the increase was such as to call for it.

Q. (By Mr. KENNEDY.) What system of taxation, among the various systems of the United States, do you favor for railroads?—A. I like the plan adopted in Kentucky and New Jersey, where the railroad commission fixes the value, because they have the means of knowing what ought to be known. I think in our State the commission can not do that. In the first place, the railroad company gives in its property to the assessor of taxes, and then there is a board of revision that goes over that and can raise or lower the taxes if it thinks proper. Then the board of revision passes on them. Now, to give an illustration of the way it is worked: The Texas and Pacific road is capitalized at about $60,000 a mile. It is valued by us at about $18,000 a mile. It is given in by them for taxes at about $8,000 a mile. They ask us to impose rates upon the people that will pay interest and dividends on $60,000 while they do not propose to pay taxes on but $8,000. That is a pretty strong illustration, but it gives a general idea of the whole thing.

Q. What is this Kentucky system you speak of?—A. The commission fixes the value. I do not assume the railroads ought to be taxed their full value, in view of the fact that no other property, as a rule, is given in at its full value; but if we could ascertain the percentage less than the full value at which other property is given in that ought to apply to our valuation of railroads also.

Q. You tax the franchise in Texas?—A. There is now a contest going on about that. It has never been done heretofore.

Q. How do you determine the value of the franchise?—A. I have never undertaken to determine that.

Q. Has anybody in Texas?—A. The county courts are now at work on that and there is litigation in several counties about it. The cases are to test this plan of valuation of the franchise.

Q. Have you an opinion as to how the value of the franchise should be obtained?—A. I have seen statements of the method, but I do not think I could state it intelligently to you. I have seen statements of the method by which they propose to reach the value of the franchise. It seems to me a little odd that the State should tax the property and the earnings. We have, I believe, a tax on the gross earnings of passenger fares and a small tax on the gross earnings of freight. If we should tax the property and then tax the earnings and then tax the franchise it would seem to me it would be going a good ways.

Q. (By Representative LORIMER.) Then you think if the property and the receipts are taxed that the franchise ought not to be?—A. I think we had better stop there; that would be my idea.

Q. (By Professor JOHNSON.) You think it would be better to levy all the taxes on the earnings than to tax the property and the earnings both? In Wisconsin the tax is on the receipts.—A. I have never undertaken to consider which of these plans would be better. Railroads with us are taxed upon their supposed value, and the average valuation in the State is somewhere in the neighborhood of $8,000 a mile. Some go as high as $10,000, and others a great deal lower.

Q. (By Representative OTJEN.) You spoke of a defect in the interstate-commerce law, made so by a decision of the court. Will you explain that a little more fully as to rate making? It was with reference to goods brought from foreign countries in comparison with domestic goods?—A. If you ever have occasion to look into that, and if you take up the opinion of the railroad commission as written by Mr. Justice Cooley, you will find it is a very elaborate and masterly opinion. It is just like a geometrical demonstration. He shows, it seems to me, beyond doubt that the authority of the United States to regulate rates is limited to the territory of the United States. The circuit court of New York sustained that opinion. The circuit court of appeals sustained that view. It was reversed under conditions that allow them to charge nearly four times as much as to certain classes of merchandise from New Orleans to San Francisco as from Liverpool or London to San Francisco. I have always understood that the jurisdiction of the United States only extended to our soil, and to the marine league from the shore. They take jurisdiction of the oceans—all of them, and of commercial states in all countries, because you see in their opinion they enumerate different countries in which there may be railroads bringing commerce to be forwarded here. It also seems to me very strange that they could take jurisdiction for such a purpose when they can take jurisdiction for no other purpose under the sun. I do not understand it. Under that, a man in London or Liverpool would make a contract for delivering merchandise at ports agreed on for Chicago. They would agree what portion should be given to the railroad bringing the merchandise to the port, what portion should be given to the ocean carrier, and what to the inland carrier. The complaint of the New York Board of Trade was that the portion which went to the inland carrier was much less than the rate that our citizens had to pay. In the dissenting opinion in that case it is very forcibly stated that that is a strong discrimination against our own merchants and our own manufacturers. Now, in addition to that, in the tenth annual report of the Interstate Commerce Commission, there is a very able argument showing that this has destroyed the power of the commission or anybody else to determine what the rates shall be in this country.

Q. (By Mr. C. J. HARRIS.) Would not an amendment to that bill regulate that matter?—A. That would do it, and I trust Congress may take it up and so amend it as to make rates uniform.

Q. (By Mr. KENNEDY.) Would you like also to see the interstate-commerce law amended so as to bring interstate railroads under the jurisdiction of the Government as national banks are now; that is, that experts may be sent out to examine the books of the interstate railroads?—A. They ought to have the power to send their experts and examine the office records. We used to have that power, and we used it. We knew morally that the roads were allowing rebates and making cut rates, but the legislature refused to give us any appropriation by which we might have the necessary investigation made to get the legal evidence of it. At the session of the legislature before the last one, we asked for $5,000 a year for two years, but stated to them that we could not tell what we wanted with it, but promised that we would return $10 for each and every one they gave us. We got the governor, and the attorney-general, and the State treasurer to unite in the request, and they finally consented to give us one appropriation of $5,000. We have already returned $67,500 in penalties, and a good many cases remaining yet. It has done a great deal to check it. That enabled our auditor to go into their offices. We have a right to demand the inspection of papers, contracts, and everything, and bring them before us and examine them as witnesses.

Q. You would like to see the interstate-commerce law amended giving the commission that power?—A. Yes; because if they can keep secret from the commission their doings there is no use for the law.

Q. You will probably get your $5,000 a year in Texas hereafter?—A. Yes; they made us an allowance this last legislature, but we do not have so much use for it. While the railroads contested our commission law very earnestly at first and carried it to the supreme court, now most of the railroads say it is a benefit to them as well as to the public, because it protects them against themselves and stops the giving of rates and the wasting of revenue.

Q. Are you familiar with the complaints against the Belt Line around Chicago?—A. No; I know there was some litigation and a decision, but I never took particular interest in that question.

Q. There is no complaint in your section of the country about it?—A. I think the cattlemen of Texas have something to do with it.

Q. Do you know the circumstances of the case?—A. I do not know that I do. I understood that there was a charge of $2 a car for bringing the cars off the roads into the city, and I think I saw a statement that the courts had reduced that to $1 a car. I am not familiar with that sufficiently to express an opinion about it.

Q. (By Professor JOHNSON.) I would like to ask if your experience leads you to believe you could enforce the imprisonment penalty?—A. I have no doubt of it; as well as you can for any other felony.

Q. Do you think a jury in this country would convict and send a man to prison for violating the law regulating transportation?—A. Well, I take it for granted they would not commit perjury, and the law requires conviction.

Q. (By Mr. C. J. HARRIS.) Did you ever have any cases of that kind in Texas?—A. None that I know of. We had a pecuniary penalty before that.

Q. (By Mr. KENNEDY.) Which of the three freight classifications is Texas in?—A. We have the Western.

Q. Do you have any conflict with the classification committee?—A. We have no special conflict, because we, in a general way, adopted their classification. But in their classification they make, in several cases, reservations in the interest of the road. Our law prohibits them from making any of these reservations. We have our classification made out and based on the Western classification, but these clauses—for instance, exempting them from liability in various cases—we strike them out of our classification.

Q. Do the shippers of Texas have an advantage over those of surrounding States?—A. They can not enforce these exceptional clauses against the people there. They have no legal force.

Q. Do you think the method by which the rates are fixed by the classification committee is the proper one? Are both sides fully heard before the committee?—A. All interests ought, of course, to be heard. The Interstate Commerce Commission has very earnestly urged uniform classification, or at least as near as can be made practical, which would be of great advantage to the public and of great convenience to the railroads also. There are different systems of classifications, as you referred to, and these give considerable annoyance.

Q. (By Representative LORIMER.) Have you any views on ticket scalping?—A. Yes; I think it ought to be prohibited.

Q. Have you any suggestion as to how to prevent it?—A. Well, yes. I have never thought about proposing a remedy. You can make it a penal offense to engage in that business.

Q. Whom would you punish, the purchaser or the seller?—A. In case we would have no witness, I would punish the scalper.

Q. Suppose the ticket is purchased by an individual and then sold on the platform to another person who is about to make a return trip; would you punish either of these two?—A. Well, that would be for legislation to determine. I would not like to make a statement about exceptions to the general rule.

Q. You know we had a bill before Congress providing for a penalty for purchasing and selling tickets that are purchased by an individual intending to make a trip, and selling it to another person who might make the whole trip or half of it?—A. Our law meets that in this way: If the person purchases a ticket and does not use it, he can go back to the office and have it redeemed.

Q. This bill also had a redemption clause in it?—A. With that clause, I would make him go to the railroad and not let him speculate.

Q. You would put him in jail if he sold it to anybody else?—A. Whatever the law said, I would put it on him.

Q. (By Mr. KENNEDY.) What do you believe to be the evil in ticket scalping?—A. It enables the railroads themselves, as a party to it, to underbid each other, and makes discriminations in that way, some having to pay full rates and some less than full rates. That is one of the evils, Then there are statements in the reports of the Interstate Commerce Commission that a great many frauds are perpetrated through the instrumentality of the ticket scalper. I do not know as I can say what they are, but the reports show the numerous cases in which frauds grow out of it.

Q. Have you studied the subject enough to know whether the railroads themselves are responsible for the system?—A. In some cases they are, because they agree with their agents to undersell other people. I do not know as I ought to say it. I think it is stated in the reports of the Interstate Commerce Commission, but I do not know it of my own personal knowledge, though I suppose it is correct. That is assigned by the Interstate Commerce Commission as one of the reasons why it should be prohibited. A railroad in Chicago in competition with others might go to a scalper and say, "You sell these tickets at such a percentage, and I will give you such a profit."

Q. You know it is the railroads that have gone to Congress asking for this legislation, and not the brokers?—A. Yes.

Q. Do you not think the railroads can break it up whenever they act unitedly upon it?—A. It seems to me they could, like all other sorts of free tickets. I do not know why they could not do it. I know the railroads have told us that they wanted free passes prohibited. I told them very plainly, "I do not suppose you do want it, because if you wanted to all you have to do is to withdraw your passes and it will be no trouble at all."

Q. What do you think of the large railroad lobby in Washington seeking the passage of the antiscalping bill and not asking to have any defects in the interstate-commerce law remedied?—A. I do not know. Maybe they think it will benefit them to get the scalping bill through and not benefit them to get the other legislation.

Q. (By Representative LORIMER.) Have you anything further to suggest?—A. I do not think of anything.

(Testimony closed.)

CHICAGO, ILL., *November 15, 1899.*

TESTIMONY OF MR. JOHN J. HYLAND,

Traffic Manager Freight Bureau, Board of Trade of the city of Chicago.

The subcommission on transportation being in session in Chicago, Representative Lorimer presiding, at 3.55 p. m., November 15, 1899, Mr. John J. Hyland was introduced as a witness, and, being duly sworn, testified concerning transportation as follows:

Q. (By Representative LORIMER.) You may state your name and place of res idence.—A. John J. Hyland, Chicago, Ill.

Q. Your business?—A. Traffic Manager of the Freight Bureau, of the Board of Trade of the city of Chicago.

The WITNESS. Before reading this paper I would like to make a few remarks. These are my own suggestions, which I believe will be approved by the majority of the members of the Chicago Board of Trade, which I have the honor to represent in traffic affairs.

Q. (By Representative LORIMER.) This is a production not of the board of trade, but of your own individual ideas?—A. Yes; that is right.

(Reading:) Although we have some grievances against the railroads, the board of trade of the city of Chicago does not at present desire to enter a formal complaint with your honorable commission.

It is, nevertheless, gratifying to this board that your kind invitation affords an opportunity to offer, through our freight bureau, a few suggestions on the subject of transportation, or, rather, on the matter of a "legalized railroad pool."

We are aware that many well-meaning persons, including some of our own members, are in favor of a legalized railroad pool, in the belief that more stable rates would obtain under a pool than under the present system of open competition.

A very large majority of our members, and, we believe, a large majority also of the general public, oppose a legalized railroad pool and favor "necessary changes in the interstate-commerce law."

We believe the law should be so amended as to give to the railroads the privilege of establishing, by mutual agreement among themselves or by arbitration, rates acceptable to all concerned, based along geographical lines or otherwise, provided, always, that such rates are just and reasonable, and to the Interstate Commerce Commission full power to regulate inland freight rates where complaint is made and the fact established of any discrimination existing against persons or localities.

The penalty for a willful violation of the law as interpreted by the commission to be placed against the corporation found guilty of such violation and not against the individual, and in cases of violation each carload or part carload shipment to constitute a separate offense, and a penalty to be imposed by a fine of double the gross earnings, at the tariff rate, for the services performed, either over one road or a combination of roads having a through line between any given points, the money collected as such penalty to be divided equally between the person or persons giving the information upon which the conviction is secured and the Government of the United States, the money thus accruing to the Government to be used in defraying the expenses of the Interstate Commerce Commission in the hearings occasioned by the railroads because of their willful violation of the law.

While the means employed to obtain information and secure conviction are open to objection, they seem to us justifiable in the interest of the public good.

With a pool established, a division of tonnage or earnings on fixed percentages between the various railroads entitled to share in the traffic must be included in the arrangement, and it will inevitably follow that some of the roads will become dissatisfied with their allotment, and, in order to be in better position to demand an increased percentage, will make private concessions in rates to a very few large shippers, that they may establish their right to an increased allotment in the pool. This is not a matter of theory, but of fact, as demonstrated by several years' experience with the workings of the Southwestern Railway Association— the strongest railroad pool ever operated in this country—and during the existence of which, rates were not always maintained in accordance with the printed tariffs.

Under a policy of open competition, as at present exists, there is really no necessity for any road to violate the law, for the reason that, if not getting a fair share of the moving traffic from a given point, the law allows, after 3 days' legal notice, the issuance of a tariff making reduced rates, and the public derives the benefit of the lower rates until the road in question has become satisfied, and again gives a 10 days' legal notice of restoration of rates to the former basis. If the long and short haul clause of the interstate-commerce act can be strictly enforced by the commission, the other roads, having enjoyed a satisfactory business, will permit their less fortunate competitor an increase in tonnage rather than jeopardize their own interests by meeting the lower published rates put in temporarily by their weaker rival.

We regard the observance of the long and short haul clause as absolutely essential to the strict maintenance of tariff rates; and if any railroad should deem it best to abandon the traffic of a certain territory rather than to reduce local rates, in observance of the long and short haul clause, there is no law to prevent; and the presumption is that other roads better entitled to that particular traffic will continue to serve the people satisfactorily. One great trouble with the railroads is their propensity to overstep legitimate boundary lines in their efforts to secure tonnage which properly belongs to other roads on account of geographical conditions.

With reference to charges usually made against the weaker lines as being the first to offer private concessions in rates, we are constrained to say that such has not been our experience; but, on the contrary, the so-called strong lines are usually the ones to lead in violating their traffic agreements and the weak lines follow at about the time the leaders are ready to make a new agreement.

We are of the opinion that a railroad pool, formed under protection of the law, whereby the railroads of this country would be permitted to pool their tonnage or their earnings, would cause to pale into insignificance all other combinations of capital commonly known as trusts.

The effects of such a combination upon the interests of the people would, indeed, be far-reaching and far from satisfactory, inasmuch as a pool would not prevent discrimination, but would restrict competition and confine the favors of the railroads to fewer individuals than under the present system of open competition. This has been experienced in railroad pools and doubtless will continue to be the experience of all such pools, whether legalized or not. The prime object of a pool is to increase the net revenue of the railroads, and we believe this would follow regardless of the interests of the people, from whom the railroads have received their valuable franchises.

We think it would be a great mistake for Congress to enact a law permitting either a tonnage or a money pool, and for the following reasons:

First. It is against public policy.

Second. Would not absolutely maintain published rates nor prevent discrimination.

Third. Would result in a minimum service at a maximum cost.

Fourth. Would, in the interest of economy, deprive of their present position thousands of men who have spent the best years of their lives in the traffic departments of the various railroads and fast-freight lines; their occupation would be gone.

Fifth. Would soon become odious and intolerable to the business men of our country.

Sixth. The railroads do not need a pool; they are doing well enough without one, their earnings at the present time and under existing conditions being generally regarded as satisfactory.

With the interstate-commerce law amended as suggested; rates agreed to and published by the railroads; a copy of every tariff filed with the commission, together with the name of some one official of each road, who alone is to be held accountable for the strict maintenance of all freight rates legally published by his road, it would not be difficult for the commission to enforce the law and make it of great benefit both to the railroads and to the public.

Q. (By Mr. KENNEDY.) You said you expressed your own opinions, though I see this paper is phrased as though you were voicing the sentiments of others. Perhaps, if you insist you are just speaking for yourself, the phrasing had better be changed by the stenographer.—A. I stated in my remarks that while these were my own opinions, I believed they met with the approval of the majority of the members of the board of trade.

Q. (By Mr. C. J. HARRIS.) He probably represents that part of the board of trade—— —A. I represent the entire board.

Q. I mean in this you represent those not in favor of pooling, and while here we will hear the other side from other witnesses.—A. Yes.

Q. (By Representative LORIMER.) As I understand it, this is all you want to say on this question of pooling?—A. That is really all I care to say at present. I think that covers the situation as I see it.

(Testimony closed.)

CHICAGO, ILL., *November 16, 1899.*

TESTIMONY OF MR. HERCULES F. DOUSMAN,

Grain shipper, Chicago, Ill.

The subcommission on transportation met at Chicago, Ill., on the 16th of November, 1899, at 10 a. m., Hon. William Lorimer presiding. Mr. Hercules F. Dousman, being duly sworn, testified as follows:

Q. Will you please state your name and residence?—A. Hercules F. Dousman, Chicago, Ill.

Q. Your place of business.—A. It has always been the board of trade.

Q. And your business?—A. Well, I am not in active business now, but for 17 or 18 years I was a grain shipper on the board of trade.

Q. (By Mr. C. J. HARRIS.) You have been a large shipper of freight in and out of Chicago?—A. I don't know that I would call myself a large shipper—a moder-·te shipper. In Chicago everybody receives more or less grain. My main business was getting it forwarded.

Q. You are familiar with the freight rates of the various lines? I would like to ask if there are any discriminations or rebates in the way of giving large shippers advantages over small ones?—A. As I told you, I have not been in active business for two years. I only know what other people tell me.

Q. In your experience has there been any trouble of that kind hitherto?—A. From the time the interstate law went into effect, for twelve months, or six months at least, everybody was on an equality. After the first six months, rebates began to be given. At the end of the first year they were quite frequent, and they have continued ever since. Prior to 1887 the only time when rates were absolutely solid, when everyone was on the same basis, was when the Vanderbilts were trying to bankrupt the West Shore road, and rates were down to 12 cents to New York. Everybody, as I understand, had the same rates.

Q. In what way were discriminations made?—A. What I got in those days was so many cents per 100 pounds, off the regular tariff, 2½ or 3 cents, whatever it might be. I feel that I have been driven out of business because I would not accept a rebate. I have never taken a rebate since the interstate law went into effect. I did not propose to put myself in the shape of a criminal, and but one man has had the impudence to offer me a rebate since that time.

Q. (By Professor JOHNSON.) Have you ever been offered favors of any other kind than rebates? I understand from what I hear that various favors have been offered.—A. No; I can not say I have.

Q. Is it not frequently the case that salaries are paid for merely nominal services?—A. It has been so reported. I have no definite information of anything of that kind.

Q. You can not say, then, that rebates are the only inducement that has ever been offered?—A. I was speaking of the time prior to the interstate law. A rebate is so much off of the freight. If the freight was 20 cents, your off rate would, perhaps, be 18 cents, which would be effected by paying back 2 or 3 cents, as the case might be.

Q. But you were in business at least ten years under the interstate-commerce law?—A. Yes, sir.

Q. What was your experience then? Were strong inducements made by the railroads to secure your shipments?—A. As I say, my position from the first was well known. I was chairman of the transportation committee of the Chicago

Board of Trade, which made some trouble for the railroads here, and I suppose I am persona non grata with the railroads here on account of that.

Q. You found that your business suffered so that you decided to go out of it?—A. I did not think that I could do business honestly.

Q. Do you think any other man can?—A. I don't know about that. Other men are doing business.

Q. I should like to have you tell us how the grain business is handled by the railroads and the lake lines. I would like to have an elementary account of the actual methods by which this grain business is handled—the grain that comes to Chicago and is shipped East from here.—A. When I came to Chicago, the grain was, I think, all consigned to Chicago; rates were not made beyond. It practically came here to be sold in Chicago, was received by one set of men called receivers, who sold it to another set of men called shippers. The receiver represented the people in the country who consigned it here—the country merchants—and the shipper either bought it for speculation on his own account or bought it here to be sold to the Eastern market, or else bought it here for someone in the Eastern market who consumed it. The elevators at that time were all situated on Western roads, and did not buy grain themselves. I think one elevator concern, when no one else was buying grain on their road, took it and sold it in the option pits—as we call them—and delivered it as soon as they could get receipts. The rates from the West were made into Chicago. There were very few through rates before the interstate law went into effect. Soon after it went into effect the elevator proprietors became grain buyers here on the market, until to-day there are practically no other buyers of grain who go on the market except elevator proprietors, and they also buy grain in the country, and send out bids for grain in the country, and the men who used to be called receivers, and received it and sold it here, have been forced to become buyers, and are bidding against each other. Of course, you understand that these elevator people are public custodians. The law of the State of Illinois gives them the right to charge three-fourths of a cent per bushel on every bushel of grain going into their house which covers ten days' storage, and that three-fourths of a cent gives them that much leverage over anyone else. They can give it away to anyone they wish. If an individual goes there and ships grain in and out he has to pay three-fourths of a cent a bushel. About the same time the railroads began to make rates from the the West through Chicago from the Mississippi River to New York, or the rate was made from Iowa, thus giving Chicago the go-by.

Q. (By Representatative OTJEN.) The grain never leaving the car?—A. Generally transferred here unless on a line car. A great deal of this grain was shipped on through billing, as it is called; that is, taking a rate from beyond, and that rate would be less to the road that brought it from the West to Chicago than the rate into Chicago. They might fix the rate from a central point in Iowa to the Mississippi River, and from the Mississippi River the percentage of the rate would make less than the local rate into Chicago. The men who used to buy the grain here to ship, on the open market, who have been going more or less to the West to buy grain themselves, are the elevator people who run it through their elevators, and there is a rate made now from the West on grain going through elevators which is a reduced rate over the local rate into Chicago.

Q. (By Professor JOHNSON.) Try to run it through the elevators to grade it down; is that the process?—A. Of course it leaves an opportunity to mix the grain.

Q. To grade it down to the actual grade at which it is sold?—A. Yes; there is more or less of clipping and cleaning, and manipulation charged by people. I guess it is fair to say that none of the Chicago grades of grain have improved at all.

Q. (By Mr. C. J. HARRIS.) How does the grading of the grain compare with other cities? Have you grades here pretty well up to the standard?—A. The standards differ in different places.

Q. How do they compare with other standards; are they as good as St. Louis, do you think?—A. I don't know anything about St. Louis grades; but to draw grain out of the elevators here the men who draw it tell me they get the lowest grades of grain. In old times cars with top grades were handled by people who had no interest in them, and the bin that received 10 cars of grain had to put up with the poor cars which got the benefit of the good ones, and it represented a pretty fair average grade. There has also at this time grown up a system of private elevators, men who own their own elevators on railroad tracks and on Eastern roads. They have on their tracks what are called transfer elevators, where they clip oats for people who wish them clipped and mix them and transfer from car to car, and, as I understand, the Eastern roads have a fixed charge for that service in their own houses and allow people owning private elevators on their tracks the same charge for transfer.

Q. What is clipping oats?—A. At the end there is a little tail like a point. That is rubbed off and the oats lay closer. It is done by machinery, and makes a heavier oat. You can get more in a car and in a bushel measure.

Q. You say most of the elevators on the railroads are owned by private concerns. What effect has that on the farmer who is selling his wheat?—A. Before you get to the farmer there stands the country buyer, who has to take the wagonload the farmer sells. The country buyer has the offer of bids from 5 to 25 grain dealers.

Q. (By Representative OTJEN.) He represents other persons?—A. No; the country buyer is the merchant. He buys the wagonloads from the farmer and makes up a carload, and every morning he gets from these people who buy postal-card bids saying they will give so much for his grain. My opinion is that on the average they don't get as much for their grain as they did in olden times, when it was consigned in open market and met the competition of all the dealers. The old-style elevators, from which the grain goes into the vessels, were all public elevators, which the law permitted to charge three-fourths of a cent. These are leased to large firms, generally.

Q. (By Mr. KENNEDY.) Are they in the combination?—A. I don't think so. They are charged with being in the combination. Sometimes they have agreed between themselves and sometimes there is a fight between them.

Q. (By Mr. C. J. HARRIS.) We have had complaints before us that out on these lines of railroad the elevator system is so controlled by the railroads that men doing business independently can not exist. Do you know anything about that?—A. In 1890, I think it was, I was the chairman of the transportation committee of the Chicago Board of Trade, and we had complaints straight along from men in the West that they could not move corn in the elevators that they had owned for years, and which they had paid for, and bring it to Chicago, but were forced to sell it to individuals. One firm, who were proprietors of an elevator on another road, were bringing corn on a certain road; they quoted every day; and one case came to me where a man said, "I have sold this man, who was the proprietor of the elevator on a rival road, so many bushels of corn; he turned around and sold it in the pit." I said, "How did it come?" He said, "It comes in over my road." The difference showed a cut of 5 cents. The Interstate Commerce Commission at that time had before it what is known as the corn rate case. The complaints were coming in so strongly that I could not help taking cognizance of them, and I went up to Washington and saw the commission in regard to it; but the time for taking testimony had passed. The time for argument was only ten days away. Colonel Morrison was chairman, and said he would be glad to hear our case on argument, but could not hear it in any other way. We got up a combination case. The railroad commissioners of Iowa, Grain Dealers' Association of Iowa, and people from Lincoln—the different State boards there interested, G. N. Lambertson, and the board of trade notified these gentlemen that the matter was going on and they were all represented. We presented our facts in regard to the postal-card bids, showing the price as it was to-day and the price as it was yesterday, and the nominal rate, and we showed that there was an actual rebate of 5 cents per hundred right along. We made such a case that the committee of the railroads, appointed to bring in their report denying the jurisdiction of the commissioners and declining to put on their rates, changed their tactics and made a report recommending to the commission that the rates be put into effect. The commission took up the case before the Federal courts and the result was two freight agents were indicted, but the case never came to trial, because, finally, on the protest of Mr. Counselman, who was one of the witnesses, that he could not testify without incriminating himself, the Supreme Court sustained it and the cases fell. Some of these men have since been obliged to go out of business on that road.

Q. Is there at the present time a fair elevator market for produce in the Western grain-raising States?—A. I should say it was a congested market; it is not a market where buyers and sellers can meet each other face to face; and the feeling in the country is that the proprietors of elevators to-day are the men who have favors that the general public does not have. I don't know whether their bids show it or not. But the fact that one man is the only buyer on a road shows that other people do not have a chance.

Q. Do you hear any complaints of not moving the cars promptly, except for people presumably connected with the elevators?—A. Not very much. I have heard of such things.

Q. Are those the complaints that used to exist some few years ago and are an echo of those days?—A. I think not. There are grounds for complaint right along.

Q. The grounds actually exist to-day?—A. Yes. A man told me day before yesterday the same thing, in relation to moving cars into Chicago, that you have in mind. He said he sold a car of corn a month before and shipped it to an Eastern road, and could get no report from it. He went to the Eastern road and they told him to go to the transfer elevator man. He did so, and was told they only receive orders to forward it two days before. For 80 days it had been lying in the yard, and in the meantime freights had advanced, I think, 5 cents per hundred.

Q. That would not be a strange thing to happen now when there is a congestion of freight and famine of cars. Was not this due to the car famine that now exists?—A. I should say not, because if a buyer wanted the grain he could give them the transfer order the day after buying it and let the railroad work it out. In this case the transfer order was not given for four weeks.

Q. Who would you think was responsible for it?—A. The Eastern roads. They have the right to charge demurrage and force the property out. That little case shows where general interests suffer from special favors. The man should have a return in a week, whereas he did not get returns for four weeks. The seller who paid the countryman's draft could not get his money back in four weeks, when he should have had it in a week, all that some special shipper might be favored.

Q. (By Representative LORIMER.) Is it your opinion that only one man buys along the line of one road because they have a special rate, or is it because they have superior facilities for handling the grain when they purchase it and can therefore do better and drive other competitors out?—A. I don't think the large concerns can do business in grain against the smaller concerns unless they are favored, for the reason that the average moderate commission merchant does his business himself and this enables him to do better by his customers than will the clerks of large concerns.

There is another thing in connection with elevator control, and the buying of grain by public elevators. The system of inspection in Chicago is run by the State. You know how in Democratic times appointments were made for political purposes. You know the character of the elevator proprietors. They are rich people. Their business is run by clerks. You know the inspectors are men appointed for political purposes, and who work for $1,000 per year. Now, I don't think any class of public servants should be exposed to such temptations as these men are placed under.

Q. What is the condition of the grain-inspection department now, so far as you know?—A. I think it is fair, so far as I know; but at the same time you can not get away from the fact that it is for the interests of certain men to have high inspection of some grain—high inspection when it comes in and low when it goes out.

Q. Are the men who are inspecting grain in Chicago generally men who have been recently appointed and never saw service before or are they the old inspectors who have served for 20 years?—A. The man in charge has been there for 20 years or more. I don't know about the men under him.

Q. Are the old inspectors there now?—A. Well, you know they were taken out, and there is the danger of a change all the time.

Q. One of the members of the railway and warehouse commission is an old inspector, who had 20 years' service before he left, and was a first-class inspector. I think he was associated with Mr. Smiley.—A. He was his assistant once.

Q. Under that sort of organization we should have fair average inspection, should we not? They have the ability, if they perform their duty faithfully.—A. Yes.

Q. Then, in your opinion, the advantage that the shippers have now or the purchasers have now is either in a rebate or an advantage that they have by reason of owning the large elevators?—A. No; the advantage that the State gives them in permitting them to charge three-fourths of a cent per bushel. Most of these elevators are owned by the railroads. They give a through rate on wheat but don't carry the grain through their own houses. They put their elevator in the hands of private parties who are dealers, and give the through rate on flour and handle it themselves, and a through rate on merchandise and handle it themselves. Now, the Canadian Pacific road—as a matter of fact, I understand have no sideshow connected with their road, but they own steamboats, elevators, dining cars, hotel, and everything connected with this business, and they say they can give a man a pass from Montreal to Vancouver and get $50 out of him on sleeping cars, hotels, and such things, and they report $1,000,000 profit from these things.

Q. (By Mr. C. J. HARRIS.) You don't mean to say that these elevators should handle this for nothing?—A. The railroads could handle it for nothing and make it a part of the through rate.

Q. The elevator should not be connected with a railroad and no special charge made for elevator service?—A. Not for their service; that is, for the service in transporting it through. If people want to hold their grain, that is different.

Q. (By Representative OTJEN.) The elevator service in carrying the freight?—A. Yes; and should be performed by people who have no interest in the property. I think it is so done at Duluth by some of the railroads there.

Q. (By Mr. C. J. HARRIS.) What proportion of freight is by water transportation, in your judgment, about Chicago?—A. That varies. The report of the secretary of the board of trade shows.

Q. I mean generally?—A. Oats, the greater part, go by rail; in summer, corn, the greater part, goes by water.

Q. Does not water competition make railroad rates very low?—A. I don't think water competition has ever made them as low as fights between the railroads.

Q. A good deal of your grain from the West comes by lake?—A. Very little. The only grain that comes by lake is wheat from Duluth for storage purposes.

Q. (By Professor JOHNSON.) There are about ten lines of steamers on the lake, are there not?—A. The trunk lines east of Buffalo each have their own lines; the New York Central, Erie, Pennsylvania, Lehigh Valley, Lackawanna; and I think the Baltimore and Ohio had a line for the last year or two, connecting at Fairport; and there is a line running to Ogdensburg.

Q. Are there any lines not owned by railroads?—A. There are boats belonging to individuals, to firms, that run as wild boats, practically like tramp steamers on the ocean.

Q. Are there any regular lines operated independently of the railroads?—A. Not that I know of.

Q. What proportion of the business is done by those so-called lake tramps?—A. I could not give you an estimate. You will have to get that of some of the vessel men.

Q. Do they constitute an important factor?—A. Yes.

Q. So far as you know, are the railroad lines worked in accordance with a rate agreement through the Lake Carriers' Association?—A. I don't think it is the Lake Carriers' Association. I think they have an association of their own—an agreement in regard to rates.

Q. That is not through the Lake Carriers' Association?—A. I think not. I think the Lake Carriers' Association embraces all the lake interests—boats that go to Lake Superior and boats that carry iron ore and lumber.

Q. Does the competition between the trunk lines take the form of competition on the lakes? Do they compete with each other vigorously?—A. I could not tell you that. I fancy they do when trade is scarce.

Q. (By Mr. C. J. HARRIS.) If you could not make satisfactory rates with these regular lines, you would have no trouble in chartering a tramp steamer to take a cargo, would you?—A. No.

Q. As a matter of fact, are not freight rates down to about bed rock, or have they not been hitherto?—A. They have been very low for several years. I have paid 23 cents a bushel for wheat from Lake Michigan to Lake Erie; it has been taken at 25 cents. The rate now is 2 cents, and has been as low as 1. Of course, that does not pay.

Q. (By Professor JOHNSON.) Do you think there is any danger of these independent boats being driven off the lakes? It has been stated to me that there was danger of the abolition of competition on the lakes, the same as on railways.—A. If the Erie Canal was out of commission I think they might.

Q. Do you think competition on the lakes depends on the Erie Canal?—A. It means an outlet for an independent shipper. Of course, they can make a contract with a railroad company on the Erie Canal.

Q. Would not the Canadian highway give them that same freight?—A. For their export business I suppose it would, and still it is a small proportion of the business that can go that way. The season is short, and even with their new canal 14 feet of water is all they have.

Q. If your statement is true, it would be a pretty strong argument for the Erie Canal.—A. I think the salvation of the grain trade rests in the Erie Canal and its independent competition.

Q. (By Mr. C. J. HARRIS.) Is there any difference between freight rates in the winter and in the summer here?—A. That depends. There has been and there has not been. Just now freight rates are higher than I think they have been since 1893. I think rates should be made to the markets. There should be fixed rates that would not change. I don't think it is a part of the duty of any freight agent or railway man to move the crops of the country. It is their business to make fair rates and hold them stable and let the merchants of the country move the crops of the country. The market price of all these commodities fluctuate. I think from here to the seaboard there should be two rates—a rate for 6 or 7 months in the winter, and a rate a little smaller for 5 or 6 months in the summer—and these rates should not change in that time.

Q. (By Representative OTJEN.) Do you think that would be practicable at all times? For instance, at the present time there is great business and freight rates are higher, are they not? Then there are times when freight rates are low, owing to the lack of business.—A. I think if you will call before you some of the managers of these railroad companies you will find that last summer rates were as low at the end of August as they have ever been, and I think you will find that the congestion here on all the roads occurred from having contracts for large amounts of freight at low rates. Since then there have been, I think, two or three advances in rates, but the congestion came from large contracts on low freights, the lowest we have ever had. For whose benefit or for what reason they were made I can not say.

Q. (By Mr. KENNEDY.) If last summer you had the lowest rates that ever obtained here, would you not naturally expect that there would be an increase in freight rates owing to the prosperous times?—A. Prosperous times in business came before the rates went down. I understand rates were as low as 11 cents to New York last summer.

Q. Was traffic as heavy as it is now?—A. Heavier, I guess, and therefore the wisdom of loading themselves up with large quantities of freight at low prices, instead of holding the rates steady and allowing the merchants to move the business of the country every day as wanted, I fail to see.

You ask if it is feasible to have railroad rates uniform. I suppose you gentlemen know that for 35 years a man could cross from Buffalo to Albany and buy a ticket from station to station just as cheap as he could buy a ticket from Buffalo to Albany, except for the penny that was given away. The rate was fixed, I think, by the act permitting the consolidation of the railroads. I don't see why the freight tariffs on all the railroads in the United States should not be as solid as that. The president of a large Chicago road said, "I wish we could nail up our tariffs on the freight boards and go about our business and know for a certainty what would happen and see how business would distribute itself; but," he said, "our people can not submit to it, as they are afraid somebody will get the advantage of them."

Q. Presidents of railroads have stated before the commission that one president admitted that the discriminations were never more flagrant than they were last year; but since the 1st of December there has been very little of it. If that is true, would you believe that it is because the railroads now have more business than they can handle and don't seek business and offer rebates or discriminations?—A. I can not tell you the philosophy of the railroad men in doing their business. I have never seen a railroad man who did his business as a merchant does.

Q. Could you state why rebates and discriminations are more flagrant in hard times than in prosperous times?—A. My experience is that they have always been the worst when there was the most stuff to move. In 1890 there was the biggest crop of corn in the West it ever had, and it was moved at the lowest price that obtained up to that time, and simply because of a fight between the railroads.

Q. (By Representative LORIMER.) Was that rate a general one?—A. No; it was not general. The people could have shipped corn in themselves and sold it in the pit; instead of that they were obliged to sell to one man, not a dealer, on their own road, but the proprietor of an elevator on another road.

Q. (By Mr. KENNEDY.) As a general thing, were rebates and discriminations made upon the solicitation of shippers, or were they offered by the railroads?—A. Prior to the interstate-commerce law everybody was seeking them.

Q. Were the railroads sending around agents and offering them?—A. Yes; that was done, and I presume it has been done since the passage of the interstate law. I once had a railroad freight agent offer me a rebate under the interstate law.

As regards the extent of these rebates, the amount paid in rebates—at the time of the Brown case in the United States Supreme Court, which forced the Pennsylvania company men to testify in a lawsuit, one of our Chicago papers stated that a railroad director or official said that the railroads of the country were paying out at least 12½ per cent of their freight receipts in rebates. Of course, that was a statement made in the public press. I don't know anything further about it.

Q. Do you know whether it is true that Mr. Armour monopolizes the buying, selling, and shipping, for domestic and export purposes, of the barley crop of the country?—A. No.

Q. Do you know who would be able to give the commission information as to that?—A. Nobody could give the statement, except Mr. Armour's own men who do the work.

Q. (By Mr. LORIMER.) Do you know whether or not barley is handled through any other elevators than Mr. Armour's in Chicago?—A. Mr. Armour's elevators handle a great deal of the barley because he has elevators on the St. Paul and Burlington roads—barley roads. A great deal of barley comes in on the Chicago and Northwestern road, and more or less on the Rock Island road.

Q. Is it handled through elevators other than Armour's?—A. I could not tell that. I suppose the proprietors of the houses in the grain business would get their share of it.

Q. Does Armour own elevators along those lines that you refer to—the Northwestern and the Rock Island?—A. Mr. Counselman is supposed to control the elevators on the Rock Island system and through the Chicago terminal company, which they represent. Weare & Co. control the elevators on the Northwestern, and I think the Great Western is also one of the Weare roads.

Q. (By Mr. C. J. HARRIS.) I understand you have paid considerable attention to the interstate-commerce law; will you give the commission your views in regard to its workings?—A. The practical effect of the interstate-commerce law has been to put the giving of favors by the railroads into fewer hands than it was before. I do not think that can be disputed or doubted.

Q. Has it lessened them?—A. I doubt it.

Q. (By Professor JOHNSON.) Will you tell us how that has been accomplished?—A. Never having been a participant, I can not tell you.

Q. What is there about the law that produces such a result?—A. Apparently the railroad gentlemen feel the necessity, since the first 6 months of the law, of giving rebates to somebody, and they give them to the people who will protect them.

Q. But they always did that, did they not? What difference has the law brought about?—A. The law has made criminal what before was not.

Q. So that they endeavor to cover it up somewhat?—A. You see that yourself.

Q. (By Mr. C. J. HARRIS.) You think while they do not give them indiscriminately, as they used to, they do give them to parties they think are responsible and will protect them?—A. Well, I tell you the statements I have read in the newspapers.

Q. Have you any particular change to suggest that would help matters?—A. Well, the only railroad rate that I know of that has been unchangeable is the one I spoke of—the passenger rate on the New York Central road. Mr. Stickney, in his book, as I recollect it—it has been a good while since I read it—gives his remedy for these things in a fixed rate per ton per mile over the country, with allowances for fixed terminal charges at the different towns, on the theory that little country stations can gather and discharge business more cheaply than the city, which is undoubtedly true. It costs a great deal more to get business through Chicago than Elgin, Rockford, or any small town. That, as I recollect it, was Mr. Stickney's remedy. That would be Congress trying its hand at its unmistakable authority to make rates.

Q. (By Professor JOHNSON.) You would advocate a legislative enactment of rates?—A. I would advocate anything that would make all the railroads of the country treat the people the way the customs-house and post-office treat the people—every man on the same basis. I think the minute you get that, all the danger from large combinations of capital will be done away with. I do not think there is an individual whose business is dangerous to his competitors, or a combination dangerous to the community at large, but that owes its formation or continued existence to special favors of some sort.

Q. (By Mr. KENNEDY.) By railroad companies?—A. Railroad companies chiefly.

Q. (By Representative OTJEN.) Transportation companies?—A. Transportation companies, yes.

Q. (By Professor JOHNSON.) Do you think in order to secure this uniformity of rates, it is necessary to have them established by law?—A. Either that or by the Interstate Commerce Commission, which comes to the same thing—Congress delegating power over the rates.

Q. What kind of control?—A. Such as will be effectual. I believe the owners of a good railroad should be protected against a poor one. I will tell you an instance, in my own experience, illustrating at least how one company tried to do some business. I was buying wheat at Duluth, which we shipped during the summer time by lake. One winter we got short and had to have some by rail, and our wheat had always been bought in one elevator on account of the difficulty of buying what we wanted. Our correspondent bought 5,000 bushels of wheat. There are two lines between Chicago and Duluth, and that wheat was directed to be shipped by one of them, simply saying that we wanted it brought to Chicago and delivered to our eastern road. The next day a clerk from the Chicago office of the railroad owning the elevator in Duluth came to me and asked to have the transportation of that wheat around by Minneapolis. I told him he could not have it. The day after the Chicago agent of that line came to me and asked for the wheat. I told him he could not have it. The next day the general freight agent of the road whose office was in St. Paul came to me and I told him he could not have it. The next day the general manager of the road came to see me and asked for the transportation of that 5,000 bushels of wheat. I said to him—I thought I had exhausted the limits of courtesy—"Can you haul that wheat any cheaper than the regular rate?" "No." "You will take it by St. Paul and transfer it there because you do not let the cars get off your own line?" "Yes." "And will give it to any one of a half dozen roads to bring it here?" "Yes." "Do you not make more out of the $2 a car you get from handling the cars at your elevators at Duluth than all that?" "I think I do." I said, "Are you not ashamed of yourself to try to take away from the road that can make a little money on it this little jag of wheat; while you take it away from our control and never let us know when we are going to get it." He said, "We are awful poor." I said, 'You will remain poor as long as you do business that way." He wanted to haul it 100 miles farther, and put it through an expensive terminal, and do the business without any profit to themselves, when this direct line could make a little. But 6 cents a bushel for hauling wheat 450 miles through the woods of Wisconsin is not a high rate. I believe the direct road should be protected against that sort of competition.

Q. In what way would you vest the rate-fixing power in a commission?—A. Give them the authority to name maximum and minimum rates, and make their order effectual at once.

Q. You mean to promulgate a general schedule of rates?—A. No; but a uniform classification over the United States, which was once attempted by the railroads, and came near being accomplished, should be made and can be made by consultation between the merchants on one side and the railroads on the other—a fair classification. Then let them make their own tariffs, subject to revision by the commission either on complaint or their own motion.

Q. Subject to the higher authority of the court?—A. Subject to review by the courts.

Q. However, upon injunctions sued out by the railroads—— —A. I should not let an injunction issue at all on a thing of that kind. Let it take its course through the courts.

Q. In accordance with the present plan?—A. Like an appeal.

Q. At the present time the commission has no power to enforce its commands?—A. I should have the commission's orders go into effect at a certain time, say 30 or 60 days after issue, and then let the railroad litigate it out.

Q. You would take away from the court the power to enjoin an enforcement of the rate?—A. I think I would. An experience of 20 years shows the railroads and the community are in no danger from any rate that anybody like the Interstate Commerce Commission may make.

Q. (By Representative OTJEN.) Can you take away from the court the power of injunction?—A. I am not a lawyer; I can not answer that.

Q. (By Professor JOHNSON.) If you could, would it not give the commission power to fix rates for several years in advance?—A. I do not see why.

Q. It takes 3 years to get a case through the Supreme Court, after you get it appealed to the higher court?—A. Emergency and constitutional cases go quickly.

Q. (By Mr. KENNEDY.) You see no obstacles in the way of uniform classifications?—A. None so serious as the ones that come from the multiplicity of classifications.

Q. (By Professor JOHNSON.) That would have to be brought about by compelling the roads to do it, or by giving the Interstate Commerce Commission power to adopt a classification?—A. Directing them to adopt it, not authorizing, but directing them to adopt it, and give time enough. We have a classification in the State of Illinois. Three or 4 years ago our board of railroad and warehouse commissioners called together the merchants, manufacturers, and railroads, and they finally agreed upon a classification that no fault has been found with.

Q. (By Mr. KENNEDY.) Do you not think there should be a different classification in the State of Illinois, where the country is level, and there is a considerable less cost of building railroads than in mountainous States?—A. That can be remedied by a different rate. I do not see why the classification should be different. You never know where you stand on a classification. Where the classification is fixed the rate should have whatever flexibility it needs. Of course the rates east from Chicago should be per ton per mile less than the rates over the mountains, but I do not see why a blanket is not a blanket, or a chest of tea a chest of tea, from the shores of the Pacific to the Atlantic, and lumber and shingles the same.

Q. Do you see any fault in the arrangement b·· which classifications are made now? Are the shippers properly represented? Do they have proper hearings before the classification committees?—A. Not being a merchant I do not know much about it. I do not think they are called upon as a rule.

Q. They are not consulted when the classification is made?—A. I think not as a rule.

Q. (By Representative LORIMER.) We have four large lines running from New York; two over the mountains—the Baltimore and Ohio and the Pennsylvania—the Lake Shore and Michigan Central not. Under your system how would you fix these rates?—A. Well, under Stickney's system the shortest road would make a little the cheapest rate, if I quote Mr. Stickney correctly, and I think I do.

Q. Then you would not take into consideration the fact that one goes over the prairie and the other over the mountains?—A. I do not think it makes any particular difference. The road that carries property the cheapest in the United States is the Chesapeake and Ohio, and that runs over mountains and through tunnels.

Q. (By Professor JOHNSON.) You do not see any reasons why differentials should be given in the case of a rate-fixing scheme such as you have described—A. I think differentials are inventions of the devil.

Q. Are they not one of the necessary inventions?—A. I do not think so.

Q. How can a line like the Grand Trunk or Baltimore and Ohio compete with the New York Central, for instance, without a differential? How can they divide the business?—A. I think you will find in business practice that any railroad that has any excuse for being a railroad, does at least 75 per cent of its business that it actually does to-day or has done for the last 10 years, better than any other railroad. That is its own business, in which it should be protected, that percentage on the average at least, that it can do better than any other railroad; that it will get more net profit out of than the balance. The other 25 per cent, which is competitive business, should be done on a straight, square rate, uniform and stable, regardless of differentials, letting the merchant take the business to his friends, to the people who do his business well—but in case one road was tied up and the other free, he would take it to the road that had the cars. Let it distribute itself naturally, and then there is no demoralization, however the rates are made.

Q. (By Mr. KENNEDY.) You are not in favor of pooling then?—A. In this instance, the Duluth case, the general manager said, "We get lots of freight from Chicago to Duluth." I said, "You are not entitled to a car." But under the pooling contract, he would come in and sandbag the direct lines and get what he called his share of it. The railroads want a pool, and I should be in favor of giving them the permission, with proper supervision of the Interstate Commerce Commission, provided they will withdraw their objection to the commission having control of rates; but they won't concede that at all.

Q. (By Representative LORIMER.) In substance, then, you are in favor of a fixed rate for a vast territory the country over, and of authorizing somebody, say the Interstate Commerce Commission, to fix that rate, a maximum and minimum?—A. Yes; but in case of contest reduce it to whatever is a fair, reasonable rate. They would have discretionary power between these two rates. I am no advocate of low rates. The business community can not get service unless the roads make money.

Q. (By Professor JOHNSON.) You say then to Mr. Lorimer's question as to the same rates for the country over that you favor it. I should infer you would divide the country into sections?—A. Yes; I see no other way, and I think that was Mr. Stickney's idea.

Q. You would have one classification for the whole country?—A. Yes.

Q. One scheme of rates for one section, and another for another; however, the classification being the same?—A. I do not say I have that scheme, but it seems to me that would accomplish the purpose of giving stable and remunerative rates.

Q. What do you think about the penal feature of the interstate commerce law?—A. While it is right, it is not expedient. The railroad men take the ground they will not furnish testimony while it will send one of their fellows to the penitentiary. They do send a man to the penitentiary for stealing a barrel of flour or a box of shoes, but the merchant who will violate the law and steal thousands of dollars must be absolved.

Q. You would change that to a money penalty?—A. A severe penalty, such as could bankrupt a railroad if they violated it.

Q. (By Mr. KENNEDY.) You mean the officers of one road will not give information against the officers of another road?—A. That is what I understand.

Q. If the penalty attached in the way of a fine on the company they would give information?—A. That is what I understand.

Q. (By Representative OTJEN.) Please explain in what way private cars are detrimental to the public welfare.—A. During the hard depression we had here in 1896 and 1897, a manager of the traffic department on an Eastern line told me, referring to the private car department of a Chicago meat firm, which has a great many private cars, that that branch of the business had paid as high as 14 per cent profit, and that his own company was then striving to keep from reducing their dividends. A man on 'change told me that he had an order for a thousand bushels of wheat and that in order to get the wheat he had to buy it in a private elevator where the switching charges would be excessive; that is, $4 or $5 a car; and to make the burden as light as possible, the freight being 4½ cents a bushel, he sent for a 1,000-bushel car, so that he could load it all in 1 car. That, of course, is not an excessive load. Now, instead of sending a 1,000-bushel car, they sent 2 cars belonging to a private car company. He said, "What does this mean?" You can figure out the transportation. The distance to this point was 415 miles and the milage on these cars, according to the published report, is three-fourths of a cent a mile, which goes to the private car companies, or $3.12 per car that the company would get on each car, or about $6.35 for the use of the 2 cars. The freight bill was $45 and the switching was $4, and if they had used a 1,000-bushel car they would have had $4 for hauling. As it was, they received $45 and paid out $8, $4 a car for switching the 2 cars, and paid the private car company at least $6.12 for the private cars, and got $30.88. Allowing the 2 cars had been there and they had no freight back, they would have had to pay about $6.25 to run the cars back. Now, the company that owned those 2 cars was the company that I referred to as having made 14 per cent on the investment. And it is on account of these things that I say I think the private car should be abolished.

Q. (By Mr. KENNEDY.) The presidents of several great railroad companies in this country have stated before us that they would like to abolish the private-car system.—A. They can not do it as long as one road uses them. If it is done it must be done by a higher power. There is a book published by the railroad companies giving the number of private cars and the people owning them.

Q. Do you know what book it is?—A. I don't know the book. There is one concern that had 10,000 private cars. Any railroad man knows what it is.

Q. (By Mr. C. J. HARRIS.) I understand these private companies have these cars.—A. No; the company I mentioned was a meat company, and that business was gone into, the private-car system, to further their own interests.

Q. (By Representative OTJEN.) They took these two cars to ship these goods in, I presume, to get other business on some other product?—A. Yes; and to the detriment of the stockholders of the road. It is simply an indirect way of cutting freights. Certainly, when railroads are earning 12 or 13 or 14 per cent they can build all the cars they need. This man that I spoke of, this traffic manager, didn't want to run these private cars, but he did not know how to get rid of them.

Q. (By Mr. KENNEDY.) Would this book that you spoke about give the number of private cars that Mr. Armour has?

A. Yes; every one in the United States.

(Testimony closed.)

CHICAGO, ILL, *November 16, 1899.*

TESTIMONY OF MR. ALEXANDER A. KENNARD,

Vice-president, Butter and Egg Board, Chicago, Ill.

The sub-commission on transportation being in session in Chicago, Representative Lorimer presiding, at 11.40 a. m., November 16, 1899, Mr. Alexander A. Kennard was introduced as a witness, and being duly sworn, testified concerning transportation as follows:

Q. (By Representative LORIMER.) Will you state your name?—A. Alexander A. Kennard.

Q. Your place of business?—A. 144 South Water street, Chicago.

Q. Your business?—A. Butter, cheese, and eggs.

Q. You represent an organization before this commission?—A. Yes; known as the butter and egg board. I am vice-president of that organization. It is the successor of the Chicago Produce Exchange. The produce exchange went out of existence and the butter and egg board succeeded to all its privileges and rights.

Q. (By Professor JOHNSON.) I think it would be well for us to have a few words in regard to what the butter and egg board does; then take up the question of transportation of its products.—A. The butter and egg board is an organization that meets daily to give opinions and vote on the market price of the products in which we deal—butter and eggs. They vote as to what the market should be daily; what is the supply and demand; and if anyone has butter and eggs to sell, it is posted on the board. If he wishes to buy, he can buy there. It is a kind of auction—not exactly that, but the transactions are made there in these perishable products. I should say that in the practice of this business, of course we have to have special railroad facilities. We have refrigerator cars, particularly in the summer time, and the rates of freight on these perishable commodities are much higher than on ordinary freight, such as garden truck and things of that sort. And, in a general way, it is considered very desirable freight for the railroads to haul and they are very glad to get hold of it. My own business, particularly the butter trade in the West here, is developing in the way of export business—trade with Great Britain, Germany, etc.

Q. (By Representative OTJEN.) Explain how many people are engaged in the business, and the capital. Give a little idea of the extent of the business.—A. In the whole United States?

Q. In this locality.—A. In this locality there are some 200 or 250 firms in this line of business. I include in this line of business country products, such as fruit and potatoes, general produce, and things of that sort. They all go together and are handled by the same persons. The trade is mostly on Randolph and South Water streets.

Q. You mean in Chicago and the country surrounding?—A. In Chicago there are about 250 engaged in that line of business.

Q. What localities do you buy from?—A. Minnesota, Wisconsin, the Dakotas, and southern Illinois.

Q. And western Missouri?—A. And western Missouri. Also some from Michigan and Indiana. and also some cheese from New York State; but the bulk of the business is done between the West and the East. Now, in fruit products we do a great deal of business with California, and that is one of the matters I want to call the commission's attention to. The railroads give us refrigerator cars; they have to do that; it is indispensable to the business, because the goods are perishable; and they charge us an extra rate of freight for refrigerator-car service; and they also charge us for icing these cars, which we think ought to be done without charge, as they get a high rate for freight. As they charge for refrigerator cars the cars might be iced.

Q. (By Professor JOHNSON.) Do any of these firms own their own cars?—A. Yes; several firms. That is another matter I wish to call to your attention later on.

Q. (By Mr. KENNEDY.) I suggest Mr. Kennard state in his own way the complaint the merchants in his line have to make against the transportation companies.—A. I have jotted down as a reminder a few notes. One of them is discrimination against shippers of freight from California. There are several large fruit concerns there—Porter Brothers Company, Earl Fruit Company, Fay Fruit Company, and there are two others I believe. These companies practically control the entire fruit-car service between California and the East; they seem to be in collusion with the railroad companies. They are mainly California concerns, but they have their branch houses and partners and so on in Chicago. Chicago is really the largest fruit-distributing center in the United States, and, I suppose, in the world, and therefore it has a very large interest in this market.

Q. Does that have to do with your business?—A. Yes. These gentlemen on our board are largely interested in this fruit business, and they have requested me to mention these items to your commission.

Q. (By Representative OTJEN.) Do the firms you spoke of own these cars?—A. The cars are controlled by them, that is, in collusion with the railroad company. They can get cars, any quantity of them, and at any time they want them.

Q. It requires special cars?—A. Special cars; and whereas a private grower or small dealer in fruit that is not identified with any of these five fruit concerns can not get cars or has to pay a considerable premium, it shuts out the smaller dealer and fruit grower. The only way he can ship his fruit is through or under the auspices of these growers, which seems to be a close corporation, and he has to pay a certain bonus to these people for the privilege of shipping his stuff so.

Q. These five firms practically control the shipments of fruit to Chicago?—A. I am so informed.

Q. (By Professor JOHNSON.) And they do that by controlling the cars?—A. Yes.

Q. (By Mr. C. J. HARRIS.) Do you know whether they have any rebates on fruits, or discriminations?—A. That I do not know, but there must be something of that nature, because anyone outside of this combination has to pay a premium in order to get these cars—$60 to $90 or more.

Q. (By Representative Otjen.) More than they have to pay?—A. More than they have to pay.

Q. (By Professor Johnson.) I do not understand how that comes about. Do these five firms own the cars?—A. Whether they own the cars or whether the railroad company owns them, I am not quite sure about that. I do not know. I only state the fact as it is said to exist.

Q. When you say they get $60 to $90 advantage over their competitor, that is equivalent to saying they are paying $60 to $90 for the use of the car?—A. Yes; I should say that would be probably the way of it.

Q. (By Mr. Kennedy.) If their competitors can live and do business at a profit, these people must have enormous profits in their business?—A. It frequently shuts out the smaller dealer and fruit grower, as I understand it.

Q. (By Representative Otjen.) Practically all the business is centered in these 5 firms?—A. They make their rates, rules, and regulations so the consumer and dealer in Chicago is practically at their mercy.

Q. (By C. J. Harris.) Of course, they have a printed rate and they hold to that?—A. The only thing that could be said against them is that they charge extra for the use of the special car—$60 to $90 for the ventilated car.

Q. (By Representative Lorimer.) The special point which it is sought to bring out is that only these 5 firms can have cars at their disposal as they call for them. The others may have them, but if they want a car at any town they pay a premium of $60 to $90 to one of these firms in order to get a car.—A. They have to be second-handed, as it were.

Q. (By Mr. C. J. Harris.) I understand they pay the $60 to $90 to the railroad company?—A. I do not know. You will have to ask these people—Porter Brothers and these companies. You will have to refer to them for full information if you wish it; I can not give it to you.

There is a complaint made in regard to excessive charge for demurrage on cars. Cars arrive in Chicago—butter, eggs, potatoes, or whatever it may be ; the consignee has only 24 hours in which to move the merchandise, and after that he is charged $1 a day. The merchants think that is too short a time and not favorable to business. They should have at least 3 days in which to move the perishable goods.

I would also say that there are times when there is considerable discrimination in markets, particularly against Chicago. In April, 1898, the railroads centering in Kansas City and points in Kansas, in the matter of carload rates on goods, rebated to shippers the local rate as between Kansas City and Chicago, instead of charging the sum of the two locals, as it is now and provided for in the tariff. The rate from Kansas City to Chicago and Chicago to New York, we will say— they take it to New York at the same rate as they would bring it to Chicago. The consequence was last year our merchants and cold-storage warehouses were really almost bare of goods that would come here except for this discrimination.

There are other discriminations, of course, which I might call to your attention. One is the rate from California to New York.

Q. Before you go any further with that, do I understand they charge as much to haul freight from Chicago to Kansas City as they do from Chicago to New York—a thousand miles farther?—A. I mean to say they charge from Kansas City to New York the same rate as from Chicago to New York.

Q. The difference is Kansas City to Chicago?—A. The rate from Kansas City to Chicago is about 45, and the rate from Chicago to New York is 65, making $1.10. Now, they take it from Kansas City to New York for 65.

Q. (By Representative Otjen.) Where does the railroad gain anything by giving Kansas City a rate as cheap as they would to Chicago, for instance? How do the railroads gain anything by the operation? I can see how it would benefit Kansas City.—A. The cut was made by railroads that did not center in Chicago by other roads that go around Chicago—and the other roads that do center in Chicago were thus compelled to make this cut in the rate.

Q. (By Mr. Kennedy.) Is it not for the purpose of controlling the business over these lines that would otherwise go to Chicago?—A. It is in a great measure to build up what is called the fast freight lines. They like to have the long haul from Chicago and Kansas City to the East. I have here a letter from one of the fast freight lines telling a party it would be greatly to his advantage to send his goods to New York instead of Chicago, as all the people in his neighborhood are sending to New York. His object is to get the haul over the New York Central, in this case, the Merchants' Dispatch. Consequently, the fast freight lines whose offices are in Chicago—their purpose seems to be to carry freight not to Chicago—but it is for the railroads themselves; they have their own refrigerator cars; and east of Chicago and east of Kansas City the Merchants' Dispatch, the Star Union line, and the Erie Dispatch get the benefit of the long haul. They are interested in trying to divert freight from Chicago.

Q. (By Professor JOHNSON.) Do these fast freight lines own their own cars?—A. Yes.

Q. And pay to the railroads?—A. Pay mileage to the railroads.

Q. This discrimination is really the result of competition between lines—between railroads from river points to the Atlantic seaboard?—A. Yes. As I understand, the fast freight lines are really a railroad within a railroad. The New York Central is a railroad and the Merchants' Dispatch is a fast freight line running over the New York Central Railroad, and they get the benefit of the high-class freights.

Q. It is not the competition of the Gulf?—A. Oh, no; the other freight lines especially.

Q. (By Mr. KENNEDY.) Do you say the Gulf competition has nothing to do with it?—A. I do not think it affects our particular business.

Q. (By Representative OTJEN.) It would be too slow for butter and eggs to go by the Gulf?—A. We have to have rapid transit, and have to have special cars, and to pay special rates.

I have been asked to call your attention to the fact that the freight rate on cheese from Wisconsin to Chicago is higher than the rate from Michigan and New York State for the same distance. That is, they haul freight going west cheaper than they do from Wisconsin and points west of there; therefore, the farmer in Wisconsin seems to be discriminated against by paying an excessive freight rate. For instance, the railroads running into Michigan and New York State will transport cheese from Utica or Buffalo to Chicago more cheaply than you can get it from the interior of Wisconsin, the same distance.

Q. Is it due to the fact that cars go west empty to a large extent?—A. That is the reason they assign for it.

Q. Cheap back freights?—A. Yes.

Q. Is that not a true reason, do you think?—A. It seems so. Yes; it seems justifiable in this case.

There is another matter suggested, and that is that there are firms and corporations that own their own private cars, and that they load these cars with merchandise of various classifications. Some of them would be third class, some first class, and fourth class, and second class, perhaps. These cars being owned by these corporations and sealed up when fully loaded, are usually subjected only to the tariff rate applicable to the lower class of freight. That is, instead of paying second class and fourth class, they pay the fourth-class rate.

Q. (By Representative OTJEN.) It is discrimination in another form?—A. Private individuals shipping butter, we will say. That would take a rate of 75 cents and would have to pay that rate in a carload or less, whereas a party shipping flour, or pork, or lard, which would be a lower class of freight, and then filling it up with butter or something else that was a higher class of freight, he can get his car through at the lower rate of freight. There must be considerable opposition to this private-car business. The merchants generally can not compete with it. They can not meet that sort of competition. The railroads haul these cars at a mileage rate instead of charging the regular rate of freight.

I want to say this. The people in my line of business feel that they are very heavily burdened by the excessive rates for telegraphic service, which is really an expensive business and a very serious item in our business, because of the sale of perishable goods; in fact the most of our business is done by telegraph; I suppose three-fourths of the business we do is done by telegraph and telephone. Therefore, we feel that it bears very heavily upon us, possibly heavier than upon anyone else. The rates are very high and the service is far from satisfactory, and we are inclined to think it is one of those things that ought to be under the control of the General Government, that is, made a part of the post-office system.

Q. (By Professor JOHNSON.) Postal telegraph, as it is sometimes called?—A. Yes; it should be under the control of the Government.

Q. (By Mr. KENNEDY.) As it is in England?—A. Yes; in England, as I know from experience. We could get a much better service and at a much lower cost. In Great Britain you can send a telegram anywhere of 10 words for 10 cents; throughout France for 11 cents; in Germany it is 12 cents; Belgium, it is 10 cents.

Q. (By Representative OTJEN.) Are the telegraph lines under the control of the government in France and Germany?—A. Yes. It is a government institution in Great Britain. The post-office department attends to the telegraph and telephone business; the same thing in Germany.

Q. (By Representative LORIMER.) Do you consider that you are in any way discriminated against by the telegraph companies?—A. No; I don't know that we are. We have not been able to feel it, and, therefore, I could not state it as a fact. It may be we are, but I don't know. However, as it is now, there is practically no competition at all. The Postal Telegraph Company and the Western Union are substantially one company; that is, they charge the same rates so far as the public generally is concerned. There is no competition any more than there would be if the two companies were under one name, and, as I say, the service is very poor. In regard to the telephone, that, too, is a serious item of expense. From what I have read and learned on the subject, I should think the Government could afford to send telegrams for one-fifth or one-tenth of what they now cost the people of the country. It is not the actual cost of the message that makes the rate so high, but it is the dividends that the company has to pay on an enormous capitalization. I saw a statement, that I believe to be reliable in every way, showing that for every $1,000 worth of stock in the Western Union Telegraph Company, the stockholder gets $3,000 per year.

Q. (By Mr. KENNEDY.) You believe the United States Government should be given the right of fixing the rate?—A. Yes. I know the Government has a cheaper rate for telegrams itself. I don't think there is any discrimination, at least there is not, so far as I know, between individuals. Of course a great many firms own private wires, and what advantage that is I don't know.

Q. Do you think the telegraph companies should give service as cheap to the individual as to the Government?—A. I don't know of any reason why the Government should not own the telephone system. I feel that if we had to do away with the post-office or the telegraph and telephone, that we could do away with the post-office so far as the business man is concerned better than we could do away with the telegraph or telephone. Of course I don't refer to private wires or anything of that kind, but to the fact that the telephone and telegraph system is more indispensable to our business than the post-office. It may be true only in our line, and that it is not true in other lines of business. But I don't think you could mention a line in which it is not indispensable; brokers, bankers, commission men, in every line of business; so far as I know there is not a line of business in which they are not just as useful as they are in our line of business.

Q. What do they charge you for a telephone?—A. One hundred and twenty dollars per year.

Q. (By Professor JOHNSON.) What suggestions have you to make in regard to the telephone service; would you have it owned by the State or by the Government?—A. I think that the telegraph and telephone systems should be incorporated in the general post-office arrangements and that they should all be under the Postmaster-General.

Q. You think the Government should maintain the service in the States?—A. Yes. I realize of course that it would cost a great many millions of dollars, and I don't know whether the country is growing so rapidly or trade is increasing so enormously as to make it pay for itself in a short time. If would probably take 10 years, or something of that sort, to get thoroughly inaugurated.

Q. (By Mr. KENNEDY.) Do you know anything about the sentiment of the business men in Chicago generally on that question?—A. I think they feel as I have expressed it; that they are not only in favor of Government service, but that they feel they are paying an exorbitant charge for the telephone and telegraph service—a charge that is far beyond the actual cost or anything of that sort. It is an enormous charge upon the amount of capital invested.

Q. Have there been no suggestions or remedies offered on the part of the business men to bring about any other condition? Has there been any organized effort to bring about any better condition?—A. I think we obtain more courtesies to-day than we did, but to go about it in the way of a business organization we feel rather helpless.

Q. You know you have to educate Congress up to these things?—A. We realize that, but everything utterly fails, and this committee, by coming around and hearing us, has made us feel that we are worth listening to, and that there is some one to hear our complaints. I would also say that the country has been very much benefited and pleased with the benefits they have received from the active interest that has been taken in our business by the Commissioner of Agriculture, and the fact that this commission as well as the Commissioner of Agriculture should look into these questions. Now there is no particular detriment to anyone and especially not to these members, and I think it will give great gratification to the citizens, and that it will be the result of our getting better service in every way. I think that we should have a commissioner of commerce as well as a Commissioner of Agriculture, to look into these questions. It would be no particular detriment to anybody, and it would give us better service.

Q. (By Professor JOHNSON.) You mean a commissioner of commerce to be made a Cabinet officer?—A. Yes; a commission with the Commissioner of Agriculture even, and it would afterwards become such an important office that it would be made a Cabinet office. There is no particular department now to look after these matters, and I think there should be one. I think we ought to have a department to be called the Commission of Commerce.

Q. (By Representative OTJEN.) A great many of the complaints or difficulties you express in your business would be corrected, would they not, if you had a commercial commission that was an interstate commission and had authority to regulate rates on the railroads, with the exception of telegraph and telephone rates?—A. I think our own Interstate Commerce Commission has authority to do that, but they don't exercise it very actively.

Q. If they had the authority, and it was so recognized, many of these difficulties would be overcome, would they not?—A. Yes; by submitting the question of freights to their revision. As the matter is now, they are not subject to anyone's supervision apparently. These tariffs are gotten out without any reference to the claims of anyone affected by them. I have been in business a great many years, and so have lots of others, and I never knew anyone who could see any good about the tariff rates. They seem to be in the hands of the railroads entirely, and whether they classify eggs in the second or fifth class, we have to submit to it.

Q. Are your associates in business members of an organization that has a representative to look after the transportation interests of the business men of Chicago?—A. Not a committee especially. That is only as it may appear to the association to be necessary.

Q. Is there not such an organization in Chicago in which a great many business men are associated and have a representative looking after their interests all the time, going to railroad companies and asking that rates be reduced, etc.?—A. I am not aware of it.

Q. (By Professor JOHNSON.) Central freight committee, I think, is what Mr. Kennedy means?—A. Yes; central traffic organization.

Q. There is the Central Traffic Association and then there is a Chicago freight committee, I believe?—A. What its functions are I don't know.

Q. (By Mr. KENNEDY.) Have they such organization in other cities, such as Philadelphia, St. Louis?—A. I think the business men of Chicago all have one.

Q. They bad for some years, did they not?—A. We had for some years what we called the Chicago Freight Bureau, representing the Board of Trade, which paid half the expenses and the merchants and manufacturers generally of Chicago paid the other half. Franklin MacVeigh was the president for some years. That has been dissolved for two or three years. The business of that was the joint interest of the merchants and manufacturers and the Board of Trade of Chicago, and if anything general came up we had a committee to meet sometimes with a railroad company, sometimes with the railroad association, and sometimes before the Interstate Commerce Commission. There is no regular organization now. I think the chief houses here in business have their own traffic man. I would say that the department at Washington has taken a very general interest in this export business of butter and cheese, about which you have asked me, in trying to develop the business between our country and Europe, and also with regard to the Philippines and China and Japan, and with some success. The business itself is quite a large one and goes into millions of dollars every year. There is a great lack of shipping facilities from the inland of this country. The only line out of New York that is available for shipments of butter and cheese, and butter more particularly—cheese don't require refrigerating like butter does, except for a short time in the year—is an American line running from New York to Southampton and other ports. Their freight rates have been almost prohibitive. They charge from New York to London a rate of 75 shillings per ton, whereas we ship from Montreal to London and the general rate is 40 shillings—35 and 40 shillings; it varies. We supply a demand from Liverpool at from 25 to 30 shillings and sometimes it runs as low as 20, and to Bordeaux generally from 30 to 35 shillings, so that a great portion of the butter of the country is carried in foreign ships before being reshipped, so that it really divides the trade in shipping to foreign countries to the disadvantage of our own interests. Of course a great many shippers going from here to various ports ship on the American line, but nearly all the lines except the American line have refrigerator facilities. The Atlantic Transport line is one of them; they have refrigerators that they own and operate. But the transportation facilities are getting more and more toward the exclusion of dairy products on account of other traffic; so that if we want to make a small shipment of butter on an American line we have to pay 75 shillings, or we can get a less rate by sending it via Montreal and having it go on a foreign ship. The result of this in connection with the encouragement that Canada is getting from the Government of England in these matters is that the Canadian trade in butter and cheese and such dairy products has developed enormously, while on the other hand our own trade is growing smaller and smaller. The actual shipments of butter and cheese from the United States to Europe are less now than they were 5 or 6 years ago or 10 years ago, whereas from Canada butter is shipped to the extent of eight times as much as it was ten or a dozen years ago, and cheese about four times as much.

Q. (By Representative OTJEN.) You ship from here to Canada instead of from here to Europe?—A. No; we ship to Europe via Canada. There is a tariff of 4 cents a pound on butter, and I think 2 cents on cheese, and we have to ship in bond from here to Montreal. Then it is taken in bond across to the other side without our having to pay a duty.

Q. (By Representative LORIMER.) Is that included in the Canadian shipments?—A. I am inclined to think it is, although the Canadian people claim they don't include American shipments in keeping the statistics of their shipments. The shipments of cheese from Montreal for the last 6 months—that is, from the 1st of May to the present time—were 1,678,330 packages, containing 60 pounds each. From New York during the same time the shipments were 254,099 packages, or about one-seventh as much. On butter from Montreal for the same time the shipments were 430,051 packages, and from New York 106,102, or a little less than one-fourth.

Q. In your opinion that is all due to the difference in the rate from our ports to Canadian ports?—A. No; not to that. There are several reasons outside of that. The first one of the reasons is that they get better freight rates than we do. That is considerable of an inducement. Another reason is that in the English markets they prefer to trade with their colonies and try and develop them, and for that reason the Canadian trade is rather favored in the English markets more than the American. Of course, we don't carry that trade, at least not to the same extent. One disadvantage we labor under is the registering with the Montreal steamers. The Canadian steamers being subsidized by the Canadian Government, they have a right to discriminate against American products. They will only take our products when they can not get the products of their own people, and they keep their freight rooms open for their own products up to within three days of sailing, so that it really shuts us out to a great extent.

Q. (By Representative OTJEN.) Then if they find they have room they take your products?—A. They only take ours when they find they have not enough of their own to make out a cargo, and they only tell us this within three days of sailing, and we have to take our chances on getting our products shipped. It is all according to whether their room is filled by Canadian products.

Q. (By Representative LORIMER.) Have you thought of any remedy?—A. I don't know of any remedy except the encouragement of our own shipping interests in this country, so as to have American steamers with carrying facilities for dairy products, instead of having to depend upon England for our ships.

Q. Build up the American merchant marine?—A. Yes. I think there are several very good reasons why that should be done, and that is one of them.

There is one other matter that I have been asked to mention to you, and that is local weights and measures, which I should like to speak of if I am not going contrary to your rules. We are put to great inconvenience from that here in Illinois. For instance, in Illinois a bushel of buckwheat weighs 52 pounds, and in Wisconsin it only weighs 50 pounds. Down in Indiana it is the same. In Michigan it is only 48 pounds. Another item is dried peaches. In Illinois 23 pounds make a bushel; in Wisconsin, 28; in Indiana, 33 pounds, and in Michigan, 28 pounds, etc., and the same way with a number of other items, so that a farmer or country merchant shipping to market really don't know what he is going to get for his produce. I submit a table showing the difference between some of the legal weights and measures in the States of Illinois, Iowa, Wisconsin, Michigan, Indiana, Missouri, New York, and Ohio.

Legal weights and measures.

[Pounds per bushel.]

Articles.	Illi-nois.	Iowa.	Wis-con-sin.	Mich-igan.	Indi-ana.	Mis-souri.	New York.	Ohio.
Apples:								
Dried	24	24	28	22	25	24	22	22
Green	50	-----	57					
Bran	20	20	20	20	-----	20	20	20
Barley	48	48	48	48	48	48	48	48
Beans:								
White	60	60	60	60	60	60	62	60
Castor	46	46	46	46	46	46	46	46
Buckwheat	52	52	50	48	50	52	48	50
Broom-corn seed	46	46	46	46	46	46	46	30
Beets	60		50					56
Carrots	55	-----	50		-----	50		50
Charcoal	22	22	22	22	22	22	22	
Coal, stone	80	80				80	-----	80
Coke	40	38						40
Corn:								
Shelled	56	56	56	56	56	56	56	56
Ear	70	70	70	70	68	70	70	68
Corn meal	48	48	48	50	50	50	50	50
Cranberries	33	-----		40	33	-----		-----
Peaches:								
Dried	28	23	28	28	33	33	32	33
Pared	40	33	28	28	33	33	-----	-----
Seed:								
Flax	56	56	56	56	56	56	55	56
Blue grass	14	14	14	14	14	14	15	10
Clover	60	60	60	60	60	60	60	60
Hungarian	48	48	48	50	-----	48	48	50
Millet	50	48	50	50	50	50	-----	50
Orchard	14	14	-----	14	14	14	14	14
Redtop	14	14	14	14	14	14	14	14
Timothy	45	45	45	45	45	45	44	45
German lupine	60							
Hemp seed	44	44	44	44	44	44	44	44
Hickory nuts	50							
Malt, barley	38	36	34	38	38	38	34	34
Mineral coal	40				70			
Middlings:								
Fine	40				40	-----		
Coarse	30				30			
Oats	32	32	32	32	32	32	32	32
Onions	57	57	57	54	48	57	57	55
Onions:								
Tops	28	28	28	28	28	28	28	25
Sets	32							
Osage orange	33							
Parsnips	55	-----	-----		55	44	-----	-----
Potatoes	60	60	60	60	60	60	60	60
Potatoes, sweet	50	46	55	56	55	56	55	50
Peas:								
Dried	60	60	60	60	60	60	60	60
In pods	32							
Pop corn	70	-----	-----		70	-----	-----	-----
Quicklime	80	80	80	80	80	80	80	-----
Rye	56	56	56	56	56	56	56	56
Salt:								
Coarse	50	50	50	50	50	50	50	50
Fine	55	50	56	56	50	50	56	50
Turnips:								
Rutabaga	55	55	56	58	55	50	55	60
White	-----	-----	42	-----	-----	42	-----	-----
Wheat	60	60	60	60	60	60	60	60

Q. (By Representative OTJEN). According to that one bushel is a little bigger in some States than in others?—A. Yes. I think everything of that kind ought to be regulated by weight instead of by measure, so that they would be uniform.

Q. (By Mr. KENNEDY). Have not the business men the remedy entirely in their own hands by purchasing by weight instead of by measure?—A. They purchase it by weight, but when it comes to Chicago—we will say a man in Wisconsin ships his potatoes, it seems a certain number of pounds of potatoes in that State constitute a bushel, and when he gets here he is going to get 3 or 4 pounds more or less, as the case may be.

Q. That is disconcerting?—A. Yes. There is no reason why it should be so any more than that the different States should have a different currency.

Q. (By Representative OTJEN). You don't know anything about the metric system of weights and measures?—A. No; I don't.

Q. You don't know whether that would be a proper thing to adopt in business here?—A. Well, it would if it was thoroughly introduced. I don't know but what it would take a long while to introduce it.

Q. It would take some time before people would understand it?—A. Yes. Another cause of complaint with us is the charges of the express companies for the stamps they put on their receipts. A man shipping to the merchants must pay for the stamp that goes on the express receipts. It is thought that the original intention of the lawmakers was that the express companies should pay for the stamp that goes on their receipts.

Q. (By Representative LORIMER.) You mean the internal-revenue stamp?— A. Yes. There was a decision by the supreme court of New York within the last few months, that the express companies should stamp their own receipts— that they should pay for the stamp on their own receipts—but that practice is not followed out here. I think, also, the telegraph companies ought to pay for the stamp on their dispatches. I believe that was the original intention of the law.

Q. (By Representative OTJEN.) You think that was the intention of Congress when the bill was passed?—A. Yes; and that the law should be amended, if necessary, so that it would take effect along the lines of the original intention.

B. (By Mr. KENNEDY.) Your association recommends that?—A. Yes; we certainly do.

CHICAGO, ILL., *November 16, 1899.*

TESTIMONY OF MR. SAMUEL H. GREELEY,

Commission merchant, Chicago, Ill.

The subcommission on transportation met at 2 p. m. November 16, 1899, at the Auditorium Hotel, Chicago, Ill., Representative Lorimer presiding. Mr. Samuel H. Greeley, being duly sworn, testified as follows:

Q. (By Representative LORIMER.) Please state your name and business.—A. Samuel H. Greeley, commission merchant, Chicago.

Q. You are a shipper, I presume, of grain here?—A. Yes.

Q. What, if any, are your complaints or criticisms of the railroad facilities given?—A. In regard to this railway situation, it seems to my mind that there are four or five different phases that are either directly or indirectly connected with the railroads in the handling of grain in this market. Primarily, I might mention railroads, bucket shops, bear speculators, and the ownership of private cars. And in order that you may get these matters placed somewhat systematically before you, I will state first in regard to public warehouses. The original intention of the State law of Illinois, and the constitution of this State was, that the public warehouseman should be a licensed servant of the people, created by virtue of the necessities of commerce, to care for the grain intrusted to him by the public in these warehouses. The growing importance of Chicago as a market center, necessitated the establishment of these warehouses for the conduct of this immense grain trade from the great West and Northwest.

The representatives of the people at Springfield early saw the importance of having a public institution to look after this large volume of trade, and therefore they created this commission for the purpose of storing the grain, and properly mixing the different grades into their proper bins as they arrived in storage; and they had no other function than to simply be the custodian of the grain for the public. But about 1887, when the interstate-commerce law was passed, the entire system of public warehousing changed. Previous to that date it was the custom of the railroads, if I am correctly informed, from my personal experience and what I have learned from others, that rebates on freight were allowed individual shippers in different portions of the country in order to draw that grain into Chicago as against any other competition that might divert it to any other market. Fearing the result of the interstate-commerce law, the railroads saw the necessity of intrusting these rebates into the hands of a single party, to protect the hauls on their lines, so they chose a man here who would necessitate the least rebate of freights, and still get the grain. Therefore, they picked out these public warehousemen, furnished them with warehouses and permitted them as merchandisers to overstep the duties for which they were created, and thus become dealers in grain. The fact that a public warehouseman is a grain dealer, as against the public, has led to a condition of affairs that has almost stifled competition for the crops in the western country.

The advantages that the warehouseman possesses over the public is that he can take his grain into the public warehouse and pay storage to himself; in other words, pay no storage, while the public pays the full advertised rates. These rates are annually posted as being so much per bushel, and the public is obliged to pay that set of rates. In addition to paying no storage whatever on his grain in these houses, he is in position, being the proprietor, to mix the better qualities of a certain grade with a poorer grade, preserving them for his own trade, and when the public calls for that particular grade, they get the worst possible sample of that grade. By virtue of the fact that he pays no storage, he can take advantage of the storage rates as against the public and give that rate away, and use it as an over competing price to get possession of the grain from the party of whom he buys it in the West. In addition to these large profits, which are enormous, resulting from the mixing of grain, together with the storage which he is not obliged to pay, this has gradually led up to a condition where competition for grain in the West has become almost dead, the details of which are set out very fully in the trial held in 1896 in the circuit court before Judge Tuley. A large number of witnesses were there examined—men familiar with the trade—and the proof was conclusive that at least 75 per cent of the grain in public warehouses sooner or later became the property of a public warehouseman. Having thus reduced competition in the West to almost a minimum, they then go to work to stifle the dealers who offer grain to the East from the Chicago market, and they are enabled to do this by offering any shipper who buys grain from these public warehouses the inferior samples, they themselves being able to quote to the same trade the better grade that they have remaining in the house; so that, having killed competition for grain in the West, and having killed the trade which offers grain to the East, it leaves them virtually with a monopoly of the grain business in this market.

Now we must not overlook the fact that a very important feature connected with the business is the fact that the public warehouseman does not aim primarily to buy the grain in the West for the sake of immediately selling it to the man in the East, but it is his intention to hoard it up in these warehouses and keep it there as long as possible, or at least so long as the speculative public is willing to buy it of him for future delivery and pay him a carrying charge. I will illustrate that by saying, for instance, that cash wheat to-day may be worth 67½ cents and wheat for May delivery may be worth in the neighborhood of 70 cents or 71. We will say, for the sake of argument, that the May wheat is 3 cents per bushel premium over the cash wheat. Now, they want to hold that grain in the elevators here just as long as people will buy grain for May delivery and pay them that premium for May wheat. Then the more grain they can carry in Chicago in these elevators the larger their profits, because the heavier tax is imposed on the man who buys it, and it continues a running tax. When May arrives it is their object not to deliver that wheat to the man who bought it for May delivery, but to force the man to sell it out, they standing ready to take it when that man is tired of the load, and sell it ahead for another deferred delivery to any other sucker who buys grain purchased on deferred delivery, and thus add another income to the carrying of the wheat in the elevator. This produces what you might term a state of enforced liquidations, enforced selling out on the part of the buying public. And we must bear in mind also that the poorer they can get the quality of the grain held in these public warehouses, so that it will barely pass the inspection grade that is applicable for a sale for future delivery, the better it suits their purpose.

It is evident that the poorer the grade is the less the public will care to take it and the more inducement is offered the public to sell it out and continue its existence in storage. It is evident to those posted in the trade that the lower they can get the values of grain the larger their profits, because the less the insurance and interest to carry it in the warehouse pending these months of future delivery for which they have it sold. Now these large stocks of grain carried in these elevators in Chicago give birth to what is known as the professional bear raider, or speculator. It encourages an army of short sellers to enter the market and sell millions upon millions of bushels of grain, taking these large stocks as a nucleus for the safety of their sales, and it brings about a condition whereby the buyer of grain for future delivery is not on a parity with the man who sells it short. It can readily be noticed in your minds that if, for instance, as at the present time, 20,000,000 bushels of wheat are held here in the Chicago market and are carried until next May, that when next May comes, these men who buy grain for future delivery being speculators and perhaps not wanting the grain at all, see this immense volume staring them in the face, and they are ready immediately, seeing that they will get it delivered to them and being of a poor quality, to dump it right out on the market. It produces a condition that forces the man who has bought it to get out of the way before the man who sells it short has to cover, so that now in the market we have got around to that condition—"when will the longs liquidate? When are the buyers going to sell out?" It is not a question of when the shorts will buy. I have stood in the pits in this market and have seen this army of short sellers hammer and hammer and hammer that market with millions upon millions of bushels of stuff, and their single solitary argument being based upon the fact that this immense volume of wheat was stored here, and that being stored it would force the man that bought it to finally liquidate; and then they buy it in at the reduced liquidating prices and secure the profit.

Not only has this large quantity of grain stored here produced these bear raiders, but it has brought into existence and made safe what is known as the bucket shop. A bucket shop is a place where a man supposes he buys grain for future delivery, but which in fact is a place wherein he goes and actually makes a bet with the proprietor of the place as to whether or not the market will advance or decline, there being no intention at all on the part of the man who conducts the bucket shop to deliver the property or receive it, as the case may be.

The existence of the bucket shops is made safe by depression in prices, and fully 75 per cent, I should say probably 90 per cent, of the business that goes into a bucket shop is buying business. If these large accumulations of grain held in Chicago by virtue of the grant of a railroad company did not exist it would not be a safe policy for a bucket shop to take the short side of a trade in making a bet on the market.

Thus indirectly a railroad company becomes a surety for a concern that should be prosecuted and in the penitentiary. They don't primarily establish the institution, but the privileges they grant really give it protection. Now, we must stop to consider the larger sense in which this subject must be looked at, and that is, What would be the effect of these large volumes of grain bought in bucket shops if they actually entered the market places?

I have heard it estimated that there are at least 10,000 bucket shops in the United States, and that they trade in 30,000,000 bushels of stuff a day. If 75 per cent of the business traded in in these bucket shops is buying business, and we could get 30,000,000 bushels of buying business on that exchange and other legitimate markets throughout the country, we would not see the condition that has been staring this country in the face for the last 12 years.

Not long ago we saw in Nebraska corn worth 8 cents per bushel. I have seen oats on the exchange in recent years at 13 cents a bushel.

In my opinion it was the constant working on the speculative public, taking away from them the tributes that purchases for future delivery necessitated, that led up to the panic of 1893, when people throughout the Western country threatened to repudiate their debts. You may talk about the tariff and free silver and other questions of importance that have come before the people in recent years as political issues, but to my mind it has been nothing more nor less than this combination on the part of the railroad companies with these warehousemen, and the effect of that combination, both directly and indirectly, upon the purchasers of this country, which has caused these political disturbances and created so much dissatisfaction.

It has finally assumed a position in the grain markets of this country where one man puts out the price for the product of the producer. On the Rock Island road you will find Charles Counselman and perhaps one or two others almost the only competitors for grain on that system. You will find on the Northwestern that there is Bartlett Frazier and the P. V. Elevator Company, and possibly one or two others. On the St. Paul you find Armour; on the Chicago, Burlington and Quincy you find Armour; and these will serve as illustrations to prove to you my former statement that the competition has been killed.

However much of an injustice this may appear to be to a Chicago commission merchant, who has been so loudly dilated upon by the warehousemen, nevertheless the fact remains true that this storage of large quantities of grain at the market center, together with the indirect favoritism shown the bucket shops, the encouragement of these bear raiders and the final killing of competition for the offering of grain East, and the purchase of grain West, have brought it right down to a condition similar to this beef business.

If I am correctly informed, these warehousemen, with the assistance of the railroads, are driving from business the country elevator dealers, and the deal is assuming such vast proportions that they are getting possession of these country stations, and as soon as that is entirely consummated on the various lines one price will go to the producers of the country and one price to the consumer.

I think this has all come out of one particular feature, and that is railroad competition. The railroads have to draw that grain, and they want a man to get it for them if it takes a special rate to do it, and he is the man that is favored, in my opinion. They go after grain not naturally tributary to Chicago. They invade territory that, by the geography of the place, it is absolutely impossible for it to come here on regular tariffs. But in competition with the Gulf and with points North, and in competition with through-billed grain that is diverted at various junction points, they are obliged, in order to protect their systems and secure this haul, to give away to some favored party the advantage to do it; and in my opinion the officials of the railroad divide the swag with the elevator proprietors, and the deal is perpetually carried on perhaps to the detriment of the stockholders of the road, although I am not prepared to state how much of a detriment that is to the stockholders.

Q. (By Professor JOHNSON.) If you have any evidence on that point I think you ought to submit it.—A. I can suggest to you the names of five men who have been in the habit of meeting every day at the close of the board of trade, for the sole purpose of arranging the combination price for grain throughout this Western territory. In my opinion those men will not deny the fact that they have entered into a pool, a combination for the purpose of establishing a set price. The public is not able to compete with that price.

It may appear to you that because these men are able to pay more for the grain than any other competitor, it is a good thing for the producer. That is the one single, solitary argument that these men have rested upon in all their trials and tribulations, both before Judge Tuley and at Springfield—that they pay more to the producer. And I will simply answer that by saying that, although they do give away a fraction perhaps more than others can to get possession of the property, when they do get possession of it they bring it into this market and put it in the elevators and adopt the policy I have previously spoken of, of hoarding it here from year to year, manufacturing it into as inferior a grade as possible, and then, while they may pay a small fraction to get possession of it, they take 5 or 10 or 15 cents per bushel off of the value of the crop.

Another feature, to my mind a very important one, is the ownership of private cars. I believe that the firm of Armour & Co., or firms in which P. D. Armour is himself interested, own between 10,000 and 20,000 private freight cars. I may be mistaken and put my estimate too high, but if any man is allowed to own a private freight car and receive, for instance, a minimum of five-eighths of a cent a mile from the railway companies for every mile the companies haul that car, or in a general way, pay a man $15 on a round trip on that car from Chicago to New York, he could lose money in the grain business and still make fortunes out of the railroad companies, and there is no possible way that competition with him can exist; and it seems to me that if there is any evil that should be taken up, either by Congress or otherwise, it should be this ownership of private cars by firms and corporations.

I have explained to you in a very general way what I consider the abuses of the greatest importance in the grain trade to-day. I have not touched particularly upon special rates of freight, although I believe every public warehouseman in the city of Chicago is receiving them. They can pay more to-day, or have recently at least, for grain in Nebraska, than they have for grain in Iowa. I believe also that they have been previously notified by the railroad companies of the existence of new tariffs 30 days in advance of the public and have contracted for the purchase of large volumes of grain long before the rates were ever generally known. I believe that is the general practice.

The Eastern roads have taken up a feature quite similar to the Western roads, and that is, they have seen the necessity of having a favored individual to look after hauling the grain from Chicago east. If I want to ship a car of corn, for instance, from Chicago to New York, and buy it on the Northwestern road here, and desire that it be sent east over the Lake Shore, it has to be transferred from a Western to an Eastern car. That transfer takes place in the transfer houses of the Eastern railroad. The railroad company puts that transfer house in the charge of a grain dealer. It is not an independent warehouse where the public can receive the accommodations which would usually devolve upon a public institution. If I want a car of oats clipped in the transfer house on its way from this market to my customer in the east, my competitor clips those oats for me. If I sell 36-pound clipped oats down east and my competitor does the clipping, I might get a 34-pound clipped oat, and not only that, I believe he possesses the ability to know the name of my customer when that car is forwarded.

I believe that Eastern railroads in this city use these parties as their chosen individuals to get special rates of freight when it is necessary for their interest.

And summed up altogether, the grain business in Chicago, which should be subject to certain conditions that are absolutely public in their nature, by which everybody should have an equal opportunity, is now monopolized by favored individuals, and competition for the crops of the country is going to pieces. We have recently seen our corn market very firm, with a demand absolutely good for all qualities, indeed so urgent that the poorest grades were at a premium over the price of better grades when the latter were not to be secured, and in the face of an urgent export demand and an urgent local demand these markets here have dropped 7 cents per bushel, dragging the cash grain down in proportion. The whole result of this large accumulation carried in these public warehouses, and the raiding of these bear forces, and the continued success of these bucket shops, has caused men who were buying in these bucket shops to think they were purchasing grain.

Now, what are the 40,000,000 farmers of this country up against? I will defy any member of this committee or any other committee to contradict by evidence or statement the facts which I have stated to you, and I also believe that the opinions which I have given are correct. They are not only my own personal opinions, but many of my statements are in the form of sworn evidence, which has been introduced in our courts and decisions obtained in our favor. We fought these public warehousemen at Springfield in an effort to enforce the fact that a public warehouseman should not deal in grain. They fled to Springfield just as soon as the courts decided that they should not deal in grain, and, in my opinion, by the use of a large volume of money, secured State legislation that to-day overrides the opinions of the supreme court of this State.

I have not touched upon the fact of the grading in grain—the attempts on the part of at least a portion of these warehousemen to influence the inspection department. I have not touched at all in reference to the weighing of grain, which to my mind is and has been for many years a source of a great deal of discomfort to western shippers.

Now, in regard to speculation in grain, whether or not that may be a fortune or a misfortune to the producers of this country—it does exist, and they have finally succeeded in killing the buying speculative public to the extent that the trade does not come in, as it used to, to support the price.

The heavy tributes that buyers are obliged to pay for grain for future delivery are so strong and embarrassing that they have finally caught on to the game, and it largely leaves the field in the possession of the men who sell it short; and the fact that these things encourage so many short sellers on the market, where the buying trade is at a disadvantage, has produced this condition of wheat in the sixties, and corn possibly in the twenties, and oats frequently under 20 cents a bushel. When we raise crops of 3,500,000,000 bushels in this country, worth from $1,000,000,000 to $2,000,000,000 annually, even at these depressed values the conditions not only force the value on the grain that comes to market, but it fixes the value on the entire crops, and, in my opinion at least, from 15 to 25 per cent of the values of the crops are taken off annually by this condition that exists by reason of a railroad company insisting that it shall practically go into the grain business.

President Stickney, of the Great Western road, admitted that his road was in the grain business, and gave the name of the company that conducted it, and that his representatives are on that floor to-day. What a pass the people are coming to, if the railroads are to become the merchandisers of the product. The difference between the price of grain in the West and in the East is the rate of freight. To my mind there is nothing short of Government ownership that can correct it. Control is impossible. To my mind it could not be done, and it is impossible for a committee of any kind, interstate commerce or otherwise, to regulate a railroad.

Railroad pooling—it would be an impossibility for them to ever stop it, because of the fact that if the railroads did pool it would never prevent one man from naming a rate to an outsider. And since the ability rests in the hands of the manager of a railroad to name the rate, there is no hope for improvement; and so far as banking on any joint agreements is concerned, these things have been tested many times and found wanting. A little illustration, I think, will serve to show you, gentlemen, the situation of the public warehouseman being a grain dealers. Suppose the collector of the port of New York should enter into and do an active business in competition with Marshall Field & Co. and J. W. Doane & Co., and should pay no import duty whatever as against these men. How long would competition exist with them? And especially if the Government should furnish him with a free custom-house, and he should be permitted to mix his goods with their goods and secure the better samples for himself and give them the poorer samples, and then give him special facilities when he shipped, in the shape of plenty of cars, rebates, etc. Where would competition exist in commercial life under such circumstances? President Stickney cited an illustration and said he didn't see why the people would not resort to arms if need be rather than submit to such a condition.

Q. (By Mr. C. J. HARRIS.) Is this elevator charge made so much a month, or how is the elevator charge arranged?—A. Three-fourths of a cent for, first the 10 days, and a quarter of a cent for each following 10 days. The storage charge remains the same and does not depreciate in proportion to the product; that is, it is so much per bushel.

Q. Is that a high charge?—A. Yes.

Q. How long has that rate been in force?—A. I think 2 or 3 years; previous to that it was slightly higher.

Q. (By Representative OTJEN.) These rates are established by the State law?—A. I believe so, the maximum. In connection with that, if I want to transfer a car of grain from the car to a boat, and do it through one of these public warehouses, and the car contains 1,600 bushels of oats, it would cost me three-fourths of a cent to make that transfer. My competitor would do it for nothing plus the cost of running the elevator.

Q. (By Professor JOHNSON.) Does your competitor own the elevators or does he rent them?—A. In some cases they own them and in some cases they are leased by the railroad company.

Q. Is not his capital sufficient to give some justification for not paying storage the same as his competitor? He owns or rents the elevator, and has a considerable capital involved in so doing. His remuneration on his capital, in one sense, is free storage, is it not?—A. In most cases, it seems to me, that the capital invested in the property is practically nothing. They are presented with the elevators by the railroad companies. In some instances they own their own elevators, and if I am correctly informed, railroad men have been the incorporators of these companies. I understand that Jay Gould was interested, and President Fish of the Illinois Central, and Russell Sage, and others.

Q. (By Mr. C. J. HARRIS.) They would not own them unless there was some profit in it some way?—A. They were incorporators. As to what their interests in the profits were I am unable to state.

Q. You think they get something back somewhere?—A. I certainly think they get a great deal back every year.

Q. (By Professor JOHNSON.) Theoretically, if a man owns an elevator, and makes use of it in his own business, he is placed differently from the other man who makes use of it?—A. There is a great injustice done the public.

Q. As a theoretical argument, I think the man ought not to pay the same for the use of his own elevator as you, an outsider, pay for it?—A. Every man should be forced to put his grain through at the same cost. If it is a public elevator, they should all be treated alike, whereas in this instance, on a car of oats I pay my competitor $12 to do my business, and he may use that $12 to my detriment.

Q. (By Representative LORIMER.) If you had money enough invested in an elevator, your own money, you would save that $12, but would not that $12 be applied as the cost of running your grain through the elevator that you own?—A. If I owned an elevator, I could probably put that grain through there for $1.50 or $2 a car, where I pay him $12.

Q. (By Mr. C. J. HARRIS.) Do you count interest on investment, rent of land, and all that?—A. As I understand it, the proprietors of the transfer elevators on the eastern lines to which I referred, receive from the railroad companies $1.50 a car for the transfer of grain and make it very profitable. So when we are obliged to pay $12 through a public warehouse——

Q. Why should the rate be that?—A. It is fixed.

Q. By State authority?—A. I think by the State a maximum.

Q. (By Representative LORIMER.) The maximum rate is fixed, but is the specfiic rate fixed?—A. I think the rate is fixed by the warehouseman within the maximum.

Q. Is the rate higher or lower than it was prior to the passage of this bill you referred to?—A. I do not know which bill you refer to.

Q. The bill which I think you said was passed in 1896 or 1897 authorizing the elevator owners to purchase grain?—A. I think they are very nearly the same.

Q. You do not know whether up or down?—A. Just about the same; not much difference.

Q. Is that information obtainable?—A. Yes, readily.

Q. If you ship a load of grain to one of these elevators, is there any way in which you can have it placed in a bin in the elevator and have it remain there, sealing the bin, and know that you are getting the same article out that you put in?—A. In theory that is supposed to be granted to the public, but, as a matter of fact, you can not get it, and it seems almost impossible to get even general storage.

Q. Is there no provision in the law for that sort of thing in this State?—A. No; I think not; nothing that will force an elevator proprietor to give you storage.

Q. You referred to the panic of 1893 and stated that it was your opinion that these railroad discriminations were what brought about that panic. You remember that that panic affected every line of industry and almost every financial house in this country, and that the most of the shops in this country, or many of them, were closed, and many of them were getting a good deal less work after that panic than before. Did you mean to attribute all that depression in trade to the discriminations of the railroads?—A. It was my intention to convey the idea that low prices for farm products in this country for so many years had finally led up to the fact that the West was almost bankrupt.

Q. Were prices low for grain in 1893?—A. Yes. Corn sold in 1893, if I remember correctly, at 19½ cents on the Chicago market—best grade, or about 1893.

Q. How about 1892?—A. I would have to become posted on that. The records are easily obtainable. About that time I think you will find wheat sold at in the forties in the Chicago market.

Q. (By Professor JOHNSON). You remember in 1892 the prices for grain were high because of the heavy foreign demand.—A. It is probable that when the prices were high they had very little for sale. It was the constant depression previous to 1893 that I think led up to the fact that the people were unable to buy goods. When you depreciate the value of farm products, you have taken the nucleus of the welfare of the people away from them.

Q. (By Representative LORIMER). You think the discriminations of the railroads brought about that condition, and that condition brought about the panic?—A. Yes; that is my opinion.

Q. And all these other conditions had practically nothing to do with it in your opinion?—A. The others probably assisted after the ball started rolling, but I believe that all resulted from these conditions.

Q. You suggest that these people are able to pay a trifle more for grain than the average trader?—A. Yes; that is correct.

Q. That means that under these conditions the farmer or producer gets a trifle more from these people than from the other traders?—A. Yes; that is correct.

Q. You say the board of trade and the bucket shops operate to reduce the price?—A. No; I would not infer that the board of trade did.

Q. The bucket shops?—A. The existence of bucket shops.

Q. And the bear raiders?—A. The bear raiders, yes.

Q. Do you mean to say that the grain is cheaper after they get through with it than it was when purchased?—A. Yes; that is the idea I mean to convey.

Q. If the elevator men pay more for it than the others pay for it, and put it in the elevator, and the bears jump on it there in the bucket shop or board of trade, and their raiding it has the effect of reducing the price, I can go in and buy at that price and can have it delivered out to me and put it into flour; then I am able to sell my flour at a less rate than I could have sold it if I had purchased the grain at the time the elevator men purchased it and before the bear raider jumped on it. Is not that the natural deduction from your statement?—A. It depreciates the value of the crop.

Q. Then the consumer purchases it for less than the farmer gets for it?—A. You may stop to consider this also, that only a small proportion of the crops are marketed, that is, sent to market; and I think figures will show that probably not to exceed 3, 4, or 5 per cent of the crop is exported.

Q. Of the wheat crop?—A. I would say the corn crop. I think a larger proportion than that of the wheat crop is exported.

Q. The wheat crop is practically all sent to market and the corn largely fed out.—A. Yes; that is it. I would convey the idea that it is a fact that the conditions here do depreciate the price.

Q. When the bears get through with it they have broken down the price?—A. When the bears get through raiding it, encouraged by these conditions, it slumps the market; oftentimes before the crop is out of the ground; they will depreciate the value of the new crop long before it exists.

Q. (By Representative LORIMER.) Now, with reference to the bucket shops and the board of trade, is it your opinion that any considerable amount of the grain that is traded in by the commission houses which have membership on the board of trade is ever actually delivered to the purchaser?—A. If you will permit me to answer in my own way, in a general way I will try to cover that point. I look at the board of trade as an institution that was founded for the purpose of facilitating business. It is a gathering of buyers and sellers, shippers and receivers. and railroad men, with all conveniences for the handling of the grain trade. By virtue of the enormity of the product handled, it seems almost necessary to buy and sell grain for future delivery, and that custom has finally become so large that it is probably the largest speculative commodity in the world. I believe that within that institution there have grown up practices among individuals by which they have prostituted their occupations by becoming criminals; and I believe that strong efforts have been made and are being made and will be made to root out from legitimate trading all such firms and men. There has grown up within that board of trade also the existence of these combinations, not a part of the board in itself, but taking advantage of the institution to transact their business; something for which the board of trade is not responsible, and which the board of trade has spent a great deal of money to abate, both in court and in the usual way in trying to enforce its rules; but I will freely admit that I believe it is true that what you may term bucket shops do exist there; that is, men who never execute their orders on the market, men who should be punished criminally for not doing so. But that is something likely to creep into any institution, like you find plenty of sinners in church, although the simile may be somewhat strained.

Q. Is it not a fact that there are hundreds of thousands, yes, millions, of bushels of grain traded in in the pit on margin deposited with the commission houses with no intention of ever actually delivering out the grain by the person who sells to the person why buys?—A. You would have to ask the men who made the trade as to their intention to deliver the property. I am not here to defend any institution. I simply know when a commission man takes an order to buy and sell grain, and he executes it on the market, he does it with the intention of buying and selling, receiving and delivering the property.

Q. You have been connected with the board of trade for a good many years. Is it, in your opinion, generally understood that the great proportion of the trading done there by the commission houses on the board of trade is simply done on margin, with the intention of buying to-day at a low price and selling to-morrow at one, two or three points raise, for the profit out of the transaction and with no intention of taking the article? Generally, I say, not specifically.—A. There are millions of bushels of grain traded in, bought and sold, and in that volume there is no doubt a great deal intended to be delivered and, it may be, a great deal that is not, but I am not prepared to say what the percentage is or is not. Nearly all my business is conducted with the intention of receiving and delivering cash grain. I am in the cash grain business. There are some men who trade there who do not own any grain and sell it; who buy grain and do not want it.

Q. When this bear you talk about sells grain, outside of the elevator owner, has he grain to deliver or does he depend on the depreciation that he hopes to bring about to buy it in?—A. No doubt he intends to buy it in as low as possible, and uses his efforts to depress the market.

Q. There are deals made where they have not the commodity?—A. That same man that sells the property may intend to deliver it, but depress the price and never do so.

Q. You suggested that this condition encouraged bears to go into the market because other men own large quantities of grain, and that being so they must sell grain that they have not got.—A. The bear is the man who wants to see a lower price after he sells short.

Q. If he sells short, he is selling something he has not got?—A. Yes.

Q. The short seller is a fellow handling an article he has not got?—A. Yes: and he is encouraged by these conditions. When he sells short he enters into a contract that is legalized.

Q. Then, as a matter of fact, there are trades on the board of trade that are as much gambling as gambling in the bucket shops?—A. No; you can not consider that a gambling trade. He has a right to sell what he has not got if he intends to get it.

Q. How do you know the bucket-shop man does not intend to deliver it?—A. Because he does not make a contract on the market that he will buy or sell.

Q. Suppose he makes a written contract with you?—A. If he makes a written contract that he will buy or deliver certain property, and it is on the market, and he does it, it is legitimate trade.

Q. Suppose he does not call on the market, but buys it somewhere else—from the farmer?—A. If he buys the grain he is doing a legitimate piece of business.

Q. Are there such bucket shops?—A. I never heard of one, and I have been in the business seventeen years.

Q. You talk about the private-car business. Is it cheaper for the railroad company to own their own cars or to rent them at the rate you talk of, or do you know?—A. I think it is cheaper to own their own cars. I think it pays the man who owns the car 25 per cent to 50 per cent per annum on the value of the car.

Q. You would prohibit a railroad company that is not well enough off to purchase its own rolling stock from renting rolling stock to supply its trade?—A. Rent it of whom?

Q. Of anybody who has it to rent; private party.—A. I believe it is a bad practice. I would prohibit it; yes.

Q. If they can get the business and do not have the cars or money to buy them, you would prevent them from renting?—A. Yes. I believe it would be the establishment of a wrong principle.

Q. Are you testing the elevator bill, that was recently passed in the legislature, in the courts?—A. The case was passed upon in 1896 by Judge Tuley, and appealed to the supreme court of the State, and Judge Tuley's opinion was approved, but pending the decision of the supreme court of the State this law was passed at Springfield. As I understand the matter now, the case is up again before Judge Tuley to enforce his injunction against the public warehouseman being a grain dealer, the original suit brought in the circuit court having been in the nature of an injunction.

Q. The old suit?—A. Yes.

Q. There is no suit pending testing present legislation?—A. No. An effort was made at the last session of the legislature to have the bill repealed, but various manipulations prevented the bill passing in the Senate after it passed the House.

Q. Have you any recommendations on which legislation could be based to prevent bear trading on the board of trade and in bucket shops, as you suggest?—A. No; I do not believe it is a good thing to prevent it. I believe all you want in regard to grain speculation is that the man who buys the grain is on an equal footing with the man who sells it short. Then these men who have the grain bought will say, "You deliver it to me," and the grain will never be carried in Chicago if they have to pay full storage rates. But when a man can hold it up here without paying storage and use that as a club to force the man who buys it to sell it out, there is the evil. Legitimate conditions no longer exist. They are artificial conditions. The grain would be in the invisible supply in the country if it had to pay full rates, and the reason would not exist for these men to hammer the market. I object to hoarding at the centers. Let the grain go through the market on its course from the producer to consumer; then let the men who want to buy grain put their money in. The bucket shops would be an impossibility without the short seller.

Q. Would a Government report in September, say, stating that the foreign crop for this year would be higher than they anticipated in July by several hundred millions, have any effect on the price if there were no elevators?—A. Well, it is hard to tell. It would depend on other speculative features that happened to be in the market at the time the Government report came out. I, myself, object to any Government report. I think it is detrimental to business.

Q. Under the law prior to 1897, in your recollection, did a Government report ever have anything to do with the bulling or bearing the price of grain?—A. I presume it has been used that way.

Q. Before this elevator system came into effect?—A. That was so long ago I do not remember. That has been in effect ever since I have been in the market myself.

Q. (By Mr. C. J. Harris.) What would be the life of a freight car?—A. I am not prepared to state.

Q. Suppose it is only four years. The wear and tear is quite great necessarily. The use of a car from here to New York and back, you state, is 15 days?—A. More or less; not far from that.

Q. Would not that be about as cheap as the railroad company could furnish the car itself? Five-eighths of a cent a mile, according to testimony we have heard, is about what it costs the railroad to run its own cars; the wear and tear, interest on the money, etc.?—A. The secretary can easily figure that out. Consider a freight car, an ordinary box car, worth $400. It takes 15 days to make the round trip to New York. How many round trips could you make in one year and how many round trips could you make in four years on that basis?

Q. In the usual run of business, you would not expect that car to make over ten or twelve round trips in a year, would you? You know practically in your shipments cars lay at either end a considerable time, are delayed on the way, and are in the repair shop, and by this, that, and the other.—A. Assuming that it makes twelve trips a year, I think you will find it makes about 50 per cent on the investment, without figuring it.

Q. (By Mr. KENNEDY.) If the private car is an evil in commerce, is it not an evil that has been brought about by the refusal or neglect of the railroads to recognize the needs of commerce and build such cars?—A. That might be. How the conditions sprang into existence I am not able to state.

Q. Were not these cars built by those men who shipped perishable freight when the railroads had no facilities for them?—A. The ownership of private cars is not confined to products which are perishable.

Q. I am speaking of meats and fruits, largely.—A. I believe these all go on the eastern trips loaded with other products.

Q. Is it not your opinion that that is what brought about the system of private cars?—A. It might have been; quite likely. But it has finally developed into handling merchandise not perishable to a very great extent. I think it could be shown on investigation that even when railroads have cars of their own that they want to use in the handling of the product the men have become so powerful in a commercial way that they can insist on the railroad company handling their cars and paying tribute.

Q. You stated, I believe, the only remedy was Government ownership?—A. Yes.

Q. And that there could not be Government control or regulation. Do you believe that it would be impossible for the Government to regulate in this way: Say that the Interstate Commerce Commission should compel the railroad companies to make public their rates, and have power to adjust these rates, and have their decision enforced. Do you think, while you are waiting for Government ownership, that there might not be alleviations in that way?—A. Well, something might come out of it, but I have no confidence whatever in railroads maintaining rates. By the very nature of the competition of railroads, cuts will continue.

Q. If the rates were made public, and they would have to be under such a law, and the Interstate Commerce Commission had power to say whether the rates were just or not, then if they were not given to all without favor the Interstate Commerce Commission would know of it?—A. I do not believe there is any law that can be made that will control a railroad.

Q. (By Professor JOHNSON.) Do you think our conditions are similar to those in Great Britain, where the rates are very stable and, on the whole, very satisfactory, under Government regulation—private railroads?—A. I believe there is a condition on the other side that for years past has educated men there to respect law and the enforcement of it.

Q. A higher moral sense?—A. A higher moral sense, yes, and the fear of justice; but with the conditions that have grown up in our country in politics, and the general condition of business and commercialism, I do not believe anything short of absolute ownership of roads will ever rectify the evil.

Q. If we are beneath these other countries in public morals, are we going to be able to work a system of Government ownership without serious difficulty?—A. I believe with Government ownership we must get to a higher system of morals, to maintain civil service before we ever endeavor to own the railroad, and see it carried out and know that we can do it.

Q. (By Mr. KENNEDY.) You mean civil-service reform?—A. Put it into operation and see that we are able to carry it out. Continue the standard in civil service, and the right to participate in political affairs. I believe it is every man's duty to participate in politics. I think a man should have the right to vote and still be employed on the railroad. I believe the system of civil service would have to be so rigid that he would perform his duties in a satisfactory manner.

Q. (By Representative LORIMER.) Do you believe Government ownership would reduce freight rates?—A. Yes; just about one-half.

Q. Have you any theory under which you think that would be done?—A. My reading in past years has led me to suppose that honestly conducted railroads, owned by the people, would give a man a round trip from here to San Francisco for about $25 or $30 in a first-class vehicle. Of course, it is impossible to tell just what the rate would be in case of Government ownership, considering the proper operation of the roads and reasonable salaries for all services rendered.

Q. (By Mr. C. J. HARRIS.) Did you ever know of any instance of the Government doing anything, running any line of business, that did not cost, perhaps, double what a private individual could do it for?—A. If the United States Post-office did not pay such heavy tribute to these railroads beyond what the actual service costs I believe there would be no private institution in the world conducted on a cheaper basis—from the knowledge that I have of what the Post-

Office Department is, although I may be greatly mistaken in that. I know in the town in which I live the people own their own waterworks and will own the gas works and I am led to believe we will get cheaper water and cheaper gas than is furnished almost anywhere else.

Q. While it is hardly material to our question, you will count the interest on the plant and all charges?—A. I see no reason why the people should not operate a thing just as cheap as any individual could operate it.

Q. (By Representative LORIMER.) The people contribute the money to the waterworks and expect no dividends; so you figure just the cost of maintenance and operation without the interest that that amount of money ought to bear?— A. When you come to compare that with railroad matters, railroad prices are a calamity compared to it.

Q. (By Mr. C. J. HARRIS.) Returning to the elevator subject, I want to ask you one question: The elevator men, whoever they may be, railroads or buyers of grain—would there be any object in their paying the farmer less for the grain than it costs him to produce it? In other words, would there be any particular object in their grinding the farmer down and getting wheat at a low price of the producer?—A. Yes; because they are carriers of grain for storage. The longer they can carry it here the more the storage. Now, it is a great deal more to his profit to carry wheat worth 50 cents than $1, because it is simply an investment. The cheaper the product the less his insurance and interest. Now, the railroad man, in my opinion, divides the profit these warehousemen make. Whether this is correct or not, they do not seem to be willing to change the system.

Q. If the elevator man controls the buying price in Nebraska, and the selling price at the other end, what difference does it make to him if he pays 75 cents a bushel in Nebraska for his wheat? He would simply charge so much more at the other end, if he regulates both ends of it.—A. He may carry it here a year, or sometimes two years, simply for storage. He does not intend to let go of that grain until he absolutely has to.

Q. If he regulates the price at each end, he can put a correspondingly high price at the other end to cover all that insurance and other charges.—A. He does when he lets it go. Sometimes they sort out this wheat and refuse to sell to Eastern buyers, except at high premiums, sometimes 15 cents a bushel, as the evidence before Judge Tuley shows. That existed sometimes in the same grades.

Q. (By Mr. KENNEDY.) Do you know anything about barley?—A. Not much.

Q. Do you know whether it is true that Mr. Armour controls or monopolizes the barley trade of the United States, and that those who want barley, for milling purposes even, have to go to him ts buy it?—A. I think he is a very important factor in the market, but I would not want to make the statement that Mr. Armour controls it, because I do not know. But I will say this, that I believe Mr. Armour is the backbone of this entire railroad combination.

Q. Do you know him personally?—A. I know his methods. I believe Mr. Armour is the man who has concocted this public warehouse scheme with the railroads, and is such a large handler of freight that he can dictate his rate of freight to any railroad in or out of Chicago, whatever it may be. That is my opinion of Mr. Armour, in brief.

Q. I have been informed that he controls the barley product of the United States absolutely; that used for domestic purposes, and for export, and that those brewers of beer who use barley malt in the manufacture of beer have to go to him for it, or to his agents. Can you suggest anybody who could give the commission information on that point?—A. I can not think of a man that would dare to state it if he knew, but I may, if I think it over. There seems to be a particular indifference to making any statements regarding that outfit, with all the unsavory record against that concern in years past.

Q. (By Representative LORIMER.) Do you know whether or not barley is held in elevators other than those owned by Armour?—A. Oh, yes; no doubt of that.

Q. (By Representative OTJEN.) In speaking of public warehouses relating to grain, you mean elevators?—A. Yes. I believe it would not be a bad plan, as a public investment, and for the convenience of the people in handling this crop, and that it would result in millions of dollars of good to the producers, if the United States Government would operate public grain warehouses.

Q. Would not a great many of these conditions relating to elevators would have to be directly under the control of the State—the State of Illinois, for instance?— A. There is so much interstate business that must necessarily go through these elevators that I do not see how it could ever be completely controlled by the State. It might to a certain extent.

Q. Could there not be a State law passed requiring all public elevator men not to engage in the buying of grain?—A. We tried to defeat that measure when they went to Springfield. They got the State legislature to pass it, and, in my opinion, that was bought with a considerable sum of money; but of course it is a law just the same.

Q. Has there been any other effort, so far as the State is concerned, to try to regulate these difficulties by having proper legislation passed?—A. I think not, except the usual laws that have existed for years on the statute books. It was a novelty previous to 1887 to see these low prices of grain: but these railroads, as it were, practically entered the grain business themselves—because it amounts to that—and since they have established these conditions and found out that in the speculative feature of it they could pile up enormous profits in addition to the freight on the property, the whole situation changed and came around as it is to-day.

Q. (By Mr. KENNEDY.) Do you know whether the Terminal Belt Railroad imposes excessive, unreasonable burdens on commerce that flows through Chicago from the West?—A. You refer to the "inner belt?"

Q. Yes.—A. I have never given that particular attention. I understand their usual charges for shipping grain around is about $3 a car.

Q. Do they not charge what they please because they are not subject to the interstate-commerce law?—A. I presume they do. I do not see where there is anything to prevent them charging what they please.

Q. Would it not be to the interest of the business men of Chicago, or Chicago, to have the State legislature compel them to charge only reasonable sums for transferring the cars from one line to another?—A. I think it would. I think $3 is too much to charge for switching anywhere in this city on a shipment from the West.

Q. (By Professor JOHNSON.) You said Congress could not interfere with these switching charges. Has not that case arisen before the Interstate Commerce Commission and been passed upon by them in the case of a Texas shipment?—A. I did not intend to be quoted as saying that the Government could not interfere.

Q. As a matter of fact, you know it does come under the interstate-commerce law as interstate shipments, and they do come before the commission?—A. I think on a shipment emanating from outside of the State of Illinois, and subject to belt switching, the Interstate Commerce Commission might have some authority.

Q. (By Mr. KENNEDY.) Their claim is the Interstate Commerce Commission has no authority because it is not an interstate road, is it not?—A. That would be a question of law I would not feel capable of deciding.

Q. (By Professor JOHNSON.) I want to know whether you make great use of the telegraphic service in your business?—A. Yes.

Q. Have you any statement to make in regard to that?—A. Yes; I believe it is a gigantic crime for a man to have a right to a private wire, just as much as for a man to own a private freight car or get a private rate. They all come in under the same head. I believe it is a crime under the United States law for the Western Union Telegraph Company to give quotations to bucket shops, those quotations being the means of fleecing the unsuspecting throughout the country.

Q. You mean to say when the telegraph company gives a private wire it does something against public policy?—A. Yes.

Q. You would be in favor of the Post-Office taking hold of the telegraphic system?—A. I would, most decidedly. I believe one of the greatest enemies of the welfare of the country rests in the telegraph companies.

Q. (By Representative OTJEN.) Do you not see any danger in turning over these vast interests to the Government and having them regulated by the Government alone?—A. Yes, I do.

Q. Do you know about how many employees are connected with the railroads of the United States, for instance?—A. In the hundreds of thousands; I am not posted exactly.

Q. About 900,000 was given to us here yesterday.—A. I do not believe Government ownership will ever make the conditions much worse than they exist to-day in commercial matters. The railroads, unquestionably, are the very foundation stones of combinations that are to-day wrecking business enterprises. Special rates are the food that they live upon, and without them they could not exist. I have been constantly in the railroad business for 17 years as regards the handling of freight and I have served on various committees, in which we have had quite heavy questions involved in regard to the regulation of rates, etc.

Q. You think even if the Interstate Commerce Commission, for instance, had full authority, by enlarging the present law so that they could revise rates and fix them, that that would not fully meet these difficulties?—A. No; because you could never prevent a man from getting a special rate.

Q. Could not the law go still further and make it a crime for the officials to give a special rate?—A. You could not cause their arrest. If you were willing to take circumstantial evidence—and we hang men on circumstantial evidence—it can be produced by the barrels. If that could be used to secure conviction, I would be willing to fall in with your proposition, but you must get the system down to the place where it would be impossible for a man to get a special rate, and I believe that is impossible.

Q. Could not that be done by giving the commission authority to investigate the transactions of railroads, and also the individuals who do business with railroads?—A. You might catch a man every 5 years, and would be lucky if you did. It is almost impossible, on a system of currency rebate, and various other means they would soon become familiar with, to bring them to justice.

Q. (By Mr. KENNEDY.) Your fear of what might happen if the railroads were placed under Government control is, I think, a reflection on the 840,000 workers in transportation in this country. Do you believe they would be any more controlled in their political convictions if the railroads were under Government control than they can be to-day; or do you think they can be controlled?—A. I would make it a crime for any influence to be used over an employee of the Government under Government ownership. We must come to the higher sense of obligation, and when the people are able to own the railroads, they will be able to see that they are properly owned.

Q. Do you think there is any foundation for the fear that the workers in transportation would belong to any one political party, or could be controlled by any one political party, in case the roads were owned by the Government?—A. Not when the people were educated up to the owning of the railroads.

Q. You know the railroad men are pretty generally educated, as far as working-men go?—A. Yes.

Q. (By Representative LORIMER.) Have you any further suggestions to make?—A. I think not.

(Testimony closed.)

CHICAGO, ILL., *November 17, 1899.*

TESTIMONY OF MR. CHARLES COUNSELMAN,

Grain and stock merchant, Chicago.

The subcommission on transportation being in session in Chicago, November 17, 1899, Representative Lorimer presiding, Mr. Charles Counselman was sworn as a witness, and testified as follows:

Q. (By Representative LORIMER.) Will you please state your name?—A. Charles Counselman.

Q. And your business?—A. I am in the grain, elevator, and stock business, in Chicago.

Q. We are informed, rather in an indirect way, that there is a combination of elevator owners in Chicago who are running their business and their elevators to the detriment of the community generally. We had a gentleman before the commission yesterday who made a statement covering the side which is more opposed to elevators, and if you will, we would like to have you state to the commission in your own way the actual condition.—A. I will be very glad to. I want to state, first, that there is no combination of any kind or nature among the elevators of Chicago, and never has been, in any manner, shape, or form. I will begin at the beginning. Some years ago the railroads had into Chicago a local rate from Western points, and a local rate out from Chicago to various Eastern points. Then these commission merchants who now claim that we have done them some injury used to receive the grain from the West on a commission largely, out of which they got probably 1 cent a bushel commission, and the grain then flowed into the elevators in the natural or normal way, so that the elevator owners at that time did not feel the necessity of being purchasers of grain in the West.

Q. (By Professor JOHNSON.) Who were the owners of the elevators at that time?—A. In our case there were the Rock Island, with which I am more intimately connected than any other; Flint, O'Dell & Co; Wheeler—I forget the old gentleman's first name—but the Wheeler family were the owners of the Northwestern properties; and the Illinois Central was controlled by Buckingham & Co.

Q. The elevators were not owned by the railroads?—A. Some of them were and some were not. The Wheelers sold out to other parties, and Flint, O'Dell & Co. sold out to me. I will relate our conversation about the matter, of which I know specifically, and I have been informed that the others had the same views controlling their actions. They concluded to sell their properties because they did not want to enter into the purchase of grain. It was a detail they did not care to enter into. They were old men and were willing to retire; so the elevators were sold out, as the case happened to be, and we were up against this proposition. The railroads then introduced a rate, a through rate from a Western point to an Eastern point, less than the sum of the locals. I want you to have these points well in your mind, because right here is the pivot to this whole matter. For instance, to illustrate clearly, a local rate from Omaha, if you choose, to Chicago, of 20 cents, and from Chicago to an Eastern point, 20 cents, the two locals making 40 cents. The railroads would then say to a party, If you throughbill that grain from Omaha to this Eastern point we will give you a rate of 38 cents, if you choose. I do not pretend to say that that was the exact figure, but to illustrate the point. So the result of that was that the Eastern buyer could come into our Western country and buy grain for Baltimore, or Philadelphia, or Newport News and pay more money for it at the Western point than we could afford to pay to bring it into Chicago on the local rate and put it out on the local rate. I had invested about $1,000,000 in elevator property. I built the South Chicago plants, which cost over $750,000, and therefore I said to myself, These railroads, by this proposition, have destroyed the earning value of my property at least 33⅓ per cent. What have I got to do? I must buy this grain and do whatever I can to fight this competition. Every other elevator man found himself in that position. Grain came in on our tracks, and comes to-day on our tracks, by the thousands of carloads that never sees an elevator, never goes near an elevator, but is sold as through-billed grain, bearing this lower rate, and that kind of grain on 'change to-day brings 1 cent to 1¼ cents, and as high as 2 cents more than the grain in here on a local billing than we can afford to pay. So, instead of the railroads helping us any, I think that they, by their through rates, have done more to destroy the value of our property than all other agencies combined. So we found that Minneapolis, with their elevator concerns, were coming down into the State of Iowa, in Northern Iowa, where I do business, and where the Northwestern run their tracks, and paying more for the grain, taking it to Minneapolis, and going out by Washburn and also Duluth, and going out by lake, and selling this grain in New England all the way from 1 cent to 1¼ cents a bushel less than we could afford to sell it here in Chicago. At St. Louis we found the Burlington road, running up into Keokuk, Iowa, was bidding in territory where I had to compete on freights to bring the grain to Chicago, taking it to St. Louis and then out by way of Newport News on this lower through rate.

So we were forced to buy grain, not only to protect the earning power of our own property, but also to keep Chicago in the front as a grain market. Now, these gentlemen—of course, their business was hurt then; there is no doubt about that; but we were no more responsible for that than you are, and are not to-day.

If we had these railroads back on the local proposition there would be no necessity for us elevator men to buy grain in the country to any great extent. It would be reduced to a minimum. It would only be in certain localities and not many places where we would have to buy as a competitive measure for Chicago. So, if these gentlemen will only use their efforts and their intelligence to help correct this proposition, which I consider the basis of all this trouble between us—it is a local affair, however—there would be no trouble between us of any nature or kind. Now, this is about a fair statement of the basic trouble.

Q. In connection with the point you have just made, I would like to ask whether it is not a fact that most of the grain from West to Chicago now starts toward Chicago on a through billing?—A. Yes.

Q. And you simply pay your proportion of the through billing?—A. No, we take that billing; and in my case I sell this grain in Europe; from the farmer I buy it. I have elevators all over the country and buy grain from the farmers, and sell it to Europe. That grain is billed by lake and rail billing, and so on 'change that is the chief way the business is done, except that which comes in locally. However, when property is billed that way they give the owner three rights. They can ship it out as lake and rail, retaining the rate; they can change it to an all-rail rate if it goes by cars, instead of by water; and they can change it to a local and stop it here, provided they pay the local rate. Everybody has that right.

Q. As a result of that practice do you get less than the local rate?—A. No, not when we stop it here. When we ship it to Europe we have the benefit of the rate, like everybody else. That is not confined to anybody. It is a public proposition by published tariffs.

Q. (By Mr. Conger.) If I understand correctly, that grain coming from the

West, bound into Chicago on a local rate, can be changed to a through rate?—A. No; I say that coming through from a Western point on a through rate it can be changed to a local.

Q. Have you an idea at all definite as to the portion of grain coming into Chicago that comes in on a through rate?—A. I could not tell you that with any accuracy, but it is pretty large, because naturally people can get more money for it because they get this low rate.

Q. So you think the greater proportion?—A. Yes. A very much larger proportion.

Q. (By Professor JOHNSON.) Do all local points west of Chicago enjoy the same advantage for this through shipping?—A. I think they do. Anybody can ship on the through export rate.

Q. How do you explain this fact, that the rates from Iowa are sometimes larger than they are from the State beyond, Nebraska?—A. I judge it is because they have less competition. That would be my judgment without knowing definitely.

Q, (By Mr. C. J. HARRIS.) You control the elevators along one line of road, we will say. Does that give the farmers a competitive market in which to sell their produce?—A. Yes. In the first place, I don't control them. That is the first point. I will tell you how that is. I build elevators through the State of Iowa and Kansas that cost me $140,000. There is no point where I have an elevator but what there are at least one or two other independent elevator proprietors buying grain. The railroads follow that idea. They will not permit anybody to have the only elevator at a point. They insist upon at least two, which is correct.

Q. What regulates the price of wheat?—A. That is a pretty hard question, of course. I was going to say to you that finally that is the agency that regulates what we can pay for the wheat. Every now and then, of course, speculation pays a higher price than we can for export. Speculation is to-day paying a higher price for wheat on the Chicago Board of Trade than we can export grain for. We can not sell it within 3 cents a bushel of what they are paying for wheat, and corn 1¼ cents. Every once in a while the people make up their minds the price is cheap, and they buy it all out of the shipping line and we can not ship it for a while. Of course that is regulated a good deal by the law of supply and demand.

Q. While these local causes might maintain prices for 2 or 3 months, in the end, sometime or other, the export price must regulate that?—A. Yes; altogether our surplus makes the price.

Q. Then, of course, what you pay the farmer at one end, plus the freight abroad, with a fair percentage for handling are the component parts?—A. Yes; that is it exactly.

Q. Do you think if these elevators did not buy wheat that the price to the farmer would be higher than it is now?—A. Very much less.

Q. We had testimony something to that effect yesterday from another source.— A. Very much less. If a man looks at it in a reasonable way, with a real sincere desire to get at the facts, he will see it. The surplus is in my judgment the lever upon which the whole crop is handled. Now, just suppose for instance that we could wipe out every central market where speculation is carried on, where men buy property for future delivery, and all this vast production of grain here was absolutely on the market to the consumer. Now, will you tell me what that consumer would pay? He would pay for it exactly as small a price as he could, and the very element of this great purchasing power in that speculation would be out of the way, and he would be conscious of the fact that he was the only buyer. I don't think you can see how low these prices would be. Look at it to-day. We are carrying millions of bushels of wheat, not only in Chicago but in other elevator centers. Speculation is carrying it. We can not sell it to-day. We are carrying that wheat by the agency of speculation until consumption overtakes it and demands it, and then it goes to consuming districts.

Q. (By Professor JOHNSON.) Does consumption have the price-fixing power or do you?—A. Consumption has to have the wheat. Suppose we try to fix it and carry all the wheat in this country. We had an illustration of this not long ago. We occupy simply the position of holding the great surplus of this country in various stages of speculative conditions until consumption requires it, and then it is sold. To-day Argentina is supplying all Europe with wheat. We can not meet their prices and we can not sell till they get through. They have no system there as we have. They have no elevators there to hold the grain and no speculative market on which elevators could hold it. The elevators could not hold it without this great market to carry it. Then, as soon as it is harvested, it is put on a vessel and sold for what it will bring, and they to-day are receiving their price for wheat because

America is held up by speculation, and is not a competitor. If our wheat in this county was put on the basis of Argentine wheat to-day and each competing for a consuming buyer, God knows what the price of wheat would be.

Q. (By Mr. KENNEDY.) Is there any speculation in Liverpool, in the wheat of Argentina and other countries, by which the price is held up, as you say it is?—A. Very little. There is none in London, which is, of course, the very great market—none in Europe. In Liverpool there is a little, but, of course, it is a very small proportion.

Q. (By Mr. CONGER.) When you say we can not compete with Argentina in Europe, do you mean that we are not now exporting?—A. That is what I mean to a very great extent.

There are some grades of wheat, like the No. 1 hard of Duluth, which is an extra fine wheat. There is more or less of that wheat going all the time. They take it because they mix it with the lower grades of Russian wheats.

Q. Does it bring a higher price?—A. Yes.

Q. Than other grades?—A. They mix that with the lower grades, so the miller has a mixed grade.

Q. You stated a few moments ago that speculation had raised the price of wheat 2 or 3 cents a bushel above the exporting point?—A. Yes.

Q. Is it in practice above the export price or only in theory? In other words, has it held up the exportation of grain?—A. It has stopped it for a while. It is only temporary, however. We generally find this condition of things along this time of year. After the first of January the Argentine shipments usually cease, or, at least, from December they are of such small proportions that they do not cut much figure. Then, the consumption, of course, of Europe is so large that they have to take Amercan wheat.

Q. In the operation of these elevators, do you store grain for the public, or for private buyers?—A. Yes; whenever they want it. We give them a special bin if they want. That is the State law. We operate here under a statute of the State of Illinois, which requires, at the request of anybody who wants to store grain in a public warehouse; that we shall furnish them special bins for their wheat or any other kind of grain.

Q. What is the practice; in other words, are these requests made frequently?—A. No; and I will tell you why. All these arguments and statements you have heard from people are old stock arguments that are put on the shelf and labeled and taken down on occasions like this. There is nothing in them. Let me show you how the grain comes to Chicago and what becomes of it. These very gentlemen who complain so loudly about these matters bring this grain to Chicago. They will have a little sample of each carload in a bag. It is brought up on 'change. It is brought to me as an elevator man, and to other elevator men. It is shown to a miller, it is shown to a shipper, it is shown to everybody, and the object of these men is to sell it to the man who will pay them the most money. If an elevator man will pay the most money he gets the grain, and if he does not pay the most money he does not get the grain. When these men sell me grain, for instance, it goes to the warehouse; it is weighed, and they present a bill with their weights and get their money. Why don't they put it in store? Because they have to accumulate 5,000 bushels before they can sell it in the option or speculative market. In doing that they have to pay storage on some of the grain, they lose the interest on their money, and they lose the insurance on the property. They save these things, and therefore the invariable rule is that the grain is sold on track, and not in the elevator. The weights are ascertained by the elevator, and they have no further interest in the property. That is the reason they will tell you why they do not own grain in the warehouse. There is nothing to prevent them from owning grain in the warehouse, but they don't want it; it costs them money.

Q. (By Professor JOHNSON.) These men say they have to pay three-fourths of a cent per bushel storage.—A. That includes the first 10 days and the receipt or delivery of the property on board cars or vessels.

Q. And they say that the men who own the elevators escape nearly all of that cost, and for that reason they are unable to compete with you. Is that true?—A. There is something in that. In other words, it is like stating that a man who owns property and who gets remuneration by his storage rates shall not have it because some other fellow is not able to own one. There is no monopoly about this elevator business. Anybody can go into it. It is very common everywhere.

Q. (By Mr. C. J. HARRIS.) Does the State regulate it?—A. It does under statute. Anyone can erect one provided he has the money to pay for it and the money afterwards to run the business.

Q. Does the State regulate anything but the price?—A. They regulate the charges; they give the privilege of charging 1¼ cents, including the delivery on cars or vessels. However, we do not charge the 1¼ cents which the statute gives us the right to do, but do it at three-fourths, the cheapest rate in the United States.

Q. (By Professor JOHNSON.) In your opinion is that a low rate?—A. It is a very low rate, inclusive of the storage, and we could not do business at that rate and make any money unless we did a considerable volume of it.

Q. (By Mr. C. J. HARRIS.) Are there loading and unloading charges besides?—A. No; nothing on earth except that. It is the cheapest rate in the United States. Minneapolis and Duluth and New York and Boston charge 1¼ cents per bushel for the same service.

Q. (By Mr. KENNEDY.) You say you do a large volume of it? Did you not say that they do not put their grain in the elevator?—A. No; they do not pay any of these charges.

Q. It is your own grain?—A. Certainly. I buy this grain, or any other man buys it, and he owns it. These men do not own any of this property, and never did.

Q. (By Representative LORIMER.) Do you mean that we shall get this impression, that unless you did a large volume of business on your own account you could not afford to do other people's business at three-quarters?—A. That is exactly what I mean to impress upon you. I do not think our elevators would be worth 25 cents on the dollar unless we did this. We can not help it. We have got to do business, and if we can not do it as public warehousemen we will do it as individuals. Every farmer and dealer in the country nowadays receives on his desk every morning card bids from a score of sources for his wheat on the track. These gentlemen hold us responsible, because these men do not want to continue to pay them a commission for selling the grain here.

Q. (By Mr. CONGER.) You have stated that anybody could go into this business?—A. Anybody can; yes.

Q. Is that strictly true? Isn't it true that you have an exclusive contract with the Rock Island, for instance?—A. No; I beg your pardon. I own and have paid for, with my own money, the elevator capacity on the Rock Island railroad for four million and a half bushels of grain. They do not own these elevators; they only own some old elevators uptown here that are used for surplus, and that is all. I do my own busines, 90-odd per cent of it. at South Chicago, on my own property that I have paid for.

Q. Have you a contract with them—that is to say, one that would prevent them from allowing some one else to build an elevator on their line of road?—A. No; not in any manner, shape, or form; never had such a contract.

Q. One would naturally conclude that if this elevator business was so extremely profitable others would want to go into the business.—A. Yes; these gentlemen make some curious statements here. Four years ago they brought this whole matter up. This is an old question here. We turned our contracts over to the Interstate Commerce Commission and said, "Look at them, and if there is anything wrong about them let us know." They said there was nothing wrong about them at all.

Q. I think I have heard it argued that the way the elevators are operated in Chicago it was to the interest of you gentlemen who owned them and operated them to keep the price of wheat down; in other words, that because of the necessarily greater premium that you would have to pay on insurance when the price was high that you could make more money when the price was low.—A. Well, that is really so ridiculous that it is hardly worth answering. We do not care anything more about the price of wheat than if we were not on the earth. I am a warehouseman. I am not a speculator. I do not speculate in grain. I buy it, bring it to Chicago, and sell it on this market, or in the Eastern market, or in Europe, or wherever I think I can get the best price. If speculation is paying a better price here to-day then I sell them the property.

Q. When you say you do not speculate, you mean in options, do you not?—A. No, I mean that literally. I have told you my method of doing business. I have a central station at Des Moines, and from every one of these little elevators in the country, every night, there is reported by telegraph the amount of various kinds of grain that I have bought and the average prices. That grain is sold at once, either for shipment East or to Europe, or in this market in Chicago. I do not hold it more than one hour after the Board of Trade opens. I am not a speculator.

Q. (By Professor JOHNSON.) You do not keep the grain in storage?—A. I do, awaiting shipment only. Some I do and some I do not. I am delivering that grain now. We hold very little in our elevators, but that is sold or expected to be sold very shortly.

Q. Do you think there is anything in the elevator business here that tends to keep a large volume of grain constantly stored here in Chicago?—A. That depends altogether upon the shipping demand.

Q. Just to bear the market?—A. I don't know anything about that. We are neither bulls nor bears. We want grain here to trade in. This market requires a large amount of grain. If they did not have it they would have a corner every month and run it up to $4 per bushel because they could not get the grain in.

Q. (By Mr. CONGER.) In the Northwest, that is, west of Minneapolis and St. Paul, I have understood that there were two or three elevator companies operating on the same line of road. It has been charged that those elevator men, or, at least, the representatives of them, would always pay the same price for grain. In other words, there was really no competition.—A. I don't know about that.

Q. You have just testified that on your line of road, at every country town where you had an elevator, there is always another elevator.—A. Always, yes.

Q. Is there any arrangement between your representative in that town and the representative of the other elevator by which you pay the same price for grain?—A. Not the slightest in the world; never has been.

Q. (By Mr. C. J. HARRIS.) You say the farmer receives quotations of prices from 15 or 20 different people every day?—A. Yes.

Q. He does not have to put his grain in the elevator; he can load it right on the cars?—A. Yes, and the railroads will furnish the cars.

Q. Those cars need not necessarily go through the elevator here, but can be sold on the track?—A. Yes, nine-tenths of them are.

Q. Did I understand you to say while yours is a public elevator the general public does not store in it?—A. No, hardly at all.

Q. Hardly at all?—A. They sell their grain on the track and get the money.

Q. (By Mr. CONGER.) Just a word further on the prices you pay for grain. It is generally a fact, is it not, that two buyers in the same town, representing different concerns—say yourself and someone else—do pay the same price for grain?—A. I don't know. Of course, it could be possible that they would make an arrangement of that sort, but my experience is that in some places it is not. For instance, I know of one place I had in my mind in Iowa that they have a competing road that is near by. They go to this road or that. These roads are not very far apart. They were paying 2 cents a bushel for corn at one point more than I could pay, and ferreting it down I discovered that the Glucose Refining Company of Chicago is buying the corn.

Q. You refer to corn now instead of wheat?—A. Yes. Wheat is a thing that you can not regulate the price of in that way, for the reason that wheat varies in quality. You as one buyer might think that the wheat is worth so much money and I might say it is not worth within 3 cents a bushel of what Mr. Conger is paying for it.

Q. (By Mr. C. J. HARRIS.) What governs the farmer ships a carload in here, and the car is on the track?—A. Do you mean its value?

Q. No, the grade of wheat?—A. Everything is inspected by the State inspector. Every carload that comes into an elevator or goes out on the track. Everything is inspected by the State of Illinois, in and out.

Q. (By Professor JOHNSON.) This statement is made in the complaint, that four men who buy on the Board of Trade meet daily at 1.15 o'clock or thereabouts and decide what price shall be paid for grain along the Northwestern, and that when that price is determined, because of your transportation facilities, through your connection with the Northwestern system, it is practically impossible for any other man to buy grain in competition with you.—A. I am rather surprised that they should make that statement, because when I tell you about it, it will be one of the worst arguments they could adduce. That is true. We do get together. Why? Because of what I told you, the competition on every point. We hire a man, and pay him a good salary, to keep posted as to what parties at other competitive points for our grain are paying, and we are determined to pay the farmer as much for grain as any city that takes it from us. That is exactly true, but the motive they do not arrive at. We are fighting for business here, and we will continue to fight.

Q. (By Mr. CONGER.) In other words, you are fighting for the Chicago market?—A. Yes, the railroads making these through rates hurt us here, and we are going to fight it in every conceivable way.

Q. (By Professor JOHNSON.) Is it true or not that you on the Northwestern system and Mr. Armour on the St. Paul system have an advantage in the shipments which other men do not possess?—A. Do you mean in the matter of shipments?

Q. So that you both pay the same price; that you make the same offer to the farmer. In other words, that you can both sell at the same price on the market, but that you can secure all the grain, practically, by paying a higher price than others can afford to pay, by reason of your transportation advantages?—A. No; we have no advantage of the transportation.

Q. Please explain; that charge is made.—A. I thought I had explained that. I don't think there is a man in Chicago who buys grain merely for the Chicago market who can compete with me, and I will tell you why. I buy this grain, as I have told you, from the farmer, and I take this export rate and I will sell that grain in any part of Europe where I can get the most money for it, and unless they are able and equipped to do that business they can not compete with me.

Q. Even though they pay exactly the same amount?—A. It don't make any difference, and you can not get legislation to control it. It is the old doctrine of socialism that wants to make the Government do everything and bar individual effort.

Q. (By Mr. Conger.) Can you tell us what the export rate is on grain to the shipper?—A. I don't know what it is just now. They raised the rates a little the 1st of the month. What the exact rate is to-day, I do not know.

Q. Is it less than the local rates to the shippers?—A. Yes, it is less.

Q. (By Mr. C. J. Harris.) What is to prevent these gentlemen who were here yesterday from sending out their quotations to various towns along these roads, whatever they are willing to pay, and having that wheat shipped in here on the track and then selling it to go on?—A. Nothing on earth. They can do that all the time.

Q. Does not that give a perfectly legitimate market to the farmer and to these other gentlemen?—A. Yes; it does. The farmer is getting the benefit of all this competition.

Q. (By Professor Johnson.) They say that you have an advantage over them in this three-quarters of a cent storage, and which is your regular price, and that you can grade wheat so as make money that they can not make?—A. That is exactly it. In other words, I am better equipped in my business than they are, and you can not make it otherwise. Now, you can not make a man who has no money as able to do business as a man who has the money.

Q. (By Representative Lorimer.) A man of energy and ability?—A. No; and a man of equal ability can not do it.

Q. (By Mr. C. J. Harris.) Unless he has the machinery?—A. Unless he has the machinery.

Q. (By Professor Johnson.) They say if they could prevent the man who owns the elevator from buying grain that everybody would be practically on the same footing.—A. I will answer that as I told you in the first instance. I want to be perfectly fair in my statement of this question and all others. If we had the local rates over the roads into Chicago, there would be no great necessity for the elevator men to buy grain. Now, if these gentlemen will address their intelligence to something of that character, they will help themselves in a material way, but you can not correct it while this thing exists. They occupy a sort of negative position in life. Everything is wrong, and nothing is right.

Q. Is it not a matter of the regulation of railroad rates?—A. It is a matter of regulation of railroad rates, if you want to eliminate the elevator man as a buyer of grain. But I think the farmer would like to have some session on that when you try to cut out from him the competition of any buyer. He don't care whether it is an elevator man or a hodcarrier who buys his grain. He wants buyers of grain on his track, and as many as he can get.

Q. (By Mr. Conger.) Would it be feasible, in your judgment, for these elevators to be owned by the railroads and by them opened to the public generally for the storage of grain; in other words, so that you and everyone else would be on an equal footing?—A. No; and I will tell you why. In the first place, the railroads do not want to go into the grain business. Their charters are against it. They are not in the grain business. In the second place, if that were the case, the elevator men of the country would be in the position that they would not have control of the speculative markets. It is pretty hard to take away individual effort in any proposition.

Q. I doubt if you get my idea. The railroad now furnishes the car that the grain is shipped in from the initial point to Chicago, or to any other destination. Now, it has been suggested that in the exercise of its functions as a transportation agent the railroad should own and operate the elevators here.—A. Yes.

Q. Not in the way of being a grain buyer, but simply in a smaller way, as they use the cars.—A. Yes.

Q. And place it at the disposition of the public.—A. Now, what would that amount to? Would the railroad amount to anything under that proposition? I own my own elevator. I buy my grain. I ask no odds of the railroad. They charge there for doing this business in their elevator. They would have to charge, would they not?

Q. They would have to make a charge.—A. All right. I buy my grain and sell it to the man who bids the most money in every part of the world. What care I about the railroad elevator. How can they compete against me there? They can not do it.

Q. Formerly there were public elevators in Chicago, were there not?—A. Yes; there are to-day.

Q. Are there any to-day?—A. Yes; any quantity of them.

Q. Do you think the proportion of public elevators, as compard with private elevators, is as large as it was two or three years ago?—A. Yes; larger now; and right on that point I suppose these gentlemen try to make you think that we want more public elevators. On the contrary, they are begging us, "For God's sake, why do you have so many public elevators here? We want to have less property here, so that we can bull and bear the market and speculate on it." And so I do not do much business in my public elevator. They raised such a howl about it that I do not want to be a public warehouseman, if it is going to interfere with my business. I am a grain merchant. I have my private warehouses where I put my grain and sell it to anyone who wants to buy it. I do not want to be a public warehouseman. There is nothing particular in it if it is going to be an obstacle in the way of my prices. It is merely incidental to the business for the accommodation of people who want to trade speculatively and have receipts that they can deliver on the market here. That is the only function of a public elevator. That is all a public elevator means. These receipts are delivered on the speculative market by indorsement, and they go from one man to another. They use our elevators for their convenience, for which we charge them this lower rate.

Q. Your testimony, then, is to the effect that there exist in Chicago plenty of public elevators for the accommodation of these gentlemen?—A. Yes; to any extent. I can nearly approximate them in my mind. I think Armour has about 10,000,000. We have 4,800,000. The Northwestern system has, I think, about 3,000,000. There are on the Alton about 5,000,000. At South Chicago, independently of my elevators, there are about 3,000,000. On the Illinois Central there are about 1,250,000. There are some others I can not just now recall. Just add that up. Twenty-three millions. You can get all the public elevators you want. Gentlemen, they do not want to do it and never did. It is only a talk they have.

Q. How much of that 23,000,000 do you suppose is in use to-day?—A. I judge about 13,000,000, possibly. I have not looked at that feature of it for some time. I may be off in that, but it is someting like that.

Q. What, approximately, would be the capacity of all of the private elevators like those belonging to yourself and Armour?—A. I should judge about 10,000,000, as nearly as I can approximate.

Q. Not more than 10,000,000?—A. Not much more than that; no. Two elevators at South Chicago—lately they have turned some of their houses into public warehouses; ten or twelve, possibly.

Q. What was the motive for turning them into private warehouses?—A. The motive was this. These gentlemen made such a howl about public warehousemen buying grain, making out the cause of their being hurt in their business; and they have been suing us under the old law, which was not clear on the subject. It was a law which was really open to two constructions as to whether a public warehouseman had a right to buy grain. And we said to ourselves, Well, all right. We are not going to be bothered so much about this. We are grain merchants, and we will use our private warehouses as we see fit. We are trading and buying. Under the public-warehouse act, everybody kept nagging us to death, so we built our private warehouses for that purpose.

Another proposition is this. Here comes grain that is dirty. It won't grade No. 1, for instance, because of the dirt in it. The grain is all right except for the dirt. The inspection department says it is No. 3. We take that grain and take the dirt out, and it makes No. 2.

Q. You testified as to 23,000,000 as the approximate capacity of the public warehouses and 10,000,000 for private warehouses. That only makes 33,000,000. Is that the entire capacity?—A. I am not just exactly positive as to the entire capacity. It may run to 40,000,000 for all I know. Some men have warehouses here that I don't know anything about. The public warehouse capacity is much larger, and whenever they want a new public warehouse for the grain or whatever they get, we will throw them wide open for them; but we feel they do not need them; they have no grain in the warehouses; they sell their grain on the market and get the money for it and have no further interest in the trade whatever; absolutely no interest.

Q. (By Professor JOHNSON.) You said a few moments ago that the railroads are not in the business of buying grain and do not want it.—A. Yes; that is my judgment.

Q. In view of the history of the Iowa Development Company and its relation with the Chicago and Great Western, and in view of the relation of the Illinois Central with the grain trade, is that statement correct?—A. I don't know anything about the relation of the Illinois Central with the grain trade.

Q. You have not kept track of the case of the Iowa Development Company?—A. I don't know the character of their custom at all.

Q. You are not familiar with the investigation of that subject?—A. No. Mr. Stickney was before the Interstate Commerce Commission, but I don't know what the result was.

Q. It has been, I think, fairly well proven that railroads were to some extent purchasers of grain—buyers and sellers of grain—bought at the initial point and sold out under shipment to Chicago, with the differentials between the two prices as their bonus.—A. I don't know anything of that kind.

Q. That was the business of the Iowa Development Company?—A. I don't know anything about that.

Q. (By Mr. KENNEDY.) Do you buy barley?—A. Yes; quite largely.

Q. Do you sell it yourself?—A. I do.

Q. Does Mr. Armour control that trade?—A. No; ridiculous! Armour control the trade? Of course not. I sell, I think, about eight or nine million bushels of barley.

Q. You have a fair share of that trade for malting purposes?—A. Certainly; it is bought and sold every day on change.

Q. You stated they could never get legislation to regulate your business.—A. I believe that is so. It was the old doctrine of socialism intended to bar individual effort.

Q. Do I understand your position is that you are opposed to this combination that is going on in the industrial world to-day?—A. I am opposed to it to the extent that they have any power to absolutely control prices. I don't mean, however, to be understood as saying that I don't believe in the consolidation idea. Now, you have pointed out a very broad question, and if you will allow me I will tell you just what I think. You can not make Government legislation that will govern any man's business or his prices, and I will tell you what I think about this thing. I appeared before the Interstate Commerce Committee of the Senate once, by request, on the subject of pooling. Now, I honestly believe that there is only one remedy for all this trouble about railroads and rebates, and that is a pooling law, which will allow these railroads to pool their interests under the control of the Interstate Commerce Commission, which has the power to protect the public in the maximum rates. Why do I believe this? Let me state this: These things are just as they are; there is no use in setting forth abstract theories; we must come down to practical things. Railroads cross the country, and you will find the most of them well equipped and in shape to render fine service, exact service, and plenty of cars. We have been dealing with these roads for some time and have no fault to find whatever with their service and mode of operation. In comes another road, not so well situated, not so well equipped, and not in a position to get so much business nor to handle it as well, and yet it must stand upon the same plane with every other road. Now, people will come in here and make long speeches to you about the railroads doing this and the railroads doing that; but here is the practical question: That road can not do business. Then what does it do? It does the only natural thing and inevitable thing it can do. It says, "We will try to equalize these advantages and we will give you a lower rate," and there you are. Someone takes that lower rate and everybody feels it in a minute in the trade. They can probably sell a little cheaper in consequence, or something or other of that kind.

Q. How does the old road protect itself against the rate adopted by this new road?—A. By meeting that rate. And things go on for a while in the same manner until after a while the same conditions obtain again and the road again puts down the rate in order to get business; and so they keep on cutting, and the rates are uncertain, and no one can predicate any business proposition upon them until that road ceases doing business or they reach some amicable understanding; or under one road goes, into the hands of receivers and operates under the protection and direction of the court. So that the inevitable logic of the whole proposition is that this bankrupt institution which started that decline in rates to get business fell into absolute bankruptcy or bankrupted the solvent road, because the solvent institution can not do business in that way; and they can not get away from these things. God knows I am for an absolute uniform rate, and I will take my chances of doing business; that is all I want and that is all I ask. People are looking for a remedy and affecting sincerity; but they don't want to stop it, because if they did there is a. way to stop it, and that is to let these roads get together and say, "Here, you are entitled to a certain proportion of this competitive freight here;" and they agree upon the proportion, and the rate is fixed, and that gets them out of trouble. Now let the Interstate Commerce Commission here say. "The rates can not be other than so and so; your power to pool shall not be used to charge an exorbitant rate." Then you have taken away from these roads the temptation to cut the rate. No necessity exists any more. They are contented to go on with their business, feeling that they get a fair proportion of freight upon which they agree, and you have stopped the cutting of rates. Of course nothing is perfect, but it would seem to me that will eliminate, I will undertake to say, 99 per cent of the trouble arising from this freight rate.

Q. Would you have this interstate-commerce law amended so that there would be no trouble about the regulation of these rates?—A. I would; yes.

Q. (By Mr. KENNEDY.) You would have the interstate-commerce law amended so as to have no question about the powers of the commission to regulate these rates?—A. I would. Now, this interstate-commerce law has done more in the last few years to restore things to an equilibrium than people know anything about. They have gone about it in a practical way.

Q. (By Mr. CONGER.) Would your proposition for a pooling arrangement do away entirely with the motives for cutting the rate? Let me suppose a case: A pool is made; and it must be done on either a tonnage or financial basis, probably a tonnage basis; and these railroads that enter into it must agree upon a proportion that each shall receive.—A. Yes.

Q. I can understand how the ambitious railroad manager, after that arrangement has been in operation for a few months, says, I do not think I have my proportion.—A. Yes.

Q. He goes out quietly and makes a rate to some large shipper—makes a rebate,. if you please.—A. Yes.

Q. And he is very soon able to demonstrate to the pool, or those who form it, that he is entitled to a larger proportion, and as long as men are controlled by motives of ambition and to get all they can I do not see how that is to be done away with at all.—A. As I told you, you can not make everything exactly perfect. I knew you would ask that question, and my answer to that is this: In any proposition where you can not have perfection you must take that which is bound to make it the best possible. I do not know any better way. In the first place, as you put it, won't it be more likely that the railroad that is trying to increase its percentage on the tonnage proposition will be the weak system, the one that did not have much freight before, and that is constantly cutting the rate to get it, that would be inclined to say, Next year I ought to have a little more tonnage. The result, in my opinion, would be, if these other strong roads feel satisfied with the present proportion, that they will say that these fellows are getting to be a continual disturbance, and the men who own the securities of the other roads will simply go to work quietly and buy control of that weak road, and stop it right there.

Q. (By Professor JOHNSON.) Then pooling will not check consolidation?—A. Unless you have pooling, consolidation will go on.

Q. And if you do have it it will go right on?—A. No; it is only liable now and then, to correct the only evil which is attachable to pools, and only in the manner of protection.

Q. (By Mr. CONGER.) In what way would you protect the public against exorbitant charges?—A. By the Interstate Commerce Commission.

Q. With what authority?—A. Absolute authority on the maximum rate.

Q. (By Mr. C. J. HARRIS.) In the case of pooling?—A. Yes. As long as you protect the public in the maximum rate, you have protected them.

Q. (By Mr. KENNEDY.) How would you protect the shipper in having his freight go over a certain line?—A. I would not have the discretion in the pool. I would let the traffic go as it is to-day. It makes no difference to the railroads; they get their proportion of the business. If it is to go over the Northwestern road, let it go over the Northwestern road.

Q. You said you were opposed to these combinations in case they would finally secure a monopoly of the trade and industry. Do you fear some of them have or may secure a monopoly?—A. Well, of course, it is quite possible.

Q. Has not the American Tin Plate Company practically secured a monopoly of that industry?—A. I should not wonder. I am interested in the packing industry on Puget Sound. I bought a large amount of tin from them the other day, and I told them I thought I would have to go into the tin business and manufacture tin. But still there is a good deal to say on the other side. If they keep the price steady, it does not make much difference. Their statement is, if they had to buy the steel to-day, they could not sell at the price they are selling to-day, and I apprehend that is true.

Q. (By Mr. C. J. HARRIS.) Are you the owner of cars yourself?—A. No, I am not. I never owned any cars.

Q. (By Mr. CONGER.) I do not know where I got the idea, but it comes to mind that I have heard it charged or said that the elevator men here in Chicago were paying more for grain in Nebraska than they were in Iowa; in other words, paying more for grain at a point where the mileage was much greater to this market. How are they able to do that, if it is done, if they do not get concessions from the railroads on these large shipments?—A. I do not know that that is true, but I will tell you my experience. Frequently I will give more for Nebraska grain than Iowa grain because of the better quality. The dry climate in Kansas and Nebraska makes a better grain to store or ship than any other. I would give more money for it any day in the week than I would for Iowa wheat.

Q. How do your prices compare on the line of road you operate on in relation to distance from this market? Do you pay as much for the grain at the farthest point as you do at a nearer point?—A. No, not exactly; but the railroads in their tariff rates for a long distance will haul grain pretty close to the local. The long haul is what they are after.

Q. Then you pay approximately as much for grain 1,000 miles as 300 miles from Chicago?—A. Yes. Look at the fish industry at Fairhaven. We can ship fish from Puget Sound to Boston at the same rate we can ship to Chicago. That is on account of these proportionate rates. Now, I have always complained about these proportionate rates, because I do not think they are right. You can start to-day a train of 50 carloads of grain; you can have in that 50-carload train 25 carloads destined to Chicago, and I will have 25 cars billed through; on the same train; identically the same service performed. When it gets to Chicago, you say, "Mr. Counselman, I wish you would clean that grain for me." "All right," I clean it. I put it out on the eastern train, and these other 25 cars come in and make up the eastern train of 50 cars. Twenty-five cars will pay, say, 38 cents on to New York; the other grain, that you had cleaned here, will pay a 40-cent rate. Now, they have performed identically the same service, but charge you the additional rate simply because you did not bill it through.

Q. The grain had to be unloaded here?—A. Yes; so did the other, but it is transferred from the western to the eastern car at their own expense.

Q. That proves to be an interesting point. I think I have heard it said or testified to that at Minneapolis the railroads make the same rate for through grain; in other words, will allow them to do that cleaning and still put it through. Do you know if that is true?—A. If it comes billed through, they do; but my assumption was you had billed it local. That is not right. The railroads ought to let it go in local and out local at the same rate.

Q. Coming back to the industrial matter; quite a number of gentlemen who have appeared before the commission in Washington have favored a national incorporation law. Have you any opinion on that matter?—A. I have not given that subject a great deal of thought. Of course, I can see it is very onerous, people having their different plants in different States, always subjected to different classes of State legislation. I should think, on the whole, national legislation might be a good thing.

Q. (By Professor JOHNSON.) Do you use the telegraph largely in your business? A. I do.

Q. Are you satisfied with the telegraph service at the present time?—A. Oh, yes.

Q. You think the rates are high?—A. I think they are very fair, indeed.

Q. (By Representative LORIMER.) Have you anything further to suggest?—Nothing.

(Testimony closed.)

CHICAGO, ILL., *November 17, 1899.*

TESTIMONY OF MR. WILLIAM H. BARTLETT,

Grain merchant, Chicago, Ill.

The Subcommission on Transportation being in session in Chicago, Representative Lorimer presiding, at 11:15 a. m., November 17, 1899, Mr. William H. Bartlett was introduced as a witness and, being duly sworn, testified concerning transportation as follows:

Q. (By Representative LORIMER.) Will you please state your name?—A. William H. Bartlett.

Q. Business?—A. Grain merchant.

Q. You sat here a part of the time and heard much that Mr. Counselman has said. Will you, in your own way, tell us what your opinions are with reference to the elevator systems in Chicago and about Chicago?—A. I did not hear what Mr. Counselman had to say relative to that. I saw, however, in the paper yesterday some statements made relative to the abuses, so called, of the elevator system, and as I have been in this grain business now almost 30 years, and have seen the elevator system, as it at present exists, grow up, I should like to call your attention to the manner of that growth. Twenty-five years ago the business at country stations was all consigned by the local dealer to some one of the larger markets—Chicago, Baltimore, New York. The local dealer paid a commission at that market, and if consigned to Chicago, the bulk of it was reconsigned to the Eastern seabord market—New York or Baltimore. There it paid another commission, and it was sold then to the exporter, who sent it abroad. I do not know but Mr. Counselman traced all this, but that was the system in vogue 20 or 25 years ago. The first change in that was when Gill & Fisher, of Baltimore, and C. H. Cummings, of Philadelphia, commenced bidding the Western dealer direct for grain, passing the markets of accumulation like Indianapolis, Toledo, Chicago, Peoria, and St. Louis. They sent direct to the country dealer and bought from him. This system was then adopted by New York, Indianapolis, Peoria, and the last market to go into it was Chicago. To-day Mr. Counselman, our firm, and others not only buy direct from the grain dealer at the country stations, eliminating the commission at Chicago, eliminating the commission at New York, and selling it direct to the consumer on the Continent and in the United Kingdom, but we also do more; we run hundreds of country elevators that buy the grain direct from the farmer, and absolutely we are the only middle men between the farmer and the foreigner who buys the grain. Certainly that change has been for the benefit of the producer. It has wiped out the commissions at the western point of accumulation; it has wiped out the commissions at the eastern point of accumulation.

The change in system in handling this grain, compelled by the action in the first place of six or seven exporting firms at the seaboard, which compelled the Chicago firms either to adopt their policy or go out of the export business, has resulted, so far at least, to the benefit of the producer in removing this commission charge at the points of accumulation. The business to-day, as handled here in Chicago, is not handled by the firms who were in business 20 years ago. Ten years ago we had no elevator in Chicago, but the necessities of the business compelled us to build elevators, one, two, and we are building a third now. Until within a week we have never had a regular house. We have been under no obligations to the Board of Trade in any way. We are simply grain merchants. We have our own houses in Liverpool and Montreal and merchandise this grain. The men who come here and complain about the elevators are generally men who have refused to adapt themselves to the change in conditions and want to have the old commission system in vogue now and levy toll at every point of accumulation on the grain as it passes through. That is not in vogue, and you can not reinstate it by legislation. The trade has gone beyond that. It is simply the old-timer railing at the business that has passed him.

Q. (By Mr. CONGER.) You said you were the owner of two elevators and building a third?—A. Yes.

Q. On what road?—A. The Elgin, Joliet and Eastern and the Western Indiana.

Q. Have you country elevators?—A. Yes.

Q. Along what road?—A. On the Santa Fe; some in Iowa, on the Northwestern; then I am interested in houses at Peoria that have them on the Central Iowa; in Terra Haute, on the Eastern Illinois, Vandalia, and Big Four; at Evansville, on the Peoria, Decatur and Evansville, and the Louisville and Nashville.

Q. Take the Santa Fe, for instance; is any other firm buying wheat along that line of road?—A. Oh, yes; we do only a small business on the Santa Fe. Our elevator in this city is not on their track.

Q. Along what other trunk lines do you operate?—A. On the Rock Island, the Chicago and Northwestern, and the Chicago Great Western.

Q. Do you buy a considerable amount of grain on the Rock Island?—A. We buy considerable on the Rock Island.

Q. Does Mr. Counselman operate on that road?—A. Yes.

Q. Is there any agreement between you and him as to the prices to be paid to the farmer?—A. Not between the firms at all.

Q. Is there any between the representatives at the local point?—A. We have no agreements; no.

Q. They usually pay the same prices?—A. Oh, yes; we do not aim to get into a fight where we can get along peaceably.

Q. There is not much competition, then? Most of these stations are limited to Counselman and yourselves?—A. We have no elevators on the Rock Island road; we buy from the dealers there.

Q. From the local dealers?—A. Yes.

Q. Do the local dealers handle very much of that grain?—A. Oh, yes; the great bulk of the grain is handled by local dealers.

Q. By local dealers?—A. Oh, yes.

Q. You and Mr. Counselman purchase of these local dealers?—A. Yes; and other firms.

Q. (By Mr. C. J. HARRIS.) Firms from other cities, I presume?—A. Yes. The Eastern exporters buy all through that country.

Q. (By Mr. CONGER.) I do not understand how you always pay the same price if there is no agreement.—A. We do not always pay the same price for the same grade, but we are regulated in our prices by the same market conditions; we are bidding for the same market and have the same freight rates, and have to meet the same competition. That naturally would bring about the same prices. We would not try to start up a fight by overbidding each other.

Q. (By Mr. C. J. HARRIS.) Owing to the price of wheat on the open market, the probability is that grain dealers from Chicago and other cities would have to pay about the same price in the local shipping points alone the line?—A. Yes. Of course, in different markets from day to day the prices will fluctuate and the grain will go to Baltimore and St. Louis instead of Chicago; they may overbid us.

Q. (By Mr. KENNEDY.) Do you usually pay the same prices as Mr. Counselman?—A. They will run about the same.

Q. Mr. Counselman admitted that 5 men get together after the close of the Board of Trade and fix the price. Is one of the men a representative of your company?—A. Yes; but that does not cover the Rock Island territory.

Q. (By Mr. CONGER.) What territory?—A. The Missouri territory west of the Missouri River, where the competition has been strongest from the Southwest. There is no agreement whatever in the territory east of the Missouri.

Q. Is that agreement sent to your representatives—about the price?—A. They do not fix the price except as between our firms; more to see that we are high enough than anything else. That is fighting ground, absolutely, west of the Missouri River, with the Southwestern concerns.

Q. (By Representative LORIMER.) Do you fix a maximum or minimum price?—A. Maximum price.

Q. In other words, you agree how much you will outbid the other fellow, or the men in the other market?—A. Yes; we have a man that specially watches the bids from the other markets and notifies us to see that we keep in line with them.

Q. (By Mr. C. J. HARRIS.) Your idea is to divert that trade to Chicago?—A. Yes; to protect the Chicago market.

Q. (By Representative LORIMER.) Do you, along your lines, every day agree that you will not pay more than a certain amount, and that less than the market price of grain; or, in other words, try to keep down the price of grain by agreeing upon a price less than the market price?—A. No; there is no idea or agreement of that kind. Our effort is to get the grain here.

Q. The effort is to go as high as you are compelled to go to take it from the purchaser who ships to another city, in order to bring it to Chicago?—A. Exactly. If the intention was to keep the price down——

Q. (Interrupting.) Why do you not agree on prices in Iowa?—A. We do not have the competition. The Southwestern lines do not compete in that territory.

Q. Do not a comparatively large number of men in Chicago purchase grain between here and the Missouri?—A. There are a half dozen firms.

Q. (By Representative LORIMER.) Then you only agree on the maximum price you will pay in the market where you have the competition; no agreement where you have no competition?—A. We have no agreement on prices east of the Missouri.

Q. (By Mr. CONGER.) Did the grain formerly from that section west of the Missouri River come almost entirely to Chicago and now go to Galveston?—A. The great bulk used to come here and to St. Louis, and is now diverted to Galveston.

Q. In other words, that competition has been a growing one, has it not?—A. Yes, right along.

Q. (By Professor JOHNSON.) Is it due Gulf competition any more than to these Southern roads to the Atlantic seaboard that do not go through Chicago, lines like the Baltimore and Ohio Southwestern, and other lines that tap that territory?—A. That is the largest competition west of the Missouri, especially in Nebraska.

Q. That is the competition you are trying to meet more than the Gulf competition proper?—A. Yes.

Q. (By Mr KENNEDY.) Have Chicago lines tapping that territory made rates to enable you to try to get that trade?—A. I have not brought a carload of wheat from Kansas, I think, for more than a year. We have had absolutely to give up that territory.

Q. Did the railroads aid you in any way to try to hold that territory?—A. Not of late.

Q. Formerly?—A. Formerly. It was a standup fight between all Chicago roads, and the Pittsburg and Gulf, and other Southern roads.

Q. (By Mr. CONGER.) That competition must have been of benefit to the farmer while it was on?—A. I presume it was. It did not benefit the road. I believe the Pittsburg and Gulf went into the hands of the receiver.

Q. (By Representative LORIMER.) You refrain from going into that territory for a reason?—A. Because we can not compete with the conditions. Whether that territory belongs by right to the Gulf, I do not know, but the fact is they are holding it now.

Q. (By Mr. C. J. HARRIS.) Is that grain shipped to Galveston exported, or does it go by water to Eastern ports?—A. It is exported direct.

Q. By Representative LORIMER.) Have they a better rate than the roads running to Chicago can make?—A. Oh, yes; the rail rate to that point plus the ocean rate, is lower than it can possibly be made by Chicago.

Q. It is the rate that excludes you from that territory?—A. That is the reason entirely. They will make a rate to the Gulf no higher than from the same stations to Chicago. Then they are on the seaboard, and we still have a rail rate to pay from here to the Atlantic seaboard.

Q. (By Mr. KENNEDY.) At what point is the line drawn where you can compete?—A. West of Kansas City it is Gulf territory, really, as far as the wheat goes. Of course, more or less corn comes here. At some seasons of the year they can not send it through the Gulf—in the germinating season.

Q. (By Mr. C. J. HARRIS.) Too hot?—A. Yes.

Q. (By Professor JOHNSON.) Your business is largely export?—A. Yes.

Q. Entirely to European points?—A. To the United Kingdom and the Continent.

Q. You ship nothing but grain; do not deal in grain products?—A. No, we do not deal in grain products.

Q. (By Mr. KENNEDY.) Are you exporting grain in large quantities at the present time?—A. Until within the last six weeks.

Q. What is the cause of the stoppage of exports in the last six weeks?—A. They overbought themselves on the fear of this war in South Africa, and that stimulated the market.

Q. In Europe?—A. In the United Kingdom and on the Continent. They were so afraid of continental complications, they all stocked up, and now they are receiving that wheat. Then again, the Argentine has been a large shipper of wheat lately. And these two factors together have held them out of the market at present.

Q. These are the two factors alone?—A. So far as I know, yes. The freight rates are now no higher—the ocean and rail rate—than they were at the time we were moving wheat.

Q. (By Professor JOHNSON.) Do you deal in corn also?—A. Oh, yes.

Q. Does any corn go on the Illinois Central to New Orleans?—A. I never heard of any going from Chicago. I have heard of some wheat, but in small quantities. As a general thing, corn is not moved out of Chicago to New Orleans.

Q. Is it probable if you were able to ship by water across the Isthmus to the Orient there would be any grain business to the Orient?—A. I should not think there would be much grain; there might be flour, but I doubt—I could not answer that.

Q. (By Mr. KENNEDY.) Has speculation put the price of wheat up beyond the export point?—A. Well, hardly, because wheat has been declining. Speculation probably does hold up the market here. The believers in high prices are, of course, the ones buying the options, and it is the option that is carrying the price. If it was not for the speculation the market would go down to the level of the bids in Europe, which would be a number of cents per bushel under the market. The speculative market is holding the price where it is now.

Q. It is a good thing for the farmer?—A. Certainly. If we did not have a speculative market to tide us over these times of depression we should have a bankrupt sale every three months. Every time we got an accumulation it would be sold under the hammer for the benefit of the European consumer.

Q. (By Professor JOHNSON.) It would seem then that speculation results in bulling prices?—A. No. When you get it too high, there are lots of people who

would think it too high and sell it down. I think that speculation brings us a fairer average of prices. We do not come to as low prices as we should without speculation, nor as high as if we had no speculation. With no stocks and a small supply we should go to the other extreme.
(Testimony closed.)

CHICAGO, ILL., *November 17, 1899.*

TESTIMONY OF MR. JOSEPH G. SNYDACKER,

Grain merchant, Chicago, Ill.

The subcommission on transportation being in session in Chicago, Representative Lorimer presiding, at 11.35 a. m., November 17, 1899, Mr. Joseph G. Snydacker was introduced as a witness, and, being duly sworn, testified concerning transportation as follows:

Q. (By Representative LORIMER.) What is your name?—A. Joseph G. Snydacker.

Q. Business?—A. Grain merchant.

Q. Are you the owner of an elevator or elevators—the concern you represent?—A. No; we do not own any elevators.

Q. Will you tell, in your own way, what information you have with reference to the grain trade and the elevator business in Chicago?—A. I think Mr. Bartlett has very correctly and accurately stated the situation and the evolution that has been going on in the grain trade for the last 20 years. I think in this business, as in every other business, there has been a survival of the fittest. The bringing of grain to the primary markets has depended entirely on the price those markets could afford to pay. It has been demonstrated that the grain could not stand the additional commissions and charges that were formerly put on it and they had to be eliminated. This enabled the various concerns that had facilities in Chicago for handling, shipping, and cleaning grain to go directly into the country and handle this grain from the farmer's hands and eliminate as many of the charges as possible.

Q. That has resulted in eliminating, to a great extent, has it not, the commission men, the so-called middle men of the business?—A. Yes. There are a few old-time commission men still in existence, but their business is not anything like what it used to be. Our firm, or the firm I used to be connected with, was in the receiving business and averaged 100 to 150 cars a day. This grain was consigned to us from all over the United States, Nebraska, Illinois, Iowa, Missouri, and even as far east as Ohio; and all that grain used to pay us a commission for selling it. The countrymen would draw on us and we would practically act as their bankers, and when we got returns on the cars we sent them a check for the proceeds. That business has been gradually declining, and instead of getting 100 to 150 cars, it came down to 5 or 10 at most. A man would have to adapt himself to the conditions as they exist to-day in competition with seaboard and other markets and cut as many charges out of the grain as he could, or die a lingering death, as a majority of the commission men are now doing.

Q. What effect has the change in system had on the price in grain to the producer?—A. I think less the number of men that the grain has to support in handling, the greater the benefit to the producer and the greater price he gets for it. The more people live off a certain car of grain, the less that grain will ultimately net to the producer and man who sells it.

Q. What effect has this change had on the price of grain to the consumer?—A. I think it has tended to cheapen it to him, too. An elevator concern will buy it in the country and deliver it to any part of Europe for probably about the same commission that the middlemen would have got 20 years ago for sending it to Chicago and having it sold there, when that would be the first of four, five, or six charges that would come out of it. Fifteen years ago we used to get 1 cent to 1¼ cents a bushel on wheat. One cent a bushel was the regular charge until within a few years ago. The live elevator concern will buy wheat or oats, and, if they can get 1 cent a bushel by buying and selling direct to the consumer on the other side they think they have a fair profit. As Mr. Bartlett stated, when the grain reached Chicago that was only the first link in the chain. It was brought here and put in the elevator, then shipped to Baltimore, New York, London, or Liverpool. It was handled by middlemen at two, three, or four points, paying all a profit.

Q. About what commission would they receive at the different points for handling under the old system?—A. The commission used to be 1 cent a bushel in these cities, but the commission for the last 5 years has been one-half cent a bushel all around. That has been the commission charged by the higher-grade firms. I think some have offered to handle oats and corn for one-fourth of a cent a bushel, and possibly wheat for a quarter of a cent a bushel.

Q. (By Professor JOHNSON.) You say you do not own any elevators. Do you use the public elevators?—A. No; we lease elevators.

Q. Then it is a mere matter of preferring to borrow money in the form of a lease?—A. Yes. We have arrangements in the country at some of the points where there are grain dealers who own their own elevators, and we pay them a certain salary a month, or commission on the grain they buy, rather than tie up our money in owning the elevators themselves.

Q. These are public elevators, are they?—A. No; we own no public elevators.

Q. (By Mr. KENNEDY.) Do you lease elevators in Chicago?—A. We have one in Chicago.

Q. Leased?—A. Yes.

Q. Do you lease the entire capacity of that elevator?—A. Yes.

Q. (By Professor JOHNSON.) Is your business mainly export or domestic?—A. Export and domestic.

Q. There has been a complaint on the part of some communities that the difference between export and domestic rates prevented the development of their domestic business. Have you any complaint to make with regard to the difference between them?—A. No; we have no particular complaint to make. I think it is a wise thing to prevent accumulations in this country, and when grain or grain products can be exported out of the country, and the prices secured, and the conditions justify it, I think it is a wise thing to have a rate that will permit the development of this business. The grain business depends on the export situation, and whenever the market here is above an export basis the situation becomes c ogged.

Q. You say it is not a disadvantage to the Eastern miller?—A. It may possibly be, but at the same time I should think if conditions in this country would warrant him in paying a high price, and he could merchandise his property, it is best for the country at large to move the grain for export when it can.

Q. (By Mr. KENNEDY.) What is your Eastern export point?—A. We take some for Montreal, some for New York, some from Philadelphia.

Q. What is the charge to New York from Chicago for export?—A. The rates vary; just at the moment I do not really know. I do not keep in close touch with the rates.

Q. (By Professor JOHNSON.) You export through New York?—A. Yes.

Q. Do you find the terminal charges there at New York are in any way a detriment to your business?—A. For some reason or other New York has been losing a great deal of its export business.

Q. (By Mr. CONGER.) Where has it been going?—A. Newport News has been getting a good share; Baltimore is getting a good share; Montreal is securing a large share. A good many years ago New York got all this export business, and these other ports were getting so small an amount that it was decided to put in a differential rate to Baltimore and Philadelphia and Newport News of 2 or 3 cents a hundred, and the result has been New York has been getting left. The roads discriminate against New York at the moment. Possibly, it may be, the charges, too, are very exorbitant, and that, in connection with the difference in rate, has been responsible for this loss of business.

Q. It does not matter to you individually whether you ship through New York or some other port?—A. Not a bit.

Q. Is it a detriment to Chicago or the central West that the railroad officials in the ring in New York should maintain this heavy terminal charge?—A. As long as we get a seaboard outlet we do not care where it is. I think that is a local matter for them to take up and fight their own battles.

Q. Do you think the railroads are treating men in your line of business equally as regards the rates, facilities, etc., or are there discriminations of any kind?—A. Well, we buy grain on half a dozen different lines coming into Chicago; we buy grain on lines east and west of Chicago, and I think it is an open field. I think a man that will adjust himself to conditions here can do business.

Q. When you have considerable shipments to make, do you inquire for the rate?—A. Yes.

Q. You do not look up the public rate, do you?—A. We know what the public rate is.

Q. (By Mr. CONGER.) You will get it for less?—A. No. At the time the bulk of this grain is shipped, during the open season of navigation, the matter of lake-and-rail rates and all-water rates is entirely a matter of trade and barter. The cheaper you can get your trade the better you are fixed to do business.

Q. (By Professor JOHNSON.) One of the greatest export shippers of grain in this country made the statement not long since that he never bothered to look up a rate; that he always got the rate quoted to him?—A. We have a man who has charge of our export department who is supposed to get a rate as cheap as any are made. Whether that is the current rate or not depends on circumstances, I presume. For instance, a certain rate is made and no grain is moving. A road may adjust its tariffs to the rate that they propose to make in order to conform their published tariffs to securing that line of businss. They will come in and contract a 100 or a 1,000 cars of grain and have that for their tariff.

Q. Of course, they can not change their tariff upward without 10 days' notice, or downward in less than 3 days?—A. No.

Q. You would not mean to testify that when the railroad wants to change its tariff to offer a special rate?——A. I would not want to testify to that extent, except that market conditions govern rates in a general way the same as they do everything else.

Q. Is it not true that most of the shipments are made on rates quoted to the man who has the shipment to make?—A. I should say that is correct.

Q. Rates are a matter of individual barter?—A. I should say that freight rates are something a road has to sell, and it has to meet conditions the same as any other merchant.

Q. It is a matter of barter and purchase?—A. I do not know that they make a rate, for I know they do not for us, but when they work for the lake-and-rail business going through the supply and demand of freight certainly fixes the prices of that rate.

Q. (By Mr. C. J. HARRIS.) Are you speaking of export rates?—A. I am talking about export rates.

Q. (By Professor JOHNSON.) I understand your statement would apply to both?—A. No; I am speaking of export rates only. The grain we send East is entirely export grain. The grain that goes to Montreal, Baltimore, New York, etc., is all exported.

Q. All you ship East is for export purposes?—A. The domestic is a small thing.

Q. (By Mr. C. J. HARRIS.) With reference to the export trade, the railroad, of course, is governed by the vessel rates in New York, which vary from month to month, so there could be no fixed export rate from Chicago.

Q. (By Professor JOHNSON.) A railroad company has no right to carry grain for A to Boston cheaper than for B, or to New York. Is not that true?—A. On local business?

Q. It may be exported again?—A. Yes: you do know.

Q. Perhaps you do?—A. Anybody does. That would be a very serious offense, to dare to divert grain for local or domestic consumption when it is billed for export and at a lower rate.

Q. You mean that a man in Boston who buys grain——A. Pays more money for domestic consumption than export.

Q. You say from the moment he purchases it in the West it is finally and certainly decided whether it is domestic or export?—A. Yes.

Q. (By Mr. CONGER.) You said it would be a serious offense; against whom?—A. It would be getting a less rate than a man is entitled to, and diverting it under false pretenses.

Q. An offense against the statutes of some State?—A. I am no lawyer; I simply know that if a man gets a lower rate for export than the domestic rate——

Q. (By Professor JOHNSON.) You get your rates quoted to you for export. Is it satisfactory to you to have these rates quoted to you, and to have them quoted to other persons, not knowing whether the other man is quoted the same rate as you get? Is that a satisfactory system?—A. It is the same method employed, for instance, about ocean tonnage when we charter a steamer.

Q. There it is unavoidable; but in case of rail rates is it a satisfactory thing to have the rate quoted and have to do business on the kind of rate you can get quoted, instead of a fixed, stable rate?—A. Any arrangement is satisfactory to us which permits us to do business.

Q. Is it as satisfactory as the other system?—A. I presume it is. It would be hard to say definitely about that.

Q. (By Mr. C. J. HARRIS.) It seems to me we are getting the two things mixed up. The export rate varies the tonnage. Anyone knows in New York you can make any rate you can, according to the vessel and the amount of freight there. That varies from day to day. Now, I think in regard to shipments locally to New York and Boston for consumption there, that you are getting the export rate and that rate mixed up.—A. No; I was very explicit about that; that rate is posted, and a man who is posted knows what that rate is.

Q. Shipments for domestic consumption are at a published rate?—A. Yes.

Q. (By Mr. KENNEDY.) Would not that be as much an offense under the interstate commerce law—to get a rate from Chicago to Boston for export as to get a rate from Chicago to Boston for domestic purposes? That is a published and public tariff?—A. I do not know how others are working on that business; I know we do it on the published tariff rate and figure on it, and fix our own prices and base our sales on those figures.

Q. For domestic or export?—A. Both export and domestic sales on that basis. When you said a rate was quoted before, I did not quite understand what you were driving at. We maintain a basis. When we sell for export we must know the basis we are working on. So I am satisfied we work on the basis of the published tariff export rates. You can not go to work and figure on the basis of a rate quoted, as you intimated, which will vary from month to month and from day to day. We could not carry on a business on that basis.

Q. (By Professor JOHNSON.) To put the question again, Is that rate you figure on the rate which is filed with the Interstate Commerce Commission or the rate the railroads publish in some daily paper?—A. I can not tell you.

Q. When you figure on the rate, where do you get the figures?—A. Our export man has a published rate which he works on.

Q. Is that supplied to him from time to time by the railroads?—A. Every time there is a change in rate he gets due notice of it. For instance, there is an advance going into effect December 1 on rates to Galveston, on rates to the Gulf.

Q. Will you testify you get no rate notifications except such as have already been sent to be filed with the Interstate Commerce Commission?—A. Will you ask the question again?

Q. Will you testify you get only such rate quotations as are filed or have been sent for filing to the Interstate Commerce Commission?—A. I should be perfectly willing to testify to that, so far as I know. Our export man is supposed to govern himself accordingly and is the man who has that matter in charge.

Q. Does he not solicit freight rates direct from the corporation?—A. No.

Q. (By Mr. KENNEDY.) Do the railroads solicit your business?—A. We keep in touch with the railroad situation all over the country.

Q. (By Representative LORIMER.) I think the original question aimed to bring out whether you got a rate on account of your connections, and, being a large dealer in grain, whether you got a rate below the published rate or below your competitor?—A. We do not. If that is the idea, I can tell you we do not.

Q. (By Mr. CONGER.) You pay the published tariff rate?—A. Yes, always.

Q. (By Representative LORIMER.) Do you know whether or not railroads file their rates with the Interstate Commerce Commission?—A. I do not.

Q. So that you would not know whether the rate quoted to you has been filed or not, as a matter of fact?—A. No.

Q. Your man, who attends to your rate, would not?—A. That is his business. You can get a through rate to Liverpool.

Q. Given by the railroad?—A. Yes.

Q. (By Mr. KENNEDY.) So much of it as is made to Boston is subject to Interstate Commerce Commission's regulation.

Q. (By Professor JOHNSON.) I am curious to know whether business men are doing business on rates that are published, or whether they are doing business by secret and special rate quotations when they have shipments to make. One of the biggest shippers in the United States made the statement that he never bothered to look up a rate, but always asked for a rate to be quoted to him, and that is the object of my question.—A. I did not quite understand what you meant, or I could have given you the information you wanted at the start as well as at the wind up.

Q. (By Mr. CONGER.) Does your firm receive any commissions from the railroads?—A. No.

Q. (By Professor JOHNSON.) Do you, as a large shipper, get any favors that others do not get?—A. I do not know what possible favors we could get.

Q. Do the railroads try to get your business and offer inducements of any kind that they do not offer men who do not have so much business?—A. Recently the difficulty has been to get the cars to ship the stuff.

Q. (By Mr. KENNEDY.) Did they ever give you such a favor as this—store your grain at the seaboard and hold it for 40, 60, or 90 days free of cost, while you were awaiting better prices?—A. We do not carry any grain at the seaboard. It is sold for export and to meet steamers and pushed right through. Having storage facilities and elevators in the West, we time our shipments so that we carry no grain at the seaboard at all.

Q. Do you ship through Peter Wright & Sons, of Philadelphia?—A. No.

Q. You make considerable use of the telegraph, do you?—A. Yes.

Q. Do you feel satisfied with the service as at present given?—A. In the main, yes.

Q. You qualify your answer somewhat.—A. Sometimes we find the service a little slow; sometimes we find where there is no competition that they are inclined to make a little higher charge than where there is competition; but, taking the entire service all over the country——

Q. Do you have a private wire? Of course, you do not see any objection to that?—A. We see no objection, or we would not have them.

Q. (By Representative LORIMER.) What is the object of a private wire?—A. We have them in our offices in the different markets and different cities, and lease the wires for so much a month, and are in constant communication with our representatives or branch houses.

Q. (By Mr. C. J. HARRIS.) That privilege is open to anyone who can pay for it?—A. Yes.

Q. Did you ever know the export rate to be lower than the rate from here to the seaboard? In other words, do they ever make an export rate at the present time less than the rate to the seaboard point—a through export rate to Liverpool?—A. I do not know about the through rate. I am inclined to think—I am not sure about it, as I do not keep in touch with the rate matter, but I am inclined to think they do make a lower rate for export grain than for domestic consumption.

Q. I understand; but I want to know whether it has ever got lower than the rate to Boston or New York—the seaboard?—A. I should answer that and say no, without absolutely being able to swear to it. I should say it was practically impossible. Of course, there is a time at the seaboard when there is an abundance of tonnage—what is known as distress room, and they sometimes carry grain practically as ballast. Instead of getting a fair rate for carrying it, rather than go out light they will take it at practically nothing—carry it for ballast.

Q. You have never heard of any from this end to Europe that were lower than the rate to the seaboard?—A. No; I do not know of it.

(Testimony closed.)

CHICAGO, ILL., *November 17, 1899.*

TESTIMONY OF MR. GEORGE H. WEBSTER,

President of the Armour Elevator Company.

The subcommission on transportation met at 2 p. m.; Chairman Lorimer presiding.

Mr. GEORGE H. WEBSTER. being duly sworn, testified as follows:

Q. (By Representative LORIMER.) Please state your name and address.—A. George H. Webster, 205 Lasalle street, Chicago.

Q. Your business, please?—A. I am president of the Armour Elevator Company at present.

Q. There has been considerable complaint about the elevator system in Chicago by the commission men, and the commission would like to have you in your own way go on and state what the actual conditions are with reference to that business.—A. I will say to that, that I am very glad of the opportunity, and have prepared and had prepared a paper which I think will cover the whole matter very comprehensively and clearly; and with your permission I should like to read it. (Witness reads paper.)

I appear in response to the invitation of your secretary, asking me for an account of the manner in which the grain business of Chicago is conducted and of the methods observed in transporting grain on the Great Lakes and of the relationship existing between lake and land carriers.

I am the president of the Armour Elevator Company, a corporation operating several large elevators in Chicago. I was a member of the firm of Armour & Co., a firm doing business in Chicago as packers of meat and provisions and dealers in grain, from 1881 to 1894, and from 1865 to 1881 I was a member of the firm of Armour, Plankinton & Co., grain and provision merchants in the city of New York.

In order that your committee may at the outset be fully informed as to the grain handling and storing facilities of Chicago, I have had prepared and submit below a list of all the grain elevators in Chicago, large and small, public and private, giving, so far as possible, the location and capacity of each and the names of the proprietors:

REGULAR PUBLIC WAREHOUSES.

Warehouses.	Operated by—	Location.	Storage capacity.
Armour A B and B annex.	Armour Elevator Co	Chicago, Milwaukee and St. Paul Rwy. and North Branch.	4,000,000
Armour F	....do	Chicago, Burlington and Quincy, and river.	1,000,000
Alton and B	G. A. Seaverns.	Chicago and Alton and river	1,800,000
Central B and annex.	Central Elevator Co	Illinois Central Rwy. and river	1,600,000
Wabash.	Chicago Elevator Co	Wabash Rwy. and South Branch.	1,5000,00
Rock Island A	C. Counselman & Co	Chicago, Rock Island and Pacific Rwy. and river.	1,0000,00
South Chicago C and annex.	South Chicago Elevator Co.	Chicago, Rock Island and Pacific and Calumet River.	3,000,000
City	Chicago Rwy. Terminal Elevator Co.	Chicago and North Western and river.	1,000,000
Union	....do	Chicago and Alton and river	2,000,000
Nebraska City	Nebraska City Packing Co.	.....do	2,500,000
National	National Elevator and Dock Co.	Chicago and Alton and river	1,000,000
St. Louis	Keith & Co	.....do	2,000,000
Calumet B	Bartlett, Frazier & Co	South Chicago, Elgin, Joliet and Eastern and Belt Rwy.	1,200,000
Peavey B		South Chicago Belt and 103d	2,000,000
Total			25,000,000
In addition there are two public warehouses, which are not regular in the sense of having qualified under the rules of the Chicago Board of Trade on the subject, viz:			
Indiana	Chicago Elevator Co	Chicago and Eastern Illinois, Wabash, and river.	1,500,000
Iowa	Chicago Rwy. Terminal Elevator Co.	Chicago and Northwestern and river.	1,500,000
Total capacity.			28,600,000

PRIVATE WAREHOUSES OF CHICAGO AND CAPACITY OF SAME.

Armour C	Armour & Co	Chicago, Burlington and Quincy, Brown and 22d streets.	1,000,000
Armour D	....do	Chicago, Burlington and Quincy, Morgan and 22d streets.	1,500,000
Armour E	....do	Chicago, Burlington and Quincy, 16th and Chicago River.	800,000
Adams	C. E. Adams	Chicago Junction Rwy., Union avenue and 40th street.	20,000
Atlantic	Lazier & Hooper	Chicago, Milwaukee and St. Paul and Weed street.	150,000
Badenoch	J. J. Badenoch	Pittsburg, Cincinnati, Chicago and St. Louis and Madison street.	160,000
Belt	Rosenbaum Bros	Belt Yards and 87th street	1,350,000
Byrnes	W. J. Byrnes & Co.	Chicago, Rock Island and Pacific and 31st st.	40,000
Calumet A	Bartlett, Frazier & Co	South Chicago, Elgin, Joliet and Eastern and Belt.	1,200,000
Calumet B	....do	.....do	1,500,000
Calumet C	....do	.....do	
Calumet A	Calumet Grain and Elevator Co.	South Chicago, Elgin, Joliet and Eastern, Pittsburg, Fort Wayne and Chicago Rwy.	175,000
Calumet B	....do	South Chicago, Baltimore and Ohio and Terminal Rwy.	175,000
Calumet C	....do	South Chicago, Chicago, Rock Island and Pacific and Belt.	150,000
Central A	Carrington, Hannah & Co	Illinois Central and South Water street.	800,000

655A——26

PRIVATE WAREHOUSES OF CHICAGO AND CAPACITY OF SAME—Continued.

Warehouses.	Operated by—	Location.	Storage capacity.
Chicago Dock Co.	A. Dickinson Co	Chicago and Alton and Taylor street.	1,000,000
Columbia	Armour & Co.	Chicago, Burlington and Quincy and Robey street.	500,000
Cragin	Chicago and O'Neill Grain Co.	Chicago, Milwaukee and St. Paul and North avenue.	70,000
Cleveland	American Linseed Oil Co.	South Chicago	400,000
Danville	Carrington, Hannah & Co.	Chicago and Alton and Ashland avenue.	400,000
Englewood	C. Counselman & Co	Chicago, Rock Island and Pacific and 63d street.	200,000
Fitchburg	Williams Grain Co	Pittsburg, Fort Wayne and Chicago and 39th street.	60,000
Fox & Bowerman.	Fox & Bowerman	Belt Line and 94th street	125,000
Farmer, Harris & Co.	Farmer, Harris & Co	Hayford	80,000
Galena	Chicago Terminal Rwy. Elevator Co.	Chicago and Northwestern and Rush street.	700,000
Grand Crossing	F. G. Ely	Illinois Central Rwy. and 77th street.	100,000
Grand Trunk	Richardson & Co	Chicago and Grand Trunk, Elsdon	100,000
Hall	American Linseed Oil Co.	Grade Crossing, Illinois Central and 76th street.	300,000
Harvey	Middle Division Elevator Co.	Harvey, Grand Trunk Rwy	50,000
Hawkeye	Stuhr Grain Co	West Hammond and Chicago Junction Rwy.	700,000
Hess	Eckhart & Swan	Carroll and Ada streets	750,000
Interstate	Interstate Elevator Co	Erie Rwy. and 50th street	100,000
Imperial	American Cereal Co	St. Charles Air Line and Dearborn	250,000
Lake Shore Transportation Co.	Churchill & Co	Lake Shore and Michigan Southern and 66th street.	125,000
Leet & Fritz		Oakdale and Belt	250,000
Livingston	Livingston & Co	Chicago, Rock Island and Pacific and 31st street.	25,000
McReynolds A	McReynolds & Co	South Chicago Belt and 106th street	1,500,000
McReynolds B	do	Wisconsin Central and Wood	1,250,000
Mabbatt	G. A. Seaverns	Chicago and Alton and Wood	1,300,000
Matteson	C. L. Dougherty	Matteson, Michigan Central Rwy	40,000
Merritt & Co	W. H. Merritt & Co	Belt Rwy. and 98th street	650,000
Metzger	American Linseed Oil Co.	Pittsburg, Cincinnati, Chicago and St. Louis and 18th street.	250,000
Michigan Central A.	T. A. Mealiff	Kensington and Michigan Central Rwy.	
Michigan Central B.	do	do	40,000
Minnesota	Armour & Co	Chicago, Milwaukee and St. Paul and Weed street.	1,200,000
Morgan	Richardson & Co	Chicago, Burlington and Quincy and Leavitt street.	100,000
Mueller	H. Mueller & Co	Pittsburg, Fort Wayne and Chicago and 55th street.	300,000
Nebraska City D.	Nebraska City Elevator Co.	Chicago and Alton and 23d street	35,000
Nickel Plate	H. G. Chase	Nickel Plate and Stony Island	50,000
Owen & Austin	W. R. Owen	Pittsburg, Cincinnati, Chicago and St. Louis and 12th street.	80,000
Peavey A.	Peavey Grain Co	South Chicago Belt and 103d street	750,000
Pennsylvania Transfer.	Requa Bros	Pennsylvania Railway and 57th street	175,000
Requa	do	Wabash and 44th street	120,000
Rock Island B.	C. Counselman & Co	Chicago, Rock Island and Pacific and 12th street.	750,000
Santa Fe A.	Richardson & Co	Santa Fe and Wood street	1,500,000
St. Paul and Fulton annex.	Not now being operated	Chicago, Milwaukee and St. Paul and river.	1,300,000
Sibley	Sibley Elevator Co	Western Indiana and 31st street	285,000
South Chicago D.	C. Counselman & Co	South Chicago, Chicago, Rock Island and Pacific and Belt.	1,000,000
Star and Crescent	Star and Crescent Milling Co.	Chicago, Milwaukee and St. Paul and Randolph street.	90,000
Truit	R. H. Truit	Western Indiana and 83d street	90,000
Wabash Transfer	R. E. Pratt & Co	Wabash Rwy. and Rockwell street	159,000
Walther	Walther & Co	Chicago, Rock Island and Pacific and Wentworth street.	35,000
Wetherill		Chicago and Alton and Quarry street.	100,000
Wright and Lawther.	American Linseed Oil Co.	Chicago and Alton and Polk street	200,000
Total			28,645,000

Under the constitution of Illinois, adopted in 1870, by Article XIII it is declared that all elevators or warehouses where grain or other property is stored for a compensation, whether the property stored be kept separate or not, are to be public warehouses, and it also provides for certain limitations upon the conduct of the business and makes it the duty of the general assembly of the State to pass necessary laws to give effect to the provisions of this article of the State constitution. In obedience to the obligation thus imposed upon it, the legislature of Illinois passed an act to regulate public warehouses, and the warehousing and inspection of grain, and to give effect to Article XIII of the constitution of the State, which act became operative on July 1, 1871. Under this law it was provided that public warehouses of Class A should embrace all warehouses, elevators, and granaries in which grain is stored in bulk, in which grain of different owners is mixed together, or in which grain is stored in such a manner that the identity of different lots or parcels can not be accurately preserved—such warehouses, elevators, or granaries being located in cities having not less than 100,000 inhabitants. The State has safe-guarded the interests of the public doing business with these regulated warehouses by a very careful system of rules and requirements which are to be observed under severe penalties for violation. It requires that licenses shall be obtained by application to, and be issued by, the circuit court of the county, permitting the applicant to carry on a public elevator business under the laws of the State, which license is revocable in a summary proceeding in such court upon the complaint of any person showing and proving a violation of the law. The warehouseman is required to give bonds to the State for the performance of his duties, and any person carrying on the business of such a public warehouseman without complying with the law is made liable to a continuing fine of from $100 to $500 per day. The law has amply provided for a system of inspection of grain, and all grain taken into such warehouses must be inspected before its reception. The law also provides a system of registration of certificates issued for grain received into such warehouses, and places the duty of executing the inspection and registration requirement of the law under the control of the State board of railroad and warehouse commissioners.

The public elevators of Chicago handle about 25 per cent of the grain which is received in Chicago, the rest being handled by the private elevators and warehouses.

In order that the standing of Chicago as a grain market from year to year may appear, I append the receipts of wheat and other grains here from the year 1880 to the present time, compared with the total production of grain in the United States for the same years:

Year.	Receipts at Chicago.		Production of United States.	
	Wheat.	Other grain.	Wheat.	Other grain.
	Bushels.	Bushels.	Bushels.	Bushels.
1880	23,541,607	127,844,513	498,550,000	2,219,644,000
1881	14,824,999	111,137,600	383,280,000	1,682,749,000
1882	23,008,596	85,197,293	504,185,000	2,195,209,000
1883	20,364,155	127,780,980	420,155,000	2,208,283,000
1884	26,397,587	110,840,000	512,764,000	2,480,115,000
1885	18,909,717	112,242,500	357,112,000	2,658,327,000
1886	16,771,743	116,535,000	457,218,000	2,384,302,000
1887	21,848,251	110,658,400	456,329,000	2,204,118,000
1888	13,438,069	141,548,700	415,863,000	2,793,874,000
1889	18,762,646	144,953,100	490,564,440	2,984,440,000
1890	14,248,770	185,191,800	399,262,000	2,120,738,000
1891	42,931,258	168,565,200	611,780,000	2,923,320,000
1892	50,234,556	175,980,700	515,949,000	2,402,051,000
1893	35,355,101	190,577,700	396,132,000	2,366,907,000
1894	25,665,902	142,883,348	460,267,000	1,975,642,000
1895	20,637,602	155,270,607	467,103,000	3,105,507,000
1896	25,818,647	193,722,000	427,684,000	3,099,906,000
1897	26,669,436	225,965,000	530,140,000	2,710,781,000
1898	38,094,804	249,309,000	675,149,000	2,747,961,000

The extension of the improved-farm acreage in the great grain belt of the Northwestern and Western States has of necessity brought about changes in the marketing of grain, just as the cost of labor, the supply and cheapness of raw material, the necessity for closer proximity to the fast-growing markets for manufactured products in the great Central and Western States, has induced so many of the seaboard manufacturers to move this way in order that they may be nearer to the base of supplies and the seat of growing demand. Before more fully considering the effect of these changes upon the grain market of Chicago, it may be of interest to look into the origin and growth of the grain or elevator storage business and of the conditions attached to the marketing of grain previous to and since the inauguration of the present system, as showing your commission the evolution that has taken place in the grain business in the past 50 years. It is within the memory of the living when the first grain was sold in Chicago. The first annual receipts of grain recorded as brought into Chicago were in 1838, when 78 bushels of wheat were received. Wheat and other grain in those days, and for a great many years after, was brought to the city in wagons by the farmers themselves and sold to the millers or grain buyers. The grain was usually marketed in bags or other receptacles convenient for manual reception and distribution. In the transferring of grain at the shipping points from the wagons, mills, cars, canal boats, or vessels in which it was received, to the cars, canal boats, or ships which should bear it to its final destination, the slow, wasteful, and expensive system of the carriage of grain upon the backs of brawny laborers was in vogue.

To gain time in the handling of grain and to reduce the expense by substituting machinery for manual labor and by handling grain in bulk was a problem solved by Mr. Joseph Dart, of Buffalo, N. Y. He first conceived the idea that this work could be as well done by machinery, and accordingly, in the year 1843, he built an elevator at the mouth of the Buffalo River, in the city of Buffalo, into which canal boats passed and were loaded and unloaded by machinery. It was a small concern compared with the mammoth structures of to-day, having a capacity of only 55,000 bushels and capable of handling 15,000 bushels in a day, but it was the origin and forerunner of the vast machinery of to-day which deposits the cereal production of the country in these huge storage bins, to be stored until sold, and by which the greatest agricultural production of the world is handled so economically, so expeditiously, and so correctly.

Horsepower was the motor power in these primitive warehouses until about 1849, when steam was substituted, and this former avenue of employment to the laborer at grain-transferring points was forever closed, as machinery has in other industries and instances displaced labor in the economy of time and expense. This change in the handling, collecting, storing, and shipping of grain was contemporaneous with the breaking to plow of the earlier of the great grain-growing States of the West and Northwest; and the cities of Chicago, St. Louis, and Milwaukee, which were the business centers of this vast territory, soon became the primary grain markets of the country, both because they were the business centers and because of their being close to inland water routes to the seaboard. It has been the unchangeable rule, where it was possible, that the grain crop of the grain belt should seek the nearest and therefore the cheapest route to market from the nearest inland lake or other water point. Aided by their superior advantages in this respect, Chicago and Milwaukee became the natural eastern terminals of the first railroads into this territory, and as naturally became the primary grain markets.

In 1849, or about that time, Mr. Hiram Wheeler built an elevator in Chicago for grain storage, near the Chicago River and Franklin street. The grain at that time was brought to Chicago by the Illinois and Michigan Canal, by cars, and in teams, and approximated 1,000,000 bushels for the year. In 1853, the first year for which the receipts are given in the board of trade reports, the receipts of grain at Chicago were: Wheat, 1,687,465 bushels; corn, 2,869,339 bushels; oats, 1,875,770 bushels; rye and barley, 278,549 bushels, or more than 6,500,000 bushels of grain in round numbers. At the time of the Chicago fire 6 elevators, with a capacity of 2,475,000 bushels, were destroyed. In 1872 the new city began its grain business with 11 elevators, having a storage capacity of 8,900,000 bushels, and during the year its receipts of grain were 84,511,000 bushels. To-day, all told, large and small, public and private, there are 81 elevators in Chicago, with a storage capacity of 57,000,000 bushels.

To build elevators is a comparatively easy matter, but to conduct them profitably in competition with neighbors, and to keep them filled with grain under existing conditions, involves an exceedingly difficult problem. True, the Western States have increased their grain production until the States of Illinois, Iowa, Indiana, Missouri, Kansas, Nebraska, Minnesota, the two Dakotas, and Wisconsin produce 55 per cent of the wheat crop, 62 per cent of the corn crop, and 67 per cent of the oats crop of this country; and if conditions of marketing had remained unchanged, Chicago, ever progressive and always prepared, would easily have commanded and handled a large part of this 2,000,000,000 bushels of grain. Changes have quite naturally occurred, however, and the growth of railroads, of cities, lake ports, banks, local mills and elevators, and other facilities which tend to disturb and shift the ordinary paths of commerce have diverted much of the grain trade from Chicago to other places more advantageously situated as to producer and consumer.

The four wheat-producing States of Kansas, Minnesota, and the two Dakotas produce 35 per cent of the wheat crop of the Union. In 1870 they were traversed by 2,658 miles of railroad; in 1896 their railroad mileage had increased to 20,357 miles. From this increase in transportation facilities inevitably followed the up-building of the small hamlet and produce-trading village, the local bank and the local mill and elevator man. Many of the numerous commercial communities of the Northwest seem to have been born in a night. Minneapolis, using more wheat in its mammoth flour mills in a year than is received for the same period in Chicago, has wrested the laurel from this city, and is to-day the greatest primary wheat market in the world. It contains 37 elevators, with a storage capacity of 28,000,000 bushels, and annually receives almost 100,000,000 bushels of wheat. Last year its receipts of grain were 120,000,000 bushels.

The city of Duluth, which had a population of 75 inhabitants in 1860, was incorporated as a city in 1869, and has survived to make jest of the sarcasm of Proctor Knott. From its humble place in 1860 it reached a population of 32,725 in 1890, and became second to Minneapolis as a wheat market. It is the Lake Superior terminus of many railroads and the head of lake navigation. It contains, with its sister city, Superior, elevator capacity for 25,000,000 bushels of grain, and handled last year 99,132,318 bushels, of which over one-half was wheat. Every water route outlet to the seaboard draws this grain trade away from the direction of Chicago, and a keen competition has developed between Chicago grain merchants and these outlets.

The annual wheat receipts at Kansas City almost equal those of Chicago, and aggregate about 24,000,000 bushels. St. Louis receives annually of wheat about 11,500,000 bushels. Peoria, Toledo, and other inland points have become largely grain trade channels and handle very large quantities, and lake cities, like Milwaukee, Detroit, Gladstone, and Manitowoc, actively compete for this trade. The grain trade has thus gone into widely separated channels, each channel growing in volume from year to year, and Chicago, to which a few years ago this stream of grain flowed by nature and from necessity and without effort on its part, is now compelled to invade the field of production and actively struggle for control. It can ask no favors and can only control trade when it meets the competition. The grain no longer seeks a market at Chicago: that market must seek the grain. It is a natural trade condition, and is a condition that exists in almost every line of trade. Competition, and the natural desire of both producer and consumer, to come closer together, to eliminate the middleman, and all unnecessary intermediate expense, have resulted in dispensing largely with commission men, brokers, and traveling solicitors.

The early business of Armour & Co. was that of country commission merchants, receiving and making advances upon shipments for sale on commission of all kinds of grain, provisions, hides, high wines, tallow, and produce generally. They have been buyers and sellers of grain for 35 years, but they have always been both aggressive and progressive, and have from time to time branched out into other lines as opportunities were presented and the progress of the times demanded. If this were not true of this firm and other Chicago packers, we should to-day be without our prestige as a packing center, and should probably be now competing with small places for hogs dressed upon the farm and sold from farmers' wagons, as we did 30 years ago, when the value of offal of slaughtered animals was lost to the producer who slaughtered and dressed his hogs for sale to the packer.

Among the general evolutions in business that the past 15 or 20 years have developed, the changes in the grain trade that have been described are no exception to the rule in other branches of trade. The methods of the provision business, and especially the export branch of it, present a very forcible example. Formerly, if a Hamburg merchant, for instance, desired to purchase 500 boxes of bacon he would cable his commission house in New York for a quotation; this agent in turn would request a quotation from another house representing Armour & Co., or some other packer in the West. This quotation would be solicited and obtained by telegraph, furnished the commission agent, and thence cabled to Hamburg. If a sale resulted, the deliveries were made in the same roundabout and expensive way, meaning two commissions in New York alone between the packer and the foreign merchant. Now, the Hamburg merchant cables to the packer direct, eliminates New York in the transaction, and the products are shipped to Hamburg from Chicago on through bills of lading, doing away with all intermediate expense. Just such facilities as these have been the prominent factors in both the grain and provision trades, enlarging their scope and magnitude by developing and opening the markets of the world. Self-interest actuates every man in conducting his business at the very least possible expense, consistent with safe business methods, whether it be in the elimination of expensive intermediaries, unnecessary labor or expense, or by any improved method, machinery, or means, and this indeed is the basis of commercial progress and success. It necessarily and frequently changes the course of trade to the injury of some and to the benefit of others, a condition that apparently will always exist.

So, too, the evolution which has taken place in the grain trade at Chicago, and doubtless also in other cities, has, no doubt, necessarily operated to interfere with the business methods of many persons. A time was when nearly every bushel of grain passed from the producer to the purchaser by the way of a commission merchant. Necessarily, a reduction in the volume of grain consigned to a commission merchant reduces his business. As the producers began to sell to local merchants direct, this reduction began. As this business grew the reduction increased; and it increased still more when it began to become general for the producer or local owner to make his own sales and dispense with the services of a middleman altogether. It is a matter for regret that so many commission merchants should find their earnings diminished. Some of them have found it wise or even necessary to engage in some other business. The majority of those affected are sensible enough to appreciate that their plight is the result of commercial conditions, precisely as many of their fellow-citizens have undergone a similar experience in other lines of business. It is, perhaps, not unnatural that some of them have become irritated and been moved to complain bitterly that they should have been made to suffer. A very few, especially in Chicago, have conceived that the blame lies on certain grain dealers, and as a result they have for years waged a war, before legislatures, in the courts, on the board of trade, in the press, on the street corner, and whenever one could be found to listen, in season and out of season, against those who formerly bought from them as commission merchants, but who find it necessary now to buy from the owner direct. If the present methods of the Chicago grain merchant are to be criticised, why not also denounce the farmer for no longer consigning his grain to the commission merchant? Why not the local grain dealer who purchases from the producer and resells to the wholesale merchant without the intervention of a middleman? These are quite as guilty as the Chicago grain merchant in bringing about the business disappointment which is complained of. Shall the farmer be compelled by law to ship to a commission merchant? Shall it be made a crime to buy from the farmer direct, or for the local dealer to make his own sale? Or for the wholesale merchant to buy from the owner in person? In what respect does the grain trade differ from any other in which such personal negotiations are now the general rule?

The fact that the leading grain merchants of Chicago are also the proprietors of or interested in elevators is not due to a purpose on their part to oppose commission merchants, much less to a desire to control the prices to be paid to producers. The situation has been forced upon them by trade conditions. The elevators were built to accommodate the great quantities of grain which formerly sought Chicago as the natural and necessary market. The situation in former years was thus graphically described in Munn v. Illinois, 94 U. S., p. 130: "The great producing region of the West and Northwest sends its grain by water and rail to Chicago, where the greater part of it is shipped by vessel for transportation to the seaboard by the Great Lakes, and some of it is forwarded by railway to the Eastern ports. * * * Vessels, to some extent, are loaded in the Chicago harbor, and sailed through the St. Lawrence directly to Europe. * * * The quantity (of grain) received in Chicago has made it the greatest grain market in the world. This business has created a demand for means by which the immense quantity of grain can be handled or stored, and these have been found in grain warehouses, which are commonly called elevators, because the grain is elevated from the boat or car, by machinery operated by steam, into the bins prepared for its reception, and elevated from the bins by a like process into the vessel or car which is to carry it on. * * * In this way the largest traffic between the citizens of the country north and west of Chicago, and the citizens of the country lying on the Atlantic coast north of Washington is in grain which passes through the elevators of Chicago. In this way the trade in grain is carried on by the inhabitants of seven or eight of the great States of the West, with four or five of the States lying on the seashore, and forms the largest part of the interstate commerce in these States."

As already indicated, in time Chicago ceased to be a tollgate for this grain. The milling industry at Minneapolis, the development of markets or extensive elevator systems, or both, at Duluth, Fort William, on Georgian Bay, at Milwaukee, Omaha, Kansas City, St. Louis, Mississippi River points, and at other cities, all combined to intrench upon Chicago's former enviable position. The resulting competition necessarily had the effect to greatly reduce the quantity of grain which naturally sought Chicago for a market. This reduction demonstrated that much of the elevator space at Chicago would necessarily lie idle the greater portion of the year. The interest on the investment would remain the same, the depreciation in the structures would continue, and the expenses of operation and maintenance would be but slightly less, whether the elevators were full or largely empty. It was but ordinary business prudence for the elevator proprietors to utilize their storage capacity. This could only be done by bringing grain to Chicago for storage. As the producers and other local owners were being induced by the efforts and advantages of competing cities to ship largely to them, the Chicago elevator proprietors had no alternative except to buy and thus to direct the point of its storage. They were enabled to do this in face of the competition which confronted them—a competition which was fatal, to a very large degree, to a commission merchant or a dealer located in Chicago, who was not similarly equipped in these respects:

1. As to private elevators, the proprietors were enabled to clean and otherwise improve the quality, and thereby the value of the grain which they had bought.

2. As to public elevators, the proprietors were enabled to include the storage charges (so far as they were above the actual expenses of operation) in the cost to them of the grain.

3. As to both classes of elevators, they were enabled to utilize the space which would otherwise have remained idle.

4. And as to both, the situation is but another illustration that a person concerned in a business finds it to his interest to himself supply the needed appliances, or, owning the appliances, to use them for products of which he is the owner. In the one case he seeks to avoid paying someone else a profit for using his appliances, and in the other he seeks to earn the profit which another would otherwise realize from such use.

This principle is not peculiar to the grain trade of Chicago. Illustrations are found in every branch of industry. The farmer supplies his own granaries, instead of storing in the local elevators; he provides his own scales, and, so far as possible, uses his own means of transportation. When it is at all possible, railroad companies and many large manufacturers mine their own coal and buy their supplies at a point nearest their own means of hauling them. Those who need ice in their business endeavor to maintain their own ice houses and refrigerating machines. Large plants install their own lighting apparatus, and so on without end. On the other hand, the producer of an agricultural product or of raw material will, if possible, transform it into a manufactured product. The farmer will make cider or distill his grain, if he can do so. The miner prefers to use his own smelter. The owner of timber lands prefers to sell in the shape of lumber. The oil producer will bend every energy to refine it and to utilize the by-products. And again, the owner of surplus space or other commodity prefers to use it if he can, and will engage in apparently extraneous pursuits to that end. A wholesale merchant will store the goods of others in his warehouse. A farmer will thresh grain, or bale hay, or gin cotton for his neighbors. An electric street railway will engage in the business of furnishing electricity for light, heat, and power for manufacturing purposes. A carrier owning terminals, wharves, and the like will permit others to use them for the sake of the compensation he can earn.

In every such case, and they are as numerous as the countless branches of human industry, the person alluded to, in a certain sense, gains an advantage over his competitors, or others engaged or interested in the same business, who are not similarly equipped. The farmer referred to can save storage, weighing, and transportation charges, which one who is less favorably equipped can not do. To the extent that he makes a profit by transforming his produce into a manufactured article he realizes a greater return than the farmer who does not pursue this course. The net returns from threshing, baling, or ginning will, in a sense, proportionately reduce the net cost of his own produce. The same results follow in all other instances which have been adverted to.

It does not at all follow, in the case of the wholesale grain merchant, because he survives or even flourishes in his business, that the result is due to special favors granted by railroad companies or to other illegal or improper practices. Indeed, the wholesale grain merchant who is also an elevator proprietor is often driven to pay the farmer or local grain dealer a larger price for grain than the current Chicago market would seem to warrant. This is not because the difference is made up by a reduced freight rate or other reprehensible practice. It is due to a number of causes and explained by a number of reasons:

1. It is because such a price is compelled to be paid in order to meet the com-

petition of other markets whose contiguity and other advantages enable them to pay the apparently higher price. Self-evidently, no more is paid than is necessary to meet the competition which exists. The Chicago dealer, like everyone else, buys as cheaply as he can.

2. In paying this high price the purchaser figures on making up the apparent excess in a number of ways. He is thereby enabled to keep his elevators filled, to make the profit that results from storing on a large scale, to save the expense of paying storage charges to some outside warehouseman, to carry on his grain business on the wholesale basis, to fill large orders, especially in foreign markets, and to make his shipments abroad by means of large cargoes.

3. In order to be in a position to accomplish these ends, the Chicago dealer must maintain himself as a buyer through a large enough territory to produce the requisite quantity. If he habitually bids less than the offers from competing markets he can not expect to get the grain. More than that, he loses his business prestige and customers by proving himself unable to compete with buyers from other markets.

4. By dealing on so large a scale and by computing the bearing of the other elements above mentioned, what seems to involve a loss is made to show, perhaps, even a profit. And at this point it should be mentioned that from his standpoint profit means the comparatively small difference of one thirty-second, one-sixteenth, one-eighth, or one-fourth of a cent a bushel.

5. Again, by buying from the owner direct the Chicago wholesale merchant, in ultimate effect, saves the compensation of an intermediate broker or commission merchant.

6. The most important element is the fact that the local price at Chicago is not the only basis from which the wholesale dealer figures his bid. He recognizes the stubborn fact that the European market fixes the price which he will obtain on a resale of his purchases. Under normal conditions he does not buy to sell to the local miller or feed dealer, but to export or to sell to an exporter. He therefore adopts the European price and computes what it will cost him to lay the article down in the foreign market. In computing this cost he takes into account that he has his own elevators and other appliances at most of the points of transshipment; that he can ship by lake or rail, or partly by each, and that he can utilize the advantage of choosing the cheapest of ocean rates; that he can ship in large quantities, or even in his own vessels, and that he can fill orders abroad in great quantities. In short, he is in a position to reap the benefit of gathering retail lots into a wholesale quantity; of shipping many purchases as one, and of himself earning much of the profit or saving much of the expense incident to the carriage to a foreign market.

It is to be borne in mind, also, that there oftentimes enters into such transaction the element of speculation, so called. On the same principle that others in nearly every branch of business buy and sell for future delivery, the Chicago grain merchant risks his judgment as to the value of grain on a given future date. He figures on making sales later on. He can only be in a position to realize his plans by actually purchasing the grain in advance and storing it in his own warehouse in the interval. His motive and plans are precisely the same as those of any other merchant who buys goods to-day, hoping that a rise in prices will enable him to reap a profit later on. Many times, therefore, the commercial spirit—the speculative instinct, if you please—will move him to pay more than the current market apparently warrants. He is buying not for to-day, nor for immediate sale, but to make a sale 90 days or more in the future. Hence he feels justified in taking the risk incidental to his bid, and especialty in territory which he would otherwise have to yield to buyers from competing cities, and in order to avert the depreciation resulting from the ownership and maintenance of an unfilled elevator.

If the local elevator man or the farmer of the interior prefers other markets or methods, there is but one remedy. His self-interest must be appealed to, and this can be done only by outbidding your competitors and making it a matter of personal advantage to him to ship his grain to a given city. The trade must conform to the varying conditions that confront it, and when it fails to meet any and all legitimate competition it necessarily declines and falls. The elevator men of Chicago were forced to face conditions of this character, and rather than run at a loss and see a great part of the grain trade completely diverted to other channels, they met this competition and are entitled to credit to no small extent for the present large annual grain receipts at this point. Whether they took the steps they did or not would make but little difference to those who formerly did a large commission business, because but for their acts the great bulk of the grain would have passed through other cities. But to a large class of men, a class to whom little attention has been directed or given in this matter, it would have been a matter of deep concern. It would mean curtailed employment to the thousands of artisans and laborers directly and indirectly engaged in grain handling and grain traffic at this city, and this is one of the great reasons why the Chicago public has so generously upheld and seconded the efforts of every man, whether elevator proprietor or grain merchant, in increasing the shipments of grain to this market.

And when all has been said, this is largely a local question. The storage of grain in Chicago elevators can not be said to enter the domain of Federal jurisdiction. It has been and is judicially declared to be a matter for State control alone. (Munn v. Illinois, 94 U. S.) Previous to the year 1897 it was considered by some of the courts of this State that, in the absence of permissive legislative authority, it was against public policy for elevator owners operating public warehouses to store grain of their own in the same bins and to mix it with the grain of others of the same grade. The legislature of Illinois at its session in 1897 enacted a law granting this permission to public warehousemen, and it is now lawful for them to store their own grain in this way, subject to the very intelligent safeguards provided in the act. Few acts of recent State legislative sessions attracted more general attention from the public and the press, or were given more earnest or free discussion than this measure. It passed the senate by the convincing vote of 34 to 11, and was no less strongly approved in the house of representatives. In the ensuing period, the opponents of the law availed themselves of every means possible to create public opposition to its continuance on the statute books, and in the session of 1899 introduced an act to repeal the law, but this act was defeated by an even more decisive vote than that by which the measure was originally enacted. The legislators in the two years' practical operation of the measure had had ample opportunity to ascertain the public sentiment as to its wisdom and propriety, and they thus know that public feeling, not only of Chicago, but of the whole State, approved their action. This deduction is particularly justified by the fact that in every instance the large majority of the votes cast in favor of this measure came from the representatives of agricultural communities of Illinois.

The elevator companies in Chicago not only have to meet the competition between themselves in order to get grain to handle, but also, as already shown, they have many prominent outside markets to compete against. This competition has made each grain firm work everything down to the finest possible margin, and has caused the elimination of a great deal of the intermediate expense which originally existed between and was borne by the farmer and the final consumer of the grain. Several years ago, a farmer who did not ship to Chicago would sell his grain to a local dealer, who operated at a small country station. As a general rule, these country stations were not plentiful and the capital of the proprietors was limited; and usually there was but one elevator and one buyer at a point, consequently he would not pay a very liberal price, but would figure on a profit of from 3 to 8 cents per bushel. Most of the farmers were unable to help themselves, as the towns were far apart and buyers scarce. With the great addition to the railroad mileage during late years and the keenness of the competition between the different roads and the building of new towns the original territory of these different grain buyers has been split up into many parts or commercial subdivisions, and at nearly all towns in the grain country there are now located from two to six buyers. The competition among these buyers is very keen, both among themselves and against other towns located but a few miles away; so that these small dealers now rarely obtain more than from one-half to 2 cents per bushel margin to pay for the expense of operating their elevators, the risk of grading, shortages, changes in the market, etc. Up to twelve or fifteen years ago, all these country elevator men consigned their grain to Chicago commission merchants, who received as a commission from one-half to 1½ cents per bushel, besides charging high rates of interest, inspection, weighing, sampling, and numerous other charges. These commission men, when they received grain, went on the board of trade and sold it to other commission men, representing Eastern buyers. The grain was transferred through the public elevators, which at that time received 1¼ cents per bushel for the first ten days' storage and one-half cent per bushel for each additional ten days. The commission man's commission and other charges were a burden added to the grain. The Chicago storage which was charged was another burden. The commission man representing the Eastern buyer charged his customer in the East from one-half to 1 cent per buhesl for buying the grain, which also added to the burden. The Eastern buyers were sometimes exporters of grain from the Atlantic seaboard cities and sometimes sold to Eastern mills; and, in a large number of cases, large shippers to Boston, New York, Philadelphia, and other Eastern cities bought the grain through their Chicago commission merchants in round lots and then resold it to different millers and smaller consumers through the East in carload lots. The exporter sold his grain abroad. In cases where the Eastern shipper bought the round lots from the Chicago market and peddled the grain out in from 1 to 5 car lots through the East, a very good margin was received. The seaboard exporters also made a very liberal commission. The charges for transferring the grain from lake vessels at Buffalo to cars was 1¼ cents per bushel. The charges at the seaboard for taking the grain from cars and putting it aboard ocean vessels were very high. Thus, the total charges in the way of commissions, middlemen's compensation, and other expenses, from the time the grain left the farmer until it reached the consumer, were very large.

It is to be at all times remembered that the ultimate market price is fixed by the foreign deficiency, and, therefore, by the European markets. In fixing this price the American producer, elevator proprietor, and grain merchant has no voice and, in the very nature of things, is powerless. That price is fixed by the competition of the entire world, as to which nothing can operate except the law of supply and demand. As the ultimate price is thus fixed, all the intermediate charges necessarily fall on the producer. The price he gets is the European market less the necessary charges incident to getting it there. The higher and more numerous these charges are the less is the price realized by the producer and, conversely, a reduction in the number or amount of these burdens increases the return to him.

By the competition of the different elevator men in the different cities, the margin of profit and the aggregate of the expenses have been very largely cut down. To begin with, in addition to the country grain dealer's margin, which has also been largely reduced, the Chicago commission man's commission has been largely eliminated and reduced, because of the fact that the elevator companies situated at the lake ports, seaboard cities, and other places buy direct from the producer or country grain dealer to so great an extent and do not figure a commission charge into the price they pay. As practically all of the concerns operate private warehouses, at times their storage charge, which is now three-fourths of a cent for the first 10 days and one-fourth of a cent for each additional 10 days, is quite often shaded in order to secure the business. The charges in public warehouses are never shaded under any circumstances. These different elevator men not only buy direct from the producers and country grain dealers, but they in turn sell direct to the Eastern consumer or miller, without any middleman in the East, so that all that expense is likewise eliminated. A large number of Western firms in Kansas City, St. Louis, Chicago, Minneapolis, and Duluth also export their grain direct to foreign dealers, thus saving the seaboard exporter's profit.

The grain business of the United States practically, at present, passes through but two hands—one, the producer, or the country elevator buyer, who receives the grain from the farmers' wagons and transfers it through his local elevator into the cars and sells the same to the elevator concern, exporter, or consumer direct. The local elevator man receives his slight charge for storage or transfer as his compensation. The balance of the original expense, which was formerly incurred, either goes to the farmer or to the consumer, according to market conditions; usually to the farmer.

At Buffalo, up to within a year or two, a charge of 1¼ cents per bushel for transferring had always been made. It is now done for one-half cent per bushel. At this point for some years the elevator companies have made a combination, not to regulate prices, but in order to secure to each his share of storage and employment. It has been the only place in the United States known to have successfully operated in that manner. The National Grain Dealers' Association, which has different organizations in different States, has attempted to prevent, in some cases, the ruinous competition among themselves and to secure a fair margin for handling grain; but all these attempts have proved failures.

The elimination of the commission charges at terminal points has caused a very bitter feeling among the commission merchants against what are now known as elevator proprietors and buyers. These commission merchants naturally feel bitter to think that they do not now receive as much of this grain as formerly and get a commission out of it as it passes through terminal points. The Chicago elevator men would be only too glad to have the same state of affairs restored which existed 15 or 20 years ago, when, on grain coming in to the grain commission men, the elevator proprietor had simply to unload the grain and receive for transferring it through his elevator 1¼ cents per bushel, with no risk, no wear and tear, and no anxiety. As it is now, in order to get any business he must go out and compete against the other terminal markets, to say nothing of his own market, and fight for the grain, handling it on small margins and taking large chances in the way of changes in the market, etc., and, finally, receive probably not half of what he formerly received without bother, or risk, or expense.

It must be borne in mind that these elevators are great, imposing, and expensive structures, nailed to the ground, and as fixed and immovable as the locality in which they exist. The grain must be brought to them, they can not follow the grain, while the commission man, movable in his person and his appliances, is fancy free to follow his vocation wherever the varying changes of grain trade may indicate a more favorable location or to change his occupation or methods at will.

The existing state of affairs has caused a large number of public elevators to cancel their licenses and to operate them as private warehouses, free from statutory control and restrictions. In most of these private warehouses machinery is placed for improving the condition of the grain; such as oat clippers, wheat cleaners, scourers, grain dryers and other appliances, which are used for bettering the quality and thus raising the grade. In the public warehouses in Chicago cleaning machinery is not allowed, and all grain must be shipped from the elevator at the same grade as it was received. In other cities the laws are different, the public elevators in Minneapolis and Duluth all having cleaning machines.

These grain-cleaning and quality-improving warehouses are beneficial to the producer and have induced the shipment of large quantities of grain to this city. The quotations on wheat grading No. 2 or No. 3 often vary from 4 to 5 cents per bushel. We will say, for instance, that two carloads of wheat are received in Chicago and inspected by the State inspector. One carload is inspected as exactly No. 3 wheat; the other is inspected as No. 3 wheat, but is pretty near No. 2. This line of wheat, thus different in actual quality, but necessarily inspected as of the same grade, is passed through the cleaning house, is improved, and what was graded as "pretty near" No. 2 wheat, on reinspection after cleaning is No. 2 wheat, is so graded and sold, and the farmer shares in the profit. In this way the No. 3 wheat which was pretty near No. 2 brought a higher price on the market than the wheat which was just No. 3. After an exhaustive judicial investigation of a similar system of grain cleaning in use in Kansas City, the Missouri supreme court not only upheld the legitimate character of the practice, but declared that it was in no sense an adulteration; that it was, in fact, a practice beneficial to all concerned, and that it could not be constitutionally interfered with. (The State ex rel Attorney-General *v*. Smith, 114 Mo., 188.) Criticism is occasionally made upon the action of the cleaning houses in turning out cleaned wheat just the grade that the rules of inspection require, or, in other words, as "line" wheat. When the cleaners meet the requirements of the law, they have done all they can be reasonably asked for, and it is nonsense to expect that a man will deliver a better grade of grain than his contract calls for. No person engaged in any other business would do so. A laborer agreeing to work 8 hours a day will not give 9 hours' work at the same price. A merchant delivers 36 inches for a yard and 16 ounces for a pound, and is not justly open to criticism for not giving more. A farmer selling live stock, grain, or other produce expects to be paid on the basis of the established standard of weights and measures. The grain merchant asks no more and can not be justly expected to take less.

It is a sufficient answer to the insinuation that the market is sometimes sought to be manipulated by large elevator proprietors or grain dealers to say that it is absolutely impossible, for the conclusive reason that the amount of grain which is grown is so immense that it is beyond the power of any one man or set of men, however powerful in other respects, to control the market for even 1 month. The effort has been repeatedly made by "plungers" and, without exception, the parties have come to grief, either losing a large amount of money or being made completely bankrupt.

The amount of grain raised in the different parts of the country is so enormous and the means of transportation are so varied, plentiful, and prompt, that manipulation at any one point is sure to attract grain from all over the United States in such large quantities, and it can be moved so rapidly, that manipulation can not be successfully carried on.

This much for "bull" manipulation for the purpose of advancing the price of grain. On the other hand, it is impossible for any interest to depress the market for the same reason that they can not successfully manipulate the market so as to advance it. If anyone in one market attempts to depreciate the value of grain at that point, it immediately becomes the target of buyers from all over the world. If the Chicago market is pushed an eighth or a quarter below that of Minneapolis or Duluth, St. Louis, Kansas City, or other markets, advantage of this fact is immediately taken by buyers.

In truth, the Chicago grain merchant can not, in any way, artificially control the prices at which he buys or those at which he sells grain. The buying price is fixed by the market value of the grain at a given point, and this market value is what the grain in question is worth at the most advantageously located market near that territory. If the Chicago merchants bid less, the grain will go to another market. So when it comes to selling, if the Chicago merchant asks more than the producers of Argentina, Russia, Egypt, India, and other grain-raising countries are willing to sell at, he will fail to sell. Of all the branches of human industry this is one in which the natural laws of supply and demand most inexorably control the prices to the producer and to the consumer.

In shipping grain from Chicago a number of routes are used. The cheapest, as a general rule, is by canal and the Great Lakes. The favorite routes are from Chicago to Buffalo, for shipment from there East via the Erie Canal and Hudson River to New York, or by rail from Buffalo or Albany to Boston, New York, Philadelphia; or from Chicago to Erie, then by rail to Philadelphia or Baltimore; from Chicago by water to Fairport, Ohio, and then to Baltimore; from Chicago to Port Huron, Sarnia, Portland, Owen Sound, Parry Sound, and Collingswood, and thence by rail through Canada to Montreal, St. Johns, Portland, or Boston; from Chicago via the Great Lakes and the Welland Canal to Prescott, Kingston, or Ogdensburg, and the transfer to barges and down the St. Lawrence River to Montreal, or taken from Ogdensburg by rail to Portland or Boston.

As a general rule these water routes are cheaper than all rail, although during the past year, for a portion of the time, the all-rail rate was as cheap as the water rate. This was partly on account of the extremely low rates by rail generally against extremely high rates by water, caused by the enormous demand for tonnage for the transportation of ores.

A new route—and one which has handled a large amount of grain during the past season—is what is known as the Canadian-Atlantic. This route is from Chicago via water to Great Lake ports, say Parry Sound, Ontario; thence by rail through Canada to a place called Coteau Point, where grain is transferred into barges and taken alongside vessels at Montreal. This route was built two years ago and has handled an enormous amount of grain. It has had a tendency to regulate to a certain extent the rates via the American all-rail lines. The traffic officials of the trunk lines have kept watch of the cost of getting grain to the seaboard via these water routes and have seen to it, as a general rule, that the all-rail tariffs were made so as to allow the railroads to compete.

The Erie Canal is a factor to a certain extent, but it is really not as great a factor as is generally supposed. It does, to a certain extent, regulate the rates which are charged by the railroads east of Buffalo and has a tendency to keep them from charging exorbitant rates. The Erie Canal's total capacity is very small compared with the amount of grain passing through Buffalo—not over about 15 per cent. This canal tonnage has decreased yearly. The cause for this is largely the fact that a great deal of agitation has been going on looking to the improvement of the Erie Canal so as to allow vessels carrying larger loads to make the passage. This has had a tendency to keep people from building additional canal boats, as when the change is made the small boats will be of little value. New York State is now agitating in a very thorough manner the improvement of the Erie Canal to such an extent as to allow boats of three or four times the present size to navigate the canal.

In my judgment just as soon as the canal is enlarged there will be a large number of canal boats built, thus increasing the tonnage of the canal to such an extent as to regulate largely the grain transportation rates of the United States. The all-rail lines east from Chicago, in order to compete with the lake and canal rates, will have to keep their rates quite low, and this will force the roads running south from Chicago and from the West to the Gulf to lower their rates also in proportion. This saving is bound to go back to the American farmer and he will get the benefit. As a matter of fact, the Western farmer and Western community are really more interested in the enlarging of the Erie Canal than New York State.

At present the Canadian routes are the cheapest, and during last season they have had all the grain they could possibly take care of at Montreal, and the lack of ocean tonnage has been the only thing which prevented Montreal from doing a much larger business. The lines from Montreal are now establishing, for the winter time, ocean lines from St. Johns and Portland, and will doubtless do a very large business via that route.

It would seem that for the benefit of the Western States the Government should use its best efforts toward improving the water routes from the West to the seaboard, as the lower the rates from the Western farmer to the foreign consumer the better the prices for grain will be to the producer.

The prominent water route is likely to remain by way of the Great Lakes. We who daily look upon one of the larger of these lakes do so without always giving full consideration to the fact that it is part of the largest body of fresh water in the world and that the merchant marine of these Great Lakes is greater than that of any nation in the world on the high seas, Great Britain and Germany alone excepted—greater than France or Norway, or any other two powers combined. This is shown by the United States Commissioner of Navigation in a recent statement. The tonnage passing through the Sault Ste. Marie annually is almost three times the tonnage in volume that passes through the Suez Canal, and grain and flour constitute over one-sixth of this tonnage and a much larger percentage in quantity of space occupied, most of the other tonnage being ores. This grain and flour comes mostly from Minneapolis via Duluth, from the elevators at Duluth and Fort William, and graphically illustrates one reason why Chicago is no longer a tollgate through which the grain of the Northwest must pass on its way to the seaboard, whether it will or not.

Some points were developed in yesterday's proceedings which perhaps should be noticed.

Barley.—It has been suggested that Armour & Co. practically control the barley market of the country. This is entirely without foundation. In fact, Armour & Co. have never done but a small business in barley, and during this year it has been less, if anything, than usual. The barley crop of the United States runs from 80,000,000 to 100,000,000 bushels per year, more than 50 per cent of which is produced in Minnesota, Wisconsin, North Dakota, and Iowa. The present holdings of Armour & Co. in barley, at all points, directly or indirectly. do not exceed ·190,000 bushels, and the aggregate amount which they have handled during the whole season has been 2,805,000 bushels.

Private cars.—The problem of private car lines does not enter into the grain trade in any respect or degree. Some four or five years ago the necessity of having large clean cars and of meeting a shortage in equipment suitable for the trade moved several grain dealers to buy a number of box cars for transporting their own grain. This never became a practice, and so far as the Armour Elevator Company is concerned the cars they then bought have long since been sold. On inquiry I am informed by those who are in a position to know that they have seen nor heard of only one single private car being used for grain at Chicago during the whole year, so that practically the use of such cars is obsolete.

Ownership of elevators.—So far as the ownership of the Armour elevators is concerned the facts are these:

The elevator known as Armour A and B was built and paid for by them and stands on ground which they own.

Elevator B annex stands on leased ground, but was built, paid for, and is owned by the Armour Elevator Company.

The Minnesota elevator and annex were built on their own land and paid for by the Armour Elevator Company.

The Columbia elevator was bought from a private owner outright.

The elevators known as Armour C, E, and F are the only ones which are leased, and as to these the Armour Elevator Company not only pays a large rental, but also assumes the obligation of operation and maintenance.

Elevator D was built and is owned by the Armour Elevator Company.

The operating expenses of these elevators run from $350,000 to $400,000 per year.

The most exhaustive investigation has failed to disclose a single instance in which a Chicago elevator proprietor has ever mixed or handled grain stored in his public elevator so as to give an advantage to himself. The theory has been that he might be tempted to do so unless the matter was controlled by law, and the Illinois act of 1897 does so control the matter that any such temptation can not be yielded to and so that any suggestions in that direction can not possibly be true.

The idea that there is the slightest connection between the course of business by elevator proprietors and the existence of " bucket shops," so called, is as novel as it is ridiculous.

For reasons already explained " bear raids " upon the market, when they are attempted at all, are based on an alleged or actual surplus of foreign production or a reduction in foreign competition, as to which elevator proprietors have neither voice, control, nor influence. To repeat, when the price at Chicago becomes depressed to any material extent, by artificial means or unfounded causes, buyers from all over the world at once turn to that market in order to absorb its offerings.

In all my long connection with them Armour & Co. have never been "short" in the grain market. Mr. Armour's unbroken policy has always been to build up and to resist and to prevent depression. They have never sold, and probably never will sell, a single bushel of grain which they have not previously bought in this or a tributary market for actual delivery.

In conclusion I desire to say that I have sought to discuss the questions under review in a broad and comprehensive manner. I recognize the high purpose of this body and appreciate the respect due to its dignity and members. Passionate denunciations and, still less, attempts to besmirch private character or business reputation are certainly not argument and seem to me to be out of place. They can only serve to bring, as they should, confusion and discredit upon those who so far forget the proprieties of the occasion as to indulge in them and thereby seek to prostitute this meeting into an opportunity for malicious slander and a display of their personal spleen and animosity. My experience has taught me that the mouths of agitators and so-called reformers do not turn and never have turned the wheels of commerce; neither can they stop the march of progress.

Q. (By Mr. KENNEDY.) Do you say that Chicago handles about 10 per cent of the grain production of the country?—A. Yes.

Q. Have you' figures to show what proportion of the grain production that is handled at Chicago enters into interstate and foreign commerce?—A. Only about one-eighth of the total corn production of this country goes abroad. So it is with wheat. It all depends upon the crops and the consumptive demand of the country.

Q. I should like to have you state what proportion of the total production comes to Chicago and is handled here. You say they handle 10 per cent of the total production. That takes into account domestic and foreign consumption?—A. I mean the total production in the country. There comes to Chicago about 10 per cent of the total production of the United States.

Q. (By Mr. LORIMER.) It is shipped abroad?—A. Yes, sir; it is shipped all over the Eastern States and abroad.

Q. (By Mr. KENNEDY.) What proportion of that which enters into interstate and foreign commerce do you get in Chicago and handle here? I don't consider that which remains in the States as entering into interstate and foreign commerce. Have you figures that will show that?—A. I have not here.

Q. Would not Chicago handle more than 10 per cent of that?—A. Chicago handles all that comes here, probably 40 per cent of what is shipped.

Q. (By Mr. CONGER.) You look upon this ownership of the elevators by grain dealers in Chicago as a matter of evolution that is necessary to the conditions and one that could not be avoided?—A. I do; yes.

Q. I want to inquire if the same evolution has taken place in other and competing markets; that is, in Minneapolis and Omaha, Kansas City, and St. Louis?—A. To the best of my knowledge and belief, it has. But this is a larger market. It permeates generally.

Q. I thought you testified that Minneapolis is now larger.—A. They receive more wheat than we do, but not more grain generally. The mills there absorb a large portion of their wheat.

Q. Do you know about these Southwestern markets, such as Kansas City, Omaha, and St. Louis? They are competitors of Chicago, are they not?—A. Yes.

Q. Do you know if the old system of commissions or operations by commission merchants is in vogue there, or has it been abandoned, as it has here?—A. They are buyers and elevator men all over this Western country, just as we are here. Without being able to answer your question from positive personal information, I think the same conditions exist as here.

Q. That is the point I wanted to bring out—whether the old commission system has been superseded by the elevator proprietor.—A. I think it is very general; it has been tending that way for some years. I have been out of the trade for several years until I went back into association with Mr. Armour a couple of years ago. I was out of it 2 or 3 years only, but I can say the evolution has been very general.

Q. (By Mr. C. J. HARRIS.) I see by your figures that 1898 was the largest year of grain receipts in the history.—A. Well, I don't know that.

Q. It struck me that way.—A. We have had two or three enormous crop years. I don't now whether that is the largest year or not. I can figure it out in a moment

Q. If it was the largest I wanted to know if there was any particular reason for it. I did not know but there might have been improved machinery or something of that nature. How much of the wheat received here goes through the elevators and how much is shipped in on the track; that is, what proportions?—A. About 25 per cent of the grain that comes here goes into the public elevators, the regular licensed elevators; the remainder goes through private elevators.

Q. It all goes through elevators, all grain that comes in here?—A. Yes, sir; practically all that comes here for sale on the market.

Q. Someone said here this morning that some grain came here in carloads and went out in carloads without going through the elevators.—A. Certainly, in through carloads; that does not necessarily change the receipts here.

Q. It was testified this morning that they did not have to pay elevator charges here.—A. There is a good deal of grain shipped from Mississippi River points and other river points on through bills of lading. The Mississippi River business operates adversely to this market; it is a discrimination of that difference.

Q. (By Mr. CONGER.) The wheat that is shipped from Mississippi River points on a through billing to New York, and passes through Chicago, is included in these figures you have just given us, is it?—A. Not through bills of lading. These figures represent only what is handled here in Chicago.

Q. In other words, the figures you have there represent the amount of grain that goes through the elevators?—A. Yes.

Q. (By Professor JOHNSON.) Do your figures for elevators here include the so-called transfer elevators owned by the railroads? There are such elevators, are there not?—A. All the elevators do a transfer business.

Q. What you call the annexes?—A. I don't think they have any special elevators for that purpose which are called annexes.

Q. (By Mr. C. J. HARRIS.) Do these country buyers who buy grain direct from the farmer pay about the market price for it there; that is to say, about what it would be worth with a fair commission for handling it?—A. I have some special knowledge about that, because I have a brother engaged in the business up in the Northwest; he tells me their average is about 2½ or 3 cents per bushel. In that they take the chances of the grain not being up to the grade, of shortages, and differences in quality, and all that sort of thing.

Q. (By Professor JOHNSON.) That is, that 2½ cents per bushel is the difference between the Chicago market price and the price paid the farmer with the transportation?—A. Yes; that is about it. In that price of course there are intermediate charges for elevator storage and handling, commission, and profit.

Q. Is there much variation or uncertainty about that transportation factor—that element of cost to the buyer? Is it a variable factor—the transportaion price?—A. Well, they have the tariff constantly before them, and I think they figure on that.

Q. The printed tariff?—A. Yes, sir.

Q. (By Mr. C. J. HARRIS.) You think the published freight rate obtains after all?—A. Yes.

Q. (By Professor JOHNSON.) Is there one tariff published for the use of the Interstate Commission and another for the use of shippers? The charge has been made that the railroads have filed a tariff sheet with the Interstate Commerce Commission, but that they have not only quoted other rates to shippers, but have published or allowed to be published other rates.—A. That is not the case, so far as I know. I don't believe it.

Q. You brought out very plainly in your paper the price you pay; now, with about what commission? In some cases would it be as low as a quarter of a cent?—A. Yes; even lower than that. That varies, of course; sometimes it is less and sometimes it is more, according to the chances we take.

Q. Would the average be a cent now?—A. I don't think it would.

Q. And with a 1 per cent commission he gets the rest of it at the other end?—A. The idea I wish to convey is that in times of sharp competition we have to fall back on a portion of this storage charge, which we assume, of three-fourths of a cent per bushel for the first 10 days, and sometimes we may have to assume the greater part of that.

Q. And of course if the wheat is held for a long time the interest on your money becomes a natural charge?—A. Becomes a factor, of course.

Q. Is the farmer getting his share at the other end?—A. Yes; I think there is no doubt about that.

Q. (By Representative LORIMER.) There is a great deal of complaint that the farmers in the West find no competition for their grain; that the so-called elevator trust controls matters so that they can sell to but one man and for one price. Do you believe that is really the complaint with farmers or is it a complaint that is put forward by the commission men of Chicago who have been injured by the new system?—A. I think the latter theory is correct. I think the farmer gets more out of it than anyone else.

Q. You think the farmer gets more under the new conditions than under the old?—A. I do; yes. I think the farmer is benefited by the present conditions. We are positive of it.

Q. (By Professor JOHNSON.) It is a fact, I believe, that Mr. Armour is a very large owner in the Milwaukee and St. Paul Railway property, and that he has a large number of elevators along that system of railroads. It has been charged, and persons have stated in my presence, that when Mr. Armour could buy grain along the St. Paul road he would do it instead of buying grain elsewhere; and it was also said that when he started out to buy grain along that line, other buyers could not buy there at the same time. I don't know whether that is true or not?—A. It is absolutely untrue. Armour & Co. own no elevators along the line of the St. Paul road except their elevators in Chicago; that is, the Minnesota terminal elevator, the Minnesota annex, and A and B and B annex on Goose Island. These are on terminals of the St. Paul, so that the grain that comes over the St. Paul, that we have no interest in, goes through them. We have no elevators along the line of the St. Paul road; we own no country elevators except, perhaps, now and then one in different sections; none on the lines of this road at all.

Q. Does the relation which Mr. Armour has with the transportion company and with the elevator company, in your opinion, cause him to receive any advantages as a shipper?—A. It does not.

Q. You think every other man has the same advantages?—A. Yes, sir; with the same facilities. If these gentlemen who have been saying ugly things about us, and about Mr. Armour personally, had the same facilities for handling their grain business they would undoubtedly avail themselves of them.

Q. I refer simply to the transportation cost.—A. No; there is nothing in that at all that I am aware of.

Q. (By Mr. CONGER.) Can an independent buyer of grain along this line of railroad reach a public elevator here in Chicago with his carload of grain without paying a switching charge?—A. I think the switching charge is very general where grain is switched to other roads, but there is none to public elevators on the same road.

Q. In other words, are there any public elevators on the line of this road at the terminal here, on the line of the St. Paul road?—A. We have two public elevators over there, and also one of our elevators is on the Burlington road here. Elevator E is a public elevator.

Q. These public elevators are at the service of the independent buyer?—A. Entirely so.

Q. (By Mr. KENNEDY.) Is there any understanding or agreement between your company and Mr. Counselman's corporation to fix the price of grain, or the buying or selling price of grain at any place?—A. There is a sort of an agreement for ascertaining the price that can safely be paid for grain west of the Mississippi River, but it does not amount to very much. It is really in the interest of Chicago, and was inaugurated for the purpose of meeting Southwestern competition.

Q. And Northwestern, too?—A. More particularly Southwestern. Not for the purpose of reducing the value of grain so much as to sustain the price. It is nothing that operates against the farmer at all; it is directly to the contrary, as I understand it.

Q. One of the operators on the board of trade who does that work is a representative of yours?—A. Yes.

Q. In conjunction with the representatives of Mr. Counselman and others?—A. Yes.

Q. It was stated here that the railroads have been the cause of the warehouse men purchasing grain on account of a discrimination that they had made against Chicago in the through rate. Is that true?—A. On account of what discrimination? Q. Discrimination against Chicago merchants.

Q. (By Mr. CONGER.) Because of the making of the through rate, which would be less than the local rate here and the local rate beyond?—A. Yes; I think it would be a factor to a certain extent.

Q. (By Mr. KENNEDY.) The testimony this morning seemed to be to the effect that the warehouse men would not be purchasers of grain now had it not been for that condition; that the railroads forced them into it.—A. I think that is so to a certain extent.

Q. (By Professor JOHNSON.) Do you think the question of rates on through billing and rates for local shipments is a serious transportation question here in the Middle West?—A. I think it is; I think there are times, however, when it is more formidable than at other times.

Q. How does it operate as regards the interests of intermediate points between the lakes and the Missouri River; do they suffer through that factor?—A. I understand they pay the local rate.

Q. And they would naturally suffer from that, would they not?—A. That would be my judgment about it; I never came in contact with that very closely, but that would be my judgment.

Q. The system, then, results in quite a serious discrimination over small places?—A. Yes. We should very much prefer to see it done away with

Q. (By Mr. KENNEDY.) I should like to state that there was no testimony given here to the effect that Mr. Armour monopolized the barley trade of the country, but a gentleman in New York who sells barley to brewers to malt throughout the country told me that Mr. Armour did control and monopolize that product and that he had to go to Mr. Armour for barley whenever he wanted it.—A. All I know is just as I have given it here. That is the actual condition of things. I heard of several things that have been presented to you and I at once volunteered the information I had. I perhaps have not succeeded, but I feel that when charges of such a nature are made against a man that I have had dealings with during the greater part of my business life, it is wrong and ought to be answered.

Q. (By Representative LORIMER.) Inquiry was made here as to whether or not Mr. Armour controlled the barley trade of the country.—A. I do not allude to that particularly, but to some other charges that were not only made yesterday, but have been made to my knowledge at a half dozen other places by the same individual. It is the same old speech.

Q. You evidently know the speech?—A. Yes; it was given before the committee at the Palmer House and before the Single Tax League; it has been given before quite a number of the meetings of the National Grain Association throughout the country, and I think I could almost repeat it myself.

Q. (By Mr. C. J. HARRIS.) I should have objected to this yesterday——.—A. When a man like Mr. Armour is called the greatest highway robber in the country, the one calling him that draws on his imagination for his facts, and it ought not to be considered for a moment.

Q. (By Professor JOHNSON.) Have you anything to do with the packing-house department of Armour & Co.?—A. No, sir; I am not a member of the firm of Armour & Co.

(Testimony closed.)

CHICAGO, ILL., *November 18, 1899.*

TESTIMONY OF MR. EDWARD P. BACON,

Representative of the Milwaukee Board of Trade.

The subcommission on transportation met at 10.10 a. m., November 18, 1899, Mr. C. J. Harris presiding.

Mr. Edward P. Bacon was introduced as a witness, and, being duly sworn, testified concerning transportation as follows:

Q. (Mr. C. J. HARRIS.) Mr. Bacon, will you give us your name and address?—A. Edward P. Bacon, Milwaukee, Wis.

Q. What is your business there?—A. I am in the grain commission business.

Q. You have been summoned before us to give us, if you have any complaints to make or any suggestion to make with reference to the workings of the interstate-commerce law, any instances of rebates or discriminations given by railroads; and we would ask you, in your own way, to give to this commission your ideas upon these subjects.—A. I will say by the way of introduction, that I have given very close attention to the working of the interstate-commerce law ever since its adoption, and have paid close attention to the important decisions of the commission, and also to the decisions of the Supreme Court in cases that have been appealed from the commission to the Supreme Court. I will say further that I took an active interest in the enactment of the interstate-commerce law. I was one of the delegates appointed by the Milwaukee Chamber of Commerce to appear before the Senate committee on the interstate-commerce act, of which Senator Cullum, I believe, was chairman, at its session here in Chicago before the passage of the act in 1885 or 1886, I believe. I was also a delegate of the Milwaukee Chamber of Commerce to the National Board of Trade for several years in succession about that time, and was a member of a committee appointed by the National Board of Trade to consider the proposed interstate-commerce act, and was appointed, also, by the National Board of Trade to confer with Senators and Members of the House of Representatives in relation to the framing of the act to conform, as far as might be, with the views of the National Board of Trade, and by that means I was brought in contact with those who were the most active in originating and framing the act. I mention these points to show that I have some knowledge of the origin and workings of the law.

I have also been chairman of a special committee of the Milwaukee Chamber of Commerce for several years which has had charge of the case brought by the Chamber of Commerce of Milwaukee before the Interstate Commerce Commission to secure the removal of what we deemed to be discriminations against Milwaukee in rates of freight on grain from points in the Northwest, as compared with rates to Minneapolis. That case was pending before the Interstate Commerce Commission 3 years before any decision was reached, and the decision was finally reached in January, 1898, in favor of the contention of the chamber of commerce, and an order was issued by the commission to the several railroads concerned (six different railroad companies operating in the Northwest), requiring a reduction of differentials to Milwaukee as compared with Minneapolis, to a basis corresponding to the differences in their distance tariff rates for corresponding distances.

Q. (By Mr. Conger.) Was that order satisfactory to Milwaukee?—A. It was.

Q. Was it obeyed promptly by the railroad companies?—A. I was coming to that. The railroad companies, some 5 months afterwards, issued tariffs reducing the differentials to about one-half the amount required in the order of the commission; still leaving the rates to Milwaukee as compared with Minneapolis disproportionate, and to such an extent as to afford Milwaukee no practical relief. It was a coincidence, I will say, perhaps, that the differentials ordered by the commission were almost exactly the same as the differences in values of grain in the two markets, Milwaukee and Minneapolis, and if the order had been fully complied with by the railway companies Milwaukee would have been thereby placed on an exact equality with Minneapolis with reference to the territory in which grain originated, and from which Milwaukee derived its wheat and a large share of its business. The Milwaukee Chamber of Commerce, in consequence, brought the matter again before the commission in the form of a supplementary complaint, and the commission appointed a hearing in Chicago shortly afterwards, at which the case was thoroughly reviewed and the commission affirmed its previous ruling and order. The railway companies, however, failed to make any further reduction in the existing differentials. Most of the roads were willing to comply fully; but one of the principal lines, consisting of the Chicago and Northwestern and the Chicago, St. Paul, Minneapolis and Omaha roads, refused to give its assent to the proposed modifications in the tariff which had been prepared and submitted for adoption by all of the lines concerned. It appears, in the arrangement between the several lines in relation to rates in competing territory, any one line has the power to veto any rate proposed. At any rate, that was the effect in this case, owing to the noncompliance of this Northwestern and Omaha line, and the rates were not put into effect.

Q. Does that grievance still exist?—A. The matter still stands in that state.

Q. What remedy would you suggest?—A. Let me say, before answering that, what has escaped me: I was about to say that the commission further took up the matter by correspondence with the Northwestern and Omaha line, hoping to secure compliance with its ruling, but thus far without any effect, and there is no apparent probability of any further result being accomplished, owing to the determined attitude of that line in resisting the equalization of rates with reference to Minneapolis and Milwaukee, its evident purpose being to favor the movement of the grain to Minneapolis in preference to Milwaukee, owing apparently to the interests of the Omaha road being more thoroughly identified with the Minneapolis than with the Milwaukee market. The ownership of the Northwestern company and the Omaha company, as this commission is probably aware, is very largely identical, and it seems to have been the policy of the Northwestern company to promote the interests of the Omaha company even at the expense of its own.

Q. (By Mr. C. J. Harris.) What do you mean by "The Omaha company?" I thought you were talking about Minneapolis.—A. The "Omaha company" is the common term by which the Chicago, St. Paul, Minneapolis and Omaha Railway is known.

Q. (By Professor Johnson.) That is the line from the south into Minneapolis and St. Paul, is it?—A. It is a line commencing at Elroy, Wis., on the Chicago and Northwestern Railway, extending northwest to Minneapolis and St. Paul, and from these cities southwest to Omaha, with two or three short branch lines in the northeastern part of Nebraska. It intersects this wheat country from which both Minneapolis and Milwaukee derive a large proportion of their wheat for milling purposes.

Q. (By Mr. Conger.) I asked you if this evil or grievance was still in existence, and you said yes; I then asked you if you had any remedy to recommend or suggest to us, or any process to suggest by which a remedy could be brought about in the way of legislation —A. The remedy which I would suggest and which, it seems to me would be effective, would be the strengthening of the powers of the Interstate Commerce Commission to such an extent as to enable it to enforce its orders. The Supreme Court, in one or two recent decisions, has denied that power to the commission which the public had generally considered that it possessed. During the first year of its existence the power was never questioned; its orders were complied with very generally.

Q. What power do you refer

make rates, but the power to enforce its rulings; or the power, upon investigation of any particular case and the determining that discrimination exists or that existing rates are unreasonable, to enforce its order as to the modification and qualification of those rates, which would be, of course, only after a full hearing of all parties concerned.

Q. (By Professor JOHNSON.) You mean to enforce its power to revise rates?—A. To revise rates and to apply and prescribe remedial rates——

Q. On particular commodities?—A. On particular commodities and in particular cases that have been brought before it in which all parties have been heard.

Q. Would it not be well to state the programme by which the commission could be vested with this power? What change in the law do you suggest?—A. I do not know that I could specify particularly just what changes in the law would be required, but I would say that the law should definitely state that the orders of the commission, after full hearing and investigation of the case, should be carried out by the carriers to whom the orders are given.

Q. (By Mr. CONGER.) Do you think it would be fair to the railroads to make that decree of the commission absolute, without any appeal?—A. There should be opportunity for appeal in order to give the parties further hearing in the case as to the existence of the facts determined or arrived at by the commission at its hearing; but if these facts are found to be as declared by the commission, then its orders should be enforced.

Q. You mean enforced pending the appeal or enforced for all time?—A. I mean should be enforced for all time. It is a question in my mind whether decisions or orders of that kind should be put into effect pending an appeal, but there are good reasons why they should, the fact being that the carriers can delay cases almost indefinitely, and by reason of that can prevent the carrying out of justice and consequently inflict upon the public the continuance of the evil for almost an indefinite period. I think, on the whole, that the commission's orders should be immediately effective, with opportunity of appeal and a reversal of the order in case it should be found by the courts to be requisite; and I believe the burden would be less if the carriers were obliged to carry out these orders pending the result of these appeals.

Q. I was going to inquire, in this case brought by Milwaukee, why you have not appealed to the courts to have the order of the commission enforced.—A. For the simple reason that the recent decisions of the Supreme Court render it utterly hopeless; that is, the Supreme Court has declared that the Interstate Commerce Commission has no power conferred upon it by the interstate-commerce act to say what rates shall be put into effect. It declares that the commission's power is limited to investigation and rendering an opinion as to whether the rates in existence are reasonable or not, and whether they are discriminative or not, and to urging their correction. It denies absolutely the power of the commission to declare what would be reasonable rates and to require the carriers to put such rates into effect.

Q. (By Mr. C. J. HARRIS.) Would not Minneapolis, through its close lake communications, have naturally a little advantage over Milwaukee in the shipment of freights?—A. The cost of transportation from Minneapolis to the seaboard exceeds the cost from Milwaukee by just about the differentials in rates that were prescribed by the Interstate Commerce Commission from points in the West to these two terminal points.

Q. (By Representative OTJEN.) By way of Duluth?—A. Yes; by way of Duluth.

Q. And if this rate were enforced or carried out it would place the two cities on an equal footing?—A. On an exact equality.

Q. (By Mr. KENNEDY.) Do you believe if the decision of the Interstate Commerce Commission were to be put into immediate effect and then an appeal allowed that the appeal would be acted upon much sooner than if the other course was pursued?—A. Unquestionably it would; it would be to the interest of the carriers to obtain a decision on appeal as early as practicable.

Q. And the other side would not obstruct?—A. They would not have any motive. On the other hand, it is to the interest of the companies to prolong the litigation to the utmost possible extent and subject the public to the burden of these discriminative rates.

Q. (By Representative OTJEN.) In case of an appeal, would you have the court review the facts or would you have the facts as found by the commission stand?—A. I think the facts as found by the commission should constitute the evidence in the case before the court. The court should pass only upon the law of the case. If the commission has made an error in the application of the law the court should pass on that; but, the commission being an expert body, having the means of investigation and inquiry, and being thoroughly familiar with all the various channels of communication and various means of competition, and everything pertaining to the making up of rates, the determination of the facts before the commission should be final.

Q. That is, the facts as found by the commission should be the facts assumed by the court?—A. That is it exactly. That reminds me, there have been cases carried to the United States court in which new evidence has been presented by the railroad companies in their defense, which has been withheld when the case was heard before the commission; evidently withheld for the purpose of prolonging the litigation and getting more time.

Q. (By Mr. C J. HARRIS.) Is that point now thoroughly digested?—A. I will go a little further into the matter of amendments of the interstate-commerce law, particularly that section about the long and short haul clause. I think that the provision should place with the commission full discretion in regard to that section, which is now limited by a provision that the rates shall be no greater for the shorter than for the longer distance, under substantially similar circumstances and conditions. Now, the commission, as a rule, under that clause "under similar circumstances and conditions," hold that only water competition changes the circumstances and conditions. In a case about a year ago, however, before the Supreme Court—the Social Circle case—the Supreme Court ruled that railroad competition was clearly a change of circumstances and conditions, which would warrant the suspension of the long and short haul clause. The Supreme Court has consequently made that clause inoperative by that ruling. Now, I claim that that provision "under substantially the same circumstances and conditions" should be stricken out entirely from that clause, making the long and short haul provision absolutely imperative except in cases in which the commission, after full consideration and hearing of all parties, believes it expedient in its own judgment to suspend it.

Q. (By Mr. CONGER.) You would make that discretionary with the commission?—A. Entirely discretionary with the commission, so that when the commission has rendered the decision in the case the railroad companies can not carry it up to any other court to determine whether the circumstances and conditions are similar or not. The commission is best qualified to judge on that point on account of its experience and its knowledge of the workings of transportation.

Q. I judge from what you said, your own idea is that only water competition would change conditions?—A. I believe the commission is eminently sound in that ruling.

Q. (By Mr. C. J. HARRIS.) You spoke about discriminations in rebates; do you want to deal further with that?—A. I wish to make a statement in regard to pooling.

Q. I have your letter here that you are in favor of that. I wish you would introduce that as a part of your testimony.—A. I will say, in regard to the proposition to legalize pooling, that I have with me a letter signed by the secretary of the Chamber of Commerce of Milwaukee, addressed to the Industrial Commission, in which he states (reading):

"I am also instructed by vote of the board of directors of this body to inform you that the chamber has at various times unqualifiedly advocated the amendment of the interstate-commerce act so as to permit pooling of railway earnings under traffic arrangements subject to approval of the Interstate Commerce Commission. It is the firm belief of the board of directors of this body, confirmed by a practically unanimous vote of the full chamber, composed of 600 business men of Milwaukee, that such an amendment will be the most effective remedy against the evils of rate cutting and favoritism to large shippers."

Q. (By Professor JOHNSON.) That letter does not say what would tend to eliminate discriminations as against localities?—A. It is only in general terms an expression of the general sentiment of the chamber of commerce.

Q. (By Mr. C. J. HARRIS.) Does that letter express your own opinion?—A. I am thoroughly in sympathy with that. I will say further, after careful consideration of the question of pooling and the arguments advanced in favor of and against it during the discussion of the law for years, I am fully of the opinion that the legalizing of pooling of railway earnings is the only practicable means of securing uniformity, equality, and stability of rates for the transportation of freight, and also the only means of avoiding discriminative rates between various points. I would, however, have the rates under pooling contracts under the control of the Interstate Commerce Commission, with absolute authority to order such changes in those rates from time to time as might be deemed best, and these orders to go into immediate effect.

Q. (By Professor JOHNSON.) You would give the railroads unlimited power to enforce their contracts with each other?—A. I would have the pooling contracts approved by the Interstate Commerce Commission before they go into effect, and the rates subject to any change that the commission might direct after they have gone into effect.

Q. (By Mr. C. J. HARRIS.) You would have the Interstate Commerce Commission provide a maximum rate above which they should not go, rather than an absolute rate; is that it?—A. No; I do not regard the fixing of maximum and minimum rates as a practical remedy or as a practical means of relief. In case of maximum rates they must necessarily be fixed high enough to cover all circumstances and conditions; and the same with minimum rates; they must be fixed so low they would never be operative. In case of maximum rates they must necessarily be higher than the rates ought to be in certain localities and under certain conditions, and for that reason it would be only an evil; but the commission should have absolute power in case of pooling contracts to determine what the rates shall be in every particular instance.

Q. (By Professor JOHNSON.) When men speak of fixing the maximum rates they mean, do they not, the fixing of a schedule for that entire classification. That is what you had in mind? While you are advocating giving the commission power to pass only upon one particular rate or a limited number of rates that may be called in question, when you speak of fixing the maximum rates the ordinary man thinks of a schedule covering the entire classification?—A. Yes.

Q. Whereas, you are talking now of giving the commission power to determine only an individual rate within a classification?—A. To determine all rates that are fixed by the railroads under their pooling arrangements. Pooling arrangements are confined to business between certain important points—certain commercial centers—and whatever rates are fixed under pooling contracts the commission should have entire control of each and every individual and separate rate. No general maximum rate can be applied to-day; they will be of no effect. I have observed the working of maximum rates to some extent, particularly in the State of Illinois. The board of railroad commissioners of Illinois have had power ever since 1873 to fix maximum rates for the State of Illinois, and they have issued from time to time complete schedules of rates and tables of classification, and specified certain rates for certain distances for certain commodities and certain classes throughout the State; the result has been that the railroad companies have very generally, under the influence of competition and owing to varying conditions in different parts of the State, fixed rates very much lower than the maximum rates prescribed by the commission, and nothwithstanding the commission has reduced its maximum rates from time to time, they can not make a scale of maximum rates that is low enough to meet the existing conditions in certain portions of the State. Generally, throughout the State, so far as I have had occasion to examine the rates—and I have had occasion to do so to a considerable extent, in Wisconsin, in comparison with Illinois—I find the actual rates enforced in the State of Illinois are very much less than the maximum rate; and it would prove to be equally the case if attempted throughout the country. It would be more so, in fact, because the field is so much larger, and so many elements of competition enter into the extensive transportation from one part of the country to another, as compared with the few that enter into that of the State of Illinois. Maximum rates for the country at large would be of less value than in the State of Illinois.

Q. (By Mr. C. J. HARRIS.) In giving the Interstate Commerce Commission such absolute powers as you suggest, do you fear that there might be at some time in that body a condition of affairs that would bankrupt all the railroads of the country? Have you looked at that side of the question at all?—A. All I have said in regard to their fixing of rates is to be understood as applying only to rates made under pooling contracts. But, to answer your question, the Supreme Court has very wisely decided—at all events, several district courts of the United States, and I think also the Supreme Court—have decided in important cases that the making of rates that are unremunerative is unconstitutional on account of their practically being confiscatory of the property. The railroads are fully protected by that principle, which is fully established.

Q. (By Professor JOHNSON.) That was brought out in Smith v. Ames?—A. Yes; particularly in that case, but there have been similar decisions in district courts of the United States in different parts of the country, and everybody admits the justice and wisdom of it.

Q. (By Mr. C. J. HARRIS.) The fact that the rate was unremunerative would have to be proved in court and the decision to that effect obtained. In the meantime that rate would be going on all the while, would it not, according to your revised plan?—A. Yes; but there must be hardships sustained somewhere, on one side or the other, and there would be less hardship if the rates were required to go into immediate effect.

Q. (By Professor JOHNSON.) The court would have the power of injunction, would it not?—A. That would be a legal question I would not pass upon.

Q. It does exercise it now, as you know?—A. There have been cases in which the enforcement of rates has been enjoined; but my point is that while it would be unjust to the railroads to be required to submit to rates prescribed by the commission which they might deem unjust and unreasonable, and were endeavoring through the courts to resist, yet the injury to the railroad companies pending the determination of the question would be very much less than if the public were left to the continued infliction of injustice and exorbitant rates for the length of time which the railroad companies could protract this litigation, which is litigation of a most difficult character.

Q. (By Mr. KENNEDY.) Is there any more probability that the railroad companies would suffer by the decision of the Interstate Commerce Commission than there is that the people and commerce of the country would suffer?—A. Not nearly as much, it seems to me. The point is well established now for their protection, which there is no probability of an attempt to overturn.

Q. They seem always to be able to have their interests taken care of better than the other side?—A. Very much.

Q. (By Mr. CONGER.) Are you familiar with the recent order of the Interstate Commerce Commission as regards the differentials between flour and wheat to the Eastern seaboard?—A. I am, to some extent, and I have something to present on that subject.

Q. Do you remember the substance of that order?—A. Yes.

Q. What was it, in brief?—A. It was that the export rate on wheat should not be more than 2 cents per hundred pounds less than the rate on flour.

Q. Do you know if the roads have complied with that order?—A. They have partially, and partially not. I have a statement which has been prepared for me by George A. Schroeder, manager of the freight bureau, Milwaukee Chamber of Commerce, which I will present as part of my testimony.

Q. Before you present that, let me ask, do you know whether the roads, in complying with that order, raised the rate on wheat for export or reduced the rate on flour for export?—A. The rates were changed on the 1st of November, which is the time of year at which rates are generally advanced between Chicago and the seaboard, and I believe they were both advanced; I am quite sure they were.

Q. On both wheat and flour?—A. On both wheat and flour.

Q. Did they make the difference 2 cents according to the order of the Commission?—A. They made that difference from points on the Mississippi River to the seaboard, but there are intermediate points from which the rates vary.

Q. The point I was bringing out—if the Interstate Commerce Commission were given this authority you speak of as regards the differences in rates, differentials between localities, between commodities and localities as well—would it not be possible for the roads interested to protect themselves by increasing the lower rate to a relative equality with the higher rate, instead of reducing the higher rate; in other words, you would allow the roads that privilege?—A. I think there are cases in which it is justifiable that it should be done. I should think the supervision of the commission over the companies would protect the public from any wrong adjustment of the rates to comply with such a decision.

Q. (By Mr. C. J. HARRIS.) Would you tell us how much the difference has been this summer between the export and the domestic rate on wheat?—A. I have not the figures with me that have been enforced during the summer, but I have those put into effect November 1. I want, here, to correct the statement I made in regard to the export and domestic rate, that the difference is 2 cents from the Mississippi River to the seaboard; I should have said from Chicago to the seaboard. This statement I have will give you pretty specific information in regard to this matter, and I will read it before going further:

The following are the present all-rail rates on export and domestic grain and grain products, as per published tariffs effective November 1, 1899.

I will say right here the rates from Chicago and Milwaukee to the seaboard are the same; they are uniform.

Q. Rail rates or lake rates?—A. Rail rates and lake and rail rates combined are always the same from the two points to all points on the seaboard.

Q. Do lake rates vary?—A. They vary continually.

Q. As you can charter them?—A. It is regulated by charter. The rates from points in the West to Milwaukee and Chicago are the same. Chicago and Milwaukee are practically one point and are so treated in the matter of rates of transportation. (Witness continues reading.)

Chicago or Milwaukee to New York:	Cents.
Export grain per 100	20
Domestic grain per 100	22
Grain products per 100	22
Mississippi River to New York:	
Export grain per 100	20
Domestic grain per 100	

The following table shows the through rates on export wheat versus the through rates on wheat to Chicago or Milwaukee plus the rate on the manufactured product:

	Export wheat.		Wheat and flour.	Differ- ence.
	Cents.		Cents.	Cents.
Columbus, Nebr., to Mississippi River.	21	Columbus to Chicago	26	
Mississippi River to New York	20	Chicago to New York	22	
Through	41	Through	48	7
Sioux City, Iowa, to Mississippi River.	21	Sioux City to Chicago	23	
Mississippi River to New York	20	Chicago to New York	22	
Through	41	Through	45	4
Sheldon, Iowa, to Mississippi River	19	Sheldon to Chicago	22	
Mississippi River to New York	20	Chicago to New York	22	
Through	39	Through	44	5
Des Moines, Iowa, to Mississippi River.	13	Des Moines to Chicago	18	
Mississippi River to New York	20	Chicago to New York	22	
Through	33	Through	40	7

The rate from Chicago or Milwaukee to New York is alike for export and domestic flour.

This shows that flour manufactured at Chicago or Milwaukee from wheat from the West, and forwarded to New York, costs 7 cents a hundred more freight in the case of Columbus, 4 cents in the case of Sioux City, 5 cents in the case of Sheldon, and 7 cents in the case of Des Moines than the freight on the wheat direct from these points of origin to New York for export, being that much disadvantage to millers in Chicago and Milwaukee.

The following table shows the through rates on export grain versus the through rates on domestic grain, based on lowest combinations:

	Export grain.		Domestic grain.	Differ- ence.
	Cents.		Cents.	Cents.
Columbus, Nebr., to Mississippi River.	21	Columbus to Mississippi River	21	
Mississippi River to New York	20	Mississippi River to New York	25.5	
Through	41	Through	45.6	5.5
Sioux City, Iowa, to Mississippi River.	21	Sioux City to Chicago	23	
Mississippi River to New York	20	Chicago to New York	22	
Through	41	Through	45	4
Sheldon, Iowa, to Mississippi River	19	Sheldon to Chicago	22	
Mississippi River to New York	20	Chicago to New York	22	
Through	39	Through	44	5
Perry, Iowa, to Mississippi River	14	Perry to Mississippi River	14	
Mississippi River to New York	20	Mississippi River to New York	25.5	
Through	34	Through	39.5	5.5
Des Moines, Iowa, to Mississippi River.	13	Des Moines to Mississippi River	13	
Mississippi River to New York	20	Mississippi River to New York	25.5	
Through	33	Through	38.5	5.5

Q. (By Mr. KENNEDY.) What is the difference between wheat shipped to New York from Chicago for the two purposes, domestic and export?—A. From Chicago and Milwaukee to New York the difference between export and domestic is 2 cents a hundred, but from original points of shipment in the interior it varies from 4 to 5½ cents.

Q. (By Mr. KENNEDY.) On through billing?—A. On through billing, yes.

Q. Is there any reason why there should be that difference as against the difference from Chicago and Milwaukee?—A. I can not see any reason why there should be that discrimination. I can see the cause of it; the purpose of it, at least, is to secure the transportation of the grain from points west of the Mississippi River to the Atlantic seaboard against the competition of the Gulf ports.

Q. It looks like a discrimination against Chicago and Milwaukee?—A. It is a discrimination in favor of export shipments. It costs the Chicago and Milwaukee millers this much more to take the wheat from the West and grind it here and forward to the seaboard, ranging from 4 to 7 cents in the points which I have named, and these points have been taken as illustrations showing the varying differences from the different points of shipment. This second table shows the discrimination against domestic grain used at the seaboard, as compared with grain exported, putting millers at the seaboard at the disadvantage of the difference in favor of the export rate.

Q. (By Mr. C. J. HARRIS.) Do you not have a milling-in-transit rate?—A. There are mill-in-transit rates, but the export grain rates are not applied to them.

Q. Domestic grain rates would be applied to them, would they not?—A. Yes; domestic grain rates are applied to milling in transit.

Q. That, at present, would be a difference of about 2 cents?—A. Yes; 2 cents difference from Chicago. But the difficulty is, that the wheat from which this flour is produced, must be obtained from these western points—the export rates of freight run, as I have shown you, from 4 to 7 cents a hundred lower.

Q. (By Mr. CONGER.) I notice you do not have Minneapolis in the table; could you tell us the situation as regards millers there? Do they labor under the same disadvantage?—A. I am not conversant with the working of rates at Minneapolis. I have only taken the operation of rates with reference to Milwaukee, and incidentally Milwaukee and Chicago, because of the rates being uniform to and from the two points. I gave Sioux City 41 and Sheldon 39 on through export; on domestic, Sioux City 45, Sheldon 44, a difference of 4 and 5 cents against the American miller.

Q. (By Mr. C. J. HARRIS.) Do you not object to the difference between the domestic and the export rate?—A. It operates very seriously to the detriment of millers in this country.

Q. Is not that export rate necessary in order to get rid of the accumulations at these various points and the surplus product of the country?—A. Not by any means; there never have been export rates until within the past two years.

Q. (By Mr. CONGER.) Why, or in what way, does this lower export rate operate to the disadvantage of the millers, if the export rate on flour was the same as the export rate on wheat?—A. It would not; but that is not the case.

Q. Then you misunderstood Mr. Harris's question. He asked if you objected to the fact that a lower rate was given on wheat and flour for export? That is, a rate lower than on domestic grain and flour?—A. If the export rate was applied to flour there would be no objection to it, so far as I can see.

Q. (By Mr. C. J. HARRIS.) The difference is only 2 cents, as you have stated, from Milwaukee at present?—A. Two cents from Milwaukee and Chicago to New York, but the cost of the wheat enters into it. The wheat must come from Western points to Chicago and Milwaukee to be manufactured into flour, and the cost of laying wheat down at Chicago, added to the cost of shipping flour to New York, makes an export expense of 4 to 7 cents a hundred pounds, on account of the domestic rate applying to wheat from the original point of shipment to Milwaukee and Chicago, as well as to the seaboard.

Q. (By Representative OTJEN.) That is a greater rate than some places west have to pay. For instance, Des Moines has to pay a less rate for the grain they receive and ship to the seaboard than Milwaukee would pay in receiving grain from the West and shipping to the seaboard?—A. That is it.

Q. (By Mr. C. J. HARRIS.) But the flour as a manufactured product ought necessarily to pay a higher classification of freight than the other.—A. That never has been the case.

Q. Is it not harder to handle, and does it not take more car room, or are there not some conditions of railroad traffic that enter into it, that demand a higher freight rate than that on grain in bulk?—A. It is possible that there is a slight difference in favor of the raw material, but the fact is that the rates for flour and wheat have always been uniform from time immemorial.

Q. (By Mr. CONGER.) Until when?—A. Until within the last two years. I am not certain when the export rates were first put in, but the great differences have been made within the past year.

Q. Do you not think the lower export rates have been a decided advantage to the producer of the grain?—A. Not at all.

Q. Why not?—A. The price of grain is fixed at the point of shipment by the freight to the principal markets. These principal markets are Minneapolis, Milwaukee, and Chicago, as far as th the interior points in the country fixes his price to the producer on the basis of the rate of freight to these points.

Q. Very well; is not the price of grain in these markets that you name fixed or at least influenced by the price of wheat at Liverpool?—A. To be sure.

Q. Then it would seem to me that the lower freight rate by which the grain from Minneapolis, Chicago, etc., could be moved to Liverpool would increase the price at this point.—A. If that were the only element of price that would be so; but price elements are innumerable, and no man can resolve them to a point which would enable him to determine what the price is going to be 24 hours hence. The price at Liverpool is only one of the elements. Sometimes the price at Liverpool is 4 or 5 cents—not as much as that perhaps, but often 3 to 4 cents less than it costs to lay the grain down in Liverpool from this country.

Q. What reason can you give?—A. Speculative influence is the principal reason.

Q. The farmer, then, sometimes gets benefits from speculation?—A. He always does. It is a mistaken idea that speculation is injurious to the farmer; it is one of the most important things in fixing the price of grain in his favor instead of against him.

Q. (By Mr. KENNEDY.) Which would European markets prefer, our grain or our flour?—A. They want both; they want grain often for the purpose of mixing with other grain in order to produce certain results in flour, and in other cases they want the manufactured product.

Q. They want grain more than they want the flour, do they not?—A: I can only judge as to that by the actual movement of the two; during the past 2 years the movement has not been far from half and half. It varies sometimes 20 per cent from that, in different years, but generally it averages about half.

Q. Following up that answer, do you believe if the rates were even for export flour and wheat there would be a greater export of flour than of wheat; you say the bulk that goes out is about the same?—A. It has been the same heretofore when there were no export rates—about an equal quantity of export flour and wheat; but the introduction of export rates on wheat without applying them to flour has changed the thing, and more wheat is going than flour, necessarily, for the reason that the miller in Great Britain or elsewhere on the other side can make his flour out of wheat that costs him less, on account of this difference in freight, than the cost to the miller here of buying his wheat and laying his flour down there. It operates to drive the miller in this country out of the manufacturing business.

Q. Have you the figures to submit showing that heretofore the export has been about equal, and that now there is a difference?—A. I have not the figures with me, but they can be readily obtained from the Treasury Department.

Q. (By Mr. C. J. HARRIS.) Has there ever been any export rate on flour corresponding to the export rate on wheat?—A. There never has been any export rate on either wheat or flour until within the past two years.

Q. My question is as to whether there ever has been any export rate on flour?—A. No, there has not been, to my knowledge, and I have kept conversant with these rates for a good many years.

Q. (By Mr. CONGER.) Your remedy for these evils would be the enlargement of the powers of the Interstate Commerce Commission?—A. That would be my remedy, yes.

Q. (By Mr. C. J. HARRIS.) Would this recommendation of the Interstate Commerce Commission of a difference of 2 cents between the export rate on manufactured goods and bulk wheat be satisfactory to you if carried out?—A. It would, so far as Milwaukee and Chicago are concerned. That would put flour and wheat on an equality. But it would not remedy the matter from the point of shipment of wheat. The difficulty lies in the fact that the wheat costs more laid down here for grinding and shipment to New York than this difference of 2 cents a hundred referred to, on account of the difference from the point of shipment to Milwaukee and Chicago being greater.

Q. (By Representative OTJEN.) On account of the discrimination from the points west?—A. That is it, yes.

Q. (By Mr. KENNEDY.) We have been speaking of the discrimination which the land carriers make against the product going abroad. Could you say whether there has heretofore been a discrimination by the ocean carriers as against flour?—A. I can not say in regard to that. I am not familiar with ocean rates as separate and distinct from other rates.

Q. (By Mr. C. J. HARRIS.) It might be the trouble is there.—A. From general knowledge I should say that rates from the seaboard across the ocean are uniform; that there is no distinction.

Q. Have you anything further to say about this, or would you pass on to discriminations and rebates?—A. I will pass on to discriminations. I wish to present a letter bearing upon the proposed amendments to the interstate-commerce law from a fellow commission merchant, of Milwaukee, Robert Eliot. Being unable to come himself, he addressed this letter to me and requested me to present it as part of my testimony.

(Whereupon the witness submitted the following communication:)

MILWAUKEE, *November 17, 1899.*

E. P. BACON, Esq., City.

DEAR SIR: Under date of November 7 I received a letter from the Industrial Commission, stating that Senator Kyle had suggested my name as one desired to give information and expression before the Industrial Commission now in session in Chicago. Owing to having taken a bad cold I am unable to go there, which I regret very much.

I was one of those deputed by the Milwaukee Chamber of Commerce, with yourself and Mr. Charles Ray, now president of the National Exchange Bank, to give expression in the same behalf before the United States Senate committee in 1885 or 1886 prior to the passage of the interstate-commerce act, said committee being composed of Senators Cullom, of Illinois; Platt, of Connecticut, and Harris, of Tennessee.

At that meeting in Chicago I was told by Senator Cullom that they had been to the Middle and Eastern State cities and to St. Louis and had had the views of prominent Chicago dealers, and that I was the only person in the United States who had advocated legalizing railway pooling under the control of the proposed Interstate Commerce Commission, in order that such control might obviate excessive charges or unjust discrimination against persons or places. Senator Cullom said that while he was impressed with the reasons given for such action, it was utterly impracticable because of adverse public opinion. I told him that time would show that there never would be any relief from secret rates or unjust preferences until the railways were permitted to enforce pooling contracts,

Since that time experience has, I think, proved the correctness of my judgment, and many commercial bodies of the United States, including the Chamber of Commerce of Milwaukee, have passed resolutions in advocacy of legalizing such traffic agreements under control of the Interstate Commerce Commission. The railway companies also have expressed themselves as willing to have the interstate-commerce act strengthened, vesting the Interstate Commerce Commission with powers to fix rates when the commission may find reason for its remedial action in that behalf, provided the power and permission to make traffic agreements as above stated be also granted.

A bill was framed in that behalf 5 or 6 years ago, and many who are deeply interested in the matter are wondering why Congress has not passed it. My solution of this question is this: Many railways have influential directors who are engaged in the grain business, or the oil business, or other branches of business, who are receiving special or preferential rates, enabling them to overcompete and drive out of business others engaged in the same branches of business, and it is the interest of such multimillionaire directors to have the present state of things continue, to wit, competition between roads, which will excuse the managers of the roads for giving these special or preferential rates when said managers have to face their directors or wealthy stockholders, because if the interstate-commerce act were strengthened and pooling legalized there could be no excuse whatever for railway managers to be giving away the earnings of their roads to some of their wealthy and poweful directors. Of course they solidly deny doing anything of this kind, but the manifestations of trade indicate it with certainty to the minds of men engaged in the business.

One method of business which, by reason of its being apparently free to all, but owing to circumstances available especially and preferentially to men operating large terminal elevators, is the monkey work of through billings, which I should be glad to have you explain to the committee. This method constitutes an unjust discrimination against the local trade and milling trade of Milwaukee and Chicago or other terminal points where it is practiced and gives advantage to the parties operating the terminal elevators. It is also an ingenious evasion of the long and short haul clause. I have wondered why the Interstate Commerce Commission has not ordered its discontinuance. I presume it to be because they do not think they have the requisite power. Then the act should be strengthened so that they will have the requisite power, and the power to enforce the long and short haul clause.

For 8 or 10 years the railway companies respected the long and short haul clause, but the courts finally turned it down by their application of the words "under similar conditions and circumstances," which were found in the act, holding that competition between railways constituted a circumstance which warranted an infraction of the long ar fully and completely as to that clause, because the railway companies can prove competition everywhere. And the consequence is many very unjust discriminations in rates by giving low rates to certain places in preference to other places.

These words should be stricken out of the interstate-commerce act, and no deviation from the long and short haul clause should be permitted except under extraordinary circumstances, such as direct juxtaposition to and competition by water routes, and then only when permitted by the Interstate Commerce Commission.

Yours, truly,

ROBERT ELIOT.

Q. Railroad discriminations and rebates.—A. In relation to the matter of rebates I will present to the commission two bids mailed to the grain dealers at Kinbrae, Minn., and Flandreau. S. Dak., on the 21st and 26th of October last, respectively, by the Milwaukee Elevator Company, a company understood to be owned wholly by a director of the Chicago, Milwaukee and St. Paul Railway Company, the points mentioned being on the Southern Minnesota division of that railway.

Q. (By Mr. KENNEDY.) Do you know his name?—A. I know his name, but I don't care to state it. I will state it if desired; P. D. Armour. I will submit these postal cards as a part of my testimony, and will say in connection with them, that the several elevator companies in Milwaukee and Chicago have been in the habit for some years past of sending bids to grain buyers in the country by means of postal cards, offering net prices at the point of shipment, which they can accept on such quantity of grain as they choose, provided the acceptance reaches the elevator proprietors before the opening of the next day's exchange; that is, 9.30 in the morning. That is stated on the postal card as a part of the condition on which the bids are made, and these prices are based on the closing of the market on the day on which they are mailed and are open for acceptance until 9.30 the next morning. And I will submit tabulated statements showing these bids and the freight, and showing the prices of the bid over the cost laid down at Milwaukee and the market value at Milwaukee at the same time. To show the correctness of the values stated at Milwaukee I will also file the daily market reports, the official daily market reports of Milwaukee on the dates mentioned.

Q. (By Representative OTJEN.) What, in substance, do these postal cards show?—A. The postal cards show the prices bid at the points mentioned, and the market reports show the value at Milwaukee at the time.

Q. And you are just going to follow that up, to show the application of it?—A. Yes; show the working out of the bids, with the cost of freight and the cost laid down at Milwaukee as compared with the value of the property at Milwaukee at the time. I will say, first, in connection with these bids, they have been sent to me by my traveling agent, and the parties who gave them to him stated that the prices named were subject to a deduction of the freight to Minneapolis and I consequently stated the freight to Minneapolis in my table which I presented. (Reads:) Prices per bushel for grain at Kinbrae, Minn., October 21, 1899, by Milwaukee Elevator Company, for shipment to Milwaukee, subject to Milwaukee inspection and dockage and Milwaukee or Chicago weights. Tariff rates of freight to Minneapolis to be deducted; showing cost laid down at Milwaukee, as compared with closing market value at Milwaukee on the same date.

Kind of grain.	Pounds per bushel.	Price bid.	Freight to Minneapolis.	Net price.	Freight to Milwaukee.	Cost at Milwaukee.	Value at Milwaukee.
		Cents.	Cents.	Cents.	Cents.	Cents.	Cents.
No. 1 northern wheat	60	66.25	8.70	57.55	12.90	70.45	69.50
No. 2 northern wheat	60	63.75	8.70	55.05	12.90	67.95	66.50
No. 3 white oats	32	22.75	4.16	18.59	6.08	24.67	24.50

Rates of freight on grain from Kinbrae, Minn., in effect the above date, as per supplementary tariff taking effect April 19, 1899, were as follows, in cents per 100 pounds:

To—	Wheat.	Other grain.
Minneapolis	14¼	13
Milwaukee	21¼	19

Prices per bushel bid for grain at Flandreau. S. Dak., October 26, 1899, by Milwaukee Elevator Company for shipment to Milwaukee, subject to Milwaukee inspection and dockage, and Milwaukee or Chicago weights; tariff rates of freight

to Minneapolis to be deducted; showing cost laid down at Milwaukee as compared with closing market value at Milwaukee the same date:

Kind of grain.	Pounds per bushel.	Price bid.	Freight to Minneapolis.	Net price.	Freight to Milwaukee.	Cost at Milwaukee.	Value at Milwaukee.
		Cents.	Cents.	Cents.	Cents.	Cents.	Cents.
No. 1 northern wheat	60	68	9.60	58.40	14.10	72.50	70.50
No. 2 northern wheat	60	66	9.60	56.40	14.10	70.50	68
No. 3 white oats	32	23.25	4.16	19.09	6.08	25.17	24.75

Rates of freight on grain from Flandreau, S. Dak., in effect above date, as per
tariff taking effect April 10, 1899, were as follows, in cents per 100 pounds:

To—	Wheat.	Other grain.
Minneapolis..	16	13
Milwaukee...	23¼	19¼

Q. What is the difference between the cost and the offer?—A. Two cents in that
instance. No. 2 northern, price to be 66. Adding freight to Milwaukee makes
it cost 70.50. Value at Milwaukee, 68 cents; 2½ cents less. No. 3 white oats 23.25
bid, making cost at Milwaukee 25.17. Value at Milwaukee, 24.75. Oats are handled on a very small margin always. Rates of freight from Flandreau to Milwaukee and Minneapolis are given in the same manner as in the previous statement.

Q. (By Mr. KENNEDY.) Do you say Mr. Armour is a director in the Chicago, Milwaukee and St. Paul Railway; does that road give him advantages over other
buyers and shippers of grain?—A. That we have no means of knowing. We
naturally infer when a man pays more for property in the country for shipment
than it will net after paying freight, that he gets his money back in some way;
and I will state in this connection that there is no means of getting that property
to the seaboard at any less expense than by billing from the points of origin to
Milwaukee and Chicago and billing it from those points to the seaboard.

Q. This territory is naturally more your territory than Chicago's?—A. Grain
from that country more naturally comes to Milwaukee.

Q. (By Mr. C. J. HARRIS.) Do I understand you to say that he made bids on it
delivered in Minneapolis?—A. No. He named a price in those bids from which
the freight to Minneapolis was to be deducted and the shipper was to receive the
difference. Mr. Armour pays the freight from the point of shipment to Milwaukee, and if he pays the tariff rates it costs what I have stated in these statements.

Q. Would not that territory more naturally ship to Minneapolis, and is not this
additional price given to divert the trade to Chicago or Milwaukee?—A. This
is competing territory between Milwaukee and Minneapolis, and the shipments
from time to time are directed to either Milwaukee or Minneapolis, according to
the price ruling in each. Sometimes it is more favorable to ship to one and sometimes to the other.

Q. (By Representative LORIMER.) The point you aim to impress on the commission is that the Milwaukee Elevator Company pays this higher price because
it has an advantage with the railroads?—A. We can not tell where they get their
money back, but the fact that they could buy the property at Milwaukee from 1
cent to 1¼ cents and 2 cents per bushel less than it would cost to lay it down at
Milwaukee, if they should pay the regular rates, would lead one to infer that
they did not pay the regular rate.

Q. Is there any advantage in owning an elevator over renting or storing grain
in a public warehouse?—A. To be sure, the owner of the elevator saves the
storage; that is, the man owning the elevator does not have to pay storage to
somebody else; but the elevators of late have been very little used for storing
grain for the trade. They have almost gone out of use for the purpose of storing
grain for the public. They are used by the proprietors to handle grain which
they buy at the original point of shipment in the country and sell to exporters
or consumers in the East.

Q. Then, without having any definite knowledge, you are of the impression that
they have advantages in railroad rates over the average shipper?—A. That is the
inevitable inference from the fact that they are paying more than they can buy
the property for at Milwaukee. · The fact of their having an elevator does not
affect the value of the property in Milwaukee. It is not worth any more in Milwaukee whether it is bought there or in the country. The property is the same,
and it is of equal value under either condition.

Q. What is the natural inference? Is it that this deduction is given over the road to Minneapolis or from Minneapolis to Milwaukee?—A. The grain bought under these bids is brought to Milwaukee. It is transported entirely over the line of the Chicago, Milwaukee and St. Paul.

Q. From the place of purchase?—A. Yes.

Q. What is the special point in compelling the owner to pay the freight to Minneapolis?—A. I can see no particular reason for putting the price in that way instead of stating the net price to the shipper at the point of shipment; but that seems to be the method pursued.

Q. (By Representative OTJEN.) Excepting that he is able to do it from the fact that he probably gets a lower rate from the railroad.—A. The question as I understand it is why the price bid was subject to a deduction of freight to Minneapolis when the property does not go to Minneapolis; that I can see no possible reason for. The more direct and more satisfactory method would be to name the price at the point of shipment. For some reason the price at Minneapolis is given, involving the necessity of deducting the freight to Minneapolis. The property is shipped to Milwaukee, the elevator company paying the freight from the point of shipment to Milwaukee, whatever it may be. I am informed by my traveling agent, who sent in these postal cards containing the bids, that the parties receiving them were in possession of letters from the Milwaukee Elevator Company to the effect that the freight to Minneapolis was to be deducted from the price named in the bids.

Q. Do any of the railroads centering in Milwaukee own their elevators?—A. The St. Paul road owns all the elevators at its terminals.

Q. Are they operating them for the road?—A. They are all leased to the Milwaukee Elevator Company, with the exception of a portion of one of the elevators known as Elevator E, which the company operates itself for storage purposes.

Q. Practically the bulk of the wheat handled through the elevators is handled by the elevators that are leased from the railroads.—A. It is handled by the Milwaukee Elevator Company. I will modify my statement as to their all being leased by the Milwaukee Elevator Company. F. Kraus & Co. lease one of the elevators, and the Milwaukee Elevator Company leases all the rest with the exception of a part of Elevator E, which is retained by the railroad company.

Q. (By Mr. C. J. HARRIS.) Is your system of public elevators much the same as exists in Chicago?—A. Substantially the same.

Q. Can the proprietors of elevators purchase grain the same as here?—A. Yes.

Q. (By Representative OTJEN.) What is he allowed per bushel for handling the grain through the elevators?—A. He buys the grain and puts it in the elevators and disposes of it to the best advantage he can.

Q. (By Mr. C. J. HARRIS.) What is the legal rate for storage?—A. There is no legal rate in the State of Wisconsin.

Q. What is the customary rate of storage?—A. The nominal rate which is charged by the St. Paul Railway Company in that part of the elevator which it operates is one-half a cent per bushel for the first 10 days and one-quarter of a cent per bushel for each additional 10 days, but in point of fact there is almost no grain put in the elevators for public storage.

Q. (By Mr. KENNEDY.) What is the belief among grain men generally as to the existence of an elevator combine in Chicago? What is the opinion at Milwaukee among the grain men of your acquaintance?—A. I don't think I can say in regard to that. There is a general impression that the owners of elevators in Chicago, as well as in Milwaukee, have advantages in the matter of rates and otherwise which are not granted to the public in general.

Q. By agreement between the railroads and elevator men of Chicago and other places?—A. Well, it is supposed to be fixed from time to time according to the varying conditions and circumstances, whatever the advantages may be. Of course, the public has no means of arriving at what is done between the railway companies and the elevator people; they can simply guess at it from results.

Q. (By Mr. C. J. HARRIS.) Do you find any such discriminations as you have presented here, apparent discriminations, in the territory which is not disputed territory with Minneapolis or other strong buying points? In other words, is this high price paid to the producer, as has been testified here, to bring that trade to Milwaukee and Chicago, where competition is very keen, we will say, with Minneapolis, and in the Southwest, with Galveston? Do you find any such conditions as you have presented in this statement in the territory that naturally comes to Milwaukee and Chicago?—A. We don't come across instances of this kind except in competing territory.

Q. Where competition is very close?—A. Whenever there are two or more roads coming into competition with each other, or paralleling each other, not only at intersecting points, but where they parallel each other, we frequently have convincing evidence that the elevator people who buy the grain have advantages, special advantages in the way of freights. Not only in the territory in which we compete with Minneapolis, but in the State of Wisconsin we find that to be the case.

Q. Would their elevator privileges or their special methods of handling this grain account for the difference in any way?—A. Not at all, because that is entirely independent of the transportation. They can buy the grain in Milwaukee and Chicago and put it in their elevators to just as good advantage as they can buy it in the country. The only advantage of buying it in the country is whatever favor they may get in a special rate of freight or by means of a rebate.

Q. (By Mr. KENNEDY.) Do you believe that it would be impossible for this or any other commission to get at the facts as to whether there is a combination between the railroads and the elevator men of Chicago by which people of the alleged combine have an advantage over the independent buyers?—A. I don't know how it could be got at. Probably the Chicago people could tell you better in regard to Chicago than I can; but it is difficult to get at what the railroads do. I have known of instances, or at least instances have been reported to me, in which sums of money have been paid by railway officials to parties receiving and handling grain without taking any receipt whatever, and paid in currency instead of checks, which covers up any possible evidence.

Q. Looking to that end, would you favor an additional amendment to the interstate-commerce act providing for Federal inspection of the business of those quasi-public corporations like railroads?—A. I would, most assuredly. I would favor the railroad companies' books being examined by experts employed by the commission, as bank books are examined by bank examiners.

Q. And have full publicity?—A. Yes, certainly; but I don't believe that would unearth the methods by which rebates are paid, because they are paid in underhanded ways which leave no trace behind them.

Q. (By Mr. C. J. HARRIS.) You have been in business a long time. Is there at the present time as much complaint about rebates and discriminations as there used to be?—A. I think there is as much complaint in general. There appears to be as much of it going on as before, but it is confined to a smaller number—that is, the beneficiaries of these privileges and advantages and rebates are very much smaller in number. They have been concentrated into fewer hands. On this subject I will say that there is room for a great deal of manipulation of rates, as it is termed, on grain, in consequence of its being billed on what are called proportional rates. Grain is billed to Milwaukee or Chicago on a rate proportional to a through rate to the seaboard, and it is taken into these elevators on the supposition that it is to be forwarded to Eastern points or exported, as the case may be. It receives the benefit of these proportional rates, and it is left entirely to the elevator people actually to forward the property to the seaboard or export it or dispose of it in any other way.

Q. Would that account at all for this difference in the rates which you have presented here, supposing that that was shipped in here on an export rate?—A. It would not in this case, for the reason that there is no export rate to our Eastern points and there is no proportional rate in effect from either of those two points.

Q. Might not that billing be by way of Minneapolis, and cover an export rate of some kind which would allow for this difference?—A. No; the property was not billed to Minneapolis. It was simply provided that the rate of freight from Minneapolis could be deducted from the published rate of freight.

Q. That is true, but supposing there was an export rate from Minneapolis to the seaboard which would allow of all this difference you suggest?—A. It would not be in any way applicable to these shipments made direct from the point to Milwaukee, and there is no way in which the wheat when it reaches Milwaukee could be benefited by it that would not apply equally to wheat brought to the Milwaukee market and put in the elevator.

Q. (By Representative OTJEN.) Regarding the ownership of private cars, do you think that the ownership of private cars is a detriment to business generally?—A. It seems to me that it is a very fruitful way of affording benefits and advantages to those who own them by paying them more for the use of the cars than they are really worth.

Q. (By Mr. C. J. HARRIS.) Are there any private cars used in the grain business now?—A. Not that I am aware of in the grain business.

Q. That is, so far as the grain business is concerned, it is done away with?—A. No; it never has been put in practical use with reference to grain.

Q. (By Mr. KENNEDY.) Is there any sentiment among the members of the Milwaukee Chamber of Commerce in favor of Government ownership of railroads or telegraph lines?—A. Not very extensively, so far as I have been able to observe.

Q. There is some?—A. There are some few who favor railroad ownership, but it is a comparatively small number.

Q. Because they believe it is the only remedy for the evils if there are any in transportation?—A. That, I think, is the reason; but personally I am opposed to public ownership and I believe that the transportation of the country could be efficiently and equitably conducted if the Interstate Commerce Commission had proper powers and its orders could be properly enforced. I should want to see that experiment effectually tried before resorting to public ownership.

Q. Do the business men of Milwaukee believe that the telegraph and telephone rates are exorbitant?—A. I have not heard any particular complaint in regard to that at Milwaukee. There is some complaint in regard to the rates charged by the telephone company, but none of any importance as to the telegraph rates have come to my knowledge. There is one point that has occurred to me and that is the making of through routes and through freight rates by the commission. I wish to say I consider it a very important and very necessary power conferred upon the commission to require the making of through freight rates between connecting lines. It often occurs that owing to individual interests of separate lines they refuse to make through rates with each other, and debar the public from the benefit of the advantages of the shortest practicable lines between two points. I believe that the interests of the people require that the railroads should be compelled to make joint rates at their intersections wherever they may be giving the public the benefit of the lowest practicable rates by the shortest line.

Q. And if they do not make them the Interstate Commerce Commission should make them for them?—A. Yes.

(The witness subsequently submitted the following, to be incorporated with his testimony:)

While the application of the export rate of freight on wheat to the transportation of flour would obviate the disadvantage under which millers in the interior of the country are now struggling, millers at seaboard points would still be subjected to a disadvantage in competition with foreign millers equal to the difference between the export and the domestic rate on wheat from points in the West to the seaboard.

In relation to grain being billed from interior points to Milwaukee or Chicago on " proportional rates "—that is, the proportion of the through rate from point of shipment to the seaboard accruing to the lines west of Milwaukee or Chicago, the grain being taken into elevators at these points presumably for transfer—I wish to say that such grain should be held " in bond " under the care of officers of the Government until so transferred, in order to insure its being actually shipped to the seaboard, for which purpose the proportional rate of freight has been applied to the grain. This rate is often from 2 to 3 cents per 100 pounds less than the rate applied to grain for local use at Milwaukee or Chicago, or shipped therefrom to other than seaboard points.

CHICAGO, ILL., *November 18, 1899.*

TESTIMONY OF MR. CHARLES S. CLARK,

Secretary Grainers' National Association and publisher of the Grainers' Journal.

The subcommission on transportation being in session on the afternoon of November 18, 1899, Chairman Lorimer presiding, Mr. Charles S. Clark was sworn and testified as follows:

Q. (By Representative LORIMER.) Please state your full name. —A. Charles S. Clark.

Q. And your business?—A. Publisher.

Q. Are you in any way connected officially with the Grain Dealers' Association?—A. I am secretary of the Grainers' National Association and publisher of the Grainers' Journal.

Q. We have information that you have decided views on a system of national grain inspection?—A. I don't know where you got that information, because those are far from my views.

Q. You have no views on that subject?—A. I am decidedly opposed to national inspection. I don't think it is practicable.

Q. You don't think it is possible?—A. It is possible, but not practicable. The grades in the quality of grain vary too much to make any classification, unless you have an endless book of rules which apply to the markets having these qualities of grain.

Q. (By Mr. C. J. HARRIS.) I understand that you had some statement to make on the inspection of grain, espcially before the commission.—A. I have not, except that, of course, if you want to know what the complaints are, I can give them to you as they have come to me. I get a good many complaints from members of the association throughout the country and reports from different markets.

Q. We should like to hear what these complaints are.—A. Of course anyone who is familiar with the grading of grain knows that it is a matter of guess, It has not been reduced to an exact science. They have flaxseed inspection reduced to an exact science; they weigh before and after they eliminate all foreign matter from the samples of seeds by means of sieves of different sized meshes. Mr. Stevens, the man who devised that scheme, has been working on the same scheme to apply to grain, but has not brought it to a point where he is ready to give it out. Several times we tried to get him to talk about it before the association and he has done so twice. He is a man who is one of the oldest grain inspectors in the country, but the detailed work of carrying out his plan has seemed to discourage him and he has given it up. The grading of grain, as I said before, is guesswork. Mr. Noble, in his speech before the national association here in October, said that if a man inspected 100 cars a day and inspected those same 100 cars to-morrow he would probably grade some of them different. It is a matter of judgment, and there are some frightful errors made. Men are not always in the same mood; they have not always the keen perception which the grain inspector is supposed to have. They will naturally err. If we could have the grading of grain reduced to an exact science, then it might be practicable to have a national inspection.

The inspection departments now value grain or classify it quite differently from what the millers do; that applies to wheat only; of course on other grains there is no one else who passes on the grade excepting the buyers or consumers; and I would say that in the matter of barley grading in Chicago the rules and grading by the official inspectors have been ignored for years by the trade. Dealers may pay some attention to the way in which the sample is classed by the department, but they don't accept it themselves; they take the sample to their offices and there pass upon it in an entirely different light—that is to say, they grade it for different characteristics. A grain inspector, if he possesses the knowledge sufficient to make a competent judge of barley, would be in the barley trade almost invariably, and although in Chicago they have some inspectors scattered all around the city to meet the demands of the barley trade to-day all the best inspectors could do would be to take a sample and submit it to a good man at the central point, as in the inspector's office here in the city. Of course the present system of barley inspecting is utterly unreliable and we pay no attention to it. And wheat. The miller values the wheat for many points or characteristics which the inspector knows nothing about; for instance, its strength as to gluten, the amount of starch contained in it, and the market he is milling for at the time. Some markets want it strong in gluten and others want it strong in starch. It depends upon what they are after for their mixtures in the blending of flours. The miller is virtually the consumer of all good wheat, but the present method of classifying wheat is such that while the miller pays a good deal of attention to the classification, still he often pays a premium for a lower grade.

As to the other grains, I know of a case here last month with an Eastern shipper. We have a number of shippers here who ship oats to one of the markets that makes a specialty of them. He bought a grade of fancy oats—that is, he bought three cars which were so much better than other grain placed in the same grade by the inspection department that he paid 4½ cents more for that grade than the ruling market price at the time. He shipped them to an Eastern market and got the profit for them because they were so much superior to the average quality for that grade.

Q. Do you have a State inspector here?—A. Yes.

Q. You say that his grading is ignored by the grain buyers?—A. No; only in the barley trade.

Q. I understood you that the men who bought and sold ignored this State inspection and went on their own private inspector's judgment largely.—A. That is on barley; yes.

Q. On barley alone?—A. Yes; on barley alone.

Q. But on the other grains they have not that difference?—A. No; the outward characteristics of the other grains are a better index of the value of the grain. In barley it is quite different. You can take barley and polish it and get good grains wherein the germinative percentage of the sample will be very low, and barley is valuable to the malster only by the percentage of it which will grow, although, of course, on its plumpness and bright color depends how clear will be the resulting product.

Q. (By Representative LORIMER.) How many official grades of oats are there?— A. I don't remember how many there are; there is the white and the mixed—I think probably there are 7 or 8.

Q. Are they numbered?—A. Yes.

Q. (By Mr. C. J. Harris.) Is there any great difference between the inspections of different cities that are buying the products? What I mean is this: Could I ship grain from a Nebraska point and get a better inspection in Minneapolis than I could in Chicago, or could I get a better inspection in St. Louis than I could in Chicago, or vice versa?—A. I have known of some shippers at points that are in territory tributary to different markets having different rules who, knowing of the methods of inspection, would invariably ship grain of certain grades or of certain qualities to certain markets. The rules governing the inspections in each one of these markets are made for the purpose of classifying the grain in the territory tributary to that market which is supposed to come to that market. For a long time—I believe until the Northwest grain trade came into this market—we had no grades provided for the classification of that grain separate from the other, such as we have now. The Northwest, Minneapolis and Duluth, have no rules governing the grades of Kansas hard wheat; that is, I think they have not. They have no use for such rules. Then there are other grades. For instance, in Texas we have the Texas rust-proof oats; you will find some of them in Kansas and all through the territories. Rules governing the grading of that grain could not be of any use in Chicago or Milwaukee or any of the Northern markets. The rules vary considerably. We had one case a year ago where Kansas City, Kans., which was under the Kansas City inspection, admitted a No. 2 wheat where the grain weighed 52 pounds and over. In Kansas City, Mo., they required 59 pounds and over. Of course that made some difference; some grain just on the line would go to Kansas City, Kans., and be graded, although most of the grain was handled by Kansas City, Mo., dealers. It worked an injustice. I think the nearer we can get uniform rules for the grading of the same grain, the better it will be for the grain trade and for everyone interested in the business. It would simplify the matter a great deal.

Q. A No. 2 wheat in St. Louis ought to be the same as a No. 2 wheat in Chicago and ought to fill the same classification requirements?—A. Yes; if it is of the same character. In St. Louis they get one quality they don't get up here and Chicago gets much wheat that never finds its way to St. Louis; and as to No. 2 wheat, Chicago has several different grades of that; that depends upon the origin of the wheat. Several years ago, I think, Kansas City received wheat from the Pacific coast, and there was a movement on foot to have a grade of Oregon wheat that would include all of the soft wheats of the Pacific coast.

Q. That is the point I wanted to bring out. It is this: That the No. 2 Kansas wheat ought to be the same No. 2 wheat in St. Louis as in Chicago; or a No. 2 Northwestern wheat ought to be the same in St. Louis as it is in Chicago. There ought to be a national uniformity on these things and I believe there is, is there not?—A. All the markets do approach uniformity in their rules, but in the carrying out of these rules they differ just as the ability of the inspectors who attempt to carry them out varies. I had a case that came into my hands as secretary of the national association here not a great while ago and is now pending, in which a southwestern Iowa shipper sold corn subject to the Peoria weights and grades. Peoria had a blockade and the grain was taken to St. Louis before being inspected, and the broker who bought it claimed the Peoria inspection, he being an active member of the Peoria Board of Trade; it is a private inspection, not a State, and he could not have it inspected there. It is well known to the trade that a State inspection is much more rigid than the Peoria inspection; these cars all graded according to the contract which they were supposed to fill, except one, and that was graded down, and the shipper refused to accept the discount for the missing grade in the St. Louis market when he had sold it subject to the Peoria inspection and weights.

Q. The producer generally sells outright to the grain buyers at the railroad point?—A. Yes.

Q. So that he has little complaint to make in regard to the inspection that exists in the cities, because his grain passes out of his hands absolutely at that point?—A. Yes.

Q. The complaints would come from the grain buyers and dealers in the cities themselves?—A. Yes.

Q. (By Representative Lorimer.) Have you anything further to suggest?—A. Nothing, I think. Of course, here is something if you can bring it about. You remember we had a bill that was introduced in Congress repeatedly for the uniform inspection of grain, but it was never enacted; it provided for the uniform classification of grain. I think if the different markets are left to themselves they will work that out; because where the grain from one territory is going to any market, that market will, out of self-interest, invariably try to make its rules about the marketing of that grain favorable to it, and can not afford to inflict any discrimination against that grain as compared with other markets. If it does, then very naturally the grain will go to the other markets. There is that influence working all the time for uniformity and the markets must eventually, I think, come closer together.

Q. As a matter of self-interest they grade it as high as possible?—A. Yes; of course the grain dealers here have not so much direct influence in the matter as they would have at Peoria, where they have private inspection. Peoria is the only market of importance west of Chicago that has private inspection. All the other places have State inspection. Toledo has the same system as Peoria and so has Cincinnati, and on Eastern markets they are not governed by State laws; but there is not enough of that private inspection to work any great injustice, because grain is not forced to take those channels, and it would not do so unless the rules were favorable to its going there.

Q. You say there was a bill introduced in Congress?—A. Yes; there was a man who was the inventor of a steel storage system, and who worked earnestly and tried to have the bill passed several times; it was introduced at two or three different sessions, I guess. It provided for the uniform classification of grain. His system was, I believe, to provide for a national inspector at Washington, who should make a chemical analysis of the grains by samples sent him from the different sections of the country. And, I believe, one of his plans was that any man could send a sample of his grain and have it classified; that is, have the inspector pass upon it as to the grade it belonged to; he could send these samples to the department at Washington, or wherever the branches might be established.

Q. (By Mr. KENNEDY.) Is your association opposed to that bill?—A. We never took any action on it. We have had several papers from different members of the association on uniform classification of grain. The members of the trade, I think, would work that out themselves in time and with probably better results than the Government ever could get, because self-interest will prompt them to carry it out carefully; and of course they are in the business all the time and know what is needed and wanted.

Q. Of what is your association constituted?—A. We have two classes of members. It is made up of commission men and country grain shippers principally. The country grain shippers are divided into two classes—that is, those who are what we call the regular members, and the attached. We have local associations wherein all the members become members of the national association; the local associations become affiliated with the national.

Q. Are the grain men of Chicago members of your association?—A. No.

Q. None of them?—A. None of them.

Q. Have you any complaint about the elevator system in Chicago?—A. Yes; we have made complaints repeatedly.

Q. Complaints have been made to your association or in your association?—A. No; never in our association. The Illinois association has sent delegations to Springfield several times to try to strengthen the old law and prevent the enactment of the new. The law itself specified that a public warehouseman should not deal in grain in his own house, which the supreme court will, I think, decide is in conflict with the constitution, article 13 of which was enacted right after the big swindle. We had false bottoms here that public warehousemen, in 1870, I think it was, say caused the enactment of that law, and all the debate and discussion which brought about the incorporation of that article in the constitution was that it was for the protection of the owner of grain, and that the warehouseman should not be recognized as a storer of grain in his own house. They could not have considered that that would ever be done, because the constitution does not specify that he shall not, and it does not recognize the possibility of that practice ever arising.

Q. (By Representative LORIMER.) Is there a case pending in the Supreme Court?—A. No; I think there is a case pending now before Judge Tuley.

Q. What case is that? Is that the case begun prior to 1896, prior to the passage of this law?—A. I think it is a case that was begun afterwards. The case begun prior to the passage of the law was upheld by the Supreme Court.

Q. (By Mr. KENNEDY.) It was stated here yesterday that the grain men of Chicago who were making complaints about these warehouses never had used them, and did not want to use them now. Do you know anything as to that?—A. You mean the commission men didn't want to use them?

Q. Yes.—A. Sometimes they have occasion to use them for their country shippers. Of course a commission man is not often an owner of grain himself; that is, he is not supposed to be. I think it would be to the best interest of the trade if we had some public warehouses which were operated as public warehouses and the people who owned them did not store grain in them. The most of the public elevators here are owned by the railroads; some of them are not.

Q. (By Representative LORIMER.) We have elevators that are exclusively public elevators, have we not?—A. There are so called.

Q. Are they not in fact?—A. I guess anyone can store grain there, provided they are not full; but the operators, I guess, generally put the grain in themselves. The impression is that most of the grain that passes through the elevators is owned by the proprietors of the elevators. Sometimes it is not.

Q. Have you heard of a cargo of grain in Chicago at any time within the last 10 years that the public elevators refused to take for storage?—A. I don't know that any case has ever arisen except when the house was full. Sometimes they have refused it. We had a case here, although I guess the house is not a regular public warehouse now. The case came up, I think it was yesterday, where the inspection department classed a grade as two or three, and it went to an elevator and they refused to accept it on that grade. Of course, the department had given that grade, but they would not take it on that classification.

Q. That was because they would be expected to turn out grain of the grade that the department had certified to, and they in fact believed it was grain of a lower grade?—A. Yes; they believed the inspector had erred.

Q. In other words, they did not refuse to take it because they wanted to exclude it?—A. No; I have not heard of that.

Q. (By Mr. C. J. Harris.) Would not that be a proper objection in some cases?—A. Most assuredly, for their own protection and the protection of the public at large.

Q. (By Mr. Kennedy.) Are these so-called public warehouses that you speak of owned by men who are the great elevator men of Chicago, like Armour and Counselman?—A. Most of them are owned by the railroads.

Q. Most of the public elevators?—A. Some of them are not, and of course they are operated by individuals. Some of the railroad elevators are operated as private elevators, showing that there is no need of so many public elevators.

(Testimony closed.)

CHICAGO, ILL., *November 18, 1899.*

TESTIMONY OF MR. EDGAR H. EVANS,

Representative of the Indianapolis Board of Trade.

The subcommission being in session in Chicago, Representative Lorimer presiding, at 12.30 p. m., November 18, 1899, Mr. Edgar H. Evans was introduced as a witness, and, being duly sworn, testified concerning transportation as follows:

Q. (By Representative Lorimer.) What is your name?—A. Edgar H. Evans.
Q. Your place of business?—A. Indianapolis.
Q. Board of trade?—A. I am a member of it.
Q. What is your business address?—A. Hoosier State Flour Mills.
Q. Are you here as a representative of the board of trade?—A. I am.
Q. Will you please state in your own way any grievances or make any suggestions that you wish, as representative of the board or for yourself?—A. I invite your attention to matters of discrimination in the first place. You may know the freight rates of past years, but I will hastily run over them to bring out the point I wish to make. On November 10, 1898, the rate of freight from Chicago to New York was 20 cents on grain and grain products. On January 12, this year, that rate was reduced to 18 cents on grain and grain products, with this exception, however, that at the port of New York there was a discrimination of 1½ cents on the hundred pounds; at the port of Philadelphia of one-half cent on the hundred pounds, owing to the change of the system of basing. This operated against the wheat miller to that extent, and the mills of the country made a protest to the traffic association, which was not regarded. On April 18 rate was made 17 cents on grain products, but on wheat and corn 11 cents, Chicago to New York. On September 18 a rate was made of 20 cents on grain products, but on grain for export 14 or 15, according to the tariff rates. On November 1 the rate was 22 cents for grain products and 20 cents on grain for export. I wish also to call your attention to the fact that from the Mississippi River, April 18, grain products were 19½ cents and wheat and corn 12 cents. On September 18, from the Mississippi River to New York the rate was 23 cents on grain products, but on grain only 15 cents, or a discrimination of 8 cents a hundred. On November 1—I think—the Interstate Commerce Commission made a decree ruling that the rate from the Mississippi River is to be 24 cents on grain products and 20 cents on grain; a difference of 4 cents. This difference is still greater at points farther west, as you have been informed this morning. Now, to illustrate the effects of this, for instance on the corn miller, as we have 2 large corn mills at Indianapolis

as well as 3 large flour mills, I wish to submit a statement given to me by a miller the Cerealine Manufacturing Company, showing the cost of corn billed from 110 per cent points west.   You will understand, Indianapolis being an interior point, its rate is a certain proportion of the Chicago to New York rate.   Indianapolis rates are generally on the same basis as Chicago, except that the interior shipper can not get the benefit of the special low rates made for export, and he is thus cut out of the trade.

Grain loaded at 110 per cent points delivered at New York for export—basis, 22 cents.

	Cost.	Per bushel.	Per 100 pounds.
		Cents.	*Cents.*
1,000 bushels Corn, at 30 cents	$300.00	30.00	53.57
Freight, 56,000 pounds, at 22.5 Cents	126.00	12.60	22.50
Delivered, New York	426.00	42.60	76.07

Same milled at Indianapolis and product forwarded to New York for domestic use:

	Cost.	Per bushel.	Per 100 pounds.
		Cents.	*Cents.*
1,000 bushels Corn, at 30 Cents	$300.00	30.00	53.57
Freight, 56,000 pounds, at 24 cents	134.40	13.44	24.00
Milling privilege, 56,000 pounds, at 1½ Cents	8.40	.84	1.50
Total	442.80	44.28	79.07
Grain delivered New York, as above	426.00	42.60	76.07
Net difference	16.80	1.68	3.00

Q. (By Mr. C. J. HARRIS.) Net difference as against what?—A. In favor of corn for export.   Now, as to its effect on flour mills—as to that I am a little more competent to speak—I would read a few letters that have been received, particularly showing the losses of business; and after this statement you can draw your own conclusions.

First, a letter from Manchester, dated September 6, 1899: "I regret that you could not see your way to book this little order, which was for the trade here.   I offered the best price I could and am unable to advance on it.   The competition of local millers renders business almost impossible at present American prices."

Next, a letter from London, dated October 31: "Sorry you could not see your way to accept our bid for 'Aurora.'   As it turns out we do not think we should have done ourselves much good if you had.   Winter wheat does not meet with the same demand it used to and is being rapidly displaced by English flour, which is in good demand.   English wheat and flour have sharply declined and lost nearly all the previous rise.   Of all the soft-wheat flours English is certainly the cheapest."

This from a Boston shipping firm which has a large export trade and also owns a mill: "Advices this morning from some of the principal ports are to the effect that local millers are turning out as good a sack of flour as any of the leading Minnesota mills, and selling it at considerably lower prices than the American mills are naming.   This scores another base hit for the mill-ruining policy of the railroads.   Hope before long something or other may turn up that will enable us to exchange more cheerful greetings."

Also a letter from Liverpool to corn mill: "But we regret there is not the slightest chance of any business at those prices.   As regards Q. M. we are very sorry indeed that English makers are gaining ground from week to week, and somehow or other are underselling us right and left.   We sincerely hope freights may soon come down again and that we can do a good business together."

To the same purport, on the 2d of August: "But it seems as if the present high freights are making it very difficult to get any orders through."

On the 25th of October, from the same firm: "Sorry there is no chance whatever to place any Q. M. at your present limit of 20/6, Liverpool.   Makers here are underselling very considerably, and we simply have to look on.   With present high freights we are afraid there is not much chance to do any business for quite a time."

From Amsterdam, August 1: "Your quotations didn't admit any business.   It seems that competing mills are ab

Q. Some of these are corn mills?—A. Yes; some are from corn mills and two from flour mills.

Q. Is there much corn meal exported?—A. The export business to my knowledge has been growing very greatly in the past 2 years, and it is now a considerable business. It is not of as long growth as the milling of flour, because the European countries have been slow to recognize the value of corn for food aside from animal food; but it is very largely on the increase, through the efforts of the State Department, beginning about 2 years ago. Now, you can see from this that the business of the mills (I speak particularly of the interior mills) has been very considerably harassed. There has never been a time in the last 20 years—I am not competent to speak of so long ago, but I have it from others who are—there never has been a time in the last 20 years when the mills, at this time of the year, have been so largely shut down or running on half time. The millers, trying to get into the foreign markets, finds the foreign markets already occupied by the British miller; then he turns his attention to the domestic market, and, of course, that is all competed for, and competition brings prices down to a limit where he can run no longer, and he shuts down his mill—as has happened in Ohio, Indiana, and Illinois—shuts down to wait until the present crisis is over. This has meant to the railroad companies a loss of the handling of the coal to run the mills; it has meant to the manufacturers the loss of the sale of mill supplies; it has meant to the men employed a loss of wages; it has meant to the milling industry at large a very serious dragging down. Many mills have had to quit the business, and if this matter is to continue, they will largely have to go out of the business. But, on the other hand, the effect on the English miller: I was told by a gentleman who has just come from Europe in the interest of his mill that the English mills are running at a rate never before known; that their profits are large and they are getting trade that the American millers had worked for years to reach. In 1870 the American millers exported only 17 per cent of the total shipments of wheat and flour; the last few years they have exported between 40 and 50 per cent, varying with crop conditions here and abroad. The effect of this I should like to give from a letter sent to a milling journal by John J. Carter, of London: "The freight discrimination against flour is no doubt working very prejudicially against the trade, and is a fine thing for the English miller. It amounts to the same as if our Government should place a duty of say 6 cents per 100 pounds and allow wheat to come in free. This is what every miller here has been agitating for for years, in order to keep American flour out of our market. It hardly seems possible that such an anomaly will be permitted by your Government to last for any length of time. Other countries are paying their manufacturers bounties in order to encourage trade."

Along the line of the suggestion of the word bounty, a St. Louis miller makes the following remark: "As a side remark it is appropriate to remind the American miller that Germany puts a prohibitive tariff on American flour, but will import something like 85,000,000 bushels of wheat from America, which American railroads will ship at reduced rates to assist the German millers and consumers, while American millers are forced into idleness."

Now, how is this to be overcome? By putting wheat and flour, grain and grain products, on the same basis. We are met with the suggestion that railroads say it costs more. That has not been sustained either in the opinion of the trade or the opinion of the Interstate Commerce Commission, and I think further investigation will show that not only is the expense of transporting flour not more, but if anything a little less. I have seen a car of wheat come in from a country town to Indianapolis, loaded by a careful shipper, and yet when it reached Indianapolis, 30 miles away, it had lost 120 bushels, for which the railroads had to pay. If it had gone to New York, the trail of wheat would have left nothing, and the railroads would have it to pay. That is not the case with flour. In case of wreckage, the wheat is thrown on the ground; it can be scooped up, but there is wood and rubbish and stones in it, and it is valueless for anything but chicken feed; flour can be gathered up in sacks or barrels, and there is no loss.

Q. Do you mean to say they would ship the flour after it had been gathered up?—A. It is in bags, and can be sold at a close approximation to its original value.

Q. If the bags are burst?—A. In that case the flour is gone; but in the same case so is the wheat. They say the cars of flour are not loaded up as heavily; if that is the point, the millers are prepared, for export or any other trade, to load to a given limit; for they have agreed to, and have done so. I took a record of 16 cars from the books of the mill, and the average was 63,000 pounds to the car; I took the record of 9 consecutive cars, which would average 65,333 pounds to the car; very few shipments of wheat will excel this. We have loaded out from our mill 80,000 pounds in one car for shipment to Philadelphia. The pretext that it will cost more is merely a pretext. When they were making this discrimination against flour from the regions in Indiana, Ohio, and Illinois, Minneapolis was getting 1¼ cents a hundred pounds less on flour than on wheat. In the first place no railroad has given a single reason that will stand, why flour, grain products, should be taken at a greater rate than grain for export. In fact, there have been numerous instances where the railroad men were opposed to it. When rates reach the low point, which was the case during the five months previous to September 18, several railroads, both East and West, refused to pro rate on that basis. I have talked with numerous railway officials, from the agents and the general managers of the roads to the traveling men who have been on the road for years and are thoroughly conversant with the situation, and without exception, in private conversation, they have agreed that the discrimination was wrong and that they would do what they could to overcome it. There was no reason that I have found to justify it. There was an explanation suggested to me by a railroad man, and it has been the only explanation that explains, and that is that some of the people are in some way or other interested in these large shipments of grain abroad. Of course, they could not lay their hands on the enormous amount of flour at once, but they can on a great amount of grain. Soliciting agents and general managers owe their position largely to the fact that they obtain a certain amount of tonnage for the railroads; whether for 2 cents or for 10 cents, they get their tonnage, and promotions are gauged that way. So long as that continues, so long will the financial interests of the railways be ignored and stockholders will have no voice. In support of that position I should like to read a letter from Mr. Ingalls. I wrote Mr. Ingalls as follows:

"Can your road and the other trunk lines afford to kill a business such as the inclosed clipping indicates? This you are doing most surely, and not simply by inches, but by long strides. At the present time there is not an export mill in the winter-wheat region, except a few that buy their wheat from first hands very cheap, that is able to do export business at any profit. There is not a mill that comes into competition with grain buyers of the East that is able to buy wheat and sell its output for foreign trade at a profit, and we are in that fix.

"Every year for the past 20 years, up to this time, we have been well sold ahead at this stage of the harvest. But what can we expect to do now? The British miller, the Dutch miller, the French miller, and the German miller are buying their wheat, bought in competition with us, at 6 cents a hundred less than we can afford to pay for it. We had hoped that the recent expostulations of the millers throughout the country and the facts brought out by the investigations of the Interstate Commerce Commission would have made the roads more reasonable. Instead of that they have adopted more arbitrary measures than ever, seeming intent to kill the milling business or, as has been hinted, in league with the large grain shippers.

"What logic there can be in giving grain the rate of 6 cents a hundred pounds less than the rate on flour for export we have not yet heard, nor can anyone, railroad man or layman, give any logical and just reason why there should be this amount of difference. We do not think your road can afford to adopt this un-American and unjust method of giving a bounty to the raw material. If the railroads are so enamored of carrying export freight at less than the domestic, and if they want to give a bounty to something, by all means give it to flour, and they will carry just as much freight and even more. All the American miller wants is to be put on the same basis, at least in approximation thereto, with the raw material, and he will take care of himself. But the discrimination that is now in operation not only robs him of his chance to live, but robs the railroads of a large amount of incidental freight.

"May we not count on your efforts to bring about a change in this at an early date? your breadth of vision and true patriotism will surely show you the folly of subjecting such a large industry as the milling interest to such unfair and unjust disadvantage."

This letter was dated July 18, 1899. In reply I received the following letter from Mr. Ingalls, dated July 20, at Hot Springs, Va.:

"I have never been in favor of this reduction in the wheat rate. What ought to be done is to raise it to the same as the flour rate, and I hope shortly the railways will get tired of their insane competition and restore the wheat rate to a paying basis, and then the flour men can live. I will do everything possible to this end."

That, from a man who stands as high as any other man in railroad circles in the country, is worthy of the attention of every railroad man, and certainly of laymen. But apparently we are not able to bring this about by appeal to the railroads. The corn men had a difficulty. It was with them that the discrimina.

tion was first made some two or three years ago. They wrote and pleaded, but to no avail. They instituted a suit, and the railroads acceded to their demands and the suit was dismissed. Not long after that the discrimination was made again, and the corn millers ever since have been enduring it.

The Winter Wheat Millers, of which I am the treasurer, came before the Traffic Association here in Chicago. We were treated very courteously, and the secretary, Mr. Tucker, afforded us every opportunity to get the information we wanted. When we talked with the individual members, they were unanimously in favor of making the change in behalf of the mills. When they went into committee, the subcommittee voted for it; but in the general committee secret influence seemed to carry it adversely by storm, and nobody seemed to be willing to open his mouth to the contrary.

The only remedy we can see is in the way of giving the Interstate Commerce Commission more power to enforce its decrees. We shall then feel certain that if we have a grievance we can come before it and present our case, and shall get the justice that we should have. As it is, we have to deal with the railroad manager. If he wishes to make an experiment, he makes it, and there is no one to say him nay. It matters not if it disturbs the whole commerce of the country and brings disaster to any line of business—he has his say. The matter should be remedied so that no railroad should be allowed to disturb the commerce of the country, as it has been in the past, by action which has been shown to be indefensible, without previous legal authority, such as would be granted under an extension of the powers of the Interstate Commerce Commission.

One further discrimination I would invite your attention to, and that is the duty levied by foreign countries on grain and grain products. With the exception of England and Holland, and, I believe, one other European country, there is a discriminating duty levied on flour as against wheat. Of course, we are a protective country ourselves and can not blame them, but every commercial treaty is merely a matter of give and take. We give France a right to bring in wines, and in return for it she simply puts on a heavier duty. We tried to get up negotiations with Brazil, where there was a large trade in flour, and she turns around and puts on a heavy duty on flour as against wheat. The consequence is the millers in Brazil are developing very rapidly, and the entire line of shipping engaged in carrying flour there has been abandoned, and the trade which could have been worked up and kept up by proper negotiations through the State Department has been lost to the country; that has to be given up or crowded into other markets now already well occupied. Of course, the Department of State has been well filled up with business the past year; perhaps that is another reason for the establishment of the Department of Commerce to look after such matters. The Winter Wheat Millers in convention on two occasions have indorsed that movement very thoroughly.

Q. (By Mr. C. J. HARRIS.) You say you have presented your case to the railroad companies without getting any relief?—A. Yes.

Q. How long has this discrimination against manufactured grain products been in existence?—A. The discrimination has been in existence only since the first of the year—it was about February 1 the tariff was finally issued, making a discrimination of a cent and a half at New York and a half cent at Philadelphia. This was first shown in Chicago before the Central Traffic Association the latter part of February, but as I show from the list of changes in rates that evidently had no effect.

Q. The railroad companies could make more by carrying the flour from 100,000 bushels of wheat to New York at 22 cents than by carrying the grain at 12 cents, could they not?—A. That is one of the absurdities of the situation. The American millers are capable of grinding all the wheat in the country; running full time, their capacity is such that they could do it; but the grain is taken away from us under such conditions that there is no chance of life.

Q. Would a difference of 2 cents, according to the decision of the Interstate Commerce Commission, be satisfactory to the millers?—A. It certainly would be much better than the other; but the objection to that is the difference of 2 cents. That is supposed to cover the difference in handling at seaboard, but it is simply a pretext for a rebate to the shipper of grain.

Q. You think for the encouragement of the American manufacturers the rate should be the same?—A. The rate should be the same as a matter of public policy, if nothing else.

Q. (By Representative OTJEN.) It has always been the same heretofore?—A. It has always been the same heretofore.

Q. (By Mr. C. J. HARRIS.) In your article you simply alluded to the traffic discrimination. You have no discriminations of a private nature in favor of one individual as against another?—A. I think there is very little of that. When any rebates are made I think they have been very general as far as any specific locality is concerned.

Q. All ship on the published rate?—A. Yes.

Q. (By Mr. KENNEDY.) You said there has been no difference heretofore between wheat shipped East for domestic use and that for export; how long since the difference was instituted?—A. There was something done in 1896.

Q. They made a difference in 1896 against flour.—A. Not against flour.

Q. Against export grain?—A. In favor of export grain as against the domestic; but I think that also carried the flour with it. At least, we did not have much trouble until this year.

Q. When was it that you could get the same rate for shipping grain to the East that you had for flour, or the same for flour that you had for grain?—A. Up to the present year.

Q. Beginning the 1st of January last?—A. Beginning exactly on the 1st of February.

Q. (By Representative LORIMER.) Have you anything further to suggest?—A. One idea came to me when a former witness was speaking of inspection. Inspection at Chicago is a matter which dealers in my country are interested in. At times it is satisfactory, at other times not; it is dishonestly rigid and dishonestly lax—rigid coming in, lax going out. There are times when we have to bring down supplies from here, and we find that we get all kinds of wheat. When we ship up we have to have gilt-edge articles.

Q. Is not the difference a difference in grading between Indianapolis and Chicago; that is to say, is No. 2 wheat in Indianapolis graded as No. 2 in Chicago, or vice versa?—A. Under normal conditions; but during the Leiter deal in wheat you could not get into Chicago unless you had a strictly gilt-edge article. Wheat which ordinarily passed at No. 2 did not then.

Q. (By Mr. C. J. HARRIS.) Would wheat inspected at Indianapolis be received here at the same grade—would the Indianapolis inspection go here in Chicago?—A. I think it would as a normal thing.

Q. (By Representative LORIMER.) What do you attribute this discrimination to?—A. It is attributed to the efforts of the railroads to get traffic from territory that does not belong to them; in other words, the competition of the Gulf is the reason for it. But whether that is a sufficient reason is a matter more for railroading.

Q. Not the inspection?—A. No; I do not see that the inspection has anything to do with it.

Q. You say the inspection is lax going out?—A. As far as Chicago is concerned.

Q. You do not attribute that to the railroads?—A. No; that is merely a matter of inspection.

Q. What do you attribute that to?—A. We were entirely at a loss to know what to attribute it to. There were different ideas advanced, but probably none of them were worthy of serious consideration.

Q. Have you known of a cargo of grain graded at Indianapolis and shipped to Chicago and graded here below the Indianapolis grade?—A. Yes.

Q. By Chicago?—A. Yes. We ship our own wheat up here considerably, and in one or two instances the grade was cut, when in our market it would have been easily received.

Q. Did you protest?—A. It was in such a shape there was nothing to do but get rid of it at once. It was during the Leiter investment, and to delay it would have been to lose all the profit in it.

Q. Have you information of other gradings from your town?—A. I have known of instances, but I could not state exactly, not being interested in them.

Q. Do you have in mind any cargo of grain shipped from Chicago to Indianapolis graded higher here than its actual grade?—A. Yes; on a number of occasions. We did not make a written protest, as it would require a great deal of debate and a great deal of work, and perhaps even then we should simply be thrown over; it would come back to the board of inspection, and it is their position to sustain the inspector. It is a common feeling all over the country; they will not ship to Chicago when they can ship to any other market at the same price.

Q. Is the inspection at Indianapolis under State supervision?—A. No; under the supervision of the board of trade.

Q. Do you know whether the State supervision is rated higher or lower than the private supervision?—A. I can only give the impressions I have gathered from others, that the State supervision is apt to be very irregular, owing to the matter of political appointments entering into it.

Q. Do you know anything about the appointments in the Chicago grain inspection?—A. No; I do not.

Q. You are not aware that most of the men here have been in the service over 20 years?—A. No.

Q. Did you hear Mr. Clark state that the Peoria grain inspection was private and a poorer inspection than the State inspection?—A. I am not acquainted with that.

Q. (By Mr. KENNEDY.) Have you spoken for the Indianapolis Board of Trade on the subject of pooling, or could you speak for them on that subject?—A. Not for the board of trade. That subject has not come up in my recollection as a board matter. The feeling among the millers, speaking for myself, is that pooling should be allowed, but only under the supervision of the Interstate Commerce Commission.

Q. (By Representative LORIMER.) Do you know that the Chicago Board of Trade has a committee known as the arbitration committee?—A. Yes.

Q. To which protests on inspection are submitted?—A. Yes.

Q. And these complaints that you have suggested with reference to the inspection were never submitted to that board?—A. No; the difference was not great, and probably not enough to make a great fuss about; but it was not equitable.

Q. What was the difference?—A. One and a half to 2 cents a bushel on a matter of 2 or 3 carloads. It would not pay to come up here and make a protest.

Q. At 1½ or 2 cents a bushel there would not be so very much difference in the grade, would there? A man might honestly make that difference in the inspection?—A. Well, when it comes to the inspection, that is all the difference between No. 2 and No. 3 wheat at times.

Q. Is there not a difference in No. 2 and in No. 3 wheat—you get one grade in No. 2 that is better than another grade of No. 2 that you may receive on the same car?—A. There is a bottom limit on No. 2, but no top limit. From a certain grade up it is No. 2.

Q. So there might be a high-grade No. 3 and a low-grade No. 3, and a low-grade No. 2 so close to the high-grade No. 3 that a man might possibly honestly make a mistake?—A. That might be done.

Q. And might that not be the case in the instances you mention, without criminal intent?—A. It is either criminal or careless.

Q. Are you in favor of a national inspection?—A. I have not given the subject much thought.

Q. Do you think it possible to have a national inspection?—A. In a modified form only; I think it would be rather impracticable, on the whole.

(Testimony closed.)

CHICAGO, ILL., *November 18, 189½.*

TESTIMONY OF MR. CHESTER A. FULLER,

Norfolk, Nebr.

The subcommission convened at 2 p. m., Representative Lorimer presiding. Mr. Chester A. Fuller was sworn, and testified concerning railroad discriminations as follows:

Q. (By Representative LORIMER.) Please state your full name, address, and business.—A. Chester A. Fuller, Norfolk, Nebr.; abstracter of titles. I will state to the commission that these remarks are in regard to the discriminations of the railroad companies in extending local freight rates to certain localities, to the detriment of rival towns, in respect to manufacturing and jobbing enterprises. The locality which I refer to is in the northeast part of Nebraska. In order to give a more definite basis of comparison let us take two towns, Norfolk and Fremont. Norfolk is credited with a population of 5,260, and was first organized about 1866. Fremont was organized about 1858, and is credited with 10,000 population. The territory tributary to Fremont is encroached on from the south and east by numerous other jobbing points, while Norfolk stands practically alone in the territory tributary to her. A circle drawn around Norfolk with a radius of 75 miles embraces no other town of equal population or railroad facilities. This region is well defined by river courses and by established railway lines. One line 485 miles long in northern Nebraska includes four tiers of counties, an empire in itself. Railroads diverge in five directions from Norfolk. Norfolk has among other thriving industries a beet-sugar factory wherein are handled annually about 32,000 tons of sugar beets, yielding a product of 3,500 tons, or 7,000,000 pounds, of the finest quality of sugar, awarded the highest standing in the recent Trans-Mississippi Exposition. Its roller mill markets its products, and a specialty known as "Wheatling," in every Western State south as far as St. Louis. A foundry and manufacturing company furnishes an improved furnace and a practical gasoline engine and employs 20 men. A creamery company, with 20 skimming stations established in surrounding towns, has a capacity of 15,000 pounds of butter per day. Here is located a State insane asylum now accomodating 300 patients, and its full capacity is not yet reached. The city, in accordance with the socialistic tendency of the present day, owns and successfully operates its own waterworks. In the grain-shipping business only one small elevator is in operation, with a capacity of 9,000 bushels, but this is explained by the fact that upward of 2,000 cattle and 18,000 sheep are fed, affording a home market for the grain raised in the immediate vicinity. Mr. W. H. Dexter, of Lowell, Mass., operates here a butter and egg refrigerator, shipping the product to his Eastern home; his complaint is that the local rate from Sioux City to Norfolk, 75 miles haul, takes the profit, and instead of. marketing in Chicago or in some other Western market, he is compelled to take advantage of the low rates between the Missouri River and the East in order to make a profit on his product.

In an educational and literary way Norfolk has a full complement of schools, including a $20,000 high school, two daily newspapers and four weeklies. Referring to the map, you will notice that Norfolk's railway location is similar to that of Lincoln, in the southeastern part of the State, indicating a commercial center, and the geography of the State amply sustains the wisdom of this opinion. Fremont operates a foundry and machine shop, a brewery marketing its beer in this section, a butter-tub cooperage factory, a creamery, saddlery and harness factory, woolen mill, mill-machine factory, three elevators, a pickle works, and factories for the manufacture of cigar boxes, wire fence, hemp, and other small factories. Fremont is accorded a rate which in effect gives it an advantage over Norfolk, in that the rate from Chicago and other eastern points to Norfolk is computed by adding to the rate to the Missouri River the additional local rate of 45 cents per hundred on first-class freight, other classes in proportion; while the rate to Fremont is the same as that to the Missouri River. The effect of this can readily be seen in that Fremont factories and jobbers can ship into territory naturally tributary to Norfolk at an advantage over Norfolk institutions of the same character equal to the difference in the rate. We are told that the rate is reasonable; that the lower rate is accorded Fremont owing to competition. The roads entering Norfolk are controlled by one system and its Pacific coast connection. We are perhaps not prepared to say that the rate is not reasonable, for the reason that water transportation is not available and the ox cart and prairie schooner are out of date. It has been suggested that whereas the rate to Norfolk from the Missouri River is based on the distance to Sioux City, a distance of 75 miles, and the same rate is accorded to Omaha, a distance of 118 miles, perhaps the rate to Norfolk should be raised to correspond to the additional distance. This might prove a means of increasing the first cost of articles laid down in Norfolk, but if the rates were equalized by making the rate to Fremont proportionate to the additional distance and in the same proportion as to points beyond it would afford some relief. Through rates are now established arbitrarily by the railroads to certain favored points. Perhaps the advantage to the public should not be questioned, with the exception of their effect in building up one locality at the expense of another, naturally more favorably situated. Were the rates established by the Government instead of at the will and pleasure of the railway managers, it is a natural conclusion that points having the same general conditions would receive equal benefits under that arrangement.

Among other things, it is noted that the rules of the Interstate Commerce Commission in reference to the publication and display of tariffs of rates are constantly violated. In regard to rebating to individuals, I have not made any particular investigation but one leading dry goods firm assures me that so long as it secures a rebate of 25 per cent at the expense of its competitors it has no objection to the present status of rates. It is a well-recognized fact of trade that the grocery business, so far as jobbing is concerned, is confined largely to houses covering a very limited amount of territory. Some 10 years ago a wholesale grocery house established a jobbing branch at Norfolk. Its receipts during the year were $155,000, and this on an average stock of $12,000. This business was conducted on a basis of 25 per cent rebate on the tariff existing at that time. Owing to a conclusion by one of the roads that it was not getting its share of this business the rebate was arbitrarily withdrawn. The company at once abandoned its local branch and handles this territory from Omaha, a distance of 118 miles. A through rate is made to Norfolk from Minneapolis, but none from Chicago except by adding the local rate to the rate to the Missouri River. This is also true of all other sources of supply in the East. I believe

Minneapolis is the only exception. The discrimination which is being practiced is detrimental not only to the immediate locality for which I speak, but in an equal measure to the East, from which we must secure our supplies, raw material, groceries, clothing, agricultural implements, etc., with which to develop this section, and especially to Chicago jobbers, who suffer because they are practically barred by the lack of the through rate.

We are told that the rate of 45 cents for 100 pounds from Sioux City and Omaha is the same as the rate to Fremont, and is a reasonable rate, and that we should not object to it; that is, 45 cents per 100 pounds, first class, from Sioux City and from Omaha to Norfolk. From Sioux City to Norfolk is 75 miles and from Omaha it is 118 miles. The railroads entering Norfolk are the Chicago, St. Paul, Minneapolis and Omaha from Sioux City, and the Fremont, Elkhorn and Missouri Valley road from Omaha; the branch of the Chicago, St. Paul, Minneapolis and Omaha road terminates at Norfolk, the other road running in is the Union Pacific. As I stated before, we are not prepared to say that this rate is not reasonable. This road here [indicating] is the northeasterly connection of the Union Pacific; they ship their coast business through here.

It has been suggested by the railroad companies, when we ask for a lower rate, that we have the 75-mile rate, but the truth of the matter is that Omaha is the base of supplies, and not Sioux City, and it is 118 miles to Omaha. As the matter now stands, Fremont enjoys a Missouri River rate, and a man shipping in his raw material from Iowa, or from Eastern points, to manufacture, gets the advantage of that rate, while the Norfolk man, if he ships from Iowa, or other Eastern points. to Sioux City, has to pay the additional local rate to get to Norfolk; that is to say, the Fremont shipper is saved the amount of the local rate from Fremont to the river.

Q. (By Mr. KENNEDY.) Where is Fremont on this map? It is pretty close to the river, is it not?—A. Yes.

The Chicago, St. Paul, Minneapolis and Omaha road has no tariff sheet hanging up in its office. No person knows what the rates are without going to the agent, and when one does he generally gets the impression that he is encroaching. They feel that perhaps he wants the rates in order to make trouble, and they don't care to have the other roads know what their rates are. The company, however, claims that it is practically complying with the law by having a card stating that the rates can be ascertained by applying to their agent, which card they have posted up in their office. In regard to reparation to individuals, I have not made any investigation along this line, I mention these things in conjunction with this question, and will say that I went down the street one day and got a list of 130 names; a large proportion of the business men pledged their moral support for the movement to secure more equitable freight rates. Many others absolutely declined to sign any such agreement to give their moral support, and they gave me to understand that they were satisfied with the treatment accorded to them by the railroad company. Then, in these particular cases, they had a rebate of 25 per cent on spring and fall orders.

It is a well-recognized fact of trade that grocery jobbing houses do the large business in their line and that a comparatively small portion of the local jobbing houses handle the goods within their territory, and the matter of freights is likely to give the retail merchant in marketing his produce a disadvantage compared with the wholesale jobbing houses and grocery jobbing houses, and the retailer has to purchase from the nearest jobbing house whatever he wants. In Iowa there are local jobbing houses scattered around all over the State, owing to the distance tariff enforced by the State board for Iowa, and they usually buy from the nearest jobbing house. These jobbing houses turn their money upward of twelve times a year, and with a very fair profit on the money invested in their business; and yet during the past and other years a smaller amount has been done from the Omaha and Sioux City houses, while the business has been handled through the nearest houses, handling their goods from Norfolk instead of from Omaha. Now, this matter has been taken up with the railroad companies. It was taken up first, I think, because there was a sentiment among the business men—while they did not want to have any hard feelings about it, they had no doubt they were discriminated against. The same road, the Chicago, St. Paul, Minneapolis and Omaha, running out of Sioux City has the rate of 22 cents for the 75-mile haul in one direction—that is, in Iowa, and except in the direction of Norfolk—the rate per ton down to the Black Hills, South Dakota, is 75 cents, or .0779 cents per ton per mile; the same local rate to David City, 78 miles, is .0641 cents per ton per mile, while from Sioux City to Beemer, 168 miles, the rate per ton is only .0524 cents per ton per mile. After going to the railroad company, they had a meeting at Omaha, inviting me and our business men down there to present our case to them, and after the first 15 minutes of conversation there was nothing said about the railroads doing the square thing and reducing the rates, except that it would mix things up for them to change the tariff, and that they would have to adjust all their rates in that part of the country if they made a change. Then the matter was taken up with the State board of transportation. The Nebraska transportation law is copied very closely, I might say it is an exact copy of the interstate-commerce law, applied, of course, to the State. The State board took the position that these roads were shipping from Sioux City to Norfolk, and Sioux City being an Iowa point, it was a matter for the Interstate Commission, and the State board had no jurisdiction, and they dismissed the complaint. At this time there is a case which is now pending on that point before the Interstate Commerce Commission and which has not been reached for a decision.

Q. (By Mr. C. J. HARRIS.) How much of a place is Fremont?—A. Fremont has about 10,000 population.

Q. Has it increased rapidly in the last 10 years?—A. It has not increased rapidly, but it is growing steadily, while Norfolk has gained little, if any, in 5 years.

Q. What is the population of Norfolk?—A. Accredited to be 5,260. Perhaps it is a little more than that now.

Q. Is it not an increasing population?—A. Very slowly.

Q. Have you any complaint to make about your grain rates in Chicago?—A. No, sir; the complaints that have been discussed by the association have not been in regard to these Eastern rates—the grain rates.

Q. Do you have a board of railroad commissioners in your State?—A. Yes. But in the State of Nebraska the constitution provides that no additional offices shall be created by the legislature without an amendment to the constitution, and in effect this has caused the State board of railroad commissioners to be made up of the governor of the State, the secretary of State, the State auditor and the State treasurer. All of the State boards are composed in the same way of the public officials; but the work is done by secretaries appointed by the governor, who make their report as to the business they have transacted to the actual board of State officers, and their action goes on record as the action of the governor and the State officers as the board.

Q. Have you laid your case before your railroad commission?—A. In the State; yes.

Q. What was their reply?—A. Their action was to dismiss the complaint, from the fact that they thought it was a matter that was out of their jurisdiction and that it was interstate-commerce business instead of local business. Their opinion was this: They told us at the time of hearing the complaint that there was certainly something wrong, and that there was some means of adjustment for it, but that they had no jurisdiction of the matter, as it was interstate business entirely, Sioux City being in Iowa.

Q. Could they not regulate the local part of it? That part of it in your own State? It would be almost entirely in the State of Nebraska, would it not?—A. No; the rate is made from Sioux City, which is out of the State of Nebraska, and the rate advances very rapidly. That is, the rate is from Sioux City, which is just across the river, a matter of a mile, perhaps, and a difference of 5 cents is made there, which is due to the bridge across the Missouri. Down at Norfolk it is a mile and a half to the switch known as Hope siding. There is a difference in that rate to Norfolk of 3 cents for that mile and a half to Hope, where there are no facilities for handling freight whatever, so they go on to Norfolk and stop and unload the freight and then go back to Hope the next morning.

Q. That is one of the terminals of the line?—A. Yes; Norfolk.

Q. I understood you to say the Interstate Commission decided you did not come under the interstate law?—A. No; you misunderstood me.

Q. I was asking for information.—A. The State commission is the only one that has passed upon it.

Q. Did I not understand you to say something about the Interstate Commission?—A. Yes; we had a case before them for consideration, but it has not come up yet.

Q. I understood you to say you had some decision from them.—A. No; that was the State commission.

Q. (By Mr. KENNEDY.) Your complaint is against the Sioux City road and not the Omaha road?—A. Both roads come in there, although they are practically the same management. The shortest haul should govern the rate in any event. If the Sioux City road would reduce its rate on the distance basis and make that their tariff, as their tariff invariably and in such proportion to other places would seem to indicate would be correct, then the Omaha road would voluntarily reduce its rates, because of the Omaha shippers, and to allow the merchants of Norfolk to purchase their supplies from them instead of going to Sioux City because of the lower rate.

Q. If you obtained your supplies from Omaha that would be in the same State and would come under your State commission. How are the rates from Omaha?— A. They are satisfactory; you can not complain of them at all on the ground of being unreasonable. I have some other items. In the discussion of this matter before our association it seemed that the creamery men were shipping butter to Sioux City by express, the belief being that the rate by express is as low as the rate by freight, and the expressman can come after the butter at the creamery and deliver it to the customer in Sioux City. Of course that was a very desirable arrangement. But as soon as the railroad company found it out they adjusted things, having the express rate raised so that the creamery men would have to ship by freight. There was a scheme devised at Norfolk, so far as the Northwestern was concerned, when the railroads became very arbitrary in the matter of freight rates, and they formed an agreement to have freight shipped from Chicago over the Illinois Central or some other road than the Northwestern, that would get the other end of the haul. That was met by the refusal of the Northwestern to receive the freight if you wanted to haul from Sioux City; in came the Omaha road, the Chicago, St. Paul, Minneapolis and Omaha road, with lines from Council Bluffs to Norfolk. By their line the distance would be perhaps 150 miles. You had to go up around by Emerson and back by Norfolk. That line still takes passengers and freight from Council Bluffs to Norfolk, but they refused to make their rate; there is no tariff made by them, and the rate would be the same from Council Bluffs to Norfolk over this 150-mile haul as it is from Sioux City over a 75-mile haul.

Q. Have the farmers of your community a competitive market for the sale of their grain; can they sell their grain to more than one dealer?—A. Yes.

Q. It is not monopolized?—A. No; there are two dealers there; one of them loads it on the car and ships it out; he has built a small elevator.

Q. He loads in cars and ships it out?—A. Yes; and the stock-feeding market furnishes a competitive market for grain, and especially for corn; they haul it out north to the surrounding towns.

Q. Do these dealers actively compete, or do they have an agreed price to pay for the grain?—A. I can not say as to that; I don't say that they compete very hard against each other, because I don't suppose they do.

Q. The farmers make no complaint?—A. I have heard none; there has been a complaint made by grain men and lumbermen that the railroads are encouraging the jobbing business in other towns from 3 to 5 miles away for the purpose of diverting the trade from Norfolk and sending it to the elevator men and lumber merchants in those adjoining towns, and in the lumber business that will eventually run some of the lumbermen out of business there. In the grain business it is for the purpose of avoiding the pooling features which are supposed to exist there, although the railroads are practically under the same management; that is, they have a different board of directors, but it is practically the same thing as one road. It is supposed that an agreement exists by which the Union Pacific receives the initial shipment, and they take 60 per cent of the tariff and divide the other 40 per cent between the two other roads, and these small elevators in control of Norfolk's grain business and the lumber dealers must submit to this for the purpose of allowing each road to handle this business separate, and without contributing to the pool.

Q. You say Norfolk has no complaint about the roads east from the State?— A. That has not been discussed in the situation; I don't know of any complaint in regard to them except——

Q. Any discrimination practiced against Norfolk?—A. Except in Fremont a man can ship his goods and market them in the Chicago market to an advantage, while at Norfolk the local rate out from the river, the Missouri River, is added to the rate between Chicago and the Missouri River; therefore, he must ship clear East in order to market his product to an advantage.

Q. Have you any opinion on the subject of pooling?—A. Only an opinion.

Q. Can you speak for the business men of Norfolk?—A. No, not as an association; I have heard individual opinions advanced; we have no proof of the pooling.

Q. I mean are you in favor or opposed to pooling?—A. I am opposed to it.

Q. Can you state your reasons for being opposed to it?—A. For the reason that while competitive practice naturally regulates these matters, pooling practically prohibits competition, or at least avoids competition.

Q. Suppose pooling was put under the supervision of the Interstate Commerce Commission and they had authority to make and adjust rates in any part of the country, would you be in favor of it then?—A. Yes; I think that under the supervision of the Interstate Commerce Commission it would be all right.

Q. Are there any complaints on the part of the Norfolk business men about the telegraphic service, particularly as to the charges made?—A. That matter has not been discussed in the business men's association; there are constant complaints as to the amount of tolls charged by the Western Union Telegraph Company on the out-of-town business, and also that the telegraph company makes the customers pay the revenue tax.

Q. Are you in favor of or opposed to Government control of the railroads and telegraph?—A. I am in favor of Government control.

Q. Do you think that expresses the sentiment of the business men of Norfolk, and that you speak for them?—A. I think the majority of them are in favor of it.

Q. Can you state your reasons for being in favor of Government ownership?—A. Only in a general way, but one reason is, that the postal service as administered by the Government is very satisfactory, both as regards the service and the cost and the condition of things among its employees. I understand the British Government operates the telegraph and telephone service exclusively, and I don't see any reason why the United States Government should not do the same thing.

Q. Have you any fear that the national Administration would undertake to perpetuate itself in office if it had control of the railroads of the country and the telegraph service; that is, if the Government owned and controlled them?—A. No.

Q. (By Representative LORIMER.) Have you anything further to suggest?—A. The rate from Sioux City; the nearest point to the Missouri River is Sioux City, and the distance from Norfolk is 75 miles by way of the Chicago, St. Paul, Minneapolis and Omaha Railroad; and we are charged the same rates for all classes of freight for that haul of 75 miles that are charged from Omaha, a haul of 118 miles; and the latter is charged at full local rates. As proof that this discrimination does exist it is only necessary to compare the rates from Sioux City to Norfolk with the rates between other points equidistant. Here are a few comparisons: The rate per ton per mile on first-class freight from Sioux City to Norfolk, 75 miles, is 12 cents; the rate per ton per mile from Sioux City to Alcester, S. Dak., 77 miles, is 0.0779; that from Lincoln to Dakota City, 78 miles, is 0.0641; while from Sioux City to Beemer, 168 miles, the rate per ton per mile is only 0.0524. These are some characteristic examples of the discrimination.

CHICAGO, ILL., *November 20, 1899.*

TESTIMONY OF MR. H. M. SAGER,

Secretary Northern Milling Company, Chicago.

The subcommission met at 2 p. m., Chairman Lorimer presiding. Mr. H. M. Sager, being duly sworn, testified as follows:

Q. (By Representative LORIMER.) Will you please state your full name?—A. H. M. Sager.

Q. And your business and place of business?—A. I am treasurer of the firm of Norton & Co., of Chicago, and also secretary of the Northern Milling Company, of Chicago; engaged in the milling business.

Q. Do you come in place of Mr. Eckhart?—A. Yes; Mr. Eckhart was unable to be here on account of a meeting of the commissioners of the sanitary board this afternoon, and requested me to take his place here.

Q. As I understand, he was going to testify as to grievances the millers of this section of the country have on domestic and export rates?—A. Yes, I believe so.

Q. Will you, in your own way, state to the commission what you have in mind with reference to these discriminations?—A. The difficulty that we labor under and that is depressing the milling industry more than any other, and that in the judgment of all millers, I believe, will destroy the milling industry so far as export business is concerned, is the discrimination practiced by the railroads (one of comparatively recent origin), whereby they give a lower rate of freight on wheat destined for export than on flour. We are obliged to sell our flour in Great Britain in direct competition with British millers who have mills at seaboard ports like Leith in Scotland and Liverpool in England and Dublin and Belfast in Ireland, and who mill very largely American wheat. They are enabled to buy that wheat in the Western part of the United States through brokers in this country, or direct from elevator proprietors, and carry it forward from point of origin to Liverpool, for a very much lower rate than the railroads grant on flour going to the same markets. That of course enables the Liverpool or London or Leith miller to offer what is practically American flour, made from American wheat, milled by English and Scotch labor, very much lower than we can offer the same product delivered in the same market. That is driving us out of that market, and if continued will ultimately destroy the American industry of milling for export. Of course we feel that the American milling industry, being one of the largest industries in the United States, representing, I believe, an investment of about $250,000,000, and paying wages to American labor to the extent of some $27,000,000 annually, ought to be protected at least so far as to have the same rates of freight that are given to the English miller on an American product. We have no protection; we ask no protection; I mean no tariff protection. Our product, of course, all goes directly abroad, and tariff protection would be of no special advantage to us. But we do ask to be placed upon the same footing with the English millers in milling American products. The discrimination in effect at present is much less than it has been all summer, because, I think, of the r ing of the Interstate Commerce Commission that was published a few weeks ago.

Very early in the present year, until the 1st of November, the discrimination was so great as to practically prevent our doing any export business at all, speaking for my own firm at least. We did very little export business at all during that time, and what little we did do was on contracts we made before the first of this year, which we were obliged to carry out. Since the 1st of December the difference between wheat rates and flour rates has been modified; but there still is a difference whereby the railroads carry wheat for export at a lower rate than flour.

Q. (By Mr. C. J. Harris.) How much was that difference during the summer?—A. I believe the tariff rate from the Mississippi River to New York for export wheat, all rail, was 10½ cents at one time. I am certain it was as low as 12 cents from the Mississippi River for export wheat, all rail. The rate at the same time on flour from Chicago to New York, for export, all rail, was 17 cents per hundred, so if the rate of 12 cents was the lowest tariff it would make a discrimination of 5 cents per hundred, in addition to which the Chicago miller has to pay the rate from the Mississippi River to Chicago. The same rate was made from the Mississippi River to New York as from Chicago to New York on wheat, but on flour we were obliged to pay the rate from the Mississippi River here, and after milling it pay the higher rate on the product from here to New York. The rate to-day on wheat for export from the Mississippi River to New York is still the same as from Chicago to New York, whereas on flour we have to pay the local rate from the Mississippi River to Chicago. I mean the miller here would pay the local rate on wheat from the Mississippi River to Chicago, and then from here east he would still have to pay a higher rate on the flour than is paid on the wheat sent east to New York from the Mississippi River.

Q. (By Mr. Kennedy.) The same rate Minneapolis would pay?—A. I am not so conversant with the rates from Minneapolis. I presume the proportion of a through rate from Minneapolis to New York for export wheat from the Mississippi River east would be the same as if we bought it in the same position at the Mississippi River, but I am not certain about that. I do not testify from positive knowledge upon that point.

Q. (By Representative Lorimer.) What is the local rate from the Mississippi River?—A. Do you mean the all-rail rate to New York?

Q. To Chicago.—A. I don't know. I believe it is about 5 cents per hundred. That would be about 3 cents per bushel.

Q. (By Mr. Kennedy.) You said you had an export rate on flour from Chicago?—A. The rate on wheat from the Mississippi River to New York is the same as the rate on wheat from Chicago to New York. The rate on flour—of course none of our flour originates west of Chicago—but speaking from the standpoint of a Chicago miller, the rate on our product from the Mississippi River would be made up of the rate from the river to Chicago, or the proportion of a through rate which they would charge, stopping it here at Chicago, plus the local rate from Chicago east on flour. That rate is higher than it would be on wheat.

Q. (By Representative Lorimer.) About 10 cents a hundred the way you figure.—A. Not at present; no. The present all-rail rate from Chicago to New York on flour is 22 cents, whether for export or for domestic consumption. But the rate on wheat, all rail, from Chicago to New York, if intended for export, is 20 cents per hundred; and they make that rate of 20 cents per hundred on wheat also applicable from the Mississippi River; so that an English miller competing with us can buy wheat at the Mississippi River and get it taken to New York for 20 cents per hundred for export, whereas we have to buy the wheat delivered at Chicago, paying the freight from the Mississippi River here, and then pay 22 cents a hundred from here to New York.

Q. Then the difference in wheat on local freight is about 5 cents, you think?—A. I believe it is about 5 cents per hundred, not 5 cents per bushel. The difference between flour and wheat would be 2 cents. I think that wou'd be it approximately.

Q. (By Mr. C. J. HARRIS.) It has been as .iigh as 10 cents during the season?— A. They made a rate during the greater part of this year as low as 12 cents, or, I believe, as low as 10¼ cents, tariff from the Mississippi River to New York on wheat for export, while the lowest rate we have had on flour from Chicago was 17 cents.

Q. (By Representative LORIMER.) So, then, you had at one time a difference of about 10 cents?—A. It made a difference of 7 cents between wheat and flour from Chicago east, besides the freight that we had to pay from the Mississippi River here. The Interstate Commerce Commission held a session in regard to that discrimination and issued a recommendation that the discrimination be stopped, and, I think, acting upon that recommendation, the railroads have modified the discrimination.

Q. (By Mr. KENNEDY.) Didn't the commission decide what the difference between wheat and flour ought to be?—A. I don't know whether they did or not. They certainly decided that there was a gross discrimination being practiced and that it should be done away with. Whether they made any special recommendation as to any difference or not I am not prepared to say. I presume they did.

Q. (By Professor JOHNSON.) I should like to ask Mr. Sager if the discrimination against the miller at the present time is not even stronger at intermediate points between Chicago and the river than it is at Chicago?—A. I really don't know. I am not acquainted with any millers between here and the Mississippi River, and don't know what their rates are.

Q. It would come about in this way, would it not: The Chicago miller in purchasing his wheat has the advantage of a competitive rate into Chicago and a competitive rate out, whereas the local miller would have the advantage of neither?— A. I think that is very likely true.

Q. I understand from what they told me in Milwaukee that the discrimination against the local millers from the Mississippi River points is very strong at present.—A. I think that is true.

Q. If that is true and is not modified will it not have a tendency to concentrate the milling interests in the large cities; that is to say, if the present condition of things is allowed to exist?—A. In so far as the millers in large centers have an advantage I think that would be true, and if this discrimination is allowed to continue my own opinion is, judging from our own business and that of those of our neighbors who have told me how it affected them, that the final outcome will be that it will lodge all of the export business in the hands of the English millers. I don't see how it can be otherwise. They at least have cheaper labor than we have, and owing to cheaper construction, owing to a less cost on account of cheaper labor in constructing mills, their plants have cost less than ours; and if they are to have the aided advantage of getting American wheat forwarded to Liverpool cheaper than an American miller can get American flour forwarded they certainly will be able to undersell us in their own market and prevent us from doing any business in those markets. At the present time we have a certain recommendation for our brands over there, and those brands are being called for, and that has prevented the American flour from being entirely shut out of the English market. But as the trade there finds by experience that they can buy flour made from the same kind of wheat raised in Minnesota and Dakota, only milled at home, and for a lower price than we can offer them that class of flour for, they will gradually work over to the English brands of American wheat flour, and that, of course, will take away all the trade the American miller has in those markets. It could not be otherwise, because the competition in the business is very keen and the margin is very small, and a difference of 5 cents a barrel, which would be 2¼ cents a hundred pounds, in selling prices, if mantained perpetually, would drive us out of the market.

Q. (By Mr. KENNEDY.) Have you an opinion as to the influences that operated to bring about this discrimination against the American miller?—A. That would be simply a matter of opinion. I never knew.

Q. Have you ever heard it discussed among millers?—A. I think millers believe, to a certain extent, that the railroads are interested in having the product go forward as wheat rather than as flour.

Q. Because they prefer to handle wheat?—A. No. I believe from interest in terminal facilities for handling the wheat; that they have interests in elevators and in the transfer facilities at the terminals whereby they have a profit on the shipment of the product as wheat that is over and above the profit that the railroad secures for simply the carrying charges. I say that is simply a matter of opinion. I am not stating it now as a matter of knowledge.

Q. Is that the general opinion among millers?—A. I believe that is the opinion of millers generally. They can not account for discrimination against American industry on any other ground than that of a selfish interest. It seems incredible that the stockholders of the railroads, ordinarily speaking, would desire to see an industry destroyed that gives them a freight both toward the West and toward the East. It seems incredible that it would be done if there was not some special object in it for interested officials. The mills are centers of population. Wherever there is a large milling center there is necessarily a large population, comprised mainly of the operators, and this gives the railroads the handling of freight toward these mills, consisting of all the supplies for the employees and of the supplies for the mills, such as barrels and sacks, machinery, coal, oil, and the thousand and one things that are used and must be brought to the mill. Then, in addition to that we give them the outbound freight, which is the same they would have handled if they handled it as wheat. Why they should discriminate against such a large industry, as they are doing, to an extent which will virtually ruin the export milling business unless the officials of the road who control its policy profit personally by it the millers can not understand; and the only way they can explain it is on the theory that the officers are interested in some way in having the product go forward as wheat. Personally, I believe that to be the case, although I can not prove it. I do not state it as a matter of fact.

Q. (By Professor JOHNSON.) Would that refer to the handling of wheat or grain in Chicago and New York both?—A. Yes; particularly at such points as Chicago, and, possibly, Minneapolis and St. Louis and the junction points, where the grain is transferred, and an elevation is earned on wheat that they would not secure on flour.

Q. Would the millers be in favor of prohibiting the owners of elevators, public elevators, from buying grain?—A. They would, decidedly; yes.

Q. I have recently heard some complaints of the price of bran raising at the same time the price of wheat was falling. Do you think that is due to the lessened output of the American mills?—A. There are several things that affect the price of bran and mill stuffs generally. For instance, a short crop of hay would create a larger demand for other feeding stuffs, and would affect the price of bran; but, generally speaking, the price of bran is more or less influenced by the activity of the mills. If the mills are all running full capacity, there is an enormous output of bran, and that makes the price of bran to American feeders lower, because we are competing with each other to sell a big product. When the milling industry is languishing, and the mills are running only part time, or not at all, the output of bran is very much curtailed, and the competition among feeders to get it puts up the price. So that, while the price of bran is influenced considerably, as I have said, by such factors as a large or small crop of hay or corn, I think it is more influenced by the ability of the mills to run full capacity.

This is a rate notice, No. 149, and it specifies the rates on grain and grain products from the Mississippi River crossing east. It gives the rates to New York at present on grain and grain products, for local New York consumption at 25½ cents from the Mississippi River; wheat for export to New York, 20 cents from the Mississippi River, or 5½ cents less than on grain or grain products for domestic consumption in New York; grain products for export, to New York, 24 cents from the Mississippi River for export than on wheat from the Mississippi River for export, or 4 cents per 100 higher on grain products from the Mississippi River for export.

Q. (By Mr. KENNEDY.) That would mean flour?—A. Grain products mean flour, yes.

Q. What is the date of the circular?—A. October 13; and it says: "Under the rates taking effect November 1 the following are the proportions of the through rates applicable from all Mississippi River crossings from East St. Louis to East Dubuque inclusive." That would practically give wheat from the Mississippi River for export a preference of 4 cents per 100 as compared with the rate on flour from the Mississippi River to New York for export.

Q. The difference is 2 cents from this point?—A. From Chicago, 2 cents. In stating it is only 2 cents you want to remember the fact the rate from the Mississippi River carries clear through on grain from the Mississippi River for export to New York, while the flour rate commences here, and the rate from the Mississippi River to Chicago has to be added.

Q. (By Mr. C. J. HARRIS.) Have you taken this up with the railroads, your millers' association, or others?—A. We have attempted to, but have not met with much encouragement. That was why it was brought before the Interstate Commerce Commission; that action was taken on the initiative of the Millers' National Association.

Q. This ruinous rate, as we understand it, has only been in operation a year, or less than a year?—A. Yes; commencing about the first of this year. Prior to that time we had a very large export business. The firm that I represent has been in the milling business since 1848—more than half a century—and ever since they entered the export trade they never have had as small an export trade as during the present year. As we are making the same class of flour and have the same friends on the other side, who continue to write that they would be very glad to handle a large volume of goods if they could do so and compete with the home millers, we think the reason is in this discrimination. If we were placed on the same footing with the English miller we believe we could still export as largely as ever. It seems to us, as millers, that looking at it purely from a national point of view it would be decidedly for the advantage of America to have this product go abroad in a manufactured form, because then you will sell all |the American labor, whereas when the English miller makes the flour the American labor is not represented at all in the selling price. In other words, we deprive American labor of all the cost of producing this product if we drive the American mills out of the export business; and of course it is a large industry. It employs hundreds of thousands of people, and they have their homes and families, and a large investment. It seems to us that Congress could protect that investment and this American industry from this unfair discrimination on the part of public servants.

Q. What have you to say in regard to the claim that it costs more to handle the flour than the grain?—A. That claim has been made; personally I do not believe it. The millers would be very glad indeed if flour could be given the same export rate as wheat upon the express condition that they load every car given to them to its fullest capacity. We can put into a 60,000 pound car 60,000 pounds of export flour—do it very often—and as we load the flour ourselves at our own expense, if we can load the car to its full capacity I can not understand why it should cost the railroad company any more to haul that car to New York than if it was loaded by the railroads at their expense with wheat and hauled to New York. The claim has been made that it costs more because the cars are not loaded as heavily as with wheat. In the domestic trade, that might be true, because American buyers as a rule buy 150 barrels to the car. But that is simply because they have that privilege. The railroads do not require us to load more than 150 barrels in a car, and until recently they allowed us to load only 125 barrels, so the trade became educated to taking these small cars, not having to pay for more than 125 or 150 barrels at a time. That is simply a matter of education, and if the rate was based on the condition that we load to the full capacity, we would load to the full capacity every time.

Q. (By Mr. KENNEDY.) Have you any suggestion as to national legislation as a remedy for the discriminations you suffer?—A. I believe the Interstate Commerce Commission understand this subject, and agree with the millers that they are suffering a great injustice, and I believe their opinion should be mandatory. If legislation could be brought about whereby the Interstate Commerce Commission, instead of merely making a recommendation, could formulate a ruling that the railroads should be obliged to obey, it would very soon relieve the situation. The millers do not ask anything unfair; they do not ask any advantage; they simply ask to be placed on an even footing with grain shippers; and I believe if they can present that matter to the Interstate Commerce Commission, and convince them that the claim is just, the Interstate Commerce Commission will formulate such a recommendation, and if that could be made obligatory on the railroads, I think it would settle the question. At present the Interstate Commerce Commission simply make a recommendation to the railroads, and the railroads acquiesce if it is to their advantage, and snap their fingers at it if it is not.

Q. (By Mr. C. J. HARRIS.) How is it that the elevators would interfere with your business, that is, interfere to your detriment, in buying wheat themselves? You do not store your wheat in their elevators, do you?—A. Yes; we do, a great deal.

Q. Do you not have your own private elevators?—A. Yes; we have our own private elevators, but we are obliged at times to buy grain here in the Chicago elevators. There are times when the local receipts are very light, and when it is to our advantage to go into the open market and buy from merchants who do their carrying in public warehouses. And, as a matter of principle, I do not think it is right for the public custodian, who is being paid for storing other people's property to be allowed also to be a merchant in similar property, which he has stored in the same warehouse, and which he controls both as custodian and owner.

Q. You can buy as cheap as the elevator man from the producer, can you not?—A. That raises a very large question. I think that we would be favored by the producer with at least as low a price on the track at the country point, but when it comes to getting that product forwarded to Chicago, I fear we should not have as favorable consideration from the railroad. That, of course, is only a matter of opinion. At all events, our experience has been that we can not buy grain and bring it to Chicago in competition with the large terminal elevator interests.

Q. Would that be due to their superior facilities in buying and handling or to some other causes?—A. I think to other causes.

Q. Do you know anything definite in regard to that?—A. No positive knowledge; it is simply an opinion that has been formed from experience, from the fact that we do not seem to be able to buy wheat in the extreme West and deliver it at any given point as cheaply as the grain elevator companies.

Q. (By Mr. KENNEDY.) Do you mill the wheat raised in the Southwest?—A. We do not. We confine ourselves entirely to spring wheat. Mr. Eckert's company, the Eckert & Swan Milling Company, mill some winter wheat.

Q. Do you know anything about a few men in Chicago getting together daily and fixing the price to be paid for wheat in certain sections of the country?—A. I believe that has existed. I think, at least, it is generally understood that such is the case.

Q. Do you understand what their object is in doing it?—A. I presume that they may not compete against one another and name too high price to the farmer.

Q. You think it is not particularly in the interest of bringing the trade to Chicago?—A. No; I do not think so.

Q. (By Professor JOHNSON.) Do you think the agreement as to prices to be paid is confined to grain originating beyond the Missouri River?—A. I do not know as to that.

. Q. You know that is the statement made by the men who made the combination; I did not know but you had reason to believe otherwise.—A. I do not know whether they effect an agreement as to the price to be paid in Iowa or not. I know it is generally understood that they meet together and reach a schedule of prices on which they are free to buy over night, but whether they limit that to special territory or not I do not know.

Q. (By Mr. C. J. HARRIS.) Suppose 4 or 5 do agree as to the price; that does not prevent you and the other firms from bidding on the same ground, does it?—A. No; certainly not.

Q. That would not prevent Minneapolis, St. Paul, and others from putting in bids?—A. Not at all.

Q. How could they agree on any price that would control the market except so far as they themselves were concerned?—A. Well, of course, they are more generally represented over a large section of the country than any individual millers or grain buyers. They make a business of quoting over night to hundreds of buyers, and if the same quotation comes in from 5 or 6 elevator people to any one of these buyers, somebody would get it that same night at that price, provided an outside industry had not happened to get that same man at that time.

Q. (By Mr. KENNEDY.) If they had the railroad facilities that you fear they have, through fixing a price they could kill competition wherever they might fix the price along such railroads?—A. Yes; so far as any advantage they might have would enable them to pay a higher price than anybody who expected to pay a different rate of freight.

Q. (By Representative LORIMER.) What per cent of the grain you use is purchased in Chicago from the elevator owners?—A. I can not tell you positively, but I should say that we are now buying in Chicago either from elevator proprietors or from other allied interests more than half of all we are grinding; probably more than three-quarters.

Q. Then for a part of your grain you are in the market with the farmer and the outside trader?—A. Yes.

Q. When you say allied interests, what are we to understand by that?—A. Well, there are interests here that call themselves, for instance, elevator companies, and there are also commission companies that are supposed to be very, very closely connected with these same elevator companies. We buy from the commission firm, and they invariably sell us the grain in the particular house with which it is supposed that firm is closely allied. So I speak of them as allied to the elevator interests, although they are separate organizations, and are maintained, usually, in separate offices; they are supposed to work together.

Q. Do they make whatever profits are made from the elevator owners, or, as commission men, from the farmer or the outside trader? In other words, are they

employees of the elevator owner or are they doing an independent business?—
A. I think they are nominally doing an independent business.

Q. Does this statement as to your purchase of grain in Chicago apply year in
and year out?—A. As to the men we are buying of here in the city? As to the
amount we are buying here?

Q. As to the amount?—A. No; that varies. There are times when we buy more
outside of Chicago than we are buying now.

Q. In large or small quantities?—A. In large quantities. There are times, for
instance, when we find it very advantageous to buy in the large centers west of
here, as for instance, in Minneapolis, or in Milwaukee, or in Omaha.

Q. Then in some degree you are competitors of the elevator owners?—A. Yes;
in a rapidly diminishing degree, though.

Q. A limited degree?—A. Yes.

Q. (By Mr. C. J. HARRIS.) You probably use how much wheat in a year?—A.
The two mills that I represent grind——

Q. I mean all the Chicago millers.—A. I estimate about 7,000,000 bushels, but
I am not giving exact figures.

Q. What proportion of the grain or wheat coming into Chicago would that be?—
A. I do not know the amount coming into this market.

Q. Would it be half?—A. Oh, no; nothing like it.

Q. (By Representative LORIMER.) Does your statement apply practically to
other millers in Chicago?—A. The question just asked me was so modified as to
cover all the wheat ground by the Chicago millers, and my reply assumes that all
the millers are running full capacity all the year; in such event they would grind
about 7,000,000 bushels. In speaking of the Chicago mills, I include one at Lock-
port, a suburb of Chicago, where one mill is located; it is considered a Chicago
mill. It buys its wheat here, and ships its flour from here, in the summer by lake.

Q. Can you get always the highest grade of No. 2 wheat from the elevators when
you want it?—A. No; they are not obliged to give us the highest grade.

Q. Do they give you the grade you ask for?—A. You say the highest grade;
there is a great difference in quality of wheat that is covered by the same grade.
For instance, in a car of No. 3 wheat there is wheat that is almost good enough
for No. 2, which is worth almost No. 2 price; and in the same car there is wheat
almost poor enough to be called No. 4, and worth very little more than the No. 4 price.
So the grade No. 3 may cover a range of 3 or 4 cents a bushel. It is on account
of the range in the value of the wheat that we consider it to be improper for warehouse men to be merchants of wheat in the public elevators, because the temptation, at least, would be very strong, if I went with an order for No. 2 wheat, and
they, at the same time. were loading out a cargo for themselves of No. 2 wheat,
to put the best wheat on their boat and the poorest on mine. Both, of course,
would have to be graded at No. 2; that is, the quality of the wheat in the poorest
delivery would have to be such as to be No. 2, according to State rules of inspection; but in that same house they may have No. 2 wheat which may be worth some
cents more, and still all be graded No. 2. We do not think it right for warehousemen to store our wheat and the wheat of a great many other people in common
bins, and have the opportunity, whether they exercise it or not, to make a selection in case they were shipping wheat for themselves.

Q. I want to know whether you as millers suffer by these opportunities that
they have to serve their own interests, and mix the wheat in that way?—A. Yes;
we believe we suffer very much.

Q. (By Mr. C. J. HARRIS.) Could you not buy from the public elevator?
There are public elevators here in Chicago, I understand.—A. In which the
proprietors are not merchants? I think nearly all the proprietors of public
elevators deal in grain; not necessarily through the elevator company, but
through these allied interests I speak of.

Q. We have had testimony here that there are public elevators; are there public
elevators or are there not?—A. Certainly, there are public elevators and private
elevators. In the private elevators the wheat is practically all owned by the proprietors, and with these elevators we have practically nothing to do. Occasionally
the owner of one of these private elevators will come to me and offer me wheat on
sample to be loaded out of his elevator, and I buy it from him on that sample, and
have dealings with him of that nature; but receipts in these so-called private elevators are not deliverable on general contracts. If I go on the board of trade to-
day and buy 10,000 bushels of wheat to be delivered in December, the man who
sells it to me must give me receipts calling for that amount of wheat in one of the
public elevators, which are entirely separate and distinct from the private elevators; but these allied companies are interested very largely in the wheat stored
in these public elevators, and what we object to is the fact that both of us may

receive on December contracts a certain amount of No. 1 wheat, the receipts all calling for the same class of wheat, and yet when I come to take my wheat out of this public elevator I have not got as good wheat as the other, who is closely allied with the elevator interests. He would be favored in the delivery of the grain. That has become so notorious that we never now accept any wheat on State inspection. We never would dream of such a thing now as sending a canal boat or train of cars to an elevator, and sending a receipt to the elevator office calling for a given amount of No. 1 wheat, and trusting to State inspection to get a fair average of that grade. But we send along with the cars or boat a private inspector, that we have to hire in addition to the State inspector fees, to see that we do not get the bottom of the grade. We can not, of course, expect to get the top of the grade, but we try to avoid getting the very bottom of the grade, and have to employ a private inspector for that purpose.

Q. If this grain is all mixed up in one bin, and another grade in another bin, would not one man be as liable to get a good carload out of it as another?— A. Yes; if it was all put in one bin; but in every elevator of any size there are hundreds of bins, and there may be a hundred bins filled with No. 1 wheat. At certain times of the year when the movement of the wheat is from the section where they have had a very, very fine crop, the cars coming in may all be put into one lot of bins at one end of the elevator perhaps. Later on there may be a large movement of wheat from another section of the country, good enough to grade No. 1, but nothing like as good as the first lot, and it is sent in and emptied into other bins; all of which could be very easily kept track of. Now, when two persons come to the elevator to take out No. 1, wheat, if one could get a cargo out of the first-mentioned bin, the difference in value might be, for a 100,000-bushel cargo, $1,000 or $2,000 between his grain and 100,000 bushels taken out of t ie other bin, although both receipts called for identically the same grade of wheat.

Q. (By Representative LORIMER.) And they are both the same grade?—A. They are both called by the same name; they are different in quality; one is the top and the other is the bottom of the grade. It is impossible, I suppose, to devise such rules that there would not be some difference in the grade, but we think all should be treated alike, and there should not be any temptation to discriminate. I mean, conceding it to be a fact that there is that temptation, we do not think the public official should be subjected to it.

Q. (By Mr. KENNEDY.) You fear the opportunity might be taken advantage of?—A. Yes.

Q. (By Mr. C. J. HARRIS.) I see this table (referring to paper previously handed to him by witness) runs from 15 to 50; the average would be about 25 or 30?—A. I specified that if they were running full capacity we could grind that amount of wheat. Unfortunately, owing to conditions, we do not run full capacity and do not grind anything like that amount.

Q. You are a serious competitor of wheat buyers for your own use?—A. Yes.

Q. (By Professor JOHNSON.) I took occasion. after Mr. Barry testified in Washington, to ask the Chief of the Bureau of Statistics to tell me whether export flour had decreased during this calendar year, or had increased as compared with the previous calendar year. I told him I got the impression from the testimony that there had been a diminution in the export of flour; he said he did not think so, and subsequently sent me the papers, which show that for the first 9 months of this year the exports of flour were heavier than for the same 9 months of the previous year.—A. That is very easily explained; for instance, in our own case, we were obliged to carry out a great many contracts early this year that were made last year, and an enormous amount of flour was exported that went to the seaboard last fall by lake and rail, and did not get away from the seaboard until January, February, and March of this year. But as far as my experience goes, and as far as the experience of the other Chicago mills goes, as I have talked with all of them, the amount of business—new business—that we have done this year in the way of making new contracts, is very, very much smaller than it has been prior to this year. Of course, contracts that we made last year, in October and as far back as August—because there are sometimes very serious delays in getting stuff forwarded from the seaboard—contracts made as far back as August, 1898, and during the balance of that year, might not go forward from the seaboard until the early part of this year. I think the movement of flour for export during this year, aside from what was contracted for last year, will show a very decided falling off.

Q. (By Mr. KENNEDY.) You are in favor, then, of increasing or enlarging the powers of the Interstate Commerce Commission?—A. Very much so.

Q. Are the millers of the country going to move in concert upon Congress for the purpose of securing legislation of that character?—A. I think they will request their Congressional Representatives to take up that matter.

Q. They are going into politics to remedy the difficulty?—A. We find we can not get the relief from the railroads unless it is made compulsory, and, of course, the only power that we know of that can make it compulsory is the United States Congress. We look to Congress to protect such a large industry, and we believe that when Congress understands a large industry is being threatened, and thousands and thousands of operatives are in jeopardy of losing their life employment, they will know the matter to be of sufficient import to take cognizance of.

Q. Have you anything to say as to industrial combinations, great industrial combinations?—A. As a matter of opinion, I believe that is simply a question of the survival of the fittest, and the tendencies are all in that direction. I do not think these industrial combinations are necessarily all bad; I think a great many of them are bad, but I think it is a very strong tendency of the times, and I think industrial combinations can effect economies that will make it very difficult in time for private properties to compete with them. Whether it is within the province of Congress to check such combinations, I am not prepared to say.

Q. Do you think they would be very serious or injurious to the public welfare if they had not the power to compel transportation favors?—A. Well, I would not say that. I do not believe in monopolies. I do not believe it would be for the advantage of the country for any industry to be exclusively in the hands of one large corporation. Personally, I am sorry to see the tendency. I should be glad to believe that the small individual proprietor was going to continue as in the past. But we must recognize facts when they are put before us, and these industrial combinations certainly can effect great economies; and if they are legal, and if they can not be controlled, I think the ultimate result will be that they will wipe out all the small competitors. While that situation is one to be deplored, I do not see how it is to be helped.

Q. (By Representative LORIMER.) You know that all the public elevators are owned by persons who own private elevators in Chicago, are they not? They are owned or controlled?—A. I think controlled. As I said before, most of the so-called public elevators are operated by the same owners or the same interests that have private elevators or that are doing a grain merchandising business. They are organized under a separate firm name or corporation; at the same time it is very well known that they work hand in glove together and their interests are at least very much alike.

Q. Have you any objection to the owners of elevators purchasing and putting grain into private elevators that are exclusively private?—A. No; I do not think we should have any right to object to a business of that kind. The only thing that we think we could properly object to is the false position in which a man places himself when he assumes to act as a public custodian of property and also as merchant of his own property in the same house. I do not see why we should object to anybody owning all the private elevators he likes.

Q. It is the public elevators you complain of?—A. It is the fact that the people who control the public warehouses act as merchants of grain, either directly or indirectly, in these same warehouses.

(Testimony closed.)

CHICAGO, ILL., *November 20, 1899.*

TESTIMONY OF MR. A. B. STICKNEY,

President of the Chicago Great Western Railway Company.

The subcommission on transportation, being in session on the afternoon of November 20, 1899, Chairman Lorimer presiding, Mr. A. B. Stickney was duly sworn, and testified as follows:

Q. (By Representative LORIMER.) Please state your name in full.—A. A. B. Stickney.

Q. And your business and place of business.—A. I am president of the Chicago Great Western Railway Company, St. Paul, Minn.

Q. (By Mr. C. J. HARRIS.) You are a resident of St. Paul?—A. Yes.

Q. We will call your attention, first, to some of the questions proposed in our topical plan of inquiry. In regard to the wages of your employees; have you had any difficulties in that respect in late years?—A. The question of wages is one that confronts us, of course, at all times; we have had no contentions, no strikes, or anything of that kind, but the employees are constantly feeling that they ought to have larger compensation, and the employers themselves say that they would have difficulty in giving it, and there is naturally a conflict going on all the time.

Q. There has been no contention in that way with your people?—A. No.

Q. You treat with organized labor for the most part?—A. We never hesitate to; we have never had any conflict that brought that matter into consideration; I never hesitate to talk over affairs of that kind with the men or anyone who requests me to meet the men or anything of that sort. I always hold myself ready to discuss that question.

Q. Have you any special regulation in regard to the hours of labor? What is the number of hours?—A. Ten hours is considered a day's work; of course you understand that different rules apply to train men, but as to the other employees, laborers on the sections and in our shops and offices, and everything of that kind, 10 hours is considered a day's work. I am not sure, however, that the office men work 10 hours.

Q. The train men run by the mile or trip?—A. Yes; and by the hour.

Q. Do you see any way in which railroads can run successfully without employing labor on Sundays?—A. Of course it would be possible; anything is possible, I suppose.

Q. Hardly probable is it, as one railroad president suggested to us in Washington?—A. It would make a revolution in things, at any rate to begin with. We don't intend to work our men Sundays any more than we consider reasonably necessary. We never work our men—that is, other than our train men—on Sunday, except in emergencies. Of course if we have a breakdown or a washout, we get it repaired as quickly as possible, and if it happens on Saturday we work Sunday on it.

Q. Have you any fund or provision for the sick or disabled that you take out of the wages of the men?—A. Nothing.

Q. Are you fully complying with the order in regard to automatic couplers, air brakes, and all these appliances required by act of Congress?—A. I think we have practically all. I should not want to say every one of our cars would have an automatic coupler on it by the 1st of January, but we shall come pretty near it; and in regard to air brakes I think we have fully complied with the law.

Q. Is it your opinion that it will be a good thing for the railroads, although it may seem harsh at the beginning perhaps?—A. I don't know; I have no very decided opinion on that.

Q. Do you think where cars are constantly being interchanged between one railroad and another that it is well that that law be complied with, and that they should all have the same high class of appliances; does it not lessen accidents?—A. So far as that goes it rests entirely on theory; theoretically these automatic couplers and air brakes are going to lessen accidents; whether they will or not, as a matter of fact, remains to be seen. I should think that up to this time it probably had not had that effect. The fact is, the effect of the application of the first ones seems to me to have been rather to increase than to diminish accidents, but I don't know but that should be expected. With the introduction of almost any new thing the first effect is usually to produce that result; but, theoretically, when men become accustomed to it, and everything is complete, I expect they will result in the saving to the railroads of a considerable amount; probably lessen the accidents to men, and probably save some property.

Q. (By Mr. KENNEDY.) You would not want to say that the number of accidents has been decreased since these appliances have been put on, would you?—A. Of course there are no statistics on that subject, and anything a man might say would be his impression rather than anything else. My impression is that up to this time they have not.

Q. Don't you have to report all accidents to the Interstate Commerce Commission at Washington?—A. I don't know; I presume so; I don't know about that. There are accidents and accidents, you know; I have known several cases where we have had accidents—I have information although I could not designate just where they were; they have come up before me—several accidents that were directly traceable to the fact that we had a part of our train equipped with them and a part not.

Q. The secretary of the Interstate Commerce Commission testified that the number of accidents has been very largely decreased since the law went into effect.—A. I have stated my impression only; I don't pretend to have exact information on that subject, and I don't know of anyone who has.

Q. Should you think it a harsh law that would compel the railroads to report to the Interstate Commerce Commission the accidents that occurred and give the details in regard to these accidents?—A. I don't think it would give much information. Now, when we have an accident on our road, any kind of an accident, say a collision; we undertake to investigate it to find out what the cause is, and when we get through we feel as if we knew very little more than we did when we commenced as to the real cause of that accident. Of course, there is a class of accidents—for instance, we have a case of this kind: Two trains have orders to meet at a certain point; the engineers and conductors all get their orders; however, the engineer of our train—that is a supposition on our part, you will see—instead of reading his order to see what it is, supposes he knows what it is and puts it in his pocket. When he gets to the station where he is to meet the other train, the conductor finds he is running right by. The conductor gets out and undertakes to stop him with the brakes and all that kind of thing, and before they can stop him the two trains come togeher and the poor fellow is killed; and, the order having been found in his pocket, we conclude that he did not read it. With such an accident as that, of course, there is no difficulty in telling what the cause of it is; but nine-tenths of the accidents that come up, you investigate and investigate and inquire and inquire, and when you get through you come to the conclusion that it is probable this car broke down—perhaps this and perhaps that; that is about all there is about it.

Q. But if the record before the commission is favorable to such a law, what I wanted to know from you was if there would be any particular objection to the railroads being required to send in more detailed information in regard to accidents than they do at the present time?—A. It would not be any particular hardship, so far as I can see, to give such information as they have; but I hardly think it would be of any particular value to the public. There will be a stack of details, and all that any railroad can gather will be the conclusion that some man has done something. It might be that or it might be anything. You know how indefinite and uncertain conclusions are when reached from insufficient evidence.

Q. (By Professor JOHNSON.) In regard to this report about accidents, the law requires you to report to the Interstate Commerce Commission the accidents which happen. That is a part of your annual report, as I understand. The statement is frequently made that these reports on the part of corporations are very inaccurate. I should like to ask you if your practice is to keep a record of these accidents and whether you attempt and in what way you attempt to render an accurate report to the commission in respect of that?—A. I am afraid I am unable to answer that question, as that is a matter I never looked into.

Q. (By Mr. C. J. HARRIS.) Passing on to the passenger rates and the subject of passes, what is your opinion in regard to the giving of passes? Is it harmful or otherwise? Have you a law in your State forbidding the giving of passes?—A. Not in Minnesota; I think not. It is very hard to answer a question like that categorically, because so many things enter into it. The most familiar illustration that I can think of is the question that divides the political parties, the question of free trade. If there never had been any protective tariff, that is one condition; but having had a protective tariff for 30 or 40 years business of all kinds is used to that tariff, and even if you undertake to root out the tariff at once you will produce a great deal of injustice and you will disturb business relations for a good while. That is the way with this pass business. If it never had been or if there was some way to get rid of it without raising too much of a disturbance, I should think it was a good thing to get rid of, and I don't know but it is anyway.

Q. As a railroad man, taking your side of it, should you prefer to be rid of it?—A. Oh, Lord, yes; it is like Congressman patronage, which I should think every Congressman would be glad to get rid of.

Q. (By Mr. KENNEDY.) Do you give passes to members of Congress and members of the State legislatures of the States through which your railroad passes?—A. We sometimes do and sometimes do not. We have no fixed rule in regard to that. I will say this; that I never had a Congressman in any district through which our road runs, so far as I can recollect, make application for a pass for himself or request it.

Q. Don't you give them to them anyway?—A. No; we do not.

Q. Do you know what the practice of railroads is generally in that respect?—A. I don't know; I think sometimes Congressmen from other parts of the country ask for passes for people, some relatives or something of that kind.

Q. (By Professor JOHNSON.) Do the members of the judiciary of Minnesota and Illinois hold passes over your road?—A. I don't think they do; I am not certain about that. If any of them ask for transportation, they get it; we don't hesitate to give to men of that class if they ask for passes; we never feel at liberty to refuse.

Q. (By Mr. KENNEDY.) You say that if members of the judiciary ask for a pass they will get it; is there any reason why a judge of a court who gets a good salary should get a pass—that is to say, is there any greater reason than why John Smith should have a pass?—A. That depends upon what you would call a good reason.

Q. Is there any reason that would not avail so far as the general public is concerned?—A. Twenty-five years ago I had charge of a little bit of a road that was a sort of a subordinate of a larger road. I had occasion to visit the president of the superior road about something, and he said: "Mr. Stickney, I see that the sheriff of this county has a pass over your road. I should like to know on what principle you gave that sheriff a pass." I said, "I did it on the principle that he was a power, and I was afraid to refuse him." "Well," he said, "I refused him." I said, "You will wish you hadn't before the year is over." Sometime afterwards, and during the year, I went into the office to see the superintendent, but he was not in; I went into the general freight agent's office, and he was not in: I went into the general manager's office, and he was not in. So I then went into the office of the president and said, "What kind of a road have you got? Your superintendent is not here, your general freight agent is not here, and your general manager is not here." He hung his head down and said: "Do you remember that conversation we had about that sheriff's pass? He has got all these men on the jury and has got them stuck for two weeks."

Q. That answer seems to indicate that railroads would be afraid to refuse for fear of the penalties?—A. I think the railroads find there is a class of men that it is to their interest not to refuse if they ask for passes.

Q. Is it not bad in morals that a judge of a court should get a pass in that way and that a private citizen could not got one?—A. I would rather not assume to be a judge of morals; let other men judge of that for themselves.

Q. Still, you say, you would like to be rid of the pass system?—A. Yes.

Q. (By Professor JOHNSON.) Would you like to have Congress prohibit the granting of passes for interstate traffic?—A. That might help things and it might not. Legislation on such things works an advantage sometimes, and sometimes it does not altogether.

Q. It seems to me that it would be useless to have such laws if you could not enforce them and punish the man who gives passes or the man who receives them.—A. Well, I don't know. I notice in England and on the Continent that they have a great many laws regulating these things, and you will see signs posted stating that such and such things are forbidden under penalty of 10 shillings or 20 shillings, and I notice they enforce these laws. Now, let Congress pass a law forbidding passes and impose a penalty of $5 or $15, or some sum like that, and there should be some possibility of enforcing it; but impose a penalty of 5 years' imprisonment or $5,000, and I don't think you are going to get the American people to enforce any such penalties.

Q. (By Mr. C. J. HARRIS.) I would like to ask you what you have to say in regard to the law preventing ticket brokerage—ticket scalping. There was such a law as that passed at the last session of Congress. What was your attitude in regard to that measure?—A. My general attitude on all of these subjects is that Congress was not created to run the business of the country, either by law or otherwise; that business is an individual function and not a Congressional function. My general attitude on all of these questions is that the best law Congress could pass on the subject is to repeal the law or laws that it has already made.

Q. That would be very true to a certain extent, though it might be too sweeping, and you would perhaps be worse off, should you not?—A. No; I am speaking of laws regulating commerce and economic affairs.

Q. Then your idea is, as I gather it, in regard to the ticket brokerage law, that it is a matter to be left to the railroads and the public to settle?—A. Yes; I am inclined to think it is.

Q. (By Mr. KENNEDY.) Do you believe the railroads could do away with the ticket brokerage business if they chose to do so?—A. I don't know how they could. If you buy a ticket from here to Washington by way of Pittsburg, and when you get to Pittsburg you conclude you want to stay there and don't want to go on to Washington, I don't see any reason why you should not sell that unused portion of the ticket, and I don't know of any reason why a man should not buy it, and buy it for his own use or to sell again; although I know that is a rather unpopular view to take of such things.

Q. You mean it is unpopular with railroad presidents?—A. Yes; I think it is.

Q. (By Professor JOHNSON.) Why is there not an objection to the man's selling that unused portion of the ticket to the public instead of selling it back to the company from which he bought it?—A. There is no feasible way to sell it back to the company.

Q. Yes; to compel the company to redeem it?—A. That is easily said; but suppose you buy a ticket from St. Paul to New York, and you go east to Chicago, and then you change your mind and want to go somewhere else. You will, say, sell that ticket back to the company. Where are you going to find the company to sell it to? I sold mine to Big John, the porter at the Grand Pacific Hotel;

he always had some one right there who would buy it from him. I can not see by what right the law could stop the sale of such tickets.

Q. (By Mr. KENNEDY.) You were speaking about selling tickets yourself to the porter; did you learn then how to make money or save money by buying tickets in that way?—A. No, it was simply—I don't pay any fare now because I travel on passes; but there was a time when I didn't and when I had to buy my tickets. I would start from home—say I was going to New York; and when I got here to Chicago I got telegrams or something of that kind so that I didn't want to go on to New York but would go back home; there I had my ticket to New York, the train was going out, and I couldn't go and hunt around to find someone who was going out on that train; so I went to the porter and said, "John, here's a ticket to New York; what will you give me for it." He said, "I will give you $15 for it," so I let him take it.

Q. Is it not a fact that by that process you reduced your fare to Chicago?— A. No, sir; I increased my fare to Chicago, although I reduced the amount that I should have lost if I had not disposed of the portion of the ticket reading from Chicago to New York.

Q. (By Mr. C. J. HARRIS.) Is it your opinion that there is anything immoral, if a man buys so much transportation, in using a portion of it and selling the remaining portion?—A. I can not see anything either illegal or immoral in it.

Q. (By Professor JOHNSON.) You say that no immoral discriminations result from the fact that the act is not immoral or illegal?—A. I don't know what you mean by illegal discriminations. I suppose I do know, too, what you mean, but I don't admit that there is any such thing as illegal discriminations.

Q. (By Mr. KENNEDY.) Is not the bulk of the business of the scalpers due to business given to them directly by the railroads?—A. I presume it is to a large extent, although I have no particular definite knowledge on that subject.

Q. (By Representative LORIMER.) The bill that was before Congress providing a penalty or imprisonment for selling an unused portion of a railroad ticket. What is your opinion, as a matter of public policy, as to the passage of a law for the punishment of a man for buying or selling the unused portion of a railroad ticket that the seller owns?—A. I should think it was a most outrageous piece of barbarism.

Q. (By Professor JOHNSON.) Is not that a pretty strong word, if he can sell it back to the company from which he bought it?—A. I know my answer might be qualified, of course. I know I occupy an unpopular position in regard to that subject among the railroad fraternity.

Q. (By Mr. C. J. HARRIS.) Does your railroad have a published tariff of rates given to the public at large?—A. If I should answer that yes or no I don't think I could be, in either event, convicted of perjury, to say the least. We have the same as other roads have. If other roads have such tariffs we have.

Q. You follow the general railroad custom in that respect?—A. Yes.

Q. (By Mr. KENNEDY.) Don't you publish a tariff and file it with the Interstate Commerce Commission at Washington?—A. That depends upon what you mean by a tariff.

Q. Freight rates?—A. There is one provision of the interstate-commerce law that requires every railway to publish a tariff of freight rates between all the stations on its own road, printed and published in a certain way. There is another provision that requires joint rates—that is to say, rates between two or more interstate railways—to be published and filed with the Interstate Commerce Commission. The clear intent of that provision, it seems to me, was that they should be published in such a way that a man of ordinary understanding by inspecting these tariffs could determine for himself just what the tariff rate was between any two points. I don't think there ever was such a tariff made. If it has got to comply with the law, the law should be made in such a way that it will embrace all of the roads of the country, and if any are left out, your law becomes of no use. If I recollect correctly, there are about 180,000 miles of railroad in this country. Say there is a station every 6 miles—and I suppose that is true—that would make 30,000 railroad stations. Now, to make a rate on one class or commodity between 30,000 stations you would have 30,000 multiplied by 15,000, and that would be 450,000,000 rates. Now, there are 6 classes in the classification; that would be 2,700,000,000. There are 12 classes; that would be 5,400,000,000 rates of classification alone. There never was such a tariff and never can be. It is not possible.

Q. (By Mr. C. J. HARRIS.) My question was in regard to public rates. What I mean by the public rate is that you would give the same rate to the public, to one and all. Whatever rate you make to one is open and public to all; not necessarily published, but in the files in each station; and if a dozen men were going to ship the same thing, they could come in and refer to your rate book and anyone of them find that rate?—A. I see that you are laboring under the same impression as almost everybody else. In the early days of the Interstate Commerce Commission, when Judge Cooley was chairman, and they were new and zealous in performing their duties, they subpœnaed the Western railways to meet them here in Chicago and exhibit their tariffs and say whether they published their rates or not, so that a man could ascertain, if he took the trouble, what the legal rate was. We met there, the traffic managers of the various roads. They were at a long table, as long as this room; and when the Interstate Commerce Commission came in each man sat there with his file of tariffs in front of him, about as large as an ordinary small trunk. The traffic manager of the Northwestern sat at the end of the table. They commenced to question him: "Have you your set here?" "Yes, they are here." "That pile?" "Yes." "How many tariffs are there?" "Well, I think there are a little over 8,000 of them." "Can an ordinary man, by inspecting these tariffs, ascertain the legal rate?" "I do not believe they could." "Can you, who are traffic manager of the road, by inspecting these tariffs, ascertain what the legal rate is?" "No; I can not." "How do you tell what the tariff rate is?" "These are distributed in cases, and we employ a lot of rate clerks whose business it is to keep track of it and say what the rates are. If I have occasion at any time to know what a rate is, I go and ask one of these boys, and he tells me, and I assume that is the tariff rate."

Well, after spending about an hour in investigation. the commission consulted together a few minutes and said: "Gentlemen, we have got something of importance to attend to, and we have concluded to adjourn this investigation until some time when we will give you notice of it." They never gave us notice of any other meeting.

Q. (By Mr. KENNEDY.) The members of the Interstate Commerce Commission have testified before our commission that the railroads do file tariff schedules with the Interstate Commerce Commission. Does your road file such a one?—A. We file the same as the others do.

Q. Can you state what that tariff is—what it embraces?—A. It is a voluminous thing. You will find in the Interstate Commerce Commission files probably 5,000 or 6,000 sheets that make up our tariffs and amendments.

Q. For your railroad alone?—A. For our railroad alone. You gentlemen might spend a year in inspecting these sheets, and I do not believe there is one of you that could come to a conclusion in his own mind as to what many of the rates are. Some of the rates may be discovered very easily, but I think a man who has not had any training would find great difficulty in discovering what many of them are. I am not speaking of our own road only, but of all the roads.

Q. If a man comes to you and wants to ship over your road and asks for your tariff sheet that pertains to the commodity that he wishes to ship, do you furnish him with your tariff slip or does he get a rate that is on that tariff slip?—A. I never see these men myself; the freight department has charge of these things.

Q. (By Mr. C. J. HARRIS.) In regard to this question of publishing rates, I was not referring so much to the one that you file with the Interstate Commerce Commission; we all understand it would be impossible for you to prepare a rate that would cover everything to every point; but here is a station, we will call it A. At that station there are certain lines of commodities shipped. When a rate on my commodity is sent to that office it not only applies to me, but to the public in general, does it not? That is, it is an open rate to all who ship that kind of commodity, the only difference being, perhaps, in regard to carload lots and less than carload lots.—A. I think that is the intention. I think it is so generally.

Q. (By Professor JOHNSON.) I should like to ask if you could legally give Mr. Harris a rate that you do not file with the commission. Could you legally give him a rate on any commodity without filing that rate with the Interstate Commerce Commission?—A. Provided it was an interstate shipment. You take a local station on our road; their shipments are largely agricultural products and very largely to one point like Chicago or Minneapolis. These rates are generally there. We intend they shall always be there, and I suppose they are. These rates almost any shipper can ascertain.

Q. Of course, you are familiar with the investigation the Interstate Commerce Commission made into the question of transportation of grain, and you know what was brought out there in regard to the way the Chicago and Northwestern secured what it deemed a fair proportion of the grain from Missouri points. As I understand, it was about the organization of the Iowa Development Company. Now, in your testimony, we should like to have information in regard to the relation of your railroad to the purchasing and selling of grain; I suppose that will be answered by giving us some account of the inception of the Iowa Development Company and its relation to the Chicago and Great Western and the grain business.—A. There is nothing that I can say on that subject that has not already been said and printed. I feel, gentlemen, that you are skimming over the surface of the real question involved in this rate question. I feel that the Interstate Commerce Commission and the general public assume certain things to be true that are not true, and regard certain theories as facts while they are nothing but theories. If you will excuse me, I will state as nearly as I can what I know. I will read from an address made by Mr. Knapp, the president of the Interstate Commerce Commission, before the National Association of Merchants and Travelers, at this hotel on the 7th of last August. I read it, not for the purpose of criticising, although I do not agree with Mr. Knapp, but because he states the general assumption more concisely than I can do it myself:

"In commercial transactions concerning actual property, the products of labor and skill, we do not want—under present economic conditions at least—uniformity of price. The producer should be free to sell for all he can get, the purchaser equally free to buy as cheap as he can. The dealer should be at liberty to make one price to one person and another price to another person, or to vary his price to the same person as and when he sees fit. In the exchange of goods there should be the utmost freedom of contract between buyer and seller, for that freedom is the essence of commercial liberty."

Now, he states there the natural law of prices, the natural law of values. He seems to assume that the dealer should be at liberty to make one price; he seems to assume that the seller makes the price of things. Now, it takes two to make a bargain, and you can not make the price of anything by publishing a tariff of prices. You can state a price; the manufacturer may, every month. get out a catalogue of the goods he manufactures, and he sets a price—probably based on what he considers the cost and a fair profit. That is his catalogue price, but that is not the price of these things unless somebody will buy them at that price. When he goes to sell them, if he can not sell them at that price, he has to accept a lower price or keep them. It takes two, the dealer and the seller. Under the present condition the manufacturer comes pretty near setting his price, but a year ago the buyer came pretty near setting the price; he said what he would give and the manufacturer had to take it. That is the condition under which prices of goods are made.

Now, you take, for instance, Marshall Field—his retail store is a one-price store. You go in there to buy anything, and he quotes you a price for it. You can not do as you would on the Bowery or in France, begin to jew him down until perhaps he would take half what he asked for it. But, if he gets a line of goods that he can not sell at that price, to-morrow he will lower that price or send them to the bargain counter; every store has got to have a bargain counter.

That is the way prices are fixed, and it is the only way they can be fixed.' You may make laws; you can pass a law that Marshall Field shall publish his price of goods, and file them with the Industrial Commission; and that there shall be a penalty of $5,000 and imprisonment if he asks, demands. or receives more or less than that. But if you enforce it, you destroy commerce, you will destroy production, you will destroy everything.

Again Mr. Knapp says: "For this reason antitrust laws, so called, are defensible, perhaps necessary. But as respects public tranportation, which is not property at all, but a service, we do want uniform charges—under like conditions—without preference or exception to any person."

Now, what we want and what we can get are two different things. That is a beautiful theory. It is a beautiful theory that the poor shall buy as cheap as the rich. During these distressing times from 1893 to 1894 there was a Jew, Strauss or some such name, who published an article in one of the magazines, showing how much more the poor paid per ton for coal, two or three times as much as the rich; and he started in to keep a store, at which he would sell coal by the bucketful as cheap as it was sold by the hundred tons. That was a nice thing to do, but the fact that he did not keep it up a great while shows that it was a charity on his part—it was not a business transaction. It is a nice thing that everybody should be treated exactly alike, but it is not done, and under our present civilization can not be done.

Q. (By Mr. KENNEDY.) Your argument, then, is that if a railroad company has transportation to sell and makes a price to-day for that transportation, a rate, and gets no business, it should be allowed to lower it to-morrow with the idea of attracting business?—A. I do not want to wait until to-morrow; do it to-day, do it right away. We have had this law in force since 1887. When it first went into effect it was very popular with the railroad companies, and an honest effort was made to put it in force; but it was a failure. It never has been enforced, and in my judgment, in the nature of things, it never can be enforced.

Another part of the law is, and Mr. Knapp speaks of that, that there shall be a just relation between the classes of freight and commodities. Now, what is that just relation? What is the basis of it? How are you going to find out what is the just relation between the rate on pig iron and the rate on stone? What is the just relation? What is it based on? What is the just relation between two places? What is that based on? How are you going to find it out? What is the basis of the just relation? What is a reasonable rate? What is that based on?

Judge Cooley, who, without speaking detrimentally of his successors, was probably the ablest man that ever occupied the position of chairman of the Interstate Commerce Commission, was certain that a reasonable rate was based on the cost of carriage; he was so certain of it that he would not listen to argument; he would not listen to anybody that suggested that by any possibility he might be wrong. There is no question but that he was wrong. The rates never were based on the cost of carriage and never can be; neither on the particular cost nor on the average cost. What are you going to base it on? Where are you going to get this reasonable rate and this true basis between the different classes? What is the true relation between the rates on first and second class goods? Is there any mathematical relation between them? If you place it on the cost of carriage, does it cost any more to haul first than second class goods, in a general way? Does it cost any more to haul a ton of pig iron than it does to haul a ton of dry goods? Certainly these rates never were and never can be based on the cost of wheelage.

Now, we have had associations; we have made an attempt to maintain these tariff rates; we have printed certain tariff rates, and have said, these are the tariff rates. What has been the result of those associations?

You recollect those Eastern trunk lines—the Joint Traffic Association. You recollect that the presidents of those trunk roads got together and were going to take the business of rate making out of the hands of the freight agents. They had a traffic association agreement and it was such a tremendous thing on paper it looked as though they had the world by the tail, so to speak. Senator Chandler got up in the Senate and denounced it as a fearful thing that was going to crush out American enterprise and everything else. I happened to be looking over some figures, and I struck some curious figures on that subject. That was dissolved by the decision of the Supreme Court in 1897, you know, and when the decision of the Supreme Court came out the stock market dropped, and investors were scared. The Financial Chronicle came out in a long article, that the "Result could only be industrial chaos;" the world was coming to an end because that traffic association had been knocked out.

Now, the object that traffic association was to hold up rates. Here is the fact I took the Lake Shore, the Michigan Central, and the Pennsylvania lines west of Pittsburg, as being most likely to reflect the influence of that organization, which was supposed to be the strongest organization we ever had. The average rate of the Lake Shore road—I picked out the four years that thing was in existence—its average rate decreased from 5.79 mills in 1894 to 5.2 mills in 1898, the Michigan Central from 6.87 in 1894 to 5.97 in 1898, the Pennsylvania west of Pittsburg from 6.5 in 1894 to 5.7 in 1898. You see the association did not maintain rates; they kept falling. Now, you take the accelerated ratio of decrease in rates during the four years of the Joint Traffic Association compared with the four years immediately preceding. During the four years the association was in existence the Lake Shore rate fell off 12.3 per cent, while during the four preceding years it fell off only 7.5 per cent; the Michigan Central rate, during the existence of the association, fell off 13.1 per cent, while during the four preceding years it fell off 1.1 per cent; the Pennsylvania west of Pittsburg rate during the four years that the traffic association was in existence fell off 12.3 per cent, while in the four preceding years it fell off less than 0.6 of 1 per cent.

Q. Please state the four years of the life of that association.—A. From 1894 to 1898, practically.

Q. (By Mr. C. J. HARRIS.) Was not that the period of depression in all lines of business?—A. Yes.

Q. Might not that account for this difference to a large extent?—A. That might account for it; but the object of the association was to maintain rates.

Q. (By Mr. KENNEDY.) You could not expect to maintain railroad rates in a period when all other rates were going down?—A. To be sure we should not; but they did. That was the intent of the organization. We should not expect it, but it was their intent to hold the rates up. Now it is a curious fact that they fell faster than they had before, in the previous year. The tendency from 1892 to 1894 was down; the panic was in 1893.

Now, this fixing of prices by law and by resolution reminds me: When I was a young man I lived in a town—here pine saw logs were the whole business. Along early in the 60s the price was $7 to $8 a thousand; but there came a year when, by reason of drought, they could not float more than 10 per cent of the logs down to market. That market produced a peculiar kind of logs known as long logs, which could not be obtained elsewhere. The result was the market price, in accordance with the market law of prices which Mr. Knapp states here, went up to $18, an unheard-of price. Those ignorant lumber men supposed that $18 was the price of logs from that time on. They had 90 per cent of their winter's cut on hand, and they went in next year extravagantly and cut more logs at a more extravagant cost than before, and the next spring they sent down 190 per cent of the year's crop to dispose of. Of course, logs went down. These gentlemen formed an agreement among themselves, an organization, and they met together every morning and resolved that the price of logs was $15 per 1,000; that is, $15 was the published tariff. Every morning during that season they met and resolved that the price was $15 per 1,000. Nobody sold any logs that season except a few fellows who had sense enough to know that $15 was not the price of logs, and they sold for what they could get. The rest of them kept their logs, and the next year every man was bankrupt. That was the result of an attempt to fix prices by resolution.

Now I will tell you, gentlemen, coming back to the transportation question, these published tariffs are not maintained, and they can not be maintained. It is an impossibility to maintain them; it can not be done. One theory is that men have got to ship their stuff by railroad, and all the railroads have to do is to get together and maintain the price. I tell you, if I was a banker, and I found a merchant that had an idea that somebody had to buy his goods, I would not allow him to do business at my bank. There is no "got to" about it. You say, a man raises wheat out in Dakota, and he has got to ship it by railroad. Yes; if he has some wheat on hand, he has probably got to ship it by the railroads, and has got to pay the price they demand; but there is no "got to" about his raising another crop of wheat in Dakota, and if the rates are so high that he can not afford to, he is not going to ship any more wheat; he is not going to raise any more wheat; and if he can not raise anything else, he will move out.

Take the flour output in Minneapolis. The traffic manager of one of the roads between here and Minneapolis said to me one day: "If the railroads could get half a cent a hundred more on that output than they do it would make $200,000 difference in the revenue of the railroads." I said: "They could not get half a cent a hundred more." He said: "We could have got that if we had stood together." Well, now, it is right hard work to look at these things as they really are. If you want to skim along the surface, that is all right, but you have got to think of a good many things at once. That rate on that flour was not a continuous rate throughout the year; it was a rate that was bobbing around, sometimes varying from half a cent sometimes to a cent, and sometimes 2 or 3 cents. It was bobbing around just the same as the price of flour bobbed around. Now, the first proposition that I want to make is this: Two and a half cents a hundred, or 5 cents a barrel, is a big profit for a mill to make; they would own the earth in a little while, if they could get somebody to guarantee them that. They can not fix the price on their flour. They have got to sell it in the market in competition with others for what they can get. In the first place, they have no storage capacity, and could not afford to store it if they had; they must keep it moving. If we maintain a uniform, steady rate, there would be some seasons when they could ship it, and some seasons when they could not. That would mean that they would run for a few months and then shut down. No mill could make money on a margin of 5 cents a barrel under such conditions; it has to be a continuous, steady output. Now, if we add another half cent a hundred, that would mean $200,000, which the millers would have to take out of their profits; the question is whether they make profit enough to stand it. I do not know that they do; they sometimes makes a profit, and some years they do not make a profit.

There are limitations about selling railroad transportation, the same as about selling anything else. It is no use to talk about a rate being reasonable, if you get a rate that nobody can pay, or only a few can pay. Of course, if a man has only one animal to ship, it does not make much difference to him whether you are charging him 5 or 10 cents more or less; but if the man has a large lot to ship, there is a limit to what he can pay. So there is a limit to what these millers can pay, and there are limits all around.

The rates of freight are fixed just the same as the prices of anything else, by agreement between the buyer and seller; and these adjustments have got to be carried on from time to time just the same as in any other business. I hear every little while of some new industry springing up. I will mention a little thing: We feed about 300,000 sheep up at St. Paul; the manure was a waste product; we had to hire teams to haul it off. We tried to get farmers to come and take it out, but they would not do it—would not haul it away for it. One day a man comes in and says: "Look here, Stickney, if you will make me a rate of so much, I will put up a factory here, and I will manufacture that stuff and ship it." I inquired into the business, about what it would cost him and what he expected to get for it, and I saw he could make a fair profit, if everything came out right, by having that rate. I corresponded, or had the freight department correspond, with the other roads, and we made him that rate, and the result has been he has been shipping a carload a day of an entirely waste product.

Now, what is the relation between the rate on that and the rate on corn? Figure it out for me. You say you must maintain a certain relation; what is the relation between that and the rate on corn?

A man finds a stone quarry. He says, I can go into that stone quarry, and I can ship that stone, and I can make so much on it. It is a local station on our road; there is no other railroad; from that point of view, he has got to ship by our road, and he has got to pay what we charge him. But he has not got to quarry that stone. That is what some people call local freight, but it is competitive just the same. There is no such thing as noncompetitive business. That was competing with some other road running in some other direction, that has got some other class of stone. By making him a certain rate, we establish a certain industry and we get some revenue out of it. What are you going to say about it? Are you going to establish a law that we shall not do it?

Q. (By Mr. C. J. Harris.) Are you in favor of pooling?—A. I am a heretic; I am in favor of anyone pooling who wants to pool; I am in favor of free trade in that way; but I am afraid that the expectations of people in regard to pooling will never be realized.

Q. While you might not obtain perfection in that way, would not that come nearer to maintaining uniform rates to all parties under the supervision of the Interstate Commerce Commission, which would see that the pool didn't get the rates too high?—A. I don't think it would have any material effect one way or the other. I don't think, in the first place, that the pool would ever be formed or could ever be formed. In the second place, if it was formed, unless it embraced everything, it would produce the very evil you want to prevent. If a pool could be formed on roads between here and St. Paul the result would be that we should hold up the commerce of St. Paul; that is, we should hold the rates so high that it would be a discrimination against St. Paul and in favor of some other city. The object of that pool would be to maintain rates, steady rates, and really high rates; I don't mean excessively high rates, but what are called normal rates. If the normal rates were held up between here and St. Paul. and there was no pool between here and Kansas City, and the normal rates were not maintained between Chicago and Kansas City, it would have the effect of subjecting the commerce of St. Paul to a disadvantage, as compared with Kansas City. We used to make pools before the law forbade it. If the other fellows got the best of us when we came to settlement we would simply say, we will not stand it; you beat me and there is no law to enforce our contract. Now, everyone or anyone can make that kind of a pool, and, if you get beat in the trade, all that you have to do is to repudiate it. When you come to form a pool out of this business, amounting to millions and millions of dollars a month and put it under a binding contract, who is going to make that contract, some freight agent of a road or some president of a road? It is a combination that amounts to a consolidation of the earnings of the road. It is a delusion; it can not be done: it will never be done.

Q. (By Mr. Kennedy.) Are you in favor of enlarging the powers of the Interstate Commerce Commission?—A. No; I think they have ample powers.

Q. Have they any powers at all?—A. I think they have all the powers they ought to have.

Q. Which is no power at all?—A. Well, I don't mean it in that sense; I don't think a commission situated and constituted as this one is should have the authority and power common to a court. You attend one of these investigations;· there are speeches and statements about the matters under consideration, but there are no rules of evidence and no cross-examination; the people come in and testify and show that they don't know anything about it and swear to their opinions, that they are so and so; they appear in the nature of the prosecutors; they are the prosecutors; they appear and give their opinions and arguments and swear to them all, and I don't want to uphold any such courts as that. The ordinary investigation before the Interstate Commerce Commission, if regarded as a trial in court. is really a farce; it has had, however, more or less educational influence. as it has talked over these things, and they have appeared in the newspapers.

Q. You say it is really a farce. Did not the Interstate Commerce Commission recently investigate the question of the export rates on flour and grain and grain products, and give an opinion, or decision rather, as to what the differentials should be upon the trunk lines? I should like to ask you whether you know what the result of the decision of the Interstate Commerce Commission on that question was, or not?—A. I don't know about the facts at all; I have read in the newspapers something about something of that kind, but I don't know what the facts are.

Q. (By Mr. C. J. HARRIS.) It has been said that the difference between the export rates on wheat and the export rates on flour varies anywhere from 8 to 10 cents per hundred. As a railroad man, is there any good reason for that; have the railroads anything to say on that subject?—A. So far as I am concerned, I don't know whether that is true, as a matter of fact, or not.

Q. The published rates would rather indicate that it was so, and if it was so I should like to know the reasons for it and whether there are any grounds for such discriminations?—A. I don't know anything about it; I don't know what the facts are or what the arguments are.

Q. You have no opinion on the subject whatever?—A. I know nothing of it.

Q. (By Mr. KENNEDY.) I should like to ask if you are in favor of having Government inspectors appointed to look into the affairs of railroads and make a report on them?—A. As I said before, I am opposed to the public or the Government meddling with private or business affairs any more than to exercise a police authority. I don't believe it is within the province of the legislature to do so.

Q. Don't you believe there is a growing sentiment among the people in favor of that sort of thing?—A. I don't know.

Q. (By Mr. C. J. HARRIS.) Would you object to the investigation of national banks on that same ground?—A. As I said once before, I am a heretic. I think it does more harm than good. I think the national-bank examiners have burst more banks than they have ever saved. I am a heretic.

Q. Under these conditions of affairs, as you have explained them here, would it or would it not be better for the Government to take hold of the railroads itself and run them?—A. I am inclined to think that if the Government owned the railroads and ran them itself you would find that even the Government itself would be controlled by these limitations that I have been speaking about. It was said in the last Census that the railroads' revenues are in the nature of a tax. That is a theory that I have developed a great deal, and I think it is so. What is the basis on which the Government raises its revenue for general purposes? They do it by levying a tariff on what they can. How do they go to work to fix the rate? They don't say it is 10 per cent on everything. They have to consider what the stuff will bear—how much they can collect. If the Government were hard up, they would have to consider every item and the rate on it which would produce the most revenue. When the Government has abundance of revenue, as our Government has, then they consider the question as a matter of public policy. They say, "We will levy a duty on steel rails of $11 per ton, not because it will produce a cent of revenue, but because we want to protect American industry." But if they were hard up for revenue, instead of making a duty of $11 per ton on steel rails they would have to see what rate per ton would bring them the greatest revenue. Eleven dollars per ton would not produce anything, while $5 might do so. Now, will $5 produce more than $2? That is the question that we shall have to consider. If the Government owned the railroads, they would have to consider this question. What rate will produce the revenue on these different things? That is the only question there is, generally. All of our railroads have to produce revenue, and the question is what rate will produce the revenue.

Q. (By Professor JOHNSON.) Do you mean to say that that would be the only question which the Government, managing its own railroads, would have to consider?—A. Yes; that is the only question that they consider; the railroad also feels that it has got to collect taxes from some source to support the road. How the articles can be made to support this rate is the question to be considered.

Q. Do you mean to say that they have to charge the maximum revenue?—A. They would have to charge—not the largest rate always; sometimes the largest rate would destroy.

Q. I mean the maximum in revenue paid?—A. They have to consider what rate on each article will produce the greatest revenue, and then fix that rate; they have to consider that just the same as they do in making the tariff.

Q. (By Mr. KENNEDY.) Would they not also consider that they would not have to give such proportions out of the proceeds as now to the directors and stockholders, and also that they could get a president for less than ten or twenty or fifty thousand dollars a year?—A. It might be foolish and expensive business for them to do it. They might save a little in salary and lose more than that somewhere else.

Q. It would be the question of the profits that are made out of the railroads going to a great many persons.—A. Small interest on the cost at any rate.

Testimony closed.

CHICAGO, ILL., *November 20, 1899.*

TESTIMONY OF MR. WILLIAM BURKE,

Grain dealer, Friend, Nebr.

The subcommission on transportation being in session in Chicago, Ill., November 20, 1899, Representative Lorimer presiding, Mr. William Burke was duly sworn, and testified as follows:

Q. (By Representative LORIMER.) Please state your full name.—A. William Burke.

Q. And your business and post-office address?—A. Grain business, Friend, Nebr.

Q. We have received information that you can give the commission some information as to the effect of the elevator system in Chicago on the price of grain to the farmer. Will you, in your own way, state what you know about the grain business before or since the establishment of the elevator system in Chicago that exists at present, and which, I presume, you are familiar with?—A. Several years ago we used to send our grain to Chicago, and sometimes with very satisfactory returns; but for the last few years we have a system whereby we sell our grain mostly to elevator men in Chicago, Burlington, St. Louis, Galveston, St. Joe, and Kansas City. We find that way rather more satisfactory to us than to try to put our grain on the market ourselves. We avoid taking our chances of the market's breaking while we are in it.

Q. What effect has this new system on the price of the grain to the farmer?—A. I think it has a good effect on the farmer; we know exactly what we can pay him—how close a margin. Several years ago we used to buy the grain on a 5-cent margin—5 cents on every bushel. We had to have a good margin to save ourselves from variations in the Chicago market. Our bids to-day don't vary very much—St. Louis and Chicago or Burlington. Some days St. Louis is half a cent ahead, some days a quarter of a cent, and some other days Kansas City is ahead.

Q. (By Mr. C. J. HARRIS.) Do you represent anyone here—that is to say, any Chicago elevator?—A. No, sir; have just one elevator.

Q. You sell to whatever men and in whatever city you can do the business; is that it?—A. Yes; we sometimes sell at Kansas City. One day last week I was offered 25 cents for oats at Kansas City, when our bids from Chicago were only 24; and there is a difference in the freight of 4 cents a hundred; the rate from Kansas City to the river is 4 cents more a hundred.

Q. Suppose that rate goes up and down between the time you sell and the time the product gets to the market?—A. That, of course, is at the sellers' risk. They give us a limited time for shipment—10 or 20 days; sometimes when the rates vary they notify us to get it there by a certain time.

Q. If that is the general custom you have no particular risk yourselves?—A. No; we don't take any risk.

Q. You say the commission has been from 5 cents up?—A. From half a cent to a cent a bushel on corn; we don't buy corn or grain of any kind over 3 cents margin; some time ago we had 5 cents and it was as high as 10 years ago, but it now runs from 2 to 3, on wheat.

Q. (By Representative LORIMER.) Are we to understand that if wheat is selling in the Chicago market to-day at 70 cents a bushel that you would bid less or more than 65 cents for it to the farmer?—A. Yes; less freight years ago, but not now.

Q. Now what do you do?—A. From 2 to 3 cents—it depends on the quality of the wheat and the grade; we have got to allow a little for shrinkage.

Q. (By Mr. C. J. HARRIS.) Are there any other elevators in your town?—A. One.

Q. Suppose the farmer does not wish to sell to the local elevator or grain buyer? What are the facilities for his shipping to these large grain centers? Are his facilities as good as yours?—A. Just the same as mine. Several of our farmers have shipped their own grain this year and last fall. They shipped wheat last fall. Of course, this year wheat is not very good; they could not clean it, and therefore they could not afford to ship it so well; they have the same rates as I do.

Q. Do you clean the wheat there?—A. Yes.

Q. (By Mr. KENNEDY.) Do the general Chicago elevators buy from the farmers in competition with you?—A. I don't think they do; I am not sure; I have not heard of their making any bids.

Q. What line of road are you on?—A. The Burlington.

Q. Is this other grain elevator man in your town an independent man, or is he connected with some elevator in Chicago?—A. No; he has an elevator on the Burlington road and also on the Grand Island and St. Joe Railway.

Q. Is he operating in connection with any of these elevator men—Counselman or others?—A. No.

Q. Is there any belief that he is connected in any way with the Burlington road?—A. No, I don't think so; he has only been open two months. It had been run and operated by another man for several years.

Q. Does he do practically the same business that you do?—A. Sometim s he is ahead and sometimes I am.

Q. Do you believe you have the same shipping facilities on the Burlington that he has?—A. I think so, yes.

Q. He has no advantage over you?—A. No; I have really got the advantage over him; I have got the larger house and better machinery.

Q. (By Mr. C. J. HARRIS.) Is there any complaint among the farmers through your country there in regard to the price they get for their wheat: that is, that they do not get a fair proportion of the price from the buyers?—A. They are satisfied in this way: they say we pay as well as other elevators and other roads.

Q. If they were not satisfied they would ship it themselves?—A. They are not satisfied unless they get a dollar a bushel for wheat, then they would be satisfied with their own transactions.

Q. But are they satisfied that they get their fair proportion? Of course we understand they think wheat is not as high as it ought to be; if they are dissatisfied, if they think they are not getting their fair proportion, they can very easily ship their own grain, can they not?—A. Yes.

Q. (By Representative LORIMER.) You say you sell to the elevator people in Chicago?—A. Yes; and in other parts of the country.

Q. If you ship your grain from your place to Chicago, do you think you get the same rate to Chicago that the large elevator owners are getting?—A. That is something I could not answer; I presume I do.

Q. Do you ship any in that way?—A. I do sometimes; yes.

Q. When your grain arrives on the market, does it appear to cost you more than the market price here?—A. By shipping here we have got to pay a cent by commission, and by selling we save that.

Q. Is that the reason you prefer to sell to the elevator men?—A. Yes; we had rather sell to the elevator men or track buyers, because we protect ourselves. We get from 12 to 15 bids every night, so that what I buy to-day I can turn out in the morning and protect myself against the market's falling. We rather like the system, and that is the way we are handling grain now.

Q. How do the people you deal with feel about it, or have you ever discussed it with them?—A. Never discussed it with them. I presume they are pleased with the system.

Q. I mean the farmers.—A. They seem to be satisfied; they are better satisfied than they were years ago when we were buying and shipping and when we had to pay the Chicago market price at that time, and when there were 7, 8, and 10 shovel grain buyers in town. Of course, the shovel house buyers did not last very long; they could not stand it. I mean those who shoveled the grain into the car without cleaning it.

Q. (By Mr. KENNEDY.) Do you send much wheat to Kansas City?—A. Quite a good market for wheat.

Q. As much as you send to Chicago?—A. More.

Q. Do you send any to Milwaukee?—A. We don't ship wheat to Milwaukee; we ship b rley to Milwaukee.

Q. Over what line do you send to Kansas City from your place?—A. Burlington.

Q. Burlington which ever way you go?—A. Yes; I had three elevators on the Grand Island road, but I sold these elevators; that is the road going from Grand Island to Kansas City and St. Joe.

Q. You spoke of your having a bid from Kansas City for a carload of oats, of a cent a bushel more than you were offered in Chicago. Did you ever get better bids for wheat in Kansas City than you got in Chicago?—A. At certain seasons of the year we do. This fall we were paid a good deal more in Kansas City than in Chicago.

Q. Why is that, do you know?—A. I could not say.

Q. Does that wheat go down the river and out by the Gulf?—A. I understand the mills of the country take the wheat and grind it into floor and send it down South.

Q. (By Professor JOHNSON.) You say you get 15 bids oftentimes in the mail or by wire?—Yes.

Q. Do you know whether the firms of Armour & Co., Counselman & Co., and others of the large grain exporters send in competitive bids?—A. Yes; they all send bids.

Q. Do these large export firms send different bids, or do they agree upon the price?—A. They vary from a cent to a cent and a half a bushel on wheat.

Q. All who are among the exporters?—A. I don't know what you mean by exporters; do you call Armour an exporter and Harris?

Q. I believe Armour handles grain?—A. I guess I don't know exactly what you mean; we get bids from Counselman, Harris, Armour, and others from Kansas City and St. Louis; they vary all the way from a cent to a cent and a half a bushel on wheat and one-half to one cent on corn.

Q. Do you get bids from Counselman?—A. No, we don't; I was thinking we did, but we don't now. We used to.

Q. (By Mr. KENNEDY.) We have had testimony here to the effect that these men get together every night and make a maximum rate.—A. It may be they do, but the bids don't show it. I don't see how they can make the rate when we get bids from Kansas City, St. Joe, Leavenworth, and once in a while from Galveston, Tex.; I have no proof that they fix the maximum rate, as their bids vary.

Q. (By Professor JOHNSON.) I think the experts agree upon that point, that they get together every 24 hours; I am curious to know who the competitive bids come from in Chicago?—A. Last Saturday night's bids from St. Louis were a cent over any Chicago bid, and it has been running that way for a month.

Q. The question is whether these large Chicago men themselves have different bids?—A. They don't all bid the same for corn, nor for wheat either.

Q. (By Mr. KENNEDY.) For wheat?—A. Nor for wheat either. They don't all give us bids on wheat. Kansas City takes all our wheat. They have not been up to Kansas City any time this year. We have not this year sold a bushel of wheat to come east; Armour & Co. and Harris & Co. are the Chicago bidders. All my wheat has gone to Kansas City; all the old wheat we shipped out to Kansas City, and they have also taken all of this year's crop.

Q. (By Professor JOHNSON.) Do you know whether it goes beyond the river?—A. It goes to Kansas City.

Q. (By Mr. KENNEDY.) You don't know where it goes to afterwards?—A. I don't know where it goes to after that, except what goes to the mills.

Q. (By Representative LORIMER.) Do you own a farm?—A. No.

Q. Have you ever been a farmer?—A. I farmed all my life until 20 years ago, when I quit it.

Q. In what section of the country?—A. Nebraska, and also Wisconsin.

Q. So you have had experience both as a farmer and as a buyer and shipper?—A. Yes; I have had a great deal of experience as a farmer; I was born and raised on a farm. I farmed 8 years in Nebraska.

Q. In your opinion are the farmers benefited or injured by this new system of elevator business in Chicago?—A. It is my opinion that they are benefited. As I said before, when we depended on the shipment of all our stuff to Chicago we bought grain on 5 cents a bushel margin, and when we now get from half a cent to a cent a bushel I think they are benefited.

Testimony closed.

CHICAGO, ILL.. *November 20, 1899.*

TESTIMONY OF MR. A. C. BIRD,

General Traffic Manager Chicago, Milwaukee and St. Paul Railway.

The subcommission on transportation being in session in Chicago, Representative Lorimer presiding, at 5.45 p. m., November 20, 1899, Mr. A. C. Bird was introduced as a witness, and, being duly sworn, testified as follows:

Q. (By Representative LORIMER.) You may state your name.—A. A. C. Bird.

Q. What is your business?—A. I am general traffic manager of the Chicago, Milwaukee and St. Paul Railway.

Q. Your post-office address is Chicago?—A. My business office is in Chicago.

Q. (By Mr. KENNEDY.) Have you a paper?—A. No, I have not; I commenced to prepare one, but I have not got it here. I took that order of proceeding of yours and selected the topics that refer to subjects that come directly under my personal observation.

Q. (By Representative LORIMER.) Will you, in your own way, cover all the points you find there that you are most familiar with?—A. The first subject that attracted my attention was No. 21, "Effects of rate wars and unrestrained rate competition upon railway employment and railway wages." Anything which tends to reduce rates must have an unfavorable effect upon everybody on the railroad company's pay roll. How much effect, or what effect, would depend largely on the degree and duration of reduced rates, either freight or passenger. It is not possible to state that definitely, but only as a general proposition, that, given any cause which seriously affects the income of the property, it must come out of the property itself, and its employees, sooner or later, in a more or less direct manner. Under 26, "The practice of giving passes and reduced rates of fare to individuals;" I do not think there could reasonably be two opinions on that subject. The practice is vicious, because it can not apply to everybody alike, and as long as it does not it must effect discrimination in favor of some people at the expense of the majority.

Q. What do you favor doing with reference to that?—A. I favor doing what the railroad companies themselves are trying to do; limiting the issuance of free or reduced transportation to the bona fide employees and dependent members of their own families. Besides that, we issue exchange passes between railroad companies, to officers and agents who are necessarily traveling on the business of their respective companies. In that case it is merely an exchange; we each receive a direct benefit. There has been quite an effort made to abolish the exchange feature; it has never succeeded, and I do not know any good reason why it should succeed. There is no particular necessity for it, because if each company limited itself to the transportation of its own officers and employees, it would pay in the one case and receive the money in the other, and I think it evens itself up.

Q. (By Mr. KENNEDY.) Mr. Spencer, of the Southern Railway Company, says he hopes for the time when even the railroad president will have to pay his fare on the railroad.—A. Other than his own?

Q. His own road; and do you not think, if the system is to be wiped out, it would be well to wipe it out entirely, and not have employees or anybody else ride on passes?—A. If that could be made practicable, I suppose it would be.

Q. Is it not just?—A. Not altogether just; generally so.

Q. The railroad is a quasi-public institution; and has the employee of the railroad any more privileges or rights than any other?—A. Traveling on the company's business he should certainly be carried free.

Q. You would limit to that?—A. I should think so; I think that is proper.

Q. (By Representative LORIMER.) Then you would make it a question of facts. You would make an employee pay when he rides over the company's road when not traveling on its business?—A. It would really lead up to corruption; he would find an excuse for traveling on the company's business. I do not see how any good can be accomplished to the public or to anybody else by drawing, or attempting to draw, the line so fine.

Q. (By Professor JOHNSON.) I think it was President Spencer's idea that these passes granted to employees were disposed of to the general public, and for that reason it could be made a matter of bookkeeping for the railroad company to require its employees to pay for that transportation.—A. I do not believe passes issued to employees of the company are issued so as to affect the traveling public. There is not one case out of thousands where an employee misuses his pass or ticket. I do not believe that is true. I never heard of a case on our road.

Q. (By Mr. KENNEDY.) What is there to prevent your line, for instance, from shutting right down on the practice and not giving passes to the State and national legislatures or judiciary? Would any injury come to your road?—A. Unless the rule was universal. If the rule could be made universal, and some means found for enforcement, there is no reason why it should not be so. I have something to say on that subject, for it is touched on later on.

No. 27, "State laws prohibiting State officials from accepting or using passes." I know of but one State that has legislated on that subject and that is Wisconsin. Its law was made at the last session. The prohibition is very sweeping, and anyone in the employ of the State in any way whatever, every official holding office, is prohibited, and the penalty for accepting and granting is severe. That law took effect early in the spring. So far as I know it has been rigidly enforced. I do not recall any other case.

Q. Florida has such a law.—A. I spoke of our territory here, and not of any other States.

Q. (By Professor JOHNSON.) Do you approve of the Wisconsin law?—A. Yes.

Q. You would like to have other States follow the Wisconsin law?—A. Yes.

Q. (By Representative LORIMER.) Except you would go further and take in everybody, including those who hold office?—A. Yes; if a common carrier allows any person or class of persons to travel free and denies the privilege to others, it can only result in discrimination.

Q. (By Mr. KENNEDY.) There is an immense amount of discrimination going on in this country then?—A. That is my judgment.

Q. (By Mr. C. J. HARRIS.) Has the giving of passes decreased to any great extent in the last few years, in your opinion?—A. I think so. I think it has, although there have been short periods—I am speaking entirely of the district about here, 8 States through which our road runs—there have been short periods when the practice has seemed to be very large, but on the whole I think there are fewer cases of free transportation through the year than there were 5 or 6 years ago.

Q. (By Professor JOHNSON.) Is the power to grant a pass given only to certain designated officials of your road?—A. Yes.

Q. What officials have that authority?—A. Up to within a short period the authority was vested solely in the second vice-president. He has recently been appointed president of the company, and the practice continues; that is the general proposition. If I wish to issue a person a pass, I can do so as the traffic manager of the road. My recollection is, however, that I have issued 3, or not over 4, this year. As a genera thing, whatever is done in free transportation. of the public is done under thelname and under the authority of the executive. I do not think, however, that is the rule in the district,

Q. (By Mr. C. J. HARRIS.) What percentage of your passenger traffic is done on passes, probably?—A. I have no means of making even an estimate.

Q. Would it be sufficient to affect passenger rates at all at the present time?—A. Free transportation from here to Omaha means $12.75, or to St. Paul, $11.50; so it does not take very many to make a substantial sum. But when you take the passenger earnings of the year, and find out how many were carried free, I imagine it would be a very small percentage.

Q. That is the testimony we have received from other roads.—A. It could not be 1 per cent, I think.

Q. I simply wanted an idea whether it was large in proportion to the whole passenger traffic, or an insignificant portion.—A. I do not think it could be figured out to show a material proportion.

Q. (By Professor JOHNSON.) During the sessions of the legislatures of the States through which you run, do you station a man at the capital with the pass-giving power?—A. That business has never come under my official supervision, and never came to my attention. Judging only by what I hear and what I see, I imagine that somebody near by can issue passes. It has never been in my jurisdiction, but has been handled, if at all, by the executive. There is no doubt that during the meetings of the various legislatures there is more or less transportation issued.

Q. (By Mr. KENNEDY.) By all the railroads?—A. All I know about.

No. 29, "Ticket brokerage." I suppose that ticket brokerage originated first from the fact that through fares for a ride over two or more railroads were less than the sum of the local rates between the several terminal points, each road having a coupon for its share of the rate, and that these unused coupons were taken up by brokers and sold at a profit, and yet at such a price that the buyer would save money on his fare. The constant effort to limit the use of through tickets has greatly reduced the profits, but there are sporadic cases now and then when low through rates are made so much less than the added locals that there is some traffic in that class of transportation yet, though not as much as formerly. Then there came to the front the dealing in 1,000-mile tickets, on the face of them nontransferable. Such a ticket is a contract with the buyer on the wholesale plan; he travels 1,000 miles in a certain number of months or days, and he gets the rebate on that ticket, which is known to everybody and published according to law. The limitations and descriptive features that have been added from time to time have restricted that traffic largely, and, I understand, in our territory there is very little scalping of 1,000-mile tickets. They have instituted a new system which has largely taken the place of that, a traveler's permit. He pays local fare, and it is put in a little book showing how much, and when he has traveled his 2,000 miles, he hands that book in, and gets the difference between what he has paid and the published rate. These tickets are interchangeable over

10 or 15 or more Western roads. He can travel over one road or another, and he goes to the person who sold him his permit to get his settlement. That is not susceptible of brokerage. It has the advantage, to a large class of mercantile houses, that by that means they can check the expense accounts of the traveling men and know where they have been. The worst feature of ticket brokerage is the connection that exists between the railroad company and the broker.

Q. Is not that the business on which the broker thrives the most?—A. It is the only business of any consequence left open to the broker. I think I can say on information and belief, with considerable positiveness, that in periods of rate disturbance, strong competition, the broker was originally allowed a reasonable commission for the sale of tickets, just as the railroad agents of connecting roads are allowed a commission. That in itself is not dangerous and not unreasonable; but it has extended and widened until, in many cases, the commission is so great that the broker can make a profit, and yet sell to the traveler at a less price than is made by the roads themselves over their own counter. Some brokers, and I think a great majority, are honest, reputable men; but there a few at least who are exceedingly dishonest, who encourge perjury and theft; that has been very clearly demonstrated.

Q. Would there be any of these forgeries in the ticket-brokerage business if the railroad companies themselves did not keep this fraternity alive by their patronage?—A. I do not think there is enough left in what you may call legitimate brokerage—the class of tickets I first referred to—to keep them alive. I do not think there is enough left in the 1,000-mile commercial ticket to allow them to keep their doors open a day.

Q. (By Mr. C. J. HARRIS.) Is there as much ticket brokerage here as there was a year ago?—A. I think there is not.

Q. (By Mr. KENNEDY.) Have not the railroads a remedy themselves without going to Congress to get legislation?—A. I think not. You take the railroads as a class, the Western and Northwestern roads from Chicago, and we are not any stronger collectively than the weakest line in the whole group. Whenever a road that is admittedly inferior, or is so regarded, makes a rate, whatever it may do to encourage business by this means, ultimately the stronger lines and those which deprecate the syftem are bound to be drawn in.

Q. So that if the weakest road in the many around here patronizes the scalper or attempts to put its business out through a broker the other roads are compelled to resort to the same practice?—A. Ultimately.

Q. (By Representative LORIMER.) If they can agree, and are honest in their agreement, that no tickets shall be turned over to brokers to handle at less than the regular rate they can do that, can they, in your opinion?—A. If they could, yes, but unfortunately it is like every other branch of business. I think the railroad people are no better and certainly no worse than people engaged in other classes of business, and the principle of competition rules just as strong, and in some cases, stronger.

Q. (By Mr. KENNEDY.) You would want Congress to interfere and make regulations for you?—A. Yes.

Q. You differ from Mr. Stickney in that respect.—A. In many respects. I have not heard Mr. Stickney's testimony in full. I think it is right that Congress should interfere. Congress assumes the right to legislate regarding railroads, as to what they shall do and as to what they shall not do. If that is the right of Congress they ought to legislate so as to give the railroads reasonable protection.

No. 32, "Unjust discriminations and undue preferences by railroads." I have a good deal to say on that subject.

Q. Are you freight or passenger traffic manager?—A. Both; general traffic manager. I presume the commission understands I am here without any conference with the executive management of our road and am giving a personal opinions only. I think I understand the policy of the company; while I am in sympathy with its policy and desires, still I am only here as an individual. I think there is a good deal of discrimination between persons, between places, and between articles.

As to discrimination between persons it is very hard to make any point with any certainty, because of the very nature of the case. On interstate traffic and on nearly all local State traffic the laws are strict, prohibitive; and on interstate business the penalties are so severe as to make it practically impossible, certainly very difficult, to get the truth. So we get our information secondhand, and generally from people whose interest it is to deceive and make us believe that competing roads are disregarding the law. I am therefore inclined to believe that there is very much less of personal discrimination than is popularly supposed to exist; but that there is some, there can be no doubt. When I came into the room Mr. Stickney was referring to the subject of discrimination between persons and articles, and I am in sympathy with his testimony to that extent. I assume that the interstate act is based upon proper ideas and conclusions, that the common carrier should not discriminate in any respect unjustly. As to personal discriminations, I have very decided opinions as to what ought to be done, although they are merely personal ideas. I think the law was drawn in such a way as to make it exceedingly difficult to convict. The penalty is largely personal. It is made an infamous crime, subject to imprisonment, and there is a natural reluctance, in the first place, on the part of one railroad to testify against another. And, further, with such a penalty, if the company or individual does violate the law he does it in such a way as would be least likely to be discovered or proven. It encourages great ingenuity in covering up. Assuming that the practice ought to be discontinued, and I certainly think it ought to be, it seems to me that the way to prevent an evil or a crime is to remove the incentive. In the case of a corporation there is only one way by which it can be punished, and that is in its pocket, its treasury. If you take the individual official, I do not know anyone in my range of acquaintances who ever wanted business bad enough to go contrary to what he believed to be the policy of his company. If you select any number of traffic men you could not find one who would venture to transgress what he believed to be an inflexible rule laid down by his management. After more than 30 years' experience in the traffic, more or less directly touching on these subjects, my conclusion is that the way to prevent it is to make the corporations themselves the agents of the law to prevent this practice. If there was a penalty assessed against the corporation for every conviction, a substantial penalty, it would be ruinous for any railway corporation to engage in this practice, absolutely ruinous if the penalty was sufficient; and the companies themselves would see to it that their employees complied with the law. I think that is the common-sense view of the case, and it is the only method, I believe, by which this law can be fully enforced. Certainly, so far as I am concerned, I would never dare to commit an act which I knew was sincerely and energetically prohibited by my company. I could not maintain my place 30 days if, by disregard of these laws, I placed my company in a position where it must suffer in its treasury.

I am associated, more or less, with the traffic men of various roads throughout the country. In many cases I am the competitor of a man who is a personal friend. I have known him for years, and have a high regard for him outside of competition and business affairs. It would take a good deal to compel or induce me to testify against these people if the result would be that they would be sent to jail. But if the Burlington, the Rock Island, or the Northwestern were cutting rates and diverting freight I should not feel the least reluctance to furnish testimony that would make it so unpleasant that they would never do it again if the penalty was in the way of a fine. That is not only my opinion, but the opinion of every traffic man of my aquaintance. It seems to me, if it is unlawful to indulge in personal preferences, that the law ought to be so framed as to make it an object for the railway companies to prevent it; in other words, remove the incentive.

Q. Do you agree with Mr. Stickney that the rates are not maintained, or do you agree with him that the rates can not be maintained?—A. I can not agree with him at all on this subject as to the maintenance of rates. I believe the law can be so changed as to bring about that result.

Q. I should judge you do believe they are not maintained.—A. As stated before, my information is based on hearsay, and the evidence almost wholly comes from people who want to produce the belief that rates are being cut. Speaking from general information and belief, I am satisfied that the rates are not maintained as the law requires; but the number of instances where it is violated, I believe, is much less than is generally supposed. The discrimination is very great, however, and so far as it goes it has this result: That when there is a discrimination by unlawful means it affects more people, it is more wide reaching in its effect, than it was before the interstate law. If an agent is going to be tempted beyond what he is able to resist, he is naturally going to find a place where he can get the greatest results. The favors will go to the man who controls the most business; the man who, perhaps, needs help less than others.

Q. What effect did the hard times have on the maintenance of rates?—A. I have theorized on that and studied the subject and heard the theories of others. It is generally supposed that when the railroad equipment is all in use in good times there is less liability to cut rates. When business is very dull some of the roads, many of them, must have about so much money anyway;

they have to have the business. I think that view is generally correct. Although there may be a very heavy movement of grain and country produce in one direction there is a temptation to manipulate rates in the opposite direction so as to load back the car. Generally speaking, however, good, heavy business steadies the rates.

Now, as to discriminations between places. I think I can safely say that 75 per cent of the rate disturbance in the West and Northwest originated primarily in the question, What is a fair relation of rates between competing markets? The interstate act does not give us any help except this: It says that rates must be reasonable. Practically, it says they must be relatively reasonable and not discriminative; but there is nothing in the law, as was said by the previous witness, in the nature of a criterion or rule by which one can determine what is a relatively reasonable rate.

Take the traffic from Chicago to St. Louis and Milwaukee to St. Paul. It has been for a number of years a bone of contention. We do not know how we are going to be able to determine that our rates are in full compliance with the act. That sort of a question applies entirely through the Northwest and Southwest. It is a continual struggle between the line from Kansas City to St. Louis, with no interest in Chicago, and the line from Kansas City to Chicago, with no interest in St. Louis. The carriers are always subject to constant complaint from the people in the terminal cities which they serve, and if a railway official, say in Chicago, fails to do that which the community here feel ought to be done to protect their commercial supremacy or equality he is a public enemy. There is no doubt that there is a great inequality of rates as between various competing distributing cities or market cities, and I think my statement that 75 per cent of our rate troubles have their origin in these questions is correct. If you will refer again to the question of rates between St. Louis and Chicago, Milwaukee and St. Paul, you will find the rate on a heavy class of goods—iron, hardware, etc.—from St. Louis is but a fraction more than the rate from Milwaukee. Milwaukee takes Chicago rates for reasons not necessary to go into here. The one is a distance of 325 miles and the other is about 600; the rates are within a cent or a half cent on the lower grade of freight, on property on which the rate is an important element in the sale of goods, articles cheap in themselves but heavy in transportation, where the rate forms a large per cent of value at destination.

We can not settle these questions, and the existence of discrimination in the tariff rate adjustment is always a strong incentive to protect your own market in some way. We have worried with that question for several years, and I suppose it has cost the railroads hundreds of thousands of dollars. The result, 5 or 6 years ago, was a compromise, which was much nearer a reasonable basis of settlement than it is to-day.

Now, we have had a number of cases where this same question has been before the Interstate Commerce Commission. I do not know of any case where the opinion and finding of the commission and its order have been fully complied with. I do not think, under the present law, the commission can expect to enforce its order unless it has power over a minimum rate as well as over a maximum rate. It can not, in the very nature of the case, create by its order and maintain a specific rate difference. For instance, in the case I have cited, the commission says there ought to be some difference between Milwaukee on the one hand and St. Louis on the other; you must make so much difference. It is comparatively an easy matter for the line from Chicago and Milwaukee to reduce its rate to St. Paul, but there is nothing to prevent the lines from St. Louis from reducing their rate just as much. There is no limit—no attempt to fix a minimum rate. Yet, since this commission under the present act can not enforce its order, I do not know whether the court could or not. So long as there is nothing to restrain the railroad company from making low rates, the very worst forms of discrimination will grow out of that very question.

That leads to the question whether the commission ought to have power to make rates; and that is a very difficult one, but this has occurred to me on that point: Neither the Interstate Commerce Commission nor the Government, nor any body the Government may choose to create, can make rates for the railroad companies in the sense in which the railroad companies now make them. They may, under complaint, thoroughly investigate by means that the law provides. The commission could, in such a case, make an order and enforce it if it had the proper authority. But this question of local discrimination can never be settled by any body now in existence until that tribunal has the power to control and limit rate reductions. It is the relative rate to this city and that city, competing cities, and the relation between articles from or to the same points, that make the real disturbance, that occupy more time of the traffic men than any other class of business that we have to deal with. There is no doubt that towns are created or destroyed by a mere matter of relation of rates. I do not think that was intended; I do not think it ought to be so.

I have dwelt somewhat at length on that point because I wished the commission to understand what it is that underlies all these questions and that leads more or less to these abuses.

Q. (By Mr. KENNEDY.) You are not in favor, then, of giving the commission these enlarged powers without giving them the power to regulate or control the minimum rate?—A. I do not think any power could be conferred on the commission that would have any materially good effect on the people unless that power was included.

Q. (By Professor JOHNSON.) The Interstate Commerce Commission is of the same belief, is it?—A. I can only answer that I had some conversation with the chairman, and my judgment is that it is in full accord with that view.[1] I think it stands to reason that the prevention of discrimination against foreign or other markets can not be controlled until that power is vested in the commission. I have been led to that belief because of my belief that Chicago is discriminated against more than any other city I know of in the United States.

Q. (By Mr. KENNEDY.) I should like to ask about these discriminations between grain and grain products that are exported; what is the cause of those discriminations?—A. I can only answer that in the form of an opinion. It has, in fact, been my belief ever since the interstate act was passed, and it is an opinion that prevails in the minds of many railroad people, that that act does not apply to export business. This is one feature of the case that wants to be kept in sight; there are conditions of competition which may, and do in some cases, apply to grain in bulk that do not apply to package freight, like flour. I think the most notable example of that is from Minneapolis to Duluth and eastward as well as from Chicago eastward, wherever the rail carriers are in competition with water carriers. I think that is true very often; it is certainly so between flour and wheat. At Minneapolis the grain comes in from the great wheat belts; it goes to the elevators at Duluth or Minneapolis, is taken up there by boats from Duluth, or by the railroads running from Minneapolis to Duluth. That is a State haul. The grain is carried usually locally to Duluth from Minneapolis, and goes to the elevator. When it reaches the port it is carried to Buffalo by boats, which are not under the interstate act; that does not apply by water. These large dealers have their elevators at lake ports, at Buffalo and some other places in New York. The grain, when it gets to Buffalo, may be distributed to the interior more or less, where it is a State matter under the New York law; it may be carried by canal, so it is all water. Carrying flour from Minneapolis is interstate traffic and comes under the act, and there is not the same class of carriers handling it as those carrying bulk wheat and grain to Buffalo. The steamship lines under the control of the trunk lines are not situated in that way, so that wheat can go at a very small cost sometimes. To what extent that justifies the differences heretofore existing I don't know.

Q. (By Mr. KENNEDY.) There were no differentials between them until last February?—A. No; not to any material extent. I don't know of any reason why there should be a material difference between the rate on flour and the rate on wheat where the rail and lake or water competition is not a direct influence, excepting in one point. Under the modern methods and arrangements wheat can be loaded quite a good deal heavier than flour in a car. In fact, I think it is loaded much heavier than flour. As a matter of fact, flour is not loaded as heavily as wheat.

Q. Suppose a car has 60,000 pounds capacity and a miller at his own expense will load 60,000 pounds of flour on that car; is there any reason why he should not have the same rate that the elevator man has?—A. In the absence of direct water competition, I know of no reason. Our own railway runs in the wheat belt through Minnesota, and we would rather have the flour manufactured at some point on the line, because it builds up local industries and we get the benefit of it. I feel the same with regard to the country at large. I don't see any reason why wheat grown in Minnesota, Iowa, and Dakota should be carried for export at so cheap a rate that the foreign miller can compete with our own miller in the manufacture of wheat into flour from wheat grown in our own country.

Q. Wheat has been carried to Buffalo in the lake steamers for many years, has it not?—A. Yes; but not to the extent that it has been in the last 4 or 5 years.

---

[1] See Eleventh Annual Report of the Interstate Commerce Commission, pp. 25, 143; Twelfth Annual Report, pp. 23-27.

Q. Is it probable that lake competition has anything to do with the matter, in view of the fact that there was no difference in the cost until last February?--A. That difference began early in this year and is a question quite separate from the one I referred to at Minneapolis. I am not able to testify positively, but my impression is that that condition grew up as a result of the controversy between or on account of the various Atlantic ports—Philadelphia, Baltimore, Boston, New York, Newport News, etc. In other words, that differentials proposition seemed to have been working to the end wherein it was shown what the effect was, and the rates were made on export business. I think there was an impression abroad that the Interstate Commerce Commission hadn't very much to say about export business, and freight competition was naturally confined more to that channel than any other. It was a fight for the supremacy.

Q. (By Professor JOHNSON.) Do you think the Eastern lines tend to stimulate the traffic in grain instead of flour because of the terminal charges at New York?—A. I don't know; I am at sea on that question: I don't think I am competent to answer it with any attempt at certainty. What effect that terminal charge has I don't know. I don't think it is a ruling basis, except perhaps with roads that connect with the trunk lines; they have to make a rate to New York on export business, and the question is how will that rate be divided. Take the rate from Kansas City to New York on grain for domestic purposes. I don't know that it makes much difference what it costs to handle it in the port there. The aggregate rate itself is what the public must consider, and that is the one that affects the welfare of the trade at large. The deduction of 1, 2, or 3 cents before prorating is a matter that concerns us very much, but I don't see how it affects the public.

Q. In this way: Might not the managers of the railways, because of being the persons who receive the terminal charges—and they are very profitable, I believe—continue to insist upo n rates that would cause the traffic to go in the shape of wheat instead of flour? It comes to the question whether or not the profits coming from these terminal charges go into the pockets of the men who determine the rates.—A. I hardly think that is true.

Q. (By Mr. C. J. HARRIS.) Would there be terminal charges on flour the same as on wheat?—A. I am not clear upon that point.

Q. I should like to ask one more question about pooling. I should like to hear what you have to say upon that subject.—A. I am very much in favor of pooling, provided sufficient authority is given to the Interstate Commerce Commission to regulate the pools and the rates made thereunder. I don't believe as an economical proposition that it would be right, or advisable at least, to legalize pooling without placing it under the supervision of a Federal commission. It has seemed to me that if pools could be legalized, and the companies could sue and be sued under the pooling contracts, if the commission had the right to legalize pools provided they approved of the rates, if the commission had the right also to discontinue a pool at any time because of the rates made by the pooling parties, then it would be beneficial to everybody. I can see only two real objections to a pool from a public standpoint; first, that the carriers would be favorable to such contracts as could be made under excessive rates; but if the commission was authorized or empowered to make a pool illegal the moment it found the rates were unreasonable, that would remove that objection. The only other objection to the pool that I think would be made, would be by people who hope in the absence of pools to get a decided advantage over someone else. As a matter of fact, the interstate act is very specific in its declaration that rates shall be reasonable; for instance, they, by inference, hold that rates, not only as between places, but as between articles and persons, shall be reasonable. But the rules are such to-day that everything which is necessary to accomplish that end is specifically prohibited. There is not a thing that the railroad company can do to comply with the spirit and purpose of the interstate act that is not made unlawful. I think that should be changed. I think there should be some way by which rates could be regulated fairly in the general interest of the carriers and the people, and so that both parties should be protected in their rights. That is all we ask. If I sit down with 3 or 4 gentlemen, freight agents or traffic managers, to discuss what rates should apply between any two competing points, it is a violation of the antitrust act, and the penalty is severe, not only upon the person, but upon the property. A fluctuating rate can not benefit anyone in the end. It is the most disastrous thing that can happen to the commercial world, and more country traders have been broken up by fluctuating rates than by excessive rates—one hundred times over. If a country merchant stocks up on staple goods when the rate is 30 cents per hundred, and by and by someone gets a rate of 15 cents per hundred, his business is gone and his profits are gone, and sometimes, more than that; his pro er y is gone, because he can not compete with the man who has purchased the same staple goods at a 15-cent-rate when he has paid 30. This has happened repeatedly. I think what the country at large needs, and is entitled to, is reasonable and stable rates. It doesn't seem to me that the country has any right to complain as long as rates are reasonable and stable.

Q. (By Mr. C. J. HARRIS.) You would advocate a pooling law, subject to the proper supervision?—A. Yes.

Q. (By Mr. KENNEDY.) I should like to ask in regard to private cars.—A. There is so very much to be said on that subject that I don't like very well to enter upon it, not having had an opportunity to reduce my opinions on the subject to order so that I can state them clearly. There is a great deal to be said, and I suppose I should say something as to how private cars originated, why they were necessary at one time, and why they are continued. There has been a great advance made in rolling stock. When I first commenced railroading, at the close of the civil war, there was a very severe penalty upon the station agent if he allowed a car to be loaded over 9 tons. Now we frequently load 30 tons, and some of the older roads load 50. The cars we have on hand now are good, serviceable cars of all suitable dimensions; that has grown up recently in the extension and enlargement of cars. Take, for instance, in the first place, a manufacturer who wants a large car and who can not get a car from the railroad that is suitable for his business. Some of the more wealthy ones put in a few private cars to accommodate their own business. Up to the present time I don't know of a railroad that has cars enough of its own to meet the emergency in the average busy season, and they are glad to take a car of a man who has it to accommodate his business. Take the furniture cars, cars of special dimensions. Then the next move of any importance was the move in the extension of the packing business, and especially that of dressed meats. I doubt very much whether it would be wise or safe for railroad companies even at this day to own or control the kind of cars which are used for the shipment of fresh meats. I have ascertained during the last 4 or 5 years that a car may appear to the uninitiated in a perfect condition for the shipment of fresh meat or dressed beef, and 24 hours' run might ruin the property. It may be a moldy car; it may be musty; perhaps it has not been properly scalded to clean away the dirt, and such a car is absolutely unsafe. If the railroad companies should own or control these cars I think it would be very expensive, and if they were required to do it now by law there would not be cars enough to handle the business, because they would have to be handled with regularity and precision, so that I am in doubt in regard to cars used for a particular purpose, especially perishable property, and more particularly fresh meats. There is no doubt that the building of private cars has grown to a very great extent, and that it is bound to be burdensome. There is neither any doubt that a large manufacturer having cars of his own, if he has not too many, can keep them running with sufficient regularity to make a profit merely from the ownership of the car. In other words, the mileage of a car that is kept going all the time is a profitable affair. Of course, that is because of the price paid. There has been some reduction in car mileage, but it is not what it should be.

Q. That is in the nature of a rebate, then?—A. I don't think the particular idea of a rebate would apply to that; he has his money invested in cars and he is entitled to something for the use of them.

Q. Is he entitled to any advantage as against any other shipper on account of the allowance made by reason of the private cars; by reason of the private cars can he ship any cheaper over a line of road than any other manufacturer can ship over the same line?—A. Well, I don't know; if a farmer has a good wagon and a good team, and another farmer has not, I don't know that the one who has a good wagon and team is doing any harm to the one who has not. If a manufacturer spends his money for the facilities that are necessary to the business, he is entitled to the benefit of the equipment he furnishes; he is entitled to a fair compensation for the equipment that is used in the business; I think that is a business proposition. If one gentleman in the grain business in Nebraska has a first-class elevator holding 50,000 or 150,000 bushels, with modern equipment for moving the grain cheaply, that does not interfere with the rights of a man who has a warehouse that will hold two or three cars.

Q. Do you think it is good public policy that one shipper is permitted to have an advantage, because he is allowed to use these private cars, as against another shipper that has not that same right and who must use the company's cars?—A. I don't feel quite competent to go into that, as that is a very serious question. I think, however, if the railroad company is not able to supply itself with cars that it needs and someone else does, then the man that does is entitled to a fair price for the use of his property.

Q. (By Representative LORIMER.) Do you think you pay more in mileage for private cars than it would cost the railroad company if they used their own cars?—A. There are different classes of private cars that are used by the railroads; the refrigirator cars and what we call the ordinary cars, the common cars that require no special treatment. For the latter we pay the owners the same price that we pay connecting railroads; I think it is 6 mills a mile; it was a cent, but a few years ago it was reduced to 6 mills. Cars that cost a few years ago, before the last rise in price, say $400 or $425, would be 6 mills for every mile run. Cars of that description make an average of about 50 or 60 miles a day in actual use. Now, the refrigirator car costs probably twice as much; while we pay $400 for the standard box-car, or $425, a well-equipped refrigirator car costs from $900 to $1,000, and it has been receiving usually 1 cent a mile. I think that is the prevailing price. It is a question of whether we are to pay more or are paying more on common cars than we ought, and more than we collect on our own cars when they are used by other people. It is all we collect when other people use our cars; in the sense that is reciprocal, I presume the price is tolerably fair.

Q. (By Mr. KENNEDY). Would not many of the railroad men of the country be glad to be rid of the private-car system if they could?—A. Undoubtedly; our company would be very glad to be rid of them. About 3 years ago we commenced to build cars. We built 10 a day for nearly a year, or the full capacity of our shop. We are now building theirs. If we had all the cars we could use we would not pay anyone else for the use of them, but we have not got them. I am in doubt as to the propriety of owning refrigerator cars for perishable property. I don't know what is best. I should regret to make the experiment of owning these cars and being responsible for their condition. But when it comes to ordinary cars it would be best for us to have all the cars we want of our own.

Q. The roads that don't appreciate or meet the requirements of commerce are largely responsible for the private ownership of private cars?—A. Very likely; none of the roads were ever yet able to meet the requirements for equipment anyway. The demand is always a little ahead. That is what causes the use of the private cars during the busy seasons. They have been very useful in this way, that we have been able to handle business we could not otherwise have obtained. I think the company should own the ordinary cars for the use of its own road, but I am in doubt as to the use of the refrigerator cars. Take Kansas City, for instance, a packing point where a large number of private cars are used. The biggest owner is the packer, who owns enough of them to take care of his business, but there is no railroad company that owns enough cars especially constructed to take its share of the business of the packers. The number of cars actually used in that particular business is much less than it would be if every company solicited that business and had a sufficient number of those particular cars to take care of its share of that business. That fact has created quite a problem in the matter. It is a practical question.

Q. Is the meat in the private cars at the owner's risk?—A. The meat in the private cars is at owner's risk excepting where there is a wreck or an unnecessary delay caused by some act for which the carrier is responsible. If the train is not wrecked and the car is moved with usual and average precision and the meat is destroyed, the individual loses; there has never been a claim under such circumstances that I know of. I have known of many cases where a train loaded with fresh meat might pass over our road with usual precision and reach its destination in due time, and when it reached its destination the meat would be unfit for use; but that is no concern of the carrier. Had we owned these cars it would have been a matter of investigation as to whether the cars were properly scalded and were put in proper order, or to show that something had not been done that ought to have been done whereby the damage was caused; and there would have been no escape from payment of damages if it could be shown that it was our fault or negligence. I think in the 17 years I have been in Chicago in this railway business we have never been asked to pay a claim for damages to property when the car went through on the ordinary time.

I want to touch more upon that question of flour and wheat for export, if you please, that the commission may know, if it desires to know, to what extent the order of the Interstate Commerce Commission has been complied with. As soon as we received that order we undertook to follow it.

Q. State what the order was.—A. The differentials ought not to be greater than 2 cents per hundred. We are dealing with the Atlantic seaboard rate now; that is the one thing that affects us. We undertook to find out what, if anything, would prevent us from complying with the order; we understood that the rate from Chicago on the Eastern lines was in violation of the commission's order.

Q. From Chicago eastward?—A. Yes; but I understand that the rates from Mississippi River points are not in line with ours, for reasons which may easily be explained to this commission. We felt compelled to make some rate from Savannah, where we cross the Mississippi River; but we can only make such rates as the Eastern trunk lines are willing to participate in. I believe that the rate on export grain from the Mississippi River to New York and other Atlantic ports is more than 2 cents less than domestic rates. We can not reduce the rate on domestic business from Savannah, where our road crosses the river, without the consent and cooperation of the Eastern roads. We can not advance the rate on export wheat from that point unless the other roads advance it from the Mississippi River crossings, or we lose the business. My recollection is that the difference between export wheat and flour from Mississippi River crossings is about 4 cents. I think that is the difference. We are prepared to comply with the law whenever it is in our power to do so. I reported that fact to the commission. We are prepared also to publish the rates which will apply on export business and to adhere to them; to adhere to the published rate. From the Missouri River to the Mississippi River we are accepting the same rates on export traffic as on domestic traffic of the same class.

Q. Is that not a farce? In view of Mr. Stickney's testimony this afternoon, it is a farce for the railroads to send their tariff sheets for filing with the Interstate Commerce Commission in Washington?—A. I can only answer that question with reference to what I have testified to. I don't think it is.

Q. You don't think it is?—A. No. If it has any effect whatever it has a good effect. The Western roads, as a rule, have an agency at Washington for the sole purpose of examining the tariffs of other roads, as they have a right to do, and as any citizen has a right to do, as it is a public office. And that has had a very beneficial effect. There have been a good many complaints—I don't know how well founded—of what is known as midnight tariffs. It was said 2 or 3 years ago that someone here issuing a tariff sent a copy to the Interstate Commission and kept a copy that was not posted up, and no one knew what the rate was, except the commissioners, on the tariffs of that company that issued them. On the other hand, I don't know of a case of that kind. I know it was very often complained of. It was often stated that that practice was prevailing, and after some conferences with the commission we hired a man and put him there as agent, and he sees every tariff that comes in and reports on it, and we find out if there is any fraud in it. I think it is beneficial. I understand that the position of the commission and the courts is that in any trial that comes up, or investigation in regard to interstate traffic, any attempt to introduce a tariff as evidence is barred unless it appears that it has been duly filed with the commission in accordance with law. I was in the United States court two weeks ago to-day, as a witness, where this issue was raised by the judge: That the tariff filed with the commission according to law stands for itself as a fact, and this will operate. If Mr. Stickney's evidence be true, there is fraud in all of that. I hope your honors will not ask me to substantiate his testimony.

I want to make a statement in regard to classification, because I think it is a matter that should have careful attention on the part of this commission, and on the part of Congress when the time comes.

I was for 3 years one of a committee of 15 that had in preparation a uniform classification. We were instigated to that work by Judge Cooley, who was then chairman of the Interstate Commerce Commission, and also by resolutions passed by the various national conventions of State and Federal commissioners. There are 3 principal classifications in the United States. One is known as the Official; that applies on the Eastern roads east of the Mississippi River and north of the Ohio River; the second is east of the Mississippi and south of the Ohio, called the Southern; the third is the one that interests us in this district, and is known as the Western. It applies generally from Chicago and St. Louis west and north; I believe it goes clear to the Pacific coast, except that there are exceptions in what is known as the commodity rate.

Q. Exceptions also made by State laws and State commissions?—A. In our district very little. Of course, the State commissioners always reserve their right to make their own classification, but as a rule they substantially conform to the Western classification. Now, we have a great variety of conditions. We find the Official classification with so many classes, 8 I think, was probably adjusted to meet the conditions in the territory in which it was applied; it fitted the business, and the business had grown up to the classification in some respects, and the classification to the business in others. So in the South and so in the West. But they were greatly at variance. We found it was necessary that we should have on freight from New York State or Pennsylvania the same classification on shipments to Mississippi River points, applying to traffic going beyond, as was made to other Mississippi River points, such as St. Louis. It was necessary to equalize not only rates but classifications, the Eastern classification being much lower in many respects, fitted to the shipping out of manufactured goods in the interest of the manufacturer shipping his goods westward. That classification was made for that purpose. But the roads from Chicago to St. Louis could not equalize the rate to Kansas City without equalizing the classification; so the basing also occurred on the crossing of the Mississippi River. The rate begins at New York and ends at the river. We apply our Western classification from the Mississippi River west, and the Eastern from the East to the Mississippi River.

To note the effect of that in one case, a shipment of whisky from Detroit to some Mississippi River crossing, our crossing at Savannah, was lower than the rate locally from Chicago to that crossing, although the Chicago distance was only 138 miles on our road, because on that classification the rate was very low and put it in the third class, while ours was comparatively high on the other classification and put it in second. So the third class from Detroit to Rock Island was less than our second class from Chicago to Rock Island. I found a case where whisky was shipped from Cincinnati to St. Paul, where the rate was less (I am speaking of carload lots) than the rate from Milwaukee to St. Paul, the latter distance being 325 miles. The whisky from Cincinnati was fourth or fifth class in small lots, and whisky at that time under Western classification was first class.

That difficulty exists more or less throughout the country. It applies to a great variety of articles. Our tariffs and classifications are made with some view of promoting business in our own territory, building up manufacturing points, and that is just exactly what the Eastern trunk lines are trying to do. They want their rates made so as to dump their surplus products in the West against new industries, and they are continually clashing. Many things are rated higher in the Official classification than in the Western classification, and vice versa. It is true also of the classification in the Southern States. So that to make a uniform classification, we had to give and take; that is all there was about it. We worked upward of three years at intervals of 3 or 4 months, sometimes 6 months, between meetings; but we kept at it until we perfected a classification which we unanimously recommended to the various roads. The roads west of Chicago agreed to accept that classifiaction if the Eastern trunk lines would, and the Southern roads agreed to accept it if the Eastern trunk lines and the Western roads would; but it was defeated by the vote of one or two, possibly three, Eastern trunk lines. I do not know who they were, but it was defeated.

Q. Defeated in the interests of Eastern manufacturers?—A. It might be uncharitable to say so, but it was defeated. My recollection is the majority of the Eastern trunk lines favored the adoption of that classification.

Now, that applies only in part to the classification. Though we should adopt that uniform classification, still the roads would have to make special commodity tariffs on grain, lumber, coal, iron ores, and that class of business—tariffs made to meet the conditions in the territory in which the tariff is to be used. It would not, in any material sense, militate against the use of tariffs as a general proposition; it would settle these difficult questions.

Q. What privileges do the business men and shippers have before the Western classification committee?—A. It has been several years since I attended a meeting of the Western Classification Association, but my understanding is the association itself chooses a representative, from each of the roads in interest, upon a subcommittee, which meets before the regular committee—whose meetings, I believe, are now held once in 6 months—and people who have any proposition to make can come before that subcommittee and make their statements in writing or orally, and they are considered. The applications are generally in the nature of demands for some special consideration for some special business; the manufacturer of some certain article finds that if he can get this special classification in his territory he can get some other person's business. Like most other propositions, they are for his own benefit against somebody else.

Q. Are they not sometimes in the nature of demonstrating whether a business can live or not?—A. Those questions are often considered, because we have frequently reduced classifications, when we did not do it because we wanted to, but because it seemed to be necessary on what appeared to be good argument. I do not understand that any business or commercial men come before the joint committee; I do not think they have recently, but they do have access to the subcommittee which passes on all these questions, and arranges them in due order and form, and makes its own statement of what it thinks ought to be done. I have received many applications myself, which I have invariably referred to the subcommittee for consideration. There would be very little progress made if these joint committees were thrown open to the public; one man wants something for his class of business, and insists that it be not granted to another.

Q. We have complaints from very large manufacturing interests in Ohio, one of the largest in the country, that the representation of the business men before these classification committees is not sufficient.—A. We do not know about that; that is the official committee, and we do not participate in it.

Nos. 44 and 45, "Joint traffic associations and pooling contracts." I have touched on pooling contracts, but not on so-called freight associations.

The term association is a misnomer, and has been for 4 or 5 years. Although it is claimed by some that what is done at these meetings might be considered to be in violation of the antitrust act, there is no other way to prevent wrong discrimination and violent fluctuation of rates, but to have some sort of conference to find out what each is going to do. Of late years nothing has been done but to discuss what ought to be done—what is proper. One man says, "I think this ought to be done, and I am going to do it unless somebody has good reasons against it." That is about all they can do at present, it is all they can amount to under the present law. If you will take the matter of rates from Omaha to Chicago, on grain alone, it is fairly illustrative of the situation. If there is not to be any unanimity of action by agreement as to rates between Omaha and Chicago, one will publish one rate and another another. Leaving entirely out of the question the effect upon the railroads of the unknown character of the rate to Omaha, the rule again touches the people east of Omaha where the long and short haul question comes in, and where the rate made by the Burlington, for instance, is the maximum for any intermediate point. There may be, without conference, a lower rate published, say, on the Rock Island, from Omaha to Chicago, than by our road. For 21 miles we are absolutely side by side; east of that point, we diverge a little, but still at a close distance, 4, 5, or 6 miles up to 10 or 12 miles apart. They would have a lower rate from Omaha than we have, and as it is a maximum rate at intermediate points, the rates at stations along their line south of ours are lower than the rates at opposite points on our road. We may not know it for a little bit, we may not find it out, but in the meantime the towns along our road are suffering a local discrimination as between themselves and other towns only a few miles away. So it goes all through the country. There is an absolute necessity of some conference, not for the purpose of making rates, but to know ourselves what the other rates are to be. I do not see how we can escape a chaotic condition without some sort of railroad conferences. I think we have pending suits amounting to over $1,000,000 for excessive rates, and the only condition on which the cases can be made, is to make it appear to the court that these rates were made by agreement between competing railroads contrary to the antitrust act. They never have been in that territory, in no instance have they been by agreement; but we have met frequently to compare freely and say what these rates are on each road. If a man says my rate is so and so, and another thinks it is too low, all he can do is to put his rate down. As to a combination of roads to maintain rates, there is nothing of the kind. Judge Shiras said, in a preliminary hearing, that if it could be made to appear that these rates were made under an agreement in restraint of competition, it was unlawful; but how much too high, it was, he said, impossible for the jury to determine. A jury may decide so and so to-day, and to-morrow the same question may arise in another case before another jury and the decision may be entirely different. There would be no stability of rates, and could not be under the jury system.

These associations are, in this district to-day, nothing but conferences to find out what has been done; they have had no power since the trans-Missouri Freight Association case.

The real point I wish to make is this: As far as the associations are concerned they do not do much good to the railroads. They help us to compare notes and get our rates reasonably in line to prevent local discrimination, but they are no permanent remedy; a man can change the rate whenever he pleases.

As to the other branch of that topic, "The policy of legalizing pools," it seems to me more essential than this. It seems to me, in conclusion, if the commission could be vested with sufficient power to regulate rates, leaving with the carriers the same right that other people have, the reasonable right to go to the courts, but in such a way as not to embarrass the proceedings or impair the usefulness of the commission, it ought to be made lawful to pool competitive business, if the commission is clothed with the power I have suggested.

A law to clothe the commission with universal power to make rates anywhere and everywhere, at all times, I think, would defeat itself.

Q. They do not desire that power?—A. I do not think the commission do—it would be inoperative. To put that immense amount of responsibility on the Interstate Commerce Commission, or upon the Government through any bureau, would, in my judgment, be absurd.

Q. If they are invested with the right to readjust rates under complaint, subject to appeal, would you have their decision go into effect immediately?—A. That treads somewhat on the legal aspect of the case; I do not feel competent to say further than this, that if the railroads are to be regulated by law they should have all the protection that other people have from legal regulation; they should have all the rights that any other citizen has, no more. I think the method of investigating and getting at the facts should be changed, and in a case of this kind the commission has made the point to good effect, that the case should go to the court on appeal with the same testimony, unless some new issue has been raised, as in ordinary practice.

I think the commission ought to be strengthened. I say this on the assumption that the law regulating railroads has come to stay, and is intended to regulate railroads to a reasonable degree. If this is so, it ought to be modified and changed, so that the commission can regulate them, and so we can get some relief from this local discrimination.

I can not but repeat that the provisions of the act, the prohibition and the penalty, have been framed in such a way as to defeat their own purpose; it seems to me that the true idea of removing an evil is to remove the cause, and I do see how you can very effectually remove the cause by laying such a severe penalty on the corporation that the corporations themselves will be the policemen or guardians of this proposition. I never heard a shipper discuss that question so far as I know. I believe that thinking business men will approve what I say.

Testimony closed.

CHICAGO, ILL., *November 21, 1899.*

TESTIMONY OF MR. C. C. EMERSON,

Produce dealer, St. Paul, Minn.

The subcommission on transportation being in session in Chicago, Representative Lorimer presiding, at 11:15 a. m., November 21, 1899, Mr. C. C. Emerson was introduced as a witness, and, being duly sworn, testified concerning transportation as follows:

Q. (By Representative LORIMER.) Will you kindly state your name, address, business, and place of business?—A. C. C. Emerson, St. Paul, Minn.; produce business; 26 East Third street.

Q. Will you, in your own way, state to the Commission any complaints that you have?—A. I do not think I would enter into the matter of rates, or very little, if at all. Our great difficulty in shipping vegetables in bulk, potatoes and other vegetables, is that we meet with great shrinkages at destination, and we feel, sometimes unjustly perhaps, the blame is on the part of the party unloading the car; and if we could have railroad supervision of the discharge of cars, a great deal of that would be saved. Another point, the Western Railway Association are very stringent in collecting their freights on loading weights rather than discharge weights, and we have quite a large number of shippers over that part of the country; there is quite a heavy traffic in that line. We should have some redress in some way; they should not accept the word of the loader as absolute fact and not give any credence to the word of the party unloading.

Q. The receiver?—A. The receiver. I think the ground for it is that the receiver or middleman is not there. The shipper loads the cars himself, or by some representative, at point of origin, and he will say, for instance, that he has loaded 600 bushels of potatoes, 36,000 pounds, into the car. The party that receives it will report back 32,000 or 34,000 pounds, as the case may be—sometimes a less shrinkage than that, and not impossibly a larger one; he produces positive proof, in his own opinion, that that is what the car contained. The railroad people, through their weighing association, insist on the payment of freight on 36,000 pounds under such conditions, they having $t_u$rne$_d$ the car over to the man who received it, in bulk, and giving no supervision whatever, no counting of the number of loads discharged from the car, or the weight of them, and leaving us with the loss of the goods if there were any, and compelling us to pay the freight on the weight as reported at the loading station.

Q. (By Mr. CONGER.) Is it not true, as a matter of fact, that there is an actual shrinkage in potatoes?—A. There is apt to be a slight shrinkage; we figure quite carefully that 2 per cent is a fair estimate of the natural shrinkage. Of course, there is more or less moisture absorbed, and more or less sand or soil that may have adhered, and may be rattled off, but in unloading cars the past season, loaded by some of my men, I have had them turn out within 100 or 200 pounds in the carload, discharge weight. It is generally conceded among shippers that 2 per cent, if proper care is given at both ends, will cover the shrinkage.

Q. How do you account for this shrinkage of 4,000 pounds, from 36,000 to 32,000 pounds?—A. There are sometimes men who are a little neglectful in their methods, and I think I can safely say that there have been cases where a load has been accidentally omitted from the report.

Q. A wagon load?—A. A wagon load has been omitted from the report because of no supervision of the party unloading.

Q. Do you think that is a proper matter for the railroads to control? Is not that a matter between the seller and the buyer?—A. It is impossible for the seller to be present. Take a man handling 10 or 20 cars a day, as more or less of us do in busy times of the year. It is impossible to have a man at the destination unloading these cars.

Q. (By Mr. C. J. HARRIS.) How would it do for the railway company to weigh the car at the terminal point? It has track scales?—A. Then they are track weights; there are great discrepancies in them.

Q. Do you find railway weights satisfactory; are they accurate?—A. Not accurate. I will give you an illustration of that that occured 2 or 3 days ago. I had a car loaded on the Milwaukee road; my own men loaded them, weighed them on team scales. They were hauled into St. Paul and weighed on Milwaukee track scales under Western railway supervision, and they made them weigh 3,710 pounds more than the team-scale weight. We ordered the car over to the Northern Pacific, and requested them to weigh them under the same conditions on their track scales, Western railway supervision, and they weighed 210 pounds more than my team scale, making a discrepancy of about 3,500 pounds between their two weights the same day.

Q. You find a discrepancy between the actual and the marked weight of the car?—A. When weighed light.

Q. This was the loaded car?—A. This was the loaded car.

Q. Now then, they took the marked weight of the car?—A. Yes.

Q. Not the actual weight?—A. In both instances, I understand. There would not be any other way but to take the marked weight of the car for tare,

Q. Is not that marked weight the weight after the car came out of the shop, and when it has been out a year, has not the actual weight changed?—A. It is very apt to be so. Very often we ask to have the car weighed empty, to find a remedy. We think that if the railroad people say, " we have hauled 600 bushels for you in the car," and compel us to pay freight on 600 bushels, on the assertion of the man that loaded it that he put that much in, they should deliver us 600 bushels.

Q. Do you have much trouble with discriminations and rebates in St. Paul, railroads giving advantages to one shipper more than to another?—A. Not very much complaint of that. I think.

Q. Less than there used to be?—A. I think we hear less of it than we used to; especially last year I know it has been very strict.

Q. Are you acquainted with the grain trade there?—A. No, I am not; it is out of my line.

Q. You have elevators in St. Paul?—A. Yes, one or two, not many; the grain trade of St. Paul is very light, except on the track.

Q. (By Mr. CONGER.) Where do these shipments of potatoes and produce, that you handle, generally originate?—A. We handle them from points on the St. Paul and Duluth, or Great Northern, the Northern Pacific, and more or less from Wisconsin, on the Wisconsin Central.

Q. The destination is St. Paul?—A. The destination is likely to be any town; our shipments are all over the country.

Q. Do you ship to Chicago?—A. Very little; some, of course, as crop conditions require the product of one locality in another. At the present time our shipments are running southeast and east, to Virginia, Washington, Louisana, Kentucky, Indiana. A great many times they go southwest: but this year the crop conditions are such that we can not get into that territory We find our greatest difficulty in the medium sized markets; the difficulty in the small markets is very slight, and in large markets, like Chicago, the railroad people do superintend the discharge of cars, and while we do get some shrinkage, they account for it by tare or something of that kind, and accept payment of freight on the basis of their discharge weights. It is all run over their team scales in markets like Chicago, St. Louis, New Orleans, and a few of the larger markets. We have the greatest difficulty in markets such as Peoria, Evansville, and other places of that size. The shippers feel if the railroads were interested with us to have the discharge of these cars superintended, so that no drayman could get a load out of the car without giving a receipt for it, then we should have a check not only on the companies, but on the freight, and might know very nearly accurately what we were doing. In other words, we should have some reason why there was a shortage from the point of shipment to destination. It is very burdensome sometimes.

Q. The railroads have a system of supervising the discharge of freight in the large markets, and you would like that extended?—A. We would like to have it extended to every station.

Q. Do you think that can be done by legislation, or must it come out of the evolution or progress—— A. (Interrupting.) I do not see why legislation would not be the remedy that we would have to look for.

Q. Do you think the railroads under the present rates could afford to have these men employed to supervise the discharge of freight?—A. I do not think it would necessitate the employment of many more men. Even if we had to pay something, we would rather pay for that supervision than not have it. We should be money ahead by having to pay a certain amount for that supervision, although we believe rates are profitable.

Q. Do you know of any specific case in your experience where shipping over the same road you have been favored with this supervision in a large market, and could not get it in a small market?—A. Yes, I could give you instances of that kind.

Q. If you can, I think you might as well do so.—A. Take the Burlington road; they give that supervision in St. Louis; they claim everything is weighed from track scales. I could give you a particular illustration of one car; I can not give you the exact number of bushels, but this particular car I shipped from Princeton, Minn., to St. Louis. The party loading it gave very good proof of putting in, say, 480 bushels. I have the written statement of the agent at St. Louis that only 420 odd bushels was discharged from the car. Of course I had to settle on that basis with both parties, the loader and the shipper, in that particular case, because I had that evidence.

Q. That was a case where supervision was not particularly satisfactory?—A. It was not as satisfactory to the loader, but it left me right. Now, whether the agent was careless in his supervision or not I would not undertake to say; but it relieved me of carrying the burden—the road accepted freight on the discharge weight.

Q. Did you have to pay the loader, or the person of whom you purchased, for 480 or 420 bushels?—A. Four hundred and twenty. He had not evidence nearly as good as I had of the discharge.

Q. The point I was getting at, the illustration I asked if you could give me, was whether the Burlington road gave this supervision in St. Louis and did not at a smaller station?—A. I am sure they do not at Peoria; for instance, they allow the cars to be turned over to the receiver there with no supervision whatever of the discharge of the car; the car is simply delivered to the buyer in bulk.

Q. In other words, your contention is that in the case cited you were able to settle with the railroad by paying freight on 420 bushels, whereas, if you had shipped that same car load to Peoria, you would have had to pay freight on 480 bushels?—A. Yes.

Q. (By Mr. C. J. HARRIS.) Have you any other complaints to make except as to potato shipments from St. Paul?—A. The minimum weight on perishable goods is quite an injury to the traffic, especially in fruits—California fruits; they have raised the minimum on that. We find that not only in the winter time, when it is not necessary to ice the refrigerator cars, but also in the summer time when it is, a car of that character heavily loaded to the roof comes in in very poor condition There is a certain amount of heat and it rises to the top, and if there is no escape it settles back and must of necessity decay the fruit. The heavy loading causes the shipper to commence icing at least 30 days earlier than under the old way of a lighter minimum. It used to be 20,000 and now it has advanced, I think, to 26,000. In the case of cars from the South in the summer time, melons, tomatoes, and all things of that kind, if a car is loaded heavily to the roof, we get very poor results; the fruit is in unsatisfactory condition. It is not only a loss on the car, but it has a demoralizing effect on the market. A carload of oranges came into St. Paul Saturday morning, loaded so you could not put another box of oranges in the car. The temperature of the car was 70° this season of the year. Fortunately, the fruit was not overripe and it did not injure it; but had it been ripe fruit, there would have been a shrinkage of from 10 per cent to 25 per cent.

Q. Are they special cars?—A. Yes; made for the purpose.

Q. Ventilated?—A. I could not tell you as to this particular shipment; I did not see it myself. I presume it was a ventilated car, a regular refrigerator car, I understand, with the ventilators open.

Q. (By Mr. CONGER.) Are these cars usually owned by the roads or by the shippers?—A. I think a large share of them are owned by these great companies like Armour cars and Fruit Growers' Express.

Q. (By Professor JOHNSON.) Does not the railroad company give you the same rate on the 26,000 as on the 20,000?—A. We must pay a higher rate for the 20,000, or pay for 26,000.

Q. You get 26 at the same rate as you would 20?—A. The rate on 20,000 is higher per 100 pounds than on 26,000. They can load into the car any number of thousands of pounds above the minimum, and pay same rate per car. In this car there were 370 boxes; not over 26,000 pounds; that was just loaded to the minimum. We find in potatoes the same difficulty—putting 30,000 the minimum. A car with 400 bushels, 3 feet deep, will carry with much less liability of decaying heat than one loaded with 500 bushels, which would necessitate loading it between 4 and 5 feet deep. While they are new and in an immature condition they are very susceptible to heat, and decay is very often caused by the necessity of loading heavy. If, unfortunately, we get a small car that we must load nearly to its capacity, that loads it very deep.

Q. (By Professor JOHNSON.) Have you made these complaints before the railway associations that have classification in charge?—A. No; we have only made these to the different general agents of the roads over which we do business.

Q. These matters of minimum and maximum carloads are determined by the classification committee, are they not?—A. I think so; I understand so.

Q. Well, would not the classification committee listen to an appeal of this kind?—A. They have not, so far.

Q. (By Mr. CONGER.) Have they been asked by you?—A. We have an association of potato shippers; it is not very old, but they went before them once in regard to this matter, and different parties, different shippers, have been before them. I myself have never been to their classification committee; I have only appealed to the roads with which I have been doing business.

Q. (By Professor JOHNSON.) Do you have a feeling that the large association of shippers, including St. Paul and Minneapolis, would not be able to secure from the railroads a modification of such a rule as this?—A. Yes; because our business extends over such a wide country and beyond these particular roads. For instance, take the Southern roads. A great many potatoes are shipped from our country to the South—Louisiana and Texas—and they turn our appeal down by saying they can not control the classification or minimum of the connecting lines. They have got to load in such a way that the connecting lines will receive the cars in the same condition; and we must protect ourselves by knowing their requirements and loading accordingly.

Q. Would a uniform classification for the whole United States, promulgated by the Interstate Commerce Commission, if necessary, answer your needs?—A. I should think so.

Q. Should you be in favor of a national uniform classification?—A. Yes; I should.

Q. Subject to the amendment and control of the Interstate Commerce Commission?—A. I think so.

Q. (By Mr. CONGER.) Do you think a uniform classification for the entire country feasible?—A. On our commodities, I do not see why not. We find now, under certain conditions sometimes, when there are no special rates in effect, that potatoes for New York and New England points take a higher classification east of Chicago than west, and consequently there is an advance in rates.

Q. Did it ever occur to you that possibly, because of the volume of shipments of a certain product in certain portions of the country, the railroads were justified in making a different classification for it?—A. Could they not reach that in their rate, making special rates covering these differences, rather than in the classification? Have they not done so?

Q. No; I think it is done generally in classification.—A. So far as I have been able to discover they have been made special rates upon occasion. For instance, at the present time the Western roads from St. Paul to Montana points have reduced their rates. Possibly they would call it through their classification, but they do not so notify us. Potatoes have been 75 cents a hundred from St. Paul to Helena. The 15th of November they notified us of a reduction in rate to 60 cents a hundred.

Q. You do not object to that, do you?—A. No; but the classification, where it is on one line of road—perhaps they just put it down. I did not look that matter up; but I think——

Q. (By Mr. C. J. Harris, interrupting.) You say a special rate?—A. A special rate.

Q. It does not come under the classification, does it?—A. Not as I understand it?

Q. (By Mr. Conger.) We were speaking about a uniform classification for the entire country. On account of the facilities for shipping potatoes in the North the roads would give them a lower classification than in the South or West; possibly again, in the South, the volume of cotton to be shipped, and consequently the facilities for handling it that the railroads possess, might be such that it could be given a lower classification than it could in the North or West. I was asking you whether you had gone into the transportation question to such an extent that you would be willing to express an opinion that uniform classification for the country is feasible?—A. I have not investigated that, I confess, as thoroughly as I might, perhaps. I have given more thought to the matter of rates, for we have had to deal with these special rates more than with classification. It is very seldom that classification is brought up; they give us joint rates from our points to different points in the country, and that has been done as crop conditions have required.

Q. (By Mr. C. J. Harris.) Do carload lots enter into classification?—A. Oh, yes.

Q. Is there any special rate made on carload lots?—A. Yes. There is one point that I intended to speak of in regard to the discharge of cars. For instance, if we load apples in barrels, they give us a count on that, but they do not on potatoes.

Q. (By Mr. Conger.) You said, I think, that the railroads had made rates to you as crop conditions required?—A. I think so; yes.

Q. I wish you would amplify a little on that, and illustrate or explain what you mean; have they given you a lower rate when crops are large than they do when the crop is small?—A. Yes; for instance, I think in 1897 we had a very heavy crop of potatoes. The prices were very low, and the existing rates at that time prohibited our crop from going to sections of the country that could use it at the price; and rates were made that would enable us to put the goods in those markets. For instance, rates were made to us at one time to New England points, Boston points, where, with the existing tariff rate, the freight was more than the value of the potatoes in Boston. The reduction of the rate was made to enable us to go in there and unload the stock at a fair price.

Q. About what was that reduction?—A. I would not be positive, but I think it was from 60 to 40 per 100 pounds.

Q. The railroads then, at that time at least, cooperated with you and the producer?—A. Certainly.

Q. (By Mr. Kennedy.) Are you permitted to see the tariff sheets whenever you desire to do so?—A. Certainly.

Q. Are the rates you g t always the ones on the tariff sheets?—A. The ones we always get; yes. Sometimes they are billed through at a higher rate than the one we get, for instance, through billing, but we ultimately get those rates.

Q. (By Mr. Conger.) Do you not sometimes get better than the tariff rates?—A. Oh, I do not remember all the past.

Q. In your opinion is rate cutting as prevalent now as it has been in the past?—A. No, I do not think it is.

Q. (By Mr. Kennedy.) It was more prevalent in hard times than in good times?—A. Yes, I think so. Perhaps more the adjusting to proper conditions than the cutting of rates. I think whenever there has been any cut it has been general.

Q. (By Mr. Conger.) Not to favored shippers?—A. Not to favored shippers.

Q. Do you think there are any shippers in your market that have advantages over others in the same line of business?—A. I think not, no.

Q. There have been at times in the past?—A. I should not wish to swear to that. I think now they are very strict and stringent in rates.

Q. Do you think it is better for all interested to have a rate to all alike, or do you think it is better to be able to get a lower rate sometimes?—A. I think it is more satisfactory to everyone to have a uniform rate, and let everyone know just what is going on. It is very unsatisfactory competition when you do not know what the other fellow is getting.

Q. When this change in rates to the East was made, or when you have been able to get a reduced rate, it being made to all alike, do you know whether that has been made by lowering the rate or changing the classification?—A. I could not tell you. My impression has been by making a special rate.

Q. Are they usually made by some one road, or by all the roads?—A. Sometimes by one road, but the others fall into line immediately.

Q. And soon meet it?—A. Yes. I think that crop illustration I was speaking of was to enforce values from the West, from Washington, to the East, at a time when we handled a great many potatoes from that section. We shipped them through, and we had a rate from Washington. The original rate was 90, and they reduced it to 60 cents, and then let in a large amount of potatoes that otherwise could not have been handled.

Q. What has been your experience as to the consequence of these reductions in rates; in other words, take 1897, when the rate was reduced from 60 to 40 cents to New England points; when the next season came was the lower rate or the higher one put in force?—A. I wish to say right here that I would not be positive about this; of course I know 40 cents was the rate of the reduction; I would not be positive; it would depend very much upon the crop condition of the country. For instance, we should not have been able to do anything this year on a 40-cent rate; it would not have let us in there at all; it has had no effect before this year.

Q. Has the tendency of the rates been upward or downward?—A. They have been very firm during the past season.

Q. By that you mean during the past 2 or 3 months?—A. Yes; there have been no special rates made.

Q. Covering a period of years, how do the rates of the past year compare with the rates of 5 or 10 years ago? In other words, do you think that transportation charges are as much now as they were 10 years ago?—A. No, sir; I don't think they are; the volume of business from our part of the country is much larger than it was 10 years ago, and rates have not been as high during the past 3 or 4 years as they were previous to that time.

Q. As I understand, then, you haven't much complaint as to the rates; your particular complaint to-day is that you wish to have the supervision of the unloading of cars?—A. Yes; we want the same supervision of goods shipped in bulk in our line that is granted where goods are shipped in packages. Carloads of apples are always checked out; we have no difficulty in checking out a carload of apples and keeping our account with the railroad people with a carload of apples shipped in barrels, but with potatoes we have not had the business checked.

Q. Do you ever ship potatoes in barrels?—A. Very infrequently, but quite often in sacks.

Q. Do you have supervision of them when they are shipped in sacks?—A. We find it much easier to get supervision of them than when they are shipped in bulk.

Q. (By Mr. C. J. HARRIS.) You make a statement of so many bags, don't you?—A. Yes; it is very seldom you can get a bill of lading indicating the number of sacks. They sometimes have a book, though they really don't account for anything, and they don't give you an absolute bill of lading; and at some of the smaller stations they don't even do that in loading.

Q. (By Mr. CONGER.) Is not right there a remedy for this whole fault; that is to say, the enactment of a law that would compel the road to give an accurate and definite bill of lading for so many pounds or so many packages, as the case might be?—A. Very likely that would cover the thing; I should expect it would. Then we should have something to go by, that we could produce as an absolute fact.

Q. It would seem to me evident that to get direct to the supervision would be a difficult thing to do, and I think many difficulties would be met with in connection with legislation; but I should think that supervision would very quickly follow the enactment of a law that would compel the railroads to give an absolute bill of lading.—A. Yes; I think that would do.

Q. The bill of lading would become a contract to deliver at destination, and the man who receives the freight should receipt for it at the place of shipment?—A. Yes, I think that would do the thing; of course that would necessitate State supervision or something of that kind, of weighing, etc., but if Congress will do that I think it would give us the remedy, especially if enforced. But there are so many different sides that it may take a long time to get it in proper shape.

Testimony closed.

CHICAGO, *November 22, 1899.*

TESTIMONY OF MR. J. H. HULBERT,

Farmer and grain dealer, Fontanelle, Iowa.

The subcommission on transportation met at 10.30 a. m., Hon. William Lorimer presiding. Mr. J. H. Hulbert, being duly sworn, testified as follows:

Q. (By Representative LORIMER.) Please state your name in full.—A. J. H. Hulbert.

Q. And your business and post-office address.—A. My post-office address is Fontanelle, Iowa; my business is what might be called that of a farmer, although I deal in grain, banking business, etc.; but my principal business is that of a farmer.

Q. Please state, in your own way, just what your information or opinions are about the present elevator system and its connection with the grain business.—A. I don't know a great deal about it, as I have not given the matter my close attention; but I should think that it was an advantage from what I know.

Q. (By Mr. C. J. HARRIS.) How long have you been in the grain buying business?—A. Seven or 8 years.

Q. On what margin or per cent of profit do you handle and buy and sell wheat at the present time?—A. We are not in a wheat country.

Q. Well, corn then?—A. Cent and a cent and a half.

Q. Eight years ago, when you first went into the business, what was the margin at which you handled it; more or less?—A. More.

Q. How much more?—A. There was not so much shelled corn to handle then as there is now, and on this we had 3 or 4 cents at that time. A great deal more now is handled as shelled corn. It comes from the farmers shelled.

Q. Did I understand you to say that the margin then would be 3 and 4 cents a bushel?—A. Yes.

Q. To what do you attribute the lessened margin at the present time?—A. When we bought it we bought it at its market value and changed it right there. At that time when we bought our corn there was snow in it; it was wet and some of it poor corn, and we had to clean it and get it ready for market.

Q. Did you shell it?—A. Yes.

Q. Does your elevator do shelling and cleaning?—No; there are four different elevators, and we have one sheller in the bunch.

Q. (By Mr. CONGER.) Did you 8 years ago?—A. Yes; it was put on a grade then.

Q. And the 3 or 4 cents margin at that time included the cost of shelling?— A. Yes; cleaning it and getting it ready for market. It was not nearly so clean then as it is now.

Q. (By Representative OTJEN.) Where is the shelling done now?—A. With the farmer.

Q. With the farmer?—A. Yes; he does it to save hauling. When it is hauled to town shelled he gets a load of 50 or 60 bushels at a time of shelled corn, whereas if the corn were not shelled he would only have 25 or 30 bushels; and then he has the cobs, which he keeps at home, and he uses a good deal of them.

Q. You are not interested in any of the elevators you speak of?—A. No; just our own.

Q. (By Mr. C. J. HARRIS.) Will you tell us to whom you sell your grain?—A. Well, the most of our grain is sold to Harris & Co., of Chicago, and we also sell— I can not remember the others—Perry, Armour, and different ones.

Q. Do you have bids from other cities?—A. Yes.

Q. How many bids do you generally get during a week?—A. I can not say how many different bids; 5 or 6; sometimes more and sometimes less; sometimes they average 1 or 2 a day. We have daily bids.

Q. Is there any truth in the statement that two or three men in Chicago, grain men, control the price of the different grains throughout the country?—A. Well, I could not say as to that.

Q. Suppose two or three men in Chicago should get together and set a price on grain, what effect would that have on other markets? Would it affect the Minneapolis, St. Louis, or Peoria markets?—A. I don't think it would.

Q. Then it would be impossible for two or three men in Chicago to set the price on grain?—A. Well, the prices range differently. In St. Louis sometimes it would be a cent a bushel higher, and at Peoria the same way, and at other times Chicago is the highest market. This firm of Harris & Co.—I don't understand their grain comes to Chicago at all; in fact, I understand that it does not.

Q. As Chicago put a low price on grains, you could, instead of shipping it there, ship to other markets; is that your understanding?—A. I understand we can sell to Harris or Armour to better advantage than we can ship it here and sell it on the track.

Q. But if they attempted to put a price on grain and should bear the market, the result would be that you would ship to other cities?—A. Yes.

Q. (By Mr. KENNEDY.) You say you can sell to them to better advantage on the track there than you can bring it to Chicago and sell it on the track here; is that what you say?—A. Yes; we sell the most of our grain on the track there—put it on the cars there.

Q. At the elevator?—A. To these two firms, yes. While the majority of it goes to these two firms, we sell some at Peoria.

Q. (By Mr. CONGER.) Are there any other local buyers in your market; in other words, do you have competition?—A. Yes.

Q. Are there more than one there in the town?—A. One visits just one town.

Q. Where does he sell?—A. To the same places as we do.

Q. In Chicago?—A. To Harris & Co., and different buyers. The American Commission Company ships to Louisville sometimes.

Q. Sometimes to Louisville?—A. Yes.

Q. When this grain is shipped to Louisville is it sold on the track at your town?—A. Yes.

Q. What exception could you make to the statement you just made, that you can sell to better advantage on the track at home than you could to send it here? In other words, is it your opinion that Armour and other grain men of Chicago—that is, the larger dealers—have a better freight rate than you can get?—A. I don't know that they have; I don't know anything about that. My idea has always been that men who buy like these Louisville men, that they buy for seaboard inspection and weights, and that they go over lines that give them a better freight rate than we can get; but I don't know.

Q. Your idea is that it is offered on track at your local market rate and then pulled out to the seaboard on another rate?—A. Yes; that is the way it is, probably. A great deal of our grain is wheat from——.

Q. (By Representative OTJEN.) It does not come here and go into the elevator, or anything of that kind?—A. No; not that I know of. We shipped grain in August, and our weights did not come in until day before yesterday. It was shipped and sold to parties in Des Moines, and it has been out since August. We just got the weights day before yesterday.

Q. (By Mr. CONGER.) That is 3 months or more?—A. Yes; it is a long time.

Q. Did you have to carry them 3 months?—A. No; we drew what is known as a bill of lading for the amount of it.

Q. Where this grain is shipped on a through bill of lading on the other road, what mention is made as to the destination in the bill of lading?—A. I could not answer that question, for I have not paid enough attention to it.

Q. What roads do they generally ship over?—A. Harris ships over the Burlington. I also think P. B. Armour has the Burlington, but I am not sure of it. I am sure Harris has.

Q. (By Professor JOHNSON.) Do they bill from your place through to the seaboard?—A. I understand so. The firm or firms we sell to bill out over the Burlington from Mississippi River. Now, we send grain to St. Louis, which is the Mississippi River terminal.

Q. Have the farmers of your section any grievances against transportation companies, so far as you know?—A. No; I don't think so.

Q. They are entirely satisfied, are they?—A. Seem to be. It is very hard to satisfy a farmer, however.

Q. What complaints do those who are not satisfied make?—A. The complaints they would make would be about cars. Sometimes it is very hard to get cars, and when you get them you have to load in 48 hours. For instance, a farmer would order his cars and shell his corn and then the cars would not come. Sometimes he would have his corn shelled a week or 10 days before he could get a car. Those are the complaints they make against the railroad companies.

Q. (By Mr. CONGER.) Is that true this year, and has it been true for several years?—A. It has been true for several years.

Q. (By Professor JOHNSON.) You say the farmer has only 48 hours in which to load his cars? That keeps him from shipping to a large extent, directly, does it not?—A. You can fill the cars in one day if you are a dealer, and have your grain right there, but the farmer can not do that.

Q. Why?—A. Because his corn is out in the country, and he can not shell his corn and bring it in in one day, and if he does bring it in maybe he can not get the cars, so it makes it difficult for him.

Q. (By Mr. KENNEDY.) Are you a member of any farmers' organization?—A. No.

Q. Have the farmers in your part of the country an organization?—A. I don't think so.

Q. The Grange has no existence there?—A. No.

Q. Have you ever shipped your grain to Chicago and sold it in the competitive market here?—A. Yes; lots of it.

Q. Could you do better under that system than under the present one?—A. I don't think so.

Q. (By Representative LORIMER.) What was the advantage of shipping it here to commission men, as against selling it to people on the track at your place?—A. Well, we got more money out of it to sell it there. It would be a cent or so a bushel more there.

Q. Did you get more by selling it at home than you would get if you shipped it here?—A. Yes.

Q. Do you know whether that condition still exists?—A. I do not.

Q. You sold it there at the Chicago market price, did you?—A. We got a card bid e er morning with daily price. Of course we compared it to the Chicago market. y

Q. (By Representative OTJEN.) Is it higher or lower than the Chicago market?—A. Take the freight out and it is higher.

Q. But if you take the transportation out it is lower than it would be in Chicago?—A. Yes.

Q. (By Mr. CONGER.) How are these dealers able to do that—to pay you more for the wheat at your market than it is worth here after the freight is paid?—A. I don't know that.

Q. Does it follow that they are able to get that grain in here at less than the tariff rates?—A. Well, I could not say as to that. I don't know anything about it. Harris or any of these elevator men can handle it to much better advantage than we can. For instance, our wheat comes right from the farmer; it is mixed up with dirt and is right from the machine; it is brought right to the car and sent to them and they can make a grade out of it. That we could not do, but they can, as they have the machinery to do it with.

Q. Is that true of corn as well?—A. Yes; to a great extent. And it is the same now about the billing of these cars of grain; they bill out at the actual weight or take the minimum car weight.

Q. The minimum?—A. Yes.

Q. Do you often put in more grain than that weight would indicate?—A. At some of the stations we weigh and put on the bill every bushel that goes in the car, and usually they are the minimum weight. On a car of 60,000 pounds we put, say, 56,000 pounds and from that to 60,000; but in the last 2 or 3 months we have been very scarce on cars and we have had instructions from the railroad company to load them 10 per cent more than the capacity.

Q. Where they were loaded in that way did they in paying the freight pay for the actual weight?—A. I suppose so.

Q. (By Mr. C. J. HARRIS.) You don't know anything about that?—A. No.

Q. You don't pay the freight?—A. No.

Q. What is corn quoted at at your place to-day, or the last quotation you have had?—A. I could not say.

Q. You don't know the freight rate per bushel here?—A. No.

Q. You say these men in Chicago pay you more for grain at your place than you could get by shipping it in here yourself—that is, that the price of grain at your place, with the freight added, is more than you could get in Chicago for it?—A. Yes.

Q. What do you base such a statement as that upon?—A. I know from what we have done. We have shipped a good deal of grain here. My recollection is that our corn rate was 17 cents—but I could not say definitely; that is my impression—for 100 pounds.

Q. Seventeen cents per 100 pounds?—A. Yes.

Q. If your price for corn at Fontanelle is 30 cents a bushel, and your freight on a bushel is 10 cents to Chicago, that makes 40 cents a bushel here in Chicago?—A. Yes.

Q. Now, do you mean to say that the market price of corn in Chicago at that time would be less than 40 cents? You say you buy on weight there and add the freight to it and ship it to Chicago, and that the price of corn in your place with the freight added amounts to more than you can sell it for in Chicago—more than the market price in Chicago?—A. Yes; that is what we think, at least.

Q. You say you don't ship your grain to Chicago now?—A. When we consigned it ourselves we sent it to Chicago, St. Louis, and Peoria.

Q. But you can tell very easily if you have a bid of so much for corn, what amount it will bring there, and you can also see what it is worth in Chicago.— A. The only way that I can explain the proposition is that they get better freight rates than we could: and they also have the faculty for cleaning and handling it.

Q. (By Representative Lorimer.) When you consign grain to Chicago to the commission men, is it received here at the same grade it would be received from you on the track by the elevator men?—A. No; it is received here and sold in its grade after inspection.

Q. Well, would that be the same grade or higher or lower than that at which the elevator men would purchase it from you on the track?—A. The grain-purchasing man don't buy third-grade grain or third-grade wheat and oats. While it comes here it will come here 4, and sometimes 2 and 3, you understand. You don't know just what you are getting here until it comes out. You ship grain here and it may be graded 2 and 3 all the time.

Q. (By Representative Otjen.) This grain that you sell on the track there—do they buy your grain uncleaned and pay you the full price for the grain, including the treating and handling?—A. They do if it inspects up to the grade.

Q. If it inspects a certain grade?—A. Yes.

Q. Then, when these buyers come to clean that grain, there would be a certain loss, would there not?—A. Yes; that is what I was trying to say.

Q. For instance, if your grade is 3, they will take it and run it through the machinery and make a No. 2 grade out of it, and the difference is all loss?—A. Yes, that is it.

Q. (By Representative Lorimer.) That disposes of the dirt, and, of course there, is some shrinkage, but they get a better grade of grain, and that more than offsets for the other losses?—A. The independent grain buyers do not attempt to change the grade there. They buy the grain in the car just as it comes from the farmer.

Chicago, Ill., *November 22, 1899*.

TESTIMONY OF MR. PAUL MORTON,

Second vice-president of the Atchison, Topeka and Santa Fe Railway Company.

The subcommission on transportation being in session on the morning of November 22, 1899, Chairman Lorimer presiding, Mr. Paul Morton was duly sworn, and testified as follows:

Q. (By Representative Lorimer.) Please state your name.—A. Paul Morton.

Q. And your business.—A. Second vice-president of the Santa Fe—the Atchison, Topeka and Santa Fe Railroad system. In charge of its commercial affairs.

Q. And your post-office address.—A. Great Northern Building, Chicago.

Q. You have prepared a statement?—A. Yes.

Q. Will you in your own way make your statement?—A. After going over this little book you sent me, I took up these various questions as they appear in the book, so that perhaps they may strike you as being somewhat scattered. I would like to read you what I have. [Reads from paper].

The effect of rate wars and unrestricted competition is injurious to the shipping community, the railroad employee, as well as to the carriers themselves.

Stability in freight rates is just as essential as unfluctuating import duties. Violent changes in rates of transportation are always accompanied by commercial distress on the part of merchants and others who have been unfortunate enough to have already laid in their stock of goods. When rates are demoralized merchants are either forced to strain their credit by buying more than they want or they have the humiliation of seeing others who have availed themselves of the low rates selling goods for less than they can with profit.

Ticket scalpers are not permitted to exist in any other civilized country than the United States, and ought not to be tolerated here. They are the cause of much dishonesty and ought to be abolished. I believe that the railroads could by united action drive them out of business. Tickets should always be sold over the counters of the railroads themselves as cheaply to the public as they are sold at times privately by some of the roads to ticket brokers. There should be national legislation on the subject to protect the traveling public as well as the railroads. In asking for legislation prohibiting scalpers the railroads are asking for nothing more than proper police regulation in the interest of themselves and the traveling public, and it ought to be given them.

The result of consolidations of small railways into large systems has been to lower the charges for transportation, improve the service rendered, and advance wages. The facts will show that the large systems of railways pay better wages as a rule than the small roads pay. As a general proposition, the employee of a large company is more justly treated and there is less favoritism shown than on the smaller lines. This is easily accounted for by the fact that on the small roads the officials in charge get better-acquainted and have more intimate relations with employees than is possible on the large systems.

Passenger rates in the United States will average lower and the service better than in any other country in the world. The rates are somewhat higher in the West than in the East, but the difference in fares is not nearly as great as the difference in density of population.

Passes are given for many reasons, almost all of which are bad ones. There should be no passes printed. Even railroad officials or employees traveling on other lines than those they work for should be required to pay fare. The chief reason that stimulates a man to ask a railroad company for a free pass is that somebody else has it. Passes are given for personal, political, and commercial reasons, and in exchange for advertising; for services and fo.· various other reasons. I am in favor of the total abolition of railroad passes, and this view is held by a large number of the railroads of the country, as will be seen by the extract, quoted below, from the proceedings of a meeting of executive officers of Western, Northwestern and Southwestern railroads, held in October last in St. Louis:

" Recommended:

" First. That all free or reduced transportation of every description, both State and interstate, with the exception of that to railroad employees, be discontinued.

" Second. That reduced or free transportation to railroad employees be very much restricted.

" Third. That a joint meeting of all the leading American lines be called for the purpose of considering this subject, with the end in view of entirely stopping the pass abuse.

" Fourth. That a copy of these recommendations be submitted to all lines, with the request that they each go on record as to their views, and, if they favor discontinuing the practice of issuing free transportation, state how many railroads they believe should subscribe to the movement in order to make it effective."

The foregoing recommendations were submitted to the executive officers of 265 railroads, representing a mileage of 184,000 miles—practically all of the mileage of the country.

Replies in favor of radical action in either abolishing or restricting the issuance of free transportation have been received from 129 of the railroads thus addressed, representing 150,590 miles.

While this indicates that a large proportion of the railroads want to shut off the free pass abuse, I doubt if anything ever comes of it until Congress passes a law prohibiting it.

There should be no unjust discriminations in rates of freight or fares in favor of individuals or localities.

Transportation is a public service and the charges are in the nature of a tax. They should be absolutely fair to all. Almost any kind of legislation that will insure this will be wise.

One great difficulty that the railroads have to contend with is the adjustment of relative rates from competing distributing points. Much money has been wasted in contending for differential rates in favor of this place or that, and there ought to be some tribunal—such as the Interstate Commerce Commission—empowered to settle such disputes. Many of the rate wars of the Western country have been caused by such contentions, and the result has generally been a restoration of old conditions, an arbitration, or a slight concession of some kind or another.

I am one of those who do not believe that the American railroads ought to put lower rates on imported or exported articles than on domestic except where forced to by foreign competition.

I think that to a very large degree the excessive competition that has existed on export traffic has been between the American carriers, and that the rates have not been justified by the competition from foreign countries. I am of the opinion that there must be some elasticity in rates on manufactured goods for export in order to extend our markets in other countries, but I do not see why these rates should in any way interfere or be considered in connection with domestic rates. We produce cereals as cheap as any other country, and such products, it seems to me, can, when exported, pay our regular domestic rates.

I make a distinction between our agricultural products and our manufactures, because in agriculture we already lead the world, while in manufactures we are only getting ready to do so.

I think freight rates are generally published and posted conspicuously in accordance with the law, but I think the posting is a good deal of a farce and an unnecessary burden on the railroads.´ I mean by that the posting in the freight offices and at the stations. I am safe in saying that there is not one intelligent man out of a hundred that can go into a railroad station, where all the tariffs of that company are properly published and posted, and. without assistance, get for his own use any given rate in any given time under 24 hours, and that he would not be sure he had it after he got it. I have been in the railroad business 25 years, and am tolerably familiar with the publication of tariffs and the making of rates, but I should hesitate to go into the office of any other railroad and try to find a rate there for myself; I don't think I could do it.

I am not in favor of governmental establishment of maximum and minimum rates, unless at the same time maximum cost of wages, rails, ties, fuel, and other supplies are arranged for. Transportation is in every respect a composite service, and unless the prices of the component parts are fixed, the idea of fixing a maximum price on the whole seems unreasonable.

Take the present situation : After several years of depression the railroads find themselves with the lowest published tariffs in force that ever existed. These have been caused by hard times and light business. The revival of trade has resulted in an advance in prices of all kinds of material. Steel rails have doubled in price and all articles of iron have made a similar advance. There has been an increase in the cost of all the supplies a railroad uses. and it is estimated, if the present prices are maintained, that it will amount to $300 per mile per annum for all the railroads in the Western country. This is equal to an increase in fixed charges; in fact, it comes ahead of interest. We have to pay our operating and maintenance charges before we pay our interest.

I think there are more freight classifications in use than there ought to be, and believe in a universal classification, although the effort to bring about such a change failed because of the various opinions respecting classification held by men from different parts of the country. The Pittsburg man was in favor of very low rates on articles of iron, because they comprised a large portion of the tonnage on his road, while the California man thought the Pittsburg man's proposition was too low, because his line in California only hauled iron incidentally and it constituted a very small proportion of his tonnage. Thus it was with many other articles. I favor the appointment of an expert commission to make a railroad classification, and believe, once adopted and adjusted to our commerce, that it would be a wise measure.

I am in favor of railroad associations and legalized pooling. The chief object of the interstate-commerce law was to prevent unjust discriminations between individuals or communities. In prohibiting pooling the same law went a very long way in obstructing the result most wished for.

Legalized pooling will come nearer creating stability in rates than anything yet proposed. It would put a premium on honesty, and make it expensive for the railroad company that cuts a rate or pays a rebate.

Legalized pooling will come nearer insuring the small shipper and the small town a fair opportunity to grow than any other plan yet proposed. It will necessitate a fair deal all around, and I contend that it is in the interest of every shipper who wants nothing but equality in freight rates.

Legalized pooling will afford protection to the railroad investor. About one-fifth of the wealth of the United States is tied up in railway securities, and this enormous property ought to be reasonably and equitably treated.

Legalized pooling among railroads is not in restraint of trade, and differs materially from legalized combinations in the sale of merchandise. The Government undertakes to regulate the railroads, and various States undertake to fix the rates to be charged. This of itself makes legalized pooling in transportation a very different proposition from a pool in other commodities where prices are fixed by individuals.

Legalized pooling will stop unrestricted and disastrous competition, and ought to result in preventing a reduction in the wages of the railroad employee. There are about 1,000,000 men directly engaged in the transportation service of the country, and they are well paid. It is of no small importance that the sources of the incomes of these men be not impaired.

Legalized pooling will give the small town a better chance to grow. There are already sufficient magnets in our large cities to induce the people from the country to leave it, and it is of great consequence that the tendency should not be stimulated by unreasonable transportation advantages.

Unless legalized pooling is authorized by Congress, the railways of the country are more than likely to pass into the hands of a few owners, and then, without being legalized, a pool of the earnings is accomplished.

In view of the poor outlook for legalized pooling, this concentration of owner- ship has already commenced. I am in favor of it, and think that such a combi- nation would insure better service to the public without any unreasonable advances in the rates. In fact I think the rates would be lower.

I believe the Interstate Commerce Commission, or some similar body, has come to stay. I am in favor of its having proper authority, and am willing, under legalized pooling, that it should be empowered to pass, subject to review, upon the reasonableness of rates. I go further than most railroad officers in stating that I should like to see all transportation, both State and interstate, subjected to the supervision of a Federal commission.

There is too much conflict between States to suit me. I do not like the idea of a State railroad commission taking action to nullify an order issued by the Inter- state Commission. I do not believe that any State should endeavor to so adjust its rates of transportation as to unjustly discriminate against shippers outside of said State. For this reason I believe the public generally, and the railroads too, would be better off if a Federal commission could pass on all matters pertaining to our inland transportation. I want to emphasize this point and to add that I doubt very much if a Federal commission can accomplish what it ought to and what will be expected of it unless it has control of State rates. The State and interstate rates are so interwoven that they must necessarily be considered together.

I am opposed to governmental ownership of railroads. Where it occurs, rates are higher and service is inferior to our own. The introduction of politics into the transportation of the country would be followed by serious complications, in my opinion.

I think the American transcontinental lines, and the American wage-earner, should be protected against the inroads of a foreign carrier. If our coastwise com- merce is to be confined to ships carrying the American flag, and foreign bottoms are to be excluded from that traffic, then I insist that the commerce by rail from one State to another should be confined to our own railroads, and that any law, or absence of laws, that permits the Canadian Pacific Railroad to carry freight from one State in the United States through the Dominion of Canada to another State in the United States is unreasonable and unfair; and especially do I think that it is altogether wrong that the Canadian Pacific line should engage in this traffic and at the same time demand that the American lines shall do the business direct and charge 10 per cent higher rates than they say they will.

There are many who believe that, left to competition and other natural laws, the railroad problem would adjust itself, and I am of that opinion; but the large majority of people do not recognize this and therefore Federal regulation is with us undoubtedly as a permanent condition.

This being the case, I think that railway construction should be subject to supervision of the Federal authorities. I do not believe that new roads should be built unless a good reason can be shown for their necessity.

One of the chief causes of our two last panics was an overconstruction of railroads. The unnecessary paralleling or duplication of lines, the invasion of territory already well served, and new railroads projected to blackmail existing lines should not be permitted.

In revising the interstate-commerce act, this should be well considered. If it is fair to regulate the transportation lines of the country, it is likewise just that they should receive ample protection.

Q. (By Mr. C. J. HARRIS.) I suppose that the legal interpretation of that post- ing was that he must keep a book of rates subject to the call of anyone—subject to inspection by the public?—A. They have them posted up around. The Inter- state Commerce Commission decided that we had to have them hung up outside of the depot office for the inspection of the public, and where anyone might come in and look at them and make out the rates if he can. Rates are published from one station to every other station, and it makes it very bulky. They are hung up all over the inside of the station principally for the average citizen to look at, and then he is obliged to ask the agent to find out what the rates really are.

Q. Do you think they would cover all the sides of a room of this size?—A. Yes.

Q. (By Professor JOHNSON.) Would it not be possible to publish these rates in such a way that they could be clearly made out?—A. It would be if they would not try to publish the rate from one station to every other station in the United

States. The railroads of the country are paying hundreds of thousands of dollars every year for the unnecessary publication of rates, I think. This is supposed to be for the information of the general public, but, as I said before, I have been in the railroad business for 25 years, and I would not trust myself to pick out the rate from one of our own tariffs. I would consult with the rate man and ask him to tell me the rate to such and such a point. The general public can not feel itself safe in undertaking to tell the rates from the published tariffs.

Q. Do you testify, then, that the rates can not be told from the schedule?—A. I think that if a man will invent a schedule from which the rates can be more intelligently understood he will be doing a great favor to the railroads. I don't believe that a universal distance tariff would do it, and I don't know of anything else that would.

Q. (By Mr. C. J. HARRIS.) There has been testimony that the rate from England on manufactured articles is less than from some American points.—A. I have known the rates from Hamburg to Denver to be less than from Chicago. I say that is unnecessary and is a reflection on the intelligence of the American railroad managers. It ought not to be. But when it comes to a rate from Hamburg to San Francisco, which can go entirely by water, it is a different thing.

Q. (By Mr. KENNEDY.) Mr. Morton, do I understand you to say there should be no unjust discriminations between communities; did you use the word unjust?—A. Yes.

Q. Are there unjust discriminations at the present time?—A. I think there are.

Q. Do you know whether there are or not?—A. I know there are.

Q. Could you specify a few instances for the benefit of the commission?—A. I prefer not to.

Q. I should like to have your idea as to what you mean by just discrimination. Is that set out in your paper, do you think?—A. I think it is a matter of fact what a just or an unjust discrimination is. The word discrimination is a broad term. It is a question of judgment. By unjust discrimination I mean preferential rates. I do not think one man should have lower rates than another under the same circumstances and conditions.

Q. Do you think a man who has one carload of grain to ship from a point in Iowa to Chicago, for instance, should have the same rate as the man who ships 100 cars?—A. That would be hardly similar conditions, but I think the one-car man should have the same rate as the 100. I think the railroad can handle 100 cars for 100 different men just as cheaply as for one man.

Q. That would not be the same for less than a carload.—A. I think the carload should be the unit. Those shipping in less than carload lots should have the same rate and those shipping in carloads should have the same rate.

Q. (By Mr. C. J. HARRIS.) Do you think there is as much discrimination as there used to be some few years ago; that is, A getting one rate and B another?—A. In one way there is more; in one way not as much. I think there are fewer people who receive the benefits of preferential rates than there used to be, but I think there is just as much business, or more, that moves on preferential rates.

Q. (By Representative LORIMER.) The cargo is greater?—A. I think so.

Q. (By Mr. C. J. HARRIS.) Do you not think that applies more to the Western roads than the Eastern?—A. No; it is pretty general; probably less of it in the South than anywhere else. That is my general observation.

Q. (By Mr. KENNEDY.) Do you agree with the president of a Western railroad, who stated that the Interstate Commerce Commission at present is a farce, and that the rates as published are not maintained?—A. I think it is very unfortunate that the Interstate Commerce Commission, as now constituted, has not more authority than it has. I do not think it is a farce by any means.

Q. (By Mr. CONGER.) Do you think the published rates are a farce?—A. No; I do not think the published rates are a farce, as a general proposition, but I think published rates are sometimes departed from by secret understandings between railroads and shippers.

Q. What methods are used to give the shipper these favors?—A. About all the methods that human ingenuity can devise.

Q. Is the payment of a commission one of the new ones?—A. That is not a new one; it is a very old one.

Q. Is it coming back into favor?—A. Not particularly. There are a great many people who think it is proper and lawful to pay commissions on tickets, and likewise legal to pay commissions on freight.

Q. (By Mr. C. J. HARRIS.) To come back to the Interstate Commerce Commission, do you not think its decisions in the way of recommendations are generally, to a certain extent, followed by the railroads?—A. They have been.

Q. Has it not had a beneficial effect in that respect?—A. I think it has. The decisions have, with very few exceptions, been followed, and they have generally been wise decisions. I am one of those who believe the Interstate Commerce Commission is the mediary between the public and the railroad, and is a good thing for both.

Q. I understand from the testimony here that it is very important that the rates should be sent on to the commission in Washington, because it gives each road a check upon the others, and is of great use to the lines themselves.—A. I think it is held properly that all rates in effect should be filed with the commission. I think that ought to be done. In what I said about rates being made public, I was referring to the posting of rates. I objected to the unnecessary filing of rates in local railroad offices where nobody can get any advantage from them.

Q. I was speaking of Washington.—A. I think that is eminently sound and ought to be done.

Q. The posting of rates you think impracticable?—A. I think it unnecessary.

Q. (By Mr. CONGER.) You refer to both passenger and freight rates?—A. I refer to freight rates; it is all right to post passenger rates.

Q. The passenger rates that are posted; that is, the schedule?—A. The local rates; if a man wants to go from a small town down here on our road to some station up in the State of Washington he will have to ask the agent what the rate is. It is impossible to post all these rates. Under the law, I suppose we are expected to do it, but in fact we do not do it: we post our own local rates.

Q. On your own line of road?—A. Yes; on our own line of road.

Q. In your testimony, where you say that the public are unable to get any intelligence from these posted rates, you referred to the freight schedule?—A. Yes.

Q. It is possible for a person of ordinary intelligence to find the passenger rate?—A. As a general thing they have a local rate, which is about 3 cents a mile; this the people know.

Q. From the schedule as posted they can get the fact?—A. Yes; I think so.

Q. (By Mr. KENNEDY.) If the officials of one railroad believe the Interstate Commerce Commission is a farce and state the rates are not maintained, we must conclude that that railroad does not maintain the rates as published?—A. You are perfectly sound in doing so.

Q. Does it follow that the railroads in the same section of country must follow the same method?—A. Unfortunately, one railroad with such ideas can come pretty near demoralizing rates for all of us. It is just a question of forbearance. It is simply a question of how much of your business you are willing to let the other fellow come in and take away from you.

Q. (By Mr. CONGER.) If the volume of business that road is carrying continues to increase, is not a war, so called, likely to follow?—A. A point is bound to be reached where things will snap. At the present time business is good, cars are scarce; we all of us have more demands for cars than we have cars, without cutting rates, and it is more a question of capacity than it is of making a bid for business in the way of cut rates; but in the long run a cut rate takes the business.

Q. Could you suggest any authority that could be given the Interstate Commerce Commission that would reach this case or similar cases?—A. It is a very difficult problem; it is a matter that we have all considered, and the only successful way of getting rid of competition of that kind is to buy it up.

Q. That means consolidation?—A. Consolidation, and perhaps another road to buy up later on.

Q. Even under present laws, are not the officials of that road liable to Government indictment for cutting rates?—A. I think so. There was a case made once. There were a few of the railroads here that started out to absolutely maintain the interstate-commerce law in every respect, with the intention that other roads should do the same thing. They made a case against one road, and the president of the road, when he was put on the stand, admitted everything that was charged. Nothing was ever done with him.

Q. It has been contended before this commission in Washington that the competing or suffering railroad or railroad officials would be more inclined to push the case against the competitor, the road that cut the rates, if the penalty of the law were made a financial one; in other words, fine rather than imprisonment. We should like your opinion on that subject.—A. I do not like the imprisonment clause of the interstate-commerce law because it is not operative, and if it was operative I should probably like it less. We should be perfectly willing to stop it if the other railroads did, and I would not hesitate, so far as I am concerned, to report other railroad men that were found cutting rates, provided everybody would do it.

Q. You are not inclined to push the cases now where there is a criminal clause?—A. I think a very heavy penalty on both the shipper receiving the cut rate and the railroad making it would be much more effective.

Q. (By Representative OTJEN.) And more easily enforced?—A. More easily enforced, and would come nearer preventing it.

Q. (By Mr. KENNEDY.) How would the shipper, in view of your former statement, know whether he was getting a cut rate and violating the law?—A. They would know. These cut rates are given on shipments of some heavy freight; they know whether it is a cut rate or not; a man who is shipping nothing but steel, or ccal, or lumber, dealing in some specialty, is better posted on the rates on that particular commodity than the railroad men are. The railroad man has got to know about everything; he has to know the rates on all kinds of commodities. There is never any question about the fact of a man's knowing whether he has a cut rate or not except in cases of mistakes that are liable to happen.

Q. (By Representative OTJEN.) You have testified that you favored legalizing pooling; of course, these restrictions would have to go with the law or they could cut just the same as they do now, could they not?—A. I think under legalized pooling the commission should have power to say what the rates should be. I think it ought to be just as incumbent on the commission to say whether a rate was unreasonably low as whether it was unreasonably high. I know of rates being made unreasonably low for the purpose of getting something that the railroad ought not to have. I have known a railroad to come in and make a rate on some commodity that it never hauled and never expected to haul, and which some other line had every reason to haul; make it so low for the purpose of getting a proportion of the business.

Q. You would, then, give the Interstate Commerce Commission authority to revise rates?—A. Prima facie, revise them. I think the railroads should have the right of appeal to the courts, the same right that any citizen would have.

Q. In case the commission decided upon a rate, you would have that stand until it could be reviewed by the court?—A. I think that is a matter that is not very material; I think that is not worth sticking for. I should personally feel as if the decision of the commission should stand temporarily, should be accepted by the railroad on the basis that the railroads were allowed to make contract obligations with each other for a division of the earnings. Of course, if we got legalized pooling there would be no way of getting railroads into the pool; there is nothing compulsory about it.

Q. (By Mr. C. J. HARRIS.) If one railroad holds out and will not go into the pool, you are entirely helpless?—A. Yes; it is then a case of fight.

Q. (By Representative OTJEN.) If, then, the Interstate Commerce Commission had authority to fix rates, you could largely correct some of these difficulties?—A. I think so.

Q. Provided there were penalties attached to the law that could be enforced?—A. Yes. The trouble with the pooling that we used to have was that it was not legalized; no railroad could commence suit against another railroad for balances; it was entirely a matter of good faith.

Q. A matter of honor, largely?—A. Yes.

Q. (By Mr. CONGER.) I was going to bring out a distinction between the power to revise the rates that it is sometimes proposed to give the Interstate Commerce Commission and the right to fix the rates in case of pool. It has been contended by some that if pooling is to be legalized the Interstate Commerce Commission should be given authority to absolutely fix the pool rate; that in cases where a pool is not entered into by the roads they should have the power of revision as regards differentials. The power of revision is practically the power to fix the rate, is it not?—A. I can conceive cases where it would not be.

Q. What protection would you give the public against exorbitant rates if pooling is to be legalized?—A. That very protection—the power of the commission to revise them.

Q. But the commission at present has no power whatever to lower or raise a rate.—A. We have not got the authority to pool either; I think the two should go together.

Q. (By Representative OTJEN). That is, the law should be amended to cover these two points?—A. Yes.

Q. (By Mr. CONGER). Some have contended that if pooling is to to be legalized the Interstate Commerce Commission should be given explicit authority to fix the rates between the points where the pool is operative; let me ask first if that would be your view?—A. My view is, they should have control of the rates; not necessarily fix them, but have power to revise them under the pooling contract. I do not believe that the Interstate Commerce Commission wants to be charged with the work of fixing the rates, but in case of complaint—in case it can be proven that the rate we are charging under this pool is higher than it ought to be, unreasonable, that the commission shall pass on it and revise it if the facts warrant.

Q. You mean have it lowered if necessary?—Yes; and I think if the case was that somebody complained a rate was too low, they should have the right to advance the rate, if they thought it was discriminating against localities.   I have known of industries starting up at some point and doing quite a business—perhaps a brickyard at St. Paul, doing a very handsome business—and the railroad would come in and make a rate abnormally low in order to bring in brick from some other place, and thereby, perhaps unjustly, discriminate against some locality. In other words, rates can be unreasonably low as well as unreasonably high.

Q. You testified in your paper that you favor an expert commission to arrange a classification schedule?—A. Yes.

Q. Now what is your idea there as to the expert commission? Should it be an official commission, or should it be one appointed by the railroads among their own traffic managers?—A. The railroads at one time appointed a universal classification committee, which consisted of representatives, as I remember, two from New England, two from the Atlantic coast, two from the Middle States, two from the far Western States, and two from the middle Western States.   I was one of the committee representing this particular section of the country. This was over 10 years ago.   As I remember, we agreed upon a classification, but it never was adopted because of these local influences I speak of.   I am inclined to think it would be to the interest of the railroads and the shipping public if an expert commission should do that work; some commission under the supervision, say, of the Interstate Commerce Commission; some body that they might appoint or select, I think they could do it better than either the railroads or the shippers could.

Q. If universal classification would be to the interest of the railroads, why did they not adopt the one prepared and presented to them?—A. I think it would have been to the interest of the railroads generally, but there were some features of the classification that some particular roads in some particular sections of the country objected to; and they did not object to the same features.

Q. Different geographical conditions?—A. The Pittsburg man wanted a very low classification on iron—iron constituting a large proportion of his tonnage; but the California man, whose road only hauled iron incidentally, objected to any such classification of iron, because his principal traffic was composed of some other commodity.

Q. Are not these conditions so various and so greatly diversified in various parts of the country that a universal classification would be practically impossible?—A. I think not.

Q. You think the railroad in California can haul iron ore, while they get but little of it, at practically the same rate as the road in Pennsylvania?—A. Iron ore is not now hauled on the classification.   In quantities it is always hauled at commodity special rate.

Q. Is that equally true of grain?—A. It is always hauled as a commodity; it appears in the tariffs under the head of grain.   That is true also of the coarser freights—lumber, salt, live stock.

Q. You think your opinion is shared by the majority of the leading railroads?—A. I find the opinions of railroad men are like the opinions of lawyers, they differ.

Q. Coming back to the question of legalizing pooling, you stated that in your opinion if pooling should be legalized rates would be lower.   Why do you think that?—A. I do not think I testified to that.   I testified that under concentration of ownership I thought rates would be lower.   My reason for thinking that is that concentration of ownership means great economies in the management and operation.   There is more money wasted in the railroad business than in any other business I know of.   We are all spending large sums of money for advertising, for soliciting freights; we each have expensive offices on Broadway in New York, say, with high-salaried agents; we are always running at certain seasons of the year unnecessary trains.   With concentration of ownership that would be unnecessary.   The service could be just as good and could be done with great economy.

Q. I think you testified that in your opinion to legalize pooling would check consolidation?—A. I say that unless legalized pooling comes concentration of ownership will come.   I think if we had had legalized pooling years ago there would have been more systems of railroads; the necessity for combination and concentration of ownership would have been less.

Q. And if we do not have it in 5 years now, we shall have fewer systems?—A.

One of three things is likely to occur—legalized pooling, concentration of ownership and consolidation of railroads, or Government control.

Q. Which of these three is the most desirable?—A. The first one.

Q. Legalized pooling?—A. That is the one we are nearest to; the second is likely to come, and it may bring the third.

Q. (By Mr. C. J. HARRIS.) Legalized pooling, under the supervision of the Interstate Commerce Commission, as I understand your testimony, would do away with discriminations?—A. I think it would; I think there would be fewer discriminations than there are now. You ask which I prefer of the three; I prefer concentration of ownership.

Q. That was what I concluded from your testimony; you think that would be the most desirable for the good of the general public, and that was what I wanted to bring out.

Q. (By Representative OTJEN.) Would not classifications by sections be practicable?—A. That is practically what we have now. There is what is called the Western classification, which, practically, is everywhere west of the Missouri River, except on transcontinental business, and there the transcontinental classification applies; then everything east of the Missouri River is the Eastern classification. There are fewer classifications now than there were 10 years ago.

Q. Is it your opinion that a universal classification would be better than the sectional classification?—A. I think it is possible to have a universal classification, but it would mean, to some extent, a readjustment of the rates. You can make the rates to fit any classification. A universal classification might be applied everywhere in the country, but the rates would be sectional.

Q. The rates might not be the same all over the country; the rates would be different in different sections of the country?—A. Yes; the rates will vary with the cost of doing business; it costs more to do business in the Rocky Mountains than in New England.

Q. The classification really has not anything to do with the rates?—A. No, not necessarily; it has a good deal to do with the rates, but the rates can be adjusted regardless of classification.

Q. (By Mr. KENNEDY.) By concentration of ownership, do you mean management by one central body of officers?—A. Not necessarily that; that would come, I think.

Q. Do you mean also by concentration of management the concentration of all the roads in one system?—A. Not necessarily.

Q. Would not that follow?—A. The roads engaged in competition for certain traffic would be concentrated; say, the transcontinental lines, or the Missouri River lines, or the lines leading to the Gulf, or the Southern lines. That might be done sectionally, and ultimately, I think, if it was done in that way, there might be a parent company that had to do with all of them.

Q. I will ask you if you do not state some of the arguments in favor of Government ownership when you speak of these great economies that would be effected by concentration of ownership in itself. Are these not the arguments used by those who favor Government ownership?—A. I think perhaps the most extravagantly managed business is the postoffice business managed by the Government. For instance, we have an agent in a town who is doing a tremendous business; he is handling thousands and thousands of dollars' worth of goods, and we pay him $125 a month; the postmaster in the same town is probably getting $300 a month. We have a station house costing us perhaps $3,000 or $4,000, and the Post-Office Department will have a Government building costing perhaps $150,000.

Q. All the people of the United States are treated alike by that system; it is superior to the railroad system in that?—A. Yes; there is no difference in the price of postage stamps; one man can get them at the same price as another; and I contend that should be so in the railroad business.

Q. If that were to come about, there would be no advocates of Government ownership, or very few at least?—A. There might be the greatest kind of discrimination in case the Government had control of the railroads and the roads got fewer.

Q. There is no such discrimination in the postal system as against sections or people?—A. Nor in import duties; custom-house rates are the same to everybody; but there are discriminations in the railroad business.

Q. (By Professor JOHNSON.) To what extent is the financial management of the railroad business being consolidated in great banking houses?—A. I think they are getting nearer together all the time, but I do not think there is any actual consolidation.

Q. To what extent does the banking house of Morgan & Co. and its allied interests control the Eastern railway systems of the country?—A. I could not answer that question; they have very little interest in the Western roads.

Q. Do you not think this concentration of financial control in big banking houses represents an important phase?—A. I think anything in the way of concentration that will do away with preferential rates, and the unrestricted competition that causes these rates, is a good thing for the community and the railroads.

Q. Do you think this concentration of financial control is having a steadying influence?—A. I think it is.

Q. Would it be a good thing for the West?—A. I think it would.

Q. Can you present figures to show the relative height of passenger rates in this country and in others?—A. I can.

Q. I should be personally glad to see this, because evidence has been submitted contrary to yours.—A. I shall be glad to submit that to you. Furthermore, in that connection, not only are the passenger rates lower in this country, but the service is superior, and the sleeping-car rates are very much lower than they are abroad. Sleeping-car rates are not only lower, but the sleeping-car accommodations in this country are infinitely better than they are on the other side.

Q. (By Mr. CONGER.) How about freight rates?—A. Freight rates are lower.

Q. (By Mr. C. J. HARRIS.) Considerably lower?—A. Considerably lower. That is the chief reason for the great inroads that we have made in capturing the markets of the world—our cheap transportation.

Q. (By Mr. KENNEDY.) You say the post-office business is the most extravagantly managed business in the country, yet we hear no complaint from the people?—A. I have no authority for that statement, except my own observation.

Q. Do you know of any considerable complaint from the people because it is a high-priced business?—A. The people are getting a good service for very little money, and I do not think many of them know that there is a big deficit ever year. As long as they are fairly treated they do not care.

Q. Do you not think if these discriminations against communities and individuals and other evils, such as the giving of passes, are not done away with through Government control that the people will be willing to stand a very extravagantly managed transportation business rather than bear these discriminations and evils?—A. Possibly; but I think it woud be extravagant. I think private individuals can conduct the transportation business for much less money than the Government can do it itself. I believe the rates would be lower; and compared with other countries that do run their own railroads the service is better and the rates lower.

Q. (By Mr. C. J. HARRIS.) Did you ever know any railroad run by any State government to be managed at all successfully from a railroad point of view or any other point? We have no State railroads here, but there are some through the South.—A. We have no State railroads in the West. I think the Michigan Central started out as a State railroad and was sold years ago to private parties.

Q. You do not know of any railroad run by the State successfully?—A. No; I do not know of any railroad run by the State.

Q. (By Representative OTJEN.) As you see it, what are the principal objections to Government or State ownership of railroads?—A. My objections all come from observations of results in countries where it obtains; the rates are higher and the service is not as good, and as the political question would be involved——

Q. (By Mr. CONGER, interrupting.) The postal service has been cited as an example of the Government operation of a public service. Now the Government carries a letter 1 mile or 3,000 miles for 2 cents; would that be possible or practicable in the railroad business?—A. I do not think so, unless the Government was prepared to meet a big deficit, as in the Post-Office Department.

Q. Would it be possible to put in a mileage rate or schedule?—A. It would be possible, but it would cause about the same kind of revolution that a very vigorous change in the tariff would, and a great deal more; the country would have to adjust itself to the change.

Q. (By Representative OTJEN.) It would disturb business for the time?—A. Very much indeed.

Q. (By Mr. CONGER.) Would a mileage tariff be practicable under individual ownership where the various lines of road are owned by different corporations?— A. It would be; it is very remote though, and I do not think anything of the kind would ever happen.

Q. You mean to testify that you think it practicable for a road in the far West, or in any sparsely settled district, to carry freight at the same rate per ton per mile, that it can be done for by the New York Central or the Pennsylvania road?—A. No. I mean to say a distance tariff is possible, but it would have to be so high to reach all the different railroads in the different sections that it is remote.

Q. (By Mr. C. J. HARRIS.) Impracticable?—A. It is possible, but improbable, very improbable.

Q. (By Mr. CONGER.) Now, in the matter of discriminations; are they ever necessary, in your judgment, in freight traffic? For instance, railroads sometimes make rates to meet crop conditions; are these things justifiable? As an illustration, if you like, yesterday it was testified before this commission that in 1897 certain of the railroads reduced their rate on potatoes from, I think, 60 to 40 cents a hundred from Minnesota to New England, because of crop conditions; was that justifiable?—A. I do not know the exact circumstances of the case, but I think crop conditions have got to be considered in making a rate.

Q. The crop conditions were that there was a very heavy crop of potatoes in Minnesota, and under existing rates they could not be moved and sold and give the producer and dealer anything for their services. Without a change in the rate a carrier would be without that traffic, and the producer would have that crop on his hands.—A. So long as the rates were made to everybody, I do not see where there is any discrimination.

Q. The point I desire to bring out is this: I think such a change in rate seems desirable, and is generally approved, or at least not disapproved; would that be possible under Government ownership, and if possible, or permitted, would it not make it possible for the party in power and controlling these rates to discriminate for or against some section of the country that was not with them?—A. No doubt about it.

Q. (By Professor JOHNSON.) How would the rates be controlled under Government ownership?—A. I presume the rates would be controlled just as the price of postage stamps is.

Q. Would it be by general legislative enactment, or by an expert commission?—A. It would have to be, I presume, just as Congress decided it; I would not undertake to say. I think the Government ownership of railroads is very remote and very undesirable. I think the complications you would get into the moment the Government undertook the control of railroads—politically commercially, and financially—would be very great.

Q. (By Mr. CONGER.) On the theory that consolidation would bring the public the best service, and also accepting your theory that legalized pooling would retard or check that, do you still think legalized pooling desirable?—A. Yes; I think legalized pooling is desirable and expedient. I do not think it is possible to have concentration of ownership for years to come.

Q. It is now going on.—A. It is now going, on, yes; and I do not see any objection to legalizing pooling even if there was a concentration of ownership. The chief object of the interstate commerce law was to prevent discriminations between communities and individuals, and legalizing pooling will assist in bringing that about.

Q. (By Mr. KENNEDY.) And that object would be subserved by having legalized pooling after you have brought about concentration of ownership?—A. There might be a concentration of ownership of the railroads in a certain section, and in some other section there might be a concentration of ownership also, but by different people. In different sections of the country the roads might be concentrated, and there might be a competition between the various systems. There is an element of market competition always in the railroad business that we have to contend with. We may have a railroad without a competitive point on it, a line with industries; people who are manufacturing sewer pipe, or brick, or articles of iron, or making salt, or doing anything in the line of industry; notwithstanding the fact there may not be a competing point on that railroad, it is competing all the time with the markets furnished by other railroads; with the product furnished by other railroads.

Q. (By Representative LORIMER.) It seems to be your idea that pooling is the nearest at hand?—A. Yes.

Q. That benefits will come more rapidly to the people by pooling, but concentration may follow and if it does follow, we shall get more benefit from that than through pooling?—A. Yes.

Q. But you believe that pooling is the most feasible because the people are probably better prepared for it at this time, and because it can be done without any financial interference. Is that the idea?—A. That is right.

Q. I think you stated that if we have a pooling act all the railroads will not necessarily go into that pool?—A. Not necessarily.

Q. And if one railroad remains out a fight would probably follow. Would you authorize the Interstate Commerce Commission to fix the rate for the road that refrains from going into the pool?—A. Yes.

Q. Then if the Interstate Commerce Commission had authority to fix the rate, and made the same rate that the pool agreed upon, how would this affect the business of the roads that had gone into the pool; or would it give the road standing out any advantage over those who had pooled?—A. I think the roads that comply with the law and maintain the published rates should be protected against a railroad that was inclined to deal with the other roads in a piratical manner.

Q. If the Interstate Commerce Commission, then, had authority to fix their rate, and fixed the same rate the pool had agreed upon, would that have the effect of protecting the pooling roads as against those standing out of the pool?—A. All the pooling roads would want would be that the road outside of it should have equality of rates—should not give secret rates, preferential rates.

Q. Could a pool exist under that condition?—A. It could; it has, prior to the interstate act. I have known of certain roads pooling their business, where there was one road outside; that is, they acted as a unit in meeting the competition of this outside line. It was the exception, though, rather than the rule. The general theory under which pools used to be made was, "One out, all out."

Q. Then you seem to think that by clothing the Interstate Commerce Commission with proper authority, the complaints of discrimination could be practically wiped out?—A. It could be very much lessened; coupled, of course, with legalized pooling.

Q. (By Mr. CONGER.) Should you have any objection to giving the Interstate Commerce Commission authority to examine the books and accounts of the railroads, by duly authorized official examiners, for the purpose of getting evidence that they had paid rebates?—A. No, I should not; I think the more publicity the better. In other words, I think it is to to the interest of the Government itself that there should be no discriminations in transportation charges.

Q. You see no objection to an official examination of books and accounts?—A. The merchants of Chicago would not stand it for a minute if they thought the merchants of New York were getting lower import duties than they were; the business men here would not tolerate the purchase of postage stamps in Washington for any less price than they pay; and here is a matter of a great deal more consequence than the postage business, or the import tariffs, where there is more or less favoritism going on which ought to be stopped.

Q. (By Mr. KENNEDY.) I should like to ask a question on the subject of ticket scalping. Is it true that the only class of trade that comes to the ticket scalpers is that which is brought by the public in the way of unused coupons, etc.; or is it true that business is furnished by the railroads themselves?—A. Of course there has always been more or less transportation furnished to the ticket brokers by dishonest employees of the railroads.

Q. What I want to ask you is, do you believe the ticket scalpers should continue in business and live on the business that is brought to them by the public and also do this business you speak of?—A. I feel that there would be fear of that. I think that if the railroads had never secretly assisted the scalpers and ticket brokers there would not be so much business as there is now.

Q. The larger per cent of the business they have is business given them by the railroads in this way, is it?—A. No; it is a less proportion of their business than the public gives them. If the railroads would combine and refuse to give business to the ticket scalpers a good many of them would be driven out of business. I think the railroads have it in their own power to make the business of the ticket broker unprofitable if they would only take the proper means to do so.

Q. (By Mr. CONGER.) Why don't they do it if they don't want it?—A. Because certain of the lines have relations with them—use them.

Q. In other words a small minority of the roads can defeat the purpose of a large majority; is that the idea?—A. Yes; it is a great wrong that these brokers should buy tickets for less money than the traveling public, and yet it is continually done. The brokers buy the tickets and make a commission on them.

Q. (By Mr. KENNEDY.) Do you favor the movement which the railroads have been making for the last few years to secure from Congress legislation on the subject, while at the same time they make absolutely no effort to secure any action by the Interstate Commerce Commission for the abolition of the pass system?—A. I believe the entire matter should be considered as one proposition. I was in favor of and have worked for an antiscalping law, but I think it is a waste of time to try to get any legislation on that subject until the entire transportation matter is taken up and the interstate-commerce law is amended.

Q. You believe it is calculated to discourage the railroads when they attempt to get this one passed?—A. No; I think the railroads are entitled to that legislation. I think it is a wise thing for the public, and I think that it should have been obtained from Congress without any asking. I think as a matter of protection of the public that it ought to be passed.

Q. You have organized labor on your lines?—A. Yes.

Q. Do you believe that it is as necessary for the laborers to combine to protect their interests as it is for the railroads to concentrate?—A. I think the organization of labor has been a benefit to labor.

Q. Has the organization of the engineers, brakemen, conductors, and trainmen generally been a benefit to the railroads also?—A. There are two sides to that question; I don't know whether it has or not. I think that is a debatable question, although I believe in the organization of labor.

Q. (By Mr. CONGER.) Is overcapitalization an evil in the railroad field?—A. My observation has been that there is or has been overcapitalization; the price of the securities has generally indicated it.

Q. Would you favor the prohibiting of the increasing of capital stock of interstate railways without permission from the Government; I mean the watering of stock by interstate railways without governmental permission?—A. I don't believe in the watering of stock; I think it is all right, though, to issue new stock for new property.

Q. Would there be objection to making it necessary to ask the permission of the Government?—A. I should say not.

Q. You think there would be no objection to that?—A. I don't think it would be necessary to ask the permission of the Government; I don't see what would be gained by it.

Q. (By Mr. C. J. HARRIS.) Do you believe the investor takes care of himself?—A. If the stock is watered the price shows it.

Q. (By Mr. CONGER.) How far has your road complied with the recent act of Congress as to automatic appliances—couplers and safety appliances?—A. Very fully; I think we have a few cars not equipped, but very few.

Q. Did you ask for the extension of time that was provided for?—A. Yes; we are one of the roads that asked for the extension. That is in the operating department, which I have little to do with, and I could not say what the facts are in regard to that, except in a general way. We have complied as well as anyone with the act of Congress.

Q. That time was extended to December 1 or January 1?—A. I really don't know. I think it was extended 2 years; I know we have complied with the law.

Q. You have or will have by that time?—A. Yes.

Q. (By Representative LORIMER.) Have you anything further to suggest?—A. Do you want to ask any questions about this conflict I spoke of between the interstate and State railway commissions?

Q. (By Mr. CONGER.) I should like to ask if you have any instances or can give us any specific information?—A. I know in a general way that there are two States that I have in mind that attempt to regulate their rates so as to confine the business to their States and to their own people; Texas is one of them.

Q. They undertake to favor the State road?—A. Yes; State road and State management and State shippers and the residents of that State generally. The Texas people tell us in so many words that they are there to protect the people of Texas, and if the rates from New York to St. Louis or Chicago are reduced by order of the Interstate Commerce Commission, or for any other reason, they will make a corresponding reduction in their rates.

Q. It is a little surprising to find that provision carried out to such an extent as it is in Texas?—A. It is a domestic tariff incidental to private protection.

Q. (By Mr. C. J. HARRIS.) It is distinguished as being against the Constitution?—A. They don't recognize that; they are States' rights people.

Q. (By Mr. CONGER.) They only feel it locally?—A. That is all.

Q. Which is the other State?—A. The grand old Republican state of Iowa has about the same idea.

Q. (By Professor JOHNSON.) How is Nebraska?—A. They go in for the same doctrine, and it is, I presume, a parent of the protective tariff.

Q. I don't think the United States Government has any remedy.—A. There is no remedy unless the Constitution is amended. And I bring up the point that it is impossible for a Federal commission to make the interstate rates of this country so long as they have no control of State rates that are so interwoven; for instance, rates from St. Louis, Mo., to Kansas City, Mo., entirely in the State of Missouri, are on the basis of rates from Chicago to Kansas City. The rates from Davenport, Iowa, to Council Bluffs, Iowa, are practically on the basis of the rates from Chicago to Council Bluffs.

Q. (By Mr. KENNEDY.) You say you believe it is a parent of the protective tariff principle; is it not more probable it is the result of the main principle of self-protection?—A. It is principally the father of the protective tariff idea.

Q. You could hardly expect anything to be a parent of the protective tariff in the State of Texas?—A. You can raise almost anything down there.

Q. (By Mr. C. J. HARRIS.) Would larger powers given to the Interstate Commerce Commission, gradually extending its territory to State lines on the transportation question, do away with this objection that you have raised to the powers of the commissions of these States? To ask the question more directly, Would not giving the Interstate Commerce Commission more power do away with that feature of it?—A. I think it might to some extent; the point I want to make is this: The shipment of grain from a point in Iowa to Burlington, Iowa, is entirely a State shipment; that is quite apt to be an interstate shipment before the grain is finally disposed of; and the shipment of cotton from Fort Worth, Tex., to the city of Galveston, entirely within the State of Texas, is quite apt to be an interstate shipment, because it is not going to be used at Galveston; it will find its way to the cotton markets of New England before it gets through. A shipment of dressed meat from Kansas City, Mo., to St. Louis, Mo., is a transportation that occurs entirely within the State of Missouri, and that dressed meat may be sold to the soldiers in Cuba before it reaches its destination. The point I make is this: I think it is impossible for the Federal commission to regulate the commerce of the country properly unless it has charge and supervision of the State shipments and State railroads which may conflict with the interstate.

Q. (By Mr. KENNEDY.) Do you know that the chairman of the Texas State railroad commission stands with you on the question of pooling?—A. I know he does; I have talked with the old gentleman a good many times on that subject.

Q. (By Mr. CONGER.) You speak of this matter as an evil; have you a remedy to suggest for it?—A. The only remedy is a Federal commission of transportation, and the declaring of this traffic to be interstate, and the putting of these roads under the authority of the Federal commission, instead of having 46 or 47 States each trying to adjust the freight rates to suit its own peculiar ideas.

Q. (By Professor JOHNSON.) Do you mean to say that Congress has the power to make such a declaration?—A. I meant to say by an amendment of the Constitution of the United States Congress could have that power. But I do mean to say that Congress can not regulate what it is supposed to have power over, that is, all interstate business, while this undercurrent of State regulation exists and conflicts.

Q. (By Mr. CONGER.) Do you not think it is a matter of lack of supervision within the State as to what shall fall under interstate commerce? For instance, take a shipment of cotton from Fort Worth to Galveston; that carload shipped from Fort Worth can not pay much more under interstate commerce than any other carload which originated at Galveston, can it?—A: Take this view of the case; under the interstate-commerce act there should be no discrimination between individuals, no preferential rates, no unjust discriminations. Here is a big shipper with 1,000 carloads of freight to ship to some interstate-commerce point from Chicago; he also has 1,000 carloads of freight to ship to various stations in the State of Illinois. He uses the State business; he sells out to the highest bidder, and in that way gets a lower rate on his interstate business than he otherwise would. Now, is not that a misuse of business entirely within the State, for the purpose of getting a preferential rate on interstate business? How is a Federal commission going to right a case of that kind, unless it has charge of the State rates?

Q. He gets a lower rate within the State because he gave the railroad the interstate-commerce business?—A. You asked me a little while ago what methods were employed to get preferred rates and discriminating rates. I told you about the methods by which a shipper could defeat the purpose of the law, and this is one of them.

Q. (By Mr. KENNEDY.) Does Congress have authority to put under the control of the commission that commerce which originates in the State with the intention of going into interstate commerce?—A. My opinion is that you can never tell when a shipment moves whether it is State or interstate transportation.

Q. That is, it may go to some point entirely within the borders of the State where it originated, and there be sent out as an interstate shipment?—A. It is quite likely to.

Q. In the case of the cotton, if it was going to the cotton mills, as there are no cotton mills in the State of Texas, you would know it was going to be interstate commerce?—A. Yes; although the cotton cloth into which it is made might be shipped from place to place in the State. There is only one other point upon which you don't cross-examine me, that is railroad construction. My testimony was that I think that in case the Federal authorities were going to regulate the railroads—and I believe they are—the subject of new construction should be passed upon. I don't believe new roads should be built unless necessity is shown for it.

Q. (By Mr. C. J. HARRIS.) That at present is entirely under State charter?—A. Yes; except in one case in Indiana.

Q. (By Mr. CONGER.) I think in all the States there are provisions intended to restrict the construction of railroads?—A. I guess there are.

Testimony closed.

CHICAGO, ILL., *November 22. 1899.*

TESTIMONY OF MR. WILLIAM J. STRONG,

Attorney-at-law, Chicago, Ill.

The subcommission on transportation convened at 2 o'clock, November 22, 1889, at Chicago, Ill., Chairman Lorimer presiding. Mr. William J. Strong, being duly sworn, testified as follows:

Q. (By Representative LORIMER.) State your full name, please.—A. William J. Strong.

Q. And your business.—A. Lawyer.

Q. We have information that you have a large collection of information with reference to blacklisting. I will ask you to state in your own way what information you have on that subject?—A. In the fall of 1895 my attention was first called to this question in the case of Fred R. Ketcham against the Chicago and Northwestern Railroad Company. The suit had been brought by other attorneys, who came to me and asked me to take the case off their hands. I had never heard of it before. They did not seem to know how, and in fact they said to me that they did not know how, to get at the question; and it interested me very much. I took up the question and began to make an investigation. I was called into the trial of the Ketcham case before Judge Edmund Burke in the fall of 1895 on 3 days' notice, with no time for preparation whatever, and introduced but four witnesses. The jury disagreed, standing 6 to 6, which necessitated a new trial. After coming into the case and seeing what there was in it I began to investigate, and put an advertisement in the Chicago Evening News asking any men who thought they had been blacklisted to come to my office and make their statements to me and bring such letters as they had that they thought were evidence of this blacklisting agreement. After spending some time, without exaggeration 3 months continuously, to the neglect of every other class of business, in taking statements of men who came to my office, I made up my mind what the agreement was; and that there was such an agreement to blacklist was apparent from the evidence which was produced before me. That evidence I formulated into a charge, which I incorporated in the amended declaration in the case; and the substance of the agreement which I claim was formed between the railroads is set forth in the pleadings in the cases which I have since brought. In the month of June, 1896, I filed some 50 cases, containing this charge of blacklisting, against nearly every railroad in the city of Chicago, I believe, with one or two exceptions, some being in the hands of receivers; and I did not bring suit against them, although I charged them with being parties to the conspiracy.

There is a voluntary association of railroads having lines running into the city of Chicago, the legal title of which is the General Managers' Association of Chicago. According to their constitution, which I have had in court, and of which I have a copy here, the object of the association is " especially the consideration of problems of management arising from the operation of railroads terminating or centering in Chicago." The beginning of this combination among railroads for the purpose of blacklisting employees was over a year before the strike of 1894, according to the testimony which I have here, in my judgment; and it has been the judgment of three different courts that it was evidence of the conspiracy. It was first mooted in March, 1893, when the committee of the General Managers' Association was appointed, the committee consisting of—I have not got their names here, but they are the general managers. I left the papers in my office, but can give you the names afterwards.

Q. (By Mr. C. J. HARRIS.) I don't think it is material.—A. I have the names; they are particular names; I have them in a number of papers I did not bring, as I did not wish to bring any more than were necessary. This committee "was appointed to tabulate the rates of pay by all roads centering in Chicago, and to report on the formation and maintenance of an employment bureau for the employment of railroad employees, and to formulate a set of rules for the government of all railroad employees, so as to bring about uniformity in those respects among all the railroads running into Chicago," being 24 roads.   These railroads, according to the testimony given by the secretary and chairman of the General Managers' Association in three different cases which I have tried, are as follows: Chicago and Eastern Illinois; the Atchison, Topeka and Santa Fe; the Baltimore and Ohio; Chicago and Erie; Chicago and Grand Trunk; Chicago and Western Indiana; Chicago, Burlington and Quincy; Chicago Great Western; Chicago, Milwaukee and St. Paul; Chicago, Rock Island and Pacific; Cleveland, Cincinnati, Chicago and St. Louis; Illinois Central; Lake Shore and Michigan Southern; Louisville, New Albany and Chicago, Michigan Central; New York, Chicago and St. Louis; Pennsylvania Company; Wisconsin Central; Union Stockyard and Transit Company; Calumet and Blue Island; Belt Railway Company of Chicago; Pittsburg, Cincinnati, Chicago and St. Louis; Pittsburg, Fort Wayne and Chicago; Chicago and Northwestern Railway Company; and the Wabash Railroad Company; being 24 railroads which were members of this General Managers Association.   In March, 1893 (the exact day I have not with me), they appointed a committee, as I have said, upon these questions, and on May 18, 1893, that committee made a report to the General Managers' Association, which I compelled them to produce in court by subpœna duces tecum, and of which the following is a copy of the material parts, to show the combination: "First, with reference to the tabulation of wages, they have classified all classes of railroad employees below the rank of division superintendent and superintendent of motive power to general master mechanic. In classifying the employees it has been necessary, in order to secure uniformity, to adopt certain terms in describing a man's employment, and the committee requests the cooperation of the general managers, in so far as possible, in using these terms instead of a special term that may be used in some particular locality. It will be found that the terms recommended by the committee are synonymous with those in use, and are only introduced so as to make the wage tables on the different roads readily comparable.

Second (and this is the important part of the subject upon which I care to give any testimony), "in the matter of the establishment of an employment bureau, the subject has been discussed at great length"—(this is stated in this report)— "and it is the opinion of the committee that such a bureau would be of advantage to the association, first, in assisting them in the procurement of men both under ordinary conditions and in times of emergency; second, in assisting the roads to guard against the employment of a man who has been proved unworthy on some other road; third," (and like a great many other insects the sting is in the tail. It says) "in abolishing the state of affairs with which we are all familiar, that is expressed when a man is disciplined, by the statement that 'your road is not the only road in Chicago,' and that employment can readily be obtained on some other road, although an offense has been committed."

That second and third clauses of the report are the reasons why they think it is a good thing to establish this employment bureau. They show, in my judgment, the purpose of this organization, namely, to abolish the state of affairs with which they are all familiar, which is expressed, when a man is disciplined, by the statement that he can readily obtain employment on some other road, and that the road he has worked for is not the only road in Chicago. That shows, in my judgment, that they attempted to get together at that time and adopt some method by which a man could not readily get work on some other road. One can readily understand that if there is a difference between an employee and his immediate superior, perhaps a personal difference—perhaps a tyrannical boss might say some things to him that a spirited man would not care to take, and he would ask for his time and tell him that he didn't have to take that kind of talk from any man, that he was a good railroad man and skilled and sober, and that his was not the only railroad in Chicago and that he could readily obtain work on some other road. They say they are familiar with that sort of statement made when they discipline a man. Now what they may be pleased to call "discipline" we don't know, except as we gather it from their different statements and writings. It may be for some trivial offense; for instance, a draw-bar pulled, and they may discipline a man by fining him 5 or 10 or 30 days or something of that kind; or if he should corner a car in the switchyard, not running it in far enough, so that a train would come along and knock off the corner; or some little accident of that kind. As has been developed in the trial of these cases, these charges against the most of these men for those offenses proved to be untrue, and they fined the wrong man; and often men in the protection of their fellow-men would refuse to disclose who the culprit was, or the one that had been negligent, and they would discipline the wrong man for it. Those conditions became very onerous to the employees in many instances. There is only one way, in my judgment, in which a man, if he had any spirit, could be made to refrain from saying that he could get work on some other road. That would be for him to gain the knowledge that he could not get work on some other railroad unless his present employer gave his consent or approval. I do not see how they were going to abolish the state of affairs in which a man of spirit would say that, unless they fixed it so that he could not get work on any other railroad, and brought that to his knowledge. Having a family dependent on him, if he knows that he can not get work on some other road, he is going to submit and say nothing about it; but unless he knows that, he is bound to make that statement, if he is a man of any spirit.

That was the foundation of the conspiracy between the railroads. Previous to that time it is a matter of history that there had been in the city of Chicago, which is the greatest railroad center in the United States, strikes and lockouts. Differences had arisen between the employees and employers; the struggle for supremacy had become bitter, and these two forces were striving to gain an advantage; the railroad men formed themselves into what they call grievance committees, and, where a man was unjustly treated, requiring of the railroads that they rescind unjust rules or fines, and preparing, in case they did not do it, to strike; that is their only remedy. On the other hand, the railroads clearly, from the testimony which I have been able to produce, determined that they would adopt some method to forever stop strikes. The railroad attorneys have clearly foreshadowed this in arguments in this case. Even in the last case I tried the attorney for the Chicago and Northwestern Railroad told the jury the time would soon come when there would be no more strikes, and asked them to keep their hands off and let the railroads and the labor unions settle this between themselves.

Other testimony was offered of the proceedings of the General Managers' Association, of which I have not an exact copy here, but which showed that the formation of this bureau was for the purpose of centralizing the employment of the men in one office. Every railroad was to send the names of its employees to that office, and that office was to keep a record of every railroad employee, and whenever a man applied to one of these railroads for employment he had to go to this office and get the O. K. of the manager of this office, thus centralizing employment.

This was brought up, I think, on June or July 20, 1893, and voted upon. Thirteen out of 20 railroads present at that meeting voted for the adoption of this thing; but the rules of the association provided that whenever any scheme was proposed that required any expenditure of money, as this did, it should not take effect unless it was unanimous. Seven having voted against it, it was defeated; to be perfectly fair with the statement about what was done.

The point of that resolution is this: They state in the opening that the subject has been discussed at great length, and they follow these three provisions with a statement like this: "Your committee is opposed to any idea of blacklisting, but it insists on the right of the different roads to know the previous history of any man who presents himself for employment." The reasoning I draw from that is that they never would have put in the word "blacklisting," immediately following this, if something preceding it had not suggested the word. Their attempt to exclude from this any idea of blacklisting was the best evidence that they knew that it meant blacklisting. There was no occasion for them to say they were opposed to blacklisting unless they did know that it meant blacklisting; the French proverb, "He who excuses, accuses," applies.

The evidence that I have gathered shows that no occasion arose to put that idea of blacklisting into effect until the strike of 1894, known as the American Railway Union strike, when the different railroad employees in this city, through the American Railway Union, sought to get the railroads to interfere and use their influence with the Pullman Company to arbitrate its differences with its employees.

Much stress is laid by the railroads upon the fact that this strike was purely a sympathetic strike, and that men strike without having any grievance of their own. They claim that because it was sympathetic it was wholly unwarranted. Of course, we reply that human sympathy is one of the noblest motives that ever prompted a body of men, and that it was entirely unselfish on their part. The public records show that within ten or twelve days after the commencement of the Pullman strike there were 1,600 families in the city of Pullman who were absolutely destitute of the necessaries of life, who had been employees of the Pullman Company from five to twenty years, and who were dependent on public charity for support; showing that these families had not been able to accumulate enough out of the pittance received by the wage-earners in all the years that they were in the employment of the Pullman Company to last them 2 weeks when on strike.

The Pullman men were members of the American Railway Union; owing to their close connection with the railroad companies, the American Railway Union sought at several conferences with the general managers to get the railroads to interfere and induce the Pullman Company to adjust or arbitrate the differences. They refused to interfere, claiming they had contracts with the Pullman Company that prevented them from interfering in any way, and that they did not propose to interfere; and then the strike was declared, for the purpose of getting the railroads to do this, the purpose of the strike being wholly to prevent the handling of Pullman cars until Mr. Pullman would arbitrate with his employees. That was the purpose of the strikers as given to me in all instances. They had no idea that it would tie up the railroad traffic of this city to any extent—only for a few days, at least, until they could get some action taken to relieve these strikers in Pullman. But the strike grew to great magnitude, and a bitter feeling was engendered between the strikers and the railroads, probably more than in any strike that ever took place in the history of this country.

There was no such destruction of property, however, as the public was given to understand. The Labor Commission investigated the strike and heard the testimony of railroad men and others, and they reported from the testimony that the railroads lost in property, including the hire of 3,000 deputy marshals and other incidental expenses, a total of $685,783. That was the total cost to all the railroads, including the hire of 3,000 deputy marshals; and the Chicago fire department, investigating the amount of loss by fires, report that the total loss by fires, including cars and all merchandise and everything else burned, was $355,612.

Q. (By Mr. C. J. HARRIS.) Have you the number of cars burned?—A. I have not the report as to the number of cars burned. There was not any such considerable number as the public was led to believe, as has been developed since in the testimony of different cases, and many of these were very old cars. I have gone into that question to some extent, as the attorneys for the railroads use this in every case they try as an excuse.

Q. (By Representative LORIMER.) The report of the fire department is included in the Labor Commission's report?—A. I think not. $355,612 by fire.

Q. (By Mr. C. J. HARRIS.) That is, outside of cars?—A. Including cars, merchandise, and everything. There was some other loss by overturning cars, repairs, and so on, but the total loss to the companies was $685,783, including the hire of United States marshals and all incidental expenses.

During this struggle Mr. John Egan was selected, as proved by the general managers themselves in a case I tried, to take charge of the whole strike and to get employees for all the different railroads. It was put in the hands of one man, which was practically the adoption of the scheme of this employment bureau. It was carried out practically when it came to the strike, as recommended here.

The first case tried was the case of Fred R. Ketcham. He charged that the railroads entered into an agreement through the general managers' association that they would not employ any man who had quit the service of any of the roads during that strike or who had committed any offense or who was a member of the American Railway Union unless that employee obtained what the railroad men commonly called a clearance, which was the approval or consent of the road that he was working for at the time that the strike broke out.

He obtained work from the Chicago Great Western just before the close of the strike; having heard of the blacklist, and to test it to see whether it was so, he obtained work from the Chicago Great Western, and made one trip as freight conductor from Chicago to Dubuque, Iowa, and back. Previous to the time when he obtained this work, about July 3, 4, or 5 of that year, Mr. J. C. Stuart, the superintendent of the Galena division, came to his house, and asked him to take out a train. Mr. Stuart testified that he was one of the first men out of 75 freight conductors that he went to to take out a train, and he told him he could have any brakeman he pleased. Ketcham said his former experience in the strike of 1891, where he had taken a train into the stock yards, with a revolver in each hand, was sufficient for him, and he did not propose to take any chances. He, at that time, was not a member of the American Railway Union, but simply stayed at home, and told Mr. Stuart that he did not feel that he was under sufficient obligation to the Chicago and Northwestern Railroad Company to jeopardize his life. Whereupon Mr. Stuart threatened him that if he would not, he would be enjoined with the blanket injunction, and would be arrested; that he felt sorry for his family, and that if he did not take out the train he would find hard work getting a job from any other road.

That prompted him to go and make this application before the strike was over. He made this one trip to Dubuque and back, and on the morning of his return he was arrested by a United States marshal and taken to the United States Court and kept in custody for a week before he could give a $3,000 bond. He had sent word by his wife to the railroad company, as an excuse, that he was sick, in order to hold his position. When he went back to the Great Western he was told by the superintendent, Mr. Kelly, that they had no further use for his services. Mr. Ketcham asked why (and this testimony is corroborated by Daniel Cash and by another man by the name of Baxter) and Superintendent Kelly told him, "Because we have received word you are a Northwestern striker." He asked if his services had not been satisfactory on the run he had made, and was told yes, that he was a first-class man, and he would like to keep him. Mr. Kelly said further: "I am obliged to discharge you, if you can not get a clearance from the Chicago and Northwestern, I should be glad to restore you; but it comes from above me. You will have to go to Stuart, and he will know what to give you."

Mr. Cash, who was also an applicant for work, then submitted this letter, which I have here, to Mr. Kelly, and Mr. Kelly said that was not a clearance. This is a letter not dated at all, but the testimony was that it was given August 6, 1894, the day the strike was declared off. Ketcham had his letter at the same time. After giving the record of his employment for about 10 years it says, at the foot: "July 8th, 1894, during A. R. U. strike, left his post and was active in persuading others to do likewise. When he returned to duty his place had been filled."

Mr. Ketcham had a letter of exactly that wording, showing 10 years' service. Mr . Kelly said that was not a clearance. Then Ketcham asked him if he was bl acklisted. Mr. Kelly said: "You can call it that or anything you've a mind to. I can not put you back to work unless you bring a clearance from the Northwestern. I am sorry, but it comes from above me."

That is the substance of the testimony of Mr. Ketcham, corroborated by Mr. Cash, Mr. Baxter not being here to testify. Mr. Kelly denied that he said all that. He admitted that he said some of it, but denied that he said he was blacklisted. Mr. Ketcham then afterwards applied to two or three roads, among them the Wabash, and showed them this letter, and although they said they needed men, they said they could not employ him, and refused to employ him.

Q. (By Mr. KENNEDY.) Can you name the other roads?—A. He applied to the Wabash—he only applied to two or three roads, and he heard everybody else was having the same experience and quit. I think he applied to the C. B. & O.; that is my remembrance.

Mr. Ketcham's testimony was corroborated in every particular by Mr. Daniel Cash. Mr. Ketcham also said he got work on the drainage canal, and worked for the city of Chicago, running a steam roller, and finally got work on the Michigan Central grain elevator, at Kensington, and just before the trial was discharged from there. The pretended cause was that business was slack, but the elevator was running full time, and there was no charge made against him for incompetency as a stationary engineer; he was a very fair engineer.

J. D. Green, a former conductor on the Illinois Central Railroad, testified that he quit during the strike, and afterwards applied for work to J. B. Strong, trainmaster of the Chicago Great Western; that Strong told him he could not hire him unless he had a clearance, and asked him if he had a clearance, and he said No, but that he could show him a lot of railroad passes showing that he was a railroad man. Strong said, "We hired a man by the name of Ketcham without a clearance and we got hell for it, and had to discharge him when we found out he had been a striker. I don't care if you have had wrecks, or accidents, or have been drunk, or anything else, if you can only bring a clearance from that strike I can hire you. We don't care whether you have been careless or anything of the kind."

He was denied employment also by the Chicago & Alton and several roads to whom he never gave a chance to make formal application. They asked if he had a clearance, and he said no.

He went to the Illinois Central after several vain efforts to get work and got a letter, which I have here, written by Mr. J. W. Higgins, superintendent of terminals of the Illinois Central, dated January 16, 1896. After searching for employment for a year and a half he got him to write a letter to Mr. C. L. Nichols, superintendent of the Chicago, Rock Island and Pacific Railway, at Blue Island, Ill., which was as follows: "Mr. J. D. Green, formerly a conductor on this road for eight years, left the service and went with the Lake Street Elevated Railroad about the time it opened, and is now desirous of making a change," covering up the fact that he quit during the strike. "As there are no vacancies in our service, business being reduced, he desires to make application to you. I think you will find Mr. Green a competent train man."

He took this letter and went to Mr. W. E. Green, train master of the Alton road, whom he knew, having failed to get work from the Rock Island. He got Mr. Green, the train master of the Alton, to write a letter on it to Mr. Willis E. Gray, general superintendent of the Alton, at Bloomington, which is as follows: "I have known the bearer, Mr. J. D. Green, for the past 6 years, and can recommend him as a first-class man in every way."

He presented that letter to Mr. Gray at Bloomington and attached it to his application for work, and Mr. Gray told him that in the morning he would report to him—he would have his application investigated; said they needed men. Finally, on February 24, he received the following letter from Mr. Gray: "Answering your communication of February 17, I beg to advise that as soon as a favorable opportunity arises I will let you hear from me as to employment. At present our business is dull and we have a good many extra men." A few days before that he had said they needed men.

A few days later Mr. Gray returned the letters, saying his application was not satisfactory, and for that reason he could not employ him. He was never able to get work on any railroad. They all said they could not hire him unless he had a clearance.

J. H. Dungan, another very important witness, testified that he had been an employee of the Northern Pacific, which is outside of the General Managers' Association, and that he had sought work from a good many railroads, but had been denied; that he had obtained temporary jobs, but was discharged because his application was rejected, until, finally he got a job at Argentine, Kans., in charge of a switch engine, and worked from the fall of 1894 through the winter of 1894 and the spring of 1895, when he was discharged and told by the yard master that it was because his application was rejected. He had referred to the Northern Pacific Railroad. He then sought to be reinstated, and wrote a letter to Mr. H. U. Mudge, general superintendent of the Atchison, Topeka and Santa Fe Railroad Company, being the road he had worked for, asking why he had been discharged after working so long and giving such satisfactory services. Previous to this he had received a letter from John Z. Roraback, superintendent of the Atchison, Topeka and Santa Fe Railroad, dated at Kansas City, March 21, 1895, on the regular form of that railroad, as follows: "This is to certify that John H. Dungan has been employed in the capacity of switchman at Argentine, Kans., on the Kansas City Terminal Division, from August 23, 1894, to March 18, 1895; was discharged on account of previous record unsatisfactory; services while here were satisfactory."

He went to Topeka and pursued Mr. Mudge, who was on the move constantly, until finally he had to write to him "on the line," on March 27, 1895. This road at that time was in the hands of the United States court, and the officials of the United States court, Aldace F. Walker, John J. McCook, Joseph C. Wilson, receivers, were in charge of the road, showing that even the officers of the United States court were a party to that conspiracy. The letter was on the regular form of the company, Eastern Grand Division: "Mr. J. H. Dungan, Argentine, Kans. Dear Sir: Acknowledging receipt of yours of the 21st, I have investigated the matter and find that immediately upon your being employed letters were written to ascertain your record with the Northern Pacific. The delay is entirely due to the fact that they neglected to reply earlier to references. It is against the policy of the receivers to have any man who was mixed up with the strike; and if we intended to do so, there are certainly a large number of men who had worked for this company who should be given preference over men from other roads. In being allowed to work five months you were more fortunate than most others, and I regret to say that I do not see my way clear to do anything further for you in this case. Respectfully, H. U. Mudge, General Superintendent."

There were so many witnesses who testified to similar experiences, and who had similar letters, that I will ask leave to incorporate, as a part of my testimony, an article which I wrote on this subject and which is published in the Arena for March, 1899, containing excerpts of the testimony of other witnesses, in order to save time. It is taken from the testimony, what I consider the material parts, and contains photographs of 4 letters and the front page of what we claim is the Illinois Central blacklist. I should like to incorporate it.

BLACKLISTING: THE NEW SLAVERY.

An American jury, composed, with one exception, of employers of men, the foreman of which was an ex-banker, and not one of whom was a member of a labor union, after a trial lasting nearly three weeks, before Judge Richard Clifford, in the circuit court at Chicago, recently returned a verdict for $21,666.33 against the Chicago and Northwestern Railway Company for blacklisting one of its former employees who left its service during the American Railway Union strike of 1894. The plaintiff in the case was Fred R. Ketcham, who had been in the employ of the road as a freight conductor for a period of about ten years preceding the strike.

The principle involved in this case was much more than personal injury or vindication; it was one of human liberty. As but $1,850 actual loss was proved, the amount allowed in excess of this sum by the verdict was for exemplary damages, or "smart money"—an emphatic assertion by the jury of this view of the case.

The character of the jury emphasizes the enormity of the offense as proved and shows what a jury of American business men think of a conspiracy to deprive a citizen of his right to earn a living in his own chosen calling. People who do not know the facts shown in this case may think the verdict excessive, but had they this knowledge they would consider it too small. The issues involved are of the highest importance, not merely to organized labor, but also to the great mass of our people, as the conspiracy was one of the most infamous ever known in this country. It is to make the facts known that this article is written.

Divested of legal verbiage, the charge was that all the railroads entering Chicago had agreed and conspired to keep each other informed of the names of all their employees who belonged to the American Railway Union or who quit work during the American Railway Union strike of 1894, and that no such employees should be employed by any of these railroads without first having a release or consent (commonly called a' "clearance") from the road by which he was last employed before the strike; that the plaintiff voluntarily left the employment of the defendant during said strike and afterwards obtained employment from the Chicago Great Western Railway, but was discharged from its employment because the defendant notified the Chicago Great Western that plaintiff was one of its strikers, and because he did not have a "clearance" from the defendant; that the plaintiff had requested such "clearance," which was refused by the defendant for the malicious purpose of preventing plaintiff from securing employment in the railroad business, for which he was well qualified, and that for said reasons the plaintiff was denied employment by all the other roads, and that by reason of said conspiracy, and for no other cause or causes, the plaintiff was prevented from securing employment in his chosen occupation as a railroad man.

It is not within the scope of this article to publish all the evidence given at the trial, but facsimiles of some of the letters introduced and excerpts from the oral testimony given will show, beyond question, that the jury were justified in finding the defendant guilty.

Benjamin Thomas, chairman of the General Managers' Association, testified that his association was a voluntary association of all railroads running into Chicago; that it was organized in 1892 and supported by contributions from all the roads belonging to it; that its meetings were held in secret; that its objects and purposes were the discussion of problems of railroad management, and that while the different roads were not legally bound to adopt the acts of the General Managers' Association, they were morally bound to do so.

The first two articles of the constitution of the General Managers' Association were then offered in evidence and are as follows:

ARTICLE I. *Title.*—This association shall be called The General Managers' Association of Chicago.

ARTICLE II. *Object.*—The object of this association shall be the consideration of problems of management arising from the operation of railroads terminating or centering in Chicago.

Here is the record of the proceedings of The General Managers' Association at its meeting of May 18, 1893, then produced:

"The chair then called for the report of the committee, to which had been referred at various times (1) Tabulation of wages; (2) employment bureau; and (3) Rules for government of employees.

"Thereupon Mr. Wall, acting chairman of said committee, read the following:

"REPORT OF COMMITTEE.

"CHICAGO, ILL.. *May 18, 1893.*
"Mr. E. ST. JOHN,
    "*Chairman General Managers' Association, Chicago Ill.*

"DEAR SIR: Your committee appointed to tabulate the rates of pay paid by all roads centering in Chicago, and to report on the formation and maintenance of an employment bureau for railroad employees, and to formulate a set of rules for the government of all railroad employees, beg leave to report:

"I. With reference to tabulation of wages: They have classified all classes of railroad employees below the rank of division superintendent and superintendent of motive power, or general master mechanic. * * * In classifying the employees, it has been necessary, in order to secure uniformity, to adopt certain terms in describing a man's employment, and the committee requests the cooperation of the general managers, in so far as possible, in using these terms instead of the special term that may be used in some particular locality. It will be found that the terms recommended by the committee are synonymous with those in use, and are only introduced so as to make the wage tables of the different roads readily comparable.

"II. The matter of the establishment of an employment bureau: The subject has been discussed at great length, and it is the opinion of the committee that such a bureau would be of advantage to the association.

"First. In assisting them in the procurement of men, both under ordinary conditions, and in times of emergency.

"Second. In assisting the roads to guard against the employment of a man who has been proved unworthy on some other road.

"Third. In abolishing the state of affairs with which we are all familiar, that is expressed, when a man is disciplined, by the statement that 'your road is not the only road in Chicago,' and that 'employment can readily be obtained on some other road,' although an offense has been committed.

"Fourth. Each railroad shall designate to the manager of the bureau the name, or names, of its officer, or officers, empowered to approve applications for employment and certificates of transfer or dismissal.

"III. On the matter referred to your committee, relating to the adoption of rules for the government of all classes of railway employees, we beg to report progress."

The plaintiff, Fred R. Ketcham, testified that he quit the employment of the defendant company during the railway union strike, and remained at home, not going near any railroad during the trouble; that about July 3 of that year Superintendent J. C. Stuart came to his house and asked him to take out a train; that he refused, as he considered it dangerous; that he was not at this time a member of the American Railway Union, but afterwards joined it about July 20; that he had been in the employ of the defendant company about ten years; that upon his refusal, Stuart "threatened him with arrest, adding that he had sympathy for his family, and that if he did not take out the train he would find hard work getting a job from any other road." Having heard of the black list, he went to the Chicago Great Western Railway and secured a situation as conductor of one of its freight trains July 28, and made one trip to Dubuque, Iowa, and back, arriving home July 31, at 5; that at 7 he was arrested by a United States marshal and kept in custody several days until he could give a bond for $3,000; but was never prosecuted, no evidence being offered against him; that August 6 he went to Superintendent Stuart and asked for a clearance, and was given a letter showing how long he had been in the employ of the Chicago and North Western, but at the bottom was the following: "Left his post during American Railway Union strike and was active in persuading others to do likewise. When he returned for duty, his place was filled." On the same day he returned to the Chicago Great Western for duty and was told by Train Master J. B. Strong and Superintendent J. A. Kelly that he was discharged, Superintendent Kelly telling him that he was a good man and he would like to keep him, but could not unless he first obtained "clearance" from the North Western. When asked why he was discharged Kelly said, "Because he had heard he was a North Western striker." Ketcham then asked where he got his information, and Kelly replied, "From the one we all get it from." Ketcham then asked if he was blacklisted, and Kelly replied, "You can call it that or anything you're a mind to. I can't put you back to work unless you bring a 'clearance' from the North Western. I am sorry, but it comes from above me."

Daniel Cash, who was with Ketcham, had a letter exactly like Ketcham's, and showed his letter to Kelly. Kelly said that was not a "clearance," so Ketcham did not show his own letter. Ketcham's testimony was corroborated by Cash.

The following facts also appeared from Ketcham's testimony. After being discharged from the Chicago Great Western he applied to several other roads for employment, but was everywhere refused, and never secured railroad employment after the strike. In the autumn of 1897 he worked as stationary engineer at the Michigan Central Railroad elevator at Kensington, but was discharged about two weeks before the trial, for the alleged cause that business was slack, though the elevator was running full time, and continued to do so after his discharge just as it had been doing previously.

J. D. Green, a former conductor on the Illinois Central Railroad, testified that after the strike he applied for work to Train Master J. B. Strong of the Chicago

ison, Topeka & Santa Fé Railroad Co

ALDACE F. WALKER, JOHN J. McCOOK, JOSEPH C. WILSON, *Receivers.*

Office of General Superintendent.

EASTERN GRAND DIVISION.

E.
Superintendent.

ASE QUOTE

255

On the Line,

Middle Division, March 2

.Dungan,

Argentine, Kansas.

(Postoffice box 69)

r:

Acknowledging receipt of yours of the 21st.   1

ted the matter and find that immediately upon your

letters were written to ascertain your record with

acific; the delay is entirely due to the fact that

to reply earlier to references.   It is against t

receivers to have any man who was mixed up with the

we intended to do so, there are certainly a large n

had worked for this company who should be given pr

n from other roads.   In being allowed to work fiv

e more fortunate than most others, and I regret to s

see my way clear to do anything further for you in

ILLINOIS CENTRAL RAILROAD COMPANY.

Office of Superintendent Terminals.

Chicago, December 23rd 189

M PRESENTED:-

The bearer, Louis Burnham, was employ

ompany from 1887 to 1892 as freight brakeman and co

892 to 1894 as switchmen in Chicago and.

uring that time he was sober, steady, performed his

factorily.   Unfortunately he was influenced to leav

e, but so far as I am aware he was not actively agg

thing to hinder the transaction of this Company's b

eve he now regrets his action, and as he has been o

long time, has an invalid wife to care for, shou

to see him given employment, and feel satisfied that

his employers a valuable man.

Great Western; that Strong told him he needed men but could not hire him unless he had an Illinois Central clearance from the strike. Strong added that he had hired a man by the name of Ketcham without a clearance and had had to discharge him, and that he (Strong) "got hell for hiring Ketcham without a clearance."

About 35 other men who had quit various roads during the strike testified that they had applied to all the roads in Chicago, were told they needed men, but were denied employment because they did not have clearances. Many of these men had letters showing years of faithful service and good habits, but whenever a letter said they had "quit during the strike" they were told "that is not a 'clearance'" and were denied employment. Some were given work and required to make out written applications showing what road they had last worked for. In a few days they were discharged, and when they asked why, were told that their "applications were rejected."

Among several letters placed in evidence as corroborating this testimony was the following significant and unequivocal official declaration of the position taken by the Wabash Railroad Company:

J. H. Dungan testified that at the time of the strike he was in the employ of the Northern Pacific Railroad, and quit with the men; that after the strike he secured successively several positions, but was discharged from each in turn because his applications were rejected; that he finally obtained a situation in Argentine, Kan., on the Atchison, Topeka and Santa Fe Railroad, put in an application referring to the Northern Pacific as the last road he had worked for, worked for about five months, when he was discharged; that he wrote the superintendent, H. U. Mudge, about it and received the reply which is reproduced herewith. This letter shows that even officials of the United States court were parties to the conspiracy.

Burnham testified that after seeking work in vain for more than a year and being denied because he had no clearance, he went to J. W. Higgins, superintendent of terminals for the Illinois Central Railroad, told him his family was starving and he could not get work without a clearance, and begged Higgins to give him a clearance, whereupon Higgins gave him the letter reproduced herewith. He asked Higgins why he (Higgins) couldn't give him employment, and Higgins said, "I can't; that's all." He went to Robert Cherry, general yard master of the Nickel Plate Railroad, and asked if he needed any men. Cherry said, "Yes; I can use a man or two. Have you a clearance?" Whereupon Burnham said, "Yes," and showed him the letter above mentioned. After reading it, Cherry said, "Burnham, that's a good letter, but it is not a clearance. I can't hire you on that letter." Burnham further testified that he had traveled all over the country and had shown that letter to railroad officials who were hiring men, yet was denied employment and had never been able to secure any employment on a railroad since the strike of 1894.

All the other witnesses related similar experiences, covering nearly every railroad in the United States. Not one of the witnesses for the plaintiff had ever committed any violence or violated any law. All were shown to be sober, careful railroad operatives, and all had good letters of recommendation from their respective roads. No charge was made save that they "had quit during the American Railway Union strike."

SUPERINTENDENT MUDGE'S EXPLANATION.

Michael Driscoll, who had first-class references for twenty-five years' service as a railroad man, testified that he left the Pittsburg, Fort Wayne and Chicago Railway during the strike, and that after the strike he secured a position from the Chicago and Western Indiana Railway by telling Mr. Warner, the superintendent, that he was in New York during the strike. He was required to make out an application and gave the name of the Pittsburg, Fort Wayne and Chicago Railroad as the road he had last worked for, having had the promise of Mr. Belz, of the Fort Wayne, that he would recommend him. After working a short time he was discharged. When he asked Mr. Warner why he was discharged, he was told that the Fort Wayne objected and that "it was the Fort Wayne which kept him from working." He called on Mr. Belz, of the Fort Wayne, and asked him to write a letter to Mr. Warner in his behalf. Belz said "if he did so it would be the price of his own head."

Frank Deyer testified that he quit the Michigan Central Railroad during the strike. He subsequently obtained several positions, but was discharged from them all because his application was rejected, though his services were entirely satisfactory. Becoming discouraged in seeking work under his own name, Deyer secured several letters belonging to his brother-in-law, W. G. Cherry, who had quit the railroad business before the strike. Under the name of W. G. Cherry he obtained a position with the Chicago and Erie in January, 1896, which he has held ever since. A similar story was told by H. F. Elliot, who testified that he was working for a railroad under an assumed name.

Andrew Stader testified as follows: He did not belong to the American Railway Union nor to any other labor organization. He had been in the employ of the defendant railway four years before the strike. When the strike broke out he was off duty on a leave of absence. He was called to take out a train to Milwaukee on the night of July 6, during the height of the trouble, and promised he would go, but when his wife, who was in a delicate condition, heard he was going, she became nervous and frightened and begged him not to go. Yielding to her entreaties, he went to the foreman and told him of his wife's condition, saying that under those circumstances he could not move the train. The foreman abused him and accused him of sympathizing with the strikers. He again reported for duty on July 10, when the master mechanic, John Heath, discharged him. After the strike he again applied to the defendant for employment, but was refused. An alderman interceded for him with General Manager Whitman, who ordered an investigation. After the investigation the superintendent had him reemployed as an extra man, and he worked as such during the winter of 1894–95, but was discharged in the spring of 1895 owing to slack business. After he was discharged and paid off he asked the master mechanic for a clearance, so that he could get work on some other road, whereupon he was given the letter reproduced herewith, which speaks for itself.

This letter is the necessary "clearance," the explicit written consent of one of the conspirators, without which employment,was, by the terms of the conspiracy, denied to any worker even suspected of the temerity of joining his fellows in a demand for better conditions. It can be explained on no other hypothesis than that the master mechanic knew that Stader must have this permission before he would be given work on any other road.

Proof was made at the trial that the superintendent and the general attorney of the Chicago and Northwestern Railway Company had tried to bribe the witness Stader to leave and not testify in the case; and a pass given him by the superintendent to Green Bay, Wis.,and return, good for 30 days, was offered in evidence. Stader has since been discharged by the Chicago and Northwestern. His testimony is believed to have cost him his place.

The secretary of the General Managers' Association testified that the general manager of the defendant railway had a copy of the proceedings of the General Managers' Association, and the defendant was notified to produce this copy for inspection, an affidavit having been filed alleging that it would show the blacklisting agreement of the railroads. The defendant refused to produce the records.

Norman Ford testified that in August, 1894, he was employed as a messenger boy in the office of J. W. Higgins, superintendent of terminals of the Illinois Central Railroad, and was instructed to make 50 mimeograph copies of a list of 524 names, containing 13 sheets; that he made the same and mailed 49 copies; that a copy was sent to the officials of the Illinois Central Railroad who hired men; also that a copy, marked "Private," was sent to every railroad in Chicago, and that he addressed and mailed these.

An original of this list was introduced in evidence. Herewith will be found a photographic reproduction of the first page of the list.

Despite this damaging documentary evidence, many railroad officials, including eight general managers, sworn by the defendant, testified they had never received or sent out such a list, that they knew of no blacklisting agreement, and had never heard blacklisting discussed in the General Managers' Association.

Almost the last witness introduced by the defendant was Mr. Atwater, of Detroit, Mich., superintendent of the Chicago and Grand Trunk Railway. He was shown the Illinois Central blacklist, and asked the stereotyped question which had been asked of all the other officials: "Did you ever see a list exactly like this in all respects, except that it was not addressed to J. T. Harrahan?" He naively replied to the railroad's attorney: "Never until I saw one in your office this morning." At last such a list had been located in the hands of a railroad official not an official of the Illinois Central, and Norman Ford was corroborated.

The defendant's attorney sought to break the force of Ford's and Atwater's testimony by the side remark that he had simply "had a copy made," insinuating that the paper which Atwater had seen was simply a transcript of the list shown in court, and not one of the sheets mailed by Ford. He did not testify to this view of the facts, though challenged to do so, obviously wishing the jury to accept it as the correct one. Next day, when plaintiff wanted to show, in rebut-

CHICAGO, April 26th /..

To May Concern;—
           This is to certify
Andrew Stader, has worked for
since July, 1890 as a loco-
adic has been laid off on acc
in business Causing redu
-er has permission to obtai
providing he can obtain a
satisfactory to himself,
if his not getting work else
return to us for service when
him. Any favors shown
appreciated,
           Yours truly
               John H
                 M. M.

Illinois Central Railroad

Chicago Terminals   DIVISION

Chicago August 25th 189

e under-noted men of Transportation.   Departme

have left the service under circumstances rendering it undesirable fo
by this Company, and should they apply to you you are requested
without first conforming to General Rule No. 686

Superintendent Term

NAMES	EMPLOYMENT	REMARK
o yard.		Participating i
John	Night Yd Master,	late A.R.U. stri
, Jas.	Asst.Night Yd Master	
, I. W		
, W. C.	Switchman,	
y, I. W.		
an, M.		
tt, Thos.		
, Geo. S.		
, W. G.		
, H.		
E. M.		
R. J.		
C. B.		
n, H. E.		
ord, A. W.		
, Jas.		
ss, T. F.		
, Jas.		
, Peter		

tal, that the list introduced in court had been in the custody of the clerk, and could not have been copied, defendant's attorney admitted that the list exhibited in court was not the original of what he had shown Mr. Atwater. He then produced a blank form of Illinois Central order No. 1324, without any date, signature, or names, and said, as a side remark, that that was what he had shown Mr. Atwater. He did not testify to this, though at the time challenged to do so, but closed his case, leaving the Ford-Atwater evidence in full force.

I go into this detail here to show the effects put forth at the trial to conceal the existence of a black list, indicating a keen sense of the significance of that device, if proved to be in use.

A jury of business men, deliberating but two and a half hours, found the defendant railway guilty as charged, thus establishing as a fact the existence of the conspiracy.

The state of affairs disclosed by the above evidence is a serious one, deserving the attention of every American citizen.

I do not believe that all the directors and stockholders of the railroads countenance this crime of their general managers. It is too atrocious to be approved by any conscientious man. If all the suffering of innocent women and children caused by this conspiracy could be laid bare; if the cases of homes sold under foreclosure, of husbands separated from wives, and of strong and willing men forced to assume false names, or driven insane by this criminal deprivation of employment, could be published, such a protest would be heard from every lover of fair play in the land that these criminal officials would be driven from power by honest stockholders and directors, and officials with some instincts of humanity put in their places.

It will not do to say that most of the men who were in the strike have been taken back, for it is not true. Out of the 30,000 in Chicago who were proved to have struck, only about 31 were proved to have been reemployed. Many of these were brought from other cities to testify for the defense. Fully one-half even of these were men who returned for work before July 10, when notified by the roads to do so; hence they were really not strikers.

If the blacklist be necessary, as some of the railroad officials claim, to prevent strikes and to enforce discipline; if private corporations can not administer our railways without depriving American citizens of the liberty guaranteed by the Constitution, without starving innocent women and children because their husbands and fathers sympathized with the American Railway Union strikers and generously tried to help them, then it is high time the Government became the owner of the railroads, put the employees under civil-service rules, and secured them in their positions during good behavior.

Strikes, to be sure, inconvenience the public, and they may be mistaken sometimes; but what other remedy have laboring men when aggrieved and refused all redress? It is important that the business interests of the country should not be interrupted, but it is more important that our citizens should be free. The victims do not complain that the roads they were working for at the time they struck did not reemploy them. They admit that the roads had a right thus to refuse them. They complain that their old employers not only refused to employ them again, but vindictively pursued them, and prevented them from getting employment anywhere else. "Once a sailor, always a sailor;" once a railroad man, always a railroad man. The most skillful railroad men in the country are usually unfitted for any other work. The public are interested in having men of this class—careful, sober, and skilled—to operate our railroads.

The evil criticised can not be justified under any of the specious excuses offered. No one questions the right of a railroad to report to another road the name of a drunken or careless employee. This is not only their right but their duty, as the public is interested in having sober and careful men operate trains. But when a railroad official sends the names of such employees to other roads than his own, it must be done in good faith and for good cause. If railways combine to keep from work men who have simply struck to better their condition, violating no law, their act becomes unlawful and dangerous to public welfare. A combination of employees to vindictively injure employers in any similar fashion would be equally wrong and unlawful. Both should be condemned as un-American, without discriminating in favor of any one class as against the other. "What is sauce for the goose is sauce for the gander."

If public conscience can be aroused the people will put a stop to this iniquity and corporations will be taught to obey the law. Corporations have their place in the industrial development of the times, being at present necessary elements in our economic system; but they should be the servants and not the masters of the people.

The street-car companies have joined in a national organization. They claim the right not only to form corporations, which are combinations of capital, but also to form a national combination of such corporations; yet they, or many of them, refuse their employees permission to form a union or any combination whatever, under penalty of dismissal. During the autumn of 1897 the Chicago City Railway Company refused to allow its employees to join a union and discharged those who did join.

A railway vice-president, in discussing these questions, recently said to the writer: " The people who own this country propose to run it." Asked if by "owners" he meant the corporations and the wealthy class, he replied: " I mean those who own the property." He then repeated the above remark and gave permission to publish it over his name. I refrain from giving his name from personal considerations. The instance merely shows the sentiment of many capitalists.

Capital can not in justice insist on its right to form combinations and deny the same right to labor. A corporation can not reasonably insist on treating with its employees only as individuals, while itself joining other corporations in disciplining laborers. Either organized capital must recognize organized labor, dealing with labor organizations as entitled to recognition like organizations of capital, or the conflict between labor and capital will produce results more serious than have yet occurred. Confronted by a great organization of capital, the individual employee is helpless. If his demands are backed up by the power of an organization of his fellows, he has some chance of securing just concessions and correcting the abuses of which he complains. When the rights of both labor and capital to organize and to act in their organized capacity are recognized, mutual concessions will be made and many of the antagonisms which now occasion strikes and lockouts will be unknown.

If our workingmen are to be independent, manly citizens, and not obsequious vassals, blacklisting must be done away with. Involving conspiracy to thwart most sacred rights, it is dangerous to public welfare and contrary to the common law.[1]

The Supreme Court of the United States, at the last term, in the case of Allgeyer v. Louisiana, held that the word "liberty," as used in the fourteenth amendment to the Federal Constitution, means not merely the right to freedom from physical restraint, but also the right to pursue any livelihood or calling. If, then, a man is denied the right of contracting for his labor, he is denied the liberty guaranteed him by the Constitution.

If a man who quits the employ of another can not get work in his chosen occupation without first obtaining the consent of the man whose employ he has left, he becomes a slave. He will not dare resist any oppression his employer may see fit to impose upon him. His wages may be cut to the starvation point; he may be called upon to work extra hours; yet he dare not complain, as he knows he can not leave and get employment elsewhere. If he protests, his employer will say: " Very well, if you don't like it, you can quit." The man having a wife and children to support will bow in submission, knowing that his master has him in his power and that he can not support his family if he is defiant, as he can not get work elsewhere without the consent of his employer.

This is slavery pure and simple, yet it is without exaggeration the condition of most railroad employees in this country to-day. The blacklisting system is also being adopted in nearly all other branches of corporate employment, such as the large packing houses, street railroads, clothing manufactories, and coal mines. It is one of the growing evils of the present era of combinations and trusts, menacing the liberty of a large class of our citizens. A recent illustration shows this. In 1897 the Chicago City Railway Company, as I have mentioned, forbade their employees to join a union, and discharged such as did join. The men having freshly in mind the terrible suffering and privations of the American Railway Union men who struck out of sympathy for the oppressed employees of the Pullman Company, also knowing that winter was coming on, yielded to the tyranny of the company rather than bring misery and distress on their wives and children.

The railroads use the blacklist not only to punish those who have been discharged, but to coerce and intimidate those still in their employ.

How long will it be, if blacklisting is allowed to continue and spread, before the laboring masses of the country, having become the helpless tools of these mighty masters, will do their bidding in the exercise of the elective franchise?

---

[1] See Cooley on Torts, page 326: "Every person has a right to make use of his labor in any lawful employment on his own behalf, or to hire it out in the service of others. This is one of the first and highest of civil rights."

We shall then have a government of corporations, by corporations, and for corporations. The wage-earner who feels his little children tugging at his coat-tails for bread, will fear in voting to assert his manhood and resist oppression. Can a republic made up of such citizens long endure? Are such mere tools fit to be electors in a government of the people? These are serious questions, which must be wisely answered by American voters at the ballot box, or the answers will be blood and revolution.

Blacklisting is thus seen to be a chief agency in fostering anarchy. It destroys manhood in citizens and makes them slaves. There must be a change. The love of liberty is too deeply rooted in the hearts of Americans long to tolerate this dangerous abuse. It is peculiarly against public policy, because when men can not find work they become paupers and public charges, if not criminals.

The conspiracy proven is the most subtle device ever devised by the brains of man to subjugate and oppress labor and make it bow to the dictates of capital.

If it is held by the courts of our land to be lawful, other employers will be swift to take advantage of it, and it will be but a short time when the liberty, independence, and patriotism of the American citizen will be but a mere tradition that our children will talk about, but not understand; and labor which hewed this nation of freemen out of the wilderness, will bow its head to the dictation of corporation bosses. The mission of the United States is to enlighten and civilize the world. It is the knight errant of liberty and justice. If it fails in its mission, the world will relapse into barbarism. This question is the greatest question facing our courts to-day. On the action of our judiciary in this case depends the salvation of the Republic, the preservation of our liberty.

WILLIAM J. STRONG.

CHICAGO.

Here is a letter introduced on the trial of the case, a letter written by the Wabash Railway to one John Snider, which was proved to be written by J. B. Barnes, superintendent of motive power and machinery of the Wabash Railway. It is proved in court to be his genuine signature. I have the original here. Mr. Snider had difficulty in getting work and wrote to Mr. Barnes asking for his record, and he gives him his record here: "February 19, 1896. John Snider, 4205 Atlantic street, Chicago, Ill. Dear Sir: Replying to yours of February 14, below please find your record while with this company: Employed as fireman October 30, 1882; promoted to switch engine February 6, 1888; resumed firing April 6, 1888, account of slack business; promoted to switch engine June 2, 1888; assigned to road engine March 25, 1893; August 1, 1892, 5 days, violation of smoke ordinance; quit July 1, 1894, giving as a reason that it was not safe to run on account of mob violence; allowed to resume work July 19, 1894; discharged August 3, 1894, for being in sympathy with strikers; worked only a short time in July and August. Yours, truly, J. B. Barnes, S. M. P. & M."

He testified he was not able to get any work on any road on account of that sympathy with strikers.

Q. These letters are all originals?—A. Yes; the signatures have all been proved in court. I have not read anything except those proved in court to be genuine signatures.

Q. (By Mr. C. J. HARRIS.) What was the gist of the statute under which you proceeded?—A. It was under the common law, not under the statute.

Q. There was no statute?—A. There is a statute in the State, but I prefer to rely on the common law as being broader. That they entered into a conspiracy the object of which was to deprive any man who committed an offense, or any man who was a member of the A. R. U. or who quit work during the strike, of the right to earn a livelihood by his trade, and by the power of their combination they were enabled to prevent them from getting work at the only trade they knew. Our claim is that that conspiracy is a criminal conspiracy and punishable as a misdemeanor. Whenever the private individual has been injured or damaged as a result of a criminal conspiracy he always has an action on the case for damages, and wherever a man has been deprived of a legal right damages are presumed. That is the theory upon which we proceeded in this case. The legal questions involved are now in the Supreme Court in the case of McDonald v. The Illinois Central Railroad Company and the Chicago and Northwestern Railway Company.

Q. What was the result in the lower court?—A. The Ketcham case? $21,666.33; and that jury was a very remarkable jury in this, that 11 out of the 12 were employers and only 1 an employee. The foreman of the jury was a banker, and there was one man on the jury who had as high as 150 to 200 men in his employ; the 1 employee was an employee of the Adams Express Company, and the other

11 were employers. They deliberated only about 2 hours, and that was over the amount of the verdict—most of the time.

As I gather it from the testimony here and from the counsel of the railroads in the trial of these cases, the objection seems to be more especially against the heads of the union; any man who was a committeeman, or who acted as a vice-president, or took any part as an official of the union, seems to have incurred the especial enmity of the railroads. Now, I gather from that that the object of the railroads is to destroy the labor union by striking at the heads of the union. No labor union can exist without officers and committeemen to do its work, and if they are to be singled out and punished, men will hesitate before accepting these positions; they have got the employees of the railroad companies to-day, probably between 900,000 and 1,000,000, absolutely terrorized. I find from the evidence brought to me outside of the men who were in the strike of 1894, men who are now employed, that they do not dare even to present a grievance any more, for fear of being discharged and blacklisted; that the punishment and suffering of the men who went out during the strike—and there were over 30,000 in the city of Chicago—has been so severe that they do not dare to form another union or present a grievance; that they are burdened with extra duties, and do not dare complain. They say that the railroad men who are now employed are afraid to exercise or assert their rights.

Q. (By Mr. CONGER.) Do you think men have been blacklisted for other offenses than participation in this strike?—A. Yes.

Q. Have you any evidence?—A. I have, but I did not bring it here, because I thought you particularly wanted to hear about this strike; any offense is sufficient. The truth is that if any man has committed any offense, no other road would employ him unless he first obtained the approval or consent of the road he last worked for.

The system by which they did that, I have been unable to prove, with one exception; the Illinois Central slopped over and sent out a list, a photograph of which I have here, in which they make the direct request that the under-noted men shall not be employed without first conforming to General Rule No. 636 of the Illinois Central, which was adopted in 1891 by nearly all the railroads, I think. It was, that no man who had been discharged from one department shall be employed by any other department, without the consent of the head of the department from which he was discharged, without the approval of the general superintendent or some other officer.

They say that only applied to their own employees, but I proved by the boy who made this mimeograph copy, that he made 50 copies of it. The Illinois Central required 27 copies to give to all their own officials. I do not claim it is improper for them to send this to their own officials, but the remarkable circumstance that comes out in the trial of the case was that 27 of these copies were required to cover their own road. The men mentioned in the upper left-hand corner, which left just 23, from this boy, Norman Ford's testimony, to make the 50. Twenty-three is the exact number required to send to every other road of the General Managers' Association; there are 24 members, and leaving the Illinois Central out, there are 23. This boy did not know how many they did send out to their own officers, but the 23 left were just enough to go around, and that he mailed it to every railroad in the city of Chicago. His testimony is unsupported except by Mr. Atwater, superintendent of the Chicago and Grand Trunk Railway, of Detroit, Mich. Mr. Atwater was at that time, I think, the superintendent of the Chicago and Grand Trunk Railway, but since, I think, the Michigan Central. He was put on the stand by the defendant and this stereotyped question was asked: "Did you ever see a list exactly like this in all respects, except that it was not addressed to J. T. Harrahan?" He said, "Never until I saw one in your office this morning." You must remember he was being asked this question by the general attorney of the Chicago and Northwestern Railroad. The inquiry arose, how did that list get to Mr. Osborne's office? The list has on it a place for addressing it, 3 lines for addressing, and the question was put: "Did you ever see a list exactly like this in all respects, except that it was not addressed to J. T. Harrahan?" I asked him if he knew who it was addressed to and he said he did not remember, but he admitted it was in all respects like the one introduced in evidence and on several sheets of paper. He said that he saw that in the office of the Chicago and Northwestern Railroad Company. They tried to break the force of that testimony by saying that they had had a copy made, but they did not produce the copy, but came in the following day with 2 sheets of paper, without any signature, no dates and no names on it, and only a sheet with names the same as on the second page of the black list, and said that was what was shown to Mr. Atwater. Next day, when the plaintiff wanted to show in rebuttal that the list introduced in court had been in the custody of the clerk and could not have been copied, defendant's attorney admitted that the list exhibited in court was not the original of what he had shown Mr. Atwater, and then produced this list without date, signature, or names, and said that was what he had shown Mr. Atwater. That was the only proof we had—Mr. Atwater's testimony—to corroborate Norman Ford as to any of those lists being found in the office of another railroad.

The system by which this was done was nearly uniform. In some instances, and in fact I think in every instance after this strike was over, most required the men to sign what they called an application. This application for work contained a lot of questions about the man's previous record, especially for the last 5 years, the last road he worked for, and what division of that road. In some instances they would put a man to work pending the result of his application, or on probation as it were, until they could learn the result of the application. The testimony of the railway managers themselves was that they had a custom of writing letters of inquiry to each other whenever a man applied for work, and of answering each other; and they claim they were exonerated from liability because they told the truth. But it was remarkable that every witness who went on the stand testified that whenever an answer came back that a man was implicated in the strike or belonged to the American Railway Union his application was rejected; and whenever one of these men showed a letter to that effect his application was rejected and he was discharged, although he might be told that his services were entirely satisfactory. The man who discharged him would withhold the reason of his discharge, or would be unable to give the reason, though he would say the orders came down from above—we assume from the general managers—and no one would know what the reasons were. The communication was, in some instances, through the telephone, and one of these men heard it over the 'phone. It is very easily seen how effective it could be made, on account of its secrecy. When a man applied for work they would send a letter and get a reply, although they never signed their names, or they would telephone and the man would be discharged. They don't say they need men any more. Before these suits were commenced and before this matter had been stirred up, they wrote these letters that I have produced here, and said a great many things that they guard against now. When a man applies now they don't say they need men; they did before the matter was agitated. Now they ask a man if he has a clearance, and if he has not they tell him they can not employ him unless he gets a clearance. That was the uniform answer—"We can not employ you unless you get a clearance"—according to the evidence of the men who gave us their sworn statements in the matter. Since these things have been agitated they don't say whether they need men or not, but they say: "We will take your application and will put you to work pending the application, and if the application is approved, all right." They did hire at the close of the strike some strikers; a great many of them, in fact. It was absolutely necessary that they should, for they could not have conducted the railroad business without them. The testimony of Mr. W. G. Brimson, of the Calumet and Blue Island, was that he secured a good many of these strikers work on other railroads. I asked him if he thought it was necessary for him to use his influence in getting them work, and he said it was, and admitted the matter, and testified that in many instances in reply to inquiries made to his road about men who had struck from his road, he left out the fact they were in the strike in order to enable them to get work. He said he did that for the express purpose of helping them to get work, and practically admitted that if the fact had been known that they were in the strike they could not have obtained work. Some of them boast now about the efforts they made to secure work for the strikers on some other road. This shows that until the consent of these men was given in some form or other, by letter or something of that kind, the men could not get work. The proof of conspiracy consists of such a mass of testimony that it is impossible to detail it before this commission. I don't know how far I ought to go in stating what I believe from the disclosures of the evidence and my analysis of it and study of it. I don't care to give my opinions about it.

Q. (By Representative LORIMER.) We should be glad to have your opinion as to a remedy.—A. It seems to me that no fair-minded man could hear this evidence and have a particle of question about the truth of the charge that there is a black-listing agreement among the railroads to prevent the employment of any man who leaves a road without its consent or who violates any discipline, unless the last road he worked for gives substantially its approval or consent.

Q. (By Representative OTJEN.) And that is practiced even now?—A. Yes; at the present time, and the system is adopted for the deliberate purpose, in my judgment, of the subjugation of labor. I don't think there is any question about it. I have never been the attorney for any labor organization or any labor union, and I recognize the tyranny of labor in many respects as much as anyone. This system is, however, so iniquitous that it practically makes slaves of the men, the worst kind of slaves—it destroys their manhood, takes away their independence, and makes them afraid to assert their rights in any way, and goes to the root, in my opinion, of civil government. No man can be a proper elector in a government of the people, for the people, and by the people who is afraid to say his soul is his own or to assert his rights in any way; and it will come to that pass, if it has not already, when they will not dare to exercise the elective franchise according to their will. I phrase it in this brief, which I filed in the Supreme Court, in one sentence: "That when my right to work depends upon the will of any man, I am that man's slave." It is insidious, because it can be worked in secret. It is difficult to prove from the fact that it can be done secretly. It can be entered into tacitly, without any formal agreement. There can be a general understanding, and it is very difficult to prove because of that fact. All the railroads having acted in the same way, and having made the same statements in regard to the same thing—denying employment to men who have the best kind of letters of recommendation, and who have rendered good service for years, and against whom there has never been a charge of carelessness—requires some explanation other than the mere fact that they did not need men, because they said they did. I will call the attention of the commission especially to one letter; it is the letter of Louis Burnham, a man with whom I am very well acquainted, and who is as ideal a personality as I ever met, in appearance, habits, dress, and manner, and everything else. He is a fine-looking fellow, about 35 years of age, and of fine health and physique and a quiet gentleman. He tried for a year and 4 months to get work; he quit during the strike. Being one of the former employees of the Illinois Central, he went to Mr. Higgins and told him he could not get work without a clearance, and begged him in a very forcible way to give him a clearance so that he could get work. Mr. Higgins gave him this letter of December 23, 1895. You will notice that the letter is eloquent in the holes that have been worn in it from the handling it has received through being carried around the country. He carried it all around the country in trying to get work, and anyone familiar with the writing can see how the letter has been worn. It reads as follows:

"ILLINOIS CENTRAL RAILROAD COMPANY,
"*December 23, 1895.*

"The bearer, Louis Burnham, was employed by this company from 1887 to 1892 as a freight brakeman and conductor; from 1892 to 1894 as a switchman in the Chicago yards. During that time he was sober, steady, and performed his work satisfactorily. Unfortunately he was influenced to leave the service, but so far as I am aware he was not actively aggressive, did nothing to hinder the transaction of this company's business. I believe he now regrets his action, and as he has been out of work a long time, has an invalid wife to care for, I would be glad to see him given employment, and feel satisfied he will make his employers a valuable man.

"J. W. HIGGINS,
"*Superintendent Terminals.*"

He was never able to get work on that letter; he was told by different railroad officials that there was reading between the lines. He went to Mr. Cherry, the yardmaster of the Nickel Plate in this city, and asked him if he needed any men. Mr. Cherry said yes, and asked him if he had a clearance, and he said yes, and handed this letter to Mr. Cherry to read. Mr. Cherry read it and said, "Burnham, that is a d——d good letter, but I can not hire you because it is not a clearance." It is something very strange when the railroads will refuse a man who presents such letters as that, when they need men; and it began to excite my curiosity to know what kind of a clearance it was that they wanted. I finally ran across this letter of Mr. Andrew Stader's, which is published here (referring to page 284 of the Arena, of March, 1899). I have long since known Mr. Stader; he is as sober and trustworthy a man as I ever met in my life. I have trusted him and never found him wanting. He was a Chicago and Northwestern fireman; he was off on a leave of absence at the time the strike broke out, and they sent for him at his house on July 3 or 4—I have forgotten the exact dates, but it was the 4th, 5th, or 6th of July—to take a train to Milwaukee and to report at the roundhouse. They have a custom of sending a call for a man at his house to let him know when they want him to go out. His wife was sick and in a delicate condition at the time when the call came for her husband, and she became frightened. When he came home she told him the caller had been there and left word for him to go down to the roundhouse, and begged him not to go. However, he went down to the round-house and reported, and told the foreman of the condition of his wife and her fears, and refused to go out unless he had protection. He really sympathized with the strikers, although he was not a member of the American Railway Union. The moment he told them he would not go out the foreman got mad and told him he was a sympathizer with the strikers, and he was discharged by the foreman and by Master Mechanic Heath. He stayed out during the rest of the strike, and when the strike was over he went back and tried to get work, but was refused it. Finally, Alderman Stanwood, of the Thirteenth Ward—I think he will corrobo-rate the story—interceded with General Manager Whitman in his behalf, and got him to make an investigation of the matter. After making a satisfactory investi-gation he was allowed to go back to work in the winter of 1894 and 1895 as an extra man, but was discharged in March of 1895. He then went to Mr. Heath—that is his testimony—and asked him to give him a clearance, so he could get work on some other road. They tried to offer an excuse for this letter, saying it was only a leave of absence, and that he was not discharged, but he testified that Mr. Heath told him he was discharged, and he said it was the custom not to pay the men except on regular pay days, if they were still with the road, but that he got his pay as soon as he was let out, and at a time when it was not the regular pay day. This letter can have no possible excuse; it can not possibly be explained unless it was the understanding that he had to have it in order to get work, because he asked for a clearance so that he could get work on some other road. This is what they gave him. [Reads letter:]

CHICAGO AND NORTHWESTERN RAILWAY COMPANY,
MOTIVE POWER DEPARTMENT,
OFFICE OF THE MASTER MECHANIC, WISCONSIN DIVISION,
Chicago, April 26, 1895.

To whom it may concern:

This is to certify that the bearer, Andrew Stader, has worked for the C. & N. W. Ry. Co. since July, 1890, as a locomotive fireman. Mr. Stader has been laid off on account of depression in business causing reduction in force. He has permis-sion to obtain work elsewhere, providing he can obtain a position that is satisfac-tory to himself, but in the event of not getting work elsewhere he can return to us for service when we have work for him. Any favors shown Mr. Stader will be appreciated.

Yours, truly, JOHN HEATH, *M. M.*

(Page 284, Arena of March, 1899.)
He has permission "to obtain work elsewhere." They had discharged him and he was laid off on account of reduction in force by reason of slack business, and yet when he asked for a clearance they gave him permission to obtain work else-where. It seems to me that it is impossible to put any two constructions upon that language.

Q. (By Mr. CONGER.) Was he able to get work on that letter?—A. He tried one or two places, but they said they did not need any men, and he went down South; he had heard that they wanted men down in the Mississippi Valley. He went down there and spent one winter, and came back and went to work for the Northwest-ern Railway Company, and never had occasion to present it to any other road for employment—that is his testimony. He has, however, since obtained work from another road on that letter.

Q. Do you think these are simply exceptional cases?—A. You can appreciate the difficulty of getting hold of a letter on which a man has secured work; the moment he gives up the letter he loses his job.

Q. How many letters have you there; you have introduced some dozen, have you not?—A. Yes.

Q. How many railroad operatives were thrown out of employment during that strike?—A. About 80,000.

Q. Would you say 100 letters out of 30,000 who didn't get employment, or something like that?—A. Yes, I think more than that.

Q. How many?—A. There are over 500 sworn statements and letters corrobora-ting them. But the fact is this Ketcham suit was commenced within a few days after the strike closed, and it warned them, so that Mr. Stewart and others said: "We will quit giving letters."

Q. There is one other thing: When did you put that advertisement in the paper?—A. In the fall, a year afterwards.

Q. After the strike?—A. Yes; they were largely scattered then.

Q. And in answer to such advertisements as that you could get 400 or 500 dissatisfied, discontented men in Chicago in any line of business, I presume?—A. If that were the situation I should have discovered it very quickly. I have made these general managers admit upon the stand that these men were first-class men; they admitted it, and could not give any reason for discharging them, or for not employing them. If you had heard the cross-examination of the general managers you could have seen that there was no excuse for these discharges, on the one hand, and for the refusal to employ by the roads, on the other. Then, another thing, railroad men are very chary about giving up such letters as these. They did not know but I might be an agent of the railroad companies trying to get these letters in order to prevent them from obtaining their rights; even to this day some of them appear to be suspicious of me. It has taken very great effort on my part to get them to have sufficient confidence in me to leave these letters with me. There are hundreds of others I could not get; I could not say how many. The men have told me of other and similar experiences, but on account of the reasons I have related I could not get them to have enough confidence in me to leave their letters with me. There are so many of them that I could not have given the matter the time to take statements from all of them.

Q. You say the railroad men are not now organized into unions?—A. No.

Q. Is there not a brotherhood of railroad trainmen?—A. Yes.

Q. And conductors, for instance?—A. The engineers are organized under Mr. Arthur, who adjusts their affairs with the railroads. They did not have much difficulty here, I understand.

Q. How about the conductors?—A. I think they belong to the Brotherhood of Railroad Trainmen; they did not do anything.

Q. Brakemen and firemen?—A. They have no organization that I know of now.

Q. (By Mr. KENNEDY.) There is a very strong organization of brakemen?—A. They belong to the organized trainmen.

Q. I mean independently, as brakemen?—A. I don't know as to that.

Q. (By Professor JOHNSON.) There are something like 30,000 railway conductors—the O. R. C.?—A. Yes, that is their organization; the Brotherhood of Railroad Trainmen takes in the trainmen, brakemen, etc. The switchmen have no organization.

Q. How long since?—A. I don't think they have ever had any since this strike. I was told by men to-day—switchmen—that a grievance committee had been appointed to go to headquarters and make a complaint, but they were afraid to go for fear of the blacklist. They were switchmen employed in the Chicago yards.

Q. What is the Junior Switchmen of American?—A. I don't know of the organization. It may be there is one, but I never happened to hear of it.

Q. (By Mr. KENNEDY.) There are departments of labor and transportation employees who are not tyrannized over so much as you describe certain classes to be—conductors and engineers, for instance.—A. Of course my experience has not extended to many of the engineers. I have among the letters that have come to me a few engineers, but not many.

Q. Members of the Brotherhood?—A. Yes. Their difficulties are adjusted by Mr. Arthur, and the railroads, from all I can learn, have so much confidence in Mr. Arthur's opinion on these questions that when he tells them a certain thing has to be done they practically do it; so I understand, although in many instances, I am told by engineers, they think that Mr. Arthur keeps them from getting their rights. He manages to be a sort of compromise between the railroads and the engineers. His influence has been very strong, and he has kept down trouble, in some ways, very ingeniously.

Q. Do you think they have in the organization as many as 80 per cent of the engineers?—A. I don't know as to that. My knowledge as to that is very limited.

Q. (By Professor JOHNSON.) What class of employees have you been dealing with?—A. Switchmen and freight conductors, passenger conductors, and brakemen.

Q. (By Representative OTJEN.) Do they include any firemen?—A. Some firemen; not many; more switchmen, brakemen, and freight conductors; a few passenger men, and a limited number of switchmen. If a person is at all familiar with the situation in Chicago he must realize that the duty of a switchman is one of the most difficult and hazardous of all the branches of railroad employment. If you were acquainted with the complicated system of switches on the railroad tracks in the city of Chicago you would see how impossible it is for a man who is not skilled to do that work and do it well.

Q. (By Professor JOHNSON.) Are the firemen who have come to you members of the Brotherhood of Locomotive Firemen?—A. I don't know.

Q. (By Mr. C. J. HARRIS.) Do you consider it tyranny for a man or a corporation to require a man asking for employment to give some sort of a statement in recommendation of himself before being employed?—A. Not if it is done in good faith and for the purpose of gaining information as to a man's skill and ability.

Q Would you hire an employee of any sort unless you knew something about him, either by letter or inquiry, beforehand?—A. That is the contention of the railroads in this fight, and our reply to that is this—that they don't ask this in good faith; and when men have presented good records, showing their qualifications, skill, and sobriety, and that they have every good quality an employer should ask in giving a man employment, and exhibited their inclination to go to work, they still deny him employment because they have combined and agreed that they will terrorize and punish these men for the purpose of preventing future strikes. If they asked it in good faith, and refused employment from a good cause, such as carelessness or drunkenness, or anything that would affect the qualifications of a railroad man, that is perfectly justifiable.

Q. If a man's recommendation or testimonial of character shows that he suddenly quit without warning or notice, and left his employer and his interests without any grievance of his own, but simply on account of sympathy with some outside party, perhaps in the Philippines, we will say, is not that—— —A. There are inside parties now, are there not?

Q. Is there not a certain amount of consideration to be given such a custom on the part of the railroads?—A. The evil complained of is this: By the power of combination, which is so vast, they are able to deprive men of the means of livelihood. You and I and every citizen are interested in having men earn a living at the trades with which they are familiar; and they have the right to work at those trades. If that right is taken from them they become paupers or criminals and fill our almshouses or our penitentiaries. It is for the welfare of the State that men should find work, if they know how to work in any special branch of business, and that they should not be deprived of that work by any power or combination. Every man should have an equal opportunity to get employment at his trade with every other man, without being forestalled by a great combination which prevents him from getting work. As I said before, that is the evil complained of. Speaking of these questions you have put to me, I would say that private considerations must step aside in the government of the people for the public welfare. I don't want to make criminals of these men and half the other men in the country. If all the men in this country who have made a mistake once in their lives were to be starved to death because of that mistake, then the most of us would be skeletons. The motive that prompted these men to strike was a most unselfish and honorable motive; it was no selfish motive; it was done to help their fellow-men. If, for actions prompted purely by sympathy for those who were downtrodden and starving to such an extent that 1,600 families were dependent upon charity within 10 days from the commencement of the strike, men are to be deprived of the right and opportunity of earning their livelihood and the livelihood of their famished families, it is time we had a new charter of liberty in this country, I think.

Q. I don't see that you have answered my question. I asked you when you hired employees if you did not either demand letters, or, by personal investigation, satisfy yourself that they had a reasonably good record.—A. I think that is perfectly proper if a man does it in his individual capacity, in good faith, and for the purpose of ascertaining whether a man has the qualifications for the job he applies for.

Q. (By Representative LORIMER.) And not in conspiracy with anyone else?—A. Not in conspiracy with somebody else and for the purpose of impoverishing him. But if it is done in pursuance of a conspiracy, not in good faith for the purpose of ascertaining a man's qualifications, but for the purpose of punishing him and setting him up as an example so that others may be terrorized, then it becomes unlawful and against public policy.

Q. (By Mr. C. J. HARRIS.) Suppose the recommendation has a serious flaw in it, such as having left his employer without any notice, or carelessness, or intemperance?—A. If you will confine it to any one of those I will answer it. If he is careless or intemperate I should say he should be excluded from employment.

Q. Suppose his record shows either one or all of these facts. It is not a conspiracy if he goes to the other men in this room and fails to find employment from them. That is the fault of his record, is it not?—A. That depends. If a man is a drunken or a careless employee the public welfare again comes in and demands that he shall be excluded. Lives and property are in danger every time we get on a train, and we have a right to know that careful and safe men are employed on the railroads. Whenever a man is denied employment by reason of such a thing affecting his qualifications I think the denial is proper.   But I have no sympathy with these sentiments, covertly expressed by you and directly expressed by the railroads, that because they were not loyal in time of need they should be forever barred from work.   I have not reached the position where I believe the railroads have the right of coercing the citizens or of attempting to subjugate them.   I believe the railroads are the servants of the American people; that they are given these franchises for the purpose of serving us, and when they attempt to exercise the right of governing us the people have a right to say something about what these public servants shall do and what methods they shall adopt in regard to the employment of men.   I will answer something further in your question which is in my mind before I forget it.   A man is not under a contract to stay a moment under the form of employment.   He can leave any day.   They exercise the right of discharging men without any notice whatever.   Your question conveys the idea that if a man exercises a similar right he is blameworthy; that if these men quit without a moment's notice it is wrong.   They are simply, in so doing, exercising a right which the railroads exercise in discharging them, and they think they have the same right that the railroads exercise.   That a man leaves a railroad without giving notice does not in any way affect his qualifications as a railroad man.   I think it is not only wrong, but iniquitous.   It is destructive of the very principles upon which this Government is founded to require men to observe regulations not observed by the roads themselves and to conspire against them.   The evil complained of could not be accomplished by individual action; it can only be effected by a combination of all, and by the power of combination they are enabled to crush the individual, who has the right of an equal contest with his fellow-men instead of being confronted by the greatest combination of brains and capital that the world ever saw.

Q. Did I understand you to say the public traveler is concerned in the question whether a man is intemperate or careless or not?—A. Yes.

Q. And that it is not concerned in these strikes?—A. I did not make any such statement; I did not intend to convey that idea.

Q. Suppose a person was passing through Chicago, as I was at that time, as a passenger through to the West, and that his car was attacked by mobs with missiles, and there were burning cars all along the line.   Is not that a matter he would be as vitally interested in as in a matter of intemperance?—A. Undoubtedly the public are interested in having public travel unimpeded; but when it comes to a question of depriving 1,000,000 men in this country of their liberty or being inconvenienced one should not be weighed against the other.

Q. One more question I want to ask.   Out of the 30,000 men who struck here I understand from your testimony that a very great number are working and have been since?—A. A great many have been taken back to work since the suits were commenced and they saw what damages they were liable to for not employing them.   In fact, they are trying their best to get witnesses to go to work and give up their cases.   In many instances they come to them and ask them to go back to work, and these men have come to me and said that their families were in such distress that they had to go back to work.   I have allowed them to dismiss their cases and go back to work.

Q. (By Mr. KENNEDY.) Is it not probable that the railroad companies could not find enough employees to do their work without employing some of that large number of strikers?—A. They had to take them in order to teach the new hands.

Q. And while there may have been a small number of cases like this, they were sufficient to teach these men who were given employment their business with the railroad company?—A. Further than that, the railroad men who were taken back were taken back by the very roads they quit.   There is another consideration.   On July 10 a notice was sent out that if they did not go back to work their places would be made vacant, and a large number went back and were reemployed.   Nobody claims that a man is blacklisted because the road by which he was employed before the strike did not hire him back.   The Northwestern striker does not complain because the Northwestern does not hire him, but because other roads do not hire him for the reason that the Northwestern line will not give its approval.   They do not complain of their former employers; they lost their rank and were willing to commence as new men, or even as extra men, but they were denied that privilege and have lost their homes.   I have the names of 12 who have been driven insane; about 20 who have been separated from their wives and families and have been made tramps; some have contracted consumption; several have frozen their feet in hunting for work.   It is a harrowing tale.   That such punishment should be meted out by the railroads, owing to the power of combination, should not be possible in a country that pretends to be free.

Q. (By Mr. CONGER.) I think you started to give us your conclusions.—A. My conclusion is, and I have not a particle of doubt, that the railroad managers have determined that they will forever prevent strikes. As a means to prevent them they have adopted this method of terrorizing, and after the men are subjugated a little more they can cut wages, they can add additional hours, and the men will not dare to resist, because they have the picture of the sufferings of those men who struck once before; and in future years the million of railway employees will become obsequious serfs.

Wendell Phillips portrayed it years ago. Referring to the evils in New England manufactories, he predicted that a new slavery, far worse than that of the negro in its effects, would be developed. It is a system of encroaching on their franchises, and this is a sample of it. If it is not stopped on the railroads it will spread to others, and it threatens the liberty of the toilers of this country.

Q. We come now to the remedy.—A. I have some very radical ideas on that question. I think there is but one real remedy. There are palliatives, like the bill which Mr. Lorimer introduced in Congress. I think his bill does not cover it. I believe I wrote Mr. Lorimer, and he did not honor me with a reply. That bill was submitted to me by Mr. Michael Driscoll, who was connected with the anti-blacklisting association, and I wrote Mr. Lorimer a letter on February 8, as follows:

"Your letter of February 5, to Michael Driscoll, containing draft of your black-listing bill, has been handed me for criticism, with the request that I write to you. After a careful examination of its provisions I am satisfied that the bill as drawn is not as good as the present common law. The exceptions in lines 13, 14, and 15 give the roads a loophole to escape punishment in every case, as it is very easy to trump up some charge of doing an unlawful act on the part of the striker. Besides, it is wrong in principle, as a man ought to be punished according to law for any unlawful act he may do and not be starved to death as a punishment, and this bill gives the railroads power to starve him, if a striker, by claiming he has done something unlawful. A bill, to do any good, should also contain a provision defining what shall be received as evidence to prove the conspiracy. I could draw such a bill, but do not desire to force my views on anyone, and I should not have written you this letter had I not been requested to do so. The railroad companies could not, in my judgment, ask any greater favor than to have this bill passed in its present shape. With all due respect, I am, very truly yours,—Wm. J. Strong."

I think that bill is entirely inadequate, and I do not think it covers the question in any way, to a practical lawyer who has tried one of the cases. It gives jurisdiction to the United States courts.

In my opinion, and I have given a good deal of study, and honest study, to it, I think there is but one remedy, only one way to settle this contest between labor and capital regarding public transportation. The only way in which that contest can be settled is for the Government to take control of the railroads and put the men on a civil-service list. Under civil-service rules we shall have independent, self-respecting citizens.

Other remedies may be suggested, but the delays in courts and the corrupting of juries—which the railroads undoubtedly do, and have the machinery for doing; it is impossible to detect it—will wear these men out in their contest to secure their rights.

Q. (By Representative LORIMER.) In the absence of Government ownership have you any remedy?—A. Make it a felony, prescribing what evidence shall be necessary to prove it, and give the United States court jurisdiction; or a board of some kind.

Q. (By Mr. KENNEDY.) Meaning the Interstate Commerce Commission, as is proposed to be done? Have you any suggestion?—A. I have not considered that proposition at all. It ought to be made a felony, and the general managers or any officers who were indicted in such a combination as that ought to be sent to the penitentiary. I do not believe any remedy will stop these men short of physical violence or incarceration. I think they are men who are so heartless and lost to the duties of citizenship that they do not care for anything short of personal violence or incarceration.

Q. (By Representative LORIMER.) What is your general opinion as to the number of men who were blacklisted in Chicago; was it half or two-thirds of the men?—A. Fully half of the men who went out here. Some of them have since been taken back to work through fear of these prosecutions. It has been very expensive to the railroads to defend these suits, and the necessities of getting skilled men has forced them to take them back. The president of the Nickel Plate, formerly superintendent of the L. S. & M. S., Mr. W. H. Canniff, testified that some of the men who went out in the strike were among the best railroad men in the United States; he admitted it on cross-examination. The evidence is clear, from all of the letters I have introduced in evidence, that there was not one of these men who have commenced suit here but had the best of qualifications, habits, and everything else. I took pains to see to that before bringing the suits. There was no excuse except that some of them were committeemen or vice-presidents of a union, and, of course, if they can hit the heads of the union they can destroy the union, because the union can not act without officers.

Q. (By Mr. CONGER.) You say the bringing of suit caused the taking back of quite a number of employees?—A. I know it has; any number of cases.

Q. Has it not had an influence in deterring them from continuing the operation of this blacklist?—A. I have evidence up to within 3 months that a blacklist is still in force for the most trivial offenses—until within 3 or 4 months of this time.

Q. Do you think this system extends all over the country?—A. The evidence shows that it extends to all the principal railroads in the United States. There are some minor lines that have not adopted it, but very few. What they call "jerk-water" roads will hire almost anybody. All the principal lines in the United States adopted this.

Q. And have it in practice to-day?—A. Yes; and even down into Mexico.

Q. (By Representative LORIMER.) Have you known of employees discharged for the same reasons that these men were discharged for, finding employment after the strike under an assumed name and continuing?—A. Yes; and a very striking instance is the case of Mr. Frank A. Dryer, who testified in this Ketcham case, that he was discharged from five or six railroads, although his services were said to have been satisfactory to them, because he did not have a clearance. He finally went to his brother-in-law, a man named W. G. Cherry, who lives on the West Side. Cherry had formerly been a railroad man and quit the railroad business in 1893. He asked Cherry for his letters which he had obtained from the railroads he had worked for, and he applied to the Erie Railroad under that assumed name, the name of W. G. Cherry, and got a position at once, and had no difficulty in retaining the position until the day he testified in the Ketcham case. Immediately after his testifying in the Ketcham case—I did not bring this fact out, that he did not give his own full name. He got off the stand and got nearly out of the court room, when he was stopped by the attorney for the railroad and asked whether he was working for a railroad company now. I had taken him in his direct testimony up to January 6, 1896. I protested against his being compelled to answer the question now, and urged the attorney to withdraw the question. The court compelled him to answer the question, and he testified that he got discouraged trying to find work under his own name, and borrowed the letters of his brother-in-law, and was working for the Erie road under that name. He was discharged immediately after that, under the pretext that his work was unsatisfactory.

I interviewed Mr. Coe the very next day; he is the general superintendent of the Erie. I asked him if he did not think it remarkable that they had discovered his incompetency at just that time; how he thought that would look to a jury; did he think it would be considered genuine or due to this disclosure? He admitted it would look pretty bad, but said that this man really had been negligent. I said, "I have come here to tell you that if you do not reinstate that man I shall have to make an example of him; this is so outrageous that I shall commence suit against your road for $100,000, and shall prosecute that case in preference to any other case on my calendar." He called me up by telephone shortly afterwards, and I met the general manager and Mr. Coe at the general counsel's office, and we had a very pleasant interview. He asked me if I did not think my threat was very violent, and if I would not agree to pass the case I had against their road if they put him back to work. I said, "I have only one case against your road, and I will pass that case, and not make you the trouble of trying it until I get these other cases through." They put him back to work the next day and he is working now. Under that agreement I passed the case I had against them until I got through with the others. I have never told about this before.

Q. (By Mr. KENNEDY.) Mr. Cherry is likely to lose his position, now, after your telling the whole story?—A. I do not know; I will tell it and take my chances. I will say further, I know of probably 60 others who are working or have worked under assumed names. I can recall one, Mr. H. F. Elliott; another, Joseph O'Day; and another, Desenfants. I know probably 50 or 60 of them; a large number.

Q. (By Representative LORIMER.) It was a similar case that caused me to introduce the blacklist law. A man and his family came down from Minneapolis and lived in the street just back of where I live. My wife found, after a while, that they were in destitute circumstances, and she investigated and found that he had been employed by the railroad company and they had discharged him. They came to the house, back and forward, and the people in the neighborhood all helped the family, and finally he said to my wife, "I have a proposition made to me by a very firm friend who is a railroad man, to change my name, and he will get employment for me, and," he said, "I do not know whether to do it or not." My wife talked to me about it, and I told her that in order to keep his family from starvation—it was apparent they would starve unless the community took hold of it—he had better change his name and get his job; and he did, and got the job and had it all winter.—A. That is true. I do not think that system of blacklisting was instituted for the purpose of punishing the men in the A. R. U. strike especially, but as a warning to strikers; that the officials made up their minds that these strikes had assumed such proportions that they must make an example of these men. They employed as many new men as they could, and used them one against another. They tried to make the punishment of these men so severe that the men in their employ would not dare to strike. It is to prevent strikes and to subjugate their men that this system is adopted.

Q. (By Professor JOHNSON.) Why is it that the large brotherhoods do not proceed vigorously against this blacklisting?—A. They are afraid to; they are even afraid to subscribe money to assist in the prosecution, and do not dare to do it for people who have applied to them, because they think they are spotters and will give them away to the railroads.

Q. (By Mr. CONGER.) Do you care to say who has borne the expense of these prosecutions?—A. It has been raised by different labor unions subscribing different amounts for writing up testimony, and most were brought without costs, and I have borne my own expenses. I have not even had enough to pay for writing up the testimony; it has cost me 2 or 8 hundred dollars.

Q. You brought Mr. Ketcham's suit on a contingent fee?—A. They are all brought on a contingent fee.

I have said to the railroads that if they would stop this I should be very glad to dismiss these cases and leave it to any man to say what fee I should have and settle all for less than it would cost them to fight the cases, and I have done everything I could. They say, practically, that they can not admit the thing exists, although in the supreme court of this State the attorneys claim they have the right to do just this thing; that they had a right to absolutely preclude any man who struck from getting work without the consent of his last employer. They say they are justified in not hiring at all, consent or no consent. They take the position that whenever a man strikes they have a right to combine to prevent him getting work, because he is not loyal. To my mind that is an assertion of sovereignty; that they shall be the judge, and nobody has a right to interfere. It is an assumption of power that I think no corporation should have in this country. They admit the men have a right to quit, and are not violating any contract or any law when they do quit.

Testimony closed.

CHICAGO, ILL., *November 22, 1899.*

TESTIMONY OF MR. F. J. O'ROURKE,

Switchman, Chicago, Ill.

The subcommission on transportation being in session on the afternoon of November 22, 1899, Representative Lorimer presiding, Mr. F. J. O'Rourke, being duly sworn, testified as follows:

Q. (By Representative LORIMER.) Please state your name.—A. F. J. O'Rourke.

Q. And your post-office address.—A. 5254 South Halstead street, Chicago.

Q. What is your business?—A. Switchman.

Q. (By Mr. KENNEDY.) Are you working as a switchman at the present time?— A. Not for the past 60 days.

Q. Will you give the name of your union?—A. Switchmen's Union of North America, No. 36.

Q. What is the membership of that lodge?—A. It is possibly 65, but I will not state positively; somewhere between 65 and 70.

Q. Have you several other local unions in Chicago?—A. Yes; 3 or 4 besides ours.

Q. (By Mr. C. J. HARRIS.) How long have you been railroading?—A. In train service since 1877, and served as an apprentice in the machine shop before that.

Q. (By Mr. CONGER.) State your experience in railroading, if you will.—A. I think the situation between the employee and employer in railroad service at the present time is this: There are 1,000,000 men engaged in operating 186,000 miles of American railroad, in which is invested one-fifth of all the invested capital in the United States. That great number should justify any one of these men in speaking upon subjects which concern their general welfare. We have had notice that an investigation is being made before the Industrial Commission. As we have been able to get at it through the press, very little attention has been given to the effect of rate raising or rate reduction upon the employees. I am thoroughly convinced from my point of observation and experience in railway service that it would be for the happier existence of railroad labor if a closer association between the employer and employee could be had, and a more complete organized union among railroad men. I am firmly convinced that all the forces which are calculated to separate them and cause antagonism between them, and hostile feelings, are wrong, and I believe those who in every way encourage it are the foes of labor. The railroad presents itself to me as being an honorable business, and should have encouragement in the means of transportation; but rate wars and rate reductions, which our present system of laws seems to encourage, place these mighty forces in opposition to each other, and consequently bring about a great deal of profitless service. I am satisfied that where labor is engaged in profitless service it diminishes the earning power of the employee. I believe that each day's labor must result in profits to the laborer and to his employer or destruction will overcome the purchaser of labor. I see our great lines paralleling each other, and employees performing service for much less than it is worth. We have some of the weak lines accepting business at figures that they can not possibly afford if they pay their employees living wages. I find big lines that prefer to move the crops from different localities at a loss rather than allow their equipment to remain idle, thus putting into effect a system under which labor is compelled to perform a profitless service; and organized labor has always been opposed to the performance of profitless service. I am free in the belief that there is a community of interest between the employer and employee, and that there should be a community of feeling. I don't know that I have any suggestions to make as to remedial legislation, but I am well satisfied of the fact in the present disorganized condition in tariff and rate wars that the earning capacity of my class of people is threatened, and if there is lacking community of feeling it is from causes which have no rightful existence.

Q. (By Representative LORIMER.) What is the remedy?—A. Men of my class are not capable of suggesting a remedy, I believe. While my associates and myself do not agree in these matters on all points, yet they have agreed with me on this one point: That railway organized labor, which is now stronger than it was ever before known to be in the history of the unions, can not possibly withhold from their employers that which they ask for themselves—the right to organize for the purpose of protecting earnings. In all rate wars, wherein lines parallel each other, they move freight at a loss, and labor is caused to be an unwilling participant in these wars. Whatever legislation would have a tendency to put a stop to irregular rates or would have a tendency to strengthen the earning power and capacity of the company would be beneficial to the man who works for it; that is the way we all feel.

Q. (By Mr. CONGER.) Is it your experience and observation that the stronger railway corporations are the better wages they pay. In other words, that the stronger ones pay better wages than the weaker?—A. The most prosperous corporation is the most agreeable one and most profitable one to work for.

Q. Your idea, then, is, if the railroads were willing to cooperate, that if pooling were legalized to the end that the roads might earn more money, organized labor would be able to secure better pay for the employees?—A. The stability of rates is essential to the general welfare of the community at large, and is of great importance to the men who perform the services.

Q. (By Professor JOHNSON.) Do you know how many local unions there are among the switchmen?—A. 158.

Q. Do you know what the membership of the Switchmen's Union is?—A. I could only give it from an impression, although I have good reason to believe that, as a lodge, we have about 7,000 members.

Q. Has the union been growing during the past 5 years?—A. Wonderfully.

Q. You reorganized in 1894 after the strike?—A. Yes; and we retained men who are connected with us now; we retained the old membership to a large extent—the old association—and have kept it alive.

Q. So it was kept in existence?—A. Yes.

Q. You have indigent relief—indigence insurance features have you?—A. Yes; that is one of the prime objects of the organization.

Q. I suppose the Switchmen's Union of America generally, as a union, has the insurance feature?—A. We have arranged with an insurance company outside of our organization, and they do all of our insurance business; have all of our members in their insurance.

Q. You differ from other railroad organizations in this respect?—A. Yes; we have completed an organization which we hope will be prosperous and not perish.

Q. When did you make this arrangement with the outside insurance company?— A. It has been completed now about 3 months.

Q. What company is that?—A. The Imperial Mystic Legion is the name of it; it is an insurance company doing business under the laws of the State of Nebraska.

Q. Is it something that has been in business for some time?—A. I am led to believe so.

Q. It is not a part of your union?—A. No.

Q. You have local relief in your local unions, have you not?—A. Yes; sick benefits.

Q. Is that in accordance with a regular system, or does it differ in different local unions?—A. The local union itself arranges that according to its own ideas.

Q. A man who is sick receives from the local union a definite, stipulated amount?—A. Yes; in case of death or injury we pay a stipulated sum.

Q. When was your last annual report?—A. Our last annual report was about— I can not give you the date, but it was some time in last May.

Q. You can get a copy of it for us, I suppose?—A. Write to J. E. Tipton, of Kansas City. Mo.

Q. (By Mr. C. J. HARRIS.) You say that the organization of railway employees is as great now as it ever was in the history of railroads; I understood you to make that statement?—A. I did; yes.

Q. (By Mr. CONGER.) Do you think as large a proportion of the employees of the railroads who live in Chicago are organized now as were organized previous to the strike here in 1894?—A. Not in these local unions; no; I don't.

Q. You are speaking, then, of the whole country?—A. I am speaking of the United States at large.

Q. (By Professor JOHNSON.) Would you count in the American Railway Union as one of the organizations?—A. I am taking them into consideration when I speak; yes.

Q. When they were in existence there were more men in railway unions than there are since they are disrupted, were there not?—A. You may be in possession of statistics and I am not; but my idea is that we have to-day more men in active service, that are members of the various unions, than there ever were before. You must remember, if you will permit me, that I should feel safe in saying that one-third of the members of the American Railway Union at that time were not in active service when they were members; it was not necessary to be in active service to be a member of that union, so that a great many of the members of that union were not in active service.

Q. (By Representative LORIMER.) What was the reason for their inactivity; why were the members not in service?—A. Scarcity of opportunity; slack business. You must remember that in the last of 1893 and the first of 1894 there was great business depression, and very little business was done.

Q. (By Professor JOHNSON.) Do you include shop men in your list; do you have all the railway service?—A. I do.

Q. They constitute a considerable per cent of the membership of the American Railway Union, don't they?—A. I think so; especially here in this immediate locality.

Q. (By Mr. CONGER.) You say you are a member of the Switchmen's Union now?—A. Yes.

Q. But you are not employed in railroading?—A. Not at the present time; no.

Q. How long since you have been?—A. Two months.

Q. What is your present business?—A. I am in business for myself.

Q. Merchandising?—A. Manufacturing.

Q. And what were you engaged in previous to 2 months ago?—A. Switchman.

Q. How long have you been engaged as a switchman?—A. I have never really been out of the business or service in the transportation department in some capacity for, say, 20 years; that is, sometimes as conductor. as brakeman, sometimes as switchman and yardmaster, yard clerk; whatever I found I could do.

Q. Were you employed in railroading at the time of the strike here?—A. No; I was sick in bed.

Q. You don't know from experience anything about this matter of blacklisting upon which we have just taken some testimony?—A. I have never felt its effects.

Q. Do you know of your own knowledge that such a system was in existence or operation?—A. I don't know that I use the word "blacklisting" as you people do. I really don't know; I know there is in effect a very well-perfected system of looking up a man's record and his character before he will be employed; whether that is blacklisting or not, it is true there is a dispute in different minds.

Q. (By Representative LORIMER.) What would you term blacklisting; what is your definition of the word "blacklist"?—A. The way I have always looked at the word "blacklist" with the railroads has been that if a man's name had been published with the different railroad lines, and he was looked upon as an objectionable character and a man they did not wish to employ, I should consider that a blacklist. A man who has his record with some other railroad showing that he has not been kept by a certain line and showing that they don't consider him worthy of employment, is blacklisted.

Q. If the information came to them otherwise than on a published list, came to them in any way, that he had been employed by a corporation and they wished no other incorporation to employ him, should you consider that a blacklist?—A. Yes; when I said published, I meant the circulation or distribution of his name.

Q. In any way?—A. Yes; that is what I meant; I didn't mean as published in the shops, anything of that kind; I meant general distribution and circulation. I should consider that blacklisting.

Q. Do you think there is such a system of blacklisting in vogue now by the railroads?—A. Yes.

Q. As this plan outlined?—A. Yes. I am satisfied of that.

Q. Do you think it is a serious complaint? Do you think it works against the laboring man?—A. No; I don't.

Q. (By Professor JOHNSON.) Why not? What is the reason for your answer?—A. I believe our present system for securing employment has a tendency to place a premium on good character and good conduct and good service, and has a tendency to shut out the fellow who is not worthy of employment.

Q. (By Mr. CONGER.) Don't you think it opens the door for railroad officials who might have a grievance against a man to shut him out of employment on any other road?—A. In that case it undoubtedly would.

Q. In that way it would be an evil system, would it not?—A. In an individual case it might. I am talking now of the general army of railroad employees in the United States. I know the situation here in Chicago has been more disagreeable than exists in any other portion of the United States.

Q. Do you think the majority of the railroad employees take the same view of the system that you do? Do you know whether a great majority do or do not condemn it?—A. That I could not say. Those among my surrounding associates, I feel sure, fully agree with the statement that I have made to you.

Q. (By Representative LORIMER.) If the union you belong to had a grievance against any railroad company and for any reason went out on a strike, and you went out in the strike with your fellow-workmen, do you believe that the railroad company that employed you would have a right to send notices to other railroad companies that you ought not to be employed because you went out on the strike? Would you believe that meritorious as a policy?—A. I have undoubtedly failed to make my statement clear; I am one of those who hope that the time has come when there will be no such thing as a strike. The men we associate with are applying for industrial peace. We believe that there is a means by which these disturbances can be avoided. I believe that in all the difficulties that take place between employers and employees, some one has to bear the expense, and in ninety-nine cases out of a hundred labor has been the one that has stood the brunt.

Q. Have you any well-developed scheme to prevent strikes?—A. I have in my own way; yes.

Q. How would you prevent them?—A. Closer association, better understanding, more harmonious dealings between employer and employee.

Q. But that is general; you have nothing specific?—A. No.

Q. (By Professor JOHNSON.) I should like to ask you whether you and other men who were not connected with the great strike of 1894 are rather more than willing that the employees who were then engaged should be kept out of the railway labor market?—A. I am free to say to you that it stands according to my mind that in the growth of the organized railway labor to-day no shelter is being given to the agitator; just to what extent the organizations may be moved along that line I don't know, and I don't care, particularly.

Q. It is a fact, is it not, that by shutting out a considerable number of men who are qualified for service the rest of the men have a chance for a better labor market; they don't have so much competition?—A. I can assure you this much, that the Switchmen's Union of North America are to-day demanding that the men in making application for membership must show as good a character as any railway company has ever asked of any man.

Q. Perhaps I don't make my question clear; I want to know whether you men who were not in the strike don't think you can get better wages by shutting out from employment those who were in the strike?—A. I don't think that question has ever been given out among the organized railway employees; I don't think it has; I have never heard of it.

Q. (By Representative LORIMER.) When a switchman submits his application for membership to your union, and you find out that he was in the strike of 1894, is he excluded from membership?—A. Well, in the majority of cases he is; but I would like to qualify that statement further by saying that we have no place in our organization for what is termed a professional agitator.

Q. (By Mr. CONGER.) Do you class every man who took part in that strike as an agitator?—A. I don't; no.

Q. But yet you do say that in the majority of cases where applications come from men who were engaged in that strike they are refused admission to your union?—A. If they were engaged, yes; but I want to qualify my statement: If they can prove to our satisfaction that they are not fomenters of strife or trouble or difficulties, and did not help to lead their coworkers into that difficulty at that time, in a majority of cases we admit them into our union.

Q. (By Representative LORIMER.) Is that a condition of the majority of the switchmen of this country, that they are agitators or fomenters of strikes?—A. No.

Q. (By Mr. CONGER.) Do your local unions all over the country follow this same rule?—A. As to that I could not say; I don't know what they do; it is what we do here in Chicago.

Q. (By Mr. KENNEDY.) Don't people who denounce organized labor look upon every one connected with it as a professional agitator in the way you speak about?—A. A great many look upon them in a false light, but we are trying to overcome that.

Q. Do you believe there were 100 persons connected with that strike in 1894 who were what you would call professional agitators?—A. I don't know; there may have been that number.

Q. You don't believe there were any more than that, do you?—A. No.

Q. Didn't more than 90 per cent of the switchmen of Chicago go out in the strike at that time?—A. I think I should be safe in saying that there were fully that many.

Q. What per cent of the men who were in that strike of 1894 are members of your union now?—A. A great number. The exact percentage I can not give you; but a great number of the switchmen who were identified with the 1894 strike in Chicago are at work in Chicago, and they are members of the organization, and they are men who are not classified as agitators.

Q. (By Representative LORIMER.) About what per cent of them?—A. I think two-thirds of them are at work.

Q. Two-thirds of the men who are working now, employed as switchmen, are members of the switchmen's organization in Chicago?—A. No, I don't understand that by your question at all; I understood by your question that you asked how many men who were in the trouble of 1894 at the present time are switchmen.

Q. Members of your organization then?—A. That I can not tell you just now.

Q. (By Mr. C. J. HARRIS.) The switchmen here, or members of your organization, or local lodges in Chicago, only organized a few months ago you say?—A. Yes.

Q. (By Mr. KENNEDY.) Do you believe the officers or members of the A. R. U. are professional agitators?—A. A great number of them.

Q. A great number?—A. Yes; especially here in Chicago.

Q. Would you say all of them?—A. No, I would not.

Q. (By Professor JOHNSON.) Were any of your local unions participants in the strike of 1894?—A. Do you mean the local lodge of switchmen in Chicago?

Q. You say you have about 65 members in your lodge; were any of these among the strikers in 1894?—A. Yes, quite a number of them.

Q. They were not debarred from membership?—A. No.

Q. Why not?—A. Because they are decent, respectable fellows.

Q. (By Representative LORIMER.) What per cent of your present lodge were among the strikers in 1894?—A. I could only answer that in the way of general belief; it would be stated on the books, but I have never made an active investigation of the matter. As I have it from those I am personally acquainted with, I judge, say one-fourth of them.

Q. (By Mr. CONGER.) And three-fourths were not?—A. Whether it amounts to more or not, I don't know; I have not investigated the case.

Q. (By Mr. KENNEDY.) What line is your lodge on; are you on any particular line, or on several lines?—A. No; we have members from different railroads.

Q. And you say you have about 60 in your lodge, and there are four or five others that you don't know the membership of—other lodges as large as yours?—A. I understand they are doing very nicely; yes.

Q. What would you say is the entire number?—A. I could not give you any idea; I know they have no heavy lodges.

Q. The others are as good as yours?—A. I do not know that; I could not say.

Q. What per cent of the switchmen in Chicago organized with your local unions here?—A. I don't believe we have a quarter of them.

Q. Are the others unorganized?—A. I know many of them are members of other organizations. A great many are members of the conductors' organizations and a great many are members of the trainmen's organizations.

Q. While they are switchmen?—A. Yes; members of the conductors' organization who did not have employment, and who came to Chicago and got employment in the yards as switchmen.

Q. Do you know how many switchmen there are in Chicago, approximately?— A. I never figured out; never asked; I judge between 900 and 1,000.

Q. And if there are five local unions, and if each had a membership of 65, you would have, approximately, 325 in the switchmen's unions, as against between 900 and 1,000 in employment in that line of work?—A. Yes.

Q. (By Mr. CONGER.) What is the attitude of the railroads toward your unions at the present time?—A. So far as I have discovered it is very friendly.

Q. Has your union or any of the local unions, so far as you know, gone to the railroad officials with grievances?—A. No; we have had no grievances up to this time.

Q. Have you had occasion to ask for better wages or better conditions, or anything of that sort?—A. Here, in the city of Chicago?

Q. Yes.—A. No.

Q. Are the wages entirely satisfactory?—A. They are.

Q. (By Mr. KENNEDY.) What are the wages?—A. They are 25 cents an hour for what they call plain switching during the day and for helping, and 27 cents at night.

Q. (By Mr. C. J. HARRIS.) That would be about what per day?—A. A great many railroads are working their men 12 hours, and some 11, and some as low as 10, and some work 15 and 16.

Q. (By Mr. KENNEDY.) Don't you think, if you take into consideration the great railroad system here in and about the city and approaching the city, that you have put the number of switchmen here rather low when you say 1,000?—A. Well, when I stated that I said I really didn't know; never had given it very much attention, and never had figured it out. I am just making an estimate as to what I judge it is.

Q. (By Representative LORIMER.) Has there been any complaint in Chicago among the railroad men for the past 5 years about wages?—A. Not that I have heard about; no.

Q. There has been no grievance as to wages since the A. R. U. strike, or for quite a while before, has there, in Chicago?—A. No; not that I know of.

Q. (By Mr. CONGER.) How do wages compare now with 2, or 3, or 4 years ago?—A. Same.

Q. No change either up or down?—A. No.

Q. (By Mr. KENNEDY.) Good times; ever any increase?—A. Gradual increase; yes; that is, a great many more men employed than there have been, and they are working more hours; that is the only increase. There are more men employed on the railroads now in America than has ever been known in the history of the railroad world; we have had good crops and have needed men and equipment to handle them.

Q. (By Mr. CONGER.) You testify that the switchmen work from 10 to 16 hours?—A. Yes.

Q. Did they work that number of hours 2, or 3, or 4 years ago?—A. If the business demanded it, they did; but business at that time did not demand it. Now the lines are more pushed with work.

Q. (By Mr. C. J. HARRIS.) Do your men prefer these long hours, or would they like to have a 10-hour limit?—A. Some prefer to go on with the long hours and make more, and others would rather have less and work only 10 or 11 hours, as it gives them more time to knock around for recreation.

Q. There is no complaint about the long hours?—A. No. If there was they might change to shorter runs.

Q. (By Representative LORIMER.) When a man makes application for admittance to your union, if you find that he is an industrious and sober man, and if you also find that he was on the strike, do you refuse him admission to your organization?—A. According to my understanding, no.

Q. (By Mr. CONGER.) I understood you to testify a short time ago that men are frequently refused admission.—A. I mean men of good, honest character, men of sobriety, and heads of families; they have a general interest in the welfare of the world at large and of the community, and are not agitators, and are not refused admittance.

Q. (By Representative LORIMER.) You said 50 per cent of those applying were refused, which would indicate that 50 per cent—— —A. (Witness.) I don't believe I made that statement, that 50 per cent of the men applying for membership were refused admission.

Q. Then you misunderstood my question.—A. I certainly did, then. If I made the statement that 50 per cent of the men who were engaged in the strike of 1894 were refused admission because they were agitators, then I did not understand the question.

Testimony closed.

CHICAGO, ILL., *November 23, 1899.*

TESTIMONY OF MR. GEORGE F. STONE,
Secretary of the Chicago Board of Trade.

The subcommission on transportation met at 11.20 a. m., November 23, 1899, in Chicago, Representative Lorimer presiding. Mr. George F. Stone was introduced as a witness, and, being duly sworn, testified concerning transportation as follows:

Q. (By Representative LORIMER.) Will you state your name in full?—A. George F. Stone.

Q. Your business and official connection?—A. Secretary of the Chicago Board of Trade.

Q. Will you, in your own way, present to the Commission what you have in mind?—A. I had in mind—it was suggested in some way, perhaps because it was a subject that I had thought of a little more than I had on a good many others— the subject of pooling. In order to save time, I have prepared a paper on the subject, which I thought would be more satisfactory than to depend on interrogatories and perhaps ill-considered replies to them. (Reading:)

Commerce consists in the exchange of commodities, generally of that which one has in superabundance for that which one needs or wishes and which is possessed by another in superabundance; or in the exchange of commodities for money, measured by the value placed upon such commodities by the possessor and agreed to as a proper valuation by the one who wishes to exchange his money for such commodities.

In either case, transportation is generally and almost without exception involved, and constitutes an important if not a preeminent factor in commerce. On the one side, transportation lines representing immense interests of a varied and important character are charged with the administration of a railway system in this country stretching, with numerous connecting lines, between the two oceans; and on the other side, an active, ambitious, and restless mercantile life, properly and legitimately sustained and promoted under the inspiration of an ambitious American citizenship.

The importance of the subject of transportation to the varied industries of the country can scarcely be exaggerated. The people of this country determined in 1887 by act of Congress that there must be a governmental supervision of railroads; that the enormous railway system of this country must not be wholly controlled by the railroads themselves; that so vast a system directly related to the welfare of the people—a people working under the inspiration of citizenship in this Republic for individual and general commercial progress and greatness— must not be absolutely dominated by those who are directly interested in its management. Wisely they thus determined, and the law stands to-day, though against it have been arrayed railroad denunciation and insidious efforts of lobbyists and legislators. It has had too often but a reluctant compliance with its mandates, and in many instances it has met with a studied and skillful evasion of its requirements.

The doctrine is unmistakably laid down that contracts, agreements, or combinations for the pooling of freights are opposed to the public welfare. In order that we may have a proper appreciation of this—one of the chief provisions of the interstate-commerce law—and of the magnitude of the evils which were sought to be removed and which led to the enactment of the pooling clause, let us look briefly at some of the conditions of transportation immediately preceding the enactment of the law.

There was great activity in railroad construction following the war, and many abuses consequent upon such activity led to the inauguration of what is known as the "Granger movement." The supporters of this movement rapidly acquired great influence, and controlled the legislatures of Illinois, Wisconsin, Iowa, and Minnesota.

Then arose in most threatening proportions an evil which became characteristic of that period, and became one of the most outrageous abuses of railway management. This movement was developed in the Eastern States. "It is doubtful whether any contrivance ever threatened to subvert long-established principles of the common law more completely than this." In a short time the baneful influences of this iniquity, extending over the whole country, exacted an enormous tribute from its commerce, exasperated merchants, exhausted heir patience, and wellnigh paralyzed every form of industry. The proposition to establish pooling is not by any means new, and we are, therefore, not left in doubt as to its effects upon the business interests of the country.

The first prominent pool was the Chicago-Omaha which was formed in 1870 and was found in its operation immensely profitable to railroads, so that in the year 1887 practically all competitive traffic was pooled. During those years business suffered, localities and shippers were discriminated against, secret rebates to a greater extent than ever before or since were granted. Discrimination in favor of industries in which some of the parties to the pool were financially interested placed other industries under great and sometimes fatal disadvantages. One of the most mischievous and demoralizing pools that were established about this time was the Southwestern Railway Association, a vampire which for a decade sucked the lifeblood of the commerce of the Missouri Valley. The Southwestern Railway Association solved the problem of how to get rid of competition and to rob the people within the letter of the law. Kansas City built a line to the South and thought she had a line that could be used to fight this pool. It had not been in operation a year before this association with subsidies had it bound hand and foot. Another outlet to the East via Omaha and Council Bluffs was also shut up, leaving the Missouri River country absolutely at the mercy of the pooling lines.

Such instances might be multiplied, but sufficient is shown to indicate the nature of railway pools; they are in restraint of trade; they prevent competition; they are monopolistic in purpose and effect; they are odious in law; they are subversive of the very interests which railways were created to conserve, viz: the general welfare, in so far as that welfare relates to the functions and obligations of a common carrier.

The law itself was largely the result of such evils which grew out of pooling. These pooling arrangements, although ostensibly for the equalization of traffic compensation, for the encouragement of feeble lines, and opposed to any unfair and unjust proportion of remuneration received by great and controlling trunk lines, degenerated into a reckless and unscrupulous abandonment of the terms of such agreement, creating confusion, distrust, an unsettling of freight rates, antagonism, and a general warfare, resulting in disaster to many of the parties to the pools, as well as to business interests generally. It is now proposed not only to cease to forbid pooling, but actually to install it in the body of the law itself. This is a high-handed proposition, and attacks the very citadel of the law, contemplating practically its overthrow. It would infect the law with a ruinous infirmity.

The United States court of appeals, in condemnation of pooling contracts, says; "The contract removes every incentive to the company to offer the public proper facilities, for there is no inducement for a railroad to furnish good service or carry at reasonable rates, when it receives as much, or more, for poor service as it would for good service and an energetic struggle for business.

President Roberts of the Pennsylvania system, at one time testified: "That under the pool there is no incentive to improve equipment and service. We get our percentage anyway. The pool suppresses activity and development." It is only proper to say that I believe President Roberts has changed his views, but I quote them notwithstanding, as I believe them sound. I do not wish to misrepresent anyone.

The New York court of appeals, in deciding against a pool of canal boats, said: "Indeed, the consequence of such a state of things would be that freighters and passengers would be ill-served just in proportion that carriers would be well paid."

The Hon. Charles A. Prouty, of the Interstate Commerce Commission, says: "The common law declares a pooling contract illegal, as against public policy; and, while there is current both in and out of Congress a good deal of nonsense upon the subject of trusts and monopolies, it is pretty generally conceded that the monopoly of a necessity should be guarded against. In this regard, I think it may be said that there are few, if any, combinations of capital which present a better opportunity for the abuse of combination than railway pooling." Again, "A transportation trust is the most dangerous of all trusts, because it absolutely dominates the situation."

It is claimed that the reduction in freight rates which has taken place during the last 25 years was accomplished by the railroads. The railroads never voluntarily reduced a rate. The forces of competition reduced rates and compelled railroads to conform to those trade conditions which all industries must recognize, if the common prosperity is to be secured and the turbulent and disintegrating effects of monopoly averted.

I warn you, gentlemen, against this concentration of power under the protection of the Government, by corporations organized for the common welfare, and I warn you in the name of the great valley of the Mississippi. The forces of competition can not be stayed; they are as irresistible as the procession of the seasons; they will break down every barrier erected in their path; they will destroy those who oppose their unhindered and beneficent sway; they will shatter all legislation that disputes their proper influence in fixing rates for the transportation of persons and property.

Competition! Under its inspiring and enlightening influence, a mighty force is imparted to human activity; it touches with its quickening power every industry and stimulates every energy of man; it arouses every capacity to increased skill and to higher and larger exercise; it studies and solves the problems presented by experience and education; it gives us products of finest quality at minimum cost; it increases luxuries and multiplies industrial facilities, reduces cost of travel and transportation, and places our products in the markets of the world without curtailing the requirements of civilized labor; it constructs a vast lake marine which astonishes the world; it spans great rivers or finds a safe and commodious way beneath their depths; it climbs the Rocky Mountains and binds together two great coasts in bonds of social and commercial life; it makes the lightning its messenger, and is in constant communication with every market throughout the world; it harnesses giant locomotives to cars freighted with commodities and drives them across the continent; it builds great steamers that plow the seas; it plants cities with warehouses, homes, schools, universities, and churches along the wonderful pathway of commerce from prairie to port. It everywhere presides over the manifold and magnificent forces of mercantile life.

When it is considered that there are more than 180,000 miles of railroad in the United States, 4,000 competitive points, 12,000,000 rates to be passed upon, and 300 pools to be supervised, no man can admit the practicability of the proposition to place pooling under the control of the commission in any sense that would protect the vast business interests of the country.

The business men of the United States are opposed to the proposition to create a vast railroad trust representing $11,000,000,000, which is one-sixth of the national wealth—a trust extending into every portion of the country, dominating railroad rates and to a large extent controlling the railway highways of the country, which highways belong to the people, were built for the people, to carry on the business of the people: under the natural and unhindered operations of commerce, adapted to its wants, subject to its demands; those demands being created by the varying conditions of the markets of the world.

The representatives of the people, in my opinion, will never vote for such a proposition. They will never dare to insult the intelligence of the people by ranging themselves upon the side of monopolistic railway management and dictation, exercised independently of the forces of competition. Let the railroads take their chances in the great world of commerce. Let competition in all the activities of business hold undisputed sway. Then will be fostered that intercourse of mankind which inspires emulation, excites and gratifies curiosity, and promotes in an important sense the commercial welfare.

This discussion is in the main because of the business depression, which has now, happily, passed away. Men in dull times try to find fault with something or somebody. No plan has been or ever will be devised for uninterrupted prosperity in any line of industry, and certainly no plan of legislation. This is not the ordained order of things in any department of business.

This Government is not only one of the people, but remember also that it is one by the people, and it will continue to be one by the people. This is a poor time and this is the last country on the face of the earth in which to trifle with the prerogatives of the people.

Men, in dull times, as I have noted, try to find fault as a natural thing with some system or somebody or some legislation or some rule ; it seems to be the experience of the business world and of men in general. The dull periods in business life, particularly those in the last 4 or 5 years, have been brought about more than anything else, I think, by excessive stocks, excessive supply, and undue proportion of the supply of things to the demand for such things. Railroads have suffered in this regard and for these causes as other departments of industry have suffered. In the case of railroads, that condition of dullness has been brought about by excess of railroads in different parts of the country, and that excessive supply of railroads, I think, was the result of the operation of the system of pooling, which encouraged building roads where the business really did not authorize the construction of such roads; by the operation of pooling, the roads that did not pay a satisfactory dividend and make a satisfactory return were aided in making a satisfactory dividend or satisfactory return by those roads that were more prosperous. Out of that condition of things there grew a larger supply of railroads than the business of the country demanded. Happily we are getting into good, prosperous times; business in almost every direction is improving, and there is less complaint. There is not to-day, I suppose, a larger supply of railroad facilities than the business and growing prosperity of the country demand. We hear less complaint on account of discrimination, less complaint of injustice in the management of railroads, less complaint of rates, when business is good, when times are prosperous; and I think that to-day, perhaps, so far as I am able to inform myself, there is very much less cause for complaint in the management of railroads and very much less unjust discrimination than there has been during the last 4 or 5 years, and perhaps during the decade just about closing.

Mr. Chairman and gentlemen, I object to pooling by railroads—

First, because it would be odious to law.

Second, it would smother competition.

Third, it would be against public policy.

Fourth, it would create a vast and dangerous monopoly under the protection of the Government itself.

Fifth, it would take away from the interstate commerce law one of its foundation pillars.

Sixth, it would be subversive of the common good and the highest interests of the people.

Seventh, it would be opposed by a great majority of the people.

Eighth, it would be class legislation.

Ninth, it would be in its every feature contrary to the genius of republican institutions and would be a constant menace to that public tranquillity which is a condition precedent to commercial prosperity.

I do not know that it is expected that any intelligent gentleman or student of political economy would advance the theory that these evils, incident to commercial life in its various departments, can be altogether cured by legislation. There is no way of making any rule or law that will give an uninterrupted prosperity to any industry, to any business, to any life. It seems to be the organic law of things that changes shall take place; that prosperity and adversity, as the preachers say—prosperity in business and dullness in business shall take place from time to time, but that in the end the force of competition will work out beneficent results.

The fact of it is that the alertness and ambitious character of American labor, the ambition of the American citizen, of the mechanic, of the scholar, are so great that we produce, as a general thing, a great deal more of our products, our manufactures, than for the time being there exists a demand for, and we get ahead of the natural law, which is that the demand should wait on supply and not the supply seek the demand.

It is a good deal like the man who went hunting and got on track of a hare and followed him as long as he could keep track of him. Presently the hare and the dog disappeared at a turn of the road, and, coming up to that place, he asked a farmer if he had seen anything of a dog and a hare. "Yes; the dog was a little ahead when they passed me." Our supply has got ahead of the demand in this country in regard to a great many of our products, and I suppose there is no doubt in the minds of many of us that this is the cause of the depression which has prevailed until very lately.

Q. (By Mr. C. J. HARRIS.) You consider perhaps the most dangerous thing in the railroad situation to the public is discrimination?—A. The discrimination, want of uniformity in rates, is undoubtedly, in my view, an unfortunate condition-

Q. It has been suggested that pooling, always with the proviso that the Interstate Commerce Commission should have power to revise the rates of a pool, set the minimum and the maximum, would perhaps do away with discriminations more than anything else. Do you believe that there is anything in that proposition?—A. I do not think that would correct the evils. I should not be in favor, in the first place, of any plan which would interfere with the natural play of the forces of competition. I do not think that the plan of permitting lawful pooling under the control of the Interstate Commerce Commission, or under the control of any bureau, would be practicable. I do not think the immense interests involved could be supervised to the extent of preventing that unjust discrimination which is liable to occur in dull times, and which does not occur to any great extent in prosperous times. I do not think it would correct that, or that any commission or any board, however able that board may be, can really control and remove the evils of which we complain.

Q. Do you think that there now exists any great discrimination in rates?—A. I do not think there is at the present time. I am not so closely in touch with trade as a merchant, but I have made special inquiry of late, and it is my conviction that there is not any very large discrimination in rates of freight at present.

Q. As secretary of the board of trade you would hear of such complaints—they would be made through you or your transportation board?—A. I certainly should hear of them if they were at all serious; but no such cases of complaint have come to me in any official way.

Q. (By Representative BELL.) If there should be a discrimination, is it not more likely to be in favor of a great railroad center like Chicago than against it? That is, if there is a general discrimination exercised, is it not usually exercised in favor of great trade centers like Chicago, for instance, over St. Louis?—A. I am not so sure about that, and yet I would not be pronounced in regard to it. My first view is that in a place like Chicago or any large city the merchants are more watchful, more alert, and commonly more sensitive to surrounding conditions than people in smaller places, and there is not apt to be, it seems to me, so much discrimination as in smaller places. I think railways would be much more cautious about allowing discriminations in any form where there was a search-light, such as public opinion furnishes in an active business community, than they would be in a place, for instance, where there was a large manufactory, one large business that stood by itself, and most of those engaged in the same kind of business were comparatively small merchants without very much influence.

Q. That would be so as between your own merchants, but how would it be as between Chicago and Kansas City, Chicago and Omaha, as to localities? That is a very important point whether one locality is to stand on its own bottom or whether it is to get the great business industries, the great corn industry, and all the great industries centered, and the business done by men interested in rail-roads who discriminate in favor of one locality as against another.—A. I should not think discriminations would more readily and more largely exist in the large than in the small cities.

Q. Do they not have favored points, generally, where the railroads try to throw the business?—A. I do not know much, really, about what they do.

Q. You know as a matter of history that when the Santa Fe went into the hands of a receiver, it was shown up that it had given in drawbacks and discriminations some $7,000,000?—A. I am not aware of that.

Q. Where did the discrimination go?—A. I do not think I am able to give you any information on that line. I certainly have no data in my possession that would enable me to do more than express my general views.

Q. I understand your chief objection to the pool by law is that it would deter competition and the incentive to improved methods?—A. Yes, generally.

Q. Is it not a fact that when the pool is maintained, the division for the succeeding year is based on what each railroad moved, in freight or passengers, the preceding year? Has not that been the system of pooling from the beginning?—A. I can not go into details about pooling arrangements or agreements, but the principle that prevades pooling, as I understand it, is that every line has a certain proportion.

Q. According to what it hauls?—A. If there is a line that does not pay a certain amount that may be agreed upon by the pool, that deficiency will be made up out of the general fund of the pool.

Q. I think you will find that every pool is built on the amount of traffic that each road carried the preceding year; its proportion is arranged according to the proportion of traffic it hauls.—A. I think that is so.

Q. Then the same incentive would necessarily exist under a Government pool that did exist under a private pool; because the more it hauls, I understand——
—A. (Interrupting.) I am not in favor of the private pool; I am not in favor of any pool at all.

Q. You do not believe that ruinous competition is good for any business?—A. You can not say as an abstract proposition, and I would not say, that anything that would bring about ruin is desirable; but I will say that on the whole, as the result of the whole thing, not taking one special time into consideration, competition brings about very many more advantages than disadvantages. There are disadvantages in any kind of a plan which you may devise. These disadvantages can not be entirely removed and may exist in any sort of a plan or any legislation, in my view; but, on the whole, I contend that the forces of competition bring about in the end salutary results, and that to deprive any business of the effect of the natural forces of competition would in the long run be ruinous.

Q. But if my assumption is right—that each individual road would share in the pool each year on the basis of the amount of freight and passengers it carried the preceding year—it would not affect in any material degree the incentive to improved methods, improved roads, improved facilities for travel and transportation. That, as I understand, is not in contemplation under Government control; it is to leave all these incentives full play. The idea is to absolutely stop this discrimination and these drawbacks, both as against communities and persons, and to make the pool lawful.—A. Yes; I understand that is the proposition.

Q. Now, have you any other reasons to urge against the advisability of a legal pool as against an illegal pool?—A. I have not any more propositions to present; but I would object to its being placed in the form " as against an illegal pool." I would not advocate pooling under any circumstances.

Q. Is it not your judgment that there is always some kind of an understood pool as between railroads, just the same as between the grocery merchant and others in the same line of business?—A. No; I do not think so; I was not aware of that.

Q. Do you not believe these pools that have been admitted to be maintained in the face of the law were illegal?—A. They have been decided to be illegal.

Q. The railroads say these are absolutely necessary for them to do the business in an orderly and honest manner, and it is argued now that they be made legal, and that a legal body take charge of them. As I understand you, your only objection of any consequence is that it destroys competition and the incentive to improve facilities. If my assumption is true, in all pooling the incentive to haul more goods and give better service, to haul more passengers and give better service, is not interfered with, because the 1st of every January the pool is made for the next year, and the proportionate amount is based on the amount that each road has hauled the preceding year.—A. You think it would not interfere?

Q. It has not among pooling companies. That is the condition of the pool. A man who has hauled one-third one year, gets one-third of the profits. If he can build up his road and get up to one-half the next year, then it will be based on one-half instead of one-third.—A. I do not think that plan would do away with the disadvantages and bring about the highest results. I suppose that we will concede that the facilities for the transportation of persons and of property, as developed in this country, have been much better—that the time of travel has been reduced to a greater extent—than in any other country.

Q. You had a greater country to develop.—A. The fact remains, they did it. It has not been because we have had a bigger country altogether. It may be ascribed to the extent of the country that we have had such a large number of miles of railway constructed, but the development of railroading, using that in the comprehensive sense, comprising conveniences, luxuries of travel, reduction of time in travel, and in various ways. These have all, in my opinion, been brought about by the play of the forces of competition in this country. Our wonderful inland commerce, our export trade, which now, happily, is increasing; these, all connected intimately with transportation, have been developed, have attained their present proportions, and have in them such promises for larger development, as a consequence of the forces of competition. I think that these have not been the result of pooling in any sense.

Q. Do you think it helps a railroad to build a parallel line beside it?—A. It may. Now, for instance, I suppose there is no doubt of this fact: That the most prosperous lines of railway, the most uniformly reliable railway lines in this country, are the great trunk lines running from the West to the Atlantic seaboard. Those lines come in direct competition with the cheap transportation along the Great Lakes and along the Erie Canal. The lesson is, and the doctrine is laid down by the experience of business men, that profits are larger upon the basis of a small percentage of profits and a large volume of trade. The railroads that feared their profits would be interfered with seriously by lake transportation have had the volume of their business increased to such an extent by lake transportation as to entirely overcome the reduction which they were forced into in rates of freight.

Q. If that be so, if the Government would take hold of this question and fix a reasonably low rate on both traffic and passengers, it would help the roads, on your theory?—A. No.

Q. I understand you to say competition did it.—A. Competition will fix these rates better than the Government can fix them, in my opinion.

Q. When the country has one railroad that can do all the business, and by the regulation of this Interstate Commerce Commission it can fix a reasonably low rate, is it not preferable to forcing a useless parallel line to come in merely for the purpose of reducing rates and convincing it that a lower rate will make more profit?—A. I think we can not abandon the theory that a man or set of men desiring to build a railroad or a steamboat must be allowed to build a steamboat or a railroad on their own responsibility and take the results.

Q. Is it not your main point that you do not believe in any Government interference with railroads at all? Is not that your contention?—A. No, I would not state that; I am only speaking on the subject of pooling. I do not think the Government or anybody, the State or the United States Government, can fix the rates of freight in such a salutary way as competition can. I think the ordinary force of business competition will, in the end, arrive at a more equitable settlement of rates than the Government could.

Q. How long do you want to wait for this? Do you believe it is right to wear out a generation or two rather than have the Government intervene?—A. I am not in favor of wearing out generations. This country has not worn out its generations in the last hundred years.

Q. We have before this commission very strong evidence that a generation has been worn out in trying to stop the rebates on shipments of oil; that when the same parties reached a country where the Government controlled the railroads they made a handsome profit. As long as they remain in their own country the independent Pure Oil Company swear they can never ship a barrel of oil in America if it goes on a single American railroad. The minute it gets into Germany, or a country where there is no discrimination, they make a handsome profit. They have been fighting that for 35 years, and the only reason, they say, is the railroad discrimination in favor of the Standard Oil Company. Do you believe it is better to go on, as we have gone on, wearing out several generations, than for the Government to step in?—A. I am not acquainted with the oil industry at all.

Q. What I was trying to reach was this: If you object to pooling under Government regulation because you would not want the Government to interfere, that would affect the validity of your testimony somewhat; you would be prejudiced against any interference of the Government, regardless of whether it would be of public benefit or not. We have a great many men in our country that are very fearful that the Government may take some steps to interfere with railroads, while every other country on the face of the earth except England has its own railroads.—A. It is reverting somewhat to the incident about the oil. I do not know why the experience with reference to oil—not doubting that it is as you say—should change the policy with regard to all the railway lines and with regard to everything else in this country.

Q. We had a witness from Cripple Creek who swore that he was interested in the Portland, one of the greatest mines in America, with some great wealthy syndicate. He is also interested with some miners in a poor mine right by the side of it; that for the Portland mine, that had ore rich enough to bear any kind of transportation charges, they got a rebate at the rate of $60,000 a year, while this poor mine over here, run by poor men, had to pay an exorbitant rate to make up that $60,000. He says it is a general thing in silver and gold mining, and we find it here and there, but the oil industry has been brought before us more generally than any other.—A. Of course I would not undertake to reconcile any or every individual case that this commission has had brought to its notice.

Q. (By Mr. KENNEDY.) Are you in favor of strengthening the Interstate Commerce Commission and giving them authority to make just rates on complaint that discriminations have been practiced?—A. I am in favor of strengthening the Interstate Commerce Commission so that upon representations and upon hearing they may say that a rate is unreasonable if it is so, and make the rate.

Q. And have their decision go into effect?—A. Have it effective.

Q. Pending an appeal to the Supreme Court?—A. Yes.

Q. (By Professor JOHNSON.) Do you know whether we have as many miles of road per square mile in this country as England and the countries of western Europe?—A. I don't think we have as many miles of road to the square mile.

Q. Does the question of discrimination, as it exists in this country, exist in

Great Britain and the countries of western Europe?—A. The complaints on discriminations are the same as here.

Q. Does the question exist there as it does here?—A. Well, I am not sure about that; I could not say.

Q. You at least have not heard that discriminations are a serious question in Great Britain and on the Continent of Europe, have you?—A. No, sir; I have not had that matter brought to my notice.

Q. Then if we don't have so many miles of road per square mile as these European countries, and these countries have practically eliminated the great railroad problems with that of discrimination, is it strictly correct to say that railroad development here is far ahead of that of any other country?—A. I don't know that it touches conclusively the proposition of our railroads in this country. Our time of railway travel and the regularity of the service is better. So far as the continental travel is concerned, I am satisfied that the time of travel here is very much quicker than on the Continent and that the facilities for passenger traffic are superior here to those there.

Q. Does your information convince you that there are more trains running over 40 miles an hour in the United States than there are in all of western Europe—that is, comparing the number of roads there with the number of roads here?—A. Comparing the number of roads there with the number of roads here, I should say that travel is quicker here than it is there. I think a commission came over here from the Continent—of course, I have not the data at my hand, but I think it was a commission from the Continent that came over here to investigate that matter—not many years ago, and I remember reading the result of the report of that commission; and it was to the effect that the time of railroad travel here was much faster. Then there are no big trunk lines abroad such as we have here.

Q. Every comparison I have seen has been a comparison between the whole United States and one country of Europe, and further than that the comparison has been only between express trains of this country as compared with one of the smaller European countries. I have not seen, but would like to ask you if you have seen, a comparison that attempted to compare our railroads as a whole with the railroad service as a whole in western Europe?—A. No; I have not seen that.

Q. Would you say that would be a fair way to make a comparison?—A. Yes; I think that would be the fairest way. I remember making quite exhaustive copies from that report, and I could easily refer to it if necessary; it shows on what lines the comparison is made and gives the prominent points in Europe, and also gives the prominent points in this country, and states the time between each one in each instance. But I have not seen a comparison upon the line that you speak of, generally.

Q. (By Mr. KENNEDY.) Coming back to America, I should like to have you state what you specifically favor in the way of amendments to the interstate-commerce law.—A. I would give them, among other things, the power to fix reasonable rates, after a hearing at which those interested in the industries to which the rates would apply could be represented. I would give them power to change existing rates if, upon hearing, the commission was convinced that they were unjust.

Q. Would you give them power to send experts to a railway office, here and there all over the country, the same as national-bank examiners are sent, to examine into the affairs of the railroad companies?—A. Yes; I think I would.

Q. (By Mr. CONGER.) Have you, in your paper, warned the commission against centralization of these big railroad properties? As I understand it, your theory is that a legal pool would hasten that centralization; am I correct in that?—A. Yes; when I spoke of centralization I used the word centralization as meaning pooling.

Q. Is not the present competition quite likely to bring about an actual consolidation of these large trunk lines, in which event the big corporation controlling all or one of the trunk lines between Chicago, for instance, and the seaboard of the East, would possess all the benefits of the pool without any legal inspection or restriction?—A. I don't think it would have that result. I don't think the avoidance of pooling would bring about that consolidation or concentration of power between different lines of road.

Q. You don't think that consolidation extends to the extreme?—A. I don't think it would follow to the extreme.

Q. (By Representative LORIMER.) Mr. Bell has suggested that in pooling a road secures its share on a basis of its traffic the previous year. Have you any opinion as to whether or not it is necessary to base their share in the same way, or can they fix it on any other basis?—A. Upon any basis, I imagine. I don't think they would be confined, in any sense, to such an arrangement.

Q. So that while probably in the past it has been based on the previous haul, they may agree upon any other scale?—A. Yes; I understand so, and think it would be possible.

Q. (By Mr. CONGER.) The point in my question that I was trying to bring out was this, that unless that basis is modified the pool would be no pool at all. The manager of some line would go right out just as he does now, or at least the opportunity would be open to him to go out, just as it is claimed they do now, and offer rebates, by which he would get more freight to carry and consequently a larger share of next year's business; in other words, there would be competing just as there is now?—A. Yes.

Q. So that I think it is a fact that while the percentage of the tonnage they do carry is used as a basis, it is modified by other interests or modified arbitrarily?—A. Yes.

Testimony closed.

CHICAGO, *November 24, 1899.*

TESTIMONY OF MR. AUGUSTINE GALLAGHER,

Representative of Merchants' Exchange, of St. Louis, Mo.

The subcommission being in session on the afternoon of November 24, 1899, Representative Lorimer presiding, Mr. Augustin Gallagher, being duly sworn, testified as follows:

Q. (By Representative LORIMER.) Please state your name in full.—A. Augustine Gallagher.

Q. And your business and post-office address.—A. I am in the publishing business in St. Louis, Mo., and represent the Merchants' Exchange of that city in this instance.

Q. (By Mr. C. J. HARRIS.) Are you prepared to go on and make a general statement, or should you prefer questioning?—A. I think I should prefer the questions, if you please.

Q. What have you to say in regard to unjust freight-rate discriminations against American flour?—A. I should like to bring the attention of the commission to the fact that we are very rapidly losing our export flour trade. The loss has been severe in recent months—from last February down to the present time. The trunk-line railways of the country published a tariff in which they established different rates for wheat and for flour, for grain and grain products. Previous to that (while, of course, cutting the grain rate whenever they felt like it) they had published the same tariff rate for wheat and flour, and it was generally understood abroad that the American miller had an equal rate on wheat and on his flour. The publication was a national transportation scandal and invited the foreign millers to bring influence to bear on the railroads to increase the export tariff on flour. The ocean carriage was largely in foreign ships and under foreign flags, and an opportunity was presented for them to lower the ocean rate on grain and increase it on flour, and this has progressed to such an extent that I fear that unless this is stopped our export flour trade will be destroyed. I am informed by well-informed men in the trade that they share this fear with me.

Q. Do you know what the difference in the tariff is in ocean trade between grain and grain products?—A. It fluctuates greatly. It will be probably 2 cents to 5 cents; and again, if there is no grain available and they get flour, they will take flour low. As a general thing the difference would range, I think, from 1 to 3 cents.

Q. And the discrimination between the two between St. Louis and the seaboard has been what?—A. It is now 7 cents per 100 pounds for flour more than for wheat. I will give you the exact figures which were in effect on November 1. It was a sort of a nice way of all the railroads to respond to the ruling of the Interstate Commerce Commission. The rate on flour from St. Louis to New York in the tariff dated November 1 is 27 cents, to Philadelphia 25 cents, and to Baltimore 24 cents; on wheat the rate to New York is 20 cents, to Philadelphia 19 cents, and to Baltimore 18½ cents.

Q. You are getting the same grain rate from St. Louis that they get from Chicago?—A. No; we are not. If we were we should be in what is known as the 100 per cent territory, whereas we are in the 116 per cent territory.

Q. (By Mr. CONGER.) Can you tell us what the rates were before November 1?—A. There has not been a large difference made by this new tariff; a very slight difference. I did not charge my memory with the exact difference, but if I remember correctly the discrimination amounted at one time to 8 cents, and previous to that it was 5 cents and before that 3; there has been a gradual increase for months.

Q. You said, I believe, that the fixing of these rates by the railroads was in order to comply in a nice way with a rule or order of the Interstate Commerce Commission; can you tell us in short what that order was?—A. The commission held a 3-months' investigation of the matter. After they got into it they found it was an enormous question. They held hearings in New York City, in Chicago, in St. Louis, and in Washington. They issued an order which ran something after this fashion. I will give you the substance of it. "We believe it is good railway policy and good business policy that wheat and flour should go at the same rate, and in case differentials are made at the seaboard in no case shall they be over 2 cents per 100 pounds." And the roads contend that they have complied with the order. The published tariff—I don't know whether it is effective or not—that is, I don't know whether they live up to it or not—but the tariff out for the 100 per cent territory is in compliance with the order, without any special recognition of the order at all. They claim that the commission has no right or authority to make such orders at will. The tariff from Chicago to-day is 2 cents higher on flour than on wheat, which would be in that way a compliance with the order. The discriminations in other parts of the country, as from St. Louis, are just as violent as before.

Q. In other words, the railroads coming into Chicago, so far as their tariff schedule is concerned, have complied with the order, whereas the roads coming into and going out of St. Louis have not complied with the order; that is your testimony?—A. Yes; that would be the effect.

Q. In this territory, in complying with this order of the Interstate Commerce Commission, that the differentials should not be more than 3 cents, did the railroads raise the then or previously existing rate on wheat for export, or did they lower the rate on flour?—A. The change was made November 1, at a time when rates generally were advanced; so that the rates on flour and wheat were advanced, if I remember aright, and on several other commodities.

Q. Your idea is that the roads raised the rate on export wheat?—A. Yes.

Q. (By Mr. C. J. HARRIS.) What have you to say of the carloads of wheat and flour; is there any difference in handling that would demand a higher rate for one than for the other?—A. It is contended by the railroads that there is, and that that is one of the reasons why they demand a higher rate. There is a domestic trade that will take flour in small carloads of 125 barrels rather than 200 barrels, particularly through the cotton States and where farmers have a few hundred hands working for them all through the South; and the same thing prevails in the Northwest. On account of this—on account of this trade taking these small carloads and the fact that the miller will often load a car with more wheat than the capacity will warrant—the railroads have an excuse to argue that it costs more to transport flour than wheat. In reality they also load more flour on a car than the capacity will warrant. That is the question we had a hearing on. It was on the question of export flour, and we introduced evidence to show that the millers had frequently loaded cars in excess of their capacity, and it was shown that they had permission from the railroad management to load the cars in excess of their capacity. It was a very simple proposition, or should have been, to anyone; because where a miller has an opportunity he would be a very foolish miller to load light cars, where he was paying for switching, when he could load heavy ones. The millers that were witnesses before the commission expressed a willingness to comply with any reasonable demand that the railroads deemed proper, if the railroads would furnish the proper equipment to do it; they complained, and very properly too, that in the matter of transportation of wheat the railroads furnished the very best of equipment, but when it come to the transportation of flour in barrels, for instance, they gave them any old car that happened to be lying around doing nothing.

Q. Gave larger cars for wheat?—A. Yes, larger cars; it was stated also that the modern equipment, the new equipment, on all the railroads is much larger than the old equipment; and, as a matter of course, the larger the cars the fewer the cars and the lower the actual cost of transportation.

Q. Is the domestic and export rate on flour the same?—A. No.

Q. There is a difference?—A. Yes; there is a difference.

Q. What is the domestic rate to New York on flour?—A. I don't know.

Q. Do you think the exportation of wheat at the rates complained of benefits the producers of grain?—A. No; I do not. That has been presented as an argument of the transportation lines. They undertook to set out that they had been making these low rates at times on that theory; that is, that they did it to take the grain out of the country because the American farmer did not have a market for his grain. In other words, they argue that they find a market for the product of the country. As a matter of fact the farmer never participates in that profit at all. This grain is bought up by buyers for a future profit; it is bought up by railroad lines and it is bought up by the elevators, and it is run out of the country by the train load, taking advantage of a rate out of which the farmer gets nothing. If there is any money in it, he merely hears of the price which it brought through the newspapers some time after the grain is gone from him, and long before that he gets for his grain exactly what the market price was at the time of his sale. That is all he ever gets; it is all anyone gets for grain and it is all anyone pays for grain.

Q. (By Mr. CONGER.) You think the price of wheat is fixed by these men, or does the market of Liverpool have something to do with it?—A. There are days when the Liverpool market will have some influence on the world's market, because the demand for the product is larger, although I think as a rule the Chicago market is the controlling feature in the grain markets.

Q. You think the Chicago grain market controls the price of wheat the world over?—A. It does to a very large extent. It is the leading speculative market of the world. Of course, the foreign markets control here, as I say, just so far as they are buyers. If there is a good demand in Liverpool—in other words, a seeking market—the foreign market will very likely influence our markets for the time being.

Q. (By Mr. KENNEDY.) You said just now that the farmer is paid for his grain just what the market price is. Is there not a charge, or at least a belief, that in some sections of the country they are paid a little more than the market price because of freight discriminations which certain grain companies or interests enjoy?—A. That happens occasionally; yes. It is not by the philanthropy of the buyer, however; that is not the basis upon which he works. It is because in a certain district there may be a competing line of railroad and also competition in the buying of the grain on that account. Of course the fellow who gets in there first will try to run all competition out of that territory if he can, and a farmer in that way may get more money; anyway sometimes the farmer gets the benefit of the competition, but it is not by reason of any philanthropy.

Q. Do the Chicago buyers invade St. Louis territory and offer the farmer more for his grain than your men can afford to pay for it?—A. No; St. Louis is a great milling center, and we always buy more wheat than Chicago on account of the milling demand.

Q. (By Mr. C. J. HARRIS.) How large is the milling interest in St. Louis?—A. We had a committee of the millers and Board of Trade of St. Louis and suburban towns for the purpose of securing some statistics to present to Congress; and we found we had a capacity of over 27,000 barrels per day, and employed 1,100 men exclusively engaged in that business outside of truck drivers, men working in the elevators, etc.

Q. Have you anything to say about the under-billing of cars?—A. That is one of the very worst evils, I think, in transportation to-day; that is one of many; I will not say it is the worst.

Q. Please state what it is.—A. It is a matter that can more properly be obtained through the railroads or lines over which the practice is permitted. I have known members of the trade—I want to ask first if it is your object to have me point out now the facts with the names, etc. Of course in getting this information——

Q. You know the general facts?—A. I have got a great deal in confidence that it would possibly not be well to publish.

Q. Give us the general facts.—A. I have had millers tell me within a week that they had been solicited by the railroad companies to ship 200 barrels of flour and bill out 125.

Q. You could not give definite proof of that?—A. The gentleman who told me didn't want to go into the matter, because he was dealing with the railroad company; but he said that if the commission deemed it necessary he would, as a matter of fact, give it.

Q. Are there any other methods of discrimination?—A. Yes; there is a straw-man and a pawnbroker system of borrowing money; that is, a system by which a railroad agent goes to a man and tells him to take a tariff and move his goods to seaboard, and they will borrow advance freight money on his shipment. In the meantime the man draws interest on his investment, and this pays a large part of the freight. That is a system that was described to me by a man who works it himself.

Q. (By Mr. CONGER.) What is the straw-man system?—A. I have a shipment of a commodity to make and I want to put it over a line that is going to give me a rebate. Instead of billing that stuff to the man I have sold it to I bill it to a fictitious man, or straw man. On the bills he is the actual shipper. I do not see him at all, don't know anything about him, but he bills the stuff to the man that I want it to go to, my customer, and it will go through all right, and by and by the straw man sends me a check for a rebate. You can not find him; at least I have not been able to do it. That was also described to me by a man who practices it.

Q. (By Mr. C. J. HARRIS.) Do you think speculation in railroad stocks is another practice of the roads?—A. Yes; my opinion on that question would simply be the reflection of what I have been told by traffic men. The securities of these roads are very slow at times, and it is very rarely that there is chance of getting any of their stock, unless it can be sold for more than it is worth. Take any of these granger roads; they are controlled by the present owners and the syndicates, and they have no intention of delivering the shares of stock, although the stocks are speculated in here and in St. Louis and everywhere all over the country. Of course the present owners have no intention of allowing the stock to pass out of their control. The present price of railroad stocks is generally considered by traffic men, so far as I know, to be out of reason—out of any correspondence to the dividends or the revenues derived from them. I don't know the history of this business, but the gentlemen who told me about it are well acquainted with it. I will mention one of them because he was before your commission; he is a very well-informed man and his name is Mr. Vanlandingham. I am told that the history of the railroads is that when the railroads get ready to dispose of their securities they encourage a rate war and in that way unload on the public, and that much money is made in hard times by speculation in these securities.

Q. (By Representative LORIMER.) To unload on the public they have to start a rate war?—A. Yes, when stocks are away up; when the stocks are high they sell out to the public on the idea that they are going up, and by and by they go down because the handling of the road is such as to depress them.

Q. After they are out?—A. Oh, certainly; after the inside speculators are out.

Q. (By Mr. CONGER.) You mentioned the billing, and then told us of other kinds of rebates and discriminations. Do you know of others than the ones you mentioned? If so, I should like to hear about them.—A. I have one case with me; I brought it along as a curiosity. I have in my safe the complete documents of the case all ready to publish; I picked them up about three years ago; I have the check the rebate was paid with, the expense bills, and everything. It was done by sending the favored shipment to shipper's order. The way I got it was this: Some clients of mine, confederates as it were, concluded with me that we would find out if there was anything of the kind going on upon a certain line. I was confident that rebates were being paid, and that a lower rate was being made to Texas by a certain railroad, and a grain buyer and a miller in —— went into this scheme. The grain buyer it seems could not very satisfactorily get any wheat along this line, but he could go to the favored shipper and buy wheat, and he found that this favored shipper would put the wheat by the carload down at a certain point he desired in Texas at a rate much lower than he could get on wheat himself and put it down there; it was shipped to that point in Texas subject to shipper's order.

Q. Addressed to themselves?—A. The shipper gives the order when it gets there, and he may forward it by the same mail. Say I bought a carload of wheat from this shipper and sent it to Texas; the man who received it, being in on the scheme, of course went and paid the freight on it. The grain man in Kansas had bought this grain from the favored shipper, who had sold it to be delivered in Texas, subject to his order. The grain man who bought it of the favored shipper sent a notice to the miller in Texas to charge the full tariff rate above the agreed price of the grain. The miller, being in the scheme, went to the freight office and paid the freight and got a receipt and found the freight was very much less than this man had stated in his notice of the tariff, and sent him a check for the difference and wrote him a letter telling him he had agreed to do. That is the method that used to be practiced a good deal. I don't know whether it is now or not; it is very hard to keep track of these cases. In fact, it is impossible, under the present system that prevails; we have no system of supervision.

Q. One witness yesterday testified that in his opinion it was the custom among some railroads to give lower rates on special articles of freight within the borders of the State in consideration of their having consigned to them a large amount of business that would be interstate commerce. Do you know anything about any such practices?—A. I could not give you any positive information; I have heard of these things, but the things I am telling you now I have investigated, so as to have positive information for you. I have no positive information along the line you mention, though I don't believe they have got a classification marked; I just happened to think that that is a way that they used to do to cut rates—to change the classification; and they have also done that in recent years.

Q. (By Representative BELL.) How is it about weights?—A. For instance, I will give you a case: Where I live we ship peaches, 4 boxes to the 100 pounds, to Salt Lake City; 350 miles farther they allow us to ship 6 boxes for 100 pounds. That is in billing, and they ship them to the railroad agent.

Q. What is the reason for that?—A. Why, they want to favor that man and lower his rates 50 per cent, or whatever per cent it is. It is understood, of course, that the railroad could punish that man if it desired to.

Q. They ship direct to the depot agent?—A. Yes; I have an intimate friend who tells me he ships 6 boxes to the 100 pounds and has to ship to the agent, while we ship 4 boxes to the 100 pounds.

Q. (By Mr. C. J. HARRIS.) What is the practice of railroads when extra tonnage is needed in grain shipments?—A. They usually go for grain; they can load it very easily and store it in large amounts; they can load up a train with it out of a house with large capacity in very short order and move it quickly.

Q. What effect does that have?—A. It tends to cutting of rates. The railroad takes advantage of the different markets where it sees they are available to millers and manufacturers; it picks them out and goes abroad, as a rule, to furnish competition there through building up the milling business in foreign countries.

Q. Do you have any complaint about the freight on millers' supplies, machinery, etc.?—A. No; we have had no complaint about that. I think it might be well to call the attention of the commission to the great volume of that business. When we have sought relief from this tearing down of the export trade, that threatens the life of the entire milling industry of the country, our argument with the railroad officials has been that we should be recognized here because the milling business furnishes the railroads with such an enormous tonnage not only on domestic, but on export business, and that this tonnage comes gradually, month after month, and is continual, and we are willing to pay good tariffs. In preparing our argument with the companies before the Interstate Commerce Commission I concluded to show the tonnage the millers were responsible for in addition to the wheat and flour. I concluded to show what the industry demands in the way of supplies used by the millers, such as coal, oil, cooperage, bags, lubricants, and the many other things that they use. Machinery was a very heavy item, paying high rates. I went to the books of about 20 mills and asked permission of the millers to secure these figures; and in some instances I wrote to the management, telling them what I wanted and asking them to have the bookkeepers give me the exact amount of the stuff that they purchased in the course of a year and the capacity of the mills. The capacity of these mills would range from 100 barrels per day to 2,000 barrels per day. One hundred barrels per day is one of the smallest mills that could engage in the business, and it is understood by millers that when you have a mill of 2,000 barrels capacity daily you have reached about the limit of industrial economy. A larger mill would not produce flour any cheaper per barrel. So I secured figures from mills of 100 barrels to 2,000 barrels capacity. I took the actual number of bushels of coal these people bought, the actual amount of machinery, bags, lumber, cooperage, oil, and all such stuff, and it amounted to 88,000 tons more than the annual grain exports of the country on a 5-year average, even including last year, with exports of 148,000,000 bushels. Now, this tonnage takes the highest local rates on every character of stuff, and the railroads make money on it. For instance, machinery and all finished products that are painted and varnished, and all that sort of thing. Take coal; I have one illustration of the cost of that from one mill in Dallas, Tex., where coal paid nine times its value in freight; and I found one in western Kansas where the coal cost ten times its value in freight.

Q. (By Mr. CONGER.) Ten times its value at the mine?—A. Yes. We are continuing to stand out against the railroads and the enforcement of these discriminations, which, besides being unjust, threaten a live industry.

Q. Do you think the railroads are justified in handling wheat for export at a lower rate than wheat for domestic use?—A. I think the roads are justified in making a lower rate for export than for domestic use.

Q. On wheat?—A. Yes.

Q. On flour. Do you think the rate should be lower on that?—A. Yes.

Q. Do you think that overproduction has any influence on the price of wheat; does a very large crop or overproduction affect prices?—A. Whenever the world has an overproduction it affects the price disastrously for wheat for the time being, although overproduction will not operate to the extent of having a depressing influence for any great length of time.

Q. When we have a surplus where is the effect felt first?—A. Most of it in Liverpool; Liverpool is the big buyer; it is the great distributing point; the Continent takes a great deal of our wheat.

Q. What I am trying to get at is this: As Liverpool is the largest buyer of our wheat and a great distributing point, whether lower transportation rates between Chicago and St. Louis and Liverpool would not give to the farmer more for his grain than he would get if these transportation rates were twice or three times what they are now.—A. If the farmer gets any benefit out of these transportation rates I don't know what it is. Of course it may be, I think it is, a question of supply and demand, and that should fix it. We have no assurance when this wheat goes abroad where it will go. It may be bought up by the Liverpool merchant, but we have no assurance that the wheat is not going to France. It will go into France under a duty of so many francs per hundred kilos, and then if the flour is exported from France that duty, which is paid by the miller, is refunded to him. He can take our wheat at a cut-rate price, take it into France and mill it without paying any duty; then export it to Great Britain, the duty being refunded to him, and take our market away from us; and when it comes to putting our flour into France it is barred.

Q. You have stated that the farmer or producer of wheat in this country receives no benefit from these lower rates on wheat or flour for export, and what I was trying to reach was your mode of reasoning by which you reached this conclusion. To that end I wanted to ask you whether, in your opinion, if it cost five times as much as it now does to transport a bushel of wheat from Chicago or St. Louis to Liverpool, the farmer could export grain or wheat. In other words, would it not cut him off?—A. Five times would be an unreasonable rate and out of proportion to the value of the stuff and out of proportion to the rates paid the world over.

Q. Does it not follow as a natural conclusion that if these rates were five times as high our exportation of grain would be practically cut off, and the result would be an oversupply here and a consequent lowering of the price of wheat all over the country?—A. I am quite willing to strike a line of principle with you, but I do not like to agree to a violent comparison of that sort.

Q. That would be, in general, the result; that would be the principle?—A. There seems to be a principle of that sort governing all business transactions.

Q. Would not the converse be true, that if the transportation rates on wheat for export were greatly reduced competition between buyers of grain would be such that the farmer would get at least a portion of the benefit?—A. In answering that question we have to take this into consideration: These men who get this low rate have the product here in their warehouses and can draw on it almost any time. Now, they may depress the market and they may not; they have it in their own hands whether to do it or not. The theory that you advance appears to be reasonable, but the facts that I advance are facts; that is the situation we complain of; it is the fact.

Q. It strikes me conjecture enters into it to some extent. I know some people contend the other way—that the farmer is actually receiving more for his grain.—A. I have heard that.

Q. (By Mr. C. J. HARRIS.) If these rates were stable and to be counted on this low rate would benefit the farmer, would it not?—A. Oh, yes; if everybody had the rate there is no question but the lower the rate the better it would be for the farmer; but then the farmer does not get the rate, and only a few people do get it.

Q. These export rates are open to all?—A. Those are not the rates we are complaining of—the 2 cents differential—although flour should be carried at the same rate.

Q. I understand what you are complaining of are these sudden, specially made rates, made at times when tonnage is particularly wanted, that the farmer does not get the benefit of?—A. That is it, exactly. I will give you an example. I am not contending against grain at all; I think it should bear its own burden, but I do not think our railroads should build up a foreign industry to hurt ourselves. I have in mind a mill; I can give the number of the tariff and the road it went over to substantiate this. These very gentlemen went to the owner; he was a big miller and could put out lots of tonnage if he took a notion. If I remember correctly, it was 17,000 bags of flour he contracted for; and you know 17,000 bags, at 400 to the car, will make quite a string of freight. He got a cut rate of 5 cents on that amount. They slapped in one of these midnight tariffs; published the tariff, and gave notice of withdrawal just as quick as he filled the contract. Now, that is a great deal to the country miller with 250 barrels a day capacity. I think the miller that gets that sort of privilege ought to be regulated just the same as the grain man who does it.

Q. I will ask you if you find any tendency on the part of your people to Government ownership?—A. I think there is a very dangerous tendency throughout the Western country. I travel a good deal over the country seeing how the crop is, and I generally travel over the territory two or three times a season. I never observed the growth of the feeling or the theory, or whatever you may call it, to be so marked as in recent months.

Q. (By Mr. CONGER.) Are the people dissatisfied?—A. The people feel that the public is not getting a square deal.

Q. Your idea is that these people are dissatisfied and advocate Government ownership because of dissatisfaction from rebates?—A. Just because they are not getting what is due them and they know that other fellows are; they are not satisfied with the way things are conducted. They have come to the conclusion that they can buy a postage stamp as cheap as anybody can, and they can go through the custom-house as cheap as anybody can, and are getting around to the idea that they could go to the station agent's office and buy a railroad ticket as cheap as anybody if Uncle Sam had control of it.

Q. Your idea is that their dissatisfaction comes not from high rates, but because the rates are unequal, and because somebody else, they think, is getting the advantage of them?—A. Yes; that is no longer theory, but facts. I want to go on record that that is no theory. Everything I have stated to you to-day is based on one or more transactions of the character described.

Q. Are you familiar with the situation in the East? Do you think the custom of giving these rebates and discriminations is as prevalent there as in the West?—A. I could not say. I am inclined to think the Trunk Line Association is a better managed body and the rates are better maintained; at least, they keep their information to themselves better than the roads in the other parts of the country.

Q. If they do discriminate the public does not know as much about it?—A. We do not hear about it as much.

Q. The point I was bringing out was this: I think it is generally believed to be a fact that the sentiment in favor of Government ownership is more general in the West than in the East, and I was wondering whether we should be justified in connecting that fact with the fact that there is more discrimination in the West than in the East?—A. Of my own knowledge I do not know. I have been informed, however, that your assumption is in line with fact; that the rate cutting is not as violent or as general. Of course, the Gulf lines inaugurate a slashing every once in a while, with their lines running down the Mississippi Valley to New Orleans and Mobile; and when grain ought to be 18 or 19 cents they go to the trade and in order to load a few ships or fill up some houses down there they put in a 10-cent cut and it upsets everything.

Q. (By Mr. C. J. HARRIS.) Have you any objection to the operation of elevators by railroads?—A. Yes; I believe the carrier that is chartered for the business of operating a railroad has no business whatever to engage in the grain business. I think his charter rights are impaired, if it was brought to an issue, in doing so.

Q. Will it not have a better effect on the prices that the producer receives, if the railroad company furnish an elevator, than if he has to go into the hands of these private elevator men?—A. I do not believe the history of trade, as conducted, will bear that out. I believe, in other words, it is the history of this business that wherever the road controls the business along its line it has a monopoly, and wherever that is the case, through the grain territory, you will find little elevators that have been abandoned for 5 or 6 years, all run down. You can tell from that what is happening. It is a sure indicator that the fellow has gone into some other business. If that man was competing at this station, it is a matter of reason to say that the farmer would get more for his stuff than when he has to deal with a monopoly.

Q. Is it your experience that competing elevators in different grain-buying points are—or did I understand you to say there are not competing elevators or grain buyers at these different points?—A. Where, for instance, a road has been shipping freight to some big grain concern that controls a big elevator system for several years, they will drive the little fellows out. Of course, when you drive the independent buyers out of the country, whether a miller or a grain dealer, you reduce the opportunity of the farmer to get a higher price for his grain.

Q. Are the natural advantages of the miller in this country as good as in any other?—A. No; the miller has some natural disadvantages that would entitle him to consideration, I think, of law-making bodies. For instance, grain going for export—I am speaking of export entirely, for I think domestic trade can be regulated by competition, as we have no imports to compete with—export grain would usually go direct from the field, and is accumulated along toward the sea. But frequently the miller, in order to get supplies, has to go out 200 or 300 miles and buy grain. There is no grain delivered in a city like St. Louis by wagon—a few thousand bushels a year, perhaps. He may even have to come to Chicago and haul the grain in and haul it back again.

Q. (By Representative LORIMER.) How about the Minneapolis miller?—A. As a general thing, they get their wheat back north of them and move it down. It is in the line of transit. Occasionally they have to buy wheat outside. They used to come to Kansas, a few years ago, but it was plain to be seen that when they had to haul wheat to Minneapolis from Kansas to keep their mills going, it was done at great cost.

Q. It pays to locate a mill in that position?—A. Indeed, it does.

Q. Is it not customary for millers to get from roads what are known as milling-in-transit rates?—A. They do in some localities. They pay a cent a hundred for it, though. I think that is a usual practice, paying a cent for the privilege.

Q. Does not that practically overcome this advantage you speak of?—A. No; it does overcome it in a sense where they do get it, and it does not where they do not get it. It is not general, only in Territories.

Q. Not general?—A. No. We have no transit privileges in St. Louis. We have to pay 1¼ cents arbitrary on that bridge.

Q. Do you mean to testify that the millers in St. Louis who do an export business pay a local rate to their mill on the wheat they use, and then pay the rate from St. Louis to the seaboard?—A. They do in a certain territory. Kansas has milling-in-transit privileges. You can buy in western Kansas and bill to the East, and stop anywhere you choose and mill it and send the flour on by paying 1 cent a hundred for the privilege.

Q. It would naturally follow, then, that the St. Louis millers get the wheat for export from this free district?—A. No; that might be the impression of one not conversant with the business. St. Louis mills, until recently, were what is known as soft-wheat mills, while in this Kansas district the majority of the product is hard wheat, which produces an entirely different kind of flour. The reputation of St. Louis mills was built upon soft-wheat flour, which they manufactured for 50 years or more for export. A mill seeking soft wheat has to go where it is to be had, and if their accustomed field has had poor crops they have had to go to Indiana, or even Ohio, or to Chicago, for wheat.

Q. And use that wheat for making flour for export?—A. Yes; use it for anything.

Q. Do you pay the local rate in?—A. They can not afford to do it. That is one of the disadvantages the miller has, and we are of the opinion that through the medium of the Interstate Commerce Commission we ought to get some relief from this discrimination, this inland or American discrimination. As it is now the St. Louis miller has to pay an export duty of 7 cents a hundred pounds, 14 cents a barrel, on his flour. He can not do it; his profit is not so great as that.

Q. It is worse from St. Louis than from Chicago?—A. Oh, yes; very much worse. Now, I want to make a suggestion or two: I think if we had a national statute that would permit an officer of the Government, such as the secret-service or the special-service agents of the Interstate Commerce Commission, to break car seals in cases of suspicion, you would get at the underbilling. What I mean is this: All he can do now is to spy around. For instance, I will furnish him a case where I am sure there is underbilling, because a man told me a mill was having stuff underbilled. That is a pretty fair sort of evidence, but it is not actual evidence and would not go in court, and you could not convict a man on it, because the other fellow would deny it. Now, if he could get the car number and the initial of the car that is going to this fellow in question, then get on a passenger train and go down to that place and wait until the car got there, and break that seal, and bring Mr. Merchant up for collusion, count the packages, and know the exact weight in the car, the merchant to avoid trouble will not confess himself guilty of fraud; he will give up his invoice and say he actually bought so much stuff in that car, and you can make a case of underbilling; but now it is very difficult to make a case—very difficult. I do not know anything about the law on that subject. I presume it is within the Constitution, policing the trade, to do such things as that. My experience in this underbilling business is that that would be the best remedy that I know of. I talked with Mr. Marchand, who has charge of that part of the work of the Interstate Commerce Commission, and he told me of the troubles he had in running these people down. For instance, he had what he considered a sure case in Louisville. The stuff went to Texas; he got evidence and had the people down there indicted, but the court decided the crime was not committed in Texas. He took it back to Louisville, got his witnesses up there, but has not got them indicted yet in Louisville, and has been at the case two years. His witnesses are getting away from him, and probably he will lose out on the case entirely.

Q. Have you any further suggestions?—A. I think uniform classification, Government supervision, interstate-commerce supervision will do away with rate-cutting in many cases where it is being done now, classification being changed to produce a cut rate.

Q. (By Mr. CONGER.) You mean a universal classification of the whole country?—A. Yes.

Q. Do you think it is practicable?—A. Yes.

Q. Without injury to the roads?—A. Yes.

Q. Do you think a railroad in California can handle iron ore as cheaply as in other places?—A. They would take that into consideration. The idea of the commission, I should think—and I have had some talk with them about it—would not be to do any injury to the lines, and they would accept such suggestions as would be needful; but the commission having adopted the classification best suited to this district, would hold it there and not change it at the instance of some extensive shipper.

Q. Any other suggestions?—A. I think not. More than that, I should be very glad to see the Interstate Commerce Commission empowered to enforce their rulings on findings of fact, the rulings to stand until reversed by the courts.

Q. (By Professor JOHNSON.) Are you in favor of substituting fines for imprisonment?—Yes; I think we should get convictions quicker by releasing the shipper unless he can be shown to be party to the fraud.

Q. Do you favor inspection of railroad accounts?—A. Yes; I do. I favor a rigid inspection. You will get the truth that way, and you will drive lots of dishonest people out of business.

Q. Do you believe in modifying the long and short haul clause so as to eliminate that wording, "substantially similar circumstances and conditions?"—A. With reference to that, I would not do anything that I conscientiously thought would injure a railway. In answering that question I would be willing, before a Congressman should vote on that matter, to take the best advice of railway representatives on the matters to be considered. They know a good deal about that themselves, and I believe when it comes to the question of making it a law they will do the fair thing. It is a big question; a great deal of evidence could be adduced on that, and a man in ignorance of the whole state of affairs might go quite wrong in expressing an opinion. But, about the inspection of records, I should be in favor of putting a stamp tax on it and putting it in the Internal Revenue Service if necessary, letting the shipper pay the tax in order to get at them because what the railroad manager is worried with to-day more than anything else is the other railroad manager. The railroads of the country want protection against each other worse than any other business I have any knowledge of; they absolutely need protection against each other, and I think before the agitation which is now on concerning transportation matters is over there will be a better understanding between the shipper and the railroad manager who wants his line conducted on absolutely fair lines, and it will result in very wise laws on the subject.

Testimony closed.

CHICAGO, ILL., *November 23, 1899.*

TESTIMONY OF MR. C. W. DICKINSON.

Manufacturer of agricultural implements, La Crosse, Wis.

The subcommission on transportation being in session in Chicago, Representative Lorimer presiding, at 2.55 p. m., November 23, 1899. Mr. C. W. Dickinson was introduced as a witness, and being duly sworn, testified concerning transportation as follows:

Q. (By Representative LORIMER.) Will you please state your name?—A. C. W. Dickinson.

Q. Your business and post-office address?—A. I live at La Crosse, Wis. I am connected with an institution for the manufacture of agricultural implements at that place.

Q. We have information that you know of some irregularities with reference to transportation in your section; will you, in your own way, tell us what your people have to say about this matter?—A. The first topic I should like to discuss is that of uniformity of classification in all parts of the country. I do not know how many different classifications there are in use in the country, but I do know of several, and we have found more or less injustice to ourselves, in our business relations, growing out of this difference in the tariffs. When I speak of "we" in this connection I mean the concern with which I am immediately connected.

Q. (By Professor JOHNSON.) Will you specify what inconveniences you have suffered?—A. Yes; a specific illustration of such an injustice arises in the difference in classification in vehicles under the Official classification and the Western classification, which governs in the territory in which we are located. For instance, under the Western classification practically all vehicles, except those of large and bulky structure, are shipped at one and one-half times first class; under the Official classification, which governs in Michigan, certain sizes of packages of vehicles are shipped as first-class. Under an arrangement of the railroad companies the classification governing at the initial point of shipment governs clear through to destination. So, while under the Western classification we should have to stand a rate of one and one-half times first class, that package can go through to a similar destination at a first-class rate. It amounts to a discrimination against the carriage manufacturer or handler in our part of the territory which is decidedly felt.

Another illustration is found in the different requirements in regard to packages. Cutters, under the Official classification, may be shipped in crates set up with the bows projecting, but no wrapping of the projecting part is required; under the Western classification, the same crating may be employed, but the bows must be wrapped—if shipped unwrapped they will take a higher rating. I had an illustration of that kind a few days ago, where the manufacturers in Michigan shipped a carload of cutters to us. When reshipped by us the bows were not wrapped, and the customer had to pay the raised classification, simply because the manufacturer, under the Official classification, was not obliged to crate as under the Western.

There is another discrimination which affects our business there, and all engaged in a business of that kind, arising out of the difference between the Western and other classifications. For instance, under the Iowa classification buggies of all kinds, packed pretty nearly in all ways, are shipped at first class; under the Illinois classification, they follow pretty closely the Official classification. The railroad companies have made a special ruling on buggies, I think brought about largely by the competition or the advantages that were afforded by manufacturers in Illinois and Iowa, whereby they have made a rate that enables the Michigan manufacturer and the manufacturers along the lake up to Manitowoc, Milwaukee, Racine, and Chicago, all getting that rate, to ship vehicles to points in Iowa at a rate that is sometimes even less than the first-class rate from Manitowoc, Milwaukee, or Racine. I specify these three towns because they are in the territory governed by the Western classification. So far as I am able to learn, that special rate, made, as I suppose, for that purpose, applies on shipments originating at any of these towns and towns taking the same rates. It is claimed by the railroad companies that that rate is made for the benefit of the manufacturers in Michigan, or the East, although the tariffs in which I have found that rate make no provision of that kind. It would seem to apply to shipments originating at these three lake-shore points I have mentioned.

We have a carriage factory at our place, and also one or two concerns shipping vehicles to many points in Iowa; where they could get a first-class rate through, the rate at our place—one and one-half times first class—amounts to more than one and one-half times the rate from these lake-shore points I have mentioned; and we think it amounts to a gross injustice to us.

I give these facts as illustrations of the principle. It seems to me that wherever there is a difference in the classification there will be more or less injustice arising from it, and that would be obviated by the adoption of a uniform classification throughout the country. I am not prepared to say that there would not be some particular instances, perhaps, where a difference in the rate arising under the classification might not be just, but throughout the very broad extent of country where these different classifications apply, the uniform classification, it seems to me, would be the proper thing. Inasmuch as the railroads themselves have adopted varying classifications in large sections of the country, I do not see how that could be brought about unless it was done by some form of governmental authority. It is quite possible, I think very likely true, that even in our territory governed by the Western classification there may be advantages to our people under that classification; but as nearly as I can reach a conclusion in the matter, it is not so. It is a very large subject of course, and one does not become posted on all the inequalities and niceties in a short time.

Q. I believe you suggested there was another subject you wanted to present?— A. Yes; it is on the subject of freight discriminations. I am not here for the purpose of making complaints against the railroad companies. I think their difficulties very largely arise out of conditions that are very difficult for them to handle; but what the business men of this country need more than anything else is not a comparative rate, but a stable rate. If we know that rates are so and so, our business enterprises can build on a rate of that kind, we know somewhere about where we stand, but so long as the railroads have the power to adjust the rates on whatever grounds they may think proper, very great hardships are sometimes produced.

I will give an illustration of what I mean in that respect. A short time ago, say about 3 years ago, our rate on agricultural implements, wagons, vehicles— carload rates—to the city of Madison, Wis., was 19 cents a hundred. La Crosse is situated to within a fraction of a mile at the same distance from Madison as Chicago is; and, of course, Racine and Milwaukee are somewhat closer; but we found we were unable to do business there. After a good deal of investigation, because our station agent did not seem to be posted on such matters, we found that from Chicago to Madison, Racine, and other towns taking these rates, the carload rate was 12½ cents. That was all we learned at that time. There was a good deal of correspondence and many interviews backward and forward among the railroads; and finally the rate from La Crosse to Madison was reduced to 12½ cents; but within a very few days after that, I discovered a tariff had been in existence for a long time, which made a rate from Madison to Chicago on the same class of goods of 8 or 8½ cents; and also a rate applying on less than carload lots on all kinds of agricultural machinery and wagons, in both directions, of 15 cents a hundred. At that time and now our first-class rate to Madison was 48 cents a hundred, and the other class rates also in proportion; but the third-class rate, if I have the figures correct, was 28 cents a hundred, while Chicago, Milwaukee, and these towns taking the same rates, had a flat rate on all kinds of agricultural machinery of 15 cents a hundred, applying in either direction.

Of course that placed us at a very great disadvantage in trying to reach that territory, which was practically, at least, as near to us as to Chicago. That rate was apparently unknown to some of the higher railroad officials; at least they disclaimed knowledge of it; and after a time the rate was abolished and the regular tariff rates were instituted—that is, the carload rate was raised to 12½ cents, and the class rates on less than carload lots, as per tariff, were instituted. That ran a very few months in that way, when one of the roads made a break again and reduced the rates to these special ones I have just indicated, to 8 or 8½ cents on the carload and 15 cents on less than carloads. That prevailed again until within the past 2 months. It was abolished about 2 months ago.

I simply call attention to these facts as illustrative of the principle that when the railroad companies are left to make the rate themselves they will, to favor special shippers under special conditions, make rates that will impose a very great hardship on other people. It seems to me that with the natural inclination of the railroad companies to get business the best way they can, the rate-making power ought to be placed under control, so that such injustices could not arise.

Q. What recommendation do you make in regard to the matter of rates?—A. It seems to me that the only way that it could be properly controlled would be to vest it in the Interstate Commerce Commission. I do not feel like making the recommendation so broad as to say the railroad companies shall not have the power to make rates, but I would at least provide that the rates may be revised by the Interstate Commerce Commission, with authority to make their rates prevail.

Q. In other words, you believe in giving the Interstate Commerce Commission that power which they think they ought to have?—A. I do, very decidedly; and if necessary to carry out the power of the Interstate Commerce Commission, I think the recommendation for the appointment of Government examiners to examine the books of railroad companies would be of great value.

Q. Do any of the industries of La Crosse and Winona have to compete with the industries at St. Paul and Minneapolis, or markets south and east?—A. There are lumber industries there that do have to compete; there are at La Crosse also. I think there are some milling industries; but I am not thoroughly posted on the condition of the milling industry in connection with rates and tariffs.

Q. You manufacture vehicles?—A. We manufacture and place a line of agricultural machinery; but there is a wagon and vehicle factory there. There is a wagon factory also at Winona; I think none at St. Paul.

Q. Do you get as favorable rates to the West and South as St. Paul and Minneapolis do?—A. No; I think not, all things considered. St. Paul is favored with commodity rates; so are we with agricultural implements shipped into La Crosse, and we are dependent on commodity rates even for raw material. I think all manufacturers in the West are dependent on commodity rates to put them in position to compete at all with manufacturers farther east; but we find we are at something of a disadvantage because of the nature of the rates. For instance, La Crosse pays 2 cents less than St. Paul under the commodity tariffs, but we pay also to St. Paul about three-fifths of the rate of freight from Chicago to St. Paul. Our commodity rate on our raw material, mostly, of course, iron and steel, is about one-half of the rate from Chicago to St. Paul on the finished product; but it takes about two carloads of raw material in the rough to make one of the finished product, and it amounts to a discrimination against us.

Q. Some years ago there was quite a strong competition between La Crosse and Eau Claire for the lumber trade, was there not?—A. Yes; and, of course, there is more or less competition between them now. The lumber industry along the Mississippi River, as far as the manufactured product is concerned, is in a languishing condition, you know; the logs are disappearing, a good many of our mills are gone, and others of the mills will have to go somewhere else for the raw product. That is true all the way up and down the Mississippi River. I think the lumbermen have felt pretty well satisfied with the way they have been treated.

Q. (By Representative BELL.) Is it a prevalent suspicion among the public that different shippers are treated differently by the railroads, different industries are treated differently, and different communities?—A. I think that is so; yes.

Q. Is there a lack of confidence in the management of railroads to-day as common carriers?—A. Yes. Now, to verify your question in regard to the differences of treatment of different localities, I may say one of the general managers very politely informed me that the rates were made on a basis that was not calculated to favor the Western manufacturer for shipping East.

Q. Has it not been the practice of certain railroads to try to build up certain trade centers?—A. Yes.

Q. How does that affect public opinion in the intermediate points; does it create dissatisfaction or is it satisfactory?—A. That is a very difficult thing for me to answer. I have not heard that discussed so very much. There are some who feel very much dissatisfied with it, and others, I think, perhaps feel as well satisfied to have a center built up where they can have their materials on short notice without a great difference in freight.

Q. How would it be between points like St. Paul and Chicago, if the railroad should feel disposed to favor one or the other? You would not expect the people of St. Paul to be satisfied if they gave Chicago a preference, or the people of Chicago if they gave to St. Paul a preference?—A. I have seen that discussed in the newspapers, more particularly, perhaps, in reference to grain rates, and my impression was there was an extreme amount of dissatisfaction. I recollect also seeing discussions in the newspapers concerning discriminations against Chicago in favor of St. Paul and Minneapolis in grain rates. Chicago seemed to feel that other industries were very sadly left behind by the railroad companies.

To state the proposition in a very broad and general way, it is quite a question, in my mind, how far a railroad is justified in making rates that will build up any one locality at the expense of another. It seems to me that when you get right down to the very broad and general underlying principles business should be built up where there are natural advantages for the business. Any discrimination on the part of a railroad in favor of another locality diverts the development of the natural locality in favor of one which is unnatural.

Q. You understand a railroad can not be built except it be on the theory that it is a public institution, do you not? The only reason why a railroad can get a right of way through your ground against your consent is that the law regards it as a public institution for the benefit of the public.—A. A public institution, qualified, of course, by——

Q. (Interrupting.) What the law calls a quasi-public institution?—A. Yes; that is so.

Q. And every man who goes into the courts for the purpose of getting a right of way across your ground or mine must show it is being built essentially for the public, in order to get it?—A. I understand that to be the case.

Q. That being the case, is it your judgment that it has the right to discriminate against any individual, any community, or any industry?—A. That question has its difficulties; as a famous statesman once said, "It is a condition and not a theory that confronts us." That is true of the business of the West to-day, especially the manufacturing business; it is largely built up by what we might call favors in the way of commodity rates for first-class freight, especially where the roads may be united upon some one town as against some other locality where the advantages are more natural. Whatever the original qualities of the proposition might be, they are very much modified by the actual condition of things to-day, in which large and prosperous communities have been built up by favors of the railroad companies. Whether it would be just to discontinue the special privileges of that kind, now that the discontinuance would result in damage to large classes and large communities, is a grave question. With this exception, I think your proposition is correct.

Q. It would be just discontinuing a wrong, and there is no reason why it should be done unless it would be a greater wrong to quit.—A. That is the question, whether it would not be a greater wrong to quit after having given a man to understand that there would be a continuation of the rates. Let me illustrate with this proposition of law; Say one goes on your ground without your knowledge and holds it, and after a while, say a period of 20 years, you try to regain possession and seize this ground.

Q. The law says they must have an undisputed possession, and claim and color of right; and has not every community been protesting all the time about this? Entered a continual protest?—A. No; I don't know that the other communities have been protesting against the conditions of the kind I am now speaking of.

Q. (By Mr. Conger.) Could you give us an illustration of some manufacturing establishment that has been built up in the West by such favoritism as you have referred to?—A. Say the iron and steel that is manufactured in the East and is not the natural product of the West.

Q. Are there many iron and steel manufacturers in the West?—A. Yes; large numbers of them.

Q. I don't mean manufacturers of steel and iron, but manufacturers of the finished product from iron and steel.—A. Yes.

Q. (By Representative Bell.) More or less manufacturing of iron and steel products, is there not? We have a plant at Pueblo, Colo., that works, I suppose, 7,000 men.—A. Yes; that is true, but they never have cut any figure in any industry that I have been connected with.

Q. They cut a great big figure in the iron and steel industry, if you will notice the product of steel rails and everything of that kind.—A. But not in the line of business I am engaged in, that of manufacturing agricultural implements. So far as I know and am concerned, the largest iron center is near us at Superior.

Q. What do you know about the production of coal and discrimination in favor of the coal companies? Do you know of any coal mine in the country that has been able to mine coal for 20 years without being connected with a railroad company? A.—My knowledge of that is all hearsay: I have heard plenty of statements that the railroads control the anthracite coal industry.

Q. Did you ever know of a man who ran a private coal mine successfully, if he was not connected with a railroad?—A. I could not answer that question; my knowledge of the question would not justify that. I don't know that it is not so.

Q. Do you believe that under the conditions under which railroads were built it is right, if they are public institutions?—A. No, I don't. I don't believe it is right that a railroad company should favor any industry as against another one.

Q. Or individual?—A. Or individual.

Q. Do you believe that it has any right to monopolize any industry because of the fact that it owns a railroad or may control transportation?—A. I do not; no.

Q. What is your experience; are people generally contented or not with the present condition of railroads and the way they are run, or is there a dissatisfaction generally?—A. That question will have to be answered. I guess, in two ways. There is something of a dissatisfaction on the part of people who are themselves shippers—business people, I mean—when they find that an injustice is done against them that results in favor of some one else. To state the proposition clearly for our own institution, I will say that it is not so much a question with us what the absolute rates are provided they are equitable as compared with those of other people with whom we come in contact. There is a large number of people who make a kick against the railroads and the conditions who really don't know whether they are justified in making a kick or not.

Q. Has it been the general opinion of the business public, and is it the general opinion now, that the railroads do assume to control the destiny of the business public, and that they may make one community and destroy another; give one man an overcheck and another man the regulation rate, etc.? Has that been the chief objection to the management of the railroads of the United States?—A. I have no personal knowledge of rebates; that is all hearsay; but no intelligent man can say that he does not hear a good deal in regard to them.

Q. Do you believe that such things as rebates should exist?—A. No; I think the rates should be alike to all.

Q. (By Mr. KENNEDY.) Do you have any traffic over the Chicago Great Western?—A. Of course we have more or less; we ship all over the West, and some of our product goes over that line.

Q. Do you think you are getting the printed tariff rates when you are shipping over that line?—A. You mean, I suppose, by that question whether we are paying the printed rates or whether our customers are paying the printed rates?

Q. Yes; according to the schedules filed with the Interstate Commerce Commission and supposed to be posted in the freight offices of that road.—A. I feel very sure, so far as we are concerned, that we pay the full tariff rates, but we have a joint rate also.

Q. You know Mr. Stickney testified here on rates and claims that the roads are not maintaining these legal rates.—A. Yes.

Q. (By Representative BELL.) What would be your suggestion as to a remedy for our railroad evils?—A. Very much against my wishes in the matter, my jugment has led me to believe that the only remedy for the troubles I believe to exist is to put all the railroads within the control of Congress, by or through the Interstate Commerce Commission or some other body, and under such restrictions that the railroad companies would not have the power to do these things which gives rise to the trouble.

Q. Why do you have any conscientious scruples against such a thing?—A. It is not my conscientious scruples; I said it was against my wishes, because I had felt that the best service ought to come from unrestricted competition.

Q. Do you believe there is such a thing as unrestricted competition in a general line of business?—A. I mean unrestricted by law.

Q. You recognize the right of the Government to control the banks, don't you?—A. National banks; yes.

Q. Is there any reason why they should not control the railroads in the same way? They are both public institutions and recognized as such, for the good of all; they are recognized as public institutions—common carriers; do you think it would be a benefit to the railroads as well as to the people to have these things settled by some general rule?—A. I am frank to say that I have reached the conclusion that not only the public but the railroads themselves would be benefited by a control outside of themselves.

Q. And it would be absolutely just, as between them and the public?—A. Probably as nearly just as anything we can reach.

Q. Do you see any other way to remedy these things?—A. No.

Q. You would recommend, then, that more power be given to the Interstate Commerce Commission to fix the rate and control it?—A. I should recommend that, I think, very readily.

Q. What is the sentiment, so far as you know, in your State on this subject? Is it in accord with yours?—A. I think so. I talked with one of the members of our board of trade—he is a very good and intelligent man and quite well posted—and he made the remark that he thought it would not be long before practically everybody would be in favor of placing the railroads under Government control. The illustration you used in regard to the similarity of national banks was brought up at that time.

Q. (By Mr. KENNEDY.) Has your State passed an antipass law?—A. Yes.

Q. That would seem to indicate that they are in favor of State regulation of railroads, would it not?—A. Yes.

Q. (By Representative BELL.) How does that work? Do you think it is enforced or not?—A. From the fact that people who have held quasi-Government positions do not have passes, I infer that it has been enforced. That has been the conclusion I have reached. I don't know anything about it, as I have not talked with the people who have received them.

Q. (By Representative LORIMER.) It only applies to public or State officials in your State?—A. Yes.

Q. Does not apply to the public at large?—A. No.

Q. (By Representative BELL.) Do you believe any individual ought to have a pass over a railroad any more than a man ought to have a frank from the post-office?—A. I don't know of anything to justify the giving of them, except, of course, to the railroad employees.

Q. Why should they have them?—A. That would be based on the broad proposition that a man who is employed ought generally to receive more favor from the company than a man who is not.

Q. If it is a public institution for the equal benefit of all and for the common welfare, then an agent of the public has no right to distribute favors.—A. Well the railroad is not really or wholly a public institution; men put large sums of money into the railroads in order to run them, and naturally they ought to have more or less voice in their management.

Q. They are built upon the theory that a railroad is built for the public, and that it is a public institution, and that the public is entitled to the same rights and privileges that any individuals are entitled to, I don't see where the roads obtain the right to give you a favor and withhold it from me. That is the question in railroading, between the people and the railroads.—A. I think that would be carrying the principle rather too far, to say that the railroads could not extend favors to its own employees. If the question was simply one between you and me, as outsiders, that would be different. It probably would be different if the employee were given such transportation facilities as would enable him to transact a profitable business and give him an advantage over you or me.

Q. Then you mean he shall only have transportation in connection with his employment?—A. No; I don't quite mean that, although, perhaps, that is it very closely. The railroad companies are in the habit of giving transportation to their employees on private trips, and giving it to their families; that is what I should call a courtesy to the employees, such as business houses are very largely in the habit of extending to their employees that they do not extend to the outsider.

Q. Is there any sentiment in your State in favor of the Government ownership of railroads?—A. Yes; I think there is. I don't mean to say, however, that it is the general sentiment, although I hear it talked of more or less.

Q. Do you know whether it is increasing or not; do you know whether there is more of such sentiment than there was a decade or two ago?—A. Yes; as compared with two decades ago, and possibly one.

Q. What do you think is causing that sentiment to grow; is it a desire to own railroads or is it because the people have been discouraged by reason of these discriminations and supposed injustice?—A. It arises, I think you might say, wholly from the fact that they think the public is not treated rightly by the railroads. I never heard a man express any opinion that the Government ought to own the railroads simply from a desire of ownership.

Q. So we must assume from that that they don't believe they can get justice in any other way?—A. I think it is fair to state that is the sentiment so far as I know. I don't mean to say it is the general sentiment, but there is a sentiment of that kind.

Q. If these shippers were to understand that the Interstate Commerce Commission would absolutely put down these discriminations between citizens, and also between localities and different industries, and that railroads would be compelled to treat everybody alike, do you think there would be any such sentiment?—A. It is very hard to tell what I believe in that respect. I think it would depend on the officials that were put in control of it for the Government. They might discriminate where the railroads discriminated; I think it is true sometimes that Government officials have wrongfully discriminated.

Q. But you would not expect that generally, would you?—A. No.

Q. You would not expect the Government officials would prohibit a man who had a private coal mine from shipping coal at a reasonable rate?—A. No, sir; as compared with rates to other people.

Q. Do you know, as a matter of history, that when men own private coal mines, even where they have given them a reasonable rate, they have refused to furnish them cars?—A. I don't know that of my own knowledge; I have seen it charged.

Q. Have you seen it in these investigations that have taken place?—A. Yes.

Q. Do you know that the charge is made everywhere, even where the States have made rates for coal and iron ore, that the railroads have always claimed to be short of cars—that they had no cars—and that that has made it practically impossible for a dealer to hold a customer?—A. I have seen that charged, but I don't know it of my own knowledge.

Q. Is it general history that these things have occurred; has it been generally rumored everywhere that the railroads had control of the coal industry of the United States?—A. That is putting it rather broader than my information would warrant; I don't know that that is the general history of the coal trade. I know it is charged very strongly that that is the history of the coal-mining industry of the East. There is a large mining district in Illinois, but I don't know that I ever heard it charged of the industry there. We have not been consumers of coal for factory purposes to any large extent; not for steam purposes anyway.

Q. (By Mr. CONGER.) Going back to the question of railroads giving passes to their employees, for a moment, I want to ask you this question: Do you know of any other institution in the country, wholesaling or retailing its goods or products, that gives special facilities to its employees for purchasing goods that are for sale;

do you know whether in dry-goods stores or clothing stores, when an employee wants dry goods or wants a suit of clothes, the firm makes a present to the employee of what he wants, the same as the railroads make presents to their employees of the transportation that is for sale?—A. It has been done in some places; I don't know that they make a general practice of it. It is quite a common thing for them to furnish their goods to their employees at less than the regular price to customers.

Q. Presenting them goods and furnishing them goods at cost would be a far different question?—A. No; not particularly; they have the right to do it——

Q. (By Representative LORIMER.) Have you known of large institutions that make presents outright to their employees?—A. Repeatedly.

Q. (By Mr. KENNEDY.) I should like to ask you if that was a well-considered reply when you said these passes were given to the employees of the railroads on the broad principle that employers show more favors to their employees than they do to others; has that been your experience? Then you used the word courtesy later on; I should like to ask you now if it is true that the employers show more favors and courtesies to their employees than to others who are not their employees?—A. I think that word was used advisedly on that subject. I did not attempt to discuss the relation of the employee of a railroad company to the railroad; but I think it is a fair statement that the railroad companies give their employees passes to make private trips, and it occurs to me that it is merely a courtesy to the employee.

Q. Don't you think that when they do this they know they are not losing any money by it? Is it not probably done by the employers, not so much in the way of a courtesy as because the service the men have rendered is such that they can well afford to give the passes?—A. I am under the impression that the higher up a man is in the service the easier it is for him to get transportation. As I say, I know very little about the pass business from personal experience.

Q. (By Representative LORIMER.) Do you know whether or not railroad employees when traveling over the road are given passes whenever they ask for them?—A. I may say yes to that, from the fact that I am acquainted with a good many railroad employees who have told me they received passes from the railroad company to go on business that I knew was personal, and not railroad business; but I never have been informed that they often receive these passes. I understand that at the present time such passes are limited to transportation over their own lines of road; although they used to be able to get transportation over almost any road in the country.

Q. Do you think it is generally understood that a railroad employee can get a pass over the road he is working for, to transact business of his own? That is, whether he is a man working for a dollar and a half a day, or whether he is the general manager of the road?—A. I don't recall any case in which a section hand got a pass in order to make a trip to transact business of his own; I do know of brakemen, conductors, and other employees of the railroads having them. Of course you understand that I am not on the inside, and if they receive them they don't come and tell me about it; so I must pass on that.

Q. Do you know of any railroad employee of any grade that was ever refused a pass after he had asked for it of the railroad for which he was working?—A. No, I have no knowledge of a refusal.

Q. So as a matter of fact, you don't know whether they give preference to the higher grade of employees or the lower grade? When I say grade of course I refer to the wages paid.—A. I feel a good deal like a man who tries to shoot something in the dark, but I will say this: Some of the higher railroad officials get annual passes, and I don't know of any of the minor employees that have received annual passes; they have trip passes. This talk is about something I don't know much about; but generally, I think the people who have had the annual passes have been the people who have been able to benefit the railroads themselves.

Q. (By Representative BELL.) Do you know whether it is a general understanding that the wealthy man, who is the man most able to pay his fare, is the man who gets the passes, and the man who is most able to pay the schedule freight rate is the man who gets the rebate?—A. Yes, I have felt that that is true; that a great number of people seem to be able to get transportation, or generally seem to, so far as I know anything about it, who don t seem to be of any value to the railroad. For instance, it might be said to be a fair proposition that a concern, whether it is an individual or corporation, that should do any favor to a railroad or furnish it with a large amount of freight would be entitled, naturally, to travel free, if anyone can. But frequently I have seen passes in the hands of people who didn't furnish the railroad companies with 10 cents' worth of business, so far as I could see.

Q. (By Representative LORIMER.) Public men, for instance?—A. Yes; public men.

Q. (By Mr. C. J. HARRIS.) Is it customary to give the newspaper men passes in your part of the country, especially?—A. I don't know of their ever giving them any. It is generally supposed, ˉ believe, that their transportation is rather in the way of mileage.

Q. (By Representative BELL.) How is it with the county commissioners? Do they get passes?—A. I could not go through the details regarding the county officials, or say how that is; I could not say that they do not get them and I could not say that they do get them.

Q. You have never obtained them for yourself and have never held any official position?—A. I remember some years ago I was in St. Joe and had occasion to go to Nebraska to a collection. The dealer I was doing business with there in St. Joe was a councilman, and I appreciated the fact very much that he was able to get transportation for me and the party who went with me, there and back.

Q. What was his business?—A. He was in my line of business. These favors are pretty scarce now, I should say; we don't hear anything of them in our place of business.

Q. (By Mr. C. J. HARRIS.) You come in contact, in your business, with the agricultural classes rather intimately, do you not?—A. To some extent, yes; by the agricultural class I suppose you mean the farmer.

Q. Well, yes. What is the condition of the farmer throughout the western part of the country at the present time? Is he getting fair prices for his products, and is he in a prosperous condition?—A. There are localities where his prices are not as great as he would like, but I think it is fair to say that the farmer in the West is prosperous to-day. I find on inquiry, where I have been during the last two years, that the farmers have the money that is in the banks. I don't do a great deal of traveling now, and of course I am not so familiar with these things. At the same time, I think it is safe for me to say that I have not seen or talked with a banker in the last two years but would say that in his locality the farmers have the money in the banks. From that I conclude they are doing well.

Q. (By Representative BELL.) How do the prices this year compare with those of last year?—A. I think, probably they are a trifle higher, but not very much.

Q. What do you mean? You don't mean that wheat or oats are higher, or potatoes are higher? You may take the lowest price—— A. I have not kept tab on the highest and lowest price; I base my assertions on what I have heard men say who have followed the markets more closely than I have done.

Q. I think you will find a great reduction in the price of wheat, oats, and potatoes; potatoes certainly so, and both oats and wheat show great reductions.— A. I have not kept tab on them, but I do remember hearing someone say—he was a newspaper man—and he said he paid, as a rule, a little more than usual; that prices were a little bit higher than usual.

Q. (By Mr. CONGER.) How about the prices of live stock, cattle, sheep, and hogs? Are they lower or higher?—A. I think they are higher.

Q (By Representative BELL.) You don't mean that they are higher now? Are you comparing them with any time during the past year?— A. I have not got the figures; I have not kept a very close tab, as I say, on these things, but I think the farmers feel very well satisfied with the prices. Horses are higher; a great deal. Hogs are higher.

Q. Horses have come up, but cattle have gone down?—A. It is a general impression, but I should say they have not. As touching on the relative prices of beef, I would say that I went to the meat market the other day and the butcher told me that the best beef was getting so much higher than it was that the people would not buy; he didn't know but he should have to go out of the business on that account; he said beef was getting to be so high that the poorer classes would not buy it. I wish to say to the commission that our people down there favor a general mileage book for travelers going over the United States or over large sections of territory, and I desire to make that statement in their behalf.

Q. (By Mr. CONGER.) What class of people are directly interested in this mileage-book question?—A. Mostly commercial men.

Q. Commercial men and employees of commercial men. Is that the idea?— A. Yes.

Q. (By Mr. C. J. HARRIS.) Would it not be difficult to arrange that mileage book so as to give the roads in sparsely settled countries and over mountains the rates they are to receive; and these roads running through thickly settled communities and on level grades, the rates they ought to receive?—A. I don't know. It seems to me that the railroad companies might adjust these things if they wanted to. For instance, the tariff rate in South Dakota is 4 cents a mile. If the traveler gets a mileage book on the roads here at the rate of 2 cents a mile—if he gets these rebates back here why should he not get them there? The theory of the 4-cent rate as against the 3-cent rate on other roads was that it is a sparsely settled country and, of course, there might be some difficulties of that kind. But the railroads always seem to be able to surmount a difficulty when they want to do so, in my experience.

Q. (By Mr. CONGER.) Do you think it would be feasible for a road to handle passengers, as an economical proposition, at as low a cost per mile per passenger in South Dakota as in New York?—A. No; I should not think that could be done.

Q. (By Representative BELL.) Why not?—A. Because they don't carry enough people at a time on a train.

Q. You mean the cost per mile would not be greater—the actual cost of running?—A. If I should figure that out, I should probably say that the cost of running the train in South Dakota would be every bit the same as the cost of running it in New York State, except, perhaps, the cost of the fuel; but I should say that the profit to be made would depend upon the number of passengers carried. If a train should only carry 100 passengers the first day's travel and the next day should arr 500, of course the railroad would make more the second day than the firstc y

Q. (By Mr. CONGER.) The question as asked was not as the Congressman put it. I asked if it would be possible to carry passengers at as low a cost per mile per passenger in South Dakota as in New York State.—A. I think it is very evident it can not be done in a sparsely settled and mountainous country as cheap as it can in the Eastern country, where there is many times as much travel and where the cost of fuel is less.

Q. To have a universal mileage book going over the entire country would work an injustice to some railroads?—A. The recommendation was not absolutely for a universal mileage book through those large and sparsely settled sections. They can carry passengers in Wisconsin or Minnesota, I think, about as cheap as they can in New York or Ohio; I don't see but there is quite as much travel in these sections of the country as there is farther east.

(Testimony closed.)

CHICAGO, ILL., *November 23, 1899.*

STATEMENT OF MR. AMOS S. MUSSELMAN,

Grand Rapids, Mich.

To the honorable subcommission on transportation of the Industrial Commission, sitting at Chicago, Ill.

GENTLEMEN: In response to your courteous invitation to appear before your body and testify relating to matters touching transportation in which Grand Rapids is interested or has just grounds for complaint, we beg leave to submit a communication on this subject and ask for it your patient indulgence and careful consideration.

1. We claim that the rate basis for Grand Rapids should be changed from 96 per cent of the Chicago rate to 90 per cent. We claim that we are justly entitled to this per cent on the actual mileage basis and that the change should be made operative on through business both to and from the East. Grand Rapids is the natural center or distributing point for western Michigan, accommodating a population of 1,500,000 people. These people and the large distributing agencies in our city have a right to demand that this inequality or unjust basis in the cost of freight be remedied.

Milwaukee, related to eastern Wisconsin as Grand Rapids is to western Michigan, has a 100 per cent basis of Chicago rate, which, by her actual mileage, she is not entitled to; and this discrimination is more apparent when the fact of cheap lake transit which is afforded to western Michigan from Chicago and Milwaukee is considered.

In 1891, when Grand Rapids was on a 100 per cent basis, our board of trade, with the good offices of the G. R. & I. R. R. Co. and the C. & W. M. R. R. officials, placed this matter before the Central Traffic Association, urging our just claims for a 90 per cent basis. This resulted in a partial remedy by our being granted a 96 per cent ratio.

While we may not have exhausted all the remedial powers within our reach to have this unjust basis righted, yet we have felt that to take this matter to the

Interstate Commerce Commission, with their lack of power to enforce compliance with their orders, would be a futile attempt and waste of energy. We therefore urge that you recommend to Congress that the powers of the Interstate Commerce Commission be enlarged and that it be given authority to make its orders mandatory and operative on any date it may name. We are of the firm opinion that with such authority vested in the commission many unjust discriminations would be speedily remedied and the people's interests better guarded and subserved.

2. As regards pooling, we think that it should be legalized under the supervision and direction of the Interstate Commerce Commission. The reasons are several: First, there could not be any inducement to cut rates, as each trunk line would be getting its agreed share of tonnage, as the tonnage would be equalized. If this were in effect we certainly should not see one of the main commodities have a 9 to 10 cent per hundredweight differential, which is the case on wheat and flour for export.

While many contend that pooling is wrong a greater portion of the shippers think otherwise, and it is the opinion of our board that pooling between the railroads would eliminate the rate cutting. Were it not for rate cutting the railroads could carry freight at a lower rate, simply because they would not be carrying a large amount of freight at less than cost to them, for which loss the rest of the freight has to make up. The Middle States, mainly Michigan, Ohio, and Indiana, are the ones most affected by these cut rates. The railroads claim they do no cutting. While they say they do not cut rates east of Chicago, they do from Chicago and from the Mississippi River points to the seaboard, and all the trunk lines carry this cut-rate freight across the Middle States and accept their proportion of this cut rate; and here is where the wrong comes in. They give low rates, as stated, from Chicago and the Mississippi River points, but not east of there, consequently the shippers of these Central States are unjustly discriminated against.

We believe the recommendations of your commission will have great weight with Congress, and as all agree that transportation matters in this country are not in an ideal condition, we respectfully submit the foregoing propositions for your consideration.

Respectfully, yours, AMOS S. MUSSELMAN,
President Grand Rapids Board of Trade.

CHICAGO, ILL., *November 24, 1899.*

TESTIMONY OF MR. JOSEPH F. TUCKER,

Chairman of the Central Freight Association.

The subcommission on transportation met at 10.10 a. m., November 24, 1899, in Chicago, Representative Lorimer presiding. Mr. Joseph F. Tucker, chairman of the Central Freight Association, was introduced as a witness, and, being duly sworn, testified concerning transportation as follows:

Q. (By Representative LORIMER.) Please state your name.—A. Joseph F. Tucker.

Q. Your post-office address and official connection.—A. Chicago; chairman of the Central Freight Association.

Q. (By Mr. C. J. HARRIS.) We would like to have a little description of the organization that you represent.—A. Our organization is composed of about 60 roads—I think 61 or 62. The boundary of our association is from Chicago west, striking the Mississippi River at Burlington, then south, around to Pittsburg, by way of the Mississippi and the Ohio, up to Buffalo, and then, crossing the Canadian frontier, up to Mackinaw, down the east bank of Lake Michigan, and back to Chicago. Within that territory there are about 60 roads, members of our association. We have bimonthly meetings and such other meetings as necessity may require. The association's organization simply provides for information of what each road is doing. There is no agreement of any kind; each road is at liberty to do as it pleases.

Q. They make, you might say, whatever rates they please?—A. Whatever rates they please.

Q. And the other roads are informed of these rates; they know what they are doing?—A. As a rule, the roads interested in any particular traffic are informed. If a case came up of necessity for reduction of rates the interested roads would individually state what they wanted, and that information would be sent out to the others.

Q. What is the condition of business in your territory at present?—A. It is very largely everything. For instance, our territory comprises the 10 large Eastern lines.

Q. What is the condition of their business at present?—A. As to rates or the condition of business?

Q. As to amount of business.—A. They have had more than they could do for the last three months.

Q. On that account there is little rate trouble?—A. I do not think there was ever a time when there was less rate trouble, and I think, as a rule, there has been more said about rate troubles than has been justified.

Q. Tell us something about these discriminations.—A. I do not know of any discriminations; I do not think any discrimination could long continue without being known to everybody.

Q. Does that apply to this charge that very large shippers get advantages over smaller ones?—A. I do not think there is any such case. Of course a man that is a large shipper and does a large wholesale business, like several packers or large grain men, naturally have more power than the smaller dealer. That is exemplified in almost every commercial transaction.

Q. What are your ideas on the legalizing of pooling?—A. I am inclined to think a legalized pool, under proper conditions, is the greatest incentive to stability and maintenance of reasonable rates. It removes any feeling, as a rule, I think, of shippers that they were not getting equal rates with their neighbors; they often think that when they really are.

Q. The great thing in railroad rates, I suppose, is that the public should have as low rates as it is possible to have and let the railroads exist and pay their expenses and interest properly. The next greatest thing to be desired is that all shippers shall be on an equality, to do away with discrimination. Would pooling do away with discrimination?—A. I think pooling will do away with it. I think it is the greatest incentive I can think of to the stability of rates. Of course the shipper feels hurt if the railroads do not equalize distances and markets. But the competition is pretty sharp among the railroads themselves. The Gulf competition opening up presents new phases, and this Montreal competition is getting to be a new factor. In fact, I think there has been a great deal of grain shipped from here during the last year for Montreal.

Q. Will that take a great deal of freight from the United States railroads?—A. It depends. It is, of course, only the surplus grain that is exported. I think it is unwise to cripple the roads so that they could not meet any competition; and then as to foreign countries' wheat, or as to any foreign competition in the way of transportation—but I am not well enough acquainted with that; the grain men ought to be able to tell you about that better than I. I think with the railroad facilities now between here and the seaboard they can successfully meet the ordinary competition. This year they have really been able to meet the competition of the lakes, but that is on account of the high rates. The rate between here and Buffalo has been as high as 3 and 4 cents a bushel; last year it was three-fourths of a cent. I think the reasonableness of rates should be left to the courts; let the railroads show that they are reasonable. I do not think it is fair to curtail a man's income, as you do when you want to dictate what the maximum rate shall be, and at the same time not help him out on his expenses.

Q. In that case what protection would the general public have against being held up by high and excessive rates?—A. I think the competition of the country would prevent any unreasonably high rates by any pool; and, secondly, I think the public should appeal to the Interstate Commerce Commission if they are unreasonable. But I think the final resort should be somewhere where the railroads could defend themselves.

Q. They would have the courts as a last resort, even if the Interstate Commerce Commission——.—A. (Interrupting.) In that case it would be a last resort.

Q. (By Professor JOHNSON.) I understand the meetings of your association are twice a month?—A. No; once in 2 months.

Q. What is the object?—A. To consult and talk over matters ; see what are the necessities of any reduction of rates or advance of rates.

Q. Who are present?—A. The general freight agents, as a rule, representing the different lines, or the freight traffic officials.

Q. (By Mr. KENNEDY.) This is the classification committee?—A. The Central Traffic Association. The classification committee is composed of 6 members of the Central Traffic Association and 9 others—there are 15 in all.

Q. (By Professor JOHNSON.) This is a successor of the Central Traffic Association?—A. Yes.

Q. You say rate questions are discussed at these meetings; these are competitive rates that are discussed?—A. Yes. Anything relating to rates is competitive; the word local is hardly to be used any more.

Q. The object of this discussion is to decide upon what rate you think you severally ought to put in force?—A. No; the individual roads settle that.

Q. Is it true, then, that individual general freight agents come there with a definite proposition as to rates?—A. No. For instance, a party asks for a rate from a certain point on brick, which is strongly competitive—a man does not care where it comes from—and the brick-interested roads come there and talk it over.

Q. He describes the situation and tells what rate that road would like to put into effect?—A. Yes.

Q. Your association takes action on that?—A. The interested lines do; yes.

Q. And make a recommendation to that line?—A. No; they state what they will do. The interested individual lines will, say, put in a rate from Hammond to Chicago of 3 cents a hundred, effective January 1.

Q. The agreement they come to is that they will charge the same rate?—A. There is no agreement; the interested lines say they will do it.

Q. Isn't there an understanding?—A. No; no understanding at all.

Q. Suppose there is an understanding that different roads are going to charge different rates on the same traffic?—A. There could not be; they will have to issue tariffs and the lowest will prevail.

Q. Suppose there is an understanding that different roads are going to charge a different tariff on the same line of competitive freight?—A. This could not be; it would be from the same point, and all the roads leading from that point will know it. These tariffs have to be filed at Washington, and we get information of all the files at Washington, and send out that information.

Q. You mean to say it is unavoidable that the competitive roads should establish the same rate?—A. It is inevitable that they would. They would have to if they did any business.

Q. That is tantamount to an agreement to charge the same rate.—A. No; I think not.

Q. In effect?—A. No; I think that if one road should make a 4-cent rate the others would have to make a 4-cent rate, or lower, to get any business.

Q. Then it is true that each individual road so reports to the association the rates it proposes to put into effect?—A. That is the usual course; yes.

Q. And if there is an objection, that is raised and discussed in your association?—A. Yes.

Q. As a natural result of that, is there not considerable pressure brought to bear on the individual members to charge a rate agreeable to all parties?—A. No; I do not think there is any pressure at all.

Q. (By Mr. KENNEDY.) Are these published rates maintained?—A. I believe rates are well maintained. I believe they are better maintained than they ever have been. Of course, it is very natural for the shipper to feel that he is not getting the lowest rate, but I think he is mistaken as a rule.

Q. You say you know of no discrimination; do you mean general or specific?—A. I mean general. I am only speaking of my own knowledge. I do not know of any cases of discrimination.

Q. Is the Chicago Great Western in your association?—A. No.

Q. (By Professor JOHNSON.) What action is taken by your association in case of a vigorous cut in the rate on the part of one member?—A. Just as other rates; meet it.

Q. (By Mr. CONGER.) By action of the association?—A. Not action of the association; individual action.

Q. (By Professor JOHNSON.) Is any effort put forth to get the individual to restore the rate?—A. If that is done, it is individual.

Q. Does the correspondence go through your association?—A. Not often.

Q. Not often; it sometimes does?—A. I do not remember any such case. The member that puts in a reduced rate does it on reflection, and usually has some good reason for it, and holds to it.

Q. You think the situation as regards rate making is radically different in your association from that before the decision of the Supreme Court in the trans-Missouri case?—A. We endeavor in our reorganization to avoid any violation of the law.

Q. (By Mr. KENNEDY.) Is it understood among the railroad men of Chicago that the Chicago Great Western enjoys a much larger volume of traffic than would naturally go to it because of the pirating of rates on the part of that company?—A. I could not speak understandingly of that; I do not know. They are in the Northwest. I was on the St. Paul some years, and the St. Paul used to bring into Minneapolis more wheat than all the other roads put together. They made what they call milling-in-transit rates, and would have a carload of wheat from Dakota stop at Minneapolis to mill, and that same rate would apply on that wheat and on the flour, with 1½ cents for stopping at Minneapolis. I do not think, in the end, any pirating of any rates will result in any increased tonnage, because it will soon be met by the competitor.

Q. Do you know whether there is truth in the statement that the public rates are not maintained and that the railroads can not maintain them?—A. I do not know how it is in the Northwest, but I should say in our association the opposite was the case.

Q. (By Representative OTJEN.) In case the railroads were allowed legally to pool, do I understand you to favor the expansion of the authority of the Interstate Commerce Commission to regulate rates; that is, to revise them?—A. Not as a finality. It seems to me that the railroads should have a reasonable hearing as to what reasonable rates were. I think the railroads would not agree to it unless there was some provision as to reasonable rates. I think there should be just as strong a law against unreasonably low rates as against unreasonably high rates.

Q. The Interstate Commerce Commission would fix the rate; in some cases it might lower it, and in other cases it might think a rate was too low. That would not preclude the right of the railroad to appeal to the courts from their decision. Do I understand you that there is any objection to that?—A. I should not think there was any. I understand from you that is the same as it is to-day. For instance, the commission makes a ruling——

Q. (Interrupting.) With the exception that they now have no authority to enforce that ruling; is not that the case?—A. Would your idea be that the railroads would have to conform to the rates under that ruling until the courts ruled otherwise?

Q. That would seem to me——A. (Interrupting.) I should not favor that.

Q. (By Professor JOHNSON.) Why not?—A. Because I do not think it would be fair for the Interstate Commerce Commission, not having in view the tonnage, and expenses, and necessities of the rate, to change the rate.

Q. (By Mr. CONGER.) Why not, if the roads had the alternative before them of not entering the pool?—A. I am only favoring a pool for the purpose of stability of rates, that is all; it would be an incentive in that direction.

Q. (By Representative OTJEN.) Even with pooling, without any supervision, how could you be certain that there was no cutting of rates and no rebates given?—A. I can only answer that by saying I am certain of but very few things. I could not be certain unless I had definite knowledge, but I believe it would remove a great many of the incentives to it.

Q. Do you think that after the Interstate Commerce Commission has given a hearing upon a certain rate there would be any great danger that they would do an injustice to the railroads?—A. I can hardly answer that. It might be so and it might be otherwise. To illustrate, take the rates to-day on grain from west of the Mississippi. The board of trade report shows that they received last year 320,000,000 bushels of grain; in 1897 they received 297,000,000 bushels. That does not look as if they were discriminated against. We have to haul that grain from west of the Mississippi in competition with the Gulf; we have to calculate the ocean rate from Galveston and New Orleans, and the extra insurance, elevator charges, and all that enters into the cost of getting that grain through the gateways and meeting the competition.

Q. Is it not to be supposed that the Interstate Commerce Commission would consider all these things in passing upon these rates?—A. They could not; no. I have sometimes thought the long and short haul clause might be abrogated. It forces, for instance, the same rate from out in the neighborhood of Kansas City to Liverpool the same as via Galveston; it forces the same rates from intermediate points where there is not the same competition, not the same necessity.

Q. (By Representative BELL.) As I understand, you see no reasonable objection to a law that would keep the railroads that were evil disposed off the people, and then keep the people off the railroads; put them on absolutely fair terms as between the public and themselves?—A. Certainly not.

Q. Do you believe in relentless competition?—A. Unrestricted competition in the end is ruin.

Q. Is it not ruinous to grocery men, farmers, laborers—any other line of business?—A. Railroading is simply a commercial transaction; it is selling transportation.

Q. I suppose in railroading you necessarily have what is known as the unreliable railroad man, the same as we have the unreliable lawyer, merchant, or men in other lines; that is, men that will break in upon agreements and start a cut that not only affects the public, but affects railroads; not only affects the railroads, but the public. If a pooling arrangement could be enacted and put under a good board, like the Interstate Commerce Commission, do you see any reason why it should not benefit the roads as well as the public?—A. I think a legalized pooling law would be a strong factor toward the maintenance of rates, and stop a good deal of the unsatisfactory feeling; yes.

Q. And I suppose there is no question but that railroad managers, traffic managers, confer and reason with one another against lowering a rate or raising a rate, just as grocery men do, or men in any other line of business, for the good of the whole?—A. They do reason together; but unlike the grocery man, perhaps, they can not go out of business, and they must meet the competition they encounter.

Q. Is it your judgment that these companies with the irreconcilable managers are a benefit to the business?—A. As I said a while ago, I think there is more said in regard to discrimination than is warranted. Between here and the East, with that immense tonnage, the lines were hauling yesterday, I think, something like 15,000 tons of grain; I think it is impossible for any shipper to have a reduced rate without everybody else knowing it very quickly.

Q. Is it possible for him to have a drawback system that you do not know?—A. Oh, yes; of course, that is possible.

Q. Mr. Huntington, I suppose you know quite well?—A. C. P. Huntingon? I know him by reputation only.

Q. He stated a while ago before the Senate committee that the Santa Fe, when it went into the hands of a receiver, developed a state of facts showing it had paid over $7,000,000 in drawbacks; now if that be true, did the other roads know it?—A. No. I should think they would know it if the Santa Fe got a greater tonnage than they would otherwise get; I think the other roads would have discovered that there was something wrong.

Q. Did they have any power to prevent it?—A. The only power would be to reduce rates.

Q. That meant ruin?—A. That meant ruin if they went far enough.

Q. Do you not believe it would be to the benefit of all reliable roads to have such a legal regulation as to absolutely prohibit that system of doing business?—A. Oh, there is no doubt of that.

Q. And it would not injure the railroad system of the country?—A. To prevent the rebates?

Q. To prevent rebates, discriminations, and special favors.—A. Oh, yes; no doubt of that, I think.

Q. Now, we have had before this commission some very glaring instances of these rebates, related by men that received the rebates. The tendency has all been to give rebates, as far as shown before us, to the men best able to pay the tariff rate. Do you believe that is morally right?—A. No.

Q. Do you approve of that?—A. No.

Q. You would also be willing to aid the people as well as the railroads in preventing such conditions?—A. Yes.

Q. (By Professor JOHNSON.) Believing these things, how can you make the statement that transportation is merely something to be sold?—A. As railroading is a commercial transaction, they sell transportation. Unlike other commercial enterprises, they are obliged to sell all at the same price. I do not think any different condition can long exist.

Q. Then, it is not something to be sold in the open market as commodities are sold; it is simply to be sold at a price equal to all?—A. Necessarily; like the open market of other goods, it would finally land in the same place.

Q. Do you think it ought to be the nation's business to say that this service is to be sold equally to all?—A. I think discriminations should stop.

Q. Do you think it is the nation's business to see that they do stop?—A. Oh, there is no doubt of that part of it.

Q. Mr. Stickney took the ground that transportation was simply something to be sold and bartered, the same as commodities.—A. I can not agree with him.

Q. (By Representative BELL.) You recognize that a railroad is a quasi-public institution?—A. Oh, yes.

Q. You are willing, and the roads with which you are associated are willing, that there be a reasonable Government regulation?—A. I could not speak for the roads. I can only give my own personal opinion.

Q. Is it your judgment that the reliable roads would approve of a just regulation on the lines you have designated?—A. Yes; that is my judgment.

Q. (By Mr. CONGER.) In fixing the rates from various cities or shipping centers in the West to the seaboard—to New York, we will say—Chicago is taken as a basis and called 100 per cent, and other cities are given a per cent, sometimes lower and sometimes higher, according to distance. Can you tell us how these rates or percentages are fixed?—A. That was reached through what was called years ago the joint rate committee. For instance, the Mississippi River was the dividing line; the western roads hauled to the east bank of the Mississippi River, and do to-day, at the same rates, and there was an equalizer put in there. The rates to these points being the same, and from these points being the same, it made the same rate through all gateways. The 100 per cent arrangement, Chicago basis—Louisville having the same basis—was, as you see, largely comparative. Thus, the east bank of the Mississippi River being 116 per cent, the west bank is plus. Some of the western lines, as you know, have small volumes of tonnage, and therefore correspondingly heavier operating expenses; that adds to that percentage basis somewhat. The eastern roads pay the western roads, for instance, out of that 116 per cent 20 per cent, and they take the balance. That is the way that was arranged, and it runs through to Buffalo. For instance, Buffalo has got, I think, two-thirds of the Chicago rate.

Q. The St. Louis rate is 116 per cent?—A. One hundred and sixteen per cent plus; that is, the bridge toll. It is arbitrary, but has to be paid.

Q. Are these rates, 100 per cent and 116 per cent, proportionate to the distances from New York to Chicago and from New York to St. Louis?—A. Yes; the 100-per-cent territory—we have a map; I wish I had it here, and it would show you at a glance. It runs up into Michigan—95 per cent up around Detroit. It is on distance.

Q. Detroit is 95 per cent?—A. I do not know what Detroit is; it is, I should think, less than 95 per cent, possibly about 85 per cent.

Q. I think Detroit is 78 per cent, not wishing to give testimony myself, however.—A. The difference in rate is a little different from the proportionate distance, for this reason, that it is fairer on a long haul to charge less per ton per mile as you increase your distance. That is, the terminal expense is the same for a haul of 50 miles as it would be for a haul of 500; so that would change the percentage a little.

Q. Do you know what the Indianapolis rate is?—A. I think the Indianapolis rate is about 100, perhaps 96; somewhere along there, I think 96 or 98; the 100 runs down to Louisville, I know.

Q. We will suppose, for illustration, that the actual distance from New York to Detroit is 72 per cent of the distance from New York to Chicago, and that the actual rate in effect is 78 per cent. That additional 6 per cent, as I understand, serves for terminal charges?—A. It would be, as I say, a less rate per ton per mile as you increase the distance.

Q. As that distance was less, the point nearer New York, that 6 per cent arbitrary would be increased?—A. Yes, to a slight degree, always, as the distance lessens.

Q. Supposing a town was exactly 90 per cent of the distance to Chicago, ought that additional terminal charge to be as much as 6 per cent?—A. It might be changed to a slight degree. I am inclined to think that Indianapolis is on the direct mileage basis.

Q. But to reduce this arbitrary charge as the distance increases would be the fair principle?—A. Yes; I think distance must necessarily be a large factor in transportation, except, perhaps, where this strong competition, like the Gulf or some other competition, comes in. Then, you have to meet the rates your neighbors set.

Q. If the distance was 90 per cent, to charge 96 per cent would be too much?—A. I do not know that I should like to say yes or no to that until I had looked into the circumstances of such a case. There might be some reasons that would govern my conclusion. But I think the original joint rate percentages were considered very carefully some 15 years ago, and were taken up on the merits of each case. It is fair to presume that any road that felt its town was hurt by 96 per cent, when it should have 92 per cent, would have stated it and it would have been corrected. We have corrected that map to some extent; not a great deal; it has lasted well.

Q. Suppose the shippers of such a town thought the rate was too high; to whom should they go for a reduction?—A. They would simply deal with the general freight agent of the initial road. For instance, Indianapolis has four or five general freight agents there—the Peoria and Eastern, the Lake Erie and Western, and others—and they would say, We are not fairly treated.

Q. That initial road, unless it had a through line of its own, would have to deal with other roads, would it not?—A. As a rule, the eastern connections of our roads take it for granted that the men that originate the business know the most about the necessities of the situation, and as a rule carry out what they suggest.

Q. Is there anything binding through your association on these roads, the connecting lines?—A. No penalty, or anything of that kind.

Q. Was this arrangement originally made through your association, the percentage arrangement?—A. That was made 15 or 20 years ago; you will see the necessity in the way of equality of

Q. Oh, yes; I see the necessity for it.—A. They have been well satisfied; there has been very little complaint about it. A rate from Chicago to New York of 20 cents carries at once that rate from Mississippi River points—116 per cent.

Q. We are to understand, then, that the burden of maintaining or reducing these rates rests principally with the road that initiates the freight?—A. Yes. To illustrate, here is Pittsburg, in the pig-iron district. Something comes up; pig iron is either advanced or reduced. The Pittsburg representatives hear the complaints of the shippers and look into the case, and, as a general rule, the shipper and the railroads meet and it is fairly considered all around.

Q. (By Representative BELL.) About that difference, I suppose you know it is the history of other lines of business. For instance, manufacturing plants get better prices nearer home, do they not, usually? For instance, a milling plant sells its surplus usually at a less price than it does the quantity necessary to supply its home customers.—A. I heard Mr. Counselman testify that he saw American flour sold in London cheaper than in New York.

Q. Is that not natural?—A. I can not understand it. Of course in other commercial transactions I presume they sell the same article. I know they do sell salt for different prices, according to the locality where it is going.

Q. Is it not your experience in all lines of business that the surplus goes for a less price than the general product?—A. Yes.

Q. For instance, here is a milling concern. They used to complain of a mill right where I lived. They said that 300 miles away they could buy the flour cheaper than they could at home. Still, I know as a matter of fact, because I was interested in it, that the flour we sold at the distant point we sold at actual cost, because we had to run, anyway, so much or shut down, and had to get rid of the surplus. Does not that cut some figure in railroading?—A. We are doing that to some extent to-day. For instance, the rate on export corn is 2 cents lower than the domestic. It is getting rid of the surplus and meeting foreign competition—meeting competition that the local interests do not meet.

Q. Is that not necessary for both railroad and consumer?—A. I think it is one of the wisest things for this country at large to move this surplus crop out.

Q. For instance, take a great iron plant, and if you may have its product for the foreign market at practically cost, that enables you to supply it with its domestic supplies, such as ores and other things that you do make a profit on?—A. I really do not know about that, but I had occasion once to contract for the surplus coal of a mine. I was with the Illinois Central then. They sold that surplus coal much cheaper than they did the general supply, and by our purchasing it—we agreed to take the surplus, whatever it was—they were enabled to keep that mine open and to keep the thing going.

Q. It developed the business at home?—A. It kept the mine open. If we had not taken that surplus the coal miner told me he could not have kept it going; and, of course, it was for our interest, as the mine was on the road, to keep it open.

Q. Do you not think that cut some figure in the shipping rate, moving the surplus?—A. Yes. Independent of that, the export traffic is very large in its volume; it loads the cars heavily, export grain and export flour also, and can be moved with fully as much profit to the railroad as other freight locally, in smaller volume.

Q. (By Mr. KENNEDY.) Would it not be good public policy on the part of railroads to place flour on the same footing with wheat, if there is an equal demand for it abroad, looking to the giving of employment to our mills and our workers in the mills?—A. I think the transportation rates should be based on the value, which carries with it the risk to the railroads; and I think also the volume has something to do with it. The law provides the carload as the unit. I think the manufactured article should always be charged more than the raw material, and, as a rule, it is of less weight.

Q. Suppose it is loaded to the capacity of the car; there will be as much in weight of the manufactured article placed in the car, and placed there at the expense of the manufacturers themselves. Ought not the railroads to haul it at the same rate as wheat?—A. Then there will come in the terminal expense and the risk. Export flour from Minneapolis loaded—I think the statistics show—about two-thirds what the wheat was loaded. To illustrate, 60,000 pounds can be loaded of corn and wheat.

Q. Millers say they can load 60,000 pounds of flour.—A. The loading being even, the only thing I can see is the value of the article moved.

Q. (By Mr. CONGER.) Might not the railroads be in part responsible for the average smaller carload, by furnishing to the millers smaller cars, and furnishing for the wheat shippers new and larger cars?—A. Those figures I saw did not take that in.

Q. What is the quality of this flour exported? Is it equal to the flour manufactured for home consumption?—A. I take it for granted you can not manufacture any article without its costing more than the raw material, taking the whole output. It must cost more than that by the cost of manufacture.

Q. That is a general rule.—A. It is a matter of evidence that that export flour bears about the same price as the wheat; but I think you would have to go into that pretty deeply to see whether they did not use the poor wheat for the export. I am inclined to think if you took the books of the miller and saw what he paid for the wheat and what he received for the flour, he must have had some profit.

Q. Might not a large proportion be in the offal?—A. That is the same thing, you know.

Q. At the same time, it would seem to me quite possible that the value of the flour is not greatly in excess of the value of the wheat, particularly as I think it is a fact, and I am inclined to think it has been testified to before the commission, that the quality of the flour exported does not equal that of the flour for home consumption.—A. I think that was the testimony, that it was of about the same price. We have a grain list; from the spirit of accommodation on the part of the railroads, perhaps because of their inability to say no, a great many articles have been added to that grain list; they run from corn products up. We are moving that at the same price as corn. But there is a risk which the railroads assume; frequently the railroads are insurers of the property. As a rule, there would be a very much lighter load. Cerealine can only load 26,000 pounds, while corn can load 60,000.

Q. (By Mr. KENNEDY.) Is there not a basis of truth in the theory of the millers that the cause of the discrimination against American flour is that the railroads are themselves merchandisers of wheat?—A. You mean owners of it? No, sir; I do not believe any such thing. I do not know anything about that, of course, but I do not credit that at all, and, as I said in speaking of competition, I do not think any such thing could long continue without those not in it knowing something about it.

Q. (By Representative BELL.) Is there not a custom also of charging a higher rate on a valuable article than on a less valuable, without considering the risk of the railroad at all, as a matter of public policy?—A. At times, on account, mainly of the necessities of the particular case. The classification is really based on the value, bulk, and risk. To illustrate, here are spring beds that are bulky; they would not be moved as cheaply as pig lead.

Q. Is not the idea of what the article will stand in transportation also considered?—A. In a particular way; yes.

Q. For instance, you take the Rocky Mountain region. There is no risk in moving the ores. They will say that ores which run so much to the ton will be moved to the smelter for $10 a ton; here is another ore that will barely stand transportation, and they say, we will move that for $6 a ton.—A. That is on account of the value; yes.

Q. That is on the theory of what the article is able to stand?—A. Yes; what the article in view of its value should pay, or is able to stand.

Q. You find that necessary in order to develop the industry of the country?—A. Oh, yes.

Q. Therefore you can not have a stated rate for bulk?—A. No; we are guided entirely by the official classification. There are three classifications, the Official, Southern, and Western; I think there is still another, the Transcontinental. These classes here are for these light, bulky, valuable articles; then, we run to six classes, and I think the Western has nine.

(Testimony closed.)

CHICAGO, *November 24, 1899.*

TESTIMONY OF MR. JOHN F. WOFFINDIN,

Chairman of Chicago East-bound Freight Committee.

The subcommission on transportation, being in session on the morning of November 24, 1899, Representative Lorimer presiding, Mr. John F. Woffindin was duly sworn and testified as follows:

Q. (By Representative LORIMER.) Please state your name in full.—A. John F. Woffindin.

Q. Your place of business, address, and official connection.—A. Monadnock Building, Chicago.

Q. Are you connected with the freight association?—A. I am chairman of the Chicago east-bound freight committee.

Q. What is the object of this organization, as to freight and freight rates?—A. Our object is that of a statistical bureau; we also keep a record of all the industries around Chicago, and what connection they have with the various roads. There are 1,200 of them, and we keep a record of their location and what it costs to make deliveries thereto. We frequently have to meet and discuss questions as they may come up in relation to our transportation on Eastern roads and the rates. We keep a record of the minimum rates so that we can at any time know what the minimum rate is from Chicago to any Eastern point.

Q. (By Professor JOHNSON.) How is this committee made up?—A. It is composed of ten Eastern trunk lines, the C. and E. I., and C., I. and L. are also members. The trunk lines are: The Baltimore and Ohio; Cleveland, Cincinnati, Chicago and St. Louis; Chicago and Erie; Grand Trunk; Lake Shore and Michigan Southern; Michigan Central; Pan Handle; Fort Wayne; New York Central, and St. Louis and Wabash.

Q. What officials of the railroads are represented?—A. The freight officials of the roads in Chicago; the assistant general freight agent, or the general freight agent, as he may have charge of the offices.

Q. (By Mr. C. J. HARRIS.) Of each road?—A. Yes.

Q. Do you have anything to do with the rate-making power?—A. No.

Q. You simply keep a record of it?—A. Yes. Of course, we have the record of the short line—the line that has the lowest rate of freight for the accommodation of business, and also a record of the other lines that have a similar rate.

Q. (By Professor JOHNSON.) In keeping this record have you watched the prices of railroads, and have you found out what the various railways are doing in the various rates; is it the object of your association to keep each member informed?—A. Yes. If a road reduces the rate we make a record of it and advise the others.

Q. Do any of the roads reduce the rate without letting you know?—A. No.

Q. Would you know anything about it if they did?—A. The probabilities are that we would know.

Q. (By Mr. KENNEDY.) You make discoveries in this direction?—A. Of course, we keep a full record of their tariffs and it would be a case of neglect on the part of my clerks if they did not report if any change was made.

Q. (By Mr. C. J. HARRIS.) What notice do they give of a change of tariff; I mean the number of days?—A. If there was no neglect in reporting I would find it out from the tariff they would send me, which would be the usual tariff they file with the Interstate Commission.

Q. (By Professor JOHNSON.) Don't you endeavor to find out in other ways than by inspection of their published tariff?—A. I don't see how we could find out in any other way. I guess we could find out from our billings in our statistical work. I think my attention would be called to it in some way if such were the fact, and rebates had been offered.

Q. (By Mr. C. J. HARRIS.) Have rates not been put down to such a minimum figure that discriminations or rebates would hardly be expected on the part of railroads for the last few years?—A. I think that is true. Last summer rates were at such a low rate that I don't think a road could possibly have discriminated without losing money.

Q. Is it your impression that there is discrimination among certain individuals by the railroads?—A. I don't know of any. I have merely learned from the reports in the papers; I don't know anything about it of my own knowledge.

Q. Do you think there is much freight discrimination?—A. I think quite probably there is, but I have no means of knowing that.

Q. Well, in your position, being entirely occupied with freight rates and transportation matters, you would be in a pretty good position to judge, would you not?—A. I don't see how I could.

Q. Have you any opinion to express on legalized pooling?—A. I don't think that I have. My views are pretty much the same as those expressed by Mr. Tucker. What I would say on that subject would be merely a repetition.

Q. Would you favor a governmental oversight of this pooling arrangement, if one should be made, through the Interstate Commerce Commission?—A. Yes, I would favor a legalized pooling, and I suppose that would have some supervision.

Q. Some governmental supervision?—A. Yes.

Q. For what term of years do you think a pool should be entered into?—A. I should say not less than five years. That is my opinion.

Q. Why do you object to a yearly change?—A. I think the difficulties attending the creating of a pool are such that the several phases and various conditions would have to be considered, and they are such that it would be impossible from year to year to change a pool and have it on the proper basis.

Q. (By Mr. KENNEDY.) Would there be anything in the way of a readjustment every year different from that of the preceding year?—A. It would depend altogether on the circumstances about changing. I think it would be better for the stability of the rates to be assured, and that the pool should have a certain tariff.

Q. (By Mr. C. J. HARRIS.) Would that, in your opinion, do away almost entirely with discrimination and the giving of rebates?—A. I think it could be so formed that it would.

Q. Illegal discriminations?—A. Yes.

Q. Would you make the penalties imprisonment or fines?—A. I don't know really that I care to express an opinion on that.

Q. Would not fines be more effective?—A. Yes; if they would enforce them and they were severe enough.

Q. (By Professor JOHNSON.) Do you think either fines or imprisonment could be imposed?—A. That would depend upon the legislature.

Q. Suppose the legislature passed a law making it an offense to cut the rate and imposed a fine for a violation of the law, do you think that it should be enforced?—A. As I said before, it depends entirely on their executive ability to carry out what they propose. I think there is no question, as a practical matter, but what it should be enforced. It would depend on the legal machinery that was employed in enforcing it.

Q. Would it require any special legal machinery to enforce it?—A. I don't know. It might be necessary. I don't see why it should be, in a penal way. I think it could be enforced.

Q. (By Mr. C. J. HARRIS.) A bill not providing for suits for damages for the breaking of the agreement, or without fines definitely set forth for each offense, would be of no effect, would it?—A. Very probably not. I think to make it operative it would have to be subject to penalties.

Q. (By Representative BELL.) You said that if there were discriminations within the last 2 years, in your judgment, the roads that did so carried the freight at a loss?—A. No; I didn't say that. I was asked the question as to whether the current published rates were so low that anything carried below that would be at a loss.

Q. I understood you to say that it would.—A. Yes; I say so now.

Q. Under the low discriminating rates?—A. I did not say that they were discriminating.

Q. If any roads should discriminate, it would usually be the weak roads, would it not? Is not that the general custom of the weaker roads?—A. That would depend on circumstances. In an ordinary way I suppose that would be true.

Q. You said they were running at a loss if they were carrying it at a lower rate than the published freight?—A. Yes.

Q. They are presumed to carry it for a reasonable rate?—A. Yes.

Q. Now a road that is running its machinery any way, and not carrying loaded cars, might lessen that loss by taking this freight at actual cost, might it not?—A. Yes, to a certain extent.

Q. Then would not a reasonable rate fixed by Congress really benefit all the strong roads and protect them against the weaker roads, who were undertaking to cut down expenses?—A. A reasonable rate might do that, certainly.

Q. You see no objection to that?—A. I see no objection provided the rate is made, not only in the interest of the public, but also with some consideration as to the rights of the roads.

Q. You don't doubt but that the action of Congress would be reasonable on both sides, do you?—A. I have no reason to suppose otherwise.

Q. Is it not your experience that the principal objection to rebates and discriminations is not so much to the rate itself as giving special favors applying to one merchant and thereby tearing down the trade of another; building up one community and tearing down another, or one industry at the expense of the destruction of another?—A. I think that is so, in a general way, yes.

Q. And that is what the real public clamor is about—that is, supposed favoritism?—A. Yes.

Q. Is it your judgement that the roads you represent would object to such a law as would put every shipper, every community, and every individual upon an equal standing as to the rates?—A. I would not like to answer for the roads, but so far as I am concerned I sse no objection to it.

Q. Is that the judgment of the reputable roads?—A. They would be, I think, very glad to have anything that would insure them stable, and at the same time reasonable, rates.

Q. You have no apprehension that a board like the Interstate Commerce Commission, appointed by the President, would be unreasonable?—A. I have no reason to suppose so, no. If the facts were properly stated before them. I would have every reason to believe their action would be reasonable.

Q. They have always been patient in hearing both sides, have they not?—A. That is my experience, yes.

Q. And it is your judgment that the roads would be willing to have the jurisdiction of the Interstate Commerce Commission so extended that they might control the business in the interest of both the people and the roads?—A. I don't think any of our roads would have any objection to any measure that would insure reasonable and permanent rates.

Q. (By Representative OTJEN.) Do you see any objection, in case of legalized pooling, to conferring authority upon the Interstate Commerce Commission to reduce rates; to lower them if they see fit, and to raise them if they see fit; to regulate the rates?—A. Of course it would be supposed that they would not take any action until after they had heard the arguments of the railroads. I could not tell without hearing the arguments of the roads. Of course, if the rates had to be reduced by some superior power, where there was a friction between what the roads might consider was the proper rate and what the public might consider was the proper rate, I don't see why the Interstate Commerce Commission should not be as able to decide on that as any other body. There would have to be some power to arbitrate these questions.

Q. (By Representative BELL.) Have you examined the Cullom bill that was introduced in the Senate?—A. No.

Q. You don't know the terms of it?—A. No.

Q. (By Professor JOHNSON.) Are you in sympathy with the movement that has been inaugurated to enlarge the powers of the Interstate Commerce Commission?—A. I have really given that matter no thought and I would not like to give an opinion upon it.

Q. As a general proposition are you opposed to it?—A. I did not expect to be asked any question of that kind; it is rather out of my line of duty, and I don't feel competent to answer.

Q. Are you in sympathy with the amendment, or opposed to it, and if so on what principle?—A. You mean in sympathy with the amendment in what way?

Q. Enlarging the power of the Interstate Commerce Commission so as to give them power to enforce their rulings?—A. I think certainly that their powers should be increased, at least so that they can be more operative than they are at the present time. That is my idea.

Q. Do you think railroad men situated as you are would be inclined to oppose such a movement?—A. I don't see why I should.

(Testimony closed.)

CHICAGO, ILL., *November 24, 1899.*

TESTIMONY OF MR. J. T. RIPLEY,

Chairman of the Western Classification Committee.

The subcommission on transportation being in session on the morning of November 24, 1899, at Chicago, Ill., Representative Lorimer presiding, Mr. J. T. Ripley was duly sworn, and testified as follows:

Q. (By Representative LORIMER.) Please state your full name.—A. J. T. Ripley.

Q. And your official connection.—A. Chairman of the Western Classification Committee.

Q. And your post-office address.—A. Chicago.

Q. Will you please state to the commission the purpose of the organization of the Western Classification Committee and its connection with railroad tariffs?—A. The purpose of the committee is to establish and maintain a freight classification for Western roads; and its relation to freight tariffs is that it forms the basis upon which rates are made. An article is presented for shipment, and it becomes necessary to examine the classification and see what class it is given in that document, and then the rate is established, the class rate being quoted on that article as the schedule of rates or tariffs on the article.

Q. (By Mr. CONGER.) How is your committee made up; is it made up of the representatives of Eastern roads? By its relation with Western railways, you mean those roads running west of Chicago?—A. Yes.

Q. Each road being equally represented?—A. Each road is represented as a road. It sends a delegate to the committee, and has presented to the committee questions which it wishes presented.

Q. What official of each road usually comes?—A. Usually the assistant freight agent, sometimes the general freight agent or the traffic manager, sometimes the commercial and general agent.

Q. Does your committee have frequent meetings?—A. Twice a year.

Q. Only twice a year?—A. As a rule we are forced to have an extra meeting; but the by-laws provide for two meetings each year.

Q. What are your duties as manager?—A. My duties as chairman are to preside at meetings, and decide questions on the construction of the classification in the interim between meetings, or rule upon new articles presented for classification which are not already provided for.

Q. And your rules are operative as soon as made and on all the roads?—A. Yes; as soon as they are published they are operative.

Q. Are there many changes in your classification from year to year, or does it remain quite permanent?—A. Constant changes are being made at these semi-annual meetings; still, the changes are not so very numerous.

Q. There are other classifications?—A. Yes; Official classifications, which go east of Chicago and the Mississippi River and north of the Ohio River; and the Southern classification, which is in effect south of the Ohio River and east of the Mississippi River, and the Western classification, which is in effect from Chicago west to the Pacific coast.

Q. Suppose freight starts in New York under the Eastern classification and comes over into your territory under a different classification; how is that rate arranged?—A. If it comes through Chicago it is rebilled under the Western classification; and that may give it a lower or higher rate.

Q. Is that much trouble to the shipper?—A. I don't think it is a source of great inconvenience to the shipper. I have not heard of any objection to it on that account.

Q. That does not cut much figure, then?—A. I think that if there is any inconvenience it would be to the carriers rather than to the shipper.

Q. (By Professor JOHNSON.) Can a shipper ship right through to the Atlantic or the Pacific coast?—A. In some instances, I understand, the property has laid over, and is not billed through; and they make other rates apply from the seaboard to the Pacific coast.

Q. (By Mr. C. J. HARRIS.) What is your idea of a universal classification that would apply to the whole of the United States?—A. I am in favor of it.

Q. Could that be done by a governmental commission?—A. I think the railroads should frame such a universal classification. The attempt was made at one time to frame such a classification; practically it was agreed upon; but there were some parties that dissented and it was not put into effect.

Q. The railroads having failed to make a uniform classification, it is hardly possible—unless it be done by the Interstate Commerce Commission, or by some other authority—that it could be made at all, is it?—A. Perhaps not, unless it was made mandatory upon the railroads to frame such a classification.

Q. (By Mr. CONGER.) In the changes that are frequently made in this Western classification, is the trend toward uniformity or in the other direction?—A. I think the trend is toward uniformity.

Q. At the time the effort was made, as you have stated, to adopt a uniform classification, did those who objected to its adoption come more from one section of the country than another?—A. Yes; I understand so.

Q. They were from what section?—A. I understand the objections were from the East, principally, although some of the Pacific coast lines thought it impracticable, I believe.

Q. (By Mr. KENNEDY.) Has a gentleman named Chapman, of Painesville, Ohio, who was before the committee last week with a scheme for uniform classification, called his scheme to your attention?—A. I never heard of it; no.

Q. (By Professor JOHNSON.) Do you know whether discriminations result from the existence of these different classifications?—A. I think we had discriminations as between markets.

Q. Please explain how such discriminations may be the result of having several classifications?—A. Well, if the Official classification makes a lower class on a given article in the northern or western division, it becomes more difficult to ship that article from Chicago to points where the Western classification governs than it otherwise would be. For instance, the Official classification goes to St. Paul—that is, on all business from all points east of Chicago and St. Paul—and the Western classification governs from Chicago to St. Paul on that article. The Western classification being higher than the Official and the Official only governing from points east of Chicago, the Chicago shipper is at a certain disadvantage in reaching that particular market. It is also lower on business going to the Mississippi River points, where the Official classification reaches. That has resulted in discrimination in favor of the Eastern shipper as against the shippers into this territory that is open to both classifications. To illustrate: if a man is shipping from a Wisconsin point to a market in either direction, he has to ship under the Western classification, whereas, if an Eastern man is shipping to the same market, he ships under the Eastern classification, and, speaking generally of the classification of the Eastern division, it is somewhat lower than the Western; and in that instance the Wisconsin shippers would be at a disadvantage.

Q. Would that be true of the Illinois territory?—A. To some extent, that is modified in Illinois. In Illinois there is a classification of freight framed by the Illinois board of railway and warehouse commissioners that is intended to offset that disability to some extent. Of course, the interstate character of commerce and competition interfers with the Illinois commission.

Q. Does not the fact that the commerce in the Illinois markets is largely interstate—does not that prevent the Illinois commission's tariff from having much effect?—A. Yes. It would not apply outside of the State.

Q. (By Mr. C. J. HARRIS.) The greater bulk of the freight would be in carloads and get the special rate, would it not, without being classified, such as wheat, coal, pork, etc.?—A. That is shipped outside of the classification; is not amenable to the classification. I don't have anything to do with the control of the rates.

Q. That, I suppose, would comprise the greater bulk of the freight, if not in value, would it not?—A. Probably it would, although I have never seen any figures made.

Q. Your classification applies to carloads?—A. Yes; and to less than carloads.

Q. (By Representative BELL.) Does your line of duty enable you to know the contests brought by the consignees of these goods through this separate classification?—A. Yes; I am apt to hear of them.

Q. Does it not result in a great many suits of replevin?—A. My impression is that it does not. Companies don't oftentimes have suits. There are oftentimes questions in dispute, and they give rise to complaints, and very often it causes delay in delivering the freight.

Q. Sometimes it results in a replevin suit, does it not?—A. Not within my observation. I don't think that is oftentimes the case.

Q. Now, in making up these classifications, what do you take into consideration?—A. Bulk and value are the two controlling features.

Q. You always consider what an article will stand, do you not?—A. That is one element, yes; represented by the value of the goods; and the element of bulk represents the accommodation furnished by the carrier and the space occupied.

Q. And also you consider what the article will stand, and the manner in which it is to be moved and used?—A. I don't think that that would be hardly a valid consideration in fixing a classification.

Q. If you were going to classify a very low grade of iron ore, a remarkably low grade; would you be liable to classify that according to its grade?—A. The element of value would be considered.

Q. But you haven't that exact.—A. The element of value don't represent all of it. Of course, the other element of bulk would be considered, inasmuch as it would enter into the amount required to make a carload, and the accomodations to be furnished.

Q. (By Mr. CONGER.) Is iron ore given two different classifications?—A. We have iron ore classified, but it is modified under the classification—under the so-called commodity rates, which are usually lower than the classification or tariff rates.

Q. It seems to me that when the railroads make two different classifications on iron ore and then pass on the quality or value thereof it would—— —A. (Interrupting.) It would complicate matters.

Q. (By Representative BELL.) Do you know of such a rate existing in the Rocky Mountains?—A. I can not say that I do, although it is my impression rates have been made based on the value of the ore.

Q. Now, do you think a uniform classification would dispense with all this trouble and annoyance to the consignee?—A. I believe it would, very largely.

Q. And do you see any reason why, when the railroads want to classify, some other power, as an arbitrator, might not do it and take into consideration all the facts, and compel the obstreperous roads to come in?—A. The framing of a classification would be a very complicated piece of work to those who have not been familiar with it, and it is doubtful whether a classification framed by the commission would give general satisfaction, at least at first. I think they might find it worse to take one of the existing classifications for the purpose of framing a new one than they would to frame an entirely new classification.

Q. You would not expect a board like the Interstate Commerce Commission to classify without taking your classification or right rates, and if they found any defects to correct them, would you?—A. No.

Q. You have no doubt but that they would take the classification of the railroads generally?—A. I think that they would find it wise to do it.

Q. If they should have a full hearing, which they would undoubtedly, and all interests should be considered, would you anticipate any injury would result to the roads from such a classification?—A. No.

Q. (By Mr. KENNEDY.) Please state what the privileges of shippers are before your committee.—A. The shippers have been demanding competition with the change in classification. They are naturally for reduction in classification, and these complaints are heard and considered at our semiannual meetings. They have the privilege of appearing before us and stating their cases.

Q. In person or by attorney?—A. In person or by delegate or attorney. The petitions are considered and passed upon by the committee.

Q. Is there much complaint on the part of shippers that their privileges are not sufficient before your commission?—A. I think there is a general satisfaction among shippers so far as the Western classification is concerned, as to their privileges of stating their cases and appearing.

Q. (By Representative OTJEN.) Did not the railroads several years ago get up a general classification which was substantially agreed to by the railroads with the exception of one or two?—A. Yes; that is correct.

Q. Of course that classsification could be taken into consideration by the commission if they saw fit to take it up?—A. Yes; it would be available.

Q. (By Mr. KENNEDY.) Can you state what roads defeated that classsfication and give us your belief as to why they did it?—A. I don't know what roads objected to it. I understood that roads in the East were the most numerous among the principal objectors; but what the reasons were that led to it, and their objections, I could not say.

Q. (By Representative OTJEN.) You think that general classification is practicable in the entire country, do you?—A. Yes; I believe it is.

Q. It is not necessary to have a classification according to the sections?—A. No.

CHICAGO, ILL., *November 24, 1899.*

TESTIMONY OF MR. JOSEPH BOOKWALTER,

Representative of Kansas City Board of Trade.

The subcommission on transportation being in session in Chicago, Representative Lorimer presiding, at 11.50 a. m., November 24, 1899, Mr. Joseph Bookwalter, representative of the Kansas City Board of Trade, was introduced as a witness, and, being duly sworn, testified concerning transportation as follows:

Q. (By Representative LORIMER.) What is your name?—A. Joseph Bookwalter.

Q. And address?—A. Kansas City.

Q. Whom do you especially represent here?—A. I am in the grain business at Kansas City and a member of the board of trade, chairman of their transportation committee; and I represent the Kansas City Board of Trade.

Q. Will you, in your own way, state to the commission the matters you have thought of with reference to transportation?—A. Well, I can only speak of the tariffs as they practically affect our business at Kansas City. We have centering in Kansas City something like 16 or 18 railways, penetrating the territory surrounding the city, and are there to receive grain on consignment or buy it in the country and sell it again, to store it, to manufacture it into flour and ship it out, both for local consumption and for export. We have a grievance or two, perhaps. Our grievance consists chiefly of this: That in all the tariffs of all the roads the rate from any local point into Kansas City and then the rate from Kansas City out to any other point is from 1 cent and up, higher than it would be from the originating point to the point to which it may be shipped—1 cent a hundred.

Q. (By Mr. CONGER.) Is that true of Kansas City only, or of many other cities of the country?—A. That is true, so far as I know, only of the Missouri River towns—Kansas City, Atchison, Leavenworth, St. Joseph.

Q. The rate on grain you are speaking of. Is not that or a similar situation true of Chicago?—A. I am not informed as to Chicago. I do not know how it may operate in Chicage, but it operates to ruin our business.

Q. (By Mr. C. J. HARRIS.) Why would it not be reasonable that 1 cent more should be charged where the freight is shipped in and unloaded and then shipped out again than if it went directly through? I understand you say that is unreasonable.—A. Yes; it is unreasonable in this: That it is sufficient to bar the business. It is particularly unreasonable with reference to us because it is not true with reference to any other local station along any of these lines in the same business. You can go west on any of these roads and buy a car of wheat and ship it to the mill or elevator at any station on that road; it is unloaded and manufactured into flour; loaded out again, and shipped to destination without any additional charge.

Q. (By Mr. CONGER.) Under a milling-in-transit rate?—A. I do not know what they call it; they permit it, and it is done.

Q. (By Representative OTJEN.) What reasons do the railroads give for the making of this additional charge for the towns you speak of?—A. They call it breaking bulk.

Q. Rehandling?—A. They may rehandle it and they may not; they may do nothing; but if it is billed to Kansas City and billed out there is an additional charge.

Q. Even if the grain never leaves the car?—A. Even if the grain never leaves the car. They are to no more terminal expense or breaking-bulk expense at Kansas City than at any other place. It may not go off their track, and may not even go out of their yard.

Q. Name some other place.—A. Take Topeka, for instance, west of Kansas City.

Q. Name some small station west of Topeka.—A. Ellsworth, perhaps.

Q. I asked you to name these towns that I might put this question, that we may have a clear understanding of the case. I understand you complain that it is possible for a buyer or handler of grain to buy a carload of wheat at Ellsworth, bill it to Topeka, there rebill it to New York at the through rate from Ellsworth; that there is no additional charge?—A. At the balance of the rate; yes.

Q. That there is no additional charge because of the rebilling or stopping at Topeka?—A. That is right.

Q. Yet if that car were bought at Ellsworth and billed to Kansas City and there rebilled to the same point they would charge you an additional rate for that rebilling?—A. Yes. Now, if there was any switching done at Kansas City there would be an additional charge for it, but for whatever switching may be done at Topeka or the intermediate point there is no additional charge. If it should leave the road over which it came and went to an elevator and went out over another road the charge would be a switching charge of $2 to $6 a car.

Q. What road or organization of roads is responsible for making this charge, this discrimination, against Kansas City, if you might call it such?—A. I do not know that any one road is more responsible than another; they are all in it. A portion of these roads do not go beyond Kansas City and can hardly be said to be grain roads; they do not take grain to Kansas City, hardly.

Q. Are there any roads running into Topeka that do not run into Kansas City?—A. No.

Q. Have these roads that run into Kansas City and also into Topeka any reason for favoring Topeka as against Kansas City that you know of?—A. Yes; I think they would make this claim: At Topeka they can feel pretty sure they will get it out on their own road to destination, while if it goes to Kansas City they might never get it again. They claim it to be their car so long as they can haul it, and therefore dictate where it shall be sold; and they make a rate that will govern that. I think, perhaps, the roads most responsible for that arrangement are the Santa Fe, the Missouri Pacific, the Rock Island, and the Burlington; but the rule applies the same to roads terminating at Kansas City from the West.

Q. (By Mr. KENNEDY.) How could they be sure of getting the grain in their own cars from Topeka eastward unless there was some understanding between the roads, since there is competition between Kansas City and Topeka? Is there not more than one road running between these two points?—A. Usually it goes into the elevator or mill on their own line. The operation of it is very effective as against us. The local mills throughout Kansas and Nebraska and Missouri sell supplies either side of us; cars will go right through Kansas City going to mill. It has been very effective, and operates in many instances to entirely destroy the business.

Q. (By Mr. CONGER.) The milling business?—A. And the grain business, both. Kansas City does not get good milling wheat. The local mills can afford to buy it and pay more than our millers can pay, because they can manufacture it for export on the same basis that our people do, and our people have the cent or more per hundred and their switching charges besides.

Q. (By Mr. KENNEDY.) One grain man in Iowa testified that because Kansas

City was a milling point they could get better prices in Kansas City at times than they could in Chicago. That would seem to indicate, if his statement is true, that they get the best class of grain there.—A. They can only do that for their local business. Kansas City is a higher market for grain than any other market for grain in the country, simply because we get so little. Take oats— hardly a car comes to Kansas City to be shipped out; 4, 5, or 6 cars of oats a day is as much as is received there, and that is consumed there, because the roads add the 1 or 2 cents to ship through Kansas City.

Q. (By Mr. C. J. HARRIS.) Do you know how much wheat Kansas City receives?—A. That is governed a good deal by the size of the crop. Last year we had about 30,000,000 out of a territory that raised 240,000,000.

Q. (By Professor JOHNSON.) Not all of that 240,000,000 was shipped out of that territory?—A. No; but we got a very small proportion of it. To give an illustration of how that will operate as affecting us, our mills, and necessarily our elevators, I wrote some letters to shippers in the country and asked them to say how many cars of wheat they had shipped from July, 1898, to July, 1899. I have not these letters with me. I did not think to bring them, and only speak from memory. From a little town like Inman, a local station on the Rock Island, a shipper shipped something like 400 cars; 54 of these came to Kansas City; 227 stopped at a mill on the way to Kansas City—large mills, grinding for export, in competition with our mills.

Q. (By Representative OTJEN.) You speak of 2 cents. Is it sometimes more than 2 cents?—A. Yes; very much more sometimes.

Q. Two cents and upward?—A. Yes; one cent and upward.

Q. How high does it go sometimes—the difference?—A. Seven or eight cents.

Q. In addition to that there is a switching charge?—A. In addition to that there is a switching charge.

Q. Which is not charged any place like Topeka and these other places you speak of?—A. Yes. Speaking of the grade of wheat that we receive, we had something over 500 cars as a result of 3 days' receipts, taking in 2 holidays and Sunday. It being a large receipt, I made inquiry of the inspection department to see what was the grade of wheat and found there was less than 2 per cent of these 500 cars that was graded wheat; it ran from "rejected" to "4" and "3."

Q. What is the reason they send inferior grades to Kansas City?—A. It is the nearest market, and it is very uncertain what they will receive for the inferior grades if they send to Galveston, New Orleans, or Chicago, and as a rule they are not in a condition for long shipment, and it is desirable to get them out of the car as soon as possible.

Q. (By Mr. CONGER.) What becomes of that wheat?—A. It goes into the elevator and is scoured and dried.

Q. Kansas City is the nearest market where that can be done?—A. Kansas City is the nearest market where that can be done and storage be obtained. I want to say that this discrimination—arbitrarily from 1 cent a hundred up, with the very narrow margin on which the grain business is now done, any difference in the charge between one and another—determines the movement of that grain; where it shall go. Not very long ago the city of New York appointed a committee to investigate as to why it was that they were not receiving as much grain for export as they previously had. Among others called before that commission was the representative of Armour & Co., who were the largest grain dealers in the country, perhaps. Mr. Armour's representative, among other things, said that their charges, lightering the grain, and lack of facilities for handling the grain from car to vessel, made additional cost enough to prevent them handling it, and incidentally said that one-sixteenth of a cent per bushel on grain will determine where it will go. I simply give that as illustrative of why any discrimination will ruin the business of any particular place.

Speaking of Nebraska, there are some peculiarities of the tariff that I jotted down as I came along on the train last night, which will illustrate what I am after. Now, this state of affairs is true of other stations on the Burlington system; I just give this one as not being different from the rest of them. There may be a difference in the mileage, but not in the tariff. This station, Wahoo, is located in a very excellent grain country, growing white oats and white corn, both of which are very valuable to us. Now, Wahoo is 229 miles from Kansas City, northwest. It is 523 miles from St. Louis. The rate from Wahoo to Kansas City is 14 cents, and to St. Louis is 14; if it goes via Kansas City to St. Louis it is 21 cents.

Q. Is it farther from Wahoo by way of Kansas City than by some other road?— A. It is 67 miles farther by the Burlington road via Kansas City than by their own through line, but they charge 7 cents extra for that 67 miles, or they do not charge anything for 294 miles. They would have earned their 14 cents by hauling 229 miles, but they haul it 294 miles farther without additional charge.

Q. Not the same road, however?—A. The same road. I took the station of Wahoo because it has a peculiar feature; it is also a station on the Union Pacific, which terminates at Kansas City. The Union Pacific rate is 14 cents to Kansas City and also to St. Louis. If it is billed through by the Union Pacific via Kansas City, they earn the 14 cents; if it is billed through by the same line which terminates at Kansas City, and must give it up to some other road, the Union Pacific gets 7 cents out of it, and they give up half what they have earned. They do not take that because they are desirous of giving up that portion, but they are forced to do it in order to make tariffs in competition with the other roads.

Q. Why does not the Union Pacific make a lower rate to Kansas City?—A. They do not want to be hammered on the back somewhere else.

Q. Your idea, then, is that the rate probably is a fair one to Kansas City, but an extremely low one to St. Louis, relatively speaking?—A. That is in part true. I think the Kansas City rate is too high and the St. Louis rate is too low. It is not so much the love of St. Louis that the 14-cent rate is made there, but Chicago is based upon the St. Louis rate, and it makes a lower rate to Chicago, and they get to haul to Chicago instead of St. Louis.

Q. (By Representative BELL.) Have these railroads any elevators in Kansas City?—A. The Burlington has no elevator.

Q. Has the Pacific?—A. The Union Pacific has; yes.

Q. (By Mr. KENNEDY.) Is it your understanding that the Burlington has elevators in Chicago?—A. We understand they have; yes.

Q. They own the elevators?—A. I can not give you positive information on that. The people of the South are great eaters of oats and white corn meal. The central portion of Nebraska, embracing this part of the country, is where the white oats are chiefly produced. They are desirable for oatmeal because they are white. Black oats and red oats are strong, and white oats are necessary for oatmeal. We have an oatmeal mill at Kansas City, but it can not get oats to run hardly any of the time; why it does not is plain from the tariffs. As I said, the rate on oats from Wahoo to Kansas City is 14 cents, that is 229 miles; the rate on oats from Wahoo to Memphis is 19 cents, 713 miles; 14 cents for 229 miles and 5 for cents 484 miles, going directly through Kansas City. If it is billed into Kansas City and then billed to Memphis it is 24 cents, 5 cents penalty for stopping at Kansas City for handling or manufacturing. The result is it goes on through and our people do not do the business. It is right on the line of road passing through the town.

Texas is a very large consumer of corn meal, and our people originally enjoyed the privilege, on the basis of through billing, of manufacturing corn meal and shipping to Texas. From Wahoo to San Antonia on corn the rate is 39 cents; if the corn is stopped at Kansas City and manufactured into meal it makes it 44 cents. The result is, the corn is shipped to Texas and manufactured in Texas, instead of being manufactured in Kansas City; 5 cents per hundred advantage is given to the mill in Texas.

Q. (By Representative OTJEN.) Is it not more expensive to ship the manufactured product than it is the raw grain?—A. I can not see any reason why it should be. It did not use to be.

Q. How long since has this been in operation, the difference between the transportation of the manufactured article and the raw grain itself?—A. I can not give you exactly the date.

Q. About how long?—A. A couple of years.

There is a little town in Kansas called Doniphan. They ship corn from Doniphan to Chicago via St. Joseph for 15 cents, 522 miles; they ship it to Chicago via Kansas City, which is 43 miles farther, at 19 cents; they ship it via Kansas City to St. Louis at 14 cents. If it is shipped to Kansas City, 50 miles, the rate is 7 cents. It is 522 miles to Chicago and 50 miles to Kansas City. One is 15 cents and the other is 7 cents.

Q. (By Mr. C. J. HARRIS.) Are these exceptional instances, or would you mean to say to this commission that Kansas City is discriminated against in favor of towns and places to this extent and proportion? If so, I can not see how you could do the volume of business in grain shipments—wheat, corn, and other products—that you do?—A. These are the extremes, ranging from 1 cent up to 7 cents, which is the highest discrimination; but there are many other stations on the Burlington system like this, running all the way down—5, 4, 3, 2, 1 cent—but anything which causes any discrimination is sufficient to bar our business.

Q. Now, is not the discrimination on some particular roads larger than on others?—A. It is all alike in the same territory.

Q. I did not know but there might be certain railroads discriminating against you.—A. We can not see any reason why the Union Pacific should charge 14 cents on a car that comes and stops at Kansas City, and 7 cents on the same car if it does not stop at Kansas City, for the same length of haul.

Speaking with reference to business, I counted up I think it was 90 days, up to yesterday, and we have averaged 3 cars of corn a day at Kansas City off the Burlington system.

Q. (By Representative OTJEN.) How much ought you to average if rates were uniform?—A. I do not know; we ought to have 150 cars, I should think, anyhow. It is a pretty small station on their road that does not ship 3 cars.

Q. Did you say the wheat that came to Kansas City amounted to 30,000,000 bushels, and that this discriminating rate has existed only within the last year or two?—A. Yes.

Q. How much business did you do prior to that time in Kansas City, in wheat, for instance?—A. It varied according to the crop; I can not tell you exactly; I have not the figures.

Q. Did it exceed the 30,000,000 of bushels?—A. Oh, it ran up as' high as 40,000,000.

Q. (By Mr. C. J. HARRIS.) You think your business in grain is falling off?—A. It is, most decidedly.

Here is the town of Humboldt, for instance. That is 120 miles from Kansas City, and 571 miles from Chicago; the rate to Kansas City is 8 cents, while the rate to Chicago is 17½ cents. Humboldt happens to be the next station from Table Rock; and according to these letters I was speaking to you about having received last year they shipped 272 cars of corn from Table Rock and 3 came to Kansas City. These were not shipped by dealers; they were shipped by farmers, who did not know any better.

Q. (By Mr. CONGER.) The 3 cars were?—A. The 3 cars; yes. The reason why I took Humboldt was because I had the figures on there day before yesterday. There was bid on track, 25¼ cents for No. 3 corn, Chicago terms. I believe the rate to Chicago is 17½ cents, that is, 9.81 cents a bushel; that would make it worth 35.30 here. The highest priced corn was worth here that day 33.5 cents. On the basis of the tariff it was worth more in Kansas City than it was in Chicago.

Q. (By Professor JOHNSON.) These points are all west of the Missouri River?—A. Yes. Now, the same relative rate is on the Missouri Pacific road in the same territory. I do not happen to have their tariff with me. While it may be said the Burlington does not necessarily bring its stuff through Kansas City, the Missouri Pacific can not avoid going through Kansas City; it is their only line.

Q. (By Mr. C. J. HARRIS.) I understood you to state that all grains were being handled on a very close margin at the present time; that would enable the farmer to get more for his produce relatively than ever before, would it not?—A. Yes.

Q. What has been the decrease in the last 10 years of the margin from the farmer to the markets?—A. I was not in the grain business as long ago as that.

Q. From your experience to the present time?—A. We used to expect always to get a half-cent margin on corn or oats, and a cent a bushel on wheat; we expect now to handle it for a quarter of a cent on corn and a half-cent on wheat.

Q. Are railroad rates lower now than when you first commenced business?—A. I do not think the local rate into Kansas City is.

Q. Are through rates to the seaboard lower?—A. I think they are, as a rule; yes.

Q. You have elevator facilities in Kansas City?—A. Yes.

Q. Are they private or public?—A. Mostly private.

Q. (By Mr. CONGER.) Have you any public elevators?—A. I think there are two.

Q. What capacity, approximately?—A. From 400,000 to 1,000,000.

Q. Do you know the total elevator capacity in Kansas City?—A. I think it is about 6,000,000.

Q. (By Mr. KENNEDY.) Who owns the private elevators?—A. They are men in business there.

Q. Not any railroad people?—A. Well, I think the understanding is they are owned by the railroads. They are operated by private parties.

Q. (By Mr. C. J. HARRIS.) Do your grain men have any complaints to make of the large private elevators buying wheat to better advantage than you, having any inside rates or discriminations that favor them particularly?—A. Yes; we do, in this, that if it continues that way we will all have to go out of business except these few people; just as this one indicates here from Humboldt.

I think I read in the paper that testimony was given before your commission by one of the large concerns here; that in view of their higher bidding out in the country the farmer was getting more for his grain than he would if they did not bid high. I simply want to say two and two make four. These large concerns can not bid any higher on the tariff than the smaller concerns, and they can not reach the business of the country nearly so cheap as the smaller concerns. To illustrate, the most of our wheat moves inside of 3 months from the time it is harvested. The local dealer at the station, besides his grain business, is engaged in the lumber and coal business, or in the grocery business, or in the dry goods business, or in the milling business—something of that kind; he is not dependent entirely on his grain operations; if he makes a half day's wages on his grain, that, along with the profit he is making at something else, makes him a business, but the man who is engaged in no other business except buying grain must make it out of the grain entirely, and there will be 5 or 6 months in the year that he has exceedingly little to do. That is not so material to the man that is in any other business, but to the man who is exclusively in the grain business it is material, and that is the case with the large concern that goes into the grain business.

Q. You claim the smaller dealer can do it as cheaply or cheaper than the larger one; what is the deduction we are to draw from that, that the large dealers get inside rates?—A. That is what we believe. The Peavey Elevator Company, of Minneapolis, operates on the Union Pacific road west of Kansas City, and is building a line of elevators. They try to buy out the local man first, if he will sell; if not, they build an elevator beside him. A few days ago they offered a quarter of a cent more for corn along the Union Pacific road than they could sell it for in Kansas City the same day.

Q. (By Mr. CONGER.) What does that indicate to your mind?—A. That indicates that there must be an advantage somewhere.

Q. (By Mr. C. J. HARRIS.) Can you say what that advantage is?—A. There could not be any freight rate in the world that would allow them to buy it out there at a quarter of a cent more than they sold it for. I mean on the basis of Kansas City; I do not mean they paid a quarter of a cent more in the country, but on the basis of the Kansas City market, freight rate considered, of course.

Q. (By Mr. CONGER.) Your idea, then, in a general way, is that the grain tributary to Kansas City, which ought naturally to go to that market, is diverted to other markets, Chicago and St. Louis?—A. Yes.

Q. In your opinion, is more diverted to Chicago, or to St. Louis, or to both?—A. I can not tell you as to that. I do not think St. Louis gets as much benefit as Chicago and the South.

Q. You have mentioned three roads, the Rock Island, Burlington, and Santa Fe, as I remember?—A. And the Missouri Pacific.

Q. I think these three that I mention are the ones that, even according to the published tariffs, distance considered, discriminate in favor of Chicago as against Kansas City?—A. Yes; they do.

Q. Had you or your people in Kansas City connected the elevator men in this city with the discrimination in any way?—A. Well, we have thought these people pay more than the market will justify; it leaves them no profit.

Q. It occurs to my mind that Mr. Counselman operates on the Rock Island, Mr. Armour on the Burlington, and Mr. Richardson on the Santa Fe, and according to your testimony they are able to get rates that haul grain 500 miles for a slight advance over the rates these roads charge to haul it to your town, 100 miles or more, even according to the published tariffs that you have mentioned?—A. Yes.

Q. Do any of these men have elevators in Kansas City?—A. Yes; Mr. Counselman operates an elevator there, and Mr. Richardson operates an elevator there.

Q. Do they do much business there?—A. It depends altogether; if it is better to send the stuff to Galveston there is very little handled in the Santa Fe elevator in Kansas City; if it is best to go to Chicago there is not a great deal handled by Mr. Counselman's elevator. There is some influence connected with the business there. Until his death, which occurred some time ago, Mr. Johnson, a son of the vice-president of the Rock Island, was Mr. Counselman's manager at Kansas City. Mr. Harris, I am told, is a brother of Mr. George B. Harris, of the Burlington, and is the chief operator on the Burlington system.

Q. You say chief operator; do you mean for Kansas City?—A. No; in the grain business. He does not do business at Kansas City. The Burlington has no elevator at this time in Kansas City. We are advised they are going to build one. The Iowa Development Company is operated and managed at Kansas City by the vice-president of the Chicago Great Western Railway.

Q. It might be well for Kansas City to interest some of these men a little more in that town, might it not?—A. If it was simply for their business, but I do not think it would do any good for the other people who are doing business there.

Referring to the Maple Leaf, there is a little peculiarity about that. I was trying to buy some oats at Shepard, Iowa, on the Maple Leaf. That is a local station, and I simply name it because I have tried it. It is 167 miles from Kansas City. The rate is 10 cents to Kansas City and the rate to St. Louis is 12 cents; it is 528 miles to St. Louis. If it is billed to Kansas City and then goes to St. Louis it is 17 cents; but they can bill it right through Kansas City for 12 cents.

Q. This distance to St. Louis means through Kansas City?—A. Yes; and it will necessarily go that way because they want to get in the full amount of their mileage; it is the terminus of their road.

Q. (By Representative OTJEN.) Do you favor legalizing pooling by the railroads?—A. Well, I am unable to answer that. I do not know.

Q. Do you know what are generally the views of business men in your section of the country regarding that subject?—A. I do not think their views are very well defined on that. Sometimes they think it would be an advantage, and other times they think it would not.

Q. Do you think there should be conferred on the Interstate Commerce Commission authority sufficient to fix the rate of railroads?—A. Yes; if it will act quickly. That is the only objection that I know of relative to the Interstate Commerce Commission, that it takes too long to act.

Q. What remedy would you have if you did not correct this matter in some way, such as by this Interstate Commerce Commission?—A. I do not know of any. The remedies, however, are too tardy.

Q. That is, the Interstate Commerce Commission takes too long a time in deciding on cases?—A. Yes.

Q. But do you not think that is largely owing to the fact that the commission has very little authority at present?—A. Well, it would seem they might exercise what authority they have a little more promptly. I think we are rapidly approaching the same condition in the grain situation that we are in most other branches of business—a trust that will absolutely control the handling, and thereby the price of the grain.

Q. What remedy do you suggest for the correction of this evil?—A. Requiring the railroads, in the first place, to attend strictly to the railroad business, and go out of the grain business, or any other kind of business; that is one way.

Q. That would also include persons who run elevators leased from railroads and who, perhaps, get special rates?—A. Yes. In the testimony before the Interstate Commerce Commission a year or two ago, involving that question, it was stated by an elevator man that the railroad company paid him as high as 4 cents per hundred for running grain through the house, as an elevator charge; that, of course, would give him the absolute control of business on that road.

Q. Well, in order to compel railroads to live up to uniform rates, they must of necessity be supervised by some sort of commission like the Interstate Commerce Commission?—A. Yes; it would seem so.

Q. And such commission ought, of necessity, to be clothed with sufficient authority to enforce its rulings?—A. It ought to.

I think it was in 1895 that we had our shortage in our corn crop, and at that time we fed out in this country 100,000,000 bushels of wheat to stock; wheat was cheaper than corn. We wiped out the immense visible supply of wheat, the immense surplus on hand, and since that time Chicago instead of Liverpool has controlled the price of wheat. Liverpool to-day goes up and down, as Chicago goes up and down; up to that time it was the other way. Now, 8 railroad systems control the grain-producing territory, and every one of these systems is going into the grain business just as rapidly as it can; and when you have got it into the hands of 8 men or 8 roads, with sufficient storage capacity to take care of the crop, it will be controlled by these people and the local dealer will have to go out of the business entirely, unless there is some remedy for that.

Q. This dealing in grain—is that done directly by the railroad?—A. I can not answer that, but there are certain persons doing business on these roads that can handle it when nobody else can.

Q. (By Mr. KENNEDY.) You think all circumstances point to it?—A. All circumstances point to it.

Q. (By Representative BELL.) Is it not the same way with the coal business?—A. I am told so, but I have not the knowledge to testify on that.

Q. Now, you seem to have a little doubt about this legal pooling; have you any doubt about there being a pool now by all these roads going into Kansas City in this case?—A. Very little doubt about it. The Union Pacific keeps up the rate of the other roads, though it ends there and has its elevators.

Q. (By Mr. KENNEDY.) You do not mean there is a pool in the sense of dividing their earnings, do you?—A. No; not that I know of.

Q. (By Representative BELL.) But as to rate and method of doing business?—A. Yes; I think so.

Q. Then, why would you have any hesitancy about a legal pool?—A. Well, as I said a moment ago, I do not know; it is a large subject. I can not tell.

Q. Do you not regard all your difficulties in Kansas City as connected with the elevators on the individual roads?—A. I think the policy has been dictated by those roads which originate the grain to compel it to go as far as possible on their lines. They have ceased to be common carriers for the public, but regard the grain as theirs, to handle for their own personal advantage, and determine where it shall be sold.

Q. You regard the 4 cents which this elevator man down there got for his grain going through the elevator as really his drawback on the freight?—A. Yes. Any elevator in Kansas City would be delighted to handle that grain for a half cent and make money out of it.

Q. (By Professor JOHNSON.) Would you apply the name of pooling to those methods of doing business?—A. It depends on what definition you give to the term.

Q. Do you define a pool in that sense?—A. I am not a railroad man. I think, perhaps, pooling is a little farther-reaching term, and reaches to the division of the profits or division of the business.

Q. (By Mr. KENNEDY.) You mean an agreement between the roads instead of pooling?—A. I think, perhaps, it would be better to term it an agreement between the roads.

Q. (By Representative LORIMER.) Do you ever pay any attention to the daily Liverpool cables on grain?—A. Yes; we get them.

Q. Within the last year or two, have they in any way affected the price of the market here?—A. Oh, they do to some extent, but their prices within the last year or two have been governed chiefly by the prices here.

Q. Have you ever known of a low cable coming here, and during that day hear it said that low cables from Liverpool put down the price of wheat in Chicago?—A. Yes.

Q. Have you ever heard of high cables coming, and hearing it said that the high cables had the effect of putting up the price of wheat in Chicago?—A. Yes; but I think those terms are used more to influence the speculative market than anything else.

Q. On these days when the cables come high, has wheat in Chicago, from your knowledge, ever risen above the previous day?—A. I can not say that I associated it in that way exactly. Very often our local market is higher than Liverpool would indicate, or lower than Liverpool would indicate, on that particular day. For instance, the foreign cable to-day will be based on what our market was yesterday. You see they are earlier in the day; they close very soon after we begin.

Q. But, as it is generally understood, have high or low cables any effect on the market here?—A. I think so; necessarily. It would have some effect on our market.

Q. Chicago, then, would not altogether control the price if it is influenced at all by the Liverpool cable?—A. The Liverpool cable is influenced by the Chicago price, and they immediately influence each other.

Q. Then it would not be entirely confined to Chicago, according to that statement?—A. Not any more than it would be confined altogether to Liverpool. Liverpool is governed by conditions in Chicago, and Chicago is governed to some extent by the conditions in Liverpool.

Q. I understood you to say that Chicago now controls the price of grain instead of Liverpool, and I want to know whether or not that is absolutely correct?—A. I believe just this, that it controls to a great deal greater extent than it ever did before. It may not absolutely control, for it is influenced by other local conditions, visible supply, etc., and their local demand will govern their market very considerably.

Q. And there are outside influences, in your opinion, which have something to do with the price of grain here?—A. Of course.

(Testimony closed.)

CHICAGO, ILL., *November 24, 1899.*

TESTIMONY OF MR. ZINA R. CARTER,

Commission and produce merchant, Chicago, Ill.

The subcommission on transportation being in session on the afternoon of November 24, 1899, Representative Lorimer presiding, Mr. Zina R. Carter was duly sworn, and testified as follows:

Q. (By Representative LORIMER.) Please state your full name.—A. Zina R. Carter.

Q. And your post-office address.—A. Chicago.

655A——37

Q. Your business.—A. Commission; produce.

Q. And any official connection you have in the city.—A. I am a member of the sanitary board.

Q. (By Professor JOHNSON.) Mr. Carter, having connection with the drainage-canal project, must have given a great deal of attention to transportation by water to and from Chicago, and information in regard to that business is what I think we have in mind.—A. Well, if I am permitted to state my views upon this——

Q. (By Representative LORIMER.) (Interrupting.) Just state them in your own way.—A. As to our water transportation I would say this, first of all, that the future growth of the industries of this country, I believe, and the opportunities for our people to compete successfully in a fair race for the commerce of the world, requires that they should have the best and cheapest methods of transportation throughout this country; and I think I can place before you a few facts which bear directly on this question, and which show conclusively that water transportation furnishes great advantages to the people of this country over the best that the railroads are able to furnish. I find in the records of the annual report of the secretary of the Board of Trade of the city of Chicago these figures: For the year 1897 the average rate of freight on corn from Chicago to New York City, via lake and canal, including the charges at Buffalo, was 4.53 cents per bushel. That was the average rate during the season of navigation; and the average of rail rate for the year, taken from the public schedules, was 11.43 cents per bushel from Chicago to New York. The average rate by lake and canal on wheat for that year 1897, including the charges at Buffalo, was 12.5 cents per bushel. In 1898 we were not able to obtain the charges at Buffalo. They were very irregular, running from three-quarters of a cent to nothing, so I have to exclude that in the calculation of the carrying charges. The charge by lake and canal for the year 1898 was 3.81 cents per bushel on corn and 4.45 cents per bushel on wheat all the way. The all-rail charge that I have for 1898 was 9.8 cents, and on wheat 12 cents. From these statistics it is very easy to deduct these facts, that on the grain that was exported by the producers of this country in the year 1898 the difference between the charges for carrying by rail and water would approximate $25,000,000 in favor of water carriage.

Q. (By Mr. CONGER.) Is that sum based on the whole crop of the country?—A. Based on the actual experience for the year 1898. It was something over 420,000,000 bushels of grain. We are not discussing in this connection, up to this time, any other character of freight.

Q. I notice these figures showing the average freight rate of the railroads are for the year, whereas the figures on the lake and canal rate are for the season of navigation.—A. True.

Q. Can you inform us whether the rail rate was lower during the season of navigation than during other times of the year?—A. Now, as regards a large part of these years which I have quoted from, I should not like to be definite. Of course I know there have been years during the summer season when the rail rate has been cut very close to the water rate; other years it has not. The average rail rate for twenty years past, as I have learned during that length of time, has been much lower during the summer than during the winter.

Q. Do you know how much lower, approximately?—A. Well, that is a matter I have not given very careful attention. I have not given it such careful attention as would enable me to state definitely, but I think it could be safely said, taking the average for 20 years, that it would be 25 per cent higher during the season of the closing of navigation than it would be during the season of water transportation.

Q. (By Professor JOHNSON.) If there is such a difference between the rail and water charge, why is it that the all-water traffic is not increased?—A. It does increase very slowly. The all-water transportation is now accomplished at a very great disadvantage, owing to the fact that the Erie Canal is not improved up to date; it is not in the condition in which it ought to be, with the commerce upon it. If it had been improved and was in such a condition now as the character of the commerce of the country at the present time demands it should be, the transportation would be at the lowest rate all water. That is the reason why a larger per cent of the trade does not go by the canal—because it is not in a condition to handle it.

Q. Still the Erie Canal can handle twice what it does now, can it not, without any improvement whatever?—A. I don't think so.

Q. Is it not a fact that the present water route is not able to compete to any large extent with the all-rail route?—A. There are the facts. Now, it is not a supposition of the mind that the man who can avail himself of a rate that is less than one-half is going to fail to do so. This year will show a difference because of the export low rates by rail, and therefore a large part of the tonnage has been drawn from the lake trade; but in 1898 the largest per cent of the grain left Chicago by water.

Q. And went as far as Buffalo or Erie points and thence by rail?—A. Yes.

Q. My point is simply this: Your figures don't prove to me conclusively that the barge traffic can compete with the rail traffic on a large scale, and I want to ask you if you can prove that.—A. Now, in connection with this, it is true that the lines of road upon which the comparisons are made are the best in the United States—the best managed roads and the best equipped roads—and they are able to make the lowest rates, and of course the canal and waterways parallel these roads. They make a relatively lower rate than a rate for the same distance into Chicago from the West.

Q. (By Mr. CONGER.) Does not the matter of time required to make a shipment have something to do with the tonnage?—A. It would, in a fluctuating market, have something to do with it sometimes; yes.

Q. Is there or is there not a very much larger amount of grain shipped from Chicago by water so far as Buffalo and other Erie points than goes to these points farther east by way of the canal?—A. Yes.

Q. Do you know how the part-water and part-rail rate compares with the all-rail rate?—A. The difference would not be as great as all-water rate. I have not the figures.

Q. Is there a difference?—A. Yes; there is a difference in favor of the water.

Q. (By Professor JOHNSON.) Have you studied the way in which the traffic over the Erie Canal is distributed?—A. Not carefully; no.

Q. I think if you were to do that that you would find the greater part of the Erie Canal traffic is distributed or rather carried on during the months when the railways are crowded with business, and are not competing with the canal for the grain trade. That would indicate to me that the canal under present conditions is not a very serious factor beyond Buffalo.—A. Well, it is very easily said that when any route of transportation runs down and fails to perform its functions with satisfaction to the people, that it loses its stand and loses its business. That is the condition to-day with the I. & N. Canal in Illinois. It no longer amounts to anything except as a distributer of freights. That is the effect that it has now because it has not been improved for years and men have simply left it.

Q. What kind of a waterway east from the Great Lakes to the seaboard would be a carrier of the large traffic?—A. Well, first of all, I think the improvement of the Erie Canal and the making of it into a deep-water channel.

Q. To what depth?—A. I believe it ought to be required to be at least 10 feet. I don't believe I have arrived at the conclusion that ship navigation of canals by the ships of the Great Lakes is likely to be brought out.

Q. The evidence is against that?—A. Yes; it is not likely to happen. One of the strong arguments against it is that the vessels are very expensive in their construction. Of course, in order to navigate the Great Lakes, and in order to make rapid progress, they are constructed with enormous power, and they can not as carriers enter the canal. Therefore a much cheaper constructed boat would answer just as well for the carrying of the heavy freight, and it would not tie up so much money. Thus it would lessen the expense of transportation. Very much of the freight at least could be more cheaply carried than by the keeping of these expensive ships in the slow method of canal navigation.

Q. That being true, the canal could be utilized as a barge canal?—A. Yes.

Q. How large would you say that barge would have to be? Would you not say it would have to be equal to a train load in order for the barge to be an economical mode of transportation?—A. The larger the barge, all other things considered—that is to say, the largest that would be practicable—would probably be the most economical—in fact there is no question about that—but then you have to fall back on the dimensions of your channel and decide upon the size of the barge accordingly. It seems to me you must presuppose a barge of a certain size in order to have a transportation generally that can compete with the train, because the train is the unit by rail, and the unit now is from 1,200 to 2,000 tons of actual burden. It seems to me that you must figure on a barge that can compete with this other agency. That must determine your waterway prism.

Q. That is to say, you don't believe it is necessary for a single barge to carry as large an amount as a train load of cars in order to compete?—A. I don't think that would naturally follow. There are many other questions of cost that would enter into it.

Q. The question of the cost does enter into it?—A. Yes. There are many other questions aside from the single question of the wages necessary to handle the barge.

Now, coming to the question of the sanitary canal. From this and numerous other facts of like character I am led to believe, in the interest of our whole country, that the channel which has now been constructed by the city of Chicago, having a depth of water of 22 feet and being 28 miles in length, and which, by reason of the large outlay of work, has been very expensive, in order to make connection with the Mississippi River, that it would be a wise policy—in fact, I believe it to be the duty of our Government—to take the work up and complete it, because it will enable the great products of the Mississippi Valley to be handled more cheaply than by any other means possible. The sanitary district has expended about $29,000,000; that is to say, it has actually paid out that money for 33 miles and over, where it has cut this channel, and the water is turned in.

Q. (By Mr. Conger.) This channel connects with the Illinois River?—A. Yes; same draft. That is, exchange has been made with the Champaign River with a view of improving the navigable features of the river, as well as to obtain additional cross sections. We are now putting in bridges at different points.

Q. (By Professor Johnson.) How deep a channel in the clear does this drainage canal make feasible?—A. The depth of the water in the drainage canal is 25 feet or less.

Q. I did not refer to that. I mean in the natural channel; about what depth is feasible to ship?—A. That is a very large question. What the practicable depth would be would depend upon the use. How to produce the best result with the money expended is a question for the engineers to decide. Major Marshall, who is the resident engineer in this city, does not believe that they will be justified in attempting what would be known as absolutely deep-water navigation, while many other men believe in that. A careful survey and estimate has been made on the cost of completing a 16-foot channel from the point where our work as a channel terminates, down through Joliet and over the Desplaines River to the Illinois River, and so on to the Mississippi River; and it falls much under $125,000,000 to complete it with a 16-foot channel.

Q. (By Mr. C. J. Harris.) And connect it with the Mississippi River?—A. Yes.

Q. (By Professor Johnson.) Is there 16 feet of water in the Mississippi River up to the mouth of the Illinois River?—A. No.

Q. That is a matter for the Mississippi River Commission, I suppose?—A. Yes.

Q. (By Mr. Conger.) Do you expect that all this volume of water that the channel is likely to put in the Mississippi River is likely to aid in giving it the required depth?—A. Yes; it will aid in giving it the required depth all the way down through the Illinois River. It will add very much to the availability of the Illinois River, and will lessen the cost necessary to give it any given depth very much. And it will assist and improve navigation in the Mississippi River. I have discussed this question with merchants of St. Louis, and men who have given the matter much thought. Last December, when in Washington attending the meeting of the National Board of Trade, I had the opportunity of discussing this question with several merchants of St. Louis, and among others the then president of the Chamber of Commerce in St. Louis, and they believe that the additional water which the sanitary canal will furnish will be of great advantage to them in time of low water.

Q. Speaking of St. Louis, has not the railroad competition practically driven the commerce from the Mississippi below St. Louis, or between St. Louis and New Orleans?—A. I think the commerce, perhaps, has grown less in the last few years. It is a question I have not been interested in and have not studied carefully.

Q. (By Mr. C. J. Harris.) What would you do with the surplus water in times of flood in the Mississippi? Will that materially add to their disasters there?—A. In time of great flood, in addition, perhaps, to the amount of water they have, the 300 cubic feet of water per minute from the canal at a time of high water would not be noticed in the Mississippi River. Of course, the volume in flood time is vast in the Mississippi.

Q. (By Mr. Conger.) What river do you connect with?—A. The Desplaines River, and very shortly after that with the Illinois.

Q. (By Representative Otjen.) What would be the object in making this canal, say, 16 feet, when in the Mississippi River there is not that depth of water?—A. I am not advocating the 16-foot channel south. But some men who have made a study of this question thoroughly believe in it, and a survey has been made along these lines, as I have stated to you.

Q. At the same time that would practically mean, it seems to me, that a ship could be taken up to some point along the Illinois River or Mississippi River, where there is a lower depth of water, and unloaded into another ship.—A. I have no doubt if you would discuss this matter with some of the men who are interested in the Mississippi River they would tell you they are in favor of deep water for the

Lower Mississippi, and that when it was completed they would have deep-water navigation the entire distance.

Q. (By Mr. C. J. HARRIS.) Would that waterway, when completed, be a dangerous rival of the Erie Canal for the shipment of grain and other supplies?—A. This waterway we are talking of now?

Q. Yes.—A. No; I don't look upon it in that way. Of course, in some respects it would add to the volume of business which is now going by the Eastern route, while at the same time under certain conditions it might work detrimentally the other way. I think the rule would be that it would add to the volume of business going by this route.

Q. (By Representative OTJEN.) This grain could be brought by water from the Mississippi River this way as well as taken the other way?—A. Yes.

Q. (By Mr. KENNEDY.) Is the Illinois River classed as a navigable river?—A. Yes.

Q. Then to deepen that the State of Illinois could not take the initiative; it would have to be done under national auspices?—A. Yes; the National Government is putting in large motors, one at Campsville and one at Lagrange, for the purpose of improving the navigable features of the Illinois River there. The United States Government has taken full charge.

Q. (By Representative LORIMER.) It has taken charge of the Chicago River?—A. Yes.

Q. Is the deepening of the water here now in charge of the United States Government?—A. Yes.

Q. (By Mr. C. J. HARRIS.) Has there been anything done in a governmental way with the Desplaines River, this connecting link between the Illinois River and your canal?—A. By the United States Government?

Q. Yes.—A. No further than making surveys. They are constructing the Hennepin Canal, but the money expended on the Hennepin Canal will be of very little service to the people of this country unless the route is improved by them in both ways, so that in coming to the river they can move freight either way. Although it was a step for a short line, it will be of very little benefit.

Q. (By Professor JOHNSON.) The Illinois and Michigan Canal is still in use?—A. Yes.

Q. It is operated by the State of Illinois, I believe?—A. Yes.

Q. (By Mr. C. J. HARRIS.) What is the prospect of the tonnage of the lakes being increased by another year so that your grain and other products will have more liberal movement by water? Is the shipbuilding being increased at all?—A. Yes; and the incentive to increase is very great at this time. The earnings this season have been very remunerative, and you can easily conclude what the result will be. I know quite a number of the largest carriers are being constructed, and I would conclude, even if I did not know that, that there would be only one result, with boats making contracts a few months since to carry ore for less than one-third of what it can be carried by rail—the result of that will be to largely increase the tonnage of the lake.

Q. What is the rate on freight by water route, or is there a combination among the owners of boats to regulate that? Is there a rate agreed upon for a season by water?—A. There never has been a successful combination on the lakes. There have been contracts, many of them, entered into which favored a certain amount of tonnage during whole seasons, but no combination including all the tonnage of the lakes. Nothing of that kind, it seems to me, at present, would be possible or feasible.

Q. Has it a charter like an ocean charter?—A. Yes.

Q. Varying in price from month to month?—A. Those who are free from contract make a special contract for every ship—every load.

Q. (By Representative OTJEN.) They follow the market?—A. Coal has been carried within the last two years from Buffalo to Chicago as low as 20 cents a ton. There was not very much carried at that rate, but there has been a great deal carried at 25, 30, and 35 cents per ton. Ore has been carried from Lake Superior points to Buffalo, and near Buffalo, and to that section of lake ports there, for 40 cents. That is, perhaps, the minimum; but great contracts have been made at 45 cents per ton.

Q. (By Mr. CONGER.) What figures have you as to the maximum?—A. For this year the maximum was $2.

Q. For ore?—A. Yes.

Q. (By Professor JOHNSON.) Then I understand there is a large number of vessel owners on the lakes?—A. Yes.

Q. And that a shipper usually has an opportunity of making a contract with several people?—A. Yes.

Q. You ship on the lakes, do you?—A. Sometimes; not extensively.

Q. How do you get your shipments billed; that is, do you charter a boat or do you go to some agent, or what is the way?—A. In grain a boat is chartered generally and loaded by one shipper. The shipper might contract with the owner, but the usual system is to contract with what is known as the vessel agent, who perhaps may be instructed to charter his vessel when he is on the road from Buffalo here. He expects it to be here on or about such a day; and it will take him from one to three days to unload; it depends upon the character of his cargo, the material he is carrying, etc. The agent desires to have a load ready for the boat when it is unloaded, so a charter or contract is made out with the agent here while the boat may be on its way.

Q. Is there much package freight on the lakes?—A. Yes.

Q. And is that shipped through the agents?—A. Yes; that is carried very largely by the regular steamship lines. The package freight—say, for instance, flour and pork, and all that sort of stuff—is carried largely by the regular lines, and they employ agents to attend to that business at all times. That business is transacted, so far as that part of it is concerned, very much the same as a railroad agent would transact it in shipping freight over a railroad.

Q. Please tell us, if you know, what the Lake Carriers' Association is, and what it does?—A. I don't happen to remember all of the things they do; but some things they try to do, for instance, is to regulate wages, and it is an association that tries to look after the interests of the lake carriers generally. I could not state the ground they try to cover, specifically.

Q. Do they have anything to do with rates?—A. Of course they would endeavor to fix a rate so far as the practice on certain lines is concerned, if they could, but they have never succeeded in fixing any rates which have stood out for any length of time.

Q. Did not this association at one time seriously consider the proposition of entering into a pool with the general traffic associations or a combination, when that was in vogue, with the Eastern traffic lines?—A. This association may have had something of that character under consideration, though it is not controlling the tonnage of the lakes. For instance, we have members of the Lake Carriers' Association who don't have any tonnage on the lakes. I know one of the leading men of Chicago who has been one of the officers of the Lake Carriers' Association, and, so far as I am aware, has not owned anything except tugs for drawing ships in here to Chicago. I don't see that the tonnage of the lake is a matter in which such members are very deeply interested, except incidentally. Of course when it is prosperous his business is good.

Q. (By Mr. CONGER.) You are a commission merchant, dealing in grain?—A. Yes.

Q. Where do you buy your grain?—A. I buy the most of my grain in Chicago.

Q. Where do you sell it?—A. Sell it in Chicago and ship some away. Largely, my trade is confined to the State and always has been.

Q. Do you ship some to New York?—A. Yes.

Q. When you do that, which kind of transportation do you use, rail or water route?—A. If I desire to ship a single carload of grain—and there is a great deal of trade done in a retail way, a carload of grain being regarded as retail—as it is already on the move, my method would be to ship by rail in order to preserve its identity.

Q. What proportion of the grain that you ship East goes by rail and what by water?—A. Nearly all the grain that I ship East goes by rail, because, as I have said to you, I have not been a large shipper. Most of my grain is sold here.

Q. For a certain class of trade—that is, the class you specify—the railroad transportation is much more desirable?—A. It would be desirable in a retail way; yes.

Q. (By Representative LORIMER.) Were you until recently the president of the Board of Trade in Chicago?—A. Yes.

Q. And you are familiar with the grain and elevator business of Chicago, are you?—A. Yes.

Q. Will you please state to the commission what you know of the elevator system as it is operated in Chicago, and its effects on the grain trade in Chicago and points tributary to Chicago?—A. Well, my knowledge of the method of management of the elevators is continuous for the past 20 years. The changes in the methods have been great. I have believed that sound business principles, correct business principles, were being violated in the elevator system of Chicago. Down to within perhaps 8 years ago the elevators of Chicago were public custodians of property, and they were paid such rate as was fixed at the beginning of each year, as a rule, for the grain placed at the beginning of the year in the elevator. The men who handled and managed these elevators were only occasionally engaged in the shipping or receiving of grain. More recently, while the elevators are still used for the purpose of storing the grain of the shipper, of the man who may ship grain from the country, or of holding the grain of the man who may purchase it here for eastern shipment, still the large part of the grain in the elevators of Chicago to-day belongs to the man who is managing the elevator and who at the same time holds a license from our court to be the custodian of public property.

Those who are thoroughly conversant with the variations in the grades of grain, and the value of different grades of the same grade of grain, will readily see that an opportunity for profit, obtained by improper methods, is within the grasp of the man who is managing the elevators and handling that part of the grain which he does not own, mixing it with his own grain. A hundred cars of grain can be inspected by the inspector, and he may be an efficient, capable man too, but you may go right out to the elevator and walk right along that line and select 8 or 10 cars of grain, especially in certain conditions of the market, that will vary from 1 to 5 or 6 cents in value from the others. Now, then, when that goes into the elevator and into one bin, the purchaser knows he will get the average of the grade as inspected, under the old system, and the result was that many dealers in grain purchased elevator receipts and took the grain from the elevator. To-day the careful man would not accept grain simply on the inspection and receipt, but he would want to see a sample of the grain itself, fearing he might be compelled to take the lowest quality known to that grade, and would be almost sure to do it every time. That is one of the preferences which is afforded the men who are handling large amounts of freight over the different lines of railroad, and it is one of the abuses which bears most heavily on men engaged in the grain business in this country, the preferences being shown by the railroad people, and that is one of t.. 'm. The railroad people in this city have built large elevators, and formerly had them managed by people who were simply managers of the elevators and custodians of other people's property. To-day, the largest receiver over a road, generally one large concern, has the use of these elevators, without doubt, at merely a nominal rent, nothing more. Another shipper or receiver who desires to place grain in that elevator must pay three-fourths of a cent for the privilege of having it handled through the elevator, and having it held 10 days. It can not go through the elevator for less than three-quarters of a cent.

Q. (By Mr. CONGER.) Are any of the public elevators managed by men who are not in the grain business?—A. I do not think there is to-day. There has been up to very recently, but to-day I do not think any of the public elevators are managed by men who are not in any way engaged in the grain business.

Q. Is there any effort being made by dealers in grain here in Chicago to correct this matter by State law?—A. Yes; much effort has been made during the past 2 or 3 years, first in the board of trade, as a body, attempting to correct conditions which they believed were a violation of correct, sound business principles. Much bad feeling was engendered by the attempt to correct it. Efforts have also been made for additional legislation, surrounding with greater safeguards the handling of public property.

Q. What is the opinion, or can you tell what would be the opinion of a majority of the members of the board of trade here on this question? Do you think you express the views of the majority of the members?—A. Yes.

Q. Has the board taken any official action on the question; have they gone on record in any way?—A. They have held elections in which that question was involved, and when the issue was made squarely they never failed to elect the officers who stood for the handling of public property by disinterested parties, by men whose only interest was the compensation which they received for caring for the property.

Q. It has been testified to before this subcommission that the present system has developed out of the necessities of the situation; that is, out of the competition between Chicago and other markets for this grain trade, and that but for the fact that these large dealers in grain had come to own their own elevators, and by dealing in grain themselves in a direct manner have thereby, because of their large operations, effected great economies—that only in that way has the prestige and supremacy of Chicago as a wheat market been maintained.—A. Now, let us analyze that and see how that looks. Here is a man that owns elevators in the country himself. He has managed these elevators for years; he has all the money that is necessary to handle his business successfully; he is thoroughly conversant with the business; and still he is absolutely forced out of business. Is it a reasonable acceptation that a man can hire every particle of his help and give his business that close, careful supervision that the other man is giving it? The reasonable explanation is that preferences are given this individual in furnishing him terminal facilities, free of charge; and the preferences he gets in rates drives the other man out of business. No man who studies that question carefully can come to any other conclusion.

Q. Is it your opinion that these large dealers in grain receive or enjoy a lower rate of freight on the grain they bring into this market than the ordinary buyer?—A. I have no doubt of it. I have investigated this question carefully, and one of the strong reasons why that is done is because if one concern can handle all the grain that is left—for the little fellows get a little here and there—but if one concern can handle all the grain, and they want to make rebates on it, they can be made to that one concern and kept from the public; if divided among a dozen, it would leak and not be kept. Now, see what the evidence of that fact is. We have men on 'Change to-day who are doing business over a certain line of road. They are purchasing grain from the men who own the country elevators. One of the men I have in mind has not been doing business with that line of road more than a year; he has not had an opportunity to become established on that line and have acquaintances and friends, which would be a great influence and factor; he has made his relations with that road in a year or such a matter, and yet that man is getting to-day perhaps nine-tenths of the grain coming in over that road. Well, if he is a skilled merchant only, why does he not get grain from the other roads? He does not; he gets it over that line of road. That is one instance, and there are others just like it. If it was caused by his great capital and great ability as a merchant, ability to send through to Europe, and all that sort of thing, he would reach out over the other lines of road; but he gets it over that one line of road and no other.

Q. We have had testimony tending to show that it is the custom for at least a number of these large buyers, some of them, to purchase grain on more than one line of road. Now, is it your opinion that as a rule, a single operator usually confines himself to one road?—A. Yes.

Q. But, to put the reverse, is it your opinion that along a given line of road there is usually but one operator?—A. There is usually the man, the firm, or organization that controls the terminal facilities in this city. They immediately branch out, and they very soon control a large percentage of the grain that goes over that line of road, and they do not do business on the other lines. They may, occasionally, do a little, but they do not do any large business, and it is almost wholly confined to the one line.

Q. (By Professor JOHNSON.) Is it not true that man is very apt to be a heavy owner in the railroad?—A. Unfortunately, we have a good many of the officers of the railroads in the grain business, and partners, and all that sort of thing.

Q. This man you had in mind was a large owner of the stock of the railroad?—A. I do not think the particular individual I was talking of has any direct connection with the railroad. I do not think he is a large stockholder in the road.

Q. (By Mr. KENNEDY.) Have you the belief that he is merely the agent of the railroad in this business?—A. No; I do not think he could be classed as a mere agent, because he is a grain merchant and has been doing a grain merchant's business in years past of a general character, just as other men in the city of Chicago have done. He has demonstrated no great ability in these years, but all at once he forms a connection with this road, and is able to go right out and get a very large part of the grain.

Q. (By Mr. CONGER.) The idea I got was that this man, in all probability, had a lower freight rate.—A. That is the point exactly.

Q. (By Professor JOHNSON.) If he was an owner in the railroad, he would be very apt to get it.—A. You gentlemen can very easily see if that was the desirable point, and that was what it led up to, the connection could be made and a half dozen silent partners could be enjoying the profits.

Q. (By Mr. CONGER.) Can you suggest a remedy for this evil? It is the purpose of this commission to recommend legislation to Congress or the various States. We have heard a great deal about the existence of the evil, and we would like to ask you, as a man of considerable information on the grain business, how to go to work to correct it?—A. Well, it is a pretty large question and requires the careful thought of the best brains of this country, and I do not know now that I have in my own mind any better method than enlarging the powers of the Interstate Commerce Commission and enforcing the law.

Q. It has been contended that if the system or custom of giving rebates could be done away with, if all discriminations to one individual or community could be eliminated from the transportation question, the evils of the trust, for instance, would be in a great measure eliminated thereby. Do you think that would apply to the grain business? In other words, if the transportation discriminations were absolutely done away with, so that men would be on an equality as rates of freight, do you think, then, this situation would be corrected?—A. In answer to your question I would like to say this: I think if that situation existed, every citizen would have all he is entitled to ask for, absolute equality before the law, and an absolute good opportunity with every man, in proportion to his energy and ability. I believe to-day that the two greatest questions affecting the interests of the American people are, first, the prevention of preferences shown by railroad companies in the matter of freght carrying; and, secondly, the prevention of overcapitalization. These are the two great questions that are before the American people to be solved. I do not think the trust, in and of itself, if founded on actual values, need frighten anybody. But when a concern can capitalize 4, 5, or 10 times the actual capital invested and float it on the community and get good money for their worthless paper, it is a pretty bad condition.

Q. Do you think the proposition to legalize pooling would have an influence to do away with these favors in transportation rates?—A. I am unalterably opposed to pooling.

Q. Under all circumstances?—A. I can not conceive of any reason why the men who invest their money in railroad construction are any more entitled to the right to be exempt from competition than any other line of business.

Q. (By Representative OTJEN.) Do you see any serious objection to legalizing pooling when it is coupled with adequate authority in the Interstate Commerce Commission to regulate freight rates, and perhaps, in addition to that, to consent to any pooling contract that the railroads may make?—A. It is certainly true that pooling, under careful supervision and restriction, would be very much less objectionable than pooling by the railroads without any restriction; there is no doubt about that, because if pools can be formed and any rate fixed which they can temporarily maintain, they can fix any price that is not absolutely prohibited.

Q. (By Mr. CONGER.) I think nearly all advocates of pooling to-day couple with it the provision that the Interstate Commerce Commission shall be given authority to fix the rate.—A. I believe that to be true; yes.

Q. Would you object to that?—A. I have never come to the conclusion that it was wise policy to permit pooling.

Q. (By Representative OTJEN.) Give us your idea why it is not?—A. First of all, of course, we have never reached the point in the supervision of railroad affairs where we could consider it from the standpoint you now suggest. That is the first and strongest reason. I am willing to admit that if the law governing the powers of the Interstate Commerce Commission were so enlarged that they could, in a measure, control the action of the companies and the rates they made, we would have arrived at a point where, perhaps, pooling would not be so objectionable; I can easily see that.

Q. (By Mr. KENNEDY.) Do you believe that, preferable to pooling, there should be supervision by the Interstate Commerce Commission in this way: A railroad company is compelled to publish its rates, and the Interstate Commerce Commission given revisionary power over those rates, to correct, upon complaint which is found to be well-grounded, inequalities, injustice in the rates, and then the finding of the commission to go into effect pending an appeal which the railroad companies may take to the Supreme Court of the United States?—A. I believe any finding which they should make should go into effect. That is the weakness of the present law. Then let the railroad company appeal from that finding, and pending the decision of the appeal, the rate fixed by the commission should stand.

Q. You would have, then, the powers which the commission was supposed to have in the first place made plain and enforcible?—A. Yes.

Q. (By Mr. C. J. HARRIS.) So far as the public are concerned, if penalties could be enforced for discriminations and rebates made on the published rate, do you think the public would be taken care of as it now stands, and no pooling law would be necessary?—A. First of all, it seems to me perfectly clear that a railroad company should be permitted to arrange its rates within reasonable restrictions. They should be fairly remunerative. Then their rates should be such that all the shippers over the line might have the advantage of the greatest business to-day. The one that goes home to the people is the preference shown. There is no doubt about it.

Q. Now, if the penalty for preferences was a heavy fine for each case, why could not these published rates be enforced by you people who are put to a disadvantage by them?—A. Well, as to the best method of bringing that character of criminals to justice that is a matter I would not care to express an opinion upon.

Q. Would not heavy fines and penalties be much more effective than this criminal prosecution and imprisonment?—A. I think very likely you would more easily obtain evidence for conviction if that were the rule.

Q. (By Mr. CONGER.) One railroad manager would be a little more willing to prosecute his competitor or the manager of another road if the punishment was one of fine rather than imprisonment?—A. Yes; no doubt about that.

Q. (By Representative BELL.) You spoke of the injury to the dealer in grain by reason of these preferences. What effect does it have on the wheat grower?--A. I think it is a well-settled law of commerce that free competition, free and open and unrestricted competition, produces the best results for the producer.

Q. Then you think the grower of wheat gets no benefit from the rebates that the preferred dealer gets?—A. I think that if the railroad company can afford to make a lower rate they should make it public and for everyone.

Q. But under the present system does the farmer benefit by these big institutions building their elevators and finding the market?—A. No, they will not in the end. It is not according to sound business principles that they will. If in the windup there is only one concern to buy their grain along the road, which is a presumable condition of affairs, they will not get a better price for their grain.

Q. You think not?—A. No, I think not.

Q. In these privileges in terminal facilities might not that be given in the way of rebate?—A. They may give it to them in any way; but these conditions exist in Chicago; the terminal facilities of the railroad companies, in many cases, facilities provided years ago, are practically given to one concern, and they immediately become large receivers over that line of road.

Q. A gentleman from the West this morning stated that he understood that a railroad company paid a dealer 4 cents for running wheat through the elevator when it was worth about a half a cent. Now, would you not regard that as a mere system of rebates—that he is making it up through the elevator charges?—A. He charged 4 cents? This was at the country point?

Q. Yes.—A. Where he received the grain?

Q. Yes.—A. And he charged the producer 4 cents a bushel?

Q. (By Mr. CONGER.) I think this was a Kansas City point and the elevator, instead of being owned by the railroad, was owned by the man, and the theory was that the railroad paid the 4 cents as a rebate on freight.—A. Yes; that was a very unusual condition of affairs, that anyone should be paying any party 4 cents a bushel for simply running grain through the elevator; and there must have been something special about it.

Q. That is what he means to say. That was the advantage given to him on the freight rate. Or, we take the oil companies that have created such a commotion in this country about discriminations. Men of one company insist that after they had hunted down the different discriminations from time to time, they found the Standard Oil Company sold the railroads all their lubricating oils, and instead of their paying the market prices, they paid three or four times the market price and centered all their trade with that one firm. As a rebate, now how would you reach a system of that kind?—A. Well, it looks to me as though these special cases which you are now describing, are all minor matters.

Q. These men state that they produce about one-tenth of the oil—the independent companies of the United States, and that they have been unable to make a profit on a single barrel of oil put on an American railroad, while, if they run it to the seaboard and ship to a foreign country where there are no discriminations, they make a handsome profit.—A. My understanding of your statement was that the rebate in this case would be the amount of oil used by this company doing the business.

Q. Instead of giving an actual rebate, it buys supplies from the company, and instead of paying the market prices it pays four or five times the market price, and they make the rebates indirectly.—A. There is a greater principle underlying this whole question, and the best any of us can do is to work determinedly along these lines. Whether or not we will ever be able to find a cure for these evils and come to a point where we will be entirely satisfied, is another question. I believe great improvements can be made over present conditions.

(Testimony closed.)

CHICAGO, ILL., *November 24, 1899.*

TESTIMONY OF MR. CHARLES A. MALLORY,

Chairman railroad committee, Chicago Live Stock Exchange.

The subcommission on transportation being in session in Chicago, Representative Lorimer presiding, at 3.30 p. m. November 24, 1899, Mr. Charles A. Mallory, chairman of the railroad committee of the Chicago Live Stock Exchange, was introduced as a witness, and being duly sworn, testified concerning transportation as follows:

Q. (By Representative LORIMER.) What is your name?—A. Charles A. Mallory.

Q. What is your business and official connection?—A. Chairman of the railroad committee of the Chicago Live Stock Exchange and treasurer and manager of the Mallory Commission Company at the Union Stock Yards, Chicago.

Q. We understand your organization has grievances, and we would like to have you state to the commission what your grievances are.—A. I was not quite positive this morning whether I would be able to come down or not, as I received word to go West, and I dictated a few of the fundamental things, and if it is the pleasure of the commission I will read them. They will probably cover all the points you will care to touch on. (Reading.)

I start out with the proposition of equal rights to all interests. Any legislation that will promote and protect all on a fair and equitable basis is most desirable. In my judgment, we have altogether too many laws, both State and national, caused largely by the lack of necessity for many of them, prepared and enacted by politicians in order that their constituents may know they are doing something, and possibly have some excuse for reelecting them to office. It is not so much the quantity of laws that we are in need of, but we should have a better quality of legislation, and then have it properly enforced.

Naturally matters pertaining to transportation business in this country, especially where much evidence is required, is very complicated to the average citizen. The courts found it impossible to cope with these matters in a satisfactory manner, owing to a lack of comprehension on the part of the courts and juries. Congress, evidently recognizing these conditions, created the Interstate Commerce Commission, with its extraordinary powers for investigation, and conducted by a board whose business it is to make themselves familiar with transportation affairs.

The law which created the Interstate Commerce Commission has proven defective in some features, and in order that the transportation companies and the public may derive benefits from their efforts, they should have proper power to enforce their findings. I believe one way to correct many of these legislative abuses will be to change existing tenures of office, laws, and methods of elections, so that no one may be elected to succeed himself, thus taking away the temptation to treat public questions with any thought of reelection.

The live-stock interests, which I have the honor to represent before your honorable body, probably have some grievances against the railroads, some of which, like many others, are doubtless more or less imaginary or the result of the generally expressed or implied sentiment against corporations; but as a rule, I believe the railroads mean to treat the live-stock shippers fairly and to treat localities as equitably as circumstances and competition will permit. From an almost national, as well as a local standpoint, our principal grievance is in what is known as the terminal charge, levied by all Western roads on all live stock consigned to Chicago. This is a charge of $2 per car, and was added to the regular tariff June 1, 1894, and is still collected by all of these roads. The only change in conditions governing the handling of live stock at Chicago on that day was the addition of a trackage charge of 80 cents per car on most of the roads, and $1.50 per car on others who used the companies' tracks a longer distance. This arbitrary charge of $2 per car, which was 50 cents per car on 3 roads and $1.20 per car on the other roads, more than the additional cost to the roads, caused the shippers all over this country to rebel against such treatment; and the Chicago Live Stock Exchange, through its railroad committee, held several sessions with the general managers of the railroads in June, 1894, and tried to convince them from a business man's standpoint that their act was not right, but without success. The chairman of this General Managers' Association stated, however, that if the company owning the tracks would take off their trackage charge they would remove the terminal charge.

We took the matter up with the Illinois Board of Railroad Commissioners, and after a full trial obtained a decision that the terminal charge was unjust, unreasonable, and illegal. The matter was afterwards brought up in the United States court in Chicago, and after a full hearing this court made a similar decision, and ordered the railroad company to desist, which they did until the court of appeals reversed the decision on a technical point. We brought the matter to the attention of the Interstate Commerce Commission, which spent considerable time in its investigations, all the roads being represented by counsel, who spent days in argument, citing authorities, etc., but the commission found the charge to be unjust, unreasonable, and illegal, and ordered the railroad companies to cease collecting it. The railroads refused to obey the order. The commission appealed to the United States court to enforce the decision, when the railroads filed a demurrer which was argued at great length and overruled. The case came up for a hearing on the 6th of this month, and after 2 days' argument, etc., the court took the case under advisement on only one of the points.

I go into this matter in detail to illustrate the necessity of some action being taken which will admit of adjustment of these and other matters pertaining to the transportation business of this country by some tribunal having the proper facilities and knowledge for making investigations, hearing complaints and enforcing decisions. During all these years of litigation, investigation, and experience in this matter, I find that it is almost impossible, under existing laws and practices, for individuals or small organizations to compete with the combined legal and financial facilities of the railroads.

Another feature that impressed me along this line was the statement made by the railroad officials at their meeting, and by one of them in his testimony before the Interstate Commerce Commission, to the effect that this terminal charge would never have been levied had no trackage charge been made, and if this trackage charge was taken off the roads would remove their terminal charge.

I think this statement of facts, which can be proven by the records of the various cases, should convince any reasonable man of the necessity of some law or other method which would not only secure prompt justice to the people but prevent any arbitrary or vindictive actions. I firmly believe that the transportation companies are entitled to proper consideration and protection at all times, the same as any other business or interest, and any legislation that will advance the various interests, secure justice based more upon right than on technicalities, and promote and lead to better harmony all around, will be acceptable to our people.

Q. (By Mr. C. J. HARRIS.) Who levy this trackage charge?—A. The Union Stock Yard and Transit Company, who owns the tracks in and about the stock yards. None of the railroads coming into Chicago own their tracks to the yards.

Q. You pay, of course, the stock yards company as well charges for putting stock in there?—A. The stock yard company have yardage and feed charges, which all stock shippers have to pay.

Q. Why do they not include their railroad trackage in that general charge? I understand if that was removed the railroads would take off this terminal charge of $2 a car.—A. The trackage charge is considered as part of the railroad charge, while the charges for yardage and feed is a stock yard company charge for their services.

Q. They are really the same company?—A. The same company practically owns the tracks that owns the stock yard, but the terminal facilities, as decided by the various courts and commissions, must be furnished by the railroad companies and must be included in their rate, and consequently the charges as levied by the stock yards company, which the shippers have to pay, have nothing to do with the railroad matter.

Q. This terminal charge has been in use since 1894?—A. Yes.

Q. The extra trackage by this stock yards company was added on at that time?—A. At the same time.

Q. (By Representative OTJEN.) As I understand, you think the interstate-commerce law should be so amended that the Interstate Commerce Commission will have authority to regulate such matters and enforce their orders?—A. Yes.

Q. (By Mr. KENNEDY.) I would like you to say if this charge is a discrimination against Chicago, which sends stock to Kansas City or other points in considerable volume.—A. Yes; it has diverted a good deal of business. It is a discrimination against Chicago to the extent of the $2; besides, the sentimental discrimination—that has been equal to 5 or 10 times that; and it is used largely by the competitors of Chicago in the same line of business. Naturally the shippers look at it in all sorts of ways that were not right, and after it had been talked over and the competitive markets had handled it in their way it became much larger than the $2 item would appear, while it does amount to considerable in the aggregate.

Q. Kansas City and these other big towns are not interested or moving with you to have this charge removed?—A. No. The Cattle Growers' Association, the largest association of its kind in this country, composed largely of Texas, Montana, and the other range people, have joined the Chicago live-stock men in their fight for the removal of this charge.

Q. (By Mr. C. J. HARRIS.) Have you any other complaints in regard to the transportation of live stock?—A. No; I do not think I have any other complaints to offer.

Q. Have you any discriminations in rates as between individuals, one man shipping his cattle for less than another—any inside rates that you know of?—A. Not that I know of. So far as I am aware, the rates on live stock are exactly the same to all shippers.

Q. Are the rates reasonable?—A. Judging from rates in the past and from the improved methods of handling the business, I should say that they would be considered reasonable. Of course there are exceptions to all rules, but I am speaking in the broad sense, and I should say they were reasonable.

Q. How does the price of stock compare now with former years?—A. The price of cattle during 1899 has been considerable higher than it has been for the past 3 or 4 years.

Q. Does that apply to hogs also?—A. The price of hogs is not so much higher. Perhaps it will average 25 to 50 cents a hundred higher, while cattle will average from $1 to $1.50 higher.

Q. To what do you attribute this rise in price—scarcity?—A. Not so much scarcity in the supply as increase in the demand. The increase in the supply has not kept pace with the increase in the demand, in my judgment, and the prospective shortage has had considerable to do with the advance also.

Q. Is there a larger consumption of meat in prosperous times over dull times, when people are not employed?—A. Oh, yes, indeed. The laboring man, in my judgment, will use a larger percentage of his earnings in prosperous times for the purchase of meat than he will at any other time; and when he is well employed at good wages he will naturally spend more for meat products than under other circumstances.

Q. (By Professor JOHNSON.) Do any of the cattle shippers own their own cars?—A. Yes; not what you might call cattle shippers, but people who ship cattle own their own cars; such people as Armour & Co., Swift & Co.; they are in the packing business, but cattle shippers also. There are no cattle shippers that are engaged exclusively in the cattle business, to my knowledge, that own cars.

Q. When they ship live cattle they ship in their own cars?—A. They do to a large extent. Of course they also ship cattle in the common or railroad cars.

Q. Does that produce a discrimination against you men who do not own your own cars?—A. I would say to the extent of whatever profit they make from the use of their own cars—tariff; so far as I know they pay tariff rates on their shipments.

Q. Have you ever thought whether they did derive very much advantage from the use of their own cars?—A. I understand the owners of private cars of all kinds derive a good revenue from the use of them.

Q. Do you ship cattle in considerable quantities?—A. We are in the live-stock commission business; we are receivers of cattle. In answer to what I think you are trying to get at, I think there are very few exclusively live-stock shippers that would handle enough business to warrant their keeping a line of cars for their own use.

Q. (By Representative OTJEN.) Do you think it is good policy to permit these private cars?—A. That is a matter that I am not familiar enough with to pass an opinion upon. As I stated, I naturally think people that do not own their own cars, and who are competing with people that do, would be at whatever disadvantage the difference in the profit might figure.

Q. Would it not seem to be more proper that a railroad company conducting a business should conduct that business by its own cars?—A. Yes.

Q. (By Representative BELL.) You were speaking of the high price of cattle in 1899. Are you aware of a shortage of cattle in the United States during the past 5 years?—A. Yes.

Q. Did that have something to do with the rise in prices?—A. Yes.

Q. Do you remember about what the shortage was?—A. I should think 10 per cent would cover it.

Q. Have you seen the figures of Mr. Mulhall, the great English statistician, as to our shortage in the past 5 years?—A. No.

Q. About how many cattle have we in the United States?—A. That is a pretty hard question to answer except from the Government report; that is the only official document we have giving the figures.

Q. The Government reports have been showing this shortage ever since the Cleveland Administration?—A. I do not know just when it dates from, but people in our line of business do not put much faith in the statistics furnished by the Government in regard to live stock.

Q. You think there has been a shortage?—A. Yes.

Q. You think that would raise the price?—A. Yes; with the tremendous increase in consumption.

Q. How have the prices been the last few weeks?—A. This last week we have had a very sharp decline in most grades of fat cattle.

Q. How has it been in stockers?—A. There has only been a small decline in stock cattle; they have been lower than usual.

Q. There has been a rupture in the market in the last few weeks?—A. The first two weeks of this month we had a fairly steady market. This week we have had an unusual decline in certain grades of cattle.

Q. It struck the Denver markets before it did you?—A. It generally strikes the markets all about the same time. The telegraph works very promptly. If Chicago declines other markets decline, and if they decline it has a sympathetic effect upon Chicago.

Q. Hogs have declined in the last few weeks?—A. Very slightly. The decline in hogs came in October, as it generally does in the fall of the year.

Q. (By Mr. KENNEDY.) Has there been a marked increase in the consumption of meats in the last year?—A. Yes.

Q. Could you state the percentage of increase?—A. I should think 25 per cent or 40 per cent over 3 years ago.

Q. What is the cause of that?—A. I should attribute it to the prosperous condition of the country and the fact that the laboring men are generally employed at fair wages, and they generally spend a good portion of their wages for meat.

Q. (By Representative BELL.) How did the war affect the meat market—the meat they supplied on the ships?—A. One part of the war affected it satisfactorily to the selling interests by advancing the price and another part of the war had a bad effect on it for quite a long time.

Q. A great deal was spoiled, was there not?—A. I do not know anything about that except what I have read in the papers.

Q. You know they had to throw overboard a good deal of meat?—A. I say I know nothing about that except what I saw in the papers.

Q. I suppose you have read also in the papers during the last few days that a great quantity of it was thrown overboard from an English ship going to South Africa?—A. Yes.

Q. We are not the only people who have to throw it overboard?—A. No.

Q. (By Representative BELL.) It affects the market, no matter who throws it overboard?—A. On that particular beef.

Q. Does it not affect all beef markets?—A. If enough of it was thrown overboard or lost in some other such way, of course it would affect the market by advancing it.

Q. (By Representative OTJEN.) As a matter of fact, the entire amount that is supposed to have been thrown over would cut very little figure in affecting the price?—A. I should say absolutely none.

Q. (By Mr. C. J. HARRIS.) It would not run one of these packing houses more than a few hours?—A. Not more than a few minutes.

Q. (By Representative LORIMER.) Would a boat load affect the market?—A. No.

Q. (By Professor JOHNSON.) If this meat had got a bad reputation—— —A. (Interrupting.) That would have a bad effect on the market, more than the actual loss of the cargo.

Q. (By Representative OTJEN.) The fear that you would lose foreign trade?—A. The sentiment that would follow the declaration that any part of the American meat was spoiled or unfit for use would naturally have a sentimental effect that would be depressing on the market. So far these times have only been temporary, because on investigation they have found that our meat products are absolutely all right.

Q. (By Representative LORIMER.) About how long do they have an effect?—A. Owing to the damage and the sentiment it causes? This one we are speaking of, regarding the investigation of army beef, lasted several months.

Q. If the throwing overboard of beef from a British ship is a fact, how much or how long will that affect the market?—A. I do not think it would affect the market at all; I do not think the trade would pay any attention to it.

We, as business men, connected with the live-stock trade, handling the product that is shipped from the range and from the feed lot to the market—we figure from the standpoint of supply and demand in the various markets. We do not go quite as far as the Agricultural Department, and figure on all the different cattle supposed to be in the United States. We have found from years of experience that this country is capable of producing anything so rapidly that by the time the years would roll around, when you might naturally expect a shortage to come, from their way of gathering statistics, other sections of the country have been industrious and increased their output to such an extent that we never come to that shortage in the market. So far as the trade and values are concerned, it is the supply and demand in the market that governs, and not what is in the country.

Q. (By Mr. KENNEDY.) The calf becomes a steer before you come to that point?—A. They are marketed a year or two earlier than they were.

Q. (By Professor JOHNSON.) As a matter of fact, are there any live-stock statistics in this country?—A. Not that we consider reliable.

Q. They are not actual counts; they are estimates?—A. I should judge so.

Q. The only counts are those made by the census?—A. Yes.

Q. (By Representative BELL.) The Agricultural Department—does it not make inquiries annually?—A. They claim to; they publish every January a supposed report of all kinds of live stock in the country.

Q. (By Mr. KENNEDY.) Without facilities for gathering that information, must it not be a matter of inquiry largely with the Agricultural Department?—A. Yes; almost entirely.

Q. (By Representative BELL.) How is it as to their other statistics?—A. I am not familiar with that.

Q. Might not we include them all and say they are all guesswork?—A. I would not want to go on record as to anything I know nothing about. They may have some facilities for finding out how much grain there is, and other things. I do not know anything about that; but so far as live stock is concerned, their statistics are of no value whatever.

Q. (By Mr. C. J. HARRIS.) So long as cattle do not have to be shipped into this country to supply the demand, and we have enough cattle raised here and shipped to the markets to supply our home demand, there could not be a shortage of cattle in this country?—A. No.

Q. There might be more or less one year than another, but there would not be what you would call a shortage so as to raise prices. Now, if we had to import cattle from other countries, that would raise the price, perhaps, would it not?— A. Yes. In my judgment these things are largely regulated by the supply and price of other live stock. For instance, when beef reaches a certain point consumption will commence to drop, and if pork is relatively lower a good deal of that consumption will take up with pork, and if mutton is still lower it will increase the demand for mutton; so we are not entirely dependent in this country on any one class of meat.

Q. (By Representative BELL.) Suppose we had 8,000,000 more cattle placed on the markets of the United States, would it raise or lower the prices of cattle?—A. It would lower the price.

Q. Then the shortage must have some effect on the price?—A. Yes; it does.

Q. (By Representative LORIMER.) Suppose we had 8,000,000 more cattle in the country than we have now, and the same amount was shipped to the market as now, what effect would that have on the market?—A. If the 8,000,000 cattle were thrown on the market all at once?

Q. If they came up in the natural way, and we were here and there shipping just as you receive now, would it affect the market?—A. I think the market would be lower with 8,000,000 more cattle in the country than there are to-day.

Q. Would it be as low as if the 8,000,000 were thrown on the market?—A. No. The temporary effect of 8,000,000 cattle on the market would be very depressing.

Q. So there would be a difference between having 8,000,000 in the country, with the regular supply shipping to market, and 8,000,000 thrown on the market?—A. Oh, yes.

Q. (By Representative BELL.) Suppose we had 8,000,000 more cattle, would they not ship more to the market?—A. Oh, yes; more of them would mature.

Q. (By Professor JOHNSON.) We are large exporters of cattle and meat products?—A. Yes.

Q. And a home supply equal to the home market would represent a tremendous shortage, would it not?—A. I do not think that I just catch your meaning.

Q. An attempt was made a moment ago by a question to show that as long as we had cattle enough to supply our own needs we could not speak of a shortage. We are supplying not only our own needs, but the foreign supply. We are large exporters, and it seems to me we would have a tremendous shortage if we could supply only our own home markets.—A. It depends a great deal to what extent you were carrying the shortage. A shortage may be less than the previous year; it may reach a point like a famine, or it may be just a few less than the last year; but, speaking with the broader view, I should say that a shortage, so called, is nothing more nor less than the natural result of the depression that the cattle market went through 2 or 3 years ago. Low prices will follow what we call generally liquidation. A great many people became discouraged because cattle were not seeing such a good market and threw them on the market.

Q. (By Representative BELL.) Do you not think the driving of cattle out of the Neutral Strip, Indian Territory, and the fencing of the Western range, whereby the ranger had to spay out of business, had some effect on the raising of cattle?— A. Yes.

Q. You handle a good many spayed cattle, do you not?—A. Yes; not during recent years, but from 1894 on we did.

Q. Did not that come from the ranges being eaten out and fenced up?—A. Yes; some of the cattle were thrown on to the market on that account, but had the price not been so low a good many of these cattle would have found places where they had feed and would have been held.

Q. You do not think high prices would make grass grow?—A. No; but it makes people hustle around and find feed more than it would with prices low. The transportation facilities are such in this country now that they can ship cattle almost any place and find feed.

Q. But the ranges are fenced up in the great West.—A. The reduction in supply of cattle on the ranges has been going down for 3, 4 or 5 years.

(Testimony closed.)

CHICAGO, ILL., *November 24, 1899.*

TESTIMONY OF MR. CHARLES W. BAKER,

Secretary of the Live Stock Exchange, Chicago, Ill.

The subcommission on transportation being in session on the afternoon of November 24, 1899, at Chicago, Ill., Representative Lorimer presiding, Mr. Charles W. Baker was duly sworn, and testified as follows:

Q. (By Representative LORIMER.) Please state your name in full?—A. Charles W. Baker.

Q. And your business?—A. Secretary of the Live Stock Exchange at the stock yards in Chicago.

Q. We understand that the people in your line have some complaint to make about the transportation companies through which you do business; will you please state what the conditions are?—A. I can only reiterate what Mr. Mallory (see testimony of preceding witness) has testified to in this regard. Mr. Mallory has covered the ground very thoroughly and carefully, and anything I would say would be cumulative evidence along that line.

Q. (By Professor JOHNSON.) Have you given any thought—you have, I suppose—to the amendment of the interstate-commerce act?—A. Yes; considerable.

Q. Are you in accord with Mr. Mallory's views?—A. Quite so; yes.

Q. Do you or not find that gentlemen in your line of business have that view generally?—A. Yes; I might go still further and say it is perfectly universal, so far as it has come within my knowledge.

Q. Is the Live Stock Association; you are secretary of that?—A. Yes.

Q. National Live Stock Association?—A. Yes; it is allied generally with the National.

Q. Does that association join with the National Millers' Association and others in the effort to secure a strong law?—A. As their representative I participated in the meeting, and will take action with them in the effort to secure remedial legislation such as we agreed upon day before yesterday.

Q. The officers of your association are in accord with the views presented and the act that was discussed there?—A. Yes; in the main I believe it meets the approval of my people.

Q. Do you remember whether that bill calls for a public accounting of the railway accounts?—A. I believe it does; I believe there is such a provision in there.

Q. (By Mr. KENNEDY.) As secretary of your organization, perhaps you are able to tell us something about this enormous shortage in cattle that was spoken of.—A. The figures we have show that some 6 years ago there were 52,000,000 cattle in the country. There are about 10,000,000 less to-day. I think 1 year there was a slight increase. I think there was an increase of about 1,750,000 in one year. But if I remember the figures now, carrying them in my head, it is my impression that the supply is now about 10,000,000 less.

Q. (By Professor JOHNSON.) How long do you think it will take. high prices to restore that deficiency?—A. About 2 years.

Q. The 10,000,000?—A. Yes; it will take longer than that, I am afraid. It would take say 3 or 4 years perhaps, with the continuance of high prices. While you can breed and put an animal on the market in 18 months or 2 years, when you come to increasing your supply, besides supplying the demand that exists all the time, it would take a little longer time to catch up. At the same time the consumption is heavier.

Q. With the high price?—A. Yes; it is constantly increasing; although I think perhaps the supply now keeps pace with the increase in population. We are spreading out all the time.

(Testimony closed.)

CHICAGO, ILL., *November 24, 1899.*

TESTIMONY OF MR. E. P. RIPLEY,

President of the Atchison, Topeka and Santa Fe Railway Company.

The subcommission on transportation being in session in Chicago, Representative Lorimer presiding, at 4.45 p. m., November 24 1899, Mr. E. P. Ripley, president of the Santa Fe Railroad Company, was introduced as a witness, and being duly sworn, testified concerning transportation as follows:

Q. (By Representative LORIMER.) Please state your name.—A. E. P. Ripley.

Q. What is your official connection?—A. President of the Atchison, Topeka and Santa Fe Railroad.

Q. If you will, you might make your statement.—A. I speak somewhat hastily upon some evidence which I saw published in the papers last night, as given here. I gather from the newspapers that it was testified here that the general sentiment of the mercantile community is averse to the pooling of the freight earnings of railway companies. That statement is, of course, a matter of opinion on the part of those who state it. My impression is that the sentiment of nearly all of the mercantile community that has had the largest dealings with the railroad companies is the other way. The statement was made here yesterday that the Chicago merchants and Chicago business men had had more or less experience with the pooling of earnings by railroads, and that it had not been satisfactory. I wish to take issue with the statement. (Reading:)

I have read the reported remarks of a witness who appeared before your board yesterday in opposition to the "pooling" idea.

Passing by a good deal of flamboyant declamation about the danger to the public from railroad combinations, which danger never existed and which never could exist, we may come to what this witness evidently thinks is the strongest case he can think of as showing the iniquity of the pool—namely, the Southwestern Traffic Association, which he says was a "vampire, which for a decade sucked the life-blood of the commerce of the Missouri Valley." How does this witness reconcile this statement with the fact that during this decade (say from 1877 to 1887) the population of Kansas City increased from 58,000 to 156,000 and that of Omaha from 25,000 to 110,000, and that not only these cities but the whole Missouri Valley and the States of Kansas and Nebraska grew and waxed fat amazingly? What evidence has he, save his naked assertion, that this association restricted trade in the slightest degree? It is true that at periodical intervals quarrels arose among the parties to this pool, and that at such times there were periods when that natural competition of which this witness thinks so highly had full sway, with the result every time of unsettling values, disarranging the plans of merchants, and working general destruction, and the reason for these disturbances was simply and solely because the pool was not legalized, because some (not all) of the courts held them to be void and unenforceable by legal process, thus relegating them to the honor of the parties as their sole support, and in the absence of legal construction of these contracts what wonder that differences of opinion and of interest worked occasional disruption? Moreover, it is absolutely untrue that the rates were advanced under this pool. It may be true that advances were at times made on certain commodities, but far more rates were reduced, and the general average for the 10 years will show a steady reduction. It is not claimed that the agreement worked perfectly or that no discriminations existed; but it is a fact that they were far less common and far less demoralizing and disastrous, alike to shipper and railroad, than those that have existed since the passage of the interstate law.

This witness quotes the opinion of various parties in opposition to the pool, but for every such opinion there can be produced 10 in favor of it, not from the ranks of railroad officers, but from merchants and shippers, State and interstate commissioners, students of modern political economy, and in fact almost all those who have dispassionately studied the problems surrounding the transportation business of this country. It is well known that the chairman of the interstate commission favors pooling under proper restrictions, as a majority of the interstate commission does, and always has from its inception. So, also, I believe, does a majority of the State commissions and a majority of the shippers of the country. The statement that the majority of the latter hold contrary opinions is pure assumption.

The statement that rates in this country ever were or ever can be too high per se is absolutely without foundation. The service performed by American railroads is admittedly the cheapest in the world, as well as the best, and no pool, however restrictive, can change the general laws of competition. No greater economic blunder can be committed than the fostering of free and unrestricted competition among carriers by rail. It tends to the aggrandizement of the few and the submerging of the many, and that portion of the interstate law which so unwisely prohibits pooling has done more to concentrate business in few hands and to drive out the small trader than could have been accomplished in a century of the old methods.

One of the ablest of the interstate commissioners has said that the prohibition of pooling defeats the whole purpose of the law; that the law prescribes uniform rates and forbids the only known plan by which rates can be kept uniform.

The fact is that the commercial world does not accept, never had, and probably never will accept the "equal rate" theory. It is just what the railroads want, but what the large shipper does not want. He will theorize that equal rates are best for all, but in his heart and in his practice he believes himself entitled to lower rates than his neighbor of less capital or less enterprise. Believing this, he is actively engaged in finding ways to evade the law, and it would be surprising indeed if he failed to succeed. The law can no more be enforced than the prohibitory laws which have so conspicuously failed. You may close the front door of the saloon, but those who are determined to get in will do so.

But the underlying fallacy of all this talk about trusts and monopolies as applied to railroad pooling is the failure to differentiate between the railroad industry of the country and other purely commercial enterprises. The demand of the railroads that they be permitted to charge reasonable rates (and nothing more has ever been asked) is treated as if it were on a parity with a demand for the legalization of a trust in any article of mechandise, and it is argued that to do this is to establish a dangerous precedent, apparently forgetful of the fact that this country has never assumed to dictate or to regulate the price of any commodity except railroad transportation, as to which it has assumed by both State and national laws to fix prices; and it certainly would appear to a reasonably fair-minded man that when the supreme authority undertakes to limit the revenues of a private corporation it owes that corporation something in the way of protection. As matters now stand, the railroads are limited in charges. forced to compete and forbidden to combine for protection, though all the world may combine against them. It is considered legitimate and praiseworthy for the employees of railroads to combine to force up wages and a crime for the railroads to combine to maintain the rates which the Government holds to be reasonable. Could injustice go further? No such restrictions are put upon any other business in this country, and no such restrictions are imposed upon railroads in any other country.

To ask for permission to pool earnings is a very modest request under the circumstances. The roads might well ask for more—as, for instance, laws prohibiting the building of unnecessary roads and confirming each existing line in the sole occupancy of its territory.

Such laws exist in other countries, and are wholly reasonable and proper if the railroad is to be considered as a public or "quasi-public" institution. In short, the whole attitude of the American people toward the railroad industry is inconsistent and dishonest. They are considered as public institutions to the extent that their users are to limit their rates, but their owners are to pay their bills. They are taxed more heavily than any other interest, and accorded nothing in return, except the so-called "right of eminent domain," which, being interpreted, means that they can force a man to sell his property at two or three times its value, and even this is nothing for which they have to thank the public, since it is a necessary concomitant to the building of railroads, which the public must have.

To conclude: The permission to pool is asked for—not as a favor, but as a right— as being not a cure-all, but as the best known remedy for discrimination as between individuals and localities, which is to-day and always has been the worst and practically the only evil with which the American railroad system can be charged, either as to present or past practice; an evil which can never be removed by laws, however drastic, but which can be largely done away with by removing all incentive to it.

Let the Government do one of three things, namely:

1. Remove all restrictions and turn the railroads loose.
2. Accord them that protection to which they are justly entitled.
3. Buy them.

The railroads are entitled, in all fairness and justice, to ask that one of these three courses be pursued. The present mixture of all the objectionable features of the three is unjust to the last degree.

My position is, if you will excuse me for advancing it—but I believe it is a part of your unfortunate positions that you are obliged to listen to everybody's opinions—a railroad is either a private corporation or it is a public corporation. If it is a private corporation solely, there is no warrant for any interference by the Government with its business; if it is a public corporation, or as some of the courts have said, a quasi public institution, it is certainly entitled to some protection at the hands of the Government. If the Government has a right to regulate, that certainly carries with it a duty to protect. The attitude of the American people toward the railroads, now, is not only grossly unfair, but absolutely dishonest. They have the restrictions without any of the protection.

In my reading of your doings, as reported in the papers, I have seen nothing except merely specific grievances here and there—instances where people thought they were aggrieved by some particular local practice. I have seen no general complaints except the question of discriminations, which everybody, all right-minded people unite to condemn, none more so than the railroads themselves. That is simply, as I see it, an almost necessary evil, in the position in which the railroads are placed.

Q. (By Mr. C. J. HARRIS.) If pools were to be formed, would they be formed for 5-year terms; as long as that?—A. That depends upon the agreement of the parties; they ought to be. The longer they are the more stable they are likely to be. Any agreement made for a year has a certain element of temporariness in it which unsettles. It ought to be made for a reasonable term, as long as possible.

Q. Would there be any objection to a revision on the part of the Interstate Commerce Commission of the rates charged by the pool?—A. Not by me. There is a difference of opinion among the railroads as to that; some of them might object. Personally I do not object. In my own judgment, there is no possible danger to the community from any extortionate rate, because there is no such thing in this country; and it is impossible. Yet I realize the public would be much better satisfied if there was some sort of buffer between them and the railroads, somebody whose mission it should be to decide disputed questions.

Q. Suppose one railroad out of four or five competing lines refused to pool, would the fact that they are obliged now to publish their rates, and if discrimination from these rates were punished by fining, and that law fully administered—would that enable a pool to exist among the four that agreed to it, even if one remained out?—A. I think it would have a very steadying effect myself. The whole proposition to establish fines instead of imprisonment would have a more deterring effect than the present arrangement does. Of course it is difficult to make an agreement where five parties are interested, without taking in the five; but a provision for the fining of the corporation for the violation of the law would make a great many more informers than under the present conditions. We live together now. We live on the same earth with all our competitors. We have to meet them from time to time, and very few men under these conditions would care to inform the authorities of anything that they might know would criminate these individuals.

Q. You think that part of the law is a failure as it now exists?—A. Absolutely. There never has been a conviction under it; or if there has been a conviction, it has been nominal.

Q. From what I could gather from your conclusion, you believe there should be a law, in the first place, to keep the people off the railroads and then one to keep the railroads off the people?—A. I think there should be some mutuality about it. You have plenty of laws to keep the railroads off the people, but you have not to keep the people off the railroads.

Q. You have seemingly a bad opinion of the people regarding the railroads. Is not that confined to a small class of people, that complain of certain injustices that certain railroads perpetrate on the people, and which rather reflect on all railroads?—A. Not at all. I am not complaining of those who complain. I am complaining of the attitude of the people at large as expressed by their laws and actions toward the railroads. I realize the railroad question in this country is not very well settled yet. So far as it is settled, as I said several times, I consider it exceedingly unjust to the railroads so far as it has taken shape.

Q. You admit that it is a great deal in railroading like it is in any other business, that a bad man in a profession rather casts a reflection on the whole profession?—A. Yes.

Q. Now, if there were a just law (and I think that is all the public demands at this time) requiring that railroads treat every community and every individual and every industry under the same conditions in the same manner, would that practically solve the railroad question?—A. If a law of that kind could be administered and properly enforced, it is all anybody wants; that is all the railroads want.

Q. We have so many instances where some railroad will favor one individual and charge a higher rate to others, that a great many suspect that is being done when it is not, probably. That has created this bad feeling.—A. That has been much more the practice, much more rife, since the attempt was made to prevent it by law than it ever was before, and naturally so.

Q. Do you not believe that if we had a law that would fix a reasonable rate—and I do not think anybody who has anything to do with the Government wants anything else than that—and see that it was enforced rigidly by the railroads—do you not think that would be better for the railroads as well as the people?—A. It certainly would be better for the railroads if all rates were enforced as published; that is what we want. It is not possible for any man, or any body of men, to fix absolutely certain rates which shall be charged under all circumstances and conditions. Conditions vary so rapidly, it is impossible, almost, to do that; and there must be a certain amount of elasticity in that; but the rates once established and once published should be changed only publicly. There is no question about that, and that portion of the law—so far as the established rates are concerned—that portion of the law is being lived up to absolutely now. The trouble, under the present conditions, is that the larger shippers, men controlling the large tonnage, believe, as they all do believe, regardless of the law or any general sentiment on the subject, that their large business entitles them to concessions. They believe that to a man; they do not admit it openly, perhaps, but that is their idea, and that is what they try to enforce; and there are comparatively few of the railroads strong enough to resist the pressure that these people bring to bear; and in my judgment it is impossible, or practically impossible, to prevent concessions being made in some way or other. There are so many ways in which it may be done—I do not like to say railroad men are expert as law breakers—but there are so many ways concessions may be made without violating the letter of the law that I regard it as impossible to arrive at a prohibition of discrimination by statute.

Q. If the spirit of the law is evaded, the law itself is transgressed?—A. Granted; but it is very difficult to apply any remedy unless the letter of the law is broken.

Q. I understand just the contrary. If the spirit of the law is evaded, there is a breach of the law. For instance, a drawback of freight indirectly to accomplish the same thing, would have as much turpitude in it as if it had been directly done?—A. But very difficult to prove, however; it would be very difficult to obtain conviction.

Q. You think the condition is practically remediless, then?—A. I think it will always be. Until it becomes to the interest of the carriers to maintain absolutely equal rates, which it is not now, concessions will continue to be made.

Q. These concessions are generally made to the men most able to pay the regular rate?—A. Yes. The tendency is, among the railroads, that the man that has the most transportation to buy is very likely to buy it the cheapest.

Q. (By Professor JOHNSON.) Do you think the railroads could withstand the pressure of the big shippers, if they were allowed to pool?—A. Under those conditions there would be no incentive for them to make any concessions to anybody.

Q. (By Representative BELL.) Do you understand, in pooling, each man should have a proportion of the business done?—A. Precisely. That is what a pool means.

Q. I thought you pooled generally on the basis of the business during the year before?—A. No; that would be a very foolish proceeding. That would be an incentive for everybody to do what he is doing now.

Q. That is the present practice?—A. There is no present practice, because there are no pools. It never was the practice when we had pools. Once in a while, some of the railroad people thought that they could, by illegitimate methods, increase their tonnage one year as a basis for demanding a larger proportion the next, but they were very seldom realized.

Q. (By Professor JOHNSON.) How would the proportion be arrived at?—A. By arbitration, as a rule; sometimes agreed to, but usually an agreement was made by which it was left to an arbitrator in case of failure to agree.

Q. (By Mr. C. J. HARRIS.) The directness of line and superior accommodations of a road—would not that lead to a larger percentage than the roundabout road?—A. Yes.

Q. No matter how much the roundabout road might get by illegitimate methods?—A. Nobody would be willing to recognize as the basis of percentage, the business done by illegitimate methods; never did.

Q. (By Representative BELL.) Under the arrangement between the Midland and the Denver and Rio Grande, have not all their traffic arrangements from Grand Junction east been made each year on the business done the year before?—A. I do not know. That is a local matter with which I am not conversant at all. I do not think, however, that is the case. In the first place, I do not think they have any pool there or any agreement.

Q. Well, they have had.—A. Perhaps, in years past.

Q. They have a joint agent?—A. They have a joint agent at Grand Junction, of course, because they have the joint use of property between Grand Junction and Glenwood. They have a joint track, but I am sure there is no agreement for any division of business there.

Q. I have always heard the railroad men there, being local men, say that one reason the competition was so sharp was that the business they did this year was the basis on which they did business the succeeding year?—A. I do not think that is true. I am not speaking of my own knowledge on that subject; I have troubles of my own, and am not altogether conversant with the business of these people out there. They occupy a stretch of joint track between Grand Junction and Glenwood—90 miles of joint track—and the expenses of that track are paid in proportion to the use of it; the expense of maintenance is in proportion to the wheelage that each company sends over it; so that every wheel each sends over there adds to his proportion of the expense. I should say, at first blush, that is the plan, but of course I do not know.

Q. (By Mr. KENNEDY.) Does your idea of legal pooling contemplate the forcing of all lines in a competitive country to go into a pool?—A. Oh, no; I would not object to that, but I do not think that is necessary. I think there are some objections to it, although I would not personally object.

Q. Then if one road remains out and indulges in pirating methods to get traffic, does not that kill your pool?—A. No; I think not. That would simply mean the others would, instead of fighting it singly fight it jointly, and fight it with legal methods. which they would be prepared to do under these circumstances. The trouble is now, when you have one party who thinks he can flock by himself, the law forbids the rest of us from combining against him. Combined, we can regulate that gentleman pretty thoroughly—singly, we are helpless.

Q. (By Professor JOHNSON.) Would you object to an examination of your accounts by a public accountant?—A. Well, that depends on what use was to be made of it afterwards. There are certain portions of the accounts of railroads that belong to the stockholders and should not be public property.

Q. The same system that applies to banking interests.—A. I do not see any objection to that.

Q. (By Mr. C. J. HARRIS.) What would be your judgment as to the possibility of the Interstate Commerce Commission making the rates for railroads; would it be possible?—A. No; because it is too much of a job, and it would be impossible for them to come in close enough contact with the wants of the mercantile community. One of the witnesses said here a few days ago that every railroad company must have a bargain counter. I disagree with that witness in almost every particular, but there is a modicum of truth in that statement that every railroad company must have a bargain counter. I do not mean he must sell transportation for less than the published rates, but he must modify his rates from time to time, and sometimes on very short order. The business is a sensitive one, and the same reasons exist for quick action in the changing of rates that exist in the selling of merchandise. There is no reason why it should not be done honestly and fairly, and everybody be advised, but it is not possible to intrust that sort of thing to a body thousands of miles away.

Q. You would have no objection to that board passing on the rate after it is fixed?—A. They have that power now, practically.

Q. In theory, would you clothe them with the power to make that effective?—A. I should be willing to that rather than the conditions we have now. It is an enormous power to intrust to any body of men, the power to fix the tremendous revenue that is involved in that thing, and yet I hardly think they would make any worse mess of it than is being made under the present conditions. That would depend very much on the personnel of the commission. I can see that a power of that kind might be subject to very great abuse. It is a larger power than is wielded by the President of the United States, or anybody in the United States.

Q. You would still have the protection of the courts?—A. Yes.

Q. And their tendency is to be conservative in all matters of that kind. The great problem you have to meet now is that of adjusting rates properly between different localities, is it not?—A. That is one of the great problems, and one that is never settled satisfactorily; that is to say, somebody is always disgruntled over it. With the best of intentions on the part of railroads, it almost always ends in a compromise, not satisfactory to anybody, and very unsatisfactory to a great many. Each railroad is interested in a particular port or particular locality, and each railroad is fighting for the supremacy of that particular port or district, and the result must be ultimately a compromise. Everything we have to-day is a compromise between opposing ideas. The endeavor has been to do the fair thing. In fact, there have been so many opposing interests that it has been impossible to do anything very unfair, but it is not an exact science.

Q. It must be a matter of compromise?—A. Of compromise and judgment.

Q. That being the case, would not a body of intelligent men, sitting as the representatives of all interests—carriers and public alike—would not such a body of men be able to assist the carriers in this judgment between conflicting interests?—A. I think so. There have been many cases where I would like to place the entire responsibility on an outside body, and have them say what is to be done; where two or three communities were warring with each other about the adjustment of rates, and the railways were between the upper and nether millstones, and could not please everybody—there have been cases where I would like to have thrown that responsibility on an outside tribunal.

Q. Then you say if the law gave the carriers power to deal with personal discriminations, and clothed the public with power to adjust, so far as may be, the conflicts between localities, the transportation problem would be largely solved?—A. It would be simplified. I do not know that it can ever be solved.

Q. (By Representative BELL.) Is it not largely settled in the Eastern States?—A. No; we can hardly say that. It is settled in certain portions of the East by the processes of amalgamation that have been going on. The lines in the East are so largely consolidated into a few hands that it is to a considerable extent settled in that way, and that is particularly the case in New England. There are practically only 2 railroad corporations in New England to-day, and yet there is less complaint there than in any part of the United States.

Q. Is it not true that as the country settles, and as the railroad business becomes settled, that it kind of settles itself in time?—A. It is true that the older a community becomes the more settled things become. It is also true that the older a community becomes the more likely they are themselves to become interested in railroad properties. I think that accounts for most of the tranquillity we find in the Eastern States—the fact that the people along the lines are interested. If the people along our lines owned a large proportion of our stock, I am satisfied we would have much less trouble than we now have. I wish they did.

Q. Now, with reference to the Government buying the roads; that is the third way. Do you think it would be possible for the Government to run the railroads in this country?—A. It would be possible. As a railroad man, I should have no objection to the Government owning the railroads. As a citizen, I should feel very unhappy about it.

Q. What do you think would be the cost of running them as compared with now?—A. I think it would cost a great deal more; no one can make an estimate of how much. There would be a certain amount of waste done away with. There is a certain amount of waste incident to all competition that would stop the moment the Government took possession, because there would be no competition. That, in the aggregate, would result in quite a large saving. But governmental methods, as we know them, and as applied to governmental affairs now, would result in a very large deficit in the operation of railroads, unquestionably. The influence of politics and politicians on the railroad business would be, I think, exceedingly disastrous, and any elective officers who were in a position to influence the policy of the railroads, and who would also be desirous of pleasing their constituents, would find the two things irreconcilable. Everybody would want a branch railroad and everybody would want as many trains as possible on it, whether they paid or not, and the price of the election of a Congressman or Senator would be his ability to get things out of the Government in the way of transportation. I think the result would be disastrous.

(Testimony closed.)

WASHINGTON, D. C., *December 6, 1899.*

TESTIMONY OF PROF. EDWIN R. A. SELIGMAN,

Professor of Political Economy and Finance in Columbia University, New York City.

The commission met at 10.55 a. m., Vice-Chairman Phillips presiding. At that time Prof. Edwin R. A. Seligman, of New York City, professor of political economy and finance in Columbia University, was introduced as a witness, and being duly sworn, testified as follows, the topical plan of inquiry on transportation being followed:

Q. (By Professor JOHNSON.) Will you give your name and post-office address?—A. My name is Edwin R. A. Seligman; my post-office address is Columbia University, New York City.

Q. In giving your testimony this morning, I think it would be best for you to present what you have to say, in a general way at least, without interruption, and then we will question you after you have presented what you have to say.—A. Mr. Chairman and Gentlemen, I understand that the special topic, or the first of the special topics on which I was expected to say something was primarily the taxation problem—the taxation of corporations and especially of transportion companies. With your leave, then, I shall say a few words about the general problem of the taxation of transportation companies, with special reference to Federal legislation and its connection with State legislation.

There are several points of view from which the problem may be approached. There is, in the first place, the general question of revenue—what amount of revenue can we or ought we to get from transportation and other corporations; and secondly, there is the point of view as to justice between the various individuals who are interested in the corporations—justice with reference to the burdens imposed upon them; and these, you see, are two different problems. Then there is another class of problems, namely, What ought to be the Federal system of taxation, if any; and what ought to be the State system; and how ought they to be dovetailed into each other?

Before going into the matter more in detail, it is perhaps unnecessary to advert to the immense importance of corporate taxation in modern times. As we all know, the wealth of the nineteenth century consists, far more largely than in past times, of what is known as personalty. The influence of land is comparatively less than in former times. Of this personalty, this personal property, by far the largest part in modern industrial conditions consists of corporate securities or investments in corporate securities, stocks and bonds, whether of transportation companies or others. And it is for this reason that the whole problem of corporate taxation, or the taxation of corporations, assumes so vast a significance as compared with former times, even with the beginning of the century, and certainly with former centuries. The problem of just taxation, therefore, is very largely, in modern America and to a less extent in almost every modern community, the problem of corporation taxation.

When we look at the question from the point of view of the Federal Government there are one or two principles that I think ought to be laid down at the very beginning, and that is, that there ought to be, as far as possible, a divorce, so far as the sources of revenue are concerned, between the Federal and the State governments. If there is any one principle which has been firmly implanted in our modern fiscal system it is that the National Government should not vie with, should not compete with, the Commonwealth governments in seeking sources of taxation; and for that reason, of course, the Federal Government has very largely depended upon the so-called indirect taxes, customs duties and internal revenue, and only in very exceptional cases has resorted to a system of taxes which—whether you would call them direct or indirect is unimportant here—have been assessed upon those subjects of taxation commonly reached by the State. It is only under the stress of war, the war of 1812 and the civil war, that there has been any conflict as regards that point.

To this general principle there is only one exception to be made. I simply mention that in passing, because it does not refer specially to this topic. That is, that under the present revenue system of the Federal Government there is one institution, one scheme, one part of the law, which seems to me very much to be deprecated, namely, the tax on inheritances, by whatever name it is called, because there the Government is trenching at once upon a form of taxation which has been developed within recent years by the States, and which, if allowed to develop, will do much to solve the whole problem of State taxation. All students, I think, of the problem, and for that matter most of the statesmen within the Commonwealths themselves where any steps have been taken toward the reform of taxation, are united in deprecating any entrance of the Federal Government upon this field of taxation, the taxation of inheritances.

Now, that being the general principle, I think it follows also that from the point of view of pure revenue the Federal Government ought not directly to tax transportation corporations. Why does that follow? Because if you look carefully at the progress in the reform of State taxation you will find that the one goal, the first step to be accomplished in the States, is the divorce between State revenues and the local revenues, and we find in all our leading Commonwealths, like New York, Pennsylvania, Massachusetts, etc., where you have the fullest and most developed industrial conditions, a well-marked tendency to derive State revenues in ever-increasing proportions from inheritances and corporations, with possibly a few other additions, gradually relegating the general property tax as such to the local divisions.

Into this general reform the Federal Government has brought a jarring and discordant element, because not only does it now levy a separate tax upon inheritances, which diminishes pro tanto the chances of the States to develop that system, but also, if the Federal Government were to tax interstate commerce through transportation companies for the purpose of independent revenue, it would most seriously and still further hamper the efforts of the separate Commonwealths to secure just taxation.

I therefore lay down, as a general principle, that there ought to be no Federal tax on transportation companies for purposes of pure revenue.

That, however, does not by any means settle the problem as to whether there ought or ought not to be a Federal tax on transportation companies, possibly for other reasons, and that brings me therefore now to the second part of the inquiry. What is the tendency in the several States with reference to the taxation of transportation and other corporations, and how can the evils which at present exist, and which seem almost insurmountable, be averted?

The chief difficulty in our Commonwealth taxation of corporations arises out of the problems of what is called double taxation. They arise, in other words, from the legal fact or fiction, whichever you may call it, that there is for all purposes and to all intents absolute State sovereignty in each Commonwealth. In the legal system, for purposes of taxation at all events, it is a fact, not a fiction, that each Commonwealth has sovereign powers. Now, what are the difficulties that arise from that legal fact, when confronted by the economic fact that economic interests are not confined to any one Commonwealth, but that the economic interests of the community are scattered throughout the country and are intertwined with all the Commonwealths, that, for instance, with the growth of industry we have corporations which may be situated legally in one State, which may have their actual property in another State, and which yet may be owned, so far as stockholders and bondholders are concerned, in a third State? Here for example, a North Dakota railway, or a railway which runs through North Dakota, whose chief officers and legal representatives may possibly be in Illinois, and whose bonds and stocks are owned in New York, which is not at all a preposterous supposition. In other words, we have, under the stress of economic development of the nineteenth century, an incongruity between economic conditions and legal facts; legally we still have the system of taxation which grew up when each community was isolated from its fellow community, and this legal situation is no longer in conformity with economic facts.

Now, what are the difficulties that arise from this curious situation? I may add, of course, that this condition of affairs is not in the least peculiar to the United States, but is found in all modern federal governments. It is found in Germany; it is found in Switzerland; it is found or will be found certainly in Australia under the new form of government; with the exception that nowhere perhaps is the legal idea of State sovereignty so strong as it is in this country. For instance, in Canada the problem does not exist at all in that way, because the provinces are not legally sovereign.

Now, the difficulty, so far as taxation is concerned, is that wherever the States attempt to tax transportation companies upon receipts—gross receipts, net receipts, or anything else in accordance with receipts—you at once run up against the rock of interstate commerce. It has been decided in a number of cases in our various States which attempt to get a State revenue from the gross receipts of corporations that, so far as domestic corporations are concerned, corporations chartered within the State, the State is at perfect liberty to levy a franchise or excise tax, however it may be called, upon the total receipts of the corporation; that is, provided the franchise is measured by the gross receipts, then it is valid. No State is at liberty to levy a tax upon gross receipts so far as those receipts are derived partly from interstate commerce. But through the fiction of the law, of course, where you call it a franchise tax or excise tax, and measure the franchise by the gross receipts, then the tax is upheld. This applies, however, only to domestic corporations. Under economic conditions to-day a large part of all corporations doing business in any State are foreign corporations; they are corporations chartered in some other State, perhaps in New Jersey or West Virginia. Now, under these conditions the courts have repeatedly held, and the Supreme Court of the United States has laid down as the law of the land, that you can not levy a franchise tax upon foreign corporations, because, of course, the State does not give a franchise except to its own corporations; a State does not give a franchise to foreign corporations; and therefore a tax of this kind levied upon foreign corporations is a tax not upon franchise but upon business, and being a tax upon business it can not be levied upon the business derived in whole or in part from interstate commerce. Therefore we have this situation in this country to-day, in all these States, more especially the more advanced and developed industrial States, and the problem will soon be the same in all the other States of the Union. It is only a question of a few decades when the industrial system will spread throughout the whole country. We have therefore this situation—that although the revenue is sought to be obtained from corporations, the great mass of corporate business can not be reached by such a tax on receipts. Some States, therefore, in order to avoid that difficulty, attempt to solve the problem by taxing corporations not on receipts but upon the valuation, or upon the capital stock, and in some cases also the bonded indebtedness. A great many of our States tax the capital stock of corporations; some, like Pennsylvania, add to the tax on capital stock a tax on bonded indebtedness.

What are the results of this conflict between legal and economic conditions in this class of cases? So far as capital stock and bonded indebtedness is concerned, it is clear at once that a difficulty arises from the fact that the capital stock may be owned or the bonds may be owned by people who are not residents of the State. The capital stock of the Pennsylvania Railway may be owned entirely or in very large part in New York or in Chicago, or *vice versa*.

What is the legal situation as regards the taxation of corporations under this, the most general form of taxation of corporations? So far as the taxation of capital stock is concerned, the courts of this country have finally reached the conclusion that it makes no difference where the stockholders live, because the tax is assessed, not upon the stockholders, but upon the capital stock. The situation would seem to be free from difficulty there, but it is not, because as soon you levy a tax on capital stock the question arises. Upon what part of the capital stock are you going to levy the tax? Here is the Western Union Telegraph Company, which ramifies through, perhaps, every State of this Union. If you levied a tax upon the entire capital stock of the Western Union corporation the Western Union Telegraph Company would be taxed fifty times; instead of being taxed once it would be taxed by each one of the fifty States upon the whole of its capital stock, which, of course, would result in the company's going out of existence. Therefore, it is easily seen that where you have a tax on capital stock, in order to realize justice you must tax only a part of the capital stock. The question then arises: what is the economically defensible part of the capital stock that is taxable in each State?

I do not wish to answer that question now, but simply to raise it and point out the difficulty and to state the problem, showing that even though you tax the capital stock you have not got over the difficulties of double taxation and the question of the diversity between economic conditions and legal facts.

What, however, is the situation with reference to the bonded indebtedness of railways? The most advanced States, as all scientists, have come to the conclusion that to tax corporations simply upon capital stock is manifestly unfair. You may have two corporations, each with $100,000 working capital; one corporation may have no bonded indebtedness at all, and the other corporation may have bonds outstanding of $200,000, double the amount of the capital stock, and the second corporation may have raised its entire working capital, in the economic sense, by selling its bonds and giving away its stock as a bonus. If, therefore, you tax only the capital stock, you would be taxing the first corporation three times as much as the second corporation; because, in the second case, where you have a total amount of $300,000—$200,000 bonds and $100,000 stock—you are taxing the corporation only upon one-third of its actual capital, while in the case of the first corporation you are taxing it upon 100 per cent. And therefore it is that all statesmen who have looked into the question, and a good many of our States that attempt to realize justice in taxation, now say that corporations must be taxed upon stocks and bonds or upon a valuation equivalent to stock plus bonds.

Now, what is the legal difficulty there? The court of the United States, in the Foreign-held Bond cases, has decided that a tax upon the bonds of a foreign corporation is a tax upon the bondholders; and consequently, since a State has sovereignty only within its own borders, no State can reach the bonds of a corporation which are held outside of that State. There at once you see the deathblow given by a legal decision which, in my humble opinion, is totally incorrect from the economic point of view, though entirely defensible from the constitutional point of view. You have a deathblow given to this whole system of taxation, because if you can tax railway bonds only so far as they are owned within the State, it will not be very long before you will have no bonds at all to tax within that State, and, as a matter of fact, you would have the same difficulties you had in the other case.

I might go on and describe other forms—although these that I have mentioned are the most important—other forms of corporate taxation in this country, to show you that in each case we run up against these legal and constitutional conditions which are not in harmony with our economic conditions. It may be laid down, of course, as a general rule that in the long run law, crystallized justice, is nothing but the outcome of social conditions. The law is simply the legal statement of the economic and social conditions of a country; and the legal system always follows the economic conditions. The economic conditions come first, and the legal conditions are gradually changed so as to be in conformity with the economic conditions.

Now, all that I have tried to point out is that we have certain economic conditions which are out of joint with our legal conditions, and that before very long we are bound to change our law to conform to our economic conditions; because, of course, we can not change economic conditions to conform to law.

The question therefore arises, in view of the chaos in our State and local systems of taxation, to which are largely due these problems of double taxation: what is the remedy? There are only two general lines on which an advance can be made. The one is to attempt to secure a uniformity of State action, if possible, through Federal pressure. I consider that one of the chief functions of this commission, not alone with reference to the taxation problem, but also with almost every other one of the problems with which you have to deal. That is to say, I consider that a great many of our existing evils in this country arise from the diversity, complexity, and opposition between our State laws, and that as long as we have our present political system, which very wisely prevents the absolute centralization of all economic powers in the Federal Government, we must try to get at the problem through a gradual unification or uniformity of State laws by pressure from above. That, applied to the problem in hand, means an attempt to do with the taxation problem what we are beginning to do with the railway problem, what we are beginning to do with the labor problem, having annual conventions of our labor commissions, our railway commissions, etc. There ought to be annual conventions of State tax commissions, where these problems might be discussed, not from the narrow point of view of State sovereignty, but from the real economic point of view of the wider economic interests of the country; and those meetings ought to be held under Federal auspices, safeguarding, of course, the interests of the Commonwealths and preventing any friction or jealousy. In that way a great deal of good could be accomplished.

If, however, that is an ideal still too remote for any practical purposes, there is one other way in which a reform of taxation in this country can be accomplished through the intervention of Federal authority. I stated some time ago that I considered it highly inadvisable for a Federal Government to levy a Federal tax on transportation or other companies for purposes of revenue. It is a question, however, whether we ought not—whether we may or not constitutionally—whether we ought not to follow the same principle that some of our State governments follow when dealing with the complications between State revenue and local revenue. In order to get around the difficulties of double taxation between counties, municipalities, etc., they levy a State tax on corporations or other subjects, and then turn back the revenue under a well-considered general system to the localities, thus avoiding the difficulties and the friction of which I speak. The question therefore arises: can the Federal Government exercise its powers of taxation by levying the tax at all events upon corporations engaged in interstate commerce, and then turn the proceeds over, according to well-considered and carefully devised rules, to the various Commonwealths, in order to help along the various Commonwealths in their struggle to adjust and reform State taxation itself.

This is the system which is pursued by other national governments. England, for instance, pursues the system in various kinds of taxes. In inheritance taxes they collect that revenue under well-settled rules and then turn over a part of the revenue to localities. So other European Governments do the same thing; and we in our own country have the precedent, of course, of the Government collecting money and then turning it over to the States—a distribution of the surplus revenue, which, of course, was not very happy as a political measure, because it was not framed on any economic line at all, but it seems that the Government has the constitutional power of getting revenue and then distributing it as it chooses.

That, therefore, would be the line of thought on which I think a consideration of the reform of taxation ought to proceed in this country. To recapitulate what has been said, to sum it up so as to state it clearly, I will just say this, that our whole system of State and local taxation is a chaos, almost worse than a chaos, in the most advanced industrial States. It is not so, of course, in the agricultural States or in the Southern States, or even perhaps in part of the West, where the old general property tax is still suitable, because the economic conditions are not the modern conditions, but the economic conditions which were true of the North and East years and years ago; but wherever we have modern industrial conditions the old general property tax is no longer defensible. We are trying to get rid of it and our advanced States are getting rid of it. There is even now a great commission sitting in New York City which—I may be permitted to say without divulging any secrets—will bring in a bill before long to reform the whole system of taxation in New York State, and it is proceeding along these general lines, although I am not at liberty to state exactly what the recommendations will be.

Now, what is true of New York will be true of all of the other States in the Union soon. Everyone agrees that in order to bring about this reform we must have a divorce of State and local revenue. Everybody agrees that if you are going to have a separate State revenue you must have it primarily from inheritances and corporations. Everybody agrees that if you have it from corporations you can not have a just system under the present conflict between legal facts and economic conditions. Ergo, I say, the conclusion is that we must so change the legal facts as to bring them into harmony with economic conditions. That can be done finally in only one of two ways, either by voluntary cooperation on the part of our State authorities, voluntary and possibly with pressure from above; or, secondly, through a certain separate or independent intervention by the Federal Government itself. Therefore, it seems to me that this problem, which at first blush seems to affect possibly only the Federal Government, is of very much wider importance because it not only affects the whole question of State and local taxation, and not only affects the question of just taxation of corporations themselves, but necessarily affects the whole question of taxation apart from that of corporations, because as soon as you solve the problem of taxation of corporations properly you are in a position where you can attack the other and perhaps more complicated problems of taxation of property.

Q. (By Professor JOHNSON.) In order to make your admirable presentation of the principles of the subject a little more concrete and to develop more details, I would like to ask you a few questions. First, I understand correctly, do I, that your objection to the taxation of inheritances is entirely from the standpoint of their taxation by the Federal Government?—A. Entirely.

Q. That is, you consider them a proper tax for the State authorities?—A. I do; and not alone proper, but a highly desirable taxation.

Q. In the taxation of gross receipts, how do the States of Illinois and Wisconsin arrive at the basis for their taxation?—A. Well, that differs, of course, with each State. In Wisconsin, if I am not mistaken, they divide the railways up according to the gross receipts per mile, and where the gross receipts are a certain number of thousand dollars per mile they tax them at a certain rate, and then it differs, high or low.

Q. Most of the railroads of Wisconsin are interstate in character. How do they determine what is subject to State taxation and what is not?—A. I am not quite sure in Wisconsin. It is some little time since I have had my attention called to that particular phase of it in Wisconsin, but my impression is that the taxes there are comparatively light, and that the interstate railways have acquiesced in the taxes imposed upon them without raising much objection. When I was speaking of that problem it was more especially cases like, for instance, Maine that I had in mind, and other States, where a large part of the revenue was sought to be obtained from this source, and where the corporations are fighting the law and have succeeded in overturning the law.

Q. If a State were to levy a tax of 4 per cent on the gross receipts of a corporation as a license tax, could that be done?—A. That brings out a point that I mentioned—that the courts of this country have tended toward a line of decisions distinguishing between domestic and foreign corporations. So far as domestic corporations are concerned, they are willing to accept a franchise tax, as it is called in some States, a license tax in other States, measured by receipts; but so far as foreign corporations are concerned, they are not willing to permit any infringement upon the law prohibiting the taxation of interstate commerce. And therefore where, as in most cases, the railways are largely foreign corporations, of course it would mean that there could be no adequate revenue from such taxes even under a license tax.

Q. In the valuation of stocks and bonds owned by a corporation, do not the States take such a proportion of the total value of the capitalization of a corporation as the mileage within the State is of the total mileage of the corporation, in some cases?—A. In some cases there has been a tendency in the last few years, notably, for instance, in taxing the express and telegraph companies in Ohio and

Illinois and a few other cases, to take only that proportion of the valuation which is employed within the State. In the case of transportation companies they measure it by mileage; but that would not apply, where the tax is imposed not upon a valuation equivalent to stocks and bonds, as in Indiana, but where the tax is imposed ipso facto upon the stock and bonds themselves, as, for instance, in New York State as well as in Pennsylvania—the tax there is imposed upon the capital stock. Now, it is true that so far as the capital stock is concerned, they levy only upon that part of it which is employed within the State; but so far as the bonds are concerned, it is complicated by this question of extra-State ownership of the bonds. That is the difficulty.

Q. If the States are to tax on valuation, that seems the only practicable way, does it not?—A. I think so.

Q. By taxing according to mileage proportionately?—A. Decidedly.

Q. (By Mr. Farquhar.) Is it possible to reach a uniformity in that class of taxation as between the States?—A. If you should tax simply railway companies within each State and then each State were to agree—which they do not by any means do at the present time—if each State were to agree to tax only that part, whether of the gross receipts or of the capital stock or anything else that you may tax, which is in proportion to the mileage within the State, then you would have to that extent uniformity between the States. But the trouble is that some States do tax that part and other States tax the whole of the capital stock.

Q. In case of States which impose an excise tax or franchise tax or the prorating by mileage, how many States tax the railroads, even back to the telegraph poles and the tools in the shops and so on? And in one or two of the States have they not taxation of township and county and State? How is it possible, even theoretically, to discover a practical way of spreading that taxation under the proposition you make?—A. I am glad you mentioned that fact, because when I was speaking of just taxation there I had reference only to the States as compared with each other. When now you come to taxation within the State I think that mileage is very far from being a just system, because, as has just been pointed out, in one city or one county you may have an immense terminal worth millions of dollars, and in another county you may have nothing but the track without any side tracks at all. Mind you, mileage does not mean trackage. Even if you were to have trackage that would be a different system from mileage, because in one county you might have four tracks, and after you have passed one station the next section might have only one, and after you have it measured up the four tracks would only amount to as much as one; and then you would have only the one line with the terminals and with the important bridges and a good many other things that might be mentioned. So that even from the point of view of State taxation, I do not think that mileage is a theoretically correct system at all.

Q. (By Professor Johnson.) Do you think, as an abstract proposition, that the taxation of receipts is a just tax?—A. From the abstract point of view, entirely irrespective of the practicability of the system, there is no doubt in my mind, that the taxation of receipts—meaning by that, however, net receipts and not gross receipts—is a more equitable system of taxation than any other, and we find that pretty much everywhere else in the world.

Q. Then if the Federal Government were to undertake taxation of interstate transportation companies, you would advise them to tax the net receipts?—A. I do not say that exactly, because the facts of the existing economic life may often invalidate an abstract principle. It may be wise abstractly to do so, and yet not wise in face of the existing relation between the individual and the government in this country, in face of the fact that our commonwealth differs from those abroad very largely in this respect, that we look upon our Government as our servant, and not as our master as they do in Germany. For instance, it is unfortunately true that one of the results following from that good principle, is that if we were to attempt to levy a tax purely upon net receipts, that probably would not result in having a just system, unless it had very careful safeguards. In other words, the great corporations could easily succeed in so scaling down the nominal net receipts that they would not have any receipts to tax. I think that if you have a tax on net receipts it must be very carefully defined; you must define net receipts as they never have been defined before, not even by the Interstate Commerce Commission, so as to obviate the possibility of diminishing the net receipts. It is largely for that reason that most of our States where they levy a tax on receipts, levy the tax on gross receipts rather than on net receipts; a system which is theoretically far less good, but which has many practical advantages.

Q. Would it be possible by careful statutory definition of net receipts, by prescription of uniformity of accounts, and by Government inspection of railway accounts, to arrive at a public knowledge of the net receipts of railway corporations?—A. I think so. I think that the main difficulty with the question of net-receipts taxation would arise not so much with transporation corporations, but with manufacturing corporations. Where you have the quasi-public corporations, the system as you outline it would very largely overcome the objections, which I have mentioned.

Q. In that connection would you advocate the prescription of uniformity of accounts on the part of the Federal Government and the public inspection of accounts of transportation corporations?—A. It seems to me that there really can be no question, not only of the advisability, but of the imperative necessity of such a system as that, because it would not only be useful for purposes of taxation, but it would be almost indispensable in a great many other questions of the relations between railways and the Government.

Q. How do you look upon taxation as one of the effective means for the regulation of transportation and industrial corporations?—A. I think that taxation has always been utilized, and will always be utilized for two purposes. Of course, I know that the extremists on both sides would take exception to that statement. My statement is that taxation is not only to be utilized for fiscal purposes, but may also be utilized for social purposes; such social purposes as are approved by the majority. In regard to that point there are really two different schools of thought throughout the world. The one is the extreme individualist, of whom we still have quite a number in this country, represented possibly most effectively by Hon. David A. Wells, who died a short time ago. He claims that taxation can be utilized only for fiscal purposes, and as soon as you utilize it for social purposes, it is not taxation, but confiscation—one of his deductions, of course, being that the protective tariff was confiscation. That was the point of view of Mr. Calhoun and others.

On the other hand, we have the socialists, the extreme socialists, who are represented in academic circles in this country and abroad by eminent men, who maintain that the difference between the nineteenth century and former centuries is that in former centuries taxes were used only for fiscal purposes; that to-day the great problem is the social problem, the economic problem, and that the taxes must be used for social purposes, and that a tax is not a tax unless it has a social object. You then have these two extremes. On the one hand you have a man who says that if a tax is used for anything but fiscal purposes the tax is not a tax, and on the other hand you have those who say if it is used for such fiscal purposes it is not a tax.

I think the great mass of scientists and statesmen will confess that the history of the world shows, and that the theory of the subject also shows, that taxation must be and may be utilized for both purposes; that, of course, the primary end of all taxation is to secure revenue, but that if, on the other hand, there is a certain desirable end to be attained, whatever the end may be, we must not shrink from utilizing taxation for that end, if the use of taxation as a means is workable. Therefore I would answer your question in that general way.

Q. You would say, then, that the regulation of trusts and interstate commerce might properly be facilitated by the agency of taxation?—A. Decidedly.

Q. (By Mr. KENNEDY.) I should like to hear an expression of your views relative to the new system of taxing corporation franchises in the city of New York, the one that was embodied in the Ford bill.—A. That is a rather special and peculiar measure, because the Ford franchise bill, or as it is now called, special franchise bill, does not affect the franchises of ordinary corporations, but only a particular aspect of some corporations. What I mean is this: There are three different rights given to corporations by Government, first, the right or the franchise to become a corporation. That is paid for in New York State, as well as most of our other States, by payments known as incorporation fees or bonus on charters, or various names of that kind. When a company incorporates, it must pay a certain fee or charge for the privilege of becoming a corporation. The second franchise which is paid for is the franchise, not to become, but to be, a corporation; not the liberty of coming into existence, but the liberty to act. That is paid for by the system of so-called franchise or license tax, as we have it in New York, Pennsylvania, and other States. That is a tax, whether upon capital stock or upon gross receipts or anything of that kind. The third kind of franchise is the one which this new New York law is attempting to reach; that is, the privilege of certain corporations in localities to make use of the streets and highways, by going either on, below or above them. It is that franchise and no other franchise which is sought to be taxed by the Ford bill, and it seems to me just as defensible to put an additional tax upon such corporations for local purposes as it is to put a general franchise tax on general corporations. The object, therefore, of the Ford franchise tax is simply to make those quasi public corporations, sometimes called municipal monopolies—the street railways, gas companies, electric light, steam heat and power companies, etc.—pay more than they are paying, simply on their capital stock for local purposes, or on their real estate, because very few of them pay on their real estate, since they do not own the streets. There is no real estate there. All. for instance, that gas companies would pay, would be on the value of the pipes beneath the street; all that the street-car companies would pay would be—if it paid at all—upon the value of the rails. Of course, they do not pay on the value of the street, because the street does not belong to them. Now, these municipal corporations pay for what is practically—what would be called in the case of a business—the good will, the good will of the business. That is to say, the value of their property as a whole is very much more than the value of their tangible assets, and the Ford franchise bill seeks to hit this difference between the value of the tangible assets, actual realty, and actual visible personalty, and the total value of the corporation.

Q. There is no attempt, then, to tax the good will that goes with the franchise the State gives a corporation to build a railroad through a State?—A. No; because that is thought to be reached by State taxes on franchises. The State has a tax on franchises, but it measures that in a peculiar way, and, moreover, the State has an additional tax on transportation companies over and above the franchise tax.

Q. You say it is measured in a peculiar way. Will you state that peculiarity?—A. In New York State they measure the general franchise tax on a corporation according to dividends. They levy the tax on capital stock in proportion to dividends, pursuing the same system that Pennsylvania formerly pursued, and finally abandoned.

Q. You understand that if the Government were to assume ownership of the railroads of the country the States would be deprived of the right to tax the property of the Government?—A. That would necessarily follow from our constitutional limitations. It does not follow abroad; they have a very curious system; but in this country, of course, no State can tax any agencies of the Federal Government. I think that would constitute, among other objections, one of the most serious objections to Government assumption of railways in this country.

Q. The States would be very jealous of that right, and would no doubt oppose the Government ownership on that ground?—A. Decidedly.

Q. (By Mr. A. L. HARRIS.) Just at this time the State of New Jersey is attracting a great deal of attention on account of her tax system. What have you to say in regard to other States adopting a similar plan?—A. The State of New Jersey has, on the whole, been very wise. I think, in fact, that the whole system of corporation law of New Jersey is, in some respects, in advance of many other States. They have taken very good advice, indeed, in framing their system in New Jersey. I know the only difficulty is that New Jersey is such a small State, and it has so few expenses in comparison with the vast interests within the State that the problem is not the same. New Jersey, you may say, fattens upon and lives upon New York City, practically; that is what it amounts to, and what properly ought to be taxed in New York, all these railways whose terminals are, economically speaking, within New York, have, legally, terminals in New Jersey, and New Jersey is therefore within its borders. The wealth and income is out of all proportion to what is really economically within it. If you were to take from New Jersey the suburbs of New York, you will find the situation a very different one in New Jersey; therefore, while the system is very good for New Jersey, and while they can get along with a very low rate of taxation, and while New Jersey does not levy any State tax at all upon property for general purposes, it is simply because of the fact that New Jersey happens to be an annex to New York City.

Q. And would it be possible to have a uniform law bearing equally upon all of the States?—A. The system of uniformity, as I said before, would have to be arranged according to carefully devised rules, and these rules ought to be framed from the point of view of the economic interests, so far as it is possible, and not in accordance with the temporary territorial and local position.

Q. Possessing the advantages she has now would New Jersey consent to uniform taxation laws?—A. Provided New Jersey would get sufficient revenue from her own State. It seems to me that the plan is feasible within certain limits. Of course, I do not wish to imply that any Federal commission or any other commission could take away from any State some of its own source of taxation. What I did mean to imply is that certain general rules can be laid down as to the division of the tax between the States—not only according to the location of the railway, but also in accordance with the rights of the stock and bond holders; in accordance, in other words, with the economic interests. They have been able to do that in Switzerland to a certain extent. They have been able to do that in Germany to a certain extent, and it seems to me that when the question is properly presented the problem is not insurmountable in this country. Of course, it would mean that certain States which now permit the domicivilization of weak corporations which are afraid to take out a charter in other States would lose that proud preeminence, but that is a thing which I think is very much to be desired in the interests of all corporate development.

Q. I see in 1897 the State of New Jersey collected from the Pennsylvania Railroad Company alone $411,000 of tax, while she had only 708 or 709 miles of road within the State of New Jersey. Is that altogether fair to the other States that have also helped to make the value of the Pennsylvania Railroad's property?— A. I think the fact that you have instanced is one example of the glaring discrepancy between our legal facts and economic conditions, and the problem is not so difficult of solution in New Jersey as might be thought, because New Jersey needs comparatively a small revenue. It is a small State, and the consequence is that its rate of tax is very much lower than, as you will see, in Pennsylvania or New York, and therefore a uniform system could very much more easily be effected there.

Q. I noticed a few days ago in the paper that the State of New Jersey had over a million dollars of the excess she had collected to turn into the school fund without taxing a single dollar of property for State purposes.—A. There are other States in this Union that do not levy any tax on property—Connecticut, for instance, and other States—and the plan under advisement, I may say, by New York is precisely to that effect, so there will be no more taxing of property.

Q. Do you think the old era of tax for State purposes, as well as other purposes, of property according to its true value in money, is not practical now?—A. I think the theory was true at a certain stage of economic development, and that was the reason why everywhere in the world at a certain stage of economic development you find the tax on general property. You find it in the Middle Ages and you find it in every country of the world at a certain stage; but when that economic stage is past that property tax is bound to go with it. In our advanced industrial communities in this country we have gotten past that stage, and it does not work. It resolves itself practically into a tax on real estate, plus a more or less wild guess at the personal property.

Q. One of the objections of the method of taxation was the difficulty of getting the true valuation of the property, was it not? A good deal of property escaped all taxation? What have you to say in regard to the present law of Illinois in regard to the reform in getting the valuation of property?—A. I say to that that Illinois is simply another example of a new broom sweeping clean. It will sweep all right for a while. All attempts to secure the desired result of equal taxation of property by making a listing system, by making the penalties more severe, work as long as everybody believes the law is going to be enforced; but it takes only a very short time for anybody to conclude that the law will not be enforced.

Q. The opinion appears to prevail among the agriculturalists of the country that they are bearing more than their share of taxation. What are your views upon that subject?—A. I think that in a great many of the States the contention is a correct one, simply for the reason that what amounts practically to a real estate tax in the rest of the State is a general property tax in the rural districts. The large cities' personal property very largely escapes because it consists mainly of corporate securities, while in the small farming districts in some of our States the chickens and the cows and the agricultural implements are taxed to the farmer as personal property. Where that is done, of course, the farmer does pay more than his share, because he has to bear his own burden and that of the city besides.

Q. The amount that goes to the State revenues is comparatively small, is it not?—A. About 15 per cent—from 13 to 15 per cent in New York State—and I should imagine perhaps a little more in some of the other States. It is pretty difficult, of course, in dealing with any economic problem, to make any generalization in regard to any part of the United States, because we forget that the United States presents this curious spectacle for the first time in the history of the world; that we are dealing with different stages of economic development. We have the frontier life in some of our States yet. We have our purely agricultural communities in some of our Southern States, and we have the most fully developed industrial communities in a few of our Eastern and Northern States. You have these three different stages of economic life existing at the same time in the country, and you can not make any generalization that covers the whole country, and that is why, therefore, I should hesitate to answer that question in regard to the whole country. That is one of the reasons why the solution of all economic problems is so much more delicate in the United States than in any of the compactly developed and complete communities of the Old World. It has taken them 1,000 or 2,000 years to get their development, which we are going through in a few decades. Some of our States have only just begun to become States—just beginning development. They are, practically, to all intents and purposes, as regards certain economic conditions, where Europe was away back in the Middle Ages.

Q. As a rule the local tax is a burden, is it not?—A. It is.

Q. And the locality that pays the tax substantially controls the amount of that tax?—A. Very largely; not entirely. There are certain obligations; but, as a general principle, I think it may be laid down.

Q. The tax problem is one of the most difficult to solve equitably that the legislator meets, is it not?—A. Yes. As long as our legislators will realize the fact, which many are beginning to realize in the most advanced States, I am glad to say, in this country—as long as they realize that you have got to attack the problem piecemeal, and you can not reform the thing all at once, the situation may be very much improved. When I say you have got to attack the problem piecemeal, I mean you have got to take one step forward at a time; and the first and most important step for the present time in this country I consider to be a divorce between State and local revenues, in order to prepare the way for reform of local revenues. You never can do that as long as you mix up State and local revenue, and it was to emphasize that point that I spoke this morning in reference to the possible interference of the Federal Government.

Q. (By Mr. RATCHFORD.) Have you noticed the recent decision of the Ohio supreme court with reference to the taxation of trusts within that State—a decision handed down some few days ago?—A. I do not think I noticed that, sir. What was the exact point?

Q. (By Mr. FARQUHAR.) You spoke of the fact that the uniformity of State action might be attained through pressure from the Federal power. How is it possible, unless the Federal power create one of these corporations, that it have any effect either on commonwealth taxation or taxation by the National Government itself?—A. I had reference more to the indirect pressure than the direct pressure. What I meant was the same sort of work being done, perhaps unconsciously, by the Interstate Commerce Commission, in influencing the State railway commissions, and thus ultimately affecting State railway legislation. There is no one at present in any of our States who looks at the problem in any but a purely local light. What I want is a body which may be induced to regard the problem in its general aspects.

Q. Do you know of any means whereby the Federal Government itself could regulate the railway corporations of this country through taxation, otherwise than by creating them?—A. If I understand the question correctly, the Federal Government has the right to tax any corporation, whether created by itself or not.

Q. Direct or indirect?—A. It would be called legally an indirect tax, although economically it would be a direct tax. This has been decided by the Supreme Court of the United States. The gross receipts' tax during the civil war, which was economically a direct tax, levied on the railways, was decided by the court to be an indirect tax and perfectly constitutional.

Q. That, however, was a state of war. I mean in a state of peace, in a normal condition of the country. How wide would you define, under the Constitution, the regulation of interstate commerce? Would you maintain that it ought not to contain within itself this taxing power?—A. Whether that is true or not, sir, the power of taxing the railways could rest upon some other clause of the Constitution. The Government now taxes inheritances; it is true that its constitutionality is being discussed at this very moment across the way (pointing to the Supreme Court), but the Government is levying taxes on other forms of business, which have been upheld. The stamp tax has been upheld only a few weeks ago as being a tax on business. There is no reason why the Government can not levy a tax on business, whether State or interstate, providing it is not levied so as to run up against the prohibition of direct taxation.

Q. What I want from you to-day would be propositions leading to some progressive gradual steps toward the regulation of this whole taxing power of corporations, and thereby leading to the regulation of trusts.—A. I thought I had covered that point in my testimony. I can repeat my own view in just a word or two. I say there are two ways in which the Government can bring its influence to bear; the one is by enacting a law providing for the calling together of annual conventions of State commissioners by inviting them. "Of course you can not compel the State to do so, but you can invite the State to do so, and by tactful arrangement I think a great deal can be accomplished in that voluntary way, and a great deal more good could be accomplished than by compulsion. The Federal Government in conjunction with the State commissioners could lay down principles which, if followed, might lead to an improvement in the system. What those principles are, I hinted at, although, of course, I did not develop them fully. That would be the only way—for the Federal Government to work hand in hand with the commissions of the States.

Q. Through the creation of a new commission, do you mean? By what agency?—A. Either a commission or an official body which would have this especial object in view. I am not prepared to say which would be more effective.

Q. (By Mr. Phillips.) You would form this commission of the taxpayers of the various States?—A. Yes; but the gentleman asked what the Federal authority would be—whether one man or a number of men. That, perhaps, is a question. That would be one way.

The second way—although I should prefer that the second way be not followed until the futility of the first had been shown—the second way would be for the Government simply to enact a law, as some of our States have already enacted laws, providing for a tax on such corporations and providing for the redistribution of this tax among the various States, in part or wholly, according to certain defined rules.

Q. (By Mr. Farquhar.) Taxation includes this general proposition—that there is a privilege granted. Every one of our interstate railroads is incorporated by a State unless we except, of course, the transcontinental. The great systems are created by States—are granted their privileges by States. What the commission want to get at is this: What position the National Government ought to take. The propositions you make on the legal status of the matter and on the economic development are seemingly antagonistic as to State and Federal taxes.—A. Of course before such a bill of any kind would be passed it would be necessary to lay down carefully the economic lines on which the bill should be framed.

Q. Much safer than legal lines?—A. Unless you have legal lines your bill will be overturned by the courts, but you have got to have economic lines when you go to work. I did not go into these matters in detail because it is not a practical proposition; but when it becomes so I shall be very glad to come before the commission. In order to save time I would say that in an essay that I have written on double taxation I have mentioned some of the fundamental principles which would have to be observed in such a bill. I shall be very glad to send the commission a copy.

Q. (By Mr. Ratchford.) Is it your opinion that when the capital stock of a corporation is increased either by appreciation of the value of the property or by what is commonly known as watered stock such increased capitalization should be taxed?—A. If the increase is a real economic increase of capital I think it should be.

Q. What is an economic increase of capital?—A. The water in the stock would not be an economic increase, because it would not increase the earning capacity of a railway.

Q. Still it has a purpose, has it not? There is a purpose behind it?—A. Oh, decidedly.

Q. If it is an appreciation in value of property, then you believe it should be taxed?—A. I think the difficulty could be easily gotten around by stating that you are going to tax the market value and not the par value. Then the difficulty settles itself, because if it is watered stock it would not increase the market value of the stock.

Q. It is believed in some cases to-day that certain corporations are capitalized for an amount two or three times as large as the actual investment. That is said to be a great evil. It is commonly called watering of the stock. Now, if that be an evil would it not be a good way to check that evil to tax them for their excess capitalization?—A. That plan in itself might be a very good one; that end would certainly be a desirable one, but the difficulty is that you would hit the good with the evil. You may strike the honest in trying to reach the dishonest, and it seems to me that the difficulty of which you speak can possibly be better reached in some other way than by the use of the power of taxation.

Q. Well, if the line between the honest corporation and dishonest one is apparent by the extent to which they water their stock, the honest corporation, it seems to me, would not be subject to taxation under that system.—A. A corporation may

655A——39

often desire to increase its capital very largely, and it might not at the first blush be apparent what the purpose is. It may seem to be water and yet not be water. We can not tell until probably some years have elapsed, when we could all see what the situation is. It often happens that a corporation needs more money to develop its fast-growing business, and an increase of capital there may be perfectly justifiable from an economic point of view. It seems to me that the Massachusetts method is the better way to deal with it.

Q. As we understand, the increase of capital in the case which we are now referring to is not an actual increase of capital. If more capital is required in the development of their business, then it is actual capital, and they would not object, it seems to me.—A. My point is that it is frequently difficult to draw the line between what is fictitious and what is actual capital, just as it is often difficult to draw the line between what is legitimate and illegitimate in speculation.

Q. Do you believe that fictitious capital creates a fictitious credit and value?—A. If you mean that an increase of capital stock, or the watering of capital stock, may sometimes be done for mere jobbing purposes, that, of course, is unfortunately true, and it may for the time being increase the credit of the stock and enable them to sell it at a higher price.

Q. Is it your opinion that franchises and State privileges, given sometimes by way of State legislation, should be taxed?—A. I think that all franchises of a quasi-public nature ought to be paid for over and above the general rate of taxation.

Q. (By Professor JOHNSON.) We shall be pleased to have you state what you wish to say in regard to the telegraph service and the public control of it.—A. I shall try to be very brief in regard to that point, gentlemen. I have only a few ideas which I want to present here touching upon the question of governmental ownership and management of the telegraph service of this country.

The general principles with which I will start out are that the problem as to governmental ownership of industry depends primarily upon the following three considerations: First, upon existence or non-existence of widespread social interests; second, the amount of capital invested, and, third, the complexity of the management. Now, what does this mean? There is no demand—ought to be no demand—in a community for the governmental assumption of any industry unless that industry is of such fundamental social importance to everyone in a community in his efforts to get a living as to justify interference by Government to that extent. No one except the socialist would, for instance, ask that the Government should take hold of a shoe factory, because after all it is a special interest. It may be true that everybody wears shoes in this country, but they do not all wear the same kind of shoes and the same quantity of shoes. So it is with every other industry. But when you come to such a thing as the postal service, for instance, everybody is agreed, with the exception of some extreme individualists in England, like Mr. Herbert Spencer and others, that it should be in public hands and not in private hands, because in a democracy everybody is supposed to read and write and everybody is also supposed to use the mails. Now, I would maintain that from simply this point of view what applies to the postal service ought to apply also to the telegraph service. Unfortunately in this country the telegraph service is not used by everyone. The charges are so high, apparently, and the conditions are such that the telegraph is used mainly for business purposes and to a very slight extent for social purposes. In other countries, where the telegraph is an adjunct to the postal system and where the rates are lower and facilities greater, people use it, as any of us know wh have traveled abroad; people use the telegraph system to a far greater extent in proportion to the intelligence and the population than we do. Therefore, from the point of view of widespread social interests, the telegraph service ought to be put on a par with the postal service. Secondly, as regards the capital invested. One reason why there is no more discussion about the governmental management of the post is that there is no capital needed. There are not any complex questions. Of course we do spend $100,000,000 a year, but we have not any large capital account. It is mostly current expense. That is wherein the postal service differs toto coelo from the railway service. Just as in the postal service you have practically no capital expended, so in the railway service, the most stupendous of all modern industries, you have the greatest possible amount of capital invested. Just as I should be most strongly opposed to governmental assumption of the railways in this country, among other reasons, for the fiscal reason that it would throw the whole budget out of gear; that the revenues and expenditures of railways would be two or three times as great as all the rest of our revenues together, and that the whole budget of the country would depend upon the success and prosperity or failure of the railway system; so, for that reason, I should be in fa,or of the governmental telegraph, because the capital, although greater than in the case of the post, is yet very slight as compared with other interests. All you have got to do is to get enough capital to put up poles and string your wires, as in case of private companies, and perhaps also to get certain rights of way in case of Government that would not be of much importance. Of course if the Government were to buy out the telegraph lines there would be a capital outlay, naturally, but even then it would be insignificant when compared with the capital invested in ordinary enterprise or the means of transportation.

As to the complexity of management. This, again, would be an insuperable bar, in my estimation, to Government management of railways, because of all businesses the railway business calls for the most delicate and careful adjustment or administration and needs and pays for the highest possible business ability. The greatest salaries in this country to-day are given to the railway presidents—salaries from $25,000 to $100,000 a year—and deservedly so, because it calls for the highest possible ability to run a railway successfully. Therefore a government could naturally not hope to compete successfully in that line of business with private individuals. It would make, under existing American conditions, more or less of a mess of it. However, in the case of the telegraph service all those difficulties vanish. There, again, you have not a complex business, but a simple business. The great end of individual initiative in industry in general is that it must have ability turned toward the reduction of the cost of production, in inventions, etc. All progress in the world consists of lowering the cost of production of commodities by driving out old processes and introducing new processes, and that method of improvement results not alone in lower prices for the community, but, as our history has amply shown, gradually higher wages for the operative as well as prosperity for the employers. In the case of the telegraph system you have not, or you have to an infinitesimal extent, this element entering. Of course there may be a new invention in telegraph machines, but the experience of even such sleepy administrations as those of France and of England shows that the telegraph service does keep on a level with the new inventions and that the telegraph operators may be put on a slightly higher scale there, but of a very different category from the regular postal officials. Therefore it seems to me, if you look at the question from these three points of view, which are the important ones—the widespread social interests, the amount of capital involved, and the complexity of the management—that all three of these considerations argue in favor of the assumption by Government of the postal telegraph, as is the case in every other country in the world, including the most improved and most democratic communities like Switzerland, like Australia, and like all other modern democracies. Of course we all know also that the telegraph was practically in Government hands at the time of the first telegraph in 1844, and that the Government decided not to go on with the telegraph business for very much the same reason that led the postmaster-general in England violently to oppose the postal reforms of Mr. Rowland Hill. They thought the whole thing would not amount to anything and did not want to commit the Government to that hazardous experiment. Yet the originator of the telegraph system, who was wise enough to forsee its natural outcome, concealed his opinion that this was a natural adjunct to the postal system, and the history of every government of the world has shown, except our own, although it may have started in private hands, that it must be brought, as in England and other countries, under Government control. The only reason, I take it, why there is not a larger and greater outcry in this country for Government assumption of the telegraph is that the abuses connected with the telegraph service are far less after all than those connected with other forms of transportation, as railways; but even then there are certain dangers, if not abuses, and the great point to be remembered is that in questions of this kind what we must seek after all is the highest social utility. It is said that if the Government ran the telegraph in this country it would not make as much money as the Western Union Telegraph. No doubt it is true; but, on the other hand, the object of the Government would be to make no profit at all, but to run the service just as the postal service is run. Any possible profits in it would reduce the rates. We all know the rates are far higher in this country. Even though we allow for the lower value of money in this country, the rates are higher in this country than abroad for short distances and for long distances, and the use of the telegraph lines and the telegraph service can not be compared in this country with the use that is made of it abroad; and, therefore, although there are not any serious abuses in the telegraph management of this country, yet at the same time it seems to me that every argument that could be made in favor of assumption of the postal service can be made in favor of assumption of the telegraph service. We do not argue about the post because the country was in possession of the post a long time before this controversy as to the desirability of Government interference on the question; but if it had not been in control of the post in the colonies or at the time of Hamilton we should have had this same question in this country as to Government posts *v.* private posts. That is simply a historical accident that we have a Government post in this country, and it is simply because the telegraph was not invented until 1844 instead of in the eighteenth or seventeenth century that we have not a postal telegraph.

Q. (By Mr. PHILLIPS.) What would be your judgment in regard to the ownership of the telephone?—A. Every argument that applies to the telegraph applies equally to the telephone, with the possible exception that in the case of the telephone it may not be desirable to have Federal control. But England passed a law only a few months ago which shows that there are a great many arguments to be advanced in favor of Federal management even of the telephone system, especially since the long-distance telephone is becoming so important a feature. England has passed a law whereby in a very few years the whole telephone system will be part of the English post-office. When I say every argument that applies to the telegraph applies to the telephone that must be taken with a modification. I think the arguments are not quite so strong for the telephone as for the telegraph, because the complexity of the management is a little greater in the telephone than in the telegraph. It requires a little more care to keep up to the level of modern science in the telephone than in the telegraph.

Q. Are there any governments now that have the telephone under their control?—A. Almost all European governments have them now.

Q. The German Government?—A. Germany, yes. In Germany, France, Norway, Switzerland, and Australia the telephone is run as a part of the postal system. In England, now, under the new law, the telephone is to be run as a part of the postal system. They still permit them another ten years continuance, but not the development of a private telephone company. The charter expires, I think, in 1911, and then the whole system will be in the hands of the English post-office.

Q. (By Mr. FARQUHAR.) In the management of the local telephone, then, would you place the postmaster, for instance, of the city in charge of the commercial and local 'phone?—A. Decidedly.

Q. How about the management of your long-distance telephone?—A. That could be arranged just as our postal service is arranged between the cities. The receiving station, of course, would always be under the management of the postmaster, and the accounts could be kept between the cities just as our postal accounts for railway transportation, etc., are arranged. Those are mere little matters of detail, which would not give any difficulty at all. But the point that I wanted to make was that the increased possible use of the long-distance telephone would argue for a national telephone rather than for a municipal telephone, and that it is that which has led England to take it up now and take the power away from the municipalities and put it into the hands of the General Government.

Q. Do you see any dangers at all in the number of Government servants and politics there?—A. Of course I assume that hand in hand with this whole system there would go a development of our civil service, a very progressive development of our civil service, a movement which the President has so wisely and so well emphasized in his message of yesterday. There have not been any great dangers politically in our postal service, it seems to me. If there have been, they have been more than counterbalanced by the political dangers that would have been if the postal service had been private. You have got to weigh and balance the good against the evil of this case. There are, of course, these possibilities of political danger in Government service.

Q. Are there not particularly political dangers where there are large amounts of money used in any governmental function?—A. That is the reason that I make so much of the second point, that the capital invested is so small, and in this business the capital invested is very small indeed; almost the entire expense is running expense. It would not be as great as that of our postal service to-day.

Q. Would your practical plan be for the Government to take over the whole of the Western Union system and the Bell telephone?—A. As soon as that could practically be done I should certainly be in favor of it.

Q. That is, you would eliminate any notion of competition there—not building a Government line in competition with any existing line?—A. I am always opposed to governmental competition with private enterprise, because, although the assumption is that the private enterprise will be brought up to the level of the governmental efficiency, the practical result is always that the governmental agent is pulled down to the level of the private. The experience of many countries has shown that. Competition between the Government and private individuals can result only disastrously to the public.

Q. Is that proposition that you are making now partly explained by the condition of railroads in France?—A. I think the best history of that instance is the history of the railways in Belgium rather than in France, because it was especially in Belgium that the competition of railways proved to be so ruinous.

Q. (By Mr. KENNEDY.) When you spoke of the running of railroads, youspoke of all these high-salaried presidents. Is it your idea that the Government would be deprived of the talent that these railroad companies now employ if they——
—A. (Interrupting.) Under our present political or democratic system I think that would inevitably follow, because our history, especially in our consular and diplomatic service, shows that you can not expect a democracy to pay as high salaries as monarchies and other countries, and with low salaries the temptation would not be great enough. They would go and finance our great trusts and they would finance our great industrial enterprises and not our railways.

Q. When you see the State of New York able to induce a great railroad president to serve in the capacity of a United States Senator for $5,000 a year, and the Government able to induce a great lawyer of the State of New York to come and act as Secretary of War, does it not seem that the inducement to enter Government service would compensate for the loss of salary, and that the Government would get all the talent that would be necessary to conduct these transportation companies?—A. Of course, it is to be understood that with the progressive advance of political ideals in this country, what you state would come more and more to be the fact; but I think we are a long way off from that condition—from the condition of the Prussian administrative service. In Prussia, I think, that is true; I hope in that respect it will be true in this country some day; and possibly the assumption by the Government of more work may lead individuals to be willing to sacrifice themselves for the public good. But under the present materialistic, and necessarily materialistic, drift of the American people, having a whole continent to conquer and necessarily developing all its productive forces, it seems to me that the weight of the influences is thrown to the other side, and not so much in political as in private business.

Q. (By Professor JOHNSON.) Have we not numerous instances of men quitting the Government service because of small salaries?—A. I think that is beyond question, and we all know that the cases mentioned by the gentlemen are the cases of men who have some means to start with. We all know of men who would have liked to accept Government positions when offered to them, but it was simply stated that they could not possibly afford to do so. It is asking a great sacrifice of a man in these days of immense opportunities for ability, to give up comfort and everything of that kind for the mere ideal end of serving the public. Only the best and highest men will do that.

Q. (By Mr. KENNEDY.) You will not say that if the Government did control the railroads it would not be able to secure all the talent that would be necessary to conduct these enterprises?—A. I should think the chances would be rather in favor of a less efficient management than you find at present under private control. What might be the case ultimately I do not pretend to say.

Q. (By Professor JOHNSON.) Will this proposition be true, that the Government would get the same talent cheaper than the private corporation?—A. That is probably true.

Q. With the evolution of our political ideals we shall be able to secure adequate talent?—A. It is simply a question, as you say, of the state of political ideals. In Germany, for instance, in Prussia, the very best men there go into public business and into administration; and in France, to a certain extent.

Q. (By Mr. RATCHFORD.) What is the experience of some of those other democracies that you spoke of—some of the European countries; has their experience been, in making their change from private ownership to public ownership, that they were unable to obtain that high development?—A. So far as telegraphs are concerned?

Q. No; railroads.—A. There is only one country in Europe that has done so, and that is Prussia. And Prussia, as I have said, is a very peculiar and exceptional case, because the Prussian civil service has always stood very high. In Prussia they have a successful income tax, for instance; and yet no one who knows the difference between political conditions in Prussia and the United States would dare to state that an income tax in this country would be as successful as it is there.

Q. How about Australia and Belgium? Are they not adding new systems of railroads, and have they not done so?—A. In Australia and in Belgium they are greatly extending their systems, but even in Australia the conditions are a little different from what they are in this country. We must remember that the drift toward governmental aid and interference in Australia has necessarily always been far greater than in this country, because of the economic conditions of Australia. Australia is a vast arid table-land, most of the country being fit only for grazing, where nature is not bountiful, and where the individual alone can scarcely cope with the difficulties of nature; and from the very beginning, in order to develop Australia, they have had to have the aid of the government in every respect. In this country we are in an entirely different sitution; this country is the most fruitful country, and the Mississippi Valley the greatest valley, on the face of the globe, and the Americans have always thought that they could develop the country most by depending on themselves. That is the fundamental political or philosophic reason why the Australian democracy has so much of what we call socialism, and why we have so little; and as long as the conditions remain such in this country, it seems to me, the legal difficulties will remain the same.

Q. One of the chief reasons you advance in opposition to governmental ownership of railroads is the enormous capital invested?—A. Yes.

Q. Is it not a fact, that in Germany the capital invested per mile of railway is many times more than it is in the United States?—A. Yes; in Germany it amounts to two or three times as much.

Q. Per mile?—A. As it does in the United States.

Q. And yet they manage successfully under Government control?—A. Oh, it must be remembered that even under private control in Prussia, the conditions were very different from what they are here, the so-called private management of the Prussian railways. The private railways of Germany were always accustomed to far greater govermental interference than we have had, and when they were bought up and lifted into the system by the Government, it was an apparently slight change. The Government had always interfered a great deal with the private railways, and they were built up under officials who were accustomed to consider questions of rates and of tariffs also.

Q. (By Mr. FARQUHAR.) Was it the same in the English and Scotch and Irish railways?—A. In England it has been less than in Germany.

Q. But they had almost supreme control of the telephones and they had almost supreme control in building roads?—A. Oh, that is so.

Q. (By Mr. RATCHFORD.) In Germany the construction of the road is much more permanent in character, and the rates for travel of passengers are much cheaper?—A. Well; the rates of the passenger fares on the whole are somewhat less than they are in this country, although it is very difficult to make a comparison, because they have the class system, and it depends on whether you are going to compare the first, second, or third class with ours. Of course, the freight rates are very much higher, because of our long-distance traffic. The passenger rates are less. On the whole, when you compare Prussia with America, I can answer best by agreeing with Professor Van der Leyen, who has written a book. He was one of the great advocates of the assumption of railways by Prussia; and he said that if he was an American he would be the most outspoken opponent of governmental railway control in this country; which shows that he sees the difference between the Prussian conditions and the American.

Q. Is it your observation that the public generally patronize their railroads more than ours are patronized?—A. No; for an entirely different reason. We must remember that in many parts of the Continent of Europe the social conditions are almost mediæval yet, and the peasants travel very little. Not so very long ago they were bound to the soil, and although they are free, yet everybody knows how slowly old conditions change; and it was mainly for this reason that the Austrian-Hungarian Government brought about such a great reduction in their system of railway charges, under the zone system, some time ago, in order to stimulate intercounty or intermunicipal travel within that State. So that I do not think we could draw any useful lesson at all from the comparison of this point in countries whose economic and social conditions are so entirely diverse as those of the United States and of Germany or Austria.

Q. (By Professor JOHNSON.) We have heard a good deal on the question of pooling pro and con, and we know very well that you have given a good deal of attention to the subject, and we should like to hear you on it.—A. Probably what I should have to say would add very little to the advice that has been presented to you by the practical men, experts on both sides. I can only state very little, which comes from a consideration and study and comparison of our system here with that of the railways in other parts of the world.

Here, of course, the general consideration with which we have to start out is that the fundamental problem is that of competition versus monopoly. It goes without saying that both systems have their good and their bad sides; and it may be well to point out in just a word how far these advantages or disadvantages would apply to the matter in hand. Now, as I take it, the great advantage of the competitive system consists in what I stated a moment ago in another connection—that competition always forces the price down to the level of the best competitor. What I mean is, that if you look at the history of any industry, you find that it is only through the force of competition that the conditions arise under which new efforts are made, under which new machines are introduced, under which the cost of production is lowered; and that all progress, therefore, which directly depends upon the lowering of the cost of production, depends indirectly upon competition between producers. It is only through competition between the producers that you have the incentive to the lowering of the cost of production. That is the immense advantage of competition, and that is why, under the competitive system in the nineteenth century, the world has been making such immense advances. Now, this very excellence of the competitive system discloses its weakness when applied to a public or quasi-public institution. Prices can be brought down and lowered only through the efforts of separate producers to get the better of each other, and to offer to their purchasers all sorts of inducements in order to widen their market. Every merchant, every manufacturer, tries, so far as he can, to get control of the market, and he tries to get control of the market by reducing his own price to that point which is consistent with any profit to him; even in some cases, if he is a shrewd man, a wise man, he does as the Standard Oil Company, for instance, has done; and in certain cases, in order to crowd out competitors, he will reduce prices for the time being below the level of the others, in order, only, to raise them a little later on.

That is the normal and the necessary condition of affairs in private industry. If I go to a woolen house in Worth street, New York, I try to ascertain what my competitor is paying for those goods and then I try to get a little lower rate; and upon my getting that lower rate or not will depend, perhaps, the success or failure of that merchant. In other words, merchants can succeed only by playing off one man against another. That is what competition means, in getting the best rates available.

Now, while that is the normal and necessary condition in ordinary economic life, when you apply that to a quasi-public institution it becomes bad instead of good, because the fundamental condition of all such quasi-public institutions connected with transportation or otherwise, is that all consumers should be put on the same level. That is just the opposite principle, therefore, of what you have in ordinary business. Ordinary competitive enterprise means preferring the one over the other. The transportation business, which is primarily a quasi-public business, if it is to be conducted according to principles of social utility, means putting everybody on the same level. In other words, the competition in transportation can be a competition not as to rates, but only as to efficiency of service; whereas, in ordinary business life, competition includes not only competition as to efficiency but also competition as to rates. Therefore, the conclusion is that competition is not so applicable to the transportation business as it is to ordinary business. It is applicable, in a certain sense, that we must seek to preserve the good side of competition, which is competition as regards efficiency, giving the best service and getting and making use of the newest appliances; but we must not have competition as regards rates.

Now, it goes without saying that the evils of this competition in transportion service are responsible for practically all the abuses of our railway system. They result in the discriminations, both personal and local, of which we continually complain. Just as in the postal service the Government does not sell to the wholesale purchaser of postage stamps at a lower rate than to the little boy who buys a 2-cent stamp, so also the railway ought not to sell to the wholesale, large, or favored shipper, at a different rate from that which it sells to the individual and defenseless man; and yet we all know that ordinary business is conducted on that very principle. The getting of wholesale business means selling differently to different individuals, according to the quantity purchased, according to individual conditions. Therefore, the conclusion is that in the transportation business competition is only relatively good, and that the bad sides of competition come out very much more clearly than they do in ordinary industry.

If you do not have competition, or if you only have modified competition, what must you have? The opposite of competition is monopoly.

The good sides and evil sides of monopoly are just as glaring. The good side of monopoly is that it prevents or it may prevent the difference in the treatment of individuals which is due to competition. Of course you may have personal discriminations through the monopolist, which are due simply to his own personal whim. So, also, we find that where railways are entire monopolies, as in some of the countries of the world, they may and often do have almost as bad a system of abuses as where the railway is entirely under the competitive system. We have only to turn to California in order to see that in a State where there is practically no competition at all, you may have just as serious evils under the monopoly system as you have under the competitive system; and we may also turn to France, where they have the division of the field of the railways, each division of the field having a monopoly of the railway system there, and we shall see a great many evils and dangers in noneffective management, lack of facilities, etc., which would not arise under the competitive system. That, however, simply means that because in a competitive industry you have the force of competition to compel improvement and to bring prices down, under a system of monopoly you must have some other power to take the place of competition in order to avoid the evils of monopoly; and that is, of course, the reason why in all real and strict monopolies governments interfere, whereas in ordinary competitive enterprises the ordinary forces of competition are supposed to be sufficient to safeguard the interests of the consumer. If you have evils under the monopoly system and evils under the competitive system the question arises, Is it not possible to devise some scheme whereby you may reduce the evils of both systems to a minimum and whereby you may increase the advantages of both systems, competition and monopoly?

Now, it is from that particular point of view that I should like to approach the question of railway pools and traffic associations. So far as I can learn from the study of the history of pools and traffic associations, both in this country and abroad, they form the best system thus far devised by human ingenuity to give us, under careful scrutiny and guidance, the advantages both of competition and of monopoly, or if you want to use instead of the word "monopoly" the word "combination." which possibly would be better, it gives the advantages both of competition and of combination. It gives the advantages of competition because even under the pooling contracts, as they exist in other parts of the world as well as in our own country, there is no cessation of competition, or ought not to be—very often is not—no cessation of competition as regards facilities.

Even under the most ironclad pooling arrangements in this country, let us say between the New York Central and the Pennsylvania, although the rates to Chicago may have been exactly the same, and although even the hours of running the trains may have been within a certain limit the same, yet each railway did what it could to increase the efficiency of its management and the pleasure of the journey so as to attract as many people as possible to it, and thus pave the way for a change in the pooling arrangement another year.

You have, therefore, under a well-devised pooling system, a retention of the advantages of competition, and you have under a well-devised pooling system an avoidance of the evils of competition so far as competition means cut rates, cut-throat competition, personal discrimination, and to a certain extent illegitimate and indefensible local discrimination. Of course, no system, whether of combination or of competition, is going to do away with local discrimination or can do away with local discrimination. Local discriminations are in the very essence of the system of railway rates, belong to the whole theory of values in economics, and they ought not to be abolished until that time comes—if it ever does come—when the railways will be run by the Government for nothing and when we shall have a uniform railway rate, just as we now have a uniform postal rate. I say that time will probably never come, because of the essential difference between the economic conditions of the railway service and those of the postal service.

Therefore, my conclusion would be that pools and traffic associations mark a natural and well-defined step forward in the progress of the railway system. That, of course, in order to avoid the evils of combination or monopoly, you must not allow the railways to do what they choose with their traffic associations or pools; but you must regulate them and keep them within certain lines. That you must make them, whether they want to or not, minister to the general public good. That they must look upon the railways not as a private business, but as a trust for the public. And that, within those lines and under a general supervision, far from pooling and traffic associations being a menace to the community, they really, so far as I can ascertain, offer the only way out of the chief evils from which we at present suffer in railway transportation. And that this is not merely a personal opinion, a fad, an idea, can be seen from the history of pools and traffic associations of all other countries of the world; and we find that in one form or another, wherever we have any vestige of competition left at all, where you have not a complete and absolute monopoly, you have these pools and traffic associations; and that even where the Government runs the railways, it forms pools and traffic associations with the railways that enter a competing

State; all of which shows that there is and must be some underlying cause which makes these things inevitable and which will compel them to endure whatever be the attitude of legislation. You may have as many laws against them as you like; if the economic forces are in favor of this institution, you will have the institution, no matter what your law. The only effect of the law may be to render secret what ought to be in the light of day; and you will thus add to the difficulties of the problem by preventing publicity and by increasing secrecy, but not in any way by doing away with the institution itself. That is, therefore, the general attitude upon it.

Q. (By Professor JOHNSON.) Do you believe in the municipalization of the street railway service, or would you have the service left in the hands of private corporations?—A. I think that everybody is agreed at present in this country that the relations between the Government and the street railways have not been close enough—I mean in an honorable, straightforward way. But it seems to me that the problem can, for the present, be attacked far better in this country by municipal regulation of street railways in the direction of greater revenue from them than by immediate governmental assumption of management. And I would base that opinion mainly on this ground, that of the three points that I have mentioned, the widespread social interest, the capital invested, and the complexity of management, the second and third apply, to a large extent, to street railways. Of course, the complexity of management in a street railway is not by any means so great as in a steam railway; it is a far smaller business; but still there is a greater complexity of management than there would be in the case of the telegraph or of waterworks or anything of that kind.

On the other hand, the capital involved is tremendous, and for that reason it seems to me that the safer plan would be to safeguard the interests of the public through governmental regulation rather than through governmental management, in the face of the immense changes that are going on at present in the methods of street railway management. We all know that we are just living in a period in which the methods of street railway management have been revolutionized, and who can tell but in another 5 or 10 years they will be revolutionized again.

If now you put it in the hands of Government, you reduce to that extent the chance that the Government will avail itself of all the new advances of science, and until we have gotten down to a condition of affairs which may be considered permanent, I should think that the argument was rather in favor of governmental control than of governmental management of street railways. I think it differs altogether in that respect; for instance, from the water supply, because in the case of the water supply there is not any question of capital involved, or not so much, and far less question of complexity of management, because the methods of management are very simple indeed. It is simply a question of getting the water and then distributing it through pipes, which is a simple matter. In the case of a railway system it is a very different matter.

Q. (By Mr. FARQUHAR.) You believe, then, in taxing the railroads all that they will stand for the benefit of the public and the general community?—A. I should not put it in that way. I should put it that the street railways ought to bear a far greater part of the municipal burdens than they do at present; that they ought to contribute far more largely than they do at present to the municipal revenues.

Q. Would there be a great difficulty there in the way of these old charters, the chartered life of these corporations, the 99-year franchise and such like? How are the municipalities going to get new taxation under these long charters?—A. We have an example of that in the new franchise tax law of which I was speaking; this new law applies to the street railways as well as to the others.

Q. An attempt was made in Ohio a short time ago to get a 99-year law through for the life of all these street corporations.—A. (Interrupting.) With a fixed rate of taxation during all that time?

Q. Yes.—A. Well, of course, that would be an argument simply against the policy of giving long leases, long iron-clad leases.

Q. And where those municipalities also, Professor, or combinations had an auction made public through public advertisements and sold these rights of franchises for their streets, when it has amounted to a large sum, has it not always been to undertake the service until they make a new arrangement?—A. That has been very frequently the result.

Testimony closed.

Whereupon at 1.25 p. m. the commission adjourned the further taking of testimony until to-morrow morning at 10.30.

WASHINGTON, D. C., *December 7, 1899.*

TESTIMONY OF MR. GEORGE R. BLANCHARD,

Late commissioner of the former Joint Traffic Association.

The commission met at 10.35 a. m., Senator Kyle presiding. Mr. George R. Blanchard, of New York City, N. Y., was introduced as a witness, and, being duly sworn, testified as follows:

Q. (By Senator KYLE.) Please state your name and address and business.

A. George R. Blanchard, late commissioner of the former Joint Traffic Association.

Senator KYLE. Mr. Blanchard, I believe has prepared carefully a statement which he is to present to the commission, and will present it in his own way from the beginning to the end, and if the commissioners discover any points they would like to have elaborated, they can make note of them, and ask questions, or defer to the close of the witness' testimony, as they see fit. You may proceed now, Mr. Blanchard.

WITNESS. (Reading:) In responding to your request for my testimony in various matters relating to land transportation charges, by rail, I premise by saying that as the general term "Science" includes many branches, so the word "Transportation" embraces multitudinous and intricate conditions of state, national and international thought, labor, development, change, discovery, disappointments, and triumphs in each of its great departmental avenues, and as each applied science has eminent specialists in its various avenues, so transportation has them in construction, operation, law, commercial relations, etc. You have, therefore, wisely divided this great general subject into topical forms, and have properly asked your witnesses to limit themselves to those subdivisions of the carrying problem as to which they are severally most experienced and informed.

As a railway traffic officer and member, chairman and commissioner of various associations, my knowledge has been greatest in the commercial channels of railway administration, and I will endeavor to limit myself thereto.

My testimony will represent my personal views, and not those of any railway company or organization.

FIRST.

JUSTIFICATION FOR DISSIMILAR FARES.

Your topical plan says, in part II, division A, paragraph 25: "Passenger rates; Differences in different parts of the United States; Causes and effects; Local and through rates."

The legitimate causes of differences in passenger fares, briefly epitomized, are—

(*a*) Because various original charters and amendments thereto, legislation and varying legal decisions in different States, originally warranted and still sanction differences in fares in various forms in adjacent as well as separated areas. For illustration, the New York Central Company is limited by law to 2 cents per passenger per mile, with some exceptions, while other roads in the same State and in other States are not.

(*b*) Dissimilar volumes of passenger traffic justify differences in fares—as, for example, those of the New Haven System contrasted with the fares of the Colorado Midland or Mobile and Ohio Companies. Five cents per mile with 10 passengers per car is not as profitable as 50 passengers per car at 2 cents per mile each. Moreover, on some lines some passenger trains may be run at a loss to aid the public convenience as well as other branches of the passenger or freight service.

(*c*) The dissimilar first costs of railway construction and, later, their varying expenses of maintenance, as when numerous high mountain elevations are to be surmounted on some lines as compared with the nearly level gradients of other routes, may justify due differences of fares. Compare, for example, the Denver and Rio Grande and the California and Oregon line in this respect with the Lake Shore and New York Central railways.

(*d*) The costs of terminal facilities and improvements, as shown by the large expense for costly lands in great cities compared with the lesser expense at smaller points, say New York contrasted with Norfolk.

The great outlay for elevated tracks in cities is also becoming a factor in this connection.

(*e*) Fares may differ in different sections as aids to freight development, as the special fares made for coal miners, lumbermen, large manufacturing concerns widely apart yet strongly competitive, etc.

(*f*) The speeds and equipments of passenger trains. The New York Central and Pennsylvania Limited trains, for example, are the most expensive in the world, having dining, buffet, apartment, and observation cars, all vestibuled, equipped with both gas and electric lighting apparatus and carrying an unusual number of employees per train—such as stenographer, barber, stewardess, special electrical engineer, etc.

By reason of the large space given to each passenger in those exceptional trains the number of passengers per car average less than one-half those per car of those carried in ordinary trains. The fewer cars per limited train are nevertheless necessary to uniform high through speed to overcome high grades and summits, differences of distance, etc., and all other trains give way to them when delays occur, thereby increasing their expense. It also costs more to maintain the costlier outfits of these swifter trains. All these elements mean lesser net earnings per car and per train mile and justify higher fares, even more than the same companies charge for travel in their regular trains at slower speed which carry many more passengers per car and per train.

For illustration, the fare by the World's Fair Special via the New York Central was fixed by arbitration at $6 above the so-called standard fare from New York to Chicago as an amount representing its speed, facilities, luxuries, etc. The steamship lines charge on the same basis and their patrons do not demur.

(*g*) Differential lines of about equal length, which compete with such superior service may perhaps justly charge lower fares for their less expensive through trains and the slower time over their longer distances. Reasonable and due concessions from the so-called standard fares—by which is meant the fares by the best equipped lines—have therefore been recognized and used to equalize these diversities until the so-called differential lines approach closer parities of time and facility, or assent to equal fares for other reasons.

(*h*) Commutation travel, being larger in volume and value and more regular—say as to and from New York City and Philadelphia and about Chicago and Boston, than between St. Louis and East St. Louis or Cincinnati and Kentucky points, etc.—justify different charges to commuters on those different lines. Low commutation fares may justify and influence the duration of standard or regular fares. It may also be just that commutation fares to and from the grand central station in New York differ from those in and out of Jersey City. New York ferriage also constitutes an item of difference in some instances.

(*i*) Some differences in fares arise from the fact that some of them are State fares, others interstate.

(*k*) Growing factors in this connection are the trolley fares parallel to some standard-gauge lines in the same general districts, but not in others. For example, there may be trolley lines in three directions from Philadelphia, and none from Louisville or Omaha. The companies thereat may justifiably make different fares on those different trains from this cause.

(*l*) The proximity of water routes. The Hudson River may particularly regulate some fares between New York and Albany; the boat lines on Long Island Sound may influence rail fares to common points on its waters, and via such points to Providence and Boston; the Ohio River between Cincinnati and Louisville, etc. The lake fares from Chicago to Milwaukee may influence those by rail between the same points. No such causes affect fares about Denver or New Orleans, yet the differences in various fares thereabouts as compared with those east or west thereof may be justified on other grounds.

(*m*) Some of the foregoing causes may operate to create different fares for 1,000, 2,000, and 5,000 mile tickets in different sections, as well as in commutation, excursion, and round trip fares, and the time periods during which various tickets are made available may also be justifiably unlike.

(*n*) Specially reduced fares for large bodies traveling together also vary in different sections. Witness dissimilar reductions to the Grand Army, the Society of Christian Endeavor, commercial conventions, the National Educational Association, etc., west of Chicago and St. Louis and south of the Ohio River as compared with those east and north thereof. The fares in the same section also differ justly for summer excursions over long distances and alternate routes and possibly over the same railways between the same points.

(*o*) Different fares are, for these and minor reasons, equitable in the same general territories as well as in separated districts, and they appear generally acceptable to interstate travelers.

(*p*) These reasonably dissimilar fares practically classify travel somewhat as it is classified abroad and somewhat as freights are classified, but each and every fare is available here to all who desire or may be entitled to use one in preference to the others or to change from one to another, as the traveler's surroundings justify or require. It is as the same travelers classify the shops where they deal in the apparel they buy, the hotels or theaters they patronize. the stage or street car they prefer to a cab, etc.

The underlying differences in the governmental import and postage tariffs are founded upon the same principles of warrantable dissimilarities—as, for example, cloths and wines differing in value for like weight, or a letter compared with a postal card occupying the same space, etc.

Why should the reasoning for the Government—i. e., the people—not govern for that essential need of the people, i. e., the railways?

(q) Some differences of through fares may be caused by the policy and action of Canadian lines as compared with ours—notably the Canadian Pacific.

(r) It is not that fares are dissimilar in different districts which caused discriminations, but the dissimilar fares on the same classes of travel in the same district.

To generalize these principal conditions, it may be said that the railways of the country tend to resolve themselves into its own natural geographical divisions:

1. East of the Hudson River and Lake Champlain.

2. The territory west thereof lying between the Great Lakes on the north, the Potomac and Ohio rivers on the south, and east, substantially, of Chicago and St. Louis.

3. All south of the Ohio and Potomac to the Gulf and east of the Mississippi River to the Atlantic Ocean.

4. All west of that group to the Missouri River or Denver meridian, forming what may be called the Rocky Mountain division.

5. All west of that group to the Pacific Ocean, constituting the transcontinental division.

6. The Canadian group, having also affiliated lines in and across the United States.

7. Our Hawaiian, Philippine, and Alaskan interests, rival to the Dominion, Isthmus, and Suez lines, which will hereafter more require special consideration and perhaps exceptional consideration as to through fares.

For the reasons adduced it is impracticable, either in usage or law, to make the fares for like general service alike in all these areas, yet the more or less justifiable disparities cited are gradually being lessened under those natural, but in many cases slowly unfolded and unenacted laws, which enlarge travel and commerce and which have operated more potentially than statutes, especially since the Windom report. These great laws are unceasing in effect, modified readily by railway administrators from constant and long experience, are equitable and comprehensive in plan, scope, and effect, and adapt themselves in due differences of measure to the variety of conditions encountered in these traffic empires. As lines extend their consolidations across former territorial borders, more uniform and lower average fares will more prevail. Witness the unification and uniformity of fares when such mergers removed the Mississippi River as a barrier to continuous travel, tickets, and baggage checks. As populations, railway amalgamations, and comprehensive betterments increase they will further justify more or swifter trains, a better general service, further concessions in fares, and a nearer approximation to uniformity of fares for each class of travel affected. Legitimate competition will then compel extensions of these liberalized facts, acts, and policies over parallel routes, as the same causes have been similarly forceful upon them in freight rates and classifications, bringing, as in the past, mutual public and corporate benefits. No statute law is needful or helpful to such advancing advantages and uniformity, because these evolutions are as natural and forceful as the sequence of the seasons from winter to harvest.

SECOND.

THE MISUSE OF PASSES.

Your paragraphs 26, 27, and 28, under the same head, relate largely to various phases of the issues and uses of passes, and I answer:

(a) Free passes are doubtless given to shippers in undue number, result in some unjustifiable discriminations in both freight and passenger traffic, and deplete due and reasonable earnings.

Nevertheless some passes issued to shippers may be regarded as justifiable. The successful merchant becomes the desirable railway director or president, and, as such, receives free travel over various lines, but railways cannot discriminate between his use of his pass for his railway and his business account. Another equally large merchant may not be so circumstanced and unintentional preferences may thus result.

(*b*) The passes issued to persons accompanying live stock are intended to secure experienced care for animals in transit.

(*c*) Some passes issued to manufacturers may be wholly or measurably compensated for in the various freight rates involved in their business, and while appearing to be free tickets are not always so. I think the two should be dissociated.

(*d*) Most passes issued for account of charitable considerations are unquestioned in purpose, but even they are liable to some abuses.

(*e*) Some press passes or reduced-fare tickets are issued in exchange for newspaper and other advertising. They constitute a convenience to the press in getting news and identifying the holders of such tickets and save the keeping of detailed accounts and the passage of moneys. It also seems desirable in these instances that each such transaction represent itself, as in the sales of other tickets.

(*f*) Exchange passes are issued for specified officers of connecting lines, car companies, etc., but I believe that if no passes were issued to anyone except officers or employees of a company and members of their own families over its own line, or for equally proper considerations, carefully limited, legislation would be measurably benefited, proper earnings saved, and discriminations in fares lessened as between persons and localities. The revenues of the freight and passenger departments would also then be more justly assigned to each as properly due. It would also tend to lessen discriminations in freight rates if the militant army of freight solicitors paid their fares on the lines of other companies which they invade in order to influence the routing, or the tariff rates, of the initial lines, who of right should specify the exact net through rates and the routes to be used. They should be paid as all their other proper expenses are paid by their employers.

(*g*) So far as the unwarrantable issue of passes to legislators and public officers is concerned, that subject can be most effectively handled by the bodies whose members accept such passes.

THIRD.

TICKET SCALPING OR BROKERAGE.

Your paragraphs 29, 30, and 31 invite consideration to ticket brokerage, commonly called "scalping," which I believe to be artificial, meretricious, and discriminating.

A mass of technical facts upon this subject and the conclusions drawn therefrom lie in the expert testimony pro and con before committees of both Houses of Congress, notably in January, 1898.

Therein it was shown that at that time 346 newspapers, substantially all the railway and steamship passenger lines of the United States, the laws of 10 States, the long example of Canada, the resolutions of numerous national, State, and mercantile associations, the resolutions of the railway commissioners of 19 States, the insistent and repeated views of the Interstate Commerce Commission, the lesson taught by every other railway country of the earth, the due protection of the large organizations to whom special fares are granted and to the railways granting them, the due observance of law, and the best moral sense of all the commercial world were all arrayed on the honest side of every phase of this question.

Per contra, ticket brokerage was defended by not over 3 railroads and 560 ticket brokers, the latter, as a class, being marshaled to perpetuate and even strengthen, by the sanction, defeat, or evasion of law, every pernicious feature and practice of the objectionable calling. Some legislators and others withheld their opposition to or gave the scalpers their indirect support mainly because they misunderstood the question or thought the railways held the cures and should apply them rather than because they sanctioned the practices of misrepresentation or wrongs abundantly proven against the guild as a whole.

The antiscalping argument stands primarily upon the unshaken ground that the proper places to buy proper railway tickets are the authorized ticket offices of the initial companies, and the only proper officers to sell them are the duly deputed agents of such starting lines or their authorized connections, and not in the private offices of self-constituted agents, having no authorized rights of representation or agency. Stock and merchandise brokers act by authority of principals, and only railway ticket brokers practice methods to reduce legal railway revenues without any due authority, because, to sell tickets cheaper than the published fares, scalpers must get them cheaper. They are therefore illegal, and such sellers must resort to every known device for personal gain.

Substantially, therefore, every dollar they realize belongs to some railway company or passenger who has been wronged to that extent.

Proceeding from these foundation principles, we oppose scalping:

(a) Because its cessation means the stoppage of many secret, fraudulent, and illegal practices, which create undue, unreasonable, and unauthorized discriminations in the passenger fares duly made, published, posted, and filed according to law.

(b) Because resold tickets cut the local fares from the points where they are sold, and thereby produce fares and differences in fares not intended or authorized by the railroads and forbidden by law. To that extent they create unjustifiable preferences between persons, localities, and also to trade bodies, conventions, and other associations moving in large numbers by extending the reduced fares granted to such bodies to persons not entitled to receive or use them.

(c) Because the closing of unauthorized brokers' offices would doubtless stop the inducements now existing to steal, alter, forge, counterfeit, or plug tickets, or issue tickets bearing fictitious indorsements as to extensions of time, and would also curb or prevent the sales of passes, advertising, editorial, and mileage tickets by sellers, buyers, and reissuers. It is also to be emphasized that it would substitute authorized and accurate information to the traveler, for the false representations now constantly made by brokers in order to sell their tickets, in respect of routes, time, change of cars, sleeping cars, checking of baggage, connections, etc. Recent tests show the great extent to which this misrepresentation still exists.

I would like to say in connection with this subject that the ticket offices of the scalpers in New York were visited recently, and in nearly all of those visited untrue or misleading representations were made in some regard as to connections, time, or some other fact in connection with the actual facilities of travel.

Q. (By Professor JOHNSON.) How could you get at that information?—A. By sending persons to the scalpers' offices to ask if such and such lines made certain connections, or did this or that, would such and such tickets be accepted on certain trains, etc., the time of trains, number of times transfers took place, and information of that general kind.

Q. And you know from sending for that information?—A. Yes. (Continued reading:)

(d) Because scalpers have induced some conductors not to cancel tickets taken up, in order that they may resell them in their scalping offices—and sometimes more than once—for their joint benefit.

(e) Because they have corrupted clerks and ticket distributors in some railway general offices by inducing them to purloin and dispose of irregularly issued tickets for a consideration.

(f) Because many scalpers operate in clear violation of law, notably in the 10 States wherein they nullify the statutes thereof.

(g) Because many scalping offices are in the nature of fences or pawn shops, both of which latter are subject to legal or police regulations and examinations, while scalpers' offices, being used for similar purposes in another commodity escape such safeguards against misuse and fraud.

(h) Because the railroad companies are held responsible for disturbing passenger conditions, which they disapprove, and which they ask the aid of law to effectually resist and prevent.

(i) Because scalpers incite railroad wars and reprisals as the best means by which they can procure the greatest number of tickets at the lowest cost and, by shifting their business from one road to another and by working in conjunction with other unauthorized or pliable agencies, they have frequently produced the serious contentions in fares which they desired.

(k) Because when a railway company decides to secretly reduce one or more classes of through fares, it dares not do it in its own offices in violation of the interstate act, of various State statutes and of the several tariffs which it has published, filed and posted pursuant thereto, but usually avails of ticket scalpers' offices to collusively violate the act, a course which involves better-intending lines in a demoralized scramble for business. I do not mean that this practice is now even considerably resorted to by the railroads. It has been gradually circumscribed, but if scalping offices were altogether abolished, or their authority required to be made legal, it would tend to the entire cessation of these joint resources and practices.

(l) Because scalpers afford no honest information or accommodations to travelers which the railroad companies do not desire to extend to all their patrons under just and uniform charges and rules, administered through their authorized bureaus of information and redemption, where they will return to the holders of unused portions of tickets all amounts exceeding the fares which duly accrue between the points which the passenger actually traverses, correct errors of their agents in selling tickets as to routes, the erroneous checking or losses of baggage, etc. Even the scalpers must send their patrons to such offices for those purposes, or substitute a show of authority made up often of fraud, ignorance, collusion, dishonesty, and depleted and unequal fares. The railroad ticket agents at all points will transmit unused coupons to the redemption bureaus and give all desired information.

(*m*) Railway companies sometimes decline to issue reduced-fare tickets of such forms as are easily manipulated because of the certainty that scalping will ensue and thus unduly extend the privilege granted to unauthorized users of such tickets. The same fear actuates some companies to impose conditions upon the faces of their special tickets and limit their durations of sale and use, whereas, if scalpers' officers were abolished, they could safely dispense with such safeguards, because the bona fide passenger would not use the methods, misrepresentations, or abuses which scalpers practice.

(*n*) The cessation of scalping would in no wise lessen the public facilities, because each company could retain the services of any experienced scalper by conferring upon him a proper appointment as agent and regulate him thereafter by the rules which govern their other agents.

(*o*) There are two organized bodies of scalpers: The American Ticket Brokers' Association and the Guarantee Ticket Brokers' Association. They have their directors, officers, agents, rules and regulations, they discuss and decide some questions of cut fares, and they adopt resolutions and deal with the property of others in which they have no direct interest, while, at the same time, under the decision of the Supreme Court, the railroad companies cannot adopt counter agreements without violating its decisions.

Moreover, the rules and decisions of the Interstate Commerce Commission do not reach scalpers' fares or practices, because they hold the railways accountable. Furthermore, the fares of the railway companies proper can only be changed by 3 days' notice as to reductions and 10 days' notice as to advances, while the scalpers can change them either way daily or hourly. In this way a railway company, acting with a scalper, can also change the fares and evade the law. There is a manifest injustice in all this which could and should be corrected by appropriate national legislation.

(*p*) Another feature of ticket brokerage has not been sufficiently urged upon public attention. If a passenger purchasing a through ticket from New York to Chicago is required or desires to discontinue his journey at Buffalo, the unused coupon west of Buffalo will be redeemed by the issuing company or its unused connection. If he takes the same unused coupon to a scalper, he is offered by him less for the ticket from Buffalo to Chicago than the railway would redeem it for. His fare from New York to Buffalo would, therefore, be more than its due amount to the extent that he received less than his remaining coupon was worth. Against this the purchasing passenger west of Buffalo may get a ticket under the legal fare but he is not entitled by law to that preference. In this way we answer the loudly vaunted public advantages of brokers and venture the further assertion that if scalping was abolished the average fares paid by passengers would not exceed those which prevail under its continuance.

(*q*) The payment of commissions by railroad companies is an inciting cause to the continuance of scalping because such commissions are often divided between scalper and passenger. The payment of commissions is justly chargeable upon the railways. Therefore I think that with the discontinuance of the one should go the stoppage of the other, and the perpetuation of either or both of the evils may prevent, in some instances, open and uniform reductions of fare more nearly to the net basis received out of the fares from which commissions and scalping must be deducted before the real or true fares are ascertained.

(*r*) I believe you would promptly advocate our view if corresponding brokerage offices were opened throughout the country for scalping freight rates through advancing, reducing, manipulating, and secretly and fraudulently altering them for the benefit of some shippers by persons utterly unauthorized to deal with such values and bills of lading. Yet I know of no act or justification in the scalping of tickets and fares which would not with equal justice warrant similar scalping in freight rates and bills of lading.

(*s*) I leave to counsel the legal arguments growing out of various decisions pro and con, some of them recent, upon this subject. I am, however, qualified to discuss it by the statement that if that law is best which is expressive of the highest justice, then an act should be passed in this respect which will secure for the mutual, personal, and commercial relations of the citizen and carrier the observance of reciprocal justice, right, and the protection of property. I also leave in their more competent hands the questions of legislative passes.

FOURTH—AS TO FREIGHT TOPICS.

GENERAL OBSERVATIONS.

You invite a very encyclopedia of information, reasoning, and conclusion as to "unjust discriminations and undue preferences," but only a hasty review is practicable now.

The first railway built in this country was in 1826, a tram, 4 miles long, to transport granite. There are now about 190,000 miles of main track, or 250,000 miles, including double, terminal, and lateral tracks.

In constructing this enormous mileage, being over one-half that of the world, within 73 years in over 3,000,000 square miles of area, covering 53 States and Territories, which were often commercially and legislatively antagonistic, depending also largely upon municipal, county, State, and national interests and assistance not always similar or concurrent, and controlled as to the most important of their earlier rates by parallel natural or artificial waters, and influenced or decided by the newness of the questions in many important aspects, many abuses crept into railway construction and subsequent administration for which legislative bodies were often equally responsible with railway organizers.

Railway promoters, therefore, operated sometimes upon questionable bases, judged both from their own or the people's interests, and competing cities, counties, States, and the General Government vied to attract intending lines, in order to secure capital, native settlers, and foreign emigrants, and thereby achieve a quickened local and national growth and international markets and interchanges. Witness the great franchises granted to the Illinois Central, Union Pacific, Texas Pacific, and other lines, the State aids to the Baltimore and Ohio and Pennsylvania railroads, etc.

Attractive charters, land grants, immunities, and exemptions from taxation, broad powers—as fixing rates and fares—public subscriptions of stocks and bonds, donations of lands and moneys, etc., were, therefore, generally sought and conceded. Then the interests of adjacent districts which failed to secure the first railways proceeded to organize and equally encourage other competing enterprises

These artificial stimulations relapsed, as do all undue elations, into mutual sobriety and regrets. Discouragements in the costs of building and in the resultant quantities of traffic, geographical and railway rivalries and other causes, then led to transportation methods and legislation often indefensible. Public contentions, restrictions and forfeitures followed by ordinance, State law, and national agitation and decisions. The changes from a people's acclaim to their opposition was shown by the enthusiasm which fired the western world when the transcontinental line opened in 1869, as compared with the adverse granger legislation which ensued largely thereafter.

Most of the first railways were constructed to first connect important objective points between which there were inadequate local traffics. The pioneer trunk line, the Baltimore and Ohio, and the first transcontinental line are instances in point. Thereafter, what with felling forests, transferring stump grounds into arable lands, opening coal mines, urging manufacturing works, etc., the intermediate traffic was developed and often became the more important resource. However many or few the bonds or stocks issued to construct such lines, their holders were compelled to await returns thereon from the slow developments of the territories traversed. To accelerate these various results some rates were made excessive and some were reduced by favoritism, but before profits were reached many of the most important railway companies defaulted upon their interest, were sold out and reorganized, and much, if not all of the so-called water was thus pressed out of them again. But bear in mind that, however much the railway promoters lost or made, the people of the countries traversed invariably benefited the most from every local and national point of view.

Moreover, the rates and fares fixed upon the opening of all the important railway lines represented their highest charges and have since been continually reduced, as has been amply and often pro en, until our patrons now enjoy the lowest rates and fares of the world, and the best and speediest average service, and American railway labor receives the highest wages in the world for less onerous duty, and for the fewer hours which constitute a day's work.

Notwithstanding these truths the public appreciation of the values of the railways as the greatest factors of home and foreign trade has constantly lessened, and municipal, State, and National legislation and taxation have increasingly restricted them or denied them the adequate consideration given, for example, to our manufacturing interests, but National and State legislatures constantly entertain, consider, or enact accumulating restrictions upon the railways, and the courts inherit, proclaim, and enforce this tendency. Within five years number-less National, State, and municipal measures have been enacted, or are now pend-ing, to reduce rates and fares, for pro rata rates, amended bills of lading, car couplers, automatic brakes and safety appliances, more protection for labor, grade crossings, speed of trains, elevated tracks in cities, reduced working hours, legis-lation as to strikes, more taxation, etc., all intended to decrease net railway revenues or having that effect, and now it is proposed to so amend the interstate law as to give the approving and veto powers over all interstate rates to five rela-tively inexperienced gentlemen, one of whom may, under the majority rule, become the political, geographical, legal, and business arbiter of the whole vast problem.

I know that the railways desire only reciprocal conditions which will represent the just equality of all shippers under like conditions and circumstances, the due relations of all United States railways and localities, and the proper recognition and adjustment of our transportation interests to those operating in adjacent foreign countries, and, still further, due respect for our nation's laws. Yet each attempt on our part to secure legislative reciprocity for so broad and mutual an internal national and international policy is met with the hypercritical judgment of the majority, that such measures are "intended to benefit only the railways," to the "injury of their patrons;" that it means a "restraint of trade," a "tend-ency to monopoly," the "cessation of competition," and is "in effect a trust," con-tentions which enlightened bodies like yours can greatly help to successfully dis-pel from the knowledge these hearings will give you.

FIFTH.

FREIGHT DISCRIMINATIONS AGAINST PERSONS.

The topical queries in your paragraphs 32 and 33 deal with the causes, extent, and manner of discriminating concessions against persons, places, and other rail-ways.

Discriminations against persons result mainly from secret rebates, which create unequal rates on direct through shipments or in combinations of rates on inward materials and outward products, so as to affect the through charges. In much less degree they arise from favoritisms in terminal facilities; quicker time in transit; unequal or hidden allowances in weights; dissimilar storage periods in cars or warehouses; preferences in supplying cars when the demand for them exceeds the supply; differences in special charges, such as switching, loading or unloading, or in cartage allowances; advantages alleged to be extended to enter-prises in which the carriers may have interests, mainly coal; paying large for-warders mileages for cars so much in excess of legal interest on the cars furnished and repairs and depreciation as to be equivalent to abatements in rates; the leas-ing of elevators to or making elevator contracts with large handlers of grain, to their exceptional advantage; the grant of undue allowances under the fictitious guise of commissions, etc., and other minor advantages granted to preferred patrons.

The effects of these wrongful methods can be briefly stated.

They uniformly upbuild the recipients thereof and as uniformly injure those who do not receive them. They are vicious, indefensible, and illegal in their con-ceptions and results, whether their results touch one or all of the producers, mid-dlemen, or consumers affected, yet they are most difficult of regulation or stoppage.

SIXTH.

THE EXTENT TO WHICH PREFERENTIAL RATES ARE GRANTED.

In paragraph 40 you ask, "To what extent are lower rates than those published granted to individuals?"

The extent to which rates are depleted by preferential rebates differs in various parts of the country or in the same sections or on the same or competing railways at different times, as the conditions more or less vary as the traffic is competitive or noncompetitive, or greater or less in quantity, the scarcity of cars, and for other reasons.

The delinquent companies never impart actual knowledge of this evil to their own commissioners more than they do to those of the Government. They are secret in agreement and payment, and I prefer not to hazard a purely conjectural answer in this important respect.

Suffice it to say that it is an evil which I think has grown steadily since about the close of the first year after the passage of the interstate act, and I believe it will continue to increase and prove more disastrous to railway revenues and to trade so long as adequate and due legislative measures for its actual and practical regulation or prevention are delayed. Mere prohibitions of the practice by providing for increased fines and penalties have not availed and never will. I discuss this subject more fully further on.

SEVENTH.

DISCRIMINATIONS AGAINST LOCALITIES.

Discriminations against places, districts, or localities usually arise out of the individual allowances just recited, because the underlying geographical bases or scales of rates have become uniform and substantially just in the territories they severally cover. For example, the scale from Chicago eastward is just; but if a large shipper of a leading commodity enjoys preferential rates therefrom, not only are other forwarders of the same commodity at the same point injured, but also both large and small forwarders—say at St. Louis on the one side and Milwaukee on the other—as well as elsewhere intermediately and in numerous directions and places. Such preferences also cause the beneficiaries to discriminate against the other railway lines from their own cities which do not concede to them like rebates.

The outside localities, shippers, and carriers thus harmed therefore often coalesce, and as they must do business under like conditions, these bad situations are extended over wider districts, involving more shippers, railways, and points and more geographical as well as individual discriminations until, in some instances, departures from the strict tariffs may have become the rule from some points, especially when business is sluggish.

Such methods also create further geographical preferences because rebates are granted mainly from the central points, which are large reservoirs of trade, and not from smaller common points or from strictly local stations. The smaller patrons from such places are therefore most discriminated against, and geographical preferences become inseparable parts of the same reprehensible system. The "long and short haul" clause is also largely nullified thereby when the duly published tariffs are depleted at the centers but maintained from shorter points en route.

More excusable or justifiable discriminations sometimes ensue from the close geographical relations of some systems to specific localities. Thus, the Canadian Pacific Company may fairly prefer and assist the cities of the Dominion, or. the Norfolk and Western would develop Norfolk, yet the acts of those lines to those points affect the carriers thereto and cities between or competitive with them. The lines reaching from St. Paul, from the West, will preferentially aid that city and Minneapolis; the Gulf lines will develop New Orleans and Galveston; the New England lines will favor Boston, and so on.

EIGHTH.

DIFFERENCES OF CHARGE IN DIFFERENT SECTIONS.

Under this head your query relates to the complications attending the geographical adjustments of domestic rates and fares between competing localities, districts and lines and routes. The differences in fares have been presented. As to freight, and taking Chicago as a pivotal point, the determination of rates in both directions, applying upon 4,000 articles moving inward and outward over many roads of unequal length, facility, time in transit, etc., between sharply contesting points, as well as the vast number of passenger fares, can hardly be calculated. Then add the number of rates and fares involved everywhere else in the nation, and you have the problem in better form for the consideration of its magnitude.

Given, further, an export shipment at Kansas City intended for London and therefore competitive via Galveston, New Orleans, Pensacola, and all the seaboard transfer points north thereof to Montreal inclusive, at various rates which affect by law the rates to interior points under the "long and short haul" clause, as well as to and through all the ports, and how difficult becomes the task to differentiate all the rates first involved and to thereafter change them promptly to meet fairly all the mercantile and railway interests involved on land and sea? The same query is good as to competitive manufactured merchandise, say at

Grand Rapids, as compared with goods sent East and West from Rochester, Harrisburg, or Atlanta, and in innumerable instances from every point in every State to every other railway point in every other State.

Taking these multiplied rates and fares together, the work which has been accomplished toward their uniform and fair solution is astonishing and one which could not have been accomplished by a governmental bureau. In no other country are such intricacies encountered, and yet our basis adjustments are generally satisfactory and would be more so if the rebates and secret allowances which impair them were stopped. It is a much greater task than all our various governmental tariffs; especially the import schedules.

These adaptations of equitable and uniform tariff bases to different districts have been mainly brought about not by law but by railway conferences, which the tendency of law now seems to forbid as if they were conspiracies against the public weal instead of solutions of wrongs, and by many interviews between railway companies and shippers or the trade bodies representing them.

Our through rate and fare formulas are generally acceptable, because complaints on this point to the carriers, who first receive them, are most rare. I venture the assertion that not one one-thousandth of our rates and fares are ever specifically questioned to or by anyone, yet a difference of one-fourth of one cent per bushel on grain between origin and delivering points may make or unmake that commerce in a wide locality, and even largely affect the volumes of our grain and flour exports. In these readjustments farmers, millers, manufacturers, elevators, railways, and inland water and the ocean lines must be considered and share. To each must accrue some moiety of burden as well as benefit, for our railways can not bear all or keep all. Therefore, as fair adjustments are the more comprehensive and difficult, the more requisite they become. Cities, interior districts, indeed States, may be as unduly injured or benefited by inconsiderate rate adjustments as by other discriminations, except that the former are open and quickest in effect.

With the substantial and fair equations of these bases there remains little to readjust geographically except to continue a watchful regard for new conditions which may justly modify previous action. For example, the increasing competition in London of South American grain, cattle, and hides with ours may warrant reconsiderations of some of our rates thereon yet not affect others so much. The English commission's advice to "watch much but prescribe little" is a good rule alike for legislatures, commissions, and railways.

Some differences of rates appear as discriminations which are not preferences. If a coal mine or a stone quarry is at the top of a mountain and the haul is all down grade, a higher rate may reasonably and justly prevail where those conditions are reversed. Quantities of tonnage are also justifiable factors of rates. So, also, is regularity of movement.

Testifying to the vastness of these questions, the last report but one of the Interstate Commission justly said:

"The freight rate is a complex problem. * * * Very few people not acquainted with the subject have any idea how difficult the solution of that problem is. Rates between points which to a superficial observer have no connection are, in fact, interdependent."

NINTH.

THE MUTUAL PREFERENCES OF SOME INTERESTS FOR EACH OTHER.

Another class of reasonable railway preferences is for parts of continuous lines to work in behalf of their whole interest. I am not aware of any public detriment thus created. For example, the Vanderbilt system operated in its entirety between New York and Chicago naturally prefers that its westward freight go to Chicago over its own rails west of Buffalo rather than those of the Grand Trunk or Erie, and that its eastward tonnage should feed and not be diverted from its own system in detriment to its own main line. I know of no arbitrary action to that end, or that they interpose any illegal hindrances to commerce or travel seeking such mutual interchange. The same is true of the Baltimore and Ohio, Pennsylvania, Grand Trunk, Erie and other systems generally.

There is another class of justifiable preferences among connecting lines. If a great system finds that one of its connections is a persistent demoralizer of rates to the general detriment of the shippers and carriers affected, for reasons of its own, that system very properly acts to prefer its own more conservative interests or connections upon good legal, business, and other grounds.

TENTH.

THE "LONG AND SHORT HAUL" CLAUSE.

You cite the "long and short haul" clause and inquire its meaning. The answer and intent are that an interstate rate or fare between any two points on a line or route operated by one or more connecting railway carriers shall not be greater on the same article moved in the same direction, under similar circumstances and conditions, between any intermediate points on the same line or route when the lesser distance is wholly included in the greater.

Stated more tersely: An interstate rate or fare made between any two points shall not be exceeded by the rate on the same article moved over the same line, in the same direction, under similar circumstances and conditions.

I regard this provision just, as to the large majority of the tonnage and travel transported, and it has done much to correct the older evils and discriminations. There are, however, some justifiable exceptions, as in the cases of traffic between intermediate points on the transcontinental routes from ocean to ocean; traffic from New York to inland points on the all-rail routes to Galveston as compared with the rail rates to Galveston made against ocean and Gulf routes and rates; through traffic across Lake Michigan at lower than all-rail rates; Asiatic shipments traversing our country to England versus Canadian routes having no similar legal limitations, some instances of differential rail and water rates, and some other causes. In such instances higher rates for short hauls may be justified both on classified articles and on specific commodities and yet work a benefit and enlargement to trade, and not its detriment or limitation. The courts have so decided in various and recent instances.

ELEVENTH.

INTERNATIONAL AND IMPORT AND EXPORT THROUGH RATES.

We must start out with one unassailable proposition. Our own people must first have all their needs supplied. All we thereafter export is a surplus, whether it be grain, cotton, cattle, or machinery. We must therefore contest for old and open new markets. That is the universal, commercial, and national demand of all countries. How then shall we do it? If we can not do it at our regular rates we must make some special rates.

Grain and other rates from Western centers to the seaboard and Gulf cities are interstate and to Montreal international, but inasmuch as grain and other articles go abroad largely, the rates on them must be adjusted with due reference to foreign markets as well as to our domestic conditions, and the two may differ essentially. The due expansion of our commerce requires the foreign markets, and all nations are contending for them. Hence certain due differences in our internal or domestic rates compared with external or export rates from many points to many others properly ensue. For example, the grain rate from Topeka to Philadelphia proper may be decided solely by local—i. e., interstate—conditions, but the foreign markets may render either a general revision of all seaboard rates or local exceptions on exported traffic necessary and just, I know of no good reason why the rate for carrying grain from Buenos Ayres to Belfast should influence or decide a rate from Burlington, Iowa, to Providence or Boston, yet it may do so. This is essentially true also on flour, cattle, meat products, cotton, tobacco, dairy products, and much exported merchandise. The same principle also holds true as to imports. The rivalries our products encounter in foreign countries also differ. They may have one result in Bremen, and another in Havre or at Marseilles as compared with Glasgow, and require American railways to accept lower inland proportional rates to all trans-Atlantic points than the local rates to the Atlantic shore points of export.

A still further view relates to competing Canadian carriers. Much of their traffic with American lines and ours with theirs is interstate; as witness traffic from Chicago to Boston and Portland via the Grand Trunk and Canadian Pacific routes. Antagonisms are, for that reason, to be avoided, not invited. An important meeting has recently been held in Canada to devise public means by which a large share of American tonnage can be secured.

If, on the contrary, we desire and receive their reasonable cooperation, which I believe is the preference of all interests, we must give them ours. If, however, their export or import rivalry should prove unreasonable we should be prepared to meet it in through oceanic shipments and without thereby involving all our local traffic rates.

These factors add intricacies to the problem confronted, because we as much desire to attract, say, Toronto traffic to New York, Boston, etc., as do they seek to carry American products to and via Montreal.

Further, touching our reduced inland rates used as proportions of import and export through rates, it is to be said that while it may in instances be to the temporary advantage or disadvantage of certain seaports to stop it, it may be greatly to the national advantage to make such thorough rates, and what may be a disadvantage to one route to-day may become a benefit to it to-morrow by changes in ocean rates only. All the steamship companies plying between our own and foreign ports usually charge higher rates on spot freight—i. e., rates for consignments originating at our ports—than they charge upon the same articles sent upon the same ships at rates which are contracted inland for direct export upon through bills of lading. Legitimate national and international causes also frequently justify inland all-rail proportions between Chicago and New York of through rail and ocean rates—say Chicago to Bremen—less than the domestic rates from and to New York proper. As, for example, our competition in Liverpool with the wheat of the Argentine Republic and the Black Sea, or in London with other flour milled elsewhere on the Continent, clearly involve transportation as well as productive and manufacturing competitions, and may require through rail and ocean rates, say from Chicago, etc., less than the sum of the land local and ocean rates, because if such through rates are not thus made much international trade may be lost to our traders, bankers, and carriers because the carriers may properly decline to reduce all their domestic tariffs to the foreign bases made necessary by these international rivalries.

In this view there appears no good reason why the rate on flour shipped from a mill at Chicago to a local consumer at New York should be reduced to the proportional rates required from Chicago to New York en route to Antwerp. If such lower through rates prevail via any one prominent American port they also involve the through rates via all other ports to make the through rates the same. Other illustrations support this view. It is deemed a beneficial competition to maintain a route from Cincinnati to Philadelphia via Toledo and Buffalo. No link in that route receives its local rates, yet I am not aware that Toledo, Detroit, or Buffalo complain of injury to their local interests because freights pass through their gates of trade at proportions less than the rates from their own warehouses. So with Pittsburg, for example. These examples are strengthened by European shipments passing, say, through Newport News, where there is a large foreign trade and but very little local tonnage.

One fact is clear. If the New York buyer for an English grain house desires to purchase a million bushels of wheat delivered in Liverpool he will pay no more for American wheat than he would for Black Sea or Argentine wheat of like grade, and it must, therefore, be delivered there at an equivalent cost. If the sum of the Chicago wheat value, plus inland tariff rail rates and ocean rates, make the total Liverpool cost of our grain the highest, then our farmers, carriers, laborers, bankers, and others will clearly lose the trade unless the competing value is equalized. The tendency of low foreign rates through is to reduce the shore point rates so that the foreign trade reduces the prices of some articles consumed here. If, therefore, the joint rail and sea carriers reduce their respective local seaboard tariff rates to and from the seaboard to meet that international contingency, I do not believe it should be deemed cause or occasion for reducing all our grain rates to the seaboard and to inter-local points, under the long and "short haul" clause, upon like traffics not competitive with any foreign markets. To require that both the seaboard local rate and the proportional ocean rate be made the same might cause some companies to go out of the foreign trade and seek only the local tonnage to make good the loss.

I do not, therefore, concede that the effects of such inland rail differences are disastrous to American interests any more than are the differences in ocean rates hurtful to the interests of the British flag. Rather the contrary, because they create aggregate national benefits, and are taken into the account in averaging annual rates. I believe the present course helps all our country's producing interests, immigration, landowners, farmers, carriers, the boards of trade, the bankers, the laborers, the elevator interests, etc. Neither the British Government nor our own interpose objections or legislate to prevent this differential as a sea practice.

This subject has received exhaustive consideration from the Interstate Commerce Commission, and although they primarily decided that the seaboard rates on domestic consignments proper should be maintained on all foreign traffic through those points, they had subsequent occasion to review that opinion, and practically announced their inability to determine or regulate the question.

They have recently considered the subject and suggested a measure of difference, thereby conceding the principle; but a difference of fixed amount is not always just via all ports alike.

The Supreme Court said, March 30, 1896 (162 U. S. Reports, 1897), in the case of the Texas and Pacific Co. v. the Interstate Commerce Commission, involving this issue: "The tribunal may and should consider the legitimate interests of the carrying companies, as of the traders and shippers. * * * The mere fact that in this case the disparity between the through and local rates was considerable, did not warrant the circuit court of appeals in finding that such disparity constitutes an undue discrimination."

TWELFTH.

UNREASONABLY HIGH RATES.

Under the title of "Unreasonable and excessive rates," your paragraph 35 asks how they are determined, the occasions therefor, their effects on places, producers, middlemen, consumers, and the public, and by what means they can be prevented.

(a) It is a misapprehension that American railway rates are usually made arbitrarily and too often excessive, because our greatly reduced tariffs are due mainly to unalterable natural competitive forces, to the changes thereafter wrought in local rates and fares by the "long and short haul" clause of the Interstate Act, supplemented by conference, discussion, tests, changes and ultimate concurrence between our own and foreign producing and consuming interests until the interstate rates now published and filed substantially conform to equity and have the public approval. No appreciable percentage of our open rates or fares are complained of to the railways, and I believe 95 per cent or more of them are satisfactory. For examples: If a coal mine is to be opened, its owners first agree with the railway as to the rate before shipping. If a large Northern manufacturing concern or a cotton mill in the South is to be built, their projectors see all the competing railways, and they finally agree on the best rates and conditions offered. So on through the list.

Therefore, I know of no standards by which to duly gauge the varying reasonableness or unreasonableness of the all-rail rates in different parts of this country. Comparisons with the rates of Canadian and Mexican rail carriers on our northern and southern borders and the success of American rail transportation lines in competing with the free water, ocean, and river routes which surround and penetrate us, or with the canal charges which are affiliated with the lakes, rivers, and the ocean, clearly establishes their reasonableness. Many of these water lines have been aided by unsecured governmental appropriations, and the successful railway competition with them also proves the lowness of the rail rates. It is commendable to assist and improve our waterways, and perhaps to leave commerce over them free, but it is not just to attack the railways for their greater national services.

The only other good standards of comparison are our former rates and fares and the all-rail rates which now prevail for land transportation in foreign countries. Judged by any and all these bases, I unhesitatingly aver that they all prove that the vast majority of all the interstate rates in the United States are reasonable. They surely are the lowest in the world, and our merchants receive therefor the quickest service, the most abundant, exceptional, and cheapest terminals and lateral service, a greater choice of routes, are granted more general recourses under our bills of lading, the most liberal settlement of claims, and have access, through reduced rates, to more foreign countries and greater varieties of legitimate and illegitimate competition than any other shippers of the earth secure.

(b) Touching the reasonableness of rates, Mr. Nimmo, the former Chief of the Bureau of Statistics, said:

"During the year ending December 31, 1893, only sixteen cases came to a formal consideration and hearing. In only one of the cases decided was the reasonableness of the rates called in question, and in that single instance the claim was decided to be not well founded." This was after the law had operated five years.

(c) I compute that there are at least three millions of freight rates and passenger fares in this country applicable to interstate traffic in both directions and including the State rates influenced thereby. When this enormous aggregate is considered, that hundreds, and often thousands, of transactions occur annually under each rate or fare, and that complaints to the Interstate and State commissions have probably not been one one-thousandth thereof, such striking facts should also challenge legislative attention in proof that our rates and fares are reasonable and just rather than unreasonable or excessive.

(*d*) Important general facts in this connection are these:

For two generations orators urged and applauded the opening of new railway lines because they would develop fallow and great arable areas, even at the high rates then current. Indeed, reductions of such former rates were sometimes publicly opposed. A State convention at Syracuse, in December, 1858, resolved: " To recommend the passage of a law by the next legislature which shall confine the railroads of this State to the business for which they were originally created " (i. e., local traffic).

(*e*) The average rate of the New York Central Company in 1858 was 3.18 cents per ton per mile, equal to 7 cents per 100 pounds on grain from Buffalo to New York. The rate now is about six (6) cents per 100 pounds. In 1873 the all-rail grain rate from Chicago to New York was 55 cents per 100 pounds. It is now not more than one-third as much.

(*f*) In 1873 the freight rates upon 70,268 miles of railway then built averaged 2.21 cents per ton per mile for 168,000,000 tons then carried. In 1895 the rate averaged 0.839 cent for 763,800,000 tons carried upon 179,162 miles of railway, producing gross freight revenues of $743,784,451, the average rate for 1873 being over 263 per cent of the rate in 1895. The rate is still lower now.

(*g*) At the average rate charged in 1873, the freight earnings in 1895 only would have been $1,215,344,000 more than they were and over $80,000,000 more than the entire indebtedness of the States and Territories in 1890. In 1895, 179,162 miles operated paid $81,375,774 in dividends, or but $454 per mile, being but 40 per cent of the dividends per mile paid in 1872. The gross mileage increased 310 per cent; the gross dividends only 26 per cent. These conditions have recently improved. Of American railway earnings in 1895, 68 per cent was derived from freights, 24 per cent from passengers, and 8 per cent from miscellaneous sources. The gross receipts upon each ton of freight moved in that year averaged 97 cents and 48 cents upon each passenger carried. The addition of but 1 cent per ton on each ton carried in 1895 would have been $7,638,000 and 1 cent on each passenger carried would have been $5,439,742, or say $13,000,000 for both, It can not be assumed as to this item that the consumer is entitled to constant reductions and that the railway shareholder is never entitled to an advance.

Apportioning the dividends paid upon stock in 1895 in the above proportions, the freight account would be chargeable with $55,335,526 and the passenger account with $19,530,187, equal to but 7.2 cents per ton and 3.6 cents per passenger carried, these figures including all distances.

(*h*) Poor's Manual for 1895 reported $5,182,122,000 of railway stock capital outstanding. The dividends on stock in that year being $81,375,774, the average rate of dividends was 1.57 per cent. The Government reports say that nothing was paid in that year on $3,475,640,253 of this stock, being 68 per cent of the whole amount outstanding.

(*i*) Had the average charge for transporting 1 ton 1 mile which obtained in 1888—the first full year of the interstate act—been charged in 1895, the freight revenues for 1895 would have been $122,223,523 more than they were. Railway taxation increased in the same period from $25,435,229 to $39,250,000, or 54 per cent, facts which seem to prove a sufficient evaporation of the " water " in stocks to satisfy the most optimistic hydraulicon.

THIRTEENTH.

COMPARISONS WITH FOREIGN RATES.

A comparison of a few of the rates charged on American and foreign railways may prove serviceable.

Edward Bates Dorsey, commenting in 1886 upon " American and British Railways Compared," said of the relative freight rates:

" The rate as given from Liverpool to Birmingham (97 miles) on grain and flour is $3.01 per gross ton, and the rate as given from Chicago to New York (1,000 miles) is $5.60 per gross ton." (It is now about $4.)

J. S. Jeans, writing on " Railroad Problems " (London, 1886), said: "English railways practically work on the same tariffs to-day they did in the infancy of the system," and " it is probable that the average ton mile rate on English railways will not be much, if any, under 1½d. (3 cents), which is just *three times* the amount charged on the principal American lines."

Our rates have been reduced since then very much more per mile than have those in England.

The average receipts of the European railways in 1890 were $9,800 per mile; ours $5,700, or but 59 per cent as much. We also had 26.5 miles of railway for every 10,000 inhabitants; Great Britain and Ireland, Germany, France, and Austria-Hungary averaged but 5.4 miles.

THROUGH FREIGHT RATES AND ROUTES.

Through freight routes and rates, referred to in your paragraph 37, need but little comment.

Through rates and fares were formerly made by adding those from point to point, charges for terminals and bridge service, etc. The responsibilities and rules of carriage of the several links in the through lines were dissimilar, uncertain, and clashing, diverse bills of lading and tickets were used, the settlements of claims were delayed and made on different bases, no road was accountable except for its own carriage under these varying rules and orders, transfers of tonnage and persons were many at numerous junctions, unequal rules of lading per car prevailed, the classifications were numerous, local, and unlike, the time in through transit was much longer, diverse rules of car service, storage, and delivery were usual, and added to these conditions the through charges were over four times those now prevailing. These facts were true of the line composed of the Hudson River Railroad to Albany, thence the New York Central and Lake Shore or Michigan Central roads to Toledo and Detroit, thence rail to Chicago, and so on beyond. They now offer more and better alternate routes to shippers than exist in any country on earth.

Such illustrations might be many times multiplied. The solutions and transformations, now almost entire, are so desirable to the railroads themselves as helps to economy in car supply and movement, return lading, relative peace with the public, swifter time, enlarged traffic, etc., that they can not again be abridged, and every change has been for the public benefit and will continue to be. So that no shippers would again favor the old semi-detached methods of carrying through freights from point to point under the warring conditions and difficulties above recited, because they now receive one through bill of lading, carrying one rate, one responsibility, and like rules, and, what is more, on much quicker time and at greatly lower rates.

These bettered facilities were the native evolutions of trade necessities, common ownerships of continuous routes, absorptions of branches, improvements at transfer stations, the betterments of terminal facilities, more uniformity in the equipments used, authentic representation by more joint agencies, the designation of specific cars for given traffics or routes, and other gradually improved smaller conditions, like the telegraph, telephone, electric light, elevators instead of staircases in warehouses, and others of the great and minor adjuncts and conveniences, developers, distributors, and pushers of improved intercourse and commerce; facts which will continue forceful and controlling hereafter, as in the past. I do not, therefore, believe that there is now any necessity for, nor any good to be accomplished by, any legislation as to continuous or additional routes. The self-interests of the carriers will provide and regulate them.

It is now the rule that lines entitled thereto receive such representation in the joint tariffs of connecting lines as may best and reasonably facilitate tonnage and travel interchanges, provided that the relations are harmonious and the compensation and divisions equal to those accruing via existing lines. To force upon the railroad companies owning the parent stems the formation of connections which may be comparatively antagonistic, weak in experience and equipment, and which will increase expenses, is not demanded by any public welfare. It should also be known that sometimes, under such a law, ulterior, unnecessary, and publicly hurtful motives might actuate the demands for such new lines. No captious proposal should, therefore, receive your indorsement that the railroad companies shall be required by law to increase their expenses in order to organize needless through lines not natural, cooperative, or complete in their affiliations, connections, or facilities, and which can not compete with others now more effectively and satisfactorily equipped. Moreover, unless new lines were equally well organized they would constitute trade hindrances rather than helps. Such a proposal also savors of requiring, by law, that the largest manufacturing concerns shall appoint as agents everybody who may apply for such an appointment.

FREIGHT CLASSIFICATIONS.

Touching dissimilar freight classifications and the causes therefor, as referred to in your paragraphs 41, 42, and 43, the subject may perhaps be made briefly clear in outline, but not in detail. I favor the consideration and adoption, if found reasonably practicable, of a uniform classification for both railway and public reasons. It is, of course, understood that, there being six classes, for example, there will be six rates between all points, ranging, for general illustration, from $1 to 60 cents per actual 100 pounds. What class an article shall be assigned to at first or transferred to thereafter, or what intermediate or commodity rate shall be made, are vital elements of rate making or fixing what the class rates shall be, and these constitute the whole question of freight tariffs. The changes therein should therefore be determined by the railroads, as they determine the original rates for each class and under the same rules, using the term "classification" as synonymous with all class-rate standards.

In the first part of my evidence I divided the United States into territorial areas in which different classes of passenger fares may justifiably prevail. Within the same areas the same or other causes may warrant differences of freight charge and classification; but other forceful general causes which influence tonnage rates should not be ignored.

For example: Where a large traffic of Western lines is in live animals their classification of live stock may reasonably differ from that applied to the smaller shipments of like animals in Alabama. So the classification of cotton in Georgia and Texas may properly differ from that used in California. The large amount of precious minerals mined in Colorado, Utah, and California, with their attendant risks and conditions, may reasonably justify classifications different from those applying to the infrequent shipments of such or other ores under a different liability over New England lines. The copper classification, or that of iron ore, may properly differ in different ore districts, depending upon quantity, regularity of movement, etc. Where there is a large and regular traffic in bituminous coal the classification may justly differ from that used upon remote lines which carry but little coal; and the classification, i. e., the rates, on anthracite and bituminous coals may differ over the same lines, depending in part on values, terminal facilities supplied, etc. The fruit classification in Florida may justly differ from that in Maine and be justifiably greater although moved in much larger quantities, because it is a principal resource in Florida and an incidental article in Maine. A class rate on lumber cut on mountains and carried down grade may justly differ from lumber rates applying all the way up grade on the same line.

The large lumber product of Michigan and Wisconsin may also justify the railroads in those States in classifying lumber differently from the classifications prevailing upon the Western plains, where but little lumber is cut.

The large concentrated manufacture of a great number of special wares in New England, largely by water power, and forming the bulk of their total outgoing interstate traffic, may justify different classifications thereon from those used in regions where manufactures are a minor resource; for example, the manufactures of New England, New York, and Pennsylvania, in comparison with those of Arizona or Florida. Similar instances could be cited as to various articles of production, such as grain, steel rails, flour, structural iron, etc., in different volumes in different sections of the country.

Some items of the classification, notably inexpensive wares like crockery, soda ash, resin, etc., are also affected by canal, ocean, and river competition more than others are; hence different classifications, as the proximity of water routes affects them.

The classification from Montreal westward to Canadian points may differ from that used from Albany, and thus affect American rates.

The transcontinental classification differs radically and with reason, because of Isthmian and Cape Horn competitions, from that used all-rail from the Atlantic seaboard to Kansas City and Memphis, or from the latter cities to Seattle.

These are some of the many salient warrants for differences in classification. Others relate to the friendly trade antagonisms of States, districts, and more extended territories; to the adjustments of the myriad differences of conditions by the considerable and necessary use of commodity tariffs and rules, which have the effect to equalize rates both as to firms and localities on important special articles, and also to provide rates intermediate between those resulting from class rates proper. For example, if the difference of 15 cents per 100 pounds, New York to Chicago, between second and third class was found too great, an intermediate, i. e., a commodity rate, may be desirable and in instances needful as an aid to equalize the railway and trade conditions otherwise created or encountered.

Many of these disparities have already been adjusted by differences of classification or by commodity rates. Any uniform classification must continue to recognize and provide for these inequalities and dissimilarities by differences of special rates or by the fixed differences of classification rates, for the cogent reason that some justifiable differences of rates will continue on certain articles which must be adjusted by some public and reasonable method. To abolish all intermediate rates would advance some and reduce other rates unnecessarily, and, in some cases, aggravate the evil sought to be corrected. Absolute uniformity is, therefore, unattainable and disturbing.

There is but little difference between the formulation of the English classification and the trunk-line classification which prevails in the United States upon about 70 to 75 per cent of its freight tonnage and earnings. In England and all other countries different causes (such as we encounter) produce like policies and assignments of classification. For example, the classification (i. e., the rate) on fruit from some Mediterranean points via rail across France and England to London necessarily differs from the locally classified rates in both France and England, because strong competition is encountered for it through carriage from Mediterranean ports by water all the way through the Straits of Gibraltar. So with wines, etc.

The continental classifications (i. e., rates) are, for the same reasons, affected by the Elbe, Rhine, Seine, and Danube rivers. The classifications also justifiably differ in some instances in those countries from points upon those streams compared with those which prevail inland thereto or therefrom.

Further, if it be published that a given article is charged from New York 65 cents, second class, to Chicago, while the classification west of Chicago would fix the west-bound rate upon the same article at $1 first class for the same distance and in the same direction, that fact would not necessarily produce a discrimination, the circumstances and conditions being dissimilar, because all like traffic would be charged a uniform rate New York to Chicago, and another uniform rate from Chicago west; yet that would not be discrimination.

If in any readjustment of the classification so as to make it uniform, the rates from Chicago to a point 1,000 miles west thereof continued unchanged, the alteration of the classification might yet operate so as to raise some and lower other rates and thus create an unreasonable rate or an unjust discrimination and require their revision or adjustment by more commodity rates. Nor would a uniform classification reconcile or dispense with legitimate differences in rates for like hauls in different districts. Notwithstanding all these reasonable issues, much good could, in my judgment, be achieved by the elimination and limitation of many commodity rates and the substitution of both local and general classifications therefor containing more classes, if some reasonable advances in rates were made in some instances in exchange for others reduced. This would produce some additional uniformity of rates and lessen some forms of inadvertent preferences.

One other view of the advocacy for a consolidated classification merits your thought and mention. I know of no pleaders for this uniformity who urge it on that ground alone. It goes, in their minds, with the desire or belief or both that a uniform classification means a reduction in rates incidental to greater mercantile convenience, but none seem to believe uniformity so essential or are so strenuous for the amalgamation as to propose or assent to any advances in rates to secure the national classification, although some interests would be required to make some concessions, if one were adopted.

As a matter of fact, interstate through rates are substantially all alike now via all like routes, and the national schedule would not make them more so because it would encounter the same sea, river, canal, and other rivalry as now, and the rates would have to be met and modified as now. For a considerable time it would require many changes in abrogating old or issuing new commodity rates. Furthermore, it would necessitate many changes in State as well as interstate procedure.

The principal causes of discrimination cited are therefore as likely to continue under a uniform classification as under various independent classifications. Diverse classifications do not cause them and a consolidated classification will not stop them.

Finally. Each of the present classifications have special adaptations to the circumstances and conditions of the business in the territories which they respectively cover, and this consideration must continue in any event we can now forecast. There are those who hold sincerely that it will increase the problem and lead to more unsteadiness in rates rather than to their solidity.

Sixteenth.

Very much that is said by and before you and elsewhere relates to misunderstood competition. I therefore submit a

CONTRAST BETWEEN RAILWAY AND TRADE COMPETITIONS.

When the term "competition" is applied to purchasing and selling transportation as it is to buying and vending goods, it is a misnomer, because, historically and instinctively, it conveys to most minds impressions of bargaining and concession. Buyers seek better terms than sellers first ask, and sellers whose capital, manufacturing facilities, control of specialties, patterns, patents, rentals, etc., differ, may, in order to secure such purchasers, sell at dissimilar prices adapted to market conditions or forecasts, the proportions of cash, notes, or credit offered in payment, their experiences with buyers' ratings, and the profits upon entire bills sold—i. e., losing on one article to make more on others. All this is commercially sanctioned, but it would be illegal and not proper in any sense to so bargain for different railway rates or exchange corn for bills of lading at false bases for the values of both, or for rival railways to grant preferences varied to accord presumably with a competing agent's estimate of a shipper's credit, the quantities forwarded, etc., or with the different capitalizations, dividends, distances, or facilities of the competitive railway lines.

Competing vendors openly misrepresent and laud their own and decry their rival's wares from market stalls and wagons, but variable freight rates and fares must not be so peddled publicly from railway wagons or privately in railway offices.

Yachtsmen "compete" for prizes with presumable rectitude, but when a yacht is purposely fouled or its spars weakened, it is not "competition" more than it would be if one railway procured the derailment of its rival's trains. It is conspiracy. This principle also holds true in athletic games, horse races, etc., because if the judges in such competitive exhibitions or of machinery, arts, etc., sell their awards, it is not "competition," but fraud.

Whatever may be the policy of the State as to prison laborers they do not fairly compete with honest toilers, nor could railways justifiably reduce the compensations of their employees to convict wages. It would not be fair competition, but a crime against honest labor.

Further, if a yacht owner, trade or art exhibitor violates the rules of his guild in its public contests, he is denounced and debarred from further competition, but if the reasonable rates, fares, and rules governing the important public functions of transportation are violated by a railway which aided to formulate them, that railway is applauded and rewarded for doing wrong by increased patronage on the trade exchanges which would dismiss their own members for lesser infractions, and the law encourages a continuance of the wrong.

This also is not competition, but a reward for illegal methods substituted for deserved punishment or penalty.

It is not, for these reasons, true competition when one or more railways unequally and secretly alter their published, uniform, and reasonable rates, fares, or rules, and which judiciously and judicially managed railways seek to legally observe in furtherance of law and the public interest as well as their own. Nor is it true competition—although it may be in a sense justifiable—when strong and well-meaning carriers, whose business has been taken by a rival at cut rates, take some legal chances to regain and keep it, because if they waited the law's inefficient aid, or any other method now usable, their shares of competitive business would be lost, perhaps permanently.

Further, if one railway company observes a reasonable tariff rate which a competing carrier reduces secretly and from which yet other rival carriers offer further rebates, it is clear that if the first rate was reasonable the last one would be unjustly low, and that such devices constitute waste, bankruptcy and discrimination. In such cases the first fair rates should clearly be restored and by united effort, if need be; nor is such unity of effort "monopoly," "conspiracy," "absolute power," or a "trust."

Assume further, one railway sturdy for uniform legal rates, the other pliant with concessions therefrom, and two shippers, one desiring to observe the law and the other to evade it. Concede then that the yielding railway grants the insistent large shipper concealed rebates. In such strife both railways will be injured—one because it loses its business, the other because it loses its profit—and one merchant will probably be ruined. Above all these, the large receiver of rebates will, phœnix-like, survive and rise, and will ultimately control his kind of business from the points whence his rebates apply and will also injure other shippers at other points affected.

If *all* railways gave but one shipper, say of grain, 1 cent per 100 pounds advantage, he might ultimately control the cereal markets of the nation. So would he if but *one* railway at each large shipping point granted him that preference, assuming that all other railways thereat stood firm for right and like rates and rules for all. Then one railway would dominate the others and constitute the monopoly.

These vicious results would differ only in degree if advantages were given by one or many railways to say five shippers at the same or different points, because the five forwarders might then attack and ruin each other and yet others, until the surviving shippers were fewer and the smaller unfavored patrons were ruined.

Further, the merchant who reduces his sale prices or pays producers more on his commodities because of his reduced rates, affects only his rivals in the same trade and locality, while railways which reduce through rates, say from St. Louis to Boston, involve the rates from St. Louis to every seaboard city. This, in turn, as required by the act, makes such through rates the maxima between numberless intermediate and many noncompetitive places. This also is not competition, but the effect of law, because the first offending line may not reach any through and local points on the other lines. In such an instance an honest adherence to the geographical scale basis of rates would also deprive competing points of their trade. All these offensive conditions come through the needless and injudicious action or willful injury of the first offending route. None of these results would ensue from true competition, but would be the effects of pernicious action and favoritisms.

When a merchant thus discriminated against fails, he retires from sight or influence, but if a railway should fail it would be required to continue in business as a chartered and obligated public agency. Indeed, it is usually said that it is then best prepared to make the lowest rates, to which other carriers must, in turn, conform or lose their traffic. Thus ensues the tortuous and anomalous logic that railway administration is the only trade in which a bankrupt line makes rates—i. e., values—for entirely solvent rivals and the only business which may be increased upon insolvent capital.

The protection of right always requires the restraint of wrong, but in transportation neither the public nor corporate right can prevail so long as both protection and restraint must come from railway cooperation. Even that is legally interdicted and the present inefficient law has so far notably failed.

For further illustration, that act requires that the actual rates shall not be "*more or less*" than the tariffs filed, thereby requiring that railway competition *shall* differ from trade competition by not making less than the announced rates, but it provides no practical aids to that legal and essential consummation.

The minority opinion in the trans-Missouri case presented this condition succinctly as follows:

"That the interstate-commerce rates, all of which are controlled by the provisions as to reasonableness, were not intended to fluctuate hourly and daily as competition might ebb and flow, results from the fact that the published rates could not be increased or reduced, except after a specified time. It follows, then, that agreements as to reasonable rates and against their secret reduction conform exactly to the terms of the act."

For these uncontroverted reasons, as well as for the convenience, restfulness, and certainty of trade, merchants who desire that rebates should cease would doubtless approve a published grain rate of 20 cents per 100 pounds from Chicago to New York, and such just regulative legislation as would sustain that rate undeviatingly until as publicly altered, rather than indorse mercantile or railway practices which connive at a concealed rate of 15 cents for large shippers. They know that such vicious discriminations render legitimate commercial competition uncertain and impossible, because vast capital, controlling traffic, may tender it in train loads to pliable railways or those which lack business, or they may shift their large tonnages from line to line or unite with other large shippers to more easily compel preferential rates. It is to be regretted that they obtain them often enough to create great discriminations and wrongs. Some shippers thus become dealers in rebated railway earnings, as much as in their own merchandise, and make large profits from their rebates, thereby growing the stronger to exact further railway allowances, to stipulate purchase prices to producers as well as sale prices to consumers, and perhaps use their combined capital and rebates to further control merchandise values on trade and financial exchanges. In such cases such shippers, and not the carriers, constitute the real transportation trusts.

It can not, therefore, be too often or too strongly shown that however much all well-intending competitive railways from each point may observe uniform and legal rates, the strongest and best disposed carriers must succumb to the objectionable conditions forced upon them by the weakest or less upright competitor.

The true purpose of the antitrust law is reversed by such methods. Not being, as the railways contend, first meant to apply to them, it is thus far adjudged that it does; yet being clearly applicable to trusts, the latter escape its effect and grow stronger from their large transactions with those carriers which grant them special advantages.

Permit a further illustration: The postal charges would be impaired if railways, express companies, and house-to-house letter carriers cut the postal rates 20 per cent, yet if real competition is the legislative desire and intent, why should individuals be restrained by law from such carriage and the public be made to pay more than they could get the same service performed for by others?

Commissioner Schoonmaker well said:

"A rate made by one line on a particular traffic must be the rate of all other lines to share in the business."

He also said:

"And this pernicious power is the creation of law, and is protected by the law upon the antiquated and once respectable theory, but now fully demonstrated fallacy, that unrestricted competition among railroads is a public benefit."

All such vicious rate-cutting methods simply sell transportation to the lowest and not, as in other trades, to the highest bidders, and are not therefore proper competition more than are auction sales of pawned, bankrupt, or damaged goods. It is the impairment or destruction of all true carrying competition and its legitimate rules, functions, agencies, and standards.

Based on these uncontroverted premises, which might be much amplified, competition properly means that when various contestants strive for a coveted consummation in any branch of endeavor they shall be governed by those rules in each which apply openly and impartially to all honorable contestants therefor, and which experiences have proven fair and essential to enable the best man, horse, yacht, machine, picture, shipper, or railroad to win under equal conditions.

When, therefore, in transportation, proper competitive forces have been fairly expressed in reasonable and uniform rates, classifications, fares, and rules, every violation of them, however small, constitutes a pernicious discrimination and should not longer receive even negative trade or national sanction.

Comprehensively and justly considered and applied yet more explicitly to railways, competition means due adjustments and readjustments of rates to conform equitably to those causes which from time to time properly control or affect them, such as rivalries with oceans, rivers, lakes, and canals, competing markets which distribute, consume, or reship, the relations of domestic and foreign localities, etc. Economies in management, longer and more numerous trains, lower grades, improved terminal facilities, better station houses, more and safer tracks and appliances, celerity of service, etc., are also true elements of legitimate emulation justly calculated to increase the business of one line against another, and also to produce lower open rates on all lines, and this true competition will never cease until human effort does.

Various interstate commissioners have strongly affirmed these views.

Judge Cooley said:

" * * * It is utterly impossible to judge of railroad competition and its effects, its usefulness, and its mischiefs by comparing it with competition as we encounter it in other lines of business."

Hon. Martin A. Knapp said:

"Deprived of special and exclusive rates, an advantage far more odious and powerful than exemptions from taxation, those trusts are shorn of their strength and divested of their supremacy."

Judge Patterson, who introduced the pooling bill of 1895, said:

"This preferential system throughout the country is gradually destroying the small and enriching the large shippers."

The great English commission of 1882 said:

"Reliance upon competition between railways to regulate rates and maintain them upon a fair basis and to prevent unjust discriminations will have to be abandoned as a failure."

Hons. A. G. Thurman, E. B. Washburn, and T. M. Cooley said in their joint report of 1882:

"The mere statement of these results is sufficient to show that this is not what in other business is known and designated as competition."

A distinguished United States Senator said in 1887:

"Competition of railroad transportation differs from every other kind of competition in the world. * * * It is not competition in trade. The railroad buys nothing of the producer; it sells nothing to the customer; it simply carries; it distributes."

The Cullom committee said:

" Competition does not prevent personal discrimination, for the evil is most conspicuous when and where competition is most active."

Judge (afterwards Senator) Howe said:

"Competition (meaning improper competition) has done more to monopolize trade or secure exclusive advantages in it than has been done by contract."

The Interstate Commerce Commission said, in its first annual report:

" Excessive and unreasonable competition is a public injury."

The convention of railway commissioners, held in Denver in August last, said, after ten years' experience with the interstate act, upon this point:

" * * * Our policy of leaving competition in transportation wholly unrestrained, just as competition in private business is unrestrained, has been steadily working out its own destruction."

This form of indiscriminate rivalry so often becomes degenerate public strife that it the more requires due control and regulation in the interest of every public and private factor involved.

Our argument is therefore bolted to the solid foundation that Congress was well advised in 1886 to sanction associations, or so-called pooling, and that the prohibition of the latter in the interstate act was a public as well as corporate error and misfortune.

This brings me to compare:

SEVENTEENTH.

GOVERNMENTAL AND RAILWAY TARIFFS.

The United States bonded debt November 1, 1896, was $847,364,460, whereas railway bonds were then about $5,641,000,000, or seven times greater.

The annual interest on the national debt was then, say $29,000,000 and about $252,000,000 on the railway bonds.

President McKinley told Congress, March 15, 1897, that the Government's gross receipts for its fiscal years 1894-95-96 were $1,072,651,000, and that they were $138,000,000 less than its expenses. He therefore specially convened a fiscal or traffic association of the States, called Congress, to say that increased import tariffs were needful to sustain the public credit and extend our trade, and the House majority concurred by 84 majority.

The railway receipts in the same period were $3,408,200,000, over three times as much, and the Interstate Commerce Commission's report for 1895 stated that $890,000,000 of railway bonds were then in default of interest, being $43,000,000 more than all the outstanding national bonds. These defaults increased in 1896. If the interest unpaid thereon averaged 5 per cent, and was three years in default, such defaults would aggregate $133,500,000, being about the same amount as the Government's deficit in the same period. During the same three years railway dividends decreased $22,000,000 more.

The prevention or correction of the railway conditions which produce discriminations then laid as fully within the power and public duty of Congress as to restore general business confidence by increased import charges.

Almost simultaneously with these national and corporate conditions the Supreme Court declared, by *one* majority, but as a minority of all the judges who had heard the cause, that an association of railways which had simultaneously decreased transportation tariffs to extend our trade should not longer agree even to that desirable public end, or to secure the uniformity, reasonableness, impartiality, publicity, and stability of charges which the Government maintains in its import, postage, internal-tax, land and consular tariffs, and which is also required in the collection of all national, State, and municipal taxes—this, too, notwithstanding the fact that the courts based their findings on the principle that we are exercising quasi and delegated governmental functions. As such, we are surely entitled to its protection in some measure—if for no other reason, than that governmental incomes are smaller and touch fewer people.

I cite some supporting illustrations:

(*a*) The Government pays uniform railway compensation in large amounts for the like carriage of its mails and stipulated prices for the transportation of its troops and supplies, yet it does not plead that "competition" is lessened, "trade restrained," or that its expenses are unduly increased because associations exist, nor does it claim and receive concealed rebates under guises falsely called "competition."

(b) As the Government is the largest patron of the railways, it is both due and consistent that all its clients should in other respects receive its legal aid to place and keep all citizens upon the same honorable plane in their transportation transactions on which it conducts its own business for the same people with the same carriers.

(c) If Government owned or rented the railways, as it does the custom-houses and post-offices, it would fix and enforce against all its patrons the uniform transportation charges which it found reasonable and made public, even by the enforcement of summary means. Such charges would not be secretly reduced, nor would that just course be then deemed "a trust," "a restraint of trade," or "a stoppage of competition." Conferences among parallel governmental lines would continue essential in order to decide and announce the intricate interstate rates and the frequent changes in them which might be required by law, by new national and international trade conditions, and by those great, legitimate, controlling, and ceaseless competitive forces which would continue as potent against governmental as corporate railways.

Railway competition, as now understood, would then clearly cease between parallel governmental carriers as it has between governmental custom-houses and post-offices, and, after the railway receipts had gone into one national purse, they would be assigned to the proper departmental incomes and expenses and their results be adjudged thereby.

A loss on one line or traffic would not be wholly justified by a gain upon another. Nevertheless, new railway lines, consolidations and combinations, carriers' antagonisms, man's faults, the rivalries of States, cities, and districts, the competition of water routes, rival foreign countries and markets, the wrongful depletions of reasonable rates by weak carriers plus strong shippers, and the struggles and reprisals which ensue and now compel corporate policies would still exist, create recurring disturbances of national rates, and invoke national cures.

(d) If, for example, the Government had purchased and operated the Union Pacific Railway under its recent foreclosure proceedings, it could only announce its competitive rates upon the large rival traffic of that great system after the conferences with other companies which it necessarily now avails of. With all its power, the Government could not maintain independent rates on that one line and secure rival traffic for it, unless its private competitors issued and maintained the same rates with equal honor and inflexibility, and clearly that railway can not do so now under a lesser sustaining power and weakening legislation. It might reduce rates and fares, but it could not even then maintain them except by cooperation with private lines. This has been found true of the competition of Government railways with private lines in Europe; therefore, the latter are alike wisely protected and to the manifest betterment, stability and security of fares, rates, and traders, as well as the carriers.

(e) The purchase and operation of the Union Pacific line would have been desirable as a stop to Congressional theorizing upon competition by bringing Senators, Representatives, and governmental officers to consider the reports of their own officers as to rates, as it did to its finance. Facts, and not theories, would then have prevailed, and the alternatives which all competitive railways must now contemplate throughout the country under any management, viz, to observe the interstate-commerce act up to the surrender of their competitive traffic to more plastic rivals, or to keep their shares of business by some of the methods employed by the latter would have been faced, not evaded. They would, perhaps, have then heeded the advice, now doubted and ignored, to legalize enforcible fair contract relations between parallel lines.

(f) When the Government publishes import tariffs it assures to all peoples, everywhere, their impartial and unabated collection. If the railways simultaneously establish reasonable, nonpreferential, and stable tariffs equally or more calculated to give effect to the same wise national policy upon what justifiable grounds can Congress deny its support to its transportation agents or representatives to enter into legally regulated joint contracts, in order that they may collect and retain such due and reasonable carrying charges, especially as it is the only plan which has everywhere proved an effective stop to undue and discriminating depletions of reasonable rates.

For further illustration import tariffs may be justly increased on some articles, but if the railways should fractionally advance their rates on the same imports it would be widely characterized as unjustifiable, monopolistic, extortionate, etc., although both increases might be alike proper or the railway increase the more so.

That one is a governmental and the other a corporate act is not a just reply, so long as it be claimed that we exercise our interstate transportation functions as trustees. Our legislators condemn railway discriminations, yet they more discriminate by withholding from those railways any measures of the protection they give rail-mill corporations, for example, although whether national revenue, credit, labor, or commerce be considered, the railways are their largest factor, and are entitled to consideration to the extent the Government would legislate rates for its own railways if they owned them.

(g) If, however, it is still desired that the transportation element of commerce be denied due protection and continue capricious, concealed and preferential as an unavoidable, permissible, or desirable factor of so-called "competition," why should not rival customs collectors rebate some parts of some import charges at competing ports of entry? Why should the whisky tax be as high at Peoria as in North Carolina, and why should postage stamps be sold at the same prices at profitable offices like New York, to large daily users of the mails, as to infrequent letter writers at small offices conducted at a loss?

Nevertheless, railway owners and managers have not succeeded in obtaining any of the adequate legal powers to meet the transportation conditions which Congress would enact for itself; and to answer that railway proprietors must, therefore, care for themselves, yet not permit them to do so legally or effectively, is the retort of theory, hostility, partiality, misconception, or inattention.

(h) As the United States do not own any railways, these grounds must be sustained by proofs drawn from other nations.

In 1874 Switzerland invited Austria-Hungary, Belgium, Germany, Italy, and the Netherlands to confer touching their competitive international railway tariffs in order that like rates, rules, bills of lading, etc., might prevail thereon via their rival routes and frontiers.

The situation in these countries was more akin to that of our own States than any other I can cite.

Further conferences in 1878, 1881, and 1886, in which private companies participated, considered the competitions of the Mediterranean and North seas and the Danube, Rhine, and other rivers, resulting in an agreement at Berne, in October, 1890, which was subsequently ratified by all the participating nations and made effective January 1, 1893.

Under that compact undue competition was ended, governmental and private rights were alike conserved, and public, stable, and reasonable charges were announced upon which to base competitive national and international traffic interchanges. Had those governments and their private railways acted upon the erroneous theories of competition held by inexperienced and hostile opponents here, they would not have thus associated or agreed, but would have fought the carrying struggle to a deplorable finish. Private corporations would have been crippled by the governments which owed them impartial protection, their intermingled strifes would have been prolonged, commercial instabilities and discriminations in rates would have continued or increased, and their several national budgets would have been involved and depleted, while the railways would meantime have deteriorated in physical condition and morale. Can there be any question which is the juster and wiser public policy, even considering trade alone?

Interstate Commissioner Schoonmaker once said:

"The lack of affirmative legal authority for such associations, the bad faith often exhibited by some of their members, and the inability either to restrain or punish delinquency have operated in another tendency—the tendency toward consolidation."

Should such "affirmative legal authority" be given and be thereafter used to antagonize the public interest, prompt repeal or amendments thereof, the interposition of the courts under amended and swifter procedures, or due enlargements of the powers of the Interstate Commerce Commission would fully protect the shippers and others involved.

EIGHTEENTH.

TRAFFIC ASSOCIATIONS.

Your paragraphs 44 and 45 inquire as to the objects, operation, and effects of traffic associations, the considerations and policy for legalizing them, subject to governmental approval and its power to abrogate them on reasonable notice.

(a) The purposes, procedures, and values of such associations have been so often presented that all else is repetition. Had it not been that the interstate act abolished and estopped all the machinery vital to their success, the voluntary associations of the railways would have to-day been its strong cooperative arms, or that commission would have been much less necessary, and the contention in the courts avoided with good results.

(*b*) It first seems just to mutually acknowledge the needs for uniformity and stability in transportation charges, that they can only be secured by those who, under law, own and administer their properties, and that such results must be secured subject to the mandates and aids of intelligent and fair law. In progressing toward these vital conclusions certain phases of association work merit and require your thought. Their effects, although always measurably good, were insufficient because they lacked affirmative legalized powers and incurred constant legal action.

Each and every contract of railway association had for its primary objects, but with more practical procedures, those of the interstate act, namely, the uniformity and stability of just and reasonable rates, the cessation of every form of concession therefrom which could operate to produce undue discriminations and the provision of workable methods to those ends.

(c) I claim to have already established the urgent need for cooperative legislative and railway procedure to cure the recited public and private evils, because neither one of those agencies ever has or ever can do it alone.

ALL GREAT INTERESTS MUST UNITE AND COOPERATE.

Cooperative railway unity is indispensable, judged by the logic of analogy. We already have various State governments, independent within limits, but the argument would be preposterous which said that national control, regulating while protecting all, is centralization and usurpation, and that there should not be a common Congress, departments, executive and judiciary. States must respect the nation, the nation the States. The civil war decided those civil issues precisely as rate wars led railways to adopt the analogy of the General Government in carrying on their local and interstate public and private functions.

The nation must have its Congress and the President his Cabinet. A government with each department pursuing its own and a different policy would be justly derided, and the responsible political party would be displaced. States have their various county governments, counties their municipalities, and municipalities their police, and every profession, business, charity, and government must concentrate the influences and authority needful to unify, equalize, and shield its different interests. Organized stock exchanges and clearing houses are indispensable to fiscal regulation and values, produce exchanges and boards of trade to mercantile prices and probity, clearing houses to banks, maritime exchanges to marine enterprises, chambers of commerce to unite varied trade interests, etc., and they are all legalized trade helps and equalizers.

Some authority must therefore exist in every calling that is central, respected, definite, and disciplinary, and that is recognized by the common or statute law, not merely as permissive, but needful public safeguards and instrumentalities, and in no other way can any work be respected or respectable, potent for good against wrong, or make its results salutary and forcible.

When, however, railways desire and endeavor to conform to these universal principles and methods, railway legislation and commissions do not hesitate enough at unsound, hostile, and deprecating laws and orders which deny the rights given every other calling.

The rates of transportation *must* be predetermined in order to be announced in accordance with law. This can only be done by conference, which is association. The forwarders of New York and Chicago can not send their wares to 8 or more railways over which different rates may prevail without knowledge as to which route offered the highest or lowest or any intermediate rates to a multitude of points. Foreknowledge is therefore more necessary to the forwarder than to the railway.

Senator Cullom's committee anticipated this vital commercial and rate condition and said in their report, as demonstrating the value of association:

"A basis of fixed rates would seem to depend upon a general predetermination of the rates to be established by the carriers interested. It seems necessary, therefore, to leave a way open by which such agreements can be made in order to avoid the constant friction that would otherwise be occasioned."

I can not state the value of railway association better than did Justice White in pronouncing the opinion of the minority of the Supreme Court in the case of the Trans-Missouri Freight Association.

He said:

"* * * Agreements as to reasonable rates and against their secret reduction conform exactly to the terms of the act."

He said also:

To secure "a uniform classification and preventing of undercutting of rates, underbilling, etc.," * * * "that agreements among carriers" * * * "were deemed not to be forbidden by law, but, on the contrary, were considered as instruments tending to secure its successful evolution."

Also:

"Even though such agreements be made with competing as well as joint lines is in accord with the plain text of the interstate-commerce act."

Finally, on the question of associations, I quote the Interstate Commerce Commission.

Its first annual report said:

"To make railroads of the greatest possible service to the country *contract* relations will be essential."

The problem is greater as the traffic of the country increases, and the wise chairman of the Interstate Commission therefore said at Denver last August:

"Nor can these beneficent ends be reached, in my judgment, without conferring upon railroad corporations privileges of association and rights of contract with each other which are denied by existing laws."

This brings us to—

NINETEENTH.

CONSIDERATIONS DUE TO THE CARRYING INTERESTS OTHER THAN THEIR GREAT REDUCTIONS IN RATES AND FARES.

(*a*) The first relates to the investors interested, which are too often ignored. The Eastern trunk lines reported in 1896 that their shareholders numbered 99,826. To this was to be added the bond and shareholders on the same and other American railroads. One Eastern line reported that 50 per cent and the Pennsylvania Railroad Company said that 40 per cent of its shareholders were women.

At the above ratio of shareholders to mileage, the total number in the union would be over 950,000. Calling the total 1,250,000 of bond and shareholders, they, with nearly 1,000,000 employees, make over 2,000,000 persons then dependent upon or interested in our railways, and the number has greatly increased since this time. Assuming each reported adult to represent 5 persons, the total number more or less affected by railway administrative, legislative, or corporate results is 10,000,000 of persons, exclusive of those interested in the manufacture or production of locomotives, cars, rails, other iron products, wheels, lumber, cross-ties, stone, paints, plushes, oils, paper, etc., or the material used by manufacturers and by the railways.

(*b*) The total number of employees of the United States Government, June 30, 1896, was only 220,594, *excluding* judicial and legislative appointees, but *including* the Army and Navy and the Marine Corps. The number of railway employees proper in 1895 was 785,034, being 88,568, or 11 per cent less than 1893, although the railway mileage had increased 4,380 miles. The number has increased through 45,000 additional miles since constructed and because of increased traffic on the old lines. The number of persons employed per mile operated in 1893 was 5.04 and but 4.38 in 1895, a reduction of over 13 per cent with even greater mileage. This has also increased since then.

(*c*) Contrasting the wages of American and foreign railway labor, the following statement of the last data I possess will suffice, as the same ratio extended substantially through other branches of railway service and continue still about the same:

Country.	Per day.		Per month.
	Engineers.	Firemen.	Conductors.
United States	$3.65	$2.05	$82.40
England	$1.25 to 1.87	$0.75 to 1.12	30.40
France	1.00 to 1.16	.75 to .83	----------
Germany	.81 to 1.25	.62 to .81	28.30
Belgium	.81 to .89	.50 to .60	----------
Holland	.83 to 1.04	.54 to .72	----------
Hungary			32.40

This comparison is yet more favorable to American railway labor when the longer hours and more onerous conditions which constitute a day's work abroad are considered.

When not only rates and fares are greatly lower, but wages and taxation are higher, American labor will justly share the net losses or the gains which may accrue in railway earnings, if the average benefit is the ruling factor, and as the tendency of legislatures and courts to reduce rates and fares continues, or is modified.

(d) There were over 30 measures pending in the Fifty-third Congress affecting railways, but one of which (the pooling amendment) being for their and the public's joint relief. That was unhappily defeated. If the public good required the recent additional import measures to protect steel and tin and other makers and workers, farmers, lumbermen, importers of silk, etc., why should not railway owners and employees be also reasonably protected in some due and well-regulated manner for like reasons, in order at least that they may collect and retain all of their just and reasonable charges and earnings? Surely it was the carriers who made effective the cheap and quick distributions of American products which are gradually giving us new international markets.

TWENTIETH.

These premises confront the question relating to legislatively sanctioned railway cooperation, called—

POOLING.

I wish it understood that I am not at this time arguing that pools be now legalized. I am striving to answer your questions. Senator Platt (of Connecticut) said truly, in 1887, "What is a pool? It is simply an agreement between competing railways to apportion the competitive business; that, and nothing more."

A distinguished Senator also pointed the Senate in 1887 to the "utter and lamentable ignorance of what pooling contracts were."

This misapprehension of the term "pooling" has caused much public distrust, because pools usually mean the sales of shares in ventures, which may be decided by chance or fraud—a horse race, for example.

Railway pools, however, or "traffic unity," or "traffic federation," or "joint purses," as they are often called abroad, really mean certainties, because the public has full and published foreknowledge of the rates and charges thereunder, and only railways incur the hazards.

Let me correct a widespread public misconception. I have never known a railway-pool agreement which specified rates, because such agreements cover fixed terms, during which many changes in rates may be required by law, by altered trade conditions, by rates to or from other points, countries, etc., while the pool itself continues in unaltered terms. Rate and tariff making are therefore wholly distinct from pooling agreements. A pooling agreement may be unchanged in any respect for twenty years, yet may involve five or one hundred rates on the same articles between the same points.

In the same manner a classification may fix the distributive rates on 4,000 articles, but it is not a pool.

Two unassailable transportation principles favor these legalized agreements— i. e., pools.

The *first* is that *some* standards of rates and fares *must* be reasonable. Being so and legally preannounced to forwarders, filed with the Interstate Commerce Commission, and uniformly collected and paid without protest by all patrons, the railways challenge proof of any possible public wrong from the divisions of their legal proceeds as the participating railways may agree, because clearly as *only the rates affect the public interest*, their apportionment during carriage or thereafter are not just public concerns any more than are the proportions in which the same railways share the costs of constructing and operating their joint double tracks, union depots, belt lines, etc.

The *second* averment follows these premises. *It is only when pools are used as the means to sustain excessive rates that they are objectionable, and then, as always, the remedy lies in the correction of the rates, and not the prohibition of pooling itself.*

SUCH AGREEMENTS BENEFICIAL TO THE PUBLIC.

Pools being indisputably for the public welfare—to the extent that they would stop the payment of preferential rebates from reasonable and just rates, charges, and fares—they have other merits.

They transfer only unconsigned or assenting tonnage or its money values from the railways in excess to those in deficit. It may be that one company has an overplus in one month and a deficit in the next month, as various causes, pendulum like, operate or recur. The associated railways are therefore the only parties who can be injured, unless it be by the stoppage of rebates to those receiving them.

The associated railways also account to each other for all the pooled traffic at the tariff rates or fares, and if rebates or commissions are nevertheless paid which produce excess tonnage or travel balances under the terms of a pool, the company—treacherously or otherwise—in excess must not only pay such rebates alone, but must also transfer its excess tonnage or pay the money balances therefor found due to its associates in deficit.

This clearly restricts rebates, because each railway and party to a pool shares the proceeds derived from the legal rates whether it carries the freight or not, and enjoys the resultant peace of management which good faith, if reenforced by law, would bring both to associated rival lines and to the public.

Pools, moreover, continue to divide the competitive traffic coming within their purview substantially in the proportions of their previous carryings of the same traffic as the public theretofore chose or preferred their routes. Under pools shippers continue to choose their routes as before, so that the traffic of dissenting forwarders is not used for tonnage equalization.

If smaller shippers assent that their freights may be used to so equalize the total joint tonnage because they thereby secure the desired parities of rates with large forwarders, that alone is a potential and conclusive argument. The largest shippers now get much the best terms, while it is the smaller ones who most need them.

Legalized pooling would also combine the facilities of the associated carriers, as if they were one company, organized to carry impartially the tonnage of a community, or as if all shippers constituted one great firm. Railways now charge all the members of one firm like rates and fares, and it would also be the best corporate and national policy for all companies to charge like rates on similar articles and tickets between the same points to all firms and persons.

Judge Cooley, as the first chairman of the commission, comprehensively, yet wisely, said in his first report:

"The more completely the whole railroad systems of the country can be treated as a unit, as if it were under one management, the greater will be its service to the public and the less the liability to unfair exactions."

The present chairman, Judge Knapp, says to the same effect:

"* * * the railroads of the country should be regarded in their entirety and treated, so far as possible, as a single system for all the purposes of regulation."

POOLING AIDS THE STABILITY OF RATES.

Pooling will, more than any other method, secure stable rates at traffic centers. They will, therefore, assist those local points dependable upon the larger ones, whereas small shippers at both central and tributary points now incur two disadvantages: They can neither compete with the preferred shippers at large adjacent cities nor can they ship as profitably against them from the small, noncompetitive points where the published rates and fares are usually held firmly.

Pooling, therefore, simply seeks to conduct competitive business upon the impartial rates and rules presumably observed at noncompetitive local points where cut rates are not allowed.

Pooling will also have the effect to increase applications for public reductions of rates which are usually considered and decided upon the merits of the causes presented rather than upon the results of concealed rebates.

Pooling affords the public the united facilities of the associated lines at times of calamity or emergency, stress of car supply, etc.

Pooling stimulates proper emulations under assured equal rates and fares, because improved facilities, speed, promptness in business methods, and courtesy are then more relied upon to secure business than the devices now too much and preferentially used instead.

Pooling will secure more uniform and rigid inspections of shipments, in order to detect false weights, misdescription of goods, etc., by which honorable merchants may be defrauded by untrusworthy shippers, and thus further tend to put all patrons upon equal shipping conditions and classifications. This form of inspection has its counterpart in the duties of the Treasury appraisers and inspectors.

Our system is equally requisite to the public security and equality.

One hundred and thirty-five thousand cases of misdescription made by westbound forwarders of the actual wares shipped were detected by the trunk-line railways at three seaboard cities in one recent year on through freights only. Add to this number those at other cities and also on local and through freights in both directions, and the total of the cases detected and known is appalling.

Pooling would diminish these practices as well as rebates and substantially stop them if legalized longer term railway agreements were authorized under which these reforms could be more thorough and permanent, rather than spasmodic and insufficient.

It is often charged that railway honesty did not prevail under pooling. To admit this is no argument against it, for pooling did not *cause* bad faith. It clearly contracted and surely aided to check it. No laws, treaties, or conventions have stopped wars, conquests, reprisals, or crimes among nations, States, corporations, or persons, but this fact renders union, laws, and better procedures of correction only the more necessary. It would be as fair an argument to allege that because under the customs laws some undervaluations, defalcations, and smuggling continue we should drop the most practical means to stop them and interdict them only by proclamation.

Importers who undervalue goods to evade the import tariffs will also misdescribe their goods to thwart uniform transportation charges. An association of merchants could not stop the practice, therefore the Government uses its power to prevent such frauds upon its revenues.

The railways can not stop its wrongs by their action alone, and are as much entitled to national aid as any other calling which invokes law for like but lesser excellent purposes.

INTERESTING POOLING DATA.

Under former pools some tonnage was transferred from road to road, but not to the extent usually conjectured. In the last year (1886) of the eastward pools from Chicago, St. Louis, Peoria, Cincinnati, Louisville, and Indianapolis all the tonnage changed from one route to another thereunder at all those points was but 2.3 per cent of the total included, and this without protests from shippers, who knew that pools were good means to secure equal rates. The cash paid by all companies therefrom to each other in money settlements did not then average 9 cents per ton, whereas cuts in through rates may average 40 cents per ton or more. Of about $12,000,000 of the freight earnings pooled at those points in that period less than $300,000, or 2½ per cent, changed hands. Over one-half that amount was thereafter returned to those companies who paid the first excess balances, because, to get their money back, they reduced their tonnage to their due apportionments thereof and not their tariff rates. No shipper or consignee was harmed by any of these results, and many were benefited.

No American railway pool can be cited which had the effect to advance rates unless to restore the unjustifiable rate-war reductions. When the Trunk Line Association was organized, in 1877, the average of the eastward and westward tariff class rates between Chicago and New York was seventy-one (71) cents per 100 pounds. When they discontinued pooling, in 1886, it was under fifty (50) cents.

None contend that pooling has fostered or that its legalization now will increase discriminations, because the agreements, declarations, purposes, and effects of pools are invariably to abolish or minimize preferences, being in this respect one with the interstate act.

TONNAGE IS NOT RESTRICTED BY POOLS.

Pooling has increased tonnage, not restricted it, because of the better general geographical adjustments of rates and their greater stability and uniformity. The westward through tonnage from New York City proper, under the pool above named, was 716,000 tons in 1877. It was 1,415,000 tons in 1893, although New York was most of that time pooled, while Boston, Philadelphia, and Baltimore were not.

Pooling has not restricted, nor can it curb, any just competition created by the laws of trade, the rivalries of seas, lakes, and rivers, or the enormous betterments of transportation conditions. Under pooling each company seeks to preserve or increase its individual strength by fair means, which is the true railway competition, and not to divert the traffic of its rivals by pernicious payments in the nature of bribes, which is false diversion and not real competition.

TRUSTS COMPARED WITH POOLS.

It is repeatedly averred that pooling will enable and encourage railroads to combine as trusts, and the Supreme Court has decided that they fall within the lines of the antitrust law, whereas all forms of pooling have been the opposites of trusts in all the respects following, viz:

Trusts are publicly antagonized because it is said that of most of them that their methods are secret and extortionate; because they combine to increase capital in order to fix and control undue prices for their products; because they strive to prevent, limit, or annihilate competition, and because they sell to the unwary watered shares, based upon the increased revenues derived from these underlying wrong principles and deeds.

Admitting these grounds of opposition, which are often untenable, these discredited features do not transpire in railway pooling.

Railway rates and fares must be publicly preannounced and published. Not so with trusts. They must not be the subjects of private preferential contracts. Trust agreements may be. Railway rates must be published before they take effect, and be filed with and receive the actual or tacit approval of a governmental commission appointed by the President, confirmed by the Senate, and which is intended to geographically and politically represent all sections and the leading parties. Not so with trusts, which may legally avoid or may evade preannouncement, publicity, and governmental review. The Interstate Commission stipulates the form in which it shall receive the detailed annual reports of railway interstate carriers and publish them to the country, and many States so require with the same companies. Not so with trusts. The railroad companies do not *control* their own through rates, but determine, announce, and change them publicly after constant reference and concessions to the controlling and ceaseless elements of natural competition: *i. e.*, water routes, foreign markets, etc., or because wavering railways compel undesirable action. Trusts make their own selling prices and conditions, and may grant various sales terms, credits, and other preferences based on quantities, responsibilities, etc. Railway prices for freight and passenger carriage must be public, reasonable, just, and uniform, and their reasonableness may be reviewed and established by the courts. Not so with the prices of trust products. Railway rates and fares are known to all competing railways. Trusts withhold prices from their rivals when practicable, and competition with them may be modified, merged, battled for, or extinguished. Trusts may so act as to restrict trade. Railways seek without exception, in their own and the public interest, to enlarge trade, and must carry all the traffic tendered for forwarding.

There is no prevention, restriction, or crushing out of competition between railways, because each competing carrier is legalized from the first charter to its last tariff, and is an ever-living agency of commerce, as much as are oceans, lakes, and rivers. The more crushed and the poorer a rival railroad becomes, the more active usually is its competition. The reverse is clearly the fact as to those who oppose trusts. Its rivals abandon business at the sinking point of lost capital. Railroads are reassessed and go on in business.

Trusts have no natural competition like that of free or publicly assisted waterways with railways. Some trusts are made and thereafter protected by the import duties of the country and find the railways their largest patrons, as in the steel industry. Railways are in no case so protected.

Trusts dictate shipping terms to railways, not the railways to the trusts, because the trusts may each day transfer their traffic from road to road in order to compel reduced rates or favoritisms. Trusts may build competing railway lines at their pleasure, under general laws, in order to achieve their purposes. Railways can not engage in the extraneous business conducted by trusts, such as the manufacture of sugar or oil. Trusts may perhaps cause furnaces, oil wells, coal and iron mines, iron mills, coke ovens, foundries, quarries, etc., to lie idle; but there are no idle railways, even under the closest pooling contract when two railways might readily carry all the tonnage offered to five. The more the tonnage offering, the more the competing carriers strive to provide the best power and cars to move it, even at reduced rates. The less the tonnage offered the more they strive for it and too often at broken rates.

Trusts advance commodity prices. It is in evidence as to every pooling contract of this country that under them rates averaged constant annual reductions.

Further, no railway would be required or could be coerced to join any pool, and if three railways of five pooled, the two which do not do so are as fully and publicly advised of the methods of the other three as if they were parties to the agreement. Not so with trusts.

POOLS DO NOT AFFECT TRUE COMPETITION.

As to voiding competition by a resort to pools. Prior to 1887 the railways could and did contract to divide money or tonnage, or both, and to maintain rates, yet not one of the disastrous results of pooling now held up to public fear ever transpired. Why, then, when they possessed this pooling power, did they not then stop parallel construction; then establish monopolies; then increase rates; then stop competition; then conduct themselves as trusts do, or, at least, then resist and stop the great annual tendency of rates downward? The enormous increase of railway mileage of the United States and the constant and voluntary rate reductions are the incontrovertible answers. The railways did not attempt these things because the unceasing forces of true competition which I have cited produced these annual reductions in rates and fares and will as surely continue to keep them the lowest of the world.

There were no water routes from Pittsburg or interior local points to Baltimore, yet they were given the benefits of the rail rates from Buffalo to New York which competed with canal rates. In other words, due competition and enlightened self-interest selfishly yet comprehensively prevailed.

As forceful then as to-day was the fact that railways sought to build up large permanent local and through tonnages at low average rates rather than to carry a smaller traffic at higher rates, and, in enlarging local freight traffic, local travel also increased to the advantage of the companies which gave it growth. This wise policy employed more labor and developed individual local traffics into a mighty volume of permanent national and international tonnage.

Pools did not even preserve former dividends on railway stocks. I challenge contradiction of the statement that every railway company in the Union which has increased its stock has reduced its average rates per ton carried. If the New York Central Company should double its bonds and shares this year, it could not, with all its own powers, plus those of its strong proprietors and allies, increase its average rates in any appreciable degree because the lines competing with it would not increase their capitalizations or rates, and the Erie Canal, the Hudson, St. Lawrence, and Mississippi rivers, and the competition of Galveston, Baltimore, Montreal, and London would prevent it. At the same time all these lines are entitled to some share of the increase in national prosperity when they pay more for all the materials they so largely consume.

FREIGHT POOLS COMPARED WITH TELEGRAPH USAGE.

The analogy of existing uniform telegraph charges to railway pooling and the results thereunder seem convincing. Simultaneously with the early construction of railways, parallel telegraphs were built; the one to transport persons and property, the other information. The telegraph companies entered into what was then, as now, falsely called "competition," in which they had rate contests, lost money, struggled for capital, and became involved with legislation. They increased their stocks and entangled interested railways. Finally the wires were substantially consolidated, both continuous and parallel lines.

When Mr. Gould made the telegraph combinations it was widely alleged by many, who also called railway pooling monstrous, that he might use the information derived from inspected messages to create syndicates and fortunes which would threaten the Republic. On the contrary, although its stock was increased, the Western Union Company proceeded to desirable economies, increased its business, reduced its charges, extended its lines, increased its facilities, achieved greater celerity in the transmission and delivery of messages, and made them more inviolate. Aside from special telegraphic charges to Government and the press, and for night messages, the rates territorially are now substantially uniform, and the users of the wires not only no longer complain of discriminations, but applaud its reduced, well-known. and unrebated charges, because they are reasonable, uniform, and stable, yet they have not as many officers as have the railways. No man believes his rival pays less than he does for a like service. Its business has become practically and promptly postal without the law which was invoked to make it so. Substantially, railways seek only corresponding rights from the same offices in order that they also may maintain the same sound principles of uniformity and nondepleted charge therefrom, to be guarded, however, in the railway instance, by due national regulation, which is not extended over the telegraphs where the Postal and Western Union companies work in accord. The telegraphic results clearly represent better commercial and public conditions without law than the disturbing railway conditions under the Interstate Commerce and Antitrust acts and decisions.

LEGALIZATION OF COOPERATION IN OTHER TRADES AND INTEREST.

As these premises and facts have not been controverted, the railways desire only the grants of duly guarded legislative authority which will remove business and legal doubts, and which are as practicable, efficient, and necessary in railway administration as to organize and conduct impartially chambers of commerce, stock, maritime, and produce exchanges, and board of trade, and to the same honorable public as well as private ends. No exercise of due private or corporate rights will create public wrongs. The same principle justifies the union and concert of counties in the State, and of the States in Congress, and of nations in international conferences, at The Hague, in world's fairs, and in political conventions, etc., to consider constitutional amendments and announce and record the will and good will of competing nations.

The New York Clearing House, with annual clearances 50 times the gross yearly receipts of the railways of the Union, has proven a national bulwark of finance, and assists all right fiscal standards, purposes, and doers.

That one of all these trade and national bodies sometimes does wrong is a reenforced argument for their necessity and benefits, because they go on organizing and acting until their principles prevail, because good agreements and deeds increase the averages of rectitude, sustain the well meaning, check the insincere or pernicious, and make and maintain right rules of human intercourse in all their channels.

TWENTY-FIRST.

AMERICAN INDORSEMENTS OF POOLING.

The extent to which pooling has been considered and favored by trade bodies, State railway commissions, and publicists and the changes in the opinions of important persons and commercial associations constitute important testimony in the railway behalf.

The Cullom committee of 1886 especially and carefully considered pooling, and of 149 persons whom it questioned 42 favored pooling generally, 26 favored legalized pools, 41 pools with legal and other restrictions, *and no witness before it offered any acceptable subtitute therefor.*

That committee reported in 1886 as follows:

"It would seem wiser to permit such agreements rather than by prohibiting them to render the enforcement and maintenance of agreed rates impracticable."

Further:

"The committee does not deem it prudent to recommend the prohibition of pooling;" and "the ostensible object of pooling is in harmony with the spirit of regulative legislation."

Still further:

"The majority of the committee are not disposed to endanger the success of the methods of regulation proposed for the prevention of unjust discriminations by recommending the prohibition of pooling."

The law which that committee first submitted therefore provided:

"Said interstate commission shall especially inquire into that method of railway management or combination known as pooling and report to Congress what, if any, legislation is advisable and expedient upon the subject."

Judge Reagan, of Texas, then chairman of the House Committee on Commerce, mainly defeated these witnesses and these recommendations of the Cullom committee. He went thence to the United States Senate, and having thereafter become a railway commissioner of Texas he frankly said:

"Further study has caused me to believe that the [fifth] section may be amended so as to benefit both the railroads and the people by allowing the railroads to enter into traffic arrangements with one another."

This recommendation was coupled with certain governmental supervision.

Among other prominent men who formerly opposed pooling but who have as frankly changed their views are Hon. Charles S. Smith, late president of the New York Chamber of Commerce; Hon. Simon Sterne, the counsel for the New York board of transportation; F. B. Thurber, of New York; Professor Atwater, of Princeton; A. B. Hepburn, chairman of the great New York State railway committee of inquiry in 1879, and many others.

The first annual report of the first Interstate Commerce Commission said:

"The scheme of pooling rates, or the earnings from traffic, was devised and put in force * * * as a means whereby steadiness in rates might be maintained."

From the same report:

"The scheme was one which was made use of in other countries, and had been found of service to the roads."

Judge Cooley, its chairman, said:

"It may therefore be taken as agreed that, so far as pooling arrangements have the correction of this subject (discriminations) in view, the purpose is commendable."

Also that:

"Without the aid of the law to enforce pooling arrangements it is not yet apparent that any scheme can be devised whereby the cutting of rates can be effectually prevented."

He also said, May 20, 1890, to a convention of State railway commissioners, in Washington:

"It may seem altogether proper that the Government should make, or permit to be made, some provisions whereby the comparatively feeble road may be supported, not entirely by the resources of the district which it serves, but to some extent also by a tax upon the business or resources of other roads. A provision to this end is not uncommon."

The Minneapolis Board of Trade said in 1892:

"The railroad pool honestly administered is the natural balance wheel of interstate commerce."

In 1893 the United States Senate requested the Interstate Commerce Commission to reconsider the subject, whereupon the latter asked commercial bodies and others as to the advisability of amending the interstate act so as to legalize "pooling contracts which would tend to diminish unlawful discriminations."

Eighty-nine answers favored that proposition, or the entire repeal of the interstate act.

In June, 1894, a conference of commercial interests in Washington, representing 23 States and 87 trade bodies, unanimously recommended the passage of the Paterson pooling bill, which was afterwards modified to more favor the public in the Foraker bill.

After seven years' experience under the interstate act pooling was also indorsed in Washington, December, 1894, by all the State railway commissions there represented, except Minnesota, at which time it was resolved:

"That competing carriers may safely be permitted to make lawful contracts with each other for the apportionment of their traffic or the earnings therefrom, provided conditions and restrictions are imposed which protect the public from excessive and unreasonable charges."

At the national convention of railroad commissioners, held in Washington in May, 1896, Hon. J. H. Reagan, of Texas, who had once defeated pooling, reported as follows:

"I have believed and do believe that the pooling of freights and division of earnings could be authorized by law and so regulated as to prevent, to a large extent, if not entirely, railroad wars and unjust discriminations in freight rates, with advantage both to the railroads and to shippers."

The committee on government ownership, control, and regulation of railways reported to the same convention without dissent:

"Congress must legalize pooling in order to make it an effectual remedy for rate wars."

The National Board of Trade has three times recommended such legislation.

All these judgments received the approval of the Fifty-third Congress, the House of Representatives, by a majority of 56, and the Senate Committee on Commerce reported the bill favorably at the same session, but it did not pass the latter body.

TWENTY-SECOND.

POOLING IN FOREIGN COUNTRIES.

Your topical plan invites mention of English precedents.

Mr. Acworth, England, said in the New York Independent (October, 1892):

"To pools properly so called there does not seem to be any popular objection. Indeed, within the last year the two great Scotch companies, the North British and the Caledonian, have agreed to a 25 years' pool of their traffic, and though there was a good deal of opposition in Glasgow when it was first announced, within the last few weeks the Glasgow traders have confessed that they were mistaken and that none of the ills which they anticipated have arisen. * * *

"As traders they see the canvassers of the different companies coming to them, hat in hand, and begging for traffic, promising a later departure, more careful handling, and more prompt delivery—it may be more generous settlements of claims. As passengers they see the companies vieing with one another in improvements, in accommodations, in frequency of service or increased speed, as well as in a score of details which make up the comforts of passenger travel. Accordingly, when the theorist comes along with his assurance that competition is extinct and that pools have done mischief, they are apt to shrug their shoulders and take not much notice."

While many of the difficulties which embarrass this issue here could be corrected by the better faith which characterizes the management of English and foreign railways generally, the closer parity of their shorter distances, their denser traffic, and their higher rates and fares all make it easier to maintain their rates on faith; nevertheless they too nave had their periods of distrust and wrong, when they found pooling between governmental lines, between governmental and private lines, and by private lines only, the best panacea therefor, unless it was governmental control or geographical apportionments of territory, both being yet more stringent forms of pooling. The dissimilarities in our conditions, the greater area of our country, our longer railway distances and systems, the great differences in the facilities and strength of our own railways and their stronger rivalries of interior and exterior water carriers, etc., the more require that good faith here be supplemented by the legislative sanction and safeguards afforded abroad.

English public railway policy was best stated by the Royal Commission of 1887, appointed to inquire into the charges, rates, and tolls of British railways. It said:

"We are of the opinion that a sound principle to act on, in the matter of working and traffic agreements between railway companies, is to allow any companies to enter into them without reference to any tribunal, upon the *sole condition* that the particulars should be made public *in the locality* and that they should be terminable by either party at the expiration of limited periods. If any such agreement contained anything contrary to the rights of the public, the court of common pleas should have a power of setting it aside at the instance of the board of trade."

Railway Rates, English and Foreign, by J. Grierson, manager of the Great Western Railway (London, 1886), said:

"Agreements for the division of traffic, or for 'pooling,' as they are termed in the United States and Canada, are not unknown in this country. Some have been sanctioned by Parliament, others have been made between the companies without any express Parliamentary authority, and have been carried out. Mr. Gladstone made, in 1851, an award apportioning, for 5 years, the receipts for traffic carried between London, York, Leeds, Sheffield, etc., between the Great Northern, London and Northwestern, and Midland railways. In 1857 he made a further award determining, for 14 years, the proportions in which the proceeds from passenger and goods traffic between the same and other places were to be divided between those companies and the Manchester company."

"The Working and Management of an English Railway," by George Findlay, manager of the London and Northwestern company (1891), said:

"There is another plan which railways sometimes adopt, which is known as 'Percentage Division of Traffic,' and which is carried out in the following manner:

Supposing that there is a certain traffic to be conveyed between two towns or districts, and that there are two or more railway companies, each having a route of its own, by which it is enabled to compete for the traffic. An agreement is made that the receipts derived from the whole of the traffic carried by all routes shall be thrown into a common fund, and that each company shall be entitled to a certain percentage of the whole.

The percentages are usually adjusted on the basis of past actual carryings."

"The Railways and Traders,' by W. M. Acworth, (London, 1891), said:

"Companies have combined, and do combine every day, but for all that they have competed, do compete, and as far as we can see at present are likely to continue to compete to the end of the chapter. Will any Lancashire trader go into the witness box and declare that the Lancashire and Yorkshire and the Northwestern never make any attempt to get hold of each other's traffic? And yet all the world knows that, from a time whereof the memory of man runneth not to the contrary, these two companies have agreed to divide the traffic at competitive points."

He further said:

"The much discussed continental agreement between the Southeastern and the Chatham and Dover, which settles the proportions in which the two companies are to share the receipts for all traffic to the Continent passing over their lines, is solemnly scheduled to an act of Parliament and has been judicially considered by every court in the country up to and including the House of Lords. Yet is it not matter of common knowledge that the Southeastern and the Chatham each fight their hardest to divert the stream of traffic from the rival line?"

The prominent case of Hare v. L. and N. W. Ry. Co. grew out of the fact that—

"Independent conterminous routes agreed to divide the profits of the whole traffic in certain fixed proportions calculated on the experience of past course of traffic. It was held that such an agreement, being *bona fide*, was not *ultra vires*."

Wood, on Railroads (London, 1894), said of this case:

"A shareholder applied, though after several years of acquiescence, for an injunction to restrain the companies from carrying out the agreement. The application was refused. The vice-chancellor considered not only that on principle such an agreement was legal, there being nothing prejudicial to either the shareholders or the public, but also that he was concluded by the judgment of Lord Cottenham, of the Court of the Queen's Bench, in the Shrewsbury Case."

The same authority said generally:

"In England it is held that 'pooling' contracts, or arrangements between competing roads by which they agree to divide their joint earnings upon certain classes of business, or even their entire earnings, are legal and valid, where it does not appear that the interests of the shareholders or the public are prejudiced thereby."

"The Mogul Steamship Company, Limited, v. McGregor, Gow & Co. et al.," grew out of a contract limiting the number of ships to be run in a certain service. Lord Bramwell said of this, in 1892:

"It does seem strange that to enforce freedom of trade, of action, the law should punish those who make a perfectly honest agreement with a belief that it is fairly required for their protection."

Professor Hadley, now president of Yale College, testified in 1885, before the Senate Select Committee on Interstate Commerce, as follows:

"It is a noticeable fact that at the time when the first series of attempts was made to check discrimination in England the first pools were arranged."

He then testified more comprehensively:

"It may be stated as a fact of history that no nation has succeeded in prohibiting discrimination and pooling at the same time. I should be willing to go further and say that, as far as I know, no law has been permanently effective in prohibiting or discouraging either discrimination or pooling, except in so far as it at the same time indirectly or directly encouraged the other.

"On the continent of Europe the worst forms of discrimination, the worst abuses from which we suffer, are, in general, efficiently prohibited, but it is generally by an organized system of pools of whose completeness we have no conception in this country, pools that are not merely recognized by law, but enforced by law. The State itself enters into such pooling contracts on account of its own lines with private lines.

"Senator PLATT of Connecticut. To what countries do your remarks apply?

"Mr. HADLEY. Chiefly to France, Belgium, and Austria; also, to a less extent, to Switzerland and Italy. In France they have never recognized railroad competition as a principle, and scarcely have had it in practice at any time; but in Belgium and Germany they have tried railroad competition, and, what is all the more striking, have given it up as producing discriminations only to be avoided by pools. About the year 1860 the railroad system of Belgium was partly in Government hands and partly in the hands of special private companies. The private companies had longer lines, but the Government had unity of management and had had the chance of first laying out its railroads and choosing the best routes. The result was an extremely even system of competition.

"Competition produced the same effects it has produced in America—good and bad. It tended to the rapid development of the country.

"It caused railroad rates to become lower in Belgium than they were or had been in any other part of Europe, or any other country except the United States. On the other hand, it caused all sorts of oppressive preferences, special rates, special contracts with private individuals; the Government itself, in spite of all the central authority could do, being a worse sinner than any of the private lines in the matter of giving special rates to individuals.

"The people would not stand that the Government road should not make money, while a private road, apparently not quite so well situated, should make money. They tried to prohibit the competition of private lines by law. It was partly ended by the absorption of the competing lines and partly by pooling arrangements.

"There is one large private company, the Belgian Grand Central, that has a most inflexible pooling contract with the Government.

"In Germany also, about the year 1870, there was a tolerable equality, in Prussia particularly, between the State railroads and the competing private lines, and there was also a system of discriminations. Just in so far as the State either consolidated with private railroads, or entered into pooling contracts with them, the discriminations were abolished, but not until then. They never had discrimination so badly in Germany as we have in America, or as badly as they had in Belgium even, but they had some, and it was only abolished by consolidation and pooling.

"At present the Prussian Government owns practically all its railroads, but there was a time when it had large pooling arrangements with private lines.

"The Austrian Government and the private railroad men have come to the conclusion that the only way they can possibly abolish discrimination is by systems of pooling. The two main cities, Vienna and Budapest, the capitols of Austria and Hungary, are connected by two railroads and the river Danube, one of these railroads having been built by the State. As soon as the second railroad was made there was this division made, which included the State road and second road and the water route, each carrying its percentage, although the water route was a natural water course, * * * and so anybody who said he would not go into a pool would ibe considered to be a very strange man, and a man who was making trouble.

"A still stronger instance, perhaps, is the Arlberg Tunnel.

"Before they had opened that road they made a percentage division between that and the existing roads by dividing the traffic at each end of the tunnel. The parties to this division were the Austrian State railroads, Austrian private railroads, Bavarian railroads, two or three Swiss private companies, railroads in other South German States, and several French companies that formed remote connections. They state themselves in all that is written on the subject that the only way of avoiding discrimination between competing points is by such percentage divisions, with the authority of.the Government."

Professor Hadley said later, in his work on "Railroad Transportation" (1886):

"With all the police power which the German Government controls, a power a hundred-fold greater than anything we have in this country, and with all its dread of irresponsible combinations, it seems that pools are not a thing which can be prevented, and that the only way to control them is to recognize them as legal and then hold them responsible for any evils which may arise under their management."

Speaking of the governmental railway policy of central Europe, he said:

"To secure obedience to this (prohibitory) system they must take away the temptation to violate it. This can only be done by a system of pooling contracts. These are accordingly legalized and enforced. They are carried on to an extent undreamed of in America. They have both traffic pools and money pools. There are pools between state roads and private roads, between railroads and water routes."

REMEDIAL LEGISLATION IMPERATIVE.

This long study and experience, the logical conclusions and usages abroad and the mutually beneficial results which followed the practical adoption of these policies in those great countries, can not be intelligently ignored in our own larger and more troublous areas by mere denunciations that the purpose is akin to monopolies, trusts, etc., although our rates average so much less than those which prevail in those nations having quasi-sanction or enforceable contracts. Here our res ma harmonious States defeat our just purposes, whereas jealous adjacent nationalities abroad assist the best solution of the problem.

OBJECTIONS TO POOLING.

The most recent authoritative criticism of pooling was made by Hon. Charles A. Prouty, of the Interstate Commerce Commission, in The Forum for December, 1897. That article was largely in answer to myself, and I have anticipated most of his grounds in other parts of this paper, but I will reply a little further.

He first conceded that "most people who have examined this question conclude that the right to make pooling contracts would, to a large extent, do away with the demoralization of rates and the consequent disastrous results to both railways and public, and that permission to make such contract should be given."

He then asks, as you do of me: "If, then, great advantage may be reasonably expected from pooling legislation, why is it that many people well informed on the subject oppose the passage of such a law?"

I now quote from his own comments, italicizing them in part, and answer them briefly:

(a) That the "enormous decrease" of railway earnings "altogether in the case of interstate traffic" is due * * * "to the action of competitive forces."

This fairly concedes all "competitive forces;" not merely "struggles" and "strifes" and "rate wars," but shows that the railways must submit to water rates also, which are the greatest "competitive forces."

(b) That * * * "there is between those (rail) carriers a continual *struggle of the fiercest kind* for competitive business" * * * "and to which * * * the above reduction is *mainly* due." * * *

A "struggle of the fiercest kind" is not competition in any due railway, national, or legislative meaning, nor have the reductions been mainly due to that cause.

"A reduction in the rates between Chicago and New York would *force down* the corresponding rates at other points." * * * "The purpose of a pooling law is to *eliminate entirely* from railway operations, with regard to the traffic which it affects, the factor of *railway* competition."

To "*force* down" corresponding rates at other points than those where the fierce struggles ensued is not competition, nor is it shown that other points are entitled to such rates by any competition, except those of markets, because many of the "other points" were local and would have but one railway.

* * * ' Let us take two points like Chicago and Kansas City. * * * They are connected by six lines of railway, with no water *connection* to complicate the situation. * * * Each of these six railroads is seeking to obtain the business which moves between the two cities. * * * When other inducements fail, it reduces the rate."

No railway pool here or abroad has ever indicated an intent, or operated in practice, to "entirely eliminate" competition. It continues, and in no case abolishes it, but it regulates it. Mr. Prouty's illustration lacks the essential logic of fact. Boats run from Kansas City to St. Louis, and *do* "complicate the situation," because they limit many important rates between Kansas City and Chicago.

"Assume that a pooling law is passed and that a pooling contract is made between these carriers." * * * "What is the objection to legalizing that contract? The common law declares it illegal as against public policy, and while there is current, both in and out of Congress, a good deal of nonsense upon the subject of trusts and monopolies" * * * "the monopoly of a necessity should be guarded against."

Rail lines Kansas City to Memphis, thence water to and via New Orleans, also govern many rates via Chicago to New York. So do rail lines Kansas City to Galveston, thence via Gulf water lines.

If, as averred, "it," i. e., *one* company, reduces not only the through rates for itself, but via all lines and all intermediate rates by the operation of law, it should not have that power. It is in no sense true competition, and if such strife ceased by pooling, and all the carriers concerned endeavored to restore and observe jointly the former agreed legal tariffs assumed to be reasonable, it would not be a monopoly more than in the first instance without a pool. The real monopoly consists in encouraging and giving one road such great power and lauding it as the victor of competition.

No pool ever dominated any traffic situation.

(c) * * * "A transportation trust is the most dangerous of all trusts, because it *absolutely dominates* the situation." * * *

"Whatever traffic passes between Chicago and Kansas City *must*, assuming them to be the only lines, pass over one of the six lines of railroad which are parties to that contract." * * * " It *can not be denied*, therefore, that this combination of railroads controls the traffic between Kansas City and Chi-

A transportation trust never has been, and cannot be formed by pooling, because the individual companies continue their rival efforts by bettered facilities, rather than by rebated rates, because of the water rivalry so often set forth and because of commercial contests involving rates. The trust view may be and is more incited and quickly secured by consolidation, which the re-cago *more absolutely than any other trust could* control a thing of common necessity, with the exception of the supply of gas, or electric light, or water."

(d) * * * 'Now at the end of six months *some one of the six lines* looks over the income sheet and ascertains that, upon a particular basis, it is not earning what it is "entitled" to.

The matter is taken up with the other members of the pool; it is agreed that the rates are too low, that they ought to be advanced somewhat; and, accordingly, an advance is made. Would or would not this be the result? If not, why?

(e) "Almost every reduction (i. e., of rates) has been a *rate-war reduction;* and who is to say whether it was justifiable or unjustifiable? * * * but let it ever be remembered that the shearing is for the wool, not for the comfort of the animal."

fusal to permit mutual contracts is now greatly stimulating. Even that form of concentration can not dominate transportation, for causes recited and reiterated, and unanswered by facts. If Mr. Vanderbilt bought every railroad leading from Chicago and St. Louis to every American port from Newport News to Boston, he would not then "dominate the issue," for New Orleans, Galveston, Pensacola, Mobile, and Savannah would still be open-door ports, and the Great Lakes and the St. Lawrence River, the Erie Canal, our laws, and Canadian rail rivalry would continue as potent and forceful as now. This seems too clear for more argument.

So if one man bought the six lines between Kansas City and Chicago and thereby made his power more absolute than any pool could, he would then be compelled to buy all the lines from Omaha, Sioux City, and St. Paul to Chicago, and from Kansas City to St. Louis, Memphis, New Orleans, and Galveston, to have anything even approaching a trust or monopoly. Even then the Missouri and Mississippi River carriers would smash his "trust."

As he asks why, I will answer: Even if some *one* company "looks over *the* income sheet" etc., it can only see its own net results. To aver that all "the other members of the pool" would nevertheless, as he predicts, regard the rates as "too low" and *all* thereupon agree to advance them for the benefit of that one company, shows how some of our public men use inexpert conjecture as the equivalent of fact and experience. No case can be adduced from any source in proof of the pure surmise advanced, and there never was such an instance in any country.

As to why the rates could not be thereupon unduly advanced, I have shown in the comment next preceding.

Elsewhere in the same article, Mr. Prouty said: "Water competition has been a potential factor in the reduction."

If "almost every reduction" of rates "has been a *rate-war reduction*," it clearly entitled the contestants to a restoration of the reasonable ante-bellum conditions.

The various railway companies, after the usual consultations between themselves and with shippers, are the more proper ones to decide if the rate was just in the first instance.

The statement is most inaccurate from national railway commissioners. It is not true that the vast reductions in rates throughout the nation on all lines in 20 years have been caused by rate wars. Those wars have been minor factors compared with the great causes I have set out; and in many instances they were greatest when there were no wars at all. As for example in the coal, iron, lumber, limestone, ore, and other leading rates of the Pennsylvania, New York Central, Illinois Central, and other systems.

(f) That it is argued "* * * that a pooling bill should be enacted because the present law is not obeyed."

The present law is not only not obeyed, but so the commission says, it is impracticable of efficient administration in its essence: i. e., the stoppage of discriminations. If to justly reenact the law with pooling legalized, *solely* because the present law is not obeyed would best stop that great abuse, that ground would alone warrant such action. That, however, is an incidental, and not at all the main argument.

Those shippers and railways who profit by non-obeyance of the law are the ones who constantly and most strenuously oppose the legalized contract proposal. They are negatively aided by law, the views set forth by Mr. Prouty and the amendments proposed. This seems inconsistent with the prior assertion that legalized contract would "eliminate competition," be more absolute "than any other trust," and would "dominate the situation."

(g) "But if the formation of this contract were legalized, would there be *nothing* to restrain these lines from an arbitrary advance in rates?"

Certainly. "Precisely the same influences which operate in other business relations would operate here." * * * "Any considerable advance in rates consequent upon the passage of a pooling bill would raise a storm of indignation which would speedily *repeal* the law itself."

If precisely the "same influences" would operate upon railways as upon trade, why should not trade and railways both be legislated for, and why are advances and greater profits in the prices of general merchandise and larger special industries hailed as proofs of national prosperity while slight advances in freight charges, largely paid by foreign consignees and senders, and caused by higher prices for material, are denounced as a cause for "storms of indignation?"

Further, if such indignation could speedily repeal the law, wherein lies the danger of a trial of such amendments to it?

(h) "In the last ten years the changes have been mostly downward. In the ten years following the enactment of a pooling law, they would be mostly up ward."

Keeping in mind the distinction between due tariff rates and undue rebated rates, this purely conjectural assertion recalls the foolish prophetic averment of the Windom Committee, appointed in 1874, entirely disproved by the later history of transportation, that national railway ownership and control were "the only means of securing and maintaining reliable and effective competition between the railways." Mr. Prouty says that government ownership keeps up rates abroad.

(i) "It may not be that the Boston and Maine would pool with a Los Angeles line, but it is *reasonably certain* that a line having its terminus at Galveston would pool with another line having its terminus in Boston."

I quote this to show another of the pure conjectures upon which a governmental railway commissioner bases an unwarranted opinion, unfounded in any fact. It is not "reasonably certain," as averred, but certainly improbable, impracticable, and without precedent either in intent or result.

(*k*) "Competition gives a low rate; but it produces a succession of evils which are deplorable. Pooling * * * puts into the hands of the carriers *absolute power* over the rate. * * *"

This induces the inquiries: What *is* a low rate, and who shall decide that question? *How* does pooling give "the carriers *absolute power over* rates" when he, himself, says elsewhere in the same article:

"Water competition has been a *potential* factor in the reduction."

"There can be no question that the rates on grain between Chicago and New York * * * is for some months a controlling element."

Also, that: "A reduction in the rates between Chicago and New York would 'force down' the corresponding rate at *other* points."

Still further, the railways have never asked for an unlimited or unregulated right to pool.

If the published rates are reasonable and are maintained by means of legalized pools at the traffic centers, they should be equally observed at local points at the same or properly graduated charges, as provided by the "long and short haul" clause of the act.

(*l*) "As water competition does not stop with the shore, so the influence of pooling contracts would not cease with the traffic to which they refer." * * * "Once give railway companies the right to make contracts by which competitive business is controlled, and you have strengthened them immensely in respect to all their business."

It is not, therefore, the addition "of immense strength," but *immense justice*, and is required by law to avoid preferences for localities. Moreover, in the present complaint that rates locally *are* maintained, while at central points they are cut. Why, again, should *not* our railways be justly strengthened, instead of continually weakened?

(*m*) "* * * that in nearly every country on the Continent where pooling is permitted the Government owns and operates either all the railways or one or more important railway lines; in the latter case, exercising a much stricter supervision over the others than we have ever deemed possible."

This clearly begs my question. No railway in Great Britain, pooled or otherwise, is owned, controlled, or operated by its Government, and the English system is constantly held up to our admiration. They are all free to "pool," and many of them do so. I have shown the British and Continental practices, and repeat the unanswered query, viz: Why does a policy, endorsed by the Governments of Europe as to the railways under governmental, or private, or blended control, wise as a means to commercial stability, uniformity, and reasonableness of national and international rates, become "unwise," "restrictive," "dominating," "absolute," "monopolistic," and creative of trusts, in America, at one-half the foreign rates?

He says that some foreign Governments "own and operate either all the railways or one or more important railway lines."

Conceded, but I do not concede that a Parliament of the goverments of Peel, or Palmerston, or Gladstone, or of Cavour, or Bismarck, or Thiers were commercially more ignorant than the Congresses of Hayes, or Cleveland, or Harrison.

Again, the statement seems to sustain rather than refute my claim that, if our

(n) Mr. Prouty asked if the Joint Traffic Association would submit to the English measure of regulation.	Government owned its railways, as the Windom committee advised we should, it would resort to the same, or an equivalent, European system to preserve equal, stable, and just rates. Mr. Prouty made no answer whatever to the striking parallels of railway with governmental or telegraph charges. I would unhesitatingly so advise, if the same rates and methods are allowed and legalized. I discuss fully elsewhere the English system.

Mr. Prouty concluded his adverse argument by stating:
"The writer does not oppose the enactment of a pooling bill." * * * "For the reasons stated by Mr. Blanchard, and for many reasons which he does not state, most people who have examined this question conclude that the right to make pooling contracts would, to a large extent, do away with the demoralization of rates, and the consequent disastrous results to both railroads and public; and that permission to make such contracts ought to be given."
He proceeds to discuss the limitations under which such authority should be granted. I present and argue them next.

Twenty-Third.

THE INTERSTATE ACT—ITS POWERS AND DEFECTS.

Your topical paragraphs 54, 55, and 56 cite the Interstate Commerce Act and the commission, their present scope and powers, their defects and the proposed remedies therefor, and invite comparisons with the authority possessed by the English Railway Commission.
The conditions which led to the act of 1886 were dealt with fully in the Windom report of 1878 and the Reagan bill of 1879, and were reported upon again more comprehensively by the Cullom committee January 18, 1886.
The last held the American railway system to eighteen (18) counts, eleven (11) of which related to discriminations, the other seven to undue rates and capitalizations, managements, classifications, and engaging in extraneous business. Time and improved procedures have substantially non-suited six of the other complaints.
The stripped fact is that the act did not protect the public and railways impartially, and was, therefore, unjust. To stimulate so-called " competition," it was not made applicable to parallel water carriers. It regarded the railways as alone responsible for all the conditions condemned, and, although it applied theoretical penalties to shippers who procured preferences it devolved the practical corrections of all transportation errors upon the railways alone.
Its provisions were all antagonistic and none remedial, nor did it create or foster that mutual interest between Government and carriers essential to its success. It held to the exploded perversion that railway warfare is synonymous with business competition. It fostered the fallacy that while rates must be alike via one railway it was desirable and legal that they be different upon rival railways to insure so-called competition, or else that, however different in facilities and conditions, all rival railways could obtain equal rates and fares. It did not recognize the palpable fact that ten different rates on ten railways were as disturbing and discriminating as ten rates on one railway, and that therefore the poorest and most reckless railway can make the competing rates for all the others.
Finally it encountered legal reverses which induced railway laxity in its observance, and it has not corrected the evils which argued for its passage. Here, more than in foreign countries, because of our greater area and more complex conditions, mere mandates against discriminations and excesses have failed and will ever fail until they give the parties affected a common interest to obey the law and because the act, *as it now stands*, does not protect upright carriers or shippers against the encroachments of others less so.

THE DEFECTS OF THE INTERSTATE ACT.

As to the defects of the act, the evidence is not only general, but official and recent.
Interstate Commissioner Clement said at Denver, August 11, 1899:
"* * * the law has not been found to mean and accomplish what its authors intended." * * *

655A——42

Mr. Clement does not explain how he has knowledge of the intent of its authors, and the Supreme Court has interpreted a different intent.

"Now, after the operation and test of this act, as slightly amended, for more than 12 years, the same causes of complaint and grievance in a large measure still exist."

Chairman Knapp, of the commission, said on the same occasion:

"The rules of conduct prescribed by the State in respect of public carriage are in many respects so indefinite as to be little more than guides, and so imperfect as to be extremely difficult of application." * * *

"* * * the railroads of the country should be regarded in their entirety and treated, so far as possible, as a single system for all the purposes of legal regulation." * * *

I remark in passing that this is the strongest form of pool.

"No just theory of legislation will proceed on the assumption that the public alone are in need of protection and that the railroads can take care of themselves. Such a view is unfair and illogical."

"The sufficient scheme of legislation, therefore, will recognize the possibility of wrongdoing on one side as well as the other, * * * and while equipping the shipper with ample protection will also furnish the carrier with all needful defenses."

"Nor can these beneficent ends be reached, in my judgment, without conferring upon the railroad corporations privileges of association and rights of contract with each other which are denied by existing laws."

Legislation framed on these wise lines can be made mutually effective, otherwise it can not.

The act has, nevertheless, secured more publicity of rates, lessened open rate-wars, has more justly scaled and equalized long and short-haul rates, both at intermediate common points and at local stations, has exercised beneficial warning or police powers, has silenced much unjust clamor against railways, has softened the railway attitude toward the public, has been mutually educational, and has been in the main well administered, but secret discriminations have not only continued, but have greatly increased. I am not, therefore, of those who believe that the commission's value is not much greater than its cost.

The insufficiencies of the act and its relapses have proceeded mainly from the legislative refusal to confirm the only practical plan commended by the Cullom report, viz, to give all well-intending shippers and carriers a joint interest and governmental authority to resist demoralizations in rates and fares by mutual contract. The adopted act followed foreign precedents, our own former usage, and the Cullom report only to this point. There it stopped. This was as if consulting physicians adhered to the discredited cures used by earlier science but disregarded the latest and best discovery for the disease treated and then blamed the patient for his relapses. It was as if Congress had refused to enact the recommendations of its own and the world's army and navy fiscal and diplomatic experts for the public welfare and security.

Railway officers and patrons can not be legislated into mutual rectitude when otherwise disposed, for even the Divine laws have not done that. They must be afforded some positive aids to betterment.

The reasons for mutual conciliation and cooperation are apparent:

Favored shippers oppose all methods to defeat rebates; weak lines will not be without business, and therefore pay drawbacks to get it; and strong lines will not permanently permit its diversion but will make the rates equal, a course which is commercially desirable, indeed essential, although it may be reluctantly and illegally done by drawbacks. Devices and concealed rates, therefore, ensue largely, which are illogically urged by some as desirable "competition" and "public benefits," whereas they are discriminations, pure and simple.

Proceeding to the failures of the act, and the best cures therefor, an amended law should, in my judgment, proceed upon very brief leading principles:

(a) That *some* standards of railway rates and fares and *some* carrying rules and conditions *must* be reasonable.

(b) That, being found reasonable in effect and being possessed with a public interest, the Government should, after such rates are filed with the commission and not by it objected to, and by direct affirmative action, aid the railway companies in their observance and enforcement as it observes and enforces its own tariffs, its arbitrations, its treaty obligations, its international postal unions, the written and unwritten laws of war, and all other expressed or implied obligations incurred on behalf of its people.

(c) That this is the essential and only means to the stoppage of the discriminations justly complained of, and the failures of the act in that respect.

These premises being unassailable, upon what defensible grounds can the nation continue to disregard the undisputed precedents, facts, and obligations involved and rely, as to the greatest agency of advancement the country possesses, upon the present inadequate and unenforced act or any amendments thereof which fail to recognize and enact these basic principles?

Twenty-Fourth.

DEPARTURES FROM THE FIRST INTENT OF THE CONSTITUTION, FROM THE ACT, AND FROM THE DECISIONS UNDER IT.

I leave to others the legal argument under this important head, but there are two or three salient points which deserve to be always remembered.

The Annapolis Constitutional Convention of 1787 declared one of its objects to be "to devise means for the uniform regulation of trade."

Its primal purpose was to prevent a State—not a carrier—from making trade discriminations against the products of other States. No railway then existed in the world, and the interstate act, especially as proposed to be amended, is not the "uniform regulation of trade," but only of one and often the smallest element of the trade. Nor is it regulation—it is control, legislation, and administration.

"The first important act of Congress respecting interstate commerce was passed June 15, 1886. It authorized railroads chartered by the several States to combine with roads of other States." "Its object was to prevent the States from impeding commerce," the commerce which the railways most desired should be interchanged.

The Cullom report of January, 1886, said: " * * * it would be inexpedient and impracticable to attempt to adjust existing inequalities by any system of rates established by legislation."

It also said: " * * * But it is questionable whether a commission, or any similar body of men, could successfully perform a work of such magnitude, involving as it would infinite labor and investigation, exact knowledge as to thousands of details, and the adjustment of a vast variety of conflicting interests."

A few months after the first commission organized it declined—in the case of Thatcher v. The Delaware and Hudson Canal Company—to fix certain rates, saying:

"It is therefore impossible to fix them in this case even if the commission had the power to fix rates generally—which it has not. Its power in respect to rates is to determine whether those which the roads impose are, for any reason, in conflict with the statutes."

The syllabus in the Texas and Pacific case v. The Interstate Commission, decided March 30, 1897, said:

"If the commission has the power of its own motion to promulgate general decrees or orders, which thereby become rules of action to common carriers, such exertion of power must be confined to the obvious purposes and directions of the statute, since Congress has not granted it legislative powers."

That the commission has not since then acquired those rate-making powers is also shown by the Denver report of August, 1899, and by the commission's urgent advocacy of the amendments now proposed. Therefore every proposal it has officially made since its organization tends and more lately intends to restrict competent railway administration to enlarge inexperienced and prejudiced control upon the dangerous margin of 1 vote, and to secure the powers not given it by the act it administers and thus far denied to it by the courts.

Twenty-Fifth.

COMPARISON WITH THE ENGLISH SYSTEM.

To intrench our position, and responsive to your topical inquiry No. 56, as well as Commissioner Prouty's inquiries of me in his Forum article, I desire to compare the existing English system with our system of supervision as the act now reads.

The Parliamentary regulation of the railways of England, Scotland, and Ireland—which, of course, does not extend over Canada or Australia—is comprised within the railway and canal traffic act of 1888, and amendments, and the previous unrepealed acts relating to the same general subject.

That act constituted a Railway and Canal Commission of two commissioners appointed upon the recommendation of the Board of Trade, to hold office during good behavior, and three ex-officio commissioners. One of the appointed commissioners *must* have railway experience and knowledge.

These constitute a court of record. The ex-officio commissioners must be judges of the superior courts—one for Scotland, one for England, and one for Ireland—each appointed by its Lord Chancellor for not less than 5 years.

Certain designated local authorities and associations may complain to this commission or appear in opposition.

I owe what follows, mainly, to the incisive arguments of Attorney Hines, of the Louisville and Nashville Railway Company, and substantially quote the language of his able paper.

The English commission " * * * is to hear and determine complaints of contraventions of the railway regulation acts. It may exercise certain powers of arbitration, and its approval is required to certain agreements between railways or railways and canals. It may also order through rates under careful restrictions provided by law, and it may, when a railway owns a canal, order changes in canal rates when necessary to prevent the diversion of traffic from the canal to the railway. It is also required to report to Parliament when, in its opinion, the working of steamboats by a railway prejudicially affects the public interest.

Though in some respects the powers of this commission exceed the powers of courts generally, yet no duties are imposed upon it which would tend to impair its fairness and judicial character. The commission does not originate complaints; it does not proceed upon its own motion; it is not charged with inquiring into the management of railways; it has no administrative supervision of any of the details of railway operation; it is not charged with detecting violations of the law or of bringing about prosecutions therefor; its duty is to hear the complaints duly brought before it by proper complainants and to determine what, if any, relief is proper under the law.

Thus, in vital respects, the Railway and Canal Commission procedure differs radically from that of the Interstate Commerce Commission. Its two appointed commissioners are appointed for life, and one of them must be of experience in railway matters. The Interstate Commerce Commissioners are appointed simply for 6 years, there is no requirement that any of them shall have railway experience, and, as a matter of fact, experience in railway matters acts as a hindrance to their appointments.

The three ex officio British commissioners are judges of the superior courts and continue to act as judges in the other superior courts when their services are not needed on the commission. All this is an additional guaranty that the proceedings of the commission will be characterized by a judicial temper, which is all important. There is no corresponding guaranty in the case of the Interstate Commission.

Perhaps an even greater guaranty of fairness and justice in the work of the English commission arises from the fact that it performs no function which would be calculated to disqualify a judge for the impartial exercise of his high office. On the other hand, the Interstate Commission is given supervision of various details of railway management; it is given and asks for more inquisitorial powers for the purpose of detecting railway violations of the law; it may institute complaints in its own name; it may cause prosecutions to be instituted to punish violations of the law. By section 12 of the interstate-commerce act, the Interstate Commission is authorized to inquire into the management of the business of carriers, and is required to keep itself informed as to the manner and method in which the same is conducted, and is given the right to obtain from the carriers full and complete information necessary to enable the commission to perform the duties and carry out the objects for which it was created. The Interstate Commission is authorized and required to execute and enforce the provisions of the act, and upon the request of the commission, it shall be the duty of any district attorney of the United States to whom the commission may apply to institute and prosecute in the proper court all necessary proceedings for the enforcement of the provisions of the act and for the punishment of all violations of it, and it may subpœna the attendance and testimony of witnesses and the production of all books, papers, etc., relating to any matter under investigation. The Interstate Commission is also given authority to institute any inquiry on its own motion in the same manner, and to the same effect, as though complaint had been made. This incites litigation rather than its avoidance, inasmuch as if the commission did not move themselves, some complaints might not be made.

Such duties and the character of detectives imposed upon the Interstate Commission and its authority to inaugurate criminal prosecutions, as well as to prosecute civil complaints on its own motion, have a strong tendency to deprive the commission of a judicial temperament, and are not conducive to the fairness and impartiality essential in judges. In all these respects, the functions of the English commission are infinitely superior. For the interstate commission, with its present varied functions, to be permitted to render judgment against a railroad would be almost like allowing a man to be convicted of murder by the grand jury which had indicted him. To give our commission the power to inaugurate complaints on its own motion, and then to hear and finally determine those complaints, would be allowing a party to be the judge in his own cause, which is contrary to one of the elementary principles of law and justice, and such anomalies would not be remedied by allowing appeals.

These comparisons show the unfitness of the Interstate Commission with its present constitution and functions, and less so when enlarged as they ask, for acting as a court, and they show that Congress never intended to give the commission general independent powers or duties, except those of an administrative body designed in some respects to assist litigants and the courts in the enforcement of the interstate act. This is made clear by a study of the debates of Congress on the subject. Indeed, the courts themselves could not have exercised them if the interstate commerce act had left its enforcement to the courts alone instead of adding the commission as an adjunct to the courts, and now that the courts have very properly refused to sanction the unwarranted assumptions, the commission demands that, while it still retains the right to act as administrative supervisor of various details of railway operations, and also the rights to act as detective, prosecutor, and complainant, it be given the powers of a court, and that its orders be enforced as the judgments of a court. The commission will appeal in vain to the railway-regulation law of England for any sanction of an arrangement so repugnant to justice.

The British railway and canal commission is empowered to award damages and, for the enforcement of its orders, has all such powers, rights, and privileges as are vested in a superior court. Since the way the English commission is constituted and the functions conferred on it all give it the dignity of a court and substantial guaranties of judicial fairness and just decisions, and since it is expressly declared to be a court, it is proper that it be given the authority of a court to carry out its orders, which are, for these reasons, entitled to as much respect as if made by any other court in the land. Notwithstanding all this, an appeal lies from its decision on all questions of law.

The Interstate Commerce Commission aspires to much greater powers for the enforcement of its orders, greatly exceeding those enjoyed by the railway and canal commission, but it wants its orders to go into effect and to remain in effect until declared unlawful by the courts, saving a power in the courts to suspend the operation of the order pending review only when on the face of the record it plainly appears that the order is erroneous in point of law or unjust or unreasonable on the facts. Since the court could seldom say that such error or injustice plainly appears simply on the face of the record, the practical result would be that the commission's orders would be in effect throughout the proceedings for review.

Instead of the railway and canal commission of England serving as a precedent for giving such powers, that commission affords a strong contrary argument. To give the Interstate Commission such powers would be about as anomalous as for one man to be detective, prosecuting attorney, and judge in the same case. Certainly, until all other functions are eliminated from the commission and transferred to some other administrative body, and until the commission is restricted solely to the hearing and determination of complaints of violations of the laws which are brought before it by proper complainants, there should be no thought of giving it the powers of a court to put its orders into effect by execution or by any means whatever, except by suit in court for their enforcement.

Even then, to be as favorably constituted for dispensing justice as is the English commission, the members should be appointed for life; some of them should be men of experience in railway matters, and some of them should be judges, in order to insure that judicial temperament which is absolutely necessary for the proper discharge of such important functions. If the commission be made a court, the Constitution of the United States will make it imperative that its members hold office during good behavior.

Not only does the Interstate Commission insist that it should be given the powers of a court to enforce its orders, but that it should be given power to make all interstate rates, rules, regulations, and classifications throughout the vast area of the United States, and hold up as an example of the practicability and propriety of such a course the railway-regulation laws of England.

We have shown how far the English railway and canal commission falls short of an argument for giving the Interstate Commerce Commission the powers of a court, and how, instead, it is an instructive argument against any such idea. Likewise, we find that the example of England, in the matter of fixing rates, is opposed to any such scheme. No provisions were made in England for fixing the rates of railways except in the charters of the various railway companies until the adoption of the traffic act of 1888, by which careful procedure was provided for revising the rates of carriers through the board of trade.

The board is a permanent committee of the privy council, established by an order in council in 1786. As now constituted, all the principal officers of the States are ex officio members, but the duties are really discharged by the president and the secretary of the board. The president is usually a member of the cabinet, being practically a cabinet minister of trade and commerce. One of its departments is the railway department, which is charged with the administrative supervision of railways in various respects, and makes inquiries into accidents, collects and publishes railway statistics, etc.

The carriers were, by the act of 1888, required to transmit to the board of trade classifications and schedules of maximum rates. The railroads were also to advertise in the newspapers and post notices at their passenger stations of their having so transmitted their schedules and classifications to that board. Thereupon the board was to hear all parties whom they considered entitled to be heard, and then, if the board agrees with the railways upon the proposed schedules, those schedules, or in the event of inability to agree, schedules prepared by the board of trade, were to be embraced in a provisional order to be transmitted to Parliament, and the board of trade was to agree on a bill confirming such provisional order. Our commission proposes to call its orders "administrative," for reasons before shown. If any objections were made to such bill, it had to be referred either to a select committee of the house in which the bill had been introduced or to a joint committee of the two houses for a hearing, and it was only when an act had been passed in pursuance of this procedure that the rates so designated should become binding upon the railways.

This system clearly recognizes that the fixing of such rates is strictly a legislative function, and as such it is exercised only by Parliament itself. Yet the Interstate Commerce Commission has used the system of railway regulation in England as an argument for conferring upon it the power to fix all interstate rates, fares and rules. Thus, according to its ambitious designs, not only is it to be a sort of superintendent of all interstate railways, and as such superior to the boards of directors and presidents, but a detective of violations of the law, a prosecutor of the railways for such violation, a party complainant against the railways, and also a court in all matters arising under the interstate commerce act, having all the powers of a court to enforce its orders, but it is also to be a legislature for the purpose of fixing the rates, fares, and rules of the carriers. Any such mingling of widely different functions is grossly inconsistent with the whole spirit of government in the United States; it would not be tolerated for a moment with respect to any other and lesser interests in the country, and is not a power given to the Treasury, Postal, Interior, State, or other branch of the Government having a Cabinet minister. Witness the recent clamor against Secretaries Gage and Hay, on the exercise of their right judgments in matters requiring legislative confirmation.

The Interstate Commission endeavors to conceal the fact that the power it seeks with reference to rates is in reality a legislative power by insisting that it would not, under the power desired, fix rates in the first instance or generally, but that it would only fix them upon complaint and after finding the existing rates unreasonable. Congress itself could not now, of course, fix rates in the first instance on any railway already in operation, because the rates have already been fixed "in the first instance." As to thereafter fixing and altering fares, rules, and rates generally, the commission's course is inconsistent with its present assertions. Although the commission now has no power to makes rates at all, it in one case assumed to make the rates on all the classes of commodities, embracing over 2,000 articles, from Chicago and Cincinnati to eight points in four Southern States, which virtually affected the rates to all points in the South, not only from Chicago and Cincinnati and other points in the northwestern and central territory, but from all points in the East as well, by the intimate inter-relation of most rates between States.

If the commission saw proper to go into such a general rate-making order as this when it had no power to make rates and so misconceive the law, it certainly will not be less modest if more and enlarged powers were actually given to it, or less liable to error.

The commission insists that adequate protection is given by the power of review by the courts; but the fact is that any such power would be wholly insufficient.

The question of the reasonableness of a rate is peculiarly one of fact, and after the commission finds the facts that the rate is unreasonable, and that the maximum and minimum rates designated by it will be reasonable, and orders those rates to be observed, this finding will make out a prima facie case. In view of the reluctance of the courts to overturn findings of fact made in pursuance of legal principles by bodies constituted for the purpose, almost the only protection the companies will have will be the right to have the orders of the commission set aside when they would result in the railroad operating at a loss, or, in other words, would result in depriving the railroad of its property without due process of law, and the railroad company would have this same protection if the rates were prescribed by Congress itself.

These considerations necessarily lead to the conclusion that the colossal and summary powers which the commission now so strenuously demands will generally be, in practical effect, just as expensive and as binding upon the railroads as the action of Congress itself in the premises. The commission may act on its own motion. It will make rates and fares generally, and fix rates in the first instance just as Congress itself might fix them in the first instance, and the power will be in effect a legislative power and a power which in England is exercised by Parliament.

Therefore to cite the example of England as an argument for conferring such powers upon the Interstate Commerce Commission is misleading and absurd. To confer upon the commission the tremendous powers which it desires, will not only make it in effect the most powerful institution in this country, with practically unlimited control, over its trade and commerce in every part, but it will obliterate those well-defined distinctions which have so long existed here between the various departments of the Government.

While the railway-regulation laws of England are relied on by the advocates of this entirely unnecessary and radical departure from the principles of our Constitution, those laws, if followed, would defeat the unwise and needless provision ambitiously longed for by the commission. Those laws afford admirable examples of careful observance of the lines of demarcation between the legislative, executive, and judicial departments, always a fundamental principle in English-speaking countries, which would be most grossly and unjustly disregarded by conferring on the Interstate Commerce Commission the tremendous and widely differing powers which it so insistently demands. Giving it such powers would, instead of leaving the commission as it intended, and an adjunct to the interstate-commerce act and the courts, make the law and the courts adjunct to the commission; and nothing would be more unlike such a remarkable condition of affairs than the consistent and well-guarded system of railway regulation in force in England.

Finally, it is important to keep other distinctions between the policy of the English Government and our own in plain view. The *first* is that the rates in Great Britain average double those in our country. The largeness of the rates reasonably influences the system and measure of regulation. Their higher rates receive the most considerate restrictive regulations. Here the lowest rates are proposed to be made subject to more stringent and inconsiderate legislation than any country of the earth exercises. The *second* is that in many details their companies receive ampler care and protection, such as policing the stations, grade crossings, invasions upon the rights of way, the contributory neglect of persons injured, penalties for securing rates by wrongdoing, the measures of damages to persons, the legality of limitations or releases, etc. The *third* is that English legislative railway policy requires that when it is proposed to construct a new and competitive railway or extend former lines to a point or district pre io s reached by one or more other companies, it shall be first demonstrated that such new line is a reasonable public requirement before parliamentary powers will be granted for its construction and operation. With us persons contemplating the like construction of parallel or competing lines are encouraged to do so under lax and the simplest of formulas, declarations, and guaranties, and when built almost universally become disturbers of the preexisting rates, fares, and regulations, in order to detach business from other companies because the mere construction of new lines adds but slowly to the antecedent traffic.

If where three lines exist a fourth is authorized and built, the original ones are entitled to have their reduced traffic reasonably cared for as being just to the business of four instead of three companies.

When a new British line is built, it also becomes a conservator of rates under the prevailing system of regulations; here it is encouraged by theory and law to become a disturber because such a course is deemed competition.

Enough surely has been shown under this general head to demonstrate that the broad, intelligent, mutual, and careful legislative policy of England is in striking contrast in every respect with the irrational, unfair, and prejudiced scheme of railway-rate control put forth by our Interstate Commerce Commission in every respect to which they both appeal commercially.

Reference is often made here to the English clearing house. As its name indicates, it clears only joint receipts and does not make or alter rates.

That body is, however, also chartered and not opposed by Parliament under substantially the general declaration that its business is to be conducted as if all the railways were one railway.

Its offices are headquarters for various rate conferences, which constitute a series of small associations possessing great value, but are not a part of its organization.

Finally, on this vital point, it is also to be recited and borne in mind that no such powers as those arrogated and asked for by our commission are conferred upon any other railway commission, board, council, or committee of any other country.

Twenty-Sixth.

SUGGESTED CHANGES IN THE ACT.

You naturally ask, in view of my criticisms of the present interstate-commerce act, and in response to your topical inquiry, what amendments I would propose for the interstate commerce act, which shall be mutual in purpose and effect, improve the administration of the law, and stop the evils of discriminations and excessive rates.

I premise by saying that I believe that the railway companies have given more cooperation and good will to the Interstate Commerce Commission than that commission has shown toward the railways. It is essential primarily that this condition be changed.

To that end I would personally favor—

(a) More frequent conferences between the railroads and the commission, in some of which—upon the initiative of the commission—perhaps interested shippers might participate.

(b) As the commission is asking us for unnecessary measures of publicity and expense, I think we should receive from them at least a monthly bulletin which would show the objections to interstate railway tariffs in use, and not leave this to exaggerated conjecture. For this purpose I would have the statement impersonal, reciting as a suggested heading, "Complaints against interstate rates, received by the Interstate Commerce Commission during the month of ———." I would show therein the rate complained of, the article to which the objectionable rate applied, and the points of shipment and receipt, without naming the railway companies complained of or the persons complaining.

I believe the tendency of this bulletin would be to cause such rates to be more closely scanned and compared before issue, as the railroads would desire to avoid being entered upon this list; competing lines would compare their rates with those complained of; shippers might the more hesitate to complain unnecessarily, and we would at last know officially the exact amount of public disaffection with rates, which I think is now greatly magnified.

(c) In my judgment the commission should be enlarged to seven members. I do not believe it possible, with the rapid expansion of the business of the country, and in view of the fact that the railroads of Puerto Rico, the Philippine Islands, and Alaska, may ultimately come within one system of regulation, that five men can by any possibility of industry and knowledge encompass the consideration of all these great and intricate questions fairly and comprehensively.

(d) I strenuously urge the right of contract. I am not now advocating the immediate grant of pooling authority, but many other contracts than pools are equally essential to uniformity of rates, rules, and regulations—such as lighterage, switching, storage, stock-yard charges, union-depot arrangements, joint tracks, joint divisions between connecting lines, etc.—every one of which are as clearly in the public interest as they are in that of the railroads. In the important matter of inspecting through cars at agreed points, that measure is, for example—and without doubt—in the clear interests of the protection of both human life and of property being transported.

(e) In other and general respects I favor substantially the general features of the Foraker bill, so called (Senate bill No. 1479, March 30, 1897).

I am aware that the people demand a supervising power, superior in some respects to the railroads themselves, and, with mutual equity kept in view, I think it a proper requirement. I think the commission should show the people what *is* mutually proper, not partisan. I think the relations between the public and the railroads are justly made up of mutual rights, but surely all the rights do not belong to the people, who do not own and who are not responsible for railway finance or management. The railroads must possess some vested rights.

I do not advocate that the railroad companies should be the exclusive and arbitrary managers of their property in all public respects, nor can I admit that five governmental officers should replace them as managers of this vast property in preference to unwise, unintelligent, and perhaps hostile constituencies. I think that conferences between the various interests should evolve a bill which every governmental and corporate fair mind should be alike willing to accept and adopt.

I favor this also because it is time that a stop was put in some measure to the confusion of authority; to the cross decisions in the lower courts; to the excessive demands of the commission on the one hand, and possibly to the excessive resistance of some railway companies on the other.

I believe the whole subject should be approached in a candid national spirit. We too much limp and jump to this end. It is not deliberately and mutually considered before action.

I wish to impress the board with my personal belief that this question is and always will be linked with a public interest; that the public has a reasonable and vital concern in transportation, as to safety appliances, the safe character of road-beds, adequate protection at public crossings, security of their persons and property, the proper accounting as to bonds, shares, etc., and in reasonable rates, rules, and fares, and the stoppage of all discriminating practices, and ought therefore to have all its rights in such particulars, but it ought to enact wise and mutual laws about them, especially as the railways are the largest factors in the prosperity of the nation.

Most of the rulings of the Interstate Commission have been accepted by the railway companies. In four years 23 of its 40 rate rulings were complied with. Nevertheless, the railway companies have felt it to be their duty to contest some of such rulings and have been justified in this conclusion by important decisions of the lower courts and of the Supreme Court in their favor.

The Interstate Commerce Commission has not shown that its proposed stringent amendments are called for by the public. They seem the notion and motion of the commission itself in most respects. The annual reports of the commission only partially show the number or nature of the complaints which come before it as to excessive rates, which, next to discriminations, constitute the only additional reason for the existence of the commission and their number is therefore magnified in the general statements.

Numerous individuals representing trade bodies urge the amendments upon the ground that the Interstate Commission will stand impartially between the railroads and the public; that it is composed of "men indisposed to favor one party any more than another," and will constitute a "board of arbitration," and that is what the "commission will be under this bill if it is passed," etc.

I demur to some of these views, because an arbitration is usually had by agreement of both parties as to the issue to be submitted and decided, and both parties have a voice in the selection of the arbitrators; also because the repeated utterances of the commission show that they have already prejudged the case in nearly every phase under which it can arise.

They will, therefore, with their proposed widely extended powers, if granted, constitute a board of prosecution rather than a board of arbitration.

It is alleged in various arguments that no amendments are proposed which give to the commission the power to make rates. This is an evasion. The power to change a rate is clearly the power to make a new rate, and from time to time thereafter to fix other new rates, i. e., changes—leaving to the carrier, therefore, only the determination of such others as may happen to please the commission. It is the power which the commission objects to on the part of the railroad, yet desires to assume and increase for itself.

Great stress is laid in various arguments upon the necessity for a tribunal standing between the shipper on the one hand and the railroad companies on the other, which shall have the power to determine the issues between the two.

The WITNESS. There is one feature of pooling contracts to which I am asked to call more specific attention than I have to-day. I have been instrumental in drawing some pooling contracts, and have been a party to many more, yet I have never seen one that held, from its first to its last word, any specific rate or fare. They refer to rates and fares then in existence or which may be from time to time made or altered. Pooling contracts, as some were made here and in England, may have been for 1 or 5 years, or more, during which time no line of the pooling agreement was changed; yet rates might have been properly and necessarily changed twenty-five times during those years. The first object, as you will readily see, was to provide a procedure adapted from past experience, whether for 1 or 30 years, to govern the division of the same business, leaving the parties thereto the opportunity under one agreement and regardless of its duration to make such changes in the contracts or rates as the succeeding conditions of policy, management, or trade might justify or require. As I have said before, there is a great misconception in the public mind that pooling contracts specify rates, and are used to maintain them. Remember also that all the forces of due competition have as much play under a pooling contract as if pools did not exist, they being simply provisos that when various rates shall have been made they shall then—whether higher or lower—come within the provisions of the joint purse memorandum as to the division between the parties of the tonnage represented by the traffic or of the earnings derived from it. I think that ought to be made initially clear to you. Of course their purpose is to maintain the various rates so adopted.

(After a recess from 12.35 to 2 p. m., the hearing of Mr. Blanchard was continued, as follows:)

Q. (By Mr. KENNEDY.) Do you believe that it is good policy to push before the national legislature a bill abolishing ticket scalping, to the exclusion of all other legislation that the people of the country and the Interstate Commerce Commission and shippers are asking for, as was done in the last session of Congress?— A. My judgment is that it is wiser that all the reforms be inaugurated and go hand in hand with each other, and that they should not be dealt with piecemeal, but comprehensively. Nevertheless the contest has been made up so fully as to scalping that, if there is liable to be any considerable delay as to the other features because of considering that one again, I am of opinion that an act passed now to discontinue scalping would be more satisfactory to us—the people and the Interstate Commerce Commission—in producing quick results; some hold that to pass it now would strengthen the hands of those who favor further legislation on other points and would be more likely to lead possibly to giving us the authority which we desire in other respects, than for us to undertake to adjust all interstate issues at once. The reverse of this view holds with others, viz, that if we fail to abolish scalping now we incur the failure of that with our further proposals hereafter. Between these views it is my conclusion that if we can we should get simultaneous action on all points. If we can not it is better to get action which would correct the one great evil of passenger traffic, which practically gets a disturbing issue away from the commission and out of the way of Congress, and will mostly work to the public good.

Q. Do you believe that the railroads themselves are responsible for the system of ticket brokerage which they seek to have abolished by the National and State legislatures?—A. Only in a small measure at present. My answer did not go this morning into all the forms or evils of ticket brokerage. We will assume, for example, that from New York there are a thousand forms of tickets which pass through what are called the western termini of the trunk lines from Toronto, on the north, to the Chesapeake & Ohio trunk line junctions, on the south. Between these junctions are a multiplicity of connections; so many that Mr. Daniels of the New York Central Railroad stated in his testimony in 1898 that there were 50,000 or more ticketed routes, as for example between the seaboard cities and Portland, Oreg.

When it comes to issuing the various class tickets by all those various roads and routes, they afford more or less opportunities for scalping. For example, a ticket from Philadelphia reading through Buffalo, from Buffalo to Cleveland, from Cleveland to Toledo, and from Toledo to Cincinnati, goes on three sides of the square, or say two-thirds the circumference of a circle. Those routes are represented by various coupons, and the longer the distance the more the opportunities for scalping. The railroad companies, starting with the public convenience and their own revenues, are therefore obliged to confront this issue; should they decline to sell those various tickets at their advertised fares or run the risks of scalping them? We will suppose a ticket sold from New York by way of Albany, Montreal and Detroit, to Cincinnati; that ticket might be scalped at Saratoga or Troy or Detroit, and again at Toledo; and while the original transaction was a legitimate one over the traveled and current routes, it nevertheless increased the liability to speculation in those tickets by selling these various cut portions at these numerous points. In that way the railroad companies have done much, by multiplying routes, to assist the scalper in his object, but always, as I aver, the public convenience entered into their issue.

Another fact that existed for years does not prevail now to the prior extent, viz, that railroad companies and scalpers assisted each other. I am familiar with the old Atlantic and Great Western Railroad, where a block of tickets, a thousand in number, for illustration, were put out from Cincinnati to New York. We will suppose the fare well maintained on the other lines on a basis of, say, $17, Cincinnati to New York, but they placed those tickets with scalpers for $14. In that way the railroad companies had direct dealings with the scalpers. In Buffalo at one time when some new lines opened through to New York perhaps over 10,000 tickets were disposed of to speculators direct, via numerous routes. Subsequently when the disturbances which such sales created were removed by a better understanding between the railway companies, the companies offered to redeem those tickets, perhaps not at the amounts which they received for them, but at a higher price than paid, that redemption fund being contributed and divided over all the lines with a view to the restoration of the rates and the public equalities of fares. The brokers, we will say, had disposed of 2,000 of those tickets; and the railways offered the brokers $2 more than they paid for the 8,000 on hand, representing a profit of say $16,000, which the public paid to the brokers, but scalpers refused to return those tickets notwithstanding that profit, believing that it was but the precursor step to stop speculation in scalping tickets; that they, nothwithstanding the large gain from that transaction, would become the losers by the aggregate general policy, and that they could sell them to travelers for an equal or greater gain.

In other cases railroad agents have undoubtedly referred passengers to scalping offices as places where, to secure business, they could buy tickets over their lines cheaper. Suppose that the fare from New York to Chicago by the Grand Trunk line in connection with the Lehigh Valley from New York is $18, while the standard fare via the New York Central routes is $20. At that difference a passenger might say, "I do not prefer the lower cost line; the difference in connections and time and in sleeping car conveniences and meals do not attract me." The ticket agent may then have said to the intending traveler, and possibly with the authority of his superior officer, "If you will go to A B, who has a scalping office, he has tickets over our road which originally started at Portland, Me., or somewhere else, through Boston to New York, and the party having used part of that ticket via New York, or elsewhere, the broker has on sale the balance of the ticket for $15." Therefore the broker gets that $3 below the fixed differential of $2. The passenger saves so much of that scalp as the broker may allow him. To that extent the railroad companies have at times referred passengers to the advantages of a scalper's office and have then shared its benefits in the way cited.

In such cases the railroad companies may formerly have been responsible directly for some of the evils, but they have now been curtailed from the fact that agents have been appointed whose special duty it is to go into these scalping offices and "test the market," as it is called; and while I dislike to bring before a body like this the use of such instrumentalities, we have availed of the most experienced experts to do this work, and out of all the mass of information they derive such facts are confirmed. Nevertheless, however much the railroad companies have formerly connived at these methods, they have been gradually eliminated, and more and more the disturbing railroad officer and scalper have been thrown on more limited resources.

A railroad president told me that his chief ticket clerk being ill and his mail, marked personal, having accumulated and caused suspicion, he caused that mail to be opened and there were found letters from three different brokers saying, in effect, "I have received from you the tickets which are to be sold in my office. The standard fare being so much, the tickets are to be sold for so much." We will suppose that the standard fare being $10 the tickets were to be sold at $7; the broker then agreed to divide the profit between the ticket clerk and the ticket scalper. In this way the chief ticket clerk was found to receive three times his salary and cut the rates of his own company. So long as scalpers can buy tickets bearing the office stamps of an authorized ticket agent they prefer it; so they use every due and undue means to get them. When they found that the railroads gradually discontinued that practice they resorted to other questionable, discriminating, and corrupt practices.

Q. If the railroads were to agree, and all abide by the agreement, to have no dealings with ticket brokers, is it probable that the ticket brokerage business would be very much curtailed, if not almost eliminated?—A. The Eastern railways had such an understanding prior to the decision of the Supreme Court, and it worked toward such good results I think that if to-day an agreement was nationally legalized by which all railroads might absolutely stop all connections with brokers that brokers' offices would continue, but in greatly curtailed extent, by reason of the ability to purchase portions of cut tickets and use the return coupons, convention and special party tickets, as they are called, and sell them to parties who are not entitled to them. This would not, however, justify the continuance of their business, especially if they had no right of agency. As, for example, if the fare from Chicago to New York is $20, the two-way rate is $40. If, instead, the companies would sell one round-trip ticket at a fare one and one-third times one standard fare that would be $26.60. To the extent the broker can induce a purchaser to use that ticket coming east for $18 and sell the return part to some party not authorized to use it for $16 they would receive $34 for that for which they paid $26, and, if a traveler presents the return portion of that ticket, the railroad companies can not, under some conditions, stop it. They can not stop to determine always whether the holder is a member of the Royal Arcanum, etc. They do undertake to get the secretary of that order, for example, to certify that the party holding such ticket was entitled to its privileges and return under the rates and rules made. But let us assume the holder sells that ticket to a broker who uses it. If the fare on mileage tickets is one and one-half cents a mile and the local fare is two cents or more per mile, the brokers would combine to buy, say a thousand of them under various names and subterfuges. By the terms of the ticket itself it is usually provided that such a ticket shall only be good when presented, say by John Richards for his passage, but he goes into one of the offices on Broadway, in New York, or on Clark street, in Chicago, and procures such a ticket, uses it part way and then sends it back to the scalper and gets a reduced fare for that part he used, or he may sell a portion of all the remainder of a ticket at first used legitimately. Again, the selling broker induces another broker to take up the ticket uncanceled and return it to him, and thereupon he divides with passenger and conductor the amount paid. In some districts, as in New England, mileage tickets are good for any holders thereof. The result is that some persons buy them and sell parts of them at advanced fares, yet under the advertised tariffs. The railroads, meantime, may have done everything they could to prevent such results. In some cases they have gone so far as to have a photograph of the holder accompany the ticket. Of course, that is an annoyance and an inconvenience to passengers, who generally care more for saving than for reform. Then, those photographs were often scratched or faded so that one could not recognize the passenger from it. Every conceivable form, as I stated this morning, of fraud and misrepresentation is therefore resorted to to evade the companies' rules and its own and the passenger's legal obligations. The one thing to do, therefore, clearly for the public interest, is that a seller of tickets shall put over his counter a certificate or authorized proof of agency from the companies for whom he purports to sell such tickets; otherwise, make it illegal for him to sell them. If a man in lower New York, say in the sugar district, said he represented the American Sugar Refining Company and offered to sell its sugars, the first thing purchasers would require would be the authority to so sell. The American Sugar Refining Company could get an injunction and arrest that man for dealing falsely in their goods and representing the wares and sales falsely. We can not arrest anybody, yet the crime against railway and traveler is as much opposed to public morals and more so.

The fact is that the law frowns at every joint measure that we have taken to protect our railroad rates and fares, and out of 36 measures pending, at one time, in Congress, as I have said before, only the pooling, scalping, and commission questions were in favor of the railroads. We are treated, although in the service of the public interest, much as if we were its enemies. Senator Chandler has repeated the following statement, substantially:

" It is the railway intention if they pool to organize a monopoly power which shall be constituted of twelve thousands of millions of capital."

A more absurd statement of intent or practicability could not be made. How can we pool a road that carries salmon and local traffic in northwestern Oregon with a road that mainly carries oranges in Florida? How could we pool a lumber railroad in Maine with a road that carries principally cotton and cattle in southwestern Texas? Yet that is the character of the misrepresentations or misinformation that constantly go abroad. I have challenged Senators and others to an open discussion of this great question and never had an acceptance or even known anything worthy to be called an argument in the case.

Q. (By Mr. KENNEDY.) You stated an instance this morning in which you said that a man who bought a ticket to a certain point and sold it beyond would not get as much from the scalpers as he would get from the railroads in redeeming that ticket. Is there not a large body of travelers in this country who buy tickets, say, at Chicago for New York—use that as an illustration—and intend to go no farther than Washington, knowing that they can sell the unused portion of that ticket at Washington to a scalper for enough to save them $1.50 or $2 on their fare—is that not a practice that prevails very largely?—A. Yes; largely.

Q. Do you believe that the custom or practice of giving passes to legislators, members of the judiciary, favored shippers, and personal friends of railroad officials, is against public morality?—A. I do; decidedly.

Q. Do you believe, then, that as long as that part of the public who are the people's servants are favored in that way that others who know how to take advantage of this system and save themselves fares should be summarily cut off and these others left to enjoy favors from the railroad companies?—A. I do not think the two questions connect with each other. The ticket which is issued to a member of Congress, or a member of the legislature, or a judge or other public officer, is supposed to go to one who represents a position of public value or public utility. It is not generally illegal to bestow such a pass. It is complimentary and does not savor of dishonest intent, nor for purposes of influencing legislation. In the other case the traveler resorts to the practice to which you refer as a deliberate evasion of the fares and rules of the railroads, and is unlawful as to the intent and depletion of uniform rates under the act. He buys a ticket at New York to go to Chicago and he deliberately sells it en route, and intends to do so when he purchases it. In the case that you cite as to members of the legislature, they do not resell or loan their tickets. Many of those tickets are also returned to the railways on the principle that the receivers can not accept those favors from the railroads. I do not think it any justification for the continuance of widespread ticket scalping in 560 brokers' offices, dealing with hundreds of thousands of travelers of all grades and stations, if a member or two of each legislature prostitutes his great public office. I do not think the one justifies the continuance of the other even if both are evils. It is an old truism that two wrongs never made a right.

Q. I do not refer to the idea that these persons who receive passes sell them; I made no allusion to the sale of passes by legislators.—A. Well, I am referring to that.

Q. (By Mr. FARQUHAR.) A person buying a ticket in New York for Chicago from a regular office—when he purchases that ticket has a certain assurance of safe carrying by the means provided for by that railroad, and also an insurance against accident attached to that ticket or whatever may befall him in being carried by common carriers between New York and Chicago. Is not that contained in every ticket that you make?—A. The assumption of that responsibility?

Q. Yes.—A. To the extent fixed by law and by usage, yes. All the tickets carry that responsibility against railroads.

Q. A buys a ticket in New York and he goes as far as Buffalo; he sells the ticket to B, a scalper—coupon ticket, say—and B sells it to a second party, C, who proceeds from Buffalo to Chicago. A railroad accident happens at Toledo or Elkhart on the line. Can that party, who is not a party to the original contract of buying the ticket, recover damages?—A. I do not know of any case of that kind that has ever been tried; but for one I should advise, if his death was caused by the neglect, fault, or error of the railroad company, that no discrimination should be made in the payment of damages merely because he was not the original buyer of the ticket. All parties who use that regular ticket do so because it is made possible by the railroad, and the holder has done nothing as yet unlawful in buying and using it. He is injured by the railroad company itself, and he ought to have the same recourse against the railroad that anybody should have, and the railroad company ought to have the same responsibility unless and until the law denies that right. Whether or not, if the case was pushed to an issue, they could successfully resist it is doubtful. There are certain cases, as in the issue of annual passes, where the pass being issued for a year specifically in favor of the person named, if that free pass is found in the hands of anybody that is not thus entitled to use it his heirs evidently should not recover if he died from railway neglect in the period of use, and I do not think he could recover any damages for injuries. On the contrary, he might be liable to arrest for misusing the ticket.

There are also some term or time tickets sold, say for half fare, for mutual considerations, in which the name of the buyer is inserted, which would, I think, come under the rule I have last suggested.

There are many cases where the railroad companies have sought to limit the use of these tickets. That is one reason for the issue of limited and unlimited tickets. A ticket good, stamped on the 13th, for a train to arrive in Chicago on the 14th offers no practicable opportunity for scalping, we will say, at Buffalo or Pittsburg. For that reason the railroad companies, in order to defeat this scalping, have reduced the fare on those limited tickets as compared with the unlimited ticket, thereby giving the holder of that ticket, for a consideration, the right to go from place to place more leisurely. And, incidental to that right, he may perhaps transfer the ticket to another purchaser, who might hold all the rights as to personal damage or the loss of baggage possessed by the first purchaser, who bought it without giving his name.

Q. As a safeguard in the matter of identification, why is not the name of every man who purchases a ticket put upon that ticket?—A. It is not practicable in the great rush of traffic.

Q. Why not?—A. In the great rush of travel there are not agents or clerks or room enough between the travelers' arrivals at stations, many at the last moment, and the departure of trains, as baggage must be checked also after the tickets are bought. In the Grand Central Station at New York, for example, there is not room enough to take the signature or name of every man and write it on his ticket. Suppose that a man comes up and says, "I want a ticket to Batavia, N. Y.," and told you his name was John Smith. It is not possible to hold that ticket in the office until the clerk is satisfied that the name placed upon it is correctly given, as a recourse against accident. Of course, at the local rates, we do not care who travels upon them; they are alike at one fare for each like ticket; they can not be scalped to yield less than local fare, nor make a profit to scalpers unless stolen, resold, altered, etc. The average time now taken in railroad ticket offices to issue the most improved form of tickets is thought too long in the one respect of writing in destinations only and punching dates. We can not have all the destinations printed, so we print all the tickets good, we will say, to Toledo, and from Toledo on they fill in writing the ultimate destination of the passenger if on the next connecting line. It may be a local station and its location and fare can not be quickly found. Then the period of use, number of train, and other data are often punched out. Those things perhaps equal 40 per cent of the force of ticket agents and of the time required in waiting, and should we put in the name of everybody and his destination the great and many inconveniences encountered make it impracticable.

There are other drawbacks. A traveler may reach a station just as the train is about to depart. Again, large numbers of trains do not stop, or stop only when flagged, at small stations by day and fewer at night, and the agents are not on hand. Men must, nevertheless, go, and such pay fare on the trains, and under such circumstances tickets could not be used unless the speed of the trains was diminished and all the small offices were open winter and summer, in some cases, through all time and all the contingencies of storm and weather. Even then passengers would be tardy.

Another proposition made, I think by Mr. Roberts, late the president of the Pennsylvania Railroad, was that every ticket should have printed upon its face the true selling price of the ticket, just as it is inserted on a freight bill of lading; that each coupon of that ticket show the portion of the whole fare which accrued to that coupon, and that there should be printed on the face of the coupon an assurance that the ticket would be redeemed at any authorized office for so much money.

That would involve an enormous amount of work, because the local State fares of the railroad companies change from time to time, sometimes very quickly, and they go to make up the through fares. This would change the through fares and the amounts to be redeemed, and if the new tickets had not been received old ones would have to be sold, and confusion would result on many lines; from many points the old tickets would be useless; the wrong amounts would be refunded; it would enormously increase the printing bills, etc.

Q. (By Mr. Kennedy.) I presume you read the decision of the court of appeals of the State of New York which declared the antiscalping law of that State unconstitutional?—A. I read it very hurriedly, but since last March, until recently, I have not attended to business by reason of ill health. That was issued during my absence, and I have only seen the general points, not the details.

Q. Can you recall one feature of the decision was that when a passenger bought a ticket of the railroad company it was his own property, to dispose of as he saw fit?—A. Yes.

Q. (By Mr. Farquhar.) But at the same time does that obviate the character of the contract between the purchaser and the railroad, even if you call it property? When you buy a ticket is it not a positive contract and agreement, and does not that second or any other party or scalper or anybody else, become a party to the contract?—A. I think that is so, and that it is equitably stated. The conditions of the purchase of the ticket seem to me to be that if the ticket is property in itself it continues to be the property of the issuing railroad company wherever it goes. For example, if it passes out of the possession of the railroad company when sold at the Grand Central Station, it is on the distinct understanding and invariable custom that it shall be taken up and again become the carriers' property in Buffalo, or wherever it reads to. Such tickets are to be taken up and returned to its general offices and have been for years. If it were not the property of the carriers the railway would not have the right to take it up and send it back to be checked against the sales, etc. The contract to transport is accomplished and ended and the contract is surrendered because the railway alone issued the evidence of contract and seems entitled to its return as proof of fulfillment.

I therefore think that the conclusion was wrong both in itself and as an incentive and support to a further wrong. I have always regarded a ticket as simply indicative of the right of the purchaser to travel on the terms indicated thereon; that it is tendered by the railroad company to the intending passenger, not as a necessary adjunct of a journey because the railway could take it up as soon as the traveler's train started, or at a gate, before it left, as on the elevated railways, nor as a requisite receipt for money paid because the amount paid is not shown. It is given into the passenger's hands simply to show connecting conductors and agents beyond and baggage checkers that the first purchaser paid the railroad company its stipulated legal fares for the privilege of traveling upon that road between stated points and upon certain trains. It seems to me it would be as well to say that when we issue bills of lading that the parties are not required to surrender them on the due performance of the contract. We do not surrender the custody of property until the goods are delivered and due receipts taken therefor, which receipts constitute the fulfillment of the obligations of the bills of lading. In some States we have a right to demand the production and surrender of the original bill of lading in order to show that the goods represented thereby were received by and delivered to the consignee of authority in good order. It seems to me the same condition arises in a ticket, for the law would not authorize the scalping of freight bills of lading and rates, and that John Jones might enjoy from Buffalo to New York the substitution of 1,000 other barrels of flour started by John Smith at Chicago. If in the sale of the evidence of the right to travel the railroad should place upon the face of any ticket onerous, unjust, unreasonable, and illegal conditions, or those disturbing to public trade, the courts would not sustain the railroads, and ought not to, but if the present practice is the result of long usage in all countries and never shown to be wrong or publicly harmful, that these conditions were before adjudged reasonable and proper for the protection of the shareholder of the railroads as well as the passengers, those considerations should have weight and not hold the railroad company to the performance of its obligation to one person as also good against the transfer of it to two, three, or four passengers.

Q. So far as the State of New York is concerned, under that decision of the court of appeals, and in the State of Illinois under a similar decision, the tickets are private property.—A. I know, but when that comes to final adjudication I do not see how it can be reasonably and justly so held. However, that is merely a layman's opinion.

Q. In carrying wheat and flour from the West to the seaboard for export they went at the same rates up to last February. Last February new schedules were made up and wheat was carried at a cheaper rate than flour. I understand that practice did not prevail until last February. Do you know why it was done at that time?—A. No; and I do not for this reason: That promptly following the decision of the Supreme Court the presidents of our companies disbanded the association. Since that time we have simply been winding up its affairs, and my active connection with the organization ceased the 1st of October, a year ago. The fact you cite in this case is entirely new to me at this moment, and, if I understand you, I do not understand any new justification.

Q. The question was involved in the case decided by the Interstate Commerce Commission some months ago, to which you referred this morning.—A. Yes; that was that the wheat which had formerly been carried to the seaboard at uniform rates, whether for export or domestic consumption, was carried for less than wheat for domestic consumption and less than the rate on flour for export. The testimony then adduced was full and clear, pro and con. I do not know any new reasons actuating that policy; it has always been so in some measure. I stated this morning that I believe that there have been circumstances and conditions which justified lower rates to the seaboard for property intended for foreign consumption than to the seaboard proper for consumption within this country, and the same reasoning holds as to the manufacture of flour, whether at Minneapolis or the seaboard. I do not comprehend why all our flour rates should be brought to the seaboard level created by competition with the British miller in Manchester. Neither he nor the American miller sell to all at the lowest price they get for any flour. Take a consumer, we will say, living in Brooklyn, the circumstances and conditions entirely dissimilar from the conditions of a consumer in Glasgow. If it came within that view, there might be defensible reasons for it, but as to the question of intentional discrimination of some American wheat against other American wheat to the same points in our own States, it would be unjustifiable from my point of view.

Q. Against American flour?—A. Yes; and American flour under the same reasoning.

Q. Would it not be in the nature of a discrimination against American labor and the American milling industry?—A. Yes, measurably, the facts being as you state; but if I knew all the facts I should be happy to explain them, and if it is the desire of the commission, I can ascertain the reasons for any recent action and communicate the facts to you. All our great manufacturers, if I understand the question, sell some products for use abroad less than for the prices obtained at home. They must do so to get the foreign markets. Perhaps the railways do so as well.

Q. (By Professor JOHNSON.) It was explained by interested parties that the trunk lines are more interested in the transportation of wheat than they are in the transportation of flour, and for that reason they are willing to make this discrimination in favor of the wheat. Have you any information on that?—A. No; nothing beyond former practices and the reasons I have partly cited. On the contrary, I have heard it represented to the railroads that they are carrying a barrel of flour which weighs 216 pounds at a price at which they were carrying 200 pounds of wheat, or 8 per cent less weight, and that the shippers made more on the flour than on the wheat, and shippers of wheat have often asked for a reduction of 16 pounds in some way to make the rates equivalent. .That was regarded not as a discrimination in the true sense of the word, but the result of long usage, and it is the intention of the carrying companies, as expressed in former resolutions, to put the two articles upon the same footing wherever practicable. The transportation of wheat, for example, by the large and independent steam and sail lake carriers is recalled, where they put grain in elevators and spout or run the grain into the boats in bulk and run the grain out of the boat at Buffalo in bulk and ship it in bulk in the cars. It is not a new question. The individual lake carriers—plus the individual canal carriers—have done all this for years and would do more of it if the railroads ceased doing it, yet the Northwestern millers have waxed fat with thrift and drawbacks. Bulk grain is the more economic proposition and gives a much larger cargo per vessel and more money per cargo than to take flour where each barrel is handled individually into and out of the boat and transferred from car to car or boat to car, and the loss of earning space caused by the circular form of the barrel, and the greater value and number of claims. All this holds good, of course, of rail transportation as well, where even a much larger percentage of wheat weight over flour weight is carried per car. I have heard these reasons advanced and urged by bulk-grain shippers, and there is truth in them. The same conditions transpire in New York Harbor, etc. There the railroads make bulk-grain deliveries under a contract with the New York Produce Exchange, by which grain was to be floated in bulk in canal boats and delivered in bulk under specific rules of grading and transfers to ocean vessels or grain warehouses. Storage is also covered by that agreement. That contract does not include flour, as all members of the New York Produce Exchange know the above differences in the transportation detail and value of the two articles, although they bear close relations to each other. The same thing might be urged to be true as to the very large and increasing list of food products made from oats and corn. They also put flour in barrels, in cloth bags and paper bags of various sizes for transportation, altering thereby the former more fixed relations of barrels, packages, and bulks, weight of. loading, etc., while bulk-grain conditions are not changed.

Q. The contention is this: That the transfer service in New York Harbor is remunerated at the rate of 3 cents per 100 pounds, and that this service is performed by a company composed largely of and controlled by the principal owners of the trunk lines, and for that reason they prefer to have the grain moved from the west in the form of wheat rather than in the form of flour. You doubtless have, or can obtain, information concerning that definite contention?—A. I have that information now and can characterize it as without foundation. There are delivering companies, not "a company," and they handle flour as well as grain, charging more on the flour. While I was vice-president of the Erie Railroad Company I made contracts for the delivery of freights about the harbor of New York at a specific rate per ton, in all cases, including grain, and on west-bound as well as eastward-bound freight. I would like to disabuse the minds of this commission of the proposition that the carrier at New York City is compensated for this terminal service at the rate of 3 cents per 100 pounds. The fact is, that freight rates to and from New York are fixed without reference to what the terminal charges there are; the rate Chicago to New York being 20 cents, the rate to Philadelphia is 18 cents, the rate to Baltimore is 17 cents. That 20 cents, with 3 cents afterwards taken into account as if it were cut out, would prove that the railroads carry freight from Chicago to Jersey City as cheap as to Baltimore, but for a considerably longer distance.

Q. (By Mr. FARQUHAR.) What is the reason for the difference?—A. The present differences were settled originally at the Brevoort House, New York, April, 1877, by the presidents of the trunk lines, every one of whom are now dead. I was present. At that time the great bulk of export property went through Boston, Montreal, Philadelphia, and Baltimore. The ports of Galveston, New Orleans, Pensacola, Norfolk, and Newport News were not then factors in the adjustment reached. Given a shipment of flour seeking through transportation from Chicago to Liverpool, it was not a transaction to the seaboard, but to Liverpool via various routes. The purpose of the railroad companies making that arrangement was to deliver freight from Chicago and elsewhere to Liverpool and elsewhere abroad at uniform rates through all ports, precisely as the rates from Chicago to New York are uniform throughout all western junctions—Pittsburg, Buffalo, Toronto, Wheeling, etc. That was the purpose set forth in the memoranda and testimony delivered to the Hepburn committee. In making these rates these were some of the elements which entered into them: In the first place, sail tonnage; in the second, steam vessels; third, lake and rail; fourth, lake and canal; finally, and in a small part only, rail and canal, the Ohio River to Cincinnati or Pittsburg, and the competition at that time, mainly as to cotton, at New Orleans.

To reach results fairly, after a long, bitter, needless, and fruitless rate war, file after file and volume after volume of rates were obtained to show what inland rates would most nearly average a parity of through rates to foreign ports upon the grain. I can only cite a few difficulties. Steamship companies and sailing vessels changed their rates, perhaps, every day, and the rates from different ports were, of course, dissimilar. I know of a case where one line changed its rates four times in one day, by reason of foreign war rumors, shortage of tonnage room, and various local causes. We could not change our rail rates four times a day from Chicago to Liverpool, affecting St. Louis, Peoria, Milwaukee, Detroit, etc., to Liverpool, yet Liverpool rates, perhaps, decided London and other European rates. Ship agents frequently made contracts for a ship in midocean, bound westward. In such cases someone had to hold the cargo until the vessel arrived. Incoming steamships were delayed at sea, etc. If a 10-day vessel was 17 days westward at sea, its return cargo might stand on the dock. Sometimes through eastward engagements were made by railways taking the risk of ocean rates, and I have known the entire inland charge to be absorbed in making such through rates good, by reason of advances in ocean rates. With only the former railroad lines and sea-going lines from the smaller number of ports of export, with orders coming from Liverpool, London, Marseilles, Brindisi, Bremen, Hamburg, Havre, and with Chicago, St. Louis, Kansas City, Milwaukee, Cincinnati, and Peoria competing for the land transportation, the problem was daily to fix a basis which we could give shippers, promptly upon application, of through and assured rates of freight between these points on a multiplicity of articles. Only a few of the entanglements of the foreign-rate problem stand before you. Therefore, after most exhaustive examinations and trials of different rates and methods; after Mr. Vanderbilt had spent or wasted millions of dollars in trying to fix a parity between New York and the ports in competition therewith, the seaboard lines abandoned fighting and entered into closer negotiations. Even then, as now, through rates can not be made on the bulk of our exports. They had to make rates to the seaboard, and to do this they had to take the past years and average all these different and conflicting rates and conditions to what would represent a just approximation. At that time 3 cents was only agreed to be a fair difference to New York higher than to Baltimore, and 2 cents as compared with Philadelphia. After so fixing the differences of rates to New York, it never was thought what the charge was at New York for handling, any more than at Chicago. The Erie company's grain lighterage in New York was then performed by the firm of McCartan & Logan, and no officer of the company had one dollar of interest in it. All its heavy freights were lightered by the New Jersey Lighterage Company. The New York Central road had employed Mr. Starin to perform their harbor service, in part, and he also performed it for the Lackawanna.

The Pennsylvania Railroad Company employs a terminal company at New York. It has been and is a favorite theory of some shippers, and was of a railway president now deceased, that there must be a personal interest hidden somewhere in this lighterage. Whether that business costs 3 cents or not is something to explain further. The Erie Railroad Company alone had 7 regular stations in New York Harbor, and had made deliveries and received freights at 105 other points; in all, 112 points, to and from which the rat s were the same as New York. It cost more then to deliver property to and from Jersey City at Staten Island, including fire and marine risks, than it cost to carry it from Milwaukee to Chicago; therefore, when the Western lines, as was then the custom, put upon their bills of lading, "Deliver to any point in lighterage limits of New York Harbor, as consignees may direct," we might as well have put on a Chicago west-bound bill, "Deliver at Milwaukee, if consignees direct." We finally advised our Western connections that they had no such right. We had abundant regular stations in New York, and would receive and deliver at any of them at the uniform New York rate; but the 105 other points must be provided for in some sense, and someone besides us should pay for it in due share. The charge, at first 8¼ cents, was subsequently reduced to 8. Now, as to who pays that charge. In a remote sense the shipper does, but the rate is not increased by that amount or any part of it to provide for it. Assuming the distance from New York to Buffalo to be one-half of the distance to Chicago—the New York Central, for example, will receive from its connections but one-half of that amount, because it is deducted from the through rate before the remainder of the rate is divided.

Q. (By Mr. KENNEDY.) A distinguished railroad president appeared before the commission in Chicago and said that the tariff schedules which were filed in freight departments and the Interstate Commerce Commission were so intricate and so technical that no shipper could possibly understand them; that he could not understand them himself, and that if he found it necessary to get information concerning them he would have to get an expert in the employ of the company to assist him. I would like to ask you if that is, in your opinion, true?—A. No; no experienced president in the country ought to have said that so broadly. Perhaps he meant rates and divisions and rules, etc. I regard rate making and rate maintaining as the most responsible and important functions a railway president can exercise. We employ experts to work out the details, but all presidents presumably understand the basis or measure and principle of rates. As to shippers, they are acute and vigilant. Many of the large forwarders in Chicago and elsewhere have their own traffic managers, as the railroads do. It is their duty to keep up, from time to time, with new roads that are opened, new rates that are published, etc. I will give you an instance: The Seaboard and Roanoke road is about to complete its line into Florida, shortening the distance. They have absorbed some lines and are building some part of a new route. That will necessitate revisions of tariffs, without doubt. In such an instance I can not understand how a president would say what you quote. He should be able to tell what will be the rate policy of his roads, and perhaps would have to get some experts to prepare tariffs for them, but he should possess knowledge that the traffic is mainly carried by other lines at open rates which he can not exceed and may reduce. There is not a shipping firm in Chicago, of any magnitude, that has not the rates in its offices. They also have the official railroad guides and directions. Then follows the classification and the rules and regulations, the forms of bills of lading, releases, and everything else requisite to enable the shipper or tariff maker to know the rates. The difficulty the president referred to, perhaps, lies in the original construction of the first rate. This being assumed, it is then a question of changes only. Both of those should receive his approval. For example, an important line has recently come to the conclusion that their material at present prices averages to cost about 50 per cent more than the same materials cost them in like quantities 2 years ago. Nobody should claim that they shall not have some increased rate compensation for that condition; every other calling has. For example: If a railroad paid last year $17.50 per ton for rails and now pays $35, except on contracts, it should make a reasonable rate advance to compensate for the greater outlays. The people should pay in part for the rails over which they and their merchandise are carried. Other concurrent causes may fortify this justice. In sending grain to the Transvaal, England may legitimately alter the price for our rail carriage of grain as well as of the grain itself. Steel rails, iron manufactures, structural material, etc., are also cases in point. When it comes to deciding the tariffs from such causes, conclusions as to rates become important, wide reaching, and intricate and a problem of duty to the public as well as to shareholders. No one man can do that, even be he an expert. I therefore favor the coming together of the shippers of iron, coal, merchandise, grain, etc., for more conferences with the railroads. We want to recognize as well as be recognized.

The unit rate is from Chicago to New York, and the rates of thousands of articles to hundreds of intermediate points depend upon that unit. What would the Interstate Commerce Commission do with propositions like that?—five men that have but small experience undertaking to cope with that and all other rate difficulties all over the United States. Surely if your Chicago witness was correct, that railway presidents can not make rates, the Interstate Commerce Commissioners can not do it. If the grain and provision rates were advanced or reduced, say from Chicago to New York, they would doubtless be followed to New Orleans and Galveston, Kansas City, St. Louis, and Louisville. That can only be done by committees and conferences at these various places adopting several rates on leading articles.

There is one fact which is important, and I would like to discuss it a moment, as I omitted it from my paper this morning.

My point relates to the extent to which discriminations in rates are caused by the frauds of shippers on the railroad companies and reacting on each other. You will be astonished, perhaps, when I tell you that last year the west-bound inspection bureau of the trunk lines from Boston, New York, and Philadelphia, and not including Baltimore or other points, discovered 270,000 misrepresentations by merchants of the goods purporting to be contained in the packages forwarded.

Upon asking the chief inspector how many of those cases he considered intentional, he said that aside from a few cases where, for example, some linoleum of certain size might have been classed different from oilcloth, that every other one of the instances was an intentional inroad upon the railroad company's rates. It must be so, for each shipper knows what he sells. Furthermore, this can not be a fraud upon the railroad companies without being a fraud upon other merchants. I have been asked how the facts were ascertained. It is by opening the packages, as the customs inspectors do. This did not include Albany, Troy, Rochester, Schenectady, Syracuse, Trenton, New Haven, or any other points—Bridgeport or Harrisburg—nor interior business, nor east-bound business, nor any territory but ours. While it is so prevalent to accuse the railroad companies of being the discriminators, I trust your body will consider this great discrimination as well.

Q. (By Mr. FARQUHAR.) Are they large shippers?—A. Some are.

Q. (By Mr. PHILLIPS.) What do you mean by opening the packages?—A. A box, really silks, may be represented to us as shirtings, the rates New York to Chicago being, let us say, 75 and 50 cents per 100 pounds, respectively. The inspectors simply pry such boxes open, taking the due responsibility therefor, and find the facts as stated. Yet the shippers know that in the event of losses they can not collect for more than the value of the articles they certified were shipped.

Q. (By Mr. FARQUHAR.) It can readily be seen where it could occur in articles of that kind, especially in hardware?—A. Speaking of hardware, an officer of an association of hardware manufacturers said to me, jocularly, at a trade dinner in New York: "It is so easy to beat your railroads. You charge manufactured brass goods at so much and iron piping at so much. I shipped a case containing only manufactured brass goods, except one piece of iron pipe joint, and I called it 'iron pipe.' It went through, and I saved about $2.30 per box to a far Western destination."

Q. (By Professor JOHNSON.) He had no more compunction?—A. No; he thought it a good joke.

Q. (By Mr. FARQUHAR.) Does not that help the question of uniform classification?—A. No; because evasions as well as detections under one classification are as easy as under another, and the more the inspections under different classifications the greater may be the chance of detection. It would assist us in other cases. The system of inspection which we have is much like that of the customhouse in identifying the character and valuations of goods under invoicing. Our inspections are carried on to a larger extent than formerly, and we are gradually circumscribing the wrongs they discover. We had over 100 inspectors a year ago, and the frauds and errors discovered paid the whole cost of the bureau 11¼ times.

Q. (By Mr. RATCHFORD.) Do the railroads seek to justify their discrimination because of the fact that advantage is taken of them by shippers in the manner in which you state?—A. Not at all.

Q. You simply make reference to that to show that the shippers who sometimes charge these discriminations are not doing the fair thing themselves?—A. That is true. I do not justify railroad companies in any preferences, excepting those that are legal and reasonable under the terms of the act, but I do not justify shippers in any, any more than in smuggling.

Q. (By Mr. PHILLIPS.) Have you any remedy to suggest in the way of remedial legislation, either to Congress or the various States, both as to shippers and to railroads?—A. The discriminations by railroads will largely cease if what I believe to be the best method is legalized, and that is the railway right of mutual contract. If we had the right to so organize for 5 years we could immediately proceed to the more comprehensive and permanent correction of these abuses. Certain companies take certain half-way measures because of this uncertain legal status and certain shippers get advantages over other shippers. Some railways think this laxity helps to build up their business against future contingencies and let such things pass and keep the regard and traffic of the shippers thus unjustly benefited. If, however, we could make long-term contracts, we could put a stop to these wrongs and act conclusively. The railroad companies would then present a more united front to both disturbing railways and shippers and discriminations would diminish. The shippers would have a more wholesome regard for the law if they knew that the railroads stood together to enforce it permanently and that it authorized us to proceed against them in this respect. That is the principal thing to be done, for we can not legislate rectitude into a man or make paper mandates prevail against lack of integrity and yet not build the machinery by which those mandates must be carried out. For example, if I alone possessed all the powers of Congress to render decisions to the effect that certain practices were wrong, they would not stop, nor could I stop them, unless I provided due means to carry those measures into due effect. The carriers in daily contact with the subject and interested practically and not as mere reformers in the upright purpose must do the work. Then we could have some united peace and some thoroughness of joint action and cooperatively stop these discriminations.

Q. That is as to the shippers?—A. That is both as to the shippers and as to ourselves. The New York Central company, for example, might not hesitate to act if it had a long term and enforceable legal contract which it could set in motion, nor then hesitate to proceed against others for the violation of joint agreements.

Then a company not as strong as the New York Central would hesitate about cutting the standard legal rates, knowing that they were going to be proceeded against, perhaps by the Interstate Commerce Commission or rival carrier under due terms, conditions, and limitations. It is impracticable to reach this wrong except by practical laws. Theoretical legislation will not do it. Let us get rid of that will-o'-the-wisp.

Q. Then have you any special form in which you would put this?—A. Nothing except the law substantially as I proposed it generally this morning.

Q. (By Mr. KENNEDY.) Is it true that some years ago the railroads of the country came very near to adopting a uniform transportation classification, and that two east-and-west trunk lines defeated it?—A. It is true that of the leading lines of the East some were prominent in opposition. It was also true that certain other lines in the South and West added their dissent, and perhaps disclosed it more after the proposal was defeated than while it was being considered. I nevertheless believe it may be brought about. When I went to the Central Traffic Association, in Chicago, as its commissioner, our eastward tariffs contained 13 classes, practically. Upon suggesting that they be reduced to 10 I was advised that they could not be so curtailed.

Subsequently, when the interstate-commerce act was passed the 13 classes were merged into 6, proving what can be done. This was exclusive of commodity rates.

I do not think a uniform classification is a cure for most of the difficulties which are complained of in that respect, but it is a help for unbroken through rates. It helps the merchant shipping now to have the classification from Chicago to New York, from Chicago to New Orleans, and another one to Galveston or San Francisco, although they differ, replaced by one classification basis.

It would be a help where 3 classifications prevailed to merge them into 1, and I would regard it as a railroad convenience and aid to have continuous through rates under some uniform classification. It will also operate to more uniform rates per mile in the tariffs.

Q. (By Professor JOHNSON.) You think, then, that uniform classification can be secured without the cooperation of the public? I understood you this morning to be opposed to the Government, through the Interstate Commerce Commission, undertaking to insist upon uniform classification.—A. Perhaps I was misunderstood or misunderstood you, on that point. I think that if the Interstate Commerce Commission were to issue a call, under law, that it contemplated taking active steps toward the unity of classification, and notify the railroads to that effect, that the railway companies would meet, as they met before, but under perhaps the more favorable auspices of time, increased prosperity of the country, etc., and it might be thus accomplished. If it be thus achieved I would not, for one, object to requiring that on and after a certain date, which allowed full consideration, the railroad companies should have a uniform classification. I have elsewhere given my views on this subject fully. That is very different from the proposal I discussed this morning, which was to give the Interstate Commerce Commission the right to say what articles should be in each class and what changes should take place from time to time in that classification, which is conferring upon them the rate-making power in the largest sense.

Q. Failing in the adoption of uniform classification by the railroads within the time limit, would you give the Interstate Commerce Commission power to prescribe it?—A. I would not object to giving them the power to say that a uniform classification should take effect within a certain time and that, failing in that, they would call for the use of a special and uniform classification.

Q. Is not that essentially what the Interstate Commerce Commission wants on that particular point?—A. On that particular point the case is well made up, if that is all they mean.

Q. (By Mr. CLARKE.) Please give us, in this connection, your idea of uniform classification.—A. That is almost impossible. There are now, I think, approximately, including the import tariffs, rates on over 4,000 articles, taking those sent locally and through and in all directions. To comprehend the original proposition of a uniform classification, the number of classes being reduced from 13 to 6, to say which one of these present classes shall then prevail in lieu of 13 over all railways, which article of the 4,000 should go into this or that class in each and all parts of the country, would be impossible without having each article before us, and discussing its merits and bearings, and even those would differ as the territories differ, as the Canadian may differ from the States' classification, much as the conditions on tickets and bills of lading may and do differ. I can not, therefore, as much as I would like to do so, answer your question satisfactorily to you or myself. There are many things to be reconciled, both in trade and railway interests, as I said this morning. The classification of cotton in the cotton producing States, the classification of wool, and the classification of zinc differ, depending upon the volumes and conditions under which they are produced and sold and carried; lead and precious ores, sheep, cattle, lumber, and all the articles which constitute the complex proposition. I should, perhaps, not be so decided in my advocacy of the general proposition if it had not approached, as Professor Johnson well says, almost a consummation at one time. At the same time, I think you overestimate the value of a uniform classification. It is desirable, but not essential, and its adoption will not stop discriminations. That goes deeper than classification and is your principal problem.

Q. It will be an aid to the shippers, I suppose?—A. It would be an aid to shippers and to the railroads also.

Q. And would it not be desirable to all that the same articles should go in the same classification in all parts of the country?—A. I think so and said so this morning, but, as I have endeavored to show, the subject bristles with difficulties. Two of them, on which I have not enlarged, are now undergoing scrutiny and publicity. One is the difference of rates between the classes, and the other is the differences between carload and less than carload rates.

Q. (By Mr. FARQUHAR.) You made a statement this morning that in your experience with all pools heretofore made, you never had rates arranged in the pools. Now, what form of pooling contract would you suggest as between roads? That is, what would be the contract features of the pool that you propose now, provided that the Congress of the United States would give you the authority?—A. I think I could dictate now, on one page of paper, a proposed pool, something like this: " The following railroads (naming them) operating from and through ———, to and through———, hereby agree that to observe and give due effect to the tariffs from time to time legally issued, they will, from———for a period of ———years from said date, divide their tonnage therefrom and thereto and the earnings produced thereby at the published rates substantially in the proportions in which the shippers have delivered it to them heretofore. The proportions in which the said business shall be carried by the several parties hereto shall be as follows: (Specifying the percentage due to each.) If any company carries more than its said proportion, it shall in the next month transfer such excess of tonnage, computed at the gross rates shown by said established tariffs, to the company or companies in deficit, or, failing to so transfer the tonnage, it shall pay money in an equal or agreed amount within 30 days thereafter."

Some details would, of course, follow, but, materially, that is all there is in a pooling contract. Now, then, comes the question of rates, which is the vital public concern. If such a contract could go out with the seal of the Government authorizing it, that is all we want, and no one has ever gainsaid its equity.

Next, as to changes in such rates: We should be authorized to get together and fix them. If we then say the rate will be 20 cents from Chicago to New York, in lieu of 18 cents, there lies the public interest. We proposed to submit all these agreements to the Interstate Commerce Commission before issue or effect, under conditions mutually protective, in some such a bill as that which I proposed here this morning and will discuss hereinafter.

Q. Maintaining the Interstate Commerce Commission in its present form with the present number of members?—A. I think the membership of that commission ought clearly to be not less than seven, for the reasons I have stated.

Q. Provided that you had this pooling system established by law, and the reconstruction or enlargement of the Interstate Commerce Commission, what would be the character of the personnel that you, as a practical railroad man, would want to see on that commission?—A. I have very strong views about that. By one of those anomalies, which I regard as unjustifiable, the present law provides that no man who owns a share of railroad stock, etc., shall become a member of this commission. The English law requires that its board shall contain someone experienced in transportation. One night, at a dinner with some officers of the Army, the effect of the interstate-commerce law upon transportation of troops and supplies for the Spanish war on the part of the Government was discussed, leading to the general discussion of the interstate law, and I said then what I now repeat, that it would be similar to appointing a committee for the purpose of making recommendations as to our coast defenses if there were a clause in such a law that there should not be an army officer on the board; or, in the increased construction of new ships, if such men as Dewey and Sampson were prohibited by law from sitting on that board.

Q. (By Professor JOHNSON.) Do you mean to say that railroad men can not be appointed on the Interstate Commerce Commission?—A. Yes; if they own stock.

Q. You would not say that a man on the commission ought to be a railroad man at the same time?—A. I think Representative Cannon made the correct statement. He reported a banking law and acknowledged he owned bank stocks. I think he is a better lawmaker because he does, and that both sides get a better and more experienced judgment. The people exact no such poverty conditions as to their Senators or Representatives, and they sit in their Houses and vote nevertheless. Such conditions ought not to disqualify any honorable man. It does not disqualify a candidate for membership on the Interstate Commission that he has received fees for arguing for or against railways as an attorney prior to his appointment. If I was sitting upon a commission I know that I would like to have a man beside me who owned railroad stock, and knew the true bearings of that interest. I would like to discuss the topics with him because he would understand the subject from that standpoint as I might claim I did from mine.

Q. Would you say that a man could be an impartial commissioner who owned stock in one of the companies of the United States?—A. I know many of them; yes. We all know of Senators who are impartial, yet own corporate securities.

Q. That seems rather impossible.—A. I know it is so regarded, but I do not.

Q. (By Mr. FARQUHAR.) In your Joint Traffic Association how many were in your main consulting board?—A. There were 32 signers of that contract, all of whom attached the seals of their companies after receiving authority to that effect from their boards. They then appointed 9 managers, so that each system, beginning with the Canadian Pacific on the north and ending with the Chesapeake and Ohio on the south, should speak for the signing roads. That was the general constituency of the board. These 9 men considered 22,000 subjects in 4 years within the territory that they covered. With all that experience and my own, and multiplying that number by passenger matters on all railroads of the country, by complications attending each and every thing relating to them, it is my judgment, without reflection upon the members of the Interstate Commission, that it would have been utterly impossible for the latter to have performed that detailed service or laid down a general rule to cover them. As a transportation man I would favor an increase in the board. I would favor a retention of the present geographical and political apportionment, and I would favor the proposition also that they hold stated meetings in different parts of the country. I would favor their right to call not only upon shippers, but railroad presidents for periodical consultations, and that they should undertake to ascertain from each what their views were as to the benefits which could be added to changes in transportation rates, fares, classifications, and rules. When I had been 8 days on the stand in New York before the Hepburn committee I wound up by favoring the appointment of a State commission, as I had done repeatedly before, for this reason, if for no other: That it would act as a buffer between the railroad companies on the one side and the intelligent public on the other; and it so turned out in practice. If A, B, C, or D has a patent safety device which he thinks should be ordered used on cars, or some one wanted an order for some safety appliance at country crossings, or if the street-railway managements favored something alleged to oppress the public, or, on the other hand, if the railroads did something that would oppress the public, that commission would, I believed, balance the contentions. The result has been that they do act to correct public misunderstandings, and they correct the railways by urging the concessions which the public should enjoy. I recently had a conversation with Mr. Hepburn, who was the chairman of that great New York committee and who is now vice-president of the Chase National Bank of New York, and asked him if he thought the mercantile community had derived any benefit from this discussion. He said he started his examination in the belief that the railways were mainly wrong. He ended finding he had misapprehended and misjudged them, and I certainly did him. So these difficulties and differences became reconciled or modified. We went over our road and collected hundreds of cases, not alone on that road where the trouble was supposed to be created, but on others where it was shown they existed. The aggregate result was of great mutual benefit.

I believe in that form of consultation now and I believe it the more, as I said in the opening remarks this morning, when such conferences take on a national character. But I believe the powers of the commission should be fully and carefully limited and defined. I do not want them to be denied access to any features that will enable them to protect the public. I want them to assist and that we aid them to that end. I want them to be clothed with the right to protect the railroads, too. These things have not gone together heretofore. The partings of the ways have had too many right angles in them.

Q. You are also aware that the American public are very jealous of the railroads?—A. Oh, yes; and that, whatever the enlargements of the functions of this Interstate Commerce Commission, that public jealousy will continue to demand increasing railway concessions to the verge of socialism or beyond it. Even when the interstate-commerce bill was being considered, judged by its terms and, more so since, by the new powers asked, I concur that this country will never wholly surrender the regulation of railroads. I do not want it conceived that I have hostility toward the Interstate Commerce Commission, although I think their new demands should in very many respects be resisted by all due argument and legal effort.

I had occasion, at a meeting of the American Board of Certified Accountants, to say that it seemed to me that the Interstate Commerce Commission was wise in providing uniform terms for the various headings, periods, and definitions of railroad companies' accounts so far as they could compass that purpose. Take the floating debt item for example.

I fancy each member of this commission, as intelligent as they are, would have a different idea and a different definition of what the floating debt of a railroad corporation really is, when it begins, matures, and what it consists of. If I buy 50 tons of iron and it is delivered, but it has not been vouchered, has that account become a floating debt in law? If I have issued a note for it which has not become due and may be renewed in part, its relation as a floating debt may be treated differently. I therefore think a uniform system is necessary to clearness and to define clear standards of credit and responsibility. I believe that the whole subject should be approached in a candid, national spirit. The one side too often says, "We want so and so and decline anything less." We all know people will never get together on that basis. We ought to have conferences, and we ought to have the cooperation of the national commission and they should have ours, within fair boundaries for both. It is only by getting together that we can accomplish good things, and then we must be prepared with olive branches as well as thorns.

Q. (By Mr. Phillips.) It has been suggested that the Government of the United States should grant charters to railroads. Have you ever given that consideration?—A. No; I have not.

Q. That the charter where the road was doing an interstate business should be granted only by the Government of the United States?—A. No; I think it better that the States shall continue to grant charters and whatever interstate traffic passes over them shall pass under due interstate regulation, as on unchartered waters. National charters would conflict constantly with the rights of the States. There are also important railroads in the country which lie wholly in one State—like the New York Central and Pennsylvania proper—a great majority of whose earnings are derived from State traffic. It would be hard to draw the line if law gave to Congress alone the right to determine the charter of a new road. If so, it would appear to carry the power over all the charges of such a railway, and this can not be constitutional, of course.

On the subject of new roads, pardon me for saying a word more.

There are too many railroads in the country. We furnish more miles of road now for every 100 persons, or 100 tons, averaged throughout the country, than any other country. I have submitted figures elsewhere in this connection, and they establish another claim to national consideration. I therefore contend that, having built so many miles for so few people, we think that these earlier roads should receive protection against newer roads unless their public necessity is made apparent, as in England. This being assured, it might more fully warrant fuller control over the rate questions at issue. In other words, if there are two railroads from Washington to Baltimore—the Pennsylvania and the Baltimore and Ohio—and a third company asked for a charter, I do not think it ought to be granted, except under the amplest needs and safeguards against reducing reasonable rates and fares. We should not be indiscriminately subjected both to new competing lines and, after they are opened, to new competing rates, especially by those who claim we are but agents of the Government and performing public duties. That being so, it becomes in a sense an attack upon the Government, as it is a clear violation of its laws. I think if Government decline such consideration to the older lines they should at least say to the new companies, in effect, "this multiplication of bonds and stocks is needless." They are equivalent to the watered stocks which we complain of so much and insistently against the older companies. At the same time, if they establish a public need for additional railroads, of course they can not be denied proper franchises.

Q. (By Mr. CLARKE.) Are you familiar with the laws of the several States regulating that subject?—A. No; I am not.

Q. In regard to public exigencies?—A. No; I am not.

Q. You are aware, I suppose, that it is embodied in some States?—A. I believe it is embodied in the Massachusetts law. I am not familiar enough to answer you affirmatively. England requires it, and the public good is manifestly conserved.

Q. (By Mr. A. L. HARRIS.) Has the pooling system been adopted in any other country?—A. Yes. In a part of the paper, which I desire to lay before you and which your Chair was good enough to allow me to bring in hereafter, I will submit that feature quite fully. That will give you an exact statement of the recent situation of pooling abroad. I invite particular attention now to the notable utterances upon the subject by Professor—now President—Hadley of Yale College.

Q. Is it the pooling system called the Joint Purse Association?—A. Called the Joint Purses in England, and so designated in the blue books, and only infrequently there called pools.

Q. (By Professor JOHNSON.) Are there pools on the Continent of Europe also?—A. There are pools in Italy, France, Germany, Austria-Hungary, and throughout the United Kingdom. For example, the London, Chatham and Dover and the Southeastern road, running from London to the Channel, have for years had the Channel passenger division—I think they call it—and yet they continue to contend for that large business actively within legitimate lines. There is also, as I remember, a pool between Glasgow and London. At first the people were in opposition to these plans, but now—as the railways give cheaper transportation and they get better facilities—the people of Glasgow have become reconciled, as they have in various districts elsewhere.

Q. (By Mr. PHILLIPS.) How do they differ from the Joint Traffic Association, with which you were connected?—A. The Joint Traffic Association was in terms almost identical in general features, but did not divide business or money as they are used abroad. This committee should perhaps better understand the difference between the English clearing house and their own joint purses and our association service. There are 2,000 or more clerks and attachés in the English clearing house service proper, and, as that name indicates, it simply clears the earnings in gross. They have stated meetings of the different district committees—the Lancashire district, the London, the Manchester, and others. These are held in the clearing house, but are not essential to its first purpose. If a railroad company desires to change a rate, it is submitted to the proper committee for the district affected, together with the reasons which fortify it, and these requests are sent to the members of such committee. The rate is not thereafter changed arbitrarily unless the competitors and connections consider and act upon it, which is showing only a due regard for all interests. If one company opposes the proposal, it goes over to the next meeting, and at the next meeting the rate can not be changed except by a two-thirds vote of the members, not of the whole conference, but that particular committee, unless the proposer acts summarily for itself, which is most rare. The changes of classification are more fully and generally reviewed. That is the way to get a new rate acted upon in England,

and the result is that every man who goes into business there is certain that he will have like and permanent rates with his fellow-merchants and railways; that there is stability and uniformity, and he knows if he wants a rate different from that in the tariff or classification, he has to go through this procedure to get it, and everybody else has to go through the same procedure. A man can not go into a railroad office there and get 2 or 3 cents paid back on freight at an hour's notice, and get a commission on tickets or scalp a fare; and yet we Americans, who clamor so loud for disturbing methods, were calling them competition, and go over there and adapt ourselves to their better procedures without any reason for demur.

At a dinner I attended in London, I asked what percentage of the entire business of the British Isles proper was carried on at established rates, and the answer was, 99 per cent or more. "Well," I said, "what becomes of the other 1 per cent?" and was told of a practice not much known in America, viz, the giving of credits for freight, which is equivalent to a drawback, but only to the extent of the rate of interest on the amount of the continuing credit. In other words, a large concern doing an immense business may be given £10,000 credit on the freight bills. In one case cited that night a large credit had run for 20 years. The railroad company was, to that extent, a partner in the business, furnishing considerable capital toward its development.

Q. What position did you occupy in the Joint Traffic Association?—A. I was its commissioner.

Q. When was it formed?—A. Three years ago last July, but it expired with the decision of the Supreme Court a year ago last October.

Q. What territory was embraced in that association?—A. Substantially all the territory south of the Great Lakes, including the peninsula in Michigan, and south of Lake Ontario and the St. Lawrence River on the north, to the Potomac on the south, taking in the Chesapeake and Ohio road, and west to St. Louis on a line drawn thence by way of the Alton road from Chicago. Subsequently the Canadian Pacific and the Grand Trunk became parties; except as to their local business, and the Canadian rates extended beyond the St. Lawrence so that we have had about 78 per cent of the tonnage of the United States and 75 per cent of the earnings of the United States in our territory, but only the freight and passenger traffic to, from, and through the western termini of the trunk lines at Buffalo, Pittsburg, etc.

Q. Were not other railroads doing business in the same geographical position almost compelled to join the association?—A. No.

Q. By force of circumstances?—A. No.

Q. They were not asked?—A. As a rule, no. They were notified by all their connections, party to the association, that the board of managers of the association would act for or with them in any case they might desire to submit, and it was also provided that any officer of a company not a member of the association in the territory had a right to appear and argue his case. For example, the lake lines, the Central of New Jersey, the Lake Erie and Western availed of this plan. The contract is on file with the Interstate Commerce Commission.

Q. (By Mr. KENNEDY.) A previous witness has said that if the railroads could have a pooling arrangement, and a company refused to go into the pool, remained out and pirated rates, that under cover of law they could combine against this other company. Did companies remaining outside of the pool pirate transportation rates; and if so, what steps did you take against those companies?—A. There have been no pools, of course, since 1887. At the time when the interstate law was approved those preexisting were promptly discontinued throughout the United States; therefore, the conditions to which you refer were prior to that time. The most notable pools that then existed were those west and east of Chicago. There were a number of roads west of Chicago that did not go into the pools and a number of roads east of Chicago that did not go into the Eastern pools. The pooling lines pooled only a small share of their whole business. For example, Buffalo to Albany, Washington to all points, Rochester to Boston were all outside the pool, etc. The pools east of Chicago were only few in number, and one pool did not cover the whole business or any considerable part of it. Chicago, Peoria, Louisville, Cincinnati, and Indianapolis, and St. Louis in that territory were the only points that were pooled, and that was east bound. Those pools represented an average of about $12,000,000 a year, the largest balance ever accruing in one year was $300,000, and two-thirds of that amount was subsequently returned to the companies that first paid it, because they reduced their tonnage so as to equalize the traffic. It was clearly not to their interest to carry the freight and then pay the proceeds to other companies. So all this clamor represented, in that great territory, about $100,000 net. Dividing $300,000 by the tonnage handled from those points, it represented the enormity and public danger of 2.2 cents per ton, while the customary rebate would not be then looked at unless it was about 50 cents per ton. The other points were not pooled eastward. For example, Cleveland was not pooled, nor Detroit, Toledo, Terre Haute, Columbus, nor any of those places. They continued to transact their business the same as they had before, and measurably with the same losses and discriminations in rates. Then the pooled cities objected to the privileges enjoyed by the smaller ones. Now it is the smaller points which demur at the discriminations given larger points. There never was a threat made against a company, to my knowledge, that if they did not go into this or that pool they could not do joint business. As to the attempts of roads outside the pooled points to demoralize business that is true, and they were assisted in it by large shippers who diverted business to such open or unpooled channels. For example, if there was a line intermediate between Chicago and Peoria, or Peoria and St. Louis, through which a connecting company or a large firm could ship its freight and avoid the pool, they took that line and its rebates. In this and every other conceivable way the outside companies, plus concurring begging shippers, sought conflicts with the pools and to defeat their just purposes. The railroad companies that were pooled had no right to force others in and did not attempt it. Nor did they care whether they were in or out if they only observed the tariff rates. We had no rights or powers of enforcing our views, and finally these causes demoralized our business. Then came the organization of the Joint Traffic Association in our territory where the same conditions existed. The Norfolk and Western road, running to and from Norfolk, was not in the association. It used the same steamships east of Norfolk that were used by the Chesapeake and Ohio, and we never interfered with them. We simply asked them to maintain the transportation rates, which were the lowest in the world. That is all there is of it. If they did so, they aided the interstate law and our own wise purposes. If they did not, they introduced conditions we jointly condemn, but can not agree to jointly abolish.

Q. Suppose pooling were legalized, and in the competitive region a great railroad remained outside that pool and pirated rates, would not the companies in the pool be compelled in self-defense to take some concerted action against that railroad?—A. Only to this extent: If pools were ever made again, more railways ought to be pooled, and from more points, for the cogent reasons just now stated. If, however, important roads on the west or east—say, of Buffalo—would not take part in the pools, from whatever motive, the pooled lines would, under those circumstances, give them notice that, inasmuch as this pool was formed to preserve equal rates, they could not receive their traffic except on the same conditions, or, in other words, not more favorable than those existing between the concurring companies. If they still refused, the pooled lines would have to stand together as to rates so as to secure them. As to any other ways of discriminating than that, I have never heard them proposed.

Q. (By Mr. A. L. HARRIS.) You say the object was to maintain the lowest possible freight rates?—A. I say the rates which are the lowest of the world. I did not say to maintain them in any other sense than the observance of legal, just, and reasonable rates.

Q. The object is to maintain living rates?—A. Yes.

Q. Does that not destroy the natural law of competition?—A. No; I went very fully into that this morning. Our plan gives, in other words, full play to that purpose. Suppose, for example, that our rate from Buffalo to New York was 10 cents a hundred, as the result of a railway warfare which reduced the rate from 15 cents. Under the right to contract we might maintain the former rate, or, say, make it 12 cents. That rate comes duly published before the Interstate Commerce Commission, who might say they saw no reason why it should not be 12 cents with the altered conditions, after considering the 10 and 15 cent rates issued under the conditions suggested. There will then be two tribunals to consider the three rates, first, the railroad companies, which have the major interest in this matter, although they can not in any case get more revenues than their environments will permit, and second, the shippers. If this rate is under 15 cents, legitimate competition has more chance to work out its own rights and show its wrongs than it had at 10 cents, because the attitude of 10 cents is not that of competition, but strife and ruinous reprisals. The general public believe that all these things are competition, but do not know about it. The shippers, however, do know. We will say, as to the Pennsylvania from Pittsburg, or the Baltimore and Ohio, that there is no water route from Pittsburg to the Potomac or Delaware rivers. That is, there are no lines parallel, as is the Erie Canal to the New York Central and other railroads from Buffalo to New York. If, therefore, the competition of the Erie Canal may be ignored, why do not the interested companies push up their rates to 15 cents from Pittsburg or Wheeling to Baltimore or Washington? It is because the unwritten law of actual competition says you can not maintain that rate. It is a natural law, and therefore beyond academic statutes which say you can not maintain against the Erie Canal from Buffalo to New York any undue rates. You have no water alongside your rails, but you have a line way off in Canada that will make a lower rate Chicago to Montreal, and you have another line from Cincinnati to Newport News which have as live an effect as if they were both adjacent to your rails. The railroad engine and the canal boat run side by side from Buffalo to New York with the West Shore Railway. That is just competition, although the State assists the canal and frowns on the railway,

Thus legitimate competition does its due work and strifes undo it and substitutes chicanery and demoralization. No mere makeshifts can adjust this issue. It must be thorough.

Q. (By Mr. CLARKE.) I would like to ask the witness about the frauds practiced by so many merchants, to which he alluded. Suppose those merchants were to combine their business, forming a vast corporation. Would their opportunity for fraud or for influencing discriminating rates be any greater than it is now?—A. Yes; for the reason that if 50 New York firms combined, like, we will say, Claflin, Arnold & Constable, and such houses as that, in dry goods, which pay 75 cents, the highest freight rate, and consolidated all their traffic on one line, they might say: "We will give you our combined business if you will not open these packages and make examinations; or, if we find you have done that, we will go to some other road, and take our traffic away from you. Our business now is in one central firm, pooled as you can not pool, and our business is worth $2,000,000 a year. The business of any one of us was worth not over $300,000 before. Now we want to be treated as a $2,000,000 concern." They might also claim rebates, special time facilities, liberality in the payment of claims, etc., and get them.

Q. If the railroads were permitted to pool lawfully, so that the contract could be enforced, would that be an effective remedy against such powerful influences of large combinations?—A. I think so; undoubtedly, in the end. It would be effective against large combinations because it would give the opposing railroads incentives for building up the smaller men by like methods if they were not discarded. In every city of which I know anything the aggregate of all smaller shipments exceeds that which comes from the principal large shippers, and the smaller shippers, whether it be west bound in dry goods or east bound in something else, are ordinarily willing that their trade shall be transferred from road to road for the purpose of equalizing rates, because through such equalization they get trade they long for but have not had equal rates to secure. I say frankly that I do not see what is going to become of the great bulk of the small dealers if the great evil of discrimination goes on increasing, nor do I see how we are going to stop it except by good faith or by pooling. The principal reason is, however, that large and small railroads will have a common incentive to maintain rates through the knowledge that then if they do not get the tonnage they will receive the money therefor. The final reason is that railroads do not desire to build up large shippers, because it enables such forwarders to combine and dictate yet more onerous transportation terms. The first has surely been more of a failure than the last. It is in the nature of a surety bond to be collected against defaulters or wrongdoers.

Q. (By Mr. FARQUHAR.) Do you believe that the adoption of legalized pooling would abolish these discriminations?—A. Substantially; particularly if we had the right to make long-term contracts, in which period we could get rid of useless officers, offices, and agents, and bad methods, and so on. When the joint traffic association was formed the original proposition was to have it continue for not less than 5 years. It finally got down to 1 year, with a year's notice, which was substantially equivalent to 2 years; but when it came to the expense of offices in Broadway the railroads could not get rid of them, because they did not know what might happen in 2 years which might leave them, or some of them, stranded for business and their traffic gone to some other road. If that feud, more farseeing because more unbelieving, was done away with and we had the legalized right to make longer contracts we would go ahead and make them and let the public and weak lines and dishonest lines see that we were in earnest and treated all shippers alike, and these discriminations would then gradually cease.

Q. You are aware of the general statement, which, I think, is very generally accepted throughout this whole country, that no trust could live that did not receive railroad discrimination. What do you say about that?—A. I never heard it so put, but it is not true. If it is true you should legalize a motive and a method to stop it, and you can not do it unless you do.

Q. Well, is it true that what are now trusts, or the great businesses of this country, whether the Standard Oil Company or others, have been built up by railroads?—A. To what extent that may be true I do not know.

Q. Has not that been accepted among railroad men as a fact?—A. It has been, unfortunately, the fact in the past that large shippers of all kinds of products have received and are now receiving advantages over other shippers. Whether that may be called fostering trusts you will judge. In some cases they may have been erected into the equivalents of trusts without incorporating them. But I can answer you, in part, by saying that if this thing keeps on they will have that effect; and if the large combined shippers find that no action is taken jointly by the Government with the railroads to stop their discriminating advantages they will unhesitatingly organize themselves into trusts or conferences. It is a very curious state of facts that the law passed against trusts does not reach or apply to them, and while it was not intended for railroads, it strenuously clutches them.

Q. You made this morning also the broad assertion that railroads do not pay rebates unasked ordinarily. The shipper does not need to go to a railroad to get a rebate, does he?—A. Yes.

Q. Up to 4 or 5 years ago have not your freight solicitors always offered them direct to the shippers, without their ever approaching an officer?—A. No; I am not aware of any such usage as that. Some companies may have sent their solicitors around to try and get freight away from some other company, and the latter may have sent theirs to keep it; but what occasion would I have, for example, as manager of one of the lines east of Chicago, to go to the largest dealer in a certain article and solicit his business and offer him a rebate when I was already getting his business at published rates? There always are, in all large cities and districts, certain railroads that, with a view of diverting business from their rivals, will go to shippers in that way; but when they go to the shipper or the shipper goes to the railroad it is the shipper who asks for the rebate and says he will change the route of his business, but that he wants so much, or the conditions desired are so and so, or that bills of lading be so granted, etc. Then the bill of lading is always made at the legal rate and the net result is arrived at by an agreement which, in every instance, makes both parties particeps criminis if one is. That is what I meant by railroads not granting these allowances unasked.

Q. (By Mr. KENNEDY.) Your solicitude as to what may befall the small shippers if this practice of railroad discrimination goes on would seem to place you somewhat in harmony with many other witnesses who have been before the commission, who, however, have testified that the railroads, through discriminations and rebates and transportation favors, are the fathers and mothers of trusts. Do you take that view of it?—A. I do not think that they are the fathers and mothers of trusts. I think the railroad owners, as capitalists, have combined more capital to help themselves in perpetuating their control of certain lines and business and to help their shippers as well as themselves; but as to being influential in forming shippers into trusts for that purpose, I think there is no railroad company in the country that does not wish to control the carrying of the traffic of trusts, because the rebates and favors granted them—falsely in the name of competition—are gradually erecting them into such dimensions that they can control the terms of shipment, what they want and what they will accept in detail, exceptional conditions in foreign freights, and so on in the chapter, and therein lies the mutual public and railway apprehension which cooperative governmental and railway methods can most effectually restrict. If these shippers have erected themselves into substantial trusts now they have done so largely by the conditions I have mentioned, and they will push their advantages. For example, Mr. Carnegie, with all his public philanthropies and high character, built a railroad from Pittsburg to Lake Erie to get lower rates than he had enjoyed as a favorite patron. That does not seem like a railway desire to build up a trust, but to avoid doing so.

Q. (By Mr. CLARKE.) Do you see a public danger in large shippers becoming heavy stockholders and directors in railroads?—A. No. I wish there were more of them. They could be reached then by the law, in the first place, and, in the second place, I think they would always be in the minority, and that the other directors would feel a keener sense of their public duty, and that the shippers who were directors would better understand the general relations of the railroad companies and carriers and their own duties to the public.

They would then necessarily lose sight of themselves as merchants, in part, in their large interests and responsibilities as carrying officers. I believe the large merchant is a large merchant because he is big enough to look at it in that way. I know some of the large owners of private enterprises who get into railway companies and make the best of directors, the most cautious and conservative of men, from the fact that they see then both sides of the issue. This is, as a vice-president of the Union Pacific road told me at one time, that perhaps the most conscientious and painstaking member of their board was Mr. Gould, who, having made his fortune by questionable methods, sought to maintain it and establish a new repute by methods that were unquestionable.

Q. (By Mr. PHILLIPS.) Have you given the subject of taxation any attention?— A. I have not the slightest. I have been so absorbed in these traffic matters that I have never seen a tax bill and never have had occasion to, and I have never paid any attention to anything of that kind.

WASHINGTON, D. C., *February 13, 1900.*

TESTIMONY OF MR. ANDREW FURUSETH,

Secretary of the Sailors' Union of the Pacific; chairman of the legislative committee, and international secretary of the Seaman's Union.

The commission met at 10.50 a. m., Vice-Chairman Phillips presiding.

Mr. ANDREW FURUSETH was introduced as a witness, and, being duly sworn, testified as follows, the topical plan of inquiry on transportation being followed:

Q. (By Mr. PHILLIPS.) You will please give us your full name and place of residence.—A. Andrew Furuseth, No. 106 Stewart street, San Francisco, Cal.

Q. What has been your occupation, and what is your occupation at present?— A. I have been a seaman since 1872, and have sailed under Norwegian, Swedish, German, Holland, English, and American flags. Since 1892 I have been engaged as secretary of the Sailors' Union of the Pacific. Being a member of that organization, I was elected to the secretaryship. On several occasions during that time I was sent to Washington in the interest of legislation for the seamen.

Q. For about how many years have you represented them in that capacity in Washington?—A. Five years.

Q. You are here now in that interest, are you?—A. I am here as representing the seamen and also the American Federation of Labor, being a member of the legislative committee of the American Federation of Labor.

Q. (By Mr. RATCHFORD.) Is your organization affiliated with the American Federation of Labor?—A. Yes; our organization is affiliated with the American Federation of Labor, and has been since 1892.

Q. (By Mr. FARQUHAR.) How many organizations of seamen are there in the United States?—A. There is one national seamen's organization only.

Q. (By Mr. PHILLIPS.) Where is their headquarters?—A. Its headquarters is in Boston.

Q. (By Mr. FARQUHAR.) What sections of the country do the seaman's union cover?—A. The Pacific coast, the Great Lakes, and the Atlantic coast.

Q. Have you any idea of the number of members that are in all these various unions?—A. I can not say exactly, but between 4 and 5 thousand; probably nearer 5 thousand than 4.

Q. How long have these unions been organized?—A. They were organized as an international union in 1892.

Q. What kind of organizations did they have before this international?—A. Local unions.

Q. How long have they been in existence?—A. On the Pacific coast from 1885; on the lakes, with short intermissions, from 1868, and on the Atlantic coast from 1890.

Q. Do you have any benefit organization in these unions, or any life insurance or mutual benefits?—A. No. We have a shipwreck benefit, and funeral benefit; that is, we bury the members. In case of shipwreck and loss of clothing, the organization pays a sum not to exceed $50 to buy a new outfit.

Q. What are the general objects of the International Seaman's Union as set forth in its constitution?—A. To improve the condition of the seamen industrially, socially, and to improve the maritime law, to get improvements in the maritime law to such an extent as to make the law a help instead of a hindrance in the development of the body of American seamen.

Q. What regulations have you in respect to wages?—A. The local organizations govern their own wages; that is, the Lakes govern the wages on the Lakes, the Atlantic on the Atlantic, and the Pacific on the Pacific.

Q. Have you a national card that is transferable from one local to another?— A. Yes.

~~~ ~~~~ ~~~~~nal card carry with it any benefits in respect to expense of travel, or what?—A. No; no traveling benefit.

Q. Then a seaman engaged in deep-sea navigation can transfer into the Lake trade, and from the Lake trade to the Pacific trade?—A. Yes.

Q. A seaman on the Lakes can transfer into the Atlantic and Pacific trade?—A. Yes.

Q. Have you any rules in respect to apprenticeship?—A. No. We are governed in that matter by law, or rather by an absence of law. Anybody whom the captain considers a seaman, is a seaman, whether he ever was to sea or not before. He can take anybody he wants.

Q. Is there a cooperation between the unions on the Atlantic seaboard, the Lakes, and the Pacific coast in respect to legislation affecting the seamen of the United States?—A. Yes, naturally so.

Q. Does that come through your executive boards or through legislative committees?—A. It comes through the convention.

Q. How frequently is your convention held?—A. We have had four conventions. The last one was on the first Monday in December, 1899.

Q. Then your legislative committees receive their instructions immediately from your convention?—A. Yes. One convention will instruct a legislative committee, and the next convention will go through what has been done, and then strike out and insert and do just as it wants with it; throw away and put together, just as it pleases.

Q. Have you an executive committee to whom these legislative committees can apply for further instructions as to the line of work that shall be carried on?—A. Yes.

Q. So there is full cooperation between the legislative committees and the executive committees?—A. Exactly.

Q. (By Mr. PHILLIPS.) We would be very glad to have you take up Part III of the plan of inquiry and give us any information you can in regard to the matter.—A. "The navigation laws as affecting the seamen." We, as seamen, hold to be responsible for the lack of American seamen, the laws such as they have been and very largely are yet. We hold that the laws themselves are responsible for the lack of seamen. Up to last year a seaman was subject to imprisonment for refusing to continue to labor in the United States as well as out of the United States. If he left his employment he was subject to being imprisoned, kept in jail for an indefinite period at his own expense, then taken on board of the vessel against his will, and compelled to proceed to sea in the vessel and do the work for which he had engaged. If, on arriving on board of the vessel, or at any later time, he refused to do the work allotted to him he was subject to penal or to corporal punishment and to being placed in irons upon short rations. On arriving in the next port, if he deserted, a certain amount of money would be offered—$10 or $15 or $20, whatever it might be—for his detection and his return to the vessel. If the master wanted to do that he had the power to do it; if the master did not want to do it he had the power to leave it alone. This law was set in motion upon a master's request.

The food—speaking about the food—that is a matter of law. It was fully 50 per cent poorer than the food provided for the prisoners in Sing Sing. It was exactly equal to the English contract scale. It was about 50 per cent below the German scale, and just about 100 per cent below the Danish scale. Seamen rations are usually a matter of law, maritime nations outside of England having recognized that the seamen can not successfully make any contracts on that matter. Their housing—that is, the forecastle, the place where the seaman live—is also a matter of law. The provision is now, and has been for a very long time, that the seamen shall be entitled to 72 cubic feet of air space, not less than 12 feet on the floor space of his forecastle; that is to say, there is a space 6 feet long that way (indicating), the length of the bunk, 6 feet high, the heighth of a man, and 2 feet wide, the width of a good big man's shoulders. That is the space allotted to each man in all the steamers of the United States. In these new sailing vessels—that is, those built or rebuilt in the last 3 years and for the future—the law has made it 100 cubic feet air space. There has been in the matter of sailing vessels an improvement. In the matter of steamers there has been none. This same space is also the space of Germany and of England, but inasmuch as they do not use any deck loads they have no special temptation to cramp and narrow the space. Houses are usually on deck, you understand, and they have no special temptation in that direction, and, therefore, though the law says 72 cubic feet in England, the actual space given is usually about 100 to 120. In the forecastle, which is certified to accommodate 32 men, there may be 24, so you see that makes a very much larger room than it would be if there were 32 men in it.

Now, the law does not provide, at present, any qualification for anyone who is a seaman; that is to say, the law does not set any standard of qualification, and does not specify any number of men to be carried in any vessel. It is left entirely with the judgment of the master or the owners of the vessel. Custom in olden times used to determine the qualification. Four years' apprenticeship is customary yet in England. Apprenticeship has been abolished in most countries. A boy goes to sea as a boy; then he becomes, in Germany, what they call a young man; then an ordinary seaman, and then an able seaman, step by step, and it usually takes him 4 years to-day before he gets certificate as an able seaman. In those vessels the custom of hiring men who have no skill is not as prevalent as it is in English and American vessels. The same condition exists as to Norway and Sweden. In Denmark the boy goes to sea as a deck boy; he becomes a young man; the second year he is at sea he will be called that; the third and fourth year he is at sea he will be called an ordinary seaman, and after he has been 4 years to sea or so, then the captain will give him a discharge as an able seaman. That is to say, the captain makes an able seaman of him. That is very often the case. In the next vessel he ships as an able seaman. In American vessels there are no qualifications at all as to standard of skill. The Navy has a standard, and a very exacting one—the old standard of years ago—and it is safe to say that no more than 15 per cent at the highest of the men engaged as seamen on the Great Lakes could come anywhere near passing the naval standard as able seamen. The vast majority can not pass the naval standard as ordinary seamen. I should judge that about one-half of the men on the Atlantic coast might pass as able seamen; about one-quarter as ordinary seamen, and about one-quarter, well, outside of any standard in the Navy, they would call them landsmen. The same rate of efficiency obtains, about, on the Pacific coast. Our law has been very peculiar, not only with reference to the skill of the seamen, but also with reference to the skill of the masters and officers. The only qualification, up until lately, for any master of an American sailing vessel was that he should be a citizen; and as far as maritime law was concerned, he might come from Montana and never have been to sea in all his life; and the same with everyone on board of the vessel. Now, this subjects the seaman to competition with anyone in a seaport who happens to be out of employment, and whom the "crimps" may induce to go to sea. In addition to that he is subject to competition from all nations and all races, in the same way as with the American on this continent. There is no restriction except as to officers, upon the nationality, upon the race, or on skill, and the result is that the wages of seamen are not really set by the seamen themselves, but it is just about the kind of wages that the idle men in the seaport can be induced to accept.

American vessels carry less men than English, German, or European continental vessels; carry less men measured by tonnage.

Q. (By Mr. RATCHFORD.) Such men as sailors and ship hands?—A. Yes; less sailors, or firemen in a steamer—anyway, less men. The only country that really has a definite law about the matter of manning vessels is New Zealand. They have an efficient manning law, enacted by the parliament, but on the Continent it is governed by custom, and as labor-saving machinery has gone in the number of men have been reduced; but it has been reduced out of proportion, so that there is really not to-day a vessel—and I am now giving what I have read from the German naval architect—he said there is not a sailing vessel efficiently manned to-day.

Q. (By Mr. FARQUHAR.) In Europe or in America?—A. In Europe or in America? Of course from my own personal knowledge and experience I know that many vessels get into serious trouble, taken aback, as we call it, the yards braced up like that, and when it strikes on a vessel that way (indicating), and when she shifts around and comes in from this side, the vessel is thrown aback. Now, the safety of the vessel depends upon quick work; and in 9 vessels out of 10 the only thing you can do is to depend on the strength of the gear and get along the best you can. The ability to swing the yards quick enough is out of the question; that can not be done to-day. Vessels that used to carry—well, we will take the *Glory of the Seas*, as an instance. The ship *Glory of the Seas* used to carry 36 men; she now carries 14. We have vessels on the Pacific coast which, while sailing in the foreign trade, carried 18 and 20 men, but now carry 10.

Q. (By Mr. PHILLIPS.) What is the cause of this reduction; is it on account of improved machinery?—A. They have usually put in a donkey winch to lift the anchor. This donkey is usually used going in and out of port; that is, for lifting the anchor and hoisting sails at once; but at sea there is no fire on the donkey, and the Armstrong patent must be resorted to.

Q. (By Mr. FARQUHAR.) Will you kindly state these improvements that have occurred.—A. Double topsail yards is one; double gallant yards is another; patent blocks are rollers—small inside rollers; softer, better rope—usually use manila rope instead of the other; then the steam donkey. Those are really all the things that have been done in that direction.

Q. (By Mr. Phillips.) Will you kindly state the number of sailors formerly required, as compared with the present time? Say 40 were required, what proportion would these new devices reduce that so as to get equal manning power now with safety?—A. I mention the ship *Glory of the Seas*. She used to carry 36 men. Twenty-four men before the mast would be a crew for her now.

Q. What did you say the crew was now?—A. Now she carries 14.

Q. (By Mr. Ratchford.) You stated that the improved devices on a vessel were largely responsible for the reduction in the number of men, and that the reduction was disproportionate.—A. Yes.

Q. Are we to understand that the labor of seamen and responsibility also has increased in the past few years?—A. Unquestionably.

Q. Have their wages increased?—A. No.

Q. Are they stationary?—A. Wages of seamen fluctuate very much. It will run from $15 in the port of New York up to $30 in the different ports.

Q. Has the general treatment of the seamen grown better or worse in the past 20 years?—A. Taking it altogether, I should say it has grown better; in some lines, at least; but there are so many things that come up in a seaman's life that it is almost impossible to put it all into one answer of that description.

Q. On the aggregate you think it has improved some?—A. Some little. In certain directions it has distinctively deteriorated; in others it has improved some. Taking it as an aggregate, you might say there has been some improvement.

Q. (By Mr. Farquhar.) What nations carry the most able seamen?—A. Holland.

Q. What is the next one? Mention them, if you can recollect them, by rank.—A. Holland would come first; Denmark would come next; Sweden would come next. I am speaking only of northern nations, because the southern nations I have no personal acquaintance with. Norway and Germany would be about the same, and in the order after the others; then England, and last, the United States.

Q. Now, do the wages enter much into the curtailment of the number of seamen on these vessels?—A. It enters in some degree; I can not say how much. When the wages go up they usually take 1 or 2 men less.

Q. Well, in respect to the wages, for instance, of Holland or Sweden, and the wages in American ships; what is the difference?—A. It depends entirely upon what kind of trade those vessels are in. Wages of seamen are governed entirely by the port, and not by the flag. Seamen's wages in New York City are the same to the American ship, and Holland ship, and German ship, and English ship, and Norwegian ship. They are able seamen's wages, irrespective of nationality; so it is with firemen. If we deal with it differently, and compare the coastwise trade of the United States with the foreign trades of the United States, or with the foreign trades of other nations, then the coast wise trade of the United States is higher than any outside of Australia.

Q. (By Mr. Ratchford.) Would you care to enumerate the different ports, so far as you are acquainted with them, and the wages paid at these ports; show the commission where the higher rate is paid, and the ports paying the lowest rate also, as far as your knowledge goes?—A. Wages in Australia and on the Pacific are generally higher than in New York; and in New York it is usually higher than in Liverpool; while in Sunderland, England, it is fully as high as in New York. Again, in Antwerp, Belgium, it is lower than in either of the places mentioned; and in Mediterranean ports usually lower still. It is different in different ports, but not different to different vessels in the same port. There are two kinds of wages, in order to make that understood. They are the coastwise wages and the deep-water wages, as we call them. Now, the coastwise wages in the city of New York are $25 per month at present; that is the highest. The highest are $25 and the lowest at present are about $18. The deep-water wages are $18 per month; at least those were the wages about 2 months ago. The wages in the San Francisco coastwise trade run from $30 to $40. There are some instances where they are $45, but they are few. In the foreign trade—deep-water—$20; the same on Puget Sound, that is, Port Townsend, Wash.; the same on the southern California coast.

Q. (By Mr. Farquhar.) You are speaking of these specific cases; they are white men's wages?—A. Yes.

Q. Not Asiatics?—A. No. Asiatics ship in Hongkong, China, and their wages are $16 Mexican. Deep-sea ship, from Hongkong or San Francisco or Puget Sound, $16 Mexican for sailors and $18 for firemen.

Q. Asiatic sailors you would class as Japanese, Chinese, and Lascars?—A. The Lascars are East India sailors; then the Chinese, then the Japanese, then the Manila men—what we call, in sailor language, the Manila man—really Tagals. The vessels that trade between Honkong and San Francisco, and Hongkong and Puget Sound and way ports, irrespective of their nationalities, whether American, British, or Japanese, ship their men in Hongkong or in Yokohama; the Japanese ship men in Japan; the English and American lines ship their men in Hongkong; and the wages are, as I said, $16 Mexican. That is permitted to our shipowners under section 20 of an act to remove certain burdens on the American merchant marine, and encourage the American carrying trade, and for other purposes, approved June 26, 1884. The substance of that section is that the master of an American vessel may ship his crew in a foreign port to come to the United States and return to any foreign port one or more trips, and he need not reship any of them in the ports of the United States; so, as far as deep-water and line steamers are concerned, whether sail or steam, there is no such thing as American wages. It is international wages; it is wages of the port where the vessel is.

Q. What is the proportion in the deep-sea marine service of these Asiatics, of the men of all nations?—A. Well, England has about one-fourth, I think; one-fourth of our merchant marine is manned by Asiatic seamen; that is, not Asiatics altogether, but including the Turks and Arabs.

Q. (By Mr. CLARKE.) Why are the sailors employed in the coastwise trade better off than those in the deep-sea trade?—A. Because in the coastwise trade, from 1874 and up to 1890, the seamen were free to quit. Being free to quit work, he was free to organize; that is one reason. Another reason is that he has to do more and harder work, and it requires a better class of men.

Q. (By Mr. RATCHFORD.) In the coastwise?—A. In the coastwise.

Q. (By Mr. PHILLIPS.) That is because of landing more frequently?—A. Yes, and handling the cargo. They carry a small number of men, and for this and several reasons want the best men they can get.

Q. (By Mr. RATCHFORD.) Taking into consideration, then, wages as between the two classes of men, you believe those in the deep-water trade are better off, do you?—A. No.

Q. Those in the coastwise trade are better off?—A. Those in the coastwise trade are indisputably better off. The wages are better, and the treatment is better.

Q. (By Mr. CLARKE.) The coastwise trade is exclusively American, is it not?—A. It is exclusively American as to vessels but not as to seamen.

Q. (By Mr. KENNEDY.) And the nationality?—A. It is open, as far as seamen are concerned. The coastwise trade is as open to the world as any other trade. There are no restrictions as to nationality, skill, or race.

Q. What is the proportion of the nationalities?—A. Well, on the Pacific coast I should think that the Scandinavians, including with them the Finns, predominate; next would be Germans, and last of all, Americans.

Q. (By Mr. RATCHFORD.) What proportion are Americans?—A. Not more than 10 per cent at most.

Q. Do the vessels in the Pacific coastwise trade that are manned by foreign nationalities float the American flag?—A. Why, of course.

Q. All the vessels in that trade float the American flag?—A. No vessel can get in the coastwise trade at all unless she floats the American flag. She can not carry passengers or cargo from one port to another unless she is built in the United States and owned in the United States and carries the American flag.

Q. (By Mr. CLARKE.) You understand that the coastwise trade is prosperous and has been from the beginning of the Government, or from the passage of the first navigation laws making it exclusively an American trade?—A. Well, the coastwise trade is prosperous; for what reasons it is prosperous I do not know, particularly. It is not manned by Americans.

Q. Do the masters of coastwise vessels have the equal opportunity to engage foreign sailors that the masters of transoceanic vessels have?—A. Certainly. That is to say, they can not go over to Liverpool to engage them there, but they engage anyone who happens to be in New York or Philadelphia, or in Boston—they must get them on the American coast somewhere. As to the proportion of Asiatic seamen, I will say Germany uses none. It is a very rare thing to have an Asiatic on a German, Scandinavian, or French vessel. The only nations who use them are England and America; that is, to any extent.

Q. (By Mr. KENNEDY.) What is the proportion of Scandinavians, German, and Americans in the Atlantic coastwise trade?—A. I should say about 10 per cent Americans, and the rest are made up of men from all over the world.

Q. Scandinavians and Germans, mostly?—A. Probably Scandinavians predominate.

Q. That is the order which the secretary of the Atlantic Coast Seamen gives them. He says, however, the majority are American citizens or have declared their intentions.—A. I am speaking of men born in the country.

Q. Are the majority American citizens or have declared their intentions to become such?—A. He has better acquaintance with that than I. I am satisfied, of course, that a great many are citizens. I know on the Pacific coast a great many were citizens. Prior to 1893 about one-half of the entire lot of coasting seamen were citizens or declared their intentions to become citizens. During 1893 and 1894, however, just about one-half of the entire personnel, as far as seamen were concerned, left the Pacific coast; and as to the proportion now I can not say.

Q. (By Mr. PHILLIPS.) You referred to "crimps." How are sailors obtained?—A. In this way: The master of the vessel, or the owner of one or more vessels, goes to or receives a visit from a marine employment agency, I should judge you would call him; we call him a shipping master. In ordinary language among us seamen he is called a "crimp;" and he makes a contract with this marine employment agent, or "crimp," to furnish a crew for him, or crews for his vessels, as the case might be. They agree about what the wages are to be, and the seamen have no more to do with it under ordinary circumstances than has the man in the moon.

The captain meets the crimp and says to him, What can I get a crew for? Well, where are you going? I am going to Cape Town, say; this being New York City. Well, $18 a month; $18 allotment to the original creditor; that is, they do not call it so; they call it advance, $18 advance and something on the side. The captain says, There are lots of men around New York at the present time; I would like to know how much you are going to pay me back out of that $18. Well, I am not going to pay you anything back. Well, then, I will go and see Jones; I guess he will give me back something, a part of the $18. So a part of the $18 or part of the amount that is given as an advance goes back to the captain of the vessel. Now, the arrangement is made between the crimp and the master of the vessel, and the crimp says he has a shipping office down South street or West street, and men come around there looking for employment. And he says, Well, I have the *None-Such;* she is going to Cape Town, and I want a crew for her; $18 a month; will you go? No, I will not. Somebody else goes around and asks for employment, and he asks them the same question. Well, they go. That is how the employment is made. If he does not get any men in that way, he speaks to the boarding master; that is, the seamen's landlord, as they call themselves. They keep boarding houses in which sailors live usually; and the shipping master speaks to them and asks, Have you any men for the *None-Such?* Oh, yes. Then it becomes a dicker between them what is going to become of the $18 or whatever advance is being paid, and if there is any blood money, what is going back of the blood money. And again, no matter how it is fixed, the sailor goes to sea for the wages that they have set, and his first month's wages goes with it. It used to be about two month's wages, but the last Congress changed it to only one, not exceeding one month's wages allotment. We have it changed; we tried to have it brought down to nothing.

Q. (By Mr. RATCHFORD.) To make that clear, that allotment is money advanced to the sailor by the shipping master?—A. No; it is money advanced by the vessel; it is money advanced by the vessel ostensibly to the sailor. The sailor must sign an order upon the vessel in favor of blank for one month's wages. He settles up with the shipping master and the shipping master draws the order after the vessel has gone to sea.

Q. Well, you spoke of some of this money being returned to the captain?—A. Yes. When the sailor has signed the order and the captain has accepted the the order, certified to its correctness, the shipping master gives the captain so much, whatever they have agreed upon.

Q. (By Mr. CLARKE.) It is a private perquisite to the captain, is it not?—A. Yes; that is a private perquisite to the captain.

Q. (By Mr. FARQUHAR.) Under the present law is not the matter of advance abolished? It was nothing but allotment.—A. That is right; the advance is abolished, but the allotment is paid now, three days after the vessel leaves port. So, while it is called an allotment, it is an advance.

Q. What is the whole amount that the sailor can make by allotment?—A. He can allot not to exceed one month of his pay now.

Q. The old way he allotted—he could mortgage everything?—A. Well, not quite that much, not to exceed $10 a month, and prior to that everything.

Q. (By Mr. CLARKE.) This allotment then practically is often divided between the sailor, boarding-house keeper, shipping master, and the captain of the vessel?—A. Exactly.

Q. (By Mr. FARQUHAR.) The allotment then is simply to pay the sailor's shore debts?—A. That is what it is meant to be.

Q. (By Mr. RATCHFORD.) Is it compulsory in case he has not any debts?—A. He can allot part of his wages to his relatives.

Q. (By Mr. FARQUHAR.) His family?—A. To his family. To the question as to whether it is compulsory, whether he has any debts or not, I should say yes. Anyone shipping out of New York or San Francisco in a deep-water vessel without taking an advance is such a rare man that I would like to see him. No matter whether he likes it or not—that cuts no figure. The shipping master must have something, and he can only get it by advance or allotment.

Q. (By Mr. RATCHFORD.) And I understand you to say that this is provided by the law?—A. Yes.

Q. If he reaches the other port within a month, or within the time necessary to render equivalent labor for the amount of money he has drawn, is he privileged to quit the vessel then?—A. He is not privileged to quit the vessel, irrespective of whether he has had any allotment or not. He can be reclaimed. A sailor that deserts in England, Africa, Australia, or China can be reclaimed. That is the term used by the law. He can be reclaimed, put in prison, and held there until the vessel is ready to put to sea, and then put on board and made to go to work. According to the Commissioner of Navigation's report, 80 men were thus reclaimed in Callao last year, in Singapore 1, and in Yokohoma 1; and 1 was punished besides; that was in Singapore.

Q. (By Mr. KENNEDY.) Do the crimp and the boarding-house keeper generally work together to keep the sailor in the toils by making him take advances, thus keeping him in debt?—A. Certainly; yes. One knows how much money he had when he came ashore, and the other governs how much money he will get when he is going; and as a usual proposition he has to spend it all before he goes to work.

Q. (By Mr. FARQUHAR.) Has your union proposed and submitted to Congress any remedial law about this matter of the crimp and the shipping master and the allotment?—A. Yes.

Q. Have you any remedies whereby those men could be taken away from these boarding-house keepers, from the parties that follow them and feed them with liquor and everything of that kind and debauch them?—A. Yes; we have. If Congress will abolish the allotment to original creditors and make a law compelling the vessel to pay the seaman one-half of what is actually due in every port where the vessel loads or delivers cargo, and give the seaman the full right to quit wherever he is, the crimp will be starved to death and have to go out of business. We say that will take place, because we know what has taken place in England, Plymouth, Portsmouth, and Sheerness, the three men-of-war ports of England, were the worst crimping dens in the United Kingdom. The admiralty decided to pay the men their wages monthly irrespective of where they happened to be, and the result of that arrangement completely wiped out the crimping dens of those three ports.

Q. (By Mr. KENNEDY.) Is it true that the crimps never ship a member of your union if they know him to be such?—A. If they can help themselves; no. That is true as a general proposition.

Q. (By Mr. RATCHFORD.) Has your organization at any time taken action upon this matter by offering protests?—A. We have been engaged in offering protests for the last 6 years and asking for legislation, and some of it has been obtained.

Q. (By Mr. PHILLIPS.) "Proposed amendments to our navigation laws; foreign navigation laws compared with ours;" what have you to propose in that regard, and what is your organization proposing?—A. The best answer to the question as to what we have to propose would be to give what we have actually drafted—a bill to amend the laws relating to American seamen and to improve the personnel of the merchant marine.

Q. You might briefly state what you propose to accomplish by this law or these amendments.—A. Well, we propose to abolish crimping altogether, as far as it can possibly be abolished by law. We propose to increase the space in the forecastle; to give the seaman one-half of what is actually due him in every port where he loads and discharges cargo, and to give the seaman the right to call for a survey of any vessel that he may happen to be in without the officers of the vessel taking part in the request; and to establish a standard of skill and experience for those who sign as able seamen; and to get a law providing for the standard or number of men to be carried by vessels according to their tonnage and rigging. Those are the contents of this bill.

Q. (By Mr. FARQUHAR.) In the case of a survey, how many of the crew do you propose shall join in the request?—A. A majority of the crew, exclusive of officers.   The manning bill proposed here is taken directly out of the recommendation made by the British commission on manning of vessels.   There was a British commission for that purpose, and after listening to some 180 expert witnesses, they made certain recommendations to Parliament; and we have taken their recommendations and put them in as our bill.   England has no manning law; Australia has.   Germany and the Scandinavian countries only have by custom; that is all. There is no specific law in any of these countries as to how many men a vessel shall carry.

Q. (By Mr. CLARKE.) When you say Australia do you mean all the Australian provinces or some one of them?—A. Well, I mean particularly New Zealand in this matter.   With reference to the reason why England appointed this commission, it was that England found that where she used to have about 20,000 apprentices, she has now less than 8,000, and there has grown to be a greater and greater scarcity of British seamen.   That is the reason they appointed this commission, and this is what the commission has to say: "Owing to unrestricted competition and the absence of any requirement as to qualification, the quest for employment in the mercantile marine has degenerated in many cases into a mere scramble in which very little consideration is bestowed on the condition of the service so long as employment is secured."

Q. What is the date of that report?—A. 1896.   Report of the committee appointed by the board of trade to inquire into the manning of British ships.

Q. (By Mr. PHILLIPS.) Upon the whole, are the foreign laws more favorable than the laws of the United States in regard to the seamen, their duties and privileges?—A. At present, taking it altogether, no.   They are much superior in some instances; in some instances they are not as good as the foreign.   In the matter of forecastles, in the matter of general treatment on board of a vessel, that has very little to do with the law.   We have a law forbidding brutality now—forbidding corporal punishment—and it is being administered, and is being used continually, all the same.   The law is being violated.   It is not a common thing at all in continental or English vessels; it is a very rare thing.   They have laws forbidding it, too, but they are better obeyed than ours.   If amendments could be made to the existing laws, such as are proposed here, our law would be up to the best.

Q. (By Mr. CLARKE.) How frequent is this corporal punishment, and what form does it take?—A. Well, it takes the form of a club—a belaying pin.   That is a stick like a policeman's club—a blow over the head with that is the most frequent kind.   We use these in the rail of a vessel to make fast ropes on, and it is very handy to take one out and use it.

Q. Is that punishment administered by the officer of the vessel at his own caprice and without any order from his superior, or without any control as to the man's offense?—A. Yes; that is right.

Q. Usually done in haste, then; sometimes in passion?—A. Always in passion, I would rather say.

Q. (By Mr. PHILLIPS.) And always by some officer of the vessel?—A. Yes.

(By Mr. KENNEDY.) I am informed that the law which was passed recently through your assistance is considered very satisfactory to the seamen, at least on the Atlantic side, if it was enforced.   The ship owners or the masters say that there never was a law enacted for the benefit of the sailors that they could not drive a horse and cart through.   I would like to ask you if that is your experience with any of those laws that have been enacted for the benefit of the sailors in this country, and how it is in other countries?—A. Well, the expression that you can "drive a horse and cart through" is generally used to signify that the law is not enforced and that it is evaded.   There are certain errors and mistakes in that law that was passed last year.   They were pointed out at the time, such as the repealing of some of the old law that had worked well.   That causes the law that was passed last year to be ineffective in some instances, just as good as useless in some instances.   That law provides that foreign vessels shipping crews in American ports shall be subject to the provisions of that act, which is that they shall pay no more than one month's allotment to original creditors; pay no more advance than that.   They violate that continually, have been violating it right along, and there is no means of getting after them, because you can not get the evidence.   They pick up some man going aboard of some vessel and take him away, and when they get to the other place, as soon as he is out of the jurisdiction of the country, then that settles it; they take away the evidence, take the evidence away with them, and unless their articles be subjected to inspection by the custom-house officers, they will no doubt continue to use that kind of means of evading the law.

Q. (By Mr. CLARKE.) If you can not get the evidence of the evasion, how do you know they do evade it?—A. We know it, because we know it afterwards when the time to prosecute is gone by. We know the evasion of the law takes place. But there is a great deal of difference between knowing a thing and being able to prove it legally.

Q. (By Mr. RATCHFORD.) Are there some beneficial features to that law?—A. Oh, yes.

Q. On the whole, it has been a benefit to the seamen?—A. On the whole. it has been a very great benefit.

Q. You speak of the law that was enacted by the Fifty-fifth Congress?—A. By the last Congress; on the whole, it has been a very great benefit.

Q. (By Mr. FARQUHAR.) Has any other nation any better law?—A. As far as that law goes, and on the points upon which it touches, no.

Q. Have you any fault to find with the law in respect to the quantity of food? You spoke of the small rations that the American seamen receive in comparison with other countries.—A. The only complaint we have in that direction is the water. We would like to have an increase in the water from 4 quarts or 1 gallon to 6 quarts, and an increase in the butter from 1 ounce to 2. That is put in this bill, and that is the only improvement in the scale of food that we desire to ask for. With those two exceptions the scale of food is perfectly satisfactory to us.

Q. Can you give the commission hereafter a comparative food scale of five or six of the nations?—A. Yes; I now submit the American, Australian, German, and Danish scales:

Scale of provisions required by law on ships of American merchant marine.

		Sunday.	Monday.	Tuesday.	Wednesday.	Thursday.	Friday.	Saturday.
Water	quarts	4	4	4	4	4	4	4
Biscuit	pound	½	½	½	½	½	½	½
Beef, salt	pounds	-----	-----	1¼	-----	1¼	-----	1¼
Pork, salt	pound	-----	1	-----	1	-----	1	-----
Flour	do	½	-----	½	-----	-----	½	-----
Canned meat	do	1	-----	-----	1	-----	-----	-----
Fresh bread		1½ pounds daily.						
Fish, dry, preserved, or fresh	pound	-----	-----	-----	-----	-----	1	-----
Potatoes or yams	do	1	1	1	1	1	1	1
Canned tomatoes	do	½	-----	-----	-----	-----	½	-----
Pease	pint	-----	-----	⅓	-----	-----	⅓	-----
Beans	do	-----	⅓	-----	⅓	-----	-----	-----
Rice	do	-----	⅓	-----	-----	-----	-----	⅓
Coffee (green berry)	ounce	¾	¾	¾	¾	¾	¾	¾
Tea	do	⅛	⅛	⅛	⅛	⅛	⅛	⅛
Sugar	ounces	3	3	3	3	3	3	3
Molasses	pint	⅓	-----	⅓	-----	⅓	-----	-----
Dried fruit	ounces	3	-----	3	-----	3	-----	-----
Pickles	pint	-----	¼	-----	¼	-----	¼	-----
Vinegar	do	-----	-----	¼	-----	-----	-----	¼
Corn meal	ounces	4	-----	-----	-----	4	-----	-----
Onions	do	4	-----	-----	-----	4	-----	4
Lard	ounce	1	1	1	1	1	1	1
Butter	do	1	1	1	1	1	1	1
Mustard, pepper, and salt sufficient for seasoning		-----	-----	-----	-----	-----	-----	-----

Scale given by the Australian United Steam Navigation Company, Limited.

	Bread.	Meat.	Flour.	Rice.	Tea.	Coffee.	Sugar.	Potatoes.	Butter.
	Lb.	*Lbs.*	*Lb.*	*Lb.*	*Oz.*	*Oz.*	*Ozs.*	*Lbs.*	*Ozs.*
Sunday	1	2¼	1	-------	¼	½	4	2	2
Monday	1	2¼	-------	¼	¼	½	4	2	2
Tuesday	1	2¼	1	-------	¼	½	4	2	2
Wednesday	1	2¼	-------	¼	¼	½	4	2	2
Thursday	1	2¼	1	-------	¼	½	4	2	2
Friday	1	2¼	-------	-------	¼	½	4	2	2
Saturday	1	2¼	-------	¼	¼	½	4	2	2

GERMAN SCALE.

[Bremen decree, March 17, 1899.]

Ration.	Daily.	Twice weekly.	Weekly.
Bread..pound..	1		
Mess beef...pounds..	1¼		
Fish...pound..		1	
Butter ....do....			1
Coffee...ounces.			6½
Tea...do.....			1¼
Water ....quarts..	4		

In addition each member of the crew must receive three-quarters of a pound of vegetables (potatoes or sauerkraut, etc.), one-quarter of a pound of dried fruit, 11 ounces of sugar or molasses, and one-half pint of vinegar weekly.

Leaving a home port, beer to the amount of 45 quarts for each of the crew must be carried, to be served out at discrimination of the master. When the ration of beer falls short from any reason, the daily ration of coffee shall be increased to 1¼ ounces.

Dried pease, beans, or oatmeal to be served in sufficient quantities.

Mess pork or bacon may be alternated or substituted with beef, at the rate of 1 pound and 1¼ pounds, respectively. After salt meat has been used for six weeks continuously, a ration of 1 pound of preserved meats twice a week must be substituted. If the ship's complement consists of ten or more hands, one extra ration of meat, fish, and water must be served.

A six months' supply of butter must be stored on board at the home port. One and a quarter pounds of lard, or 1 pint of olive oil, or an additional ration of 1¼ pounds of beef, or 6 ounces of bacon may be substituted for butter.

DANISH SCALE.

Ration.	Weekly.	Ration.	Weekly.
Bread ....pounds..	7	Coffee...........................pound..	¾
Mess pork......................do....	1½	Sugar ....do....	¾
Mess beef......................do....	3	Tea ....ounce..	¼
Butter ....pound..	1	Barley (pearl) ... .pint..	1
Codfish ....do....	1	Beer ....gallons..	1¼

Water in sufficient quantities, without waste.

Potatoes, pickles, cabbage, horse-radish, or dried or preserved vegetables must be gi en at least twice a week at sea and in port.

Fresh mess, consisting of at least one-half pound of preserved meat, without bones, and one-half pound of bouilli, must be given once a week at sea.

The ration of hard bread may be substituted by soft wheat or rye bread at the rate of 7 pounds or 10½ pounds each, respectively.

Instead of butter may be given one-half pound of olive oil, with the necessary vinegar, or 2 pounds of mess pork.

Whenever the circumstances of the voyage will permit, the stipulated ration of beer must be kept on board. Under other circumstances wine may be substi-tuted at the rate of one-half pint per day, or grog (French brandy or rum) at the rate of 1 gill per day, or Danish corn brandy at the rate of one-half gill per day.

Mustard, salt, vinegar, sirup, prunes, and dried fruit must be given daily in sufficient quantities.

Q. Is there any question about the quality of the food?—A. Well, of course, we are not getting the new scale. In the deep-water vessels they are not giving it; they are not giving it even in some of the coastwise vessels. It has not come into general operation. Just as in a vessel on the Atlantic coast, where the men insisted upon having the scale, the master gave it to them without cooking it. He says, "The law does not provide for cooking it."

Q. What is the permanency of employment in the Continental and English marine? Do men ship and do they perform work on the same vessel for, say, 10, 12, or 14 years?—A. No.

Q. How long?—A. No; usually about a year or two. They ship for a year.

Q. But you take what are called the liners, freight and passenger, what is the average time of employment on those continental or English ships?—A. That I do not know. 1 have never sailed on them.

Q. Is there as much shiftiness of employment with the European marine as there is with the American?—A. I could not say.

Q. Have any of the other nations this right that you contend for—that a seaman shall ship for a certain point and then have his discharge, whether he makes the return port or not?—A. No.

Q. Is the American better?—A. On that point it is better than most of them, except England. The English law gives the seaman the right to quit in England, but with the other nations, after having shipped and left the home port, he can not quit at all; he becomes a deserter and can be taken back.

Q. What are the penalties for desertion of a ship?—A. Penalties for desertion at the present time? There is really no penalty for desertion in a home port. The sailor has a right to quit in the home port; simply takes his clothes with him and goes. He leaves all the money he has earned behind him. That is the penalty.

Q. That is the forfeiture?—A. He forfeits what money he has earned. That is the penalty. In a foreign port he is taken back as I stated.

Q. Now, in the case of a sailor being left sick or in a hospital, say at Hongkong or elsewhere, what are the provisions of this Government for the return of that sailor through the consul or commercial agent?—A. Congress appropriates annually a certain amount of money for the return of sick and disabled seamen; and being left behind by a vessel in some place where the consul can not ship him, and left on the consul's hands in that way, he can be returned to the United States at the expense of the United States. Congress appropriates money for that purpose.

Q. (By Mr. CLARKE.) Therefore to protect the United States it is not necessary that there should be a law requiring a sailor to return in the vessel that he shipped upon from American ports?—A. It would be much better for him if they would abolish the return to the United States and leave the sailor free to quit.

Q. Well, how about the Government?—A. Well, the Government would not have any expense then.

Q. (By Mr. PHILLIPS.) And leave the sailor free to quit?—A. Leave the sailor free to quit and to get his money, too.

Q. (By Mr. CLARKE.) I think I have recently seen a statement by a consul that a great many sailors who have left their vessels become dependent, and he has to help sustain them, and then help them back to the United States at the expense of the Government. Is it desirable that that condition of things should be avoided?—A. It does not strike me as being of any importance at all. These men are in all probability driven out of the vessels they were in, without receiving any money for the work they had done. They came ashore and went to some boarding house or some place and then they were thrown on their own resources, afterwards thrown out by these boarding masters, and the result was that they were destitute. Now, if they had received no allotment when they shipped and had received the money that was due them when they quit, they would have had money enough to live on until they could get another vessel, and would not be in need of any charity either from the United States or from individuals.

Q. Why do you say they were probably driven out of the vessels?—A. Because vessels lying in a port waiting for cargo, do not keep the men on board. The law of 1884 provides that the master may discharge the men if they consent to be discharged, by paying them what is due them. Now, sometimes the master will not do that; he will not pay them what is due them. They will ask to be discharged and he will say "no." He will treat them in such a way that they will have to get out of the vessel and leave the money behind them.

Q. You mean that they are driven out by bad treatment?—A. Yes.

Q. And that this is a scheme of the master of the vessel to save money?—A. Yes.

Q. Well, can you provide against that by law?—A. By saying that when a man leaves a vessel he receives all the money he has earned.

Q. (By Mr. RATCHFORD.) How frequently do sailors receive their wages now, under our present system?—A. With an average good master of a vessel, when he comes into a port like Singapore or Hongkong, if he does not want to keep them on board, he says, "Well, any of you that want your money can get it;" and he takes them to the consul and pays them off,-and they go.

Q. That is entirely left with the master?—A. The payment. He can not go to the master and say "I want to quit the vessel and get my money." If the master does not want to give him his discharge and his money, he can not get it. If the master wants to give him his discharge and his money and he refuses to take it, he will leave in a week or two without it invariably, because then the treatment becomes such that he will be glad to leave the vessel.

Q. Could you state one or more cases in which the master of the vessel has held money or wages of his men for an unusual length of time?—A. The way that the articles are signed nowadays—and I do not know how far back the practice extends—is, no money except at the master's option; shipped for 12 months and no money except at the master's option. Go to the master and ask for some money and he says "no." I have been 6 months on board of a vessel and could not get a cent. I have been again in other vessels where I would get whatever money I wanted—that is, reasonably, whatever money I wanted ; and that is the experience of every sailor. As a usual thing, when the master refuses to give a sailor any money he means by that, "You better get out of here." He refuses him that money in order to drive him out of the vessel.

Q. (By Mr. CLARKE.) Why does a man sign a contract that he will serve without money except at the master's option?—A. Because he has no option in the matter.

Q. That is to say he is poor and ignorant and perhaps—— —A. (Interrupting.) He is not necessarily ignorant but he is poor. I am a sailor—know my work, I can do it on board of a vessel—taking me as an instance: I refuse to sign that kind of a contract. There is a man who has never been to sea in his life, knows nothing at all about the life he is going to lead, knows nothing at all about the kind of vessel he is going on board of, knows nothing about the work he is going to do. He is asked, "Will you go on board of the vessel and work for those wages and sign that kind of a contract?" "Yes." So it is purely a question of how many men there are around that seaport who can be coaxed to go to sea. The man who says he will not sign that kind of a contract will stay ashore.

Q. Do you see any objection from your point of view to a law that would require the wages to be paid regularly?—A. None whatever. That is what we have been asking for.

Q. (By Mr. FARQUHAR.) Would you have very serious objections, on the part of a married man who ships and there is an allotment of $10 a month for his family? Why is it not proper that that family should be safeguarded against this man's expenditures in foreign ports and away from home?—A. I think it is proper. Of course, there should be an allotment in the case of a married man. We are not opposed to any allotment to an immediate and dependant relative; not at all. Allotments of that description given to wife, mother, and children are proper allotments, and it would be a hardship, a very great hardship, upon seamen to have that abolished. We would not see that abolished. It is the allotment to the original creditor that we want to have abolished, because he is not a creditor at all in nine cases out of ten.

Q. (By Mr. RATCHFORD.) Do our statutes now provide for the establishing of homes for aged and disabled sailors?—A. No.

Q. Would not such a statute be very desirable?—A. There is one such institution in the United States now; that is Snug Harbor, in New York. It is an excellent institution, does an immense amount of good, and, of course, as a sailor, I would not say that it would not be a good thing on the part of the United States to establish those kind of things; but I doubt whether it would be a proper thing to do. Under our existing law I am sure it would not be a proper thing to do, because all the sailors of the world would have an opportunity to go in there.

Q. Well, is it not to be presumed that if such institutions were established in America they would be for American sailors?—A. Answering your question generally, I would say this: We have not discussed this particular question that you bring up, and I can not speak for the sailors' union upon that subject; but, taking it generally, we look on those questions as eleemosynary institutions, and, though they are a good thing, they have a tendency in the wrong direction. The idea that the sailors' union has had right along is to clear away all the laws that make a kind of a child out of a sailor, to put him on his own resources, stand him on his own legs, and tell him, "Now, take care of yourself, and if you can not, why, that is all the worse for you."

Q. We are speaking of when he gets too old, for instance, to have any legs to stand on; taking care of him in old age or in disability.—A. In case of disability, there are marine hospitals now, and they are very good things. And there is also established, on the recommendation of Surgeon-General Wyman, down in Arizona, I think it is, or in New Mexico, a farm where consumptives are sent and placed up in the dry atmosphere; and that is an excellent institution. It will probably save hundreds upon hundreds of lives in years to come, because consumption is extremely prevalent amongst the seamen, owing to the crowded quarters in which they live.

Q. Now, you speak of marine hospitals. Have the sailors, both in the deep water and in the coastwise trade and on the lakes, access to these marine hospitals?—A. Yes.

Q. (By Mr. FARQUHAR.) How do they contribute to them?—A. They do not contribute to them now. We used to contribute 40 cents a month to these hospitals until the passage of the law of 1884, when that was wiped out, and it comes out of the tonnage dues or tonnage taxes on the vessels.

Q. (By Mr. RATCHFORD.) You spoke of the New York home; how is that maintained?—A. A gentleman, who died years and years ago, willed a farm on Manhattan Island to establish an institution for old and disabled seamen, to be called Snug Harbor. Well, the land that he willed to this institution has grown so enormously in value that the institution is extremely rich and can do very much; but you see it is a bequest.

Q. (By Mr. FARQUHAR.) It is private benevolence?—A. It is private benevolence.

Q. (By Mr. RATCHFORD.) How is it supported?—A. From the same source. It does not cost the sailors or the Government or the State anything.

Q. (By Mr. CLARKE.) How is the consumptives' home in New Mexico or Arizona supported?—A. It is supported by the United States Government.

Q. (By Mr. FARQUHAR.) Marine-Hospital Service?—A. Marine-Hospital Service.

Q. (By Mr. PHILLIPS.) We will pass to topic 65, "Proportion of American vessels engaged in our foreign commerce as compared with vessels under foreign flags so engaged." Have you any information on that question?—A. Well; statistics would give such information as was valuable much more closely and reliably than I could possibly give it.

Q. Tramp steamers are different from liners?—A. The tramp steamer is a vessel that goes anywhere where she can get anything to do—carries cargo anywhere, from one port to another. She goes anywhere where the traffic carries her and brings her.

Q. Do you have any information in regard to the number of those as compared to the liners?—A. I do not think we have any under the American flag.

Mr. KENNEDY. I would suggest that the witness glance over the plan of inquiry and pick out any topic upon which he desires to speak.

The WITNESS. The question has often been raised, Why do not American boys go to sea?

To begin with, because there is not any prospect for a man to make a living and keep a family by going to sea. The wages of the seamen have been stationary, while the wages of men working ashore have increased. The cost of living has increased in about the ratio of improvement in the wages, and the result is that the seaman's wages is not sufficient to keep himself, far less keep a family. Now, a boy may go to sea out of romance; he may read Captain Marryat and the rest of the writers, and get into his head that he wants to be a sailor; and he goes to sea and makes one or two trips, and he finds out what the sea is, what kind of a life it is, what kind of work he has to do, what kind of wages he is likely to receive when he is a grown man, and he says, "There is nothing in this for me," and he quits and looks around for something else to do. And it is the same, not only in the United States, but in other countries. Norway used to furnish an enormous amount of seamen. When I first went to sea, the wages of the seamen in purchasing power was such that he was really better off than the ordinary mechanic at shore. Ninety per cent of them were married, had little homes of their own in the little gullies along the seacoast, or wherever they might happen to be, and their homes were neater and usually a little better furnished than those of the ordinary mechanic. Now, the condition of shore employment has increased in that country to such an extent that the standard of living of the shore mechanic has risen vastly above that of the seaman, and the boy does not go to sea any more as he used to. The Norwegian vessels are now very largely filled with Swedes and Finns. Take English vessels. Englishmen used to go to sea just for the same reason and under the same conditions. The wages of the English sailor to-day runs between £4 and £6 a month—between $20 and $30 a month. That is the English wages around England; it is anything between those figures. Now, he can make a great deal more wages and be at home with his family, if he has one; or he can afford to furnish himself with one and stay home with them and get better wages by working at something ashore. The boy who has the stuff in him to be a sailor must be healthy physically, and must have a fair average intelligence, or else he is no good at sea; and in order that he may remain at sea, or be willing to go to sea, the conditions of sea life must be such as to give him the inducement, or at least give him the ability to live in the same way as his neighbors do—come up to the ordinary standard of living of everybody around him; everybody that he knows and has been brought up with. Now, sea life will not do that; it will not keep those who go to sea for any length of time. On an average now the sailor goes from port to port looking for something else to do. He comes into New York and gets paid off with $30 or $40 or $50 after a long trip. The first thing he does after he comes into New York is not, as shore people think, go and get drunk; not at all. There is much less drunkenness than people who do not know have any idea of. People ashore have a tendency to say that any man they see drunk around the water front of a seaport city is a sailor. In a majority of the cases he is not. The sailor goes ashore and looks around, and goes up around the city, goes into the employment offices and other places and looks to see whether there is anything else to do, and if there is anything he can get to do he is glad to quit the sea. He becomes a bridge builder, he becomes an architectural iron worker. I suppose that 75 per cent of the men who work at architectural iron work at New York, Philadelphia, Boston, and Chicago are sailors.

Q. (By Mr. FARQUHAR.) You mean the fitters?—A. These men that put up this architectural iron work. He becomes a bridge builder on the railways; becomes a gripman on the street cars. Going to sea, he learns certain things; he learns to keep his head cool and his feet warm, as we call it at sea; to have his presence of mind with him. He works with both hands; or he steadies himself with one hand; balances his body with his feet; works for the vessel with the other hand and thinks. If he can not do that he is no good at sea; he is a burden on the vessel instead of really an efficient man. Well, a man who gets accustomed to that—to think and work at the same time—receives a certain training that makes him a valuable man in other employments, particularly in such employment as street cars. It is very much like the steering of a vessel; very much like it. And so it is with all kinds of work in a vessel, where you must use your hands and your brain and meet new conditions all the time. The real training of the sailor consists in these things, and that makes him capable of doing other work. He comes ashore in New York and he finds that architectural iron workers get $3.50 a day, and he gets employment among them, and he says, "Good-bye sea; I am done with you." Now, that is the meaning of all that, and it is the meaning of it in England. Along with this case there comes this additional thing, that that which will not produce sufficient for the living of a family is looked down upon by everybody; and at the present time there is no calling so looked down upon in this country and in England as the seafaring calling—as going to sea. The ordinary man ashore speaks about the sailor as a poor fellow; he would not go to sea if he could do anything else; he is not worth any more anyway; that is all he is good for. That is about the idea, and he loses social caste by going to sea, loses the respect of the people whom he has been associated with. That tends to prevent men from going to sea.

Q. (By Mr. PHILLIPS.) Have you any remedy for that?—A. Improving the general condition of the men in such a way that it is brought upon a level with the earning capacity and general condition of the rest of the ordinary mechanics.

Q. (By Mr. FARQUHAR.) Is it in a wage way that you would have that done—more privileges or better wages?—A. In both ways it will have to be. Wages could be permitted to attend to themselves. Wages would tend to settle themselves if the sailor were given the opportunity to help himself; but the trouble is that he is not given that opportunity; he has not been permitted to organize.

Q. (By Mr. KENNEDY.) He could not formerly?—A. He could not organize because anybody who can not quit can not organize. If you can not strike you can not organize. Take away the right to strike and you take away all that organization is worth. In order to make an organization effective you must be able to quit work. That is one thing, and, then, there is this: He goes away 2 or 3 or 4 months. Once a man is on board of a vessel, irrespective of whether he has any skill or ability or not, he must remain there because the vessel is at sea, so that the competion that he is subjected to is much more fierce than that of the ordinary man; and, in addition to all that, the actual sailor has to do the work for this kind of people; it puts more work on his shoulders, and makes his life still harder; and some stop and say, I am going to quit.

Q. (By Mr. FARQUHAR.) Suppose the Seamen's Union of America here did order and get an advance of, say, 20 per cent in wages; do you think there is any way in the world that the continental wages could be raised to equal that?—A. Of course. All sailors' wages are on a level. England will be forced to change the condition of her seamen; absolutely forced to do it. Her national life will compel her to do it. Military and naval experts to-day put that down as beyond any doubt. I will show you what a naval expert says (reading from newspaper clipping): "The discussion is said to have narrowed to Great Britain, Japan, and the United States, and one paper holds that England and the United States will soon be checked in the increase of their navies by the question of manning their ships."

Q. (By Mr. CLARKE.) Will the reforms which you propose make the running of vessels any more expensive?—A. Yes; it will make them a little more expensive.

Q. Now, if American vessels become more expensive to operate, can they compete with foreign vessels and get business?—A. There is much that would go in answer to that. Take the condition of England. The cost of running an English vessel is greater than the cost of running an Italian vessel, and yet England can more than compete with Italy. The cost, altogether, of running a vessel includes so many things that the wages of the men employed in the vessel forms only a small part of it; and whether the improvement of the seamen's condition and the increase of the seamen's pay would materially affect the cost of running a vessel, is more than I can say at present. I should judge that it would affect it to some extent.

Q. (By Mr. PHILLIPS.) Would it affect it more in sailing vessels than in steam vessels?—A. No; I do not think so.

Q. (By Mr. RATCHFORD.) Is it not to be supposed that the increased wages and improved condition and treatment of the men would result in a better class of service and a better class of men?—A. No doubt.

Q. And in that way counteract the increased cost?—A. That used to be the case when, some 50 years ago, the American merchant marine was practically supreme upon the water. Faster vessels and better manned, it was said, and the better stowing of cargoes and the better care taken of cargoes, and the speedier and quicker, the shorter time required to bring them from place to place, caused the American vessels to get a higher rate than other nations, I believe. I have seen that stated. I do not know whether it is so or not, but I believe it is true.

Q. (By Mr. FARQUHAR.) Independent of the extra cost to the ship in its being manned, is not the great loss to the ship the lack of employment—lying by?—A. Lack of employment, of course.

Q. Is not that the great loss to the ship, entirely independent of what you pay in wages, insurance, or anything else?—A. I suppose so. However, somebody else can count the cost of running a vessel, and all that kind of thing; somebody else is much more fitted to give that to the commission than I could.

Q. (By Mr. PHILLIPS.) Would not that be true in regard to the labor employed? Does not the seaman's loss of time enter into it very largely, and might that not be one reason why the sea is being deserted and people are seeking employment on land?—A. It is one of the reasons, of course, but it is not by any means the main reason. The main reasons are those I gave—the condition of the vessel, the small pay, the small crews carried, and so on.

Q. (By Mr. CLARKE.) If something is done to make the American merchant marine more profitable, so that it can pay better wages and in other respects improve the condition of the sailors, would that meet it fully unless you have some legislation such as you propose?—A. I do not think it would follow at all. I have never seen, whether in good times or in bad, any master of a vessel paying any more than he had to pay, or giving any better food than he had to, as a general proposition. The general proposition is that if the wages were $25 a month he would want men for $20; it does not make any difference how much his vessel earned.

Q. Whatever is done, then, by way of encouragement of the American merchant marine, you think, should be done on condition that they will at the same time provide for an improved condition of the seamen?—A. I suppose you have in mind at the present time the general talk about improving the American merchant marine by subsidies, and that is a matter upon which I do not care to go into any discussion of, except to say that none of the schemes that I have seen so far, or heard discussed so far, has anything in it that would in anyway increase the number of real American sailors, or cause any American boy to go to sea, or stay at sea, or in anyway make it any easier for the merchant marine or Navy to obtain real American sailors.

Q. You would think, however, that some of these measures might be taken to increase the business of the American merchant marine?—A. Yes; probably.

Q. Well, then, if these measures were accompanied by such measures as you suggest for the improvement of the condition of the sailors, you think it would be of general benefit to the country?—A. Then the improvement, so far as the sailor is concerned, would come from the measures accompanying the measure, and not from the original measure.

Q. But the original measure might tend to make it easier or possible for the vessels to comply with the condition of improvement which you suggest?—A. That would make it easier. If the earning capacity of the vessel was increased, I suppose it would be easier to pay better wages.

Q. (By Mr. FARQUHAR.) Do you think the bounties proposed in these subsides, in these bills. to the fishing fleet are going to be of any advantage in bringing more into that, and then ultimately augmenting the marine?—A. The bounty given seamen?

Q. Yes.—A. No; not a bit of it.

Q. You think it will be simply absorbed where it is?—A. The seaman, instead of getting $20 a month, will get $19 a month from the man who hires him and $1 from the Government. It is simply another way of subsidizing the vessel; that is all; adding so much to the subsidy paid to the owner of the vessel, and will not do the sailor one iota of good. There is just a doubt in our minds as seamen, a very grave doubt, as to whether that section which proposes to subsidize the fishermen in that way does not at the same time make the seaman subject to be impressed. Being in the service of the Government, recorded by the Government, and having received the Government's money, and having done that under a general bill under which everything else that receives any money is taken by the Government, the proposition seems fair that he, after receiving money, should be taken by the Government. And that is one of the reasons why the convention of the seamen which met in Chicago condemned that bill. If they strike out section 7 and make a proviso in section 14 that contracts entered into between the vessel and seamen should be abrogated if the vessel was taken into the United States service, and if the words "and seamen" were stricken out of the title, it would have nothing to do with seamen, and seamen would not care whether it passed or did not pass.

Q. They object only so far as it affects them directly?—A. In so far as it affects us and is a menace to our liberty.

Q. But there is no objection to the general principle of building a merchant marine?—A. Of course not. It may be a question as to just the best way to do it; but that the seaman is in favor of the increase of the merchant marine, of course, goes without saying.

Q. (By Mr. KENNEDY.) You object to it because you fear that if the bill is enacted into law it would force your patriotism or the patriotism of your craft instead of leaving you free to exhibit it in your own way as other citizens are?—A. It might be put in that shape and answered yes. We think the seamen of the United States have always been willing to volunteer when needed; they have always volunteered as freely as any other people, and why any press gang should be sent after the seamen any more than any other people we can not understand.

(After a recess from 1.03 to 2.15 p. m., the hearing of Mr. Furuseth was resumed, as follows:)

The WITNESS. The manning of vessels ought to be important to the public for this reason—that in passenger vessels, whether they be sailing on the lakes, on the Western coast, or crossing the Atlantic, none of them has sufficient life-saving apparatus to take care of the people on board in case of wreck or disaster of any kind; and there are not enough seamen actually skilled men to handle those that exist. The great loss of life in such cases as the La Bourgogne and Elbe arises from this particular point. It usually takes place between 4 and 6, or between 3 and 6, in the morning. It is called by the name of "the graveyard watch," and it is said by the seamen that the graveyard is then open—if the men are over-worked and do not get the necessary sleep. About 4 o'clock in the morning is when one watch goes off and another watch goes on deck, and is the most danger-ous time. Those who go on deck have had but 4 hours sleep that night, and are usually far from awake when they take charge of the vessel. Anything happen-ing just then is sure to cause a large loss of life in a passenger vessel, and a loss corresponding to the number of actually skilled men that the vessel has got. Thus, it is a matter of common knowledge or record that the Cunard Line of steamers sailing out of Great Britain has never lost any passengers, whereas the White Star and other vessels sailing in the same trade have lost passengers repeatedly.

Q. (By Mr. FARQUHAR.) On that point suppose you state how the 24 hours are divided?—A. The 24 hours are divided in 7 watches. The crew, to begin with, is divided into 2 watches. They are called the starboard and port watch. The star-board watch, say, will go on duty, take charge of the deck at 12 o'clock noon. They will hold the deck until 4 o'clock p. m., and then the port watch takes charge of the deck at 4 p. m. and holds it until 6. The starboard watch takes charge at 6 and holds it until 8. The port watch takes charge at 8 and holds it until 12, and the starboard watch takes charge at 12 and holds it until 4. The port watch takes charge at 4 and holds it until 8, and the starboard watch goes on at 8 and stays on until 12. This completes the 24 hours.

Now, there is in some vessels—passenger vessels and others—a custom of keeping the men on deck during the daytime. They should not. When they are not on watch, they should be asleep. But they say that it is too much sleep, and so the afternoon watch, from 12 to 4 in the afternoon, is very often used to have both watches on deck. This gives too little sleep and rest, and makes the men too much subject to sleepiness to be effective either at the wheel or on the lookout during the night.

There is another custom growing up, and it is only of late origin, which is called the kalashi watch; that is, all hands on deck all day, and called out at any time when they are wanted during the night, leaving on deck only a watchman, a lookout man, and the wheelman, and, of course, the officers on the bridge. If a disaster happens to vessels of that description, the men go out from the forecastle half asleep; they go out in the light and are half blinded, and for the first 15 minutes are practically useless, and thus increase the danger to the passengers and to the vessel; and at the same time, of course, it makes it much harder for the men to work hard all day and be called out at night.

Another matter that is of considerable importance, the British commission says, and as practical seamen we know it is true, is that no man is actually capable of proper lookout or proper work at the wheel for more than 2 hours at a time. In any case it means intense watchfulness, and to be more than 2 hours at it is too long. In a storm and on very serious occasions, 1 hour is long enough, and sometimes too long. I have myself come away from the wheel feeling as though I had been through a sickness, absolutely useless for hours afterwards.

One of the reasons why they use kalashi watches is that vessels can thus be run with 2 or 3 men less than they otherwise would have to have, and it means to the particular owner in question the saving of the wages of 2 or 3 men. This system is in use at present on practically everyone of the passenger steamers sailing on the Eastern coast of the United States. It is largely in use on the Pacific coast, but not to such an extent as on the Eastern coast, and it is a system which has not been applied in Europe. On the Great Lakes men stand at the wheel for 4 hours, sometimes as much as 6 hours. That is in an ordinary freight steamer. I do not know what time they have in the passenger steamers running between Buffalo and Duluth.

Now, these improvements are matters which the seamen themselves can not deal with, under existing conditions at least—with the existing law—and the British commission has dealt with it succinctly in this book here [indicating] under the several heads of "Seamen seldom examine ships," "Particular in articles insufficient," "Results of breach of contract." There are some matters here that I would like to ask permission to have inserted, because it deals particularly with this subject. If agreeable, I will read it.

Mr. PHILLIPS. You might state the substance of it.

The WITNESS. It says that the seamen can not deal with these matters, because they do not know what kind of vessel they are going in. They do not ship always in the port in which they join the vessel. Thus, a vessel lying at New York may go to Boston—send to Boston for her men—or to Philadelphia. The men go aboard in New York while the vessel is lying out in the bay, and the men who go on board have no idea at all as to what manning the vessel should have, or as to what kind of vessel it is, or what kind of men they are going to go with; and the vessel may be undermanned, she may have but one-half the crew she ought to have, but if they work hard enough and are particularly lucky, do not run across any gales or have any accidents, they may see in one trip that the crew they have taken the vessel across or down or up the coast with, as the case may be, at this time is a sufficient crew for the future. This is what the two articles state in substance. They are as follows:

"41. Owing to unrestricted competition and the absence of any requirement as to qualification, the quest for employment in the mercantile marine has degenerated in many cases into a mere scramble, in which very little consideration is bestowed on the conditions of service so long as employment is secured. Articles of agreement containing particulars respecting the ship, the voyage, the crew, and the provisions are indeed read over to the parties by a superintendent of mercantile marine before being signed, and it has been suggested that if a seaman or fireman is not content with the information contained in the articles he has it in his power to examine the vessel for himself. The weight of the evidence shows conclusively that such an examination is in practice seldom made, as the seamen and firemen are generally under the impression that if they were inquisitive they 'would not be wanted,' and when men are taken out in tugs, or shipped at night, or engaged at another port and sent by train, such an examination is out of the question.

"42. The conditions and circumstances of sea service differ in fact so widely from those of any employment ashore that there is not, and can not be under existing circumstances, such a thing as a contract entered into on equal terms by employers and employed. It has been declared by the witnesses who have given evidence on behalf of shipowners that there are various considerations, not even referred to in the articles of agreement, which must be taken into account in determining a proper crew for a ship, such as rig, sail area, steering gear, winches, number of fires, coal consumption, position of bunkers, etc. In signing articles the seaman can have no adequate knowledge of such considerations nor of the extent of work to which he binds himself, and he has subsequently practically no appeal. It is greatly to the credit of the general body of shipowners that their position in dealing with the sailor is not frequently taken advantage of, but such virtue is scarcely to be expected from every member of a large body, and it is therefore incumbent on the State to provide reasonable safeguards for the seamen in those respects in which he can not practically help himself.

"43. A case may be quoted illustrative of the conditions and results of a contract entered into in the United Kingdom in time of labor disputes. The crew of a vessel signed articles at Liverpool to join at Newport, but were actually put on board from a tug in Barry Roads. After sailing, the crew came to the conclusion that the ship was undermanned and refused duty on the master refusing to accede to their demands to put into the nearest port. The ship eventually put into Bahia, where the men were tried by a naval court for 'insubordination, refusal of duty, combining to disobey lawful commands, neglecting duty, impeding navigation of the ship and progress of the voyage,' and 18 of them were sentenced to imprisonment at Bahia for 10 weeks each, and one for 12 weeks. The court did not express any opinion as to the plea of undermanning, although both the mates admitted that the vessel was undermanned. It is, however, immaterial to the present inquiry whether this particular vessel was or was not undermanned. The case is illustrative of the manner in which contracts for sea service are sometimes entered into. Men are brought from a distance and put on board ships at night without an opportunity being afforded them of judging as to the state of the ship or her requirements as to manning. By working for their lives they may succeed in reaching their destination, and thus they will have established their number as a proper crew for the vessel until a further reduction is made; but should they refuse to fulfill their contract, which may perhaps involve excessive risk and work for a whole year, they may, as in this case, be thrown into a foreign prison."

Here is a document that was issued by the British merchant shipping—"Reports of certain foreign and colonial ports respecting the desertion of seamen from British ships, presented to both Houses of Parliament by command of Her Majesty, 1899."

The report from one of the consuls, the consul at Nagasaki, Japan, goes closer into the condition and feeling of seamen, and the circumstances and hardships that cause them to quit going to sea, than any other of these parties. I have never seen anything that states it so clearly as this does, and it is not very lengthy. It deals with the subject of not being permitted to go ashore. It deals with the subject of not being permitted to receive any money while lying in port; being kept on board of the vessel all the time, and kept at work all the time; lying out in the bay under the hot sun of the Tropics, etc., and the general condition on board the vessel, and the desire that each one has to go out of the vessel. And he suggests to the British Government certain important changes in existing conditions.

The report above described follows:

"*Memorandum by Mr. J. H. Longford, Her Majesty's consul at Nagasaki, Japan, on the desertion of seamen from British ships.*

"The question of the desertion of seamen from British merchant ships has recently attracted attention in the House of Commons, and instructions have been given by the secretary of state to Her Majesty's consuls at the principal ports in the United States to report upon it. The local conditions of Japan are such that, although attempts to desert are pro rata as frequent on the part of merchant seaman in Japan as they are in the United States ports, they are rarely successful, the difficulties either of temporary concealment or of final escape being such that the men guilty of them are almost invariably arrested and returned to their ships before their departure from the port. In almost all these cases there are present two characteristics—that they take place from sailing ships and among the members of the crew who are of British birth. The desertion or attempted desertion of a seaman from a steamer, not only from those of well-known and wealthy lines, in which the same picked men continue to be employed from voyage to voyage and year to year, but even from those of the ocean-tramp type, is so rare as to be practically unknown; while it is almost equally rare that several attempts are not made by the seamen of every sailing ship manned by non-Asiatic crews which enters a Japanese port after a long voyage. Even in cases where no serious attempt at desertion is made, the offense of absence without leave is frequently committed, involving to the seamen guilty of it both loss of wages and liability for fines and expenses incurred in connection with their arrest and imprisonment.

"Having for several years past, when at ports at which the opportunity has been afforded, given special attention to the subject of merchant seamen; and having, through an active participation in the management of sailors' homes, been brought into much closer connection with many of them and thereby learned more of their condition than I could have hoped for in the ordinary course of official duties, I trust I may venture, though uninvited, to offer some opinions on the subject which has been referred to Her Majesty's consuls at other places, and on the circumstances which my experience gives me strong grounds for believing to be its primary cause.

"In the annual report on the trade and shipping of Hakodate for the year 1890 I dealt with the subject at length, and the report at the time both received the commendation of the secretary of state and was extensively quoted from and commented on in the English press generally, and especially in that portion of it mainly devoted to shipping. I have unfortunately not now a copy of that report to refer to, but I pointed out in it certain disabilities under which merchant seamen labored, the removal or amelioration of which would, I considered, tend greatly to the general improvement of their condition and consequent popularity of their service. Since then a new and exhaustive merchant shipping act has come into operation, but not one of these disabilities is dealt with in it, and they still remain, as I consider them, main causes why the merchant sailing service— the only school in which competent seamen can be made—is, as is undoubtedly the case, yearly becoming less popular with British subjects. They were, shortly stated: (1) No alteration in the scale of provisions that had been in use for many years; (2) enforced total abstinence; (3) the absence of any right to shore leave when in port, or to part payment, prior to the arrival of the ship at the final port of discharge, of wages already earned.

"The first of these disabilities—the scale of provisions—has since the publication of my former report been discussed by the Seamen's Union, and also been the subject of investigation by a committee of the House of Commons, and as the result of inquiries made by the latter (the merchant shipping victualing scale committee, 1892), a scale was recommended somewhat more liberal and in a slight degree more varied than that in common use. A list of substitutes and equivalents of articles that might from time to time be used in lieu of those mentioned in the scale was also drawn up, and still more a weekly bill of fare, which provided a diet of very palatable nature, varying each day, was also drawn up as a suggestion, the latter, I believe, having been largely adopted from one already in use in American ships. Since then a printed form has been provided on the articles of British ships for the insertion of this bill of fare, but though every master to whom I have spoken on the subject has unhesitatingly expressed his opinion that its adoption would be an undoubted boon to the men, an immense improvement on their present diet, and involve very little extra cost to the owners, not one instance has yet come to my knowledge in which it was either entered on the articles, or even without that formality availed of for the men. Not only that, even the recommendations for the improvement of the scale on the articles have, so far as my experience goes, been entirely without result. In steamers men are, as a rule, fed liberally and well, the short duration of their sea runs admitting of frequent supplies of fresh meat and vegetables. In some sailing ships preserved potatoes and vegetables, currants, pickles, calavances are occasionally dealt out, but the scale of provisions in the articles, to which alone the men have a legal claim and which in many ships is all that is allowed to them, continues to be exactly the same as it was 30 or 50 years ago—the same unvarying round of salt beef and salt pork—notwithstanding the immense advances that have in that period been made in the science of preserving and the cheapness at which preserved meats, fruits, and vegetables in great variety and of the best quality can now be supplied in large quantities. Lime juice continues to be the sole antiscorbutic. Fruit while at sea is unknown to the English sailor. Preserved potatoes and vegetables are furnished to him neither universally nor continuously, and his daily food is the same in quantity and quality whether in the North

Atlantic in midwinter, or becalmed, it may be, on the equator. Thirty years ago this may have been necessarily so, but at the present day there can be no reason, scarcely even that of economy from its strictest point, why the sailor should not have a varied and palatable diet suited even to the different climate conditions to which he is subject. But he can never rely on this until the entry is made a sine qua non on the articles, the present form of which admits of this being most easily done.

"The board of trade has, perhaps, done all that is in its power to remedy this disability, and its final removal must be left to arrangements between ship-owners and their crews, or to the Seamen's Union; but the others under the above headings might very easily be removed by regulations under section 114 of the merchant shipping act, 1894, though it is possible that a very slight alter-ation might be required in the terms of paragraphs (d) and (g) of clause 2 of the section. All these disabilities are already provided for in the regulations for Her Majesty's navy, and these specific regulations might, mutatis mutandis, be included in the printed conditions of agreements with the crews in the form approved of by the board of trade.

"The question of total abstinence is one of so controversial a nature that it can scarcely be expected that any suggestion for the removal of its enforcement on the merchant seaman would meet with unanimous approval from those who are most ready to consider his interests. But longer experience has only served to confirm my previous opinion that the issue of a daily dole of spirits to mer-chant seamen, who cared to take it, would have the best effects—either spirits or malt liquors—for continuous periods of from 4 to 6 months or longer. The con-sequence is, that on arrival in port the fullest indulgence is given to a craving intensified by long deprivation. Whole outfits of clothes are exchanged for the vilest spirits, either on shore or over the ship's side, and the most degrading exhi-bitions given of drunkenness in its worst forms. The system of a daily ration of spirits works well in Her Majesty's navy; the number of total abstainers in the Navy is pro rata incomparably higher than in the merchant service, so that it can not be considered as fatal to the cause of temperance : and it is difficult to understand why a system which is so well suited to one should be entirely inap-plicable to the other service.

"Both the above points, however—those of diet and total abstinence—fade into insignificance as compared with the grievous hardship very frequently suffered by sailors of merchant sailing ships in consequence of the third—one in which they are entirely at the mercy of their respective masters, and one which is, in my experi-ence, by a long way the chief incentive to desertion, and to the minor offense of absence without leave. Fortunately, it is one which can arouse no controversy, and the advocacy of its removal can give no offense. It is at the present day exceptional for any of the ships of Her Majesty's navy to be ever at sea or in any place where leave, however, under the special circumstances, men have been necessarily con-fined to the ship for such a period, it is the invariable custom, immediately on arriving at any port, the circumstances of which admits of their landing, to give general leave, in alternate watches for 48 hours; and in a recent visit to Japanese ports by one squadron of Her Majesty's fleet on the China station this period was extended to 96 hours, every man in every ship in the squadron having thus enjoyed an unbroken period of 4 days on shore. When a ship remains continu-ously in one port, all men of first-class character are practically permitted to go ashore on every alternate evening, with leave until 7 o'clock on the following morn-ing. Twice in each week, on Thursday and Saturday afternoons, general leave is given every man who is not on the defaulters' list, thus getting on shore for an afternoon and night at least once in every week. The men receive their wages monthly, and they are, therefore, seldom without both money and the opportunity to spend it on shore as they please. Their lives, too, on board ship are character-ized by every physical and mental comfort that the most thoughtful care can pro-vide for them. The lower deck of one of Her Majesty's ships, with its airiness in summer and its warmth in winter, its perfect sanitation and cleanliness, its abundant room and ample provision of mess furniture, could no more be com-pared to the forecastle of a merchant sailing ship than could the lodging of a respectable mechanic and his family in a model dwelling in London to the over-crowded dens in St. Giles or Whitechapel rookeries. The abundant and whole-some food can be supplemented at most moderate cost with anything, with the single exception of intoxicating liquor, that taste can fancy, from the ship's can-teen, which is in itself a small cooperative store, managed by the men themselves, under the presidency of an officer. Concerts, variety entertainments, and theat-rical performances are constantly organized. There is always a good ship's library, and abundant supplies of magazines and papers are handed on from the officers' messes. Officers and men alike take part in cricket, football, sailing matches, and athletic sports, and, generally speaking, nothing whatever that can be done is left undone to promote relaxation and amusement, the whole result being that the men are thoroughly contented with their service, and that there are few better specimens of Her Majesty's subjects than the naval blue jacket.

"In merchant steamers, which now are, at least in the Eastern trade, seldom at sea for more than a fortnight continuously, it has grown to be a custom little less forcible than a regulation to permit the men to go ashore while in port, in alternate watches, every evening after 6 o'clock, when the day's work is done, and for the whole of Sundays when once the ordinary morning scrubbing and polishing are finished. The whole voyage, out and home, of a steamer rarely exceeds 6 months, at the end of which a man is paid the balance of his wages in full; and not only in all large lines, but in nearly all steamers, it is the custom also to make him reasonable advances, at his option, from month to month. Nominally, the old board of trade regulation diet is preserved as in sailing vessels, but in practice little use is made of it, no more, perhaps, than makes it even an agreeable variety on the constant supply of fresh provisions and vegetables that the short runs at sea admit of being provided.

"The consequence is that in the merchant steam service, as well as in the navy, the men, having every reason to be contented with their service, and never being wholly without money or reasonable leave, abuse neither. Their savings banks' accounts are numerous and substantial, and an attempt at desertion on the part of, or a charge of being absent without leave against, a seaman of a merchant steamer is as exceptional as it is frequent against those of merchant sailing vessels, notwithstanding that there is an immense inferiority in the total number of the latter.

"During the last 8 weeks more than 6,000 sailors of Her Majesty's navy have had liberal shore leave in this port, without one single charge of any kind for misconduct on shore having been preferred against them. Cases of intoxication were seen among them here and there, but their number was small in proportion to that of the whole on shore, and not one was of a nature to require the interference of the police. In the case of one British sailing ship that visited and remained some time in this port during the last 8 months, the practice of the steam service of giving leave in alternate watches every evening and on Sundays was adopted by the master, with satisfactory results.

"But the practice in most sailing ships is quite the reverse of this. As a rule, ships arrive in Japanese ports, after a voyage of from 4 to 6 months' duration, from Cardiff or Philadelphia, and they remain continuously in port for any period of from 1 to 2 months. All leave and advances of wages are, during this period, entirely at the option of the master; and, as a concrete instance of the rigor with which their power is sometimes exercised by masters in this respect, I may mention the case of a large iron sailing ship now in this harbor, which arrived from Cardiff with a cargo of coal after a voyage of 4 months' duration. The ship lies less than half a mile from the shore, in full view of the town, with picturesque green hills on both sides, and her stay in port will last for, at the very least, one full month. The master refused any leave, but said he might give some prior to the ship's departure from the port as soon as she was ready for sea. In the meantime all the men were to be detained on board for a whole month, occupied during the day in scraping and painting the ship's sides, in the full glare of an Eastern sun in August, without a particle of protection against it in the shape of either awning or proper head covering, choked with the fine, penetrating dust that Cardiff coal gives out during unloading, and both themselves and the ship in a constant state of most grimness. On being remonstrated with very forcibly on this line of conduct, the master consented to give both short leave and a small advance of wages, but this was not until the ship had been in port for a full fortnight and until after several of the men had broken out of the ship, and one, at least, had attempted to dessert, and to raise money had not only sold all of his own clothing, but some of his shipmates, for less than one-tenth of its value. This is by no means an isolated instance, and in cases where leave is given advances of money already earned by the men are often made only under such conditions as prevent the latter enjoying more than half their benefit. One glaring instance of injustice in this respect was quoted in my previous report, and I believe both that such an instance was not exceptional and that similar ones are occurring at the present day, and, strange to say, not a single word of complaint as to their injustice is ever made by the seaman.

"What are the consequences of such a line of conduct? Forecastle life in a sailing ship is utterly devoid of every semblance of the smallest approach to the comfort that the poorest agricultural laborer enjoys in England, with the single

655A——45

exception that the men, if coarsely and monotonously, are at the same time substantially fed. The men are confined in small, ill-ventilated spaces. In heavy weather at sea even this limited space must all be kept closely shut, and the atmosphere in the Tropics, with damp clothes and oilskins hung everywhere in it to dry, must then be little short of horrible. Neither tables, crockery, nor cutlery is provided, lighting is of the scantiest description, and the food is eaten from a tin pannikin on the men's knees, seated either on a bunk or a chest.

"Books, papers, or magazines are unknown on board, nor is any provision of any kind made for the amusement of the men in such leisure hours as they may have. Can it be wondered at that human nature revolts at such experience unnecessarily prolonged, and that, refused leave and money, the men lend a ready ear to the blandishments of crimps and grogshop keepers, and if they do not desert, forfeiting all their wages for the sake of a week's ease on shore, the cost of which has to be paid from advances on reemployment in another ship, incur the penalties of being absent without leave and obtain money by selling the whole of their kit for one-tenth its value. Recklessness, the feeling that there is no future for them, encourages them in the most abandoned dissipation, and exhibitions on shore of degrading drunkenness, in the full view of jeering natives of the lower orders, are a deep cause of humiliation to their fellow countrymen residing on the spot. And even if the man continues in one ship till the end of his original engagement, and is finally paid off with a balance £50 or £60 to his credit, what is the too frequent result? Totally unaccustomed to money, he knows not how to use a large sum, and falling a ready prey to sharpers of every description, a week or a fortnight sees him as poor as ever and forced again to take any employment that offers itself to him. Had this balance been only half what it is, and had he been accustomed during his service to the regular use of small sums, a small portion would probably satisfy his immediate requirements, and the facilities of the board of trade savings banks be used for the disposal of the remainder.

"Writing after a long experience of seamen and after having given much thought and attention to their circumstances, I can have no hesitation in stating my strong belief that a complete reform in these points, and especially in those of leave of absence and advances of wages, would tend very greatly to the improvement of the conditions of the merchant seaman's life on board sailing ships, and thereby render him more contented and law abiding than he now is. The character of the British sailor has, it is to be remarked, entirely changed during the last 30 years from what it was in the days when steam had not yet commenced to figure as a serious factor in ocean navigation, or even when it was as yet only in its infancy as such. His old peculiar dress—the blue guernsey, wide trousers, and oilskin hat worn on the back of his head—have entirely disappeared and are replaced by clothes little distinguishable from those worn by a shore mechanic, and with his dress have gone his old simplicity of character, the jovial good humor and rollicking sportiveness that made him on his trips on shore at once a pet and a wonder to the rest of the community. When on shore now he only too often appears a loafer, sunk in debauchery and sodden with drink (I am writing only of those in sailing ships), an object of disgust or at best of compassion to all who see him. He has no yarns to tell, no songs to sing, his conversation and thoughts are mainly confined to his grievances. He is more often than not a sea lawyer with a keen sense of what privileges or rights the law gives him, but with an equally keen sense of how few and limited those rights and privileges are. No longer the trustful child that he was in former days, he feels that he is still treated as a child, bound by restrictions and liabilities that would not be tolerated for a year in any other trade in life, and liable for the slightest breach of those restrictions to the treatment and penalties of a criminal. Once committed to the sea life, other openings are practically closed to him, and for better or worse he is bound to it as long as he lives. Its hardships, its rapid changes of climate, with total absence of provisions for adapting himself to those changes, render his life comparatively short; but it is no longer a merry one. Now and then a drunken spree, a short space of liberty, lawful or unlawful; if the latter, enjoyed only as a hunted fugitive and purchased by the sacrifice of what it has taken months of hard and dangerous work to earn, are its sole bright spots, and the inevitable end is, if not an early death, too often the workhouse. Is it to be wondered at that when the conditions of the life of not to say a skilled mechanic—and such is the proper prototype on shore of a trained and skilled seaman—but even of an ordinary laborer are compared with these, that in the present day, when education is widespread, mercantile marine life should fail to attract any but those who are committed to it when they are too young to choose for themselves, or who have altogether failed in other lines? And how different might be the case is shown by that in the Navy. Every improvement I have suggested exists and has existed for many years in the latter, and the consequence is that recruiting for it never fails and that desertion is as rare in the one as it is the reverse in the other. Nor is there any lack of competent men, of excellent men, for service in steam lines, who, if they no longer appear in their old sailor's garb, afford when on shore the spectacle of a steady, respectable, well-to-do English workman, just as much as the sailor of the sailing ship often does the reverse.

"Several of the disabilities which I have mentioned exist also in the mercantile marine of the United States. 'Going on shore in foreign ports is prohibited, except by permission of the master,' and 'no grog allowed, and none 'to be brought on board by the crew,' are conditions printed on the articles of American ships, and are, I presume, therefore universal. And a third condition, 'no money will be advanced to crew aboard except at master's option,' is also frequently added in writing. But American merchant seamen receive higher wages than English, their accommodation is better and their diet is, in nearly all ships, incomparably better and more varied."

Dealing with the matter of laws that provide for a penalty for desertion, I would like to add to what I said about that before: We used to say in former years, I have shipped; I have engaged myself with so and so; I have shipped with such and such a vessel. To-day it is changed; and I have heard them state, "I have sold myself." The feeling that the sailor does not belong to himself, that his body does not belong to him, that he belongs to the ship just as much as the mainmast or the anchor does, and that somebody can go after him, put a reward on him, and bring him back just as if he had run away from prison—that feeling that the sailor has to-day makes him particularly bitter, and it is so well known in seaports that that is the usual condition, and that that is being done, that the sailor is looked upon as not equal to other men on that account. We tried to overcome that matter by an appeal to the Supreme Court under the thirteenth amendment, but the court ruled against us; held that the seaman does not come under the thirteenth amendment to the Constitution; that the thirteenth amendment does not apply to seamen at all. The feeling, however, has been since that the statutes under which that decision was given ought to be wiped out, and the House would have wiped them out altogether last year if it had not run up against the Senate on the subject. At the present time it remains only in the foreign port. Thus a seaman in a port of Asia, Japan, China, Australia, Africa, or Europe is yet in the condition that when he goes ashore and does not turn up again, the captain issues a reward for him; publishes a reward if he wants him very badly, and he is met, took up, and brought on board by the police under treaties with foreign countries and under the statutes here. And inasmuch as the seamen are the only ones who are subject to that, it becomes so much the more onerous; men feel it more than if other people were in the same condition. One of the first things that ought to be done to give the sailor the idea that he is as good as other men, has as good a right as other men, is to give him the right to go, wherever the vessel is lying in the harbor.

Q. (By Mr. Farquhar.) If that was made the contract, that they could go just as soon as they got to port, would there be a great difficulty and delay to the vessel in securing a new crew?—A. None whatever.

Q. Did you ever know of cases where the whole crew desired to leave the ship, unless in extraordinary circumstances?—A. No; under ordinary circumstances the whole crew would not want to leave.

Q. Then if it were an open contract that they might leave the ship at the port of destination or port of touch, do you think there are sufficient sailors to be found in those ports to man the ship again without unnecessary delay?—A. Yes; I do. The usual thing is to pay the sailors or to drive them out, and then let the vessel lay there without any sailors until she is ready to go to sea again, and then go and hire new ones. Where there is a port where there are no vessels coming, of course, the sailor would not want to leave—such as a port in some little island in the southern Pacific, or some place like that. The sailor would not want to leave; he would be marooning himself if he did.

Now, on the matter of the coastwise trade. The coastwise trade is absolutely protected from any interference or any competition of foreign vessels. The seamen in the coastwise trade are in absolutely the same condition as if they were in the foreign trade. There is no difference. The result of that has been that even in the protected coastwise trade, lake trade, there are practically no Americans, and there are comparatively few men who stay in the trade any great length of time. They come and go. Out on the California coast men will come from deep water, stay a year or two, or three or four years, and go again. There are comparatively few who stay altogether. They are usually men who have attachments there, or they get attached to a place for some other reason than that the party wants employment there.

Q. (By Mr. RATCHFORD.) Is it acceptable to your organization, so far as its influence is concerned, that the wages of sailors be fixed at the port from which they ship, regardless of their nationality?—A. We have never given any thought to that matter. It is a matter of such settled custom for years and years back that no one can remember it ever to have been otherwise.

Q. (By Mr. FARQUHAR.) In other words, a sailor is a sailor independent of his nationality?—A. Yes.

Q. (By Mr. RATCHFORD.) It has also been a custom, I suppose, for a long time, in the nature of things, that the unemployed sailors in every port practically fixed the rate of wages?—A. Certainly; the unemployed sailors and the unemployed—I was pretty near saying soldiers—but the unemployed who are neither sailors nor soldiers.

Q. Would-be sailors?—A. Yes; the unemployed would-be sailors; that is right.

Q. (By Mr. FARQUHAR.) Is there much use for the old style able-bodied seamen on the steam marine?—A. Yes; he is just as necessary now as he ever was. "Able-bodied seaman" does not mean being able to rig a vessel. The rigger can do that, and yet be useless when he gets to sea. An able seaman is a man accustomed to the sea; a healthy man in his active years accustomed to the seas who has received the peculiar training that makes it possible for him to apply his wits to the conditions as they come, and he is just as necessary now as he was in the days of the sailing ship. A naval officer told me on the Pacific coast that they had found that out in the Cuban war that the actual seaman was the one that had any value; that the landsman taken on board a vessel was simply lumber.

Q. In the cutting down of the crew, which has occurred within the last 20 or 25 years, has it not been the fact that the ordinary seaman is the person who has suffered most?—A. Yes; that is true. Vessels do not carry ordinary seamen any more. American vessels do not carry ordinary seamen or boys any more. What are called American seamen are foreign seamen, who are just at the present time sailing under the American flag.

Q. (By Mr. RATCHFORD.) I want to ask a question with reference to the comparative wages paid in the Pacific coast trade to American seamen and to the Asiatic seamen. According to your testimony American seamen are paid from $30 to $40, and in some cases $45.—A. Yes.

Q. While the Asiatic seamen are paid about $16 in Mexican money?—A. Yes.

Q. I want to ask whether the American seaman finds any opportunities open to him to obtain employment as long as it is possible to secure the cheaper class?—A. No; he does not. The vessels that go to Hongkong—the old vessels that trade between Hongkong, China, and San Francisco and Puget Sound—all those vessels, whether under the American flag or the English flag, or Japanese flag, sign all their men in China or Japan. They carry white quartermasters and white officers, but not any white sailors or white firemen or in the steward's department. There is no employment to be obtained in these vessels at all, except as quartermasters.

Q. How do you account for the great difference in the wages of the seamen?—A. It is due to the different ports in which they are signed and the different kind of men.

Q. In other words, supply and demand, I suppose?—A. And then, of course, they must carry more Chinamen than they would white men; they carry about double. English vessels that carry Kalashis carry about 3 times as many of them as they do of white men.

Q. To do the same work?—A. Yes.

Q. In the end they are no cheaper, are they?—A. I don't know. They could not be a great deal cheaper—a little, perhaps. Those that carry them say they are more amenable to discipline; they are not so apt to get drunk or to leave the vessel; they are more docile; for all of these several reasons. Whether these reasons are real good reasons or not I do not know.

Q. Well, is it a fact that they do not require the same care or the same living as American seamen?—A. They are usually fed on their own kind of food—rice, and curry of different kinds. Of course their food costs much less than that of white men.

Q. Do they attain the same high standard of skill as American seamen as a rule?—A. No. Where it comes to where real seamen are needed in a storm or in disaster of any kind, then they are useless, practically.

Q. (By Mr. PHILLIPS.) Why so?—A. Because they have not the self-control, nor the coolness, nor the courage, nor the strength of the average white man.

Q. (By Mr. RATCHFORD.) There is a large proportion of them Chinamen, is there not?—A. Of those that come to San Francisco and Puget Sound, yes.

Q. They are not reached by the exclusion laws, are they, this class?—A. No.
Q. Then the sailor has no protection from these laws?—A. Absolutely none. Nor from the immigration laws. He is always exempted. When the exclusion law was passed he was exempted, and when the immigration law was passed he was again exempted.

Q. You spoke in the early part of your testimony about a higher standard of skill, or something to that effect, among seamen. Could you, in closing your testimony, explain as fully as you care to what you would advise or suggest along these lines to cover the points not yet touched upon? There are no qualifications provided, I presume.—A. The only qualification that is provided in this bill, and it has the English commission's recommendations for it, is that the seaman signed be an able seaman; must be more than 18 years of age; must have served 3 years at sea on deck; he must have 3 years' experience.

Q. That bill has become a law?—A. No. That is what we propose. It is hard to specify just what he shall be able to do; that would hardly be possible.
(Testimony closed.)

WASHINGTON, D. C.,
Monday, February 19, 1900.

TESTIMONY OF MR. CHARLES H. KEEP,

Secretary of the Lake Carriers' Association and of the Buffalo Merchants' Exchange.

The commission met at 10.55 a m., Vice-Chairman Phillips presiding.
Mr. CHARLES H. KEEP, of Buffalo, N. Y., was introduced as a witness, and, being duly sworn, testified as follows, the topical plan of inquiry on transportation being followed:

Q. (By Representative LORIMER.) Will you state your name and official connection with organizations, together with the names of the organizations?—A. Charles H. Keep, secretary of the Lake Carriers' Association and Buffalo Merchants' Exchange.

Q. Will you give the commission a little history of the Lake Carriers' Association, that it may know the purpose of the organization?—A. My own connection with the Lake Carriers' Association has lasted about 11 years. The association was in existence for 3 or 4 years before that time. I can not tell you the exact date on which it was formed. It began in a small way. A few of the managers of the principal fleets of vessels on the Great Lakes saw that there were various questions coming up from time to time in which vessel owners had common interests, in such matters as the building of needed light-houses and the legislation with reference to channels; some such matters as that principally; and they decided that they would form a little organization to act together in matters of common concern. That organization was formed. In the first instance it was comprised principally of owners who lived at Buffalo, N. Y., and gradually owners from other places have joined the association. About the same time another organization called the Cleveland Vessel Owners' Association was formed at Cleveland. That organization had a slightly different purpose; it was largely to look after business matters connected with the running of their boats, and particularly the supplying of labor to their boats, and they opened shipping offices at Cleveland and put shipping masters in charge, employment officers, to get men for the boats. The two associations ran along side by side, sometimes taking a little different view of things, until finally about 1890. on some matter, I do not remember exactly what it was, the Carriers' Association favored one thing and the Cleveland Vessel Owners favored just the opposite; and out of that grew in 1891 the consolidation of the two organizations into the Lake Carriers' Association; and since that time the Lake Carriers' Association has been the only vessel owners' association on the lakes. It has comprised most of the tonnage there and has general charge of the questions in which vessel owners act together. At the present time the work of the association is to interest itself in legislative matters relating to the lakes, opposing hostile legislation, endeavoring to get needed channel improvements and needed improvements in the aids to navigation, the supplying of necessary private lights and the maintenance of necessary shipping offices. The lake waterway being an international waterway and the Canadian government not having a great interest in the commerce, there are quite a number of places in which there are not sufficient lights on the Canadian side; and the Lake Carriers' Association has built the requisite lights, and contracts each year with light keepers to keep the lights there. There are certain places on the American side where they do the same thing. They maintain shipping offices for the furnishing of men to vessels at a number of ports on the lakes—Chicago, South Chicago, Milwaukee, Cleveland, Toledo, Ashtabula, and Buffalo.

Q. Is your association interested in any proposed legislation now before Congress?—A. We are always interested in river and harbor bills, appropriations for light-houses and life-saving stations, and matters of that kind. Aside from that we have no special interest in any legislation now be ore Congress.

Q. Have you anything in mind that you wish to give to the commission concerning your business, any grievances?—A. No; I do not think we have. I may say that the lake business is so thoroughly understood, its magnitude and importance so thoroughly understood now by Congress that the matter is in a very different shape now from what it was when the Lake Carriers' Association was first organized. We have only to present our requests to Congress to insure a good hearing of them, and we try not to present any unless we have such an overwhelming case that it will appeal to the favorable action of Congress. The whole policy of the association since it was formed has been to act upon a few things, and only those things which they thought they were entitled to and could get. We entirely exclude all matters of local improvement and attend only to matters of general concern.

Q. Are the people that you represent getting into any controversy, especially with reference to their employees, or have they had any recently?—A. No; they are having none now and have had none recently; there has been very little trouble of that kind on the lakes since my connection with the transportation.

Q. No trouble on either side?—A. There has been some little trouble, but nothing of great importance.

Q. Would you mind stating to the commission what that trouble was?—A. The question of union and nonunion labor has come up once or twice, but only in spots and in a small way. The schooner *Mabel Wilson* lay at the breakwater at Buffalo with a crew of nonunion men on her, and a boat load of union men went out from the city and pulled off the crew and assaulted the captain. We took that matter up and two of the ringleaders we sent to State's prison—punished in the United States court and sent to State's prison.

Q. What was the original cause of that?—A. Only the unwillingness of the union men to see a nonunion crew on the boat. I know of no other cause.

Q. Not one of the wages paid?—A. No; none at all. The Lake Carriers' Association from time to time issues a card, called its wages card, of the wages that they will pay to the different classes of employees; and that card is raised in good times and lowered in poor times. There has been little or no dissatisfaction with it of late years; we have had very little controversy, almost no controversy. with labor. During such seasons as 1898 the wages were very much lower than they were in 1899, which was a much more prosperous year; and this year the wages card will undoubtedly show a higher rate of wages than it did in the spring of last year.

Q. (By Mr. RATCHFORD.) In this case that you speak of did the union employees refuse to work for the rate of wages that were paid to that crew?—A. I can not tell you. I do not know anything about the hiring of men for any particular vessels, and I have no recollection or knowledge of the facts in that regard of that particular vessel. I do not remember the cause of the controversy. I only remember the assault and the arrest and the prosecution and punishment of the ringleaders. It was under the new act of Congress, I think, which had then made the laws of the high seas applicable to the lakes.

Q. And you do not know the cause of the controversy?—A. I do not know the cause of the controversy.

Q. (By Mr. KENNEDY.) You recognize committees from organized seamen?—A. Yes.

Q. Do they have any voice in determining this rate of wages stated on this card?—A. They sometimes send in communications when they know that the wages card is about to be made or altered. They sometimes send in communications stating their wishes and these communications are taken into consideration.

Q. Are all the vessels on the lakes bound by this rate of wages that you fix and send out?—A. The rate is a maximum rate. Members of the association only are bound by it at all; members of the association are not supposed to pay more than the card rate for the various classes of employees.

Q. (By Representative LORIMER.) Do they frequently pay less?—A. Sometimes, yes. The card rate is understood to be the maximum rate. The law of supply and demand enables owners to get their men at less.

Q. (By Mr. SMYTH.) What proportion of the seamen on the lakes are organized?—A. I can not tell you. Their organizations have not been very active of late years. They have a seamen's union, a fireman's union, and an engineer's organization.

Q. (By Representative LORIMER.) When this scale that you speak of is made up, do I understand that you say it is made up by the association members?—A. Made up by the executive committee of the association, and changed when they may deem it necessary from time to time.

Q. And the employees either accept that or not, or else there is trouble?—A. They have accepted it. As far as I know it has been satisfactory to them.

Q. (By Mr. FARQUHAR.) Is not this high rate of wages of seamen governed a great deal by the freight rates that are established?—A. Yes: the policy of the vessel owners has been to raise wages and pay liberal wages in good times, and during very hard times, when the vessels can not make any money, to reduce the wages; and they have expected that the men would recognize the fairness and justice of that arrangement, and they have done so.

Q. (By Representative LORIMER.) Now, when they have been compelled to reduce wages, have they had any controversy with the men on account of reduction?—A. Very little; no.

Q. So it is generally satisfactory all around?—A. So far as I know it is generally a satisfactory arrangement.

Q. (By Mr. FARQUHAR.) Now, in the loading and unloading of vessels around at these variout ports, there are unions of stevedores. The trouble you have had at Buffalo, was not that from the parties that made these contracts, outside parties?—A. The grain shovelers' trouble at Buffalo—they are in no respect employees of the Lake Carriers' Association. They are employees of a stevedore contractor. The Lake Carriers' Association makes a contract with some individuals to do the necessary shoveling for the elevators of grain at Buffalo, for the entire season; and the contractor had some trouble with his men.

Q. There were two unions at Buffalo at that time, were there not?—A. Yes.

Q. Both contending for the same rate of wages?—A. Yes. The question was not in its final form a question of wages at all.

Q. It was as to the parties to the contract?—A. Largely a question of personal animosity, it turned into in the end. The men belonging to one of the organizations there declined to work for the contractor of the Lake Carriers' Association on any terms. That was their position for some time.

Q. (By Representative LORIMER.) Would you mind telling the commission what you know about that trouble?—A. The last annual report of the Lake Carriers' Association, of which I have a copy here, contains a pretty full account of that controversy. There is a page or two that I might either read or submit.

Q. If it is not a very lengthy matter, we would like to have you read it.—A. (Reading:)

"The contract for shoveling grain at Buffalo during the season of 1899 was awarded at the last annual meeting to W. J. Conners, of Buffalo. It became apparent before navigation opened that there was to be a labor controversy at Buffalo between the contractor and the shovelers. It is not necessary to recite here the history of the differences of opinion between the contractor and the shovelers. It is enough to confine ourselves to the position taken by the Lake Carriers' Association and to recite the part which it took in the troubles at Buffalo during the early part of the season of navigation.

"The greater proportion of the grain fleet arrived in Buffalo on the 3d and 4th of May."

That is, the fleet that was loading all winter at Western ports—as soon as the Straits of Mackinaw were opened they came down and arrived in Buffalo. (Reading:)

"The work of unloading the boats proceeded very slowly. At no time was the work of unloading entirely discontinued, but the force of men employed was much smaller than under ordinary circumstances. Whatever form the differences between the contractor and his men had taken in the first instance, soon after the opening of navigation the shovelers took the position that they would not work under the contract system, but that they would return to the system of shoveling grain under boss scoopers at the different elevators, which had prevailed before the contract system was put into effect. Under these circumstances the executive committee of the Lake Carriers' Association, at their meeting in Cleveland on May 3, adopted the following resolution:

"'Whereas the system of grain shoveling in vogue at Buffalo for three seasons past had operated to correct many abuses; has furnished good wages to the men actually doing the work; saved vessels from delays and extortions and been of marked advantage to the grain trade of Buffalo, and for the mutual advantage of the shoveler and the vessel this system should continue; and

" ' Whereas a contest has been excited in Buffalo to do away with this system and compel a return to the old system with all the abuses:

" ' *Resolved*, That the members of the Lake Carriers' Association have confidence that their contractor, W. J. Conners, is ready and willing to give the men fair treatment and the same wages as last year, and that they stand by Mr. Conners in this contest and insist on the performance of the work under his contract.'

" On the 5th of May a conference was held at the Iroquois Hotel in Buffalo between members of the executive committee of the Lake Carriers' Association and a delegation from Local No. 51, headed by President McMahon. This meeting was practically held under the auspices of the New York State board of mediation and arbitration. Messrs. Goulder, Wilson, Coulby, Corrigan, and Brown attended on behalf of the Lake Carriers' Association. The various labor interests in Buffalo were represented by officers, and a number of elevator men were in attendance. The position of the Lake Carriers' Association was stated by Mr. Goulder to the effect that the association had entered into a contract with Mr. Conners; that he had given them a bond for the faithful performance of the contract, and that the association had determined to stand by its contractor and by the contract system.

" On Saturday, May 6, another conference was held at the Iroquois Hotel, at which representatives of the Lake Carriers' Association, the State board of mediation and arbitration, representatives of the elevator association, and all the various labor organizations of Buffalo were present. At this conference a paper was drawn up and signed by the various interests, proposing a basis of settlement. This basis included the preservation of the contract with Mr. Conners, abolishing the saloon evil, the appointment of an inspector to see that the saloon evil was abolished, in fact, the abolition of all dummies from the pay rolls, and strict supervision in this regard by the inspector. This proposition, though signed by prominent labor leaders in Buffalo as a basis of settlement, was rejected at a meeting of the shovelers, after which the Lake Carriers' Association, through Mr. Goulder, made a statement showing that they had made earnest efforts to settle the trouble in a manner satisfactory to the scoopers and contractor, and had submitted what they considered a fair proposition to the scoopers, which they had refused to hear. In this statement Mr. Goulder suggested for the first time the name of Bishop Quigley, of Baffalo, to act as arbitrator."

Bishop Quigley was the Roman Catholic bishop of Buffalo. (Reading:)

" On the 7th of May Bishop Quigley agreed to endeavor to reconcile the contending parties, and on Monday, May 8, a prolonged conference was held at the house of Bishop Quigley, at which were present, in addition to the bishop, representatives of the Lake Carriers' Association, New York state board of mediation, International Longshoremen's Union, Buffalo Local No. 51. Little progress toward an agreement was made at this conference. During several days thereafter conferences were held at the house of Bishop Quigley, and on Saturday, May 13, a basis of agreement was arrived at and put in writing, and signed by Mr. Goulder, for the Lake Carriers' Association, and the attorney for the shovelers. The basis of settlement agreed upon was as follows:

" First. That the price of $1.85 per thousand bushels should be paid to the men actually doing the work of shoveling, with not exceeding one foreman at each elevator leg; no other person to participate therein.

" Second. Each gang to select a timekeeper from its own number.

" Third. The timekeeper and inspector provided for at the conference to have free access to bills of lading and other documents showing the quantity of grain e evated.

" Fourth. Wages to be paid at elevator offices.

" Fifth. No bar bill or other accounts to be deducted from wages.

" Sixth. No boss or paymaster to be directly or indirectly connected with any saloon.

" Seventh. An inspector to be appointed by the bishop to see that the provisions of the agreement were carried out, and to report any violation to the bishop and to the Lake Carriers' Association; the inspector to be removable by the bishop with power to appoint another, if necessary, to be paid by the Lake Carriers' Association.

" Eighth. Bishop Quigley to have power to appoint a disinterested arbitrator to hear and finally determine complaint.

"Although this agreement was entered into by all parties to the controversy, upon the following Monday morning the scoopers did not return to work as expected, alleging acts on the part of the contractor inconsistent with the agreement. Representatives of the Lake Carriers' Association, therefore, gave out a statement that they had entered into an agreement which provided a remedy for every abuse and evil that had been complained of by the men; that they had done all they possibly could to put an end to the labor trouble at Buffalo, and not having been successful in inducing the men to go to work, they could only withdraw from further negotiations, leaving Bishop Quigley to deal with the matter as he saw fit. Meanwhile, the steam shovels and a force of two to three hundred men were steadily at work in unloading grain at Buffalo, and giving, under peculiarly difficult circumstances, as good dispatch to vessels as was possible. Meantime, also, without participation by representatives of the Lake Carriers' Association, various questions between the contractor and men, such as the selection of bosses, the temporary suspension of objectionable bosses, and the employment of men not members of local 51, had been the subject of negotiations between the contractor and shovelers, and on the 23d of May the settlement of these questions was so far advanced that the men returned to work at all the elevators. Bishop Quigley appointed Timothy P. Donovan inspector, to see that the various terms of agreement which had been arrived at by all parties were faithfully carried out, and to report any complaints of violation of the agreement to Bishop Quigley or his representative."

That is the history of that; there was no trouble after that.

Q. (By Representative LORIMER.) Can you give the commission the number of vessels and the tonnage that moves down the Great Lakes?—A. Yes. On the 30th of June, 1899, the total number of vessels on the lakes was 3,162, and their tonnage was 1,446,348 tons. That was out of a total of 22,728 vessels of all kinds in the United States. The total marine tonnage of the United States was 4,864,-238 tons. A little less than one-third of the tonnage of the whole country is on the lakes.

Q. Have you information that would tend to show the number of American vessels and the tonnage used in ocean commerce?—A. Well, you mean by ocean commerce coastwise and others?

Q. Yes.—A. I can give you those figures in a moment; that is, practically the whole tonnage of the country, less that of the lakes and the Western rivers. The tonnage of the country is divided into 4 classes: The Atlantic and Gulf coasts, the Pacific coast, the Northern lakes, and Western rivers. Now, the total tonnage in 1899 was 4,864,238, of which the Atlantic and Gulf coasts had 2,614,869, the Lakes 1,446,348, the Pacific coast 539,937, and the Western rivers 263,084. Those are the figures, but in a way they are somewhat misleading. Now, there is a total number of vessels on the Lakes of 3,162. That includes boats, harbor tugs, scows, steamers, canal boats, river excursion boats, and all that. We have in the Lake Carriers' Association about 600 vessels out of the 3,162, but their tonnage is a little over 1,000,000 tons out of 1,400,000 tons that make the whole.

Q. They are practically the carriers, then?—A. They are the carriers; the freight carriers.

Q. And your association has practically all the carrying tonnage within the association?—A. There are some exceptions, but we have probably somewhere from four-fifths to nine-tenths of the whole freight-carrying tonnage.

Q. Many of those vessels are owned by the large railroad transportation companies, are they not?—A. Some of them are; not a large proportion.

Q. Have you any idea of what percentage?—A. I can tell you. Out of about 600 vessels in the Lake Carriers' Association 72 are owned or controlled by companies having affiliations of some kind with the railroads.

Q. What is the tonnage?—A. The tonnage of those vessels—the tonnage given by the Government's reports—is what is called gross tonnage, and our tonnage that we keep in our books, and on which our association is supported by tax, is what is called the net registered tonnage. Those boats have a net registered tonnage of 122,000 out of a net registered tonnage in the association of 760,000, a little less than one-sixth of the association.

Q. (By Mr. KENNEDY.) Are the fleets of the iron and steel manufacturers in your association?—A. Yes.

Q. (By Mr. RATCHFORD.) What railways are interested in those vessels?—A. I have a list of those boats here. The Great Northern Line, which is connected with the Great Northern Railroad, has 8 vessels, of which 6 are freight and 2 passenger. The Canadian Atlantic Transit Company has 5 vessels; the vessels are American; the company is Canadian. The Western Transit Company, which is affiliated with the New York Central, has 13 vessels. The Anchor Line, affiliated with the Pennsylvania, has 16 vessels. The Wabash Line, 4 vessels. Ogdensburg Transit Company, which is the Central Vermont Line, 8. The Soo Line, which is the St. Paul, Minneapolis and Sault Ste. Marie Railroad, 5. The Union

Steamboat Company (vessels) is affiliated with the Erie Railroad. The Lehigh Valley Transportation Company (vessels) is the Lehigh Valley Railroad fleet. The Lackawanna also has a line. Now, I may say that those are all what we call on the lakes package freight boats. They are engaged in different business altogether from the ordinary lake vessel. The ordinary lake vessel is built to carry bulk freights, either coal, or ore, or lumber, or grain. The package boats have an extra deck. They have a hold in which they carry grain or coal and then a between decks in which they carry package freight; and they are built to carry miscellaneous merchandise for what is called the lake and rail route; that is, a New York Central agent in Chicago will contract for some freight to be taken through to New York by lake and rail. They use the Western Line of steamers from Chicago to Buffalo and then the New York Central from Buffalo to New York.

Q. Are any of the grain boats affiliated with the railroads?—A. A few owners build their boats with the decks so that they may charter them for the season to some of these companies that are short of boats; but that is rather disappearing from the lakes. The great object with the lake vessel owner in building a boat is the speedy handling of cargo, and if the boat is to be engaged most of the year in bulk-freight business, such as coal or ore, the deck is in the way of the handling process; so they build their boats without any between decks.

Q. Speaking of ore, do you know of any railroads, or any trust, or any corporation other than the transportation companies that own and control their own boats for the shipping of ore?—A. Many of the mining companies have separate companies organized for owning vessels, and those vessels usually have some affiliation with the owners of the mines. The stock may be identically owned, or may be to a certain extent owned by the same interests—the stock in the mines, the stock in the steel company, and the stock in the boats.

Q. Has the Standard Oil Company a line of boats?—A. My impression is that they have just one tank boat on the lakes that is engaged in carrying oil in bulk from Chicago to Duluth.

Q. Are they engaged in the shipping of ore?—A. No; Mr. Rockefeller has ore interests, but the Standard Oil Company has not, as far as I know.

Q. (By Mr. PHILLIPS.) You understand that Mr. Rockefeller has, and not the Standard Oil Company?—A. That is my understanding.

Q. Well, who built what are called the whaleback boats of recent years?—A. The inventor of the whaleback was a man named Alexander McDougall. He lived in Duluth and he interested some New York capitalists in a shipyard, and he built a fleet of whalebacks, or a fleet of whalebacks was built by a company called the American Barge Company. They have a fleet of about 80 boats.

Q. Who is the principal owner of that fleet?—A. I can not tell you that, but it is supposed that that fleet has been bought by Mr. Rockefeller since the close of navigation last fall.

Q. Bought entirely?—A. I think he had some interest in them before, but it is understood that he is the owner of that fleet now.

Q. Well, are those the boats that handle the Carnegie or the Bessemer ore?—A. No; the Carnegie ore has been handled quite largely by the fleet of the company called the Bessemer Steamship Company. That company is owned by Mr. Rockefeller.

Q. Do you know whether Mr. Carnegie proposes now to carry his ore or not?—A. Some half dozen boats are now building for the Carnegie people.

Q. This Carnegie line connects with the railroad built by Mr. Carnegie from some ports on the lakes to his works?—A. There is a railroad built from Conneaut, Ohio, to Pittsburg—the Pittsburg, Bessemer and Lake Erie Railroad, I think it is called—on which Mr. Carnegie has much of his ore carried. It is carried by the Bessemer boats to Conneaut.

Q. Could you state what effect the building of these whaleback boats has had on the other boats and people engaged in shipping?—A. The whaleback boats are not the largest boats by any means on the lakes. There are other boats which are larger.

Q. But upon those built in recent years by these other companies, have they had any great effect on the people doing this business, the building of these large boats, whalebacks and others?—A. It is impossible to state what effect they have had on the smaller boats. The smaller boats have made a great deal of money this year; have had a very prosperous year. They have had this year perhaps as prosperous a year as they ever have had.

Q. For a time did it effect other shippers?—A. 1897 and 1898 were dull years, but in 1899 there was a great deal of freight to be carried by vessels. There was a good deal of tonnage that had been contracted for the season at a very low rate, and the larger vessels that had contracts to carry throughout most of the season had to carry for a low rate. although the vessels that had not contracted for the season were getting extremely high rates. The variation was as great as that between 60 cents a ton and $2 a ton—60 cents a ton, the season contract rate, which was made in the winter of 1898 and 1899, and $2 the highest going rate from day to day that prevailed for quite a time during the navigation season of 1899.

Q. (By Mr. SMYTH.) These larger boats require an additional number of firemen and an additional number of seamen?—A. Yes; they employ more men than the smaller. There are more men in the engine room. But the advantage of the large boat is that with a comparatively small increase in the expense of running, comparatively small increase in the crew, the carrying capacity is greatly increased.

Q. Are these large boats built for any special trade?—A. The ore trade is the great trade of the lakes; it is more than twice what the total grain trade is and more than twice the coal trade. The great item in the carrying of freight on the lakes is the ore.

Q. That business has very largely increased in the last few years?—A. Immensely; there were about 20,000,000 net tons of ore carried on the lakes in 1899.

Q. These large boats, then, were built to meet the demand, I suppose, for tonnage for carrying this ore?—A. Yes; that is what they were built for.

Q. (By Representative LORIMER.) Do you know what percentage of the traffic was ore last year?—A. The total traffic on the lakes is a thing that no man can give, and there are no records that can enable you to say what the total amount of traffic carried on the lakes is. The traffic to and from Lake Superior—a record of that is kept at the entrance to Lake Superior, the Soo Canal—and that traffic of Lake Superior is about half of the total traffic on the lakes. I can give you the proportions of the different commodities in the Lake Superior traffic, and from that a deduction can be made as to how the proportions run in the entire lake traffic. The total freight traffic through the Soo Canal last season was 25.255.810 tons, and of that 15.328,000 tons, or about 60 per cent, was ore.

Q. That would be the total tonnage of ore, then, would it not, about 15,000,000?—A. No; there is ore also shipped from Escanaba in Lake Michigan and from Gladstone in Lake Michigan.

Q. Could you give the commission an idea of the tonnage shipped on Lake Michigan, of ore?—A. The total shipments by lake of iron ore in the season of 1899 were 17,901,000 gross tons, or a little over 20,000,000 net tons, and of that 17,901,000 gross tons the shipments by ports were as follows: Escanaba, which is in Lake Michigan, 3,720,218 tons; Gladstone. which is in Lake Michigan, 381,457 tons. The other ports are all in Lake Superior. So that of that 18,000,000 tons, about 4,000,000 were shipped from Lake Michigan and about 14,000.000 from Lake Superior. That 14,000,000 tons would be 15,500,000 tons if converted into net tons.

Q. About the ownership of the mines along the lakes; do you know who own them?—A. I do not. I have no information as to that.

Q. Will you give the commission the grain traffic on the lakes for last year?—A. I can give you the Buffalo traffic, which is probably about 80 per cent of the total grain traffic on the lakes; that is, the traffic in the Georgian Bay, to Erie, Ogdensburg, and down the St. Lawrence, is about one-fourth of the traffic to Buffalo. There was a falling off in the grain traffic on the lakes last year, due principally to two causes. The first of these causes was the prolonged labor controversy at Buffalo, in the spring of the year, which shortened the season; and the second and more important cause was the extremely high rates prevailing for the carriage of iron ore. The steel companies were so anxious to get ore that they bid the freights up to get boats, and, of course, the grain trade could get no boats without bidding against the rates the ore people were offering. This raised the grain freight so materially that the railroads, who find it difficult to compete with the lake trade in seasons of low rates, were able to compete actively last season when the freights were so high, and a considerable quantity of grain was diverted last year from the lakes to the all-rail route. I will give you the figures for last year and the year before, which was the largest year in the history of the grain trade. The grain receipts in Buffalo in 1899 were 153,000,000 bushels and 10,000,000 barrels of flour; in 1898 they were 12,500,000 barrels of flour and 204,000,000 bushels of grain.

Q. Have you the other commodities on the list?—A. Yes.

Q. Will you kindly give those to the commission?—A. I have a complete statement of the imports by lakes at Buffalo and the coal exports.

Q. Have you the exports of coal there on that list?—A. The shipments of coal from Buffalo last year were the largest in the history of the port.

Q. (By Mr. RATCHFORD.) Have you the imports of coal from points in Canada to the United States?—A. The movement is the other way. There is quite a shipment of coal from the United States to Canada, but there is no coal received from Canada into the United States by lake.

Q. (By Representative LORIMER.) If you can, will you just give us the total?—A. Well, I can not give you the total of the trade. I can give you the Buffalo business. There was shipped last year from Buffalo 2,648,425 tons of anthracite coal by lake, and 126,140 tons of bituminous. Buffalo is the principal port of anthracite shipment by lake, and it is just beginning to be a small shipping point for bituminous coal; but the most of the bituminous that is shipped by lake is shipped from ports farther west—Cleveland, Toledo, and Ashtabula.

Q. That is shipped to all ports?—A. Shipped to all ports, most of it American, and some of it Canadian. There is coal shipped on Lake Ontario from Charlotte and Oswego and other ports to Toronto, and other points in Canada.

Q. You do not know what that amounts to?—A. I can not tell you about that.

Q. Do you know the percentage of vessels now owned by individuals?—A. Very few vessels are owned by individuals. Vessels are becoming too large and expensive. A group of men will get together and build a boat, but as a rule they organize a company and the boat is owned by the corporation. The corporation, however, consists of a few individuals who perhaps own other vessels in different proportions, and organize a separate company for each new boat.

Q. There are very few boats now being sailed by their owners?—A. Very few.

Q. Have you any idea of what percentage of vessels are sailed by the owners?—A. Some of the smaller lumber schooners; that is all.

Q. A few years ago a great many of the vessels on the lakes were owned by individuals, were they not?—A. I have no knowledge. That is before my connection with the lake business. The class of tonnage was totally different from what it is now.

Q. (By Mr. FARQUHAR.) I think the commission would like to have some knowledge of these freight rates for this season, and say for last season. We have the tonnage, and we have every other feature now, but we have no notion of these great raises in freight rates, and what caused the increase of the rates, for instance, on ore; and if you have figures that are official, or as near official as they can be, the commission would like to have them.—A. The freight rate on the lakes varies from day to day. The high rates prevailed through the season of 1899 solely because there was a great demand for boats. Every furnace in the territory dependent on lake ores was in operation at full capacity, and the demand for ore was very great, and the demand for boats to move it was very great, and the freight rates went up automatically.

Q. Have you a table of freight rates for 1898 and 1899?—A. I have the grain figures for 1898 and 1899, and they will serve equally well with the ore. There is a relation between them that is a fixed one. If the grain freights were higher than the ore freights why it would immediately be equalized; boats would leave one trade for the other. I will take the rate from Chicago to Buffalo on grain. In 1898 the highest rate was 3¼ cents on wheat, and the lowest 1¼. The average for the season was 1½.

Q. Is that in the bushel, or what?—A. That is per bushel. In 1899 the highest was 3¾, the lowest 1⅞, and the average 2¼.

Q. What is the minimum rate at which the railroads can compete with boats at Chicago?—A. I can not say. I have no knowledge.

Q. You suggested that on account of the high rates the railroads handled a great deal of the grain trade?—A. That is an inference from the fact that the rate was much higher and the grain movement by lake decreased.

Q. You have no idea about what was the minimum rate at which the railroads could compete?—A. No.

Q. (By Mr. A. L. HARRIS.) Has your association anything to do with fixing freight rates?—A. Nothing whatever.

Q. (By Mr. FARQUHAR.) Well, are the freight rates fixed on the exchanges of the various cities?—A. The freight rates are largely fixed from time to time by the supply and demand of vessels at the shipping ports, as far as grain is concerned. So far as ore is concerned, what is called wild tonnage is decreasing all the time, and what is called season tonnage is increasing all the time. The greater part of the ore—the carriage of it down the lakes—is contracted for by contracting it in large bulks during the winter to be carried during the next season. The reason for that is easily seen. In the first place, as soon as the ore is sold the tendency is to cover the ore, cover the freights by chartering tonnage to carry it, and the two transactions go on together. Then, in the next place, so far as the vessel is concerned, the owner of a vessel that carries 1,000 or 2,000 tons may be willing to take his chances on getting cargoes from trip to trip during the seasons; but if a man owns a boat that carries 7,000 or 8,000 tons, his boat carries so much more that he can not as easily pick up loads when he wants to, and safety requires that he should take a block of cargo to be carried, and take it during the winter, and get the vessel something to do during the summer; so that the owners of a large class of tonnage are inclined to contract for the season and not take chances on wild-trip rates. The owners of smaller boats are willing to take that chance.

Q. (By Representative LORIMER.) Is it generally understood what class of freight Mr. Rockefeller intends to carry with the boats that he has purchased, or are they to be put in the general shipping business, do you know?—A. They are what are called ore boats. They are built for the ore business. As a matter of fact, the Rockefeller boats carry ore, like most of the large boats, during the midsummer and per a s carry a load or two of grain in the fall of the year, before the close of navigation, and perhaps a load or two in the spring before the ore movement begins. In the first place, the Straits of Mackinaw sometimes open before the St. Marys River opens and boats will carry a load of grain from Chicago to Buffalo before the ore trade opens. And in the fall of the year the ore is full of moisture, and as soon as the extreme cold weather comes it freezes in the ore pockets and it becomes difficult to load vessels, whereas grain can still be loaded from elevators into the vessels, and many of the vessels carry one or two loads of grain in the fall of the year after they have closed up their ore contracts and before they go into winter quarters.

Q. What percentage of ore is carried by boats that are presumed to be owned directly or indirectly by the mine owners?—A. I can form no estimate of that whatever. I have no knowledge.

Q. (By Mr. FARQUHAR.) What is the character of the return cargo of those boats from the Eastern ports to the Western—the return cargo?—A. Very many of them return light. Coal is the only large item of west-bound shipment on the lakes.

Q. Do the ore boats take coal as a return cargo?—A. Very often. Many of them return light.

Q. Do the grain boats take a return cargo at all?—A. Very often. The east-bound movement is two or three time as large as the west-bound movement. Therefore the majority of the fleet returns light.

Q. (By Representative LORIMER.) Has there been any discussion in your association on the opening of the drainage canal and the probable effect of it on the lake levels?—A. There has. We have had the general subject of lake levels under discussion in our association. There is no question but what the opening of the drainage canal will affect the lake level. The only question is about the amount. This has been estimated to be about 3 inches by Major Marshall, the engineer at Chicago. Other engineers have estimated that the drainage canal would lower the lake level of Lakes Huron and Michigan by 7 or 8 inches.

Q. Has your association had any discussion as to what effect that would have on commerce, on the boats that are now used in transportation over the lakes?—A. We have had the whole matter up in connection with other projects for diverting the water. There is at the present time building at Sault Ste. Marie, Mich., a power canal which is to draw water from the St. Marys River or out of the basin of Lake Superior above the rapids and return it to that river below the rapids. Now, as that canal is built proposing to pass a volume of water equal to nearly 50 per cent of the entire flow of the St. Marys River at low-water stage, the engineer of the power company has estimated that if no compensatory works to obstruct the flow in the rapids were built, that canal would lower the level of Lake Superior 2 feet before a condition of equilibrium was again established. The company proposes to build compensatory works in the St. Marys River to obstruct the flow over the rapids by an amount equal to that which they take through the canal. Our association had a hearing before the River and Harbor Committee last Friday morning, on the question of necessary legislation to protect the interests of navigation there, and not permit the level of Lake Superior and the available draft of water in all its harbors and in the canal at the head of the lock there to be affected. It was shown by figures to the River and Harbor Committee that a diminution of 1 inch in the available draft of water would amount to $150,000 a year to the vessels, net loss.

Q. Have they discussed any legislation on account of the drainage canal at Chicago?—A. Not in connection with that project especially; but the question of legislation on the whole subject of the control of lake levels is one of the questions before the association now. The most serious effect, I might say, so far as we can see it at the present time, is the effect on the harbor of Chicago itself. It is making a dangerous current in the Chicago River, and it has lowered the draft through that river in which the drainage is carried off—the water in the upper part of Chicago River is lowered 2 feet. It has lowered it over the Washington street tunnel, which is one of the places where the draft of vessels is limited, by about 6 inches.

Q. If dredging was done at the mouth of the canal to bring it to a depth of 21 feet, would there be any complaint on the part of the vessels?—A. You mean if the draft of the water into the drainage canal from Lake Michigan was very largely increased?

Q. Yes; if the draft was made 21 feet.—A. Yes; it would have very serious effects on the lake navigation. No question about it.

Q. You know that Congress passed a law two years ago providing that the draft in Chicago River should be made 21 feet. Do you think that if the law is put into operation it will have a very serious effect on the lake?—A. On Chicago River?

Q. The lake level?—A. Well, the improvement of the Chicago River without any increased draft of water through the drainage canal would have no effect on the lake navigation. It would be simply a harbor improvement. It would be for the advantage of the lake navigation.

Q. (By Mr. KENNEDY.) I would like to ask if the members of your association have taken any interest in the proposition to make the drainage canal navigable for vessels of light draft? Of course, it is merely a matter of discussion so far.—A. We have taken no action upon that; have not had that brought to us at all.

Q. Have you any idea what the sentiment of your association would be on a proposition of that kind, if it should take legislative shape?—A. I think it would be solely a question as to whether it would increase the amount of water abstracted from Lake Michigan through the canal.

Q. (By Mr. PHILLIPS.) Under the head of No. 71 in this plan of inquiry there is a question as to "effect of the closing of lake navigation on rates of transportation between the Mississippi Valley and the seaboard; importance as a factor in maintaining reasonable rates; efforts to control freight rates on the Great Lakes; methods employed to that end." Could you give us information on that?—A. I can not give any definite information on that point further than to say that the railroads do not make the differences that they formerly did in their rates between the season of navigation and the winter season. That is as far as I can go. I can not give you any information on that.

I have a little information here on the subject of shipbuilding that I thought might be of interest—shipbuilding on the lakes. There are at the present time under construction in the lake shipyards vessels having an estimated carrying capacity of 185,500 tons and a cost of $8,902,000. These are now building in the lake shipyards and will come out during the coming season. That is the greatest carrying capacity and value of ships that was ever built on the Great Lakes in any one year.

Q. (By Mr. KENNEDY.) Are these American vessels?—A. There are one or two Canadian vessels, but they are small and affect the totals only in the smallest way. I think, so far as I know, out of the $8,902,000 value of the ships now building less than $400,000 is Canadian and $8,500,000 American. In 1898, at the same time, vessels were building aggregating 71,400 tons capacity, and having a value of $2,974,000. That shows the very great activity in ship building now prevailing on account of the prosperous season last year on the lakes. Instead of $3,000,000 value of vessels there are $9,000,000 value of vessels now building, and they are the largest type of vessels that have ever been constructed on the lakes. I will read a description of the first two being built by the American Ship Building Company at Loraine: Length over all, 498 feet; breadth, 52 feet; depth, 30 feet; approximate value, $360,000; estimated capacity in gross tons on 18-foot draft of 7,900 tons; quadruple expansion engines, 1,800 horsepower.

Q. Are many of them of the whale-back type?—A. No; none at all.

Q. (By Mr. FARQUHAR.) Are many of the whale backs being built now?—A. None. A 500 footer—that is the first 500 footer we have seen on the lakes—is coming out the coming season. These are practically all steel boats; there are very few wooden boats building.

Q. (By Mr. PHILLIPS.) Is there any reason why they are not building whale backs?—A. The company that built the whale backs is now building one boat. I think, which is not a whale back; and no other company excepting that has ever built a whale back.

As showing the growth of the steel construction on the lakes, I will say that in 1886 there were 6 steel vessels on the Great Lakes; in 1891 there were 89; in 1899 there were 296.

Q. (By Mr. KENNEDY.) How many are building now, or did you state?—A. About 30 now building this winter, most of them of very large size—boats costing all the way from barges costing from $175,000 to $200,000 and steamers costing as high as $360,000.

Q. Could many of these vessels be availed of for military purposes in case of war?—A. I could not state.

Q. Could not be equipped?—A. That is a question I could not answer.

Q. (By Mr. PHILLIPS.) What is the capacity of the largest vessels in tonnage on the lakes?—A. Those vessels now building by the American Ship Building Company at Loraine—498 feet long, steamers—have a carrying capacity on 18-foot draft of water of 7,900 gross tons, which is about 9,000 net tons.

Q. What amount of tons would the largest vessel carry 10 years ago, as compared with those you named now?—A. The largest cargo brought from the upper lakes down to Lake Erie, down to 1891, was 3,527 tons, and the largest cargo that passed through the St. Marys Falls Canal last year (1899) was 8,215 tons.

Q. Could you tell about the difference in the freight rate during that period—along about that period—and at present?—A. Last year's freight rates were high. A better comparison, as showing the course of freight rates downward as the vessels increased, would be the rates of 1898 as compared with 1890.

Q. We would be glad to have that comparison.—A. The rates on ore in 1891 from Lake Superior ports to Lake Erie ports varied during different parts of the season from 90 cents a ton to $1.50 a ton, the average for 1891 being about $1.15 or $1.20. In 1898 the large proportion of the iron ore was brought down at 65 cents. The vessel has to pay for loading and unloading out of these freights.

Q. (By Mr. KENNEDY.) Can you make a comparison between the freight rate for a given number of years and the wages paid on these vessels? For instance, you state that the rate last year for freight was very high; I would like to know if the rate of wages was correspondingly high.—A. I have not the data for that; I can not give it to you.

Q. Will not your cards that you say you send out from year to year show that?—A. Yes; and if I had the cards here I could form some estimate; but I haven't them.

Q. (By Mr. PHILLIPS.) Could you furnish that information to the commission?—A. I presume I could send you cards showing the rate of wages last year, in the season of high freight rates, and in the year before, which was a season of low ones.

Q. (By Mr. KENNEDY.) Will you do that; put it in your testimony?—A. Yes. The cards change variously during the year. The cards are based on supply and demand to a certain extent, as well as the rates of freight. When men get scarce a higher card goes into effect.

Q. Is not that true also of freight rates?—A. Yes; they change the same way. The Lake Carriers' Association has never since its organization undertaken the slightest interference with the natural law of supply and demand as far as freight rates are concerned. On ore the freight rate is largely now a season rate, for reasons I have already stated. On grain the freight rate fluctuates from time to time, purely and simply on the question of supply and demand of boats. The rate may rise one-fourth cent at Chicago for a shipment of corn to Buffalo because the boats are scarce, and it may go back the next day. It operates entirely and under the control absolutely of competition.

Q. No doubt these figures you have in regard to the rates in force during the last year will show that the lake traffic people enjoyed great prosperity. Have the men that work on the boats been enjoying a proportionate share of that prosperity?—A. I will try and send you a set of the cards. I might say in that regard, however, that the prosperity of the season of 1898 was very unequally distributed on the lakes on account of this question of season contracts. Many of the vessels had tied up their tonnage at a very low rate for the greater part of last season, and they did not get the profit out of the season that the vessels did that got the going rate for the season. Now, during the coming season the contract rate is higher than last year, and the vessels that tie up at the contract rate for next season will do much better than those who tied up to it last season. The owner of the smaller vessels had the best profits last year, because, rather than tie up his boat at a low rate for the season, he took his chances on the wild rate, and he got the high rates last year, whereas the man with the large carrying capacity did not dare to trust to trip charters, and as a rule he tied up his boat under a season contract at the lower rate.

Q. (By Mr. FARQUHAR.) Is it not a fact that it is almost impossible to make an average as to seamen's wages on the lakes for the season, or as to freight rates?—A. Yes.

Q. Have you ever known of an average being made?—A. No.

Q. Fluctuations are of such character that it is utterly impossible to take two figures and divide at either extreme?—A. Yes; you can not do it. The freight rate may be the prevailing rate for two weeks, for example, on grain in Chicago, and it may be so high as to shut off the business; and it may go down one-fourth cent, and in a few days there might be more business done than during that two weeks. So, taking into account the time they remained in effect and the amount of trade during the time they remained in effect, no true average can be obtained.

Q. Is the passenger business on the lakes growing?—A. The passenger business on the lakes is growing.

Q. You have some exclusively passenger boats?—A. Yes.

Q. What is the size of the boats?—A. The Great Northern Railroad have two passenger boats nearly 400 feet long and costing them about $800,000 each running between Buffalo and Duluth, and making the round trip in 6½ days—2,000 miles. They are fitted with the very best accommodations in every respect, as luxurious as the best ocean liners, and they carry not a pound of freight. They are very large twin-screw vessels, and built exclusively for the passenger service.

Q. Do they carry a large number of passengers?—A. The season is short. They do not go into operation until early in June; generally stop running in September; but they are crowded during that season.

Q. (By Mr. KENNEDY.) Tourist traffic?—A. Tourist traffic. Then there is another class of vessels that are doing a large passenger business in connection with the package freight business, such as the boats between Buffalo and Cleveland, between Cleveland and Detroit, night service between Detroit and Mackinaw, and night service between Chicago and Mackinaw, and Chicago and Milwaukee.

Q. (By Mr. PHILLIPS.) Is there considerable service between the United States and Canada?—A. There is a line running from the mouth of the Niagara River to Toronto—one or two boats daily in the summer time—a passenger business of considerable size. That is the only international service—that and the ferry service at Detroit, except on the St. Lawrence River.

Q. (By Mr. FARQUHAR.) Are the facilities of navigation at the Soo now large enough to take care of the whole traffic of Lake Superior?—A. They need very extensive improvement, just as soon as they can get at it. There were two blockades in the Soo River this last season, which cost the vessels a million dollars in delay. The Soo channels in several places are only 300 feet wide. They are running boats down there 500 feet long. In one case last summer the steamer *Geoffrey Houghton*, of the Bessemer Company, broke her wheel chains just as she was approaching a turn, at a point called the "Sailor's Encampment," where the channel is only 300 feet wide. She was towing a large barge and had 7,000 or 8,000 tons of cargo; she swerved and stuck her nose in the bank and her stern swung across, and the barge came down and collided with the steamer and sunk her. It took about 5 days to get her out of the channel, and it cost the vessels about three-quarters of a million dollars in time.

Q. Is there more than one channel from the Soo down to Lake Huron?—A. Practically only one—what is called the Hay Lake Channel. There was an old channel from the Soo down to Lake Huron, which had about 14½ or 15 feet of water. The Government has since constructed what is known as the Hay Lake Channel, which cuts off the old channel, and the available draft of vessels through the Hay Lake Channel is about 18 feet. The old channel is therefore practically not available. Although there is 15 feet of water, it is not available for the class of vessels now running. So when this vessel, the *Geoffrey Houghton*, sank in the channel she tied up the tonnage. The other boats were heavily loaded and could not go through the old channel.

Q. What are the proposed improvements?—A. Two plans are proposed; one to widen the channel where it is now 300 feet to a minimum of 600 feet, and have no points where it is less than 600 feet; the other is to diverge from the present channel, just below the "Sailors' Encampment," and make the West Neebish Channel, leaving the old channel 300 feet wide and making a new one 300 feet wide. The latter is the plan which the vessel men favor, as you can not blockade two channels at once. It is only a question of time when we will get 600-foot boats which will blockade a 600-foot channel; but you can not blockade two 300-foot channels with one disaster.

Q. Is the Hay Lake Channel navigable at night?—A. Yes; the boats not loaded to full capacity come up; but where they are very heavily loaded they will not dare go down at night. They wait until daylight, or plan their trips so as to reach the river in the daytime.

Q. Have you any comparative figures of the traffic through the Soo locks and through the Suez Canal?—A. I have a table showing a comparison between the Soo and the Suez Canal, as far as traffic is concerned. The last figures for the Suez were 1897. The traffic through that canal, in ship tonnage, was 7,899,373 tons. During the same year the traffic through the St. Marys Falls Canal was 18,982,755 tons. The traffic of the St. Marys Falls Canal has since increased so that the vessel tonnage through it in 1899 was 21,958,347 tons, about 2¾ times the traffic of the Suez Canal, and the St. Marys Falls Canal is open less than 8 months in the year.

Q. Your facilities for loading and unloading in port are considerably more than they were 6 or 8 years ago, are they not?—A. The methods of unloading and loading boats are constantly improving. The lake season being a short one, and the vessels being only in commission about two-thirds of the year, the question of dispatch in port is one of great importance to the boats. The machinery has been very greatly improved in the last few years for the handling of cargo.

Q. How long would the detention of a boat be now for unloading, supposing you got her docked on arrival?—A. A vessel could come into Buffalo with 260,000 or 270,000 bushels of wheat and be unloaded—she might arrive in the early morning, have her cargo unloaded and get a load of coal and get out the same night.

Q. (By Mr. RATCHFORD.) When does the lake season begin?—A. With the opening of the Straits of Mackinaw; about the 20th of April.

Q. Is there not a specified time in which the insurance takes place?—A. Not for the opening. As a rule the insurance expires on a certain day, but season insurance begins when the straits are reported open.

Q. Formerly did not the insurance on a boat begin some time about the middle of May and end about the last of October?—A. Not so far as I know. That must have been long before my connection with the lake business.

Q. (By Mr. PHILLIPS.) What day does insurance end now?—A. There has been some variation in that of late years. Some of the policies expire the 1st of December, some the 5th, some run as late as the 12th. They expire at noon of any one of those days. If the vessel is on a voyage at that time the insurance covers her until she completes the voyage.

Q. (By Mr. FARQUHAR.) Is there any fault found with the terminal or transfer charges at Buffalo now with respect to grain?—A. That is a rather hard question to answer. There is always fault found with all charges, but the charges at Buffalo have been decreased during the last 2 years; and those that know what the charges are now, I think, are not inclined to find fault with them. The transfer charge on grain at Buffalo is only one-half cent per bushel now.

Q. Is there any combination of the elevators at Buffalo?—A. There is an elevator association; yes.

Q. How many working elevators does that association control?—A. Last season there were no elevators in the association except working elevators.

Q. Are these elevators combined with reference to a division of profits?—A. The elevator association last season was an association solely of working elevators, having rail connections; houses that were not working or that were situated on islands and that could only unload into canal boats and not into railroad cars, were not in the association. The elevators in the association are some of them owned by individuals, some by companies, and some by railroads.

Q. (By Mr. PHILLIPS.) Is this association a joint stock concern?—A. I think not.

Q. (By Mr. FARQUHAR.) Is it a pooling arrangement?—A. It is a pooling arrangement.

Q. How much of the elevator business of Buffalo does it control?—A. It did almost all the business last year. A few of the canal houses, not taken into the association transacted a little business in taking grain out of vessels and loading it into canal boats—but the association did practically all the business.

Q. Do the trunk lines have their own elevators?—A. They have; most of them. The New York Central has its elevators; the Erie has its elevators; I think the Lehigh Valley has none; the Lackawanna, I think, has one small elevator; the Great Northern Railroad has its own elevator, and the Pennsylvania Railroad has an elevator.

Q. You say the charge is now one-half cent?—A. Yes. That includes the elevation of the grain and 10 days' storage.

Q. What was the old rate?—A. The old rate was seven-eighths cent.

Q. How long did seven-eighths cent remain as the rate there in Buffalo?—A. I can not tell you the number of years; quite a number of years prior to 1898. In 1898 there was no association and no fixed rate. In 1899 an elevator association was again formed and the rate was made one-half cent. It had never been lower than seven-eighths cent before.

Q. Is the commerce of the Erie Canal increasing or decreasing?—A. Decreasing.

Q. What is the reason; railroad competition?—A. Railroads have improved their service and lowered their rates, and the canal itself has not been improved for a long period of time. The canal-boat business has not been a profitable or prosperous business, so there have not been any new boats built. Even if freight rates materially advance now, there are no boats to do any large business on the canal. The number of boats on the canal in condition to carry grain cargo is decreasing every year as the boats get older, and there are no new boats being built. The Erie Canal must, therefore, in a few years drop out of the grain business altogether unless some radical change in the condition of the canal is made.

Q. What was the rate on wheat to Buffalo last season?—A. It is difficult to say; I can not answer. Most of it is contracted through from the West, including lake and rail. It is impossible to say what the rail rate east of Buffalo is.

Q. You are not aware of any rates made from Buffalo through to New York?—A. There are rates called " ex-lake rates " from Buffalo to New York, but I can not tell you what they are. They vary according to the rail situation.

Q. So you would say it is impossible for the canal, in its present condition and the character of the freight carriers on the canal, to compete with railroads?—A. It certainly is impossible.

Q. What is the position of your firms: is it favorable to the improvement of the canal?—A. Favorable toward an adequate improvement of the canal. I think the general understanding among lake men and well-posted transportation people in Buffalo is that the canal should either be abandoned or adequately improved. A small improvement would be of no use; it must be built over practically—modernized.

Q. Are you aware of any sentiment of the farmers of the Northwest in respect to the improvement of this canal?—A. There has been a sentiment in the West for a deep waterway from the lakes to the East.

Q. A ship canal?—A. A ship canal. Probably that same sentiment would be in favor of a barge canal if it could be shown that a barge canal could handle the freight as economically as a ship canal. Major Simons made a pretty exhaustive study of the question, and he has reached the conclusion that freight can be carried from the lakes to the sea much more cheaply by barge than by ship canal. In other words, to put the expensive lake ship into the canal with its great number of locks and stops and slow progress would be a more expensive way of carrying the grain than in barges built cheaply. The extra transfer would be more than made up by the fact that you were carrying the grain all the time in a vessel best adapted to that use; that you were carrying on the lakes in a vessel built just right for the lake service, and on the canal in a vessel best adapted to the canal, and on the ocean in a vessel best adapted for ocean service. In a boat adapted to all of these services you would lose in efficiency.

Q. You had a commission in New York that passed on this matter?—A. The State commission has just reported to the governor, urging the improvement of the Erie Canal by making it 11 feet deep, with an available draft of water for boats of 10 feet, and capable of handling boats 25 feet wide and 150 feet long, with 10 feet draft of water, with all the single locks arranged so as to take in 2 of these boats at once. The idea is that the boats would be handled with 1 canal steamboat pushing 1 barge ahead of it, and towing 2 behind, 1,000 tons to the load, making the total tow 4,000 tons.

Q. And the prospective cost of that is reported as how much, by the commission?—A. For the improvement of the Erie Canal proper about $58,500,000, and for the Oswego Canal, the completion of what is called the Seymour plan, some $3,500,000 more, making a total cost of $62,000,000.

Q. This great commerce of the inland lakes and the prosperity that has come to those cities and States, and the development of all these lines, has come from the legislation, has it not, of the National Government, so far as navigation is concerned?—A. Originally there was only about 9 feet of water in the shallow parts of the St. Marys and Detroit rivers; and, of course, it was by the improvement of the channels and harbors that this traffic was made possible.

Q. (By Mr. PHILLIPS.) It was done by the General Government?—A. Yes.

Q. (By Mr. FARQUHAR.) What is the depth at the lowest points between Duluth and Buffalo, now?—A. The Government is engaged in the dredging of a 20 and 21 foot channel; 20 feet in still water and 21 feet when subject to wave action; but up to date the available draft is 18 feet on the average.

Q. What is the highest tonnage you can use on 18 feet?—A. The largest vessels will carry about 9,000 tons of freight. The vessels now building and that will be out this spring will carry about 9,000 tons. Up to the present time the largest cargo has been about 8,300 tons.

Q. Are you acquainted with the United States statute that protects all lake navigation and lake trade?—A. (Reading.) " Section 4 of the act of 1817. No goods, wares, or merchandise shall be imported under penalty of forfeiture thereof from one port of the United States to another port thereof in a vessel belonging wholly or in part to a subject of any foreign power; but this clause shall not be construed to prohibit the sailing of any foreign vessel from one to another part of the United States, provided no goods, wares, or merchandise, other than those imported in such vessels from such foreign port, and which shall not be unladen, shall be carried from one port or place to another in the United States." It is a general provision for the protection of the coastwise trade

Q. Is not that really the foundation of the great lake trade, the fact that the Canadians can not interfere with your commerce?—A. It is impossible to say what proportion of the commerce the Canadians would have carried on but for that statute. I might say they do not carry on much of the foreign commerce on the lakes. The commerce between American and Canadian ports is almost entirely in the hands of American vessels.

Q. The Canadian tonnage cuts a small figure?—A. Very small, indeed.

Q. Can you give the figures?—A. To show the proportion between the business done by the American and the Canadian vessels: During the season of 1899, through the St. Marys Falls Canals, American vessels carried 96.9 per cent of the freight and the Canadian 3.1 per cent.

Q. The Canadians have their own canal, have they not?—A. Yes. They have the free use of our canal and we have the free use of theirs. While the most of our vessels take the American canal, if they find they are going to be subjected to delay they go to the other lock. There is no charge by the Government for the use of the canal. Some years ago a question arose between the Lake Carriers' Association and the Canadian government as to the right of the Canadian government to make certain regulations that they were making at the Welland Canal. They were charging a toll of 20 cents per ton on all freight carried through the Welland Canal, but if they carried the freight to Montreal they rebated 18 cents of the 20 cents, while if it stopped at Ogdensburg or some other American port they rebated nothing. The Lake Carriers' Association called the attention of the State Department to the matter and complained of it as a violation of the treaty of Washington between the United States and Great Britain. The State Department took the ground that our contention was well-founded, and complained to the Canadian government, and the result was that, no relief being obtained, our Government made discriminating tolls for a short time at the St. Marys Falls Canal against Canadian vessels. That was before the foreign lock was completed, and as a result of that one season the discrimination at the Welland Canal was abolished and a uniform rate of 10 cents was made whether the grain went to Montreal or Ogdensburg.

Q. (By Mr. FARQUHAR.) Has there ever been any effort made to control freight rates on the lakes by any kind of combination? Do you think it is possible that any combination could last over one season?—A. No effort has ever been made, so far as I know, and it would be a very difficult matter. The boats are owned by a great variety of individuals and companies and the business has always been on a competitive basis. No attempt has been made to control it, and nobody has ever thought they could control it. There was some talk 2 or 3 years ago, during a very dull season, when vessels were tying up at the docks and making no money, about an effort to get the vessel owners together and agree on a minimum freight; that no one would carry at less than the minimum rate; but no progress was made and it was given up as impossible. Aside from that I never heard of any attempt to control freight rates.

Q. From your preliminary remarks as to what the association was and what purpose it had, borne out by your answers, it might be inferred that the association, possibly, is a monopoly itself.—A. It owns no vessels and is not engaged in the transportation business. It is simply an association of vessel owners to act together in matters of common interest. They never have taken up the question of freights.

Q. Has not the Lake Carriers' Association's purpose been to gain from Congress and from the National Government aids in the way of navigation laws?—A. That has been one of its principal purposes; but it has existed for the purpose of carrying on the necessary private lights, maintaining these shipping offices and contracting with contractors for uniform prices for loading and unloading lake freights of various kinds.

Q. Now, where the Government had neither erected nor maintained a light at any point, and navigation needed that light, did the Lake Carriers' Association establish one and maintain the expense of it?—A. In some cases. Not in all cases; but at vital points in the St. Marys River and Detroit River and St. Clair River, where vessels were going through crowded, narrow channels, and where lights were needed in the water, or on the Canadian shore, and were not supplied by our Government or the Canadian government, we have supplied them at our own expense.

Q. (By Mr. SMITH.) How many?—A. It varied from season to season. A number that we used to maintain have since been taken over by our Government; but there are at least 6 lights in the Lower Detroit River which we have maintained for the last 10 years.

(Testimony closed.)

ARGUMENT OF DAVID J. LEWIS (CUMBERLAND, MD.)

IN FAVOR OF THE PURCHASE AND OPERATION BY THE GOVERN-
MENT OF RAILWAYS ENGAGED IN INTERSTATE COMMERCE.

THE UNITED STATES INDUSTRIAL COMMISSION,
  Subcommission of Transportation, Washington, D. C.

GENTLEMEN: In response to the letter of the Hon. J. L. Kennedy, dated February 23, 1899, suggesting that he thought "testimony" from me "on the subject of
transportation would be very valuable to the Industrial Commission," I beg leave
herewith to present my views on the subject of railway transportation. I observe
in your syllabus on transportation, section No. 58, the query, "Ownership and operation by the United States of railroads engaged in interstate commerce, arguments
for and against it." My contribution is intended as an argument in favor of the
governmental ownership of all railways so engaged in interstate commerce. An
impartial investigation of the subject has convinced me that the following great
attainments may be secured:

First. The just security of the capital invested upon the basis of its commercial
worth. Precarious securities will become things of the past.

Second. Uniformity and equality of freight rates among shippers; the elimination of quasi natural discriminations as well as willful.

Third. A half-cent passenger rate per mile over the entire country.

Fourth. An 8-hour day for all railway workers; and the consequent employment of 165,000 of the unemployed to fill this one-fifth reduction in time.

Fifth. The greater development of the natural resources of the country by a
sensible application of the capital now invested in "parallels," etc.

Sixth. A juster distribution of railway mileage to the population and area of the
several States; the grossest inequality is the necessary effect of the present system.

Seventh. The establishment of a system of postal express, which it seems might
be conducted, in conjunction with the post-office, at half the present cost to the
public.

Eighth. The institution of accident insurance for passengers, employees, and
freight under certain limitations.

Ninth. The emancipation of public men from the evil influences of railway
"politics," and the attainment of free elections.

Tenth. The adoption by the Government of punitive freight rates, when considered necessary to destroy existing trusts and discourage the formation of others.

It will be observed from the reading of the following chapters that, first, the
real railway owners are justly protected; second, the shipping interests of the
country fully secured under the assurance of equal freight rates; third, that the
800,000 railway employees will be engaged by the prospect of an 8-hour workday;
fourth, that the general public will be profited by the half-cent-a-mile passenger
rate, while, fifth, every patriotic mind must be deeply impressed with the certainty of a better railway development of the entire country, the safety of railway
travelers and employees, a system of railway accident insurance, the institution
of postal express, and, finally, the elimination forever from our industrial and
political systems of discriminations in rates, rebates to favored shippers, etc., on
the one hand, and passes, railway lobbies, alliances with trusts, railway politics,
the corruptions of legislatures, etc., which have made the history of our country
in the last 30 years almost too sickening for patriotism to read.

It is submitted that no just interest of either the railway owners or the public
is attacked, while all the American people are favorably engaged by the attainments which I believe are easily reached. Independently of the conclusions
deduced from a study of the data of railway economics shown in the Interstate
Commerce Commission's reports, we have the definite and uniform experience of
more than a half dozen different nations who own and operate their respective
railways. Germany, Austro-Hungary, Belgium, British India, and each of the
Australian colonies have shown, by their experience, the complete consistency
and practicability of low passenger rates, equality of freight rates, reduced hours
of labor, perfect freedom from "politics" under State ownership and operation
of their railways.

A very dark prospect is presented to this and coming generations unless we imitate their prudence in our own country. It is now a fact recognized by all observant citizens that the "pass" evil, the legislative lobby, the interference in primaries and elections, the general preference of "trust" shippers over their fellow competitors, and the treasonable influence exerted by railway managers upon their dependent employees during elections, have each and all become permanent features of modern business, legislation, politics, and private railway management and ownership.

Can merely regulative and repressive legislation cure these evils inherent in our present system of railways? Twenty years of attempted regulation and repression answer no. It is in the hope that they may be cured by the only means competent to cure them, namely, the elimination of private interests, that I have submitted my testimony in favor of government ownership to your commission.

It is always a fair question in a republic, "Will this proposal be popular among the people?" My uniform conversation with them leads me to emphatically answer yes. They have long despaired of good from the present system, and while the studious generally commend the governmental assumption of powers, which have long since outgrown the coexisting powers of the Republic, the others have become accustomed to look rather to some ill-determined day of revolutionary accounting. Looking to analogous proposals we do know that municipal ownership and operation of varied industries, ranging from water, electric, gas, and street-railway enterprises, have not lost a single election in any city in the United States, and have been attended in their practical operation by the most gratifying success.

It is in the hope that your honorable commission will not hesitate to recommend any proposal which convinces your judgments of its value, and in the belief that the perpetuation of the collective interests of a people is the first duty of a citizen, I submit to your commission my testimony under the invitation you have so kindly given me.

Respectfully submitted.   DAVID J. LEWIS.
CUMBERLAND, MD., *March 3, 1899.*

THE RAILWAYS AND THE STATES.

[Extract from speech of James A. Garfield in Congress, June 22, 1874.]

Since the dawn of history, the great thoroughfares have belonged to the people, have been known as the king's highways, or the public highways, and have been open to the free use of all, on payment of a small uniform tax or toll, to keep them in repair. But now the most perfect, and by far the most important roads known to mankind, are owned and managed as private property by a comparatively small number of private citizens.

In all its uses the railroad is the most public of all our roads; and in all the objects to which its work relates, the railroad corporation is as public as any corporation can be. But in the start it was labeled a private corporation; and, so far as its legal status is concerned, it is now grouped with eleemosynary institutions and private charities, and enjoys similar immunities and exemptions. It remains to be seen how long the community will suffer itself to be a victim of an abstract definition.

*   *   *   *   *   *   *

It is painfully evident from the experience of the last few years, that the efforts of the States to regulate their railroads have amounted to little more than feeble annoyance. In many cases the corporations have treated such efforts as impertinent meddling, and have brushed away legislative restrictions as easily as Gulliver broke the cords with which the Lilliputions attempted to bind him.

In these contests the corporations have become conscious of their strength, and have entered upon the work of controlling the States. Already they have captured some of the oldest and strongest of them; and these discrowned sovereigns now follow in chains the triumphal chariot of their conquerors. And this does not imply that merely the officers and representatives of States have been subjected to the railways, but that the corporations have grasped the sources and fountains of power, and control the choice of both officers and representatives.

*   *   *   *   *   *   *

The consolidation of our great commercial companies, the power they wield and the relations they sustain to the State and to the industry of the people, do not fall far short of Fourier's definition of commercial and industrial feudalism. The modern barons, more powerful than their military prototypes, own our greatest highways and levy tribute at will on all our vast industries. And, as the old feudalism was finally controlled and subordinated only by the combined effort of the kings and the people of the free cities and towns, so our modern feudalism can be subordinated to the public good only by the great body of the people, acting through their governments by wise and just laws.

I.—RAILWAY CAPITAL.

The real railway capitalist, that is, the bona fide owner of railway stocks or bonds, is, I believe, to be first considered in any general legislation or social measures undertaken with relation to our railroads. I refer, of course, to the people who have in fact invested their money in this form of property, and who are entitled presumably to the same fruits of abstinence usually accorded to other investors. That there is an immense amount of such capital so invested in railways, that it is the most useful in the economic sense, that it deserves the same respect in which we hold other acquisitions of wealth, not even the crimes and misdoings of some railway managers .will lead me to deny. Let me say, then, that I propose to treat these owners of property just as I should treat any other investor or investment; that is, as the general commercial world would treat them if it desired to purchase their property.

It is a fact that railway investments, permanent though the subject-matter is, have been almost the most precarious property in all the range of public securities. One should not expect this charge to be true. The railway is itself more permanent than houses and land; banks may go under, great droughts may palsy the harvests of labor, forms of government themselves vacilate, while the railroad and its traffic is almost as constant as the currents of the sea. Laid deep and induring in the soil of the continent they are physical facts more lasting in character than other property, and yet experience teaches us that the stock and bond holders of American railways are the most uncertain and perhaps the least recompensed of all its capitalists.

The reason for this must be found in some other explanation than the subject, matter of his investment. That we believe is even more constant than any other species of property. The reason we believe to be the inefficiency of private railway ownership and management.

THE INSTABILITY OF RAILWAY CAPITAL.

At this point I invite the reader's attention to a list of the 30 principal railway systems of the country, operating 95,270 miles of road, for the purpose of showing the almost frightful instability of railway capital. (The fractions are omitted.)

Name of railway.	Miles operated.	Stock, 1897.		Stock, 1898.		Bonds, 1897.		Bonds, 1898	
		H.	L.	H.	L.	H.	L.	H.	L.
Atchison, Topeka and Santa Fe	6,946	13	9	19	10	90	78	100	85
Chicago, Burlington and Quincy	7,180	102	69	125	85	120	115	118	113
Baltimore and Ohio	2,048	21	9	72	12	90	76	118	80
Chicago Great Western	930	20	3	18	9				
Chicago, Milwaukee and St. Paul	6,153	102	69	120	83				
Chicago and Northwestern	6,486	132	101	143	113				
Chicago, Rock Island and Pacific	3,571	97	60	114	80				
Chicago, St. Paul, Minneapolis and Omaha	1,492	89	47	94	65	142	128	163	138
Denver and Rio Grande	1,698	14	9	21	10	113	108	112	108
Erie	2,271	19	11	16	11	95	88	94	84
Great Northern	4,698	141	120	180	122				
Illinois Central	4,140	110	91	115	96	113	110	115	109
Lake Erie and Western	890	22	13	23	12	104	99	106	95
Lehigh Valley	1,255	32	20			106	102	105	100
Louisville and Northern	5,028	63	40	65	44	103	99	108	101
Missouri, Kansas and Texas	2,147	16	10	14	10	88	82	92	82
Missouri Pacific	5,368	40	10	46	22	98	68	110	93
New York Central and Hudson River	2,395	115	92	124	105	121	117	119	113
Northern Pacific	4,502	22	11	61	35	96	85	103	90
Reading	2,515	29	16	23	15	86	80	89	77
Rio Grande Western	520	25	14	32	23	84	70	93	78
Southern Pacific	6,664	23	13	35	12	105	90	112	100
Southern Railway	5,232	12	7	10	7	95	87	106	87
St. Louis Southwestern	1,223	7	1	·7	3	76	59	85	70
Toledo, Peoria and Western	248					73	60	80	69
Texas and Pacific	1,499	15	18	20	8	98	85	110	98
Union Pacific	4,888	27	4	36	23	105	101	124	115
Union Pacific, Denver and Gulf	901	11	1	13	3	52	45	88	48
Wabash Railway	1,936	.9	4	9	6	108	101	114	104
Wisconsin Central	938	4	1	4	1	38	31	7	4
Total	95,270								

The total railway capital is seen to fluctuate in stocks anywhere from 30 to 300 per cent, and in bonds from 5 to 100 per cent, in each of both years. Is this fair to the people who must invest their savings in railways? For somebody must. It certainly is not good for them, when the principal fluctuates considerably above. the expected interest. It may be contended that these quotations represent but a part of the capital, and that the larger part never changes hands. That is a mistake. According to Henry Clews & Co.'s statement for 1897, more than 50,000,000 shares of railway stock were sold on the New York Stock Exchange in that year alone, being more than the full equivalent of the total railway stock. In the same year $500,000,000 of railway bonds were sold in the New York Stock Exchange alone. Crediting London (and an immense amount of railway securities are held there), Paris, Boston, Philadelphia, Baltimore, Chicago, San Francisco, and other cities together with an equal amount for that year, it seems certain the full equivalent of our railway stock and at least one-quarter of the bonds were covered twice. But can there be any question that sales on the Stock Exchange fix the price? Suppose the whole stock or bonds were offered, would they bring more or fluctuate less? Now, as to the proposed form of capital which it is designed should replace the present, will it fluctuate? The question answers itself.

Of course, Government capital will eliminate this evil, an evil that honest investors should at once correct. For just as this great field of vacillating values is redeemed by the substitution of stable capital, the gambler will give place to the savings bank and sober thrift. The lottery has long been recognized as a crime against society. What, then, can be said for that railway capital which necessitates a condition as much worse as it is infinitely greater in proportion. The stock exchange may not be blamed. It is the character of the stocks and bonds, which, inspiring alternately hope and fear, demoralizes alike the minds of great and humble. This instability creates fortune hunters who in other circumstances would be willing to live by their work instead of their wits.

Railway stocks and bonds constitute about 75 per cent of this gambling media, and if they were redeemed as proposed a like reduction of this crime and folly must result. Besides, this proposal would seem to guarantee the perfection of capital by eliminating all hazard. It delivers this great body of active wealth from the hands of anarchy and plants it forever in the realm of security. But grant that many who thrive in stock gambling may be forced to work, will not those who fought so fiercely for financial stability in 1896 apply their influence to correct the prodigious disorder which dominates the railway capital of to-day?

It will not be denied that two railways, operating in a district where one can meet the needs of society, represent only waste of capital, waste of labor, current expenditures, a double system of capital and expenditures, which, not enlarging the supply of traffic, must either result in advanced rates to support these charges or fall with ruinous havoc upon the real owners of the road. If they indeed compete, this only hastens and aggravates the disaster which a false principle applied to railway capital naturally insures. On the other hand, human selfishness can not be safely trusted with a monopoly in the railway business any more than in any other where men's interests conflict. Not a State constitution but does inhibit the granting of a monopoly, and yet competition in the railway business is as impossible, I was going to say, as a struggle between the planets. The people will not permit monopoly or a trusting of the interests involved, and competition will, if in fact indulged in, destroy all the capital invested.

My proposal, then, is this: That the whole people of the United States become the owners of our railway capital, and thus establish complete harmony of interests. That is, that the capital now invested in the 183,000 miles of railway be bought by the Government at its market value, and the railways then operated on the general principles of our Post-Office. This would not be a monopoly; every citizen would be a stockholder and equally enjoy the advantages flowing from such ownership and management.

The owners of railways should not object to this; they would secure for their property its full market value, in cash, which they could invest in the bonds of the United States, or in such other property as they may think proper. It was Daniel Webster, I think, who said, "If a thing can be done, a wise man who knows it can be ought to be able to tell us how it can be done." I shall now endeavor to indicate "how" it can be done.

The first question which will occur to the thinking reader is, "To buy the railways the Government must know how much they are worth; how can it determine their value?" Switzerland, Great Britain, and other countries have recently answered that question.

The method adopted in Switzerland (1898) in the purchase by that Government of her railways was to take the net profits of the railroads for 10 years, add them together, then divide by 10 to get the annual average profits, and then capitalize such profits at from 4 to 5 or 6 per cent. Thus suppose the average annual net profits were $1,000,000; this sum capitalized at 5 per cent would make the capital invested $20,000,000, which would thus be the full value of a railroad yielding such annual profits. Let us then apply this very just and commercial standard to American railways, and find what they are worth on the markets of the world, and what it would cost to purchase them.

At this point, then, let us see what the net profits upon American railways have been, i. e. the interest on bonds and the dividends on stock. The following tables are taken from Poor's Railroad Manual:

Miles of railroads operated, capital invested, earnings, and dividends in the United States from 1871 to 1897.

[Prepared by John P. Meany, editor of Poor's Railroad Manual.]

Year.	Miles operated.	Capital and funded debt (stock and bonds).	Earnings.				Dividends paid.
			Gross.	Net.	From freight.	From passengers.	
1871	44,614	$2,664,627,645	$403,329,209	$141,746,404	$294,430,322	$108,898,886	$56,456,681
1872	57,523	3,159,423,057	465,241,055	165,754,373	340,931,785	132,809,270	64,418,157
1873	66,237	3,784,543,034	526,419,935	183,810,562	389,035,508	137,384,427	67,120,709
1874	69,273	4,221,763,594	520,466,016	189,570,958	379,466,935	140,999,081	67,042,942
1875	71,759	4,415,631,680	508,065,505	185,506,488	363,960,294	139,105,271	74,294,208
1876	73,508	4,468,591,935	497,257,959	186,452,752	361,137,376	136,120,583	68,099,668
1877	74,112	4,568,597,248	472,909,272	170,976,897	342,859,222	130,050,050	58,536,312
1878	78,960	4,590,048,793	490,103,351	187,575,167	365,466,061	124,637,290	53,629,868
1879	79,009	4,715,136,465	525,690,577	218,544,909	386,676,108	142,336,191	61,681,470
1880	82,146	5,239,548,218	613,733,610	255,557,555	467,748,928	147,658,603	77,115,871
1881	92,971	6,055,798,785	701,780,982	272,406,787	551,968,477	173,356,642	93,344,190
1882	104,988	6,692,998,547	764,251,399	278,009,565	506,367,247	196,218,220	101,441,491
1883	110,381	7,155,205,297	817,376,576	295,737,078	549,756,695	206,837,258	101,662,548
1884	115,671	7,373,967,813	770,668,892	268,080,557	506,925,375	206,790,701	98,244,835
1885	128,280	7,518,864,803	765,310,519	286,488,963	519,690,992	200,883,911	76,112,105
1886	125,144	7,810,125,828	822,191,949	297,311,615	550,359,054	211,929,857	80,094,138
1887	136,956	8,302,586,330	931,385,154	331,135,676	636,666,228	240,542,876	78,943,041
1888	145,333	8,977,758,747	950,622,008	297,363,677	639,200,723	251,356,187	78,948,041
1889	158,689	9,231,276,871	992,046,319	317,963,074	665,962,331	259,439,231	79,531,863
1890	157,976	9,645,696,585	1,078,835,339	341,696,389	734,821,783	272,320,961	88,575,705
1891	164,262	9,981,977,522	1,125,534,815	350,807,370	754,185,910	290,799,696	89,009,757
1892	170,607	10,270,074,077	1,169,036,840	352,817,405	794,526,500	293,557,476	93,862,412
1893	173,361	10,531,802,079	1,207,106,026	358,648,918	808,494,668	311,042,870	94,295,815
1894	176,221	10,663,380,481	1,066,943,358	317,757,399	700,477,409	275,352,190	83,478,669
1895	179,154	10,830,033,035	1,092,395,437	323,196,464	743,784,451	260,929,741	81,685,774
1896	180,891	10,716,805,536	1,125,632,095	332,333,756	770,424,013	265,313,258	81,364,854
1897	181,133	10,859,239,923	1,128,546,666	338,170,195	780,351,939	253,557,986	82,630,989

Finances of railroads—Continued. Passengers and freight carried, etc.

Year.	Passengers carried.	Passengers carried 1 mile.	Average receipts per passenger per mile.	Freight carried.	Freight carried 1 mile.	Average receipts per ton per mile.
			Cents.	Tons.	Tons.	Cents.
1882	375,391,812	10,484,363,728	1.85	360,490,375	39,302,209,249	1.24
1883	312,686,641	8,541,309,674	2.42	400,453,439	44,064,923,445	1.22
1884	334,570,766	8,778,581,061	2.36	399,074,749	44,725,207,677	1.13
1885	351,427,688	9,183,673,956	2.20	437,040,099	49,151,894,469	1.06
1886	382,284,973	9,659,608,294	2.19	482,245,254	52,802,070,529	1.04
1887	428,225,513	10,570,306,710	2.28	552,074,752	61,561,069,996	1.08
1888	451,353,655	11,190,613,679	2.25	590,857,353	65,428,005,988	.98
1889	494,808,421	11,964,726,015	2.17	619,165,630	68,677,278,992	.97
1890	520,439,082	12,521,565,649	2.17	691,344,437	79,192,985,125	.93
1891	558,015,802	13,316,925,239	2.18	704,398,609	81,210,154,523	.98
1892	575,769,678	13,584,343,804	2.17	730,605,011	84,418,197,180	.94
1893	597,056,539	14,979,847,458	2.07	757,464,480	90,552,087,290	.89
1894	569,660,216	13,600,531,635	2.08	674,714,747	82,219,900,498	.88
1895	529,756,259	12,609,082,551	2.07	755,799,883	88,587,770,801	.84
1896	535,120,756	13,054,840,243	2.03	773,868,716	93,885,853,694	.82
1897	504,106,205	12,494,958,000	2.08	788,385,448	97,842,569,150	.80

Finances of railroads—Continued.   Passengers and freight carried, etc.—Cont'd.

Year.	Interest paid on bonds and other debt.	Dividends paid on stock.	Interest per cent of bonds and debt.	Dividends per cent of stock.	Earnings per mile of railroad in operation.		Percentage of expenses to earnings.
					Gross.	Net.	
	Dollars.	*Dollars.*			*Dollars.*	*Dollars.*	
1878	103,160,512	53,629,368	4.16	2.34	6,207	2,376	61.73
1879	112,235,515	61,681,470	4.53	2.57	6,653	2,741	58.80
1880	107,866,828	77,115,371	4.00	2.84	7,471	3,111	58.36
1881	128,587,302	93,344,190	4.16	2.94	7,548	2,930	61.18
1882	152,931,300	101,441,491	4.39	2.92	7,283	2,649	63.62
1883	171,774,984	101,662,548	4.58	2.77	7,405	2,679	63.82
1884	176,694,302	93,208,835	4.54	2.48	6,663	2,318	65.21
1885	185,986,991	77,672,105	4.65	2.02	6,265	2,185	65.12
1886	187,358,581	80,094,138	4.53	2.04	6,570	2,376	63.84
1887	202,009,042	90,018,458	4.54	2.18	6,861	2,444	64.45
1888	205,288,021	78,943,041	4.20	1.77	6,540	2,045	68.72
1889	216,877,898	79,531,863	4.23	1.81	6,455	2,068	67.95
1890	224,499,571	83,575,705	4.13	1.80	6,822	2,162	68.33
1891	228,572,703	89,099,757	4.14	1.85	6,852	2,136	68.83
1892	236,502,579	93,862,412	4.16	1.93	6,852	2,068	69.82
1893	244,965,446	94,295,815	4.14	1.88	6,963	2,069	70.29
1894	242,147,714	83,473,689	4.04	1.64	6,054	1,803	70.22
1895	247,895,884	81,685,774	4.09	1.58	6,097	1,804	72.41
1896	250,411,950	81,364,854	4.35	1.54	6,223	1,837	71.48
1897	236,680,114	82,630,989	4.09	1.52	6,203	1,867	69.91

From the foregoing is seen what the net profits have been for a long number of years.   The total interest paid on funded debt during five years (1893–1897) was $1,222,101,108, and the average for each year was just $244,420,221.   During same period the dividends paid on stock amounted to $423,456,101, from which should be deducted $81,817,018 deficits for the years 1894–1897, making the true net profits applicable to stock $341,639,083, or an average for each year of $68,327,816. Thus we have—

Average interest paid on funded debt, etc., for five years (1893–1897)
  equals $244,420,221, which capitalized at 5 per cent would make
  the bonds worth $4,888,404,420
Average dividends paid on stock during five years (1893–1897),
  $68,327,816, which capitalized at 6 per cent would make all the
  stock worth 1,138,796,934
Average rents paid (1896) for equipment, track yards, terminals,
  buildings, etc., equals $18,463,371, which capitalized at 12 per cent
  equals investment of... 221,561,856

Thus the entire funded debt, stock, and rented property would be
  capitalized at... 6,248,763,200

I shall treat this amount for simplicity's sake as six and a half billion dollars throughout the testimony.

I have selected five years, instead of ten as in Switzerland, because the amount of railway capital has not changed materially in that time, as may be seen from the preceding tables.

As to the rate at which I have capitalized the bonds, it may be said that some roads borrow at a lower rate than 5 per cent.   My answer is that the rate, while not true of particular roads, is true for the whole.   Looking over Haight and Freeze's Investment Guide for 1898, I find that while 81 companies have succeeded in borrowing at 4 per cent, yet 193 companies pay 5 per cent, and still 244 more pay 6 per cent and over.   So that I believe a 5 per cent capitalization expresses the truth for the value of the total funded debt of all railways.   In adjusting with the bondholders of a particular road, the settlement would be governed by the exact rate of such road, whether greater or less.   As to the 6 per cent capitalization for stock, the same observations apply.   The purpose is to be just to the owners.   But in order to do this commercial methods must guide us.   On the markets of the world a property is worth just what its income will capitalize. That is the test applied here.

It should be explained to those not acquainted with commercial methods in computing values of stocks and bonds that they may be worth on the market either more or less than their face value.   If stocks, for example, pay 6 per cent., they are at par; if they pay at the rate of 3 per cent only, then they are worth about 50 cents on the dollar; bonds (railroad mortgages) usually command about an average interest of 5 per cent, and are at par when such interest is regularly paid; if the interest is only half paid, the bonds sink correspondingly in value.   As a rule, securities sell on the market according to the rate of profits they annually pay, with certainty, and their values have no relation to what they cost, whether more or less than their quoted price. It would be unjust, therefore, to adopt any other standard for computing the values of railway stocks or bonds when the owners bought them on the market by commercial standards; and it would be equally unjust for such owners to ask any higher price for such stock and bonds than they are quoted at as productive securities.

Now, I have indicated how the Government might determine the value of the railroads as an entirety. The reports of the Interstate Commerce Commission, compiled from the sworn accounts made by the companies themselves, show exactly the capitalized values of all railway bonds and stocks as shown above. The next query a thinking man will make is, "How will you determine the value of the stock and bonds of each particular railway?" My answer is just precisely as we have determined it for the whole. It will take time and labor, of course; all business endeavors do. But having determined what it should pay for the roads as a whole, i. e., what their stocks and bonds are commercially worth, the Government would then take immediate possession of all the roads, and settle with individuals at its leisure, paying them usual profits during such delay.

I say it would take time to investigate the books of each company and determine from its average annual net profits the value of its stock and bonds. There are about 1,985 different companies. A year or two would suffice.

Now, I want to ask, is not this proposal perfectly just to the owners of the railways? It would substitute an absolutely certain Government bond for their precarious bonds or stock. Surely, then, real stockholders and bondholders can have no objection, as such, to the Government ownership of our railroads.

I will not cite cases as to what their lot at present is, and for years back has been. The American public knows their sad history only too well. The common stock of the Baltimore and Ohio Railroad sold some years ago, I am told, as high as $200 the share, while in the last three years it has been as low as $8. This is but one road; but very few of them can tell another tale. The rule is that railway securities are the most precarious and uncertain of all securities on the market. It is for that reason the stock gambler can mimic the marvels of Aladdin. For example, the Commission's report shows that for the year 1896, railway stock amounting to $3,667,503,195 paid no dividends. It is a mistake to suppose that none of this stock represents a real investment. A large portion actually was paid for. Then the same report shows that $860,559,442 in amount of their bond indebtedness paid no interest whatever; that another billion paid only from 1 to 3 per cent. I append hereto that statement to show how deeply concerned the investors of this country should be in any just proposal having for its object a fair and certain return to the people who put their savings in railway property.

The Interstate Commission reports show for the years 1895 and 1894, dividends paid to stock of $85,961,500 and $101,607,264. It would thus appear that my statement of average annual profits on stock were too low. But if the reader will notice in 1895 the deficit was $29,845,241, and in 1894 the deficit was $45,851,294, and in 1897 just $6,120,483. Thus the average dividend is about as stated. Just think of the viciousness of paying dividends that have never been earned, and refusing to pay the expenses of operation, in order to pay such false dividends. Suppose a bank did this? Would not the Government at once close its business?

The series of summaries which follows is designed to show the amount of dividends paid on railway stocks, and of interest paid on railway bonds. This information is presented in such a manner as to show the amount of stocks paying no dividends and of bonds paying no interest, as also the amounts paying at the several rates named.

Condensed statement of stocks and funded debt, classified by rate of dividend or interest, 1896.

Per cent paid.	Stocks.	Per cent of total stocks.	Funded debt (exclusive of equipment trust obligations).	Per cent of total funded debt.
Nothing paid	$3,667,503,194	70.17	$860,559,442	16.26
From 1 to 2	38,603,850	.74	233,556,980	4.42
From 2 to 3	138,160,882	2.64	438,582,638	8.29
From 3 to 4	87,569,321	1.68	420,346,647	7.95
From 4 to 5	290,062,078	5.55	1,270,172,756	24.01
From 5 to 6	356,305,879	6.82	1,138,564,031	21.52
From 6 to 7	204,150,574	3.91	573,997,946	10.85
From 7 to 8	228,890,610	4.37	302,806,486	5.72
From 8 to 9	142,144,170	2.72	19,816,000	.38
From 9 to 10	5,405,736	.10	15,217,795	.29
10 and above	68,230,475	1.30	16,412,900	.31
Total	5,226,527,269	100	5,290,033,571	100

It will be observed that under present management honest and dishonest stock and bonds fare alike in the matter of dividends and interest. Stock and bonds for which you have paid full value are just as liable to receive or not receive profits as the like investments representing only water and fraud. It is true as a general proposition that the bonded indebtedness represents the actual rock-bottom value of the roads, while the stock represents only the chicanery of promoters and managers, used principally to gain control of the roads.

Again, bonds of railways no longer represent a fixed security, although supported by mortgage; for the courts will not allow the bondholders, like other mortgagees, to sell the mortgaged roads to make their money.

It would appear then that no class of persons could be more interested in asking for Government ownership than the real owners of American railways. Besides, investigation will show that all the life insurance companies and other corporate investors require some more satisfactory and safe line of securities than the present railways offer. The change advocated would provide them with the best securities the world knows. Six and a half billion dollars in United States bonds would be ample investments for all that class of investors, growing every year more numerous, who ask a certain rather than a high return.

It may be urged by the overcautious that the financial operation involved in the issue of enough securities to purchase the railway capital ($6\frac{1}{2}$ billions of dollars) would be too great for the Government. The answer is that only a change in the form of the present holdings would be rendered necessary; at least 60 per cent of the present holders would but exchange securities; the market would lie in the displacement of the old stocks and bonds. Such an issue would in no true sense involve the Government in debt; the railway asset would fully balance the liability. Taxation would not be required either for interest or principal; so that none of the elements of indebtedness proper would belong to this operation.

Finally, there can be no reasonable question that the United States of America might market such an issue, independently of the special market created by the extinction of the old railway securities. And this could be done at the $2\frac{1}{2}$ per cent interest rate proposed, by fixing the term of maturity at either fifty or a hundred years. She has already borrowed at a 2 per cent rate, and those bonds, although payable at the option of the Government, are quoted at par (May 24, 1899). But it is inquired, Would that be true of a $6\frac{1}{2}$ billion dollar issue? In answer to this question, let us look to the experience of some other country, some country not esteemed as stable as our own.

I refer to France. Her public debt now amounts to 31,094,356,744 francs, which, estimating the franc at 19 cents in our money, equals a debt of $5,907,927,781.36. The population of France is less than 39,000,000, making the per capita debt about $162. Our population, according to Government estimates, will just double that in 1900; so that, adding the proposed issue to the subsisting debt, the whole would be something less than $100 per head. Well, France pays 3 per cent and her bonds are above par. It would seem that the stationary point of interest on absolutely sound and immediately and universally convertible securities is somewhere between 2 and $2\frac{1}{2}$ per centum. That is the lowest point at which men will be willing to abstain from the immediate enjoyment of their wealth. These conditions may be realized by France, Germany, Great Britain, or our own country. It would seem then that the experience of France is conclusive as to our ability to float the required issue, even regarding it as a submergence into debt. It only remains to suggest that these bonds could be invested with the privilege of being exchanged for Treasury notes in time of monetary panic, and be reissued by the Treasury on presentation of an equivalent amount of such Treasury notes. This would provide the elastic feature so much desired in our currency.

A parting word to the railway capitalist. You know not what the future may have in store for you. Your turn may come next in a bond or stock disaster which will steal away in a single day a quarter or half or nearly all of your stock or bond investment. The Supreme Court has warned you that the roads can not legally combine into traffic agreements to maintain rates. They must compete, and thus destroy each other. You know the temptation to which each road is subject in its suicidal struggle for the other's lifeblood—to wit, its business. I think it may be safely said that the people will not allow the roads to combine under private capital. How black and hopeless then must be the future for the railway capitalist.

II. Uniform Freight Rates.

The demand for uniformity in freight rates has its basis in the right to equal justice. To deny this uniformity to the shipper is as unjust as to deny him equality before the law. Moreover, it is not merely a question of individual justice, but of national concern. If an anarchy of freight rates is to be the lot of American shippers, prudence would dictate that no investments be made except under circumstances of the most extraordinary promise. Men will not invest their capital when a varying freight rate may destroy it in a day, or when such uncertainty destroys the basis of their confidence. Thus national industry will suffer; and thus uniformity of freight rates becomes the most pressing requirement of an industrial country. Congress has recognized this exigency by constituting the Board of Interstate Commerce. It will be admitted, I think, that so far as obtaining the desired object is concerned that board has itself confessed in each of its annuals a complete failure. The reason for this is hardly abstruse. It is found in the differing needs and situation of each particular road. Let us look at the facts.

It costs a given amount by reason of location, distance between points, past management, amount of traffic, population, etc., to construct and maintain a particular road. Another road commanding all or some of the same points of traffic supply may cost immensely less or immensely more; thus, conditions being different, uniformity of rates under the present system is impracticable; the contending roads are not equal, and can not enter the contest as equals. Then, again, when some road has sole control of a point of traffic, but at other points a competition is kept up, the point thus monopolized is discriminated against in order to supply the deficiency at the competitive point; or indeed for any other motive that may inspire the managers of 1,000 different companies among which such uniformity is sought.

It is thus seen that a railway company commanding the traffic of a given town or district holds the power of life and death over its commercial relations with the balance of the world. The roads being unequal, their accommodations to the point of traffic must be unequal, thus effecting, whether intentionally or otherwise, a substantial discrimination against such town or city. This is a defect of their nature that no amount of just or wise management on their part can repair.

I shall not go into a long indictment of the discriminations of a voluntary character which have made the cry for uniformity of rates the most urgent requirement of the last 20 years. The real owners of railways must regret this condition as much as the general public. Of the purposed discriminations which have succored the childhood and nursed into vigorous being the principal trust, the Standard Oil Company, of this country, I will speak somewhat later on.

Again the thinking man will ask, How can public ownership attain the object desired? Namely, uniformity.

The interstate commerce reports show that the number of tons of freight carried 1 mile (average) was 95,139,022,225 in 1897; that the number carried an average of 1 mile in 1896 was 95,328,360,278, being practically the same freight carried in both years. The average earnings from the freight service for the whole country was for each ton of freight carried just 8.6 mills in 1896, while in 1897 the average charge per ton per mile was 8.1 mills. Now it being thus well known what the average freight rate is, not only for the whole country, but in each of the ten districts into which the Commissioners have divided the Union, this average rate may be adopted by the Government for the determination of what uniform rate it will employ in the transport of freight—that is, generally speaking, that uniform rate would be about 8 mills per ton per mile. Good results in one instance could be made to correct the deficiencies in others; so that single control and management might equalize and reduce to uniformity the freight rates for the entire country.

It would be found, no doubt, this in matters of freight some differentiation would be practicable in the different freight zones. It is not desired that freight should be carried like letters, without reference to actual cost of the service. But perfect uniformity certainly can be reached by this proposal just as certainly as it is impossible of realization under the anarchy of railroad interests which now dominate the freight traffic. By the way, no complaint of discrimination is ever made in Germany. Why? Manifestly because the reasons which make uniformity impossible here, conflicts of railroad interests, have been removed there by Government ownership and regulation.

The consensus of opinion, I believe, would concede that Government ownership, and that alone, can achieve a perfect equality of rates. Certainly 1,000 different managements can not, even if they desired. Moreover, 10 years of experience have shown us that this object can not be gained through mere measures of repression by the board of commerce. If anyone will take the trouble to read their reports, he will be satisfied on this point. The commission can not bring about a uniform classification, much less such rates. Hear them—report, 1897:

"As often as this commission has had occasion to refer to the subject of a uniform basis for rate schedules over the whole country, whether in annual reports, opinions rendered, correspondence had, or personal conferences, it has not failed to emphasize the importance and indeed the necessity for such uniformity. A single classification is regarded essential to insure compliance with the law, and to promote greater economy in the administration and conduct of transportation; it is therefore in the interests of the carriers themselves. In no other way, it is believed, can the patrons of the roads, both shippers and consumers, obtain that actual justice and equal treatment which the act to regulate commerce was designed to secure.

"But since nothing has been done by them (the companies) in this direction for more than a half dozen years, since nothing is now being done or attempted, and it is evident that there is not likely to be any effort on their part to accomplish this reform, it becomes the duty of the commission to impress upon Congress the gravity of the situation, to point out the apparent indifference of the carriers generally to the reiterated requests of the public, the Congress, and the commission, and to emphasize the necessity for a single classification as the basis for equal rates.

"These considerations of the necessity for reform in this regard, the universal demand for a uniform classification, the ten years of appeal to the carriers, by the commission and by Congress, to adopt a consolidated and single system for the whole country, the 'representations' by the carriers themselves, their former efforts to that end, the energy at one time displayed by them, and the apparent apathy that marks their attitude toward the subject to-day, all lead the commission to the renewed recommendation that Congress provide for such uniformity by prompt and appropriate legislation."

The rates and classification should be as uniform as the railway gauge. On the subject of rates, the reader is referred to the last section of the testimony.

III. Cheap Passenger Rates and Railway Economics.

A full examination of railway data, such as may be found in the exhaustive reports of the Interstate Commission, will satisfy anyone that the passenger service of the United States is relatively too costly; and that the high rates maintained for passenger transport almost defeat the utility of this agency of travel for a large portion of the American people. One acquainted with comparative railway freight rates of Europe must concede that ours are as cheap if not the cheapest in the world. No valid complaint can be made of this average rate if discriminations, natural and willful, were eliminated. If two wholesalers or shippers in the same city or at different points are uniformly served, it will be found they will not complain of freight rates, however high. If, on the contrary, one is served at necessary cost and the other at half cost, it is plain that the former is as much injured as if doubly charged; for he is prevented from engaging with his competitor on terms of equality. Thus equal rather than unjustly low rates is the desideratum among shippers.

It is quite different in the passenger service. There the amount of traffic is not fixed by the definite commercial needs of the people. The amount of freight would not be appreciably enlarged by a great reduction in the carrying cost. The amount of coal and wheat, etc., for railway traffic is reasonably certain, being limited to the determined physical needs of men. But travel on railways is a variant quantity, depending as much upon the cost of such service as the need of locomotion. it was found by the Austro-Hungary Government that upon reducing fares 40 per cent the traffic increased 50 per cent; and so I think it may be argued that if the passenger rates were reduced to an average charge of one-half cent per mile for each passenger, the number of passenger miles would increase from the 13,000,000,-000 carried in 1896 to at least 26,000,000,000. The percentage of increase would even then be smaller than was found in the experience of Austro-Hungary; for there the reduction was only 40 per cent and the increase 50 per cent, while here che reduction would amount to more than three-fourths of present rate.

Nor would the increased traffic occasion any sensible increase of the cost. The Interstate Commerce Commission's report shows that the average number of persons carried in each train was 42 for the year 1896. It seems this number could be doubled without affecting the cost of carriage by the Government. A full train is as easily hauled as an empty one; and thus, generally speaking, the cost of the passenger service would be precisely the same whether 13,000,000,000 or 26,000,000,000 of passenger miles were accomplished.

Besides, this general reduction would but slightly reduce the revenues of the railways when compensated by the costless and immense increase of traffic set forth above. Charging an average rate of 2.019 or 2 cents and 2 mills a mile, as they did in 1896, the service only netted them on the 13,000,000,000 passenger miles $266,562,533, while the 26,000,000,000 miles at one-half cent would have brought $130,000,000; and yet such a reduction would add immensely to the traveling facilities of 70,000,000 of people. Let those who would willfully stand in the way of such a consummation speak out their objections or clear the path. Railways were peculiarly ordained for social accommodations, and the most efficient management for that purpose is entitled to demand control. As we have seen, the real owners of the roads can have no valid objections; they would be better off with Government than railway bonds. Shippers are clamoring for a uniformity of freight rates which only public ownership can attain, and now the entire public, it is seen, may be secured a half cent a mile fare. Shall then a stubborn crowd of railway managers (not owners) defy the interests of every class of citizenship merely to perpetuate their grip upon managerial powers?

Little need be said as to the educational and refining influence of general travel. This method of passenger service would bring the entire continent under the command of a laborer's weekly pay. At least 90 per cent of even the American people have never seen the Capitol, or even one of our principal cities. It is a social crime to needlessly continue such a state of things. And what more effective agency for socializing our citizenship can be suggested than a cheap method of intercommunication. By this means alone can men find suitable location for their individual tastes and needs. The crowding of the colored population in the South might at least be considerably relieved; and laborers might move from place to place in harmony with the local demands of the labor market.

The prime purpose of public railways, like the post-office, would be service. It is almost marvelous what great ends may be accomplished when this principle governs and the consideration of "profit" is eliminated. Institution or method counts for almost as much as individuality; and we shall see how completely the advantages of each are realized by means of public railways.

At this point I deem it necessary to show what I conceive will be the revenues derivable under public ownership, what the necessary expenditures will amount to, and generally to consider income and expenditures under the present and under the projected system. For this purpose I shall rely wholly upon the reports of the Commerce Commission.

Here are its summaries for 1896:

Summary showing number of employees, total yearly amount paid each class, and average daily compensation of each kind of employee for the year ending June 30, 1896. Railway mileage covered, 181,982.

Class.	Number of employees.	Amount paid each Class.	Daily wages.
General officers	5,372	$12,497,957	$9.19
Other officers	2,718	5,301,119	5.96
General office clerks	26,828	19,037,816	2.21
Station agents	29,728	17,050,117	1.73
Other station men	75,919	39,076,478	1.62
Enginemen	35,851	41,854,307	3.65
Firemen	36,762	23,724,854	2.06
Conductors	35,457	26,758,485	3 05
Other train men	64,806	38,379,035	1.90
Machinists	29,272	19,312,746	2.28
Carpenters	38,846	22,948,585	2.03
Other shopmen	95,613	48,497,887	1.69
Section foremen	30,372	17,097,882	1.70
Other track men	169,664	54,521,113	1.17
Switchmen, flagmen, and watchmen	44,266	24,950,907	1.74
Telegraph operators and dispatchers	21,682	13,695,587	1.93
Employees—account floating equipment	5,502	3,221,290	1.94
All other employees and laborers	88,467	43,398,416	1.65
Total	826,620	468,824,531	....

Summary showing amount of work done and receipts therefrom.

Work done.	1896.	Source of income.	1896.
Passengers carried	511,722,737	Passenger revenue...............	$266,562,533
Passengers carried 1 mile.......	13,049,007,233	Mail.............................	32,379,819
Passengers carried 1 mile per		Express..........................	24,880,383
mile of line.....................	71,705	Other earnings, passenger	
Tons carried	765,891,385	service........................	6,691,279
Tons carried 1 mile	95,328,360,278	Freight revenue	786,415,837
Tons carried 1 mile per mile line.	523,832	Other earnings, freight service.	3,885,890
Passenger train mileage..........	332,854,218	Other earnings from operation.	28,574,237
Average number of passengers		Unclassified	579,398
in train..........................	39		
Average journey per passenger,		Total earnings from oper-	
miles	25.50	ation	1,150,169,376
Freight train mileage............	479,500,170		
Average number of tons in			
train	198.81		
Average haul per ton	124.47		

Item.	1896.	Item.	1896.
Revenue per passenger per		Revenue per train mile, all	
mile ....cents..	2.019	trains.......................	$1.39.567
Revenue per ton of freight per		Average cost of running a train	
mile......................cents..	.806	1 mile, all trains ....cents..	93.838
Revenue per train mile, passen-		Percentage of operating expen-	
ger trains.......................	$0.98.591	ses to operating income	67.20
Revenue per train mile, freight			
trains............................	1.63.337		

Summary of railway accidents—United States.

Kind of accident.	Employees.		Others.	
	Killed.	Injured.	Killed.	Injured.
Coupling and uncoupling	229	8,457	....	....
Falling from trains and engines	472	3,898	....	....
Overhead obstructions...	63	358	....	....
Collisions	178	1,047	27	77
Derailments	117	659	39	79
Other train accidents	53	486	43	68
At highway crossings..	24	160	611	1,025
At stations...	92	1,471	354	639
Other causes..	633	13,433	3,332	3,956
Total..	1,861	29,969	4,406	5,845

Summary showing classifications of operating expenses of railways in the United States for the year ending June 30, 1896.

Maintenance of way and structures:
1. Repairs of roadway $77,501,102
2. Renewals of rails 10,419,393
3. Renewals of ties 21,855,268
4. Repairs and renewals of bridges and culverts 16,347,620
5. Repairs and renewals of fences, road crossings, signs, and cattle guards 4,049,534
6. Repairs and renewals of buildings and fixtures.............. 12,948,641
7. Repairs and renewals of docks and wharves.................. 1,948,636
8. Repairs and renewals of telegraphs 972,446
9. Stationery and printing... 193,913
10. Other expenses 2,684,407

Total 148,920,960

Maintenance of equipment:

11. Superintendence	$4,807,224
12. Repairs and renewal of locomotives	43,150,823
13. Repairs and renewal of passenger cars	15,990,268
14. Repairs and renewals of freight cars	51,910,309
15. Repairs and renewals of work cars	1,049,314
16. Repairs and renewals of marine equipment	1,245,109
17. Repairs and renewals of shop machinery and tools	8,753,775
18. Stationery and printing	291,116
19. Other expenses	8,321,494
Total	125,519,432

Conducting transportation:

20. Superintendence	12,494,620
21. Engine and roundhouse men	70,243,683
22. Fuel for locomotives	69,786,920
23. Water supply for locomotives	4,988,998
24. Oil, tallow, and waste for locomotives	2,734,331
25. Other supplies for locomotives	1,655,556
26. Train service	56,182,337
27. Train supplies and expenses	11,233,426
28. Switchmen, flagmen, and watchmen	29,732,359
29. Telegraph expenses	14,273,549
30. Station service	55,647,544
31. Station supplies	5,731,378
32. Switching charges—balance	2,567,074
33. Car mileage—balance	14,821,688
34. Hire of equipment	2,326,142
35. Loss and damage	5,591,312
36. Injuries to persons	6,060,690
37. Clearing wrecks	909,188
38. Operating marine equipment	5,958,607
39. Advertising	3,014,518
40. Outside agencies	11,308,133
41. Commissions	1,211,298
42. Stock yards and elevators	910,321
43. Rents for tracks, yards, and terminals	12,602,109
44. Rents of buildings and other property	3,625,237
45. Stationery and printing	4,443,871
46. Other expenses	8,945,620
Total	414,000,539

General expenses:

47. Salaries of general officers	8,751,208
48. Salaries of clerks and attendants	10,171,801
49. General office expenses and supplies	2,243,415
50. Insurance	3,215,625
51. Law expenses	5,233,788
52. Stationery and printing (general offices)	1,189,892
53. Other expenses	2,484,106
Total	33,289,835

Recapitulation of expenses:

54. Maintenance of way and structures	148,920,960
55. Maintenance of equipment	125,519,432
56. Conducting transportation	414,000,539
57. General expenses	33,289,835
Grand total	[1] 721,730,766

[1] Excludes $51,258,278, unclassified.

Summary of receipts under Government ownership of railways.

Passenger miles traveled, 26,000,000,000 at one-half cent per mile..	$130,000,000
Tons carried 1 mile, 95,328,360,278, at 8⁸₁₀ mills per ton per mile..	786,615,837
Receipts from mail service in 1897, $33,754,466	32,379,819
Receipts from express service	25,880,383
Other earnings from passenger service	6,691,279
Other earnings from freight service	3,885,890
Other earnings from operation (not classified)	28,574,237
Income unclassified	579,898
Total receipts under public ownership	1,013,606,843

Summary showing expenditures under public operation.

Expenditures for maintenance of way and structures	$148,920,960
Expenditures for maintenance of equipment	125,019,432
Expenditures for conducting transportation	414,000,539
Expenditures for general expenses	33,289,835
Unclassified expenditures	51,258,278
Total as per experience of all roads for 1896	772,989,044
Interest at 2½ per cent on $6,502,186,396. United States century bonds employed to purchase bonds, stock, and rented property as set forth in this work	162,534,659
Appropriation to sinking fund to pay off this indebtedness in 100 years	25,000,000
Reduction of number of hours of labor from 10 to 8, by employing one-fifth greater number of men, namely, 165,324, at same wages hitherto paid for ten hours, namely, one-fifth of $452,025,455, excluding officers	90,205,090
To raising daily wages of 169,664 trackmen from $1.17 to $1.30 per day of eight hours	6,000,000
Indemnity of $2,000, paid to each employee killed, average for 1896 being 1,861	3,722,000
Indemnity of $5,000, paid each passenger killed on roads, average being 238 in 1896	1,190,000
Total expenses (without deduction of savings)	1,062,545,793

Savings.

The following deductions must, however, be made from expenditures for operation:

Salaries of 1,500 railway presidents; superintendents discharge their duties	$12,000,000
Law expenses; present law officers in employ of Government would suffice, besides 90 per cent. of litigation would disappear	5,233,788
Advertising would, of course, be unnecessary	3,014,518
"Commissioners to seek for business"	1,211,298
Three-eighths of salaries of general officers; uniform management would dispense with these	3,000,000
Insurance. No receipts credited by me from this source on "gross receipts"	3,215,625
Savings on printing and stationery; resulting from uniformity, etc. (one-half)	4,300,000

Rent, hire, equipment, track yards, terminals, buildings. other property rented; all these items are funded in purchased price of roads, see page 6, being items 34, 43 in summary operating expenses	$18,463,288
Item 40 "Outside agencies"	11,308,133
Savings from abolition of Traffic Association	2,000,000
Exclusive use of shortest routes	15,000,000
Consolidation, depots, staffs, etc	8,000,000
Savings by uniformity of rolling stock, accounts, machinery, manufacture; innumerable economies of a vast company, under single control, etc	15,000,000
Avoiding strikes and cultivating better spirit with employees	3,000,000
Abolition of fund for legislation, corruption, lobbies, etc	10,000,000
Elimination of pass evil, etc.	5,000,000
Elimination of private cars, etc	1,000,000
Total saving	$120,746,642
Total net cost of operation, interest, sinking fund, insurance, etc	$941,799,151
Net surplus and revenue for the Government from annual operation	71,807,692

It will be remarked that a great uniformity prevails in the annual amount of business done, as well as in the receipts derived from this immense business. Examination will show that the amount of the passenger traffic has not varied more than 7 per cent since 1890, while the freight business has preserved a slight increase from year to year. Accidents, wages, rates, and all other features of these totals for the United States maintain the same general uniformity from year to year.

This fact means much. It enables the railroad economist, like the life insurance expert, to predict results and predicate all reasonable conclusions thereon. This is indeed the key to efficient economy in railway management. While on one road the most inexplicable variability of results will follow the year's operations, yet when the entire system is considered conclusions are as constant as the principles of mathematics. For a comparative study of this subject, drop a card to the Commerce Commission for its annual abstract.

It is thus seen that, basing calculations upon the unquestioned data of past railway receipts and adopting an average freight rate of 8.6 mills, together with an average passenger rate of one-half cent per mile, and the other incidental receipts, the Government would realize $1,013,606,843. At the same time, it is seen that, accepting the present cost of operating these roads, that is, $772,899,044, and adding thereto the annual interest charge of the $6,500,000,000 of bonds necessary to purchase the entire system (along with the reduction of the hours of labor from 10 to 8 per diem and the consequent employment of 165,324 additional men, and the insurance provided) that the Government would still be ahead, on comparison of annual receipts and expenditures, the immense sum of $71,807,712.

It should be observed that 40 millions of this balance is the savings resulting from the elimination of State taxation. Under the proposed plan this revenue would go to the General Government, and not to the States. In view of the ever-increasing difficulty of securing Federal revenues, and the easy methods available to the States, I believe the General Government might well retain this revenue. Besides, would it be wise to leave the railroads subject to taxation by 45 States, and about 2,000 different county and municipal bodies? Even if Federal jurisprudence should permit such an exercise of the powers of taxation, I think it would be much better for the States to resign this power in the interest of the common weal.

It will be observed by the reader who has followed the business statement of the roads as at present conducted, and the second statement giving a forecast of its necessary finances under public ownership, that I have adopted nothing but the experience of the railways themselves, saving some half a dozen items in which it is claimed immense savings must result from such public operation.

In the statement of "Summary of receipts under Government ownership" I assume that the passenger traffic would increase from 13 billions of miles traveled to 26 billions, and that no appreciable increase of expenses would result.

First, would passenger traffic so double? It will be observed that the rate charged for such service would be reduced from 2¼ cents to one-half cent per mile. That reduced fares augment the traffic every excursion will testify; but I want the reader to consider the definite experience of Hungary on this very point.

Hungary owns and operates her railways as public property, and here is what the British consul, Sir A. Nicolson, said of a general reduction of passenger fares in that country:

"The year 1889 will be noteworthy in the history of Hungarian railways, as it witnessed the introduction of the zone tariff on all Hungarian state railways. I have on former occasions reported on this subject, so that it is needless to go into details, beyond mentioning that since the introduction of the new cheap traffic on the 1st of August, 1889, to the 31st of December, 1889, the passenger traffic increased by over 3,000,000 persons, and the gross receipts by over £50,000. As the total number of passengers annually carried by Hungarian railways has not heretofore exceeded 15,500,000, the largest increase in five months is remarkable, and would appear to be of good augury for the permanent success of the new system. It is said that no extra expense has been incurred, and in fact that economies have been affected in the ticket-issuing department, owing to the facilities now afforded for obtaining tickets at post-offices, and other places in towns."

Such, then, has been the effect among the circumscribed population of Hungary; there the reduction of rates was about one-half and the augmentation of traffic about 50 per cent, and the gross receipts are said to have increased $250,000. Can there be any doubt, then, that a corresponding increase of the passenger traffic would result here if the cost of travel were reduced four-fifths? Not much. I consider this point settled.

But it may be argued you have allowed nothing extra for carrying this increased traffic.

Well that also seems to have been the effect of the change in Hungary, according to the consul quoted above. Let us see why this fact can be true:

The interstate-commerce reports show that the average number of passengers in each train moved in 1896 was 39 passengers; in 1895, 38; in 1894, 44; and in 1893, 42; 1892, 42; 1891, 41. The report does not give the passenger capacity of the average train, but we may safely place it at 3 cars to the train. Allowing 50 passengers to the car we would thus have a carrying capacity of 150 persons for each train, or 275 per cent more than has been used during the last 7 years. It appears that only 28 per cent of the passenger capacity is actually employed; and as a consequence that the 28 per cent have to pay for the other 72 per cent, who are, perhaps prevented from taking the empty seats reserved for them by the high rate which private management exacts. Now, it is patent that an empty train is as expensive to haul as one loaded to its full capacity. One hundred and fifty passengers, each weighing 150 pounds would equal about 11 tons. An engineer or fireman could not tell whether such a burden got on or off at the last station. The conductor service would, of course, remain the same, and so all other services worthy of account.

Then so far as "receipts under Government ownership" are concerned, may I not say I am justified in assuming an immensely increased passenger traffic, with no appreciable augmentation of expenditures on that account.

As this is the only item in "receipts" which differs from the past experience of the companies themselves, I think I may safely pass on to the account for "expenditures and maintenance," etc.

It will be observed that in estimating the amount of necessary expenses I have adopted the past experience of the companies, just as in the account showing "receipts."

The first item of difference in "public expenditures," as compared with the past expenses, is a saving of $165,000,000 in the annual interest charge. That results from the simple and indisputable fact that the United States Government can borrow money at one-half the rate at which nearly 2,000 disorganized, struggling, mismanaged frequently, and antagonistic railways can. The 3 per cent bonds of the United States are now quoted at from 8 to 9 per cent above their face value; and I believe there can be no doubt that bonds to the amount of $6,500,000,000, providing a safe investment for 100 years, would be easily negotiated at a 2½ per cent rate of interest. Thus the interest charge would unquestionably be cut in two, and $165,000,000 annually saved.

The next items of difference are two charges to expenses of operation, involving an outlay of $90,205,090 and $6,000,000, respectively. The first is over and above the amount now paid, and is incurred in order to reduce the hours of labor from

10 to 8 per diem for all employees except officers. I do not intend to grow eloquent on this topic, but I should like to emphasize the prudence of alleviating the damages and dangers of railway industry by this greatly needed reform. The resulting safety to life and property, the immense opportunities which this reduction of hours would open to those relieved (800,000 men and their family associations), and, over and above all, the 165,000 now unemployed, who would thus find means of decent self-support, are subjects which I shall only suggest in their infinite potentialities of individual betterment and national progress.

Besides, it may be taken for granted that society would not conduct the railways upon the minimum wage scale. Some reduction of hours of labor or increase of wages would be among the most worthy ends at which the nation might aim. Indeed, the railway workers may safely expect that, like their brother workers of the post-office, they will be paid according to their work, not according to the barometer of the overcrowded labor market.

I have added $6,000,000 to the expenditures to cover an increase of wages for trackmen, of from $1.17 to 1.30, numbering about 170,000 in the United States. Small wages may not always make small men, but only herculean character will be able to feed, clothe, and educate an average family of 5 on $1.17 a day. If one stops to consider the awful labors of these trackmen, burned by the heat of summer and frozen by our winter winds, working 10 hours with bent backs from "morn to noon, from noon to dewy eve," it would seem that the railway manager who first established this rate and thus compelled his competitors to follow him, has a heart that "would shame hell in its palmiest days." This increase of wages to the trackmen would be in addition to the reduction of the day's work from 10 to 8 hours.

I have also allowed an item to cover insurance for employees, allowing them $2,000 when killed in the course of their employment. This subject needs no argument, and I will make none. An allowance of $5,000 is made for each passenger killed. An allowance of $2,000 to the non-trespassers who may be killed upon the railways should also be made. So great a loss is too much for the individuals composing a family alone to bear; and where the deceased is himself innocent, society may well make this appropriation for the people killed on her railways. Some distinction might be made between children and others, but that some provision ought to be made above that provided by suits for negligence most men will agree.

I now come to the "savings" which it appears to me would result from the unified management of railways. Why do railways insist upon a uniform gauge? Is it not for the economy it inaugurates? Now, it does seem to me that uniformity of management will be equally prolific of advantage in the active operation of the roads. The first item of this kind which I submit would be saved is $12,000,000 for some 1,500 railway presidents. This does not imply that we believe the roads will be able to get along without competent brains and training to superintend them. Outside of this item, some $10,000,000 is allowed for "superintendence." The fact is that railway presidents in most instances represent the financing rather than the actual management of railroads. The superintendents are usually trained railroaders, while the president is the fellow with the largest amount of stock.

There are exceptions, doubtless, but with uniformity and no clashing of interests among the different branches it is readily seen that the "railroad president" function will pass away. Superintendence, of course, will be even more useful than now, in its highest sense, but the item for that has not been impaired by this deduction. Law expenses, advertising, commissions, amounting altogether to about $12,500,000 (see statement), would absolutely pass away. Litigation, the biggest element, is the child of private interests in railways, and whatever remained could be attended to by the regular officers of the Government. As to insurance, the Government would do its own; besides, nothing has been credited in "receipts" for this item, which would make it, therefore, an improper charge. I have cut the item for stationery in two. With uniformity in the forms of stationery and their manufacture in large amounts at least 50 per cent could be saved.

The next item is $18,463,288, which is credited as a saving on rent, hire, equipment track yards, terminals, and other property rented by the companies. All this has been funded and is charged up in the 6¼ billions, which would purchase all this rented property, so far as necessary, along with the roads themselves; so that this item can not be disputed.

Here follow 9 items, amounting to 70 millions, all of which speak for themselves. They are of necessity more or less conjectural as to details, but the principle upon which they would certainly be saved is the unquestionable value of associative labor and capital over antagonistic and anarchic effort. Every trust seeking to combine and prevent division of those engaged in the same business is a living proof of the eternal value of cooperation and the futility of conflict; besides, in the statement of "expenditures" by the present companies, you will find an item of $52,000,000 charged up to operating expenses which can not be classified, that is, the character of which the companies have refused to make known to the Interstate Commission. They may have some reason for this. It seems to be the money spent by the roads to get business, etc.

Let me say that I am not alone in my contention of the certainty of the savings to be effected in "operating expenses." I beg leave to append the estimate of a railway man who has written upon this subject. Mr. C. Wood Davis, formerly general freight and passenger agent on a Chicago road, in his work in favor of Government ownership makes the following estimate of the savings which would result:

From consolidation of depots and staffs	$20,000,000
From exclusive use of shortest routes	25,000,000
Saved on free passes	30,000,000
From the abrogation of the commission evil	20,000,000
By dispensing with high-priced managers and staffs	4,000,000
By disbanding traffic associations	4,000,000
Dispensing with presidents, etc	25,000,000
By abolishing all but local office solicitors, etc	15,000,000
Of five-sevenths of the advertising account	5,000,000

A few of Mr. Davis's estimates far exceed what my study of the interstate commerce reports would lead me to believe might be realized. He computes a total of 160 millions as being within the economies of railway operation by the Government, with all the innumerable eliminations which must follow.

My effort has been in all cases to discount rather than dilate or amplify the savings on public operation, and I am firmly of the opinion that I have understated the economies which must certainly follow the introduction of universal principles into the management of our great railway system.

IV. Future Railway Development.

The statement given above shows a balance in the railway treasury each year of some $70,000,000. In this connection we should not forget how important the railway is to modern life. It has taken the place of the public roads for every purpose of practical life; and if our country is to develop, it can only be by a prudent and steady extension of her railway service. I should suggest, therefore, the importance of some competent guaranty in this matter. We are so accustomed to regarding our immense railway mileage that we forget the immense tracts of country that have no such accommodations, and whose resources are rendered, thus, beyond the reach of men.

It is an old saying that "we have twice too many railways, and yet not half enough." I have no complete data at hand going to show the amount of socially unnecessary railways, but the useless duplications of competing roads must indeed be great. In Allegany County, Md., where I write this paper, there are four railways when two would abundantly meet the needs for which railways, like public highways, should be built. Perhaps one-fourth of the capital now invested in railways is wasted in such duplication.

This, however, is only a suggestion of what must continue to happen if the roads are to remain in private hands. For example, a road now running from Cumberland, Md., to Baltimore is in the hands of receivers, presumably because the traffic will not sustain the regular bonded interest charge. And yet it is now in contemplation by certain "West Virginia interests" to parallel the Baltimore and Ohio Railroad along this very line.

Thus is railway capital systematically wasted by "private interests" which are incompetent to realize the highest needs of society. Who would suggest paralleling the county roads? And where is the political economist who must not recognize in railway duplication a prodigious waste of the national resources?

We know that private interests have seemed to justify this improvidence in the past, and it can not reasonably be expected that this inherent defect of private railway capital will pass away but with the "interest" of its master. In short, nothing but the General Government ownership of the railways can reconcile the national demands of political economy with the highest service and advantage to the individual citizen; so that the proposal of this work stands finally confirmed if only with reference to the general claims of national economy of capital.

How different the situation would be if social service were the only test applied in railway building as well as management. The building of new railways should be determined by general considerations of social and national character. Say a given mileage to a given amount of territory and population. The average mileage to the 10,000 of population for the United States as a whole is just 26 miles; and yet the actual distribution of mileage throughout the country bears no sort of harmony with any unit of comparison. This fact is another inherent shortcoming of private railways. Only social as opposed to private methods can correct it.

Comparison showing unequal distribution of railway mileage in fourteen States.

Name of State.	Railroad mileage to the 10,000 inhabitants.	Population to 100 square miles.	Railway mileage to 100 square miles.	Per cent of difference.
California	37.38	775	3.24	
Florida	71.38	722	5.76	77
Utah	59.08	253	1.67	
North Dakota	123.18	260	3.59	113
North Carolina	19.29	3,330	7.19	
Wisconsin	32.65	3,098	11.32	57
Maryland	11.14	10,572	13.19	
Ohio	21.23	9,010	21.41	62
Kentucky	14.55	4,647	7.56	
New Hampshire	28.67	4,181	13.42	83
Arkansas	20.22	2,127	4.82	
Minnesota	42.26	1.664	7.74	81
Missouri	22.04	3,898	9.62	
Iowa	39.82	3,446	15.36	70

I have thus shown that in the comparison for some 14 States Florida, under identical conditions with California, has 77 per cent greater mileage; North Dakota 113 per cent greater than Utah; Wisconsin 57 per cent greater than North Carolina; Ohio 62 per cent greater than Maryland; Kentucky 83 per cent less than New Hampshire; Arkansas 81 per cent less than Minnesota, and Missouri 70 per cent less than Iowa. The States compared are in effect identical in their population to the area compared, except that in each case the State having such excess, in the distribution of mileage, has the smaller population to the area, thus still further augmenting the excess enjoyed. It is true that the railway manager is in no sense responsible for this discrimination against States. Private interests build for themselves not for society. And yet the discrepancy is so terrific that if such a policy were attempted in taxation the suffering States would, indeed, secede.

Yet, still the discrimination in the distribution of railway mileage is quite, if not fully, as disastrous to the States named as if they were compelled to pay all the taxes of the favored ones. This subject has not hitherto, so far as I can find, been studied by any public man. It certainly deserves their attention. A great deal of this excessive distribution to some States may consist of "parallels" and useless duplication. In that case the inequality could be readily remedied under public ownership. No roads would be built but from social considerations.

States and counties thinking themselves entitled to greater railway accommodation could bond themselves to cover the cost of construction of new roads under the supervision and to be operated by the General Government; if the roads were justified by the supply of traffic, then the prudence of their construction would appear, when the General Government would assume the bonds. If such roads failed to pay more than the cost of operation, the local body would have to remain liable and accept the responsibility of its own desires. At the same time they could not be sufferers; for the construction of a road, even at the points of low traffic, would inure to their benefit in improved land values, which could thus be made to bear the burdens of the investment. Some objection has been made to nationalization on the ground that "political roads" would be built where the traffic would not justify it. I am quite sure the institution outlined above would prevent that. The local body should be made first responsible; and only in the event of the traffic justifying the investment, i. e., paying cost of operation and interest, should the Government accept responsibility. In this way the needed new roads would be built by local initiative and responsibility, and the Government preserved harmless.

Thus again we see the anarchism which prevails in railway distribution; only to be compared with an equal anarchism of rates, fares, dividends, and public service. There is no data obtainable, but I would wager a dare that there is no such disproportion in the distribution of the public roads of the United States. There is as little reason for one as the other; and besides the immense development that would result from devoting the capital now used for useless duplications of railways to opening up accommodation for the backwoods farmers and others, an equally great object would be attained in preserving some principle of balance in railway distribution.

I think, then, I may safely add "Development of the country" as one of the urgent arguments in favor of railway socialization.

V. SAFETY OF RAILWAY PASSENGERS AND EMPLOYEES.

I only desire to suggest on this topic that the difference between the number of deaths and injuries on American railways, as compared with the same in Germany and Austria-Hungary (government railways), is enough to intimate mayhem and murder as the principal object of railroad management on this side of the Atlantic. The figures are for the year 1890 in each country, the average journey being 24 miles in this country and 16 miles in the others.

	Number.	Killed.		Injured.	
		Number.	Proportion.	Number.	Proportion.
Passengers carried:					
United States	492,430,865	286	1: 1,721,786	2,425	1: 203,064
Germany	426,056,250	46	1: 9,262,092	236	1: 1,805,323
Austria-Hungary	68,638,938	4	1: 17,109,734	53	1: 1,291,300
Men employed:					
United States	749,301	2,451	1: 306	22,396	1: 33
Germany	340,553	454	1: 750	2,011	1: 169
Austria-Hungary	166,463	156	1: 1,067	570	1: 292
Other persons:					
United States		3,598		4,206	
Germany		226		205	
Austria-Hungary		163		110	

RECAPITULATION.

	Total killed.	Total injured.
United States	6,335	29,027
Germany	726	2,452
Austria-Hungary	223	733

Is this terrible comparison justly drawn between public and private ownership of railways? I candidly believe it is.

About a year ago, when the railways applied to the Interstate Commerce Commission for an extension of the time to complete the air-brake and patent coupler appliances, it was argued that the poorer railways could not afford to expend the money necessary under the law. Of course, it would be almost useless for the more solvent roads to do it unless the conditions were made universal in this respect: and so with "poor railways" (and such, indeed, many of them are, 10 per cent in the hands of receivers, etc.) these great measures of safety, with even an act of Congress commanding them to be done, have dragged along from year to year defying every consideration of humanity and of law.

But if the railways were the property of the people that act of Congress would have been an appropriation, and in 2 years these great measures would have been finally realized as facts. I do not propose to denounce the individual roads for this neglect, nor grow eloquent over the carnage and slaughter. But this state of things must stop. If there is any other means than public operation which can achieve this end I have not heard of it.

I only want to add on this topic a common observation. Many of the accidents are attributed to overwork. I believe that the reduction of the day's work from 10 to 8 hours will completely remove this trouble.

Besides, when the roads are socialized improvements in safety appliances can at once be utilized. Only the fact of their utility needs be satisfactorily determined; after that the improvement would follow, of course.

VI. A SYSTEM OF RAILWAY ACCIDENT INSURANCE.

The principle of insurance is designed to eliminate the dominion of chance and accident over the lives of individual workers. It is eminently just that, where a person accepts a particular work for himself and society, when the unforeseen happens his partner society should share with him, according to their relative capacity, the losses as well as the profits of the enterprise. Whether consciously or not it is a fact that the railway employee and society are partners, and the terrible afflictions which the former has to bear ought to be distributed as far as possible ratably to the partnership liability. It is shamefully unjust that the relatively weak individual should bear alone "the slings and arrows of outrageous fortune." All civilized Governments recognize the obligations of society in this respect by providing pensions for the victims of their only great industry—war, war hardly as ferocious to legs and lives as the railway traffic.

Here is the proof. (United States.)

Table of railway carnage.

Year.	Killed.	Injured.	Year.	Killed.	Injured.
1888	5,282	25,888	1893	7,346	40,393
1889	5,823	26,309	1894	6,447	31,889
1890	6,335	28,027	1895	6,136	33,748
1891	7,029	33,881	1896	6,267	31,814
1892	7,147	36,652	Total	57,812	288,601

Does this difference between public and private management arise out of personal malevolence of railways on this side of the water? Certainly not. It arises out of a difference of methods. What is the only known difference of method? Ours are private railways and the German "government" owned and operated. So much for the value of institution. Individuality may enjoy a great helpmeet in wise methods or institutions. It will be remarked by the reader that there is a striking uniformity of death and accident during 9 years given, taking substantial increase into account. That is accounted for by the increased number of men at work. Now, this fact of uniformity is of invaluable importance in the scheme of railway insurance proposed. With a practical foreknowledge of what is going to happen in the way of accident, the Government could well discharge the duty of society in this partnership of the laborer and the public well-being.

I shall not indicate here what compensation should be made in each class of accidents. It should be liberal and yet not so great as to induce indifference to personal safety, as some might argue. What I particularly desire to say is that, under the Government, certain and adequate insurance could be had because it would be master of all the facts. Under the dispensation of 1,985 different railway companies no half satisfactory provision can be made. My proposal is that the Government should bear half the cost of sustaining sufficient insurance; the employee should bear the other half. That in addition thereto crippled employees should have an opportunity to educate themselves for the sedentary employments about railways, should pass examinations as to their fitness to hold clerical positions, and that, other things being equal, they should enjoy a preference for the employment for which they were fit.

It may be said in answer that so far as insurance is essential it exists in the numerous casualty companies which are anxious to write policies. That is so, but they are so grossly inefficient that they defeat the purpose of insurance. I mean by the charge of inefficiency that they charge more than two prices for their insurance, and thus place it beyond the reach of the pressing poverty of the more than half million railroaders who need it. Besides, the railways should pay one-half of the insurance, a thing they will never do while some of them are too poor to employ patent couplers and air brakes, saving legs and lives instead of insuring them.

I have said the casualty companies are inefficient because of their charges. There are some 29 of these companies in this country, and here is their business statement for the year 1898:

Summary of 29 companies, taken from Standard Publishing Company, insurance statistics.

Gross assets	$49,866,711
Gross liabilities	30,779,473
Surplus to policy holders	19,107,244

Premiums received during 1897	$16,018,536
Dividends paid during 1897	604,132
Losses paid during 1897	6,393,741
Gross amount at risk December 31, 1897	2,672,380,735

It will be observed that they charged $16,018,536 in premiums; while all they paid out to the insured was $6,393,741. Every casualty company will show this low ratio of "losses" to "premiums." Eighteen hundred and ninety-seven is in no sense an exceptional year. It thus appears that they only paid back to the people who sought their insurance 39 per cent of what they exacted for insurance: in other words, the railway employee would have to pay 60 per cent more than actually necessary to cover the actual cost of his insurance. It is patent that railway insurance of railway subjects would not cost more than 6 per cent to administer it in conjunction with the railway finances. It only costs that amount to administer the "sick, invalid, old age, and accident insurance" carried on by the German Government for its laboring population. (See Fourth Special Report, Commissioner of Labor, Washington, D. C.)

Now, if you add to the 39 per cent 6 per cent, to cover governmental cost of administration, the total cost will be just 42 per cent of the sum now necessary with the casualty companies. Dividing that between the railroads and the individual employee the cost would be just 21 per cent, or one-fifth of the amount now necessary to insure with casualty companies and secure compensation for his individual loss.

At the same time the traveling public could avail itself of this institution, and have the fortunate travelers cooperate with the unfortunate in amending pecuniarily the misadventures of railway locomotion.

I need hardly argue that the present companies will never adequately correct this great evil. The "fellow-servant" rule of law excuses them absolutely from any responsibility to their employees, and when a passenger or a freight disaster happens the sufferer has usually a lawsuit instead of insurance. If he secures a verdict he divides it with his lawyers, unless it has previously been consumed in appeals to higher courts.

VII. POSTAL EXPRESS.

The demand for a parcel post and Government assumption of the express system has long attained the point of almost universal desire. Of its convenience for commerce and the accommodation of the people I shall not think it necessary to speak. My remarks upon this subject will be confined to showing that if the Government should undertake the railways this service would follow, as a matter of course. I think I shall be able to show, besides, that the express service under these circumstances could be conducted at half the present cost to the general public; that allowing the same railway charge for carrying, which is at present paid by the express companies, and adding thereto the cost of distribution in connection with the post-office, the service would be almost as greatly improved in the matter of delivery as in the reduction of rates.

Mr. Weir, president of the Adams Express Company, stated before a committee of the United States Senate that the usual compensation paid by the company to the railroads was "not less than 40 per cent of the gross receipts;" they guaranteed that; that in some cases it might rise to 50 or even 60 per cent. (See Congressional Record, May 6, 1898, and Senator Pettigrew's speech of that date.)

It would appear that more than half of the cost of express service goes to other sources than railway carriage, viz. to independent offices, warehouses, staff officers, accounts, dividends, handsome salaries, etc. The only service performed by them which is of social utility is delivery by wagons in the larger cities.

It is readily seen that if conducted between a government railway and a government post-office this necessary service could be reduced to its most efficient and economical basis: and the necessary cost of delivery in connection with postal matter decreased so that the whole service might be had for just 50 per cent of the present cost.

Besides, the present express companies carry on a wasteful (socially) competition with each other. This means the multiplication of rents, accounts, dividends, salaries, wagons, etc., all of which would be eliminated by the socialization of the service. For example: An intelligent driver of an express wagon in a town of some 18,000 people, upon being asked as to the number of wagons necessary for the delivery of express matter, replied: "We have altogether 5 wagons running; there are 2 different companies. If one company had the whole business 3 delivery wagons would do the work just as well." This is the testimony of a man who knew whereof he spoke, but did not know the writer's object in asking the question. I consider it fair to expect that the post-office could conduct this service, in connection with public railways, at about one-half of the rate now required by the private companies.

I will not argue this question further. It is merely incidental to the proposal for public railways. If we should get them the express system would come as a matter of course. If we can not get the railways, I fear the express service had as well be left where it is; for the example of the carrying of the mails and the charge exacted therefor under private ownership of the railways leads me to think that instead of ' 40 per cent" the railways would secure about 80 per cent for carrying the express, and thus in effect defeat the other economies of postal management.

VIII. A SYSTEM OF RAILWAY CIVIL SERVICE.

I believe no person has ever advocated public railways but in the same breath to demand the most rigid enforcement of genuine civil service. I should, indeed, be quite the last to omit this requirement, urgent in every public employment, but especially urgent in the operation of a system so intimately concerned in our industrial, social, individual, and national life. I conceive the system of civil service to aim at the maintenance of merit in the active work of the Government. In that respect I regard the system of railway civil service not so much a measure tending to insure as high an order of ability and devotion as we hitherto have had, but as an adjunct to the service which must immensely improve it over what we have known in the past.

Consider a few suggestions on this point. As a matter of course, all the interferences with legislatures, county and city public functionaries, courts, as many believe, as well as Congress, will pass away with the private interests which inspire them. Passes, discriminations, overbonding and stocking, building upon one community at the expense of another, etc., must disappear with the interests which render them profitable. We have only one possible apprehension left then. "The roads will get into politics." I think it but a fair question to ask, Where are they now? What is meant by this objection is that employment will become a matter of partisan selection.

Well, let us see what this can mean at worst. Out of the 826,620 men employed in 1896 only 5,372 were general officers. Other officers were 2,718, and here the "offices" cease, unless clerks (26,828) and station agents (29,723) are included. Of offices, about one-half would be abolished as unnecessary, so that at most there would remain not more than 5,000. I believe no one will contend that the other 820,000 employees would be in danger from this influence. No firemen, enginemen, station men, conductors, train men, machinists, carpenters, shopmen, track men, etc., would be in peril of their employment from political desires at Washington. Thus it is seen that the subject-matter of railway employment does not offer the same temptations as other activities of the public service. Besides the "offices" which are now dealt out to the friends and relations of the railway "president" and "board of directors," being incidents of private ownership of stock, etc., will be dropped, and thus the only nook which your "office seeker" could fill will be out of reach. Real and responsible appointments could not be taken except by those who had spent their lives in the railway service. Nature would protect us from the attack of the office seekers. There would be no "offices" to give. Not even your sleek politician could dispatch a train, adjust a schedule, and I do not think we should stand in any peril from his desire to engineer or watch a switch. If he endeavored to foist himself on the railway management, an indignant public, solicitous of their lives and limbs, would either ridicule or hound him off the earth.

The fact is that the elimination of "private interests" would remove the possibility of this abuse. The general public knows that this evil exists to-day in its very worst form in private railway management. The railway president, who is he? Not 10 in 100 are experienced railway workers. Their merits and appointments are usually ascertained by their "stock." They are not selected; they appoint themselves, and hold their positions as long as they hold their stock. And in other cases are they not systematically chosen to "protect certain interests?" Saving a few small roads and the Pennsylvania Railroad, your railroad president is invariably the representative of "certain interests," not a railroad man, but the agent of a clique. How seldom, very seldom, do we see a railway president who "rose from the ranks up."

I need hardly say that under public ownership, with an efficient commission having charge of all the "superintending service," great lawyers and great bankers, adepts in their own calling, would not be seen in such appointments. A system of rules could be readily arranged providing for competitive examination in knowledge of railway operation linked to life service as a railway worker; and thus confining the "superintending service" to real railway men, your politician would be effectually excluded. The commission would also have charge of freight rates, passenger fares, the building of new roads. When the limit of their ability to attend to their duties had been reached, other boards with definite powers and duties would begin. Each member might be sworn, like a judge, to allow no consideration but merit and the good of the service to influence him in his conduct or appointments.

With the railway service confined to railway men, no one being eligible to advancement but some railway man who had passed the required examination, and who, as in the post-office, had least errors marked to him in his last department, the possibility of partisan selection is, I submit, effectually removed.

But let us see what a vista of hope this arrangement would insure the railroader. The head of the service being supplied exclusively from the service itself, every railroader of spirit, intelligence, sobriety, and ambition might look forward to promotion, and we can readily see how this spur would wake to life the latent energies, aptitudes, and ambitions of almost the entire railway service. Their promotion should be made conditional upon their attaining the highest marks in their previous functions, along with the required preparation for the one to which they seek advancement; and in this way the most powerful motives of human nature could be brought into play for the perfection of railway operation.

The merit system? Yes. Not because we desire the roads run as well as now, merely, but because we desire to cure the nepotism which is more rampant in railway management to-day than it is in any of the departments of the public service. We desire civil service for the same reason we desire lower passenger rates, and we propose public ownership because we know it alone will give us both.

With the systematizing of this great service on the lines of the highest economy will come a tendency to a thorough renovation of all the public departments. Not that they are more in need of it than the private enterprises of the country, for I am sure it will be found upon enlightened comparison of the public service with the private that the palm of highest efficiency must be rendered to the post-office as on the whole the best-managed industrial enterprise in the United States. Look over the list of annual failures shown in the Government's business annuals and there will be found an average bankruptcy among private business enterprises of some $200,000,000 every year for the last 20. And this terrific waste and ravage does not include "the bad debts" of an individual character, but only such failures as are of general concern and are reported to Dun and Bradstreet. It is far from true that the business of the Government is less successful than that of private enterprise. The opposite assertion is nearer just.

I have only to add under this title that no difficulty has been found among other nations in applying economic methods to public railway management. In Germany, Austria, Hungary, Belgium, India, Japan, New Zealand, Victoria, New South Wales, Russia, and, indeed, in all countries that have tried the proposal of this work. no word of discouragement is heard on the matter of "civil service." People naturally expect a rigid management on just business principles, and in no single case has there been a word of complaint.

But this should make us none the less urgent in the demand for nonpartisan control of the department of railways; and, let me say again, the idea has never been advanced but in conjunction with the emphatic requirement of such a principle.

IX. The Test of Past Experience.

"Experience is the best of teachers. We are always prone to look for precedents." The facts are that every possible species of political government has made the experiment of public ownership—some 54 different countries now owning their railways, either in the whole or in part.

One of the first features observable in the results of this system is the complete absence of the corruption and monopolies which grow out of our system.

Another is the fact that in some countries the railway traffic is made a source of political revenue. In Germany in 1890 the net profits were 38¼ per cent of the entire railway receipts, or $119,159,147.51 revenue, and this immense sum was turned into the imperial treasury. It is attested, too, that the net profits of the German system have increased 41 per cent during the 10 years, while wages are said to have been increased 1.21 per cent over the wages of private management. On third-class fare in that country one may ride 4 miles for a cent, and 10 miles on the Berlin road for a like amount.

The experience of Belgium is like that of Germany, according to Vail, who has written an excellent work on this subject. There fares and freight rates have been reduced one-half and wages of employees doubled under government operation. The net profits for 1891 were $11,313,175. In New Zealand the roads yielded a net profit of $2,179,473 in 1893, while the advantages which are said to have accrued to the colony in cheapened transportation are inestimable.

In New South Wales the government owns 2,351 miles of railways, which in 1893 returned a profit of $9,565,868. The value added to public lands would more than pay the entire cost of her roads. This is equally true of all the other Australian colonies. In Australia one may ride 1,000 miles first class for $6.50, while workingmen may ride 3 miles for 1 cent. Yet wages are from 25 to 30 per cent higher than in this country, while the working-day is but 8 hours.

In Russia some 6,800 miles are public, which, together with the new Siberian line, make 11,000 miles. This entire distance may be covered for $50, being less than a half cent per mile, through an unsettled and almost uncivilized country. The net return to the Government in 1891 was $25,000,000. All the other railways revert to the Czar in periods from 35 to 85 years. Workingmen there regularly ride at the cheap rate of $6 for 2,000 miles. In France the railways revert to the republic in specified periods.

The experience of Austria-Hungary tallies with the rest. Her net profits from railways in 1888 were $50,457,822. But since that year immense changes have been made. The "zone" has been substituted mainly for the per mile rate, each zone increasing in breadth as the total journey is an extended one. Mrs. Marion Todd, in her work "Railways of Europe and America," gives an exhaustive description of this institution.

Thus we have the project tried and tested by every kind of government. Whether in the most radical democracies, like the Australian colonies, or in the most untoward despotism, like that of Russia, whether among the people professing the endowments of western civilization or among the Hindoos or Japanese, the experience of each and all attests the immense advantage, as well as the practicability, of the public railway. Institutional lines can not, then, be drawn upon its advocates, for under every kind of political institution has this system been tried with the one result, elimination of the rottenness of irresponsible private power and an immensely augmented public service. Experience, then, would seem to favor nationalization.

Professor Ely informs us that, without exception, every man he met in Germany considered the test of experience as demonstration of the superiority of public ownership. "Even those who were once bitterly opposed to the undertaking are now convinced of their error, and no one wishes to return to private ownership."

It seems, then, in our case that it is only a question of being behind the age.

X. Trusts—Destruction by Punitive Freight Rates.

It has become almost a universal principle in pathology that the most effective method for curing a disease is to be found in the inoculation of the patient with its virus. The business men and observers of events well know that the parent of trusts has uniformly been a preferential freight rate. The Standard Oil is a well-known example of this fact; and anyone who cares to know the definite relations of this company to preferential freight rates may be well referred to a most excellent work by Henry D. Lloyd, entitled "Wealth against the Commonwealth."

It has been seen in the last 10 years that civil prohibitions are simply meaningless as against those great combinations of wealth. In the last few days we have seen offered to the attorney-general of the State of Ohio a straight bribe large enough to have subsidized ninety-nine of every hundred known kings in history. Monnett has proved stronger than the Standard Oil, but I am afraid to think how many have in the past and how many will in the future yield under so prodigious a burden. How few have ever stopped to consider that moral endurance, like physical endurance, has its well-defined limits; that while some may bear the small burden and others the greater, that still for the great mass of the human race the limit of endurance is reached far below the point at which these great monsters can disburse their bribes. Moral endurance has its limits, just like physical endurance; and while a strong man may bear up under a burden of 500 pounds, yet if the load is raised to a ton in weight he will be crushed to atoms. Little wonder is there that the moral instincts of the masses have taken fright at these omnipotent forces of corruption; and great indeed should be the anxiety of Americans in every station to curb and overpower these organizations, already more potent than any of the peace powers of the Republic.

To this end I have but one suggestion to make. If preferential freight rates were the means of lending economic strength to these great monsters, then punitive freight rates may most certainly be made the means of their undoing. Let there be a commission whose duty shall be to determine when an industrial organization has become a trust. With the Government owning the railroads (and this suggestion is only made upon that condition), the production of such trusts could be so discriminated against, on the principle of our protective tariffs, that the trusts must soon give way. The commission having determined that certain subjects of transportation were the productions of a trust, it could then issue its orders to every freight agent in the Union, commanding them to impose 100 per cent additional for the transportation of such freight, or prohibit its transportation entirely, if it were found that consumers might rely upon another market. In this way society would be meeting one economic fact with another; and history should have taught us by this time that economic factors are the only ones with which to do intelligent battle with other economic factors. A punitive or prohibitive freight rate would so harass the operations of the trust that it could not reach its market, and voluntary dissolution would follow the application of such a force.

These trusts have been recognized by the statutes of the Union and by the common law from time immemorial as crimes against the law. The suggestion, therefore, that such measures as punitive and prohibitive freight rates might be unconstitutional is hardly called for. The Constitution certainly was designed to punish crime and not to protect it. The clause therein relating to interstate commerce applies to legitimate and laudable commerce, to be determined by Congress, and where an article or manufactured product were being unlawfully produced and vended the Congress, in the interest of interstate commerce, would have the clear and unquestioned power to prohibit such traffic. The Louisiana lottery is an example of constitutional principles when applied to unlawful avocations; so that I do not perceive any valid legal objection to the practice of punitive and prohibitory freight rates.

I think it is not an assumption to say that if the proposal of Government railways were supported only by the incidental prospect of the discouragement and destruction of trusts, the American people would be nearly unanimous in favor of this measure. Certainly they have long despaired of lawsuits under antitrust legislation, for they well know that the administrators of the law are helpless in their practical impotency as against malefactors who possess the only active powers of effective government—that is, direct power over the millions of their fellow-citizens.

X. Objections Considered.

I now come to the consideration of the few objections which, when an objector is found, are sometimes made against the proposed system of national railways.

The most general of these is the one expressed in the aphorism "The least government is the best government." I do not think this maxim applicable to the subject; for in a literal sense railway administration is hardly government. The adage was born in another age, in response to censorships, government expurgatorials, imprisonment for debt, State religion, and all the trying annoyances of monarchical governments in the centuries past. It can not justly be quoted against coordination and cooperation, which, in the interest of economy, it is here sought to introduce.

But, in another sense, suppose it is admitted that the proposed transformation will place upon the roads the complexion of government—let us see what will be gained or lost.

I think it can not be denied that the systematic exercise of power by any set of persons over another number of persons is in itself "government," whether the arm of power is exerted in the name of the Government or not. Substance must be looked to, and not the mere forms of speech. Now, this being true, what are the facts in relation to private railways?

The facts are that more than four-fifths of a million of American citizens are employed by these private railways. They are dependent on their employment for the physical means of subsistence. Their necessities are their highest laws, and any power that can consciously govern their necessities can govern them. The interests or prejudices of the superior may make it desirable for him to do this frequently; to do it systematically; to make it a matter of employment or no employment if the employee, thus dependent, refuses to submit. When it becomes a question between the man's subsistence and his independence, we well know how we would act ourselves, and we well know that the vast majority of the employees thus put in terrible jeopardy may yield to what the hour seems to indicate as most convenient. He will not, as a rule, make an individual sacrifice merely for "his rights" and lose his living. A family and a lot already sufficiently reduced in its proportions make his "rights" and his necessities come in fatal conflict, and he feels that he can not retain the one and secure the other. With this power over the lives of 800,000 citizens, do the companies "govern?" If not, what name shall we give to the systematic acts of effective railway power?

For example, the writer knows of a supposed "relief fund" conducted in connection with one of our largest railways. The motives which inspired its foundation were in all probability just enough. The purpose was to raise a fund to compensate the widows and orphans as well as the injured—made such by the railway accident carnage of our system.

Every employee on penalty of his job was compelled to subscribe to this fund. Some government, I should say. After some years a surplus of $600,000 was accumulated from the excessive levies made by the company. Every provision was ostensibly made so that the accumulations should be safe, etc. A few years ago a receiver took charge of the railway, and found that the $600,000 had been swallowed up by the managers who preceded; and there is not a man in the employ of that company to-day who would dare inquire what has become of the "widow and orphans' fund"—nor will the reorganizers pay it. I refer to the former management of the Baltimore and Ohio Railroad.

Thus, it indeed becomes a question what is the least government? The managers, of course, say "ours." The love of power is deeply planted in the human breast, and the managers prefer to continue their "governing."

Does not the principle "the least government" require the transfer of this system to the hands of that institution which has no desire to oppress, no motive to plunder, no earthly reason for "governing" in the railway business any more than in the post-office?

The least government is the best government, and the least government is that with the least motive for oppression, plunder, waste of railway resources, etc.; and with these motives will pass the abuses and possibilities of too much governing.

The assertion that the roads would get into politics is met in the chapter on "Civil service." It would be almost trite to speak of how far they are now in politics. Lawson, in his text-book on railway law, gives it as his opinion, after examination of the decisions of the supreme court of Pennsylvania, that "the Pennsylvania Railroad Company seems to run that court with the same facility that it runs its trains." Politics is an important branch of the present dispensation. Railway interests daily come in conflict with the concerns of society. Taxes, rights of way, laws of negligence, grants of rights of way to competitors, and a thousand different elements make the private management think it necessary to go into "politics." Sometimes they have to "put up" to be served. Congressmen, legislators, governors, judges, tax assessors and their election are all of the deepest concern to your private railway. "In politics!" A politician would call you an idiot if you forgot to consider "the railway influence." As a general proposition every officeholder, sheriff, deputy, select magistrate, judges of lower and higher courts, all State officers, legislators, congressmen, lobbyists, indeed every officer from constable to the cabinet are the special recipients of their passes, the coin current of the railway realm. With this currency they succeed in establishing a disposition, unconscious perhaps, in their favor. If the pass does not work, something bigger is proffered, so big that, as Brice has said, "ordinary virtue turns pale." This is the inevitable consequence of the immense interests at stake, and railway managers will resort to this as long as these powerful incentives remain—i. e., as long as the exigencies of private railways exist.

I am not one of those who believe that a railway manager is necessarily a corruptionist. He does just what other speculators do in smaller affairs. The trouble is that in his case a single "coup" shakes and shatters the social fabric; his subject-matter is so great, like that of the East India Company, that entire races suffer from his operations. His doings are shifted from the circle of individual consequence to that where society itself feels the weight of his hand. The fact is that your petty stock-jobbing concerns are schools of training for him; he mostly comes through that form of chrysalis, and will emerge into your railway sultan. The remedy lies not, then, in measures of Sunday-school restraint and legislative restriction. The temptation of the "inside" on a rising or falling stock market will always prove too much; if the vaccillations do not come frequently enough he will produce them by artifice. You can not, therefore, redeem private railway management without reforming society to its depths; and the only relief predicable is that which advocates the removal of the subject-matter entirely away from the private passions and interests which dominate the railways now.

That the railways are now deeply immersed in politics to the infinite demoralization of public virtue, while the Post-Office, with nearly 200,000 employees in its service, is comparatively free from politics, I believe no one can gainsay.

Show me a single instance of the Post-Office trying to bribe a public officer or anyone else? And if there is now and then a slight change of incumbency does the service suffer; can society. complain?

But it is patent that the nation will insist upon a much more rigid enforcement of civil service as to railways; and even if there were some change now and then in administrative heads, would that be without daily and hourly precedent under the present form?

But I shall quit arguing a point so plain, for it is quite clear that with the elimination of private motives from the service its economical administration would be as free from this objection as the great postal service.

It may be objected that this project is "unconstitutional;" that the present powers of the National Government would not permit it to assume such ownership.

GOVERNMENT OWNERSHIP CONSTITUTIONAL.

I have omitted to state that the power of Congress to construct, establish, and maintain interstate railways has been set at rest by numerous decisions of the court of last resort. In 1888 the case of California v. The Central Pacific Railroad Company was decided. It involved the validity of the old acts of Congress incorporating the Pacific roads. Judge Bradley, speaking for the whole court in that case, said:

"The power to construct, or to authorize individuals or corporations to construct national highways and bridges from State to State is essential to the complete control and regulation of interstate commerce. Without authority in Congress to establish and maintain such highways and bridges it would be without authority to regulate one of the most important adjuncts of commerce. This power in former times was exerted to a very limited extent, the Cumberland or National road being the most notable instance. * * * But since, in consequence of the expansion of the country, the multiplication of its products, and the invention of railroads and locomotion by steam, land transportation has so vastly increased, a sounder consideration of the subject has prevailed and led to the conclusion that Congress has plenary power over the whole subject. Of course, the power of Congress over the Territories, and its power to grant franchises exercisable therein are and ever have been undoubted. But the wider power was very freely exercised, and much to the general satisfaction, in the creation of the vast system of railroads connecting the East with the Pacific, traversing States as well as Territories, and employing the agency of States as well as Federal corporations." (127 U. S. Reports, 156.)

In the year 1892, in the case of Monongahela Navigation Company v. United States, a full court again says:

"Notice to what the opposite view would lead: A railroad between Columbus, Ohio, and Harrisburg, Pa., is an interstate highway, created under franchises granted by the two States of Ohio and Pennsylvania, franchises not merely to construct but to take tolls for the carrying of passengers and freight. In its exercise of its supreme power to regulate commerce, Congress may condemn and take that interstate highway, etc. It may be suggested that the cases are not parallel in that in the present (a river) there is a natural highway; while in that suggested it is wholly artificial. But the power of Congress is not determined by the character of the highway. They are simply the means and instruments of commerce, and the power of Congress to regulate commerce carries with it power over all the means and instrumentalities by which commerce is carried on." (Justice Brewer, in 148 U. S. Rep., 342. See also Cherokee Nation v. Southern Kans. R. Co., 135 U. S., 641; Luxton v. North River Bridge Co., 153 U. S., 526; Western U. T. Co. v. Pendleton, 122 U. S., 347, and numerous other cases.)

The power of Congress to condemn existing roads has also been affirmatively determined. See Monongahela Navigation Company v. United States, as above given; likewise that corporate franchises may be condemned, and that such proceedings would not interfere with the inviolability of contracts. West River Bridge Company v. Town of, etc. (6 Howard, U. S., 507). The General Government possesses the power of eminent domain, etc. (Kohl v. United States; see 91 U. S., 367.) Congress might authorize an entry and the taking possession of the roads immediately, by providing a remedy against the Government for just compensation. (American and English Encyclopedia of Law, second edition, vol. 10, p. 1139, and 2 McCreary, 203; 4 Fed. Rep., 298; and Cherokee Nation v. Southern Kansas Railroad Company, 135 U. S., 641.)

These leading cases have been noted and approved by the Supreme Court in the following cases: Covington, etc., v. Sanford (164 U. S., 594); United States v.

Stanford (161 U. S., 410; 162 U. S., 494; Re Debs, 158 U. S., 565; 166 U. S., 322–323; 162 U. S., 91, and especially 98 U. S., 708).

Congress, then, has the unquestioned constitutional power to maintain the railways; to acquire them by condemnation of the franchises and property of the present owners, and may take possession of the same by a simple act of Congress, and provide for the payment of the owners in due time, when the market value of the roads is properly determined. The organic law presents no obstacles to the immediate realization of national railways.

Again it may be said by some that it is not within the sphere of government to operate railways. But the practice of three-fourths of the nations of the world is against this contention. It is not only within their sphere, but they are doing it. How about the Post-Office, the Weather Bureau, the schools and public roads? Some profess to believe that the state should only act as a policeman. But why should it act as a policeman? Obviously because it alone can do it efficiently and with due regard to social justice. In short, because the state can discharge that function better than the private citizen.

It may not be out of place to note what John Stuart Mill, one of the noblest and wisest of mankind, thought upon this subject. Discussing the exceptions to the doctrine of "laissez faire" he says:

"In attempting to enumerate the necessary functions of government, we find them to be considerably more multifarious than most people are at first aware of. * * * We sometimes, for example, hear it said that Governments ought to confine themselves to affording protection against force and fraud, etc. But why should people be protected by their Government, that is by their own collective strength, against violence and fraud, and not against other evils, except that the expediency is more obvious?" And again: " The third exception which I shale notice, to the doctrine that government can not manage the affairs of individualsl as well as individuals themselves, has reference to the great class of cases in which the individuals can only manage the concern by delegated agency, and in which the so-called private management is, in point of fact, hardly better entitled to be called management by the persons interested than administration by a public officer. Whatever is left to spontaneous agency, or can only l e done by joint-stock associations, will often be as well and sometimes better done, as far as the actual work is concerned, by the state. * * * Against the very ineffectual security afforded by meetings of stockholders and by their individual inspection and inquiries, may be placed the greater publicity and more active discussion and comment, to be expected in free countries, with regard to affairs in which the General Government takes part. There are many cases in which the agency of whatever nature by which a service is performed is certain from the nature of the case to be virtually single: in which a practical monopoly * * * can not be prevented from existing. I have already adverted more than once to the case of the gas and water companies, among which, although perfect freedom is allowed to competition, none really takes place, and practically they are found to be even more irresponsible and unapproachable by individual complaints than the Government. * * * This applies to the case of a road, a canal, or a railway. These are always in the greatest degree practical monopolies." (Political Economy, Vol. II.)

I think it is clear that the state can operate the railways better than private interests, and thus there is the same justification for Government railways as Government police. It will be found that men's ideas of the sphere of government spring mainly from their prejudices and party associations, rather than from a calm analysis of the functions of government. Whether the active forces of society shall be exerted in this or in that case depends on the facts of the case. If they are such as to demand social intervention, that alone being adequate to social need, then society should do its duty and assume its full responsibilities. Railways are far from being individual affairs; they are national in character and consequence. Only the nation is strong enough to control them; and that, as experience has shown, can not be done but by owning them. The Government is but the common agent of society to conserve its interests where the individual units can not act efficiently for themselves. Unless this is so government should be abolished and supremacy left to the strongest, and the lex talionis set in general operation.

"Government administration of the roads will be costlier than the present." And it ought to be in some respects. Any railway manager who offers an employee less than a dollar for a day's work, such as navvies sometimes receive, is an anarchist at heart, infinitely dangerous to the country of Washington. But this fact has been provided for in advance, and $90,000.000 are set to this account for the general reduction of the hours of labor from ten to eight. No government could or should desire to run the roads on the minimum wage plan, but rather with a view to the greatest social service.

But, as I have shown, instead of being costlier, one-half of the interest charge can be saved, and about one hundred millions besides in the economies which will result from the unification of the 1,985 different companies. These economies must increase from year to year, for the Government can take advantage of every labor-saving device and improvement, saying nothing of the immensely increased social service. To show that government service is not necessarily "costlier" I append a statement giving relative cost of service in some nine different European countries. Private railways and public, for the same countries, alone are compared. The table is taken from Todd's Railways of Europe and America.

Countries.	State line.	Companies line.
	Per cent.	*Per cent.*
Germany	9.40	13.10
Austria-Hungary	6.50	8.47
Belgium	5.05	10.13
Denmark	6.89	5.77
Italy	6.49	8.76
Norway	7.80	7.00
Holland	5.30	10.35
Roumania	4.40	10.80
Russia	9.27	13.70

"The roads should be left to the free action of competition." We have seen that in order to pay interest on the investment and cost of operation it is necessary, in 90 per cent of the country, that a road should secure all the traffic. Two roads mean two bad ones, poorly equipped, cheaply paid labor, business disaster, no interest, no dividends; finally combination or agreement as to rates—a monopoly at last. No law can make it other than profitable for the roads to agree rather than fight and waste their resources. Sound economy of capital and labor requires that social service rather than "competition" should be the aim of railway administration. The railways themselves are against competition. They have had a bill introduced in Congress known as "the pooling law," which seeks to drive away forever the principle of competition, and to combine them for the purpose of profit. If they should succeed in this object we should then have a private corporation collecting more revenue each year than all the city, county, State, and Federal governments, and dispensing more in interest and dividends every year than the United States does to administer the Government, while it would have on its pay roll an army of voters larger in numbers than the commands of both Grant and Lee. And experience has shown us that private owners cow and vote them. This cannot be fairly said of the post-office. Who would own the Government then? Is it not better that the people should own both the roads and the Government? And "competition," where would it be? "Gentle shepherd, tell me where."

Now all these objections were singly and collectively made before the Government of Germany assumed the ownership of the roads, and each and all of them have happily proved to be invalid. Professor Cohn, of the University of Göttingen, says that in Germany the question of state ownership and management has been settled by the test of experience.

To sum up, then, there are some 10 great objects which can certainly be secured by nationalization of the railways:

(1) The perfect security of the capital invested; precarious railway securities must pass away. A vast body of certain investment will arise instead.

(2) Uniformity and equality of freight rates throughout the different freight zones; all shippers will enjoy equal opportunities, the national desire of 20 years. Only this system can cure quasi natural as well as willful discriminations.

(3) A half-cent passenger rate per mile over the entire country. A volume would be necessary to describe the resulting educational, industrial, and social advantages.

(4) An 8-hour day for all railway workers; trackmen elevated from helotism; the immediate use of all safety appliances. A volume more would be needed to state the benefits to the workmen and society at large which must result from the introduction of these principles and the employment of 165,000 additional men, now tramping the streets of our towns and cities begging for work.

(5) The greater development of the resources of the country by a wise application of the capital now wasted in "parallels."

(6) A juster distribution of railway mileage as between the different States; the grossest discrimination and inequality is the practical effect of the present system.

(7) The emancipation of public men from the influence and evils of "railway

corruption and politics." I do not mean this as denunciation, but as my sober judgment of the unavoidable consequence of leaving such prodigious power and temptations to the natural selfishness of at most a very few men. Moral endurance, like physical strength, is a limited quantity; nations should take competent notice of this fact by abridging the artificial power of "positions."

(8) The establishment and operation of a postal express; that I tried to show might be the means of reducing the cost of the express service 50 per cent. The advantages to commerce are beyond computation.

(9) The gradual inauguration of a system of accident insurance for passengers, employees, and, perhaps, to cover losses of freight.

(10) The availability of punitive freight rates to destroy or discourage monopolies.

Besides, this great body of capital thus released, in effect, from the railways, could be used to build up the country in various directions.

Now, in view of all these great ends I desire to ask, in perfect candor, those who have hitherto opposed this proposal (and they are among the most powerful), are you not in honor bound, by the great gifts with which our common country has enriched you, to examine again, perhaps a little more impartially and generously, a proposition which will mean so much for this generation and the countless generations destined to live their lives in this quarter of the globe? Are a few aphorisms of doubtful validity, such as "least government," "not in the sphere of government," and "may get into politics" more to you than the collective interests of an entire race? You know how received ideas have been shaken up by modern science; do you not think this great topic worth a frank study from the other standpoint, the claims of society? I believe you do, and if your interest could be earnestly engaged I am quite certain a great problem could be settled right.

I might occupy as many more pages in narrating the history of railway scandal in the last 20 years. I do not desire to "play with the feelings" of the reader, who in all probability is as well acquainted with that subject as rehearsal could make him.

I now desire to refer the reader to the sources from which this work has been compiled. The Interstate Commerce reports, most excellently edited and reliably prepared from the accounts of the companies, are my principal sources of information. They may be had for any year since 1888 from the courteous members of the board. This board has succeeded in achieving a greater purpose than was contemplated by its founders. It has settled, by its reports, this whole question from the standpoint of political economy in favor of nationalization.

THE FUTILITY OF REGULATION.

Even those who have opposed the Government assumption of the railways have not denied the intolerable evils of private ownership. Their hopes of betterment are, however, based upon the idea that the Government should merely interfere and regulate the traffic. This suggestion of compromise between two irreconcilable powers and two discordant interests can only meet, has only met, the fate common in attempts to balance two inherent enemies. As a matter of a priori argument it would seem clear that a regulation of the railways must be premised upon a set of conditions which can never exist among some 1,000 different companies. Uniformity of practice, rates, classifications, etc., presupposes common interests, aims, and conditions. No rule can be made on any material matter as to which the violation will not be more advantageous than the observance to a considerable number of the regulated railways. Therefore the temptation will come to violate, and such a violation throws the whole outfit into anarchy. But this "regulation" has been tried. Let the regulators narrate their grief. (Report Interstate Commerce Commission, 1898, p. 6):

"There is, therefore, a constant temptation to obtain it at any cost. Now, the rates between two competitive points have been published. The manager of one road finds that business has abandoned his line, and he believes that it is moving by a rival route. He can draw but one inference, and that is that his competitor has secretly reduced the rate. Under these circumstances what shall he do? Shall he maintain the published rate and thereby abandon the business? But that means disaster to his road, the loss of his reputation as manager, and ultimately of his employment. What most managers actually do is to get the business by making whatever rate is necessary. * * * Meanwhile the situation has become intolerable, both from the standpoint of the public and the carriers. Tariffs are disregarded, discriminations constantly occur, the price at which transportation can be obtained is fluctuating and uncertain. Railroad managers are distrustful of each other and shippers all the while in doubt as to the rates secured by their competitors. Enormous sums are spent in purchasing business and secret rates accorded far below the standard of published charges. The general public gets little benefit from these reductions, for concessions are mainly confined to the heavier shippers. All this augments the advantages of large capital and tends to the injury and often to the ruin of smaller dealers. These are not only matters of gravest consequence to the business welfare of the country, but they concern in no less degree the higher interests of public morality."

The commission, then, confesses the disorder. But it also confesses that it is beyond regulation. I shall quote freely from its reports, for they contain the sanction of experience, the highest reason. (See Report 1897, pp. 32 to 47.)

FAILURE TO MAINTAIN PUBLISHED RATES.

"If the act were amended in accordance with the foregoing suggestions, we believe it would in the main secure the establishment and publication of just and reasonable tariffs. If such rates are published, shippers will see to it that they are not charged too much. This, however, is but half the problem. It is one thing to secure the publication of a proper rate and another thing to secure adherence to it. Discrimination may be occasioned not only by charging too much, but as well by charging too little. We are constrained to believe that one of the worst features in' the present situation arises from a departure from the published rate in favor of particular shippers, and that this might continue to be so.

"It is well understood that the statute at the present time makes it a criminal offense, punishable by fine or imprisonment, for an officer or agent of a railroad company to receive for like service less from one shipper than from another. It is also a crime, punishable in the same manner, if any shipper takes a rate less than the published rate. It was assumed when these provisions of the law were enacted that they would secure compliance with the open rate. It speedily began to be said, however, that carriers did not maintain their rates, and the commission undertook the investigation of complaints of this character; but upon inquiring of those persons who had knowledge of the transactions, either as agents of the carrier or as shippers, objection was made that the witness could not be obliged to criminate himself and was, therefore, not compelled to answer. This left the commission entirely without power to obtain evidence of offenses of this character, since neither the shipper who received the rate nor the railroad official who gave it could be compelled to testify to the fact. In order to meet this difficulty, the law was so amended as to exempt the witness from all further prosecution for that offense, and this provision was held in the Brown case to be a constitutional one.

"The Brown decision was announced in April, 1896, and thereupon railroad managers immediately became loud in their protests that whatever might have occurred in the past, upon the strength of the notion that it could not be discovered, should no longer occur, and that rates from then on would be scrupulously maintained. It soon began to be said, however, that conditions were becoming much the same as they had been before. Railroad men themselves tacitly admitted that rates were not maintained. The press openly charged it. and what inquiries the commission could make led us to the same conclusion. Finally, for the purpose of ascertaining what could be developed in the way of investigation, we began that inquiry into grain rates between the West and the Atlantic seaboard which is referred to in another part of this report. It is only proposed to observe here in reference to that inquiry that it was participated in by the several members of the commission in person; that those officers of the different railroad companies engaging in that traffic, who must have known had the rate been departed from, were called before us and compelled to give evidence under oath. That evidence was, without exception, that the rate had been in all cases maintained.

"Now, these gentlemen must have known whereof they spoke. Their testimony covers a period in which rates of the kind involved were said to have been more than ordinarily disturbed, and that testimony shows that during all that time and in reference to all those shipments the published tariff was scrupulously exacted. Nevertheless, there are strong reasons for believing that the fact is otherwise. Those who are in a position to know say that this is so. Railroad managers themselves, with one accord, declare it to be so. Facts which are morally convincing, although not of a character to secure a legal conviction, lead us to the same opinion. We have no doubt that at the present time very large quantities of competitive traffic are carried at other than published rates.

"The effect of this rate cutting is most unfortunate. Incidentally it prefers the large to the small shipper. Rebates can not be given to-day as they were before the passage of this act, nor as they were before the Brown decision even.

Various devices are resorted to. Only a few can know of the transaction. The whole matter must be covered up and kept secret, with the result that the large shipper, the trust, the monopoly, is able to secure the concession, while the small shipper is obliged to pay the published rates, and this concession, while at the present time small as a rule in individual instances, is often very large in the aggregate.

"But the most unfortunate feature of the whole situation is the fact that it often prevents the honest shipper from doing business at all. It being a crime to accept less than the published rate, one who believes that the law of the land should be obeyed can not accept a reduction from that rate. It is only the dishonest trader that can and does accept it. This concession is often the only profit in the transaction. A margin of a cent a bushel on grain when handled in large quantities for export is considered a fair one, and this is not a large nor unusual concession in the freight rate. The result is therefore that not only is the honest dealer at a disadvantage, but he may be absolutely prohibited from engaging in that business.

"The same thing is true with the carrier. It is a crime for the agent of the railroad company to give this concession in rates, and no honest man can be, on behalf of the railroad company, a party to such a transaction ; so that the carrier which would obey the law is deprived of the business that legitimately belongs to it.

"It is not suggested that railroad managers wantonly violate the law in this respect. As a rule, they are apparently anxious to obey it. The failure to do so not only makes them criminals, but inflicts enormous losses upon the properties they represent. Why, then, should not rates be maintained ? 'Because,' says the carrier, 'this law, under existing conditions, puts it into the power of the dishonest railway and the dishonest shipper to compel every competing railway and every competing shipper to be dishonest also or withdraw from the business.' The shipper declares : 'If I pay the published rate, I must close my warehouse.' The carrier asserts : 'If I exact the published rate, the traffic which belongs to me goes to my rival and my stockholders are without dividends.'

"It is difficult to conceive a graver charge than this or a more outrageous situation than that which is assumed to justify the charge. To what extent that situation actually prevails the commission has no definite knowledge. That it exists to a considerable extent seems certain ; that there is pressing need of a remedy can not be denied. The carriers insist that such a remedy lies in the enactment of a pooling bill, which they earnestly demand."

As to "pooling" and its wisdom the commission does not agree. I quote again:

POOLING.

"As to the wisdom of this legislation the commission is not agreed. In the first place, we do not agree as to the probable effect of such a law. There is no precedent by which we can be fairly guided as to the result. * * *

"At the same time it must be remembered that if pooling produces any beneficial result it necessarily does so at the expense of competition. It is only by destroying competition that the inducement to deviate from the published rate is wholly removed, and it is only to the extent that competition is actually destroyed that beneficial results can be expected. Notwithstanding the specious arguments of carriers to the contrary, this is and must be the fact. By the legalizing of pooling the public loses the only protection which it now has against the unreasonable exactions of transportation agencies. We are all agreed that the enormous power which such a measure would place in the hands of railroad companies ought not to be granted, unless the exercise of that power is properly restrained in advance. * * * The members of the Interstate Commerce Commission wish to say in the strongest possible terms that they are unanimous in the opinion that to overturn the trans-Missouri decision, to repeal the fifth section and enact in its place a pooling bill, thereby permitting and inviting unlimited combination between carriers, would be little better than a crime against the people of the United States, unless this tribunal, or some other tribunal, is at the same time invested with adequate powers of control, and that nothing less in degree than those outlined in this report or their equivalent would be adequate."

That is, a system of regulation, etc., of the "poolers" shall be tried again. I do not mean to speak disparagingly of the members of that board. The public has not sufficiently, in my opinion, appreciated the high integrity of its labors— labors none the less trying, arduous, or commendable because unattended with the desired results. It is, indeed, extremely gratifying to know that men may be obtained in the public service for a small pittance to pass upon subjects of such immense financial proportions without a single suggestion of impropriety or partiality in 10 long years.

But to come again to the pooling project. The railways want that. The commission believe it would be a crime unless accompanied with adequate power of control, etc. It is not claimed that pooling would prevent discrimination in favor of "large capital," i. e., trusts and the like. And of what avail would it be to the people? There would be none of the economies of a single organization as against one thousand. The old line of expense would remain intact. Its object is to maintain rates and protect the railway owners from the disadvantages of competition. Under such circumstances we might see some 4 billions of railway stock now cursed to barreness by its parents, "water and fraud," rise into predatory vitality again. How much better to proceed the entire way, as has been done in Germany and some 50 countries, and own and operate them on principles which everyone concedes should control. Common ownership and common interests will secure us every end deemed so desirable. The commission admits that transportation is a governmental function. (Report 1898, pp. 19, 20).

"While railway transportation in this country is carried on by private capital, it is essentially a Government function. This appears from the necessary conditions of railroad construction. It is a universal maxim that private property can not be taken for private uses, but only for the public use. Yet no railroad can be built without the appropriation of private property. It equally appears from the relation of the carrier's business to the community. A merchant may sell to one customer for one price and to another customer for another price, as best subserves his interest, without violating any sense of right and wrong, but it is to-day universally felt that the rates of public transportation should be uniform to all. As we have already said, the railway is, from its very nature, in respect to the greater part of its business, a virtual monopoly. The essential feature of a Government function or of a monopoly is that it excludes the idea of competition, and this notion prevails in almost every civilized country to-day."

Moreover, the railway managers will not consent to accept the pooling arrangement when incumbered by the conditions, the absence of which the commission considers a crime against the people. Milton H. Smith, president of the Louisville and Nashville Railroad Company, in the North American Review for April, declares that "it might be decidedly better that the Government should acquire the roads" than to submit to the rate-making power in the commission.

Very respectfully submitted.

DAVID J. LEWIS.

CUMBERLAND, MD., *May 25, 1899.*

STATEMENT OF MR. WALTER E. WEYL,

On American and European Passenger Rates.

The following table shows in a general way the contrast between the passenger traffic of America and that of European and East Indian railways. The number of passengers on American railways is less than that on British and German railways, and in proportion to population the American people take a considerable smaller number of trips than do the English or Germans, or indeed the French, Belgians, or Swiss. The average distance traveled per passenger, however, is considerably greater in the United States than in the States of Western Europe, and the total number of miles traveled by all passengers on American railways is greater than that for any other country, although in pro ortion to population it is only about as great as that of Germany or France and prpbably considerably less than that of Great Britain, while in proportion to our total mileage our passenger traffic is quite insignificant. Our receipts per passenger are considerably higher than those of other countries, our fares averaging 2 cents, while those of Europe average generally from three-fourths cent to 1¼ cents. The peculiarity of American traffic, however, is that high fares are associated with empty trains (as may be seen from a comparison of the receipts in the various sections of the United States), and the receipts per passenger train made on European railways are not much below those on American railways.

The comparison often made between the day-coach service in America and the first-class cars on the Continent is defective since, as the following table shows, the great mass of travel in Europe is in the third or fourth class. The comparison between first-class in America and third-class in Europe shows a superior service in American lines and a cheaper service in European roads. India offers the example of exceedingly poor and remarkably cheap service, together with good returns to the railways.

The accompanying statement has been compiled from the most trustworthy accessible resources, and it is to the best of my knowledge and belief correct.

WALTER E. WEYL.

DISTRICT OF COLUMBIA, *City of Washington:*

Sworn to and subscribed before me this 21st day of December, 1899.

S. OLVIA MOORE,
[SEAL.]   *Notary Public, District of Columbia.*

Country.	Year.	Number of passengers (in millions).	Number of passenger miles (in millions).	Number of passengers per head of population. a	Number of passenger miles per head of population. a	Average length of trip in miles.	Receipts per passenger.	Receipts per passenger per mile.	Number of passengers per train.	Revenue per passenger train mile. b	Passenger density. (Ton miles divided by miles of railroad.)	Freight density. (Ton miles divided by miles of railroad net tons.)
						M.	Cts.	Cts.		Cts.		
Germany	1897-8	692.5	10,058	a 13.2	192	14.5	15.7	1.08	71	77	342,000	661,000
United Kingdom	1897	c1,060.4	....	c27.0	....	17.4	......	......	...	...	283,000	373,000
France	1897	396.7	7,227	10.3	188	18.3	27.8	1.17	...	...	289,000	373,000
India d	1897	151.2	5,931	0.5	20	39.2	e11.4	e.27	e189	e62	289,000	234,000
United States	1898	501.2	13,880	{ 8.0 / g(6.6)	{ 214 / g(189)	26.7	{ f9.0 / 52.6	{ f.25 / 1.97	{ f215 / 39	{ f60 / 77	72,000	618,000

a On the basis of the last preceding census.
b Including passenger fares alone and not including receipts from mail, express, or other revenues often associated with passenger receipts.
c Not including season-ticket travel.
d Rupee taken at 21 cents. See United States Consular Reports. According to the value of the rupee the receipts of Indian railways in gold would be 50 per cent greater than the figures here given.
e Broad-gauge railways.
f Meter-gauge railways.
g On the basis of an estimated population of 76,000,000 for the year 1899.

Divisions of passenger travel in various classes in various countries.

Country.	Year.	Per cent of all passengers in class.					
		1.	2.	3.	4.	Military class.	Total.
Germany	1898	0.37	9.5	60.8	27.63	1.7	100
Switzerland	1897	.94	14.47	84.59			100
Belgium (state)	1897	3.07	10.19	86.74			100
India:							
Broad gauge	1897	.5	28	4.8	91.9		100
Meter gauge	1897	.3	1.4	1	97.3		100
Norway	1898	.1	7.3	92.6			100
Sweden (state)	1897	.3	13.2	84.8		1.7	100
Denmark	1898	.6	12.7	86.7			100
United Kingdom	1898	3.1	6.2	90.7			100
Italy	1892	4	24.3	71.7			100

INQUIRY CONCERNING LEGISLATION AFFECTING RAILWAY LABOR.

The questions in the commission's "Inquiry concerning legislation affecting railway labor" are set out together below. The answers thereto follow, each being marked to correspond to the question to which it is a reply.

I.

What legislation, if any, would you recommend the States and Congress to enact concerning the employment and discharge of railway employees?

1. Legislation to insure to employees the right to membership in their brotherhoods and associations.

2. Legislation regarding blacklisting.

3. Would it be advisable to regulate by law the conditions under which railway employees may be discharged?

4. Please suggest such other legislation as you may think advisable concerning employing and discharging railway employees.

II.

Is it desirable to regulate by State or Federal legislation the hours of labor in any branches of the railway service? If so, what legislation would you suggest?

III.

1. What legislation, if any, would you recommend for the purpose of limiting the power of the State and Federal courts to issue injunctions in cases of disputes between railway companies and their employees?

2. Should there be a limit put upon the power of Federal courts to imprison for contempt?

3. Would it be desirable to allow only the Attorney-General of the United States to invoke the equitable jurisdiction of the Federal courts in controversies between common carriers of interstate commerce and their employees concerning wages and terms of employment where irreparable injury is threatened?

IV.

1. What State and Federal legislation would you recommend for the modification of the common-law provision exempting the employing railway company from liability for damages received by an employee as the result of the negligence of a "fellow-servant?"

2. Would it be possible, and would it be desirable, to require Federal courts to follow the rules of law laid down by State courts in cases involving injuries to railway employees?

V.

Is the law of June 1, 1898, concerning conciliation and arbitration, satisfactory? If it is unsatisfactory, what changes would you recommend?   In discussing the law, will you please state, among other things, what you thinkconcerning—
(a) The feasibility or pra ti a i it of compulsory arbitration.
(b) The desirability of additional legislation regarding the relief departments established by railway companies.

VI.

What additional State and Federal legislation, if any, do you desire on the subject of safety appliances?

VII.

If any State or Federal legislation that you may think desirable is not suggested by the foregoing questions, will you please state what you think that legislation should be?

REPLY FROM THE CHIEF EXECUTIVE OFFICERS OF BROTHERHOOD OF LOCOMOTIVE ENGINEERS, BROTHERHOOD OF LOCOMOTIVE FIREMEN, ORDER OF RAILWAY CONDUCTORS, BROTHERHOOD OF RAILWAY TRAINMEN, AND ORDER OF RAILROAD TELEGRAPHERS.·

AUGUST 18, 1899.

To the Sub-Commission on Transportation of the Industrial Commission.

GENTLEMEN: Answering the inquiries bearing upon the subject of "Legislation affecting railway labor," we submit the following suggestions. We desire that this evidence shall be understood as supplementary to that prepared by us and submitted during the early days of the hearing before the commission (see p. 64). We further desire to be understood as speaking from the standpoint of the employees composing our organizations, and as reflecting the consensus of the opinions which are held by them.

I.

1. We believe that the right of a railway employee to hold membership in a reputable and lawful organization of his choice should be as inalienable as his right to worship God according to the dictates of his conscience.
Our organizations are permitted by and are recognized in the laws of the United States. The jurisdiction of Congress over interstate railroads is unquestioned. To the credit of the vast majority of the railway managers be it said that it is the sentiment and the actions of a very few which render any legislation on this subject desirable.
We believe that discrimination of any kind on the part of an officer of a railway against an employee or an applicant for employment on account of membership in a lawful organization should be met with a punishment so swift, so sure, and so severe as to not only prevent a repetition of the act on the part of that particular employer, but to afford an object lesson which will have a salutary and the desired effect upon others who may be similarly inclined.
By reference to section 10 of the act of June 1, 1898, commonly termed the "arbitration law," it will be seen that this point was sought to be covered. If that enactment can be strengthened or reenforced we should be greatly pleased to see it done.
2. It will be seen that section 10 of the act of June 1, 1898, just referred to, makes "blacklisting" a misdemeanor. We are of the opinion that existing laws, State and national, are sufficient to prevent any open blacklisting of exemployees. It will probably be impossible to entirely stop the secret practice unless a penalty sufficiently severe to make fear of the penalty outweigh the desire to violate the law can be attached. We favor such a penalty.
3. We may well doubt the advisability of such legislation. Our organizations afford pretty full protection against unjust dismissals of our members, except where in a few instances the employees have no thorough organization and are not permitted, through fear of loss of employment, to perfect such organization.
4. We reaffirm the statement in our first answers (see page 66): "Railroad companies have recently adopted with practical unanimity the requirement of a

searching physical examination of all applicants for employment, under which the man who has suffered amputation of a portion of a hand or foot, or who has suffered from some other injury while in the service of some railway company, is refused employment by other companies. If a man who has sustained such injury, which in reality does not prevent or hinder him from performing in an able manner the duties of his position, or who has attained a certain age which leaves him the prime of life yet to be lived, is to be refused employment under the operation of a rule adopted in concert or contemporaneously by the railroads, it seems but fair that the employee should look to the railroads for compensation for his injury or pension for his age." Moral obligations, even though strong and weighty, are not always met and cheerfully discharged. This moral obligation should be laid upon the railway companies and should also be made a legal obligation which could not be evaded.

II.

The necessity of changing train and engine crews at established points where terminal facilities are provided renders it impracticable to arbitrarily fix the hours of labor of train and engine men. We think the hours of labor of yard and office men should be shortened, and we think they could reasonably be fixed by law. For train dispatchers and yard employees in large or busy yards, 8 hours should constitute a day. In all other classes of service 10 hours should be recognized as a day's work, and all time on duty in excess of 10 hours for a day's pay should be paid for as extra or overtime.

We would suggest an act specifying the legal workday as above and legalizing claims for extra pay for extra hours worked.

III.

1. In addition to the provisions incorporated in the act of June 1, 1898, we think it would be well to enact substantially the following:

"*Be it enacted by the Senate and House of Representatives of the United States of America in Congress assembled,* That contempts of court are divided into two classes, direct and indirect, and shall be proceeded against only as hereinafter prescribed.

"SEC. 2. That contempts committed during the sitting of the court or of a judge at chambers, in its or his presence or so near thereto as to obstruct the administration of justice, are direct contempts. All other are indirect contempts.

"SEC. 3. That a direct contempt may be punished summarily without written accusation against the person arraigned, but if the court shall adjudge him guilty thereof a judgment shall be entered of record in which shall be specified the conduct constituting such contempt, with a statement of whatever defense or extenuation the accused offered thereto and the sentence of the court thereon.

"SEC. 4. That upon the return of an officer on process or an affidavit duly filed, showing any person guilty of indirect contempt, a writ of attachment or other lawful process may issue and such person be arrested and brought before the court; and thereupon a written accusation setting forth succinctly and clearly the facts alleged to constitute such contempt shall be filed and the accused required to answer the same by an order which shall fix the time therefor and also the time and place for hearing the matter. The court may, on proper showing, extend the time so as to give the accused a reasonable opportunity to purge himself of such contempt. After the answer of the accused, or if he refuse or fail to answer, the court may proceed at the time so fixed to hear and determine such accusation upon such testimony as shall be produced. If the accused answer the trial shall proceed upon testimony produced as in criminal cases, and the accused shall be entitled to be confronted with the witnesses against him; but such trial shall be by the court, or, in its discretion, upon application of the accused, a trial by jury may be had as in any criminal case. If the accused be found guilty judgment shall be entered accordingly, prescribing the punishment.

"SEC. 5. That the testimony taken on the trial of any accusation of indirect contempt may be preserved by bill of exceptions, and any judgment of conviction therefor may be reviewed upon direct appeal to or by writ of error from the Supreme Court, and affirmed, reversed, or modified as justice may require. Upon allowance of an appeal or writ of error execution of the judgment shall be stayed upon the giving of such bond as may be required by the court or a judge thereof, or by any justice of the Supreme Court.

"SEC. 6. That the provisions of this act shall apply to all proceedings for contempt in all courts of the United States except the Supreme Court; but this act shall not affect any proceedings for contempt pending at the time of the passage thereof."

We believe the criminal laws are brought into contempt and lose much of their vitality by the liberal use of the process of injunction restraining men from doing those things which the law prohibits their doing. We repeat that it is much better to depend upon the code and let all men understand that the laws as contained in the code are to be applied alike to all, and are to be enforced without further warning in the shape of injunction, mandamus, or in other form.

2. The dignity of the courts must be upheld and their decisions be enforceable and enforced. For an act of open or violent contempt, committed in the presence of the court, the court should have power to summarily punish. But even then the foundations of our form of government and jurisprudence would be strengthened if an appeal were open for the offender. Judges, though chosen with a view to their especial fitness for the position, are human. If they do in reality possess the judicial mind which they are supposed to possess would they not prefer that an appeal be open for the offender, to the end that the court might be relieved of the charge that unnecessarily severe punishment had been meted out because of the sole jurisdiction of the court?

In cases of alleged contempt, consisting of acts committed outside of the presence of the court a trial by jury should be permitted, if demanded by accused, and appeal to the higher court should be permitted.

3. Where men simply exercise their inalienable right to cease work under an employer or conditions which are no longer satisfactory or acceptable, and where due regard for the public safety is exercised, as is always the case with the men in whose name we speak, we see no occasion for the intervention of the Federal courts. The courts have, not infrequently, interfered with restraining orders under the plea of threatened irreparable injury, when the injury was neither threatened nor irreparable if inflicted.

We invite a careful review of the records in connection with the restraining order issued in December, 1893, by Judge Jenkins of the Federal court in Wisconsin on request of the receiver of the Northern Pacific Railroad, the hearings on motion to modify said writ, the hearing on appeal to the appellate court, and the Congressional investigation of Judge Jenkins's act. We also invite careful review of similar order issued shortly thereafter by Judge Dundy, of Nebraska, on petition of the receivers of the Union Pacific Railway, and the subsequent proceedings in the Federal courts. It will be found that the only injury that "threatened" at that time existed solely in the minds of the receivers.

IV.

1. We have seen no proposed legislation on this subject which seemed more comprehensive and concise than the proposed bill referred to by Mr. E. A. Moseley in his testimony before your commission, and found on page 81 of that printed testimony.

2. We are inclined to doubt the possibility of taking such jurisdiction away from the Federal courts. We believe it would be much better for all concerned if the decision of some court could be made the rule and be followed in all cases to which it could be justly applied. If that were done all interested would understand alike and the hope that another court could differ in opinion from the one whose decision had been handed down would not encourage the prosecution of doubtful cases or the stubborn defense of such as were not doubtful.

V.

The act of June 1, 1898, has not as yet been given a fair test. It must depend for its vitality very largely upon the vigorous and interested way in which the commissioners, who are charged with the duty of invoking its conciliatory provisions and its arbitration features, take hold of any case which is brought to their attention. If dignified with earnestness on part of the Government officials, we believe the law to be pregnant with good. We have no suggestions as to changes in it to offer at this time.

(a) We do not believe that the decision of a board or court, involving the relations between employer and employee, in the appointment of which the parties most at interest have no voice, is or ever can be arbitration. When compulsion comes in, the spirit of arbitration steps out. We do not see how "compulsory arbitration" can be indulged in without creating "involuntary servitude," and that when it is not a "punishment for crime."

(*b*) Our ideas on relief associations are expressed in our former testimony. (See p. 67 of the printed testimony.) The act of June 1, 1898, makes it unlawful to make membership in such an association a condition of employment. If the association were in fact " voluntary," there would be little in it to criticise.

VI.

We think the existing law sufficient for the present. After the time within which its terms must be complied with has passed, it may develop that additional legislation, State or national, will be necessary or desirable.

VII.

As of great value in compiling accurate data, and as a guide to intelligent conclusion as to the necessity for legislation on any subject originating in or connected with railroad accidents, the causes and responsibilities therefor, we heartily recommend the enactment of the amendment to the act of March 2, 1893, introduced in the Senate of the Fifty-fifth Congress by Senator Pettigrew, known as Senate bill No. 3244, and referred to by Mr. Moseley in his testimony before your commission. (See pp. 37, 38, this volume.)

Yours, very truly,

E. E. CLARK,
Grand Chief Order of Railway Conductors.

P. M. ARTHUR,
Grand Chief Brotherhood of Locomotive Engineers.

F. P. SARGENT,
Grand Master Brotherhood of Locomotive Firemen.

P. H. MORRISSEY,
Grand Master Brotherhood of Railway Trainmen.

W. V. POWELL,
Grand Chief Order of Railway Telegraphers.

REPLY OF MR. F. W. ARNOLD,

Grand Secretary and Treasurer Brotherhood of Locomotive Firemen.

PEORIA, ILL., *August 10, 1899.*

The Subcommission on Transportation,
Industrial Commission, Washington, D. C.

SIRS: I take pleasure in replying to your recent request for answers to certain interrogatories:

I.

1. I would recommend that Congress enact a law giving employees the right to join an organization of their classes for the purpose of better protecting their interests intellectually, socially, morally, and financially.

2. I would recommend a stringent law against blacklisting, so called, as it is clearly un-American, unfair, and unjust. The present law is not complete, nor does it answer the purpose.

3. I think that a railway employee, who has devoted the greater part of his life, and faithfully, to his trade or calling, and who arrives at an age that is regarded by the railroad corporation as objectionable, should not be discharged for that cause alone, and thrown upon his own, generally meager, resources. Also that an employee who has faithfully performed his duties for a long term of years, and who has reached an age that prohibits him from starting successfully in some other walk, should not be discharged simply because he has violated some ordinary rule of the corporation, unless, perhaps, it be of the most serious possible character.

II.

I should judge it highly desirable and necessary that there be Federal legislation regulating the hours of continuous labor on railways, that employees may secure such rest as will enable them to perform their work with safety to themselves, the public, and to the property of their employer. Men on locomotives can not be regarded as safe men unless they have a reasonable number of hours of rest each day.

III.

1. I would recommend the passage of the bill that has been before Congress for several years, but which has been side tracked on various occasions, by others than employees, and known as the "contempt" bill. It provides substantially for two kinds of contempt, and was first drawn up by the late Senator Daniel Voorhees, of Indiana. The two kinds of contempt shall be known as "direct contempt" and "indirect contempt." "Direct contempt" shall be that committed within the knowledge of the court and should be punishable by fine only. "Indirect contempt" shall be that committed without the knowledge of the court and shall be tried by jury, the punishment for which should be by fine.

2. I think courts should not be given the right to imprison for contempt committed without their knowledge. From a humane standpoint I think imprisonment for contempt in any particular belongs to the dark ages, since punishment by fine would be, in my opinion, quite as efficacious.

3. I can not say.

IV.

1. I would recommend for State and Federal legislation a law that is now embodied in a bill known as the "Employees Liability" bill, which corrects the shameless injustice in the present law which exempts railway corporations from liability for damages received by an employee as the result of the negligence of a fellow-servant.

2. I should think it possible, and certainly desirable, that Congress should require Federal courts to follow the rules of law laid down by State courts in cases involving injuries to railway employees, and I think it equally desirable that Congress enact a law making a uniform amount of damages recoverable in all States and Territories alike where an employee has received injuries, followed by death, as the result of the negligence of a fellow-servant, and an unstated amount where injuries, amounting to total and permanent disability, have been received under like circumstances.

V.

The law of June 1, 1898, so far as I have been able to observe its application, is satisfactory.

a. I do not regard as feasible or practicable any such thing as compulsory arbitration.

b. I would recommend that Congress enact a law which will prohibit a railway corporation, by threat, insinuation, or innuendo, or in any other manner, to require an employee to involuntarily become a member of or join a relief association or department in order that such employee shall remain in the service of such corporation.

VI.

I have no suggestions to offer in reply to this question.

VII.

I would recommend that Congress enact a law giving to all labor organizations (strictly so) that are not organized nor conducted for profit a right to carry on an insurance business, not for profit, strictly among its members, without the requirement of incorporating, nor of licensing in any State except the State where the headquarters of the organization may be located, and that after procuring such license such organization shall have standing in any court in any State or Territory.

Very respectfully, yours,   F. W. ARNOLD,
                                         Grand Secretary and Treasurer.

REPLY OF MR. JOHN T. WILSON,

Grand Chief of the Brotherhood of Railroad Trackmen of America.

St. Louis, Mo., *August 12, 1899.*

The Subcommission on Transportation, Industrial Commission, Washington, D. C.

Sirs: I reply as follows to your favor of 19th ultimo with a list of questions inclosed, which were prepared for the purpose of completing the Industrial Commission's inquiry concerning "Legislation affecting railway labor, etc.":

I.

1. When a railway company, through any of its officers or agents, is charged and found guilty of interfering with or discriminating against any of its employees on account of their connection with their brotherhoods, it should be fined not less than $10 nor more than $25,000 dollars in each case; 10 per cent of the fine to be awarded to the prosecuting witness and 10 per cent to the prosecuting attorney, the balance to revert to the school fund of the State in which conviction is secured.

A few days ago I received a letter containing the following paragraph: "My husband is dead. He would have kept in good standing with your order, but he was afraid the company would find it out and discharge him. I am a sickly woman, not able to work. I have 5 small children. We were unable to save anything during his lifetime, and if the brotherhood does not help me, God only knows what will become of us."

2. The system of blacklisting is conducted with so much privacy that I hardly think it possible to enact and enforce laws to abolish the evil. I do not think that very many railway managers would condescend to blacklist an employee without he had shown himself to be reckless, unreliable, or unworthy of trust.

3. As railway employees are frequently discharged without just cause by minor officials who have but little, if any, sense of honor or justice, they (the minor officials) should only be permitted to suspend employees under their jurisdiction and should be required to report the cause of suspension to the general manager. The suspended employee should always be given an opportunity to make a statement in his own behalf. The manner in which the Government employees in the United States Mail Service are dismissed would, I think, be a good rule for railway companies to adopt; always making the general manager of the road the highest tribunal to appeal to and permitting his decision to be final.

Last month I was informed by a section foreman on the Union Pacific Railway that the foremen under the jurisdiction of the roadmaster for whom he was working received a letter from their roadmaster insisting upon them to subscribe for a paper known as the Roadmaster and Foreman, and advising them to send him $4 for a year's subscription. The subscription price of the paper is $1 a year. It is customary with the publishers to give roadmasters 20 per cent for collecting subscriptions; therefore the roadmaster charged his men $3.20 each for sending 80 cents of their money to the Roadmaster and Foreman. The foreman who reported the matter to me says: "I think I am the only foreman out of 38 who did not send him $4, and on account of failing to do so I don't feel at all secure in my position. If you refer to the robbery through the columns of the Trackmen's Advance Advocate, please don't mention my name, as it would be sure to cost me my job."

There are a great many similar cases. Something should be done to protect the weak against the avarice of the strong.

4. All applicants for responsible positions on railways, and especially foremen and roadmasters, whose duty it is to protect life and property by keeping the track in proper condition, should always be subjected to an examination which will give evidences of their fitness to fill the positions applied for, of their reliability, etc., before being permitted to enter upon the discharge of their duties.

We frequently read in newspapers reports of bridges going down with trains, trains jumping the track, turning over on curves, of a score or more people losing their lives, etc., and that the officials were unable to discover the cause of the catastrophe. In such cases, as a rule, the real causes are incompetent men in charge of the track, or not a sufficient number of men on a section to keep the track in safe running condition.

Railway companies should be required to employ men enough year in and year out to keep their track in proper order at all times. At the present time it is customary with the railway companies to discharge from 50 to 75 thousand of their track men in the fall of the year, at a time when it is hard to obtain employment. They are turned out to tramp, beg, starve, steal, and become criminals. Horses receive better treatment from their owners than a great many railway track men receive from their employers.

II.

All railway employees not engaged in operating trains should not be required to work more than 8 hours out of 24 except in cases of emergency. Time served at emergency work should be paid for at regular rates. On account of the nature of the work performed by track men, car inspectors, repairers, shopmen, they will be as much fatigued after pegging away for 8 hours as men engaged in operating trains will be after being on duty 10 or 12 hours.

II.I

1. I think all judges requested to issue injunctions in cases of disputes between railway companies and their employees should be compelled to follow the example set by Judge Caldwell, in the case of the Union Pacific Railway v. Its Employees, tried at Omaha, Nebr., March, 1894; and that the dissenting opinion of the same judge, in the case of Hopkins v. Oxley Stave Company (28 C. C. A. Reports, 108), should be enacted into law and made applicable to all disputes between railway companies and their employees. In case either party believes the judge to be biased and that he will not render a just decision, they should have a right to have the disputed questions of fact in the case tried by a jury, whose findings of fact should be binding on the court, as in ordinary cases.

Give railway employees an opportunity to present their side of the question in court, treat them as equals and not as inferiors of corporations, and they will always submit to the decisions of an unbiased court or jury.

2. Federal judges should have the power to maintain the dignity of their courts, compel witnesses to answer questions, etc., and to compel railway companies and railway employees to abide by their decisions or the decisions of a jury, provided they are rendered in accordance with the suggestions above made in answer to question 1 of Section III.

3. No; this would be vesting too much power in the hands of an officer, who is not elected, but appointed. With the limitations upon the powers of Federal judges, suggested in answer to question 1, Section III, the right to invoke the jurisdiction of the Federal courts could safely be left to the parties interested.

IV.

The fellow-servant laws enacted by the different States vary very much. As railway employees are not permitted to say who their fellow-servants shall be, but must be coworkers with anyone the company sees fit to employ, I think railway companies should be held responsible for damages to their employees the same as they are to nonemployees. A uniform law to govern these matters should be enacted by Congress, and all of the States should enact a similar law.

V.

The law of June 1, 1898, concerning conciliation and arbitration, seems to be satisfactory to railway employes engaged in the operation of trains. According to the Twelfth Annual Report of the Interstate Commerce Commission only 226,617 of the 823,476 railway employees are engaged in train service; therefore, 596,859 railway employees have no protection under the law referred to. The men engaged by railway companies to operate their trains are well organized. The railway officials recognize their power, which causes them to prefer to settle all grievances with them amicably, and especially so unless they think they can invoke the aid of the Government and overawe their trainmen by the use of injunction proceedings.

(a.) While I am not in favor of compulsory arbitration, and am unalterably opposed to strikes, if justice can be obtained in any other way, I believe the Interstate Commerce Commission should constitute a tribunal before which all classes of railway employees, from the president of the board of directors down to the men who spike the rails and tamp the ties, could go and present their grievances concerning traffic rates, wages, hours of labor, or conditions of employment, without fear of being discharged. Under such an arrangement, in case a class of employees fail to have their grievances satisfactorily adjusted by railway officials, they could place them before the commission, whose duty it would be to determine what is right and just under the circumstances, and their award becoming a document of public record would do a great deal toward influencing railway companies to deal fairly with employees who are being mistreated and oppressed under the present system, which is to pay wages and deal out justice to their employees in proportion to the organized force they have to demand them.

(b) Railway companies having relief departments should not be permitted to manage them in such a way as to prevent injured employees, or the beneficiaries of employees killed by the negligence of the company, from collecting the amount of damages they are justly entitled to. On March 10, 1899, the Atlantic Coast Line organized a relief department. In their book of rules, by which members of the relief department are to be governed, page 42, rule 64, appears the following:

"In case of injury to a member, he may elect to accept the benefits in pursuance of these regulations, or to prosecute such claims as he may have at law against the company or any companies associated therewith in the administration of their relief departments. The acceptance by the member of benefits for injury shall operate as a release and satisfaction of all claims against the company and all other companies associated therewith, as aforesaid, for damages arising from or growing out of such injury; and further, in the event of the death of a member, no part of the death benefit shall be due or payable unless and until good and sufficient releases shall be delivered to the superintendent of all claims against the relief department, as well as against the company and all other companies associated therewith, as aforesaid, arising from or growing out of the death of a member, such releases having been duly executed by all who might legally assert such claim; and further, if any suit shall be brought against the company or any other company associated therewith, as aforesaid, for damages arising from or growing out of injury or death occurring to a member, the benefits otherwise payable, and all obligations of the relief department and of the company created by the membership of such member in the relief fund, shall thereupon be forfeited, without any declaration or other act by the relief department or the company; but the superintendent may, in his discretion, waive such forfeiture upon condition that all pending suits shall first be dismissed. If a claim for damages on account of injuries shall be settled by the company without suit, such settlement shall release the relief department and the company from all claims for benefits on account of such injuries."

In their handbook of questions and answers concerning the relief department, they ask the question, "Are members debarred from bringing suit against the company?" and answer it in the following manner: "They are not. They have the same right in this respect that they would have if they were not members. The injured member may either accept the benefits of the fund or rely upon the issue of a suit. He can not do both." (Reg. 64.)

By examining the rates charged by the company, I find that they charge $36 a year on $1,000 insurance and for a few dollars weekly benefits, provided in each case that members shall not receive anything for the first week's sickness; thus, you see, employees of the Atlantic Coast Line Railway system are caused to believe that in order to be secure in their positions they must join the company's relief department, pay exorbitant rates for insurance, then, in case they are injured, in order to collect insurance money that they have paid the company at least a third more than it is worth or that it would cost them in other concerns, they must sign a release, exonerating the company from all blame.

A railway company having a relief department, withholding insurance money which has been paid for by an employee until he signs a release, should be fined not less than ten nor more than twenty-five thousand dollars in each case where conviction is secured.

VI.

It seems the railway companies are doing all they reasonably can to equip their rolling stock with the best safety appliances that have been invented.

VII.

First, the Interstate Commerce Commission should determine passenger and freight rates to be charged by all interstate roads. In fixing the rate to be charged by each road they should be governed by the amount of money actually invested in building and equipping the road, cost of operating, and the amount of traffic. In each case the rate should be fixed high enough to enable the road to pay all necessary and legitimate expenses and reasonable wages to all employees, etc., and leave margin enough to pay stockholders reasonable dividends on the money invested.

Second, the issuing of free transportation should be restricted to railway employees and Government employees in the Railway Mail Service. Companies issuing passes to other parties should be fined heavily.

The issuing of passes by railway companies to men of political influence has done a great deal to prejudice the public against railway enterprises, and to corrupt society, especially politicians.

The railway companies of the United States give away millions of dollars in passes annually, and, as a rule, they extend favors to those who can well afford to buy tickets.

Third, the occupation of ticket scalpers should be abolished, and the rates fixed by the Interstate Commerce Commission should be maintained by all interstate roads. The States should enact similar laws for the government of roads not under the jurisdiction of the Interstate Commerce Commission. Stop those unnecessary leaks from the railway companies' earnings, and on the majority of roads the cost of transportation can be reduced, all the employees can be paid reasonable wages, it will not be necessary for any of them to work an unreasonable number of hours in any one day, and the men who have invested their money in railway enterprises will receive reasonable profits on their investments. . Railways should be blessings to and civilizers of the people. They should not be operated in such a way as to keep up strife between citizens and to corrupt society.

Fourth, the Interstate Commerce Commission should incorporate in their annual reports the amount of wages paid to employees in each class on each road.

Yours, truly,

JOHN T. WILSON,
Grand Chief, Brotherhood of Railroad Trackmen of America.

REPLY OF MR. W. H. RONEMUS,

Grand Chief of the Brotherhood of Railway Carmen.

CEDAR RAPIDS, IOWA, *August 29, 1899.*

The Subcommission on Transportation,
  Industrial Commission, Washington, D. C.

SIRS: I reply as follows to your favor of August 4, with a list of questions inclosed for the purpose of completing the Industrial Commission's inquiry concerning"legislation affecting railway labor, etc:"

I.

1. When a railway company through any of its officers or agents is charged and found guilty with or discriminating against any of its employees on account of their connection with their brotherhoods, not less or more than $25,000 in each case; 10 per cent of the fine to be awarded to the prosecuting witness and 10 per cent to the prosecuting attorney, the balance to revert to the school fund of the State in which conviction is secured.

2. I believe the causes for blacklisting will gradually disappear altogether, brought about by the general organization of the employees, as the unreliable will not generally be admitted to the organizations, and by the general recognition of organizations the cause for discontent from this source will become less with time. If it becomes necessary to further legislate against the practice, I believe such legislation can be secured; but under the present circumstances I would not recommend such further legislation.

3. The conditions under which employees may be discharged should be regulated by legislation. Good reasons for the discharge should be given and be approved by a competent officer of the employer, and the discharged employee should have the opportunity to state his side of the case.

The practice exists in some instances of favored friends of department foremen being shown partiality, and worthy and efficient workmen being either discharged or their tenure of position made so undesirable that they are driven to severing their connection with a company, and often can not again secure employment for a considerable length of time.

Railway companies being subject to and deriving rights by States, being granted charter to do business within the State, the States should likewise protect its citizens against unjust discriminations against its citizens by corporations. I think such legislation would cause many injustices, both toward railway companies and employees, to be wiped out. If companies were made responsible for the unjust discrimination against employees on the part of department foremen, very few, if any, employees would suffer discharge without good and sufficient reasons.

4. In the first place no one should be employed for any position of responsibility without having been subjected to a prescribed examination submitted by the head of the department in which the man is employed. The railway service, being of the most importance to the public, no careless, intemperate, untrustworthy, or unreliable person should be installed in a position of trust. A violation of well-selected rules, especially if persisted in, should be cause for dismissal, but no reliable, temperate, and efficient employee should be discharged to make room for one untried in the service.

II.

Humanity to man, the welfare of society, and the best interests of the nation, physically, morally, and intellectually, most emphatically demand as short a work day as is consistent with the best interests of the country and its business. This is true of all kinds of manual toil, but especially is it true of such work as is performed by men in the car department of railroads of the country. While there is not a general demand on the part of these men at the present time for shorter hours, the reason for such seeming satisfaction with 10 and 12, and often more hours per day, is more owing to the men being fearful lest their meager earnings at less hours per day will not assure the life and comfort of the dear ones at home.

I think that in every department where it is possible to do so 8 hours should be considered a maximum day's work. In most classes of shopwork in the car department men would perform almost, if not entirely, as much work in 8 as in 10 hours. The work in most cases being of such a nature that with 8 hours of constant bending, twisting of the body, and lifting, the physical forces of most men become so exhausted that the remaining time they are compelled to work is not productive of much result.

In most cases the hours could well be reduced to 8, and where it could not at once it could be arranged that the utmost exertions of man's physical strength should not be evoked for a greater consecutive time.

III.

1. No injunction should be issued until the employees have had an opportunity to answer after the application for injunction has been made. Either the State or Federal court, or a commission created for that purpose (I would favor a special commission), should determine whether or not cause exists for injunction. Injunctions against men who have committed no actual offense, and who do not contemplate such, for the asking, without proper hearing of both sides, seems to me un-American and discriminating.

2. I believe it would be unnecessary to limit the power of the court in enforcing its orders when made under the provisions above advocated.

The tendency to disobey the order of the court would become less, if it were not entirely obviated. If the employee has the opportunity to be heard before being condemned, he could not reasonably be accused of contempt.

3. The parties to the controversy should apply to the special commission, if necessary, to invoke the jurisdiction of the Federal court, and through such commission such invocation should be made. One-man power should not be vested in any official.

IV.

1. I do not think the employing company should be exempt from liability for damages received by a fellow-employee as the result of the negligence of a fellow-servant. The employing company selecting the fellow-servant and issuing his instructions should be responsible for his actions while in the discharge of his duties as a fellow-servant or employee. By making the company liable for damages received as the result of the negligence of a fellow-servant, the greatest care would be used in employing men to fill the various positions.

The most reliable men being employed in all departments would reduce the number of injuries sustained to a minimum.

2. In deciding cases involving injuries to employees I think Federal courts should, as nearly as consistent, follow the decisions of State courts, based upon statutory enactments of law of the State in which the injury was sustained.

V.

Not having a copy of the law of June 1, 1898, concerning conciliation and arbitration, I can not venture to approve or disapprove the same. I believe, however, there should be a national arbitration board before whom either side in a controversy, feeling that he had been oppressed or was about to be so oppressed, could state his grievances and secure recommendations that would approve or disapprove the grievance complained of. The approval or disapproval of the commission, or board, to be considered as notice to the public as to the merits of the demands of the respective parties. This would act as a mediator in many instances, no doubt, and the force of public opinion would do much to prevent unimportant or ridiculous questions being carried up thus far.

Previous to 1898 some railway companies maintained relief departments by retaining a certain per cent of the employees' wages to maintain same. It was compulsory on every applicant for a position in any department to make application for insurance through this department. A man might be rejected because of the rigid examination, and was therefore denied employment. Many worthy and competent applicants for employment have thereby been prevented from securing employment because of some minor physical ailment. This, it seems to me, worked an injustice to those who could not thus secure employment, when they were in every way qualified to fill a good position and support their families.

There can be no reasonable objection offered to railway companies maintaining relief departments, but no applicant for employment should be so discriminated against as to be denied employment on technicalities. Neither should participation in any relief association bar any employee from collecting damages for injuries received because of such participation. I think most relief associations are more expensive to the employee than the same amount of insurance can be carried for in the brotherhood of which such employee is or should be a member. The organization of the various brotherhoods is made permanent and of the greatest good through their insurance features. Insurance is furnished to members at actual cost and can not be forfeited except by the negligence of the member in paying dues or assessments. The compulsory participation in the railway companies' relief associations prevents many of the poorly paid employees from taking advantage of the cheap and in every case good insurance offered by the organization of their craftsmen.

VI.

Car repairers are subjected to many inconveniencies and hardships which could be overcome to a great extent by railway companies furnishing proper places to have their cars repaired in. I refer more particularly to what may be termed rush work, such as a car being disabled while in transit and necessitating repairs at the nearest division point where a force of inspectors and repairers are retained.

The universal arrangement seems to be to run all defective cars on the repair track, where the loaded cars necessary to be repaired must be quickly disposed of. To make the necessary repairs men are required to keep at work constantly, regardless of rain, hail, sleet, mud, and all other inconveniences of the weather, exposing themselves to the cold blasts of the wind and rain, or snow in winter, and sitting or lying in the mud during the wet weather in summer. The nature of the work will not admit of postponing it until the storm subsides or until the sun shines more warmly. No other class of men are thus at the mercy of the weather so much as car repairers. Time must be made by the cargo of freight; the cars must be ready for the next train starting out. The work must be done and under the present conditions it must be accomplished out on the track under the tropical sunshine, the storm of wind, sleet, rain, or snow.

It seems to me that it could not be unreasonable to ask that railway companies be required to erect suitable sheds over at least a part of the repair track, where the men could be sheltered from the storm and snow. Without proper sheds to work under men are in many cases rendered ill and unfit for service for days to come.

I would, therefore, have proper shelter for workmen, classed as safety appliances. This may seem a little ridiculous to anyone not familiar with the duties and requirements of the car repairer, but it is not so to the men who are compelled to render a day's work during all kinds of weather. It can not be expected that railway companies can protect their employees against the inconveniences occasioned by nature in general, but the exposed condition of the average repair track needs attention. Men can render a better service to the company with the repair track properly inclosed to keep out the storm. Men are not competent to perform the regular day's work in a day where they become chilled from wet and cold; and it would, in my opinion, be a saving to the companies to provide as comfortable and well-equipped regular repair tracks as is consistent with a reasonable outlay for the appliance suggested.

VII.

First, the Interstate Commerce Commission should determine passenger and freight rates to be charged by the interstate roads. In fixing the rate to be charged by each road, they should be governed by the amount of money actually invested in building and equipping the road, cost of operating, and amount of traffic.

In each case the rate should be fixed high enough to enable the road to pay all necessary and legitimate expenses, and reasonable wages to all employees, etc., and leave margin enough to pay stockholders reasonable dividends on the money invested.

Second, the issuing of free transportation should be restricted to railway employees and Government employees in the Railway Mail Service. Companies issuing passes to other parties should be fined heavily.

The issuing of passes in my opinion should be entirely done away with outside of employees while in the discharge of their duties; and a uniform rate on all railways should be adopted for railway employees and their families of 1 cent per mile, so that all employees could avail themselves of a 1-cent per-mile rate at any or all times. This I think would be profitable to the employees as well as the railroads.

Respectfully, yours,   W. H. RONEMUS,
    Grand Chief of the Brotherhood of Railway Carmen of America.

REPLY OF MR. ALDACE F. WALKER,

Chairman of the Board of Directors of the Atchison, Topeka and Santa Fe Railway Company.

59 CEDAR STREET,
New York City, September 21, 1899.

UNITED STATES INDUSTRIAL COMMISSION,
    Washington, D. C.

GENTLEMEN: I have received your questions connected with legislation affecting railway labor, and take pleasure in stating my views.

I do not favor any legislative action whatever on the subjects enumerated in your circular. Very many matters which are put forward as affording occasion for special legislation will right themselves in due time if let alone. Many other such matters originate in the natural strife of antagonistic social, commercial, or industrial forces; legislative interference on either side will do more harm than good. Such questions present a shifting equilibrium; sometimes the scale appears to turn one way, sometimes another, but in the long run they are self-corrective through the working of natural agencies. Legislative interference can not be otherwise than bungling. It is like a crowbar thrust into the main-spring of a watch.

It is not safe to attempt to devise new legislation as a remedy for every real or fancied grievance. Laws should assert general principles with the least possible detail. Our present system of law—the English common law and equity juris-prudence—molded and adapted by the judiciary of this country since the American Revolution to fit republican conditions, will work out as near absolute justice as anything that man can devise. Unfortunately its principles have been constantly tampered with by special legislative rules framed to meet special cases. The effort to legislate in detail has almost become a mania. The world would wag its way and all civil rights would be well preserved if Congress and State legisla-tures would devote themselves strictly to questions respecting the carrying on of their respective governmental machinery and would cease attempting to lay down new rules to be observed at common law or in equity. So much of this has already been done that rights and duties have become unsettled and uncertain. I protest against more. I will answer your questions categorically.

I.

I would recommend no legislation concerning the employment and discharge of railway employes. Under our form of government there is no such thing as labor which is not contract labor. All service is a matter of contract, the terms of which are agreed upon between employers and employees as individuals. The nation or the State can not rightfully interfere. Paternalism is next door to socialism. State control involves State protection of the interests subjected to control. Let us either have State ownership or freedom of contract. Any attempt at this time to interfere on either side by way of legislation will inevitably do harm.

1. I do not understand the question. Employees now have the right to membership in as many brotherhoods and associations as they choose. Possibly cases are referred to where rules of brotherhoods have been so framed as to conflict with the rights of employers, and where objection may have been made to membership in particular brotherhoods on account of particular requirements exacted from their members, which, if accepted, would interfere with and perhaps destroy the reciprocity which is essential to freedom of contract. No law should be passed which directly or indirectly would tend to cut off the equal rights of employers and employees in framing and carrying out the contract of service.

2. Blacklisting is largely an imaginary grievance. If a servant is unfaithful, it is not only the right, but the duty, of the master to tell the truth upon inquiry. If he tells untruth he is liable to make full compensation at the common law. If he tells the truth it protects faithful employees, and it is absolutely in their interest that this should be done.

3. It would not be advisable to regulate by law the conditions under which railway employees may be discharged. Their service is one involving the safety of life and property at every moment. The employer is pecuniarily responsible for every act of the employee. The public has every interest in holding railroad companies to their full duty. This responsibility, justly placed upon railroad corporations, involves the necessity that they be absolutely let alone in the choice and retention of their servants. They carry the responsibility and must have corresponding freedom of action. Suppose, under State laws, an employee were retained against the desire of the employer, would the State relieve the employer from liability in case of accident arising from the negligence of such an employee? If any legislation on this subject is to be had, it must provide fully for such a case as that. The State must take the full responsibility of its act.

4. I have no suggestions to make on this subject. I am not aware that anyone is asking for legislation to protect employers. Legislation of a paternal character in behalf of employees is apparently in view. When freedom of contract is interfered with, either on behalf of one party or the other, the sphere of useful legislation is exceeded, especially so when the proposed legislation is in aid of the party which is frequently (if not usually) the stronger of the two, when the struggle comes.

II.

I see no occasion for legislation respecting hours of railway labor. Children are not employed. Overtime is paid for under schedules agreed on with the men. They are usually glad of a chance to work overtime, and if they can get a few more dollars per month in this way why should they not be allowed to do so? Moreover, when trains are delayed it would be impossible to tie them up at the expiration of any stated hour of service. It may be said that there is danger of impaired service resulting from tired and sleepy employees. Such cases, however, are very exceptional—snow blockades, etc.—and the liability of the employer to respond in damages in all such cases is an adequate safeguard.

III.

I see no reason for interfering with the well-established rules of equity covering the issuance of injunctions, punishment for contempt, etc. I have heard much clamor on this subject, but have yet to hear of any actual wrong being worked, except, possibly, in one or two cases in preliminary proceedings, which were reversed on appeal, and where the final judgment of the higher court stands as an enduring precedent. Our courts may be trusted to work out the proper system for treating this subject under well-established rules of general application. Error sometimes may be made by decisions in the courts of first instance, but the body of law is composed of decisions of the courts of last resort. I do not know of any such decisions that legislatures can safely overturn.

IV.

I am not sufficiently familiar with this subject to have an opinion as to whether the common-law rules respecting injuries resulting from the negligence of fellow-servants should be modified by statutes. I am aware that some States have done this. It is a special legislative topic which I have not studied.

V.

I have no faith in the usefulness of laws concerning conciliation and arbitration. Eight years ago I published an article containing my view on this subject, from which I submit the following extracts, which are as true now as when the article was written:

"An arbitration is the nonjudicial determination of a controversy by a tribunal organized for the special purpose by mutual agreement. Its sanction lies in a preliminary consent of the parties to be bound by its result. It is a contract, and is enforceable as a contract, and not otherwise. When two men submit their differences to arbitration the unanimous judgment of the board (unless it be specially provided that a majority may decide) becomes conclusive; not through any inherent value of its own, but solely by virtue of the agreement to refer. Without such an agreement arbitration does not exist. Compulsory arbitration is a contradiction of terms. The essential idea of arbitration is the assent of both parties thereto; without such assent it is naught. What is apparently desired by persons who use the phrase 'compulsory arbitration' is the establishment of some tribunal before which either party to a labor controversy may cite the other party for a final decision of the matter. This would not be an arbitration, but a judicial proceeding; the court thus established would require new process of execution adequate to compel workmen to labor in future at a scale fixed and to compel manufacturers to operate their property in order to provide employment for their men; powers which do not seem compatible with our republican institutions.

"There are some things which, from their nature, can not be arbitrated. The State can not arbitrate with an alleged criminal a question of larceny or of arson. Subjects of special statutory regulation, in cases where a judicial procedure has been established by law, also must be handled by the courts, pursuant to the methods prescribed.

"Before the suggestion of arbitration can properly be entertained there must exist a fair question of disagreement upon which the arbitrator may exercise his judicial faculty, either by ascertaining the right of a doubtful matter or by the employment of discretion in the adjustment of conflicting rights. When no doubt is conceded to exist there is nothing for an arbitrator to decide. If a man lays claim to my farm not under any question of colorable title, but because he wants it for his own, I may very properly decline to admit the existence of a controversy. By every standard of ethics I should be justified not only in refusing to arbitrate, but in kicking him off the place. If the question concern the employment of labor and the claim be asserted that no workmen shall be hired who do not belong to a given labor union, there is nothing in such a demand which calls for arbitration, for every employer has an inherent and essential right to employ whom he will, and every laborer has a right to work, whether he belongs to a union or no. A merchant would be justified in refusing to arbitrate the price of his goods; he may fix his own price, and the customer may take them or leave them. In the foregoing cases and many others the person upon whom the claim is made may properly repudiate the existence of any just demand and may defend his position by force if force is used against him.

"Here we meet the argument that the use of physical force is at all times to be deplored; that it results in pain and distress; that might is not always right; that violence is the argument of the brute; that human nature should find some other method of solving its contests; that, whether the dispute be between nations, between classes, or between individuals, a resort to force is essentially wrong and is inevitably to be condemned. But is this position a sound one? What is the ultimate ratio decidendi among men but physical power? Even the decision of a court, if not voluntarily conformed to, is executed by a sheriff. If his single hand is insufficient, he calls upon his posse. If the power of the county fails, the armed force of the State must assist him. So of controversies between nations. If a fair question of doubt is raised, modern ideas have introduced the possibility of arbitration. But how is the award to be enforced except by war, and how is war to be avoided in case absolute rights are trampled on? The same is true in respect to contentions between individuals. A man's house is his castle, which he may defend by force. If his own hands are too weak, he may hire the strength of his fellows. It is true that in cases where a mob seeks to take possession of the property of a railroad corporation, a manufacturer, or a miner it would be possible for the party thus attacked to submit for the time being to eviction and to wait for legal process of restoration, with an award of uncollectible damages. But human nature is not so constituted. Such conduct would be craven and disgraceful. Moreover, in organized society man owes a duty to his fellows, and in the long run the minimum of strife is found where rights are most jealously defended.

"The intensity which prevails in labor disturbances at the present time is apparently due to the fact that certain fundamental questions are in process of settlement, which can be settled only by force. Strikers are seeking to ascertain how far they will be suffered to go in the employment of violence to prevent the operation of the properties which they have left and to prevent the introduction of other workmen to take their place. There is no arbitrable question in either proposition. These matters permit of no dispute. The fact is being rapidly demonstrated that strikers shall not employ violent measures to prevent the operation of railroads and manufacturing establishments in their absence or to prevent the employment of other workmen in their place, These questions can only be settled by vis major, and when it is once perceived that the superior power will be employed in every like case, those particular features of strikes will disappear. There is no other way out of it.

"It is worth while to look a little closer into the theory and the history of strikes in order to ascertain just where arbitration may properly come in. No one can question the right of a workman to strike. Unless he is a slave his labor is voluntary, and he may cease if he will. But when he has left his bench and announced his purpose to do no more labor until his demands are complied with he is no longer an employee of his former employer. In common speech it is often said that the workmen employed in such and such an industry are on a strike; but if they have struck they are not employed. They perform no services and earn no wages. They have exercised their undoubted right to cease from both. The contract of employment has been terminated by their own act. They have no lien upon the property and no rights against its owners. They may negotiate for reinstatement, but they may not interfere with its operation at other hands. All this seems too simple to require statement, but the contrary view has been broadly claimed. The sympathy of the American people naturally goes out in behalf of every effort on the part of laborers to better their condition. We are proud of high wages paid and exult over every advance in the scale. The feeling is becoming prevalent, and is supported by many sympathetic and vigorous writers, that the workingman has some personal interest in the plant where his labor is performed other than and different from his right to be paid for his labor. It is difficult to see any logical foundation for this claim. Certainly at the outset capital provides the plant and the laborers first employed come in as strangers. In what way do subsequent years of remunerated toil change their relation to it? The workman is a seller of his strength and his skill. He endeavors to get the best price obtainable for his commodity. The market value of labor, theoretically at least, is controlled by the same principle which dominates the value of every other merchantable product. It is fixed by competition. Strikes, as they were first employed, presented to the employer the alternative of the stoppage of his industry or assent to the demands of his workmen. The question was a simple one. Could he fill their places with other workmen at the old rates of compensation or at less if the strike was against a proposed reduction? The striking workmen took the risk of outside competition, and often with entire safety; for the labor market was restricted to narrow localities and the skill required was limited to few. In these modern times movement in every direction is free and cheap. The market from which employers may procure labor is the whole country. It would be the whole world but for restrictive laws. This fact led to the introduction of labor unions, formed for the purpose of restricting and controlling competition in the sale of labor. Their members agree upon the wages they will accept and refuse to enter into vacancies caused by strikes on the part of their associates. To this extent they are within their right. Combinations for mutual protection against disastrous and ruinous competition by the use of legitimate methods are as proper on the part of workmen as of other members of society. The principle involved is the same in respect to all, and the same rules must be applied. Parties making such combinations are always liable to underbidding by outsiders, and this chance is the risk of the game. Excessive and unhealthy competition can be restrained and ameliorated by combination, but competition can not be extinguished by combination unless every possible present and future competitor is included. In attempting to regulate the competition of laborers the supply has often been too great for trade unions to control. Argument was at first employed to prevent other workmen not members of the union from taking vacant jobs. By easy steps argument changes to abuse and reason is replaced by violence. The trouble is not with the strike itself, but with the methods of the strikers. The peace of the Commonwealth requires that all this illegitimate excess should be restrained. The rights of workmen who are not members of the unions are too readily forgotten. The rights of employers whose tender of employment has been rejected are ignored. Thus once more we reach a point where the power of the State must repel force by violent means. We are beyond the scope of any agency save the exercise of strength sufficient to keep the peace and to protect every citizen in his rights.

"Arbitration is often available in disputes between employees and employers, but the difficulties surrounding its use are many. In the first place there is a doubt as to what considerations may be admitted to control the result. The employer insists that his balance sheet is foreign to the case, and that the only question is the competitive value of the labor under consideration; and he therefore refuses to make known the cost of his product. Nevertheless, the profits of business are often given as an occasion for an advance in wages by liberal-minded employers who feel themselves able to pay a higher scale and who are grateful to their men for their skill and persevering industry. The broad and generous treatment which has again and again been extended to American workmen is thus made the basis of a claim against other employers which strict legal right hardly supports. The theory of profit sharing has also been introduced in many quarters with a view to securing permanence, efficiency, and good will on the part of the employed; and its value in that direction has again and again been proved. We must not forget, however, that it is a concession and not a right. There can be no interest in profits claimed as a right which does not involve a corresponding liability for losses, unless by virtue of a special contract; and while a scale of wages has often been conceded in which the prospective profits of employers has formed an element, the question whether a wage arbitration should enter upon the field has not yet been answered definitely in the affirmative.

"There are also some other grounds for a feeling of reluctance on the part of employers to arbitrate the claims of their workmen, whether of wages, of hours, or of conditions under which the labor is to be performed. The sympathy of every board of arbitrators is sure to be with the weaker party. If any argument can be found for improving the condition of the workmen, it is almost certain to be applied. Arbitrators are bound by no rules of law in reaching their conclusions, but are entitled to make their award in accordance with what they may consider to be ex æquo et bono. They are not required to give any reasons whatever for their decisions. The universal tendency of arbitrators is to 'split the difference,' a process which will inevitably yield something to the laborer. In an arbitration of this kind there will inevitably be advantages upon the side of the workmen, and an employer who voluntarily submits such questions to an arbitration board often feels that he takes his life in his hands, especially in cases where the continued payment of heavy fixed charges stands between him and bankruptcy. Moreover, it is difficult to find men to whom such questions as these may be prudently submitted. The judges of our courts are presumed to stand upon a high plane of rectitude and impartiality, and yet even our judges are often criticised. When an effort is made to go into the business world and constitute an arbitration board through the selection of an umpire, by an agreement arrived at between one party named in the interest of the workman and another party named in the interest of the employer, the chances involved are great. The pecuniary risk is much heavier on the part of the employer than of the laborer. The hazard of the latter is measured by his individual interest in the result. Of the former it is the same, multiplied by the total number of men affected, and intensified by the fact that there is no conpensation for added business risks or participation in resulting business losses.

" There is always, also, the question whether both parties are equally concluded by the result. The employer is always bound. The laborer, on the other hand, is not concluded by the acts of a voluntary ' union,' from which he may at any time withdraw, and whose transactions are sometimes regulated by a committee or controlled by a single and autocratic ' chief.' The employer may therefore properly insist upon something more than negotiation with an ' order,' to the end that the result of an arbitration may affect both parties equally; and he may well refuse to admit the interference of strangers in negotiations with his workmen.

"Notwithstanding all the inequalities which have been suggested, it is nevertheless undoubtedly true that so long as labor controversies are in process of negotiation and before employment has been terminated and business suspended by a strike, employers may often well accept a proposal for an arbitration of such differences as do not involve the surrender of any essential right. If adverse claims are made in good faith, not arising from mercenary avariciousness on the one part or from the interference of the walking delegate or other outside manipulator on the other, a resort to arbitration may often be a happy method of attaining that just medium between conflicting claims and interests which negotiation often fails to reach through the too stubborn assertion of the ultimatum.

"Unfortunately, however, the workingman on his part apparently seems averse to accepting arbitration as a method of settling his disputes. Again and again arbitration boards have been organized at State expense for the determination of labor troubles; but except in rare cases the effort has been wholly futile. They are repudiated by the very class whose interests they were designed to serve. Even the arrangement provided by the Congress of the United States for the settlement of controversies affecting interstate commerce through a national provision for the payment of arbitrators and the tender of an official arbitration has proved to be wholly unavailing. Arbitration is apparently not wanted by the laborers themselves, and is seldom even thought of by them until a strike has proceeded so far as to become apparently a failure. There are reasons for this also. When an arbitration decides adversely on the workman's claim the result is more impressive than the ordinary result of failure in systematic litigation, where it is accepted as a necessity that one or the other party must lose his cause. An unsuccessful arbitration leads to a sweeping condemnation of the system of arbitration as a whole, and the feeling at once becomes general that no good can be accomplished in that way. This feeling is fostered by the managers of labor unions who find their usefulness and their employment in strikes and the entanglements which attend them; who have devised the sympathetic strike as part of their recognized machinery; who are valued in proportion to the disturbances which they create, and who are defeated in every case of peaceful settlement which is reached without their interference. The unwisdom of this attitude is now clearly perceived by the more intelligent and thoughtful leaders of labor. One and another have broken away from the belief that unlawful violence can help their cause and have affirmed a common interest of labor with capital, trusting to moral agencies and to sound reason for the maintenance of their rights. With those less reasonable the controversy is now waging, and we can but hope that when their methods are shown to be nugatory—when it has been demonstrated that excess will inevitably be controlled and punished, while conciliatory and peaceful negotiations will surely win public opinion and support, there will arise a disposition to employ some other agent than violence to accomplish that betterment of conditions for which the workingman is constantly and rightly struggling, and a determination to tender the tribunal of voluntary arbitration again and again. Among business men the remark is often heard that one can not refuse to 'leave the question out,' the meaning being that where there is a fair question of difference as to which some settlement must be made the decision of a court is only the judgment of a man or a group of men at the best, and delays should be avoided by a more summary procedure; or, again, that in cases not apt for the decision of judicial tribunals an arbitration is desirable for the termination of strife and for affording an opportunity for the claimant to make good his standing if he can. This feeling may well be taken advantage of by the laboring man, and a persistent effort in this direction may properly replace the present crude and too often unlawful methods undertaken by him for the amelioration of his condition."

Very truly, yours,

ALDACE F. WALKER.

REPLY OF MR. JOHN H. MURPHY,

Attorney at law, Denver, Colo.

I.

1. Section 10 of an act entitled "An act concerning carriers engaged in interstate commerce and their employees," approved June 1, 1898, reads as follows:

"That any employer subject to the provisions of this act, and any officer, agent, or receiver of such employer who shall require any employee, or any person seeking employment, as a condition of such employment, to enter into an agreement, either written or verbal, not to become or remain a member of any labor corporation, association, or organization, or shall threaten any employee with loss of employment, or shall unjustly discriminate against any employee because of his membership in such labor corporation, association, or organization, or who shall require any employee or any person seeking employment, as a condition of such employment, to enter into a contract whereby such employee or applicant for employment shall agree to contribute to any fund for charitable, social, or benefit purposes, to release such employer from legal liability for any personal injury by reason of any benefit received from such fund beyond the proportion of the benefit arising from the employer's contribution to such fund, or who shall, after having discharged an employee, attempt to conspire to prevent such employee from obtaining employment, or who shall, after the quitting of an employee, attempt to conspire to prevent such employee from obtaining employment, is hereby declared to be g ilt of a misdemeanor, and, upon conviction thereof in any court of the United States of competent jurisdiction in the district in which such offense was committed, shall be punished for each offense by fine of not less than one hundred dollars or not more than one thousand dollars.

Many of the States have penal statutes making it unlawful for employers to coerce, intimidate, or use any other methods calculated to prevent employees from belonging to their brotherhoods or to associations of laboring men. Both the United States and State statutes on this subject are violated with impunity, and such laws appear to be impotent to afford a remedy for the evil sought to be suppressed or to protect the rights intended to be preserved to the employee. There is one trunk line of railways running out of Chicago, westward, which maintains a large detective corps for the purpose of ascertaining whether or not an employee does or is about to become a member of a labor organization, and if he has, or is likely to become a member the company watches for a convenient time to discharge him; the dismissal, however, being placed on some other grounds than the fact of his affiliation with labor organizations. So many subterfuges can be used for the purpose of getting rid of employees on account of their membership in these organization that it would be almost impossible to enact, under the present system of hiring and discharging, a law that can be enforced. Perhaps if all such laws were amended so as to make it criminal to procure or furnish evidence of the employee's membership in a labor organization to anyone other than the membership thereof, it would make the law as perfect and complete as it is possible to frame such measures.

It is not desired by the foregoing statement to convey the idea that railway corporations in general are antagonistic to the railway brotherhoods; for, on the contrary, the greater number of them offer no opposition, and a few trunk lines, being particularly observant of the benefits which have accrued to them by reason of the existence of the brotherhoods on their road, encourage their existence in many ways.

2. This question is one that is as difficult to deal with as the question respecting the protecting of employees in their right to belong to their brotherhoods. Nearly all of the States and the section of the United States statute quoted, supra, makes blacklisting a penal offense, but owing to the difficulty of getting evidence which would convict one guilty of the offense the laws are ineffectual. It has always been permissible in law for a master to give a statement concerning a servant to an inquiring employer or prospective employer. Such statement, however damaging to the servant, if truthful, may be lawfully made. But this is pernicious and works a great injustice, because a bare statement of certain happenings or acts of a servant unexplained may make him appear as a very undesirable employee, but an explanation may relieve him in the eyes of a fair, prospective employer from blame; so to prevent this injury and blacklisting of all kinds in a more effectual way it should be made unlawful for any corporation or individual to furnish a statement to any other employer, or other person, concerning an employee without first furnishing the employee with a true copy of it. At present statements are promiscuously furnished without the employee knowing anything about their contents, and therefore he is unable to explain or refute false statements which may be made against him. However, the remedy for the present evil will be more fully disclosed in answer to subdivision three.

3. After much observation and consideration of this question by anyone the answer given will certainly be, yes. It is only about a quarter of a century ago when nearly every family conducted a sort of a manufacturing institution so far as necessary to provide crude things for their wants. Sheep were shorn, wool washed, carded, spun, woven into cloth, and cut and sewed into garments by the members of the one household; even the head of the household was usually a shoemaker or cobbler, or he could build a house, do blacksmithing, and like work,

At the present day few people can do more than one thing well. The crude work of the man of many years ago will, at the present day, not be acceptable to any person. He could now find no employment. Therefore it is necessary to follow one or two things and perfect oneself in doing them in order to find and retain employment.

The railroads of the country have numerous departments, and generally the degree of skill required in each department requires strong, active bodies and the highest faculty of the mind to be exercised, and so exacting are the duties in a single department that as a general thing the average man is not only not able to acquire knowledge or fit himself up for other duties in life, but he is unable to acquire knowledge which would enable him to readily fill any of the other departments, and so if discharged, unless he can find work at his usual vocation, it is exceedingly difficult for him to obtain a livelihood. It is to the interest of railroad companies—to the interest of the public in general—to let men work in such places and at such work where the result of their labor is of the highest productive quality and greatest productive quantity. The wealth of the community or nation is, after all, but the combined wealth of the individuals. Every day that the individual workman is out of employment is a day forever lost to himself and indirectly a day lost to the community and nation, and frequent loss of employment finally leaves him in his old age, together with his family, dependent upon the county for support.

Railway companies are owned by a few individuals, and it is not often that those who are real stockholders of the company do the superintending of the various departments, and often the person entrusted in the position of "superintending employee" has his own friends to reward and enemies often to punish, or through some whim or caprice, discharges a faithful and valuable servant to the company, which it would really be to the interest of the company to keep at work; therefore, it would be well to have a labor court in which the employee, if he felt aggrieved, could demand a hearing, and if he was unjustly discharged, he should have a decree in his favor, at the cost of the offending party, that he be permitted to return to his accustomed duties. If he was justly discharged, the cost should be paid by him. This in no way, of course, would prevent a railway company from discharging any employee who was detrimental to the service or for the purpose of curtailing expenses, or from abandoning any department that it was desirable to abandon. On some roads a few of the brotherhoods were strong enough to have been able to enter into a contract with the company to the effect that any member of their organization shall not be discharged without a hearing, and if it is found that he was unjustly discharged, then, in such a case, the company shall pay him full time which he lost during his term of discharge.

Investigation has revealed this rule to be beneficial, both to the classes of employees which it affects and the company, for, on the one hand, men do not work under the nervous tension and strain that no matter how efficient their services may be, through whim or caprice of some individual having temporary authority over them, they will be sent adrift any day, but they rest assured that on performing their duty they may stay in the service of the company continually, and thus they strive to do their duty and reach higher perfection in their work, realizing at all times that it is the one sole condition of their continued employment.

The companies under such contracts, find that they get the highest degree of service and operate their road more cheaply and are able to enforce the highest degree of discipline. As an illustration why this would be beneficial, cases might be cited that occurred years ago before the brotherhoods were in position to influence their members for good or afford material assistance when employees were discharged for trivial offenses and discharged without any hearing. It caused recklessness to grow upon them, and if they got into a little difficulty, or if some of the company's property was accidentally destroyed, they would realize that such meant discharge, and many of them did not save property which might have been saved, or try to lessen the damage or injury in any way whatever; but this certainly is now otherwise since the advent of the brotherhoods and since employees realize that they will be tried fairly and their acts adjudicated impartially. In connection with this matter it might be further urged that railroads are affected with public interest. They get the most valuable franchises from the public; the lives and property of thousands of the public are constantly in the keeping of railways, and therefore the public are interested in having the highest degree of efficiency, and it is further and vitally interested in not permitting a railroad company to have the best service of various individuals for a long number of years, and when they are unable to discharge any other duties acceptably other than the vocation which they have learned, that they be not wrongfully and unwarrantably discharged, and perhaps become a public charge themselves or their families.

II.

Railway work is exacting and exhaustive, especially the work required for the movement of trains, and perhaps the reason that the degree of exhaustion is not more noticed by the public is because the feebler class of mankind do not seek employment in this branch of industrial undertaking, and if they do seek employment, they are generally rejected, so it is only the more strong, healthy, and robust constitutions that come into the service. Therefore, such employees are enabled to stand numerous hardships. Still, for the interest of the public who patronize railroad companies and for their individual safety, men should not be permitted to be on duty more than 12 hours in any 24, except in cases of emergency or other unavoidable occurrence, and in yards and machine shops and in all other departments where the service will not be impaired by one set of employees relieving another, 8 hours a day should constitute a day's work. It is to the interest of the State to have good, healthy, robust citizens, so that they will be capable of bearing arms should the State need their service, and that they will be capable of self-support; also, that they have more time in which to cultivate their mental faculties, and thus generally advance the interest of the race. At the present time society seems to be moving along at such a feverish pace that many evils seem to be creeping in, causing cynics to be everywhere, and nervous and puny forms to appear on all sides. Numerous suicides are being committed and a large army of people are coming to have no fixed purpose or aim in life. They make a feeble attempt to do one thing, then, growing easily discouraged, quit it and attempt to do another with like results, thus wasting away their life, not accomplishing anything useful. Shorter hours of labor will undoubtedly tend to remedy this condition much to the interest of the general welfare and even to the employer. The employer will be benefited, because men with clear minds and fresh bodies produce more and better work within a given time than it is possible for men to do who are kept overworked all the time. It is within the power of Congress to legislate upon this subject.

III.

1. Legislation should be enacted which would take away the power from judges or courts to issue ex parte injunctions in all strike cases. Where an injunction is issued it is in general, if not always, forbidding acts to be done which are already under the statutes of the States made criminal, and therefore there are ample means for reaching any wrong done against the railroad company by putting the law of the State in operation; but by proceeding by injunction the equity power of the court is substituted for the criminal process provided for by the State, and thus the right of trial by jury guaranteed by the Constitution is subverted.

2. The answer is emphatically that there should be a law greatly modifying and limiting the power of the courts in this direction. The framers of the Constitution, having in view the history of centuries, showing how the rights and liberties of people were disregarded and how they were imprisoned on shallow pretext growing out of malice or intrigue, believed it was absolutely necessary to preserve and afford to everyone likely to be committed to jail, on any charge, the right of trial by jury. Now, when an injunction is issued in a labor strike, it commands certain individuals to refrain from doing a thing which the State law already declares, in most cases, to be criminal. If it is alleged that the injunction is violated, the persons violating it are brought before the very judge who issued it, and while, of course, he does not punish them for the crime alleged to have been committed, he does punish them for disobeying the mandate contained in the injunction, and it is clear that before he can so punish them he must adjudge that they have committed certain acts, which, if true, would be criminal and would also subject them to the penal laws of the State. So he sends them to jail, and they suffer the same punishment as if they were tried and convicted under the penal laws of the State. They may be tried under the penal law, and can not plead such term of imprisonment as once in jeopardy.

But to point out another phase of the question we may suggest that in order to convict the person under the penal laws of the State of doing the acts mentioned in the injunction, the prisoner would have to be found guilty beyond a reasonable doubt. All the strict laws of evidence in criminal cases might be invoked for his protection, but there is nothing, not even a fair preponderance of the evidence which necessarily governs the judge sitting in judgment of the person charged with violating the mandate of the court; so the judge may at once become prosecutor, judge, and jury. The average judge is human, and when it is said that the order which he issued is violated he is very much biased against those who dared to disregard his authority and dignity, and he is very much inclined indeed to allow his human nature to enter into the judicial determination of the case. Granting injunction in labor cases, where the criminal law of the land is sufficient to meet the exigency, is simply substituting the equity power, which originally was so sparingly exercised by courts of chancery, and which was intended only to afford relief where the law was deficient or inadequate, for that of the criminal law. It subjects one to double punishment for the same act, viz., violating the laws of the State and the mandate of the court. It deprives one of the benefit of the strict rules of evidence of criminal cases, and in short, it violates and contravenes the very spirit and genius of the Constitution, and, therefore, acts of contempt should be limited to those committed in the very presence of the court. All other alleged acts of contempt should be tried by a jury under the rules governing criminal procedure.

3. It is difficult to answer such a question. Should the Attorney-General be prejudiced against labor, and as many of them have been employed by corporations before and during the time of their incumbency of that high office, they certainly would not be very fair toward the employees—throwing the influence of their high office in favor of the corporations might only tend to influence courts all the more against the best interest of the employee. However, if the Attorney-General is fair and unprejudiced, and equally fair to both parties in the controversy, his presence in cases of this kind could not but tend to promote justice, but before he would be useful in such a case it would be absolutely necessary to cause him to cut off all relationship with corporations before engaging in the duties of his office.

IV.

1. A general uniform law should be enacted making all common carriers liable for the negligence of a fellow-servant the same as the master is liable to the employee for his own negligence. This rule is not an injustice upon the master, for he selects, governs, and directs each employee; but as to the employee himself, he has no choice in the selection of his fellow-servant, and usually little, if anything, to do with governing or controlling the action of such fellow-servant, and is very often at the mercy, so far as his safety depends, of the fellow-servant. For these reasons the master should be held responsible.

2. As a general thing the Federal courts do follow the rules laid down by State courts as to the admission of evidence and the administering of State laws respecting personal injuries, and, of course, it is most desirable that the Federal courts when administering the law of any particular State should follow the rules laid down by the highest courts of such State in the same manner that they would follow the rules laid down by the Supreme Court of the United States in administering the Constitution or the laws of the United States.

V.

It is unwise for lawyers, perhaps, on an occasion like this to discuss a law which has been enacted by Congress, but apparently has not in any manner been tested by the courts, and as the law of 1898 has not been in any respects called into question as far as we know, we will not attempt to give any opinion on it.

A. Respecting the feasibility or practicability of compulsory arbitration, we unhesitatingly state that it seems both practicable and feasible. In the first place, corporations are but the creatures of law. They must accept conditions imposed upon them by the State, and if the State should see fit to impose upon each corporation a condition that, on it being given a charter, it should submit to arbitration in matters arising between the corporation and its employees which could not be amicably settled, it would certainly tend to solve a vexed problem. Any corporation which would not accept such a condition should not be given a charter, and the States which have retained the power to amend or modify the charters of any corporation are in as good position to force all existing corporations to accept such a law as those which may be organized hereafter. The general public has a great interest at stake respecting the operation of a railroad, for every contract that is made is based on normal conditions, and a strike occurring may upset all conditions existing at the time contracts were entered into between individuals who have no connection with the railroad as far as managing them or dealing with the employees is concerned, and therefore on account of it being such a great public concern and capable of inflicting so much injury on the public, both the employer and the employee should be compelled to submit to arbitration. Besides, the railroads' interest is growing larger each year, and consequently each year affects the general public to a greater extent; besides, by preventing strikes it would be one method of preserving the peace and general stability of affairs throughout the country as well as preventing the corporations from oppressing the employees, or vice versa.

Your, struly,

JOHN H. MURPHY

LIST OF WITNESSES.

INDEX OF TESTIMONY.

Freight rates, etc.—Continued.
  Unreasonableness, discussed, etc.—Continued.
    Judged only by comparison............... Newcomb, 99; Clements, 153, 161
    Effect of, importance.. Newcomb, 101
    Live stock, reasonable.. Mallory, 588
    Local rates, discussed. Vanlandingham, 201, 202; Callaway, 226; Cowen, 318
    Mill supplies, reasonable .... Gallagher, 543
    Should be settled by courts.................................... Tucker, 558
  Water routes, rates, and effect of competition .... Knapp, 134, 144;
                        Clements, 155; Vanlandingham, 203,
                        206, 207; Callaway, 225; Spencer, 276
  Western manufacturers not favored .... Dickinson, 550
Freight traffic:
    Transportation of, chief purpose of railways .... Newcomb, 95
    Fast-freight lines, nature and relations to railways............. Newcomb, 98;
                        Prouty, 151, 152
    Grain and provisions, importance of............................. Callaway, 232
    Receipts from... Lewis, 728, 732
      Under Government ownership, estimated.................... Lewis, 737–741
    Volume .... Lewis, 728, 732
      Uniformity of... Lewis, 738
    Through transportation, increase and importance................. Newcomb, 99
Fremont, Nebr.:
    Discriminations in favor of .... Fuller, 441, 442
Frogs of switches:
    Blocking .... Moseley, 38; Clark, 115
Fruit:
    Discriminations in transportation............................... Kennard, 363
Galveston. (See *Gulf ports.*)
Garfield, James A.:
    On Government ownership of railroads........................... Lewis, 725
General Managers' Association, Chicago:
    Membership.. Strong, 504
    Proposed blacklisting agreements............................. Strong, 504, 509
    Action on terminal charge on live stock at Chicago............. Mallory, 587
General property tax:
    Character and working...................... Seligman, 599, 602, 603, 607
Germany:
    Government ownership of railroads .... Spencer, 279; Seligman, 614; Lewis, 747
    Management less satisfactory.................................. Spencer, 279
    Difficulty of double taxation in .... Seligman, 600
    Pooling in .... Blanchard, 651
Gladstone, Mich.:
    Iron-ore shipments .... Keep, 715
Government ownership:
    Three criteria for determining desirability .... Seligman, 610
    Competition between Government and private enterprise undesirable
                        Seligman, 612, 613
    Low salaries would cause loss of highest talent................ Seligman, 613
    Extravagance .... Newcomb, 102; Morton, 497
    Postal service approved by practically all.................... Seligman, 610
      A historical accident....................................... Seligman, 612
    Telegraphs and telephones, advocated .... Seligman, 610–612
Government ownership of railroads:
    Discussed—
      Generally .... Newcomb, 102
      Favored.. Greeley, 379; Lewis, 724–757
      Desirable for Prussia, not for United States .... Seligman, 614
      Experiences of States and cities, unsuccessful .... Spencer, 283
      Deprecated .... Wilson, 51;
                        Knapp, 145; Callaway, 239; Ingalls, 287; Reagan,
                        347; Fish, 338; Ripley, 598; Seligman, 606, 610–614
    Advantages—
      Generally .... Lewis, 724
      Eight-hour day .... Lewis, 739, 740
      Blacklisting checked by .... Strong, 513
      Stability of securities.................................... Lewis, 726, 727